Dutcher

P9-CJE-499

TEACHER'S EDITION

Prentice Hall Biology

Kenneth R. Miller, Ph.D.
Professor of Biology
Brown University
Providence, Rhode Island

Joseph Levine, Ph.D.
Science Writer and Producer
Concord, Massachusetts

Copyright © 2002 by Pearson Education, Inc., Upper Saddle River, New Jersey 07458.
All rights reserved. Printed in the United States of America. This publication is protected by copyright, and permission should be obtained from the publisher prior to any prohibited reproduction, storage in a retrieval system, or transmission in any form or by any means, electronic, mechanical, photocopying, recording, or likewise. For information regarding permission(s), write to: Rights and Permissions Department.

ISBN 0-13-050742-3
3 4 5 6 7 8 9 10 05 04 03 02 01

Upper Saddle River, New Jersey
Glenview, Illinois
Needham, Massachusetts

Contents in Brief

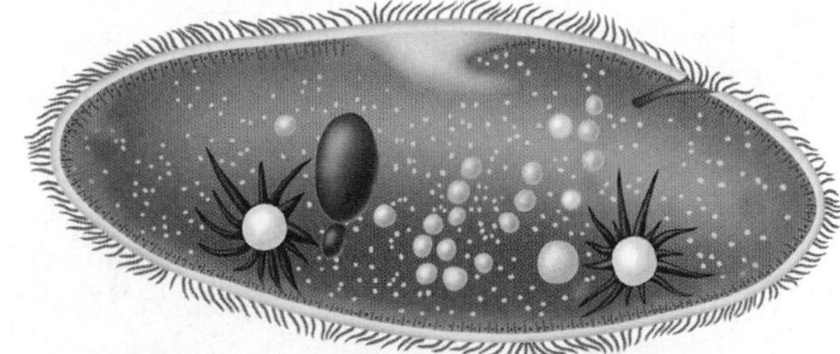

Overview of Teacher's Edition

A bold new vision for biology

One program that ensures success for all students

Instructional approach makes biology accessible

A student edition that promotes understanding

As you have just read, the production of NADPH and ATP requires ... the photosynthetic ... produce these ... in **Figure 9–4**. The relationship betwe... reactions is shown in **Figure 9–5**. **In the ligh... reactions, the energy of sunlight is captured ... to make energy-storing compounds.** If NADPH ... store large amounts of energy over long peri... photosynthesis might stop with th... tion. Th... called the **light-**

The second stage of photosynthesis is called the **light-independent reactions**. This stage uses the energy stored in NADPH and ATP to produce glucose. Glucose is more stable than either NADPH or ATP and is able to store more energy than either of these compounds. In fact, one molecule of glucose stores approximately 100 times more energy ... phate group in

• KEY CONCEPTS ICONS

Clearly identified ***before, during,*** and ***after*** every section. Key concept icons encourage students to focus on the big ideas of biology.

Guide for Reading

Key Concepts

- What events occur during the light-dependent reactions of photosynthesis?
- How are the light-independent reactions and the light-dependent reactions related?

Vocabulary

light-dependent reactions
light-independent reactions
photosystem
electron transport
Calvin cycle

Reading Strategy: Previewing Visuals

Before you read, preview Figure 8–7 to get an overview of the two major stages of photosynthesis. As you read, make a list of the reactants and products of each of these major stages of photosynthesis.

• BUILT-IN READING SUPPORT—

At the start of every section, the ***Guide for Reading*** helps all students master concepts and provides strategies to improve reading comprehension.

FIGURE 9–5 PHOTOSYNTHESIS: An Overview

The process of photosynthesis includes the light-dependent reactions as well the light-independent reactions (Calvin cycle). Both sets of reactions take place in the chloroplast, shown here.

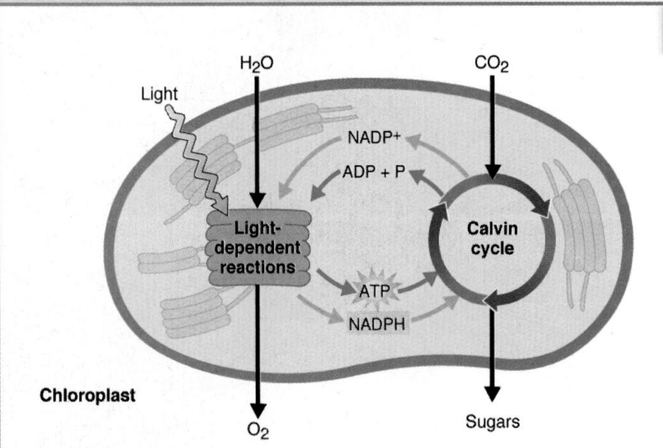

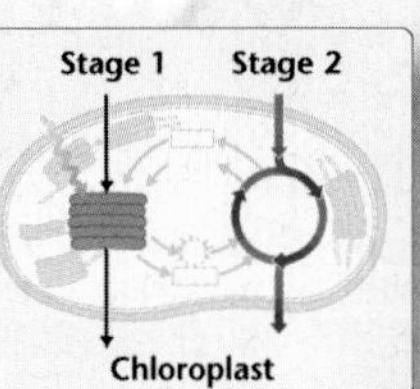

*To understand the different stages of reactions in photosynthesis refer to **Figure 9–6** and **Figure 9–7**.*

• VISUALLY REINFORCED CONTENT—

Visual overviews of complex processes are shown with breakout drawings detailing the specifics of the process—providing students with a visual anchor to the narrative. Students read, see, and ultimately understand and retain the fundamentals of biology.

to all students

Flexible support package helps you reach and motivate all students

• BIOLOGY iTEXT—

Interactive Student Edition online with animations and simulations helps students visualize tough-to-understand concepts. Also includes assessments to help students review and master content.

• GUIDED READING AND STUDY WORKBOOK—

Linked directly to every section in the Student Edition, provides a wide range of question formats, promotes and enhances study skills, and builds a record of students' work to use as a study aid for quizzes and tests!

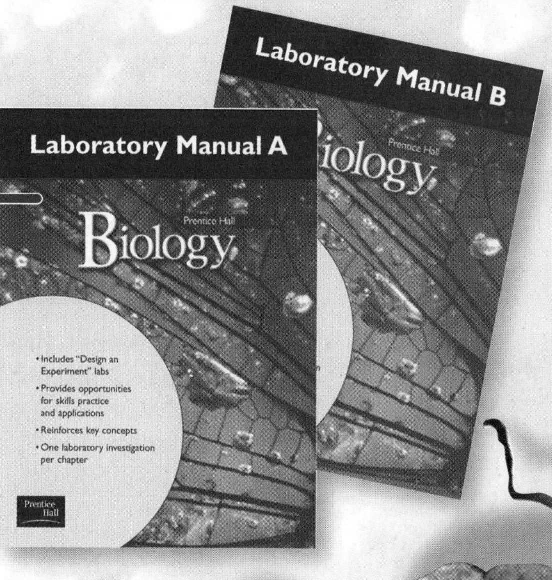

Laboratory Manual B
Laboratory Manual A
Prentice Hall
Biology
• Includes "Design an Experiment" labs
• Provides opportunities for skills practice and applications
• Reinforces key concepts
• One laboratory investigation per chapter
Prentice Hall

• 2 LEVELS OF LABS

Choice of two lab manuals—quantitative/analytical or more conceptual labs—gives you the option of customizing your lab program to meet the needs of all learners.

• PRENTICE HALL BIOLOGY WEB SITE—

Includes additional support for every chapter! Student activities, data sharing, chapter assessment, and teacher support are a few of the many resources you'll find!
www.phschool.com

Approach to assessment helps you quickly monitor student progress

Resources that ensure test-taking success

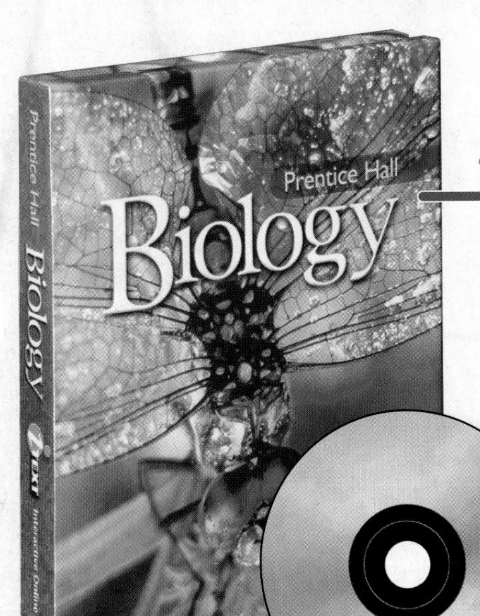

• BIOLOGY iTEXT—

In addition to electronic animations and simulations, this breakaway resource provides a wealth of assessment tools. Students can monitor their progress at point-of-use—with ongoing assessment, helpful hints, and instant feedback. Available on CD and through our web site.

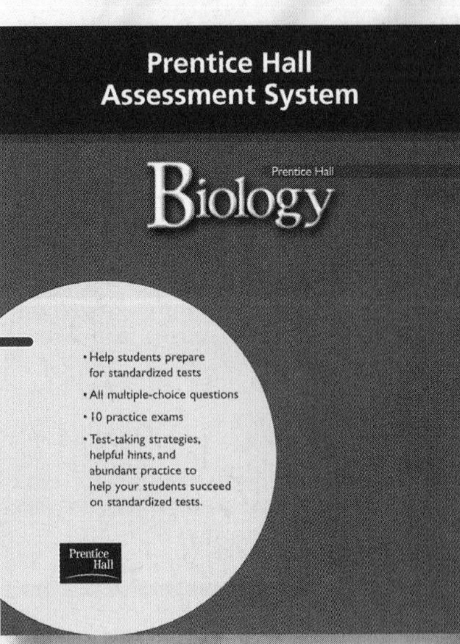

Prentice Hall
Assessment System
Prentice Hall
Biology
• Help students prepare for standardized tests
• All multiple-choice questions
• 10 practice exams
• Test-taking strategies, helpful hints, and abundant practice to help your students succeed on standardized tests.
Prentice Hall

• PRENTICE HALL ASSESSMENT SYSTEM—

This complete assessment system gives your students the strategies, confidence, and practice they need to succeed on state and national tests.

Computer Test Bank

Prentice Hall

Biology

• Provides different levels of questions for those students with different needs
• Enables you to select, modify, and sequence test questions
• Includes over 2,900 objective and essay questions
• Questions are correlated to chapter objectives

Prentice Hall

PRENTICE HALL

Test Bank CD-ROM

Version 2.0 Mac/Win Technical Support 1-800-234-5TEC

www.phschool.com

Biology

THIRD EDITION

• COMPUTER TEST BANK CD-ROM—

Tailor tests to your classroom needs by creating your own test or editing an existing test from the bank of 4600 questions!

Assess student understanding— right at point-of-use in the student text

Responsive

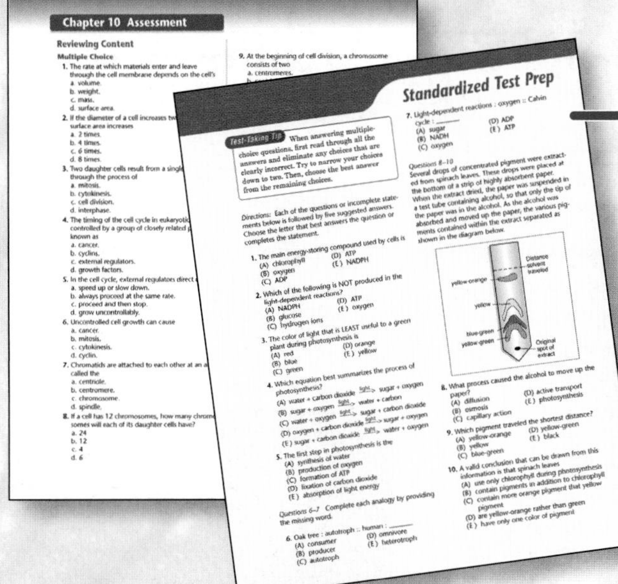

• VARIED, ONGOING ASSESSMENT—

Section assessments, chapter assessments, and standardized test practice in every chapter allow you to assess student understanding at the time that's right for you.

where chlorophyll does not, thus allowing more of the available light energy to be used. After light energy is absorbed by one of the pigment molecules in a photosystem, the energy is passed from one pigment molecule to the next until it reaches a special pair of chloro...

...all the photosystem...
the special pair of chlorophyll molecu...

CHECKPOINT *What is the role of photosystems?*

• CHECK POINT QUESTIONS—

Appearing throughout the Student Edition, encourage students to reflect back on what they have read, confirming and reinforcing understanding of the material just covered.

▼ **Figure 9–4** Plant cells contain chloroplasts, where photosynthesis occurs. **Posing Questions** ***What part of a plant cell absorbs light energy?***

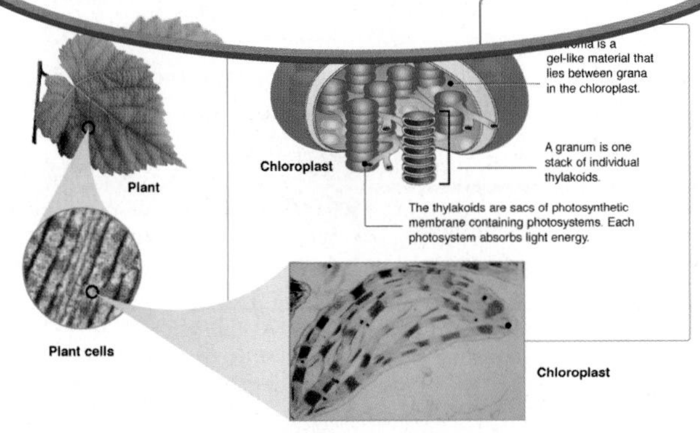

• CAPTION QUESTIONS—

Maximize photos and graphics in the Student Edition. Caption questions enhance students' critical thinking skills and deepen their understanding of chapter content.

• PRENTICE HALL BIOLOGY WEB SITE—

Provides additional self-assessment opportunities. **www.phschool.com**

Organization and support resources

Flexible resource package meets your specific teaching needs

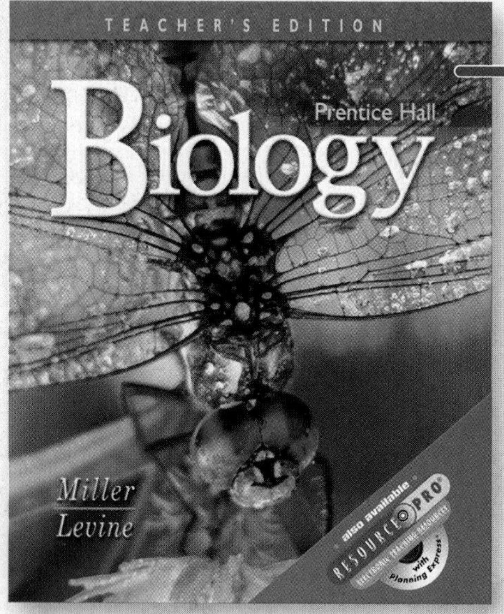

• TEACHER'S EDITION

Provides all the point-of-use help you need to maximize learning and minimize planning time. From dynamic demonstration ideas and alternative strategies to helpful background notes, Prentice Hall *Biology* gives you all the support you need in an easy to follow 3-step format.

RESOURCE PRO
USER'S GUIDE
PRENTICE HALL
Prentice Hall
Biology
Prentice Hall

• RESOURCE PRO® CD-ROM—

The ultimate lesson planning and scheduling tool. Resource Pro provides instant electronic access to all program print resources by topic, chapter, or concept. Powerful planning program lets you customize your course by the day, week, or month!

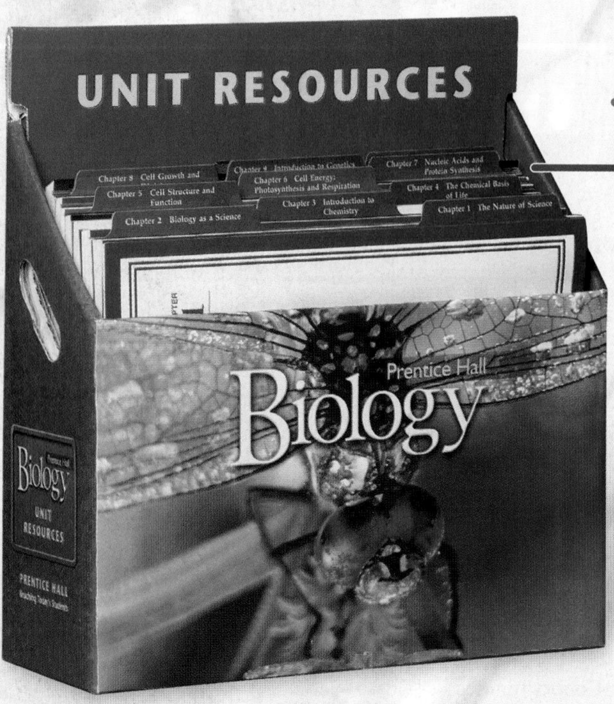

• CONVENIENTLY ORGANIZED UNIT RESOURCES

Contain section reviews, vocabulary reviews, graphic organizers, chapter enrichment, lab work sheets, and answer keys. Adaptable organization by chapter saves you time!

• SCIENCE NEWS CONNECTION—

Weekly science content updates on the web keep you and your students current!

KEEP CURRENT WITH . . .
SCIENCE NEWS®
A Science Service Publication

www.phschool.com
As you read this unit, learn about ongoing research and discoveries related to these questions by visiting the *Science News* Web site.

Adaptable

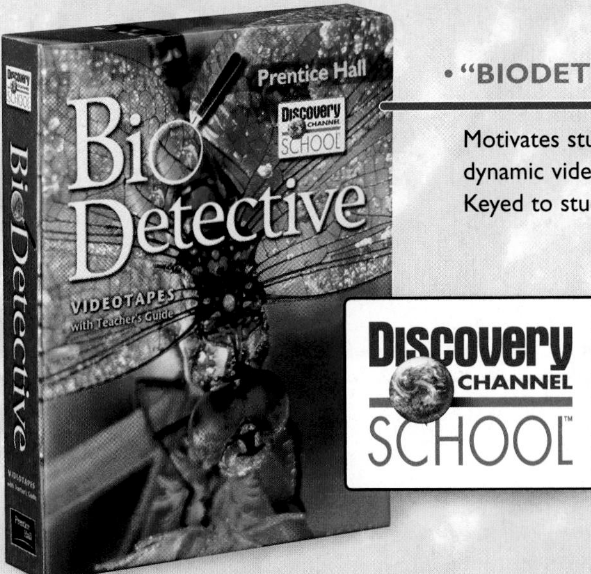

• **"BIODETECTIVES" VIDEOS—**

Motivates students to apply what they learn in dynamic video segments to real-world problems. Keyed to student text.

• **VIDEOTAPE LIBRARY—**

Animations reinforce difficult-to-understand concepts.

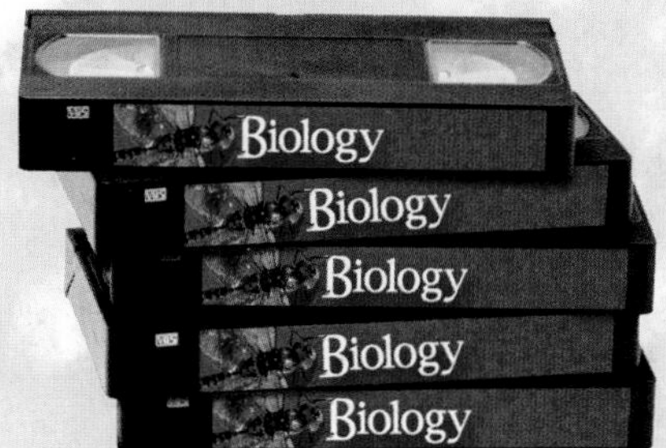

PRESENTATION ASSISTANT PLUS

Transparency & CD-ROM package puts hundreds of dynamic teaching images at your fingertips!

• **OVER 600 TEACHING TRANSPARENCIES—**

Referenced at point-of-use in the Teacher's Edition and organized by chapter/unit, the transparencies provide support for every section in the book. Help students visualize tough-to-understand concepts. Include interest grabbers, section outlines, and colorful four-color art.

FIGURE 9–5 PHOTOSYNTHESIS: An Overview

The process of photosynthesis includes the light-dependent reactions as well the light-independent reactions (Calvin cycle). Both sets of reactions take place in the chloroplast, shown here.

Light, H_2O, CO_2, NADP+, ADP + P, Light-dependent reactions, Calvin cycle, ATP, NADPH, Chloroplast, O_2, Sugars

Stage 1, Stage 2, Chloroplast

*To understand the different stages of reactions in photosynthesis refer to **Figure 9–6** and **Figure 9–7**.*

PRESENTATION ASSISTANT PLUS
Transparencies with Presentation Pro™ CD-ROM
Prentice Hall Biology

• **PRESENTATION™ PRO CD-ROM**

Provides electronic access to over 600 teaching transparencies, allowing you to create custom presentations at the click of a mouse.

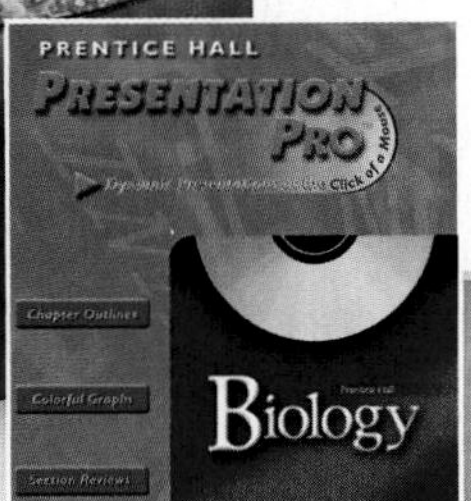

A bold, new vision for biology

Prentice Hall *Biology* ©2002 comprehensive support resources

- Student Edition
- Teacher's Edition
- Unit Resources
- Laboratory Manual A, Student Edition
- Laboratory Manual A, Teacher's Edition
- Laboratory Manual B, Student Edition
- Laboratory Manual B, Teacher's Edition
- Guided Reading & Study Workbook
- Guided Reading & Study Workbook, Teacher's Edition
- Resource Pro® CD-ROM
- Presentation Assistant Plus:
  - Presentation Pro CD-ROM
  - Transparency Package
- Computer Test Bank Booklet
- Computer Test Bank CD-ROM
- Lab Assessment & Scoring Guide
- Issues & Decision Making
- Biotechnology Manual
- Chapter Tests: Levels A & B
- Prentice Hall Biology Web site with Science News
- Biology iText 
- BioDetectives Videos 
- Videotape Library

Pacing Guide

Planning for Classroom Diversity

The Pacing Guide below suggests one way to schedule your instructional time for Basic (students who need additional help), Average (all students), and Enriched (students who need to be challanged) students.

Week	Basic	Average	Enriched
	Chapters	Chapters	Chapters
1	1	1	1
2	2-1, 2-2, 2-3	2	2-1, 2-2, 2-3
3	3	3, 4-1	2-4
4	4-1, 4-2	4-2, 4-3, 4-4	3, 4
5	4-3, 4-4	5, 6-1, 6-2, 6-3	5, 6
6	5	7	7
7	6	8-1, 8-2	8-1, 8-2
8	7	9	8-3
9	8-1, 8-2	10	9
10	9	11	10
11	10-1, 10-2	12-1, 12-2, 12-3, 12-4	11
12	11-1, 11-2, 11-3	13-1, 13-2, 13-3	12-1, 12-2
13	11-4	13-4, 14	12-3, 12-4, 12-5
14	12-1, 12-2	15, 16-2, 16-3	13
15	12-3	17-3, 17-4	14
16	13-1, 13-2, 13-4	18	15
17	14-1, 14-2	19	16
18	15-1, 15-3	20	17
19	16-1, 16-2	21	18
20	17-3, 18-2	22	19
21	19, 20-1	23-1, 23-2	20
22	21-1, 21-3	23-3, 23-4	21
23	22-1, 22-5, 23-1	24-1, 24-2, 25	22
24	24-2, 24-3, 25-2, 25-3	26, 27	23
25	26, 27	27-3, 27-4	24, 25
26	28-1, 28-4, 29-2	28, 29	Invertebrate survey 26,27
27	30	30	Invertebrate survey 28
28	31	31	Invertebrate survey 29
29	32-1, 32-3, 33-3	32	Vertebrate survey 30- 31
30	34	33	Vertebrate survey 32-33
31	35-1, 35-2, 35-4, 35-5	34, 35	34, 35
32	36	36	36
33	37	37	37
34	38	38	38
35	39	39	39
36	40	40	40
Total	**36 Weeks**	**36 Weeks**	**36 Weeks**

1 Week = 2 1/2 blocks or 5 periods

Thematic Approaches

The Pacing Guide below suggests one way to schedule your instructional time for each of the four themes listed.

Week	Molecular Biology and Biotechnoloy Chapters	Phylogenetic Evolution Chapters	Human Survey Chapters	Ecology Chapters
1	1	1-1,1-2	1	1, 6-3
2	2-1, 2-2, 2-3	1-3, 1-4	2	2
3	2-4	2-1, 2-2	3, 4	3, 8-1
4	7, 23-5	2-3, 2-4	5, 6	8-2, 8-3, 9-1
5	8-1, 8-2	3-4	7	9-2, 4-1, 4-2
6	8-3	5	9	4-3, 4-4
7	9-1, 23-4	6-1, 6-3	10	5
8	9-2	7	11	6
9	10	9	11	7
10	11	10	12-1, 12-2, 12-3	10
11	12-1, 12-2	11	12-4, 12-5	19
12	12-3, 12-4, 12-5	12	13	20
13	13-1, 13-2	13	14	21
14	13-3, 13-4	14	30-1, 32-1, 32-2	15, 16-2
15	14-1, 14-2	15-1, 15-2	32-3	17-3, 17-4
16	14-3, 14-4	15-3	33-1, 33-2	18
17	34, 35	16-1, 16-2	34	22
18	36	16-3, 17-1, 17-2	35-1, 35-2	23-1, 23-2
19	37	17-3, 17-4	35-3, 35-4, 35-5	23-3, 23-4
20	38	18	36-1	24-1, 24-2, 25
21	39	19	36-2, 36-3	26, 27-1, 27-2
22	40	20	37-1, 37-2	27-3, 27-4
23	15	21	37-3	27-3, 27-4
24	16	22	38-1, 38-2	28-1, 27-4 29
25	17	23	38-3	30
26	18	8	39-1, 39-2	31
27	Microorganism and fungi	26	39-3, 39-4	32
28	and ecology survey Ch. 19, 20, 21, 3, 4, 5, 6 Instructor's	27-1, 27-2	40-1, 40-2	33
29	Choice of Material	27-3, 27-4	40-3, 40-4	34
30	22-1, 22-2, 22-3	28	Evolution 15, 16, 17	11
31	24, 25	29	Microorganism	12
32	Invertebrate Survey	30	Survey 19, 20, 21, 22, 23, 24, 25	13
33	Ch. 26, 27, 28, 29 Teacher's	31	Plant Survey 26, 27	14
34	Choice of Material	32	Invertebrate Survey 28, 29	Project
35	30-31	33	Vertebrate Survey	
36	32, 33	34	30-2, 30-3, 31, 33-3	
Total	**36 weeks**	**36 weeks**	**36 Weeks**	**33 + Project**

1 Week = 2 1/2 blocks or 5 periods

National Science Education Standards

Correlation to National Science Education Standards

Life Science Content Standard	Chapter/Section/Page
Unifying Concepts and Processes	
• Systems, order, and organization	Ch. 1: Sec. 1-3; Ch. 2: Sec. 2-1, Sec. 2-3; Ch. 3: Sec. 3-1, Sec. 3-2, Sec. 3-3; Ch. 4: Sec. 4-2, Sec. 4-3, Sec. 4-4; Ch. 7: Sec. 7-1, Sec. 7-2, Sec. 7-4; Ch. 11, Sec. 11-2; Ch. 12, pp. 291-294, pp. 311-312; Ch. 15: Sec. 15-3; Ch. 17: p. 440; Ch. 18, Sec. 18-1, Sec. 18-2, Sec. 18-3; Ch. 23: Sec. 23-1; Ch. 26: pp. 660-663; Ch. 35: Sec. 35-1; Appendix E
• Evidence, models, and explanation	Ch. 1: Sec. 1-1, Sec. 1-2, Sec. 1-3 pp. 22-23, Sec. 1-4; Ch. 3: pp. 65-66; Ch. 7: pp. 169-170; Ch. 8: pp. 204-206; Ch. 11: Sec. 11-1, Sec. 11-2, Sec. 11-5; Ch. 12: Sec. 12-1; Ch. 15: Sec. 15-2, Sec. 15-3; Ch. 16: p. 383; pp. 400-401; Ch. 17: Sec. 17-1; Ch. 32, pp. 838-841
• Change, constancy, and measurement	Ch. 1: Sec. 1-4; Ch. 2: Sec. 2-1, Sec. 2-2 pp. 42-43, Sec. 2-4; Ch. 3: Sec. 3-2, Sec. 3-3; Ch. 4: Sec. 4-1, Sec. 4-2; Ch. 5: Sec. 5-1, Sec. 5-2, Sec. 5-3; Ch. 6: Sec. 6-2, Sec. 6-3; Ch. 8: Sec. 8-1, Sec. 8-2 p. 206; Ch. 9: pp. 230-232; Ch. 10: Sec. 10-1, Sec. 10-2; Ch. 11: Sec. 11-3; Ch. 12: Sec. 12-3, Sec. 12-4; Ch. 13: Sec. 13-1; Ch. 15: Sec. 15-2; Ch. 16: Sec. 16-1, Sec. 16-2, Sec. 16-3; Ch. 17: Sec. 17-1, Sec. 17-3, Sec. 17-4; Ch. 18: pp. 454-455; Ch. 28: pp. 729; Ch. 33: Sec. 33-2; Ch. 34: pp. 878-879; Ch. 35: pp. 895-896; Appendix C
• Evolution and Equilibrium	Ch. 1: pp. 19-20; Ch. 2: pp. 52-53; Ch. 3: Sec. 3-3; Ch. 4: Sec. 4-2; Ch. 5: p. 122, Sec. 5-2; Ch. 7: Sec. 7-3; Ch. 8: Sec. 8-1, Sec. 8-3 p. 214; Ch. 9: p. 232; Ch. 10: Sec. 10-3; Ch. 12: Sec. 12-4; Ch. 15; Ch. 16: Sec. 16-2, Sec. 16-3; Ch. 17: Sec. 17-3, Sec. 17-4; Ch. 18: Sec. 18-2, Sec. 18-3; Ch. 22: p. 553-555, p. 560, p. 566; Ch. 23: Sec. 23-5; Ch. 25: Sec. 25-2, Sec. 25-3; Ch. 26: pp. 660-663; Ch. 28: pp. 716; Ch. 29: Sec. 29-1; Ch. 30: pp. 772-773, pp. 782-783; Ch. 31: pp. 798-799, p. 807; Ch. 32: p. 821, p. 832, pp. 836-841; Ch. 33: Sec. 33-1, Sec. 33-2; Ch. 34: p. 872
• Form and function	Ch. 2: Sec. 2-3; Ch. 4: Sec. 4-3, Sec. 4-4; Ch. 7: pp. 171-172, Sec. 7-2, Sec. 7-4; Ch. 8: p. 208; Ch. 15: pp. 384-385; Ch. 19: pp. 471-473, pp. 482-483; Ch. 20: pp. 497-500, pp. 506-507, pp. 510-512, pp. 516-519; Ch. 21: pp. 527-528, p. 530; Ch. 22: pp. 556-557, pp. 561-562, pp. 564-565, p. 569; Ch. 23: Sec. 23-1, Sec. 23-2, Sec. 23-3, Sec. 23-4, Sec. 23-5 p. 601; Ch. 25: Sec. 25-3; Ch. 26: pp. 664-667, pp. 670-672; Ch. 27: pp. 684-686, p. 690, pp. 695-696, pp. 702-704; Ch. 28: pp. 716-719, pp. 727-728, pp. 735-736; Ch. 29: Sec. 29-2; Ch. 30: pp. 774-778, pp. 784-787; Ch. 31: pp. 800-802, pp. 808-812; Ch. 32: pp. 822-827, pp. 834-835; Ch. 33: Sec. 33-3
CONTENT STANDARD A • Science as Inquiry	
• Abilities necessary to do scientific inquiry	Ch. 1: Sec. 1-1, Sec. 1-2, p. 23, Sec. 1-4; Ch. 3: p. 65; Inquiry Activities, Analyzing Data, Problem Solving, Quick Labs, Real-World Labs, Design-an-Experiment Labs, and Exploration Labs: Chapters 1-40; Appendix A; Appendix B; Appendix C; Appendix D
• Understandings about scientific inquiry	Ch. 1: Sec. 1-1, Sec. 1-2, Sec. 1-4; Ch. 3: p. 65; Technology & Society: Chapters 1-40; Careers: Chapters 1-40; Appendix A
CONTENT STANDARD B • Physical Science	
•Structure of atoms	Ch. 2: Sec. 2-1, Sec. 2-2, Sec. 2-3, Sec. 2-4

Correlation to National Science Education Standards

Life Science Content Standard	Chapter/Section/Page
• Structures and properties of matter	Ch. 2: Sec. 2-1, Sec. 2-2, Sec. 2-3; Ch. 12: pp. 291-294
• Chemical reactions	Ch. 2: Sec. 2-4; Ch. 8: Sec. 8-3; Ch. 9: pp. 222-224, Sec. 9-2; Ch. 38: Sec. 38-1
• Motions and forces	Ch. 2: pp. 38-39; Ch. 4: Sec. 4-1; Ch. 7: Sec. 7-3; Ch. 35: Sec. 35-2
• Conservation of energy and increase in disorder	Ch. 2: Sec. 2-4; Ch. 3: pp. 72-73; Ch. 4: Sec. 4-1, Sec. 4-3, pp. 98-99, p. 104, Sec. 4-4
• Interactions of energy and matter	Ch. 1: p. 18; Ch. 3: Sec. 3-2, Sec. 3-3; Ch. 4: pp. 94-97, Sec. 4-3; Ch. 8: Sec. 8-1, Sec. 8-2 pp. 206-207, Sec. 8-3; Ch. 9: Sec. 9-1, Sec. 9-2; Ch. 25: Sec. 25-2; Ch. 34: p. 878; Ch. 38: Sec. 38-1
LIFE SCIENCE CONTENT STANDARD C • The Cell	
• Cells have particular structures that underlie their functions.	Ch. 7: p. 171, Sec. 7-2, Sec. 7-3; Ch. 8: p. 202-203, Sec. 8-3; Ch. 9: Sec. 9-1, Sec. 9-2; Ch. 10: Sec. 10-2, p. 251
• Most cell functions involve chemical reaction.	Ch. 2: Sec. 2-4; Ch. 7: pp. 177-180, p. 182; Ch. 8: Sec. 8-1, Sec. 8-3; Ch. 9: Sec. 9-1, Sec. 9-2; Ch. 38: Sec. 38-1
• Cells store and use information to guide their functions.	Ch. 2: pp. 47-48; Ch. 7: Sec. 7-2; Ch. 10: p. 241, p. 244; Ch. 12: Sec. 12-2, Sec. 12-3
• Cell functions are regulated.	Ch. 7: Sec. 7-3; Ch. 10: Sec. 10-1, Sec. 10-3; Ch. 12: Sec. 12-4; Ch. 14: pp. 344-348, pp. 350-352
• Plant cells contain chloroplasts, the site of photosynthesis.	Ch. 1: p. 18; Ch. 3: pp. 67-68; Ch. 7: pp. 180; Ch. 8: p. 206, Sec. 8-3, p. 232; Ch. 19: p. 474
• Cells can differentiate, and complex multicellular organisms are formed as a highly organized arrangement of differentiated cells.	Ch. 1: p. 17; Ch. 7: Sec. 7-4; Ch. 10: p. 253; Ch. 11: Sec. 11-4; Ch. 12: Sec. 12-4; Ch. 23: Sec. 23-1; Ch. 26: pp. 660-661; Ch. 39: Sec. 39-4 pp. 1016-1019
Molecular Basis of Heredity	
• In all organisms, the instructions for specifying the characteristics of the organisms are carried in DNA.	Ch. 1: p. 17; Ch. 2: pp. 47-48; Ch. 10: p. 244; Ch. 12: pp. 291-294, Sec. 12-2, Sec. 12-3; Ch. 13: Sec. 13-2; Ch. 14: Sec. 14-1; Ch. 16: pp. 394-396
• Most of the cells in a human contain two copies of each of 22 different chromosomes. In addition, there is a pair of chromosomes that determine sex.	Ch. 7: Sec. 7-2; Ch. 10: Sec. 10-2, Sec. 10-3; Ch. 11: Sec. 11-4, Sec. 11-5; Ch. 14: Sec. 14-1, Sec. 14-2; Ch. 39: p 1016
• Changes in DNA (mutations) occur spontaneously at low rates.	Ch. 12: pp. 306-308, p. 312; Ch. 13: pp. 320-321; Ch. 14: pp. 346-348; Ch. 16: Sec. 16-1, Sec. 16-2; Ch. 18: Sec. 18-2, p. 455; Ch. 40: Sec. 40-4, pp. 1046-1047
Biological Evolution	
• Species evolve over time.	Ch. 1: p. 20; Ch. 4: Sec. 4-2; Ch. 5: Sec. 5-1, Sec. 5-2; Ch. 13: pp. 320-321; Ch. 15: Sec. 15-3; Ch. 16: Sec. 16-1, Sec. 16-2, Sec. 16-3; Ch. 17: Sec. 17-1, Sec. 17-3, Sec. 17-4; Ch. 18: Sec. 18-2; Ch. 20, pp. 495-496; Ch. 22: pp. 553-554; Ch. 25: Sec. 25-3; Ch. 28: p. 716; Ch. 29: Sec. 29-1; Ch. 30: pp. 772-773, pp. 782-783; Ch. 31: pp. 798-799, p. 807; Ch. 32: p. 821, p. 832, pp. 836-841; Ch. 33: Sec. 33-1

Correlation to National Science Education Standards

Life Science Content Standard	Chapter/Section/Page
• The great diversity of organisms is the result of more than 3.5 billion years of evolution that has filled every available niche with life forms.	Ch. 4: pp. 91-92, pp. 99-105, Sec. 4-4; Ch. 6: p. 152; Ch. 15: Sec. 15-1, Sec. 15-2, Sec. 15-3; Ch. 16: Sec. 16-2, Sec. 16-3; Ch. 17; Ch. 18: Sec. 18-2; Ch. 21: Sec. 21-2; Ch. 22: p. 553-555, pp. 570-571; Ch. 26: pp. 660-663; Ch. 28: p. 716, p. 726; Ch. 29: Sec. 29-1; Ch. 30: pp. 768-769, pp. 772-773, pp. 782-783; Ch. 31: pp. 798-799, p. 807; Ch. 32: p. 821, p. 826-827, Sec. 32-2, Sec. 32-3 pp. 836-837; Ch. 33: Sec. 33-1
• Natural selection and its evolutionary consequences provide a scientific explanation for the fossil record of ancient life forms, as well as for the striking molecular similarities observed among the diverse species of living organisms.	Ch. 15: p. 371, Sec. 15-3; Ch. 16; Ch. 17: Sec. 17-1, Sec. 17-3, Sec. 17-4; Ch. 18: pp. 452-455, p. 458; Ch. 25: Sec. 25-3; Ch. 26: p. 660; Ch. 29: pp. 746-747; Ch. 30: p. 768; Ch. 31: p. 807; Ch. 32: pp. 836-837; Ch. 33: Sec. 33-1
• The millions of different species of plants, animals, and microorganisms that live on Earth today are related by descent from common ancestors.	Ch. 6: p. 152; Ch. 15: Sec. 15-3; Ch. 16: Sec. 16-3; Ch. 17: Sec. 17-4; Ch. 18: p. 447, Sec. 18-2, Sec. 18-3; Ch. 22: p. 554; Ch. 26: p. 660; Ch. 29: Sec. 29-1; Ch. 30: pp. 768-769; Ch. 31: p. 807; Ch. 32: p. 836; Ch. 33: Sec. 33-1
• Biological classifications are based on how organisms are related.	Ch. 3: p. 64; Ch. 18; Ch. 19: pp. 471-473; Ch. 20: p. 496, Sec. 20-2, Sec. 20-3, Sec. 20-4 pp. 510-512, Sec. 20-5 pp. 516-519; Ch. 21: Sec. 21-2; Ch. 22: pp. 555-557, pp. 561-562, pp.566-568, Sec. 22-5; Ch. 26: p. 657, p. 664, p. 669, pp. 672-674; Ch. 27: p. 683, pp. 686-689, p. 694, pp. 697-698, p. 701, pp. 705-707; Ch. 28: p. 715, Sec. 28-2, pp. 726-729, p. 734, pp. 737-738; Ch. 29: p. 747-749; Ch. 30: Sec. 30-1, Sec. 30-2 p. 771, pp. 778-780, Sec. 30-3 p. 782, p. 788; Ch. 31: p. 797, pp. 803-805, p. 806, pp. 812-813; Ch. 32: p. 821, Sec. 32-2, Sec. 32-3; Ch. 33: Sec. 33-1
Interdependence of Organisms	
• The atoms and molecules on Earth cycle among the living and nonliving components of the biosphere.	Ch. 3: Sec. 3-2, Sec. 3-3; Ch. 4: Sec. 4-1, Sec. 4-2, p. 90
• Energy flows through ecosystems in one direction, from photosynthetic organisms to herbivores to carnivores and decomposers.	Ch. 1: p. 18; Ch. 3: Sec. 3-2; Ch. 8: p. 201; Ch. 21: Sec. 21-3, pp. 537-538; Ch. 26: Sec. 26-1; Ch. 33: Sec. 33-3: p. 858
• Organisms both cooperate and compete in ecosystems.	Ch. 3: Sec. 3-1; Ch. 4: Sec. 4-2, Sec. 4-3 p. 108; Ch. 5: Sec. 5-2; Ch. 6: p. 153; Ch. 20: p. 503, pp. 508-509, pp. 519-520; Ch. 21: Sec. 21-3; Ch. 24: p. 619; Ch. 25: Sec. 25-3; Ch. 26: p. 667, p. 675; Ch. 27: p. 699-700, p. 708; Ch. 28: pp. 730-733, p. 738; Ch. 30: p. 789; Ch. 31: p. 814; Ch. 34: Sec. 34-2
• Living organisms have the capacity to produce populations of infinite size, but environments and resources are finite.	Ch. 5; Ch. 6: p. 144, p. 159; Ch. 15: p. 377; Ch. 20: pp. 508-509
• Human beings live within the world's ecosystems. Increasingly, humans modify ecosystems as a result of population growth, technology, and consumption.	Ch. 5: Sec. 5-3; Ch. 6; Ch. 13; Ch. 19: p. 480-481; Ch. 20: p. 515; Ch. 22: p. 559; Ch. 24: pp. 624-626; Ch. 26: pp. 674-675; Ch. 27: p. 700; Ch. 30: p. 787, p. 789; Ch. 31: p. 805, p. 814

Correlation to National Science Education Standards

Life Science Content Standard	Chapter/Section/Page
Matter, Energy, and Organization in Living Systems	
• **All matter tends toward more disorganized states. Living systems require a continuous input of energy to maintain their chemical and physical organizations.**	Ch. 1: p. 18; Ch. 3: Sec. 3-1; Ch. 7 : Sec. 7-4, pp. 191-192; Ch. 8: Sec. 8-1, Sec. 8-2, Sec. 8-3; Ch. 9: Sec. 9-1, Sec. 9-2
• **The energy for life primarily derives from the sun.**	Ch. 3: pp. 67-68; Ch. 8: pp. 201-202; Ch. 38: pp. 971-973
• **The chemical bonds of food molecules contain energy.**	Ch. 9: pp. 221-222, Sec. 9-2; Ch. 38: Sec. 38-1
• **The complexity and organization of organisms accommodate the need for obtaining, transforming, transporting, releasing, and eliminating the matter and energy used to sustain the organism.**	Ch. 7: Sec. 7-4; Ch. 8: pp. 202-203; Ch. 9: Sec. 9-2; Ch. 19: pp. 474-478, 482-486; Ch. 20: pp. 497-500, 505-507; Ch. 22: pp. 551-552, 558-559, 561-563, 564-566; Ch. 23; Ch. 25: Sec. 25-1, 25-3; Ch. 26: pp. 657-659, Sec. 26-2, pp. 669-672; Ch. 27: pp. 683-686, 689-690, 694-696, 701-704; Ch. 28: pp. 715-719, 727-728, 734-736; Ch. 29: Sec. 29-2; Ch. 30: pp. 774-778, 784-787; Ch. 31: pp. 800-802, 808-812; Ch. 32: pp. 822-827; Ch. 33: Sec. 33-3
• **The distribution and abundance of organisms and populations in ecosystems are limited by the availability of matter and energy and the ability of the ecosystem to recycle materials.**	Ch. 3: Sec. 3-2; Ch. 4: pp. 92-97, Sec. 4-3, Sec. 4-4; Ch. 5: Sec. 5-2; Ch. 6: Sec. 6-2, Sec. 6-3
• **As matter and energy flow through different levels of organization of living systems—cells, organs, organisms, communities—and between living systems and the physical environment, chemical elements are recombined in different ways.**	Ch. 1: Sec. 1-3, p. 21; Ch. 3: Sec. 3-3; Ch. 4: Sec. 4-2; Ch. 7: Sec. 7-4, pp. 192-193; Ch. 8: pp. 202-203
Behavior of Organisms	
• **Multicellular animals have nervous systems that generate behavior.**	Ch. 26: Sec. 26-3, pp. 671-672; Ch. 27: Sec. 27-1, p. 685, Sec. 27-2, p. 690, Sec. 27-3, p. 696, Sec. 27-4, pp. 702-704; Ch. 28: Sec. 28-1, pp. 716-719, Sec. 28-3, pp. 727-733, Sec. 28-4, pp. 735-736; Lab: Ch. 28; Ch. 35: Sec. 35-2, Sec. 35-3, Sec. 35-4
• **Organisms have behavioral responses to internal changes and to external stimuli.**	Ch. 25: Sec. 25-2; Ch. 28: pp. 732-733, 739, 789; Lab: Ch. 29; Ch. 34: Sec. 34-1
• **Like other aspects of an organism's biology, behaviors have evolved through natural selection.**	Ch. 15: Sec. 15-3, pp. 380-382; Ch. 34: Sec. 34-1, pp. 880-882
• **Behavioral biology has implications for humans, as it provides links to psychology, sociology, and anthropology.**	Ch. 32: Sec. 32-3; Ch. 34: Sec. 34-1; Ch. 35: Sec. 35-3
CONTENT STANDARD D • Earth and Space Science	
• **Energy in the Earth system**	Ch. 3: Sec. 3-2; Ch. 4: Sec. 4-1

Correlation to National Science Education Standards

Life Science Content Standard	Chapter/Section/Page
• Geochemical cycles	Ch. 3: Sec. 3-3; Ch. 19: Sec. 19-1, p. 474
• Origin and evolution of the Earth system	Ch. 15: pp. 374-375; Ch. 17: Sec. 17-1, Sec. 17-2, Sec. 17-3
• Origin and evolution of the universe	
CONTENT STANDARD E • Science and Technology	
• Abilities of technological design	Ch. 13; Ch. 14: Sec. 14-3; Ch. 19: pp. 480-481; Ch. 24: Sec. 24-3
• Understandings about science and technology	Ch. 1: pp. 24-29; Ch. 3: pp. 66; Ch. 13; Ch. 24: Sec. 24-3; Ch. 32: p. 842
CONTENT STANDARD F • Science in Personal and Social Perspectives	
• Personal and community health	Ch. 19: pp. 479-481, 486-488; Ch. 20: pp. 501-502; Ch. 27: pp. 690-693; Ch. 35: Sec. 35-5; Ch. 37: pp. 949-950, 961-963; Ch. 38: Sec. 38-1; Ch. 40
• Population growth	Ch. 5: Sec. 5-1, Sec. 5-3
• Natural resources	Ch. 6: Sec. 6-2
• Natural and human-induced hazards	Ch. 6: Sec. 6-2, Sec. 6-3
• Environmental quality	Ch. 4; Ch. 6
• Science and technology in local, national, and global challenges	Ch. 3: pp. 66; Ch. 6: Sec. 6-4; Ch. 13; Ch. 14: Sec. 14-3; Ch. 19: pp. 480-481; Ch. 24: Sec. 24-3
CONTENT STANDARD G • History and Nature of Science	
• Science as a human endeavor	Ch. 1: pp. 5-6
• Nature of scientific knowledge	Ch. 1: pp. 3-5, 8-1, 14-15
• Historical perspectives	Ch. 1: pp. 11-13; Ch. 6: pp. 140-143, 145-146, 156-157; Ch. 7: pp. 169-171; Ch. 8: Sec. 8-12; Ch. 11: Sec. 11-1; Ch. 12: pp. 287-290, 292-293; Ch. 13: p. 319; Ch. 15: Sec. 15-1, Sec. 15-2; Ch. 17: pp. 424; Ch. 18: Sec. 18-1; Ch. 19: pp. 479-480; Ch. 24: pp. 624-625; Ch. 28: pp. 730-731; Ch. 32: pp. 838-839

Correlation to the Benchmarks for Literacy

Benchmarks for Science Literacy	Chapters
1 The Nature of Science	
1A The Scientific World View	1, 3, 5, 6, 11, 12, 15, 17; Appendix A
1B Scientific Inquiry	1, 2, 3, 11, 12, 13, 14, 15; all Inquiry Activities, Quick Labs, Real-World Labs, Design-an-Experiment Labs, and Exploration Labs in Ch. 1-40; Appendix A
1C The Scientific Enterprise	1, 2, 11, 12, 13, 14, 16, 18, Appendix B, Appendix D
2 The Nature of Mathematics	
2A Patterns and Relationships	3, 4, 5, 11, 12, Appendix E; all Analyzing Data Features
2B Mathematics, Science, and Technology	1, 13; Technology and Society: Ch. 3, 10, 18, 24, 26, 34, 36; Appendix C; all Analyzing Data Features
2C Mathematical Inquiry	2, 5, 6, 9, 10, 11, 12, 16; Quick Lab: Ch. 14, 17; Analyzing Data: Ch. 1, 12, 17, 30, 38; Problem Solving: Ch. 11, 22, 31; Exploration Lab: Ch. 1, 5, 15, 17, 27, 31
3 The Nature of Technology	
3A Technology and Science	3, 10, 12, 13, 14, 18, 20, 24, 26, 34, 36
3B Design and Systems	1, 6, 24; Labs: Ch. 2, 6, 8, 13, 20, 24, 28, 29, 34, 37, 38
3C Issues in Technology	5, 6, 12, 13, 14; Technology & Society: Ch. 3, 10, 11, 18, 24, 26, 34; Issues in Biology: Ch. 1, 5, 9, 13, 14, 16, 20, 25, 27, 32, 40
4 The Physical Setting	
4A The Universe	1
4B The Earth	2, 3, 4, 5, 6
4C Processes that Shape the Earth	3, 4, 6, 8, 9, 16, 17, 21, 22
4D Structure of Matter	2, 3, 7, 8, 9, 12, 13, 17, 18, 19
4E Energy Transformations	2, 3, 4, 5, 6, 7, 8, 9, 17, 19, 20, 21, 23, 25, 26, 27, 28, 29, 30, 31, 32, 33, 34, 37, 38
4F Motion	2, 7, 9, 10, 12, 13, 25, 26, 27, 28
4G Forces of Nature	2, 3, 4, 12, 13, 25
5 The Living Environment	
5A Diversity of Life	1, 3, 5, 18, 19, 20, 21, 22, 26, 27, 28, 29, 30, 31, 32, 33
5B Heredity	7, 11, 12, 14, 16, 17, 40
5C Cells	2, 7, 8, 9, 10, 11, 12, 19, 27, 37, 40
5D Interdependence of Life	3, 4, 5, 6, 21
5E Flow of Matter and Energy	2, 3, 4, 6, 7, 21
5F Evolution of Life	15, 16, 17, 18, 20, 22, 26, 28, 29, 30, 31, 32, 33
6 The Human Organism	
6A Human Identity	2, 11, 12, 14, 32
6B Human Development	10, 11, 32, 35, 39
6C Basic Functions	35, 36, 37, 38, 39, 40
6D Learning	32, 34, 35
6E Physical Health	9, 13, 14, 19, 20, 21, 36, 37, 38, 40; Issues in Biology: Ch. 16, 25
6F Mental Health	35, 37
7 Human Society	
7A Cultural Effects on Behavior	5, 6
7B Group Behavior	1, 6, 34, 35, 40

Correlation to the Benchmarks for Literacy

Benchmarks for Science Literacy		Chapters
7C	Social Change	5, 6, 17, 20, 28, 32, 40
7D	Social Trade-Offs	5, 6; Issues in Biology: Ch. 5, 15, 32, 40
7E	Political and Economic Systems	5, 6; Issues in Biology: Ch. 13, 14, 40
7F	Social Conflict	5, 6, 14, 15; Issues in Biology: Ch. 1, 5, 32, 40
7G	Global Interdependence	3, 6, 17, 19, 22, 32, 40
8	**The Designed World**	
8A	Agriculture	6, 11, 12, 13, 22, 23, 24, 25
8B	Materials and Manufacturing	1, 2, 6, 20, 21; Technology & Society: Ch. 22, 23, 24, 26, 36
8C	Energy Sources and Use	2, 3, 4, 6, 8, 9, 17
8D	Communication	34, 35
8E	Information Processing	1, 3, 6, 12, 35; all Analyzing Data Features; all Labs.
8F	Health Technology	2, 10, 13, 14, 19, 20, 26, 34, 35, 36, 37, 40
9	**The Mathematical World**	
9A	Numbers	1, 2, Appendix C; all Analyzing Data Features; all Labs
9B	Symbolic Relationships	1, 3, 4, 5, 6, 11, 17, 24, 25, 26, 33, 40
9C	Shapes	2, 7, 10, 12
9D	Uncertainty	2, 5, 11, 16, 19, 23, 26, 32, 39
9E	Reasoning	1, 2, 4, 6, 12, 15, 17, 21, 24, 26, 37; all Analyzing Data Features
10	**Historical Perspectives**	
10A	Displacing the Earth from the Center of the Universe	
10B	Uniting the Heavens and Earth	4
10C	Relating Matter & Energy and Time & Space	2, 8, 9, 18
10D	Extending Time	15, 16, 17
10E	Moving the Continents	15, 17, 18, 32
10F	Understanding Fire	2, 4, 6
10G	Splitting the Atom	2
10H	Explaining the Diversity of Life	3, 11, 15, 16, 17, 18, 32
10I	Discovering Germs	1, 5, 12, 19, 21, 27, 28, 40
10J	Harnessing Power	5, 6, 7, 8, 9
11	**Common Themes**	
11A	Systems	3, 4, 8, 9, 23, 35, 36, 38, 39, 40
11B	Models	2, 11, 12, 14, 15, 17, 33, 36, 37; Appendix A
11C	Constancy and Change	2, 3, 4, 5, 6, 7, 10, 11, 13, 15, 16, 17, 22, 24
11D	Scale	1, 2, 5, 7, 19; Appendix C
12	**Habits of the Mind**	
12A	Values and Attitudes	1, 13, 14, 18; all Inquiry Activities
12B	Computation and Estimation	1, 4, 6, 16, 24, 25, Appendix C; all Design-an-Experiment Labs
12C	Manipulation and Observation	1, 3, Appendix A; Appendix D; all Labs
12D	Communication Skills	2, 6, 8, 13, 14, 20, 24, 27, 28, 30, 32, 33, 34
12E	Critical-Response Skills	13, 14, 16, 20, 21, 27, 32, 34, 35, 40, Appendix A

Inquiry Skills Chart

Science Process Skills

The Prentice Hall *Biology* program provides comprehensive practice and assessment of science skills, with an emphasis on the process skills necessary for inquiry. The chart lists the skills covered in the program and cites page numbers where each skill is covered.

	Labs and Activities	Caption and Assessment Questions
Observing	81, 125, 200, 206, 215, 240, 242, 411, 466, 470, 521, 531, 543, 573, 601, 603, 608, 613, 627, 677, 695, 718, 739, 753, 798, 843, 861, 937, 965, 982, 991, 996, 1020, 1049	44, 132, 170, 302, 326, 347, 349, 382, 502, 526, 537, 780, 944
Inferring	18, 27, 29, 37, 54, 70, 81, 93, 125, 133, 151, 155, 179, 228, 235, 238, 262, 298, 340, 392, 403, 408, 411, 416, 437, 441, 463, 489, 508, 521, 531, 543, 550, 563, 565, 573, 578, 581, 592, 601, 620, 649, 662, 674, 675, 695, 718, 719, 753, 775, 791, 796, 815, 820, 835, 848, 855, 856, 861, 937, 961, 965, 970, 982, 1028	2, 4, 8, 12, 48, 58, 79, 84, 94, 107, 118, 123, 136, 164, 172, 188, 198, 208, 213, 214, 218, 244, 249, 258, 280, 284, 294, 323, 326, 338, 372, 377, 407, 409, 416, 430, 431, 435, 438, 444, 466, 476, 498, 502, 524, 532, 535, 546, 554, 559, 588, 598, 599, 602, 606, 608, 616, 626, 630, 638, 642, 652, 663, 675, 680, 685, 699, 706, 712, 721, 728, 730, 738, 742, 745, 750, 762, 769, 770, 774, 777, 778, 779, 781, 783, 787, 794, 800, 801, 802, 818, 825, 836, 868, 894, 905, 907, 914, 918, 925, 940, 963, 968, 972, 975, 978, 984, 994, 1030, 1033, 1041, 1047, 1052
Predicting	19, 42, 62, 81, 88, 181, 123, 133, 138, 151, 155, 161, 200, 228, 235, 340, 368, 387, 403, 408, 550, 565, 603, 608, 632, 759, 787, 848, 855, 935, 982, 990, 1023, 1049	22, 39, 43, 58, 80, 84, 99, 114, 125, 136, 143, 145, 158, 164, 187, 193, 198, 249, 258, 267, 302, 307, 316, 338, 348, 364, 381, 390, 414, 492, 524, 528, 576, 630, 652, 684, 712, 762, 805, 818, 918, 929, 930, 934, 940, 946, 956, 968, 1008, 1052
Measuring	603	32
Calculating	27, 133, 179, 298, 351, 387, 392, 416, 420, 437, 441, 787, 977	32, 73, 132, 154, 164, 198, 243, 258, 265, 286, 394, 811
Classifying	27, 62, 70, 88, 168, 411, 453, 462, 463, 494, 578, 593, 632, 656, 674, 766, 820, 920	63, 69, 84, 118, 124, 140, 173, 466, 492, 516, 524, 546, 555, 576, 680, 723, 742, 780, 794, 804, 826, 830, 831, 849, 868, 896, 1048
Using Tables and Graphs	79, 115, 118, 133, 151, 235, 387, 437, 453, 674, 707, 709, 739, 787, 825, 855	118, 132, 164, 364, 396, 401, 420, 546, 547, 631, 726, 818, 1031

Science Process Skills (continued)

	Labs and Activities	Caption and Assessment Questions
Using Models	53, 242, 255, 281, 313, 351, 361, 387, 441, 486, 662, 811, 865, 915, 937, 964, 965, 1023, 1039	58, 84, 127, 189, 243, 258, 316, 326, 404, 414, 444, 524, 794, 868, 940, 968, 994, 1002
Posing Questions	62, 463, 550, 1023, 1049	6, 364, 680, 731, 818, 825
Designing Experiments	54, 81, 113, 133, 161, 195, 215, 235, 335, 508, 521, 543, 603, 649, 675, 759, 825, 964, 990, 991	32, 58, 118, 164, 218, 249, 252, 258, 284, 414, 444, 492, 606, 630, 680, 742, 794, 868, 918, 94 968, 994
Formulating Hypotheses	19, 54, 70, 81, 118, 161, 235, 335, 379, 489, 531, 565, 573, 608, 632, 724, 796, 811, 942, 954, 960, 964, 965, 990	58, 84, 118, 146, 151, 159, 164, 218, 281, 338, 364, 390, 400, 414, 428, 502, 524,546, 572, 576, 594, 602, 612, 630, 671, 673, 680, 702, 712, 762 777, 789, 811, 827, 857, 868, 940, 994, 1052
Forming Operational Definitions	113, 168, 335, 462, 494, 656, 990	222, 794, 853
Controlling Variables	161, 990	32, 775, 808, 818, 822
Analyzing Data	42, 93, 100, 115, 118, 138, 161, 228, 255, 335, 368, 403, 411, 420, 441, 489, 521, 543, 603, 811, 835, 915, 1049	32, 131, 218, 286, 742, 918, 968
Drawing Conclusions	23, 27, 29, 54, 79, 81, 93, 115, 123, 125, 133, 161, 195, 206, 215, 220, 228, 255, 268, 281, 306, 313, 351, 361, 408, 411, 441, 446, 470, 486, 489, 508, 521, 543, 573, 601, 613, 620, 627, 637, 640, 649, 662, 615, 682, 707, 708, 718, 739, 744, 759, 775, 791, 815, 843, 848, 890, 905, 913, 915, 937, 954, 960, 965, 970, 977, 991, 1020, 1028, 1043, 1049	139, 213, 371, 385, 390, 422, 546, 565, 600, 646, 667, 680, 693, 707, 728, 733, 775, 808, 818, 822, 902, 947, 958, 989
Communicating Results	23, 281, 361	58, 293, 492, 529, 542
Evaluating and Revising	23, 42, 54, 81, 215, 235, 335, 441, 603, 865, 965, 1049	2, 32, 378, 390, 449, 524, 606

Critical Thinking Skills

	Labs and Activities	Caption and Assessment Questions
Comparing and Contrasting	79, 113, 179, 195, 240, 313, 335, 392, 463, 550, 563, 649, 675, 753, 759, 766, 791, 815, 843, 865, 930	10, 14, 27, 32, 39, 47, 84, 99, 118, 136, 142, 164, 172, 183, 189, 198, 203, 214, 224, 232, 238, 249, 258, 284, 286, 299, 312, 316, 329, 338, 353, 385, 404, 425, 430, 440, 444, 466, 476, 492, 502, 520, 526, 536, 539, 546, 576, 583, 630, 680, 707, 712, 724, 736, 738, 742, 762, 773, 784, 786, 794, 802, 806, 809, 837, 853, 856, 868, 903, 968, 999, 1038, 1040, 1052
Applying Concepts	37, 79, 113, 123, 179, 195, 238, 255, 268, 306, 392, 411, 463, 592, 613, 621, 905, 930, 935, 982, 991, 1023, 1043	5, 7, 15, 22, 28, 36, 41, 53, 65, 90, 91, 118, 127, 130, 136, 141, 146, 160, 164, 188, 210, 218, 231, 262, 266, 275, 278, 284, 308, 320, 329, 338, 344, 364, 373, 385, 390, 396, 406, 410, 414, 425, 429, 444, 450, 455, 461, 466, 474, 475, 480, 481, 487, 492, 524, 529, 532, 540, 542, 546, 562, 566, 568, 576, 606, 623, 630, 652, 663, 672, 680, 687, 712, 722, 724, 742, 758, 762, 781, 785, 794, 810, 814, 826, 837, 841, 864, 868, 909, 912, 918, 927, 929, 930, 936, 940, 968, 980, 984, 989, 994, 1002, 1013, 1022, 1033, 1036, 1039, 1044, 1052
Interpreting Graphics	37, 408, 575, 576, 577, 592, 620, 637, 724, 913, 935, 1043	11, 25, 32, 52, 53, 58, 68, 71, 75, 77, 78, 84, 125, 136, 148, 150, 174, 182, 188, 189, 207, 209, 213, 218, 221, 225, 230, 238, 248, 258, 273, 277, 284, 291, 292, 303, 309, 316, 325, 341, 345, 348, 350, 356, 359, 363, 370, 383, 384, 414, 422, 425, 438, 439, 450, 452, 457, 461, 491, 493, 496, 500, 523, 524, 525, 545, 546, 554, 555, 570, 576, 579, 586, 596, 606, 607, 608, 611, 626, 630, 651, 652, 653, 661, 666, 687, 692, 712, 713, 717, 718, 733, 741, 742, 745, 752, 761, 763, 768, 770, 776, 794, 801, 807, 824, 827, 832, 868, 940, 951, 952, 959, 973, 974, 976, 977, 981, 994, 998, 1010, 1015, 1019, 1021, 1037, 1052

Critical Thinking Skills (continued)

	Labs and Activities	Caption and Assessment Questions
Making Judgments	787, 843, 913	118, 164, 189, 205, 333, 338, 342, 360, 364, 390, 458, 466, 487, 492, 546, 1052
Problem Solving	23, 161, 390, 553, 825	58, 269, 274, 284, 321, 338, 390, 444, 492, 509, 606, 652, 762, 1052
Using Analogies	235, 905	45, 58, 80, 136, 143, 169, 198, 209, 218, 232, 312, 316, 326, 364, 496, 805, 918, 943, 953

Information Organizing Skills

	Chapters
Concept Maps	30, 48, 67, 116, 123, 134, 144, 162, 172, 274, 294, 336, 412, 441, 464, 490, 583, 621, 678, 710, 740, 792, 816, 844, 866, 916, 938, 955, 1033, 1050
Compare Contrast Tables	7, 15, 39, 172, 333, 360, 477, 522, 543, 570, 588, 599, 760, 789, 864
Venn Diagrams	48, 193, 214, 278, 299, 476, 896
Flowcharts	11, 12, 82, 99, 216, 282, 314, 326, 332, 347, 362, 520, 628, 692, 827, 900, 966, 989, 992
Cycle Diagrams	56, 256, 258, 786

Master Materials List

Item	*Quantity	Chapter
Adhesive notes: white, red, yellow	1 of each color	40-2 QL
Agar plate, sterile	1 2 3	16 Lab 19 IA 19 Lab
Alcohol, isopropyl	10 mL	32 Lab
Alcohol, 70%	200 mL	16 Lab
Algae culture, *Chlorella*	1	3 Lab
Aluminum foil	Strip	5 Lab, 8 IA, 26 Lab
Amylase solution, 1%	20 mL	37 Lab, 38 Lab
Annatto coloring (achiote seed extract)	2–5 drops	39 IA
Antibiotic paper disks	4	16 Lab
Ants, live from 3 different colonies		28 Lab
Ants, live from same species		28 Lab
Aphids, pea	20	3-2 QL
Apples (different varieties)	5	13 IA
Apron	1 per student	7 Lab, 10 QL, 31 Lab, 36 Lab, 38 Lab
Aquarium net	1	34 Lab
Aquarium water	2 liters	34 Lab
Aquarium with live fish	1	4 IA, 30-2 QL
Arthropod exoskeleton	2–3	29 IA
Arthropod specimens or pictures	4 or 5	28 IA
Artichoke	1	23 IA
Bacterial culture, liquid	1	16 Lab, 19 Lab
Balance	1	30 Lab, 31 Lab
Ball and socket joint	1	36 IA
Balloon, large, round	6 1	31-2 QL 37 Lab
Balloon, small, round	1	37 Lab
Balloons, red, yellow, blue	3 of each color	40-2 QL
Battery (6V) and wires with alligator clips	1	35 Lab

Item	*Quantity	Chapter
Beads	20 12	10 Lab 6-2 QL
Beads, pop, 4 colors	12 (4 of each color)	12 IA
Beads, red	33	16 IA
Beads, white	67	16 IA
Beaker, 50-mL	5	2 Lab
Beaker, 100-mL	1	5 Lab, 6 Lab
Beakers, 100-mL	3	17 Lab
Beaker, 150-mL	1	10 QL, 23 Lab
Beaker, 250-mL	1	17 QL, 17 Lab, 23 QL, 28 QL, 37 QL, 39 IA
Beaker, 400-mL	1	8 Lab
Beaker, 1000-mL	1	4 Lab, 6 QL, 16 IA, 30 Lab
Bean plant in flower	1	24 Lab
Beans, lima	10 2	15 IA, 21 IA 5 Lab
Beans, red	15	14-2 QL
Beans, seedlings in small pots or cups	2	3-2 QL
Beans, white	5	14 QL
Beetles, ladybird (ladybug)	4	3-2 QL
Bell	1	34IA
Benedict's solution	25 mL	38 Lab
Bird breast bone	1	31 Lab
Bird leg or bone	1	31 Lab
Biuret reagent	50 mL	32 Lab
Bleach	50 mL	36-2 QL
Blocks	20	1-IA
Blocks, wooden	4	28-3 QL
Blood, animal	1–3 drops	7 Lab
Bologna, slice	1/2 slice	29 Lab
Bone, bird breastbone	1	31 Lab
Bone, bird leg	1	31 Lab
Bone, bird (cut section)	1	31 Lab
Bone, mammal (cut section)	1	31 Lab
Bottle, plastic, 1L	1	37 Lab

Key: **IA**=Inquiry activity **QL**=Quick lab **Lab**=End-of-Chapter Lab

*=Quantities per group

Item	*Quantity	Chapter
Box, clear plastic	1	34 Lab
Brassica plant in flower	1	24 Lab
Bread, moldy	1 piece	21-2 QL
Brine shrimp	1	29 Lab
Broccoli	1	15-3 QL, 15 Lab
Bromthymol blue solution	2–5 drops	8 Lab, 9-2 QL
Brussels sprouts	1	15-3 QL, 15 Lab
Butter	1 tablespoon	2 IA
Cabbage	1	15-3 QL, 15 Lab
Cabbage, Chinese, chopped	1 handful	9 Lab
Calcium chloride solution, concentrated	50 mL	24 Lab
Calculator	1	11-2 QL, 31 Lab, 37 Lab
Candle	1	9 IA
Cardboard box	1	25-2 QL
Cardboard box dividers	2	25-2 QL
Cardboard tubes	2	38-2 QL
Carmine dye	a few granules	20-2 QL
Cauliflower	1	15-3 QL, 15 Lab
Celery, raw with leaves	3 stalks	23-4 QL
Cellophane, blue, red, and green	1 sheet of each	8 Lab
Chicken neck, disinfected	1	33 IA
Chicken wing, raw bleached	1	36-2 QL
Chlorella culture	1 drop	20-2 QL
Chlorophyll solution	T	8-2 QL
Clam, live	1	29-2 QL
Coin	1	15 Lab
Coleus plant, large or 4 branches	1	25 Lab
Container, air tight	2	21 Lab
Container, plastic, small	1	29-2 QL
Cotton, balls	1	20 Lab
Cotton swab	1	23-4 QL

Item	*Quantity	Chapter
Cotton swabs, sterile	3	19 Lab
Coverslips	1 box per class	4 Lab, 5 Lab, 7 Lab, 20 IA, 20-2 QL, 20 Lab, 21 Lab, 22-3 QL, 22 Lab, 24-2 QL 24 Lab, 32 Lab
Craft materials (clay, cardboard, etc.)	See investigation.	19-3 QL
Crayfish, live	1	21, Lab, 22-3 Lab, 28 IA, 29-2 QL, 29 Lab
Crickets, live	1	28-3 QL
Cups, paper	1 4	17-1 QL 4-1 QL
Cups, paper (small)	3	6-2 QL
Cups, paper (medium)	1 12 2	6-2 QL 25 Lab 5-2 QL
Cups, paper (large)	1	6-2 QL
Cups, plastic	2	14-2 QL, 30-2 QL, 36 Lab, 37-2 QL, 38-2 QL
Dialysis tubing, 1 inch diameter	15 cm	36 Lab
Dissecting microscope	1	27-1 QL, 27-3 QL, 39-4 QL
Dissecting probe	1	24 Lab, 31 Lab, 33 IA
Dissecting tray	1	27 Lab,
Dowels, wooden	1	19 Lab
Dropper pipette	1 2 4	1 Lab, 2 Lab, 20 IA, 22-3 QL, 22 Lab, 24-2 QL, 24 Lab, 27-3 QL, 27 Lab, 28-4 QL, 30-2 QL, 32 Lab, 36 Lab, 3 Lab, 5 Lab, 20-2 QL, 20 Lab, 21 Lab, 26 Lab, 29 Lab, 2-2 QL, 4 Lab, 20 Lab
Earthworm, live	1	27-3 QL
Earthworm, live or photo	1	27-1 QL, 28 IA, 29 Lab

Key: **IA**=Inquiry activity **QL**=Quick lab **Lab**=End-of-Chapter Lab *=Quantities per group

Master Materials List *(continued)*

Item	*Quantity	Chapter
Ecosystem	1	4 IA
Egg, hard boiled and peeled	2	10-2 QL
Eggs, instant fish kit	1	1-QL
Egg, raw	1	31 IA, 37 Lab
Egg white, cooked	1	38 Lab
Egg yolk, cooked	1	29 Lab
Euglena culture, concentrated	1	8 IA
Faucet, single-lever	1	36 IA
Fern plant, living	1	22 IA, 22 Lab
Fern frond with sori	1	22-3 QL
Fibers, various	10	32 Lab
Field guide, ants	1	28 Lab
Filter paper, circles	2	30 Lab
Filter paper, disks		2 Lab, 6 Lab, 36 Lab
Filter paper, square	1	36 Lab
Fish, betta, male	1	34 Lab
Fish, dissected	1	30 IA
Fish food		30-2 QL
Fish, fresh water	5 grams	30 Lab
Fish, live	1	30-2 QL
Fish, male betta	1	34 Lab
Fish, salt-water	5 grams	30 Lab
Flashlight	1	9 IA
Flower	1	24-2 QL
Flowering plant, living	1	22 IA
Flower pot containing soil	1	25 QL
Fluorescein, dilute or Glo Germ oil		40 IA
Food coloring, any color	1	23-4 QL, 29-2 QL, 30-2 QL
Food coloring, blue	10 drops	10-1 QL
Forceps	1	2 Lab, 7 Lab, 8 Lab, 16 Lab, 17 Lab, 20 Lab, 21 Lab, 22 Lab, 24-2 QL, 24 Lab, 32 Lab, 36-2 QL
Forceps, long	1	17 Lab
Frog, early embryos	2–4	39-4 QL
Frog egg	2–4	31 IA
Fruit	5 different kinds	18 IA
Funnels	2	30 Lab
Garlic, sliced or crushed		9 Lab
Glass rod	1 4	30 Lab 32 Lab
Gloves, heat resistant	1 per student	38 Lab
Glue		10 Lab, 19-3 QL, 19 Lab
Graduated cylinder, 10-ml	1	5 Lab, 9 QL, 30 Lab,
Graduated cylinder, 25-mL	1 3	2 Lab, 2QL 17 Lab
Graduated cylinder, 50-mL	1	3 Lab, 36 Lab
Graduated cylinder, 100-mL	1	5 Lab, 6 Lab
Graduated cylinder, 250-mL	1	31 Lab
Grass clippings	1 handful	4 Lab
Grasshopper, live or photo	1	28 IA
Hand lens	1	1 IA, 6 Lab, 16 IA, 17 IA, 19 Lab, 22 IA, 22-3 QL, 22 Lab, 28 Lab, 30 IA, 33 IA
Hinge	1	36 IA
Hot plate	1	37 Lab
Hydra culture	1	29 Lab
Hydra, brown	1	26 Lab
Hydra, green	1	26 Lab
Hydrochloric acid solution, 0.2%	20 mL	38 Lab
Hydrogen peroxide solution, 1%	100 mL	2 Lab
Ice bath	1	2 Lab
Incubator	1 per class	19 Lab
Index cards, white unruled	1 3 25	7-2 QL, 35 Lab 33 QL 11 Lab

Key: **IA**=Inquiry activity **QL**=Quick lab **Lab**=End-of-Chapter Lab *=Quantities per group

Item	*Quantity	Chapter
Ink, India	1 drop	23 Lab
Iodine solution	1 or 2 drops 25 mL	7 Lab 8 Lab
Jars, wide mouth, large	2	3-2 QL
Juice, apple	10 mL	2-2 QL
Juice, lemon	10 mL	2-2QL
Lamp, desk, 40 watt	1	27 Lab
Lancelet, preserved	11	30 IA
Leaves, dried	1 handful	4 Lab
Leaves, freshly collected	5-10	18 IA, 18 Lab
Len, concave	1	35 Lab
Lens, convex	2	35 Lab
Light bulb (6 Volt) and socket	1	35 Lab
Light, ultra violet (battery-operated)	1	40 IA
Litmus paper, blue		30 Lab
Liver, raw & puree	1 oz	2 Lab
Mammal bone	1	31 Lab
Marker, felt tip	1	11 Lab
Measuring spoons 1.25-mL (1/4 teaspoon)	1	9 Lab
Meter stick	1	35 Lab
Methyl cellulose	1	20 IA
Microorganisms chart or book	1	4 Lab
Microscope, compound	1	1 Lab, 4 Lab, 5 Lab, 7 IA, 7 Lab, 10 IA, 10 Lab, 20-2 QL, 20 IA, 20 Lab, 21-2 QL, 21 Lab, 22-3 QL, 22 Lab, 24-2 QL, 32 Lab
Microscope, dissecting	1	27-3 QL, 27 Lab, 28 Lab, 29 Lab
Millipede, live or photo	1	28IA
Mirror, small		34 Lab
Modeling clay	1 pkg.	19 Lab, 26-1 QL, 33 Lab, 35 Lab

Item	*Quantity	Chapter
Moss plant, living	1	22 IA, 22 Lab
Mousetraps (plastic)	3	35-3 QL
Mushroom	1	21 IA
Newspaper	1	1 Lab
Noisemaker (bell or clicker)	1	34 IA
Oil, vegetable	20 mL	39 IA
Onion, raw	1	7 Lab, 23 IA
Onion, red	1	7 Lab
Organisms, diverse specimens		26IA
Packing tape		35-3 QL
Paintbrush, small	1	24 Lab
Paper bag, brown	1	22-3 QL
Paper, construction (assorted colors)	2–4 sheets	16-2 QL, 19 Lab, 34 Lab, 39 Lab
Paper, construction-black	1 sheet	8 Lab, 19 Lab, 27 IA, 27 Lab, 35 Lab
Paper, construction-green, gray, purple, red, tan, and yellow	1 sheet of each color	12 Lab
Paper, graph	1 sheet	51A, 14 Lab, 15 IA, 17-1 QL
Paper, loose leaf	1–2 sheets	32-3 QL, 34-2 QL
Paper towels		2 QL, 7 Lab, 8 Lab, 10-1 QL,13 Lab, 21 Lab, 23 Lab, 27 Lab, 30 Lab, 36-2 QL, 36 Lab, 38-2 QL
Paper, white unlined	2 sheets	17-1 QL
Paramecium caudatum culture	1 per class	20-2 QL, 20 Lab
Peanuts in the shell	1	22-3 QL
Pencils, colored	2	4 Lab, 8-2 QL, 14 Lab, 35 IA
Pencils, glass marking	1	2 IA, 2 Lab, 3 Lab, 4 Lab 6 Lab, 8 Lab, 9 QL, 13 Lab, 16 Lab, 19 IA, 19 Lab, 26 Lab, 30 Lab, 32 Lab, 38 Lab
Pencil with eraser	1	27 IA

Key: IA=Inquiry activity **QL**=Quick lab **Lab**=End-of-Chapter Lab *=Quantities per group

Master Materials List *(continued)*

Item	*Quantity	Chapter
Pepsin solution, 1%	20 mL	38 Lab
Petri dish	1	2 Lab, 23 Lab, 27 Lab, 28 Lab, 29 Lab
Petri dishes	2 3 4 5	6 Lab 28 Lab 13 Lab 8 Lab
Petroleum jelly		23-4 QL
pH paper		2-2 QL, 6 Lab, 9 Lab
Phenolphthalein indicator solution	20 mL	36 Lab
Photo easels (cardboard)	2	35 Lab
Pins, dissecting	1	40-2 QL
Pipe cleaners	1 pkg. per class	10 Lab, 19 Lab
Planarian	1	27 IA, 27-1 QL, 29 Lab, 28 IA
Plants, desert (cactus or succulents)	2-4 per class	25 IA
Plants, rainforest (African violet)	2-4 per class	25 IA
Plant (small) in dark, opaque container	1	9 IA
Plastic box, clear	1	34 Lab
Plastic foam balls	1	19 Lab
Plastic or paper plate	1	31 IA
Plastic sandwich bags, resealable,	2	9 Lab
Pollen nutrient solution	20 mL	24 Lab
Pollen nutrient solution without Ca	20 mL	24 Lab
Potato chip, baked	1 chip	38 IA
Potato chip, regular	1 chip	38 IA
Potato, cooked	1/2	38 Lab
Potato, raw	1	23 IA
Pots, plant	2	3-2 QL, 13 Lab
Pot with soil	1	25-2 QL
Potted plant	1	8 Lab
Prepared slide, crossed fibers	1	1 Lab
Probe, blunt metal	1	29 Lab
Pump, balloon (hand powered)	1	31-2 QL
Razor blade, single-edged or scalpel	1	27-1 QL, 36-2 QL, 38 Lab
Red chili pepper, chopped		9 Lab
Rooting compound (auxin powder)		25 Lab
Rubber bands	2 1	3-2 QL 27 IA
Rubber cement		32 Lab
Rubber stopper, no hole	6	2 IA, 38 Lab
Rubber stopper, one hole #3	1	2 IA, 37 Lab
Ruler, metric (15 cm)	1	16-2 QL, 16 Lab
Ruler, metric (30cm)	1	10-1 QL, 12 Lab, 16 Lab, 19-3 QL, 19 Lab, 23-4 QL, 23 Lab, 25 Lab, 27 Lab, 34-2 QL, 35-3 QL, 36 Lab, 37 Lab, 38-2 QL, 38 Lab
Ruler, transparent, 15 cm, plastic	1	1 Lab, 17 IA
Rutabaga	1	15-3 QL, 15 Lab
Safety goggles	1 pair per student	7 Lab, 8 Lab, 31 Lab, 35-3 QL, 36 Lab, 38 Lab
Sand	2 cups	4-1 QL, 6-2 QL
Salt, non-iodized	2.5 mL (1/2 teaspoon)	9 Lab
Salt solution 25 %	1–5 drops	7 Lab
Salt solution, 0.5 %	10 mL	20 Lab
Salt solution, 1.0 %	10 mL	20 Lab
Scalpel	1	2-2 QL, 7 Lab, 10-1 QL, 18 IA, 21 Lab, 22-3 QL, 23-4 QL, 24-2 QL, 25 Lab, 36-2 QL, 38 Lab

Key: **IA**=Inquiry activity **QL**=Quick lab **Lab**=End-of-Chapter Lab *=Quantities per group

Item	*Quantity	Chapter
Scissors	1	1 Lab, 8 Lab, 10 Lab, 11 Lab, 12 Lab, 13 QL, 14 Lab,16-2 QL, 19-3 QL, 19 Lab, 21 Lab, 25-2 QL, 30 Lab, 33 Lab, 34-2 QL, 35-3 QL, 36-2 QL, 36 Lab, 37 Lab, 38-2 QL, 38 Lab
Screening, flexible	2 pieces	3-2 QL
Seeds, apple or orange	1	24 IA
Seeds, burr type	1	24 IA
Seeds, bean	20 4 10 100	5-2 QL 23 Lab, 25-2 QL 15 IA, 21 Lab 17 Lab
Seeds, corn	10	21 Lab
Seeds dandelion	1	24 IA
Seeds, gymnosperm cones	1	24 IA
Seeds, irradiated	10	13 Lab
Seeds, maple	1	24 IA
Seeds, non-irradiated	10	13 Lab
Seeds, peas	200	17 Lab
Seeds, radish or mustard	100	6 Lab
Seeds, rice	20	4-1 QL
Seeds, rye	10	4-1 QL
Seeds, wheat	10	21 Lab
Seltzer tablet	1	37-3 QL
Shale billets from Green River, CO	1	17 IA
Shells, mollusk	2–3	29 IA
Shower head arm mount	1	36 IA
Silver nitrate solution	10 mL	30 Lab
Slides, microscope, depression	1	39 IA
Slides, microscope, glass	1 box per class	1 Lab, 4 Lab, 7 Lab, 20 IA, 20-2 QL, 20 Lab, 21-2 QL, 21 Lab, 22-2 QL, 22 Lab, 24-2 QL, 24 Lab, 27 Lab, 32 Lab

Item	*Quantity	Chapter
Slides, prepared, bacteria	1	1 Lab, 7 IA
Slide, prepared, bacteria *Spirillum volutans*	1	1 Lab
Slide, prepared, crossed fibers	1	1 Lab
Slide, prepared, frog embryos	1	39-4 QL
Slide, prepared, frog muscle	1	10 IA
Slide, prepared, grass leaf	1	10 IA
Slide, prepared, human cheek cells	1	7 Lab
Slide, prepared, human muscle	1	10 IA
Slide, prepared, leaf cross section	1	7 IA
Slide, prepared, nerve cells	1	7 IA
Slide, prepared, onion root tip	1	10 Lab
Slide, prepared, paramecium	1	7IA
Slide, prepared, root cross section	1	1 Lab
Slide, prepared, stem cross section	1	1 Lab, 7 IA
Slide, prepared, tree leaf, whole mount	1	10 IA
Snail, live, land	1	27 Lab
Soap, liquid	1 mL	2 IA
Sodium bicarbonate (baking soda)	10 mL	30 Lab, 36 Lab
Soil, potting	1 large bag per class	4-1 QL, 4 Lab, 5-2 QL, 13 Lab, 25 Lab
Soy sauce	10 mL	2 IA
Specimens for classification	1 set	18 Lab
Spectroscope	1	8-2 QL
Spider, live	1	28 IA
Spoon, tea	1	10-1 QL, 17 Lab
Stain, aniline blue	1–2 drops	21 Lab
Stain, methylene blue	1	5 Lab
Starch	10 mL	2-2 QL
Starfish, live or photo	1	28IA

Key: IA=Inquiry activity **QL**=Quick lab **Lab**=End-of-Chapter Lab

*=Quantities per group

Master Materials List *(continued)*

Item	*Quantity	Chapter
Sticks, ice cream	2–4	34 Lab
Stopper	2	3 Lab
Stop watch	1	37 IA
Straw, large, clear plastic	1	27-3 QL
Straws, small	2	9-2 QL
Straw, soda	2	33 Lab
Strep A diagnostic kit	1	40 Lab
String	30 cm	8 Lab, 30 Lab, 35-3 QL
Sugar	10 grams	2 IA
Sulfuric acid, dilute (0.1 N)	10 mL	6 Lab
Tape, duct		29 Lab, 35-3 QL
Tape, masking		6-2 QL, 14-2 QL, 19 IA, 25-2 QL, 33 Lab, 31-2 QL
Tape, measuring	1	
Tape, packing		35-3 QL
Tape, transparent		8 Lab, 10 Lab, 11 Lab, 12 Lab, 13-2 QL, 16-2 QL, 16 Lab, 19-3 QL, 19 Lab, 21-2 QL, 26 Lab, 27 IA, 30 Lab, 34 Lab, 35 Lab
Teeth, mammal (incisors, canines, molars)	1-5	32 IA
Telephone book page	1	11-2 QL
Terrarium	1	4 IA, 28-3 QL
Test tube (150 mm)	8	2 IA, 5 Lab, 8 Lab, 9-3 QL
Test tubes	4	30 Lab
Test-tubes, large, with stoppers	2	3Lab, 39 IA 8 Lab, 38 lab, 39 IA
Test tubes, small	2 4	9-2 QL 32 Lab
Test-tubes, small, with screw caps	8	8 IA, 26 Lab
Test-tube holder	1	38 Lab
Test-tube rack	1	3 lab, 5 Lab, 8 IA, 26 Lab, 32 Lab, 38 Lab
Thermometer	3 1	2 Lab 9 Lab, 19 Lab
Tissues, facial	1 box per class	32 Lab
Tofu	1 teaspoon	2 IA
Toothpicks	1 box per class	19 Lab, 20-2 QL, IA, 23 Lab, 25 Lab, 33 Lab, 40-2 QL
Trisodium phosphate 10% solution	10 mL	3 Lab
Tub, plastic	2	2 Lab
Vinegar	100 mL	30 Lab
Watch, or clock with a second hand	1	2 Lab, 9-2 QL, 16-2 QL, 17 Lab, 20 Lab, 27 Lab, 28 Lab, 31-2 QL, 34 Lab, 37 IA
Watch glass	1	29 Lab
Water bath, boiling water	1 per class	38 Lab
Water bath, hot	1	32 Lab
Water bath, warm	1 per class	2 Lab
Water, distilled	600 mL 50 mL	30 Lab 7 Lab
Water, non-chlorinated (aged)	600 mL 1 gallon 2–5 drops	4 Lab 30-2 QL 27-3 QL
Water, pond	50 mL 1–2 drops	3 Lab, 26 Lab 20 IA
Water, spring	10 mL–50mL	8 IA, 27 IA, 29-2 QL
Water, sterile	10 mL	40 Lab
Yarn, any color	30 cm	10 Lab
Yarn, 2 shades of red, 2 shades of green	80 cm of each color	11 Lab

Key: **IA**=Inquiry activity **QL**=Quick lab **Lab**=End-of-Chapter Lab

*=Quantities per group

Prentice Hall Biology

Kenneth R. Miller, Ph.D.
Professor of Biology
Brown University
Providence, Rhode Island

Joseph Levine, Ph.D.
Science Writer and Producer
Concord, Massachusetts

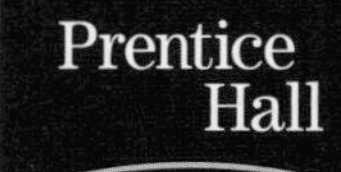

Upper Saddle River, New Jersey
Glenview, Illinois
Needham, Massachusetts

Prentice Hall Biology

Print Components

Student Edition
Teacher's Edition
Laboratory Manual A
Laboratory Manual A,
 Annotated Teacher's Edition
Laboratory Manual B
Laboratory Manual B,
 Annotated Teacher's Edition
Teaching Resources
Guided Reading and Study Workbook
Cuaderno de orientación al estudio y
 a la lectura
Guided Reading and Study Workbook,
 Annotated Teacher's Edition
Chapter Tests: Levels A and B
Pruebas de los capítulos
Computer Test Bank
Biotechnology Manual
Prentice Hall Assessment System
Laboratory Assessment With
 Scoring Guide
Issues and Decision Making

Technology

Presentation Assistant Plus
 Teaching Transparencies Package
 Prentice Hall Presentation Pro CD-ROM
Biology iText CD-ROM
Biology iText Web Site
BioDetectives Videotapes With BioDetectives:
 Investigations in Forensics
Prentice Hall Web Site With *Science News*®
Resource Pro
Computer Test Bank CD-ROM
ABC Videotapes

Ackowledgments appear on page 1110, which constitutes an extension of this copyright page.

Copyright © 2002 by Pearson Education, Inc., Upper Saddle River, New Jersey 07458.
All rights reserved. Printed in the United States of America. This publication is protected by copyright, and permission should be obtained from the publisher prior to any prohibited reproduction, storage in a retrieval system, or transmission in any form or by any means, electronic, mechanical, photocopying, recording, or likewise. For information regarding permission(s), write to: Rights and Permissions Department.

Discovery Channel School™ is a registered trademark of Discovery Communications, Inc. DBA The Discovery Channel.

Science News® is a registered trademark of Science Services, Inc.

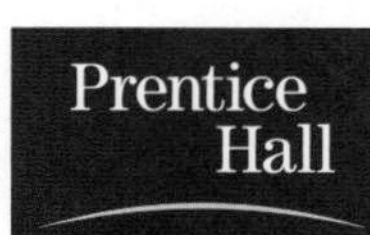

ISBN 0-13-050730-X
4 5 6 7 8 9 10 05 04 03 02 01

About the Authors

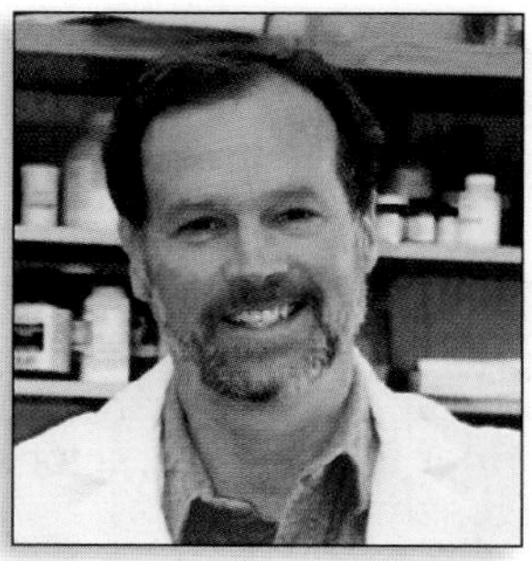

Kenneth R. Miller grew up in Rahway, New Jersey, attended the local public schools, and graduated from Rahway High School in 1966. Miller attended Brown University on a scholarship and graduated with honors. He was awarded a National Defense Education Act fellowship for graduate study, and earned his Ph. D. in Biology at the University of Colorado. Miller is Professor of Biology at Brown University in Providence, Rhode Island, where he teaches courses in general biology and cell biology.

Miller's research specialty is the structure of biological membranes. He has published more than 70 research papers in journals such as *CELL, Nature,* and *Scientific American*. In 1999, he wrote the popular trade book *Finding Darwin's God.*

Miller lives with his wife, Jody, on a small farm in Rehoboth, Massachusetts. He is the father of two daughters, one of whom is a wildlife biologist. He swims competitively in the masters' swimming program and umpires high school and collegiate softball.

Joseph S. Levine was born in Mount Vernon, New York, where he attended public schools. He earned a B.S. in Biology at Tufts University, a master's degree from the Boston University Marine Program, and a Ph.D. at Harvard University. His research has been published in scientific journals ranging from *Science* to *Scientific American*, and in several academic books. He taught introductory biology, marine ecology, and neurobiology for six years at Boston College.

After receiving a Macy Fellowship in Science Broadcast Journalism at WGBH-TV, Levine dedicated himself to improving public understanding of science. His popular scientific writing has appeared in five trade books and in magazines such as *Smithsonian*, *GEO*, and *Natural History*. He has produced science features for National Public Radio and has designed exhibit programs for state aquarium projects in Texas, New Jersey, and Florida.

Since 1987, Levine has served as scientific advisor at WGBH, where he worked on *NOVA* programs and on projects including the film *Cocos: Island of Sharks* and the series *The Secret of Life*. Most recently, he served as Science Editor for *The Evolution Project*.

Levine and his family live in Concord, Massachusetts, a short distance from Thoreau's Walden Pond.

Consultants

Reading Consultant

Bonnie Armbruster, Ph.D.
Department of Curriculum and Instruction
University of Illinois
Champaign, IL

Safety Consultant

Douglas Mandt
Lab Safety Consultant
Edgewood, WA

Lab Activity Consultant

Paul C. Johnson
University of New Hampshire
Durham, NH

Activity Writers

Kathy Laney
Hicksvillle HS
Hicksville, OH

Neo/SCI
Rochester, NY

Patsye Peebles
Louisiana State University Lab School
Baton Rouge, LA

Herbert L. Saxon, Ed.D.
Ball State University
Muncie, IN

Content Reviewers

J. David Archibald, Ph.D.
Professor of Biology
Curator of Mammals
San Diego State University
San Diego, CA

David M. Armstrong
Professor
Environmental, Population, and Organismic Biology
University of Colorado
Boulder, CO

Katharine Atkinson
Associate Professor of Cell Biology
Department of Cell Biology and Neuroscience
University of California
Riverside, CA

David L. Brautigan
Director, Center for Cell Signaling
Professor, Microbiology and Medicine (Endocrinology)
University of Virginia
Charlottesville, VA

Elizabeth Coolidge-Stolz, MD
Medical Writer
North Reading, MA

Dr. Darleen A. DeMason
Botany and Plant Sciences
University of California, Riverside
Riverside, CA

Elizabeth De Stasio
Raymond H. Herzog
Professor of Science and Associate Professor of Biology
Lawrence University
Appleton, WI

Betsey Dyer
Professor of Biology
Wheaton College
Norton, MA

Milton Fingerman
Professor of Biology
Department of Ecology and Evolutionary Biology
Tulane University
New Orleans, LA

Katherine Glew
Assistant Professor
University of Puget Sound
Tacoma, WA

Deborah L. Gumucio, Ph.D.
Associate Professor
Department of Cell and Developmental Biology
University of Michigan Medical School
Ann Arbor, MI

Paul R. Haberstroh, Ph.D.
Assistant Professor of Chemical Oceanography
Department of Marine Science
University of Hawaii at Hilo
Hilo, HI

Evan B. Hazard, Ph.D.
Professor Emeritus of Biology
Bemidji State University
Bemidji, MN

Donald C. Jackson
Professor of Physiology
Brown University
Providence, RI

Jeremiah N. Jarrett
Assistant Professor
Department of Biological Sciences
Central Connecticut State University
New Britain, CT

Kirk Johnson
Curator of Paleontology
Denver Museum of Nature and Science
Denver, CO

Ted Johnson, Ph.D.
Professor of Biology
St. Olaf College
Northfield, MN

Joe Leverich, Ph.D.
Professor
Biology Department
St. Louis University
St. Louis, MO

Martin K. Nickels, Ph.D.
Professor of Physical Anthropology
Illinois State University
Normal, IL

Gerald P. Sanders, Sr.
Biology Publishing Consultant
Former Biology Instructor at Grossmont College
El Cajon, CA

Ronald L. Sass, Ph.D.
Professor of Biology, Chemistry, and Education
Department of Ecology and Evolutionary Biology
Rice University
Houston, TX

David Scholnick
Assistant Professor
Eckerd College
St. Petersburg, FL

Dr. Dilbagh Singh
Professor of Biology
Blackburn College
Carlinville, IL

Bruce A. Wilcox
Affiliate Faculty
University of Hawaii
Kailua, HI

Alan C. Yen
Research Fellow
Harvard University
Cambridge, MA

Bruce A. Young
Professor of Biology
Department of Biology
Lafayette College
Easton, PA

Edward J. Zalisko
Professor of Biology
Illinois Professor of the Year, 2000
Blackburn College
Carlinville, IL

High School Reviewers and Contributing Writers

John Bartsch
Amsterdam High School (retired)
Amsterdam, NY

Myron E. Blosser
Harrisonburg High School
Harrisonburg, VA

James Boal
Natrona County High School
Casper, WY

Jan Bowersox
Nathan Hale High School
Seattle, WA

LouEllen Parker Brademan
Potomac Senior High School
Dumfries, VA

Heidi Busa
Marcellus High School
Marcellus, NY

Dr. Charles E. Campbell
Burbank High School
Burbank, CA

Robert Campbell
Wilson Classical High School
Long Beach, CA

Mary P. Colvard
Cobleskill-Richmondville High School
Cobleskill, NY

Don Morris Curry
Silverado High School
Las Vegas, NV

Liz Dann
Phoenix Country Day School
Paradise Valley, AZ

Bob Demmink
East Kentwood High School
Kentwood, MI

Eloise Farmer
Torrington High School
Torrington, CT

Steve Ferguson
Lee's Summit High School
Lee's Summit, MO

Diedre Galvin
Ridgewood High School
Ridgewood, NJ

Dennis Glasgow
Little Rock School District
Little Rock, AR

Ruth Gleicher
Niles West High School
Skokie, IL

John E. Gonzales
Temescal Canyon High School
Lake Elsinore, CA

Dick Jordan
Timberline High School
Boise, ID

Marion LaFemina
Ridgewood High School
Ridgewood, NJ

Janice Lagatol
Fort Lee High School
Fort Lee, NJ

Sue Madden
Chippewa Valley High School
Clinton Township, MI

Gregory W. McCurdy
Salem High School
Salem, IN

Lynne M. McElhaney
LeFlore High School
Mobile, AL

Tamsen Knowlton Meyer
Boulder High School
Boulder, CO

Francis K. Mustapha
Snider High School
Fort Wayne, IN

Duane Nichols
Alhambra High School
Alhambra, CA

Joe E. Nunley, Jr.
Riverdale High School
Murfreesboro, TN

Richard K. Orgeron
Carencro High School
Lafayette, LA

Tracy Rader
Fulton Jr. High School
Indianapolis, IN

Dr. Thomas P. Rooney
Father Judge High School
Philadelphia, PA

Linda S. Samuels
Dana Hall School
Wellesley, MA

Jorge E. Sanchez
Green Valley High School
Henderson, NV

Sheila Smith
Terry High School
Terry, MS

Brenda Waldon
Clayton County Public Schools
Morrow, GA

Audra J. Williams
Sprayberry High School
Marietta, GA

Activity Testers

Diane Clark
Monticello High School
Charlottesville, VA

Lucy M. Fern
Ridgewood High School
Ridgewood, NJ

Laine Gurley, Ph.D.
Rolling Meadows High School
Rolling Meadows, IL

Patricia Anne Johnson
Ridgewood High School
Ridgewood, NJ

Wade Mercer
Fairhill School
Dallas, TX

Dwight Taylor
Goldenview Middle School
Anchorage, AK

Contents

UNIT 4 Genetics 260–365

UNIT 5 Evolution 366–467

UNIT 7 Plants 548–653

UNIT 8 Invertebrates 654–763

UNIT 9 Chordates 764–887

UNIT 10 The Human Body 888-1053

Labs and Activities

Inquiry Activity

Opportunities for exploration and inquiry before reading

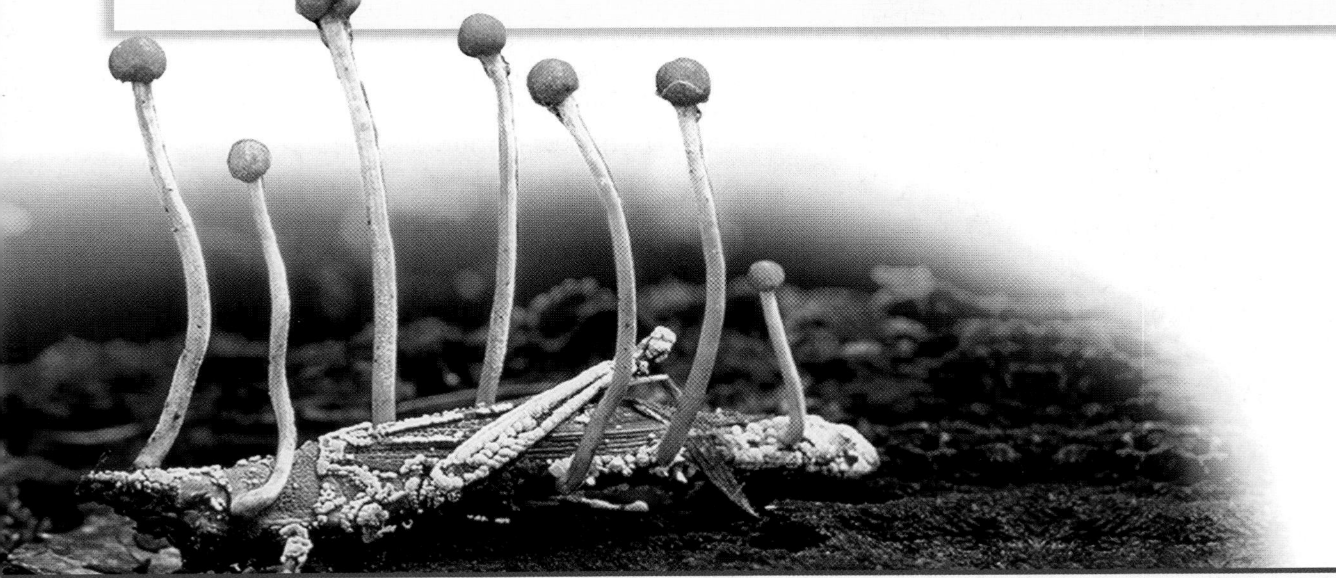

Quick Lab

Activities that reinforce key biological concepts

Real-World Lab

Labs that demonstrate everyday applications of biological concepts

Design an Experiment

Labs that build key science skills

Exploration

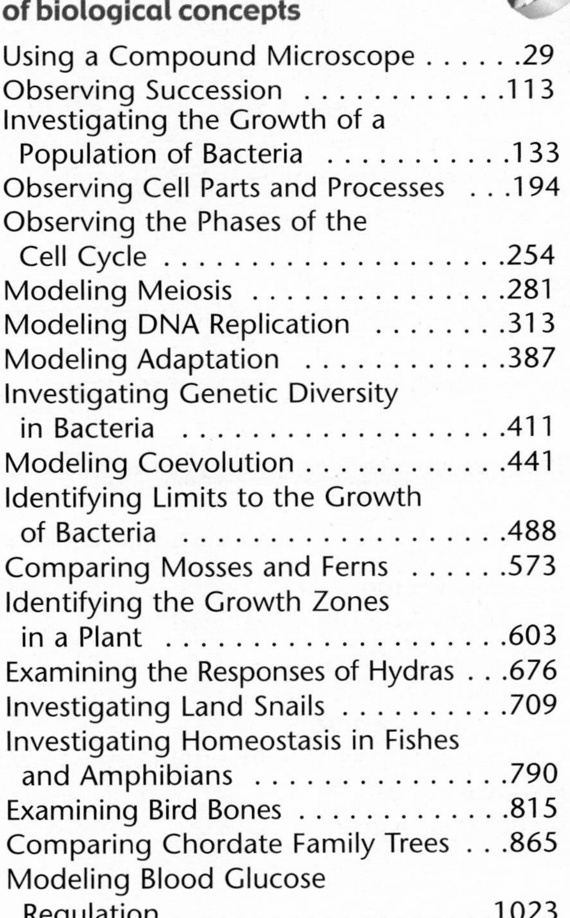

Labs that provide in-depth exploration of biological concepts

Analyzing Data

Activities that provide students opportunities to interpret data and draw conclusions

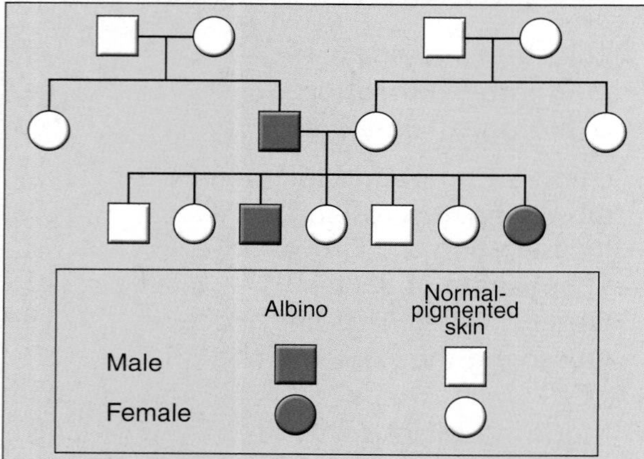

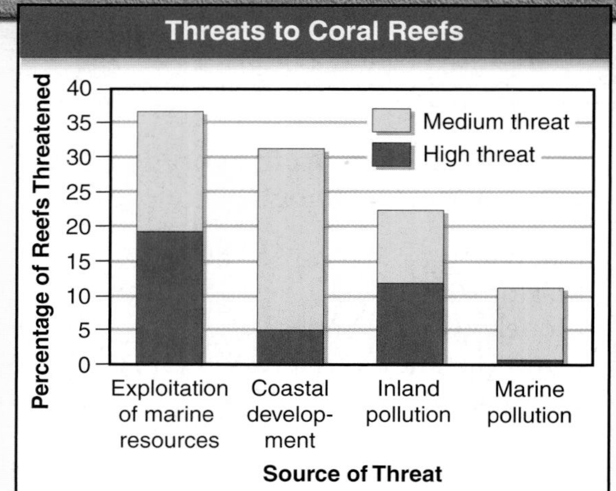

Problem Solving

Activities that build critical-thinking skills

Features

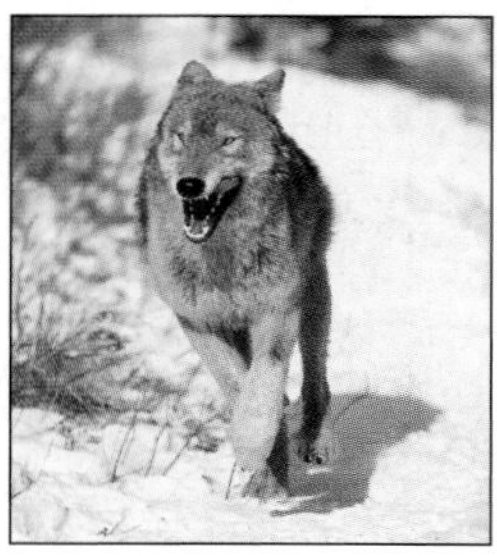

Features that relate content to current issues

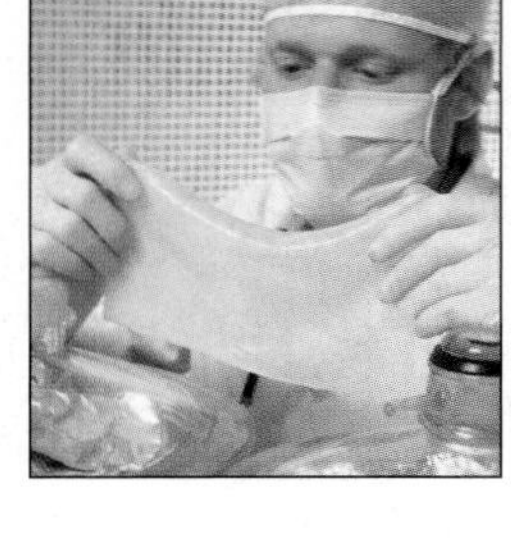

Features that relate content to current technological advances

Biology and History

Time lines that place biology in a social and historical context

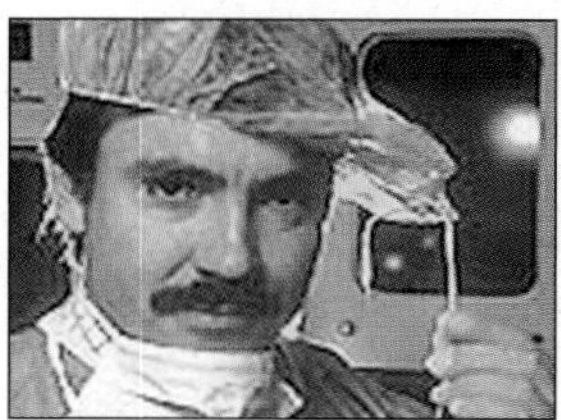

Careers in Biology

Relates biology to actual occupations

Joe Levine and I wrote this book for a very simple reason: We wanted to let you in on a secret. Biology isn't just a "subject" in school. Biology is the science of life itself. Biology is the study of what makes an eagle fly, a flower bloom, or a caterpillar turn into a butterfly. It's the study of ourselves—of how our bodies grow and change and respond to the outside world, and it's the study of our planet, a world transformed by the actions of living things. Of course, you might have known some of this already. So, what's the secret?

The secret is that you've come along at just the right time. In all of human history, there has never been a moment like the present, a time when we stood so close to the threshold of answering the most fundamental questions about the nature of life. You belong to the first generation of students who can read the human genome almost as your parents might have read a book or a newspaper. You are the first students who will grow up in a world that has a chance to use that information for the benefit of humanity, and you are the very first to bear the burden of using that knowledge wisely.

If all of this seems like heavy stuff, it is. But there is another reason we wrote this book, and we hope that is not a secret at all. Science is fun! Biologists aren't a bunch of serious, grim-faced, middle-aged folks in lab coats who think of nothing but work. In fact, most of the people we know in science would tell you honestly, with broad grins on their faces, that they have the best jobs in the world. They would say there's nothing that compares to the excitement of doing scientific work, and that the beauty and variety of life make every day a new adventure.

We agree, and we hope that you'll keep something in mind as you begin the study of biology. You don't need a lab coat or a degree or a laboratory to be a scientist. What you do need is an inquiring mind, the patience to look at nature carefully, and the willingness to figure things out. We've filled this book with some of the latest and most important discoveries about living things, but we hope we've also filled it with something else: our wonder, our amazement, and our sheer delight in the variety of life itself. Come on in, and enjoy the journey!

Sincerely,

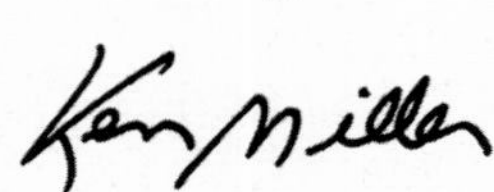

What do you think about biology? Are you interested in the natural world and the workings of your body? Or could you care less, and do you find yourself wondering "What's in it for me?" However you think, Ken and I wrote this book to convince you that biology is exciting, fascinating—and important to you. In fact, biology is more important to the daily lives of all humans today than it has ever been.

Why? You could answer in three words: "We are one." Now, this is a science text, so this statement isn't meant in any kind of "touchy-feely" or "New Age" way. "We" means all living things on earth. And "are one" means that all of us are tied together more tightly, in more different ways, than anyone ever dreamed of until recently. That's what biology tells us.

All forms of life—from bacteria to palm trees to humans are based on information written in a single, universal code carried in our genes. As biologists "read" those genes, they find nearly identical instructions directing life's processes in all of us. That's why medical researchers can learn about human diseases—diseases that may strike you or your family—by studying yeast. We are one on the molecular level.

All organisms interact with one another and with the environment in ways that create our planet's web of life. Organisms make tropical rain forests and coral reefs, prairies and swamps—and farms and cities. Our interactions involve not only each other—but also the winds and ocean currents that tie our planet together. Human activity can change, and is changing, local and global environments in ways that alter our ability to produce food and protect ourselves from diseases. We are one on the global ecological level.

All organisms change over time as they adapt to their surroundings. If humans alter the environment, we encourage other organisms to change. When we deploy antibiotics against bacteria, they develop resistance to our drugs. If we use pesticides against insects, they become immune to our poisons. We are one in our ability to evolve over time.

Those are the kinds of connections you will find in this book. Microscopic. Enormous. Amusing. Threatening. But always fascinating. That's why—no matter where you start off in your attitude about biology—we think you are in for some surprises!

Sincerely,

Joe Levine

See the book as a whole.

Knowing the chapter organization makes studying easier.

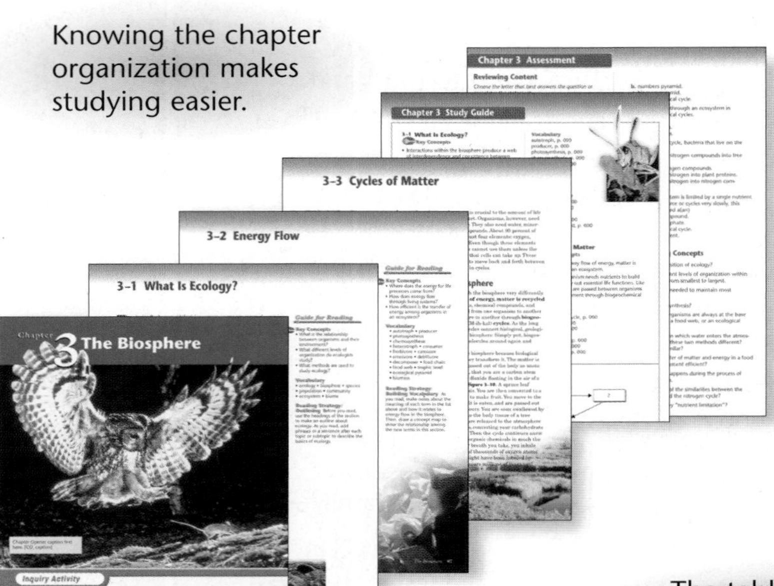

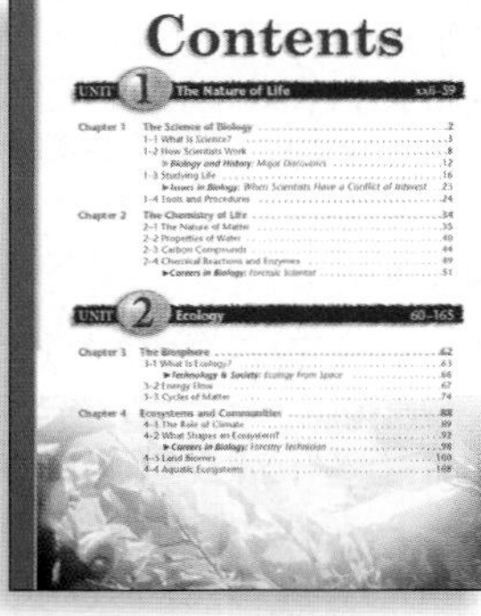

The table of contents, glossary, and index help you find specific topics.

Read for mastery.

Key Concepts are clearly identified.

Guide for Reading

Key Concept
- What factors limit population growth?

Vocabulary
limiting factor
density-dependent limiting factor
density-independent limiting factor
predator-prey relationship

Reading Strategy: Predicting Before you read, preview the diagram in **Figure 5–5.** Predict how each factor might limit the growth of a population. As you read, note whether your predictions were correct or incorrect.

level. These factors operate most strongly when a population is large and dense, and do not usually affect small, scattered populations. **Density-dependent limiting factors include competition, predation, parasitism, and disease.**

CHECKPOINT *What is a density-dependent limiting factor?*

5–2 Section Assessment

1. **Key Concept** List three density-dependent factors and three density-independent factors that can limit the growth of a population.
2. What is the relationship between competition and population size?
3. If an entire lynx population disappears, what is likely to happen to the hare population on which it preys?
4. **Critical Thinking Applying Concepts** Give an example of a density-independent limiting factor that has affected a human population. Describe how this factor changed the human population.

iTEXT **Assessment** Use iText to review the important concepts in Section 5–2.

MAKING CONNECTIONS

Biotic and Abiotic Factors Study the factors that limit population growth in **Figure 5–5.** Classify each factor as either biotic or abiotic. (*Hint:* Refer to the information on biotic and abiotic factors in Section 4–2.)

Monitor your progress.

Use concrete strategies for active learning.

Visualize the content.

Photographs

Photographs of real-world examples make topics memorable.

Figure 16–16 The eastern meadowlark (left) and western meadowlark (right) have overlapping ranges. They do not interbreed, however, because they have different mating songs. **Applying Concepts** ***What type of reproductive isolation does this situation illustrate?***

Caption questions reinforce knowledge and deepen understanding.

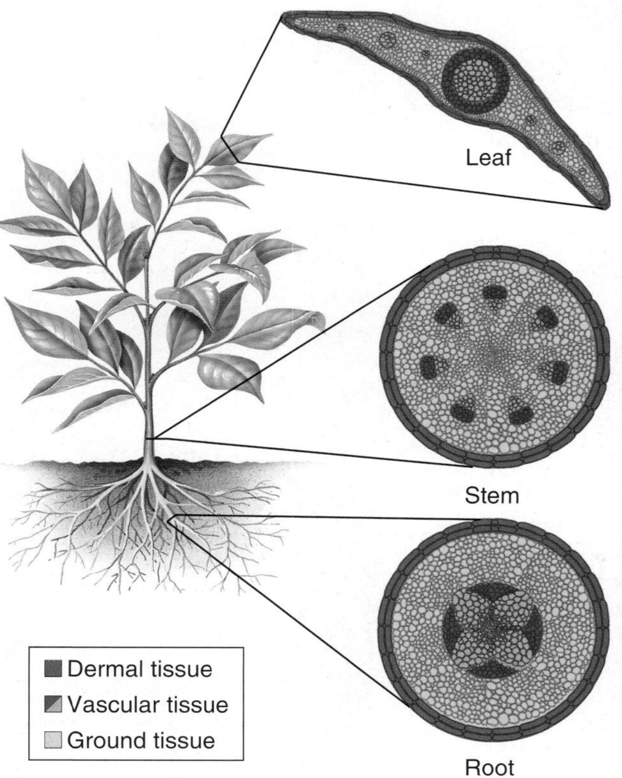

Diagrams

Diagrams break down complex ideas and demonstrate abstract processes.

Prepare for assessment.

Practice with varied question formats from standardized tests.

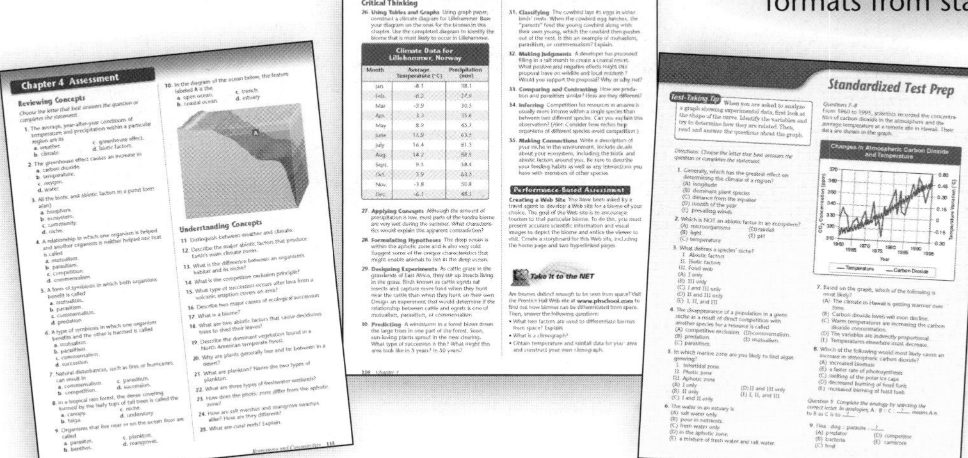
Chapter 4 Assessment

Reviewing Concepts

Understanding Concepts

Chapter 4 Assessment

Critical Thinking

Climate Data for Lillehammer, Norway

Performance-Based Assessment

Take It to the NET

Standardized Test Prep

Test-Taking Tip

Review each chapter with a variety of question formats.

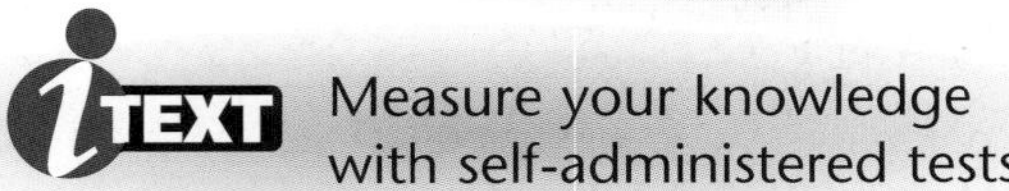

Measure your knowledge with self-administered tests.

Unit 1

Dear Colleague,

"Want to write a textbook?" That was the starting point of a conversation between the two of us that went on for months. Did we really want to do this? Did we have the time? And, finally, would it make a difference? You can guess, we're sure, how we answered those questions.

Trying to cover the enormous scope of the biological sciences in a single textbook is at once a terrifying and an exhilarating experience. More than once, we felt the task was beyond us. From time to time, we had to seek out fellow scientists to point the way, to help us identify key concepts, and even to encourage us with assurances that the task was worth completing.

More often, however, we felt a sense of amazement. Like you, we have chosen careers as biologists, and perhaps like you, we emerged from our formal educations with a sense that we had mastered the field. We were wrong about that, of course, and continuing to discover just how wrong we were has been one of the delights of our lives.

Students can be overwhelmed by the sheer amount of information presented in any biology course, and it's easy to see why. From ecology to systematics, from genetics to the nervous system, there's just so much to learn. The false impression students can get from such studies, of course, is that biology has pretty much come to an end, that just about everything has been figured out. Scientists, they might be tempted to conclude, are very smart people who are proud of what they know and are embarrassed by ignorance. Scientists, a student once told us, are ashamed to admit there's anything they don't know.

That student's assertion couldn't have been more wrong. What really turns a scientist on isn't knowledge,

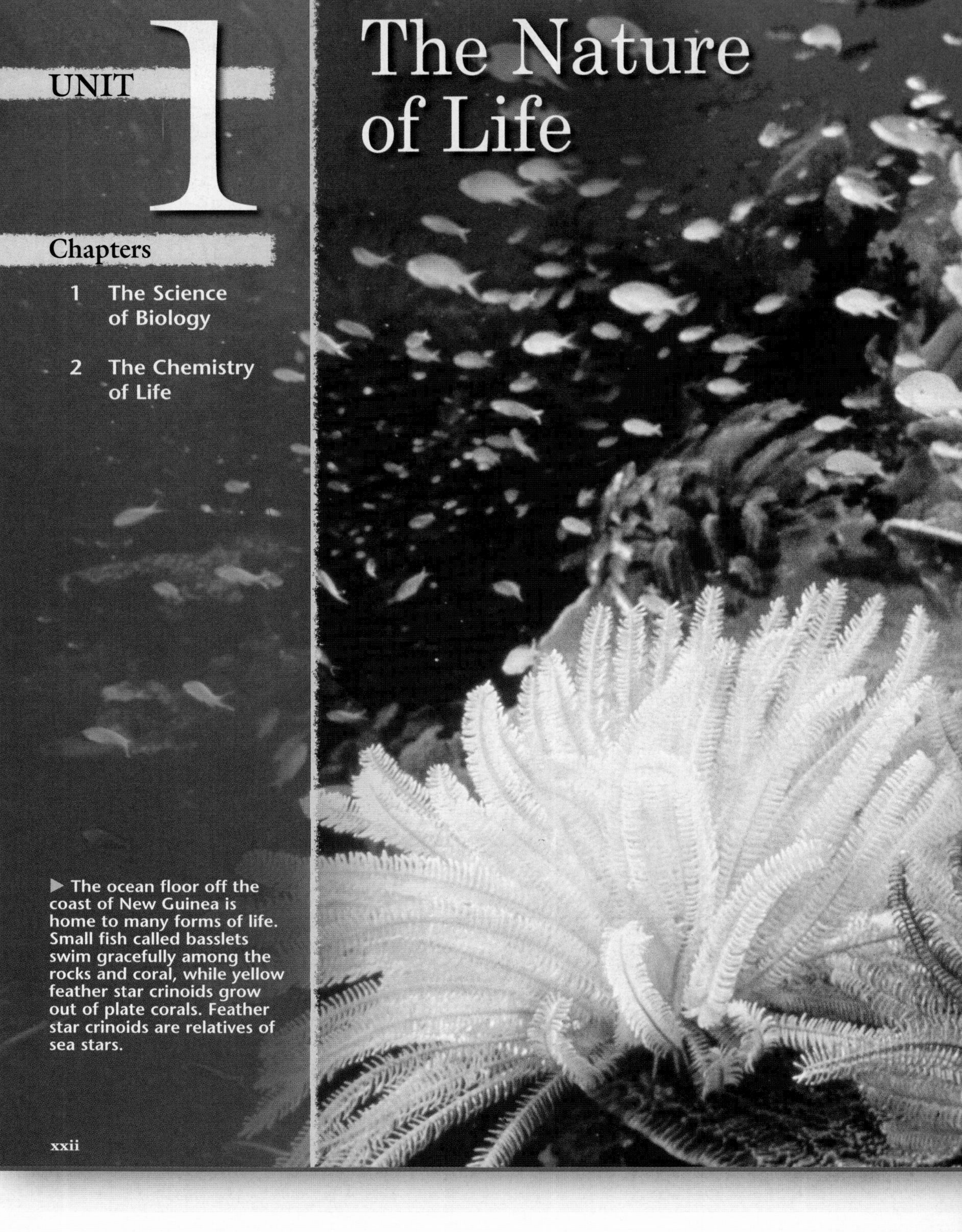

▶ The ocean floor off the coast of New Guinea is home to many forms of life. Small fish called basslets swim gracefully among the rocks and coral, while yellow feather star crinoids grow out of plate corals. Feather star crinoids are relatives of sea stars.

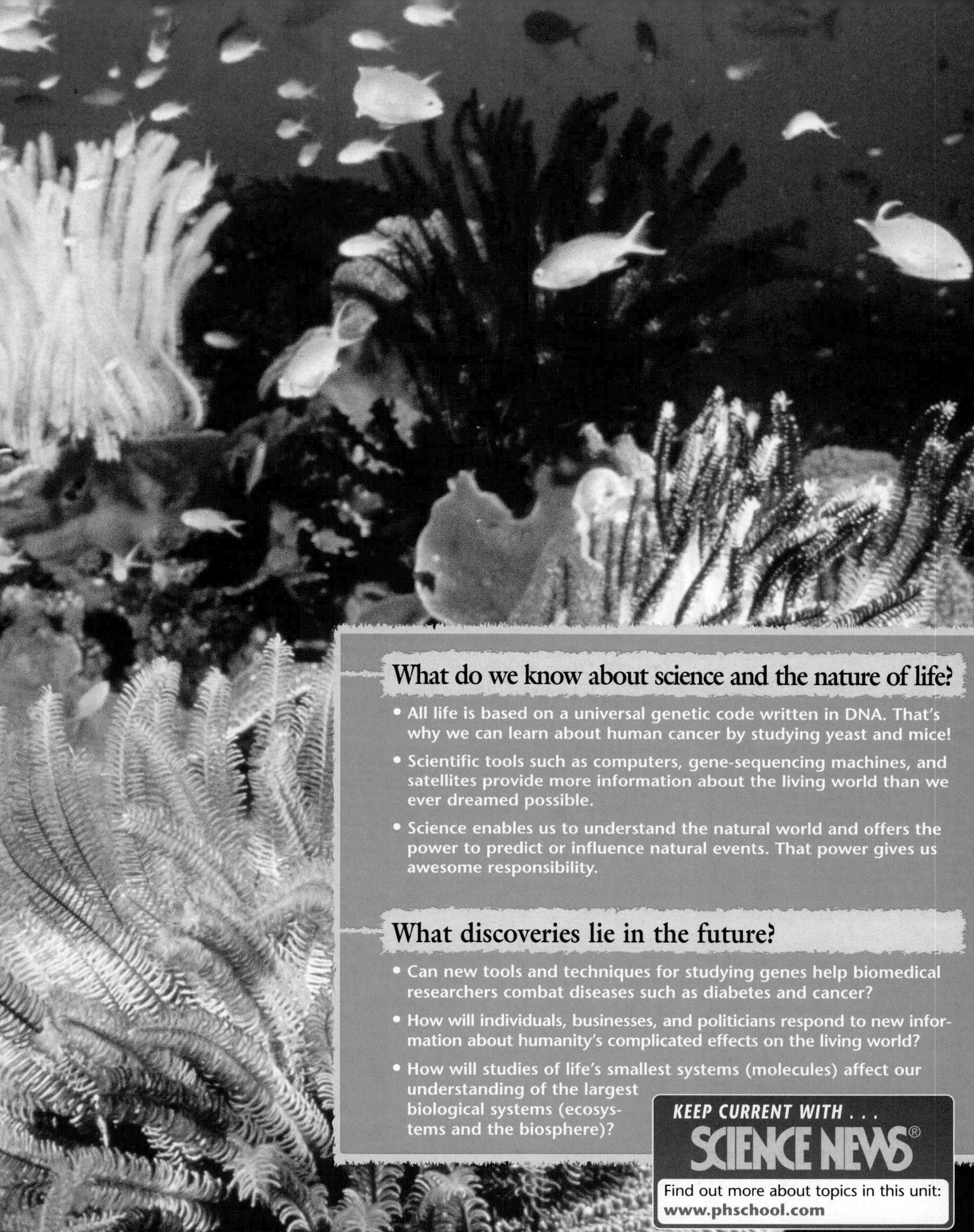

What do we know about science and the nature of life?

- All life is based on a universal genetic code written in DNA. That's why we can learn about human cancer by studying yeast and mice!
- Scientific tools such as computers, gene-sequencing machines, and satellites provide more information about the living world than we ever dreamed possible.
- Science enables us to understand the natural world and offers the power to predict or influence natural events. That power gives us awesome responsibility.

What discoveries lie in the future?

- Can new tools and techniques for studying genes help biomedical researchers combat diseases such as diabetes and cancer?
- How will individuals, businesses, and politicians respond to new information about humanity's complicated effects on the living world?
- How will studies of life's smallest systems (molecules) affect our understanding of the largest biological systems (ecosystems and the biosphere)?

KEEP CURRENT WITH . . .
SCIENCE NEWS®
Find out more about topics in this unit: **www.phschool.com**

but ignorance. A field that is pretty well figured out is the last thing that most scientists want to hear about. What's exciting is what we don't know, the unsolved problem, the inexplicable observation, the unexplored territory. We wrote this book, in large measure, to make this clear.

Scientists are, by nature, optimists. They believe that nature, ultimately, can be understood, and that helping to achieve such understanding is one of the most important things a human being can do in life. We members of the scientific community—you and we—also carry around a little trade secret that the general public never quite seems to notice: namely, that biology is fun. There's no point in keeping that a secret from your students, and this is a second reason we wrote this book.

We hope that you will view this book as a resource, as something that you can draw upon to enlighten, to excite, and even to amuse your students. If you find the book useful, we'll be happy. But, we hope you will go well beyond that. We live in remarkable times, and your students are growing up in what historians may come to regard as the most exciting decades in the history of biology. We spared no effort in trying to make that clear, and we know you will do the same.

In the final analysis, teachers are not only part of the scientific community—you are the most important part of it. You are the nurturers of new talent, the caretakers of youthful curiosity; you are the inspirations that fill the scientific enterprise with hope, energy, and vigor. We regard ourselves as your partners in that effort, and we hope you'll feel the same way. We hope you'll share your thoughts, suggestions, and criticisms of this textbook with us, because we know we'll learn from them. And we thank you most especially for the honor of sharing your classroom with us.

SCIENCE NEWS®

Have students visit the Prentice Hall Web site at **www.phschool.com** to find the most current information on biology and its tools and techniques.

Sincerely,

Ken Miller

Joe Levine

Chapter Planner 1 The Science of Biology

Section and Section Objectives	Time	Activities and Labs
1–1 What Is Science?, pp. 3–7 **1.1.1** ***Explain*** what the goal of science is. **1.1.2** ***Explain*** what a hypothesis is.	**1 period (1/2 block)**	**SE:** ***Inquiry Activity,*** Can your procedure be replicated?, p. 2 **TE:** ***Build Science Skills,*** p. 4 **TE:** ***Build Science Skills,*** p. 5
1–2 How Scientists Work, pp. 8–15 **1.2.1** ***Describe*** how scientists test hypotheses. **1.2.2** ***Explain*** how a scientific theory develops.	**2 periods (1 block)**	**SE:** ***Biology and History,*** Major Discoveries, pp. 12–13
1–3 Studying Life, pp. 16–22 **1.3.1** ***Describe*** some characteristics of living things. **1.3.2** ***Explain*** how life can be studied at different levels.	**2 periods (1 block)**	**TE:** ***Build Science Skills,*** p. 16 **SE:** ***Quick Lab,*** What are the characteristics of living things?, p. 19 **SE:** ***Issues in Biology,*** When Scientists Have a Conflict of Interest, p. 23
1–4 Tools and Procedures, pp. 24–28 **1.4.1** ***Describe*** the measurement system most scientists use. **1.4.2** ***Explain*** how light microscopes and electron microscopes are similar and different. **1.4.3** ***Describe*** two common laboratory techniques. **1.4.4** ***Explain*** why it is important to work safely in biology.	**1 period (1/2 block)**	**TE:** ***Meet Diverse Needs,*** p. 25 **SE:** ***Analyzing Data,*** Bacterial Reproduction, p. 27 **SE:** ***Exploration,*** Using a Compound Microscope, p. 29
Chapter Assessment, pp. 30–33	**1 period (1/2 block)**	

ACTIVITY PLANNER

SE: ***Inquiry Activity,*** p. 2; (15 min.); set of 10 interlocking blocks, screen

TE: ***Build Science Skills,*** p. 4; (10 min.); moldy piece of bread or slice of cheese in a sealed plastic bag

TE: ***Build Science Skills,*** p. 5; (15 min.); boxes with different arrangement of partitions, marbles

TE: ***Build Science Skills,*** p. 16; (15 min.); watch or clock with second hand, living animal

SE: ***Quick Lab,*** p. 19; (15 min.); hand lens, dormant brine shrimp eggs, water, hatched brine shrimp eggs, covered bowls

TE: ***Meet Diverse Needs,*** p. 25; (15 min.); microscope

SE: ***Exploration,*** p. 29; (45 min.); compound microscope, microscope slide, newspaper or other small-print text, scissors, dropper pipette, prepared slide of bacteria, coverslips, prepared slide of crossed fibers, transparent 15-cm plastic ruler, prepared slide of root or stem

PLANNING KEY

Ability Levels

B Basic	For students who need additional help
A Average	For all students
E Enriched	For students who need to be challenged

Components

SE	Student Edition	**GRSW**	Guided Reading and Study Workbook	**IDM**	Issues and Decision Making
TE	Teacher's Edition	**CT**	Chapter Tests: Levels A and B	**CTB**	Computer Test Bank
LMA	Laboratory Manual A	**PHAS**	PH Assessment System	**PA**	Presentation Assistant Plus
LMB	Laboratory Manual B	**LA**	Lab Assessment with Scoring Guide	**BD**	BioDetectives Videotape
TR	Teaching Resources	**BTM**	BioTechnology Manual	**iT**	iText
IF	Investigation in Forensics				

Program Resources	Assessment	Media and Technology
TR: Section Review 1–1 B A **GRSW:** Section 1–1 B A **IDM:** 1–1 A E	**SE:** 1–1 Section Assessment, p. 7 **TR:** Section Review 1–1	**PA:** 1–1 Interest Grabber, Section Outline, Observation or Inference **iT:** Section 1–1
TR: Section Review 1–2 B A **GRSW:** Section 1–2 B A **IDM:** Issues and Decisions 2 A E	**SE:** 1–2 Section Assessment, p. 15 **TR:** Section Review 1–2	**PA:** 1–2 Interest Grabber, Section Outline, Flowchart, Figure 1–8, Figure 1–10, Figure 1–11 **iT:** Section 1–2
TR: Section Review 1–3 B A **GRSW:** Section 1–3 B A	**SE:** 1–3 Section Assessment, p. 22 **TR:** Section Review 1–3	**PA:** 1–3 Interest Grabber, Section Outline, Characteristics of Life, Figure 1–21 **iT:** Section 1–3
LMA: Chapter 1 Lab A E **LMB:** Chapter 1 Lab B A **TR:** Section Review 1–4 B A Chapter 1 Exploration B A E **GRSW:** Section 1–4 B A	**SE:** 1–4 Section Assessment, p. 28 **TR:** Section Review 1–4	**PA:** 1–4 Interest Grabber, Section Outline, Making a Graph From a Data Table **iT:** Section 1–4
	SE: Chapter 1 Assessment, pp. 30–33 **TR:** Chapter Vocabulary Review, Graphic Organizer **CT:** Chapter 1 Test **CTB:** Chapter 1 Test **PHAS:** Practice Test	**CTB:** Chapter 1 Test **iT:** Chapter 1 Assessment

PRESSED FOR TIME?

To Preview the Chapter
- Introduce students to Key Concepts and Vocabulary terms in each section.
- Assign the Reading Strategies for each section.

To Cover the Chapter Quickly
- Have students read all of Section 1–1, Designing an Experiment in Section 1–2, Characteristics of Living Things in Section 1–3, and all of Section 1–4.
- Assign the 1–1 Section Review and the 1–4 Section Review, questions 1–6 and 8–10 in Chapter 1 Assessment, and questions 1–6 in Chapter 1 Standardized Test Prep.

To Review the Chapter
- Assign Sections 1–1 through 1–4 in the Guided Reading and Study Workbook.
- Assign Section Reviews for 1–1 through 1–4 and the Chapter Vocabulary Review for Chapter 1 in the Teaching Resources.

ENGAGE/EXPLORE

Inquiry Activity

Objective Students will be able to infer that a scientific procedure should be written in such a way that it can be replicated by other scientists.

Skill Focus Inferring

Materials set of 10 interlocking blocks, cardboard screen

Time 15 minutes

Advance Prep Divide the class into teams, and provide teams with identical sets of 10 interlocking blocks.

Strategies
- Make sure each team contains students with a variety of abilities.
- Check to see that each team is writing its directions without being observed by any other teams.

Expected Outcomes Most teams will write some directions that are unclear or misleading. Students will infer that directions should be carefully written so that other people can understand and replicate the procedure.

Think About It

1. A typical response might suggest that the writer of the directions should assume that the reader has never seen what is being described. The writer should describe each step in precise, specific language to avoid confusion.
2. Writing procedures that can be replicated allows other scientists to repeat the experiment to see if the same results occur every time.

Assess Prior Knowledge

Display several pictures of natural environments that show a variety of organisms, including various plants and animals. These pictures might be of a rain forest or a wetland, which are environments that contain a diversity of life. Ask students to choose one of the pictures to examine closely. Then, have each student compile a list of 20 questions a biologist might ask about the organisms in the picture.

Chapter 1 The Science of Biology

Researchers paired this wood ant and microchip to show their relative sizes. A scanning electron microscope was used to make this image, which has been artificially colored.

Inquiry Activity

Can your procedure be replicated?

Procedure

1. Behind a screen, assemble 10 blocks into an unusual structure. Write directions that others can use to replicate that structure without seeing it.
2. Exchange directions with another team. Replicate the team's structure by using its directions.
3. Compare each replicated and original structure. Identify which parts of the directions were clear and accurate, and which were unclear or misleading.

Think About It

1. **Evaluating and Revising** How could you have written better directions?
2. **Inferring** Why is it important that scientists write procedures that can be replicated?

HISTORY OF SCIENCE

The science of biology in ancient Greece
Although the word *biology* was not used until the early nineteenth century, the science of life has a history of thousands of years. Alcmaeon, a Greek physician born in about 535 B.C., is the first person known to have studied the human body in a scientific way. He discovered the optic nerve, and he speculated that the brain was the center of intellectual activity. The Greek philosopher Aristotle, born in 384 B.C., was a meticulous observer of living things, and he classsified over 500 animal species in a strict hierarchy. He even proposed a theory of progressive change among animals—an early suggestion of evolution.

1–1 What Is Science?

One ancient evening, lost in the mists of time, someone looked into the sky and wondered for the first time: What are those lights? Where did plants and animals come from? How did I come to be? Since then, humans have tried to answer those questions. At first, the answers our ancestors came up with involved tales of magic or legends like the one that inspired the art in **Figure 1–1**. Then, slowly, humans began to explore the natural world using a scientific approach.

What Science Is and Is Not

What does it mean to say that an approach to a problem is scientific?  **The goal of science is to investigate and understand nature, to explain events in nature, and to use those explanations to make useful predictions.**

Science has several features that make it different from other human endeavors. First, science deals only with the natural world. Second, scientists collect and organize information in a careful, orderly way, looking for patterns and connections between events. Third, scientists propose explanations that can be tested by examining evidence. In other words, **science** is an organized way of using evidence to learn about the natural world. The word *science* also refers to the body of knowledge that scientists have built up after years of using this process.

Guide for Reading

Key Concept
- What is the goal of science?

Vocabulary
science
observation
data
inference
hypothesis

Reading Strategy: Making Comparisons As you read, list steps that scientists use to solve problems. After you read, compare the methods you use to solve problems with those used by scientists.

◀ **Figure 1–1** A Navajo artist, Harrison Begay, produced this painting called *Creation of North Sacred Mountain.* It shows the first woman and man interacting with nature.

SECTION RESOURCES

Print:
- ***Teaching Resources,*** Section Review 1–1
- ***Guided Reading and Study Workbook,*** Section 1–1

Technology:
- ***iText,*** Section 1–1

Section 1–1

1 FOCUS

Objectives

1.1.1 ***Explain*** what the goal of science is.
1.1.2 ***Explain*** what a hypothesis is.

Guide for Reading

Vocabulary Preview

Have students write the vocabulary words, dividing each into its separate syllables as best they can. Remind students that each syllable usually has only one vowel sound. The correct syllabications are: sci•ence, ob•ser•va•tion, da•ta, in•fer•ence, hy•poth•e•sis.

Reading Strategy

Tell students that they should write at least one phrase about how a scientist works for each of the blue heads in the section.

2 INSTRUCT

What Science Is and Is Not

Build Science Skills

Applying Concepts Divide the class into small groups, and ask each group to propose an explanation for why it rains without including any scientific thinking in their explanation. Groups might propose that clouds are crying, that there is an invisible river in the sky, or that an invisible rain god pours water on Earth when angry. Once each group has agreed upon an explanation, have a member from each present it to the class. Then, ask: **Suppose someone does not believe your explanation. Could you supply evidence to support your explanation?** *(For almost all explanations, the answer will be no.)* **Why not?** *(There is no way to gather evidence, there is no way to observe a cloud that is "crying," and so on.)* Emphasize that scientists propose explanations that can be tested by examining evidence.

1–1 (continued)

Evidence Based on Observation

Build Science Skills

Observing Several days or weeks before students begin this chapter, prepare a slice of bread or cheese so that by the day students read this section it has become moldy. Place the moldy bread or cheese in a sealed plastic bag. Show it to the class and ask: **What do you see?** *(Typical answers might mention seeing a slice of bread with green spots, seeing a section of moldy cheese, and so on.)* **Can you describe in detail what you see?** *(Observations should include the color and texture of the mold, the extent to which it covers the cheese, and whether the mold is in solid patches or small spots.)* **What questions would you as a biologist pose after seeing the mold?** *(Possible questions: What caused the mold? How long has the mold been there? Is the mold alive? Will the mold cover more of the bread or cheese? Does all bread or cheese get moldy?)*

Interpreting the Evidence

Meet Diverse Needs

Have students with limited English proficiency look up the word *inference* in a dictionary and discuss the definitions they find. Explain that in everyday speech, the word is often misused. In correct usage, *imply* and *infer* are like *give* and *take*—one person gives or implies, and another person takes or infers. A person "implies" by suggesting something without saying it explicitly. A listener "infers" that suggestion by interpreting what is said. Similarly, in science an inference is an interpretation of what the evidence "says." In science, though, the inference must be a logical interpretation, not a mere feeling about the evidence. **Limited English proficiency**

▲ **Figure 1–2** **The goal of science is to investigate and understand nature.** The first step in this process is making observations. This researcher is observing the behavior of a manatee in Florida.

Evidence Based on Observation

Science starts with observation. **Observation** involves using one or more of the senses—sight, hearing, touch, smell, and sometimes taste—to gather information. The information gathered from observations, such as those being made in **Figure 1–2,** is called evidence, or **data.**

Observations can be classified into two types. Quantitative observations involve numbers, for example, counting or measuring objects. An example of a quantitative observation is *There are seven birds at the feeder.* Qualitative observations involve characteristics that cannot be easily measured or counted, such as color or texture. A qualitative observation could be *One of the birds has a red head.* As scientists make observations, they try to be objective and avoid bias, which is a preference for a particular, predetermined point of view.

Interpreting the Evidence

An observation alone has little meaning in science, because the goal is to understand what was observed. Scientists usually follow observations with inferences. An **inference** is a logical interpretation based on prior knowledge and experience. For example, researchers might sample water from a reservoir, as shown in **Figure 1–3.** If samples collected from different parts of the reservoir are all clean enough to drink, the researchers may infer that all the water in the reservoir is safe to drink.

◀ **Figure 1–3** Researchers testing water for lead pollution cannot test every drop, so they check small amounts, called samples. **Inferring** *How might a local community use such scientific information?*

TIME SAVER **PRESENTATIONS MADE EASY!**

The Presentation Assistant Plus contains the Prentice Hall Presentation Pro and the Transparencies, which provide easy-to-follow visual support for every step of this lesson. If you have a computer presentation station, use Prentice Hall Presentation Pro Section 1–1, or use the transparencies listed here.

Section 1–1: **Interest Grabber**
Section Outline
Observation or Inference

Explaining the Evidence

Suppose a group of people became ill with an unknown kind of infectious disease after attending a large public event. Health professionals would want to know how the people contracted the disease. They might form several hypotheses. A **hypothesis** is a possible explanation for a set of observations or an answer to a scientific question. In everyday settings, a hypothesis can be stated about any topic or idea. In science, a hypothesis is useful only if it can be tested.

In the infectious disease example, health professionals might propose several competing hypotheses: (1) The disease was spread by human contact. (2) The disease was spread through insect bites. (3) The disease was spread through contaminated air, water, or food. Evidence could be gathered to test each of these hypotheses. The incorrect hypotheses would be ruled out, and the correct explanation would eventually be found.

Scientific hypotheses may be developed and tested in different ways, often by researchers working in teams like the one in **Figure 1–4.** Hypotheses may arise from prior knowledge, logical inferences, or imaginative guesses. The testing may sometimes be done by making further observations or through careful questioning. Discovering how infected individuals contracted a disease, for instance, might require surveying what they did before developing the disease symptoms. Often, however, a hypothesis is tested through a controlled experiment, a procedure you'll learn about in the next section. The tests of a hypothesis may support it, or suggest that the hypothesis is partly true but needs to be revised. The tests may even prove that the hypothesis is wrong. No matter what the outcome, a tested hypothesis has value in science because it helps researchers advance scientific knowledge.

CHECKPOINT *How do scientists develop hypotheses?*

KEEP CURRENT WITH . . . SCIENCE NEWS®

To find out more about the topics in this chapter, go to: **www.phschool.com**

◀ **Figure 1–4** Researchers often work in teams, combining imagination and logic to develop and test hypotheses. **Applying Concepts** *How do scientists decide whether to accept or reject a hypothesis?*

Explaining the Evidence

SCIENCE NEWS®

Encourage students to visit **www.phschool.com** for the most current information on this topic.

Build Science Skills

Formulating Hypotheses Divide the class into small groups, and give each group a "mystery box." Prepare each box ahead of time, each with a different arrangement of partitions and each containing one or more marbles. Explain to groups what the boxes contain, in general terms. Tell students their task is to formulate a hypothesis about the specific arrangement of partitions in their group's box. Have them tilt, turn, and tap the box to move the marbles inside so that sounds and sensations will provide clues about the internal arrangement. Each group should make a sketch of its hypothesis of how the partitions are arranged inside its mystery box. Then, groups should make a list of what further tests could be performed to support or refute the hypothesis, short of opening the box. (Students may have the misconception that hypotheses are always confirmed, because the activities they have done in science classes were usually designed to support a hypothesis.)

BIO INSIGHTS — FACTS AND FIGURES

Evidence can be misused

There have been times in human history when scientific evidence or apparent evidence has been misused to serve the ends of racial prejudice and sexual bias. For example, the Swiss-American biologist Louis Agassiz (1807–1873) expressed the racist belief that non-European peoples were inferior to Europeans. Other scientists at the turn of the nineteenth century shared his view. They accepted unsubstantiated or inaccurate data to try to support their ideas. In the late nineteenth century, a group of scientists called craniologists made measurements of brain and skull size to prove that women were intellectually inferior to men. These "scientific studies" were cited in attempts to deny women equal rights. Today, scientists know that among humans, brain size has nothing to do with intelligence.

Answers to . . .

CHECKPOINT *Hypotheses may arise from prior knowledge, logical inferences, or imaginative guesses.*

Figure 1–3 *The leaders of a community might use the test results to warn residents about lead pollution, take steps to prevent or remedy pollution problems, or assure residents that the water is safe to drink.*

Figure 1–4 *Scientists accept or reject a hypothesis by evaluating the outcome of a controlled experiment.*

A Scientific View of the World

Use Community Resources

Scientists from the community can provide students with firsthand knowledge about careers in science. Invite a local scientist to speak to the class about his or her career and about looking at the world with a scientific view. Also, identify some local people with careers related to science. As much as possible, mention individuals of different ethnicities and backgrounds, especially women, with whom students can relate. These neighbors will help students see that they too can enter careers in science. Keep in mind that some findings of modern science as well as some types of scientific experiments may be incompatible with the beliefs of certain ethnic or religious groups. The support of respected members of the community of different cultural backgrounds may help promote understanding.

Meet Diverse Needs

Encourage students who need an extra challenge to investigate the discovery in 1996 of human bones on a bank of the Columbia River. These remains, named Kennewick man, were from a man who lived in the area over 9000 years ago. The find was hailed as significant by archaeologists and other scientists, who looked forward to detailed analysis. But, the remains were claimed by Native Americans for burial. A court battle followed. Have students investigate this controversy and what it says about how the scientific view of the world is sometimes opposed by other perspectives. **Learning modality: verbal**

Science and Human Values

Use Community Resources

Invite a university biologist and a member of the local clergy to address the class on an issue related to science, such as research using stem cells, cloning, or laws about endangered species. Ask the speakers to talk about how people who share their viewpoints might confront such an issue.

A Scientific View of the World

People often think about everyday events in a scientific way. Suppose a car won't start. Perhaps it's out of gas. A glance at the fuel gauge tests that idea. Perhaps the battery is dead. An auto mechanic can use an instrument to test that idea. A logical person would continue to look for a mechanical explanation, testing one possible explanation after another until the cause of the problem was identified.

All scientists, including the researcher in **Figure 1–5,** bring the same kind of problem-solving attitude to their work. They consider the whole universe a system in which basic rules apply to all events, small or large. Scientists assume that those rules can be discovered through scientific inquiry. They collect data as a means of achieving their goal—a better understanding of nature. For scientists, science is an ongoing process, not the discovery of an unchanging, absolute truth. Scientific findings are always subject to revision as new evidence is developed.

In keeping with this approach to pursuing knowledge, certain qualities are desirable in a scientist: curiosity, honesty, open-mindedness, skepticism, and the recognition that science has limits. An open-minded person is ready to give up familiar ideas if the evidence demands it. A skeptical person continues to ask questions and looks for alternative explanations. Scientists are persuaded by logical arguments that are supported by evidence. Despite recognizing the power of science, scientists know that science has definite limits. Science cannot help you decide whether a painting is beautiful or cheating on a test is wrong.

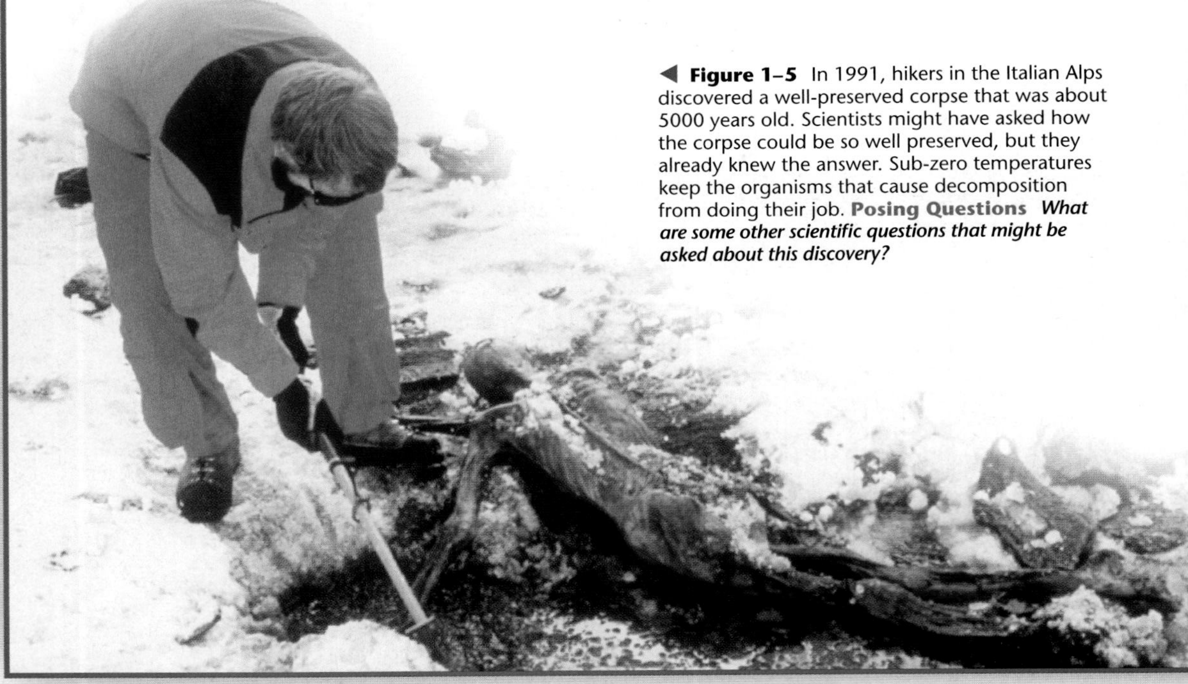

◀ **Figure 1–5** In 1991, hikers in the Italian Alps discovered a well-preserved corpse that was about 5000 years old. Scientists might have asked how the corpse could be so well preserved, but they already knew the answer. Sub-zero temperatures keep the organisms that cause decomposition from doing their job. **Posing Questions** ***What are some other scientific questions that might be asked about this discovery?***

FACTS AND FIGURES

Ötzi the Ice Man

The human remains shown in Figure 1–5 were discovered at the end of a warm summer in a barren Alpine pass near the Italian-Austrian border. Carbon-14 testing showed that the man had died some 5300 years earlier, during the Neolithic Age. He was named Ötzi the Ice Man because he was found in the Ötzal Alps and he had been preserved in glacial ice since his death. The unusually warm summer of 1991 had melted ice on the pass and exposed the body to view. Ötzi now lies on display at the South Tyrol Museum of Archaeology in Bolzano, Italy. Researchers have done many studies on Ötzi, including some using X-rays and CAT scans. Chemical analysis of a tiny clump at the top of his colon showed that he had eaten food from a nearby valley just eight hours before he died. His last meal had been a cracker-hard, unleavened bread made from einkorn wheat.

Science and Human Values

Most of this textbook deals with the workings of biological science. The importance of science, however, reaches far beyond the scientific world. Today, scientists contribute information to discussions about health and disease, and about the relationship between human beings and the rest of the living world.

Make a list of things that you need to understand to protect your life and the lives of others close to you. Chances are that your list will include drugs and alcohol, smoking and lung disease, AIDS, cancer, and heart disease. Other questions focus on public health and the environment. How can we best use antibiotics to make sure that those "wonder drugs" keep working for a long time? How much of the information in your genes should you be able to keep private? Should communities produce electricity using fossil fuels, nuclear power, or hydroelectric dams? How should chemical wastes be disposed of? Who should be responsible for their disposal? The people in **Figure 1–6** are expressing their concern about the effect of pollution on Earth.

All of these questions involve scientific information. For that reason, an understanding of science and the scientific approach is essential to making intelligent decisions about them. None of these questions, however, can be answered by science alone. They involve the society in which we live and the economy that provides jobs, food, and shelter. They may require us to consider laws and moral principles. In our society, scientists alone do not make final decisions—they make recommendations. Who makes the decisions? We, the citizens of our democracy do—when we vote to express our opinions to elected officials. That is why it is more important than ever that everyone understand what science is, what it can do, and what it cannot do.

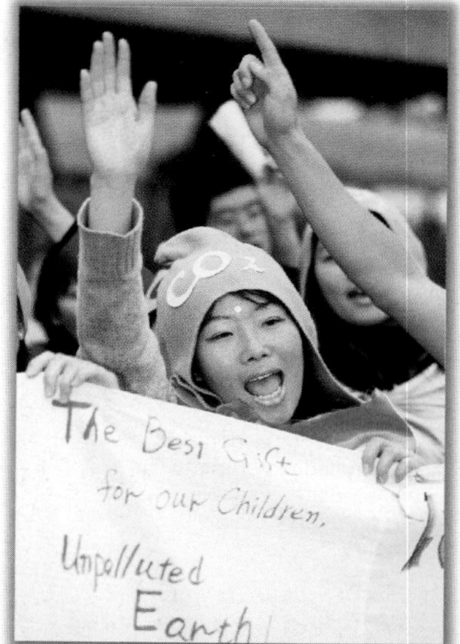

▲ **Figure 1–6** How people treat the environment is an issue involving science and human values. This protester shows her concern about the amount of carbon dioxide in the atmosphere. **Applying Concepts** *How is science involved in this discussion? How are values involved?*

1–1 Section Assessment

1. **Key Concept** What does science study? What does it not study?
2. What does it mean to describe a scientist as skeptical? Why is skepticism considered a valuable quality in a scientist?
3. What is the main difference between qualitative and quantitative observations?
4. Is a scientific hypothesis accepted if there is no way to prove that the hypothesis is wrong? Explain your answer.
5. **Critical Thinking Making Judgments** Suppose a community proposes a law to require the wearing of seatbelts in all moving vehicles. How could science play a role in the decision?

iTEXT **Assessment** Use iText to review the important concepts in Section 1–1.

ALTERNATIVE ASSESSMENT

Making a Table
List the five main senses—vision, hearing, smell, taste, and touch—and give an example of an observation that can be made using each sense. Then, add at least one inference that could be made from each observation.

3 ASSESS

Evaluate Understanding

Have students write an explanation in their own words of what a hypothesis is and the three ways in which a hypothesis may arise.

Reteach

Direct students' attention to the manatee pictured in Figure 1–2, and ask students at random to explain what quantitative and qualitative observations a biologist might make about this animal.

ALTERNATIVE ASSESSMENT

Students should list an observation and a logical inference for each sense. For example, if you see wet pavement, it may have rained or someone may have washed a car in that location. If you hear a bird sing, it may be singing to mark a territory or attract a mate. If a tabletop feels sticky, someone may have spilled syrup on the table.

Use iText to review the key concepts in Section 1–1.

1–1 Section Assessment

1. Science is the study of the natural world, the search for patterns and connections between events. Science does not address questions that cannot be tested, such as whether an object is beautiful or an action is ethical.
2. Skepticism requires that scientists maintain a questioning attitude and look for alternative explanations. It is valuable because findings are always subject to revision as new evidence develops.
3. Qualitative observations involve characteristics that cannot be measured or counted.
4. It is not a scientific hypothesis, because a hypothesis is useful only if it can be tested.
5. Sample answer: Science could determine whether the wearing of seatbelts would decrease the number of deaths or the severity of injuries caused by automobile accidents.

Answers to . . .

Figure 1–5 *Typical answers might include: Was the corpse male or female? How did the person die? How old was the person? Where might the person have been going at the time that he or she died?*

Figure 1–6 *A typical answer might suggest that science is involved in determining the amount of carbon dioxide in the atmosphere, the sources of that gas, and the consequences to the environment of an increase in atmospheric carbon dioxide. Values are involved in deciding the importance of those consequences and what steps society should take to prevent or remedy any harmful effects.*

Section 1–2

1 FOCUS

Objectives

1.2.1 ***Describe*** how scientists test hypotheses.
1.2.2 ***Explain*** how a scientific theory develops.

Guide for Reading

Vocabulary Preview

Have students preview the section's Vocabulary terms by skimming the text, finding the boldfaced terms, and writing down the definitions of each in their notebooks.

Reading Strategy

Have students make an outline of the section, using the blue heads as the first level of the outline and the green heads as the second level. Explain that the third and, possibly, fourth levels of the outline should be supporting details of the topics suggested by the heads.

2 INSTRUCT

Designing an Experiment

Meet Diverse Needs

Help at-risk students and students with limited English proficiency understand the term *spontaneous generation* by having them use a dictionary to look up the definition of each of the two words in the term. Discuss what it means to be "spontaneous" in class and how that meaning of the word is related to the meaning used in biology. Emphasize that *generation* in this context is related to the verb *to generate,* which means to bring into existence.
Limited English proficiency

1–2 How Scientists Work

Guide for Reading

Key Concepts
- How do scientists test hypotheses?
- How does a scientific theory develop?

Vocabulary
spontaneous generation
controlled experiment
manipulated variable
responding variable
theory

Reading Strategy: Outlining As you read, make an outline of the main steps in a controlled experiment.

Have you ever noticed what happens to food that is left in an open trash can for a few days in summer? Creatures that look like worms appear on the discarded food. These creatures are called maggots. For thousands of years people have been observing maggots on food that is not protected. The maggots seem to suddenly appear out of nowhere. Where do they come from?

Designing an Experiment

People's ideas about where some living things come from have changed over the centuries. Exploring this change can help show how science works. Remember that what might seem obvious now was not so obvious thousands of years ago.

About 2300 years ago, the Greek philosopher Aristotle made extensive observations of the natural world. He tried to explain his observations through reasoning. During and after his lifetime, people thought that living things followed a set of natural rules that were different from those for nonliving things. They also thought that special "vital" forces brought some living things into being from nonliving material. These ideas, exemplified by the directions in **Figure 1–7,** persisted for many centuries. About 400 years ago, some people began to challenge these established ideas. They also began to use experiments to answer their questions about life.

▼ **Figure 1–7** About 2000 years ago, a Roman poet wrote these directions for producing bees. **Inferring** ***Why do you think reasonable individuals once accepted the ideas behind this recipe?***

Recipe for Bees

1. Kill a bull during the first thaw of winter.
2. Build a shed.
3. Place the dead bull on branches and herbs inside the shed.
4. Wait for summer. The decaying body of the bull will produce bees.

Stating the Problem For many years, observations seemed to indicate that some living things could just suddenly appear: Maggots showed up on meat; mice were found on grain; and beetles turned up on cow dung. Curious about what they saw, people wondered how these events happened. They were, in their own everyday way, identifying a problem to be solved: How do new living things, or organisms, come into being?

Forming a Hypothesis For centuries, people accepted the prevailing explanation for the sudden appearance of some organisms, that some life somehow "arose" from nonliving matter. The maggots arose from the meat, the mice from the grain, and the beetles from the dung. Scholars of the day even gave a name to the idea that life could arise from nonliving matter—**spontaneous generation.** In today's terms, the idea of spontaneous generation can be considered a hypothesis.

In 1668, Francesco Redi, an Italian physician, proposed a different hypothesis for the appearance of maggots. Redi had observed that these organisms appeared on meat a few days after flies were present. He considered it likely that the flies laid eggs too small for people to see. Thus, Redi was proposing a new hypothesis—flies produce maggots. Redi's next step was to test his hypothesis.

SECTION RESOURCES

Print:
- ***Teaching Resources,*** Section Review 1–2
- ***Guided Reading and Study Workbook,*** Section 1–2
- ***Issues and Decision Making,*** Issues and Decisions 2

Technology:
- ***iText,*** Section 1–2

Setting Up a Controlled Experiment In science, testing a hypothesis often involves designing an experiment. The factors in an experiment that can change are called variables. Examples of variables include equipment used, type of material, amount of material, temperature, light, and time.

Suppose you want to know whether an increase in water, light, or fertilizer can speed up plant growth. If you change all three variables at once, you will not be able to tell which variable is responsible for the observed results. **Whenever possible, a hypothesis should be tested by an experiment in which only one variable is changed at a time. All other variables should be kept unchanged, or controlled.** This type of experiment is called a **controlled experiment.** The variable that is deliberately changed is called the **manipulated variable.** The variable that is observed and that changes in response to the manipulated variable is called the **responding variable.**

Based on his hypothesis, Redi made a prediction that keeping flies away from meat would prevent the appearance of maggots. To test this hypothesis, he planned the experiment shown in **Figure 1–8.** Notice that Redi controlled all variables except one—whether or not there was gauze over each jar. The gauze was important because it kept flies off the meat.

CHECKPOINT *What was the responding variable in Redi's experiment?*

▼ **Figure 1–8 In a controlled experiment, only one variable is tested at a time.** Redi designed an experiment to determine what caused the sudden appearance of maggots (photograph, below). In his experiment, the manipulated variable was the presence or absence of the gauze covering. The results of this experiment helped disprove the hypothesis of spontaneous generation.

Redi's Experiment on Spontaneous Generation

OBSERVATIONS: Flies land on meat that is left uncovered. Later, maggots appear on the meat.

HYPOTHESIS: Flies produce maggots.

PROCEDURE

Controlled Variables: jars, type of meat, location, temperature, time

Manipulated Variable: gauze covering that keeps flies away from meat

Responding Variable: whether maggots appear

Several days pass.

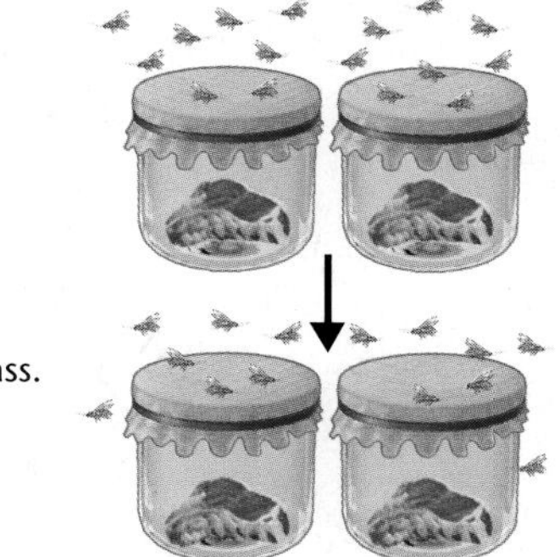

CONCLUSION: Maggots form only when flies come in contact with meat. Spontaneous generation of maggots did not occur.

PRESENTATIONS MADE EASY!

The Presentation Assistant Plus contains the Prentice Hall Presentation Pro and the Transparencies, which provide easy-to-follow visual support for every step of this lesson. If you have a computer presentation station, use Prentice Hall Presentation Pro Section 1–2, or use the transparencies listed here.

Section 1–2:

Interest Grabber
Section Outline
Flowchart
Figure 1–8
Figure 1–10
Figure 1–11

Use Visuals

Figure 1–8 Ask students: **What was Redi's hypothesis?** *(Flies produce maggots.)* **Why did he design an experiment that tested only one variable?** *(He designed such an experiment to make sure that any differences he observed during the experiment were caused by that single variable.)* **What was the manipulated variable in Redi's experiment?** *(Whether or not there was gauze over each jar)* **What is the difference that you can see between the two setups?** *(After several days, maggots appear on the meat in the uncovered jars, but no maggots appear on the meat in the covered jars.)*

Build Science Skills

Designing Experiments Show students an example or photo of moldy bread. Explain that mold will grow on bread that is exposed to air at room temperature. Then, ask each student to design an experiment to test the effects of water and sunlight on the growth of bread mold. Tell students that they may use up to four slices of bread and any materials available in the classroom. Ask that they state the problem, formulate a hypothesis, and identify the manipulated variable and the control in the proposed experiment. Discuss various experimental designs as a class. Then, defer any experiments that look promising until students study molds in Chapter 21. At that time, encourage students to carry out their experiments in small groups.

Answers to . . .

CHECKPOINT *The responding variable was whether maggots appeared.*

Figure 1–7 *A typical response might suggest that without controlled experiments, such a recipe could seem logical based on prior observations.*

Build Science Skills

Designing Experiments Divide the class into small groups, and have each group consider this question: Does the amount of sleep a student gets affect how well the student does in school? Ask each group to design an experiment that would address that question. Point out that they should state the problem, form a hypothesis, describe a controlled experiment, and describe how the results could be recorded and analyzed.

Publishing and Repeating Investigations

Demonstration

Display a number of periodicals and science journals for students to study, including issues of *Science* and *Nature.* Go over two or three of the experiments described, pointing out the hypothesis, the manipulated variable, the responding variable, the control, the results, and the conclusion for each experiment. Then, divide the class into small groups and assign each group an experiment in one of the journals to analyze according to the experimental process described in their textbook.

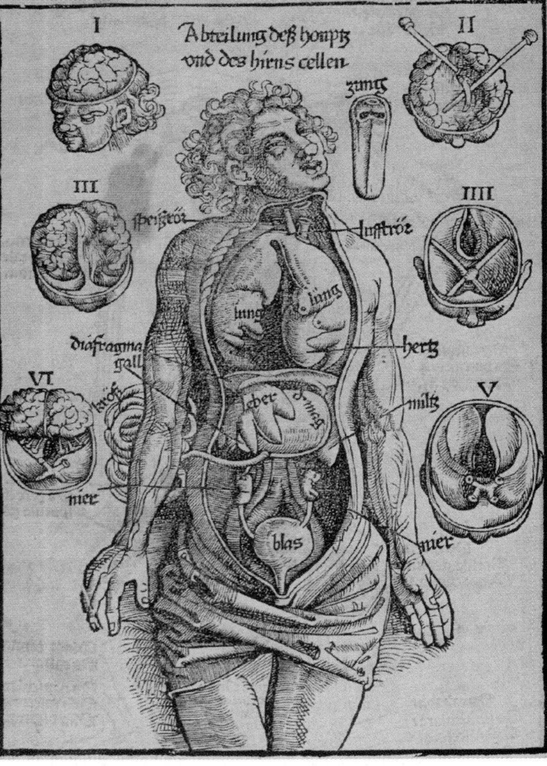

▲ **Figure 1–9** For centuries, the workings of the human body remained a mystery. Gradually, scientists observed the body's structures and recorded their work in drawings like this. **Comparing and Contrasting** *How does this drawing compare with the modern illustrations in Unit 10?*

Recording and Analyzing Results
Scientists usually keep written records of their observations, or data. In the past, data were usually recorded by hand, often in notebooks or personal journals. Sometimes, drawings recorded certain kinds of observations more completely and accurately than a verbal description could. The drawing in **Figure 1–9** was made in Austria in the fifteenth century. Today, researchers may record their work on computers. Online storage often makes it easier for researchers to review the data at any time and, if necessary, offer a new explanation for the data. Scientists know that Redi recorded his data because copies of his work were available to later generations of scientists. His investigation showed that maggots appeared on the meat in the control jars. No maggots appeared in the jars covered with gauze.

Drawing a Conclusion Scientists use the data from an experiment to evaluate the hypothesis and draw a conclusion. That is, they use the evidence to determine whether the hypothesis was supported or refuted. In Redi's case, his results supported his hypothesis. He therefore concluded that the maggots were indeed produced by flies.

As scientists look for explanations for specific observations, they assume that the patterns in nature are consistent. Thus, Redi's results could be viewed not only as an explanation about maggots and flies but also as a refutation of the hypothesis of spontaneous generation.

Publishing and Repeating Investigations

A key assumption in science is that experimental results can be reproduced because nature behaves in a consistent manner. When one particular variable is manipulated in a given set of variables, the result should always be the same. In keeping with this assumption, scientists expect to test one another's investigations. Thus, publishing a description of an experiment is an essential part of science. Today's researchers often report their work in a scientific journal. Other scientists review the experimental procedures to make sure that the design was without flaws. They often repeat experiments to be sure that the results match those already obtained. In Redi's day, scientific journals were not common, but he wrote about his work in a book that included a description of his investigation and its results.

HISTORY OF SCIENCE

An emphasis on experimentation
Galileo Galilei (1564–1642) is generally considered to have established the modern scientific method, as demonstrated in his investigations. Some stories about Galileo cannot be verified, including the one about the Leaning Tower of Pisa, but his approach to the study of nature is beyond question. He challenged Aristotle's view that the natural state of a body was at rest, a view accepted for 2000 years. Galileo's discovery of Jupiter's moons supported the Copernican model of the solar system. His emphasis on experimentation as the way to prove the validity of ideas was part of the broader movement of free thought and skepticism that was characteristic of the European Renaissance.

Needham's Test of Redi's Findings Some later tests of Redi's work were influenced by an unexpected discovery. About the time Redi was carrying out his experiment, Anton van Leeuwenhoek (LAY-vun-hook) of the Netherlands was preparing lenses that let him magnify tiny objects. He was not trying to discover new types of life, but that is what he found—a world of tiny moving objects in rainwater, pond water, and dust. Inferring that these objects were alive, he called them "animalcules," or tiny animals. He made drawings of his observations and shared them with other scientists. This discovery had a major effect on the arguments about spontaneous generation. For the next 200 years or so, scientists could not agree on whether the animalcules were alive or how they came to exist.

In the mid-1700s, John Needham, an English scientist, used an experiment involving animalcules to attack Redi's work. Needham claimed that spontaneous generation could occur under the right conditions. To prove his claim, he sealed a bottle of gravy and heated it. He claimed that the heat had killed any living things that might be in the gravy. After several days, he examined the contents of the bottle and found it swarming with activity. "These little animals," he inferred, "can only have come from juice of the gravy."

Spallanzani's Test of Redi's Findings An Italian scholar, Lazzaro Spallanzani, read about Redi's and Needham's work. Spallanzani thought that Needham had not heated his samples enough and decided to improve upon Needham's experiment. **Figure 1–10** shows that Spallanzani boiled two containers of gravy, assuming that the boiling would kill any tiny living things, or microorganisms, that were present. He sealed one jar immediately and left the other jar open. After a few days, the gravy in the open jar was teeming with microorganisms. The sealed jar remained free of microorganisms.

How did Spallanzani's investigation improve upon Needham's work?

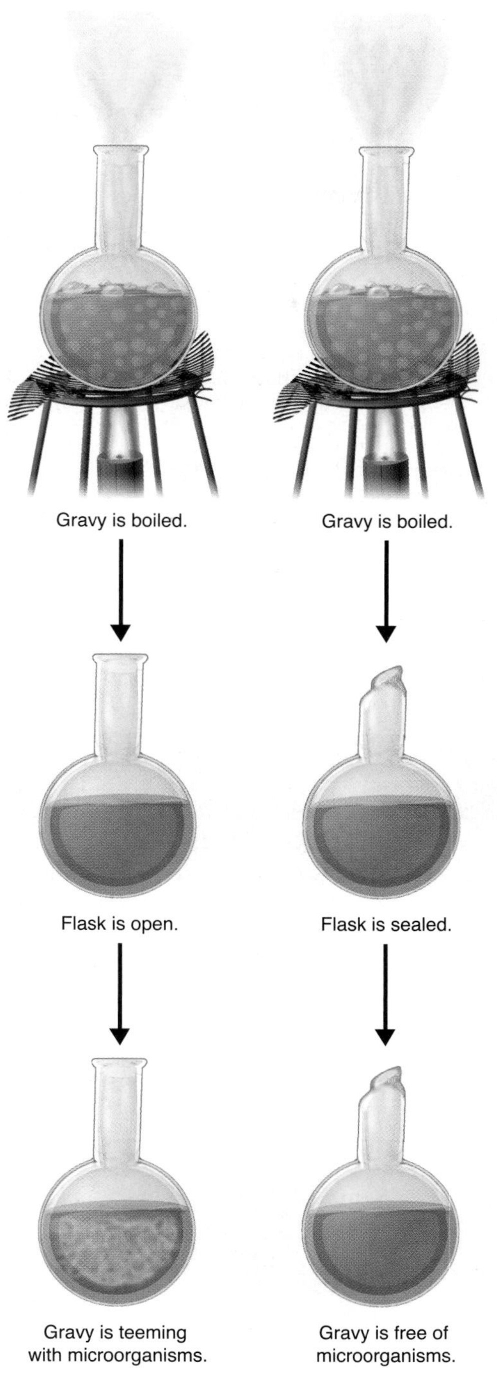

Gravy is boiled.
Gravy is boiled.
Flask is open.
Flask is sealed.
Gravy is teeming with microorganisms.
Gravy is free of microorganisms.

▶ **Figure 1–10** Spallanzani's experiment showed that microorganisms will not grow in boiled and sealed gravy but will grow in boiled gravy that is left open to the air. **Interpreting Graphics** *What variable was controlled in this experiment?*

Build Science Skills

Applying Concepts After students have read about Needham's test of Redi's findings, ask: **What was Needham's hypothesis in his experiment?** *(Spontaneous generation could occur under the right conditions.)* **In what way did he change Redi's experiment?** *(Needham heated a sealed bottle of gravy. Redi never used heat in his experiment.)* **What assumption did Needham make that made his results invalid?** *(He assumed that heating the gravy killed all the "animalcules." That assumption was wrong.)* **What is the result when a scientist draws a conclusion from data that are derived from an invalid assumption?** *(The conclusion is flawed.)*

Use Visuals

Figure 1–10 Ask students: **What was Spallanzani's hypothesis?** *(Boiling would kill any tiny living things in gravy, and no growth of organisms would occur in a sealed flask.)* **Is boiling the manipulated variable in Spallanzani's experiment? If not, what is?** *(Boiling was not the manipulated variable; the manipulated variable was whether or not the flask was sealed.)* **What variables were kept the same, or controlled, in his experiment?** *(Same gravy, same boiling, same flasks, same time)*

BIO INSIGHTS
HISTORY OF SCIENCE

Water teeming with "animalcules"
Anton van Leeuwenhoek had a passion for tiny things. During a lifetime of investigation, he studied the structure of muscle, skin, hair, tooth scrapings, and various small insects. His famous discovery of "animalcules" occurred late in the summer of 1674 when he returned home from boating on a local lake with a sample of the water. That water was cloudy, and most people at the time thought that such cloudiness was caused by a heavy dew. But, when Leeuwenhoek used one of the lenses he had mounted as a microscope, he was surprised to see that the water was teeming with tiny organisms, so many that it was cloudy with them. This and other discoveries made him world-famous. Perhaps his most remarkable discovery was made in 1676 when he described tiny organisms that are now known to have been bacteria.

Answers to . . .

CHECKPOINT *Spallanzani boiled the gravy, assuming that boiling would kill any microorganisms.*

Figure 1–9 *Students' answers will vary. A typical comparison might suggest that modern illustrations are much more realistic and accurate.*

Figure 1–10 *The main controlled variable was the boiling of the gravy.*

Use Visuals

Figure 1–11 Ask students: **What was the hypothesis Pasteur tested in his experiment?** *(As long as broth is protected from microorganisms, it will remain free of living things.)* **Why did Pasteur boil the broth at the beginning of this experiment?** *(To kill any microorganisms in the broth)* **What was the purpose of the curved neck in Pasteur's setup?** *(The curved neck allowed air into the flask but not microorganisms.)*

Biology and History

After students have read about the discoveries, add any general events to the time line that students can recall from other classes, such as the first performance of *Hamlet* in 1602, the Declaration of Independence in 1776, the beginning of the U.S. Civil War in 1861, and the assassination of President Kennedy in 1963. Discuss how each of the discoveries included in the time line changed both science and society. Ask students if there are any other major scientific discoveries they would add to the time line.

Writing Activity

Make sure some students are writing reports about each of the discoveries included on the time line. Explain that for each of the scientists listed, students could probably find a biography in the library. Advise them to look for specialized books in the library's reference section that focus on scientific biography.

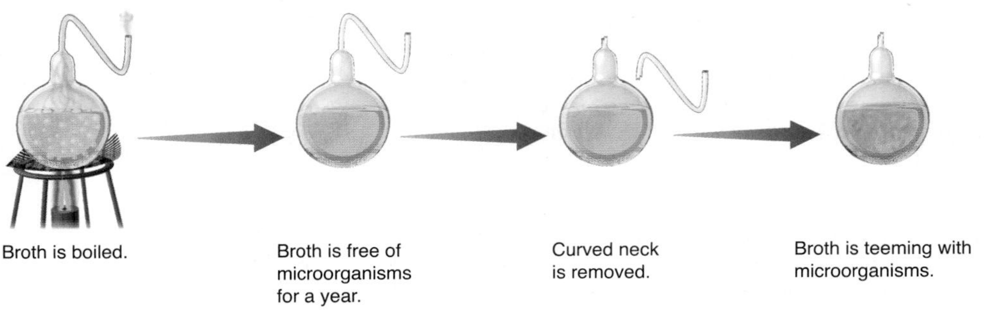
Broth is boiled.
Broth is free of microorganisms for a year.
Curved neck is removed.
Broth is teeming with microorganisms.

▲ **Figure 1–11** Pasteur's experiment showed that boiled broth would remain free of microorganisms even if air was allowed in, as long as dust and other particles were kept out. **Inferring** *Why did microorganisms grow after Pasteur broke the neck of the flask?*

Spallanzani concluded that nonliving gravy did not produce living things. The microorganisms in the unsealed jar were offspring of microorganisms that had entered the jar through the air. This experiment and Redi's work supported the hypothesis that new organisms are produced only by existing organisms.

Pasteur's Test of Spontaneous Generation Well into the 1800s, scientists continued to argue for the spontaneous generation hypothesis. Some supporters of the hypothesis argued that air was a necessary factor in the process of generating life because air contained the "life force" needed to produce new life. They pointed out that Spallanzani's experiment was not a fair test because air had been excluded from the sealed jar.

Biology and History

Major Discoveries

The history of biology includes discoveries about the structure of the human body, the nature of cells, how species evolve, ways to fight deadly diseases, and what molecule determines hereditary traits. You will learn about these discoveries as you study this textbook.

1500 — 1600 — 1700

1520 Suleiman I becomes sultan of the Ottoman Empire

1543 **Andreas Vesalius** Vesalius publishes *On the Structure of the Human Body,* the first accurate and detailed study of human anatomy.

1628 **William Harvey** Harvey is the first scholar to describe the circulation of blood. He shows how blood pumped through blood vessels returns to the heart and is recirculated.

1649 Charles I of England is executed by Parliament

1673 **Anton van Leeuwenhoek** Van Leeuwenhoek perfects the simple microscope and observes cells and microorganisms. Four years later, he discovers protozoa.

BIO INSIGHTS — HISTORY OF SCIENCE

The dawn of modern science
Andreas Vesalius (1514–1564) was a physician from Brussels, Belgium. Because dissection of human cadavers was forbidden in northern Europe, Vesalius moved to Italy in the 1530s, where he taught anatomy at universities and performed numerous dissections. One of his achievements was to demonstrate that men and women had the same number of ribs—the common belief had been that men had one fewer rib than women, because Eve was created from Adam's rib. In 1543, Vesalius published his book on human anatomy. It contained outstanding illustrations, many of which were done by a student of the great Italian painter Titian. In this groundbreaking work, Vesalius showed the human body in natural positions. It ended the influence of the Greek physician Galen, whose works on anatomy had dominated scientific thinking since the second century.

In 1864, an ingenious French scientist, Louis Pasteur, found a way to settle the argument. He designed a flask that had a long curved neck, as shown in **Figure 1–11.** The flask remained open to the air, but microorganisms from the air did not make their way through the neck into the flask. Pasteur showed that as long as the broth was protected from microorganisms, it remained free of living things. About a year after the experiment began, Pasteur broke the neck of the flask, and the broth quickly became filled with microorganisms. His work convinced other scientists that the hypothesis of spontaneous generation was not correct. In other words, Pasteur showed that all living things come from other living things. This change in thinking represented a major shift in the way scientists viewed living things.

The Impact of Pasteur's Work During his lifetime, Pasteur made many discoveries related to microorganisms. He saved the French wine industry, which was troubled by unexplained souring of wine, and the silk industry, which was endangered by a silkworm disease. Moreover, he began to uncover the very nature of infectious diseases, showing that they were not inexplicable events but the result of microorganisms entering the bodies of the victims. Pasteur is considered one of biology's most remarkable problem solvers.

✓CHECKPOINT *What improvement did Pasteur make to Redi's experiment?*

Writing Activity

Find out more about one of these discoveries. Research the person or people who made the discovery and how they did it. Write a one-page report detailing your findings.

1815 Napoleon is defeated at Waterloo

1859 **Charles Darwin** Darwin publishes *On the Origin of Species,* stating that all forms of life have evolved into their present state over the course of millions of years.

1881 **Louis Pasteur** Pasteur develops the first vaccine against anthrax, a deadly bacterial disease that affects both animals and humans.

1914 Germany invades Belgium; World War I begins

1953 **James Watson and Francis Crick** Watson and Crick determine the structure of DNA. They, along with fellow scientist Maurice Wilkins, win the Nobel Prize, in 1962, for their discovery.

1992 Soviet Union is dissolved

1800 1900 2000

Meet Diverse Needs

After reading about the experiments of Redi, Spallanzani, and Pasteur, some students may be confused about the steps a scientist takes in carrying out an experiment. To review these steps, use the following activity. Write the steps on a set of index cards. Place the cards face down on a desk or table. Have each student pick a card at random. Ask the students to line themselves up so that the steps they have drawn are in the correct order. Then, have students take turns describing each step. **Learning modality: kinesthetic**

Build Science Skills

Applying Concepts Point out that a jar of mayonnaise or pasta sauce is kept on a grocery store shelf or in a cupboard at home unrefrigerated. But, after the top is opened and a portion of the contents are used, the jar must be kept in a refrigerator to keep it from spoiling. Ask students: **What can you infer from Pasteur's work about why an opened jar must be kept in a refrigerator?** *(Pasteur showed that all living things come from other living things, and opening the jar exposes the contents to organisms in the air, just as breaking the neck of the flask did in his experiment.)* Have students write a description of a controlled experiment they might carry out that would test the hypothesis that organisms would grow in an opened jar of food.

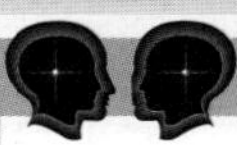

TEACHER TO TEACHER

Before introducing Pasteur's test of spontaneous generation, I have students carry out a simulation of his experiment. Students fill three pre-cleaned test tubes with 5–10 mL of nutrient broth. Tube A is left open. Tube B is loosely fitted with an autoclaved rubber stopper, which is always handled with an alcohol-cleaned forceps. Tube C is fitted with a rubber stopper pierced with a bent piece of glass tubing that has also been autoclaved. The three tubes are heated in a boiling-water bath for at least 30–40 minutes and then observed daily for about one week. Students look for signs of turbidity. Tube A will show growth within a day or two. Tubes B and C will stay sterile.

—*Gregory W. McCurdy,*
Biology Teacher
Salem High School,
Salem, IN

Answers to . . .

✓CHECKPOINT *He used a flask with a long curved neck to allow air to enter the flask, but not microorganisms.*

Figure 1–11 *The curved neck prevented microorganisms from making their way into the flask. Once the neck of the flask was broken, microorganisms could get to the broth, where the microorganisms multiplied.*

When Experiments Are Not Possible

Build Science Skills

Classifying Have each student write down two topics related to biology that he or she would like to investigate and develop one hypothesis related to each topic. Divide the class into small groups, and ask each group to classify the hypotheses of each of its members according to whether a controlled experiment could be used in testing them. If the answer is no, challenge groups to explain how each hypothesis could be investigated in a way in which scientists could discover reliable patterns that could add to scientific knowledge.

How a Theory Develops

Address Misconceptions

Discuss with students how the word *theory* is used in everyday speech. One dictionary definition of the word lists *conjecture* and *speculation* as synonyms. Point out that people often use the word *theory* when they are really referring to a hypothesis—for example, "I have a theory about why the washing machine doesn't work."

Build Science Skills

Comparing and Contrasting Ask students to look for examples from the print or electronic media where the term *theory* is used. Have them determine for each example whether the usage represents the scientific meaning of theory or its meaning in everyday speech.

▲ **Figure 1–12** In animal field studies, such as the observation of wild elephants, scientists usually try to work without making the animals aware that humans are present. **Comparing and Contrasting** *How do animal field studies differ from controlled experiments?*

When Experiments Are Not Possible

It is not always possible to do an experiment to test a hypothesis. For example, to learn how animals in the wild interact with others in their group, researchers carry out field studies. It is necessary to observe the animals without disturbing them, as shown in **Figure 1–12.** Ethical considerations prevent certain experiments, such as determining the effect on people of a chemical suspected of causing cancer. In such cases, medical researchers may choose volunteers who have already been exposed to the chemical. For comparison, they would study a group of people who have not been exposed to the chemical.

When researchers design such alternative investigations, they try to maintain the rigorous thinking associated with a controlled experiment. They often study large groups of subjects so that small differences do not produce misleading results. They try to identify as many relevant variables as possible so that most variables are controlled. For example, in a study of a cancer-causing chemical, they might exclude volunteers who have other serious health problems. By exerting great care in planning these kinds of investigations, scientists can discover reliable patterns that add to scientific knowledge.

CHECKPOINT *Why are controlled experiments sometimes impossible?*

How a Theory Develops

As evidence from numerous investigations builds up, a particular hypothesis may become so well supported that scientists consider it a **theory.** That is what happened with the hypothesis that new organisms come from existing organisms. This idea is now considered one of the major ideas in science. It is called biogenesis, meaning "generating from life."

You may have heard the word *theory* used in everyday conversations as people discuss ideas. Someone might say, "Oh, that's just a theory," to criticize an idea that is not supported by evidence. **In science, the word *theory* applies to a well-tested explanation that unifies a broad range of observations.** A theory enables scientists to make accurate predictions about new situations.

FACTS AND FIGURES

An established principle

In common speech, the word *theory* is often used to mean an unverified assumption, in contrast to a fact—something that exists or is known to have happened. In scientific usage, a theory is an overarching generalization that explains, and is supported by, a broad range of observation and experimentation. Thus, the germ theory of disease is not an assumption but an established principle of modern science. This confusion about the meaning of the term is often heard in debates about the theory of evolution, with those who oppose the teaching of that theory attacking it on the basis that it is unproven, or "just a theory." In fact, the opposite is closer to the truth. There is so much evidence for evolution that it has become an established principle, or a scientific theory.

Figure 1–13 **A theory is a well-tested explanation that unifies a broad range of observations.** The theories of plate tectonics and evolution help explain why marsupials such as the koala (top) and kangaroo (below) can be found only in Australia.

Sometimes more than one theory is needed to explain a particular circumstance. For example, why are the marsupial mammals in **Figure 1–13** found only in Australia? An answer lies with the theories of plate tectonics and evolution. Millions of years ago, Australia, Antarctica, and South America were joined. During that time, most marsupials disappeared from North and South America. Some marsupials ended up in Australia. After the continents separated, the marsupials in Australia survived and evolved because they did not have to compete with other types of mammals. You will study the theory of evolution in Unit 5.

A useful theory may become the dominant view among the majority of scientists, but no theory is considered absolute truth. As new evidence is uncovered, a theory may be revised or replaced by a more useful explanation. Sometimes, scientists resist a new way of looking at nature, but over time new evidence determines which ideas survive and which are replaced. Thus, science is characterized by both continuity and change.

1–2 Section Assessment

1. **Key Concept** Why is Redi's experiment on spontaneous generation considered a controlled experiment?
2. **Key Concept** How does a scientific theory compare with a scientific hypothesis?
3. Explain the hypothesis of spontaneous generation.
4. How did the design of Pasteur's flask help him successfully refute the hypothesis of spontaneous generation?
5. **Critical Thinking Applying Concepts** What problem might arise if a researcher fails to control the relevant variables in an experiment?

Assessment Use iText to review the important concepts in Section 1–2.

ALTERNATIVE ASSESSMENT

Making a Table
Compare the experiments done by Redi, Spallanzani, and Pasteur. Identify the problem each experiment was designed to solve. State the conclusion of each experiment.

3 ASSESS

Evaluate Understanding

Focus students on Pasteur's experiment. Then, call on students at random to state the problem Pasteur identified, explain what his hypothesis was, describe his controlled experiment, analyze the results of that experiment, and explain what conclusion he drew.

Reteach

Review Redi's experiment by having students revisit Figure 1–8. Then, have students write a description of the experiment as if they were Redi writing to a colleague. Emphasize that they should identify the problem to be solved, write a hypothesis, explain how a controlled experiment was set up, analyze the results, and draw a conclusion.

ALTERNATIVE ASSESSMENT

Students' tables should list each of the three experiments described in the section. Redi—Problem: do flies produce maggots; Conclusion: maggots are produced by flies. Spallanzani—Problem: does boiling and sealing a jar of gravy prevent the growth of microorganisms; Conclusion: boiling and sealing prevent microorganism growth. Pasteur—Problem: does a flask designed to allow air but not microorganisms to enter prevent growth of microorganisms in broth; Conclusion: air without microorganisms does not support the growth of microorganisms.

Use iText to review the key concepts in Section 1–2.

1–2 Section Assessment

1. Redi controlled all variables but one—whether or not there was gauze over each jar.
2. A hypothesis is a possible explanation for a set of observations or an answer to a scientific question. A theory is a well-tested explanation that unifies a broad range of observations.
3. Life can arise from nonliving matter.
4. The design of the flask allowed air into the jar of broth but protected the broth from microorganisms. This design was a response to those who said air contained the "life force" needed to produce new life.
5. If an experiment has more than one manipulated variable, any observed differences cannot be attributed to a single variable.

Answers to . . .

CHECKPOINT *Ethics prevent most experiments with humans. In field studies, researchers try not to disturb systems that they observe.*

Figure 1–12 *In field studies, researchers observe relationships among identified variables but do not manipulate the variables.*

Section 1–3

1 FOCUS

Objectives

1.3.1 ***Describe*** some characteristics of living things.

1.3.2 ***Explain*** how life can be studied at different levels.

Guide for Reading

Vocabulary Preview

Pronounce each of the vocabulary words for the class, and have students repeat the pronunciation in unison. Note any words that students with limited English proficiency have trouble pronouncing and work with them to correct their problems.

Reading Strategy

Students should write one sentence describing each of the eight characteristics listed on page 16. You might have students rewrite the items in the list and revise their sentences as they read the section.

2 INSTRUCT

Characteristics of Living Things

Build Science Skills

Comparing and Contrasting Divide the class into small groups, and allow each group to examine two objects: a watch or clock with a working second hand and an active, living animal such as a fish or an insect. Ask groups to compare the two, noting similarities and differences. Have group members collaborate on writing a paragraph explaining what makes one object a living thing and the other object not.

1–3 Studying Life

Guide for Reading

Key Concepts
- What are some characteristics of living things?
- How can life be studied at different levels?

Vocabulary
biology
cell
sexual reproduction
asexual reproduction
metabolism
homeostasis
evolve

Reading Strategy: Summarizing As you read, make a list of the properties of living things. Write one sentence describing each property.

Beneath the sparkling waves near a South Pacific island, divers carry cameras and underwater notepads as they crisscross a coral reef. Outside an Antarctic research station, a lone figure searches the ice around her for signs of life. In a high-security facility in Atlanta, a man dressed like an astronaut passes through a double airlock into a sterile laboratory. Sweltering in the heat and humidity of sub-Saharan Africa, volunteers collect blood samples from women and children with AIDS. What do these people have in common? They are biologists.

The word *biology* means the study of life. (The Greek word *bios* means "life," and *-logy* means "study of.") **Biology** is the science that seeks to understand the living world. A biologist is someone who uses a scientific method to study living things. The work of biologists can be quite varied, because organisms are complex and vary so greatly.

Characteristics of Living Things

Are the firefly and the fire in **Figure 1–14** alive? They are both giving off energy. Describing what makes something alive is not easy. No single characteristic is enough to describe a living thing. Also, some nonliving things share one or more traits with living things. Mechanical toys, automobiles, and clouds move around, for example, whereas mushrooms and trees live their lives in one spot. Other things, such as viruses, exist at the border between organisms and nonliving things. (You'll read more about viruses in Chapter 19.)

Despite these difficulties, it is possible to describe what most living things have in common. **Living things share several characteristics. These characteristics include the following:**

- **Living things are made up of units called cells.**
- **Living things reproduce.**
- **Living things are based on a universal genetic code.**
- **Living things grow and develop.**
- **Living things obtain and use materials and energy.**
- **Living things respond to their environment.**
- **Living things maintain a stable internal environment.**
- **Taken as a group, living things change over time.**

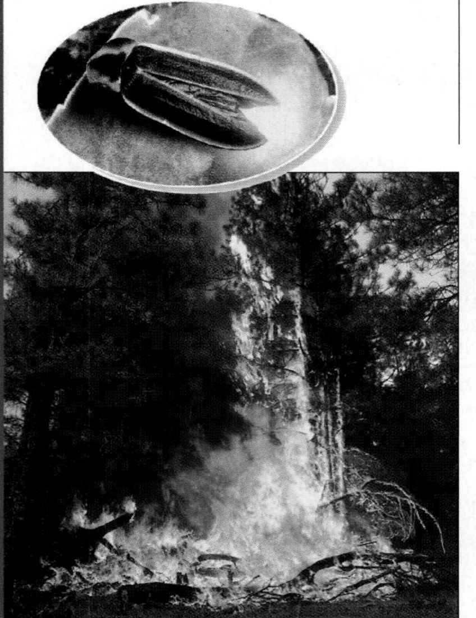

Figure 1–14 A Colorado firefly beetle (top) has all of the characteristics of living things. Even though fire (bottom) uses materials and can grow as living things do, fire is not alive because it does not have other characteristics of living things.

SECTION RESOURCES

Print:
- ***Teaching Resources,*** Section Review 1–3
- ***Guided Reading and Study Workbook,*** Section 1–3

Technology:
- ***iText,*** Section 1–3

Made Up of Cells Living things, or organisms, are made up of small, self-contained units called cells. A **cell** is a collection of living matter enclosed by a barrier that separates the cell from its surroundings. Cells are the smallest units of an organism that can be considered alive. Cells can grow, respond to their surroundings, and reproduce. Despite their small size, cells are complex and highly organized.

Many living things consist of only a single cell and are therefore called unicellular organisms. (The Latin prefix *uni-* means "one," so *unicellular* means "single-celled.") Many of the microorganisms involved in Spallanzani's and Pasteur's experiments were unicellular organisms.

The organisms you are most familiar with—for example, animals and plants—are multicellular. You can see one type of multicellular organism in **Figure 1–15.** (The Latin prefix *multi-* means "many." Thus, *multicellular* means "many-celled.") Multicellular organisms contain hundreds, thousands, or even trillions of cells. The cells in these organisms are often remarkably diverse, existing in a variety of sizes and shapes. In some multicellular organisms, each type of cell is specialized to perform a different function. The human body alone is made up of at least 85 different cell types. You will learn more about cells in Chapter 7.

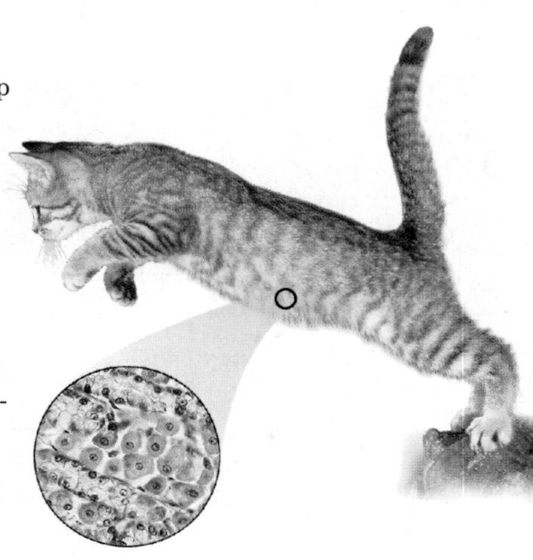

▲ **Figure 1–15** **Living things are made of cells.** Cats and most other familiar organisms are made of many cells. The inset shows cells from a cat's stomach (magnification: 500×).

Reproduction All organisms produce new organisms through a process called reproduction. There are two basic kinds of reproduction: sexual and asexual. The vast majority of multicellular organisms—from maple trees to birds and humans—reproduce sexually. In **sexual reproduction,** two cells from different parents unite to produce the first cell of the new organism. In **asexual reproduction,** the new organism has a single parent. In some forms of asexual reproduction, a single-celled organism divides in half to form two new organisms. In the type of asexual reproduction shown in **Figure 1–16,** a portion of an organism splits off to form a new organism.

CHECKPOINT *What is sexual reproduction?*

Based on a Genetic Code Offspring always resemble their parents. With asexual reproduction, offspring and their parents have the same traits. With sexual reproduction, offspring differ from their parents in some ways. However, there are limits to these differences. Flies produce flies, dogs produce dogs, and seeds from maple trees produce maple trees.

Explaining how organisms inherit traits is one of the greatest achievements of modern biology. Biologists now know that the directions for inheritance are carried by a molecule called deoxyribonucleic acid, or DNA. With minor exceptions, the DNA genetic code determines the inherited traits of every organism on Earth. You will learn how this is possible in Unit 4.

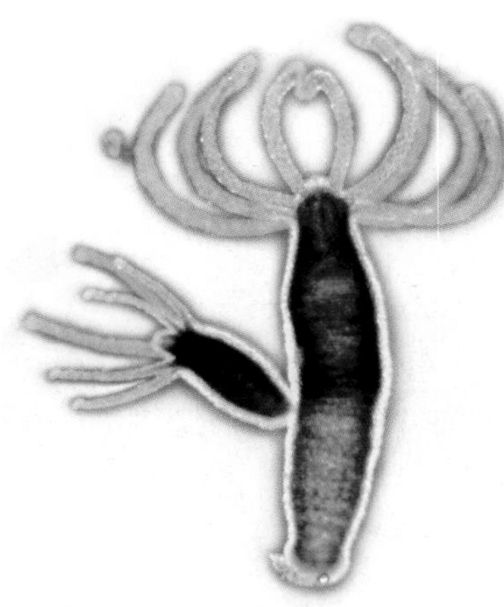

▲ **Figure 1–16** **All living things reproduce.** Here, one hydra is being formed from another through a type of asexual reproduction called budding. Shortly, the new organism will break away from the parent and live independently.

Build Science Skills

Comparing and Contrasting Ask students to compare the two organisms shown in the figures on this page, the cat in Figure 1–15 and the hydra in Figure 1–16. Explain that a hydra is a freshwater animal in the same animal phylum as the jellyfish. Ask students: **What characteristics of life do both of these organisms exhibit?** *(Both exhibit all the eight characteristics of life. Students should note that the cat is made of cells and that the hydra reproduces. Allow students to speculate about how each animal exhibits the other characteristics.)* **How are these two living things similar, and how are they different?** *(They are similar in that they are both animals. They are different in size, shape, structure, and habitat, among many other ways.)*

Meet Diverse Needs

Explain to students with limited English proficiency that the prefix *a-* means "not" or "without." Point out that the only difference between the terms *sexual reproduction* and *asexual reproduction* is the prefix *a-* at the beginning of the second term. Ask: **What does *asexual reproduction* literally mean?** *(Reproduction without sex, or "not" sexual reproduction)* **Limited English proficiency**

PRESENTATIONS MADE EASY!

The Presentation Assistant Plus contains the Prentice Hall Presentation Pro and the Transparencies, which provide easy-to-follow visual support for every step of this lesson. If you have a computer presentation station, use Prentice Hall Presentation Pro Section 1–3, or use the transparencies listed here.

Section 1–3:

Interest Grabber
Section Outline
Characteristics of Life
Figure 1–21

Answer to . . .

CHECKPOINT *In sexual reproduction, two cells from different parents unite to produce the first cell of a new organism.*

1–3 (continued)

Build Science Skills

Comparing and Contrasting Emphasize to students the difference between growth in living and growth in nonliving things. A good comparison to make is the growth of a child compared with that of a garbage heap. Point out that as a child eats food—pasta, fruits, vegetables, meat—he or she grows. In contrast, if you were to throw the same foods into a pile, the garbage heap would also grow. Ask: **Based on the example given, how would you compare the growth of living and nonliving things?** *(Answers may include the concepts of assimilation and organization, development of specific structures, and/or organized growth rather than a "pile.")* **Do organisms always grow and develop at the same rate?** *(Most students will know that organisms don't.)* **When do organisms stop growing and developing?** *(The process goes on at different rates but does not completely stop until death.)*

Use Visuals

Figure 1–18 Ask students: **How does the chameleon obtain the energy it needs to live?** *(It eats the grasshopper and other organisms for the energy stored in their bodies.)* **Where do you think the grasshopper obtained the energy it needed to live?** *(It obtained energy from plants it ate.)* **Where did the plants the grasshopper ate obtain the energy they needed to live?** *(From the sun through the process of photosynthesis)* Point out that all the living things on Earth ultimately obtain the energy they need from the energy of sunlight, as students will learn in greater detail in subsequent chapters.

Figure 1–17 **All living things grow and develop.** These photographs show how a spicebush swallowtail butterfly develops from an egg into a caterpillar (larva), a pupa, and, finally, an adult butterfly.

Growth and Development Each type of organism has a distinctive life cycle—a particular pattern of growth and change that occurs over the organism's lifetime. For some microorganisms, the main change that occurs is growth, an increase in size. All organisms grow during at least part of their lives.

Another type of change may occur, however. The life cycle of many kinds of multicellular organisms involves a process called development. The flies you read about earlier in Redi's experiment started life as eggs and became maggots (larvae) before becoming the familiar adult flies. **Figure 1–17** shows how a spicebush swallowtail butterfly changes before it becomes an adult. These changes are examples of development. During this process, the cells in an organism not only increase in number but also become different, or differentiate.

Need for Materials and Energy Think of what an organism needs as it grows and develops. Just as a building grows taller because workers use energy to assemble new materials, an organism uses energy and a constant supply of materials to grow, develop, and reproduce. The chameleon in **Figure 1–18,** for example, gets the materials it needs by eating smaller animals. Organisms also need materials and energy just to stay alive. The combination of chemical reactions through which an organism builds up or breaks down materials as it carries out its life processes is called **metabolism.**

All organisms take in selected materials that they need from their surroundings, or environment, but the way they obtain energy varies. Plants, some bacteria, and most algae obtain their energy directly from sunlight. Through a process called photosynthesis, these organisms convert light into a form of energy that is stored in certain molecules. That stored energy is ready to be used when needed.

Most other organisms rely on the energy stored during photosynthesis. Some organisms, such as grasshoppers and sheep, obtain their energy by eating plants and other photosynthesizing organisms. Other organisms, such as birds and wolves, get energy by eating the grasshoppers or sheep. And some organisms, called decomposers, obtain energy from the remains of organisms that have died.

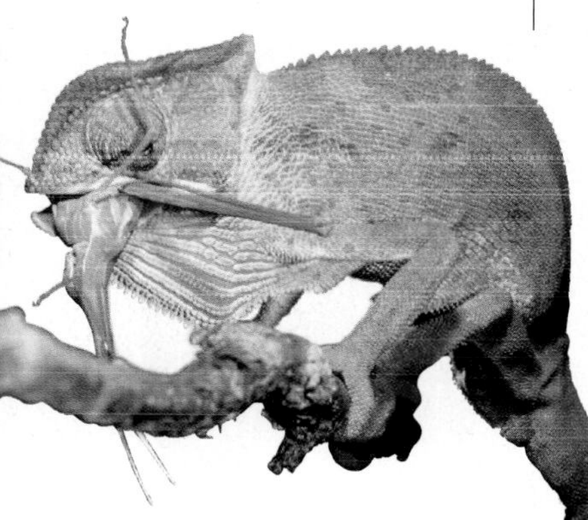

▲ **Figure 1–18** **Living things obtain and use materials and energy.** This chameleon has captured a large grasshopper, whose body will provide energy and a supply of materials needed for growth.

What is metabolism?

FACTS AND FIGURES

From largest to smallest
All organisms grow and develop. Yet how much growth and development occurs varies tremendously among living things. The largest animal alive is the blue whale, which can be as long as 30 meters and weigh as much as 130 metric tons—the equivalent of 30 elephants. The largest living thing is the giant sequoia, which can reach heights of over 100 meters. The smallest living thing is a type of bacteria known as *Mycoplasma,* which can be almost as small as 1000 nanometers in length. Viruses can be as small as 10 nanometers, but they are not considered living things. The smallest protozoans are about 10,000 nanometers, or 1 micron, in length.

Response to the Environment Organisms live in constantly changing environments. Variables such as the amount of light and the temperature change from day to day and from season to season. Other nearby living and nonliving things may change. An organism may make changes to its environment as well. Each organism responds to these changes in its own way.

A plant seed, for example, can germinate only when there is sufficient water and the ground is warm enough. The new leaves and stems that develop grow up toward light. The roots respond to gravity and grow down into the soil. Meanwhile, the plant takes in water and certain materials from the soil. It takes other materials from the air. The plant may provide shelter for insects and food for rabbits. Even after the plant dies, its remains become part of the very environment in which it once lived.

Maintaining Internal Balance The changes that happen in an organism are complex. A plant, for example, may take in water at one time and give off water at another. The plant may even take in and give off water at the same time. It may need large amounts of energy at one moment and have extra energy to store at another. Yet, while the plant lives, it maintains a certain internal consistency. The process by which organisms keep their internal conditions relatively stable is called **homeostasis** (hoh-mee-oh-STAY-sis). The condition of homeostasis is constantly being threatened by changes in the environment, such as shifting temperatures and changing light. The bird in **Figure 1–19** maintains a fairly constant body temperature during cold winters and hot summers. If homeostasis is disrupted in a major way, an organism cannot survive.

▲ **Figure 1–19** **Living things maintain an internal stability.** Despite the cold temperatures of this robin's environment, its body temperature remains fairly constant, partly because its feathers provide a layer of insulation and partly because of body heat it produces.

Quick Lab

What are the characteristics of living things?

Materials hand lens, unknown objects (dry), same objects soaked in water

Procedure 

1. Examine the dry unknown object your teacher provides. Record your observations.
2. **Predicting** In step 3, you will observe the same kind of object after it has been soaked in water. Write a prediction describing what you expect to see.
3. Examine one of the objects that has been soaking in water for a period of time. Record your observations. Wash your hands when you have finished.

Analyze and Conclude

1. **Evaluating** Was the prediction you made in step 2 correct? Explain your answer.
2. **Inferring** Were the objects you observed in step 1 living or nonliving? Were the objects you observed in step 3 living or nonliving? Use the observations you made as supporting evidence for your answers.
3. **Formulating Hypotheses** Suggest one or more ways to explain the differences between the dry and wet objects.
4. **Formulating Hypotheses** In what kind of natural environment might the objects you observed in this lab be found?

Quick Lab

Objective Students will be able to infer some characteristics of living things.

Skill Focus **Formulating Hypotheses**

Materials hand lens, dormant brine shrimp eggs, water, hatched brine shrimp eggs, bowls covered with fabric

Time 15 minutes

Advance Prep Obtain dormant brine shrimp eggs—also called "sea monkeys"—from a biological supply house. A day, or at least several hours, before the activity begins, put some of the dormant eggs in water so that students can observe live hatchlings in step 3.

Safety Make sure students wash their hands after handling the dormant eggs or live shrimp.

Strategy Have the hatchlings in bowls covered with fabric and stationed around the classroom. After students have written their predictions, uncover the bowls and invite students to observe.

Expected Outcomes Students will recognize that the line between living and nonliving is not as clear as they might have thought.

Analyze and Conclude

1. Answers will depend on students' predictions. Most students will not have predicted that the objects they observed in step 1 would become live shrimp or anything else alive.
2. Students should recognize that the objects they observed in step 3 were alive and infer that the objects they observed in step 1 were also alive.
3. Accept any reasonable response, provided that the arguments are logical and based on observation.
4. Students might correctly infer from their observations that these organisms are native to a tidal environment, where the eggs can remain dormant when they are dry.

BIO INSIGHTS **HISTORY OF SCIENCE**

A constant "internal milieu"

In 1851, French physiologist Claude Bernard (1813–1878) discovered that nerves in an animal's body control the dilation and constriction of blood vessels. He observed that on hot days the blood vessels of the skin become dilated, whereas on cold days those same blood vessels become constricted. Bernard concluded that the function of these changes has to do with regulating the body's internal temperature. On hot days, dilated blood vessels radiate heat away from the body. On cold days, constricted vessels conserve body heat. Thus, even when the external environment changes, an animal has a way of maintaining a constant "internal milieu." His concept of the maintenance of an internal balance within an animal is incorporated in the modern concept of homeostasis, which literally means "same condition."

Answer to . . .

✓CHECKPOINT *Metabolism is the combination of chemical reactions through which an organism builds up or breaks down materials as it carries out its life processes.*

Use Visuals

Figure 1–20 Ask students: **What does it mean in your everyday life when you become "adapted" to a situation?** *(You adjust to the situation by making small changes in the way you act or feel.)* **How could an organism such as a plant become "adapted" to a changing environment?** *(Some students might suggest that plants could somehow adjust to dryness or coldness by growing new structures.)* Explain that the biological term *adaptation* implies changes over time—a great deal of time. An individual organism doesn't adapt; rather, a group of organisms changes over time.

Branches of Biology

Meet Diverse Needs

To introduce this topic to at-risk students, play a game of 20 questions with the class. Think of a familiar plant or animal, such as a dandelion, an ant, or a sparrow. Tell students that you are thinking of a certain organism and that they are allowed 20 yes-or-no questions to determine what this organism is.
As the game progresses, you might suggest questions to the class; do not let them stray too far from the correct answer. Tell students that whether they realized it or not, they were conducting a scientific investigation. They were presented with a problem, and they needed to ask the right questions to reach a solution. Emphasize that in science, answers are often available—it's figuring out the right questions that is difficult.
Learning modality: verbal

Figure 1–20 **Taken as a group, all living things change over time.** If you suddenly moved most plants to this Namibian desert (left), they would be killed by the heat and lack of water. But a few types of plants have become adapted to these hot and dry conditions, surviving periods of drought to grow and flower after a rainfall (right).

Evolution Although individual organisms experience many changes during their lives, the basic traits they inherited from their parents usually do not change. As a group, however, any given kind of organism can **evolve,** or change over time.

Over a few generations, the changes in a group may not seem significant. But over hundreds of thousands or even millions of years, the changes can be dramatic. The ability of certain plants, such as those in **Figure 1–20,** to survive periods without water is one example. Another example concerns fishes. Scientists study deposits containing the remains of animals that lived long ago to learn about the evolution of organisms. From the study of very early deposits, scientists know that at one time there were no fishes in Earth's waters. Yet, in more recent deposits, the remains of fishes and other animals with backbones are abundant. The ability of a group of organisms to change over time is invaluable for survival in a world that is always changing. You will read about the processes of evolution in Unit 5.

Branches of Biology

The diversity of life is so great that no biologist can study everything, so biology is often organized into branches, or divisions. Some divisions are based on the type of organism being studied. Zoologists study animals. (The prefix *zoo-* means "animal.") Botanists study plants. (*Botanikos* means "plants.") Others study life from a particular perspective. Ethologists study animal behavior. (*Ethos-* means "custom.") Paleontologists study life as it was in the past. (*Paleo-* means "ancient.")

The study of biology can also be approached based on the idea that life can be studied at different levels of organization. Each level is a system made up of smaller parts. Each system may, in turn, be part of a larger system. The levels can differ in both size and complexity. **The many levels at which life can be studied include molecules, cells, organisms, populations of a single organism, communities of populations living in the same area, and the biosphere.** Some of the levels of organization of interest to biologists are summarized in the table in **Figure 1–21.**

FACTS AND FIGURES

Branches of biology
The branches of biology are too numerous to list. Zoologists, botanists, paleontologists, and ethologists are just a few of the great variety of biologists. Biochemists study the chemistry of living things. Geneticists study heredity and variation among organisms. Cytologists, or cell biologists, study the structure and function of cells. Ecologists study the interaction of organisms in ecosystems. Microbiologists study the structure and function of microorganisms. The list goes on, and those mentioned are just the biologists who pursue knowledge in what is sometimes called theoretical science. There are also many biologists who work in applied or practical science, including physicians, medical researchers, wildlife managers, foresters, and agricultural researchers, to name just a few.

Levels of Organization		
Biosphere	The part of Earth that contains all ecosystems	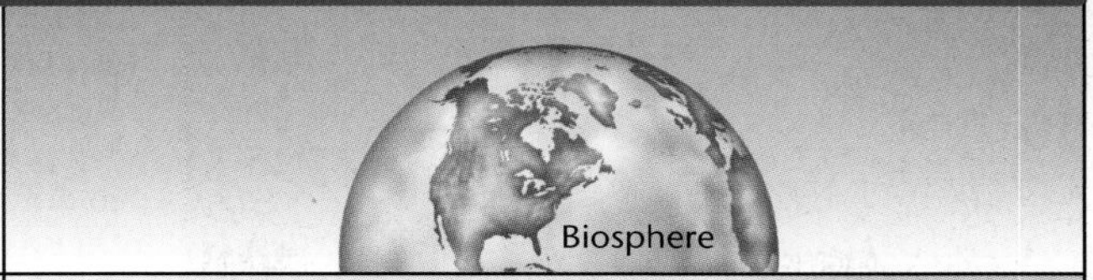 Biosphere
Ecosystem	Community and its nonliving surroundings	 Hawk, snake, bison, prairie dog, grass, stream, rocks, air
Community	Populations that live together in a defined area	 Hawk, snake, bison, prairie dog, grass
Population	Group of organisms of one type that live in the same area	 Bison herd
Organism	Individual living thing	 Bison
Groups of Cells	Tissues, organs, and organ systems	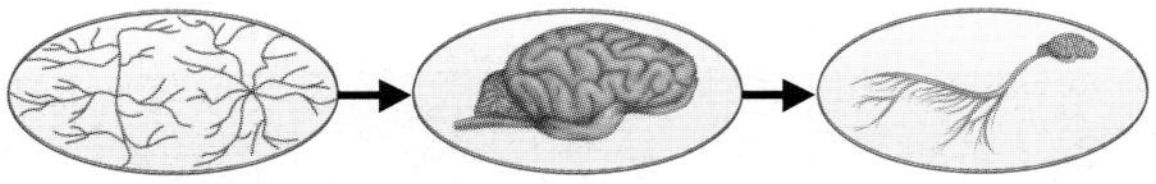 Nervous tissue → Brain → Nervous system
Cells	Smallest functional unit of life	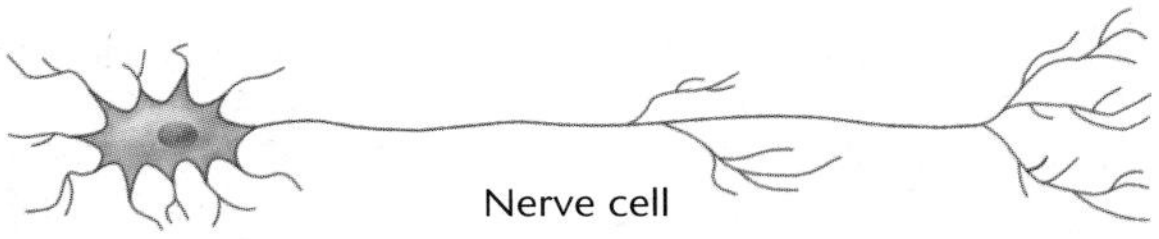 Nerve cell
Molecules	Groups of atoms; smallest unit of most chemical compounds	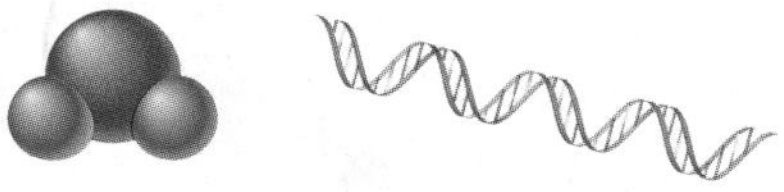 Water, DNA

Figure 1–21 **Living things may be studied on many different levels.** The largest and most complex level is the biosphere. The smallest level is the molecules that make up living things.

Use Visuals

Figure 1–21 Make sure students understand the hierarchy implied in the figure: molecular, cellular, multicellular, organism, population, community, ecosystem, and biosphere. Have students use a dictionary to clarify the meaning of these terms. Then, ask students to make a graphic organizer that could represent relationships among the terms, such as a series of larger and larger circles.

Build Science Skills

Posing Questions Display the same pictures of natural environments that students examined for the Assess Prior Knowledge activity on page 2. Ask students again to choose one of the pictures to examine closely and to compile a list of 20 questions a biologist might ask about the organisms in the picture. Explain that these questions could concern anything from the molecular level to the biosphere level. Have students compare the 20 questions they wrote after having read these sections with the 20 questions they wrote previously.

Biology in Everyday Life

Build Science Skills

Applying Concepts Ask students to choose a commercial product that they use every day, such as a certain soap, type of makeup, kind of chewing gum, or brand of deodorant. Ask them to explain in a paragraph how they could use what they have learned so far in this chapter to find out how the product affects their body and whether it could be harmful in some way.

3 ASSESS

Evaluate Understanding

Have students explain in writing how a cat, such as the one shown in Figure 1–15, exhibits all of the characteristics of living things.

Reteach

Point out a living thing and a nonliving thing in the classroom, such as a computer and a fish in an aquarium. Have students compare and contrast the two using the eight characteristics of living things.

MAKING CONNECTIONS

Students could observe whether the object ingests or excretes materials, whether it increases in size over time, and whether it responds to changes in its environment.

Use the iText to review the key concepts in Section 1–3.

▲ **Figure 1–22** Progress in biology has meant huge improvements in health not just for you and your family but, in some societies, for pets as well. **Predicting** ***How do you expect advances in biology to change health care during your lifetime?***

Biology in Everyday Life

As you begin studying biology, you may be thinking of it as just another course, with a textbook to read plus labs, homework, and tests. It's also a *science* course, so you may worry that it will be too difficult. But you will see that more than any other area of study, biology touches your life every day. In fact, it's hard to think of anything you do that isn't affected by it. It helps you understand and appreciate every other form of life, from pets such as the dog in **Figure 1–22** to dinosaurs no longer present on Earth. It provides information about the food you need and the methods for sustaining the world's food supplies. It describes the conditions of good health and the behaviors and diseases that can harm you. It is used to diagnose and treat medical problems. It identifies environmental factors that might threaten you, such as disposal of wastes from human activities. More than any other science, biology helps you understand what affects the quality of your life.

Biologists do not make the decisions about most matters affecting human society or the natural world; citizens and governments do. In just a few years, you will be able to exercise the rights of a voting citizen, influencing public policy by the ballots you cast and the messages you send public officials. With others, you will make decisions based on many factors, including customs, values, ethical standards, and scientific knowledge. Biology can provide decision makers with useful information and analytical skills. It can help them envision the possible effects of their decisions. Biology can help people understand that humans are capable of predicting and trying to control their future and that of the planet.

1–3 Section Assessment

1. **Key Concept** Describe five characteristics of living things.
2. **Key Concept** What topics might biologists study at the community level of organization?
3. Compare sexual reproduction and asexual reproduction.
4. What biological process includes chemical reactions that break down materials?
5. What happens to an organism if its homeostasis is disrupted and not restored?
6. **Critical Thinking Applying Concepts** Try to think of a nonliving thing that satisfies each characteristic of living things. Does any nonliving thing have all the characteristics of life?

Assessment Use iText to review the important concepts in Section 1–3.

MAKING CONNECTIONS

Making Observations
List some observations that could be made to determine whether an object that is not moving is living or nonliving. Refer to Section 1–1.

1–3 Section Assessment

1. Made up of cells; reproduce; are based on a genetic code; grow and develop; obtain and use materials and energy; respond to their environment; maintain a stable internal environment; as a group, change over time
2. Biologists might identify all the populations living in a given area, study the interactions between a predator and its prey, or investigate how a change in the size of one population affects the sizes of other populations.
3. In sexual reproduction, offspring have the same traits as their single parent. In sexual reproduction, offspring are not identical to either of their two parents.
4. Metabolism
5. The organism could not survive.
6. No nonliving thing would satisfy all the characteristics of life, because by definition that thing would be considered as living.

Answer to . . .

Figure 1–22 *A typical response might suggest that researchers will find cures for many diseases.*

When Scientists Have a Conflict of Interest

Science Advisors Were Paid Industry Consultants Two scientists testifying at a public hearing about the safety of a new pesticide today admitted that they had once worked for the pesticide's manufacturer. Both researchers denied that their testimony was influenced by the company. However, neither scientist had disclosed the relationship before giving a recommendation.

Scientists are expected to be completely honest about their investigations. Doctors are expected to place the welfare of their patients first. Yet, conflicts of interest can often threaten the credibility of a researcher. A conflict of interest exists when a person's work can be influenced by personal factors such as financial gain, fame, future work, or favoritism.

The Viewpoints

Regulation Is Necessary

Some scientists argue that, because the public must be able to trust the work of science, some rules are essential for preserving scientific integrity. Every profession should regulate its members, and every science publication should have strict rules about avoiding conflicts of interest. In any published work, announcements of potential conflicts should be required. In some cases, scientists should avoid or be forbidden to do work that involves personal gain in addition to the usual payment for doing the work. Some form of government regulation may be needed.

Regulation Is Unnecessary

Other scientists insist that conflict-of-interest regulations are unnecessary for the majority of researchers, who are honest and objective about their work. It is unfair to assume that a researcher's discoveries would be different because a particular organization has paid for an investigation. In fact, without additional funding from some organizations, new drugs or new techniques would never have been developed. So, it is important that scientists be allowed to investigate any topic, especially when it would help others.

You Decide

1. **Defining the Issue** When might scientists have a conflict of interest? Are financial incentives more dangerous to a scientist's objectivity than other conflicts of interest? Explain.
2. **Analyzing the Viewpoints** How might the views about a possible conflict of interest differ among a group of scientists, a science journal editor deciding to publish a scientist's work, the company employing a scientist, and people seeking information from a scientist?
3. **Forming Your Opinion** How do you think this problem of possible conflicts of interest should be decided? Include information or reasoning that answers people with the opposite view.
4. **Role-Playing** Suppose doctors who own a company developing a new medicine want their patients to help test the medicine. Let one person represent a doctor, a second person a patient, and a third person a medical reporter asking: Should the patients take part in the tests?

After students have responded to question 4 in You Decide, have student volunteers role-play the situation for the class. Follow that by a class discussion of the issue. Then, ask each student to write a statement about his or her own assessment on such a conflict of interest.

You Decide

1. A conflict of interest exists when a person's work can be influenced by personal factors such as financial gain, future work, favoritism, or fame. Students should provide an example for each of kind of conflict of interest when stating their opinions on whether financial reasons are more dangerous to a scientist's objectivity.

2. A typical response might suggest that a science journal and people seeking information from a scientist would have the greatest interest in avoiding possible conflicts of interest, because a journal's reputation depends on the validity of published research and a person seeking information wants only unbiased data.

3. A typical response might suggest that journals and professional organizations should adopt strict guidelines about conflicts of interest and that there should even be some government regulation. Students should back their positions with logical arguments.

4. Have students write a dialogue that includes viewpoints from the doctor and the patient, with the reporter questioning each. The reporter might press the doctor on whether owning the company is a conflict of interest that would invalidate the test. The reporter might ask the patient whether the doctor can be trusted and whether the test will be conducted in a safe way.

BIO INSIGHTS — BACKGROUND

Reasons to be concerned

There are no sciencewide rules about reporting conflicts of interest, nor is there government regulation requiring biologists to do so. Various publications and professional organizations have their own code of ethics. In recent years, there has been a growing concern about how such conflicts might be affecting scientific research, especially the great amount of research done in universities. By 1997, U.S. companies were spending $1.7 billion a year on university-based science and engineering research. By the late 1990s, more than 90 percent of companies connected to the life sciences had some kind of relationship with scientists who worked in universities. In 1992, the ten top research universities received $170 million in product royalties. Yet, in a survey of science journals, 142 of 210 journals did not publish a single disclosure of a conflict of interest in 1997.

Section 1–4

1 FOCUS

Objectives

1.4.1 ***Describe*** the measurement system most scientists use.
1.4.2 ***Explain*** how light microscopes and electron microscopes are similar and different.
1.4.3 ***Describe*** two common laboratory techniques.
1.4.4 ***Explain*** why it is important to work safely in biology.

Guide for Reading

Vocabulary Preview

Have students write a definition of what they think each of the Vocabulary terms means before they read the section. As they read the section, they should revise their definitions as needed.

Reading Strategy

Before students read, have them skim the section to identify the main ideas. As they read the section, have them make a list of the supporting details for each main idea.

2 INSTRUCT

A Common Measurement System

Meet Diverse Needs

All students should be somewhat familiar with the metric system, but at-risk students may not have the facility necessary to use the system with confidence. To reinforce students' ability to make and use metric measurements, prepare a set of flashcards that students can use to learn equivalent units of metric measure. For example:

- 1 kilometer = *(1000)* meters
- 0.45 liter = *(450)* milliliters
- 5000 milligrams = *(5)* grams
- 130 meters = *(0.13)* kilometer
- 2500 milliliters = *(2.5)* liters
- 0.017 grams = *(17)* milligrams

Learning modality: logical/mathematical

1–4 Tools and Procedures

Guide for Reading

Key Concepts
- What measurement system do most scientists use?
- How are light microscopes and electron microscopes similar? How are they different?

Vocabulary
metric system
microscope
compound light microscope
electron microscope
cell culture
cell fractionation

Reading Strategy: Using Graphic Organizers As you read, create a table that lists the procedures discussed in this section. List one example of what biologists can accomplish using each procedure.

Imagine being one of the first people to see living things through a magnifying glass. How surprised you would have been to discover a a whole new realm of life! Could there still be other types of life that remain undiscovered today because the right tools are not available?

Tools play a major role in science. Electronic balances measure the mass of objects with great precision. Microscopes and telescopes make it possible to observe objects that are very small or very far away. With powerful computers, scientists can store and analyze vast collections of data. Biologists have even devised procedures that help them unlock the information stored in the DNA of different organisms.

A Common Measurement System

Because researchers need to replicate each other's experiments and most experiments involve measurements, scientists need a common system of measurement. **Most scientists use the metric system when collecting data and performing experiments.** The **metric system** is a decimal system of measurement whose units are based on certain physical standards and are scaled on multiples of 10. A revised version of the original metric system is called the International System of Units, or SI. The abbreviation SI comes from the French *Le Système International d'Unités.*

Because the metric system is based on multiples of 10, it is easy to use. Notice in **Figure 1–23** how the basic unit of length, the meter, can be multiplied or divided to measure objects and distances much larger or smaller than a meter. The same process can be used when measuring volume and mass. You can learn more about the metric system in Appendix C.

▶ **Figure 1–23** **Scientists usually use the metric system in their work.** This system is easy to use because it is based on multiples of 10.

Common Metric Units

Length	Mass
1 meter (m) = 100 centimeters (cm) 1 meter = 1000 millimeters (mm) 1000 meters = 1 kilometer (km)	1 kilogram (kg) = 1000 grams (g) 1 gram = 1000 milligrams (mg) 1000 kilograms = 1 metric ton (t)
Volume	**Temperature**
1 liter (L) = 1000 milliliters (mL) 1 liter = 1000 cubic centimeters (cm^3)	0°C = freezing point of water 100°C = boiling point of water

TIME SAVER

SECTION RESOURCES

Print:
- ***Laboratory Manual A,*** Chapter 1 Lab
- ***Laboratory Manual B,*** Chapter 1 Lab
- ***Teaching Resources,*** Section Review 1–4, Chapter 1 Exploration
- ***Guided Reading and Study Workbook,*** Section 1–4

Technology:
- ***iText,*** Section 1–4

Water Released and Absorbed by Tree

Time	Absorbed by Roots (g/h)	Released by Leaves (g/h)
8 AM	1	2
10 AM	1	5
12 PM	4	12
2 PM	6	17
4 PM	9	16
6 PM	14	10
8 PM	10	3

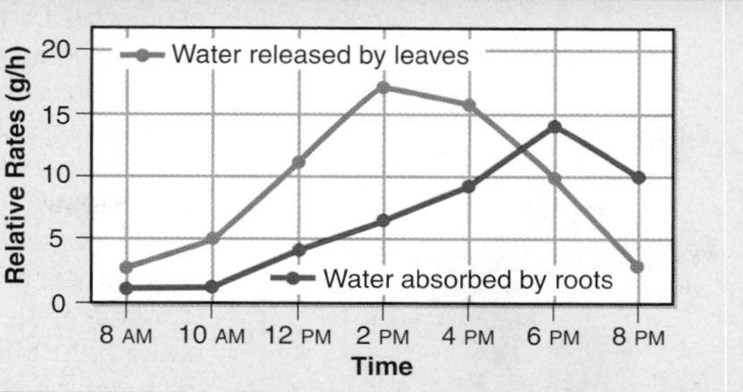

▲ **Figure 1–24** One way to record data from an experiment is by using a data table. Then, the data may be plotted on a graph to make it easier to interpret. **Interpreting Graphics** *At what time of day is the rate of water released by leaves equal to the rate of water absorbed by roots?*

Analyzing Biological Data

When scientists collect data, they are often trying to find out whether certain factors changed or remained the same. Often, the simplest way to do that is to record the data in a table and then make a graph. Although you may be able to detect a pattern of change from a data table like the one in **Figure 1–24**, a graph of the data can make a pattern much easier to recognize and understand.

In science today, the amount of data being produced by biologists is so huge that no individual can look at more than a tiny fraction of it. To make sense of the data, biologists often turn to computers. For example, computers help determine the structure of molecules. They also allow biologists to search through DNA sequences, find significant regions of the molecule, and discover how organisms are affected by that region. At the opposite end of the scale, computers are essential to every step of data gathering by satellite, including analyzing satellite data and presenting the results. Analyses of satellite data are used to make predictions about complex phenomena such as global climate changes.

✓CHECKPOINT *How can a graph help biologists analyze data?*

Microscopes

When people think of scientific tools, one of the first tools that comes to mind is the microscope. **Microscopes** are devices that produce magnified images of structures that are too small to see with the unaided eye. **Light microscopes produce magnified images by focusing visible light rays. Electron microscopes produce magnified images by focusing beams of electrons.** Since the first microscope was invented, microscope manufacturers have had to deal with two problems: What is the instrument's magnification—that is, how much larger can it make an object appear compared to the object's real size? And how sharp an image can the instrument produce?

Word Origins

Microscope comes from the Greek words *micro-*, meaning "small," and *skop-*, meaning "see." So, *microscope* means an instrument for looking at very small objects. **What do you think the word *microorganism* means?**

Analyzing Biological Data

Use Visuals

Figure 1–24 Direct students' attention to the graph in the figure. Then, ask: **On which axis is time recorded?** *(On the horizontal axis, or x-axis)* **On which axis are the relative rates recorded?** *(On the vertical axis, or y-axis)* **What pattern does the graph show at a glance about water given off and taken in by a tree?** *(The water released by leaves peaks at 2 PM; the water absorbed by roots peaks at 6 PM.)*

Microscopes

Word Origins

The word *microorganism* means "small living thing."

Meet Diverse Needs

Most students will remember some things about microscopes from previous science courses, but there is likely to be a wide range of proficiencies in the class. This is the time to get out the microscopes and have a hands-on review of the parts and their functions. Have students work with partners to practice naming parts, describing functions, and demonstrating proper handling and use. **Learning modality: tactile**

PRESENTATIONS MADE EASY!

The Presentation Assistant Plus contains the Prentice Hall Presentation Pro and the Transparencies, which provide easy-to-follow visual support for every step of this lesson. If you have a computer presentation station, use Prentice Hall Presentation Pro Section 1–4, or use the transparencies listed here.

Section 1–4:

Interest Grabber
Section Outline
Making a Graph From a Data Table

Answers to . . .

✓CHECKPOINT *A graph of collected data can make a pattern much easier to recognize and understand.*

Figure 1–24 *The rate of water released by leaves is equal to the rate of water absorbed by roots at around 5 PM.*

Build Science Skills

Making Judgments Point out that all microscopes have limits of resolution. Explain that as the magnifying power of a light microscope is increased, more and more detail can be seen, at least up to a certain point. Detail is lost and objects get blurry beyond that point, which is called the limit of resolution. Resolution is the capability to distinguish the individual parts of an object. Ask students: **If you are looking at feathers or insect legs under a microscope, how important is excellent resolution?** *(Not very important, because you are looking at overall structure)* **What if you are looking at slides of plant or animal cells?** *(Resolution is now very important, because detail is important.)* **Name some obvious advantages to looking at living rather than dead specimens under the microscope.** *(Advantages include the ability to observe living color, movement, and reactions to stimuli.)*

Build Science Skills

Applying Concepts Give students a list of the following topics, and ask them which kind of microscope, if any, would best serve the topic's investigation, with an explanation of why that kind would serve best.

- **The feeding habits of unicellular protozoa** *(A light microscope, because the organisms are small and would need to be studied alive)*
- **The surface of a red blood cell** *(A scanning electron microscope, because it would be best for looking at surfaces)*
- **The feeding habits of a house cat** *(No microscope is necessary to observe the behavior of an animal as large as a cat.)*
- **The interior structures of a cell** *(A transmission electron microscope, because it would be best for looking at a very thin specimen)*

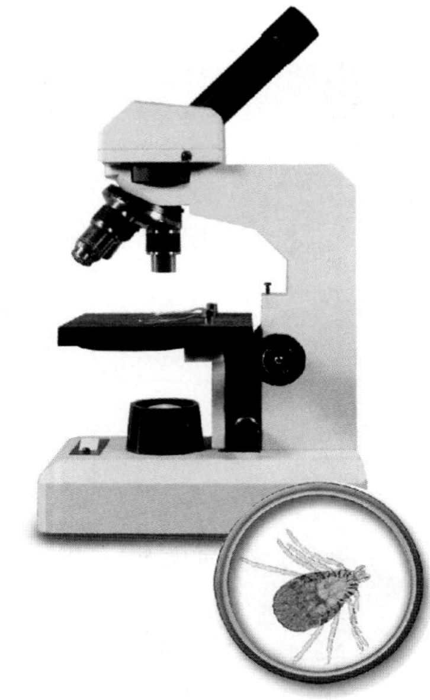

▲ **Figure 1–25** **Light microscopes produce magnified images by focusing visible light rays.** The tick shown in the inset is magnified about 10 times.

Light Microscopes The most commonly used microscope is the light microscope. Light microscopes can produce clear images of objects at a magnification of about 1000 times. **Figure 1–25** shows a compound light microscope similar to those in many high school laboratories. **Compound light microscopes** allow light to pass through the specimen and use two lenses to form an image. In addition to studying specimens of dead organisms or their parts, light microscopes make it possible to observe some tiny organisms and cells while they are still alive. You can refer to Appendix D to learn how to use a compound light microscope.

Biologists have developed techniques and procedures to make light microscopes more useful. Chemical stains, also called dyes, can show specific structures in the cell. Fluorescent dyes have been combined with video cameras and new optical techniques to produce moving three-dimensional images of processes such as cell movement. Computer processing of the video signals from such microscopes even makes it possible to follow the movements of cell parts and materials within the cell in real time.

Electron Microscopes Light microscopes can produce sharp images of objects only when the objects are larger than 0.2 micrometers, or about $\frac{1}{50}$ the diameter of a typical cell. To study smaller objects, biologists developed electron microscopes in the 1950s. **Electron microscopes** focus beams of electrons on specimens. These microscopes can form images of objects 1000 times smaller than those visible under a light microscope. Because light from the visible spectrum is not involved, untouched electron microscope images have no color.

Biologists use two main types of electron microscopes. Transmission electron microscopes (TEMs) shine a beam of electrons through a thin specimen. Scanning electron microscopes (SEMs) run a pencil-like beam of electrons back and forth across the surface of a specimen. SEMs produce realistic—and often dramatic—three-dimensional images of the surfaces of objects. The image of the ant in **Figure 1–26** was produced by a scanning electron microscope. Despite their power, however, electron microscopes cannot be used to study live specimens. Samples for TEM and SEM work must be completely dried out before they are placed in the vacuum inside the microscope. This means that only dead and preserved cells can be observed. Living specimens would be killed by the processes that are used to prepare the sample.

✓CHECKPOINT *What are microscopes used for?*

◀ **Figure 1–26** **Electron microscopes produce images by focusing beams of electrons.** This image of an ant on a blade of grass was created using a scanning electron microscope. The color, not part of the original image, was added artificially.

FACTS AND FIGURES

Electron microscopes
In both transmission electron microscopes and scanning electron microscopes, the lenses are made of electromagnets, which gather and focus the beam of electrons. The beam of electrons is produced by heating a filament. For an image to be produced, the path of the electrons must be unobstructed. Therefore, the samples are placed in a vacuum instead of in air. Objects must be extremely thin—less than 0.1 micron—to be examined by a TEM, because the TEM produces an image by passing a beam of electrons through an object. The electrons then either produce an image on a fluorescent screen or produce a permanent image on photographic film. Objects examined by an SEM need not be thin, because the electrons are picked up by detectors after bouncing off the specimen, and the detectors provide the data necessary to form an image on a monitor.

Analyzing Data

Bacterial Reproduction

Bacteria are tiny microorganisms that can reproduce by dividing into two. The graph shows the results of an experiment on the effect of temperature on bacterial reproduction. At the beginning, three populations of bacteria, all of the same type, were of equal size. Each population was kept at a different temperature for 4 days.

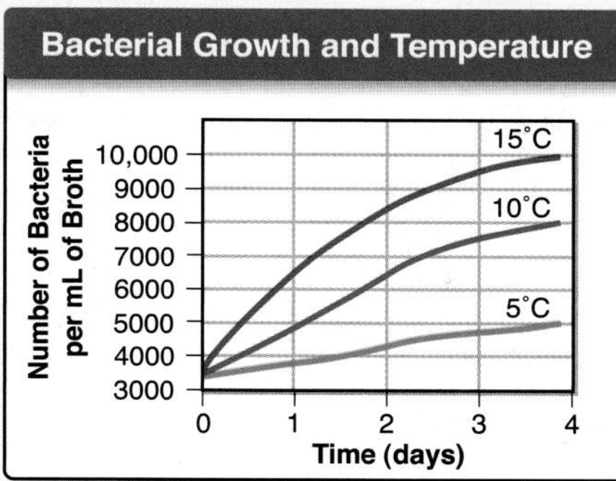

1. **Classifying** What variable did the researcher change during this experiment?
2. **Inferring** What do the shapes of the curves tell you about the changes in population size?
3. **Calculating** For the bacteria kept at 15°C, how did population size change during the experiment?
4. **Drawing Conclusions** What effect did the different temperatures have on the growth of the bacterial populations?
5. **Going Further** Suppose some bacteria used in this experiment were kept at a temperature of 100°C (the temperature of boiling water). Would you expect the population sizes to increase even faster than at 15°C? Explain your reasoning.

Laboratory Techniques

Biologists use a variety of techniques to study cells. Two common laboratory techniques are cell culturing and cell fractionation.

Cell Cultures To obtain enough material to study, biologists like the one in **Figure 1–27** sometimes place a single cell into a dish containing a nutrient solution. The cell is able to reproduce so that a group of cells, called a **cell culture,** develops from the single original cell. Cell cultures can be used to test cell responses under controlled conditions, to study interactions between cells, and to select specific cells for further study.

Cell Fractionation Suppose you want to study just one part of a cell. How could you separate that one part from the rest of the cell? Biologists often use a technique known as **cell fractionation** to separate the different cell parts. First, the cells are broken into pieces in a special blender. Then, the broken cell bits are added to a liquid and placed in a tube. The tube is inserted into a centrifuge, which is an instrument that can spin the tube up to 20,000 times per minute. Spinning causes the cell parts to separate, with the most dense parts settling near the bottom of the tube and the least dense parts rising toward the top. A biologist can then remove the specific part of the cell to be studied by selecting the appropriate layer.

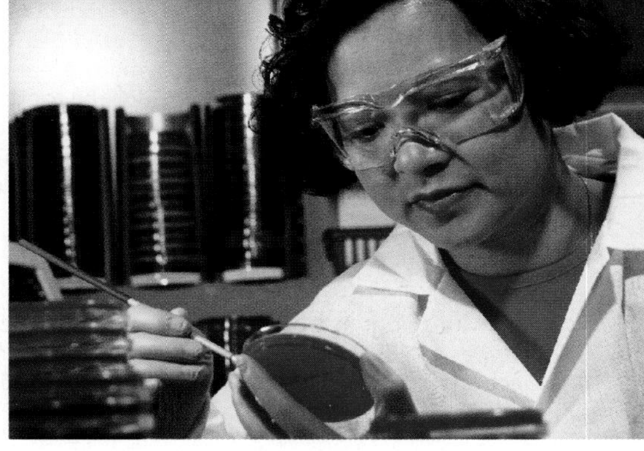

▼ **Figure 1–27** This researcher is preparing a cell culture by transferring bacteria to a solid that contains nutrients, which will enable the bacteria to reproduce. **Comparing and Contrasting** *How do the results of a cell culture differ from the products of cell fractionation?*

BIO INSIGHTS — HISTORY OF SCIENCE

From the kitchen to the lab

The ability to study bacteria in a laboratory is crucial for understanding their structure and function. Robert Koch (1843–1910), a German bacteriologist, was the first to perfect a method of doing so. The growth medium he first used was beef broth. The addition of the protein gelatin to the broth solidified the medium, but a problem remained. Many bacteria could digest the gelatin, and the result was the formation of little puddles in the medium, making it difficult to study the bacteria. The answer came in 1881 when the wife of one of Koch's coworkers told Koch about the agar-agar she used in cooking as a solidifying agent. Koch discovered that this substance, produced by the red alga *Gelidium,* could not be digested by bacteria. Agar—the current term for agar-agar—has been used in laboratories as a culture medium ever since.

Laboratory Techniques

Analyzing Data

The experiment described here is typical of how cell cultures of bacteria and other microorganisms are studied to test responses under controlled conditions. In this study, researchers might be investigating the optimum growth temperature of a bacterial species. The specific range of temperatures in which bacteria can grow varies among species. Some species, called psychrophiles, can grow at temperatures below 0°C. Other species, called thermophiles, grow at temperatures approaching the boiling point of water and are incapable of growth below 45°C. The most common bacteria, called mesophiles, have an optimum growth temperature between 25°C and 40°C.

Answers

1. Temperature
2. The population of bacteria at 5°C grew slowly and steadily. At 10°C, the popultation grew rapidly at first; the rate of growth decreased after about two days. The population at 15°C grew most rapidly at first; the rate of growth slowed steadily after a day and the population appears to have leveled off at about four days.
3. The population size grew from about 3500/mL of broth at the start of the experiment to 10,000/mL at the end.
4. The bacterial population grew most at the highest temperature and grew least at the lowest temperature.
5. Students might suggest that population size would increase even faster than at 15°C, because the graph shows that the higher the temperature, the more the bacterial growth. Because 100°C is the boiling point of water, students may say that the bacteria would not survive at 100°C.

Answers to . . .

CHECKPOINT *Microscopes are used to produce images of structures that are too small to see with the unaided eye.*

Figure 1–27 *The product of a cell culture is a group of cells. The products of cell fractionation are layers containing different cell parts.*

1–4 (continued)

Working Safely in Biology

Demonstration

To acquaint students with the laboratory in which they will be working, point out the location of the water, the nearest fire extinguisher, and the first aid equipment. Explain the procedures to follow in case of fire, accident, or injury. You may wish to make instructions for display in the lab. Show how to use safety goggles and heat-resistant gloves. Show some of the equipment students will use in the lab, including glassware, microscopes, heating devices, chemicals, knives, and scalpels. For each piece of equipment, ask: **What is the safety symbol associated with this item?** *(Some students may be familiar with common safety symbols.)* Point out and discuss the safety symbols used in their textbook and laboratory manuals.

3 ASSESS

Evaluate Understanding

Call on students at random to explain the differences in structure and image obtained from a compound light microscope, a TEM, and a SEM.

Reteach

Have students look at the image on page 2. Ask them to tell how they know the image was made by a SEM and not a light microscope or a TEM.

Take It to the NET

Time lines should include such microscopes as Janssens's from the 1590s, Leeuwenhoek's from the 1670s, and some made in Europe in the 1700s and 1800s. For additional information, visit **www.phschool.com**

Use iText to review the key concepts in Section 1–4.

Answer to . . .

Figure 1–28 *To protect themselves from exposure to nuclear wastes*

Working Safely in Biology

Scientists working in a laboratory or in the field like those in **Figure 1–28** are trained to use safe procedures when carrying out investigations. Laboratory work may involve flames or heating elements, electricity, chemicals, hot liquids, sharp instruments, and breakable glassware. Laboratory or field work may involve contact with living or dead organisms—not just the plants, animals, and other living things you can see but other organisms you cannot see without a microscope.

Whenever you work in your biology laboratory, it's important for you to follow safety precautions as well. Before performing any activity in this course, study the safety rules in Appendix B. Before you start any activity, read all the steps, and make sure that you understand the entire procedure, including any safety precautions that must be followed. The single most important rule for your safety is simple: Always follow your teacher's instructions and the textbook directions exactly. If you are in doubt about any part of an activity, always ask your teacher for an explanation. And, because you may be in contact with organisms you cannot see, it is essential that you wash your hands thoroughly after every scientific activity. Remember, you are responsible for your own safety and that of your teacher and classmates. If you are handling live animals, you are responsible for their safety as well.

▼ **Figure 1–28** These workers are cleaning up Rocky Flats, a Colorado site once used for producing nuclear weapons. **Applying Concepts** *Why must they wear heavy protective gear?*

1–4 Section Assessment

1. **Key Concept** Why do scientists use a common system of measurement?
2. **Key Concept** What is the difference in the way light microscopes and electron microscopes produce images?
3. Describe the technique and purpose of cell fractionation.
4. What types of objects can be studied with a light microscope? What types can be studied with an electron microscope?
5. **Critical Thinking Applying Concepts** It has been said that many great discoveries lie in wait for the tools needed to make them. What does this statement mean to you? If possible, include an example in your answer.

Assessment Use iText to review the important concepts in Section 1–4.

Take It to the NET

Construct a time line of the early types of microscopes. Include photographs or drawings of the microscopes. Use the links provided in the Biology area at the Prentice Hall Web site for help in completing this activity: **www.phschool.com**

1–4 Section Assessment

1. They need to replicate each other's experiments, which often involve measurements.
2. Light microscopes produce images by focusing visible light rays, whereas electron microscopes produce images by focusing beams of electrons.
3. In cell fractionation, cells are broken into pieces, added to a liquid, and placed in a tube. The tube is spun in a centrifuge, where the cell parts are separated into layers according to density. This technique is done to study just one part of a cell.
4. Light microscopes and electron microscopes can be used to study dead and preserved specimens. Only light microscopes can be used to study living organisms or cells.
5. Sample answer: More advanced tools might reveal parts of living things never observed before. Students may list discoveries that required the development of microscopes.

Exploration

Using a Compound Microscope

Microscopes are widely used in biology. In this investigation, you will use a compound microscope to determine the positions and sizes of objects. Before you begin, read Appendix D on pages 1064–1065 and practice the procedures described there.

Problem

What kinds of information can a compound microscope provide?

Materials

- compound microscope
- microscope slide
- newspaper or other small-print text
- scissors
- dropper pipette
- coverslips
- prepared slide of crossed fibers
- transparent 15-cm plastic ruler
- prepared slide of root or stem
- prepared slide of bacteria

Skills

Observing, Measuring, Calculating

Procedure  

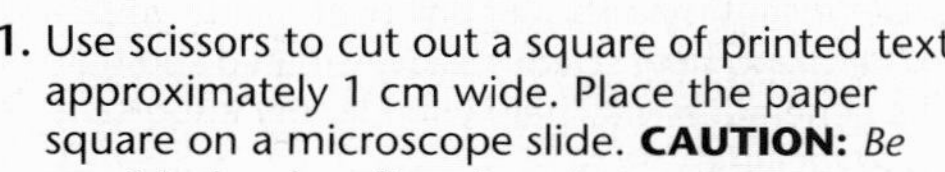

1. Use scissors to cut out a square of printed text approximately 1 cm wide. Place the paper square on a microscope slide. **CAUTION:** *Be careful when handling sharp instruments.*
2. Use a dropper pipette to place a drop of water on the paper square. Add a coverslip. Place the slide on the stage of a compound microscope. Use the stage clips to hold the slide in place.
3. Use the low-power objective to bring the letters on the paper square into focus. Slowly move the slide in different directions along the stage. Record how the image changes when you move the slide.
4. Observe a prepared slide of crossed fibers through the low-power objective. Use the fine adjustment to focus up and down through the area where the fibers cross. Record the order of the fibers, from top to bottom.
5. Observe a transparent ruler through the low-power objective. Use the ruler to measure the diameter of your field of view. Record this distance and the magnification of the low-power objective.
6. Calculate and record the diameter of the field of view through the other objectives. For example, if a 4× objective has a field of 2 mm (2000 micrometers), then a 10× objective will have a field of $(4 \div 10) \times 2$ mm = 0.8 mm (800 micrometers).
7. Examine a prepared slide of a plant stem or root at low and high powers. The small round shapes you see are cells. Use the field diameters you calculated in step 6 to estimate and record the size of a typical plant cell. For example, if 4 cells fit across an 800-micrometer field, then each cell is 200 micrometers long.
8. Repeat step 7 with a prepared slide of bacteria.

Analyze and Conclude

1. **Applying Concepts** What are the advantages of using the high-power objective? What are the disadvantages?
2. **Inferring** Some plant diseases are caused by bacteria. Could bacteria injure plants by consuming plant cells? By entering plant cells? Explain.
3. **Drawing Conclusions** In what ways did the microscope alter the image in step 3? How did moving the slide affect the image?
4. **Drawing Conclusions** In what order were the fibers arranged on the slide you observed in step 4?

Go Further

Measuring With your teacher's permission, use the microscope to observe one of your hairs and estimate its width.

Exploration

Objective Students will be able to draw conclusions about the kinds of information that a compound microscope can provide.

Skills Focus **Observing, Measuring, Calculating, Drawing Conclusions**

Time 45 minutes

Alternative Materials Students may use inexpensive stage micrometers, which are available from science supply houses.

Teaching Tips

- At low power, most compound light microscopes have a field of view with a diameter of about 1.4 millimeters.
- Explain to students that the millimeter is usually too large a unit for microscopic calculations. Normally, biologists use the micrometer (μm); 1 μm = 1/1000 mm.
- Legal notices in a newspaper are an ideal size for this activity.

Procedure

5. Make sure students are using the low-power objective for this step. Explain how to estimate the diameter of the field of view. Have students place the ruler on the microscope stage and focus on the lines that divide the ruler into millimeters. Then, have them move the ruler so that one of these lines is at the left edge of the field of view. Students should add the number of whole millimeters—usually one—to the estimated fraction of a millimeter left over at the right.

Expected Outcomes Students will become familiar with the low-power and high-power objectives of a compound microscope and learn how the image moves as they move a slide.

Go Further

Encourage students to observe a hair under the microscope, and discuss how to estimate its width. Generally, students should compare the width of the magnified hair with the diameter of the field of view they've already calculated. For example, if the hair takes up about a third of the field of view and the diameter of that field is 375 micrometers, then the width of the hair is 125 micrometers.

Analyze and Conclude

1. Advantages include the greater magnification of the image. Disadvantages include that the image is relatively darker when viewed with a high-power lens and that the size of the field of vision decreases as magnification increases.

2. Students should infer that bacteria could injure plants by entering plant cells but not by consuming them, because observation showed that bacteria are much smaller than plant cells.

3. The microscope magnified the printed text. As students moved the slide, they should have observed the image moving in the opposite direction. For instance, if the slide is moved to the left, the image moves to the right.

4. Students should be able to distinguish the order of the fibers.

Chapter 1 Study Guide

Study Tip

Divide the class into pairs, and have each pair make a list of review questions that incorporates all the Key Concepts and Vocabulary terms from the four sections. Ask that they answer the questions on separate sheets of paper. Then, have pairs of students exchange lists of questions. Once students have had time to answer the questions, have the same pairs exchange answer keys.

Thinking Visually

1. Hypotheses
2. Observations
3. Field studies

Chapter 1 Assessment

Reviewing Content

1. c **5.** a **9.** d
2. a **6.** b **10.** a
3. b **7.** b
4. c **8.** d

Understanding Concepts

11. The goal of science is to investigate and understand nature, to explain events in nature, and to use those explanations to make useful predictions.

12. An observation uses senses to gather information; an inference is an interpretation based on prior knowledge and experience.

13. A hypothesis is an explanation for a set of observations or an answer to a scientific question.

14. A hypothesis may arise from prior knowledge, logical inferences, or imaginative guesses.

15. Scientists should test only one variable at a time so that only one observable factor affects the outcome of the experiment.

Chapter 1 Study Guide

1–1 What Is Science?

 **Key Concept**

- The goal of science is to investigate and understand nature, to explain events in nature, and to use those explanations to make useful predictions.

Vocabulary
science, p. 3
observation, p. 4
data, p. 4
inference, p. 4
hypothesis, p. 5

1–2 How Scientists Work

 **Key Concepts**

- Whenever possible, a hypothesis should be tested by an experiment in which only one variable is changed at a time. All other variables should be kept unchanged, or controlled.
- In science, the word *theory* applies to a well-tested explanation that unifies a broad range of observations.

Vocabulary
spontaneous generation, p. 8
controlled experiment, p. 9
manipulated variable, p. 9
responding variable, p. 9
theory, p. 14

1–3 Studying Life

 **Key Concepts**

- Living things share characteristics including cellular organization, reproduction, a universal genetic code, growth and development, use of materials and energy, response to their environment, and maintaining an internal stabiity.
- Living things can be studied at different levels of organization, from the molecular level to the biosphere.

Vocabulary
biology, p. 16
cell, p. 17
sexual reproduction, p. 17
asexual reproduction, p. 17
metabolism, p. 18
homeostasis, p. 19
evolve, p. 20

1–4 Tools and Procedures

Key Concepts

- Most scientists use the metric system when collecting data and doing experiments.
- Light microscopes produce magnified images by focusing visible light rays. Electron microscopes produce images by focusing beams of electrons.

Vocabulary
metric system, p. 24
microscope, p. 25
compound light microscope, p. 26
electron microscope, p. 26
cell culture, p. 27
cell fractionation, p. 27

Thinking Visually

Make a concept map that shows some ways scientists think and work. You can start with the partial concept map shown below or create your own. Recalling how scientists investigated spontaneous generation may help you identify important ideas to include.

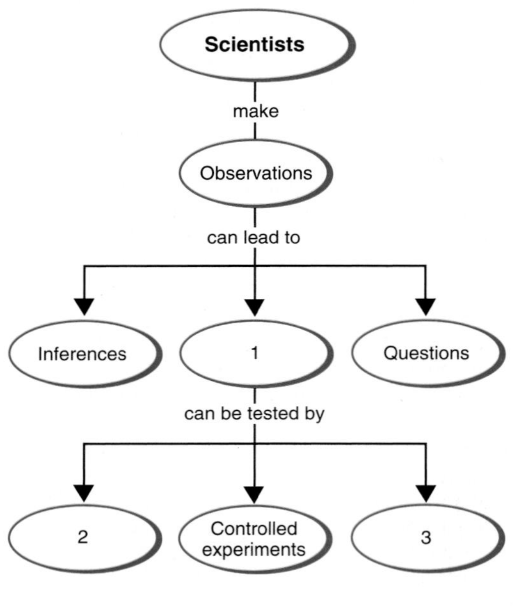

CHAPTER RESOURCES

Print:
- ***Teaching Resources,*** Chapter Vocabulary Review, Graphic Organizer
- ***Chapter Tests: Levels A and B,*** Chapter 1 Test
- ***PH Assessment System,*** Practice Test

Technology:
- ***Computer Test Bank,*** Chapter 1 Test
- ***iText,*** Chapter 1 Assessment

Chapter 1 Assessment

Reviewing Content

Choose the letter that best answers the question or completes the statement.

1. Which of the following statements about the image shown below is not an observation?
   a. The insect has three legs on the left side.
   b. The insect has a pattern on its back.
   c. The insect's pattern shows that it is poisonous.
   d. The insect is green, white, and black.

2. The statement "the worm is 2 cm long" is a(n)
   a. quantitative observation.
   b. qualitative observation.
   c. inference.
   d. hypothesis.
3. An inference is
   a. the same as an observation.
   b. a logical interpretation of an observation.
   c. a statement involving numbers.
   d. a way to avoid bias.
4. To be useful in science, a hypothesis must be
   a. measurable. c. testable.
   b. observable. d. correct.
5. The term *spontaneous generation* means that
   a. living things can arise from nonliving matter.
   b. living things arise from other living things.
   c. a maggot is part of the life cycle of a fly.
   d. living things evolve over time.
6. Which of the following statements about a controlled experiment is true?
   a. All the variables must be kept the same.
   b. Only one variable is tested at a time.
   c. Scientists always use controlled experiments.
   d. Controlled experiments cannot be performed on living things.
7. A scientific theory is
   a. another word for hypothesis.
   b. a well-tested explanation that unifies a broad range of observations.
   c. the same as the conclusion of an experiment.
   d. the first step in a controlled experiment.
8. The process in which two cells from different parents unite to produce the first cell of a new organism is called
   a. homeostasis. c. asexual reproduction.
   b. development. d. sexual reproduction.
9. The process by which organisms keep their internal conditions relatively stable is called
   a. metabolism. c. evolution.
   b. a genome. d. homeostasis.
10. An instrument that produces images by focusing light rays is called a
    a. light microscope.
    b. transmission electron microscope.
    c. scanning electron microscope.
    d. electronic balance.

Understanding Concepts

11. What is the goal of science?
12. How does an observation about an object differ from an inference about that object?
13. How does a hypothesis help scientists understand the natural world?
14. Describe three possible ways in which a hypothesis may arise.
15. Why is it advantageous for scientists to test only one variable at a time during an experiment?
16. Distinguish between a variable and a control.
17. What steps are involved in making a conclusion?
18. Why is publishing the design and results of an experiment considered an essential part of science?
19. Describe the impact Pasteur's work had on the scientific community.
20. What must happen for a hypothesis to become a theory?
21. How are unicellular and multicellular organisms alike? How are they different?
22. Give an example of changes that occur during the life cycle of a multicellular organism.
23. Why do scientists find it helpful to use the metric system?
24. How can a graph of data be more informative than a table of the same data?
25. What is a cell culture? How can a cell culture be useful to biologists?

HOMEWORK GUIDE

Section:	Questions:
Section 1–1	1–4, 11–14, 28, 35
Section 1–2	5–7, 15–20, 32, 33, 35
Section 1–3	8, 9, 21, 22
Section 1–4	10, 23–27, 29–31, 34

Chapter 1 Assessment (continued)

16. A variable is a factor being tested or changed. A control includes those factors that remain constant.

17. Scientists use data from experiments to evaluate a hypothesis and draw a conclusion; that is, they use the data to support or refute the hypothesis.

18. Publishing the design and results of an experiment are important so that other scientists can review the procedures and test the results by repeating the experiment.

19. Pasteur showed that all living things come from other living things, which was a major shift in how scientists viewed living things. He also demonstrated that infectious diseases were not inexplicable events but the result of microorganisms entering the bodies of their victims.

20. For a hypothesis to become a theory, it must be supported by extensive observation and experimentation.

21. Unicellular and multicellular organisms are alike in that they all perform eight life functions or characteristics. They are different in that unicellular organisms are one-celled and multicellular organisms have more than one cell.

22. During its life cycle, a fly goes through these stages: egg → larva → adult fly.

23. The metric system is easy to use because it is based on multiples of 10 and is universally accepted by scientists.

24. A graph of data can be more informative than a chart because patterns of change are usually more easily seen in a graph.

25. A cell culture is a group of cells produced when a single cell is placed in a nutrient solution and allowed to reproduce. Scientists can use cell cultures to test cell responses under controlled conditions, to study interactions between cells, and to select specific cells for future study.

Chapter 1 Assessment

Critical Thinking

26. Check to be sure that students' measurements are in millimeters.

27. 1500 grams

28. Science is both an organized process for gathering, organizing, and analyzing information and the body of knowledge that results from the scientific process.

29. The magnification is better with an electron microscope, but an electron microscope cannot be used to study organisms while they are alive. A light microscope produces magnified images by focusing a readily available source—visible light. With a video camera attached, a light microscope can provide three-dimensional images of some cell processes.

30. Student answers should reflect the idea that the number of organisms depends upon the time. Graph #1: As the time increased, so did the number of organisms. Graph #2: There was an increase in the number of organisms, then a decline in the population. Graph #3: There were spikes in the population, followed by declines. The second spike was the most noticeable. Graph #4: The number of organisms remained constant.

31. Student answers should include a manipulated variable, a responding variable, and the relationship between the variables.

32. Check to be sure the experiment has one manipulated variable and a control.

33. The other key variables may be responsible for the observed outcome of the experiment.

34. (1) Safety goggles; (2) Animal safety; (3) Breakage; (4) Electric shock; (5) Sharp object: (6) Heat-resistant gloves.

35. Check students' writing for an understanding of a scientific attitude.

Chapter 1 Assessment

Critical Thinking

26. **Measuring** Estimate or use a ruler to find the length and width of this book in millimeters.

27. **Calculating** Give an animal's mass in grams if its measured mass is 1.5 kilograms.

28. **Evaluating** Why is it misleading to describe science as a collection of facts?

29. **Comparing and Contrasting** What are some advantages and disadvantages of light microscopes and electron microscopes?

30. **Analyzing Data** The following graphs show the sizes of four different populations over a period of time. Write a sentence summarizing what each graph shows.

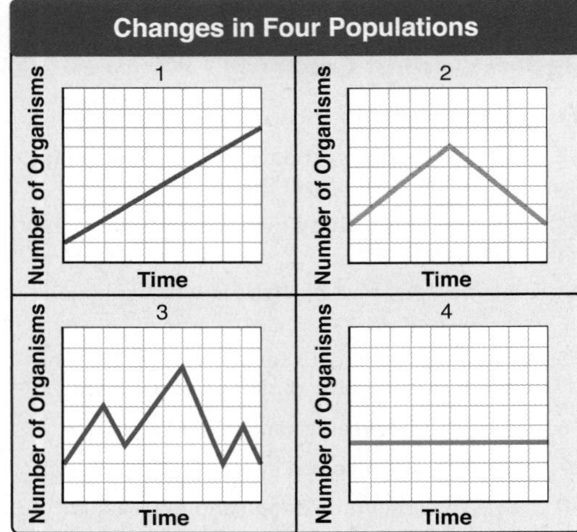

31. **Comparing and Contrasting** Graphs of completely different events can have the same appearance. Select one of the graphs from question 30 and explain how the shape of the graph could apply to a different set of events.

32. **Designing Experiments** A young animal normally grows larger no matter what food it eats. Suggest an experiment that would show whether one type of food was better than another at helping an animal to grow faster.

33. **Controlling Variables** Explain why you cannot draw a conclusion about the effect of one variable in an investigation when the other key variables are not controlled.

34. **Interpreting Graphics** Each of the following safety symbols might appear in a laboratory activity in this book. Describe what each symbol stands for. (*Hint:* Refer to Appendix B.)

35. **Making Connections** Use the information in Section 1–2 to explain how having a scientific attitude might help you in everyday activities, for example, in trying to learn a new skill. Describe your ideas in your journal.

Performance-Based Assessment

Planning an Experiment Many people add fertilizers to house or garden plants. Make a hypothesis about whether you think these fertilizers really help plants grow. Next, design an experiment to test your hypothesis. Include in your plan what variable you will test and what variables you will control. Then, listen to other students' plans. Which plans would properly test their hypotheses?

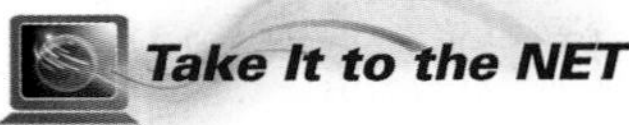

Where can you learn about different careers in biology? Go to the Prentice Hall Web site at **www.phschool.com** to find out. Then, answer the following questions:

- List five different careers in biology and describe what skills are needed for those careers.
- For each of the five careers, list the training and education that is needed.
- Choose one career that you would be interested in pursuing. Write down three questions that you have about that career. How might you go about finding the answers to those questions?

Performance-Based Assessment

Student answers should include a testable hypothesis and a description of a controlled experiment in which the variable to be tested and the variables to be controlled are listed.

Standardized Test Prep

Test-Taking Tip Before taking a standardized test, it helps to become familiar with the format of the test, including the different question types. One helpful method is to complete practice tests, such as this one.

Questions 1–2 Complete each analogy by selecting the correct letter. In analogies, A : B :: C : __?__ *means* A is to B as C is to __?__.

1. Sexual reproduction : two parents :: asexual reproduction : __?__
(A) two parents
(B) two cells
(C) one nonliving thing
(D) one parent
(E) one cell

2. One gram : 1000 milligrams :: one meter : __?__
(A) 1000 millimeters
(B) 1 millimeter
(C) 1 kilometer
(D) 1 milliliter
(E) 1000 meters

Directions: Choose the letter that best answers the question or completes the statement.

Questions 3–4

A researcher investigated two groups of fruit flies. Population A was kept in a 0.5-L container. Population B was kept in a 1-L container.

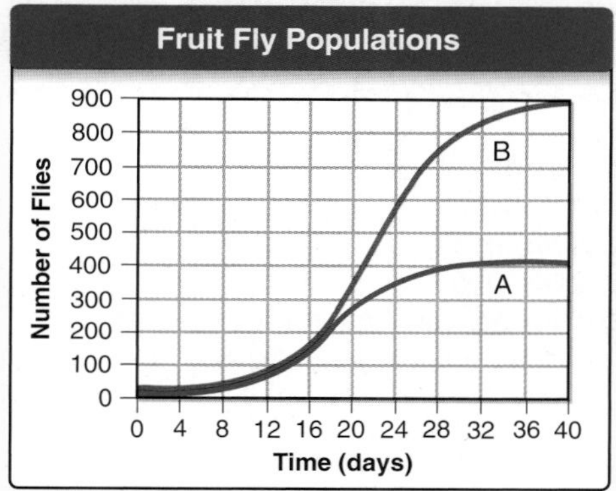

3. The manipulated variable was the
(A) number of flies.
(B) number of groups studied.
(C) time in days.
(D) difference in time per group.
(E) size of the containers.

4. Which of the following is a logical inference based on the contents of the graph?
(A) The flies in Group B were healthier than those in Group A.
(B) A fly population with more available space will grow larger than a population with less space.
(C) If Group B were observed for 40 more days, the size of the population would double.
(D) In 40 more days, the sizes of both populations would decrease at the same rate.
(E) The pattern shown in this graph is true only for fruit flies.

Questions 5–6

Once a month, a pet owner recorded the mass of her puppy in a table. When the puppy was 3 months old, she started to feed it a "special puppy food" she saw advertised on TV.

Change in a Puppy's Mass Over Time

Age (months)	Mass at Start of Month (kg)	Change in Mass per Month (kg)
2	5	—
3	8	+3
4	13	+5

5. According to the table, which statement is true?
(A) The puppy's mass increased at the same rate for each month shown.
(B) The puppy's increase in mass during month 4 was greater than 4 kg.
(C) The puppy added more mass during month 2 than during month 3.
(D) The puppy added more mass during month 3 than during month 2.
(E) No accurate statements are possible unless you know the data from the first month.

6. All of the following statements about the pet owner's study are true EXCEPT
(A) The owner made quantitative observations.
(B) The owner used the metric system.
(C) The owner recorded data.
(D) The owner could graph the data.
(E) The owner conducted a controlled experiment.

Standardized Test Prep

1. D **2.** A **3.** E **4.** B **5.** B **6.** E

Take It to the NET

• Students should list specific skills that are required for each career, such as collecting and analyzing data, investigating and evaluating programs, and assessing impacts.

• Students should list the years of training or education required and describe the type of training or education—for example, technical school, community college, or a Ph.D program.

• Students may include questions about the job outlook, specific colleges or programs of study, how to contact people in the field for interviews, volunteer opportunities, and salary range. Encourage students to find answers to their questions if they have a high level of interest in particular careers. Encourage students to visit

www.phschool.com

Chapter Planner 2 The Chemistry of Life

Section and Section Objectives	Time	Activities and Labs
2–1 The Nature of Matter, pp. 35–39 **2.1.1** ***Identify*** the three subatomic particles found in atoms. **2.1.2** ***Explain*** how all of the isotopes of an element are similar and how they are different. **2.1.3** ***Explain*** what chemical compounds are. **2.1.4** ***Describe*** the two main types of chemical bonds.	**1 period (1/2 block)**	**SE:** ***Inquiry Activity,*** Do large and small molecules behave exactly alike?, p. 34 **TE:** ***Build Science Skills,*** p. 35 **TE:** ***Meet Diverse Needs,*** p. 36 **SE:** ***Careers in Biology,*** Forensic Scientist, p. 37
2–2 Properties of Water, pp. 40–43 **2.2.1** ***Explain*** why water molecules are polar. **2.2.2** ***Differentiate*** between solutions and suspensions. **2.2.3** ***Explain*** what acidic solutions and basic solutions are.	**1 period (1/2 block)**	**TE:** ***Demonstration,*** p. 41 **SE:** ***Quick Lab,*** Are foods acidic or basic?, p. 42
2–3 Carbon Compounds, pp. 44–48 **2.3.1** ***Describe*** the functions of each group of organic compounds.	**1 periods (1/2 block)**	**TE:** ***Build Science Skills,*** p. 45
2–4 Chemical Reactions and Enzymes, pp. 49–53 **2.4.1** ***Explain*** how chemical reactions affect chemical bonds in compounds. **2.4.2** ***Describe*** how energy changes affect how easily a chemical reaction will occur. **2.4.3** ***Explain*** why enzymes are important to living things.	**1 period (1/2 block)**	**TE:** ***Demonstration,*** p. 49 **SE:** ***Analyzing Data,*** How does pH affect an enzyme?, p. 51 **TE:** ***Build Science Skills,*** p. 52 **TE:** ***Build Science Skills,*** p. 53 **SE:** ***Design an Experiment,*** Investigating the Effect of Temperature on Enzyme Activity, pp. 54–55
Chapter Assessment, pp. 56–59	**1 period (1/2 block)**	

ACTIVITY PLANNER

SE: ***Inquiry Activity,*** p. 34; (10 min.); tofu, soy sauce, butter, soap, cornstarch, sugar, teaspoon, 6 test tubes with stoppers, water

TE: ***Build Science Skills,*** p. 35; (15 min.); model of an atom, toothpicks, gumdrops

TE: ***Meet Diverse Needs,*** p. 36; (10 min.); marbles of 2 different colors

TE: ***Demonstration,*** p. 41; (10 min.); flask, 25 g sugar, masking tape, stirring rod, metric ruler

SE: ***Quick Lab,*** p. 42; (15 min.); pH paper, solid foods and fruit juices, paper towel, scalpel, dropper pipette, plastic gloves

TE: ***Build Science Skills,*** p. 45; (20 min.); Lugol's solution, dropper, soda cracker, potato, white bread, oatmeal, granulated sugar, test tubes

TE: ***Demonstration,*** p. 49; (10 min.); baking soda, vinegar, 3 beakers

TE: ***Build Science Skills,*** p. 52; (15 min.); toothpicks, clock or watch with second hand

TE: ***Build Science Skills,*** p. 53; (10 min.); padlock, key

SE: ***Design an Experiment,*** pp. 54–55; (45 min.); liver, petri dish, dropper pipette, 1% H_2O_2, graduated cylinder, beakers, filter paper, forceps, glass-marker, ice and warm water baths, thermometers, watch

PLANNING KEY

Ability Levels

(B) **Basic**	For students who need additional help
(A) **Average**	For all students
(E) **Enriched**	For students who need to be challenged

Components

SE	Student Edition	**GRSW**	Guided Reading and Study Workbook	**IDM**	Issues and Decision Making
TE	Teacher's Edition	**CT**	Chapter Tests: Levels A and B	**CTB**	Computer Test Bank
LMA	Laboratory Manual A	**PHAS**	PH Assessment System	**PA**	Presentation Assistant Plus
LMB	Laboratory Manual B	**LA**	Lab Assessment with Scoring Guide	**BD**	BioDetectives Videotape
TR	Teaching Resources	**BTM**	BioTechnology Manual	**iT**	iText

Program Resources	Assessment	Media and Technology
TR: Section Review 2–1 (B) (A) **GRSW:** Section 2–1 (B) (A) **IDM:** 2–1	**SE:** 2–1 Section Assessment, p. 39 **TR:** Section Review 2–1	**PA:** 2–1 Interest Grabber, Section Outline, An Element in the Periodic Table, Figure 2–3, Figure 2–4 **BD** "John Toms" **iT:** Section 2–1
TR: Section Review 2–2 (B) (A) **GRSW:** Section 2–2 (B) (A)	**SE:** 2–2 Section Assessment, p. 43 **TR:** Section Review 2–2	**PA:** 2–2 Interest Grabber, Section Outline, pH scale, Figure 2–9 **iT:** Section 2–2
LMA: Chapter 2 Lab (A) (E) **LMB:** Chapter 2 Lab (B) (A) **TR:** Section Review 2–3 (B) (A) **GRSW:** Section 2–3 (B) (A)	**SE:** 2–3 Section Assessment, p. 48 **TR:** Section Review 2–3	**PA:** 2–3 Interest Grabber, Section Outline, Concept Map, Figure 2–11, Figures 2–13 and 2–14, Figures 2–16 and 2–17 **iT:** Section 2–3
TR: Section Review 2–4 (B) (A) Chapter 2 Design an Experiment (B) (A) (E) **GRSW:** Section 2–4 (B) (A)	**SE:** 2–4 Section Assessment, p. 53 **TR:** Section Review 2–4	**PA:** 2–4 Interest Grabber, Section Outline, Effect of Enzymes, Figure 2–19, Figure 2–21 **iT:** Section 2–4 
	SE: Chapter 2 Assessment, pp. 56–59 **TR:** Chapter Vocabulary Review, Graphic Organizer **CT:** Chapter 2 Test **CTB:** Chapter 2 Test **PHAS:** Practice Test	**CTB:** Chapter 2 Test **iT:** Chapter 2 Assessment

PRESSED FOR TIME?

To Preview the Chapter

- Introduce students to Key Concepts and Vocabulary terms in each section.
- Assign the Reading Strategies for each section.

To Cover the Chapter Quickly

- Have students read all of Section 2–1; Figures 2–6, 2–9, and 2–10 in Section 2–2; all of Section 2–3; and Chemical Reactions, Energy in Reactions, and Enzymes in Section 2–4.
- Assign 2–1 Section Review and 2–3 Section Review, as well as questions 1–3 and 5–9 in Chapter 2 Assessment and questions 1–3 and 5–10 in Chapter 2 Standardized Test Prep.

To Review the Chapter

- Assign Sections 2–1, 2–3, and 2–4 in the Guided Reading and Study Workbook.
- Assign Section Reviews for 2–1, 2–3, and 2–4 and the Chapter Vocabulary Review for Chapter 2 in the Teaching Resources.

Chapter 2

ENGAGE/EXPLORE

Inquiry Activity

Objective Students will be able to draw the conclusion that large molecules are less soluble in water than smaller related molecules.

Skill Focus **Drawing Conclusions**

Materials tofu, soy sauce, butter, soap, cornstarch, sugar, teaspoon, 6 test tubes with stoppers, water

Time 10 minutes

Advance Prep You can obtain each of the substances used in the activity at a grocery store.

Safety Caution students to make sure that the stopper is secure in the test tube before they shake it.

Strategies

- Explain that it is not important to add an exact amount of each material to the water, though students should not add too much. They should add about 1 teaspoon of each substance.
- Point out that the soy protein in tofu is the same protein that is broken down into amino acids to make soy sauce.

Expected Outcomes Students should observe that soy sauce, soap, and sugar dissolve in water, whereas tofu, butter, and starch do not.

Think About It

1. Soy sauce, soap, and sugar
2. The large molecules are less soluble than the smaller molecules.

Assess Prior Knowledge

To assess students' knowledge of basic chemistry, write this chemical equation on the board:

$C_6H_{12}O_6 + 6O_2 \rightarrow CO_2 + H_2O$

Ask students to write everything they know about this equation, including the compounds involved and how many atoms of each element are in each molecule. Also, ask students to balance the equation. *(Students may know that this is the summary equation for cellular respiration, in which glucose reacts with oxygen to produce carbon dioxide and water. Students should balance the equation as follows: $C_6H_{12}O_6 + 6O_2 \rightarrow 6CO_2 + 6H_2O$)*

Chapter 2 The Chemistry of Life

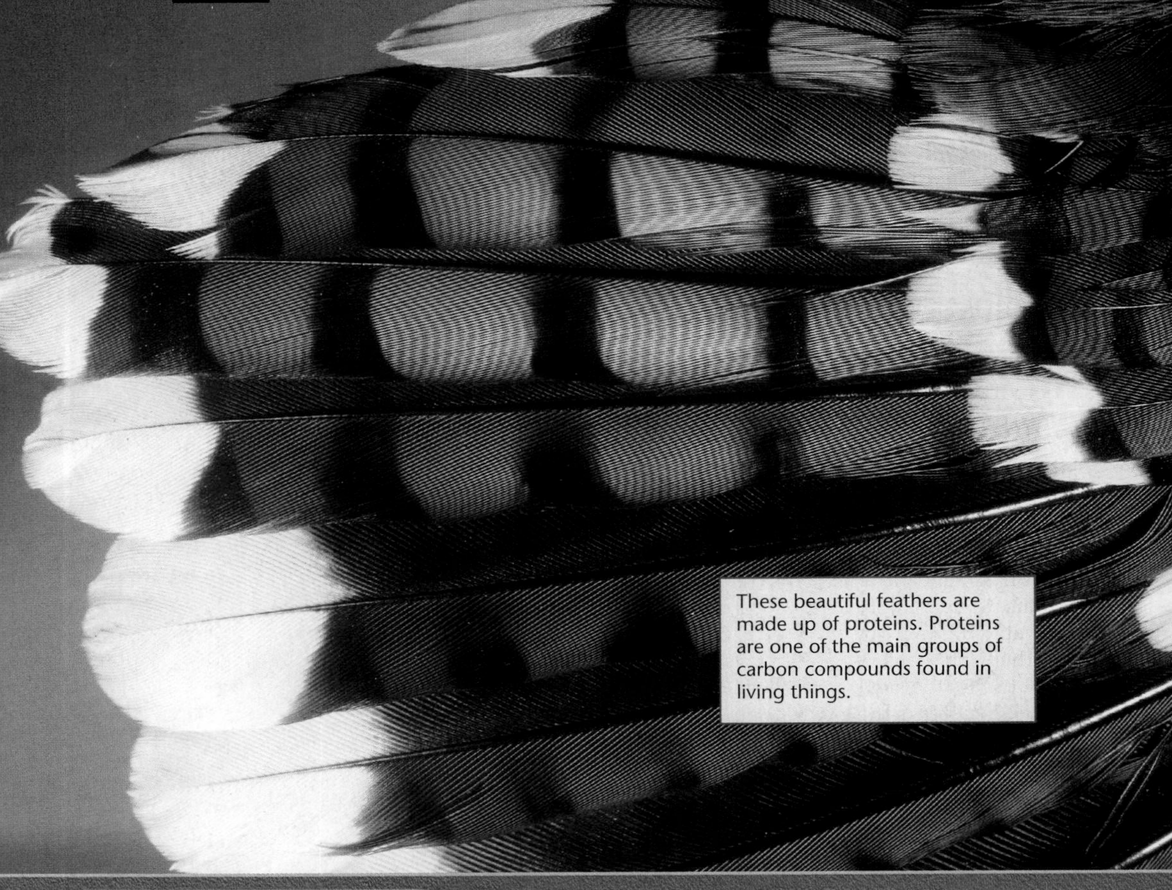

These beautiful feathers are made up of proteins. Proteins are one of the main groups of carbon compounds found in living things.

Inquiry Activity

Do large and small molecules behave exactly alike?

Procedure

1. Label six test tubes as follows: tofu, soy sauce, butter, soap, starch, and sugar. Place a tiny amount of each sample in the appropriate test tube.
2. Half-fill each test tube with water. Stopper the test tubes. Shake each test tube for 2 minutes. Record your observations of each test tube.

Think About It

1. **Observing** Which substances dissolved easily in water?
2. **Drawing Conclusions** Tofu, starch, and butter consist mostly of large molecules (protein, starch, and fat, respectively). Soy sauce, sugar, and soap contain smaller molecules that are related to the large molecules. Are the large molecules more or less soluble than the smaller molecules?

FACTS AND FIGURES

Biochemistry—the chemistry of life
Chemistry is the study of the composition and properties of substances, as well as the changes that substances can undergo. One major branch of chemistry is called organic chemistry, which is the study of organic compounds, or compounds that contain carbon. Inorganic chemistry is the rest of chemistry, or the study of all compounds that don't contain carbon, except for the oxides of carbon and the carbonates. Biochemistry is the study of the chemicals of living things and the changes that those chemicals undergo; that is, it is the chemistry of life, the focus of this chapter. Biochemistry is primarily concerned with organic chemistry and the structure and reactions of carbohydrates, lipids, nucleic acids, and proteins. It is also concerned with some inorganic compounds such as water and carbon dioxide.

2–1 The Nature of Matter

Life depends on chemistry. When you eat food or inhale oxygen, your body uses these materials in chemical reactions that keep you alive. Just as buildings are made from bricks, steel, glass, and wood, living things are made from chemical compounds. If the first task of an architect is to understand building materials, then the first job of a biologist is to understand the chemistry of life.

Atoms

The study of chemistry begins with the basic unit of matter, the **atom.** The Greek word *atomos,* which means "unable to be cut," was first used to refer to matter by the Greek philosopher Democritus nearly 2500 years ago. Democritus asked a simple question: If you take an object like a stick of chalk and break it in half, are both halves still chalk? The answer, of course, is yes. But what happens if you go on? Suppose you break it in half again and again and again. Can you continue to divide without limit, or does there come a point at which you cannot divide the fragment of chalk without changing it into something else? Democritus thought that there had to be a limit. He called the smallest fragment the atom, a name scientists still use today.

Atoms are incredibly small. Placed side by side, 100 million atoms would make a row only about 1 centimeter long—about the width of your pinkie! Despite its extremely small size, an atom contains subatomic particles that are even smaller. **Figure 2–1** shows the subatomic particles in a helium atom. **The subatomic particles that make up atoms are protons, neutrons, and electrons.** Protons and neutrons have about the same mass. However, protons are positively charged particles (+) and neutrons carry no charge. Their name is a reminder that they are neutral particles. Strong forces bind protons and neutrons together to form the **nucleus,** which is at the center of the atom.

The **electron** is a negatively charged particle (–) with 1/1840 the mass of a proton. Electrons are in constant motion in the space surrounding the nucleus. They are attracted to the positively charged nucleus but remain outside the nucleus because of the energy of their motion. Because atoms have equal numbers of electrons and protons, and because these subatomic particles have equal but opposite charges, atoms are neutral.

Guide for Reading

Key Concepts
- What three subatomic particles make up atoms?
- How are all of the isotopes of an element similar?
- What are the two main types of chemical bonds?

Vocabulary
atom
nucleus
electron
element
isotope
compound
ionic bond
ion
covalent bond
molecule
van der Waals forces

Reading Strategy: Using Prior Knowledge Before you read, write down what you already know about atoms, elements, and compounds. As you read, note the main new concepts you learn.

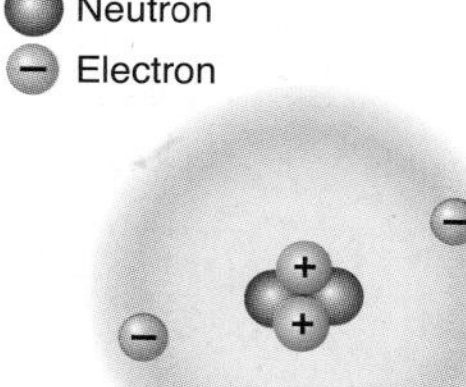

▶ **Figure 2–1** **Helium atoms contain protons, neutrons, and electrons.** The positively charged protons and uncharged neutrons are bound together in the dense nucleus, while the negatively charged electrons move in the space around the nucleus.

SECTION RESOURCES

Print:
- ***Teaching Resources,*** Section Review 2–1
- ***Guided Reading and Study Workbook,*** Section 2–1
- ***Issues and Decision Making,*** 2–1

Technology:
- **BioDetectives Videotape**, "John Toms"
- ***iText,*** Section 2–1

Section 2–1

1 FOCUS

Objectives

2.1.1 ***Identify*** the three subatomic particles found in atoms.
2.1.2 ***Explain*** how all of the isotopes of an element are similar and how they are different.
2.1.3 ***Explain*** what chemical compounds are.
2.1.4 ***Describe*** the two main types of chemical bonds.

Guide for Reading

Vocabulary Preview
Before students read the section, ask them to find each Vocabulary term and preview its meaning.

Reading Strategy
Encourage students to refer back regularly to their initial thoughts about atoms, elements, and compounds, editing their sentences as they revise their thinking in light of the section's discussion.

2 INSTRUCT

Atoms

Build Science Skills

Using models Display a model of an atom, and have students identify the nucleus, protons, neutrons, and electrons. Then, have students build their own models of atoms, using toothpicks and gumdrops. Assign each student one or more of the elements mentioned in this section—helium, hydrogen, oxygen, carbon, sodium, and chlorine—and elements that will be discussed in future sections, such as nitrogen and calcium. Stress that all models have limitations. In the Figure 2–1 drawing, for example, electrons are shown as equal in size to the more massive protons and neutrons, and the constant motion of the electrons cannot be shown.

2–1 (continued)

Elements and Isotopes

Make Connections

Chemistry Display a wall-sized periodic table of elements and review with students the information it contains. Focus first on the names and symbols. Explain that new elements are assigned three-letter symbols until they are officially named. Ask: **How are the elements arranged in the table?** *(In order by increasing atomic number)* Remind students that the atomic number equals the number of protons in an atom. **What else does the atomic number equal?** *(The number of electrons in the atom)* Use the table to discuss the average atomic masses and the concept of a weighted average after students have learned about isotopes.

Meet Diverse Needs

Help at-risk students grasp the concept of isotopes by using marbles of two different colors. Have dark-colored marbles represent protons and light-colored marbles represent neutrons. Place six of each color of marble in a student's hand, and explain that this represents the nucleus of a carbon-12 atom. Add a light-colored marble to the hand, and ask: **What do the marbles now represent?** *(The nucleus of a carbon-13 atom)* **How many electrons does this isotope of carbon contain?** *(The isotope has six electrons.)* Add another dark-colored marble to the hand, and ask: **Is the nucleus the marbles now represent a nucleus of a carbon isotope?** *(No. Carbon isotopes always have six protons.)* **Which element has seven protons?** *(Nitrogen)* **Learning modality: tactile**

Elements and Isotopes

A chemical **element** is a pure substance that consists entirely of one type of atom. More than 100 elements are known, but only about two dozen are commonly found in living organisms. Elements are represented by a one- or two-letter symbol. C, for example, stands for carbon, H for hydrogen, and Na for sodium. The number of protons in an atom of an element is the element's atomic number. Carbon's atomic number is 6, meaning that each atom of carbon has six protons and, consequently, six electrons.

Isotopes Atoms of an element can have different numbers of neutrons. For example, some atoms of carbon have six neutrons, some have seven, and a few have eight. Atoms of the same element that differ in the number of neutrons they contain are known as **isotopes.** The sum of the protons and neutrons in the nucleus of an atom is called its mass number. Isotopes are identified by their mass numbers. **Figure 2–2** shows the subatomic composition of carbon-12, carbon-13, and carbon-14 atoms. The weighted average of the masses of an element's isotopes is called its atomic mass. "Weighted" means that the abundance of each isotope in nature is considered when the average is calculated. **Because they have the same number of electrons, all isotopes of an element have the same chemical properties.**

Radioactive Isotopes Some isotopes are radioactive, meaning that their nuclei are unstable and break down at a constant rate over time. The radiation these isotopes give off can be dangerous, but radioactive isotopes have a number of important scientific and practical uses.

For example, geologists can determine the ages of rocks and fossils by analyzing the isotopes found in them. Radiation from certain isotopes can be used to treat cancer and to kill bacteria that cause food to spoil. Radioactive isotopes can also be used as labels or "tracers" to follow the movements of substances within organisms.

▼ **Figure 2–2 Because they have the same number of electrons, these isotopes of carbon have the same chemical properties.** The difference among the isotopes is the number of neutrons in their nuclei.

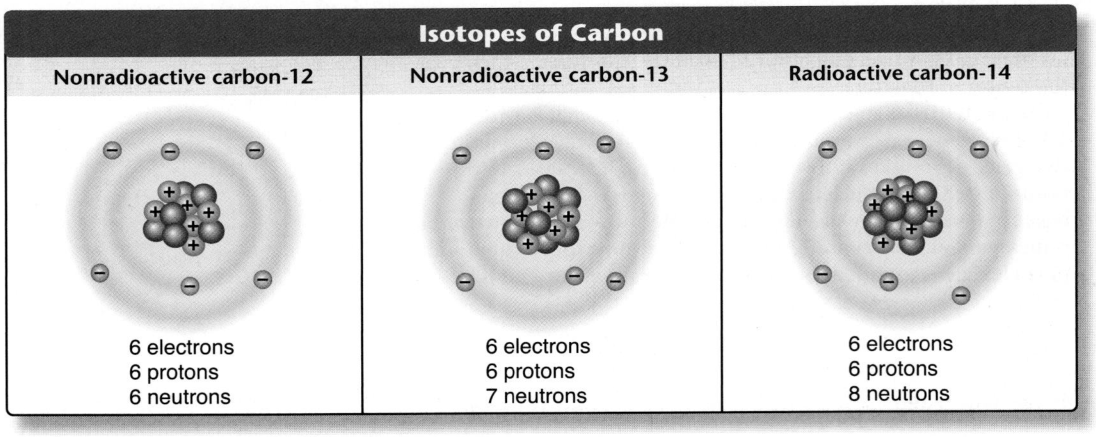

Isotopes of Carbon		
Nonradioactive carbon-12	Nonradioactive carbon-13	Radioactive carbon-14
6 electrons 6 protons 6 neutrons	6 electrons 6 protons 7 neutrons	6 electrons 6 protons 8 neutrons

PRESENTATIONS MADE EASY!

The Presentation Assistant Plus contains the Prentice Hall Presentation Pro and the Transparencies, which provide easy-to-follow visual support for every step of this lesson. If you have a computer presentation station, use Prentice Hall Presentation Pro Section 2–1, or use the transparencies listed here.

Section 2–1:

Interest Grabber
Section Outline
An Element in the Periodic Table
Figure 2–3
Figure 2–4

Careers in Biology

Forensic Scientist

Job description: work as a forensic scientist for local, state, or federal investigative agencies in order to conduct scientific forensic examinations in criminal investigations

Education: a bachelor's degree in science—biology, physics, chemistry, metallurgy; some states require several years of forensic laboratory experience

Skills: analytical, computer literate, detail oriented, capable of taking meticulous notes, logical, and capable of preparing evidence for presentation in court as well as testifying as an expert witness

Highlights: You have the opportunity to use logic and science to solve unique or unusual problems in criminal investigations.

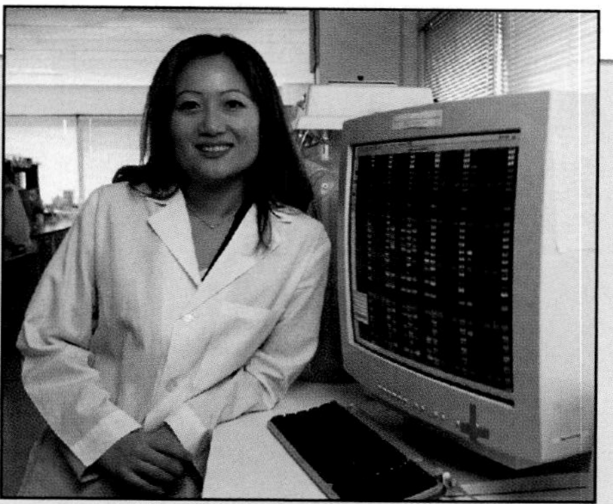

Kelly Yi, who is pictured here, chose forensic science when DNA analysis was just beginning to be accepted as evidence in court. "Everything in forensic science deals with basic principles," she explains.

To find out more about forensic science, view the videotape "History's Mystery: An Introduction to Forensic Science."

Chemical Compounds

In nature, most elements are found combined with other elements in compounds. A chemical **compound** is a substance formed by the chemical combination of two or more elements in definite proportions. Scientists show the composition of compounds by a kind of shorthand known as a chemical formula. Water, which contains two atoms of hydrogen for each atom of oxygen, has the chemical formula H_2O. The formula for table salt, NaCl, indicates that the elements from which table salt forms—sodium and chlorine—combine in a 1 : 1 ratio.

The physical and chemical properties of a compound are usually very different from those of the elements from which it is formed. For example, hydrogen and oxygen, which are gases at room temperature, can combine explosively and form liquid water. Sodium is a silvery metal that is soft enough to cut with a knife. It reacts explosively with cold water. Chlorine is very reactive, too. It is a poisonous, greenish gas that was used to kill many soldiers in World War I. Sodium and chlorine combine to form sodium chloride (NaCl), or table salt. Sodium chloride is a white solid that dissolves easily in water. As you know, sodium chloride is not poisonous. In fact, it is essential for the survival of most living things.

What information is contained in a chemical formula?

HISTORY OF SCIENCE

Same element, different atoms

In the early nineteenth century, British chemist John Dalton expounded a number of postulates about matter, including that all atoms of a given element are identical. His work had tremendous influence. About a century later, though, scientists working on radioactive decay detected scores of atoms that seemed to refute Dalton's postulate. English chemist Frederick Soddy provided a solution. In working with neon atoms, he found some atoms with a mass number of 20 and others with a mass number of 22. He suggested that atoms with both mass numbers can be considered neon because they have the same number of protons, even though they have different numbers of neutrons in their nuclei. Because both types of atoms could occupy the same place on the periodic table, he called them isotopes, from the Greek words for "same" and "place."

Careers in Biology

When a criminal investigation is needed, forensic scientists—also called criminalists—examine, compare, and analyze various types of physical evidence, including blood and other body fluids, hair and fibers, DNA and fingerprints.

- An entry-level job as a forensic scientist usually requires a bachelor's degree in forensic science or some other science.
- To analyze blood evidence at a crime scene, for instance, a forensic scientist might first determine whether the blood is human. If the blood is human, further steps might include determining the ABO blood type, examining the blood for various genetic markers, and analyzing the blood spatter.

Resources

Encourage interested students to contact a local university to see if it has a degree program in forensic science and what the program entails. Students might also contact a local police department and ask to talk to a forensic scientist or criminalist.

Encourage students to view "John Toms" on the BioDetectives Videotape.

Chemical Compounds

Address Misconceptions

Many students may think that the smallest unit of every compound is a molecule. Chemists use the term *molecule* to describe the smallest unit of compounds whose atoms are joined by covalent bonds. You may want to note that atoms of some elements can join with other atoms of the same element and form molecules—hydrogen and oxygen, for example. For ionic compounds, the formula represents the lowest whole-number ratio of ions in the compound.

Answer to . . .

CHECKPOINT *The types of elements that are in the compound and the ratio in which atoms of those elements combine*

2–1 (continued)

Chemical Bonds

Build Science Skills

Using Models Arrange two circles of eight chairs each. The circles should be next to each other, about 1 meter apart. Then, invite nine students to take seats in one circle and seven students to take seats in the other. One student invited to sit in a circle will be left without a chair. Encourage that student to walk around the circle of eight chairs, looking for a place to sit. Then, ask: **How can this student's problem be resolved?** *(The student could sit in the empty seat in the other circle of chairs.)* **Assume the student is an electron. If the student takes a seat in the other circle, what kind of bond is being modeled?** *(An ionic bond, because the electron is transferred)*

Use Visuals

Figure 2–3 Explain that an element's chemical properties are determined by the number and location of the electrons in its atoms. Ask: **Why does the transfer of an electron occur between a sodium atom and a chlorine atom?** *(The sodium atom, which has only one electron in its outermost level, easily loses that electron. The chlorine atom, which has seven electrons in its outermost level, easily gains an electron.)* Explain that the ions are more stable than the neutral atoms because their outermost levels are filled with electrons. Ask: **What is an ionic bond?** *(The attraction between two oppositely charged ions)* Students may notice that the name for the ion formed from a chlorine atom has an *-ide* ending. This is true for all monatomic negative ions.

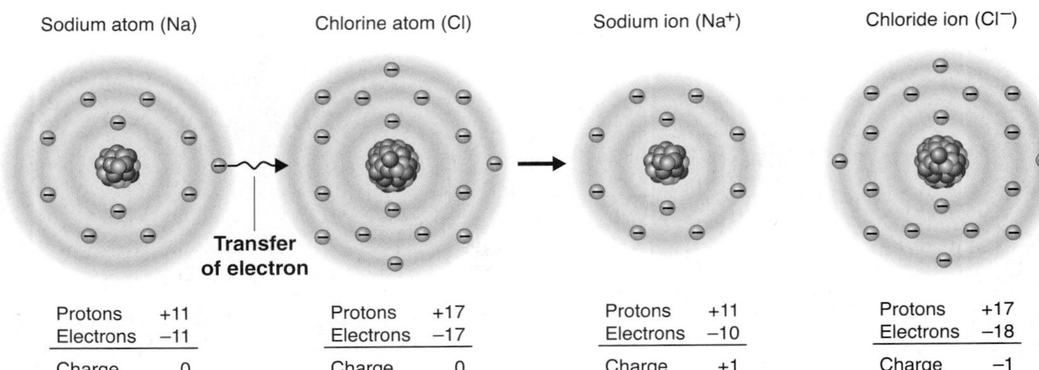

▲ **Figure 2–3** **The chemical bond in which electrons are transferred from one atom to another is called an ionic bond.** The compound sodium chloride forms when sodium loses its valence electron to chlorine.

Chemical Bonds

The atoms in compounds are held together by chemical bonds. Much of chemistry is devoted to understanding how and when chemical bonds form. Bond formation involves the electrons that surround each atomic nucleus. The electrons that are available to form bonds are called valence electrons. **The main types of chemical bonds are ionic bonds and covalent bonds.**

Ionic Bonds An **ionic bond** is formed when one or more electrons are transferred from one atom to another. Recall that atoms are electrically neutral because they have equal numbers of protons and electrons. An atom that loses electrons has a positive charge. An atom that gains electrons has a negative charge. These positively and negatively charged atoms are known as **ions.**

Figure 2–3 shows how ionic bonds form between sodium and chlorine in table salt. A sodium atom easily loses its one valence electron and becomes a sodium ion (Na^+). A chlorine atom easily gains an electron and becomes a chloride ion (Cl^-). In a salt crystal, there are trillions of sodium and chloride ions. These oppositely charged ions have a strong attraction. The attraction between oppositely charged ions is an ionic bond.

Covalent Bonds Sometimes electrons are shared by atoms instead of being transferred. What does it mean to "share" electrons? It means that the moving electrons are located in a region between the atoms where the orbitals of the atoms overlap. A **covalent bond** forms when electrons are shared between atoms. When the atoms share two electrons, the bond is called a single covalent bond. Sometimes the atoms share four electrons and form a double bond. In a few cases, atoms can share six electrons and form a triple bond.

The structure that results when atoms are joined together by covalent bonds is called a molecule. The **molecule** is the smallest unit of most compounds. The diagram of a water molecule in **Figure 2–4** shows that each hydrogen atom forms a single covalent bond with the oxygen atom.

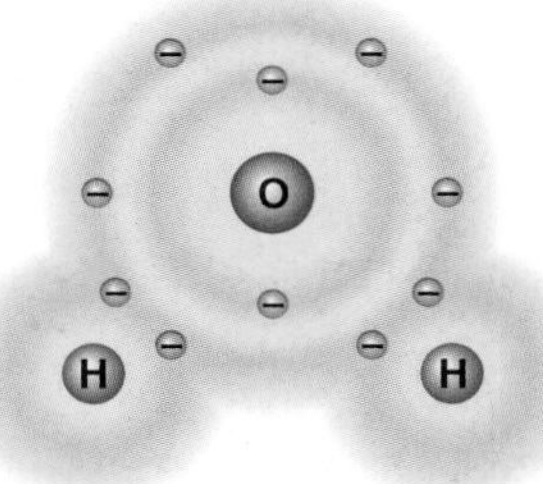

▲ **Figure 2–4** **The chemical bond in which electrons are shared between atoms is called a covalent bond.** In a water molecule, each hydrogen atom shares two electrons with the oxygen atom.

FACTS AND FIGURES

Valence is the key to bonds

Atoms don't bond in haphazard ways. The number of valence electrons that occupy the outermost energy level of an atom determines the number and types of bonds that the atom can form. In the periodic table, elements are placed into columns called groups. Elements in the same group have the same number of valence electrons. For example, elements in group 4A have four valence electrons. Metallic elements on the left side of the table tend to lose electrons; nonmetallic elements on the right side of the table tend to gain electrons when they react with metals or share electrons when they react with another nonmetal. When the outermost energy level is filled through the transfer or sharing of electrons, the atom or ion formed is stable. Inert gases are extremely unreactive because their atoms have filled outermost energy levels. Some, such as helium, do not form any compounds.

Van der Waals Forces Because of their structures, atoms of different elements do not all have the same ability to attract electrons. Some atoms have a stronger attraction for electrons than do other atoms. Therefore, when the atoms in a covalent bond share electrons, the sharing is not always equal. Even when the sharing is equal, the rapid movement of electrons can create regions on a molecule that have a tiny positive or negative charge.

When molecules are close together, a slight attraction can develop between the oppositely charged regions of nearby molecules. Chemists call such intermolecular forces of attraction **van der Waals forces,** after the scientist who discovered them. Although van der Waals forces are not as strong as ionic bonds or covalent bonds, they can hold molecules together, especially when the molecules are large.

People who keep geckos as pets have already seen van der Waals forces in action. These remarkable little lizards can climb up vertical surfaces, even smooth glass walls, and then hang on by a single toe despite the pull of gravity. How do they do it? No, they do not have some sort of glue on their feet and they don't have suction cups.

A gecko foot like the one shown in **Figure 2–5** is covered by as many as half a million tiny hairlike projections. Each projection is further divided into hundreds of tiny, flat-surfaced fibers. This design allows the gecko's foot to come in contact with an extremely large area of the wall at the molecular level. Van der Waals forces form between molecules on the surface of the gecko's foot and molecules on the surface of the wall. The combined strength of all the van der Waals forces allows the gecko to balance the pull of gravity. When the gecko needs to move its foot, it peels the foot off at an angle and reattaches it at another location on the wall.

▼ **Figure 2–5** Van der Waals forces help geckos to grip smooth, vertical surfaces. **Applying Concepts** *Explain why a similar technique could not work for humans.*

Use Visuals

Figure 2–5 Ask: **Are van der Waals forces stronger than ionic or covalent bonds?** *(No, they are much weaker.)* **How can such weak forces keep a gecko attached to a smooth vertical surface despite the gecko's weight?** *(The combined strength of all the van der Waals forces that form between molecules on the gecko's hairlike projections and the surface of the wall balance the pull of gravity.)*

2–1 Section Assessment

1. **Key Concept** Describe the structure of an atom.
2. **Key Concept** Why do all isotopes of an element have the same chemical properties? In what way do isotopes of an element differ?
3. **Key Concept** What is a covalent bond? An ionic bond?
4. What is a compound? How are compounds related to molecules?
5. How do van der Waals forces hold molecules together?
6. **Critical Thinking Comparing and Contrasting** How are ionic bonds and van der Waals forces similar? How are they different?

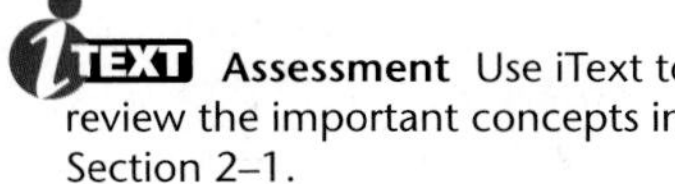

Assessment Use iText to review the important concepts in Section 2–1.

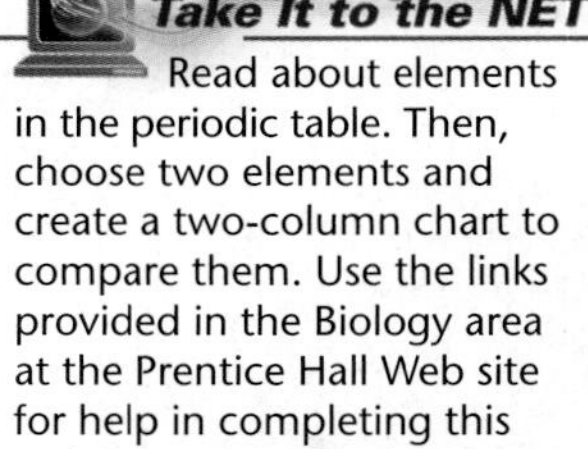

Take It to the NET

Read about elements in the periodic table. Then, choose two elements and create a two-column chart to compare them. Use the links provided in the Biology area at the Prentice Hall Web site for help in completing this activity: **www.phschool.com**

2–1 Section Assessment

1. Atoms have a nucleus made up of protons and neutrons. Electrons are in constant motion in the space around the nucleus.
2. They have the same number of electrons. They differ in number of neutrons.
3. A covalent bond forms when electrons are shared between atoms. An ionic bond forms when electrons are transferred.
4. A compound is a substance formed by the combination of two or more elements in definite proportions. A molecule is the smallest unit of most compounds.
5. When the sharing of electrons is unequal, a molecule has regions that are charged. An attraction can occur between oppositely charged regions of nearby molecules.
6. In both cases, particles are held together by attractions between opposite charges, but the attractions are stronger between the ions than they are between the molecules.

3 ASSESS

Evaluate Understanding

Call on students at random to define each of the section's Vocabulary terms. Then, ask students to explain the difference between the chemical bond in a water molecule and the chemical bond in table salt.

Reteach

Have students write answers to the three Key Concept questions listed on the first page of the section.

Take It to the NET

Students can choose any two elements in the periodic table and click on them for a list of statistics ranging from appearance to cost per 100 g. Students' charts should compare the two elements on at least five different characteristics. As students work on their charts, help them link an element's place on the periodic table with its characteristics and help them identify trends across the periods. For additional information, visit **www.phschool.com**

Use iText to review the key concepts in Section 2–1.

Answer to . . .

Figure 2–5 *Even if human toes and fingers had hairlike projections, the surface area would not be sufficient to generate a combined force that could support a human's weight.*

Section 2–2

1 FOCUS

Objectives

2.2.1 ***Explain*** why water molecules are polar.
2.2.2 ***Differentiate*** between solutions and suspensions.
2.2.3 ***Explain*** what acidic solutions and basic solutions are.

Guide for Reading

Vocabulary Preview

Challenge students to divide the Vocabulary terms into three groups of related words. *(Cohesion, adhesion; mixture, solution, solute, solvent, suspension; pH scale, acid, base, buffer)*

Reading Strategy

Figure 2–7 shows that hydrogen bonds form between polar water molecules. Figure 2–9 shows that an ionic compound can dissolve in water because its ions are attracted to the polar water molecules, which surround and separate the ions.

2 INSTRUCT

The Water Molecule

Use Visuals

Figure 2–7 Point out that water is the most abundant compound in most living things, making an understanding of the chemical makeup of water extremely important for understanding how living things function. Then, ask: **What kind of bonds join the atoms in a water molecule?** *(Covalent bonds)* **Are the hydrogen atoms bonded to each other?** *(No, each is bonded to the oxygen atom.)* **Why is the hydrogen end of the molecule positive and the oxygen end negative?** *(In a water molecule, the electrons are shared unequally. At any moment, there is a greater probability of finding the shared electrons near the oxygen atom than near the hydrogen atoms.)*

2–2 Properties of Water

Guide for Reading

Key Concepts
- Why are water molecules polar?
- What are acidic solutions? What are basic solutions?

Vocabulary
cohesion
adhesion
mixture
solution
solute
solvent
suspension
pH scale
acid
base
buffer

Reading Strategy: Using Visuals Before you read, preview **Figure 2–7** and **Figure 2–9.** As you read, note how these two figures are related.

After several days in space, one of the first astronauts to travel to the moon looked back longingly at Earth and marveled at its distant beauty. If there are other beings who have seen Earth, he said, they must surely call it "the blue planet." The astronaut was referring to the blue appearance of the water in the oceans, which cover three fourths of Earth's surface. Water is also the single most abundant compound in most living things.

Water is one of the few compounds that is a liquid at the temperatures found over much of Earth's surface. Unlike most substances, water expands as it freezes. Thus, ice is less dense than liquid water, which explains why ice floats on the surface of lakes and rivers. If the ice sank to the bottom, the situation would be disastrous for fish and plant life in regions with cold winters, to say nothing of the sport of ice skating!

The Water Molecule

Like all molecules, a water molecule (H_2O) is neutral. The positive charges on its 10 protons balance out the negative charges on its 10 electrons. However, there is more to the story.

Polarity With 8 protons in its nucleus, an oxygen atom has a much stronger attraction for electrons than does the hydrogen atom with a single proton in its nucleus. Thus, at any moment, there is a greater probability of finding the shared electrons near the oxygen atom than near the hydrogen atom. Because the water molecule has a bent shape, as shown in **Figure 2–6**, the oxygen atom is on one end of the molecule and the hydrogen atoms are on the other. As a result, the oxygen end of the molecule has a slight negative charge and the hydrogen end of the molecule has a slight positive charge.

A molecule in which the charges are unevenly distributed is called a polar molecule because the molecule is like a magnet with poles. **A water molecule is polar because there is an uneven distribution of electrons between the oxygen and hydrogen atoms.** The negative pole is near the oxygen atom and the positive pole is between the hydrogen atoms.

◀ **Figure 2–6** **The unequal sharing of electrons causes the water molecule to be polar.** The hydrogen end of the molecule is slightly positive and the oxygen end is slightly negative.

SECTION RESOURCES

Print:
- ***Teaching Resources,*** Section Review 2–2
- ***Guided Reading and Study Workbook,*** Section 2–2

Technology:
- ***iText,*** Section 2–2

Hydrogen Bonds Because of their partial positive and negative charges, polar molecules such as water can attract each other, as shown in **Figure 2–7.** The charges on a polar molecule are written in parentheses, (–) or (+), to show that they are weaker than the charges on ions such as Na^+ and Cl^-. The attraction between the hydrogen atom on one water molecule and the oxygen atom on another water molecule is an example of a hydrogen bond. Hydrogen bonds are not as strong as covalent or ionic bonds, but they are the strongest of the bonds that can form between molecules.

A single water molecule may be involved in as many as four hydrogen bonds at the same time. The ability of water to form multiple hydrogen bonds is responsible for many of water's properties. **Cohesion** is an attraction between molecules of the same substance. Because of hydrogen bonding, water is extremely cohesive. Water's cohesion causes molecules on the surface of water to be drawn inward, which is why drops of water form beads on a smooth surface. Cohesion also explains why some insects and spiders can walk on a pond's surface, as shown in **Figure 2–8.**

Adhesion is an attraction between molecules of different substances. Have you ever been told to read the volume in a graduated cylinder at eye level? The surface of the water in the graduated cylinder dips slightly in the center because the adhesion between water molecules and glass molecules is stronger than the cohesion between water molecules. Adhesion between water and glass also causes water to rise in a narrow tube against the force of gravity. This effect is called capillary action. Capillary action is one of the forces that draw water out of the roots of a plant and up into its stems and leaves. Cohesion holds the column of water together as it rises.

CHECKPOINT *How are cohesion and adhesion similar? Different?*

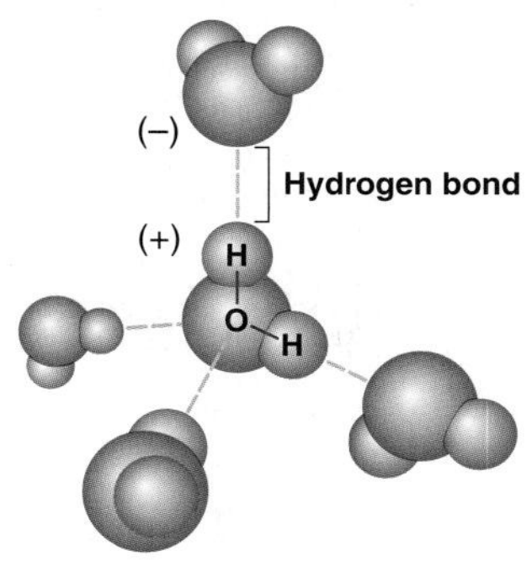

▲ **Figure 2–7** The illustration shows the hydrogen bonds that form between water molecules. **Applying Concepts** *Why are water molecules attracted to one another?*

Solutions and Suspensions

Water is not always pure—it is often found as part of a mixture. A **mixture** is a material composed of two or more elements or compounds that are physically mixed together but not chemically combined. Salt and pepper stirred together constitute a mixture. So do sugar and sand. Earth's atmosphere is a mixture of gases. Living things are in part composed of mixtures involving water. Two types of mixtures that can be made with water are solutions and suspensions.

▶ **Figure 2–8** Cohesion is responsible for enabling this tarantula to rest on the water's surface. **Observing** *How does the tarantula's physical structure help it to stay afloat?*

Meet Diverse Needs

Explain that *cohesion* and *adhesion* are both derived from Latin verbs meaning "to stick." A subtle difference between the terms—reflected in their scientific definitions—can be found in their prefixes. The prefix *co-* means "common," and the prefix *ad-* means "toward." Point out that *cohesion* means an attraction, or "sticking," between molecules that have properties "in common." *Adhesion* means an attraction, or "sticking," from one substance "toward" another. **Limited English proficiency**

Solutions and Suspensions

Demonstration

Show students that when a solution is formed, the solute seems to disappear and yet takes up space. First, pour 225 mL of water into a 250-mL flask. Mark the level of the water with masking tape, and make sure students note this level. Then, stir in 25 g of sugar, which will dissolve almost immediately. Ask: **Is there any evidence that the sugar dissolved into the water?** *(Most students will note that the solution is transparent.)* Have students check to see if the level of the liquid is at the same height as before, as marked by the tape. Use a metric ruler to show that the liquid's level is about 1 cm higher than before, indicating that the sugar is present in the solution.

Answers to . . .

CHECKPOINT *Cohesion and adhesion are similar because they are attractions between molecules, but cohesion occurs between molecules of the same substance and adhesion occurs between molecules of different substances.*

Figure 2–7 *Water molecules are polar, meaning they have regions with partial positive and negative charges.*

Figure 2–8 *Because of its multiple legs, a tarantula's mass is distributed over a large area on the surface of the water, which means that the pull of gravity is limited at any one location on the surface.*

TIME SAVER PRESENTATIONS MADE EASY!

The Presentation Assistant Plus contains the Prentice Hall Presentation Pro and the Transparencies, which provide easy-to-follow visual support for every step of this lesson. If you have a computer presentation station, use Prentice Hall Presentation Pro Section 2–2, or use the transparencies listed here.

Section 2–2: 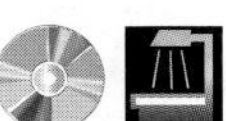 

Interest Grabber
Section Outline
pH scale
Figure 2–9

Acids, Bases, and pH

Quick Lab

Objective Students will be able to conclude whether foods are acidic or basic.

Skill Focus Evaluating and Revising

Materials pH paper, solid foods and fruit juices, paper towel, scalpel, dropper pipette, plastic gloves

Time 15 minutes

Advance Prep Obtain a variety of foods for students to test, including orange juice, lemon juice, tomato juice, egg white, meat, fish, fruits, and vegetables. For the test to work, the samples must be moist.

Safety Demonstrate safe cutting techniques, such as holding the sample behind the cutting edge when using the scalpel.

Strategies
- Ask students to write down their predictions.
- Make sure each student constructs a data table to record the pH of each sample. This simple table needs only two columns, headed Sample and pH.
- Review how pH paper acts as an indicator: a base turns red litmus paper blue; an acid turns blue litmus paper red.
- Either supply a pipette for each liquid or have students use one pipette and clean it between samples.

Expected Outcomes Students should discover that most foods are acidic.

Analyze and Conclude
1. Most of the samples were acidic.
2. Students were correct if they predicted that most foods are acidic.

Use Visuals

Figure 2–10 Have students copy the pH scale in Figure 2–10 onto a sheet of notebook paper, including the substances given as examples. Challenge students to use other references to add substances found in living things to the scale.

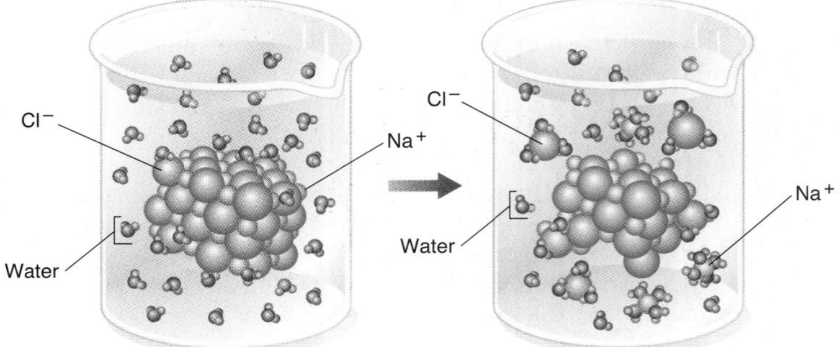

▶ **Figure 2–9** When an ionic compound such as sodium chloride is placed in water, water molecules surround and separate the positive and negative ions. **Interpreting Graphics** *What happens to the sodium ions and chloride ions in the solution?*

Quick Lab

Are foods acidic or basic?

Materials pH paper, samples of food, paper towel, scalpel, dropper pipette, plastic gloves

Procedure 

1. **Predicting** Predict whether most foods are acidic or basic.
2. Tear off a small piece of pH paper for each sample you will test. Place these pieces on a paper towel.
3. Construct a data table in which you will record the name and pH of each food sample.
4. Use a scalpel to cut a piece off each solid. **CAUTION:** *Be careful not to cut yourself. Do not eat the food.* Touch the cut surface of each sample to a square of pH paper. Use a dropper pipette to place a drop of any liquid sample on a square of pH paper. Record the pH of each sample in your data table.

Analyze and Conclude

1. **Analyzing Data** Were most of the samples acidic or basic?
2. **Evaluating** Was your prediction correct?

Solutions If a crystal of table salt is placed in a glass of warm water, sodium and chloride ions on the surface of the crystal are attracted to the polar water molecules. Ions break away from the crystal and are surrounded by water molecules, as illustrated in **Figure 2–9.** The ions gradually become dispersed in the water, forming a type of mixture called a solution. All the components of a **solution** are evenly distributed throughout the solution. In a salt–water solution, table salt is the **solute**—the substance that is dissolved. Water is the **solvent**—the substance in which the solute dissolves. Water's polarity gives it the ability to dissolve both ionic compounds and other polar molecules, such as sugar. Without exaggeration, water is the greatest solvent on Earth.

Suspensions Some materials do not dissolve when placed in water but separate into pieces so small that they do not settle out. The movement of water molecules keeps the small particles suspended. Such mixtures of water and nondissolved material are known as **suspensions.** Some of the most important biological fluids are both solutions and suspensions. The blood that circulates through your body is mostly water, which contains many dissolved compounds. However, blood also contains cells and other undissolved particles that remain in suspension as the blood moves through the body.

Acids, Bases, and pH

A water molecule can react to form ions. This reaction can be summarized by a chemical equation in which double arrows are used to show that the reaction can occur in either direction.

$$H_2O \rightleftharpoons H^+ + OH^-$$

$$\text{water} \rightleftharpoons \text{hydrogen ion} + \text{hydroxide ion}$$

How often does this happen? In pure water, about 1 water molecule in 550 million reacts and forms ions. Because the number of positive hydrogen ions produced is equal to the number of negative hydroxide ions produced, water is neutral.

HISTORY OF SCIENCE

pH—a simpler way of expression

In 1909, the Danish chemist Søren Sørensen introduced the expression *pH*, or *p*otential of *H*ydrogen. A pH value represents the concentration of hydrogen ions in solution, an important factor in many chemical reactions. Before Sørensen's suggestion, chemists had to deal with negative logarithms of the concentration of the ions, such as a concentration of 1.0×10^{-4} moles/liter. Today, that would be expressed as a pH of 4, which is about the pH of wine. Pure water has a pH of 7, which means that the concentration of H^+ ions equals the concentration of OH^- ions. That is, there is about one ten-millionth of a mole of H^+ ions per liter of water and the same number of OH^- ions. If an acid is added to the water, the H^+ ions outnumber the OH^- ions, and the pH of the solution decreases. The opposite occurs if a base is added to the water.

The pH scale Chemists devised a measurement system called the **pH scale** to indicate the concentration of H^+ ions in solution. As **Figure 2–10** shows, the pH scale ranges from 0 to 14. At a pH of 7, the concentration of H^+ ions and OH^- ions is equal. Pure water has a pH of 7. Solutions with a pH below 7 are called acidic because they have more H^+ ions than OH^- ions. The lower the pH, the greater the acidity. Solutions with a pH above 7 are called basic because they have more OH^- ions than H^+ ions. The higher the pH, the more basic the solution. Each step on the pH scale represents a factor of 10. For example, a liter of a solution with a pH of 4 has 10 times as many H^+ ions as a liter of a solution with a pH of 5.

Acids Where do all those extra H^+ ions in a low-pH solution come from? They come from acids. An **acid** is any compound that forms H^+ ions in solution. **Acidic solutions contain higher concentrations of H^+ ions than pure water and have pH values below 7.** Strong acids tend to have pH values that range from 1 to 3. The hydrochloric acid produced by the stomach to help digest food is a strong acid.

Bases A **base** is a compound that produces hydroxide ions (OH^- ions) in solution. **Basic, or alkaline, solutions contain lower concentrations of H^+ ions than pure water and have pH values above 7.** Strong bases, such as lye, tend to have pH values ranging from 11 to 14.

Buffers The pH of the fluids within most cells in the human body must generally be kept between 6.5 and 7.5. If the pH is lower or higher, it will affect the chemical reactions that take place within the cells. Thus, controlling pH is important for maintaining homeostasis. One of the ways that the body controls pH is through dissolved compounds called buffers. **Buffers** are weak acids or bases that can react with strong acids or bases to prevent sharp, sudden changes in pH.

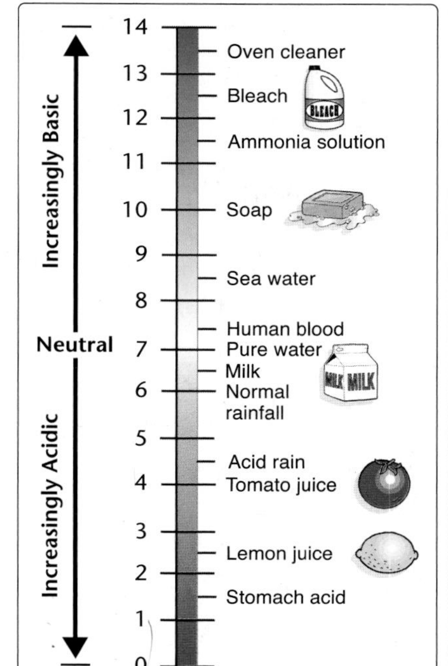

▲ **Figure 2–10** **The concentration of H^+ ions determines whether solutions are acidic or basic.** The most acidic material on this pH scale is stomach acid. The most basic material on this scale is oven cleaner.

2–2 Section Assessment

1. **Key Concept** Use the structure of a water molecule to explain why it is polar.
2. **Key Concept** Compare acidic and basic solutions in terms of their H^+ ion and OH^- ion concentrations.
3. What is the difference between a solution and a suspension?
4. What does pH measure?
5. **Critical Thinking Predicting** The strong acid hydrogen fluoride (HF) can be dissolved in pure water. Will the pH of the solution be greater or less than 7.0?

iTEXT **Assessment** Use iText to review the important concepts in Section 2–2.

ALTERNATIVE ASSESSMENT

Making Analogies
Use the following pairs of terms to develop a set of word analogies: hydrogen bonds and polarity; cohesion and adhesion; solvent and solute.

Address Misconceptions

Students might mistakenly conclude that all water has a pH of 7. Explain that only pure water has a neutral pH. Normal rain water, for example, can have a pH as low as 5.6, making it slightly acidic. As rain falls, it reacts with CO_2 in the atmosphere and forms carbonic acid, which lowers the pH of the rain. Acid rain has an even lower pH due to reactions between water and oxides of nitrogen and sulfur, which are pollutants found in air. Ask volunteers to collect rain or melt snow and use pH paper to check on the acidity of local precipitation.

3 ASSESS

Evaluate Understanding

Ask students to write a paragraph that explains how the concentration of hydrogen ions determines the acid–base properties of a solution. Students should discuss how water reacts and forms ions, the difference between acids and bases, and the significance of the pH scale.

Reteach

Use Figure 2–9 to review the section's key concepts, including the polarity of water molecules, how this polarity gives water the ability to interact with other particles, how sodium and chloride ions become evenly dispersed in water to form a solution, and why some solutions are neutral, some are acidic, and others are basic.

ALTERNATIVE ASSESSMENT

Students' word analogies need not be limited to the listed vocabulary words. Students could incorporate other pairs of terms, such as solutions and suspensions or acids and bases.

2–2 Section Assessment

1. The hydrogen atoms form covalent bonds with the oxygen atom. Because of oxygen's greater attraction for electrons, there is an unequal distribution of electrons. The oxygen end of the bent water molecule is negative; the hydrogen end is positive.
2. Per volume, there are more H^+ ions than OH^- ions in an acidic solution and more OH^- ions than H^+ ions in a basic solution.
3. In a solution, all components are evenly distributed. In a suspension, undissolved particles are suspended in the mixture and can settle out over time.
4. The pH scale measures the concentration of H^+ ions in a solution.
5. The pH will be less than 7.0.

Use iText to review the key concepts in Section 2–2.

Answer to . . .

Figure 2–9 *They become evenly dispersed in the water.*

Section 2–3

1 FOCUS

Objective

2.3.1 ***Describe*** the functions of each group of organic compounds.

Guide for Reading

Vocabulary Preview

As students read, have them make a concept map using the section's Vocabulary terms, excluding the words *monomer* and *polymer.* In the initial oval, they should write *Four Groups of Organic Compounds in Living Things.* Then, students should add Vocabulary terms to their concept map as they read the section.

Reading Strategy

Explain that the boldfaced sentences are the key ideas. In writing their summaries, students should use key words from the key ideas, as well as any boldfaced Vocabulary terms.

2 INSTRUCT

The Chemistry of Carbon

Make Connections

Chemistry Remind students that a stable carbon atom would have eight electrons in its outermost level. Then, ask: **How many electrons would a carbon atom have to gain to fill its outermost level?** *(Four)* Point out that such a transfer is unlikely. Instead, carbon completes its outermost level by sharing electrons and forming four covalent bonds. The atoms that carbon most often forms bonds with, besides other carbon atoms, are hydrogen, oxygen, and nitrogen. Have students look for these elements in the compounds discussed in this section. (Finding a definition of organic chemistry that does not require exceptions is difficult. The definition given in the text excludes methane—which is represented by a molecular drawing in Figure 2–11—and compounds derived from methane, but it includes the vast majority of organic compounds.)

2–3 Carbon Compounds

Guide for Reading

Key Concept
- What are the functions of each group of organic compounds?

Vocabulary
monomer
polymer
carbohydrate
monosaccharide
polysaccharide
lipid
nucleic acid
nucleotide
ribonucleic acid (RNA)
deoxyribonucleic acid (DNA)
protein
amino acid

Reading Strategy: Summarizing As you read, find the key ideas. Write down a few key words from each main idea. Then, use the key words in your summary. Reread your summary, keeping only the most important ideas.

Until the early 1800s, many chemists thought that compounds created by organisms—organic compounds—were distinctly different from compounds in nonliving things. In 1828, a German chemist was able to synthesize the organic compound urea from a mineral called ammonium cyanate. Chemists soon realized that the principles governing the chemistry of nonliving things could be applied to living things. Scientists still use the term *organic chemistry,* but now it describes something a little different. Today, organic chemistry is the study of all compounds that contain bonds between carbon atoms.

The Chemistry of Carbon

Is carbon so interesting that a whole branch of chemistry should be set aside just to study carbon compounds? It is indeed, for two reasons. First, carbon atoms have four valence electrons. Each electron can join with an electron from another atom to form a strong covalent bond. Carbon can bond with many elements, including hydrogen, oxygen, phosphorus, sulfur, and nitrogen.

Even more important, a carbon atom can bond to other carbon atoms, which gives carbon the ability to form chains that are almost unlimited in length. These carbon-carbon bonds can be single, double, or triple covalent bonds. Chains of carbon atoms can even close upon themselves to form rings, as shown in **Figure 2–11.** Carbon has the ability to form millions of different large and complex structures. No other element even comes close to matching carbon's versatility.

▼ **Figure 2–11** Carbon can form single, double, or triple bonds with other carbon atoms. Each line between atoms in a molecular drawing represents one covalent bond. **Observing** ***How many covalent bonds are there between the carbon atoms in acetylene?***

Methane

Acetylene

Butadiene

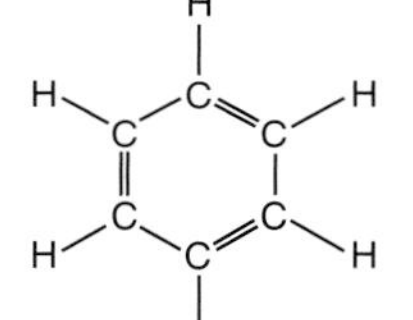

Benzene

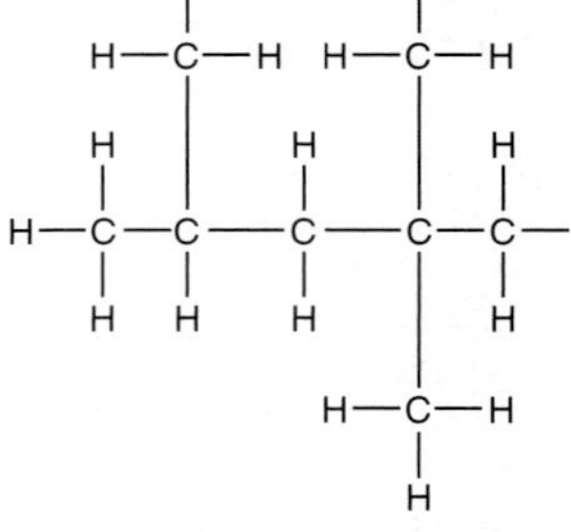

Isooctane

SECTION RESOURCES

Print:
- ***Laboratory Manual A,*** Chapter 2 Lab
- ***Laboratory Manual B,*** Chapter 2 Lab
- ***Teaching Resources,*** Section Review 2–3
- ***Guided Reading and Study Workbook,*** Section 2–3

Technology:
- ***iText,*** Section 2–3

Macromolecules

Many of the molecules in living cells are so large that they are known as macromolecules, which means "giant molecules." Macromolecules are made from thousands or even hundreds of thousands of smaller molecules.

Macromolecules are formed by a process known as polymerization (pah-lih-mur-ih-ZAY-shun), in which large compounds are built by joining smaller ones together. The smaller units, or **monomers,** join together to form **polymers.** The monomers in a polymer may be identical like the links on a metal watch band, or the monomers may be different like the beads in a multicolored necklace. **Figure 2–12** illustrates the formation of a polymer from more than one type of monomer.

It would be difficult to study the millions of organic compounds if they were not classified into groups. **Four groups of organic compounds found in living things are carbohydrates, lipids, nucleic acids, and proteins.**

CHECKPOINT *What is polymerization?*

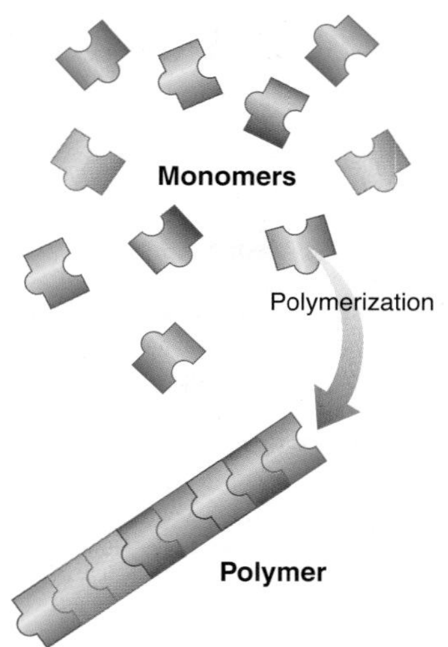

▲ **Figure 2–12** When small molecules called monomers join together, they form polymers, or large molecules. **Using Analogies** *How are monomers similar to links in a chain?*

Carbohydrates

Carbohydrates are compounds made up of carbon, hydrogen, and oxygen atoms, usually in a ratio of 1 : 2 : 1. **Living things use carbohydrates as their main source of energy. Plants and some animals also use carbohydrates for structural purposes.** The breakdown of sugars, such as glucose, supplies immediate energy for all cell activities. Living things store extra sugar as complex carbohydrates known as starches. As shown in **Figure 2–13,** the monomers in starch polymers are sugar molecules.

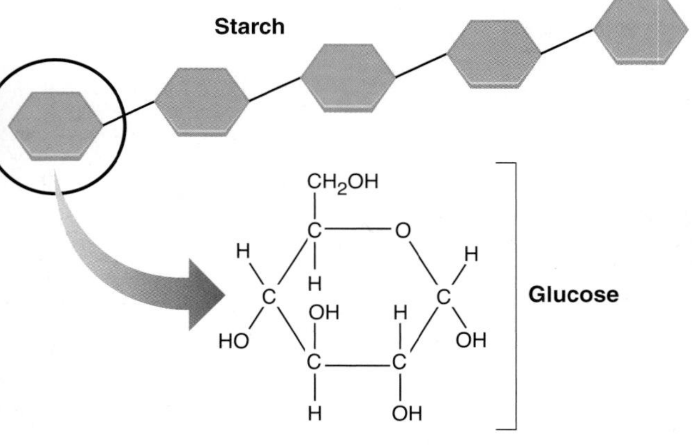

Figure 2–13 **Starches and sugars are examples of carbohydrates that are used by living things as a source of energy.** Starches form when sugars join together in a long chain.

Macromolecules

Use Visuals

Figure 2–12 After you introduce the four types of macromolecules, have students revisit Figure 2–12. Ask: **Which type of macromolecule could this drawing represent?** *(Students might say that the monomers represent different amino acids or nucleotides or sugars.)* Explain that plant starch, glycogen, and cellulose contain only glucose monomers. The drawing cannot represent a lipid because lipids are not polymers.

Build Science Skills

Using Tables and Graphs Have students make a compare/contrast table entitled Four Groups of Organic Compounds. Column heads should include Group Name, Chemical Composition, Examples, and Function in Living Things. As students read the rest of the section, they should use the table to organize the information they learn about the groups of macromolecules.

Carbohydrates

Build Science Skills

Observing Divide the class in pairs, and give each pair Lugol's solution, a dropper, test tubes, soda crackers, and several other foods, including a potato section, white bread, oatmeal, and granulated sugar. Explain that Lugol's solution is an indicator of starch—if the solution turns dark blue or black, starch is present. Then, have pairs test the foods for the presence of starch. For example, they should place pieces of soda crackers in a test tube, add 5 drops of Lugol's solution, and observe whether it darkens. Students should observe that all the foods listed contain starch except granulated sugar.

TIME SAVER — PRESENTATIONS MADE EASY!

The Presentation Assistant Plus contains the Prentice Hall Presentation Pro and the Transparencies, which provide easy-to-follow visual support for every step of this lesson. If you have a computer presentation station, use Prentice Hall Presentation Pro Section 2–3, or use the transparencies listed here.

Section 2–3:

Interest Grabber
Section Outline
Concept Map
Figure 2–11
Figures 2–13 and 2–14
Figures 2–16 and 2–17

Answers to . . .

CHECKPOINT *The process in which monomers are joined together to form larger molecules called polymers*

Figure 2–11 *Three*

Figure 2–12 *Like links in a chain, monomers are either identical or closely related units that connect together to form a larger structure.*

Word Origins

The term *monosaccharide* means "single sugar"; the term *polysaccharide* means "many sugars."

Build Science Skills

Applying Concepts Display photos of various foods that contain high amounts of carbohydrates, including milk, potatoes, and fruits. Explain that milk contains the carbohydrates lactose and galactose, fruits contain fructose, and potatoes contain starch. Ask: **What is the source of these carbohydrates?** *(Energy from sunlight)* **What function do these carbohydrates serve in living things?** *(They store energy.)*

Lipids

Use Visuals

Figure 2–14 After students study the structural formula of a lipid, ask: **What are the components of a lipid?** *(Glycerol and fatty acids)* **Would you describe the lipid shown in the structural formula as saturated, unsaturated, or polyunsaturated?** *(It is unsaturated because there is a single double bond in each fatty acid chain. Fatty acids with only one double bond are called monounsaturated.)* Then direct students' attention to the photo, and ask: **Which is more likely to be polyunsaturated, a solid fat or a liquid oil?** *(Oils usually contain more unsaturated fatty acids.)*

Use Community Resources

Invite a dietician to address the class about why some fats are an important part of a healthy diet and why foods with a high fat content should be avoided. Ask the speaker to explain which fats are harmful and which aren't, and which common foods have a high content of harmful fats. Make sure students ask about saturated, unsaturated, and polyunsaturated fats in foods.

Word Origins

Monomer comes from the Greek words *monos*, meaning "single," and *meros*, meaning "part." *Monomer* means "single part." The prefix *poly-* comes from the Greek word *polus,* meaning "many," so *polymer* means "many parts." **The word *saccharide* comes from the Latin word *saccharum,* meaning "sugar." What do you think the terms *monosaccharide* and *polysaccharide* mean?**

Single sugar molecules are also called **monosaccharides** (mahn-oh-SAK-uh-rydz). Besides glucose, monosaccharides include galactose, which is a component of milk, and fructose, which is found in many fruits.

The large macromolecules formed from monosaccharides are known as **polysaccharides.** Many animals store excess sugar in a polysaccharide called glycogen, or animal starch. When the level of glucose in your blood runs low, glycogen is released from your liver. The glycogen stored in your muscles supplies the energy for muscle contraction and, thus, for movement.

Plants use a slightly different polysaccharide, called plant starch, to store excess sugar. Plants also make another important polysaccharide called cellulose. Tough, flexible cellulose fibers give plants much of their strength and rigidity. Cellulose is the major component of both wood and paper, so you are actually looking at cellulose as you read these words!

Lipids

Lipids are a large and varied group of biological molecules that are generally not soluble in water. **Lipids** are made mostly from carbon and hydrogen atoms. The common categories of lipids are fats, oils, and waxes. **Lipids can be used to store energy. Some lipids are important parts of biological membranes and waterproof coverings.** Steroids are lipids as well. Many steroids serve as chemical messengers.

Many lipids are formed when a glycerol molecule combines with compounds called fatty acids, as shown in **Figure 2–14.** If each carbon atom in a lipid's fatty acid chains is joined to another carbon atom by a single bond, the lipid is said to be saturated. The term *saturated* is used because the fatty acids contain the maximum possible number of hydrogen atoms.

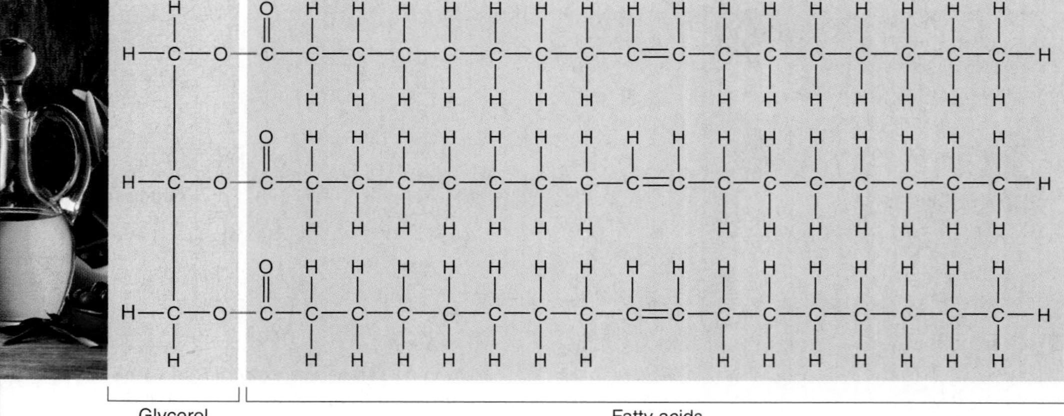

▼ **Figure 2–14** **Lipids are used to store energy.** Lipid molecules are made up of fatty acids and glycerol. Liquid lipids, such as olive oil, contain mainly unsaturated fatty acids.

BIO INSIGHTS — FACTS AND FIGURES

Mono-, di-, and polysaccharides

The names of carbohydrates usually end in the suffix *–ose*. This includes glucose, which is the most common monosaccharide. Its formula is $C_6H_{12}O_6$, which conforms to the general formula of all carbohydrates: $C_x(H_2O)_y$. This general formula shows the derivation of *carbohydrate*, which means "carbon hydrate." Glucose is formed when a carbon compound, carbon dioxide, reacts with water. Monosaccharides, such as glucose, are important nutrients for cells, as evidenced by the central role glucose has in cellular respiration. Fructose and galactose are other monosaccharides. When a covalent bond links two monosaccharides, the result is called a disaccharide. An example is lactose, a sugar in milk. Polysaccharides, which include glycogen, starch, and cellulose—the most abundant organic chemical on Earth—can contain thousands of monosaccharides linked together.

If there is at least one carbon-carbon double bond in a fatty acid, the fatty acid is said to be unsaturated. Lipids whose fatty acids contain more than one double bond are said to be polyunsaturated. If the terms *saturated* and *polyunsaturated* seem familiar, you have probably seen them on food package labels. Lipids such as olive oil, which contains unsaturated fatty acids, tend to be liquid at room temperature. Cooking oils, such as corn oil, sesame oil, and peanut oil, contain polyunsaturated lipids.

Nucleic Acids

Nucleic acids are macromolecules containing hydrogen, oxygen, nitrogen, carbon, and phosphorus. Nucleic acids are polymers assembled from individual monomers known as nucleotides. **Nucleotides** consist of three parts: a 5-carbon sugar, a phosphate group, and a nitrogenous base, as shown in **Figure 2–15.** Individual nucleotides can be joined by covalent bonds to form a polynucleotide, or nucleic acid.

Nucleic acids store and transmit hereditary, or genetic, information. There are two kinds of nucleic acids: **ribonucleic acid (RNA)** and **deoxyribonucleic acid (DNA).** As their names indicate, RNA contains the sugar ribose and DNA contains the sugar deoxyribose.

CHECKPOINT *What are the three parts of a nucleotide?*

Proteins

Proteins are macromolecules that contain nitrogen as well as carbon, hydrogen, and oxygen. Proteins are polymers of molecules called **amino acids.** Amino acids are compounds with an amino group ($-NH_2$) on one end and a carboxyl group ($-COOH$) on the other end.

Figure 2–16 shows one reason why proteins are among the most diverse macromolecules. More than 20 different amino acids are found in nature. All 20 amino acids are identical in the regions where they may be joined together by covalent bonds. This uniformity allows any amino acid to be joined to any other amino acid—by bonding an amino group to a carboxyl group.

Nitrogenous base

Phosphate group

5-carbon sugar

▲ **Figure 2–15 Nucleic acids store and transmit genetic information.** The monomers that make up a nucleic acid are nucleotides. Each nucleotide has a 5-carbon sugar, a phosphate group, and a nitrogenous base.

Nucleic Acids

Meet Diverse Needs

To help at-risk students understand nucleic acids, ask: **What are the three basic parts of a nucleotide?** *(A 5-carbon sugar, a phosphate group, and a nitrogenous base)* Explain that each nucleotide in DNA contains one of four nitrogenous bases—adenine, guanine, cytosine, and thymine. The sequence of the nucleotides in a DNA molecule determines the information that it contains. Point out that the English alphabet contains only 26 letters, but different combinations of letters make virtually limitless numbers of words. Likewise, different combinations of the four nucleotides make endless numbers of different DNA molecules. **Learning modality: verbal**

Proteins

Use Visuals

Figure 2–16 Ask: **Which parts of an amino acid are the same in every amino acid?** *(The amino group, $-NH_2$, and the carboxyl group, $-COOH$)* Make sure students understand what composes the R group in alanine and serine. Ask: **In what ways are R groups different?** *(Some are acidic, some are basic, some are polar, and some are nonpolar.)* Stress that the joining of one amino acid to another, amino group to carboxyl group, creates a product that still has an amino group on one end and a carboxyl group on the other.

Amino Acids

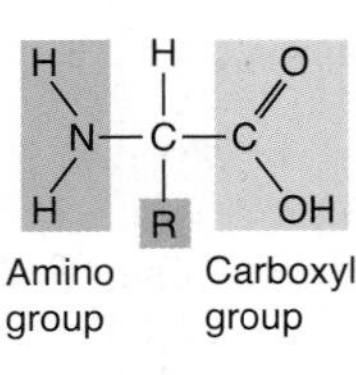

General structure

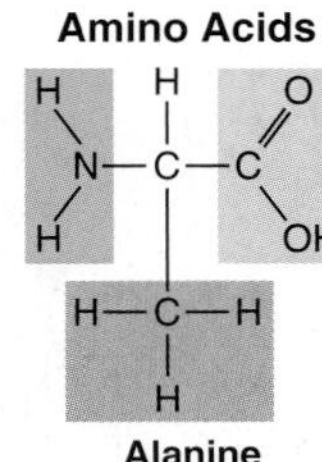
Alanine

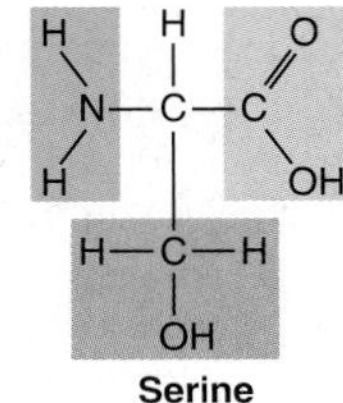
Serine

▶ **Figure 2–16** Amino acids are the monomers of proteins. All amino acids have an amino group at one end and a carboxyl group at the other end. What distinguishes one amino acid from another is the R-group section of the molecule. **Comparing and Contrasting** *How are proteins and carbohydrates similar? How are they different?*

BIO INSIGHTS **FACTS AND FIGURES**

Proteins serve many functions

The word *protein* is derived from a Greek word meaning "first or primary," and this class of molecules was so named because proteins are of "prime importance" in living things. They are so important because they have so many functions. As enzymes, they catalyze biological chemical reactions. Other proteins provide structural support, such as the protein collagen in bones and muscles. Proteins are important parts of cell membranes, where they play a role in reaction cycles such as the citric acid cycle. Proteins such as insulin function as hormones, regulating body metabolism. Actin and myosin are the proteins responsible for muscle contraction. The antibodies that protect against foreign invaders are proteins. Some proteins function as nutrient-storage molecules. Proteins are even used as toxins by some microorganisms.

Answers to . . .

CHECKPOINT *A 5-carbon sugar, a phosphate group, and a nitrogenous base*

Figure 2–16 *Carbohydrates and proteins are both polymers. The monomers in carbohydrates are monosaccharides. The monomers in proteins are amino acids.*

Make Connections

Health Science Have students list foods that contain high amounts of protein, such as meats, fish, dairy products, and beans. Ask: **Why is it important to have an adequate amount of protein for a healthy diet?** *(Proteins perform numerous functions.)* Ask: **How can one group of compounds have so many different functions?** *(The diversity of amino acids and four levels of organization account for proteins with properties suited to a myriad of biological tasks.)* The four levels of organization in proteins are called primary, secondary, tertiary, and quaternary.

3 ASSESS

Evaluate Understanding

Ask students to use their understanding of monomers, polymers, and polymerization to write an explanation of how polysaccharides, nucleic acids, and proteins are formed. They should use monosaccharides, nucleotides, and amino acids to explain polymerization.

Reteach

Ask a volunteer to explain what macromolecules are. Ask another student to list the four main groups of organic compounds found in living things. Then, call on students at random to explain the functions of each group of organic compounds in living things.

MAKING CONNECTIONS

Each level in a system is made up of smaller parts and is part of a larger system. For example, a nucleotide is made up of a sugar, a phosphate group, and a nitrogenous base. A nucleotide is part of a nucleic acid molecule. The nucleic acid molecule is larger and more complex than the nucleotide, which is larger and more complex than its three components.

Use the iText to review the key concepts in Section 2–3.

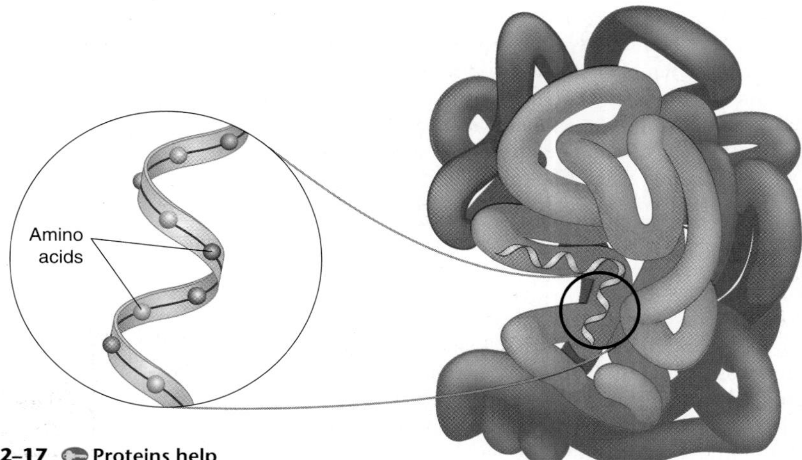

▲ **Figure 2–17** **Proteins help to carry out chemical reactions, transport small molecules in and out of cells, and fight diseases.** Proteins are made up of chains of amino acids folded into complex structures.

The portion of each amino acid that is different is a side chain called an R-group. Some R-groups are acidic and some are basic. Some are polar and some are nonpolar. Some contain carbon rings. The instructions for arranging amino acids into many different proteins are stored in DNA. Each protein has a specific role. **Some proteins control the rate of reactions and regulate cell processes. Some are used to form bones and muscles. Others transport substances into or out of cells or help to fight disease.**

Proteins can have up to four levels of organization. The first level is the sequence of amino acids in a protein chain. Second, the amino acids within a chain can be twisted or folded. Third, the chain itself is folded. If a protein has more than one chain, they have a specific arrangement in space as illustrated by the red and blue structures in **Figure 2–17.** Van der Waals forces and hydrogen bonds help maintain a protein's shape. In the next section, you will learn why a protein's shape is so important.

2–3 Section Assessment

1. **Key Concept** Name four groups of organic compounds found in living things.
2. **Key Concept** Describe at least one function of each group of organic compounds.
3. What properties of carbon explain carbon's ability to form many different macromolecules?
4. **Critical Thinking Applying Concepts** Explain why proteins are polymers but lipids are not.

iTEXT Assessment Use iText to review the important concepts in Section 2–3.

MAKING CONNECTIONS

Levels of Organization
Use what you learned about levels of organization in Section 1–3 to discuss the levels of organization in macromolecules.

2–3 Section Assessment

1. Carbohydrates, lipids, nucleic acids, and proteins
2. Living things use carbohydrates as their main source of energy. Plants and some animals also use them for structural purposes. Fats can be used to store energy. Other lipids are parts of biological membranes and waterproof coverings. Nucleic acids store and transmit hereditary information. Proteins control the rate of chemical reactions, regulate cell processes, form tissues, transport substances, and help to fight disease.
3. Each carbon atom can form 4 covalent bonds, and carbon atoms can bond with other carbon atoms.
4. Proteins are made up of amino acid monomers joined in long chains. Although fatty acid chains may be mistaken for monomers, only three fatty acids can attach to a glycerol molecule.

2–4 Chemical Reactions and Enzymes

Living things, as you have seen, are made of chemical compounds—some simple and some complex. The influence of chemistry doesn't stop, however, with the study of the composition of living organisms. To get the whole story, you have to look further. Chemistry isn't just what life is made of—chemistry is also what life does. Everything that happens in an organism—its growth, its interaction with the environment, its reproduction, and even its movement—is based on chemical reactions.

Guide for Reading

Key Concepts
- What happens to chemical bonds during chemical reactions?
- How do energy changes affect whether a chemical reaction will occur?
- Why are enzymes important to living things?

Vocabulary
chemical reaction
reactant
product
activation energy
catalyst
enzyme
substrate

Reading Strategy: Building Vocabulary After you read, write a phrase or sentence using your own words to define or describe each boldfaced word in the section.

Chemical Reactions

A **chemical reaction** is a process that changes one set of chemicals into another set of chemicals. Some chemical reactions occur slowly, such as the combination of iron and oxygen to form an iron oxide called rust, shown in **Figure 2–18.** Other reactions occur quickly. When hydrogen gas is ignited in the presence of oxygen, the reaction is rapid and explosive. The elements or compounds that enter into a chemical reaction are known as **reactants.** The elements or compounds produced by a chemical reaction are known as **products. Chemical reactions always involve the breaking of bonds in reactants and the formation of new bonds in products.**

One example of an important chemical reaction that occurs in your body involves carbon dioxide. Your cells constantly produce carbon dioxide as a normal part of their activity. This carbon dioxide is carried to your lungs through the bloodstream, and then is eliminated as you exhale. However, carbon dioxide is not very soluble in water. The bloodstream could not possibly dissolve enough carbon dioxide to carry it away from your tissues were it not for a chemical reaction. As it enters the blood, carbon dioxide reacts with water to produce a highly soluble compound called carbonic acid, H_2CO_3.

$$CO_2 + H_2O \longrightarrow H_2CO_3$$

This reaction enables the bloodstream to carry carbon dioxide to the lungs. In the lungs, the reaction is reversed.

$$H_2CO_3 \longrightarrow CO_2 + H_2O$$

This reverse reaction produces carbon dioxide gas, which is released as you exhale.

▶ **Figure 2–18 Chemical reactions always involve changes in chemical bonds.** The iron in these chain links gradually combined with oxygen to produce a compound known as rust.

SECTION REVIEW

Print:
- ***Teaching Resources,*** Section Review 2–4, Chapter 2 Design an Experiment
- ***Guided Reading and Study Workbook,*** Section 2–4

Technology:
- ***iText,*** Section 2–4

Section 2–4

1 FOCUS

Objectives

2.4.1 ***Explain*** how chemical reactions affect chemical bonds in compounds.

2.4.2 ***Describe*** how energy changes affect how easily a chemical reaction will occur.

2.4.3 ***Explain*** why enzymes are important to living things.

Guide for Reading

Vocabulary Preview

Before students read the section, call on volunteers to pronounce each word in the vocabulary list. Correct any mispronunciations.

Reading Strategy

Students should focus their attention on the section's Vocabulary terms, not the words in the boldfaced Key Concepts. Before writing a definition using their own words, students might use the glossary at the back of their books. Explain that often words are defined in context within a section. The glossary definition sometimes provides a more general definition.

2 INSTRUCT

Chemical Reactions

Demonstration

To show students what a chemical reaction looks like, use baking soda and vinegar. In separate beakers, mix 5 mL of baking soda with 120 mL of water and 5 mL of vinegar with 120 mL of water. Have students observe that nothing extraordinary happens when these substances are mixed. Then, in a third beaker, mix 5 mL of baking soda with 5 mL of vinegar. Students should observe that this third mixture produces foaming and fizzling, indicating that a gas is produced in a chemical reaction.

Energy in Reactions

Use Visuals

Figure 2–19 Have students compare the graphs representing the two types of chemical reactions. Then, ask: **Compare the energy of the products and reactants in the two types of reactions.** (In an energy-absorbing reaction, the products have more energy than the reactants. In an energy-releasing reaction, the products have less energy than the reactants.) **Which type of reaction is more likely to be spontaneous?** *(An energy-releasing reaction)*

Demonstration

Help students understand that enzymes lower the activation energy needed to get a reaction going by using the analogy of a book on the edge of a table. Show students that the book will not fall off the table without a push, which is the activation energy in this case. Then, place some kind of wedge under one side of the book, in such a way that the book is slanted off the edge of the table. Now, the push, or activation energy, needed to make the book fall is much less. Likewise, an enzyme lowers the activation energy needed to begin a chemical reaction.

Energy in Reactions

Energy is released or absorbed whenever chemical bonds form or are broken. Because chemical reactions involve breaking and forming bonds, they involve changes in energy.

Energy Changes Some chemical reactions release energy, and other reactions absorb energy. Energy changes are one of the most important factors in determining whether a chemical reaction will occur. **Chemical reactions that release energy often occur spontaneously. Chemical reactions that absorb energy will not occur without a source of energy.** An example of an energy-releasing reaction is hydrogen gas burning, or reacting, with oxygen to produce water vapor.

$$2H_2 + O_2 \longrightarrow 2H_2O$$

The energy is released in the form of heat, and sometimes—when hydrogen gas explodes—light and sound.

The reverse reaction, in which water is changed into hydrogen and oxygen gas, absorbs so much energy that it generally doesn't occur by itself. In fact, the only practical way to reverse the reaction is to pass an electrical current through water to decompose water into hydrogen gas and oxygen gas. Thus, in one direction the reaction produces energy, and in the other direction the reaction requires energy.

What significance do these energy changes have for living things? In order to stay alive, organisms need to carry out reactions that require energy. Thus, every organism must have a source of energy to carry out chemical reactions. Plants get their energy by trapping and storing the energy from sunlight in energy-rich compounds. Animals get their energy when they consume plants or other animals. Humans release the energy needed to grow tall, to breathe, to think, and even to dream through the chemical reactions that occur when humans metabolize, or break down, digested food.

Activation Energy Even chemical reactions that release energy do not always occur spontaneously. That's a good thing because if they did, the pages of this book might burst into flames. The cellulose in paper burns in the presence of oxygen and releases heat and light. However, the cellulose will burn only if you light it with a match, which supplies enough energy to get the reaction started. Chemists call the energy that is needed to get a reaction started the **activation energy.** As **Figure 2–19** shows, activation energy is a factor in whether the overall chemical reaction releases energy or absorbs energy.

CHECKPOINT *What is activation energy?*

▼ **Figure 2–19 Chemical reactions that release energy often occur spontaneously. Chemical reactions that absorb energy will occur only with a source of energy.** The peak of each graph represents the energy needed for the reaction to go forward. The difference between this required energy and the energy of the reactants is the activation energy.

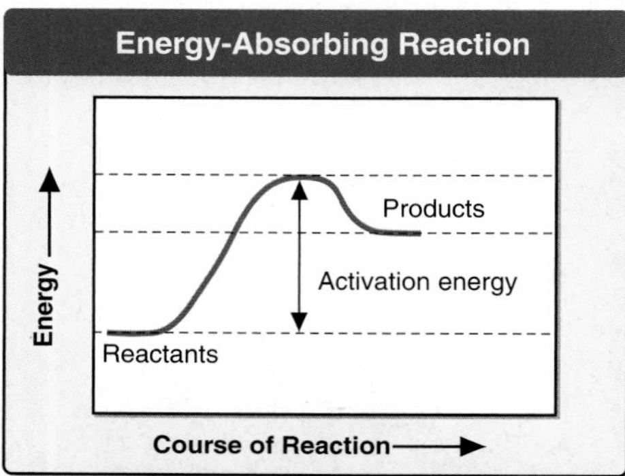

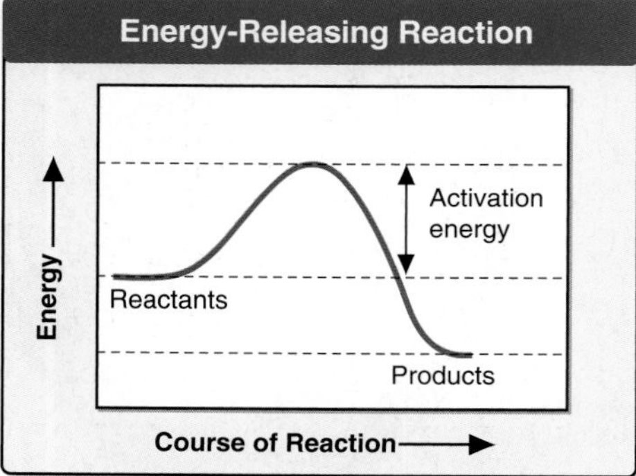

PRESENTATIONS MADE EASY!

The Presentation Assistant Plus contains the Prentice Hall Presentation Pro and the Transparencies, which provide easy-to-follow visual support for every step of this lesson. If you have a computer presentation station, use Prentice Hall Presentation Pro Section 2–4, or use the transparencies listed here.

Section 2–4:   
Interest Grabber
Section Outline
Effect of Enzymes
Figure 2–19
Figure 2–21

Analyzing Data

How does pH affect an enzyme?

Catalase is an enzyme that helps decompose the toxic hydrogen peroxide that is produced during normal cell activities. The products of this reaction are water and oxygen gas. The pressure of the oxygen gas in a closed container increases as oxygen is produced. Any increase in the rate of the reaction will cause an increase in the pressure of the oxygen.

The purple line on the graph represents the normal rate of the reaction in a water solution of hydrogen peroxide and catalase. The red line represents the rate of reaction when an acid is added to the solution. The blue line represents the rate of reaction when a base is added to the solution.

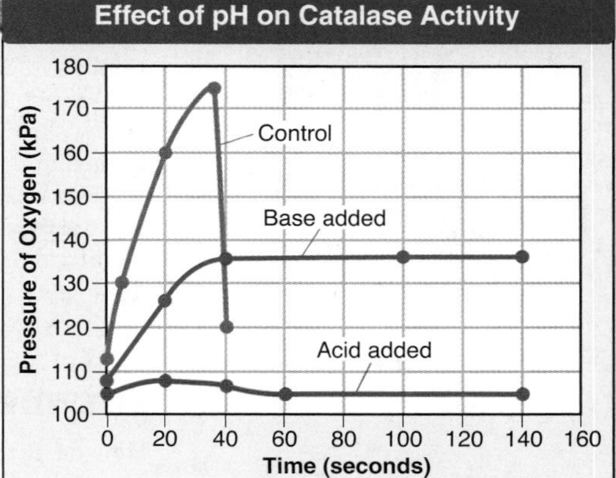

1. **Applying Concepts** What variable is plotted on the *x*-axis? What variable is plotted on the *y*-axis?
2. **Interpreting Graphics** How did the rate of reaction change over time in the control reaction?
3. **Inferring** Suggest an explanation for the change in the control reaction at about 40 seconds.
4. **Interpreting Graphics** How does the presence of a base affect the rate of the reaction? How does the presence of an acid affect the rate?
5. **Drawing Conclusions** What effect do acids and bases have on the enzyme catalase?
6. **Going Further** Predict what would happen if vinegar were added to a water solution of hydrogen peroxide and catalase.

Enzymes

Some chemical reactions that make life possible are too slow or have activation energies that are too high to make them practical for living tissue. These chemical reactions are made possible by a process that would make any chemist proud—cells make catalysts. A **catalyst** is a substance that speeds up the rate of a chemical reaction. Catalysts work by lowering a reaction's activation energy.

Enzymes are proteins that act as biological catalysts. **Cells use enzymes to speed up chemical reactions that take place in cells.** Like other catalysts, enzymes act by lowering the activation energies, as illustrated by the graph in **Figure 2–20.** Lowering the activation energy has a dramatic effect on how quickly the reaction is completed. How big an effect? Remember the reaction in which carbon dioxide combines with water to produce carbonic acid.

$$CO_2 + H_2O \longrightarrow H_2CO_3$$

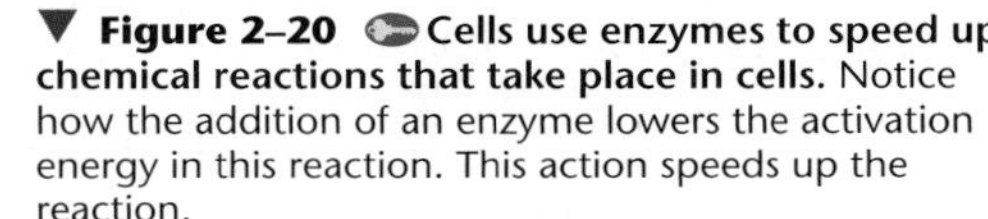

▼ **Figure 2–20 Cells use enzymes to speed up chemical reactions that take place in cells.** Notice how the addition of an enzyme lowers the activation energy in this reaction. This action speeds up the reaction.

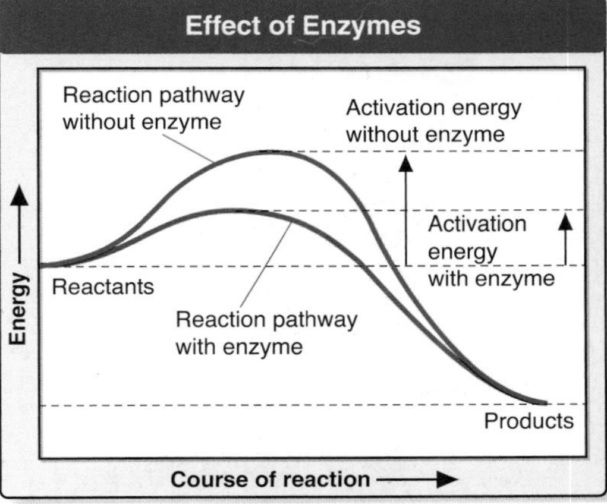

Analyzing Data

Write the equation for the reaction on the chalkboard:

$2H_2O_2 \rightarrow O_2 + 2H_2O$

Explain that the pressure of oxygen gas is a measure of the amount of oxygen produced. The slope of the graphs is an indication of the rates of the reactions.

Answers

1. Time is plotted on the *x*-axis and pressure of oxygen on the *y*-axis.
2. The rate was very rapid at first and then dropped off dramatically after about 40 seconds.
3. Students may suggest that the hydrogen peroxide was used up or that the reaction is reversible.
4. With added base, the rate of reaction slowed down; with added acid, there is almost no reaction.
5. A base inhibits the enzyme so that it is less effective. An acid may deactivate the enzyme so that the reaction cannot take place.
6. Because vinegar is an acid, it would inhibit and possibly destroy the catalyst.

Enzymes

Use Visuals

Figure 2–20 Have students study the graph and explain its subject as well as what its axes represent. Then, ask: **What does the graph show would be the effect if enzymes were not available within a cell?** *(Without enzymes, reactions would need more activation energy to get started.)* **Would a reaction take a longer or shorter time with an enzyme?** *(A shorter time)* Explain that an enzyme may accelerate a reaction by a factor of 10^{10}, making it 10 billion times faster.

TEACHER TO TEACHER

To help students understand the action of enzymes, I have them do a lab in which they investigate bromelin, an enzyme in pineapple that breaks down certain proteins. Students mix liquid gelatin and fresh pineapple in one test tube, liquid gelatin and canned pineapple in a second, liquid gelatin and meat tenderizer in a third, and plain liquid gelatin in a fourth. After refrigerating the mixtures overnight, they let all four test tubes sit out at room temperature for 20 minutes and then assess each for how much the liquids have jelled.

—*LouEllen Parker Brademan, Teacher*
Potomac Senior High School, Dumfries, VA

Answer to . . .

CHECKPOINT *Activation energy is the energy that is needed for a reaction to begin.*

SCIENCE NEWS®

Encourage students to visit
www.phschool.com
for the most current information on this topic.

Build Science Skills

Using models Have students model the action of enzymes by carrying out the "chemical reaction" of breaking toothpicks in half. Divide the class into groups, each with an increasing number of students. Group 1 should have two students, group 2 should have three students, and so on. Give each group 200 toothpicks, and ask one member to be a timer. The other students in each group represent enzyme molecules, and the toothpicks represent substrate molecules in a chemical reaction. Then, at your signal, all groups should begin breaking their toothpicks in half. The timer for each group should record the time it takes for the group to break all the toothpicks. Compare the times of each group. Students will find that the more "enzyme molecules" available, the faster the reaction is completed.

Enzyme Action

Use Visuals

Figure 2–21 Ask: **What are the substrates in this reaction?** *(Glucose and ATP)* **What are the products?** *(ADP and glucose-6-phosphate)* **How does the presence of an enzyme affect this reaction?** *(The enzyme speeds up the reaction.)* **What do the three arrows at the top left indicate?** *(Two arrows indicate that both products are released. The third arrow indicates that the enzyme is free to find new substrate molecules and start a new reaction cycle.)*

KEEP CURRENT WITH . . . SCIENCE NEWS®

To find out more about the topics in this chapter, go to: **www.phschool.com**

Left to itself, this reaction is so slow that carbon dioxide might build up in the body faster than the bloodstream could remove it. Your bloodstream contains an enzyme called carbonic anhydrase that speeds up the reaction by a factor of 10 million. With carbonic anhydrase on the job, the reaction takes place immediately and carbon dioxide is removed from the blood quickly.

Enzymes are very specific, generally catalyzing only one chemical reaction. For this reason, part of an enzyme's name is usually derived from the reaction it catalyzes. Carbonic anhydrase gets its name because it catalyzes the reaction that removes water from carbonic acid.

Enzyme Action

How do enzymes do their jobs? For a chemical reaction to take place, the reactants must collide with enough energy so that existing bonds will be broken and new bonds will be formed. If the reactants do not have enough energy, they will be unchanged after the collision.

The Enzyme-Substrate Complex Enzymes provide a site where reactants can be brought together to react. Such a site reduces the energy needed for reaction. The reactants of enzyme-catalyzed reactions are known as **substrates.**

▼ **Figure 2–21** The enzyme hexokinase converts the substrates glucose and ATP into glucose-6-phosphate and ADP. **Predicting** ***What happens to the hexokinase after the products are released?***

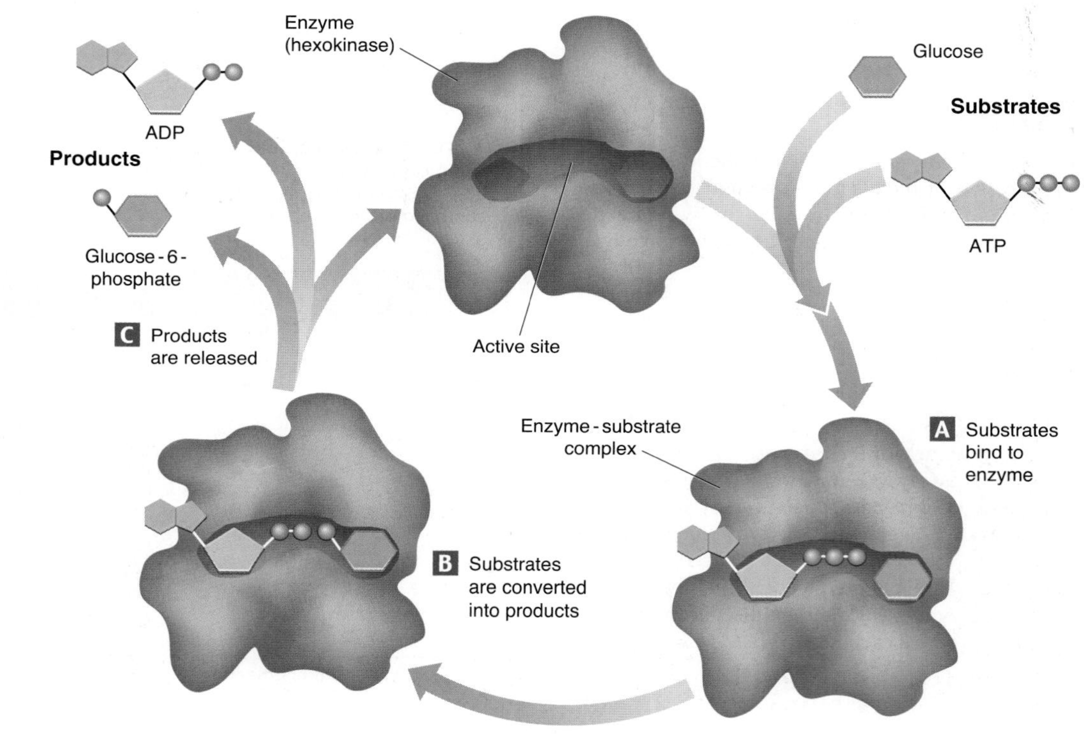

FACTS AND FIGURES

Just the right temperature
Each enzyme works best—that is, its reaction rate is fastest—at an optimal temperature. Enzymes in the human body generally function best near body temperature, or 35–40°C. Below an enzyme's optimal temperature, the reaction is slower. But, if the temperature rises above the optimal temperature, the reaction speed drops sharply because the high temperature disrupts the chemical bonds in the enzyme, which changes its shape; that is, the enzyme undergoes denaturation and is no longer functional. This is what occurs when the body has a high fever. Because denaturation is not reversible, a temperature higher than 44°C usually causes death. Enzymes in other organisms have different optimal temperatures. The bacteria in the hot springs of Yellowstone National Park, for instance, contain enzymes with optimal temperatures as high as 100°C.

Figure 2–21 provides an example of an enzyme-catalyzed reaction. The enzyme is hexokinase. The substrates are glucose and ATP. During the reaction, a phosphate group is transferred from ATP to the glucose molecule. Recall that each protein has a specific, complex shape. The substrates bind to a site on the enzyme called the active site. The active site and the substrates have complementary shapes. The fit is so precise that the active site and substrates are often compared to a lock and key.

Figure 2–22 shows a substrate fitting into an active site on an enzyme. The enzyme and substrate are bound together by intermolecular forces and form an enzyme-substrate complex. They remain bound together until the reaction is done. Once the reaction is over, the products of the reaction are released and the enzyme is free to start the process again.

Regulation of Enzyme Activity Because they are catalysts for reactions, enzymes can be affected by any variable that influences a chemical reaction. Enzymes, including those that help digest food, work best at certain pH values. Many enzymes are affected by changes in temperature. Not surprisingly, those enzymes produced by human cells generally work best at temperatures close to 37°C, the human body's core temperature.

Cells can regulate the activities of enzymes in a variety of ways. Most cells contain proteins that help to turn key enzymes "on" or "off" at critical stages in the life of the cell. Enzymes play essential roles in regulating chemical pathways, making materials that cells need, releasing energy, and transferring information.

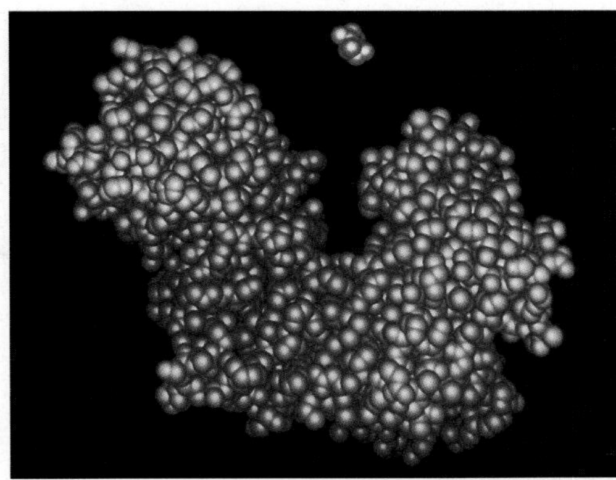

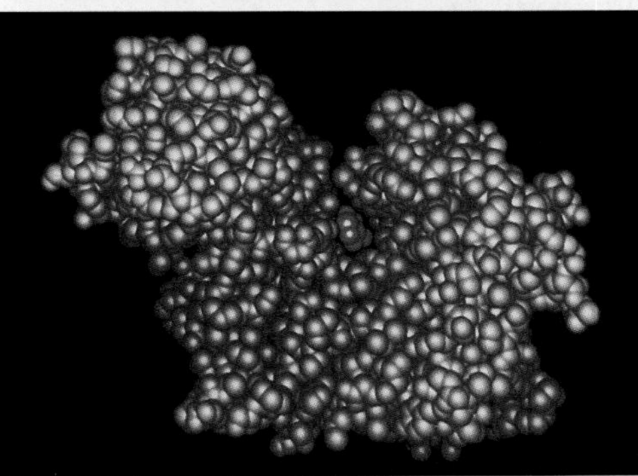

▲ **Figure 2–22** This space-filling model shows how a substrate binds to an active site on an enzyme. **Interpreting Graphics** *What happens after the substrate binds to the enzyme?*

2–4 Section Assessment

1. **Key Concept** What happens to chemical bonds during chemical reactions?
2. **Key Concept** Describe the role of energy in chemical reactions.
3. **Key Concept** What are enzymes, and how are they important to living things?
4. Describe how enzymes work, including the role of the enzyme-substrate complex.
5. **Critical Thinking Applying Concepts** A change in pH can change the shape of a protein. How might a change in pH affect the function of an enzyme such as hexokinase?

iTEXT **Assessment** Use iText to review the important concepts in Section 2–4.

ALTERNATIVE ASSESSMENT

Modeling a Process
Make a model that demonstrates how an active site and a substrate are like a lock and a key. Write a paragraph referring to your model that explains how enzymes work.

Build Science Skills

Using Analogies As students watch, open a large padlock with its key. Ask: **In a chemical reaction, which of these is like the enzyme and which is like the substrate?** *(The padlock is like the enzyme and the key is like the substrate.)* **Which place on this padlock is like an active site?** *(The keyhole)* Direct students' attention to Figure 2–22. Ask: **How is inserting a key into a lock different from the formation of an enzyme-substrate complex?** *(The enzyme changes its shape when it binds to the substrate.)*

3 ASSESS

Evaluate Understanding

Direct students' attention to Figure 2–21, and ask them to write as full a description as possible of the chemical reaction that is illustrated. They should mention the substrates and the products, the enzyme involved, how the enzyme lowers the activation energy, and the formation of the enzyme-substrate complex.

Reteach

Call on student volunteers to explain what a chemical reaction is, the energy changes involved in reactions, and how enzymes affect the rate of biochemical reactions.

ALTERNATIVE ASSESSMENT

Provide students with a variety of materials, including modeling compound, fabric, sponges, construction paper, and papier-mâché. Labels on the model should include *enzyme, active site, and substrate.* Paragraphs should explain how the model demonstrates the enzyme function.

2–4 Section Assessment

1. Bonds are broken in reactants and new bonds are formed in products.
2. Some chemical reactions release energy, and other chemical reactions absorb energy. Energy changes determine how easily a chemical reaction will occur.
3. Enzymes are biological catalysts. Living cells use enzymes to speed up virtually every important chemical reaction that takes place in cells.
4. Substrates, the reactants of an enzyme-catalyzed reaction, attach to the enzyme at an active site and form an enzyme-substrate complex. Once the complex is formed, the enzyme helps convert substrate into product.
5. A change in pH could change the shape of hexokinase. This change would diminish or possibly eliminate the ability of glucose and ATP to bind to the active site on the enzyme.

Use iText to review the key concepts in Section 2–4.

Answers to . . .

Figure 2–21 *It is free to form a new enzyme-substrate complex.*

Figure 2–22 *The substrate reacts and forms one or more products.*

Design an Experiment

Objective Students will be able to design an experiment to investigate how temperature affects the rate of an enzyme-catalyzed reaction.

Skills Focus **Formulating Hypotheses, Predicting**

Time 45 minutes

Advance Prep

- Improvise controlled-temperature baths using a plastic dish-washing tub filled with either ice water or warm water. A student volunteer can be stationed to check the temperature of the water with a thermometer, adding hot or cold water periodically to maintain a desired temperature.
- Liver puree, which you can prepare by mixing cut-up pieces of raw liver with a little distilled water in a blender, is often very concentrated in catalase. Before the lab, check the enzyme's activity by running through the procedure. Dilute the puree with distilled water, as necessary, to manipulate the time needed to float the disks into the measurable range. Refrigerate until ready to use.

Safety Caution students to be careful with the hydrogen peroxide, especially when they are pouring 25 mL of hydrogen peroxide solution into the 50-mL beaker.

Pre-Lab Discussion Have students review the discussion of catalysts in Section 2–4 and read the procedure for this lab. Then, ask: **How are enzymes essential for living things?** *(Living things use enzymes to speed up virtually every important chemical reaction that takes place in cells.)* **The action of what enzyme is investigated in this lab?** *(The enzyme catalase)* **What does catalase do in liver cells?** *(It helps break down hydrogen peroxide formed in cells into water and oxygen gas.)* **When you design your experiment, what will the manipulated variable be?** *(Temperature)* **What will the data be that you'll collect for your data table?** *(How many seconds it takes the filter-paper disk to float to the top of the liquid at various temperatures of the liver puree)*

Design an Experiment

Investigating the Effect of Temperature on Enzyme Activity

Almost all chemical reactions that occur in living organisms are catalyzed by enzymes. Many factors in a cell's environment affect the action of an enzyme. In this investigation, you will design an experiment to determine the effect of temperature on an enzyme-catalyzed reaction.

Problem
How does temperature affect the rate of an enzyme-catalyzed reaction?

Materials

- raw liver
- petri dish
- dropper pipette
- 1% hydrogen peroxide solution
- liver puree
- 25-mL graduated cylinder
- 5 50-mL beakers
- filter-paper disks
- forceps
- glass-marking pencil
- ice bath
- 3 thermometers
- warm water bath
- clock or watch with second hand

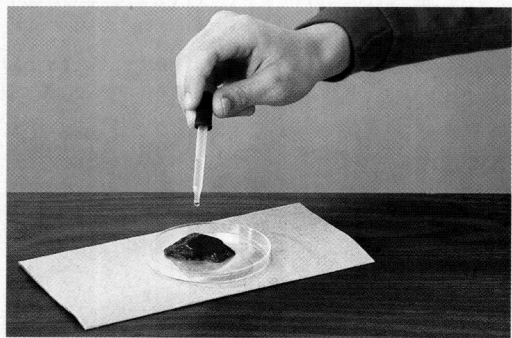

Skills
Formulating Hypotheses, Predicting

Design Your Experiment

Part A: Observe the Catalase Reaction

1. Place a small piece of raw liver in an open petri dish. Use a dropper pipette to put a drop of hydrogen peroxide solution on the liver. **CAUTION:** *Hydrogen peroxide can be irritating to skin and eyes. If you spill any on yourself or your clothes, wash it off immediately and tell your teacher.* Observe what happens. Liver contains the enzyme catalase, which breaks down hydrogen peroxide (H_2O_2) formed in cells to water (H_2O) and oxygen gas (O_2). When hydrogen peroxide is broken down by catalase, bubbles of oxygen gas are released.
2. To measure the activity of catalase, use a graduated cylinder to place 25 mL of hydrogen peroxide solution in a 50-mL beaker.
3. Use forceps to dip a filter-paper disk in liver puree. Place the filter-paper disk on a paper towel for 4 seconds to remove any excess liquid.
4. Use the forceps to place the filter-paper disk at the bottom of the beaker of hydrogen peroxide solution. Observe the filter-paper disk and record the number of seconds it takes to float to the top of the liquid.

Part B: Design an Experiment

5. **Formulating Hypotheses** Develop a hypothesis about how temperature will affect the rate at which catalase breaks down hydrogen peroxide. Record your hypothesis.

6. **Designing Experiments** Design an experiment to test your hypothesis. Your experimental plan should include a prediction of the result based on your hypothesis, and any appropriate controls and replications (repetitions). Be sure to identify all manipulated, responding, and controlled variables in your experimental plan.
7. Construct a data table in which to record the results of your experiment. Perform your experiment only after you have obtained your teacher's approval of your plan.
8. Make a graph of the results of your experiment. Plot temperature on the x-axis and the variable by which you measured catalase activity on the y-axis.

Analyze and Conclude

1. **Inferring** How does the time required for a catalase-soaked, filter-paper disk to float reflect the amount of catalase activity in the solution?
2. **Evaluating and Revising** How did temperature affect catalase activity? Was your prediction confirmed?
3. **Drawing Conclusions** Many mammals, including cattle and pigs, have body temperatures close to 37°C. Does your graph indicate that catalase is most active close to the temperature at which it exists in a living animal?

Go Further

Design an Experiment Catalase is also found in potatoes. Design an experiment using potato puree instead of liver puree to determine the temperature at which potato catalase is most active.

Procedure

1. Demonstrate how to use a dropper pipette to put a drop of hydrogen peroxide solution on the piece of liver. When students perform this action, they should observe bubbles of oxygen appear in the hydrogen peroxide solution.

3. Demonstrate how to dip the filter-paper disk in the liver puree and then place it on a paper towel.

5., 6. Ask students to write down their hypothesis, prediction, and experimental design. Check these to make sure students are on the right track before they proceed.

7. Make sure each student or group has constructed a good data table in which to record the necessary data.

8. Graphs should show a rise until about 40°C and then a sharp decline.

Expected Outcomes Students should discover that temperature has an effect on enzyme activity. Their data should show that catalase is most active near 40°C.

Go Further

Most students' experiments will be similar to the experimental design in this lab, with a substitution of potato puree for liver puree. Students should include a prediction and appropriate controls and replications.

Analyze and Conclude

1. Catalase catalyzes a reaction that releases oxygen gas. Bubbles of oxygen form around the filter-paper disk, lifting it to the surface of the liquid. The more active the enzyme, the more quickly the bubbles are produced.

2. Students should observe that increasing the temperature increases the activity of catalase up to about 40–45°C.

3. Students' graphs should indicate that catalase is most active close to the 37°C body temperature of a living animal, because catalase is most active near 40°C.

Chapter 2 Study Guide

Study Tip

Divide the class into four groups, and have the members of each group collaborate in writing study questions tied to one of the four sections in the chapter. The questions should cover all the Key Concepts and Vocabulary terms in the section. Each group should also produce an answer key. Then, provide each student with a list of the questions developed by all four groups. Students should answer the questions, and then check their answers against the answer keys.

Thinking Visually

Students' cycle diagrams should be similar to that shown in Figure 2–21. Each cycle diagram should include this sequence of events: an enzyme attaches, or binds, to substrates at the enzyme's active site, creating an enzyme-substrate complex; the substrates become the reactants in a chemical reaction, which yields products; the products are released from the enzyme. Students should include arrows between the events, showing a continuous process. The diagram becomes a cycle with arrows that show the release of products and another arrow that shows that the enzyme begins the process anew.

Chapter 2 Assessment

Reviewing Content

1. c **5.** b **8.** c
2. d **6.** d **9.** a
3. b **7.** c **10.** d
4. b

Understanding Concepts

11. Elements are composed of atoms. Compounds are composed of atoms of two or more elements combined in definite proportions.

12. Radioactive isotopes are isotopes whose nuclei are unstable and break down at a constant rate over time. Radioactive isotopes are used in determining the ages of rocks, treating cancer, killing bacteria in food, and following the movements of substances within organisms.

13. Atoms in a compound are held together by a chemical bond.

14. Two electrons are shared in a single covalent bond, four in a double bond, and six in a triple bond.

Chapter 2 Study Guide

2–1 The Nature of Matter

Key Concepts

- The subatomic particles that make up atoms are protons, neutrons, and electrons.
- Because they have the same numbers of electrons, all isotopes of an element have the same chemical properties.
- The main types of chemical bonds are covalent bonds and ionic bonds.

Vocabulary

- atom, p. 35 • nucleus, p. 35 • electron, p. 35
- element, p. 36 • isotope, p. 36
- compound, p. 37 • ionic bond, p. 38
- ion, p. 38 • covalent bond, p. 38
- molecule, p. 38 • van der Waals forces, p. 39

2–2 Properties of Water

Key Concepts

- A water molecule is polar because there is an uneven distribution of electrons between the oxygen and hydrogen atoms.
- Acidic solutions contain higher concentrations of H^+ ions than pure water and have pH values below 7.
- Basic, or alkaline, solutions contain lower concentrations of H^+ ions than pure water and have pH values above 7.

Vocabulary

- cohesion, p. 41 • adhesion, p. 41 • mixture, p. 41
- solution, p. 42 • solute, p. 42 • solvent, p. 42
- suspension, p. 42 • pH scale, p. 43 • acid, p. 43
- base, p. 43 • buffer, p. 43

2–3 Carbon Compounds

Key Concepts

- Four groups of organic compounds found in living things are carbohydrates, lipids, nucleic acids, and proteins.
- Living things use carbohydrates as their main source of energy. Plants and some animals also use carbohydrates for structural purposes.
- Lipids can be used to store energy. Some lipids are important parts of biological membranes and waterproof coverings.
- Nucleic acids store and transmit hereditary, or genetic, information.
- Some proteins control the rate of reactions and regulate cell processes. Some proteins build tissues such as bone and muscle. Others transport materials or help to fight disease.

Vocabulary

- monomer, p. 45 • polymer, p. 45
- carbohydrate, p. 45 • monosaccharide, p. 46
- polysaccharide, p. 46 • lipid, p. 46
- nucleic acid, p. 47 • nucleotide, p. 47
- ribonucleic acid (RNA), p. 47
- deoxyribonucleic acid (DNA), p. 47
- protein, p. 47 • amino acid, p. 47

2–4 Chemical Reactions and Enzymes

Key Concepts

- Chemical reactions always involve the breaking of bonds in reactants and the formation of new bonds in products.
- Chemical reactions that release energy often occur spontaneously. Chemical reactions that absorb energy will not occur without a source of energy.
- Cells use enzymes to speed up chemical reactions that take place in cells.

Vocabulary

- chemical reaction, p. 49 • reactant, p. 49
- product, p. 49 • activation energy, p. 50
- catalyst, p. 51 • enzyme, p. 51 • substrate, p. 52

Thinking Visually

Create a cycle diagram that shows how enzymes work. Use the following terms in your cycle diagram: *enzyme, substrate, enzyme-substrate complex, active site, reactants, products.*

CHAPTER RESOURCES

Print:

- ***Teaching Resources,*** Chapter Vocabulary Review, Graphic Organizer
- ***Chapter Tests: Levels A and B,*** Chapter 2 Test
- ***PH Assessment System,*** Practice Test

Technology:

- ***Computer Test Bank,*** Chapter 2 Test
- ***iText,*** Chapter 2 Assessment

Chapter 2 Assessment

Reviewing Content

Choose the letter that best answers the question or completes the statement.

1. The positively charged particle in an atom is the
   a. neutron. **c.** proton.
   b. ion. **d.** electron.

2. Two or more different atoms are combined in definite proportions in any
   a. symbol. **c.** element.
   b. isotope. **d.** compound.

3. A covalent bond is formed by the
   a. transfer of electrons. **c.** gaining of electrons.
   b. sharing of electrons. **d.** losing of electrons.

4. When you shake sugar and sand together in a test tube, you cause them to form a
   a. compound. **c.** solution.
   b. mixture. **d.** suspension.

5. A compound that produces hydrogen ions in solution is a(an)
   a. salt. **c.** base.
   b. acid. **d.** polymer.

6. In polymerization, complex molecules are formed by the joining together of
   a. macromolecules. **c.** polymers.
   b. carbohydrates. **d.** monomers.

7. Which formula represents an amino acid?

a.
```
     H   H   H   OH  H   H
     |   |   |   |   |   |
  H—C—C—C—C—C—C=O
     |   |   |   |   |
     OH  OH  OH  H   OH
```

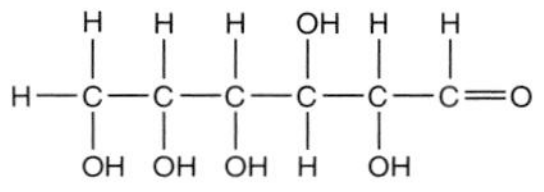

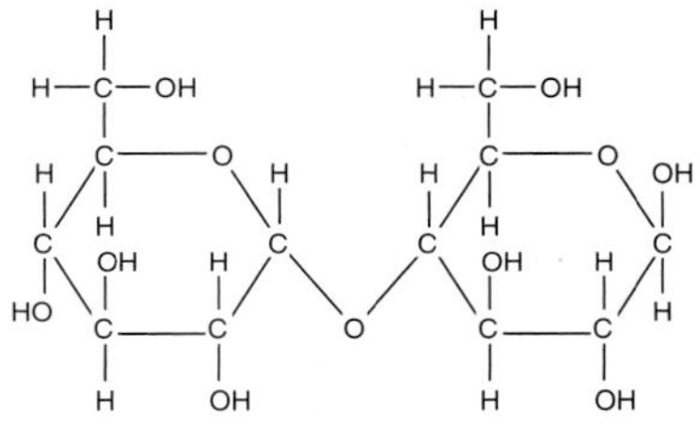

b.
```
     H                        H
     |                        |
  H—C—OH                 H—C—OH
     |                        |
     C———O     H         H    C———O    OH
  H /       \  |          |  /      \   |
   |  H      \ |          | / H      \  |
   C  |       C           C   |       C
   |\ OH  H  / \         / \  OH  H  /|
 HO | |   | /   \       /   \ |   | / | H
    C———C        O          C———C
    |     |                 |     |
    H     OH                H     OH
```

c.
```
     H  H  O
     |  |  ||
  H—N—C—C—OH
        |
     H—C—H
        |
        H
```

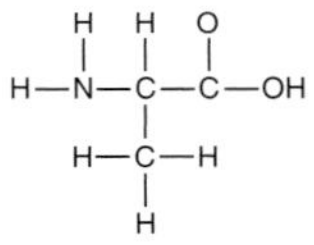

d.
```
     H   H   OH  OH  H   H
     |   |   |   |   |   |
  H—C—C—C—C—C—C=O
     |   |   |   |   |
     OH  OH  H   H   OH
```

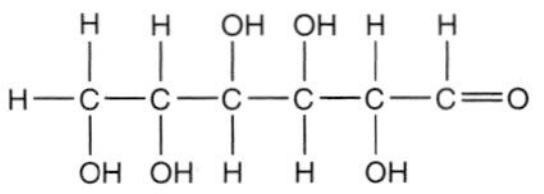

8. Proteins are polymers formed from
   a. lipids.
   b. carbohydrates.
   c. amino acids.
   d. nucleic acids.

9. An enzyme speeds up a reaction by
   a. lowering the activation energy.
   b. raising the activation energy.
   c. releasing energy.
   d. absorbing energy.

10. In a chemical reaction, a reactant binds to an enzyme at a region known as the
    a. catalyst.
    b. product.
    c. substrate.
    d. active site.

Understanding Concepts

11. Explain the relationship among atoms, elements, and compounds.
12. What is a radioactive isotope? Describe two scientific uses of radioactive isotopes.
13. How are atoms in a compound held together?
14. Distinguish among single, double, and triple covalent bonds.
15. Explain the properties of cohesion and adhesion. Give an example of each property.
16. What is the relationship among solutions, solutes, and solvents?
17. How are acids and bases different? How do their pH values differ?
18. Explain the relationship between monomers and polymers, using polysaccharides as an example.
19. Identify three major roles of proteins.
20. Describe the parts of a nucleotide.
21. Name the two basic kinds of nucleic acids. What sugar does each contain?
22. What is a chemical reaction?
23. Describe the two types of energy changes that can occur in a chemical reaction.
24. What relationship exists between an enzyme and a catalyst?
25. Describe some factors that may influence enzyme activity.

TIME SAVER

HOMEWORK GUIDE

Section:	Questions:
Section 2–1	1–3, 11–14
Section 2–2	4, 5, 15–17, 26, 30, 32, 35, 37
Section 2–3	6–8, 18–21, 29, 31, 34
Section 2–4	9, 10, 22–25, 27, 28, 33, 34, 36

Chapter 2 Assessment (continued)

15. Cohesion is an attraction between molecules of the same substance. An example is drops of water forming beads on a smooth surface. Adhesion is an attraction between molecules of different substances. An example is capillary action.

16. A solution is a mixture in which one substance is dissolved in another. The solute is the substance that is dissolved. The solvent is the substance in which the solute is dissolved.

17. An acid is any compound that produces H^+ ions in solution; acidic solutions have pH values below 7. A base is a compound that produces hydroxide ions (OH^-) in solution; basic solutions have pH values above 7.

18. Polymers are large macromolecules made up of smaller molecules called monomers. For example, monomers called monosaccharides are joined together to form polymers called polysaccharides.

19. Proteins control the rate of chemical reactions, regulate cell processes, form tissues, transport substances, and help fight disease.

20. Nucleotides consist of a 5-carbon sugar, a phosphate group, and a nitrogenous base.

21. The two basic kinds are ribonucleic acid (RNA), which contains the sugar ribose, and deoxyribonucleic acid (DNA), which contains the sugar deoxyribose.

22. A chemical reaction is a process that changes one set of chemicals into another set of chemicals.

23. Some chemical reactions release energy, and others absorb energy.

24. An enzyme is a biological catalyst.

25. Factors that can influence enzyme activity include pH, temperature, and proteins in cells that help turn key enzymes "on" and "off" at critical stages.

Critical Thinking

26. Adding a base to the solution would increase its pH, because a base produces hydroxide ions in solution and basic solutions have pH values above 7.

27. To carry out all life processes, living things need the energy released in the chemical reactions involved in digesting food.

28. The total product was doubled when the temperature of the reaction increased from 25°C to 35°C, and it decreased to almost zero when the temperature was increased to 45°C. Enzymes work best at certain temperatures. Students should hypothesize that the enzyme involved in this reaction works best at about 35°C, and a much higher temperature inhibits the enzyme's function.

29. Students might suggest trying to dissolve the solid in water. Lipids are generally not water soluble. They also might suggest warming the solid to see if it would soften, which solid lipids tend to do when heated.

30. The mixture could be separated by adding water. The sodium chloride would dissolve in the water, whereas the silica would not. The salt could be retrieved by filtering the mixture and evaporating the filtrate.

31. The name indicates that carbohydrates contain carbon and the elements in water, oxygen and hydrogen.

32. The diagram should show that hydrogen and chlorine form a covalent bond. Students can use the chlorine atom in Figure 2–3 as a starting point and pair up one of the seven electrons in its outer level with hydrogen's single electron.

33. If the temperature or pH were changed, the shape of the enzyme hexokinase could change. It might lose its ability to bind with the substrates, glucose and ATP, and an enzyme-substrate complex would not form. As a result, the enzyme would not speed up the reaction.

34. Students might refer to the structural formulas for glucose, on page 45, and for an amino acid, on page 47, and then use a reference book for illustrations of three-dimensional models of these substances.

Chapter 2 Assessment

Critical Thinking

26. **Predicting** Suppose you wanted to increase the pH of a solution. What could you add to the solution to increase the pH? Explain your prediction.

27. **Inferring** Why is it important that energy-releasing reactions take place in living organisms?

28. **Interpreting Graphics** The bar graph shows the total amount of product from a chemical reaction performed at three different temperatures. The same enzyme was involved in each case. Describe the results of each reaction. How can you explain these results?

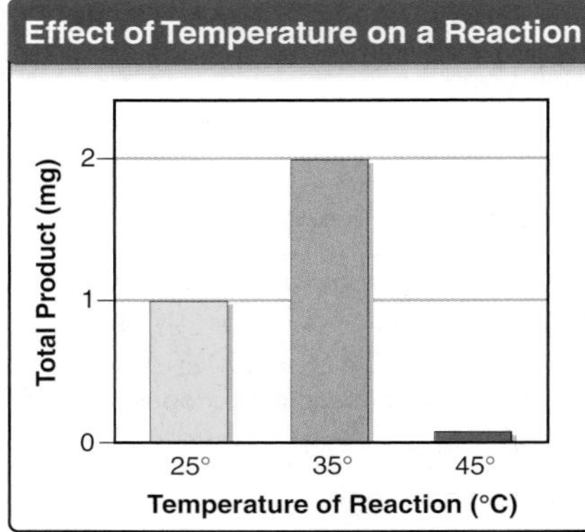

29. **Designing Experiments** Suggest one or two simple experiments to determine whether a solid white substance is a lipid or a carbohydrate. What evidence would you need to support each hypothesis?

30. **Problem Solving** Silica is a hard, glassy material that does not dissolve in water. Suppose sodium chloride is accidently mixed with silica. Describe a way to remove the sodium chloride.

31. **Inferring** Explain what the name "carbohydrate" might indicate about the chemical composition of sugars.

32. **Using Models** Make a diagram like the one in Figure 2–4 to show how chlorine and hydrogen form from the compound hydrogen chloride, HCl.

33. **Predicting** Changing the temperature or pH can change an enzyme's shape. Describe how changing the temperature or pH might affect the function of the enzyme in **Figure 2–21.**

34. **Making Models** Make three-dimensional models of organic compounds such as single sugars and amino acids. Refer to illustrations in this textbook or in other reference books.

35. **Predicting** As part of the digestive process, the human stomach produces hydrochloric acid, HCl. Sometimes excess acid causes discomfort. In such a case, a person might take an antacid such as magnesium hydroxide, $Mg(OH)_2$. Explain how this substance can reduce the amount of acid in the stomach.

36. **Using Analogies** Explain why a lock and key is used to describe the way an enzyme works. Describe any ways in which the analogy is not perfect.

37. **Making Connections** Refer back to Chapter 1 to review the way scientists work. Then, describe an experiment that would test the effects of pH on a plant species.

Performance-Based Assessment

Writing a Speech At a yearly convention, individual atoms describe their recent experiences. Assume you are an oxygen atom that began the year in an O_2 molecule, then spent time in a water molecule, in a hydroxide ion, and in carbonic acid. Write a speech describing the chemical reactions you experienced and the other molecules you met along the way.

Amino acids are the monomers in proteins. Visit the Prentice Hall Web site at **www.phschool.com** to find out more about the chemistry of amino acids. Then, answer the following questions:

- Which element is in the center of an amino acid?
- What is the difference between D-amino acids and L-amino acids?
- What is a peptide bond?
- What do the primary and secondary structures of a protein refer to?

Take It to the NET

- Carbon
- L and D, which stand for left and right, refer to the arrangement of the groups attached to the central carbon atom of the amino acid. D-amino acids have been synthesized in the laboratory, but only L-amino acids occur naturally in proteins.
- A bond that joins amino acids together
- The primary structure is the sequence of amino acids. The secondary structure refers to the three-dimensional shape of a polypeptide chain.

For additional information, visit

www.phschool.com

Standardized Test Prep

Test-Taking Tip As you briefly scan the questions, mark those that may require pure guesswork on your part and save them for last. (Do not write in this book.) Use whatever time you have left for those questions to eliminate as many answers as possible through reasoning.

Directions: Choose the letter that best answers the question or completes the statement.

1. Which one of the following is NOT an organic molecule found in living organisms?
(A) protein
(B) nucleic acid
(C) carbohydrate
(D) sodium chloride
(E) lipid

2. Which combination of particle and charge is correct?
(A) proton: positively charged
(B) electron: positively charged
(C) neutron: negatively charged
(D) proton: negatively charged
(E) electron: no charge

3. In which of the following ways do isotopes of the same element differ?
(A) in number of neutrons only
(B) in number of protons only
(C) in numbers of neutrons and protons
(D) in number of protons and in mass
(E) in number of neutrons and in mass

Questions 4–6 Each of the lettered choices below refers to the following numbered statements. Select the best lettered choice. A choice may be used once, more than once, or not at all.

(A) Cohesion
(B) Adhesion
(C) Catalysts
(D) Reactants
(E) Products

4. An attraction between different substances

5. Lower a chemical reaction's activation energy

6. The elements or compounds that enter into a chemical reaction

Questions 7–8 Study the graph at the top of the next column to answer the questions that follow.

The enzyme catalase speeds up the chemical reaction that changes hydrogen peroxide into oxygen and water. The amount of oxygen given off is an indication of the rate of the reaction.

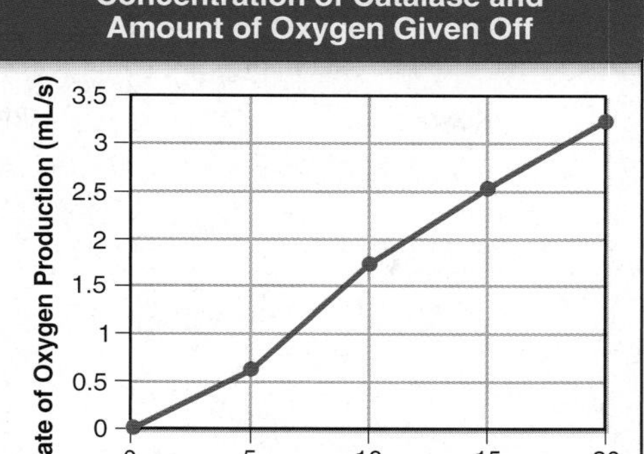
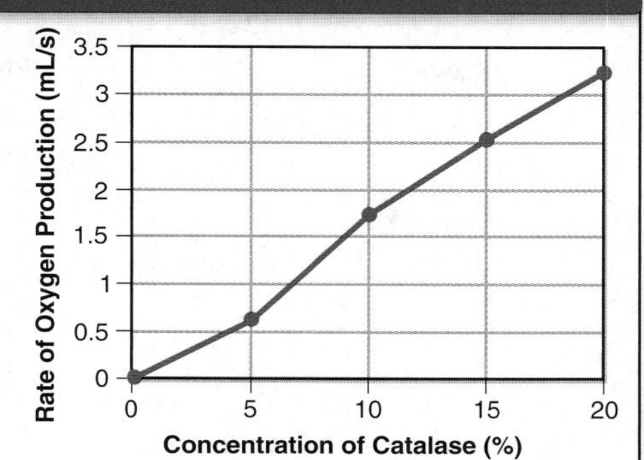

7. Based on the graph, what can you conclude about the relationship between enzyme concentration and reaction rate?
(A) Reaction rate decreases with increasing enzyme concentration.
(B) Reaction rate increases with decreasing enzyme concentration.
(C) Reaction rate increases with increasing enzyme concentration.
(D) The variables are indirectly proportional.
(E) The variables are not related.

8. Which concentration of catalase will produce the fastest reaction rate?
(A) 0%
(B) 5%
(C) 10%
(D) 15%
(E) 20%

Questions 9–10 Complete each analogy by selecting the correct letter. In analogies, A : B :: C : __?__ *means* A is to B as C is to __?__.

9. Saturated fat : single bonds :: polyunsaturated fat : __?__.
(A) covalent bonds
(B) ionic bonds
(C) chemical bonds
(D) double bonds
(E) no bonds

10. Protein : amino acids :: nucleic acid : __?__.
(A) acids
(B) bases
(C) nucleotides
(D) ribose sugars
(E) fatty acids

Standardized Test Prep

1. D **2.** A **3.** E **4.** B **5.** C **6.** D **7.** C **8.** E **9.** D **10.** C

(continued from page 58)

35. Students should infer that magnesium hydroxide is a base. The base reacts with the acid in the stomach, and forms a product that is not acidic.

36. The fit of an enzyme and a substrate at the enzyme's active site is so precise that the substrate is like a key and the enzyme is like a lock. Like a key in a lock, only a substrate of a certain shape can fit into the active site of the enzyme. What occurs when a key is inserted into a lock is a physical process, unlike what occurs at an active site, which is a chemical process.

37. All responses should reflect an understanding of how scientists design an experiment using this procedure: stating the problem, forming a hypothesis, setting up a controlled experiment, recording and analyzing results, and drawing a conclusion. A typical experiment might involve observing differences in several plants' growth, with the pH of the soil being the manipulated variable.

Performance-Based Assessment

A good speech will be both imaginative and scientifically accurate. Students should describe these events: being a part of an O_2 molecule, being in a polar water molecule with two hydrogen atoms, experiencing the decomposition of a water molecule into a hydrogen ion and a hydroxide ion, and being in the blood when carbon dioxide and water react and produce carbonic acid. Students should demonstrate knowledge of chemical compounds, chemical bonds, solutions, and chemical reactions.

Unit 2

Dear Colleague,

Even those of us who love animals feel uncomfortable staring into the maw of a hungry crocodile. Why? Because they offer an unusual reminder that humans don't always have to be at the top of the food chain.

As modern Americans, of course, we are rarely reminded that food chains and other ecological processes even exist. Few of us grow our own vegetables. Fewer still think about where our chicken, beef, or veal dinners come from. And VERY few of us give a second thought to where our wastes go when we flush the toilet. Many of us are so isolated from the day-to-day workings of the biosphere that we forget them altogether. The only time we think about food chains, nutrient cycles, or rainfall is during food shortages, droughts, or floods. In other words, we ignore our planet's life-support systems unless or until they malfunction.

That level of ecological illiteracy is a pity. It's a shame that more people don't realize just how fascinating ecology really is. Imagine a carbon atom from your breath, wafted out to sea, absorbed by phytoplankton, settled into sediments, driven beneath the crust, belched out of a volcano, and becoming part of the global atmospheric greenhouse that has stabilized Earth's temperatures since life began. Imagine populations of insects and plants—predators and prey, parasites and hosts—growing and reproducing, passing through cycles of increase and decrease, rarely going extinct, yet never taking over the planet either.

These days, ecological illiteracy can be dangerous, too, because humans have become the most powerful force for change in the world. We transport more materials and use more energy than any other multicellular species. Our actions have even

UNIT 2 Ecology

Chapters

▶ Like all living things, alligators such as this one are involved in interactions with other living things (trees and vines) and with their physical surroundings (water, air, and climate).

60

begun to affect the workings of vital systems, such as the ozone layer and the global greenhouse. This is not a healthy state of affairs. But there is an alternative. If enough people understand ecological principles well enough to work with them, the result can be profoundly positive.

What do we know about ecology?
• Biologists have discovered entire ecosystems living in the total darkness of the ocean floor, 1.6 kilometers beneath the surface.
• Global temperatures are rising. Plants and animals on land and in the sea are already responding to these warmer temperatures.
• Ecosystems around the world are under stress from human activities and from the introduction of "weed" species that have been introduced far from their natural ranges.
What discoveries lie in the future?
• What effects will rising temperatures have on the environment? Can humans take any actions to stop the trends of global warming?
• Can humans learn how to produce the food and energy that they need while preserving the environment?
• What steps can be taken to preserve biodiversity?
KEEP CURRENT WITH . . .
SCIENCE NEWS®
Find out more about topics in this unit:
www.phschool.com

On a national level, the Clean Air and the Clean Water acts fundamentally improved American air and water quality. Levels of lead in rivers and streams, for example, have fallen dramatically.

On a local level, the town I live in has wisely set aside nearly half its land area (much of it wetland) for conservation. It was no coincidence that when a multiyear drought forced mandatory water rationing in surrounding communities, our wells did not run dry.

On a personal level, I am delighted with a food chain currently in action near my son's bedroom. To my great satisfaction, platoons of beneficial insects—ladybugs, lacewings, predatory mites, and a beetle named *Cryptolaemus*—are munching their way through armies of aphids, spider mites, and mealybugs that had been devouring my "pet" plants. The Web sites of beneficial insect dealers supplied information on niche requirements for each predator, so I could select the correct species for my conditions of temperature and humidity. Those "good bugs" cost little more than the pesticides that I would have needed to do the same job. I can rest easy, knowing that I have protected my plants from herbivores without exposing my son to pesticides. Now, that's a food chain I can live with!

I hope these examples help inspire you to teach this unit vigorously. If enough of us teach our students that human society is part of the biosphere, that biological diversity is a treasure, that clean air and water and soil are invaluable resources, that old-growth forests are different from tree farms, and that all life is connected, our students and their descendants will enjoy a happier and healthier future.

Sincerely,

Joe Levine

SCIENCE NEWS®

Have students visit the Prentice Hall Web site at

www.phschool.com

to find the most current information on ecology.

Chapter Planner 3 The Biosphere

Section and Section Objectives	Time	Activities and Labs
3–1 What Is Ecology?, pp. 63–65 **3.1.1** ***Identify*** the levels of organization that ecologists study. **3.1.2** ***Describe*** the methods used to study ecology.	1 period (1/2 block)	**SE:** ***Inquiry Activity,*** How do organisms affect one another's survival?, p. 62 **SE:** ***Technology & Society,*** Ecology From Space, p. 66
3–2 Energy Flow, pp. 67–73 **3.2.1** ***Identify*** the source of energy for life processes. **3.2.2** ***Trace*** the flow of energy through living systems. **3.2.3** ***Evaluate*** the efficiency of energy transfer among organisms in an ecosystem.	2 periods (1 block)	**TE:** ***Build Science Skills,*** p. 67 **SE:** ***Quick Lab,*** How is a food chain organized?, p. 70 **TE:** ***Build Science Skills,*** p. 71
3–3 Cycles of Matter, pp. 74–80 **3.3.1** ***Describe*** how matter cycles among the living and nonliving parts of an ecosystem. **3.3.2** ***Explain*** why nutrients are important in living systems. **3.3.3** ***Describe*** how the availability of nutrients affects the productivity of ecosystems.	2 periods (1 block)	**TE:** ***Make Connections,*** p. 76 **TE:** ***Meet Diverse Needs,*** p. 78 **SE:** ***Analyzing Data,*** Farming in the Rye, p. 79 **SE:** ***Real-World Lab,*** Identifying a Limiting Nutrient, p. 81
Chapter Assessment, pp. 82–85	1 period (1/2 block)	

ACTIVITY PLANNER

SE: ***Inquiry Activity,*** p. 62; (10 min.)

TE: ***Build Science Skills,*** p. 67; (20 min.); heavy wrapping or butcher paper, meter stick, balance, various classroom objects

SE: ***Quick Lab,*** p. 70; (15 min.); 2 wide-mouth jars, 2 pieces of flexible screening, 2 rubber bands, 2 bean seedlings in small pots or paper cups, pea aphids, ladybird beetles

TE: ***Build Science Skills,*** p. 71; (25 min.); at least 25 pictures of producers and different-level consumers; masking tape; colored yarn

TE: ***Make Connections,*** p. 76; (15 min.); one empty vitamin container for each pair of students

TE: ***Meet Diverse Needs,*** p. 78; (15 min.); variety of materials for making models of chemical formulas

SE: ***Real-World Lab,*** p. 81; (15 min. for setup); dropper pipette, algae culture, 2 test tubes with stoppers, test tube rack, 50-mL graduated cylinder, pond water, glass-marking pencil, 10% trisodium phosphate solution

PLANNING KEY

Ability Levels

- **B Basic** For students who need additional help
- **A Average** For all students
- **E Enriched** For students who need to be challenged

Components

SE	Student Edition	**GRSW**	Guided Reading and Study Workbook	**IDM**	Issues and Decision Making
TE	Teacher's Edition	**CT**	Chapter Tests: Levels A and B	**CTB**	Computer Test Bank
LMA	Laboratory Manual A	**PHAS**	PH Assessment System	**PA**	Presentation Assistant Plus
LMB	Laboratory Manual B	**LA**	Lab Assessment with Scoring Guide	**BD**	BioDetectives Videotape
TR	Teaching Resources	**BTM**	BioTechnology Manual	**iT**	iText
IF	Investigations in Forensics				

Program Resources	Assessment	Media and Technology
TR: Section Review 3–1 B A **GRSW:** Section 3–1 B A	**SE:** 3–1 Section Assessment, p. 65 **TR:** Section Review 3–1	**PA:** 3–1 Interest Grabber, Section Outline, Compare/Contrast Table, Figure 3–2 **iT:** Section 3–1
TR: Section Review 3–2 B A **GRSW:** Section 3–2 B A	**SE:** 3–2 Section Assessment, p. 73 **TR:** Section Review 3–2	**PA:** 3–2 Interest Grabber, Section Outline, Photosynthesis and Chemosynthesis, Figure 3–5 **iT:** Section 3–2
LMA: Chapter 3 Lab A E **LMB:** Chapter 3 Lab B A **TR:** Section Review 3–3 B A Chapter 3 Exploration B A E **GRSW:** Section 3–3 B A **IDM:** 3–1 A E	**SE:** 3–3 Section Assessment, p. 80 **TR:** Section Review 3–3	**PA:** 3–3 Interest Grabber, Section Outline, Ecological Pyramids, Figure 3–3, Figure 3–14 **BD:** *Pfiesteria:* A Killer in the Water **iT:** Section 3–3 Discovery Channel School
	SE: Chapter 3 Assessment, pp. 82–85 **TR:** Chapter Vocabulary Review, Graphic Organizer **CT:** Chapter 3 Test **CTB:** Chapter 3 Test **PHAS:** Practice Test	**CTB:** Chapter 3 Test **iT:** Chapter 3 Assessment

PRESSED FOR TIME?

To Preview the Chapter
- Have students read the Key Concepts in Sections 3–1 and 3–2.
- Assign the Reading Strategy for Section 3–3.

To Cover the Chapter Quickly
- Have students study Figure 3–2 and read Levels of Organization on page 64 in Section 3–1, read pages 67–70 in Section 3–2, and read all of Section 3–3.
- Assign questions 1 and 2 in 3–2 Section Assessment, question 1 in 3–3 Section Assessment, and questions 11–16, 18, and 21 in Chapter 3 Assessment.

To Review the Chapter
- Assign Sections 3–2 and 3–3 in the Guided Reading and Study Workbook.
- Assign the Chapter Vocabulary Review for Chapter 3 in Teaching Resources.

ENGAGE/EXPLORE

Inquiry Activity

Objective Students will be able to identify relationships among various types of organisms they have observed in their immediate environment.

Skill Focus **Classifying, Predicting**

Time 10 minutes

Strategies

- Emphasize to students that they should list specific types of organisms, not broad categories such as "trees" or "birds."
- If students have difficulty identifying different kinds of relationships, let them brainstorm ideas in a class discussion.

Expected Outcome Students should be able to identify at least five different types of common organisms and at least two different types of relationships among them, for example: feeding relationships; using plants for nesting sites, shelter, and hiding places; and creating favorable conditions for other organisms (for example, earthworms aerating soil).

Think About It

1. Students should identify most plants and several first- and second-order consumers as providing energy and nutrients to other organisms.
2. All other organisms would die, since they are dependent on plants either directly (as first-order consumers) or indirectly (as higher-order consumers, scavengers, or decomposers).
3. Accept all reasonable answers. *Sample answer:* Changes are difficult to predict because there are so many variables.

Brain Teaser

Challenge students' thinking by asking: **How do animals benefit plants?** *(Possible responses include: Some animals disperse plant seeds. Decomposers break down animal wastes and the remains of dead organisms into simpler substances that provide nutrients for plants. Some plants are nurtured and protected by humans.)*

Chapter 3 The Biosphere

A tawny owl prepares to seize a mouse. The mouse is carrying a berry in its mouth as it runs along a fallen, moss-covered tree trunk. The owl, the mouse, the tree trunk, and the moss are all members of this forest ecosystem.

Inquiry Activity

How do organisms affect one another's survival?

Procedure

1. Make a list of all the types of organisms, including plants, humans, insects, and so on, that you have seen near your home or school.
2. Make a diagram that shows how the organisms on your list interact with one another.

Think About It

1. **Classifying** Which organisms on your list provide energy or nutrients to the others?
2. **Predicting** What would you expect to happen if all the plants on your diagram died? Explain your answer.
3. **Posing Questions** Why is it difficult to make accurate predictions about changes in communities of organisms?

FACTS AND FIGURES

Earth's biosphere

In Earth's biosphere, populations of organisms interact not only with one another but also with the three major divisions of the abiotic environment: the lithosphere (the soil and rock of Earth's crust), the atmosphere (the gases surrounding Earth), and the hydrosphere (all of Earth's water, whether gaseous, liquid, or frozen, fresh or saline). Earth's biosphere is a closed system. Nothing leaves or enters—except energy from the sun, the ultimate source of all life on Earth. Much more solar energy reaches Earth each day than is needed to support Earth's producers. Most of the "extra" energy is absorbed or reflected by Earth's surface and atmosphere. In fact, only about 1 percent of the solar energy that reaches Earth's producers is converted to chemical energy through the process of photosynthesis. That 1 percent, however, is sufficient to produce about 170 billion tons of organic matter every year!

3–1 What Is Ecology?

The stories flash across television screens, radios, newspapers, and the Internet nearly every day. "Floods hit the Midwest!" "Southwest wildfires char thousands of acres!" "Florida's Everglades faces drought!" "Great Lakes battle marine invaders!" What do floods, raging wildfires, and droughts have in common? What are "marine invaders," and why do they pose problems in lakes? Every one of these headline-grabbing events involves interactions between organisms and their environment. To understand the changes that occur as a result of such interactions, scientists turn to a branch of biology called ecology.

Interactions and Interdependence

Ecology (ee-KAHL-uh-jee) is the scientific study of interactions among organisms and between organisms and their environment, or surroundings. The word *ecology* was coined in 1866 by the German biologist Ernst Haeckel. Haeckel based this term on the Greek word *oikos,* meaning house, which is also the root of the word *economy.* Haeckel saw the living world as a household with an economy in which each organism plays a role.

Nature's "houses" come in many sizes—from single cells to the entire planet. The largest of these houses is called the biosphere. The **biosphere** contains the combined portions of the planet in which all of life exists, including land, water, and air or atmosphere. It extends from about 8 kilometers above Earth's surface to as far as 11 kilometers below the surface of the ocean.

Interactions within the biosphere produce a web of interdependence between organisms and the environment in which they live. Whether it occurs on top of a glacier, in a forest like the one in **Figure 3–1,** or deep within an ocean trench, the interdependence of life on Earth contributes to an ever-changing, or dynamic, biosphere.

Guide for Reading

Key Concepts
- What different levels of organization do ecologists study?
- What methods are used to study ecology?

Vocabulary
ecology
biosphere
species
population
community
ecosystem
biome

Reading Strategy: Asking Questions Before you read, rewrite the headings in this section as *how, what,* or *why* questions about ecology. Then, as you read, write brief answers to your questions.

▶ **Figure 3–1** Organisms and their environment are interdependent. This giant land snail could not survive without plants and algae to eat, and the plants and algae could not grow unless bacteria and other organisms helped recycle nutrients in the water and soil. **Classifying** *List the organisms that you see in the photograph. Then list the nonliving parts of the environment with which the organisms interact.*

SECTION RESOURCES

Print:
- ***Teaching Resources,*** Section Review 3–1
- ***Guided Reading and Study Workbook,*** Section 3–1

Technology
- ***iText,*** Section 3–1

Section 3–1

1 FOCUS

Objectives

3.1.1 ***Identify*** the levels of organization that ecologists study.
3.1.3 ***Describe*** the methods used to study ecology.

Guide for Reading

Reading Strategy

Before students begin their outlines, point out that one major topic below each heading is identified by bold type preceded with the key symbol. Encourage students to rephrase the Key Concepts in their own words. Also point out the boldfaced Vocabulary terms and their definitions.

2 INSTRUCT

Interactions and Interdependence

Make Connections

Earth Science Call on a volunteer to read the definition of *ecology* aloud. Ask: **What nonliving things in their environment do organisms interact with?** *(Sunlight, air, water, soil, rocks)* **In what ways are these nonliving things essential to organisms?** *(Accept all reasonable descriptions of how abiotic factors meet organisms' needs.)*

Build Science Skills

Applying Concepts Point out that no organism exists in isolation but that all types of organisms on Earth depend on one another for their survival. Ask: **What evidence do you see that people in our society today are aware of the interdependence of living things?** *(Laws have been enacted to reduce air, water, and land pollution and to protect endangered species. People are encouraged to conserve natural resources through recycling and in other ways.)*

Answer to . . .

Figure 3–1 *The snail, ferns, mosses, and other plants are organisms. They interact with the rocks, water, air, and light.*

Levels of Organization

Meet Diverse Needs

Visual learners would benefit from creating posters or bulletin board displays similar to Figure 3–2, but showing different examples of the six levels of organization. Students can draw the illustrations themselves or use pictures they have cut or photocopied from magazines and books. Have students work in small groups, and encourage each group to focus on a different biome. Have students scan Sections 4–3 and 4–4 to identify major biomes. **Learning modality: visual**

SCIENCE NEWS®

Encourage students to visit **www.phschool.com** for the most current information on this topic.

▲ **Figure 3–2** **The study of ecology ranges from the study of an individual organism to populations, communities, ecosystems, biomes—and finally, to the entire biosphere.** The information that ecologists gain at each level contributes to our understanding of natural systems.

KEEP CURRENT WITH . . . SCIENCE NEWS®

To find out more about the topics in this chapter, go to: **www.phschool.com**

Levels of Organization

To understand relationships within the biosphere, ecologists ask questions about events and organisms that range in complexity from a single individual to the entire biosphere. The many levels of organization that ecologists study are shown in **Figure 3–2.**

Some ecologists study interactions between a particular kind of organism and its surroundings. Such studies focus on the species level. A **species** is a group of organisms so similar to one another that they can breed and produce fertile offspring. Other ecologists study **populations,** or groups of individuals that belong to the same species and live in the same area. Still other ecologists study **communities,** or assemblages of different populations that live together in a defined area.

Ecologists may study a particular ecosystem. An **ecosystem** is a collection of all the organisms that live in a particular place, together with their nonliving, or physical, environment. Larger systems called biomes are sometimes studied by teams of ecologists. A **biome** is a group of ecosystems that have the same climate and dominant communities. The highest level of organization that ecologists study is the entire biosphere itself.

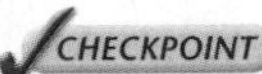
CHECKPOINT *What is an ecosystem?*

TIME SAVER — PRESENTATIONS MADE EASY!

The Presentation Assistant Plus contains the Prentice Hall Presentation Pro and the Transparencies, which provide easy-to-follow visual support for every step of this section. If you have a computer presentation station, use Prentice Hall Presentation Pro for Section 3–1, or use the transparencies listed here.

Section 3–1: **Interest Grabber**
Section Outline
Compare/Contrast Table
Figure 3–2

Ecological Methods

Ecologists use a wide range of tools and techniques to study the living world. Some, like the scientists in **Figure 3–3**, use binoculars and field guides to assess changes in plant and wildlife communities. Others use studies of DNA to identify bacteria in the mud of coastal marshes. Still others use radio tags to track migrating wildlife or use data gathered by satellites.

Regardless of the tools they use, scientists conduct modern ecological research using three basic approaches: observing, experimenting, and modeling. All of these approaches rely on the application of scientific methods to guide ecological inquiry.

Observing Observing is often the first step in asking ecological questions. Some observations are simple: What species live here? How many individuals of each species are there? Other observations are more complex and may form the first step in designing experiments and models.

Experimenting Experiments can be used to test hypotheses. An ecologist may set up an artificial environment in a laboratory to imitate and manipulate conditions that organisms would encounter in the natural world. Other experiments are conducted within natural ecosystems.

Modeling Many ecological phenomena occur over long periods of time or on such large spatial scales that they are difficult to study. Ecologists make models to gain insight into complex phenomena such as the effects of global warming on ecosystems. Many ecological models consist of mathematical formulas based on data collected through observation and experimentation. The predictions made by ecological models are often tested by further observations and experiments.

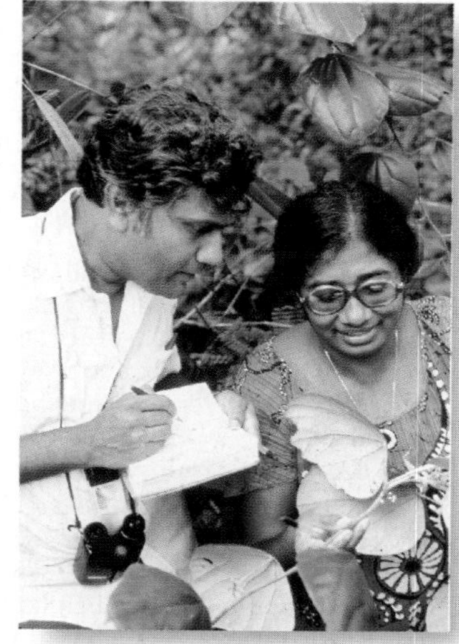

▲ **Figure 3–3** **The three fundamental approaches to ecological research involve observing, experimenting, and modeling.** These ecologists are studying a rain forest ecosystem in Sri Lanka. They are using field observations to collect data on vines and other plants.

3–1 Section Assessment

1. **Key Concept** List the six different levels of organization that ecologists study, in order from smallest to largest.
2. **Key Concept** Describe the three basic methods of ecological research.
3. Identify two ways in which you interact with each of the three parts of the biosphere—land, water, and air—every day.
4. **Critical Thinking Applying Concepts** Suppose you wanted to know if the water in a certain stream is safe to drink. Which ecological method(s) would you choose, and why?

iTEXT Assessment Use iText to review the important concepts in Section 3–1.

Take It to the NET

Visit three different ecological institutions on the Web. Then, make a table that shows the level of organization, location, and method(s) of study that each group uses. Use the links provided in the Biology area at the Prentice Hall Web site for help in completing this activity: **www.phschool.com**

Ecological Methods

Build Science Skills

Classifying Divide the class into groups of three, and have each group list one specific example of each ecological method, with all three examples relating to the same type of ecosystem. Then, let groups exchange lists and identify the ecological method that each example represents.

3 ASSESS

Evaluate Understanding

Using the diagrams they drew for the Inquiry Activity on page 62, have students write a paragraph describing how the organisms shown in the diagram depend on one another and on nonliving things in their environment.

Reteach

Call on one student to name an individual organism, a second student to identify the population to which the organism belongs, a third student to describe the community of which the population is a part, and a fourth student to describe the community's ecosystem. Repeat this procedure until every student has had at least one turn.

Take It to the NET

For additional information, visit **www.phschool.com**

iTEXT

Use iText to review the key concepts in Section 3–1.

3–1 Section Assessment

1. Species, population, community, ecosystem, biome, biosphere
2. Observing involves using the senses to gather information and may include using tools and recording data. Experimenting involves testing hypotheses in a laboratory or natural ecosystem. Modeling involves making representations of objects, events, processes, and relationships.
3. Student answers should give examples of interactions with land, water, and air.
4. Observing—i.e., testing a water sample in a lab to determine whether it is safe.

Answer to . . .

CHECKPOINT A collection of all the various organisms that live in a particular place, together with their nonliving environment

After students have read this feature, you might want to discuss one or more of the following:

- From their previous learning, students may know how the destruction of forests affects the global carbon-oxygen cycle and water cycle. Have them share this information in a class discussion. Then, ask: **Why is it important for ecologists to be aware of forest destruction? How do you think they would use this information?**
- Discuss the role of phytoplankton in the carbon-oxygen cycle. (You may want to have students preview Energy From the Sun on page 68.)
- Encourage interested students to research satellite systems besides those described in this feature and share the information with the class in brief oral reports accompanied by pictures similar to those on this page. Discuss how each type of system could assists ecologists in their studies of ecosystems.

Exploring Ecology From Space

Modern research in global ecology would not be possible if all its tools were earthbound. Studies on a planetary scale require enormous data-gathering networks. Through a process called remote sensing, satellites extend the range of information that ecologists can collect within the biosphere.

Remote-sensing satellites are fitted with optical sensors that can scan several bands of the electromagnetic spectrum and convert those bands into electrical signals. The signals are run through a computer and converted into digital values, which are used to construct an image.

Remote sensing provides detailed images of essentially every square meter of Earth's surface. How else could scientists view all the world's lakes and oceans to see where concentrations of algae are the highest? Or view areas of destroyed forests in places like the Amazon Basin or northern Russia?

Global Change

The false-color image below was assembled from data gathered by NASA's Sea-viewing Wide Field-of-view Sensor (SeaWiFS) Project. The project's goal is to study factors that affect global change and to assess the oceans' role in the global carbon cycle, as well as other chemical cycles. The different ocean colors indicate varying concentrations of microscopic algae. Blue represents the least amount of algae, and red the highest amount. On land, the dark green areas have the most vegetation, while gold land areas have the least.

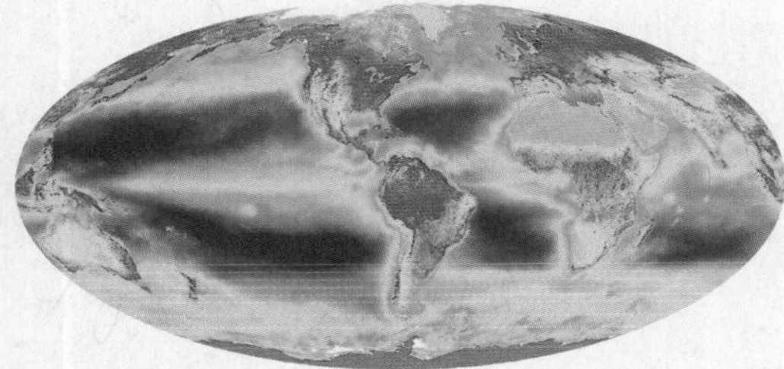

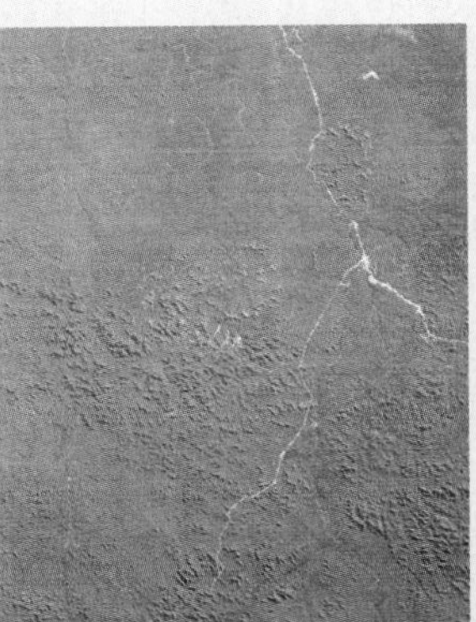

Rain Forest Destruction

Remote sensing is a powerful tool for ecologists monitoring the destruction of the world's rain forests. The two satellite images above show one tract of land in Brazil's rain forest. The image on the right was taken 11 years after the one on the left. Red areas show healthy vegetation, while light blue areas show urban areas and deforested land—land where forests have been cut down. Notice the feathered or fishbone pattern of deforestation in the right-hand photo. This pattern typically occurs because the cutting of forests begins along roads and then fans out.

Satellite images like these allow ecologists to estimate the rate at which rain forest destruction is occurring. They also add to scientists' understanding of the complex issues involved in this global problem. This information can help ecologists in their work with local governments to slow the destruction of these vital ecosystems.

On Your Own

Find out more about the use of satellites in ecological studies. Log on to the Prentice Hall Web site at **www.phschool.com**.

BIO INSIGHTS — FACTS AND FIGURES

Terra in space

Launched on December 18, 1999, and costing $1.3 billion, the school bus–sized Terra has been described as "a sort of Hubble Space Telescope aimed at Earth." But the amount of data that Terra collects each day—about 100,000 encyclopedia volumes' worth—roughly equals the amount of data collected by the Hubble telescope in one year.

Terra circles 705 kilometers above Earth's surface in a polar orbit that carries it past the equator at 10:30 AM each day, when cloud cover over Earth's landmasses is minimal. The satellite's five instruments monitor Earth's radiation balance, sea surface temperatures, levels of greenhouse gases, changes in land cover use, ice sheet volume, and atmospheric chemistry. Data from Terra also may have practical applications, such as managing crops and coastal fisheries and assessing natural hazards such as volcano activity, earthquakes, floods, and fires.

3–2 Energy Flow

At the core of every organism's interaction with the environment is its need for energy to power life's processes. Consider, for example, the energy that ants use to carry objects many times their size, or the energy that birds use to migrate thousands of miles. Think about the energy that you need to get out of bed in the morning! The flow of energy through an ecosystem is one of the most important factors that determines the system's capacity to sustain life.

Producers

Without a constant input of energy, living systems cannot function. **Sunlight is the main energy source for life on Earth.** Of all the sun's energy that reaches Earth's surface, only a small amount—less than 3 percent—is used by living things. This seemingly small amount is enough to produce as much as 3.5 kilograms of living tissue per square meter a year in some tropical forests.

In a few ecosystems, some organisms obtain energy from a source other than sunlight. **Some types of organisms rely on the energy stored in inorganic chemical compounds.** For instance, mineral water that flows underground or boils out of hot springs and undersea vents is loaded with chemical energy.

Only plants, some algae, and certain bacteria can capture energy from sunlight or chemicals and use that energy to produce food. These organisms are called **autotrophs.** Autotrophs use energy from the environment to fuel the assembly of simple inorganic compounds into complex organic molecules. These organic molecules combine and recombine to produce living tissue. Because they make their own food, autotrophs, like the kelp in **Figure 3–4**, are also called **producers.** Both types of producers—those that capture energy from sunlight and those that capture chemical energy—are essential to the flow of energy through the biosphere.

Guide for Reading

Key Concepts
- Where does the energy for life processes come from?
- How does energy flow through living systems?
- How efficient is the transfer of energy among organisms in an ecosystem?

Vocabulary
- autotroph • producer
- photosynthesis
- chemosynthesis • heterotroph
- consumer • herbivore
- carnivore • omnivore
- detritivore • decomposer
- food chain • food web
- trophic level
- ecological pyramid • biomass

Reading Strategy: Building Vocabulary As you read, make notes about the meaning of each term in the list above and how it relates to energy flow in the biosphere. Then, draw a concept map to show the relationships among the new terms in this section.

▼ **Figure 3–4** Sunlight falls on a dense kelp forest off the coast of California. **Kelp is an autotroph that uses energy from the sun to produce living tissue.**

SECTION RESOURCES

Print:
- ***Teaching Resources,*** Section Review 3–2
- ***Guided Reading and Study Workbook,*** Section 3–2

Technology
- ***iText,*** Section 3–2

Section 3–2

1 FOCUS

Objectives

3.2.1 ***Identify*** the source of energy for life processes.
3.2.2 ***Trace*** the flow of energy through living systems.
3.2.3 ***Evaluate*** the efficiency of energy transfer among organisms in an ecosystem.

Guide for Reading

Vocabulary Preview

To help students understand related terms in this section, write the following sets of words and word parts on the board.
Set 1: *photo-, chemo-, synthesis*
Set 2: *herb-, carn-, omni-, detritus, -vore*
Have students look up the meaning of each word or part in a dictionary and list them. As students read the section and make notes about the terms, they can check the text's definitions against this list.

Reading Strategy

Students' concept maps could be titled "Energy Flow" and begin with autotrophs, or producers, which make food through photosynthesis or chemosynthesis. Then, students should add the various types of heterotrophs to their concept maps and show how the various types of organisms are interrelated, using the terms *food chain, food web, trophic level,* and *ecological pyramid.*

2 INSTRUCT

Producers

Building Science Skills

Measuring Have groups of students cut out one-square-meter pieces of heavy wrapping or butcher paper. Next, let each group use a balance and various common objects in the classroom to measure out 3.5 kg of mass, then place the objects on the paper square. Encourage the groups to examine one another's piles of objects. Emphasize that each pile represents the amount of living tissue produced per square meter each year in a tropical forest.

Make Connections

Chemistry On the board, write the chemical equation for photosynthesis:

$$6CO_2 + 6H_2O \xrightarrow[\text{energy}]{\text{light}} C_6H_{12}O_6 + 6O_2$$

Ask: **Which element does each letter in the formulas stand for?** *(C for carbon; O, oxygen; H, hydrogen.)* Explain that the equation can be read as "Six molecules of carbon dioxide and six molecules of water combine in the presence of light energy to yield one molecule of glucose and six molecules of oxygen." Ask: **Why are the numbers needed in the equation?** *(Without numbers, the equation wouldn't be balanced.)* If students are not familiar with this concept, write the equation on the board and then cross out the balanced pairs—6 carbon atoms (6C) on the left and 6 carbon atoms (C_6) on the right; 18 oxygen atoms ($6O_2$ + 6O) on the left and 18 (O_6 + $6O_2$) on the right; 12 hydrogen atoms ($6H_2$) on the left and 12 (H_{12}) on the right.

Consumers

Meet Diverse Needs

For students who learn best through handling materials, provide pictures of a wide variety of organisms, and let students physically sort the pictures into two piles—producers and consumers—and then sort the consumers into piles representing the four subcategories of herbivores, carnivores, omnivores, and decomposers. **Learning modality: kinesthetic**

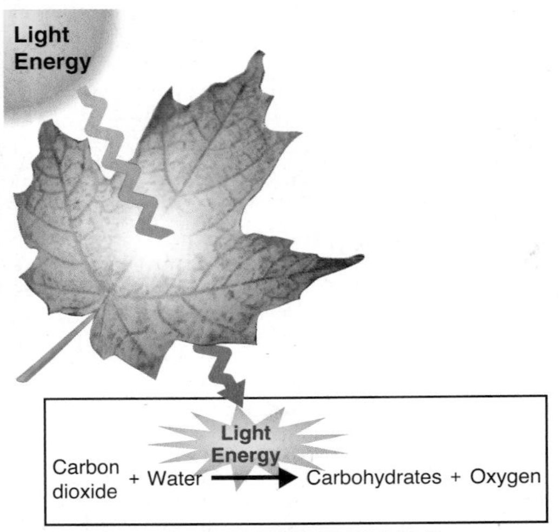

Light Energy
Light Energy
Carbon dioxide + Water → Carbohydrates + Oxygen

PHOTOSYNTHESIS IN PLANTS

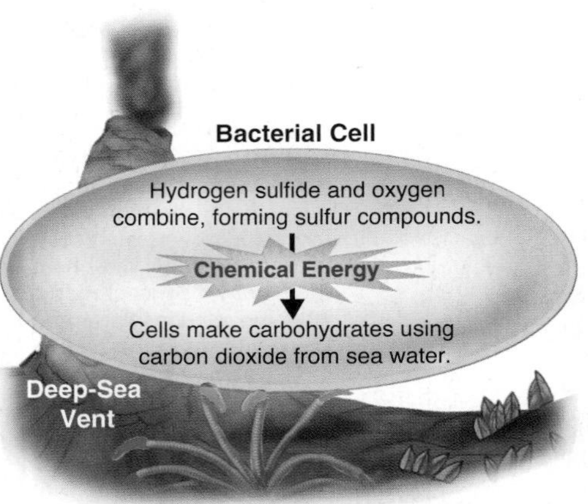

Bacterial Cell
Hydrogen sulfide and oxygen combine, forming sulfur compounds.
Chemical Energy
Cells make carbohydrates using carbon dioxide from sea water.
Deep-Sea Vent

CHEMOSYNTHESIS IN SULFUR BACTERIA

▲ **Figure 3–5** **Sunlight is the main energy source for life on Earth. Some types of organisms rely on the energy stored in inorganic chemical compounds.** Plants use the energy from sunlight to carry out the process of photosynthesis. Other autotrophs, such as sulfur bacteria, use the energy stored in chemical bonds for chemosynthesis. In both cases, energy-rich carbohydrates are produced.

Energy From the Sun The best-known autotrophs are those that harness solar energy through a process known as photosynthesis. During **photosynthesis,** these autotrophs use light energy to power chemical reactions that convert carbon dioxide and water into oxygen and energy-rich carbohydrates such as sugars and starches. This process, shown in **Figure 3–5,** is responsible for adding oxygen to—and removing carbon dioxide from—Earth's atmosphere. In fact, were it not for photosynthetic autotrophs, the air would not contain enough oxygen for you to breathe!

On land, plants are the main autotrophs. In freshwater ecosystems and in the sunlit, upper layers of the ocean, algae are the principal autotrophs. Photosynthetic bacteria, the most common of which are called cyanobacteria (sy-an-oh-bak-TEER-ee-uh), are important in certain wet ecosystems such as tidal flats and salt marshes.

Life Without Light Although plants are the most visible and best-known autotrophs, some autotrophs can produce food in the absence of light. Such autotrophs rely on energy within the chemical bonds of inorganic molecules such as hydrogen sulfide. When organisms use chemical energy to produce carbohydrates, the process is called **chemosynthesis** (kee-moh-SIN-thuh-sis). This process is performed by several types of bacteria. Surprisingly, these bacteria represent a large proportion of living autotrophs. Some chemosynthetic bacteria live in very remote places on Earth, such as volcanic vents on the deep-ocean floor and hot springs in Yellowstone Park. Others live in more common places, such as tidal marshes along the coast.

✓CHECKPOINT *What is the difference between photosynthesis and chemosynthesis?*

Consumers

Many organisms—including animals, fungi, and many bacteria—cannot harness energy directly from the physical environment as autotrophs do. The only way these organisms can acquire energy is from other organisms. Organisms that rely on other organisms for their energy and food supply are called **heterotrophs** (HET-ur-oh-trohfs). Heterotrophs are also called **consumers.**

PRESENTATIONS MADE EASY!

The Presentation Assistant Plus contains the Prentice Hall Presentation Pro and the Transparencies, which provide easy-to-follow visual support for every step of this section. If you have a computer presentation station, use Prentice Hall Presentation Pro for Section 3–2, or use the transparencies listed here.

Section 3–2:

Interest Grabber
Section Outline
Photosynthesis and Chemosynthesis
Figure 3–5

There are many different types of heterotrophs. **Herbivores** obtain energy by eating only plants. Some herbivores are cows, caterpillars, and deer. **Carnivores,** including snakes, dogs, and owls, eat animals. Humans, bears, crows, and other **omnivores** eat both plants and animals. **Detritivores** (dee-TRYT-uh-vawrz), such as mites, earthworms, snails, and crabs, feed on plant and animal remains and other dead matter, collectively called detritus. Another important group of heterotrophs, called **decomposers,** breaks down organic matter. Bacteria and fungi such as the one in **Figure 3–6** are decomposers.

▲ **Figure 3–6** This fungus, growing on the forest floor, is a decomposer that obtains nutrients by breaking down dead and decaying plants and animals. It is called a coral fungus because of its color and shape. **Classifying** ***Is the fungus a producer or a consumer?***

Feeding Relationships

What happens to the energy in an ecosystem when one organism eats another? That energy moves along a one-way path. **Energy flows through an ecosystem in one direction, from the sun or inorganic compounds to autotrophs (producers) and then to various heterotrophs (consumers).** The relationships between producers and consumers connect organisms into feeding networks based on who eats whom.

Food Chains The energy stored by producers can be passed through an ecosystem along a **food chain,** a series of steps in which organisms transfer energy by eating and being eaten. For example, in a prairie ecosystem, a food chain might consist of a producer—such as grass—that is fed upon by an herbivore—such as a grazing antelope. The herbivore is in turn fed upon by a carnivore—such as a coyote. In this situation, the carnivore is only two steps removed from the producer.

In some marine food chains, such as the one in **Figure 3–7,** the producers are microscopic algae that are eaten by very small organisms called zooplankton (zoh-oh-PLANK-tun). The zooplankton, in turn, are eaten by small fish, such as herring. The herring are eaten by squid, which are ultimately eaten by large fish, such as sharks. In this food chain, the top carnivore is four steps removed from the producer.

▼ **Figure 3–7** **Food chains show the one-way flow of energy in an ecosystem.** In this marine food chain, energy is passed from the producers (algae) to four different groups of consumers.

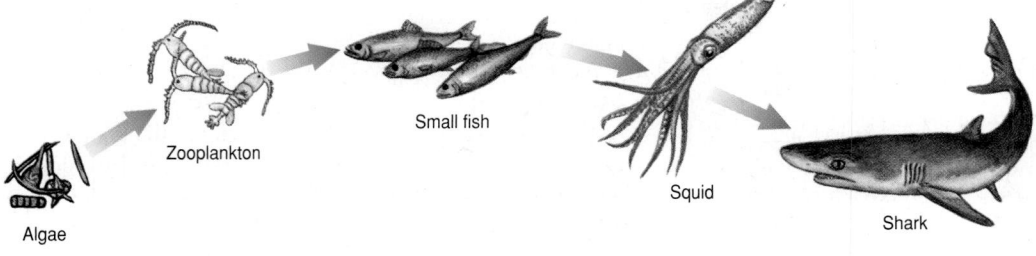

Feeding Relationships

Build Science Skills

Applying Concepts Show students some acorns, sunflower seeds, or other common type of seeds, and ask: **Where did these seeds come from?** *(A plant)* **What kind of animal might eat these seeds?** *(Depending on the type of seeds used, a squirrel, chickadee, mouse, or chipmunk might eat them.)* **What kind of animal might eat the animal that ate the seeds?** *(A larger carnivore such as a fox, hawk, or coyote)* **What is the feeding relationship that you just described called?** *(A food chain)* **What happens to energy in the food chain?** *(Energy is transferred from the organism being eaten to the organism doing the eating.)* **What was the original source of energy in the food chain?** *(The sun)*

FACTS AND FIGURES

Energy moves up the chain

In nature, simple "straight line" food chains are rare, primarily because few species eat or are eaten by only one other species. Nevertheless, a food chain is a useful model for studying the transfer of energy and materials in an ecosystem.

All food chains on land begin with producers that use light energy to synthesize organic compounds. Primary consumers are herbivores that feed directly on the producers. Above the primary consumers are secondary consumers, then tertiary consumers, and, in some food chains, quaternary consumers. Not many food chains extend beyond four consumer levels. Decomposers (also known as saprotrophs), detritivores, and parasites—organisms that live in or on other organisms and obtain energy from them—can occupy any level of a food chain.

Answers to . . .

Photosynthesis uses light energy. Chemosynthesis uses the energy stored in chemical bonds.

Figure 3–6 *A consumer*

Quick Lab

Objective Students will be able to describe the organization of a simple food chain.

Skill Focus **Classifying**

Materials 2 wide-mouth jars, 2 pieces of flexible screening, 2 rubber bands, 2 bean seedlings in small pots or paper cups, pea aphids, ladybird beetles

Time 15 minutes for initial setup, 5 minutes per day for one week to observe and record

Advance Prep
- About two weeks before students do this activity, plant bean seeds in pots or paper cups. Each group will need two seedlings. Plant extras in case some plants do not thrive.
- Aphids and ladybird beetles may be collected outdoors or ordered from a biological supply house. Ladybird beetles also may be available at garden centers as natural pest-controls. If the organisms are collected outdoors, make sure they are returned to their original locations at the conclusion of the activity.

Safety Caution students to handle organisms without harming them.

Strategies
- Make the aphids and ladybird beetles available to students in a central distribution center.
- You may want to let students examine the aphids with magnifiers before they place them in the jars.

Expected Outcome See Analyze and Conclude number 1 below.

Analyze and Conclude
1. In the jar without ladybird beetles, the uncontrolled aphids harmed (or perhaps killed) the seedling. In the jar with ladybird beetles, the seedling was less damaged and survived longer. The ladybird beetles helped protect the seedling by eating some of the aphids that were feeding on it.
2. The seedlings are producers; the aphids and ladybird beetles are consumers.

Word Origins

Hetero- means "other, different," and *auto-* means "self." Thus, *heterotroph* refers to an organism that feeds on other organisms, and *autotroph* refers to one that produces its own food.

Quick Lab

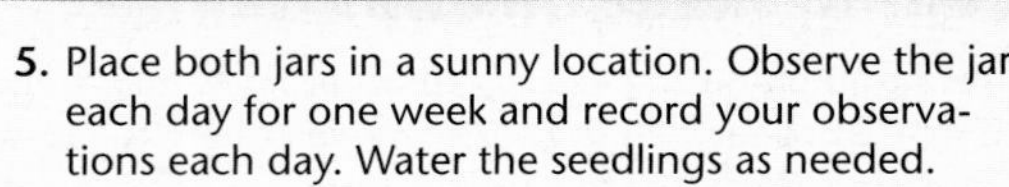

How is a food chain organized?

Materials 2 wide-mouth jars, 2 pieces of flexible screening, 2 rubber bands, 2 bean seedlings in small pots or paper cups, pea aphids, ladybird beetles

Procedure
1. Place a potted bean seedling in each of the two jars.
2. Add 20 aphids to one jar and cover the jar with screening to prevent the aphids from escaping. Use a rubber band to attach the screening to the jar.
3. Add 20 aphids and 4 ladybird beetles to the second jar. Cover the second jar as you did the first one.
4. **Formulating Hypotheses** Record your hypothesis about how the presence of the ladybird beetles will affect the survival of the aphids and the bean seedling. Also, record your prediction of what will happen to the organisms in each jar during the next week.
5. Place both jars in a sunny location. Observe the jars each day for one week and record your observations each day. Water the seedlings as needed.

Analyze and Conclude
1. **Observing** What happened to the aphids and the seedling in the jar without the ladybird beetles? In the jar with the ladybird beetles? How can you explain this difference?
2. **Classifying** Identify each organism in the jars as a producer or a consumer.

Food Webs In most ecosystems, feeding relationships are more complex than can be shown in a food chain. Consider, for example, the relationships in a salt marsh. Although some producers—including marsh grass and other salt-tolerant plants—are eaten by water birds, grasshoppers, and other herbivores, most producers complete their life cycles, then die and decompose. Decomposers convert the dead plant matter to detritus, which is eaten by detritivores, such as sandhoppers. The detritivores are in turn eaten by smelt and other small fish. Some of those consumers will also eat detritus directly. Add mice, larger fish, and hawks to the scenario, and feeding relationships can get very confusing!

When the feeding relationships among the various organisms in an ecosystem form a network of complex interactions, ecologists describe these relationships as a **food web.** A food web links all the food chains in an ecosystem together. The food web in **Figure 3–8,** for example, shows the feeding relationships in a salt-marsh community.

Trophic Levels Each step in a food chain or food web is called a **trophic level** (TRAHF-ik). Producers make up the first trophic level. Consumers make up the second, third, or higher trophic levels. Each consumer depends on the trophic level below it for energy.

Word Origins

Trophic originates from the Greek word *trophe,* which means "food or nourishment." **What do you think are the original meanings of the words *heterotroph* and *autotroph?***

CHECKPOINT *What is a food web?*

BIO INSIGHTS — FACTS AND FIGURES

Two types of food webs

There are two basic types of food webs: grazing food webs and detrital food webs. A grazing food web begins with photosynthesizing plants, algae, or phytoplankton. A detrital food web begins with decomposers and detritivores. It is the detrital type of food web that enables nutrients to be recycled in ecosystems.

Decomposers and detritivores obtain energy by breaking down organic wastes and the remains of dead organisms. This process releases simple inorganic molecules such as mineral salts, carbon, nitrogen, phosphorous, and potassium, making these nutrients available for reuse by producers and, eventually, all other organisms in the ecosystem. Without decomposers and detritivores, such essential elements would remain in animal wastes and dead organisms permanently.

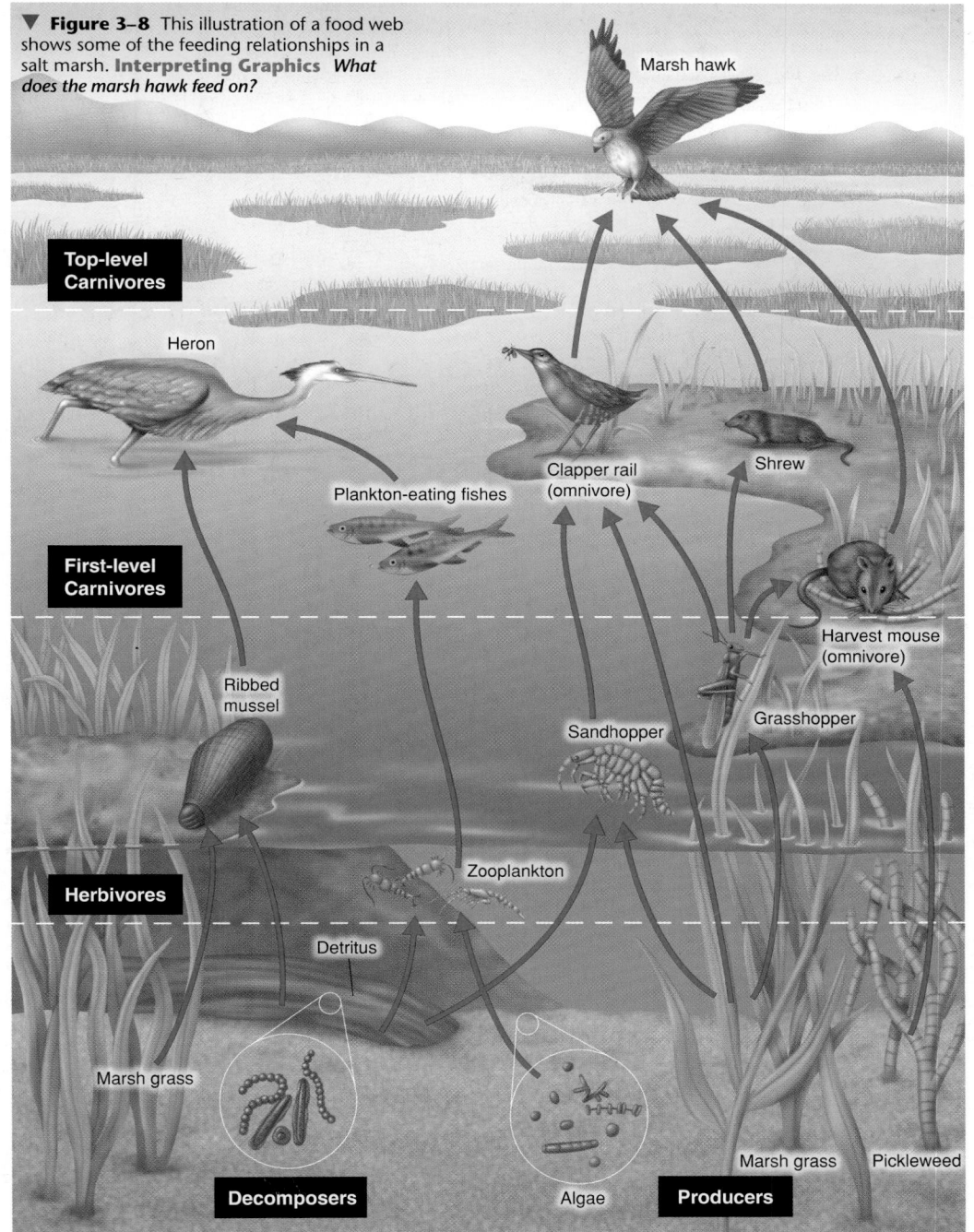

▼ **Figure 3–8** This illustration of a food web shows some of the feeding relationships in a salt marsh. **Interpreting Graphics** *What does the marsh hawk feed on?*

Use Visuals

Figure 3–8 To help students deal with the complexity of the food web, call on different students in turn to name the organisms in one food chain, beginning with a producer and working upward to the final consumer. For example, students might identify a food web including algae, zooplankton, plankton-eating fishes, heron.

Build Science Skills

Making Models Obtain at least 25 pictures of organisms—producers and different-level consumers—that could be found in an ecosystem other than the one shown in Figure 3–8. Tape the pictures in random order on the classroom walls, desktops, and other surfaces. Give each student a small ball of colored yarn and several small pieces of masking tape. Then, let four or five students at a time connect pictures with yarn to show different food chains. Students may crisscross the room with the yarn so the food web becomes quite complex. When every student has had a turn, let the class examine the results. Ask: **What is the name for this pattern of feeding relationships?** *(A food web)* **How is a food web different from a food chain?** *(A food web contains many overlapping food chains, so it is much more complex than a single food chain.)*

TEACHER TO TEACHER

I have students make a food web poster for a particular ecosystem or biome. The food web must contain at least five food chains consisting of a producer, a primary consumer, and a secondary consumer. Each consumer must be labeled as an herbivore, carnivore, omnivore, or decomposer. At least one predator-prey relationship must be shown. Five abiotic factors also must be included and labeled.

The posters may be drawn free-hand, or students may cut and paste pictures from magazines or computer printouts. I usually have students explain their posters to the class in oral presentations.

LouEllen Parker Brademan
Teacher
Potomac Senior High School
Dumfries, Virginia

Answers to . . .

CHECKPOINT *A food web is the network of feeding relationships in an ecosystem.*

Figure 3–8 *Birds and small mammals*

Ecological Pyramids

Make Connections

Mathematics Draw students' attention to the energy pyramid in Figure 3–9. Explain that the amount of energy available in food is measured in calories. One calorie is the amount of energy needed to raise the temperature of 1 gram of water 1°C. Scientists usually refer to the energy content of food in units of kilocalories. One kilocalorie equals 1,000 calories. A kilocalorie is also expressed as a Calorie, with a capital C. Then, pose the following problem: **Suppose that the base of this energy pyramid consists of plants that contain 450,000 Calories of food energy. If all the plants were eaten by mice and insects, how much food energy would be available to those first-level consumers?** *(45,000 Calories)* **If all the mice and insects were eaten by snakes, how much food energy would be available to the snakes?** *(4,500 Calories)* **If all the snakes were eaten by a hawk, how much food energy would be available to the hawk?** *(450 Calories)* **How much food energy would the hawk use for its body processes and lose as heat?** *(405 Calories—90 percent of 450)* **How much food energy would be stored in the hawk's body?** *(45 Calories)*

Build Science Skills

Applying Concepts Point out the exception described in the text of a numbers pyramid. Ask: **What would be the shape of a numbers pyramid for the forest?** *(The pyramid's base, representing the trees, would be much smaller than the second section, representing the insects that feed on the trees.)*

Energy Pyramid
Shows the relative amount of energy available at each trophic level. Organisms use about 10 percent of this energy for life processes. The rest is lost as heat.

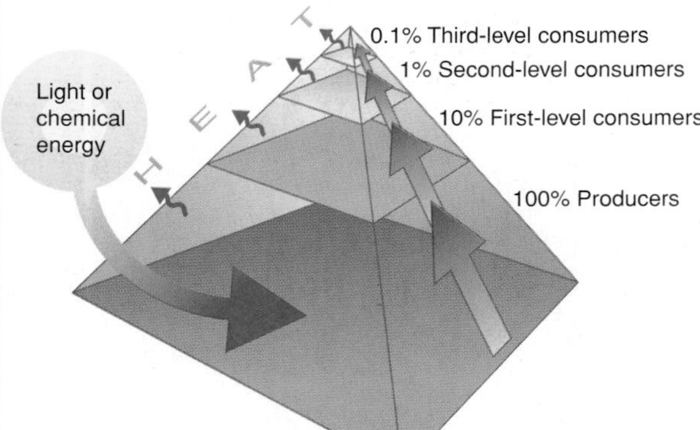

Biomass Pyramid
Represents the amount of living organic matter at each trophic level. Typically, the greatest biomass is at the base of the pyramid.

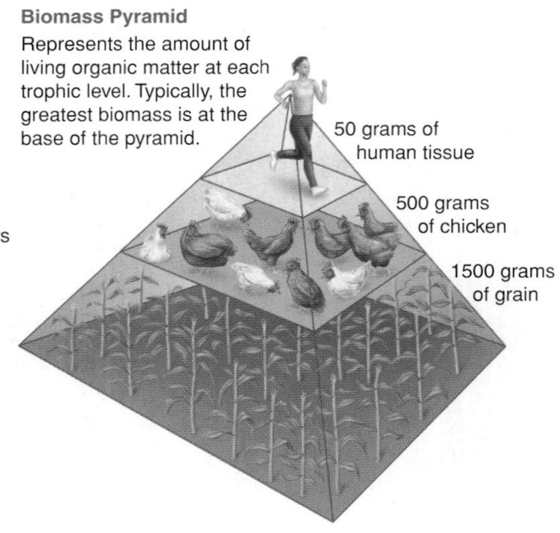

Ecological Pyramids

The amount of energy or matter in an ecosystem can be represented by an ecological pyramid. An **ecological pyramid** is a diagram that shows the relative amounts of energy or matter contained within each trophic level in a food chain or food web. Ecologists recognize three different types of ecological pyramids: energy pyramids, biomass pyramids, and pyramids of numbers. **Figure 3–9** shows an example of each type.

Energy Pyramid Theoretically, there is no limit to the number of trophic levels that a food chain can support. But there is one hitch. Only part of the energy that is stored in one trophic level is passed on to the next level. This is because organisms use much of the energy that they consume for life processes, such as respiration, movement, and reproduction. Some of the remaining energy is released into the environment as heat. **Only about 10 percent of the energy available within one trophic level is transferred to organisms at the next trophic level.** For instance, one tenth of the solar energy captured by grasses ends up stored in the tissues of cows and other grazers. Only one tenth of that energy—10 percent of 10 percent, or 1 percent total—is transferred to the humans that eat the cows. Thus, the more levels that exist between a producer and a top-level consumer in an ecosystem, the less energy that remains from the original amount.

Biomass Pyramid The total amount of living tissue within a given trophic level is called **biomass.** Biomass is usually expressed in terms of grams of organic matter per unit area. A biomass pyramid represents the amount of potential food available for each trophic level in an ecosystem.

BIO INSIGHTS **BIOLOGY UPDATE**

The rule of 10
The textbook's discussion of energy pyramids states that only about 10 percent of the energy available at each trophic level in a food chain is transferred to organisms at the next higher trophic level. This "rule of 10," which was based on early studies of aquatic ecosystems, is useful as a general approximation. However, it does not apply uniformly to all food chains.

More recent studies have demonstrated that energy efficiency varies between trophic levels in a food chain and between different food chains. In fact, these recent studies have yielded approximations of energy efficiency ranging from a low of 0.05 percent to a high of 20 percent.

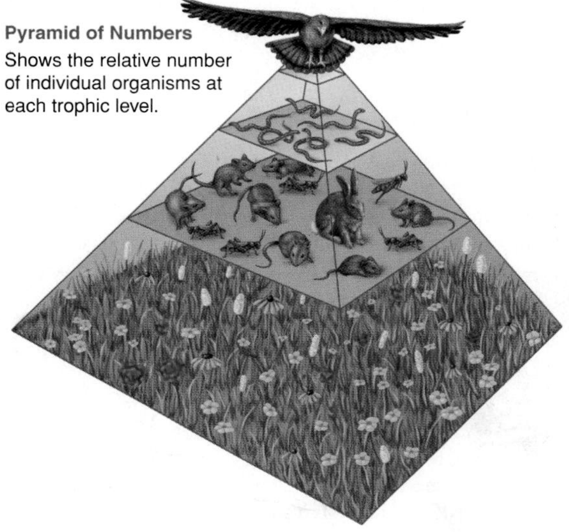

Pyramid of Numbers
Shows the relative number of individual organisms at each trophic level.

◀ **Figure 3–9** Ecological pyramids show the decreasing amounts of energy, living tissue, or number of organisms at successive feeding levels. The pyramid is divided into sections that represent each trophic level. The area of each level symbolizes the amount of energy or matter remaining at that level. **Because each trophic level harvests only about one tenth of the energy from the level below, it can support only about one tenth the amount of living tissue.**

Pyramid of Numbers Ecological pyramids can also be based on the numbers of individual organisms at each trophic level. For some ecosystems, such as the meadow shown in **Figure 3–9** above, the shape of the pyramid of numbers is the same as that of the energy and biomass pyramids. This, however, is not always the case. In most forests, for example, there are fewer producers than there are consumers. A single tree has a large amount of energy and biomass, but it is only one organism. Many insects live in the tree, but they have less energy and biomass. Thus, a pyramid of numbers for a forest ecosystem would not resemble a typical pyramid at all!

3–2 Section Assessment

1. **Key Concept** What are the two main forms of energy that power living systems?
2. **Key Concept** Briefly describe the flow of energy among organisms in an ecosystem.
3. **Key Concept** What proportion of energy is transferred from one trophic level to the next in an ecosystem?
4. Show the following as a food chain: omnivore, autotroph, herbivore.
5. **Critical Thinking Calculating** Draw an energy pyramid for a five-step food chain. If 100 percent of the energy is available at the first trophic level, what percentage of the total energy is available at the highest trophic level?

iTEXT Assessment Use iText to review the important concepts in Section 3–2.

MAKING CONNECTIONS

Characteristics of Living Things Review what you learned in Chapter 1 about an organism's needs for materials and energy. Then describe how the following organisms meet their energy needs: a caterpillar, a plant, a snake, and a fungus.

3 ASSESS

Evaluate Understanding

Have each student draw and label a food web for a specific ecosystem of his or her choice. Tell students that the web should contain at least four food chains and that each food chain should consist of at least three organisms.

Reteach

Display a list of organisms that would be found in a specific ecosystem. Call on students in turn to identify each organism as a producer or a consumer. Write *P* or *C* next to each organism's name. Then, have students further classify each consumer as an herbivore, carnivore, or omnivore; write *H, C,* or *O* next to each name. As a final step, have students in turn link together any three organisms—a producer, an herbivore, and a carnivore—in a food chain.

MAKING CONNECTIONS

A caterpillar obtains energy and materials by eating plants. A plant obtains energy and synthesizes carbohydrates through photosynthesis. A snake obtains energy and materials by eating other animals. A fungus may obtain energy from the decaying remains of other organisms.

Use iText to review the key concepts in Section 3–2.

3–2 Section Assessment

1. Solar energy is harnessed by autotrophs that conduct photosynthesis. Chemical energy—the energy within the chemical bonds of inorganic molecules—is harnessed by autotrophs that conduct chemosynthesis.
2. Students should describe a one-way flow of energy from autotrophs (producers) to consumers—first herbivores, then carnivores and/or omnivores.
3. In general, about 10 percent
4. Autotroph→herbivore→omnivore
5. Students' pyramids should show 100 percent of the energy available at the first (producer) level, 10 percent at the second level, 1 percent at the third level, 0.1 percent at the fourth level, and 0.01 percent at the fifth level.

Section 3–3

1 FOCUS

Objectives

3.3.1 ***Describe*** how matter cycles among the living and nonliving parts of an ecosystem.
3.3.2 ***Explain*** how nutrients are important in living systems.
3.3.3 ***Describe*** how the availability of nutrients affects the productivity of ecosystems.

Guide for Reading

Vocabulary Preview

Figure 3–11, page 75, introduces seven vocabulary terms. Two of the terms, *evaporation* and *transpiration*, are explicitly defined in the text. The meanings of the remaining five terms—*condensation, precipitation, runoff, seepage*, and *uptake*—can be inferred from their context. As students read about the water cycle on page 75, have them look for sentences that relate to the terms and copy them on a sheet of paper. Finally, using the sentences they copied as a basis, students can extrapolate a "formal" definition for each term. Have students share their definitions in a class discussion.

Reading Strategy

Have students make their own simplified cycle diagrams of the water cycle, carbon cycle, nitrogen cycle, and phosphorus cycle.

2 INSTRUCT

Recycling in the Biosphere

Build Science Skills

Inferring After students have read Recycling in the Biosphere, point out the sentence that begins *You are soon swallowed by a dung beetle. . . .* Ask: **How can a molecule that's swallowed by a dung beetle "combine into"—or become part of—the body tissue of a tree shrew and then an owl?** *(The tree shrew takes in the molecule when it eats the dung beetle, then an owl takes in the molecule when it eats the tree shrew.)*

3–3 Cycles of Matter

Guide for Reading

Key Concepts
- How does matter move among the living and nonliving parts of an ecosystem?
- How are nutrients important in living systems?

Vocabulary
biogeochemical cycle
evaporation
transpiration
nutrient
nitrogen fixation
denitrification
primary productivity
limiting nutrient
algal bloom

Reading Strategy: Using Visuals Before you read, preview the cycles shown in **Figures 3–11, 3–13, 3–14,** and **3–15.** Notice how each diagram is similar to or different from the others. As you read, take notes on how each chemical moves through the biosphere.

Energy is crucial to an ecosystem. But all organisms need more than energy to survive. They also need water, minerals, and other life-sustaining compounds. In most organisms, more than 95 percent of the body is made up of just four elements: oxygen, carbon, hydrogen, and nitrogen. Although these four elements are common on Earth, organisms cannot use them unless the elements are in a chemical form that cells can take up.

Recycling in the Biosphere

Energy and matter move through the biosphere very differently. **Unlike the one-way flow of energy, matter is recycled within and between ecosystems.** Elements, chemical compounds, and other forms of matter are passed from one organism to another and from one part of the biosphere to another through **biogeochemical cycles.** As the long word suggests, biogeochemical cycles connect *bio*logical, *geo*logical, and *chemi*cal aspects of the biosphere.

Matter can cycle through the biosphere because biological systems do not use up matter, they transform it. The matter is assembled into living tissue or passed out of the body as waste products. Imagine, for a moment, that you are a carbon atom in a molecule of carbon dioxide floating in the air of a lowland marsh like the one in **Figure 3–10.** The leaf of a blueberry bush absorbs you during photosynthesis. You become part of a carbohydrate molecule and are used to make fruit. The fruit is eaten by a caribou, and within a few hours, you are passed out of the animal's body. You are soon swallowed by a dung beetle, then combined into the body tissue of a hungry shrew, which is then eaten by an owl. Finally, you are released into the atmosphere once again when the owl exhales. Then, the cycle starts again.

Simply put, biogeochemical cycles pass the same molecules around again and again within the biosphere. Just think—with every breath you take, you inhale hundreds of thousands of oxygen atoms that might have been inhaled by dinosaurs millions of years ago!

▼ **Figure 3–10** **Matter moves through an ecosystem in biogeochemical cycles.** In this Alaskan wetland, matter is recycled through the air, the shrubs, the pond, and the caribou—as it is used, transformed, moved, and reused.

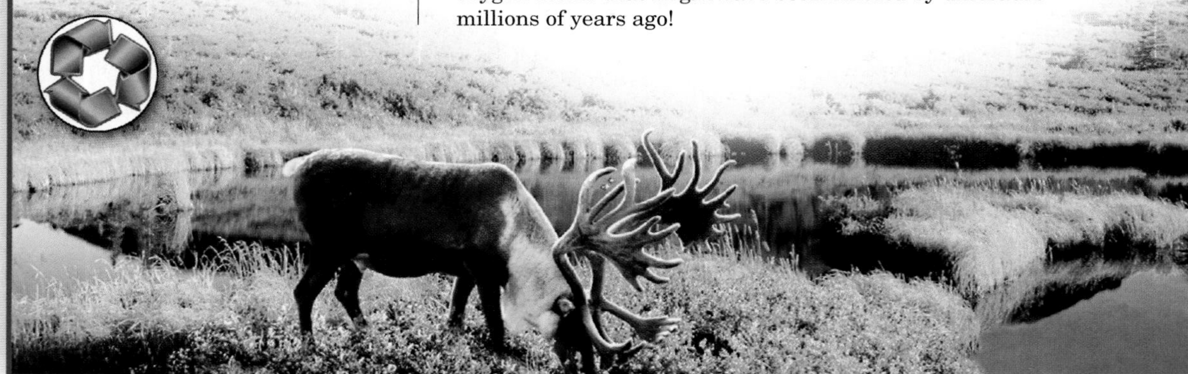

SECTION RESOURCES

Print:
- ***Laboratory Manual A,*** Chapter 3 Lab
- ***Laboratory Manual B,*** Chapter 3 Lab
- ***Teaching Resources,*** Section Review 3–3, Chapter 3 Exploration
- ***Guided Reading and Study Workbook,*** Section 3–3
- ***Issues and Decision Making,*** 3–1

Technology
- ***BioDetectives Videotape,*** *Pfiesteria:* A Killer in the Water
- ***iText,*** Section 3–3

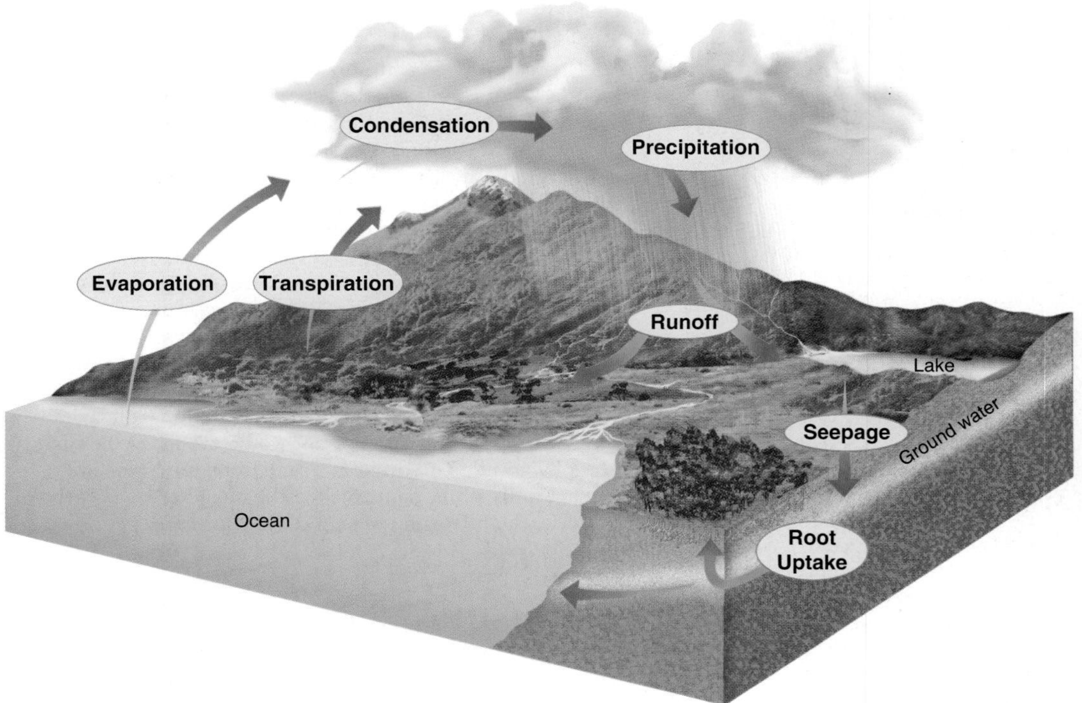

▲ **Figure 3–11** This diagram shows the main processes involved in the water cycle. Scientists estimate that it can take a single water molecule as long as 4000 years to complete one cycle. **Interpreting Graphics** ***What happens to the water that evaporates from oceans and lakes?***

The Water Cycle

All living things require water to survive. Where does all this water come from? It moves between the ocean, atmosphere, and land. As **Figure 3–11** shows, water molecules enter the atmosphere as water vapor, a gas, when they evaporate from the ocean or other bodies of water. The process by which water changes from liquid form to an atmospheric gas is called **evaporation** (ee-vap-uh-RAY-shun). Water can also enter the atmosphere by evaporating from the leaves of plants in the process of **transpiration** (trans-puh-RAY-shun).

During the day, the sun heats the atmosphere. As the warm, moist air rises, it cools. Eventually, the water vapor condenses into tiny droplets that form clouds. When the droplets become large enough, the water returns to Earth's surface in the form of precipitation—rain, snow, sleet, or hail.

On land, much of the precipitation runs along the surface of the ground until it enters a river or stream that carries the runoff back to an ocean or lake. Rain also seeps into the soil, some of it deeply enough to become ground water. Water in the soil enters plants through the roots, and the water cycle begins anew.

CHECKPOINT *How are evaporation and transpiration related?*

The Water Cycle

Meet Diverse Needs

Students with limited English proficiency may be unfamiliar with some of the terms used in Figure 3–11 and in the text description of the water cycle. Call on different students in turn to read aloud each sentence or set of sentences in the text that describes one process in the water cycle. (For example, the first two sentences in the second paragraph describe evaporation. The first, second, and third sentences in the second paragraph describe condensation.) After each process's text is read aloud, have students find that stage in Figure 3–11 and rephrase the text in their own words, either in writing or in an oral discussion. **Limited English proficiency**

Build Science Skills

Comparing and Contrasting Emphasize that transpiration by plants releases water vapor, a gas, into the air, not liquid water. Ask: **What process in humans and other mammals also releases water vapor into the air?** *(Respiration)* **How are transpiration in plants and respiration in mammals different?** *(Sample answer: Mammals have specialized organs that are involved in respiration—the lungs, diaphragm, bronchial tubes, and so forth—but plants do not have "breathing" organs.)*

PRESENTATIONS MADE EASY!

The Presentation Assistant Plus contains the Prentice Hall Presentation Pro and the Transparencies, which provide easy-to-follow visual support for every step of this section. If you have a computer presentation station, use Prentice Hall Presentation Pro for Section 3–3, or use the transparencies listed here.

Section 3–3:

Interest Grabber
Section Outline
Ecological Pyramids
Figure 3–13
Figure 3–14

Answers to . . .

CHECKPOINT *Evaporation is part of the process of transpiration.*

Figure 3–11 *The water vapor rises into the atmosphere, then cools and condenses to form clouds.*

Nutrient Cycles

Make Connections

Health Science For each pair of students, provide an empty vitamin container with its nutrition label intact. Try to provide a mix of vitamins for adults, for young children, and for infants. (You may want to ask students in advance to bring in containers from home.) Ask: **What types of information are given on the nutrition label?** *(The serving size, the total number of servings in the container, the specific nutrients in the pills or drops, the amount of each nutrient in one serving, and the percentage of daily value each amount represents.)* **What do you think a "daily value" is?** *(How much of a nutrient a person should take in each day)* **What does "percentage of daily value" mean?** *(How much of the daily value is in one serving of the vitamin)* Ask students if they recognize the names of any of the nutrients listed on the label and whether they know the nutrients' common dietary sources and their functions in maintaining good health. Depending on the extent of students' knowledge, you may want to suggest that they research this information and share their findings in posters or brief oral presentations.

▲ **Figure 3–12 Like all living organisms, the owl monkey needs nutrients to build tissues and carry out essential life functions.** This monkey, which is found in Central and South America, obtains most of its nutrients by eating plants.

Nutrient Cycles

The food you eat contains energy, but it also contains important chemicals that sustain you. Together, all the chemical substances that an organism, like the owl monkey in **Figure 3–12,** requires to live are called **nutrients.** You can think of nutrients as the body's building blocks.

Every living organism needs nutrients to build tissues and carry out essential life functions. Like water, nutrients are passed between organisms and the environment through biogeochemical cycles. In many ecosystems, nutrients are often in short supply. Thus, recycling nutrients is essential for these ecosystems to keep functioning. Nutrient cycling also prevents many chemicals from reaching concentrations that would otherwise be toxic, or harmful, to organisms. Three nutrient cycles play especially prominent roles in the biosphere: the carbon cycle, the nitrogen cycle, and the phosphorus cycle.

CHECKPOINT *What is a nutrient?*

The Carbon Cycle Carbon is especially important to living systems because it is the key ingredient in all living organisms. Carbon is also found in the oceans, in the air, and in certain types of rocks. However, of all the carbon on Earth, less than 1 percent actively circulates within the biosphere.

Like water, carbon cycles between the various components of the biosphere. There are four different kinds of processes involved in the carbon cycle:

- biological processes, such as photosynthesis, respiration, and decomposition of plants and animals;
- geochemical processes, such as the release of carbon dioxide (CO_2) gas to the atmosphere by volcanoes;
- mixed biogeochemical processes, such as the burial of carbon-rich remains of organisms and their conversion into coal and petroleum (fossil fuels) by the pressure of the overlying earth; and
- human activity, including mining, the burning of fossil fuels, and the cutting and burning of forests.

Scientists identified these processes decades ago. Now we face an urgent need to know more about them. For example, how much carbon is released into the atmosphere by human activity? How do other components of the carbon cycle respond to changes in atmospheric carbon levels? What is the capacity of the ocean to absorb excess carbon dioxide? You will learn more about the effects of human activity on the carbon cycle later in this unit.

FACTS AND FIGURES

The rain in Spain, and elsewhere
Huge quantities of water cycle between Earth's surface and atmosphere. Hydrologists estimate that about 390,000 cubic kilometers of water evaporate from Earth's surface and enter the atmosphere each year.

Viewed globally, precipitation falls fairly evenly on Earth's surface. Considering all forms of precipitation, about 77 percent falls on oceans and about 23 percent on land. However, this same proportion does not hold true for water that evaporates from Earth's surface: 84 percent of the water in the atmosphere comes from oceans and only 16 percent from land. The reason for the difference in proportions is simple: about 7 percent of the precipitation that falls on land runs off into streams and rivers and is carried to oceans.

Figure 3–13 shows how these processes move carbon through the biosphere. In the atmosphere, carbon is present as carbon dioxide gas. Carbon dioxide is released into the atmosphere by volcanic activity, by respiration, by human activities such as the burning of fossil fuels, and by the decomposition of organic matter. Plants take in carbon dioxide and use the carbon to build carbohydrates during photosynthesis. The carbohydrates are passed along food webs to animals and other consumers. In the ocean, carbon is also found, along with calcium and oxygen, in calcium carbonate, which is formed by many marine organisms. Calcium carbonate can also be formed chemically in certain marine environments. This chalky, carbon-based compound accumulates in marine sediments and in the bones and shells of organisms. Eventually these compounds break down and the carbon returns to the atmosphere.

▼ **Figure 3–13** Carbon is found in several large reservoirs in the biosphere. In the atmosphere, it is found as carbon dioxide gas; in the oceans as dissolved carbon dioxide; on land in organisms, rocks, and soil; and underground as coal, petroleum, and calcium carbonate rock. **Interpreting Graphics** ***What are the main sources of carbon dioxide in the ocean?***

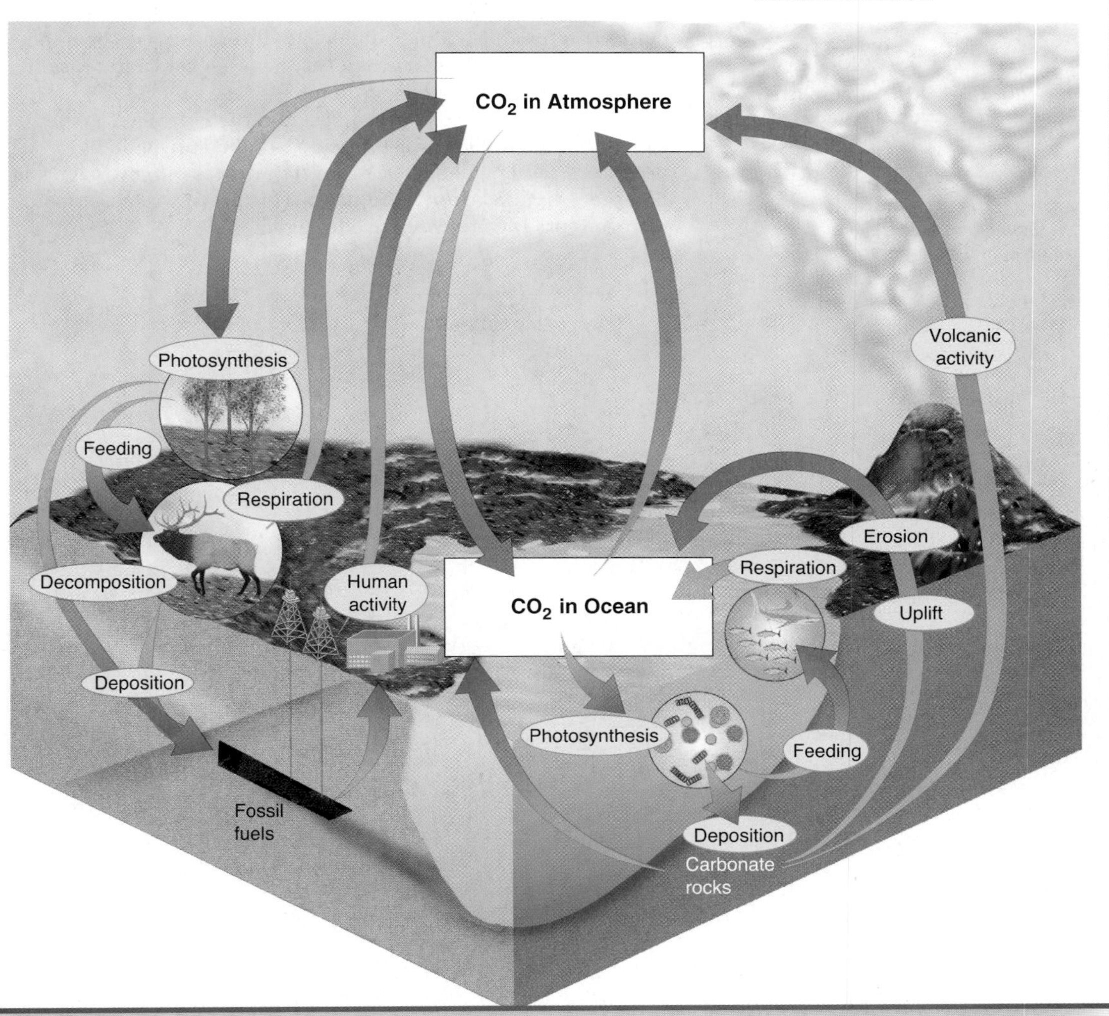

Use Visuals

Figure 3–13 Call on different students in turn to "translate" the diagram's pictures, labels, and arrows into complete, descriptive sentences. For example, the circled picture of trees, the arrows, and the *Photosynthesis* label on the left side of the diagram can be expressed as, "During photosynthesis, plants take in carbon dioxide from the atmosphere and release oxygen." The circled picture of the elk with two arrows can be translated as, "During respiration, animals take in oxygen given off by plants and release carbon dioxide into the atmosphere," and, "When animals die and decompose, carbon is released into the soil." Continue until all the processes in both pathways have been described this way.

BIO INSIGHTS

FACTS AND FIGURES

The carbon pool

Scientists estimate the biosphere's total carbon pool to be approximately 49,000 metric gigatons. (1 metric gigaton equals 10^9 metric tons.) Of that total, 71 percent is contained in Earth's oceans, mainly in the form of carbonate and bicarbonate ions. Fossil carbon comprises 22 percent of the total pool. An additional 3 percent is contained in dead organic matter and phytoplankton, and another 3 percent is held in terrestrial ecosystems. The remaining 1 percent is held in the atmosphere, circulated, and used in photosynthesis.

The carbon that is contained in organic molecules—such as the wood in trees—may not be recycled back to the abiotic environment for several hundred years or even longer. Carbon compounds found in coal that formed from ancient trees, for example, are the products of photosynthesis that occurred millions of years ago.

Answers to . . .

CHECKPOINT *Any chemical substance that an organism requires to live*

Figure 3–13 *Respiration by ocean animals, precipitation containing dissolved carbon dioxide, erosion of carbonate rocks formed from the skeletons of ocean organisms such as corals*

Make Connections

Chemistry Write the chemical formulas for atmospheric nitrogen (N_2), ammonia (NH_3), the nitrate ion (NO_3^-), and the nitrite ion (NO_2^-) on the board. Ask students: **Which element is symbolized by each letter in these formulas?** *(N is the symbol for nitrogen; H for hydrogen, and O for oxygen.)* **What do the small numbers mean?** *(The small numbers tell how many atoms of the element are in one molecule or ion of the substance.)* **What atoms make up one molecule of atmospheric nitrogen?** *(Two atoms of nitrogen)* **One molecule of ammonia?** *(One atom of nitrogen and three atoms of hydrogen)* **The nitrate ion?** *(One atom of nitrogen and three atoms of oxygen)* **The nitrite ion?** *(One atom of nitrogen and two atoms of oxygen)*

Meet Diverse Needs

Students who learn best by handling materials would benefit from making models of the four chemical formulas of the different forms of nitrogen. Provide a variety of materials, and let each student choose the type of model to make. For example, two-dimensional models could be made with circles cut from colored construction paper and glued to a larger sheet. Three-dimensional models could be made with clay balls of different colors held together with toothpicks. Students can use their models as they study the nitrogen cycle in Figure 3–14. **Learning modality: tactile**

Use Visuals

Figure 3–14 The "translation" procedure described on page T77 for Figure 3–13 would also work well with this diagram. For example, the part of the diagram that illustrates nitrogen fixation by bacteria could be described as, "In nitrogen fixation, bacteria in the soil and on plant roots change atmospheric nitrogen into ammonia."

The Nitrogen Cycle All organisms require nitrogen to make amino acids, which in turn are used to build proteins. Many different forms of nitrogen occur naturally in the biosphere. Nitrogen gas (N_2) makes up 78 percent of Earth's atmosphere. Nitrogen-containing substances such as ammonia (NH_3), nitrate ions (NO_3^-), and nitrite ions (NO_2^-) are found in the wastes produced by many organisms and in dead and decaying organic matter. Nitrogen also exists in several forms in the ocean and other large water bodies. Human activity adds nitrogen to the biosphere in the form of nitrate—a major component of plant fertilizers.

Figure 3–14 shows how the different forms of nitrogen cycle through the biosphere. Although nitrogen gas is the most abundant form of nitrogen on Earth, only certain types of bacteria can use this form directly. Such bacteria, which live in the soil and on the roots of plants called legumes, convert nitrogen gas into ammonia in a process known as **nitrogen fixation.** Other bacteria in the soil convert ammonia into nitrates and nitrites. Once these products are available, producers can use them to make proteins. Consumers then eat the producers and reuse the nitrogen to make their own proteins.

When organisms die, decomposers return nitrogen to the soil as ammonia. The ammonia may be taken up again by producers. Other soil bacteria convert nitrates into nitrogen gas in a process called **denitrification.** This process releases nitrogen into the atmosphere once again.

▼ **Figure 3–14** The atmosphere is the main reservoir of nitrogen in the biosphere. Nitrogen also cycles through the soil and through the tissues of living organisms. **Interpreting Graphics** *What are the main nitrogen-containing nutrients in the biosphere?*

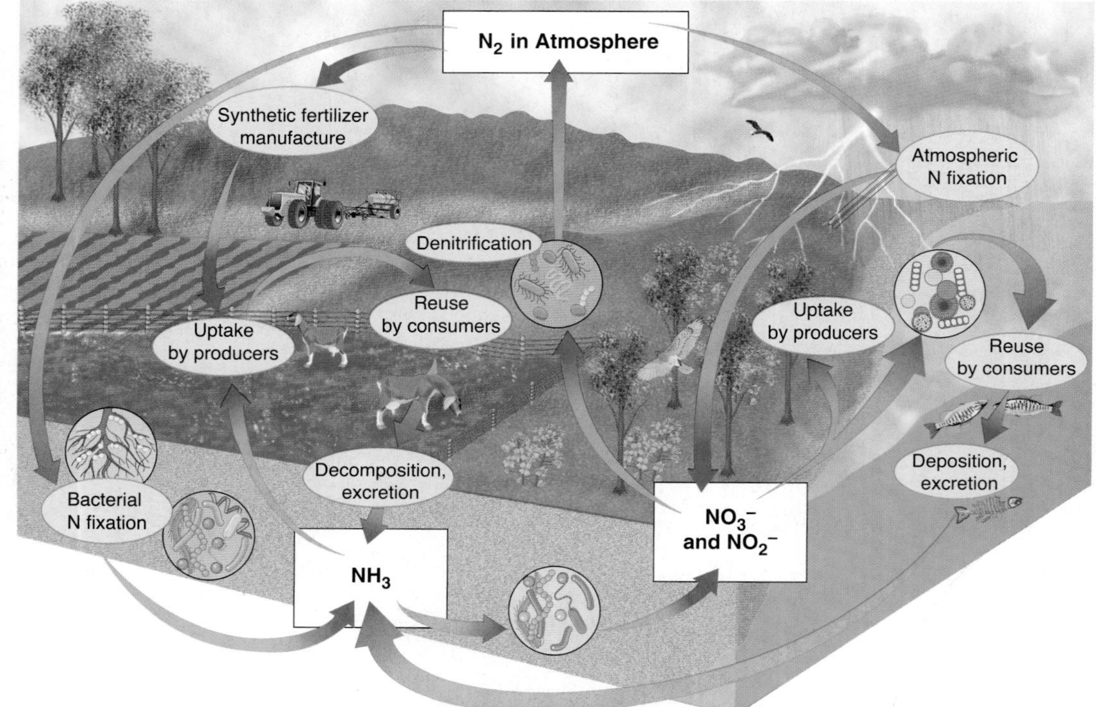

BIO INSIGHTS — FACTS AND FIGURES

The scarcity of nitrogen

Although about 80 percent of the air surrounding Earth is nitrogen gas (N_2), usable forms of the element are scarce in ecosystems. The reason for this is that the two atoms in atmospheric nitrogen are held together by triple covalent bonds that only lightning, volcanic action, and certain bacteria can break. In addition, the ammonia, nitrite, and nitrate formed by nitrifying bacteria are very susceptible to leaching and runoff, which carry away nitrogen dissolved in the water.

Nitrifying bacteria use nitrogenase, an enzyme, to break the covalent bonds in N_2 molecules. Nitrogenase functions only when it is isolated from oxygen. On land, nitrogen-fixing bacteria accomplish this by living inside oxygen-excluding nodules or layers of insulating slime on plant roots. In aquatic ecosystems, cyanobacteria—the primary nitrogen-fixers—have specialized cells called heterocysts that exclude oxygen.

Analyzing Data

Farming in the Rye

Rye and other grasses are able to grow fairly well in nutrient-poor soils. Sometimes, farmers grow crops of rye grass and then plow them under the soil to decay. This practice helps to increase crop yields of other plants. Farmers may also plow under legumes such as peas, vetch, and lentils. Legumes are plants that have colonies of nitrogen-fixing bacteria living in nodules on the plant roots.

In an effort to determine which practice produces the best crop yields, scientists performed an experiment in Georgia. They grew corn on land that had previously received one of five treatments. Three fields had previously been planted with three different legumes. A fourth field had been planted with rye grass. The fifth field was left bare before the corn was planted. None of the fields received fertilizer while the corn was growing. The table shows how much corn was produced per hectare of land (kg/ha) in each field. One hectare is equivalent to 10,000 square meters.

Corn Production

Previous Crop	Average Yield of Corn (kg/ha)
Monantha vetch	2876
Hairy vetch	2870
Austrian peas	3159
Rye grass	1922
None	1959

1. **Using Tables and Graphs** Use the data in the table to create a bar graph.
2. **Comparing and Contrasting** Compare the effect of growing legumes to that of growing grass on the yield of corn. How do the yields differ from the yield on the field that had received no prior treatment?
3. **Analyzing Data** Which treatment produced the best yield of corn? The worst yield?
4. **Applying Concepts** Based on your knowledge of the nitrogen cycle, how can you explain these results?

The Phosphorus Cycle Phosphorus is essential to living organisms because it forms part of important life-sustaining molecules such as DNA and RNA. Although phosphorus is of great biological importance, it is not very common in the biosphere. Unlike carbon, oxygen, and nitrogen, phosphorus does not enter the atmosphere. Instead, phosphorus remains mostly on land in rock and soil minerals, and in ocean sediments. There, phosphorus exists in the form of inorganic phosphate. As the rocks and sediments gradually wear down, phosphate is released. On land, some of the phosphate washes into rivers and streams, where it dissolves. The phosphate eventually makes its way to the oceans, where it is used by marine organisms.

As **Figure 3–15** shows, some phosphate stays on land and cycles between organisms and the soil. When plants absorb phosphate from the soil or from water, the plants bind the phosphate into organic compounds. Organic phosphate moves through the food web, from producers to consumers, and to the rest of the ecosystem.

CHECKPOINT *Where is most of the phosphorus stored in the biosphere?*

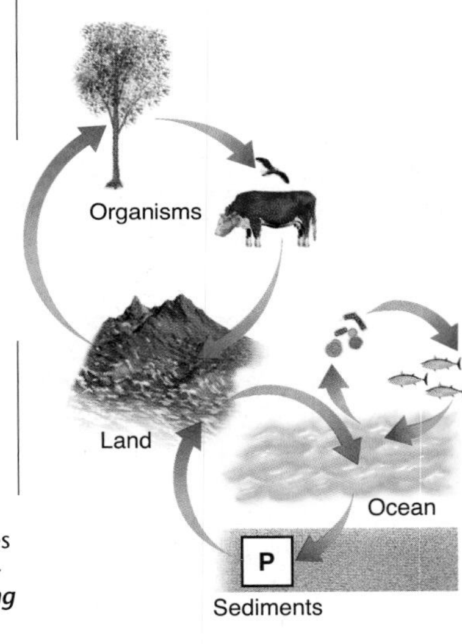

▶ **Figure 3–15** Phosphorus in the biosphere cycles among the land, ocean sediments, and living organisms. **Inferring** *How is phosphorus important to living organisms?*

Analyzing Data

Help students understand the experiment procedure by asking: **Why was fifth field left bare?** *(It was the control in the experiment. If the corn in the fifth field grew as well as or better than the corn in any of the other fields, the researchers would know that the previous year's plantings in those other fields did not increase corn productivity.)*

Answers

1. Students could plot plant names on the vertical axis and yields on the horizontal axis; use different increments for the yield axis; and/or arrange the crops in sequence from highest to lowest yield or from lowest to highest.
2. Growing legumes the previous year significantly increased the crop yields. Growing rye did not increase yields. In fact, the bare field's yield was slightly higher than the field planted with rye.
3. The legumes—particularly the Austrian peas—produced the highest yields. Rye produced the lowest yield.
4. The corn plants benefitted greatly when the soil was enriched with nitrogen fixed by legumes the previous year.

Build Science Skills

Comparing and Contrasting Point out the terms *inorganic* and *organic* in the description of the phosphorus cycle. Encourage students to consult science dictionaries and chemistry textbooks to determine the difference between organic and inorganic compounds and report their findings to the rest of the class. (See Facts and Figures below.)

BIO INSIGHTS — FACTS AND FIGURES

What makes a compound organic?

Organic compounds are often defined simply as compounds that contain carbon. However, not all carbon-containing compounds are considered organic. Carbon dioxide and hydrocarbons such as methane and propane are prime examples of carbon compounds that are not organic. A more precise definition of an organic compound is: a compound that contains carbon and is constructed in living cells.

A carbon atom has four electrons in its outer shell—but the shell is capable of holding eight electrons. For this reason, a carbon atom can form covalent bonds with as many as four atoms of other elements. Carbon atoms are usually joined together in a ring or chain that forms a stable "backbone" for building molecules. Such structures are not present in simple inorganic compounds such as carbon dioxide.

Answers to . . .

CHECKPOINT *In rock and soil minerals and in ocean sediments*

Figure 3–14 *Ammonia, nitrate, and nitrite*

Figure 3–15 *Phosphorous is part of energy-producing and life-sustaining molecules in living organisms.*

3–3 (continued)

Nutrient Limitation

Build Science Skills

Making Judgments Call attention to the paragraph about farmers' use of fertilizers. Ask: **How might the use of fertilizers harm ecosystems nearby?** *(Runoff from the fields could carry fertilizers to bodies of water and cause algal blooms there.)* Have students discuss the pros and cons of fertilizer use. Then, let two teams debate the issue.

3 ASSESS

Evaluate Understanding

Make one photocopy of Figure 3–11 (the water cycle), Figure 3–13 (the carbon cycle), and Figure 3–14 (the nitrogen cycle). Cover the diagrams' labels with white tape, and then use these "masters" to make a set of copies for students to add labels.

Reteach

Have each student write a brief description of each cycle discussed in the section referring to Figures 3–11, 3–13, 3–14, and 3–15. Let students share their work in a class discussion and correct any errors or omissions in one another's descriptions.

ALTERNATIVE ASSESSMENT

Students' reports should focus on the problem of algae blooms. Excess phosphorus stimulates explosive growth of algae, which die and are consumed by bacteria. This process depletes oxygen in the water, killing aquatic organisms.

Use iText to review the key concepts in Section 3–3.

Answer to . . .

Figure 3–16 *Bacteria in a lake consume dead algae and deplete oxygen in the lake just as excess food in a fish tank is consumed by bacteria that deplete oxygen in the water.*

▲ **Figure 3–16** When an aquatic ecosystem receives a large input of a limiting nutrient, the result is often an increase in the number of producers. Here, an extensive algal bloom covers the shoreline of Tule Lake in California. **Using Analogies** *How is this situation similar to the one that occurs in a fish tank in which the fish have been overfed?*

Nutrient Limitation

Ecologists are often interested in the **primary productivity** of an ecosystem, which is the rate at which organic matter is created by producers. One factor that controls the primary productivity of an ecosystem is the amount of available nutrients. If a nutrient is in short supply, it will limit an organism's growth. When an ecosystem is limited by a single nutrient that is scarce or cycles very slowly, this substance is called a **limiting nutrient.**

Farmers, who are well aware of this phenomenon, apply fertilizers to their crops to boost their productivity. Fertilizers usually contain three important nutrients—nitrogen, phosphorus, and potassium. These nutrients help plants grow larger and more quickly than they would in unfertilized soil.

The open oceans of the world can be considered nutrient-poor environments compared to the land. Sea water contains at most only 0.00005 percent nitrogen, or 1/10,000 of the amount typically found in soil. In the ocean and other saltwater environments, nitrogen is often the limiting nutrient. In some areas of the ocean, however, silica or even iron can be the limiting nutrient. In streams, lakes, and freshwater environments, phosphorus is typically the limiting nutrient.

When an aquatic ecosystem receives a large input of a limiting nutrient—for example, runoff from heavily fertilized fields—the result is often an immediate increase in the amount of algae and other producers. This result is called an **algal bloom**. Why do algal blooms occur? There are more nutrients available, so the producers can grow and reproduce more quickly. If there are not enough consumers to eat the excess algae, conditions can become so favorable for growth that algae cover the surface of the water. Algal blooms, like the one shown in **Figure 3–16,** can sometimes upset the health of an ecosystem.

3–3 Section Assessment

1. **Key Concept** How does the way that matter flows through an ecosystem differ from the way that energy flows?
2. **Key Concept** Why do living organisms need nutrients?
3. Describe the path of nitrogen through its biogeochemical cycle.
4. Explain how a nutrient can be a limiting factor in an ecosystem.
5. **Critical Thinking Predicting** Based on your knowledge of the carbon cycle, what do you think might happen if vast areas of forests are cleared?

iTEXT **Assessment** Use iText to review the important concepts in Section 3–3.

ALTERNATIVE ASSESSMENT

Writing a Report
Use library materials or the Internet to research the problems of excess phosphorus in freshwater ecosystems. Write a short report, illustrated by a drawing or photograph, about the effect of excess phosphorus on a lake, stream, or river.

3–3 Section Assessment

1. Energy flows just one way through an ecosystem: from producers to consumers. Matter moves through the water, carbon, nitrogen, and phosphorous cycles.
2. Organisms need nutrients to build tissues and carry out essential life functions.
3. Bacteria in the soil and on plant roots convert atmospheric nitrogen into ammonia. Other soil bacteria then convert the ammonia to nitrates and nitrites, which are taken in by producers and then by consumers that eat the producers. Decomposers convert the nitrogen in animal wastes and dead organisms into ammonia. Soil bacteria break down the nitrates and nitrites into nitrogen gas, which are released into the atmosphere.
4. A nutrient in short supply limits the growth of organisms and ecosystem productivity.
5. Less carbon dioxide would be removed from the atmosphere by plants.

Real-World Lab

Identifying a Limiting Nutrient

Limiting nutrients control the growth of organisms in many ecosystems. Excess nutrients can promote the growth of weeds, disease-causing bacteria, and other undesirable organisms. In this investigation, you will determine whether phosphate is a limiting nutrient for the growth of algae.

Problem Does the supply of phosphate limit the growth of algae?

Materials

- dropper pipette
- algae culture
- 2 test tubes with stoppers
- test-tube rack
- 50-mL graduated cylinder
- pond water
- glass-marking pencil
- 10% trisodium phosphate solution

Skills Formulating Hypotheses, Predicting

Procedure     

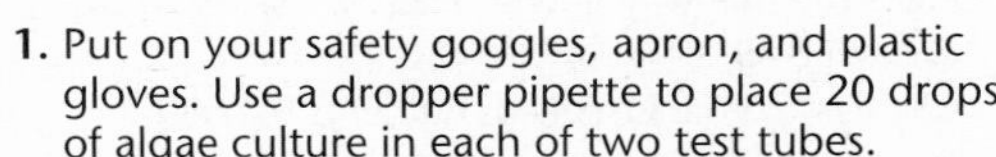
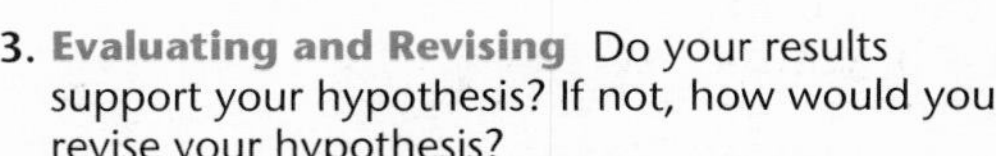

1. Put on your safety goggles, apron, and plastic gloves. Use a dropper pipette to place 20 drops of algae culture in each of two test tubes.
2. Use a 30-mL graduated cylinder to add 19 mL of pond water to each test tube.
3. Use the glass-marking pencil to label one test tube "control" and the other test tube "phosphate." Use a dropper pipette to add 2 drops of trisodium phosphate to the "phosphate" test tube. **CAUTION:** *Trisodium phosphate can injure your skin. Do not get it on your skin or touch your face after handling it.*
4. Stopper both test tubes and place them in a sunny place.
5. **Formulating Hypotheses** Record your hypothesis of how phosphate will affect the growth of the algae if it is a limiting nutrient. Also, record your prediction of how the two test tubes will appear after 7 days.
6. Observe the two test tubes each day for the next week. Record your observations each day, including a labeled sketch of each test tube.

Analyze and Conclude

1. **Observing** How did the added phosphate affect the growth of the algae?
2. **Drawing Conclusions** Do your results indicate that phosphate is a limiting nutrient for algae?
3. **Evaluating and Revising** Do your results support your hypothesis? If not, how would you revise your hypothesis?
4. **Predicting** Some detergents are labeled as environmentally safe because they contain little or no phosphate. What might you expect to see in a river or lake that contains high levels of phosphate detergents?

Go Further

Designing Experiments Select another nutrient and design an experiment to determine whether it is a limiting nutrient for the growth of algae. With your teacher's permission, conduct the experiment and share your findings with the class.

To find out more about how scientists investigate algal blooms, view the videotape "*Pfiesteria:* A Killer in the Water."

Analyze and Conclude

1. The phosphate greatly increased algae growth.
2. Yes.
3. Answers will vary depending on students' hypotheses.
4. Water that contains high levels of phosphate detergents would have algae blooms.

Encourage students to view the Bio Detectives videotape entitled, "*Pfiesteria:* A Killer in the Water."

Real-World Lab

Objective Students will be able to determine that the supply of phosphate is a limiting factor in the growth of algae.

Skills Focus **Formulating Hypotheses, Predicting**

Time 15 minutes for initial setup; follow-up of 5 minutes each day for 7 days to observe and record

Advance Prep

- Obtain a culture of *Chlorella.* Within four days, this alga will show more visible growth with phosphate than would other algae species such as *Spirogyra* or *Chlamydomonas.*
- **CAUTION:** Wear goggles, plastic gloves, and a lab apron while preparing the trisodium phosphate solution. In a beaker, completely dissolve 10 g of trisodium phosphate in about 80 mL of distilled or deionized water (*not* tap water). Transfer the solution to a 100-mL graduated cylinder and add enough water to bring the total to 100 mL.

Safety Make sure that students wear plastic gloves, goggles, and lab apron when handling the trisodium phosphate solution. Properly dispose of chemicals.

Pre-Lab Discussion
Ask students to describe what a limiting nutrient is in their own words. Then, have students read the complete procedure.

Teaching Tips

- Dispense the trisodium phosphate solution to students in small dropper bottles.
- Tell students to label the pair of test tubes with their initials so they can readily identify them.

Procedure
5. Sample hypothesis: The added phosphate will cause the algae in that test tube to grow more rapidly than the algae in the test tube without added phosphate. Sample prediction: The test tube with added phosphate will have more algae in it than the other test tube.

Expected Outcome The liquid in the test tube with added phosphate should be significantly cloudier and greener than the liquid in the test tube without added phosphate.

Chapter 3 Study Guide

Study Tip

For each section of the chapter, have students read the Key Concepts that are listed. Then have them review the chapter text for any concepts that they do not fully understand. Next, students can define each vocabulary term in their own words and check their definitions against the text's definitions. Tell students that when they check the text, they should read all the related text, not just the sentence that defines the boldfaced vocabulary term.

Thinking Visually

1. Autotroph (or Producer)
2. Consumer (or Carnivore)
3. Decomposer

Chapter 3 Assessment

Reviewing Content

1. c	**5.** c	**9.** d
2. b	**6.** c	**10.** d
3. c	**7.** a	
4. b	**8.** d	

Understanding Concepts

11. The scientific study of interactions among organisms and between organisms and their environment

12. Individual organism, population, community, ecosystem, biome, biosphere

13. Scientists use models to gain insight into ecological changes that are too complex or too long-range to study directly.

14. Sunlight is the ultimate source of energy in most ecosystems.

15. The process in which producers use chemical energy to produce carbohydrates

16. Autotrophs, such as plants, make their own food using the energy in sunlight or chemical bonds. Heterotrophs, such as animals, must rely on other organisms for energy and food.

17. A heterotroph that breaks down organic matter; bacteria, fungi

18. Autotrophs (producers)

Chapter 3 Study Guide

3–1 What Is Ecology?

Key Concepts

- To understand the various relationships within the biosphere, ecologists ask questions about events and organisms that range in complexity from a single individual to a population, community, ecosystem, or biome, or to the entire biosphere.
- Scientists conduct modern ecological research according to three basic approaches: observing, experimenting, and modeling. All of these approaches rely on the application of scientific methods to guide ecological inquiry.

Vocabulary

ecology, p. 63
biosphere, p. 63
species, p. 64
population, p. 64
community, p. 64
ecosystem, p. 64
biome, p. 64

3–2 Energy Flow

Key Concepts

- Sunlight is the main energy source for life on Earth. In a few ecosystems, some organisms rely on the energy stored in inorganic chemical compounds.
- Energy flows through an ecosystem in one direction, from the sun or inorganic compounds to autotrophs (producers) and then to various heterotrophs (consumers).
- Only about 10 percent of the energy available within one trophic level is transferred to organisms at the next trophic level.

Vocabulary

autotroph, p. 67
producer, p. 67
photosynthesis, p. 68
chemosynthesis, p. 68
heterotroph, p. 68
consumer, p. 68
herbivore, p. 69
carnivore, p. 69
omnivore, p. 69
detritivore, p. 69
decomposer, p. 69
food chain, p. 69
food web, p. 70
trophic level, p. 70
ecological pyramid, p. 72
biomass, p. 72

3–3 Cycles of Matter

Key Concepts

- Unlike the one-way flow of energy, matter is recycled within and between ecosystems.
- Every living organism needs nutrients to build tissues and carry out essential life functions. Like water, nutrients are passed between organisms and the environment through biogeochemical cycles.

Vocabulary

biogeochemical cycle, p. 74
evaporation, p. 75
transpiration, p. 75
nutrient, p. 76
nitrogen fixation, p. 78
denitrification, p. 78
primary productivity, p. 80
limiting nutrient, p. 80
algal bloom, p. 80

Thinking Visually

Using information from this chapter, complete the following flowchart:

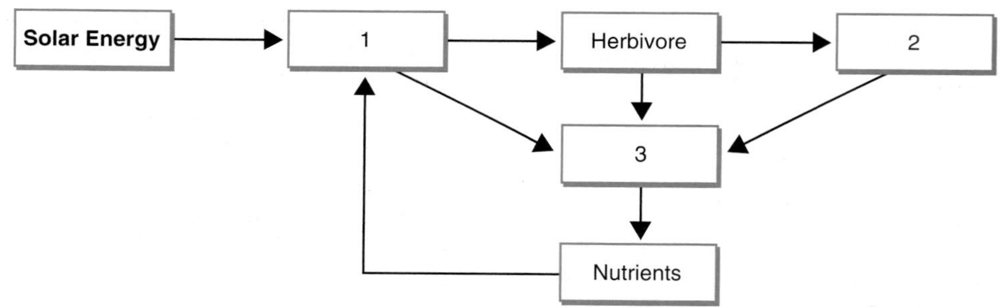

CHAPTER RESOURCES

Print:

- ***Teaching Resources,*** Chapter Vocabulary Review, Graphic Organizer
- ***Chapter Tests: Levels A and B,*** Chapter 3 Test
- ***Assessment Plus,*** Practice Test

Technology

- ***Computer Test Bank,*** Chapter 3 Test
- ***iText,*** Chapter 3 Assessment

Chapter 3 Assessment

Reviewing Content

Choose the letter that best answers the question or completes the statement.

1. All of life on Earth exists in a region known as
   a. an ecosystem.
   b. a biome.
   c. the biosphere.
   d. ecology.
2. Groups of different species that live together in a defined area make up a(an)
   a. population.
   b. community.
   c. ecosystem.
   d. biosphere.
3. Autotrophs are organisms that
   a. rely on other organisms for their energy and food supply.
   b. consume plant and animal remains and other dead matter.
   c. use energy they take in from the environment to convert inorganic molecules into complex organic molecules.
   d. obtain energy by eating only plants.
4. The series of steps in which a large fish eats a small fish that has eaten algae is a
   a. food web.
   b. food chain.
   c. pyramid of numbers.
   d. biomass pyramid.
5. Which of the following organisms is a decomposer?

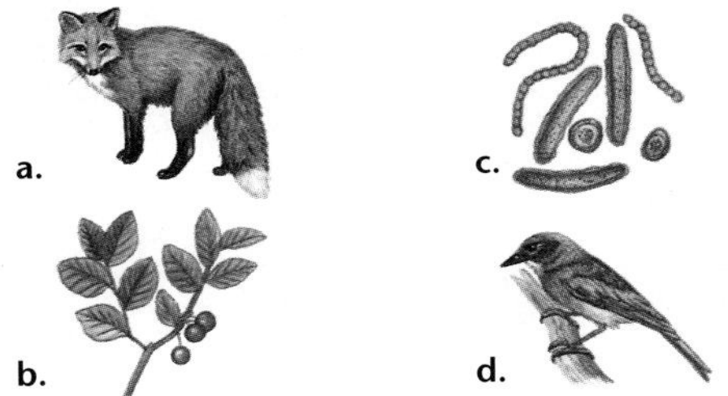

6. The total mass of living tissue at each trophic level can be shown in a(an)
   a. energy pyramid.
   b. pyramid of numbers.
   c. biomass pyramid.
   d. biogeochemical cycle.
7. Nutrients move through an ecosystem in
   a. biogeochemical cycles.
   b. water cycles.
   c. energy pyramids.
   d. ecological pyramids.
8. In the nitrogen cycle, bacteria that live on the roots of plants
   a. break down nitrogen compounds into nitrogen gas.
   b. denitrify nitrogen compounds.
   c. change nitrogen gas into plant proteins.
   d. change nitrogen gas into ammonia.
9. Which biogeochemical cycle does NOT involve a stage where the chemical enters the atmosphere?
   a. the water cycle
   b. the carbon cycle
   c. the nitrogen cycle
   d. the phosphorus cycle
10. When an ecosystem is limited by a single nutrient that either is scarce or cycles very slowly, this substance is called a(an)
    a. nitrogen compound.
    b. organic phosphate.
    c. biogeochemical cycle.
    d. limiting nutrient.

Understanding Concepts

11. What is the definition of ecology?
12. Name the different levels of organization within the biosphere, from smallest to largest.
13. How do scientists use modeling to study ecological changes?
14. How is sunlight important to most ecosystems?
15. What is chemosynthesis?
16. Distinguish between autotrophs and heterotrophs. Give an example of each.
17. What is a decomposer? Provide an example.
18. Which group of organisms is always found at the base of a food chain or food web?
19. What is an ecological pyramid? Describe the three different types of ecological pyramids.
20. Why is the transfer of energy and matter in a food chain only about 10 percent efficient?
21. What is a biogeochemical cycle?
22. List two ways in which water enters the atmosphere in the water cycle.
23. Explain the process of nitrogen fixation.
24. What are some of the similarities between the carbon cycle and the nitrogen cycle?
25. What is meant by "nutrient limitation?"

HOMEWORK GUIDE

Section:	Questions:
Section 3–1	1, 2, 11–13
Section 3–2	3–7, 14–20, 27, 30, 32
Section 3–3	8–10, 21–26, 28, 29, 31, 33

19. An ecological pyramid is a diagram that shows the relative amounts of energy or matter contained within each trophic level of a food chain or food web. An energy pyramid shows the amount of energy available from one trophic level to the next. A biomass pyramid shows the total amount of living tissue within each trophic level. A numbers pyramid shows the number of individual organisms at each trophic level.

20. Organisms use some of the energy they consume for life processes, and most is released into the environment as heat.

21. A repeating series of processes that passes the same molecules around again and again within the biosphere

22. Evaporation, transpiration

23. Bacteria in the soil and on plant roots convert nitrogen gas into ammonia. Other soil bacteria then convert the ammonia to nitrates and nitrites, which are taken in by producers and then by consumers that eat the producers. Decomposers convert the nitrogen in animal wastes and dead organisms into ammonia. Soil bacteria break down the nitrates and nitrites into nitrogen gas, which is released into the atmosphere.

24. In both cycles, the atmosphere is a major reservoir. Both cycles involve plants as transformers of the nutrients.

25. If a nutrient is in short supply, the organism's growth will be limited.

Critical Tinking

26. The fertilizer was carried into the stream with runoff and promoted the growth of algae. The algae depleted oxygen in the water. Without oxygen, the fish died.

27. Accept all food chains that begin with a producer and end with the student.

28. Students' answers should be logical and should provide some insights into the importance of water conservation.

29. As the rainfall amount increases, plant productivity also increases. Other factors that affect plant growth are the amount of sunlight, the types and amounts of nutrients in the soil, and the number of herbivores eating the plants.

30. Earthworm: detritivore; bear: omnivore; cow: herbivore; snail: detritivore; owl: carnivore; human: omnivore

31. The fish would decompose, releasing nutrients into the soil for use by the plants.

32. Several different food chains are possible. Make sure students identify a producer at the first level, an herbivore at the second level, and a carnivore at the third level.

33. Biogeochemical cycles pass molecules of essential nutrients among Earth's atmosphere, land, oceans and other bodies of water, and living organisms. In these cycles, complex substances are broken down into simple materials, transformed into forms that living organisms can use, and again assembled into complex substances such as proteins and carbohydrates.

Performance-Based Assessment

Make sure each food web begins with producers and includes several consumers.

Chapter 3 Assessment

Critical Thinking

26. Formulating Hypotheses Ecologists discovered that trout were dying in a stream that ran through some farmland where nitrogen fertilizer was used on the crops. How might you explain what happened?

27. Using Models Describe a food chain of which you are a member.

28. Problem Solving Water is a vital commodity. What are several ways in which you see water being wasted in your community? Can you offer some suggestions that will help limit the amount of wasted water? Can water consumption be reduced without a change in lifestyle?

29. Analyzing Data The graph below shows the effect of annual rainfall on the rate of primary productivity in an ecosystem. What happens to productivity as rainfall increases? What factors other than water might affect primary productivity?

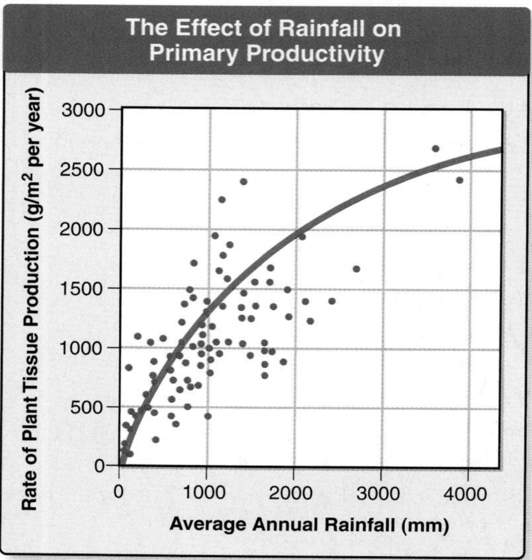

30. Classifying Classify each of the following as an herbivore, a carnivore, an omnivore, or a detritivore: earthworm, bear, cow, snail, owl, human.

31. Inferring Native Americans taught European settlers to bury pieces of fish with the seeds of corn they planted. Why might this practice ensure a good harvest?

32. Using Models Create flowcharts that show four different food chains in the food web shown below.

33. Making Connections Describe how biogeochemical cycles provide organisms with the raw materials necessary to synthesize complex organic compounds. Refer back to Chapter 2 for help in answering this question.

Performance-Based Assessment

Make a Poster With a piece of string, mark off an area of about 4 m^2 in the schoolyard or your own backyard. Create a poster that shows a food web of the organisms that you identify in the ecosystem you have sectioned off. Present your poster to the class.

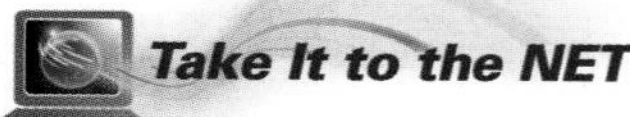

Take It to the NET

What does ecology have to do with you? Visit the Prentice Hall Web site at **www.phschool.com** to learn about ecology's role in human society. Then, answer the following questions:

- What are two examples of how ecological knowledge has helped improve the environment?
- What are three ways in which ecological knowledge helps to protect human health?
- What are four ways that we can use ecological knowledge to help manage natural resources?

Take It to the NET

• Reduced water pollution from laundry detergents and fertilizers. (In the 1960s, ecological research identified two of the major causes of poor water quality in lakes and streams—P and N—which were found in large amounts in laundry detergents and fertilizers. Armed with this information, citizens could make choices that helped restore the quality of many lakes and streams.)

• Control of non-native or introduced species invasions. (At first, highly toxic chemicals, which also poisoned other animals, were used to control introduced pests. By studying the pests' life cycles, ecologists devised less toxic approaches to control their numbers.)

• Protection of natural services. (Ecologists discovered that marshes and wetlands filter toxins and other impurities from water.)

Standardized Test Prep

Test-Taking Tip As you briefly scan the questions, identify those that may require pure guesswork on your part and save them for last. Then, use your time on those questions to reason through them and eliminate incorrect choices. Note: Do not write in this book.

Directions: Choose the letter that best answers the question or completes the statement.

1. A group of individuals belonging to a single species that live together in a defined area is termed a(an)
(A) population.
(B) ecosystem.
(C) community.
(D) biome.
(E) biosphere.

2. Which of the following is NOT true about matter in the biosphere?
(A) Matter is recycled in the biosphere.
(B) Biogeochemical cycles transform and reuse molecules.
(C) The total amount of matter decreases over time.
(D) Water and nutrients pass between organisms and the environment.
(E) The lack of a specific nutrient can reduce primary productivity.

3. Which is a source of energy for Earth's living things?
I. Wind energy
II. Sunlight
III. Chemical energy
(A) I only
(B) II only
(C) I and II only
(D) II and III only
(E) I, II, and III

4. In addition to herbivores, another type of consumer is a(an)
I. Carnivore
II. Omnivore
III. Detritivore
(A) I only
(B) II only
(C) I and II only
(D) II and III only
(E) I, II, and III

5. Human activities, such as the burning of fossil fuels, cycle carbon through the carbon cycle. Which other processes also participate in the carbon cycle?
I. Biological processes such as photosynthesis
II. Geochemical processes such as the release of gas from volcanoes
III. Mixed biogeochemical processes such as the formation of fossil fuels
(A) I only
(B) II only
(C) I and II only
(D) II and III only
(E) I, II, and III

Questions 6–7

The diagrams below represent the amount of biomass and the numbers of organisms in an ecosystem.

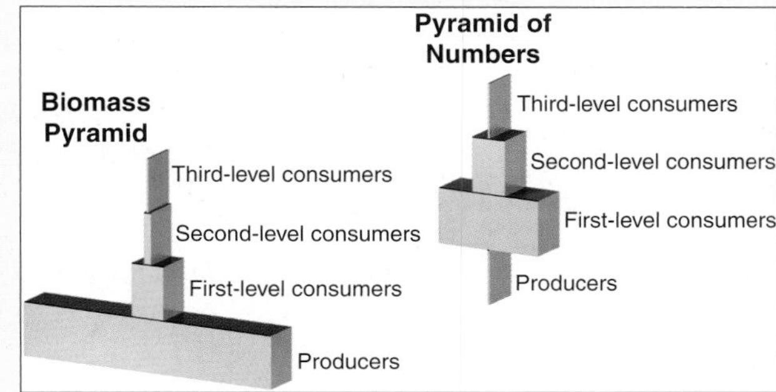

6. What is true about the pyramid of numbers?
I. First-level consumers compose the greatest number of individuals.
II. There are more third-level consumers than second-level consumers.
III. There are more producers than first-level consumers.
(A) I only
(B) II only
(C) I and III only
(D) II and III only
(E) I, II, and III

7. What can you conclude based on the two pyramids?
I. The producers are probably small, like single-celled algae in a body of water.
II. The producers are probably large, like trees in a forest.
III. No reasonable conclusion can be drawn from the information given.
(A) I only
(B) II only
(C) I and II only
(D) II and III only
(E) I, II, and III

Standardized Test Prep

1. A **2.** C **3.** D **4.** E **5.** E **6.** A **7.** B

Take It to the NET

• Biomedical treatments. (Ecologists have discovered that many plants and animals produce chemicals that can be used to treat human diseases.)
• Control of Lyme Disease. (Ecological studies of the connections between acorns, deer, mice, and ticks have helped ecologists predict the likelihood of infection from Lyme disease and issue public health warnings.)
• Endangered species protection
• Improved forestry management
• Biological control of agricultural pests
• Protection of nursery grounds and breeding areas for fish populations

For additional information, visit

www.phschool.com

Chapter Planner 4 Ecosystems and Communities

Section and Section Objectives	Time	Activities and Labs
4–1 The Role of Climate, pp. 87–89 **4.1.1** ***Identify*** the causes of climate. **4.1.2** ***Explain*** how Earth's temperature range is maintained. **4.1.3** ***Identify*** Earth's three main climate zones.	1 period (1/2 block)	**SE:** ***Inquiry Activity,*** What relationships exist in an ecosystem?, p. 86 **TE:** ***Build Science Skills,*** p. 88 **TE:** ***Meet Diverse Needs,*** p. 88
4–2 What Shapes an Ecosystem?, pp. 90–97 **4.2.1** ***Explain*** how biotic/abiotic factors influence an ecosystem. **4.2.2** ***Identify*** interactions that occur within communities. **4.2.3** ***Describe*** how ecosystems recover from a disturbance.	2 periods (1 block)	**SE:** ***Quick Lab,*** How do abiotic factors affect different plant species?, p. 91 **TE:** ***Demonstrations,*** pp. 92, 94 **SE:** ***Careers in Biology,*** Forestry Technician, p. 95
4–3 Land Biomes, pp. 98–105 **4.3.1** ***Explain*** what microclimates are. **4.3.2** ***Identify*** the characteristics of major land biomes.	2 periods (1 block)	**TE:** ***Build Science Skills,*** p. 103
4-4 Aquatic Ecosystems, pp. 106–112 **4.4.1** ***Identify*** the factors that govern aquatic ecosystems. **4.4.2** ***Identify*** the two types of freshwater ecosystems. **4.4.3** ***Describe*** the characteristics of the marine zones.	2 periods (1 block)	**TE:** ***Demonstration,*** p. 107 **TE:** ***Meet Diverse Needs,*** p. 108, 110 **SE:** ***Analyzing Data,*** Ecosystem Productivity, p. 111 **SE:** ***Exploration,*** Observing Succession, p. 113
Chapter Assessment, pp. 114–117	1 period (1/2 block)	

ACTIVITY PLANNER

SE: ***Inquiry Activity,*** p. 86; (15 min.); small ecosystem

TE: ***Build Science Skills,*** p. 88; (5 min.); penlight, graph paper

TE: ***Meet Diverse Needs,*** p. 88; (5 min.); paper plate, pencil

SE: ***Quick Lab,*** p. 91; (15 min.; observation and recording each day for 2 weeks); rye and rice seeds, sand, potting soil, paper cups

TE: ***Demonstration,*** p. 92; (20 min.); string, uncolored and colored toothpicks

TE: ***Demonstration,*** p. 94; (15 min. for setup); dishpan, gravel, soil, shallow dish, water, grass seed, mixed birdseed

TE: ***Build Science Skills,*** p. 103; (15 min.); photographs of animals characteristic of each major land biome

TE: ***Demonstration,*** p. 107; (20 minutes); aquarium, freshwater plants and animals, water, rocks, mud, sand, soil

TE: ***Meet Diverse Needs,*** p. 110; (15 minutes); variety of ocean organisms

SE: ***Design an Experiment,*** p. 113; (10 min. for setup, 20 min. every 2 days for 2 weeks); 1000-mL beaker, soil, grass clippings, dried leaves, 600-mL aged water, 4 coverslips, 4 glass slides, 4 dropper pipettes, microscope, guide for identifying microorganisms

PLANNING KEY

Ability Levels

B Basic	For students who need additional help
A Average	For all students
E Enriched	For students who need to be challenged

Components

SE	Student Edition	**GRSW**	Guided Reading and Study Workbook	**IDM**	Issues and Decision Making
TE	Teacher's Edition	**CT**	Chapter Tests: Levels A and B	**CTB**	Computer Test Bank
LMA	Laboratory Manual A	**PHAS**	PH Assessment System	**PA**	Presentation Assistant Plus
LMB	Laboratory Manual B	**LA**	Lab Assessment with Scoring Guide	**BD**	BioDetectives Videotape
TR	Teaching Resources	**BTM**	BioTechnology Manual	**iT**	iText

Program Resources	Assessment	Media and Technology
TR: Section Review 4–1 B A **GRSW:** Section 4–1 B A	**SE:** 4–1 Section Assessment, p. 89 **TR:** Section Review 4–1	**PA:** 4–1 Interest Grabber, Section Outline, Greenhouse Effect, Figure 4–3 and Figure 4–4 **iT:** Section 4–1
LMA: Chapter 4 Lab A E **LMB:** Chapter 4 Lab B A **TR:** Section Review 4–2 B A **GRSW:** Section 4–2 B A	**SE:** 4–2 Section Assessment, p. 97 **TR:** Section Review 4–2	**PA:** 4–2 Interest Grabber, Section Outline, Abiotic and Biotic Factors, Figure 4–6 **iT:** Section 4–2
TR: Section Review 4–3 B A **GRSW:** Section 4–3 B A **IDM:** 4–1 A E	**SE:** 4–3 Section Assessment, p. 105 **TR**: Section Review 4–3	**PA:** 4–3 Interest Grabber, Section Outline, Compare/Contrast Table, Figure 4–11 **iT:** Section 4–3
TR: Section Review 4–4 B A Chapter 4 Exploration B A E **GRSW:** Section 4–4 B A	**SE:** 4–4 Section Assessment, p. 112 **TR:** Section Review 4–4	**PA:** 4–4 Interest Grabber, Section Outline, Freshwater Pond Ecosystem, Figure 4–15 **iT:** Section 4–4
	SE: Chapter 4 Assessment, pp. 114–117 **TR:** Chapter Vocabulary Review, Graphic Organizer **CT:** Chapter 4 Test **CTB:** Chapter 4 Test **PHAS:** Practice Test	**CTB:** Chapter 4 Test **iT:** Chapter 4 Assessment

PRESSED FOR TIME?

To Preview the Chapter
- Have students read What Is Climate? on page 87, Biotic and Abiotic Factors on page 90, The Major Biomes on page 99, and the three introductory paragraphs on page 106.

To Cover the Chapter Quickly
- Have students do the Reading Strategy for Section 4–1, page 87; read pages 90–93 of Section 4–2; review the land biome descriptions on pages 100–104; and read all of Section 4–4.

To Review the Chapter
- Assign Sections 4–1 through 4–4 in the Guided Reading and Study Workbook.
- Assign the Chapter Vocabulary Review for Chapter 4 in Teaching Resources.

ENGAGE/EXPLORE

Inquiry Activity

Objective Students will be able to identify relationships among different organisms and between organisms and nonliving factors in a model ecosystem.

Skill Focus Classifying

Materials terrarium, aquarium, or other small ecosystem

Time 15 minutes

Advance Prep If you do not already have a suitable small ecosystem in your classroom, prepare one before students do this activity. Set up the ecosystem sufficiently ahead of time so you are sure that it is fairly stable and the organisms are surviving well.

Strategy Provide times throughout the class period for pairs or small groups of students to take turns observing the ecosystem.

Expected Outcome Students should be able to identify some relationships between different organisms and between organisms and nonliving parts of the ecosystem.

Think About It

1. Answers will vary depending on the type of ecosystem and the kinds of organisms in it. Students should note any feeding relationships, competition, or nurturing behavior they observe. They also should identify organisms' interactions with air, water, sunlight, nutrients in the soil, and other nonliving factors.
2. Predictions will vary but should indicate differences due to the producers no longer adding energy to the ecosystem.

Assess Prior Knowledge

Determine whether students already understand the difference between climate and weather by asking them to define each term in their own words. Acknowledge all responses without comment, but encourage discussion by asking: **What do you think of [student's] definition? Do you agree? Is there something you think should be added?** Suggest that students note their definitions and compare them with those given in the text when they read Section 1.

Chapter 4 Ecosystems and Communities

In a tropical rain forest in Belize, Central America, a jaguar drinks from a pool.

Inquiry Activity

What relationships exist in an ecosystem?

Procedure

1. Observe a terrarium, aquarium, or other small ecosystem that your teacher provides.
2. Use your observations to construct a diagram (similar to a concept map) showing all the relationships that exist among the parts of the ecosystem.
3. Indicate on your diagram which relationships involve nonliving parts of the ecosystem.

Think About It

1. **Classifying** What types of relationships did you find among the organisms? What types of relationships did you find between the organisms and the nonliving parts of their environment?
2. **Predicting** How might your diagram change if the ecosystem were in the dark for a week?

HISTORY OF SCIENCE

Exploring the world
Prevailing winds and ocean currents played a vital role in world explorations of the fifteenth through eighteenth centuries. In some cases, sailors followed prevailing winds and currents to reach their desired location. In many cases, however, explorers encountered new lands by chance when they were carried off their intended course by unexpected winds or currents. Some voyagers met with difficulty or disaster when their ships entered the equatorial area of calm winds known as the doldrums or when they had to sail against prevailing winds and currents.

4–1 The Role of Climate

If you live in Michigan, you know better than to try to grow banana trees in your backyard. Bananas are tropical plants that need plenty of water and heat. They cannot survive in freezing temperatures. It may not be as obvious, however, that cranberries will not grow in the Rio Grande Valley of Texas. Cranberries need plenty of water and a cold rest period. They cannot tolerate the months of very hot weather that frequently occur in the Rio Grande Valley.

Bananas and cranberries, like many other organisms, require a specific set of environmental conditions in order to grow. Bananas need warm temperatures, and cranberries thrive in cool temperatures. What produces the wide range of environmental conditions that shapes the communities in which organisms live?

Guide for Reading

Key Concepts
- How does the greenhouse effect maintain the biosphere's temperature range?
- What are Earth's three main climate zones?

Vocabulary
- weather • climate
- greenhouse effect • polar zone
- temperate zone • tropical zone

Reading Strategy: Outlining Before you read, use the headings in this section to make an outline about climate. As you read, fill in the subtopics and smaller topics. Then, add phrases or a sentence after each subtopic to provide key information.

What Is Climate?

In the atmosphere, temperature, precipitation, and other environmental factors combine to produce weather and climate. **Weather** is the day-to-day condition of Earth's atmosphere at a particular time and place. The weather where you live may be clear and sunny one day but cloudy and cold the next. **Climate,** on the other hand, refers to the average, year-after-year conditions of temperature and precipitation in a particular region.

Climate is caused by the interplay of many factors, including the trapping of heat by the atmosphere, the latitude, the transport of heat by winds and ocean currents, and the amount of precipitation that results. The shape and elevation of landmasses also contribute to global climate patterns.

The energy of incoming sunlight drives Earth's weather and helps determine climate. As you might expect, solar energy has an important effect on the temperature of the atmosphere. At the same time, the presence of certain gases in the atmosphere also has an effect on its temperature.

The Greenhouse Effect

Temperatures on Earth remain within a range suitable for life as we know it because the biosphere has a natural insulating blanket—the atmosphere. **Carbon dioxide, methane, water vapor, and a few other atmospheric gases trap heat energy and maintain Earth's temperature range.** These gases perform a function similar to that of the glass windows of a greenhouse. Just as the glass keeps the greenhouse plants warm, so these gases trap the heat energy of sunlight inside Earth's atmosphere. The natural situation in which heat is retained by this layer of greenhouse gases is called the **greenhouse effect,** shown in **Figure 4–1.**

▼ **Figure 4–1 Carbon dioxide, water vapor, and several other gases in the atmosphere allow solar radiation to enter the biosphere but slow down the loss of heat to space.** These greenhouse gases cause the greenhouse effect, which helps maintain Earth's temperature range.

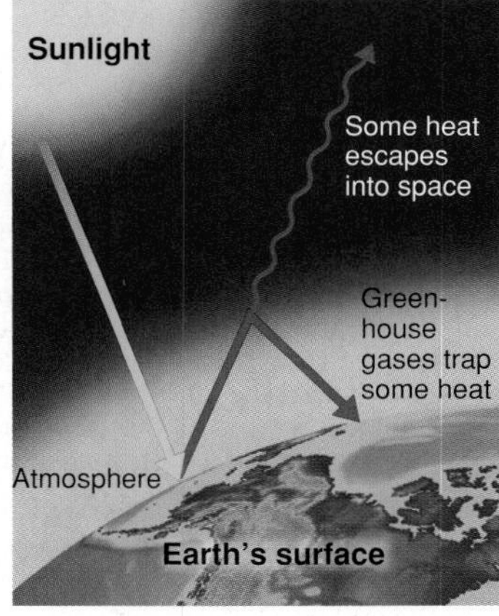

SECTION RESOURCES

TIME SAVER

Print:
- ***Teaching Resources,*** Section Review 4–1
- ***Guided Reading and Study Workbook,*** Section 4–1

Technology
- ***iText,*** Section 4–1

Section 4–1

1 FOCUS

Objectives

4.1.1 ***Explain*** how Earth's temperature range is maintained.

4.1.2 ***Identify*** Earth's three main climate zones.

Guide for Reading

Vocabulary Preview

Review the term *latitude* by asking students to describe what the term refers to. (*The distance north and south of the equator*) Display a large world map or globe, and have a volunteer point out the latitude lines on it.

Reading Strategy

Pair students who are not strong readers with proficient readers who can help them select main ideas, subtopics, and relevant details for the outline.

2 INSTRUCT

What Is Climate?

Use Community Resources

Encourage students to interview older family members and friends to find out what the climate was like in their area 25, 50, or more years ago. Instruct students to take notes during the interview. In class, let students compare notes to see whether the people they interviewed agree about climate changes in their lifetimes.

The Greenhouse Effect

Make Connections

Physics Ask: **In what forms does Earth receive solar energy?** *(As heat and light)* **Besides radiation, how is heat transferred?** *(By conduction [transfer from molecule to molecule within an object] and by convection [transfer in currents of air or a fluid])* **What causes the greenhouse effect?** *Earth's atmosphere traps much of the energy from the sun, raising the temperature of the atmosphere.*

The Effect of Latitude on Climate

Build Science Skills

Using Models To model sunlight striking Earth in the three main climate zones, students can hold a penlight very close to a sheet of graph paper and shine it on the paper from three different angles: 90°, 60°, and 30°. Tell students that at each angle, they should note the shape of the lighted section and the number of squares in it. Have students compare the shapes of the lighted sections on the paper with the shapes shown in Figure 4–2. Ask: **Which climate zone does each angle represent?** *(90°, tropical zone; 60°, temperate zone; 30°, polar zone)*

Heat Transport in the Biosphere

Meet Diverse Needs

The following activity is particularly suitable for students who learn best through physical activity. Give each pair of students a paper plate. Have one student hold a finger on the center of the plate while slowly turning the plate with the other hand. The second student should put the point of a pencil near the center of the plate and draw a line straight to the plate's edge. Students will see that the line drawn on the plate is not straight but curved, due to the plate's rotation. Explain that Earth's rotation has the same effect on winds and currents. **Learning modality: kinesthetic**

Greenhouse gases allow solar energy to penetrate the atmosphere in the form of sunlight. Much of the sunlight that hits the surface of our planet is converted into heat energy and then radiated back into the atmosphere. However, those same gases do not allow heat energy to pass out of the atmosphere as readily as light energy enters it. Instead, the gases trap heat inside Earth's atmosphere. If these gases were not present in the atmosphere, Earth would be 30 Celsius degrees cooler than it is today.

The Effect of Latitude on Climate

Because Earth is a sphere that is tilted on its axis, solar radiation strikes different parts of Earth's surface at an angle that varies throughout the year. At the equator, the sun is almost directly overhead at noon all year. At the North and South poles, however, the sun is much lower in the sky for months at a time. Look at **Figure 4–2**, and you will see that differences in the angle of sunlight directed at different latitudes result in the delivery of more heat to the equator than to the poles. The difference in heat distribution with latitude has important effects on Earth's climate zones.

As a result of differences in latitude and thus the angle of heating, Earth has three main climate zones: polar, temperate, and tropical. The **polar zones** are cold areas where the sun's rays strike Earth at a very low angle. These zones are located in the areas around the North and South poles, between 66.5° and 90° North and South latitudes. The **temperate zones** sit between the polar zones and the tropics. Because temperate zones are more affected by the changing angle of the sun over the course of a year, the climate in these zones ranges from hot to cold, depending on the season. The **tropical zone,** or tropics, is near the equator, between 23.5° North and 23.5° South latitudes. The tropics thus receive direct or nearly direct sunlight year-round, making the climate almost always warm. **Figure 4–2** shows Earth's main climate zones.

CHECKPOINT *What effect does latitude have on climate?*

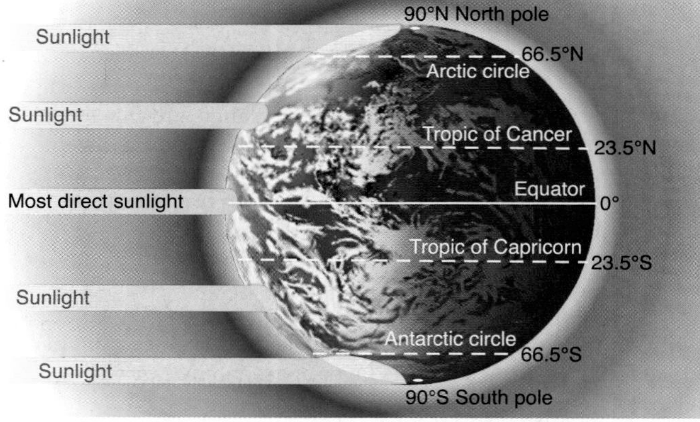

▶ **Figure 4–2** **Earth has three main climate zones.** These climate zones are caused by the unequal heating of Earth's surface. Near the equator, energy from the sun strikes Earth almost directly. Near the poles, the sun's rays strike Earth's surface at a lower angle. The same amount of solar energy is spread out over a larger area, heating the surface less than at the equator.

TIME SAVER — PRESENTATIONS MADE EASY!

The Presentation Assistant Plus contains the Prentice Hall Presentation Pro and the Transparencies, which provide easy-to-follow visual support for every step of this section. If you have a computer presentation station, use Prentice Hall Presentation Pro for Section 4–1, or use the transparencies listed here.

Section 4–1:

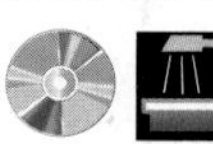

Interest Grabber
Section Outline
Greenhouse Effect
Figure 4–3 and Figure 4–4

Heat Transport in the Biosphere

The unequal heating of Earth's surface drives winds and ocean currents, which transport heat throughout the biosphere. Winds form because warm air tends to rise and cool air tends to sink. Consequently, air that is heated near the equator rises. At the same time, cooler air over the poles sinks toward the ground. The upward movement of warm air and the downward movement of cool air create air currents, or winds, that move heat throughout the atmosphere, from regions of sinking air to regions of rising air. The prevailing winds, shown in **Figure 4–3,** bring warm or cold air to a region, affecting its climate.

Similar patterns of heating and cooling occur in Earth's oceans. Cold water near the poles sinks and then flows parallel to the ocean bottom, eventually rising again in warmer regions through a process called upwelling. Meanwhile, surface water is moved by winds. In both cases, the water flow creates ocean currents. Like air currents, ocean currents transport heat energy within the biosphere. Surface ocean currents warm or cool the air above them, thus affecting the weather and climate of nearby landmasses.

Continents and other landmasses can also affect winds and ocean currents. Landmasses can interfere with the movement of air masses. For example, a mountain range causes a moist air mass to rise. As this happens, the air mass cools and moisture condenses, forming clouds that bring precipitation to the mountains. Once the air mass reaches the far side of the mountains, it has lost much of its moisture. The result is a rain shadow—an area with a dry climate—on the far side of the mountains.

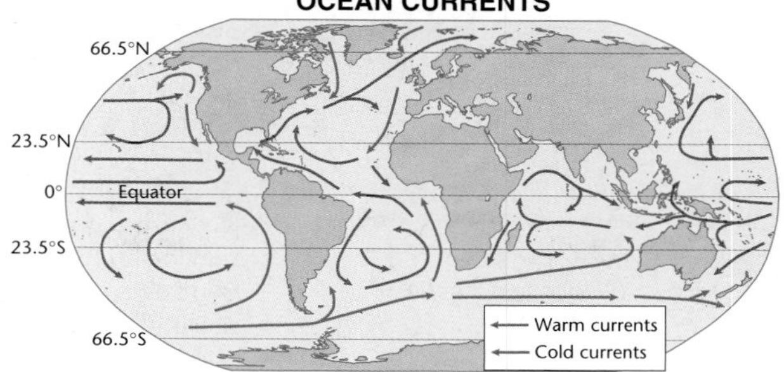

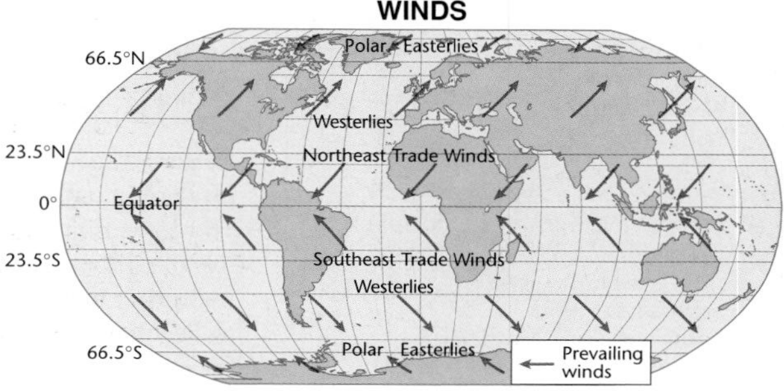

▲ **Figure 4–3** Earth's ocean currents (top) and winds (bottom) interact to help produce Earth's climates. The curved paths of some currents and winds are the result of Earth's rotation. **Interpreting Maps** *In what direction do cold currents in Earth's oceans generally move?*

4–1 Section Assessment

1. **Key Concept** What is the greenhouse effect?
2. **Key Concept** Describe Earth's three main climate zones.
3. What are the main factors that determine Earth's climate?
4. Describe two ways in which heat is transported in the biosphere.
5. **Critical Thinking Applying Concepts** What might conditions on Earth be like without the greenhouse effect?

iTEXT Assessment Use iText to review the important concepts in Section 4–1.

ALTERNATIVE ASSESSMENT

In Your Community
Ask an older friend or family member about a time of extreme precipitation or drought in your region. Find newspaper articles about the event and write a brief summary.

3 ASSESS

Evaluate Understanding

Call on students at random to identify the major climate factors discussed in this section and explain how each factor helps determine climate.

Reteach

Start a simple diagram of the greenhouse effect by drawing a curving section of Earth's surface on the board. Then, have different students in turn add features and labels to the drawing to explain the greenhouse effect step by step.

ALTERNATIVE ASSESSMENT

Encourage students to make photocopies of any old photographs or drawings they find as they research information. Give each student an opportunity to present his or her summary to the class.

Use iText to review the key concepts in Section 4–1.

4–1 Section Assessment

1. Greenhouse gases trap heat inside Earth's atmosphere.
2. Tropical zone: near equator; receives direct or nearly direct sunlight year-round. Polar zones: near North and South poles; receive the sun's rays at a low angle. Temperate zones: between the other two zones; receive sunlight at changing angles during the year.
3. The trapping of heat by the atmosphere, latitude, the transport of heat by winds and ocean currents, and the amount of precipitation that results
4. Winds and ocean currents
5. Sample answer: Earth would be much cooler.

Answers to . . .

CHECKPOINT *Regions at higher latitudes receive less heat energy per unit area than do regions near the equator. As a result, the temperate and polar zones have cooler climates than the tropical zone.*

Figure 4–3 *Cold currents generally move in curving paths toward the equator.*

Section 4–2

1 FOCUS

Objectives

4.2.1 ***Explain*** how biotic and abiotic factors influence an ecosystem.

4.2.2 ***Identify*** the interactions that occur within communities.

4.2.3 ***Describe*** how ecosystems recover from a disturbance.

Guide for Reading

Vocabulary Preview

The text provides pronunciations for most of the new Vocabulary terms in this section. Encourage students to use a dictionary to look up the phonetic spellings of the words for which pronunciations are not given, convert those spellings to the system used in this text (using the chart at the beginning of the Glossary), and include the phonetic spellings when they list the boldfaced terms.

Reading Strategy

Students often confuse the terms *symbiosis, mutualism,* and *commensalism.* To help them understand and remember the distinctions, have them look up the derivations of the words in a dictionary and note the derivations when they list the boldfaced terms.

2 INSTRUCT

Biotic and Abiotic Factors

Build Science Skills

Applying Concepts Point out to students that in any ecosystem, removing biotic elements can dramatically affect the ecosystem's abiotic conditions. For example, the trees in a forest hold topsoil with their roots, shade the soil, contribute organic matter to the soil in the form of dead leaves, and return water to the atmosphere through evaporation and transpiration. Removing trees from the forest ecosystem reduces these benefits. Ask students to suggest other examples of removing biotic elements from an ecosystem. For each example, have the class describe the possible effects on the ecosystem's abiotic elements.

4–2 What Shapes an Ecosystem?

Guide for Reading

Key Concepts
- How do biotic and abiotic factors influence an ecosystem?
- What interactions occur within communities?
- What is ecological succession?

Vocabulary
biotic factor
abiotic factor
habitat
niche
resource
competitive exclusion principle
predation
symbiosis
mutualism
commensalism
parasitism
ecological succession
primary succession
pioneer species
secondary succession

Reading Strategy: Building Vocabulary Before you read, preview new vocabulary terms by skimming the section and making a list of the boldfaced terms. Leave space to make notes as you read.

If you ask an ecologist where a particular organism lives, that person might say the organism lives on a Caribbean coral reef, or in an Amazon rain forest, or in a desert in the American Southwest. Those answers provide a kind of ecological address not unlike a street address in a city or town. An ecological address, however, tells you more than where an organism lives. It tells you about the climate the organism experiences and what neighbors it is likely to have. But what shapes the ecosystem in which an organism lives?

Biotic and Abiotic Factors

Ecosystems are influenced by a combination of biological and physical factors. The biological influences on organisms within an ecosystem are called **biotic factors.** These include the entire living cast of characters with which an organism might interact, including birds, trees, mushrooms, and bacteria—in other words, the ecological community. Biotic factors that influence a bullfrog, for example, might include the tiny plants it eats as a tadpole, the herons that eat the adult frog, and other species that compete with the bullfrog for food or space.

Physical, or nonliving, factors that shape ecosystems are called **abiotic factors** (ay-by-AHT-ik). For example, the climate of an area includes abiotic factors such as temperature, precipitation, and humidity. Other abiotic factors are wind, nutrient availability, soil type, and sunlight. For example, the bullfrog in **Figure 4–4** is affected by abiotic factors such as the availability of water and the temperature of the air. **Together, biotic and abiotic factors determine the survival and growth of an organism and the productivity of the ecosystem in which the organism lives.** The area where an organism lives is called its **habitat.** A habitat includes both biotic and abiotic factors.

CHECKPOINT *Give an example of an abiotic factor.*

◀ **Figure 4–4** **Like all ecosystems, this pond is shaped by a combination of biotic and abiotic factors.** The bullfrog, plants, and other organisms in the pond are biotic factors. The water, air, and the rock on which the bullfrog sits are abiotic factors.

SECTION RESOURCES

Print:
- ***Laboratory Manual A,*** Chapter 4 Lab
- ***Laboratory Manual B,*** Chapter 4 Lab
- ***Teaching Resources,*** Section Review 4–2
- ***Guided Reading and Study Workbook,*** Section 4–2

Technology
- ***iText,*** Section 4–2

Quick Lab

How do abiotic factors affect different plant species?

Materials presoaked rye and rice seeds, sand, potting soil, 4 paper cups

Procedure 

1. Use a pencil to punch three holes in the bottom of each cup. Fill 2 cups with equal amounts of sand and 2 cups with the same amount of potting soil.
2. Plant 5 rice seeds in one sand-filled cup and 5 rice seeds in one soil-filled cup. Plant 5 rye seeds in each of the other 2 cups. Label each cup with the type of seeds and soil it contains.
3. Place all the cups in a warm, sunny location. Each day for 2 weeks, water the cups equally and record your observations of any plant growth. **CAUTION:** *Wash your hands well with soap and warm water after handling plants or soil.*

Analyze and Conclude

1. **Analyzing Data** In which medium did the rice grow best—sand or soil? Which was the better medium for the growth of rye?
2. **Inferring** Soil retains more water than sand, providing a moister environment. What can you infer from your observations about the kind of environment that favors the growth of rice? The growth of rye?
3. **Drawing Conclusions** Which would compete more successfully in a dry environment—rye or rice? In a moist environment?

The Niche

If an organism's habitat is its address, its niche is its occupation. A **niche** (NITCH) is the full range of physical and biological conditions in which an organism lives and the way in which the organism uses those conditions. For instance, part of the description of an organism's niche includes its place in the food web. Another part of the description might include the range of temperatures that the organism needs to survive. The combination of biotic and abiotic factors in an ecosystem often determines the number of different niches in that ecosystem.

A niche includes the type of food the organism eats, how it obtains this food, and which other species use the organism as food. For example, a mature bullfrog catches insects, worms, spiders, small fish, or even mice. Predators such as herons, raccoons, and snakes prey on bullfrogs.

The physical conditions that the bullfrog requires to survive are part of its niche. As amphibians, bullfrogs spend their lives in or near the water of ponds, lakes, and slow-moving streams. A bullfrog's body temperature varies with that of the surrounding water and air. As winter approaches, bullfrogs burrow into the mud of pond or stream bottoms to hibernate.

The bullfrog's niche also includes when and how it reproduces. Female bullfrogs lay their eggs in water during the warmer months of the year. The young frogs, called tadpoles, live in the water until their legs and lungs develop.

PRESENTATIONS MADE EASY!

The Presentation Assistant Plus contains the Prentice Hall Presentation Pro and the Transparencies, which provide easy-to-follow visual support for every step of this section. If you have a computer presentation station, use Prentice Hall Presentation Pro for Section 4–2, or use the transparencies listed here.

Section 4–2: **Interest Grabber**
Section Outline
Abiotic and Biotic Factors
Figure 4–6

Quick Lab

Objective Students will be able to describe how abiotic factors affect growth in different species of plants.

Skill Focus **Drawing Conclusions**

Materials rye and rice seeds, sand, potting soil, 4 paper cups

Time 15 minutes for setup; brief observation and recording each day for 2 weeks

Advance Prep Soak the rice and rye seeds in water overnight.

Strategies

- Have students place the cups in trays or other shallow containers to hold any water, sand, and soil that may leak from the holes.
- Emphasize that except for the type of soil and type of seeds in each cup, all variables must be kept the same for all four cups.

Expected Outcome Rice seeds will not grow well in the sand-filled cup because the water drains out and leaves the sand too dry. Rye seeds should grow well in soil or sand.

Analyze and Conclude

1. Both types of seeds will be more successful in soil. However, the effect on rice will be more pronounced.
2. Rice requires a moister environment than rye does. Rye can tolerate dry conditions better than rice can but also benefits from an ample supply of water.
3. Rye will be more successful than rice in dry conditions. Rice will be more successful than rye in moist conditions.

The Niche

Address Misconceptions

Students sometimes misunderstand what a niche is, believing it to be a part of an ecosystem. Use simple analogies to clarify the meaning of the term. For example, each player on a baseball team has a specific niche—a different role to play. Ask students to suggest other analogies.

Answer to . . .

CHECKPOINT *The example should be any nonliving factor, such as air, water, soil, or rocks.*

Community Interactions

Demonstration

Mark off a 3-meter-square area with masking tape or string. Scatter 25 uncolored toothpicks (or other small objects) and 25 colored toothpicks over the area. Explain that the toothpicks represent two different species of insects. Choose two students to represent different species of lizards that eat both types of insects. At a signal from you, the two lizards start catching insects of both types. Signal the lizards to stop after 5–10 seconds, and ask them to count their insects. Rescatter the toothpicks and repeat the activity, but this time have one lizard eat only uncolored insects and the other lizard eat only colored insects. Compare the insect counts from the two different methods. Ask the "lizards": **Was it easier to catch insects when you were competing with each other or when you each had a different food?** *(When each had a different food)* Also ask the other students to describe competitive behaviors they observed.

Build Science Skills

Problem Solving Emphasize that any given ecosystem has only a certain amount of space, food, water, and other life essentials. Ask: **If one organism is involved in direct competition for life essentials, what are the possible outcomes for that organism?** *(The organism may win the struggle and survive, or it may lose the struggle and die.)* **Is there any other alternative for organisms that are in competition with other organisms?** *(If the competition is between different yet similar species, the organisms may change in ways that will decrease competition. In this way, both species may survive.)*

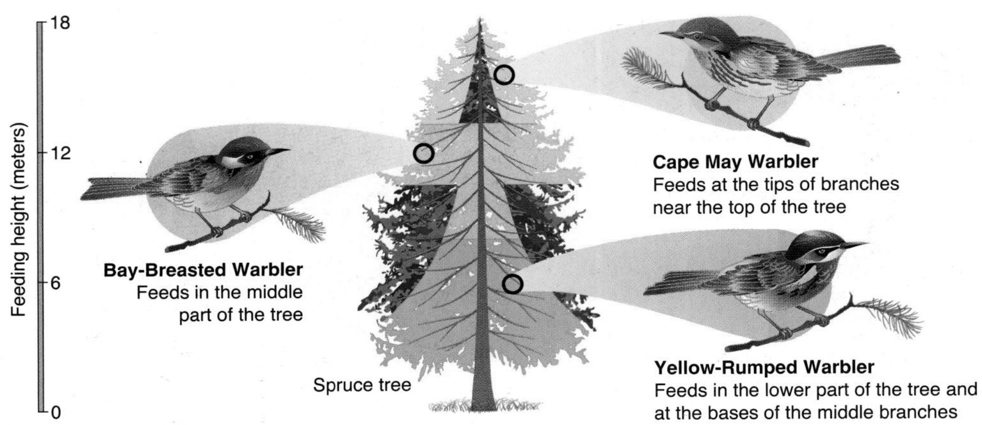

▲ **Figure 4–5** Each of these warbler species has a different niche in its spruce tree habitat. By feeding in different areas of the tree, the birds avoid competing with one another for food. **Inferring** *What would happen if two of the warbler species occupied the same niche?*

As you will see, no two species can share the same niche in the same habitat. However, different species can occupy niches that are very similar. For instance, the three species of North American warblers shown in **Figure 4–5** live in the same spruce trees but feed at different elevations and in different parts of those trees. The species are similar, yet each warbler has a different niche within the forest.

CHECKPOINT *What is a niche?*

Community Interactions

When organisms live together in ecological communities, they interact constantly. These interactions help shape the ecosystem in which they live. **Community interactions, such as competition, predation, and various forms of symbiosis, can powerfully affect an ecosystem.**

Competition Competition occurs when organisms of the same or different species attempt to use an ecological resource in the same place at the same time. The term **resource** refers to any necessity of life, such as water, nutrients, light, food, or space. In a forest, for example, broad-leaved trees such as oak or hickory may compete for sunlight by growing tall, spreading out their leaves, and blocking the sunlight from shorter trees. Similarly, two species of lizards in a desert might compete by attempting to eat the same type of insect.

Direct competition in nature often results in a winner and a loser—with the losing organism failing to survive. A fundamental rule in ecology, the **competitive exclusion principle,** states that no two species can occupy the same niche in the same habitat at the same time. Look again at the distribution of the warblers in **Figure 4–5.** Can you see how this distribution avoids direct competition among the different warbler species?

HISTORY OF SCIENCE

The competitive exclusion principle
The competitive exclusion principle was first postulated by Russian ecologist G. F. Gause in 1934. In laboratory experiments, Gause studied the effect of interspecific competition on two closely related species of protists. When he cultured the two species separately, both populations grew rapidly and then leveled off at the culture's carrying capacity. When he cultured the two species together, however, one species apparently had a competitive edge in obtaining food, and the other species was driven to extinction in the culture. Gause concluded that two species so similar that they compete for the same limited resources cannot coexist in the same place. His conclusion was later confirmed by further studies.

Predation An interaction in which one organism captures and feeds on another organism is called **predation** (preh-DAY-shun). The organism that does the killing and eating is called the predator (PRED-uh-tur), and the food organism is the prey. Cheetahs are active predators with claws and sharp teeth. Their powerful legs enable them to run after prey. Other predators, such as anglerfishes, are more passive. An anglerfish has a fleshy appendage that resembles a fishing lure, which it uses to draw unsuspecting prey close to its mouth.

Symbiosis Any relationship in which two species live closely together is called **symbiosis** (sim-by-OH-sis), which means "living together." Biologists recognize three main classes of symbiotic relationships in nature: mutualism, commensalism, and parasitism. Examples of these three relationships are shown in **Figure 4–6.**

In **mutualism** (MYOO-choo-ul-iz-um), both species benefit from the relationship. Many flowers, for example, depend on certain species of insects to pollinate them. The flowers provide the insects with food in the form of nectar, pollen, or other substances, and the insects help the flowers reproduce.

In **commensalism** (kuh-MEN-sul-iz-um), one member of the association benefits and the other is neither helped nor harmed. Small marine animals called barnacles, for example, often attach themselves to a whale's skin. The barnacles perform no service to the whale, nor do they harm it. Yet, the barnacles benefit from the constant movement of water past the swimming whale, because the water carries food particles to them.

In **parasitism** (PAR-uh-sit-iz-um), one organism lives on or inside another organism and harms it. The parasite obtains all or part of its nutritional needs from the other organism, called the host. Generally, parasites weaken but do not kill their host, which is usually larger than the parasite. Tapeworms, for example, are parasites that live in the intestines of mammals. Fleas, ticks, and lice live on the bodies of mammals, feeding on the blood and skin of the host.

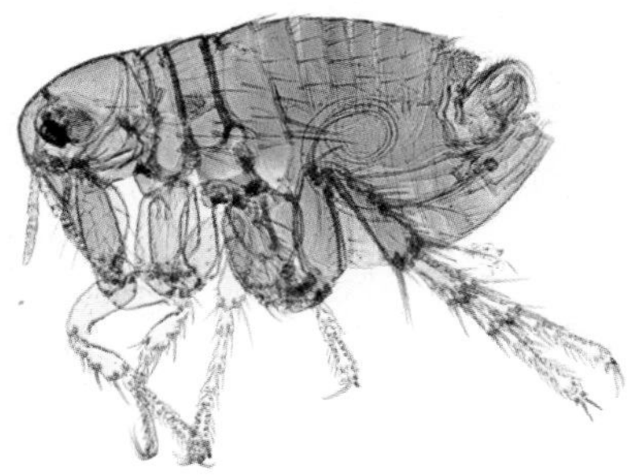

Figure 4–6 Mutualism—both species benefit (top): The ant cares for the aphids and protects them from predators. The aphids produce a sweet liquid that the ant drinks. Commensalism—one species benefits; the other is neither helped nor harmed (center): The orchid benefits from its perch in the tree as it absorbs water and minerals from rainwater and runoff, but the tree is not affected. Parasitism—one species benefits while the other is harmed (bottom): A flea feeds on the blood of its host, which can be harmed by diseases the flea carries. **Predicting** ***What would happen to the aphids if the ant died?***

Build Science Skills

Problem Solving Explain that under normal conditions, prey populations seldom become extinct as a result of predation. Tell students to imagine an ecosystem in which a predator species has killed off an entire prey species. Ask: **What would the possible consequences be for the predators?** *(They would run out of food and die, they would have to change their eating habits and find other prey, or they would have to move to another area where that prey species still survives.)*

Meet Diverse Needs

Students who need an additional challenge could do independent research on the various types of defenses that have evolved in prey species as protection against predators. Such defenses include camouflage, mechanical defenses (quills or thorns, for example), chemical defenses such as toxins and caustic agents (perhaps combined with warning coloration), and mimicry. Encourage students to share their findings with the class in oral reports, posters, or displays. **Learning modality: verbal**

Build Science Skills

Applying Concepts Have each student list examples of symbiotic relationships that he or she knows from previous learning or has researched. In a class discussion, ask volunteers to describe examples without identifying the type of symbiosis each example represents. After each description, challenge other students to identify the relationship as mutualism, commensalism, or parasitism.

BACKGROUND

Predation and diversity

In nature, predator species rarely kill and eat all their prey species, which would reduce community diversity. In fact, studies have shown that predation can actually help maintain diversity. One example of this process involves the gray wolf, a top predator in its ecosystem. Where wolves were hunted to extinction, such as in many parts of North America, populations of deer and other herbivores increased dramatically. As these populations overgrazed the vegetation, many plant species that could not tolerate such grazing pressure disappeared from the ecosystem. In turn, many insects and small animals that depended on the plants for food also disappeared. The elimination of wolves thus produced an ecosystem with considerably less species diversity.

Answers to . . .

CHECKPOINT *The full range of physical and biological conditions in which an organism lives and the way in which the organism uses those conditions*

Figure 4–5 *Most likely, one warbler species would be more successful in that niche, and the other species would not survive.*

Figure 4–6 *Without the ants, the aphids could be eaten by predators.*

Ecological Succession

Demonstration

The following activity models stages of succession described on this page. Elicit student volunteers to help you create the model. Put a 2.5-cm layer of gravel in the bottom of a dishpan, and cover with a 10-cm layer of soil. Make a pond by sinking a shallow dish into the soil so its top is even with the soil surface. Put a 1-cm layer of soil in the bottom of the pond. Slowly pour water into the dishpan until the pond is completely full and the soil around it is wet. Sprinkle a handful of grass seeds over the entire dishpan. Leave the dishpan near a sunny window. Every 3 to 4 days, sprinkle grass seeds over the dishpan again. Lightly water the soil to keep it damp, but do not refill the pond or clean it out. Over time, the pond will become shallower and will eventually fill in with growing grass. When this has occurred, sprinkle a handful of mixed birdseed over the dishpan once a week for two weeks. The birdseed plants, which will be larger than the grass plants, represent the gradual invasion of shrubs and trees and the succession from a meadow to a forest.

Build Science Skills

Problem Solving Ask: **What types of human activities can disturb an ecosystem and cause succession?** *(Examples include logging, strip mining, draining a marsh, clearing woodland to grow crops or graze livestock, removing a beaver dam, and the like.)*

Ecological Succession

On the time scale of a human life, some ecosystems may seem stable. The appearance of stability is often misleading, because ecosystems and communities are always changing. Sometimes, ecosystems changes in response to an abrupt disturbance, such as a severe storm. At other times, change occurs as a more gradual response to natural fluctuations in the environment. **Ecosystems are constantly changing in response to natural and human disturbances. As an ecosystem changes, older inhabitants gradually die out and new organisms move in, causing further changes in the community.** This series of predictable changes that occurs in a community over time is called **ecological succession.** Sometimes succession results from slow changes in the physical environment. A sudden natural disturbance from human activities, such as clearing a forest, may also be a cause of succession.

Primary Succession On land, succession that occurs on surfaces where no soil exists is called **primary succession.** For example, primary succession occurs on the surfaces formed as volcanic eruptions build new islands or cover the land with lava rock or volcanic ash. Primary succession also occurs on bare rock exposed when glaciers melt.

In **Figure 4–7,** you can follow the stages of primary succession after a volcanic eruption. When primary succession begins, there is no soil, just ash and rock. The first species to populate the area are called **pioneer species.** The pioneer species on volcanic rocks are often lichens (LY-kunz). A lichen is made up of a fungus and an alga and can grow on bare rock. As lichens grow, they help break up the rocks. When they die, the lichens add organic material to help form soil in which plants can grow.

CHECKPOINT *What are pioneer species?*

▼ **Figure 4–7** Primary succession occurs on newly exposed surfaces, such as this newly deposited volcanic rock and ash. A volcanic eruption destroys the previous ecosystem (1). The first organisms to appear are lichens (2). Mosses soon appear, and grasses take root in the thin layer of soil (3). Eventually, tree seedlings and shrubs sprout among the plant community (4). **Predicting** *What types of animals would you expect to appear at each stage, and why?*

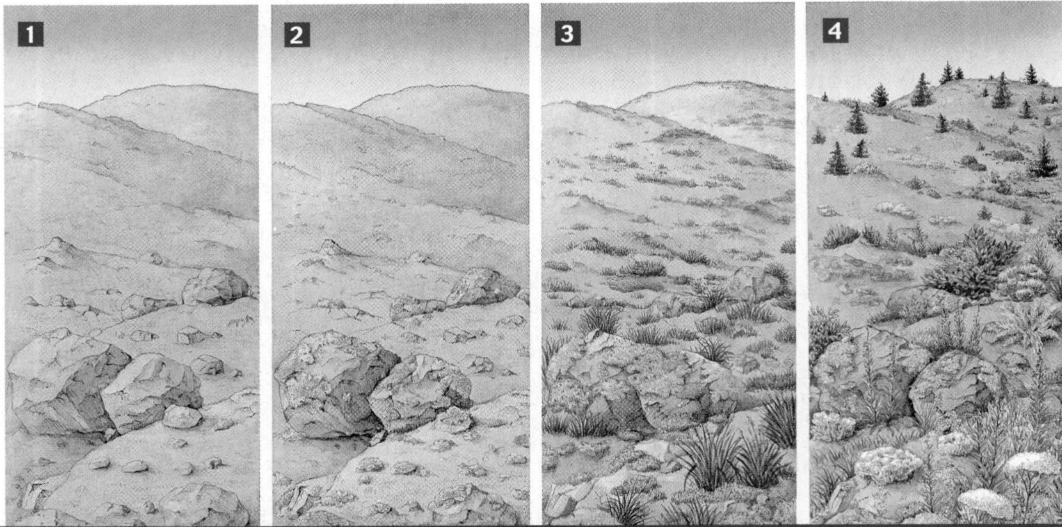

BIOLOGY UPDATE

Succession and chance

Many ecologists once believed that succession was an orderly and predictable process. Today, they realize that random, unpredictable events may influence which species succeed and which die off after a disturbance. For example, random variables such as the season of year the disturbance occurs, the wind direction and rainfall immediately after the disturbance, and which organisms are in an active stage of their breeding cycle can change the succession of a community after a fire, volcanic eruption, or other major disturbance. Ecologists have also found that climax communities are often not as stable as they were once thought to be. In studying coral reefs and tropical rain forests, for example, researchers find shifting patchworks of early, middle, and late successionary communities.

Secondary Succession When a disturbance of some kind changes an existing community without removing the soil, then **secondary succession** can follow. Secondary succession occurs when land cleared and plowed for farming is abandoned. It also occurs when wildfire burns woodlands. **Figure 4–8** shows a wildfire in Yellowstone National Park that led to secondary succession after the fire. Fires set by lightning occur naturally in many ecosystems. Certain plants have adapted to a regular cycle of fire and regrowth. Their seeds will not sprout unless exposed to fire.

Ecologists used to think that the process of succession in a given area always proceeded in certain specific and predictable stages and ended with a mature, stable community that did not undergo further succession. This stage was referred to as a "climax community." Old-growth forests in the Pacific Northwest and ancient cypress swamps in Alabama, Georgia, Louisiana, and Arkansas were considered climax communities. Although these communities may appear to be permanent, they too undergo change. Long-term climate change and introduction of nonnative species can profoundly affect these communities.

▲ **Figure 4–8** Wildfires in Yellowstone National Park in 1988 quickly led to secondary succession. **Observing** *What are some characteristics of the ecosystem in the photograph that might help to explain the occurrence of the Yellowstone fires?*

Careers in Biology

Forestry Technician

Job description: work outdoors to help maintain, protect, and develop forests (by planting trees, fighting insects and diseases that attack trees, and controlling soil erosion)

Education: two- or four-year college degree in forestry, wildlife, or conservation; summer work in parks, state and national forests; and private industry provides on-the-job training

Skills: knowledge of the outdoors and basic safety precautions; communication skills for working with the public; keen observational skills; physical fitness for jobs that require walking long distances through forests

Highlights: help to manage and conserve forest biomes by analyzing data, planting trees, and managing fires when necessary; contribute to people's enjoyment of outdoor recreation

Belva Fry said this about seeing grown trees she planted: "I love tree planting—working physically hard, then going back later to where you planted and seeing trees about 20 feet tall on the hillside. You know you really did something."

Take It to the NET

For more career information, visit the Prentice Hall Web site at **www.phschool.com**.

TEACHER TO TEACHER

To help students understand ecological succession, have them interview an older family member or neighbor who has lived in their neighborhood for a long time. Ask the person to describe how the neighborhood has changed over time. Make sure that students ask the following questions. 1.) Have areas that were formerly grassy been paved or developed? 2.) Have any farms, parks, or lots returned to their wild state? Have students write a summary of their interview and then, share it with the class.

—*Deidre Galvin,*
Biology Teacher
Ridgewood High School,
Ridgewood, NJ

Careers in Biology

Encourage students to use library resources to find out how to get started in a forestry career. Suggest that they present their findings in posters that include information such as the geographic locations where forestry professionals work, specific courses that are necessary, areas of research, and issues in the industry.

Resources Society of American Foresters; International Union of Forestry Research Organizations; U.S. Department of Agriculture Forest Service

Take It to the NET

For additional information, visit **www.phschool.com**

Use Community Resources

Invite students to cite examples of natural or human disturbances they have seen in their area. Emphasize that the disturbance need not be a large-scale event, such as cutting down all the trees in an area of woodland, but could be on a small scale—for example, homeowners removing thorny bushes from a narrow strip of land between their houses. Ask students to describe any changes they observed after the disturbance or, if the disturbance is very recent, to predict changes they think will occur over time. Take the class to a disturbed site, if feasible, or ask students to visit a site on their own periodically to observe changes that occur during the school year.

Answers to . . .

CHECKPOINT *The first species to populate an area at the beginning of the process of primary succession*

Figure 4–7 *Stage 2: insects and spiders are carried in by the wind; stage 3: rodents that feed on these arthropods and new grasses; stage 4: larger mammals and birds that feed on rodents*

Figure 4–8 *In the photograph, students can observe that there are dead tree trunks on the ground that could provide fuel for a fire. In addition, the grass looks brown, suggesting dry conditions that would increase the risk of fire.*

Meet Diverse Needs

Students who learn best when material is organized logically would benefit from creating a concept map or flowchart to summarize the steps in succession described in Figure 4–9 and the text on succession in a marine ecosystem. Have students work in small groups. Let each group decide on the type of graphic organizer to create, but instruct students that the organizer must include the major phases of succession (for example: *dead whale sinks to ocean floor*), the changes that occur in each phase *(whale carcass decays)*, and the types of organisms that make up the community in each phase *(scavengers and decomposers)*. Display the organizers so groups can compare their approaches. **Learning modality: logical/mathematical**

Build Science Skills

Interpreting Graphics Collect, or ask students to find, several sets of photographs that show areas soon after a disturbance and at intervals as succession occurs. Good subjects for such photos include areas affected by a volcanic eruption or forest fire, such as the areas mentioned in the student text. Photos of succession after the eruption of Mount St. Helens are also widely available. Display each set of photos in random order, and have students identify the correct order. For each set, also ask: **How were you able to determine the correct order?** *(Sample answer: by the types and sizes of the plants growing in the area)*

SCIENCE NEWS®

Encourage students to visit **www.phschool.com** for the most current information on this topic.

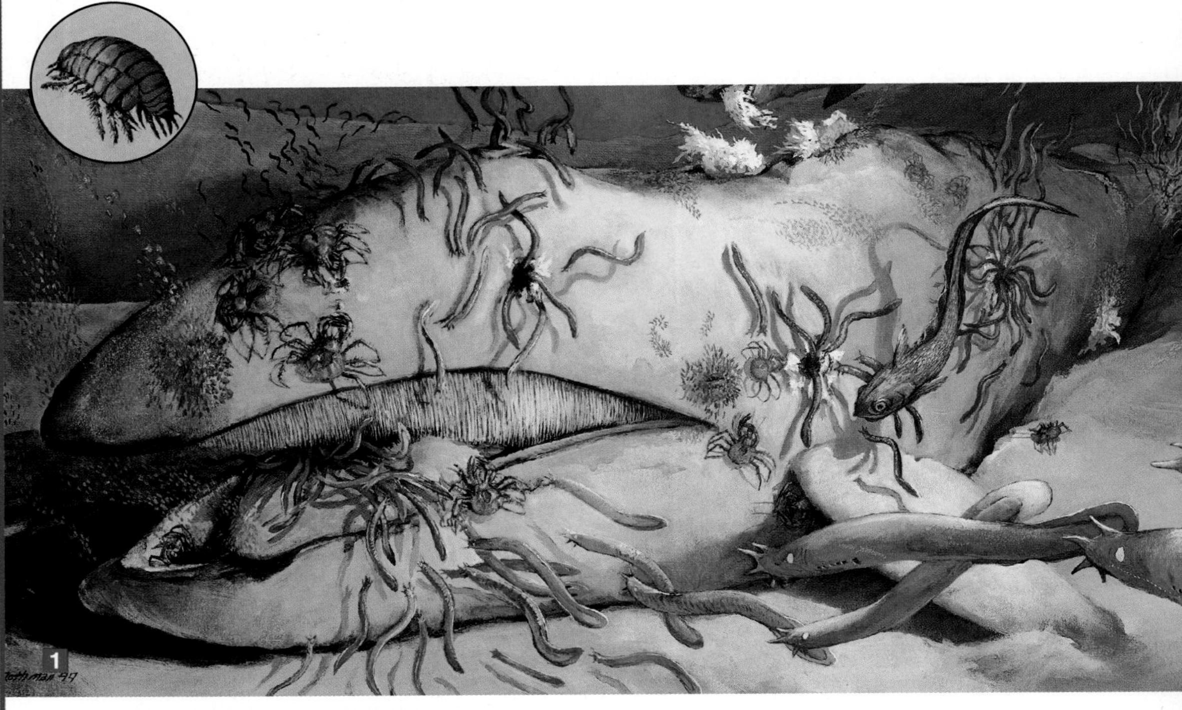

Figure 4–9 Ecosystems are constantly changing in response to disturbances. In natural environments, succession occurs in stages. A dead whale that falls to the ocean floor is soon covered with scavengers, including tiny crustaceans called amphipods (inset), hagfish, crabs, and shrimp. After a time, only bare bones are left. The bones contain oil that supports several types of deep-sea bacteria. In the next stage of succession, the bacteria provide energy and nutrients for a different community of organisms, such as limpets, marine worms, and marine snails (inset), that live on the bones and in the surrounding sediments.

Succession in a Marine Ecosystem Succession can occur in any ecosystem—even in the permanently dark, deep ocean. In 1987, scientists found an unusual community of organisms living on the remains of a dead whale in the deep waters off the coast of southern California. At first, ecologists did not know what to make of this extraordinary community. After several experiments and hours of observation, the ecologists found that the community represented a stage in succession amid an otherwise stable and well-documented deep-sea ecosystem. Since that discovery, several more whale carcasses have been found in other ocean basins with similar organisms surrounding them. **Figure 4–9** illustrates three stages in the succession of a whale-fall community.

1 The disturbance that causes this kind of succession begins when a large whale, such as a blue or fin whale, dies and sinks to the normally barren ocean floor. The whale carcass attracts a host of scavengers and decomposers, including amphipods (inset), hagfishes, and sharks, that feast on the decaying meat.

2 Within a year, most of the whale's tissues have been eaten. The carcass then supports only a much smaller number of fishes, crabs, marine snails (inset), and other marine animals. The decomposition of the whale's body, however, enriches the surrounding sediments with nutrients, forming an oasis of sediment dwellers, including many different species of marine worms.

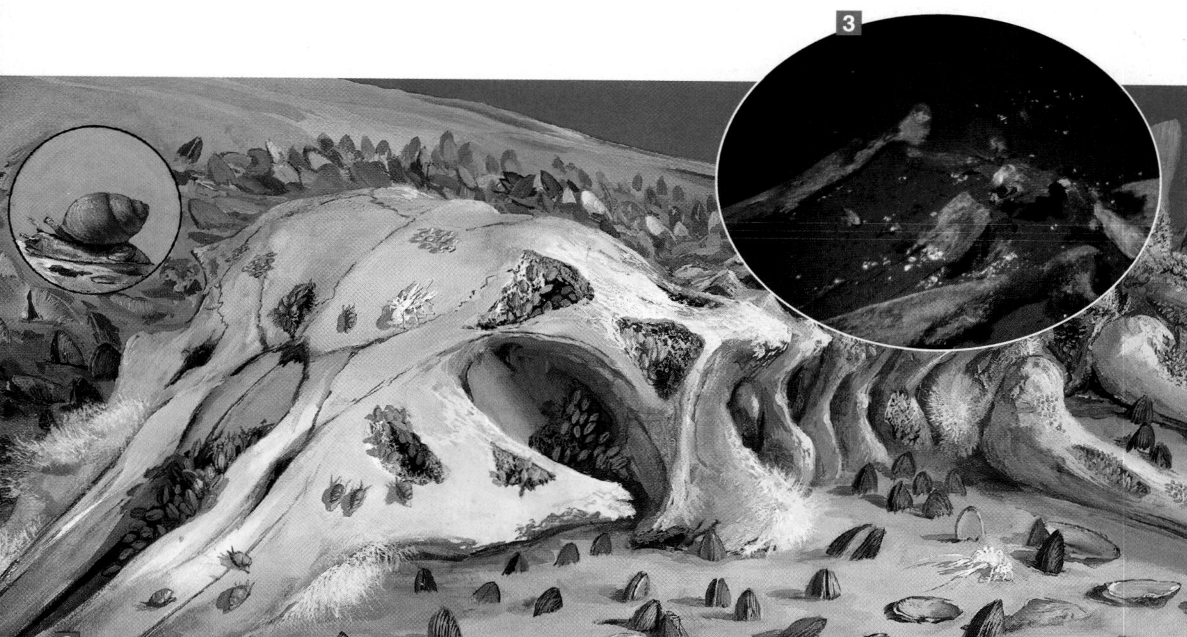

3 When only the whale's skeleton remains, a third community moves in. Heterotrophic bacteria begin to decompose oils inside the whale bones. In doing so, they release chemical compounds that serve as energy sources for other bacteria that are chemosynthetic autotrophs. The chemosynthetic bacteria, in turn, support a diverse community of mussels, limpets, snails, worms, crabs, clams, and other organisms that live on the bones and within the nearby sediments.

4–2 Section Assessment

1. **Key Concept** What is the difference between a biotic factor and an abiotic factor?
2. **Key Concept** Name three types of community interactions that can affect an ecosystem.
3. **Key Concept** What is the difference between primary succession and secondary succession?
4. How is an organism's niche determined?
5. **Critical Thinking Comparing and Contrasting** How are the three types of symbiotic relationships different? How are they similar?

iTEXT **Assessment** Use iText to review the important concepts in Section 4–2.

ALTERNATIVE ASSESSMENT

Creative Writing
Use the information from this section to write a short story about an ecosystem that is disturbed and undergoes succession. Include a flowchart with your story to show the main stages of change.

3 ASSESS

Evaluate Understanding

Have each student select an example of succession—either one described in the student text or one of his or her own choice—and write a brief description of the sequence of changes that the ecosystem could undergo. As an alternative, students could draw sketches to show the changes.

Reteach

Using photographs of ecosystems that you have selected from other chapters in this textbook or from other sources, have students list the biotic and abiotic factors in each ecosystem.

ALTERNATIVE ASSESSMENT

Let students use any ecosystem and any kind of disturbance of their choice. In general, students' stories should include information about a change in the biotic or abiotic factors in a stable ecosystem, resulting in succession. Students should chronicle the gradual changes that return the ecosystem to a climax community. If students have a hard time getting started, suggest that they begin by making a flowchart of steps in succession for a particular ecosystem, then use the flowchart as an outline for the story.

Use iText to review the key concepts in Section 4–2.

4–2 Section Assessment

1. A biotic factor is a living organism. An abiotic factor is nonliving.
2. Competition, predation, and symbiosis
3. Primary succession occurs where any previously existing ecosystem has been removed. The area is then colonized by pioneer species, and soil forms, allowing more plants and animals to move in. Secondary succession occurs after an ecosystem has been disturbed by natural events or human activities. As secondary succession takes place, the disturbed area comes to resemble its surroundings.
4. An organism's niche is determined by the physical and biological conditions in its environment and how it uses those conditions.
5. In mutualism, both species benefit. In commensalism, only one species benefits while the other is neither helped nor harmed. In parasitism, one species benefits while the other is harmed.

Section 4–3

1 FOCUS

Objectives

4.3.1 ***Explain*** what microclimates are.

4.3.2 ***Identify*** the characteristics of the major land biomes.

Guide for Reading

Vocabulary Preview

Have students recall the definition of *climate* they learned earlier. Write *microclimate* on the board, and draw a box around the prefix *micro-*. Ask a volunteer to find the meaning of the prefix in a dictionary. *Micro-* means "small"; thus the term *microclimate* literally means "small climate"—a climate that exists over a small area.

Reading Strategy

Encourage students to create a table for recording the characteristics of each biome. Suggest that they include the following columns: *Name of Biome, Temperature, Precipitation, Soil Type, Dominant Plants, Dominant Animals,* and a final column labeled *Other Characteristics* in which to record any information that does not fit in the previous columns.

2 INSTRUCT

Climate and Microclimate

Use Community Resources

Take students on a tour of the school grounds or immediate neighborhood to look for microclimates. Examples might include a south-facing embankment along a roadway, the sunny south side and shaded north side of a building, and the shaded, damp environment beneath a group of trees. Encourage students to check each microclimate periodically and note any changes—for example, spring flowers blooming along a building's south side.

4–3 Land Biomes

Guide for Reading

Key Concept
- What are the unique characteristics of the world's major land biomes?

Vocabulary
- biome • microclimate
- canopy • understory
- deciduous • coniferous
- humus • taiga
- permafrost

Reading Strategy: Using Visuals Before you read, preview **Figure 4–11.** Write down the names of the different biomes. As you read, examine the photographs and list the main characteristics of each biome.

Our planet is home to an amazing diversity of organisms that live in many different ecosystems—from frozen, treeless expanses near the North Pole to steaming tropical forests with trees that tower higher than the Statue of Liberty. Sometimes, it is useful to classify the bewildering variety of ecosystems into a manageable number of categories. To do this, ecologists may use the concept of biomes. A **biome** is a particular physical environment that contains a characteristic assemblage of plants and animals.

For example, the temperate grassland biome occupies large areas of flat or rolling land in regions with dry, temperate climates on several continents. This biome generally receives too little rainfall for forests to grow, but does support grasses and wildflowers and large herds of herbivores.

Climate and Microclimate

Climate is especially important in determining the characteristics of a biome. The two main factors that determine a region's climate—temperature and precipitation—can be summarized on a graph called a climate diagram. Study the general climate diagram in **Figure 4–10,** because you will encounter similar diagrams on the next few pages.

Climate conditions can vary over much smaller distances than you might imagine. Mountains, forests, oceans, lakes, and other natural features can influence the climate in a small area within a biome. The climate within a small area that differs significantly from the climate around it is called a **microclimate.** In California, for example, certain streets within the city of San Francisco are often blanketed with thick fog, yet the sun shines just a few blocks away. Parts of California's northern coast are covered with lush redwood forests, while areas a short distance inland are desertlike, spotted with cacti and other drought-resistant plants. Even a small park, if it is usually sunnier or windier than nearby areas, can have its own microclimate.

CHECKPOINT *What is a microclimate?*

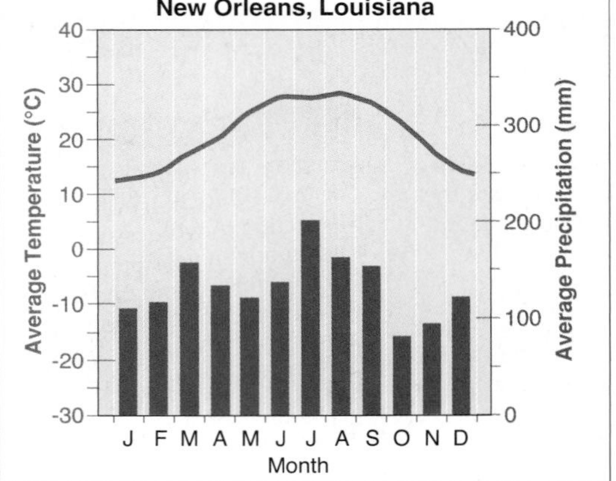

◀ **Figure 4–10** Climate diagrams show the average temperature and precipitation at a given location during each month of the year. In this graph, and the others to follow, temperature is plotted as a red line. Precipitation is shown as vertical bars. **Interpreting Graphics** ***What is the approximate average temperature and precipitation in New Orleans during the month of July?***

SECTION RESOURCES

Print:
- ***Teaching Resources,*** Section Review 4–3
- ***Guided Reading and Study Workbook,*** Section 4–3
- ***Issues and Decision Making,*** 4–1

Technology
- ***iText,*** Section 4–3

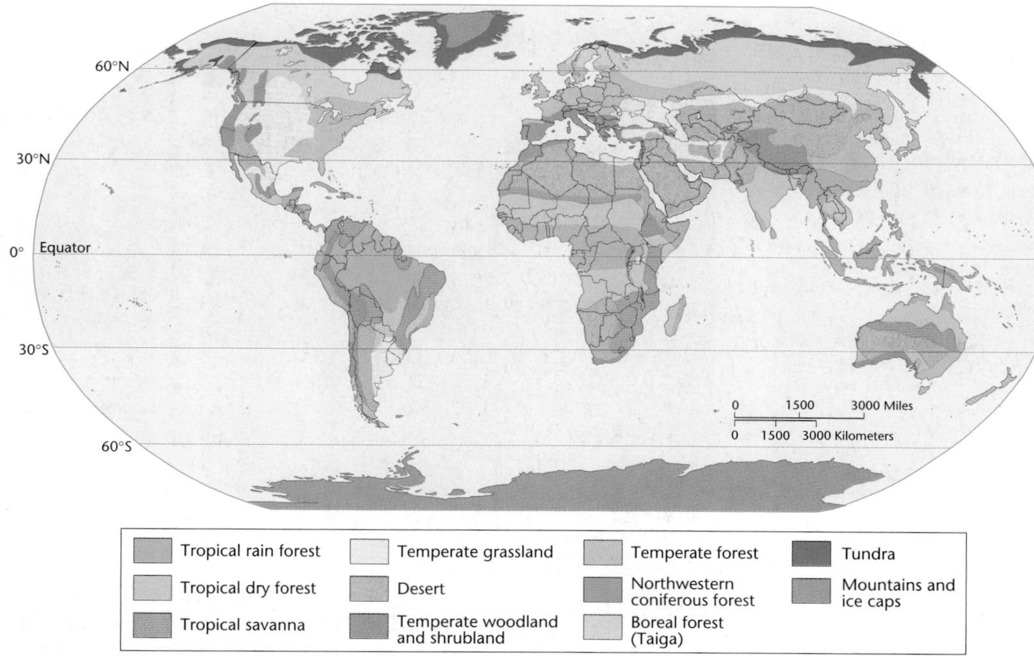

The Major Biomes

Ecologists recognize at least ten different biomes. **The world's major land biomes include tropical rain forest, tropical dry forest, tropical savanna, desert, temperate grassland, temperate woodland and shrubland, temperate forest, northwestern coniferous forest, boreal forest, and tundra. Each of these biomes is defined by a unique set of abiotic factors—particularly climate—and has a characteristic ecological community.** The map in **Figure 4–11** shows the natural geographic distribution of these major biomes. Be aware, however, that this is just one of many different systems that are used to classify biomes. The map does not take into account changes made by human activity, which you will read about in a later chapter.

The boundaries between the biomes may appear to be sharp on the map. On the ground, however, there are often transitional areas between biomes. In these transitional areas, one biome's plants and animals gradually become less frequent, while the organisms characteristic of the adjacent biome become more frequent. In addition, the community structure of a particular biome will differ slightly, depending on location and elevation above sea level. For this survey, you will study an example of each major biome from a specific location and elevation. You will begin in the tropics and finish at the poles.

▲ **Figure 4–11** This map shows the locations of the world's major land biomes. Other parts of Earth's surface are classified as mountains or ice caps. **Each biome has a characteristic climate and community of organisms.** These characteristics are shown in the pages that follow.

The Major Biomes

Build Science Skills

Interpreting Tables and Graphs To ensure that students understand the format of a climate diagram, ask questions about Figure 4–10, such as the following: **In which month does New Orleans have the least precipitation?** *(October)* **The most precipitation?** *(July)* **What general trend do you see in the average monthly temperatures throughout the year?** *(Temperatures are lowest in winter, rise through the spring, are highest in summer, and decline through the fall and early winter.)*

Use Visuals

Figure 4–11 Direct students' attention to the map and ask: **Which biomes are found in the United States, not including Alaska and Hawaii?** *(Temperate grassland, desert, temperate woodland and shrubland, northwestern coniferous forest and temperate forest)* **Which biomes are found in Alaska?** *(Temperate forest, boreal forest, and tundra)* **Which biome do you predict is found in Hawaii? Why?** *(Tropical rain forest; Hawaii's location near the equator and surrounded by ocean produces a hot, wet climate.)*

Build Science Skills

Inferring Direct students to look back at Figure 4–2 on page 88 and compare it with Figure 4–11 on this page. Ask: **Why do you think scientists classify land biomes into 10 categories when there are only three major climate zones on Earth?** *(Conditions vary somewhat within each climate zone, so several biomes are necessary to characterize each climate zone accurately.)*

PRESENTATIONS MADE EASY!

The Presentation Assistant Plus contains the Prentice Hall Presentation Pro and the Transparencies, which provide easy-to-follow visual support for every step of this section. If you have a computer presentation station, use Prentice Hall Presentation Pro for Section 4–3, or use the transparencies listed here.

Section 4–3: **Interest Grabber**
Section Outline
Compare/Contrast Table
Figure 4–11

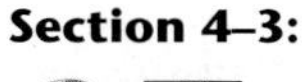

Answers to . . .

CHECKPOINT *A climate that exists over a small area and that is different from the climate of the surrounding region.*

Figure 4–10 *During the month of July in New Orleans, the average temperature is 25°C and the average precipitation is 200 mm.*

Build Science Skills

Comparing and Contrasting Guide students through the wealth of information on pages 100–104 by having them focus on a single factor at a time across all the biomes. For example, first have students compare the biomes' temperature ranges and sequence them from lowest to highest. *(Tundra, boreal forest, temperate forest, northwestern coniferous forest, temperate grassland, temperate woodland and shrubland, desert, tropical savanna, tropical rain forest, tropical dry forest)* Then, have students compare the biomes' precipitation and sequence those amounts from lowest to highest. *(Desert and tundra, boreal forest, temperate woodland and shrubland, temperate grassland, temperate forest, tropical savanna, tropical dry forest, northwestern coniferous forest, tropical rain forest)* Next, have students compare the types of plants that are dominant in each biome and, finally, the dominant animals. Discuss any biome features or organisms that are unfamiliar to students. Encourage students to share any personal experiences they have had with different land biomes.

Meet Diverse Needs

Particularly for students who learn best through visual means, supply field guides in book or CD-ROM format so students can see what each biome and its characteristic plants and animals look like. Note that CD-ROM programs may also include interesting sound effects and video clips. **Learning modality: visual**

Tropical Rain Forest

Tropical rain forests are home to more species than all other land biomes combined. The leafy tops of tall trees—extending up to 70 meters above the forest floor—form a dense covering called a **canopy.** In the shade below the canopy, a second layer of shorter trees and vines forms an **understory.** Organic matter that falls to the forest floor quickly decomposes and the nutrients are recycled.

- **Abiotic factors:** hot and wet year-round; thin, nutrient-poor soils
- **Dominant plants:** broad-leaved evergreen trees; ferns; large woody vines and climbing plants; orchids and bromeliads
- **Dominant wildlife:** herbivores such as sloths, tapirs, and capybaras; predators such as jaguars; anteaters; monkeys; birds such as toucans, parrots, and parakeets; insects such as butterflies, ants, and beetles; piranhas and other freshwater fishes; reptiles such as frogs, caymans, boa constrictors, and anacondas
- **Geographic distribution:** parts of South and Central America, Southeast Asia, parts of Africa, southern India, and northeastern Australia

Tropical Dry Forest

Tropical dry forests grow in places where rainfall is highly seasonal rather than year-round. During the dry season, nearly all the trees drop their leaves to conserve water. A tree that sheds its leaves during a particular season each year is called **deciduous.**

- **Abiotic factors:** generally warm year-round; alternating wet and dry seasons; rich soils subject to erosion
- **Dominant plants:** tall, deciduous trees that form a dense canopy during the wet season; drought-tolerant orchids and bromeliads; aloes and other succulents
- **Dominant wildlife:** tigers; monkeys; herbivores such as elephants, Indian rhinoceros, hog deer; birds such as great pied hornbill, pied harrier, and spot-billed pelican; insects such as termites; reptiles such as snakes and monitor lizards
- **Geographic distribution:** parts of Africa, South and Central America, Mexico, India, Australia, and tropical islands

BACKGROUND

What's soil got to do with it?
Soil is a mixture of rock, mineral ions, and organic matter. Each land biome tends to have a characteristic soil type. The top layer of soil in tropical rain forest biomes is acidic, with light-colored humus. The subsoil consists of iron and aluminum compounds mixed with clay. The soil in desert biomes is dry, brown to reddish brown with variable accumulations of clay, calcium carbonate, and soluble salts. A humus-mineral mixture exists in a thin layer of topsoil.

Tropical Savanna

Receiving more seasonal rainfall than deserts but less than tropical dry forests, tropical savannas, or grasslands, are characterized by a cover of grasses. Savannas are spotted with isolated trees and small groves of trees and shrubs. Compact soils, fairly frequent fires, and the action of large animals such as rhinoceros prevent some savanna areas from turning into dry forest.

- **Abiotic factors:** warm temperatures; seasonal rainfall; compact soil; frequent fires set by lightning
- **Dominant plants:** tall, perennial grasses; sometimes drought-tolerant and fire-resistant trees or shrubs
- **Dominant wildlife:** predators such as lions, leopards, cheetahs, hyenas, and jackals; aardvarks; herbivores such as elephants, giraffes, antelopes, and zebras; baboons; birds such as eagles, ostriches, weaver birds, and storks; insects such as termites
- **Geographic distribution:** large parts of eastern Africa, southern Brazil, northern Australia

Desert

All deserts are dry—in fact, a desert biome is defined as having annual precipitation of less than 25 centimeters. Beyond that, deserts vary greatly, depending on elevation and latitude. Many undergo extreme temperature changes during the course of a day, alternating between hot and cold. The organisms in this biome can tolerate the extreme conditions.

- **Abiotic factors:** low precipitation; variable temperatures; soils rich in minerals but poor in organic material
- **Dominant plants:** cacti and other succulents; creosote bush and other plants with short growth cycles
- **Dominant wildlife:** predators such as mountain lions, gray foxes, and bobcats; herbivores such as mule deer, pronghorn antelope, desert bighorn sheep, and kangaroo rats; bats; birds such as owls, hawks, and roadrunners; insects such as ants, beetles, butterflies, flies, and wasps; reptiles such as tortoises, rattlesnakes, and lizards
- **Geographic distribution:** Africa, Asia, the Middle East, United States, Mexico, South America, and Australia

Build Science Skills

Communicating Divide the class into ten groups, and assign a different biome to each group. Tell students that each group is to serve as the "class experts" on its assigned biome. Let each group's members divide responsibilities among themselves however they wish. For example, one student could handle abiotic factors, another student the dominant plants, and a third student the dominant animals. Encourage groups to do research to gain additional information about the biomes. Provide an opportunity for each group to present its biome to the class, share additional information they have gathered, and answer other students' questions.

Address Misconceptions

Most students—in fact, most people in general—think that all deserts are hot as well as dry. Emphasize that it is the amount of precipitation, not the temperature range, that distinguishes the desert from other biomes. Encourage students to find out about cold deserts, including the high-altitude deserts of Mongolia and China and the Great Basin in the western United States.

BIO INSIGHTS — FACTS AND FIGURES

Convergent evolution

Plants and animals that appear to be quite similar often are found in similar environments but in widely separated parts of the world. For example, a member of the cactus family that grows in deserts of the southwestern United States is similar in appearance to a member of the spurge family that grows in the deserts of southwestern Africa. It would seem that these plants have evolved from a common ancestor, but this is not the case. The two species evolved from plants that are not related. This phenomenon of similar yet unrelated species occurring in different parts of the world is known as convergent evolution.

4–3 (continued)

Build Science Skills

Comparing and Contrasting Have students refer back to the biome map in Figure 4–11 on page 99. Ask: **Which biome makes up the largest portion of the continental United States?** *(Temperate grassland)* Then, direct students to review the climate diagrams and text descriptions of the temperate grassland biome on this page and the tropical savanna biome on page 101. Ask: **What is the major similarity between these two biomes?** *(The dominant plants are grasses.)* **What are the major differences in the two biomes' climate?** *(The savanna gets more rainfall and has a greater range between the highest and lowest amounts. Savanna temperatures are higher but less variable than temperate grassland temperatures.)*

Meet Diverse Needs

As students read through the biome descriptions, encourage those who are not yet proficient in English to create a glossary of any unfamiliar terms they encounter. Suggest that they write the English term first, followed by its translation or equivalent in the students' first language. Encourage students to use the glossary as a reference tool; do not treat the words as vocabulary terms to be memorized. **Limited English proficiency**

Temperate Grassland

Characterized by a rich mix of grasses and underlaid by some of the world's most fertile soils, temperate grasslands—such as plains and prairies—once covered vast areas of the midwestern United States. Since the development of the steel plow, however, most have been converted to agricultural fields. Periodic fires and heavy grazing by large herbivores maintain the characteristic plant community.

- ▶ **Abiotic factors:** warm to hot summers; cold winters; moderate, seasonal precipitation; fertile soils; occasional fires
- ▶ **Dominant plants:** lush, perennial grasses and herbs; most are resistant to drought, fire, and cold
- ▶ **Dominant wildlife:** predators such as coyotes and badgers—historically included wolves and grizzly bears; herbivores such as mule deer, pronghorn antelope, rabbits, prairie dogs, and introduced cattle—historically included bison; birds such as hawks, owls, bobwhite, prairie chicken, mountain plover; reptiles such as snakes; insects such as ants and grasshoppers
- ▶ **Geographic distribution:** central Asia, North America, Australia, central Europe, and upland plateaus of South America

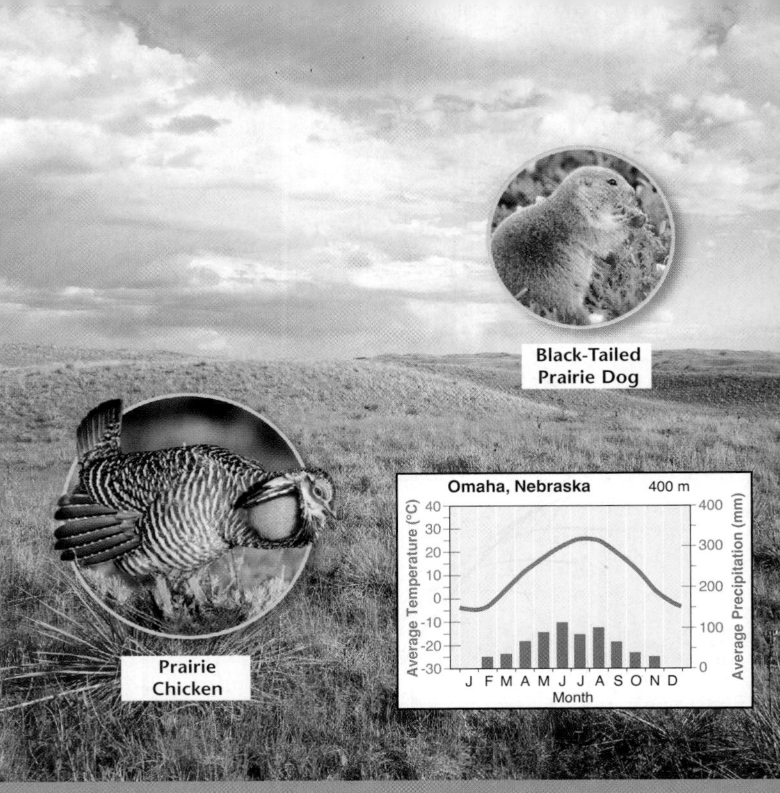

Temperate Woodland and Shrubland

This biome is characterized by a semiarid climate and a mix of shrub communities and open woodlands. In the open woodlands, large areas of grasses and wildflowers such as poppies are interspersed with oak trees. Communities that are dominated by shrubs are also known as chaparral. The growth of dense, low plants that contain flammable oils makes fires a constant threat.

- ▶ **Abiotic factors:** hot, dry summers; cool, moist winters; thin, nutrient-poor soils; periodic fires
- ▶ **Dominant plants:** woody evergreen shrubs with small, leathery leaves; fragrant, oily herbs that grow during winter and die in summer
- ▶ **Dominant wildlife:** predators such as coyotes, foxes, bobcats, and mountain lions; herbivores such as blacktailed deer, rabbits, squirrels, and mice; birds such as hawks, California quail, western scrub jay, warblers and other songbirds; reptiles such as lizards and snakes; butterflies; spiders
- ▶ **Geographic distribution:** western coasts of North and South America, areas around the Mediterranean Sea, South Africa, and Australia

BACKGROUND

More on soil

The topsoil of temperate grassland biomes tends to be dark, alkaline, and rich in humus. This topsoil layer extends downward for more than a meter. Because topsoil formed on grasslands is often very fertile, most of the world's crops are grown on grassland soils. The subsoil consists of clay and calcium compounds. Soil in the boreal forest biomes is often quite acidic.

Temperate Forest

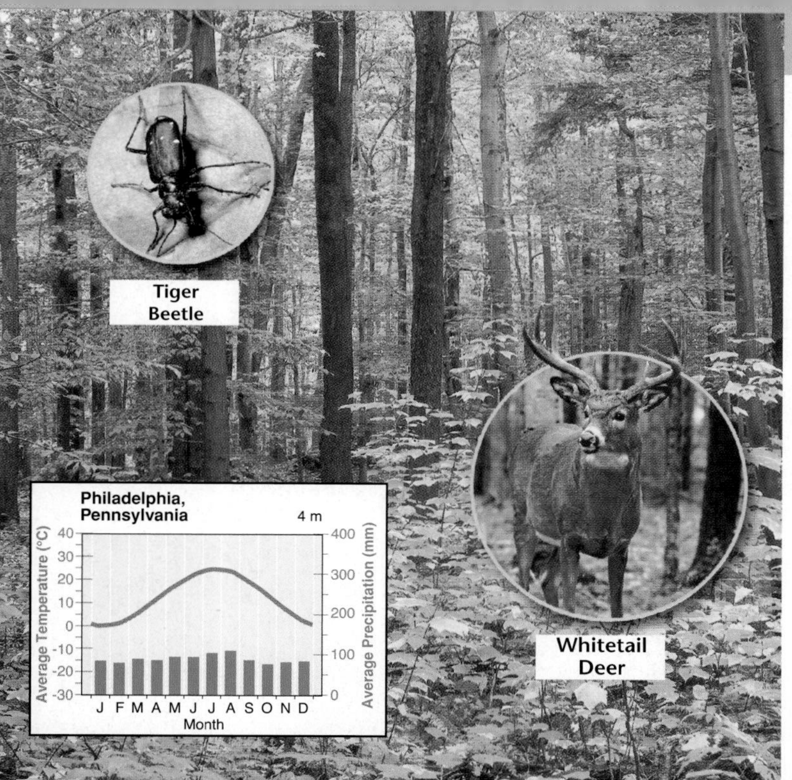

Temperate forests contain a mixture of deciduous and coniferous (koh-NIF-ur-us) trees. **Coniferous** trees, or conifers, produce seed-bearing cones and most have leaves shaped like needles. These forests have cold winters that halt plant growth for several months. In autumn, the deciduous trees shed their leaves. In the spring, small plants burst out of the ground and flower. Soils of temperate forests are often rich in **humus** (HYOO-mus), a material formed from decaying leaves and other organic matter that makes soil fertile.

- **Abiotic factors:** cold to moderate winters; warm summers; year-round precipitation; fertile soils
- **Dominant plants:** broadleaf deciduous trees; some conifers; flowering shrubs; herbs; a ground layer of mosses and ferns
- **Dominant wildlife:** Deer; black bears; bobcats; nut and acorn feeders, such as squirrels; omnivores such as raccoons and skunks; numerous songbirds; turkeys
- **Geographic distribution:** eastern United States; southeastern Canada; most of Europe; and parts of Japan, China, and Australia

Northwestern Coniferous Forest

Mild, moist air from the Pacific Ocean provides abundant rainfall to this biome. The forest is made up of a variety of conifers, ranging from giant redwoods along the coast of northern California to spruce, fir, and hemlock farther north. Moss often covers tree trunks and the forest floor. Flowering trees and shrubs such as dogwood and rhododendron are also abundant. Because of its lush vegetation, the northwestern coniferous forest is sometimes called a "temperate rain forest."

- **Abiotic factors:** mild temperatures; abundant precipitation during fall, winter, and spring; relatively cool, dry summer; rocky, acidic soils
- **Dominant plants:** Douglas fir, Sitka spruce, western hemlock, redwood
- **Dominant wildlife:** bears; large herbivores such as elk and deer; beavers; predators such as owls, bobcats, and members of the weasel family
- **Geographic distribution:** Pacific coast of northwestern United States and Canada, from northern California to Alaska

BIO INSIGHTS — FACTS AND FIGURES

Layers of plant growth

In a temperate forest, there may be up to five layers of plant growth. The tallest trees make up the canopy layer; often this layer consists of only one or two dominant species. Under the canopy is a layer of shorter trees called the understory. Below the understory is a shrub layer made up of short, branching, woody plants. An herb layer consisting of grasses, ferns, and annual wildflowers grows close to the ground. Finally, there is the ground layer, which consists of mosses, fungi, and leaf litter.

Build Science Skills

Applying Concepts Point out that the temperate forest biome in northeastern regions of North America and Asia is noted for its strikingly colored fall foliage. If students do not live in an area that experiences this seasonal change, urge them to collect photographs of fall foliage. Also suggest that they obtain booklets and other tourist guides that describe the best times and locations for foliage viewing at different latitudes within the biome.

Build Science Skills

Classifying Collect photographs of various types of animals that are characteristic of each major land biome. Number the photographs, and display them in random order. Working individually or in pairs, students should try to determine the biome(s) in which each animal might live. In a followup class discussion, let students compare their choices and explain their reasoning.

4–3 (continued)

Build Science Skills

Drawing Conclusions Focus students' attention on the climate diagram for the tundra biome. Ask: **In terms of precipitation throughout the year, which other biome does the tundra most resemble?** *(The desert biome)* Have students look back at the biome map on page 99. Ask: **Why does the tundra biome have the lowest temperatures of all the biomes?** *(The tundra is the farthest north of all biomes, so it receives the sun's rays at the lowest angles and for the shortest periods of time.)*

Other Land Areas

Make Connections

Earth Science Display a large world map that shows Earth's major mountain ranges. Have students locate the color-coded mountain areas on the biome map in Figure 4–11, page 99, then find those areas on the large map and list the names of the mountain ranges. Separate groups could investigate each range's characteristics—the heights of its tallest peaks, the temperature ranges and dominant organisms at various elevations, and other data. Encourage students to also search out interesting facts about the ranges, such as the 1998 discovery of mummified children on high Andean peaks or tales of the elusive Yeti ("abominable snowmen") high in the Himalayas. Let groups share their findings in oral reports, illustrated displays, or three-dimensional models.

Boreal Forest

Along the northern edge of the temperate zone are dense evergreen forests of coniferous trees. These biomes are called boreal forests, or **taiga** (TY-guh). Winters are bitterly cold, but summers are mild and long enough to allow the ground to thaw. The word *boreal* comes from the Greek word for "north," reflecting the fact that boreal forests occur mostly in the Northern Hemisphere.

- **Abiotic factors:** long, cold winters; short, mild summers; moderate precipitation; high humidity; acidic, nutrient-poor soils
- **Dominant plants:** needleleaf coniferous trees such as spruce and fir; some broadleaf deciduous trees; small, berry-bearing shrubs
- **Dominant wildlife:** predators like lynx and timberwolves and members of the weasel family; small herbivorous mammals; moose and other large herbivores; beavers; songbirds and migratory birds
- **Geographic distribution:** North America, Asia, and northern Europe

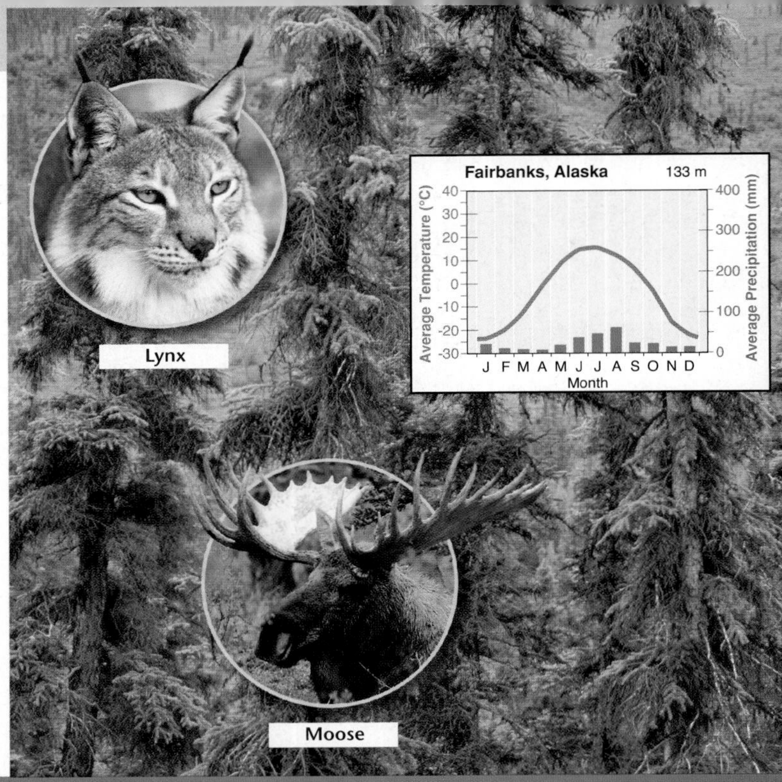

Tundra

The tundra is characterized by **permafrost,** a layer of permanently frozen subsoil. During the short, cool summer, the ground thaws to a depth of a few centimeters and becomes soggy and wet. In winter, the topsoil freezes again. This cycle of thawing and freezing, which rips and crushes plant roots, is one reason that tundra plants are small and stunted. Cold temperatures, high winds, the short growing season, and humus-poor soils also limit plant height.

- **Abiotic factors:** strong winds; low precipitation; short and soggy summers; long, cold, and dark winters; poorly developed soils; permafrost
- **Dominant plants:** ground-hugging plants such as mosses, lichens, sedges, and short grasses
- **Dominant wildlife:** a few resident birds and mammals that can withstand the harsh conditions; migratory waterfowl, shore birds, musk ox, Arctic foxes, and caribou; lemmings and other small rodents
- **Geographic distribution:** northern North America, Asia, and Europe

FACTS AND FIGURES

Oases in the tundra

As an example of the tundra's extreme dryness: In the Arctic regions north of mainland Canada, less than 15 cm of precipitation falls annually—about the same amount as falls in the desert regions of Arizona. Such dryness, coupled with intense cold, makes the tundra a barren place. Yet, like the oases in deserts, there are areas where living things can survive and even thrive. Some of these areas are sheltered valleys that are protected from bitterly cold winds. Other areas are meadows with an abundant water supply that can support large numbers of animals.

Other Land Areas

Some areas of land on Earth do not fall neatly into the major biome categories described on the previous pages. These areas include mountain ranges and polar ice caps.

Mountain Ranges Mountain ranges can be found on all continents. On mountains like the one in **Figure 4–12,** the abiotic and biotic conditions vary with elevation. As you move up from base to summit, temperatures become colder and precipitation increases. Therefore, the types of plants and animals also change. If you were to climb the Rocky Mountains in Colorado, for example, you would begin in a grassland. Then, you would pass through an open woodland of pines. Next, you would hike through a forest of spruce and other conifers. Near the summit, you would reach open areas of wildflowers and stunted vegetation resembling tundra. In the Canadian Rockies, ice fields occur at the peaks of some ranges.

Polar Ice Caps The icy polar regions that border the tundra are cold year-round. Outside of the ice and snow, plants and algae are few but do include mosses and lichens. In the north polar region, the Arctic Ocean is covered with sea ice, and a thick ice cap covers most of Greenland. Polar bears, seals, insects, and mites are the dominant animals. In the south polar region, the continent of Antarctica is covered by a layer of ice that is nearly 5 kilometers thick in some places. There, the dominant wildlife includes penguins and marine mammals.

▲ **Figure 4–12** Washington's Mount Rainier towers above the tree line. **Applying Concepts** *Based on what you have seen in the previous pages, which biome lies at the base of this mountain?*

4–3 Section Assessment

1. **Key Concept** List the major land biomes and give one characteristic feature of each.
2. How are biomes classified?
3. What are the two types of tropical forest? How do they differ?
4. How might the presence of a mountain range affect the types of plants and animals found in an area?
5. **Critical Thinking Inferring** What characteristics would you expect tundra animals to have?

Assessment Use iText to review the important concepts in Section 4–3.

ALTERNATIVE ASSESSMENT

Creating Artwork
Choose one of the land biomes discussed in this section. Then, depict the biome in a piece of artwork. Include the biome's characteristic plant and animal life in your art.

4–3 Section Assessment

1. Students should list the major biomes along with one characteristic of each biome from the text on pages 100–104.
2. By their climate, which is determined by precipitation and temperature
3. Tropical rain forests have higher temperatures and more rainfall annually than do tropical dry forests.
4. Animals found in mountain ranges must be adapted to the generally cooler, wetter conditions that are found there.
5. Sample answer: Tundra animals need to be well insulated with thick coats of fur/hair or layers of feathers.

3 ASSESS

Evaluate Understanding

Briefly describe characteristics of various biomes, and call on students at random to identify each one. For example, if you say, "High temperatures that do not vary much throughout the year," students should identify the biome as a tropical rain forest or a tropical savanna. Base your descriptions on the information presented on pages 100–104 of the student text.

Reteach

Make overhead transparencies of the climate diagrams for each of the land biomes. Project the diagrams in any order. For each diagram, call on one student to summarize the diagram's information about temperature and precipitation *(for example, "High temperatures and heavy rainfall year-round")*, and call on a second student to identify the biome.

ALTERNATIVE ASSESSMENT

This activity can be completed individually or in small groups. Provide students with a variety of materials to choose from, including basic art supplies, modeling clay, pasta shapes, pipe cleaners, fabric, and construction paper. You might also encourage students to bring materials from home, or you might coordinate this activity with an art class at your school. Encourage students to be creative but accurate in depicting the biomes.

iTEXT

Use iText to review the key concepts in Section 4–3.

Answer to . . .

Figure 4–12 *Boreal forest*

Section 4–4

1 FOCUS

Objectives

4.4.1 ***Identify*** the factors that govern aquatic ecosystems.

4.4.2 ***Identify*** the two types of freshwater ecosystems.

4.4.3 ***Describe*** the characteristics of the marine zones.

Guide for Reading

Vocabulary Preview

Point out the words *photic* and *aphotic* in the vocabulary list on this page. Explain that *phot-* in these words means the same thing as the prefix *photo-* in words such as *photograph.* Ask: **What does the prefix *photo-* mean?** *("Light")* **What does the prefix *a-* in the word *aphotic* mean?** *("Not" or "without")* **What do you think the terms *photic* and *aphotic* mean?** *("With light" and "without light")* Tell students to check their predictions when they encounter these words in the text.

Reading Strategy

As with the land biomes in Section 4–3, have students set up a table for recording the similarities and differences they find as they read about aquatic ecosystems. Suggest that they divide the "Marine Ecosystems" section of the table into two subsections so they can keep separate notes on the photic and aphotic zones.

2 INSTRUCT

Freshwater Ecosystems

Use Community Sources

Have students consult road maps to find the locations and names of any freshwater ecosystems—lakes, ponds, rivers, or streams—in their area. If possible, arrange a trip to one of these locations so students can observe its characteristics and the types of organisms living there.

4–4 Aquatic Ecosystems

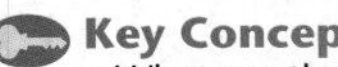

Key Concepts
- What are the main factors that govern aquatic ecosystems?
- What are the two types of freshwater ecosystems?
- What are the characteristics of the different marine zones?

Vocabulary
- plankton • phytoplankton
- zooplankton • wetland
- estuary • detritus • salt marsh
- mangrove swamp
- photic zone • aphotic zone
- zonation • coastal ocean
- kelp forest • coral reef
- benthos

Reading Strategy: Making Comparisons As you read, write down statements about similarities and differences among the different types of aquatic ecosystems.

Nearly three fourths of Earth's surface is covered with water, so it is not surprising that many organisms make their home in aquatic habitats. Oceans, streams, lakes, and marshes—indeed, nearly any body of water—contain a wide variety of communities. These aquatic communities are governed by biotic and abiotic factors, including light, nutrient availability, and oxygen.

Aquatic ecosystems are determined primarily by the depth, flow, temperature, and chemistry of the overlying water. In contrast to land biomes, which are grouped geographically, aquatic ecosystems are often grouped according to the abiotic factors that affect them. One such factor is the depth of water, or distance from shore. The depth of water, in turn, determines the amount of light that organisms receive. Water chemistry refers primarily to the amount of dissolved chemicals—especially salts, nutrients, and oxygen—on which life depends. For example, communities of organisms found in shallow water close to shore can be very different from the communities that occur away from shore in deep water. One abiotic factor that is important both to land biomes and aquatic ecosystems is latitude. Aquatic ecosystems in polar, temperate, and tropical oceans all have distinctive characteristics.

▼ **Figure 4–13** The Menominee River in Michigan is a flowing-water ecosystem. **Like all aquatic ecosystems, this river's communities are determined by the depth, flow, and chemistry of the water.**

Freshwater Ecosystems

It may surprise you to know that only 3 percent of the surface water on Earth is fresh water. **Freshwater ecosystems can be divided into two main types: flowing-water ecosystems and standing-water ecosystems.**

Flowing-Water Ecosystems Rivers, streams, creeks, and brooks are all freshwater ecosystems that flow over the land. Organisms that live there are well adapted to the rate of flow. Some insect larvae have hooks that allow them to take hold of aquatic plants. Certain catfish have suckers that anchor them to rocks. Trout and many other fishes have streamlined bodies that help them move with or against the current.

Flowing-water ecosystems like the river in **Figure 4–13** originate in mountains or hills, often springing from an underground water source. Near the source, the turbulent water has plenty of dissolved oxygen but little plant life. As the water flows downhill, sediments build up and enable plants to establish themselves. Farther downstream, the water may meander more slowly through flat areas, where turtles, beavers, or river otters make their homes.

SECTION RESOURCES

Print:
- ***Guided Reading and Study Workbook,*** Section 4–4

Technology
- ***iText,*** Section 4–4

Standing-Water Ecosystems Lakes and ponds are the most common standing-water ecosystems. In addition to the net flow of water in and out of these systems, there is usually water circulating within them. This circulation helps to distribute heat, oxygen, and nutrients throughout the ecosystem.

The relatively still waters of lakes and ponds provide habitats for many organisms, such as plankton, that would be quickly washed away in flowing water. **Plankton** is a general term for the tiny, free-floating or weakly swimming organisms that live in both freshwater and saltwater environments. See **Figure 4–14** for examples. Single-celled algae, or **phytoplankton** (FYT-oh-plank-tun), are supported by nutrients in the water and form the base of many aquatic food webs. Planktonic animals, or **zooplankton** (ZO-oh-plank-tun), feed on the phytoplankton.

CHECKPOINT *What are phytoplankton?*

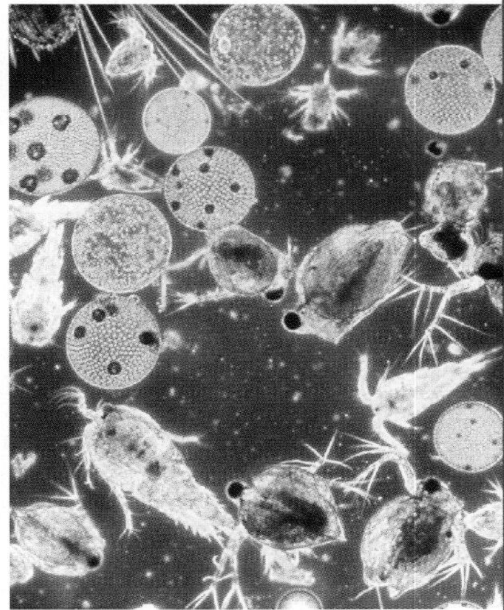

▲ **Figure 4–14** Both freshwater and saltwater ecosystems often include plankton. This photograph shows phytoplankton, zooplankton, and larger animals called water fleas. **Predicting** *What might happen to an aquatic food web if phytoplankton were removed from the ecosystem?*

Freshwater Wetlands A **wetland** is an ecosystem in which water either covers the soil or is present at or near the surface of the soil for at least part of the year. The water in wetlands may be flowing or standing, or fresh, salty, or brackish—a mixture of fresh and salt water. Many wetlands are very productive ecosystems that serve as breeding grounds for insects, fishes and other aquatic animals, amphibians, and migratory birds.

The three main types of freshwater wetlands are bogs, marshes, and swamps. Bogs typically form in depressions called "kettle holes" left by ice sheets that melted thousands of years ago. Thick mats of sphagnum moss grow in bogs, where the water tends to be very acidic. Marshes are shallow wetlands along rivers. Marshes may be under water for all or part of the year. Marshes often contain cattails, rushes, and other tall, grasslike plants. Water flows slowly through swamps, which often look like flooded forests. The presence of trees and shrubs is what distinguishes a swamp from a marsh.

Some wetlands, such as the swamp shown in **Figure 4–15**, are wet year-round. Other kinds of wetlands, however, may not always be covered in standing water. Such areas may be classified as wetlands because they have certain kinds of soils and are wet enough to support a specific community of water-loving plants and animals.

▼ **Figure 4–15** **Freshwater ecosystems can be divided into two main types: flowing-water ecosystems and standing-water ecosystems.** Although this swamp along the Loxahatchee River in Florida appears stagnant, water actually flows through it slowly. The swamp is home to turtles, otters, alligators, and herons that live among the bald cypress trees.

Build Science Skills

Comparing and Contrasting
As suggested for land biomes, guide students through the information in this section by having them focus on one factor at a time—temperature range, light, oxygen and nutrient availability, and characteristic organisms—across all the aquatic ecosystems. Discuss any unfamiliar organisms, and provide field guides so students can do further research. Also, encourage students to share any personal experiences they have had with different aquatic biomes.

Demonstration

Collect several different types of freshwater plants and animals to set up a classroom aquarium. Also collect some abiotic elements—water, rocks, mud, sand, and the like—so the organisms will have as natural an environment as possible. Make sure you or students return all organisms to their original location at the end of this unit.

Use Community Resources

Emphasize that a particular area of land is classified as a wetland not by whether it has water on it at any particular time of the year but by its soil type and the plants found there. In fact, many freshwater wetlands are dry for a good part of the year, so people may not even recognize them as wetlands. If a wetland exists near the school, take the class to observe it. Caution students to be very careful walking in the area, as many wetland plants are fragile and the soil, if damp, can be easily compacted. Do not allow students to collect any plants, animals, or abiotic materials.

PRESENTATIONS MADE EASY!

The Presentation Assistant Plus contains the Prentice Hall Presentation Pro and the Transparencies, which provide easy-to-follow visual support for every step of this section. If you have a computer presentation station, use Prentice Hall Presentation Pro for Section 4–4, or use the transparencies listed here.

Section 4–4: **Interest Grabber**
Section Outline
Freshwater Pond Ecosystem
Figure 4–15

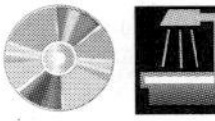

Answers to . . .

CHECKPOINT *Single-celled algae*

Figure 4–14 *The consumers would die off because there would be no more producers to sustain them.*

4–4 (continued)

Estuaries

Build Science Skills

Comparing and Contrasting Have students describe similarities and differences between the types of organisms found in freshwater ecosystems and those found in estuaries. Then, ask: **Do the same species of aquatic organisms live in both ecosystems?** *(No)* **Why not?** *(Estuaries are saltwater ecosystems. Species usually are adapted to live in either a saltwater environment or a freshwater environment, not both.)*

Marine Ecosystems

Build Science Skills

Predicting Draw a horizontal line on the chalkboard to represent the surface of the ocean. Then, draw a diagonal line slanting downward, and mark it to indicate ocean depths of 50 meters, 100 meters, 200 meters, 1000 meters, 2000 meters, and 10,000 meters. Invite students to relate what they already know about marine organisms. Then, ask: **What factors do you think determine the types of organisms that live at different depths in the ocean?** *(Most students will realize that available light is a major factor. Accept all responses without comment at this time.)*

Meet Diverse Needs

Most students probably will have had personal experience with freshwater ecosystems, but few will have observed any marine ecosystems beyond the intertidal zone. To help students comprehend the text description of marine zones, provide a wide variety of visual resources—photographic books, nature magazines, videotapes, and CD-ROM programs—so students can see what the different zones and their organisms look like. **Learning modality: visual**

Word Origins

A detritivore is an organism that eats detritus.

Word Origins

Detritus is a Latin word meaning "worn away." In ecology, detritus refers to particles that have worn away from decaying organic material. **If the Latin word *vorare* means "to devour," what is a *detritivore*?**

Estuaries

Estuaries (ES-tyoo-ehr-eez) are wetlands formed where rivers meet the sea. Estuaries thus contain a mixture of fresh water and salt water, and are affected by the rise and fall of ocean tides. Many are shallow, so sufficient sunlight reaches the bottom to power photosynthesis. Primary producers include plants, algae, and both photosynthetic and chemosynthetic bacteria. Estuary food webs differ from those of more familiar ecosystems because most primary production is not consumed by herbivores. Instead, much of that organic material enters the food web as detritus. **Detritus** is made up of tiny pieces of organic material that provide food for organisms at the base of the estuary's food web. Organisms that feed on detritus include clams, worms, and sponges.

Estuaries support an astonishing amount of biomass, although they usually contain fewer species than freshwater or marine ecosystems. Estuaries serve as spawning and nursery grounds for commercially important fishes and for shellfish such as shrimps and crabs. Many young animals feed and grow in estuaries, then head out to sea to mature, and return to reproduce. Many waterfowl use estuaries for nesting, feeding, and resting during migrations.

Salt marshes are temperate-zone estuaries dominated by salt-tolerant grasses above the low-tide line, and by seagrasses under water. Salt marshes like the one shown in **Figure 4–16** (left) are (or were once) found along great stretches of Eastern North America from Southern Maine to Georgia. One of the largest systems of connected salt marshes in America surrounds the Chesapeake Bay estuary in Maryland.

Mangrove swamps, shown in **Figure 4–16** (right), are coastal wetlands that are widespread across tropical regions, including southern Florida and Hawaii. Here, the dominant plants are several species of salt-tolerant trees, collectively called mangroves. Seagrasses are also common below the low-tide line. Like salt marshes, mangrove swamps are valuable nurseries for fish and shellfish. The largest mangrove area in the continental United States is Florida's Everglades National Park.

Figure 4–16 Salt marshes occur in estuaries along seacoasts in the temperate zone. Salt-tolerant grasses are the dominant plants in this salt marsh (left) along the coast of Mount Desert Island in Maine. Mangrove swamps (right) occur in bays and estuaries along tropical coasts. The stiltlike roots of mangrove trees trap sediment that accumulates as mud behind the trees. This allows other plants to take root and helps to build the mangrove forest out from the shoreline. **Predicting** ***Would you expect to find mangrove swamps or salt marshes on a coast exposed to large ocean waves? Explain.***

FACTS AND FIGURES

Bottoms up!

A problem that occurs in aquatic ecosystems is that nutrients tend to sink below the photic zone so organisms cannot use them. In lakes, strong winds usually mix the water. In oceans, deep nutrient-rich water rises to the photic zone in a process called upwelling. In upwelling, winds carry surface water away from land. Bottom water with valuable nutrients is pulled up into the photic zone to replace the surface water that has been moved out to sea. These nutrients support vigorous and rapid growth of phytoplankton, which provide the basis for marine food webs. Upwelling occurs only in certain places on Earth, including the western coasts of North America and South America.

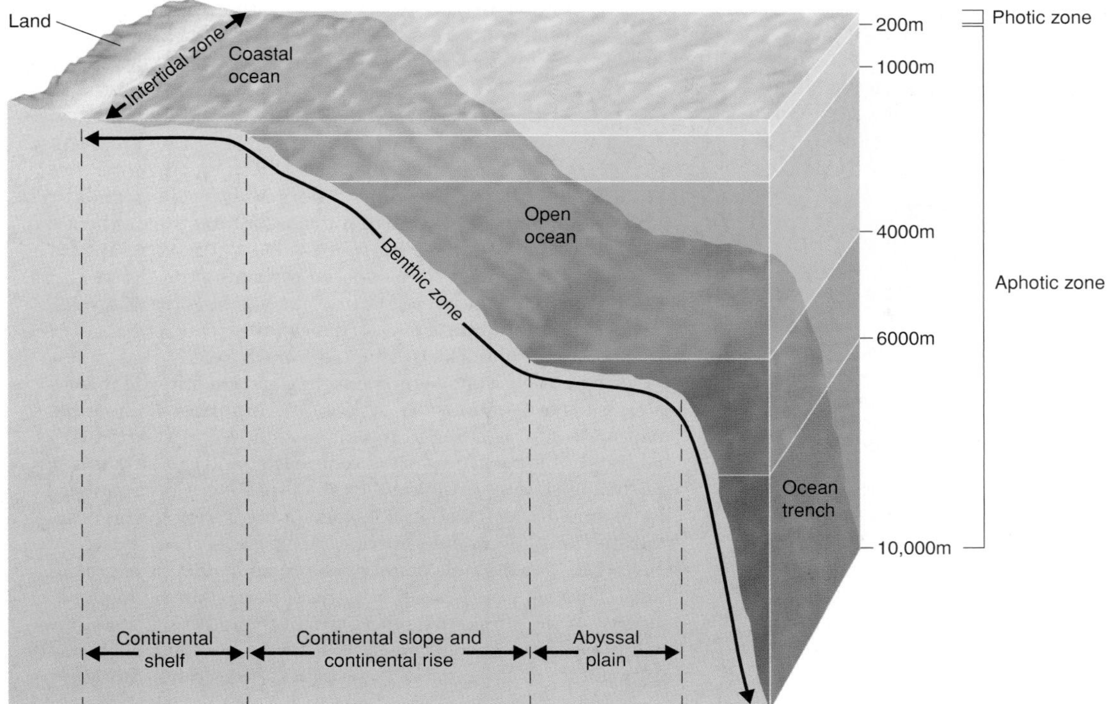

▲ **Figure 4–17 The ocean can be divided into zones based on light penetration and into zones based on depth and the distance from shore.** Each zone contains a characteristic assemblage of organisms.

Marine Ecosystems

Unless you are an avid diver or snorkeler, it takes some imagination to picture what life is like in the vast, three-dimensional ocean. Sunlight penetrates only a relatively short distance through the surface of the water. Photosynthesis is limited to this well-lit upper layer known as the **photic zone** (FOH-tihk). Only in this relatively thin surface layer—typically down to a depth of about 200 meters—can algae and other producers grow. Below the photic zone is the **aphotic zone** (ay-FOH-tihk), which is permanently dark. Chemosynthetic autotrophs are the only producers that can survive in the aphotic zone.

There are several different classification systems that scientists use to describe marine ecosystems. **In addition to the division between the photic and aphotic zones, marine biologists also divide the ocean into zones based on the depth and distance from shore: the intertidal zone, the coastal ocean, and the open ocean.** Each of these zones supports distinct ecological communities. The benthic zone covers the ocean floor and is, therefore, not exclusive to any of the other marine zones. **Figure 4–17** shows a generalized diagram of the marine zones.

CHECKPOINT *What factor is absent in the aphotic zone?*

Build Science Skills

Problem Solving Explain that three main factors determine the types of marine organisms that live at different depths: available sunlight, water temperature, and water pressure. Ask: **At what depth do you think sunlight is most abundant?** *(Near the surface)* **How does this factor affect where organisms live?** *(Organisms that conduct photosynthesis live near the surface, as do many animals that depend on those organisms for food.)* **At what depth would you expect water temperatures to be the warmest? Why?** *(Near the surface, because sunlight warms the water there)* **How do you think water pressure changes with ocean depth?** *(Pressure increases as depth increases.)* **How would this factor affect where organisms live?** *(Most organisms cannot withstand great pressure on their bodies, so they must live near the surface.)* **Based on sunlight, temperature, and pressure, at which depth would you expect to find the greatest abundance of organisms?** *(Near the surface)* Point out that ocean life is also abundant in areas near shore.

Use Visuals

Figure 4–17 Have students locate the intertidal zone, coastal ocean, open ocean, and benthic zone on the figure and identify the characteristic organisms pictured for each of the four zones. Ask: **What are the abiotic characteristics of each zone?** (*Intertidal zone: extreme changes in conditions from being submerged in sea water to being exposed to air, sunlight, and heat; subject to waves and currents. Coastal ocean: receives sunlight. Open ocean: surface receives sunlight; deep ocean has high pressure, frigid temperatures, and total darkness. Benthic zone: includes ocean floor, various ocean depths, and deep-sea vents.*) **What are the two horizontal zones of marine ecosystems?** (*Photic zone and aphotic zone*) **What kind of producers are found in each of these zones?** (*Photic zone: photosynthetic autotrophs; aphotic zone: chemosynthetic autotrophs*)

Answers to . . .

CHECKPOINT *Sunlight*

Figure 4–16 *No. Large ocean waves would make it impossible for the roots of salt marsh grasses or mangrove trees to remain anchored.*

Meet Diverse Needs

For students who learn best through handling objects, try to provide a variety of once-living ocean organisms for students to examine. Possibilities include dried sea stars and sea urchins, seashells, crab and lobster shells, dried kelp and other seaweed, pieces of coral, and dried, pickled, or fresh squid or octopus. Challenge students to sort the objects into groups based on the zones in which the living organisms are found. **Learning modality: tactile**

▲ **Figure 4–18** **The main divisions in the ocean based on depth and distance from shore are the intertidal zone, the coastal ocean, and the open ocean.** Along the coast of Vancouver Island in Canada, low tide reveals sea stars, seaweed, and other organisms adapted to life in the intertidal zone.

Intertidal Zone Organisms that live in the intertidal zone are exposed to regular and extreme changes in their surroundings. Once or twice a day, they are submerged in sea water. The remainder of the time, they are exposed to air, sunlight, and temperature changes. Often, organisms in this zone are battered by waves and sometimes by strong currents.

There are many different types of intertidal communities. One of the most interesting is the rocky intertidal, shown in **Figure 4–18,** which exists in temperate regions where exposed rocks line the shore. There, barnacles and seaweed permanently attach themselves to the rocks. Other organisms, such as snails, sea urchins, and sea stars, cling to the rocks by their feet or suckers.

Competition among organisms in the rocky intertidal zone often leads to zonation (zoh-NAY-shun). **Zonation** is the prominent horizontal banding of organisms that live in a particular habitat. In the rocky intertidal zone, each band can be distinguished by differences in color or shape of the major organisms. For example, a stripe of black algae might grow at the highest high-tide line, followed by encrusting barnacles. Lower down, clusters of blue mussels might stick out amid clumps of green algae. This zonation is similar to the pattern that you might observe as you climb up a mountain. In the intertidal zone, however, zonation exists on a smaller vertical scale—just a few meters compared to the kilometers you would ascend on a mountain.

Coastal Ocean The **coastal ocean** extends from the low-tide mark to the outer edge of the continental shelf, the relatively shallow border that surrounds the continents. The continental shelf is often shallow enough to fall mostly or entirely within the photic zone, so photosynthesis can usually occur throughout its depth. As a result, the coastal ocean is often rich in plankton and many other organisms.

One of the most productive coastal ocean communities is the kelp forest. **Kelp forests** are named for their dominant organism: a giant brown algae that can grow at extraordinary rates—as much as 50 centimeters a day. Huge forests of this seaweed are found in cold-temperate seas around the world, including those along the coasts of California and the Pacific Northwest. Kelp forests, like the one shown in **Figure 4–19,** support a complex food web that includes snails, sea urchins, sea otters, a variety of fishes, seals, and whales.

CHECKPOINT *What is the coastal ocean?*

◀ **Figure 4–19** Kelp forests are ecosystems that occur in coastal oceans swept by cold-water currents. The long strands of giant kelp create a habitat that shelters a variety of fishes and other organisms. This kelp forest off the coast of California is part of a larger zone of kelp forests found along the western coast of North America from Alaska to Mexico. **Comparing and Contrasting** *How is a kelp forest like a forest on land?*

BACKGROUND

The ocean floor

The benthic zone, or ocean floor, extends from the high-tide mark to the deepest part of the ocean. Life in this zone consists of sessile and motile organisms. These organisms are distributed from near the shore to the depths of the ocean and they play an important role in the ocean's food chain. Plants found in the benthic zone can live only in the photic zone, or area where sunlight can penetrate (30 to 200 meters below the ocean's surface). The portion of the benthic zone that is between 4000 meters and 6000 meters deep is known as the abyssal zone. The surface of the abyssal zone is covered with mud and organic debris. For the most part, food is in short supply. However, there are fishes (rattails), echinoderms, mollusks, and burrowing worms. In areas around hydrothermal vents (volcanic hot springs), clumps of bacteria growing on rocks use the hydrogen sulfide as an energy source. Living on these bacteria are filter-feeding animals such as giant clams and giant tube worms (up to 3.7 meters long).

Coral Reefs In the warm, shallow water of coastal, tropical oceans are coral reefs, among the most diverse and productive environments on Earth. **Coral reefs** are named for the coral animals whose hard, calcium carbonate skeletons make up their primary structure. As you can see in **Figure 4–20,** an extraordinary diversity of organisms flourishes in these spectacular habitats.

Coral animals are tiny relatives of jellyfish that live together in vast numbers. Most coral animals are the size of your fingernail, or even smaller. Each one looks like a small sack with a mouth surrounded by tentacles. These animals use their tentacles to capture and eat microscopic creatures that float by. Coral animals cannot grow in cold water or water that is low in salt.

Coral animals live in symbiosis with algae contained within the body of each coral animal. The algae carry out photosynthesis, supplying nutrients to the corals. In turn, the coral animals provide a framework on which the algae grow. Below 40 meters, not enough light penetrates the water for algae to grow. For this reason, almost all growth in a coral reef occurs within 40 meters of the surface.

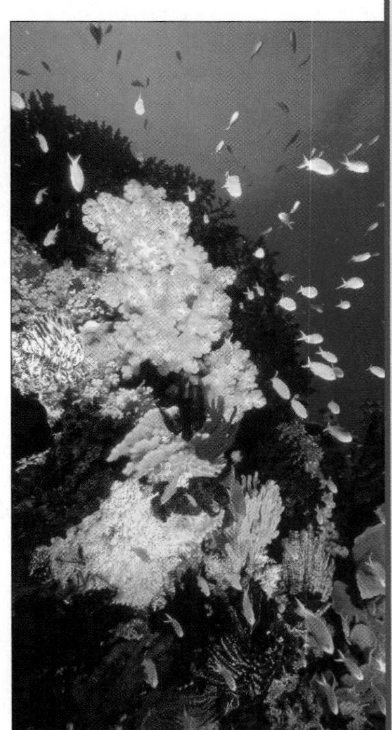

▶ **Figure 4–20** This coral reef off the island of New Britain in the Pacific Ocean supports a dazzling variety of corals and fishes. Some coral reefs in the Pacific have been damaged by crown-of-thorns starfish, which prey on corals. Reefs are most abundant around islands and along the eastern coasts of continents. In the United States, only the coasts of southern Florida and Hawaii have coral reefs. **Applying Concepts** ***In what types of community interactions are coral animals involved?***

Analyzing Data

Ecosystem Productivity

The data table on the right compares the primary productivity of some of the world's ecosystems. Use the data table to answer the following questions.

1. **Using Tables and Graphs** Construct a bar graph to display the data. Use different colors to distinguish aquatic and land ecosystems.
2. **Analyzing Data** According to your graph, which ecosystem is most productive? Use what you know to explain that fact.
3. **Inferring** Although the open ocean is among the least productive ecosystems, it contributes greatly to the overall productivity of the biosphere. How can this situation be explained?
4. **Applying Concepts** What are two abiotic factors that might account for the differences in productivity among the land ecosystems in the table? (*Hint:* Review the relevant biomes on pages 100–104.)

Productivity of Aquatic and Land Ecosystems

Ecosystem	Average Primary Productivity (grams of organic matter produced per sq. meter per year)
Aquatic Ecosystems:	
Coral reef	2500
Estuary	1800
Lake	500
Open ocean	125
Land Ecosystems:	
Tropical rain forest	2200
Temperate forest	1250
Tropical savanna	900
Tundra	90

Analyzing Data

Before students graph the data, have them review the characteristics of the listed types of ecosystems.

1. Students should choose a scale for the axis of the graph representing average primary productivity that is large enough to enable them to graph the data accurately.

2. Coral reef ecosystems are the most productive. Students may infer that reefs are so productive because they are near the top of the photic zone.

3. The area of the open ocean far exceeds the area occupied by all the other ecosystems put together.

4. Latitude and precipitation are both factors that affect the productivity of the land ecosystems in the table. Ecosystems that are drier (tropical savanna) or closer to the polar zones (tundra) are less productive.

Build Science Skills

Using Analogies Direct students to consider what they learned about mountains when they studied land biomes in the previous section. Then, ask: **How is the benthic zone like an upside-down mountain?** *(Sample answer: As you go up a mountain, temperatures become colder and precipitation increases, producing different conditions at different elevations. Similarly, as you go farther down in the ocean and the water depth increases, pressure also increases, available sunlight decreases, and temperatures become colder, producing different zones along the ocean floor.)*

Answers to . . .

✓CHECKPOINT *The part of the ocean that extends from the low tide mark to the outer edge of the continental shelf.*

Figure 4–19 *Students' comparisons should include the idea that the producers in a kelp forest ecosystem—giant kelp—have a function similar to the producers in a forest on land.*

Figure 4–20 *Coral animals are involved in predation both as predators on microscopic sea creatures and as prey of the crown-of-thorns starfish. They are also involved in a mutualistic symbiotic relationship with algae. Students might also infer that corals are involved in competition and are affected by parasitism and disease.*

4–4 (continued)

Meet Diverse Needs

Students who need an additional challenge might enjoy researching and reading about Sylvia Earle, a marine biologist who has earned international recognition for her pioneering studies of hydrothermal vents and the unique organisms found there. Encourage students to share their findings in posters, oral reports, mock radio shows, or skits. **Learning modality: verbal**

3 ASSESS

Evaluate Understanding

As you did with land biomes in the previous section, describe various aquatic ecosystems and ocean zones, and call on students at random to identify each one. Limit your descriptions to the information contained in this section.

Reteach

Have students work cooperatively to construct a bulletin board display showing the different kinds of aquatic ecosystems and ocean zones discussed in this section, using pictures they have drawn themselves or photocopied. Have students label the names of the aquatic ecosystems and ocean zones, their major characteristics, and the types of organisms found in each.

Students should color the ocean regions to match the false color images provided on the Web site. For additional information, visit **www.phschool.com**

Use iText to review the key concepts in Section 4–4.

▲ **Figure 4–21 The main divisions in the ocean based on depth and distance from shore are the intertidal zone, the coastal ocean, and the open ocean.** In the open ocean, the swordfish (top) can sometimes be seen swimming near the surface, yet these fish can also dive to more than 600m to prey on fishes of the deep ocean. Some types of octopus (bottom) live in the depths of the open ocean, although other types live in shallow coastal waters.

Open Ocean The open ocean, often referred to as the oceanic zone, begins at the edge of the continental shelf and extends outward. It is the largest marine zone, covering more than 90 percent of the surface area of the world's oceans. The open ocean ranges from about 500 meters deep along continental slopes to more than 11,000 meters at the deepest ocean trench. Organisms in the deep ocean are exposed to high pressure, frigid temperatures, and total darkness.

Typically, the open ocean has very low levels of nutrients and supports only the smallest producers. Productivity is generally low. Still, because of the enormous area, most of the photosynthetic activity on Earth occurs in the part of the open ocean within the photic zone. Fishes of all shapes and sizes dominate the open ocean. The swordfish and the octopus in **Figure 4–21** are just two examples of the organisms found in this zone. Marine mammals such as dolphins and whales also live there but must stay close to the surface to breathe.

Benthic Zone The ocean floor contains organisms that live attached to or near the bottom, such as sea stars, anemones, and marine worms. Scientists refer to these organisms as the **benthos.** That is why the ocean floor is called the benthic zone. This zone extends horizontally along the ocean floor from the coastal ocean through the open ocean.

Benthic ecosystems often depend on food from organisms that grow in the photic zone, particularly the producers. Animals that are attached to the bottom or do not move around much, such as clams and sea cucumbers, feed on pieces of dead organic material, or detritus, that drift down from the surface waters. Near deep-sea vents, where superheated water boils out of cracks on the ocean floor, dwell chemosynthetic primary producers that support life without light and photosynthesis.

4–4 Section Assessment

1. **Key Concept** List three characteristics that determine the structure of aquatic ecosystems.
2. **Key Concept** How are standing-water ecosystems similar to flowing-water ecosystems? How are they different?
3. **Key Concept** List six distinct ecological zones that can be found in the ocean. Give two abiotic factors for each zone.
4. Define a wetland and an estuary.
5. **Critical Thinking Predicting** How might the damming of a river affect an estuary at the river's mouth?

Assessment Use iText to review the important concepts in Section 4–4.

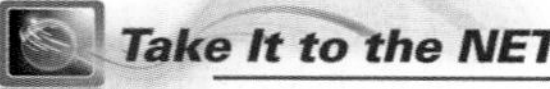

Read about the productivity of the world's oceans. Then, print out a map of the oceans and color-code the regions of highest productivity. Use the links provided in the Biology area at the Prentice Hall Web site for help in completing this activity: **www.phschool.com**

4–4 Section Assessment

1. The depth, flow, and chemistry of the overlying water
2. Similar: freshwater ecosystems; water contains oxygen and nutrients. Different: Water in a flowing-water ecosystem moves rapidly near the source and slows near the mouth. Water in a standing-water ecosystem has little net flow, but circulates within the system.
3. Photic zone, aphotic zone, intertidal zone, coastal ocean, open ocean, benthic zone and the abiotic factors for each discussed in the text
4. A wetland is an ecosystem in which the roots of plants are submerged. An estuary is an ecosystem in which a freshwater source meets the ocean.
5. Without fresh water from the river, the brackish estuary water would become saltier, changing the kinds of organisms that could survive in that ecosystem.

Exploration

Observing Succession

The most obvious examples of succession involve large organisms, such as plants and animals, that are easily seen. In this investigation, you will determine whether succession also occurs in a community of microorganisms.

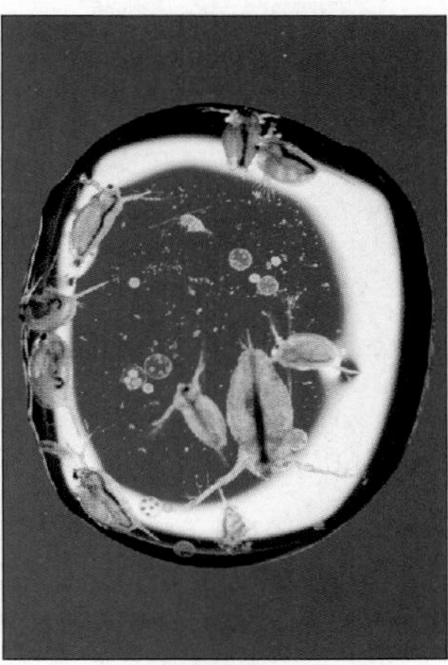

Problem

What changes occur in a microscopic community over time?

Materials

- 1000-mL beaker or large jar
- soil
- grass clippings
- dried leaves
- 600-mL aged water
- 4 coverslips
- 4 glass slides
- 4 dropper pipettes
- microscope
- reference book or chart for identifying common microorganisms

Skills

Using Graphs, Analyzing Data

Procedure

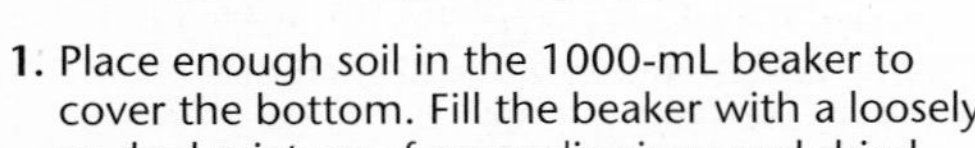

1. Place enough soil in the 1000-mL beaker to cover the bottom. Fill the beaker with a loosely packed mixture of grass clippings and dried leaves and add the aged water.
2. Set the beaker aside in a cool place where it can remain undisturbed for 24 hours.
3. After 24 hours, check the water for signs of life. For example, a strong odor or cloudy water is evidence of bacterial growth; fuzzy growths or threads indicate the presence of mold; and a green tint is due to algae. Record your observations.
4. Use a dropper pipette to transfer a drop of water from the beaker to a microscope slide. Add a coverslip.
5. Examine the slide under the low-power objective of the microscope to locate any microorganisms. Then, switch to high power. Use a reference book or chart to identify the organisms. Record the date and your observations, including labeled drawings, the number of each type of organism in your field of view, and the magnification.
6. Repeat steps 4 and 5 with water samples from several different areas of the beaker.
7. Repeat steps 3 through 6 every day for 2 weeks. Note any changes in the number or types of organisms in the beaker.

Analyze and Conclude

1. **Using Graphs** Make a graph of the population of each type of organism. Plot time on the *x*-axis and number of organisms per field of view on the *y*-axis.
2. **Observing** How did the number and variety of organisms in the beaker change over the 2-week period?
3. **Analyzing Data** What kinds of organisms appeared first in the microscopic water community? Which appeared last? How can you explain these changes?
4. **Drawing Conclusions** Do your observations support the idea that succession occurs in communities of microorganisms? Explain your answer.

Go Further

Analyzing Data With your teacher's approval, set up a simple community of only a few known species of microorganisms. Observe the community for two weeks and try to explain any evidence of succession that you observe.

Analyze and Conclude

1. Graphs will vary depending on the numbers and types of organisms that appear over the two-week observation period.

2. Typically, bacteria are most numerous at first, followed by heterotrophic protists, microscopic animals, and algae.

3. Successional sequences will vary. Bacteria often appear first, followed by small protists and eventually larger predatory protists. The bacteria decompose the organic material present in the culture and support the populations of protists that prey on them. Larger protists and occasionally small animals appear later; these organisms may include some that prey on the protists.

4. Yes. The changes in types and numbers of microscopic organisms observed during the two-week period are evidence of succession.

Exploration

Objective Students will be able to identify changes that occur in a microscopic community as it undergoes succession

Skills Focus **Using Graphs, Analyzing Data**

Time 10 minutes for setup, 20 minutes every 2 or 3 days for 2 weeks for observation and recording

Advance Prep For each group, fill a 600-mL beaker with tap water. Leave the beakers undisturbed for 48 hours so any gases harmful to microscopic organisms can evaporate.

Alternative Materials To shorten the time required to complete the activity, prepare several hay infusions 5 to 10 days apart, and let students observe samples of all the infusions on the same day.

Pre-Lab Discussion Ask students to recall the meaning of the term *succession.* Have them read the introductory paragraph, the problem, and the complete procedure. Ask: **What kinds of organisms do you think you'll see?** *(Sample answers: bacteria, mold, algae, protists)*

Teaching Tips

- Circulate as students prepare the slides and use the microscopes to ensure that they are following correct procedures.
- During the first week, show students how to stain a specimen with methylene blue to make bacteria more visible.
- After the first week, offer students methyl cellulose or cotton fibers to slow down motile protists for observation.

Expected Outcome In general, no odor or organisms will become evident until day 4. By day 7, *Volvox, Spirogyra,* and *Paramecium* may be visible. By day 14, numerous fast-moving protists may appear. Between days 14 and 21, small numbers of nematodes, *Paramecium,* and *Spirostomum* and many small ciliates will probably be seen.

Go Further

A community containing *Paramecium,* yeast as food, and the predatory protist *Didinium* can undergo succession within 2 to 6 weeks.

Chapter 4 Study Guide

Study Tip

This chapter presents a large number of Vocabulary terms—both the terms that are boldfaced and defined in the sections and other terms that may be unfamiliar to students. Have students prepare vocabulary flash cards, each card with a term written on one side and its definition written on the other side. Let students use these flash cards to quiz each other in pairs or small groups.

Thinking Visually

Student concept maps should indicate that community interactions affect ecosystems, which are made up of biotic and abiotic factors; and that abiotic factors include light, oxygen, and nutrients.

Chapter 4 Assessment

Reviewing Concepts

1. b **2.** b **3.** b **4.** d **5.** a **6.** b **7.** d **8.** a **9.** b **10.** a

Understanding Concepts

11. Climate: year-to-year conditions of temperature and precipitation within a particular region. Weather: day-to-day conditions of Earth's atmosphere at a particular time and place.

12. Temperature, precipitation, humidity, wind, nutrient availability, soil type, and sunlight

13. An organism's habitat is *where* it lives. Its niche is *how* it lives, or its occupation. A niche is the full range of physical and biological conditions in which an organism lives and the way in which the organism uses those conditions.

14. According to the competitive exclusion principle, no two species can occupy the same niche.

15. Primary succession, because the volcanic eruption has destroyed any ecosystem that previously existed at that location

Chapter 4 Study Guide

4–1 The Role of Climate

Key Concepts

- Carbon dioxide, methane, water vapor, and a few other atmospheric gases trap heat energy and maintain Earth's temperature range.
- As a result of differences in latitude and thus the angle of heating, Earth has three main climate zones: polar, temperate, and tropical.

Vocabulary
- weather, p. 87 • climate, p. 87
- greenhouse effect, p. 87 • polar zone, p. 88
- temperate zone, p. 88 • tropical zone, p. 88

4–2 What Shapes an Ecosystem?

Key Concepts

- Together, biotic and abiotic factors determine the survival and growth of an organism and the productivity of the ecosystem in which the organism lives.
- Community interactions, such as competition, predation, and various forms of symbiosis, can powerfully affect an ecosystem.
- Ecosystems are constantly changing in response to natural and human disturbances. As an ecosystem changes, older inhabitants gradually die out and new organisms move in, causing further changes in the community.

Vocabulary
- biotic factor, p. 90 • abiotic factor, p. 90
- habitat, p. 90 • niche, p. 91 • resource, p. 92
- competitive exclusion principle, p. 92
- predation, p. 93 • symbiosis, p. 93
- mutualism, p. 93 • commensalism, p. 93
- parasitism, p. 93 • ecological succession, p. 94
- primary succession, p. 94 • pioneer species, p. 94
- secondary succession, p. 95

4–3 Land Biomes

Key Concept

- The world's major land biomes include tropical rain forest, tropical dry forest, tropical savanna, temperate grassland, desert, temperate woodland and shrubland, temperate forest, northwestern coniferous forest, boreal forest, and tundra. Each of these biomes is defined by a unique set of abiotic factors—particularly climate—and has a characteristic ecological community.

Vocabulary
- biome, p. 98 • microclimate, p. 98
- canopy, p. 100 • understory, p. 100
- deciduous, p. 100 • coniferous, p. 103
- humus, p. 103 • taiga, p. 104
- permafrost, p. 104

4–4 Aquatic Ecosystems

Key Concepts

- Aquatic ecosystems are determined primarily by the depth, flow, temperature, and chemistry of the overlying water.
- Freshwater ecosystems can be divided into two main types: flowing-water ecosystems and standing-water ecosystems.
- In addition to the division between the photic and aphotic zones, marine biologists also divide the ocean into zones based on the depth and distance from shore: the intertidal zone, coastal ocean, and the open ocean.

Vocabulary
- plankton, p. 107 • phytoplankton, p. 107
- zooplankton, p. 107 • wetland, p. 107
- estuary, p. 108 • detritus, p. 108
- salt marsh, p. 108 • mangrove swamp, p. 108
- photic zone, p. 109 • aphotic zone, p. 109
- zonation, p. 110 • coastal ocean, p. 110
- kelp forest, p. 110 • coral reef, p. 111
- benthos, p. 112

Thinking Visually

Using information from this chapter, create a concept map that includes the following terms: *abiotic factors, biotic factors, community interactions, predation, competition, symbiosis, nutrients, ecosystems, light, oxygen.*

TIME SAVER CHAPTER RESOURCES

Print:
- ***Teaching Resources,*** Chapter Vocabulary Review, Graphic Organizer
- ***Chapter Tests: Levels A and B,*** Chapter 4 Test
- ***PH Assessment System,*** Practice Test

Technology
- ***Computer Test Bank,*** Chapter 4 Test
- ***iText,*** Chapter 4 Assessment

Chapter 4 Assessment

Reviewing Concepts

Choose the letter that best answers the question or completes the statement.

1. The average, year-after-year conditions of temperature and precipitation within a particular region are its
   a. weather. c. greenhouse effect.
   b. climate. d. biotic factors.
2. The greenhouse effect causes an increase in
   a. carbon dioxide.
   b. temperature.
   c. oxygen.
   d. water.
3. All the biotic and abiotic factors in a pond form a(an)
   a. biosphere.
   b. ecosystem.
   c. community.
   d. niche.
4. A relationship in which one organism is helped and another organism is neither helped nor hurt is called
   a. mutualism.
   b. parasitism.
   c. competition.
   d. commensalism.
5. A form of symbiosis in which both organisms benefit is called
   a. mutualism.
   b. parasitism.
   c. commensalism.
   d. predation.
6. A type of symbiosis in which one organism benefits and the other is harmed is called
   a. mutualism.
   b. parasitism.
   c. commensalism.
   d. succession.
7. Natural disturbances, such as fires or hurricanes, can result in
   a. commensalism. c. parasitism.
   b. competition. d. succession.
8. In a tropical rain forest, the dense covering formed by the leafy tops of tall trees is called the
   a. canopy. c. niche.
   b. taiga. d. understory.
9. Organisms that live near or on the ocean floor are called
   a. parasites. c. plankton.
   b. benthos. d. mangroves.
10. In the diagram of the ocean below, the feature labeled **A** is the
   a. open ocean. c. trench.
   b. coastal ocean. d. estuary.

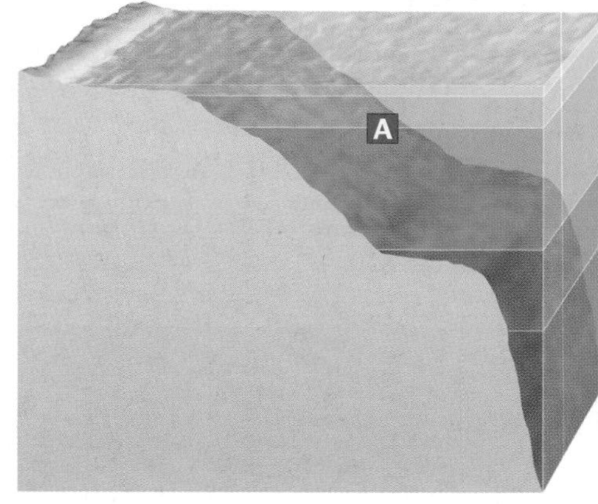

Understanding Concepts

11. Distinguish between weather and climate.
12. Describe the major abiotic factors that produce Earth's main climate zones.
13. What is the difference between an organism's habitat and its niche?
14. What is the competitive exclusion principle?
15. What type of succession occurs after lava from a volcanic eruption covers an area?
16. Describe two major causes of ecological succession.
17. What is a biome?
18. What are two abiotic factors that cause deciduous trees to shed their leaves?
19. Describe the dominant vegetation found in a North American temperate forest.
20. Why are plants generally few and far between in a desert?
21. What are plankton? Name the two types of plankton.
22. What are three types of freshwater wetlands?
23. How does the photic zone differ from the aphotic zone?
24. How are salt marshes and mangrove swamps alike? How are they different?
25. What are coral reefs? Explain.

HOMEWORK GUIDE

Section:	Questions:
Section 4–1	1, 2, 11, 12
Section 4–2	3–7, 13–16, 29, 31, 33–35
Section 4–3	8, 17–20, 26, 27, 30
Section 4–4	9, 10, 21–25, 28, 32

16. Natural disturbances such as hurricane or fire, or human activities

17. A physical environment that has its own particular kinds of plants and animals

18. Deciduous trees in the tropical dry forest biome shed their leaves to conserve water. In the temperate forest biome, deciduous trees shed their leaves to survive the cold winters.

19. Broadleaf deciduous trees, coniferous trees, flowering shrubs, herbs, lichens, mosses, and ferns

20. Lack of precipitation. Annual precipitation is less than 25 centimeters.

21. Plankton are tiny, free-floating or weakly swimming algae and animals that occur in both freshwater and salt-water environments. Examples: single-celled algae (phytoplankton), and planktonic animals called zooplankton.

22. Bogs are formed in depressions that fill with water that is often very acidic. Sphagnum moss frequently grows in bogs. Marshes are shallow wetlands along rivers. Cattails and rushes often grow in marshes, which may be flooded for all or part of the year. Swamps are flooded forests through which water flows slowly.

23. The photic zone is the thin surface layer of the ocean that light can penetrate so that photosynthesis can occur. The aphotic zone is the permanently dark zone immediately below the photic zone.

24. Both salt marshes and mangrove swamps are coastal ecosystems that are influenced by tides. Salt marshes are flat, muddy areas that often surround estuaries and bays. Mangrove swamps occur only in warm climates.

25. Coral reefs are large structures made up of the calcium carbonate skeletons of coral animals that live in the warm, shallow waters of tropical oceans.

Chapter 4 Assessment

Critical Thinking

26. Check students' diagrams. They should appear similar to the diagrams on pages 102 through 107. The biome that is most likely to occur in Lillehammer is the boreal forest biome.

27. During the short, cool summers in the tundra, the ground thaws to a depth of a few centimeters and becomes soggy and wet.

28. The aphotic zone is permanently dark. Plants and animals would need to be able to manufacture and obtain food without photosynthesis.

29. Students' experiments will vary but should demonstrate an understanding of the concepts of mutualism, parasitism, and commensalism.

30. This situation represents an example of secondary succession. In 5 years, the sun-loving plants may predominate, although seedlings of new trees may have begun to grow. In 50 years, the trees will have matured, re-establishing the forest ecosystem.

31. The cowbird's behavior is an example of parasitism. The cowbird benefits from having its young nurtured by the parasitized species, which is harmed because some of its offspring are pushed out of the nest and do not survive.

32. Students' answers should demonstrate an understanding of the positive and negative effects of salt marsh development. Students' answers should also give reasons as to why they do or do not support the proposal.

33. In both predation and parasitism, one organism is feeding on another. In predation, the predator kills its prey. In parasitism, the parasite lives off a live host.

34. No two species can occupy the same niche in the same habitat. Individuals within a single species living in the same niche would compete for the same resources.

35. Students' answers should demonstrate an understanding of biotic and abiotic factors in your area.

Chapter 4 Assessment

Critical Thinking

26. Using Tables and Graphs Using graph paper, construct a climate diagram for Lillehammer. Base your diagram on the ones for the biomes in this chapter. Use the completed diagram to identify the biome that is most likely to occur in Lillehammer.

Climate Data for Lillehammer, Norway

Month	Average Temperature (°C)	Precipitation (mm)
Jan.	-8.1	38.1
Feb.	-6.2	27.9
Mar.	-3.9	30.5
Apr.	3.3	35.6
May	8.9	45.7
June	13.9	63.5
July	16.4	81.3
Aug.	14.2	88.9
Sept.	9.5	58.4
Oct.	3.9	63.5
Nov.	-3.8	50.8
Dec.	-6.1	48.3

27. Applying Concepts Although the amount of precipitation is low, most parts of the tundra biome are very wet during the summer. What characteristics would explain this apparent contradiction?

28. Formulating Hypotheses The deep ocean is within the aphotic zone and is also very cold. Suggest some of the unique characteristics that might enable animals to live in the deep ocean.

29. Designing Experiments As cattle graze in the grasslands of East Africa, they stir up insects living in the grass. Birds known as cattle egrets eat insects and capture more food when they hunt near the cattle than when they hunt on their own. Design an experiment that would determine if the relationship between cattle and egrets is one of mutualism, parasitism, or commensalism.

30. Predicting A windstorm in a forest blows down the large trees in one part of the forest. Soon, sun-loving plants sprout in the new clearing. What type of succession is this? What might this area look like in 5 years? In 50 years?

31. Classifying The cowbird lays its eggs in other birds' nests. When the cowbird egg hatches, the "parents" feed the young cowbird along with their own young, which the cowbird then pushes out of the nest. Is this an example of mutualism, parasitism, or commensalism? Explain.

32. Making Judgments A developer has proposed filling in a salt marsh to create a coastal resort. What positive and negative effects might this proposal have on wildlife and local residents? Would you support the proposal? Why or why not?

33. Comparing and Contrasting How are predation and parasitism similar? How are they different?

34. Inferring Competition for resources in an area is usually more intense within a single species than between two different species. Can you explain this observation? (*Hint:* Consider how niches help organisms of different species avoid competition.)

35. Making Connections Write a description of your niche in the environment. Include details about your ecosystem, including the biotic and abiotic factors around you. Be sure to describe your feeding habits as well as any interactions you have with members of other species.

Performance-Based Assessment

Creating a Web Site You have been asked by a travel agent to develop a Web site for a biome of your choice. The goal of the Web site is to encourage tourism to that particular biome. To do this, you must present accurate scientific information and visual images to depict the biome and entice the viewer to visit. Create a storyboard for this Web site, including the home page and two hyperlinked pages.

Are biomes distinct enough to be seen from space? Visit the Prentice Hall Web site at **www.phschool.com** to find out how biomes can be differentiated from space. Then, answer the following questions:

- What two factors are used to differentiate biomes from space? Explain.
- What is a climograph?
- Obtain temperature and rainfall data for your area and construct your own climograph.

Performance-Based Assessment

Students' storyboards will vary but should include a general overview of the chosen biome, its abiotic and biotic factors, and examples of the dominant plants and wildlife that live there.

Standardized Test Prep

Standardized Test Prep

1. C 4. A 7. A
2. A 5. C 8. E
3. E 6. E 9. C

Test-Taking Tip When you are asked to analyze a graph showing experimental data, first look at the shape of the curve. Identify the variables and try to determine how they are related. Then, read and answer the questions about the graph.

Directions: Choose the letter that best answers the question or completes the statement.

1. Generally, which has the greatest effect on determining the climate of a region?
(A) longitude
(B) dominant plant species
(C) distance from the equator
(D) month of the year
(E) prevailing winds

2. Which is NOT an abiotic factor in an ecosystem?
(A) microorganisms
(B) light
(C) temperature
(D) rainfall
(E) pH

3. What defines a species' niche?
I. Abiotic factors
II. Biotic factors
III. Food web
(A) I only
(B) III only
(C) I and III only
(D) II and III only
(E) I, II, and III

4. The disappearance of a population in a given niche as a result of direct competition with another species for a resource is called
(A) competitive exclusion.
(B) predation.
(C) parasitism.
(D) commensalism.
(E) mutualism.

5. In which marine zone are you likely to find algae growing?
I. Intertidal zone
II. Photic zone
III. Aphotic zone
(A) I only
(B) II only
(C) I and II only
(D) II and III only
(E) I, II, and III

6. The water in an estuary is
(A) salt water only.
(B) poor in nutrients.
(C) fresh water only.
(D) in the aphotic zone.
(E) a mixture of fresh water and salt water.

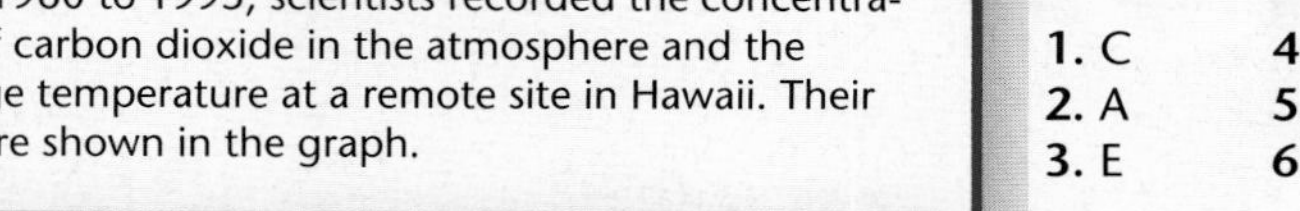

Questions 7–8
From 1960 to 1995, scientists recorded the concentration of carbon dioxide in the atmosphere and the average temperature at a remote site in Hawaii. Their data are shown in the graph.

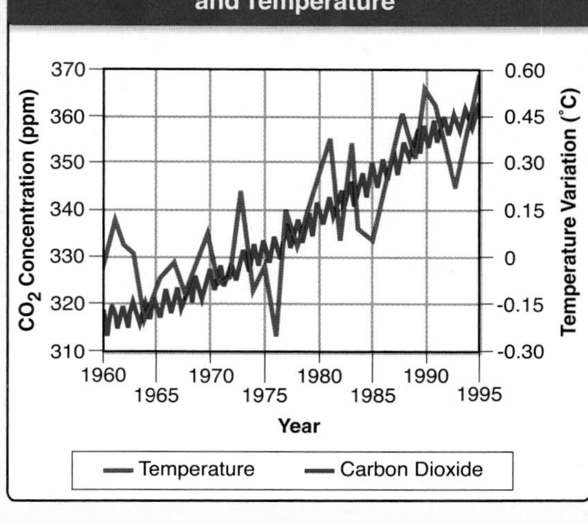

7. Based on the graph, which of the following is most likely?
(A) The climate in Hawaii is getting warmer over time.
(B) Carbon dioxide levels will soon decline.
(C) Warm temperatures are increasing the carbon dioxide concentration.
(D) The variables are indirectly proportional.
(E) Temperatures elsewhere must decrease.

8. Which of the following would most likely cause an increase in atmospheric carbon dioxide?
(A) increased biomass
(B) a faster rate of photosynthesis
(C) melting of the polar ice caps
(D) decreased burning of fossil fuels
(E) increased burning of fossil fuels

Question 9 Complete the analogy by selecting the correct letter. In analogies, A : B :: C : __?__ *means* A is to B as C is to __?__ .

9. Flea : dog :: parasite : __?__
(A) predator
(B) bacteria
(C) host
(D) competitor
(E) carnivore

Take It to the NET

• Different biomes can almost be separated out by location and "greenness" alone. Tropical rain forests are a mix of light and dark green in the center of the map, tropical savannas are light green, deciduous forests are light green towards the upper and lower parts of the map, deserts are yellowish everywhere, boreal forests are mostly dark green, and tundras are mostly pinkish.

• A plot of average temperature and precipitation during the year at a particular location

• Students can obtain this information from a local television or radio station and the U.S. Geological Survey.

For additional information, visit

www.phschool.com

Chapter Planner 5 Populations

Section and Section Objectives	Time	Activities and Labs
5–1 How Populations Grow, pp. 119–123 **5.1.1** ***List*** the characteristics used to describe a population. **5.1.2** ***Identify*** factors that affect population size. **5.1.3** ***Differentiate*** between exponential and logistic growth.	**1 period (1/2 block)**	**SE:** ***Inquiry Activity,*** How do populations grow?, p. 118 **TE:** ***Meet Diverse Needs,*** p. 122 **SE:** ***Analyzing Data,*** Population Trends, p. 123
5–2 Limits to Growth, pp. 124–127 **5.2.1** ***Identify*** factors that limit population growth. **5.2.2** ***Differentiate*** between density-dependent and density-independent limiting factors.	**1 period (1/2 block)**	**SE:** ***Quick Lab,*** How does competition affect plant growth?, p. 125 **TE:** ***Meet Diverse Needs,*** p. 126 **SE:** ***Issues in Biology,*** Does the Gray Wolf Population Need Protection?, p. 128 **SE:** ***Exploration,*** Investigating the Growth of a Population of Bacteria, p. 133
5–3 Human Population Growth, pp. 129–132 **5.3.1** ***Describe*** how the size of the human population has changed over time. **5.3.2** ***Explain*** why population growth rates differ in countries throughout the world.	**1 period (1/2 block)**	
Chapter Assessment, pp. 134–137	**1 period (1/2 block)**	

ACTIVITY PLANNER

SE: ***Inquiry Activity***, p. 118; (15 min.); graph paper

TE: ***Meet Diverse Needs***, p. 122; (15 min.); box of 100 paper clips for each group

SE: ***Quick Lab***, p. 125; (15 min. for setup); bean seeds, 2 paper cups, potting soil

TE: ***Meet Diverse Needs***, p. 126; (10 min.); 1 index card for each student, 4 labeled *owl* and the rest labeled *mouse*

SE: ***Exploration***, p. 133; (5 min. for setup, 10–20 min./day for 5 days, 30 min. on day 6); 2 lima beans, 2 dropper pipettes, 100-mL beaker, coverslips, microscope slides, 10-mL graduated cylinder, 100-mL graduated cylinder, methylene blue stain, microscope, test tube rack, 4 test tubes, aluminum foil

PLANNING KEY

Ability Levels

B **Basic**	For students who need additional help
A **Average**	For all students
E **Enriched**	For students who need to be challenged

Components

SE	Student Edition	**GRSW**	Guided Reading and Study Workbook	**IDM**	Issues and Decision Making
TE	Teacher's Edition	**CT**	Chapter Tests: Levels A and B	**CTB**	Computer Test Bank
LMA	Laboratory Manual A	**PHAS**	PH Assessment System	**PA**	Presentation Assistant Plus
LMB	Laboratory Manual B	**LA**	Lab Assessment with Scoring Guide	**BD**	BioDetectives Videotape
TR	Teaching Resources	**BTM**	BioTechnology Manual	**iT**	iText
IF	Investigations in Forensics				

Program Resources	Assessment	Media and Technology
TR: Section Review 5–2 B A **GRSW:** Section 5–1 B A	**SE:** 5–1 Section Assessment, p. 123 **TR:** Section Review 5–1	**PA:** 5–1 Interest Grabber, Section Outline, Concept Map, Figure 5–4 **iT:** Section 5–1
TR: Section Review 5–2 B A **GRSW:** Section 5–2 B A **IDM:** Issues and Decisions 48 A E	**SE:** 5–2 Section Assessment, p. 127 **TE:** Section Review 5–2	**PA:** 5–2 Interest Grabber, Section Outline, Effect of a Density-Dependent Factor on a Population, Figure 5–7 **iT:** Section 5–2
LMA: Chapter 5 Lab A E **LMB:** Chapter 5 Lab B A **TR:** Section Review 5–3 B A Chapter 5 Exploration B A E **GRSW:** Section 5–3 B A **IDM:** Issues and Decisions 47 A E	**SE:** 5–3 Section Assessment, p. 132 **TE:** Section Review 5–3	**PA:** 5–3 Interest Grabber, Section Outline, Human Population Growth, Figure 5–13 **iT:** Section 5–3
	SE: Chapter 5 Assessment, pp. 134–137 **TR:** Chapter Vocabulary Review, Graphic Organizer **CT:** Chapter 5 Test **CTB:** Chapter 5 Test **PHAS:** Practice Test	**CTB:** Chapter 5 Test **iT:** Chapter 5 Assessment

PRESSED FOR TIME?

To Preview the Chapter

- Have students do the Reading Strategies for Sections 5–1, 5–2, and 5–3. Make sure students save their work for completion as they read the chapter.

To Cover the Chapter Quickly

- Have students read Section 5–1, exclusive of Analyzing Data on page 123; read all of Section 5–2; and review Figures 5–10 and 5–12 and their captions.
- Assign questions 2 and 3 in 5–1 Section Assessment, questions 1 and 2 in 5–2 Section Assessment, and questions 1 and 2 in 5–3 Section Assessment.

To Review the Chapter

- Assign Sections 5–1 and 5–2 in the Guided Reading and Study Workbook.
- Assign the Chapter Vocabulary Review for Chapter 5 in Teaching Resources.

ENGAGE/EXPLORE

Inquiry Activity

Objectives Students will be able to calculate the size of a population over time, given its rate of reproduction, and construct a graph based on the calculations.

Skill Focus Graphing, Formulating Hypotheses

Materials graph paper

Time 15 minutes

Strategies

- You may want to allow students to use calculators.
- Watch for common errors in calculations. In particular, students may forget that in each generation, only about half of the population will be female.

Expected Outcome 6 offspring in one year, 18 in two years, 54 in three years, 162 in four years, 486 in five years

Think About It

1. The graph's shape is a curve that rises at an increasing rate.
2. In 10 years: about 120,000 rabbits; 20 years: about 7 billion rabbits
3. They would eventually eat all the available food, and the population would decrease as rabbits died of starvation.
4. Natural predators, disease, and limited supplies of food and water limit rabbit populations. In addition, not all offspring survive to maturity, and some adults do not reproduce.

Brain Teaser

Tell students to think about the plant populations in the park. Ask: **Once the original pair of rabbits started reproducing, what would happen to the plant populations, and why?** *(They would start decreasing, because the rabbits would eat them.)* **If the rabbits started to die off because there weren't enough plants to eat, what would happen to the plant populations, and why?** *(The plant populations would start to increase, because there would be fewer rabbits to eat them.)*

Chapter 5 Populations

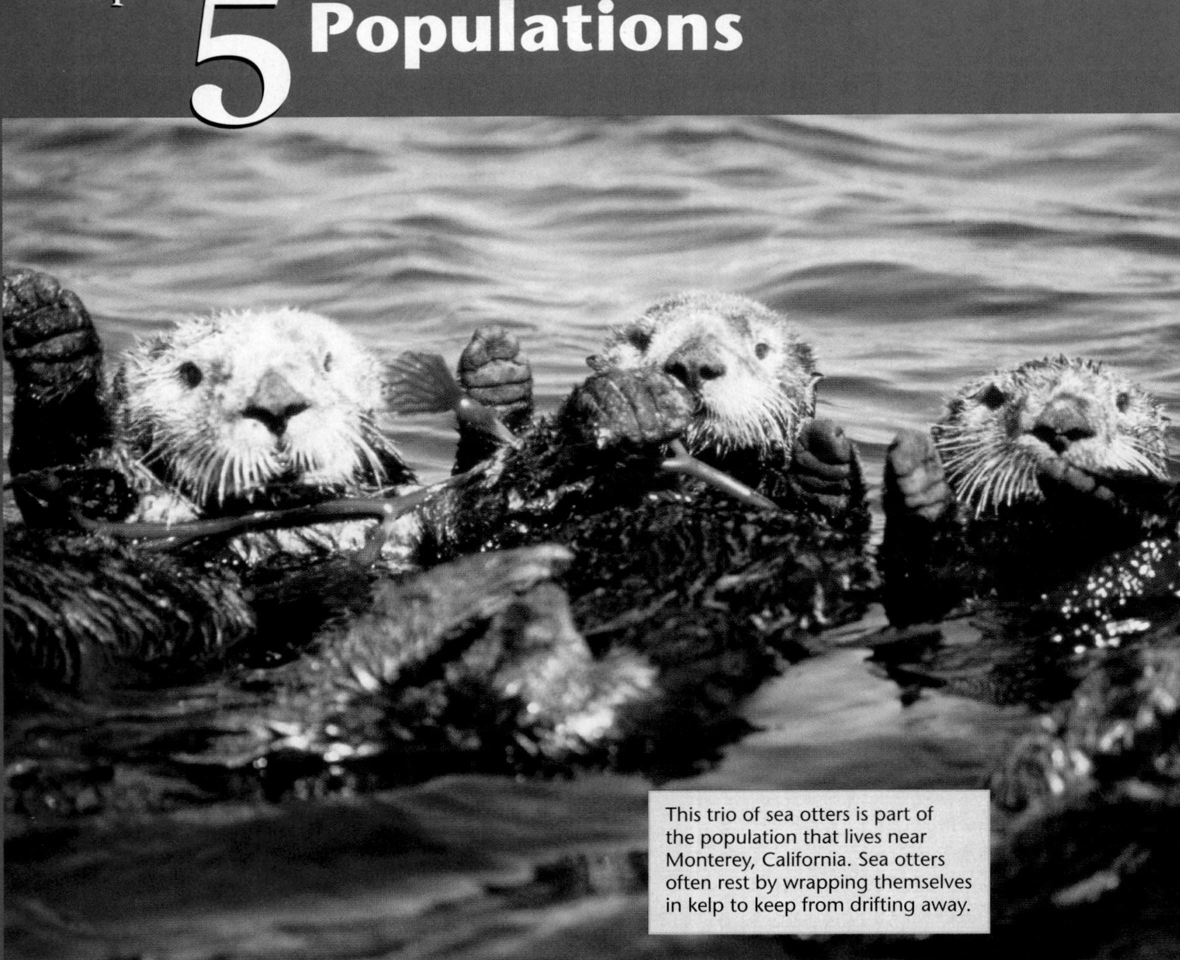

This trio of sea otters is part of the population that lives near Monterey, California. Sea otters often rest by wrapping themselves in kelp to keep from drifting away.

Inquiry Activity

How do populations grow?

Procedure

1. Suppose that one mated pair of rabbits in a park can produce a litter of 6 offspring each year. Assume that all the members of one generation reproduce each year and that no rabbits die. Calculate how many offspring would be produced each year for 5 years.
2. Construct a graph of your data. Plot time on the *x*-axis and population on the *y*-axis.

Think About It

1. **Analyzing Data** Describe the shape of your graph.
2. **Using Graphs** Use your graph to predict the population of rabbits in 10 years and in 20 years.
3. **Predicting** What would eventually happen to the population of rabbits if they were not able to leave the park?
4. **Formulating Hypotheses** How can you explain the fact that Earth is not covered by rabbits?

5–1 How Populations Grow

Sea otters are important members of the kelp forest community of America's Pacific Northwest coast. This "forest" is made up of algae called giant kelp, which have stalks up to 30 meters long, as well as smaller types of kelp. The kelp forest provides habitat for a variety of animals. Sea otters need lots of energy to stay warm in cold water, so they eat lots of their favorite food: sea urchins. Sea urchins, in turn, feed on the kelp.

The relationships along this food chain set the stage for a classic tale of population growth and decline. A century ago, otters were nearly eliminated by hunting. Sea urchin populations increased greatly, and kelp forests nearly disappeared. Why? Because the kelp was eaten down to the bare rock by hordes of sea urchins! The future of the kelp forests looked grim. Then sea otters were declared an endangered species and were protected from hunting. With hunters out of the picture, otter populations recovered. Sea urchin numbers dropped dramatically. Kelp grew back. But now, some otter populations are shrinking again because otters are being eaten by killer whales. To better understand why populations such as these change as they do, we turn to the study of population biology.

Guide for Reading

Key Concepts

- What characteristics are used to describe a population?
- What factors affect population size?
- What are exponential and logistic growth?

Vocabulary

population density
immigration
emigration
exponential growth
logistic growth
carrying capacity

Reading Strategy: Asking Questions Before you read, rewrite the headings in the section as *how, why,* or *what* questions about populations. As you read, write down the answers to your questions.

Characteristics of Populations

Several terms can be used to describe a population in nature. **Three important characteristics of a population are its geographic distribution, density, and growth rate.** A fourth characteristic, the population's age structure, will be discussed later in this chapter. Geographic distribution, or range, is a term that describes the area inhabited by a population. The range can vary in size from a few cubic centimeters occupied by bacteria in a rotting apple to the millions of square kilometers occupied by migrating whales in the Pacific Ocean.

Population density is the number of individuals per unit area. This number can vary tremendously depending on the species and its ecosystem. The population of saguaro cactus in the desert plant community shown in **Figure 5–1,** for example, has a low density, whereas other plants in that community have a relatively high density.

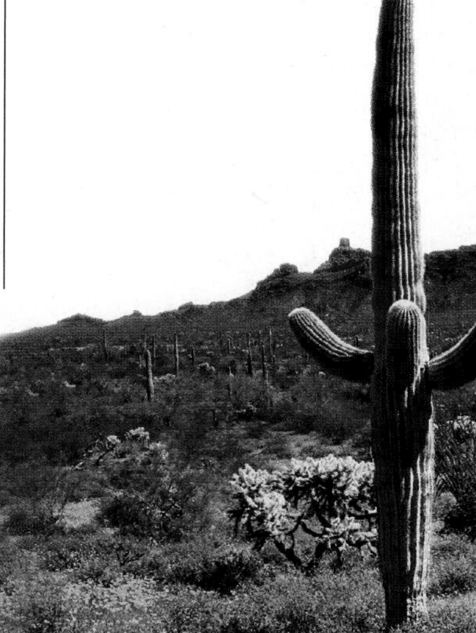

▶ **Figure 5–1** The tall saguaro cactuses in this Arizona desert have a low population density compared to the smaller desert plants. **Density is one of the main characteristics that describe a natural population. Other characteristics of populations are their geographic distribution and growth rate.**

SECTION RESOURCES

Print:

- ***Teaching Resources,*** Section Review 5–1
- ***Guided Reading and Study Workbook,*** Section 5–1

Technology:

- ***iText,*** Section 5–1

Section 5–1

1 FOCUS

Objectives

5.1.1 ***List*** the characteristics used to describe a population.
5.1.2 ***Identify*** factors that affect population size.
5.1.3 ***Differentiate*** between exponential and logistic growth.

Guide for Reading

Vocabulary Preview

To prepare students for the term *population density,* ask: **How many people are in this classroom?** *(Make sure students include you in the count.)* **What is the room's area?** *(Let students measure the room and calculate its area in square meters.)* **How many people are there in the room per square meter?** *(Have students divide the number of people by the room's area.)* Then, explain that the number of people per square meter is the density of the population in the room.

Reading Strategy

Suggest that students write their questions and the answers in outline format, with enough detail and explanation of terms so the outline can be used later as a study tool.

2 INSTRUCT

Characteristics of Populations

Make Connections

Mathematics Give students the equation for calculating population density:

$$\text{Population density} = \frac{\text{Number of individuals}}{\text{Unit area}}$$

Then, pose the following math problem for them to solve: **Suppose there are 150 bullfrogs living in a pond that covers an area of 3 square kilometers. What is the density of the bullfrog population?** *(50 bullfrogs per square kilometer)* Challenge students to make up similar problems for the rest of the class.

5–1 (continued)

Population Growth

Meet Diverse Needs

Use the following mnemonic device to help students, particularly those with limited English proficiency, understand and remember the difference between immigration and emigration. Write both terms on the board, draw a box around *migration* in each word, and ask students to define this part in their own words. Students will probably suggest "traveling from one place to another" or something similar. Tell students that when they see the prefix *im-*, they can think of the word "in," so *immigration* means "in-migration." When they see the prefix *e-*, they can think of the word "exit," so *emigration* means "out-migration." **Limited English proficiency**

Build Science Skills

Applying Concepts Explain that populations can experience negative growth as well as positive growth. Then, pose the following problem: **Suppose that the total penguin population in Figure 5–2 was 1200 at the beginning of the year and 1600 at the end of the year. What was the population's growth rate?** *(An increase of 400 penguins per year)* **Suppose 250 penguin chicks died during the year. What was the population's growth rate?** *(A net increase of 150 penguins per year)* **Suppose that 200 adult penguins also died during the year. What was the population's growth rate?** *(A net decrease—negative growth—of 50 penguins per year)*

Word Origins

Immigration is formed from the Latin prefix *in-*, meaning "in," and *migrare,* meaning "to move from one place to another." **If the Latin prefix *e-* means "out," then what does *emigration* mean?**

Population Growth

Natural populations may stay the same size from year to year. But a population can grow rapidly, as sea otter populations did when they were first protected from hunting. Populations can also decrease in size, as otter populations are doing now because of predation by killer whales. But just how do interacting factors such as these influence population growth?

Three factors can affect population size: the number of births, the number of deaths, and the number of individuals that enter or leave the population. Simply put, a population will increase or decrease in size depending on how many individuals are added to it or removed from it.

Generally, populations grow if more individuals are born than die in any period of time. For some organisms, such as the penguins in **Figure 5–2,** being born may actually mean hatching. Plants can add new individuals as seeds sprout and begin to grow.

A population can grow when its birthrate is greater than its death rate. If the birthrate equals the death rate, the population stays more or less the same size. If the death rate is greater than the birthrate, the population shrinks. Sea otter populations grew when hunting stopped, because their death rate dropped. Those same otter populations are shrinking now because killer whales have raised the death rates of otters again.

Immigration (im-uh-GRAY-shun), the movement of individuals into an area, is another factor that can cause a population to grow. **Emigration** (em-uh-GRAY-shun), the movement of individuals out of a population, can cause a population to decrease in size. Wildlife biologists studying changes in populations of animals such as grizzly bears and wolves must consider immigration and emigration. For example, emigration can occur when young animals approaching maturity leave the area where they were born, find mates, and establish new territories. A shortage of food in one area may also lead to emigration. On the other hand, populations can increase by immigration as animals in search of mates or food arrive from outside.

▼ **Figure 5–2** This king penguin population has grown in size due to the recent births of chicks, recognizable by their downy brown feathers. **Population size is affected by the number of births, the number of deaths, and the number of individuals that enter or leave the population.**

PRESENTATIONS MADE EASY!

The Presentation Assistant Plus contains the Prentice Hall Presentation Pro and the Transparencies, which provide easy-to-follow visual support for every step of this section. If you have a computer presentation station, use Prentice Hall Presentation Pro for Section 5–1, or use the transparencies listed here.

Section 5–1: **Interest Grabber**
Section Outline
Concept Map
Figure 5–4

Exponential Growth

If a population has abundant space and food, and is protected from predators and disease, then organisms in that population will multiply and the population size will increase. Let's conduct an imaginary investigation to understand how growth under ideal conditions might occur. Suppose you put a single bacterium in a petri dish. Supply it with enough nutrients and incubate the culture with the right amount of heat, moisture, and light. How will the population change over time?

Bacteria reproduce by splitting in half. If the bacteria have a doubling time of 20 minutes, then within 20 minutes the first bacterium will divide to produce 2 bacteria. Twenty minutes later, the 2 bacteria will divide to produce 4. After another 20 minutes, there will be 8 bacteria. In another hour, there will be 64 bacteria, and in two more hours there will be 512. And in just one day, this colony of bacteria will grow to an astounding size of 4,720,000,000,000,000,000,000. What would happen if this growth pattern continued for several days without slowing down? Bacteria would cover the planet!

Figure 5–3 shows a graph with the size of the bacterial population plotted against time. As you can see, the pattern of growth is a J-shaped curve. The J-shaped curve indicates that the population is undergoing exponential (eks-poh-NEN-shul) growth. **Exponential growth** occurs when the individuals in a population reproduce at a constant rate. At first, the number of individuals in an exponentially growing population increases slowly. Over time, however, the population becomes larger and larger until it approaches an infinitely large size. **Under ideal conditions with unlimited resources, a population will grow exponentially.**

With a doubling time of 20 minutes, some bacteria have the fastest rates of reproduction among living things. Populations of other species grow more slowly. For example, a female elephant can produce an infant only every 2 to 4 years, then the offspring take about 10 years to mature. But as you can see in **Figure 5–3,** in the unlikely event that all the offspring of a single pair of elephants survived and reproduced for 750 years, there would be more than 20 million elephants!

CHECKPOINT *What is exponential growth?*

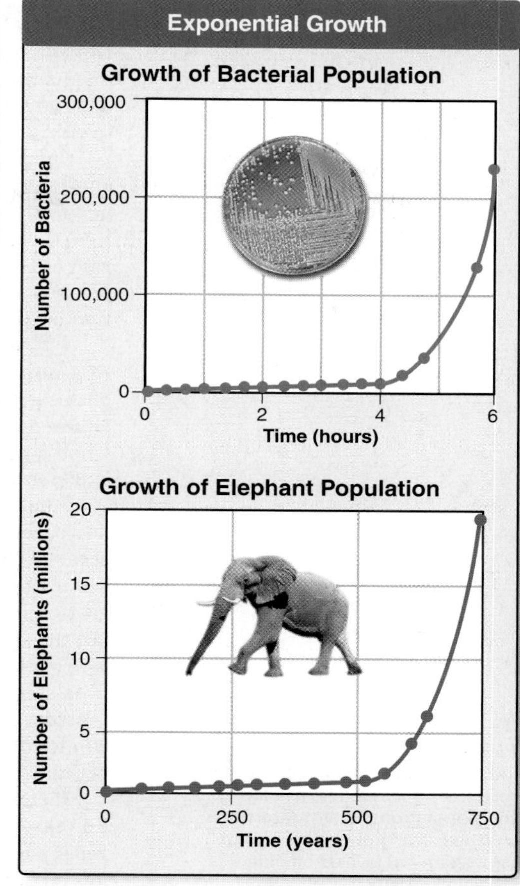

▲ **Figure 5–3 In the presence of unlimited resources, and in the absence of predation and disease, a population will grow exponentially.** Both of these hypothetical graphs show the characteristic J-shape of exponential population growth. Of course, there are many reasons why populations—whether bacteria or elephants—do not usually grow exponentially for very long.

Exponential Growth

Use Visuals

Figure 5–3 Have students study the two graphs; then, ask: **How are these graphs alike?** *(Both plot time on the horizontal axis and number of organisms on the vertical axis, and the curve on both graphs is J-shaped.)* **Besides showing different types of organisms, how do the graphs differ?** *(The size of the population is given in hundreds of thousands for bacteria and in millions for elephants. The elapsed time is in hours for bacteria and in hundreds of years for the elephants.)* **What do these differences indicate?** *(Bacteria reproduce very rapidly in a short period of time, but elephants reproduce much more slowly over a long period of time.)* **What is another major difference between the reproduction of bacteria and that of elephants?** *(Bacteria reproduce asexually; every bacterium is capable of producing two bacteria. Elephants reproduce sexually; two parents—a male and a female—are needed to produce one offspring.)*

Word Origins

Emigration means "out-migration."

BIO INSIGHTS — FACTS AND FIGURES

Biotic potential

The biotic potential of a species is defined as the size a population would reach if all offspring were to survive and produce young. In order for this to happen, conditions would have to be ideal; there would have to be enough food and living space to support the population, and there would have to be no factors present that would limit population growth. An illustration of biotic potential is given in the text: two elephants, under ideal conditions, would produce more than 20 million descendents after 750 years. In actuality, no population ever reaches its biotic potential. The factors that prevent this ideal growth are called limiting factors, or environmental resistance.

Answer to . . .

CHECKPOINT *Growth that occurs when a population reproduces at a constant rate*

Logistic Growth

Use Visuals

Figure 5–4 Ask: **How frequently did the yeast population double?** *(Every 7 to 10 hours)* **How long did it take the yeast population to reach its carrying capacity?** *(About 32 hours)* **Based on the number of cells produced in 50 hours, would you say that yeast populations increase quickly or slowly?** *(Quickly, but not as rapidly as bacteria)*

Meet Diverse Needs

The following activity, which models exponential and logistic growth, is particularly helpful with students who learn best when concepts are "translated" into visual form. Divide the class into small groups, and give each group a box of 100 paper clips. Tell students that the clips represent amoebas, one-celled organisms that reproduce simply by splitting in half. Have students lay out paper clips in a branching dichotomous "tree" to represent exponential growth through six generations. (*The results will be: Generation 1: 1 amoeba; Generation 2: 2 amoebas; Generation 3: 4 amoebas; Generation 4: 8 amoebas; Generation 5: 16 amoebas; and Generation 6: 32 amoebas.*)

Next, have each group model logistic growth by repeating the procedure, this time removing clips to represent deaths, as follows: Generation 1: 1 amoeba; Generation 2: 2 amoebas; Generation 3: 4 amoebas, remove 1; Generation 4: 6 amoebas, remove 2; Generation 5: 8 amoebas, remove 3; and Generation 6: 10 amoebas. Have students compare the number of organisms in the last generation of both models. **Learning modality: visual**

Logistic Growth

Obviously, neither bacteria nor elephants cover the planet. This means that exponential growth does not continue in natural populations for very long. What might cause population growth to stop or to slow down?

Suppose that a few animals are introduced into a new environment. At first, as the animals begin to reproduce, the population increases slowly. Then, because resources are unlimited, the population grows exponentially. In time, however, the rate of population growth begins to slow down. This does not mean that the size of the population has dropped. The population is still growing, but at a much slower rate.

As resources become less available, the growth of a population slows or stops. The general, S-shaped curve of this growth pattern, called logistic growth, is shown in **Figure 5–4** in a yeast population. **Logistic growth** occurs when a population's growth slows or stops following a period of exponential growth. How might this happen?

Population growth may slow down when the birthrate decreases, when the death rate increases, or when both events occur at the same rate. Similarly, population growth may slow down when the rate of immigration decreases, the rate of emigration increases, or both. When the birthrate and death rate are the same, or when the rate of immigration is equal to the rate of emigration, then population growth will slow down or even stop for a time. Note that even when the population growth is said to stop, the population is still rising and falling somewhat, but the ups and downs average out around a certain population size.

If you look again at **Figure 5–4**, you will see a horizontal line through the region of the graph where the growth of the yeast population has leveled off. The point at which that line intersects the y-axis tells you the size of the population when the average growth rate reaches zero. That number, in turn, represents the largest number of individuals—in this case, yeast cells—that a given environment can support. Ecologists call this number the **carrying capacity** of the environment for a particular species.

If you examine natural populations of familiar plant and animal species, you will find that many of them follow a logistic growth curve. In the natural world there are many factors that can slow the growth of a population. The factors that limit population growth are discussed in the next section.

▼ **Figure 5–4** This graph shows the S-shaped curve of logistic growth in a population of yeast cells. **As resources become less available, the population growth rate slows or stops.** The growth of this yeast population has leveled off at its carrying capacity.

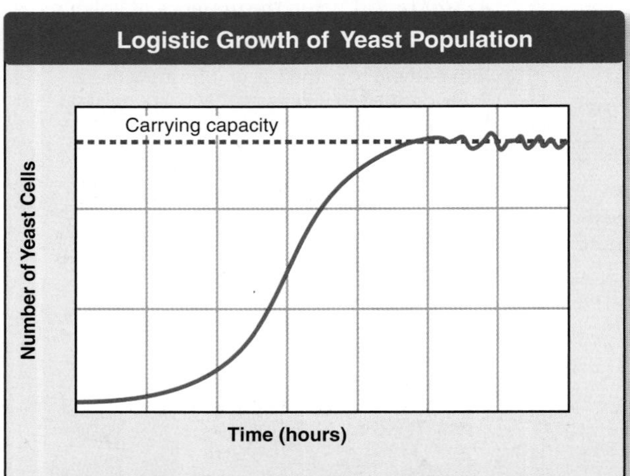

Analyzing Data

Population Trends

Do fruit flies and rabbits show similar trends in population growth?

1. **Tables and Graphs** Make a graph using the data in each data table. One graph will show the growth rate of a fruit fly population. The other graph will show the growth rate of a population of rabbits.
2. **Analyzing Data** What type of growth pattern is exhibited by the fruit fly population? Is it the same type of growth as in the rabbit population? Explain.
3. **Drawing Conclusions** Does either graph indicate that there is a carrying capacity for the population? If so, when does the population reach its carrying capacity? What is the maximum number of individuals that can be supported at that time?
4. **Predicting** Animals such as foxes and cats often prey on rabbits. Based on the growth curve of the rabbit population, what might have happened if a group of predators moved into the rabbits' habitat during the tenth generation and began eating the rabbits?

Fruit Fly Population Growth

Days	Number of Fruit Flies
5	10
10	50
15	100
20	200
25	300
30	310
35	320
40	320

Rabbit Population Growth

Generations	Number of Rabbits
1	100
2	105
25	1000
37	1600
55	2400
72	3350
86	8000
100	13,150

Analyzing Data

Before students create their graphs, help them decide on appropriate intervals for the *x*- and *y*-axes.

Answers

2. The fruit fly population exhibits logistic growth, while the rabbit population exhibits exponential growth. Limiting factors must have affected the growth of the fruit fly population but not the growth of the rabbit population.
3. The graph of the fruit fly population seems to reach its carrying capacity at 35 days, when 320 individuals can be supported.
4. With predators added, the rabbit population would exhibit logistic growth, not exponential growth, and the population's growth would slow, stop, or decrease in later generations.

5–1 Section Assessment

1. **Key Concept** List three characteristics that are used to describe a population.
2. **Key Concept** What factors can change a population's size?
3. **Key Concept** What is the difference between exponential growth and logistic growth?
4. What is meant by population density?
5. Define carrying capacity.
6. **Critical Thinking Inferring** What factors might cause the carrying capacity of a population to change?

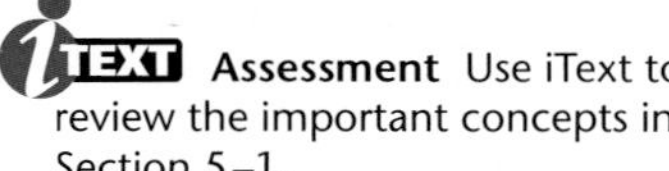

Assessment Use iText to review the important concepts in Section 5–1.

ALTERNATIVE ASSESSMENT

Using Graphic Organizers Draw a concept map that shows how populations grow. Include the following terms: exponential growth, logistic growth, birthrate, death rate, immigration, emigration. Add any other terms that you think are useful to complete the map.

5-1 Section Assessment

1. Geographic distribution, population density, growth rate
2. Births, deaths, immigration, emigration
3. Exponential growth occurs when the population grows at a constant rate. Exponential growth occurs only under ideal conditions (ample space and food; protection from predators and disease). Logistic growth occurs when a population's growth rate slows or stops following a period of exponential growth.
4. The number of individuals per unit area
5. The largest number of individuals that a given environment can support
6. Accept all reasonable answers. Sample answer: A natural disaster such as a forest fire, flood, or hurricane might reduce the amount of resources available to a population.

3 ASSESS

Evaluate Understanding

Have students explain why the graph curves for exponential growth and logistic growth are different shapes and also identify some factors that cause population growth to slow or stop.

Reteach

Have each student draw two simplified graphs—one for exponential growth and the other for logistic growth—with each graph including only the correct shape of the curve and two axes labeled *Number* and *Time.* Have students compare their graphs with those in their textbook and make any necessary corrections in the shapes of the curves.

ALTERNATIVE ASSESSMENT

Students' concept maps will vary but should show logical connections between terms.

Use iText to review the key concepts in Section 5–1.

Section 5–2

1 FOCUS

Objectives

5.2.1 ***Identify*** factors that limit population growth.

5.2.2 ***Differentiate*** between density-dependent and density-independent limiting factors.

Guide for Reading

Vocabulary Preview

To prepare students for the new Vocabulary terms *density-dependent* and *density-independent,* ask them to recall the definition of *population density* that they learned in Section 5–1. *(The number of individuals per unit of area)*

Reading Strategy

Suggest that students record their predictions in writing, leaving space below each one to note whether the prediction was correct or incorrect. In the case of incorrect predictions, have students correctly note how those limiting factors affect a population's growth.

2 INSTRUCT

Limiting Factors

Use Visuals

Figure 5–5 For each of the limiting factors shown in the diagram, have students suggest examples that are already familiar to them—for example, weeds and crop plants competing for light, space, and nutrients in a vegetable garden; the predator-prey relationship of a toad eating a moth; and so on. As students cite examples, have a volunteer list them on a large sheet of paper. Save the list for use again later in Evaluate Understanding, page 127.

5–2 Limits to Growth

Guide for Reading

Key Concept
- What factors limit population growth?

Vocabulary
limiting factor
density-dependent limiting factor
predator-prey relationship
density-independent limiting factor

Reading Strategy: Predicting Before you read, preview the diagram below. Predict how each factor might limit the growth of a population. As you read, note whether your predictions were correct.

Now that you know a few things about population growth, think again about the sea otter example in the beginning of the previous section. When a sea otter population declines, something has changed the relationship between the birthrate and the death rate, or between the rates of immigration and emigration. For instance, in part of the sea otter's range, the death rate of sea otters is increasing because killer whales are eating the otters. Predation by killer whales creates a situation that reduces the growth of the sea otter population.

Limiting Factors

Recall from Chapter 3 that the primary productivity of an ecosystem can be reduced when there is an insufficient supply of a particular nutrient. Ecologists call such substances limiting nutrients. A limiting nutrient is an example of a more general ecological concept: a limiting factor. In the context of populations, a **limiting factor** is a factor that causes population growth to decrease.

Some of the limiting factors that can affect a population are shown in **Figure 5–5.** Those limiting factors that affect a population more strongly as the population grows larger are shown with purple arrows. Factors that limit a population's growth regardless of the population's size are shown with green arrows.

▼ **Figure 5–5** Many different factors can limit population growth. **Inferring** *How might each of these factors increase the death rate in a population?*

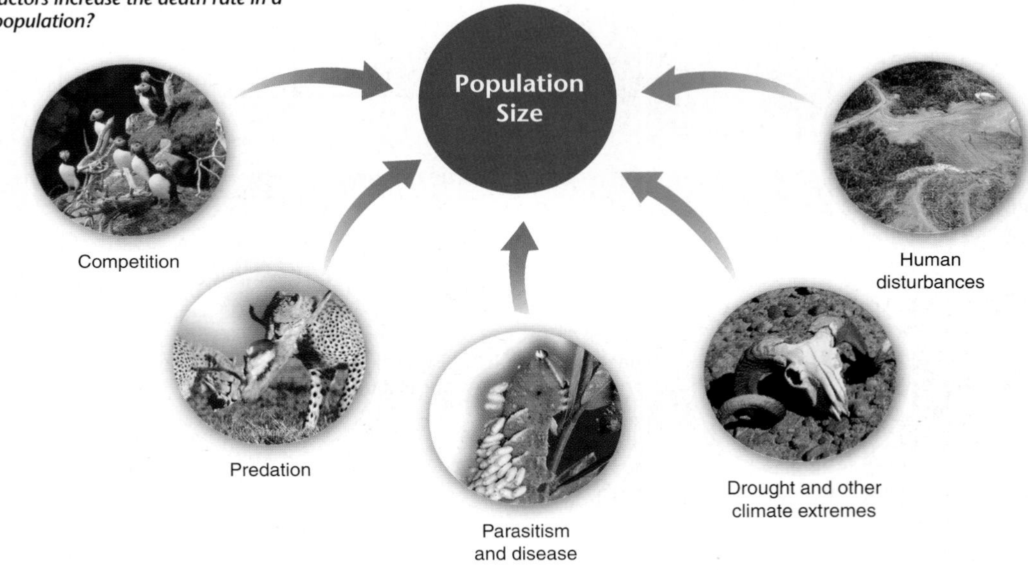

SECTION RESOURCES

Print:
- ***Teaching Resources,*** Section Review 5–2
- ***Guided Reading and Study Workbook,*** Section 5–2
- ***Issues and Decision Making,*** Issues and Decisions 48

Technology
- ***iText,*** Section 5–2

Density-Dependent Factors

A limiting factor that depends on population size is called a **density-dependent limiting factor.** Density-dependent factors become limiting only when the population density—the number of organisms per unit area—reaches a certain level. These factors operate most strongly when a population is large and dense. They do not affect small, scattered populations as greatly. **Density-dependent limiting factors include competition, predation, parasitism, and disease.** An example of competition can be seen in **Figure 5–6.**

Competition When populations become crowded, organisms compete, or struggle, with one another for food, water, space, sunlight, and other essentials of life. It is easy to see why competition among members of the same species is a density-dependent limiting factor. The more individuals that live in an area, the sooner they will use up the available resources. Likewise, the fewer the number of individuals, the more resources that are available to them, and the less they must compete with one another.

Competition can also occur between members of different species. This type of competition is a major force behind evolutionary change. When two species compete for the same resources, both species are under pressure to change in ways that decrease their competition. Over time, the species may evolve to occupy separate niches. That is because, as you may recall, no two species can occupy the same niche in the same place at the same time.

CHECKPOINT *What is a density-dependent limiting factor?*

Quick Lab

How does competition affect plant growth?

Materials bean seeds, 2 paper cups, potting soil

Procedure 

1. Label two paper cups 3 and 15. Use a pencil to make several holes in the bottom of each paper cup. Fill each paper cup two-thirds full with potting soil. Plant 3 bean seeds in cup 3, and plant 15 bean seeds in cup 15.
2. Water both cups so that the soil is moist but not wet. Put them in a location that receives bright indirect light. Water the cups equally as needed.
3. Count the seedlings every other day for 2 weeks. **CAUTION:** *Wash your hands with soap and warm water before leaving the lab.*

Analyze and Conclude

Observing What differences did you observe between the two cups?

◀ **Figure 5–6** The Atlantic puffin lives in large colonies along the coast of eastern North America from Maine north into the Arctic. Puffins nest in burrows dug into the sides of cliffs. Because nesting sites are limited, puffins must compete for space. **Competition is a density-dependent limiting factor. Other density-dependent factors are predation, parasitism, and disease.**

Density-Dependent Factors

Quick Lab

Objective Students will be able to determine that crowding is a limiting factor in plant growth.

Skill Focus Drawing Conclusions

Materials bean seeds, 2 paper cups, potting soil

Time 15 minutes for initial setup, followed by observation and recording for 2 weeks

Strategy Remind students that the only variable that should be different between the two cups is the number of seeds planted. Ask: **What variables should you keep the same in both cups?** *(The depth at which the seeds are planted, the amount of water the cups are given, the amount of sunlight the cups receive, temperature)*

Expected Outcome The uncrowded seedlings will thrive. The crowded seedlings will show limited growth, and some may die.

Analyze and Conclude

1. The seedlings in cup 15 will be smaller and less robust than those in cup 3, and some may die.

TIME SAVER — PRESENTATIONS MADE EASY!

The Presentation Assistant Plus contains the Prentice Hall Presentation Pro and the Transparencies, which provide easy-to-follow visual support for every step of this section. If you have a computer presentation station, use Prentice Hall Presentation Pro for Section 5–2, or use the transparencies listed here.

Section 5–2:  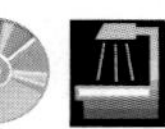
Interest Grabber
Section Outline
Effect of a Density-Dependent Factor on a Population
Figure 5–7

Answers to . . .

CHECKPOINT *A factor that limits population growth only when the population's density reaches a certain level*

Figure 5–5 *Each of the factors that limit population growth could cause deaths of individuals. Accept all reasonable responses.*

Use Visuals

Figure 5–7 Make sure students understand that two separate sets of data are plotted on the graph: the blue line represents the numbers of wolves labeled on the graph's left vertical axis, and the red line represents the numbers of moose labeled on the right vertical axis.

Make Connections

Mathematics Present the following math problems: **In order to survive, a 50-kilogram wolf needs to eat about 2700 kilograms of moose per year. The average mass of a moose is about 385 kilograms; males have more mass, females less. How many "average" moose does a wolf need to eat each year?** *(About 7)* **If there are 8 wolves in a pack, how many moose does the pack need to eat each year?** *(About 56)*

Meet Diverse Needs

Give four students index cards labeled *owl*, and give the remaining students cards labeled *mouse*. At your signal, the "owls" should collect cards from the "mice" one at a time until no more "mice" remain. Ask: **Which limiting factors did you model, and which population did each factor affect?** *(Competition affected the "owls"; predation affected the "mice.")* **Learning modality: kinesthetic**

Density-Independent Factors

Build Science Skills

Applying Concepts Ask: **Does the graph in Figure 5–7 show a crash in either population?** *(Yes; the wolf population from 1980 to 1982 and the moose population from 1995 to 1996)* Read the caption and then ask: **What combination of density-dependent and density-independent factors may have caused the crash in the wolf population?** *(Decline in the moose population; unusually deep winter snows could have made it difficult for the wolves to hunt; parasites or disease could have weakened or killed the wolves.)*

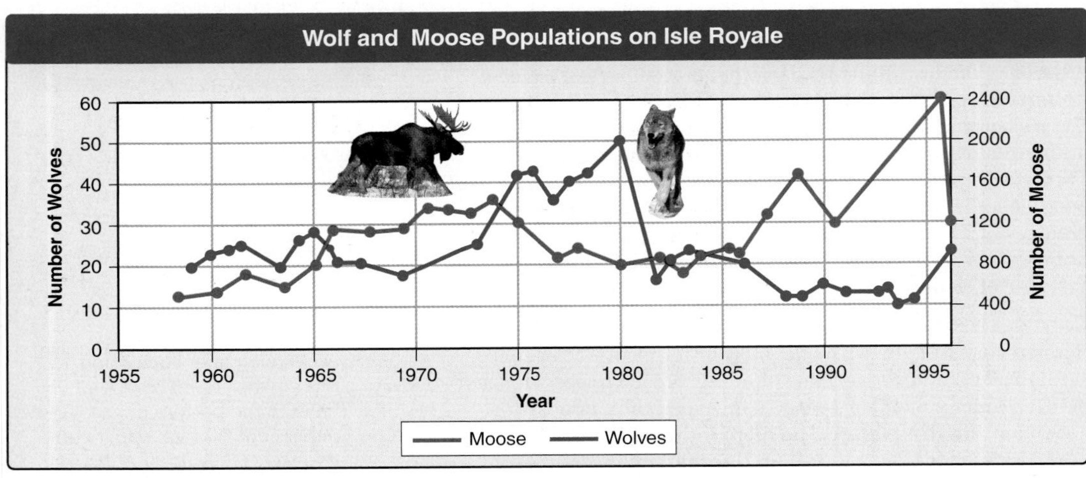

▲ **Figure 5–7** The relationship between moose and wolves on Isle Royale illustrates how predation can affect population growth. Other factors can come into play. In this example, the moose population was affected by changes in food supply, and the wolf population was affected by disease. **Interpreting Graphics** ***How are the increases and decreases in the moose population related to the changes in the wolf population?***

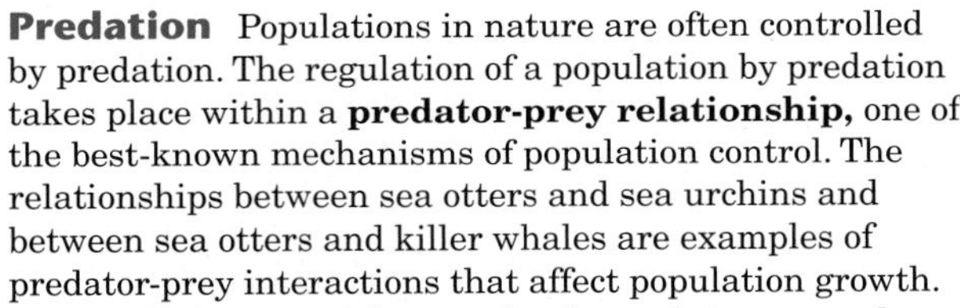

Predation Populations in nature are often controlled by predation. The regulation of a population by predation takes place within a **predator-prey relationship,** one of the best-known mechanisms of population control. The relationships between sea otters and sea urchins and between sea otters and killer whales are examples of predator-prey interactions that affect population growth.

A well-documented example of a predator-prey relationship is the interaction between wolves and moose on Isle Royale, an island in Lake Superior. The graph in **Figure 5–7** shows how periodic increases in the moose population—the prey—on Isle Royale are quickly followed by increases in the wolf population—the predators. As the wolves prey on the moose, the moose population falls. The decline in the moose population is followed, sooner or later, by a decline in the wolf population because there is less for the wolves to feed upon. A decline in the wolf population means that the moose have fewer enemies, so the moose population rises again. This cycle of predator and prey populations can be repeated indefinitely.

Parasitism and Disease Parasites can also limit the growth of a population. Parasitic organisms range in size from microscopic, disease-causing bacteria to tapeworms 30 centimeters or more in length. These organisms are similar to predators in many ways. Like predators, parasites take nourishment at the expense of their hosts, often weakening them and causing disease or death. The wasp cocoons in **Figure 5–8,** for example, can weaken or kill many caterpillars.

◀ **Figure 5–8** This larval sphinx moth has been attacked by a parasitic wasp. The wasp inserted its eggs beneath the moth's skin. After hatching, the wasp larvae fed on their host internally until they appeared as white cocoons on its back. **Predicting** ***How might the wasp larvae affect the sphinx moth population?***

TEACHER TO TEACHER

Use a short video clip of a forest fire, such as the National Park Service's video of fires in Yellowstone Park. Then, read one or two actual news articles that describe the fire and its effects.

Divide the class into groups of three or four, and assign each group the task of developing a management plan to study the ecological damage caused by the fire and help re-establish plant and animal populations in the burned area. Students should research the following information: the types of populations living in the area before and after the fire; the initial and current size of each population; resources now available to the populations and resources no longer available; and possible steps to help reintroduce populations. Give each group an opportunity to explain its plan to the class.

Brenda Waldon
Biology Teacher
Clayton County Public Schools,
Morrow, Georgia

Density-Independent Factors

Density-independent limiting factors affect all populations in similar ways, regardless of the population size. **Unusual weather, natural disasters, seasonal cycles, and certain human activities—such as damming rivers and clear-cutting forests—are all examples of density-independent limiting factors.** In response to such factors, many species show a characteristic crash in population size. After the crash, the population may build right up again or it may stay low for some time.

For some species, storms or hurricanes can nearly extinguish a population. For example, thrips, aphids, and other insects that feed on plant buds and leaves might be washed out by a heavy rainstorm. Extremes of cold or hot weather also can take their toll on a population, regardless of the population's density. A severe winter frost, for example, can kill giant saguaro cacti in the Arizona desert. In some areas, periodic droughts can affect entire populations of grasses. Such events can, in turn, affect the populations of consumers within the food web.

Environments are always changing, and most populations can adapt to a certain amount of change. Populations often grow and shrink in response to such changes. Major upsets in an ecosystem, however, can lead to long-term declines in certain populations. Human activities have caused some of these major upsets, as you will soon read.

▶ **Figure 5–9** A drought can result in the abrupt decrease of a population, regardless of its size. **Droughts and other natural disasters are density-independent limiting factors. So are many human activities, such as clear-cutting forests.**

5–2 Section Assessment

1. **Key Concept** List three density-dependent factors and three density-independent factors that can limit the growth of a population.
2. What is the relationship between competition and population size?
3. If an entire lynx population disappears, what is likely to happen to the hare population on which it preys?
4. **Critical Thinking Applying Concepts** Give an example of a density-independent limiting factor that has affected a human population. Describe how this factor changed the human population.

iTEXT Assessment Use iText to review the important concepts in Section 5–2.

MAKING CONNECTIONS

Biotic and Abiotic Factors Study the factors that limit population growth in **Figure 5–5.** Classify each factor as either biotic or abiotic. (*Hint:* Refer to the information on biotic and abiotic factors in Section 4–2.)

3 ASSESS

Evaluate Understanding

Display the list of examples that the class created at the beginning of this section (Use Visuals, page 124). Call on students at random to identify each example as density-dependent or density-independent.

Reteach

Have students work in groups of three, with each student responsible for writing a brief description of how one of the three density-dependent limiting factors discussed in the text can limit a population's growth. Let the group members share their descriptions and offer corrections and improvements.

Making Connections

Density-dependent limiting factors, such as competition, predation, parasitism, and disease, can be classified as biotic factors. Density-independent limiting factors, such as drought and other climate extremes as well as human disturbance to ecosystems, can be classified as abiotic factors. Some students may argue that human disturbance should be considered a biotic factor for the reason that humans are organisms interacting with other organisms. At the same time, however, human disturbances such as building roads, filling wetlands, or clearing forests cause large-scale changes in the physical environment that should be considered abiotic factors.

Use iText to review the key concepts in Section 5–2.

5–2 Section Assessment

1. Density-dependent: competition, predation, parasitism, disease; density-independent: unusual weather, natural disasters, seasonal cycles, human activities
2. When populations become larger and more crowded, organisms must compete with one another for food, water, space, sunlight, and other essential resources.
3. The hare population would probably undergo explosive growth.
4. Accept all reasonable responses. Sample answer: A prolonged drought, with its associated crop loss, could cause deaths, financial hardship, and emigration to other countries.

Answers to . . .

Figure 5–7 *As the moose population increased, the wolf population increased. Decreases in the moose population were followed by decreases in the wolf population.*

Figure 5–8 *Predation by wasp larvae would reduce the growth rate of the sphinx moth population.*

Encourage students to research current nature publications to gather more detailed information on both sides of this issue. If students live in an area where ranchers or farmers suffer losses due to wolf predation, suggest that they interview affected people and research local newspaper articles to learn more.

You may wish to let students work in several small groups, with some groups representing ranchers and others representing conservationists and other stakeholders. Give the groups time to discuss their points of view and their reasoning. Then, hold a mock meeting in which each side presents its view to the "government official." (You may want to role-play the official yourself.)

You Decide

1. Students should accurately describe the status of U.S. wolf populations in the past and today.
2. Students' lists will vary and may include researched information as well as information included in this feature.
3. Accept opinions on both sides of the issue so long as students defend their choices with reasonable explanations.

Does the Gray Wolf Population Need Protection?

Feds Reconsider Status of Gray Wolf The federal government is preparing to announce that the gray wolf, which was once nearly extinct in the United States, is abundant enough in some states that it no longer needs the strict protection required under the Endangered Species Act. The change would mean that wolves that pose a threat to human affairs could be chased away or legally shot by government agents.

Wolves were once widely distributed around the world, occupying almost every habitat except tropical jungles. Today, however, wolves occupy only a fraction of their former range. In 1973, the Endangered Species Act was passed by the United States Congress to protect declining populations of gray wolves from becoming extinct. At the time, there were only about 400 wolves in the lower 48 states. By 1999, the population had swelled to an estimated 3500 individuals scattered mostly throughout the Rocky Mountains and Great Lakes areas.

Classifying the status of animals is a judgment call. In some cases, the judgment is easy. For instance, the California condor population now includes only a few remaining members and is clearly in great danger. With other species, such as the gray wolf, the situation is much more complex. How should the gray wolf be classified—and therefore managed—in the United States?

The Viewpoints

Keep the Endangered Classification

People who want to keep the gray wolf's status as an endangered species say that most of its former habitat in the 48 contiguous states is unsuitable due to human encroachment. Proponents of this view cite the fact that only after wolves were given protection under the Endangered Species Act did the wolf population in the United States begin to increase. There is concern that human persecution and loss of habitat will restrict gray wolves to more remote areas, or reduce their habitat even further, unless federal protection continues.

Reclassify the Wolf and Remove Federal Protection

Opponents of the endangered species classification counter that in states like Minnesota, the gray wolf population is growing at a rate of 4 to 5 percent each year. These people are confident that, because the populations are increasing at a healthy rate, the wolves no longer need federal protection. Ranchers are concerned that, at the current growth rate, wolves will encroach on their livestock. Many feel strongly that landowners should have the right to protect themselves from potential losses. The protection of wolves currently costs the United States government over $200,000 per year. If the wolves could be legally hunted and trapped, the money that would be saved could be used to help protect other, more endangered species.

You Decide

1. **Defining the Issue** In your own words, explain the issues surrounding the classification and management of the gray wolf in the United States.
2. **Analyzing the Viewpoints** List the pros and cons of each option as they relate to both humans and wolves. Consider the different perspectives of landowners, conservationists, and other stakeholders.
3. **Forming Your Opinion** Should the federal status of the gray wolf change? Why or why not?

5–3 Human Population Growth

How quickly is the world's human population growing? In the United States and other developed countries, the current growth rate is very low. In some developing countries, the human population is growing at a rate of nearly 3 people per second. Because of this bustling growth rate, the human population is well on its way to reaching 9 billion within your lifetime.

Guide for Reading

Key Concepts
- How has the size of the human population changed over time?
- Why do population growth rates differ in countries throughout the world?

Vocabulary
demography
demographic transition
age-structure diagram

Reading Strategy: Asking Questions Before you read, preview the graphs in **Figures 5–10**, **5–12**, and **5–13.** Make a list of questions about the graphs. As you read, write down the answers to your questions.

Historical Overview

Like the populations of many other living organisms, the size of the human population tends to increase with time. For most of human existence, the population grew slowly. Life was harsh, and limiting factors kept population sizes low. Food was scarce. Incurable diseases were rampant. Until fairly recently, only half the children in the world survived to adulthood. Because death rates were so high, families had many children, just to make sure that some would survive.

About 500 years ago, the human population began growing more rapidly. Agriculture and industry made life easier and safer. The world's food supply became more reliable, and essential goods could be shipped around the globe. Improved sanitation, medicine, and health care dramatically reduced the death rate and increased longevity. At the same time, birthrates in most places remained high. With these advances, the human population experienced exponential growth, as shown in **Figure 5–10.**

▼ **Figure 5–10** **The size of the human population has increased over time.** After a long, slow start, the worldwide population grew exponentially following improvements in medicine, sanitation, agriculture, energy use, and technology.

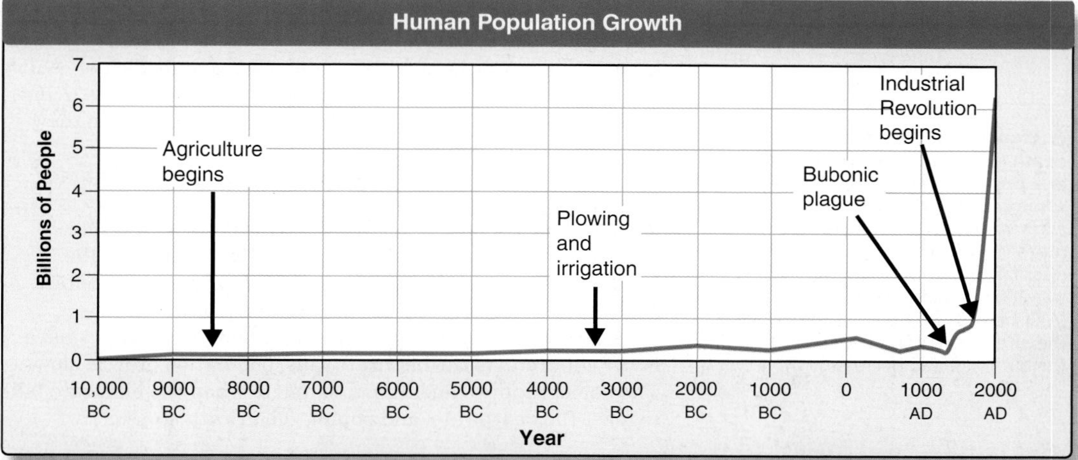

SECTION RESOURCES

Print:
- ***Laboratory Manual A,*** Chapter 5 Lab
- ***Laboratory Manual B,*** Chapter 5 Lab
- ***Teaching Resources,*** Section Review 5–3
- ***Guided Reading and Study Workbook,*** Section 5–3
- ***Issues and Decision Making,*** Issues and Decisions 47

Technology
- ***iText,*** Section 5–3

Section 5–3

1 FOCUS

Objectives

5.3.1 ***Describe*** how the size of the human population has changed over time.
5.3.2 ***Explain*** why population growth rates differ in countries throughout the world.

Guide for Reading

Vocabulary Preview

Students with limited English proficiency would benefit from scanning the section's text to identify any unfamiliar words and terms—not only the boldfaced Vocabulary terms but others such as *essential goods* and *sanitation.* Have students record the terms and their dictionary definitions for use as a reference as they read the section.

Reading Strategy

To help students get started, let the entire class brainstorm ideas for items in each column. Draw a simple table on the board, and record students' suggestions as they make them. Also, explain that some of the items they list in the "want to learn" column may not be covered in the section, so they may want to do further reading.

2 INSTRUCT

Historical Overview

Build Science Skills

Predicting Ask: **If you extended the graph in Figure 5–10 thousands of years into the future, what do you think the curve would look like, and why?** *(Although a few students may say that the steep rise would continue, most will realize that at some point, Earth's carrying capacity for the human population would be reached, and population growth would slow and remain steady or might even drop—forming the S-shaped curve typical of logistic growth.)*

Patterns of Population Growth

Use Community Resources

Encourage small groups of students to research the demographics of their own city or town over a certain period of time. Statistics on births, deaths, total population, and other demographic data may be available from town/city hall, a library, county or state officials, or even real estate agencies. Suggest that the groups make graphs to share their findings.

Use Visuals

Figure 5–11 Make sure students understand what the photographs represent by asking them to identify the "positive change" shown and explain how the change has affected population growth. For example, the photograph showing a health worker giving an injection of vaccine to an infant represents medical advances that have significantly reduced death rates. Reduced death rates have in turn resulted in reduced birthrates.

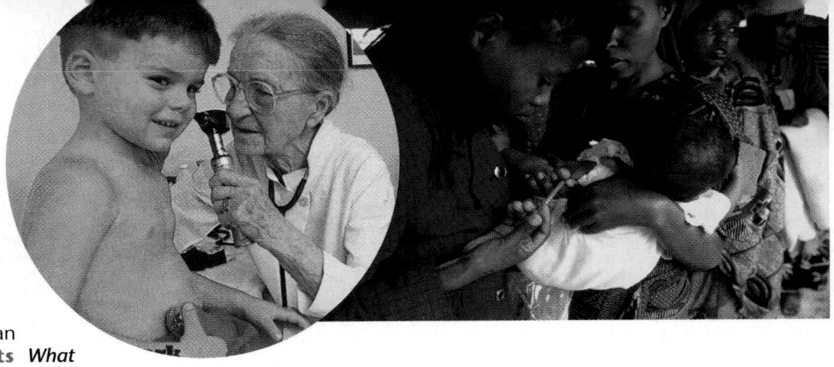

Figure 5–11 Medical advances can lead to a dramatic drop in a population's death rate. Dr. Leila Denmark (left), the oldest known practicing physician in the United States, helped invent the whooping cough vaccine in 1936. A health-care worker in Rwanda (right) vaccinates an infant. **Applying Concepts** *What other advancements can reduce a population's death rate?*

Patterns of Population Growth

The human population cannot keep growing exponentially forever, because Earth and its resources are limited. The question is, when and how will our population growth slow? Two centuries ago, English economist Thomas Malthus observed that human populations were growing rapidly. Malthus predicted that such growth would not continue indefinitely. Instead, according to Malthus, war, famine, and disease would limit human population growth.

Today, scientists have identified a variety of other social and economic factors that can affect human populations. The scientific study of human populations is called **demography** (duh-MAH-gruh-fee). Demography examines the characteristics of human populations and attempts to explain how those populations will change over time. **Birthrates, death rates, and the age structure of a population help predict why some countries have high growth rates while other countries grow more slowly.**

The Demographic Transition Over the past century, population growth in the United States, Japan, and much of Europe has slowed dramatically. Demographers have developed a hypothesis to explain this shift. According to this hypothesis, these countries have completed the **demographic transition,** a dramatic change in birth and death rates.

Throughout most of history, human societies have had high death rates and equally high birthrates. As countries modernize, however, advances in nutrition, sanitation, and medicine result in more children surviving to adulthood and more adults living to old age. These changes lower the death rate and begin the demographic transition.

As you can see in **Figure 5–12,** when the death rate first begins to fall, birthrates remain high. During this phase of the demographic transition, births greatly exceed deaths, and population increases rapidly. This was the situation in the United States from 1790 to about 1910. Many parts of South America, Africa, and Asia are still in this phase.

As societies continue to modernize, however, families have fewer children. As the birthrate falls, population growth slows. The demographic transition is complete when the birthrate falls to meet the death rate, and population growth stops.

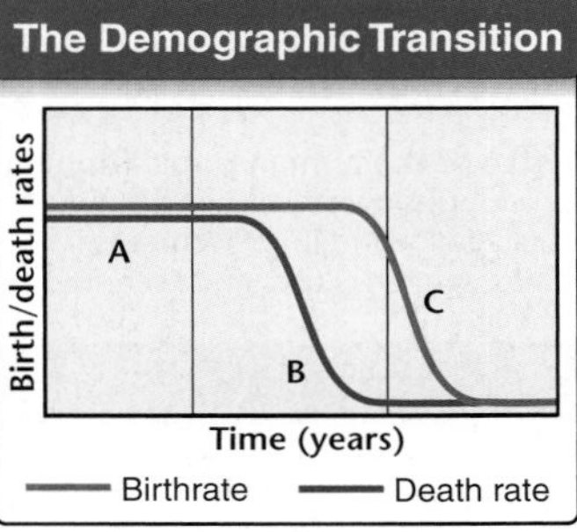

▲ **Figure 5–12** **Birthrates, death rates, and the age structure of a population help predict why some countries have high growth rates while other countries grow more slowly.** Birthrates and death rates fall during the demographic transition. Initially, both rates are high (A). Then, the death rate drops while the birthrate remains high (B). Finally, the birth rate also decreases (C).

PRESENTATIONS MADE EASY!

The Presentation Assistant Plus contains the Prentice Hall Presentation Pro and the Transparencies, which provide easy-to-follow visual support for every step of this section. If you have a computer presentation station, use Prentice Hall Presentation Pro for Section 5–3, or use the transparencies listed here.

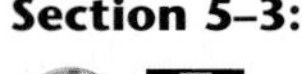

Section 5–3: **Interest Grabber**
Section Outline
Human Population
Figure 5–13

So far, the demographic transition has happened in only a few countries. Despite the trend in the United States, Europe, and Japan, the worldwide human population is still growing exponentially. Most people live in countries that have not yet completed the demographic transition. Much of the population growth today is contributed by only 10 countries, with India and China in the lead, where birthrates remain high.

Age Structure Population growth depends, in part, on how many people of different ages make up a given population. Demographers can predict future growth using models called **age-structure diagrams,** or population profiles, which graph the numbers of people in different age groups in the population.

Consider **Figure 5–13,** which compares the age structure of the United States population with that of Rwanda. In the United States, there are nearly equal numbers of people in each age group. This age structure predicts a slow but steady growth rate for the near future. In Rwanda, on the other hand, there are many more young children than teenagers, and many more teenagers than adults. This age structure predicts a population that will double in about 30 years.

CHECKPOINT *What are age-structure diagrams?*

KEEP CURRENT WITH . . . SCIENCE NEWS®

To find out more about the topics in this chapter, go to: **www.phschool.com**

▼ **Figure 5–13** These graphs compare the age structure of the U.S. population with the population of Rwanda. Each bar in the age-structure diagram represents individuals within a 5-year group. Males are to the left of the center line, and females are to the right. **Analyzing Data** ***How do the United States and Rwanda differ in the percentages of 10- to 14-year-olds in the population?***

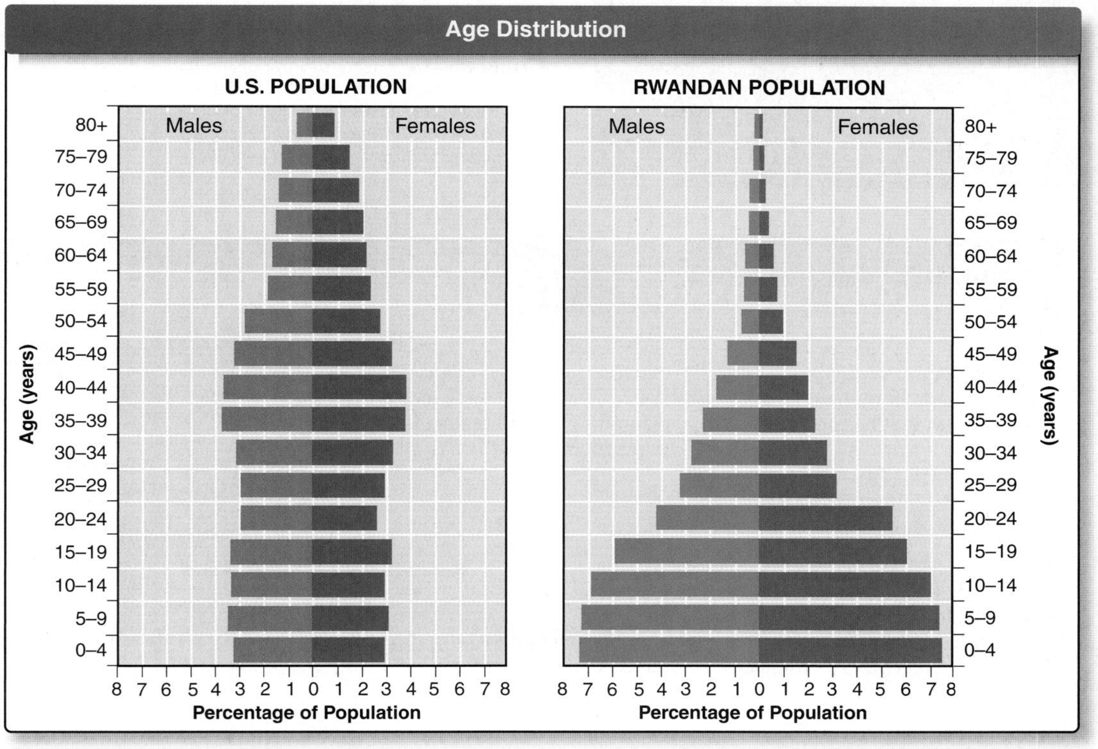

Age Distribution

U.S. POPULATION | RWANDAN POPULATION

Males | Females

Age (years): 80+, 75–79, 70–74, 65–69, 60–64, 55–59, 50–54, 45–49, 40–44, 35–39, 30–34, 25–29, 20–24, 15–19, 10–14, 5–9, 0–4

8 7 6 5 4 3 2 1 0 1 2 3 4 5 6 7 8

Percentage of Population

FACTS AND FIGURES

Controlling human population

Two examples illustrate the complexities of controlling human population growth in developing nations. In India, government-sponsored population control programs have not done well, due largely to family resistance. In desperation, the government enacted a law subjecting some men to compulsory sterilization. Public outrage was so great that the law was rescinded. India's population continues to grow.

China has instituted the most extensive family planning program in the world. Couples who pledge to have only one child are given extra food, better housing, free medical care, and salary bonuses. Couples who break this pledge lose their benefits. These policies have curtailed explosive population growth. However, growth is still rapid, due primarily to the large number of women in or entering their reproductive years.

SCIENCE NEWS®

Encourage students to visit **www.phschool.com** for the most current information on this topic.

Build Science Skills

Interpreting Graphics Focus students' attention on the right-hand graph in Figure 5–13 and ask: **What overall trend do you see in Rwanda's population growth?** *(Every five-year population group is larger than the previous group.)* **Why would this age structure predict a large population increase in the future?** *(With each five-year group having more women entering their child-bearing years, the rate of population growth would increase.)* **If you compare the top halves of the two graphs, what can you tell about Rwanda's population?** *(Death rates of older people are higher in Rwanda than in the United States. People in Rwanda do not live as long as people in the United States. In the United States, women tend to live longer than men; in Rwanda, men tend to live longer than women.)*

Answers to . . .

CHECKPOINT *Graphs that represent the numbers of people in different age groups in a population*

Figure 5–11 *Improved health care increases life expectancy and lowers infant and childhood mortality, which decreases the death rate. With fewer deaths, the birthrate may also decrease.*

Figure 5–13 *In the United States, 10-to-14-year-olds make up about 6.5 percent of the population, and in Rwanda they make up about 14 percent of the population. The difference is about 7.5 percent—about 3.5 percentage points for males and 4 percentage points for females.*

5–3 (continued)

Future Population Growth

Build Science Skills

Making Judgments Ask: **What two opposing points of view about future population growth are expressed in the last paragraph?** *(One view is stated in the sentence that begins "Many ecologists suggest . . ." The other view is stated in the last sentence.)* Let students meet in small groups to brainstorm ideas about both viewpoints. Then, choose two teams of volunteers to debate the viewpoints for the class.

3 ASSESS

Evaluate Understanding

Have students write a paragraph explaining, in their own words, why the human population grew very slowly for many thousands of years and why the growth increased dramatically about 500 years ago.

Reteach

If students have difficulty answering any of the Section Assessment questions, have them reread the related text material and then work in small groups to quiz one another and offer corrections.

Have students visit **www.phschool.com** to find the projected sizes of the human population in 2025 and 2050.

Use iText to review the key concepts in Section 5–3.

◀ **Figure 5–14** This photograph shows a bustling street in a city in India, which has one of the world's fastest growing populations. **Inferring** ***What would you expect an age-structure diagram for India to look like?***

Future Population Growth

To predict how the worldwide human population will grow in the near future, demographers must take into account the age structures of every country. Current projections suggest that by the year 2025, the world's population will reach 7.8 billion. By 2050, the population may reach more than 9 billion people. There is evidence, however, that the growth rate may level off, or even slow down, by that time. This may happen if countries that are currently growing rapidly move toward the demographic transition. One such country, India, is shown in **Figure 5–14**.

Will human population growth continue at its current rate, or will it level out to a logistic growth curve and become stable? Many ecologists suggest that if the growth of the human population does not slow down, there could be serious and lasting damage to the environment as well as to the global economy. On the other hand, many economists assert that science, technology, and positive changes in society will help to control those negative impacts.

5–3 Section Assessment

1. **Key Concept** Describe the general trend of human population growth that has occurred over time.
2. **Key Concept** What factors explain why populations in different countries grow at different rates?
3. What is demography?
4. Describe the demographic transition and explain how it might affect a country's population growth rate.
5. **Critical Thinking Evaluating** Why do you think age-structure diagrams can help predict future population trends?

iTEXT Assessment Use iText to review the important concepts in Section 5–3.

Take It to the NET

Read about world population growth. Then, create a bar graph comparing the world's population in 2000 and projections for 2025 and 2050. Use the links provided in the Biology area at the Prentice Hall Web site for help in completing this activity: **www.phschool.com**

Answer to . . .

Figure 5–14 *Students may infer that the age-structure diagram for India might resemble that for Rwanda in Figure 5–13 on p. 131. A population profile in which there are large numbers of individuals in younger age groups is predictive of rapid growth.*

5–3 Section Assessment

1. For tens of thousands of years, the human population grew very slowly. Then, about 500 years ago, the population started to grow exponentially and increased dramatically.
2. Birthrates, death rates, and the age structure of a population
3. The scientific study of human populations
4. When the demographic transition begins, the birthrate and the death rate are high. Then, the death rate drops while the birthrate remains high. Finally, the birthrate also falls. After the demographic transition, a population's growth rate would be very low, and could even be negative.
5. Age-structure diagrams include data on younger individuals in age groups that will contribute to population growth as members of those groups mature.

Exploration

Investigating the Growth of a Population of Bacteria

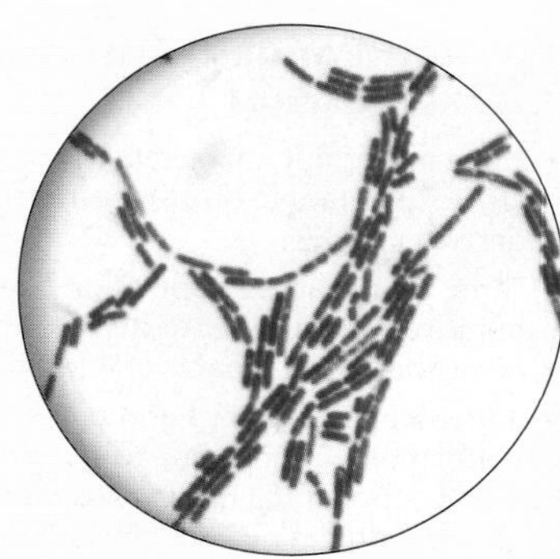

Bacteria are convenient for laboratory studies of populations because they are small in size and reproduce rapidly. In this investigation, you will examine the growth of a bacterial culture.

Problem **What happens to a population that depends on limited resources?**

Materials

- 2 lima beans
- 2 dropper pipettes
- 100-mL beaker
- coverslips
- microscope slides
- 10-mL graduated cylinder
- 100-mL graduated cylinder
- methylene blue stain
- microscope
- test-tube rack
- 4 test tubes
- aluminum foil

Skills Calculating, Using Tables and Graphs

Procedure

1. Before you begin, review the rules for sterile procedure with your teacher.
2. Wash your hands. Put on your plastic gloves. Then, to start a bacterial culture, put 2 lima beans into a 100-mL beaker. Add 50 mL of water. Allow this mixture to sit for 48 hours.
3. Construct a data table with four columns and five blank rows. At the top of the table, label the columns "Day," "Bacteria Observed," "Dilution Factor," and "Bacteria Present."
4. After 48 hours, use a dropper pipette to place a drop of the culture on a microscope slide. Add a coverslip. Place a drop of methylene blue stain on the slide next to the coverslip. Lightly touch a paper towel on the opposite side of the coverslip to draw the stain under the coverslip.
5. Use the high-power objective of a microscope to locate some bacteria. If you can count the bacteria in your field of view, go to step 7. If there are too many bacteria to count, go to step 6.
6. Use a dropper pipette to put 1 mL of the culture into a 10-mL graduated cylinder. Add 9 mL of water to the graduated cylinder. Empty the graduated cylinder into a test tube. This procedure dilutes the culture by a factor of 10. Examine the diluted sample under the microscope as in step 5. If there are still too many bacteria to count, dilute the sample again in the same way. Stop diluting when you can count the bacteria. Each time you dilute, multiply the dilution by 10.
7. Record the number of bacteria and the dilution factor in your data table. If you did not dilute, the dilution factor is 1. To determine the number of bacteria present, multiply the number of bacteria you observed by the dilution factor.
8. Cover the beaker with aluminum foil and set it aside overnight. Wash your hands when you are finished.
9. **Predicting** Record a prediction of how the population of bacteria will change.
10. Repeat steps 5 through 8 every day for 5 days.

Analyze and Conclude

1. **Using Tables and Graphs** Make a graph of the data from your data table. When did the population grow most quickly? Most slowly?
2. **Drawing Conclusions** How can you explain the changes in population growth?
3. **Inferring** What caused the changes in the population growth rate?

Go Further

Designing Experiments Design an experiment to investigate how a change in the food supply affects the growth of a bacterial population. With your teacher's approval, carry out your experiment.

Analyze and Conclude

1. In a typical logistic pattern, the bacteria population will grow quickly at first and then will slow, stop, or decrease.

2. As the population grew, it consumed the food supply and produced toxic wastes that reduced growth.

3. The accumulation of toxic wastes and consumption of the food supply reduced population growth. Organisms that prey on bacteria also may have begun to infiltrate the culture.

Exploration

Objective Students will be able to infer how limited resources affect a bacteria population.

Skills Focus Calculating, Using Tables and Graphs

Time 5 minutes for initial setup, then 10–20 minutes each day for five days, 30 minutes on sixth day

Pre-Lab Discussion Remind students that they saw a graph showing the growth of a bacteria population early in this chapter. Ask: **Did the graph's curve indicate exponential growth or logistic growth?** *(Exponential growth)* If students cannot recall the term, let them look back at page 121. Then, have students read the procedure, and address any questions they have.

Teaching Tips

- If students have limited experience using a microscope, show them the correct technique. Also demonstrate how to prepare the slide, add the stain, and use the dropper pipette.
- As students conduct their counts in Steps 3–5, circulate among them to help with any processes that cause difficulty.

Procedure

3. You may want to draw a sample data table on the board or an overhead transparency for students to copy.

5. Point out the photograph of bacteria on this page, which will give students an idea of what to look for.

9. Remind students to record their predictions. Most students will probably predict that the bacteria population will increase.

Expected Outcome During the first few days, the bacteria count will increase. However, at some point near the end of the observation period, bacteria will start to die off as toxic wastes accumulate and the food supply becomes exhausted.

Go Further

Check students' plans to make sure that their experiments will not cause rampant overgrowth of bacteria or development of mold.

Chapter 5 Study Guide

Study Tip

Have students work in pairs to review the Key Concepts and the Vocabulary for each section. Students might first quiz each other on the Key Concepts, with one student reading the text statement but omitting the key terms, and the other student supplying the terms. For the first Key Concept in Section 5–1, for example, the first student would say, "The main characteristics of a population are . . .," and the second student would identify the characteristics. A similar approach can be used to review vocabulary.

Thinking Visually

1. Density-dependent factors
2. Density-independent factors
3. Competition
4. Unusual weather or seasonal cycles

Chapter 5 Study Guide

5–1 How Populations Grow

 **Key Concepts**

- Three important characteristics of a population are its geographic distribution, density, and growth rate.
- Three factors affect population size: the number of births, the number of deaths, and the number of individuals that enter or leave the population.
- Under ideal conditions and unlimited resources, a population will continue to grow in a pattern called exponential growth. As resources are used up and population growth slows or stops, the population exhibits logistic growth.

Vocabulary

population density, p. 119
immigration, p. 120
emigration, p. 120
exponential growth, p. 121
logistic growth, p. 122
carrying capacity, p. 122

5–2 Limits to Growth

 **Key Concepts**

- Density-dependent limiting factors include competition, predation, parasitism, and disease.
- Unusual weather, natural disasters, seasonal cycles, and certain human activities—such as damming rivers and clear-cutting forests—are all examples of density-independent limiting factors.

Vocabulary

limiting factor, p. 124
density-dependent limiting factor, p. 125
predator-prey relationship, p. 126
density-independent limiting factor, p. 127

5–3 Human Population Growth

Key Concepts

- Like the populations of many other living organisms, the size of the human population tends to increase with time.
- The characteristics of populations, and the social and economic factors that affect them, explain why some countries have high population growth rates while populations of other countries grow slowly or not at all.

Vocabulary

demography, p. 130
demographic transition, p. 130
age-structure diagram, p. 131

Thinking Visually

Using information from this chapter, complete the following concept map:

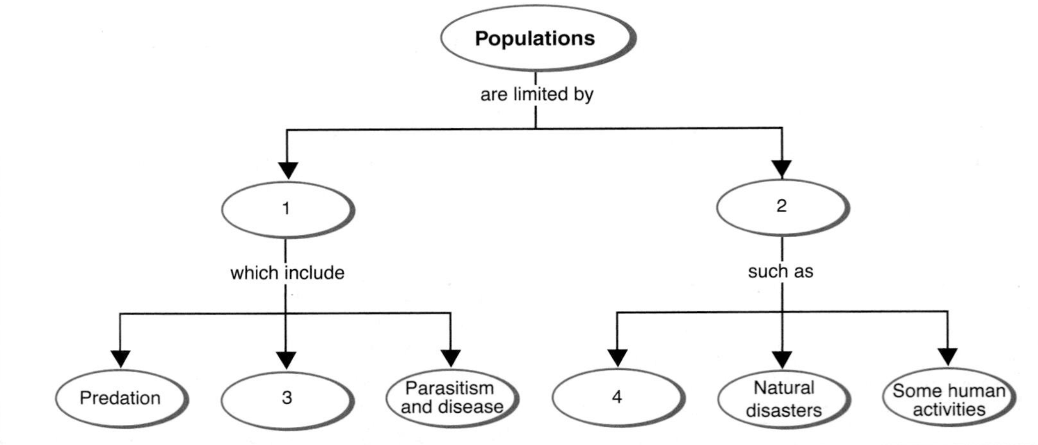

Chapter 5 Assessment

Reviewing Content

1. c	**5.** b	**9.** d
2. c	**6.** a	**10.** a
3. b	**7.** b	
4. b	**8.** a	

Understanding Concepts

11. The movement of individuals into an area occupied by an existing population is called immigration. Emigration occurs when individuals move out of a population.

12. The graphs should show the characteristic J-shape of exponential population growth as illustrated in Figure 5-3 on page 121.

13. Logistic growth occurs when a population's growth rate slows or stops following a period of exponential growth. Population growth may slow down when the birthrate decreases or the death rate increases, or when both events occur at the same rate. Population growth may also slow down when the rate of immigration decreases, the rate of emigration increases, or both.

TIME SAVER — SECTION RESOURCES

Print:

- ***Teaching Resources,*** Chapter Vocabulary Review, Graphic Organizer
- ***Chapter Tests: Levels A and B,*** Chapter 5 Test
- ***PH Assessment System,*** Practice Test

Technology

- ***Computer Test Bank,*** Chapter 5 Test
- ***iText,*** Chapter 5 Assessment

Chapter 5 Assessment

Reviewing Content

Choose the letter that best answers the question or completes the statement.

1. The number of individuals of a single species per unit area is known as
   a. carrying capacity. c. population density.
   b. logistic growth. d. population growth rate.
2. The movement of individuals into an area is called
   a. demography. c. immigration.
   b. carrying capacity. d. emigration.
3. The range or area occupied by a population is its
   a. growth rate.
   b. geographic distribution.
   c. age structure.
   d. population density.
4. The graph below represents
   a. carrying capacity.
   b. exponential growth.
   c. logistic growth.
   d. limiting factors.

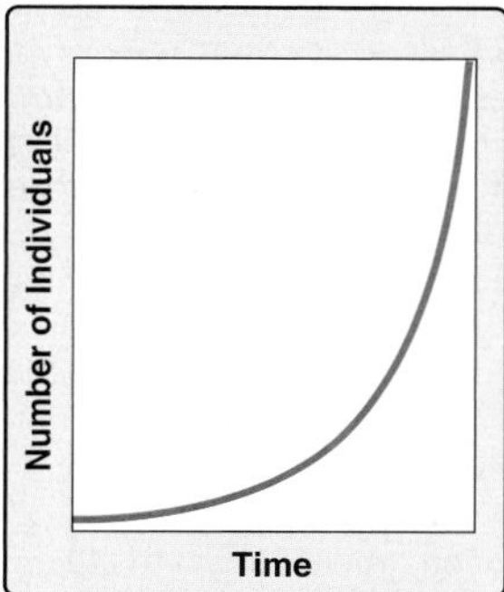

5. The maximum number of organisms of a particular species that can be supported by an environment is called
   a. logistical growth.
   b. carrying capacity.
   c. exponential growth.
   d. population density.
6. If a population grows larger than the carrying capacity of its environment, the
   a. death rate may rise.
   b. birthrate may rise.
   c. death rate may fall.
   d. immigration rate may increase.
7. Density-independent limiting factors include
   a. predation. c. competition.
   b. hurricanes. d. parasitism.
8. A limiting factor that depends on population size is called a
   a. density-dependent limiting factor.
   b. density-independent limiting factor.
   c. predator-prey relationship.
   d. parasitic relationship.
9. The scientific study of human populations is called
   a. immigration.
   b. emigration.
   c. demographic transition.
   d. demography.
10. The demographic transition is complete when
    a. population growth stops.
    b. the birthrate is greater than the death rate.
    c. the death rate begins to fall.
    d. the death rate is greater than the birthrate.

Understanding Concepts

11. Distinguish between immigration and emigration.
12. Sketch the exponential growth curve of a hypothetical population.
13. Describes the conditions under which logistic growth occurs.
14. What is carrying capacity? Give an example.
15. How might the introduction of a limiting nutrient in a pond affect the carrying capacity of that pond?
16. Describe the long-term effects of competition on populations of two different species competing for the same resources.
17. Describe how a predator-prey relationship can be a mechanism of population control.
18. How do parasites serve as a density-dependent limiting factor?
19. Explain how density-independent limiting factors can affect populations.
20. How can you account for the fact that the human population has grown more rapidly during the past 500 years than throughout its previous history?
21. What is the significance of the demographic transition in studies of the human population?
22. How does the age structure of a population affect its growth rate?

TIME SAVER HOMEWORK GUIDE

Section:	Questions:
Section 5–1	1–6, 11–14, 23, 33
Section 5–2	7, 8, 15–19, 24, 25, 27–32
Section 5–3	9, 10, 20–22, 26

Chapter 5 Assessment (continued)

14. Carrying capacity represents the largest number of individuals that a given environment can support. For example, the carrying capacity of Isle Royale for moose is determined by a number of factors, including the food supply and predators on the island.

15. The addition of a limiting nutrient to a pond would most likely increase the productivity of the pond's ecosystem.

16. Over time, two different species competing for the same resources will probably evolve to occupy separate niches. Another possibility is that the population of the species that is less successful in competing for resources will fall toward zero.

17. The rise in the population of the prey would normally be followed by a rise in the predator population. As the population of predators rises, the population of prey declines. Since there is less prey available, the population of predators also declines. This cycle repeats itself and functions as a means of population control.

18. As a host population becomes more dense, diseases caused by parasites can become limiting. The larger the host population, the more likely that parasites will be able to travel from one suitable host to another.

19. Density-independent factors have similar effects on all individuals in a population regardless of the population's density. Examples include the effects of a prolonged drought, a killing frost, or a flood.

20. Human population began growing more rapidly 500 years ago due to favorable growth conditions. Advances in agriculture and industry made life easier. The world's food supply became more reliable, and essential goods could be shipped around the globe. Improved sanitation, medicine, and health care dramatically reduced the death rate and increased longevity. Simultaneously, the birthrate remained high.

21. Demographic transition is a prediction of population changes based on an analysis of changes in birthrate.

22. Populations with nearly equal numbers will have a slow, but steady growth rate for the near future. Populations with many more young children and teenagers will increase dramatically in the near future.

Chapter 5 Assessment

Critical Thinking

23. Since the communicable virus is more likely to spread when people are crowded together, it is density-dependent.

24. In most cases, it will have a greater effect on the population of a small ecosystem. A small population will be more susceptible to serious damage from a density-independent limiting factor such as a flood or storm.

25. Because there are relatively small numbers of individuals in younger age groups, the population of Sweden is likely to stay about the same or even decline over the next 50 years.

26. The growth curve of a small town made up of mostly senior citizens would show a decline in population. A growth curve of a small town made up of newly married couples would show an increase in population.

27. The carrying capacity of a population is affected by limiting factors such as competition, predation, parasitism, disease, climate, drought, and human disturbances. Likewise, the carrying capacity of a city's roads depends on such limiting factors as the number and width of roads, the number of intersections, and the number of vehicles traveling on the road.

28. If there is a sudden increase in food for the prey, the population of predators would probably increase as well. An increase in food for prey would allow for a greater number of prey. More predators would then be supported.

29. In parasitic and predator-prey relationships, one member of the relationship benefits, while the other is harmed or killed.

30. The population of fish would most likely decrease due to a decrease in the size of the ecosystem. The decreased size would provide a smaller amount of resources.

31. A demographer would ask questions such as: "Have changes in society, such as access to health care and medicines, lowered the death rate?" and "Does the birthrate remain high, or are there signs that the birthrate is falling?"

Chapter 5 Assessment

Critical Thinking

23. **Applying Concepts** Why might a contagious virus that causes a fatal disease be considered a density-dependent limiting factor?

24. **Inferring** Would a density-independent limiting factor have more of an effect on population size in a large ecosystem or in a small ecosystem? Explain.

25. **Predicting** Study the age-structure diagram for Sweden below. Then predict how Sweden's rate of population growth is likely to change over the next 50 years.

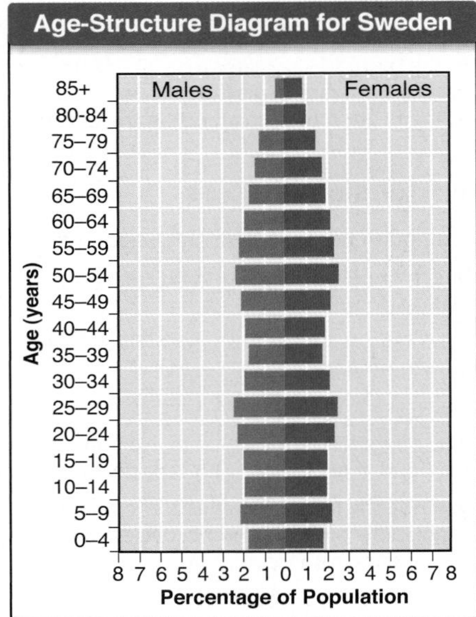

26. **Comparing and Contrasting** Describe the most likely population growth curve you would expect to see in a small town made up mainly of senior citizens. Compare this growth curve to that of a small town made up of newly married couples in their twenties.

27. **Using Analogies** How is the carrying capacity of a city's roads similar to the carrying capacity of an ecosystem?

28. **Predicting** What will happen to a population of predators if there is a sudden increase in food for the prey? Explain.

29. **Comparing and Contrasting** How is the relationship between parasites and their hosts similar to a predator-prey relationship?

30. **Applying Concepts** If the water level of a river drops, how might that affect a fish population living in that river?

31. **Posing Questions** What questions would a demographer need to answer in order to determine whether a country is approaching the demographic transition?

32. **Making Connections** Nitrogen is a limiting factor in aquatic ecosystems. Suppose that runoff from a field washes nitrogen-rich fertilizer into a pond containing a population of algae. Predict how the fertilizer will affect the carrying capacity of the pond for algae. (*Hint:* Refer to the information on limiting nutrients in Section 3–3.)

Performance-Based Assessment

Multimedia Presentation Create a visual presentation that describes how limiting factors regulate population growth. Be sure to distinguish between density-dependent limiting factors and density-independent limiting factors.

How is population growth similar to the growth of your savings account? Visit the Prentice Hall Web site at **www.phschool.com** to learn more about how populations grow. Then answer the following questions:

- How does population growth compare to the way money grows when interest is left to compound over time?
- What is the most crucial difference between compound interest and population growth?
- Why is it easier to interpret population data in graphs than data presented in table format?

Standardized Test Prep

Test-Taking Tip To answer questions that have different combinations of Roman numerals as answer choices, you must evaluate each Roman numeral separately in relation to the question. Then, look to see which answer choice corresponds to the numerals you have selected.

Directions: Choose the letter that best answers the question or completes the statement.

1. The total change in a population's size over time is
(A) immigration
(B) emigration
(C) birthrate and death rate
(D) population growth rate
(E) population density

2. Which factors increase the size of a population?
I. Emigration
II. Birthrate
III. Immigration
(A) I only
(B) III only
(C) I and III only
(D) II and III only
(E) I, II, and III

3. Which of the following is NOT an example of a density-dependent limiting factor?
(A) natural disasters
(B) predators
(C) parasites
(D) competitors
(E) diseases

4. Which of the following are necessary to complete the demographic transition?
I. the birthrate increases
II. the death rate falls
III. the birthrate falls
(A) I only
(B) II only
(C) III only
(D) II and III only
(E) I, II, and III

Question 5 Complete the following analogy by selecting the correct letter. In analogies, A : B :: C : ? *means* A is to B as C is to ?.

5. J-shaped curve : exponential ::
S-shaped curve : ______?______
(A) demographic
(B) predation
(C) logistic
(D) limiting factor
(E) immigration

Questions 6–8 Use the graph below to answer the following questions.

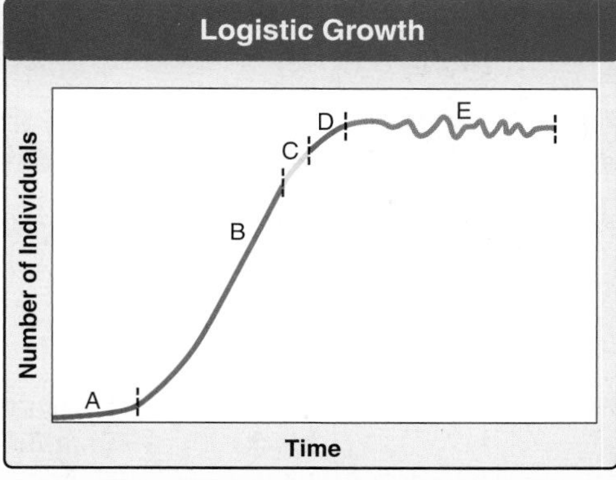

6. What is true of the time interval marked E in the graph?
I. Carrying capacity has been reached.
II. Birthrate equals death rate.
III. Population is growing.
(A) I only
(B) II only
(C) III only
(D) I and II only
(E) I, II, and III

7. Which time interval(s) in the graph shows exponential growth?
(A) D and E
(B) A and B
(C) C and D
(D) E only
(E) A only

8. Which time interval(s) in the graph depicts the effects of limiting factors on population?
(A) A only
(B) A and B
(C) C, D, and E
(D) C and D
(E) C only

Questions 9–12 Each of the lettered choices below refers to the following numbered statements. Select the best lettered choice. A choice may be used once, more than once, or not at all.

(A) Limiting factor
(B) Logistic growth
(C) Carrying capacity
(D) Exponential growth
(E) Population density

9. Birthrate = death rate

10. Slows the growth of a population

11. Number of individuals per unit area

12. Population grows at a constant rate

Standardized Test Prep

1. D **2.** D **3.** A **4.** D
5. C **6.** D **7.** B **8.** C
9. C **10.** A **11.** E **12.** D

(continued from page 136)

32. The fertilizer washing into the pond would increase the level of a limiting factor in the pond ecosystem—nitrogen. This would increase the carrying capacity of the pond and probably lead to rapid growth of the algae population.

Performance-Based Assessment

Visuals will vary but should include density-independent factors, such as fire, seasonal cycles, and natural disasters, and density-dependent factors, such as competition, predation, parasitism, and disease.

Take It to the NET

- When interest is compounded, the account earns interest on the accumulating interest as well as on the original principle. This is similar to the process of exponential growth, in which each generation "accumulates" offspring that in turn reproduce to increase the total population.
- Population growth rates can change because of deaths, immigration, emigration, or many other factors, whereas interest rates are usually held constant.
- Trends are easily seen on a graph.

For additional information, visit
www.phschool.com

Chapter Planner 6 Humans in the Biosphere

Section and Section Objectives	Time	Activities and Labs
6–1 A Changing Landscape, pp. 139–143 **6.1.1** ***Describe*** human activities that can affect the biosphere.	**1 period (1/2 block)**	**SE:** ***Inquiry Activity,*** What happens to household trash?, p. 138
6–2 Renewable and Nonrenewable Resources, pp. 144–149 **6.2.1** ***Explain*** how environmental resources are classified. **6.2.2** ***Describe*** how human activities affect land, air, and water resources.	**2 periods (1 block)**	**TE:** ***Demonstration,*** p. 148 **TE:** ***Build Science Skills,*** p. 148
6–3 Biodiversity, pp. 150–156 **6.3.1** ***Define*** biodiversity and explain its value. **6.3.2** ***Identify*** current threats to biodiversity. **6.3.3** ***Describe*** the goal of conservation biology.	**2 periods (1 block)**	**TE:** ***Build Science Skills,*** p. 151 **SE:** ***Quick Lab,*** How does biological magnification occur?, p. 153 **SE:** ***Biology and History,*** Success in Conservation, pp. 154–155
6–4 Charting a Course for the Future, pp. 157–160 **6.4.1** ***Explain*** how human activities contribute to global changes.	**1 period (1/2 block)**	**SE:** ***Analyzing Data,*** Banning CFCs, p. 158 **SE:** ***Design an Experiment,*** Observing the Effects of Acid Rain, p. 161
Chapter Assessment, pp. 162–165	**1 period (1/2 block)**	

ACTIVITY PLANNER

SE: ***Inquiry Activity,*** p. 138; (20 min.); bag containing dry trash

TE: ***Demonstration,*** p. 148; (15 min.); large freezer bag filled with car exhaust

TE: ***Build Science Skills,*** p. 148; (15 min.); samples of rainwater, sample of tapwater, litmus paper

TE: ***Build Science Skills,*** p. 151; (15 min.); graph paper, string, ruler

SE: ***Quick Lab,*** p. 153; (15 min.); paper cups (3 small, 1 medium, and 1 large), 1 L-beaker, sand, 12 beads, masking tape

SE: ***Design an Experiment,*** p. 161; (45 min. to design and set up experiment, 5 min./day for observation and recording); diluted sulfuric acid, filter paper, glass-marking pencil, 2 petri dishes, 100-mL graduated cylinder, 100 seeds (mustard or radish), pH paper, 2 100-mL beakers, hand lens

PLANNING KEY

Ability Levels

B	**Basic**	For students who need additional help
A	**Average**	For all students
E	**Enriched**	For students who need to be challenged

Components

SE	Student Edition	**GRSW**	Guided Reading and Study Workbook	**IDM**	Issues and Decision Making
TE	Teacher's Edition	**CT**	Chapter Tests: Levels A and B	**CTB**	Computer Test Bank
LMA	Laboratory Manual A	**PHAS**	PH Assessment System	**PA**	Presentation Assistant Plus
LMB	Laboratory Manual B	**LA**	Lab Assessment with Scoring Guide	**BD**	BioDetectives Videotape
TR	Teaching Resources	**BTM**	BioTechnology Manual	**iT**	iText

Program Resources	Assessment	Media and Technology
TR: Section Review 6–1 B A **GRSW:** Section 6–1 B A	**SE:** 6–1 Section Assessment, p. 143 **TR:** Section Review 6–1	**PA:** 6–1 Interest Grabber, Section Outline, Concept Map **iT:** Section 6–1
LMA: Chapter 6 Lab A E **TR:** Section Review 6–2 B A **GRSW:** Section 6–2 B A	**SE:** 6–2 Section Assessment, p. 149 **TR:** Section Review 6–2	**PA:** 6–2 Interest Grabber, Section Outline **iT:** Section 6–2
TR: Section Review 6–3 B A **GRSW:** Section 6–3 B A	**SE:** 6–3 Section Assessment, p. 156 **TR:** Section Review 6–3	**PA:** 6–3 Interest Grabber, Section Outline, Species Diversity, Figure 6–18 **iT:** Section 6–3
LMB: Chapter 6 Lab B A **TR:** Section Review 6–4 B A Chapter 6 Exploration B A E **GRSW:** Section 6–4 B A **IDM:** 6–1 A E	**SE:** 6–4 Section Assessment, p. 160 **TR:** Section Review 6–4	**PA:** 6–4 Interest Grabber, Section Outline, Chemistry of Ozone Destruction, Figure 6–19 **iT:** Section 6–4
	SE: Chapter 6 Assessment, pp. 162–165 **TR:** Chapter Vocabulary Review, Graphic Organizer **CT:** Chapter 6 Test **CTB:** Chapter 6 Test **PHAS:** Practice Test	**CTB:** Chapter 6 Test **iT:** Chapter 6 Assessment

PRESSED FOR TIME?

To Preview the Chapter
- Have students preview the major headings (in blue) and subheadings (green) in all three sections, then review the following figures and answer any caption questions: Figures 6–8, 6–13, 6–19, and 6–20.

To Cover the Chapter Quickly
- Have students read pages 140–143 in Section 6–1, pages 144–145 in Section 6–2, pages 150–153 in Section 6–3, and all of Section 6–4.
- Assign question 1 in 6–1 Section Assessment, questions 2 and 3 in 6–2 Section Assessment, questions 1 and 2 in 6–3 Section Assessment, and question 1 in 6–4 Section Assessment.

To Review the Chapter
- Assign Sections 6–1 through 6–4 in the Guided Reading and Study Workbook.
- Assign the Chapter Vocabulary Review for Chapter 6 in Teaching Resources.

Chapter 6

ENGAGE/EXPLORE

Inquiry Activity

Objective(s) Students will be able to suggest ways to reduce the amount of household trash produced.

Skill Focus Evaluating

Materials bag of dry trash

Time 20 minutes

Advance Prep For each group, prepare a large plastic garbage bag containing about 2 kg of dry trash, apportioned as follows: 0.94 kg paper and cardboard; 0.34 kg leaves and yard clippings; 0.15 kg glass; 0.18 kg metal; 0.22 kg plastic; and 0.17 kg wood. Make sure all glass, metal, and wood items are in the form of safe, unbroken items and all containers are empty and clean.

Safety Have students wear safety goggles, aprons, and plastic gloves.

Expected Outcome Allow students some leeway in how they sort the items so long as they can offer reasonable explanations for their choices.

Think About It

1. About half the material is paper and paper products. Yard waste is about 17 percent, and metal, glass, and plastic each account for about 10 percent. This is a typical household mixture, although the proportions may vary for some homes.
2. Some of the material may be recycled. The rest is usually buried in a landfill or burned. Substances that leach out of landfills can become pollutants.
3. Students might suggest recycling, reducing their use of some materials, and reusing some items.

Brain Teaser

Challenge each student group to choose one item from the trash they sorted and list as many ways as they can think of for reusing the item. Encourage students to be creative in devising possible uses. Have groups share their ideas with the class.

Chapter 6 Humans in the Biosphere

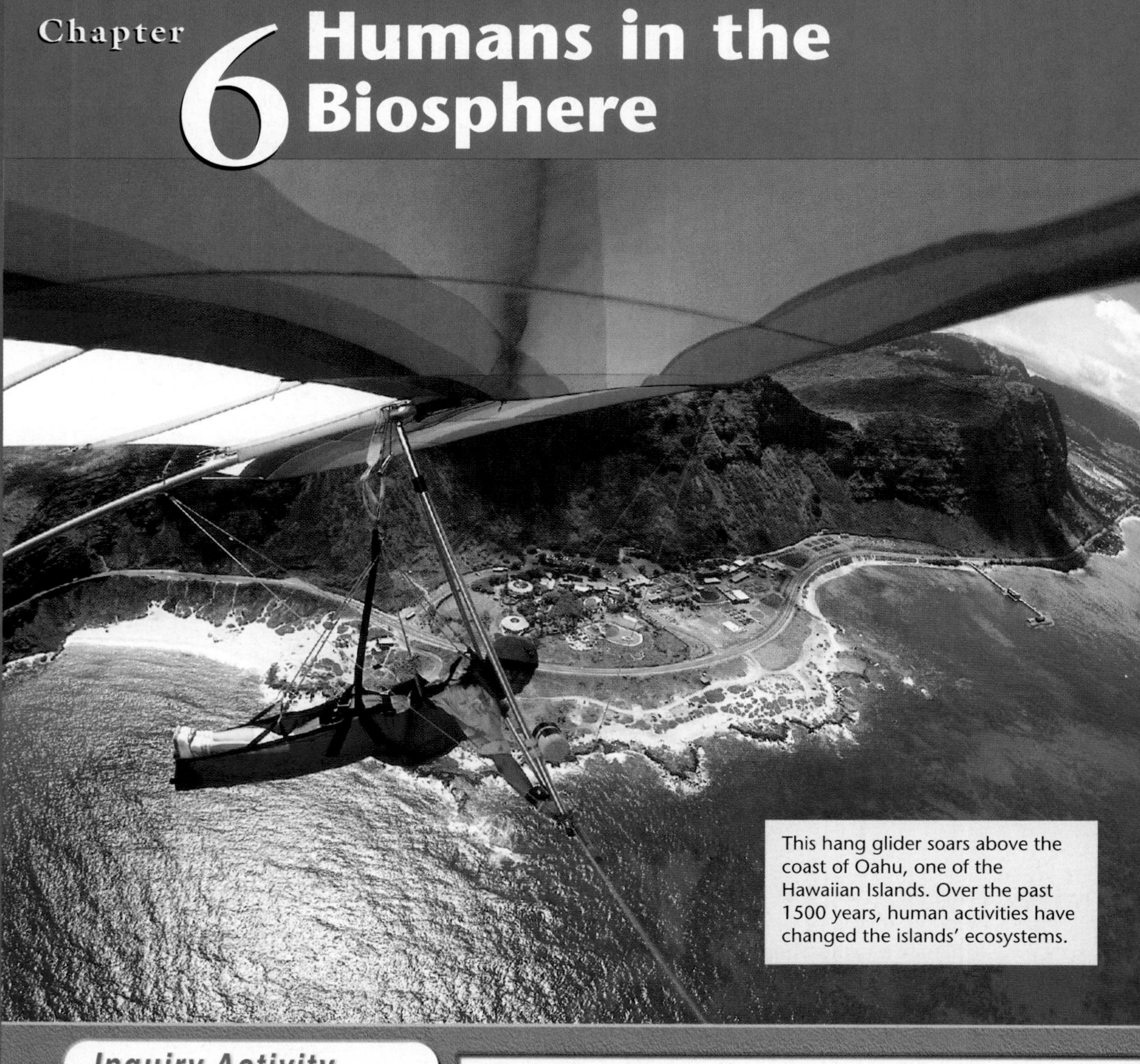

This hang glider soars above the coast of Oahu, one of the Hawaiian Islands. Over the past 1500 years, human activities have changed the islands' ecosystems.

Inquiry Activity

What happens to household trash?

Procedure

1. Examine the contents of a bag containing roughly the amount of dry trash produced per person each day in the United States.
2. Sort the trash into items that can be reused, items that can be recycled, items that can be composted, and items that must be discarded because they cannot be recycled or composted.

Think About It

1. **Analyzing Data** Which materials make up most of the trash? Does this reflect the amount and types of trash you produce?
2. **Predicting** What do you think happens to the trash you produce? What effect does trash have on the environment?
3. **Evaluating** List three ways you can reduce the amount of trash you produce.

6–1 A Changing Landscape

About 1600 years ago, human settlers from Polynesia began arriving on the island chain called Hawaii. As an island people, they were accustomed to living in limited space. Their farming and fishing practices were guided by centuries of accumulated wisdom. To cut down a coconut palm, a person had to plant two palm trees to take its place. Laws prohibited fishing for certain species during spawning season.

Even though their customs taught respect for the land, these early settlers changed the ecology of the Hawaiian Islands. From the forested mountaintops to the ocean's fringing reefs, a wide range of ecosystems and many unique species were used for basic needs such as food, medicine, wood, and fiber. Pigs and other nonnative species that the Polynesians brought to Hawaii altered many native communities. By the time Captain Cook came ashore in 1778, about 60 species of native birds were already extinct. The arrival of Europeans changed the islands even more, introducing ranching, predators, and disease.

The Hawaii of today is very different from what it was long ago. Vast tracts of land have been cleared to grow pineapples and sugar cane. Large areas have been paved for housing, schools, and industry. Ground water has been tapped for irrigation, depleting water resources in many places. In addition to the reduction—by two thirds—of native bird species, like the one in **Figure 6–1,** an enormous number of land snails, plants, insects, and hundreds of other native Hawaiian species are gone. Imported plants and animals have crowded out many of the remaining native species.

Guide for Reading

Key Concept

- What types of human activities can affect the biosphere?

Vocabulary
subsistence hunting
agriculture
green revolution
monoculture

Reading Strategy: Finding Main Ideas
As you read, make a list of facts that support the statement "The spreading influence of humans can and does affect the biosphere."

Earth as an Island

The history of humans in Hawaii offers an important lesson for the twenty-first century. In a sense, Earth, too, is an island. All of the organisms—including humans—that live on Earth share a limited resource base. We all depend on the natural ecological processes that sustain these resources. The human population is still growing, but the planet we live on is not. Along with this growing population come increasing demands on Earth's air, water, land, and living things.

Understanding how humans interact with the biosphere is crucial to protecting these resources. It requires you to remember all that you have learned about energy flow, chemical cycling, climate, and population-limiting factors. You must also understand how scientific models can be used to make predictions about complex systems. It is also important to realize why studies of islands like Hawaii are important to people who don't live on an island—or don't think they do.

▼ **Figure 6–1** The iiwi, or Hawaiian honeycreeper, is one of the most beautiful birds in Hawaii. Like many native species in Hawaii, the iiwi is becoming scarce. Disease, habitat loss, and predation by introduced animals have taken their toll on the species. **Drawing Conclusions** *Based on the photograph, what can you conclude about the iiwi's niche?*

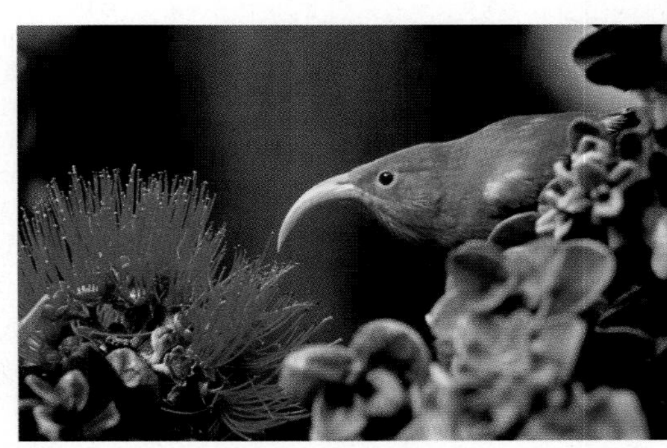

SECTION RESOURCES

Print:

- ***Teaching Resources,*** Section Review 6–1
- ***Guided Reading and Study Workbook,*** Section 6–1

Technology:

- ***iText,*** Section 6–1

Section 6–1

1 FOCUS

Objective

6.1.1 ***Describe*** human activities that can affect the biosphere.

Guide for Reading

Vocabulary Preview

Suggest that students use Word Origins on page 141 and a dictionary to derive the literal meaning of the Vocabulary term *monoculture.*

Reading Strategy

To help students focus on main ideas that support the statement, have them divide a sheet of paper into two columns. In the first column, they can write the types of human activities identified in this section as affecting the biosphere. In the second column, they can write sentences or phrases found in the text that explain how those activities affect the biosphere.

2 INSTRUCT

Earth as an Island

Build Science Skills

Predicting Have students recall the definition of *carrying capacity,* introduced in Chapter 5. *(Carrying capacity is the largest number of individuals that an environment can support.)* Then, explain that many biologists feel that in the not-too-distant future, the human population may reach or exceed the carrying capacity of Earth. Ask: **What do you think would be the consequences of exceeding Earth's carrying capacity for the human population?** *(Students will probably mention overcrowding; shortages of food, water, and fuel; malnutrition; increased disease; and the like.)*

Answer to . . .

Figure 6–1 *Based on the unusual shape of its beak, the bird seems to depend on nectar that is deep within curved flowers.*

Human Activities

Build Science Skills

Applying Concepts Point out that although many of the factors affecting the global environment are not under our control, each person can make a difference in the quality of the environment. Encourage students to list environmental problems and then brainstorm actions that they and their families can take to help resolve those problems. Students' suggestions might include conserving resources by recycling and by reducing total consumption, educating others about the issues, and voting on legislation.

Hunting and Gathering

Build Science Skills

Inferring Ask: **What are some of the disadvantages of relying on hunting and gathering to obtain all the food you need?** *(Sample answers: You may have to move your home to follow animals that are used for food. Without being cared for by humans, plants may die from drought.)*

▲ **Figure 6–2** People of the Paleolithic, or Stone Age, relied on hunting and gathering for their existence. This cave painting from Northern Spain shows ancient hunters slaying a herd of deer with bows and arrows. **Hunting and gathering are among the many human activities that have changed the biosphere.**

▼ **Figure 6–3** Like his Stone Age predecessors, this modern subsistence hunter from the Asmat tribe in New Guinea uses bows and spears. Other subsistence hunters may use modern tools like guns or motorized vehicles. **Predicting** *What effects might subsistence hunters have on the environment in which they live?*

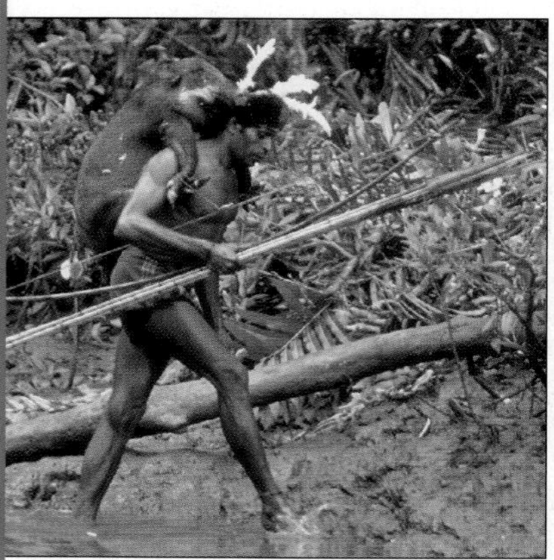

Human Activities

Industry and technology give humans a strong advantage in competing with other species for limited resources such as food, energy, and space. According to a recent study, human activity uses as much energy as all of Earth's other multicellular species combined. Today, humans are the most important source of environmental change on the planet.

Because humans take part in local and global food webs and chemical cycles within the biosphere, human activities can change the flow of energy in an ecosystem and reduce the ability of ecosystems to recycle nutrients. **Among the human activities that have transformed the biosphere are hunting and gathering, agriculture, industry, and urban development.**

Hunting and Gathering

For most of human history, hunting and gathering was the primary means of survival. Early humans hunted birds and other animals and fished in rivers and oceans. They gathered wild seeds, fruits, and nuts. Some peoples were nomadic, traveling great distances to take advantage of movements and cycles of natural plant and animal populations.

Hunters and gatherers lived in small groups. Yet, even prehistoric hunter-gatherers, like the ones who created the cave painting in **Figure 6–2,** changed the environment. They built dams to divert water and burned grasslands to encourage the growth of certain plants. Some scientists hypothesize that when human hunters arrived in North America about 12,000 years ago, they caused one of the major mass extinctions of large animals—including woolly mammoths, giant ground sloths, and sabertooth cats. Even species you wouldn't think of as living in North America—cheetahs, zebras, and yaks, for example—disappeared within one or two thousand years of human arrival there.

Today, groups of people in scattered parts of the world, from the Arctic to Central Africa, still follow the hunter-gatherer way of life to some degree. These groups supplement their diet with the meat of wild animals through **subsistence hunting.** Modern subsistence hunters, like the one in **Figure 6–3,** make relatively few demands on the environment. However, nearly all modern subsistence hunters use some form of technology, such as guns, snowmobiles, or manufactured tools.

CHECKPOINT *What is subsistence hunting?*

PRESENTATIONS MADE EASY!

The Presentation Assistant Plus contains the Prentice Hall Presentation Pro and the Transparencies, which provide easy-to-follow visual support for every step of this section. If you have a computer presentation station, use Prentice Hall Presentation Pro for Section 6–1, or use the transparencies listed here.

Section 6–1: **Interest Grabber**
Section Outline
Concept Map

Agriculture

During thousands of years of foraging, early hunter-gatherers learned how plants grew and ripened and discovered which ones were useful for food and medicines. They then began planting seeds near human settlements. By the end of the last ice age—about 11,000 years ago—humans began the practice of farming, or **agriculture.** Soon, villagers in different regions of the world were growing wheat, rice, and millet in nearby fields. From these regions, agriculture spread in many directions as people planted other varieties of seeds.

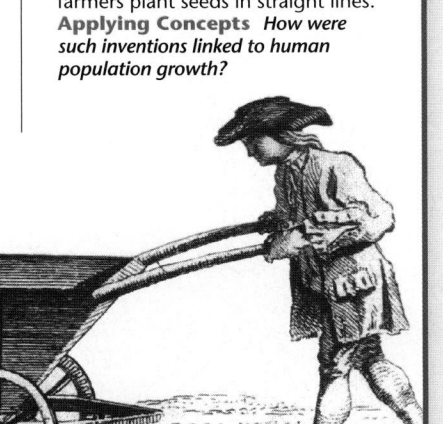

The spread of agriculture was an important event in human history because it provided people with one of their most basic needs—a dependable supply of food. With a stable and predictable food source, humans began to gather in larger settlements, such as towns and cities, and to develop elements of civilization such as government, laws, and writing.

Domestication of Animals Over the next few thousand years, as crops improved and farming methods became more reliable, farmers began to keep herds of domesticated animals, including sheep, goats, cows, pigs, horses, and dogs. These animals supplied humans with milk, meat, hides, wool, companionship, and the energy to do work. With the cultivation of both plants and animals, however, came many ecological changes. Overgrazing by goats, cows, and other herbivores changed grassland ecosystems to scrub, eroded soils, and put large demands on water supplies.

From Traditional to Modern Agriculture Historical farming practices continued successfully for thousands of years. Between 1450 and 1700, world exploration and discovery led to an exchange of foods that greatly influenced farming and nutrition around the globe. In the 1800s, advancements in science and technology set the stage for a remarkable change in agriculture. Large-scale watering, or irrigation; new crop varieties; and the invention of farm machines—like the seed drill shown in **Figure 6–4**—for plowing, planting, and harvesting helped farmers to increase their yields tremendously.

Word Origins

Agriculture is a combination of the Latin words *ager,* meaning "a field," and *cultura,* meaning "care." *Agriculture* is the science and art of farming, which includes the cultivation of field soils, production of crops, and the raising of livestock. **If the prefix *agro-* has the same meaning as *agri-,* what do you think the definition of the noun *agrochemical* is?**

▼ **Figure 6–4** By the 1700s, most Europeans relied on simple tools and animal-drawn plows and vehicles to work the land. This illustration shows a farmer guiding a four-wheeled seed drill as his horse pulls it across a field. The seed drill was invented to help farmers plant seeds in straight lines. **Applying Concepts** ***How were such inventions linked to human population growth?***

Agriculture

Word Origins

An agrochemical is a chemical that is used to improve the growth and health of crops or livestock.

Use Community Resources

Encourage students who are interested in careers in agriculture to research farming practices in your area. Sources of information include 4-H clubs, state and county agricultural agencies, and agricultural organizations listed in the *Encyclopedia of Associations,* including its separate volumes *Regional, State and Local Organizations* for different regions. Let students present their findings to the class in oral reports, posters, or bulletin board displays.

Meet Diverse Needs

Role-playing is an effective learning tool, particularly for students who learn best through the spoken word. Have students work in five teams. Divide the four paragraphs on this page and the description of the green revolution on the next page among the five teams. Have each team create a skit in which they role-play farmers describing the agricultural practices of their assigned era. **Learning modality: verbal**

Answers to . . .

✓CHECKPOINT *A modern-day way of life in which people supplement their diet by hunting wild animals for meat.*

Figure 6–3 *Subsistence hunting may affect the animal populations on which subsistence hunters depend for food.*

Figure 6–4 *Improved agricultural methods and technology increased crop yields, which in turn supported increased numbers of humans.*

6–1 (continued)

Build Science Skills

Making Judgments Draw students' attention to Figure 6–5 and its caption. Then, ask: **What are the advantages of using agricultural machines such as tractors and harvesting combines?** *(Vast acreages can be plowed, sown, and harvested in less time and with fewer people, enabling farmers to produce large crops.)* **What are the disadvantages of such machines?** *(Accept a variety of responses, including their initial cost, costs of repairs and maintenance, increased energy resources they use, the exhaust gases they release into the air, and their noise.)*

Using Community Resources

Encourage students to interview farm owners and managers who represent different viewpoints and approaches, including both those farmers who employ green revolution practices such as using chemical fertilizers and pesticides, and those who rely on organic practices with low environmental impact. Students could then stage a debate for the rest of the class.

The Green Revolution By the 1950s, the fast-growing human population was overstraining the world's food supply. In a global effort to increase food production, governments and scientists introduced new, intensive farming practices that greatly increased yields of rice, wheat, and other crops. This effort is now known as the **green revolution.**

The green revolution depended on several strategies to increase crop yields. The central strategy was the development of new, highly productive varieties of major food crops. Crop breeders developed new plant varieties called "miracle strains" that improved harvests. Another strategy was to use a method called **monoculture.** This method called for large fields to be cleared, plowed, and planted with a single crop year after year. To support these fields, farmers relied on irrigation to provide needed water, chemical fertilizers to boost plant growth, and pesticides to control unwanted species. Farmers also replaced human and animal power with heavy equipment and machinery, as shown in **Figure 6–5.**

The benefits of the green revolution to human society were enormous. The new farming practices increased food production in many places and helped to prevent food shortages worldwide. For the first time in years, densely populated countries such as China and India were able to feed their populations. Within 20 years, Mexican farmers increased the production of wheat tenfold. Because of the green revolution, global food production has more than doubled in the past 50 years.

In many places, green revolution techniques continue to be successful. However, the constant use of these techniques has also caused problems. Intensive farming can deplete energy and water supplies. Monoculture allows many pest species, such as the cabbage white butterfly, to reproduce on a vast scale. In turn, farmers spray their crops with pesticides that carry potentially harmful chemicals. The application of fertilizers can interfere with food webs and biogeochemical cycles. Clearly, other techniques are needed to supply the world with food while protecting the biosphere from further harm.

✓CHECKPOINT *What was the green revolution?*

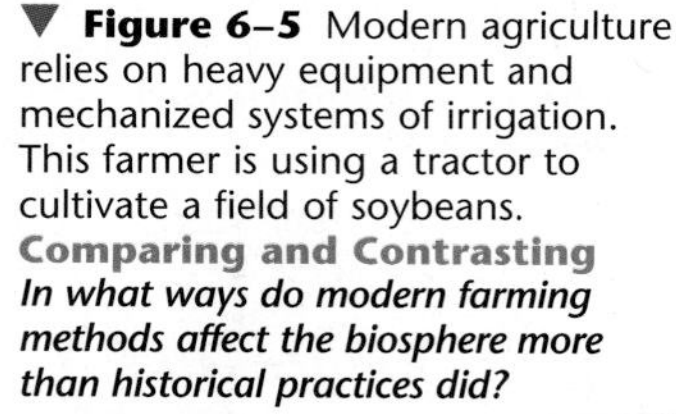

▼ **Figure 6–5** Modern agriculture relies on heavy equipment and mechanized systems of irrigation. This farmer is using a tractor to cultivate a field of soybeans. **Comparing and Contrasting** *In what ways do modern farming methods affect the biosphere more than historical practices did?*

Industrial Growth and Urban Development

Human society and its impact on the biosphere were transformed by the Industrial Revolution, which added machines and factories to civilization during the 1800s. That revolution led to the combination of industrial productivity and scientific know-how that provides us with most of the conveniences of modern life, from the homes we live in and the clothes we wear to the electronic devices we use in work and play. Mass-produced farm machinery makes efficient, large-scale agriculture possible. Automobiles give us mobility. Of course, to produce and power these machines, we need energy. We obtain most of this energy from fossil fuels—coal, oil, and natural gas.

For years, our cities and industries could grow rapidly and cheaply because they discarded wastes from manufacturing and energy production into the air, water, and soil. Meanwhile, as urban centers became crowded, many people moved from the cities to the suburbs. The result was the growth of suburbs and suburban sprawl, or the spread of suburban communities across the American landscape, as shown in **Figure 6–6**. Industrial development and the growth of cities and suburbs are closely tied to the high standard of living that so many Americans enjoy.

Many ecologists, however, are concerned about the effects of human activity on both local and global environments. Certain kinds of industrial processes pollute air, water, and soil. Dense human communities produce wastes that must be disposed of. Suburban sprawl consumes farmland and natural habitats, placing additional stress on plant and animal populations and on the biosphere's life-support systems. Can we learn to control these harmful effects of human activity while preserving—or even improving—our standard of living? This is the enormous challenge that you and your children face.

Figure 6–6 In the United States today, most people live and work either in cities or in the suburbs that surround them. The continued spread of suburbs is now referred to as suburban sprawl. **Problem Solving** ***List some ways that problems associated with suburban sprawl can be prevented.***

6–1 Section Assessment

1. **Key Concept** List three types of human activities that can affect the biosphere. For each activity, give one environmental cost and one benefit.
2. What is the difference between early hunter-gatherers and modern subsistence hunters?
3. What did agriculture provide that changed the course of human history?
4. Name three results of the Industrial Revolution.
5. **Critical Thinking Predicting** How might improved agricultural practices in a developing nation affect that nation's human population?

iTEXT Assessment Use iText to review the important concepts in Section 6–1.

ALTERNATIVE ASSESSMENT

Mapping Suburban Sprawl Are there signs of suburban sprawl in your community? Map out some of the residential areas, shopping malls, and industrial parks in your community. Then, write a brief paragraph telling how suburban sprawl has made life in your community better or worse.

6–1 Section Assessment

1. Sample answers: Agriculture: cost—uses large amount of water; benefit—increased food production. Industry: cost—toxic wastes; benefit—large-scale production of products. Urban development: cost—destruction of habitat; benefit—housing and jobs for large numbers of people.
2. Early hunter-gatherers killed available animals and collected foods without the benefit of sophisticated tools. Modern subsistence hunting involves using technology such as guns and manufactured tools.
3. A dependable supply of food
4. Sample answer: Reliance on fossil fuels; increased use of mineral resources; large-scale production of manufactured goods
5. Sample answer: With a reliable food supply, children are more likely to survive to adulthood, so families might have fewer children.

Industrial Growth and Urban Development

Build Science Skills

Comparing and Contrasting Prompt students' thinking about what their world might be like in the future by discussing the changes they have already witnessed in their lifetime—for example, conversion of agricultural land to housing, shopping centers, or office buildings; highway construction; rehabilitation of vacant land or old buildings in cities.

3 ASSESS

Evaluate Understanding

Have each student write a brief paragraph identifying one type of human activity that has changed the biosphere and describing an example of that activity's effect.

Reteach

Write the headings Hunting and Gathering, Agriculture, and Industry and Urban Development on the board. Ask students to find in the text examples for each category of how human activities have changed the biosphere.

ALTERNATIVE ASSESSMENT

Encourage students to be honest about the effects of suburban sprawl on their community and to consider its positive effects as well. For example, development has most likely brought conveniences that it would be difficult to do without.

Use iText to review the key concepts in Section 6–1.

Answers to . . .

CHECKPOINT *A global effort to increase food production through the development of new, highly productive varieties of major food crops.*

Figure 6–5 *The modern use of fertilizers and pesticides can cause pollution.*

Figure 6–6 *Accept all reasonable responses. Some students may suggest that development in suburbs should be more compact, to preserve farmland and open space, and linked to public transit to reduce traffic congestion and the need to build more highways.*

Section 6–2

1 FOCUS

Objectives

6.2.1 ***Explain*** how environmental resources are classified.

6.2.2 ***Describe*** how human activities affect land, air, and water resources.

Guide for Reading

Vocabulary Preview

Help students understand the terms *aquaculture, deforestation,* and *desertification* by writing the words on the board, using lines or boxes to indicate the word parts (roots, prefixes, and suffixes). Then, have students use a dictionary to find the meaning of each word part.

Reading Strategy

Have students divide a sheet of paper into two columns. They can list the section's Vocabulary terms in one column and the definitions in the other column. This chart should assist students when they draw the concept map for the terms.

2 INSTRUCT

The Tragedy of the Commons

Meet Diverse Needs

Role-playing the villagers described in the first paragraph could benefit many students. Divide the class into groups of three to discuss the tragedy of the commons, with one student representing the viewpoint of a villager who wants to keep grazing cattle on the commons, another student representing a villager who wants to have all the cattle removed from the commons, and the third student representing a town official who is trying to find a compromise between the two people. After students have discussed the issue, ask for volunteers to role-play a meeting in which the villagers and the official find a solution. **Learning modality: verbal**

6–2 Renewable and Nonrenewable Resources

Guide for Reading

Key Concepts
- How are environmental resources classified?
- What effects do human activities have on natural resources?

Vocabulary
- renewable resource
- nonrenewable resource
- sustainable use
- soil erosion • desertification
- deforestation • aquaculture
- smog • pollutant • acid rain

Reading Strategy: Building Vocabulary
As you read, make notes about the meaning of each new term in the list above. Then, draw a concept map to show the relationships among the terms in this section.

A few hundred years ago, villagers in England grazed their cattle on a pasture in the town center called the *commons,* which the king provided free. The villagers were quick to realize that whoever grazed the most cattle on the commons would reap the biggest reward. People added more and more cattle to their herds, and soon, there were too many animals eating the grass in the commons. People did not remove their cattle because those who did sacrificed personal profits while others continued to gain. The herders were locked into a system that eventually led to their ruin. They kept adding cattle until, eventually, the commons was destroyed. Was this a lesson for the modern world?

The Tragedy of the Commons

Generally speaking, a resource is something that can be drawn upon to take care of a need. When an environmental resource is owned by many people in common, or by no one, it is called a common resource. In 1968, environmentalists spoke about the *tragedy of the commons.* What was the tragedy? It was the notion that any resource that is open to everyone—such as the air or parts of the oceans—will eventually be destroyed because everyone can use the resource, but no one is responsible for preserving it. When people are not compelled to preserve resources for the welfare of future generations, the tragedy of the commons occurs.

Regardless of whether they are held in common, environmental resources can be classified into two types: renewable and nonrenewable. A tree is an example of a renewable resource, because a new tree can grow in place of an old tree. **Renewable resources** can regenerate and are therefore replaceable. However, a renewable resource is not necessarily unlimited. Fresh water, for example, is a renewable resource that can easily become limited by drought or overuse.

▼ **Figure 6–7 Natural resources can be classified as renewable or nonrenewable.** The grass growing in these pastures is a renewable resource—as long as the number of sheep grazing there is limited.

A **nonrenewable resource** is one that cannot be replenished by natural processes. The fossil fuels coal, oil, and natural gas are nonrenewable resources. Fossil fuels formed over hundreds of millions of years from deeply buried organic materials. When these fuels are depleted, they are gone forever.

The classification of a resource as renewable or nonrenewable depends on its context. Although a single tree is renewable, a population of trees in a forest ecosystem—on which a community of organisms depends—may not be renewable, because that ecosystem may change forever once those trees are gone.

CHECKPOINT *What is the "tragedy of the commons"?*

SECTION RESOURCES

Print:
- ***Laboratory Manual A,*** Chapter 6 Test
- ***Teaching Resources,*** Section Review 6–2
- ***Guided Reading and Study Workbook,*** Section 6–2

Technology:
- ***iText,*** Section 6–2

Sustainable Use

How can people be sure that renewable resources will be available for future generations? The concept of sustainable use is one answer to this question. **Sustainable use** is a way of using natural resources at a rate that does not deplete them. **Human activities affect the supply and the quality of renewable resources, including resources such as land, forests, ocean resources, air, and water.** A sustainable system operates without causing long-term harm to the ecological resources on which it depends. Unless sustainable strategies are used, human activities can damage or deplete these resources.

Sustainable practices are based on principles of ecology as well as economics. Those principles can be applied to agriculture, fisheries, land development, and other human activities. One example of sustainable use in agriculture is the management of unwanted species by understanding their interactions with other organisms and the environment. The ladybug in **Figure 6–8** is used in biological pest control in place of pesticides.

▲ **Figure 6–8** Alternative methods of pest control, such as the use of beneficial insects, are often an appropriate choice in sustainable agriculture. The ladybug in this photograph is eating an unwanted pest—a black aphid. **Applying Concepts** *Why is biological pest control preferable to the use of pesticides?*

▼ **Figure 6–9** **Human activities affect the supply and the quality of renewable resources, including resources such as land, forests, ocean resources, air, and water.** In dry regions, human activities, such as farming practices that fail to protect the soil, can contribute to desertification.

Land Resources

Land is a resource that provides space for cities and suburbs and raw materials for industry. Land is also important for the soils in which crops are grown. If managed properly, soil is a renewable resource. Soil, however, can be permanently damaged if it is mismanaged.

Food crops grow best in fertile soil, which is a mixture of humus, sand, clay, and rock particles. Most of the humus that makes soil fertile is in the uppermost layer of the soil, called topsoil. Good topsoil absorbs and retains moisture yet allows excess water to drain. It is rich in nutrients but low in salts. Such soil is produced by long-term interactions between the soil and plants growing in it. Much agricultural land in the American Midwest, for example, was once covered by prairie ecosystems that produced and maintained a meter or more of very fertile topsoil. Deep roots of long-lived grasses held soil in place against rain and wind.

Plowing the land removes the roots that hold the soil in place. This increases the rate of **soil erosion**—the wearing away of surface soil by water and wind. A typical field on the High Plains of the Midwest loses roughly 47 metric tons of topsoil per hectare every year! In certain parts of the world with dry climates, a combination of farming, overgrazing, and drought has turned once productive areas into deserts—a process called **desertification.** There are, however, a variety of sustainable-use practices that can guard against these problems. One practice is contour plowing, in which fields are plowed across the slope of the land to reduce erosion. Other strategies include leaving the stems and roots of the previous year's crop in place to help hold the soil and planting a field with rye rather than leaving it unprotected from erosion.

Sustainable Use

Use Community Resources

Encourage students to visit local nurseries, greenhouses, and garden centers to see if they sell natural "pest controllers" such as ladybugs and praying mantises. Also suggest that students ask about plants (nasturtiums, for example) that are used to repel insect pests in gardens.

Land Resources

Make Connections

Environmental Science Explain that when land is overgrazed by livestock, the grasses die and are replaced by scrub, weeds, and toxic plants that do not provide good pasture. The death of grasses with wide-branching roots increases runoff of precipitation, causing soil erosion. Overgrazing also ruins wildlife habitats. For example, livestock trample the fertile areas that border streams, killing plants, causing erosion of the stream banks, and making the water too muddy to support aquatic life. Encourage students to interview local ranchers and farmers or do library research to find out how damage from grazing can be minimized. (Methods include moving herds at intervals, which allows grass in the grazed area to regrow. Controlled burning destroys scrub brush and toxic plants without harming grass, whose roots sprout anew.)

PRESENTATIONS MADE EASY!

The Presentation Assistant Plus contains the Prentice Hall Presentation Pro and the Transparencies, which provide easy-to-follow visual support for every step of this section. If you have a computer presentation station, use Prentice Hall Presentation Pro for Section 6–2, or use the transparencies listed here.

Section 6–2: **Interest Grabber**
Section Outline
Chemistry of Ozone Destruction
Figure 6–13

Answers to . . .

CHECKPOINT *The "tragedy of the commons" is the idea that any resource that is open to everyone will eventually be destroyed, because everyone will use the resource but no one is responsible for conserving it.*

Figure 6–8 *Biological pest control does not cause pollution that can enter the food chain and harm other organisms.*

Forest Resources

Build Science Skills

Applying Concepts Have students review Figure 3–16, the diagram of the phosphorus cycle, in Chapter 3. Explain that one consequence of the loss of forests is disruption of the phosphorus cycle. Normally, the rate of phosphorus loss from an undisturbed ecosystem is low. The removal of trees, however, causes a great deal of rainwater and snowmelt to wash over the soil as runoff. Large amounts of nutrients are washed away in this runoff.

Build Science Skills

Predicting Encourage students to share any experiences with national forests and parks. Explain that these areas are one of the ways in which the federal government has sought to preserve and protect our forests and the wildlife living there. Explain that trees in national forests are available for logging on a regulated basis, but that national parks are protected from all commercial exploitation of their resources. Ask: **Do you think that these forests would remain as they are if the area were not set apart as a national forest or park? Why or why not?** *(Probably not, because the forests would probably be more extensively logged or destroyed to make room for industry, mining, housing, farming, or other uses.)*

Forest Resources

Earth's forests are an important resource for the products they provide and for the ecological functions they perform. People use the wood from forests to make products ranging from homes to paper. In many parts of the world, wood is still burned as fuel for cooking and heating. But living forests also provide a number of important ecological services. Forests have been called "lungs of the Earth" because they remove carbon dioxide and produce oxygen. Forests also store nutrients, provide habitats and food for organisms, moderate climate, limit soil erosion, and protect freshwater supplies.

Whether a forest can be considered a renewable resource depends partly on the type of forest. For example, the temperate forests of the northeastern United States can be considered renewable. Most of these forests have been logged at least once in the past and have grown back naturally. However, today's forests differ somewhat in species composition from the forests they replaced.

Other forests, such as those in Alaska and the Pacific Northwest, are called old-growth forests because they have never before been cut. Worldwide, about half of the area originally covered by forests and woodlands has been cleared. Only about one fifth of the world's original old-growth forests remain. Because it takes many centuries to produce old-growth forests, they are in effect nonrenewable resources. Old-growth forests often contain a rich variety of species. When logging occurs in these forests, the irreplaceable species they contain are lost.

▼ **Figure 6–10** Planting new trees is one way to counteract the effects of deforestation. **Applying Concepts** *What are two ways in which reforestation might affect the biosphere?*

Loss of forests, or **deforestation,** has several effects. Deforestation can lead to severe erosion as soil is exposed to heavy rains. Erosion also can wash away nutrients in the topsoil. Grazing or plowing after deforestation can cause permanent changes to local soils and microclimates that in turn prevent the regrowth of trees—even after human disturbance has stopped. For example, certain tropical soils exposed by deforestation have changed chemically to a hard, bricklike material called laterite.

There are a variety of sustainable-use strategies for forest management. In some forests, mature trees can be harvested selectively to promote the growth of younger trees and preserve the forest ecosystem. Increasingly, foresters plant, manage, harvest, and replant tree farms in places where forests have already been cut, as shown in **Figure 6–10.** Tree farms can now be planted and harvested efficiently, making them fully renewable resources. Tree geneticists are also breeding new, faster-growing tree varieties that produce high-quality wood.

What is deforestation?

BIO INSIGHTS **FACTS AND FIGURES**

Trading forests for food
During the past 200 years, forest land in the United States has been reduced by approximately 20 percent. This amounts to an area of woodland about equal to the size of Texas. Forest land worldwide has been reduced by 20 percent in just the past 30 years. Many of these forests were cleared to grow crops for food—a need that no doubt continues to increase rapidly in developing nations.

Most of the land suitable for agriculture has already been cleared for that use. This means that in the years to come, the need for more food to feed a growing human population will have to be met in some other way.

Ocean Resources

Earth's oceans are particularly valuable for the food resources they contain. People depend on the ocean as a major source of protein, both from finfish (such as cod) and from shellfish (such as shrimp). Yet, despite modern technology, people still obtain most food from the sea by hunting and gathering!

Throughout the second half of the twentieth century, larger fishing boats with better gear for locating and catching fish were deployed around the world. As you can see in **Figure 6–11,** the annual world fish catch grew from about 20 million tons to more than 90 million tons between 1950 and 1990. This growth led many to believe that the oceans' food supply was endless. But by the 1970s, more effort was needed to catch the same amount of fish. More sophisticated equipment, and many more boats, were put to work. Fish catches kept rising—for a time.

As fishing has increased, however, fish stocks in many fisheries are being harvested faster than they can reproduce. This situation, called overfishing, can destroy a fishery. For example, Peru's anchovy fishery was once one of the most productive in the world. At the fishery's peak, overfishing stressed the system so much that fish populations collapsed. Decades later, the fishery has still not recovered. Other important species, including halibut, cod, salmon, Atlantic herring, and Alaskan king crab, have also been overfished.

One approach to sustainable use of fisheries is to limit the catch of fish populations stressed by overfishing. To prevent population collapse, portions of Georges Banks and other Atlantic fishing grounds have been closed temporarily. Researchers hope to give fish populations a chance to recover. One problem with this approach is that open ocean waters and their animals lie in international waters, outside the legal control of any single country. For that reason, they are a good example of a common resource that everyone wants but no one has the incentive to manage properly.

As wild-caught fishes become scarce, people have turned to another sustainable-use strategy: **aquaculture,** or the farming of aquatic organisms. Aquaculture can be an efficient way to produce animal protein. If not properly managed, aquaculture can pollute water with fish wastes and can damage local aquatic ecosystems. However, more environment-friendly aquaculture techniques are steadily being developed.

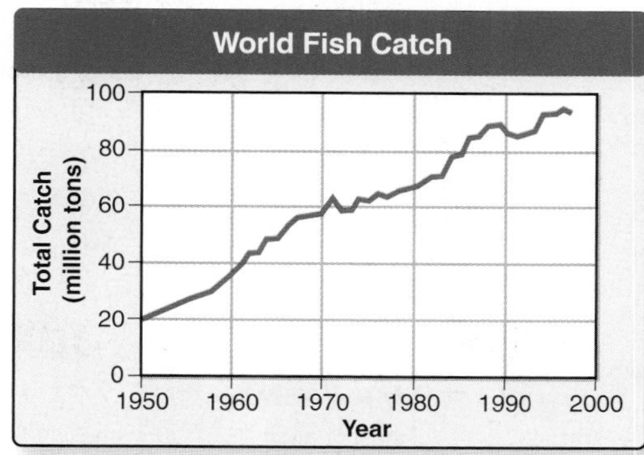

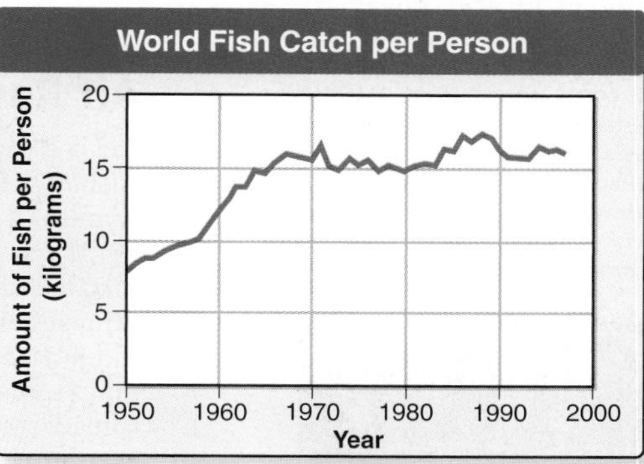

Figure 6–11 Despite the increase in the total amount of fish caught each year, the supply of fish per person has stayed the same. Stocks of fishes like the Atlantic cod (below) are nearly depleted. **Predicting** *If the world's total fish catch levels off but the human population keeps growing, what might happen to the amount of fish per person?*

Codfish

Ocean Resources

Build Science Skills

Applying Concepts Have interested students work as a group to learn about the fishing industry in the United States. Encourage students to find out about the history of the fishing industry as well as the various types of fishes that are caught and sold in different parts of the United States today. Have students present their findings to the class in the form of an oral report. Also ask the group to prepare a map that shows where various types of fishes are found.

Use Community Resources

Designate several pairs of students to interview the owners or managers of fish stores and the managers of fish and seafood departments in local supermarkets. Encourage students to gather the following information: Which types of fish being sold in the store are caught in the wild, and which are raised on fish farms? Is there a price difference between wild and farmed fish? Which wild fish are abundant? Which are harder for the store to obtain? After the interviews, let the student pairs meet as a group to share their findings and prepare an oral report to share with the class.

Answers to . . .

CHECKPOINT *The loss of forests*

Figure 6–10 *Sample answer: Reforestation would prevent further soil erosion and provide habitats for forest animals.*

Figure 6–11 *The amount per person would drop.*

Air Resources

Demonstration

Tie a 4-liter heavy-duty freezer-type bag over the end of the cold tailpipe of your car and start the engine. Turn the car off after 10 seconds or so, seal the bag tightly closed, and bring it to class. Let students use hand lenses to examine the emission particles in the bag. Point out that this bag of pollution is from only one car that ran for only 10 seconds. Ask students to imagine the amount of particles that would be released by hundreds or even thousands of vehicles during a morning commute.

Build Science Skills

Analyzing Data Have students collect samples of rainwater from various outdoor locations, test each sample's pH level with litmus paper, and compare the pH level with that of a sample of tapwater. Explain that all rainwater is slightly acidic (pH 6–7) due to naturally occurring carbon dioxide in the air. However, a sample with a pH of less than 6 qualifies as acid rain.

Water Resources

Use Community Resources

Invite students to share any experiences they may have had with local water pollution. Ask a member of your local health board to visit the class and tell students about problems with water pollution that have been encountered in your immediate area, the state, or the region. Make sure the guest also discusses whether and how any pollution problems are being resolved.

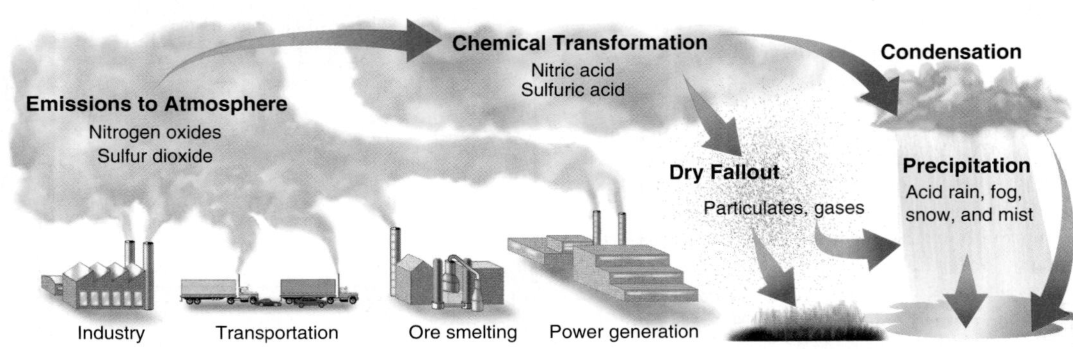

Figure 6–12 Acid rain results from the chemical transformation of nitrogen and sulfur products that come from human activities. The face of the statue (below) shows damage from acid rain. **Interpreting Graphics** *What pathways do the chemicals in atmospheric emissions take on their way to becoming acid rain?*

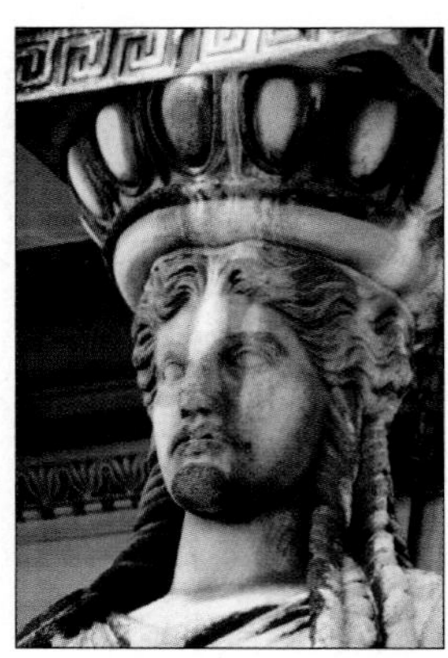

Air Resources

Air is a common resource that we use every time we breathe. Although it's easy to take air for granted, preserving air quality remains a challenge for modern society.

If you live in a large city, you have probably seen **smog,** a mixture of chemicals that occurs as a gray-brown haze in the atmosphere. Smog is primarily due to automobile exhausts and industrial emissions. Because it threatens the health of people and animals with asthma or respiratory conditions, smog is considered a pollutant. A **pollutant** is a harmful material that can enter the biosphere through the land, air, or water.

The burning of fossil fuels can release pollutants that cause smog and other problems in the atmosphere. Potentially toxic chemicals, like nitrates, sulfates, and particulates (pahr-TIK-yoo-lits), are especially troublesome in large concentrations. Particulates are microscopic particles of ash and dust that can enter the nose, mouth, and lungs, causing health problems over the long term. Today, most industries use technology to control emissions from factory smokestacks. Strict automobile emission standards and clean-air regulations have improved air quality in many American cities, but air pollution is an ongoing problem in other parts of the world.

Many combustion processes, such as the burning of fossil fuels, release acidic gases containing nitrogen and sulfur compounds into the atmosphere. When these gases combine with water vapor in the air, they form drops of nitric and sulfuric acids. These strong acids can drift for miles before they fall as **acid rain.** Acid rain can kill plants by damaging their leaves and changing the chemistry of soils and standing-water ecosystems. Acid rain may also dissolve and release toxic elements, such as mercury, from the soil, freeing those elements to enter other portions of the biosphere. **Figure 6–12** shows the processes that lead to the formation of acid rain.

CHECKPOINT *What is a pollutant?*

BIO INSIGHTS **FACTS AND FIGURES**

The Clean Water Act

Pressure by concerned voters resulted in the passage by Congress of the Water Pollution Control Act of 1972. This act and its amendments, now called the Clean Water Act, empower the federal government to set minimum water quality standards for rivers and streams. The Act also allows individual states to pass stricter laws if they wish.

The Act prohibits the discharge of any pollutant into a waterway unless a permit is first obtained from the state. The permit system sets specific pollutant limits on a facility-by-facility basis.

The Act gives the Environmental Protection Agency the power to impose deadlines for compliance with the law and to fine industries and municipalities that do not comply. Fines may go as high as $10,000 per day; repeat offenders may be fined up to $50,000 per day and may receive a prison term.

Water Resources

Americans use billions of gallons of fresh water daily for everything from drinking and washing to watering crops and making steel. Although water is a renewable resource, the total supply of fresh water is limited. For this reason, protecting water supplies from pollution and managing society's ever-growing demand for water are major priorities.

Pollution such as the oil spill in **Figure 6–13** threatens water supplies in several ways. Improperly discarded chemicals can enter streams and rivers. Wastes discarded on land can seep through soil and enter underground water supplies that we tap with wells. Domestic sewage, which is the wastewater from sinks and toilets, contains nitrogen and phosphorous compounds that can encourage the growth of algae and bacteria in aquatic habitats. Sewage can also contain microorganisms that can spread disease among humans and animals. In this country, most cities and towns now treat their sewage to make it environmentally safer.

One way of ensuring the sustainable use of water resources is to protect the natural systems involved in the water cycle. For example, wetlands such as swamps can help to purify the water passing through them. As water flows slowly through a swamp, densely growing plants filter certain pollutants out of the water. Similarly, forests and other vegetation not only hold soil in place but help to purify the water that seeps into the ground or runs off into rivers and lakes.

As demand for water grows rapidly in many parts of the United States, water conservation is becoming an increasingly important aspect of sustainable use. There are many strategies for conserving water—in homes, industry, and agriculture. More than three quarters of all water consumed in this country is used in agriculture, so conservation in this area can save large amounts of water. For example, drip irrigation delivers water directly to plant roots. This reduces the amount of water lost through evaporation.

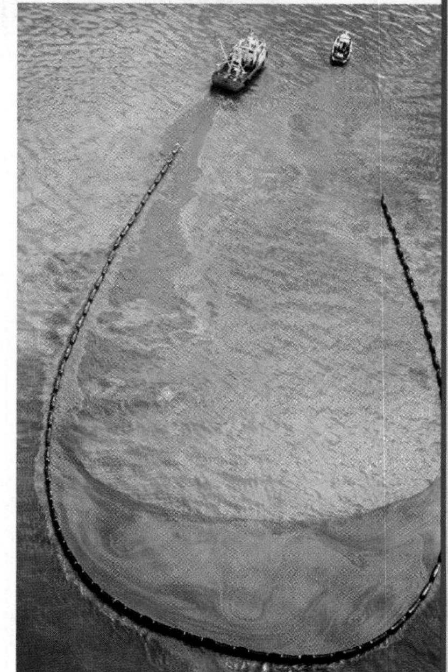

▲ **Figure 6–13** Trawlers clean up an oil spill caused by a disaster at sea. A system of floats called booms helps keep the oil from spreading during the cleanup process. **Formulating Hypotheses** ***What factors might improve the cleanup of an oil spill at sea?***

3 ASSESS

Evaluate Understanding

Call on students at random to name harmful human activities discussed in the section and identify each activity's effects on the biosphere.

Reteach

Name different natural resources, and ask students to identify each as renewable or nonrenewable. Then, have students describe ways they can help to conserve resources.

Use iText to review the key concepts in Section 6–2.

Take It to the NET

For additional information, visit **www.phschool.com**

6–2 Section Assessment

1. **Key Concept** What is the difference between a renewable and a nonrenewable resource?
2. **Key Concept** List two human activities that affect land resources, and explain the changes that can result. Do the same for air and water resources.
3. How does the decline in world fisheries represent a "tragedy of the commons"?
4. **Critical Thinking Applying Concepts** Describe sustainable-use strategies to manage forests as a renewable resource.

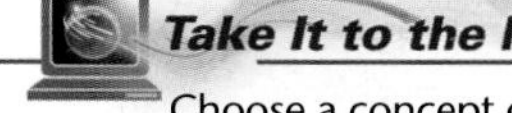

Assessment Use iText to review the important concepts in Section 6–2.

Take It to the NET

Choose a concept of sustainable use that is not described in this section. Explain how the features of sustainable use apply to the activity. If you need help, use the links provided in the Biology area at the Prentice Hall Web site: **www.phschool.com**

6–2 Section Assessment

1. A renewable resource can regenerate and is therefore replaceable. A nonrenewable resource cannot be replenished by natural processes.
2. Check students' responses for logical cause-and-effect relationships.
3. Areas of the ocean that are in international waters are being overfished because no one is responsible for regulating the harvesting of fish.
4. Selective harvesting of mature trees and tree farming are two approaches to the sustainable use of forests.

Answers to . . .

CHECKPOINT *A harmful material that can enter the biosphere through the land, air, or water*

Figure 6–12 *The gases combine with water vapor to form drops of nitric acid and sulfuric acid. These acids can drift long distances before they fall as acid rain.*

Figure 6–13 *Sample answer: Calm weather, small size of the spill, installing booms quickly*

Section 6–3

1 FOCUS

Objectives

6.3.1 ***Define*** biodiversity and explain its value.
6.3.2 ***Identify*** current threats to biodiversity.
6.3.3 ***Describe*** the goal of conservation biology.

Guide for Reading

Vocabulary Preview

Write the following terms on the board, and underline the parts as shown here: *habitat fragmentation, invasive species,* and *biological magnification*. Have students find the definition of each underlined part in a dictionary. Then, ask them to tell what they think the entire vocabulary term means. Encourage students to write down their predicted definitions and make any necessary corrections when they encounter the terms in the text.

Reading Strategy

Encourage students to vary their questions so they don't simply keep repeating "What is . . ." for most headings. For example, the heading on page 153 could be rewritten as "How do introduced species affect biodiversity?" or "Why are introduced species a threat to biodiversity?"

2 INSTRUCT

The Value of Biodiversity

Build Science Skills

Classifying Have each student find out about one specific example of how biodiversity is valuable to society. Tell students that the example should relate to agriculture, medicine, recreation, industry, or general health. After students have completed their research, let them meet in groups that are organized according to those fields and share their findings. Suggest that each group prepare a poster to summarize the information.

6–3 Biodiversity

Guide for Reading

Key Concepts
- What is the value of biodiversity?
- What are the current threats to biodiversity?
- What is the goal of conservation biology?

Vocabulary
biodiversity
ecosystem diversity
species diversity
genetic diversity
extinction
endangered species
habitat fragmentation
biological magnification
invasive species
conservation

Reading Strategy: Asking Questions Before you read, rewrite the headings in the section as *how, why,* or *what* questions about biodiversity. As you read, write brief answers to your questions.

Those of us who love nature find much to admire in the many forms of life that surround us. We marvel at the soaring flight of an eagle, the majestic movements of a whale, and the colors of spring wildflowers. "Variety," the saying goes, "is the spice of life." But variety in the biosphere gives us more than just interesting things to look at. Human society takes part in local and global food webs and energy cycles, and depends on both the physical and biological life-support systems of our planet. For that reason, our well-being is closely tied to the well-being of a great variety of other organisms—including many that are neither majestic nor beautiful to our eyes.

The Value of Biodiversity

Another word for variety is diversity. Therefore, biological diversity, or **biodiversity,** is the sum total of the genetically based variety of all organisms in the biosphere. **Ecosystem diversity** includes the variety of habitats, communities, and ecological processes in the living world. **Species diversity** refers to the number of different species in the biosphere. So far, biologists have identified and named about 1.5 million species and estimate that millions more may be discovered in the future. **Genetic diversity** refers to the sum total of all the different forms of genetic information carried by all organisms living on Earth today. Within each species, genetic diversity refers to the total of all different forms of genes present in that species. You will read about genetic information later in the book.

Biodiversity is one of Earth's greatest natural resources. Species of many kinds have provided us with foods, industrial products, and medicines—including painkillers, antibiotics, heart drugs, antidepressants, and anticancer drugs. For example, the rosy periwinkle plant in **Figure 6–14** is the source of substances used to treat certain cancers. The biodiversity represented by wild plants and animals is a kind of "library" of genetic information upon which humans can draw for future use. For example, most crop plants have wild relatives with useful traits such as resistance to disease or pests. When biodiversity is lost, potential sources of material with significant value to the biosphere and to humankind may be lost with it.

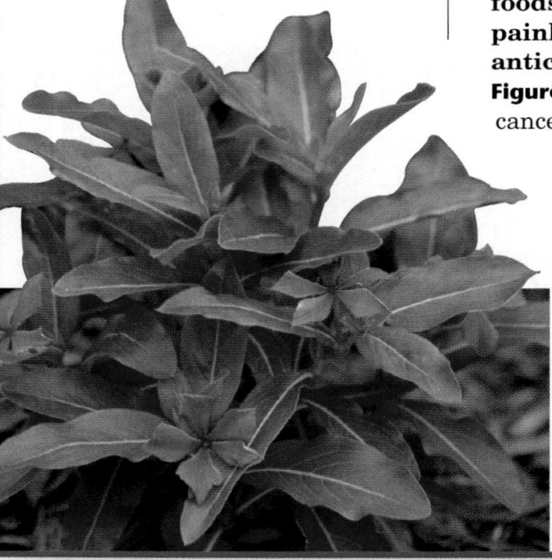

◀ **Figure 6–14** **Biodiversity is one of Earth's greatest natural resources. Species of many kinds have provided us with foods, industrial products, and medicines.** The rosy periwinkle is a pink-petaled flowering plant native only to an island off the coast of Africa. The substances produced by this plant are used in modern medicine.

SECTION RESOURCES

Print:
- ***Teaching Resources,*** Section Review 6–3
- ***Guided Reading and Study Workbook,*** Section 6–3

Technology
- ***iText,*** Section 6–3

Threats to Biodiversity

Human activity can reduce biodiversity by altering habitats, hunting species to extinction, introducing toxic compounds into food webs, and introducing foreign species to new environments. As human activities alter ecosystems, this may lead to the extinction of species. **Extinction** occurs when a species disappears from all or part of its range. A species whose population size is declining in a way that places it in danger of extinction is called an **endangered species.** As the population of an endangered species declines, the species loses genetic diversity—an effect that can make it even more vulnerable to extinction.

Habitat Alteration and Fragmentation

When land is developed, natural habitats may be destroyed. As habitats disappear, the species that live in those habitats vanish. In addition, development often splits ecosystems into pieces, a process called **habitat fragmentation.** As a result, remaining pieces of habitat become biological "islands." We usually think of islands as bits of land surrounded by water. But a biological island can be any patch of habitat surrounded by a different habitat. New York's Central Park is an island of trees and grass in a sea of concrete. In suburbs, patches of forest can be surrounded by farms, houses, and shopping malls. Habitat islands are very different from large, continuous ecosystems. The smaller the "island," the fewer species can live there, the smaller their populations can be, and the more vulnerable they are to further disturbance or climate change.

CHECKPOINT *What is habitat fragmentation?*

Demand for Wildlife Products

Throughout history, humans have pushed some animal species to extinction by hunting them for food or other products. During the 1800s, hunting caused the extinction of species such as the Carolina parakeet, shown in **Figure 6–15**, and the passenger pigeon.

Today, in the United States, endangered species are protected from hunting. Hunting, however, still threatens populations of rare animals in parts of Africa, South America, and Southeast Asia. Some species are hunted for meat, fur, or hides. Others are hunted because people think that their body parts such as horns or gall bladders have medicinal properties. The Convention on International Trade in Endangered Species, often referred to as CITES, bans international trade in products derived from an agreed-upon list of endangered species. It is, however, often difficult to enforce laws in remote wilderness areas.

▲ **Figure 6–15 Human activity can reduce biodiversity by altering habitats, hunting species to extinction, introducing toxic compounds into food webs, and introducing foreign species to new environments.** The Carolina parakeet was once common in the southeastern United States. This colorful bird was hunted to extinction by the early twentieth century because its feathers were in demand to decorate hats.

TIME SAVER **PRESENTATIONS MADE EASY!**

The Presentation Assistant Plus contains the Prentice Hall Presentation Pro and the Transparencies, which provide easy-to-follow visual support for every step of this section. If you have a computer presentation station, use Prentice Hall Presentation Pro for Section 6–3, or use the transparencies listed here.

Section 6–3:  
Interest Grabber
Section Outline
Species Diversity
Figure 6–18

Threats to Biodiversity
Build Science Skills

Classifying Explain that endangered species are those considered to be in immediate danger of extinction. Ask: **What is extinction?** *(The dying out of an entire species so it no longer exists on Earth)* **Once a species becomes extinct, will it ever reappear?** *(No)* Explain that other organisms are considered to be endangered or threatened species.

Habitat Alteration and Fragmentation
Build Science Skills

Using Models The following activity models the relationship between a habitat's perimeter and its interior area. Direct students as follows: On a sheet of graph paper, draw two irregularly shaped "islands"—one large and one much smaller. Measure each habitat's perimeter by laying a string along its outline and then measuring the string with a ruler. Count the squares in each habitat. (Count more than half a square as one square, and do not count less than half a square.) For each habitat, divide the number of interior squares by the number of perimeter units, rounding off to the nearest tenth. The result will be the ratio of perimeter units to interior-area units. Have students compare the two ratios. Ask: **Which habitat has more interior area per unit of perimeter?** *(Regardless of the habitats' actual sizes, the larger one will always have more interior area per unit of perimeter.)*

Demand for Wildlife Products
Meet Diverse Needs

Some endangered species are still abundant in some areas, but their numbers have decreased in other areas where they were also abundant in the past. Encourage interested students to do independent research and compile lists of endangered and threatened species worldwide. Other students may wish to research endangered species that are in demand commercially for food, medicines, or other uses.

Answers to . . .

CHECKPOINT *The splitting of habitat into small, isolated "islands"*

6–3 (continued)

Pollution

Meet Diverse Needs

Some students, particularly those who are not proficient in English, may have difficulty differentiating between the terms *bioaccumulation* and *biological magnification.* Emphasize that bioaccumulation occurs within an individual organism as it repeatedly ingests a harmful substance over time, while biological magnification occurs in a series of organisms in a food chain as each organism eats many contaminated organisms at a lower trophic level. **Limited English proficiency**

Use Visuals

Figure 6–16 Use the DDT example illustrated in the diagram to clarify the effect of biomagnification on an entire ecosystem. Remind students that food webs can be very complex; let them look again at Figure 3–9 on page 11 to see one example. Explain that when biomagnification kills organisms at one trophic level, the organisms at both lower and higher trophic levels are also affected. For example, biomagnification may reduce the number of top-level predators in an ecosystem. This can lead to a series of events that will upset the balance of the entire ecosystem.

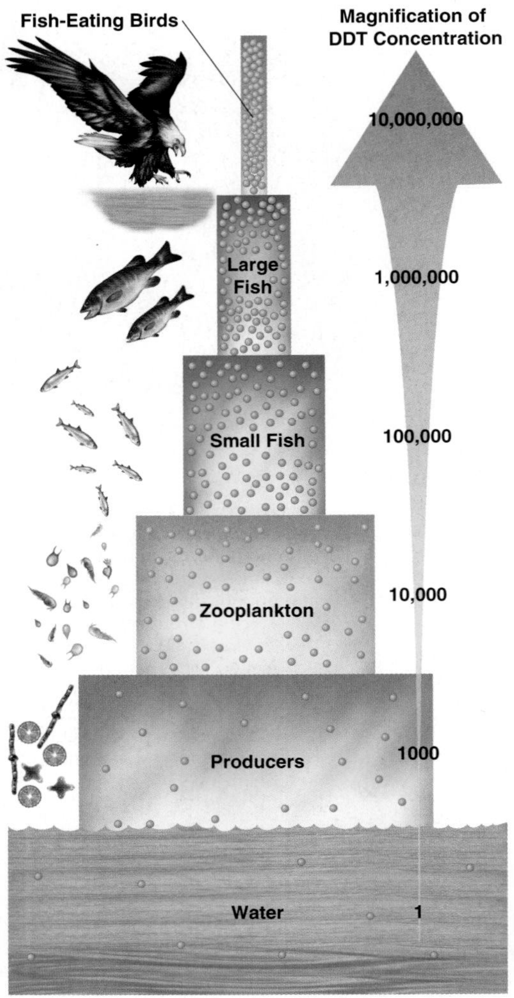

▲ **Figure 6–16** In the process of biological magnification, the concentration of a pollutant such as DDT—represented here by orange dots—is multiplied as it passes up the food chain from producers to consumers. By the time it reaches the top-level consumers, shown here as fish-eating birds, the amount of DDT in biological tissues can be magnified nearly 10 million times. **Calculating** *By what number is the concentration of DDT multiplied at each successive trophic level?*

Pollution

Many forms of pollution can threaten biodiversity, but one of the most serious problems occurs when toxic compounds accumulate in the tissues of organisms. The history of DDT, one of the first widely used pesticides, explains the situation well. At first, DDT seemed to be a perfect pesticide. It remains active for a long time, kills many different insects, and is cheap enough to be sprayed widely to control agricultural pests and disease-carrying mosquitoes.

When DDT was sprayed, it drained into rivers and streams at low concentrations that seemed harmless. But DDT has two properties that make it hazardous. First, DDT is nonbiodegradable, which means that it is not broken down by metabolic processes in bacteria, plants, or animals. Second, when DDT is picked up by organisms, they do not eliminate it from their bodies. As a result, something unexpected happens. DDT is picked up, concentrated, and stored by aquatic plants and algae. When herbivores eat those plants, they concentrate DDT to levels ten times higher than levels found in plants! When carnivores eat herbivores, the toxic substance is concentrated further, as shown in **Figure 6–16.** In this process, called **biological magnification,** concentrations of a harmful substance increase in organisms at higher trophic levels in a food chain or food web. Biological magnification affects the entire food web, although top-level carnivores are at highest risk.

In 1962, biologist Rachel Carson wrote a book called *Silent Spring* that alerted people to the dangers of biological magnification. The widespread spraying of DDT over many years had threatened populations of many animals—especially fish-eating birds like the osprey, brown pelican, and bald eagle—with extinction. One effect of DDT was to make eggs of these birds so fragile that the eggs could not survive intact. By the early 1970s, DDT was banned in the United States and in most other industrialized countries. In the years since, scientists have noted a marked recovery in the populations of birds that had been affected. Bald eagles, for example, can once again be seen around rivers, lakes, and estuaries in the lower 48 states.

CHECKPOINT *What is biological magnification?*

Quick Lab

How does biological magnification occur?

Materials paper cups (3 small, 1 medium, and 1 large); 1-L beaker; sand; 12 beads; masking tape

Procedure 

1. Use a pencil to punch five holes in the bottom of each paper cup. Place tape over the outsides of the holes. The small cups represent grasshoppers, the medium-sized cup represents an insect-eating lizard, and the large cup represents a hawk.
2. Half-fill each small cup with sand and 4 beads. The sand represents food. The beads represent a chlorinated pesticide.
3. Hold each small cup over a beaker to catch the sand and remove the tape. The sand that flows out of the cup represents digested food. Record the number of beads in each cup.
4. To model the effects of biological magnification on the lizard, empty the contents of the three small cups into the medium-sized cup. Repeat step 3 with the medium-sized cup.
5. With two classmates, empty the three medium-sized cups into a large cup to model a hawk eating the lizard. Repeat step 3 with the large cup.

Analyze and Conclude

1. **Inferring** Which animals accumulated the most pesticide?
2. **Predicting** Which level of the food chain is most affected by biological magnification?

Introduced Species

One of the most important threats to biodiversity today comes from an unexpected source: apparently harmless plants and animals that humans transport around the world either accidentally or intentionally. Introduced into new habitats, these organisms often become **invasive species** that reproduce rapidly. Invasive species increase their populations because their new habitat lacks the parasites and predators that control their population "back home."

Hundreds of invasive species, including the one in **Figure 6–17,** are already causing ecological problems in the United States. Zebra mussels, an aquatic pest, were imported from Europe during the 1980s. They spread through the Great Lakes and several major rivers. These mussels reproduce and grow so quickly that they cause major ecological changes and are driving several native species close to extinction. There are also many examples on land. One European weed, the leafy spurge, now infests millions of hectares of grasslands across the Northern Great Plains, where it displaces native plants.

▶ **Figure 6–17** **Human activity can reduce biodiversity by introducing foreign species to new environments.** Native to South America, nutrias have become pests in coastal areas of the southeastern United States. These furry rodents eat water plants that protect fragile shorelines from erosion. This destroys the habitats of species native to those ecosystems.

FACTS AND FIGURES

Costa Rica's megareserves

The Central American nation of Costa Rica has become a world leader in the effort to slow ecosystem destruction. In exchange for reductions in its international debt, the Costa Rican government has established eight megareserves—extensive regions that include one or more undisturbed areas surrounded by buffer zones that are used by people for economic gain.

The buffer zones provide a steady, lasting supply of forest products, water, and hydroelectric power, and also support sustainable agriculture and ecotourism. Destructive practices that are incompatible with long-term ecosystem stability are prohibited in these zones. Costa Rica expects its megareserve system to maintain at least 80 percent of the country's native species. In addition, its thriving ecotourism industry is a significant source of income for the country.

Quick Lab

Objective Students will be able to create a model of biological magnification

Skill Focus Inferring, Predicting

Materials paper cups (3 small, 1 medium, and 1 large); 1-L beaker; sand; 12 beads; masking tape

Time 15 minutes

Advance Preparation

- Use large beads that will not fall through the holes in the cups. Buttons or marbles can be substituted for the beads. Use waxed paper cups (plastic or foam cups will not puncture cleanly).

Strategies

- Before students begin, discuss the model with them to make sure they understand what each material represents.
- Have students set up a data table for recording results.

Expected Outcome Starting with 4 beads in each "grasshopper" cup, the "lizard" cup will contain 12 beads, and the "hawk" cup 36 beads.

Analyze and Conclude

1. The hawks
2. The highest trophic level

Introduced Species

Build Science Skills

Applying Concepts Make a list of invasive species that compete with native species in the United States. (Examples: starlings; zebra mussels in the Great Lakes; kudzu in Southeastern states; Varroa mites killing honeybees; Dutch elm disease killing trees; Asian long-horned beetles attacking New England maples; Eurasian milfoil choking lakes and ponds; phragmites and purple loosestrife crowding out native wetland plants; Mexican boll weevil attacking cotton crops; and cheatgrass crowding out native grasses in the West.) Give a copy of the list to each small group, and have students find out where each species originated, how it was transported to the United States, and what problems it causes.

Answers to . . .

CHECKPOINT *The increasing concentration of a harmful substance in organisms at higher trophic levels in a food chain*

Figure 6–16 *A factor of 10*

SCIENCE NEWS®

Encourage students to visit **www.phschool.com** for the most current information on this topic.

Biology and History

Call on fluent readers to read aloud the descriptive paragraphs on the time line. Then, divide the class into nine groups, and assign a different time-line topic to each group. Challenge each group to prepare some sort of presentation—a debate, a role-play, or a taped radio show, for example—to dramatize the topic for the class.

Writing Activity

Encourage students to focus on endangered species found in their state or region. If students have difficulty identifying such species, let them choose threatened species instead.

Meet Diverse Needs

Encourage students who need an extra challenge to make an enlarged version of the Biology and History time line on a wall of the classroom. Then, have students research other conservation milestones and add them to the time line. Students can draw their own pictures or photocopy ones in books and magazines, then write a paragraph explaining the milestone. **Learning modality: verbal**

KEEP CURRENT WITH . . . SCIENCE NEWS®

To find out more about the topics in this chapter, go to: **www.phschool.com**

Conserving Biodiversity

Most people would like to preserve Earth's biodiversity for future generations. In ecology, the term **conservation** is used to describe the wise management of natural resources, including the preservation of habitats and wildlife. The modern science of conservation biology seeks to protect biodiversity. To do so requires detailed information about ecological relationships—such as the way natural populations use their habitats—and integrates information from other scientific disciplines, such as genetics, geography, and natural resource management.

Strategies for Conservation Many conservation efforts are aimed at managing individual species to keep them from becoming extinct. Some zoos, for example, have established captive breeding programs, in which young animals are raised in protected surroundings until the population is stable, then are later returned to the wild. This strategy has succeeded with a few species, including the black-footed ferret.

Today, conservation efforts focus on protecting entire ecosystems as well as single species. Protecting an ecosystem will ensure that the natural habitats and the interactions of many different species are preserved at the same time. This effort is a much bigger challenge. Governments and conservation groups worldwide are working to set aside land, or expand existing areas, as parks and reserves.

Biology and History

Success in Conservation

Human activity can have a dramatic impact on the biosphere, to the point where other forms of life are threatened. Many efforts have been made to protect and preserve Earth's natural environments.

1850 — 1900

1854 **Henry David Thoreau** Thoreau recommends the preservation of wildlife. In his book *Walden,* he cautions against seeking to dominate nature and suggests living in harmony with it.

1872 Yellowstone becomes the world's first national park.

1896 **Harriet Hemenway** Hemenway and her cousin, Minna Hall, petition in Boston for legislation to prevent the extinction of birds due to unregulated hunting. By refusing to buy or wear plumed hats, the two cousins are among the first founders of the conservation movement.

1900 **Lacey Act** Enacted by the U.S. Congress, the Lacey Act is the first major national conservation law. Transporting illegally killed animals across state borders becomes a federal crime.

HISTORY OF SCIENCE

The Endangered Species Act
Originally passed in 1973 and updated in 1982, 1985, and 1988, the Endangered Species Act prohibits the sale or purchase of any product made from a species that has been listed by the U.S. government as endangered or threatened. In 1989, the U.S. Fish and Wildlife Service (FWS) listed 461 foreign species and 271 domestic species of animals as endangered. The list of threatened animals included 37 foreign species, 51 domestic species, and 10 species that reside in both the United States and other countries. For each species listed as endangered or threatened, the Act requires FWS officials to choose a suitable habitat and design a recovery plan. The recent effort to re-establish populations of wolves in Yellowstone National Park is one example of such a recovery plan.

The United States has an extensive system of national parks, forests, and other protected areas. Few of these, however, were designed with ecological principles in mind. As a result, these areas may not be large enough, or contain the right resources, to protect biodiversity. Marine sanctuaries are being designated to protect marine resources, such as coral reefs and marine mammals. Ecologists are realizing, however, that even these areas may not be enough to conserve the world's biodiversity.

Challenges in Conservation Sometimes, the need to protect biodiversity is greatest in countries that are least able to do so. The destruction of tropical rain forests, for example, is the single greatest threat to biodiversity on land. Most rain forests are located in developing countries, where conservation goals must be weighed against the survival needs of the human population.

Protecting species and ecosystem diversity in many places around the world is an enormous challenge. As part of the effort to locate problem areas and set up a list of priorities, conservation biologists often identify "hot spots," 25 of which are shown in **Figure 6–18** on page 156. Each hot spot is a place where significant numbers of habitats and species are in immediate danger of extinction as a result of human activity. The hot-spot strategy may help scientists and governments to focus their efforts to make and enforce laws that protect habitats and prevent or regulate hunting.

✓CHECKPOINT *What do conservation biologists mean by a "hot spot"?*

1933
Civilian Conservation Corps
President Roosevelt establishes the CCC, providing work in reforestation, prevention of soil erosion, and park and flood control projects. The "tree army" renews the nation's forests by planting an estimated 3 billion trees.

1938
Benny Goodman brings new style to jazz music.

1950

1966
Endangered Species Preservation Act
This act allows for the identification of and research on endangered species. Seven years after passing, the act was expanded to protect plants and to prohibit threats to endangered species.

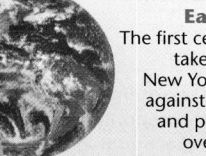

1970
Earth Day
The first celebration takes place in New York to rally against pollution and population overgrowth.

1972
National Marine Sanctuaries Act
The Secretary of Commerce is empowered to designate marine ecosystems as preservation or conservation areas.

1992
Earth Summit
A United Nations conference in Brazil seeks international solutions for environmental issues, including the worldwide loss of species.

2000

Writing Activity

Choose and research a specific endangered species and its habitat. Then, write a letter to the editor of your local newspaper stating the problem and offering one or more possible conservation efforts for that species.

Use Community Resources

Contact local and state chapters of various conservation groups to see if they would provide speakers to visit the class. Ask each speaker to describe the group's efforts to preserve wildlife and ecosystems in your area. Also encourage the visitors to bring brochures, posters, and other materials to leave with students. If you are able to locate several such speakers, you might want to have them all visit at the same time for a Conservation Fair in the classroom.

Meet Diverse Needs

Have students work in teams to create a mural entitled *Extinction Is Forever* to display in the classroom or a school hallway. Tell students that the goal of the display should be to dramatize the plight of endangered and threatened species and to motivate anyone viewing the display to become more concerned about protecting those species. **Learning modality: visual**

Answer to . . .

✓CHECKPOINT *An area where habitats and species are in danger of extinction because of human activity*

6–3 (continued)

Make Connections

Earth Science Let students take turns using a large world globe to find the "hot spots" that are highlighted on the map in Figure 6–18. If they present oral reports for the Alternative Assessment activity on this page, they could point out each ecosystem's location on the globe.

3 ASSESS

Evaluate Understanding

Call on students at random to identify one type of human activity that threatens biodiversity and to explain the effects of that activity.

Reteach

Have students prepare written or tape-recorded statements in which they discuss what it means to be a "citizen of Earth." For example, students might write a set of "eco-laws" that a good global citizen would follow or might create a bill of rights for all living things.

MAKING CONNECTIONS

Consult with your school's or town's librarian to make sure adequate sources are available for students' research.

Use iText to review the key concepts in Section 6–3.

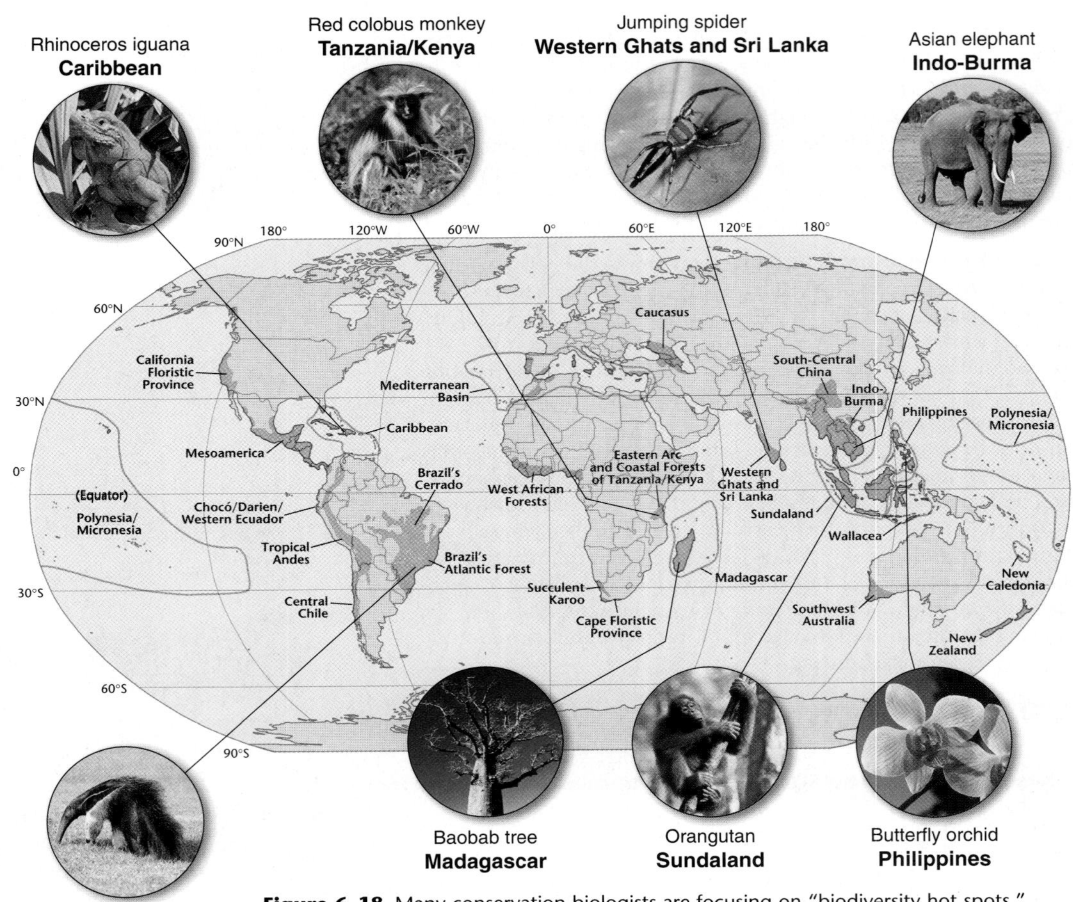

Figure 6–18 Many conservation biologists are focusing on "biodiversity hot spots," where the biodiversity of these unique ecosystems is threatened. The 25 identified hot spots are shown in orange on the map. **By focusing on protecting specific ecosystems, biologists hope to preserve global biodiversity.**

6–3 Section Assessment

1. **Key Concept** Why is biodiversity worth preserving?
2. **Key Concept** List four different ways in which humans are decreasing biodiversity.
3. **Key Concept** What is the current focus of conservation biologists worldwide?
4. Explain the relationship between habitat size and species diversity.
5. **Critical Thinking Predicting** What problems could result if an endangered species were introduced into a nonnative habitat?

iTEXT Assessment Use iText to review the important concepts in Section 6–3.

MAKING CONNECTIONS

Exploring Biomes
Review biomes in Chapter 4. Then, choose one of the hot spots shown above. Find out about the biome in which these unique ecosystems and endangered species occur. Report on your findings and suggest specific actions that can be taken to preserve the biome's biodiversity.

6–3 Section Assessment

1. Biodiversity is worth preserving because it is one of Earth's greatest natural resources and has provided us with foods, industrial products, and medicines.
2. By altering or fragmenting habitats, causing species extinction through hunting, polluting ecosystems, and introducing nonnative species
3. Protecting entire ecosystems as well as single species
4. The smaller the habitat's size, the fewer the number of species that can live there.
5. Sample answer: The endangered species might not be able to compete with native species in that habitat, and it would die out entirely.

6–4 Charting a Course for the Future

For most of human history, environmental change was a local affair. For example, many animals in the Hawaiian islands became extinct after humans arrived there. Yet, the effect of these extinctions on the biosphere at large was negligible. Since your parents and grandparents were born, however, global human population has grown from around 2.5 billion to more than 6.1 billion! Today, much of Earth's land surface has been altered by human activity. What's more, our species now uses as much energy and transports almost as much material as all of Earth's other multicellular species combined. We have become the most important source of environmental change.

 **As we enter the twenty-first century, many biologists are concerned about the biological effects of two types of global change: the thinning, or depletion, of the ozone layer and global warming.** Understanding these phenomena requires that you remember what you have learned about global climate and weather, energy flow, nutrient cycling, population growth, and factors that limit population size. It also requires that you understand how scientific models make predictions about the complex systems that make up the biosphere. One such system is Earth's atmosphere.

Guide for Reading

Key Concept
- What are two types of global change of concern to biologists?

Vocabulary
ozone layer
global warming

Reading Strategy: Summarizing As you read, find the key concept in the section. Write down a few words or phrases from the key concept, then use them in a summary of Section 6–4.

Ozone Depletion

Between 20 and 50 kilometers above Earth's surface, the atmosphere contains a concentration of ozone gas—the **ozone layer.** Molecules of ozone consist of three oxygen atoms. Although ozone at ground level is a pollutant, the naturally occurring ozone layer serves an important function. It absorbs a good deal of harmful ultraviolet, or UV, radiation from sunlight before it reaches Earth's surface. You may know that overexposure to UV radiation is the principal cause of sunburn. You may not know that exposure to UV can also cause cancer, damage eyes, and decrease organisms' resistance to disease. Intense UV radiation can also damage tissue in plant leaves and even phytoplankton in the oceans. Thus, by shielding the biosphere from UV light, the ozone layer serves as a global sunscreen.

Beginning in the 1970s, scientists found evidence from satellite data and other measurements that the ozone layer was in trouble. The first problem sign was a gap or "hole" in the ozone layer over Antarctica during winter. Over the past 20 years, that hole has been growing larger and lasting longer, as shown in **Figure 6–19.** A similar ozone hole has also appeared over the Arctic. By 1995, that northern ozone hole had grown enough to expose parts of the United States to higher-than-normal levels of UV.

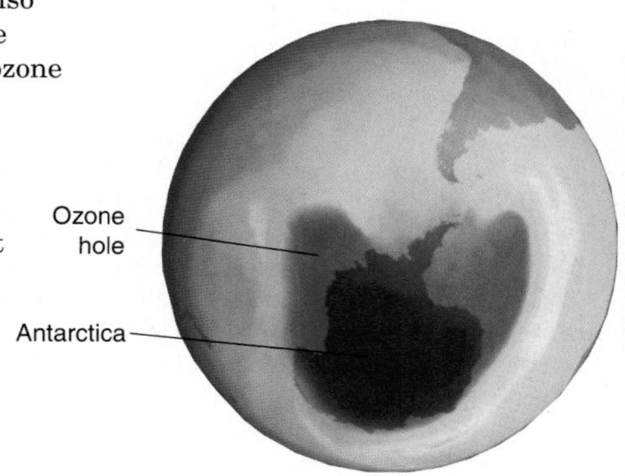

▼ **Figure 6–19** **Many biologists are concerned about the thinning, or depletion, of the ozone layer.** This image, taken by satellite in October 1999, shows the thinning of the ozone layer in the Southern Hemisphere. The image is color-coded, with yellow being the area with the highest concentration of ozone and blue the lowest. The ozone hole is the bright blue area surrounding Antarctica.

Section 6–4

1 FOCUS

Objective

6.4.1 ***Explain*** how human activities contribute to global changes.

Guide for Reading

Vocabulary Preview

Discuss with students the molecular structure of ozone (O_3) and make sure that they understand that its molecules are different from the diatomic oxygen molecules (O_2) in the atmosphere.

Review the greenhouse effect (Chapter 4). Ask: **What would happen to the temperature of the atmosphere if the proportion of greenhouse gases increased?** (*The atmosphere would become warmer—hence, the term* global warming.)

Reading Strategy

Students who are not fluent in written English would benefit from being paired with fluent readers who can help them identify main ideas and select relevant words and phrases.

2 INSTRUCT

Ozone Depletion

Making Connections

Earth Science Have students draw diagrams to scale that show the main layers of Earth's atmosphere, then shade the area occupied by the ozone layer. Ask: **Which layer contains most of the mass of the atmosphere?** *(The troposphere, which extends from 0 to 12 km above the surface)* **In which layer does the ozone layer occur?** *(The stratosphere, which extends from the top of the troposphere to about 50 km above the surface)*

TIME SAVER **SECTION RESOURCES**

Print:
- ***Laboratory Manual B,*** Chapter 6 Lab
- ***Teaching Resources,*** Section Review 6–4
- ***Guided Reading and Study Workbook,*** Section 6–4
- ***Issues and Decision Making,*** 6–4

Technology:
- ***iText,*** Section 6–4

Analyzing Data

Make sure students understand that the three differently colored branching lines represent the three different possibilities identified in the graph's key.

Answers

1. Companies continued to make—and people continued to use—aerosol spray cans containing CFCs.
2. If CFCs are not restricted, chlorine content will increase dramatically over the next 40 years. If countries follow the Montreal Protocol, chlorine content will rise more slowly but will eventually equal the "without restrictions" level. If CFCs are banned, chlorine content will decline, eventually falling to 1970 levels.

◀ **Figure 6–20** The ultraviolet light that causes sunburn is known to be a cause of skin cancer. The thinning of the ozone layer resulting from ozone depletion could lead to higher rates of this disease. **Using Analogies** *State an analogy that explains the similarity between sunblock and the ozone layer.*

We now know that this problem is caused by compounds called chlorofluorocarbons (klawr-oh-FLAWR-uh-kar-bunz), or CFCs. CFCs were once widely used as propellants in aerosol cans, in the production of plastic foams, and as coolants in refrigerators, freezers, and air conditioners. In the intense cold of the polar atmosphere, CFCs act as catalysts that enable UV light to break apart ozone molecules. The United States has joined many other nations in an international agreement to phase out the use of CFCs. Those already present in the atmosphere will linger for some time. Even in temperate latitudes, it is still important for people to protect themselves from overexposure to UV light, as shown in **Figure 6–20.**

CHECKPOINT *What is ozone depletion?*

Analyzing Data

Banning CFCs

A layer of ozone is normally present in Earth's upper atmosphere, or stratosphere. The ozone layer prevents much of the ultraviolet light emitted by the sun from reaching Earth's surface. In the 1970s, scientists discovered an ozone hole over the Southern Hemisphere, which was caused by the introduction of chlorofluorocarbons into the atmosphere.

In the lower atmosphere, CFCs are stable. However, when CFCs are carried into the stratosphere, UV rays bombard them and break them apart. This process causes a series of chemical reactions that break down the ozone molecules into ordinary oxygen, which offers no protection from UV light at all.

In 1987, environmental experts from around the world met to address the problem of Earth's changing ozone layer. Forty-six nations signed an agreement called the Montreal Protocol, which called for an immediate reduction in production and use of CFCs. The following year, the United States passed a law to phase out the use of CFCs in aerosol cans by 2000. The members of the Montreal Protocol met again in 1990 and agreed to end the use of all CFCs by the year 2000.

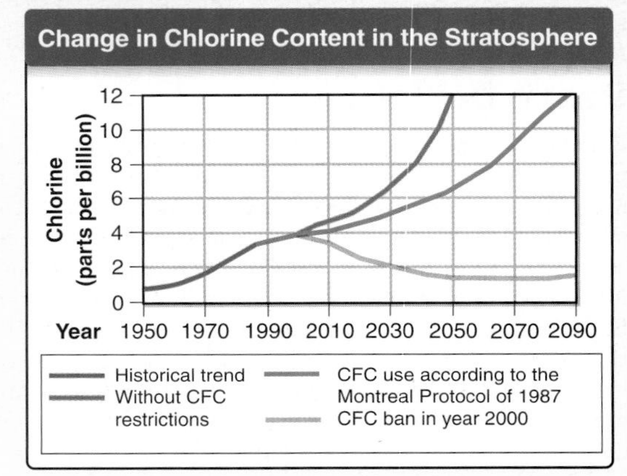

The graph shows the rise and predicted fall of the amount of chlorine from CFCs in Earth's stratosphere for three different scenarios of CFC use. Use the graph to answer the questions that follow.

1. **Inferring** In the years that immediately followed the signing of the Montreal Protocol, chlorine levels continued to rise. What might have caused the rise?
2. **Predicting** Explain the three different future scenarios shown on the graph.

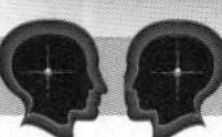

TEACHER TO TEACHER

I use the following activity to demonstrate the effects of ozone depletion. Ahead of time, I prepare a sufficient amount of yeast culture so each team can partially fill three or more petri dishes. The cultures can be started in large test tubes with baker's yeast in a sugar solution. I ask students to bring in sunscreen lotions of their choice, preferably several with different SPF ratings. Each team uses a microscope to get a rough population count of yeast in the starting culture. Students pour the culture into petri dishes and cover them. Then, they smear a different sunscreen on each cover. After exposing the dishes to direct sunlight or a sunlamp for a certain amount of time, students take a rough count of yeast in each dish and compare the counts with the starting counts.

Tamsen Meyer
Biology Teacher
Boulder High School,
Boulder, CO

Global Warming

Any change in Earth's climate can have a profound effect on the biosphere. That's why many ecologists and biologists are concerned about evidence of an increase in the temperature of Earth's atmosphere and oceans.

The term used to describe this increase in the average temperature of the biosphere is **global warming.** Over the past 120 years, global temperatures have risen 0.5 degrees Celsius. Scientists have evidence that temperatures between 1980 and 2000 rose at a faster rate than during the previous 100 years. The 1990s were the hottest decade ever recorded, and each year of that decade was among the hottest 15 years since record keeping began in 1880. Global warming has even affected Earth's ice caps, as shown in **Figure 6–21.**

What is the cause of global warming? The most widely accepted hypothesis is that human activities have caused global warming by adding carbon dioxide and other greenhouse gases such as methane to the atmosphere. As a result, the global atmospheric greenhouse is retaining more heat. Atmospheric concentrations of carbon dioxide have been rising for 200 years. During this period, the burning of fossil fuels, combined with the cutting down and burning of forests, has been adding carbon dioxide to the atmosphere faster than the carbon cycle can remove it.

Not everyone agrees about the causes of global warming. Some scientists think that the rise in global temperature may be part of natural variations in climate. Even scientists who do accept that global warming is a result of human activities admit that it is difficult to predict just how global temperatures will change in the future. The most recent computer models suggest that average global surface temperature will increase by about 1 to 2 degrees Celsius by the year 2050.

Scientists around the world are trying to model the possible effects of global warming on the biosphere. If global warming continues at current rates, the polar ice caps will continue to melt and sea levels could rise enough to flood some low-lying coastal areas. Storms and other weather disturbances could become more frequent and more severe. Several climate models also suggest that parts of North America may experience more serious droughts during the summer growing season.

All these changes in climate and weather are abiotic factors that affect ecosystems and the geographic distributions of species. Environmental change favors certain species of both plants and animals—such as weeds, insects, and rodents—that flourish in a wide range of conditions and reproduce and spread relatively quickly. At the same time, other species with very specific requirements for heat and moisture might be unable to survive. In addition, health scientists are concerned that warmer temperatures could increase the geographic distribution and abundance of some species that carry diseases, such as the mosquitoes that transmit malaria.

▼ **Figure 6–21** **Biologists are also concerned about global warming.** This map of the Arctic is based on images taken by satellites in 1979 and 1999. Sea ice in the Arctic Ocean has receded so quickly that some scientists suggest that, within the next 50 years, the ice could disappear completely.

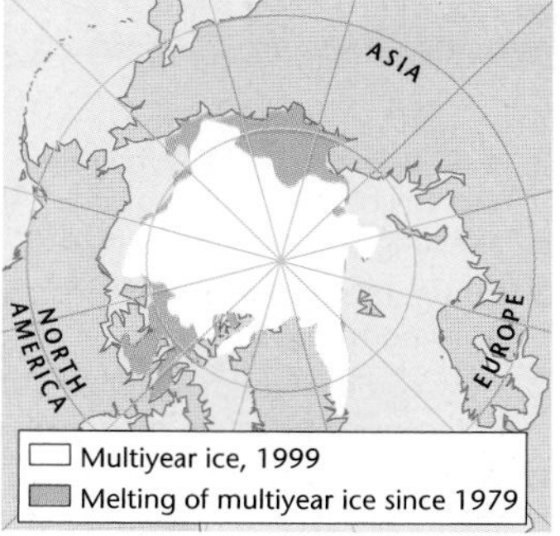

Global Warming

Use Visuals

Figure 6–21 Have students examine the map and read the caption. Then ask: **What do you think will happen if polar ice continues to melt?** *(Sea levels would rise, and oceans would flood low-lying land areas, including many coastal regions in the United States.)*

Address Misconceptions

Students may think that an average climate change of only a degree or two would have little impact. Many researchers agree that even slight global warming could cause storms to increase in strength and cause shifts in wind patterns that affect local temperatures and rainfall. Encourage students to find out about recent climatic events such as floods and droughts in the United States and elsewhere and the effects of those events on the human population.

PRESENTATIONS MADE EASY!

The Presentation Assistant Plus contains the Prentice Hall Presentation Pro and the Transparencies, which provide easy-to-follow visual support for every step of this section. If you have a computer presentation station, use Prentice Hall Presentation Pro for Section 6–4, or use the transparencies listed here.

Section 6–4: **Interest Grabber**
Section Outline
Sustainable Agriculture
Figure 6–21

Answers to . . .

CHECKPOINT *Thinning of the ozone layer resulting from release of chlorofluorocarbons into the atmosphere*

Figure 6–20 *Students' analogies should include the idea that the ozone layer acts as a sunblock to filter out harmful UV light.*

6–4 (continued)

The Value of a Healthy Biosphere

Build Science Skills

Problem Solving Tell students to imagine that they are conservation biologists, local developers, and town officials who are meeting to discuss the need to preserve natural areas in their community. Have students meet in small groups to outline the major points they would want to make. Let students role-play the meeting.

3 ASSESS

Evaluate Understanding

Have each student write two paragraphs: one explaining why it's important to stop releasing chlorofluorocarbons into the atmosphere, the other discussing the probable causes and possible long-term effects of global warming.

Reteach

Have small groups of students create an illustrated pamphlet designed to inform other students about one of the major topics in this section.

ALTERNATIVE ASSESSMENT

Students should have no difficulty finding sources that express different opinions about global warming and the ozone hole. Make sure students note that more data are needed before scientists can make firm predictions about climate change.

Use iText to review the key concepts in Section 6–4.

Answer to . . .

Figure 6–22 *Most students will probably classify the ecological services as renewable resources, although some may argue that certain services are not renewable unless they are managed wisely.*

Ecosystem Services
Solar energy
Production of oxygen
Storage and recycling of nutrients
Regulation of climate
Purification of water and air
Storage and distribution of fresh water
Food production
Nursery habitats for wildlife
Detoxification of human and industrial waste
Natural pest and disease control
Management of soil erosion and runoff

▲ **Figure 6–22** Human society depends on healthy, diverse, and productive ecosystems because of the environmental and economic benefits they provide. **Classifying** ***Should the ecosystem services in the chart be considered renewable or nonrenewable resources? Explain.***

The Value of a Healthy Biosphere

A healthy biosphere provides us with many valuable goods and services. The goods include the raw materials for foods, medicines, and many other products. The services include temperature control, water purification, soil formation, and other services listed in **Figure 6–22.**

Is there any way that people can help maintain the health of the biosphere without drastically changing their lifestyles? The answer is yes. People can make wise choices in the use of resources and in the disposal or recycling of materials. Energy conservation is probably the most important shift that a society can make. Most people, without seriously affecting their quality of life, could better insulate their homes and offices, purchase cars that are more fuel-efficient, and recycle. Collectively, the actions of individuals can make a difference in the health of the biosphere.

You will face a great challenge as you come of age in America in the twenty-first century. It will be your responsibility to help build a sustainable global economy—one that can improve the living conditions of people worldwide without harming the global environment. Understanding that humans are part of the ecosystems they inhabit is only the first step in charting that course for the future. Each of us affects the biosphere with everything we do, from driving a car or eating hamburgers to heating or air-conditioning our houses.

Studies examining the impact of our choices are not about predicting disaster. The biosphere is strong. Humans are clever. We have great ability to deal with change. But we do need to pay attention to what we are doing. The results of your choices in these matters will affect life on Earth for generations to come.

6–4 Section Assessment

1. **Key Concept** What are two major global changes affecting the biosphere today?
2. Why is the ozone layer important to living things?
3. How could a worldwide increase in temperature affect organisms?
4. What actions can people take in their daily lives to help preserve a healthy biosphere?
5. **Thinking Critically Predicting** Ultraviolet light is known to have a harmful effect on phytoplankton. Given this fact, how might depletion of the ozone layer affect an aquatic ecosystem?

iTEXT Assessment Use iText to review the important concepts in Section 6–4.

ALTERNATIVE ASSESSMENT

Comparing Media Locate five print, radio, television, or Internet sources about global warming or the ozone hole. What attitudes and opinions are expressed in these sources? Compare them with the information in this section.

6–4 Section Assessment

1. The thinning of the ozone layer and global warming
2. The ozone layer absorbs ultraviolet light from the sun that can harm organisms.
3. The effects of global warming include rising sea level, which could affect coastal ecosystems, and changes in climate that could affect the geographical distribution of species. Some species might be able to extend their ranges, while others might become extinct.
4. Recycling and energy conservation are two actions that people can take to help protect the health of the biosphere.
5. Phytoplankton are the producers that form the base of food webs in many aquatic ecosystems. If they were harmed by ultraviolet light, then all the other organisms in the food web would also be harmed.

Design an Experiment

Observing the Effects of Acid Rain

Acid rain is formed when the combustion of fossil fuels releases gases containing nitrogen and sulfur compounds into the atmosphere. It can damage crops, forests, soil, and buildings. In this investigation, you will design and perform an experiment to simulate and test the effect of acid rain on the germination of seeds.

Problem

How does acid rain affect the germination of seeds?

Materials

- diluted sulfuric acid
- filter paper
- glass-marking pencil
- 2 petri dishes
- 100-mL graduated cylinder
- 100 seeds (mustard or radish)
- pH paper
- 2 100-mL beakers
- hand lens

Skills

Designing Experiments, Controlling Variables

Design Your Experiment

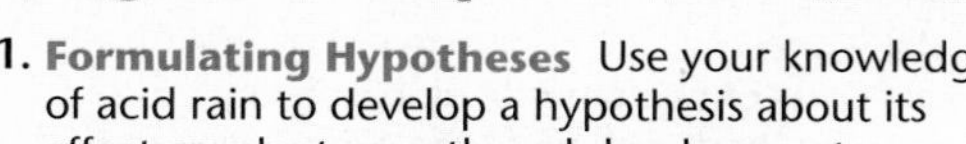

1. **Formulating Hypotheses** Use your knowledge of acid rain to develop a hypothesis about its effect on plant growth and development. Record your hypothesis.
2. **Predicting** Record a prediction about how acid rain will affect seed germination.
3. Design an experiment to test your prediction. It is not practical in the classroom to expose some plants to acid rain and others to nonacid rain. You will need to choose a way to simulate acid rain.
4. Check your experimental design to make sure you are testing only one variable and have included any necessary controls. Construct any data tables you will need to use for recording the results of your experiment. With your teacher's approval, carry out your experiment.

Analyze and Conclude

1. **Analyzing Data** What percentage of your control seeds germinated? What percentage of your acid-treated seeds germinated?
2. **Drawing Conclusions** What do your results imply about the short-term effects of acid rain?
3. **Predicting** Would you expect acid rain to injure plants after they have completed germination? Explain your answer.

Go Further

Problem Solving Conduct research and report to the class on the various methods used in industry to reduce the amounts of sulfur dioxide and nitrogen oxides being emitted into the atmosphere.

Analyze and Conclude

1. Actual counts and percentages will vary. Fewer acid-treated seeds will germinate than control seeds.
2. Acid rain inhibits seed germination.
3. Yes. If acid rain has a negative effect on seeds, it would probably injure young plants as well.

Design an Experiment

Objective Students will be able to determine how acid rain affects seed germination.

Skills Focus **Designing Experiments, Controlling Variables**

Time 45 minutes to design and set up experiment; 5 minutes each day for observation and recording

Advance Prep To prepare the diluted sulfuric acid, dilute 10 mL of 0.1 N H_2SO_4 in water to a total of 1 L. **CAUTION:** *Always add acid to water, never water to acid.* Check the pH. Add additional 0.1 N sulfuric acid to bring the pH down to 3 or 4.

Safety Wear goggles, lab apron, and plastic gloves when you prepare the diluted acid.

Pre-Lab Discussion Have students read the entire lab and ask any questions they may have about how they are to proceed. Review the difference between a testable hypothesis and a prediction.

Teaching Tips

- Have students work in groups of three or four.
- Circulate among the groups to check that they provide a safe and contained method of simulating acid rain, account for all variables that must be controlled, and plan data tables that will allow regular, detailed recording.

Expected Outcome The seeds exposed to acid rain will not germinate as well as those not exposed.

Go Further

Alert your school or town librarian to the topic of students' research so appropriate books can be set aside.

Chapter 6 Study Guide

Study Tip

Divide the class into four groups, and assign one section to each group. Tell students that each group will serve as the "class experts" on the assigned sections. Also, explain that they can divide the section's material among the group members in any way they wish. Encourage students to think of the kinds of questions other students might ask and to be prepared to answer them. Encourage groups to meet at least once to review their understanding of the sections.

Thinking Visually

1. Renewable
2. Nonrenewable

Chapter 6 Assessment

Reviewing Content

1. c	5. d	9. c
2. d	6. b	10. b
3. c	7. d	11. a
4. c	8. b	

Understanding Concepts

12. The greatest source of change in the biosphere is human activity.

13. The green revolution, which took place globally, introduced farming strategies such as high-yield varieties of major food crops, which greatly increased agricultural production.

14. Advantages of the Industrial Revolution were that it raised the standard of living for humans through such milestones as the invention of machines and the building of roads; disadvantages of industrialization include threats to the environment such as habitat loss, land erosion, and pollution.

15. By changing the balance of carbon and oxygen in the atmosphere, deforestation can hasten the greenhouse effect.

16. Examples of environmental pollutants include sewage dumped into streams, oil spills at sea, pesticides that enter the food chain, and acidic gases from burning fossil fuels.

17. Biodiversity is the sum total of the variety of organisms in the biosphere.

Chapter 6 Study Guide

6–1 A Changing Landscape

Key Concept

- Among the human activities that have transformed the biosphere are hunting and gathering, agriculture, industry, and urban development.

Vocabulary
- subsistence hunting, p. 140 • agriculture, p. 141
- green revolution, p. 142 • monoculture, p. 142

6–2 Renewable and Nonrenewable Resources

Key Concepts

- Regardless of whether they are held in common, environmental resources can be classified into two types: renewable and nonrenewable.
- Human activities affect the supply and the quality of renewable resources, including resources such as land, forests, ocean resources, air, and water.

Vocabulary
- renewable resource, p. 144
- nonrenewable resource, p. 144
- sustainable use, p. 145 • soil erosion, p. 145
- desertification, p. 145 • deforestation, p. 146
- aquaculture, p. 147 • smog, p. 148
- pollutant, p. 148 • acid rain, p. 148

6–3 Biodiversity

Key Concepts

- Biodiversity is one of Earth's greatest natural resources. Many species have provided us with foods, industrial products, and medicines—including painkillers, antibiotics, heart drugs, antidepressants, and anticancer drugs.
- Human activity can reduce biodiversity by altering habitats, hunting species to extinction, introducing toxic compounds into food webs, and introducing foreign species to new environments.
- Today, conservation efforts focus on protecting entire ecosystems as well as single species. Protecting an ecosystem will ensure that the natural habitats and interactions of many different species are preserved at the same time.

Vocabulary
- biodiversity, p. 150 • ecosystem diversity, p. 150
- species diversity, p. 150 • genetic diversity, p. 150
- extinction, p. 151 • endangered species, p. 151
- habitat fragmentation, p. 151
- biological magnification, p. 152
- invasive species, p. 153 • conservation, p. 154

6–4 Charting a Course for the Future

Key Concept

- Many biologists are concerned about the biological effects of two types of global change: the thinning, or depletion, of the ozone layer and global warming.

Vocabulary

ozone layer, p. 157

global warming, p. 159

Thinking Visually

Using information from this chapter, complete the following concept map:

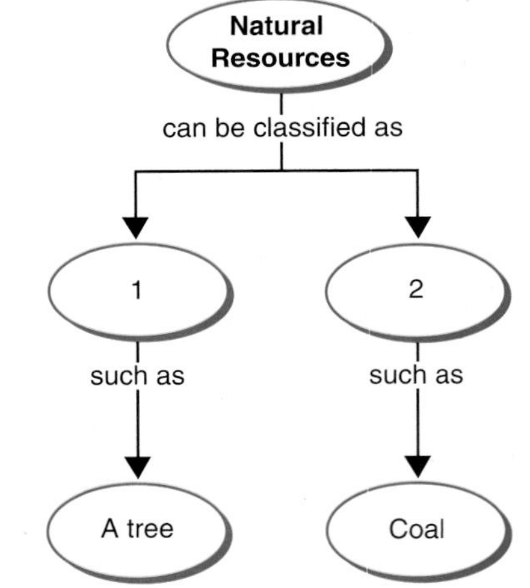

CHAPTER RESOURCES

Print:
- ***Teaching Resources,*** Chapter Vocabulary Review, Graphic Organizer
- ***Chapter Tests: Levels A and B,*** Chapter 6 Test
- ***PH Assessment Plus,*** Practice Test

Technology:
- ***Computer Test Bank,*** Chapter 6 Test
- ***iText,*** Chapter 6 Assessment

Chapter 6 Assessment

Reviewing Content

Choose the letter that best answers the question or completes the statement.

1. Modern hunter-gatherers are called
   a. farmers. c. subsistence hunters.
   b. herders. d. suburban sprawlers.
2. Which of the following human activities was NOT important in transforming the biosphere?
   a. agriculture
   b. industry
   c. urban development
   d. aquaculture
3. A resource that cannot be replenished by natural processes is called
   a. common. c. nonrenewable.
   b. renewable. d. conserved.
4. The conversion of a previously soil-rich area to a sandy desert is called
   a. habitat fragmentation.
   b. deforestation.
   c. desertification.
   d. acid rain.
5. The burning of fossil fuels may cause all of the following EXCEPT
   a. acid rain. c. smog.
   b. global warming. d. the ozone hole.
6. The sum total of the variety of organisms on Earth is referred to as
   a. ecosystem. c. forest.
   b. biodiversity. d. agriculture.
7. When land development divides a habitat into isolated "islands" of the original area, the result is called
   a. deforestation. c. bioaccumulation.
   b. reforestation. d. fragmentation.
8. A species that enters an environment where it has not lived before is called a(an)
   a. endangered species. c. threatened species.
   b. invasive species. d. predator.
9. A species whose population size is declining so rapidly that it could soon become extinct is said to be
   a. nonnative. c. endangered.
   b. fragmented. d. invasive.
10. The concept of using natural resources at a rate that does not deplete them is called
   a. conservation. c. reforestation.
   b. sustainable use. d. successful use.
11. Examine the food web below and determine which of the following organisms would accumulate the highest levels of a chlorinated pesticide.
   a. hawk c. frog
   b. rabbit d. grasses

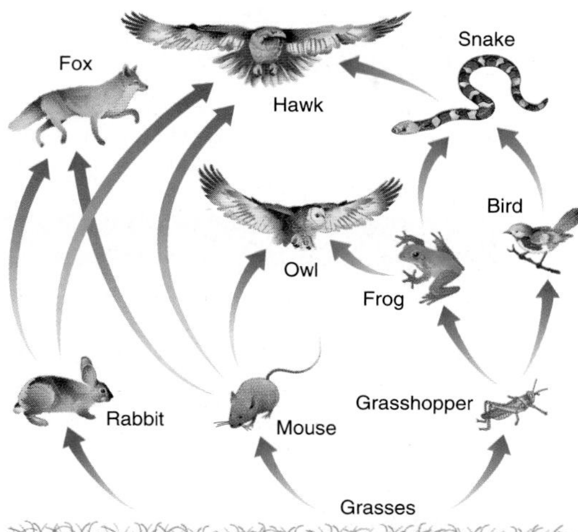

Understanding Concepts

12. What has been the greatest source of change in the biosphere?
13. What was the green revolution, and where did it occur?
14. What were the advantages and disadvantages of the Industrial Revolution?
15. How does deforestation contribute to the greenhouse effect?
16. List three examples of an environmental pollutant.
17. Define biodiversity.
18. Give an example of biological magnification. How does it occur?
19. Describe the process by which chlorofluorocarbons deplete the ozone layer.
20. Speaking ecologically, what is conservation? What is the role of conservation biology?
21. Name four natural services that ecosystems provide for the biosphere.

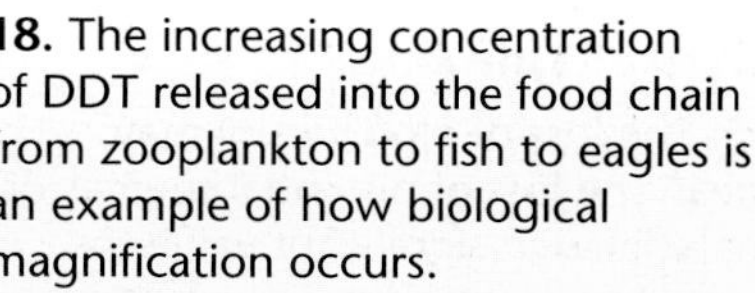

18. The increasing concentration of DDT released into the food chain from zooplankton to fish to eagles is an example of how biological magnification occurs.

19. CFCs are carried into the upper atmosphere, where UV rays break them apart. A series of chemical reactions follows, breaking down ozone into ordinary oxygen.

20. Conservation is the wise management of natural resources, including the preservation of habitats and wildlife.

21. Student may name any four of the services listed in the chart on page 160: conversion of solar energy to matter, production of oxygen, storage and recycling of nutrients, regulation of climate, and so on.

TIME SAVER

HOMEWORK GUIDE

Section:	Questions:
Section 6–1	1, 2, 12–14, 24, 27
Section 6–2	3–4, 10, 16, 26, 28, 30, 32, 33
Section 6–3	6–9, 11, 17, 18, 20, 22, 23, 29, 31, 34
Section 6–4	5, 15, 19, 21, 25

Critical Thinking

22. The loss of biodiversity may mean the loss of potential sources of material with significant value to humans. Students may suggest examples such as the loss of plants that can be used for medicines.

23. Species diversity refers to the number of species in the biosphere, and ecosystem diversity refers to the variety of different habitats, communities, and ecological processes that occur on Earth.

24. Suburban sprawl has resulted in habitat fragmentation and loss. Use of fossil fuels has caused air pollution and contributed to global warming.

25. a. The change in temperature, expressed in °C, is plotted on the *y*-axis. The unit 0.0 represents the global temperature in 1850. **b.** The world temperature change in 2000 was +0.7, or 7 degrees higher than in 1850. **c.** The data between 1970 and 2000 show an overall increase in temperature. **d.** The graph by itself does not predict the pattern of global warming in the future, because many different variables interact to produce temperature averages for a given year and can also modify climate trends in unpredictable ways.

26. Toxic chemicals in oil wastes that enter ground water or topsoil could have adverse effects on plant life or contaminate well water and be carried to streams, lakes, and oceans.

27. Students may hypothesize that because the cotton crop was made up of plants that were all the same in their inability to resist disease, the new disease was able to sweep through and destroy the cotton crop.

28. Students' experiments should compare erosion of soil that is protected in various ways with erosion of unprotected soil.

29. To determine the concentration at each trophic level, multiply by 10. Thus, Ist level=40 ppm; 2nd level=400 ppm; 3rd level=4,000 ppm; 4th level=40,000 ppm; 5th level=400,000 ppm.

Chapter 6 Assessment

Critical Thinking

22. Predicting How might the loss of biodiversity adversely affect humans?

23. Comparing and Contrasting Explain the difference between species diversity and ecosystem diversity.

24. Applying Concepts How has suburban sprawl and the increased use of fossil fuel created problems for the biosphere?

25. Using Tables and Graphs Study the graph below that shows the change in global temperature from 1850 to 2000. Use the graph to answer the questions.

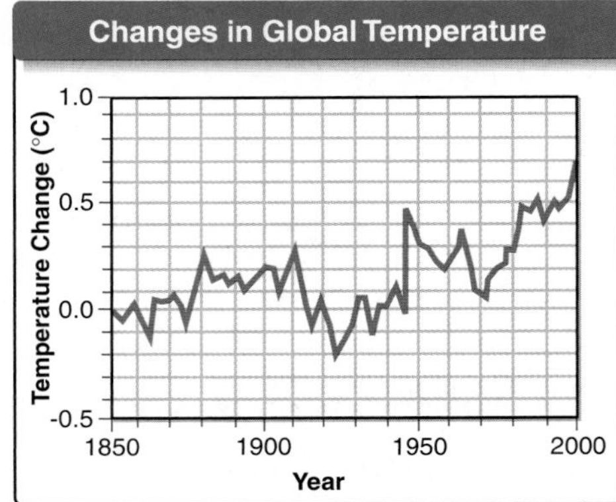

a. In your own words, explain what is plotted on the *y*-axis. What does the unit 0.0 represent?
b. How much did temperature change between 1850 and 2000?
c. Describe the trend in the data between 1970 and 2000.
d. Does this graph predict the pattern of global warming in the future? Why or why not?

26. Predicting What might happen if a container holding waste oil ruptured and the waste entered the ground water or topsoil?

27. Formulating Hypotheses A monoculture of cotton was planted in the 1980s in many southern states. A new disease invaded the cotton plants, almost completely destroying them. Explain how monoculture contributed to the effect of the disease.

28. Designing Experiments Can covering soil with mulch or compost near the bases of plants help to reduce soil erosion? Design an experiment to answer the question.

29. Calculating The concentration of a toxic chemical is magnified 10 times at each trophic level. What will be its concentration in organisms at the fifth trophic level if producers store the substance at concentrations of 40 parts per million?

30. Making Judgments Water is often referred to as Earth's most important natural resource. Do you agree? Why or why not?

31. Predicting What effect might destroying the eucalyptus trees in Australia have on the koalas that live there and eat only eucalyptus leaves?

32. Inferring Lakes that are affected by acid rain often appear clear and blue. Why might this be so?

33. Formulating Hypotheses Different grades of coal contain different amounts of sulfur. Explain why burning low-sulfur coal can reduce acid rain.

34. Making Connections What environmental factors make high levels of biodiversity possible in most coastal waters? Refer to the discussion of abiotic and biotic factors in Chapter 4 if you need help answering this question.

Performance-Based Assessment

Designing an Educational Pamphlet The State Department of Education has decided that all students in grade five will complete an extensive unit on "Humans in the Biosphere." You have been asked to design a pamphlet to distribute to the fifth-graders' parents that explains the importance of this curriculum decision and outlines the contents of the unit. The pamphlet must be scientifically accurate and contain illustrations. Create a thumbnail sketch of your pamphlet, including an outline of topics and images.

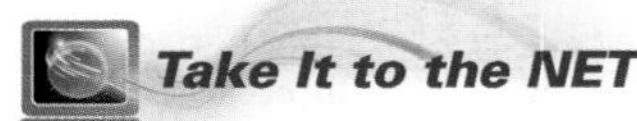

What kinds of organisms are invading your region? Visit the Prentice Hall Web site at **www.phschool.com** to find out about invasive species in the United States. Then, answer the following questions:

- How much do invasive species cost taxpayers each year?
- What is the main way that invasive species are transported and introduced to nonnative areas?
- Choose three invasive species and describe the nature of the problems they are causing today.

Performance-Based Assessment

Student pamphlets should include highlights of the key concepts of the chapter: the effect of humans on the biosphere, renewable and nonrenewable resources, biodiversity, and sustainable use.

Standardized Test Prep

Test-Taking Tip When evaluating multiple-choice answers, be sure to read all of the answer choices, even if the first choice seems to be the correct one. By doing so, you can make sure that the answer you chose is the best one.

Directions: Choose the letter that best answers the question or completes the statement.

1. What is always true of a renewable resource?
   I. It is unlimited.
   II. It is replaceable by natural means.
   III. It can regenerate quickly.
   (A) I only
   (B) II only
   (C) I and III only
   (D) II and III only
   (E) I, II, and III
2. Which of the following is NOT a renewable resource?
   (A) wind
   (B) sunlight
   (C) water
   (D) fossil fuels
   (E) trees
3. Which of the following is NOT an effect of deforestation?
   (A) global warming
   (B) decreased productivity of the ecosystem
   (C) soil erosion
   (D) increased ground-water levels
   (E) mudslides
4. The sum total of the variety of organisms in the biosphere is called
   (A) biodiversity.
   (B) species diversity.
   (C) ecosystem diversity.
   (D) genetic diversity.
   (E) bioaccumulation.
5. Which is NOT a characteristic of the sustainable use of natural resources?
   (A) instability
   (B) flexibility
   (C) appropriate technology
   (D) efficiency
   (E) productivity
6. Ozone is made up of
   (A) water.
   (B) hydrogen.
   (C) nitrogen.
   (D) oxygen.
   (E) chlorine.

Questions 7–8 Complete each analogy by selecting the correct letter. In analogies, A : B :: C : ___?___ *means* A *is to* B *as* C *is to* ___?___.

7. Ozone depletion : CFCs :: deforestation : ___?___
   (A) ozone
   (B) suburban sprawl
   (C) aquaculture
   (D) soil erosion
   (E) pollution
8. Endangered species : extinction :: soil erosion : ___?___
   (A) mudslides
   (B) fertilizers
   (C) monoculture
   (D) desertification
   (E) acid rain

Questions 9–10 Use the information below to answer the questions that follow.

Fire ants first arrived in the United States in 1918, probably on a ship traveling from South America to Alabama. The maps show the geographic location of the U.S. fire ant population in 1953 and 1994.

1953

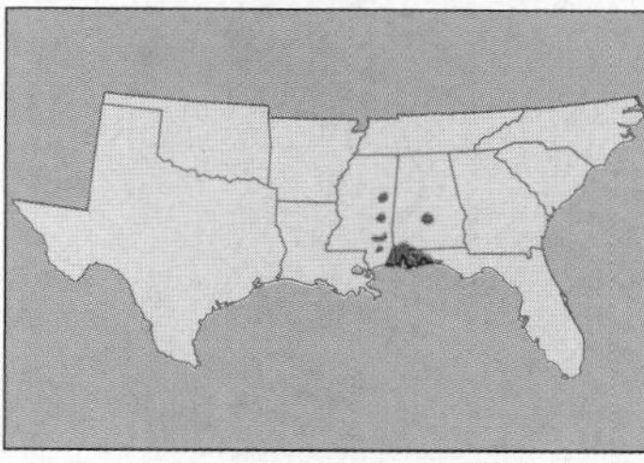

1994

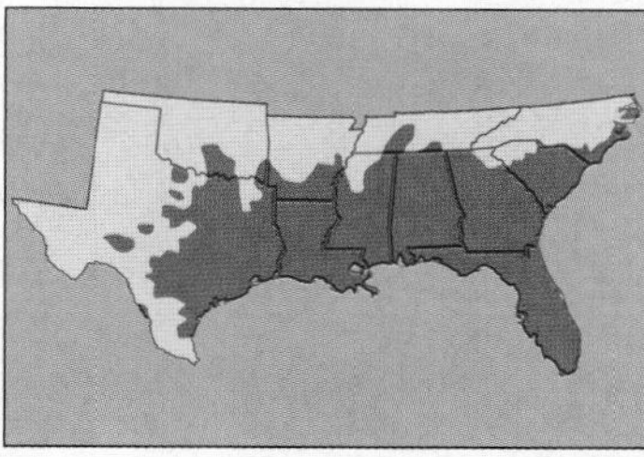

9. Based on the maps, what can you conclude about fire ants in the United States?
   (A) They reproduce slowly.
   (B) They are a native species of the United States.
   (C) They are an invasive species.
   (D) Their numbers are declining.
   (E) They do not compete with other ant species.
10. By 2010, fire ants are likely to
    (A) occupy Florida only.
    (B) have reached their carrying capacity.
    (C) die out.
    (D) return to South America.
    (E) have spread to a larger area.

Standardized Test Prep

1. D
2. D
3. D
4. A
5. A
6. D
7. B
8. D
9. C
10. E

30. Students may agree because water is essential to all life, including those forms of life that humans depend on for their food and other needs. Organisms are made up of at least 50% to 90% water; all biochemical reactions occur in a watery environment; photosynthesis requires water; and without water, recycling of nutrients would be impossible.

31. Destroying the eucalyptus trees might cause the extinction of koalas, for whom eucalyptus leaves are the main source of food.

32. Acid rain might change the water chemistry of the lake, destroying life forms such as algae that can make lake water look cloudy.

33. Sulfur dioxide, which forms when sulfur-containing coal is burned, helps produce sulfuric acid, a component of acid rain. Low-sulfur coal produces less of the dioxide than high-sulfur coal, and thus less sulfuric acid and less acid rain.

34. The productivity of an ecosystem in which organisms live, and hence the potential variety of species (i.e. the level of biodiversity), depends on the ecosystem's abiotic and biotic factors. Most coastal waters are in the photic zone. As a result, they receive plenty of solar energy for the producers that support the food chain. In addition, runoff from rivers and streams may bring nutrients to coastal waters that also increase the productivity of coastal ecosystems. Finally, estuaries, the intertidal zone, and the coastal ocean provide varied habitats that encourage biodiversity.

Take It to the NET

- The total annual cost of invasive species in the United States have been estimated to be nearly $125 billion.
- Humans deliberately and accidentally disperse invasive species to nonnative areas.
- Students can find information on an entire index of invasive species at www.invasivespecies.gov Web site. Students can profile any of the following or other species featured on the Web site: Asian longhorn beetle, zebra mussel, fire ants, purple loosestrife, Brazilian waterweed, and kudzu. For additional information, visit

www.phschool.com

Unit 3

Dear Colleague,

I can still remember the first time I looked through a microscope and saw a living cell. It was in Mr. Zong's ninth grade biology class in my home town in New Jersey. After carefully instructing us in the proper use of the microscope, our teacher placed a drop of water on every student's slide and told us to have a look.

I couldn't believe my eyes. Glistening creatures swam across the field of view. They twisted and turned, I thought, almost as if they were alive. I think I said that out loud, because I can remember Mr. Zong's deep, gentle laugh and a pat on my shoulder. "They *are* alive, Kenny! They're alive just like you and me."

Mr. Zong was famous among my classmates at Rahway High for his devotion to the "practicum" style of exam. Every other Friday, we walked into the classroom to be confronted by 30 "stations," one at the desk of every student. Each station had a specimen—a leaf, a butterfly, a seed, or a drop of water under a microscope. Taped to each desk was a question about that specimen.

We had 90 seconds to look at the specimen, read the question, and write down an answer. Then, we each moved on to the next station. No timeouts, no chances to go back. Forty-five minutes went by like a flash.

At first, I feared these semiweekly exams. After a while, however, I grew to love the challenge. In a way, I suppose, we sensed the passion in our teacher's insistence that the mysterious world of nature held stories—great stories. We students, he thought, could be expected to read, to learn, and then to tell those stories from the material of life itself.

UNIT 3 Cells

Chapters

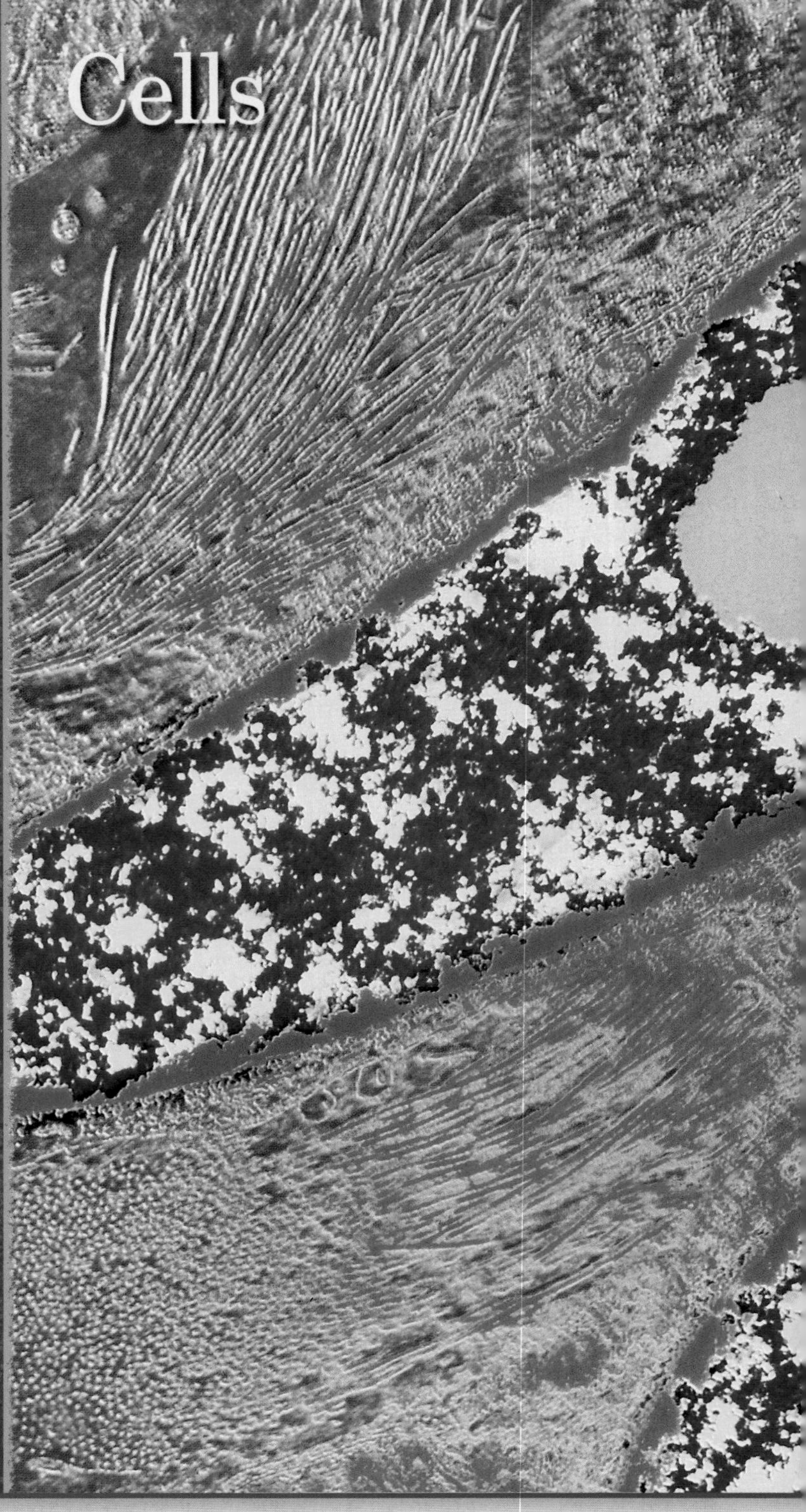

▶ This color-enhanced photograph shows two long cell nuclei (colored blue and yellow) from a human sarcoma, or cancer of the connective tissue. Cancer occurs when cells multiply uncontrollably and destroy healthy tissue. The round, orange structure near the middle of each nucleus is the nucleolus, or little nucleus.

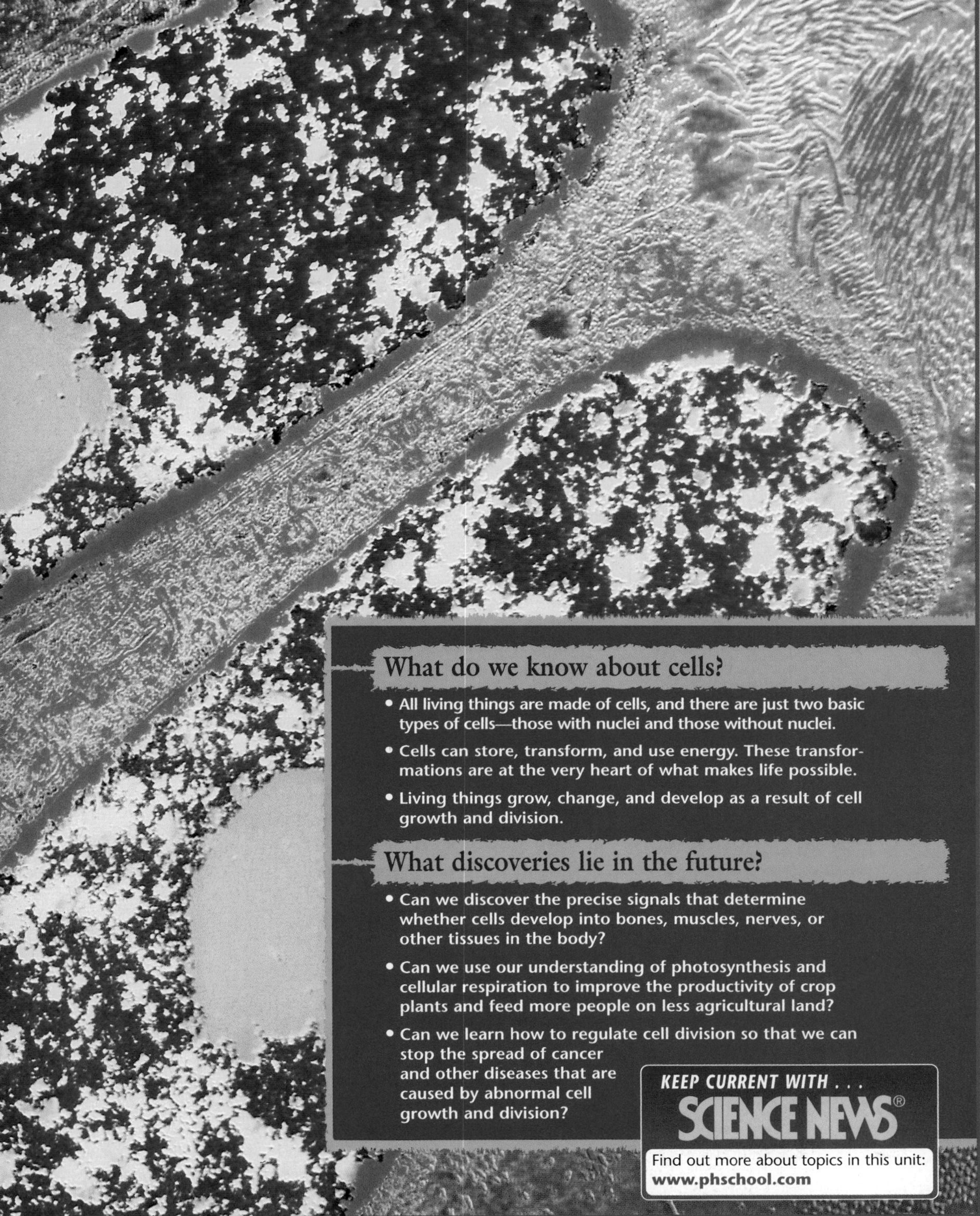

What do we know about cells?

- All living things are made of cells, and there are just two basic types of cells—those with nuclei and those without nuclei.
- Cells can store, transform, and use energy. These transformations are at the very heart of what makes life possible.
- Living things grow, change, and develop as a result of cell growth and division.

What discoveries lie in the future?

- Can we discover the precise signals that determine whether cells develop into bones, muscles, nerves, or other tissues in the body?
- Can we use our understanding of photosynthesis and cellular respiration to improve the productivity of crop plants and feed more people on less agricultural land?
- Can we learn how to regulate cell division so that we can stop the spread of cancer and other diseases that are caused by abnormal cell growth and division?

KEEP CURRENT WITH . . .
SCIENCE NEWS®
Find out more about topics in this unit:
www.phschool.com

As fall turned toward winter, I remember my parents' surprise when I told them what I hoped to find under our Christmas tree that year—a microscope.

Only a few weeks later, I had transformed a tiny corner of the room I shared with my brother into a miniature laboratory. A tiny desk lamp glowed day and night, providing energy for nearly a dozen test-tube colonies of *Euglena*. At the end of the year, those cells would become a science project, the very first research I would ever do on my own.

I won second place that year in our school's science fair for my study of light's effect on the growth of *Euglena*. Although I have long since misplaced the ribbon my project was given, I hope I never lose the greater gift that came from a year of study in Paul Zong's classroom—a sense of amazement that returns every time I sit down at a microscope in my laboratory.

I hope that you and your students will find some of that amazement written into the pages of this unit. As a cell biologist, I especially hope to give students an appreciation of the roles that cells play in every aspect of life. In these four chapters, we have done our best to explain how cells live and grow, how they transform energy, and how they pass information along from one generation to the next.

I have been lucky enough to make biology my career, using the electron microscope as my primary research tool. Not all of your students can expect to do this, of course. But we can hope that with your guidance, each and every one of them will experience the same thrill I did when they focus their microscopes on living cells for the very first time.

Sincerely,

Ken Miller

SCIENCE NEWS®
Have students visit the Prentice Hall Web site at
www.phschool.com
to find the most current information on cells.

Chapter 7 Planner — Cell Structure and Function

Section and Section Objectives	Time	Activities and Labs
7–1 Life Is Cellular, pp. 169–172 **7.1.1** ***Explain*** what the cell theory is. **7.1.2** ***Name*** the basic cell structures. **7.1.3** ***Describe*** prokaryotes and eukaryotes.	**1 period (1/2 block)**	**SE: *Inquiry Activity,*** What is a cell?, p. 168 **SE: *Biology and History,*** A History of the Cell, pp. 170–171
7–2 Cell Structures, pp. 173–183 **7.2.1** ***Describe*** the main function of the cell wall. **7.2.2** ***Describe*** the function of the cell nucleus. **7.2.3** ***Identify*** the main roles of the cytoskeleton. **7.2.4** ***Describe*** the functions of the major cell organelles.	**3 periods (1 1/2 blocks)**	**TE: *Build Science Skills,*** p. 174 **TE: *Build Science Skills,*** p. 178 **SE: *Quick Lab,*** How can you make a model of a cell?, p. 179
7–3 Movement Through the Membrane, pp. 184–189 **7.3.1** ***Identify*** the main functions of the cell membrane. **7.3.2** ***Describe*** what happens during diffusion. **7.3.3** ***Explain*** the processes of osmosis, facilitated diffusion, and active transport.	**2 periods (1 block)**	**TE: *Build Science Skills,*** pp. 186, 189 **TE: *Demonstration,*** p. 187 **SE: *Analyzing Data,*** Crossing the Cell Membrane, p. 188 ***SE: Real-World Lab,*** Observing Cell Parts and Processes, pp. 194–195
7–4 The Diversity of Cellular Life, pp. 190–193 **7.4.1** ***Describe*** cell specialization. **7.4.2** ***Identify*** the organization levels in multicellular organisms.	**1 period (1/2 block)**	**SE: *Careers in Biology,*** Histotechnologist, p. 192 **TE: *Build Science Skills,*** p. 192
Chapter Assessment, pp. 196–199	**1 period (1/2 block)**	

ACTIVITY PLANNER

SE: *Inquiry Activity,* p. 168; (15 min.); microscopes, prepared slides of plant leaf or stem cross-section, nerve cell, bacteria, and paramecia

TE: *Build Science Skills,* p. 174; (15 min.); prepared slides of animal cell and plant cell, microscope

TE: *Build Science Skills,* p. 178; (20 min.); paramecium culture, yeast, Congo red, slide, coverslip, toothpick, microscope, dropper pipette

SE: Quick Lab, p. 179; (20 min.); variety of craft supplies, index cards

TE: *Build Science Skills,* p. 186; (20 min.); cornstarch, plastic sandwich bag, tie, 2 beakers, iodine, dropper pipette

TE: *Demonstration,* p. 187; (15 min.); paramecium culture, petri dish, microprojector, distilled water

TE: *Build Science Skills,* p. 189; (5 min.); board, books, tennis ball

SE: *Real-World Lab,* pp. 194–195; (90 min.); safety goggles, lab apron, forceps, red onion, scalpel, 4 glass slides, dropper pipette, 4 coverslips, iodine solution, paper towel, microscope, prepared slide of human cheek cells, concentrated salt solution, distilled water, animal blood, plastic gloves

TE: *Build Science Skills,* p. 192; (10 min.); photographs, diagrams, or prepared slides of specialized cells

PLANNING KEY

Ability Levels

B **Basic**	For students who need additional help
A **Average**	For all students
E **Enriched**	For students who need to be challenged

Components

SE	Student Edition	**GRSW**	Guided Reading and Study Workbook	**IDM**	Issues and Decision Making
TE	Teacher's Edition	**CT**	Chapter Tests: Levels A and B	**CTB**	Computer Test Bank
LMA	Laboratory Manual A	**PHAS**	PH Assessment System	**PA**	Presentation Assistant Plus
LMB	Laboratory Manual B	**LA**	Lab Assessment With Scoring Guide	**BD**	BioDetectives Videotape
TR	Teaching Resources	**BTM**	BioTechnology Manual	**iT**	iText
IF	Investigations in Forensics				

Program Resources	Assessment	Media and Technology
TR: Section Review 7–1 B A **GRSW:** Section 7–1 B A	**SE:** 7–1 Section Assessment, p. 172 **TR:** Section Review 7–1	**PA:** 7–1 Interest Grabber, Section Outline, Prokaryotic and Eukaryotic Cells **iT:** Section 7–1
TR: Section Review 7–2 B A **GRSW:** Section 7–2 B A	**SE:** 7–2 Section Assessment, p. 183 **TR:** Section Review 7–2	**PA:** 7–2 Interest Grabber, Section Outline, Venn Diagram Figure 7–5, Figure 7–7 **iT:** Section 7–2
LMA: Chapter 7 Lab A E **TR:** Section Review 7–3 B A **GRSW:** Section 7–3 B A	**SE:** 7–3 Section Assessment, p. 189 **TR:** Section Review 7–3	**PA:** 7–3 Interest Grabber, Section Outline, Facilitated Diffusion, Figure 7–15, Figure 7–17, Figure 7–20 **iT:** Section 7–3
LMB: Chapter 7 Lab B A **TR:** Section Review 7–4 B A Chapter 7 Real-World Lab B A E **GRSW:** Section 7–4 B A	**SE:** 7–4 Section Assessment, p. 193 **TR:** Section Review 7–4	**PA:** 7–4 Interest Grabber, Section Outline, Levels of Organization **iT:** Section 7–4
	SE: Chapter 7 Assessment, pp. 196–198 **TR:** Chapter Vocabulary Review, Graphic Organizer **CT:** Chapter 7 Test **CTB:** Chapter 7 Test **PHAS:** Practice Test	**CTB:** Chapter 7 Test **iT:** Chapter 7 Assessment

TIME SAVER — PRESSED FOR TIME?

To Preview the Chapter
- Introduce students to Key Concepts and Vocabulary terms in each section.
- Assign the Reading Strategies for each section.

To Cover the Chapter Quickly
- Have students read all of Section 7–1; Figure 7–5 and the subsections Nucleus and The Cell as a Factory in Section 7–2; Figures 7–15, 7–16, 7–17, 7–19, and 7–20 in Section 7–3; and all of Section 7–4.
- Assign Section Reviews for 7–1 through 7–4, as well as questions 1–10 in Chapter 7 Assessment and questions 1–11 in Chapter 7 Standardized Test Prep.

To Review the Chapter
- Assign Sections 7–1 through 7–4 in the Guided Reading and Study Workbook.
- Assign Section Reviews for 7–1 through 7–4 and the Chapter Vocabulary Review for Chapter 7 in the Teaching Resources.

ENGAGE/EXPLORE

Inquiry Activity

Objectives Students will be able to
- form an operational definition of the term *cell*
- classify the cells they observe into two or more groups

Skills Focus **Forming Operational Definitions, Classifying**

Materials microscope, prepared slides of plant leaf or stem cross-section, nerve cell, bacteria, and paramecia

Time 15 minutes

Advance Prep If slides of some types of cells are unavailable, substitute slides of other types of cells or use photographs of different cell types. You may want to have students prepare fresh-mount slides of plant sections and microorganisms.

Strategy Set up the slides on microscopes around the room, and have students rotate through the stations to look at each slide.

Expected Outcomes Students should recognize that there are differences in structure and complexity among cells.

Think About It

1. Students should write a concise definition of *cell.* Sample definition: A cell is a structure within a living thing that has a definite boundary enclosing the material inside.

2. Typically, students might classify cells into plant cells and other cells, or into cells with and without nuclei.

Assess Prior Knowledge

Display a three-dimensional model of a cell, or use an overhead projector to display an enlarged photo of a eukaryotic cell. Then, challenge students to name any structures they think they recognize in the cell. Encourage debate about the names and the functions of various structures in the cell. Ask students: **Is this an animal cell or a plant cell?** *(Answers will depend on the displayed cell. Accept any reasonable explanation of why they classify it one way or another.)*

Chapter 7 Cell Structure and Function

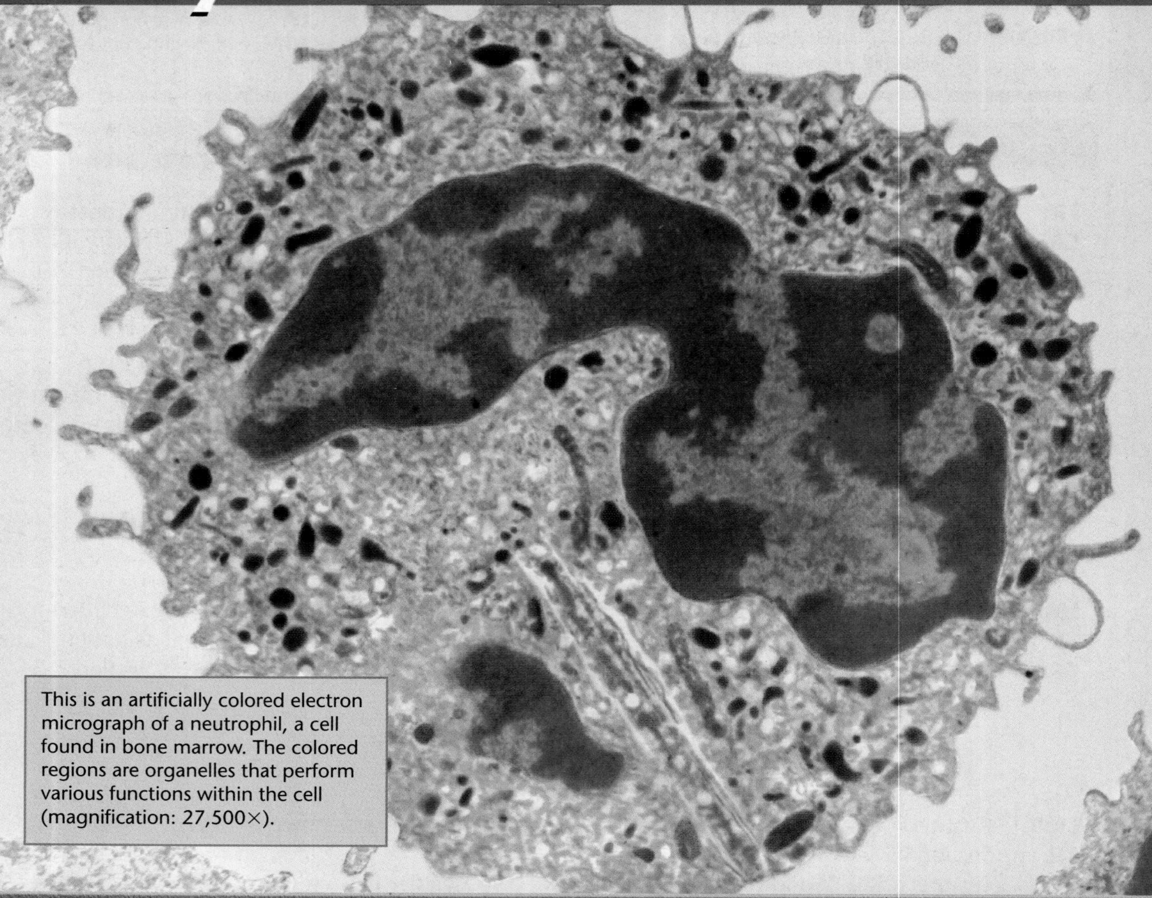

This is an artificially colored electron micrograph of a neutrophil, a cell found in bone marrow. The colored regions are organelles that perform various functions within the cell (magnification: 27,500×).

Inquiry Activity

What is a cell?

Procedure

1. Look through a microscope at a slide of a plant leaf or stem cross section. **CAUTION:** *Handle the microscope and slide carefully to avoid breaking them.* Sketch one or more cells. Record a description of their features, such as shape and internal parts.
2. Repeat step 1 with slides of nerve cells, bacteria, and paramecia.
3. Make a list of characteristics that all of the cells have in common. List some differences among the cells.

Think About It

1. **Forming Operational Definitions** Use your observations to write a definition of "cell."
2. **Classifying** Classify the cells you observed into two or more groups. Explain what characteristics you used to put each cell in a particular group.

HISTORY OF SCIENCE

Whatever happened to protoplasm?
At one time, practically everyone was taught that the fluid material of the cell was something called protoplasm, a colloid whose wonderful properties accounted for many of the unique abilities of the cell. The term actually means "first fluid," and it reflects the idea that the composition of a living cell is something so extraordinary that the common laws of chemistry cannot explain it. This is an idea whose time has passed. As biologists began to explore the composition of the cell with modern tools, it became increasingly clear that the properties of the cell could be explained in other ways. Instead of protoplasm, we now speak of cytoplasm, or "cell fluid," a term that encompasses all the complexity of the contents of the cell outside of the nucleus.

7–1 Life Is Cellular

Look closely at a part of a living thing, and what do you see? Hold a blade of grass up against the light, and you see tiny lines running the length of the blade. Examine the tip of your finger, and you see the ridges and valleys that make up fingerprints. Place an insect under a powerful dissecting microscope, and you see the intricate structures of its wings and the spikes and bristles that protect its body. As interesting as these close-up views may be, however, they're only the beginning of the story. Look closely at **Figure 7–1,** and you'll see that there is a common structure that makes up every living thing—the cell.

Guide for Reading

 **Key Concepts**

- What is the cell theory?
- What are the characteristics of prokaryotes and eukaryotes?

Vocabulary
cell
cell theory
cell membrane
cell wall
nucleus
cytoplasm
prokaryote
eukaryote
organelle

Reading Strategy: Finding Main Ideas
As you read, look for evidence to support the statement "The cell theory revolutionized how biologists thought about living things."

The Cell Theory

The first lenses were used in Europe in the late 1500s by merchants who needed to determine the quality of cloth. They used their magnifying lenses to examine the quality of the thread and the precision of the weave in a bolt of cloth. From these simple glass lenses, combinations of lenses were put together. In Holland in the early 1600s, two useful instruments were constructed: the telescope and the microscope. In the 1600s, Dutch businessman Anton van Leeuwenhoek (LAY-vuhn-hook) became one of the first people to use a microscope to study nature. Using only a single powerful lens, van Leeuwenhoek crafted instruments that could produce magnified images of very small objects. His simple microscope enabled him to see things that no one had ever seen before. He was the first person, for example, to see tiny living organisms in a drop of water. Van Leeuwenhoek carefully observed the living things in pond water and made detailed drawings of each kind of organism.

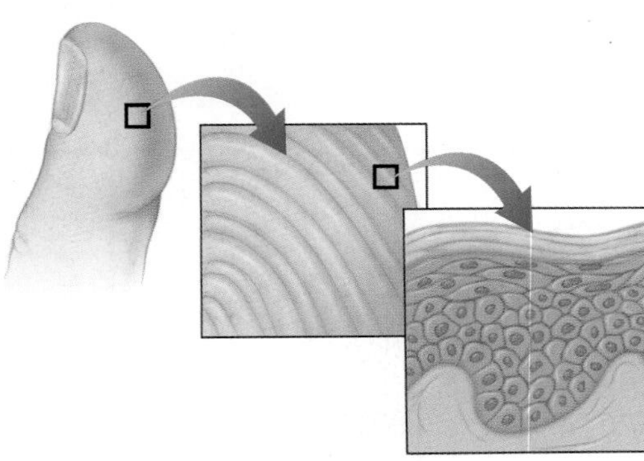

◀ **Figure 7–1** Like all living things, you are made up of cells. This illustration shows that even a portion of your thumb contains cells. **Using Analogies** *How is a cell in an organism similar to a brick in a building? How is it different?*

SECTION RESOURCES

Print:

- ***Teaching Resources,*** Section Review 7–1
- ***Guided Reading and Study Workbook,*** Section 7–1

Technology:

- ***iText,*** Section 7–1

Section 7–1

1 FOCUS

Objectives

7.1.1 ***Explain*** what the cell theory is.
7.1.2 ***Name*** the basic cell structures.
7.1.3 ***Describe*** prokaryotes and eukaryotes.

Guide for Reading

Vocabulary Preview

Have students write the Vocabulary terms, dividing each into its separate syllables as best they can. Remind students that each syllable usually has only one vowel sound. The correct syllabications are: cell the•o•ry, cell mem•brane, cell wall, nu•cle•us, cy•to•plasm, pro•kar•y•ote, eu•kar•y•ote, or•gan•elle

Reading Strategy

Ask students to make an outline of the section, using the blue heads as their first level of the outline.

2 INSTRUCT

The Cell Theory

Build Science Skills

Posing Questions Divide the class into small groups, and give each group a variety of drawings and photos of cells taken from numerous sources, such as college textbooks and Internet sites. These cells should include both unicellular organisms and cells from plants and animals. Have each group make drawings of the various cells, labeling any structure they recognize. Then, ask each group to brainstorm a list of questions about these cells that they expect will be answered as they read the chapter.

Answers to . . .

Figure 7–1 *An organism is formed by the cells that compose it, just as a building is formed by the bricks that compose it.*

Biology and History

Discuss the contributions of each of the scientists leading up to the formulation of the cell theory. Be sure that students understand the importance of the individual accomplishments. It is also important that students understand the time span involved. Ask: **How did each observation influence the next scientist's work?** *(Answers will vary, but generally one clearly influenced the next. The microscope was essential to the discovery of the cell. Both van Leeuwenhoek and Hooke used early microscopes to observe cells and unicellular organisms. Schwann elaborated Schleiden's findings, and so on.)*

Writing Activity

Help students find appropriate books and Web sites as they investigate new discoveries about cells. Explain that the branch of biology that focuses on cells and their structures is called cytology, and the branch that is concerned with one-celled organisms is called microbiology. Encourage students to find out what scientist discovered each of the organelles they learn about in Section 7–2 and when the discovery was made.

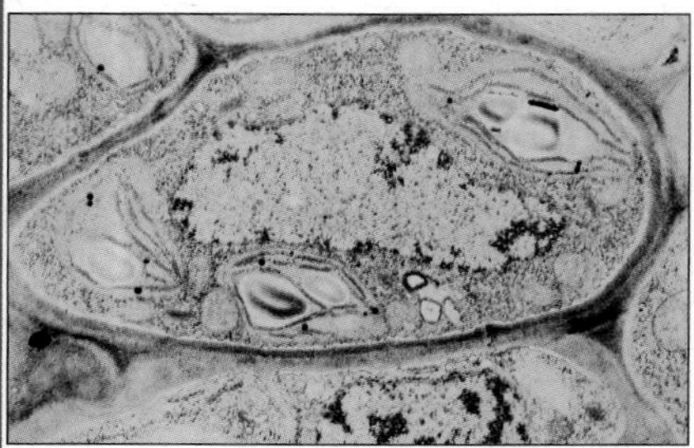

(magnification: 12,000×)

▲ **Figure 7–2** **The cell theory states that cells are the basic units of all living things.** This cell is from a plant leaf.

In 1665, English physicist Robert Hooke used one of the first light microscopes to look at thin slices of plant tissues. One of these, a slice of cork, especially caught his eye. Under the microscope, cork seemed to be made of thousands of tiny chambers. Hooke called these chambers "cells," because they reminded him of a monastery's tiny rooms, which were also known as cells. The term *cell* is used to this day. Hooke's discovery stimulated other scientists to search for cells in other living things. Before long, it became apparent that **cells** were the basic units of all forms of life. **Figure 7–2** shows a typical plant cell.

In 1838, German botanist Matthias Schleiden (SHLY-dun) concluded that all plants are made of cells. The next year, another German scientist, Theodor Schwann, concluded that animals are also made of cells. Rudolf Virchow (FUR-koh), a German physician, studied cell reproduction. In 1855, he summarized years of research by stating, "Where a cell exists, there must have been a preexisting cell. . . ."

The discoveries of these and other biologists are summarized in the **cell theory,** one of the fundamental concepts of biology. **The cell theory states the following:**

- **All living things are composed of cells.**
- **Cells are the basic units of structure and function in living things.**
- **New cells are produced from existing cells.**

Biology and History

A History of the Cell

The observations and conclusions of many scientists helped to develop the current understanding of the cell.

1600

1607
English settlers found colony at Jamestown, Virginia

1665
Robert Hooke
Hooke publishes his book *Micrographia,* which contains his drawings of sections of cork as seen through one of the first microscopes.

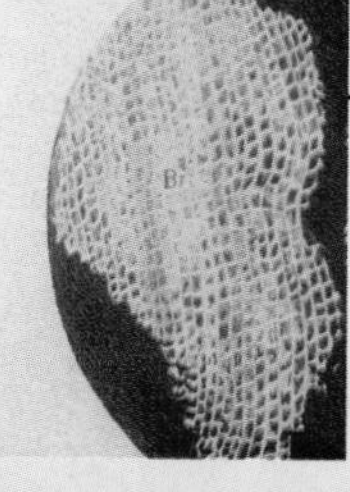

1674
Anton van Leeuwenhoek
Leeuwenhoek observes tiny living organisms in drops of pond water through his simple microscope.

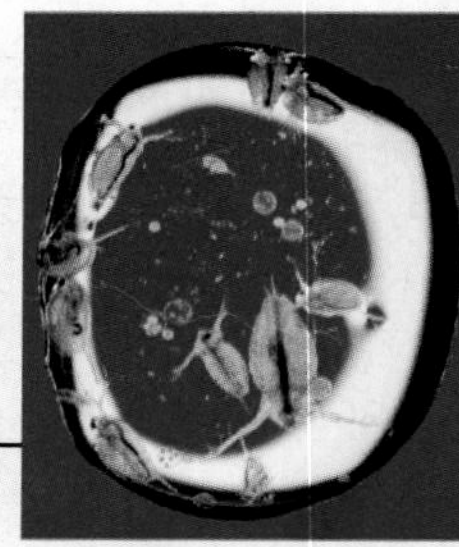

1700

PRESENTATIONS MADE EASY!

The Presentation Assistant Plus contains the Prentice Hall Presentation Pro and the Transparencies, which provide easy-to-follow visual support for every step of this lesson. If you have a computer presentation station, use Prentice Hall Presentation Pro Section 7–1, or use the transparencies listed here.

Section 7–1: **Interest Grabber**
Section Outline
Prokaryotic and Eurkaryotic Cells

Basic Cell Structures

Cells come in many shapes and sizes. Although typical cells range from 5 to 50 micrometers in diameter, the tiniest bacteria are only 0.2 micrometers across. These bacteria are so small that they are difficult to see, even with the aid of the most powerful light microscope. In contrast, the giant amoeba, *Chaos chaos,* may reach 1000 micrometers in diameter—large enough to be seen without a microscope.

Despite differences in cell size and shape, certain structures are common to most cells. All cells have a cell membrane and cytoplasm. The **cell membrane** is a thin, flexible barrier around the cell. Many cells also have a strong layer around the cell membrane known as a **cell wall.** Cell walls and cell membranes support and protect cells, while allowing them to interact with their surroundings.

Some cells also have a **nucleus** (plural: nuclei), a large structure that contains the cell's genetic material and controls the cell's activities. The material inside the cell membrane—but not including the nucleus—is called the **cytoplasm.** The cytoplasm contains many important structures. You will read about these structures, as well as more about the cell membrane, cell wall, and nucleus, in the next section.

CHECKPOINT ***What is the cytoplasm?***

KEEP CURRENT WITH . . . SCIENCE NEWS®

To find out more about the topics in this chapter, go to: **www.phschool.com**

Writing Activity

Use the library or the Internet to find more information about new discoveries concerning the cell or its structures. Then, present the discovery to your classmates in the form of an oral report.

1800 — 1900 — 2000

1838 **Matthias Schleiden** Schleiden concludes that all plants are made up of cells.

1839 **Theodor Schwann** Schwann concludes that all animals are made up of cells.

1855 **Rudolph Virchow** Virchow proposes that all cells come from existing cells, completing the cell theory.

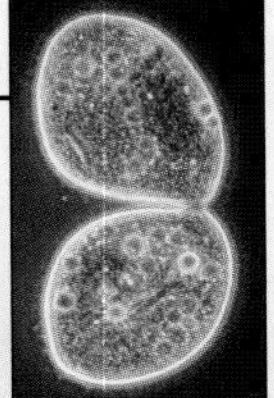

1931 **Janet Plowe** Plowe demonstrates that the cell membrane is a physical structure, not an interface between two liquids.

1945 World War II ends

1970 **Lynn Margulis** Margulis proposes the theory that certain organelles, tiny structures within some cells, were once free-living cells themselves.

BIO INSIGHTS — HISTORY OF SCIENCE

Hooke's observations
Robert Hooke (1635–1703) was the son of an English minister and a graduate of Oxford University. He did important work in mechanics and physics, and he became one of the most prominent microscopists of his time. The cork he observed through a compound microscope he had built was taken from the bark of an oak tree. Rectangular and boxlike cork cells are produced in woody plants as the woody stem increases its girth. Cork cells are dead at maturity, and thus Hooke was not looking at living cells when he gave them a name. Hooke never fully understand the significance of his findings, and it was some 150 years before the term *cell* took on its current meaning.

Basic Cell Structures

Address Misconceptions

Many students have the misconception that a common egg, such as a chicken egg, is one cell. Some students might believe that the egg yolk is the nucleus and the egg white is the cytoplasm, while others may think that the yolk is the complete cell. Explain that an unfertilized egg does have only one cell, but that cell consists of a small, whitish disk at the top of the yolk. This disk can be seen if the yolk is carefully separated from the rest of the egg. When an egg is fertilized, that cell begins to divide and multiply. The yolk serves as nourishment for the developing embryo.

Make Connections

Mathematics Explain to students that cells are so small that the basic metric unit of length, the meter, has no usefulness in measuring cells. Ask: **What is one thousandth of a meter called?** *(1 millimeter)* Explain that 1 micrometer (μm) is one thousandth of 1 millimeter. Ask: **How long is 1 micrometer in terms of meters?** *($1\ \mu m = 1/1000 \cdot 1/1000\ m = 1/1{,}000{,}000\ m$)* Thus, a micrometer is one millionth of a meter. Scientists use a unit called the nanometer (nm) to measure cell structures. A nanometer is 1/1000 of a micrometer.

SCIENCE NEWS®

Encourage students to visit **www.phschool.com** for the most current information on this topic.

Answer to . . .

CHECKPOINT *The cytoplasm is the material inside the cell membrane but does not include the cell nucleus.*

7–1 (continued)

Prokaryotes and Eukaryotes

Use Visuals

Figure 7–3 Ask students: **What is the main difference between prokaryotic cells and eukaryotic cells?** *(Eukaryotic cells contain a nucleus; prokaryotic cells do not.)* **Do bacterial cells contain a nucleus?** *(No. All bacteria are prokaryotes.)* **What else do eukaryotic cells contain that prokaryotic cells don't?** *(Eukaryotic cells contain organelles, which are specialized structures that perform important cellular functions.)*

3 ASSESS

Evaluate Understanding

Call on students at random to define each of the basic cell structures: cell membrane, cell wall, nucleus, and cytoplasm. Then, ask volunteers to explain the difference between prokaryotes and eukaryotes.

Reteach

Reinforce students' understanding of the three ideas that make up the cell theory by having them write statements that apply those ideas to specific living things.

ALTERNATIVE ASSESSMENT

Students' charts will vary, but they should include most of the information contained in the subsection Prokaryotes and Eukaryotes. Encourage students to add to their charts as they continue reading the chapter.

Use iText to review the key concepts in Section 7–1.

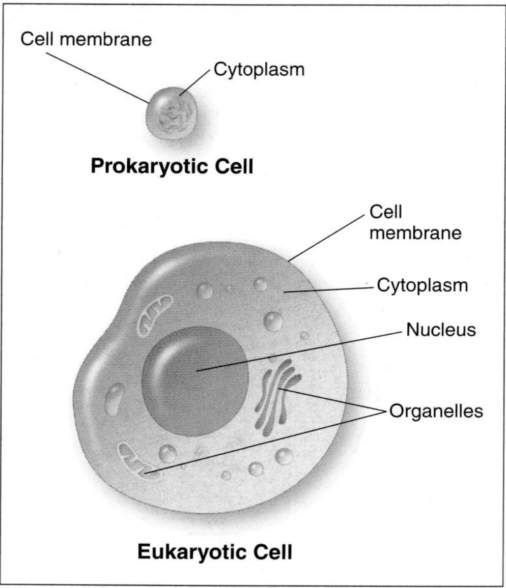

▲ **Figure 7–3** **Biologists divide cells into two categories: eukaryotes and prokaryotes. The cells of eukaryotes have a nucleus, but the cells of prokaryotes do not.**

Prokaryotes and Eukaryotes

Biologists divide cells into two categories: eukaryotes and prokaryotes. The cells of eukaryotes have a nucleus, but the cells of prokaryotes do not. The differences between the cells of prokaryotes and those of eukaryotes are shown in **Figure 7–3.**

Prokaryotes The cells of prokaryotes (proh-KAR-ee-ohts) are generally smaller and simpler than the cells of eukaryotes. **Prokaryotes** have cell membranes and cytoplasm but do not contain nuclei. All bacteria are prokaryotes. Examples of prokaryotes include *Escherichia coli,* which live in your intestines, and *Staphylococcus aureus,* which can cause skin infections.

Even though they are relatively simple, prokaryotes carry out every activity associated with life. They grow, reproduce, and respond to changes in the environment. Some even move by gliding along surfaces or swimming through liquids!

Eukaryotes Unlike the cells of prokaryotes, the cells of **eukaryotes** (yoo-KAR-ee-ohts) do contain nuclei. In addition to a nucleus, a cell membrane, and cytoplasm, most cells of eukaryotes contain dozens of other specialized structures, called **organelles,** that perform important cellular functions. Although some eukaryotes live solitary lives as single-celled organisms, many are large, multicellular organisms. All plants, animals, and fungi, and many microorganisms, are eukaryotes.

7–1 Section Assessment

1. **Key Concept** What three statements describe the cell theory?
2. **Key Concept** What is the main characteristic that distinguishes eukaryotes from prokaryotes?
3. When Hooke first used the term *cell,* did he intend to have it apply to living material? Explain your answer.
4. Name two structures that all cells have.
5. **Critical Thinking Inferring** If microscopes had not been invented, do you think the cell theory would have been developed? Explain your answer.

iTEXT Assessment Use iText to review the important concepts in Section 7–1.

ALTERNATIVE ASSESSMENT

Constructing a Chart Make a two-column chart comparing prokaryotes with eukaryotes. In the first column, list the features of prokaryotes. In the second column, list the features of eukaryotes.

7–1 Section Assessment

1. All living things are composed of cells. Cells are the basic units of structure and function in living things. New cells are produced from existing cells.
2. The cells of eukaryotes have a nucleus, but the cells of prokaryotes do not.
3. Some students may suggest that Hooke did intend to have it apply to living material, because he used it to describe tiny chambers in cork from a living plant.
4. All cells have a cell membrane and cytoplasm.
5. Sample answer: The cell theory would not have been developed because biologists would not have been able to observe cells in living things without the aid of a microscope.

7–2 Cell Structures

At first look, the image of a cell as seen by the electron microscope seems chaotic, as shown in **Figure 7–4.** The cell is filled with membranes, granules, fibers, and other structures. Look closely, however, and patterns begin to emerge. To see the patterns more clearly, let's look, one at a time, at some structures that are common to eukaryotic cells, such as those of plants and animals.

Cell Wall

Cell walls are found in many organisms, including plants, algae, fungi, and nearly all prokaryotes. Animal cells, however, do not contain cell walls. The cell wall lies outside the cell membrane. Most cell walls allow water, oxygen, carbon dioxide, and other substances to pass through them. **The main function of the cell wall is to provide support and protection for the cell.**

Most cell walls are made from fibers of carbohydrate and protein. The cell produces these substances, which are then released at the surface of the cell membrane. There, they are assembled to form the wall. Plant cell walls are made mostly of cellulose, a tough carbohydrate fiber. Cellulose is the principal component of both wood and paper. Every time you pick up a sheet of paper, you are holding the stuff of cell walls in your hands.

Guide for Reading

Key Concept
- What are the functions of the major cell structures?

Vocabulary
chromatin
chromosome
nucleolus
nuclear envelope
cytoskeleton
microtubule
microfilament
ribosome
endoplasmic reticulum
Golgi apparatus
lysosome
vacuole
chloroplast
mitochondrion

Reading Strategy: Building Vocabulary
Before you read, preview new vocabulary by skimming the section and making a list of the boldfaced terms. Leave space to make notes as you read.

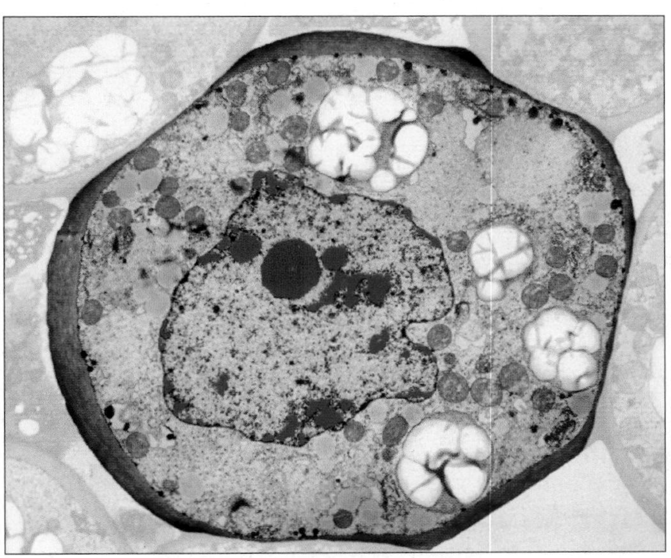

(magnification: 1500×)

◀ **Figure 7–4** This electron micrograph of a plant cell shows the different types of structures that are found in cells. The cell has been artificially colored so that you can distinguish one structure from another. The green structure encircling the cell is the cell wall. **The cell wall supports and protects the cell.**

Section 7–2

1 FOCUS

Objectives

7.2.1 ***Describe*** the main function of the cell wall.
7.2.2 ***Describe*** the function of the cell nucleus.
7.2.3 ***Identify*** the main roles of the cytoskeleton.
7.2.4 ***Describe*** the functions of the major cell organelles.

Guide for Reading

Vocabulary Preview

Pronounce each vocabulary word and have students repeat the pronunciation as a class. Pay special attention to words that are difficult for students with limited English proficiency.

Reading Strategy

To help students begin their understanding of the differences between plant cells and animal cells, have them preview Figure 7–5 and answer the caption question.

2 INSTRUCT

Cell Wall

Build Science Skills

Using Models Divide the class into small groups, and have groups make a labeled, two-dimensional drawing of a typical cell. First, have groups meet before reading the section to discuss what the inside of a cell might contain. Then, ask groups to meet again after learning about the structures of a cell to make the labeled drawing.

TIME SAVER **SECTION RESOURCES**

Print:
- ***Teaching Resources,*** Section Review 7–2
- ***Guided Reading and Study Workbook,*** Section 7–2

Technology:
- ***iText,*** Section 7–2

7–2 (continued)

Build Science Skills

Predicting Ask students what specific functions a one-celled organism would need to carry out in order to live. Then, divide the class into small groups, and ask each group to make a table of predictions about what structures would likely be found inside a one-celled organism. The table should have two columns: Necessary Function and Structure Needed to Carry Out Function.

Use Visuals

Figure 7–5 Encourage students to make copies of these labeled illustrations in their notebooks. As they learn about the various structures that make up a cell, they can add definitions and descriptions of functions for each of the labels. Point out that when they have completed this task, they will have made the best possible tool for review.

Build Science Skills

Comparing and Contrasting
Set up microscope stations at several locations around the room, and provide prepared slides of an animal cell and a plant cell at each location. Have students make labeled drawings of each and write a paragraph comparing and contrasting the two types of cells.

FIGURE 7–5 PLANT AND ANIMAL CELLS

Both plant and animal cells contain a variety of organelles. Some structures are specific to either plant or animal cells. Others are found in both types of cells. **Interpreting Graphics** ***What structures do plant cells have that animal cells do not?***

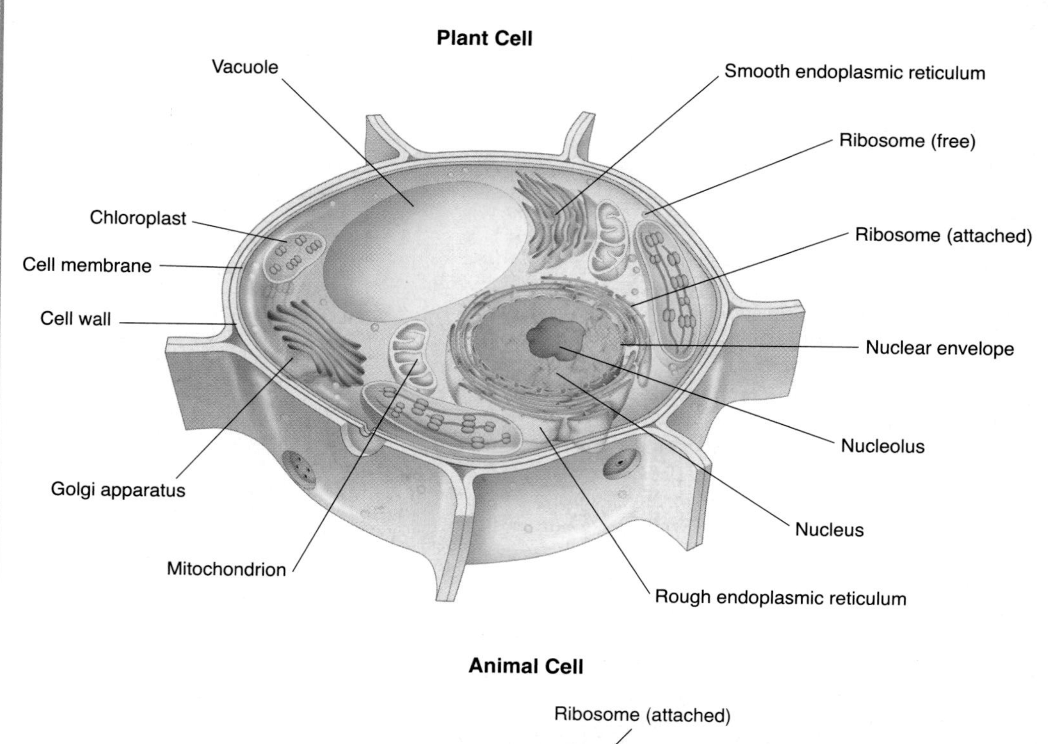

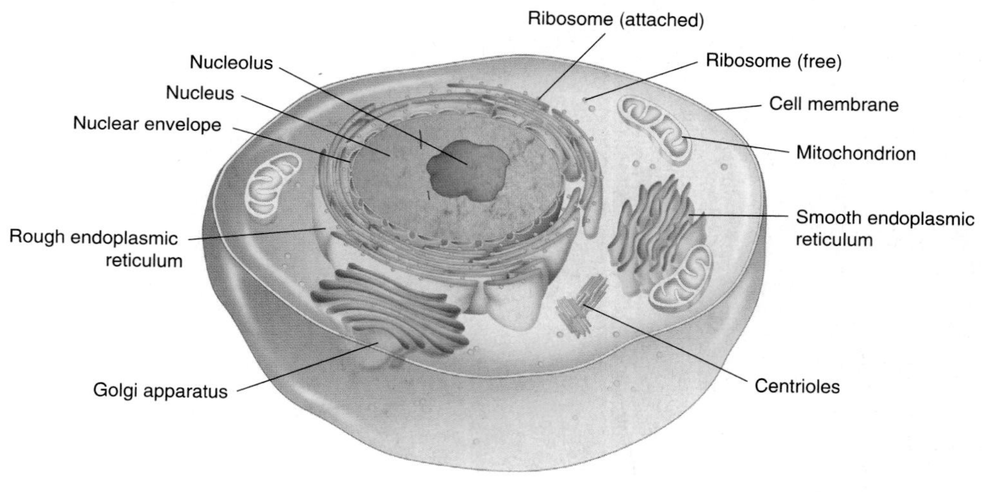

PRESENTATIONS MADE EASY!

The Presentation Assistant Plus contains the Prentice Hall Presentation Pro and the Transparencies, which provide easy-to-follow visual support for every step of this lesson. If you have a computer presentation station, use Prentice Hall Presentation Pro Section 7–2, or use the transparencies listed here.

Section 7–2:

Interest Grabber
Section Outline
Venn Diagram
Figure 7–5
Figure 7–7

Figure 7–6 The Nucleus

The nucleus controls most cell processes and contains the hereditary information of DNA. The DNA combines with protein to form chromatin, which is found throughout the nucleus. The small, dense region in the nucleus is the nucleolus.

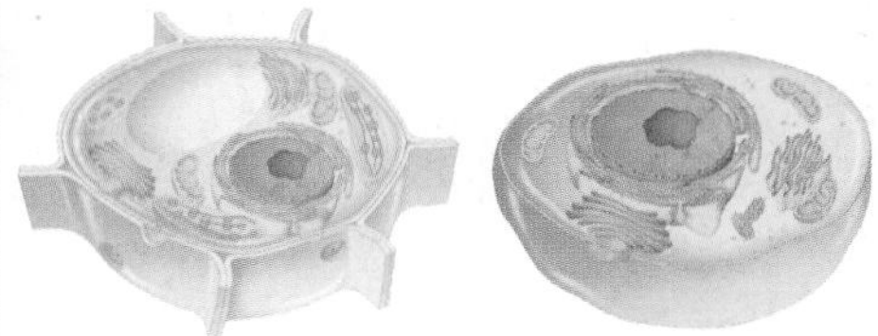

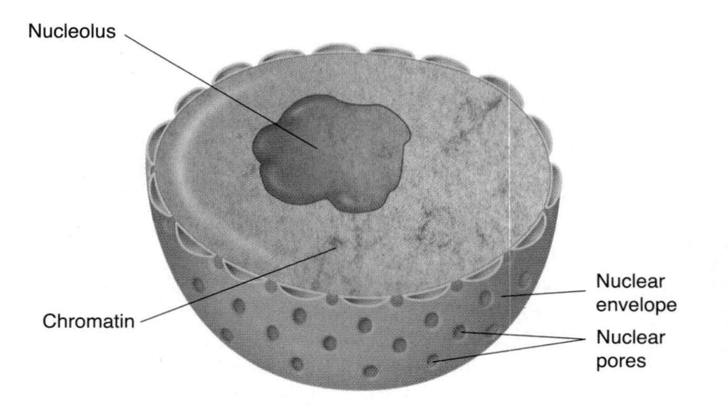

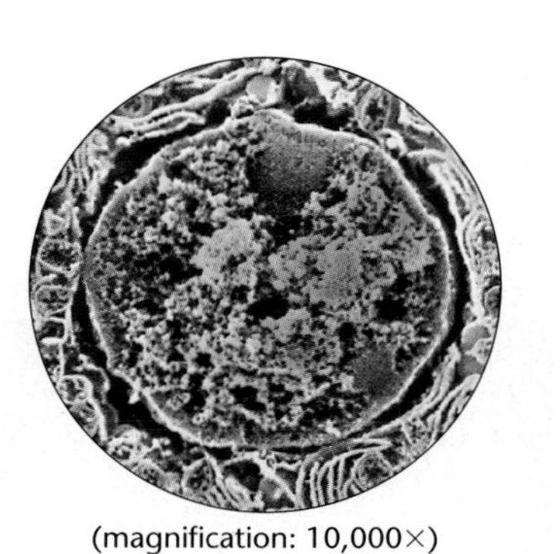

(magnification: 10,000×)

Nucleus

When the Scottish botanist Robert Brown first identified the nucleus in 1831, he immediately had a sense that this organelle was doing something important. Today, biologists know that Brown was right. **The nucleus controls most cell processes and contains the hereditary information of DNA (deoxyribonucleic acid).** Almost all eukaryotic cells, including the plant and animal cells shown in **Figure 7–5,** contain a nucleus.

The structure of the nucleus is shown in **Figure 7–6.** The nucleus contains nearly all of the cell's DNA. This substance holds the coded instructions for making proteins and other important molecules. The nucleus is important because making proteins is one of the main functions of cells.

Chromatin and Chromosomes The granular material visible within the nucleus is called **chromatin.** It consists of DNA bound to protein. Most of the time, chromatin is spread throughout the nucleus. When a cell divides, however, chromatin condenses to form **chromosomes** (KROH-muh-sohms). These are distinct, threadlike structures containing the genetic information that is passed from one generation of cells to the next.

CHECKPOINT *What kind of information do chromosomes hold?*

Nucleus

Use Visuals

Figure 7–6 Ask students: **What is the nucleolus?** *(It is a small, dense region of the nucleus where the assembly of ribosomes begins.)* **Where is the DNA that a nucleus contains?** *(The DNA is part of the chromatin, which is spread throughout the nucleus most of the time.)* **Why is DNA important?** *(It contains the genetic information that is passed on from one generation to the next. It holds coded instructions for making proteins and other molecules.)* Point out that the genetic information is the coded instructions for making molecules.

Build Science Skills

Inferring Remind students that prokaryotes do not contain a nucleus. Then, ask: **If the nucleus controls most cell processes in eukaryotes, how can prokaryotes live without a nucleus?** *(Some students might suggest that the lives of prokaryotes aren't as complex as those of eukaryotes. Others might correctly infer that the most important part of a nucleus is the DNA it contains, and prokaryotes have DNA without having a nucleus.)*

BIO INSIGHTS — HISTORY OF SCIENCE

The nucleus controls the cell

During the 1930s and 1940s, researchers performed a series of experiments that demonstrated the link between a cell's nucleus and the physical characteristics of the cell. Two species of *Acetabularia* algae were used in the experiments. This marine alga, though 5 cm long, consists of a single cell. Each cell includes a holdfast at the bottom, a stalk, and a cuplike cap at the top, and the cell's nucleus is in the holdfast. The two species that were used had different-shaped caps. Researchers cut the cap off one cell, removed the nucleus from its holdfast, and transplanted a nucleus from a cell of the second species into the holdfast of the first cell. The cell regenerated a new cap, and researchers cut off that one. Eventually, the cap that grew was the shape of the cap from the second species, from which the transplanted nucleus came, and not the shape of the first cap.

Answers to . . .

CHECKPOINT *Chromosomes hold the genetic information passed on from one generation of cells to the next.*

Figure 7–5 *Plant cells have a cell wall, a vacuole, and chloroplasts.*

Cytoskeleton

Meet Diverse Needs

Help students with limited English proficiency better understand the structures of the cell by explaining the meanings of difficult words in the descriptions of the structures. To reinforce their understanding of the nuclear envelope, explain that *pore* derives from a Greek word for "passage," and a pore is a minute opening through which materials pass. To help students understand the structure of the cytoskeleton, explain that *cyto-* means "cell" and the cytoskeleton is the "skeleton of the cell"—analogous but not the same as our own bony skeleton. Point out that a filament is a thread-like material. Thus, students can think of the cytoskeleton as composed of protein threads that hold the cell together. Also explain that *tubule* means "a very slender tube" and *micro-* means "minute." Thus, a microtubule might be described as a minute, slender tube. **Limited English proficiency**

Build Science Skills

Using Analogies Show students a photo of a house that's being built, with only the foundation laid and the basic frame constructed. Builders call this initial stage "framing" the house. Ask: **How is this house frame like a cell's cytoskeleton?** *(Just as a cytoskeleton is a network of protein filaments that helps a cell maintain its shape, the frame of a house is a network of boards and timbers that forms the shape of the house.)*

Nucleolus Most nuclei also contain a small, dense region known as the **nucleolus** (noo-KLEE-uh-lus). For many years, the function of the nucleolus was a mystery. Scientists now know, however, that this is where the assembly of ribosomes begins. Ribosomes aid in the production of proteins within the cell.

Nuclear Envelope The nucleus is surrounded by a double-membrane layer called the **nuclear envelope.** The nuclear envelope is dotted with thousands of nuclear pores, which allow material to move into and out of the nucleus. The nucleus sends a steady stream of RNA and other information-carrying molecules to the rest of the cell through the nuclear pores.

Cytoskeleton

Some cells have a structure—the **cytoskeleton**—that helps to support the cell. **The cytoskeleton is a network of protein filaments that helps the cell to maintain its shape. The cytoskeleton is also involved in many forms of cell movement.**

The cytoskeleton is made up of a number of important structures, including microtubules and microfilaments, as **Figure 7–7** shows. **Microtubules** are hollow tubes of protein about 25 nanometers in diameter. They maintain cell shape and can also serve as "tracks" along which organelles are moved.

Microtubules are especially important in cell division, in which they help to separate chromosomes. In animal cells, microtubules form a pair of structures known as centrioles. Plant cells do not have centrioles.

In some cells, bundles of microtubules form hairlike projections from the cell surface known as cilia and flagella that enable cells to swim rapidly through liquids. Cilia and flagella can produce considerable force; in some cells, cilia move almost like the oars of a boat, pulling or pushing cells through the water.

The cytoskeleton also includes microfilaments. **Microfilaments** are long, thin fibers that function in the movement and support of the cell. Microfilaments are about 7 nanometers in diameter—much narrower than microtubules. Like microtubules, microfilaments form extensive networks in some cells. Microfilaments also produce a tough, flexible framework that supports the cell.

Another function performed by the cytoskeleton is moving organelles within the cell. The cell contains scores of motor proteins that can attach to organelles and generate force to move them along microtubules or microfilaments.

(magnification: 1000×)

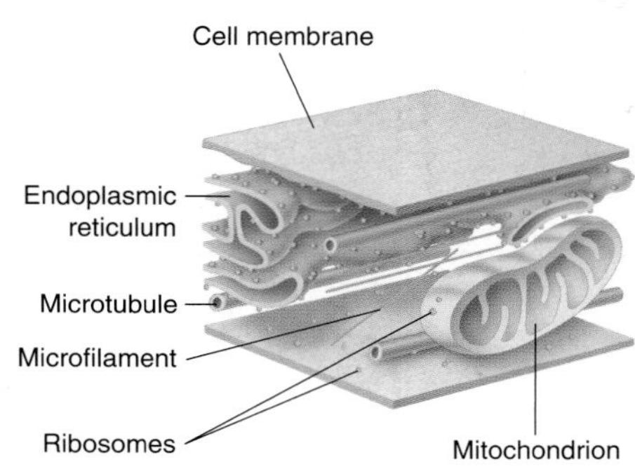

▲ **Figure 7–7** **The cytoskeleton is a network of protein filaments that helps the cell to maintain its shape and is involved in many forms of cell movement.** The photograph shows the microtubules of kidney cells. Microtubules are part of the cytoskeleton and maintain cell shape.

CHECKPOINT *What are microtubules and microfilaments?*

HISTORY OF SCIENCE

Learning from sea urchin nuclei
The German cytologist Theodor Boveri (1862–1915) performed an experiment before the invention of microdissection that demonstrated the importance of the nucleus. By vigorous shaking, Boveri removed the nuclei from the eggs of sea urchins of the genus *Spahaerechinus.* He then fertilized the eggs (which had no nuclei) with sperm from sea urchins of the genus *Echinus.* In a practical sense, fertilization resulted in the substitution of one nucleus for another. The larvae that developed had only the traits of *Echinus*, even though the sperm contributed little more than a tiny bit of nucleus to the developing organism.

FIGURE 7–8 ENDOPLASMIC RETICULUM

The endoplasmic reticulum is the organelle in which components of the cell membrane are assembled and some proteins are modified. The endoplasmic reticulum illustrated is called rough endoplasmic reticulum because of the ribosomes on its surface.

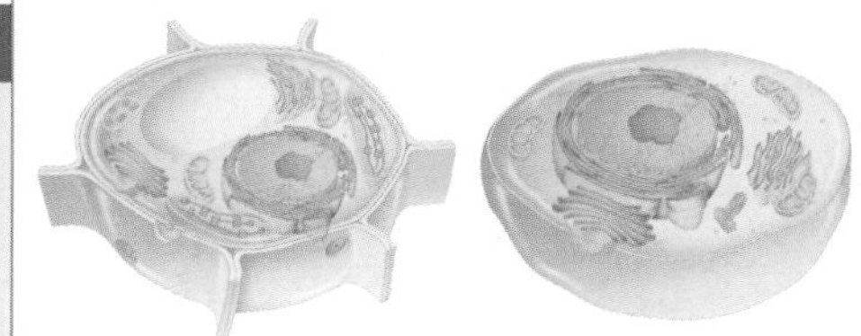

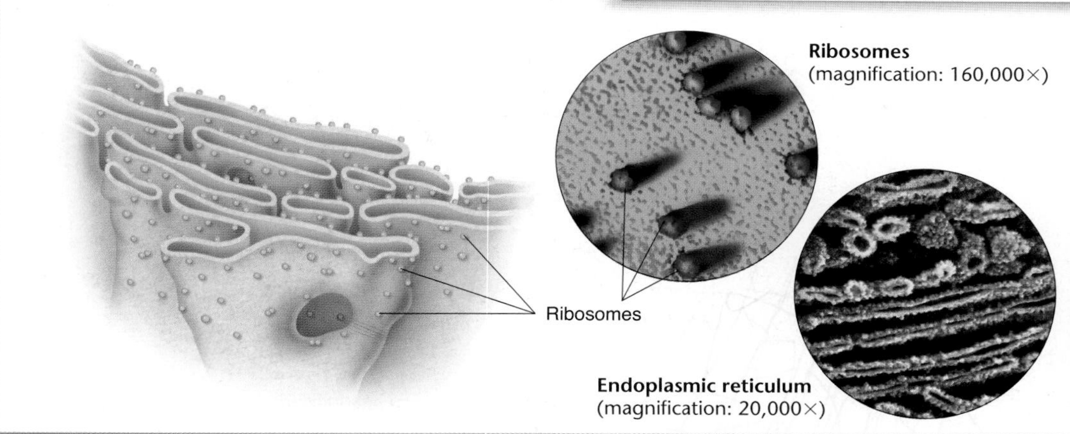

Organelles in the Cytoplasm

The cytoplasm contains many important structures. Because many of these structures act almost as though they were specialized organs in their own right, they are known as organelles, or "little organs."

Ribosomes One of the most important jobs carried out in the cell is making proteins. Proteins are assembled on **ribosomes,** small particles made of RNA (ribonucleic acid) and protein. Ribosomes are about 0.025 micrometers in diameter. Ribosomes produce proteins following coded instructions that come from the nucleus.

Endoplasmic Reticulum Eukaryotic cells also contain an internal membrane system known as the **endoplasmic reticulum** (en-doh-PLAZ-mik rih-TIK-yuh-lum), or ER. **The endoplasmic reticulum is the organelle in which components of the cell membrane are assembled and some proteins are modified.**

The part of the endoplasmic reticulum that is involved in the synthesis of proteins is called rough endoplasmic reticulum (rough ER). The rough endoplasmic reticulum has this name because of the ribosomes that stud its surface, as shown in **Figure 7–8.** Newly made proteins move directly from these ribosomes into the rough endoplasmic reticulum, where they may be chemically modified.

Organelles in the Cytoplasm

Meet Diverse Needs

Draw the outlines of a plant cell and an animal cell on the chalkboard, and include and label the nucleus, the cell membrane, and the cytoplasm. Have students make a copy of these cells in their notebooks. Then, as each of the cell organelles is discussed in class, add labeled structures to the cells on the chalkboard and have students add them to their own drawings. **Learning modality: visual**

Use Visuals

Figure 7–8 Ask students: **What are ribosomes composed of?** *(RNA and protein)* **Where are ribosomes produced?** *(In the nucleolus)* **What do ribosomes produce?** *(Proteins)* **What happens to these proteins after they're produced by ribosomes?** *(They move directly into the endoplasmic reticulum, where they may be chemically modified.)* **If this were an illustration of smooth endoplasmic reticulum, how would it be different?** *(The ER would not have ribosomes on its surface.)* **What is the function of smooth ER?** *(In many cells, the smooth ER contains collections of enzymes that perform specialized tasks, such as the synthesis of lipids.)*

FACTS AND FIGURES

Is a ribosome an organelle?

Some students may wonder whether a ribosome fits the definition of organelle. Other organelles, such as mitochondria and vacuoles, are enclosed by membranes, but ribosomes are tiny structures without membranes. The truth is that biologists do not have an official definition of what does or does not qualify as an organelle. The working definition, though, is that an organelle is a specialized structure that carries out a specific function. By that definition, ribosomes qualify. These protein-synthesizing structures are the most numerous of a cell's organelles. A growing *E. coli* cell, for instance, contains about 15,000 ribosomes. A eukaryotic cell, normally larger than a prokaryotic cell, often has many times that number. The more proteins a cell must make to carry out its functions, the more ribosomes it has.

Answer to . . .

CHECKPOINT *Microtubules are hollow tubes of protein about 25 nanometers in diameter. They maintain cell shape and can also serve as "tracks" along which organelles are moved. Microfilaments are long, thin fibers that function in the movement and support of the cell.*

Use Visuals

Figure 7–9 Students often confuse the Golgi apparatus with the endoplasmic reticulum, because both are usually represented as folded membranes within the cytoplasm. Ask: **How does the function of the Golgi apparatus differ from the function of the endoplasmic reticulum?** *(In the Golgi apparatus, carbohydrates and lipids are attached to proteins. In the endoplasmic reticulum components of the cell membrane are assembled and some proteins are modified. Ribosomes are also associated with ER, not the Golgi apparatus.)*

Build Science Skills

Observing Divide the class into small groups, and give each group access to a paramecium culture and a yeast suspension, as well as to a microscope slide, coverslip, toothpick, dropper pipette, and microscope. (Prepare the yeast suspension by adding a pinch of Congo red indicator to a thick mixture of yeast and water. Then, bring it to a gentle boil for 5 minutes. Cool before using. Transfer some paramecium culture from the stock culture at least a day ahead of time, and then limit the food supply to the transferred culture.) Have each group prepare a slide of live paramecia using the dropper pipette. Students should focus the slide under the low-power objective of the microscope. They should then obtain a small sample of the yeast solution. The indicator in the solution is red above pH 5 and blue below pH 3. The next step is to use a toothpick to transfer a small drop of yeast suspension to the edge of the slide and observe the paramecia under the microscope for 5 minutes. (*Students should observe that the paramecia sweep the yeast through their oral grooves and form vacuoles to enclose it. The vacuoles become blue at first and eventually red, as lysosomes fuse with the vacuole and release acids that digest the yeast.*)

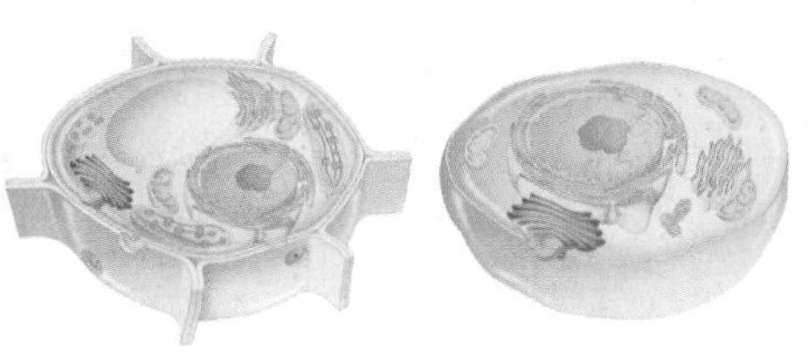

Figure 7–9 Golgi Apparatus

Enzymes in the Golgi apparatus attach carbohydrates and lipids to proteins. Notice the stacklike membranes that make up the Golgi apparatus in this scanning electron micrograph of an olfactory bulb cell.

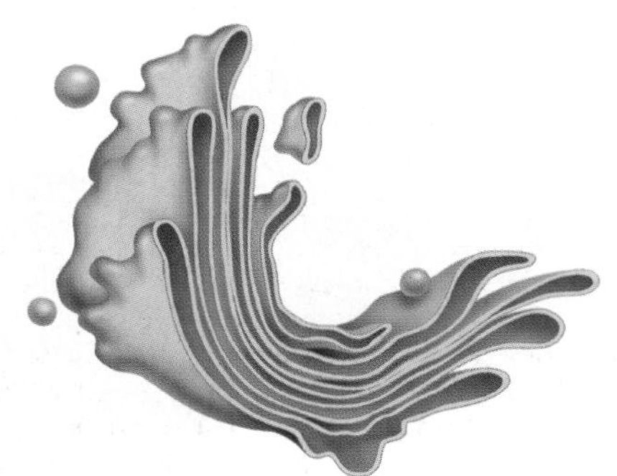

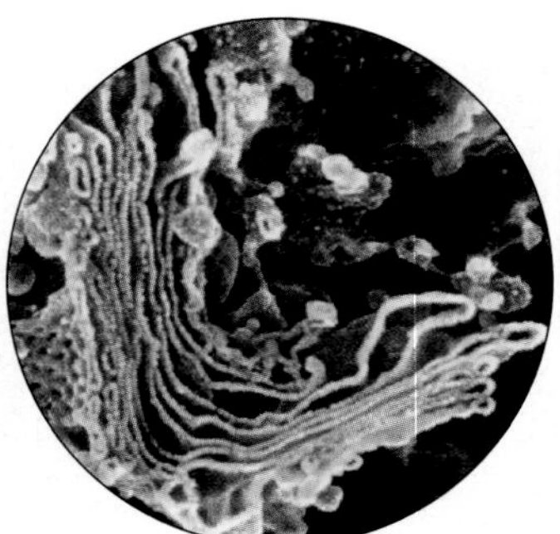

(magnification: 25,000×)

Proteins that will be released from the cell are modified in the rough endoplasmic reticulum, as are many membrane proteins. Other cellular proteins are made by "free" ribosomes, which are not attached to any membrane.

The other part of the endoplasmic reticulum, the smooth endoplasmic reticulum (smooth ER), does not have ribosomes on its surface. In many cells, the smooth endoplasmic reticulum contains collections of enzymes that perform specialized tasks, such as the synthesis of lipids.

CHECKPOINT *What distinguishes rough ER from smooth ER?*

Golgi Apparatus Proteins produced by the rough endoplasmic reticulum move into a stack of membranes called the **Golgi apparatus,** shown in **Figure 7–9.** The Golgi apparatus was named after the Italian biologist Camillo Golgi, who discovered it. **Enzymes in the Golgi apparatus attach carbohydrates and lipids to proteins.** From the Golgi apparatus, proteins are then sent to their final destinations.

Lysosomes **Lysosomes** (LY-suh-sohmz) are small organelles filled with enzymes. One function of lysosomes is to break down lipids, carbohydrates, and proteins from food into particles that can be used by the rest of the cell.

FACTS AND FIGURES

Important products of the Golgi apparatus One of the most important cell components packaged and distributed by the Golgi apparatus is material for the membranes of the cell and its organelles. Lysosomes, which are essentially membranous bags, are products of the Golgi apparatuses. These bags enclose enzymes that would destroy the cell if they were not surrounded by membrane. An example of how lysosomes function in cells can be seen in the way paramecia digest their food. Upon contact with a food organism or some other particle, the paramecium envelops the food in a vacuole. Lysosomes then fuse with the vacuole and release acids. The acids quickly digest the contents of the vacuole.

Quick Lab

How can you make a model of a cell?

Materials variety of craft supplies, index cards

Procedure

1. Your class is going to make a model of a plant cell using the whole classroom. Either with a partner or in a small group, decide what cell part or organelle you would like to model.
2. Using materials of your choice, make a three-dimensional model of the cell part or organelle you chose. Make the model as complete and as accurate as you can.
3. Label an index card with the name of your cell part or organelle and list its main features and functions. Attach the card to your model.
4. Attach your model to an appropriate place in the room. If possible, attach your model to another related cell part or organelle.

Analyze and Conclude

1. **Inferring** Why does a plant cell have so many different organelles?
2. **Calculating** Assume that a typical plant cell is 50 micrometers wide. Calculate the scale of your classroom cell model. (*Hint:* Divide the width of the classroom by the width of a cell, making sure to use the same units.)
3. **Comparing and Contrasting** How is your model cell part or organelle similar to the real cell part or organelle? How is it different?

Lysosomes also help break down organelles that have outlived their usefulness. Lysosomes perform the vital function of removing debris that might otherwise accumulate and clutter up the cell.

Vacuoles Cells often store materials such as water, salts, proteins, and carbohydrates in saclike structures known as **vacuoles** (VAK-yoo-ohlz). Many plant cells have a single large, central vacuole filled with liquid, as shown in **Figure 7–10.** Pressure in these central vacuoles makes it possible for plants to support heavy structures such as leaves and flowers. Vacuoles are also found in single-celled organisms and in animals. Smaller vacuoles, especially those involved in transporting substances within the cell, are often also called vesicles.

CHECKPOINT *What are two functions of vacuoles?*

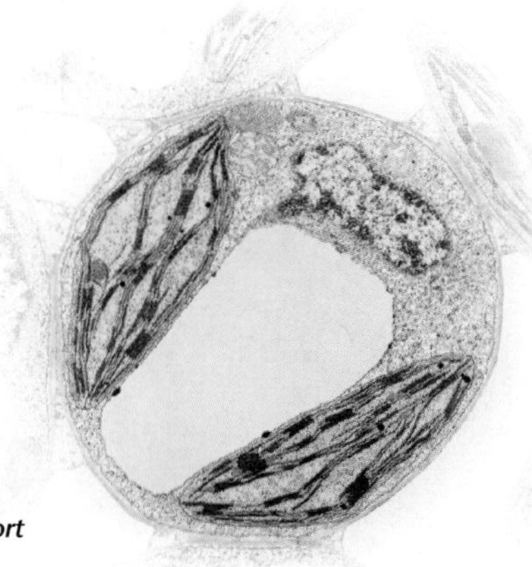

▶ **Figure 7–10** The large blue structure in the center of this *Coleus* plant cell is a vacuole. Vacuoles store water, salts, proteins, and carbohydrates. **Applying Concepts** *How do vacuoles help to support plant structures?*

(magnification: about 3000×)

Quick Lab

Objective Students will make models of cell organelles and a large class model of a cell.

Skill Focus Using models

Materials craft supplies, index cards

Time 20 minutes

Advance Prep Collect a variety of craft supplies, including scissors, construction paper, cardboard tubes, plastic bags, yarn, glue, beads, and so on.

Safety Caution students about the use of pins and about standing on chairs as they hang up their models. Supervise them as they do so.

Strategies

- You may want students to build a model of a different kind of cell. A model of a plant cell is suggested because plant cells have a great variety of structures and organelles.
- Make sure at least one group is working on these major structures: cell wall, cell membrane, nucleus, microtubules, microfilaments, ribosomes, smooth ER, rough ER, Golgi apparatus, lysosomes, vacuoles, mitochondria, and chloroplasts.

Expected Outcomes Students will make models of plant-cell structures and arrange them to form a complete cell.

Analyze and Conclude

1. The cell carries out many different processes, and each organelle has a different function within the cell.

2. Scales will vary depending on the size of the cell model. A typical scale, assuming that the classroom is 5 m across, would be 5/0.00005 (50 micrometers = 0.00005 meters), or 100,000 : 1.

3. The model should be similar in shape and structure to a real cell part. The model is different in that it is much larger, is made of different materials, and does not function.

Answers to . . .

CHECKPOINT *Only rough ER has ribosomes that stud its surface. Smooth ER does not have ribosomes on its surface.*

CHECKPOINT *Vacuoles store materials and help support structures.*

Figure 7–10 *The pressure of a central vacuole in cells makes it possible for plants to support structures such as leaves and flowers.*

7–2 (continued)

Use Visuals

Figure 7–11 Direct students' attention to the labeled drawing of a chloroplast. Ask: **What process can animal cells not carry out because they do not contain chloroplasts?** *(Animal cells can't carry out photosynthesis.)* Emphasize that chloroplasts are found not only in plant cells but also in some other organisms, as students will learn in later chapters. Then, ask: **Why are chloroplasts green?** *(They contain a green pigment.)* Explain that the green pigment is essential to the process of photosynthesis. Make sure students take note of the stacks of photosynthetic membranes, about which they will learn more in Chapter 8.

Build Science Skills

Using Analogies Explain to students that mitochondria have long been called the "powerhouses" of cells. Ask: **What is a "powerhouse"?** *(A powerhouse is another name for a power plant, which produces electricity for cities and regions.)* **How is a mitochondrion like a powerhouse?** *(A powerhouse produces the electricity needed to power all of the lights, appliances, electronic devices, and tools needed for a modern society to function. Likewise, a mitochondrion produces the high-energy compounds needed by the cell to use in growth, development, and movement.)*

FIGURE 7–11 CHLOROPLAST

Chloroplasts use the energy from sunlight to make energy-rich food molecules. The cells of plants and some other organisms contain chloroplasts, whereas animal and fungal cells do not. The photograph shows a chloroplast from a *Phleum pratense* plant.

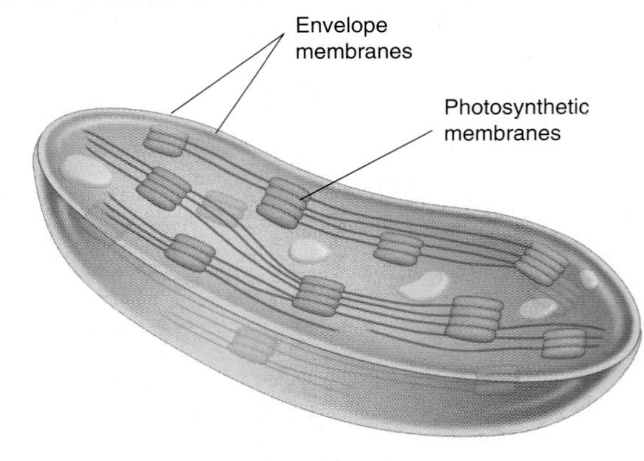

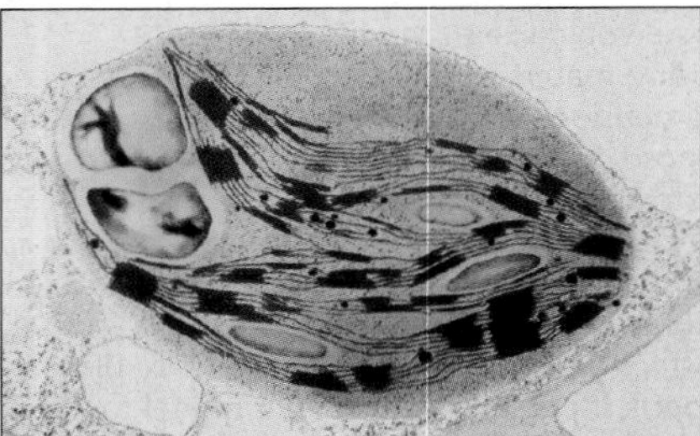

(magnification: 9000×)

Chloroplasts The **chloroplasts** (KLAWR-uh-plasts) are found in plants and some other organisms. Animal and fungal cells do not contain chloroplasts. **Chloroplasts use the energy from sunlight to make energy-rich food molecules in a process known as photosynthesis.**

As **Figure 7–11** shows, chloroplasts are bounded by two envelope membranes and contain large stacks of photosynthetic membranes. The green pigment chlorophyll is located in the photosynthetic membranes.

CHECKPOINT *What types of cells contain chloroplasts?*

Mitochondria The **mitochondria** (myt-oh-KAHN-dree-uh; singular: mitochondrion) are organelles that release energy from stored food molecules. **Mitochondria use energy from food to make high-energy compounds that the cell can use to power growth, development, and movement.**

Like chloroplasts, mitochondria are enclosed by two envelope membranes, an outer membrane and an inner membrane. The inner membrane is folded, as shown in **Figure 7–12.** Mitochondria are found in nearly all eukaryotic cells, including those of plants and algae.

TEACHER TO TEACHER

When I introduce the structure of the cell, I try to analogize the cell with the students' city. Taking this analogy a step further, I organize a cooperative learning activity in which I ask teams of students to "create" an imaginary city that correlates cell structures with city components. Teams should include most of the organelles in their city. For example, they might use a mitochondrion as the local power plant or microtubules as major thoroughfares.

For this activity, each team will need a large sheet of paper or poster board for drawing the city, as well as colored pencils or similar materials. If possible, have teams display their work and explain their "creations" to the class.

—*Jorge E. Sanchez,*
Biology Teacher
Green Valley High School,
Henderson, NV

Figure 7–12 Mitochondrion

Mitochondria use energy from food to make high-energy compounds that the cell can use to power growth, development, and movement. Note that mitochondria, such as the one shown here from an intestinal cell, have two membranes. The inner membrane, which is folded, is the place where the high-energy compounds are produced.

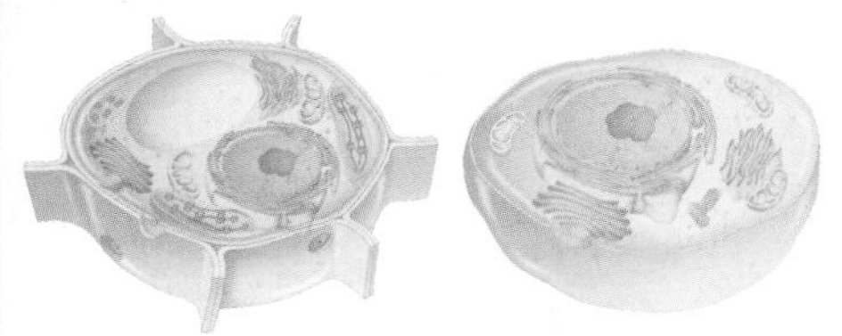

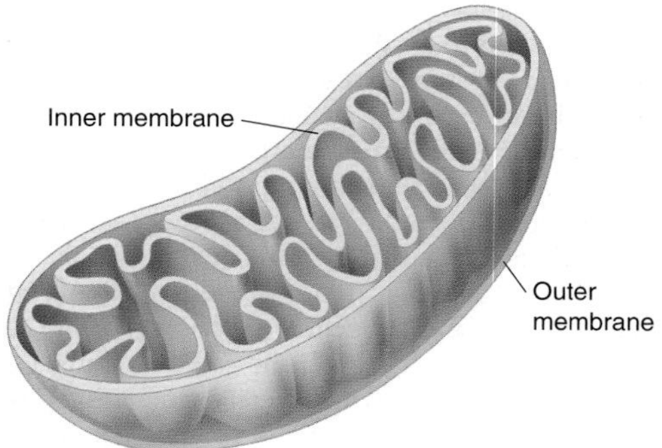

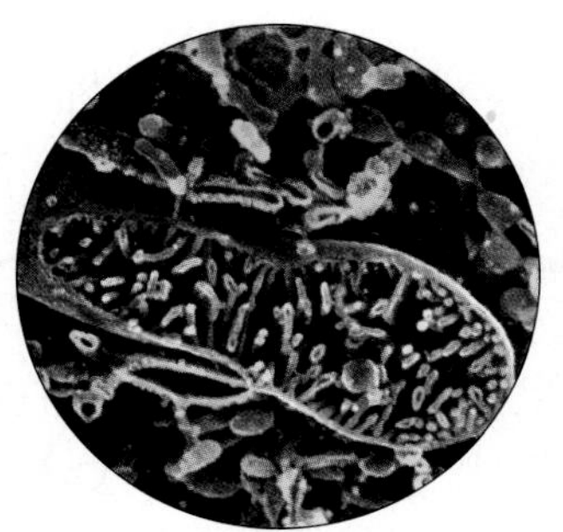

(magnification: about 1000×)

Organelle DNA

Unlike other organelles, chloroplasts and mitochondria contain some of their own genetic information in the form of DNA. These small DNA molecules contain information that is essential for the normal function of both organelles. The American biologist Lynn Margulis has suggested that mitochondria and chloroplasts are actually the descendants of ancient prokaryotes. Her idea is that the prokaryotic ancestors of these organelles formed relationships with early eukaryotic cells that benefited both cells. As these relationships developed, DNA in the cell nucleus took over more and more of the genetic information of each organelle. Mitochondrial DNA, according to this idea, is just the remnant of the genetic information of the bacteria from which mitochondria are descended.

Whether Margulis's idea is correct or not, one of the most interesting aspects of mitochondria is the way in which they are inherited. In humans, all or nearly all of our mitochondria come from the cytoplasm of the ovum, or egg cell. This means that when your relatives are discussing which side of the family should take credit for your best characteristics, you can tell them that you got your mitochondria from Mom!

Organelle DNA

Use Visuals

Figure 7–12 After students have studied the figure, ask: **What is wrong with this statement: Plant cells contain chloroplasts, and animal cells contain mitochondria.** *(There is nothing false about the statement, but it wrongly suggests that only plant cells contain chloroplasts and only animal cells contain mitochondria. Some eukaryotic cells other than plant cells contain chloroplasts. Almost all eukaryotic cells, including plant cells, contain mitochondria.)* Explain that students will learn more about the function of mitochondria when they study cellular respiration in Chapter 9.

Build Science Skills

Applying Concepts Have students make flowcharts that explain how eukaryotic cells might have developed from prokaryotic cells. Encourage interested students to investigate this theory further in other texts and then to add details to their flowcharts.

Word Origins

You would find the prologue at the beginning of the book, because *prologue* means "before the telling of the story."

Bio Insights: Facts and Figures

The origin of eukaryotes?
The idea that chloroplasts and mitochondria originated in symbiotic relationships among prokaryotic cells is called the endosymbiotic theory. According to this theory, which was extensively developed by biologist Lynn Margulis, the ancestors of eukaryotic cells were smaller species of prokaryotes living within larger species of prokaryotes. Chloroplasts possibly originated when cyanobacteria became established in larger prokaryotes either as parasites or as prey that were not digested. Mitochondria were once possibly anaerobic heterotrophs that found "safe harbor" inside larger prokaryotes as the world became increasingly aerobic. As the host and symbionts over time became more and more interdependent, the organisms merged to become a single organism.

Answer to . . .

Checkpoint *Chloroplasts are found in plant cells and some other organisms.*

The Cell as a Factory

Build Science Skills

Using Analogies Have students turn back to the illustrations of the plant and animal cells in Figure 7–5. Call on students at random to describe the function of a cell structure and then compare it to a part of a factory. For example, ask: **What is the Golgi apparatus, and what part of a factory is it like?** *(The Golgi apparatus is a stack of membranes where carbohydrates and lipids are attached to proteins by enzymes. It is like a factory's customization shop, where finishing touches are put on products before they are ready to leave the factory.)*

Meet Diverse Needs

Encourage students who need an extra challenge to work together in writing a short play based on the analogy of the cell as a factory. Explain to students that a good play needs some conflict or danger. The "factory" might be under economic threat or some environmental threat. Students should try to include the function of as many parts of the factory, or cell organelles, as possible. Once the play has been written, encourage the students to recruit class members to act out the play. **Learning modality: verbal**

Comparing Cells

Use Visuals

Figure 7–14 Ask students: **Which kind of cells are bacteria?** *(Prokaryotes)* **Can eukaryotic cells be one-celled organisms?** *(Yes. Some eukaryotes live solitary lives as single-celled organisms.)* **Which organelles in eukaryotic cells may be descended from prokaryotes?** *(Chloroplasts and mitochondria)*

The Cell as a Factory

Now that you have read about how each part of the cell functions, let's look at how the cell as a whole works. In some respects, a eukaryotic cell is very much like a factory. Although cells perform many different functions, one of the most important jobs carried out in the cellular "factory" is making proteins. **Figure 7–13** shows how manufacturing proteins in the cell is like manufacturing a product in a factory.

The walls and roof of a factory building are supported by steel or concrete beams and columns. Some cells also have a supporting structure—the cytoskeleton. A factory needs a transportation system to move parts and machines from one end of the building to the other, and so does a cell. This is another function performed by the cytoskeleton.

In the same way that the main office controls a large factory, the nucleus is the control center of the cell. In a factory, the main office sends instructions out to the factory floor. In a cell, the nucleus sends a steady stream of RNA and other information-carrying molecules to the rest of the cell. RNA contains instructions that tell the cell what type of protein to make. The instructions travel to ribosomes. Each ribosome is like a factory machine turning out proteins on orders that come from its "boss"—the nucleus.

▼ **Figure 7–13** The way in which proteins are made in cells is similar to the way products are made in factories. Like a cell, a factory has a control center, support structures, an assembly area, and a power supply. **Interpreting Graphics** ***What part of a factory corresponds to the mitochondria of a cell?***

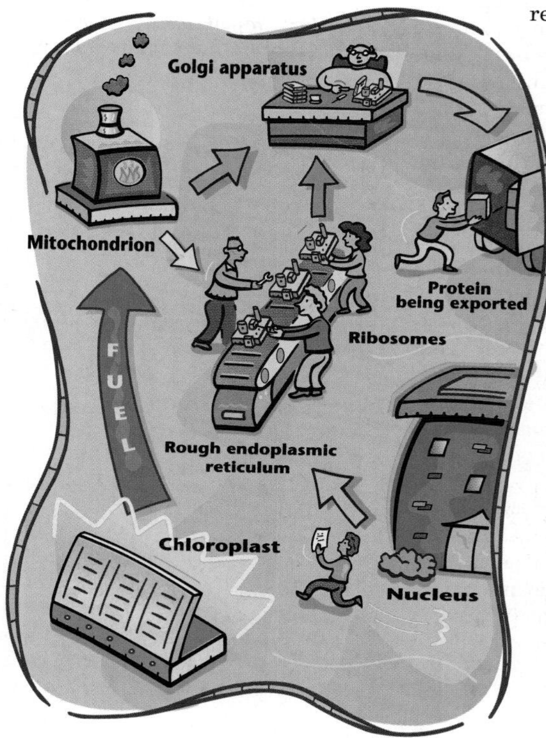

From the ribosomes, proteins that will be released from the cell move to the Golgi apparatus, which attaches carbohydrates and lipids to them to prepare the proteins for their roles. The Golgi apparatus is a bit like a factory's customization shop, where the finishing touches are put on products before they are ready to leave the factory. From the Golgi apparatus, proteins are then "shipped" to their final destinations.

Only one thing remains to complete the picture of the cell as a busy factory—a source of energy. Cells cannot be hooked up to the local power company, of course, so they get their energy from two organelles: mitochondria and chloroplasts. Some cells contain chloroplasts, which use energy from the sun to make food molecules. Thus, chloroplasts are the biological equivalents of solar power plants. Mitochondria then use these molecules to produce high-energy compounds that the cell can use immediately. In this way, the mitochondria are like a factory's oil-burning furnace.

✓CHECKPOINT ***How is the nucleus like the main office of a factory?***

TEACHER TO TEACHER

When teaching cell structure, I ask small groups of students to research the structure and function of a specific organelle, using a variety of sources, including college texts and relevant Internet sites. The members of each group work together to prepare a report to the class, complete with a detailed model of the organelle they researched. I have groups present their reports in the form of a justification of the importance of their organelles to their "parent organization," Cell Industries, with the understanding that they might be "downsized" if they don't make their case convincingly. Groups must cite the source of any information they present. The models students make are creative, and they are a strong learning reinforcement tool.

—Tamsen K. Meyer
Biology Teacher
Boulder High School,
Boulder, CO

A Comparison of Cells			
Structure	Prokaryotic Cells	Eukaryotic Cells	
		Animal	Plant
Cell Membrane	Yes	Yes	Yes
Cell Wall	Yes	No	Yes
Nucleus	No	Yes	Yes
Ribosomes	Yes	Yes	Yes
Endoplasmic Reticulum	No	Yes	Yes
Golgi Apparatus	No	Yes	Yes
Lysosomes	No	Yes	No
Vacuoles	No	Small or none	Yes
Mitochondria	No	Yes	Yes
Chloroplasts	No	No	Yes
Cytoskeleton	No	Yes	Yes

▲ **Figure 7–14** This table shows the main similarities and differences among different types of cells. **Comparing and Contrasting** *How are prokaryotic and eukaryotic cells similar? How are they different?*

Comparing Cells

Figure 7–14 summarizes the main differences among cells. The greatest distinction among types of cells is between prokaryotes and eukaryotes. Prokaryotic cells have cell membranes but do not have nuclei. Eukaryotic cells are much larger than prokaryotic cells and contain nuclei. They also contain more highly specialized organelles, including the endoplasmic reticulum, Golgi apparatus, and mitochondria. There are also large differences between plant and animal cells. Plant cells contain cell walls, large vacuoles, and chloroplasts. Animal cells do not have cell walls or chloroplasts.

7–2 Section Assessment

1. **Key Concept** Describe the functions of the endoplasmic reticulum, Golgi apparatus, chloroplast, and mitochondrion.
2. What does the cell wall provide for a cell?
3. Describe the role of the nucleus in the cell.
4. What are two functions of the cytoskeleton?
5. How is a cell like a factory?
6. **Critical Thinking Inferring** If you examine an unknown cell under the microscope and discover that the cell contains chloroplasts, what could you infer about the organism from which the cell came?

iTEXT Assessment Use iText to review the important concepts in Section 7–2.

ALTERNATIVE ASSESSMENT

Creating Artwork
Create a work of art—such as a painting or sculpture—depicting a plant or animal cell in cross section. Include all the different organelles described in this section that would be found in that type of cell. Label each organelle in your artwork.

3 ASSESS

Evaluate Understanding

Have students make a Venn diagram to show organelles that are found only in prokaryotic cells, those that are found only in eukaryotic cells, and those that are found in both types of cells.

Reteach

Ask students to make a compare/contrast table that lists all the parts of a typical cell, including nucleus and organelles. Column heads might include Name, Structure, and Function.

ALTERNATIVE ASSESSMENT

Encourage students to be creative yet accurate in their painting or sculpture. Provide them with a variety of materials to choose from, including paints, paintbrushes, plastic bags, balloons, various pasta shapes, pipe cleaners, gelatin, and pieces of fabric and construction paper. Also, have students bring materials from home. (*Students might use a plastic bag or balloon for the cell membrane, different pasta shapes for parts of the cytoskeleton and different organelles, and so on.*)

Use iText to review the key concepts in Section 7–2.

Answers to . . .

CHECKPOINT *In the same way that the main office controls a large factory, the nucleus is the control center of the cell.*

Figure 7–13 *Mitochondria are like a factory's furnace.*

Figure 7–14 *Similar: Both kinds of cells have a cell membrane and ribosomes; both prokaryotic cells and plant cells have a cell wall. Different: Eukaryotic cells have many structures that prokaryotic cells do not have, including a nucleus, ER, Golgi apparatus, lysosomes, vacuoles, mitochondria, chloroplasts, and cytoskeleton.*

7–2 Section Assessment

1. Cell membrane components are assembled, and some proteins are modified, in the ER. Enzymes in the Golgi apparatus attach carbohydrates and lipids to proteins. Chloroplasts use sunlight to make food molecules. Mitochondria use energy from food to make high-energy compounds.
2. The main function of the cell wall is to provide support and protection for the cell.
3. The nucleus controls most cell processes and contains DNA.
4. The cytoskeleton is a network of protein filaments that helps the cell maintain its shape. The cytoskeleton is also involved in many forms of cell movement.
5. Students' responses should reflect an understanding of the comparisons made in the subsection The Cell as a Factory.
6. It would either be a plant or another organism that carries out photosynthesis.

Section 7–3

1 FOCUS

Objectives

7.3.1 ***Identify*** the main functions of the cell membrane.
7.3.2 ***Describe*** what happens during diffusion.
7.3.3 ***Explain*** the processes of osmosis, facilitated diffusion, and active transport.

Guide for Reading

Vocabulary Preview

Suggest that students preview the meaning of the Vocabulary terms in the section by skimming the text to find the boldfaced words and their meanings.

Reading Strategy

Before students read, have them skim the section to identify and make a list of the main ideas. Then, as they read the section they should write down supporting details for each main idea.

2 INSTRUCT

Cell Membrane

Use Visuals

Figure 7–15 Ask students: **What does it mean that a cell membrane has a "lipid bilayer"?** *(A cell membrane is composed of two layers of lipid molecules.)* **What do the blue molecules represent in the illustration of the cell membrane?** *(They represent carbohydrate chains attached to the outside of the protein molecules that run through the lipid bilayer.)* Explain that these carbohydrate molecules are particularly important in cell recognition. Nearly all cells have special carbohydrate molecules on their surfaces—cell markers—that are unique to their type, their individual, and their species.

7–3 Movement Through the Membrane

Guide for Reading

Key Concepts
- What are the main functions of the cell membrane?
- What happens during diffusion?
- What is osmosis?

Vocabulary
- lipid bilayer
- concentration • diffusion
- selective permeability
- osmosis • facilitated diffusion
- active transport • endocytosis
- phagocytosis • exocytosis

Reading Strategy: Summarizing As you read, make a list of the ways in which substances can move through the cell membrane. Write one sentence describing each process.

When you begin to study a country, one of the first things you may do is draw a map of the country's borders. Before you can learn anything about a nation, it's important to understand where it begins and where it ends. The same principle applies to cells. Among the most important parts of a cell are its borders, which separate the cell from its surroundings. The boundary of the cell is the cell membrane.

Cell Membrane

The cell membrane regulates what enters and leaves the cell and also provides protection and support. The cell takes in food and water and eliminates wastes through the cell membrane.

The core of nearly all cell membranes is a double-layered sheet called a **lipid bilayer.** Lipid bilayers form by themselves when certain kinds of lipids are dissolved in water. The bilayer gives cell membranes a tough, flexible structure that forms a strong barrier between the cell and its surroundings.

In addition to lipids, most cell membranes contain protein molecules that run through the lipid bilayer. Carbohydrate molecules form chains that are attached to the outer surfaces of these proteins. There are so many kinds of molecules attached to most cell membranes that scientists call the membrane a "mosaic" of different molecules. A mosaic is a work of art made of individual tiles or other pieces assembled to form a picture or design.

The structure of a cell membrane is shown in **Figure 7–15.** As you will see, some of the proteins form channels and pumps that help to move material across the cell membrane. Many of the carbohydrates act like chemical identification cards, allowing cells to identify one another.

▼ **Figure 7–15** **The cell membrane regulates what enters and leaves the cell and also provides protection and support to the cell.** This illustration of the cell membrane shows that it is made up of a lipid bilayer in which proteins are embedded.

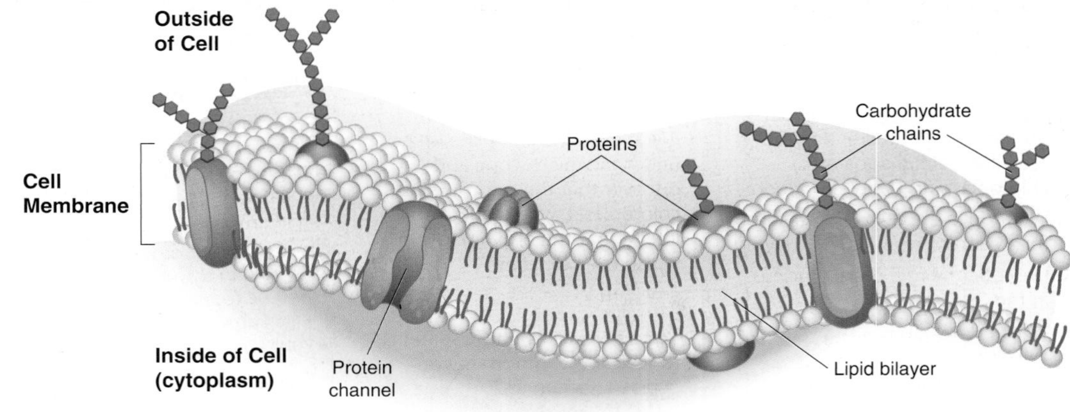

SECTION RESOURCES

Print:
- ***Laboratory Manual A,*** Chapter 7 Lab
- ***Teaching Resources,*** Section Review 7–3
- ***Guided Reading and Study Workbook,*** Section 7–3

Technology:
- ***iText,*** Section 7–3

Diffusion

Every living cell contains a liquid interior and is surrounded by liquid. Even in the dust and heat of a desert, the cells of cactus plants, scorpions, and vultures are bathed in liquid. The cell membrane separates the solution that surrounds the cell from the solution within the cell. One of the most important functions of the cell membrane is to regulate the movement of molecules from one side of the membrane to the other.

The cytoplasm of a cell is a solution of many different substances in water. Recall that a solution is a liquid mixture of two or more substances in which the molecules of the substances are evenly mixed. The substances dissolved in the liquid are called solutes. The **concentration** of a solution is the mass of solute in a given volume of solution, or mass/volume. For example, if you dissolved 12 grams of salt in 3 liters of water, the concentration of the solution would be 12 g/3 L, or 4 g/L (grams per liter).

In a solution, molecules move constantly. They collide with one another and tend to spread out randomly through space. As a result, the molecules tend to move from an area where they are more concentrated to an area where they are less concentrated, a process known as **diffusion** (dih-FYOO-zhun). When the concentration of the solute is the same throughout a solution, the system has reached equilibrium. **Diffusion causes many substances to move across a cell membrane but does not require the cell to use energy.**

What do diffusion and equilibrium have to do with biological membranes? Suppose two substances are present in unequal concentrations on either side of a membrane, as shown in **Figure 7–16.** The substance that can cross the membrane will tend to move toward the area where it is less concentrated until equilibrium is reached. Then, the concentration of the substance on both sides of the membrane will be the same. Even after equilibrium is reached, individual molecules continue to move rapidly across the membrane in both directions. Roughly equal numbers of molecules move in each direction, however, so there is no further change in concentration on either side.

CHECKPOINT *When is equilibrium reached in a solution?*

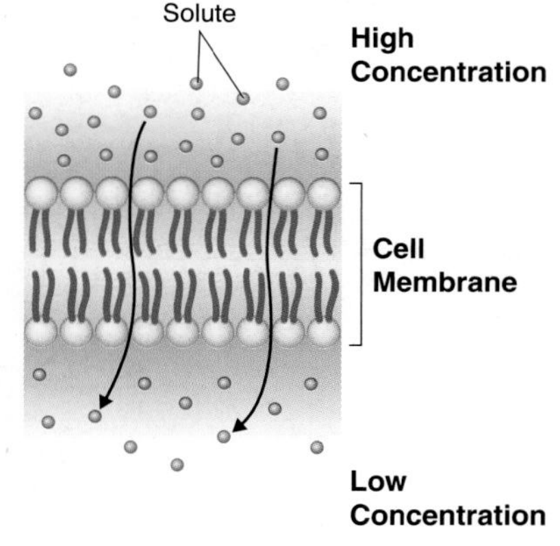

▶ **Figure 7–16** Diffusion is the process by which molecules of a substance move from areas of higher concentration to areas of lower concentration. **Diffusion is also responsible for the movement of some materials across cell membranes.**

Diffusion

Build Science Skills

Using Models Have students act out the process of diffusion. To begin, group class members at the classroom door. Then, tell them to spread out through the classroom in such a way that no two students are closer to each other than to any other students. Discuss how molecules randomly spread out through a liquid or a gas.

PRESENTATIONS MADE EASY!

The Presentation Assistant Plus contains the Prentice Hall Presentation Pro and the Transparencies, which provide easy-to-follow visual support for every step of this lesson. If you have a computer presentation station, use Prentice Hall Presentation Pro Section 7–3, or use the transparencies listed here.

Section 7–3: **Interest Grabber**
Section Outline
Facilitated Diffusion
Figure 7–15
Figure 7–17
Figure 7–20

Answer to . . .

CHECKPOINT *When the concentration of the solute is the same throughout a solution, the system has reached equilibrium.*

7–3 (continued)

Osmosis

Use Visuals

Figure 7–17 Ask students: **Is this membrane permeable to water? Explain how you know.** *(It is permeable to water, because the illustration shows that water molecules can pass through the membrane.)* **How does the figure show that there is a high concentration of water on one side of the membrane and a low concentration on the other side?** *(The bottom side has many sugar molecules mixed with water molecules, and the top side has fewer sugar molecules. Therefore, there is a higher concentration of water molecules on the top side.)* **How is osmosis related to diffusion?** *(Osmosis is the diffusion of water through a selectively permeable membrane.)*

Word Origins

A hypertonic solution is stronger, or more concentrated, than another solution.

Build Science Skills

Using Models Divide the class into small groups. Tell students that iodine is an indicator of starch. Then, have groups follow these steps to observe a model of how osmosis works in cells.

- In a beaker, stir in 10 milliliters (2 teaspoons) of starch in 125 milliliters of water. Pour about half of that mixture into a plastic sandwich bag, and secure it with a tie.
- Fill a second beaker with 250 milliliters of water, and add 15 drops of iodine.
- Place the sandwich bag of water and starch into the beaker of water and iodine. Note any changes after 20 minutes.
- While waiting, add 8 drops of iodine to the rest of the water-starch mixture in the first beaker, and note any changes that occur.

Students should observe a change in color to blue-black inside the sandwich bag and in the first beaker. However, the water outside the bag remains clear, because water and iodine molecules can pass through the selectively permeable bag, whereas the starch molecules cannot.

Osmosis

Not all substances can cross biological membranes. If a substance is able to diffuse across a membrane, the membrane is permeable (PER-mee-uh-bul) to that substance. A membrane is said to be impermeable to those things that cannot pass across it. Most biological membranes are **selectively permeable,** meaning that some substances can pass across them and others cannot.

A process called **osmosis** allows water molecules to pass easily through most biological membranes. **Osmosis is the diffusion of water through a selectively permeable membrane.**

How Osmosis Works Like the cell membrane, the membrane in **Figure 7–17** is permeable to water but impermeable to sugar. There is a concentrated sugar solution on one side of the membrane and a dilute sugar solution on the other side. Although water molecules move in both directions across the membrane, there is a net movement of water into the compartment containing the concentrated sugar solution. That means more water is moving into this compartment than out of it. Why? Water, like other substances, tends to diffuse from a region where it is highly concentrated to one where it is less concentrated. The compartment with the dilute sugar solution starts out with the highest concentration of water.

Water will move across the membrane until equilibrium is reached. At that point, the concentrations of water and sugar will be the same on both sides of the membrane. When this happens, the two solutions will be isotonic, which means "same strength." When the experiment began, the more concentrated sugar solution was hypertonic, which means "above strength." The dilute sugar solution was hypotonic, or "below strength."

Word Origins

Hypotonic comes from the Greek word *hupo,* meaning "under" and the New Latin word *tonicus,* meaning "tension" or "strength." So a hypotonic solution is less strong, or less concentrated, than another solution. **If *hyper* means "over," how would you describe a hypertonic solution?**

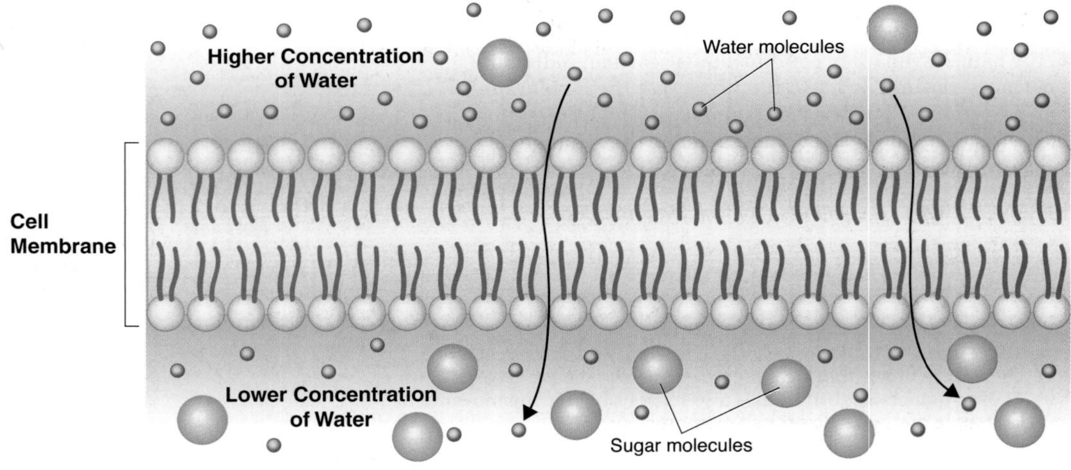

▼ **Figure 7–17 Osmosis is the diffusion of water through a selectively permeable membrane.** In this illustration, there is a higher concentration of water outside the cell than inside it. As a result, water molecules move across the membrane into the cell.

SCIENCE UPDATE

Water finds its way

Osmosis is easy to observe in cells, yet it was long a mystery as to how water can cross membranes so quickly. Water is a polar molecule, and as such it is not lipid soluble and should not be expected to cross a lipid bilayer. Many puzzled physical chemists suggested that biochemists should look for some kind of channels in the membrane. In the late twentieth century, such channels were in fact discovered. These channels, which are membrane-spanning proteins, are named aquaporins. They have been found in scores of cells, and some scientists think that they might be present in nearly all cells. Their discovery is so recent that a detailed analysis of how they work may be years away.

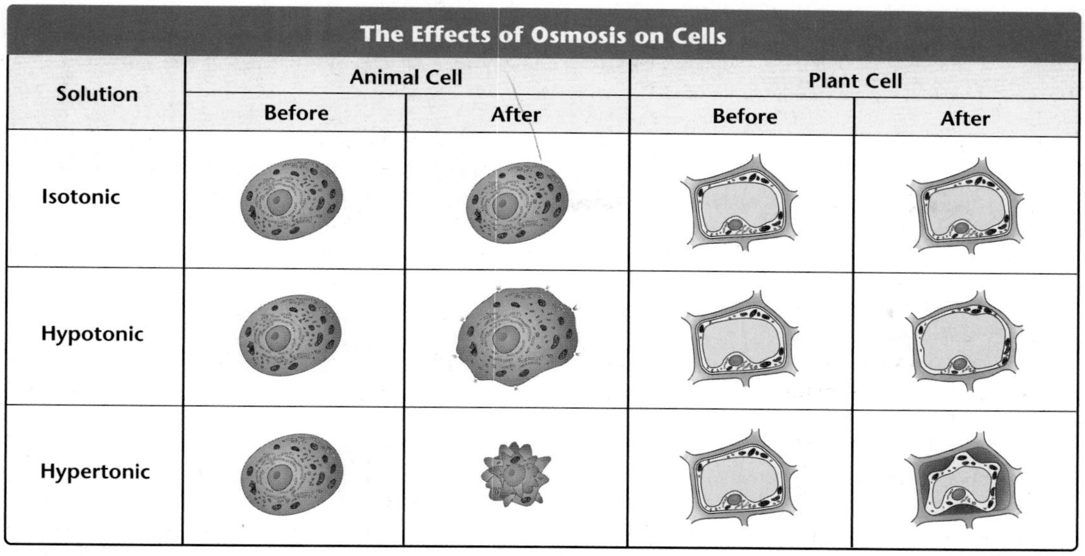

Solution	Animal Cell		Plant Cell	
	Before	After	Before	After
Isotonic				
Hypotonic				
Hypertonic				

Table title: **The Effects of Osmosis on Cells**

▲ **Figure 7–18** Cells placed in an isotonic solution neither gain nor lose water. In a hypotonic solution, animal cells swell and burst. The vacuoles of plant cells swell, pushing the cell contents out against the cell wall. In a hypertonic solution, animal cells shrink, and plant cell vacuoles collapse. **Predicting** ***What would happen to the animal cell in the hypertonic solution if it were placed in pure water?***

Osmotic Pressure Osmosis exerts a pressure known as osmotic pressure on the hypertonic side of a selectively permeable membrane. Osmotic pressure can cause serious problems for a cell. Because the cell is filled with salts, sugars, proteins, and other molecules, it will almost always be hypertonic to fresh water. That means that osmotic pressure should produce a net movement of water into a typical cell that is surrounded by fresh water. If this happens, the volume of a cell will increase until the cell becomes swollen, as shown in **Figure 7–18.** Eventually, it may burst like an overinflated balloon.

Fortunately, cells in large organisms are not in danger of bursting. Most cells in such organisms do not come in contact with fresh water. Instead, the cells are bathed in fluids, such as blood, that are isotonic. These isotonic fluids have concentrations of dissolved materials roughly equal to those in the cells themselves.

Other cells, such as plant cells and bacteria, which do come into contact with fresh water, are surrounded by tough cell walls. The cell walls prevent the cells from expanding, even under tremendous osmotic pressure. However, the increased osmotic pressure makes the cells extremely vulnerable to injuries to their cell walls.

Still other cells use a mechanism to pump out the water that is forced in by osmosis. For example, some single-celled organisms have a structure called a contractile vacuole. By contracting rhythmically, the contractile vacuole pumps excess water out of the cell. This process is an example of homeostasis, the maintenance of a controlled internal environment.

✔CHECKPOINT *How do cell walls protect cells from osmotic pressure?*

Build Science Skills

Applying Concepts Ask students to consider this real-life circumstance. A homeowner contracts a lawn company to add fertilizer to the lawn in order to make the grass grow better. This process is normally done by spraying a mixture of fertilizer and water onto the lawn. Ask: **What would happen if too much fertilizer and too little water were sprayed onto the lawn?** *(Students may know that the grass would appear to be burned.)* **Can you suggest what happened to the cells of the grass?** *(They lost water because of the concentrated solution of fertilizer around them.)* **In that case, was the fertilizer-water mixture hypotonic or hypertonic compared to the grass cells?** *(The mixture was hypertonic compared to the grass cells.)*

Demonstration

Place a small number of paramecia in a petri dish on a microprojector. Have students observe the paramecia as you discuss contractile vacuoles, which some unicellular organisms have to pump water out of the cell. Flood the environment of the paramecia with distilled water. As students continue to observe, point out the action of the contractile vacuoles. Ask: **What was added to the dish?** *(Pure water)* **How do you know?** *(The action of the contractile vacuoles increased.)* **What will eventually happen to the paramecia?** *(They will explode.)* **Why?** *(The vacuoles cannot keep up with the inward movement of water because of osmosis.)* **What would happen if a small amount of salt water were added?** *(Vacuole action would probably return to normal.)*

FACTS AND FIGURES

Penicillin works by osmosis
Penicillin, one of the most important antibiotic drugs in the history of medicine, depends on osmosis for its killing action. Penicillin inhibits an enzyme with which many bacteria produce chemical cross-links in their cell walls. This leads to the formation of a weakened cell wall that cannot stand the stress of osmotic pressure. Gradually, the cell wall becomes weaker and weaker until it breaks, and the bacterium bursts under the inrush of water caused by osmosis.

Answers to . . .

✔CHECKPOINT *Cell walls prevent the cells from expanding, even under tremendous osmotic pressure.*

Figure 7–18 *The volume of the cell would increase until it became swollen. Eventually, it could burst like an overinflated balloon.*

Facilitated Diffusion

Analyzing Data

Answers

1. Students may predict that water will diffuse most quickly because it is the smallest and glucose will diffuse most slowly because it is the largest.

2. Students' hypotheses may include: The smaller a molecule is, the faster it diffuses.

3. Students' experiments should be designed to test their hypotheses and control variables.

4. Students may suggest that temperature affects the rate of diffusion.

Analyzing Data

Crossing the Cell Membrane

The cell membrane regulates what enters and leaves the cell and also provides protection and support. The core of nearly all cell membranes is a double-layered sheet called a lipid bilayer. Most materials entering the cell pass across this membrane by diffusion. The graph shows the sizes of several molecules that can diffuse across a lipid bilayer.

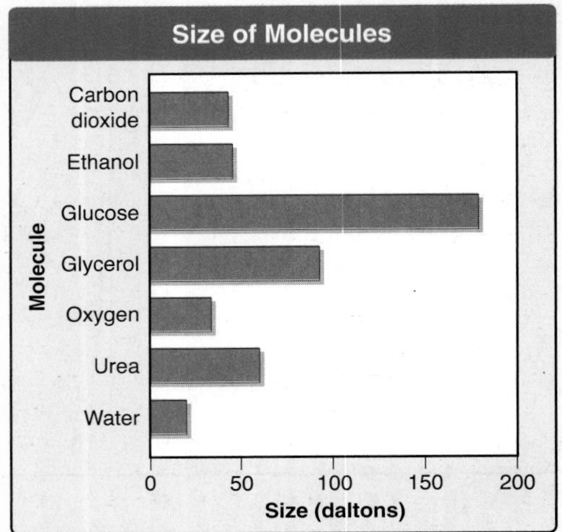

1. **Predicting** Which substances do you think will diffuse across the lipid bilayer most quickly? Most slowly? Explain your answers.
2. **Formulating Hypotheses** Formulate a hypothesis about the relationship between molecule size and rate of diffusion.
3. **Designing Experiments** Design an experiment to test your hypothesis.
4. **Going Further** What other factors do you think might affect the rate of diffusion? (*Hint:* Review Chapter 2.)

Facilitated Diffusion

Some molecules, including alcohol, water, and small lipids, can move through the lipid bilayer and diffuse directly across the cell membrane. Other molecules cannot cross the lipid bilayer but do diffuse across the membrane. How do they do this?

Many membranes have protein channels that allow molecules to cross the membrane. In red blood cells, for example, a specific protein that spans the membrane has an internal channel that allows glucose to pass right through it. Only glucose can pass through this channel, and it can move through in either direction. This membrane protein is said to facilitate, or help, the diffusion of glucose across the membrane. The process, which is shown in **Figure 7–19,** is known as **facilitated diffusion** (fuh-SIL-uh-tayt-ud dih-FYOO-zhun). Hundreds of different protein channels have been found that allow ions, sugars, and salts to cross various membranes.

Although facilitated diffusion is fast and specific, it is still diffusion. Therefore, a net movement of molecules across a cell membrane will occur only if there is a higher concentration of the molecules on one side than on the other side. This movement does not require the addition of energy.

High Concentration
Glucose molecules
Cell Membrane
Protein channel
Low Concentration

▲ **Figure 7–19** During facilitated diffusion, molecules such as glucose that cannot cross the cell membrane's lipid bilayer directly move through protein channels instead. **Applying Concepts** *Why does facilitated diffusion not require the cell to use energy?*

FACTS AND FIGURES

Protein molecules and active transport
One of the most important examples of active transport is known as the sodium potassium pump, in which sodium ions are maintained at a lower concentration inside the cell and potassium ions are maintained at a higher concentration inside the cell. The active transport by protein molecules of these ions is central to the production of electrical impulses by nerve cells. At one time, scientists thought that the protein molecules actually rotated as they transported substances through the cell membrane, picking up their parcels on the outside and dumping them on the inside. Now, scientists think that the transported molecules are somehow squeezed through the transport proteins, as the proteins change their configuration to accommodate their riders.

Active Transport

Often, material moves across a cell membrane against a concentration difference, as shown in **Figure 7–20.** The material moves from an area of lower concentration to an area of greater concentration, in a process called **active transport.** Active transport requires the input of energy, hence the term "active."

Active transport of small molecules is often compared to a pump. Most animal cells, for example, have membrane proteins that pump sodium ions (Na^+) out of the cell and pump potassium ions (K^+) in. Like any pump, these transport proteins require energy to move ions against the forces of diffusion. Because of the sodium-potassium pump, the insides of most animal cells have a low concentration of sodium but a high concentration of potassium.

In another type of active transport, large amounts of material are transported through movements of the cell membrane. One of these movements, called **endocytosis** (en-doh-sy-TOH-sis), is the process of taking material into the cell by means of infoldings, or pockets, of the cell membrane. The pocket that results breaks loose from the outer portion of the cell membrane and forms a vacuole within the cytoplasm. Large molecules, clumps of food, and even whole cells can be taken up by endocytosis.

When large particles are taken into the cell by endocytosis, the process is called **phagocytosis** (fag-oh-sy-TOH-sis). In phagocytosis, extensions of cytoplasm surround and engulf large particles.

As you might expect, cells are also able to send material out of the cell. The removal of large amounts of material from a cell is known as **exocytosis** (ek-soh-sy-TOH-sis). During exocytosis, the membrane of the vacuole surrounding the material fuses with the cell membrane, forcing the contents out of the cell.

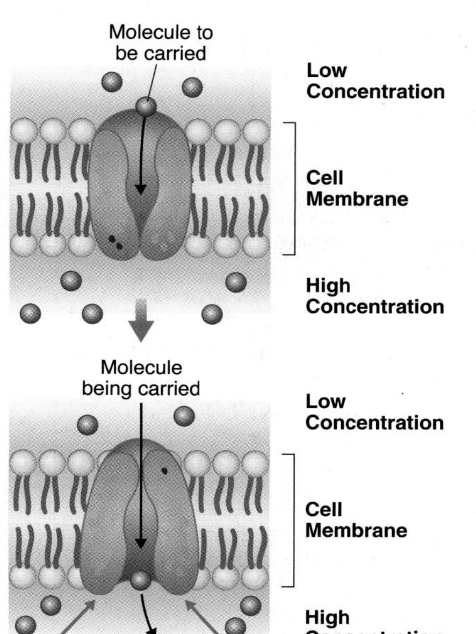

▲ **Figure 7–20** Active transport of molecules and ions against a concentration difference requires transport proteins and energy. **Interpreting Graphics** *What is happening in the illustration?*

7–3 Section Assessment

1. **Key Concept** What processes are made possible by the cell membrane?
2. **Key Concept** How does diffusion affect cells?
3. **Key Concept** Describe how water moves during osmosis.
4. What is the basic structure of a cell membrane?
5. **Critical Thinking Comparing and Contrasting** How does active transport differ from diffusion?

iTEXT Assessment Use iText to review the important concepts in Section 7–3.

Take It to the NET

As a graphic designer, you are asked to create an animation that shows osmosis and the selective permeability of a membrane. Make a storyboard that shows the main steps in your animation. Use the links provided in the Biology area at the Prentice Hall Web site for help in completing this activity: **www.phschool.com**

Active Transport

Build Science Skills

Using Analogies Set up a ramp using a board propped up on one end by a stack of books. Then, as students observe, roll a ball down the ramp and push it back up again. Ask: **Which is like facilitated diffusion and which is like active transport, rolling the ball down the ramp or pushing it up? Explain.** *(Rolling the ball down is like facilitated diffusion, because neither requires addition of energy. Pushing the ball back up is like active transport, because it requires addition of energy.)*

3 ASSESS

Evaluate Understanding

Make up a list of fictitious substances. Have students describe the method of transport a cell would use to move each substance through the cell membrane and why. Students need not be accurate; what you are looking for is correct reasoning.

Reteach

Have students write definitions of diffusion, osmosis, facilitated diffusion, and active transport. Then, discuss ways in which they are similar and ways in which they are different.

Take It to the NET

Make sure that the students' storyboards show the concepts of osmosis and selective permeability accurately.

Use the iText to review the key concepts in Section 7–3.

7–3 Section Assessment

1. The cell membrane allows materials to enter and leave the cell.
2. Diffusion causes many substances to move across a cell membrane without the cell's using energy.
3. Water tends to diffuse from a region where it is highly concentrated to one where it is less concentrated. Water will move across a membrane until equilibrium is reached.
4. The core of nearly all cell membranes is a double-layered sheet called a lipid bilayer. Most cell membranes contain protein molecules that run through the lipid bilayer, and carbohydrate molecules are attached to these proteins. There are so many molecules attached to the membrane that scientists call the membrane a mosaic of molecules.
5. Active transport requires the input of energy, but diffusion does not require additional energy.

Answers to . . .

Figure 7–19 *The molecules are moving from an area of high concentration to an area of low concentration.*

Figure 7–20 *A molecule is moving across the cell membrane from an area of low concentration to an area of high concentration with the help of a transport protein.*

Section 7–4

1 FOCUS

Objectives

7.4.1 ***Describe*** cell specialization.
7.4.2 ***Identify*** the organization levels in multicellular organisms.

Guide for Reading

Vocabulary Preview

On the chalkboard, make a concept map entitled Cell Specialization, using the section's Vocabulary terms. The map should show this hierarchy: cell, tissue, organ, organ system.

Reading Strategy

Have the students rewrite the section's blue headings as questions. Then, have them answer those questions as they read the section.

2 INSTRUCT

Unicellular Organisms

Use Visuals

Figure 7–21 Have students read the caption and study the unicellular organisms. Then, ask: **Which of these unicellular organisms are prokaryotic and which are eukaryotic?** *(The yeast cells and the* Volvox aureus *are eukaryotic. The bacterium* Leptospira interrogans *is prokaryotic.)*

7–4 The Diversity of Cellular Life

Guide for Reading

Key Concepts
- What is cell specialization?
- What are the four levels of organization in multicellular organisms?

Vocabulary
cell specialization
tissue
organ
organ system

Reading Strategy: Using Visuals Before you read, preview **Figure 7–23.** As you read, note the different levels of organization in the body.

Earth is sometimes called a living planet, and for good reason. Living things are found in every corner of the globe—above and below its surface, and deep within its seas. The diversity of life is so great that you might have to remind yourself just how similar the different forms of life really are. All cells, no matter how different they may seem, use the same basic chemistry. This does not, however, mean that all living things are the same. Cells are specialized to perform certain tasks, either as individuals or as parts of larger organisms.

Unicellular Organisms

Cells are the basic living units of all organisms, but sometimes a single cell is a little more than that. Sometimes, a cell *is* the organism. A single-celled organism is also called a unicellular organism. Unicellular organisms do everything that you would expect a living thing to do. They grow, respond to the environment, and reproduce. In some ways, unicellular organisms dominate life on Earth. Some examples of unicellular organisms are shown in **Figure 7–21.**

Unicellular organisms include both prokaryotes and eukaryotes. Prokaryotes, especially bacteria, are remarkably adaptable. Bacteria live almost everywhere—in the soil, on leaves, in the ocean, in the air, and even within the human body.

Many eukaryotes also spend their lives as single cells. Some types of algae, which contain chloroplasts and are found in oceans, lakes, and streams around the world, are single-celled. Yeasts, or unicellular fungi, are also widespread. Yeasts play an important role in breaking down complex nutrients, which makes them available for other organisms. People use yeasts in making bread and other foods.

A few organisms stretch the concept of unicellularity. Some species of protists and algae are colonial. Colonial organisms live in groups of individuals of the same species that are attached to one another but have few specialized structures.

Figure 7–21 Yeasts are unicellular fungi often used in breadmaking. The *Volvox aureus* cells shown are actually individual alga cells that live together in a colony. The spiral-shaped bacterium *Leptospira interrogans* causes a serious disease in humans.

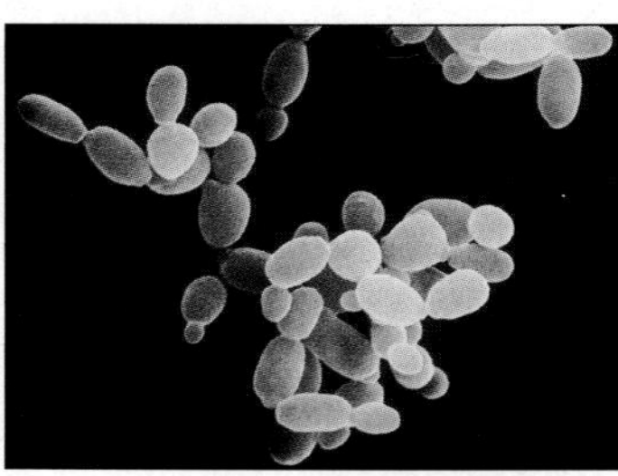

Yeast (magnification: 34,000×)

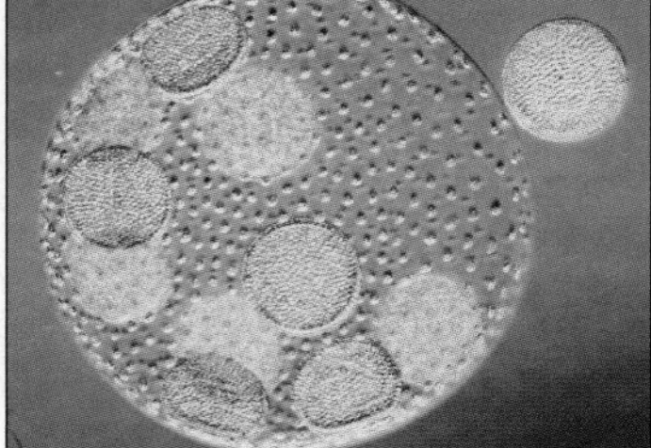

Volvox aureus (magnification: 250×)

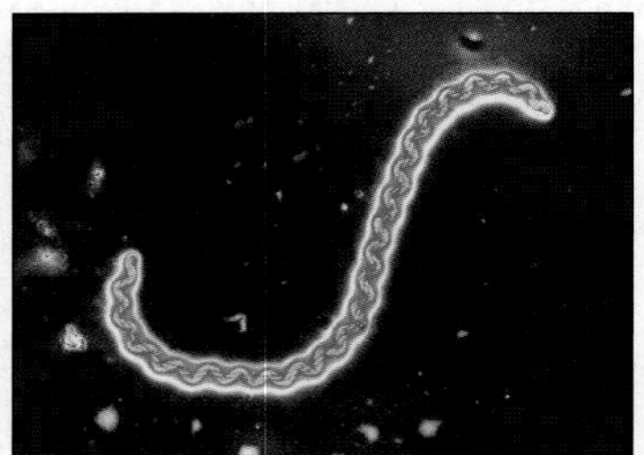

Leptospira interrogans (magnification: 27,000×)

SECTION RESOURCES

Print:
- ***Laboratory Manual B,*** Chapter 7 Lab
- ***Teaching Resources,*** Section Review 7–4
- ***Guided Reading and Study Workbook,*** Section 7–4

Technology:
- ***iText,*** Section 7–4

Figure 7–22 Cell Specialization

Cells in multicellular organisms are specialized to perform particular functions within the organism. Red blood cells transport oxygen throughout the body. Pancreatic cells produce compounds such as insulin that the body needs. Nerve cells transmit information from one part of the body to another. Muscle cells contract and relax to move parts of the body.

Red Blood Cells (magnification: 13,000×)

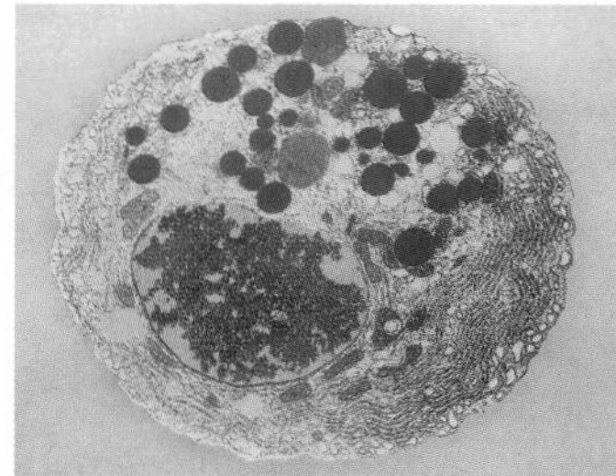

Pancreatic Cell (magnification: 4000×)

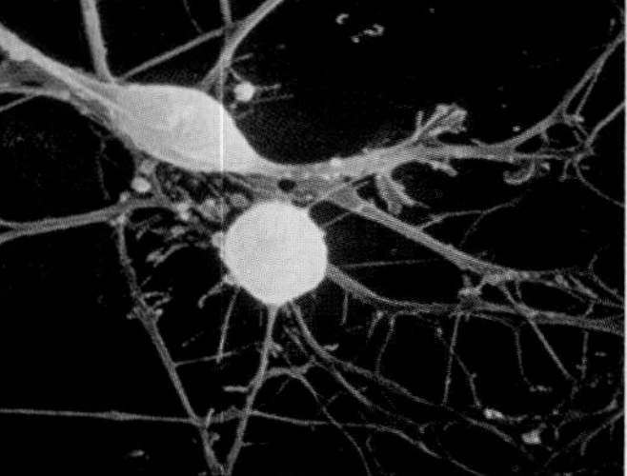

Nerve Cells (magnification: 8900×)

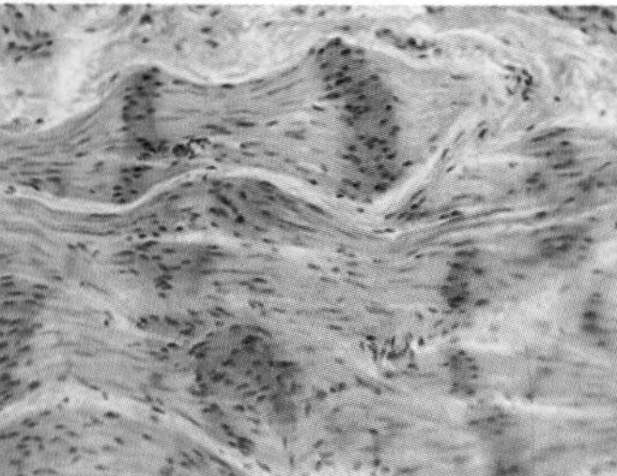

Muscle Cells (magnification 90×)

Multicellular Organisms

The cells of multicellular organisms, such as human beings, do not live on their own. They are interdependent, like the members of a baseball team. Each player has a function that contributes to the success of the team. Organisms that are made up of many cells that work together are called multicellular organisms. Multicellular organisms have **cell specialization,** or separate roles for each type of cell. **Cells in multicellular organisms are specialized to perform particular functions within the organism.** Some cells are specialized to move, others to react to the environment, and still others to produce substances that the organism needs. The human body contains scores of different cell types. Look at **Figure 7–22** to get an idea of specialized cells in the human body.

Pancreatic cells are a good example of cell specialization. These cells are specialized to produce protein enzymes that make it possible to digest food. To perform this function, these cells contain enormous amounts of the organelles involved in protein synthesis—rough endoplasmic reticulum, Golgi apparatus, and clusters of storage vacuoles loaded with protein.

Multicellular Organisms

Use Visuals

Figure 7–22 Discuss with students how each of the cells shown is specialized, carrying out only one or a few particular functions within the organism. Have students contrast these cells with those shown in Figure 7–21. Emphasize that the cells of unicellular organisms must carry out all the essential functions of life, whereas the cells of multicellular organisms are specialists.

Build Science Skills

Using Analogies Introduce students to an analogy between the way cells evolved toward greater specialization and the way society evolved toward greater specialization during the Industrial Revolution. Just as cells became specialized to perform particular functions, people left their generalized lives in rural areas to take jobs in urban industries that produced particular goods or fulfilled particular functions. Challenge students to develop this analogy, either in a class discussion or in individual essays.

TIME SAVER — PRESENTATIONS MADE EASY!

The Presentation Assistant Plus contains the Prentice Hall Presentation Pro and the Transparencies, which provide easy-to-follow visual support for every step of this lesson. If you have a computer presentation station, use Prentice Hall Presentation Pro Section 7–4, or use the transparencies listed here.

Section 7–4:

Interest Grabber
Section Outline
Levels of Organization

Careers in Biology

- Tim Morken's formal professional name is written in this way: Tim Morken, BA, EMT(MSA), HTL(ASCP). The initials after his name indicate that he has a bachelor's degree, is certified to use an electron microscope, and has a histotechnology certificate from the American Society of Clinical Pathologists (ASCP).
- Tim Morken is excited about the new uses of technology in his field. Have students find out what kind of technology is being used by histotechnologists at a local hospital, clinic, or university. Students can gather information by interviewing a local histotechnician or administrator.

Resources Have interested students contact a local college or university to see if it has a certified histotechnology program. They might also gather information about this career by contacting the National Society for Histotechnology.

Take It to the NET

For additional information, visit **www.phschool.com**

Levels of Organization

Build Science Skills

Applying Concepts Show students photographs, diagrams, or slides of various specialized cells. Discuss their specialization and what makes them uniquely suited to their function. For example, you might show human red blood cells. Then, ask: **How would you describe the shape of these cells?** *(They all have a disklike shape.)* **What important function do red blood cells have?** *(Students may know that red blood cells carry oxygen.)* Contrast these cells with cells from epithelial tissue. Elicit from students the idea that epithelial cells are closely packed and regular in appearance, a structure that suits their function of protection.

Careers in Biology

Histotechnologist

Job Description: work in a hospital laboratory, research institution, industrial laboratory, or government agency to prepare slides of body tissues for microscopic examination using special dyes and more advanced techniques, such as an electron microscope

Education: a bachelor's degree from a certified histotechnology program or a bachelor's degree with emphasis in biology and chemistry and one year's experience under a board-certified pathologist to become eligible for national certification exam, leading to a histotechnologist (HTL) certification

Skills: background in biology, anatomy, pathology, and/or chemistry; manual dexterity; attention to detail; good organizational skills; strong writing skills; computer literacy

Highlights: "There are many sides to histotechnology that make the field wide open for people with a variety of interests and skills," says Tim Morken. You will have the opportunity to learn new techniques and use cutting-edge technology as the field is changing. "One hospital I have heard about has no pathologists of its own and instead puts microscope slides on a robotic microscope with a video camera, all controlled and viewed by a pathologist in a distant city!"

"In our laboratory we deal with the most unusual (and deadly) infectious agents on the planet," says Tim Morken. "We are diagnosing and investigating these organisms with cutting-edge molecular biology technology."

Take It to the NET

For more career information, visit the Prentice Hall Web site at **www.phschool.com**.

Levels of Organization

Biologists have identified levels of organization that make it easier to classify and describe the cells within an organism. **The levels of organization in a multicellular organism are individual cells, tissues, organs, and organ systems.** These levels of organization are shown in **Figure 7–23.**

Cells The organization of the cells of the body creates a division of labor among those cells that makes multicellular life possible. Specialized cells such as nerve and muscle cells are able to exist because other cells are specialized to obtain the food and oxygen that those cells need.

This specialization and interdependence is one of the remarkable attributes of living things. Appreciating this is an important step in understanding the nature of living things.

Tissues In multicellular organisms, cells—the first level of organization—are organized in specialized groups called tissues. A **tissue** is a group of similar cells that perform a particular function. The collection of cells that produce digestive enzymes in the pancreas makes up one kind of tissue. This also applies to cells in the eye that respond to light and the contractile cells in muscle.

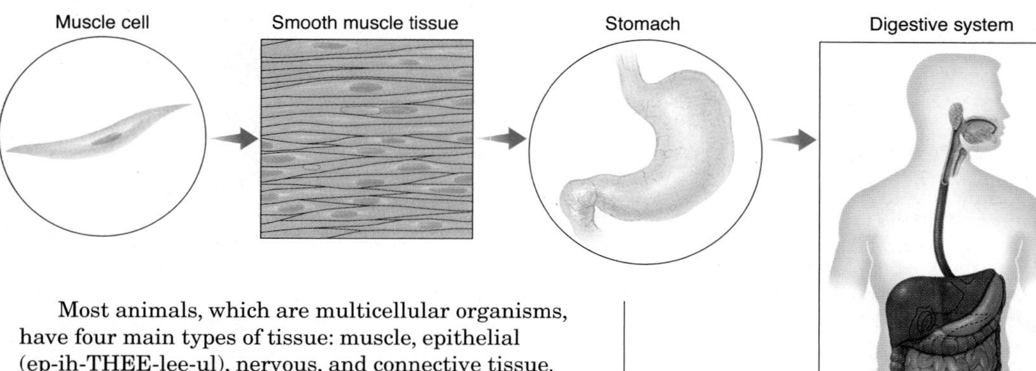

▲ **Figure 7–23** **The levels of organization in a multicellular organism are individual cells, tissues, organs, and organ systems.** In this example, muscle cells make up smooth muscle tissue, which, along with other tissues, makes up the stomach, an organ. The stomach in turn is part of an organ system, the digestive system.

Most animals, which are multicellular organisms, have four main types of tissue: muscle, epithelial (ep-ih-THEE-lee-ul), nervous, and connective tissue. Epithelial tissues, such as skin, cover or line body surfaces. Connective tissues include bone, blood, cartilage, and lymph.

CHECKPOINT *What is a tissue?*

Organs Many tasks within the body are too complicated to be carried out by just one type of tissue. In these cases, many groups of tissues work together as an **organ.** For example, each muscle in your body is an individual organ. Within a muscle, however, there is much more than muscle tissue. There is nerve tissue, and there is connective tissue, which connects different parts of the body. Each tissue performs an essential task to help the organ function.

Organ Systems In most cases, organs must complete a series of specialized tasks. A group of organs that work together to perform a specific function is called an **organ system.** There are 11 major organ systems in the human body, including the muscular, skeletal, circulatory, and nervous systems. You will discover more about organ systems in the human body in Unit 10.

7–4 Section Assessment

1. **Key Concept** In what kinds of organisms is cell specialization a characteristic?
2. **Key Concept** List the levels of biological organization from most simple to most complex.
3. Which level of organization is represented by the eye?
4. Give two examples of an organ system.
5. **Critical Thinking Predicting** Muscle cells have a large number of which organelle?

iTEXT **Assessment** Use iText to review the important concepts in Section 7–4.

ALTERNATIVE ASSESSMENT

Using Analogies

There are different levels of organization in many areas, for example, school and government. Use an area of your life such as school, sports, or extracurricular activities as an example to construct an analogy to explain the levels of organization in living organisms.

Meet Diverse Needs

To reinforce the concept of levels of organization for at-risk students, play a game of Name That Cell, Tissue, Organ, or System. Give students as many examples as you can in random order. Ask them to identify whether the example is a cell, a tissue, an organ, or an organ system. **Learning modality: verbal**

3 ASSESS

Evaluate Understanding

Ask students to explain the levels of organization involved in touch. (*A typical response might mention individual nerve cells, or receptors; brain tissue; the brain; the nervous system.*)

Reteach

Direct students' attention to Figure 7–22 on page 191. Ask them which level of organization is represented by the cells shown. (*Individual cells*) Then, for each kind of specialized cell, discuss the tissue, organ, and organ system of which that cell is a part.

ALTERNATIVE ASSESSMENT

Make sure that each student's analogy appropriately relates an area of the student's life to the levels of organization in living things.

Use iText to review the key concepts in Section 7–4.

7–4 Section Assessment

1. Multicellular organisms have cell specialization.
2. Individual cells, tissues, organs, organ systems
3. The eye represents the organ level of organization, because groups of tissues work together to help the organ function.
4. Students might cite two of the following: muscular system, skeletal system, circulatory system, and nervous system.
5. Muscle cells have a large number of mitochondria, because mitochondria release energy from stored food molecules and muscle cells need great amounts of energy to do the tasks they do.

Answer to . . .

CHECKPOINT *A tissue is a group of similar cells that perform a particular function.*

Real-World Lab

Objective Students will be able to draw conclusions about how the differences in structure between plant and animal cells affect the ways they respond to hypertonic and hypotonic solutions.

Skill Focus Observing, Comparing and Contrasting, Drawing Conclusions

Time 90 minutes (45 minutes for each part)

Advance Prep Order prepared slides of human cheek cells and sterile heparinized sheep blood well in advance. Prepare the concentrated salt solution by dissolving 25 grams of sodium chloride (NaCl) in enough warm water to make a total of 100 milliliters of solution. Obtain or prepare a solution of "photographer's hypo," or 158 grams of sodium thiosulfate ($Na_2S_2O_3$) per liter of water. This solution will remove iodine stains from clothes and hands safely and quickly. Practice the procedure for staining the piece of onion on the slide so you can demonstrate the process to students.

Alternative Materials Other prepared slides of animal cells can be used instead of human cheek cells, as long as the cells' nuclei are clearly visible under the microscope.

Safety

- If students should spill any of the iodine solution, instruct them to quickly wash it off with plenty of water. Do not allow students to use chipped glass slides.
- Use sterile animal blood from a biological supply company.
- Students should be very careful when handling animal blood. Be sure that students wear goggles, disposable plastic gloves, and lab aprons. Make sure to properly dispose of the gloves.

Exploration

Observing Cell Parts and Processes

A cell's structures affect how it responds to changes in its environment. In this investigation, you will observe the differences between plant and animal cells. You will then determine how plant and animal cells are affected by hypertonic and hypotonic solutions and relate those effects to the cells' structures.

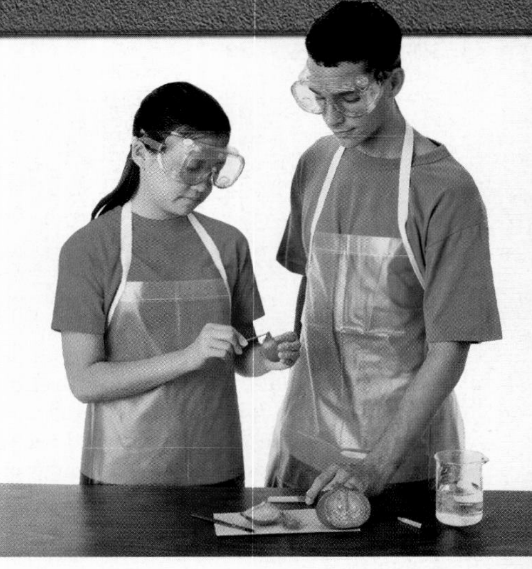

Problem

How do the differences in structure between plant and animal cells affect how they are affected by hypertonic and hypotonic solutions?

Materials

- forceps
- piece of red onion
- scalpel
- 4 glass slides
- dropper pipette
- 4 coverslips
- iodine solution
- paper towel
- microscope
- plastic gloves
- prepared slide of human cheek cells
- concentrated salt solution
- distilled water
- treated animal blood

Skills

Observing, Comparing and Contrasting, Drawing Conclusions

Procedure

Part A: Plant and Animal Cell Structures

1. Put on safety goggles and a lab apron. Using forceps, peel a thin layer from the inner surface of a piece of a red onion, as shown in the photograph.
2. Use a scalpel to cut a small piece out of the layer you removed. **CAUTION:** *The scalpel is very sharp. Handle it carefully and make sure to cut away from yourself.*
3. Place the piece of onion in the center of a glass slide. Add a drop of water to the piece of onion and cover it with a coverslip.
4. Use a dropper pipette to place a drop of iodine solution at one end of the coverslip. **CAUTION:** *Iodine can stain skin and clothing. Be careful not to spill it on yourself.* Hold a piece of paper towel near the opposite edge of the coverslip, as shown in the diagram. This will draw the iodine under the coverslip, where it will stain the onion cells.
5. Examine your slide under the low-power objective of the microscope. **CAUTION:** *Microscopes and slides are fragile. Handle them carefully.* Sketch one cell and label any structures you recognize.
6. Carefully switch to high power and observe the cell again. Try to identify other cell structures and add them to your sketch with appropriate labels.
7. Repeat steps 5 and 6 using prepared slides of human cheek cells.

Part B: Effects of Hypertonic and Hypotonic Solutions

8. Repeat steps 1 to 3 to prepare another onion cell wet mount. Using the same method as in step 4, add a drop of concentrated salt solution to the slide and use a paper towel to draw it under the coverslip.

Analyze and Conclude

1. Onion cells are generally rectangular, with some variation in size and shape. Cheek cells are flat and roughly circular. The onion cells have rigid cell walls and distinct nuclei, both of which stain with iodine. Students may be able to see vacuoles in the centers of onion cells and dark spots (other organelles) outside the nucleus. The cheek cells do not have cell walls. Students should be able to see cell membranes as well as the nucleus within each cell. They may also see other dark spots (other organelles). Cell walls protect the cell and provide support. The nucleus directs cell activities and is where genetic material is stored. Vacuoles store water and other materials. Cell membranes regulate what enters and leaves the cell.

2. Plant and animal cells both have cell membranes and nuclei. Plant cells have cell walls, whereas animal cells do not.

3. The concentration of water was greater inside the cells than in the salt solution, so osmotic pressure moved water out of the cells. The cytoplasm of the cells then shrank away from the cell walls.

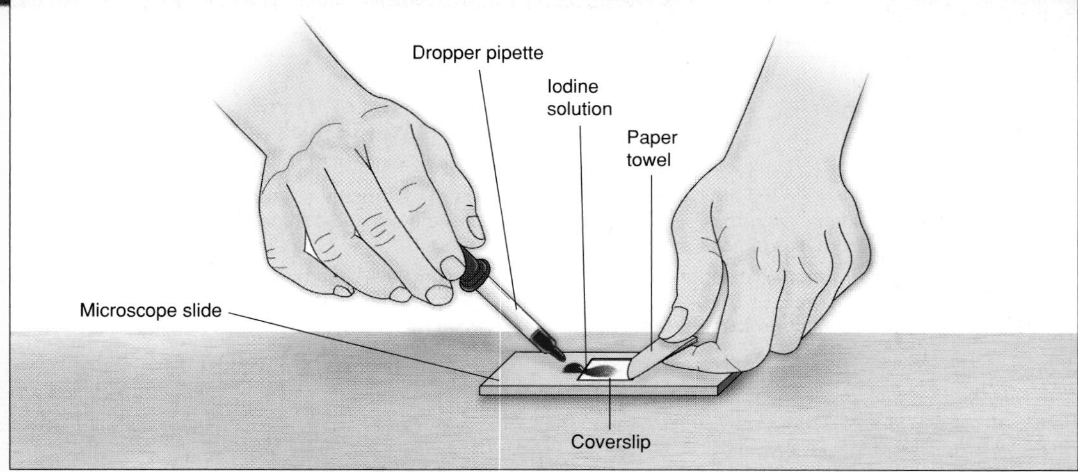

9. Observe the onion cells under the microscope under both low power and high power. Record your observations.
10. Put on your plastic gloves. Prepare a wet-mount slide using treated animal blood. **CAUTION:** *Use only blood samples provided by your teacher.* Do not add water as you did with the onion cells.
11. Observe the blood cells under the microscope under low power and high power. Sketch one cell and label any structures you recognize.
12. Using the same method as in step 4, add a drop of concentrated salt solution to the slide and use a paper towel to draw it under the coverslip.
13. Observe the blood cells under the microscope under both low power and high power. Record your observations. Rinse out the dropper pipette with distilled water.
14. Prepare another wet-mount slide of blood cells. This time, add a drop of distilled water to the slide and draw it under the coverslip.
15. Observe the blood cells under the microscope under both low power and high power. Record your observations.
16. Remove the plastic gloves and discard them according to your teacher's instructions. Wash your hands thoroughly with warm water and soap.

Analyze and Conclude

1. **Applying Concepts** Describe the general shapes of the onion cells and the cheek cells you observed in Part A. What structures did you see in the onion cells? The cheek cells? Describe the functions of each of the structures you saw.
2. **Comparing and Contrasting** How are plant and animal cells similar in structure? How are they different?
3. **Drawing Conclusions** Explain your observations in step 9 in terms of osmosis.
4. **Drawing Conclusions** Explain your observations in steps 13 and 15 in terms of osmosis.
5. **Applying Concepts** What part of the cell is involved in the processes you observed in steps 9, 13, and 15? Explain your answer.
6. **Comparing and Contrasting** Why don't onion cells burst when they are in distilled water? Relate your answer to the differences between plant and animal cells.

Go Further

Designing Experiments Design one or more experiments to test the effects of hypotonic and hypertonic solutions on other cells. Make sure to write a hypothesis for each experiment and control all variables. Get your teacher's permission before carrying out your experiments.

Prelab Discussion Have students read through the lab. Answer any questions they have about materials and procedure. Then, ask: **Why is the iodine solution used to stain the piece of onion?** *(The iodine will make some of the cell structures more visible under the microscope.)* **What is osmosis?** *(Osmosis is the diffusion of water through a selectively permeable membrane.)* **How do differences in the concentration of molecules of a substance affect diffusion across a cell membrane?** *(Diffusion across a cell membrane occurs as molecules of a substance move from areas of high concentration to areas of lower concentration.)*

Teaching Tips
- Review the proper use of a microscope before students perform this lab.
- If microscopes include a mirror rather than a built-in light source, make sure students do not use sunlight as a light source, because doing so could damage their eyes.

Procedure

Part A

1. Demonstrate how to peel a thin layer from the inner surface of a piece of red onion.

4. Demonstrate how to hold a piece of paper towel near the opposite edge of a coverslip in order to draw the iodine under it.

Part B

10. Demonstrate how to prepare a wet-mount slide using animal blood.

13. Make sure students rinse out the dropper pipette with distilled water.

Expected Outcomes
- In Part A, students should observe and draw the cell membranes and nuclei of the plant and animal cells and the cell wall of the plant cell.
- In Part B, students should observe that the plant and animal cells shrink in the concentrated salt solution, while only the animal cells expand in the distilled water.

Go Further

A typical experiment will be similar to the steps in Part B of this lab. You may want to suggest that students design their experiments with protists or bacteria in mind.

4. In step 13, the cells shrank. Because the concentration of water was greater inside the cells than in the salt solution outside the cells, osmotic pressure moved water out of the cells. In step 15, the cells expanded, and some may have burst. Because the concentration of water was greater in the distilled water than inside the cells, osmotic pressure moved water into the cells.

5. The cell membrane was involved. Water moves in and out of the cell by osmosis through the cell membrane.

6. The cell walls of the onion cells are strong enough to keep the cells from bursting. Animal cells do not have cell walls, so they may burst.

Chapter 7 Study Guide

Study Tip

Divide the class into small groups, and have each group generate a list of questions about the Vocabulary terms and the Key Concepts for each of the four sections. When groups have completed their lists, have groups exchange lists of questions. Each group should end up with a list of questions for each section from four different groups. Ask the students in each group to collaborate in answering the questions they received from other groups.

Thinking Visually

Typically, a student's concept map will label the first level Movement Into and Out of a Cell. The next level should include Diffusion and Active Transport. A line from Diffusion should connect to Osmosis and Facilitated Diffusion. Lines from Active Transport should connect to Endocytosis and Exocytosis. A line from Endocytosis should connect to Phagocytosis.

Chapter 7 Study Guide

7–1 Life Is Cellular

Key Concepts

- The cell theory states that all living things are composed of cells, cells are the basic units of structure and function in living things, and new cells are produced from existing cells.
- Biologists divide cells into two categories: eukaryotes and prokaryotes. The cells of eukaryotes have a nucleus; the cells of prokaryotes do not.

Vocabulary
- cell, p. 170 • cell theory, p. 170
- cell membrane, p. 171 • cell wall, p. 171
- nucleus, p. 171 • cytoplasm, p. 171
- prokaryote, p. 172 • eukaryote, p. 172
- organelle, p. 172

7–2 Cell Structures

Key Concepts

- The main function of the cell wall is to provide support and protection for the cell.
- The nucleus controls most cell processes and contains the hereditary information of DNA.
- The cytoskeleton is a network of protein filaments that helps the cell to maintain its shape. The cytoskeleton is also involved in many forms of cell movement.
- The endoplasmic reticulum is the organelle in which components of the cell membrane are assembled and some proteins are modified.
- Enzymes in the Golgi apparatus attach carbohydrates and lipids to proteins.
- Chloroplasts use the energy from sunlight to make energy-rich food molecules, a process known as photosynthesis.
- Mitochondria use energy from food to make high-energy compounds that the cell can use to power growth, development, and movement.

Vocabulary
- chromatin, p. 175 • chromosome, p. 175
- nucleolus, p. 176 • nuclear envelope, p. 176
- cytoskeleton, p. 176 • microtubule, p. 176
- microfilament, p. 176 • ribosome, p. 177
- endoplasmic reticulum, p. 177
- Golgi apparatus, p. 178 • lysosome, p. 178
- vacuole, p. 179 • chloroplast, p. 180
- mitochondrion, p. 180

7–3 Movement Through the Membrane

Key Concepts

- The cell membrane regulates what enters and leaves the cell and also provides protection and support.
- Diffusion causes many substances to move across a cell membrane but does not require the cell to use energy.
- Osmosis is the diffusion of water through a selectively permeable membrane.

Vocabulary

lipid bilayer, p. 184
concentration, p. 185
diffusion, p. 185
selective permeability, p. 186
osmosis, p. 186
facilitated diffusion, p. 188
active transport, p. 189
endocytosis, p. 189
phagocytosis, p. 189
exocytosis, p. 189

7–4 The Diversity of Cellular Life

Key Concepts

- Cells in multicellular organisms are specialized to perform particular functions within the organism.
- The levels of organization in a multicellular organism are individual cells, tissues, organs, and organ systems.

Vocabulary

cell specialization, p. 191
tissue, p. 192
organ, p. 193
organ system, p. 193

Thinking Visually

Use the information in this chapter to create a concept map about the ways substances can move into and out of cells. Use the following terms in your concept map: *diffusion, osmosis, facilitated diffusion, active transport, phagocytosis, endocytosis, exocytosis.*

Chapter 7 Assessment

Reviewing Content

1. d	**5.** c	**9.** d
2. b	**6.** a	**10.** a
3. b	**7.** d	
4. b	**8.** c	

Understanding Concepts

11. Robert Hooke observed cork slices and named cells. Matthias Schleiden concluded that all plants are made of cells. Theodor Schwann concluded that all animals are made of cells. Rudolf Virchow concluded that all cells come from preexisting cells.

12. Both prokaryotic and eukaryotic cells contain cytoplasm and a cell membrane. Both types of cells carry out life processes of growth, reproduction, and response. All bacteria are prokaryotes. Eukaryotes also contain a nucleus and cell organelles. All plants, animals, fungi, and many microorganisms are eukaryotes.

CHAPTER RESOURCES

Print:
- ***Teaching Resources,*** Chapter Vocabulary Review, Graphic Organizer
- ***Chapter Tests: Levels A and B,*** Chapter 7 Test
- ***PH Assessment System,*** Practice Test

Technology:
- ***Computer Test Bank,*** Chapter 7 Test
- ***iText,*** Chapter 7 Assessment

Chapter 7 Assessment

Reviewing Content

Choose the letter that best answers the question or completes the statement.

1. In many cells, the structure that controls the cell's activities is the
   a. cell membrane. c. nucleolus.
   b. organelle. d. nucleus.
2. Despite differences in size and shape, all cells must have cytoplasm and a
   a. cell wall. c. mitochondrion.
   b. cell membrane. d. nucleus.
3. If a cell of an organism contains a nucleus, the organism is a(an)
   a. plant. c. animal.
   b. eukaryote. d. prokaryote.
4. Distinct threadlike structures containing genetic information are called
   a. ribosomes. c. nuclei.
   b. chromosomes. d. mitochondria.
5. The organelle that makes energy available for the cell is the
   a. nucleolus. c. mitochondrion.
   b. chromosome. d. chloroplast.
6. Cell membranes are constructed mainly of
   a. lipid bilayers. c. carbohydrate gates.
   b. protein pumps. d. free-moving proteins.
7. The movement of water molecules across a selectively permeable membrane is known as
   a. exocytosis. c. endocytosis.
   b. phagocytosis. d. osmosis.
8. A substance that moves across a cell membrane without using the cell's energy tends to move
   a. away from the area of equilibrium.
   b. away from the area where it is less concentrated.
   c. away from the area where it is more concentrated.
   d. toward the area where it is more concentrated.
9. Which cell is best suited to transmit information through the human body?

a. 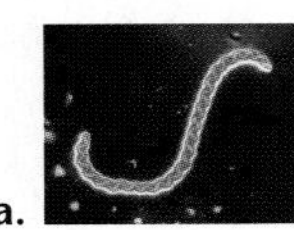

c. 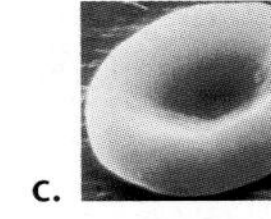

b. 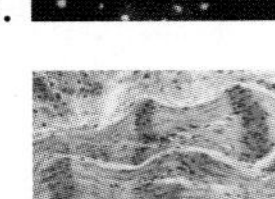

d. 

10. A tissue is composed of a group of
    a. similar cells.
    b. related organelles.
    c. organ systems.
    d. related organs.

Understanding Concepts

11. Make a table to summarize the contributions made to the cell theory by Robert Hooke, Matthias Schleiden, Theodor Schwann, and Rudolf Virchow.
12. How are prokaryotic and eukaryotic cells alike? How do they differ?
13. Draw a cell nucleus. Label and give the function of the following structures: chromatin, nucleolus, and nuclear envelope.
14. Name and describe the two types of structures that make up the cytoskeleton.
15. What is the function of ribosomes?
16. What happens in the rough endoplasmic reticulum?
17. Describe the role of the Golgi apparatus.
18. Which two organelles contain their own DNA? What hypothesis has Lynn Margulis proposed to account for the presence of DNA in these organelles?
19. Briefly describe the structure of a cell membrane. How does the cell membrane affect the contents of a cell?
20. What is meant by the concentration of a solution? Give a specific example of concentration involving volume and mass.
21. Describe the process of diffusion. Name and describe the condition that exists when the diffusion of a particular substance is complete.
22. What is the relationship between osmosis and diffusion? By definition, what's the only substance that can carry out osmosis?
23. Using the example of a sugar solution, explain what is meant by an isotonic solution.
24. Name and describe the cell structure that helps prevent damage to certain cells when they are subjected to high osmotic pressure.
25. Use an example to describe the relationship among cells, tissues, organs, and organ systems.

TIME SAVER — HOMEWORK GUIDE

Section:	Questions:
Section 7–1	1–3, 11, 12
Section 7–2	4, 5, 13–18, 29, 31, 34, 35
Section 7–3	6–8, 19–24, 26–28, 30
Section 7–3	9, 10, 25, 32, 33

13. chromatin—granular material within nucleus consists of DNA bound to protein; nucleolus—small dense region where the assembly of ribosomes begins; nuclear envelope—a double membrane layer containing many pores that allow materials to move into and out of the nucleus

14. Microtubules are hollow tubes of protein that maintain cell shape and serve as "tracks" along which cell organelles are moved. Microfilaments are long, thin fibers that function in the movement and support of the cell.

15. Ribosomes produce proteins following coded instructions that come from the nucleus.

16. Ribosomes are found on the rough ER surface; newly made proteins move from these ribosomes to the rough ER, where they may be chemically modified.

17. The Golgi apparatus contains enzymes that attach carbohydrates and lipids to proteins.

18. Mitochondria and chloroplasts contain their own DNA. Lynn Margulis has suggested that mitochondria and chloroplasts are descendants of ancient prokaryotes.

19. The core of the cell membrane is made up of a lipid bilayer. Protein molecules, which have carbohydrates attached to them, run through this layer. The proteins form channels and pumps that enable materials to move across the cell membrane.

20. The concentration of a solution is the mass of solute in a given volume of solution, or mass/volume. For example, if you dissolved 12 grams of salt in 3 liters of water, the concentration of the solution would be 12 g / 3 L, or 4 grams per liter.

21. Diffusion is the process that allows substances to move across a cell membrane without using the cell's energy. Substances tend to move from an area of greater concentration to an area of lesser concentration. When the concentration of a substance is the same on both sides of the membrane, equilibrium is reached.

22. Osmosis is the diffusion of water through a selectively permeable membrane. Only water can move by osmosis.

23. Water will move across a membrane until equilibrium is reached. When that happens, the concentration of a water and sugar solution will be the same on both sides of the membrane. The two solutions are isotonic, or the same strength.

24. Cell walls help prevent damage to cells when they are subjected to high osmotic pressure. Cell walls provide support, preventing the cells from expanding.

25. Muscle cells make up smooth muscle tissue, which is part of the stomach, an organ. The stomach and other organs make up the digestive system.

Critical Thinking

26. The water level on the left side will increase, and the water level on the right side will decrease. This is a result of water's moving from an area of higher concentration to an area of lower concentration.

27. Solution A is more concentrated because there are 3 grams of salt per liter compared to the 2 grams per liter in Solution B.

28. The blood cells would shrink. The water in the solution is less concentrated than the water inside the cells. The water inside the cells would move across the membrane until equilibrium was reached.

29. Because muscle cells are responsible for movement, they require more energy than skin cells. Therefore, skin cells contain fewer mitochondria.

30. Most students will develop an experiment in which the rate of diffusion of food coloring is observed by dropping equal amounts of food coloring into each beaker. Make sure that students identify the control (water at room temperature).

31. The cell wall gives the plant cell structure and shape, whereas an animal cell has an irregular shape. Chloroplasts give the plant cell its green color and allow it to carry out photosynthesis.

Chapter 7 Assessment

Critical Thinking

26. **Predicting** The beaker in the diagram has a selectively permeable membrane separating two solutions. Assume that the salt molecules can pass freely through the membrane. Will the water level on either side of the membrane change? Explain your answer.

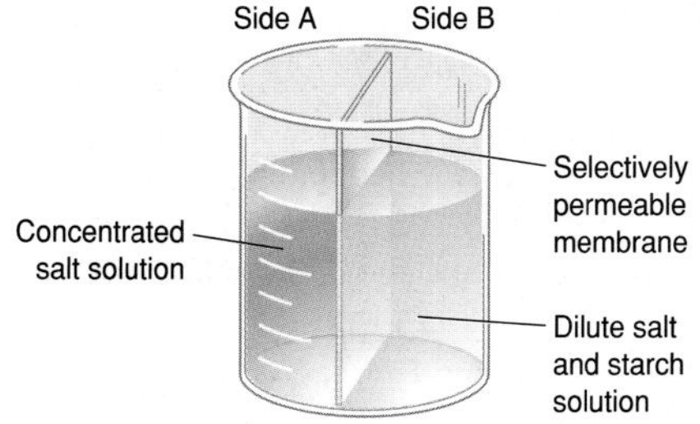

27. **Calculating** Which salt solution is more concentrated, solution A, which contains 18 g of salt in 6 L of water, or solution B, which contains 24 g of salt in 12 L of water? Explain.

28. **Predicting** What would happen to a sample of your red blood cells if they were placed into a hypotonic solution? Explain your prediction.

29. **Inferring** Would you expect skin cells to contain more or fewer mitochondria than muscle cells? Explain your answer.

30. **Designing Experiments** You are given vegetable coloring and three beakers. The first beaker contains water at room temperature, the second beaker contains ice water, and the third beaker contains hot water. Design an experiment to determine the effects of temperature on the rate of diffusion. Be sure to state your hypothesis and to include a control.

31. **Comparing and Contrasting** Describe how the characteristics of a plant cell differ from those of an animal cell because plant cells contain cell walls and chloroplasts.

32. **Inferring** The pancreas, an organ present in certain animals, produces enzymes used elsewhere in the animals' digestive systems. Which cell structure(s) might produce those enzymes? Explain your answer.

33. **Comparing and Contrasting** How does a unicellular organism differ from the single cell of a multicellular organism?

34. **Using Analogies** Compare a cell to a factory, as in the chapter, or to something else, such as a school. (For example, a cell has a nucleus, and a school has a principal.) Use that analogy to describe the function of different parts of the cell.

35. **Making Connections** In Chapter 2, you learned about four categories of carbon compounds called the "molecules of life." Explain where some of those compounds are found in a typical cell.

Performance-Based Assessment

Prepare to Debate One day, unicellular organisms got tired of being referred to as simple organisms by the multicellular organisms. They felt that they should be recognized as complex individuals and challenged the multicellular organisms to a debate. As a unicellular organism, what arguments would you use to defend your position?

How do illustrations of cell organelles compare to the real things? Visit the Prentice Hall Web site at **www.phschool.com** to find out more about the parts of a plant cell. Then, answer the following questions:

- What are the indentations in the inner mitochondrial membrane called? What is the inner space called? What processes occur in each location?
- What is a thylakoid? Use the "zoom" action for a closer look. Describe the difference, if any, between the illustration and the electron micrograph of the thylakoids.
- Compare the nuclear pores in the illustration of the nucleus to those in the photograph taken through an electron micrograph.

Performance-Based Assessment

Student answers should be scientifically accurate. Students' answers should demonstrate an understanding of the complex life processes that go on inside a cell.

Take It to the NET

- The indentations in the inner mitochondrial membrane, called cristae, are clearly shown in the micrograph. The inner fluid-filled space is called the mitochondrial matrix. The cristae are the sites where NADH oxidation, electron transport, and oxidative phosphorylation occur. The matrix stores Krebs cycle enzymes and is responsible for carbon dioxide production and generation of NADH and other reductants.

Standardized Test Prep

Test-Taking Tip When you answer a question based on experimental data, read the description of the experiment carefully to determine the steps followed. Then, try to see if there are any trends in the data. For example, "if x increases, what happens to y?"

Directions: Choose the letter that best answers the question or completes the statement.

1. Animals cells have all of the following EXCEPT
(A) mitochondria. (D) a cell membrane.
(B) chloroplasts. (E) Golgi apparatus.
(C) a nucleus.

2. The nucleus includes all of the following structures EXCEPT
(A) cytoplasm. (D) nucleolus.
(B) nuclear envelope. (E) chromatin.
(C) DNA.

3. In a typical cell placed into fresh water, osmotic pressure produces
(A) active transport.
(B) a net movement of water out of the cell.
(C) a net movement of water into the cell.
(D) protein synthesis.
(E) no change.

4. Which of the following are sometimes found attached to the endoplasmic reticulum?
(A) chloroplasts (D) nuclei
(B) mitochondria (E) ribosomes
(C) vacuoles

5. Which process always involves the movement of materials from inside the cell to outside the cell?
(A) phagocytosis (D) exocytosis
(B) endocytosis (E) osmosis
(C) diffusion

Questions 6–7 Complete each analogy by selecting the correct letter. In analogies, A : B :: C : __?__ *means* A is to B as C is to __?__.

6. Connective tissue : bone :: epithelial tissue : __?__
(A) cartilage (D) nerves
(B) muscles (E) blood
(C) skin

7. Support : cell wall :: energy release : __?__
(A) cytoskeleton (D) ribosomes
(B) nucleus (E) mitochondria
(C) Golgi apparatus

8. Which of the following is NOT an example of active transport?
I. Facilitated diffusion
II. Osmosis
III. Diffusion
(A) I only (D) II and III only
(B) III only (E) I, II, and III
(C) I and II only

9. Which of the following is an example of a eukaryote?
I. Plant
II. Bacterium
III. Fungus
(A) I only (D) II and III only
(B) II only (E) I, II, and III
(C) I and III only

Questions 10–11

In an experiment, plant cells were placed in sucrose solutions of varying concentrations. The rate at which the plant cells absorbed sucrose from the solution was then measured for the different concentrations. The results are summarized in the graph.

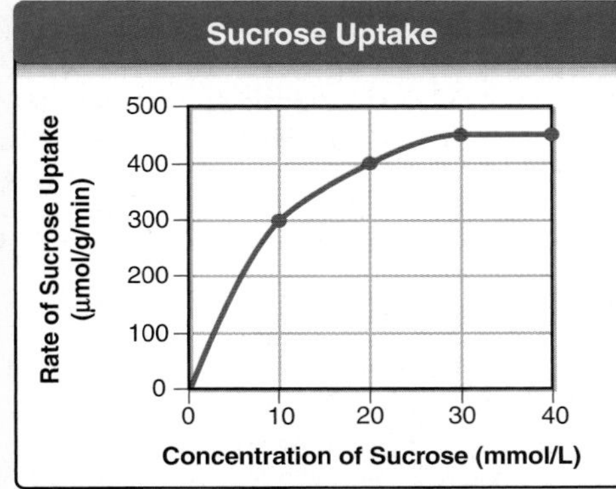

10. In each experiment, there was a positive sucrose uptake. Sucrose probably entered the cells by means of
(A) endocytosis. (D) phagocytosis.
(B) osmosis. (E) active transport.
(C) exocytosis.

11. The graph shows that as the concentration of sucrose increases from 10 to 30 mmol/L, the plant cells
(A) take in sucrose more slowly.
(B) take in sucrose more quickly.
(C) fail to take in more sucrose.
(D) secrete sucrose more slowly.
(E) secrete sucrose more quickly.

Standardized Test Prep

1. B **2.** A **3.** C **4.** E **5.** D **6.** C **7.** E **8.** E **9.** C **10.** E **11.** B

Chapter 7 Assessment (continued)

32. Ribosomes are responsible for making proteins. Because enzymes are proteins, the ribosomes would be present in the pancreas.

33. The single cell of a unicellular organism performs all the life processes of the organism. It is in direct contact with the outer environment and can take in and release substances as needed. The single cell of a multicellular organism is specialized to carry on certain functions for the whole organism. It is dependent upon the other cells to obtain needed substances and complete other life processes.

34. Students should demonstrate an understanding of the functions of different parts of the cell.

35. Carbohydrates are found in the mitochondria, where they are converted into high-energy compounds. Lipids are found in the cell membrane, made up of the lipid bilayer. Proteins are found in ribosomes, where they are manufactured. Nucleic acids are found in the cells' chromosomes, where genetic information is stored.

- A thylakoid is a membrane in which the most important processes of photosynthesis take place. The inside view of the illustration shows the thylakoids in even stacks, or grana, each containing three to seven membranes of approximately the same width. The stacks are parallel to each other and are spaced at regular intervals. On the other hand, the stacks (grana) shown in the EM are not parallel but occur at various angles within the cell and at irregular intervals. The thylakoids in the EM are of varying width, and parts of some membranes extend beyond the stack.
- In both the drawing and the micrograph, the nuclear pores are equidistantly spaced over the nuclear envelope.

For additional information, visit

www.phschool.com

Chapter Planner 8 Photosynthesis

Section and Section Objectives	Time	Activities and Labs
8–1 Energy and Life, pp. 201–203 **8.1.1** ***Explain*** where plants get the energy they need to produce food. **8.1.2** ***Describe*** the role of ATP in cellular activities.	**1 period (1/2 block)**	**SE:** ***Inquiry Activity,*** How do organisms capture and use energy?, p. 200
8–2 Photosynthesis: An Overview, pp. 204–207 **8.2.1** ***Explain*** what the experiments of van Helmont, Priestley, and Ingenhousz reveal about how plants grow. **8.2.2** ***State*** the overall equation for photosynthesis. **8.2.3** ***Describe*** the role of light and chlorophyll in photosynthesis.	**1 period (1/2 block)**	**SE:** ***Biology and History,*** Understanding Photosynthesis, pp. 204–205 **SE:** ***Quick Lab,*** What colors of light does chlorophyll absorb?, p. 206
8–3 The Reactions of Photosynthesis, pp. 208–214 **8.3.1** ***Describe*** the structure and function of a chloroplast. **8.3.2** ***Describe*** what happens in the light-dependent reactions. **8.3.3** ***Explain*** what the Calvin cycle is. **8.3.4** ***Identify*** factors that affect the rate at which photosynthesis occurs.	**2 periods (1 block)**	**TE:** ***Demonstration,*** p. 210 **SE:** ***Analyzing Data,*** p. 213 **SE:** ***Design an Experiment,*** Investigating Photosynthesis, p. 215
Chapter Assessment, pp. 216–219	**1 period (1/2 block)**	

ACTIVITY PLANNER

SE: ***Inquiry Activity,*** p. 200; (10 min.); 2 test tubes, aluminum foil, *Euglena* in water

SE: ***Quick Lab,*** p. 206; (15 min.); spectroscope, test tube of chlorophyll solution, colored pencils or markers

TE: ***Demonstration,*** p. 210; freshly picked green leaf, bowl, water

SE: ***Design an Experiment,*** p. 215; (60 min.); scissors, black construction paper, potted plant, tape, cellophane (blue, red, and green), 5 large test tubes, glass-marking pencil, forceps, 400-mL beaker, 5 petri dishes, iodine solution, paper towels

PLANNING KEY

Ability Levels

- **B Basic** — For students who need additional help
- **A Average** — For all students
- **E Enriched** — For students who need to be challenged

Components

SE	Student Edition	**GRSW**	Guided Reading and Study Workbook	**IDM**	Issues and Decision Making
TE	Teacher's Edition	**CT**	Chapter Tests: Levels A and B	**CTB**	Computer Test Bank
LMA	Laboratory Manual A	**PHAS**	PH Assessment System	**PA**	Presentation Assistant Plus
LMB	Laboratory Manual B	**LA**	Lab Assessment with Scoring Guide	**BD**	BioDetectives Videotape
TR	Teaching Resources	**BTM**	BioTechnology Manual	**iT**	iText
IF	Investigations in Forensics				

Program Resources	Assessment	Media and Technology
TR: Section Review 8–1 B A **GRSW:** Section 8–1 B A	**SE:** 8–1 Section Assessment, p. 203 **TR:** Section Review 8–1	**PA:** 8–1 Interest Grabber, Section Outline, ATP, Figure 8–3 **iT:** Section 8–1
LMA: Chapter 8 Lab A E **LMB:** Chapter 8 Lab B A **TR:** Section Review 8–2 B A **GRSW:** Section 8–2 B A	**SE:** 8–2 Section Assessment, p. 207 **TR:** Section Review 8–2	**PA:** 8–2 Interest Grabber, Section Outline, Photosynthesis: Reactants and Products, Figure 8–5 **iT:** Section 8–2
TR: Section Review 8–3 B A Chapter 8 Design an Experiment B A E **GRSW:** Section 8–3 B A **BTM:** Lab 17, Issue 4 A E	**SE:** 8–3 Section Assessment, p. 214 **TR:** Section Review 8–3	**PA:** 8–3 Interest Grabber, Section Outline, Concept Map, Figure 8–7, Figure 8–10, Figure 8–11 **iT:** Section 8–3
	SE: Chapter 8 Assessment, pp. 216–219 **TR:** Chapter Vocabulary Review, Graphic Organizer **CB:** Chapter 8 Test **CTB:** Chapter 8 Test **PHAS:** Practice Test	**CTB:** Chapter 8 Test **iT:** Chapter 8 Assessment

PRESSED FOR TIME?

To Preview the Chapter
- Introduce students to Key Concepts and Vocabulary terms in each section.
- Assign the Reading Strategies for each section.

To Cover the Chapter Quickly
- Have students read all of Section 8–1, read The Photosynthesis Equation and Figure 8–4 in Section 8–2, and Figures 8–7, 8–10, and 8–11 in Section 8–3.
- Assign the 8–1 Section Assessment and questions 1–14 in Chapter 8 Assessment and questions 1–10 in Chapter 8 Standardized Test Prep.

To Review the Chapter
- Assign the Section Reviews for 8–1 through 8–3 in the Guided Reading and Study Workbook.
- Assign Section Reviews for 8–1 through 8–3 and the Chapter Vocabulary Review for Chapter 8 in the Teaching Resources.

Chapter 8

ENGAGE/EXPLORE

Inquiry Activity

Objective Students will be able to infer that photosynthetic organisms obtain energy from sunlight.

Skill Focus **Predicting, Inferring**

Materials 2 test tubes, aluminum foil, *Euglena* in water

Time 10 minutes

Advance Prep Pour a culture containing *Euglena* into all the test tubes. Cover the test tubes completely with foil. Tear a small hole in the foil on the sides of half the test tubes. Set up the test tubes a day in advance so that the organisms will distribute accordingly.

Safety Remind students to handle the glass test tubes carefully.

Strategies

- Make sure that the test tubes are in bright light.
- Show students a test tube with a *Euglena* culture so they know what to look for.

Expected Outcome Students should observe that the *Euglena* congregate near the hole in the foil where they can get light.

Think About It

1. In the completely covered test tube, the *Euglena* are evenly distributed. In the test tube with the hole in the foil, the *Euglena* should all be near the hole. The *Euglena* are drawn to the hole because of the light.
2. Light is the source of energy for the *Euglena*.

Assess Prior Knowledge

Challenge students to recall their observations of patterns of plant growth in parks and backyards. Ask: **Why don't bushes or other trees usually grow underneath large trees?** *(There's not enough sunlight for such plants to grow.)* **Why do plants need sunlight to grow?** *(Plants need sunlight to make food.)* Then, ask students to describe their understanding about how this food-making process occurs.

Chapter 8 Photosynthesis

This leaf is carrying out photosynthesis, which converts light energy into chemical energy that the grasshoppers can use.

Inquiry Activity

How do organisms capture and use energy?

Procedure

1. Obtain two test tubes wrapped in foil. Note the hole in the foil surrounding one test tube.
2. **Predicting** The test tubes contain *Euglena*, photosynthetic microorganisms that have chloroplasts and can move. Record your prediction of where in each test tube you will find *Euglena.*
3. Without shaking or disturbing the contents of the test tubes, carefully remove the foil. Record where *Euglena* are located in each test tube.

Think About It

1. **Observing** What pattern did you observe in the distribution of the *Euglena?* Why do you think they behave this way?
2. **Inferring** What is the source of energy that powers the *Euglena*'s swimming?

FACTS AND FIGURES

Photosynthesis drives carbon cycle
Photosynthesis is an integral part of one of the important biogeochemical cycles, the carbon cycle. Essentially, the carbon cycle consists of the complementary processes of photosynthesis and cellular respiration. Autotrophs, such as plants, produce carbohydrates using the carbon in carbon dioxide. Both autotrophs and heterotrophs, such as grasshoppers that eat plants, use those carbohydrates in cellular respiration, a product of which is carbon dioxide. In this way, carbon continually circulates through Earth's ecosystems. There is no corresponding cycle of energy, though. The energy captured from sunlight by photosynthetic organisms is used and released in the cellular respiration of living things. This energy is ultimately dissipated as heat. The energy used by living things must be continually replenished through photosynthesis.

8–1 Energy and Life

Energy is the ability to do work. Nearly every activity in modern society depends on one kind of energy or another. When a car runs out of fuel—more precisely, out of the chemical energy in gasoline—it comes to a sputtering halt. Without electrical energy, lights, appliances, and computers stop working.

Living things depend on energy, too. Sometimes, the need for energy is easy to see. It is obvious that energy is needed to play soccer or other sports. However, there are times when that need is less obvious. For example, when you are sleeping, your cells are busy using energy to build new proteins and amino acids. Clearly, without the ability to obtain and use energy, life would cease to exist.

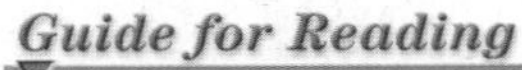

 **Key Concepts**
- Where do plants get the energy they need to produce food?
- What is the role of ATP in cellular activities?

Vocabulary
autotroph
heterotroph
adenosine triphosphate (ATP)

Reading Strategy: Asking Questions Before you read, study the diagram in **Figure 8–3.** Make a list of questions about the diagram. As you read, write down the answers to your questions.

Autotrophs and Heterotrophs

Where does the energy that living things need come from? The simple answer is that it comes from food. Originally, though, the energy in most food comes from the sun. **Plants and some other types of organisms are able to use light energy from the sun to produce food.** Organisms such as plants, which make their own food, are called **autotrophs** (AW-toh-trohfs).

Other organisms, such as animals, cannot use the sun's energy directly. These organisms, known as **heterotrophs** (HET-uh-roh-trohfs), obtain energy from the foods they consume. Impalas, for example, eat grasses, which are autotrophs. Other heterotrophs, such as the leopard shown in **Figure 8–1,** obtain the energy stored in autotrophs indirectly by feeding on animals that eat autotrophs. Still other heterotrophs—mushrooms, for example—obtain food by decomposing other organisms. To live, all organisms, including plants, must release the energy in sugars and other compounds.

Figure 8–1 **Autotrophs use light energy from the sun to produce food.** These impalas get their energy by eating grass, while this leopard gets its energy by eating impalas and other animals. Impalas and leopards are both heterotrophs.

SECTION RESOURCES

Print:
- ***Teaching Resources,*** Section Review 8–1
- ***Guided Reading and Study Workbook,*** Section 8–1

Technology:
- ***iText,*** Section 8–1

Section 8–1

1 FOCUS

Objectives

8.1.1 ***Explain*** where plants get the energy they need to produce food.

8.1.2 ***Describe*** the role of ATP in cellular activities.

Guide for Reading

Vocabulary Preview

Explain that the term *autotroph* comes from the Greek words *autos,* meaning "self," and *trophe,* meaning "food." Therefore, an autotroph is an organism that makes food for itself. Ask: **If *heteros* means "other," what does *heterotroph* mean?** *(A heterotroph is an organism that gets food from others.)*

Reading Strategy

Have students write a question for each head and subhead. For example, they might ask, "What are autotrophs and heterotrophs?" As students read the section, encourage them to write the answer to each question. Students can use their questions and answers as a study guide.

2 INSTRUCT

Autotrophs and Heterotrophs

Build Science Skills

Classifying Divide the class into small groups and have each group brainstorm a list of types of living things. Then, ask the groups to classify each type of living thing according to whether it is an autotroph or a heterotroph. After the groups have made their classifications, ask whether they found it difficult to classify any type of organism. Some students may know that certain bacteria–chemoautotrophs–are classified as autotrophs but do not obtain energy from the sun.

Chemical Energy and ATP

Address Misconceptions

Some students may have difficulty with the concept that natural processes occur automatically when materials and conditions are right. Ask: **Do cells "think" about the life processes they carry out?** *(Some students might suggest that the nucleus is the "brain" of the cell, so maybe the nucleus directs cell processes in the same way a human brain directs body movements.)* Point out that cells have no thoughts. Although we often speak of how a cell "uses" energy or of how a cell can "add" a phosphate group, these words should not suggest that cells decide when or how to act.

Use Visuals

Figure 8–2 Ask: **What does an ATP molecule consist of?** *(Adenine, ribose, and three phosphate groups)* **What do the lines between these parts of the molecule represent?** *(Chemical bonds)* **What would be the result if the third phosphate group were removed?** *(The remaining molecule would be ADP, and removing the third phosphate group would release energy.)*

Make Connections

Chemistry Use a large spring to help students understand the release of energy that occurs when the third phosphate group of ATP is removed. Explain that the "tail" of three phosphate groups is unstable and that the bonds that hold the phosphate groups together have high potential energy. In a sense, they are like a compressed spring. The chemical change that occurs when a phosphate group is removed and new products are formed is like letting that spring go. Energy is released as the spring relaxes—that is, as the spring changes from an unstable condition to a more stable condition. Likewise, the products of the chemical change that ATP undergoes are more stable than ATP itself, and energy is released in the process.

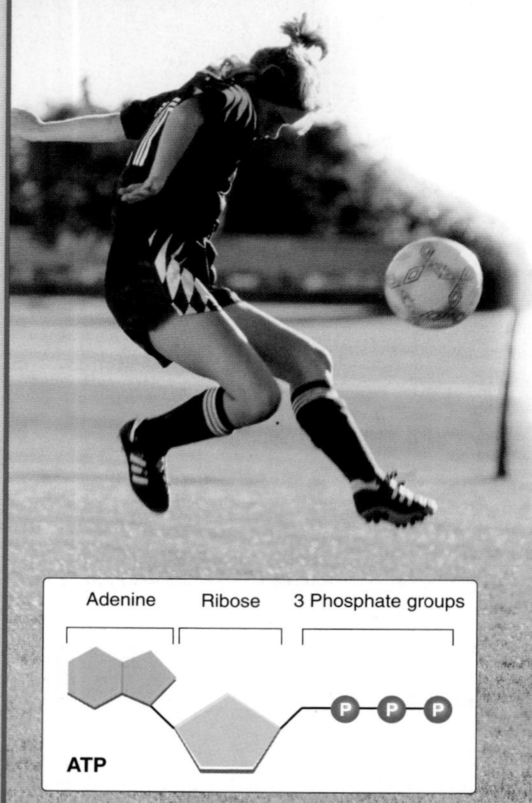

▲ **Figure 8–2 ATP is used by all types of cells as their basic energy source.** The energy needed by the cells of this soccer player comes from ATP.

Chemical Energy and ATP

Energy comes in many forms, including light, heat, and electricity. Energy can be stored in chemical compounds, too. For example, when a candle burns, carbon and hydrogen in the wax combine with oxygen from the air to produce water and carbon dioxide. This process releases energy in the form of light and heat.

ATP and ADP The activities of the cell are powered by chemical fuels. One of the principal chemical compounds that living things use to store energy is **adenosine triphosphate** (uh-DEN-uh-seen try-FAHS-fayt), abbreviated **ATP.** As **Figure 8–2** shows, an ATP molecule consists of a nitrogen-containing compound called adenine, a 5-carbon sugar called ribose, and three phosphate groups.

Adenosine diphosphate (ADP) has a structure that is similar to ATP but with one important difference: ADP has two phosphate groups instead of three. This difference is the key to the way in which cells store energy. When a cell has energy available, it can store small amounts of energy by adding a phosphate group to ADP molecules, producing ATP molecules, as shown in **Figure 8–3.** In a way, ATP is like a fully charged battery, ready to power the machinery of the cell.

CHECKPOINT *What is the difference between ATP and ADP?*

Releasing Energy From ATP The energy stored in ATP is released when ATP is converted into ADP and a phosphate group. Because a cell can add and subtract a third phosphate group, it has a way of storing and releasing energy as needed. ATP carries just enough energy to power a variety of cellular activities. **The characteristics of ATP make it an exceptionally useful molecule that is used by all types of cells as their basic energy source.**

Using Biochemical Energy Cells use the energy provided by ATP in a number of ways. One way is active transport. Many cell membranes contain a sodium-potassium pump that moves sodium ions (Na^+) out of the cell and potassium ions (K^+) into it. A single ATP molecule provides enough energy to cause the pump to move three sodium ions and two potassium ions in different directions.

TIME SAVER — PRESENTATIONS MADE EASY!

The Presentation Assistant Plus contains the Prentice Hall Presentation Pro and the Transparencies, which provide easy-to-follow visual support for every step of this section. If you have a computer presentation station, use Prentice Hall Presentation Pro for Section 8–1, or use the transparencies listed here.

Section 8–1: **Interest Grabber**
Section Outline
ATP
Figure 8–3

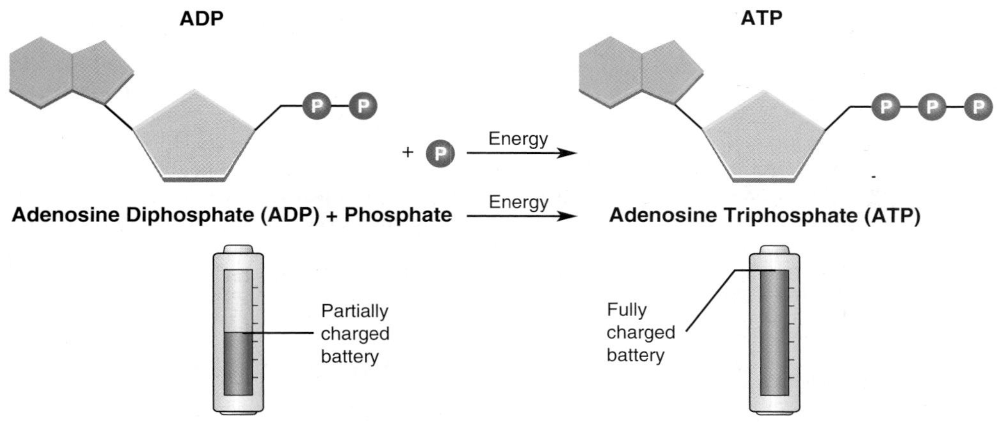

▲ **Figure 8–3** ATP can be compared to a fully charged battery because both contain stored energy, whereas ADP resembles a partially charged battery. **Predicting** *What happens when a phosphate group is removed from ATP?*

ATP also powers movement within the cell. Cell organelles are moved along microtubules by motor proteins that use the energy of ATP to generate force. When enough ATP is available, the organelle moves quickly along the microtubule.

ATP and Glucose

Most cells have only a small amount of ATP, enough to last for only a few seconds of activity. Why is this? Even though ATP is very efficient at transferring energy, it is not very good for storing large amounts of energy over the long term. In fact, a single molecule of the sugar glucose stores more than 90 times the chemical energy of a molecule of ATP. Therefore, it is more efficient for cells to keep only a small supply of ATP on hand. Cells can regenerate ATP from ADP as needed by using the energy in carbohydrates like glucose.

8–1 Section Assessment

1. **Key Concept** What is the ultimate source of energy for plants?
2. **Key Concept** What is ATP and what is its role in the cell?
3. Describe cellular activities that use the energy released by ATP.
4. How do autotrophs obtain energy? How do heterotrophs obtain energy?
5. **Critical Thinking Comparing and Contrasting** With respect to energy, how are ATP and glucose similar? How are they different?

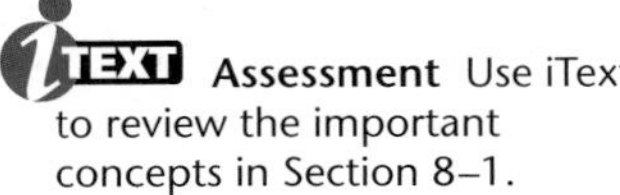

Assessment Use iText to review the important concepts in Section 8–1.

ALTERNATIVE ASSESSMENT

Making a Poster
Find an area near your school with several types of plants. Without disturbing any of the organisms, identify any relationships between the autotrophs and the heterotrophs. Create a poster showing these relationships that are present in your community.

8–1 Section Assessment

1. The sun
2. ATP stands for adenosine triphosphate, which is one of the principal chemical compounds that living things use to store energy.
3. Active transport and movement within the cell
4. Autotrophs obtain energy by making their own food. Heterotrophs obtain energy from the foods they consume.
5. Similar: both store chemical energy for a cell. Different: a single molecule of glucose stores more than 90 times the chemical energy of an ATP molecule.

ATP and Glucose

Meet Diverse Needs

Some at-risk students may have difficulty understanding why cells keep only a small supply of ATP on hand. To clarify, display numerous coins and a number of paper bills of varying denominations. Explain that molecules of ATP are like the coins—coins are very useful, but too many of them fill a pocket fast. The paper money is like glucose—the bills represent much more value than an equal mass of coins. **Learning modality: visual**

3 ASSESS

Evaluate Understanding

Call on students at random to explain the difference between autotrophs and heterotrophs. Then, ask other students to explain the difference between ATP and ADP, describe how cells store and release energy, and explain why cells contain only a small amount of ATP.

Reteach

Have pairs of students work together to make a sequence of labeled illustrations that show how energy is stored and released through the addition and removal of a phosphate group. Students can use the illustration of the ATP molecule in Figure 8–2 as a basis for their sequence.

ALTERNATIVE ASSESSMENT

Some relationships students might identify include that autotrophs provide food and shelter for some heterotrophs and heterotroph wastes provide nutrients for autotrophs.

Use iText to review the key concepts in Section 8–1.

Answers to . . .

CHECKPOINT *ATP has three phosphate groups; ADP has two.*

Figure 8–3 *ADP is formed, and stored energy is released.*

Section 8–2

1 FOCUS

Objectives

8.2.1 ***Explain*** what the experiments of van Helmont, Priestley, and Ingenhousz reveal about how plants grow.

8.2.2 ***State*** the overall equation for photosynthesis.

8.2.3 ***Describe*** the role of light and chlorophyll in photosynthesis.

Guide for Reading

Vocabulary Preview

Have students write the vocabulary words, dividing each into its separate syllables as best they can. Remind students that each syllable usually has only one vowel sound. The correct syllabications are: pho•to•syn•the•sis, pig•ment, chlo•ro•phyll.

Reading Strategy

Students' summaries should describe the findings of van Helmont, Priestley, and Ingenhousz and explain that plants use the energy of sunlight to convert water and carbon dioxide into oxygen and high-energy sugars. They should also describe the role of light and chlorophyll in photosynthesis.

2 INSTRUCT

Investigating Photosynthesis

Meet Diverse Needs

To help at-risk students grasp the basic problem faced by researchers centuries ago, draw a large tree on the board with leaves and roots. Point to the roots and ask: **What could trees obtain from underground that could help them grow?** *(Minerals, water)* Point to the leaves and ask: **What could trees obtain from the air that could help them grow?** *(Students might suggest oxygen or other gases. Some may mention light.)* Ask for their opinions about answers to the questions in the text about where a tall tree gets its mass. **Learning modality: verbal**

8–2 Photosynthesis: An Overview

Guide for Reading

Key Concepts
- What did the experiments of van Helmont, Priestley, and Ingenhousz reveal about how plants grow?
- What is the overall equation for photosynthesis?
- What is the role of light and chlorophyll in photosynthesis?

Vocabulary
photosynthesis
pigment
chlorophyll

Reading Strategy: Summarizing As you read, find the key ideas under each blue head. Write down a few key words from each key idea. Then, use the key words in your summary.

The study of energy capture and use begins with photosynthesis. In the process of **photosynthesis,** plants use the energy of sunlight to convert water and carbon dioxide into oxygen and high-energy carbohydrates—sugars and starches. The experiments of many scientists have contributed to the modern understanding of the process of photosynthesis.

Investigating Photosynthesis

Research into photosynthesis began centuries ago with a simple question: When a tiny seedling grows into a tall tree with a mass of several tons, where does the tree's increase in mass come from? From the soil? From the water? From the air?

Van Helmont's Experiment In the 1600s, the Belgian physician Jan van Helmont devised an experiment to find out if plants grew by taking material out of the soil. Van Helmont determined the mass of a pot of dry soil and a small seedling. Then, he planted the seedling in the pot of soil. He watered it regularly. At the end of five years, the seedling, which by then was a small tree, had gained about 75 kg. The mass of the soil,

Biology and History

Understanding Photosynthesis

Many scientists have contributed to understanding how plants carry out photosynthesis. Early research focused on the overall process. Later researchers investigated the detailed chemical pathways.

1600

1643 

Jan van Helmont After careful measurements of a plant's water intake and weight increase, van Helmont concludes that trees gain most of their mass from water.

1689 Peter the Great becomes czar of Russia

1700

1771 
Joseph Priestley Using a bell jar, a candle, and a plant, Priestley finds that the plant releases a substance that keeps the candle burning—a substance that we now know is oxygen.

1776 United States Declaration of Independence signed

1779 **Jan Ingenhousz** Ingenhousz finds that aquatic plants produce oxygen bubbles in the light but not in the dark. He concludes that plants need sunlight to produce oxygen.

TIME SAVER — SECTION RESOURCES

Print:
- ***Laboratory Manual A,*** Chapter 8 Lab
- ***Laboratory Manual B,*** Chapter 8 Lab
- ***Teaching Resources,*** Section Review 8–2
- ***Guided Reading and Study Workbook,*** Section 8–2

Technology:
- ***iText,*** Section 8–2

however, was almost unchanged. Van Helmont concluded that most of the mass the plant gained had come from water, because that was the only thing that he had added to the pot.

Van Helmont's experiment accounts for the "hydrate," or water, portion of the carbohydrate produced by photosynthesis. But where does the carbon of the "carbo-" portion come from? Although van Helmont did not realize it, carbon dioxide in the air made a major contribution to the mass of his tree. The carbon in carbon dioxide is used to make sugars and other carbohydrates in photosynthesis. Van Helmont had only part of the story, but he had made a major contribution to science.

Priestley's Experiment More than 100 years after van Helmont's experiment, the English minister Joseph Priestley performed an experiment that would give another insight into the process of photosynthesis. Priestley took a candle, placed a glass jar over it, and watched as the flame gradually died out. Something in the air, Priestley reasoned, was necessary to keep a candle flame burning. When that substance was used up, the candle went out. That substance was oxygen.

Priestley then found that if he placed a live sprig of mint under the jar and allowed a few days to pass, the candle could be relighted and would remain lighted for a while. The mint plant had produced the substance required for burning. In other words, it released oxygen.

CHECKPOINT *What did Priestley discover about photosynthesis?*

Word Origins

Photosynthesis comes from the Greek words *photo,* meaning "light" and *synthesis* meaning "putting together." Therefore, *photosynthesis* means "using light to put something together," specifically, carbohydrates. *Chemo* means "having to do with chemicals or chemical reactions." **What do you think *chemosynthesis* means?**

Writing Activity

Use the Internet or a library to find out more about the experiments conducted by one of these scientists. Then, write a summary of the scientist's experiments as it might appear in a newspaper story of the time. Give your story a headline.

1800 — 1900 — 2000

1836
Republic of Texas formed after Texans defeat Mexico at the Battle of San Jacinto

1845
Julius Robert Mayer
Mayer proposes that plants convert light energy into chemical energy.

1941
Samuel Ruben
Martin Kamen
Ruben (pictured) and Kamen use isotopes to determine that the oxygen liberated in photosynthesis comes from water.

1948
Melvin Calvin
Calvin traces the chemical path that carbon follows to form glucose. These light-independent reactions are also known as the Calvin cycle.

1992
Rudolph Marcus
Marcus wins the Nobel Prize in chemistry for describing the process by which electrons are transferred from one molecule to another in the electron transport chain.

TIME SAVER PRESENTATIONS MADE EASY!

The Presentation Assistant Plus contains the Prentice Hall Presentation Pro and the Transparencies, which provide easy-to-follow visual support for every step of this section. If you have a computer presentation station, use Prentice Hall Presentation Pro for Section 8–2, or use the transparencies listed here.

Section 8–2:

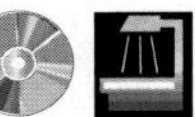

Interest Grabber
Section Outline
Photosynthesis: Reactants and Products

Word Origins

Chemosynthesis means "using chemical reactions to put something together."

Biology and History

Invite student volunteers to read aloud to the class the annotations on the time line. Encourage students to add to the time line by suggesting historical events that took place near in time to one of the discoveries mentioned. For each contribution to the understanding of photosynthesis mentioned in the time line, challenge students to suggest how that discovery might have provided the basis for the next.

Writing Activity

Encourage students to look for descriptions of these experiments in books about photosynthesis, the history of biology, and college-level textbooks, as well as at Internet sites that specialize in biology. Provide several examples of news articles about medical and other scientific breakthroughs from a large daily newspaper.

Build Science Skills

Designing an Experiment Divide the class into small groups and challenge them to design an experiment similar to the experiment that Joseph Priestley did in the 1700s. They should keep this concept in mind: plant photosynthesis produces oxygen that animals need to breathe, while animal and plant respiration produces carbon dioxide that plants need in photosynthesis. Ask students to list the materials they would need and write a step-by-step procedure.

Answers to . . .

CHECKPOINT *Priestley discovered that a plant releases a substance that keeps a candle burning. This substance, oxygen, is released during photosynthesis.*

8–2 (continued)

The Photosynthesis Equation

Quick Lab

Objective Students will be able to conclude that red and blue light are most strongly absorbed by chlorophyll, and therefore are most important in photosynthesis.

Skills Focus **Predicting, Observing, Inferring, Drawing conclusions**

Time 15 minutes

Safety Heat alcohol only in a well-ventilated area, away from flames and sparks. Remind students not to look at the sun with their spectroscopes.

Advance Prep Prepare a chlorophyll extract by heating green leaves in alcohol with a hot-water bath. Fluorescent lamps are ideal for this activity because their spectra consist of only a few well-separated bands.

Strategy Ask students what color of light they see when they look at the chlorophyll and which colors are missing.

Expected Outcome Students should observe that the chlorophyll extract most strongly absorbs red and blue light and transmits green light.

Analyze and Conclude

1. Chlorophyll most strongly absorbs red and blue light.
2. Chlorophyll absorbs most colors of light other than green, so green is all that is left to see.
3. Red and blue light are most important in photosynthesis because they are most strongly absorbed by chlorophyll.

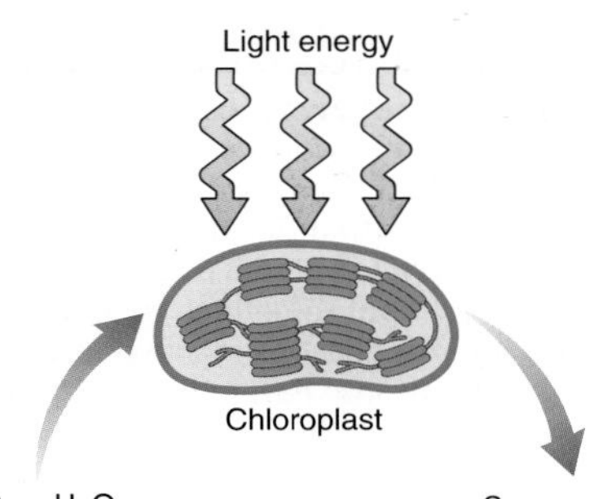

▲ **Figure 8–4** **Photosynthesis is a series of reactions that uses energy from the sun to convert water and carbon dioxide into sugars and oxygen.** Photosynthesis takes place in a plant organelle called the chloroplast.

Jan Ingenhousz Later, the Dutch scientist Jan Ingenhousz showed that the effect observed by Priestley occurred only when the plant was exposed to light. The results of Priestley's and Ingenhousz's experiments showed that light is necessary for plants to produce oxygen. **The experiments performed by van Helmont, Priestley, Ingenhousz, and other scientists reveal that in the presence of light, plants transform carbon dioxide and water into carbohydrates and release oxygen.**

The Photosynthesis Equation

Because photosynthesis usually produces 6-carbon sugars ($C_6H_{12}O_6$) as its final products, the overall equation for photosynthesis can be shown as follows:

$$6CO_2 + 6H_2O \xrightarrow{\text{light}} C_6H_{12}O_6 + 6O_2$$

$$\text{carbon dioxide} + \text{water} \xrightarrow{\text{light}} \text{sugar} + \text{oxygen}$$

Photosynthesis uses the energy of sunlight to convert water and carbon dioxide into oxygen and high-energy sugars. Plants then use the sugars to produce complex carbohydrates such as starches. Plants obtain carbon dioxide from the air or water in which they grow. The overall process of photosynthesis is shown in **Figure 8–4.**

Quick Lab

What colors of light does chlorophyll absorb?

Materials spectroscope, test tube of chlorophyll solution, colored pencils or markers

Procedure 

1. **Predicting** Write a prediction about which colors of light chlorophyll absorbs.
2. Observe a lamp through a spectroscope. Use colored pencils to draw the spectrum that you see.
3. As you observe the spectrum, hold a test tube of chlorophyll solution in front of the spectroscope. Draw the spectrum and mark the differences from the spectrum you observed in step 2. **CAUTION:** *Be careful when handling glassware.*

Analyze and Conclude

1. **Observing** Which colors of light does chlorophyll absorb most effectively? Was your prediction correct?
2. **Inferring** How do chlorophyll and light interact to produce a green color?
3. **Drawing Conclusions** Which part of the visible spectrum do you think is most important in photosynthesis? Explain the reasons for your answer.

HISTORY OF SCIENCE

Priestley's experiment "purifies" air
Joseph Priestley (1733–1804), a British Unitarian minister, never formally studied science. His interest in science began when he met Benjamin Franklin in London in 1766. For one of his many experiments, Priestley devised an apparatus that consisted of enclosed containers of air sealed at the bottom by a trough of water. He discovered that a burning candle in one of the closed containers caused the air to become "impure," eventually putting out the flame. He also found that a mouse placed inside the container of "impure" air died. He expected the same to happen to a sprig of spearmint. Much to his surprise, instead of dying the plant flourished. Furthermore, he discovered that the plant "purified" the air, since after leaving the plant in the space for several weeks, a candle would burn or a mouse could live in the same enclosed space.

Light and Pigments

Although the equation tells you that water and carbon dioxide are required for photosynthesis, it does not tell you how plants use these low-energy raw materials to produce high-energy sugars. To answer that question, you have to know how plants capture the energy of sunlight. **In addition to water and carbon dioxide, photosynthesis requires light and chlorophyll, a molecule in chloroplasts.**

Energy from the sun travels to Earth in the form of light. Sunlight, which your eyes perceive as "white" light, is actually a mixture of different wavelengths of light. Many of these wavelengths are visible to your eyes and make up what is known as the visible spectrum. Your eyes see the different wavelengths of the visible spectrum as different colors.

Plants gather the sun's energy with light-absorbing molecules called **pigments.** The plants' principal pigment is **chlorophyll** (KLAWR-uh-fil). There are two main types of chlorophyll: chlorophyll *a* and chlorophyll *b*.

As **Figure 8–5** shows, chlorophyll absorbs light very well in the blue and red regions of the visible spectrum. However, chlorophyll does not absorb light well in the green region of the spectrum, which is why plants are green. Plants also contain red and orange pigments such as carotene that absorb light in other regions of the spectrum.

Because light is a form of energy, any compound that absorbs light also absorbs the energy from that light. When chlorophyll absorbs light, much of the energy is transferred directly to electrons in the chlorophyll molecule, raising the energy levels of these electrons. These high-energy electrons make photosynthesis work.

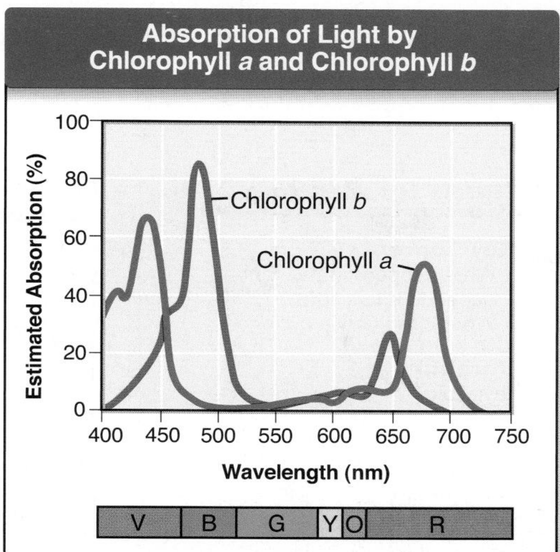

▲ **Figure 8–5 Photosynthesis requires light and chlorophyll, which absorbs light energy.** In the graph, notice how chlorophyll *a* absorbs light in the violet and red regions of the visible spectrum, while chlorophyll *b* absorbs light in the blue and red regions of the visible spectrum.

8–2 Section Assessment

1. **Key Concept** What did van Helmont, Priestley, and Ingenhousz discover about plant growth?
2. **Key Concept** Describe the process of photosynthesis, including the reactants and products.
3. **Key Concept** Why are light and chlorophyll needed for photosynthesis?
4. Why are plants green?
5. **Critical Thinking Predicting** How well would a plant grow under pure yellow light? Explain your answer.

iTEXT Assessment Use iText to review the important concepts in Section 8–2.

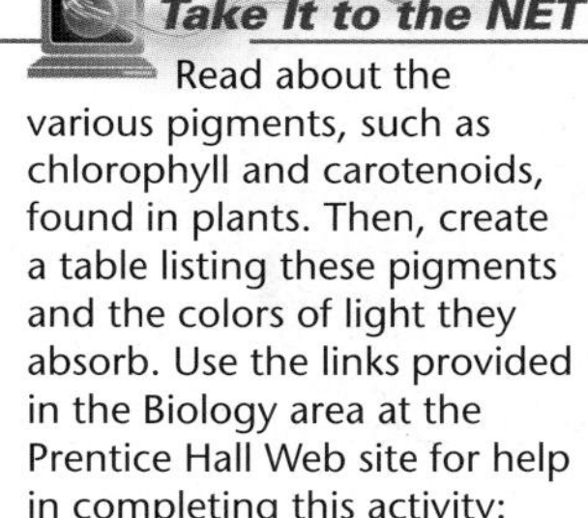

Take It to the NET

Read about the various pigments, such as chlorophyll and carotenoids, found in plants. Then, create a table listing these pigments and the colors of light they absorb. Use the links provided in the Biology area at the Prentice Hall Web site for help in completing this activity: **www.phschool.com**

8–2 Section Assessment

1. Van Helmont discovered that water was involved in increasing the mass of a plant. Priestley discovered that a plant produces the substance in air required for burning. Ingenhousz discovered that light is necessary for plants to produce oxygen.
2. Photosynthesis uses the energy of sunlight to convert water and carbon dioxide into oxygen and high-energy sugars.
3. Light provides the energy needed to produce high-energy sugars. Chlorophyll absorbs light, and the energy of that absorbed light makes photosynthesis work.
4. The chlorophyll in plants does not absorb light well in the green region of the visible spectrum.
5. The plant would not grow well because neither chlorophyll *a* nor chlorophyll *b* absorbs much light in the yellow region of visible light.

Light and Pigments

Build Science Skills

Using Tables and Graphs After students have examined the graph in Figure 8–5, ask: **How does the color spectrum at the bottom relate to the graph itself?** *(Each of the colors of the visible spectrum has a characteristic range of wavelengths, as designated on the horizontal axis of the graph.)* **In what region of the spectrum does chlorophyll *b* absorb light best?** *(In the blue region)* Challenge students to convert the data in the graph into a data table that shows, for example, the estimated absorption of chlorophyll *a* and chlorophyll *b* at 550 nm.

3 ASSESS

Evaluate Understanding

Have students write a paragraph, using their own words, that explains how plants produce high-energy sugars through the process of photosynthesis. Call on students at random to read their paragraphs.

Reteach

Ask students to make a labeled drawing based on Figure 8–4 but with more realistic objects, including a leafy tree, the sun, and clouds in the sky (visually representing the atmosphere). Ask that they use arrows and symbols in their drawing to show the same equation for photosynthesis that Figure 8–4 does.

Take It to the NET

Students' charts could include the accessory pigments anthocyanins, anthoxanthins, carotenoids (including carotenes and xanthophylls), fucoxanthins, and phycobilins. Accessory pigments generally absorb different wavelengths of light than the chlorophyll pigments absorb. For additional information, visit **www.phschool.com**

Use iText to review the key concepts in Section 8–2.

Section 8–3

1 FOCUS

Objectives

8.3.1 ***Describe*** the structure and function of a chloroplast.
8.3.2 ***Describe*** what happens in the light-dependent reactions.
8.3.3 ***Explain*** what the Calvin cycle is.
8.3.4 ***Identify*** factors that affect the rate at which photosynthesis occurs.

Guide for Reading

Preview Vocabulary

Before reading, have students find each vocabulary word in the section and preview its meaning.

Reading Strategy

Suggest that students write a summary of the information in Figures 8–7, 8–10, and 8–11. Have them revise their summaries after reading the section.

2 INSTRUCT

Inside a Chloroplast

Use Visuals

Figure 8–6 Have student volunteers read the annotations for the parts of a chloroplast. Then, with students' help, make a Venn diagram on the board that shows the relationships among a granum, thylakoids, and photosystems. The diagram should show a thylakoid within a granum, and photosystems within the thylakoid. Then, ask: **Within the chloroplast, where do the light-dependent reactions occur, and where does the Calvin cycle occur?** *(The light-dependent reactions occur within the thylakoid membranes, and the Calvin cycle occurs in the stroma.)* Have students locate these places on the figure.

8–3 The Reactions of Photosynthesis

Guide for Reading

Key Concepts
- What happens in the light-dependent reactions?
- What is the Calvin cycle?

Vocabulary
thylakoid
stroma
NADP⁺
light-dependent reactions
ATP synthase
Calvin cycle

Reading Strategy: Using Visuals Before you read, preview **Figures 8–7, 8–10,** and **8–11.** As you read, notice where in the chloroplast each stage of photosynthesis takes place.

The requirements of photosynthesis were discovered in the 1800s. It was not until the second half of the 1900s, however, that biologists unraveled the complex reactions that allow plants to use the energy of sunlight to produce carbohydrates.

Inside a Chloroplast

In plants and other photosynthetic eukaryotes, photosynthesis takes place inside chloroplasts. The chloroplasts, shown in **Figure 8–6,** contain saclike photosynthetic membranes called **thylakoids** (THY-luh-koydz). Thylakoids are arranged in stacks known as grana (singular: granum). Thylakoids contain clusters of chlorophyll and other pigments and protein known as photosystems that are able to capture the energy of sunlight.

To understand photosynthesis, scientists break the reaction into two stages: the light-dependent reactions and the light-independent reactions, or Calvin cycle. The relationship between these two sets of reactions is shown in **Figure 8–7.** The light-dependent reactions take place within the thylakoid membranes. The Calvin cycle takes place in the **stroma,** the region outside the thylakoid membranes.

Figure 8–6 In plants, photosynthesis takes place inside chloroplasts. **Observing** *What color are the thylakoids, and why?*

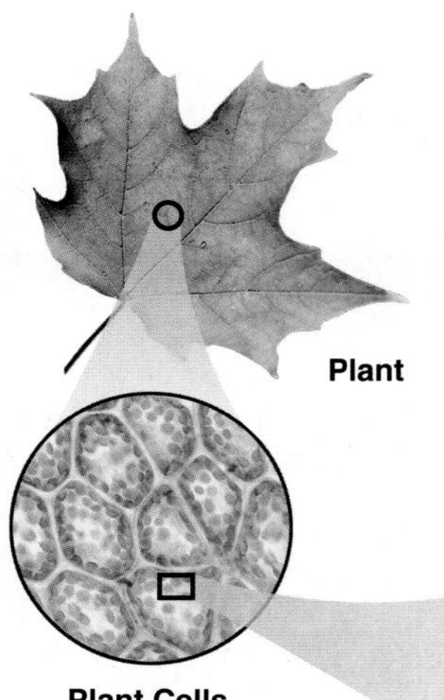

Plant
Plant Cells
(magnification: 500×)

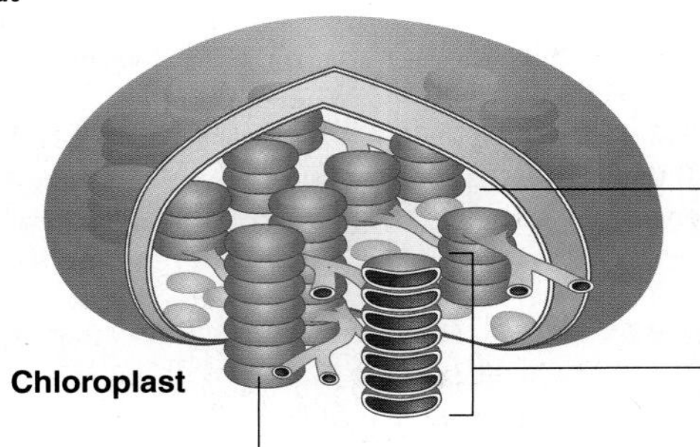

Chloroplast
The stroma is the space outside the thylakoid membranes.
A granum is a stack of thylakoids.
Photosystems, clusters of pigment and protein that absorb light energy, are found in saclike photosynthetic membranes called thylakoids.

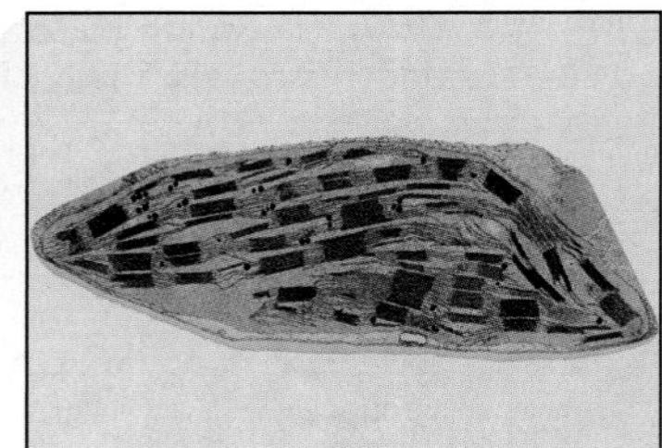

Chloroplast
(magnification: 10,000×)

TIME SAVER

SECTION RESOURCES

Print:
- ***Teaching Resources,*** Section Review 8–3, Chapter 8 Design an Experiment
- ***Guided Reading and Study Workbook,*** Section 8–3
- ***Biotechnology Manual,*** Lab 17, Issue 4

Technology:
- ***iText,*** Section 8–1

Figure 8–7 Photosynthesis: An Overview

The process of photosynthesis includes the light-dependent reactions as well as the Calvin cycle. **Interpreting Graphics** *What are the products of the light-dependent reactions?*

Light, H_2O, CO_2, $NADP^+$, ADP + P, Light-Dependent Reactions, Calvin Cycle, ATP, NADPH, Chloroplast, O_2, Sugars

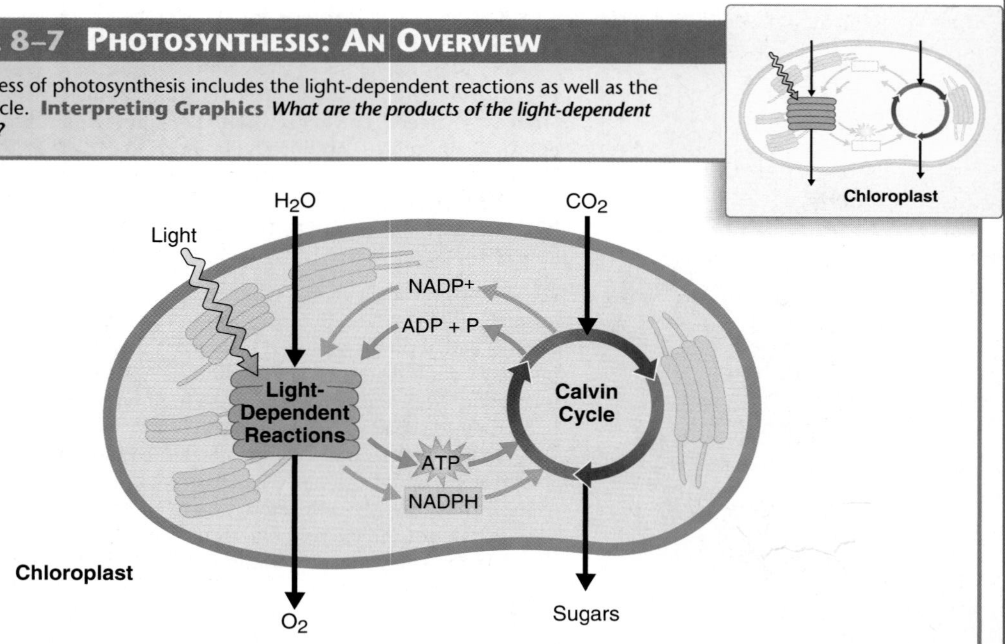

NADPH

When sunlight excites electrons in chlorophyll, the electrons gain a great deal of energy. These high-energy electrons require a special carrier. Think of a high-energy electron as being similar to a red-hot coal from a fireplace or campfire. If you wanted to move the coal from one place to another, you wouldn't pick it up in your hands. You would use a pan or bucket—a carrier—to transport it, as shown in **Figure 8–8.** Cells treat high-energy electrons in the same way. Instead of a pan or bucket, they use electron carriers to transfer high-energy electrons from chlorophyll to other molecules. A carrier molecule is a compound that can accept a pair of high-energy electrons and transfer them along with most of their energy to another molecule.

One of these carrier molecules is a compound known as **$NADP^+$** (nicotinamide adenine dinucleotide phosphate). The name is complicated, but the job that $NADP^+$ has is simple. $NADP^+$ accepts and holds 2 high-energy electrons along with a hydrogen ion (H^+). This converts the $NADP^+$ into NADPH. The conversion of $NADP^+$ into NADPH is one way in which some of the energy of sunlight can be trapped in chemical form.

The NADPH can then carry high-energy electrons produced by light absorption in chlorophyll to chemical reactions elsewhere in the cell. These high-energy electrons are used to help build a variety of molecules the cell needs, including carbohydrates like glucose.

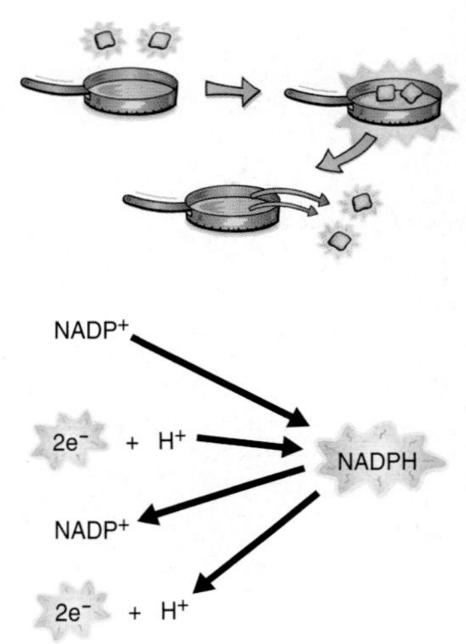

▲ **Figure 8–8** When $NADP^+$ accepts a pair of high-energy electrons, it becomes NADPH. **Making Analogies** *How are the electrons similar to the hot coals?*

NADPH

Make Connections

Chemistry Remind students that an ion is an atom or group of atoms that has a positive or negative charge because it has lost or gained electrons. Ask: **If an ion has more protons than electrons, is its charge positive or negative?** *(Positive)* Point out that $NADP^+$ is a positive ion, which explains why it can accept a negative electron. Then, ask: **What does a hydrogen atom consist of?** *(One proton and one electron)* **If a hydrogen atom loses its electron, what is the result?** *(A hydrogen ion, or H^+)*

Use Visuals

Figure 8–7 After students have studied the figure and read the caption, have them answer the questions on a sheet of paper. **What materials come into the chloroplast that are used in the light-dependent reactions?** *(Light and H_2O)* **What material comes into the chloroplast that is used in the Calvin cycle?** *(CO_2)* **What material moves out of the chloroplast from the light-dependent reactions?** *(O_2)* **What materials move out of the chloroplast from the Calvin cycle?** *(Sugars)* **What materials move from the light-dependent reactions to the Calvin cycle?** *(ATP and NADPH)* **What materials move from the Calvin cycle back to the light-dependent reactions?** *($NADP^+$ and ADP + P)*

Presentations Made Easy!

The Presentation Assistant Plus contains the Prentice Hall Presentation Pro and the Transparencies, which provide easy-to-follow visual support for every step of this section. If you have a computer presentation station, use Prentice Hall Presentation Pro for Section 8–3, or use the transparencies listed here.

Section 8–3:

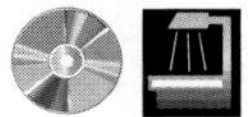

Interest Grabber
Section Outline
Concept Map
Figure 8–7
Figure 8–10
Figure 8–11

Answers to . . .

Figure 8–6 *The thylakoids are green because they contain the green pigment chlorophyll.*

Figure 8–7 *The products of the light-dependent reaction are O_2, ATP, and NADPH.*

Figure 8–8 *Both the electrons and the coals have a lot of energy and require a carrier to be transported.*

Light-Dependent Reactions

Make Connections

Physics Ask students: **Does light radiate in waves or particles?** *(Some students may say waves, others particles.)* Explain that light has both the properties of waves and the properties of a stream of particles. A particle of light is called a photon, and some photons have more energy than others. The amount of energy in a photon depends on the wavelength; the shorter the wavelength, the more energy a photon has. Explain that when a photon of a certain amount of energy—a certain wavelength—strikes a molecule of chlorophyll, the energy of that photon is transferred to an electron in that chlorophyll molecule.

Demonstration

To reinforce the concept that the light-dependent reactions produce oxygen as a product, pick a green leaf from a live plant and submerge it in a bowl of water. Have students observe the leaf. Wait about 30 minutes, and have students again observe the leaf. They should see that bubbles have formed on the underside of the leaf. Explain that the process of photosynthesis continued after the leaf was picked. Ask: **What gas is released by plants during the process of photosynthesis?** *(Oxygen gas)* **In what form does the oxygen originally enter the plant cells?** *(Oxygen enters plant cells as part of water molecules.)*

Light-Dependent Reactions

As you might expect from their name, the **light-dependent reactions** require light. That is why plants like the one in **Figure 8–9** need light to grow. The light-dependent reactions use energy from light to produce ATP and NADPH. **The light-dependent reactions produce oxygen gas and convert ADP and NADH⁺ into the energy carriers ATP and NADPH.** Look at **Figure 8–10** to see what happens at each step of the process.

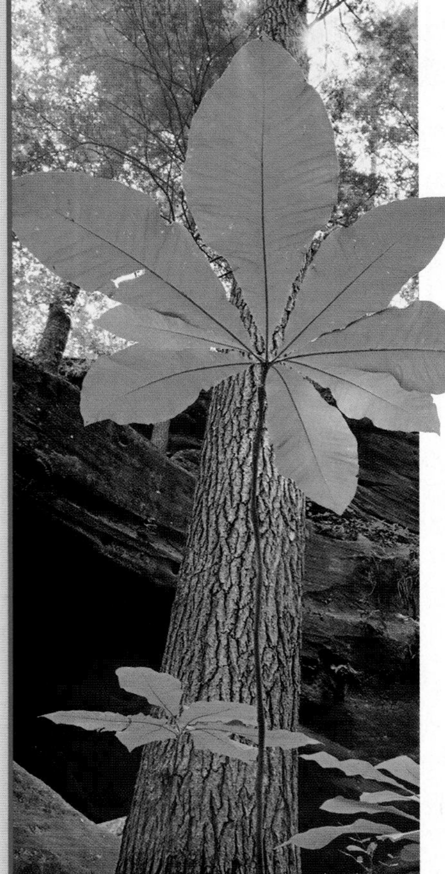

▲ **Figure 8–9** Like all plants, this seedling needs light to grow. **Applying Concepts** *What stage of photosynthesis requires light?*

A Photosynthesis begins when pigments in photosystem II absorb light. The first photosystem in the light-dependent reactions is called photosystem II because it was discovered after photosystem I. Energy from the light is absorbed by electrons, increasing their energy level. These high-energy electrons are passed on to the electron transport chain.

As light continues to shine, does the chlorophyll run out of electrons? No, it does not. The thylakoid membrane contains a system that provides new electrons to chlorophyll to replace the ones it has lost. These new electrons come from water molecules (H_2O). Enzymes on the inner surface of the thylakoid membrane break up each water molecule into 2 electrons, 2 H^+ ions, and 1 oxygen atom. The 2 electrons replace the high-energy electrons that chlorophyll has lost to the electron transport chain. The oxygen is eventually released into the air as oxygen gas (O_2). The 2 H^+ ions are released inside the thylakoid membrane.

B High-energy electrons move through the electron transport chain from photosystem II to photosystem I. Energy from the electrons is used by the molecules in the electron transport chain to transport H^+ ions from the stroma into the inner thylakoid.

C Pigments in photosystem I use energy from light to reenergize the electrons. $NADP^+$ then picks up these high-energy electrons at the outer surface of the thylakoid membrane, plus a H^+ ion, and becomes NADPH.

D As a result of the H^+ ions released during water-splitting and electron transport, the inside of the thylakoid membrane becomes positively charged and the outside becomes negatively charged. The difference in charges across the membrane provides the energy to make ATP.

E H^+ ions cannot cross the membrane directly. However, the membrane contains a protein called **ATP synthase** (SIN-thays) that allows H^+ ions to pass through it. As H^+ ions pass through this protein, the protein rotates like a turbine being spun by water in a hydroelectric power plant. As it rotates, ATP synthase binds ADP and a phosphate group together to produce ATP.

✓CHECKPOINT *What are the roles of the two photosystems?*

TEACHER TO TEACHER

When I introduce photosynthesis to students, I first present information about the physical properties of light, especially how light can be thought of as either waves or photons. This information both sparks the interest of students and helps them understand how the light-dependent reactions work. Then, I move on to the biochemistry of photosynthesis. Students often get bored quickly with the specifics of the chemical reactions. Turning their attention to an illustration of chloroplast structure can help renew interest in the biochemistry. Using paper chromatography to identify the different pigments in plants also helps students understand photosynthesis.

—*Greg McCurdy,*
Biology Teacher
Salem High School,
Salem, IN

Figure 8–10 Light-Dependent Reactions

The light-dependent reactions use energy from sunlight to produce ATP, NADPH, and oxygen. The light-dependent reactions take place within the thylakoid membranes of chloroplasts.

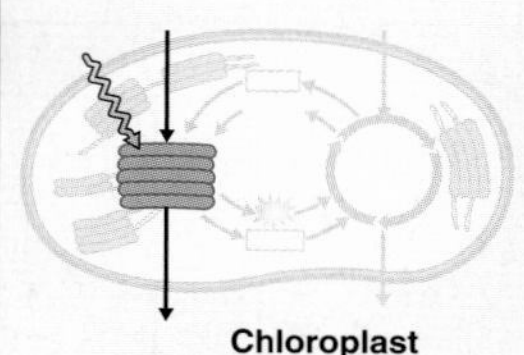

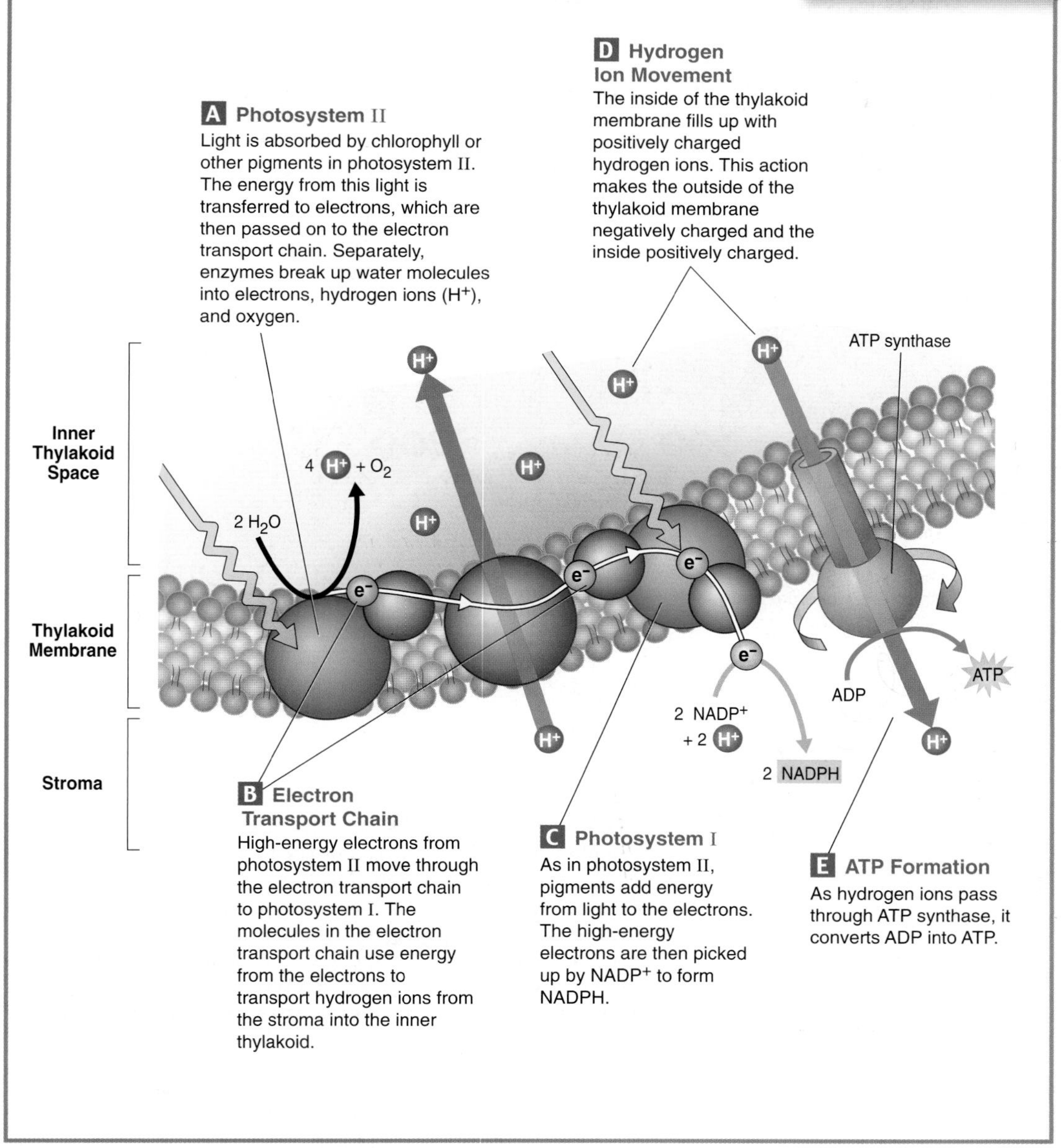

Inner Thylakoid Space

Thylakoid Membrane

Stroma

2 H_2O

4 H^+ + O_2

H^+

e^-

2 $NADP^+$ + 2 H^+

2 NADPH

ADP

ATP

ATP synthase

A Photosystem II
Light is absorbed by chlorophyll or other pigments in photosystem II. The energy from this light is transferred to electrons, which are then passed on to the electron transport chain. Separately, enzymes break up water molecules into electrons, hydrogen ions (H^+), and oxygen.

B Electron Transport Chain
High-energy electrons from photosystem II move through the electron transport chain to photosystem I. The molecules in the electron transport chain use energy from the electrons to transport hydrogen ions from the stroma into the inner thylakoid.

C Photosystem I
As in photosystem II, pigments add energy from light to the electrons. The high-energy electrons are then picked up by $NADP^+$ to form NADPH.

D Hydrogen Ion Movement
The inside of the thylakoid membrane fills up with positively charged hydrogen ions. This action makes the outside of the thylakoid membrane negatively charged and the inside positively charged.

E ATP Formation
As hydrogen ions pass through ATP synthase, it converts ADP into ATP.

Use Visuals

Figure 8–10 Have students study the figure and read the caption. Then, ask: **Where are these light-dependent reactions occurring?** *(Within the thylakoid membrane of a chloroplast)* **Where is water broken down?** *(Water is broken down on the inner surface of the thylakoid membrane.)* Point out that the reactions move from left to right on the figure, from photosystem II through the electron transport chain to photosystem I. **Where are two places that chlorophyll absorbs the energy of sunlight?** *(In photosystem II and photosystem I)* **Where and how is ATP produced in this process?** *(ATP is produced as H^+ ions pass through ATP synthase, as shown to the right of photosystem I.)* **How is NADPH produced in this process?** *(NADPH is produced when $NADP^+$ picks up high-energy electrons from photosystem I at the outer surface of the thylakoid membrane.)*

Facts and Figures

How photosystems I and II differ

In the thylakoid membranes, the pigments and carrier molecules are packed together in granules called photosynthetic units. About 300 molecules of chlorophyll are packed together in each unit. The photosynthetic units made almost completely with chlorophyll *a* and very little chlorophyll *b* are called photosystem I. Units with about equal amounts chlorophyll *a* and *b* are called photosystem II. A main difference in function between photosystem I and photosystem II is that the chlorophyll molecules of photosystem II get their replacement electrons from water, while those in photosystem I do not. Getting electrons from water makes the process very efficient, because water is an abundant and "cheap" resource compared to other molecules in the cell—so "cheap" that the cell strips it of electrons and protons and then "throws away" the oxygen.

Answers to . . .

CHECKPOINT *In photosystem II, energy from light is absorbed by chlorophyll and transferred to electrons, and then these high-energy electrons are passed on to the electron transport chain. In photosystem I, pigments use energy from light to reenergize the electrons.*

Figure 8–9 *The light-dependent reactions of photosynthesis require light.*

8–3 (continued)

The Calvin Cycle

Use Visuals

Figure 8–11 Have students study the figure and read the caption. Then, ask: **Where does the Calvin cycle take place?** *(It takes place in the stroma, outside the grana.)* **What enters the Calvin cycle from the atmosphere?** *(Six CO_2 molecules)* Ask a volunteer to describe where on the figure those molecules enter the cycle. Then, ask another volunteer to point out where in the cycle ATP and NADPH become involved. Ask: **Where do the ATP and NADPH come from?** *(Both ATP and NADPH come from the light-dependent reactions.)* Emphasize that the Calvin cycle uses the energy of those high-energy molecules from the light-dependent reactions to keep the cycle going. Ask: **What is the product of this cycle?** *(A 6-carbon sugar)* Have a volunteer describe where on the cycle the 6-carbon sugar is produced. Ask: **How is the cycle completed?** *(The cycle is complete when the remaining 3-carbon molecules are converted back into 5-carbon molecules, which are ready to combine with new carbon dioxide molecules to begin the cycle again.)*

Meet Diverse Needs

To help both students with limited English proficiency and at-risk students, divide the class into pairs, matching students who are having difficulty with those who have shown a grasp of the details of photosynthesis. Ask the pairs to quiz each other on the details of the two stages, using Figures 8–10 and 8–11 as their primary resources. **Learning modality: verbal**

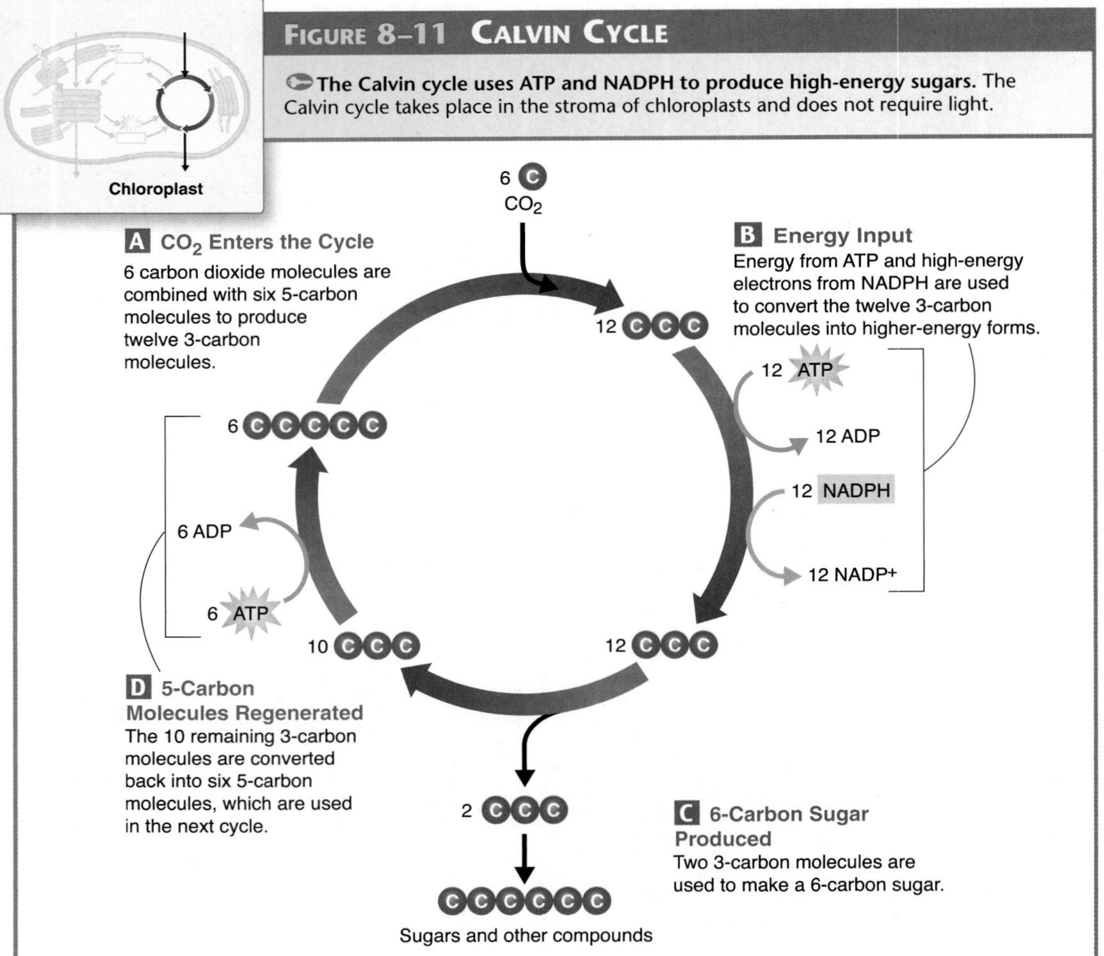
Chloroplast
6 C
CO_2
A CO_2 Enters the Cycle
6 carbon dioxide molecules are combined with six 5-carbon molecules to produce twelve 3-carbon molecules.
B Energy Input
Energy from ATP and high-energy electrons from NADPH are used to convert the twelve 3-carbon molecules into higher-energy forms.
12 CCC
12 ATP
12 ADP
12 NADPH
12 NADP+
12 CCC
6 CCCCC
6 ADP
6 ATP
10 CCC
D 5-Carbon Molecules Regenerated
The 10 remaining 3-carbon molecules are converted back into six 5-carbon molecules, which are used in the next cycle.
2 CCC
C 6-Carbon Sugar Produced
Two 3-carbon molecules are used to make a 6-carbon sugar.
CCCCCC
Sugars and other compounds

FIGURE 8–11 CALVIN CYCLE **The Calvin cycle uses ATP and NADPH to produce high-energy sugars.** The Calvin cycle takes place in the stroma of chloroplasts and does not require light.

The Calvin Cycle

The ATP and NADPH formed by the light-dependent reactions contain an abundance of chemical energy, but they are not stable enough to store that energy for more than a few minutes. During the **Calvin cycle,** plants use the energy that ATP and NADPH contain to build high-energy compounds that can be stored for a long time. **The Calvin cycle uses ATP and NADPH from the light-dependent reactions to produce high-energy sugars.** The Calvin cycle is named after the American scientist Melvin Calvin, who worked out the details of this remarkable cycle. Because the Calvin cycle does not require light, these reactions are also called the light-independent reactions. Follow **Figure 8–11** to see how the Calvin cycle works.

BIO INSIGHTS

HISTORY OF SCIENCE

Same stages, different names

In the early 1900s, British plant physiologist F. F. Blackman concluded that photosynthesis occurs in two stages, a stage that depends on light followed by a stage that can take place in darkness. The terms *light reactions* and *dark reactions* have been commonly used for the two stages since that time. Yet, the term *dark reactions* implies that those reactions can occur only in darkness, which is not at all the case. It's just that the dark reactions don't depend on sunlight to occur. To avoid this ambiguity, the authors of many modern textbooks have labeled the two stages the *light-dependent reactions* and the *light-independent reactions.* The authors of this textbook have gone a step further toward clarity by labeling the light-independent reactions the *Calvin cycle,* the name of the series of reactions that make up the light-independent reactions in most photosynthetic organisms.

A Six carbon dioxide molecules enter the cycle from the atmosphere. The carbon dioxide molecules combine with six 5-carbon molecules. The result is twelve 3-carbon molecules.

B The twelve 3-carbon molecules are then converted into higher-energy forms. The energy for this conversion comes from ATP and high-energy electrons from NADPH.

C Two of the twelve 3-carbon molecules are converted into two similar 3-carbon molecules. These 3-carbon molecules are used to form various 6-carbon sugars and other compounds.

D The remaining ten 3-carbon molecules are converted back into six 5-carbon molecules. These molecules combine with six new carbon dioxide molecules to begin the next cycle.

The Calvin cycle uses six molecules of carbon dioxide to produce a single 6-carbon sugar molecule. As photosynthesis proceeds, the Calvin cycle works steadily, turning out energy-rich sugars and removing carbon dioxide from the atmosphere. The plant uses the sugars for energy and to build more complex carbohydrates such as starches and cellulose, which it needs for growth and development. When other organisms eat plants, they can also use the energy stored in carbohydrates.

CHECKPOINT *What are the main products of the Calvin cycle?*

KEEP CURRENT WITH . . . SCIENCE NEWS®

To find out more about the topics in this chapter, go to: www.phschool.com

SCIENCE NEWS®

Encourage students to visit www.phschool.com for the most recent information on this topic.

Build Science Skills

Comparing and Contrasting Have students compare what happens in the light-dependent reactions of photosynthesis with what happens in the Calvin cycle. This could be done by each student in written form or orally in class discussion. Students should particularly compare the reactants and products of each series of reactions.

Analyzing Data

Rates of Photosynthesis

The rate at which a plant carries out photosynthesis depends in part on its environment. Plants that grow in the shade, for example, carry out photosynthesis at low levels of light. Plants that grow in the sun, such as desert plants, typically carry out photosynthesis at much higher levels of light.

The graph compares the rates of photosynthesis between plants that grow in the shade and plants that grow in the sun. It shows how the rate of photosynthesis changes with the number of micromoles of photons per square meter per second (μmol photons/m^2/s), a standard unit of light intensity.

Rates of Photosynthesis

1. **Interpreting Graphics** When light intensity is below 200 μmol photons/m^2/s, do sun plants or shade plants have a higher rate of photosynthesis?
2. **Drawing Conclusions** Does the relationship in question 1 change when light intensity increases above 400 μmol photons/m^2/s? Explain your answer.
3. **Inferring** The average light intensity in the Sonoran Desert is about 400 μmol photons/m^2/s. According to the graph, what would be the approximate rate of photosynthesis for sun plants that grow in this environment?
4. **Going Further** Suppose you transplant a sun plant to a shaded forest floor that receives about 100 μmol photons/m^2/s. Do you think this plant will grow and thrive? Why or why not? How does the graph help you answer this question?

Analyzing Data

Have student volunteers explain what is measured on the vertical axis and the horizontal axis of this graph. Tell students that understanding the unit of measure for the rate of photosynthesis is not as important as recognizing that the rate increases in units of 5 along the vertical axis.

Answers

1. Shade plants
2. Yes; above 400 μmol photons/m^2/s, sun plants have a higher rate of photosynthesis than shade plants.
3. 13 μmol CO_2 consumed/m^2/s
4. The graph shows that a sun plant's rate of photosynthesis would decrease dramatically from its normal rate if transplanted to a shaded forest, from 13 μmol CO_2 consumed/m^2/s at 400 μmol photons/m^2/s to only about 4 μmol CO_2 consumed/m^2/s at 100 μmol photons/m^2/s.

BIO INSIGHTS — HISTORY OF SCIENCE

Calvin's investigation

In the late 1940s, University of California biochemist Melvin Calvin worked out the details of the sequence of reactions that now bears his name. For this investigation, Calvin exposed cells of *Chlorella,* a unicellular green alga, to carbon dioxide that contained the radioactive isotope carbon-14. After a short time, he dropped the algae into boiling alcohol, killing the cells and stopping the reactions at that point. He then identified the compounds in the dead cells that contained carbon-14, reasoning that these compounds were involved in the process of photosynthesis. By varying the time between exposure and killing the cells, Calvin was able to work out the steps in the light-independent reactions, or the Calvin cycle. For this work, Calvin received the 1961 Nobel Prize in chemistry.

Answers to . . .

CHECKPOINT *The main products of the Calvin cycle are high-energy sugars.*

8–3 (continued)

Factors Affecting Photosynthesis

Use Community Resources

Have students brainstorm a list of questions to ask a staff member at a local arboretum or conservatory about factors that limit or enhance plant growth. Ask a student volunteer to contact the person to set up an appointment for an interview. Have that student and one or two others use the list of questions as a basis for the interview. Then, have the interviewers make an oral report to the class.

3 ASSESS

Evaluate Understanding

Call on students at random to define or explain each of the section's vocabulary words. Encourage other students to add to any definition or explanation given by one of their classmates.

Reteach

Ask student volunteers to orally describe parts of Figure 8–10 and 8–11, in the sequence in which the light-dependent reactions and the Calvin cycle occur.

ALTERNATIVE ASSESSMENT

In their flowcharts, students should illustrate as many steps as they can find in the section, including events in both stages of photosynthesis. Some students may have 20 or more steps. After students have completed the task, post the flowcharts around the room and invite volunteers to present their work to the class.

Use iText to review the key concepts in Section 8–3.

Answer to . . .

Figure 8–12 *They both have a waxy coating on their leaves that reduces water loss.*

Factors Affecting Photosynthesis

Many factors affect the rate at which photosynthesis occurs. Because water is one of the raw materials of photosynthesis, a shortage of water can slow or even stop photosynthesis. Plants that live in dry conditions, such as desert plants and conifers, have a waxy coating on their leaves that reduces water loss.

Temperature is also a factor. Photosynthesis depends on enzymes that function best between 0°C and 35°C. Temperatures above or below this range may damage the enzymes, slowing down the rate of photosynthesis. At very low temperatures, photosynthesis may stop entirely. The conifers shown in **Figure 8–12** can carry out photosynthesis only on sunny days.

The intensity of light also affects the rate at which photosynthesis occurs. As you might expect, increasing light intensity increases the rate of photosynthesis. After the light intensity reaches a certain level, however, the plant reaches its maximum rate of photosynthesis. The level at which light intensity no longer affects photosynthesis varies from plant type to plant type.

Figure 8–12 Both temperature and the availability of water can affect rates of photosynthesis. Desert plants such as this Joshua tree (above) are adapted to survive with little water. During the cold winter months these conifers (below) may only occasionally carry out photosynthesis. **Comparing and Contrasting** *What do both plants shown have that helps them conserve water?*

8–3 Section Assessment

1. **Key Concept** Summarize the light-dependent reactions.
2. **Key Concept** What reactions make up the Calvin cycle?
3. What is the function of NADPH?
4. How is light energy converted into chemical energy during photosynthesis?
5. **Critical Thinking Inferring** Can the complete process of photosynthesis take place in the dark? Explain your answer.

iTEXT Assessment Use iText to review the important concepts in Section 8–3.

ALTERNATIVE ASSESSMENT

Making a Flowchart
Construct a flowchart that illustrates the steps of photosynthesis. Begin with the energy of sunlight and end with the production of sugars. Include as much detail as possible in the numerous steps.

8–3 Section Assessment

1. The light-dependent reactions produce oxygen gas and convert ADP and $NADP^+$ into the energy carriers ATP and NADPH.
2. The Calvin cycle uses ATP and NADPH from the light-dependent reactions to produce high-energy sugars.
3. The main function of NADPH is to carry high-energy electrons produced by light absorption in chlorophyll to chemical reactions elsewhere in the cell.
4. Light energy is converted into chemical energy by the pigments in the chloroplast.
5. The complete process of photosynthesis cannot take place in the dark because the light-dependent reactions of photosynthesis must have light to occur.

Design an Experiment

Investigating Photosynthesis

If only part of a leaf receives light, does the whole leaf perform photosynthesis? What if a leaf receives only light of one color? You are going to design an experiment to test the effects of colored light on photosynthesis.

Problem **How do different colors of light affect the process of photosynthesis?**

Materials

- scissors
- black construction paper
- potted plant
- tape
- blue, red, and green cellophane
- 5 large test tubes
- glass-marking pencil
- forceps
- 400-mL beaker
- 5 petri dishes
- iodine solution
- paper towels

Skills Predicting, Formulating Hypotheses

Design Your Experiment

1. **Predicting** During photosynthesis, starch accumulates in leaves. Record your prediction of how keeping part of a leaf in darkness will affect starch accumulation.
2. Cut two pieces of black construction paper large enough to cover half of one leaf of the plant.
3. Sandwich half of the leaf between the two squares of black paper and tape the paper in place as shown.
4. **Formulating Hypotheses** Develop a hypothesis that predicts how the color of light will affect photosynthesis. Record your hypothesis.
5. Design an experiment to test your hypothesis. Have your teacher check your plan. Set up your experiment using leaves from the same plant as in step 3.
6. Leave your plant in a sunlit area for 2 days.
7. Cut off each experimental leaf and one leaf that was not treated. Roll up each leaf and put it in a large test tube. Label each tube and petri dish with the treatment the leaf received.
8. Before you test the leaves for starch, the chlorophyll must be removed from the leaves. Your teacher will add alcohol to your test tubes and heat them in hot water. **CAUTION:** *Alcohol is toxic and flammable, and its fumes are irritating.* When the color has disappeared from each leaf, use forceps to swirl each leaf in a beaker of water. Place it in a labeled petri dish.
9. Cover each leaf with iodine solution. Iodine solution stains starch blue or black. **CAUTION:** *Iodine is corrosive and irritating to the skin and can stain clothes and skin.*
10. After 1 minute, use forceps to gently swirl each leaf in the beaker of water and lay the leaf flat on a paper towel.
11. Observe each leaf and record your observations.

Analyze and Conclude

1. **Observing** Which leaves contained starch? Which did not? Was your prediction about the leaf covered in black paper correct? Explain your answer.
2. **Evaluating** What effect did each color of light have on the leaves? Was your hypothesis correct?
3. **Drawing Conclusions** Use your knowledge of chlorophyll to explain your results.

Go Further

Designing an Experiment Where is starch found in the multicolored leaves of a coleus plant? With your teacher's approval, perform an experiment to find out. Explain your results.

Design an Experiment

Objective Students will be able to relate the effectiveness of different colors of light in photosynthesis to the absorption spectrum of chlorophyll.

Time 30 minutes on each of two days

Advance Prep Use geraniums (or other uniformly green-leafed plants) with plenty of leaves so that covering and removing leaves will not harm the plants. Keep the plants in darkness for about two days before the activity begins to remove any starch stored in the leaves. Construct a hot-water bath by placing student's test tubes in a large beaker of water on a hot plate.

Safety Heat the sample tubes in a hot-water bath in a fume hood or other well-vented area. Wear safety goggles and thermal gloves when handling the hot-water bath. Spilled iodine can be removed from hands and clothing with a solution of 12.5 g/L of sodium thiosulfate ($Na_2S_2O_3$—photographer's "hypo").

Teaching Tips

- In step 5, the cellophane should not cover the leaves so tightly that gas exchange is blocked.
- To save time and alcohol, you can dispense with test tubes and heat all leaves that are treated identically as a batch in one beaker of alcohol.

Expected Outcome Leaves that are not covered or are covered by red or blue cellophane contain starch. Leaves that are covered by black paper or green cellophane contain little or no starch.

Analyze and Conclude

1. The uncovered leaf and the leaves covered with red and blue cellophane contain starch, while the leaves covered with black paper or green cellophane contain little or no starch. Black paper or green cellophane prevents the right color of light from reaching the chlorophyll, thus preventing photosynthesis.
2. The blue and red cellophane did not affect photosynthesis. The green cellophane reduced the amount of starch produced by the leaf. Students should explain why their hypothesis was or was not correct.
3. Chlorophyll absorbs red and blue light, but not green light. The leaves covered by red and blue cellophane received the energy they needed for photosynthesis to occur and produced starch. The leaf covered by green cellophane received little light energy the chlorophyll could use, and thus produced little starch.

Go Further

Most students' experiments will involve testing different locations on a coleus leaf for the presence of starch. Students should find that the green leaf parts contain starch while the white leaf parts do not, because only the green parts contain chlorophyll.

Chapter 8 Study Guide

Study Tip

Divide the class into pairs and have students quiz each other about the vocabulary words and key concepts.

Thinking Visually

1. Water
2. Light-dependent reactions
3. Oxygen

Chapter 8 Assessment

Reviewing Content

1. b	**5.** c	**9.** b
2. b	**6.** a	**10.** a
3. b	**7.** d	
4. d	**8.** a	

Understanding Concepts

11. Autotrophs are able to obtain energy by making their own food. Heterotrophs obtain their energy by consuming food.

12. An ATP molecule consists of a nitrogen-containing compound called adenine, a sugar called ribose, and three phosphate groups.

13. ATP resembles a fully charged battery because it can yield energy when the third phosphate group is removed, also forming ADP. ADP is like a partially charged battery that can be recharged when energy is added to link a third phosphate group, reforming ATP.

14. A single molecule of glucose stores more than 90 times the energy stored by ATP. However, ATP, which transfers energy quickly, is used by the cell as an immediate source of energy.

15. Priestley discovered that plants produced a substance needed to burn candles, now known to be oxygen. Ingenhousz found that plants produce oxygen only when exposed to light.

16. Carbon dioxide+ water → sugars + oxygen

17. Plant pigments absorb energy from light and transfer it to electrons involved in photosynthesis.

Chapter 8 Study Guide

8–1 Energy and Life

Key Concepts

- Plants and some other types of organisms are able to use light energy from the sun to produce food.
- The characteristics of ATP make it an exceptionally useful molecule that is used by all types of cells as their basic energy source.

Vocabulary

autotroph, p. 201
heterotroph, p. 201
adenosine triphosphate (ATP), p. 202

8–2 Photosynthesis: An Overview

Key Concepts

- The experiments performed by van Helmont, Priestley, Ingenhousz, and other scientists reveal that in the presence of light, plants transform carbon dioxide and water into carbohydrates and release oxygen as a byproduct.
- Photosynthesis uses the energy of sunlight to convert water and carbon dioxide into oxygen and high-energy sugars.
- In addition to water and carbon dioxide, photosynthesis requires light and chlorophyll, a molecule found in chloroplasts.

Vocabulary

photosynthesis, p. 204
pigment, p. 207
chlorophyll, p. 207

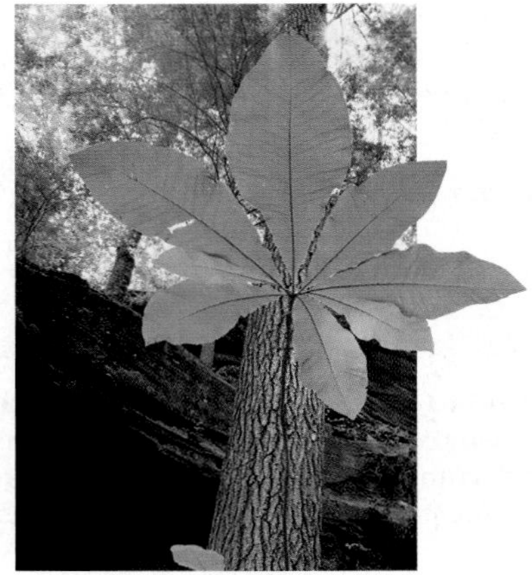

8–3 The Reactions of Photosynthesis

Key Concepts

- The process of photosynthesis includes the light-dependent reactions as well as the Calvin cycle.
- The light-dependent reactions produce oxygen gas and convert ADP and NADH$^+$ into ATP and NADPH. The light-dependent reactions occur in different areas of the thylakoid, called photosystem I and photosystem II.
- The Calvin cycle uses ATP and NADPH from the light-dependent reactions to produce high-energy sugars. The Calvin cycle is also known as the light-independent reactions.

Vocabulary

thylakoid, p. 208
stroma, p. 208
NADP$^+$, p. 209
light-dependent reactions, p. 210
ATP synthase, p. 210
Calvin cycle, p. 212

Thinking Visually

Using the information in this chapter, complete the following flowchart about photosynthesis:

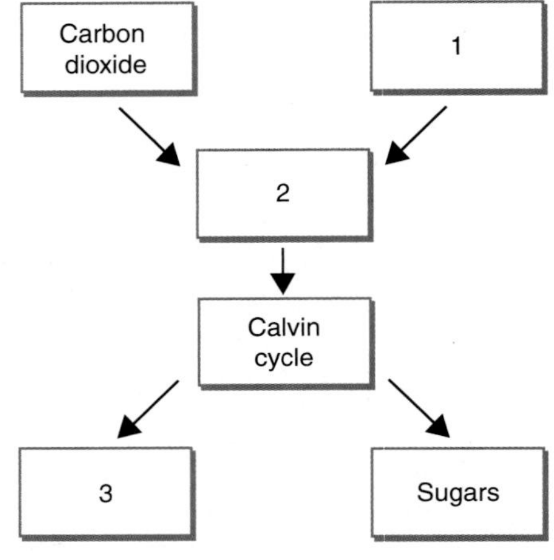

CHAPTER RESOURCES

Print:

- ***Teaching Resources,*** Chapter Vocabulary Review, Graphic Organizer
- ***Chapter Tests: Levels A and B,*** Chapter 8 Test
- ***PH Assessment System,*** Practice Test

Technology:

- ***Computer Test Bank,*** Chapter 8 Test
- ***iText,*** Chapter 8 Assessment

Chapter 8 Assessment

Reviewing Content

Choose the letter that best answers the question or completes the statement.

1. Which of the following are autotrophs?
   a. impalas c. leopards
   b. plants d. mushrooms
2. One of the principal compounds that living things use to store energy is
   a. DNA. c. H_2O.
   b. ATP. d. CO_2.
3. Which scientist concluded that most of a growing plant's mass comes from water?
   a. Priestley c. Ingenhousz
   b. van Helmont d. Calvin
4. In addition to light and chlorophyll, photosynthesis requires
   a. water and oxygen.
   b. water and sugars.
   c. oxygen and carbon dioxide.
   d. water and carbon dioxide.
5. The leaves of a plant appear green because chlorophyll
   a. reflects blue light.
   b. absorbs blue light.
   c. does not absorb green light.
   d. absorbs green light.
6. The products of photosynthesis are
   a. sugars and oxygen.
   b. sugars and carbon dioxide.
   c. water and carbon dioxide.
   d. hydrogen and oxygen.
7. Which organelle contains chlorophyll?

a. 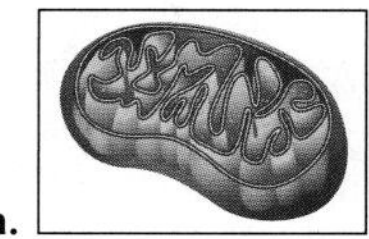
c. 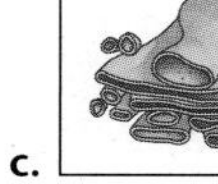
b. 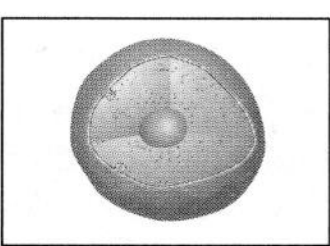
d. 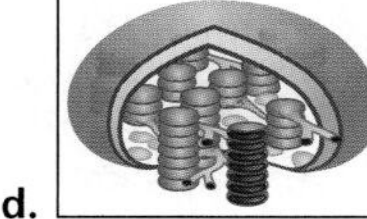

8. The first process in the light-dependent reactions of photosynthesis is
   a. light absorption.
   b. electron transport.
   c. oxygen production.
   d. ATP formation.
9. Which substance from the light-dependent reactions of photosynthesis is the source of energy for the Calvin cycle?
   a. ADP c. H_2O
   b. NADPH d. pyruvic acid
10. The light-independent reactions of photosynthesis are also known as the
    a. Calvin cycle. c. Ingenhousz cycle.
    b. Priestley cycle. d. van Helmont cycle.

Understanding Concepts

11. How do heterotrophs and autotrophs differ?
12. Describe the three parts of an ATP molecule.
13. Use the analogy of a battery to explain how energy is stored in and released from ATP.
14. Compare the amounts of energy stored by ATP and glucose. Which compound is used by the cell as an immediate source of energy?
15. How were Priestley's and Ingenhousz's discoveries about photosynthesis related?
16. Write the basic equation for photosynthesis using the names of the starting and final substances of the process.
17. What role do plant pigments play in the process of photosynthesis?
18. Identify the structures labeled A, B, C, and D. In which structure(s) do the light-dependent reactions occur? In which structure(s) does the Calvin cycle take place?

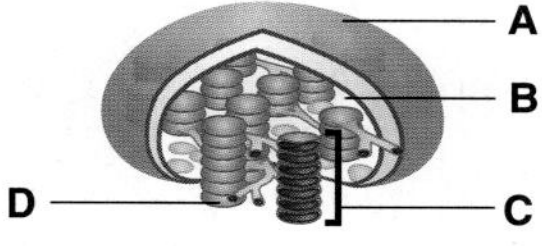

19. Explain the role of $NADP^+$ as an energy carrier in photosynthesis.
20. What is the role of ATP synthase? How does it work?
21. Summarize what happens during the Calvin cycle.
22. How do the events in the Calvin cycle depend on the light-dependent reactions?
23. Describe three factors that affect the rate at which photosynthesis occurs.

18. A: chloroplast; B: stroma; C. granum; D: thylakoid. The light-dependent reactions take place in the thylakoids. The Calvin cycle takes place in the stroma.

19. $NADP^+$ carries energy by holding two electrons and a hydrogen ion. It carries the stored energy to other reactions that help build sugar molecules.

20. ATP synthase is a protein found in the thylakoid membrane that allows H^+ ions to pass through it. As H^+ ions pass through this protein, it rotates and binds ADP and a phosphate group together to produce ATP.

21. During the Calvin cycle, plants use the energy that ATP and NADPH contain to build high-energy compounds that can be stored for a long time. The Calvin cycle uses six molecules of carbon dioxide to produce a single 6-carbon sugar molecule.

22. The Calvin cycle uses the ATP and NADPH produced during the light-dependent reactions to produce high-energy sugars.

23. Factors that affect the rate of photosynthesis include the temperature, the amount of available water, and the intensity of light.

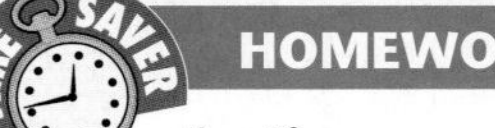

HOMEWORK GUIDE

Section:	Questions:
Section 8–1	1, 2, 11–14, 27
Section 8–2	3–6, 15–17, 32
Section 8–3	7–10, 18–26, 28–31

Chapter 8 Assessment

Critical Thinking

24. The chlorophyll may be broken down by the cooling temperatures or the changing light, so the green color disappears. A leaf then shows the color of its remaining pigment(s).

25. Some students may build on the analogy of the battery from the chapter. Others may develop a new analogy. For example, ADP is like a ball at the bottom of the hill. Moving the ball to the top of the hill is like adding a phosphate group and making ATP. The ball now has the energy to roll downhill and move other objects in its path. ATP has energy to help change molecules.

26. No step of the Calvin cycle depends directly on light. Instead it uses energy stored in the molecules ATP and NADPH.

27. Students' answers may include: Start with two samples of the same amount and type of pond algae in water. Put one sample in the dark and the other in a location that receives daylight, keeping the temperatures the same. After two weeks, compare the two samples to determine the amount and health of the algae.

28. a. The graph shows a curve that descends from left to right. The farther the light is from the plant, the fewer bubbles were produced.
b. 10 cm. **c.** The closer the plant is to the light, the more oxygen is produced. This occurs because more light energy is reaching the algae cells and thus is available for photosynthesis.

29. At first, photosynthesis would take place during daylight, but it would stop when the water was used up. If no more water was added, the plant might die.

30. Because the Indian pipe plant has no chlorophyll or other pigment involved in photosynthesis, it probably cannot make its own food. Therefore, it must obtain food from other sources the way a heterotroph does. Perhaps it absorbs partly decayed food in the soil.

Chapter 8 Assessment

Critical Thinking

24. Formulating Hypotheses Some plant leaves contain yellow and red pigments as well as chlorophyll. In the fall, those leaves may become red or yellow. Suggest an explanation for those color changes.

25. Using Analogies Develop an analogy to explain ATP and energy transfer to a classmate who does not understand the concept.

26. Interpreting Graphics The Calvin cycle is sometimes described as the light-independent reactions. Study **Figure 8–11** on page 212 and give evidence to support the idea that the Calvin cycle does not depend on light.

27. Designing an Experiment Design an experiment that uses pond water and algae to demonstrate the importance of light energy to pond life. Be sure to identify the variables you will control and the variable you will change.

28. Analyzing Data A water plant placed in a bright light gives off bubbles of oxygen. In the laboratory, you notice that if the light is placed at different distances from the plant, the rate at which the plant produces bubbles changes. Your data are shown in the following table.

Oxygen Production

Distance From Light (cm)	Bubbles Produced per Minute
10	39
20	22
30	8
40	5

a. On graph paper, plot the data on a line graph. Describe the trend. When the light was farther from the plant, did the number of bubbles produced increase or decrease? Explain.
b. At what distance is gas production at its highest?
c. What relationship exists between the distance from the plant to the light and the number of bubbles produced? Explain your answer.

29. Predicting Suppose you water a potted plant and place it by a window in an airtight jar. Predict when photosynthesis might occur over the next few days. Would you expect the pattern to change if the plant were left there for several weeks? Explain.

30. Inferring Examine the photograph of the Indian pipe plant shown below. What can you conclude about the ability of the Indian pipe plant to make its own food? Explain your answer.

31. Formulating Hypotheses Many of the sun's rays may be blocked by dust or clouds formed by volcanic eruptions or pollution. What are some possible short-term and long-term effects of this on photosynthesis?

32. Making Connections Recall what you learned about the flow of energy through an ecosystem. Explain how photosynthesis relates to that flow.

Performance-Based Assessment

Creative Writing Imagine that you are an oxygen atom and two of your friends are hydrogen atoms. Together, you make up a water molecule. Describe the events and changes that happen to you and your friends as you journey through the light-dependent reactions and Calvin cycle of photosynthesis. Include illustrations with your description.

Why is it important to study photosynthesis? Visit the Prentice Hall Web site at **www.phschool.com** to find out some of the ways in which the study of photosynthesis is important. Then, answer the following questions:

- In what ways do people use the products of photosynthesis in their everyday lives?
- How might research into photosynthesis help scientists increase the amount of food that farmers are able to produce?
- How can we use the products of photosynthesis to help reduce levels of harmful air pollutants?

Performance-Based Assessment

Stories and illustrations will vary, but all students should include the basic events of the photosynthesis. Students should recognize that both the oxygen atom and the hydrogen atoms enter a chloroplast together as a molecule of water, H_2O. The writer, as the oxygen atom, will split from the friends, the hydrogen atoms, in the first stage of photosynthesis and leave the plant as oxygen gas. The hydrogen atoms will become involved in the formation of NADPH, the production of ATP, and the production of high-energy sugars in the Calvin cycle.

Standardized Test Prep

Test-Taking Tip In tests, analogies compare pairs of items, such as *kitten : cat :: puppy :* __?__. Before looking at the possible answers, identify how the first pair is related. For example, since a kitten is a young cat, the relationship is *baby : adult,* so the correct answer is *puppy : dog.*

Questions 1–2 Complete each analogy by selecting the correct letter. In analogies, A : B :: C : __?__ *means* A is to B as C is to __?__.

1. Oak tree : autotroph :: human : __?__
   (A) consumer
   (B) producer
   (C) autotroph
   (D) omnivore
   (E) heterotroph
2. Light-dependent reactions : oxygen :: Calvin cycle : __?__
   (A) sugar
   (B) NADH
   (C) oxygen
   (D) ADP
   (E) ATP

Directions: Choose the letter that best answers the question or completes the statement.

3. One of the main energy-storing compounds used by cells is
   (A) chlorophyll.
   (B) oxygen.
   (C) ADP.
   (D) ATP.
   (E) NADPH.
4. Which of the following is NOT produced in the light-dependent reactions of photosynthesis?
   (A) NADPH
   (B) sugars
   (C) hydrogen ions
   (D) ATP
   (E) oxygen
5. Which equation best summarizes the process of photosynthesis?
   (A) water + carbon dioxide $\xrightarrow{\text{light}}$ sugars + oxygen
   (B) sugars + oxygen $\xrightarrow{\text{light}}$ water + carbon
   (C) water + oxygen $\xrightarrow{\text{light}}$ sugars + carbon dioxide
   (D) oxygen + carbon dioxide $\xrightarrow{\text{light}}$ sugars + oxygen
   (E) sugars + carbon dioxide $\xrightarrow{\text{light}}$ water + oxygen
6. The color of light that is LEAST useful to a plant during photosynthesis is
   (A) red.
   (B) blue.
   (C) green.
   (D) orange.
   (E) violet.
7. The first step in photosynthesis is the
   (A) synthesis of water.
   (B) production of oxygen.
   (C) formation of ATP.
   (D) breakdown of carbon dioxide.
   (E) absorption of light energy.
8. In a typical plant, all of the following factors are necessary for photosynthesis EXCEPT
   (A) chlorophyll.
   (B) light.
   (C) oxygen.
   (D) carbon dioxide.
   (E) water.

Questions 9–10

Several drops of concentrated pigment were extracted from spinach leaves. These drops were placed at the bottom of a strip of highly absorbent paper. After the extract dried, the paper was suspended in a test tube containing alcohol so that only the tip of the paper was in the alcohol. As the alcohol was absorbed and moved up the paper, the various pigments contained in the extract separated as shown in the diagram below.

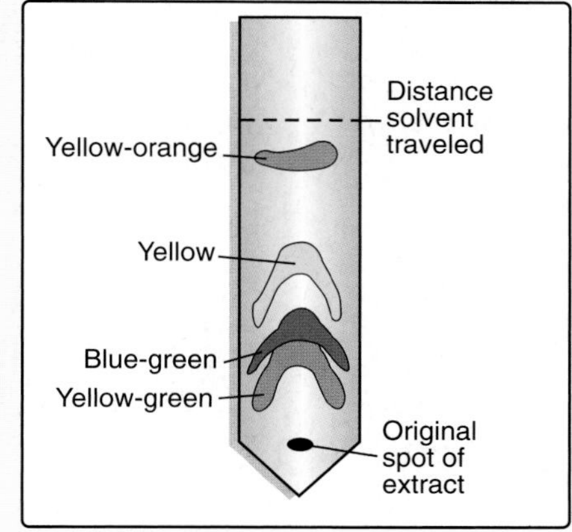

9. Which pigment traveled the shortest distance?
   (A) yellow-orange
   (B) yellow
   (C) blue-green
   (D) yellow-green
   (E) black
10. A valid conclusion that can be drawn from this information is that spinach leaves
    (A) use only chlorophyll during photosynthesis.
    (B) contain several pigments.
    (C) contain more orange pigment than yellow pigment.
    (D) are yellow-orange rather than green.
    (E) have only one color of pigment.

1. E **2.** A **3.** D **4.** B **5.** A **6.** C **7.** E **8.** C **9.** D **10.** B

Chapter 8 Assessment (continued)

31. Short-term effects: Less light will reach photosynthetic organisms, so less photosynthesis will occur, and those organisms may grow more slowly. Long-term effects: Some autotrophs could die because they lack the food and energy they need; then heterotrophs that depend on those autotrophs could experience starvation and death.

32. In autotrophs, the process of photosynthesis captures energy from sunlight and uses it to produce high-energy sugars. This energy passes from one organism to another in an ecosystem as organisms eat and are eaten.

Take It to the NET

• Food comes either directly or indirectly from plants, which capture the sun's energy through photosynthesis. The fossil fuels used to heat homes and power vehicles are the result of photosynthesis. Almost all plant and animal products are the direct or indirect result of photosynthesis.

• Food production might be increased in two ways through such research. First, scientists might be able to develop plants that are more efficient in capturing the sun's energy, increasing the energy contained in each plant. Second, scientists might be able to create herbicides that are more efficient in destroying weeds.

• Research may provide scientists with the means to design energy converters that rely on photosynthetic processes to convert carbon dioxide and sunlight into useful energy sources. For additional information, visit

www.phschool.com

Chapter Planner 9 Cellular Respiration

Section and Section Objectives	Time	Activities and Labs
9–1 Chemical Pathways, pp. 221–225 **9.1.1** ***Explain*** what cellular respiration is. **9.1.2** ***Describe*** what happens during the process of glycolysis. **9.1.3** ***Name*** the two main types of fermentation.	**2 periods (1 block)**	**SE:** ***Inquiry Activity,*** How do living things release energy?, p. 220 **TE:** ***Build Science Skills,*** p. 224 **SE:** ***Problem Solving,*** A Family Recipe, p. 224
9–2 The Krebs Cycle and Electron Transport, pp. 226–232 **9.2.1** ***Describe*** what happens during the Krebs cycle. **9.2.2** ***Explain*** how high-energy electrons are used by the electron transport chain. **9.2.3** ***Identify*** three pathways the body uses to release energy during exercise. **9.2.4** ***Compare*** photosynthesis and respiration.	**3 periods (1–1/2 block)** **1 period (1/2 block)**	**SE:** ***Quick Lab,*** How does exercise affect cellular respiration?, p. 231 **SE:** ***Issues in Biology,*** Should Creatine Supplements Be Banned?, p. 233 **SE:** ***Real-World Lab,*** Making Kimchi, pp. 234–235
Chapter Assessment, pp. 236–239		

ACTIVITY PLANNER

SE: ***Inquiry Activity,*** p. 220; (15 min.); an electric device such as a flashlight, a chemically fueled device such as a candle, a live or preserved animal, a small plant in an opaque container

TE: ***Build Science Skills,*** p. 224; (5 min.); piece of leavened bread, piece of unleavened bread

SE: ***Quick Lab,*** p. 231; (15 min.); 2 small test tubes, glass marking pencil, 10-mL graduated cylinder, bromthymol blue solution, 2 straws, clock or watch with second hand

SE: ***Real-World Lab,*** pp. 234–235; (40 min., weekly follow-up); 2 resealable plastic sandwich bags, chopped Chinese cabbage, noniodized salt, 2.5-mL (1/2 teaspoon) measuring spoon, pH-indicator paper, thermometer

PLANNING KEY

Ability Levels

B **Basic**	For students who need additional help
A **Average**	For all students
E **Enriched**	For students who need to be challenged

Components

SE	Student Edition	**GRSW**	Guided Reading and Study Workbook	**IDM**	Issues and Decision Making
TE	Teacher's Edition	**CT**	Chapter Tests: Levels A and B	**CTB**	Computer Test Bank
LMA	Laboratory Manual A	**PHAS**	PH Assessment System	**PA**	Presentation Assistant Plus
LMB	Laboratory Manual B	**LA**	Lab Assessment With Scoring Guide	**BD**	BioDetectives Videotape
TR	Teaching Resources	**BTM**	BioTechnology Manual	**iT**	iText
IF	Investigations in Forensics				

Program Resources	***Assessment***	***Media and Technology***
TR: Section Review 9–1 B A **GRSW:** Section 9–1 B A	**SE:** 9–1 Section Assessment, p. 225 **TR:** Section Review 9–1	**PA:** 9–1, Interest Grabber, Section Outline, Chemical Pathways, Figure 9–2, Figure 9–3, Figure 9–4 **iT:** Section 9–1
LMA: Chapter 9 Lab A E **LMB:** Chapter 9 Lab B A **TR:** Section Review 9–2 B A Chapter 9 Real-World Lab B A E **GRSW:** Section 9–2 B A	**SE:** 9–2 Section Assessment, p. 232 **TR:** Section Review 9–2	**PA:** 9–2 Interest Grabber, Section Outline, Flowchart, Figure 9–6, Figure 9–7 **iT:** Section 9–2
	SE: Chapter 9 Assessment, pp. 236–239 **TR:** Chapter Vocabulary Review, Graphic Organizer **CB:** Chapter 9 Test **CTB:** Chapter 9 Test **PHAS:** Practice Test	**CTB:** Chapter 9 Test **iT:** Chapter 9 Assessment

PRESSED FOR TIME?

To Preview the Chapter

- Introduce students to Key Concepts and Vocabulary terms in each section.
- Assign the Reading Strategies for each section.

To Cover the Chapter Quickly

- Have students read all of Section 9–1 and read Figures 9–6 and 9–7, and Comparing Photosynthesis and Respiration in Section 9–2.
- Assign the Section Reviews for 9–1 and 9–2 and questions 1–10 in Chapter 9 Assessment and questions 1–10 in Chapter 9 Standardized Test Prep.

To Review the Chapter

- Assign the Section Reviews for 9–1 and 9–2 in the Guided Reading and Study Workbook.
- Assign Section Reviews for 9–1 and 9–2 and the Chapter Vocabulary Review for Chapter 9 in the Teaching Resources.

ENGAGE/EXPLORE

Inquiry Activity

Objective Students will be able to formulate hypotheses for how organisms release energy from food.

Skill Focus **Using Tables and Graphs, Formulating Hypotheses**

Materials an electric device such as a flashlight, a chemically fueled device such as a candle, a live or preserved animal, a small plant in an opaque container

Time 15 minutes

Advance Prep Decide in advance which items will be provided to each group or student. To stimulate discussion, provide different examples of each type of item to different groups or students.

Safety If you provide some kind of flame-producing device, do not permit matches or other fire hazards to be present in the room.

Strategies

- Display a blank table with labeled columns on the board or with an overhead projector.
- Present items in order of difficulty, such as: electrical device, chemically fueled device, animal specimen, plant.

Expected Outcomes Students will identify the energy sources of various living and nonliving things. They will also identify the energy-releasing mechanisms of nonliving things and speculate about how living things release energy.

Think About It

1. Students will find it easier to describe how nonliving devices use energy because the energy sources those devices use are familiar to students.

2. Responses will vary depending on students' prior knowledge. Typical answers might include food, carbohydrates, and glucose.

3. A typical hypothesis might suggest that organisms release energy from food through a chemical process within cells.

Chapter 9 Cellular Respiration

Athletes get the energy they need from the breakdown of glucose during cellular respiration.

Inquiry Activity

How do living things release energy?

Procedure

1. Draw a table with 5 rows and 4 columns. Label the columns from left to right: Item, Activities, Energy Source, and How Energy Is Released.
2. Fill in each row of your table for every item your teacher provides.
3. Complete your table, using yourself for the last item.

Think About It

1. **Using Tables and Graphs** Was it easier to describe how organisms use energy or how nonliving devices use energy?
2. **Using Tables and Graphs** What is the most common energy source for organisms?
3. **Formulating Hypotheses** How do you think organisms release the energy they need?

FACTS AND FIGURES

Respiration—converting ADP into ATP
Organisms pay a price in energy for the cellular work they do, including movement, molecular synthesis, active transport, and so on. Most of the energy used is gained through the conversion of ATP molecules into ADP molecules. To keep everything going, cells must convert the ADP molecules back into ATP molecules, and they do this mostly through the process of cellular respiration. For example, a working muscle cell converts ADP into ATP at a rate of about 10 million molecules per second. To accomplish this conversion, cells use the chemical energy stored in food.

9–1 Chemical Pathways

When you are hungry, how do you feel? If you are like most people, your stomach may seem empty, you might feel a little dizzy, and above all, you feel weak. The sensations produced by hunger vary from one person to the next, but the bottom line is always the same. Our bodies have a need for food, and they have their own ways of telling us when we need it.

Food provides living things with the chemical building blocks they need to grow and reproduce. Food serves as a source of raw materials from which the cells of the body can synthesize new molecules. Most of all, food serves as a source of energy.

Chemical Energy and Food

How much energy is actually present in food? Quite a lot. One gram of the sugar glucose ($C_6H_{12}O_6$), when burned in the presence of oxygen, releases 3811 calories of heat energy. A **calorie** is the amount of energy needed to raise the temperature of 1 gram of water 1 Celsius degree. The Calorie (capital "C") that is used on food labels is a kilocalorie, or 1000 calories. Cells, of course, don't "burn" glucose. Instead, they gradually release the energy from glucose and other food compounds.

This process begins with a pathway called **glycolysis** (gly-KAHL-ih-sis). Glycolysis releases only a small amount of energy. If oxygen is present, glycolysis leads to two other pathways that release a great deal of energy. If oxygen is not present, however, glycolysis is followed by a different pathway.

Guide for Reading

 **Key Concepts**
- What is cellular respiration?
- What happens during the process of glycolysis?
- What are the two main types of fermentation?

Vocabulary
calorie
glycolysis
cellular respiration
NAD+
fermentation
anaerobic

Reading Strategy: Asking Questions Before you read this section, rewrite the headings as *how, why,* or *what* questions about releasing energy. Then, as you read, write brief answers to your questions.

Figure 9–1 Living things get the energy they need from food. Both plant and animal cells carry out the final stages of cellular respiration in the mitochondria.

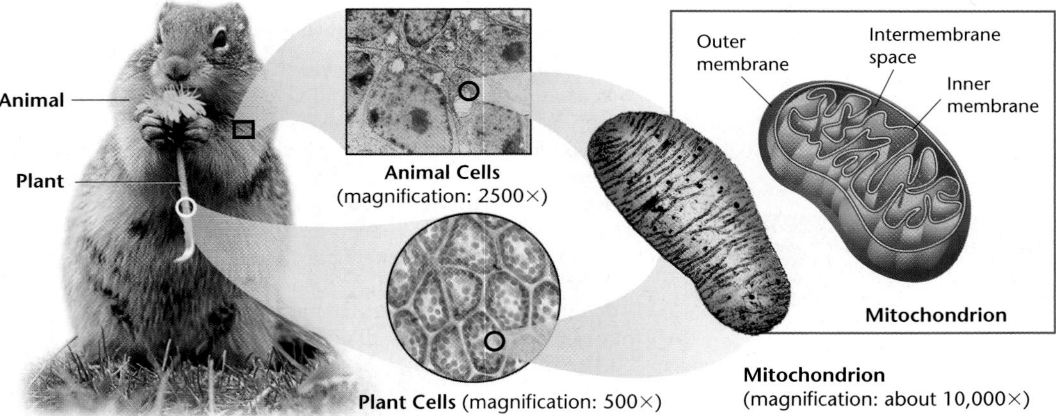

SECTION RESOURCES

Print:
- ***Teaching Resources,*** Section Review 9–1
- ***Guided Reading and Study Workbook,*** Section 9–1

Technology:
- ***iText,*** Section 9–1

Section 9–1

1 FOCUS

Objectives

9.1.1 ***Explain*** what cellular respiration is.

9.1.2 ***Describe*** what happens during the process of glycolysis.

9.1.3 ***Name*** the two main types of fermentation.

Guide for Reading

Vocabulary Preview

Call on volunteers to pronounce the section's vocabulary words. Correct any mispronunciations, and then have all students pronounce each word together.

Reading Strategy

Students should write a question for each head and subhead. For example, they might write, "How are chemical energy and food related?" Encourage students to write an answer to each question as they read the section.

2 INSTRUCT

Chemical Energy and Food

Use Visuals

Figure 9–1 Ask: **How would you describe the inner mitochondrial membrane?** *(It is convoluted, with many turns and folds.)* **What is the space between the inner and outer membranes called?** *(Intermembrane space)*

Overview of Cellular Respiration

Meet Diverse Needs

To help both students with limited English proficiency and at-risk students, draw a large cell on the board. Within the cell, draw a nucleus, a chloroplast, and a mitochondrion. Then, ask students to point to and identify where in the cell photosynthesis occurs *(chloroplast)*, glycolysis occurs *(cytoplasm)*, and cellular respiration occurs *(mitochondrion)*. **Learning modality: visual**

Use Visuals

Figure 9–2 Have students study the figure. Then, ask: **Where does the glucose used in respiration come from?** *(Cells obtain glucose mainly by breaking down carbohydrates such as starch.)* **How do you know that this series of reactions occurs in the presence of oxygen?** *(If there were no oxygen present, then fermentation would occur, not cellular respiration.)* **What does glycolysis supply to the Krebs cycle and to the electron transport chain?** *(It supplies pyruvic acid to the Krebs cycle and high-energy electrons via NADH to the electron transport chain.)* **What stages of cellular respiration occur in mitochondria?** *(The Krebs cycle and the electron transport chain)*

SCIENCE NEWS®

Encourage students to visit **www.phschool.com** for the most current information on this topic.

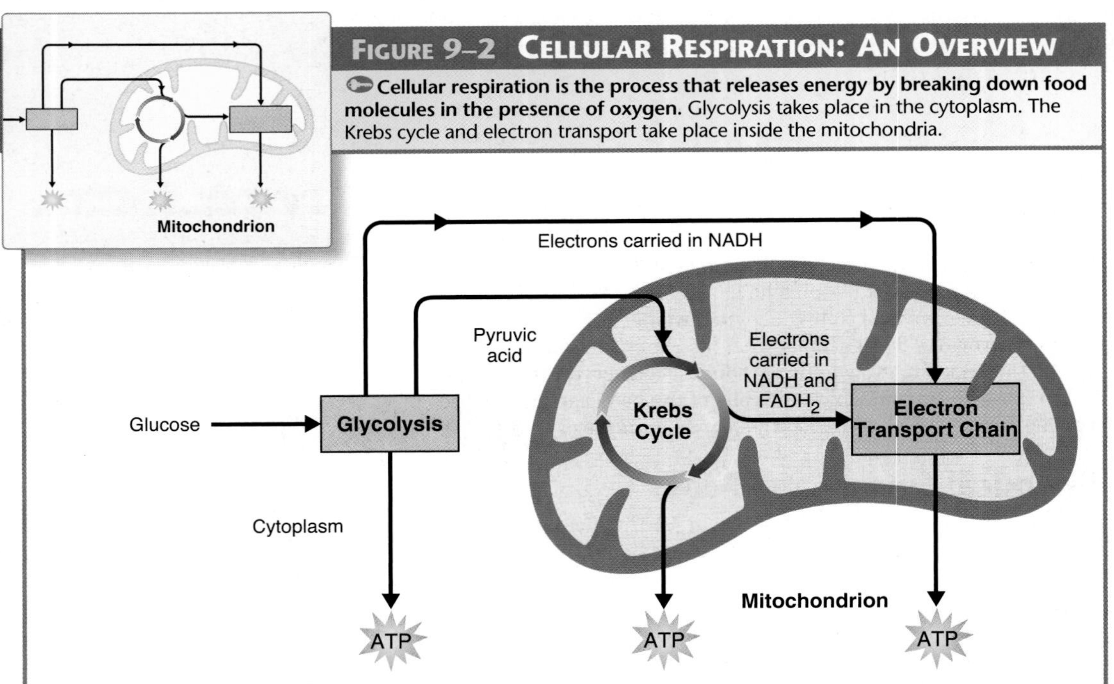

FIGURE 9–2 CELLULAR RESPIRATION: AN OVERVIEW **Cellular respiration is the process that releases energy by breaking down food molecules in the presence of oxygen.** Glycolysis takes place in the cytoplasm. The Krebs cycle and electron transport take place inside the mitochondria.

Overview of Cellular Respiration

In the presence of oxygen, glycolysis is followed by the Krebs cycle and the electron transport chain. Glycolysis, the Krebs cycle, and the electron transport chain make up a process called **cellular respiration.** **Cellular respiration is the process that releases energy by breaking down food molecules in the presence of oxygen.** The equation for cellular respiration is:

$$6O_2 + C_6H_{12}O_6 \longrightarrow 6CO_2 + 6H_2O + \text{Energy}$$

oxygen + glucose ⟶ carbon dioxide + water + energy

As you can see, cellular respiration requires a food molecule such as glucose and oxygen, and gives off carbon, water, and energy. Do not be misled, however, by the simplicity of this equation. If cellular respiration took place in just one step, all of the energy from glucose would be released at once, and most of it would be lost in the form of light and heat. Clearly, a living cell has to control that energy. It can't simply start a fire—it has to release the explosive chemical energy in food molecules a little bit at a time. The cell needs to find a way to trap those little bits of energy by using them to make ATP. As you will see, that is exactly what the cell does.

The three main stages of cellular respiration are shown in **Figure 9–2.** Each of the three stages captures some of the chemical energy available in food molecules and uses it to produce ATP.

KEEP CURRENT WITH . . . SCIENCE NEWS®

To find out more about the topics in this chapter, go to: **www.phschool.com**

TIME SAVER — PRESENTATIONS MADE EASY!

The Presentation Assistant Plus contains the Prentice Hall Presentation Pro and the Transparencies, which provide easy-to-follow visual support for every step of this section. If you have a computer presentation station, use Prentice Hall Presentation Pro for Section 9–1, or use the transparencies listed here.

Section 9–1:

Interest Grabber
Section Outline
Chemical Pathways
Figure 9–2
Figure 9–3
Figure 9–4

Glycolysis

The first set of reactions in cellular respiration is glycolysis. **Glycolysis is the process in which one molecule of glucose is broken in half, producing two molecules of pyruvic acid, a 3-carbon compound.** The process of glycolysis is shown in **Figure 9–3.**

ATP Production Even though glycolysis is an energy-releasing process, the cell needs to put in a little energy to get things going. At the pathway's beginning, 2 molecules of ATP are used up. In a way, those 2 ATP molecules are like an investment that pays back interest. In order to earn interest from a bank, first you have to put money into an account. Although the cell puts 2 ATP molecules into its "account" to get glycolysis going, when glycolysis is complete, 4 ATP molecules have been produced. This gives the cell a net gain of 2 ATP molecules.

NADH Production One of the reactions of glycolysis removes 4 high-energy electrons and passes them to an electron carrier called **NAD^+,** or nicotinamide adenine dinucleotide. Like $NADP^+$ in photosynthesis, each NAD^+ accepts a pair of high-energy electrons. This molecule, known as NADH, holds the electrons until they can be transferred to other molecules. By doing this, NAD^+ helps to pass energy from glucose to other pathways in the cell.

Although the energy yield from glycolysis is small, the process is so fast that cells can produce thousands of ATP molecules in just a few milliseconds. Besides speed, another advantage is that glycolysis itself does not require oxygen. This means that glycolysis can supply chemical energy to cells when oxygen is not available.

However, when a cell generates large amounts of ATP from glycolysis, it runs into a problem. In just a few seconds, all of the cell's available NAD^+ molecules are filled up with electrons. Without NAD^+, the cell cannot keep glycolysis going, and ATP production stops.

CHECKPOINT *What does glycolysis break down?*

Word Origins

Glycolysis comes from the Greek word *glukus,* meaning "sweet," and the Latin word *lysis,* which indicates a process of loosening or decomposing. Thus, *glycolysis* means "breaking glucose." **If *hydro* means "water," what do you think the term *hydrolysis* means?**

▼ **Figure 9–3** Glycolysis is the first stage in cellular respiration. **During glycolysis, glucose is broken down into 2 molecules of pyruvic acid.**

Glycolysis

Word Origins

Hydrolysis means "breaking down water."

Meet Diverse Needs

Some at-risk students may not be familiar with interest-bearing bank accounts. To clarify the analogy used in the text, show students a bank statement of a savings account. Point out that a person has to deposit money into the account in order to earn interest, just as a cell must put 2 ATPs into the "account" to earn the interest of additional ATPs. **Learning modality: visual**

Use Visuals

Figure 9–3 Have students study the process of glycolysis, and then, ask: **Where in the cell does glycolysis take place?** *(In the cytoplasm)* Remind students that the cell must expend energy to get the process going. Ask: **Where in the figure does it show that the cell is using energy to start glycolysis?** *(During the breakdown of glucose, 2 molecules of ATP change to 2 molecules of ADP.)* Have a volunteer point out where in the process 2 NAD^+ molecules accept electrons. Then, ask: **NAD^+ is an electron carrier in this process. What is an electron carrier?** *(An electron carrier is a compound that can accept a pair of high-energy electrons and transfer them along with most of their energy to another molecule.)* **Glycolysis is an energy-releasing process. Where in this figure does it show energy being released?** *(On the right side of the figure, 4 ATP molecules are produced from 4 ADP molecules using the energy released from the breakdown of the glucose molecule.)*

TEACHER TO TEACHER

When I introduce cellular respiration to students, I take a novel approach that sounds "off the wall," but it works. We first look at the overall equation for cellular respiration. I have the students take note of the products, and then, we work backwards. With this approach, I find that my students come away with a greater understanding of the total process and also have greater retention of the basic concepts. I do a fermentation lab with my students using a variety of juices, including orange, grape, prune, apple, pineapple, and even diet cola. In addition, we make breads using different sugars and compare the weights of the resulting doughs. (CO_2 is a heavy gas.)

—*Greg McCurdy, Biology Teacher, Salem High School, Salem, IN*

Answer to . . .

CHECKPOINT *Glycolysis breaks down a molecule of glucose into 2 molecules of pyruvic acid.*

9–1 (continued)

Fermentation

Build Science Skills

Comparing and Contrasting Display to students a piece of leavened bread and a piece of unleavened bread. Ask: **What is the difference between the two breads?** *(The unleavened bread is thinner than the leavened bread and has no holes, while the leavened bread is thicker than the unleavened bread and has little holes in it.)* Explain that *leaven* means "to raise," and so *unleavened* bread is bread that didn't rise when baked. Ask: **What was added to the leavened bread that made it rise?** *(Yeast)* **What process did the yeast carry out that caused the bread to rise?** *(Alcoholic fermentation)*

Problem Solving

Bread recipes are often precise about ingredients, though where and how to allow the dough to rise is often left up to the cook. Students may focus on the amount of yeast or flour, or they may want to focus on the conditions of the place where the dough is left to rise. This activity might be more appropriate for small groups than for individual students.

Defining the Problem A typical definition of the problem: How can the production of bubbles of carbon dioxide be increased during the making of bread?

Organizing Information Students should know that temperature affects the action of enzymes, and that temperature affects the processes of living things such as yeast. They should also understand that the amount of food available for a living thing to use will affect the outcome. Students should write a prediction for each factor listed.

Creating a Solution A typical experiment might identify temperature as the manipulated variable.

Presenting Your Plan Encourage students to include as many details as possible on their posters. Allow time for students or groups to present their experiments to the class.

Fermentation

When oxygen is not present, glycolysis is followed by a different pathway. The combined process of this pathway and glycolysis is called fermentation. **Fermentation** releases energy from food molecules in the absence of oxygen.

During fermentation, cells convert NADH to NAD^+ by passing high-energy electrons back to pyruvic acid. This action converts NADH back into the electron carrier NAD^+, allowing glycolysis to continue producing a steady supply of ATP. Because fermentation does not require oxygen, it is said to be **anaerobic.** The term *anaerobic* means "not in air." **The two main types of fermentation are alcoholic fermentation and lactic acid fermentation.**

Alcoholic Fermentation Yeasts and a few other microorganisms use alcoholic fermentation, forming ethyl alcohol and carbon dioxide as wastes. The equation for alcoholic fermentation after glycolysis is:

$$\text{pyruvic acid} + \text{NADH} \longrightarrow \text{alcohol} + CO_2 + NAD^+$$

Alcoholic fermentation produces carbon dioxide as well as alcohol. Alcoholic fermentation causes bread dough to rise. When yeast in the dough runs out of oxygen, it begins to ferment, giving off bubbles of carbon dioxide which form the air spaces you see in a slice of bread. The small amount of alcohol produced in the dough evaporates when the bread is baked.

Problem Solving

A Family Recipe

You have opened a bakery, selling bread made according to your family's favorite recipe. Unfortunately, most of your customers find your bread too heavy. You need to make your bread more appealing to your customers. Before bread is baked, yeast cells in the dough ferment some of the carbohydrate in the flour, producing bubbles of carbon dioxide. These bubbles cause the dough to rise and give bread its light, spongy structure. How can you make your bread lighter?

Define the Problem In your own words, write down what problem you are trying to solve.

Organizing Information The process of fermentation is a series of chemical reactions catalyzed by enzymes. Review what you've learned about such reactions. Make a list of factors, such as temperature and the amounts of yeast and flour in the dough, that might affect the process of fermentation. Predict how each factor will affect the rate of fermentation.

Creating a Solution Write a detailed description of an experiment that could determine if changing the conditions of the fermentation would make the bread lighter. Identify each of your variables. What controls and experimental treatments will you use?

Presenting Your Plan Make a poster showing the procedures in your proposed experiment and explain it to your classmates.

FACTS AND FIGURES

Yeast leavens bread through fermentation
Yeast and other organisms that can carry out both fermentation and cellular respiration, including many kinds of bacteria, are called facultative anaerobes. Human muscle cells also behave as facultative anaerobes. What happens to the end product of glycolysis—pyruvic acid—depends on whether oxygen is present. If there is no oxygen, then fermentation begins.

Baker's yeast, *Saccharomyces cerevisiae,* is the most common organism used to leaven bread. Sourdough bread is leavened by lactobacilli and other lactic-acid bacteria found in flour and milk. Chemicals can also be used to leaven bread. Yeast multiplies best between temperatures of about 27°C and 43°C. It is dormant below 10°C, and it dies at temperatures above 49°C.

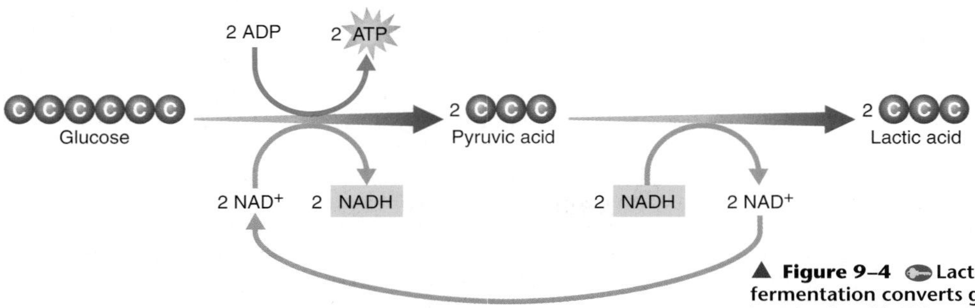

▲ **Figure 9–4 Lactic acid fermentation converts glucose into lactic acid.** This type of fermentation occurs in human muscle cells during strenuous exercise when breathing cannot supply the cells with enough oxygen.

Lactic Acid Fermentation In many cells, the pyruvic acid that accumulates as a result of glycolysis can be converted to lactic acid. Because this type of fermentation produces lactic acid, it is called lactic acid fermentation. This process regenerates NAD^+ so that glycolysis can continue, as shown in **Figure 9–4.** The equation for lactic acid fermentation after glycolysis is:

$$\textbf{pyruvic acid} + \textbf{NADH} \longrightarrow \textbf{lactic acid} + \textbf{NAD}^+$$

Lactic acid is produced in your muscles during rapid exercise when the body cannot supply enough oxygen to the tissues. Without enough oxygen, the body is not able to produce all of the ATP that is required. When you exercise vigorously by running, swimming, or riding a bicycle as fast as you can, the large muscles of your arms and legs quickly run out of oxygen. Your muscle cells rapidly begin to produce ATP by lactic acid fermentation. The buildup of lactic acid causes a painful, burning sensation. This is why muscles may feel sore after only a few seconds of intense activity.

9–1 Section Assessment

1. **Key Concept** Describe the process of cellular respiration.
2. **Key Concept** What are the products of glycolysis?
3. **Key Concept** Name the two main types of fermentation.
4. What is a calorie? A Calorie?
5. How is the function of NAD^+ similar to that of $NADP^+$?
6. **Critical Thinking Comparing and Contrasting** How are lactic acid fermentation and alcoholic fermentation similar? How are they different?

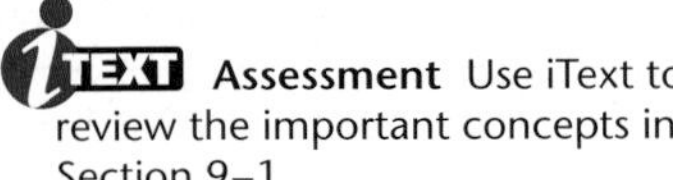

Assessment Use iText to review the important concepts in Section 9–1.

Take It to the NET

Read about fermented foods that are consumed by humans. Then, make a data table that lists each food and its source (before fermentation). Use the links provided in the Biology area at the Prentice Hall Web site for help in completing this activity: **www.phschool.com**

9–1 Section Assessment

1. Cellular respiration is the process that releases energy by breaking down molecules in food in the presence of oxygen.
2. Glycolysis produces 2 molecules of pyruvic acid, 2 molecules of ATP, and 2 molecules of NADH.
3. Alcoholic fermentation and lactic acid fermentation
4. A calorie is the amount of energy required to raise the temperature of 1 gram of water 1 Celsius degree. A Calorie is 1000 calories.
5. Both are electron carriers.
6. Similar: Both provide energy to cells in the absence of oxygen. Different: Alcoholic fermentation produces alcohol, carbon dioxide, and NAD^+; while lactic acid fermentation produces lactic acid and NAD^+.

Use Visuals

Figure 9–4 Have students study the process shown in the figure. Point out that the process of glucose breaking down and giving off energy in the figure is similar to the process shown in Figure 9–3. Then, ask: **What is missing from this series of reactions that makes the process anaerobic?** *(There is no oxygen in the process.)* Point out that this pathway shows how an electron carrier behaves cyclically. In lactic acid fermentation, 2 NADH molecules become 2 NAD^+ molecules, resupplying the cell with the electron carriers needed in glycolysis.

3 ASSESS

Evaluate Understanding

Call on students at random to explain what occurs during glycolysis. Then, ask students to write the equations for alcoholic fermentation and lactic acid fermentation.

Reteach

Have students make three simple flowcharts, using words in each box that explain the processes of glycolysis, alcoholic fermentation, and lactic acid fermentation. Tell students they can use Figures 9–3 and 9–4 for reference.

Take It to the NET

Sample data table:

Fermented Food	Source
Bread	Sugar
Yogurt	Milk
Cheese	Milk
Kimchi	Cabbage and other vegetables
Pickles	Cucumbers

Use iText to review the key concepts in Section 9–1.

Section 9–2

1 FOCUS

Objectives

9.2.1 ***Describe*** what happens during the Krebs cycle.
9.2.2 ***Explain*** how high-energy electrons are used by the electron transport chain.
9.2.3 ***Identify*** three pathways the body uses to release energy during exercise.
9.2.4 ***Compare*** photosynthesis and respiration.

Guide for Reading

Vocabulary Preview

Explain that a prefix is a letter or group of letters placed at the beginning of a word to change its meaning. Remind students that *anaerobic* means "not in air." Explain that the prefix *an* means "not." Then, have a volunteer explain what the vocabulary word *aerobic* means. (*"in air"*)

Reading Strategy

Before students read the section, have them examine Figures 9–6 and 9–7 and make a list of questions about what they see. Then, as they study the text, they can write answers to their questions.

2 INSTRUCT

The Krebs Cycle

Address Misconceptions

Many students will know the term *respiration* as a synonym for breathing, or the inhalation and exhalation of air. Point out that the process described in this chapter is called *cellular respiration* to avoid confusion and to stress the idea that this process occurs on the cellular level. Explain that they will soon understand that breathing and cellular respiration are connected, because cellular respiration requires oxygen, which enters the body when you breathe.

9–2 The Krebs Cycle and Electron Transport

Guide for Reading

Key Concepts
- What happens during the Krebs cycle?
- How are high-energy electrons used by the electron transport chain?

Vocabulary
aerobic
Krebs cycle
electron transport chain

Reading Strategy: Using Visuals Before you read, review **Figure 9–2** on page 222. Then preview **Figures 9–6** and **9–7.** As you read, notice where the Krebs cycle and electron transport take place.

At the end of glycolysis, about 90 percent of the chemical energy that was available in glucose is still unused, locked in the high-energy electrons of pyruvic acid. To extract the rest of that energy, the cell turns to one of the world's most powerful electron acceptors—oxygen. Oxygen is required for the final steps of cellular respiration. Because the pathways of cellular respiration require oxygen, they are said to be **aerobic.**

As you know, the word *respiration* is often used as a synonym for breathing. This is why we have used the term "cellular respiration" to refer to energy-releasing pathways within the cell. The double meaning of respiration points out a crucial connection between cells and organisms: The energy-releasing pathways within cells require oxygen, and that is the reason we need to breathe, to respire.

The Krebs Cycle

In the presence of oxygen, pyruvic acid produced in glycolysis passes to the second stage of cellular respiration, the **Krebs cycle.** The Krebs cycle is named after Hans Krebs, the British biochemist who demonstrated its existence in 1937. **During the Krebs cycle, pyruvic acid is broken down into carbon dioxide in a series of energy-extracting reactions.** Because citric acid is the first compound formed in this series of reactions, the Krebs cycle is also known as the citric acid cycle.

▲ **Figure 9–5** Hans Krebs won the Nobel Prize in 1953 for his discovery of the citric acid cycle, or Krebs cycle.

A The Krebs cycle begins when pyruvic acid produced by glycolysis enters the mitochondrion. One carbon atom from pyruvic acid becomes part of a molecule of carbon dioxide, which is eventually released into the air. Two of the 3 carbon atoms are joined to a compound called coenzyme A to form acetyl-CoA. (The acetyl part of acetyl-CoA is made up of 2 carbon atoms, 1 oxygen atom, and 3 hydrogen atoms.) Acetyl-CoA then adds the 2-carbon acetyl group to a 4-carbon molecule, producing a 6-carbon molecule called citric acid.

B As the cycle continues, citric acid is broken down into a 4-carbon molecule, more carbon dioxide is released, and electrons are transferred to energy carriers. Follow the reactions in **Figure 9–6,** and you will see how this happens. First, look at the 6 carbon atoms in citric acid. One is removed, and then another, releasing 2 molecules of carbon dioxide and leaving a 4-carbon molecule. This 4-carbon molecule is then ready to accept another 2-carbon acetyl group, which starts the cycle all over again.

Next, look for ATP. For each turn of the cycle, a molecule equivalent to ATP is produced. Finally, look at the electron carriers. For each turn of the cycle, 5 pairs of high-energy

SECTION RESOURCES

Print:
- ***Teaching Resources,*** Section Review 9–2
- ***Guided Reading and Study Workbook,*** Section 9–2
- ***Laboratory Manual A,*** Chapter 9 Lab
- ***Laboratory Manual B,*** Chapter 9 Lab

Technology:
- ***iText,*** Section 9–2

Figure 9–6 The Krebs Cycle

During the Krebs cycle, pyruvic acid from glycolysis is used to make carbon dioxide, NADH, ATP, and $FADH_2$.

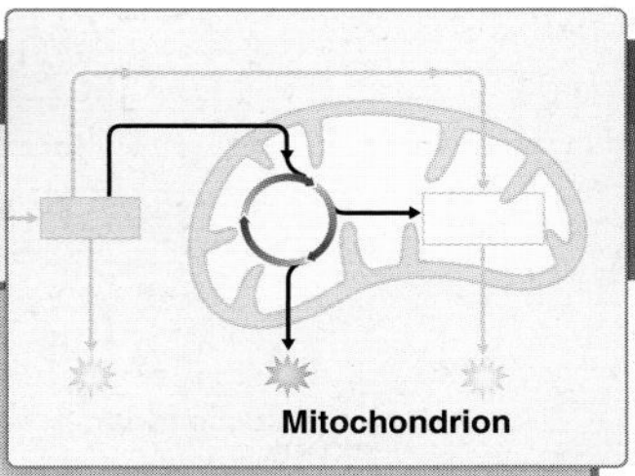

Mitochondrion

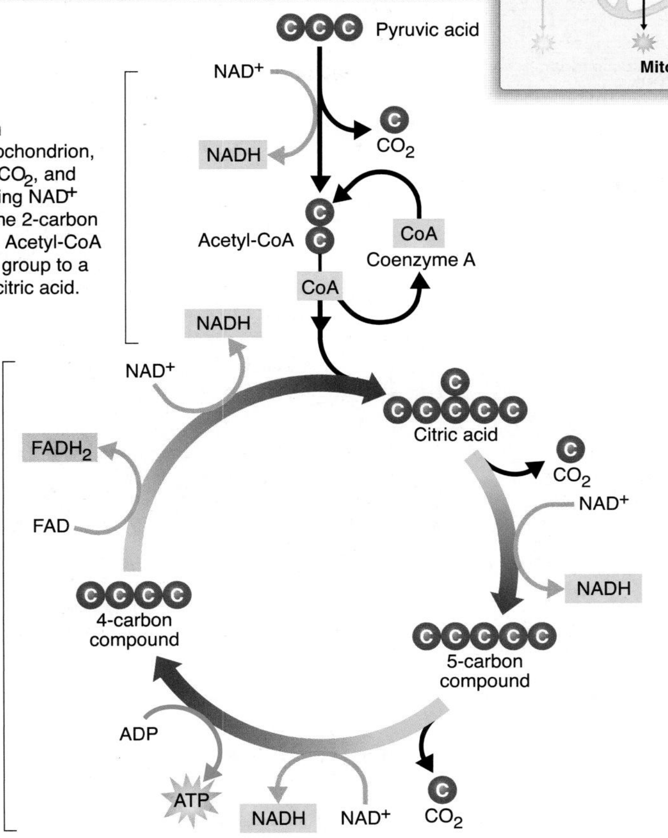

A Citric Acid Production
As pyruvic acid enters the mitochondrion, a carbon is removed, forming CO_2, and electrons are removed, changing NAD^+ to NADH. Coenzyme A joins the 2-carbon molecule, forming acetyl-CoA. Acetyl-CoA then adds the 2-carbon acetyl group to a 4-carbon compound, forming citric acid.

B Energy Extraction
Citric acid is broken down into a 5-carbon compound, then into a 4-carbon compound. Along the way, two more molecules of CO_2 are released, and electrons join NAD^+ and FAD, forming NADH and $FADH_2$. In addition, one molecule of ATP is generated. The energy tally from one molecule of pyruvic acid is 4 NADH, 1 $FADH_2$, and 1 molecule of ATP.

Pyruvic acid
NAD^+
NADH
CO_2
Acetyl-CoA
CoA
Coenzyme A
CoA
NADH
NAD^+
Citric acid
CO_2
NAD^+
NADH
$FADH_2$
FAD
4-carbon compound
5-carbon compound
ADP
ATP
NADH
NAD^+
CO_2

electrons are captured by 5 carrier molecules: 4 NADH molecules and 1 $FADH_2$. FAD (flavine adenine dinucleotide) and $FADH_2$ are molecules similar to NAD^+ and NADH, respectively.

What happens to each of these Krebs cycle products? First, the carbon dioxide released is the source of all the carbon dioxide in your breath. Every time you exhale, you expel the carbon dioxide produced by the Krebs cycle. Next, the ATP produced directly in the Krebs cycle can be used for cellular activities. However, what does the cell do with all those high-energy electrons in carriers like NADH? In the presence of oxygen, those high-energy electrons can be used to generate huge amounts of ATP.

CHECKPOINT *Why is the Krebs cycle also known as the citric acid cycle?*

Use Visuals

Figure 9–6 Have students study the cycle of reactions, and then, ask: **Where does this cycle take place in the cell?** *(The Krebs cycle takes place in the mitochondrial matrix.)* Point out that the pyruvic acid produced in glycolysis moves from the cytoplasm through two membranes, the outer and inner membranes of a mitochondrion. Ask a volunteer to indicate the three places in the cycle where carbon dioxide is produced. Ask: **How many ATP molecules are generated for every one turn of the Krebs cycle?** *(One—Actually, GTP is made during the Krebs cycle. However, because GTP is rapidly converted into ATP by the cell, this book portrays the molecule as ATP.)* **Where is most of the chemical energy in pyruvic acid transferred as a result of the cycle?** *(Most of the energy is transferred to the electron carriers, NAD^+ and FAD^+, producing 4 NADHs and 1 $FADH_2$.)*

Make Connections

Environmental Science Emphasize that the carbon dioxide produced in the Krebs cycle moves out of organisms as waste through exhalation and other processes. This gas becomes part of the atmosphere and becomes available for intake by plants for use in photosynthesis. Encourage students who need challenges to prepare a presentation to the class about the carbon cycle, which is the cycle of carbon through Earth's environment.

PRESENTATIONS MADE EASY!

The Presentation Assistant Plus contains the Prentice Hall Presentation Pro and the Transparencies, which provide easy-to-follow visual support for every step of this section. If you have a computer presentation station, use Prentice Hall Presentation Pro for Section 9–2, or use the transparencies listed here.

Section 9–2:

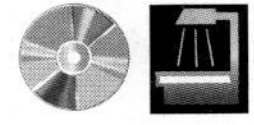

Interest Grabber
Section Outline
Flowchart
Figure 9–6
Figure 9–7

Answer to . . .

CHECKPOINT *The Krebs cycle is also known as the citric acid cycle because citric acid is the first compound formed in this series of reactions.*

Electron Transport

Meet Diverse Needs

To help students with limited English proficiency, review the names and abbreviations of the electron carriers by writing them on the board and pronouncing their names: nicotinamide adenine dinucleotide (NAD^+) and flavine adenine dinucleotide (FAD). Call on volunteers to explain that the ions accept high-energy electrons to form NADH and $FADH_2$. Make sure students recognize by the abbreviations when the carriers are carrying high-energy electrons and when they are not.

Use Visuals

Figure 9–7 After students have studied the figure, ask: **Where does the third stage of respiration take place?** *(Within the inner mitochondrial membrane)* **Where is the intermembrane space?** *(The space between the outer membrane and the inner membrane)* Emphasize that the NADH and $FADH_2$ molecules are a product of the Krebs cycle. Then, ask: **What happens that causes NADH to change to NAD^+ and $FADH_2$ to change to FAD?** *(The electron carriers give up their high-energy electrons to the carrier proteins on the electron transport chain.)* **What happens to those electrons?** *(They are passed from one carrier protein to the next.)* **Where does the energy come from that moves hydrogen ions into the intermembrane space?** *(The energy comes from the electrons moving down the electron transport chain.)* **How is the difference in charge on either side of the membrane used to produce ATP molecules?** *(The charge differences cause H^+ ions to pass through ATP synthase in the membrane, and the energy released during the passing converts ADP molecules into ATP molecules.)*

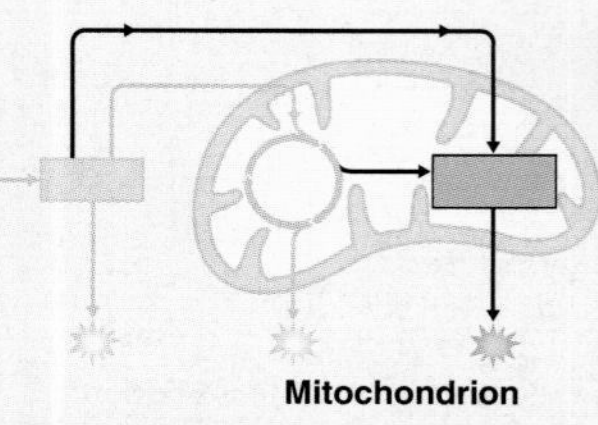

FIGURE 9–7 ELECTRON TRANSPORT CHAIN

The electron transport chain uses high-energy electrons from the Krebs cycle to convert ADP into ATP.

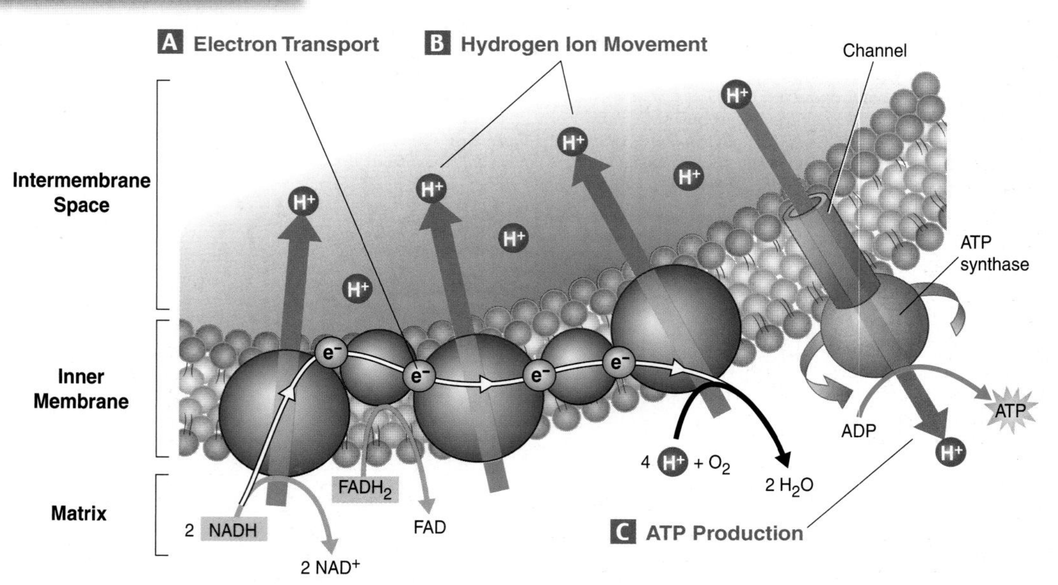

Electron Transport

As we have just seen, the Krebs cycle spins round and round, generating high-energy electrons that are passed to NADH and $FADH_2$. What's next? The electrons are passed from those carriers to the **electron transport chain.** **The electron transport chain uses the high-energy electrons from the Krebs cycle to convert ADP into ATP.** The beauty of the electron transport chain is the way in which it couples the movement of high-energy electrons with the production of ATP. Look at **Figure 9–7** to see how this happens.

A High-energy electrons from NADH and $FADH_2$ are passed into and along the electron transport chain. In eukaryotes, the electron transport chain is composed of a series of carrier proteins that is located in the inner membrane of the mitochondrion. In prokaryotes, the same chain is in the cell membrane. High energy electrons are passed from one carrier protein to the next. At the end of the electron transport chain is an enzyme that combines electrons from the electron chain with hydrogen

HISTORY OF SCIENCE

Hans Krebs discovers a cycle

Hans Krebs (1900–1981) grew up in Germany the son of a Jewish physician. In 1933, he was forced to leave Germany because of the Nazi persecution of the Jewish people. Krebs spent the rest of his life in Great Britain, where he taught and did research at universities. In 1937, he worked out the details of a cycle of chemical reactions in the breakdown of sugar in living organisms, a cycle in which citric acid is formed. He did most of his research about this cycle on pigeon tissues. His work was initially met with disbelief—the prestigious journal *Nature* rejected his paper on the findings. His discovery of what came to be called the Krebs cycle is of great importance in understanding cell metabolism. For his work, Krebs shared the 1953 Nobel Prize in medicine and physiology.

ions and oxygen to form water. If you're still wondering why we need oxygen, here's why: oxygen serves as the final electron acceptor of the electron transport chain. Thus oxygen is essential for getting rid of low-energy electrons and hydrogen ions, the wastes of cellular respiration.

B Every time 2 high-energy electrons transport down the electron transport chain, their energy is used to transport hydrogen ions (H^+) across the membrane. During electron transport, H^+ ions build up in the intermembrane space, making it positively charged. The other side of the membrane, from which those H^+ ions have been taken, is now negatively charged.

C How does the cell use the charge differences that build up as a result of electron transport? The inner membranes of the mitochondria contain protein spheres called ATP synthases. As H^+ ions escape through channels into these proteins, the ATP synthases spin. Each time it rotates, the enzyme grabs a low-energy ADP and attaches a phosphate, forming high-energy ATP. On average, each pair of high-energy electrons that moves down the electron transport chain provides enough energy to convert 3 ADP molecules into 3 ATP molecules.

CHECKPOINT *What is the role of ATP synthase?*

The Totals

How much chemical energy does cellular respiration yield from a single molecule of glucose? Recall that glycolysis produces just 2 ATP molecules per glucose. In the absence of oxygen, that is all the energy that a cell can extract from each molecule of glucose.

In the presence of oxygen, everything changes. As **Figure 9–8** shows, the Krebs cycle and electron transport enable the cell to produce 34 more ATP molecules per glucose molecule, in addition to the 2 ATP molecules obtained from glycolysis. This means that 18 times as much ATP can be generated from glucose in the presence of oxygen. The final wastes of cellular respiration are water and carbon dioxide.

How efficient is the process of cellular respiration? The 36 ATP molecules the cell makes per glucose represent about 38 percent of the total energy of glucose. That might not seem like much, but it means that the cell is actually more efficient at using food than the engine of a typical automobile is at burning gasoline. What happens to the remaining 62 percent? It is released as heat, which is one of the reasons your body feels warmer after vigorous exercise, and you do not freeze in winter.

▼ **Figure 9–8** The complete breakdown of glucose through cellular respiration, including glycolysis, results in the production of 36 molecules of ATP. **Interpreting Graphics** *How many molecules of ATP are produced during glycolysis?*

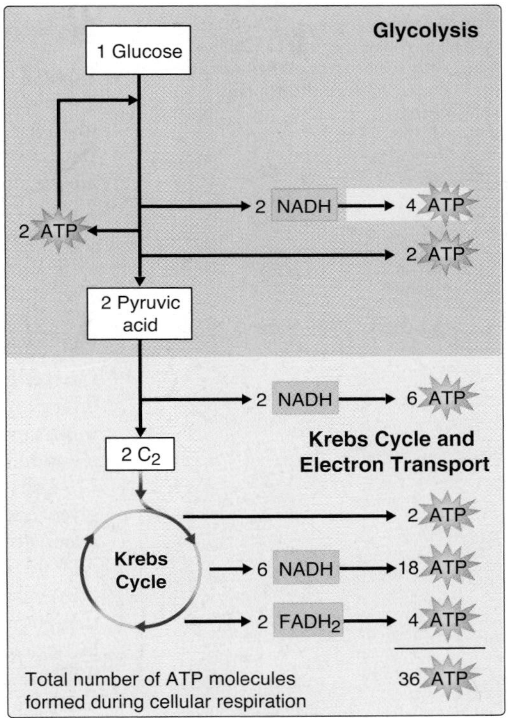

FACTS AND FIGURES

Releasing energy in a series of steps
The final product of the electron transport chain is water, or H_2O. If hydrogen and oxygen gas were allowed to combine directly, there would be a great release of wasted energy. Instead, the cell uses a chain of carrier molecules, mostly proteins, embedded in the inner mitochondrial membrane to release the energy of electrons in a series of steps. At each step, the electrons lose a little bit of their energy. The flow of electrons along the chain begins, for example, when a NADH molecule passes two electrons and two protons to the first carrier protein. The two protons pass into the intermembrane space, making it positively charged. As the process continues, the electrons lose their energy and protons are pumped from the matrix out through the membrane. ATP is made when the H^+ ions are "pushed" back through the membrane, a process called chemiosmosis.

Make Connections

Chemistry Remind students that a positive ion has fewer electrons than protons. Since a hydrogen atom contains only one electron and one proton, a positive hydrogen ion is simply one proton. Positive ions are attracted to negative ions, or ions with more electrons than protons. That attraction is the basis of ionic bonds. Explain to students that one of the reasons the hydrogen ions move through the membrane is that there is a relatively greater number of negatively charged hydroxide ions in the mitochondrial matrix.

The Totals

Use Visuals

Figure 9–8 Students may ask why 4 ATPs in glycolysis are shown in a pale green box. The reason is that the 2 NADH molecules are transported to the electron transport chain, where they are used to make ATP. So, those 4 ATPs are counted under the total for the Krebs cycle and electron transport, not glycolysis. Students may also ask why each NADH from glycolysis produces only 2 ATPs, while each NADH from the Krebs cycle and electron transport produce 3 ATPs. The reason is that energy must be used to import the NADHs from glycolysis from the cytoplasm into the mitochondrion.

Build Science Skills

Calculating Explain to students that 1 mole of glucose (about 180 g) contains about 686 kilocalories of energy. A mole is the SI unit of the amount of a substance. Remind students that 1 kilocalorie = 1000 calories. Then, ask: **How much energy does respiration yield from 1 mole of glucose?** *(686 kilocalories × 0.38 = 261 kilocalories)* **How much energy is lost to heat?** *(686 kilocalories × 0.62 = 425 kilocalories; or 686 kilocalories – 261 kilocalories = 425 kilocalories)*

Answers to . . .

CHECKPOINT *ATP synthase uses energy from H^+ ions to convert ADP into ATP.*

Figure 9–8 *Glycolysis produces 2 ATP molecules per glucose molecule.*

Energy and Exercise

Make Connections

Health Science Encourage student volunteers to research the differences between aerobic exercise and anaerobic exercise and the benefits of each. Have the students prepare a presentation to the class.

Build Science Skills

Predicting After students have read the section Energy and Exercise, give them a list of sports and activities, including weight lifting, playing soccer, dancing, taking a long walk, cutting the grass, running a sprint, and running a marathon. For each activity, ask students to predict how much the muscles doing that activity would use lactic acid fermentation or cellular respiration as a source of energy.

Use Community Resources

Invite an aerobics exercise instructor to address the class and explain his or her understanding of the benefits of aerobic and anaerobic exercise. A day before the presentation, encourage students to brainstorm a list of questions to ask the instructor.

▲ **Figure 9–9** During a race, runners rely on the energy supplied by ATP to make it to the finish line. **Applying Concepts** *When runners begin a race, how do their bodies obtain energy?*

Energy and Exercise

Bang! The starter's pistol goes off, and the runners push off their starting blocks and sprint down the track. The initial burst of energy soon fades, and the runners settle down to a steady pace. After the runners hit the finish line, they walk around slowly and breathe deeply to catch their breaths.

Let's look at what happens at each stage of the race in terms of the pathways the body uses to release energy. To obtain energy, the body uses ATP already in muscles and new ATP made by lactic acid fermentation and cellular respiration. At the beginning of a race, the body uses all three ATP sources, but stored ATP and lactic acid fermentation can only supply energy for a limited time.

Quick Energy What happens when your body needs lots of energy in a hurry? In response to sudden danger, quick actions might make the difference between life and death. To an athlete, a sudden burst of speed might win a race.

Cells normally contain small amounts of ATP produced during glycolysis and cellular respiration. When the starting gun goes off in a footrace, the muscles of the runners contain only enough of this ATP for a few seconds of intense activity. Before most of the runners have passed the 50-meter mark, that store of ATP is nearly gone. At this point, their muscle cells are producing most of their ATP by lactic acid fermentation. These sources can usually supply enough ATP to last about 90 seconds. In a 200- or 300-meter sprint, such as in **Figure 9–9**, this may be just enough to reach the finish line.

FACTS AND FIGURES

Aerobic and anaerobic training
During strenuous exercise, usually both aerobic and anaerobic pathways are at work in supplying muscles with ATP, though the percentage of each varies by the sport. For example, the quick and all-out action of lifting a heavy weight is 100 percent anaerobic. Running a marathon, by contrast, is about 99 percent aerobic. Playing soccer or basketball is about 20 percent anaerobic and 80 percent aerobic. Athletes can improve ATP production through training. Anaerobic training, including sprints and similar bursts of energy, can increase the level of glycogen in the muscles and increase tolerance of lactic acid. Aerobic training, including long runs, can increase the size and number of mitochondria in muscles and increase the delivery of oxygen to muscles by improving the heart and lungs. Thus, both types of training are beneficial.

Fermentation produces lactic acid as a byproduct. When the race is over, the only way to get rid of lactic acid is in a chemical pathway that requires extra oxygen. For that reason, you can think of a quick sprint building up an oxygen debt that a runner has to repay after the race with plenty of heavy breathing.

Long-Term Energy What happens if a race is longer? How does your body generate the ATP it needs to run 2 kilometers or more, or to play in a soccer game that lasts more than an hour? For exercise longer than about 90 seconds, cellular respiration is the only way to generate a continuing supply of ATP. Cellular respiration releases energy more slowly than fermentation, which is why even well-conditioned athletes have to pace themselves during a long race or over the course of a game. Your body stores energy in muscle and other tissues in the form of the carbohydrate glycogen. These stores of glycogen are usually enough to last for 15 or 20 minutes of activity. After that, your body begins to break down other stored molecules, including fats, for energy. This is one reason why aerobic forms of exercise such as running, dancing, and swimming are so beneficial for weight control.

CHECKPOINT *Why do runners breathe heavily after a race?*

Quick Lab

How does exercise affect cellular respiration?

Materials 2 small test tubes, glass marking pencil, 10-mL graduated cylinder, bromthymol blue solution, 2 straws, clock or watch with second hand

Procedure 

1. **Predicting** Record your prediction of how exercise will affect your body's production of carbon dioxide.
2. Label two test tubes A and B. Put 10 mL of water and a few drops of bromthymol blue solution in each test tube. Carbon dioxide causes bromthymol blue to turn yellow or green.
3. Your partner will time you during this step. When your partner says "go," slowly blow air through a straw into the bottom of test tube A. **CAUTION:** *Do not inhale through the straw.*
4. When the solution changes color, your partner should say "stop," and then record how long the color change took.
5. Jog in place for 1 minute. **CAUTION:** *Do not do this if you have a medical condition that interferes with exercise. If you feel faint or dizzy, stop immediately and sit down.*
6. Repeat steps 3 and 4 using test tube B.
7. Trade roles with your partner. Repeat steps 2 to 6.

Analyze and Conclude

1. **Analyzing Data** How did exercise affect the time for the solution to change color?
2. **Inferring** What process in your body produces carbon dioxide? How does exercise affect this process?
3. **Drawing Conclusions** Was your hypothesis correct? Explain your answer.

Quick Lab

Objective Students should conclude that exercise increases the body's production of carbon dioxide.

Skill Focus Analyzing Data, Inferring, Drawing Conclusions

Time 15 minutes

Safety Warn students not to inhale or swallow the bromthymol blue solution.

Strategy

- Demonstrate how to slowly blow air through a straw into a test tube that contains water and bromthymol blue solution.
- If students have difficulty understanding the significance of their results, have them think about which process in their own cells produces carbon dioxide and how that process is important to their survival. Then, have them think about how the rate of that process changes during exercise.

Expected Outcome Students should observe that the bromthymol blue solution changes color more rapidly after exercise than before exercise.

Analyze and Conclude

1. The time decreased after exercise.
2. Cellular respiration produces carbon dioxide. Exercise increases the rate of cellular respiration.
3. Those students were correct who predicted that exercise would increase the body's production of carbon dioxide.

FACTS AND FIGURES

Using alternative fuels in cellular respiration Glucose is a common fuel for cells. Starch is broken down into glucose by the digestive system. Humans and many other animals store glycogen in their liver and muscle cells, and glycogen also can be changed into glucose. But, glucose is not the only fuel. For example, proteins and fats can also be used. Proteins are broken down into their constituent amino acids, and then modified amino acids are fed into the Krebs cycle with the help of enzymes. Fats, whether taken in with food or stored in the body, provide excellent fuel for respiration. The fatty acids of fats are broken down and carried into the mitochondrial matrix by special transport proteins, and then they enter the Krebs cycle in fragments as acetyl-CoA. Fats yield much more energy than glucose. A gram of fat produces more than double the ATP that a gram of carbohydrate does.

Answers to . . .

Figure 9–9 *Their bodies obtain energy from ATP already in muscles and new ATP made by lactic acid fermentation and cellular respiration.*

CHECKPOINT *They need extra oxygen to get rid of lactic acid that has built up in their muscles.*

Comparing Photosynthesis and Cellular Respiration

Build Science Skills

Using analogies Draw a hill on the board, and write *glucose* at the top of the hill. Then, tell students that photosynthesis might be considered as an "uphill" process, while cellular respiration could be considered a "downhill" process.

3 ASSESS

Evaluate Understanding

Call on students at random to describe the steps in the process of cellular respiration, one at a time.

Reteach

Have students re-examine Figures 9–6 and 9–7. Ask each student to write a description of those figures using as many details from the section as possible.

ALTERNATIVE ASSESSMENT

Students should use Figure 9–6 to find the main events in the Krebs cycle, including citric acid production and energy extraction. They should use Figure 9–7 to find the main events in the electron transport chain, including electron transport, hydrogen ion movement, and ATP production. On their posters, students should show that the Krebs cycle occurs inside the mitochondrion and the electron transport chain occurs within the inner mitochondrial membrane.

Use iText to review the key concepts in Section 9–2.

Answer to . . .

Figure 9–10 *The energy is "saved" and can be "withdrawn" when the body needs it.*

Comparing Photosynthesis and Cellular Respiration

	Photosynthesis	Cellular Respiration
Function	Energy storage	Energy release
Location	Chloroplasts	Mitochondria
Reactants	CO_2 and H_2O	$C_6H_{12}O_6$ and O_2
Products	$C_6H_{12}O_6$ and O_2	CO_2 and H_2O
Equation	$6CO_2 + 6H_2O \rightarrow C_6H_{12}O_6 + 6O_2$	$6O_2 + C_6H_{12}O_6 \rightarrow 6CO_2 + 6H_2O$

▶ **Figure 9–10** Photosynthesis and cellular respiration can be thought of as opposite processes as shown in the chart. **Using Analogies** ***How is the chemical energy in glucose similar to money in a savings account?***

Comparing Photosynthesis and Cellular Respiration

Photosynthesis and cellular respiration are almost opposite processes. Earlier in this chapter, the chemical energy in carbohydrates was compared to money in a savings account. Photosynthesis is the process that "deposits" energy. Cellular respiration is the process that "withdraws" energy. The equations for photosynthesis and cellular respiration are the reverse of each other.

Photosynthesis removes carbon dioxide from the atmosphere, and cellular respiration puts it back. Photosynthesis releases oxygen into the atmosphere, and cellular respiration uses that oxygen to release energy from food. As **Figure 9–10** shows, the products of photosynthesis are similar to the reactants of cellular respiration. The products of cellular respiration are the reactants of photosynthesis. Cellular respiration takes place in all eukaryotes and some prokaryotes. Photosynthesis, however, occurs only in plants, algae, and some bacteria.

9–2 Section Assessment

1. **Key Concept** What happens to pyruvic acid during the Krebs cycle?
2. **Key Concept** How does the electron transport chain use the high-energy electrons from the Krebs cycle?
3. Why is cellular respiration considered to be much more efficient than glycolysis alone?
4. How many molecules of ATP are produced in the entire breakdown of glucose?
5. **Critical Thinking Comparing and Contrasting** Compare photosynthesis and cellular respiration. How are they similar? How are they different?

iTEXT Assessment Use iText to review the important concepts in Section 9–2.

ALTERNATIVE ASSESSMENT

Organizing Information Using **Figure 9–6** and **Figure 9–7** as guides, prepare a poster showing the main events of the process of cellular respiration. For each event, show the reactant and products and where in the mitochondrion the event occurs. Use your poster to explain cellular respiration to a classmate.

9–2 Section Assessment

1. Pyruvic acid is broken down into carbon dioxide in a series of energy-extracting reactions.
2. The electron transport chain uses the high-energy electrons from the Krebs cycle to convert ADP into ATP.
3. Cellular respiration enables the cell to produce 34 more ATP molecules per glucose molecule in addition to the 2 ATP molecules obtained from glycolysis.
4. 36
5. Similar: They both involve a series of chemical reactions that take place in cells. Different: They are almost opposite processes.

Should Creatine Supplements Be Banned?

Many athletes now use a dietary supplement called creatine to enhance their performance. Creatine may improve athletic performance but critics point to potentially serious side effects as a reason to control its use.

Although muscle cells contain only enough ATP for a few seconds of intense activity, most have a reserve nearly twice as large in the form of a molecule called creatine phosphate. When the muscle goes to work and starts to use up its available ATP, phosphates are transferred from creatine phosphate directly to ADP, regenerating ATP in a matter of milliseconds. The more creatine phosphate a muscle contains, the longer it can sustain intense activity. Hoping to increase their capacity for strong, short-term muscle contractions, many athletes have added creatine to their diets. Should athletes be allowed to use creatine supplements?

The Viewpoints

Creatine Supplements Should Be Allowed

Creatine is a natural substance found in human cells and in foods such as meat. Taken in recommended doses, creatine helps build muscle strength and performance, which can mean the difference between winning and losing. When athletes have followed instructions on container labels, no serious side effects have been reported. The risks are small and the rewards of winning are large enough to justify its use.

Creatine Supplements Should Be Banned

Like any natural substance, creatine can be abused. Creatine is known to cause water loss, putting the athletes who use it at risk for dehydration, muscle injury, diarrhea, kidney failure, and perhaps even death. Because creatine is considered a dietary supplement and not a drug, the Food and Drug Administration (FDA) has never determined its safety. Until a truly safe dose has been determined by careful scientific studies, athletes should not be allowed to use creatine.

You Decide

1. **Defining the Issue** In your own words, describe at least two major issues involved in the controversy surrounding the use of creatine to enhance athletic performance.
2. **Analyzing the Viewpoints** List the key arguments expressed by the proponents and critics of using creatine as a dietary supplement. What is known? What is not known? What are the benefits? What are the risks?
3. **Forming Your Opinion** Should athletes be allowed to take creatine to enhance performance? Weigh the pro and con arguments. Research to find out if some professional sports have banned the use of creatine by athletes. What were the reasons for this decision? Do some arguments outweigh others? Which arguments? Explain your answer.
4. **Writing an Editorial** Write an editorial for a sports magazine that takes a stand on creatine. Your editorial should persuade your readers that your opinion is justified.

Activity After students have read the feature, divide the class into small groups and allow time for discussion. Then, have each group prepare questions for an interview with one of the following: the coach of one of the high school teams, a physician associated with high school teams, a high school athlete, a salesperson at a health food store that sells creatine supplements, and a professor in the health or physical education department of a local college or university.

Work with each group to decide whom students want to talk to and how to go about setting up the interview. Encourage students to write several questions they want to ask and anticipate asking follow-up questions.

After completing the interview, group members should collaborate in preparing a report to the class. Encourage students to research additional information to include in their report. Once all groups have given their reports, lead a class discussion of what students learned from the various sources.

You Decide

1. Two issues include: (1) health risks involved in taking creatine supplements, and (2) how allowing the use of the supplements will pressure all athletes into using it in order to compete.
2. Students should list the key arguments discussed in the feature, including increasing strength and performance and possibly causing damage to health.
3. Some students may argue for taking the supplements, some may argue against, while others may be ambivalent. No matter which position a student takes, he or she should back up the opinion with facts and logic.
4. Students' editorials should concisely state their opinions, with good arguments for their positions.

BIO INSIGHTS **BACKGROUND**

The creatine connection

Muscle cells have two backup systems when oxygen is in short supply. One is lactic acid fermentation, but before that begins a muscle uses up its supply of a compound called creatine phosphate. That molecule can transfer its phosphate to ADP in the reaction: creatine phosphate + ADP → ATP + creatine. A good diet usually supplies an adequate amount of creatine. Meat and fish contain large quantities. In muscle cells, creatine is changed into creatine phosphate. Creatine supplements add to the amount already supplied in a good diet. Some research has shown that taking a recommended dose of creatine supplement can increase the level of creatine phosphate in muscles 10–20 percent, which can increase energy levels in muscles 2.5–10 percent. Research is incomplete about the health risks of taking the supplement.

Real-World Lab

Objective Students will be able to draw a conclusion about how fermentation affects pH.

Skills Focus **Drawing Conclusions**

Time 40 minutes the first day; 10 minutes a day on one day in each of the following 4 weeks

Advance Prep Most of the materials are available at a local supermarket. Chinese cabbage is also sold at Asian food stores. Chop the cabbage in advance.

Alternative Materials Regular cabbage can be used if Chinese cabbage is unavailable.

Safety Acetic acid and other compounds produced during fermentation may irritate students' eyes. Using larger lab groups and fewer bags of fermenting cabbage will reduce the quantities of these compounds.

Pre-Lab Discussion Have students read the entire procedure, and answer any questions they have about the lab. Then, ask: **What is the purpose of this lab?** (*To measure the chemical changes of fermentation*) **What types of fermentation occur in making kimchi, and what are the products of those processes?** (*Both lactic acid and alcoholic fermentation occur. The products are lactic acid, carbon dioxide, and alcohol.*)

Teaching Tips

- Discuss with students how to construct the graph of their results.
- Demonstrate how to unseal the bags and expel any air.
- Show students how to use pH indicator paper to measure the pH of the liquid.

Procedure

1. Some students may correctly hypothesize that production of lactic acid will reduce the pH of the kimchi.

Real-World Lab

Making Kimchi

In this investigation, you will make a popular Korean side dish known as kimchi. Kimchi is made by allowing microorganisms to ferment Chinese cabbage. The main microorganism involved is a bacterium called Lactobacillus. *This bacterium mainly carries out lactic acid fermentation. Some species of* Lactobacillus *and other microorganisms on the cabbage carry out alcoholic fermentation. All of these microorganisms occur naturally on the surface of the Chinese cabbage. As these microorganisms ferment the Chinese cabbage, turning it into kimchi, you will measure the chemical changes that occur during this process. You will use your knowledge of fermentation to explain the observations that you make.*

Problem **How does fermentation affect pH?**

Materials

- 2 resealable plastic sandwich bags
- chopped Chinese cabbage
- noniodized salt
- 2.5-mL (1/2 teaspoon) measuring spoon
- pH-indicator paper
- thermometer

Skills Predicting, Measuring, Drawing Conclusions

Procedure

1. **Formulating Hypotheses** Recall that pH is a measure of how acidic or basic a solution is. Bases have pH levels between 7 and 14, and acids have pH levels between 0 and 7. Formulate a hypothesis that explains how fermentation leads to changes in pH. Record your hypothesis and your prediction of how the pH of the kimchi will change as it ferments.
2. Put one resealable plastic bag inside the other. Half-fill the inner bag with chopped cabbage. Add 2.5 mL of salt. Seal both bags and turn them upside down several times to mix the ingredients.
3. Unseal the bags and press down on them to expel any air. Then, reseal the bags. Label the plastic bags containing the kimchi with your name and place them in a cool area where they will remain undisturbed. Copy the data table shown. Measure and record the air temperature in your copy of the data table.
4. Each day, observe the kimchi in the bags. Record your observations of any changes in the appearance of the kimchi or the bags in your data table. When a small amount of liquid appears in the bottom of the inner bag, open the bags. **CAUTION:** *Do not eat the kimchi.*

Data Table

Day	pH	Temperature	Observations
1			
8			
15			
22			
29			

5. Use pH-indicator paper to measure the pH of the liquid. Record the pH in your data table.
6. Press out any gas in the bags and reseal them. Return the bags to the cool area and leave them undisturbed for a week.
7. One week after you first measured the pH, repeat steps 5 and 6. Then, move the bags containing the kimchi to a refrigerator. Record the temperature of the refrigerator in your data table. Continue to observe the kimchi and record its pH every week for 4 weeks.

Analyze and Conclude

1. **Using Tables and Graphs** Use your data table to construct a graph showing the relationship between pH and time. Describe how the pH of the kimchi changed over time.
2. **Inferring** What substance do you think was responsible for the change in pH? What process could have produced this substance?
3. **Evaluating and Revising** Was your prediction correct? What changes would you make in your hypothesis as a result of your observations?
4. **Inferring** Did you see any evidence that a gas was produced or consumed in the bags? If so, what was this gas? What process was responsible for this change? Explain the reasons for your answers.

Go Further

Designing an Experiment Yogurt is made from milk using microorganisms that carry out lactic acid fermentation. Describe an experiment you could do to determine how a factor, such as temperature or sugar concentration, affects the fermentation of yogurt. Your description should state your hypothesis; identify all variables; and explain how the outcome of the experiment could support or contradict your hypothesis.

Take It to the NET Visit the Prentice Hall Web site at **www.phschool.com**. Enter your data on time, pH, and temperature. Look at the data entered by other students around the country. Basing your conclusion on the data, how do you think temperature affects the rate of fermentation by the microorganisms in the kimchi?

Expected Outcome The pH of the kimchi will gradually drop as *Lactobacillus* produces lactic acid and carbon dioxide.

Go Further

A typical experiment might involve investigating how temperature affects fermentation by measuring changes in pH over time in two or more batches, each kept at a different temperature.

Take It to the NET Have students visit **www.phschool.com** to pool and analyze data with students nationwide.

Analyze and Conclude

1. Students' graphs should have pH on the *y*-axis and time on the *x*-axis. The pH should decline from about 7 on Day 1 to about 4 on Day 29.
2. Lactic acid caused the change in pH. It was produced by the *Lactobacillus* during lactic acid fermentation. Production of carbon dioxide also helped to acidify the mixture.
3. Students predicted correctly if they predicted that the pH of the kimchi would decline. Students should revise their hypothesis if it was incorrect.
4. Students should have observed an accumulation of gas in the bags, evidence that gas was produced. They should infer that the gas was carbon dioxide, and they should also infer that the process responsible for gas production was alcoholic fermentation, because the sealed bags eliminated the possibility of oxygen being involved in the process.

Chapter 9 Study Guide

Study Tip

Have students make vocabulary flashcards by writing a vocabulary word on one side of a card and its definition on the other side.

Thinking Visually

1. glucose
2. glucose and oxygen
3. glycolysis, several others
4. glycolysis, Krebs cycle, electron transport
5. either carbon dioxide and alcohol or lactic acid
6. carbon dioxide, water
7. 2
8. 36

Chapter 9 Assessment

Reviewing Content

1. c **4.** c **7.** c **10.** b
2. b **5.** b **8.** b
3. b **6.** b **9.** a

Understanding Concepts

11. A calorie is the amount of energy needed to raise the temperature of 1 gram of water 1 Celsius degree. Cells break down high-calorie molecules in a series of steps, releasing the stored energy a small amount at a time.

12. During glycolysis, glucose is broken down into two molecules of pyruvic acid. The other products are ATP molecules and high-energy electrons that are picked up by NAD^+.

13. After glycolysis, if oxygen is available, a cell might carry out the rest of cellular respiration. If oxygen is not available, some cells carry out the rest of fermentation.

14. $6O_2 + C_6H_{12}O_6 \rightarrow 6CO_2 + 6H_2O$; oxygen + glucose → carbon dioxide + water

15. Student diagrams should be similar to Figure 9–2.

16. NAD^+ picks up high-energy electrons produced during glycolysis, forming NADH. The large number of high-energy electrons quickly fill all of the cell's available NAD^+ molecules. Without NAD^+, the cell cannot keep glycolysis going, and ATP production stops.

Chapter 9 Study Guide

9–1 Chemical Pathways

Key Concepts

- Cellular respiration is the process that releases energy by breaking down food molecules in the presence of oxygen.
- Glycolysis is the process in which one molecule of glucose is broken in half, producing two molecules of pyruvic acid, a 3-carbon compound.
- Glycolysis captures two pairs of high-energy electrons with the carrier NAD^+. Because glycolysis does not require oxygen, it supplies chemical energy to cells when oxygen is not available.
- The two main types of fermentation are alcoholic fermentation and lactic acid fermentation.
- In the absence of oxygen, yeast and a few other microorganisms use alcoholic fermentation, forming ethyl alcohol and carbon dioxide as wastes.
- Animals cannot perform alcoholic fermentation, but some cells, such as human muscle cells, can convert glucose into lactic acid. This is called lactic acid fermentation.

Vocabulary

calorie, p. 221
glycolysis, p. 221
cellular respiration, p. 222
NAD^+, p. 223
fermentation, p. 224
anaerobic, p. 224

9–2 The Krebs Cycle and Electron Transport

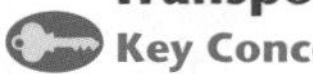

Key Concepts

- During the Krebs cycle, pyruvic acid is broken down into carbon dioxide in a series of energy-extracting reactions.
- The electron transport chain uses the high-energy electrons from the Krebs cycle to convert ADP into ATP.
- The products of photosynthesis are similar to the reactants of cellular respiration. The products of cellular respiration are the reactants of photosynthesis.

Vocabulary

aerobic, p. 226
Krebs cycle, p. 226
electron transport chain, p. 228

Thinking Visually

Using the information in this chapter, complete the following compare-and-contrast table about fermentation and cellular respiration:

Comparing Fermentation and Cellular Respiration

Characteristic	Fermentation	Cellular Respiration
Starting reactants	1	2
Pathways involved	3	4
End products	5	6
Number of ATP molecules produced	7	8

CHAPTER RESOURCES

Print:

- ***Teaching Resources,*** Chapter Vocabulary Review, Graphic Organizer
- ***Chapter Tests: Levels A and B,*** Chapter 9 Test
- ***PH Assessment System,*** Practice Test

Technology:

- ***Computer Test Bank,*** Chapter 9 Test
- ***iText,*** Chapter 9 Assessment

Chapter 9 Assessment

Reviewing Content

Choose the letter that best answers the question or completes the statement.

1. In cells, the energy available in food is used to make an energy-rich compound called
   a. water. c. ATP.
   b. glucose. d. ADP.
2. The first step in releasing the energy of glucose in the cell is known as
   a. alcoholic fermentation. c. Krebs cycle.
   b. glycolysis. d. electron transport.
3. The process that releases energy from food in the presence of oxygen is
   a. synthesis.
   b. cellular respiration.
   c. ATP synthase.
   d. photosynthesis.
4. Which organisms perform cellular respiration?

a.  b.  c.  d. 

   a. only c c. all of the above
   b. only a and c d. only a and b
5. The net gain of energy from glycolysis is
   a. 4 ATP molecules.
   b. 2 ATP molecules.
   c. 8 ADP molecules.
   d. 3 pyruvic acid molecules.
6. Because fermentation takes place in the absence of oxygen, it is said to be
   a. aerobic.
   b. anaerobic.
   c. cyclic.
   d. essential to oxygen production.
7. The Krebs cycle takes place within the
   a. chloroplast.
   b. nucleus.
   c. mitochondrion.
   d. cytoplasm.
8. The electron transport chain uses the high-energy electrons from the Krebs cycle to
   a. produce glucose.
   b. convert ADP to ATP.
   c. produce acetyl-CoA.
   d. produce GTP.
9. A total of 36 molecules of ATP are produced from 1 molecule of glucose as a result of
   a. cellular respiration.
   b. glycolysis.
   c. alcoholic fermentation.
   d. lactic acid fermentation.
10. During heavy exercise, the buildup of lactic acid in muscle cells results in
    a. alcoholic fermentation. c. the Calvin cycle.
    b. oxygen debt. d. the Krebs cycle.

Understanding Concepts

11. What is a calorie? How do cells use a high-calorie molecule such as glucose?
12. How is glucose changed during glycolysis? What products are produced as a result of glycolysis?
13. What are the two pathways that might follow glycolysis? What factor can determine which of those pathways a cell might follow?
14. Use formulas to write a chemical equation for cellular respiration. Label the formulas with the names of the compounds.
15. Draw and label a mitochondrion surrounded by cytoplasm. Indicate where glycolysis, the Krebs cycle, and the electron transport chain occur.
16. How is NAD^+ involved in the products of glycolysis? What happens to a cell's NAD^+ when large numbers of high-energy electrons are produced in a short time?
17. Which two compounds react during fermentation? Which of these compounds passes high-energy electrons to the other?
18. Write equations to show how lactic acid fermentation compares with alcoholic fermentation. Which reactant(s) do they have in common?
19. How are fermentation and cellular respiration similar? What is the main difference between their starting compounds?
20. Summarize what happens during the Krebs cycle. What happens to the high-energy electrons generated during the Krebs cycle?
21. How is ATP synthase involved in making energy available to the cell?
22. When runners race for about 20 minutes, how do their bodies obtain energy?

17. Pyruvic acid and NADH react together as NADH passes high-energy electrons to pyruvic acid.

18. Lactic acid fermentation:
glucose $\rightarrow$ lactic acid
Alcoholic fermentation:
glucose $\rightarrow$ alcohol + CO_2
Both have glucose as the reactant.

19. Fermentation and cellular respiration are both processes that break down glucose and release the energy stored in the molecule. Both start with the process of glycolysis, which produces pyruvic acid. Cellular respiration requires oxygen as a reactant. Fermentation occurs without oxygen.

20. During the Krebs cycle, pyruvic acid is broken down into carbon dioxide in a series of reactions that give off energy. The high-energy electrons that are produced are picked up by a series of electron carriers, and the energy is used to convert ADP into ATP.

21. ATP synthase is a large protein through which hydrogen ions (H^+) pass, converting ADP into high-energy ATP.

22. At the beginning of a race, runners' energy comes from ATP that is present in their muscles and that is produced by lactic acid fermentation. When runners race for about 20 minutes, their bodies use cellular respiration to use stored carbohydrates to make ATP.

HOMEWORK GUIDE

Section:	Questions:
Section 9–1:	1–6, 11–19, 25, 27, 29, 31, 32
Section 9–2:	7–10, 20–24, 26, 28, 30

Chapter 9 Assessment

Critical Thinking

23. 1 CO_2 and H_2O
2 cellular respiration

24. In a eukaryotic cell, cellular respiration begins in the cytoplasm where glycolysis takes place, and then the pyruvic acid produced during glycolysis passes into the mitochondria where cellular respiration is completed. In a prokaryotic cell, the electron transport chain occurs within the cell membrane.

25. Bacteria that live without oxygen probably obtain energy through fermentation, because that process releases energy without involving oxygen.

26. An increased number of mitochondria in muscle cells would enable an individual to obtain energy from cellular respiration at a faster rate, so the individual might perform energy-requiring activities more quickly than others or for a longer period.

27. Yeast cells would probably grow more rapidly when they perform cellular respiration, because 18 times more ATP can be generated in the presence of oxygen than in anaerobic conditions.

28. Sample answer: Start with two groups of healthy volunteers who do not exercise regularly. Test their initial responses during intense activity, using the same definition of muscle discomfort for all. Monitor one group as they exercise regularly for a specific period, and then test both groups again to see whether the groups differ.

29. Lactic acid is produced by muscles when the supply of oxygen is insufficient, so the presence of lactic acid indicates that the heart did not receive the oxygen it needed.

Chapter 9 Assessment

Critical Thinking

23. Interpreting Graphics Complete the following concept map showing the flow of energy in photosynthesis and cellular respiration.

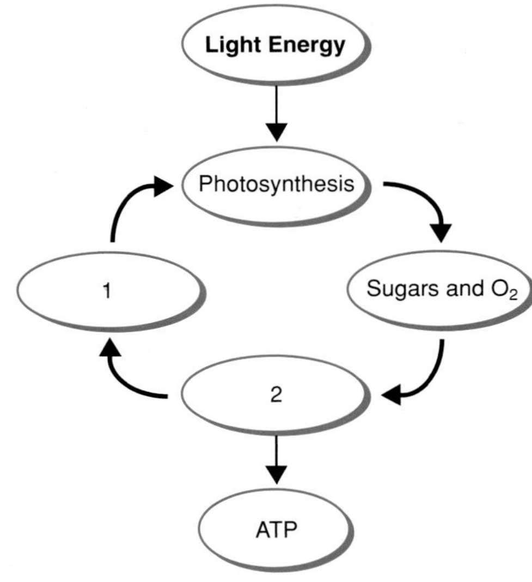

24. Comparing and Contrasting Where does cellular respiration take place in a eukaryotic cell? In a prokaryotic cell?

25. Inferring Certain types of bacteria thrive in conditions that lack oxygen. What does that fact indicate about the way they obtain energy?

26. Predicting In certain cases, regular exercise causes an increase in the number of mitochondria in muscle cells. How might that situation improve an individual's ability to perform energy-requiring activities?

27. Formulating Hypotheses Yeast cells can carry out both fermentation and cellular respiration, depending on whether oxygen is present. In which case would you expect yeast cells to grow more rapidly? Explain.

28. Designing an Experiment Would individuals who carry out regular aerobic exercise suffer less muscle discomfort during intense exercise than other individuals? Outline an experiment that could answer this question.

29. Inferring To function properly, heart muscle cells require a steady supply of oxygen. After a heart attack, small amounts of lactic acid are present. What does this evidence suggest about the nature of a heart attack?

30. Applying Concepts Carbon monoxide (CO) molecules bring the electron transport chain in a mitochondrion to a stop by binding to an electron carrier. Use this information to explain why carbon monoxide gas kills organisms.

31. Using Analogies Expand the analogy of deposits and withdrawals of money used in the chapter, or develop another analogy. Using that analogy, write a short paragraph to explain cellular respiration.

32. Making Connections In Chapter 3, you learned that certain substances are involved in chemical cycles. Draw a sketch showing how cellular respiration fits into one of those cycles.

Performance-Based Assessment

Creating Diagrams Make one or more diagrams with labels or captions to show how two athletes get energy when the first athlete runs for 30 seconds and the second athlete runs for 20 minutes. Be sure to show whether the energy is produced by an aerobic process or by an anaerobic process.

Why is knowledge of cellular respiration and fermentation important to sports physiologists? Visit the Prentice Hall Web site at **www.phschool.com** to learn more about sports and cellular processes. Then, answer the following questions:

- Which three metabolic systems are important in understanding the limits of physical activity?
- Under optimal conditions, how many minutes of muscle activity can anaerobic metabolism produce?
- Which metabolic system provides you with the most endurance? Which system is most important for giving extra power during intermediate races, such as a 200-meter run?
- Which system functions almost exclusively in weight lifting? Tennis? Cross-country skiing?

Performance-Based Assessment

Diagrams of the 30-second run should show that runners use the ATP that was already present in the muscles as well as that produced by lactic acid fermentation. Diagrams of the 20-minute run should show runners using carbohydrates to release energy through cellular respiration.

Standardized Test Prep

Test-Taking Tip To answer questions that have different combinations of roman numerals as answer choices, evaluate each roman numeral separately in relation to the question. Then, determine which answer choice corresponds to the numerals you have selected.

Directions: Choose the letter that best answers the question or completes the statement.

1. What raw materials are needed for cellular respiration?
   (A) glucose and carbon dioxide
   (B) glucose and oxygen
   (C) carbon dioxide and oxygen
   (D) oxygen and lactic acid
   (E) carbon dioxide and water
2. What happens during the Krebs cycle?
   (A) Hydrogen ions and oxygen form water.
   (B) The cell releases a small amount of energy through fermentation.
   (C) Each glucose molecule is broken down into two molecules of pyruvic acid.
   (D) Hydrogen ions build up on one side of the mitochondrial membrane.
   (E) Pyruvic acid is broken down into carbon dioxide in a series of reactions.
3. Which of the following is needed to begin the process of glycolysis?
   (A) ATP (D) pyruvic acid
   (B) NADP (E) carbon dioxide
   (C) NADH
4. In eukaryotic cells, most of cellular respiration takes place in the
   (A) nuclei. (D) cell walls.
   (B) cytoplasm. (E) centrioles.
   (C) mitochondria.
5. What substance produced by alcoholic fermentation makes bread dough rise?
   (A) oxygen (D) water
   (B) lactic acid (E) alcohol
   (C) carbon dioxide
6. Which process(es) include glycolysis?
   I. Alcoholic fermentation
   II. Lactic acid fermentation
   III. Cellular respiration
   (A) I only (D) II and III only
   (B) III only (E) I, II, and III
   (C) I and II only
7. The human body can use all of the following as energy sources EXCEPT
   (A) ATP in muscles. (D) alcoholic fermentation.
   (B) glycolysis. (E) cellular respiration.
   (C) lactic acid fermentation.
8. Which of the following best represents the waste products of cellular respiration?
   (A) CO_2 (D) CO_2 and H_2O
   (B) H_2O (E) CO_2 and O_2
   (C) O_2

Questions 9–10 The graph below shows the rate of alcoholic fermentation for yeast at different temperatures.

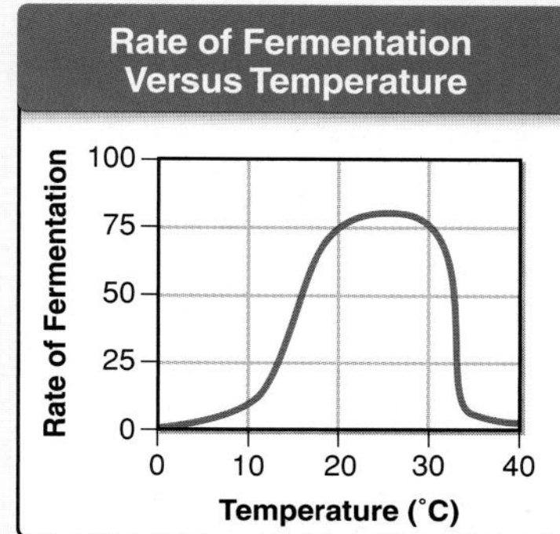

9. What is the relationship between the rate of fermentation and temperature?
   (A) The rate of fermentation continually increases as temperature increases.
   (B) The rate of fermentation continually decreases as temperature increases.
   (C) The rate of fermentation increases with temperature, then it rapidly decreases.
   (D) The rate of fermentation decreases with temperature, then it increases.
   (E) There is no relationship between the rate of fermentation and temperature.
10. Which statement(s) could explain the data shown in the graph?
    I. The molecules that regulate fermentation break down at temperatures above 30°C.
    II. The yeast begins releasing carbon dioxide at 30°C.
    III. The yeast cannot survive at temperatures above 30°C.
    (A) I only (D) II and III only
    (B) II only (E) I, II, and III
    (C) I and III only

Standardized Test Prep

1. B	**5.** C	**9.** C
2. E	**6.** E	**10.** C
3. A	**7.** D	
4. C	**8.** D	

(continued from p. 238)

30. An organism cannot continue to live without a constant supply of energy, which is provided by the Krebs cycle and the electron transport chain. Any event that cuts off that energy supply will cause the death of the organism.

31. Students' analogies should include parallels to the capture of energy, the storage of energy, and the gradual release of energy for use by the cell(s). Sample answer: Electrical energy can be used to move skiers to the top of a mountain. The skiers now have stored energy because of their position. They can remain at the top of the mountain or ski down in short trips, stopping along the way.

32. Students may sketch the carbon cycle in which plants absorb light, convert light energy to chemical energy, and store energy in sugars during photosynthesis. The sugars may be used by the plants or taken in as food by other organisms. Energy is extracted from the sugars during respiration, and carbon dioxide is given off as a product.

Take It to the NET

- The phosphagen system, the glycogen lactic acid system, and the aerobic system
- The glycogen lactic acid system can provide 1.3 to 1.6 minutes of maximal muscle activity under ideal conditions.
- The aerobic system provides unlimited time (as long as nutrients last). Thus, the aerobic system is used for prolonged athletic activity. The glycogen lactic system provides 1.3 to 1.6 minutes of endurance and is important for giving extra power during intermediate races such as 200- to 800-m runs. The phosphagen system provides only 8 to 10 seconds of endurance.
- Weight lifting—phosphagen system, almost entirely; Tennis—glycogen lactic acid system; Cross-country skiing—aerobic system

For additional information, visit

www.phschool.com

Chapter 10 Planner — Cell Growth and Division

Section and Section Objectives	Time	Activities and Labs
10–1 Cell Growth, pp. 241–243 **10.1.1** ***Explain*** the problems that growth causes for cells. **10.1.2** ***Describe*** how cell division solves the problems of cell growth.	**1 period (1/2 block)**	**SE: *Inquiry Activity,*** How do organisms grow?, p. 240 **TE: *Build Science Skills,*** p. 241 **SE: *Quick Lab,*** What limits the sizes of cells?, p. 242
10–2 Cell Division, pp. 244–249 **10.2.1** ***Name*** the main events of the cell cycle. **10.2.2** ***Describe*** what happens during the four phases of mitosis.	**2 periods (1 block)**	**TE: *Demonstration,*** p. 244 **TE: *Meet Diverse Needs,*** p. 245 **TE: *Build Science Skills,*** p. 246 **TE: *Meet Diverse Needs,*** p. 247 **SE: *Analyzing Data,*** Life Spans of Human Cells, p. 249 **SE: *Exploration,*** Observing the Phases of the Cell Cycle, pp. 254–255
10–3 Regulating the Cell Cycle, pp. 250–252 **10.3.1** ***Identify*** a factor that can stop cells from growing. **10.3.2** ***Describe*** how the cell cycle is regulated. **10.3.3** ***Explain*** how cancer cells are different from other cells.	**1 period (1/2 block)**	**SE: *Technology & Society,*** Stem Cells: Promises and Problems, p. 253
Chapter Assessment, pp. 256–259	**1 period (1/2 block)**	

ACTIVITY PLANNER

SE: *Inquiry Activity,* p. 240; (15 min.); microscope, prepared slides of cells from large and small plants and similar tissues from large and small animals

SE: *Build Science Skills,* p. 241; (15 min.); 2 boxes of different sizes, metric ruler

SE: *Quick Lab,* p. 242; (15 min.); 2 peeled hard-boiled eggs, blue food coloring, 150-mL beaker, scalpel, spoon, paper towels, metric ruler

TE: *Demonstration,* p. 244; (5 min.); 2 pipe cleaners, pin

TE: *Build Science Skills,* p. 246; (15 min.); copies of pictures of each phase of mitosis

TE: *Build Science Skills,* p. 247; (20 min.); microscope, paramecium culture, slide, dropper pipette

TE: *Meet Diverse Needs,* p. 247; (15 min.); pipe cleaners, string

SE: *Exploration,* pp. 254–255; (50 min.); microscope, prepared slides of onion root tips, scissors, tape or glue, craft materials such as beads, yarn, and pipe cleaners

PLANNING KEY

Ability Levels	
(B) **Basic**	For students who need additional help
(A) **Average**	For all students
(E) **Enriched**	For students who need to be challenged

Components

SE	Student Edition	**GRSW**	Guided Reading and Study Workbook	**IDM**	Issues and Decision Making
TE	Teacher's Edition	**CT**	Chapter Tests: Levels A and B	**CTB**	Computer Test Bank
LMA	Laboratory Manual A	**PHAS**	PH Assessment System	**PA**	Presentation Assistant Plus
LMB	Laboratory Manual B	**LA**	Lab Assessment With Scoring Guide	**BD**	BioDetectives Videotape
TR	Teaching Resources	**BTM**	BioTechnology Manual	**iT**	iText
IF	Investigations in Forensics				

Program Resources	*Assessment*	*Media and Technology*
TR: Section Review 10–1 (B) (A) **GRSW:** Section 10–1 (B) (A)	**SE:** 10–1 Section Assessment, p. 243 **TR:** Section Review 10–1	**PA:** 10–1 Interest Grabber, Section Outline, Ratio of Surface Area to Volume in Cells **iT:** Section 10–1
LMA: Chapter 10 Lab (A) (E) **LMB:** Chapter 10 Lab (B) (A) **TR:** Section Review 10–2 (B) (A) **GRSW:** Section 10–2 (B) **BTM:** Lab 3	**SE:** 10–2 Section Assessment, p. 249 **TR:** Section Review 10–2	**PA:** 10–2 Interest Grabber, Section Outline, Concept Map, Figure 10–4, Figure 10–5 **iT:** Section 10–2
TR: Section Review 10–3 (B) (A) Chapter 10 Exploration (B) (A) (E) **GRSW:** Section 10–3 (B) **IF:** Investigation 3	**SE:** 10–3 Section Assessment, p. 252 **TR:** Section Review 10–3	**PA:** 10–3 Interest Grabber, Section Outline, Control of Cell Division, Figure 10–8 **iT:** Section 10–3 **BD:** Skin Cancer: Deadly Cells Discovery Channel School
	SE: Chapter 10 Assessment, pp. 256–259 **TR:** Chapter Vocabulary Review, Graphic Organizer **CT:** Chapter 10 Test **CTB:** Chapter 10 Test **PHAS:** Practice Test	**CTB:** Chapter 10 Test **iT:** Chapter 10 Assessment

PRESSED FOR TIME?

To Preview the Chapter
- Introduce students to Key Concepts and Vocabulary terms in each section.
- Assign the Reading Strategies for each section.

To Cover the Chapter Quickly
- Have students read the first page and Figure 10–2 of Section 10–1, The Cell Cycle and Figures 10–5 and 10–6 in Section 10–2, and Controls on Cell Division and Figure 10–8 in Section 10–3.
- Assign the Section Review 10–2, questions 1–10 in Chapter 10 Assessment, and Chapter 10 Standardized Test Prep.

To Review the Chapter
- Assign Sections 10–1 through 10–3 in the Guided Reading and Study Workbook.
- Assign Section Reviews for 10–1 through 10–3 and the Chapter Vocabulary Review for Chapter 10 in the Teaching Resources.

ENGAGE/EXPLORE

Inquiry Activity

Objective Students will be able to observe that the number and size of cells are about the same in small organisms as in large organisms.

Skill Focus **Observing, Comparing and Contrasting**

Materials microscope, prepared slides of cells from large and small plants and similar tissues from large and small animals

Time 15 minutes

Advance Prep Set up microscope stations at several locations around the classroom. Select prepared slides of corresponding tissues in large and small organisms, such as grass blades and tree leaves, as well as muscle tissue from a small and a large vertebrate.

Safety Caution students to handle prepared slides carefully.

Strategy Circulate among students to make sure they are focusing their microscopes correctly.

Expected Outcome Students should determine that growth in multicellular organisms is due mostly to an increase in cell number, not cell size.

Think About It

1. Students should observe that cells of small and large plants are about the same size and cells from small and large animals are about the same size.
2. A typical statement might suggest that there is a greater number of cells in large organisms than in small organisms, but the size of cells is about the same.

Assess Prior Knowledge

Ask students: **How would you describe the process by which a multicellular organism increases its size?** *(Accept all reasonable responses. Many students might suggest that the organism's cells grow larger.)* Point out that all the cells that students know about are quite small. Then, ask: **Why do cells stay small?** *(Some students might suggest that cells stay small because they are programmed to be small by their DNA.)*

Chapter 10 Cell Growth and Division

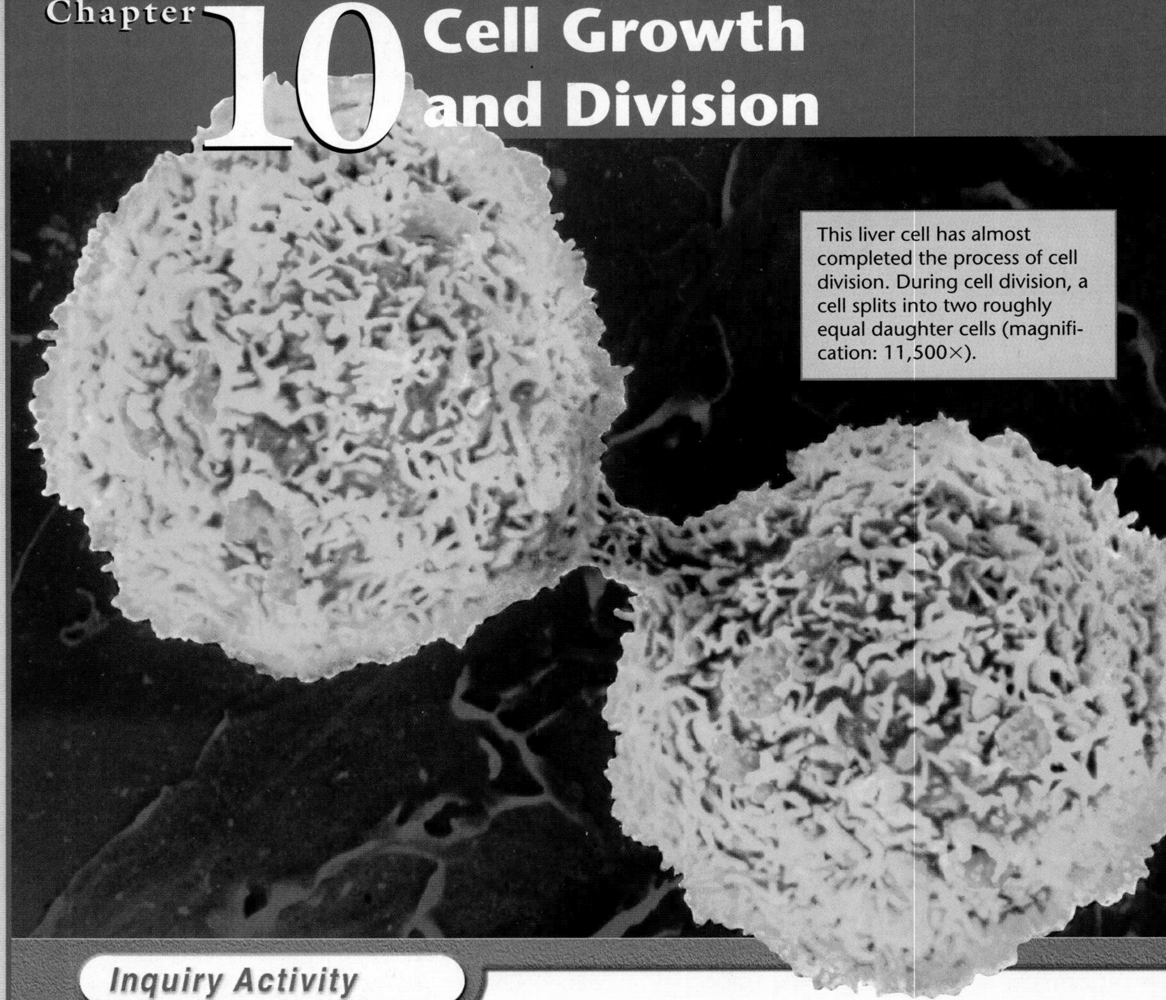

This liver cell has almost completed the process of cell division. During cell division, a cell splits into two roughly equal daughter cells (magnification: 11,500×).

Inquiry Activity

How do organisms grow?

Procedure

1. Use a microscope to compare the sizes of similar cells in large and small plants. For example, you might compare the leaf cells of grass to the leaf cells of a tree. Be sure to use the same magnification when comparing the sizes of the cells.
2. Use a microscope to compare the sizes of cells in similar tissues from small and large animals, such as muscle tissue from a frog and from a human.

Think About It

1. **Observing** Are the cells of the small plant larger or smaller than those of the large plant? Are the cells of the small animal larger or smaller than those of the large animal?
2. **Comparing and Contrasting** Make a general statement that compares the number and size of cells in small organisms to those in larger organisms.

HISTORY OF SCIENCE

Human cells that keep dividing

To study cell division for medical and other purposes, biologists need human cells that continue to divide in culture in the laboratory. Yet, finding such cells proved difficult. In 1951, researchers at Johns Hopkins University tried to culture a line of cells that would continue to live and multiply. Every cell sample they tried died out in a few weeks, because normal mammalian cells will divide only 20–50 times in culture before they die. Finally, cells from one sample kept dividing week after week, and eventually, year after year. These were called HeLa cells after their original source, a young Baltimore woman named Henrietta Lacks. The sample had been taken from a malignant tumor in her body. Unfortunately, she died a few months later, but HeLa cells have been grown since that time in laboratories around the world.

10–1 Cell Growth

When a living thing grows, what happens to its cells? Does an animal get larger because each cell increases in size or because it produces more of them? In most cases, living things grow by producing more cells. On average, the cells of an adult animal are no larger than those of a young animal—there are just more of them.

Limits to Cell Growth

There are two main reasons why cells divide rather than continuing to grow indefinitely.  **The larger a cell becomes, the more demands the cell places on its DNA and the more trouble the cell has moving enough nutrients and wastes across the cell membrane.**

DNA "Overload" As you may recall, the information that controls a cell's function is stored in a molecule known as DNA. In eukaryotic cells, DNA is found in the nucleus of the cell. When a cell is small, the information stored in that DNA is able to meet all of the cell's needs. But as a cell increases in size, it usually does not make extra copies of DNA. If a cell were to grow without limit, an "information crisis" would occur.

To help understand why a larger cell has a more difficult time functioning efficiently than a smaller cell, compare the cells to a growing town. Suppose a small town has a library with a few thousand books. If more people move into the town, the town will get larger. There will be more people borrowing books, and sometimes people may have to wait to borrow popular titles. Similarly, a larger cell would have to make greater demands on its available genetic "library." In time, the cell's DNA would no longer be able to serve the increasing needs of the growing cell.

Exchanging Materials There is another reason why the size of cells is limited. You may recall that food, oxygen, and water enter a cell through its cell membrane. Waste products leave in the same way. The rate at which this exchange takes place depends on the surface area of the cell, which is the total area of its cell membrane. However, the rate at which food and oxygen are used up and waste products are produced depends on the cell's volume. Understanding the relationship between a cell's volume and its surface area is the key to understanding why cells must divide as they grow.

Guide for Reading

Key Concept
- What problems does growth cause for cells?

Vocabulary
cell division

Reading Strategy: Asking Questions Before reading this section, rewrite each blue heading as a *what, where,* or *how* question. Then, as you read, fill in the answer to each question.

▼ **Figure 10–1** Living things grow by producing more cells. Although the adult snail is larger than the young snail, the cells of both are the same size.

SECTION RESOURCES

TIME SAVER

Print:
- ***Teaching Resources,*** Section Review 10–1
- ***Guided Reading and Study Workbook,*** Section 10–1

Technology:
- ***iText,*** Section 10–1

Section 10–1

1 FOCUS

Objectives

10.1.1 ***Explain*** the problems that growth causes for cells.

10.1.2 ***Describe*** how cell division solves the problems of cell growth.

Guide for Reading

Vocabulary Preview

Before students read the section, ask for volunteers to define *cell division.*

Reading Strategy

Have students preview Figure 10–2 and write an explanation of the implications the data in the table have for cell size and growth. Then, after they read the section, have them revise their explanation.

2 INSTRUCT

Limits to Cell Growth

Build Science Skills

Drawing conclusions Divide the class into small groups, and give each group two cardboard boxes, one larger than the other. Ask each group to use a metric ruler to find the surface area of each box and then, the volume of each box. After students have collected data, ask them to compare the difference in surface area between the boxes and the difference in volume between the boxes. Challenge students to draw a conclusion about whether surface area or volume increases more rapidly as the size of a box increases. Students should discover that volume increases more rapidly than surface area.

Quick Lab

Objective Students will be able to use a model to explain why a cell cannot continue to grow indefinitely.

Skill Focus Observing, Using Models

Materials 2 peeled hard-boiled eggs, blue food coloring, 150-mL beaker, scalpel, spoon, paper towels, metric ruler

Time 15 minutes

Advance Prep Boil eggs the day of the activity, two per group of students. Blue coloring works best, though other colors can be used. You may want to cut egg cubes ahead of time.

Strategies
- Food coloring will diffuse farther if the eggs are warm.
- To investigate the ratio of surface area to volume further, have students measure the volume of water that the whole egg and the egg cube each displace in a graduated cylinder. Have them measure the surface area of each by wrapping aluminum foil tightly around the material, leaving no wrinkles and cutting away any overlap. They can trace the resulting pieces of foil onto graph paper and count the squares within each tracing.

Expected Outcome Students should find that the food coloring diffuses almost to the center of the egg cube but just through the surface of the whole egg.

Analyze and Conclude

1. The coloring almost reaches the center of the egg cube but moves only a few millimeters into the whole egg.
2. Just as the food coloring entered the eggs, food must enter a living cell, and wastes must be removed. The food coloring diffused into more of the egg cube than the whole egg because the egg cube had a smaller ratio of surface area to volume than the whole egg. Similarly, a very large cell would not have a large enough surface area for substances to move easily into and out of the cell.

sa $6 cm^2$
vol $1 cm^3$

$24 cm^2$
$8 cm^3$

$54 cm^2$
$27 cm^3$

Ratio of Surface Area to Volume Imagine a cell that is shaped like a cube, like those in **Figure 10–2.** If this cell has a length of 1 cm, its surface area would be equal to length × width × number of sides, or 1 cm × 1 cm × 6 = 6 cm^2. The volume of the cell would be equal to length × width × height, or 1 cm × 1 cm × 1 cm = 1 cm^3. To obtain the ratio of surface area to volume, divide the surface area by the volume. In this case, the ratio of surface area to volume would be 6 / 1, or 6 : 1.

If the length of the cell doubled, what would happen to the cell's surface area compared to its volume? The cell's surface area would be equal to 2 cm × 2 cm × 6 = 24 cm^2. The volume would be equal to 2 cm × 2 cm × 2 cm = 8 cm^3. The cell's ratio of surface area to volume would be 24 / 8, or 3 : 1.

What if the length of the cell triples? The cell's surface area now would be 3 cm × 3 cm × 6 = 54 cm^2. The volume would be 3 cm × 3 cm × 3 cm = 27 cm^3. The ratio of surface area to volume would be 54 / 27, or 2 : 1.

Note that the volume increases much more rapidly than the surface area, causing the ratio of surface area to volume to decrease. This decrease creates serious problems for the cell.

To use the town analogy again, suppose the small town has a two-lane main street. As the town grows, more people will use this street. The main street leading through town, however, has not increased in size. As a result, people will encounter more traffic as they enter and leave the town. A cell that continues to grow larger would experience similar problems. It would be more

Quick Lab

What limits the sizes of cells?

Materials 2 peeled hard-boiled eggs, blue food coloring, 150-mL beaker, scalpel, spoon, paper towels, metric ruler

Procedure  

1. Place 100 mL of water in a beaker. Add 10 drops of blue food coloring, and stir with a spoon. **CAUTION:** *Food coloring may stain hands and clothing.*
2. Use the scalpel to cut through the middle of 1 hard-boiled egg. **CAUTION:** *Be careful with the scalpel.* Remove the yolk. Cut an 8-mm cube from the thickest part of the egg white.
3. Place the egg cube and a peeled hard-boiled egg gently into the beaker of food coloring and water. Allow the eggs to sit in the beaker for 10 minutes.
4. After 10 minutes, use a spoon to carefully remove the egg cube and the whole egg from the beaker, and place them on a paper towel. Cut the egg cube in half. Clean the scalpel blade and cut the whole egg in half. Measure how far the blue color penetrated the egg cube and the whole egg.

Analyze and Conclude

1. **Observing** How close to the centers of the egg cube and the whole egg did the color reach?
2. **Using Models** Compare the whole egg and the egg cube to cells to explain why a cell cannot continue to grow indefinitely.

TIME SAVER — PRESENTATIONS MADE EASY!

The Presentation Assistant Plus contains the Prentice Hall Presentation Pro and the Transparencies, which provide easy-to-follow visual support for every step of this section. If you have a computer presentation station, use Prentice Hall Presentation Pro for Section 10–1, or use the transparencies listed here.

Section 10–1: 
Interest Grabber
Section Outline
Ratio of Surface Area to Volume in Cells

Ratio of Surface Area to Volume in Cells			
Cell Size	1 cm,  1 cm, 1 cm	2 cm, 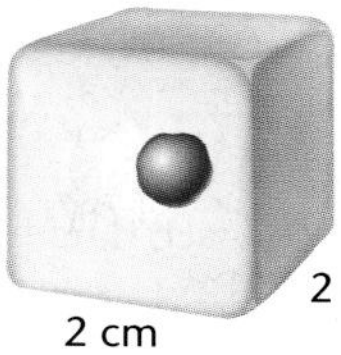 2 cm, 2 cm	3 cm, 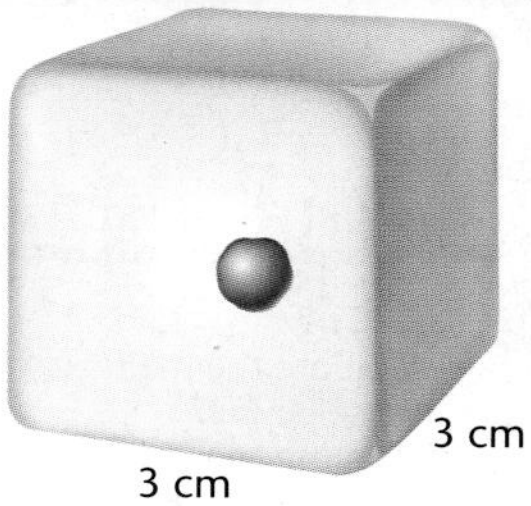 3 cm, 3 cm
Surface Area (length x width x 6)	1 cm x 1 cm x 6 = 6 cm^2	2 cm x 2 cm x 6 = 24 cm^2	3 cm x 3 cm x 6 = 54 cm^2
Volume (length x width x height)	1 cm x 1 cm x 1 cm = 1 cm^3	2 cm x 2 cm x 2 cm = 8 cm^3	3 cm x 3 cm x 3 cm = 27 cm^3
Ratio of Surface Area to Volume	6 / 1 = 6 : 1	24 / 8 = 3 : 1	54 / 27 = 2 : 1

▲ **Figure 10–2 As the length of a cell increases, its volume increases faster than its surface area. The resulting decrease in the cell's ratio of surface area to volume makes it more difficult for the cell to move needed materials in and waste products out.**

difficult for a larger cell to get oxygen and nutrients in and waste products out. This problem is one reason why cells do not grow much larger even if the organism of which they are a part does.

Cell Division Before it becomes too large, a growing cell divides forming two "daughter" cells. The process by which a cell divides into two new daughter cells is called **cell division.**

Before cell division occurs, the cell replicates, or copies, all of its DNA. This replication of DNA solves the problem of information storage because each daughter cell gets one complete set of genetic information. Thus, each daughter cell receives its own genetic "library." Cell division also solves the problem of increasing size by reducing cell volume. Each daughter cell has an increased ratio of surface area to volume. This allows efficient exchange of materials with the environment.

10–1 Section Assessment

1. **Key Concept** Give two reasons why cells divide.
2. How is a cell's DNA like the books in a library?
3. What is the solution to the problems caused by cell growth?
4. As a cell increases in size, which increases more rapidly, its surface area or its volume?
5. **Critical Thinking Calculating** Calculate the surface area, volume, and ratio of surface area to volume of an imaginary cubic cell with a length of 4 cm.

iTEXT Assessment Use iText to review the important concepts in Section 10–1.

MAKING CONNECTIONS

Stability and Equilibrium Select two cell organelles and describe how their functions might be impaired if the cell were to become too large. *Hint:* A review of Chapter 7 may help you with this task.

10–1 Section Assessment

1. The larger a cell becomes, the more demands the cell places on its DNA and the more trouble the cell has moving enough nutrients and wastes across the cell membrane.
2. The information that controls a cell's function is stored in DNA, just as information needed by the public is stored in the books of a library. A cell's DNA, then, is a "genetic" library.
3. Before a growing cell becomes too large, it undergoes cell division, forming two "daughter" cells.
4. Its volume
5. The surface area is 96 cm^2, the volume is 64 cm^3, and the ratio of surface area to volume is 96/64 = 3 : 2.

Make Connections

Mathematics Some students may have limited experience with ratios. Explain that a ratio is a measure of the relative size of two quantities, expressed as a proportion or as a fraction. A ratio can be expressed as a fraction, such as *1/2,* or with a colon, such as *1 : 2.* Like a fraction, a ratio can be reduced to the lowest numbers, and thus 50 : 25 is reduced to 2 : 1. Ask: **What is the ratio of vowels to consonants in the alphabet?** *(5 : 21)*

Use Visuals

Figure 10–2 Have students compare the largest cell and the smallest cell in the figure. Ask: **Which of the two cells has the greatest volume?** *(The larger cell)* **Which of the two has the greatest surface area?** *(The larger cell)* Point out that both volume and surface area increase with cell size. Then, ask: **What causes the problem for a cell as it grows in size?** *(The problem is caused by the surface area relative to the cell's volume, or the ratio of surface area to volume.)*

3 ASSESS

Evaluate Understanding

Ask students to write a paragraph that explains why a cell in the human body never grows as large as a fist.

Reteach

Tell students that an imaginary cubic cell has doubled, from a length of 3 mm to a length of 6 mm. Have them calculate the ratio of surface area to volume for each cell. *(The first cell has a ratio of 2 : 1; the larger cell has a ratio of 1 : 1.)*

MAKING CONNECTIONS

Sample student answer: The function of a mitochondrion might be impaired because it might not be able to get enough oxygen from outside the cell. Similarly, a chloroplast might not be able to get enough water from outside the cell.

Use iText to review the key concepts in Section 10–1.

Section 10–2

1 FOCUS

Objectives

10.2.1 ***Name*** the main events of the cell cycle.

10.2.2 ***Describe*** what happens during the four phases of mitosis.

Guide for Reading

Vocabulary Preview

Ask students at random to pronounce the vocabulary words in the order in which they appear. Correct any mispronunciations.

Reading Strategy

Suggest that students write a summary of the information in Figure 10–5. Then, have them revise their summaries after reading the section.

2 INSTRUCT

Chromosomes

Address Misconceptions

Some students may think that there is a chemical or structural difference between chromosomes and chromatids. Explain that there is really no difference between chromosomes and chromatids except that the chromatids are in pairs. Biologists vary the terminology to avoid saying that an organism has "double" the number of "chromosomes," because each kind of organism has a specific number of chromosomes. A chromatid again becomes a chromosome when the sister chromatids separate during anaphase.

Demonstration

Reinforce students' understanding of chromatids and centromeres by using two pipe cleaners and a pin. Show students a pipe cleaner and explain that it represents a chromosome. As you explain the process of duplication of chromosomes during interphase, pick up another pipe cleaner of the same size and wind it around the first one. Then, push a pin through the contact joint of the two pipe cleaners and explain that the pin represents a centromere.

10–2 Cell Division

Guide for Reading

Key Concepts
- What are the main events of the cell cycle?
- What are the four phases of mitosis?

Vocabulary
chromatid
centromere
interphase
cell cycle
mitosis
prophase
centriole
spindle
metaphase
anaphase
telophase
cytokinesis

Reading Strategy: Outlining As you read this section, outline the major events of the cell cycle. Write a few sentences to describe the activity of chromosomes as they progress through each part of the cell cycle.

What do you think would happen if a cell were simply to split into two, without any advance preparation? Would each daughter cell have everything it needed to survive? Because each cell has only one set of genetic information, the answer is no. Every cell must first copy its genetic information before cell division begins. Each daughter cell then gets a complete copy of that information.

In most prokaryotes, the rest of the process of cell division is a simple matter of separating the contents of the cell into two parts. Although eukaryotic cells divide in a similar way, their greater complexity makes eukaryotic cell division a more involved process.

Chromosomes

In eukaryotic cells, the genetic information that is passed on from one generation of cells to the next is carried by chromosomes. Chromosomes are made up of DNA—which carries the cell's coded genetic information—and proteins. The cells of every organism have a specific number of chromosomes. The cells of fruit flies, for example, have 8 chromosomes; human cells have 46 chromosomes; and carrot cells have 18 chromosomes.

Chromosomes are not visible in most cells except during cell division. This is because the DNA and protein molecules that make up the chromosomes are spread throughout the nucleus. At the beginning of cell division, however, the chromosomes condense into compact, visible structures that can be seen through a light microscope.

Well before cell division, each chromosome is replicated, or copied. Because of this, when they become visible at the beginning of cell division, each chromosome consists of two identical "sister" **chromatids** (KROH-muh-tidz), as shown in **Figure 10–3.** Each pair of chromatids is attached at an area called the centromere (SEN-troh-meer). **Centromeres** are usually located near the middle of the chromatids, although some lie near the ends. A human body cell entering cell division contains 46 chromosomes, each of which consists of two chromatids.

CHECKPOINT *When are chromosomes visible?*

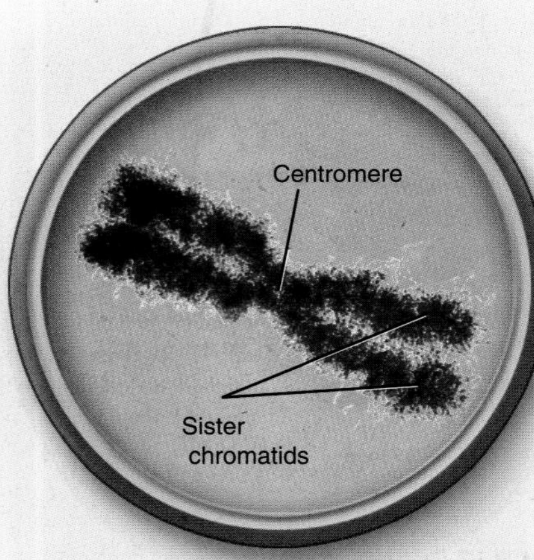

◀ **Figure 10–3** This is a human chromosome shown as it appears through an electron microscope. Each chromosome has two sister chromatids attached at the centromere. **Inferring** ***Why are the sister chromatids identical?***

SECTION RESOURCES

Print:
- ***Laboratory Manual A,*** Chapter 10 Lab
- ***Laboratory Manual B,*** Chapter 10 Lab
- ***Teaching Resources,*** Section Review 10–2
- ***Guided Reading and Study Workbook,*** Section 10–2
- ***Biotechnology Manual,*** Lab 3

Technology:
- ***iText,*** Section 10–2

The Cell Cycle

At one time, biologists described the life of a cell as one cell division after another separated by an "in-between" period of growth called **interphase.** We now appreciate that a great deal happens in the time between cell divisions, and use a concept known as the cell cycle to represent recurring events in the life of the cell. The **cell cycle** is the series of events that cells go through as they grow and divide. **During the cell cycle, a cell grows, prepares for division, and divides to form two daughter cells, each of which then begins the cycle again.** The main events of the cell cycle are shown in **Figure 10–4.**

The cell cycle consists of four phases. Two of these are so important that they are used as landmarks to define everything else. One of these phases is the M phase. During the M phase, **mitosis** (my-TOH-sis)—the division of the cell nucleus—and cytokinesis take place. The other important phase—the S phase—is the copying of the chromosomes. When the cell copies the chromosomes, it synthesizes, or makes, a duplicate set of DNA. Between the M and S phases are G_1 and G_2. The *G* in the names of these phases stands for "gap," but the G_1 and G_2 are definitely not periods when nothing takes place. They are actually periods of intense growth and activity.

Events of the Cell Cycle

During the normal cell cycle, interphase can be quite long, whereas the actual division of the cell takes place quickly. Interphase is divided into three phases: G_1, S, and G_2.

The G_1 phase is a period of activity in which cells do most of their growing. During this phase, cells increase in size and synthesize new proteins and organelles.

G_1 is followed by the S phase, in which chromosomes are replicated and the synthesis of DNA molecules takes place. Key proteins associated with the chromosomes are synthesized during the S phase. Usually, once a cell enters the S phase and begins the replication of its chromosomes, it completes the rest of the cell cycle including mitosis.

When the DNA replication is completed, the cell enters the G_2 phase. G_2 is usually the shortest of the three phases of interphase. During the G_2 phase, many of the organelles and molecules required for cell division are produced. When the events of the G_2 phase are complete, the cell is ready to enter the M phase and begin the process of cell division.

▼ **Figure 10–4** **During the cell cycle, the cell grows, replicates its DNA, and divides into two daughter cells.**

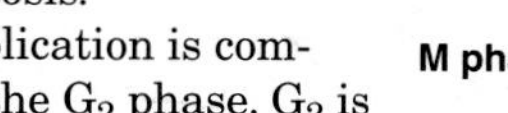

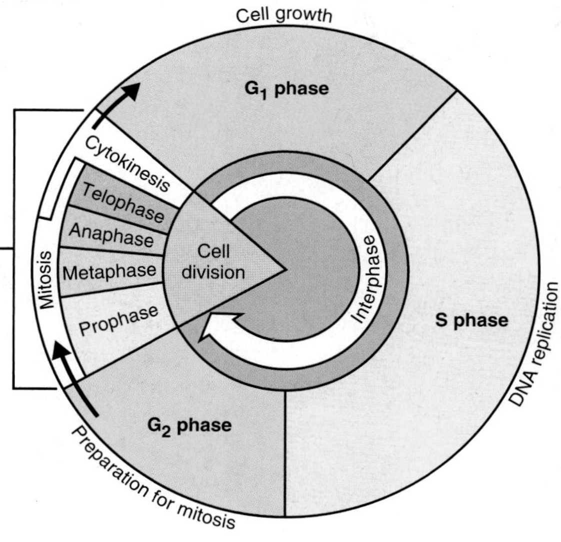

The Cell Cycle

Use Visuals

Figure 10–4 After students have examined the figure, ask: **What are the four phases of the cell cycle?** *(G_1 phase, S phase, G_2 phase, and M phase)* **If you were to divide the cell cycle into two parts, what would they be?** *(Interphase and cell division)* Explain that this is called a cycle because the process is continuous through generations of cells, and one phase leads into the next. Then, ask: **For each individual cell, when does the cell cycle begin?** *(When the daughter cells form, at the end of the M phase, or after cytokinesis has occurred)*

Events of the Cell Cycle

Meet Diverse Needs

Divide the class into eight groups, making sure that each group contains a mix of gifted, at-risk, and limited English proficiency students. Assign one group the G_1 phase, a second group the S phase, a third group the G_2 phase, four groups one of the four phases of mitosis, and the eighth group cytokinesis. Explain that together, the groups will make a wall-length cartoon strip that shows the events in the cell cycle. Give each group four frames—four large sheets of paper—for its part of the total cartoon sequence. Advise group members to work together to plan what should be shown in the four frames, which should contain cartoon figures that creatively tell the story of that part of the cell cycle. When all groups have completed their work, tape all cartoons in sequence across the side of the classroom. **Learning modality: visual**

TIME SAVER **PRESENTATIONS MADE EASY!**

The Presentation Assistant Plus contains the Prentice Hall Presentation Pro and the Transparencies, which provide easy-to-follow visual support for every step of this lesson. If you have a computer presentation station, use Prentice Hall Presentation Pro for Section 10–2, or use the transparencies listed here.

Section 10–2: **Interest Grabber**
Section Outline
Concept Map
Figure 10–4
Figure 10–5

Answers to . . .

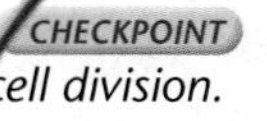

CHECKPOINT *They are visible during cell division.*

Figure 10–3 *Before cell division, each chromosome is duplicated. The sister chromatids, therefore, are identical because they are duplicates of each other.*

10–2 (continued)

Mitosis

Build Science Skills

Predicting Divide the class into small groups, and give each group a packet of pictures, each of which represents a phase of mitosis. To make each packet, copy photos or illustrations from a college textbook, eliminating any labels. Challenge each group to make a prediction about how mitosis proceeds by placing the pictures in the correct sequence. Then, have groups present their predictions to the class.

Use Visuals

Figure 10–5 Explain that this figure shows each event in the cell cycle in two ways, as a photomicrograph and as a labeled illustration. Ask: **When are the cell's chromosomes copied during the cell cycle?** *(During the S phase of interphase)* **What function does the spindle serve during mitosis?** *(The spindle helps separate the chromosomes.)* Have students look back at Figure 10–4, and ask: **Does cytokinesis start when telophase ends?** *(No. The figure shows that cytokinesis ends after telophase, but it begins during mitosis.)* Explain that cytokinesis overlaps mitosis and usually begins during telophase. Finally, have students use the figure to make their own drawings of each phase of the mitosis.

Meet Diverse Needs

To help students better understand the terminology of the cell cycle, have them look up these prefixes in a dictionary: *inter-, pro-, meta-, ana-,* and *telo-*, which mean, respectively, "between," "before," "after," "backward," and "end." With the meanings of these prefixes in mind, have students explain the meanings of each of the names of the phases of mitosis. **Limited English proficiency**

Mitosis

Biologists divide the events of mitosis into four phases: prophase, metaphase, anaphase, and telophase. Depending on the type of cell, the four phases of mitosis may last anywhere from a few minutes to several days. As you read about each phase of mitosis, look at **Figure 10–5.**

Prophase The first and longest phase of mitosis, **prophase,** can take as much as 50 to 60 percent of the total time required to complete mitosis. During prophase, the chromosomes become visible. The **centrioles** (SEN-tree-ohlz), two tiny structures located in the cytoplasm near the nuclear envelope, separate and take up positions on opposite sides of the nucleus.

▼ **Figure 10–5** Most eukaryotic cells go through a regular cycle of interphase, mitosis, and cytokinesis. **Mitosis has four phases: prophase, metaphase, anaphase, and telophase.** The events shown here are typical of animal cells. The photographs shown are from a developing whitefish embryo (magnification: 625×).

Centrioles
Nuclear envelope
Chromatin
Interphase
The cell grows and replicates its DNA and centrioles.

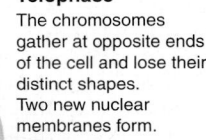

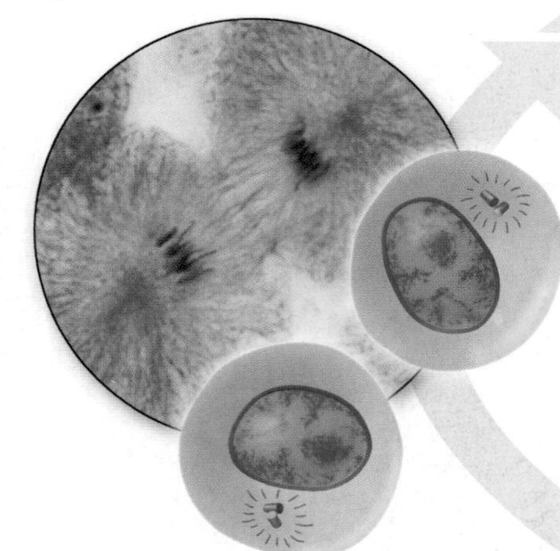
Cytokinesis
The cytoplasm pinches in half. Each daughter cell has an identical set of duplicate chromosomes.

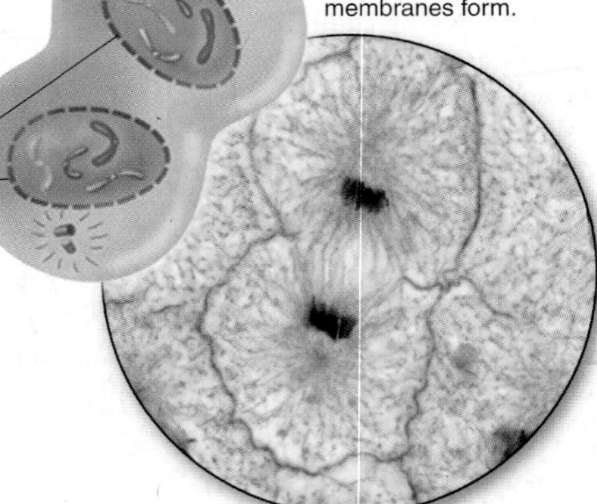
Telophase
The chromosomes gather at opposite ends of the cell and lose their distinct shapes. Two new nuclear membranes form.
Nuclear envelope reforming

BIO INSIGHTS

FACTS AND FIGURES

The evolution of mitosis

Prokaryotes generally reproduce by binary fission, during which the circular DNA chromosome replicates, both duplicates attach to the cell membrane, and the cell splits at its midsection. Eukaryotes—much more complicated organisms—needed a more complex process, and mitosis evolved. Clues to the intermediary steps in this evolution can be seen in some unicellular algae. During cell division in dinoflagellates, for instance, the nuclear envelope does not break down, as it does during mitosis. Rather, the chromosomes duplicate and attach to the nuclear membrane. Microtubules pass through cytoplasmic tunnels in the nucleus, which eventually splits in a process much like binary fission. In diatoms, another type of algae, a spindle forms from microtubules within the nucleus, which then splits into two nuclei.

The centrioles lie in a region called the centrosome that helps to organize the **spindle,** a fanlike microtubule structure that helps separate the chromosomes. During prophase, the condensed chromosomes become attached to fibers in the spindle at a point near the centromere of each chromatid. Interestingly, plant cells do not have centrioles, but still organize their mitotic spindles from centrosomes.

Near the end of prophase, the chromosomes coil more tightly. In addition, the nucleolus disappears, and the nuclear envelope breaks down.

CHECKPOINT *What is the function of the spindle?*

KEEP CURRENT WITH . . . SCIENCE NEWS®

To find out more about the topics in this chapter, go to: **www.phschool.com**

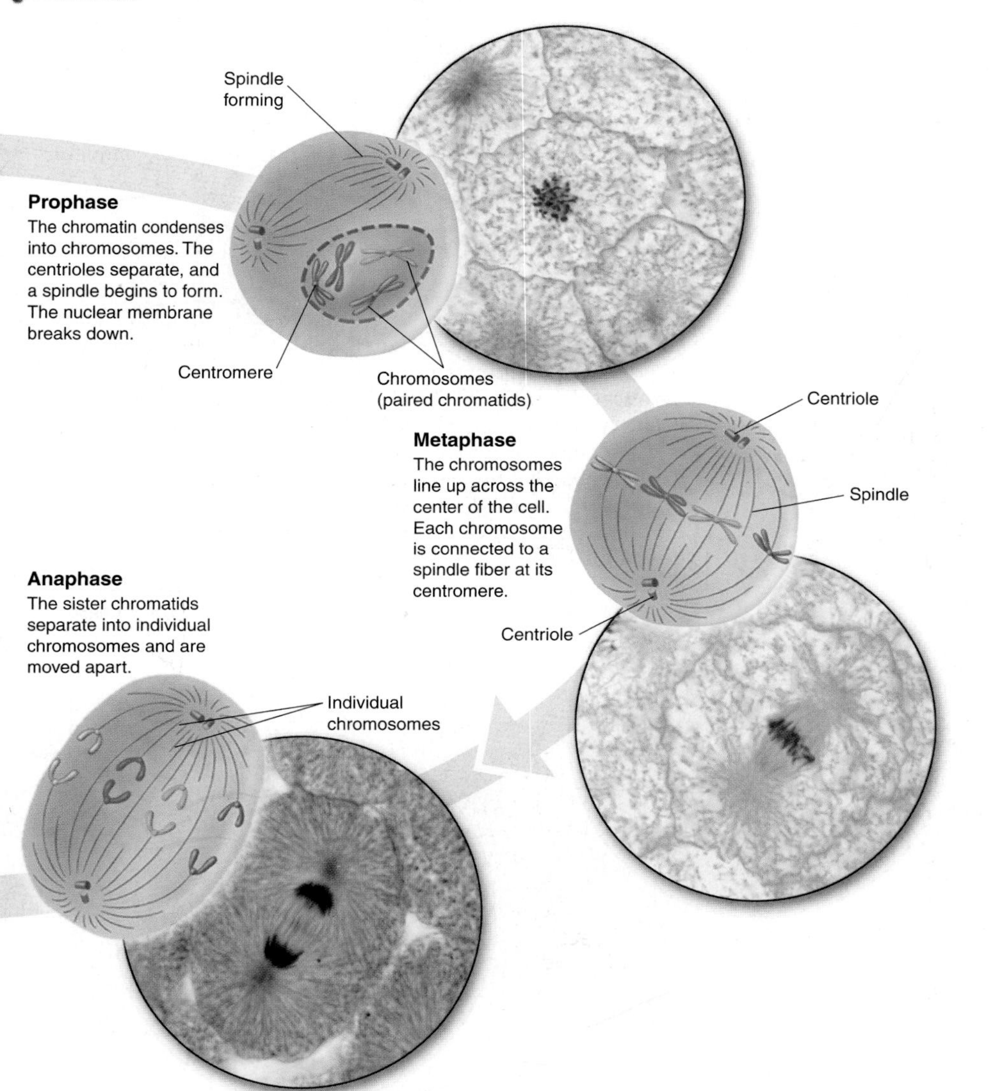

Spindle forming
Prophase
The chromatin condenses into chromosomes. The centrioles separate, and a spindle begins to form. The nuclear membrane breaks down.
Centromere
Chromosomes (paired chromatids)
Centriole
Metaphase
The chromosomes line up across the center of the cell. Each chromosome is connected to a spindle fiber at its centromere.
Spindle
Centriole
Anaphase
The sister chromatids separate into individual chromosomes and are moved apart.
Individual chromosomes

SCIENCE NEWS®

Encourage students to visit **www.phschool.com** for the most current information on this topic.

Build Science Skills

Observing Set up microscope stations around the room, and provide a paramecium culture. Ask each student to make a slide from the culture. Have students examine their slides, using low power, to find any paramecia that are pinched in the middle or that look like "double cells." When such an example is found, the student should switch to high power and make a sketch of the organism. Students should also write a short description of what they think is occurring.

Meet Diverse Needs

Divide the class into small groups, and give each group pieces of pipe cleaner and string. Have each group form a cell with the string and use the pipe cleaners for chromosomes. Then, call on student volunteers to explain what occurs during prophase, metaphase, anaphase, and telophase. As a student explains each event, group members should manipulate their materials to model that phase of mitosis. Circulate among the groups to correct any misconceptions. **Learning modality: tactile**

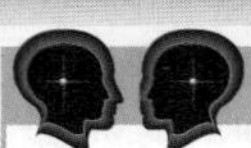

TEACHER TO TEACHER

To reinforce students' understanding of the processes of mitosis, I have them manipulate common materials as they mirror the sequence of phases. I supply them with a paper towel to represent the cell, gummy worms (which are bicolored) to represent chromosomes, and toothpicks to represent spindle fibers. They use plastic knives to cut the gummy worms, making sister chromatids. For mitosis, they organize a spindle with toothpicks on opposite sides of the towel (prophase), line up the chromosomes (metaphase), separate the chromosomes into two groups (anaphase), form the chromosomes into clusters (telophase), and split the paper towel in two (cytokinesis).

—Sheila Smith,
Biology Teacher
Terry High School,
Terry, MS

Answer to . . .

CHECKPOINT *The spindle helps separate the chromosomes.*

Cytokinesis

Word Origins

The word *cytotoxic* means "related to something poisonous to a cell."

Analyzing Data

Many students have the misconception that mitosis occurs regularly in all cells. The information in the data table will help address that mistaken notion.

Answers

1. Most white blood cells are needed by the body only for a short time to fight infection, so they do not have to be long-lived.
2. Because cardiac muscle cells and neurons cannot divide, injuries to the heart or spinal cord cannot heal through the production of new heart or nerve cells. In contrast, because the cells of smooth muscle can divide, an injury to smooth muscle may be able to heal through cell division.
3. A typical hypothesis might suggest that cells lining the digestive system, where chemical and mechanical digestion occur, are more apt to be destroyed or damaged by these processes.
4. A typical prediction will correctly suggest that cancer cells are long-lived and can divide, because cancer cells are almost "immortal" and divide uncontrollably.

Metaphase The second phase of mitosis, **metaphase,** often lasts only a few minutes. During metaphase, the chromosomes line up across the center of the cell. Microtubules connect the centromere of each chromosome to the poles of the spindle.

Anaphase **Anaphase** is the third phase of mitosis. During anaphase, the centromeres that join the sister chromatids separate, allowing the sister chromatids to separate and become individual chromosomes. The chromosomes continue to move until they have separated into two groups near the poles of the spindle. Anaphase ends when the chromosomes stop moving.

Telophase Following anaphase is **telophase,** the fourth and final phase of mitosis. In telophase, the chromosomes, which were distinct and condensed, begin to disperse into a tangle of dense material. A nuclear envelope re-forms around each cluster of chromosomes. The spindle begins to break apart, and a nucleolus becomes visible in each daughter nucleus. Mitosis is complete. However, the process of cell division is not complete.

CHECKPOINT *What happens during anaphase?*

Word Origins

Cytokinesis comes from the Greek words *kytos,* meaning "hollow vessel," and *kinesis,* meaning "motion." The prefix *cyto-* refers to cells, so *cytokinesis* means movement within the cell. **What do you think the term *cytotoxic* means?**

Cytokinesis

As a result of mitosis, two nuclei—each with a duplicate set of chromosomes—are formed, usually within the cytoplasm of a single cell. All that remains to complete the M phase of the cycle is **cytokinesis** (sy-toh-kih-NEE-sis), the division of the cytoplasm itself. Cytokinesis usually occurs at the same time as telophase.

Cytokinesis can take place in a number of ways. In most animal cells, the cell membrane is drawn inward until the cytoplasm is pinched into two nearly equal parts. Each part contains its own nucleus and cytoplasmic organelles. In plants, a structure known as the cell plate forms midway between the divided nuclei, as shown in **Figure 10–6.** The cell plate gradually develops into a separating membrane. A cell wall then begins to appear in the cell plate.

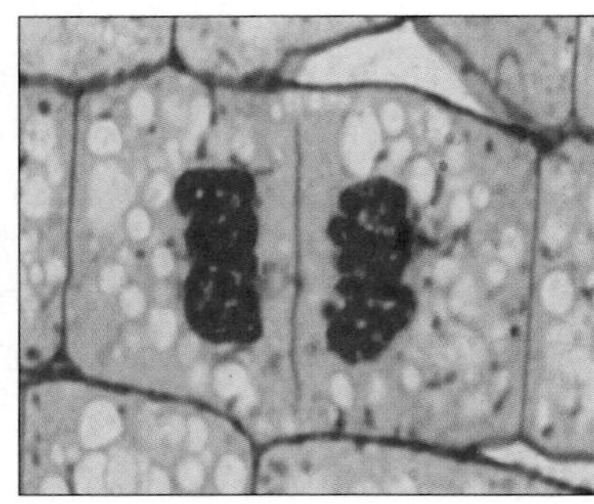

(magnification: 2200×)

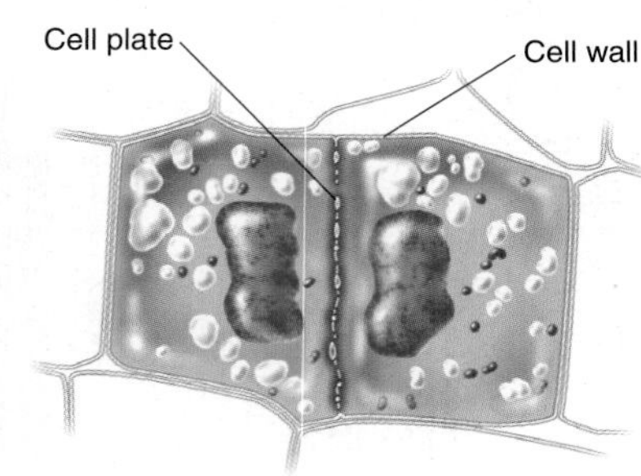

▶ **Figure 10–6** During cytokinesis in plant cells, the cytoplasm is divided by a cell plate. The thin line you can see between the two dark nuclei in this electron micrograph of onion cells dividing is the cell plate forming. **Interpreting Graphics** ***What structure forms between the divided nuclei?***

FACTS AND FIGURES

How long does a cell cycle take?
The time it takes for a cell to complete a cell cycle, called the generation time, varies widely among cells. The minimum time for a complete cell cycle is about 10 minutes. It takes about 2 hours for cells to divide in a newly forming sea urchin. In animal and plant cells that are actively growing, generation time is often between 8 and 10 hours. The generation time for a bean cell is 19 hours; the G_1 phase lasts about 5 hours, the S phase lasts about 7 hours, the G_2 phase lasts about 5 hours, and the M phase lasts about 2 hours. The generation time for a mouse cell is about 22 hours; the G_1 phase lasts about 9 hours, the S phase lasts about 10 hours, the G_2 phase lasts about 2 hours, and the M phase lasts about 1 hour. Many mature cells, such as nerve and red blood cells, never divide; they are said to be in the G_0 phase, which is much like the G_1 phase.

Analyzing Data

Life Spans of Human Cells

Like all organisms, cells have a given life span from birth to death. In multicellular organisms, such as humans, the health of the organism depends on cells not exceeding their life span. This is especially true of cells that tend to divide rapidly. If these cells did not die on schedule, overcrowding of cells would occur, causing uncontrolled growth that would be life-threatening.

The data table shows the life spans of various human cells. It also contains information about the ability of the cells to multiply through cell division.

1. **Inferring** White blood cells help protect the body from infection and disease-producing organisms. How might their function relate to their life span?
2. **Comparing and Contrasting** Based on the data, how are the consequences of injuries to the heart and spinal cord similar to each other? How are they different from the consequences of injuries to smooth muscle?
3. **Formulating Hypotheses** Propose a hypothesis to account for the data related to the cell life spans of the lining of the esophagus, small intestine, and large intestine.

Life Spans of Various Human Cells

Cell Type	Life Span	Cell Division
Lining of esophagus	2–3 days	Can divide
Lining of small intestine	1–2 days	Can divide
Lining of large intestine	6 days	Can divide
Red blood cells	Less than 120 days	Cannot divide
White blood cells	10 hours to decades	Cannot divide
Smooth muscle	Long-lived	Can divide
Cardiac (heart) muscle	Long-lived	Cannot divide
Skeletal muscle	Long-lived	Cannot divide
Neuron (nerve cell)	Long-lived	Most do not divide

4. **Going Further** Cancer is a disease related to cell life span and cell division. If cancer cells were added to the data table, predict what would be written under the columns headed "Life Span" and "Cell Division." Explain the reasoning underlying your predictions.

10–2 Section Assessment

1. **Key Concept** Name the main events of the cell cycle.
2. **Key Concept** Describe what happens during each of the four phases of mitosis.
3. Describe what happens during interphase.
4. What are chromosomes made of?
5. How do prokaryotic cells divide?
6. **Critical Thinking Comparing and Contrasting** How is cytokinesis in plant cells similar to cytokinesis in animal cells? How is it different?

iTEXT Assessment Use iText to review the important concepts in Section 10–2.

Take It to the NET

Read about the relationship between the enzyme telomerase and the process of cell division. Then, construct a time line of the scientists who contributed to this discovery. Use the links provided in the Biology area at the Prentice Hall Web site for help in completing this activity: **www.phschool.com**

3 ASSESS

Evaluate Understanding

Ask students to look at the pie chart in Figure 10–4. Then, call on volunteers to describe the events in each phase of interphase and each phase of mitosis.

Reteach

Have students make a flowchart of the cell division, including what occurs in each of the four phases of mitosis as well as in cytokinesis.

Take It to the NET

Students should find information on the following scientists: Howard Cooke, M. A. Blasco, Thomas Cech, Jerry Shay, and Woodring Wright. The time line should extend from 1986 to 1998. For additional information, visit

www.phschool.com

Use iText to review the key concepts in Section 10–2.

10–2 Section Assessment

1. A cell grows, prepares for division, and divides to form two daughter cells.
2. Students should describe what happens during prophase, metaphase, anaphase, and telophase, as in Figure 10–5.
3. Students should describe what happens during the G_1 phase, S phase, and G_2 phase.
4. DNA, which carries the cell's coded genetic information, and proteins
5. A prokaryotic cell first copies its genetic information before cell division begins. In most prokaryotes, the rest of the process of cell division is a simple matter of separating the contents of the cell into two parts.
6. Cytokinesis is the division of the cytoplasm in both types of cells. The difference is that in plant cells a cell plate forms midway between the divided nuclei.

Answers to . . .

CHECKPOINT The centromeres that join the sister chromatids split, allowing the sister chromatids to separate. The chromosomes continue to move until they separate into two groups near the poles of the spindle.

Figure 10–6 *A cell wall forms in the cell plate.*

Section 10–3

1 FOCUS

Objectives

10.3.1 ***Identify*** a factor that can stop cells from growing.
10.3.2 ***Describe*** how the cell cycle is regulated.
10.3.3 ***Explain*** how cancer cells are different from other cells.

Guide for Reading

Vocabulary Preview

Have students write the vocabulary words, dividing each into its separate syllables as best they can. Remind students that each syllable usually has only one vowel sound. The correct syllabications are: cy·clin, can·cer.

Reading Strategy

Before they read, have students skim the section to find the Key Concepts and copy each onto a note card. Then, as they read, they should make notes of supporting details.

2 INSTRUCT

Controls on Cell Division

Use Visuals

Figure 10–7 Ask: **What happened to the cells between the first petri dish and the second petri dish?** *(The cells divided until a thin layer of cells covered the bottom of the dish.)* Explain that researchers then removed cells from the center of the petri dish, as shown in the third dish. Ask: **What caused the difference shown between the third and fifth petri dishes?** *(The cells began dividing again until they filled the empty space.)* **Why didn't the cells keep dividing until they spilled over the edge of the petri dish?** *(When the cells came into contact with other cells, they responded by not growing.)*

10–3 Regulating the Cell Cycle

Guide for Reading

Key Concepts

- How is the cell cycle regulated?
- How are cancer cells different from other cells?

Vocabulary
cyclin
cancer

Reading Strategy: Summarizing Summarizing helps you understand and remember what you read. Write a main-idea statement for each section. When you have finished the section, compare your statements with those in the study guide.

One of the most striking aspects of cell behavior in a multicellular organism is how carefully cell growth and cell division are controlled. Not all cells move through the cell cycle at the same rate. In the human body, most muscle cells and nerve cells do not divide at all once they have developed. In contrast, the cells of the skin and digestive tract, and cells in the bone marrow that make blood cells, grow and divide rapidly throughout life. Such cells may pass through a complete cycle every few hours. This process provides new cells to replace those that wear out or break down.

Controls on Cell Division

Scientists can observe the effects of controlled cell growth in the laboratory by placing some cells in a petri dish containing nutrient broth. The nutrient broth provides food for the cells. Most cells will grow until they form a thin layer covering the bottom of the dish, as shown in **Figure 10–7.** Then, the cells stop growing. When cells come into contact with other cells, they respond by not growing.

If cells are removed from the center of the dish, however, the cells bordering the open space will begin dividing until they have filled the empty space. These experiments show that the controls on cell growth and cell division can be turned on and off.

Something similar happens within the body. When an injury such as a cut in the skin or a break in a bone occurs, cells at the edges of the injury are stimulated to divide rapidly. This action produces new cells, starting the process of healing. When the healing process nears completion, the rate of cell division slows down, controls on growth are restored, and everything returns to normal.

▼ **Figure 10–7** Cells in a petri dish will continue to grow until they come into contact with other cells. **Applying Concepts** *What would happen if the cells continued to divide?*

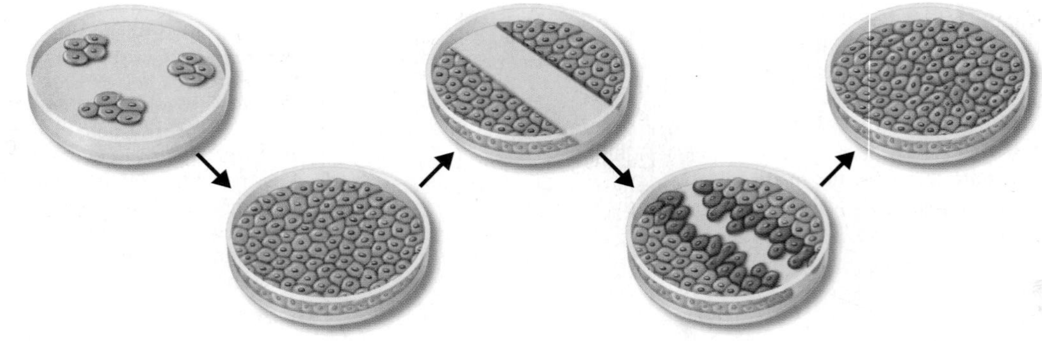

SECTION RESOURCES

Print:

- ***Teaching Resources,*** Section Review 10–3, Chapter 10 Exploration
- ***Guided Reading and Study Workbook,*** Section 10–3

Technology:

- ***iText,*** Section 10–3

Cell Cycle Regulators

For many years, biologists searched for a substance that might regulate the cell cycle—something that would "tell" cells when it was time to divide, duplicate their chromosomes, or enter another phase of the cycle. In the early 1980s, biologists found the substance.

Several scientists, including Tim Hunt of Great Britain and Mark Kirschner of the United States, discovered that cells in mitosis contained a protein that when injected into a nondividing cell, would cause a mitotic spindle to form. Such an experiment is shown in **Figure 10–8.** To their surprise, they discovered that the amount of this protein in the cell rose and fell in time with the cell cycle. They decided to call this protein **cyclin** because it seemed to regulate the cell cycle. Investigators have since discovered a family of closely related proteins known as cyclins. **Cyclins regulate the timing of the cell cycle in eukaryotic cells.**

The discovery of cyclins was just the beginning. More recently, dozens of other proteins have been discovered that also help to regulate the cell cycle. There are two types of regulatory proteins: internal regulators and external regulators.

CHECKPOINT *What are cyclins?*

Internal Regulators Proteins that respond to events inside the cell are called internal regulators. For example, several regulatory proteins make sure that a cell does not enter mitosis until all its chromosomes have been replicated. Another regulatory protein prevents a cell from entering anaphase until all its chromosomes are attached to the mitotic spindle.

External Regulators Proteins that respond to events outside the cell are called external regulators. External regulators direct cells to speed up or slow down the cell cycle. Growth factors are among the most important external regulators. They stimulate the growth and division of cells, and are especially important during embryonic development and wound healing. Molecules found on the surfaces of neighboring cells often have an opposite effect, causing cells to slow down or stop their cell cycles. These signals prevent excessive cell growth and keep the tissues of the body from disrupting each other.

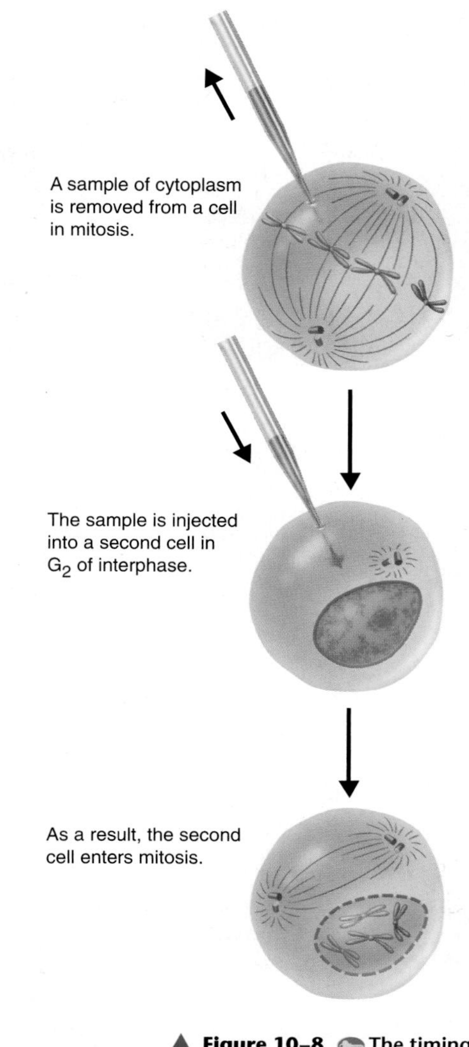

A sample of cytoplasm is removed from a cell in mitosis.
The sample is injected into a second cell in G_2 of interphase.
As a result, the second cell enters mitosis.

▲ **Figure 10–8 The timing of the cell cycle is regulated by cyclins.** When cytoplasm from a cell in mitosis is injected into another cell, the second cell enters mitosis. The reason for this effect is a protein called cyclin, which triggers cell division.

Cell Cycle Regulators

Use Visuals

Figure 10–8 Emphasize that this sequence shows an experiment carried out by scientists who were researching what regulates the cell cycle. Ask: **How can you tell that the first cell shown is in mitosis?** *(The illustration shows that a spindle has formed and the chromosomes are lined up across the middle of the cell. The cell is therefore in metaphase.)* **How can you tell that the second cell shown is in interphase?** *(The illustration shows that the nuclear envelope is intact.)* **How can you tell that the third cell shown has begun mitosis?** *(The chromosomes are visible, and the spindle has begun to form. This is prophase.)* **What caused the second cell to enter mitosis?** *(The cyclin injected into the second cell from the first cell caused the second cell to enter mitosis.)*

Build Science Skills

Designing Experiments Divide the class into small groups, and ask each group to design an experiment to test the following hypothesis: Substance C regulates when a cell begins each phase of the cell cycle. Groups' experiments will vary. Each group, though, should designate Substance C as the variable in its experiment. A typical experiment will focus on either increasing or decreasing the amount of Substance C at various points in the cell cycle and then observing what effect this has on the cell.

TIME SAVER PRESENTATIONS MADE EASY!

The Presentation Assistant Plus contains the Prentice Hall Presentation Pro and the Transparencies, which provide easy-to-follow visual support for every step of this lesson. If you have a computer presentation station, use Prentice Hall Presentation Pro for Section 10–3, or use the transparencies listed here.

Section 10–3:

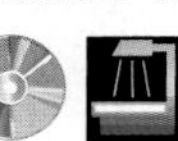

Interest Grabber
Section Outline
Control of Cell Division
Figure 10–8

Answers to . . .

CHECKPOINT *Cyclins are proteins that regulate the timing of the cell cycle in eukaryotic cells.*

Figure 10–7 *The cells would form more layers and possibly grow out of the petri dish.*

Uncontrolled Cell Growth

Encourage students to view "Skin Cancer: Deadly Cells" on the BioDetectives Videotape.

Use Community Resources

Invite a representative of a local cancer support group to address the class about the causes, symptoms, and treatments of various kinds of cancer. A day before the speaker makes the presentation, discuss with students the kinds of questions they might ask, and then have each student write two or three questions.

3 ASSESS

Evaluate Understanding

Call on students at random to explain what controls cell division, what regulates the cell cycle, and why cancer cells are different from normal cells in the body.

Reteach

Have students write a few paragraphs that could be used in a pamphlet given to the public. The purpose of the pamphlet is to explain the regulation of cell division and how cancer cells have lost the growth control that normal body cells have.

ALTERNATIVE ASSESSMENT

The strategies of student-designed drugs will vary. They should, however, function to interrupt the cell cycle and prevent cell division.

Use iText to review the key concepts in Section 10–3.

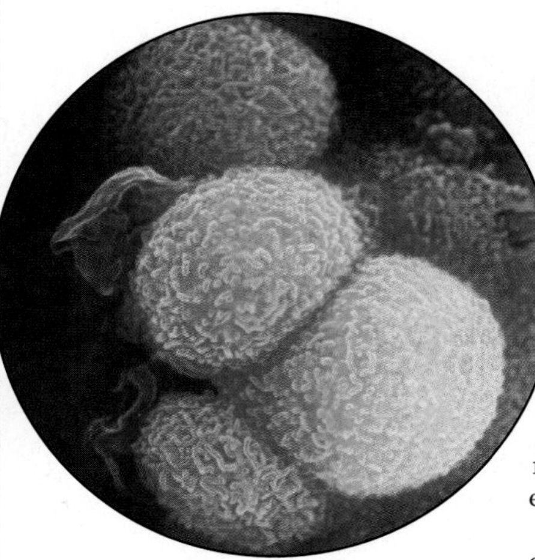

(magnification: 6900×)

▲ **Figure 10–9** **Cancer cells do not respond to the signals that would normally stop them from dividing.** Masses of cancer cells form tumors that can damage normal tissues. These cancer cells are from a cancer tumor in the large intestine.

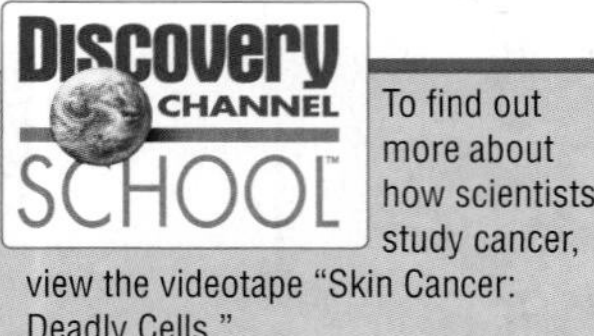

To find out more about how scientists study cancer, view the videotape "Skin Cancer: Deadly Cells."

Uncontrolled Cell Growth

Why is cell growth regulated so carefully? The principal reason may be that the consequences of uncontrolled cell growth in a multicellular organism are very severe. **Cancer,** a disorder in which some of the body's own cells lose the ability to control growth, is one such example. **Cancer cells do not respond to the signals that regulate the growth of most cells. As a result, they form masses of cells called tumors that can damage the surrounding tissues.** Cancer cells may break loose from tumors and spread throughout the body, disrupting normal activities and causing serious medical problems or even death. **Figure 10–9** shows typical cancer cells.

What causes the loss of growth control that results in cancer? The various forms of cancer have many causes, including smoking tobacco, radiation exposure, and even viral infection. All cancers, however, have one thing in common: The control over the cell cycle has broken down. Some cancer cells will no longer respond to external growth regulators, while others fail to produce the internal regulators that ensure orderly growth.

An astonishing number of cancer cells have a defect in a gene called p53, which normally halts the cell cycle until all chromosomes have been properly replicated. As a result, chromosome damage builds up in such cells. This damage causes the cells to lose the information needed to respond to signals that would normally control their growth.

Cancer is a serious disease. Understanding and combating cancer remains a major scientific challenge, but scientists at least know where to start. Cancer is a disease of the cell cycle, and conquering cancer will require a much deeper understanding of the processes that control cell division.

10–3 Section Assessment

1. **Key Concept** What chemicals regulate the cell cycle? How do they work?
2. **Key Concept** What happens when cells do not respond to the signals that normally regulate their growth?
3. How do cells respond to contact with other cells?
4. Why can cancer be considered a disease of the cell cycle?
5. **Critical Thinking Formulating Hypotheses** Write a hypothesis about what you think would happen if cyclin were injected into a cell that was in mitosis.

iText Assessment Use iText to review the important concepts in Section 10–3.

ALTERNATIVE ASSESSMENT

Designing an Anticancer Drug

Imagine that you are developing a drug that will inhibit the growth of cancer cells. Use your knowledge of the cell cycle to describe how the drug would target and prevent the multiplication of cancer cells. Use the Internet to compare your anticancer treatment with those currently in use.

10–3 Section Assessment

1. Cyclins regulate the timing of the cell cycle in eukaryotic cells. Cyclin causes a mitotic spindle to form and triggers cell division.
2. Such cells, called cancer cells, form masses of cells called tumors that can damage the surrounding tissues.
3. Normal cells respond by not growing.
4. Cancer is a disorder in which some of the body's cells lose the ability to control growth, and the cell cycle is the series of events that cells go through as they grow and divide.
5. A typical hypothesis might suggest that the cyclin would have no effect because the cell was already in mitosis.

Stem Cells: Promises and Problems

Every cell in the human body, including muscle cells, neurons, and blood cells, developed from a single fertilized cell. The cells that form during the first few divisions after fertilization can potentially become any type of cell in the body. During development before birth, however, most cells become differentiated, which means that some cells become bone cells, others become skin cells, and still others become cells in blood vessels.

Once a cell becomes a specific type of cell, it remains that way—it cannot be changed into another type of cell. Some cells, however, do not become specialized. These cells, called stem cells, can develop into any number of specialized cells. Stem cells are abundant in developing embryos, but adults also have stem cells. Stem cells in the bone marrow, for example, can produce more than a dozen types of blood cells that are used to replace those lost due to normal wear and tear.

Stem Cells in Medicine

Although your body produces billions of new cells every day, it is not always able to produce the right kind of cell to replace those damaged by injury or disease. For example, the body is not able to produce new neurons to repair spinal cord injuries, such as those that cause paralysis. Because of this, there is no way for doctors to restore movement and feeling to people who are paralyzed.

Stem cells may be the perfect solution to this problem. Recently, researchers have found that implants of stem cells can reverse the effects of brain injuries in mice. There is hope that the same will hold true for humans and that a similar technique can be used to reverse brain and spinal cord injuries in humans. It may also be possible to use stem cells to grow new liver tissue, to replace heart valves, and to reverse the effects of diabetes.

Sources of Stem Cells

Stem cells can easily be collected from embryonic tissue, but research with human embryos raises serious moral and ethical issues. The fact that embryonic tissue is genetically different from that of a person who might need a stem cell transplant presents a problem, too. The immune system of a transplant recipient might reject the stem cells, causing the transplant to fail. Is there any way to solve these problems?

A breakthrough in stem cell research may be at hand. Using stem cells from adults, researchers have shown that bone marrow stem cells can sometimes develop into nerve cells, and that brain stem cells can develop into blood cells. Experiments like these may usher in an era in which doctors literally grow new parts—replacement tissues—from a person's own cells.

On Your Own

Research the latest information on stem cell research by visiting the Prentice Hall Web site at **www.phschool.com**. Write a brief report of your findings.

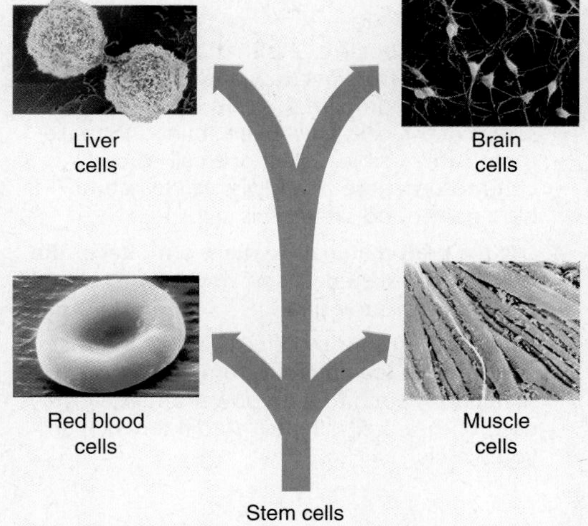

After students have read this feature, you might want to do one or more of the following:

- Lead a discussion about how cells become differentiated as an embryo grows.
- Ask students to hypothesize why adults don't have stem cells that can give rise to every kind of cell in the body.
- The use of stem cells has many applications in medicine. Diseases that might benefit from stem-cell therapy include heart disease, arthritis, Parkinson's disease, Alzheimer's disease, and diabetes. Stem cells might also be used in treating such conditions as stroke, burns, and spinal-cord injuries. Discuss with students how stem cells might be useful in treating each of these diseases and conditions.
- Although researchers are working on ways to derive stem cells from adult cells, the primary sources of stem cells are still embryos and fetal tissue. Lead a discussion about the moral and ethical objections to using such cells in research and therapy.

On Your Own

Encourage students to visit **www.phschool.com** for the most current information on this topic.

FACTS AND FIGURES

Three kinds of stem cells

A human fertilized egg has the potential to form a whole organism, and therefore the egg and the cells that result from early cell division are called totipotent stem cells. About five days after fertilization, the cells develop into a blastocyst, with an outer layer of cells and an inner cell mass. The inner cells go on to form almost all the tissues of the human body, although they don't have the potential to form a whole organism. They are called pluripotent stem cells. These cells eventually specialize further to become stem cells that can give rise to specific kinds of cells. For example, a blood stem cell can give rise to both red and white blood cells, and a skin stem cell can give rise to different kinds of skin cells. These stem cells are called multipotent stem cells, and they are present in adults. For most medical purposes, pluripotent stem cells are used.

Exploration

Objective Students will be able to observe what the phases of the cell cycle look like in a typical plant cell.

Skills Focus **Classifying, Using Models**

Time 50 minutes

Advance Prep Assemble a variety of materials for students to make their models, including index cards, beads, yarn, pipe cleaners, licorice, and gum drops.

Prelab Discussion Have students read the procedure and ask any questions they have about materials or about what they are to do. Then, ask: **In the data table, why are the phases listed in that sequence?** *(That is the sequence in which those phases occur in the cell cycle.)* **Of the phases listed in the table, which do you predict will have the greatest number of cells once you have made your observations?** *(Many students will predict that interphase will have the greatest number, because it encompasses most of the cell cycle.)*

Teaching Tips

- Circulate among students as they work, asking such questions as: What do you think is going on in this phase? What phases are you seeing the most?
- You may want to calculate class averages and compare them to the results of individuals or groups to demonstrate the importance of sample size.

Procedure

1. Help students find the root tips on the slides.

2. Make sure that students are looking at the meristematic cells on the slides. Point out the darkly stained chromosomes.

6. Discuss with students how to choose 25 cells at random. They could choose 25 cells that are touching or randomly point to 25 cells. Ensure that they are careful not to choose a cell twice.

Exploration

Observing the Phases of the Cell Cycle

In a growing root, the cells at the tip of the root are constantly dividing. Because each cell divides independently of the others, a root tip contains many cells at different phases of the cell cycle. This makes a root tip an excellent tissue in which to study the cell cycle. In this investigation, you will identify and describe the phases of the cell cycle in root tip cells.

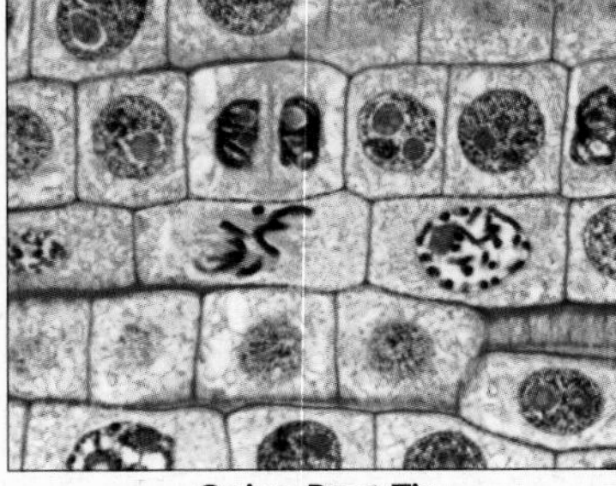

Onion Root Tip
(magnification: 700×)

Problem **What do the phases of the cell cycle look like in a typical plant cell?**

Materials

- microscope
- prepared slides of onion root tips
- scissors
- tape or glue
- craft materials such as beads, yarn, and pipe cleaners

Skills Classifying, Using Models

Procedure

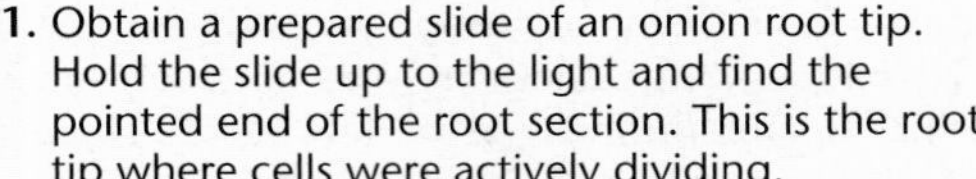

1. Obtain a prepared slide of an onion root tip. Hold the slide up to the light and find the pointed end of the root section. This is the root tip where cells were actively dividing.
2. Place the slide on the microscope stage with the root tip pointing away from you. Using the low-power objective, adjust the focus of the microscope until the root tip is clearly visible. Just above the root tip is a region that contains many new small cells. The larger cells of this region were in the process of dividing when the slide was made. These are the cells you will be observing.
3. Observe the boxlike cells that are arranged in rows. Scan across one row and down to the next row to compare the cells. The chromosomes of the cells have been stained to make them easily visible. Select one cell whose chromosomes are clearly visible. Switch to high power and sketch this cell.
4. Use the craft materials to make a model of the cell that you sketched, showing how its chromosomes are arranged.
5. Select at least four more cells whose internal appearances are different from the first cell you sketched. Switch to high power and sketch each of these cells. Repeat step 4 for each cell you sketch.
6. On a separate sheet of paper, make a copy of the data table shown. Choose 25 root tip cells at random and decide which phase of the cell cycle each is in. Record the number of cells in each phase in your copy of the data table. If you find that some cells appear to be between two phases, record those observations as well.
7. Look closely at your sketches and models. Arrange the models in order to represent the process of cell division.
8. Refer to **Figure 10–5** on pages 246 and 247 to determine whether you have ordered the phases of the cell cycle correctly. Correct the order of your models, if necessary, and label each of the models and sketches with the name of the phase it represents. Use the models to explain the process of cell division to another student.

Data Table

Phase	Number of Cells
Interphase	
Prophase	
Metaphase	
Anaphase	
Telophase	

Sample Data Table

Phase	Number of Cells
Interphase	19
Prophase	3
Metaphase	1
Anaphase	1
Telophase	1

Analyze and Conclude

1. **Analyzing Data** Do your results indicate that there were more cells in some phases than in others? Identify the most common phase(s) and explain what these differences in numbers of cells might mean.
2. **Drawing Conclusions** What evidence did you observe that shows mitosis is a continuous process, not a series of separate events?
3. **Using Models** Describe what is happening in each phase of your cell models.
4. **Applying Concepts** Cells in the root divide many times as the root grows longer and thicker. With each cell division, the chromosomes are divided between two daughter cells, yet the number of chromosomes in each cell does not change. What process ensures that the normal number of chromosomes is restored after each cell division? During which part of the cell cycle does this process occur?

Go Further

Making Models In muscle cells, mitosis is not always followed by cell division. Instead, repeated cycles of mitosis result in long, tubular cells with many nuclei. These cells are called muscle fibers. Make a model that shows how mitosis occurs in a muscle fiber.

Take It to the NET Go to the Prentice Hall Web site at **www.phschool.com** and follow the links for this lab. Add your data to the pool of data from students across the country. Compare your numbers of cells in the various phases to those of other students. Why might they be different?

Expected Outcome Students will identify and make models of the phases of the cell cycle, and they will determine that most of the onion cells are in interphase.

Go Further

Students' models should show that cells repeatedly proceed through the four phases of mitosis but that cytokinesis never occurs.

Take It to the NET

Have students visit the Prentice Hall Web site to pool and analyze data with students nationwide. For more information, visit **www.phschool.com**

Analyze and Conclude

1. Most students will observe that more cells are in interphase than any other phase of mitosis, the reason being that interphase is the longest phase of the cell cycle.

2. Students should observe that many cells appear to be in intermediate phases rather than in a specific mitotic phase.

3. Students should describe what is happening to cells in the four phases of mitosis.

4. The duplication of chromosomes during the S phase of the cell cycle ensures that each daughter cell has the normal number of chromosomes after cell division.

Chapter 10 Study Guide

Study Tip

Divide the class into pairs, and have students quiz each other about the vocabulary words and the chapter concepts.

Thinking Visually

1. The cell grows and duplicates its DNA and centrioles.
2. The chromosomes line up across the middle of the cell.
3. The sister chromatids separate into individual chromosomes and move apart.
4. The cell membrane pinches the cytoplasm in half.

Chapter 10 Assessment

Reviewing Content

1. d	**5.** c	**9.** a
2. c	**6.** a	**10.** a
3. b	**7.** b	
4. c	**8.** b	

Understanding Concepts

11. During cell division, a cell divides into two new daughter cells.

12. When a cell is small, the information stored in its DNA is able to meet all of the cell's needs. But if a cell were to grow without limit, an "information crisis" would occur.

13. Cell volume is the amount of material inside the cell. Surface area is the total area of the cell's membrane. Ratio of surface area to volume is the surface area divided by the volume.

14. A cell's ratio of surface area to volume decreases as a cell grows larger. This means that the area available for diffusion decreases, as well. Thus, if a cell grows too large, it is unable to take in all needed materials and expel all its wastes. These problems impose limits on the growth of a cell.

15. Well before cell division, each chromosome is duplicated. At the beginning of cell division, each chromosome consists of two identical sister chromatids.

16. Together, interphase and cell division make up the cell cycle.

Chapter 10 Study Guide

10–1 Cell Growth

Key Concept

- The larger a cell becomes, the more demands the cell places on its DNA and the more trouble the cell has moving enough nutrients and wastes across the cell membrane.

Vocabulary
cell division, p. 243

10–2 Cell Division

Key Concepts

- During the cell cycle, a cell grows, prepares for division, and divides to form two daughter cells, each of which then begins the cycle again.
- Biologists divide the events of mitosis into four phases: prophase, metaphase, anaphase, and telophase.
- During prophase in animal cells, the centrioles separate and take up positions on opposite sides of the nucleus.
- During metaphase, the chromosomes line up across the center of the cell. Microtubules connect the centromere of each chromosome to the poles of the spindle.
- During anaphase, the centromeres that join the sister chromatids split, allowing the sister chromatids to separate and become individual chromosomes.
- In telophase, the chromosomes, which were distinct and condensed, begin to disperse into a tangle of dense material.
- Cytokinesis is the division of the cytoplasm.

Vocabulary
chromatid, p. 244
centromere, p. 244
interphase, p. 245
cell cycle, p. 245
mitosis, p. 245
prophase, p. 246
centriole, p. 246
spindle, p. 247
metaphase, p. 248
anaphase, p. 248
telophase, p. 248
cytokinesis, p. 248

10–3 Regulating the Cell Cycle

Key Concepts

- Cyclins regulate the timing of the cell cycle in eukaryotic cells.
- Cancer cells do not respond to the signals that regulate the growth of most cells. As a result, they form masses of cells called tumors that can damage the surrounding tissues.

Vocabulary
cyclin, p. 251
cancer, p. 252

Thinking Visually

Using the information in this chapter, complete the following cycle diagram of the cell cycle.

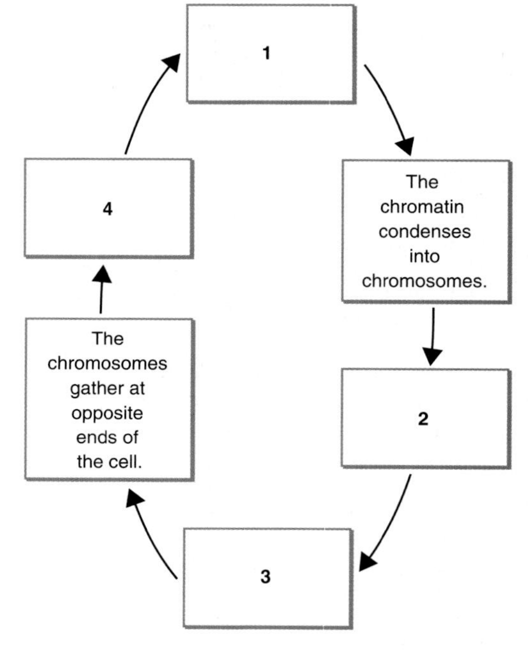
1
The chromatin condenses into chromosomes.
2
3
The chromosomes gather at opposite ends of the cell.
4

CHAPTER RESOURCES

Print:
- ***Teaching Resources,*** Chapter Vocabulary Review, Graphic Organizer
- ***Chapter Tests: Levels A and B,*** Chapter 10 Test
- ***PH Assessment System,*** Practice Test

Technology:
- ***Computer Test Bank,*** Chapter 10 Test
- ***iText,*** Chapter 10 Assessment

Chapter 10 Assessment

Reviewing Content

Choose the letter that best answers the question or completes the statement.

1. The rate at which materials enter and leave through the cell membrane depends on the cell's
   a. volume. c. mass.
   b. weight. d. surface area.
2. The process of cell division results in
   a. sister chromatids. c. two daughter cells.
   b. mitosis. d. unregulated growth.
3. Pairs of identical chromatids are attached to each other at an area called the
   a. centriole. c. spindle.
   b. centromere. d. chromosome.
4. If a cell has 12 chromosomes, how many chromosomes will each of its daughter cells have after mitosis?
   a. 4 c. 12
   b. 6 d. 24
5. At the beginning of cell division, a chromosome consists of two
   a. centromeres. c. chromatids.
   b. centrioles. d. spindles.
6. The phase of mitosis during which chromosomes become visible and the centrioles separate from one another is
   a. prophase. c. metaphase.
   b. anaphase. d. telophase.
7. Metaphase is best illustrated in which figure?

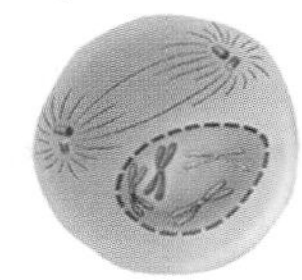
a.

c.

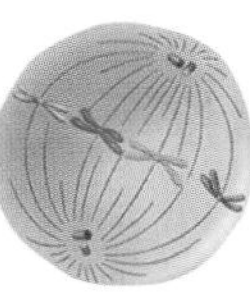
b.

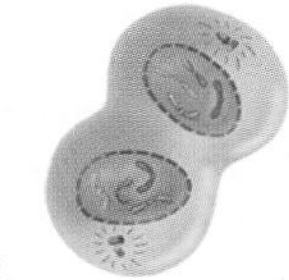
d.

8. The timing of the cell cycle in eukaryotic cells is controlled by a group of closely related proteins known as
   a. chromatids. c. centromeres.
   b. cyclins. d. centrioles.
9. In the cell cycle, external regulators direct cells to
   a. speed up or slow down the cycle.
   b. remain unchanged.
   c. proceed and then stop the cycle.
   d. grow uncontrollably.
10. Uncontrolled cell division occurs in
    a. cancer. c. cytokinesis.
    b. mitosis. d. cyclin.

Understanding Concepts

11. Summarize what happens during the process of cell division.
12. Explain how a cell's DNA can limit the cell's size.
13. Describe what is meant by each of the following terms: *cell volume, cell surface area, ratio of surface area to volume.*
14. How is a cell's potential growth affected by its ratio of surface area to volume?
15. Describe how a cell's chromosomes change as a cell prepares to divide.
16. What is the relationship between interphase and cell division?
17. Summarize what happens during interphase.
18. Explain how the following terms are related to each other: *DNA, centromere, chromosome, chromatid.*
19. List the following events in the correct sequence, and describe what happens during each event: anaphase, metaphase, prophase, and telophase.
20. After cytokinesis, how does the number of chromosomes in the two new cells compare with the number in the original cell?
21. Summarize what happens during the cell cycle.
22. When some cells are removed from the center of a tissue culture, will new cells replace the cells that were removed? Explain.
23. Describe the role of cyclins in the cell cycle.
24. Why is it important that cell growth in a multicellular organism be regulated so carefully?
25. How do cancer cells differ from noncancerous cells?

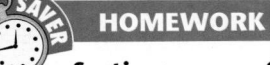

HOMEWORK GUIDE

Section:	**Questions:**
Section 10–1:	1, 2, 11–14, 26, 27
Section 10–2:	3–7, 15– 21, 29–35
Section 10–3:	8–10, 22–25, 28

17. During interphase, a cell increases in size, synthesizes new proteins and organelles, duplicates its chromosomes, and prepares for cell division by producing needed organelles and molecules.

18. The genetic information that is passed on from one generation of cells to the next is carried by chromosomes, which are made up of DNA. Before cell division, chromosomes are duplicated, so that each chromosome consists of two identical "sister" chromatids. Each pair of chromatids is attached at an area called the centromere.

19. Prophase: Chromatin condenses into chromosomes; centrioles separate; spindle begins to form; nuclear membrane breaks down. Metaphase: Chromosomes line up across middle of cell with spindle fibers connected to their centromeres. Anaphase: Sister chromatids separate and move apart. Telophase: Chromosomes gather at opposite ends of cell and lose distinct shape; new nuclear membranes form.

20. The number of chromosomes in each of the two cells equals the number in the original cell.

21. A cell grows, prepares for division, and divides to form two daughter cells, each of which then begins the cycle again.

22. Yes, new cells will replace the removed cells because of the process of cell division, which will continue until the new cells come in contact with other cells. When that occurs, cell division will stop.

23. Cyclins regulate the timing of the cell cycle in eukaryotic cells.

24. The consequences of uncontrolled cell growth are severe, as, for example, in cancer.

25. Cancer cells do not respond to the signals that regulate the growth of most cells. As a result, they form masses of cells called tumors that can damage the surrounding tissues.

Critical Thinking

26. Students' models should demonstrate that as the size of a cube increases, its volume increases faster than its surface area. As a result, the ratio of surface area to volume decreases as the size of the cube increases.

27. Surface area = $5 \text{ mm} \times 5 \text{ mm} \times 6 = 150 \text{ mm}^2$. Volume = $5 \text{ mm} \times 5 \text{ mm} \times 5 \text{ mm} = 125 \text{ mm}^3$.
Ratio of surface area to volume = $150/125 = 6:5$.

28. The structures that might play a major role are the chromosomes, because the chromosomes carry the genetic information from one cell to another. Any defect in chromosomes can be passed on from a cancerous cell to daughter cells.

29. A typical experiment might suggest comparing the rate of cell division over time in the same kind of plant cell at various temperatures.

30. The cell is in metaphase. It most resembles that of a tiger because there is no evidence of a cell wall, as there would be in the cell of a tree. Also, this cell has centrioles at opposite ends of the spindle, and plant cells do not have centrioles.

31. The presence of many nuclei indicates that mitosis has occurred repeatedly without cytokinesis having occurred, because there is still only one cell.

32. Cell division is similar in animal and plant cells. In prophase, though, plant cells do not have centrioles, as animal cells do. Plant cells organize their mitotic spindles from regions known as centrosomes. Also, during cytokinesis in most animal cells, the cell membrane moves inward until the cytoplasm is pinched into two nearly equal parts. In plant cells, a cell plate forms midway between the divided nuclei and gradually develops into a separating membrane. A cell wall then appears in the cell plate.

33. Because nerve cells seldom undergo mitosis, the body is usually unable to repair damage to parts of the nervous system.

Chapter 10 Assessment

Critical Thinking

26. Using Models Use paper, blocks, or another material to create three-dimensional models demonstrating how the ratio of surface area to volume changes as the size of a cube changes.

27. Calculating Calculate the surface area, volume, and ratio of surface area to volume of an imaginary cubic cell with a length of 5 mm.

28. Inferring Recall the functions of the different structures in a eukaryotic cell. Which of those structures might play a major role in the development of cancer cells? Explain.

29. Designing an Experiment A classmate suggests that temperature might affect the rate of mitosis in plant cells. Design an experiment to test this hypothesis.

30. Interpreting Graphics The diagram below shows a phase of mitosis. Identify the phase and indicate whether the cell most resembles that of a tree or a tiger. Explain your answer.

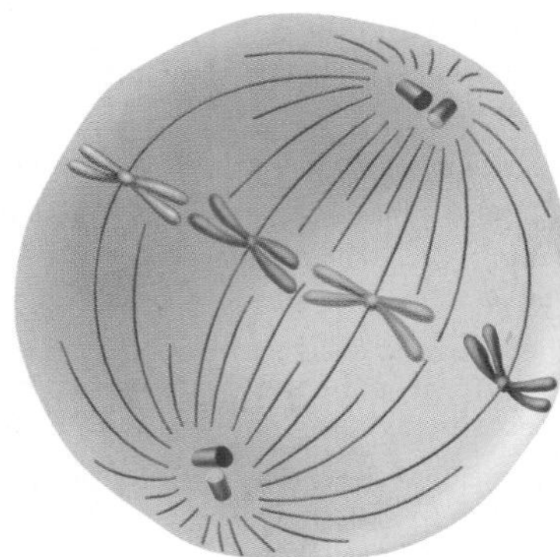

31. Formulating Hypotheses Some cells are multinucleated, or have several nuclei within the cytoplasm of a single cell. Considering the events in a typical cell cycle, how might multinucleated cells form?

32. Comparing and Contrasting Describe the differences between cell division in an animal cell and cell division in a plant cell.

33. Predicting The nerve cells in the human nervous system seldom undergo mitosis. Predict how well you think the body is able to repair damage to parts of the nervous system.

34. Formulating Hypotheses Each type of eukaryotic organism has a characteristic number of chromosomes. All human cells, for example, have 46 chromosomes in their nuclei; fruit fly cells have 8 chromosomes. How might a particular type of organism be affected if this pattern were not repeated in each generation?

35. Making Connections Recall what you learned about the characteristics of life in Chapter 1. How is cell division related to one or more of those characteristics?

Performance-Based Assessment

Demonstrate the Cell Cycle A flip-book consists of pages of sequential drawings that when flipped, appear to move. Create a flip-book movie of the steps in the cell cycle. Be sure to show what happens to the chromosomes at each step. Exchange your flip-book with another student. Look at the other student's movie, and write a review of it.

Take It to the NET

When the cell cycle goes awry, cancer can result. Visit the Prentice Hall Web site at **www.phschool.com** to find out more about cancer. Then, answer the following questions:

- What are the four different categories of cancer?
- List four prefixes used in naming cancers and explain the meaning of each.
- Describe the two mechanisms by which cancers are spread through the body.
- What is the difference between a benign tumor and a malignant tumor?

Performance-Based Assessment

Students' flip books should include several illustrations for each of the four phases of the cell cycle, including several pages for each phase of mitosis. Those pages illustrating mitosis should be similar to the illustrations in Figure 10–5. The flip books should illustrate all the major events in the cell cycle on pages 246–247. Initiate a way that students can exchange flip books at random, such as drawing names out of a hat. Students should evaluate a flip book by deciding how well the flip-book movie puts across the events of the cell cycle.

Standardized Test Prep

Test-Taking Tip If after reading all of the answer choices you are not sure which one is correct, eliminate the choices that you know are wrong. Then, select your answer from the remaining choices.

Directions: Choose the letter that best answers the question or completes the statement.

1. Which of the following is NOT related to a cell's ratio of surface area to volume?
(A) cell size
(B) rate of growth
(C) number of nuclei
(D) efficiency of cell's transport of oxygen
(E) efficiency of cell's transport of nutrients

2. Which family of proteins regulates the timing of the cell cycle in eukaryotes?
(A) chromatids
(B) chromosomes
(C) nutrients
(D) DNA and RNA
(E) cyclins

3. Which of the following is NOT a phase of mitosis?
(A) anaphase
(B) metaphase
(C) telophase
(D) prophase
(E) interphase

4. Chromatids are attached to each other at the
(A) nucleus.
(B) centriole.
(C) centromere.
(D) cell plate.
(E) cell membrane.

5. In the cell cycle, the period between cell divisions is called
(A) interphase.
(B) prophase.
(C) G_3 phase.
(D) telophase.
(E) cytokinesis.

Questions 6–7 Each of the lettered choices below may refer to the following numbered statements. Select the best lettered choice.

(A) Mitosis
(B) Cell cycle
(C) Cytokinesis
(D) Cancer
(E) Interphase

6. a process in which unregulated cell division occurs

7. a process of cytoplasmic division

8. series of events that cells go through as they divide and grow

9. the division of the cell nucleus

Questions 10–12

The spindle fibers of a dividing cell were labeled with a fluorescent dye. At the beginning of anaphase, a laser beam was used to stop the dye from glowing on one side of the cell, thereby marking the fibers, as shown in the second diagram. The laser did not inhibit the normal function of the fibers.

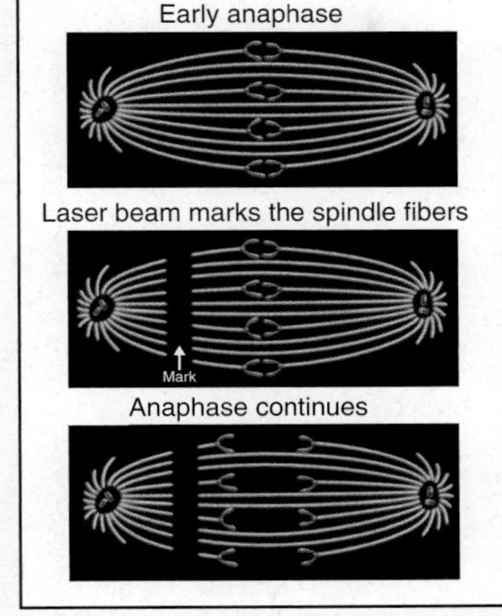

10. This experiment tests a hypothesis about
(A) how chromosomes migrate during cell division.
(B) how fluorescent dyes work in the cell.
(C) the effect of lasers on cells.
(D) the effect of lasers on fluorescent dye.
(E) why cells divide.

11. The diagram shows that the spindle fibers
(A) shorten on the chromosome side of the mark.
(B) lengthen on the chromosome side of the mark.
(C) shorten on the centriole side of the mark.
(D) lengthen on the centriole side of the mark.
(E) do not change in size on either side of the mark.

12. A valid conclusion that can be drawn from this experiment is that
(A) centrioles pull chromosomes toward the poles of the cell.
(B) chromosomes do not migrate in the presence of dye.
(C) lasers inhibit the migration of chromosomes.
(D) chromosomes migrate only when treated with dye.
(E) chromosomes travel along the fibers toward the poles of the cell.

Standardized Test Prep

1. C	**5.** A	**9.** A
2. E	**6.** D	**10.** A
3. E	**7.** C	**11.** A
4. C	**8.** B	**12.** E

Chapter 10 Assessment (continued)

34. If the pattern were not constant, each type of organism could not stay the same, and there would be no species continuity.

35. Students might mention that organisms are made of units called cells and that organisms grow and develop as their cells divide.

Take It to the NET

• Carcinomas, which arise from cells that cover external and internal body surfaces; sarcomas, which arise from cells in the body's supporting tissues; lymphomas, which arise in the lymph nodes; and leukemias, which are cancers of the blood cells.

• Student answers may include *adeno-* (gland), *chrondro-* (cartilage), *erythro-* (red blood cell), *hemangio-* (blood vessels), *hepato-* (liver), *lipo-* (fat), *lympho-* (lymphocyte), *melano-* (pigment cell), *myelo-* (bone marrow), *myo-* (muscle), and *osteo-* (bone).

• Invasion is the direct migration and penetration by cancer cells into neighboring tissues. Metastasis is the ability of cancer cells to penetrate into lymphatic and blood vessels, circulate through the bloodstream, and then invade normal tissues elsewhere in the body.

• A malignant tumor is one that can spread to other parts of the body, while a benign tumor does not spread.

www.phschool.com

Unit 4

Dear Colleague,

The year was 1963, and the news article was from Stockholm. My teacher reserved a small bulletin board right next to the blackboard for newspaper clippings that dealt with science, and this particular one caught my eye. It seemed that three people named Watson, Crick, and Wilkins had just received a Nobel Prize for unraveling the structure of DNA.

A few days after the article appeared, our teacher took some time to tell us a little about DNA and about something he called the "double helix" model. To tell the truth, I was a little confused. Our textbook barely mentioned DNA, and it was only our teacher's enthusiasm that made me remember this as something important.

As the years went by, I came to appreciate the clippings on that bulletin board more and more. Not everything worth knowing, it was clear, was in the textbook. One of the most exciting things about the sciences—and biology in particular—is how quickly things can change.

In the 1970s, I had the good fortune to start my professional career in the same building in which Allan Maxam and Walter Gilbert first developed their technique for reading the sequence of DNA. Such techniques, Gilbert would later point out, might well revolutionize the study of genetics. Before long, it became clear that such talk was, if anything, an understatement.

In 1999, one of my colleagues returned from a conference and handed me a shiny computer disk. On that disk was the complete DNA sequence of the fruit fly *Drosophila melanogaster*. In just a few months of intensive work, a private laboratory had sequenced the genome of the most important of all organisms for the study of genetics. Only a bit more than a year later, the human genome followed.

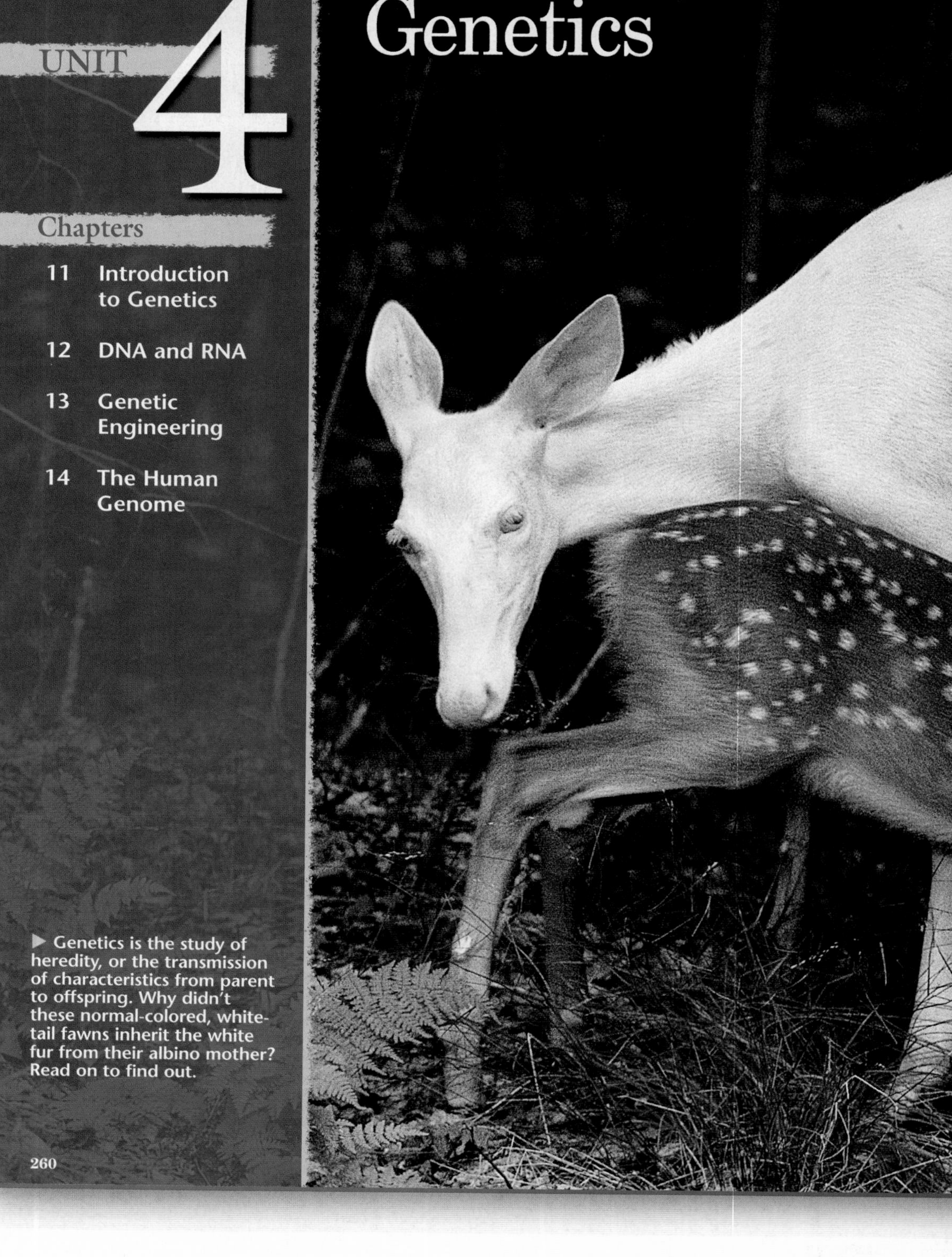

UNIT 4 Genetics

Chapters

▶ Genetics is the study of heredity, or the transmission of characteristics from parent to offspring. Why didn't these normal-colored, white-tail fawns inherit the white fur from their albino mother? Read on to find out.

260

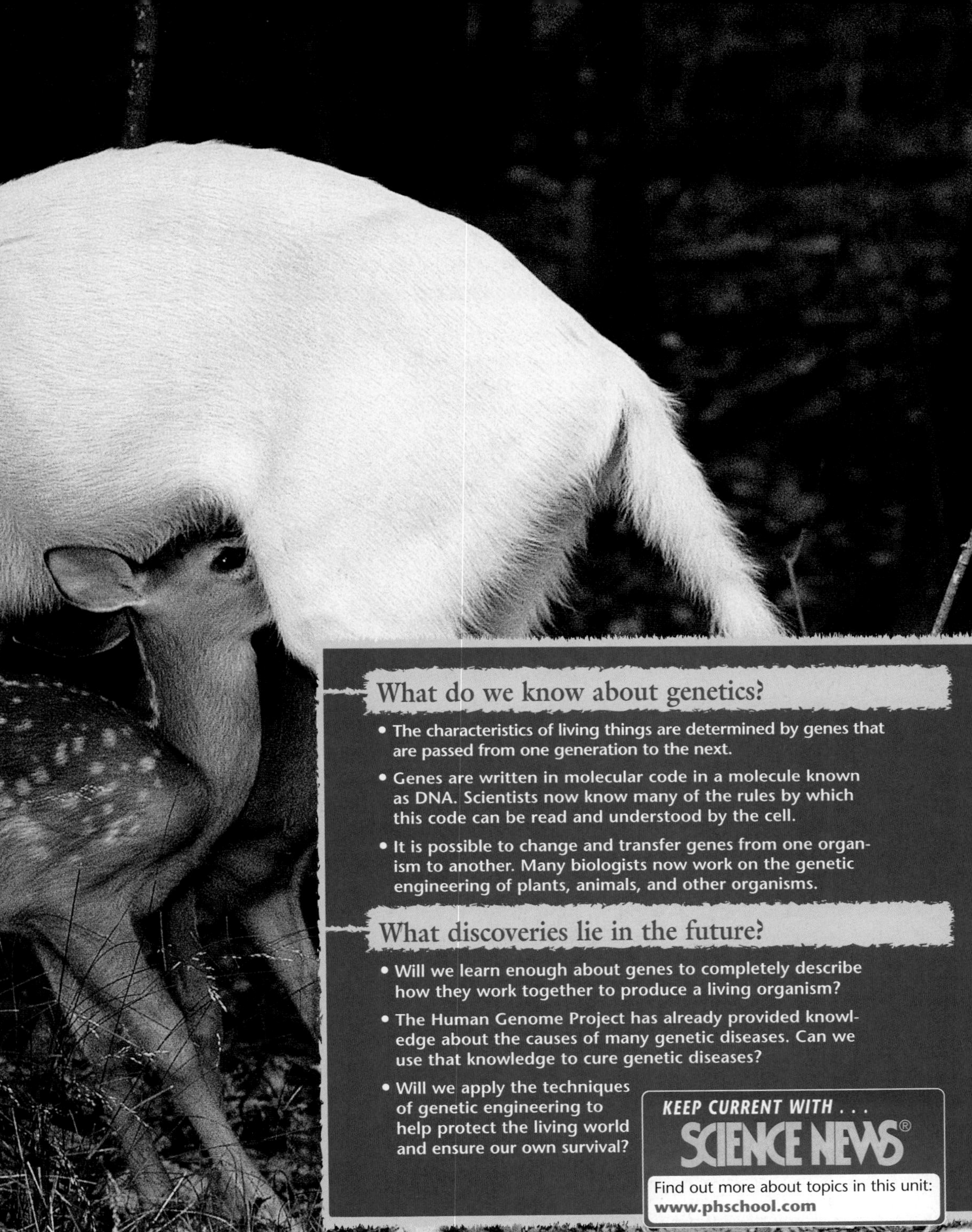

What do we know about genetics?
• The characteristics of living things are determined by genes that are passed from one generation to the next.
• Genes are written in molecular code in a molecule known as DNA. Scientists now know many of the rules by which this code can be read and understood by the cell.
• It is possible to change and transfer genes from one organism to another. Many biologists now work on the genetic engineering of plants, animals, and other organisms.
What discoveries lie in the future?
• Will we learn enough about genes to completely describe how they work together to produce a living organism?
• The Human Genome Project has already provided knowledge about the causes of many genetic diseases. Can we use that knowledge to cure genetic diseases?
• Will we apply the techniques of genetic engineering to help protect the living world and ensure our own survival?
KEEP CURRENT WITH . . .
SCIENCE NEWS®
Find out more about topics in this unit:
www.phschool.com

Today, you or I or any of your students can sit down at a computer and access the DNA sequences of each and every human chromosome. We can test for many genetic disorders, hope to cure at least a few of them, and routinely insert new genes into bacteria, plants, and laboratory animals.

In every respect, we are living not only in a new century but also in a truly new world. Our students will spend most of their lives in what may eventually come to be known as the Biological Century. They'd better be prepared.

Where does that preparation start? Well, in many respects, it starts with us—a scientific community composed of researchers and teachers. We owe it to each of our students to teach them what science has learned. That's important work. However, we must also keep in mind that it's just as important to teach them *how* science learns. That's where the bulletin board in *your* classroom comes in.

As Joe Levine and I rushed to put the finishing touches on this unit, the very first detailed annotations of the human genome were published. We had just enough time to write much of that new information, including the first informed estimate of the number of human genes, into this unit.

Try as we might, however, we cannot predict the future, and that's one of the many places where you come in. At best, this book should serve as a starting point for you and for your students. Where you go from this starting point is up to you. I hope, however, whether you use a newspaper clipping or a Web page, you'll find a way to convey to your students the same thing my biology teacher showed me. The future isn't in the book—it's up there on the board that changes every day.

Sincerely,

Ken Miller

SCIENCE NEWS®

Have students visit the Prentice Hall Web site at **www.phschool.com** to find the most current information on genetics.

Chapter Planner 11 Introduction to Genetics

Section and Section Objectives	Time	Activities and Labs
11–1 The Work of Gregor Mendel, pp. 263–266 **11.1.1** ***Describe*** how Mendel studied inheritance in peas. **11.1.2** ***Summarize*** Mendel's conclusion about inheritance. **11.1.3** ***Explain*** the principle of dominance. **11.1.4** ***Describe*** what happens during segregation.	1 period (1/2 block)	**SE:** ***Inquiry Activity,*** Are traits inherited?, p. 262 **TE:** ***Build Science Skills,*** p. 263 **TE:** ***Demonstration,*** p. 265 **TE:** ***Build Science Skills,*** p. 266
11–2 Probability and Punnett Squares, pp. 267–269 **11.2.1** ***Explain*** how geneticists use the principles of probability. **11.2.2** ***Describe*** how geneticists use Punnett squares.	1 period (1/2 block)	**TE:** ***Make Connections,*** p. 267 **SE:** ***Quick Lab,*** How are dimples inherited?, p. 268 **TE:** ***Build Science Skills,*** p. 269
11–3 Exploring Mendelian Genetics, pp. 270–274 **11.3.1** ***Explain*** the principle of independent assortment. **11.3.2** ***Describe*** other inheritance patterns that exist aside from simple dominance. **11.3.3** ***Explain*** how Mendel's principles apply to organisms.	1 period (1/2 block)	**TE:** ***Build Science Skills,*** p. 270 **SE**: ***Problem Solving,*** Producing True-breeding Seeds, p. 271 **TE:** ***Demonstration,*** p. 274
11–4 Meiosis, pp. 275–278 **11.4.1** ***Contrast*** chromosome number of body cells and gametes. **11.4.2** ***Summarize*** the events of meiosis. **11.4.3** ***Contrast*** meiosis and mitosis.	1/2 period (1/4 block)	**TE:** ***Demonstration,*** p. 277 **SE:** ***Exploration,*** Modeling Meiosis, p. 281
11–5 Linkage and Gene Maps, pp. 279–280 **11.5.1** ***Identify*** the structures that actually assort independently. **11.5.2** ***Explain*** how gene maps are produced.	1 period (1/2 block)	**TE:** ***Build Science Skills,*** p. 279
Chapter Assessment, pp. 282–285	1 period (1/2 block)	

ACTIVITY PLANNER

SE: ***Inquiry Activity,*** p. 262; (10 min.)

TE: ***Build Science Skills,*** p. 263; (15 min.); flowers, scissors, dissecting microscope, compound microscope, slide, tweezers, coverslips

TE: ***Demonstration,*** p. 265; (10 min.); P and F_1 corn cobs for a single trait

TE: ***Build Science Skills,*** p. 266; (15 min on two days; 10 days apart); F_2 corn seeds, potting soil, water, aluminum pans

TE: ***Make Connections,*** p. 267; (15 min.); bag, different-colored items

SE: ***Quick Lab,*** p. 268; (15 min.); page from phone book, calculator

TE: ***Build Science Skills,*** p. 269; (15 min.); coin, or bag with 2 or 3 beads

TE: ***Build Science Skills,*** p. 270; (10 min.); starchy F_1 corn cobs

TE: ***Demonstration,*** p. 274; (15 min on two days; 2 weeks apart); wild-type fruit flies, fruit flies with vestigial wings, microscope, fruit fly growth medium, culture jars, ether, jar with mineral oil, paint brush, index cards

TE: ***Demonstration,*** p. 277; (10 min.); pipe cleaners, beads, scissors, tape

TE: ***Build Science Skills,*** p. 279; (10 min.); pipe cleaners, beads

SE: ***Exploration,*** p. 281; (45 min.); yarn, scissors, tape, cards, marker

PLANNING KEY

Ability Levels

B	**Basic**	For students who need additional help
A	**Average**	For all students
E	**Enriched**	For students who need to be challenged

Components

SE	Student Edition	**GRSW**	Guided Reading and Study Workbook	**IDM**	Issues and Decision Making
TE	Teacher's Edition	**CT**	Chapter Tests: Levels A and B	**CTB**	Computer Test Bank
LMA	Laboratory Manual A	**PHAS**	PH Assessment System	**PA**	Presentation Assistant Plus
LMB	Laboratory Manual B	**LA**	Lab Assessment With Scoring Guide	**BD**	BioDetectives Videotape
TR	Teaching Resources	**BTM**	BioTechnology Manual	**iT**	iText
IF	Investigations in Forensics				

Program Resources	Assessment	Media and Technology
TR: Section Review 11–1 B A **GRSW:** Section 11–1 B A	**SE:** 11–1 Section Assessment, p. 266 **TR:** Section Review 11–1	**PA:** 11–1 Interest Grabber, Section Outline, Principles of Dominance, Figure 11–3 **iT:** Section 11–1
TR: Section Review 11–2 B A **GRSW:** Section 11–2 B A	**SE:** 11–2 Section Assessment, p. 269 **TR:** Section Review 11–2	**PA:** 11–2 Interest Grabber, Section Outline, *Tt* × *Tt* Cross **iT:** Section 11–2
LMA: Chapter 11 Lab B A **LMB:** Chapter 11 Lab B A **TR:** Section Review 11–3 B A **GRSW:** Section 11–3 B A	**SE:** 11–3 Section Assessment, p. 274 **TR:** Section Review 11–3	**PA:** 11–3 Interest Grabber, Section Outline, Concept Map, Figure 11–10, Figure 11–11 **iT:** Section 11–3
TR: Section Review 11–4 B A **GRSW:** Section 11–4 B A	**SE:** 11–4 Section Assessment, p. 278 **TR:** Section Review 11–4	**PA:** 11–4 Interest Grabber, Section Outline, Crossing-Over, Figure 11–15, Figure 11–17 **iT:** Section 11–4
TR: Section Review 11–5 B A Chapter 11 Exploration B A E **GRSW:** Section 11–5 B A **BTM:** LAB 2 A E	**SE:** 11–5 Section Assessment, p. 280 **TR:** Section Review 11–5	**PA:** 11–5 Interest Grabber, Section Outline, Comparative Scale of Gene Mapping, Figure 11–19 **iT:** Section 11–5
	SE: Chapter 11 Assessment, pp. 282–285; **TR:** Chapter Vocabulary Review, Graphic Organizer; **CT:** Chapter 11 Test; **CTB:** Chapter 11 Test; **PHAS:** Practice Test	**CTB:** Chapter 11 Test **iT:** Chapter 11 Assessment

PRESSED FOR TIME?

To Preview the Chapter
- Introduce students to Key Concepts and Vocabulary in each section.
- Encourage students to study all chapter figures and captions.

To Cover the Chapter Quickly
- Have students read all of Sections 11–1 and 11–2, Independent Assortment in Section 11–3, all of Section 11–4, and Gene Linkage in Section 11–5.
- Assign the Section Reviews 11–1, 11–2, and 11–4; questions 1–5, 7–9, 12, 13, 16–28, and 30 in Chapter 11 Assessment; and questions 1–3, 6, 9–12 in Chapter 11 Standardized Test Prep.

To Review the Chapter
- Have students study Figure 11–15 and complete the flowchart in the Chapter 11 Study Guide.
- Assign Section Reviews 11–1 through 11–5 and Chapter Vocabulary Review in the Teaching Resources.

ENGAGE/EXPLORE

Inquiry Activity

Objective Students will be able to infer whether traits are inherited.

Skill Focus Inferring

Time 10 minutes

Strategies

- Help students identify examples of widow's peak vs. straight hairline, attached earlobes vs. free earlobes, and gapped vs. ungapped front teeth.
- Ask students if these traits run in families. Follow by inquiring exactly what that means, soliciting the idea that "you get them from your parents."

Expected Outcomes Students will recognize two or more forms of a trait and infer that these traits are inherited from parents.

Think About It

1. Yes; parents

2. Genes are passed from generation to generation, but they are not all expressed in every generation. If students mention adoption as an explanation, remind them that the question asks only about biological relatives.

Brain Teaser

Challenge students to explain how two brown rabbits could have white offspring. *(Accept all reasonable responses. The parents are heterozygous for fur color. The white offspring inherited both recessive alleles, thereby showing the recessive coat color.)* Challenge students to predict the coat color of offspring produced in a cross between two white rabbits. *(All offspring will be white.)* Revisit this question at the end of the chapter. Invite student volunteers to explain whether or not they would change their prediction and why.

Chapter 11 Introduction to Genetics

The varied colors of these parakeets result from differences in their genetic makeup.

Inquiry Activity

Are traits inherited?

Procedure

1. Look at your classmates. Note how they vary in the shape of the front hairline, the space between the two upper front teeth, and the way in which the earlobes are attached.
2. Make a list of the different forms of these traits that you have observed in the class or among other people you know.

Think About It

1. **Inferring** Could these traits be inherited? From whom could they be inherited?
2. **Inferring** How is it possible that these traits could be found in a person and his or her biological grandparents but not in the biological parents?

HISTORY OF SCIENCE

Changing theories of inheritance

Greek philosophers were the first to theorize how traits are passed from parent to offspring. Their theory of pangenesis explained that body fluids were composed of a mixture of particles secreted from all organs of the body. New individuals formed from a blend of male and female fluids. The discovery of eggs and sperm in the seventeenth century led to the theory of preformation—sex cells contain preformed miniatures of the adult. This theory was disproved by Caspar Wolff's work with chicken embryos. So when Darwin was developing an explanation for the mechanism of evolution, he took the ancient Greek idea of pangenesis and expanded it to include the inheritance of acquired characters. He theorized that as parts of the body changed, so did the pangenes (particles) that they produced.

11–1 The Work of Gregor Mendel

What is an inheritance? To most people, it is money or property left to them by a relative who has passed away. That kind of inheritance is important, of course. There is another form of inheritance, however, that matters even more. This inheritance has been with you from the very first day you were alive—your genes.

Every living thing—plant or animal, microbe or human being—has a set of characteristics inherited from its parent or parents. Since the beginning of recorded history, people have wanted to understand how that inheritance is passed from generation to generation. More recently, however, scientists have begun to appreciate that heredity holds the the key to understanding what makes each species unique. As a result, **genetics,** the scientific study of heredity, is now at the core of a revolution in understanding biology.

Guide for Reading

Key Concepts
- What is the principle of dominance?
- What happens during segregation?

Vocabulary
- genetics • true-breeding
- trait • hybrid • gene • allele
- segregation • gamete

Reading Strategy: Finding Main Ideas As you read, find evidence to support the following statement: Mendel's ideas about genetics were the beginning of a new area of biology.

Gregor Mendel's Peas

The work of an Austrian monk named Gregor Mendel was particularly important to understanding biological inheritance. Gregor Mendel was born in 1822 in what is now the Czech Republic. After becoming a priest, Mendel spent several years studying science and mathematics at the University of Vienna. He spent the next 14 years working in the monastery and teaching at the high school. In addition to his teaching duties, Mendel was in charge of the monastery garden. In this ordinary garden, he was to do the work that changed biology forever.

Mendel worked with garden peas. Like many plants, pea plants use parts of their flowers to reproduce. The male part of each flower produces pollen—which contains male sex cells. The female part of the flower produces eggs—female sex cells.

When pollen fertilizes an egg cell, a seed for a new plant is formed. Pea plants normally reproduce by self-pollination, in which pollen fertilizes the egg cells in the very same flower. Seeds that are produced by self-pollination inherit all of their characteristics from the single plant that bore them. In effect, they have only one parent.

When Mendel took charge of the monastery garden, he had several different stocks of pea plants. These peas were **true-breeding,** meaning that if they were allowed to self-pollinate, they would produce offspring identical to themselves. One stock of seeds would produce only tall plants, another only short plants. One stock produced only green seeds, another only yellow seeds. These true-breeding plants were the basis of Mendel's experiments.

▲ **Figure 11–1** Gregor Mendel's experiments with pea plants laid the foundations of the science of genetics.

SECTION RESOURCES

Print:
- ***Teaching Resources,*** Section Review 11–1
- ***Guided Reading and Study Workbook***, Section 11–1

Technology:
- ***iText,*** Section 11–1

Section 11–1

1 FOCUS

Objectives

11.1.1 ***Describe*** how Mendel studied inheritance in peas.
11.1.2 ***Summarize*** Mendel's conclusion about inheritance.
11.1.3 ***Explain*** the principle of dominance.
11.1.4 ***Describe*** what happens during segregation.

Guide for Reading

Vocabulary Preview

Help students become comfortable with the language of genetics by showing them how the vocabulary words are related to one another. For example, a true-breeding individual is the opposite of a hybrid; an allele is one form of a gene, and genes specify particular traits. Construct a word web on the board to show these relationships.

Reading Strategy

Students should incorporate Mendel's research approach, as well as his results and interpretations as support for the main idea.

2 INSTRUCT

Gregor Mendel's Peas

Build Science Skills

Observing Give students lilies, tulips, freesia, or other flowers with large stamens and pistils. Instruct them to cut off the stamens and pistils with small scissors and examine them under a dissecting microscope. If students carefully section the anther and the pistil, they may be able to observe pollen and egg cells on microscope slides with a compound microscope. Encourage students to draw labeled diagrams of their flowers.

Build Science Skills

Classifying Explain that much of Mendel's success came from his choice of experimental organism. Pea plants are useful for genetic study because they have many contrasting characters, they reproduce sexually, their crosses can be controlled, they have short life cycles, they produce a large number of offspring, and they are easy to handle in a laboratory. Invite students to use these same criteria to evaluate other organisms, such as humans, fruit flies, bacteria, oak trees, dogs, and mice. For each organism, students should explain why or why not it would be useful for genetic study. *(Fruit flies, bacteria, and mice are most useful.)*

Meet Diverse Needs

Encourage at-risk students and students with limited English proficiency to begin a glossary of vocabulary words for this chapter. Students should write the meanings of the vocabulary words in their own words, as well as in their native language. Help students work out phonetic spellings for the words they have trouble pronouncing correctly. Also encourage students to illustrate their glossaries. **Limited English proficiency**

Genes and Dominance

Use Visuals

Figure 11–3 Review the results of Mendel's crosses. Ask: **Why was Mendel surprised when the offspring had the character of only one of the parents?** *(In Mendel's time, people thought that characters of the parents blended to form the offspring.)*

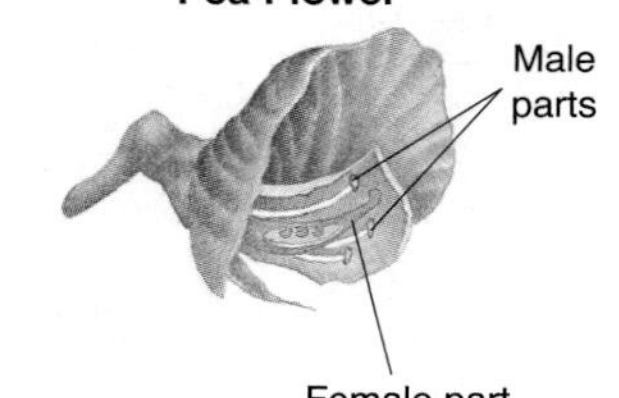

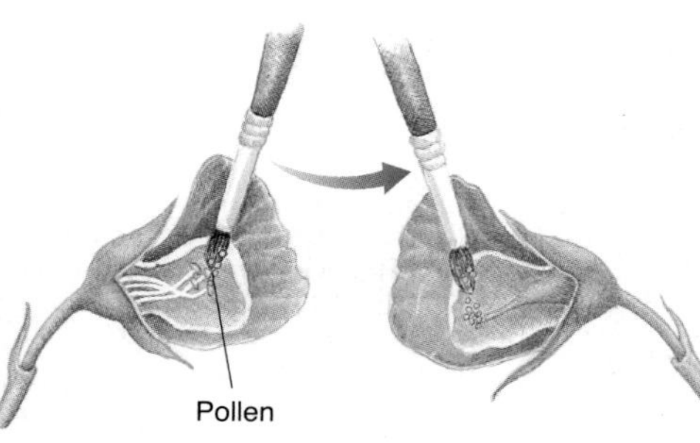

◀ **Figure 11–2** To cross-pollinate pea plants, Mendel cut off the male parts of one flower and then dusted it with pollen from another flower. **Applying Concepts** *How did this procedure prevent self-pollination?*

However, pea plants can also cross-pollinate. In cross-pollination, male sex cells in pollen from the flower on one plant fertilize the egg cells of a flower on another plant. The seeds produced from cross-pollination have two plants as parents.

To perform his experiments, Mendel had to select the pea plants that he would mate with each other. Therefore, he had to prevent the pea flowers from self-pollinating and control their cross-pollination. How did Mendel accomplish this task? First, he cut away the male parts of a flower. Then, he dusted that flower with pollen from a second flower, as shown in **Figure 11–2**. The resulting seeds were crosses between the two plants.

Genes and Dominance

Mendel studied seven different pea plant traits. A **trait** is a specific characteristic, such as seed color or plant height, that varies from one individual to another. Each of the seven traits Mendel studied had two contrasting characters, for example, green seed color and yellow seed color. Mendel crossed plants with each of the seven contrasting characters and studied their offspring. Mendel called each original pair of plants the P (parental) generation. He called the offspring the F_1, or "first filial," generation. *Filius* is the Latin word for "son." The offspring of crosses between parents with different traits are called **hybrids.**

▼ **Figure 11–3** When Mendel crossed plants with contrasting characters for the same trait, the resulting offspring had only one of the characters. **From these experiments, Mendel concluded that some alleles are dominant and others are recessive.**

Mendel's Seven F_1 Crosses on Pea Plants

	Seed Shape	Seed Color	Seed Coat Color	Pod Shape	Pod Color	Flower Position	Plant Height
P	Round X Wrinkled	Yellow X Green	Gray X White	Smooth X Constricted	Green X Yellow	Axial X Terminal	Tall X Short
F_1	Round	Yellow	Gray	Smooth	Green	Axial	Tall

PRESENTATIONS MADE EASY!

The Presentation Assistant Plus contains the Prentice Hall Presentation Pro and the Transparencies, which provide easy-to-follow visual support for every step of this section. If you have a computer presentation station, use Prentice Hall Presentation Pro for Section 11–1, or use the transparencies listed here.

Section 11–1:

Interest Grabber
Section Outline
Principle of Dominance
Figure 11–3

What were those F_1 hybrid plants like? Did the characters of the parent plants blend in the offspring? Not at all. To Mendel's surprise, all of the offspring had the character of only one of the parents, as shown in **Figure 11–3.** In each cross, the character of the other parent seemed to have disappeared.

From this set of experiments, Mendel drew two conclusions. Mendel's first conclusion was that biological inheritance is determined by factors that are passed from one generation to the next. Today, scientists call the chemical factors that determine traits **genes.** Each of the traits Mendel studied was controlled by one gene that occurred in two contrasting forms. These contrasting forms produced the different characters of each trait. For example, the gene for plant height occurs in one form that produces tall plants and in another form that produces short plants. The different forms of a gene are called **alleles** (uh-LEELZ).

Mendel's second conclusion is called the principle of dominance. **The principle of dominance states that some alleles are dominant and others are recessive.** An organism with a dominant allele for a particular form of a trait will always have that form. An organism with a recessive allele for a particular form of a trait will have that form only when the dominant allele for the trait is not present. In Mendel's experiments, the allele for tall plants was dominant and the allele for short plants was recessive. The allele for yellow seeds was dominant, while the allele for green seeds was recessive.

Segregation

Mendel wanted the answer to another question: Had the recessive alleles disappeared, or were they still present in the F_1 plants? To answer this question, he allowed all seven kinds of F_1 hybrid plants to produce an F_2 (second filial) generation by self-pollination. In effect, he crossed the F_1 generation with itself to produce the F_2 offspring, as shown in **Figure 11–4.**

KEEP CURRENT WITH . . . SCIENCE NEWS®

To find out more about the topics in this chapter, go to: **www.phschool.com**

▼ **Figure 11–4** When Mendel allowed the F_1 plants to reproduce by self-pollination, the traits controlled by recessive alleles reappeared in about one fourth of the F_2 plants in each cross. **Calculating** ***What proportion of the F_2 plants had a trait controlled by a dominant allele?***

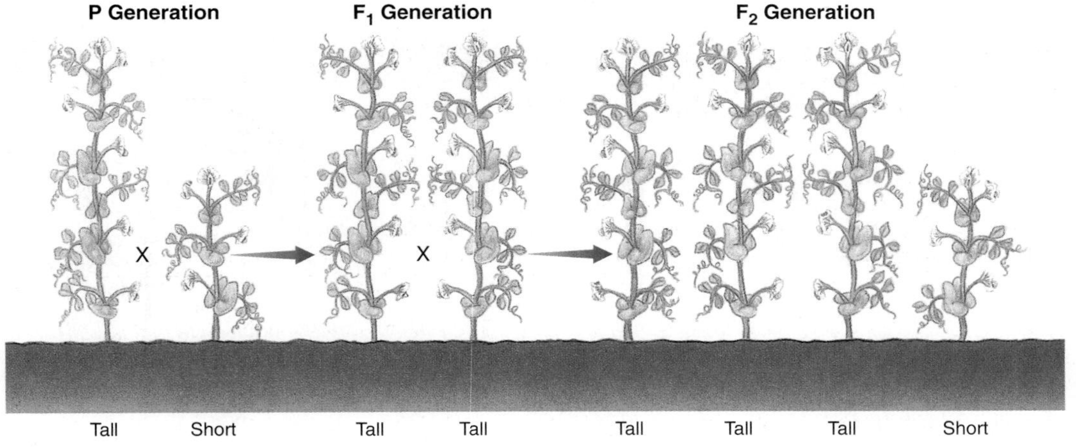

HISTORY OF SCIENCE

Methods of Mendel's success

Mendel was the first scientist of his time to obtain successful results from inheritance studies because of the methods he employed. In fact, his methods continue to be used today. Mendel studied only one trait at a time. He also took the time to verify that the parent plants were true-breeding for the particular trait he was studying. Mendel used a quantitative approach to analyze his results. He counted the number of offspring from every cross and used statistical analysis to interpret his numbers. Most important, Mendel formulated hypotheses to explain his results, and he developed experimental tests to confirm them.

SCIENCE NEWS®

Encourage students to visit **www.phschool.com** for the most current information on this topic.

Demonstration

Display the parental corn cobs and the F_1 corn cobs produced in a cross between purple *(R/R)* corn and yellow *(r/r)* corn, as well as those produced in a cross between starchy *(Su/Su)* corn and sweet *(su/su)* corn. Have students identify the alleles of the gene for each cross, and which allele is dominant and which is recessive.

Segregation

Use Visuals

Figure 11–4 Walk students through the crosses that Mendel set up as they are illustrated in the figure. Ask: **Did Mendel cross-pollinate F_1 plants to get F_2 plants?** *(No, he allowed them to self-pollinate.)* **Was the recessive allele for shortness lost in the F_1 generation?** *(No, it was masked by the dominant allele for tallness.)* **Are the F_1 plants true-breeding?** *(No, they did not produce offspring identical to themselves.)* Have student volunteers identify the gametes that each plant would produce in the P generation and in the F_1 generation.

Address Misconceptions

Some students might think it is impossible for two tall pea plants to produce short pea plants. For these students, review the cross as shown in Figure 11–4. Make sure they see that the tall pea plants came from a tall plant crossed to a short plant. Ask: **Why aren't any offspring short?** *(The allele for tallness is dominant and masks the allele for shortness.)* **Why do these plants have an allele for shortness?** *(One of their parents was short and could contribute only alleles for shortness to its offspring.)*

Answers to . . .

Figure 11–2 *The flower no longer had its own source of pollen.*

Figure 11–4 *Three fourths*

Build Science Skills

Calculating Instruct students to plant F_2 corn seeds produced in a cross between two plants heterozygous for green and white color *(Gg)*. When the seeds sprout, students should get a mixture of green plants and white plants. Ask: **Which allele is dominant?** *(Green)* **Which is recessive?** *(White)* **How do you know?** *(More green plants)* Have students calculate the ratio of green plants to white plants. Discuss how their results compare to Mendel's. *(The class should have a ratio close to 3 green : 1 white.)*

3 ASSESS

Evaluate Understanding

Assign students a trait in pea plants. Have them set up a cross as Mendel did to show the F_1 and F_2 offspring. Students should identify the dominant and recessive alleles.

Reteach

Help student devise a flowchart that outlines Mendel's method for his breeding experiments in pea plants. Encourage students to include as many vocabulary words as possible.

ALTERNATIVE ASSESSMENT

Students' diagrams should be similar to Figures 11–3 and 11–5. Segregation of alleles ensures that each gamete carries only a single copy of each gene.

Use iText to review the key concepts in Section 11–1.

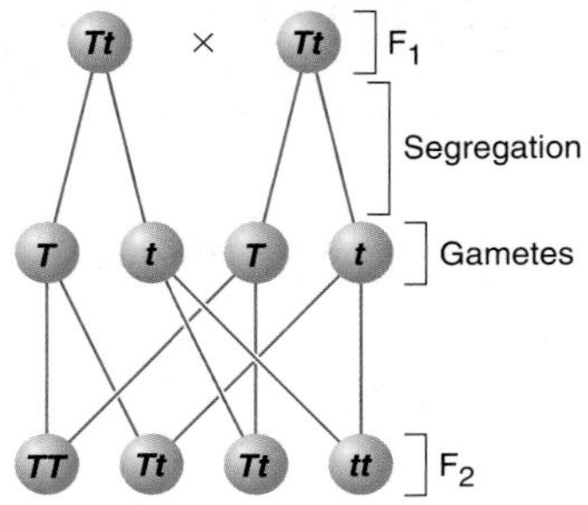

▲ **Figure 11–5 During gamete formation, alleles are segregated from each other so that each gamete carries only a single copy of each gene. Each F_1 plant produces two types of gametes—those with the allele for tallness and those with the allele for shortness.** The alleles are paired up again when gametes fuse during fertilization.

The F_1 Cross The results of the F_1 cross were remarkable. The traits controlled by the recessive alleles reappeared! Roughly one fourth of the F_2 plants showed the trait controlled by the recessive allele. Why did the recessive alleles seem to disappear in the F_1 generation and then reappear in the F_2 generation? To answer this question, let's take a closer look at one of Mendel's crosses.

Explaining the F_1 Cross To begin with, Mendel assumed that a dominant allele had masked the corresponding recessive allele in the F_1 generation. However, the trait controlled by the recessive allele showed up in some of the F_2 plants. This reappearance indicated that at some point the allele for shortness had been separated from the allele for tallness. How did this separation, or **segregation,** of alleles occur? Mendel suggested that the alleles for tallness and shortness in the F_1 plants were segregated from each other during the formation of the sex cells, or **gametes** (GAM-eets). Did that suggestion make sense?

Let's assume, as perhaps Mendel did, that the F_1 plants inherited an allele for tallness from one parent and an allele for shortness from the other parent. Because the allele for tallness is dominant, all the F_1 plants are tall. **When each F_1 plant flowers, the two alleles are segregated from each other so that each gamete carries only a single copy of each gene. Therefore, each F_1 plant produces two types of gametes—those with the allele for tallness and those with the allele for shortness.**

Look at **Figure 11–5** to see how alleles are separated during gamete formation and then paired up again in the F_2 generation. A capital letter T represents a dominant allele. A lowercase letter t represents a recessive allele. The result of this process is an F_2 generation with new combinations of alleles.

11–1 Section Assessment

1. **Key Concept** What are dominant and recessive alleles?
2. **Key Concept** What is segregation? What happens to alleles during segregation?
3. What did Mendel conclude determines biological inheritance?
4. Describe how Mendel cross-pollinated pea plants.
5. **Critical Thinking Applying Concepts** Why were true-breeding pea plants important for Mendel's experiments?

iTEXT Assessment Use iText to review the important concepts in Section 11–1.

ALTERNATIVE ASSESSMENT

Using Visuals
Use a diagram to explain Mendel's principles of dominance and segregation. Describe why it is important for the alleles to segregate during gamete formation.

11–1 Section Assessment

1. Dominant allele: allele whose form of a trait always shows up in an organism if the dominant allele is present; recessive allele: allele whose form of a trait shows up only when the dominant allele is not present
2. Separation of alleles; the alleles are separated so that each gamete carries only a single copy of each gene.
3. Factors that are passed from one generation to the next
4. Mendel cut away the male parts of one flower, then dusted it with pollen from another flower.
5. True-breeding pea plants have two identical alleles for a gene, so in a genetic cross each parent can contribute only one form of a gene.

11–2 Probability and Punnett Squares

Whenever Mendel performed a cross with pea plants, he carefully counted the offspring. Every time Mendel repeated a particular cross, he obtained similar results. For example, whenever Mendel crossed two plants that were hybrid for stem height (*Tt*), about three fourths of the resulting plants were tall and about one fourth were short. Mendel realized that the principles of probability could be used to explain the results of genetic crosses.

Genetics and Probability

The likelihood that a particular event will occur is called **probability.** As an example of probability, consider an ordinary event like the coin flip shown in **Figure 11–6.** There are two possible outcomes: The coin may land heads up or tails up. The chances, or probabilities, of either outcome are equal. Therefore, the probability that a single coin flip will come up heads is 1 chance in 2. This is 1/2 or 50 percent.

If you flip a coin three times in a row, what is the probability that it will land heads up? Because each coin flip is an independent event, the probability of each coin's landing heads up is 1/2. Therefore, the probability of flipping three heads in a row is:

$$\frac{1}{2} \times \frac{1}{2} \times \frac{1}{2} = \frac{1}{8}.$$

As you can see, you have 1 chance in 8 of flipping heads three times in a row. That the individual probabilities are multiplied together illustrates an important point—past outcomes do not affect future ones.

How is coin flipping relevant to genetics? The way in which alleles segregate is completely random, like a coin flip.  **The principles of probability can be used to predict the outcomes of genetic crosses.**

CHECKPOINT *What is the probability that a tossed coin will come up tails twice in a row?*

Guide for Reading

Key Concept
- How do geneticists use the principles of probability?

Vocabulary
probability
Punnett square
homozygous
heterozygous
phenotype
genotype

Reading Strategy: Building Vocabulary Before you read, preview the list of new vocabulary words. Predict the relationship between phenotype and genotype. As you read, check to see if your predictions were correct.

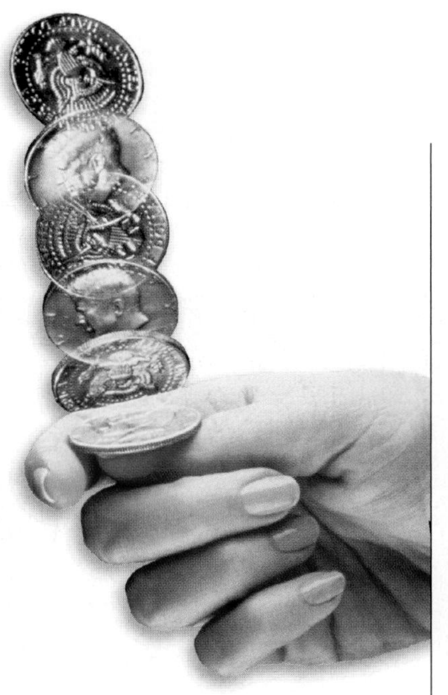

▶ **Figure 11–6** The mathematical concept of probability allows you to calculate the likelihood that a particular event will occur. **Predicting** *What is the probability that the coin will land heads up?*

SECTION RESOURCES

Print:
- ***Teaching Resources,*** Section Review 11–2
- ***Guided Reading and Study Workbook,*** Section 11–2

Technology:
- ***iText,*** Section 11–2

Section 11–2

1 FOCUS

Objectives

11.2.1 ***Explain*** how geneticists use the principles of probability.
11.2.2 ***Describe*** how geneticists use Punnett squares.

Guide for Reading

Vocabulary Preview

Ask: **What suffix do the words *homozygous* and *heterozygous* share?** (-zygous) Tell students that *-zygous* means "yoked" or "joined," and the prefix *homo-* means "same." Also explain that a homozygous organism has two identical alleles for a certain gene. Ask: **If *hetero-* means "other," what does *heterozygous* describe?** *(An organism with two different alleles for a gene)*

Reading Strategy

Encourage students to write down the main headings of the section before they begin reading. Tell them to leave room below each heading to record important ideas as they read.

2 INSTRUCT

Genetics and Probability

Make Connections

Mathematics Give student pairs a paper bag that has 4 identical items that differ in color. The items should be the same shape and size. Ask: **What is the probability of picking a red item?** *(1/4 or 25 percent)* **Of picking a red item two times in a row?** *(1/4 × 1/4 = 1/16)* Then, instruct students to pick an item from the bag 20 times, then 50 times. Ask: **Did your results equal your calculated probabilities?** *(The more times students pick from the bag, the closer their actual results will be to the predicted probability.)*

Answers to . . .

CHECKPOINT *25 percent*

Figure 11–6 *50 percent*

Punnett Squares

Quick Lab

Objective Students will be able to conclude how dimples are inherited.

Materials copy of page from telephone book, calculator

Time 15 minutes

Advance Prep Photocopy several pages from a telephone book.

Strategies
- Demonstrate the use of a 4-digit number to represent the genotypes of the parents in a genetic cross.
- Show students how to set up and use Punnett squares, if necessary.

Expected Outcomes Students will determine the probability of having a child with dimples based on the genotypes of the parents. Calculated probabilities will vary depending on the genotypes of the parents.

Analyze and Conclude

1. Class averages will vary but will usually be close to 75 percent dimples, the result of a cross between two heterozygotes.
2. 100 percent

Meet Diverse Needs

Challenge at-risk students to write an instructional manual for using Punnett squares. Students should include a labeled diagram of a Punnett square in their manual, as well as step-by-step directions on how to use one and why Punnett squares are useful tools for geneticists. **Learning modality: logical/mathematical**

Probability and Segregation

Address Misconceptions

Beginning genetics students often misinterpret probable genotypic and phenotypic ratios as actual numbers of offspring. Provide opportunities to calculate "actual" ratios using F_2 corn cobs or experimental data. Students should set up Punnett squares and compare the predicted ratios with the "actual" ratios.

Quick Lab

How are dimples inherited?

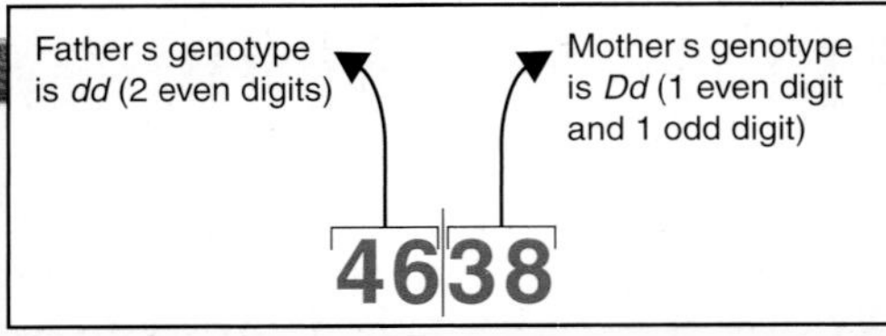
Father s genotype is *dd* (2 even digits)
Mother s genotype is *Dd* (1 even digit and 1 odd digit)
4638

Materials copy of page from telephone book, calculator

Procedure

1. Write the last 4 digits of any telephone number. These 4 random digits represent the gene that determines whether a person will have dimples. Odd digits represent the allele for the dominant trait of dimples. Even digits stand for the allele for the recessive trait of no dimples.
2. Use the first 2 digits to represent a certain father's genotype. Use the symbols *D* and *d* to write his genotype, as shown in the example.
3. Use the last 2 digits the same way to find the mother's genotype. Write her genotype.
4. Use **Figure 11–7** as an example to construct a Punnett square for the cross of these parents. Then, using the Punnett square, determine the probability that their child will have dimples.
5. Determine the class average of the percent of children with dimples.

Analyze and Conclude

1. **Applying Concepts** How does the class average compare with the result of a cross of two heterozygous parents?
2. **Drawing Conclusions** What percentage of the children will be expected to have dimples if one parent is homozygous for dimples *(DD)* and the other is heterozygous *(Dd)?*

Tt

Tt	*T*	*t*
T	*TT* 25%	*Tt* 25%
t	*Tt* 25%	*tt* 25%

▲ **Figure 11–7** **The principles of probability can be used to predict the outcomes of genetic crosses.** This Punnett square shows the probability of each possible outcome of a cross between hybrid tall *(Tt)* pea plants.

Punnett Squares

The gene combinations that might result from a genetic cross can be determined by drawing a diagram known as a **Punnett square.** The Punnett square in **Figure 11–7** shows one of Mendel's segregation experiments. The types of gametes produced by each F_1 parent are shown along the top and left sides of the square. The possible gene combinations for the F_2 offspring appear in the four boxes that make up the square. The letters in the Punnett square represent alleles: capital letters for dominant alleles and lowercase letters for recessive alleles. In this example, *T* represents the dominant allele for tallness and *t* represents the recessive allele for shortness.

Organisms that have two identical alleles for a particular trait—*TT* or *tt* in this example—are said to be **homozygous** (hoh-moh-ZY-gus). Organisms that have two different alleles for the same trait are **heterozygous** (het-er-oh-ZY-gus). Homozygous organisms are true-breeding for a particular trait. Heterozygous organisms are hybrid for a particular trait.

All of the tall plants have the same **phenotype,** or physical characteristics. They do not, however, have the same **genotype,** or genetic makeup. The genotype of one third of the tall plants is *TT,* while the genotype of two thirds of the tall plants is *Tt.* The plants shown in **Figure 11–8** have the same phenotype but different genotypes.

TIME SAVER — PRESENTATIONS MADE EASY!

The Presentation Assistant Plus contains the Prentice Hall Presentation Pro and the Transparencies, which provide easy-to-follow visual support for every step of this section. If you have a computer presentation station, use Prentice Hall Presentation Pro for Section 11–2, or use the transparencies listed here.

Section 11–2: **Interest Grabber**
Section Outline
***Tt* × *Tt* Cross**

Probability and Segregation

Look again at **Figure 11–7.** One fourth (1/4) of the F_2 plants have two alleles for tallness *(TT)*; 2/4, or 1/2, of the F_2 plants have one allele for tallness and one allele for shortness *(Tt)*. Because the allele for tallness is dominant over the allele for shortness, 3/4 of the F_2 plants should be tall. Overall, there are 3 tall plants for every 1 short plant in the F_2 generation. Thus, the ratio of tall plants to short plants is 3 : 1. This assumes, of course, that Mendel's model of segregation is correct.

Did the data from Mendel's experiments fit his model? Yes. The predicted ratio—3 dominant to 1 recessive—showed up consistently, indicating that Mendel's assumptions about segregation had been correct. For each of his seven crosses, about 3/4 of the plants showed the trait controlled by the dominant allele. About 1/4 showed the trait controlled by the recessive allele. Segregation did indeed occur according to Mendel's model.

Probabilities Predict Averages

Probabilities predict the average outcome of a large number of events. However, probability cannot predict the precise outcome of an individual event. If you flip a coin twice, you are likely to get one head and one tail. However, you might also get two heads or two tails. To be sure of getting the expected 50 : 50 ratio, you would have to flip the coin many times.

The same is true of genetics. The larger the number of individuals, the closer the resulting offspring numbers will get to expected values. If an F_1 generation contains just three or four offspring, it may not match Mendelian predictions. When an F_1 generation contains hundreds or thousands of individuals, however, the ratios usually come very close to matching expectations.

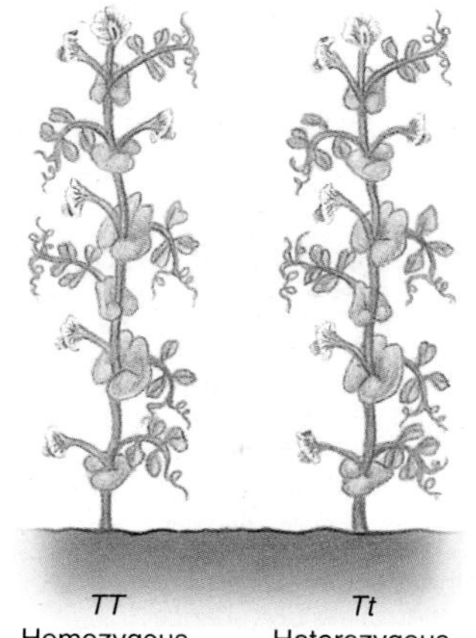

▲ **Figure 11–8** Although these plants have different genotypes (*TT* and *Tt*), they have the same phenotype (tall). **Predicting** ***If you crossed these two plants, would their offspring be tall or short?***

11–2 Section Assessment

1. **Key Concept** How are the principles of probability used to predict the outcomes of genetic crosses?
2. What is probability?
3. What is a Punnett square?
4. Define the terms *genotype* and *phenotype.*
5. **Critical Thinking Problem Solving** An F_1 plant that is homozygous for shortness is crossed with a heterozygous F_1 plant. What is the probability that a seed from the cross will produce a tall plant? Use a Punnett square to explain your answer.

iTEXT Assessment Use iText to review the important concepts in Section 11–2.

ALTERNATIVE ASSESSMENT

Drawing Punnett Squares

Imagine that you came upon a tall pea plant similar to those Mendel used in his experiments. How could you determine the plant's genotype with respect to height? Draw two Punnett squares to show your answer.

Probabilities Predict Averages

Build Science Skills

Designing Experiments Give students a coin or a bag with 2 or 3 beads that differ in color. Ask them to design an experiment to show that probabilities cannot predict the outcome of an individual event.

3 ASSESS

Evaluate Understanding

Assign students different traits in peas. Then, instruct them to set up a Punnett square to show the cross between two heterozygous pea plants for their trait. Students should give both the genotypic and phenotypic ratio of the offspring.

Reteach

Give student pairs a list of genetic crosses between parents of various genotypes. Instruct pairs to use Punnett squares to show the possible outcomes of the crosses.

ALTERNATIVE ASSESSMENT

The genotype of the tall pea plant is determined by allowing the plant to self-pollinate. If the plant is heterozygous, there is a 25 percent chance that an offspring will be short. If the plant is homozygous, then all offspring will be tall. Students should draw Punnett squares to show both possibilities.

Use iText to review the key concepts in Section 11–2.

11–2 Section Assessment

1. The way in which the alleles segregate is completely random, and probability allows the calculation of the likelihood that a particular event will occur.
2. The likelihood that a particular event will occur
3. A diagram that shows the gene combinations that might result from a genetic cross
4. Genotype: genetic makeup; phenotype: physical characteristics
5. 50 percent; Punnett square:

	t	*t*
T	*Tt*	*Tt*
t	*tt*	*tt*

Answer to . . .

Figure 11–8 *The offspring would be 100 percent tall.*

Section 11–3

1 FOCUS

Objectives

11.3.1 ***Explain*** the principle of independent assortment.
11.3.2 ***Describe*** inheritance patterns aside from dominance.
11.3.3 ***Explain*** how Mendel's principles apply to all organisms.

Guide for Reading

Vocabulary Preview

Explain that the prefix *poly-* means "more than one." Ask: **What do you think a polygenic trait is?** *(A trait controlled by more than one gene)*

Reading Strategy

Before students read the section, suggest that they read the captions and study the art and diagrams in each figure.

2 INSTRUCT

Independent Assortment

Build Science Skills

Applying Concepts Give students F_1 corn cobs produced in a dihybrid cross between homozygous purple, starchy and yellow, sweet parents *(R/r Su/su)*. Ask: **Which traits are controlled by dominant alleles?** *(Purple and starchy)* Then, have students construct a Punnett square to show all the possible gametes and offspring from the cross.

11–3 Exploring Mendelian Genetics

Guide for Reading

Key Concepts
- What is the principle of independent assortment?
- What inheritance patterns exist aside from simple dominance?

Vocabulary
independent assortment
incomplete dominance
codominance
multiple alleles
polygenic traits

Reading Strategy: Finding Main Ideas Before you read, draw a line down the center of a sheet of paper. On the left side, write down the main topics of the section. On the right side, note supporting details and examples.

After showing that alleles segregate during the formation of gametes, Mendel wondered if they did so independently. In other words, does the segregation of one pair of alleles affect the segregation of another pair of alleles? For example, does the gene that determines whether a seed is round or wrinkled in shape have anything to do with the gene for seed color? Must a round seed also be yellow?

Independent Assortment

To answer these questions, Mendel performed an experiment to follow two different genes as they passed from one generation to the next. Mendel's experiment is known as a two-factor cross.

The Two-Factor Cross: F_1 First, Mendel crossed true-breeding plants that produced only round yellow peas (genotype *RRYY*) with plants that produced wrinkled green peas (genotype *rryy*). All of the F_1 offspring produced round yellow peas. This shows that the alleles for yellow and round peas are dominant over the alleles for green and wrinkled peas. A Punnett square for this cross, shown in **Figure 11–9**, shows that the genotype of each of these F_1 plants is *RrYy*.

This cross does not indicate whether genes assort, or segregate, independently. However, it provides the hybrid plants needed for the next cross—the cross of F_1 plants to produce the F_2 generation.

Figure 11–9 Mendel crossed plants that were homozygous dominant for round yellow peas with plants that were homozygous recessive for wrinkled green peas. All of the F_1 offspring were heterozygous dominant for round yellow peas. **Interpreting Graphics** ***How is the genotype of the offspring different from that of the homozygous dominant parent?***

rryy (top); *RRYY* (left)

	ry	*ry*	*ry*	*ry*
RY	*RrYy*	*RrYy*	*RrYy*	*RrYy*
RY	*RrYy*	*RrYy*	*RrYy*	*RrYy*
RY	*RrYy*	*RrYy*	*RrYy*	*RrYy*
RY	*RrYy*	*RrYy*	*RrYy*	*RrYy*

TIME SAVER

SECTION RESOURCES

Print:
- ***Laboratory Manual A,*** Chapter 11 Lab
- ***Laboratory Manual B,*** Chapter 11 Lab
- ***Teaching Resources,*** Section Review 11–3
- ***Guided Reading and Study Workbook,*** Section 11–3

Technology:
- ***iText,*** Section 11–3

The Two-Factor Cross: F_2 Mendel knew that the F_1 plants had genotypes of *RrYy*. In other words, the F_1 plants were all heterozygous for both the seed shape and seed color genes. How would the alleles segregate when the F_1 plants were crossed to each other to produce an F_2 generation? Remember that each plant in the F_1 generation was formed by the fusion of a gamete carrying the dominant *RY* alleles with another gamete carrying the recessive *ry* alleles. Did this mean that the two dominant alleles would always stay together? Or would they "segregate independently," so that any combination of alleles was possible?

In Mendel's experiment, the F_2 plants produced 556 seeds. Of these, 315 seeds were round and yellow and another 32 were wrinkled and green, the two parental phenotypes. However, 209 of the seeds had combinations of phenotypes—and therefore combinations of alleles—not found in either parent. This clearly meant that the alleles for seed shape segregated independently of those for seed color—a principle known as **independent assortment.** Put another way, genes that segregate independently—such as the genes for seed shape and seed color in pea plants—do not influence each other's inheritance. Mendel's experimental results were very close to the 9 : 3 : 3 : 1 ratio that the Punnett square shown in **Figure 11–10** predicts. Mendel had discovered the principle of independent assortment. **The principle of independent assortment states that genes for different traits can segregate independently during the formation of gametes.**

RrYy × RrYy	*RY*	*Ry*	*rY*	*ry*
RY	*RRYY*	*RRYy*	*RrYY*	*RrYy*
Ry	*RRYy*	*RRyy*	*RrYy*	*Rryy*
rY	*RrYY*	*RrYy*	*rrYY*	*rrYy*
ry	*RrYy*	*Rryy*	*rrYy*	*rryy*

F_2 Generation

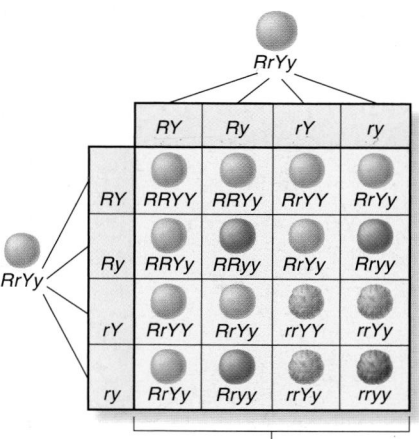

▲ **Figure 11–10** **When Mendel crossed plants that were heterozygous dominant for round yellow peas, he found that the alleles segregated independently to produce the F_2 generation.**

Problem Solving

Producing True-Breeding Seeds

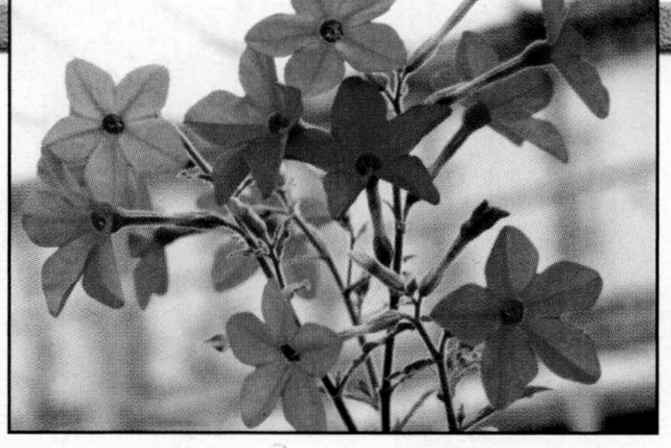

Imagine that you work for a company that specializes in ornamental flowers. One spring, you find an ornamental tobacco plant with beautiful lavender flowers, a color you are sure will be in high demand. Knowing that tobacco plants are self-pollinating, you harvest seeds from it. A test plot of the seeds planted the following season fails to impress your boss. Of the 106 test plants, 31 have white flowers. Is there a way to develop seeds guaranteed to produce only lavender flowers?

Defining the Problem Describe the problem that must be solved to make the lavender-flowered plants a commercial success.

Organizing Information The first lavender flower produced offspring with both lavender and white flowers when allowed to self-pollinate. Use your knowledge of Mendelian genetics, including Punnett squares, to draw conclusions about the nature of the allele for lavender flowers.

Creating a Solution Write a description of how you would begin with seeds from your test plot and produce seeds guaranteed to produce 100 percent lavender plants. Keep in mind that a single tobacco plant can produce as many as 1000 seeds.

Presenting Your Plan Prepare a step-by-step outline of your plan, including Punnett squares when appropriate. Present the procedure to your class as you would a business plan.

PRESENTATIONS MADE EASY!

The Presentation Assistant Plus contains the Prentice Hall Presentation Pro and the Transparencies, which provide easy-to-follow visual support for every step of this section. If you have a computer presentation station, use Prentice Hall Presentation Pro for Section 11–3, or use the transparencies listed here.

Section 11–3: **Interest Grabber**
Section Outline
Concept Map
Figure 11–10
Figure 11–11

Use Visuals

Figure 11–10 Have students give the phenotypic and genotypic ratios of the offspring for the cross shown in the figure. Ask: **What phenotypes would you observe if the alleles did not segregate independently?** *(Round, yellow seeds and wrinkled, green seeds)*

Problem Solving

The 106 test plants were the result of the self-fertilization, or selfing, of the original lavender-flowering plant. Because the male and female gametes came from the same plant, they have the same genotype. You can compare this to the F_1 crosses set up by Mendel.

Defining the Problem
Develop true-breeding, or homozygous, lavender-flowering plants.

Organizing Information
The allele for lavender flowers is dominant. The lavender-flowering plant is heterozygous. Students should show Punnett squares for selfing a homozygous plant (would expect only one flower color) and a heterozygous plant (would expect two colors in a 3:1 ratio).

Creating a Solution
The best plans will suggest collecting seeds from many plants with lavender flowers and sowing them in separate plots, one plot for seeds produced by each plant. If enough plants are tested, at least one will produce offspring with only lavender flowers. Sow seeds from these plants to be absolutely sure the plants are true-breeding.

Presenting Your Plan
The best plans will include a step-by-step outline of the procedure to collect lavender-flowering tobacco plants that is genetically sound. The plan should include Punnett squares to support the genetic predictions of the crosses.

Answer to . . .

Figure 11–9 *The offspring are heterozygous.*

A Summary of Mendel's Principles

Meet Diverse Needs

Divide the class into pairs, mixing at-risk students with students who clearly understand the concepts. Challenge pairs to role-play in which one person poses as a talk-show host or news reporter and the other poses as Gregor Mendel. The news reporter should ask Mendel about his findings and how his principles have formed the basis for modern genetics. Make sure students have a chance to switch roles. **Learning modality: verbal**

Beyond Dominant and Recessive Alleles

Use Visuals

Figure 11–11 Ask: **What phenotypic ratio would you expect to see if two heterozygous plants with pink flowers were crossed?** *(1 red: 2 pink: 1 white)* Explain that for alleles that show incomplete dominance, the alleles work together to produce a "dosage effect." For example, if a plant has one allele for red pigment and one allele for no pigment (which produces white flowers), then only half as much red pigment is produced, making the flowers pink.

Build Science Skills

Using Models Challenge students to devise a model that shows the difference between incomplete dominance and codominance. One way to do this is to use paper and crayons. In incomplete dominance, two colors are blended together to form a new color. In codominance, the two individual colors are still distinctly visible; they are not blended together.

A Summary of Mendel's Principles

Mendel's principles form the base on which the modern science of genetics has been built. These principles can be summarized as follows:

- The inheritance of biological characteristics is determined by individual units known as genes. In organisms that reproduce sexually, genes are passed from parents to their offspring.
- In cases in which two or more forms of the gene for a single trait exist, some forms of the gene may be dominant and others may be recessive.
- In most sexually reproducing organisms, each adult has two copies of each gene—one from each parent. These genes are segregated from each other when gametes are formed.
- The alleles for different genes usually segregate independently of one another.

Beyond Dominant and Recessive Alleles

Despite the importance of Mendel's work, it would be a mistake to characterize the principles he discovered as "laws," because there are important exceptions to most of them. For example, not all genes show simple patterns of dominant and recessive alleles. In most organisms, genetics is more complicated, because the majority of genes have more than two alleles. In addition, many important traits are controlled by more than one gene. **Some alleles are neither dominant nor recessive, and many traits are controlled by multiple alleles or multiple genes.**

▲ **Figure 11–11** **Some alleles are neither dominant nor recessive.** In four o'clock plants, for example, the alleles for red and white flowers show incomplete dominance. Heterozygous *(RW)* plants have pink flowers—a mix of red and white coloring.

Incomplete Dominance A cross between two four o'clock *(Mirabilis)* plants shows one of these complications. The F_1 generation produced by a cross between red-flowered *(RR)* and white-flowered *(WW)* plants consists of pink-colored flowers *(RW)*, as shown in **Figure 11–11.** Which allele is dominant in this case? Neither one. Cases in which one allele is not completely dominant over another are called **incomplete dominance.** In incomplete dominance, the heterozygous phenotype is somewhere in between the two homozygous phenotypes.

Codominance A similar situation is **codominance,** in which both alleles contribute to the phenotype of the organism. For example, in cattle the allele for red hair is codominant with the allele for white hair. Cattle with both alleles are roan, or pinkish brown, because their coats are a mixture of both red and white hairs. In certain varieties of chickens, the allele for black feathers is codominant with the allele for white feathers. Heterozygous chickens appear speckled with black and white feathers.

BIO INSIGHTS **HISTORY OF SCIENCE**

Testing to identify F_1 genotypes
Mendel was very thorough in his methodology, so it really comes as no surprise that he devised a method to test his hypotheses in various ways. One method he used, which is used frequently by geneticists today, has come to be known as the testcross. A testcross is used to identify the genotype of F_1 hybrids. For this cross, F_1 hybrids are crossed back to the parent with the trait controlled by the recessive allele. When Mendel used a testcross for his F_1 offspring, he expected to observe approximately equal numbers of offspring with the traits controlled by the dominant and recessive alleles. That is what he observed. Today, a testcross is used to determine whether an individual with the phenotype controlled by the dominant allele is heterozygous or homozygous. If the individual is homozygous, none of the offspring will have the phenotype controlled by the recessive allele.

Figure 11–12 Coat color in rabbits is determined by a single gene that has at least four different alleles. Different combinations of alleles result in the four colors you see here. **Interpreting Graphics** ***What allele combinations can a chinchilla rabbit have?***

Full color: CC, Cc^{ch}, Cc^{h}, or Cc

Chinchilla: $c^{ch}c^{h}$, $c^{ch}c^{ch}$, or $c^{ch}c$

Himalayan: $c^{h}c$ or $c^{h}c^{h}$

Albino: cc

Key

- C = full color; dominant to all other alleles
- c^{ch} = chinchilla; partial defect in pigmentation; dominant to c^{h} and c alleles
- c^{h} = Himalayan; color in certain parts of body; dominant to c allele
- c = albino; no color; recessive to all other alleles

Multiple Alleles Many genes have more than two alleles and are therefore said to have **multiple alleles.** This does not mean that an individual can have more than two alleles. It only means that more than two possible alleles exist in a population. One of the best-known examples is coat color in rabbits. A rabbit's coat color is determined by a single gene that has at least four different alleles. The four known alleles display a pattern of simple dominance that can produce four possible coat colors, as shown in **Figure 11–12.** Many other genes have multiple alleles, including the human genes for blood type and eye color.

Polygenic Traits Many traits are produced by the interaction of several genes. Traits controlled by two or more genes are said to be **polygenic traits,** which means "having many genes." For example, at least three genes are involved in making the reddish-brown pigment in the eyes of fruit flies. Different combinations of alleles for these genes produce very different eye colors. Polygenic traits often show a wide range of phenotypes. For example, the wide range of skin color in humans comes about partly because more than four different genes probably control this trait.

CHECKPOINT *What are multiple alleles?*

Address Misconceptions

Students might try to apply the ideas of simple dominance to other types of gene expression. Give students many different examples of incomplete dominance, codominance, multiple alleles, and polygenic traits. Collect pictures for students to compare the various phenotypes.

Meet Diverse Needs

At-risk students might find it helpful to develop a table in which they list the five different patterns of gene expression (including simple dominance), along with descriptions and examples of each. Encourage students to include Punnett squares that illustrate potential phenotypic ratios of offspring for each pattern of inheritance. **Learning modality: visual**

Use Visuals

Figure 11–12 Explain that coat color in rabbits does show a pattern of simple dominance among four alleles. Have students study the genotypes of the rabbits in the figure. Challenge them to arrange the alleles for coat color in order from the most dominant to the least dominant. *($C > c^{ch} > c^{h} > c$)* Then, have students make up genetic crosses for coat color in rabbits and exchange them with partners. Partners should solve the problems using Punnett squares.

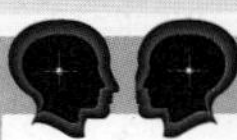

TEACHER TO TEACHER

When I teach introductory genetics, I find that students often lose interest studying only the inheritance of traits in pea plants. To keep them more interested, I like to relate inheritance to their world and insert many examples of human traits. Some human traits that show simple dominance include cystic fibrosis (recessive), freckles (dominant), and widow's peak (dominant). Blood type is controlled by 3 alleles in which A (I^A) and B (I^B) are codominant, and both are dominant over O (ii). I devise genetic problems using these and other human traits for students to practice setting up Punnett squares and identifying genotypes and phenotypes.

James Boal,
Biology Teacher
Natrona County High School,
Casper, WY

Answers to . . .

CHECKPOINT *Genes that have more than two alleles*

Figure 11–12 $c^{ch}c^{h}$, $c^{ch}c^{ch}$, or $c^{ch}c$

Applying Mendel's Principles

Demonstration

Set up crosses between wild-type fruit flies and fruit flies with vestigial wings. Allow students to observe the parents of the cross and the F_1 offspring. Ask: **Which trait is controlled by a dominant allele?** *(Normal wings)* Then, have student volunteers diagram a Punnett square on the board to predict the phenotypic ratio of the F_2 offspring. Count all the F_2 progeny from the cross and have students compare the actual phenotypic ratio with the predicted ratio.

3 ASSESS

Evaluate Understanding

Play a game in which you ask student teams to solve various problems in genetics—from identifying the pattern of inheritance, such as simple dominance, incomplete dominance, or multiple alleles, to predicting the outcome of dihybrid crosses.

Reteach

Students can make flashcards for each of the vocabulary words. Student pairs can quiz each other on the meanings of the words.

ALTERNATIVE ASSESSMENT

Students' problems should follow the rules of genetics and include correct and complete answers. Have pairs of students exchange and try to solve each other's problems.

Use iText to review the key concepts in Section 11–3.

Answer to . . .

Figure 11–13 *They are small, easy to keep in the laboratory, and produce large numbers of offspring in a short time.*

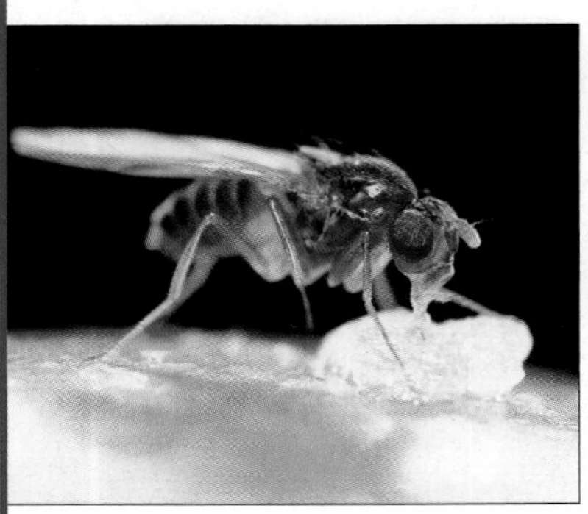

▲ **Figure 11–13** The common fruit fly is a popular organism for genetic research. **Inferring** *Why are fruit flies easier to use for genetic research than large animals, such as dogs?*

Applying Mendel's Principles

Mendel's principles don't apply only to plants. At the beginning of the 1900s, the American geneticist Thomas Hunt Morgan decided to look for a model organism to advance the study of genetics. He wanted an animal that was small, easy to keep in the laboratory, and able to produce large numbers of offspring in a short period of time. He decided to work on a tiny insect that kept showing up, uninvited, in his laboratory. The insect was the common fruit fly, *Drosophila melanogaster,* shown in **Figure 11–13.**

Morgan grew the flies in small milk bottles stoppered with cotton gauze. Morgan found that he could breed a new generation of flies every 14 days. A single pair of flies could produce as many as 100 offspring. *Drosophila* was an ideal organism for genetics because it could produce plenty of offspring, and it did so quickly. Before long, Morgan and other biologists had tested every one of Mendel's principles and learned that they applied not just to pea plants but to other organisms as well.

Mendel's principles also apply to humans. The basic principles of Mendelian genetics can be used to study the inheritance of human traits and to calculate the probability of certain traits appearing in the next generation.

In 1900, Archibald Garrod, a British doctor, discovered that the pattern of inheritance of a rare disorder known as alkaptonuria fit the Mendelian pattern. Before long, a wide variety of human genes had been discovered. One of these is a gene for skin pigmentation. The gene's dominant allele *(A)* produces skin coloration. Individuals who are homozygous for the recessive form of the allele *(a)* have albinism, meaning that they lack the pigment melanin that gives human skin its color.

If two people with normal skin color have a child with albinism, what are the odds that a second child will also have albinism? By constructing a Punnett square, you can see that there is a 1 in 4 probability that their next child will also have albinism.

11–3 Section Assessment

1. **Key Concept** Explain what *independent assortment* means.
2. **Key Concept** Describe two inheritance patterns besides simple dominance.
3. What is the difference between incomplete dominance and codominance?
4. Why are fruit flies an ideal organism for genetic research?
5. **Critical Thinking Problem Solving** A geneticist crosses a pea plant that is true-breeding for round green seeds *(RRyy)* with one that is true-breeding for wrinkled yellow seeds *(rrYY)*. Construct a Punnett square to show the results of this cross.

iTEXT Assessment Use iText to review the important concepts in Section 11–3.

ALTERNATIVE ASSESSMENT

Problem Solving Construct a genetics problem to be given as an assignment to a classmate. The problem must test incomplete dominance, codominance, multiple alleles, or polygenic traits. Your problem must have an answer key that includes all of your work.

11–3 Section Assessment

1. Genes for different traits do not influence each other's inheritance.
2. Answers include descriptions for any two of the following: incomplete dominance, codominance, multiple alleles, or polygenic traits.
3. In incomplete dominance, the heterozygous phenotype is somewhere between the two homozygous phenotypes. In codominance, the heterozygous phenotype has characteristics coded for by both alleles.
4. They are small, easy to keep in the laboratory, and produce large numbers of offspring in a short period of time.
5. All offspring will be *RrYy.* Punnett squares should be constructed like the one in Figure 11–9, except parental gametes are *Ry* and *rY.*

11–4 Meiosis

Gregor Mendel did not know where the genes he had discovered were located in the cell. Fortunately, his predictions of how genes should behave were so specific that it was not long before biologists were certain they had found them. Genes are located on chromosomes in the cell nucleus.

Mendel's principles of genetics require at least two things. First, each organism must inherit a single copy of every gene from both its "parents." Because each pea plant has two "parents," each plant must carry two complete sets of genes. Second, when an organism produces its own gametes, those two sets of genes must be separated from each other so that each gamete contains just one set of genes. This means that when gametes are formed, there must be a process that separates the two sets of genes so that each gamete ends up with just one set. Although Mendel didn't know it, gametes are formed through exactly such a process.

Guide for Reading

Key Concepts
- What happens during the process of meiosis?
- How is meiosis different from mitosis?

Vocabulary
homologous
diploid
haploid
meiosis
tetrad
crossing-over

Reading Strategy: Using Visuals Before you read, preview **Figure 11–15.** As you read, note what happens at each stage of meiosis.

Chromosome Number

As an example of how this process works, let's consider the fruit fly, *Drosophila.* A body cell in an adult fruit fly has 8 chromosomes, as shown in **Figure 11–14.** Four of the chromosomes came from the fruit fly's male parent, and 4 came from its female parent. These two sets of chromosomes are **homologous** (hoh-MAHL-uh-guhs), meaning that each of the 4 chromosomes that came from the male parent has a corresponding chromosome from the female parent.

A cell that contains both sets of homologous chromosomes is said to be **diploid,** which means "two sets." The number of chromosomes in a diploid cell is sometimes represented by the symbol 2N. Thus for *Drosophila,* the diploid number is 8, which can be written 2N = 8. Diploid cells contain two complete sets of chromosomes and two complete sets of genes. This agrees with Mendel's idea that the cells of an adult organism contain two copies of each gene.

By contrast, the gametes of sexually reproducing organisms, including fruit flies and peas, contain only a single set of chromosomes, and therefore only a single set of genes. Such cells are said to be **haploid,** which means "one set." For *Drosophila,* this can be written as N = 4, meaning that the haploid number is 4.

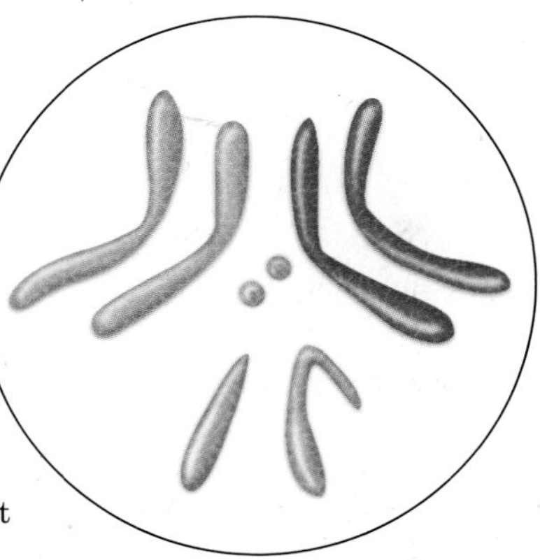

▶ **Figure 11–14** These chromosomes are from a fruit fly *(Drosophila).* Each of the fruit fly's body cells has 8 chromosomes.

SECTION RESOURCES

Print:
- ***Teaching Resources,*** Section Review 11–4
- ***Guided Reading and Study Workbook,*** Section 11–4

Technology:
- ***iText,*** Section 11–4

Section 11–4

1 FOCUS

Objectives

11.4.1 ***Contrast*** the chromosome number of body cells and gametes.
11.4.2 ***Summarize*** the events of meiosis.
11.4.3 ***Contrast*** meiosis and mitosis.

Guide for Reading

Vocabulary Preview

Explain that the prefix *hapl-* comes from the Greek word *haplous,* which means "single." The word *haploid* refers to cells that have a single set of chromosomes. Ask: **If the prefix *diplo-* means "double," what does the word *diploid* refer to?** (A cell with two sets of chromosomes)

Reading Strategy

Before students read the section, encourage them to preview the vocabulary words by finding the boldfaced terms in the section and listing them. Tell students to leave space on their lists to make notes as they read.

2 INSTRUCT

Chromosome Number

Meet Diverse Needs

Review the location of chromosomes in the cell. Diagram a pair of homologous chromosomes in a cell. Then, work backward to show how one chromosome came from the mother and one from the father. Point out the location of a gene. Show how it can have two alleles. Ask: **What would happen if gametes were also 2N?** *(Offspring would have 4N chromosomes.)* **Learning modality: visual**

Phases of Meiosis

Use Visuals

Figure 11–15 Have volunteers use their own words to describe what is occurring during each step of meiosis. Ask: **Which cell is diploid?** *(The original cell)* **Which cell is haploid?** *(The daughter cells of meiosis I through the daughter cells of meiosis II)* Discuss the difference between the divisions in meiosis I and meiosis II. Make sure students understand that homologous chromosomes separate during meiosis I and the centromeres and chromosome copies separate during meiosis II.

Address Misconceptions

Some students might confuse mitosis and meiosis. The most difficult point to understand is that the daughter cells produced after meiosis I are already haploid; they contain only one set of chromosomes. Have students compare diagrams of mitosis and meiosis. Point out that DNA replication occurs in prophase I; however, the chromosome copies do not separate until meiosis II. Also point out that the division in meiosis II is like that of mitosis—centromeres divide to separate the chromosome copies. Emphasize that meiosis occurs only in cells that form gametes; it does not occur in body cells.

Meet Diverse Needs

Have at-risk students and students with limited English develop a flowchart that shows the phases of meiosis. Students can base their flowcharts on Figure 11–15, but should draw their own diagrams and use their own words to describe what is occurring during each step. Students with limited English may make notes in their native language. **Limited English proficiency**

Figure 11–15 **During meiosis, the number of chromosomes per cell is cut in half through the separation of the homologous chromosomes.** The result of meiosis is 4 haploid cells that are genetically different from one another and from the original cell.

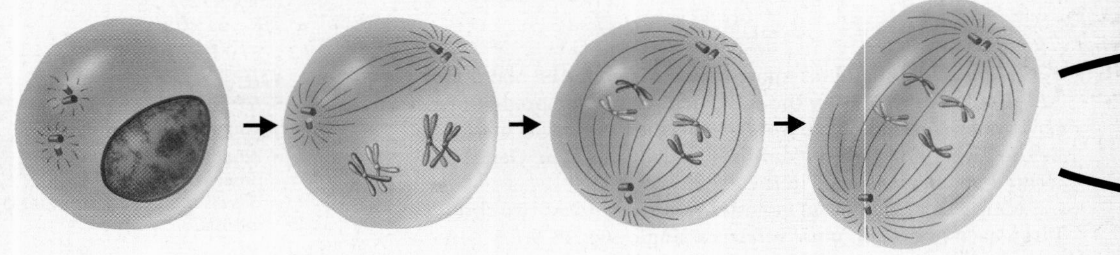

MEIOSIS I

Interphase I
Cells undergo a round of DNA replication, forming duplicate chromosomes.

Prophase I
Each chromosome pairs with its corresponding homologous chromosome to form a tetrad.

Metaphase I
Spindle fibers attach to the chromosomes.

Anaphase I
The fibers pull the homologous chromosomes toward opposite ends of the cell.

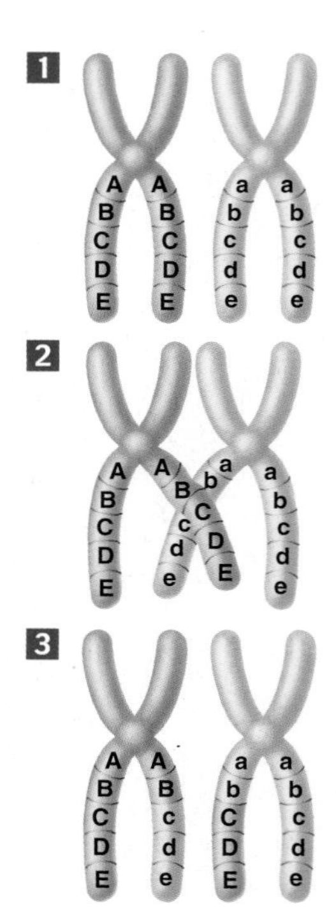

◀ **Figure 11–16** During prophase I of meiosis, homologous chromosomes may cross over and exchange portions of their chromatids. **Interpreting Graphics** *How does crossing-over affect the alleles on a chromatid?*

Phases of Meiosis

How are haploid (N) gamete cells produced from diploid (2N) cells? That's where **meiosis** (my-OH-sis) comes in. **Meiosis is a process of reduction division in which the number of chromosomes per cell is cut in half through the separation of homologous chromosomes in a diploid cell.**

Meiosis usually involves two distinct stages: the first meiotic division, called meiosis I, and the second meiotic division, called meiosis II. By the end of meiosis II, the diploid cell that entered meiosis has become 4 haploid cells. **Figure 11–15** shows the details of meiosis in an organism that has a diploid number of 4 (2N = 4).

CHECKPOINT *What is meiosis?*

Meiosis I Prior to meiosis I, each chromosome is replicated. The cells then begin to divide in a way that looks similar to mitosis. In mitosis, the 4 chromosomes line up individually in the center of the cell. The 2 chromatids that make up each chromosome then separate from each other.

In prophase of meiosis I, however, each chromosome pairs with its corresponding homologous chromosome to form a structure called a **tetrad.** There are 4 chromatids in a tetrad. This pairing of homologous chromosomes is the key to understanding meiosis.

TIME SAVER **PRESENTATIONS MADE EASY!**

The Presentation Assistant Plus contains the Prentice Hall Presentation Pro and the Transparencies, which provide easy-to-follow visual support for every step of this section. If you have a computer presentation station, use Prentice Hall Presentation Pro for Section 11–4, or use the transparencies listed here.

Section 11–4: **Interest Grabber**
Section Outline
Crossing-Over
Figure 11–15
Figure 11–17

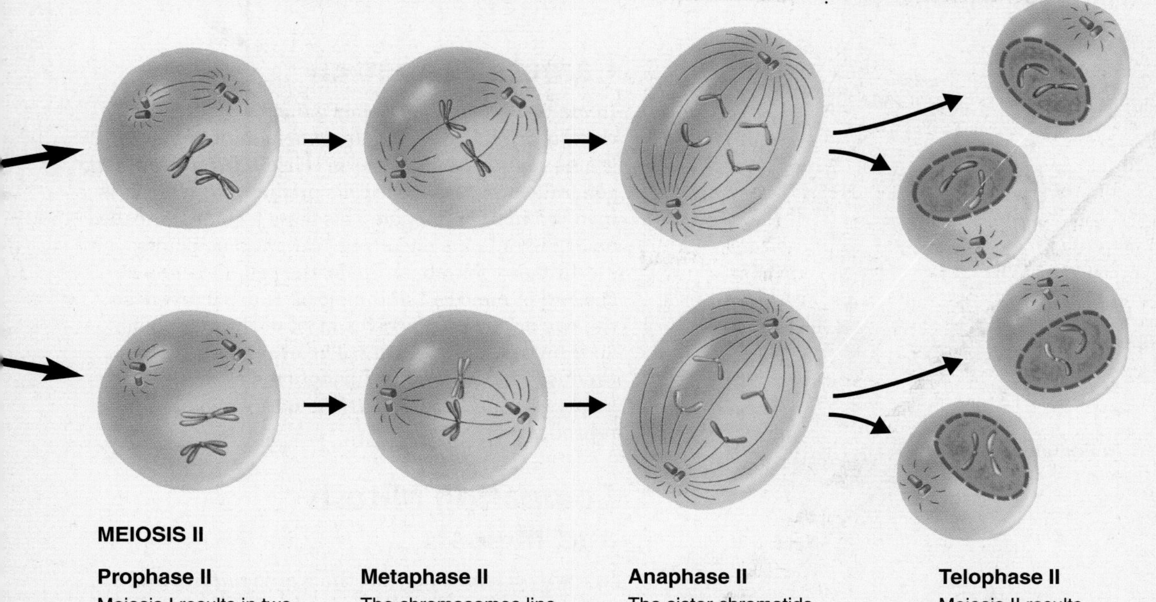

MEIOSIS II
Prophase II
Meiosis I results in two haploid (N) daughter cells, each with half the number of chromosomes as the original cell.
Metaphase II
The chromosomes line up in a similar way to the metaphase stage of mitosis.
Anaphase II
The sister chromatids separate and move toward opposite ends of the cell.
Telophase II
Meiosis II results in four haploid (N) daughter cells.

As homologous chromosomes pair up and form tetrads in meiosis I, they may exchange portions of their chromatids in a process called **crossing-over.** Crossing-over, shown in **Figure 11–16,** results in the exchange of alleles between homologous chromosomes and produces new combinations of alleles.

What happens next? The homologous chromosomes separate, and two new cells are formed. Although each cell now has 4 chromatids (as it would after mitosis), something is different. Because each pair of homologous chromosomes was separated, neither of the daughter cells has the two complete sets of chromosomes that it would have in a diploid cell. Those two sets have been shuffled and sorted almost like a deck of cards. The two cells produced by meiosis I have sets of chromosomes and alleles that are different from each other and from the diploid cell that entered meiosis I.

Meiosis II The two cells produced by meiosis I now enter a second meiotic division. Unlike the first division, neither cell goes through a round of chromosome replication before entering meiosis II. Thus, each of the cell's chromosomes has 2 chromatids. During metaphase II of meiosis, 2 chromosomes line up in the center of each cell. In anaphase II, the paired chromatids separate. Each of the four daughter cells produced in meiosis II receives 2 chromatids. Those four daughter cells now contain the haploid number (N)—just 2 chromosomes each.

Build Science Skills

Applying Concepts Challenge students to draw diagrams of meiosis that show how seed color and seed shape in Mendel's peas are traits whose genes assort independently. Make sure students realize that the genes for seed shape and seed color are on different chromosomes. Ask: **If the genes for seed shape and seed color had not assorted independently, what could you assume about the genes for these traits?** *(The genes for these traits are located on the same chromosome.)*

Demonstration

Use pipe cleaners of different colors to show how a tetrad forms from two homologous chromosomes. Connect sister chromatids together by threading 2 pipe cleaners through a bead. Ask: **What structure does the bead represent?** *(Centromere)* Overlap the pipe cleaners to simulate crossing over. Then, cut and tape the pipe cleaners to simulate the breaking and recombination of chromosomes to form the genetically different chromatids. Discuss the significance of crossing-over. Elicit from students that crossing-over increases genetic diversity. Ask: **Will crossing-over cause a different phenotype in the offspring of true-breeding parents?** *(No, the homologous chromosomes are homozygous for the particular trait because they have the same allele for the gene that encodes the trait. Crossing-over will cause portions of the chromosomes to be mixed, but if the alleles are identical, crossing-over is not detected.)*

BIO INSIGHTS — FACTS AND FIGURES

Clarifying the language of mitosis and meiosis After DNA replication prior to the start of mitosis or meiosis, a chromosome is described as being composed of two sister chromatids. The sister chromatids have exactly the same DNA sequence, unless a mistake was made during replication. These two chromatids are held together by centromeres. When the centromeres divide, the chromatids separate soon after. Note that the chromosome number is not reduced. This is the division that occurs in mitosis and meiosis II. During meiosis I, the homologous chromosomes separate. This division changes the cell from a diploid state to a haploid state because each resulting cell has only one set of chromosomes. These chromosomes, however, still consist of two sister chromatids that will be separated during meiosis II.

Answers to . . .

CHECKPOINT *Meiosis is a process of reduction division in which the number of chromosomes per cell is cut in half through the separation of chromosomes in a diploid cell.*

Figure 11–16 *The alleles can be moved to different chromatids.*

Gamete Formation

Use Visuals

Figure 11–17 Use the illustrations to help students see the end results of meiosis. Emphasize that the cells are haploid after meiosis I. Ask: **In what cells does meiosis occur?** *(Only in cells of the reproductive organs that will form gametes)*

Comparing Mitosis and Meiosis

Build Science Skills

Use Analogies Challenge students to explain how making two copies of a story is analogous to mitosis. *(The pages are copied, then collated into two separate, complete stories.)* Discuss how this analogy can be applied to meiosis. *(The pages are copied, the even and odd pages are separated, and then the two groups of pages are collated separately to make four groups of half stories.)*

3 ASSESS

Evaluate Understanding

Have students list the stages of meiosis in order and describe what occurs during each stage.

Reteach

Have students review Figure 11–15. Then, instruct them to diagram the movement of chromosomes as a cell goes through the stages of meiosis.

MAKING CONNECTIONS

For sister chromatids, students' models should show two strands of yarn or other material joined together near the center. Models of homologous chromosomes should show separate pairs of identical chromosomes. Chromosomes can be either with their sister chromatids or without them.

Use iText to review the concepts in Section 11–4.

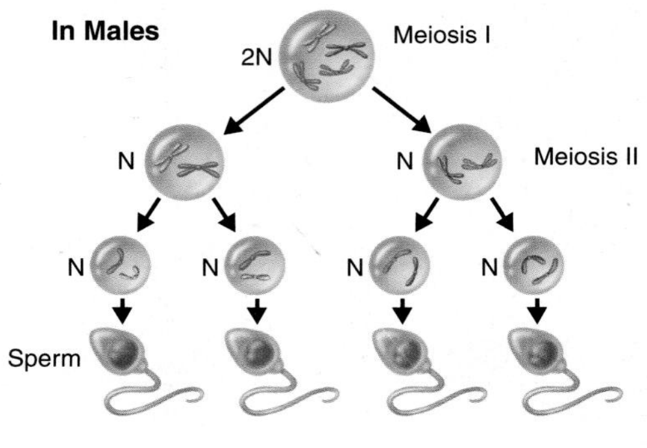

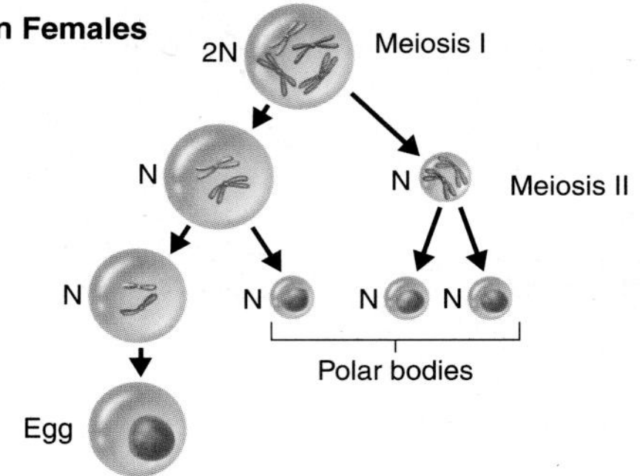

▲ **Figure 11–17** **Meiosis produces four genetically different haploid cells.** In males, meiosis results in four equal-sized gametes called sperm. In females, only one large egg cell results from meiosis. The other three cells, called polar bodies, usually are not involved in reproduction.

Gamete Formation

In male animals, the haploid gametes produced by meiosis are called sperm. In some plants, pollen grains contain haploid sperm cells. In female animals, generally only one of the cells produced by meiosis is involved in reproduction. This female gamete is called an egg in animals and an egg cell in some plants.

In many female animals, the cell divisions at the end of meiosis I and meiosis II are uneven, so the egg or egg cell receives most of the cytoplasm, as shown in **Figure 11–17.** The other three cells produced in the female during meiosis are known as polar bodies and usually do not participate in reproduction.

Comparing Mitosis and Meiosis

In a way, it's too bad that the words *mitosis* and *meiosis* sound so much like each other, because the two processes are very different. **Mitosis results in the production of two genetically identical diploid cells, whereas meiosis produces four genetically different haploid cells.**

A diploid cell that divides by mitosis gives rise to two diploid (2N) daughter cells. The daughter cells have sets of chromosomes and alleles that are identical to each other and to the original parent cell. Meiosis, on the other hand, begins with a diploid cell but produces four haploid (N) cells. These cells are genetically different from the diploid cell and from one another.

11–4 Section Assessment

1. **Key Concept** Describe the main results of meiosis.
2. **Key Concept** What are the principal differences between mitosis and meiosis?
3. What do the terms *diploid* and *haploid* mean?
4. What is crossing-over?
5. **Critical Thinking Applying Concepts** In human cells, 2N = 46. How many chromosomes would you expect to find in a sperm cell? In an egg cell? In a white blood cell? Explain.

iTEXT Assessment Use iText to review the important concepts in Section 11–4.

MAKING CONNECTIONS

Modeling
Using materials found around the house, create a model that illustrates the difference between sister chromatids and homologous pairs of chromosomes. You may want to refer to Chapter 10 for help.

11–4 Section Assessment

1. Four haploid cells genetically different from each other and from the original cell
2. Mitosis produces two genetically identical diploid cells; meiosis produces four genetically different haploid cells.
3. Diploid: two sets of chromosomes; haploid: one set of chromosomes
4. Homologous chromosomes pair up and form tetrads, which may exchange portions of their chromatids, resulting in the exchange of alleles between the homologous chromosomes.
5. Both sperm and egg cells have 23 chromosomes because they are gametes, which are haploid cells. A white blood cell has 46 chromosomes because it is a diploid body cell.

11–5 Linkage and Gene Maps

If you thought carefully about Mendel's principle of independent assortment as you analyzed meiosis, one question might have been bothering you. It's easy to see how genes located on different chromosomes assort independently, but what about genes located on the same chromosome? Wouldn't they generally be inherited together?

Guide for Reading

Key Concept

- What structures actually assort independently?

Vocabulary

gene map

Reading Strategy: Predicting Before you read, preview **Figure 11–19.** Predict how a diagram like this one can be used to determine how likely genes are to assort independently. As you read, note whether or not your prediction was correct.

Gene Linkage

The answer to these questions, as Thomas Hunt Morgan first realized in 1910, is yes. Morgan's research on fruit flies led him to the principle of linkage. After identifying more than 50 *Drosophila* genes, Morgan discovered that many of them appeared to be "linked" together in ways that, at first glance, seemed to violate the principle of independent assortment. For example, a fly with reddish-orange eyes and miniature wings, like the one shown in **Figure 11–18,** was used in a series of crosses. The results showed that the genes for those traits were almost always inherited together and only rarely became separated from each other.

Morgan and his associates observed so many genes that were inherited together that before long they could group all of the fly's genes into four linkage groups. The linkage groups assorted independently, but all of the genes in one group were inherited together. *Drosophila* has four linkage groups. It also has four pairs of chromosomes, which led to two remarkable conclusions. First, each chromosome is actually a group of linked genes. Second, Mendel's principle of independent assortment still holds true. **It is the chromosomes, however, that assort independently, not individual genes.**

How did Mendel manage to miss gene linkage? By luck, or by design, six of the seven genes he studied are on different chromosomes. The two genes that are found on the same chromosome are so far apart that they also assort independently.

▼ **Figure 11–18** The genes for this fruit fly's reddish-orange eyes and miniature wings are almost always inherited together. The reason for this is that the genes are close together on a single chromosome. **Chromosomes assort independently, not individual genes.**

Gene Maps

If two genes are found on the same chromosome, does this mean that they are linked forever? Not at all. Crossing-over during meiosis sometimes separates genes that had been on the same chromosome onto homologous chromosomes. Crossover events occasionally separate and exchange linked genes and produce new combinations of alleles. This is important because it helps to generate genetic diversity.

TIME SAVER — SECTION RESOURCES

Print:

- ***Teaching Resources,*** Section Review 11–5, Chapter 11 Exploration
- ***Guided Reading and Study Workbook,*** Section 11–5
- ***Biotechnology Manual,*** Lab 2

Technology:

- ***Presentation Assistant Plus,*** Interest Grabber, Section Outline, Comparative Scale of Gene Mapping, Figure 11–19
- ***iText,*** Section 11–5

Section 11–5

1 FOCUS

Objectives

11.5.1 ***Identify*** the structures that actually assort independently.

11.5.2 ***Explain*** how gene maps are produced.

Guide for Reading

Vocabulary Preview

Have student volunteers describe what a map is. Elicit the fact that maps show the locations of places and things. Ask: **What do you think a gene map is?** *(It shows the locations of genes on a chromosome.)*

Reading Strategy

As students read, encourage them to write down the main ideas that lead them to determine whether or not their prediction was correct.

2 INSTRUCT

Gene Linkage

Build Science Skills

Using Models Students can construct a model of a chromosome with beads threaded on a pipe cleaner. The beads represent genes, and the pipe cleaner represents the chromosome. Challenge students to demonstrate why genes linked to the same chromosome do not assort independently. Ask: **Why would two genes located far apart on the same chromosome assort independently?** *(Crossing-over causes the genes to act as though they are located on two different chromosomes, and they assort independently during meiosis.)*

Gene Maps

Use Visuals

Figure 11–19 As students study the gene map, ask: **Would you expect more crossing-over events to occur between star eye and speck wing or between star eye and black body? Explain.** *(Star eye and speck wing; because these genes are located farther apart, it is more likely that a*

11–5 (continued)

crossing-over event will occur between them.) Explain that recombination rates are calculated by determining the percentage of recombinants produced in a cross. Recombinant offspring have a phenotype that is different from either parent. For example, in a cross between a homozygous male with a black body *(bb)* and vestigial wings *(vv)* and heterozygous female *(BbVv)* with a brown body and normal wings, most of the F_2 offspring will look like either parent. However some of the offspring, about 20%, will have either a black body and normal wings or a brown body and vestigial wings.

3 ASSESS

Evaluate Understanding

Draw a hypothetical gene map on the board. Have students tell which genes would have high frequencies of crossing-over and which would not.

Reteach

Have students diagram a crossing-over event to show how genes that are located close together have a lower frequency of recombination than genes that are located far apart.

Take It to the NET

B.A. degree from Kentucky State College (1886), Ph.D. from Johns Hopkins University (1890), appointment at Columbia University (1904), discovery of the white-eyed mutation in the fruit fly, *Drosophila* (1910), publication of *The Mechanism of Mendelian Heredity* (1915), appointment at the California Institute of Technology (1928), and award of the Nobel Prize in Physiology or Medicine (1933). For additional information, visit **www.phschool.com**

Use iText to review the concepts in Section 11–5.

Answer to . . .

Figure 11–19 *The "purple eye" gene is located at 54.5.*

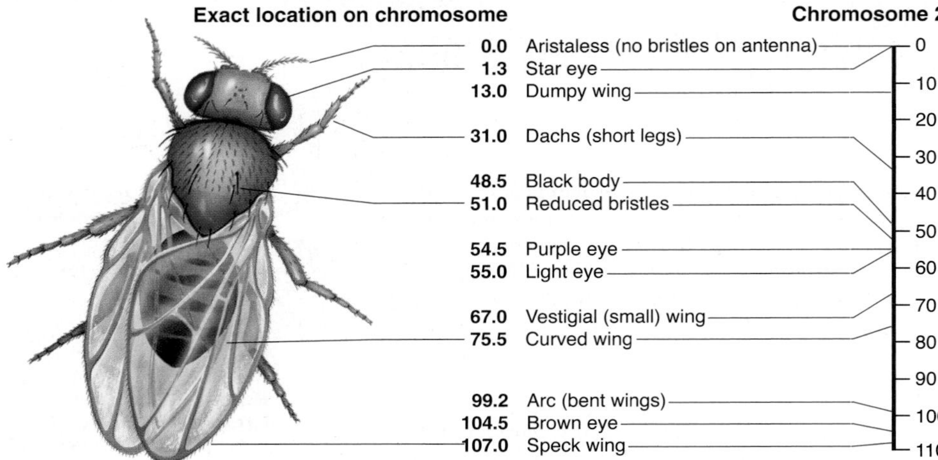

▲ **Figure 11–19** This gene map shows the location of a variety of genes on chromosome 2 of the fruit fly. The genes are named after the problems abnormal alleles cause, not the normal structure. **Interpreting Graphics** *Where on the chromosome is the "purple eye" gene located?*

In 1911, a Columbia University student was working part time in Morgan's lab. This student, Alfred Sturtevant, hypothesized that the rate at which crossing-over separated linked genes could be the key to an important discovery. Sturtevant reasoned that the farther apart two genes were, the more likely they were to be separated by a crossover in meiosis. The rate at which linked genes were separated and recombined could then be used to produce a "map" of distances between genes. Sturtevant gathered up several notebooks of lab data and took them back to his room. The next morning, he presented Morgan with a **gene map** showing the relative locations of each known gene on one of the *Drosophila* chromosomes, as shown in **Figure 11–19**. Sturtevant's method of using recombination rates, which measure the frequencies of crossing-over between genes, has been used to construct genetic maps, including maps of the human genome, ever since.

11–5 Section Assessment

1. **Key Concept** How does the principle of independent assortment apply to chromosomes?
2. What are gene maps, and how are they produced?
3. How does crossing-over make gene mapping possible?
4. **Critical Thinking Inferring** If two genes are on the same chromosome but usually assort independently, what does that tell you about how close together they are?

iText Assessment Use iText to review the important concepts in Section 11–5.

Take It to the NET

For his pioneering research on fruit flies, Thomas Hunt Morgan won a Nobel Prize. Create a time line that shows at least four highlights of Morgan's life as a scientist. Use the links provided in the Biology area at the Prentice Hall Web site for help in completing this activity: **www.phschool.com**

11–5 Section Assessment

1. It is the chromosomes that assort independently, not individual genes.
2. A gene map shows the relative locations of genes on a chromosome. The frequency of crossing-over between genes is used to produce a map of distances between genes.
3. The farther apart two genes are, the more likely they are to be separated during a crossover in meiosis. Therefore, the frequency of crossing-over is equal to the distance between two genes.
4. The two genes are located very far apart from each other.

Exploration

Modeling Meiosis

Meiosis results in 4 new cells, each containing half the number of chromosomes in the original cells. Using the procedures below, you will build a model to demonstrate the process of meiosis and explore how it can lead to genetic changes.

Problem **What happens to the chromosomes in cells during meiosis?**

Materials

- 4 colors of yarn (2 shades of red and 2 shades of green)
- scissors
- transparent tape
- index cards
- felt-tip marker

Skills Using Models, Communicating Results

Procedure

1. You will use yarn and index cards to model each stage of meiosis. Use 2 shades of red yarn to represent one homologous pair of chromosomes and 2 shades of green yarn to represent another pair. Use an index card to represent a cell.
2. Cut 2 pieces of yarn about 5 cm long from each color of yarn. Each piece of yarn will represent a chromatid.
3. Tape pieces of red and green yarn to an index card to show the appearance of two tetrads in a cell at the beginning of meiosis.
4. Tape pieces of yarn to additional index cards to model the numbers and positions of the chromosomes and cells at each stage of meiosis. Be sure to include an example of crossing-over at the correct stage. Use a felt-tip marker to label each card with the name of the stage it represents.
5. Arrange the finished cards to show the complete process of meiosis. Label the stages at which genetic segregation and crossing-over occur and chromosome number changes.
6. Use your cards to explain the process of meiosis to a classmate. Then, trade roles and have your classmate use his or her models to explain the process of meiosis to you.

Analyze and Conclude

1. **Using Models** What is the result of the first meiotic division (meiosis I)?
2. **Using Models** What is the result of the second meiotic division (meiosis II)?
3. **Drawing Conclusions** How does meiosis lead to increased genetic variation?
4. **Predicting** How would the gametes be affected if a pair of chromatids failed to separate in the second meiotic division?

Go Further

Using Models Make a second set of models that shows the differences between the formation of sperm and the formation of eggs.

Exploration

Objective Students will be able to use models to show what happens to the chromosomes in cells during meiosis.

Skills Focus **Using Models, Communicating Results, Predicting**

Time 45 minutes

Alternative Materials Yarn of any color may be used. However, use two shades of one color and two shades of another color.

Pre-Lab Discussion Discuss how gametes form. Ask: **Why is it important for gametes to have only half the number of chromosomes that body cells have?** *(When gametes combine, the zygote has the proper number of chromosomes.)*

Teaching Tips

- Refer students to Figure 11–15 as a guide for constructing their models.
- Students should use the lighter shade of yarn to represent the chromosomes that come from one parent and the darker shade to represent the chromosomes from the other parent. Chromosome copies should be the same shade.
- Circulate among students to make sure they understand what homologous chromosomes and chromatids are.

Procedure

5. Student models should look similar to the diagrams in Figure 11–15. Crossing-over occurs during prophase I. Segregation, or the separation of alleles, occurs during anaphase I. The chromosome number becomes haploid at the end of meiosis I.

Expected Outcomes Students will have constructed a usable model for meiosis.

Analyze and Conclude

1. Two cells with a haploid number of duplicated chromosomes
2. Four cells, each with a haploid number of chromosomes
3. Crossing-over redistributes the alleles for genes, so the resulting chromosomes are different from the parental chromosomes. Homologous chromosomes align randomly during metaphase I, so chromosomes from each parent are combined in the gametes. The production of haploid gametes requires the joining of two gametes (that are usually genetically different) to produce viable offspring.
4. One gamete would have an extra copy of a chromosome, and another gamete would not have any copies of that chromosome.

Go Further

In sperm formation, all 4 daughter cells develop into sperm cells, whereas in egg formation, only one daughter cell develops into an egg. In most species, the polar bodies die.

Chapter 11 Study Guide

Study Tip

Give students various problems in genetics where they must identify genotypes and phenotypes of parents and offspring, identify patterns of inheritance, or predict the outcomes of crosses with Punnett squares.

Thinking Visually

1. Each chromosome pairs with its corresponding homologous chromosome.

2. Spindle fibers pull homologous chromosomes toward opposite ends of the cell.

3. Sister chromatids separate and move toward opposite ends of the cell.

Chapter 11 Assessment

Reviewing Content

1. c	**5.** c	**9.** d
2. a	**6.** d	**10.** b
3. a	**7.** d	
4. c	**8.** d	

Understanding Concepts

11. (1) The inheritance of biological characteristics is determined by genes. (2) Where there are two or more forms of the gene for a single trait, some forms of the gene may be dominant and others recessive. (3) In most sexually reproducing organisms, each adult has one allele for each gene from each parent. These two alleles are segregated when gametes form. (4) The alleles for different genes usually segregate independently.

12. Probability is the likelihood that an event will occur. This principle can be used to predict the outcomes of genetic crosses.

Chapter 11 Study Guide

11–1 The Work of Gregor Mendel

Key Concepts

- The principle of dominance states that some alleles are dominant and others are recessive.
- When each F_1 plant flowers, the two alleles are segregated from each other so that each gamete carries only a single copy of each gene. Therefore, each F_1 plant produces two types of gametes—those with the allele for tallness and those with the allele for shortness.

Vocabulary

- genetics, p. 263 • true-breeding, p. 263
- trait, p. 264 • hybrid, p. 264
- gene, p. 265 • allele, p. 265
- segregation, p. 266 • gamete, p. 266

11–2 Probability and Punnett Squares

Key Concept

- The principles of probability can be used to predict the outcomes of genetic crosses.

Vocabulary

- probability, p. 267 • Punnett square, p. 268
- homozygous, p. 268 • heterozygous, p. 268
- phenotype, p. 268 • genotype, p. 268

11–3 Exploring Mendelian Genetics

Key Concepts

- The principle of independent assortment states that genes for different traits can segregate independently during the formation of gametes.
- Some alleles are neither dominant nor recessive, and many traits are controlled by multiple alleles or multiple genes.

Vocabulary

independent assortment, p. 271
incomplete dominance, p. 272
codominance, p. 272
multiple alleles, p. 273
polygenic traits, p. 273

11–4 Meiosis

Key Concepts

- Meiosis is a process of reduction division in which the number of chromosomes per cell is cut in half through the separation of homologous chromosomes in a diploid cell.
- Mitosis results in the production of two genetically identical diploid cells, whereas meiosis produces four genetically different haploid cells.

Vocabulary

- homologous, p. 275 • diploid, p. 275
- haploid, p. 275 • meiosis, p. 276
- tetrad, p. 276 • crossing-over, p. 277

11–5 Linkage and Gene Maps

Key Concept

- The chromosomes assort independently; individual genes do not.

Vocabulary

gene map, p. 280

Thinking Visually

Using the information in this chapter, complete the following flowchart about meiosis.

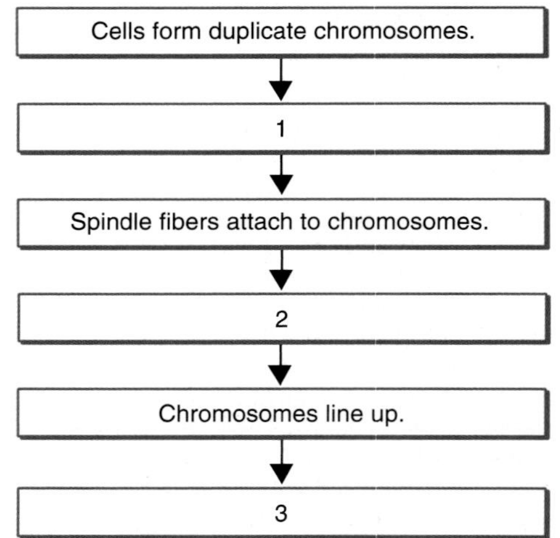

Cells form duplicate chromosomes.
1
Spindle fibers attach to chromosomes.
2
Chromosomes line up.
3

CHAPTER RESOURCES

Print:

- ***Teaching Resources,*** Chapter Vocabulary Review, Graphic Organizer
- ***Chapter Tests: Levels A and B,*** Chapter 11 Test
- ***PH Assessment System,*** Practice Test

Technology:

- ***Computer Test Bank,*** Chapter 11 Test
- ***iText,*** Chapter 11 Assessment

Chapter 11 Assessment

Reviewing Content

Choose the letter that best answers the question or completes the statement.

1. Different forms of a gene are called
   a. hybrids. c. alleles.
   b. dominant factors. d. recessive factors.
2. If a homozygous tall pea plant and a homozygous short pea plant are crossed,
   a. the recessive trait disappears.
   b. the offspring are of medium height.
   c. no hybrids are produced.
   d. all the offspring are short.
3. A Punnett square is used to determine the
   a. probable outcome of a cross.
   b. actual outcome of a cross.
   c. result of segregation.
   d. result of meiosis.
4. Organisms that have two identical alleles for a particular trait are said to be
   a. hybrid. c. homozygous.
   b. heterozygous. d. dominant.
5. The physical characteristics of an organism are its
   a. genetics. c. phenotype.
   b. heredity. d. genotype.
6. A situation in which a gene has more than two alleles is known as
   a. complete dominance.
   b. codominance.
   c. polygenic dominance.
   d. multiple alleles.
7. The illustration below represents what stage of meiosis?
   a. prophase I c. telophase I
   b. anaphase II d. metaphase I

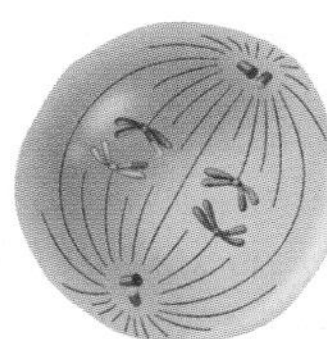

8. Unlike mitosis, meiosis results in the formation of
   a. two haploid cells.
   b. three diploid polar bodies.
   c. four diploid gamete cells.
   d. four haploid gamete cells.
9. To maintain the chromosome number of an organism, the gametes must
   a. become diploid.
   b. become recessive.
   c. be produced by mitosis.
   d. be produced by meiosis.
10. A gene map shows
   a. the number of possible alleles for a gene.
   b. the relative locations of genes on a chromosome.
   c. where chromosomes are in a cell.
   d. how crossing-over occurs

Understanding Concepts

11. List the four basic principles of genetics that Mendel discovered in his experiments. Briefly describe each of these principles.
12. What is probability? How does probability relate to genetics?
13. In pea plants, the allele for yellow seeds is dominant to the allele for green seeds. Predict the genotypic ratio of offspring produced by crossing two parents heterozygous for this trait. Draw a Punnett square to illustrate your prediction.
14. How do multiple alleles and polygenic traits differ?
15. Why can multiple alleles provide many different phenotypes for a trait?
16. If an organism has five pairs of chromosomes, how many different gametes could it produce without crossing-over? Explain your answer.
17. In rabbits, *B* is an allele for black coat and *b* is an allele for brown coat. Write the genotypes for a rabbit that is homozygous for black coat and another rabbit that is heterozygous for black coat.
18. Describe the process of meiosis.
19. Compare the phases of meiosis I with the phases of meiosis II in terms of the number and arrangement of the chromosomes.
20. Explain why it is chromosomes, not individual genes, that assort independently.

HOMEWORK GUIDE

Section:	**Questions:**
Section 11–1	1, 22, 23
Section 11–2	2–5, 12, 13, 17, 21, 25–28, 30
Section 11–3	6, 11, 14, 15, 20, 29
Section 11–4	7–9, 16, 18, 19, 24
Section 11–5	10

13. 1 *YY* : 2 *Yy* : 1 *yy*

	Y	y
Y	YY	Yy
y	Yy	yy

14. A gene has multiple alleles if it has more than two alleles. Two or more genes control polygenic traits.

15. A single gene that has more than two possible alleles in a population can display a pattern of simple dominance that can produce several phenotypes.

16. Each pair of homologous chromosomes can segregate in two different ways, so there are 2^5 (2 x 2 x 2 x 2 x 2), or 32 possible gametes.

17. Homozygous black coat: *BB*; heterozygous black coat: *Bb*

18. Meiosis is a process of reduction division in which the number of chromosomes per cell is cut in half and homologous chromosomes in a diploid cell are separated.

19. In meiosis I, DNA replication occurs. Then, after forming tetrads and crossing over, duplicated homologous chromosomes line up and are pulled by spindle fibers toward opposite ends of the cell to form two haploid daughter cells with chromosomes composed of two chromatids. In Meiosis II, DNA replication does not occur, duplicated chromosomes (consisting of two chromatids) line up in the center of each cell. Then, the chromatids separate to form four haploid daughters with chromosomes composed of only one chromatid.

20. It is the chromosomes that are separated during gamete formation.

Chapter 11 Assessment

Critical Thinking

21. By crossing the white ram to a black ewe; if any offspring are black, then the white ram is heterozygous

22. Horse breeders hope that the resulting offspring may inherit the genes that enabled its parent to win the derby.

23. The allele for black coat color is dominant over the allele for brown, and the black rabbit is homozygous for black coat color.

24.

	Mitosis	Meiosis
Number of cells produced	2	4
Type of cell	body	gamete
Chromosome number	diploid (2N)	haploid (N)

25. Both parents are heterozygous.

26. The predicted outcome of the cross is 50% rough and 50% smooth. However, since the result of each fertilization (joining of egg and sperm) is independent of any previous fertilization, it is possible for all offspring to have smooth coats.

27. *Tt* and *tt*; The genotype *TT* could not have been present; if it were, all the offspring would be tall.

28. The probability is (1 − 3/4)/7 = 1/28.

29. The color helps the ptarmigan hide from predators. In winter, its white coat color blends in with its snowy surroundings. In summer, its brown coat blends in with the surroundings.

30. Punnett squares would be used to predict the possible outcomes of a cross when writing the hypothesis.

Chapter 11 Assessment

Critical Thinking

21. Designing Experiments In sheep, the allele for white wool *(A)* is dominant over the allele for black wool *(a)*. How would you determine the genotype of a white ram, or male sheep?

22. Inferring Explain why horse breeders will pay a lot of money to breed one of their horses with a horse that has won the Kentucky Derby.

23. Formulating Hypotheses Suppose you found out that a mating between a black rabbit and a brown rabbit produced all black offspring. Propose a hypothesis to explain the color of the offspring.

24. Comparing and Contrasting Design and complete a table to compare and contrast meiosis and mitosis.

25. Applying Concepts In dogs, the allele for short hair is dominant over the allele for long hair. Two short-haired dogs are the parents of a litter of eight puppies. Six puppies have short hair, and two have long hair. What are the genotypes of the parents?

26. Applying Concepts In guinea pigs, the allele for a rough coat *(R)* is dominant over the allele for a smooth coat *(r)*. A heterozygous guinea pig *(Rr)* and a homozygous recessive guinea pig *(rr)* have a total of nine offspring. The Punnett square for this cross shows a 50 percent chance that any particular offspring will have smooth coats. Explain how all nine offspring can have smooth coats.

	R	*r*
r	*Rr*	*rr*
r	*Rr*	*rr*

27. Inferring Suppose Mendel crossed two pea plants and got both tall and short offspring. What could have been the genotypes of the two original plants? What genotype could not have been present?

28. Problem Solving Suppose that there is a 3/4 probability that it will be sunny on any given day. What is the probability that a person's birthday in the year 2010 will fall on a cloudy Tuesday?

29. Interpreting Graphics Genes that control hair or feather color in some animals are expressed differently in the winter than in the summer. How might such a difference in expression be beneficial to the ptarmigan shown below?

30. Making Connections In what step of a scientific method would you use a Punnett square?

Performance-Based Assessment

Creative Writing You are a writer for a TV station. The producer asks you to write a series that takes the viewer on an imaginary voyage back in time. Each week, a famous person in history will be visited. The show is designed to provide insight into the work of the person being interviewed and to give the viewers a feel for the events of that era. The first person you visit will be Gregor Mendel. Write a script for this program.

Have you ever heard the phrase "a horse of a different color?" Visit the Prentice Hall Web site at **www.phschool.com** to find out what this phrase means in terms of genetics. Then, answer the following questions:

- How is the color of a horse's coat determined?
- What does the *W* gene control? The *E* gene?
- What will a horse that is genotype *wwEE* look like?
- If a mare with the genotype *wwee* is crossed with a *wwEE* stallion, what proportion of the foals will have the ability to form black hair?

Performance-Based Assessment

Scripts will vary, but should describe Mendel's work, including his experimental design and results, his principles, and how his principles are relevant to modern genetics.

Test-Taking Tip

To complete an analogy, write a sentence that uses the two given words of the first pair. Then, rewrite the sentence with the third given word and a blank. Try each of the answer choices in the blank to see which one works best. If more than one answer choice seems to fit, refine the original sentence and repeat the process.

Directions: Choose the letter that best answers the question or completes the statement.

1. What happens to the chromosome number during meiosis?
(A) It doubles.
(B) It stays the same.
(C) It halves.
(D) It becomes diploid.
(E) It quadruples.

2. Which ratio did Mendel find in his F_2 generation?
(A) 3 : 1
(B) 1 : 3 : 1
(C) 1 : 2
(D) 1 : 9
(E) 3 : 4

3. During which phase of meiosis is the chromosome number reduced?
(A) anaphase I
(B) metaphase I
(C) telophase I
(D) prophase II
(E) telophase II

4. Two pink-flowering plants are crossed. The offspring flower as follows: 25% red, 25% white, 50% pink. What pattern of inheritance does flower color in these flowers follow?
(A) dominance
(B) multiple alleles
(C) incomplete dominance
(D) recessiveness
(E) polygenic traits

5. Which of the following is used to construct a gene map?
(A) chromosome number
(B) litter count
(C) rate of meiosis
(D) recombination rate
(E) number of generations

6. Alleles for the same trait are separated from each other during the process of
(A) mitosis.
(B) meiosis I.
(C) meiois II.
(D) interphase.
(E) metaphase II.

Questions 7–8

A student calculates the recombination frequency of genes A, B, C, and D on one chromosome. The recombination frequencies are as follows: C-D: 25 map units; A-B: 12 map units; B-D: 20 map units; and A-C: 17 map units.

7. Assuming the student's calculations are correct, how many map units apart are genes A and D?
(A) 5
(B) 8
(C) 10
(D) 12.5
(E) 15

8. Which gene map best reflects the student's data?

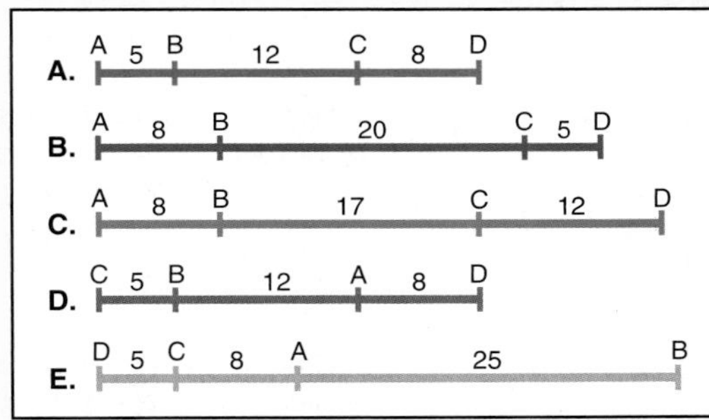

Complete the anology by selecting the correct letter. In analogies, A : B :: C : __?__ means A is to B as C is to __?__.

9. Mitosis : diploid daughter cells :: meiosis : __?__
(A) egg cells
(B) sperm cells
(C) four daughter cells
(D) haploid daughter cells
(E) tetraploid daughter cells

Questions 10–12 Each of the lettered choices below refers to the following numbered statements. Select the best lettered choice. A choice may be used once, more than once, or not at all.

(A) Phenotype
(B) Hybrids
(C) Genotype
(D) Homozygotes
(E) Multiple alleles

10. Offspring of crosses between parents with different traits
11. Appearance due to genetic makeup
12. Having two identical alleles for a given gene

Standardized Test Prep

1. C	**5.** D	**9.** D
2. A	**6.** B	**10.** B
3. A	**7.** B	**11.** A
4. C	**8.** D	**12.** D

Take It to the NET

• The color of a horse's coat is determined by the interaction of a number of different genes.

• The *W* gene controls whether or not any pigment can be deposited in a horse's hair. The *E* gene determines whether or not a horse will have black pigment in its hair.

• The horse will be fully pigmented. It will have black pigment in its skin, but its hair pigment will appear red.

• A two-factor cross will show that all the offspring will have genotype *wwEe*. Therefore, all of the foals will have the ability to form black pigment in their skin and hair.

For additional information, visit

www.phschool.com

Chapter Planner 12 DNA and RNA

Section and Section Objectives	Time	Activities and Labs
12–1 DNA, pp. 287–294 **12.1.1** ***Summarize*** the relationship between genes and DNA. **12.1.2** ***Describe*** the overall structure of the DNA molecule.	**2 periods (1 block)**	**SE:** ***Inquiry Activity,*** How do codes work?, p. 286 **TE:** ***Demonstration,*** p. 291 **SE:** ***Biology and History,*** Discovering the Role of DNA, pp. 292–293
12–2 Chromosomes and DNA Replication, pp. 295–299 **12.2.1** ***Summarize*** the events of DNA replication. **12.2.2** ***Relate*** the DNA molecule to chromosome structure.	**1 period (1/2 block)**	**TE:** ***Demonstration,*** p. 295 **SE:** ***Analyzing Data,*** Genome Replication, p. 296 **TE:** ***Build Science Skills,*** p. 297 **SE:** ***Exploration,*** Modeling DNA Replication, p. 313
12–3 RNA and Protein Synthesis, pp. 300–306 **12.3.1** ***Tell*** how RNA differs from DNA. **12.3.2** ***Name*** the three main types of RNA. **12.3.3** ***Describe*** transcription and the editing of RNA. **12.3.4** ***Identify*** the genetic code. **12.3.5** ***Summarize*** translation. **12.3.6** ***Explain*** the relationship between genes and proteins.	**2 periods (1 block)**	**TE:** ***Demonstration,*** p. 302 **TE:** ***Build Science Skills,*** p. 303 **SE:** ***Quick Lab,*** How does a cell interpret DNA?, p. 303
12–4 Mutations, pp. 307–308 **12.4.1** ***Contrast*** gene mutations and chromosomal mutations.	**1 period (1/2 block)**	
12–5 Gene Regulation, pp. 309–312 **12.5.1** ***Describe*** a typical gene. **12.5.2** ***Describe*** how *lac* genes are turned off and on. **12.5.3** ***Explain*** how most eukaryotic genes are controlled. **12.5.4** ***Relate*** gene regulation to development.	**1 period (1/2 block)**	**TE:** ***Meet Diverse Needs,*** p. 311
Chapter Assessment, pp. 314–317	**1 period (1/2 block)**	

ACTIVITY PLANNER

SE: ***Inquiry Activity,*** p. 286; (15 min.); 12 pop beads of four colors

TE: ***Demonstration,*** p. 291; (15 min.); paper clips, beads, safety pins

TE: ***Demonstration,*** p. 295; (10 min.); ball of string, about 1 meter

TE: ***Build Science Skills,*** p. 297; (15 min.); yarn, beads, dowels, film canister

SE: ***Exploration,*** p. 313; (45 min.); construction paper (tan, gray, green, yellow, red, and purple), metric ruler, scissors, transparent tape

TE: ***Demonstration,*** p. 302; (10 min.); string, marker, scissors, tape, yarn

TE: ***Build Science Skills,*** p. 303; (30 min.); building set or colored blocks

TE: ***Meet Diverse Needs,*** p. 311; (20 min.); pipe cleaner, marker, paper-clips, beads

PLANNING KEY

Ability Levels

B **Basic**	For students who need additional help
A **Average**	For all students
E **Enriched**	For students who need to be challenged

Components

SE	Student Edition	**GRSW**	Guided Reading and Study Workbook	**IDM**	Issues and Decision Making
TE	Teacher's Edition	**CT**	Chapter Tests: Levels A and B	**CTB**	Computer Test Bank
LMA	Laboratory Manual A	**PHAS**	PH Assessment System	**PA**	Presentation Assistant Plus
LMB	Laboratory Manual B	**LA**	Lab Assessment With Scoring Guide	**BD**	BioDetectives Videotape
TR	Teaching Resources	**BTM**	BioTechnology Manual	**iT**	iText
IF	Investigations in Forensics				

Program Resources	Assessment	Media and Technology
LMA: Chapter 12 Lab A E **LMB:** Chapter 12 Lab B A **TR:** Section Review 12–1 B A **GRSW:** Section 12–1 B A **BTM:** Labs 4, 5, 6	**SE:** 12–1 Section Assessment, p. 294 **TR:** Section Review 12–1	**PA:** 12–1 Interest Grabber, Section Outline, Percentage of Bases in Four Organisms, Figure 12–2, Figure 12–4, Figure 12–5, Figure 12–7 **iT:** Section 12–1
TR: Section Review 12–2 B A **GRSW:** Section 12–2 B A	**SE:** 12–2 Section Assessment, p. 299 **TR:** Section Review 12–2	**PA:** 12–2 Interest Grabber, Section Outline, Prokaryotic Chromosome Structure, Figure 12–10, Figure 12–11 **iT:** Section 12–2
TR: Section Review 12–3 B A **GRSW:** Section 12–4 B A	**SE:** 12–3 Section Assessment, p. 306 **TR:** Section Review 12–3	**PA:** 12–3 Interest Grabber, Section Outline, Concept Map, Figure 12–12, Figure 12–14, Figure 12–17, Figure 12–18 **iT:** Section 12–3
TR: Section Review 12–4 B A **GRSW:** Section 12–4 B A	**SE:** 12–4 Section Assessment, p. 308 **TR:** Section Review 12–4	**PA:** 12–4 Interest Grabber, Section Outline, Gene Mutations: Substitution, Insertion, and Deletion, Figure 12–20
TR: Section Review 12–5 B A Chapter 12 Exploration B A E **GRSW:** 12–5 B A **BTM:** Lab 13 A E	**SE:** 12–5 Section Assessment, p. 312 **TR:** Section Review 12–5	**PP:** 12–5 Interest Grabber, Section Outline, Typical Gene Structure **iT:** Section 12–5
	SE: Chapter 12 Assessment, pp. 314–317; **TR:** Chapter Vocabulary Review, Graphic Organizer; **CT:** Chapter 12 Test; **CTB:** Chapter 12 Test; **PHAS:** Practice Test	**CTB:** Chapter 12 Test **iT:** Chapter 12 Assessment

PRESSED FOR TIME?

To Preview the Chapter

- Instruct students to find all of the Vocabulary terms in the chapter and write a definition for each.
- Have students look at the chapter figures and read the captions.

To Cover the Chapter Quickly

- Have students read The Structure of DNA in Section 12–1 and all of Sections 12–2 and 12–3.
- Assign the 12–2 and 12–3 Section Reviews.

To Review the Chapter

- Assign Sections 12–1 through 12–5 in the Guided Reading and Study Workbook.
- Assign Section Reviews for 12–1 through 12–5 and the Chapter Vocabulary Review for Chapter 12 in the Teaching Resources.

Chapter 12

ENGAGE/EXPLORE

Inquiry Activity

Objective Students will be able to determine how codes work.

Skills Focus **Using Models, Calculating, Analyzing Data**

Materials 12 pop beads of four different colors

Time 15 minutes

Strategies
- Explain to students that each letter of the word should have its own combination of bead colors.
- Students should connect their pop beads to form a chain that represents the encoded word.

Expected Outcomes Students will devise a code in which two colors represent one letter.

Think About It

1. Each letter must be encoded by a sequence of at least two beads.
2. A two-bead code can represent 16 different letters. ($4 \times 4 = 16$)
3. Yes, a three-bead code could represent 64 different letters. ($4 \times 4 \times 4 = 64$)

Assess Prior Knowledge

To find out what students already know about DNA and RNA, ask: **What organelle is known as the "control center" of the cell?** *(Nucleus)* **What structures are found in the nucleus?** *(Chromosomes)* **What are located on chromosomes?** *(Genes)* **What are chromosomes composed of?** *(DNA wound around proteins)* **How do genes and chromosomes control the activity of a cell?** *(By producing proteins that regulate cellular functions or become part of the cell structure)*

Chapter 12 DNA and RNA

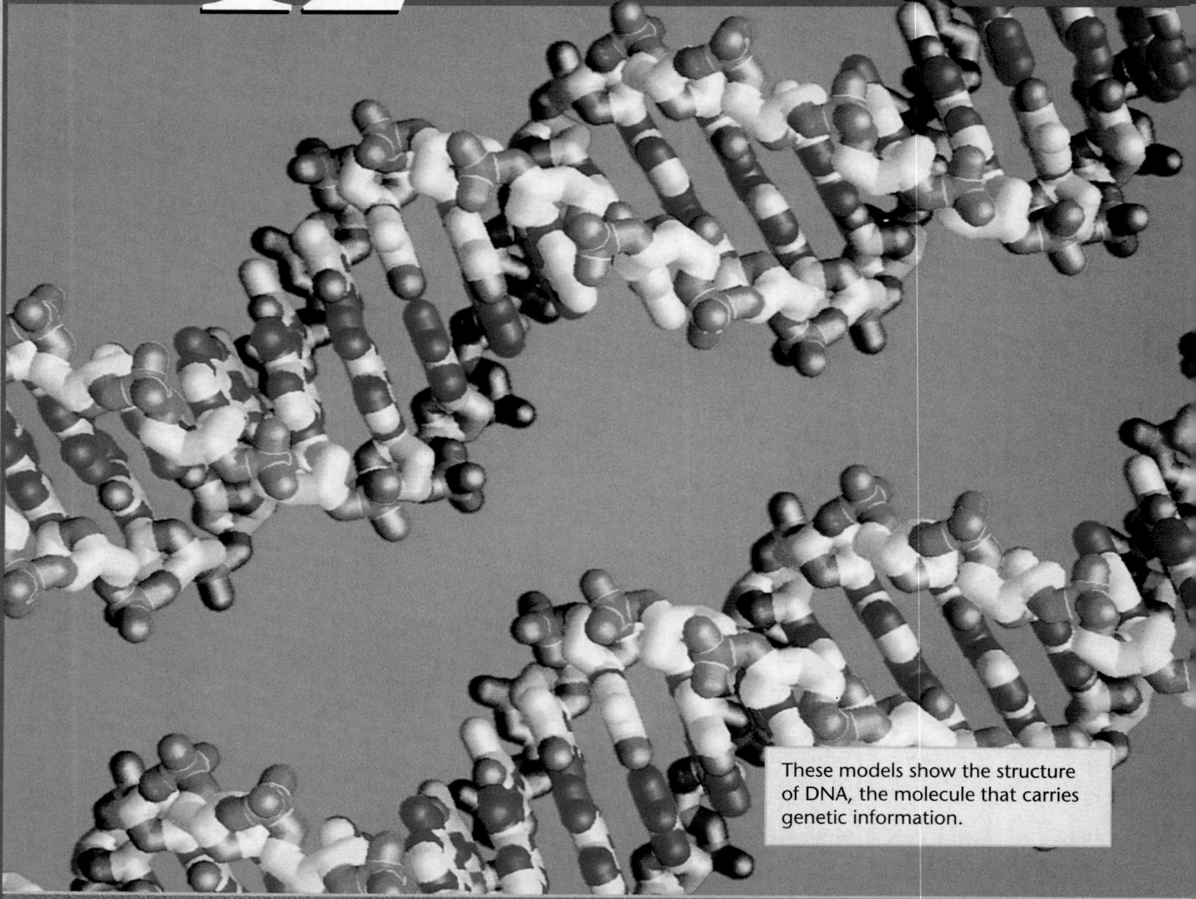

These models show the structure of DNA, the molecule that carries genetic information.

Inquiry Activity

How do codes work?

Procedure

1. Obtain 12 pop beads of four different colors.
2. Select a word that contains at least five different letters from the text on the next page. Use your beads to develop a code for your word.
3. Exchange your code and your coded bead chain with a classmate. Use the classmate's code to decipher his or her word.

Think About It

1. **Using Models** How were you able to encode five different letters using only four colors?
2. **Calculating** How many different letters could you encode by using two beads to stand for each letter used in your message?
3. **Analyzing Data** Could you encode the whole alphabet by using three beads for each letter?

HISTORY OF SCIENCE

The search for genes

After Mendel's work was rediscovered in the 1900s, two scientists, Walter Sutton and Thomas Hunt Morgan, showed that genes are the units of heredity and are located on chromosomes. In the 1940s, George Beadle and Edward Tatum showed that genes control the structure and function of an organism by directing the synthesis of enzymes, which were known to control chemical reactions in cells. Soon, scientists wanted to know the structure of genes. They already knew that chromosomes were made up of proteins and DNA. Most scientists then believed that genes were composed of proteins, because proteins were important to the chemical processes of the cell. They thought the chemical structure of DNA was too simple to contain all the information needed to direct cell processes.

12–1 DNA

How do genes work? What are they made of, and how do they determine the characteristics of organisms? Are genes single molecules, or are they longer structures made up of many molecules? In the middle of the 1900s, questions like these were on the minds of biologists everywhere.

To truly understand genetics, biologists first had to discover the chemical nature of the gene. If the structures that carry genetic information could be identified, it might be possible to understand how genes control the inherited characteristics of living things.

Griffith and Transformation

Like many stories in science, the discovery of the molecular nature of the gene began with an investigator who was actually looking for something else. In 1928, British scientist Frederick Griffith was trying to figure out how bacteria make people sick. More specifically, Griffith wanted to learn how certain types of bacteria produce a serious lung disease known as pneumonia.

Griffith had isolated two slightly different strains, or types, of pneumonia bacteria from mice. Both strains grew very well in culture plates in his lab, but only one of the strains caused pneumonia. The disease-causing strain of bacteria grew into smooth colonies on culture plates, whereas the harmless strain produced colonies with rough edges. The differences in appearance made the two strains easy to distinguish.

Guide for Reading

Key Concepts
- What did scientists discover about the relationship between genes and DNA?
- What is the overall structure of the DNA molecule?

Vocabulary
transformation
bacteriophage
nucleotide
base pairing

Reading Strategy: Summarizing As you read, find the key ideas for the text under each blue heading. Write down a few key words from each main idea. Then, use the key words in your summary. Revise your summary, keeping only the most important ideas.

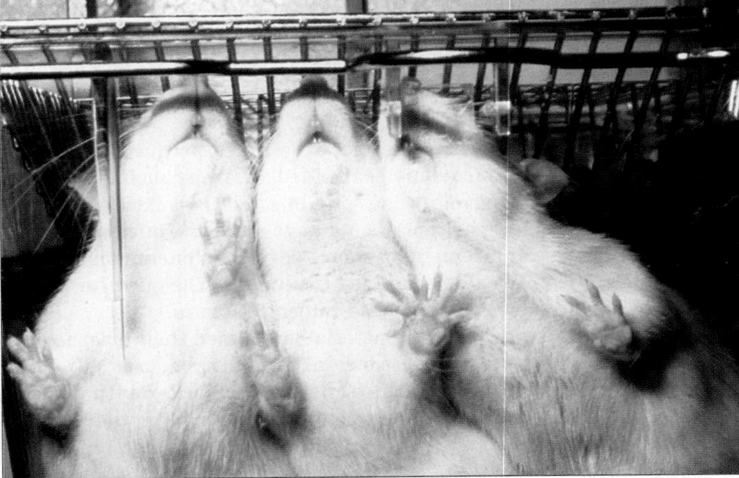

◀ **Figure 12–1** White mice like these are commonly used in scientific experiments.

SECTION RESOURCES

Print:
- ***Laboratory Manual A,*** Chapter 12 Lab
- ***Laboratory Manual B,*** Chapter 12 Lab
- ***Teaching Resources,*** Section Review 12–1
- ***Guided Reading and Study Workbook,*** Section 12–1
- ***Biotechnology Manual,*** Labs 4, 5, 6

Technology:
- ***iText,*** Section 12–1

Section 12–1

1 FOCUS

Objectives

12.1.1 ***Summarize*** the relationship between genes and DNA.
12.1.2 ***Describe*** the overall structure of the DNA molecule.

Guide for Reading

Vocabulary Preview

Read the Vocabulary terms aloud to the class. Then, invite students to write the words and divide them into syllables as best they can. The correct syllabications are trans•for•ma•tion, bac•te•ri•o•phage, nu•cle•o•tide, base pair•ing.

Reading Strategy

Before students read the section, have them write a question for each of the section heads. As they read for key ideas to summarize the section, they should also write the answers to the questions.

2 INSTRUCT

Griffith and Transformation

Build Science Skills

Posing Questions Engage students in a discussion about the scientific question that Griffith originally set out to answer. Explain that Griffith set out to learn whether or not a toxin produced by the bacteria was the cause of pneumonia. Brainstorm a list of scientific questions that Griffith might have asked when he designed his experiment. Write the questions on the board. Work together as a class to decide which questions could serve as the basis for scientific inquiry and which could not.

Use Visuals

Figure 12–2 Review Griffith's transformation experiment. Ask: **What was Griffith trying to learn when he set up this experiment?** *(How bacteria caused pneumonia)* Encourage students to evaluate Griffith's experimental design and discuss the controls he used. Then, ask: **How did Griffith show that the disease-causing bacteria were killed by the heat?** *(He tried to grow them in a petri dish. If the bacteria grew, then he knew that he had not killed them.)* **What result was Griffith expecting when he injected the mixture of live harmless bacteria and heat-killed disease-causing bacteria?** *(He expected the mice to live.)*

Make Connections

Health Science Poll the class to find out who remembers getting immunizations for tetanus and diphtheria. Find out if anyone knows why he or she received the immunizations and how they work. Explain that for these diseases, the immunizations are actually toxoids, or inactivated toxins. These diseases are not caused by the bacteria themselves but by toxins that the bacteria produce. Ask: **Why do you think it's important to learn how bacteria cause disease?** *(To find a cure for the disease or a means to prevent it)* Explain that Griffith set up his experiment to show that a toxin produced by the bacteria causes pneumonia. It was later learned that pneumonia is caused instead by bacterial growth damaging healthy lung tissue.

Meet Diverse Needs

Help students with limited English proficiency to assemble a glossary of terms for this chapter. They can include phonetic spellings of words, formal definitions, and definitions in their own words. Use synonyms or mnemonics to help with meanings. Also encourage students to use illustrations and phrases from their native languages. **Limited English proficiency**

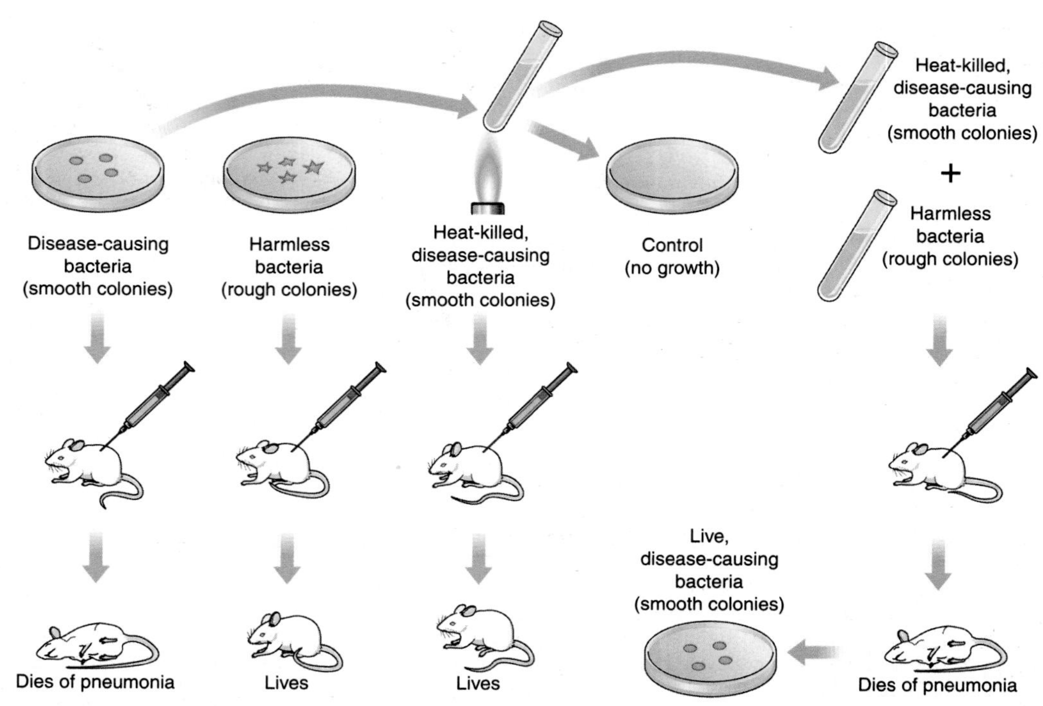

▲ **Figure 12–2** Griffith injected mice with four different samples of bacteria from the smooth and rough colonies. When injected separately, neither heat-killed, disease-causing bacteria nor live, harmless bacteria killed the mice. The two types injected together, however, caused fatal pneumonia. Some factor from the dead bacteria had "transformed" the harmless bacteria into disease-causing ones. **From this experiment, biologists inferred that genetic information could be transformed from one bacterium to another.**

Griffith's Experiments When Griffith injected mice with the disease-causing strain of bacteria, the mice developed pneumonia and died. When mice were injected with the harmless strain, they didn't get sick at all. Griffith wondered if the disease-causing bacteria might produce a poison.

To find out, he took a culture of these cells, heated the bacteria to kill them, and injected the heat-killed bacteria into mice. The mice survived, suggesting that the cause of pneumonia was not a chemical poison released by the disease-causing bacteria. The results of Griffith's experiments are shown in **Figure 12–2.**

Transformation Griffith's next experiment produced an amazing result. He mixed his heat-killed, disease-causing bacteria with live, harmless ones and injected the mixture into mice. By themselves, neither should have made the mice sick. But to Griffith's amazement, the mice developed pneumonia and many died. When he examined the lungs of the mice, he found them filled with the disease-causing bacteria.

Somehow the heat-killed bacteria had passed their disease-causing ability to the harmless strain. Griffith called this process **transformation** because one strain of bacteria (the harmless strain) had apparently been changed into another (the disease-causing strain). Griffith hypothesized that when the

TIME SAVER — PRESENTATIONS MADE EASY!

The Presentation Assistant Plus contains the Prentice Hall Presentation Pro and the Transparencies, which provide easy-to-follow visual support for every step of this section. If you have a computer presentation station, use Prentice Hall Presentation Pro for Section 12–1, or use the following transparencies.

Section 12–1:

Interest Grabber
Section Outline
Percentage of Bases in Four Organisms
Figure 12–2
Figure 12–4
Figure 12–5
Figure 12–7

live, harmless bacteria and the heat-killed bacteria were mixed together, some factor was transferred from the heat-killed cells into the live cells. That factor, he hypothesized, might contain a gene with the information that could change harmless bacteria into disease-causing ones.

Avery and DNA

In 1944, a group of scientists led by Canadian biologist Oswald Avery at the Rockefeller Institute in New York decided to repeat Griffith's work. They did so to determine which molecule in the heat-killed bacteria was most important for transformation. If transformation required just one particular molecule, that might well be the molecule of the gene.

Avery and his colleagues made an extract, or juice, from the heat-killed bacteria. They then carefully treated the extract with enzymes that destroyed proteins, lipids, carbohydrates, and other molecules, including the nucleic acid RNA. Transformation still occurred. Obviously these molecules were not responsible for the transformation. If they had been, transformation would not have occurred, because the molecules would have been destroyed by the enzymes.

Avery and the other scientists repeated the experiment, this time using enzymes that would break down DNA. When they destroyed the nucleic acid DNA in the extract, transformation did not occur. There was just one possible conclusion. DNA was the transforming factor. **Avery and other scientists discovered that DNA is the nucleic acid that stores and transmits the genetic information from one generation of an organism to the next.**

The Hershey-Chase Experiment

Scientists are a skeptical group. It usually takes several experiments to convince them of something as important as the chemical nature of the gene. The most important of these experiments was performed in 1952 by two American scientists, Alfred Hershey and Martha Chase. They studied viruses, nonliving particles smaller than a cell that can infect living organisms.

Bacteriophages One kind of virus that infects and kills bacteria is known as a **bacteriophage** (bak-TEER-ee-uh-fayj), which means "bacteria eater." **Figure 12–3** shows a typical bacteriophage. Bacteriophages are composed of a DNA or RNA core and a protein coat. When a bacteriophage enters a bacterium, the virus attaches to the surface of the cell and injects its DNA into it. The viral genes act to produce many new bacteriophages, and they gradually destroy the bacterium. When the cell splits open, hundreds of new viruses burst out.

CHECKPOINT *What is a bacteriophage?*

KEEP CURRENT WITH . . . SCIENCE NEWS®

To find out more about the topics in this chapter, go to: **www.phschool.com**

▼ **Figure 12–3** A bacteriophage is a type of virus that infects and kills bacteria. This image shows two T2 bacteriophages (purple) invading an *E. coli* cell (green). **Comparing and Contrasting** *How large are viruses compared with bacteria?*

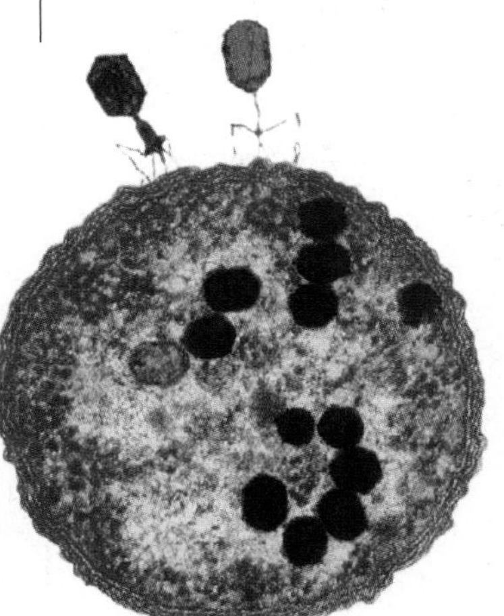

(magnification: 25,000×)

Avery and DNA

Build Science Skills

Designing Experiments Challenge students to diagram the experiments conducted by Avery and his group to repeat Griffith's work. Students should identify the variable in the experiment. *(The enzyme used to destroy a certain molecule.)* Make sure students realize that Avery used only one enzyme at a time. Explain that for these experiments, they didn't need mice because they had developed a test for the presence of transformed bacterial cells that could be done in a test tube. Ask: **How did this experiment show that it was DNA and not any other molecule?** *(Transformation occurred every time, except when DNA was destroyed.)*

SCIENCE NEWS®

Encourage students to visit **www.phschool.com** for the most current information on this topic.

The Hershey-Chase Experiment

Demonstration

Diagram on the board the process by which a bacteriophage infects and replicates in bacteria. Show how the bacteriophage injects its DNA into a bacterium and how DNA incorporates itself into the bacterial DNA (which is usually circular). Explain that the bacterium is tricked into thinking that the viral DNA is its own and begins to make the bacteriophage's DNA and proteins. These parts assemble into new bacteriophages and burst out of the bacterial cell, killing it in the process. If possible, find electron micrographs of this process to show to students.

BIO INSIGHTS — HISTORY OF SCIENCE

Scientists are a skeptical bunch

Now, Avery's results show without a doubt that DNA makes up genes. However, in 1944 the results were questionable. Then, inheritance in bacteria was just beginning to be studied. Scientists didn't know if bacteria had genes like those in more complex organisms. And even if DNA were the hereditary substance in bacteria, it might not be the hereditary substance in more complex organisms. DNA was still considered a very simple molecule. Scientists were more excited about Hershey and Chase's results with bacteriophages in 1952. By that time, genetic studies showed that bacteriophages had properties of heredity similar to those of more complex organisms. Also, experiments showed that DNA was more complex than originally thought.

Answers to . . .

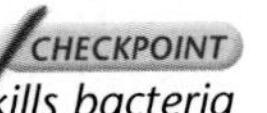 *A virus that infects and kills bacteria*

Figure 12–3 *Viruses are smaller.*

Use Visuals

Figure 12–4 Use the diagram to discuss Hershey and Chase's experimental design. Make sure students understand that the radioactive elements can be easily observed in the laboratory. Ask: **How were Hershey and Chase able to determine whether bacteriophages injected DNA or protein into bacteria?** *(By growing the bacteriophages in cultures containing either ^{32}P or ^{35}S so that the bacteriophage DNA or protein would be labeled in a way that was easy to follow)* **If a bacteriophage injected protein into a bacterial cell, what results would they have expected?** *(Only bacteriophages labeled with ^{35}S would cause bacteria to contain the radioactive label. Bacteriophages labeled with ^{32}P would not result in radioactive bacteria.)*

Make Connections

Chemistry Explain that radioactive elements are unstable isotopes of an element. Diagram an atom of hydrogen on the board with one proton in the nucleus and one electron. Add one neutron to the nucleus. Ask: **Now what element is this?** *(It's still hydrogen, but it is an isotope of hydrogen, deuterium.)* Add another neutron to the nucleus, and ask a volunteer to tell what element it is now. *(Another hydrogen isotope, tritium)* Point out that the three isotopes of hydrogen all have the same chemical properties—they each have one proton and one electron. However, they have very different physical properties because of their differences in mass. Ask: **What causes their mass to be different?** *(Neutrons)* **Do neutrons affect the chemical properties of an element? Why not?** *(No, they are not charged particles; they do not repel or attract other particles.)* Explain that tritium is an unstable, radioactive isotope because its nucleus tends to break down and release small particles of energy. This release of energy is called radioactivity.

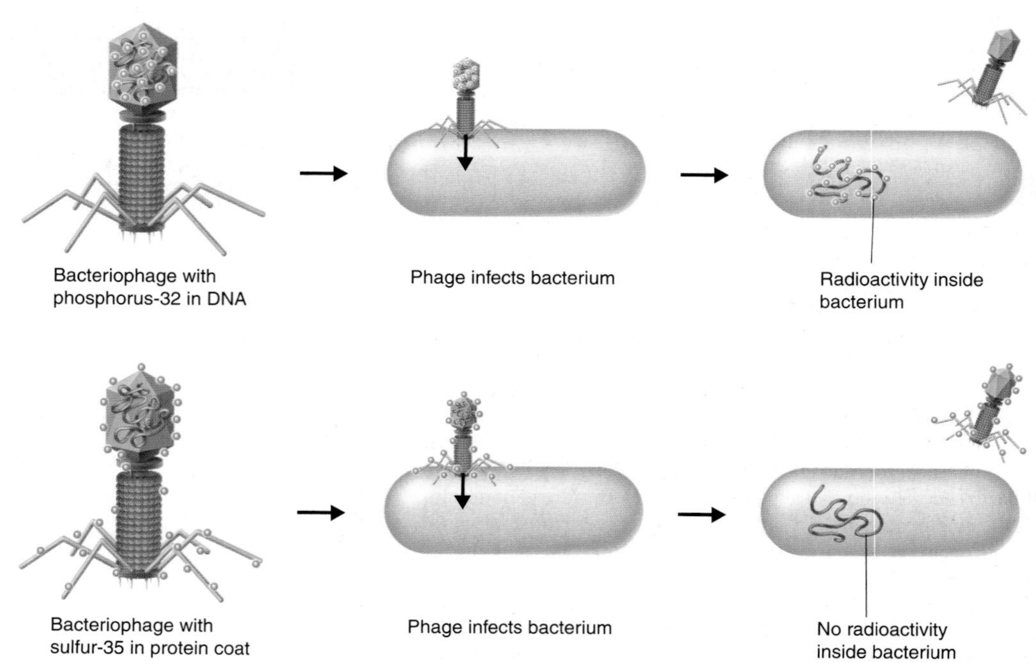

▲ **Figure 12–4** Alfred Hershey and Martha Chase used different radioactive markers to label the DNA and proteins of bacteriophages. The bacteriophages injected only DNA into the bacteria, not proteins. **From these results, Hershey and Chase concluded that the genetic material of the bacteriophage was DNA.**

Radioactive Markers Hershey and Chase reasoned that if they could determine which part of the virus—the protein coat or the DNA core—entered the infected cell, they would learn whether genes were made of protein or DNA. To do this, they grew viruses in cultures containing radioactive isotopes of phosphorus-32 (^{32}P) and sulfur-35 (^{35}S). This was a clever strategy because proteins contain almost no phosphorus and DNA contains no sulfur. The radioactive substances could be used as markers. If ^{35}S was found in the bacteria, it would mean that the viruses' protein had been injected into the bacteria. If ^{32}P was found in the bacteria, then it was the DNA that had been injected.

The Hershey-Chase experiment is shown in **Figure 12–4.** The two scientists mixed the marked viruses with bacteria. Then, they waited a few minutes for the viruses to inject their genetic material. Next, they separated the viruses from the bacteria and tested the bacteria for radioactivity. Nearly all the radioactivity in the bacteria was from phosphorus (^{32}P), the marker found in DNA. **Hershey and Chase concluded that the genetic material of the bacteriophage they infected with bacteria was DNA, not protein.**

CHECKPOINT *What part of the virus did the Hershey-Chase experiment show had entered the bacteria?*

BIO INSIGHTS **FACTS AND FIGURES**

Radioisotopes—a tool for biologists
Biologists commonly use radioisotopes—radioactive isotopes—to learn about cell processes, because they can be substituted into biochemical reactions without changing the chemistry of the reaction. Radioactive isotopes are unstable and break apart or "decay" into a stable form. Because of this decay, their presence can be detected. When they decay, two different kinds of particles are given off—alpha particles, which are 2 neutrons and 2 protons, and beta particles, which are high-speed electrons. In some cases, gamma rays are also given off. Gamma rays are electromagnetic waves of energy that act like X-rays. This is the component of radiation that damages tissues.

The Structure of DNA

You might think that knowing genes were made of DNA would have satisfied scientists, but that was not the case at all. Instead, they wondered how DNA, or any molecule for that matter, could do the three critical things that genes were known to do: First, genes had to carry information from one generation to the next; second, they had to put that information to work by determining the heritable characteristics of organisms; and third, genes had to be easily copied, because all of a cell's genetic information is replicated every time a cell divides. For DNA to do all of that, it would have to be a very special molecule indeed.

DNA is a long molecule made up of units called **nucleotides.** As **Figure 12–5** shows, each nucleotide is made up of three basic parts: a 5-carbon sugar called deoxyribose, a phosphate group, and a nitrogenous (nitrogen-containing) base. There are four kinds of nitrogenous bases in DNA. Two of the nitrogenous bases, adenine (AD-uh-neen) and guanine (GWAH-neen), belong to a group of compounds known as purines. The remaining two bases, cytosine (SY-tuh-zeen) and thymine (THY-meen), are known as pyrimidines. Purines have one ring in their structures, whereas pyrimidines have two rings. Because of this, adenine and guanine are larger molecules than cytosine and thymine.

The backbone of a DNA chain is formed by sugar and phosphate groups of each nucleotide. The nitrogenous bases stick out sideways from the chain. The nucleotides can be joined together in any order, meaning that any sequence of bases is possible.

If you don't see much in **Figure 12–5** that could explain the remarkable properties of the gene, don't be surprised. In the 1940s and early 1950s, the leading biologists in the world thought of DNA as little more than a string of nucleotides. They were baffled, too. The four different nucleotides, like the 26 letters of the alphabet, could be strung together in many different ways, so it was possible they could carry coded genetic information. However, so could many other molecules, at least in principle. Was there something more to the structure of DNA?

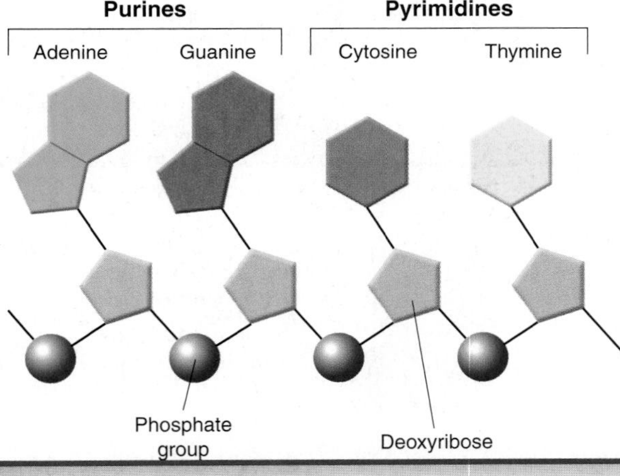

◀ **Figure 12–5** DNA is made up of a series of monomers called nucleotides. Each nucleotide has three parts: a deoxyribose molecule, a phosphate group, and a nitrogenous base. There are four different bases in DNA: adenine, guanine, cytosine, and thymine. **Interpreting Graphics** *How are the nucleotides joined together to form the DNA chain?*

FACTS AND FIGURES

The one-way direction of DNA
Bonds join the deoxyribose sugars of the nucleotides to form the backbone of the DNA molecule. These bonds occur between the 3′-OH group of one deoxyribose sugar and the 5′-OH group of the neighboring deoxyribose. The numbers 3′ and 5′ refer to the position number of each carbon in the deoxyribose sugar. This gives the DNA molecule polarity, meaning that the nucleotides attach to each other in the same direction. One end of the DNA molecule has a 5′-OH group and the other end has a free 3′-OH. When DNA base sequences are written, the base sequence is always written in the 5′ to the 3′ direction. Thus, the sequence AGCT is different from the sequence TCGA. The opposite strand DNA in a molecule has opposite polarity. It runs in the 3′ to 5′ direction.

The Structure of DNA

Build Science Skills

Predicting Challenge students to predict how DNA is able to carry out the three critical things that genes were known to do. Have them write their predictions in their lab manuals. When you complete the chapter, have students check their predictions to see if they are correct. Encourage students to share the facts or inferences on which they based their predictions.

Meet Diverse Needs

At-risk students might have difficulty comprehending the structure of the DNA molecule because they cannot sort through the vocabulary. Have students make concept maps to show the basic parts of the DNA molecule. Make sure they include nucleotide, deoxyribose, phosphate group, nitrogenous base, purine, pyrimidine, adenine, guanine, cytosine, and thymine. **Learning modality: visual**

Demonstration

Demonstrate what a polymer is by linking together paper clips to make a chain. Explain that a polymer is a very large molecule made up of repeating units that are bonded together. The individual paper clips act as the repeating units of the polymer chain. You can make the polymer chain more complex by making the repeating unit more complex, for example, by adding beads or safety pins to the paper clips. Ask: **How many basic units does DNA have?** *(Three: deoxyribose, a phosphate group, and a nitrogenous base)* Explain that polymers can be very strong and flexible and have a variety of uses. For example, nylon is a polymer.

Answers to . . .

✓CHECKPOINT *The DNA*

Figure 12–5 *By the deoxyribose sugar and the phosphate group*

Biology and History

Tell students that the DNA and RNA molecules were discovered not long after Mendel published his ideas about inheritance. Discuss the length of time it required for scientists to make the connection between DNA and genes and why it took so long to establish the molecular basis of inheritance. Then, focus on the short period of time between Avery's work and Watson and Crick's proposal for the DNA molecule.

Writing Activity

Students' essays should describe the research activities of James Watson or Francis Crick since the early 1950s. They might write something similar to a time line, or they might write a summary. Students should mention what the scientist they choose is doing now.

Percentages of Bases in Four Organisms

Source of DNA	A	T	G	C
Streptococcus	29.8	31.6	20.5	18.0
Yeast	31.3	32.9	18.7	17.1
Herring	27.8	27.5	22.2	22.6
Human	30.9	29.4	19.9	19.8

▲ **Figure 12–6** Erwin Chargaff showed that the percentages of guanine and cytosine in DNA are almost equal. The same is true for adenine and thymine. **Interpreting Graphics** *Which organism has the highest percentage of adenine?*

Chargaff's Rules One of the puzzling facts about DNA was a curious relationship between its nucleotides. Years earlier, Erwin Chargaff, an American biochemist, had discovered that the percentages of guanine [G] and cytosine [C] bases are almost equal in any sample of DNA. The same thing is true for the other two nucleotides, adenine [A] and thymine [T], as shown in **Figure 12–6.** The observation that [A] = [T] and [G] = [C] became known as Chargaff's rules. Despite the fact that DNA samples from organisms as different as bacteria and humans obeyed this rule, neither Chargaff nor anyone else had the faintest idea why.

X-Ray Evidence In the early 1950s, a British scientist named Rosalind Franklin began to study DNA. She used a technique called X-ray diffraction to get information about the structure of the DNA molecule. Aiming a powerful X-ray beam at concentrated DNA samples, she recorded the scattering pattern of the X-rays on film. Franklin worked hard to make better and better patterns from DNA until the patterns became clear.

Biology and History

Discovering the Role of DNA

Genes and the laws of heredity were discovered before scientists identified the molecules that genes are made of. With the discovery of DNA, scientists have been able to explain how genes are replicated and how they function.

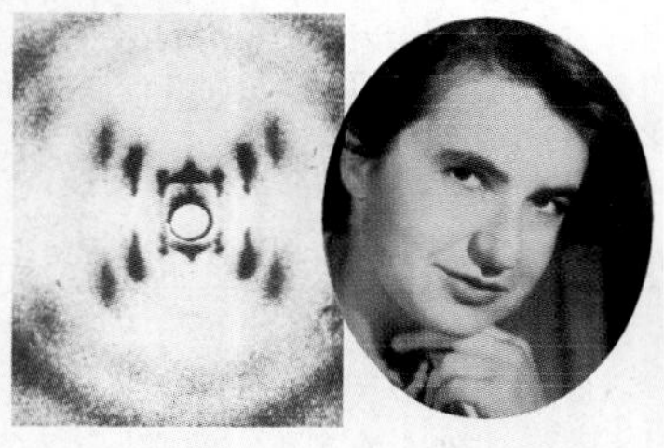

1900

1913 Henry Ford introduces the first assembly line.

1928 **Frederick Griffith** Griffith discovers that a factor in heat-killed, disease-causing bacteria can "transform" harmless bacteria into ones that can cause disease.

1944 **Oswald Avery** Avery's team determines that genes are composed of DNA.

1950

1951 **Linus Pauling Robert Corey** Pauling and Corey determine that the structure of a class of proteins is a helix.

1952 **Rosalind Franklin** Franklin studies the DNA molecule using a technique called X-ray diffraction.

HISTORY OF SCIENCE

Watson and Crick's discoveries
When Watson and Crick were ready to announce their double-helix model in 1953, they made drawings of DNA and sent their paper to *Nature* magazine. They ended their first paper by writing, "It has not escaped our notice that the specific pairing we have postulated immediately suggests a possible copying mechanism for the genetic material." Within a few weeks, Watson and Crick had written another paper describing the copying mechanism.

By itself, Franklin's X-ray pattern does not reveal the structure of DNA, but it does carry some very important clues. The X-shaped pattern in the time-line photograph shows that the strands in DNA are twisted around each other like the coils of a spring, a shape known as a helix. The angle of the *X* suggests that there are two strands in the structure. Other clues suggest that the nitrogenous bases are near the center of the molecule.

CHECKPOINT *What technique did Franklin use to study DNA?*

The Double Helix At the same time that Franklin was continuing her research, Francis Crick, a British physicist, and James Watson, an American biologist, were trying to understand the structure of DNA by building three-dimensional models of the molecule. Their models were made of cardboard and wire. They twisted and stretched the models in various ways, but their best efforts did nothing to explain DNA's properties.

Then, early in 1953, Watson was shown a copy of Franklin's remarkable X-ray pattern. The effect was immediate. In his book *The Double Helix,* Watson wrote: "The instant I saw the picture my mouth fell open and my pulse began to race." Watson reported the pattern's clues to Crick at once. Within weeks, Watson and Crick had figured out the structure of DNA. They published their results in a historic one-page paper in April of 1953. **Watson and Crick's model of DNA was a double helix, in which two strands were wound around each other.**

Meet Diverse Needs

Students who would like an extra challenge can read *The Double Helix: A Personal Account of the Discovery of the Structure of DNA* by James Watson. This book gives students insight into the everyday work of a scientist. After students read the book, invite them to discuss what they think of the story and the people involved. Remind them that they read only one viewpoint of the story, and challenge them to consider how Rosalind Franklin might tell the same story. Encourage students to read *Rosalind Franklin and DNA: A Vivid View of What It Is Like to Be a Gifted Woman in an Especially Male Profession* (Anne Sayre, 1975). **Learning modality: verbal**

Writing Activity

Do research in the library or on the Internet to find out what James Watson or Francis Crick has worked on since discovering the structure of DNA. Organize your findings about the scientist's work and write a short essay describing it.

1953
James Watson Francis Crick
Watson and Crick develop the double-helix model of the structure of DNA.

1960
Sydney Brenner
Brenner and other scientists show the existence of messenger RNA.

1977
Walter Gilbert
Gilbert, Allan Maxam, and Frederick Sanger develop methods to read the DNA sequence.

2000
Human Genome Project
The Human Genome Project—an attempt to sequence all human DNA—is essentially complete.

2000

Answers to . . .

CHECKPOINT *X-ray diffraction*

Figure 12–6 *Yeast*

12–1 (continued)

Use Visuals

Figure 12–7 As students study the diagram, point out that the dotted lines represent the hydrogen bonds that hold together the two DNA strands. Ask: **How does the number of hydrogen bonds relate to Chargaff's rules?** *(Adenine and thymine cannot bond to either guanine or cytosine, because the number of possible hydrogen-binding sites is not equal.)*

3 ASSESS

Evaluate Understanding

Devise a trivia game for the class in which teams of three to four students work together to answer questions about the discovery of DNA and its structure.

Reteach

Encourage students to draw their own diagram of the DNA molecule using Figure 12–7 as a guide. Students should label all parts of the molecule.

MAKING CONNECTIONS

Students can choose the experiments of Griffith, Avery or Hershey and Chase for their flowcharts. You might divide the class into thirds to ensure that each experiment is covered. Organizers should include the procedure and the conclusions of each experiment.

Use iText to review the key concepts in Section 12–1.

▶ **Figure 12–7 DNA is a double helix in which two strands are wound around each other.** Each strand is made up of a chain of nucleotides. The two strands are held together by hydrogen bonds between adenine and thymine and between guanine and cytosine.

Nucleotide
Hydrogen bonds
Sugar-phosphate backbone

KEY
Adenine (A)
Thymine (T)
Cytosine (C)
Guanine (G)

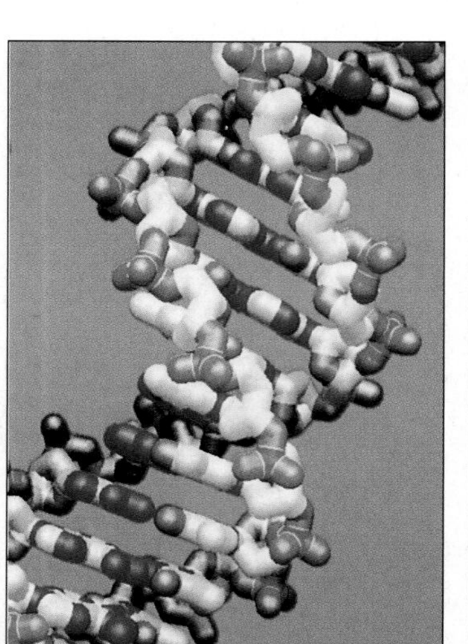

A double helix looks like a twisted ladder or a spiral staircase. The double helix accounted for many of the features in Franklin's X-ray pattern but did not explain what forces held the two strands together. Watson and Crick found the answer. They discovered that hydrogen bonds could form between certain nitrogenous bases and provide just enough force to hold the two strands together. As **Figure 12–7** shows, hydrogen bonds can form only between certain base pairs—adenine and thymine and guanine and cytosine. Once they saw this, they also realized that this principle, called **base pairing,** explained Chargaff's rules. Now there was a reason that [A] = [T] and [G] = [C]. For every adenine in a double-stranded DNA molecule, there had to be exactly one thymine molecule; for each cytosine molecule, there was one guanine molecule.

12–1 Section Assessment

1. **Key Concept** List the conclusions Griffith, Avery, Hershey, and Chase drew from their experiments.
2. **Key Concept** Describe Watson and Crick's model of the DNA molecule.
3. What are the four kinds of bases found in DNA?
4. How did Watson and Crick's model explain why there are equal amounts of thymine and adenine in DNA?
5. **Critical Thinking Inferring** Why did Hershey and Chase grow viruses in cultures that contained both radioactive phosphorus and radioactive sulfur? What might have happened if they had used only one radioactive substance?

iTEXT Assessment Use iText to review the important concepts in Section 12–1.

MAKING CONNECTIONS

Scientific Methods
Using either Griffith's, Avery's, or Hershey-Chase's experiment as an example, develop a flowchart that shows the scientific process. Be sure to identify each process. (*Hint:* You may wish to review Chapter 1, which describes the scientific method.)

12–1 Section Assessment

1. Griffith and Avery: genes were probably made of DNA; Hershey and Chase: genetic material of bacteriophage was DNA, not protein.
2. DNA is a double helix in which two strands are wound around each other.
3. Adenine, thymine, guanine, cytosine
4. Hydrogen bonds can form only between certain base pairs—adenine and thymine and guanine and cytosine.
5. So that both the viral DNA and viral proteins would be marked; they would not have been able to trace the location of the unmarked molecule in the bacterial cell, and would not have conclusive results.

12–2 Chromosomes and DNA Replication

DNA is present in such large amounts in many tissues that it's easy to extract and analyze. But where is DNA found in the cell? How is it organized? Where are the genes that Mendel first described a century and a half ago?

DNA and Chromosomes

Prokaryotic cells lack nuclei and many of the organelles found in eukaryotes. Their DNA molecules are located in the cytoplasm. Most prokaryotes have a single circular DNA molecule that contains nearly all of the cell's genetic information. This large DNA molecule is usually referred to as the cell's chromosome, as shown in **Figure 12–8.**

Eukaryotic DNA is a bit more complicated. Many eukaryotes have as much as 1000 times the amount of DNA as prokaryotes. This DNA is not found free in the cytoplasm. Eukaryotic DNA is generally located in the cell nucleus in the form of a number of chromosomes. The number of chromosomes varies widely from one species to the next. For example, diploid human cells have 46 chromosomes, *Drosophila* cells have 8, and giant sequoia tree cells have 22.

DNA Length DNA molecules are surprisingly long. The chromosome of the prokaryote *E. coli,* which can live in the human colon, contains 4,639,221 base pairs. The length of such a DNA molecule is roughly 1.6 mm, which doesn't sound like much until you think about the small size of a bacterium. A typical bacterium is less than 1.6 µm in diameter, so the DNA molecule must be folded into a space only one one-thousandth of its length.

Guide for Reading

Key Concept
- What happens during DNA replication?

Vocabulary
chromatin
histone
replication
DNA polymerase

Reading Strategy: Asking Questions Before you read, study the diagram in **Figure 12–11.** Make a list of questions about the diagram. As you read, write down the answers to your questions.

▼ **Figure 12–8** Most prokaryotes, such as this *E. coli* bacterium, have only a single circular chromosome. This chromosome holds most of the organism's DNA.

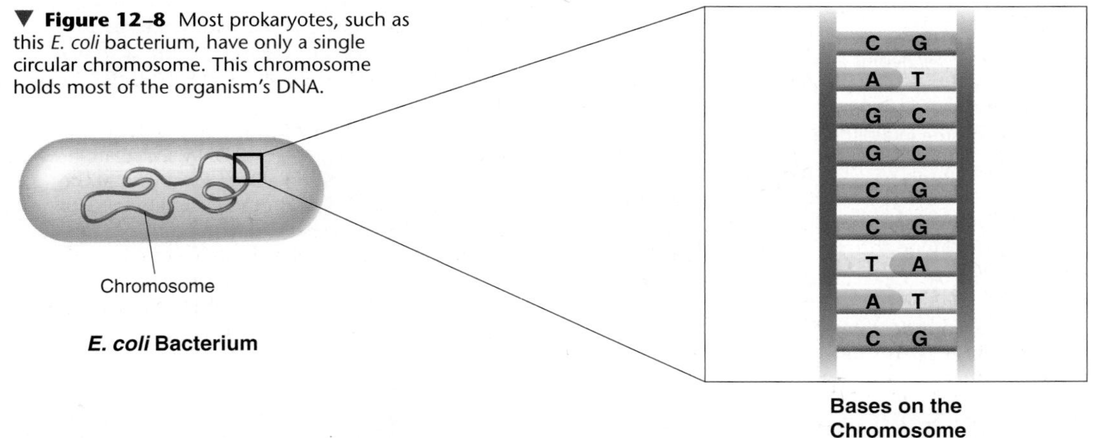

SECTION RESOURCES

Print:
- ***Teaching Resources,*** Section Review 12–2
- ***Guided Reading and Study Workbook,*** Section 12–2

Technology:
- ***iText,*** Section 12–1

Section 12–2

1 FOCUS

Objectives

12.2.1 ***Summarize*** the events of DNA replication.
12.2.2 ***Relate*** the DNA molecule to the chromosome structure.

Guide for Reading

Vocabulary Preview

Explain that the suffix *-ase* is used to denote molecules that are enzymes, proteins that catalyze biochemical reactions. Challenge students to look carefully at the word *DNA polymerase.* Ask: **Based on the root of the word, what do you think DNA polymerase does?** *(It synthesizes the DNA molecule by adding individual nucleotides to the DNA polymer.)*

Reading Strategy

Encourage students to preview all diagrams in this section before reading. For Figure 12–11, have students list questions for the diagram and write answers to those questions as they read.

2 INSTRUCT

DNA and Chromosomes

Demonstration

To give students an idea of how large a DNA molecule is compared to the cell into which it is packed, show students a ball formed from a piece of string that is about 1 meter long. Then, draw a circle on the board that has a diameter of about 1 mm. If needed, review the metric equivalents so that students can see the relationship between micrometers and millimeters (10^{-3} to 1) and millimeters to meters (also 10^{-3} to 1). Explain that the string represents the DNA molecule that must fit inside the circle drawn on the board. Encourage students to speculate how the DNA molecule is able to fit into the cell and why it is so long.

Analyzing Data

Diagram on the board how circular DNA in *E. coli* looks during DNA replication by drawing a double-stranded circle with two replication bubbles moving around the circle. Explain that the replication process is a continuous process, so while the leading edge of the replicating DNA is separating, the regions that have already been replicated are hydrogen-bonding back together. Explain that the new double-stranded DNA molecule is composed of a newly synthesized strand and an original strand.

Answers

1. About 2,319,610 bases (Number of bases divided by 2)
2. About 1,933 bases per second (Half the number of bases divided by 20 to give bases per minute, then divide by 60 to get bases per second)
3. Almost 18 (17.96) days. (Divide 3 billion by 1,933 to get seconds required, then divide by 3600 to get hours, then divide by 24 to get days.) Most students will think that this length of time is not reasonable.
4. Students should suggest that a very large number of DNA replication complexes work simultaneously to copy human DNA. About 431 replication complexes are needed. (One complex requires about 18 days (17.96), or about 25,866 minutes divided by 60 minutes to give the number of complexes required.)

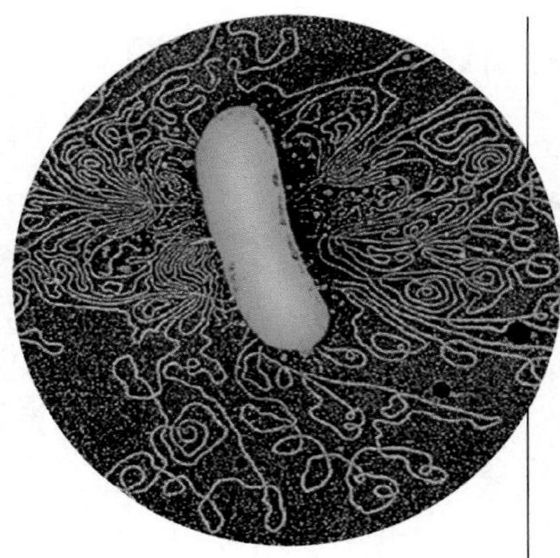

▲ **Figure 12–9** The DNA in a bacterium is about 1000 times as long as the bacterium itself. It must therefore be very tightly folded. **Making Analogies** *Compare DNA in a bacterium to jamming rope into a backpack.*

To get a rough idea of what this means, think of a large school backpack. Then, imagine trying to pack a 300-meter length of rope into the backpack! **Figure 12–9**, which shows DNA spilling out from a ruptured bacterium, indicates how dramatically the DNA must be folded to fit within the cell.

Chromosome Structure The DNA in eukaryotic cells is packed even more tightly. A human cell contains almost 1000 times as many base pairs of DNA as a bacterium. This means that the nucleus of a human cell contains more than 1 meter of DNA. Even the smallest human chromosome contains more than 30 million base pairs of DNA, making its DNA nearly 10 times as long as many bacterial chromosomes. How is so much DNA folded into tiny chromosomes? The answer can be found in the composition of eukaryotic chromosomes.

Eukaryotic chromosomes contain both DNA and protein, tightly packed together to form a substance called **chromatin.** Chromatin consists of DNA that is tightly coiled around proteins called **histones,** as shown in **Figure 12–10.** Together, the DNA and histone molecules form a beadlike structure called a nucleosome. Nucleosomes pack with one another to form a thick fiber, which is shortened by a system of loops and coils.

During most of the cell cycle, these fibers are dispersed in the nucleus so that individual chromosomes are not visible. During mitosis, however, the fibers of each individual chromosome are drawn together, forming the tightly packed chromosomes you can see through a light microscope in dividing cells. The tight packing of nucleosomes may help separate chromosomes during mitosis. There is also some evidence that changes in chromatin structure and histone-DNA binding are associated with changes in gene activity and expression.

Analyzing Data

Genome Replication

Replication of the 4,639,221 base pairs of DNA in the bacterium *E. coli* begins at a single point and continues in both directions until the entire circular chromosome is copied. The bacterium can complete replication of its chromosome in as little as 20 minutes.

1. **Calculating** Two DNA replication complexes move around the *E. coli* chromosome. Approximately how many bases are copied by each complex during the replication process?
2. **Calculating** Calculate the number of bases that must be copied per second by each replication complex in order to replicate the entire *E. coli* genome in 20 minutes.
3. **Calculating** Calculate how long a single replication complex moving at the same speed as an *E. coli* complex would take to copy the DNA of a single human cell. (*Hint:* Refer to your answer to question 2.)
4. **Inferring** The human genome consists of approximately 3 billion base pairs of DNA. Calculate how long a single replication complex moving at the same speed as an *E. coli* complex would take to copy the DNA of a single human cell. Does this length of time seem reasonable to you? (Assume that a human replication complex works at the same speed as an *E. coli* replication complex. Refer to your answer to question 3.)

PRESENTATIONS MADE EASY!

The Presentation Assistant Plus contains the Prentice Hall Presentation Pro and the Transparencies, which provide easy-to-follow visual support for every step of this section. If you have a computer presentation station, use Prentice Hall Presentation Pro for Section 12–2, or use the transparencies listed here.

Section 12–2: **Interest Grabber**
Section Outline
Prokaryotic Chromosome Structure
Figure 12–10
Figure 12–11

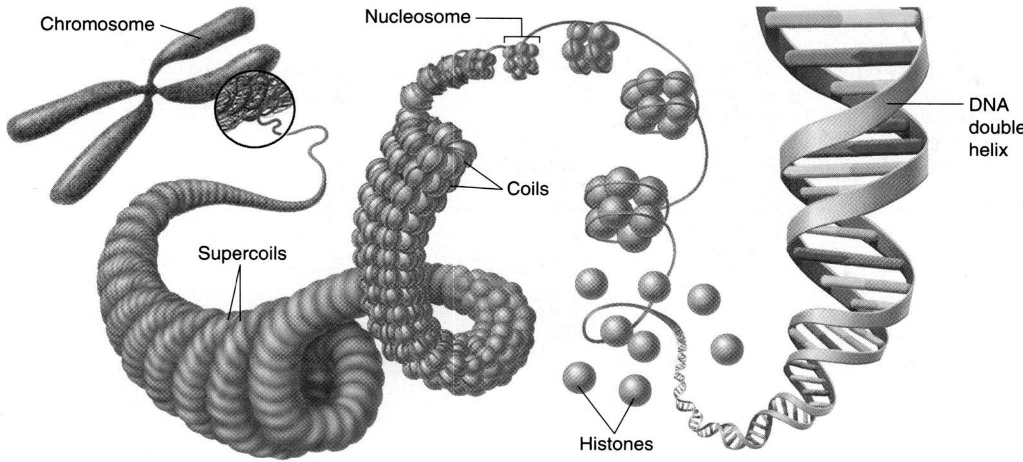

▲ **Figure 12–10** Eukaryotic chromosomes contain DNA wrapped around proteins called histones. The strands of nucleosomes are tightly coiled and supercoiled to form chromosomes. **Interpreting Graphics** *What is each DNA-histone complex called?*

What do nucleosomes do? Nucleosomes seem to be able to fold enormous lengths of DNA into the tiny space available in the cell nucleus. This is such an important function that the histone proteins themselves have changed very little during evolution—probably because mistakes in DNA folding could harm a cell's ability to reproduce.

More recently, biologists have discovered that nucleosomes may play a role in regulating how genes are "read" to make proteins. The first step in activating certain genes has turned out to be a rearrangement of their nucleosomes. By opening up regions of DNA that previously were hidden, these chromatin rearrangements can allow different genes to be "read," changing which proteins are produced.

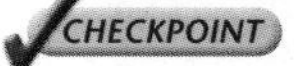 *What is chromatin?*

DNA Replication

When Watson and Crick discovered the double helix structure of DNA, there was one more remarkable aspect that they recognized immediately. The structure explained how DNA could be copied, or replicated. Each strand of the DNA double helix has all the information needed to reconstruct the other half by the mechanism of base pairing. Because each strand can be used to make the other strand, the strands are said to be complementary. If you could separate the two strands, the rules of base pairing would allow you to reconstruct the base sequence of the other strand.

DNA Replication

Meet Diverse Needs

At-risk students will benefit from a review of where DNA replication occurs and when it occurs in the cell. First, show students a picture of a bacterial cell and an animal cell. Ask: **Where is the DNA located?** *(In cytoplasm of bacterial cell; in nucleus of animal cell)* **Where does DNA replication occur?** *(In cytoplasm of bacterial cell; in nucleus of animal cell)* Then, discuss situations in which the cell would need copies of its DNA molecule. Elicit from students that replication occurs when new cells are needed, either during healing and growth (mitosis) or during the production of sex cells (meiosis). **Learning modality: verbal**

Build Science Skills

Using Models Give students a very long piece of yarn (30–50 cm), some beads, short wooden dowels, and a film canister. Challenge students to use the materials to help them fit the yarn inside the container, making sure that the yarn can be unwound fairly easily. Encourage students to make comparisons between their models and chromatin.

FACTS AND FIGURES

Straight talk about nomenclature
Chromatin is a general term that describes a substance that is made up of DNA, histone and nonhistone proteins, and some RNA that is identified by its special staining properties. Chromosomes are composed of chromatin. Chromosomes have specific structures. Bacteria usually have a single circular chromosome. Multicellular plants and animals have rod-shaped chromosomes. A chromatid is found only in duplicated chromosomes after DNA replication has occurred in the S phase of the cell cycle. A chromatid is each of the two subunits of the chromosome that becomes visible during prophase of mitosis and meiosis.

Answers to . . .

CHECKPOINT *Chromatin is DNA and protein tightly packed together.*

Figure 12–9 *Both situations involve packing a very long, narrow material (the DNA or rope) into a compact space (the bacterium or backpack).*

Figure 12–10 *A nucleosome*

Use Visuals

Figure 12–11 As students examine the diagram of DNA replication, have volunteers explain what a complementary strand of DNA is and what happens when the DNA molecule unzips. *(Hydrogen bonds break.)* Discuss how the strand being copied acts as a template for the new strand being synthesized. Ask: **Why is the new strand complementary to the original strand?** *(It is made up of a base sequence of purines and pyrimidines that match, or base pair, with the sequence of purines and pyrimidines of the original strand.)*

Build Science Skills

Applying Concepts Divide the class into pairs. Instruct each student to write a base pair sequence for one strand of DNA. Partners should exchange their DNA sequences with each other and write the sequence of the complementary strand. Monitor students to be sure they understand the process.

Figure 12–11 **During DNA replication, the DNA molecule produces two new complementary strands following the rules of base pairing. Each strand of the double helix of DNA serves as a template for the new strand.** The electron micrograph shows a double strand of human DNA.

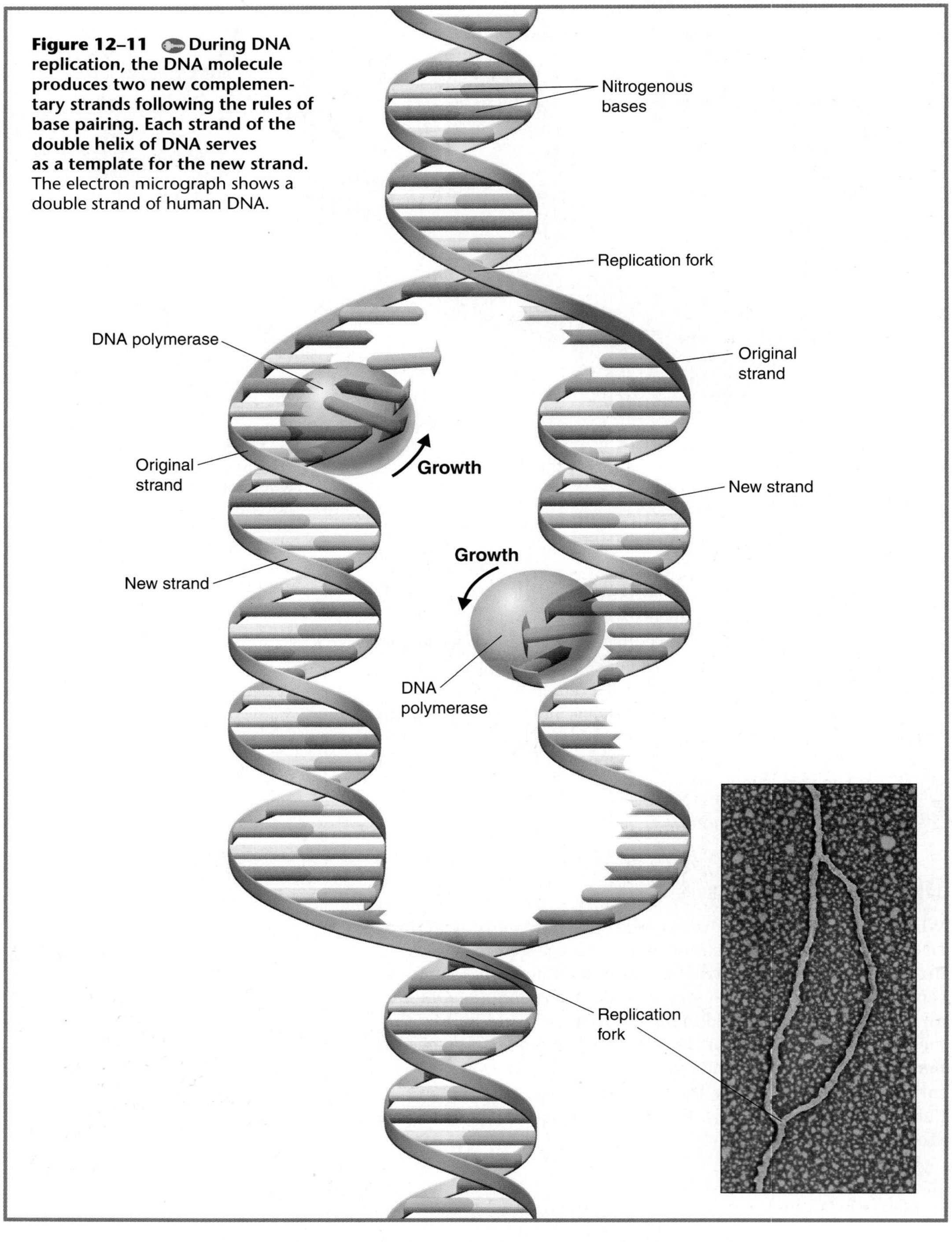

FACTS AND FIGURES

Where other genes are located

All the genes in a cell are not located in the nucleus, although for many years, scientists thought they were. Then, scientists noticed that a few genes seem to follow a pattern of inheritance that is quite unusual for genes in the nucleus. Could those genes be located somewhere else in the cell? In the 1970s, researchers found that mitochondria and chloroplasts have their own DNA molecules, containing anywhere from 10 to 50 genes. These genes code for proteins found in the organelles, some of them quite important.

In 1989, Douglas Wallace of Emory University in Atlanta discovered a mitochondrial disorder known as Leber disorder—a rare condition that leads to blindness. Since then, six more human mitochondrial genetic disorders have been discovered.

Duplicating DNA Before a cell divides, it duplicates its DNA in a copying process called **replication.** This process ensures that each resulting cell will have a complete set of DNA molecules. **During DNA replication, the DNA molecule separates into two strands, then produces two new complementary strands following the rules of base pairing. Each strand of the double helix of DNA serves as a template, or model, for the new strand.**

In most prokaryotes, DNA replication begins at a single point in the chromosome and proceeds, often in two directions, until the entire chromosome is replicated. In the larger eukaryotic chromosomes, DNA replication occurs at hundreds of places. Replication proceeds in both directions until each chromosome is completely copied. The sites where separation and replication occur are called replication forks.

How Replication Occurs DNA replication is carried out by a series of enzymes. These enzymes "unzip" a molecule of DNA. The unzipping occurs when the hydrogen bonds between the base pairs are broken and the two strands of the molecule unwind. Each strand serves as a template for the attachment of complementary bases.

For example, a strand that has the bases TACGTT produces a strand with the complementary bases ATGCAA. The result is two DNA molecules identical to each other and to the original molecule. Note that each DNA molecule resulting from replication has one original strand and one new strand.

DNA replication involves a host of enzymes and regulatory molecules. You may recall that enzymes are highly specific. For this reason, they are often named for the reactions they catalyze. The principal enzyme involved in DNA replication is called **DNA polymerase** (PAHL-ih-mur-ayz) because it polymerizes individual nucleotides to produce DNA. DNA polymerase also "proofreads" each new DNA strand, helping to maximize the odds that each molecule is a perfect copy of the original DNA.

12–2 Section Assessment

1. **Key Concept** Explain how DNA is replicated.
2. Where and in what form is eukaryotic DNA found?
3. How are the long DNA molecules found in eukaryotes packed into short chromosomes?
4. How are histones related to nucleosomes?
5. What is the role of DNA polymerase in DNA replication?
6. **Critical Thinking Comparing and Contrasting** How is the structure of chromosomes in eukaryotes different from the structure of chromosomes in prokaryotes?

iTEXT **Assessment** Use iText to review the important concepts in Section 12–2.

ALTERNATIVE ASSESSMENT

Creating a Venn Diagram Make a Venn diagram that compares the process of DNA replication in prokaryotes and eukaryotes. Compare the location, steps, and end products of the process in each kind of cell.

12–2 Section Assessment

1. The DNA molecule separates into two strands, which serve as templates against which the new strands are made, following the rules of base pairing.
2. In the cell nucleus as chromosomes
3. DNA is tightly wound around histones, forming nucleosomes. Nucleosomes are tightly coiled and supercoiled to form chromosomes.
4. Nucleosomes are composed of DNA wound around histones
5. Polymerizes individual nucleotides to produce DNA
6. Prokaryotes: single, circular DNA molecule; eukaryotes: many chromosomes composed of tightly coiled DNA and histones

3 ASSESS

Evaluate Understanding

Ask students to describe the steps that occur in the process of DNA replication. Ask other students to explain how DNA is packaged to fit inside cells.

Reteach

Have students review Figure 12–10 and Figure 12–11. Encourage them to draw a diagram that combines the ideas described in each figure. Remind students to clearly label their diagrams.

ALTERNATIVE ASSESSMENT

In the Venn diagrams, students should describe prokaryotic DNA replication as beginning at a single point and occurring in the cytoplasm. Eukaryotic DNA replication begins in hundreds of places at once and occurs in the nucleus. DNA replication in both eukaryotes and prokaryotes proceeds in both directions, results in two identical strands of DNA, and so on. You might use the diagrams to emphasize that the process of DNA replication is very similar in the two types of cells.

Use iText to review the key concepts in Section 12–2.

Section 12–3

1 FOCUS

Objectives

12.3.1 ***Tell*** how RNA differs from DNA.
12.3.2 ***Name*** the three main types of RNA.
12.3.3 ***Describe*** transcription and the editing of RNA.
12.3.4 ***Identify*** the genetic code.
12.3.5 ***Summarize*** translation.
12.3.6 ***Explain*** the relationship between genes and proteins.

Guide for Reading

Vocabulary Preview

Ask: **What does it mean to transcribe something?** *(To write a copy of it)* Explain that in transcription, DNA is transcribed to produce a molecule of RNA. Ask: **What does it mean to translate something?** *(To express something in another language)* Explain that the message encoded by RNA is translated into a protein sequence during the process of translation.

Reading Strategy

Encourage students to preview all the figures in the section by carefully reading the captions and studying the diagrams. Remind students to refer to the diagrams while reading the section.

2 INSTRUCT

The Structure of RNA

Meet Diverse Needs

Encourage students who would like an additional challenge to learn more about the structure of RNA. Have them find out how its differences from DNA cause it to behave in a chemically different way. Have students summarize their findings in a Venn diagram or other graphic organizer. **Learning modality: logical/mathematical**

12–3 RNA and Protein Synthesis

Guide for Reading

Key Concepts
- What are the three main types of RNA?
- What is transcription?
- What is translation?

Vocabulary
messenger RNA
ribosomal RNA
transfer RNA
transcription
RNA polymerase
promoter
intron
exon
codon
translation
anticodon

Reading Strategy: Using Visuals Before you read, preview **Figure 12–18.** As you read, notice what happens in each step of translation, or protein synthesis.

The double helix structure explains how DNA can be replicated, or copied, but it does not explain how a gene works. As you will see, genes are coded DNA instructions that control the production of proteins within the cell. The first step in decoding these genetic messages is to copy part of the nucleotide sequence from DNA into RNA, or ribonucleic acid. These RNA molecules then carry out the process of making proteins.

The Structure of RNA

RNA, like DNA, consists of a long chain of nucleotides. As you may recall, each nucleotide is made up of a 5-carbon sugar, a phosphate group, and a nitrogenous base. There are three main differences between RNA and DNA: The sugar in RNA is ribose instead of deoxyribose, RNA is generally single-stranded, and RNA contains uracil in place of thymine.

You can think of an RNA molecule as a disposable copy of a segment of DNA. In many cases, an RNA molecule is a working copy of a single gene. The ability to copy a single DNA sequence into RNA makes it possible for a single gene to produce hundreds or even thousands of RNA molecules.

Types of RNA

RNA molecules have many functions, but in the majority of cells most RNA molecules are involved in just one job—protein synthesis. The assembly of amino acids into proteins is controlled by RNA. **There are three main types of RNA: messenger RNA, ribosomal RNA, and transfer RNA.** The structures of these molecules are shown in **Figure 12–12.**

▼ Figure 12–12 The three main types of RNA are messenger RNA, ribosomal RNA, and transfer RNA. Ribosomal RNA is combined with proteins to form ribosomes.

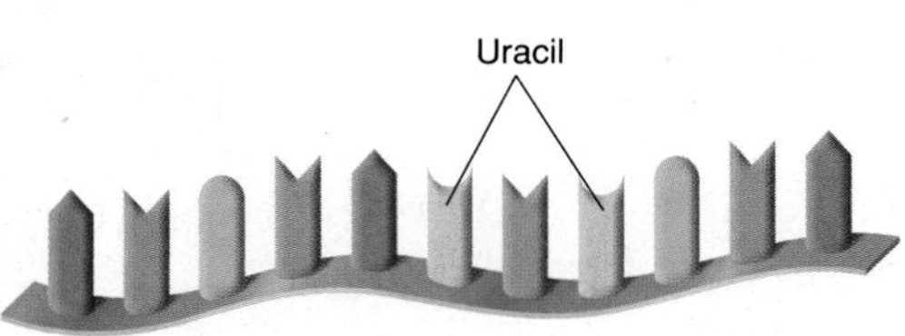

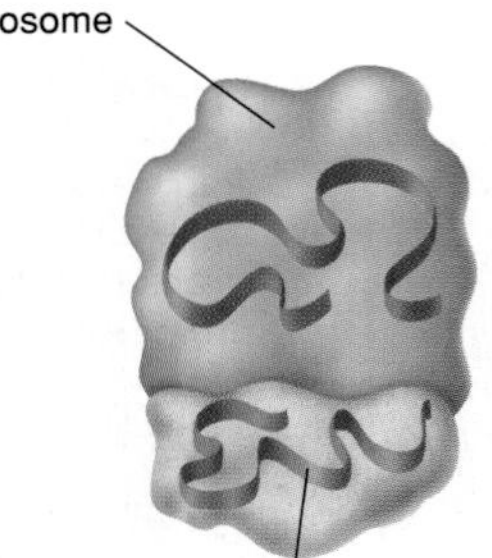

SECTION RESOURCES

Print:
- ***Teaching Resources,*** Section Review 12–3
- ***Guided Reading and Study Workbook,*** Section 12–3

Technology:
- ***iText,*** Section 12–3

Most genes contain instructions for assembling amino acids into proteins. The RNA molecules that carry copies of these instructions are known as **messenger RNA** (mRNA) because they serve as "messengers" from DNA to the rest of the cell.

Proteins are assembled on ribosomes. Ribosomes are made up of several dozen proteins, as well as a form of RNA known as **ribosomal RNA** (rRNA).

During the construction of a protein, a third type of RNA molecule transfers each amino acid to the ribosome as it is specified by coded messages in mRNA. These RNA molecules are known as **transfer RNA** (tRNA).

CHECKPOINT *What are ribosomes made of?*

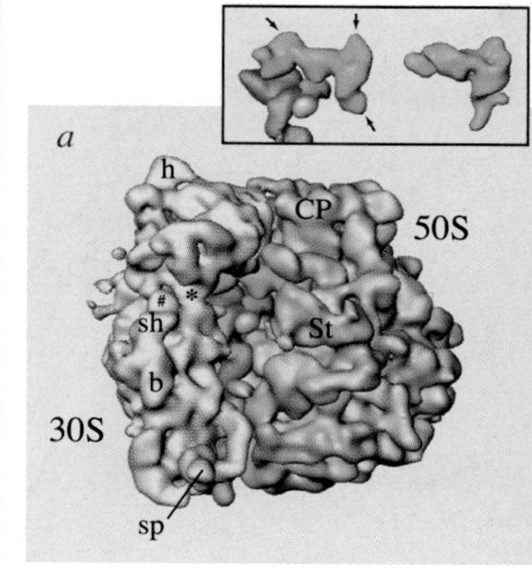

▲ **Figure 12–13** This computer-generated image of an actual ribosome was made using neutron and X-ray diffraction.

Transcription

RNA molecules are produced by copying part of the nucleotide sequence of DNA into a complementary sequence in RNA, a process called **transcription.** Transcription requires an enzyme known as **RNA polymerase** that is similar to DNA polymerase. **During transcription, RNA polymerase binds to DNA and separates the DNA strands. RNA polymerase then uses one strand of DNA as a template from which nucleotides are assembled into a strand of RNA.** The process of transcription is shown in **Figure 12–14.**

How does RNA polymerase "know" where to start and stop making an RNA copy of DNA? The answer to this question begins with the observation that RNA polymerase doesn't bind to DNA just anywhere. The enzyme will bind only to regions of DNA known as **promoters,** which have specific base sequences. In effect, promoters are signals in DNA that indicate to the enzyme where to bind to make RNA. Similar signals in DNA cause transcription to stop when the new RNA molecule is completed.

▼ **Figure 12–14 During transcription, RNA polymerase uses one strand of DNA as a template to assemble nucleotides into a strand of RNA.**

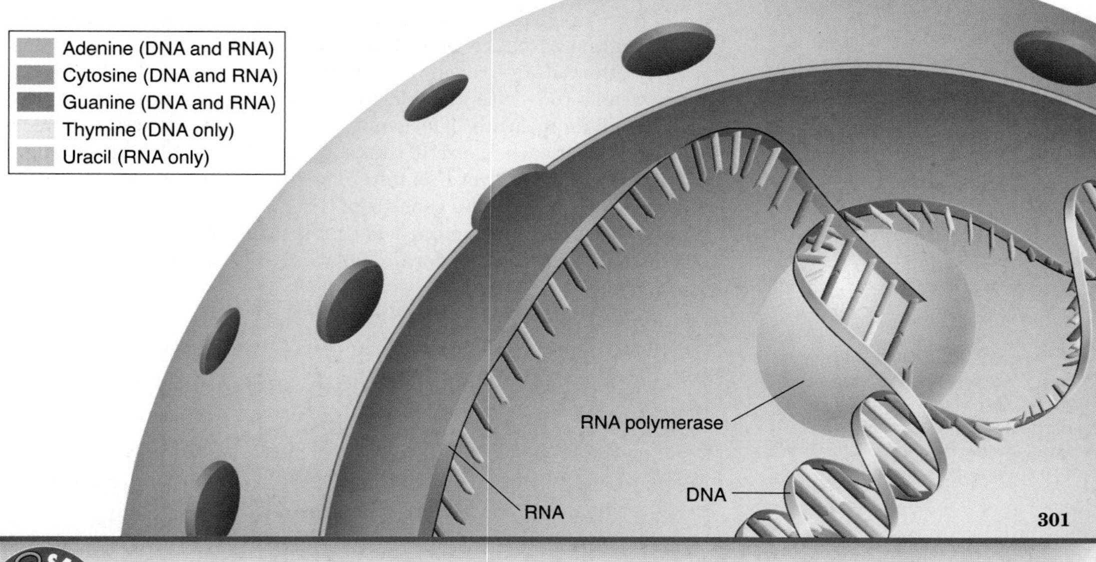

Types of RNA

Build Science Skills

Predicting Explain that each type of RNA has a specific job in the process of making proteins. Have students examine the structures of each type of RNA molecule. Either provide diagrams of your own or have students look at the diagrams in Figure 12–12. From the structures of each type of RNA, challenge students to predict what function that RNA has in protein synthesis. Students should write their predictions and their reasons for making them. After studying transcription and translation, have students review their predictions.

Transcription

Use Visuals

Figure 12–14 As students study the diagram, ask: **Where is DNA located in the eukaryotic cell?** *(In the nucleus)* **Where does transcription take place?** *(In the nucleus)* **Where does protein synthesis take place?** *(In the cytoplasm)* Discuss the role of mRNA and its significance as a copy of DNA. Challenge students to consider why DNA stays inside the nucleus and produces expendable copies of RNA that leave the nucleus to direct protein synthesis.

Address Misconceptions

Some students might think that mRNA is transcribed from DNA and then processed into tRNA and/or rRNA. Review the roles and the structures of each form of RNA. Point out that rRNA and tRNA must bind to other proteins in the cytoplasm of the cell before they are activated. Emphasize that mRNA is transcribed only from genes that encode proteins. Ribosomal RNA and transfer RNA are transcribed from other genes that cannot be translated into proteins.

TIME SAVER **PRESENTATIONS MADE EASY!**

The Presentation Assistant Plus contains the Prentice Hall Presentation Pro and the Transparencies, which provide easy-to-follow visual support for every step of this section. If you have a computer presentation station, use Prentice Hall Presentation Pro for Section 12–3, or use the transparencies listed here.

Section 12–3:

Interest Grabber
Section Outline
Concept Map
Figure 12–12
Figure 12–14
Figure 12–17
Figure 12–18

Answer to . . .

CHECKPOINT *Proteins and rRNA*

RNA Editing

Demonstration

Show students what occurs during RNA editing by using a length of string to represent the pre-mRNA molecule. Color the string with markers to show which segments are introns and which are exons. Remind students that this process occurs in the nucleus before the mRNA moves into the cytoplasm. Demonstrate that the introns form loops so that the exons are situated next to each other. Cut the introns off with scissors and tape together the adjacent exons. Then tape yarn to both ends of the string to represent the cap and the tail added to the mRNA sequence before it leaves the nucleus.

The Genetic Code

Build Science Skills

Applying Concepts Give student pairs different sequences of DNA, and tell them that a mutation has occurred in the sequence that changed one of the nucleotide bases. Have students show two possible sites for this mutation, one that affects the protein product and one that does not. Ask students to explain how the genetic code can help prevent some DNA mutations from affecting an organism's phenotypes. *(The mutations changed a nucleotide base, but the resulting codon specifies the same amino acid as the original codon.)*

Use Visuals

Figure 12–17 Encourage students to closely examine the genetic code in the diagram. Make sure students are reading the diagram correctly to decode a codon. Ask: **What amino acid is specified by CAU?** *(Histidine)* **What is the codon for tryptophan?** *(UGG)* **What are two possible codons for glutamine?** *(CAG, CAA)* **What amino acid is usually the first amino acid of a protein?** *(Methionine)* **How do you know?** *(AUG is the start codon.)*

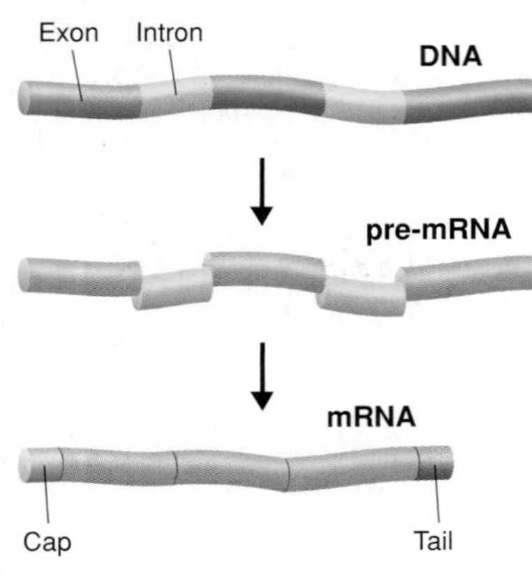

▲ **Figure 12–15** Many RNA molecules have sections, called introns, edited out of them before they become functional. The remaining pieces, called exons, are spliced together. Then, a cap and tail are added to form the final RNA molecule. **Predicting** ***What do you think would happen if the introns were not removed from the pre-mRNA?***

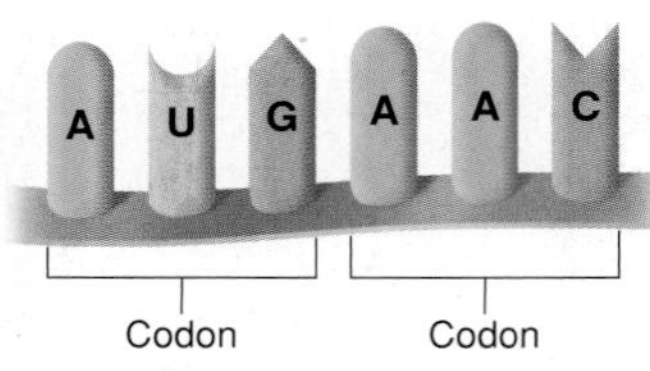

▲ **Figure 12–16** A codon is a group of three nucleotides on messenger RNA that specify a particular amino acid. **Observing** ***What are the three-letter groups of the two codons shown here?***

RNA Editing

Like a writer's first draft, many RNA molecules require a bit of editing before they are ready to go into action. A few, including some of the rRNA molecules that make up ribosomes, are produced from larger RNA molecules that are cut and trimmed to their final sizes. Surprisingly, large pieces are removed from the RNA molecules transcribed from many eukaryotic genes before they become functional. These pieces, known as **introns,** or intervening sequences, are cut out of RNA molecules while they are still in the cell nucleus. The remaining portions, called **exons,** or expressed sequences, are then spliced back together to form the final mRNA. This process is shown in **Figure 12–15.**

Why do cells use energy to make a large RNA molecule and then throw parts of it away? That's a good question, and biologists still do not have a complete answer to it. Some RNA molecules may be cut and spliced in different ways in different tissues, making it possible for a single gene to produce several different forms of RNA. Other biologists have suggested that introns and exons may play a role in evolution. This would make it possible for very small changes in DNA sequences to have dramatic effects in gene expression.

CHECKPOINT *What are introns and exons?*

The Genetic Code

Proteins are made by joining amino acids into long chains called polypeptides. Each polypeptide contains a combination of any or all of the 20 different amino acids. The properties of proteins are determined by the order in which different amino acids are joined together to produce polypeptides. How, you might wonder, can a particular order of nitrogenous bases in DNA and RNA molecules be translated into a particular order of amino acids in a polypeptide?

The "language" of mRNA instructions is called the genetic code. As you know, RNA contains four different bases: A, U, C, and G. In effect, the code is written in a language that has only four "letters." How can a code with just four letters carry instructions for 20 different amino acids? The genetic code is read three letters at a time, so that each "word" of the coded message is three bases long. Each three-letter "word" in mRNA is known as a codon, as shown in **Figure 12–16.** A **codon** consists of three consecutive nucleotides that specify a single amino acid that is to be added to the polypeptide. For example, consider the following RNA sequence:

UCGCACGGU

This sequence would be read three bases at a time as:

UCG-CAC-GGU

The codons represent the different amino acids:

UCG-CAC-GGU

Serine-Histidine-Glycine

FACTS AND FIGURES

RNA wobble

Cells do not produce 61 tRNA molecules—one for each codon. Most cells produce between 22 and 30 kinds of tRNA. The third nucleotide base in a codon is often called the wobble position, because the strength of the bond between the codon and the anticodon is weak. Because of this weakness, Chargaff's rules can be broken, and bases that would not normally pair up, do. This wobble effect is evident in the genetic code. In many cases, the first two bases are the most important in specifying an amino acid. It often does not matter what the third base is.

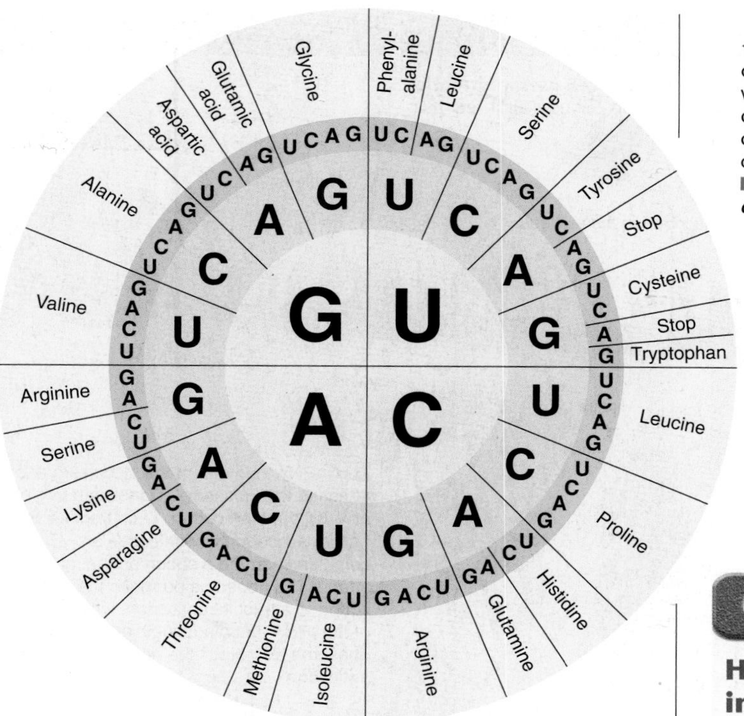

◀ **Figure 12–17** The genetic code shows the amino acid to which each of the 64 possible codons corresponds. To decode a codon, start at the middle of the circle and move outward. **Interpreting Graphics** ***For what amino acid does the codon UGC code?***

Because there are four different bases, there are 64 possible three-base codons ($4 \times 4 \times 4 = 64$). **Figure 12–17** shows all 64 possible codons of the genetic code. As you can see, some amino acids can be specified by more than one codon. For example, six different codons specify the amino acid leucine, and six others specify arginine.

There is also one codon, AUG, that can either specify methionine or serve as the initiation, or "start," codon for protein synthesis. Notice also that there are three "stop" codons that do not code for any amino acid. Stop codons act like the period at the end of a sentence; they signify the end of a polypeptide.

Translation

The sequence of nucleotide bases in an mRNA molecule serves as instructions for the order in which amino acids should be joined together to produce a polypeptide. However, anyone who has tried to assemble a complex toy knows that instructions generally don't do the job themselves. They need something to read them and put them to use. In the cell, that "something" is a tiny factory called the ribosome.

Quick Lab

How does a cell interpret DNA?

Procedure

1. A certain gene has the following sequence of nucleotides:
   GACAAGTCCACAATC
   Write this sequence on a sheet of paper.
2. From left to right, write the sequence of the mRNA molecule transcribed from this gene.
3. Look at **Figure 12–17.** Reading the mRNA codons from left to right, write the amino acid sequence of the polypeptide translated from the mRNA.
4. Repeat step 3, reading the codons from right to left.

Analyze and Conclude

1. **Appying Concepts** Why did steps 3 and 4 produce different polypeptides?
2. **Drawing Conclusions** Do cells usually decode nucleotides in one direction only or in either direction?

Translation

Build Science Skills

Using Models Give small groups of students a diagram of a simple object to build using colored blocks or other building sets. Explain that the diagram must stay in one spot and the building materials and building site must be in a different spot. Instruct students to devise a method by which they can build the object accurately despite the distance between the building plan and site.

Quick Lab

Objective Students will be able to conclude how a cell interprets DNA.

Skills Focus **Applying Concepts, Drawing Conclusions**

Time 15 minutes

Strategy Diagram a molecule of DNA on the board, or show students a three-dimensional model of one. Show students that ends of the DNA are different and that the molecule is directional. Discuss the importance of the directionalism of DNA and how it affects the sequence of amino acids making up proteins.

Expected Outcomes Students should conclude that translation in both directions yields two different amino acid sequences.

Analyze and Conclude

1. The mRNA sequence is not the same in both directions. Reading the sequence backward specifies a different amino acid sequence.
2. Cells usually decode nucleotides in only one direction.

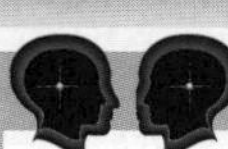

TEACHER TO TEACHER

To help my students better understand how DNA encodes proteins, I like to give them a worksheet on which they practice transcribing and translating DNA. More specifically, I instruct them to write the mRNA sequence of the DNA, then write the tRNA anticodon sequence that is complementary to the mRNA. However, instead of using amino acids, I substitute words so that students produce a sentence instead of a protein sequence. I like to make up sentences such as "I love biology." or "Biology is often fun." I also instruct students to write their own DNA molecules and have their lab partners decode them.

—James Boal,
Biology Teacher
Natrona County High School,
Casper, WY

Answers to . . .

✔CHECKPOINT *Introns: intervening sequences of RNA; exons: expressed sequences of mRNA*

Figure 12–15 *The protein would be made incorrectly.*

Figure 12–16 *AUG, AAC*

Figure 12–17 *Cysteine*

12–3 (continued)

Use Visuals

Figure 12–18 As students study the process of translation in the diagram, discuss the roles of mRNA, tRNA, and rRNA. Explain that ribosomes begin translation by binding to mRNA at an initiation site, which includes the start codon, AUG. Also point out that as soon as the initiation site is open on mRNA, another ribosome binds to it and begins translating another polypeptide. Make sure students understand where translation occurs within the cell *(in the cytoplasm)*.

FIGURE 12–18 TRANSLATION

During translation, or protein synthesis, the cell uses information from messenger RNA to produce proteins. The cell uses all three main forms of RNA during this process.

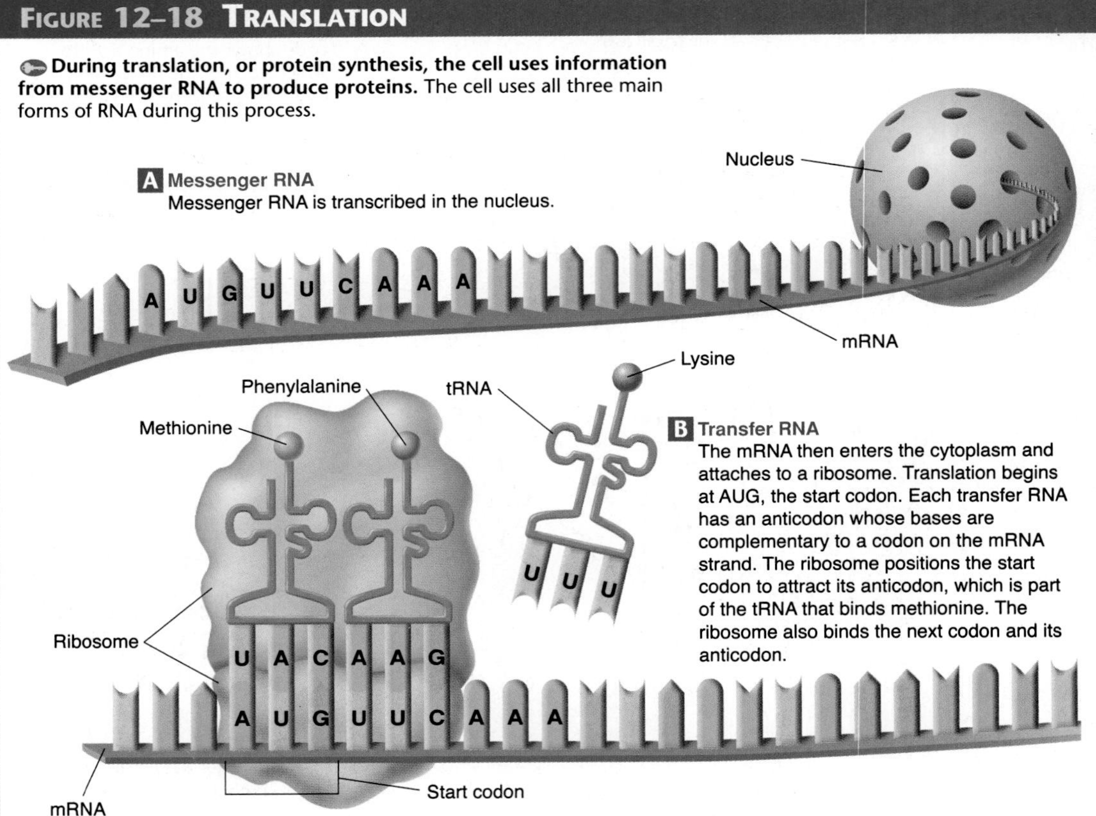
Nucleus
A Messenger RNA
Messenger RNA is transcribed in the nucleus.
A U G U U C A A A
mRNA
Lysine
Phenylalanine
tRNA
Methionine
B Transfer RNA
The mRNA then enters the cytoplasm and attaches to a ribosome. Translation begins at AUG, the start codon. Each transfer RNA has an anticodon whose bases are complementary to a codon on the mRNA strand. The ribosome positions the start codon to attract its anticodon, which is part of the tRNA that binds methionine. The ribosome also binds the next codon and its anticodon.
U U U
Ribosome
U A C A A G
A U G U U C A A A
Start codon
mRNA

The decoding of an mRNA message into a polypeptide chain (protein) is known as **translation.** Translation takes place on ribosomes. **During translation, the cell uses information from messenger RNA to produce proteins.** Refer to **Figure 12–18** as you read about translation.

A Before translation can occur, messenger RNA must first be transcribed from DNA in the nucleus and released into the cytoplasm.

B Translation begins when an mRNA molecule in the cytoplasm attaches to a ribosome. As each codon of the mRNA molecule moves through the ribosome, the proper amino acid is brought into the ribosome and attached to the growing polypeptide chain. The ribosome does not "know" which amino acid to match to each codon. That's the job of transfer RNA. Each tRNA molecule has an amino acid attached to one end and a region of three unpaired bases at the other. The three bases on the tRNA molecule, called the **anticodon,** are complementary to one of the mRNA codons.

BIO INSIGHTS

FACTS AND FIGURES

The importance of protein synthesis
The synthesis of proteins is a carefully orchestrated and controlled process that begins with a coded message on a DNA molecule. The cell goes to a lot of trouble to synthesize proteins correctly because proteins define what the cell looks like, how it functions, how it grows, and how it passes this information to its daughter cells. Some of the specific roles played by proteins include enzymatic action, transport, motion, protection, support, communication, and regulation.

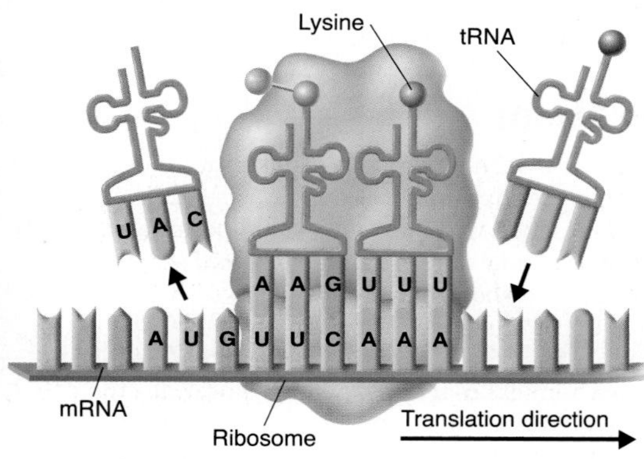

C The Polypeptide "Assembly Line"
The ribosome joins the two amino acids—methionine and phenylalanine—and breaks the bond between methionine and its tRNA. The tRNA floats away, allowing the ribosome to bind to another tRNA. The ribosome moves along the mRNA, binding new tRNA molecules and amino acids.

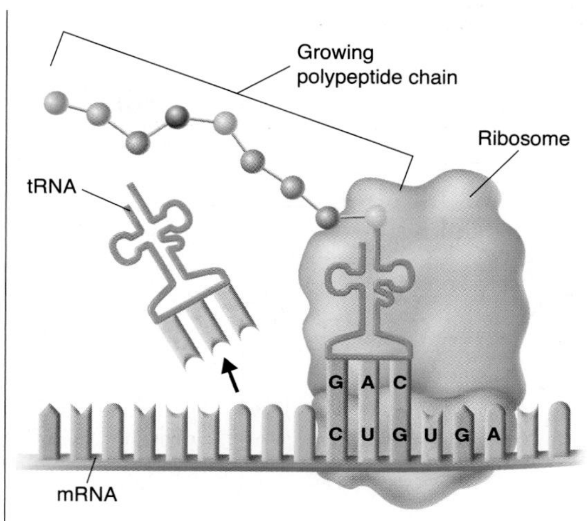

D Completing the Polypeptide
The process continues until the ribosome reaches one of the three stop codons. The result is a growing polypeptide chain.

In the case of the tRNA molecule for methionine, the anticodon bases are UAC, which pair with the methionine codon, AUG. The ribosome has a second binding site for a tRNA molecule for the next codon. If that next codon is UUC, a tRNA molecule with an AAG anticodon would fit against the mRNA molecule held in the ribosome. That second tRNA molecule would bring the amino acid phenylalanine into the ribosome.

C Like an assembly line worker who attaches one part to another, the ribosome forms a peptide bond between the first and second amino acids, methionine and phenylalanine. At the same time, the ribosome breaks the bond that had held the first tRNA molecule to its amino acid and releases the tRNA molecule. The ribosome then moves to the third codon, where a tRNA molecule brings it the amino acid specified by the third codon.

D The polypeptide chain continues to grow until the ribosome reaches a stop codon on the mRNA molecule. When the ribosome reaches a stop codon, it releases the newly formed polypeptide and the mRNA molecule, completing the process of translation.

Meet Diverse Needs

Encourage at-risk students to devise a flowchart in which they describe the steps in the process of translation. Students should also identify the molecules involved and describe their function. Students can include illustrations in their flowcharts to help them better visualize the process. **Learning modality: visual**

12–3 (continued)

The Roles of RNA and DNA

Genes and Proteins

Meet Diverse Needs

Encourage students who need a challenge to find out the different classes of proteins and how they function in an organism. Students can create a table that includes the type of protein, its function, and some examples of that protein class. Encourage students to share their results with the class. Discuss how genes that specify these proteins contribute to the phenotype of an organism. **Learning modality: verbal**

3 ASSESS

Evaluate Understanding

Invite student volunteers to give the steps in the processes of transcription and translation. Write the steps on the board in the form of a flowchart.

Reteach

Have students study the process of translation in Figure 12–18. Instruct them to describe the roles of mRNA, tRNA, and rRNA in the synthesis of proteins. Make sure students know where transcription and translation occur in the cell.

ALTERNATIVE ASSESSMENT

Students' résumés should clearly describe the functions of each type of RNA.

Use iText to review the key concepts in Section 12–3.

The Roles of RNA and DNA

You can compare the different roles played by DNA and RNA molecules in directing protein synthesis to the two types of plans used by builders. A master plan has all the information needed to construct a building. But builders never bring the valuable master plan to the building site, where it might be damaged or lost. Instead, they prepare inexpensive, disposable copies of the master plan called blueprints. The master plan is safely stored in an office, and the blueprints are taken to the job site. Similarly, the cell uses the vital DNA "master plan" to prepare RNA "blueprints." The DNA molecule remains in the safety of the nucleus, while RNA molecules go to the protein-building sites in the cytoplasm—the ribosomes.

Genes and Proteins

Gregor Mendel might have been surprised to learn that most genes contain nothing more than instructions for assembling proteins. He might have asked what proteins could possibly have to do with the color of a flower, the shape of a leaf, a human blood type, or the sex of a newborn baby.

The answer is that proteins have everything to do with these things. Remember that many proteins are enzymes, which catalyze and regulate chemical reactions. A gene that codes for an enzyme to produce pigment can control the color of a flower. Another enzyme-specifying gene helps produce a red blood cell surface antigen. This molecule determines your blood type. Genes for certain proteins can regulate the rate and pattern of growth throughout an organism, controlling its size and shape. In short, proteins are the keys to almost everything that living cells do.

12–3 Section Assessment

1. **Key Concept** List the three main types of RNA.
2. **Key Concept** What happens during transcription?
3. **Key Concept** What happens during translation?
4. Describe the three main differences between RNA and DNA.
5. **Critical Thinking Applying Concepts** Using the genetic code, identify the amino acids that have the following messenger RNA strand codes: UGGCAGUGC.

iText Assessment Use iText to review the important concepts in Section 12–3.

ALTERNATIVE ASSESSMENT

Descriptive Writing
An RNA molecule is looking for a job in a protein synthesis factory, and it asks you to write its résumé. This RNA molecule is not yet specialized and could, with some structural changes, function as either mRNA, tRNA, or rRNA. The résumé you create should reflect the qualifications needed for each type of RNA.

12–3 Section Assessment

1. Messenger RNA, transfer RNA, ribosomal RNA
2. RNA polymerase binds to DNA, separates the strands, and then uses one strand as a template to assemble RNA.
3. The cell uses information from messenger RNA to produce proteins.
4. The sugar in RNA is ribose instead of deoxyribose; RNA is generally single-stranded; RNA contains uracil in place of thymine.
5. Tryptophan-glutamine-cysteine

12–4 Mutations

As precise as they are, every now and then cells make mistakes in copying their own DNA, inserting an incorrect base or sometimes even skipping a base as the new strand is put together. These mistakes are called mutations, from the Latin word *mutare,* meaning "to change." **Mutations** are changes in the DNA sequence that affect genetic information. Like the mistakes that people make in their daily lives, mutations come in many shapes and sizes. **Gene mutations result from changes in a single gene. Chromosomal mutations involve changes in whole chromosomes.**

Gene Mutations

Some gene mutations involve several nucleotides, but the majority involve just one. Mutations that affect one nucleotide are called **point mutations** because they occur at a single point in the DNA sequence. Some point mutations simply substitute one nucleotide for another. These substitutions generally, although not always, change one of the amino acids in a protein.

When a point mutation involves the insertion or deletion of a nucleotide, much bigger changes result. Remember that the genetic code is read in groups of three bases known as codons. What happens if a nucleotide is deleted? The base is still read in groups of three, but now the groupings are shifted for every codon that follows. Inserting an extra nucleotide has a similar effect. Changes like these are called **frameshift mutations** because they shift the "reading frame" of the genetic message. By changing the reading frame, frameshift mutations affect every amino acid that follows the point of the insertion or deletion, as shown in **Figure 12–19.** Such mutations can alter a protein so that it is unable to perform its normal functions.

Guide for Reading

Key Concept
- What are gene mutations and chromosomal mutations?

Vocabulary
mutation
point mutation
frameshift mutation

Reading Strategy: Using Visuals Before you read, preview **Figure 12–19** and **Figure 12–20.** As you read, notice the changes that occur in gene and chromosomal mutations.

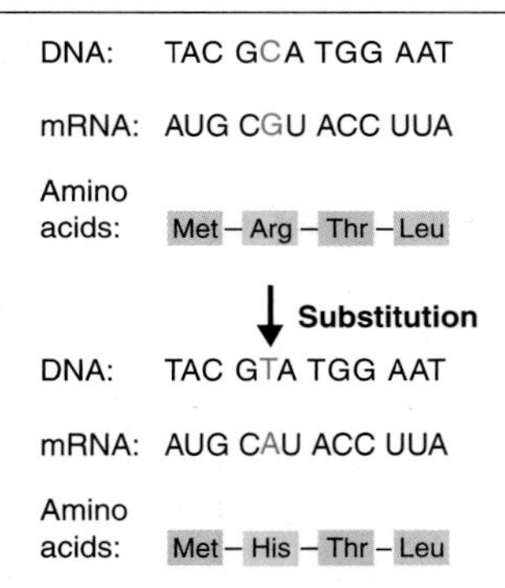

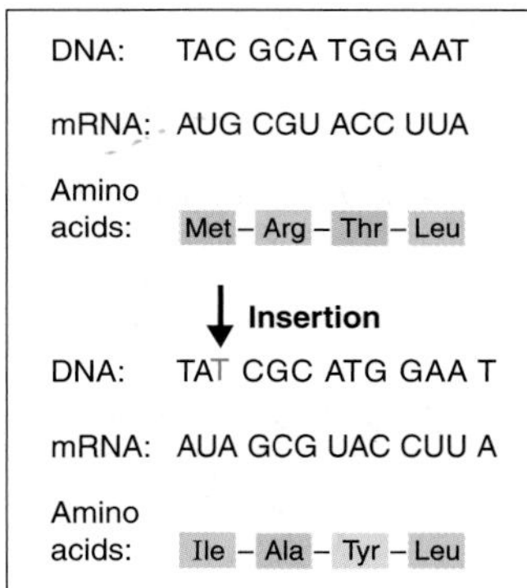

Figure 12–19 **Gene mutations result from changes in a single gene.**

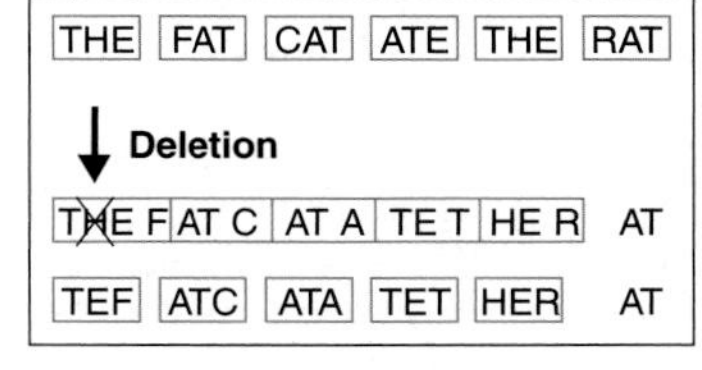

SECTION RESOURCES

Print:
- ***Teaching Resources,*** Section Review 12–4
- ***Guided Reading and Study Workbook,*** Section 12–4

Technology:
- ***iText,*** Section 12–4
- ***Presentation Assistant Plus,*** Interest Grabber; Section Outline; Gene Mutations: Substitution, Insertion, and Deletion; Figure 12–20

Section 12–4

1 FOCUS

Objective

12.4.1 ***Contrast*** gene mutations and chromosomal mutations.

Guide for Reading

Vocabulary Preview

Some students will already know what a mutation is. Ask: **What is a mutation?** *(A change in the DNA sequence that affects genetic information)* Ask: **What do you think a point mutation is?** *(A mutation that affects only one nucleotide)*

Reading Strategy

Encourage students to preview **Figures 12–19** and **12–20** and note the changes that occur in gene and chromosomal mutations.

2 INSTRUCT

Gene Mutations

Build Science Skills

Comparing and Contrasting Encourage students to compare point mutations and frameshift mutations. First, have students write a DNA sequence and show how it is changed by a point mutation and a frameshift mutation. Then, have students compare the mRNA sequence and the protein sequence produced by both "mutated" DNA sequences. Discuss which type of mutation causes more damage and why. *(Frameshift, because it changes all the codons after the point of the mutation)*

Chromosomal Mutations

Meet Diverse Needs

Have at-risk students develop an "owner's manual" for a eukaryotic cell in which they write step-by-step instructions for creating chromosomal mutations. Students should describe how a deletion, duplication, inversion, and translocation occur in the cell's chromosomes. **Learning modality: logical/mathematical**

12–4 (continued)

Make Connections

Health Science Explain to students that chromosomal mutations occur in humans, causing various genetic disorders. One disorder, Down syndrome, is caused when a person has three copies of chromosome 21. Have students compare a normal human karyotype with that of one with Down syndrome. Show students how this mutation occurs when chromosomes fail to separate properly during metaphase I of meiosis.

3 ASSESS

Evaluate Understanding

Ask: **What kinds of mutations can occur in organisms?** *(Gene mutations—point and frameshift mutations; chromosomal mutations)* Have students describe how these mutations affect the proteins produced by the cell.

Reteach

Have students review Figures 12–19 and 12–20 and describe the types of mutations. Make sure that students understand the difference between gene mutations and chromosomal mutations.

Take It to the NET

Students should create concept maps that show the different kinds of gene and chromosomal mutations. Make sure students have correctly linked the types of mutations. For additional information, visit **www.phschool.com**

Use iText to review the key concepts in Section 12–4.

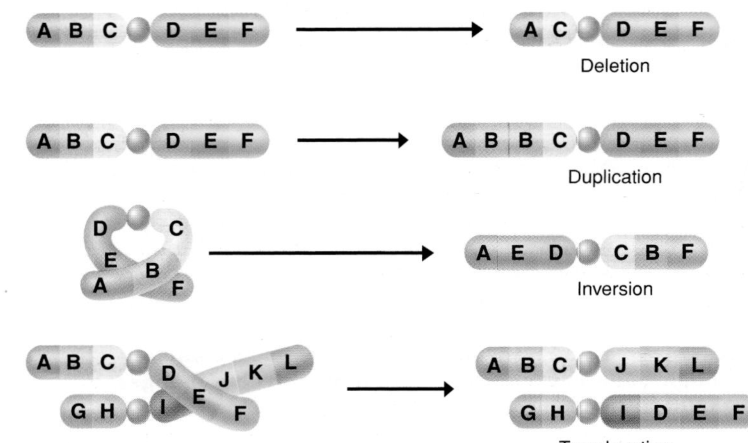

▶ **Figure 12–20** **Chromosomal mutations involve changes in whole chromosomes.**

Chromosomal Mutations

A chromosomal mutation involves changes in the number or structure of chromosomes. Chromosomal mutations may change the locations of genes on chromosomes and even the number of copies of some genes.

Figure 12–20 shows four types of chromosomal mutations. A deletion involves the loss of all or part of a chromosome. The opposite of a deletion is a duplication, in which a segment of a chromosome is repeated. When part of a chromosome becomes oriented in the reverse of its usual direction, the result is an inversion. A translocation occurs when part of one chromosome breaks off and attaches to another, nonhomologous, chromosome. In most cases, nonhomologous chromosomes exchange segments so that two translocations occur at the same time.

12–4 Section Assessment

1. **Key Concept** What is a gene mutation? What is a chromosomal mutation?
2. What is a point mutation?
3. What are two kinds of frameshift mutations?
4. What are four types of chromosomal mutations?
5. **Critical Thinking Inferring** The effects of a mutation are not always visible. How might a biologist determine whether a mutation has occurred and, if so, what type of mutation it is?

iTEXT Assessment Use iText to review the important concepts in Section 12–4.

Take It to the NET

Find out more about the kinds of mutations that can occur in DNA. Then, create a concept map linking each kind of mutation. Use the links provided in the Biology area at the Prentice Hall Web site for help in completing this activity: **www.phschool.com**

12–4 Section Assessment

1. Gene mutations result from changes in a single gene. Chromosomal mutations involve changes in whole chromosomes.
2. A point mutation is a mutation that occurs at a single point in the DNA sequence.
3. Two kinds of frameshift mutations are insertions and deletions.
4. Four kinds of chromosomal mutations are deletions, duplications, inversions, and translocations.
5. A researcher could compare the DNA sequence of normal DNA to that of the mutated DNA. The base sequence should reveal the type of mutation.

12–5 Gene Regulation

Only a fraction of the genes in a cell are expressed at any given time. An expressed gene is a gene that is transcribed into RNA. How does the cell determine which genes will be expressed and which will remain "silent"? A close look at the structure of a gene provides some important clues.

At first glance, the DNA sequence of a gene is nothing more than a confusing jumble of the four letters that represent the bases in DNA. However, if we take the time to analyze those letters, patterns emerge. Molecular biologists have found that certain DNA sequences serve as promoters, binding sites for RNA polymerase. Others serve as start and stop signals for transcription. In fact, cells are filled with DNA-binding proteins that attach to specific DNA sequences and help to regulate gene expression. A typical gene might look something like **Figure 12–21**.

As we've seen, there is a promoter just to one side of the gene. But what are the "regulatory sites" next to the promoter? These are places where other proteins, binding directly to the DNA sequences at those sites, can regulate transcription. The actions of these proteins help to determine whether a gene is turned on or turned off.

Guide for Reading

Key Concepts
- How are *lac* genes turned off and on?
- How are most eukaryotic genes controlled?

Vocabulary
operon
operator
hox gene

Reading Strategy: Outlining Before you read, use the headings of the section to make an outline about gene regulation. As you read, fill in subtopics and smaller topics. Then, add phrases or a sentence after each subtopic to provide key information.

Gene Regulation: An Example

How does an organism "know" whether to turn a gene on or off? The common bacterium *E. coli* provides us with a perfect example of how gene expression can be regulated. The 4288 protein-encoding genes in this bacterium include a cluster of three genes that are turned on or off together. A group of genes that operate together is known as an **operon**. Because these genes must be expressed in order for the bacterium to be able to use the sugar lactose as a food, they are called the *lac* operon.

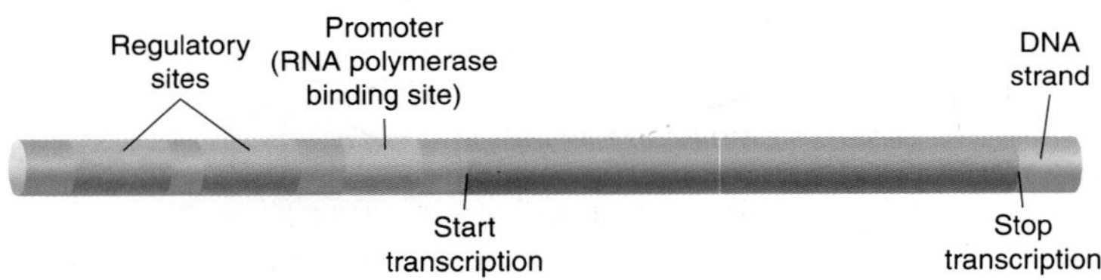

GAATTCTAATCTCCCTCTCAACCCTACAGTCACCCATTTGGTATATTAAAGATGTGTTG
TCTACTGTCTAGTATCCCTCAAGTAGTGTCAGGAATTAGTCATTTAAATAGTCTGCAAG
CCAGGAGTGGTGGCTCATGTCTGTAATTCCAGCACTGGAGAGGTAGAAGTGGGAG
GACTGCTTGAGCTCAAGAGTTTGATATTATCCTGGACAACATAGCAAGACCTCGTCT
CTACTTAAAAAAAAAAAAATTAGCCAGGCATGTGATGTACACCTGTAGTCCCAGCTAC
TCAGGAGGCCGAAATGGGAGGATCCCTTGAGCTCAGGAGGTCAAGGCTGCAGTGA
GACATGATCTTGCCACTGCACTCCAGCCTGGACAGCAGAGTGAAACCTTGCCTCAC
GAAACAGAATACAAAAACAAACAAACAAAAAACTGCTCCGCAATGCGCTTCCTTGAT
GCTCTACCACATAGGTCTGGGTACTTT

◀ **Figure 12–21** A typical gene includes start and stop signals, with the nucleotides to be translated in between. The DNA sequence shown is only a very small part of an actual gene. **Interpreting Graphics** ***What is the function of the promoter?***

TIME SAVER — SECTION RESOURCES

Print:
- ***Teaching Resources,*** Section Review 12–5, Chapter 12 Exploration
- ***Guided Reading and Study Workbook,*** Section 12–5
- ***Biotechnology Manual,*** Lab 13

Technology:
- ***iText,*** Section 12–5

Section 12–5

1 FOCUS

Objectives

12.5.1 ***Describe*** a typical gene.
12.5.2 ***Describe*** how *lac* genes are turned off and on.
12.5.3 ***Explain*** how most eukaryotic genes are controlled.
12.5.4 ***Relate*** gene regulation to development.

Guide for Reading

Vocabulary Preview

Read aloud the vocabulary words to the class. Classify the words so that students have a sense of their meaning. For example, explain that *hox gene* is the name of a specific gene, but *expressed gene* is a general description used for any gene to describe whether it is in the process of being translated or not.

Reading Strategy

As students complete their outlines, encourage them to include sketches of the diagrams in the section. Students should label the sketches as they are labeled in the text.

2 INSTRUCT

Gene Regulation: An Example

Use Visuals

Figure 12–21 As students examine the structure of a typical gene in the diagram, have volunteers describe the function of each part. Ask: **What codon sequence would you expect to find in the mRNA at the place where transcription starts?** *(AUG, the start codon)* **At the place where transcription ends?** *(Any one of the three stop codons—UAA, UAG, or UGA)* **What kinds of molecules bind to the regulatory sites of genes?** *(DNA-binding proteins)* **What is the action of these proteins on genes?** *(They turn genes off or on.)*

Answer to . . .

Figure 12–21 *It's the RNA polymerase binding site.*

12–5 (continued)

Use Visuals

Figure 12–22 Reinforce the operation of the *lac* operon by diagramming the illustration on the board while students follow along in their textbooks. Ask: **When is the repressor protein bound to the operator?** *(When lactose is not present)* **Can transcription occur when the repressor is bound to the operator?** *(No)* **Why not?** *(The repressor protein blocks RNA polymerase from binding to the promoter.)* **How does the presence of lactose help start transcription of the *lac* genes?** *(Lactose binds to the repressor protein, causing it to release from the operator site, and RNA polymerase can bind to the promoter.)*

Build Science Skills

Inferring Help students realize how elegantly the cell is able to control its production of proteins involved in the utilization of lactose. Challenge students to make inferences about why the cell has evolved such an elaborate method of gene regulation. Have them consider why regulating the production of proteins that utilize lactose is advantageous to the cell. They can also consider why it is not advantageous to produce the *lac* proteins continuously.

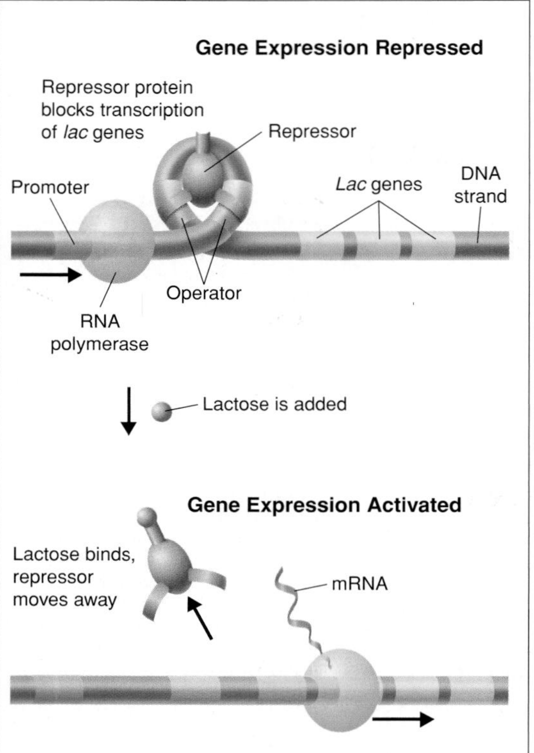

▲ **Figure 12–22** **The *lac* genes in *E. coli* are turned off by repressors and turned on by the presence of lactose.** When lactose is not present, the repressor binds to the operator region, preventing RNA polymerase from beginning transcription. Lactose causes the repressor to be released from the operator region.

Why must *E. coli* turn on the *lac* genes in order to use lactose for food? Lactose is a compound made up of two simple sugars, galactose and glucose. To use lactose for food, the bacterium must take lactose across its cell membrane and then break the bond between glucose and galactose. These tasks are performed by proteins coded for by the genes of the *lac* operon. This means, of course, that if the bacterium is grown in a medium where lactose is the only food source, it must transcribe the genes and produce these proteins. On the other hand, if grown on another food source, such as glucose, it would have no need for these proteins.

Remarkably, the bacterium almost seems to "know" when the products of these genes are needed. **The *lac* genes are turned off by repressors and turned on by the presence of lactose.** How is the bacterium so smart? The answer tells us a great deal about how genes are regulated.

On one side of the operon's three genes are two regulatory regions. In the promoter (P), RNA polymerase binds and then begins transcription. The other region is the **operator** (O). *E. coli* cells contain several copies of a DNA-binding protein known as the *lac* repressor, which can bind to the O region. As **Figure 12–22** shows, when the *lac* repressor binds to the O region, RNA polymerase is prevented from binding to the promoter. In effect, the binding of the repressor protein turns the operon "off" by preventing the transcription of its genes.

If the repressor protein is always present, then how are the *lac* genes turned on in the presence of lactose? Besides its DNA binding site, the *lac* repressor protein has a binding site for lactose itself. When lactose is added to the medium, a few of the sugar molecules diffuse into the cell and bind to the repressor proteins. The binding of lactose causes the repressor protein to change shape in a way that completely alters its DNA-binding site, causing the repressor to fall off the operator. Now, with the repressor no longer bound to the O site, RNA polymerase can bind to the promoter and transcribe the genes of the operon.

This simple system allows the cell automatically to turn the *lac* genes on and off as needed. The *lac* operon is an example of the ways in which prokaryotic genes are regulated. Many other genes are also regulated by repressor proteins, while others use proteins that enhance the rate of transcription. In some systems, regulation occurs at the level of protein synthesis. Regardless of the actual system involved, the result is the same: Cells are able to turn their genes on and off as needed.

CHECKPOINT *What is the function of the operator region?*

PRESENTATIONS MADE EASY!

The Presentation Assistant Plus contains the Prentice Hall Presentation Pro and the Transparencies, which provide easy-to-follow visual support for every step of this section. If you have a computer presentation station, use Prentice Hall Presentation Pro for Section 12–5, or use the transparencies listed here.

Section 12–5: **Interest Grabber**
Section Outline
Typical Gene Structure

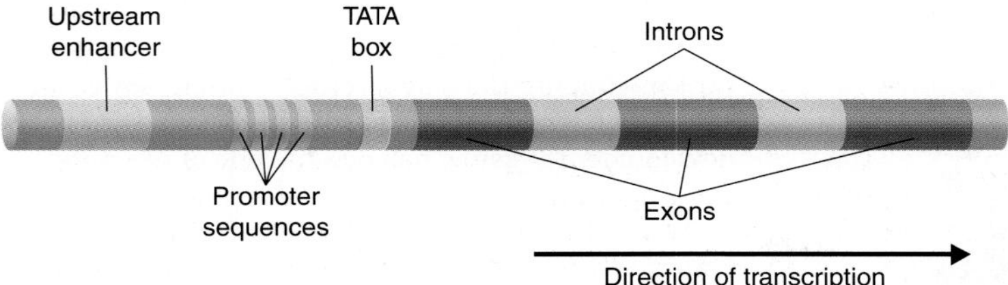

◀ **Figure 12–23** **Eukaryotic genes are more complex than prokaryotic genes.** Many eukaryotic genes include a sequence called the TATA box that may help position RNA polymerase.

Eukaryotic Gene Regulation

The general principles of gene regulation in prokaryotes also apply to eukaryotic cells, although there are some important differences. Operons are generally not found in eukaryotes. **Most eukaryotic genes are controlled individually and have regulatory sequences that are much more complex than those of the *lac* operon.**

Figure 12–23 shows some of the features of a typical eukaryotic gene. One of the most interesting is a short region of DNA about 30 base pairs long, with a sequence of TATATA or TATAAA, before the start of transcription. This region is found before so many eukaryotic genes that it even has a name: the "TATA box." The TATA box seems to help position RNA polymerase by marking a point just before the point at which transcription begins. Eukaryotic promoters are usually found just before the TATA box, and they consist of a series of short DNA sequences.

Genes are regulated in a variety of ways by enhancer sequences located before the beginning of transcription. An enormous number of proteins can bind to different enhancer sequences, which is why eukaryotic gene regulation is so complex. Some of these DNA-binding proteins enhance transcription by opening up tightly packed chromatin. Others help to attract RNA polymerase. Still other proteins block access to genes, much like prokaryotic repressor proteins.

Why is gene regulation in eukaryotes more complex than in prokaryotes? Think for a moment about the way in which genes are expressed in a multicellular organism. The genes that code for liver enzymes, for example, are not expressed in nerve cells. Keratin, an important protein in skin cells, is not produced in blood cells. Cell specialization requires genetic specialization, but all of the cells in a multicellular organism carry the complete genetic code in their nucleus. Therefore, for proper overall function, only a tiny fraction of the available genes needs to be expressed in cells of different tissues throughout the body. The complexity of gene regulation in eukaryotes makes this specificity possible.

Meet Diverse Needs

Give at-risk students more opportunities to model the regulation of the *lac* operon by having them model the action of the repressor protein, lactose, and RNA polymerase on the *lac* operon. Students can use a pipe cleaner to represent the *lac* operon and beads connected to paperclips to represent the repressor protein, RNA polymerase, and lactose. Students might wish to use a marker to color-code the promoter, the operator, and the *lac* genes on the pipe cleaner. Encourage them to base their models on Figure 12–22. **Learning modality: kinesthetic**

Eukaryotic Gene Regulation

Address Misconceptions

Many students might think that all genes are expressed in all cells of a eukaryotic organism. Help students understand that not every gene is expressed in every body cell. Explain that the pancreas secretes many digestive enzymes, such as amylase, to help break down foods. The gene for amylase is expressed in the pancreas in order to synthesize the enzyme. However, cells in bone marrow have no reason to produce amylase. The gene for amylase in bone cells is always turned off because these cells do not need to secrete amylase.

Answer to . . .

CHECKPOINT *The operator is a region to which a repressor can bind, preventing transcription of the genes.*

12–5 (continued)

Regulation and Development

Build Science Skills

Formulating Hypotheses Challenge students to devise a hypothesis that describes how a hox gene might be regulated. Suggest that they review the way in which eukaryotic genes are regulated to help them get started. Encourage students to diagram the method of regulation that they hypothesize.

3 ASSESS

Evaluate Understanding

Instruct students to make a compare/contrast table in which they compare and contrast the regulation of gene expression in prokaryotes and eukaryotes.

Reteach

Have students diagram the regulation of the *lac* operon, using the diagram in Figure 12–22. Students should label the diagram with the parts of the operon and describe the functions of each part. Encourage students to describe these functions.

ALTERNATIVE ASSESSMENT

Encourage students to work with a partner to brainstorm analogies. In one possible analogy, students might compare the *lac* operon to a lamp, in which the promoter is the electricity, the operator is the lamp socket, the repressor is the lamp switch in the "off" position, and lactose is the lamp switch in the "on" position. Even if student analogies do not carry through all of the components of the *lac* operon, students will internalize the main concepts of the model in the process of creating the analogy.

Use iText to review the key concepts in Section 12–5.

Answer to . . .

Figure 12–24 *Rear section*

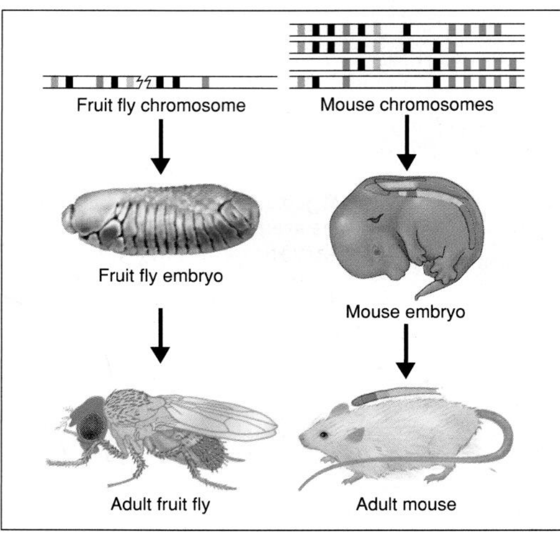

▲ **Figure 12–24** In fruit flies, a series of hox genes along a chromosome determines the basic structure of the fly's body. Mice have very similar genes on four different chromosomes. **Interpreting Graphics** ***What section of the bodies of flies and mice is coded by the genes shown in blue?***

Regulation and Development

Regulation of gene expression is especially important in shaping the way a complex organism develops from a single fertilized cell. In fact, the study of developmental genes has become one of the most exciting areas in all of biology.

Why all the excitement? Molecular studies of embryos have shown that a series of genes, known as the **hox genes,** controls the organs and tissues that develop in various parts of the embryo. These genes determine an animal's basic body plan. How important are these genes? A mutation in one of these "master control genes" can completely change the organs that develop in specific parts of the body. Mutations affecting the hox genes in the fruit fly, *Drosophila,* for example, can replace the fly's antennae with a pair of legs growing right out of its head!

In flies, the hox genes are located side by side in a single cluster, arranged in the exact order in which they are expressed in the body, as shown in **Figure 12–24.** Remarkably, similar clusters exist in the DNA of other animals, including humans. The function of the hox genes in humans seems to be almost the same as it is in flies—to tell the cells of the body which organs and structures they should develop into as the body grows. Careful control of expression in these genes is essential for normal development.

The striking similarity of genes that control development has a simple scientific explanation: Common patterns of genetic control exist because all these genes have descended from the genes of common ancestors. One such gene, called Pax 6, controls eye growth in *Drosophila.* A similar gene was found to guide eye growth in mice and other mammals. When a copy of the mouse gene was inserted into the "knee" of a *Drosophila* embryo, the resulting fruit fly grew an eye on its leg! The fly gene and the mouse gene are similar enough to trade places and still function—even though they come from animals that have not shared a common ancestor in at least 600 million years.

12–5 Section Assessment

1. **Key Concept** How is the *lac* operon regulated?
2. **Key Concept** Describe how most eukaryotic genes are controlled.
3. What is a promoter?
4. Why are only a limited number of genes expressed in each cell of a multicellular eukaryote?
5. **Critical Thinking Comparing and Contrasting** How is the way hox genes are expressed in mice similar to the way they are expressed in fruit flies? How is it different?

iTEXT Assessment Use iText to review the important concepts in Section 12–5.

ALTERNATIVE ASSESSMENT

Making an Analogy Make an analogy to demonstrate the different components of the *lac* operon. Then, explain in a short paragraph—using your analogy—how the *lac* operon works.

12–5 Section Assessment

1. It is turned off by repressors and turned on by the presence of lactose.
2. Most are controlled individually and have regulatory sequences that are much more complex than those of the *lac* operon.
3. The region of mRNA where RNA polymerase binds and starts transcription
4. Because of cell specialization in eukaryotes, many proteins are needed only in specific types of cells. All genes do not need to be expressed in all cells.
5. The genes themselves are very similar and have the same function. In fruit flies, the genes are located on one chromosome. In mice, the genes are spread among four chromosomes.

Exploration

Modeling DNA Replication

Living cells make exact copies of DNA molecules that are passed on to each daughter cell during cell division. In this investigation, you will model DNA replication.

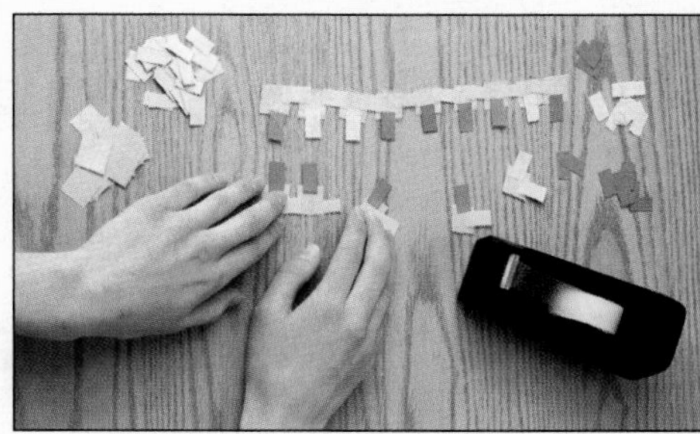

Problem How is DNA replicated?

Materials

- construction paper (tan, gray, green, yellow, red, and purple)
- metric ruler
- scissors
- transparent tape

Skills Using Models

Procedure

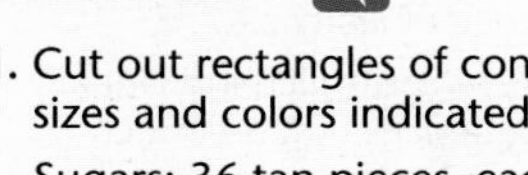

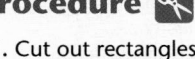

1. Cut out rectangles of construction paper in the sizes and colors indicated below:

   Sugars: 36 tan pieces, each 2 cm × 2 cm

   Phosphates: 36 gray pieces, each 1 cm × 2 cm

   Adenines (A): 12 green pieces, each 1 cm × 2 cm

   Thymines (T): 12 yellow pieces, each 1 cm × 2 cm

   Guanines (G): 6 red pieces, each 1 cm × 2 cm

   Cytosines (C): 6 purple pieces, each 1 cm × 2 cm
2. To model a nucleotide, tape together a phosphate group, a sugar, and a guanine molecule (G) (see **Figure 12–5** on page 291).
3. Assemble eight additional nucleotide models with the following nitrogenous bases: 3 thymines (T); 3 adenines (A); 2 cytosines (C).
4. To model a single strand of DNA, tape the sugar of each nucleotide to the phosphate group of the next nucleotide in the following order: G T T A C A A T C.
5. Construct a strand of DNA that is complementary to the first strand. Tape the nucleotides of the second strand together as you did in step 4. Record the positions of the bases in both strands of your model.
6. Place the two strands side by side so that their complementary nucleotides face each other. Do not tape the two strands together. Write "original" on each strand.
7. Separate the two strands. Simulate the action of DNA polymerase by constructing a new complementary strand for each original strand.
8. Tape the bases of each new strand to the complementary bases of its matching strand.

Analyze and Conclude

1. **Comparing and Contrasting** Compare the new double-stranded DNA models with your original DNA model. Are their nucleotide sequences identical?
2. **Using Models** After a cell's DNA is replicated, the cell may divide in two. Each new cell receives one copy of the original cell's DNA. According to your model, how are the new strands and the original strands divided between the two new cells?
3. **Drawing Conclusions** How does the pairing of complementary bases help ensure that the nucleotide sequence is copied accurately during DNA replication?
4. **Drawing Conclusions** What problems would you expect to occur if DNA was not copied accurately as it is replicated?

Go Further

Using Models Before DNA can be replicated, the DNA double helix must be unwound so that the enzymes involved in this process can make contact with the bases. The enzyme DNA polymerase adds the correct complementary nucleotides to the growing new strands. Modify your model or make a new model to show how these processes occur.

Exploration

Objective Students will be able to use models to determine how DNA is replicated.

Skills Focus **Using Models**

Time 45 minutes

Prelab Discussion Review how DNA is replicated. Invite volunteers to describe the steps in the process. Ask: **How does the structure of DNA make it easy to copy?** *(The weak hydrogen bonds holding the two strands are easily broken to separate the strands. The sequence of base pairs specifies the synthesis of a new strand because of Chargaff's base-pairing rules.)*

Teaching Tip Monitor students as they construct their models to make sure they understand how the DNA molecule is assembled.

Procedure

4. The color sequence of the DNA model should be red-yellow-yellow-green-purple-green-green-yellow-purple.

5. Color sequence should be purple-green-green-yellow-red-yellow-yellow-green-red.

Expected Outcomes Students should construct two strands of DNA that have a complementary sequence to the two original DNA strands.

Go Further

Student models will vary but should show how the DNA molecule forms a helical structure. Students should also construct a model of DNA polymerase out of paper, showing how it moves along the DNA strand to add the correct nucleotide to the growing new strand.

Analyze and Conclude

1. Yes, the new DNA sequence should be identical to the original sequence.

2. Each cell receives a DNA molecule consisting of a new strand and an original strand.

3. Only one complementary nucleotide fits in place opposite each nucleotide in the original strand, so the new strand consists of the complementary sequence to the original strand.

4. Mutations would occur that might affect the functions of the proteins specified by the DNA sequence. These mutations could affect the life of the cell.

Chapter 12 Study Guide

Study Tip

Have students make a glossary for the Vocabulary terms in which they use their own words for the definitions. Also encourage students to use illustrations or mnemonics to help them remember meanings.

Thinking Visually

1. The mRNA enters the cytoplasm and attaches to a ribosome.

2. The tRNA anticodon matches with the mRNA codon in the ribosome. The ribosome assembles the amino acids brought by tRNA.

Chapter 12 Assessment

Reviewing Content

1. c	**4.** c	**7.** b	**10.** b
2. d	**5.** a	**8.** c	
3. b	**6.** d	**9.** b	

Understanding Concepts

11. Genes carry information from one generation to the next, determine heritable characteristics, and are replicated easily.

12. DNA is a long molecule made up of nucleotides. Each nucleotide has three parts: a 5-carbon sugar called deoxyribose, a phosphate group, and a nitrogenous base. The four nitrogenous bases are adenine and guanine, which are purines, and cytosine and thymine, which are pyrimidines.

13. Chargaff's rules suggested that adenine bonds only to thymine and cytosine bonds only to guanine.

14. Base pairing is the principle that hydrogen bonds form only between certain base pairs—A and T and C and G. In DNA replication, base pairing ensures that the complementary strands produced are identical to the original strands.

15. It has a single, circular DNA molecule that contains nearly all of the cell's genetic information.

16. Each new DNA molecule has one strand from the original molecule and one new strand. Both new molecules are identical to the original one.

Chapter 12 Study Guide

12–1 DNA

Key Concepts

- Avery and other scientists discovered that DNA is the nucleic acid that stores and transmits the genetic information from one generation of an organism to the next.
- Hershey and Chase concluded that the genetic material of the bacteriophage they infected with bacteria was DNA, not protein.
- Watson and Crick's model of DNA was a double helix, in which two strands were wound around each other.

Vocabulary
- transformation, p. 288 • bacteriophage, p. 289
- nucleotide, p. 291 • base pairing, p. 294

12–2 Chromosomes and DNA Replication

Key Concept

- During DNA replication, the DNA molecule separates into two strands, then produces two new complementary strands following the rules of base pairing. Each strand of the double helix of DNA serves as a template, or model, for the new strand.

Vocabulary
- chromatin, p. 296 • histone, p. 296
- replication, p. 299 • DNA polymerase, p. 299

12–3 RNA and Protein Synthesis

Key Concepts

- There are three main types of RNA: messenger RNA, ribosomal RNA, and transfer RNA.
- During transcription, RNA polymerase binds to DNA and separates the DNA strands. RNA polymerase then uses one strand of DNA as a template from which nucleotides are assembled into a strand of RNA.
- During translation, the cell uses information from messenger RNA to produce proteins.

Vocabulary
- messenger RNA, p. 301 • ribosomal RNA, p. 301
- transfer RNA, p. 301 • transcription, p. 301
- RNA polymerase, p. 301 • promoter, p. 301
- intron, p. 302 • exon, p. 302 • codon, p. 302
- translation, p. 304 • anticodon, p. 304

12–4 Mutations

Key Concept

- Gene mutations result from changes in a single gene. Chromosomal mutations involve changes in whole chromosomes.

Vocabulary
mutation, p. 307
point mutation, p. 307
frameshift mutation, p. 307

12–5 Gene Regulation

Key Concepts

- The *lac* genes are turned off by repressors and turned on by the presence of lactose.
- Most eukaryotic genes are controlled individually and have regulatory sequences that are much more complex than those of the *lac* operon.

Vocabulary
operon, p. 309
operator, p. 310
hox gene, p. 312

Thinking Visually

Using the information in this chapter, complete the following flowchart about protein synthesis:

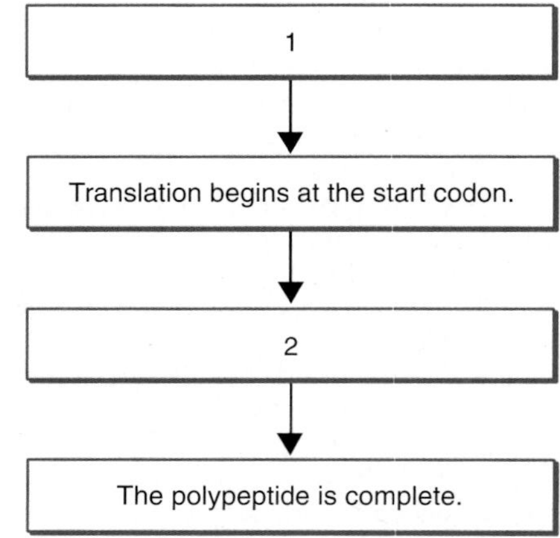
1
Translation begins at the start codon.
2
The polypeptide is complete.

TIME SAVER — CHAPTER RESOURCES

Print:
- ***Teaching Resources,*** Chapter Vocabulary Review, Graphic Organizer
- ***Chapter Tests: Levels A and B,*** Chapter 12 Test
- ***PH Assessment System,*** Practice Test

Technology:
- ***Computer Test Bank,*** Chapter 12 Test
- ***iText,*** Chapter 12 Assessment

Chapter 12 Assessment

Reviewing Concepts

Choose the letter that best answers the question or completes the statement.

1. The process by which one strain of bacteria is apparently changed into another strain is called
   a. transcription. c. transformation.
   b. translation. d. replication.
2. Bacteriophages are
   a. tiny bacteria. c. coils of RNA.
   b. enzymes. d. viruses.
3. A nucleotide does NOT contain
   a. a 5-carbon sugar.
   b. polymerase.
   c. a nitrogen base.
   d. a phosphate group.
4. In prokaryotes, DNA molecules are located in the
   a. nucleus. c. cytoplasm.
   b. ribosome. d. histone.
5. The diagram below shows the process of DNA
   a. replication. c. translation.
   b. transcription. d. transformation.

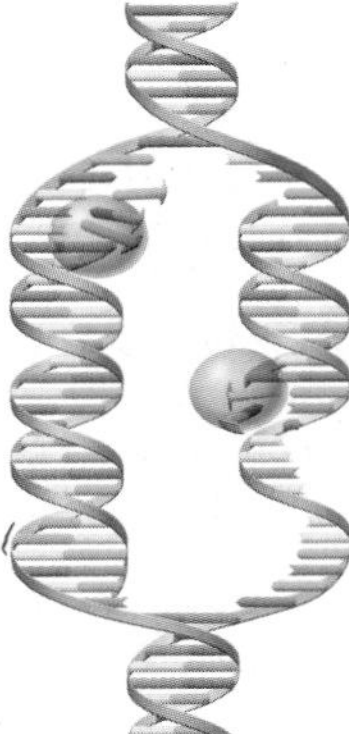

6. The main enzyme involved in linking individual nucleotides into DNA molecules is
   a. transfer RNA. c. RNA polymerase.
   b. ribose. d. DNA polymerase.
7. The process by which the genetic code of DNA is copied into a strand of RNA is called
   a. translation. c. transformation.
   b. transcription. d. replication.
8. In messenger RNA, each codon specifies a particular
   a. nucleotide. c. amino acid.
   b. purine. d. pyrimidine.
9. Changes in the DNA sequence that affect genetic information are known as
   a. replications. c. transformations.
   b. mutations. d. prokaryotes.
10. An expressed gene is one that
    a. functions as a promoter.
    b. is transcribed into RNA.
    c. codes for proteins.
    d. is made of mRNA.

Understanding Concepts

11. As scientists tried to discover the nature of genes, what three critical gene functions had they identified?
12. Describe the structure of a DNA nucleotide.
13. Explain how Chargaff's rules helped Watson and Crick model DNA.
14. What is meant by the term *base pairing*? How is base pairing involved in DNA replication?
15. Describe the appearance of DNA in a typical prokaryotic cell.
16. When a DNA molecule is replicated, how do the new molecules relate to the original molecule?
17. Describe the relationship between DNA, chromatin, histones, and nucleosomes.
18. What is the difference between exons and introns?
19. What is a codon?
20. What is an anticodon? How does it function?
21. If a code on a DNA molecule for a specific amino acid is CTA, what would be the messenger RNA codon? The transfer RNA anticodon?
22. Explain why controlling the proteins in an organism controls the organism's characteristics.
23. Name two major types of mutations. What do they have in common? How are they different? Give an example of each.
24. Describe how the RNA polymerase is positioned in a eukaryotic cell.
25. Describe the role of an operon in a prokaryotic cell, and give an example of how an operon works.

17. Nucleosomes are made up of DNA wrapped around histones. Chromatin is long chains of nucleosomes.

18. Exons are sections of messenger RNA. Introns are sections of pre-mRNA that are removed when mRNA is formed.

19. A codon consists of three nucleotides that specify a single amino acid that is to be added to a polypeptide. The source of the codon's message is DNA. Each codon stands for a specific amino acid.

20. An anticodon consists of the three bases on the tRNA molecule that are complementary to a mRNA codon. Anticodons determine which tRNA binds to the codon on mRNA, and thus which amino acid is attached to the polypeptide chain.

21. GAU; CUA

22. Proteins are responsible for catalyzing and regulating chemical reactions, as well as regulating the rate and pattern of growth. These actions help determine an organism's characteristics.

23. Gene and chromosomal; both change the DNA sequence that affects genetic information. Gene mutations involve a change in one or several nucleotides in a single gene, whereas chromosomal mutations involve changes in the number or structure of whole chromosomes.

24. RNA polymerase is positioned along DNA in the nucleus.

25. An operon regulates gene expression. In the *lac* operon, the *lac* genes are turned off by a repressor that binds to the operator, blocking RNA polymerase from the promoter. When lactose is present, it binds to the repressor, causing it to release from the operator, allowing RNA polymerase to transcribe the *lac* genes.

TIME SAVER — HOMEWORK GUIDE

Section:	Questions:
Section 12–1	1–3, 11–14, 26, 27
Section 12–2	4–6, 15–17, 28
Section 12–3	7, 8, 18–22, 24, 33, 34
Section 12–4	9, 23, 32
Section 12–5	10, 25

Critical Thinking

26. Griffith heated a culture of the disease-causing strain, which killed the bacteria but did not destroy the DNA. When he mixed the heat-killed, disease-causing bacteria with the live, harmless bacteria, the DNA from the disease-causing bacteria was picked up by the live bacteria. The disease-causing DNA began replicating and was passed on to new bacteria cells. The new bacteria cells were disease-causing because of their DNA. These bacteria caused pneumonia in the mice.

27. Students' models should look like Figure 12–7 on page 294 when viewed from the side and like the photograph of the X-ray diffraction pattern of DNA in the Biology and History feature on page 292 when viewed from the top. The "X" is what some of the nucleotide "rungs" look like when viewed from the top.

28. DNA replication is similar to photocopying because an exact duplicate is made. DNA replication is different because the strands are templates for the production of two DNA molecules. Each new molecule contains half the original molecule. In photocopying, the copy is an entirely new image and the original is preserved intact.

29. UGGCAGUG; AGCGUGCA

30. Additional amino acids would be added to the protein, and it would probably not function properly in the cell.

31. In genetics, transcription is the process by which a complementary strand of RNA is produced from DNA. It is similar to its meaning in ordinary language in that the order of DNA nucleotides is written out. In genetics, translation refers to the decoding of the RNA "message." In ordinary language, it refers to the similar process of converting one language into another.

32. Chromosomal mutations that occur during meiosis affect the gametes and will appear in the offspring. Mitotic chromosomal mutations will affect only a few body cells.

Chapter 12 Assessment

Critical Thinking

26. Interpreting Graphics Look back at Griffith's experiment, shown in **Figure 12–2** on page 288. Describe the occasion in which the bacterial DNA withstood conditions that killed the bacteria. Describe what happened to the DNA from that point until the end of the experiment.

27. Using Models Franklin's X-ray photographs told Watson and Crick that the distance between the two "backbones" of DNA is constant along the length of the molecule. Create a simple model of a twisted ladder to represent DNA, and show how this model relates to the *X* in Franklin's photos.

28. Using Analogies Is photocopying a document similar to DNA replication? Think of the original materials, the copying process, and the final products. Explain how the two processes are alike. Identify major differences.

29. Applying Concepts Suppose you start with two DNA strands: ACCGTCAC and TCGCACGT. Use the "rules" of base pairing to list the bases on messenger RNA strands transcribed from those DNA strands.

30. Predicting Examine the first intron in the diagram below. What difference would result in the protein produced by the messenger RNA if that intron were not removed but instead functioned as an exon?

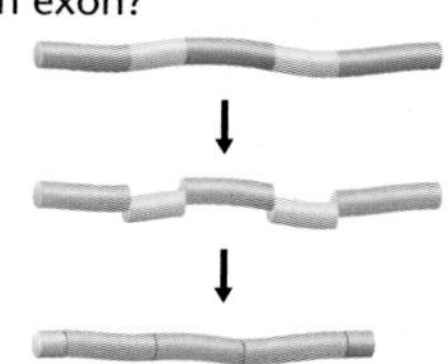

31. Using Analogies The word *transcribe* means "to write out," and the word *translate* means "to express in another language." Review the meanings of *transcription* and *translation* in genetics. How do the technical meanings of these words relate to meanings of the words in ordinary language?

32. Comparing and Contrasting How does the possible impact of a chromosomal mutation that occurs during meiosis differ from that of a similar event that occurs during mitosis?

33. Predicting A researcher identifies the nucleotide sequence AAC in a long strand of RNA inside a nucleus. In the genetic code, AAC codes for the amino acid asparagine. When that RNA becomes involved in protein synthesis, will asparagine necessarily appear in the protein? Explain.

34. Making Connections Recall what you learned about mitosis in Chapter 10 and meiosis in Chapter 11. Describe how a given amount of a cell's DNA might be alike or different after each process was complete.

Performance-Based Assessment

Make a Model Make a three-dimensional model representing protein synthesis. Your "protein" should be a sequence of three different amino acids. Show the DNA molecule and the related RNA molecules that would be involved in producing your protein.

Take It to the NET

Want to learn more about the genetic code and protein synthesis? Visit the Prentice Hall Web site at **www.phschool.com**. Then, answer the following questions:

- What is the "central dogma" of molecular biology? Summarize this in four steps.
- Why is the genetic code said to be degenerate?
- Describe the three possible ways that DNA can replicate.
- List four steps in the control of gene expression. When does each step occur?

Performance-Based Assessment

Check student models for structural accuracy of DNA, mRNA, and tRNA. Student models should reflect an understanding of the roles of DNA and RNA in protein synthesis and the significance of codons and anticodons in the process.

Take It to the NET

- The central dogma of molecular biology is the transcription of DNA into RNA, which is then translated into proteins. The steps are replication, transcription, processing or mRNA, and translation.

- An amino acid can correspond to more than one codon.

Standardized Test Prep

Test-Taking Tip When asked to find the solution to a problem, such as the complementary sequence of DNA or RNA, first solve the problem on scratch paper. Then, compare your answer with the options provided.

Directions: Choose the letter that best answers the question or completes the statement.

1. During replication, which sequence of nucleotides would bond with the DNA sequence TATGA?
   (A) TATGA
   (B) UAUGA
   (C) ATACT
   (D) AUAGA
   (E) ATACA
2. In which of the following ways does RNA differ from DNA?
   (A) RNA contains uracil and deoxyribose.
   (B) RNA contains ribose and thymine.
   (C) RNA contains uracil and ribose.
   (D) RNA contains adenine and ribose.
   (E) RNA contains uracil, adenine, and ribose.
3. Which of the following nucleotide(s) bond(s) with adenine?
   (A) thymine only
   (B) uracil only
   (C) cytosine and guanine
   (D) thymine and uracil
   (E) thymine, uracil, and cytosine
4. The process of decoding mRNA into a polypeptide chain is known as
   (A) transformation.
   (B) transpiration.
   (C) translation.
   (D) transcription.
   (E) translocation.
5. Which of the following does NOT describe the structure of DNA?
   (A) double helix
   (B) nucleotide polymer
   (C) sugar-phosphate backbone
   (D) contains adenine-uracil pairs
   (E) double stranded
6. What did Hershey and Chase's work show?
   (A) Genes are probably made of DNA.
   (B) Genes are probably made of protein.
   (C) Genes are made of both DNA and protein.
   (D) Viruses contain DNA but not protein.
   (E) Bacteria contain DNA but not protein.

Questions 7–8

A scientist analyzed several DNA samples to determine the relative proportions of purine and pyrimidine bases. Her data are summarized in the table below.

Percentages of Bases in Three Samples

Sample	G	C	A	T
A	35	35	15	15
B	40	10	40	10
C	25	25	25	25

7. Which sample(s) support(s) the base-pairing rules?
   (A) Sample A only
   (B) Sample B only
   (C) Sample C only
   (D) Samples A and C
   (E) Samples A, B, and C
8. If the scientist had analyzed mRNA rather than DNA, what percentage of uracil would you expect to find in Sample B?
   (A) 10
   (B) 25
   (C) 35
   (D) 40
   (E) 80

Question 9 Complete the following analogy by selecting the correct letter. In analogies, A : B :: C : ___?___ means A is to B as C is to ___?___.

9. Map directions : photocopier :: DNA : ___?___.
   (A) translation
   (B) transformation
   (C) transcription
   (D) protein synthesis
   (E) replication

Questions 10–12 Each of the lettered choices below refers to the following numbered statements. Select the best lettered choice. A choice may be used once, more than once, or not at all.

(A) Mutation
(B) Genetic code
(C) Protein synthesis
(D) Double helix
(E) Transcription

10. RNA molecules are produced by copying part of the nucleotide sequence of DNA into a complementary sequence in RNA.
11. mRNA codons that are used to make proteins
12. Heritable change in the DNA sequence that affects genetic information

Standardized Test Prep

1. C **2.** C **3.** D **4.** C **5.** D **6.** A **7.** D **8.** A **9.** E **10.** E **11.** B **12.** A

33. No, asparagine will not necessarily appear in the protein. The sequence may be part of two adjacent codons that specify different amino acids, or it may be part of an intron.

34. During mitosis, the cell's DNA is replicated and each daughter cell receives a copy. Each new cell has the same amount of DNA as the original cell. During meiosis, the final cells receive only half the amount of DNA that was in the original cell.

• Conservative replication would leave intact the original DNA molecule and generate a completely new molecule. Dispersive replication would produce two DNA molecules with sections of both old and new DNA interspersed along each strand. Semiconservative replication would produce molecules with both old and new DNA, but each molecule would be composed of one old strand and one new one.

• (1) Transcriptional control occurs during transcription of a DNA sequence into RNA; (2) RNA processing control occurs during the formation of mRNA; (3) Translation control occurs during the translation of mRNA to protein; (4) Protein activity control occurs when the protein becomes inactive.

For additional information, visit

www.phschool.com

Chapter Planner 13 Genetic Engineering

Section and Section Objectives	Time	Activities and Labs
13–1 Changing the Living World, pp. 319–321 **13.1.1** ***Explain*** the purpose of selective breeding. **13.1.2** ***Describe*** two techniques used in selective breeding. **13.1.3** ***Tell*** why breeders try to induce mutations.	**1 period (1/2 block)**	**SE:** ***Inquiry Activity,*** Can you improve plant breeding?, p. 318 **SE:** ***Design an Experiment,*** Investigating the Effects of Radiation on Seeds, pp. 334–335
13–2 Manipulating DNA, pp. 322–326 **13.2.1** ***Explain*** how scientists manipulate DNA.	**1 period (1/2 block)**	**TE:** ***Demonstration,*** p. 324 **SE:** ***Quick Lab,*** How are restriction enzymes used?, p. 326
13–3 Cell Transformation, pp. 327–329 **13.3.1** ***Summarize*** what happens during transformation. **13.3.2** ***Explain*** how you can tell if a transformation experiment has been successful.	**1 period (1/2 block)**	**TE:** ***Meet Diverse Needs,*** p. 329 **SE:** ***Issues in Biology,*** Do Genetically Modified Foods Need Stricter Controls?, p. 330
13–4 Applications of Genetic Engineering, pp. 331–333 **13.4.1** ***Describe*** the usefulness of some transgenic organisms to humans. **13.4.2** ***Summarize*** the main steps in cloning.	**1 period (1/2 block)**	
Chapter Assessment, pp. 336–339	**1 period (1/2 block)**	

ACTIVITY PLANNER

SE: ***Inquiry Activity,*** p. 318; (10 min.); 5 apples of different varieties

SE: ***Design an Experiment,*** pp. 334–335; (45 min.); irradiated seeds and nonirradiated seeds of the same species, petri dishes, paper towels, plant pots with soil, glass-marking pencil

TE: ***Demonstration,*** p. 324; (20 min. on two days); prepared kit for DNA restriction analysis and gel electrophoresis

SE: ***Quick Lab,*** p. 326; (20 min.); construction paper, scissors, transparent tape

TE: ***Meet Diverse Needs,*** p. 329; (15 min.); pipe cleaners or pop beads of different colors

PLANNING KEY

Ability Levels	
B **Basic**	For students who need additional help
A **Average**	For all students
E **Enriched**	For students who need to be challenged

Components

SE	Student Edition	**GRSW**	Guided Reading and Study Workbook	**IDM**	Issues and Decision Making
TE	Teacher's Edition	**CT**	Chapter Tests: Levels A and B	**CTB**	Computer Test Bank
LMA	Laboratory Manual A	**PHAS**	PH Assessment Plus	**PA**	Presentation Assistant Plus
LMB	Laboratory Manual B	**LA**	Lab Assessment With Scoring Guide	**BD**	BioDetectives Videotape
TR	Teaching Resources	**BTM**	BioTechnology Manual	**iT**	iText
IF	Investigations in Forensics				

Program Resources	*Assessment*	*Media and Technology*
TR: Section Review 13–1 B A **GRSW:** Section 13–1 B A	**SE:** 13–1 Section Assessment, p. 321 **TR:** Section Review 13–1	**PA:** 13-1 Interest Grabber, Section Outline, Concept Map **iT:** Section 13–1
LMA: Chapter 13 Lab A E **LMB:** Chapter 13 Lab B A **TR:** Section Review 13–2 B A **GRSW:** Section 13–2 B A **BTM:** Issue 1; Lab 8, 9, 12 **IF:** Investigation 4	**SE:** 13–2 Section Assessment, p. 326 **TR:** Section Review 13–2	**PA:** 13–2 Interest Grabber, Section Outline, Restriction Enzymes, Figure 13–6, Figure 13–7, Figure 13–8 **iT:** Section 13–2
TR: Section Review 13–3 B A **GRSW:** Section 13–3 B A **BTM:** Concept 5, 7; Lab 14, 15	**SE:** 13–3 Section Assessment, p. 329 **TR:** Section Review 13–3	**PA:** 13-3 Interest Grabber, Section Outline, Knockout Genes, Figure 13–9, Figure 13–10 **iT:** Section 13–3
TR: Section Review 13–4 B A Chapter 13 Design an Experiment B A E **GRSW:** Section 13–4 B A **IDM:** Issues and Decisions 18 A E **BTM:** Lab 17; Issue 4	**SE:** 13–4 Section Assessment, p. 333 **TR:** Section Review 13–4	**PA:** 13-4 Interest Grabber, Section Outline, Flowchart, Figure 13–13 **iT:** Section 13–4
	SE: Chapter 13 Assessment, pp. 336–339 **TR:** Chapter Vocabulary Review, Graphic Organizer **CT:** Chapter 13 Test **CTB:** Chapter 13 Test **PHAS:** Practice Test	**CTB:** Chapter 13 Test **iT:** Chapter 13 Assessment

PRESSED FOR TIME?

To Preview the Chapter
- Instruct students to read the Key Concepts and Vocabulary terms in each section.
- Have students examine all the figures in the chapter and read their captions.

To Cover the Chapter Quickly
- Have students read all of Sections 13–1, 13–2, and 13–3.
- Assign the Section Assessments for 13–1, 13–2, and 13–3.

To Review the Chapter
- Review the concept map in the Chapter 13 Study Guide.
- Assign Sections 13–1, 13–2, 13–3, and 13–4 in the Guided Reading and Study Workbook.

ENGAGE/EXPLORE

Inquiry Activity

Objective Students will be able to determine how to improve plant breeding.

Skills Focus **Formulating Hypotheses**

Materials 5 apples of different varieties

Time 10 minutes

Advance Prep Purchase five different varieties of apples at a grocery store or fruit market.

Strategy You might want students to use a cloth tape measure or string to determine the circumference of the apples at their widest point.

Expected Outcomes Students will identify the apple varieties that they consider to be best in color, shape, and size.

Think About It

1. Crossbreed the existing varieties until a hybrid with the desired traits is developed.

2. Isolate the genes that encode the desirable traits from the different apple varieties. These genes can be combined in one of the apple varieties to produce a new apple variety.

Brain Teaser

Challenge students to consider how a sheep that is 12 years old can have an identical twin that is only 4 years old. *(The 4-year-old sheep is a clone of the older sheep.)* To help students get started, first discuss with them what identical twins are. *(Two individuals that are genetically identical.)* If students cannot solve the puzzle, write the puzzle on the board and revisit it periodically while studying this chapter.

Chapter 13 Genetic Engineering

This animal is part goat and part sheep. It was created by mixing together cells from separate embryos and then implanting the mixed embryo into a surrogate mother.

Inquiry Activity

Can you improve plant breeding?

Procedure

1. Examine 5 apples of different varieties. Record the color, shape, and size of each apple.
2. Record your choices of the varieties that you consider best in color, shape, and size.

Think About It

1. **Formulating Hypotheses** How could you produce an apple that has the best traits of all 5 varieties?
2. **Formulating Hypotheses** Most apple trees do not produce fruit until they are about 15 years old. How could you use your knowledge of DNA to produce a new variety of apple more quickly?

HISTORY OF SCIENCE

Giant steps in genetics

From the time Watson and Crick discovered the structure of the DNA molecule in 1953, it took ten years for researchers to crack the genetic code. Ten years later, in the early 1970s, researchers first developed the techniques for manipulating DNA, including the use of restriction enzymes and gel electrophoresis. In the late 1970s, researchers successfully engineered bacteria to produce insulin and interferon. In 1982, the first drug produced by recombinant bacteria—insulin—was approved for use on people. It was also in 1982 that researchers were successful in transferring genes between plant and animal species. In the early 1990s, researchers began inserting DNA into human patients to treat genetic diseases. In 2001, the human genome had been sequenced.

13–1 Changing the Living World

Visit a dog show, and what do you see? Dogs of every breed imaginable, distinguished from one another by an enormous range of characteristics. Striking contrasts are everywhere—the size of a tiny Chihuahua and that of a massive great Dane, the short coat of a Labrador retriever and the curly fur of a poodle, the long muzzle of the wolfhound and the pug nose of a bulldog. The differences among breeds of dogs are so great that someone who had never seen such animals before might think that many of these breeds are different species. They're not, of course, but where did such differences come from? What forces gave rise to the speed of a greyhound, the courage of a German shepherd, and the herding instincts of a border collie?

Guide for Reading

Key Concepts
- What is the purpose of selective breeding?
- Why might breeders try to induce mutations?

Vocabulary
selective breeding
hybridization
inbreeding
polyploid

Reading Strategy: Outlining Before you read, write down the blue headings of the section. As you read, list the important information under each heading.

Selective Breeding

The answer, of course, is that *we* did it. Humans have kept and bred dogs for thousands of years, always looking to produce animals that might be better hunters, better retrievers, or better companions. By **selective breeding,** allowing only those animals with desired characteristics to produce the next generation, humans have produced the many different breeds on display at a dog show.

Humans use selective breeding to pass desired traits on to the next generation of organisms. Nearly all domestic animals—including horses, cats, and farm animals—and most crop plants have been produced by selective breeding. American botanist Luther Burbank (1849–1926) may have been the greatest selective plant breeder of all time. He developed the disease-resistant Burbank potato, which was later exported to Ireland to help fight potato blight and other diseases. During his lifetime, Burbank developed more than 800 varieties of plants.

Hybridization As one of his tools, Burbank used **hybridization,** crossing dissimilar individuals to bring together the best of both organisms. Hybrids, the individuals produced by such crosses, are often hardier than either of the parents. In many cases, Burbank's hybrid crosses combined the disease resistance of one plant with the food-producing capacity of another. The result was a new line of plants that had the characteristics farmers needed to increase food production. **Figure 13–1** shows hybrid daisies developed using Burbank's techniques.

▼ **Figure 13–1** **Humans use selective breeding to pass desired traits on to the next generation of organisms.** Luther Burbank used selective breeding to develop these Shasta daisies, a popular variety.

SECTION RESOURCES

Print:
- ***Teaching Resources,*** Section Review 13–1
- ***Guided Reading and Study Workbook,*** Section 13–1

Technology:
- ***iText,*** Section 13–1

Section 13–1

1 FOCUS

Objectives

13.1.1 ***Explain*** the purpose of selective breeding.
13.1.2 ***Describe*** two techniques used in selective breeding.
13.1.3 ***Tell*** why breeders try to induce mutations.

Guide for Reading

Vocabulary Preview

Read aloud the vocabulary terms for this section. Invite students to identify parts of the words that give clues about the words' meaning. For example, *hybrid-* gives a clue to the meaning of *hybridization,* and the prefix *poly-* gives a clue to the meaning of the word *polyploid.*

Reading Strategy

Instruct students to include the green subheadings from the section in their outlines. Remind students to include at least one piece of information for each green subhead. Also encourage them to add information to their outlines that is described in the figure captions, especially if the caption has a Key Concept.

2 INSTRUCT

Selective Breeding

Build Science Skills

Designing Experiments Challenge student pairs to develop a breeding plan to improve the traits of any domestic organism. Students should choose the organism and describe a way to improve the organism. In other words, students should choose a real problem or real characteristics. (*Some examples include purebred dogs that do not have hip dysplasia, roses resistant to fungal diseases, or oak trees resistant to gypsy moths.*) If students need help getting started, refer them to Mendel's breeding experiments with peas. Have students present their breeding plans to the class.

Use Visuals

Figure 13–2 Have students look at the puppies in the photograph and ask: **How can you tell that these puppies are inbred?** *(They all look identical.)* Discuss how the puppies might look instead if they were hybrids. Ask: **What differences might these puppies have if they were hybrids?** *(Differences in coloring, fur, shape and size of body; might look different from mother)*

Meet Diverse Needs

Review the vocabulary of selective breeding with at-risk students and students with limited English proficiency. Relate the terms *hybridization* and *inbreeding* to the Mendelian terms *true-breeding* and *hybrid.* Ask: **How would you produce a homozygous individual, by hybridization or inbreeding?** *(Inbreeding)* **A heterozygous individual?** *(Hybridization)* **Limited English proficiency**

Increasing Variation

Address Misconceptions

Emphasize that creating mutants is a totally random process because of the action of the mutagens—chemicals or radiation used to cause mutations. The offspring that survive the mutagenic effects may have mutations that either are not detectable or are not useful to the researcher. Because of the laws of probability, researchers must create thousands of mutants before they can isolate the particular one they are searching for.

Building Science Skills

Applying Concepts Explain that researchers also induce mutations to learn the function of a protein. By comparing the structure and function of the normal individual to those of the mutant, they can elucidate the protein's function. Challenge students to set up a protocol to determine the function of a known protein. They should describe the expected phenotype of a mutant based on the protein's function.

▶ **Figure 13–2** Inbreeding is required to maintain the characteristics of pedigreed dogs, such as these golden retrievers. However, inbreeding has also increased the breed's susceptibility to diseases and deformities. **Applying Concepts** *What other animals are likely to be inbred?*

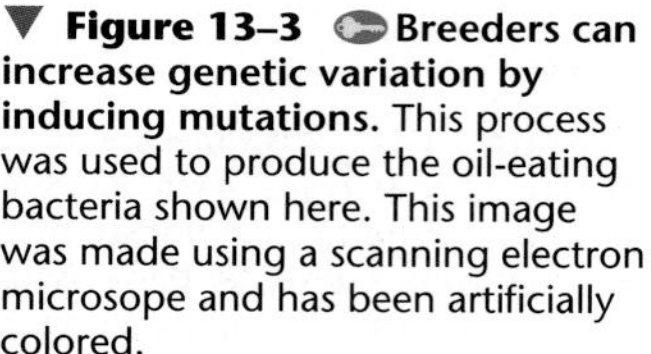

Inbreeding To maintain the desired characteristics of a line of organisms, breeders often use a technique known as inbreeding. **Inbreeding** is the continued breeding of individuals with similar characteristics. The many breeds of dogs—from beagles to poodles—are maintained by inbreeding. Inbreeding helps to ensure that the characteristics that make each breed unique will be preserved. The golden retrievers shown in **Figure 13–2** are an example of inbred animals.

Although inbreeding is useful in retaining a certain set of characteristics, it does have its risks. Most of the members of a breed are genetically similar. Because of this, there is always a chance that a cross between two individuals will bring together two recessive alleles for a genetic defect. Serious problems in many breeds of dogs, including blindness and joint deformities in German shepherds and golden retrievers, have resulted from excessive inbreeding.

✓CHECKPOINT *What is inbreeding?*

▼ **Figure 13–3** **Breeders can increase genetic variation by inducing mutations.** This process was used to produce the oil-eating bacteria shown here. This image was made using a scanning electron microsope and has been artificially colored.

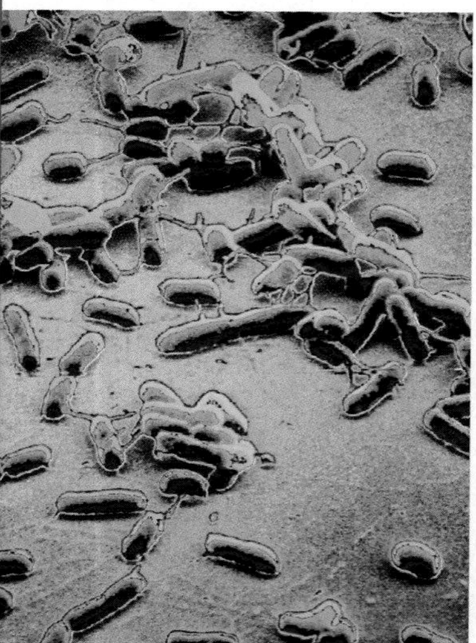

(magnification: 6200×)

Increasing Variation

Selective breeding would be nearly impossible without the wide variation that is found in natural populations. This is one of the reasons biologists are interested in preserving the diversity of plants and animals in the wild. However, sometimes breeders want more variation than exists in nature. **Breeders can increase the genetic variation in a population by inducing mutations, which are the ultimate source of genetic variability.**

As you may recall, mutations are inheritable changes in DNA. Mutations occur spontaneously, but breeders can increase the mutation rate by using radiation and chemicals. Many mutations are harmful to the organism. With luck and perseverance, however, breeders can produce a few mutants—individuals with mutations—with desirable characteristics that are not found in the original population.

TIME SAVER

PRESENTATIONS MADE EASY!

The Presentation Assistant Plus contains the Prentice Hall Presentation Pro and the Transparencies, which provide easy-to-follow visual support for every step of this section. If you have a computer presentation station, use Prentice Hall Presentation Pro for Section 13–1, or use the transparencies listed here.

Section 13–1: **Interest Grabber**
Section Outline
Concept Map

Producing New Kinds of Bacteria This technique has been particularly useful with bacteria. Their small size enables millions of organisms to be treated with radiation or chemicals at the same time. This increases the chances of producing a useful mutant. Using this technique, scientists have been able to develop hundreds of useful bacterial strains. It has even been possible to produce bacteria that can digest oil, as shown in **Figure 13–3,** and are thus useful in cleaning up oil spills.

Producing New Kinds of Plants Drugs that prevent chromosomal separation during meiosis have been particularly useful in plant breeding. Sometimes these drugs produce cells that have double or triple the normal number of chromosomes. Plants grown from such cells are called **polyploid** because they have many sets of chromosomes. Polyploidy is usually fatal in animals. However, for reasons that are not clear, plants are much better at tolerating extra sets of chromosomes. Polyploidy may instantly produce new species of plants that are often larger and stronger than their diploid relatives. **Figure 13–4** shows some polyploid day lilies. Many important crop plants have been produced in this way, including bananas and many varieties of citrus fruits.

Word Origins

Polyploid comes from the Greek words *polus,* meaning "many," and *-ploos,* meaning "fold." So *polyploid* means "many-fold" or "many times." **How many sets of chromosomes do you think a triploid plant has?**

▶ **Figure 13–4** The day lilies at the right are examples of polyploid plants. New species of plants are produced when the chromosome number is doubled or tripled. **Applying Concepts** ***Are any of the fruits and vegetables that you regularly eat polyploid?***

13–1 Section Assessment

1. **Key Concept** Give one example of selective breeding.
2. **Key Concept** Relate genetic variation and mutations to each other.
3. How might a breeder induce mutations?
4. What is polyploidy?
5. **Critical Thinking Problem Solving** Suggest ways that plants could be altered to improve the world's food supply.

iTEXT **Assessment** Use iText to review the important concepts in Section 13–1.

ALTERNATIVE ASSESSMENT

Interviewing an Expert
Interview a person who breeds plants or animals. Find out what kinds of techniques the person uses. What traits does he or she try to select for? Why?

Word Origins

A triploid plant has three sets of chromosomes.

3 ASSESS

Evaluate Understanding

Describe some breeding situations, and invite students to classify each as an example of hybridization or inbreeding. Have students describe the effects of genetic variation on selective breeding.

Reteach

Have students make a concept map to show the relationships among selective breeding, hybridization, inbreeding, and increasing variation. Encourage students to write notes on the maps to clarify meanings of words and concepts.

ALTERNATIVE ASSESSMENT

Possible experts include an agriculture teacher or 4-H club member, a dog or cat breeder, a person from a local plant nursery, a county extension agent, a zookeeper, or a pet-shop worker who breeds fishes, rodents, or other animals. Have students prepare interview questions beforehand. Encourage them to develop a graphic organizer, poster, videotape, or other device to share what they learned with the class.

Use iText to review the key concepts in Section 13–1.

13–1 Section Assessment

1. Nearly all domestic animals, including horses, cats, and farm animals, and most crop plants have been produced by selective breeding.
2. Mutations are the ultimate source of genetic variation.
3. By using radiation and chemicals
4. The condition of having many sets of chromosomes
5. Students might suggest producing plants that require less fertilizer; resist drought, diseases, pests, and cold weather; produce more nutritious or abundant crops.

Answers to . . .

CHECKPOINT *Continued breeding of individuals with similar characteristics*

Figure 13–2 *Any domesticated animal*

Figure 13–4 *Bananas, citrus fruits*

Section 13–2

1 FOCUS

Objectives

13.2.1 ***Explain*** how scientists manipulate DNA.

Guide for Reading

Vocabulary Preview

Explain that the word *recombinant* is an adjective that came from the word *recombination.* Discuss what recombination is (creation of new DNA molecules by inserting different DNA sequences).

Reading Strategy

As students read the section, encourage them to answer the questions or correct their predictions made while previewing the figures.

2 INSTRUCT

The Tools of Molecular Biology

Build Science Skills

Using Analogies Challenge student pairs to develop an analogy for the process researchers use to manipulate DNA. In their analogies, students should point out the similarities to the methods used in genetic engineering. Encourage students to develop a graphic organizer, poster, computer presentation, or videotape to present their analogy to the class.

13–2 Manipulating DNA

Guide for Reading

Key Concept
- How do scientists make changes to DNA?

Vocabulary
genetic engineering
restriction enzyme
gel electrophoresis
recombinant DNA
polymerase chain reaction (PCR)

Reading Strategy: Previewing Graphics Before you read this section, examine the figures. Read the titles and captions, and identify questions about or predict relationships among the techniques illustrated.

Until very recently, animal and plant breeders could not modify the genetic code of living things. They were limited by the need to work with the variation that already exists in nature. Even when they tried to add to that variation by introducing mutations, the changes they produced in the DNA were random and unpredictable. Imagine, however, that one day biologists were able to go right to the genetic code, rewrite an organism's DNA, and make any changes they wanted. Imagine that biologists could swap genes at will from one organism to another, designing new living things to meet specific needs. That day, as you may know from scientific stories in the news, is already here.

How are changes made to DNA? **Scientists use their knowledge of the structure of DNA and its chemical properties to study and change DNA molecules. Different techniques are used to extract DNA from cells, to cut DNA into smaller pieces, to identify the sequence of bases in a DNA molecule, and to make unlimited copies of DNA.** Understanding how these techniques work will help you develop an appreciation for what is involved in genetic engineering.

The Tools of Molecular Biology

Suppose you had a computer game you wanted to change. Knowing that the characteristics of that game are determined by a coded computer program, how would you set about rewriting parts of the program? To make such changes, a software engineer would need a way to get the program out of the computer, read it, make changes in it, and then put the modified code back into the game. **Genetic engineering,** making changes in the DNA code of a living organism, works almost the same way.

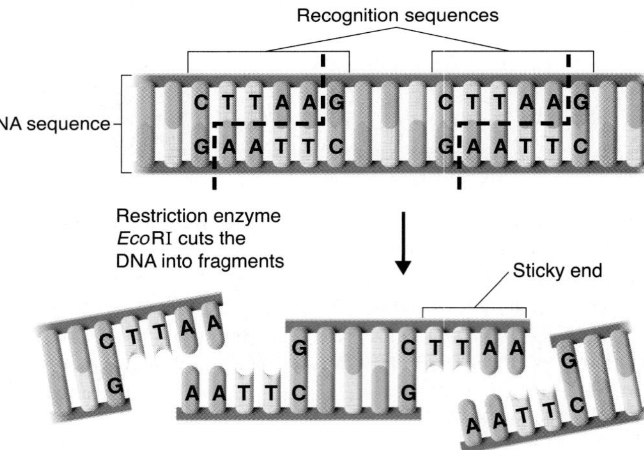

▶ **Figure 13–5** **Molecular biologists have developed different techniques that allow them to study and change DNA molecules.** This drawing shows how restriction enzymes are used to edit DNA. The restriction enzyme *Eco*RI, for example, finds the sequence CTTAAG on DNA. Then, the enzyme cuts the molecule at each occurrence of CTTAAG. Different restriction enzymes recognize and cut different sequences of nucleotides on DNA molecules.

SECTION RESOURCES

Print:
- ***Laboratory Manual A,*** Chapter 13 Lab
- ***Laboratory Manual B,*** Chapter 13 Lab
- ***Teaching Resources,*** Section Review 13–2
- ***Guided Reading and Study Workbook,*** Section 13–2
- ***Biotechnology Manual,*** Issue 1; Lab 8, 9, 12
- ***Investigations in Forensics,*** Investigation 4

Technology:
- ***iText,*** Section 13–2

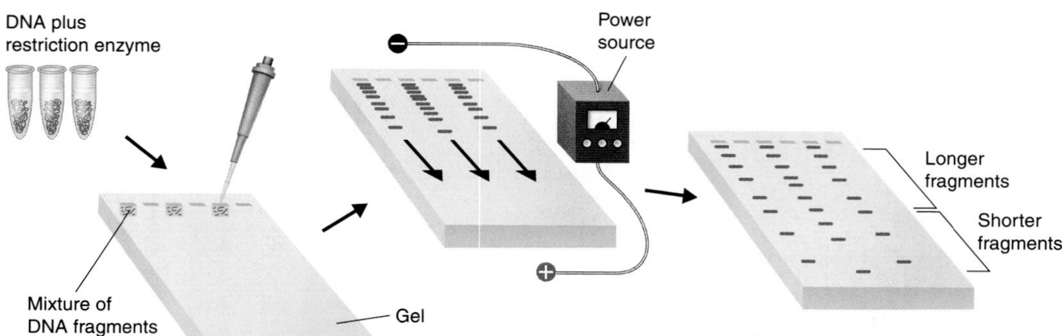

▲ **Figure 13–6** Gel electrophoresis is used to separate DNA fragments. First, restriction enzymes cut DNA into fragments. The DNA fragments are then poured into wells on a gel, which is similar to a thick piece of gelatin. An electric voltage moves the DNA fragments across the gel. Because longer fragments of DNA move through the gel more slowly, they do not migrate as far across the gel as shorter fragments of DNA. Based on size, the DNA fragments make a pattern of bands on the gel. These bands can then be compared with other samples of DNA. **Inferring** ***What kinds of information might the bands from two different DNA sources provide?***

DNA Extraction How do biologists get DNA out of a cell? DNA can be extracted from most cells by a simple chemical procedure: The cells are opened and the DNA is separated from the other cell parts.

Cutting DNA DNA molecules from most organisms are much too large to be analyzed, so biologists cut them precisely into smaller fragments using restriction enzymes. Hundreds of **restriction enzymes** are known, and each one cuts DNA at a specific sequence of nucleotides. As shown in **Figure 13–5,** restriction enzymes are amazingly precise. Like a key that fits only one lock, a restriction enzyme will cut a DNA sequence only if it matches the sequence precisely.

Separating DNA How can DNA fragments be separated and analyzed? One way, a procedure known as gel electrophoresis (ee-lek-troh-fuh-REE-sis), is shown in **Figure 13–6.** In **gel electrophoresis,** a mixture of DNA fragments is placed at one end of a porous gel, and an electric voltage is applied to the gel. When the power is turned on, DNA molecules, which are negatively charged, move toward the positive end of the gel. The smaller the DNA fragment, the faster it moves. Gel electrophoresis can be used to compare the genomes of different organisms or different individuals. It can also be used to locate and identify one particular gene out of the millions of genes in an individual's genome.

Using the DNA Sequence

Once DNA is in a manageable form, its sequence can be read, studied, and even changed. Knowing the sequence of an organism's DNA allows researchers to study specific genes, to compare them with the genes of other organisms, and to try to discover the functions of different genes and gene combinations. The following are some techniques scientists use to read and change the sequence of DNA molecules.

Use Visuals

Figure 13–6 Walk students through the processes of preparing DNA for gel electrophoresis. Also use Figure 13–5 to make sure students understand the action of restriction enzymes. Then, discuss the steps in gel electrophoresis. Ask: **Why do DNA molecules move through a gel?** *(They are negatively charged and are attracted, or pulled, to the positive end of the gel that is set up with an electric voltage.)* **Where are the shorter DNA fragments located on a completed gel?** *(At the end of the gel.)* **Why?** *(The shorter fragments move much faster.)*

Meet Diverse Needs

Have at-risk students devise a flowchart that shows the steps to prepare DNA for gel electrophoresis, as well as the protocol for setting up and running a gel. Encourage students to add diagrams to the flowcharts and add detailed notes to help them understand the procedures. **Learning modality: visual**

PRESENTATIONS MADE EASY!

The Presentation Assistant Plus contains the Prentice Hall Presentation Pro and the Transparencies, which provide easy-to-follow visual support for every step of this section. If you have a computer presentation station, use Prentice Hall Presentation Pro for Section 13–2, or use the transparencies listed here.

Section 13–2:

Interest Grabber
Section Outline
Restriction Enzyme
Figure 13–6
Figure 13–7
Figure 13–8

Answer to . . .

Figure 13–6 *Possible answers include differences in the DNA sequences of the two sources and the relative sizes of particular genes.*

Using the DNA Sequence

Demonstration

Demonstrate DNA restriction analysis and gel electrophoresis for the class. Some biological supply companies have prepared kits that contain restriction enzymes, DNA, agarose gel materials, electrophoresis equipment, and all the other supplies and detailed instructions required for this procedure. You might wish to perform a restriction map analysis in which a DNA sequence is cut separately with two different restriction enzymes and then cut with a mixture of the two enzymes. These three different samples are run together on a gel along with a sample of uncut DNA and marker DNA with fragments of known lengths. From the bands on the gel, the order of the fragments in the DNA sequence can be determined.

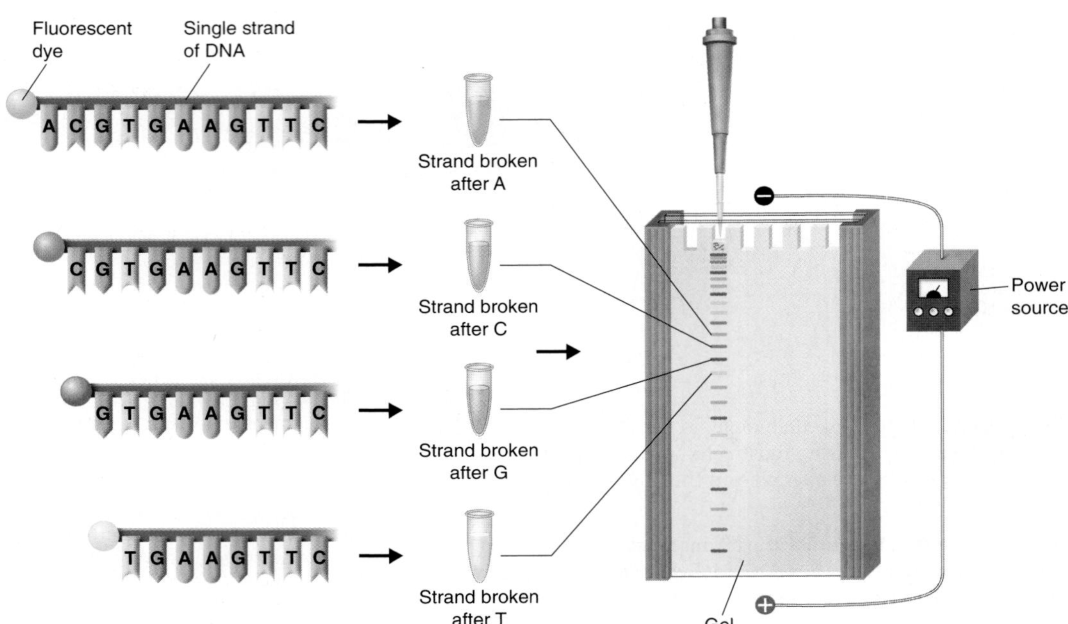

▲ **Figure 13–7 Knowing the sequence of an organism's DNA allows researchers to study specific genes.** In DNA sequencing, a complementary DNA strand is made using a small proportion of fluorescently labeled nucleotides. Each time a labeled nucleotide is added, it stops the process of replication, producing a short color-coded DNA fragment. When the mixture of fragments is separated on a gel, the DNA sequence can be read directly from the gel.

Reading the Sequence In many laboratories, "reading" a DNA sequence is now an automated process. **Figure 13–7** shows one technique for reading DNA. Small, single-stranded pieces of DNA are placed in test tubes with an enzyme that can make a complementary DNA strand by using the original DNA strand as a template. A supply of the 4 nucleotide bases found in DNA is then added, along with a small amount of one of the bases that has been labeled with a fluorescent dye. When the enzyme adds one of the labeled bases, the new DNA strand is terminated—producing a short DNA fragment tagged with the colored dye of the last base added.

When this is done for all 4 bases, each labeled with a different color, a series of tiny DNA fragments is generated. These DNA fragments are color-coded according to the fluorescent dye that has been added at the very end. These fragments are then separated according to size, often by gel electrophoresis. The pattern of colored bands tells the exact sequence of bases in the DNA.

Cutting and Pasting DNA sequences can be changed in a number of ways. Short sequences can be assembled using laboratory machines known as DNA synthesizers. "Synthetic" sequences can then be joined to "natural" ones using enzymes that splice DNA together. The same enzymes make it possible to take a gene from one organism and attach it to the DNA of another organism. Such DNA molecules are sometimes called **recombinant DNA** because they are produced by combining DNA from different sources.

TEACHER TO TEACHER

To help students understand how restriction enzymes work, I like to give them a sentence, such as "My twin sister Sherry, older brother Larry, and I all went to the shopping mall to purchase a gift for our mother and new baby brother Harry." Then, I tell half the class to cut the sentence using a restriction enzyme that cuts between "rr." I instruct the other half to cut the sentence between "he." Next, I have both groups compare the sizes and numbers of fragments by arranging the fragments on a grid according to their lengths. Finally, I have them cut the same sentence using both enzymes and compare the grid pattern with the pattern produced when using the enzymes singly.

—Mary Colvard,
Biology Teacher,
Cobleskill-Richmondville High School,
Cobleskill, NY

Making Copies In order to study genes, biologists often need to make many copies of a particular gene. Like a photocopy machine stuck on "print," a technique known as **polymerase chain reaction (PCR)** allows biologists to do exactly that. **Figure 13–8** shows how PCR works.

The idea behind PCR is surprisingly simple. At one end of a piece of DNA a biologist wants to copy, he or she adds a short piece of DNA that is complementary to a portion of the sequence. At the other end, the biologist adds another short piece of complementary DNA. These short pieces are known as "primers" because they provide a place for the DNA polymerase to start working.

The DNA is heated to separate its two strands, then cooled to allow the primers to bind to single-stranded DNA. DNA polymerase starts making copies of the region between the primers. Because the copies themselves can serve as templates to make still more copies, just a few dozen cycles of replication can produce millions of copies of the DNA between those primers.

Where did Kary Mullis, the American inventor of PCR, find a DNA polymerase enzyme that could stand repeated cycles of heating and cooling? Mullis found it in bacteria living in the hot springs of Yellowstone National Park—a perfect example of the importance of biodiversity to biotechnology.

CHECKPOINT *What is a polymerase chain reaction?*

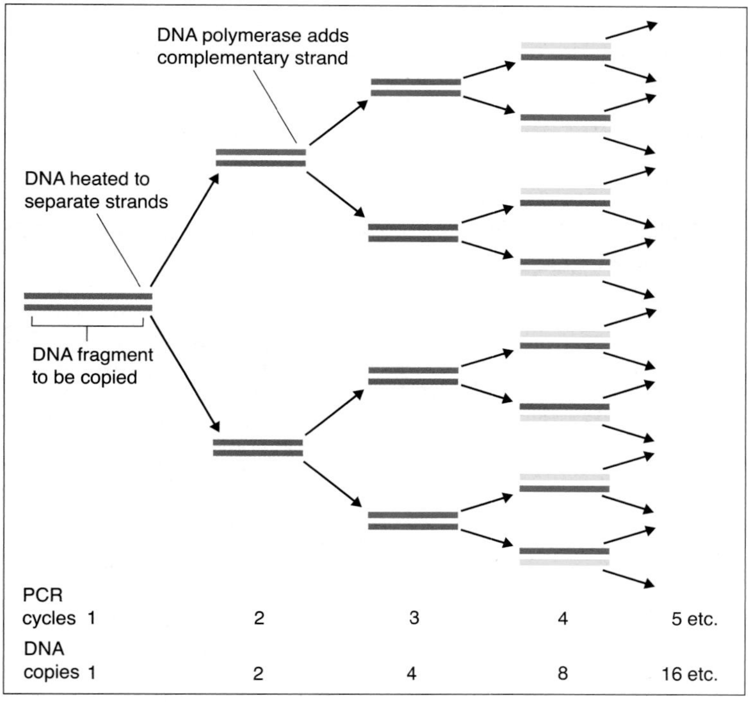

◀ **Figure 13–8** Polymerase chain reaction (PCR) is used to make multiple copies of genes. **Calculating** *How many copies of the DNA will there be after six cycles?*

KEEP CURRENT WITH . . . SCIENCE NEWS®

To find out more about the topics in this chapter, go to: **www.phschool.com**

SCIENCE NEWS®

Encourage students to visit **www.phschool.com** for the most current information on this topic.

Address Misconceptions

Students might not fully understand how so many different-sized bands can be produced in a sequencing gel. Diagram the process on the chalkboard, beginning with preparing the small, single-stranded piece of DNA that is to be sequenced. Make sure students realize that more than one piece of this DNA is in the test tube. Emphasize that all nucleotides required to form the complementary strand are in the test tube; however, only a small percentage of the nucleotides are marked with the fluorescent dye. Remind them of the laws of probability to explain why a complementary sequence of every length from one nucleotide to the complete sequence is produced in the reaction. Use a short nucleotide sequence of 5 bases to demonstrate this idea on the board. Correlate the length of the marked complementary strand with the band on a gel.

BIO INSIGHTS — FACTS AND FIGURES

The randomness of inserting DNA

There is one aspect of the DNA insertion technique that is still not completely understood. When DNA is injected into animal and plant cells, sometimes it is inserted into a host cell chromosome and sometimes it is not. Although researchers are trying to develop ways of targeting DNA to a particular place on one of the chromosomes, as yet it is not understood exactly what happens inside a cell to cause the injected DNA to take up permanent residence. Therefore, in most experiments researchers insert DNA into hundreds or thousands of cells, hoping that the new DNA will be successfully maintained in a few of them.

Answers to . . .

CHECKPOINT *A technique in which biologists can make many copies of a particular gene*

Figure 13–8 *32*

Quick Lab

Objective Students will model how restriction enzymes are used.

Skills Focus **Observing, Using Models, Inferring**

Materials construction paper, scissors, transparent tape

Time 20 minutes

Advance Prep To increase the chance of students finding a matching cut site, provide them with several 50-base sequences that include one or more cut sites.

Expected Outcomes Students will construct recombinant DNA models.

Analyze and Conclude

1. Answers will depend on students' sequences.
2. Yes; complementary single-stranded ends that will join together are produced only when cut with the same enzyme.
3. The single-stranded, or sticky, ends produced by *Eco*RI and *Bam*I easily form hydrogen bonds with complementary bases in another strand. The blunt ends produced by *Hae*III don't have a complementary sequence to "grab" onto.

3 ASSESS

Evaluate Understanding

Have students describe what is occurring in each figure in the section.

Reteach

Have students develop a table about the procedures and uses of each technique for manipulating DNA.

Use iText to review the key concepts in Section 13–2.

Take It to the NET

Students should clearly describe a safe procedure for using PCR to isolate and visualize DNA.

For additional information, visit **www.phschool.com**

Quick Lab

How are restriction enzymes used?

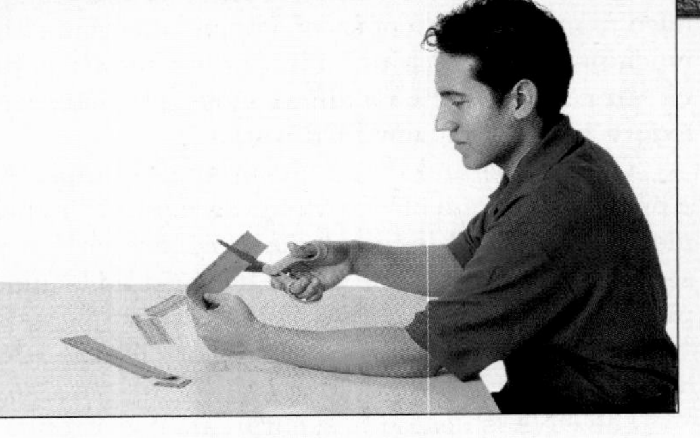

Materials construction paper, scissors, transparent tape

Procedure

1. Write a 50-base double-stranded DNA sequence using the letters A, C, G, and T in random order. Include each of the base sequences shown below at least once in your 50 base-pair sequences.
2. Make 3 copies of your double-stranded sequence on three different-colored strips of paper.
3. Use the drawings below to see how the restriction enzyme *Eco*RI would cut your double-stranded sequence. Use scissors to cut 1 copy of the sequence as *Eco*RI would.

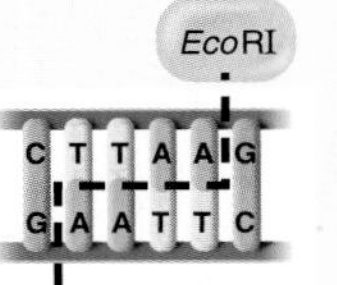

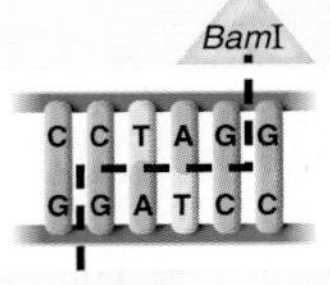

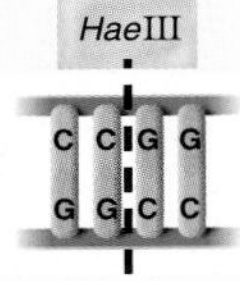

4. Use the procedure in step 3 to cut apart another copy of your sequence as the restriction enzyme *Bam*I would. Cut apart the third copy as the restriction enzyme *Hae*III would.
5. To model the building of recombinant DNA, tape the single-stranded end of one of your pieces of DNA sequences to a complementary, single-stranded end of one of a classmate's pieces. This will form a single, long DNA molecule.

Analyze and Conclude

1. **Observing** Which restriction enzyme produced the most pieces? The fewest pieces?
2. **Using Models** Were the two pieces you joined cut by the same restriction enzyme? Must both pieces of DNA be cut by the same restriction enzyme before they are joined? Explain your answer.
3. **Inferring** Why are *Eco*RI and *Bam*I better choices than *Hae*III for cutting pieces of DNA to be joined?

13–2 Section Assessment

1. **Key Concept** Describe the process scientists use to manipulate DNA.
2. Why might a scientist want to know the sequence of a DNA molecule?
3. How does gel electrophoresis work?
4. Which technique can be used to make multiple copies of a gene? What are the basic steps in this procedure?
5. **Critical Thinking Using Analogies** How is genetic engineering like computer programming?

iTEXT **Assessment** Use iText to review the important concepts in Section 13–2.

Take It to the NET

Design an experiment to carry out PCR in your kitchen at home. Include a list of materials, safety precautions, and a step-by-step procedure that you could follow. Use the links provided in the Biology area at the Prentice Hall Web site for help in completing this activity: **www.phschool.com**

13–2 Section Assessment

1. Biologists use various tools to extract, read, edit, and reinsert DNA into living organisms, including DNA extraction, restriction enzymes, gel electrophoresis, sequencing DNA, and PCR.
2. To study specific genes, compare them with the genes of other organisms, and discover the functions of different genes
3. An electric voltage is used to separate DNA fragments placed in a porous gel by their sizes.
4. PCR; short pieces of complementary DNA are added to each end of a DNA sequence. DNA is heated, then cooled, and DNA polymerase makes copies of the sequence.
5. Both rely on a code that can be manipulated to change the function of the system.

13–3 Cell Transformation

It would do little good to modify a DNA molecule in the test tube if it were not possible to put that DNA back into a living cell and make it work. This sounds tricky, and it is, but you have already seen an example of how this can be done. Remember Griffith's experiments on bacterial transformation? **During transformation, a cell takes in DNA from outside the cell. This external DNA becomes a part of the cell's DNA.**

Today, biologists understand that Griffith's extract of heat-killed bacteria must have contained DNA fragments. When he mixed those fragments with live bacteria, a few of them actually took up the DNA molecules. This suggests that bacteria can be transformed simply by placing them in a solution containing DNA molecules—and indeed they can.

Guide for Reading

Key Concepts
- What happens during cell transformation?
- How can you tell if a transformation experiment has been successful?

Vocabulary
plasmid
genetic marker

Reading Strategy: Summarizing As you read, take notes on how each kind of cell can be transformed. After you read, go back to your notes and compare the different techniques.

Transforming Bacteria

Figure 13–9 shows how bacteria can be transformed using recombinant DNA. The foreign DNA is first joined to a small, circular DNA molecule known as a **plasmid.** Plasmids are found naturally in some bacteria and have been very useful for DNA transfer. Why? The plasmid DNA has two essential features. First, it has a DNA sequence that serves as a bacterial origin of replication. If the plasmid containing the foreign DNA manages to get inside a bacterial cell, this sequence ensures that it will be replicated.

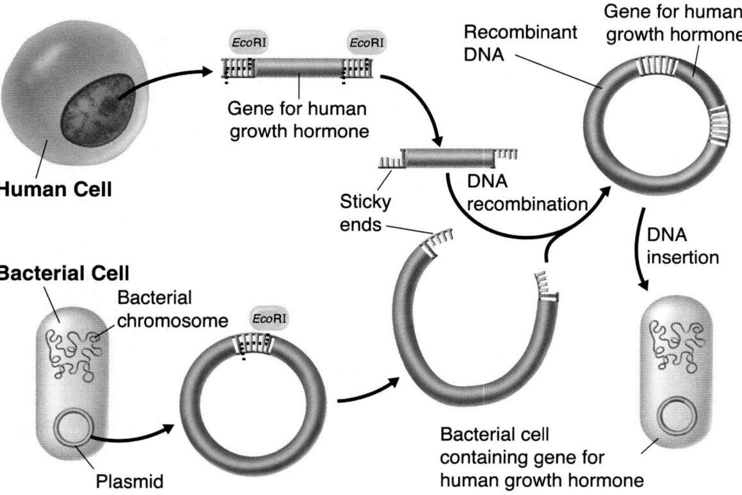

◀ **Figure 13–9 During transformation, a cell incorporates DNA from outside the cell into its own DNA.** One way to make recombinant DNA is to insert a human gene into bacterial DNA. The new combination of genes is then returned to a bacterial cell, and the bacteria can produce the human protein.

SECTION RESOURCES

Print:
- ***Teaching Resources,*** Section Review 13–3
- ***Guided Reading and Study Workbook,*** Section 13–3
- ***Issues and Decision Making,*** Issues and Decisions 18
- ***Biotechnology Manual,*** Concept 5, 7; Lab 14, 15

Technology:
- ***iText,*** Section 13–3

Section 13–3

1 FOCUS

Objectives

13.3.1 ***Summarize*** what happens during transformation.
13.3.2 ***Explain*** how you can tell if a transformation experiment has been successful.

Guide for Reading

Vocabulary Preview

Explain that the word *plasmid* is derived from the prefix *plasm-,* which refers to the cytoplasm in the cell, and the suffix *-id,* which means particle. Then, ask: **Where do you think a plasmid is located?** *(In the cytoplasm of a cell)* **What do you think a plasmid is?** If students can't answer this question, explain that it's a small, circular piece of DNA.

Reading Strategy

Encourage students to include in their notes sketches of the diagrams of the three kinds of transformation.

2 INSTRUCT

Transforming Bacteria

Use Visuals

Figure 13–9 Go through the procedure of producing recombinant DNA as it is outlined in the diagram. Make sure students know that a plasmid is a small, circular piece of DNA found in some bacteria. Bacteria will readily take up plasmids under the right conditions. Ask: **Why must both the plasmid and the human gene be cut with the same restriction enzyme?** *(So that both DNA sequences have sticky ends that are complementary to each other.)* **How do you think the human gene was isolated from the DNA in a human cell?** *(The gene was isolated by cutting the band of DNA out of a gel.)*

13–3 (continued)

Build Science Skills

Applying Concepts Challenge student pairs to brainstorm a list of reasons why researchers might transform bacteria in the course of their studies. Students should describe how bacterial transformation is useful in the experiment. Make a class list of these uses and add to or subtract from the list as you continue with the chapter.

Transforming Plant Cells

Use Visuals

Figure 13–10 As students study the procedure diagrammed in the figure, point out that the transformed bacteria are mixed in a test tube with plant cells before the plant cells are plated out onto a petri dish. As with bacteria, genetic markers are used so that only transformed plant cells will grow on the petri dish. Individual plant colonies are removed from the petri dish and placed in a special growing medium where they will grow into a plant. Ask: **How do you think researchers inactivate the tumor-producing gene on the plasmid?** *(They remove part of the gene sequence—create a mutation—that inactivates the gene.)*

Second, the plasmid has a **genetic marker**—a gene that makes it possible to distinguish bacteria that carry the plasmid (and the foreign DNA) from those that don't. Genes for resistance to antibiotics, compounds that can kill bacteria, are commonly used as markers. A marker makes it possible for researchers to mix recombinant plasmids with a culture of bacteria, add enough DNA to transform one cell in a million, and still be able to "find" that cell. After transformation, the culture is treated with an antibiotic. Only those rare cells that have been transformed survive—because only they carry a resistance gene.

CHECKPOINT *What is a genetic marker?*

Transforming Plant Cells

Many plant cells can be transformed by using a process that takes advantage of a bacterium. In nature, this bacterium inserts a small DNA plasmid that produces tumors into a plant's cells, as shown in **Figure 13–10.** Researchers have discovered that they can inactivate the tumor-producing gene and insert a piece of foreign DNA into the plasmid. The recombinant plasmid can then be used to infect plant cells.

▼ **Figure 13–10** The bacterium *Agrobacterium tumefaciens* can be used to introduce foreign DNA into plant cells. **If the transformation is successful, the DNA will be integrated into one of the cell's chromosomes.**

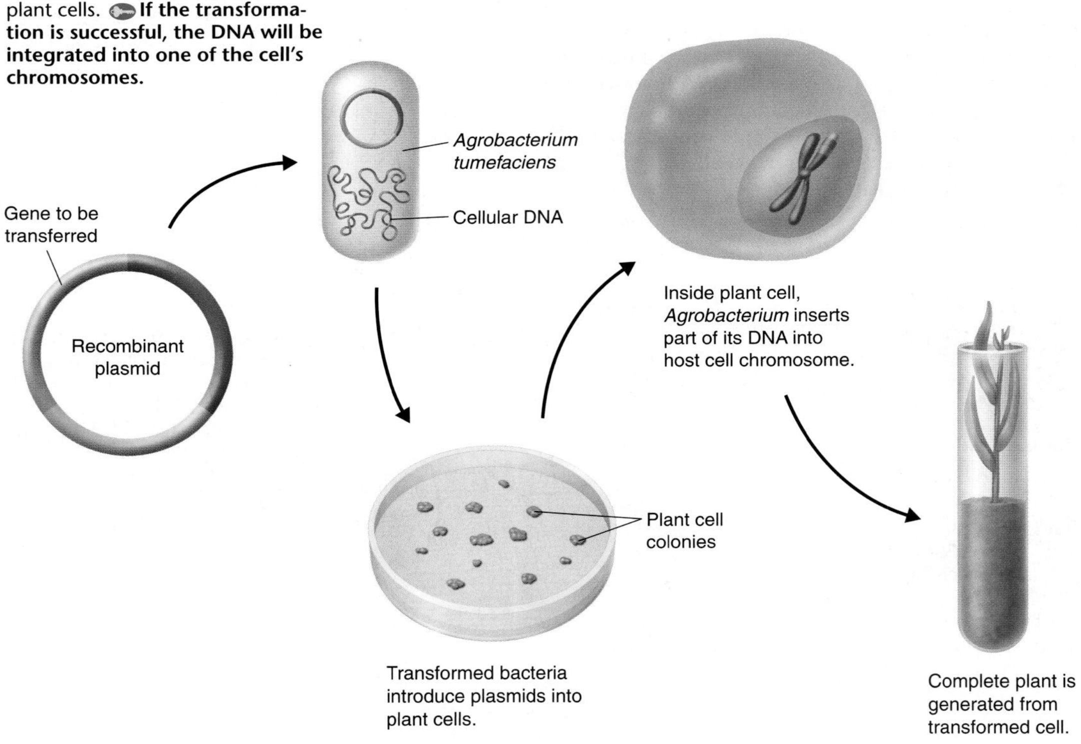
Gene to be transferred
Recombinant plasmid
Agrobacterium tumefaciens
Cellular DNA
Inside plant cell, Agrobacterium inserts part of its DNA into host cell chromosome.
Plant cell colonies
Transformed bacteria introduce plasmids into plant cells.
Complete plant is generated from transformed cell.

PRESENTATIONS MADE EASY!

The Presentation Assistant Plus contains the Prentice Hall Presentation Pro and the Transparencies, which provide easy-to-follow visual support for every step of this section. If you have a computer presentation station, use Prentice Hall Presentation Pro for Section 13–3, or use the transparencies listed here.

Section 13–3: **Interest Grabber**
Section Outline
Knockout Genes
Figure 13–9
Figure 13–10

When their cell walls are removed, plant cells in culture will sometimes take up DNA on their own. DNA can also be injected directly into some cells. Cells transformed by either procedure can be cultured to produce adult plants. **If transformation is successful, the recombinant DNA is integrated into one of the chromosomes of the cell.**

Transforming Animal Cells

Animal cells can be transformed in some of the same ways as plant cells. Many egg cells are large enough that DNA can be directly injected into the nucleus. Once inside the nucleus, enzymes normally responsible for DNA repair and recombination may help to insert the foreign DNA into the chromosomes of the injected cell. Like bacterial plasmids, the DNA molecules used for transformation of animal and plant cells contain marker genes that enable biologists to identify which cells have been transformed.

Recently, it has become possible to "knock out" particular genes by careful design of the DNA molecules used for transformation. As **Figure 13–11** shows, DNA molecules can be constructed with two ends that will sometimes recombine with specific sequences in the host chromosome. Once they do, the host gene between those two sequences may be lost ("knocked out") or specifically replaced with a new gene. This kind of gene replacement has made it possible to pinpoint the specific functions of genes in many organisms, including mice.

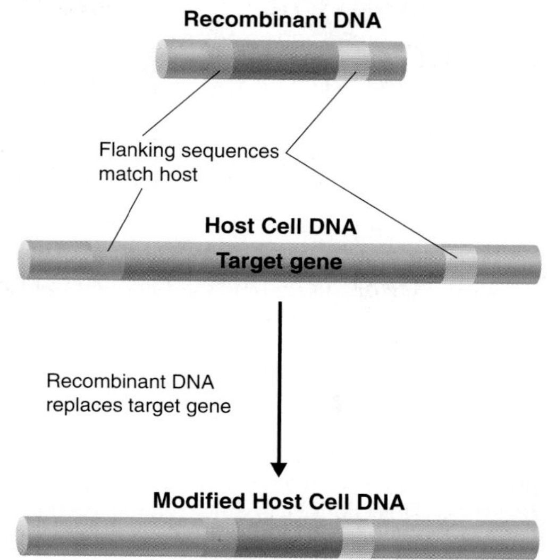

▲ **Figure 13–11** Recombinant DNA can replace a gene in an animal's genome. The ends of the recombinant DNA recombine with sequences in the host cell DNA. When the recombinant DNA is inserted into the target location, the host cell's original gene is lost or knocked out of its place. **Applying Concepts** ***How might this technique be used to treat disorders caused by a single gene?***

Transforming Animal Cells

Meet Diverse Needs

Have at-risk students model the changes made to the DNA molecule when an animal cell is transformed. Students can use different-colored pipe cleaners or pop beads. While students demonstrate what occurs to the chromosome, encourage them to narrate the process. **Learning modality: kinesthetic**

3 ASSESS

Evaluate Understanding

Have students devise a table in which they compare and contrast the process of transformation in bacteria, plant cells, and animal cells. Make sure students describe how the processes are similar and how they are different.

Reteach

Have students review the procedures for transforming bacteria, plant cells, and animal cells by diagramming the procedure for each. For each step of the procedure, students should explain what is occurring. They can use the figures in the section as guides.

13–3 Section Assessment

1. **Key Concept** What is transformation?
2. **Key Concept** How can you tell if a transformation experiment has been successful?
3. How are genetic markers related to transformation?
4. What are two features that make plasmids useful for transforming cells?
5. **Critical Thinking Comparing and Contrasting** Compare the transformation of a prokaryotic cell with the transformation of a eukaryotic cell.

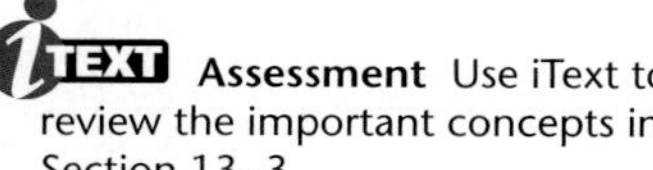
Assessment Use iText to review the important concepts in Section 13–3.

ALTERNATIVE ASSESSMENT

Writing an Experimental Protocol
Imagine that you are a genetic engineer. Determine what your next project will be. Then, write up the steps you will follow and what your intended result will be.

ALTERNATIVE ASSESSMENT

Help students get started by suggesting that they first determine what their end product will be. Then, students can write the protocol. Students might choose the techniques described in this section, as well as in the previous section.

Use iText to review the key concepts in Section 13–3.

13–3 Section Assessment

1. A process in which a cell incorporates DNA from outside the cell into its own DNA
2. A genetic marker makes it possible to distinguish a cell that has been transformed from those that have not.
3. The DNA of the marker is integrated into one of the cell's chromosomes.
4. They have DNA sequences that serve as bacterial origins of replication, and they have genetic markers.
5. Transformation in eukaryotic cells is more complex than in prokaryotic cells. Students should compare transformation in bacteria with either the plasmid technique used in plants or the "knock-out" technique used in animals.

Answers to . . .

CHECKPOINT *Gene that makes it possible to distinguish bacteria that carry the plasmid and foreign DNA*

Figure 13–11 *The mutated gene causing the disorder can be replaced by the normal gene.*

After students have read the feature, invite them to learn more about this issue. First, encourage students to learn how genetically modified foods are produced. Then, have them research one specific example of a genetically modified food. They should learn what genes were added to the plant or animal and why the plant or animal was altered. They should learn what benefit or improvement researchers were trying to make. Finally, have students present their findings to the class. Encourage the class to debate the pros and cons of each example.

You Decide

1. Sample answers: The critics think that genetically modified food might cause dangerous, unexpected effects on people and could pose a hazard to the environment. The proponents think the foods can be beneficial to people by providing additional nutrients that are otherwise missing from their diets and beneficial to the environment by reducing the need for pesticides and fertilizers.
2. Risks: could cause unexpected effects on people, such as allergic reactions; could kill beneficial insects; could cause antibiotic-resistant bacteria; could produce weeds that don't respond to herbicides. Benefits: provide essential vitamins; higher yields could help prevent famine in some parts of world; eliminate need for chemical pesticides; could be inexpensive sources for medicines, fuels, and plastics
3. Students should give sound reasons to support their opinions.
4. The letter from the farmer should include reasons GM plants are beneficial. The letter from the company president should address the points brought up in the farmer's letter and also include reasons for opposition to GM plants.

Do Genetically Modified Foods Need Stricter Controls?

Since they were first introduced in 1994, bioengineered, or genetically modified (GM), crops have become common in the American supermarket and diet. Most GM plants are engineered to produce pest-killing chemicals or to resist weed-killing chemicals. For example, in 1998, 20 percent of U.S. corn crops contained a gene for *Bt-toxin*, a natural insecticide that protects corn plants from the European corn borer, a major insect pest. *Bt*-corn, as this GM corn is called, enables farmers to produce more food on fewer acres, increasing food production and profits.

Many consumers, however, are concerned about the long-term impact of these crops. The European Union, for example, has effectively stopped the import of many GM food crops and required that others be prominently labeled as genetically modified. Should GM foods be more tightly controlled?

The Viewpoints

GM Foods Need Tighter Controls

Some people are concerned that GM foods might have unexpected effects on people. For example, GM corn approved only for animal feed has appeared accidentally in tortillas. The corn contains a protein that could cause allergic reactions in people. The contaminated tortillas show that GM crops can get mixed in with non-GM crops.

Genetically modified crops also could pose a hazard to the environment. Plants engineered to produce insecticides can kill beneficial insects as well as pests. Antibiotic-resistance genes used as markers could spread into the environment, resulting in antibiotic-resistant bacteria. Pollen from GM plants might transfer genes to wild plants, resulting in "super weeds" that are impossible to control with weed killers. The spread of natural pesticide genes into wild plants might harm beneficial insects, such as bees and butterflies.

GM Foods Do Not Need More Controls

Recently developed GM food crops contain essential vitamins that are lacking in the diets of many people. For example, golden rice contains genes from daffodils and bacteria that greatly increase its content of beta-carotene, which the body uses to make vitamin A. The high productivity and nutritional benefits of GM crops are especially important in developing countries, where their use may prevent famine and ease human suffering.

Because they increase production and eliminate the need for chemical pesticides, GM crops can be beneficial to the environment. Someday, GM plants could be inexpensive sources of medicines, fuels, and plastics. If GM products are more strictly controlled, companies might give up researching new applications for GM plants.

You Decide

1. **Defining the Issue** In your own words, explain the major issues about GM foods.
2. **Analyzing the Viewpoints** What are the risks and benefits of GM plants?
3. **Forming Your Opinion** Are stricter regulations needed? Give reasons for your opinion.
4. **Role-Playing** Suppose you are a farmer trying to sell your GM crop. The company that usually purchases your crop has decided not to use GM crops. Write a letter to the company explaining your position. Then, take the role of company president and respond to the farmer's letter.

13–4 Applications of Genetic Engineering

As you have just read, the technology of genetic engineering makes it possible to transfer DNA sequences, including whole genes, from one organism to another. Does this mean that genes from organisms as different as animals and plants can be made to work in each other? American researcher Steven Howell and his associates at the University of California at San Diego provided the answer to that question in 1986. They isolated the gene for luciferase, an enzyme that allows fireflies to glow, and inserted it into tobacco cells. When whole plants were grown from the recombinant cells and the gene was activated, the plants glowed in the dark, as you can see in **Figure 13–12.** The fact that the gene for luciferase works perfectly in a plant shows that the basic mechanisms of gene expression are shared by plants and animals.

Guide for Reading

Key Concept
- How are transgenic organisms useful to human beings?

Vocabulary
transgenic
clone

Reading Strategy: Monitoring Your Understanding Make a table with three columns. Before you read, write what you already know about cloning in the first column. Under the next heading, write down what you want to learn about cloning. After you read, write down what you learned about cloning in the last column.

Transgenic Organisms

The universal nature of genetic mechanisms makes it possible to construct organisms that are **transgenic,** meaning that they contain genes from other organisms. Using the basic techniques of genetic engineering, a gene from one organism can be inserted into cells from another organism. These transformed cells can then be used to grow new organisms. Don't think for a moment that transgenic organisms are of interest only to scientists. **Genetic engineering has spurred the growth of biotechnology, a new industry that is changing the way we interact with the living world.**

Transgenic Microorganisms Because they reproduce rapidly and are easy to grow, transgenic bacteria now produce a host of important substances useful for health and industry. The human forms of proteins such as insulin, growth hormone, and clotting factor were once rare and expensive. Bacteria transformed with the genes for human proteins now produce these important compounds cheaply and in great abundance. People with insulin-dependent diabetes are now treated with pure human insulin produced by human genes inserted into bacteria. In the future, transgenic microorganisms may produce substances designed to fight cancer, as well as the raw materials for plastics and synthetic fibers.

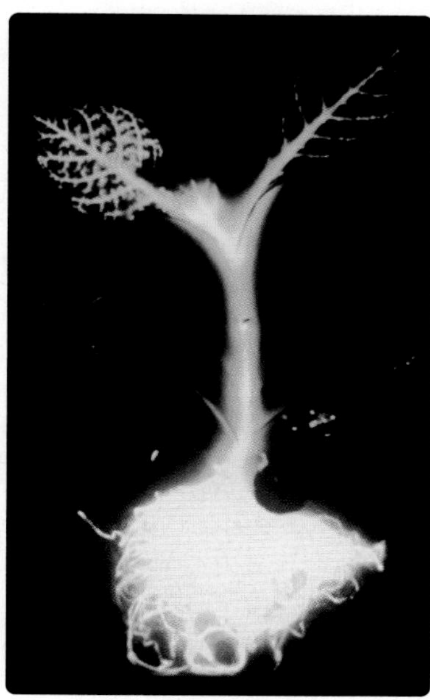

▶ **Figure 13–12** **Genetic engineering has changed the way we interact with living things.** This transgenic tobacco plant, which glows in the dark, was produced by transferring a gene from a firefly into a tobacco cell.

TIME SAVER — SECTION RESOURCES

Print:
- ***Teaching Resources,*** Section Review 13–4
- ***Guided Reading and Study Workbook,*** Section 13–4
- ***Issues and Decision Making,*** 13–1
- ***Biotechnology Manual,*** Lab 17; Issue 4

Technology:
- ***iText,*** Section 13–4

Section 13–4

1 FOCUS

Objectives

13.4.1 ***Describe*** the usefulness of some transgenic organisms to humans.

13.4.2 ***Summarize*** the main steps in cloning.

Guide for Reading

Vocabulary Preview

Challenge students to infer the meaning of the word *transgenic* by first explaining that the prefix *trans-* means "across or beyond." Write students' inferences on the board, and review them as you study the section. After completing the section, compare the inferences with the actual meaning.

Reading Strategy

Encourage students to make a list of the events involved in cloning. You might also want students to add diagrams to their list of events.

2 INSTRUCT

Transgenic Organisms

Build Science Skills

Using Models Challenge students to create a model of a transgenic organism. Encourage them to be creative. Students may choose a bacterium, a plant, or an animal. If possible, try to get a mixture of organisms in the class. Students can use various materials to create a three-dimensional organism, or they can simply diagram the organism. In either case, students must describe what gene or genes were inserted into the organism, how the foreign gene or genes affect the phenotype of the organism, and how this new phenotype is beneficial. Have students present their models to the class.

13–4 (continued)

Meet Diverse Needs

At-risk students might need help making the transition from manipulating DNA molecules to engineering new organisms. Have these students make flowcharts that show the steps in developing a transgenic organism. Remind them that first the DNA fragment to be inserted into the organism must be constructed. Then, one of the transformation techniques described in Section 13–3 must be used, depending on whether the transgenic organism they are describing is a bacterium, a plant, or an animal. **Learning modality: visual**

Address Misconceptions

Students might have the mistaken idea that performing genetic engineering techniques and transformations is easy. Emphasize that these procedures are complicated and often fail for no apparent reasons. For example, scientists might inject 50 mouse eggs with DNA before one egg survives to form a living, developing embryo. Encourage students to read articles about the experiments described in the section to learn the success rates of the procedures.

Transgenic Animals Transgenic animals have been used to study genes and to improve the food supply. Strains of mice have been produced with human genes that make their immune systems act similarly to those of humans. This allows scientists to study the effects of diseases on the human immune system. Transgenic livestock have been produced with extra copies of growth hormone genes. Such animals grow faster and produce meat that is less fatty than that from ordinary animals. Efforts are now underway to produce transgenic chickens that will be resistant to the bacterial infections that sometimes cause food poisoning.

In the future, transgenic animals might also provide us with an ample supply of our own proteins. Several labs have engineered transgenic sheep and pigs that produce human proteins in their milk, making it easy to collect and refine the proteins.

Transgenic Plants Transgenic plants are now an important part of our food supply. In the year 2000, 52 percent of the soybeans and 25 percent of the corn grown in the United States were transgenic, or genetically modified (GM). Many of these plants contain genes that produce a natural insecticide, so the crops do not have to be sprayed with synthetic pesticides. Others have genes that enable them to resist weed-killing chemicals, allowing farmers to grow more food by controlling weeds.

▼ **Figure 13–13** In early 1997, Dolly made headlines as the first clone of an adult mammal. **Applying Concepts** *Why did Dolly not look like her foster mother?*

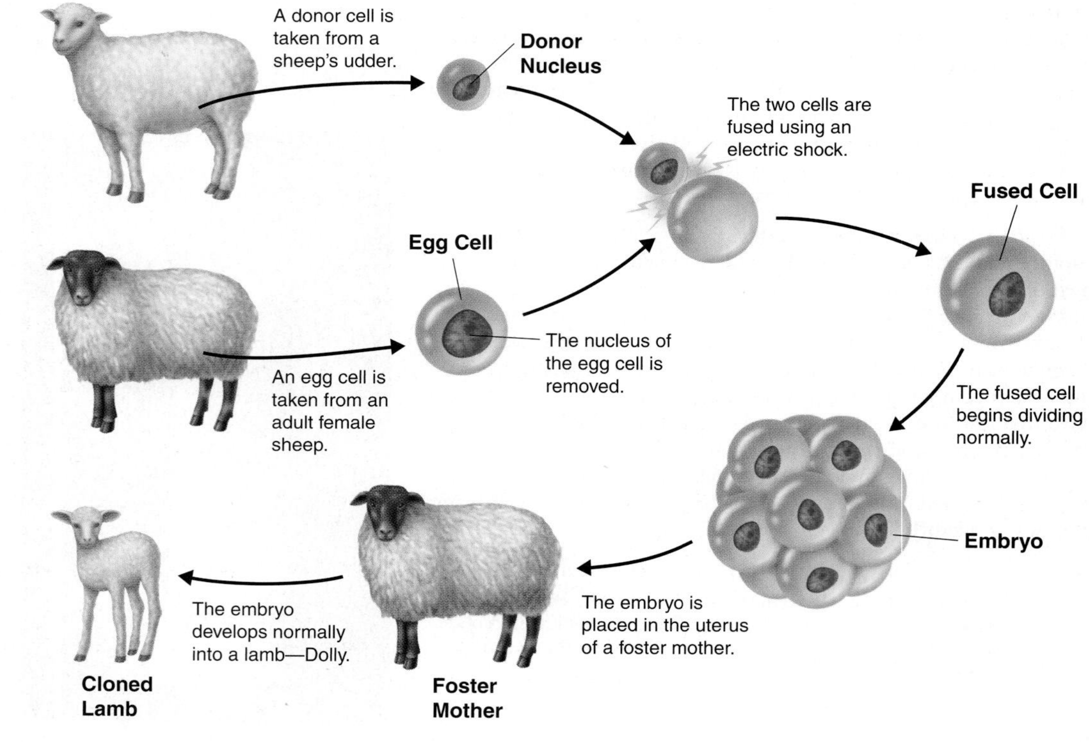
A donor cell is taken from a sheep's udder.
Donor Nucleus
The two cells are fused using an electric shock.
Fused Cell
Egg Cell
The nucleus of the egg cell is removed.
An egg cell is taken from an adult female sheep.
The fused cell begins dividing normally.
Embryo
The embryo is placed in the uterus of a foster mother.
The embryo develops normally into a lamb—Dolly.
Cloned Lamb
Foster Mother

TIME SAVER — PRESENTATIONS MADE EASY!

The Presentation Assistant Plus contains the Prentice Hall Presentation Pro and the Transparencies, which provide easy-to-follow visual support for every step of this section. If you have a computer presentation station, use Prentice Hall Presentation Pro for Section 13–4, or use the transparencies listed here.

Section 13–4:

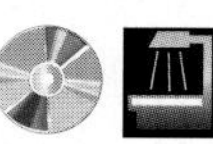

Interest Grabber
Section Outline
Flowchart
Figure 13–13

Transgenic plants may soon produce human antibodies that can be used to fight disease; plastics that can now be produced only from petroleum; and foods that are resistant to rot and spoilage. One of the most important new developments in GM foods is a rice plant that adds vitamin A to rice, the major food for billions of the world's people.

Cloning

A **clone** is a member of a population of genetically identical cells produced from a single cell. Cloned colonies of bacteria and other microorganisms are easy to grow, but this is not always true of multicellular organisms, especially animals. For many years, biologists wondered if it might be possible to clone a mammal—to use a single cell from an adult to grow an entirely new individual that is genetically identical to the organism from which the cell was taken. After years of research, many scientists had concluded that this was impossible.

In 1997, Scottish scientist Ian Wilmut stunned biologists by announcing that he had cloned a sheep. How did he do it? **Figure 13–13** shows the basic steps. In Wilmut's technique, the nucleus of an egg cell is removed. The cell is fused with a cell taken from another adult. The fused cell begins to divide and the embryo is then placed in the reproductive system of a foster mother, where it develops normally. The sheep, which Wilmut named Dolly, is shown in **Figure 13–14.** Cloned cows, pigs, mice, and other mammals have been produced by similar techniques. Cloned animals are not necessarily transgenic, but researchers hope that cloning will enable them to make copies of transgenic animals that produce genetically engineered substances that will have medical or scientific value.

Cloning may indeed find wide use in medical and scientific research and even in helping to save endangered species. Cloning, however, also raises serious ethical issues, including the possibility that sooner or later someone may attempt to clone a human being.

▲ **Figure 13–14** The adult sheep is Dolly, the first mammal cloned from an adult cell. The lamb is Dolly's first offspring, called Bonnie. The fact that Dolly was cloned did not affect her ability to produce a live offspring. **Inferring** ***Why might it be important for cloned animals to be able to reproduce?***

13–4 Section Assessment

1. **Key Concept** List one practical application for each of the following: transgenic bacteria, transgenic animals, transgenic plants.
2. What is a transgenic organism?
3. What basic steps were followed to produce Dolly?
4. **Critical Thinking Making Judgments** List reasons you would or would not be concerned about eating genetically modified food.

iTEXT **Assessment** Use iText to review the important concepts in Section 13–4.

ALTERNATIVE ASSESSMENT

Conducting a Survey
Survey at least ten people about their viewpoints on cloning animals. Include classmates, friends, relatives, and teachers. Organize your results into a chart.

13–4 Section Assessment

1. Sample answers: transgenic bacteria—produce human proteins for medical use, produce materials for plastics; animals—study genes, improve food supply, provide human proteins; plants—improve food supply, produce human antibodies, produce plastics
2. An organism that contains genes from other organisms
3. The nucleus of an egg cell is removed and replaced with a nucleus taken from another adult. This egg is then placed in the reproductive system of a foster mother, where it develops normally.
4. Some may be concerned because the foods might have unknown effects on humans. Others will not be concerned because they think the genetic modifications will not affect humans.

Cloning

Use Visuals

Figure 13–13 Go through Ian Wilmut's procedure for producing a clone of a sheep. Discuss how this procedure is similar to and different from transformation. Point out that Dolly is not a transgenic animal because she does not have any DNA sequences from a different organism. Her DNA is exactly the same as the DNA from the donor sheep. Also relate the cloning procedure to meiosis and fertilization, having volunteers point out which cells are diploid (donor nucleus) and which are haploid (egg cell nucleus).

3 ASSESS

Evaluate Understanding

Have students draw diagrams to show how a transgenic organism is produced and how a clone is produced.

Reteach

Instruct students to make a table to describe the uses and the examples of transgenic microorganisms, animals, and plants.

ALTERNATIVE ASSESSMENT

Charts will depend on the viewpoints of the people interviewed. However, all charts should include at least ten different people and their viewpoints, either for or against cloning animals. Students should summarize their findings in the charts, but may also include specific quotes that exemplify typical responses.

Use iText to review the key concepts in Section 13–4.

Answers to . . .

Figure 13–13 *Dolly received all of her genetic material from the donor sheep, not from the foster mother.*

Figure 13–14 *To make it possible to pass on the desired trait to future generations*

Design an Experiment

Objective Students will be able to investigate whether plants grown from irradiated seeds have more mutations.

Skill Focus **Forming Operational Definitions**

Time 45 minutes

Advance Prep Purchase irradiated seeds from a biological supply company, or arrange to have your seeds irradiated at a local university or medical clinic.

Safety

- Make sure students wear disposable plastic gloves when handling seeds, plants, or soil. Dispose of the gloves properly.

Prelab Discussion Review with the class how mutations can be induced in DNA. Remind students that radiation, or exposure to X-rays, damages the DNA molecule. Then, encourage students to brainstorm a list of mutations that they might observe in the plants grown from irradiated seeds. If no one mentions it, point out that lethality is one possibility. In other words, they might observe a lower germination rate in irradiated seeds. Finally, go over the procedure with students and answer any questions they have.

Teaching Tips

- Review each group's experimental design before students proceed with their experiment. Make sure their data table is organized properly to record the observations that they plan to record.
- Place the petri dishes in a warm, dark place while the seeds are germinating. After germination, move the petri dishes into direct light.

Expected Outcomes Students should observe that irradiated seeds have variable growth and development, whereas nonirradiated seeds grow and develop normally.

Design an Experiment

Investigating the Effects of Radiation on Seeds

Mutations occur naturally in all organisms. However, an organism's mutation rate increases when it is exposed to certain chemicals or types of radiation. In this investigation, you will design an experiment to test the effects of X-ray exposure on seeds.

Problem **Do plants grown from irradiated seeds show evidence of increased mutation?**

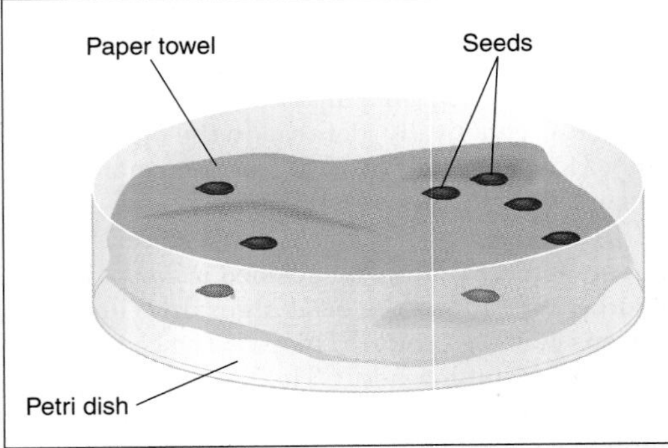

Materials

- irradiated seeds and nonirradiated seeds of the same species
- petri dishes
- paper towels
- plant pots with soil
- glass-marking pencil

Skills Forming Operational Definitions

Design Your Experiment 

Part A: Plan the Experiment

1. **Designing Experiments** Working with two of your classmates, design an experiment to test the hypothesis that radiation increases the rate of mutation in seeds.
2. Discuss your experimental plan with your group. Make certain that you have identified and controlled all important variables and included both irradiated and control seeds in your experimental plan.
3. You will not be able to observe mutations in DNA directly. What observations or measurements can you make that will provide evidence of the number of mutations that have occurred in a seed? With your group, plan what observations you will use to estimate the number of mutations that have occurred in a seed.
4. Design a data table in which to record your observations.
5. Show your experimental plan to your teacher. Once your teacher approves your plan, begin your experiment.

Part B: Carry Out Your Experiment

6. To grow the seeds, follow any instructions that are on the seed packages. If there are no instructions, line a petri dish with a paper towel for each experimental group of seeds. Place the seeds in the petri dishes and cover the seeds with water, as shown in the diagram above. **CAUTION:** *Wash your hands well with warm water and plenty of soap after handling seeds, plants, or soil and before leaving the laboratory.*
7. Place the covers on the petri dishes to protect the seeds from mold and bacteria. Record everything you do to the seeds.
8. Use a glass-marking pencil to label each petri dish. Every petri dish that you use in this experiment should be identified by a different label that includes your name. Store the petri dishes in the location that your teacher designates.
9. Record your observations of each group of seeds every day for 2 weeks. Add water to the petri dishes as necessary to keep the seeds moist.
10. After 2 weeks, carefully transfer the young plants from the petri dishes to pots of soil. Water each pot after you have transferred plants into it. Label each pot with your name and the kind of plants it contains.
11. Place the potted plants in sunlight or under a fluorescent lamp as your teacher directs. Water the plants regularly. Continue to observe the plants daily, according to your experimental plans, for the next 2 weeks. Record your observations each day.

Analyze and Conclude

1. **Comparing and Contrasting** What differences did you observe between the irradiated seeds and the nonirradiated seeds?
2. **Designing Experiments** How could you best determine whether a seed contains mutant DNA?
3. **Forming Operational Definitions** What kinds of observations did you decide to use as evidence of mutations? Explain why you think that these observations are reliable evidence of mutations.
4. **Analyzing Data** What evidence did you see of mutations? Did the irradiated seeds show evidence of more mutations than the nonirradiated seeds?
5. **Formulating Hypotheses** Mutations sometimes cause part of an otherwise healthy-looking leaf or other plant part to appear abnormal. Did you see abnormal-looking areas on any plants? Would you expect this kind of mutation to be inherited? Explain your answer.
6. **Evaluating** What explanations, other than mutation, can you think of for the differences you observed between the irradiated seeds and the nonirradiated seeds?

Go Further

Observing Compare the chromosomes of irradiated and nonirradiated plants to see whether radiation can damage chromosomes. To do this, collect several root tips from plants in each experimental group. Place each root tip on a microscope slide with a drop of methylene blue stain and add a coverslip. Press gently on the coverslip with the handle of a dissecting probe to flatten the root tip. Observe this sample with a microscope to find dividing cells in which the chromosomes are visible.

Go Further

Students might observe that cells from irradiated plants have different numbers of chromosomes or different sizes of chromosomes or no difference in the chromosomes from nonirradiated plants.

Analyze and Conclude

1. Observations will vary. Some irradiated seeds will grow into plants that look the same as those from nonirradiated seeds. Other irradiated seeds will produce plants with very different phenotypes, or they may not grow at all.

2. A seed that produces an abnormal plant probably has mutant DNA.

3. Students should show evidence of understanding that mutations often cause random, usually damaging, changes in growth and development.

4. Observations will vary, but irradiated seeds will probably produce plants with more mutations than nonirradiated seeds, if they grow at all.

5. Observations will vary, but this type of damage is common in irradiated plants. Localized damage is often a sign of a mutation in somatic (non-gamete) cells. These mutations are not inherited because they do not affect the genes of the gametes.

6. Possible explanations include that the seeds contained mutant DNA before they were irradiated; the seeds were not produced by homozygous parents; or the seeds were subjected to different environmental conditions.

Chapter 13 Study Guide

Study Tip

Have students develop a crossword puzzle, word search, or other word puzzle that incorporates the Vocabulary terms and some of the Key Concepts. Students can exchange their puzzles and solve them.

Thinking Visually

1. Selective Breeding
2. Genetic Engineering
3. Hybridization

Chapter 13 Assessment

Reviewing Content

1. c	**5.** a	**9.** a
2. a	**6.** b	**10.** a
3. c	**7.** c	
4. a	**8.** c	

Understanding Concepts

11. Hybridization: cross dissimilar organisms; inbreeding: breed similar organisms; both involve selecting to breed organisms with the desired characteristics.

12. By inducing mutations with chemicals or radiation

13. The condition in which cells have many sets of chromosomes; it may instantly produce new plant species that are larger and stronger.

14. Both have codes that can be isolated and altered to change the characteristics of the game or the organism.

15. With restriction enzymes that recognize and cut specific nucleotide sequences of DNA

16. Gel electrophoresis enables scientists to separate and analyze DNA fragments, to compare genomes of different individuals and organisms, and to identify a specific gene.

17. A DNA molecule produced by combining DNA from other sources

Chapter 13 Study Guide

13–1 Changing the Living World

Key Concepts

- Humans use selective breeding to pass desired traits on to the next generation of organisms.
- Breeders can increase the genetic variation in a population by inducing mutations, which are the ultimate source of genetic variability.

Vocabulary
selective breeding, p. 319
hybridization, p. 319
inbreeding, p. 320
polyploid, p. 321

13–2 Manipulating DNA

Key Concepts

- Scientists use their knowledge of the structure of DNA and its chemical properties to study and change DNA molecules. Different techniques are used to extract DNA from cells, to cut DNA into smaller pieces, to identify the sequence of bases in a DNA molecule, and to make unlimited copies of DNA.
- Knowing the sequence of an organism's DNA allows researchers to study specific genes, to compare them with the genes of other organisms, and to try to discover the functions of different genes and gene combinations.

Vocabulary
genetic engineering, p. 322
restriction enzyme, p. 323
gel electrophoresis, p. 323
recombinant DNA, p. 324
polymerase chain reaction (PCR) , p. 325

13–3 Cell Transformation

Key Concepts

- During transformation, a cell takes in DNA from outside the cell. This external DNA becomes a part of the cell's DNA.
- If transformation is successful, the recombinant DNA is integrated into one of the chromosomes of the cell.

Vocabulary
plasmid, p. 327
genetic marker, p. 328

13–4 Applications of Genetic Engineering

Key Concepts

- Using the basic techniques of genetic engineering, a gene from one organism can be inserted into cells from another organism. These transformed cells can then be used to grow new organisms.

Vocabulary
transgenic, p. 331
clone, p. 333

Thinking Visually

Using the information in this chapter, complete the following concept map.

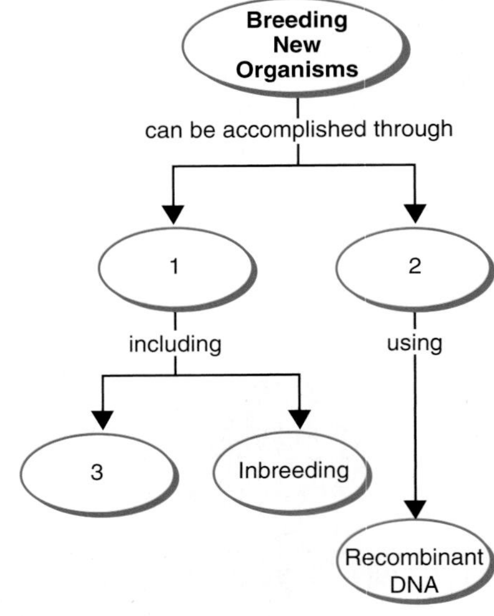

CHAPTER RESOURCES

Print:

- ***Teaching Resources,*** Chapter Vocabulary Review, Graphic Organizer
- ***Chapter Tests: Levels A and B,*** Chapter 13 Test
- ***PH Assessment System,*** Practice Test

Technology:

- ***Computer Test Bank,*** Chapter 13 Test
- ***iText,*** Chapter 13 Assessment

Chapter 13 Assessment

Reviewing Content

Choose the letter that best answers the question or completes the statement.

1. A cross between dissimilar individuals to bring together their best characteristics is called
   a. genetic engineering. c. hybridization.
   b. inbreeding. d. sequencing.

2. Crossing individuals with similar characteristics so that those characteristics will appear in the offspring is called
   a. inbreeding. c. hybridization.
   b. electrophoresis. d. genetic engineering.

3. Varieties of purebred dogs are maintained by
   a. selective breeding. c. inbreeding.
   b. hybridization. d. genetic engineering.

4. Changing the DNA of an organism is called
   a. genetic engineering.
   b. hybridization.
   c. selective breeding.
   d. inbreeding.

5. DNA can be cut into shorter sequences by proteins known as
   a. restriction enzymes.
   b. plasmids.
   c. mutagens.
   d. clones.

6. What has been produced in the drawing below?
   a. a clone c. a genome
   b. recombinant DNA d. a species

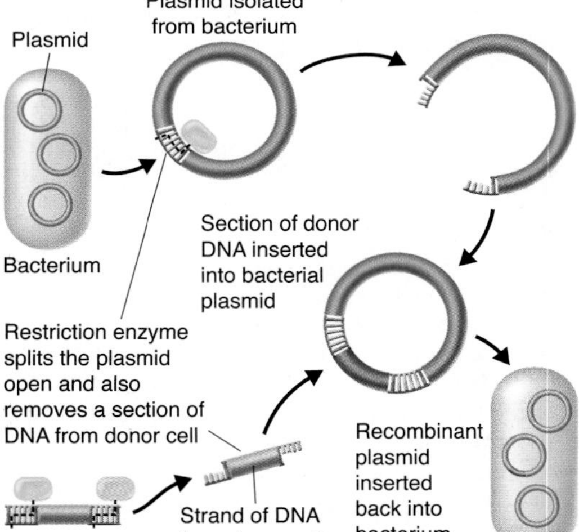
Plasmid isolated from bacterium
Plasmid
Bacterium
Section of donor DNA inserted into bacterial plasmid
Restriction enzyme splits the plasmid open and also removes a section of DNA from donor cell
Recombinant plasmid inserted back into bacterium
Strand of DNA from donor cell

7. When cell transformation is successful, the recombinant DNA
   a. undergoes mutation.
   b. is treated with antibiotics.
   c. is integrated into a chromosome.
   d. becomes a plasmid.

8. Bacteria often contain small circular molecules of DNA known as
   a. clones. c. plasmids.
   b. restriction enzymes. d. hybrids.

9. Organisms that contain genes from other organisms are called
   a. transgenic. c. donor organisms.
   b. mutagenic. d. cloned organisms.

10. A member of a population of genetically identical cells produced from a single cell is a
    a. clone. c. mutant.
    b. plasmid. d. sequence.

Understanding Concepts

11. Compare hybridization and inbreeding. Why are they considered forms of selective breeding?
12. How do breeders produce new genetic variations not found in nature?
13. What is polyploidy? When is this condition useful?
14. Explain why genetic engineering can be compared to reprogramming a computer game.
15. How are large DNA molecules cut up?
16. What role does gel electrophoresis play in the study of DNA?
17. What is recombinant DNA?
18. Describe what occurs during a polymerase chain reaction (PCR).
19. What happens during cell transformation? What are some types of cells that have been transformed?
20. Explain what genetic markers are, and describe how scientists use them.
21. What did the successful transfer of the luciferase gene from an animal to a plant indicate about the functioning of genes?
22. What is a transgenic organism? Explain how transgenic bacteria have been useful.
23. How did Ian Wilmut clone the sheep known as Dolly?
24. Explain how a transgenic plant differs from a hybrid plant.

18. A short piece of complementary DNA—a primer—is added to both ends of the DNA fragment to be copied. The DNA is heated to separate the two strands, then cooled. DNA polymerase makes copies of the region between the two primer sequences. The copies also serve as templates to make more copies.

19. A cell takes in DNA from outside the cell, and the external DNA becomes a part of the cell's DNA. Bacteria and plant and animal cells are types of cells that have been transformed.

20. Genetic markers make it possible to distinguish bacteria that carry plasmids and foreign DNA from those that do not; genetic markers are inserted into plasmids so that scientists can identify transformed bacteria.

21. That the basic mechanisms for gene expression are shared by plants and animals

22. An organism that contains genes from other organisms; produce important substances for health and industry

23. Ian Wilmut removed the nucleus of an egg cell and replaced it with a nucleus taken from a cell from another adult. This egg was then placed in the reproductive system of a foster mother, where it developed normally.

24. A transgenic plant contains DNA from another organism via genetic engineering. A hybrid plant contains DNA only from both parents via fertilization.

TIME SAVER — HOMEWORK GUIDE

Section:	Questions:
Section 13–1	1–3, 11–13, 27, 29
Section 13–2	4–6, 14–18, 28, 36, 38
Section 13–3	7, 8, 19–21, 26, 31, 33, 34
Section 13–4	9, 10, 22–25, 30, 32, 35–37

Chapter 13 Assessment

Critical Thinking

25. They can be produced relatively inexpensively in large quantities; they are the actual human protein; and they are pure.

26. No, the change involves body (somatic) cells, not germ cells.

27. Answers should involve crossing the different varieties of roses and selecting the offspring with the desired traits for further crosses. For example: cross the pink and yellow roses until a thornless plant with sweet-smelling flowers is obtained. Cross this plant with purple roses until thornless plants with sweet-smelling purple flowers are obtained. Inbreed these plants until the traits breed true.

28. T-A-C-G-C-T-T-T-T-C-G-C-A-A-A-G-A-C-C-T-G-C-C-A-G-T-G-A-T-T

29. Breeding techniques require little technology and take much time. It is also difficult to achieve the desired combination of traits. Genetic engineering requires extensive training and expensive equipment. Specific combinations of traits can be made, and traits from organisms that cannot be crossed naturally can be combined.

30. Students' opinions should display an understanding of genetic engineering.

31. DNA from one organism can be inserted into another, and the gene is successfully expressed to produce the same protein.

32. The blood proteins that people need could be produced by bacteria that have been transformed with the human gene that encodes the needed protein.

33. Sample answers: Transgenic microorganisms might produce substances designed to fight cancer, as well as the raw materials for plastics and synthetic fibers. Transgenic animals might provide humans with sources of human proteins. Transgenic plants might produce human antibodies that can be used to fight disease, foods that are resistant to spoilage, and foods that contain extra vitamins.

Chapter 13 Assessment

Critical Thinking

25. Applying Concepts Describe one or more advantages of producing needed proteins such as insulin through genetic engineering.

26. Inferring If a human patient's bone marrow cells were removed, altered genetically, and reimplanted, would the change be passed on to the patient's children? Explain your answer.

27. Problem Solving Suppose a plant breeder has a thornless rose bush with scentless pink flowers, a thorny rose bush with sweet-smelling yellow flowers, and a thorny rose bush with scentless purple flowers. How might the plant breeder develop a purebred variety of thornless sweet-smelling purple roses?

28. Problem Solving The following fragments were obtained when a gene that consists of ten codons was cut by restriction enzymes. What is the sequence of bases in the gene? (*Hint:* Look for overlapping sections on the fragments.)

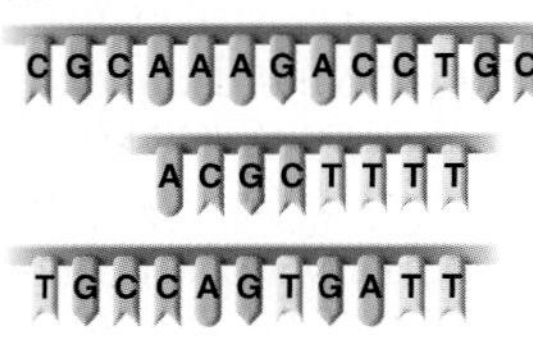

29. Comparing and Contrasting Compare the advantages and disadvantages of breeding techniques and genetic engineering.

30. Making Judgments Should genetic engineering be performed directly on humans? If so, under what circumstances? Explain your answer.

31. Formulating Hypotheses Almost every organism has DNA that is made of the same four nucleotides and translated by the same genetic code. Explain why this fact is significant in cell transformation.

32. Inferring People who receive blood transfusions have a low risk of being exposed to HIV. How could genetic engineering eliminate this risk?

33. Predicting Predict three ways in which you think genetically engineered organisms will be used in the future.

34. Applying Concepts Bacteria and human beings are very different organisms. Why is it possible to combine their DNA and use a bacterium to make a human protein?

35. Applying Concepts Your friend proposes that with the techniques of genetic engineering, biologists should be able to produce an organism with any combination of characteristics. For example, they could create an animal with the body of a frog and the wings of a bat. Do you think this is a reasonable proposal? Explain your answer.

36. Comparing and Contrasting Compare the tools used to edit DNA to the tools used to edit computer programs.

37. Making Connections To produce a transgenic animal, a scientist typically transforms an unfertilized egg cell. Use what you know about cells and the development of multicellular organisms to explain why that is done, and what happens afterward.

Performance-Based Assessment

Persuasive Writing Your local newspaper has published an editorial against the use of genetic engineering. The editorial states that genetic engineering is still too new to use, while traditional selective breeding can accomplish anything that genetic engineering can do. Write a letter to the newspaper either in support of the newspaper's position or against it. Use actual examples of genetic engineering to make your points.

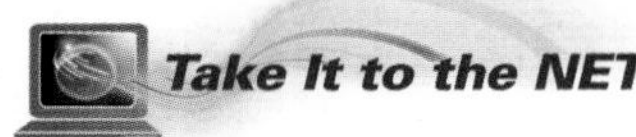

What kinds of foods are the result of selective breeding? Visit the Biology area of the Prentice Hall Web site at **www.phschool.com** to learn about some of the foods that have been produced using selective breeding techniques. Then, answer the following questions:

- Name three fruits that have been developed using selective breeding.
- What is a paradox walnut tree?
- Why did Luther Burbank develop spineless cactuses?

Performance-Based Assessment

Students should support their positions with examples of genetic engineering. They should demonstrate an understanding of both selective breeding and genetic engineering and the advantages and disadvantages of each.

Standardized Test Prep

Test-Taking Tip For questions containing the words NOT or EXCEPT, begin by eliminating each answer choice that *does* fit the characteristic in question. After eliminating all but one of the choices, check to see that your answer is correct by confirming that it does *not* fit the characteristic in question.

Directions: Choose the letter that best answers the question or completes the statement.

1. Which of the following can be used to increase genetic variation?
   I. inbreeding
   II. genetic engineering
   III. inducing mutations
   (A) I only
   (B) II only
   (C) I and III only
   (D) II and III only
   (E) I, III, and III
2. Which of the following characteristics does NOT apply to a plasmid?
   (A) made of DNA
   (B) in bacterial cells
   (C) circular
   (D) accepts foreign DNA
   (E) in animal cells

Questions 3 and 4

A researcher chooses a plasmid with a gene that confers resistance to the antibiotic ampicillin. She isolates and inserts a human gene that codes for a protein into the plasmid. Next, she transforms bacteria using the plasmid. She then cultures the new bacteria on a nutrient medium containing ampicillin.

3. What can the researcher conclude about the bacteria that grow on the nutrient medium?
   I. They are resistant to ampicillin.
   II. They contain recombinant DNA.
   III. They contain a human gene.
   (A) I only
   (B) II only
   (C) I and III only
   (D) II and III only
   (E) I, II, and III
4. Which of the following would indicate that the bacteria contain the human gene?
   I. They are resistant to ampicillin.
   II. They produce the human protein encoded by the human gene.
   III. They produce ampicillin.
   (A) I only
   (B) II only
   (C) I and III only
   (D) II and III only
   (E) I, II, and III

Questions 5–9 Each of the lettered choices below refers to the following numbered statements. Select the best lettered choice. A choice may be used once, more than once, or not at all.

(A) Gel electrophoresis
(B) Plasmid
(C) Polymerase chain reaction
(D) Knock-out gene
(E) DNA synthesizer

5. Used to insert new genes into plant cells
6. Replaced or deleted gene
7. Assembles short sequences of DNA
8. Makes many copies of a DNA sample
9. Separates DNA fragments

Questions 10–11

The graph below shows the number of accurate copies of DNA produced by polymerase chain reaction (PCR).

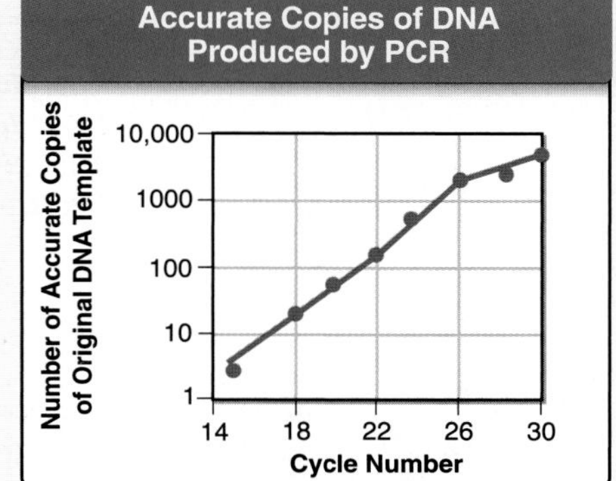

10. What can you conclude about cycles 18–26?
    (A) PCR produced accurate copies of template DNA at an exponential rate.
    (B) The amount of DNA produced by PCR doubled with each cycle of the reaction.
    (C) The DNA copies produced by PCR were not accurate copies of the original DNA template.
    (D) A and B only
    (E) A and C only
11. Based on the graph, which of the following might have happened between cycles 26 and 28?
    (A) PCR stopped producing accurate copies of the template.
    (B) The rate of the reaction slowed down.
    (C) All the template DNA was used up.
    (D) A and C only
    (E) B and C only

Standardized Test Prep

1. D	**5.** B	**9.** A
2. E	**6.** D	**10.** A
3. A	**7.** E	**11.** B
4. B	**8.** C	

Chapter 13 Assessment (continued)

34. All DNA contains the same four nucleotides and is translated by the same mechanism and genetic code, so the DNA from a bacterium could be used to make a human protein.

35. Students should disagree. Possible explanations include: too many genetic differences exist between frogs and bats. It is too difficult to control the expression of so many genes in such a specific location.

36. Scientists use tools to extract, read, edit, and reinsert DNA into living organisms. Some of these tools use a power source that enables a chemical reaction to take place. When editing computer programs, programmers use a source of power; however, the changes that take place are electronic, rather than chemical.

37. Students' answers should reflect an understanding of genetic engineering.

Take It to the NET

- Possible answers include nectarines, freestone peaches, plums, nuts, and plumcots.
- A fast-growing walnut tree; it is a paradox because walnuts are hardwoods and hardwoods are slow-growing trees.
- He thought spineless cactuses would make excellent cattle feed, and he thought it would create a productive use for deserts.

For additional information, visit

www.phschool.com

Chapter Planner 14 The Human Genome

Section and Section Objectives	Time	Activities and Labs
14–1 Human Heredity, pp. 341–348 **14.1.1** ***Identify*** the types of human chromosomes in a karyotype. **14.1.2** ***Explain*** how sex is determined. **14.1.3** ***Explain*** how pedigrees are used to study human traits. **14.1.4** ***Describe*** examples of the inheritance of human traits. **14.1.5** ***Explain*** how small changes in DNA cause genetic disorders.	2 periods (1 block)	**SE:** ***Inquiry Activity,*** Can you predict chin shape?, p. 340 **SE:** ***Problem Solving,*** Using a Pedigree, p. 343
14–2 Human Chromosomes, pp. 349–354 **14.2.1** ***Identify*** characteristics of human chromosomes. **14.2.2** ***Describe*** some sex–linked disorders and explain why they are more common in males than in females. **14.2.3** ***Explain*** the process of X–chromosome inactivation. **14.2.4** ***Summarize*** nondisjunction and the problems it causes.	1 period (1/2 block)	**TE:** ***Address Misconceptions,*** p. 350 **SE:** ***Quick Lab,*** How is colorblindness transmitted?, p. 351 **TE:** ***Build Science Skills,*** p. 352 **SE:** ***Issues in Biology,*** Who Controls Your DNA?, p. 354
14–3 Human Molecular Genetics, pp. 355–360 **14.3.1** ***Summarize*** methods of human DNA analysis. **14.3.2** ***State*** the goal of the Human Genome Project. **14.3.3** ***Describe*** how researchers are attempting to cure genetic disorders.	1 period (1/2 block)	**TE:** ***Demonstration,*** p. 357 **SE:** ***Careers in Biology,*** Geneticist, p. 359 **SE:** ***Real-World Lab,*** Modeling DNA Probes, p. 361
Chapter Assessment, pp. 362–365	1 period (1/2 block)	

ACTIVITY PLANNER

SE: ***Inquiry Activity,*** p. 340; (10 min.)

TE: ***Address Misconceptions,*** p. 350; (10 min.); charts used to diagnose colorblindness

SE: ***Quick Lab,*** p. 351; (20 min.); 2 plastic cups, 3 white beans, black marker, red bean

TE: ***Build Science Skills,*** p. 352; (20 min.); prepared slides of female cells with Barr bodies and cells without Barr bodies

TE: ***Demonstration,*** p. 357; (15 min.); yarn, scissors

SE: ***Real-World Lab,*** p. 361; (45 min.); graph paper, scissors, colored pencil or marker

PLANNING KEY

Ability Levels

- **B Basic** For students who need additional help
- **A Average** For all students
- **E Enriched** For students who need to be challenged

Components

SE	Student Edition	**GRSW**	Guided Reading and Study Workbook	**IDM**	Issues and Decision Making
TE	Teacher's Edition	**CT**	Chapter Tests: Levels A and B	**CTB**	Computer Test Bank
LMA	Laboratory Manual A	**PHAS**	PH Assessment System	**PA**	Presentation Assistant Plus
LMB	Laboratory Manual B	**LA**	Lab Assessment With Scoring Guide	**BD**	BioDetectives Videotape
TR	Teaching Resources	**BTM**	BioTechnology Manual	**iT**	iText
IF	Investigations in Forensics				

Program Resources	Assessment	Media and Technology
LMA: Chapter 14 Lab A E **LMB:** Chapter 14 Lab B A **TR:** Section Review 14–1 B A **GRSW:** Section 14–1 B A **BTM:** Lab 10; Issues 2, 3 A E	**SE:** 14–1 Section Assessment, p. 348 **TR:** Section Review 14–1	**PA:** 14–1 Interest Grabber, Section Outline, Concept Map, Figure 14–3, Figure 14–4, Figure 14–8 **iT:** Section 14–1
TR: Section Review 14–2 B A **GRSW:** Section 14–2 B A **IDM:** Issues and Decisions 7 A E	**SE:** 14–2 Section Assessment, p. 353 **TR:** Section Review 14–2	**PA:** 14–2 Interest Grabber, Section Outline, Nondisjunction, Figure 14–13 **BD:** "Coming Home: A Nation's Pledge" **iT:** Section 14–2 DISCOVERY CHANNEL SCHOOL
TR: Section Review 14–3 B A Chapter 14 Real-World Lab B A E **GRSW:** Section 14–3 B A **IDM:** Issues and Decisions 9, 10, 11, 12 A E **BTM:** Labs 2, 11, 12; Concepts 2, 3, 4, 6 A E	**SE:** 14–3 Section Assessment, p. 360 **TR:** Section Review 14–3	**PA:** 14–3 Interest Grabber, Section Outline, Locating Genes, Figure 14–18, Figure 14–21 **iT:** Section 14–3
	SE: Chapter 14 Assessment, pp. 362–365 **TR:** Chapter Vocabulary Review, Graphic Organizer **CT:** Chapter 14 Test **CTB:** Chapter 14 Test **PHAS:** Practice Test	**CTB:** Chapter 14 Test **iT:** Chapter 14 Assessment

PRESSED FOR TIME?

To Preview the Chapter

- Have students read the Key Concepts and Vocabulary terms in each section.
- Have students examine all the figures in the chapter and read their captions.

To Cover the Chapter Quickly

- Have students read Human Chromosomes and Human Traits in Section 14–1; Sex-Linked Genes, X-Chromosome Inactivation, and Chromosomal Disorders in Section 14–2; and all of Section 14–3.
- Assign the 14–3 Section Assessment.

To Review the Chapter

- Review the concept map in the Chapter 14 Study Guide.
- Assign Sections 14–1, 14–2, and 14–3 in the Guided Reading and Study Workbook.

Chapter 14

ENGAGE/EXPLORE

Inquiry Activity

Objective Students will be able to predict chin shape with Punnett squares.

Skills Focus Predicting

Time 10 minutes

Strategy Use photographs of famous people to demonstrate cleft and uncleft chins. Emphasize that cleft chin is used here as an illustrative example. In practice, the inheritance of traits such as cleft chin is a complex process affected by other factors in addition to Mendel's laws. Students should not assume that they can analyze their own or anyone's ancestry simply by examination of such traits.

Expected Outcomes Students will use Punnett squares to predict that the parents will have a 25 percent chance of having a child with a cleft chin.

Think About It

1. Punnett squares give the possible genotypic and phenotypic ratios of the offspring of a cross. No; the Punnett square suggests that the parents have a 1 in 4, or 25 percent, chance of their fourth child's having a cleft chin.
2. 25 percent; Each child is the result of an independent combination of chromosomes from each parent. The phenotype of one child does not affect the phenotype of the next.

Brain Teaser

List on the board the phenotypes of the following members of a family. The mother, father, one son, and the two daughters have normal vision. The other son is colorblind. The mother's mother, two sisters, and three brothers have normal vision, but the mother's father is colorblind. The father's mother, father, sister, and three brothers all have normal vision. Challenge students to determine how the allele for colorblindness is inherited. *(The mother has one X chromosome that carries the allele for colorblindness, which she inherited from her father.)* Continue working on the puzzle throughout the chapter until students are able to successfully solve it.

Chapter 14 The Human Genome

The children in this family have some traits that are similar to their mother's and some that are similar to their father's.

Inquiry Activity

Can you predict chin shape?

Procedure

1. Two parents with cleft chins, both heterozygous for cleft chin *(Cc)*, have three children with cleft chins. The parents are sure that their fourth child will not have a cleft chin. Draw a Punnett square to see if this is possible.
2. Determine the probability that the fourth child will have a cleft chin.

Think About It

1. **Using Models** What information does a Punnett square give? Does the Punnett square support the parents' prediction? Explain your answer.
2. **Predicting** If these parents have a fifth child, what are the chances that the child will have a cleft chin? Explain your answer.

14–1 Human Heredity

"Know thyself" was once a philosopher's first instruction to his students, and it still applies today. Of all the living things that inhabit this remarkable world, there is one in particular that has always drawn our interest, one that has always made us wonder, one that will always fire our imagination. That creature is, of course, ourselves, *Homo sapiens.*

Scientists once knew much less about humans than about other organisms. Until very recently, human genetics lagged far behind the genetics of "model" organisms such as fruit flies and mice. That, however, has changed. Scientists are now on the verge of understanding human genetics at least as well as they understand that of some other organisms. From that understanding will come a new responsibility to use that information wisely.

Guide for Reading

Key Concepts
- How is sex determined?
- How do small changes in DNA cause genetic disorders?

Vocabulary
karyotype
sex chromosome
autosome
pedigree
polygenic

Reading Strategy: Using Prior Knowledge Before you read, write down what you already know about the inheritance of traits. As you read, compare the information in the text to your notes.

Human Chromosomes

What makes us human? Biologists can begin to answer that question by taking a look under the microscope to see what is inside a human cell. To analyze chromosomes, cell biologists photograph cells in mitosis, when the chromosomes are fully condensed and easy to see. The biologists then cut out the chromosomes from the photographs and group them together in pairs. A picture of chromosomes arranged in this way is known as a **karyotype** (KAR-ee-uh-typ).

The chromosomes shown in **Figure 14–1** are from a typical human body cell, which contains 46 chromosomes. Each of us began life when a haploid sperm, carrying just 23 chromosomes, fertilized a haploid egg, also with 23 chromosomes. The diploid zygote, or fertilized egg, contained the full complement of 46 chromosomes.

Two of those 46 chromosomes are known as **sex chromosomes,** because they determine an individual's sex. Females have two copies of a large X chromosome. Males have one X and one small Y chromosome. To distinguish them from the sex chromosomes, the remaining 44 chromosomes are known as autosomal chromosomes, or **autosomes.** To quickly summarize the total number of chromosomes present in a human cell, both autosomes and sex chromosomes, biologists write 46XX for females and 46XY for males.

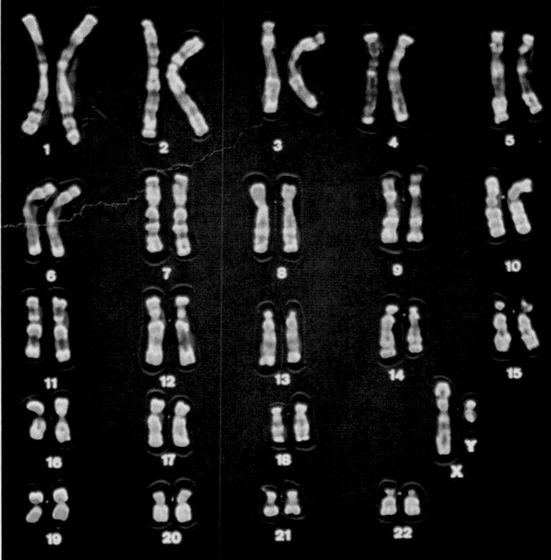

▶ **Figure 14–1** These human chromosomes have been cut out of a photograph and arranged to form a karyotype. **Interpreting Graphics** *How is the X chromosome different from the Y chromosome?*

SECTION RESOURCES

Print:
- ***Laboratory Manual A,*** Chapter 14 Lab
- ***Laboratory Manual B,*** Chapter 14 Lab
- ***Teaching Resources,*** Section Review 14–1
- ***Guided Reading and Study Workbook,*** Section 14–1
- ***Biotechnology Manual,*** Lab 10; Issues 2, 3

Technology:
- ***iText,*** Section 14–1

Section 14–1

1 FOCUS

Objectives

14.1.1 ***Identify*** the types of human chromosomes in a karyotype.
14.1.2 ***Explain*** how sex is determined.
14.1.3 ***Explain*** how pedigrees are used to study human traits.
14.1.4 ***Describe*** examples of the inheritance of human traits.
14.1.5 ***Explain*** how small changes in DNA cause genetic disorders.

Guide for Reading

Vocabulary Preview

Explain that the word *autosome* is the opposite of the term *sex chromosome.* Challenge students to infer the meaning of the word *autosome. (A chromosome that is not a sex chromosome)* Also find out what students think the sex chromosomes are and correct any misconceptions they have.

Reading Strategy

As students read this section, encourage them to write at least one main idea from each subsection under a blue heading. Remind students to include information given in figure captions.

2 INSTRUCT

Human Chromosomes

Use Visuals

Figure 14–1 As students examine the karyotype in the figure, ask: **Is this individual male or female?** *(Male)* **How do you know?** *(There is one X chromosome and one Y chromosome.)* Point out that the chromosomes are arranged by size. Encourage students to make inferences about why this is so. *(For organizational purposes, making it easier to see abnormalities)* Explain that the human chromosomes were originally assigned numbers based on their sizes and positions in a karyotype.

Answer to . . .

Figure 14–1 *The X chromosome is longer.*

Meet Diverse Needs

Have at-risk students review Figure 12–10 on page 297. Make sure students can relate the structure of human chromosomes to the structure of the DNA molecule they learned about in Chapter 12. Emphasize that human DNA is manipulated using the same techniques described in Chapter 13. **Learning modality: visual**

Human Traits

Use Visuals

Figure 14–3 Copy the pedigree from Figure 14–3 on the board. Have student volunteers identify the symbols used in the chart—circles, squares, and vertical and horizontal lines. Explain that carriers are heterozygous for the trait and do not exhibit the trait. Emphasize that pedigree charts are most often used by geneticists when tracking the inheritance of genetic disorders, such as hemophilia or colorblindness. They are used to help parents understand the probability of having a child with a genetic disorder.

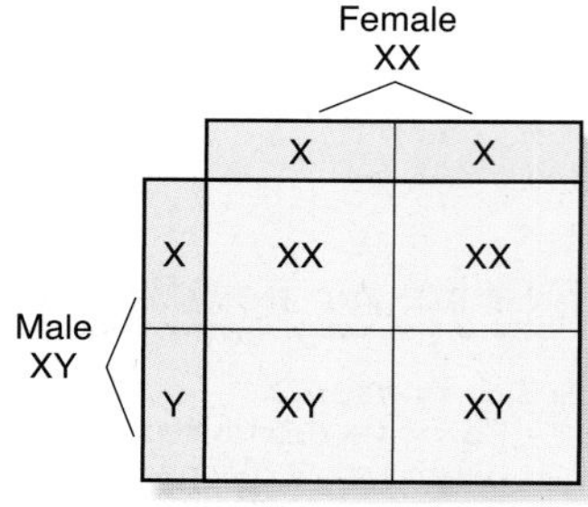
Female
XX
X
X
Male
XY
X
XX
XX
Y
XY
XY

▲ **Figure 14–2** **Egg cells contain a single X chromosome. Sperm cells contain either one X chromosome or one Y chromosome.** Approximately half of the zygotes are XX (female) and half are XY (male).

As you can see in **Figure 14–2**, males and females are born in a roughly 50 : 50 ratio because of the way in which sex chromosomes segregate during meiosis. **All egg cells carry a single X chromosome (23X). However, half of all sperm cells carry an X chromosome (23X) and half carry a Y chromosome (23Y). This ensures that just about half of the zygotes will be 46XX and half will be 46XY.**

Like the chromosomes of other eukaryotes, human chromosomes contain both DNA and protein. Each chromosome contains a single, double-stranded DNA molecule. Human genes are coded directly in the sequences of nucleotides in DNA.

CHECKPOINT
What is a karyotype?

Human Traits

As you read in Chapter 12, human genes are inherited according to the same principles that Gregor Mendel discovered working with garden peas. However, in order to apply Mendelian genetics to humans, biologists must identify an inherited trait controlled by a single gene, which is not always easy. First, they must establish that the trait is actually inherited and not the result of environmental influences. Then, they have to study how the trait is passed from one generation to the next. A **pedigree** chart, which shows the relationships within a family, can be used to help with this task.

The pedigree in **Figure 14–3** shows how a trait is transmitted through three generations of a family. Females who have one allele for the trait are only carriers, while males who have one allele express the trait. In the first row, a female carrier marries a male who does not carry the trait. They have four children: a female carrier, a female who does not carry the trait, a male with the trait, and a male who does not carry the trait. The female carrier child also marries a male who does not carry the

▼ **Figure 14–3** This drawing shows what the symbols in a pedigree represent. **Interpreting Graphics** *What is the sex of the last person in the second row? Does that person have the trait?*

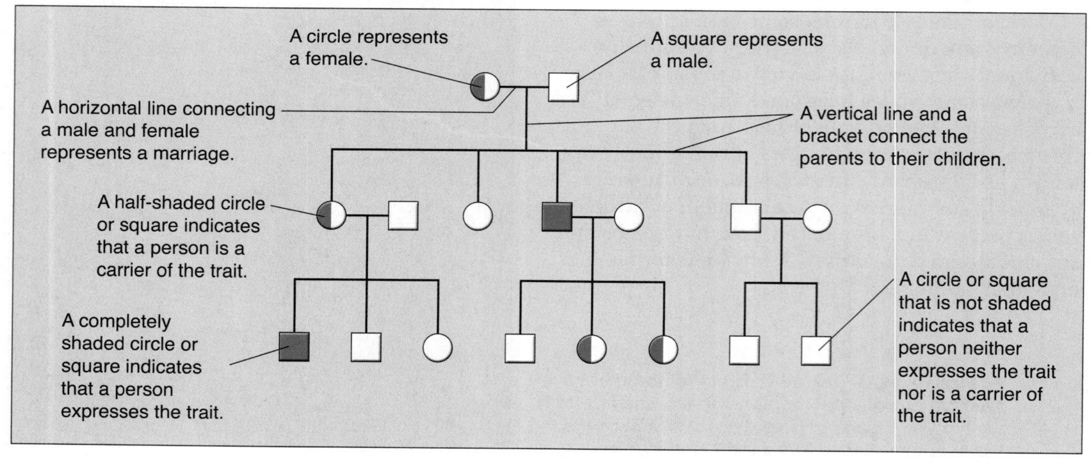
A circle represents a female.
A square represents a male.
A horizontal line connecting a male and female represents a marriage.
A vertical line and a bracket connect the parents to their children.
A half-shaded circle or square indicates that a person is a carrier of the trait.
A completely shaded circle or square indicates that a person expresses the trait.
A circle or square that is not shaded indicates that a person neither expresses the trait nor is a carrier of the trait.

TIME SAVER **PRESENTATIONS MADE EASY!**

The Presentation Assistant Plus contains the Prentice Hall Presentation Pro and the Transparencies, which provide easy-to-follow visual support for every step of this section. If you have a computer presentation station, use Prentice Hall Presentation Pro for Section 14–1, or use the transparencies listed here.

Section 14–1:

Interest Grabber
Section Outline
Concept Map
Figure 14–3
Figure 14–4
Figure 14–8

trait, and has children: a male with the trait, a male who does not carry the trait, and a female who does not carry the trait.

Unfortunately for folks who would like to settle burning issues, like which side of the family is responsible for your good looks, some of the most obvious human traits are almost impossible to associate with single genes. There are two reasons for this. First, things you might think of as single traits, such as the shape of your eyes or ears, are actually **polygenic,** meaning they are controlled by many genes. Second, many of your personal traits are only partly governed by genetics. Remember that the phenotype of an organism is only partly determined by its genotype. Many traits are strongly influenced by environmental, or nongenetic, factors, including nutrition and exercise. For example, even though a person's maximum possible height is largely determined by genetic factors, nutritional improvements in the United States and Europe have increased the average height of these populations about 10 centimeters over their average height in the 1800s.

Although it is important to consider the influence of the environment on the expression of some genes, it must be understood that environmental effects on gene expression are not inherited; genes are. Genes that are denied a proper environment in which to reach full expression in one generation can, in a proper environment, achieve full potential in a later generation.

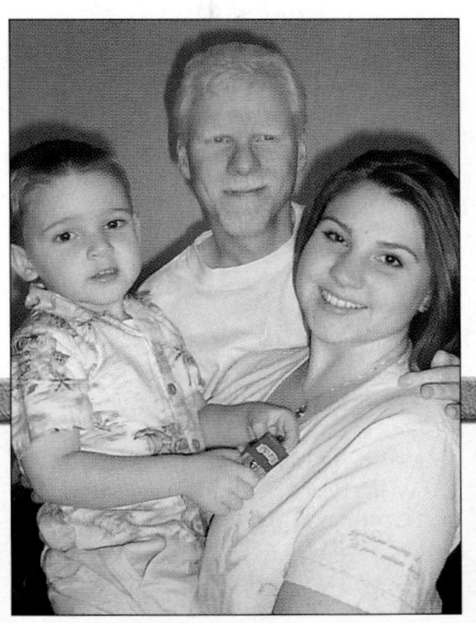

Problem Solving

Using a Pedigree

Imagine that you are a genetic counselor. The pedigree shown illustrates the inheritance of albinism in three generations of a family. A couple from the family have come to you for advice about how the trait is inherited. Your task is to determine whether the allele for albinism is dominant or recessive.

Defining the Problem Define the problem that must be solved to determine whether the allele is dominant or recessive.

Organizing Information Copy the pedigree and the key onto a piece of paper. Label each person on the pedigree with his or her phenotype: normal-pigmented skin or albino.

Creating a Solution Write down how you would analyze the pattern in the inheritance of the albinism trait. Use what you know about patterns of inheritance to determine what information is most important. Describe how you will use your analysis to infer the genotype of as many individuals as possible.

Presenting Your Plan Prepare a step-by-step outline of your plan. Present the plan to your class as if you were explaining the process to the couple involved.

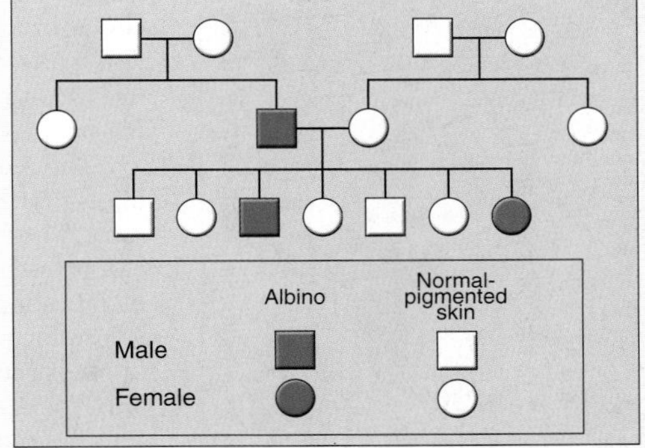

Problem Solving

Defining the Problem Are heterozygotes albino or normal-pigmented?

Organizing Information Students should copy the pedigree onto their own papers and label each individual as normal-pigmented or albino. If students are having trouble interpreting the pedigree, suggest that they use Figure 14–3 as a model.

Creating a Solution To analyze the pattern in the inheritance of the albinism trait, students should assume that the allele for the trait is dominant, then observe the phenotypes in the pedigree to see if they match that pattern of inheritance. Then, they should do the same for the recessive inheritance pattern. Students can use Punnett squares to help them make inferences about genotypes and phenotypes. By assigning the known genotypes to individuals first, students can work backward and make assumptions about the genotypes of some individuals. For normal-pigmented individuals that are heterozygous, they will not be able to assign definitive genotypes. Students should conclude that the allele for albinism is recessive.

Presenting Your Plan Students should explain why they think the allele for the trait is recessive. Plans should include phenotypes of first- and third-generation individuals as part of their explanations. Students might present a pedigree to show how the phenotypes of the family would be different if the allele for the trait were dominant. They might also present a Punnett square to show the probability of the couple's having another albino child.

BIO INSIGHTS — FACTS AND FIGURES

Multiple genes, multiple phenotypes
Polygenic traits include height, skin color, and eye color. None of the genes for a polygenic trait are dominant. Each gene has an active allele and an inactive allele. Active alleles have an additive effect on the phenotype. Inactive alleles do not affect the phenotype. Because of these additive effects, a continuous range of phenotypes is possible. Environmental conditions also affect the phenotype of polygenic traits. For example, height and weight are affected by nutrition, disease, and exercise.

Answers to . . .

CHECKPOINT *A picture of chromosomes arranged in pairs*

Figure 14–3 *Female; no.*

Human Genes

Build Science Skills

Applying Concepts Give students genetics practice problems that involve the blood group genes. Ask: **What blood groups would you expect the children to have if their parents are group A and group B?** *(1 AB: 1 A: 1B: 1 O)* **If this couple has Rh+ blood, could they have a child with Rh− blood? Explain.** *(Yes; if both parents are heterozygous; Rh+/Rh−.)* **Could a child with group A blood have parents that have group O and group B blood?** *(No, this couple can only have children with group O and group B blood.)* Encourage students to make up their own problems and trade them with other students to solve.

Make Connections

Health Science Explain the importance of transfusing the correct blood group into an individual. On the board, diagram a group A blood cell with "A" antigens on the outside of the cell. Do the same for a group B blood cell. The group O blood cell does not have any antigens. Explain that if group A or group B blood were given to a group O person, the immune system would recognize the blood cells as foreign because of the different antigens on the cells' surfaces. The immune system would produce antibodies against these blood cells and destroy them. Then, challenge students to infer why people with group AB blood are called universal acceptors, while people with group O blood are called universal donors. Ask: **What blood group do you think blood centers want the most?** *(Group O, because it has no antigens and it can be given to any blood group without causing an antibody reaction.)*

▶ **Figure 14–4** This table shows the relationship between genotype and phenotype for the ABO blood group. It also shows which blood types can safely be transfused into people with other blood types. **Applying Concepts** ***Why are there four different phenotypes, even though there are six different genotypes?***

Blood Groups

Phenotype (Blood Type)	Genotype	Antigen on Red Blood Cell	Safe Transfusions	
			To	From
A	I^AI^A or I^Ai	A	A, AB	A, O
B	I^BI^B or I^Bi	B	B, AB	B, O
AB	I^AI^B	A and B	AB	A, B, AB, O
O	ii	none	A, B, AB, O	O

Human Genes

The human genome—our complete set of genetic information—includes tens of thousands of genes. The DNA sequences on these genes determine many characteristics, from the color of your eyes to the detailed structures of proteins within your cells. The exploration of the human genome is now a major scientific undertaking. By 2000, the DNA sequence of the human genome was almost complete.

Until recently, the identification of a human gene took years of scientific work. Studying the genetics of our species is not easy. Humans have long generation times and a complex life cycle, and they produce, at least compared with peas and fruit flies, very few offspring. Still, in a few cases, biologists were able to identify genes that directly control a single human trait. Some of the very first human genes to be identified were those that control blood type.

Blood Group Genes Human blood comes in a variety of genetically determined blood groups. Knowing a person's blood group is critical because using the wrong type of blood for a transfusion during a medical procedure can be fatal. A number of genes are responsible for human blood groups, but the best known are the ABO blood groups and the Rh blood groups.

The Rh blood group is determined by a single gene with two alleles—positive and negative. *Rh* stands for "rhesus monkey," the animal in which this factor was discovered. The positive (Rh+) allele is dominant, so persons who are Rh+/Rh+ or Rh+/Rh- are said to be Rh-positive. Individuals with two Rh- alleles are Rh-negative.

The ABO blood group is more complicated. There are three alleles for this gene, I^A, I^B, and i. Alleles I^A and I^B are codominant. These alleles produce molecules known as antigens that can be recognized by the immune system on the surface of red blood cells. As **Figure 14–4** shows, individuals with alleles I^A and I^B produce both antigens, making them blood type AB. The i allele is recessive. Individuals with alleles I^AI^A or I^Ai produce only the A antigen, making them blood type A. Those with I^BI^B or I^Bi alleles are type B. Those who are homozygous for the i allele (ii) produce no antigen, and are said to have blood type O.

▼ **Figure 14–5** This medical worker is drawing blood from a patient. The blood will be tested to see what types of blood can safely be transfused into the patient. **Applying Concepts** ***Why is blood typing so important?***

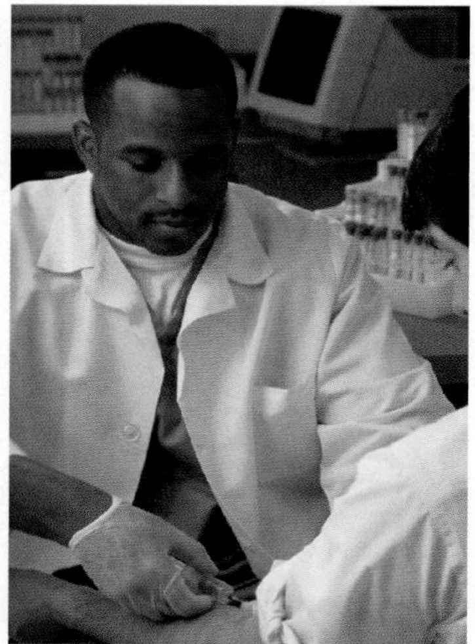

TEACHER TO TEACHER

I usually have students choose a human genetic mutation or disorder and research it. I encourage them to use the Internet, printed materials, or interviews. I ask them to learn about the genetics behind the condition, including the condition's pattern of inheritance and its frequency of occurrence in the population. Students must also learn about the specifics of the condition, such as its phenotype, any cures, treatments, or life-altering measures—diet, medications, exercise—to survive the condition. After students complete their research, I invite them to share their knowledge with the class in short presentations. This process seems to make the terminology and the genetics more understandable to students.

—Myron E. Blosser, Biology Teacher Harrisonburg High School, Harrisonburg, VA

When a medical worker refers to blood groups, he or she usually mentions both groups at the same time. For example, if a patient has AB-negative blood, it means the individual has I^A and I^B alleles from the ABO gene and the Rh- allele from the Rh gene.

Recessive Alleles Many human genes have become known through the study of genetic disorders. **Figure 14–6** lists some common genetic disorders. In most cases, the presence of a normal, functioning gene is revealed only when an abnormal or nonfunctioning allele affects the phenotype.

One of the first genetic disorders to be understood this way was phenylketonuria (fen-ul-ket-oh-NOOR-ee-uh), or PKU. People with PKU lack the enzyme that is needed to break down phenylalanine. Phenylalanine is an amino acid found in milk and many other foods. If a newborn has PKU, phenylalanine may build up in the tissues during the child's first years of life and cause severe mental retardation. Fortunately, newborns can be tested for PKU and then placed on a low-phenylalanine diet that prevents most of the effects of PKU. PKU is caused by a recessive allele carried on chromosome 12.

Many other disorders are also caused by autosomal recessive alleles. One is Tay-Sachs disease, which is caused by an allele found mostly in Jewish families of central and eastern European ancestry. Tay-Sachs disease results in nervous system breakdown and death in the first few years of life. Although there is no treatment for Tay-Sachs disease, there is a test for the allele. By taking this test, prospective parents can learn whether they are at risk of having a child with the disorder.

▼ **Figure 14–6** This table shows the major symptoms of some well-known genetic disorders. **Interpreting Graphics** *Which disorder causes galactose to accumulate in the tissues?*

Some Autosomal Disorders in Humans

Type of Disorder	Disorder	Major Symptoms
Disorders caused by recessive alleles	Albinism	Lack of pigment in skin, hair, and eyes
	Cystic fibrosis	Excess mucus in lungs, digestive tract, liver; increased susceptibility to infections; death in childhood unless treated
	Galactosemia	Accumulation of galactose (a sugar) in tissues; mental retardation; eye and liver damage
	Phenylketonuria (PKU)	Accumulation of phenylalanine in tissues; lack of normal skin pigment; mental retardation
	Tay-Sachs disease	Lipid accumulation in brain cells; mental deficiency; blindness; death in early childhood
Disorders caused by dominant alleles	Achondroplasia	Dwarfism (one form)
	Huntington's disease	Mental deterioration and uncontrollable movements; appears in middle age
	Hypercholesterolemia	Excess cholesterol in blood; heart disease
Disorders caused by codominant alleles	Sickle cell disease	Sickled red blood cells; damage to many tissues

Meet Diverse Needs

Students with limited English proficiency can organize the details for the genetic disorders described in this section by using colored index cards. Students should choose a separate color for each pattern of inheritance: recessive, dominant, and codominant. Instruct students to list the main characteristics of each disorder on a separate card. They may include notes in their native languages, if they wish. **Limited English proficiency**

Build Science Skills

Designing Experiments Challenge students to outline an experimental protocol that uses genetic engineering techniques to cure phenylketonuria. Encourage students to review the techniques in genetic engineering that they learned about in Chapter 13 and to apply those techniques to treating a human genetic disorder. Have students point out the steps in their protocol that will be especially difficult to carry out.

FACTS AND FIGURES

Achondroplasia

Achondroplasia is a type of dwarfism in which the affected person never reaches a height greater than 4 feet 4 inches tall. When long bones develop in an affected child, cartilage forms in such a way that the arms and legs end up being disproportionately short. About 1 in every 10,000 individuals is affected by achondroplasia.

Answers to . . .

Figure 14–4 *Because the allele for no antigens, i, is recessive to I^A and I^B.*

Figure 14–5 *Using the wrong type of blood for a transfusion could be fatal.*

Figure 14–6 *Galactosemia*

14–1 (continued)

Building Science Skills

Posing Questions Make sure students realize that the genetic disorders they are learning about were not always known to be inherited. Doctors were the first to try to treat and characterize these disorders, and it was through their observations that they identified these disorders as inheritable. Challenge students to imagine that they are doctors who have identified a disorder that has not been identified before. Instruct them to develop a list of questions that will help them determine whether the disorder is due to an inherited gene, an environmental factor such as poor nutrition, or infection by bacteria or viruses.

From Gene to Molecule

Use Visuals

Figure 14–9 Have students compare and contrast the shapes of the normal red blood cells and the sickle-shaped red blood cells. Discuss how the shape of the sickle cells affects their movement through capillaries. Ask: **Why don't the heterozygous individuals suffer from sickle cell disease?** *(They have normal-shaped red blood cells moving through their bodies.)*

Dominant Alleles Not all genetic disorders are caused by recessive alleles. You may recall that the effects of a dominant allele are expressed even when the recessive allele is present. Therefore, if you have a dominant allele for a genetic disorder, it will be expressed. Two examples of genetic disorders caused by autosomal dominant alleles are a form of dwarfism known as achondroplasia (ay-kahn-droh-PLAY-zhuh) and a nervous system disorder known as Huntington's disease. Huntington's disease causes a progressive loss of muscle control and mental function until death occurs. People who have this disease generally show no symptoms until they are in their thirties and forties, when the gradual damage to the nervous system begins.

Codominant Alleles Sickle cell disease, a serious disorder found in 1 in 500 African Americans, is caused by a codominant allele. As you will read, the reason for the high incidence of sickle cell in the United States is a story that links genetics, human history, and molecular biology.

✓CHECKPOINT *What type of allele causes Huntington's disease?*

From Gene to Molecule

How do the actual DNA sequences in genes affect phenotype so profoundly? What is the link between the DNA bases in the allele for a genetic disorder and the disorder itself? For many genetic disorders, scientists are still working to find the answer. But for two disorders, the connection is understood very well indeed. **In both cystic fibrosis and sickle cell disease, a small change in the DNA of a single gene affects the structure of a protein, causing a serious genetic disorder.**

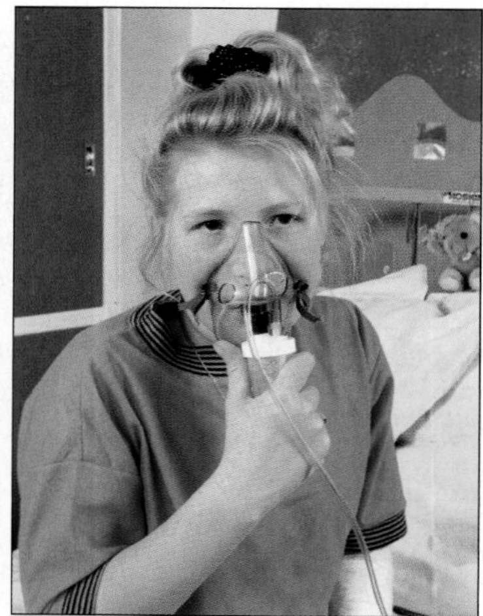

▲ **Figure 14–7** This girl is inhaling a fine mist through a nebulizer. The medication in the mist thins the mucus in the lungs, making breathing easier. **Inferring** *Why is it important for people with CF to thin the mucus in their lungs?*

Cystic Fibrosis Cystic fibrosis, or CF, is a common fatal genetic disease. Cystic fibrosis is most common among people whose ancestors came from Northern Europe. The disease is caused by a recessive allele on chromosome 7. Children with cystic fibrosis have serious digestive problems. In addition, they produce a thick, heavy mucus that clogs their lungs and breathing passageways. The disease takes a heavy toll. Only about half of the children born with cystic fibrosis survive into their 20s.

Cystic fibrosis involves a very small genetic change. Most cases of cystic fibrosis are caused by the deletion of 3 bases in the middle of a sequence for a protein, as shown in **Figure 14–8.** This protein normally allows chloride ions (Cl^-) to pass across biological membranes. The deletion of these 3 bases removes just one amino acid from this large protein, causing it to fold improperly. Because of this, the cells do not transport the protein to the cell membrane, and the misfolded protein is destroyed. Unable to transport chloride ions, tissues throughout the body malfunction. People with one normal copy of the allele are unaffected, because they can produce enough of the chloride channel protein to allow their tissues to function properly.

FACTS AND FIGURES

Founder effect and Huntington's disease
The frequency of Huntington's disease has been higher in South Africa than in any other part of the world. Researchers have discovered that all affected persons in South Africa were directly or indirectly descended from an adult male from the Netherlands who settled there in 1658.

This phenomenon of one or a few individuals with a genetic abnormality causing the establishment of a new population is known as the founder effect. The founder effect is most likely to occur in remote areas where the total population is relatively small.

▼ **Figure 14–8** **Cystic fibrosis is usually caused by the deletion of three bases in the DNA of a single gene.** As a result, the body does not produce normal CFTR, a protein needed to transport chloride ions. Cystic fibrosis causes serious digestive and respiratory problems.

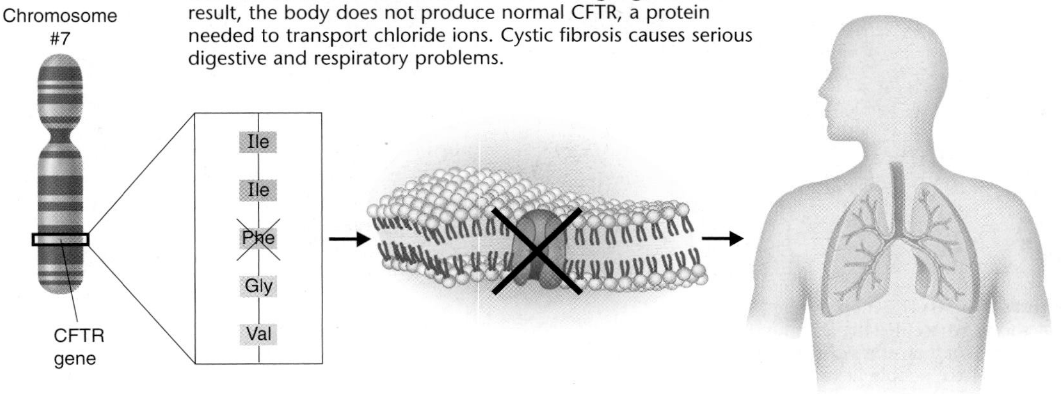

Chromosome #7

CFTR gene

Ile

Ile

Phe

Gly

Val

A The most common allele that causes cystic fibrosis is missing 3 DNA bases. As a result, the amino acid phenylalanine is missing from the CFTR protein.

B Normal CFTR is a chloride ion channel in cell membranes. Abnormal CFTR cannot be transported to the cell membrane.

C The cells in the person's airways are unable to transport chloride ions. As a result, the airways become clogged with a thick mucus.

Sickle Cell Disease Sickle cell disease is a common genetic disorder found in African Americans. Sickle cell disease is characterized by the bent and twisted shape of the red blood cells, like those shown in **Figure 14–9.** These sickle-shaped red blood cells are more rigid than normal cells and tend to get stuck in the capillaries, the narrowest blood vessels in the body. As a result, blood stops moving through these vessels, damaging cells and tissues beyond the blockage. Sickle cell disease produces physical weakness and damage to the brain, heart, and spleen. In some cases, it may be fatal.

Hemoglobin is the protein that carries oxygen in the blood. The normal allele for this gene differs very little from the sickle cell allele—just one DNA base is changed. This change inserts the amino acid valine in place of glutamic acid. As a result, the abnormal hemoglobin is somewhat less soluble than normal hemoglobin. Any decrease in blood oxygen levels causes many of the hemoglobin molecules to come out of solution and stick together. The stuck-together molecules form long chains and fibers that produce the characteristic shape of sickled cells.

Why do so many African Americans carry the sickle cell allele? Most African Americans can trace their ancestry to west central Africa. Malaria, a serious parasitic disease that infects red blood cells, is common in this region of Africa. People who are heterozygous for the sickle cell allele are generally healthy. In addition, they have the benefit of being resistant to malaria. The relationship between the incidence of malaria and the presence of the sickle cell allele is shown in **Figure 14–10** on the next page.

▼ **Figure 14–9** These red blood cells contain the abnormal hemoglobin characteristic of sickle cell disease. **Observing** *How is this cell different from a normal red blood cell?*

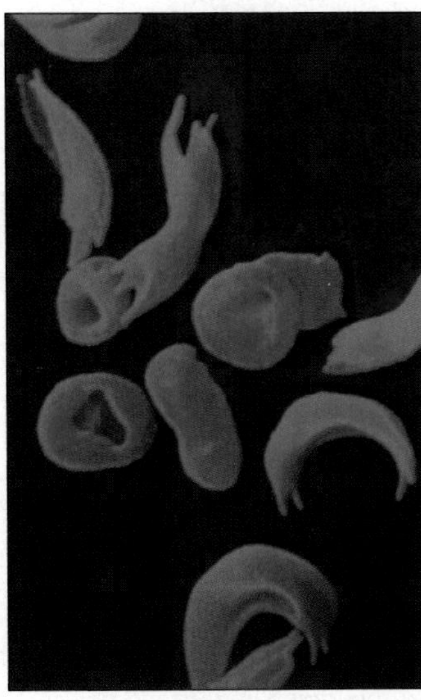

(magnification 1800×)

Meet Diverse Needs

Students who would like an extra challenge might be interested in learning more about sickle cell disease. Challenge them to learn the biochemistry of the disease, why the abnormal hemoglobin causes the blood cell to collapse, and why heterozygotes are resistant to malaria. Encourage students to summarize their findings on a poster and present it to the class. **Learning modality: verbal**

BIO INSIGHTS — FACTS AND FIGURES

Fetal hemoglobin and sickle cell disease
Hemoglobin F is the form of hemoglobin found only in developing fetuses. This form of hemoglobin is different from the adult form of hemoglobin and is not affected by the sickle cell mutation. Unfortunately, production of hemoglobin F is stopped a few months after the birth of a baby. Some scientists think that hemoglobin F could provide a key to better medical treatment for sickle cell patients.

Answers to . . .

CHECKPOINT *A dominant allele*

Figure 14–7 *Thinning the mucus makes it easier for people with CF to breathe.*

Figure 14–9 *The sickle cells have elongated, sickle shapes.*

Build Science Skills

Using Models Challenge student pairs to create a model that shows why an allele is dominant or recessive. Their model may be a diagram, a short skit with props, or three-dimensional structures. The models should show how the role of the gene's protein product and the action of the normal protein versus the mutant protein determine whether the mutant allele is dominant or recessive.

3 ASSESS

Evaluate Understanding

Quiz students about the pattern of inheritance of the human genetic traits described in the section. Give them sample genetic problems that they can solve with Punnett squares to predict probabilities of couples' having children with specific genotypes or phenotypes.

Reteach

Review the karyotype in Figure 14–1. Make sure students know the difference between autosomes and sex chromosomes and can identify them on the karyotype.

ALTERNATIVE ASSESSMENT

If students have a difficult time finding a family to use for their pedigree, you might allow them to fabricate one. Students should use the standard pedigree symbols used in this section in their pedigrees and include a key.

Use iText to review the key concepts in Section 14–1.

Answer to . . .

Figure 14–10 *The area where malaria is common is similar to the area where people have the sickle cell allele.*

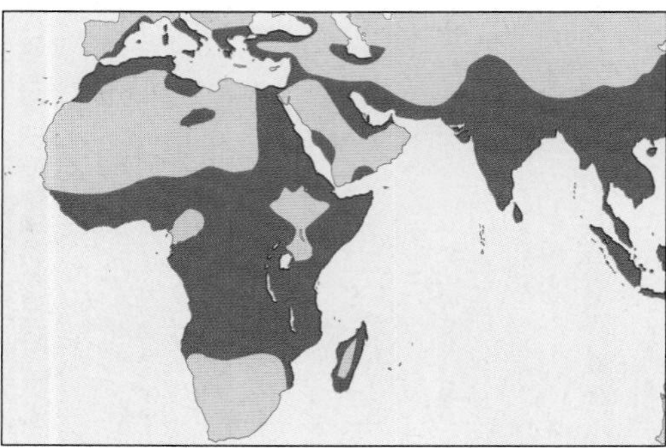

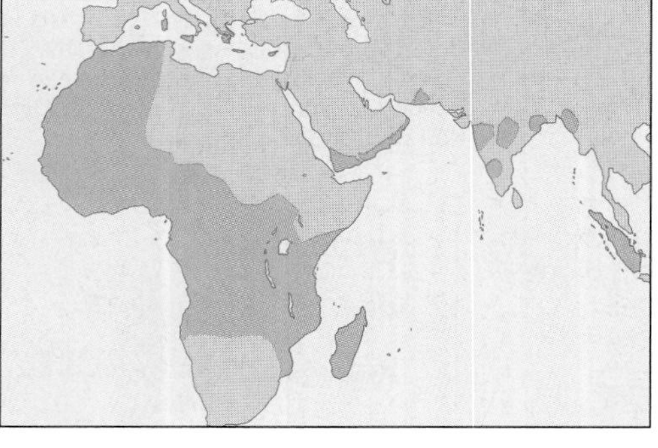

Figure 14–10 The map on the left shows where malaria is common. The map on the right shows regions where people have the sickle cell allele. **Interpreting Graphics** *What is the relationship between malaria and the sickle cell allele?*

Low oxygen levels cause some red blood cells to become sickle shaped. When the body destroys the sickled cells, it gets rid of the parasite at the same time. Because of this, in parts of the world such as west central Africa, where malaria is a major threat to health, the sickle cell allele is actually beneficial in heterozygous persons.

Dominant or Recessive? What makes an allele dominant, recessive, or codominant? CF and sickle cell disease show biologists that it all depends on the nature of a gene's protein product and its role in the cell. In the case of CF, just one copy of the normal allele can supply cells with enough chloride channel proteins to function. Because of this, the normal allele is considered dominant over the recessive CF allele.

The allele for normal hemoglobin was once also considered dominant over the sickle cell allele, but biologists now know that this situation is more complex. An individual with both normal and sickle cell alleles has a different phenotype—resistance to malaria—from someone with only normal alleles. Therefore, the sickle cell alleles are thought to be codominant because both alleles contribute to the phenotype.

14–1 Section Assessment

1. **Key Concept** What are sex chromosomes? What determines whether a person is male or female?
2. **Key Concept** Using an example, explain how a small change in a person's DNA can cause a genetic disorder.
3. How does studying genetic disorders such as PKU help biologists understand normal alleles?
4. What are some problems biologists face in studying human inheritance?
5. **Critical Thinking Predicting** If a woman with type O blood and a man with type AB blood have children, what are the children's possible genotypes?

iTEXT Assessment Use iText to review the important concepts in Section 14–1.

ALTERNATIVE ASSESSMENT

Drawing a Pedigree Choose a family and a trait that you can trace through three generations. For example, you might choose dimples in a celebrity's family. Find out who in the family has had the trait and who has not. Then, draw a pedigree to represent the family history of the trait.

14–1 Section Assessment

1. X and Y chromosomes; Females have two X chromosomes; males have one X and one Y chromosome.
2. In both cystic fibrosis and sickle cell disease, a small change in the DNA of a single gene affects the structure of a protein, causing a serious genetic disorder.
3. Many human genes have become known through the study of genetic disorders.
4. Humans have long generation times and a complex life cycle, and they produce few offspring.
5. $I^{A}i$ and $I^{B}i$

14–2 Human Chromosomes

A human diploid cell contains more than 6 billion nucleotide pairs of DNA—6 billion individual characters of the genetic code. To get an idea of how long a complete human DNA sequence actually is, consider the following: In this textbook, there are approximately 1500 letters on each page. If a complete human DNA sequence were to be written in the same-size type as this textbook, it would constitute a book more than 4 million pages long.

Despite its size, all of this information is neatly packed into the 46 chromosomes present in every diploid human cell. In its own way, each of these chromosomes is like a library containing hundreds or even thousands of books. Although biologists are many decades away from mastering the contents of those books, biology is now in the early stages of learning just how many books there are and what they deal with.

Guide for Reading

Key Concepts
- Why are sex-linked disorders more common in males than in females?
- What is nondisjunction, and what problems does it cause?

Vocabulary
sex-linked gene
nondisjunction

Reading Strategy: Outlining Before you read, use the headings of the section to make an outline about human chromosomes. As you read, write a sentence under each head to provide key information.

Human Genes and Chromosomes

Chromosomes 21 and 22 are the smallest human autosomes. Chromosome 22 contains approximately 43 million DNA bases. Chromosome 21 contains roughly 32 million bases. These chromosomes were the first two human chromosomes whose sequences were determined. Their structural features seem to be representative of other human chromosomes.

Chromosome 22 contains as many as 545 different genes, some of which are very important for health. Genetic disorders on chromosome 22 include an allele that causes a form of leukemia and another associated with neurofibromatosis, a tumor-causing disease of the nervous system. However, chromosome 22 also contains long stretches of repetitive DNA that do not code for proteins. These long stretches of repetitive DNA are unstable sites where rearrangements occur.

The structure of chromosome 21 is similar. It contains about 225 genes, including one associated with amyotrophic lateral sclerosis (ALS), also known as Lou Gehrig's disease. Chromosome 21 also has many regions with no genes at all.

As exploration of the larger human chromosomes continues, molecular biologists may gradually learn more about how the arrangements of genes on chromosomes affect gene expression and development.

As you may recall, genes located on the same chromosome are linked, meaning that they tend to be inherited together. This is also true for human genes, so each human chromosome represents a distinct linkage group. You also read earlier that linked genes may be separated by recombination during meiosis; this applies to human chromosomes, as well.

▲ **Figure 14–11** Lou Gehrig died at age 37 of ALS. ALS causes a progressive loss of muscle control due to the destruction of nerves in the brain and spinal cord.

SECTION RESOURCES

Print:
- ***Teaching Resources,*** Section Review 14–2
- ***Guided Reading and Study Workbook,*** Section 14–2
- ***Issues and Decision Making,*** 7
- ***Biotechnology Manual,*** Labs 2, 11, 12; Concepts 2, 3, 4, 6

Technology:
- ***BioDetectives Videotape,*** "Coming Home: A Nation's Pledge"
- ***iText,*** Section 14–2

Section 14–2

1 FOCUS

Objectives

14.2.1 ***Identify*** characteristics of human chromosomes.
14.2.2 ***Describe*** some sex-linked disorders and explain why they are more common in males than in females.
14.2.3 ***Explain*** the process of X-chromosome inactivation.
14.2.4 ***Summarize*** nondisjunction and the problems it causes.

Guide for Reading

Vocabulary Preview

Write the word *nondisjunction* on the board. Challenge students to identify the prefixes in the word. Ask: **What does *junction* mean?** *(Joining together)* Add the suffix *dis-*, and ask: **What does *disjunction* mean?** *(The act of separating)* Finally, challenge students to infer the meaning of *nondisjunction. (The act of not separating)*

Reading Strategy

Encourage students to add the green subheadings to their outlines and write a sentence under each. Remind students to include information in their outlines that is presented in figure captions.

2 INSTRUCT

Human Genes and Chromosomes

Use Visuals

Figure 14–12 As students study the chromosomes in the figure, explain that the banding pattern does not mark the location of specific genes but echoes the chromosome banding pattern when certain stains are added to condensed chromosomes. Students can observe this banding pattern on the chromosomes in the karyotype in Figure 14–1.

Sex-Linked Genes

Use Visuals

Figure 14–13 Discuss the symbols used in the Punnett square and relate them to pedigree. Ask: **Why is the circle for the mother shaded only halfway?** *(She is heterozygous for the trait and is a carrier.)* **Would you expect the colorblind son to have sons who are colorblind?** *(No, the son can pass only the Y chromosome to his sons.)* **What is the probability that the daughter who is a carrier will have a colorblind son if she marries a man with normal vision?** *(25%)*

Build Science Skills

Using Models Challenge student pairs to design a pedigree that traces the inheritance of colorblindness in a family over several generations. Students can invent the family and the affected individuals. Then, students should write three questions about their pedigree and the inheritance of colorblindness. Have groups exchange pedigrees and answer the questions.

Address Misconceptions

Students might think that colorblind people see the world only in black and white. Show students charts used to diagnose colorblindness. Explain that a colorblind person either cannot see the object in the pattern or might see a different object. Help students realize that people who are red-green colorblind do see objects as blue or yellow or shades of red; they cannot see objects as green.

X Chromosome

Duchenne muscular dystrophy

Melanoma

X-inactivation center

X-linked severe combined immunodeficiency (SCID)

Colorblindness

Hemophilia

Y Chromosome

Testis-determining factor

▲ **Figure 14–12** Genes on X and Y chromosomes are called sex-linked genes. **Interpreting Graphics** ***Which chromosome carries more genes?***

Sex-Linked Genes

Is there a special pattern of inheritance for genes located on the X chromosome or the Y chromosome? The answer is yes. Because these chromosomes determine sex, genes located on them are said to be **sex-linked genes.** Many sex-linked genes are found on the X chromosome, as shown in **Figure 14–12.** More than 100 sex-linked genetic disorders have now been mapped to the X chromosome. The human Y chromosome is much smaller than the X chromosome and appears to contain only a few genes.

Colorblindness Three human genes associated with color vision are located on the X chromosome. In males, a defective version of any one of these genes produces colorblindness, an inability to distinguish certain colors. The most common form of this disorder, red-green colorblindness, is found in about 1 in 10 males in the United States. Among females, however, colorblindness is rare—only about 1 female in 100 has colorblindness. Why the difference?

Males have just one X chromosome. Thus, all X-linked alleles are expressed in males, even if they are recessive. In order for a recessive allele, such as the one for colorblindness, to be expressed in females, there must be two copies of the allele, one on each of the two X chromosomes. This means that the recessive phenotype of a sex-linked genetic disorder tends to be much more common among males than among females. In addition, because men pass their X chromosomes along to their daughters, sex-linked genes move from fathers to their daughters and may then show up in the sons of those daughters, as shown in **Figure 14–13.**

Figure 14–13 **X-linked alleles are always expressed in males, because males have only one X chromosome.** Males who receive the recessive X^c allele all have colorblindness. Females, however, will have colorblindness only if they receive two X^c alleles.

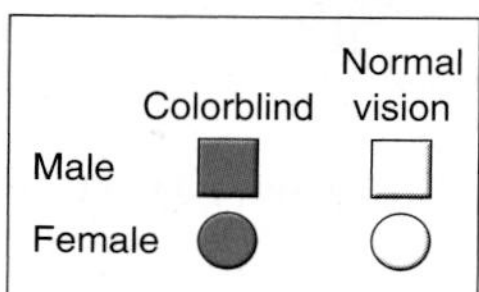

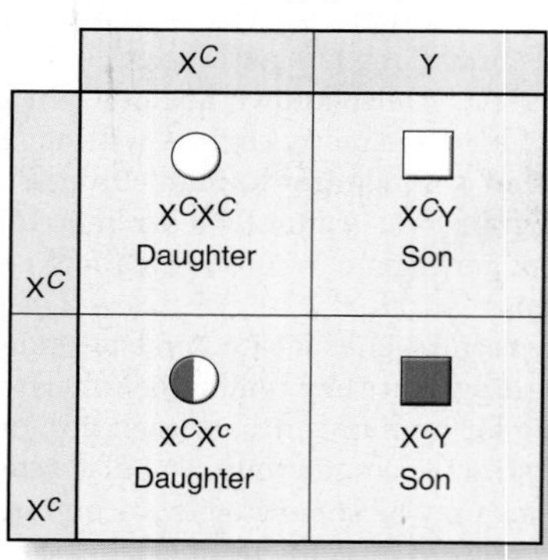

PRESENTATIONS MADE EASY!

The Presentation Assistant Plus contains the Prentice Hall Presentation Pro and the Transparencies, which provide easy-to-follow visual support for every step of this section. If you have a computer presentation station, use Prentice Hall Presentation Pro for Section 14–2, or use the transparencies listed here.

Section 14–2: **Interest Grabber**
Section Outline
Nondisjunction
Figure 14–13

Quick Lab

How is colorblindness transmitted?

Materials 2 plastic cups, 3 white beans, black marker, red bean

Procedure

1. On a sheet of paper, draw a data table with the column headings "Trial," "Colors," "Sex of Individual," and "Number of X-Linked Alleles." Draw 10 rows under the headings and fill in the numbers 1 through 10 under "Trial." Use the marker to label one cup "father" and the other "mother."
2. The white beans represent X chromosomes. Use the marker to mark a dot on 1 white bean to represent the X-linked allele for colorblindness. Place this bean, plus 1 unmarked white bean, into the cup labeled "mother."
3. Mark a black dot on 1 more white bean. Place this bean, plus 1 red bean, into the cup labeled "father." The red bean represents a Y chromosome.
4. Close your eyes and pick one bean from each cup to represent how each parent contributes a sex chromosome to a fertilized egg.
5. In your data table, record the color of each bean and the sex of an individual who would carry this pair of sex chromosomes. Also record how many X-linked alleles the individual has. Put the beans back in the cups they came from.
6. Determine whether the individual would have colorblindness.
7. Repeat steps 4 to 6 for a total of 10 pairs of beans.

Analyze and Conclude

1. **Using Models** Why did you select one bean from each cup?
2. **Drawing Conclusions** How do the sex chromosomes keep the numbers of males and females roughly equal?
3. **Calculating** Share your data with your classmates. Calculate the class totals for each table column. How many females were colorblind? How many males? How would you explain these results?

Hemophilia Hemophilia is another example of a sex-linked disorder. Two important genes carried on the X chromosome help control blood clotting. A recessive allele in either of these two genes may produce a disorder called hemophilia (hee-moh-FIL-ee-uh). In hemophilia, a protein necessary for normal blood clotting is missing. About 1 in 10,000 males is born with a form of hemophilia. People with hemophilia can bleed to death from minor cuts and may suffer internal bleeding from bumps or bruises. Fortunately, hemophilia can be treated by injections of normal clotting proteins.

Duchenne Muscular Dystrophy Duchenne muscular dystrophy (DIS-truh-fee) is a sex-linked disorder that results in the progressive weakening and loss of skeletal muscle. People with Duchenne muscular dystrophy rarely live past early adulthood. In the United States, one out of every 3000 males is born with Duchenne muscular dystrophy. Duchenne muscular dystrophy is caused by a defective version of the gene that codes for a muscle protein. Researchers in many laboratories are trying to find a way to treat or cure this disorder, possibly by inserting a normal allele into the muscle cells of Duchenne muscular dystrophy patients.

What causes Duchenne muscular dystrophy?

BIO INSIGHTS — FACTS AND FIGURES

Hemophilia and royalty
The frequency of hemophilia was much higher among the royal families of nineteenth-century Europe than among the general population. This was probably due to the fact that these families often intermarried. Queen Victoria of England was a carrier of the disease, as were two of her daughters. At one time, it was calculated that of Victoria's 69 descendants, 18 were either affected males or female carriers.

Quick Lab

Objective Students will be able to model how colorblindness is transmitted.

Skills Focus **Using Models**

Materials 2 plastic cups, 3 white beans, black marker, red bean

Time 20 minutes

Strategies

- After students read the procedure, ask: **Is either parent colorblind?** *(Yes, the father)* **Is the mother heterozygous or homozygous for colorblindness?** *(Heterozygous)* **Is she a carrier?** *(Yes, she has one allele for colorblindness)*
- Remind students to keep their eyes closed while picking the beans so that they choose randomly.

Expected Outcomes Students will conclude that colorblindness occurs more frequently in males because they have only one copy of the X chromosome.

Analyze and Conclude

1. Each parent contributes one chromosome to its offspring.

2. There is a 50 : 50 chance that a child will receive an X or Y chromosome from the father.

3. About 50% of the females will be colorblind and about 50% of the males will be colorblind. The mother is heterozygous, so her sons have a 50% chance of inheriting the X chromosome that carries the allele for colorblindness. The father is colorblind, so the daughters have a 50% chance of inheriting X chromosomes from both parents that carry the allele for colorblindness.

Answers to . . .

CHECKPOINT *A defective gene that codes for a muscle protein*

Figure 14–12 *The X chromosome*

14–2 (continued)

X-Chromosome Inactivation

Build Science Skills

Observing Set up microscope stations with slides of animal body cells that have Barr bodies. Encourage students to draw their observations, labeling the cell cytoplasm, nucleus, nucleoplasm, chromosomes, and Barr bodies. Then, give students two unknown slides and challenge them to identify which slide came from a female.

Chromosomal Disorders

Use Visuals

Figure 14–15 Ask: **What phase of meiosis is illustrated by the first cell?** *(Metaphase I)* If necessary, review meiosis so that students remember that in meiosis I, homologous chromosomes separate to produce a haploid cell and that in meiosis II, chromosome copies (or sister chromatids) separate. Ask: **What types of gametes are produced when nondisjunction occurs?** *(Gametes that have two copies of the chromosome and gametes with no copies of it)*

▲ **Figure 14–14** This cat's fur color is controlled by a gene on the X chromosome. **Drawing Conclusions** *Is the cat shown a male or a female?*

X-Chromosome Inactivation

Females have two X chromosomes, but males have only one. If just one X chromosome is enough for cells in males, how does the cell "adjust" to the extra X chromosome in female cells? The answer was discovered by the British geneticist Mary Lyon. In female cells, one X chromosome is randomly switched off. That turned-off chromosome forms a dense region in the nucleus known as a Barr body. Barr bodies are generally not found in males because their single X chromosome is still active.

The same process happens in other mammals. In cats, for example, a gene that controls the color of coat spots is located on the X chromosome. One X chromosome may have an allele for orange spots and the other may have an allele for black spots. In cells in some parts of the body, one X chromosome is switched off. In other parts of the body, the other X chromosome is switched off. As a result, the cat's fur will have a mixture of orange and black spots, as shown in **Figure 14–14.** Male cats, which have just one X chromosome, can have spots of only one color. By the way, this is one way to tell the sex of a cat. If the cat's fur has three colors—white with orange and black spots, for example—you can almost be certain that it is female.

▼ **Figure 14–15** **Nondisjunction causes gametes to have abnormal numbers of chromosomes.** The result of nondisjunction may be a chromosome disorder such as Down syndrome.

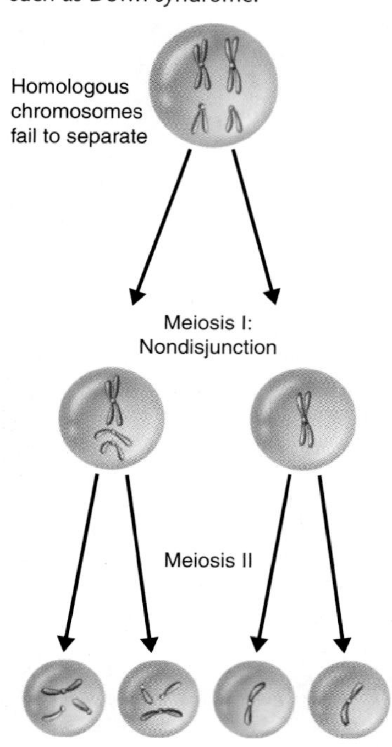

Chromosomal Disorders

Most of the time, the mechanisms that separate human chromosomes in meiosis work very well, but every now and then something goes wrong. The most common error in meiosis occurs when homologous chromosomes fail to separate. This is known as **nondisjunction,** which means "not coming apart." Nondisjunction is illustrated in **Figure 14–15.** **If nondisjunction occurs, abnormal numbers of chromosomes may find their way into gametes, and a disorder of chromosome numbers may result.**

Down Syndrome If two copies of an autosomal chromosome fail to separate during meiosis, an individual may be born with three copies of a chromosome. This is known as a trisomy, meaning "three bodies." The most common form of trisomy involves three copies of chromosome 21 and is called Down syndrome. **Figure 14–16** shows a karyotype of a person with Down syndrome. In the United States, approximately 1 baby in 800 is born with Down syndrome. Down syndrome produces mild to severe mental retardation. It is also characterized by an increased susceptibility to many diseases and a higher frequency of some birth defects.

Why should an extra copy of one chromosome cause so much trouble? That is still not clear, and it is one of the reasons scientists have worked so hard to learn the DNA sequence for chromosome 21. Now that researchers know all of the genes on the chromosome, they can begin experiments to find the exact genes that cause problems when present in three copies.

BIO INSIGHTS HISTORY OF SCIENCE

Barr bodies

Barr bodies were named for Murray Barr, who first observed them in the nerve cells of female cats in 1949. It was not until the early 1960s that Mary Lyon proposed that one X chromosome is randomly inactivated. In body cells, she observed that one X chromosome replicated later than the other. The late-replicating X chromosome is inactivated when the embryo implants in the uterine wall. All body cells have the same inactivated X chromosome as the embryonic cell from which they were derived.

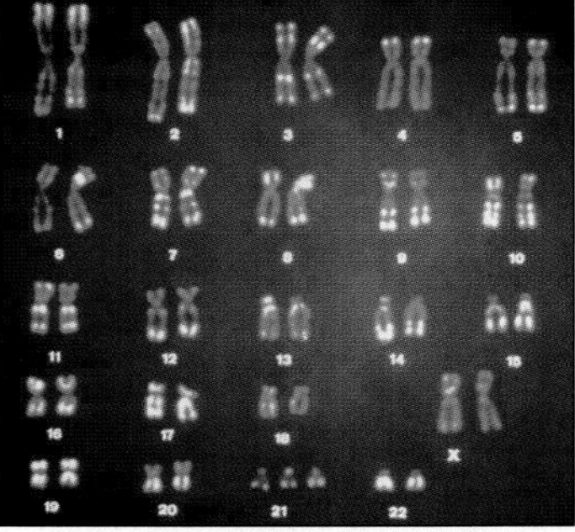

Figure 14–16 The karyotype on the right is from a person with Down syndrome. Down syndrome causes mental retardation and various physical problems. People with Down syndrome can, however, lead active, happy lives. **Observing** ***What is different in this karyotype as compared with the karyotype on page 341?***

Sex Chromosome Disorders Disorders also occur among the sex chromosomes. Two of these abnormalities are Turner's syndrome and Klinefelter's syndrome.

In females, nondisjunction can lead to Turner's syndrome. A female with Turner's syndrome inherits only one X chromosome (genotype XO). Women with Turner's syndrome are sterile because their sex organs do not develop at puberty.

In males, nondisjunction causes Klinefelter's syndrome (genotype XXY). The extra X chromosome interferes with meiosis and usually prevents these individuals from reproducing. Cases of Klinefelter's syndrome have been found in which individuals were XXXY or XXXXY. There have been no reported instances of babies being born without an X chromosome, indicating that the X chromosome contains genes that are vital for normal development.

These sex chromosome abnormalities point out the role of the Y chromosome in sex determination. The Y chromosome contains a sex-determining region that is necessary to produce male sexual development, even in combination with several X chromosomes. However, if this region of the Y chromosome is absent, the embryo develops as a female.

14–2 Section Assessment

1. **Key Concept** Why are sex-linked disorders more common in males than in females?
2. **Key Concept** How does nondisjunction cause chromosome number disorders?
3. List at least two examples of human sex-linked disorders.
4. Describe two sex chromosome disorders.
5. **Critical Thinking Comparing and Contrasting** Distinguish between sex-linked disorders and sex chromosome disorders.

iTEXT **Assessment** Use iText to review the important concepts in Section 14–2.

ALTERNATIVE ASSESSMENT

Animating Nondisjunction
Make a flip book to animate nondisjunction during meiosis. First, make a series of 6 to 10 drawings that gradually show the process of nondisjunction. Then, put the process in motion by flipping the pages with your thumb.

Meet Diverse Needs

Have students who need to review meiosis and nondisjunction draw diagrams to show how Turner's syndrome or Klinefelter's syndrome can occur. Make sure students realize that nondisjunction occurs during the formation of the egg cell or sperm cell. You might also have students draw Punnett squares to show the possible genotypes produced in a cross between a normal sex cell and a cell in which nondisjunction has occurred. **Learning modality: visual**

3 ASSESS

Evaluate Understanding

Have students construct a concept map that summarizes the concepts described in this section. Students should include the Vocabulary terms and Key Concepts in the map.

Reteach

Have students use Punnett squares to model how sex-linked traits are transmitted from parents to offspring. Challenge students to show how a dominant sex-linked allele has a different pattern of inheritance from a recessive sex-linked allele.

ALTERNATIVE ASSESSMENT

Provide students with card stock, or index cards without lines. Students should draw a minimum of six drawings that show incrementally the failure of one pair of homologous chromosomes to separate (anaphase I) or the failure of one pair of chromatids to separate (anaphase II).

Use iText to review the key concepts in Section 14–2.

14–2 Section Assessment

1. Males have just one X chromosome. Thus, all X-linked alleles are expressed in males, even if they are recessive.
2. Chromosomes fail to separate, causing gametes to have abnormal numbers of chromosomes.
3. Answers include colorblindness, hemophilia, and Duchenne muscular dystrophy.
4. A female with Turner's syndrome has only one X chromosome and is sterile. A male with Klinefelter's syndrome has one or more extra X chromosomes and is usually sterile.
5. Sex-linked disorders are caused by alleles of genes carried on either the X or Y chromosome. Sex chromosome disorders are caused by nondisjunction, or sex chromosomes failing to separate correctly during meiosis.

Answers to . . .

Figure 14–14 *The cat is female.*

Figure 14–16 *It has three copies of chromosome 21.*

Encourage one group of students to learn what companies or agencies are interested in knowing about an individual's DNA. Students should find out what the motives of these agencies and companies are. Have another group of students learn about medical records and who has access to that information. A third group of students can research how DNA information has allegedly been used to discriminate against individuals. Have each group present its findings to the class. Then, have a class discussion about the pros and cons of keeping DNA information private.

You Decide

1. The issues are whether individuals have the right to control their DNA and what are legitimate uses for DNA samples.
2. Accept all reasonable answers. Justified: Employers use DNA information as a record of employees' identity, as in the case of the military. Withhold: Individuals are concerned that DNA information could be used against them, causing them to lose promotions or even their jobs.
3. Students will have different opinions, but all opinions should include reasonable explanations.
4. Some students might think the insurance company has a right to test for cystic fibrosis so that it can decide not to insure a family carrying the allele to prevent a profit loss. Others might think the insurance company does not have the right to test for the cystic fibrosis allele, because DNA information is private and should not be used to discriminate against an individual.

Who Controls Your DNA?

April 16. Cpl. John C. Mayfield and Cpl. Joseph Vlacovsky were found guilty of disobeying a lawful order. The U.S. Department of Defense requires DNA samples for a database that could be used to identify soldiers' remains. The two Marines refused.

At their court martial, the two Marines argued that DNA samples could be examined for genes related to disease or even behavior and, therefore, the database was an invasion of privacy. As a result of the concerns raised by this case, the U.S. Department of Defense has changed its policies. It now destroys DNA samples upon request when an individual leaves military service. Do people have a right to control their own DNA samples?

The Viewpoints

DNA Information Is Not Private

As the court recognized, the U.S. Department of Defense had good reasons for requiring that DNA samples be taken and stored. Furthermore, DNA sequences are no more private and personal than fingerprints or photographs, which are taken by private and government agencies all the time. An employer has a right to take and keep such information. Individuals should have no reason to fear the abuse of such databases.

DNA Information Is Private and Personal

The use of DNA for personal identification by the military may be justified. An individual's genetic information, however, is a private matter. A recent study at Harvard and Stanford universities turned up more than 200 cases of discrimination because of genes individuals carried or were suspected of carrying. Employers with DNA information might use it to discriminate against workers who carry genes they suspect might cause medical or behavioral problems. Individuals must have the right to control their own DNA and to withhold samples from such databases.

You Decide

1. **Defining the Issue** What are the major issues regarding DNA databases?
2. **Analyzing the Viewpoints** Are there any circumstances in which an employer might be justified in demanding DNA samples from its employees? Why might an employee wish to withhold such samples?
3. **Forming Your Opinion** Should the control of DNA databases be a matter of law, or should it be a matter to be negotiated between people, their employers, and insurance companies?
4. **Persuasive Speaking** Suppose you were a doctor working as a consultant to a health insurance company. The insurance company is trying to decide whether to test adults for cystic fibrosis alleles before agreeing to insure their families. What advice would you give to the company about this?

To find out about military uses of DNA, view the videotape "Coming Home: A Nation's Pledge."

Encourage students to view "Coming Home: A Nation's Pledge" on the BioDetectives Videotape.

14–3 Human Molecular Genetics

Watson and Crick took the first step in making genetics a molecular science when they discovered the double-helical structure of DNA in 1953. Today, the transformation they started is complete. The exploration of human genes is now a major scientific undertaking. Biologists can now read, analyze, and even change the molecular code of genes.

Human DNA Analysis

The roughly 6 billion base pairs you carry in your DNA are a bit like an encyclopedia with thousands of volumes. In principle, biologists would like to know everything the volumes contain, but as a practical matter there isn't enough time to read all of them. Nonetheless, if you've used an encyclopedia you've already learned one of the ways to handle huge amounts of information—you find a way to look up only what you need. In an encyclopedia, you can use an index or an alphabetical list of articles, but in the genome, biologists have to use a different technique. As you might suspect, biologists search the volumes of the human genome using DNA sequences.

Testing for Alleles If two prospective parents suspect they might be carrying recessive alleles for a genetic disorder such as cystic fibrosis (CF) or Tay-Sachs disease, how could they find out for sure? Because the Tay-Sachs and CF alleles have slightly different DNA sequences from their normal counterparts, a variety of genetic tests have been developed that can spot those differences. Sometimes these genetic tests use labeled DNA probes to detect specific sequences found in disease-causing alleles. Some tests use other techniques to detect alleles, including looking at changes in restriction enzyme cutting sites and differences in the lengths of normal and abnormal alleles.

Genetic tests are now available for hundreds of disorders, making it possible to determine whether prospective parents risk passing such alleles to their children. In an increasing number of such cases, DNA testing can pinpoint the exact genetic basis of a disorder, making it possible to develop more effective therapy and treatment for individuals affected by genetic disease.

Guide for Reading

Key Concepts
- What is the goal of the Human Genome Project?
- What is gene therapy?

Vocabulary
DNA fingerprinting

Reading Strategy: Finding Main Ideas As you read, find evidence to support the following statement: The influence of human molecular genetics on society is growing rapidly.

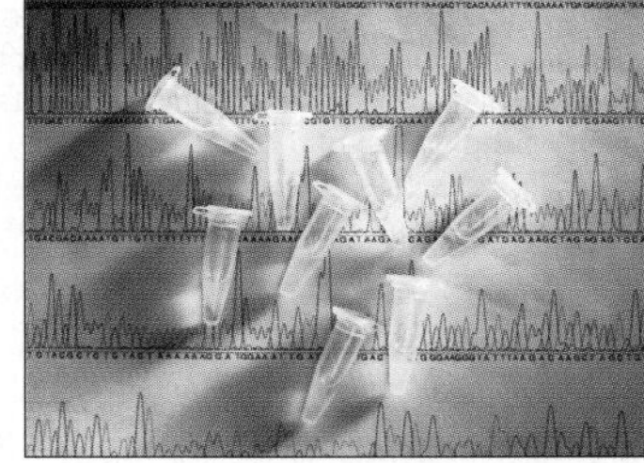

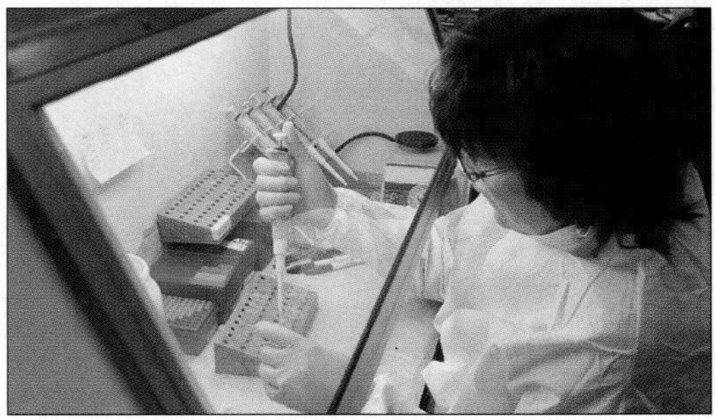

▶ **Figure 14–17** This laboratory worker is preparing a report on DNA evidence. The inset shows vials of DNA lying on a printout of a DNA analysis chart.

SECTION RESOURCES

Print:
- ***Teaching Resources,*** Section Review 14–3, Chapter 14 Real-World Lab
- ***Guided Reading and Study Workbook,*** Section 14–3
- ***Issues and Decision Making,*** Issues and Decisions 9, 10, 11, 12

Technology:
- ***iText,*** Section 14–3

Section 14–3

1 FOCUS

Objectives

14.3.1 ***Summarize*** methods of human DNA analysis.
14.3.2 ***State*** the goal of the Human Genome Project.
14.3.3 ***Describe*** how researchers are attempting to cure genetic disorders.

Guide for Reading

Vocabulary Preview

Invite student volunteers to describe what a fingerprint is and what it is used for. Then, challenge them to make inferences about what DNA fingerprinting is. List the inferences on the board, and narrow them down to two or three. Revisit this list throughout the section, if necessary, until the class correctly defines the term.

Reading Strategy

Instruct students to write the statement from the text onto a sheet of paper. As they read, students should list under the statement the evidence that supports it.

2 INSTRUCT

Human DNA Analysis

Build Science Skills

Designing Experiments Challenge students to write the steps in a protocol in which they test for the allele of a gene that causes a genetic disorder using restriction enzymes and gel electrophoresis. Students who need an extra challenge can list the steps to testing for alleles using a labeled DNA probe. Encourage students to use what they learned in Chapter 13. They might also wish to use the Internet to find additional resources.

14–3 (continued)

Use Visuals

Figure 14–18 Go over the steps in the procedure used in DNA fingerprinting. Have volunteers describe what occurs in each step. Make sure all students understand which DNA sequences are being targeted and how restriction enzymes are used to find similarities and differences between DNA samples. Ask: **Why is DNA fingerprinting more accurate if the samples are cut with more than one restriction enzyme?** *(There is a greater chance of finding differences in the sequences, which translates to restriction fragments of varying sizes.)*

Use Community Resources

Invite a forensic expert to the class to describe how DNA evidence is used in criminal cases. Suggest that the expert describe how DNA evidence is collected at the crime scene and how it is manipulated in the laboratory. Before the expert visits the class, have students brainstorm questions to ask the expert. Encourage students to ask their questions during the expert's presentation.

Figure 14–18 DNA fingerprinting can be used to determine whether blood, sperm, or other material left at a crime scene matches DNA from a suspect. **Interpreting Graphics** ***In the DNA fingerprint below, does the DNA fingerprint from the evidence (E) match suspect 1 (S1) or suspect 2 (S2)?***

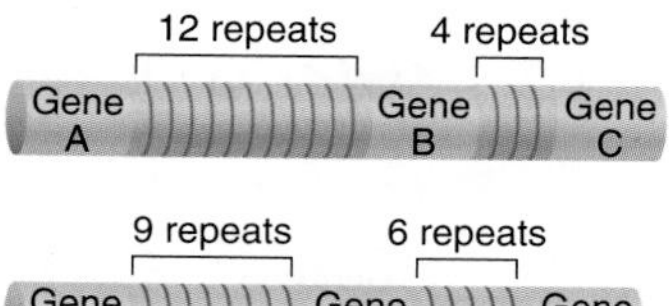

A Chromosomes contain large amounts of DNA called repeats that do not code for proteins. This DNA varies from person to person. Here, one sample has 12 repeats between genes A and B, while the second sample has 9 repeats.

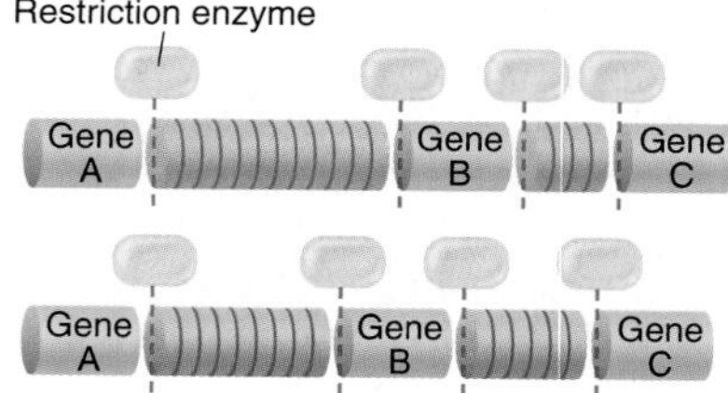

B Restriction enzymes are used to cut the DNA into fragments containing genes and repeats. Note that the repeat fragments from these two samples are of different lengths.

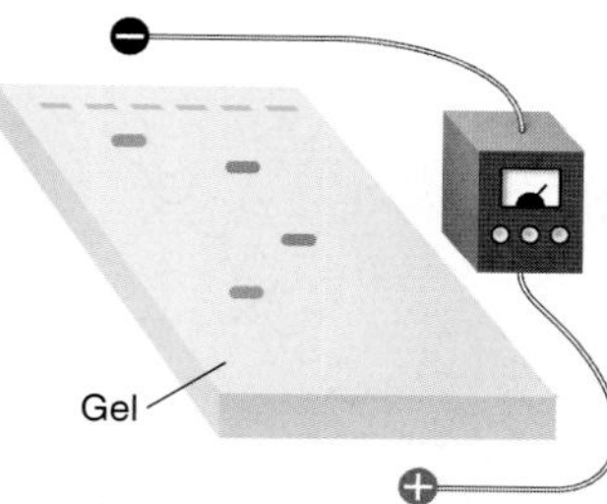

C The DNA fragments are separated according to size using gel electrophoresis. The fragments containing repeats are then labeled using radioactive probes. This produces a series of bands—the DNA fingerprint.

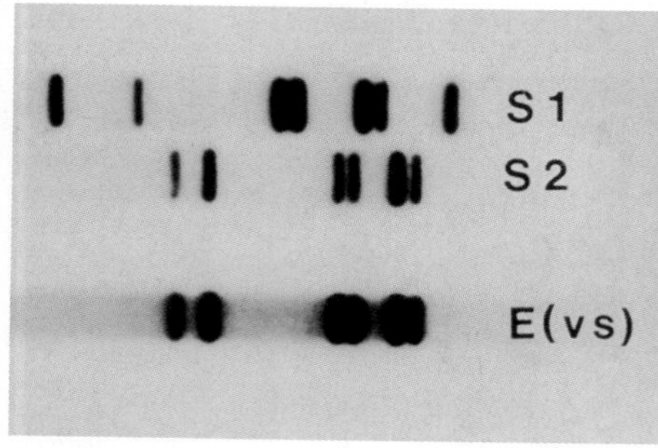

DNA fingerprint

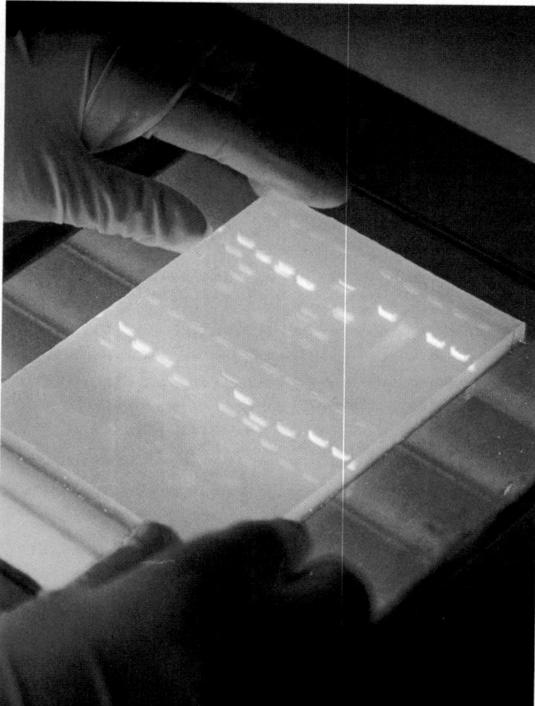

Gel electrophoresis

TIME SAVER **PRESENTATIONS MADE EASY!**

The Presentation Assistant Plus contains the Prentice Hall Presentation Pro and the Transparencies, which provide easy-to-follow visual support for every step of this section. If you have a computer presentation station, use Prentice Hall Presentation Pro for Section 14–3, or use the transparencies listed here.

Section 14–3:

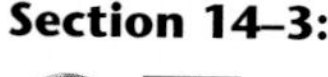

Interest Grabber
Section Outline
Locating Genes
Figure 14–18
Figure 14–21

DNA Fingerprinting The great complexity of the human genome ensures that no individual is exactly like any other. Molecular biology has used this biological fact to add a powerful new tool called **DNA fingerprinting** to the identification of individuals. Unlike other forms of testing, DNA fingerprinting does not analyze the cell's most important genes, which are largely identical among most people. Rather, DNA fingerprinting analyzes sections of DNA that have little or no known function but vary widely from one individual to another.

Figure 14–18 shows how DNA fingerprinting works. A small sample of human DNA is cut with a restriction enzyme. The resulting fragments are separated by size using gel electrophoresis. Fragments containing these highly variable regions are then detected with a DNA probe, revealing a series of DNA bands of various sizes. If enough combinations of restriction enzymes and probes are used, a pattern of bands is produced that can be distinguished statistically from the pattern of any other individual in the world, except, of course, for an identical twin. DNA samples can be obtained from blood, sperm, and even hair strands with small pieces of tissue at the base.

DNA fingerprinting has been used in the United States since the late 1980s. The reliability of DNA evidence has helped convict criminals as well as overturn many convictions. The precision that molecular biology brings to the justice system is good news not only for those who are victims of crime but also for those who have been wrongly convicted.

KEEP CURRENT WITH . . . SCIENCE NEWS®

To find out more about the topics in this chapter, go to: **www.phschool.com**

The Human Genome Project

Advances in DNA sequencing technologies at the close of the twentieth century made it possible, for the first time, to sequence entire genomes. At first, biologists worked on relatively small genomes, such as those of viruses and bacteria. The DNA sequence of the common bacterium *Escherichia coli,* which was determined in 1996, contains "only" 4,639,221 base pairs, making it just about as long as this textbook if it were printed on paper in a readable typeface. The genomes of even the simplest eukaryotic organisms are much larger, and the human genome is more than a thousand times as large.

Despite the problem of size, in 1990, scientists in the United States and other countries began the Human Genome Project. **The Human Genome Project is an attempt to sequence all human DNA.** Along the way, investigators completed the genomes of several other organisms, including yeast, a single-celled eukaryote, and *Drosophila melanogaster*—the fruit fly. In June 2000, scientists announced that the DNA sequence of the human genome was essentially complete.

▲ **Figure 14–19** **The Human Genome Project is an attempt to sequence all human DNA.** Dr. Francis Collins and Dr. Craig Venter, who headed the public and private portions of the project, jointly announced the essential completion of the human genome sequence.

The Human Genome Project

SCIENCE NEWS®

Encourage students to visit **www.phschool.com** for the most current information on this topic.

Demonstration

Demonstrate to students how sequencing the human genome was much like putting together a puzzle or solving a word puzzle. Copy on the board the X chromosome and its genes from Figure 14–12 on page 350. Make up short sequences of DNA on the board and assign them to various places on the X chromosome. Explain that these sequences are the "markers" sequenced by government scientists. Then, demonstrate the "shotgun" sequencing method by cutting up into very short pieces a length of yarn that represents the X chromosome. Choose four or five of these short yarn pieces, and give each a DNA sequence. Write the sequences on the board. Set it up so that students can determine where the DNA segments from the yarn fragments are located on the X chromosome based on the marker sequences.

Meet Diverse Needs

Students who would like an extra challenge might wish to learn about the actual human DNA sample that was sequenced. Have them find out if this DNA came from only one person or if it was a mixture of many people. Also have them find out how scientists plan to handle the fact that every human individual has a different DNA sequence. Encourage students to present their findings to the class. **Learning modality: verbal**

BIO INSIGHTS — HISTORY OF SCIENCE

The beginning of the genomic race

The Human Genome Project officially began in 1990 with two ultimate goals: identify and map every gene to its chromosome and determine the entire DNA sequence for the human genome. Research centers, universities, and private companies in the United States and around the world began work on this multibillion-dollar project, which was first estimated to take 20 years to complete. The first step of the project was completed in 1993, when a group in France completed a rough map of genetic markers for the entire genome. These markers were used to help researchers map the locations of various DNA fragments.

Answer to . . .

Figure 14–18 *It matches suspect 2.*

Careers in Biology

- High school students interested in genetics should take courses in biology, chemistry, and physics, as well as English and math. College students should choose majors such as biochemistry, biology, or chemistry.
- Dr. Royal encourages students interested in studying genetics to also learn about research going on in the social sciences, such as anthropology, history, and psychology, because the study of genetics is beginning to affect these disciplines as well.

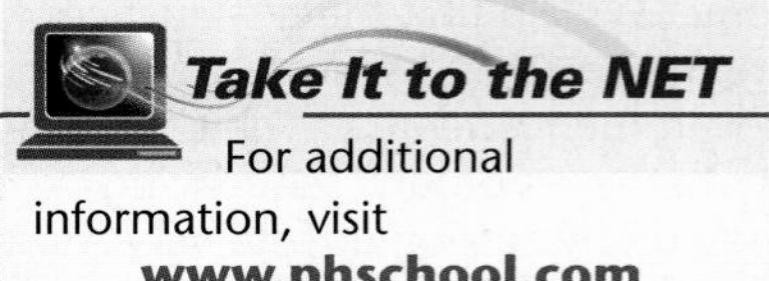

For additional information, visit **www.phschool.com**

Rapid Sequencing How did they do it? First, government scientists laid the groundwork by carefully sequencing widely separated regions of DNA on each chromosome. These "markers" made it possible to find the proper positions of other DNA sequences between them. Scientists at a private company then used a technique known as "shotgun" sequencing in which randomly generated fragments of DNA were automatically sequenced without any thought as to where they might fit into the entire sequence. High-speed computers then found overlapping regions between the fragments and positioned them relative to known markers to assemble the final sequence.

When the Human Genome Project was completed in June 2000, investigators began to count the genes in the sequence. First estimates that it might contain as few as 31,000 genes surprised many scientists. The fruit fly *Drosophila* contains approximately 14,000 genes, and the tiny worm *Caenorhabditis elegans* contains roughly 20,000. Many researchers had expected to find more, and how so few genes manage to produce an organism as complex as a human being now becomes a central question for biologists. In nearly every respect, the interesting part of exploring the human genome is just beginning.

Searching for Genes Molecular biologists continue to hunt for genes as they search through the genome's 24 volumes of information (22 autosomal chromosomes and the 2 sex chromosomes). They can locate genes in several ways. One of these ways is to find a so-called open reading frame. An open reading frame is a series of DNA bases that can produce part of a working mRNA sequence. The mRNA coding regions of most genes are interrupted by introns. Therefore, investigators also have to find the special DNA sequences that mark the boundaries between introns and exons in order to follow the gene through its complete length. When the process is complete, researchers can often pinpoint the gene's promoter, as well as the "start" and "stop" sites for transcription, as shown in **Figure 14–20.**

▼ **Figure 14–20** Researchers exploring the human genome can use DNA sequences to locate many genes. Promoters are sequences in which RNA polymerase can bind to DNA. On either side of a typical gene are other DNA sequences that may serve as signals for RNA polymerase to start and stop transcription, as shown below. **Interpreting Graphics** ***In which direction would RNA polymerase move in transcribing the gene shown below?***

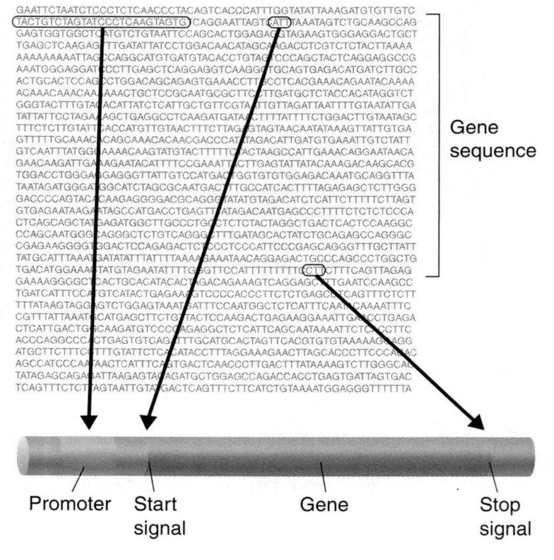

Research groups around the world are now hard at work analyzing the huge amount of information in the DNA sequence, looking for genes that may provide useful clues to some of the basic properties of life. In addition to its scientific significance, understanding the structure and control of key genes may have commercial value. Biotechnology companies are rushing to find genetic information that may be useful in developing new drugs and treatments for diseases.

A Breakthrough for Everyone One of the most remarkable things about genome research is the open availability of nearly all its data. From its very beginning, data from publicly supported research on the human genome have been posted

Careers in Biology

Geneticist

Job Description: work in the laboratories of universities or large companies doing molecular-level research, or work in a clinic collecting family histories and counseling parents with children who have a genetic disorder or who are at risk for contracting a genetic disorder

Education: a master's or doctor's degree in genetics or related field; some medical research positions require a medical degree, as well

Skills: good verbal and written communication skills, analytical, detail-oriented, self-motivated, organized, curious, and able to meet deadlines

Highlights: You have the opportunity to discover new genes or patterns of heredity that can help treat or cure genetic disorders or to make sure that these types of discoveries are put into practice to improve public health.

Dr. Charmaine Royal focuses on "looking at issues in genetic research related to African Americans." Dr. Royal says her "desire to help people and to relieve suffering in general are what drive me to do what I do. My desire is for all of society to benefit from genetic research."

Take It to the NET

For more information, visit the Prentice Hall Web site: **www.phschool.com**

on the Internet on a daily basis. Yes, that means that if you have access to the Internet, you can read the latest genome data and, if you wish, analyze it. The Web site for this textbook provides a direct link to the Human Genome Project.

Gene Therapy

One of the most obvious uses of information about the human genome would be to cure genetic disorders by gene therapy. Gene therapy is the process of changing the gene that causes a genetic disorder. **In gene therapy, an absent or faulty gene is replaced by a normal, working gene.** This way, the body can make the correct protein or enzyme it needs, which eliminates the cause of the disorder.

The first authorized attempt to cure a human genetic disorder by gene transfer occurred in 1990. Then, in 1999, a young French girl was apparently cured of an inherited immune disorder when cells from her bone marrow were removed, modified in the laboratory, and then placed back in her body.

Figure 14–21 shows one of the ways in which researchers have attempted to practice gene therapy. Viruses are often used because of their ability to enter a cell's DNA. The virus particles are modified so that they cannot cause disease. Then, a DNA fragment containing a replacement gene is spliced to viral DNA. The patient is then infected with the modified virus particles, which should carry the gene into cells to correct genetic defects.

Gene Therapy

Use Visuals

Figure 14–21 Help students understand the procedure of gene therapy. Encourage them to compare it to animal cell transformation. Ask: **What is used to carry the DNA into the cell instead of a plasmid?** *(A virus)* **Why doesn't the virus cause disease in an individual?** *(The viral DNA has been modified to prevent the virus from causing disease.)* Remind students about the control of gene expression in eukaryotes. Ask: **Would all body cells produce hemoglobin?** *(No, only cells in which hemoglobin is produced would express the hemoglobin gene.)* **Why do researchers inject the hemoglobin gene into bone marrow cells and not into muscle cells or skin cells?** *(Muscle and skin cells do not produce hemoglobin; the hemoglobin gene is not expressed in these cells. It is expressed only in bone marrow cells, where red blood cells are produced.)*

HISTORY OF SCIENCE

Transforming human cells

The first federally approved transfer of cells with foreign genes into a human occurred in May, 1989, at the Clinical Center of the National Institutes of Health in Bethesda, Maryland.

Cancer-fighting cells into which a foreign gene had been inserted were infused into the bloodstream of a cancer patient who had volunteered for the experiment. The primary purpose of the manipulation was to make the cells easily identifiable so that doctors could track them in the patient's body. The patient was not expected to benefit directly.

The cells, tumor-infiltrating lymphocytes, had been taken from the patient's cancerous tissue and treated in the laboratory to increase their numbers and, thus, their ability to attack the cancer tissue.

Answer to . . .

Figure 14–20 *It moves from the promoter to the stop signal.*

Ethical Issues in Human Genetics

Build Science Skills

Making Judgments Have groups work together to devise a set of guidelines for the use of the human genome. Make sure students understand the consequences of the guidelines they develop.

3 ASSESS

Evaluate Understanding

Challenge students to choose a topic in genetics and briefly describe its implications for society. Challenge them to explain how an understanding of science will help them make informed decisions.

Reteach

Have students design a flowchart to show the steps in gene therapy. They should also include the steps required to engineer the virus that carries the human gene. Students can use Figure 14–21 as a guide.

Take It to the NET

Questions may include how the test results might help in planning for the future; what are the benefits and disadvantages of knowing and not knowing whether the disease has been inherited; what other problems might occur as a result of the testing; how might the news affect one's family; and if the results are positive, what can they do to avoid triggering the disorder. For additional information, visit **www.phschool.com**

Use iText to review the key concepts in Section 14–3.

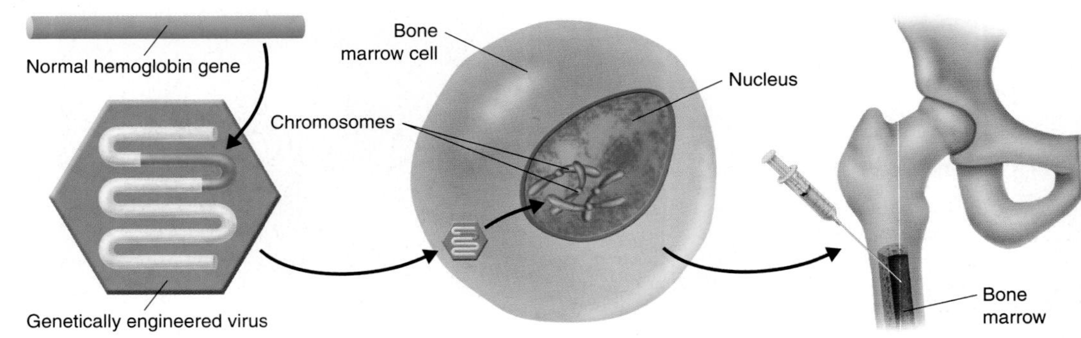

▲ **Figure 14–21** **Gene therapy is the process of changing the genes that cause a genetic disorder.** This drawing shows how a virus can be used to deliver the gene for normal hemoglobin into a person's bone marrow.

Unfortunately, gene therapy experiments have not always been successful. Attempts to treat cystic fibrosis by spraying genetically engineered viruses into the breathing passages have not produced a lasting cure. For all the promise it holds, in most cases gene therapy remains a high-risk, experimental procedure.

Ethical Issues in Human Genetics

It would be marvelous to be able to cure hemophilia or other genetic diseases. But if human cells can be manipulated to cure disease, should biologists try to engineer taller people or change their eye color, hair texture, sex, blood group, or appearance? What will happen to the human species if we gain the opportunity to design our bodies? What will be the consequences if biologists develop the ability to clone human beings by making identical copies of their cells? These are questions with which science will rapidly force society to come to grips.

The goal of biology is to gain a better understanding of the nature of life. The more biologists understand life, the more they will be able to manipulate it. As biologists' power over nature increases, society will have to learn to use wisely the tools that science has given it. Our society will have to develop a thoughtful and ethical consensus of what should and should not be done with the human genome. Scientists alone should not be expected to assume all of the responsibility for these decisions. Society in its entirety should have to deal with these questions.

14–3 Section Assessment

1. **Key Concept** What is the Human Genome Project?
2. **Key Concept** Describe how gene therapy works.
3. Name two common uses for DNA testing.
4. Describe how molecular biologists identify genes in sequences of DNA.
5. **Critical Thinking Making Judgments** Do you think it should be legal for people to use genetic engineering to affect their children's characteristics? Give reasons for your answer.

iTEXT Assessment Use iText to review the important concepts in Section 14–3.

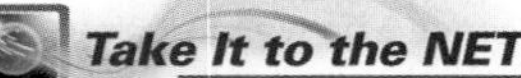

Take It to the NET

Read about genetic counseling. Prepare questions you might ask a genetic counselor if you were seeking advice on getting tested for an inherited disease. Use the links provided in the Biology area at the Prentice Hall Web site for help in completing this activity: **www.phschool.com**

14–3 Section Assessment

1. An attempt to sequence all human DNA
2. Doctors attempt to cure genetic disorders by placing copies of healthy genes into cells that lack them.
3. To detect alleles for a genetic disorder and to identify individuals
4. By looking for promoters, which are binding sites for RNA polymerase, a "start" site, a "stop" site, and DNA sequences that mark the boundaries between introns and exons
5. Accept all reasonably supported answers.

Real-World Lab

Modeling DNA Probes

A DNA probe is a short, single-stranded DNA molecule bound to a fluorescent dye that makes the probe visible. Because the probe is single stranded, it can bind to other DNA that has a complementary sequence. To find a specific DNA sequence, scientists mix a probe with an unknown DNA sample. The probe will only bind to a DNA sample that has a complementary sequence, showing where the desired sequence is. In this lab, you will model how scientists use DNA probes.

Problem

How do DNA probes help to identify individuals?

Materials

- graph paper
- scissors
- colored pencil or marker

Skills

Using Models, Classifying

Procedure 

Individual 1	ATCTCGAGACTGATAGGCTCTAAGCTCGAG
Individual 2	ATTGGCCACTCGAGACGTTGGCCAAGTCCG
Individual 3	ATGACCATGGCCAGGCTCGAGCTGATGACG
Individual 4	ATATGGCCATTGCTCGAGTGGCCAGATCCG
Individual 5	ACTCGAGGTCCCTCGAGTGTAGGCTCATCG

1. DNA sequences from five individuals are shown. Copy each individual's number and DNA sequence onto graph paper, putting one letter from the DNA sequence into each square. Skip five lines between each sequence and the next one.
2. Copy the following sequence for a six-base DNA probe onto graph paper, as you did the DNA sequences in step 1: T C C G A G
3. Fill in the square that follows the probe sequence with a colored pencil or marker to represent the fluorescent dye bound to the probe.
4. Cut out the strip of graph paper that represents the probe and its attached fluorescent dye.
5. Move the probe along each individual's DNA sequence. As you do so, look for parts of the DNA sequences that are complementary to the probe's sequence.
6. Circle the part of any individual's DNA sequence that is complementary to the sequence of the DNA probe.
7. Record the numbers of the individuals who were identified by the DNA probe.
8. Choose one of the five individuals, and construct a new DNA probe that will identify only that individual. Write out the DNA sequence of this new probe as you did in step 2. Your new probe does not have to be six bases long.
9. Cut out your new probe and exchange it for one written by a classmate.
10. Repeat steps 5 and 6 with the probe you received to identify the individual that your classmate selected.

Analyze and Conclude

1. **Observing** What DNA sequence is complementary to the sequence of the probe shown in step 2?
2. **Classifying** Which individual(s) was (were) identified by the DNA probe given in step 2?
3. **Using Models** Is it possible for the same DNA probe to identify more than one individual? Explain your answer.
4. **Drawing Conclusions** Would DNA probes with longer or shorter sequences be more likely to identify only one individual? Explain your answer.

Go Further

Using Models Restriction enzymes cut DNA at specific base sequences. Make a model of a DNA probe and a restriction enzyme. Use your models to show how DNA probes and restriction enzymes could be used together to create DNA fingerprints for the five individuals shown.

Analyze and Conclude

1. A G G C T C

2. Individuals 1, 3, and 5

3. Yes, if the complementary sequence occurs in more than one individual's DNA, then the probe will bind to the DNA of all those individuals.

4. Longer, because the longer the probe sequence is, the less often the complementary sequence is likely to occur

Real-World Lab

Objective Students will be able to use models to determine how DNA probes help to identify individuals.

Skills Focus **Using Models, Classifying**

Time 45 minutes

Prelab Discussion After students read the procedure, review what a complementary sequence is. Write several DNA sequences on the board, and have student volunteers give the complementary sequence of each.

Teaching Tips

- Use quarter-inch graph paper so that students have room to write.
- Have students write the complementary sequence under the DNA sequence of the probe.
- Suggest that students circle or highlight the complementary sequences in the individuals' DNA with the colored pencil or marker.
- Remind students to read the DNA sequence from left to right.

Procedure

7. Individuals 1, 3, and 5

10. Answers depend on the probe sequence written by students.

Expected Outcomes Students should observe that the DNA probe identified individuals 1, 3, and 5.

Go Further

Students should specify the DNA sequence that is cut by their restriction enzymes. They should cut the DNA samples from the individuals with the restriction enzymes (using scissors), then order the fragments by size. Only the fragments with the complementary sequence to the probe will be highlighted. Individuals will show different bands that are highlighted.

Chapter 14 Study Guide

Study Tip

Write each Vocabulary term on a separate card, as well as a question for each Key Concept. Place the cards into a hat or a bowl. Have students draw a card and either give the definition of the word or answer the question. Continue until all the cards have been used.

Thinking Visually

1. Autosomes

2.–5. Tay-Sachs disease, achondroplasia, Huntington's disease, sickle cell disease (or any other disorder listed in Figure 14–6 on page 345)

6.–7. Colorblindness, Duchenne muscular dystrophy

Chapter 14 Assessment

Reviewing Content

1. b	**5.** d	**9.** a
2. a	**6.** a	**10.** a
3. c	**7.** d	
4. b	**8.** c	

Understanding Concepts

11. Biologists photograph cells in mitosis, cut out the chromosomes from the photographs, and group them together in pairs.

12. The sex chromosomes determine an individual's sex; the remaining chromosomes are autosomal.

13. A pedigree shows how the genetic disorder has been passed from one generation to the next. This information can be used to predict the likelihood of having a child with the disorder.

14. Mothers 1 and 6 are carriers. Person 3 can pass his affected X chromosome only to his daughters; his sons inherit his Y chromosome and an X chromosome from their mother.

15. No, because people with blood type A do not have the I^B allele.

Chapter 14 Study Guide

14–1 Human Heredity

Key Concepts

- All egg cells carry a single X chromosome (23X). However, half of all sperm cells carry an X chromosome (23X), and half carry a Y chromosome (23Y). This ensures that just about half of the zygotes will be 46XX (female), and half will be 46XY (male).
- In both cystic fibrosis and sickle cell disease, a small change in the DNA of a single gene affects the structure of a protein, causing a serious genetic disorder.

Vocabulary
karyotype, p. 341
sex chromosome, p. 341
autosome, p. 341
pedigree, p. 342
polygenic, p. 343

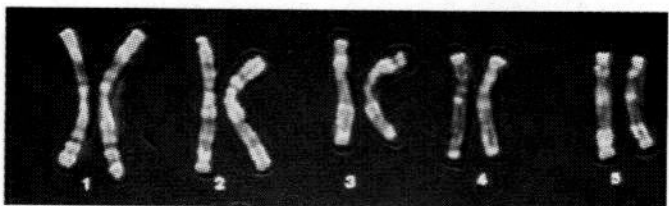

14–2 Human Chromosomes

Key Concepts

- Males have just one X chromosome. Thus, all X-linked alleles are expressed in males, even if they are recessive.
- Nondisjunction causes gametes to have abnormal numbers of chromosomes, which in turn causes a chromosome number disorder.

Vocabulary
sex-linked gene, p. 350
nondisjunction, p. 352

14–3 Human Molecular Genetics

Key Concepts

- The Human Genome Project is an attempt to sequence all human DNA.
- In gene therapy, an absent or faulty gene is replaced by a normal, working gene.

Vocabulary
DNA fingerprinting, p. 357

Thinking Visually

Using the information in this chapter, complete the following concept map about chromosome disorders:

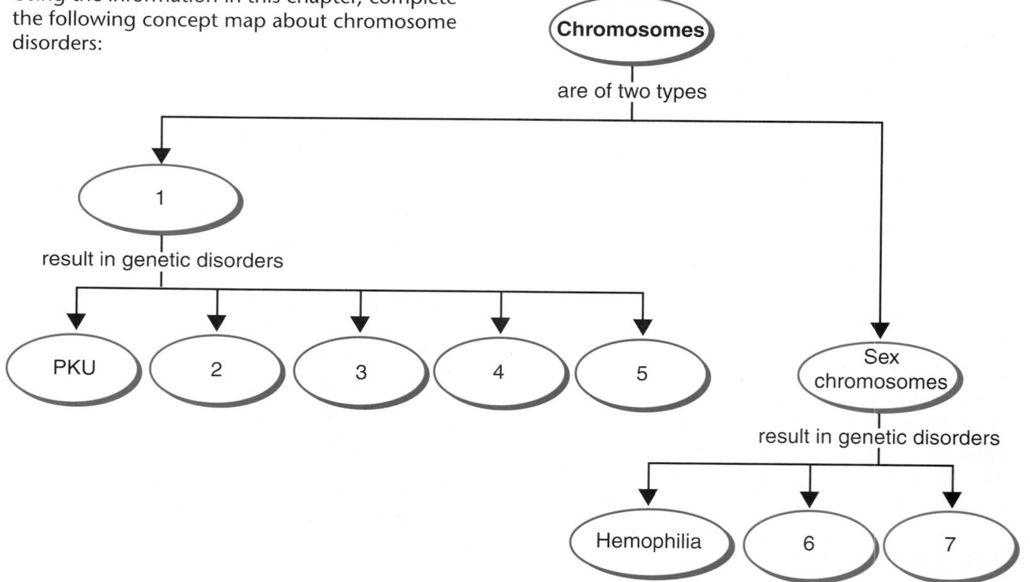

CHAPTER RESOURCES

Print:
- ***Teaching Resources,*** Chapter Vocabulary Review, Graphic Organizer
- ***Chapter Tests: Levels A and B,*** Chapter 14 Test
- ***Prentice Hall Assessment System,*** Practice Test

Technology:
- ***Computer Test Bank,*** Chapter 14 Test
- ***iText,*** Chapter 14 Assessment

Chapter 14 Assessment

Reviewing Content

Choose the letter that best answers the question or completes the statement.

1. A normal human diploid zygote contains a full set of
   a. 23 chromosomes.
   b. 46 chromosomes.
   c. 44 chromosomes.
   d. XXY chromosomes.

2. A chart that traces the inheritance of a trait in a family is called a(an)
   a. pedigree.
   b. karyotype.
   c. genome.
   d. autosome.

3. Traits that are caused by the interaction of many genes are said to be
   a. polyploid.
   b. linked.
   c. polygenic.
   d. autosomal.

4. An example of a trait that is determined by multiple alleles is
   a. Huntington's disease.
   b. ABO blood groups.
   c. Down syndrome.
   d. hemophilia.

5. Most sex-linked genes are found on the
   a. Y chromosome.
   b. O chromosome.
   c. YY chromosomes.
   d. X chromosome.

6. Hemophilia is a genetic disorder that is
   a. sex-linked.
   b. sex-influenced.
   c. fairly common.
   d. more common in women than men.

7. Which parental pair could produce females with colorblindness?
   a. homozygous normal-vision mother, father with colorblindness
   b. mother with colorblindness, normal-vision father
   c. heterozygous normal-vision mother, normal-vision father
   d. heterozygous normal-vision mother, father with colorblindness

8. A common genetic disorder characterized by bent and twisted red blood cells is
   a. cystic fibrosis.
   b. hemophilia.
   c. sickle cell disease.
   d. muscular dystrophy.

9. Which of the following techniques takes advantage of repeated DNA sequences that do not code for proteins?
   a. DNA fingerprinting
   b. DNA sequencing
   c. genetic engineering
   d. rapid sequencing

10. The process of attempting to cure genetic disorders by placing copies of healthy genes into cells that lack them is known as
    a. gene therapy.
    b. DNA fingerprinting.
    c. rapid sequencing.
    d. the Human Genome Project.

Understanding Concepts

11. Describe how a karyotype is prepared.

12. What is the difference between autosomes and sex chromosomes?

13. How can a family pedigree be helpful in determining the probability of having a child with a genetic disorder?

14. In the pedigree below, the shaded symbols indicate people who have hemophilia. Which mothers certainly are carriers? Why did the sons of person 3 not inherit the trait?

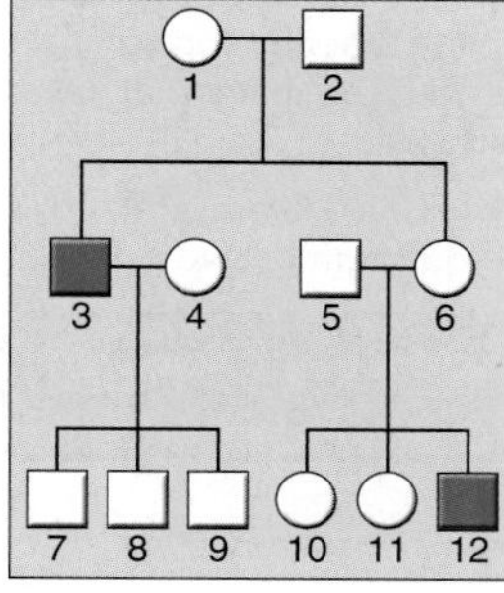

15. Is it possible for a person with blood type alleles I^A and I^B to have blood type A? Explain your answer.

16. Explain the significance of the Rh factor in blood groups.

17. Describe the symptoms present in an individual with Tay-Sachs disease.

18. What determines whether an allele is dominant, recessive, or codominant?

19. What is a chromosomal disorder? Name one chromosomal disorder that can result from nondisjunction.

20. Describe the process of DNA fingerprinting.

21. Describe what is meant by the term *rapid sequencing.*

22. How does an open reading frame help molecular biologists search for genes?

16. Giving a person a transfusion of blood with the wrong Rh factor could be fatal.

17. Tach-Sachs disease causes nervous-system breakdown and death.

18. The nature of the gene's protein product and its role in the cell

19. A chromosomal disorder occurs when abnormal numbers of chromosomes find their way into the gametes. Chromosomal disorders resulting from nondisjunction include Down syndrome, Turner's syndrome, and Klinefelter's syndrome.

20. A small sample of DNA is cut with restriction enzymes. The fragments are separated by size using electrophoresis. Fragments containing highly variable regions of DNA are detected with a DNA probe.

21. It is a sequencing technique in which widely separated regions of DNA on each chromosome are first sequenced. Then, randomly generated fragments of DNA are automatically sequenced. High-speed computers then find overlapping regions between the fragments and position them relative to the known markers to assemble the final sequence.

22. An open reading frame helps biologists find the gene's promoter, as well as the "start" and "stop" sites for transcription.

TIME SAVER

HOMEWORK GUIDE

Section:	**Questions:**
Section 14–1	1–4, 11–18, 23–26, 29, 31
Section 14–2	5–8, 19, 27, 28, 32, 33
Section 14–3	9, 10, 20–22, 30

Critical Thinking

23. Neither parent has the disease because the Tay-Sachs allele is recessive. They have a 1 : 4 chance of having a child with Tay-Sachs disease and a 1 : 2 chance of having a healthy child who will carry the Tay-Sachs allele.

24. Like a tree, a pedigree has family branches that further divide into smaller branches, which lead to individual leaves, or persons.

25. A genetic disorder caused by a dominant allele is very likely to cause death before the individual reproduces and passes on the allele. The allele tends to be eliminated from the gene pool. Recessive alleles can be hidden in heterozygous carriers.

26. One hypothesis is that sickled red blood cells lack a substance *P. falciparum* needs to live. Another is that when the body destroys the sickled red blood cell, it also destroys *P. falciparum.*

27. There is a 50 percent chance that either a son or a daughter will have the disorder.

28. 0.1%; 0.2%; 1.0%; 8.0%; The incidence of Down syndrome increases with the age of the mother.

29. The incidence of malaria might increase because more individuals would be susceptible.

30. Information from the Human Genome Project can be used to study human diseases. Possible student judgments include that society will have to develop a thoughtful and ethical consensus of what should and should not be done with the human genome.

31. Parents who wish to determine the likelihood of passing certain genes on to their offspring might undergo allele testing, have their family pedigree constructed, or have their karyotypes done.

32. Possible genotypes of the parents of a male child with colorblindness are X^CX^c and X^CY, X^CX^c and X^cY, X^cX^c and X^CY, or X^cX^c and X^cY.

33. All three disorders are caused by the nondisjunction of chromosomes during meiosis.

Chapter 14 Assessment

Critical Thinking

23. Predicting Two prospective parents learn that they each carry one allele for Tay-Sachs disease. Why does neither of them suffer from Tay-Sachs disease? If they decide to have children, what are the chances they will have a baby with Tay-Sachs disease? What are the chances that one of their healthy children will carry the Tay-Sachs allele?

24. Using Analogies How is a tree analogous to a family pedigree?

25. Applying Concepts Why are genetic disorders caused by dominant alleles less common than genetic disorders caused by recessive alleles?

26. Formulating Hypotheses *Plasmodium falciparum,* a protist, causes a fatal form of malaria. Propose a hypothesis to explain why *P. falciparum* can live in red blood cells that contain normal hemoglobin but not in red blood cells that contain the sickle cell allele.

27. Predicting A man with colorblindness marries a woman who is a carrier of the disorder. Determine the probability that any son will have the disorder. Determine the probability that any daughter will have the disorder.

28. Using Tables and Graphs Study the graph and answer the question below.

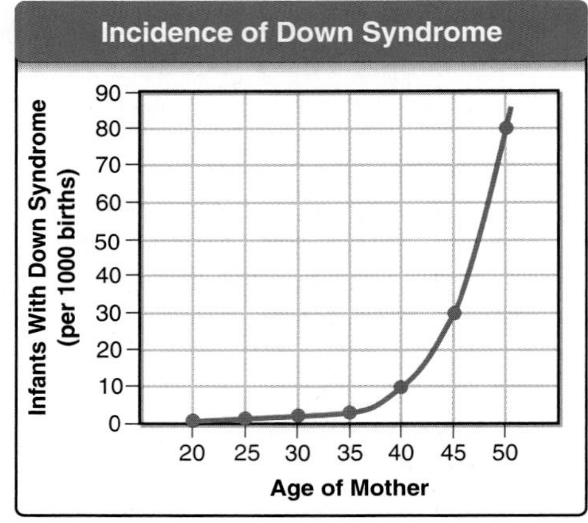

What percent of children born to women under age 30 has Down syndrome? Age 35? Age 40? Age 50? What can you infer about how the age of the mother is related to the incidence of Down syndrome?

29. Formulating Hypotheses Suppose that techniques of genetic engineering make it possible to eliminate the sickle cell allele. What effect might such action have on people in areas where malaria is still common?

30. Making Judgments What impact will the Human Genome Project have on society? Do you think the project is valuable? Explain your answer.

31. Applying Concepts What steps can parents take to determine the likelihood of passing certain genes on to their offspring? Cite specific examples.

32. Predicting What are the possible genotypes of the parents of a male child with colorblindness?

33. Making Connections Explain the relationship between meiosis and Down syndrome, Turner syndrome, and Klinefelter's syndrome. (*Hint:* You may wish to refer to Chapter 11.)

Performance-Based Assessment

Interviewing a Geneticist Your career ambition is to be a science reporter. You are sent by your school newspaper to interview a geneticist who works with human genetic disorders. Prepare a script of the questions you would like answered.

What do we know about the human genome? Visit the Prentice Hall Web site at **www.phschool.com** to explore the current results of the Human Genome Project. Then, answer the following questions:

- How many nucleotide bases are in the human genome sequence?
- What proportion of nucleotides are exactly the same in all people?
- How much of the human genome actually codes for proteins?
- What is the ratio of mutations in males and females? What is one explanation for this difference?
- What is "junk DNA"? What important clues does it hold?

Performance-Based Assessment

Some questions that students might wish to pose include the following: What are the most commonly occurring genetic disorders? How are they inherited? What effects do they have on the body? Can they be detected by genetic screening methods? Can they be treated? If so, how?

Standardized Test Prep

Standardized Test Prep

1. D
2. B
3. C
4. B
5. B
6. E
7. C

Test-Taking Tip When interpreting a pedigree, first read through all the generations given. Then, go back and assign (either mentally or on scratch paper) a possible genotype to each person represented in the pedigree. Use Punnett squares to test your assigned genotypes to ensure that they could produce each successive generation's phenotypes.

Directions: Choose the letter that best answers the question or completes the statement.

1. Which of the following can be observed in a person's karyotype?
   I. Colorblindness
   II. Trisomy 21
   III. Turner's syndrome
   (A) I only
   (B) III only
   (C) I and II only
   (D) II and III only
   (E) I, II, and III

2. Which of the following conditions is caused by a sex-linked gene?
   I. Klinefelter's syndrome
   II. Down syndrome
   III. Muscular dystrophy
   (A) I only
   (B) III only
   (C) I and II only
   (D) II and III only
   (E) I, II, and III

3. A child has colorblindness. Which genotype-phenotype combination is NOT possible in the child's parents?
   (A) The father does not carry the allele and does not have colorblindness.
   (B) The mother carries one allele but does not have colorblindness.
   (C) The father carries one allele but does not have colorblindness.
   (D) The father carries one allele and has colorblindness.
   (E) The mother carries two alleles and has colorblindness.

4. A woman is homozygous for A-negative blood type. A man has AB-negative blood type. What is the probability that the couple's child will be type B-negative?
   (A) 0%
   (B) 25%
   (C) 50%
   (D) 75%
   (E) 100%

Questions 5–7

A student traced a widow's peak hairline in her family. Based on her interviews and observations, she drew the following pedigree:

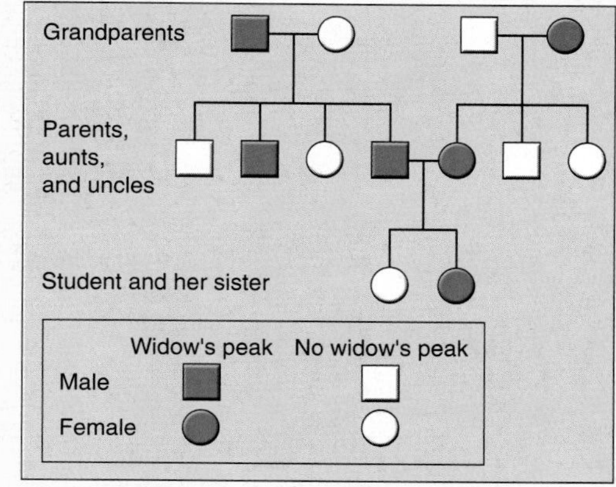

5. Which pattern(s) of inheritance are consistent with the pedigree?
   I. Sex-linked
   II. Complete dominance
   III. Codominance
   (A) I only
   (B) II only
   (C) I and II only
   (D) II and III only
   (E) I, II, and III

6. What are the probable genotypes of the student's parents?
   (A) Mother—*Ww;* Father—*ww*
   (B) Mother—*ww;* Father—*ww*
   (C) Mother—*WW;* Father—*Ww*
   (D) Mother—*WW;* Father—*WW*
   (E) Mother—*Ww;* Father—*Ww*

7. The student does not have a widow's peak hairline, but her sister does. What are the girls' probable genotypes?
   (A) Student—*Ww;* her sister—*ww*
   (B) Student—*WW;* her sister—*Ww*
   (C) Student—*ww;* her sister—*Ww*
   (D) Student—*ww;* her sister—*ww*
   (E) Student—*Ww;* her sister—*Ww*

Take It to the NET

- 3164.7 million (approximately 3.2 billion)
- 99.9 percent
- less than 2 percent
- The ratio of mutations in males and females is 2 : 1. One reason for the higher mutation rate in males is that there are a greater number of cell divisions involved in the formation of sperm than in the formation of eggs.
- Repeated sequences, or "junk DNA," make up at least 50 percent of the human genome. Repetitive sequences are thought to have no direct functions, but they shed light on chromosome structure and dynamics. They hold important clues about evolutionary events and can help chart mutation rates.

For additional information, visit

www.phschool.com

Unit 5

Dear Colleague,

Blue feet and comical mating behaviors make these boobies among the most obvious of the birds that nest in the Galápagos Islands. Although they raise their young on islands, boobies feed at sea and often fly great distances over open water. That's why booby species found in the Galápagos are common from Mexico to Ecuador, and some live as far north as southern California.

That's also why boobies, though amusing, are not of special interest to evolutionary biologists. The most intriguing Galápagos species, such as tortoises and ground finches, *don't* like to travel through or over open water. Island populations of those species are reproductively isolated from others of their kind and can therefore evolve into unique forms in ways that teach us how evolution works.

Galápagos finches and tortoises ranked high among the inspirations for Darwin's theory of evolution by natural selection—described by leading scientists as the "single most important scientific idea that anyone has ever had." During the century and a half since Darwin's day, as new branches of science have appeared and matured, scientists have gathered evidence beyond Darwin's wildest dreams. Any of that evidence—from biochemistry, molecular genetics, geology, and physics—could have either confirmed or negated Darwin's work. Astonishingly, all those new data have not only supported and reinforced Darwin's insight but have strengthened and expanded it so that evolutionary theory now informs every aspect of biological thought, from global ecology to human genome studies. Evolutionary change is now as well documented as anything we have ever learned in science.

UNIT 5

Evolution

Chapters

▶ Named after the color of their feet, the blue-footed boobies belong to the most common of the three species of boobies found on the Galápagos Islands. Blue-footed boobies are known for their hunting, which involves diving headfirst into the ocean.

366

"But why," you might ask, "is evolutionary theory really *that* important to teach, and to teach properly?" There are many answers, but here are a few points most relevant to high school biology.

Science attempts to describe events in the natural world based on phenomena that we can observe, measure, and replicate. It tries to explain the past in terms of events and processes we can observe today.

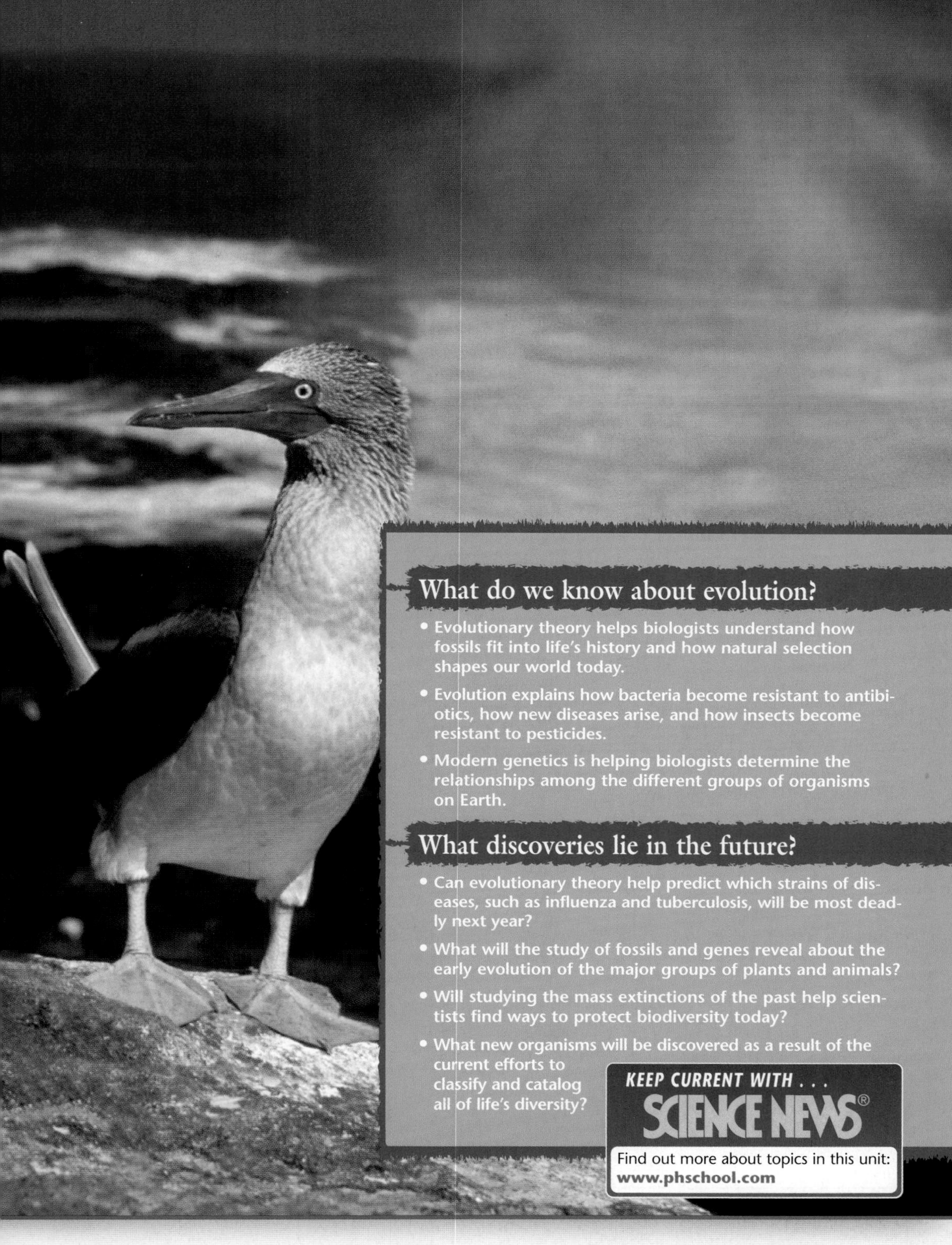

What do we know about evolution?
• Evolutionary theory helps biologists understand how fossils fit into life's history and how natural selection shapes our world today.
• Evolution explains how bacteria become resistant to antibiotics, how new diseases arise, and how insects become resistant to pesticides.
• Modern genetics is helping biologists determine the relationships among the different groups of organisms on Earth.
What discoveries lie in the future?
• Can evolutionary theory help predict which strains of diseases, such as influenza and tuberculosis, will be most deadly next year?
• What will the study of fossils and genes reveal about the early evolution of the major groups of plants and animals?
• Will studying the mass extinctions of the past help scientists find ways to protect biodiversity today?
• What new organisms will be discovered as a result of the current efforts to classify and catalog all of life's diversity?
KEEP CURRENT WITH . . .
SCIENCE NEWS®
Find out more about topics in this unit:
www.phschool.com

Science also attempts to make useful predictions about future events in the same way. That's what science is all about, and that is *all* that science is about. Evolutionary biology uses Darwinian theory to produce scientific explanations and predictions about certain kinds of events in the living world around us.

How, for example, do bacteria become resistant to antibiotics? They evolve under pressure from natural selection. In fact, one physician wrote that humanity would be in a lot better shape with regard to bacteria and antibiotics "if doctors had been taught in medical schools as much about Darwin as they learned about Pasteur." What is the best scientific explanation for the heartbreaking reality that we have not yet been able to develop either a vaccine or a cure for AIDS? The fact is, the human immunodeficiency virus is evolving even faster than bacteria.

But more than simply providing *descriptions* of these phenomena, evolutionary theory enables us to make valuable *predictions* about how living systems will respond to human activity. Evolutionary theory is now informing new treatments for AIDS, new approaches to the production and use of antibiotics, and new strategies for using insecticides against agricultural pests. These and other applications, which hold great promise for humanity, explain why having an understanding of evolution is vital to making informed judgments about many issues in the modern world.

The goal of this unit is to help students understand the evolutionary worldview. As scientists and teachers, we believe very strongly that the purpose of education is to promote understanding, not to compel belief. That applies to evolution, too, which, if properly taught, should *never* threaten the beliefs of students. As biologists, we genuinely feel, as Darwin wrote, there is ". . . grandeur in this view of life." We hope you agree.

Sincerely,

Joe Levine

SCIENCE NEWS®

Have students visit the Prentice Hall Web site at **www.phschool.com** to find the most current information on evolution.

Chapter Planner 15 Darwin's Theory of Evolution

Section and Section Objectives	Time	Activities and Labs
15–1 The Puzzle of Life's Diversity, pp. 369–372 **15.1.1** ***Describe*** the voyage of the *Beagle.* **15.1.2** ***Identify*** Charles Darwin's contribution to science. **15.1.3** ***Describe*** the pattern Darwin observed among organisms of the Galápagos Islands.	**1 period (1/2 block)**	**SE: *Inquiry Activity,*** Do lima beans show variation?, p. 368 **TE: *Demonstration,*** p. 370
15–2 Ideas That Shaped Darwin's Thinking, pp. 373–377 **15.2.1** ***State*** how Hutton and Lyell described geological change. **15.2.2** ***Identify*** how Lamarck thought species evolve. **15.2.3** ***Describe*** Malthus's theory of population growth.	**2 periods (1 block)**	**SE: *Biology and History,*** Origins of Evolutionary Thought, pp. 374–375 **TE: *Demonstration,*** p. 377
15–3 Darwin Presents His Case, pp. 378–386 **15.3.1** ***List*** events leading to Darwin's publication of *On the Origin of Species.* **15.3.2** ***Describe*** how natural variation is used in artificial selection. **15.3.3** ***Explain*** how natural selection is related to species' fitness. **15.3.4** ***Identify*** evidence Darwin used to present his case for evolution. **15.3.5** ***State*** Darwin's theory of evolution by natural selection.	**3 periods (1 1/2 blocks)**	**SE: *Quick Lab,*** New vegetables from old?, p. 379 **TE: *Build Science Skills,*** p. 382 **TE: *Demonstration,*** p. 382 **SE: *Exploration,*** Modeling Adaptation, p. 387
Chapter Assessment pp. 388–391	**1 period (1/2 block)**	

ACTIVITY PLANNER

SE: *Inquiry Activity,* p. 368; (15 min.); 10 lima beans, ruler, calculator, graph paper

TE: *Demonstration,* p. 370; (5 min.); 10 peanuts in the shell

TE: *Demonstration,* p. 377; (10 min.); green pepper

SE: *Quick Lab,* p. 379; (20 min.); various *Brassica* vegetables

TE: *Build Science Skills,* p. 382; (5 min.); taxonomic chart

TE: *Demonstration,* p. 382; (15 min.); several beakers, water, several small objects such as leaves and shells, sand and soil mixture

SE: *Exploration,* p. 387; (45 min.); coin

PLANNING KEY

Ability Levels

B Basic	For students who need additional help
A Average	For all students
E Enriched	For students who need to be challenged

Components

SE	Student Edition	**GRSW**	Guided Reading and Study Workbook	**IDM**	Issues and Decision Making
TE	Teacher's Edition	**CT**	Chapter Tests: Levels A and B	**CTB**	Computer Test Bank
LMA	Laboratory Manual A	**PHAS**	PH Assessment Systems	**PA**	Presentation Assistant Plus
LMB	Laboratory Manual B	**LA**	Lab Assessment with Scoring Guide	**BD**	BioDetectives Videotape
TR	Teaching Resources	**BTM**	BioTechnology Manual	**iT**	iText

Program Resources	Assessment	Media and Technology
TR: Section Review 15–1 A B **GRSW:** Section 15–1 A B	**SE:** 15–1 Section Assessment, p. 372 **TR:** Section Review 15–1	**PA:** 15–1 Interest Grabber, Section Outline, Giant Tortoises of the Galápagos Islands, Figure 15–1 **iT:** Section 15–1
TR: Section Review 15–2 A B **GRSW:** Section 15–2 A B	**SE:** 15–2 Section Assessment, p. 377 **TR:** Section Review 15–2	**PA:** 15–2 Interest Grabber, Section Outline, Movement of Earth, Figure 15–7 **iT:** Section 15–2
LMA: Chapter 15 Lab E A **LMB:** Chapter 15 Lab A B **TR:** Section Review 15–3 A B Chapter 15 Exploration A B E	**SE:** 15–3 Section Assessment, p. 386 **TR:** Section Review 15–3	**PA:** 15–3 Interest Grabber, Section Outline, Concept Map, Figure 15–14, Figure 15–15 **iT:** Section 15–3
GRSW: Section 15–3 A B **IDM:** 15–1 E A	**SE:** Chapter 15 Assessment, pp. 389–391 **TR:** Chapter Vocabulary Review, Graphic Organizer **CT:** Chapter 15 Test **CTB:** Chapter 15 Test **PHAS:** Practice Test	**CTB:** Chapter 15 Test **iT:** Chapter 15 Assessment

PRESSED FOR TIME?

To Preview the Chapter

- Introduce students to Key Concepts and Vocabulary terms in each section.
- Assign the Reading Strategies for each section.

To Review the Chapter

- Assign the Section Review 15–1 through 15–3 in the Guided Reading and Study Workbook.
- Assign the Section Review for 15–1 through 15–3 and the Chapter Vocabulary Review for Chapter 15 in the Teaching Resources.

To Cover the Chapter Quickly

- Have students read all of Section 15–1, the Biology and History time line in Section 15–2, and Summary of Darwin's Theory in Section 15–3.
- Assign the Section Review 15–1, questions 1, 2, 3, 10, 11, 12, 13, 25, 27, and 31 in Chapter 15 Assessment, and questions 1, 2, 3, 4, and 7 in Chapter 15 Standardized Test Prep.

Chapter 15

ENGAGE/EXPLORE

Inquiry Activity

Objective Students will be able to measure, calculate, and analyze differences in length of a sample of lima beans and predict how the data are affected by sample size.

Skills Focus **Analyzing Data, Predicting**

Materials 10 lima beans, ruler, calculator, graph paper

Time 15 minutes

Strategy
Students can write their measurements in pencil directly on each lima bean.

Expected Outcome Students should find slight differences in length of the lima beans in their sample.

Think About It
1. Most lima beans are close to the average length.
2. Students should predict that a graph of data from the entire class would have the same general shape but a smoother curve.

Brain Teaser

Show students pictures of several different species of familiar animals in which the feet or other means of locomotion are visible. Ask: **What different ways do these animals use to move about?** *(Students should state the means of locomotion, for example, a robin flies or a rabbit hops.)* **What traits does each animal have that help it move about as it does?** *(Students should identify the traits. For example, robins have wings for flying and rabbits have large hind legs for hopping.)* Conclude by telling students that observing variation such as this was instrumental in Darwin's developing his theory of evolution.

Chapter 15 Darwin's Theory of Evolution

If you look closely at the top of what appears to be a leaf in the center of this photograph, you can see a head. This walking-leaf insect is a superb example of camouflage. Charles Darwin developed an explanation for how such camouflage may have developed.

Inquiry Activity

Do lima beans show variation?

Procedure
1. Count out 10 lima beans and measure the length of each in millimeters. Record your results in a data table.
2. Combine your data with the data of two other classmates. Place all the data on one graph. Plot the length on the x-axis and the number of beans of each length on the y-axis.

Think About It
1. **Analyzing Data** Calculate the average length of the beans. Are most lima beans close to the average length?
2. **Predicting** How do you think a graph of data from the entire class would be different from your graph of data?

HISTORY OF SCIENCE

How Darwin became a naturalist
Charles Darwin came from a family of doctors, and he almost became one, too. Both his father and grandfather were doctors, and they urged him to follow in their footsteps. Charles started out in medical school but soon found that he did not like it. He then went to theological school to study to become a minister. Darwin had always been interested in nature, so he also took courses in biology and geology. These courses were the extent of his formal training as a naturalist when he applied for a job on the *Beagle*. Darwin was not the most qualified applicant, but he was hired anyway, perhaps because the captain, Robert Fitzroy, thought Darwin would make a good companion for the five-year voyage.

15–1 The Puzzle of Life's Diversity

Nature presents scientists with a puzzle. Humans share the Earth with millions of other kinds of organisms of every imaginable shape, size, and habitat. This variety of living things is called biological diversity. How did all these different organisms arise? How are they related? These questions make up the puzzle of life's diversity.

What scientific explanation can account for the diversity of life? The answer is a collection of scientific facts, observations, and hypotheses known as evolutionary theory. **Evolution,** or change over time, is the process by which modern organisms have descended from ancient organisms. A **theory** is a well-supported testable explanation of phenomena that have occurred in the natural world.

Voyage of the *Beagle*

The individual who contributed more to our understanding of evolution than anyone was Charles Darwin. Darwin was born in England on February 12, 1809—the same day as Abraham Lincoln. Shortly after completing his college studies, Darwin joined the crew of the H.M.S. *Beagle*. In 1831, he set sail from England for a voyage around the world. His route is shown in **Figure 15–1.** Although no one knew it at the time, this was to be one of the most important voyages in the history of science. **During his travels, Darwin made numerous observations and collected evidence that led him to propose a revolutionary hypothesis about the way life changes over time.** That hypothesis, now supported by a huge body of evidence, has become the theory of evolution.

Guide for Reading

Key Concepts
- What was Charles Darwin's contribution to science?
- What pattern did Darwin observe among organisms of the Galápagos Islands?

Vocabulary
evolution • theory
fossil

Reading Strategy: Using Visuals Before you read, examine **Figure 15–1.** Find the British Isles, where Darwin's journey began, then trace his route. Write a statement describing his travels.

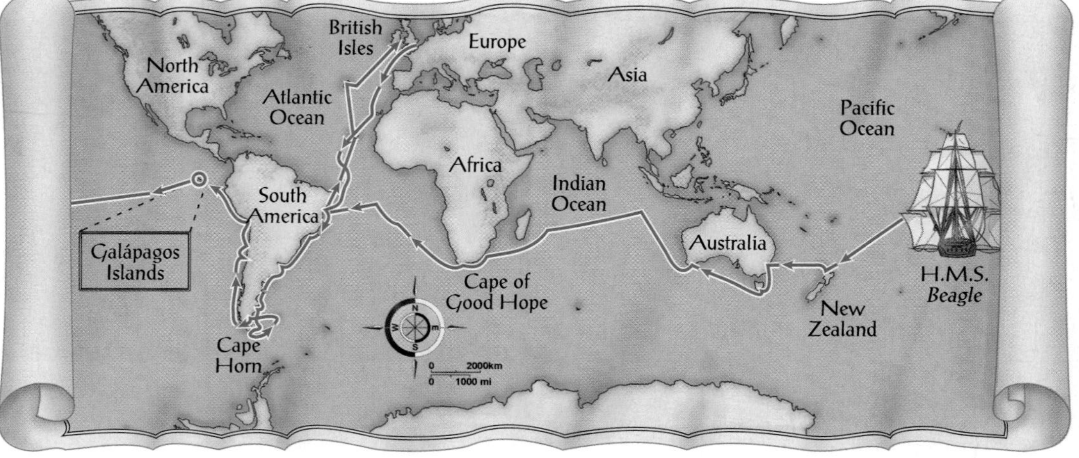

▼ **Figure 15–1** On a five-year voyage on the *Beagle,* Charles Darwin visited several continents and many remote islands. **Darwin's observations led to a revolutionary theory about the way life changes over time.**

SECTION RESOURCES

TIME SAVER

Print:
- ***Teaching Resources,*** Section Review 15–1
- ***Guided Reading and Study Workbook,*** Section 15–1

Technology:
- ***iText,*** Section 15–1

Section 15–1

1 FOCUS

Objectives

15.1.1 ***Describe*** the voyage of the *Beagle.*
15.1.2 ***Identify*** Charles Darwin's contribution to science.
15.1.3 ***Describe*** the pattern Darwin observed among organisms of the Galápagos Islands.

Guide for Reading

Vocabulary Preview

Challenge students to predict how the three vocabulary terms are related. Then, have them check to see if they were correct after they read the section.

Reading Strategy

Questions Darwin asked himself on the journey include: Why were there no rabbits in Australia and no kangaroos in England? Why had some species disappeared, and how were they related to living species? Had animals living on different Galápagos Islands once been members of the same species?

2 INSTRUCT

Address Misconceptions

Students may hold the misconception that because evolution is called a theory, it is no more likely to be true than any other explanation for biological diversity. Point out that a theory is a well-tested concept that is supported by evidence. Explain that scientists do not dispute the fact that evolution has occurred because so much evidence supports it. The only thing that is "theoretical" about evolution is exactly how it happens.

Voyage of the *Beagle*

Use Visuals

Figure 15–1 Have students use the figure to trace Darwin's voyage as they read about it in the chapter.

Darwin's Observations

Demonstration

Most discussions of diversity use animals as examples. Give students a chance to examine patterns of diversity in plants. Provide each student with a sample of 10 peanuts in the shell. Have students examine the shells carefully to find differences in size, shape, color, texture, and other observable characteristics. Ask: **Did you find any two peanut shells that were exactly alike?** *(Students are highly unlikely to find two identical peanut shells.)*

Meet Diverse Needs

Give students who need extra challenges a chance to learn more about what Darwin observed on the voyage of the *Beagle*. Suggest that they obtain a copy of Darwin's publication, *On the Origin of Species*, and find passages in which Darwin described his observations of plants and animals in South America and on the Galápagos Islands. Urge students to put Darwin's observations in their own words and share them with the class in a written report. If possible, students should illustrate their report with copies of Darwin's original drawings. **Learning modality: verbal**

Wherever the ship anchored, Darwin went ashore to collect plant and animal specimens that he added to an ever-growing collection. At sea, between bouts of seasickness, he studied his specimens, read the latest scientific books, and filled many notebooks with his observations and thoughts. Darwin was well educated and had a strong interest in natural history. His curiosity and analytical nature were ultimately the keys to his success as a scientist. During his travels, Darwin came to view every new finding as a piece in an extraordinary puzzle: a scientific explanation for the diversity of life on this planet.

Darwin's Observations

Darwin knew a great deal about the plants and animals of his native country. But he saw far more diversity during his travels. For example, during a single day in a Brazilian forest, Darwin collected 68 different beetle species—despite the fact that he was not even searching for beetles! He began to realize that an enormous number of species inhabit the Earth.

Patterns of Diversity Darwin was intrigued by the fact that so many plants and animals seemed remarkably well suited to whatever environment they inhabited. He was impressed by the many ways in which organisms survived and produced offspring. He wondered if there was some process that led to such a variety of ways of reproducing.

Darwin was also puzzled by where different species lived—and did not live. He visited Argentina and Australia, for example, which had similar grassland ecosystems. Yet, those grasslands were inhabited by very different animals. Also, neither Argentina nor Australia was home to the sorts of animals that lived in European grasslands. For Darwin, these patterns posed challenging questions. Why were there no rabbits in Australia, despite the presence of habitats that seemed perfect for them? Similarly, why were there no kangaroos in England?

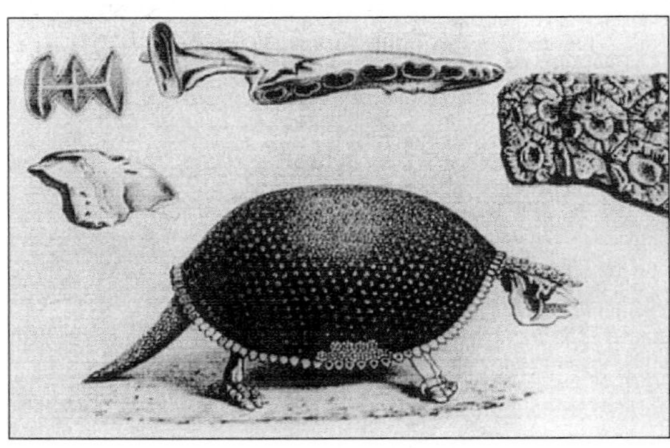

Figure 15–2 Many of the fossils that Darwin discovered resembled living organisms but were not identical to them. The glyptodon, an extinct animal known only from fossil remains, is an ancient relative of the armadillo of South America. **Comparing and Contrasting** ***What are some similarities and differences between these two types of animals?***

TIME SAVER: PRESENTATIONS MADE EASY!

The Presentation Assistant Plus contains the Prentice Hall Presentation Pro and the Transparencies, which provide easy-to-follow visual support for every step of this section. If you have a computer presentation station, use Prentice Hall Presentation Pro for Section 15–1, or use the transparencies listed here.

Section 15–1:

Interest Grabber
Section Outline
Giant Tortoises of the Galápagos Islands
Figure 15–1

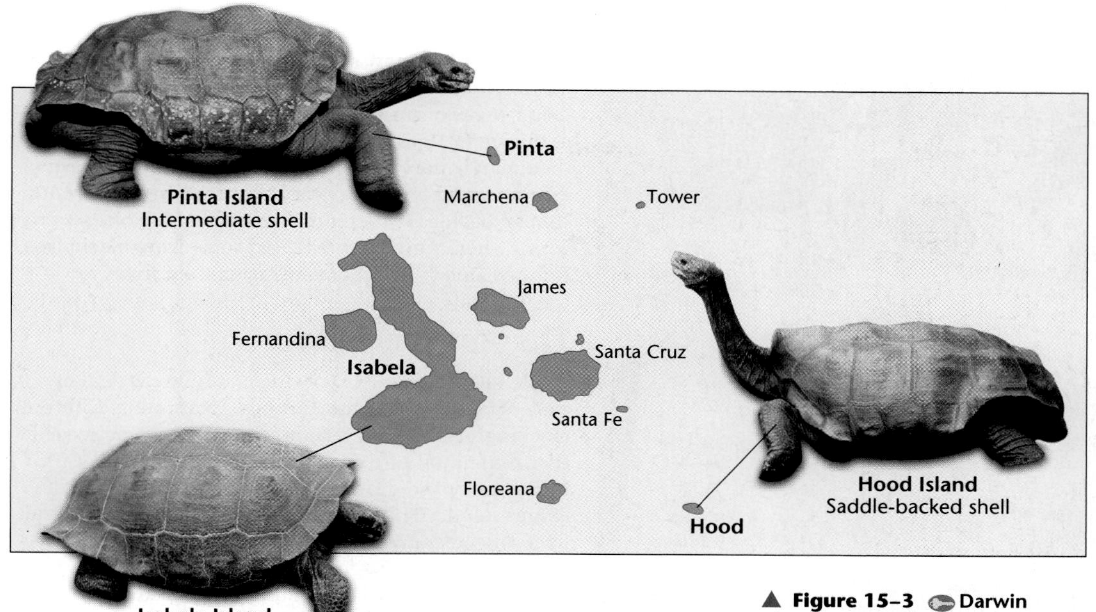

▲ **Figure 15–3** **Darwin observed that the characteristics of many animals and plants varied noticeably among the different Galápagos Islands.** Among the tortoises, the shape of the shell corresponds to different habitats. The Hood Island tortoise (right) has a long neck and a shell that is curved and open around the neck and legs, allowing the tortoise to reach the sparse vegetation on Hood Island. The tortoise from Isabela Island (lower left) has a dome-shaped shell and a shorter neck. Vegetation on this island is more abundant and closer to the ground. The tortoise from Pinta Island has a shell that is intermediate between these two forms.

Living Organisms and Fossils Darwin soon realized that living animals represented just part of the puzzle posed by the natural world. In many places during his voyage, Darwin collected the preserved remains of ancient organisms, called **fossils.** Some of those fossils resembled organisms that were still alive, as shown in **Figure 15–2.** Others looked completely unlike any creature he had ever seen. As Darwin studied fossils, new questions arose. Why had so many of these species disappeared? How were they related to living species?

The Galápagos Islands Of all the *Beagle*'s ports of call, the one that influenced Darwin the most was a group of small islands located 1000 km west of South America. These are the Galápagos Islands. Darwin noted that although they were close together, the islands had very different climates. The smallest, lowest islands were hot, dry, and nearly barren. Hood Island, for example, had sparse vegetation. The higher islands had greater rainfall and a different assortment of plants and animals. Isabela Island had rich vegetation that tortoises could easily reach.

Darwin was fascinated in particular by the land tortoises and marine iguanas that lived in the Galápagos. He learned from the vice-governor of the islands that the giant tortoises varied in predictable ways from one island to another, as shown in **Figure 15–3.** The shape of a tortoise's shell could be used to identify which island a particular tortoise inhabited. Darwin later admitted in his notes that he "did not for some time pay sufficient attention to this statement."

CHECKPOINT *How did the fossils Darwin observed compare with the living organisms he studied?*

To find out about an unusual theory about life on the Galápagos Islands, view the videotape "The Galápagos Islands: A Glimpse Into the Past."

Build Science Skills

Inferring Help students appreciate why the Galápagos Islands were such an important influence on Darwin. Point out how different some of the islands are from one another in climate and other environmental features, despite their close proximity. If possible, show students pictures taken on different Galápagos Islands that illustrate these differences, or challenge students to find pictures and bring them to class. Ask: **What traits do you think an animal might need to survive on a hot, dry, rocky island?** *(Students might describe traits that help conserve water, provide protection from the sun, or make use of scarce food resources.)* **What traits might an animal need to survive on an island with a lot of rainfall and vegetation?** *(Students might describe traits that help the animal move around in trees or tolerate dim, damp conditions.)* Conclude by pointing out that the sharply contrasting environments on the Galápagos Islands and the different animals found on them helped Darwin see how evolution could occur.

Make Connections

Earth Science Explain to students that climate on the Galápagos Islands varies with elevation. Ask: **Why do you think the islands are drier at lower elevations and wetter at higher elevations?** *(At higher elevations, the air is cooler and cannot hold as much moisture, which causes clouds and precipitation.)*

Encourage students to view "The Galápagos Islands: A Glimpse Into the Past" on the BioDetectives Videotape.

BIO INSIGHTS — FACTS AND FIGURES

Galápagos Islands
The 15 Galápagos Islands lie almost 1000 km off the coast of South America. They have a total land area of about 7800 square km, or about three quarters the land area of the Hawaiian Islands. The Galápagos were formed by volcanoes that rise out of the ocean at different elevations, from barely above sea level to 1500 m above the sea. About 10,000 people live on the islands, which are best known for their unusual animals, including the giant tortoises for which the islands were named. The largest species weigh more than 230 kg. The Galápagos also have an unusual history. They were once known as the Enchanted Isles, and pirates buried their treasure there. Ships also abandoned mutineers on the islands. During World War II, the United States established a military base on the Galápagos to guard the Panama Canal.

Answers to . . .

CHECKPOINT *Some fossils resembled organisms that were still alive, while others looked completely unlike any creature Darwin had ever seen.*

Figure 15–2 *Both animals have a type of shell that covers their bodies. The armadillo's covering consists of overlapping plates, whereas the glyptodon's covering consists of one entire piece.*

15–1 (continued)

The Journey Home

Build Science Skills

Inferring Challenge students to make inferences about what a particular species of animal needs to survive. Remind students that a species is a group of organisms with similar characteristics that produces fertile offspring when bred. Point out that not only the physical characteristics of an organism help it to survive, but also its behaviors and relationship with its environment. Have each student choose a particular organism and list its characteristics that help it to survive. Encourage students to share their lists in a class discussion.

3 ASSESS

Evaluate Understanding

Call on students at random to explain in their own words what the vocabulary terms mean.

Reteach

Work with students to develop a list of examples of the different types of biological diversity that Darwin observed.

Take It to the NET

Students should prepare a persuasive letter that lists the reasons why Darwin's presence would be useful to the expedition, and shows Darwin's enthusiasm as a volunteer. Above-average students should make reference to Darwin's previous experience and specific scientific interests. For additional information, visit **www.phschool.com**

Use iText to review the key concepts in Section 15–1.

▲ **Figure 15–4** Darwin's notebooks and some of the finch specimens he collected have been preserved for today's scientists to study. **Inferring** *What might modern scientists learn from examining evidence collected by earlier investigators?*

Darwin also saw several types of small, ordinary-looking brown birds hopping around, looking for seeds. As an eager naturalist, he collected several specimens, as shown in **Figure 15–4.** However, he did not find them particularly unusual or important. As Darwin examined the birds, he noted that they had differently shaped beaks. He thought that some of the birds were wrens, some were warblers, and some were blackbirds. But he came to no other conclusions—at first.

The Journey Home

While heading home, Darwin spent a great deal of time thinking about his findings. Examining different mockingbirds from the Galápagos, Darwin noticed that individual birds collected from the island of Floreana looked different from those collected on James Island. They also looked different from individuals collected on other islands. Darwin also remembered what the vice-governor had told him about the tortoises. Although Darwin did not immediately understand the reason for these patterns, he had stumbled across an important finding. **Darwin observed that the characteristics of many animals and plants varied noticeably among the different islands of the Galápagos.** After returning to England, Darwin began to wonder if animals living on different islands had once been members of the same species. According to this hypothesis, these separate species would have evolved from an original South American ancestor species after becoming isolated from one another. Was this possible? If so, it would turn people's view of the natural world upside down.

15–1 Section Assessment

1. **Key Concept** What did Darwin's travels reveal to him about the number and variety of living species?
2. **Key Concept** How did tortoises and birds differ among the islands of the Galápagos?
3. What is evolution? Why is evolution referred to as a theory?
4. What is a fossil?
5. **Critical Thinking Inferring** Darwin found fossils of many organisms that were different from any living species. How would this finding have affected his understanding of life's diversity?

iText Assessment Use iText to review the important concepts in Section 15–1.

Take It to the NET

Read the preface to Charles Darwin's book, *The Voyage of the Beagle*. Then, write a letter to Captain Fitz Roy, as Darwin might have written it, expressing the wish to volunteer for the voyage. Use the links provided in the Biology area at the Prentice Hall Web site for help in completing this activity: **www.phschool.com**

15–1 Section Assessment

1. Darwin's travels showed him that the diversity of living species was far greater than he had previously known.
2. Each Galápagos island had its own type of tortoises and birds that were clearly different from the tortoises and birds on other islands.
3. Evolution, or change over time, is the process by which modern organisms have descended from ancient ones. Evolution is referred to as a theory because it is a well supported explanation of phenomena that have occurred in the natural world.
4. A fossil is the preserved remains of an ancient organism.
5. It would have greatly increased his estimates of biological diversity.

15–2 Ideas That Shaped Darwin's Thinking

If Darwin had lived a century earlier, he might have done little more than think about the questions raised during his travels. But Darwin's voyage came during one of the most exciting periods in the history of Western science. Explorers were traversing the globe, and great thinkers were beginning to challenge established views about the natural world. Darwin was powerfully influenced by the work of these scientists, especially those who were studying the history of Earth. In turn, he himself greatly changed the thinking of many scientists and nonscientists. Some people, however, found Darwin's ideas too shocking to accept. To understand how radical Darwin's thoughts appeared, you must understand a few things about the world in which he lived.

Most Europeans in Darwin's day believed that the Earth and all its forms of life had been created only a few thousand years ago. Since that original creation, they concluded, neither the planet nor its living species had changed. A robin, for example, has always looked and behaved as robins had in the past. Rocks and major geological features were thought to have been produced suddenly by catastrophic events that humans rarely, if ever, witnessed.

By the time Darwin set sail, numerous discoveries had turned up important pieces of evidence. A rich fossil record, including the example in **Figure 15–5,** was challenging that traditional view of life. In light of such evidence, some scientists even adjusted their beliefs to include not one but several periods of creation. Each of these periods, they contended, was preceded by a catastrophic event that killed off many forms of life. At first, Darwin accepted these beliefs. But he began to realize that much of what he had observed did not fit neatly into this view of unchanging life. Slowly, after studying many scientific theories of his time, Darwin began to change his thinking dramatically.

Guide for Reading

Key Concepts
- How did Hutton and Lyell describe geological change?
- According to Lamarck, how did species evolve?
- What was Malthus's theory of population growth?

Reading Strategy: Finding Main Ideas
As you read about the individuals who influenced Darwin's thinking, write a sentence briefly describing what Darwin learned from each one.

▶ **Figure 15–5** This engraving, made around 1850, shows the fossil remains of a giant sloth from South America. During the 1800s, explorers were finding the remains of numerous animal types that had no living representatives. **Inferring** ***What did such fossil evidence indicate about life in the past?***

Section 15–2

1 FOCUS

Objectives

15.2.1 ***State*** how Hutton and Lyell described geological change.
15.2.2 ***Identify*** how Lamarck thought species evolve.
15.2.3 ***Describe*** Malthus's theory of population growth.

Guide for Reading

Reading Strategy

Students should list Hutton, Lyell, Lamarck, and Malthus. Before students read the section, have them look at the figures, read the captions, and write down each Key Concept they find in the captions. As they read the section, they should match each Key Concept they listed with a related Key Concept in the text.

2 INSTRUCT

Address Misconceptions

With the rapid pace of technological change today, students may not appreciate how revolutionary the idea of evolution was in Darwin's time. Point out that, from ancient times, most people believed that all living things were created by a divine being and that, once created, living things remained unchanged.

SECTION RESOURCES

Print:
- ***Teaching Resources,*** Section Review 15–2
- ***Guided Reading and Study Workbook,*** Section 15–2

Technology:
- ***iText,*** Section 15–2

Answers to . . .

Figure 15–4 *They can learn how the earlier investigators formed their ideas based on the evidence they had. They might also interpret the evidence in new ways.*

Figure 15–5 *That some organisms from the past had no modern representatives, and that some organisms may have become extinct*

An Ancient, Changing Earth

Use Visuals

Figure 15–6 Call students' attention to the figure and have them read the caption. Ask: **How did Hutton's and Lyell's proposals about Earth support Darwin's ideas about the changes he had observed in living things?** *(Hutton and Lyell proposed that Earth had changed. This helped support Darwin's idea that living things change. Hutton and Lyell also proposed that Earth was millions of years old. This provided the long time span Darwin thought was needed for changes in living things to occur.)*

Biology and History

Point out to students that most of the dates in the time line refer to the dates of publications that influenced Darwin. After students read the time line, suggest that they refer back to it as they read about each of the scientists in the text. Doing so will help students appreciate the role each scientist played in the evolution of Darwin's theory.

Writing Activity

Students might write about how similar Darwin's and Wallace's theories are. They also might write about how different the backgrounds and careers of the two men were. Wallace came from a large family with little money and only went to grammar school, whereas Darwin came from a small, well-to-do family and graduated from college. Darwin became one of the most famous scientists of all time for his theory of evolution, whereas Wallace has never been very well known, despite the fact that his theory of evolution predated Darwin's theory.

▲ **Figure 15–6** These huge rocks, which are composed of sandstone, show distinct layers that were laid down over millions of years. **Hutton and Lyell cited geological features such as these rocks as evidence that Earth is many millions of years old. Geological processes acting millions of years ago continue to shape Earth in the present.**

An Ancient, Changing Earth

During the eighteenth and nineteenth centuries, scientists examined Earth in great detail. They gathered information suggesting that Earth was very old and had changed slowly over time. Two scientists who formed important theories based on this evidence were James Hutton and Charles Lyell. **Hutton and Lyell helped scientists recognize that Earth is many millions of years old, and the processes that changed Earth in the past are the same processes that operate in the present.**

Hutton's Theory of Geological Change

In 1795, the geologist James Hutton published a detailed theory about the geological forces that have shaped Earth. He proposed that layers of rock, such as those in **Figure 15–6**, form very slowly. Also, some rocks are moved up by forces beneath Earth's surface. Others are buried, and still others are pushed up from the sea floor to form mountain ranges. The resulting rocks, mountains, and valleys are then shaped by a variety of natural forces—including rain, heat, and cold temperatures. Most of these geological processes operate extremely slowly, often over millions of years. Hutton, therefore, proposed that Earth had to be much more than a few thousand years old.

Biology and History

Origins of Evolutionary Thought

The groundwork for the modern theory of evolution was laid during the 1700s and 1800s. Charles Darwin developed the central idea of evolution by natural selection, but others before and during his time also built essential parts of the theory.

1750

1773 Boston Tea Party

1785 **James Hutton** Hutton proposes that Earth is shaped by geological forces that took place over extremely long periods of time. He estimates Earth to be millions—not thousands—of years old.

1787 The United States Constitution is signed.

1798 **Thomas Malthus** In his *Essay on the Principle of Population,* Malthus predicts that the human population will grow faster than the space and food supplies needed to sustain it.

1800

1809 **Jean-Baptiste Lamarck** Lamarck publishes his theory of the inheritance of acquired traits. The theory is flawed, but he is one of the first to propose a mechanism explaining how organisms change over time.

PRESENTATIONS MADE EASY!

The Presentation Assistant Plus contains the Prentice Hall Presentation Pro and the Transparencies, which provide easy-to-follow visual support for every step of this section. If you have a computer presentation station, use Prentice Hall Presentation Pro for Section 15–2, or use the transparencies listed here.

Section 15–2: **Interest Grabber**
Section Outline
Movement of Earth
Figure 15–7

Lyell's *Principles of Geology* Just before the *Beagle* set sail, Darwin had been given the first volume of geologist Charles Lyell's book, *Principles of Geology*. Lyell stressed that scientists must explain past events in terms of processes that they can actually observe, since processes that shaped the Earth millions of years earlier continue in the present. Volcanoes release hot lava and gases now, just as they did on an ancient Earth. Erosion continues to carve out canyons, just as it did in the past.

Lyell's work explained how awesome geological features could be built up or torn down over long periods of time. Lyell helped Darwin appreciate the significance of geological phenomena that he had observed. Darwin had witnessed a spectacular volcanic eruption. Darwin wrote about an earthquake that had lifted a stretch of rocky shoreline—with mussels and other animals attached to it—more than 3 meters above its previous position. He noted the fossils of marine animals displaced many feet above sea level. Darwin then understood how geological processes could have raised these rocks from the sea floor to a mountaintop.

This understanding of geology influenced Darwin in two ways. First, Darwin asked himself: If the Earth could change over time, might life change as well? Second, he realized that it would have taken many, many years for life to change in the way he suggested. This would have been possible only if the Earth were extremely old.

CHECKPOINT *What are some ways the Earth has changed over time?*

Writing Activity

Use the library or the Internet to find out more about Darwin and Wallace. Write a dialogue between these two men, where the conversation shows the similarities in their careers and theories.

Charles Darwin Darwin sets sail on the H.M.S. *Beagle*, a voyage that would provide him with vast amounts of evidence that lead to his theory of evolution.

1831

1833

Charles Lyell In the second and final volume of *Principles of Geology*, Lyell explained that processes occurring now have shaped Earth's geological features over long

1849 California Gold Rush

1850

Alfred Wallace Wallace writes to Darwin, speculating on evolution by natural selection, based on his studies of the distribution of plants and animals. Darwin presents Wallace's essay to the Linnaean Society.

1858

1859 Darwin publishes *On the Origin of Species.*

1861 The United States Civil War begins.

Meet Diverse Needs

Challenge gifted students to research Count Georges Louis-Leclerc de Buffon, the 18th-century French naturalist who influenced Darwin with his voluminous writings about the changing nature of species. Suggest that students try to locate some of Buffon's original works and skim them to find passages that might have influenced Darwin's ideas about evolution. Ask students to share their findings with the rest of the class in an oral report. **Learning modality: verbal**

Make Connections

Earth Science Help students appreciate how slowly geological forces such as erosion occur. Ask: **How did the Grand Canyon form?** *(Through the erosion of rock layers by the Colorado River)* Tell students that the Colorado River has been eroding Earth's surface at a rate of about 0.3 m per millennium, which is actually a rather rapid rate of erosion. Point out that the Grand Canyon is as deep as 1800 m in some places. Ask: **About how long did it take the Colorado River to erode the Grand Canyon to this depth?** *(About six million years)*

Use Community Resources

Have students visit a local road bed, ravine, rock outcrop, or other site where sedimentary layers have been exposed to view by construction activities or by natural processes, such as erosion or faults. Challenge students to predict how long it took for the sediments in each layer to be deposited and turned into rock. If possible, arrange to have a geologist from a local college, university, or state department of natural resources meet with your class at the site to explain how the exposed layers were formed and how long it took them to form.

BIO INSIGHTS — HISTORY OF SCIENCE

In Darwin's shadow

Alfred Russel Wallace was born in 1823 in Wales. He received only six years of formal education but was very well read. His first job, as a surveyor, gave him practical experience in the natural world and furthered his love of nature. Wallace began his career as naturalist in 1848, when he went on an expedition to the Amazon River basin. There, he spent four years traveling, collecting, mapping, and writing. He later went to Malaysia, where he spent eight years involved in the same pursuits. His evolutionary theory, which is strikingly similar to Darwin's, was developed during this time. Because Wallace was a vocal proponent of unpopular social and religious views, he never held a permanent academic position. Part-time jobs and a small inheritance allowed him to spend much of his time writing. By the time he died in 1913, he had over 700 publications and two honorary doctorate degrees.

Answer to . . .

CHECKPOINT *Geological features on Earth have been built up and torn down over long periods of time through processes such as volcanic activity, earthquakes, and erosion.*

Lamarck's Theory of Evolution

Address Misconceptions

The way evolution is often discussed may lead students to hold the misconception that scientists today still view evolution as a Lamarckian process. Give students the following example, which is typical of what they might read in a textbook: "The bird evolved a larger beak." This sounds as though an individual bird has intentionally changed its biological traits. Ask: **What would be a more accurate way of stating this?** *(Over many generations, the bird species gradually evolved larger beaks.)*

Build Science Skills

Designing Experiments Challenge students to design an experiment to test Lamarck's theory of the inheritance of acquired traits. Students' experimental designs should include a hypothesis, procedure, and possible outcomes. Ask: **What species would you use, and what variable would you test?** *(Answers will vary depending on students' experimental designs. In one well-known experiment, scientists cut off the tails of adult mice and then observed whether the offspring of the mice also had short tails.)* Have students explain how the different possible outcomes of their experiment would or would not support Lamarck's theory.

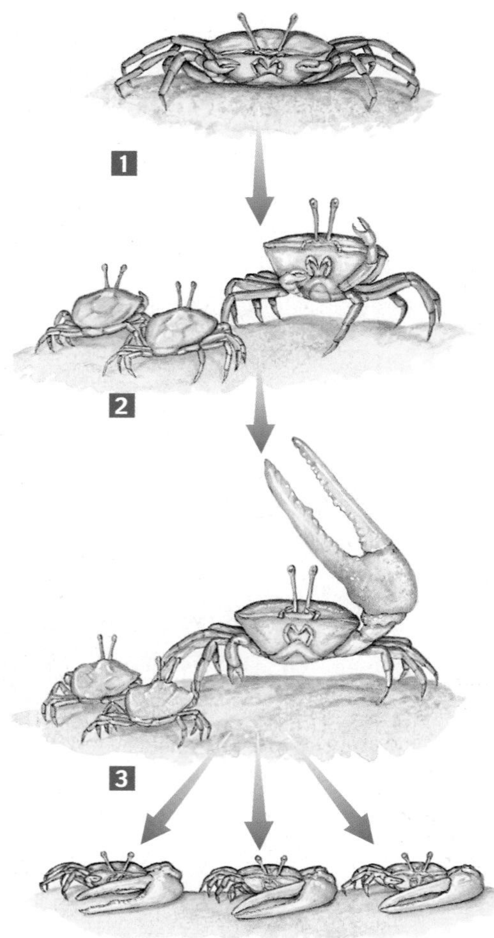

▲ **Figure 15–7 One explanation for evolution proposed that the selective use or disuse of an organ led to a change in that organ that was then passed on to offspring.** This proposed mechanism is shown here applied to fiddler crabs. (1) The male crab uses its small front claw to attract mates and ward off predators. (2) Because the front claw has been used repeatedly, it becomes larger. (3) The acquired characteristic, a larger claw, is then passed on to the crab's offspring. This explanation, proposed by Lamarck in 1809, was found to be incorrect.

Lamarck's Theory of Evolution

One of the best-known scientific theorists to precede Darwin was the French naturalist Jean-Baptiste Lamarck. Lamarck was among the first scientists to recognize that living things have changed over time—and that all species were descended from other species. He also realized that organisms were somehow adapted to their environments. In 1809, the year that Darwin was born, Lamarck published his theory of how organisms changed over time. **Lamarck proposed that by selective use or disuse of organs, organisms acquired or lost certain traits during their lifetime. These traits could then be passed on to their offspring. Over time, this process led to change in a species.**

Tendency Toward Perfection Lamarck proposed that all organisms have an innate tendency toward complexity and perfection. As a result, they are continually changing and acquiring features that help them live more successfully in their environments. In Lamarck's view, for instance, the ancestors of birds acquired an urge to fly. Over many generations, birds kept trying to fly, and their wings increased in size and became more suited to flying.

Use and Disuse Because of this tendency toward perfection, Lamarck proposed that organisms could alter the size or shape of particular organs by using their bodies in new ways. For example, by trying to use their front limbs for flying, birds could eventually transform those limbs into wings. Conversely, if a winged animal did not use its wings—an example of disuse—the wings would decrease in size over generations and finally disappear.

Inheritance of Acquired Traits Like many biologists of his time, Lamarck thought that acquired characteristics could be inherited. For example, if during its lifetime an animal somehow altered a body structure, leading to longer legs or fluffier feathers, it would pass that change on to its offspring. By this reasoning, if you spent much of your life lifting weights to build muscles, your children would inherit big muscles, too.

Evaluating Lamarck's Theory Lamarck's theory of evolution, illustrated in **Figure 15–7,** is incorrect in several ways. Lamarck, like Darwin, did not know how traits are inherited. He did not know that an organism's behavior has no effect on its inheritable characteristics. However, Lamarck was one of the first to develop a scientific theory of evolution and realize that organisms are adapted to their environments. In this way, he paved the way for the work of later biologists.

CHECKPOINT *According to Lamarck, how did bird flight evolve?*

BIO INSIGHTS — HISTORY OF SCIENCE

Lamarck's successes and failures
French naturalist Jean-Baptiste Lamarck began his career as a botanist. He spent many years collecting and studying plants, and he wrote numerous books and articles on his research. Lamarck was also a museum curator and one of the originators of the modern concept of the museum collection. In addition, he coined the terms *invertebrate* and *biology*. In 1801, Lamarck's carefully researched book, *System of Invertebrate Animals,* presented a revision of the Linnaean classification of invertebrates that is still accepted by most scientists today. Unfortunately, some of Lamarck's other publications were based more on fancy than fact, including his 1809 *Zoological Philosophy*, in which he discusses the inheritance of acquired traits. Because of these other publications, Lamarck became a scientific outcast, and he died a poor, lonely man.

Answer to . . .

CHECKPOINT *Lamarck thought that bird ancestors repeatedly used their small wings, causing an increase in wing size that was passed on to offspring. Over many generations, the wings became more powerful, eventually producing modern birds capable of efficient flight.*

Population Growth

Another important influence on Darwin came from the English economist Thomas Malthus. In 1798, Malthus observed that babies were being born faster than people were dying. **Malthus reasoned that if the human population continued to grow unchecked, sooner or later there would be insufficient living space and food for everyone.** The only forces he observed that worked against this growth were war, famine, and disease. Conditions in nineteenth-century England, illustrated in **Figure 15–8,** reinforced Malthus's somewhat pessimistic view of the human condition.

When Darwin read Malthus's work, he realized that this reasoning applied even more strongly to plants and animals than it did to humans. Why? Because humans produce far fewer offspring than most other species do. A mature maple tree can produce thousands of seeds in a single summer, and one oyster can produce millions of eggs each year. If all the offspring of almost any species survived for several generations, they would overrun the world.

Obviously, this has not happened, because continents are not covered with maple trees, and oceans are not filled with oysters. The overwhelming majority of a species' offspring die. Further, only a few of those offspring that survive succeed in reproducing. What causes the death of so many individuals? What factor or factors determine which ones survive and reproduce, and which do not? Answers to these questions became central to Darwin's explanation of evolutionary change.

▶ **Figure 15–8** **Malthus proposed that war, famine, and disease limited the growth of human populations.** He supported his theory with the evidence he observed in the streets of London.

15–2 Section Assessment

1. **Key Concept** What two ideas from geology were important to Darwin's thinking?
2. **Key Concept** According to Lamarck, how did organisms acquire traits?
3. **Key Concept** According to Malthus, what factors limited population growth?
4. Why has Lamarck's theory of evolution been rejected?
5. **Critical Thinking Inferring** Malthus formed his theory by studying factors that control the population growth of humans. How might factors operating on organisms in nature differ from those of Malthus's theory?

iTEXT Assessment Use iText to review the important concepts in Section 15–2.

ALTERNATIVE ASSESSMENT

Give a Talk Imagine that you are either James Hutton or Charles Lyell addressing an audience of their time. Give a talk explaining your ideas, noting what your listeners will consider new and different.

Population Growth

Demonstration

Help students appreciate the tremendous reproductive potential of organisms. Have each student or small group count all the seeds in a green pepper that has been cut in half. Then, ask: **How many seeds would there be in one generation if all the seeds in your pepper grew into plants that each produced the same number of seeds?** *(There would be x^2 seeds, where x is the number of seeds in the original pepper.)* Challenge students to calculate how many seeds there would be in two generations. *(There would be $(x^2)^2$, or x^4 seeds.)* Conclude by saying that, if pepper plants actually reproduced at their potential rate, there would be billions of offspring in just a few generations.

3 ASSESS

Evaluate Understanding

Read each of the Key Concepts in the section, leaving the names *Hutton, Lyell, Lamarck,* or *Malthus* blank. Call on students at random to fill in the correct name.

Reteach

Using the chalkboard or an overhead transparency, work with students to create a concept map summarizing the contributions of other scientists to Darwin's ideas about evolution.

ALTERNATIVE ASSESSMENT

Audiences of the time thought that Earth was just a few thousand years old and that all major geological changes occurred in the past. Hutton proposed that Earth was millions of years old. Lyell stressed that the forces shaping Earth are the same in the present as in the past.

15–2 Section Assessment

1. Earth is very old, and the same processes that shaped Earth millions of years ago continue in the present.
2. Lamarck thought that organisms acquired traits by using their bodies in new ways. For example, birds might transform their front limbs into wings by trying to use the limbs for flying.
3. Malthus thought that war, famine, and disease limited population growth.
4. Lamarck's theory was discredited because evidence shows that acquired characteristics are not inherited.
5. Factors operating on organisms in nature might include competition and predation instead of famine and war.

Use iText to review the key concepts in Section 15–2.

Section 15–3

1 FOCUS

Objectives

15.3.1 ***List*** events leading to Darwin's publication of *On the Origin of Species.*
15.3.2 ***Describe*** how natural variation is used in artificial selection.
15.3.3 ***Explain*** how natural selection is related to species' fitness.
15.3.4 ***Identify*** evidence Darwin used to present his case for evolution.
15.3.5 ***State*** Darwin's theory of evolution by natural selection.

Guide for Reading

Vocabulary Preview

Have students think of examples of each of the concepts in the vocabulary list. As they read the section, they should check to see if their examples are suitable.

Reading Strategy

Suggest that students write the headings and subheadings in outline form and fill in details under each topic as they read the section.

2 INSTRUCT

Publication of *On the Origin of Species*

Build Science Skills

Making Judgments Tell students that Darwin's reluctance to publish his work is a good example of how science is influenced by its social context. Help students appreciate this by challenging them to think of similar examples from today. Ask: **What current areas of scientific research are controversial, much as evolution was controversial in Darwin's time?** *(Possible answers include cloning, genetic engineering, and research involving animals or human fetal tissue.)*

15–3 Darwin Presents His Case

Guide for Reading

Key Concepts
- How is natural variation used in artificial selection?
- How is natural selection related to a species' fitness?
- What evidence of evolution did Darwin present?

Vocabulary
natural variation
artificial selection
struggle for existence
fitness
adaptation
survival of the fittest
natural selection
descent with modification
common descent
homologous structure
vestigial organ

Reading Strategy: Building Vocabulary As you read, write a phrase or sentence in your own words to define each boldfaced term.

When Darwin returned to England in 1836, he brought back specimens from around the world. Subsequent findings about these specimens soon had the scientific community abuzz. Darwin learned that his Galápagos mockingbirds actually belonged to three separate species found nowhere else in the world! Even more surprising, the brown birds that Darwin had thought to be wrens, warblers, and blackbirds were all finches. They, too, were found nowhere else. The same was true of the Galápagos tortoises, the marine iguanas, and many plants that Darwin had collected on the islands. Each island species looked a great deal like a similar species on the South American mainland. Yet, the island species were clearly different from the mainland species and from one another.

Publication of *On the Origin of Species*

Darwin began filling notebooks with his ideas about species diversity and the process that would later be called evolution. However, he did not rush out to publish his thoughts. Recall that Darwin's ideas challenged fundamental scientific beliefs of his day. Darwin was not only stunned by his discoveries, he was disturbed by them. Years later, he wrote, "It was evident that such facts as these . . . could be explained on the supposition that species gradually became modified, and the subject haunted me." Although he discussed his work with friends, he shelved his manuscript for years and told his wife to publish it in case he died.

In 1858, Darwin received a short essay from Alfred Russel Wallace, a fellow naturalist who had been doing field work in Malaysia. That essay summarized the thoughts on evolutionary change that Darwin had been mulling over for almost 25 years! Suddenly, Darwin had an incentive to publish his own work. At a scientific meeting later that year, Wallace's essay was presented together with some of Darwin's work.

◀ **Figure 15–9** Each zebra inherits genes that give it a distinctive pattern of stripes. Those visibly different patterns are an example of natural variation in a species. **Formulating Hypotheses** ***What might be some inherited variations that are not visible?***

SECTION RESOURCES

Print:
- ***Laboratory Manual A,*** Chapter 15 Lab
- ***Laboratory Manual B,*** Chapter 15 Lab
- ***Teaching Resources,*** Section Review 15–3, Chapter 15 Exploration
- ***Guided Reading and Study Workbook,*** Section 15–3
- ***Issues and Decision Making,*** 15–3

Technology:
- ***iText,*** Section 15–3

Darwin began writing in earnest. Eighteen months later, in 1859, he published the results of his work: *On the Origin of Species.* In his book, he proposed a mechanism for evolution that he called natural selection. He then presented evidence demonstrating that the process of evolution has been taking place for millions of years—and continues in all living things. Darwin's work caused an immediate sensation. Many people considered his arguments to be brilliant, while others strongly opposed and even ridiculed his message. But what did Darwin actually say?

CHECKPOINT *What event motivated Darwin to publish his ideas?*

Natural Variation and Artificial Selection

Darwin began his explanation of evolution by abandoning the idea of a species as perfect and unchanging. He argued that **natural variation,** defined as differences among individuals of a species, is found in all types of organisms. Variation is present in species in nature, as shown in **Figure 15–9,** and in farm crops and livestock. Some cows gave more milk than others, for example, and some plants bore larger fruit than others. Darwin proposed that much of this variation could be inherited, or passed on to the next generation. Today, the fact that variation exists seems obvious. We can easily observe it in so many living things. In Darwin's day, however, it was revolutionary to suggest that variation was a major feature of life.

Despite all his world travels, Darwin actually made some of his greatest progress on evolutionary theory by studying the work of English farmers and breeders. He noted that breeders routinely used variation to improve their crops and livestock. Through a technique called selective breeding, they would determine which individuals to use for breeding based on the natural variation that they found. Only the largest hogs, the fastest horses, or the cows that gave the most milk were selected to produce offspring. Darwin termed this process **artificial selection.** Using artificial selection, breeders were able to produce a wide range of plants and animals that looked very different from their ancestors. **In artificial selection, nature provided the variation among different organisms, and humans selected those variations that they found useful.** Artificial selection is still used today to shape a variety of traits, as shown in **Figure 15–10.**

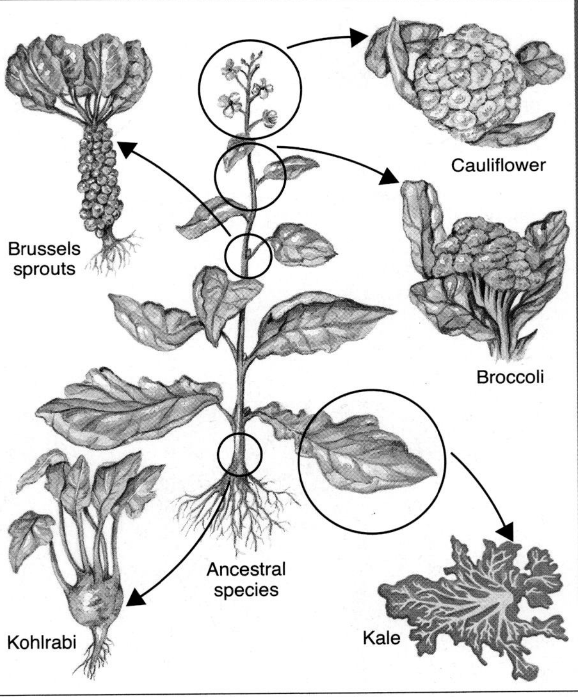

▶ **Figure 15–10** **In the process of artificial selection, humans select from among the naturally occurring variations in a species.** This process can lead to great differences. In some cases, a single ancestral species has given rise to a variety of modern plants.

Quick Lab

New vegetables from old?

Materials various *Brassica* (cabbage family) vegetables

Procedure
Examine each of the vegetables and compare them. Determine which organ of the ancestral plant breeders may have chosen to produce each vegetable.

Analyze and Conclude
Formulating Hypotheses Choose one of the vegetables. Explain how breeders might have produced that variety from the ancestor plant, shown below.

Natural Variation and Artificial Selection

Quick Lab

Objective Students will be able to formulate hypotheses to explain how breeders modify plant organs to develop new vegetables.

Skill Focus **Formulating Hypotheses**

Materials various *Brassica* vegetables

Time 20 minutes

Advance Prep Obtain a variety of fresh *Brassica* vegetables, such as broccoli, Brussels sprouts, cauliflower, cabbage, and rutabaga.

Strategy
After students have completed the procedure, challenge them to recall what selective breeding is. (If necessary, prompt them to review Section 13–1.) Then encourage them to observe the ancestral species in Figure 15–10.

Expected Outcome Students should hypothesize that plants in the ancestral species must have shown great variation, for example, some probably had larger leaves or flowers. Breeders would have selected plants with similar traits and crossed them to produce new vegetables. Students may also suggest that chemicals were used to produce polyploid plants.

TIME SAVER — PRESENTATIONS MADE EASY!

The Presentation Assistant Plus contains the Prentice Hall Presentation Pro and the Transparencies, which provide easy-to-follow visual support for every step of this section. If you have a computer presentation station, use Prentice Hall Presentation Pro for Section 15–3, or use the transparencies listed here.

Section 15–3:
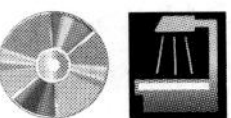
Interest Grabber
Section Outline
Concept Map
Figure 15–14
Figure 15–15

Answer to . . .

Figure 15–9 *Answers may include: differences in speed of the animal, physical strength, resistance to disease, vision, hearing, and so on.*

Evolution by Natural Selection

Meet Diverse Needs

Tell students that in Darwin's book, *On the Origin of Species*, he defined natural selection in the following terms: "I have called this principle, by which each slight variation, if useful, is preserved, by the term Natural Selection." Ask: **What was Darwin referring to when he wrote "each slight variation, if useful"?** *(Each adaptation, or inherited characteristic that increases an organism's chance of survival)* **What did Darwin mean by "is preserved"?** *(Is selected for, by being passed on to successive generations)* **Learning modality: verbal**

Use Community Resources

Arrange for students to visit a local zoo, wildlife preserve, or museum of natural history. Challenge small groups of students to identify adaptive traits in ten different animal species. Tell students to consider behavioral as well as biological traits. After the visit, urge groups to share their lists of adaptive traits. In the case of traits for which the adaptive significance is not obvious, ask: **Why do you think the trait is adaptive?** *(Answers will vary depending on the species and trait identified. For example, students might say that an orangutan's long arms are adaptive because they help the animal swing through trees in its arboreal habitat.)*

Address Misconceptions

The phrase "struggle for existence" may lead to the misconception that the struggle is a physical contest in which bigger or stronger individuals always win. Challenge students to think of situations in which smaller, weaker individuals might be winners, for example, because small size helps them hide from predators or survive with less food.

Evolution by Natural Selection

Darwin's next insight was to compare processes in nature to artificial selection. By doing so, he developed a scientific hypothesis to explain how evolution occurs. This is where Darwin made his greatest contribution—and his strongest break with the past.

The Struggle for Existence Darwin was convinced that a process like artificial selection worked in nature. But how? He recalled Malthus's work on population growth. Darwin realized that high birth rates and a shortage of life's basic needs would eventually force organisms into a competition for resources. The **struggle for existence** means that members of each species compete regularly to obtain food, living space, and other necessities of life. In this struggle, the predators that are faster or have a particular way of ensnaring other organisms can catch more prey. Those prey that are faster, better camouflaged, or better protected, such as the porcupine shown in **Figure 15–11,** can avoid being caught. This struggle for existence was central to Darwin's theory of evolution.

Survival of the Fittest A key factor in the struggle for existence, Darwin observed, was how well suited an organism is to its environment. Darwin called the ability of an individual to survive and reproduce in its specific environment **fitness.** Darwin proposed that fitness is the result of adaptations. An **adaptation** is any inherited characteristic that increases an organism's chance of survival. Successful adaptations, Darwin concluded, enable organisms to become better suited to their environment and thus better able to survive and reproduce. Adaptations can be physical characteristics, such as a porcupine's sharp quills, or more complex features, such as behavior in which some animals live and hunt in groups.

▼ **Figure 15–11** Survival of the fittest can take many different forms. For one species, it may be an ability to run fast, whereas for another species, it may be behavioral tactics that it uses to outsmart predators. For the porcupine, sharp quills make a powerful, hungry predator back away from an attack. **Inferring** ***What other types of characteristics might increase chances of survival?***

TEACHER TO TEACHER

I like to take my class to the gym and play "survival of the fittest." Several physical exercises are set up to test for different athletic abilities, such as jumping, crawling, running, and dodging. The "winners" are likely to have adaptations for their speciality areas. For example, students who excel in crawling through tight openings are likely to be smaller than average. This activity highlights individual uniqueness and is a great springboard for discussion of adaptations that increase fitness.

—*Dick Jordan,*
Biology Teacher
Timberline High School,
Boise, ID

◀ **Figure 15–12** Each of these baby tanagers has its own set of inherited traits that affect its survival. A stronger bird may take food from a weaker sibling. A faster bird may escape predators more easily. Only those birds that survive and reproduce have the chance to pass their traits to the next generation. **Over time, natural selection results in changes in the inherited characteristics of a population.**

The concept of fitness, Darwin argued, was central to the process of evolution by natural selection. Generation after generation, individuals compete to survive and produce offspring. The baby birds in **Figure 15–12,** for example, compete for food and space while in the nest. Because each individual differs from other members of its species, each has unique advantages and disadvantages. Individuals with characteristics that are not well suited to their environment—that is, with low levels of fitness—either die or leave few offspring. Individuals that are better suited to their environment—that is, with high levels of fitness—survive and reproduce most successfully. This was a process that Darwin called **survival of the fittest.**

Because of its similarities to artificial selection, Darwin referred to the survival of the fittest as **natural selection.** In both artificial selection and natural selection, only certain individuals of a population produce new individuals. However, in natural selection, the traits being selected—and therefore increasing over time—contribute to an organism's fitness in its environment. Natural selection also takes place without human control or direction. **Over time, natural selection results in changes in the inherited characteristics of a population. These changes increase a species' fitness in its environment.** Natural selection cannot be seen directly; it can only be observed as changes in a population over many successive generations.

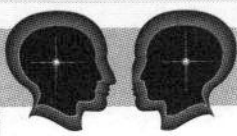

What did Darwin mean when he described certain organisms as "more fit" than others?

Descent With Modification Darwin proposed that over long periods, natural selection produces organisms that have different structures, establish different niches, or occupy different habitats. As a result, species today look different from their ancestors. Each living species has descended, with changes, from other species over time. He referred to this principle as **descent with modification.**

KEEP CURRENT WITH . . . SCIENCE NEWS®

To find out more about the topics in this chapter, go to: **www.phschool.com**

Build Science Skills

Applying Concepts Divide the class into small groups. Instruct each group to brainstorm ways Earth might change over the next thousand years. For example, there might be an increase in harmful compounds such as sulfur dioxide in the atmosphere, or oxygen-producing plants might become nearly extinct. Have each group select an organism living today and explain how it might evolve to adapt to the changes. The groups should describe or sketch specific adaptations in their organism. Invite each group to share its ideas with the class.

Address Misconceptions

Students may hold the misconception that if a trait is favored by natural selection, it must be adaptive in every respect. Provide an example to make the point that some adaptive traits have drawbacks as well as benefits. Show students a picture of (or have them imagine) a deer with large antlers. Tell students that the antlers help the deer to compete for a mate and, therefore, to reproduce. However, a deer uses energy to produce the antlers and they may get in the way when the deer tries to run through thick woods or feed in dense brush. Obviously, the reproductive advantage of antlers outweighs these risks to survival.

SCIENCE NEWS®

Encourage students to visit **www.phschool.com** for the most current information on this topic.

TEACHER TO TEACHER

I like to use a make-believe scenario to illustrate natural selection. I have students pretend that a small group of humans is rocketed at "warp speed" to Planet X, without any books, weapons, or technology. Planet X has no ozone layer to protect its surface from cancer-causing ultraviolet radiation, but native plants and animals have evolved to live safely there. Below the surface, the planet has a network of underground tunnels, just a meter high, that are inhabited by carnivorous predators. I challenge students to describe how descendants of the group of humans would look and act after evolving for 100,000 years on Planet X.

—Dennis Glasgow,
Biology Teacher
Little Rock School District,
Little Rock, AR

Answers to . . .

CHECKPOINT *He meant organisms that are better suited to survive in their environment.*

Figure 15–11 *Possible answers include characteristics that help the organism evade predators, such as a chameleon's ability to change color, or characteristics that help the organism obtain resources, such as a giraffe's long neck.*

Build Science Skills

Applying Concepts Find a taxonomic chart that classifies living things. Give a copy to each student and point out the major taxonomic groups, including the kingdoms, phyla, and classes. Explain that the classification is based on similarities in traits among living organisms. The classification also shows how different kinds of organisms are related to one another. It represents the "tree of life" mentioned in the text. Have students look closely at one of the lineages in the chart, such as the lineage that leads to the species *Homo sapiens*. Check their interpretation of the chart as a record of evolution by asking: **To which family do humans belong?** *(The hominid family)* **Which other families are most closely related to the hominids?** *(The pongids, or great apes, and the hylobatids, or lesser apes)* **What type of animal was the common ancestor of humans and apes?** *(A hominoid)*

Evidence of Evolution

Demonstration

Half fill some beakers with water. Place a small leaf, shell, or other object in the bottom of each beaker. As students observe, gradually add a couple of handfuls of a mixture of sand and soil to each beaker. Do not stir or shake the beakers. Have students observe the beakers again at the end of class and once a day for the next two days. Then, ask: **What happened to the leaves, shells, and other objects?** *(They became covered with deposits of sediment.)* Point out that this is also what happens to organisms when they die and fall into ponds or lakes. Explain how the pressure of water and additional deposits eventually turns the sediments into rock. Ask: **What might eventually happen to organic remains that are covered over with sediments?** *(They turn into fossils.)*

Descent with modification also implies something else: that all living organisms are related to one another. Look back in time, and you will find common ancestors shared by tigers, panthers, and cheetahs. Look farther back, and you will find ancestors that these felines share with horses, dogs, bats, and primates. Farther back still are the common ancestors of mammals, birds, alligators, and fishes. If we look far enough back, the logic concludes, we could find the common ancestors of all living things. This is the principle known as **common descent.** According to this principle, all species—living and extinct—were derived from common ancestors.

Carry the concepts of descent with modification and common descent to their logical conclusion, and what do they produce? A single "tree of life" that links all living things on Earth. Darwin conceived of this idea long before he published his theory of evolution.

Evidence of Evolution

With this unified, dynamic theory of life, Darwin could finally explain many of the observations he had made during his travels aboard the *Beagle*. He presented these observations as evidence of the process of evolution. **Darwin argued that living things have been evolving on Earth for millions of years. Evidence for this process could be found in the fossil record, the geographical distribution of living species, homologous structures of living organisms, and similarities in early development.**

The Fossil Record It was well known in Darwin's time that fossils were the remains of ancient life and that different layers of rock had been formed at different times in Earth's history.

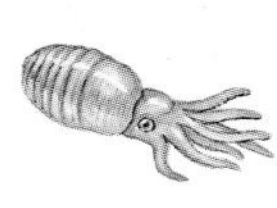

▼ **Figure 15–13** **Darwin argued that the fossil record provided evidence that living things have been evolving for millions of years.** Sometimes the fossil record includes similar, intermediate forms of a group of organisms that together suggest gradual modification over time. The four organisms shown here are all cephalopods, a group that includes octopi and squid. Fossil evidence indicates that these organisms gradually evolved a longer, more coiled shell.

HISTORY OF SCIENCE

Monkeys old and new

Until a few decades ago, scientists had long believed that Old and New World monkeys diverged from a common prosimian ancestor at least 50 million years ago. According to this view, the two primate groups became separated as Africa and South America drifted apart, but they evolved many of the same traits because of their similar tropical arboreal habitats. This interpretation was challenged in the 1970s by Richard Hoffstetter, an anthropologist, who theorized that Old and New World monkeys evolved from a common monkey ancestor much more recently. According to Hoffstetter, small numbers of monkeys accidentally rafted on fallen trees across the Atlantic Ocean from Africa to South America, after the two continents had already drifted apart. Later, genetic evidence was found to support Hoffstetter's theory, which is accepted by most experts today.

However, few people viewed the fossil record as Darwin did, as a detailed record of evolution. Darwin proposed that Earth was hundreds of millions—rather than thousands—of years old. During this time, he stated, countless species of many different forms had appeared on Earth, lived for a time, and then vanished. Fossils that had formed in the different layers of rock were evidence of this gradual change over time. In fact, by examining fossils from sequential layers of rock, one could view how a species had changed and produced different species over time, as shown in **Figure 15–13.**

Geographic Distribution of Living Species Remember that many parts of the biological puzzle that Darwin saw on his *Beagle* voyage involved living organisms. After Darwin discovered that those little brown birds he collected in the Galápagos were all finches, he began to wonder how they came to be similar, yet distinctly different from one another. Each species was slightly different from every other species. They were also slightly different from the most similar species on the mainland of South America. Could the island birds have changed over time, as populations in different places adapted to different local environments? Darwin struggled with this question for a long time. He finally decided that all these birds could have descended with modification from a common mainland ancestor.

There were other parts to the living puzzle as well. Recall that Darwin found entirely different species of animals on the continents of South America and Australia. Yet, when he looked at similar environments on those continents, he sometimes saw different animals that had similar structures and behaviors. Darwin's theory of descent with modification made scientific sense of this part of the puzzle as well. Species now living on different continents, as shown in **Figure 15–14,** had each descended from different ancestors. However, because some animals on each continent were living under similar ecological conditions, they were exposed to similar pressures of natural selection. Because of these similar selection pressures, different animals ended up evolving certain striking features in common.

CHECKPOINT *How can two species that look very different from each other be more closely related than two other species that look similar to each other?*

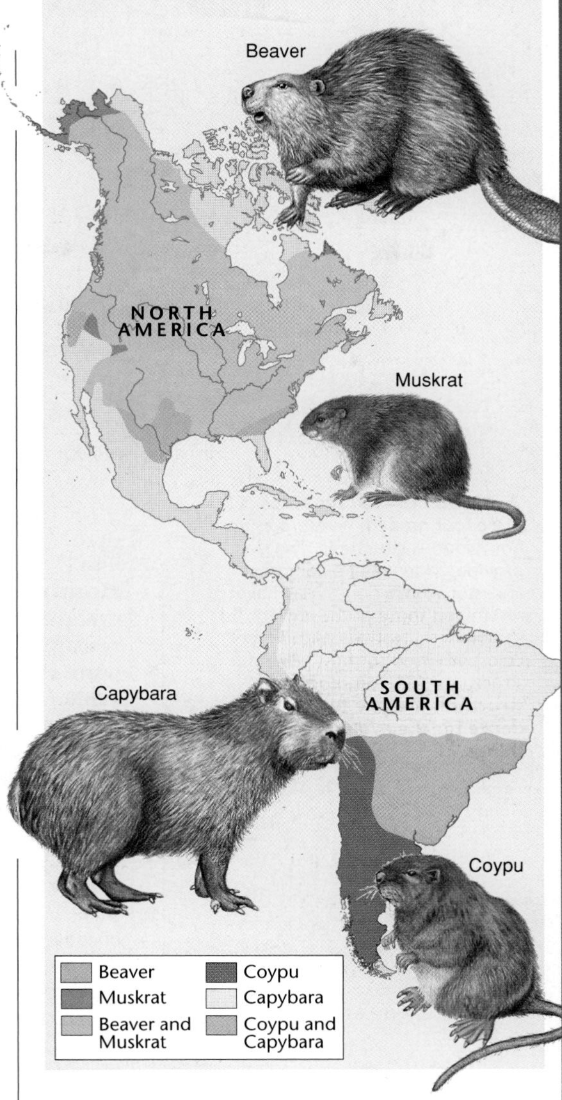

▲ **Figure 15–14** The existence of similar but unrelated species was a puzzle to Darwin. Later, he realized that similar animals in different locations were the product of different lines of evolutionary descent. Here, the beaver and the capybara are similar species that inhabit similar environments of North America and South America. The South American coypu also shares many characteristics with the North American muskrat. **Interpreting Graphics** ***Which animal has a larger geographical range, the coypu or the muskrat?***

Build Science Skills

Using Analogies Explain to students that the evolution of shared traits in unrelated species because of similar environments is called convergent evolution. Give students a chance to see how convergent evolution works by using an analogy similar to one that Darwin himself suggested. Have small groups of students brainstorm several ways to solve the same problem, such as improving traffic flow in the school or decreasing crowding in the classrooms. Tell students to be creative as they brainstorm ideas. After several minutes, have the groups share their ideas and identify those that are similar. Ask: **What do the different groups represent in terms of convergent evolution?** *(Unrelated species)* **What do the similar ideas represent?** *(Similar adaptations)* **What does the common problem that the groups worked on represent?** *(Similarities in the environments of the unrelated species)*

Meet Diverse Needs

Give students who need extra challenges an opportunity to learn more about convergent evolution. Have students research the convergent evolution of marsupial and placental mammals. *(They will learn that marsupials evolved to fill most of the same niches in Australia that placental mammals evolved to fill throughout the rest of the world.)* Ask students to share what they learn with the class by creating a poster that compares examples of convergent species of marsupial and placental mammals.

BIO INSIGHTS FACTS AND FIGURES

Comparing DNA
Instead of comparing homologous structures or embryos, a more direct way of determining evolutionary relationships among species is to compare the sequence of nitrogenous bases in their DNA. The same four nitrogenous bases—adenine, guanine, cytosine, and thymine—occur in the DNA of all living things on Earth. However, the exact sequence of nitrogenous bases is unique to each species. The sequence of bases is more similar in closely related species than in species that are not as closely related, and scientists can use this information to estimate how long it has been since two species shared a common ancestor. Since the 1990s, scientists have also been able to sequence the DNA of fossils to determine how extinct organisms were related to each other and to their living descendants.

Answers to . . .

CHECKPOINT *Regardless of their appearance, two species are closely related when they share a common ancestry. If one of those species experienced natural selection in a particular kind of environment, such as a desert, it may look similar to some unrelated desert species from a different location.*

Figure 15–14 *Muskrat*

Build Science Skills

Applying Concepts Help students understand homologous structures by contrasting them with analogous structures. Tell students that homologous structures are similar because they were inherited from a common ancestor, whereas analogous structures are similar because they evolved to fulfill the same function in unrelated species. Challenge students to apply the concepts by asking: **Are bat wings and butterfly wings homologous or analogous structures?** *(Analogous)*

Use Visuals

Figure 15–15 Call students' attention to the figure. Ask: **What similarities in the limbs suggest that they developed from the same basic structure?** *(The number and placement of the bones)* **How is the form of each limb adapted for a specific type of movement?** *(Students might say, for example, that the thin, light bones of a bat's wing help it to fly and the thick, strong bones of a whale's flipper help it to swim.)*

Build Science Skills

Classifying Challenge students to use the information in the text to create a graphic organizer to classify the following animals according to their similarities and differences: crocodiles, lizards, robins, hawks, bats, and whales. *(Students' graphics should show that crocodiles are most closely related to lizards, robins to hawks, and bats to whales. Graphic organizers also should show that robins and hawks are more closely related to crocodiles and lizards than they are to bats and whales.)* Urge students to share their work with the class. Then, ask: **Would you expect the vestigial limb bones of a snake to be more like the bones of a bird's wing or a rabbit's leg?** *(A bird's wing)*

Word Origins

Homomorphic structures are different structures that have the same, or similar, shapes.

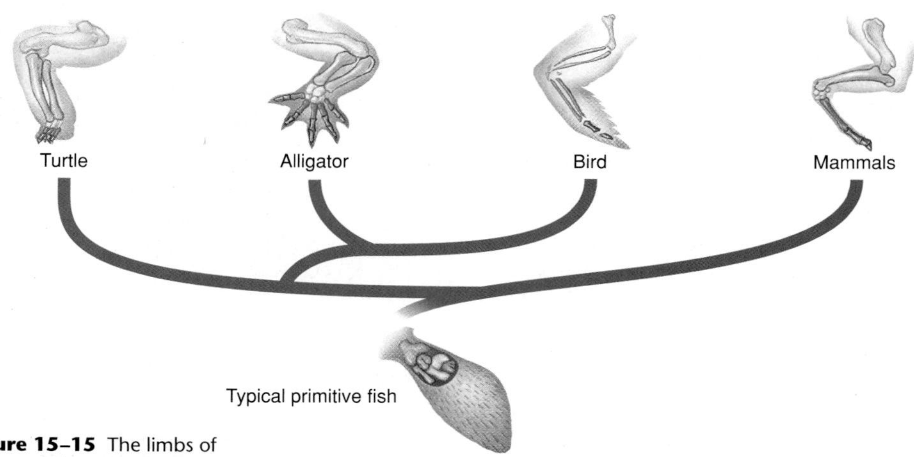

▲ **Figure 15–15** The limbs of these four modern vertebrates are homologous structures. They provide evidence of a common ancestor whose bones may have resembled those of the ancient fish shown here. Notice that different colors are used to show related structures. **Homologous structures are one type of evidence for the evolution of living things.**

Homologous Body Structures Further evidence of evolution can be found in living animals. By Darwin's time, researchers had noticed striking similarities among the body parts of animals with backbones. For example, they described similarities among the bones of different vertebrates, such as reptiles, birds, and mammals. Some of these limbs are arms, whereas others are wings, legs, or even flippers. The limbs differ greatly in form and function, yet they are all constructed from the same basic bones, as shown in **Figure 15–15.**

What is the scientific explanation for these similarities? Each of these limbs has adapted in ways that enable organisms to survive in different environments. Despite these different functions, however, these limb bones all develop from the same clumps of cells in growing embryos. Structures such as these, which have different mature forms but develop from the same embryonic tissues, are called **homologous structures** (hoh-MAH-luh-gus). Homologous structures provide strong evidence that all four-limbed animals with backbones have descended, with modifications, from common ancestors.

There is still more information to be gathered from homologous structures. If we compare the front limbs, we can see that all bird wings are more similar to one another than any of them are to bat wings. Other bones in bird skeletons most closely resemble the homologous bones of certain reptiles—including crocodiles and extinct reptiles such as dinosaurs. The bones that support the wings of bats, by contrast, are more similar to the front limbs of humans, whales, and other mammals than they are to those of birds. These similarities and differences help biologists group animals according to how recently they last shared a common ancestor.

Not all homologous structures serve important functions. The organs of many animals are so reduced in size that they are just vestiges, or traces, of homologous organs in other species.

Word Origins

Homologous, from the Greek words *homos,* meaning "same," and *legein,* meaning "say," describes similar body structures that come from a common ancestor. **If the word *morphe* means "shape," what are homomorphic structures?**

FACTS AND FIGURES

Clues to evolution

Many species of animals have vestigial organs. A familiar example is the human appendix. Some mammalian species such as koalas need an appendix for digestion, but the organ plays no role in human digestion. Humans also have a set of miniature tailbones at the base of the spine, even though humans obviously do not have tails. In addition, the muscles that move the ears are vestigial in humans. Vestigial organs often persist in a species indefinitely because they are unaffected by natural selection. Natural selection can increase the frequency of useful traits and decrease the frequency of harmful traits, but it cannot change the frequency of traits that have little or no effect on an organism's ability to survive and reproduce.

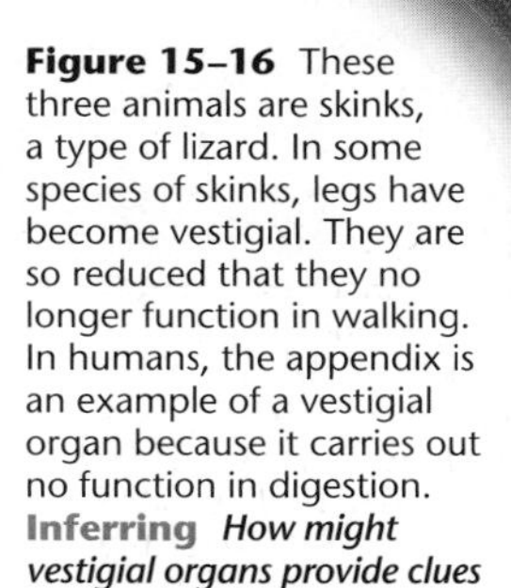

These **vestigial organs,** shown in **Figure 15–16,** may resemble miniature legs, tails, or other structures. Why would an organism possess organs with little or no function? One possibility is that the presence of a vestigial organ may not affect an organism's ability to survive and reproduce. In that case, natural selection would not cause the elimination of that organ.

Figure 15–16 These three animals are skinks, a type of lizard. In some species of skinks, legs have become vestigial. They are so reduced that they no longer function in walking. In humans, the appendix is an example of a vestigial organ because it carries out no function in digestion. **Inferring** *How might vestigial organs provide clues to an animal's evolutionary history?*

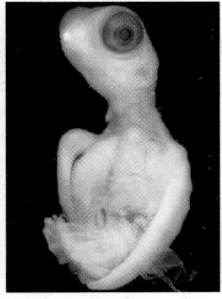

Similarities in Early Development The early stages, or embryos, of many animals with backbones are so similar that they can be hard to tell apart. This does not mean that a human embryo is ever identical to a fish or a bird embryo. However, as you can see in **Figure 15–17,** many embryos look especially similar during early stages of development. What do these similarities mean?

There have, in the past, been incorrect explanations for these similarities. Also, the great biologist Ernst Haeckel fudged some of his drawings to make the earliest stages of some embryos seem more similar than they actually are! Errors aside, however, it is clear that the same groups of embryonic cells develop in the same order and in similar patterns to produce the tissues and organs of all vertebrates. These common cells and tissues, growing in similar ways, produce the homologous structures discussed earlier.

CHECKPOINT *How can biologists use the idea of homologous structures to determine whether particular species are closely related?*

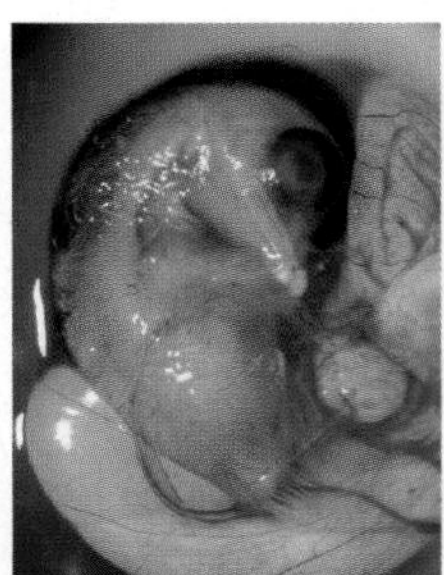

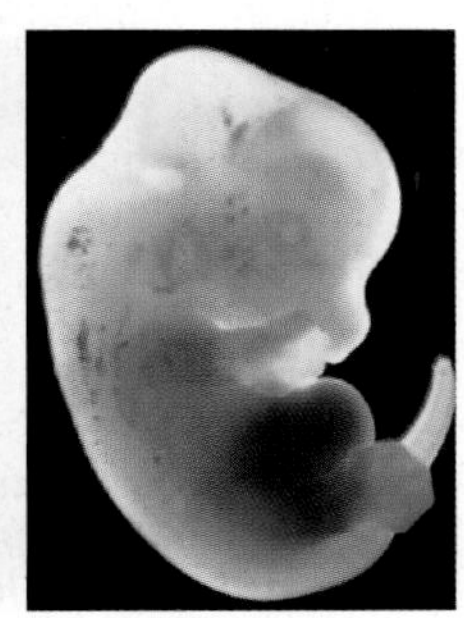

Chicken Turtle Rat

Figure 15–17 In their early stages of development, chickens, turtles, and rats look similar, providing evidence that they shared a common ancestry. **Drawing Conclusions** *How could a study of these embryos help show the relationships among animals with backbones?*

Meet Diverse Needs

Give enriched students an opportunity to learn more about the evolution of homologous and analogous structures by reading Stephen J. Gould's fascinating book, *The Panda's Thumb.* After they finish the book, challenge students to summarize a few of the most interesting examples that Gould describes, including the panda's "thumb." Urge them to share the examples with the class in an oral report. **Learning modality: verbal**

Build Science Skills

Inferring Tell students that similarities and differences in the DNA of different species are used to reconstruct evolutionary relationships. Ask: **Why do DNA comparisons provide the most direct evidence of evolutionary relationships?** *(Because DNA is passed directly from common ancestors to their descendants and controls the development of other traits.)*

FACTS AND FIGURES

Comparative embryology explained

The explanation for embryonic similarities in organisms that are very different as adults lies with the timing of gene action. All of an organism's genes are not active at the same time. In addition, those that are active during early development are less subject to change than those that are active later. This is because mutations occurring early in development have such far reaching effects that they tend to be lethal. Therefore, they are not passed on to successive generations. Mutations occurring later in development, on the other hand, tend to have more limited effects, so they are less likely to be lethal and more likely to be passed on. Thus, genes controlling later development are more subject to evolutionary change, explaining why humans and chickens are so different at later stages despite their similarity as embryos.

Answers to . . .

CHECKPOINT *The greater the similarities among homologous structures, the more recently particular species last shared a common ancestor.*

Figure 15–16 *A specific vestigial organ suggests that an organism's ancestor once used that organ.*

Figure 15–17 *Embryos of less closely related species would likely look different earlier in their development, while embryos of more closely related species probably look similar for longer periods.*

15–3 (continued)

Summary of Darwin's Theory

Meet Diverse Needs

Have students make a concept map to summarize Darwin's theory. Check that their illustrations of "the struggle for existence" show intraspecific competition and not interspecific predation. **Learning modality: visual**

3 ASSESS

Evaluate Understanding

Ask students to make a compare/contrast table listing similarities and differences between artificial and natural selection and giving examples of each.

Reteach

Write each of the following concepts on the chalkboard and review its meaning: *fitness, adaptation, natural selection, struggle for existence, survival of the fittest,* and *descent with modification.* Then, have students write a paragraph in which they use each concept to explain how populations of organisms become suited for their environments.

ALTERNATIVE ASSESSMENT

Students' newspaper articles should explain Darwin's theory in simple terms that are understandable to readers with no background knowledge of evolution. Their articles should outline how heritable traits that help organisms survive and reproduce tend to be passed on to successive generations and, therefore, to increase in frequency in populations.

Use iText to review the key concepts in Section 15–3.

Answer to . . .

Figure 15–18 *Based on Darwin's theory, you could observe how these species are adapted to survive and reproduce in their environments.*

▲ **Figure 15–18** Darwin published *On the Origin of Species* almost 150 years ago. Today, his theory of evolution continues to be upheld in all areas of biology. **Applying Concepts** ***New species are continually being discovered. How could you use Darwin's theory to learn more about these new species?***

Summary of Darwin's Theory

Darwin's theory of evolution presented a new view of life, summarized below. This view, profoundly different from anything known in nineteenth-century England, continues to be upheld by research today. Many would still agree with Darwin, who wrote, "There is grandeur in this view of life, [that] from so simple a beginning, endless forms most beautiful and wonderful have been and are being evolved."

1. Individual organisms in nature differ from one another. Some of this variation is inherited.
2. Organisms in nature produce more offspring than can survive, and many of those that survive do not reproduce.
3. Because more organisms are produced than can survive, members of each species must compete for limited resources.
4. Because each organism is unique, each has different advantages and disadvantages in the struggle for existence.
5. Individuals best suited to their environment survive and reproduce most successfully. The characteristics that make them best suited to their environment are passed on to offspring. Individuals whose characteristics are not as well suited to their environment die or leave fewer offspring.
6. Species change over time. Over long periods, natural selection causes changes in the characteristics of a species, such as in size and form. New species arise, and other species disappear.
7. Species alive today have descended with modifications from species that lived in the past.
8. All organisms on Earth are united into a single tree of life by common descent.

15–3 Section Assessment

1. **Key Concept** How is artificial selection dependent on variation in nature?
2. **Key Concept** The theory of evolution by natural selection explains, in scientific terms, how living things evolve over time. What is being selected in this process?
3. **Key Concept** What types of evidence did Darwin use to support his theory of change over time?
4. What is the "struggle for existence"? How was this idea based on Malthus's work?
5. **Critical Thinking Comparing and Contrasting** Compare and contrast Darwin's theory of evolution with that of Lamarck. How are they similar? How are they different?

iTEXT Assessment Use iText to review the important concepts in Section 15–3.

ALTERNATIVE ASSESSMENT

Writing a Newspaper Article

Write a brief newspaper article reporting on the meeting of the Linnaean Society, where Darwin's and Wallace's hypotheses of evolution were first presented. Explain the theory of evolution by natural selection for an audience who knows nothing about the subject.

15–3 Section Assessment

1. Nature provides the variation, and humans select the variations that are useful.
2. The traits that help an organism survive in a particular environment
3. The fossil record, geographic distribution of species, homologous structures, and similarities in early development
4. The struggle for existence is competition between members of the same species for food, living space, and other needs. The more limited the food and other resources, the greater the competition. Malthus had argued that war, famine, and disease keep human population numbers in check.
5. Both stated that species become adapted to their environments. Lamarck thought organisms acquire and pass on certain traits. Darwin thought that, over time, natural selection causes a change in the inherited characteristics of a population.

Exploration

Modeling Adaptation

In this game, three families land on an alien planet. At home, the Hunter family survived by hunting in the cold north. The Seeder family farmed the temperate zone. The Fisher family lived on a tropical island. In this investigation, you will model how well each family survives in a new environment.

Problem **How do organisms survive in new habitats?**

Material

- coin

Skills Using Models, Using Tables and Graphs, Calculating

Procedure

1. Work in groups of three, with each member playing a Hunter, Seeder, or Fisher.
2. Flip a coin. Record the result as 1 for heads, 0 for tails. Toss the coin three more times to produce a series of four 1s and 0s. This 4-digit number is the code for your new habitat.
3. If the first digit in your code is 1, you live in a hot area. If it is 0, the climate is cold. If the second digit is 1, the climate is wet. If it is 0, it's dry. If the third digit is 1, you have a dry cave to live in. If it is 0, you sleep under the stars. If the last digit is 1, there is enough food. If it is 0, food is scarce. Record a description of your habitat.
4. Find your family in the table below. Then, record each number in your row that falls under a heading that describes your habitat (hot or cold and so forth). Record the total of these 4 numbers. This total represents the energy you have accumulated from your food.
5. Subtract 8 from your total to model the energy you must use to survive. If you don't have enough energy to do this, you're out of the game. The player with the most energy wins. Record the score and habitat of each family.
6. **Predicting** Record a prediction of what would happen if you reversed each player's habitat code by changing all the 1s to 0s and the 0s to 1s.
7. Reverse your habitat code as described in step 6. Play a second round with these conditions.

Analyze and Conclude

1. **Comparing and Contrasting** In which habitat were you most successful? Was it similar to your home environment?
2. **Using Models** The numbers in the table are different for each family. How did this fact help you model the survival of different organisms?
3. **Drawing Conclusions** Is one habitat best for all players? Explain in terms of adaptation.

Go Further

Revise the game to reflect the different conditions of summer and winter. Then, demonstrate your game to the class.

Energy Points for Survival

	Temperature		Water		Shelter		Food	
	Cold	Hot	Dry	Wet	None	Cave	Scarce	Plenty
Hunter	8	-2	0	4	-6	7	-5	8
Seeder	0	3	2	2	-1	2	-2	6
Fisher	-5	8	-2	5	0	1	-1	4

Exploration

Objective Students will be able to use a model to determine how adaptations affect survival of organisms in new habitats.

Skills Focus **Using Models, Using Tables and Graphs, Calculating**

Time 45 minutes

Advance Prep Before assigning the lab, you may want to play a round of the game by yourself to get a feel for how it works.

Teaching Tips

Have students read the entire procedure. Then, ask:

- **Why do the Hunters score the most points in a cold habitat?** *(Because they are adapted to a cold environment)*
- **Why do the Fishers score the least points in a cold habitat?** *(Because they are adapted to a hot habitat)*

Procedure

6. Have groups share their results by recording their scores and habitats on the board or a transparency.

Go Further

For summer, students might give the Fisher family more energy points, because they have adaptations for heat. For winter, students might give the Hunter family more energy points, because they have adaptations for cold. For both seasons, students might give the Seeder family fewer energy points, because they lack adaptations for heat or cold.

Analyze and Conclude

1. Answers will vary by family. Each family will be most successful in a habitat that is similar to its home environment.
2. The different numbers in the table for each family reflect differences in their adaptations. In nature, different organisms have different adaptations that help them to survive in their environments.
3. No, because the players have different adaptations that are suited for some environments but not others.

Chapter 15 Study Guide

Study Tip

Suggest that students review their answers to the Key Concept questions in the section assessments. Divide the class into pairs and have students quiz each other on definitions of the vocabulary words.

Thinking Visually

Check students' tables. See pp. 382–385.

Chapter 15 Assessment

Reviewing Content

1. c **2.** a **3.** a **4.** a **5.** d **6.** b **7.** a **8.** a **9.** c **10.** b

Understanding Concepts

11. Evolution, or change over time, is the process by which modern organisms have descended from ancient organisms. An example is a population of predators in which the fastest animals passed on their traits to new generations.

12. Darwin observed fossils, some of which resembled living organisms and others that were unlike any organisms he knew; that organisms everywhere seemed remarkably well suited to their environments; and that similar organisms, such as tortoises, were different on each island.

13. Darwin's visit to the Galápagos Islands convinced him that new species might arise from existing species over time.

14. Hutton proposed that Earth had to be millions—not thousands—of years old. Lyell argued that the same forces change Earth in the present as in the past, so scientists should explain Earth's history in terms of processes that are observable in the present.

15. Lamarck said that structures that are used develop and are passed on to offspring, whereas structures that are not used are not passed on.

Chapter 15 Study Guide

15–1 The Puzzle of Life's Diversity

Key Concepts

- During his travels, Charles Darwin made numerous observations and collected evidence that led him to propose a revolutionary hypothesis about the way life changes over time.
- Darwin observed that the characteristics of many animals and plants varied noticeably among the different islands of the Galápagos.

Vocabulary
evolution, p. 369
theory, p. 369
fossil, p. 371

15–2 Ideas That Shaped Darwin's Thinking

 **Key Concepts**

- Hutton and Lyell helped scientists realize that Earth is many millions of years old, and the processses that changed Earth in the past are the same processes that operate in the present.
- Lamarck proposed that by selective use or disuse of organs, organisms acquired or lost certain traits during their lifetime. These traits could then be passed on to their offspring. Over time, this process led to change in a species.
- Malthus reasoned that if the human population continued to grow unchecked, sooner or later there would be insufficient living space and food for everyone.

15–3 Darwin Presents His Case

Key Concepts

- In artificial selection, nature provides the variation among different organisms, and humans select those variations that they find useful.
- Over time, natural selection results in changes in the inherited characteristics of a population. These changes increase a species' fitness in its environment.
- Darwin argued that living things have been evolving on Earth for millions of years. Evidence for this process could be found in the fossil record, the geographical distribution of living species, homologous structures of living organisms, and similarities in early development.

Vocabulary
natural variation, p. 379
artificial selection, p. 379
struggle for existence, p. 380
fitness, p. 380
adaptation, p. 380
survival of the fittest, p. 381
natural selection, p. 381
descent with modification, p. 381
common descent, p. 382
homologous structure, p. 384
vestigial organ, p. 385

Thinking Visually

Use the information in this chapter to complete the table below.

Evidence of Evolution

Type of Evidence	Example	What Evidence Reveals
The fossil record	1	2
Geographic distribution of living species	3	4
Homologous body structures	5	6
Similarities in early development	7	8

TIME SAVER — CHAPTER RESOURCES

Print:

- ***Teaching Resources,*** Chapter Vocabulary Review, Graphic Organize
- ***Chapter Tests: Levels A and B,*** Chapter 15 Test
- ***PH Assessment System,*** Practice Test

Technology:

- ***Computer Test Bank,*** Chapter 15 Test
- ***iText,*** Chapter 15 Assessment

Chapter 15 Assessment

Reviewing Content

Choose the letter that best answers the question or completes the statement.

1. Who observed variations in the characteristics of animals and plants on the different islands of the Galápagos?
   a. James Hutton c. Charles Darwin
   b. Charles Lyell d. Thomas Malthus
2. In addition to observing living organisms, Darwin studied the preserved remains of ancient organisms, called
   a. fossils. c. homologous structures.
   b. adaptations. d. vestigial organs.
3. Which of the following ideas proposed by Lamarck was later found to be incorrect?
   a. Acquired characteristics can be inherited.
   b. All species were descended from other species.
   c. Living things change over time.
   d. Organisms are adapted to their environments.
4. Differences among individuals of a species are referred to as
   a. natural variation. c. natural selection.
   b. fitness. d. adaptation.
5. Which would an animal breeder use to produce cows that give more milk?
   a. overproduction
   b. genetic isolation
   c. acquired characteristics
   d. artificial selection
6. An inherited characteristic that increases an organism's ability to survive and reproduce in its specific environment is called
   a. a vestigial organ. c. speciation.
   b. adaptation. d. radiation.
7. The concept that each living species has descended, with changes, from other species over time is referred to as
   a. descent with modification.
   b. artificial selection.
   c. theory of acquired characteristics.
   d. natural selection.
8. Fitness is a result of
   a. adaptations. c. common descent.
   b. artificial selection. d. variation.
9. Structures that have different mature forms but develop from the same embryonic tissue are
   a. vestigial organs.
   b. adaptations.
   c. homologous structures.
   d. fossils.
10. The diagram below best illustrates
    a. Lamarck's theory of evolution.
    b. Darwin's theory of evolution.
    c. Malthus's principles.
    d. Lyell's theory about past changes.

Understanding Concepts

11. Explain what is meant by the term *evolution,* and give an example.
12. Describe three of Darwin's observations about animals in South America and on the Galápagos Islands.
13. How did the visit to the Galápagos Islands affect Darwin's thoughts on evolution?
14. How did Hutton's and Lyell's views of Earth differ from that of most people of their time?
15. Explain Lamarck's principle of use and disuse.
16. How does natural variation affect evolution?
17. What is artifical selection? How did this concept influence Darwin's thinking?
18. Distinguish between fitness and adaptation. Give an example of each.
19. How is the process of survival of the fittest related to a population's environment?
20. How does Darwin's principle of descent with modification explain the characterisitics of today's species?
21. What does fossil evidence show about evolution?
22. What evidence of evolution can be found in the geographic distribution of living animals? Give an example.
23. What is a vestigial organ? Give an example.
24. How do scientists use similarities in early development as evidence for evolution?
25. Summarize the main ideas in Darwin's theory.

HOMEWORK GUIDE

Section:	Questions:
Section 15–1	1, 2, 11–13
Section 15–2	3, 14, 15
Section 15–3	4–10, 16–25, 26–35

16. Natural variation results in evolution by natural selection because it leads to differences in fitness among individuals.

17. Artificial selection is the process by which humans select certain naturally occurring variations to use in breeding new plants and animals. Darwin thought that a similar process in nature could explain how organisms change over time.

18. Fitness is the ability of an individual to survive and reproduce in its specific environment. An example is a lion that has sharp teeth and claws, and can run fast. An adaptation is any inherited characteristic that increases an organism's chance of survival. An example is a porcupine's quills.

19. In the survival of the fittest, individuals that are best suited to their environment survive and reproduce most successfully.

20. Descent with modification explains why organisms living today may be different from their ancestors, for example, by having different structures.

21. Fossils that formed in different layers of rock provide evidence of the way species changed over time.

22. Evidence of evolution in living animals includes the existence of unrelated organisms from different locations that share traits because they evolved from similar environments. An example is the beaver in North America and the capybara in South America.

23. A vestigial organ is an organ, such as the human appendix, that is reduced in size and no longer has a function.

24. Similarities in the early development of different species have been used as evidence that the species evolved from a common ancestor.

25. Variations occur within populations, and some of the variations are favorable. More offspring are produced than can survive, and individuals with favorable variations are more likely to survive. Because of this, changes accumulate in populations over long periods of time.

Critical Thinking

26. Answers may vary. Students who disagree might say that there are still variations in fitness in humans, so natural selection is still operating to shape human evolution.

27. Giraffes with slightly longer necks could reach plant materials that those with shorter necks could not reach and, therefore, would have a better chance of surviving and passing on their genes. Over many generations of natural selection, the long necks of modern giraffes evolved.

28. The few mosquitoes that were resistant to DDT survived and reproduced, whereas those that were not resistant were killed by the insecticide. The succeeding populations of mosquitoes were more resistant to DDT.

29. Their survival might depend on whether predators were present and whether the food supply was adequate.

30. Most endangered species are endangered because human actions have reduced their fitness by changing or destroying their habitats. Protecting endangered species—for example, by preserving their habitats or providing them with nesting sites—may restore the natural conditions.

31. Vegetation on Hood Island is sparse, so tortoises with longer necks had a better chance of obtaining food, surviving, and reproducing—thus producing offspring with longer necks. Vegetation on Isabela Island is abundant and close to the ground, so tortoises with short necks were able to find food, survive, and reproduce.

32. It is not a new species, because it can breed with other dogs and produce fertile offspring.

33. The similar hormones are homologous traits. They were inherited from a common ancestor but now have different functions.

34. A whale could have vestigial hip and leg bones, because the ancestral vertebrate had them.

35. Darwin did not understand how traits were passed from parents to offspring. Mendel explained that traits were determined by "factors" that were inherited from the parents.

Chapter 15 Assessment

Critical Thinking

26. Evaluating Decide if you agree or disagree with the following statement and write a paragraph supporting your position: Since civilized humans no longer live in natural environments, natural selection is no longer operating to shape human evolution.

27. Applying Concepts Explain how natural selection might have produced the modern giraffe from short-necked ancestors.

28. Formulating Hypotheses DDT is an insecticide that was first used in the 1940s to kill mosquitoes and stop the spread of malaria. At first, it was very effective. However, over a period of years, people began to notice that it was becoming less and less effective. A possible explanation for this was that the insects were becoming resistant to the DDT. Explain how the resistance may have evolved.

29. Predicting Although wild turkeys can fly, domesticated turkeys cannot. Suppose that a population of domesticated turkeys escaped from a farm into a new environment. Give examples of environmental conditions that might determine whether that population would survive over time.

30. Making Judgments Is protecting an endangered species upsetting the process of natural selection? Explain your answer.

31. Applying Concepts Charles Darwin discovered that different types of tortoises lived on the different Galápagos Islands. Two of those types are shown below. Darwin learned that each type of tortoise was adapted to feed on the vegetation that was characteristic of its particular island. Use **Figure 15–3** and what you learned about Darwin's theory to explain how the different types of tortoises may have evolved.

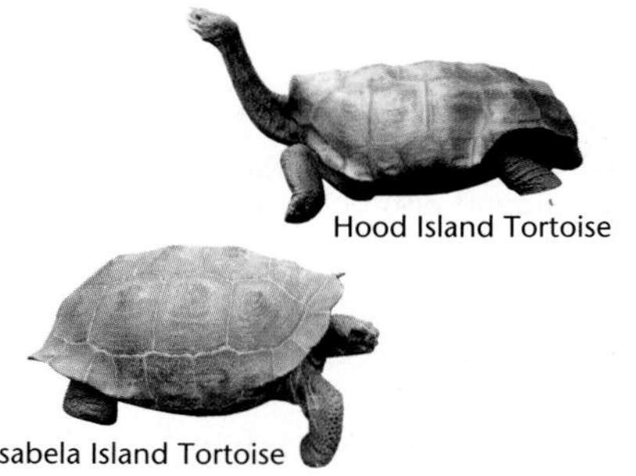

32. Problem Solving Dog breeders occasionally find that the result of a cross between two dog breeds is a totally new breed. Is the new type of dog a new species? Explain.

33. Applying Concepts A protein similar to the mammalian hormone prolactin, which stimulates the production of milk, is found in amphibians and birds. In amphibians, such as newts, the prolactin causes the animals to seek water when they lay eggs. In birds, such as pigeons, the prolactin causes them to regurgitate material from the crop to feed their young. How might the similarities and differences among these proteins be explained?

34. Applying Concepts A whale flipper and a human arm are considered homologous. Do you think a whale might have vestigial hip and leg bones? Explain.

35. Making Connections Refer back to Chapter 11 to refresh what you learned about Mendel. If Mendel and Darwin had met, how might Mendel have helped Darwin develop his theory? Include parts of Mendel's theory in your answer.

Performance-Based Assessment

Creative Writing Select an adaptation of a plant or animal. Write a scenario explaining how the trait might have evolved according to Lamarck, then write a second scenario using Darwin's ideas. Present your essay, and challenge classmates to identify the theory on which each scenario is based.

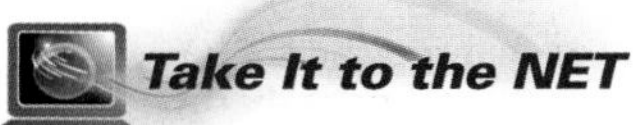

Dozens of people paved the way for Darwin's theory, and countless others have expanded on it. Visit the Prentice Hall Web site at **www.phschool.com** to learn more about the history of evolutionary thought. Then, answer the following questions:

- Who was the first to hypothesize that fossils were once-living organisms that had been buried at a time before the mountains were raised? When was that person born?
- Who is Carl Linnaeus? What is he most famous for?
- What controversial event occurred between Alfred Russel Wallace and Charles Darwin?
- Why was Thomas Henry Huxley nicknamed "Darwin's Bulldog?"

Performance-Based Assessment

Students' first scenario should explain that the adaptive trait was acquired through use and then inherited by future generations. Their second scenario should explain that the adaptive trait was present in the population and it increased in the population over time because it enhanced the survival or reproduction of individuals with the trait.

Standardized Test Prep

Test-Taking Tip If you have trouble answering a question, make a mark beside it and go on. (Do not write in this book.) You may find information in later questions that will allow you to eliminate some answer choices in your unanswered question.

Directions: Choose the letter that best answers the question or completes the statement.

1. Which scientist formulated the theory of evolution through natural selection?
(A) Charles Darwin
(B) James Hutton
(C) Charles Lyell
(D) Jean-Baptiste Lamarck
(E) Alfred Russel Wallace

2. The ability of an individual organism to survive and reproduce in its natural environment is called
(A) natural selection.
(B) evolution.
(C) adaptation.
(D) descent with modification.
(E) fitness.

3. The French scientist Jean-Baptiste Lamarck proposed which of the following theories?
I. Species do not change over time.
II. Species change over time.
III. A single organism can acquire traits over its lifetime that are then passed to its offspring.
(A) I only
(B) II only
(C) I and II only
(D) II and III only
(E) I, II, and III

4. Which of the following is an important concept in Darwin's theory of evolution by natural selection?
I. Struggle for existence
II. Survival of the fittest
III. Descent with modification
(A) I only
(B) II only
(C) I and II only
(D) II and III only
(E) I, II, and III

5. Which of the following does NOT provide evidence that living things have been evolving for millions of years?
(A) fossil record
(B) natural variation within a species
(C) geographical distribution of living things
(D) homologous structures of living organisms
(E) similarities in early development

6. A farmer's use of the best livestock for breeding is an example of
(A) natural selection.
(B) artificial selection.
(C) fitness.
(D) common descent.
(E) extinction.

Question 7 Complete the analogy by selecting the correct letter. In analogies, A : B :: C : ___?___ *means* A is to B as C is to ___?___.

7. Evolutionary theory : Darwin :: geological theory : ___?___
(A) Lamarck
(B) Lyell
(C) Wallace
(D) Malthus
(E) Linnaeus

Questions 8–9

The birds shown below are two species of the 13 species of finches Darwin found on the Galápagos Islands.

Woodpecker finch

Large ground finch

8. What process produced the two different types of beaks shown?
(A) artificial selection
(B) natural selection
(C) geographical distribution
(D) inheritance of acquired traits
(E) disuse of the beak

9. The large ground finch obtains food by cracking seeds. Its short, strong beak is an example of
(A) the struggle for existence.
(B) the tendency toward perfection.
(C) the inheritance of acquired traits.
(D) an adaptation.
(E) a vestigial organ.

Standardized Test Prep

1. A	**4.** E	**7.** B
2. E	**5.** C	**8.** B
3. D	**6.** B	**9.** D

Take It to the NET

• Loenardo da Vinci, born 1452.

• Carl Linnaeus, also known as Carl von Linné or Carolus Linnaeus, is often called the Father of Taxonomy. His system for naming, ranking, and classifying organisms is still in wide use today.

• In 1858, Wallace penned an essay on the "survival of the fittest" and sent it to Darwin. Charles Lyell and Joseph Hooker, two of Darwin's close friends, decided to present Wallace's essay to the next meeting of the Linnean Society without obtaining Wallace's permission first.

• Huxley, one of the first adherents of Darwin's theory of evolution by natural selection, was a passionate defender of Darwin's theory.

For additional information, visit
www.phschool.com

Chapter Planner 16 Evolution of Populations

Section and Section Objectives	Time	Activities and Labs
16–1 Genes and Variation, pp. 393–396 **16.1.1** ***Explain*** what a gene pool is. **16.1.2** ***Identify*** the main sources of inheritable variation in a population. **16.1.3** ***State*** what determines the number of phenotypes for a given trait.	1 period (1/2 block)	**SE:** ***Inquiry Activity,*** Does sexual reproduction affect genotype ratios?, p. 392 **TE:** ***Build Science Skills,*** p. 396 **SE:** ***Exploration,*** Investigating Genetic Diversity in Bacteria, p. 411
16–2 Evolution as Genetic Change, pp. 397–402 **16.2.1** ***Explain*** how natural selection affects single-gene and polygenic traits. **16.2.2** ***Describe*** genetic drift. **16.2.3** ***List*** the five conditions needed to maintain genetic equilibrium.	2 periods (1 block)	**TE:** ***Meet Diverse Needs,*** p. 400 **TE:** ***Build Science Skills,*** p. 400 **SE:** ***Quick Lab,*** Can the environment affect survival?, p. 401 **SE:** ***Issues in Biology,*** Should the Use of Antibiotics Be Restricted?, p. 403
16–3 The Process of Speciation, pp. 404–410 **16.3.1** ***Identify*** the factors involved in the formation of new species. **16.3.2** ***Describe*** the process of speciation in the Galápagos finches.	1 period (1/2 block)	**SE:** ***Analyzing Data,*** How Are These Fish Related?, p. 408
Chapter Assessment, pp. 412–415	1 period (1/2 block)	

ACTIVITY PLANNER

SE: ***Inquiry Activity,*** p. 392; (10 min.); 33 red beads, 67 black beads, 1-L beaker

TE: ***Build Science Skills,*** p. 396; (15 min.); tape measure

SE: ***Exploration,*** p. 411; (15 min., 30 min.); liquid bacterial culture, sterile swabs, sterile agar plate, glass-marking pencil, antibiotic paper disks, forceps, transparent tape, 70% alcohol, metric ruler, dilute bleach solution and plastic container for clean-up and disposal

TE: ***Meet Diverse Needs,*** p. 400; (10 min.); different-colored paper squares

TE: ***Build Science Skills,*** p. 400; (15 min.); 10 beans each of 5 different types

SE: ***Quick Lab,*** p. 401; (20 min.); scissors, construction paper (several colors), transparent tape, 15-cm ruler, watch with a second hand

PLANNING KEY

Ability Levels

(B)	**Basic**	For students who need additional help
(A)	**Average**	For all students
(E)	**Enriched**	For students who need to be challenged

Components

SE	Student Edition	**GRSW**	Guided Reading and Study Workbook	**IDM**	Issues and Decision Making
TE	Teacher's Edition	**CT**	Chapter Tests: Levels A and B	**CTB**	Computer Test Bank
LMA	Laboratory Manual A	**PHAS**	PH Assessment System	**PA**	Presentation Assistant Plus
LMB	Laboratory Manual B	**LA**	Lab Assessment with Scoring Guide	**BD**	BioDetectives Videotape
TR	Teaching Resources	**BTM**	BioTechnology Manual	**iT**	iText
IF	Investigations in Forensics				

Program Resources	*Assessment*	*Media and Technology*
LMA: Chapter 16 Lab (A) (E) **TR:** Section Review 16–1 (B) (A) **GRSW:** Section 16–1 (B) (A)	**SE:** 16–1 Section Assessment, p. 396 **TR:** Section Review 16–1	**PA:** 16–1 Interest Grabber, Section Outline, Relative Frequencies of Alleles, Figure 16–3, Figure 16–4 **iT:** Section 16–1
LMB: Chapter 16 Lab (B) (A) **TR:** Section Review 16–2 (B) (A) **GRSW:** Section 16–2 (B) (A)	**SE:** 16–2 Section Assessment, p. 402 **TR:** Section Review 16–2	**PA:** 16–2 Interest Grabber, Section Outline, Genetic Drift, Figure 16–6, Figure 16–7, Figure 16–8 **iT:** Section 16–2
TR: Section Review 16–3 (B) (A) **GRSW:** Section 16–3 (B) (A) **IDM:** Issues and Decisions 16 (A) (E)	**SE:** 16–3 Section Assessment, p. 410 **TR:** Section Review 16–3	**PA:** 16–3 Interest Grabber, Section Outline, Concept Map **BD:** "The Galápagos Islands" **iT:** Section 16–3 Discovery Channel School
	SE: Chapter 16 Assessment, pp. 412–415 **TR:** Chapter Vocabulary Review, Graphic Organizer **CT:** Chapter 16 Test **CTB:** Chapter 16 Test **PHAS:** Practice Test	**CTB:** Chapter 16 Test **iT:** Chapter 16 Assessment

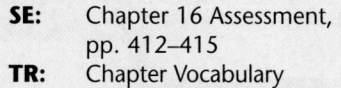

PRESSED FOR TIME?

To Preview the Chapter
- Have students read the headings and boldfaced sentences in each section.
- Have students study the figures and read the captions.

To Cover the Chapter Quickly
- Have students read all of Section 16–1, the introduction and Natural Selection on Single-Gene Traits in Section 16–2, and the introduction and Speciation of Darwin's Finches in Section 16–3.
- Assign the Section Assessments 16–1 and 16–3, questions 1–4, 9–14, 17, 18, 22, 24, 25, and 30–34 in Chapter 16 Assessment, and questions 1, 2, and 6–8 in Chapter 16 Standardized Test Prep.

To Review the Chapter
- Assign Sections 16–1 through 16–3 in the Guided Reading and Study Workbook.
- Assign the Section Reviews for 16–1 through 16–3 and the Chapter Vocabulary Review for Chapter 16 in the Teaching Resources.

Chapter 16

ENGAGE/EXPLORE

Inquiry Activity

Objective Students will be able to calculate genotype ratios in a model population and compare them with Mendelian ratios.

Skills Focus Calculating, Comparing and Contrasting

Materials 33 red beads, 67 black beads, 1-L beaker

Time 10 minutes

Strategy Provide a data table on the chalkboard where students can pool their results.

Expected Outcome Genotype ratios calculated from the individual samples will vary, but the ratios calculated from the pooled data for the class should be very close to 4:4:1.

Think About It

1. For the pooled data, there should be an approximate ratio of four homozygous black offspring to four heterozygous offspring to one homozygous red offspring.
2. No, because a 1:2:1 ratio would be expected only if there were equal numbers of red and black beads.
3. The genotype ratios would change only slightly because you are selecting from the same pool of alleles.

Assess Prior Knowledge

Introduce inheritable traits by explaining that they are traits controlled by genes. Then, ask: **In what ways are you like your parents?** *(Students might mention physical traits such as hair color and behavioral traits such as sense of humor.)* **Which traits do you think you inherited?** *(Students are likely to know that most physical traits are largely inherited but may not realize that many behavioral traits, including personality and IQ, are also at least partly inherited.)* Explain that in this chapter students will learn how inheritable traits evolve in populations.

Chapter 16 Evolution of Populations

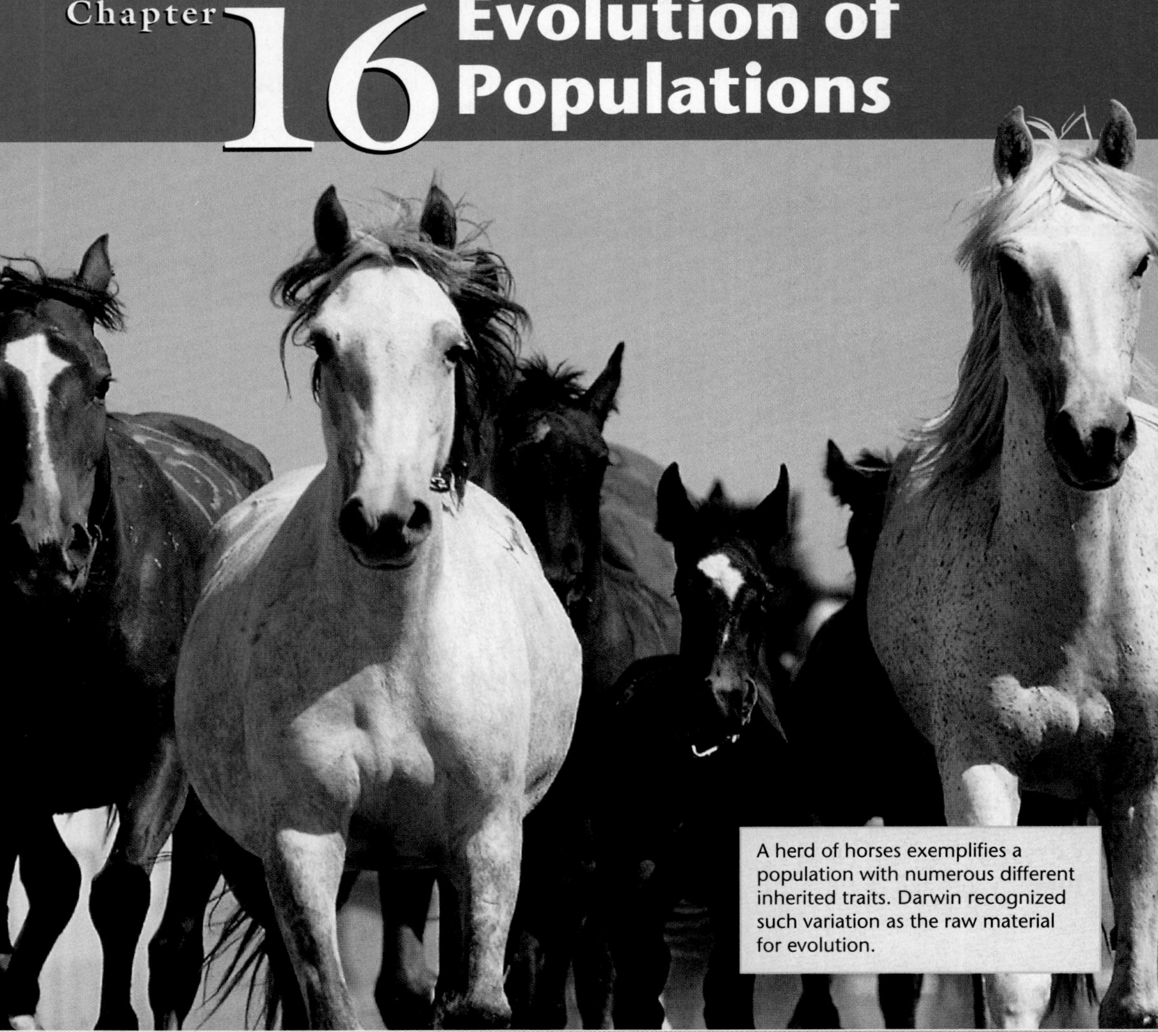

A herd of horses exemplifies a population with numerous different inherited traits. Darwin recognized such variation as the raw material for evolution.

Inquiry Activity

Does sexual reproduction change genotype ratios?

Procedure

1. Put 33 red and 67 black beads in a 1-L beaker to represent two alleles of a certain gene in a population.
2. To model the genotype of an offspring, remove two beads. Record the genotype. Return the beads.
3. Repeat step 2 for a total of 10 offspring. Add your data to the class total.

Think About It

1. **Calculating** What was the genotype ratio of the offspring?
2. **Comparing and Contrasting** Was the genotype ratio the same as the 1 : 2 : 1 genotype ratio for a cross between two heterozygotes (*Aa* × *Aa*)? Explain.
3. **Predicting** If you repeated this activity over and over, would you expect the genotype ratios to change? Explain.

16–1 Genes and Variation

As you look at the babies in **Figure 16–1,** you will immediately notice many differences among the individuals, such as different size and skin color. The babies also differ in terms of less visible characteristics, such as agility, the ability to fight off disease, and a host of behavioral traits.

Some of those differences are inheritable, which means that they can be passed from one generation to the next. Such differences provide the raw material for natural selection. Over time, those differences that help organisms survive and reproduce in their environment become more common. Meanwhile, differences that are not as beneficial become less common.

Darwin's Ideas Revisited

As Darwin developed his theory of evolution following his return to England in 1836, he worked under a serious disadvantage. He did not know how heredity worked. Although Mendel's work on inheritance was published in the 1860s, which was during Darwin's lifetime, its importance was not recognized until after 1900. Without an understanding of heredity, Darwin was unable to explain two important factors. First, he did not know the source of the variation that was so central to his theory. Second, he could not explain how inheritable traits were passed from one generation to the next.

It was more than fifty years before biologists could begin to determine the details of how evolution takes place. About 1910, biologists began to realize that genes carry the information that determines traits. With this knowledge, they were able to combine Mendel's work on inheritance with Darwin's work on evolutionary theory. Today, genetics, molecular biology, and evolutionary theory work together to explain how inheritable variation appears and how natural selection operates on that variation. This progress in evolutionary theory allows biologists to explain—much more completely than Darwin ever could—how evolution takes place.

Guide for Reading

Key Concepts
- What are the main sources of inheritable variation in a population?
- What determines the numbers of phenotypes for a given trait?

Vocabulary
gene pool
relative frequency
single-gene trait
polygenic trait

Reading Strategy: Building Vocabulary
Before you read, make a list of the vocabulary terms above. As you read, take notes about the meaning of each term.

▼ **Figure 16–1** **There are two main sources of genetic variation: mutations and the gene shuffling that results from sexual reproduction.** Each of these babies has inherited a collection of traits. Some, such as hair color, are visible, while others, such as the ability to resist certain diseases, are not.

SECTION RESOURCES

Print:
- ***Laboratory Manual A,*** Chapter 16 Lab
- ***Teaching Resources,*** Section Review 16–1
- ***Guided Reading and Study Workbook,*** Section 16–1

Technology:
- ***iText,*** Section 16–1

Section 16–1

1 FOCUS

Objectives

16.1.1 ***Explain*** what a gene pool is.
16.1.2 ***Identify*** the main sources of inheritable variation in a population.
16.1.3 ***State*** what determines the number of phenotypes for a given trait.

Guide for Reading

Vocabulary Preview

Help students understand the Vocabulary terms by reviewing the terms *gene (segment of DNA that codes for a particular protein)* and *allele (one of a number of different forms of the same gene for a specific trait).*

Reading Strategy

Suggest that students preview the section by studying the figures and reading the captions. Advise them to look for Key Concepts in the captions.

2 INSTRUCT

Darwin's Ideas Revisited

Meet Diverse Needs

Review the dates of publication of Darwin's theory of evolution (1859) and Mendel's work on inheritance (1866). Explain that the synthesis, or merging, of these two ideas did not occur until the mid-1930s. Central figures in the development of what has been called the "Synthetic Theory of Evolution" included several scientists from around the world: Theodosius Dobzhansky, Ronald Fisher, J.B.S. Haldane, Sewall Wright, and Sergei Chetverikov. Challenge interested students to learn more about the lives and works of any or all of these important scientists. Encourage students to share what they learn with the class. **Learning modality: verbal**

16–1 (continued)

Gene Pools

Use Visuals

Figure 16–2 Explain that the gene pool modeled in the drawing is a simplification of reality. In a real gene pool, each person has alleles for thousands of different genetic traits, not just one. Help students understand the concept of relative allele frequency by asking: **If the relative frequency of the B allele decreased in the gene pool, what would happen to the relative frequency of the other allele?** *(It would increase in frequency, because the total of the two frequencies must remain 100 percent.)*

Sources of Genetic Variation

Address Misconceptions

Perhaps because mutations are often the subjects of science fiction, many people have misconceptions about them. One misconception is that most mutations have drastic effects on the organism, for example, by causing major physical deformities. Point out that most mutations involve only minor changes in the DNA and that many mutations do not lead to visible changes in the phenotype. Add that most people carry hundreds of mutations that have little or no effect on their fitness. Avoid giving students the impression that most mutations are harmless, however. Explain that some minor changes in DNA can have drastic effects on the organism. For example, the allele that codes for sickle cell hemoglobin differs by just one codon from the allele that codes for normal hemoglobin, yet a person with two sickle cell alleles suffers from a life-threatening disease that affects virtually every organ of the body.

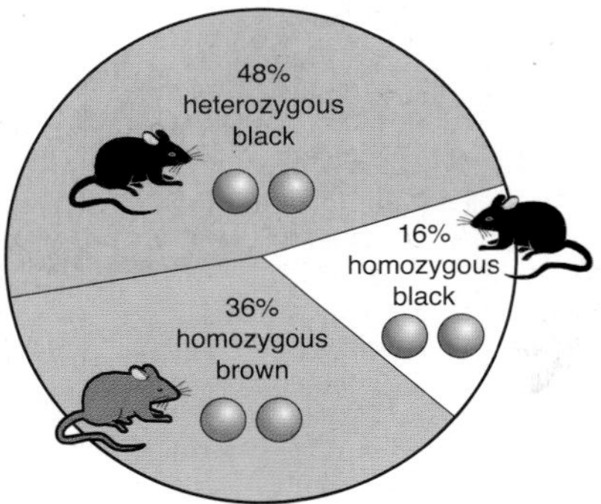

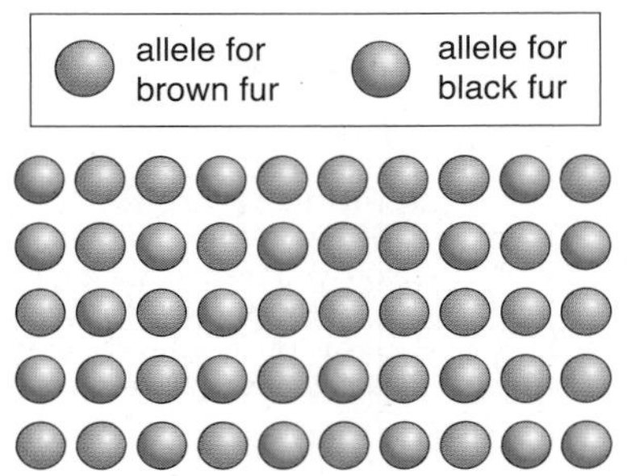

▲ **Figure 16–2** When scientists determine whether a population is evolving, they may look at the sum of the population's alleles, or its gene pool. This diagram shows the gene pool for fur color in a population of mice. **Calculating** *Here, in a total of 50 alleles, 20 alleles are B (black), and 30 are b (brown). How many of each allele would be present in a total of 100 alleles?*

Gene Pools

Today, biologists studying evolution often focus on a particular population. Recall that a population is a collection of individuals of the same species in a given area. Because all members of a population can interbreed, they share a common group of genes, called a gene pool. A **gene pool** is the combined genetic information of all the members of a particular population.

A gene pool typically contains two or more alleles—or forms of a certain gene—for each inheritable trait. For example, a mouse population may have two alleles for fur color, as shown in **Figure 16–2.** The gene pool for that trait is the combination of all the alleles in the population.

The **relative frequency** of an allele is the number of times that allele occurs in a gene pool compared with the number of times other alleles occur. Frequencies are often expressed in percents. Here, for example, 40 percent of the alleles are *B* (black fur).

Sources of Genetic Variation

Biologists can now explain how variation is produced. **The two main sources of genetic variation are mutations and the genetic shuffling that results from sexual reproduction.**

Mutations A mutation is any change in a sequence of DNA. Mutations can occur because of mistakes in the replication of DNA or as a result of radiation or chemicals in the environment. Mutations can be limited to one or a few bases of DNA, or they can affect lengthy segments of a chromosome.

Mutations do not always affect an organism's phenotype—its physical, behavioral, and biochemical characteristics. For example, a DNA codon altered by a point mutation from GGA to GGU will still code for the same amino acid, glycine. As a result, that mutation has no effect on the organism's phenotype. Many mutations do produce changes in an organism's phenotype, however. Some of these mutations can affect an organism's fitness, or its ability to survive and reproduce in its environment. Other mutations may have no effect on fitness.

Gene Shuffling Mutations are not the only source of inheritable variation. You do not look exactly like your biological parents, even though they provided you with all your genes. You probably look even less like any brothers or sisters you may have. Yet, no matter how you feel about your relatives, mutant genes are not primarily what makes them so different from you.

TIME SAVER — PRESENTATIONS MADE EASY!

The Presentation Assistant Plus contains the Prentice Hall Presentation Pro and the Transparencies, which provide easy-to-follow visual support for every step of this section. If you have a computer presentation station, use Prentice Hall Presentation Pro for Section 16–1, or use the transparencies listed here.

Section 16–1:

Interest Grabber
Section Outline
Relative Frequencies of Alleles
Figure 16–3
Figure 16–4

Most inheritable differences are due to gene shuffling that occurs during the production of gametes. Recall that each chromosome moves independently during meiosis. As a result, the 23 pairs of chromosomes found in humans can produce 8.4 million different combinations of genes!

Another process, crossing over, can also occur during meiosis. Crossing over further increases the number of different genotypes that can appear in offspring. Recall that a genotype is an organism's genetic makeup. When alleles are recombined during sexual reproduction, they can produce dramatically different phenotypes. Thus, sexual reproduction is a major source of variation within many populations.

Sexual reproduction can thus produce many different phenotypes, but it does not change the relative frequency of alleles in a population. To understand why, compare a population's gene pool to a deck of playing cards. Each card represents an allele found in the population. The exchange of genes during gene shuffling is similar to shuffling a deck of cards. Shuffling leads to different types of hands, but it can never change the relative numbers of aces, kings, or queens in the deck. The probability of drawing an ace off the top of the deck will always be 4 in 52, or one thirteenth (4/52 = 1/13). No matter how many times you shuffle the deck, this probability will remain the same. Similarly, sexual reproduction produces many different combinations of genes, but in itself it does not alter the relative frequencies of each type of allele in a population.

CHECKPOINT *What are the sources of inheritable variation?*

Single-Gene and Polygenic Traits

Inheritable variation can be expressed in a variety of ways. **The number of phenotypes produced for a given trait depends on how many genes control the trait.** Among humans, a widow's peak—a downward dip in the center of the hairline—is a **single-gene trait.** It is controlled by a single gene that has two alleles. As a result, variation in this gene leads to only two distinct phenotypes, as shown in **Figure 16–3.** As you can see, the frequency of phenotypes caused by a single gene is represented on a bar graph. This graph shows that the presence of a widow's peak may be less common in a population than the absence of a widow's peak, even though the allele for a widow's peak is the dominant form. In real populations, allele frequencies may not match Mendelian ratios.

Word Origins

Gene comes from the Greek word *gignesthai,* meaning "to be born," and refers to factors that produce an organism. The prefix *poly-* comes from the Greek word *polys,* meaning "many," so *polygenic* means "having many genes." The prefix *mono-* means "one." **What do you think the term *monogenic* means?**

Figure 16–3 In humans, having a widow's peak (left) or not having a widow's peak (right) is controlled by a single gene with two alleles. As a result, only two phenotypes are possible. **The number of phenotypes a given trait has is determined by how many genes control the trait.**

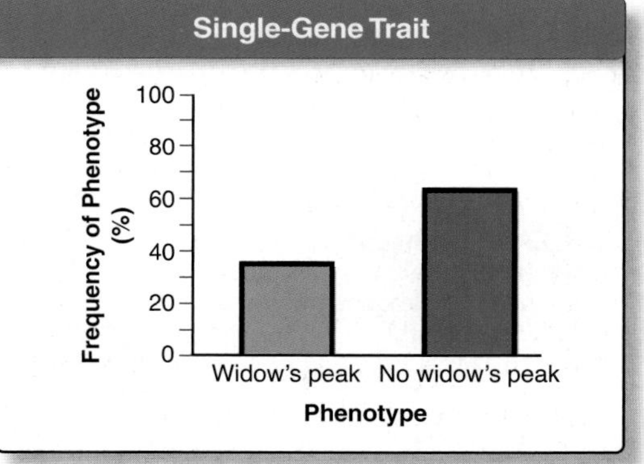

Meet Diverse Needs

At-risk students may benefit from a review of meiosis. Refer them to the diagram of meiosis in Figure 11–15 on page 276. Point out that gene shuffling refers to the cross-over event that occurs during the first stage of meiosis. Discuss how crossing-over exchanges alleles between chromosomes so that the chromosomes that are passed on to the offspring are different from chromosomes that were inherited from the parents. **Learning modality: visual**

Single-Gene and Polygenic Traits

Word Origins

Monogenic means having a single gene.

Demonstration

Find students with and without widow's peaks to demonstrate this trait. Then, explain that there are a number of other single-gene traits that are easy to see and that are either present or absent in individuals because of dominance. Invite students to demonstrate each of the following single-gene traits (or their absence) to the class: tongue rolling (the ability to fold up the sides of the tongue into a pea-shooter shape); and attached ear lobes (ear lobes with no notch or indentation where they are attached to the side of the face). Challenge students to count the number of phenotypes in the class for each of the traits and then draw a graph for each trait like the graph in Figure 16–3 for widow's peak.

Answers to . . .

CHECKPOINT *Mutations and the genetic shuffling that results from sexual reproduction*

Figure 16–2 *40* B *and 60* b

16–1 (continued)

Build Science Skills

Using Tables and Graphs Measure and record the height of each student in class, and have students use the data to create a bar graph showing the distribution of students by height in the class. After the graph is completed, ask: **How does the bar graph for the class compare with a normal distribution?** *(Like a normal distribution, the bar graph for the class should have more individuals at or near the average height and increasingly fewer students at shorter and taller heights.)*

3 ASSESS

Evaluate Understanding

Have students calculate the relative frequencies of the three ABO blood group alleles in a population in which there are 40 I^A alleles, 60 I^B alleles, and 100 *i* alleles. *(The frequencies are 0.2, 0.3, and 0.5, respectively.)*

Reteach

Have students draw two graphs, one to show the frequency of phenotypes for a hypothetical single-gene trait and the other to show the frequency of phenotypes for a hypothetical polygenic trait. Review why the two graphs differ as they do.

MAKING CONNECTIONS

Independent assortment means that genes segregate independently during gamete formation. This means that sexual reproduction results in a large amount of genetic variation.

Use iText to review the key concepts in Section 16–1.

Answer to . . .

Figure 16–4 *It indicates that the height of most people is at or near the average, with a small number of individuals at either extreme.*

Figure 16–4 The graph below shows the distribution of phenotypes that would be expected for a trait if many genes contributed to the trait. The photograph shows the actual distribution of heights of a group of young men. **Using Tables and Graphs** *What does the shape of the graph indicate about height in humans?*

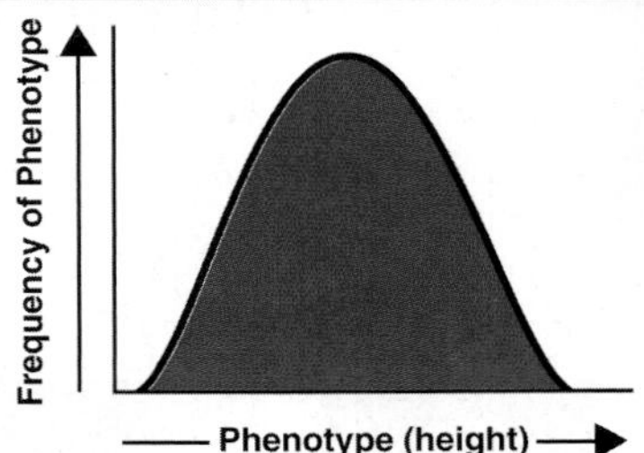

Most traits are controlled by two or more genes and are, therefore, called **polygenic traits.** Each gene of a polygenic trait often has two or more alleles. As a result, one polygenic trait can have many possible genotypes and even more possible phenotypes.

Height in humans is one example of a polygenic trait. You can sample phenotypic variation in this trait by measuring the height of all the students in your class. You can then calculate the average height of this group. Many students will be just a little taller or shorter than average. Some of your classmates, however, will be very tall or very short. If you graph the number of individuals of each height, you may get a graph similar to the one in **Figure 16–4.** The symmetrical bell-like shape of this curve is typical of polygenic traits. A bell-shaped curve is also called a normal distribution.

16–1 Section Assessment

1. **Key Concept** What two processes can lead to inherited variation in populations?
2. **Key Concept** How does the range of phenotypes differ between single-gene traits and polygenic traits?
3. What is a gene pool? How are allele frequencies related to gene pools?
4. **Critical Thinking Applying Concepts** How could you distinguish between a species in which there is a lot of variation and two separate species?

iTEXT Assessment Use iText to review the important concepts in Section 16–1.

MAKING CONNECTIONS

Genetics How does the process known as independent assortment relate to the genetic variation that results from sexual reproduction? (*Hint:* Refer to Chapter 11.)

16–1 Section Assessment

1. Mutations and the genetic shuffling that results from sexual reproduction
2. Single-gene traits have only two distinct phenotypes. Polygenic traits can have many possible phenotypes.
3. A gene pool is the combined genetic information of all members of a particular population. Allele frequencies are the number of times certain alleles occur in a particular gene pool compared with other alleles.
4. Members of the same species live together in populations and reproduce together. Members of different species do not.

16–2 Evolution as Genetic Change

Natural selection does not act directly on genes. Instead, it acts on phenotypes. Natural selection affects which individuals having different phenotypes survive and reproduce and which do not. In this way, natural selection determines which alleles are passed from one generation to the next. Thus, even though natural selection does not operate directly on genes, it can change the relative frequencies of alleles in a population over time.

But exactly what factors change the relative frequencies of alleles in a population? In a deck of cards, it is any situation that causes certain cards to be added to or removed from the deck. In genetic terms, any factor that causes alleles to be added to or removed from a population will change the relative frequencies of alleles. Whenever an individual dies without reproducing, its genes are removed from the population. But if an individual produces many offspring, the proportion of that individual's genes in the gene pool will increase. In genetic terms, evolution is any change in the relative frequencies of alleles in a population's gene pool. Thus, evolution acts on populations, not on individuals.

Natural Selection on Single-Gene Traits

Natural selection on single-gene traits can lead to changes in allele frequencies and thus to evolution. Imagine a population of brown lizards in which mutations produce red and black forms, as shown in **Figure 16–5.** Consider how various conditions might affect lizard survival. If the population lives in an area with dark soil, the red lizards might be easier for predators to see. They would be less likely to survive and reproduce, and over time would pass fewer copies of the allele for red coloring to future generations. That allele could even disappear from the gene pool completely.

Guide for Reading

Key Concepts

- How does natural selection affect single-gene and polygenic traits?
- What is genetic drift?
- What five conditions are needed to maintain genetic equilibrium?

Vocabulary

directional selection
stabilizing selection
disruptive selection
genetic drift
founder effect
Hardy-Weinberg principle
genetic equilibrium

Reading Strategy: Outlining Before you read, use the headings to make an outline. As you read, add a sentence after each heading to provide key information.

▼ **Figure 16–5 Natural selection on single-gene traits can lead to changes in allele frequencies and thus to evolution.** Organisms of one color, for example, may produce fewer offspring than organisms of other colors.

Effect of Color Mutations on Lizard Survival

Initial Population	Generation 10	Generation 20	Generation 30
80%	80%	70%	40%
10%	0%	0%	0%
10%	20%	30%	60%

TIME SAVER SECTION RESOURCES

Print:

- ***Laboratory Manual B,*** Chapter 16 Lab
- ***Teaching Resources,*** Section Review 16–2
- ***Guided Reading and Study Workbook,*** Section 16–2

Technology:

- ***iText,*** Section 16–2

Section 16–2

1 FOCUS

Objectives

16.2.1 ***Explain*** how natural selection affects single-gene and polygenic traits.
16.2.2 ***Describe*** genetic drift.
16.2.3 ***List*** the five conditions needed to maintain genetic equilibrium.

Guide for Reading

Vocabulary Preview

Challenge students to predict what the Vocabulary terms *directional selection, stabilizing selection,* and *disruptive selection* refer to. They should check to see if their predictions were correct after they read the section.

Reading Strategy

When completing their outlines, students should pay special attention to the boldfaced terms and sentences.

2 INSTRUCT

Natural Selection on Single-Gene Traits

Use Visuals

Figure 16–5 Ask: **Besides a mutation for red color, what other mutation occurred in the lizard population?** *(A mutation for black color)* **How does color affect the fitness of the lizards?** *(Both red and brown lizards are less fit than black lizards.)* **What do you predict the lizard population will look like by generation 50? Explain.** *(Students are likely to say that the lizard population will have more black lizards, fewer brown lizards, and no red lizards by generation 50. They should describe the environmental conditions that would support their prediction.)*

Natural Selection on Polygenic Traits

Build Science Skills

Applying Concepts Point out how polygenic traits show continuous variation rather than falling into discrete, all-or-nothing categories like single-gene traits. Ask: **Besides height and birth weight, what are some other polygenic traits that show continuous variation?** *(Other human polygenic traits that show continuous variation include body proportions such as limb length, biochemical traits such as skin pigmentation, and behavioral traits such as intelligence.)*

Build Science Skills

Inferring Explain that polygenic traits are often susceptible to environmental influences. In fact, a shift in the environment can lead to a corresponding shift in the phenotypes of a polygenic trait, which can mimic directional selection. Give students an example. Explain that, during the 1900s, average height in the United States increased because of environmental factors. Ask: **What environmental factors do you think led to this shift in phenotype?** *(The increase in average height has been attributed largely to changes in diet and health care that maximized growth potential.)*

Suppose that the black lizards in **Figure 16–5** are able to absorb more heat on cold days. If the extra heat allows them to move more quickly on cold days, the lizards may be better able to avoid predators. The new allele for a black body would increase an individual's fitness. Black lizards might then leave behind more offspring than other lizards. The relative frequency of the allele for a black body could, therefore, increase.

It is also possible that a particular color change, such as from brown to gray, would have no effect on the lizard's fitness. In that case, the allele that produces this trait will not be under pressure from natural selection, and its frequency will remain unchanged.

Natural Selection on Polygenic Traits

When traits are controlled by more than one gene, the effects of natural selection are more complex. As you learned earlier, the action of multiple alleles on traits produces a range of phenotypes that often fit a bell curve. The fitness of individuals close to one another on the curve is not very different. But fitness can vary a great deal from one end of a curve to the other. Where fitness varies, natural selection can act. **Natural selection can affect the distributions of phenotypes in any of three ways: directional selection, stabilizing selection, or disruptive selection.**

Directional Selection When individuals at one end of the curve have higher fitness than individuals in the middle or at the other end, **directional selection** takes place. This situation causes the entire curve to move as the character trait changes. In other words, evolution causes an increase in the number of individuals with the trait at one end of the curve.

One observed example of directional selection was an increase in the average size of the beaks in a particular species of Galápagos finches. During a period when food became scarce, the finches had to compete for food. Birds with larger beaks were better able to survive and reproduce. As a result, the average size of the beaks increased, as shown in **Figure 16–6.**

▼ **Figure 16–6 Directional selection occurs when individuals at one end of the curve have higher fitness than individuals in the middle or at the other end.** In this example, birds with larger beaks were able to survive more successfully than other birds during a period when food was scarce. In the graph on the right, the dotted line shows the original graph. The solid line shows how the distribution of phenotypes has changed as a result of selection.

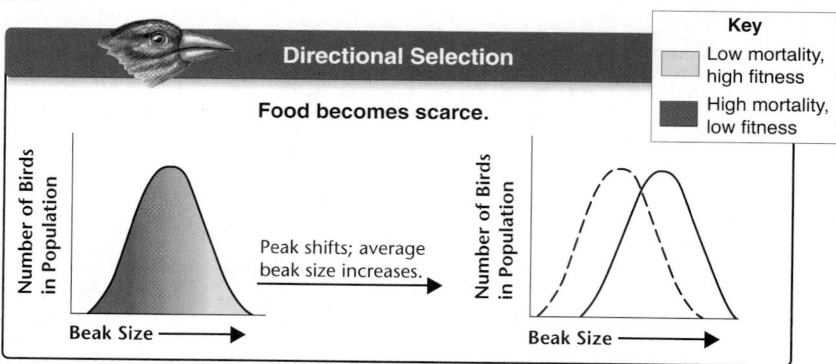

PRESENTATIONS MADE EASY!

The Presentation Assistant Plus contains the Prentice Hall Presentation Pro and the Transparencies, which provide easy-to-follow visual support for every step of this section. If you have a computer presentation station, use Prentice Hall Presentation Pro for Section 16–2, or use the transparencies listed here.

Section 16–2:

Interest Grabber
Section Outline
Natural Selection on Polygenic Traits
Figure 16–6
Figure 16–7
Figure 16–8

Stabilizing Selection When individuals near the center of the curve have higher fitness than individuals at either end of the curve, **stabilizing selection** takes place. This situation keeps the center of the curve at its current position, but it narrows the overall graph.

As shown in **Figure 16–7,** the weight of human infants at birth is under the influence of stabilizing selection. Human babies born much smaller than average are likely to be less healthy and thus less likely to survive. Babies that are much larger than average are likely to have difficulty being born. The fitness of these larger or smaller individuals is, therefore, lower than that of more average-sized individuals.

Disruptive Selection When individuals at the upper and lower ends of the curve have higher fitness than individuals near the middle, **disruptive selection** takes place. In such situations, selection acts most strongly against individuals of an intermediate type. If the pressure of natural selection is strong enough and lasts long enough, this situation can cause the single curve to split into two. In other words, selection creates two distinct phenotypes.

For example, suppose a population of birds lives in an area where medium-sized seeds become less common and large and small seeds become more common. Birds with unusually small or large beaks would have higher fitness. As shown in **Figure 16–8,** the population might split into two subgroups: one that eats small seeds and one that eats large seeds.

CHECKPOINT *How do stabilizing selection and disruptive selection differ?*

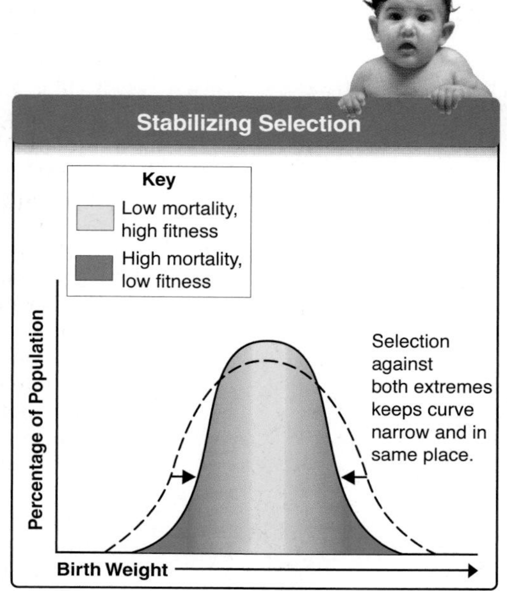

▲ **Figure 16–7** **Stabilizing selection takes place when individuals near the center of a curve have higher fitness than individuals at either end.** This example shows that human babies born at an average weight are more likely to survive than babies born either much smaller or much larger than average.

▼ **Figure 16–8** **When individuals at the upper and lower ends of the curve have higher fitness than individuals near the middle, disruptive selection takes place.** In this example, average-sized seeds become less common, and larger and smaller seeds become more common. As a result, the bird population splits into two subgroups specializing in eating different-sized seeds.

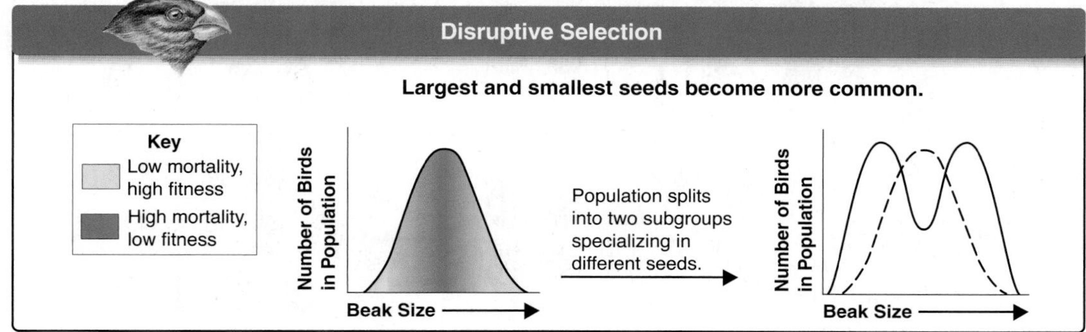

Demonstration

Show students illustrations of monarch and viceroy butterflies. Challenge them to detect any visible differences between the two species. Explain that monarch butterflies are avoided by bird predators because they taste bitter and that viceroy butterflies are avoided by bird predators because they resemble the bitter-tasting monarch butterflies, a situation called mimicry that has evolved through natural selection. Ask: **If monarch butterflies evolved white spots instead of orange spots, what do you think would happen to viceroy butterflies?** *(If a mutation for white spots occurred in viceroy butterflies, natural selection would cause the trait to increase in frequency.)*

Use Visuals

Figure 16–7 Ask: **If the fitness of phenotypes at both ends of the curve were to decrease even more, how would it affect the shape of the curve?** *(The curve would become narrower.)* **If medical advances could prevent problems for high birth weight babies but not for low birth weight babies, how might the curve change then?** *(There might be a shift in the curve toward higher birth weights, or at least a broadening of the curve at the high end.)*

Answer to . . .

CHECKPOINT *Stabilizing selection is selection for individuals at the center of the curve. It keeps the center of the curve at its current position. Disruptive selection is selection for individuals at the upper and lower ends of the curve. It splits the curve in two.*

Genetic Drift

Meet Diverse Needs

Students can experience "genetic drift" by playing the role of alleles in a population of organisms. Have students wear different-colored paper squares to represent different alleles of a trait. Help them choreograph genetic drift occurring as part of a population colonizes a new environment. They should demonstrate the loss of some alleles at random during this process. **Learning modality: kinesthetic**

Build Science Skills

Using Models Divide the class into groups, and provide each group with a bowl containing ten beans each of five different types, such as pinto, kidney, navy, white, and lima beans. Challenge groups to brainstorm a way to use the beans to model genetic drift. *(One way is by randomly selecting only some of the beans from the bowl to represent alleles in the next generation.)* Ask: **How would you show with your model that genetic change had occurred?** *(By calculating the relative frequencies of the different types of beans in the next generation to show that their frequencies had changed)*

SCIENCE NEWS®

Encourage students to visit **www.phschool.com** for the most current information on this topic.

Genetic Drift

Natural selection is not the only source of evolutionary change. In small populations, an allele can become more or less common simply by chance. Recall that genetics is controlled by the laws of probability. These laws can be used to predict the overall results of genetic crosses in large populations. However, the smaller a population is, the farther the results may be from what the laws of probability predict. This kind of random change in allele frequency is called **genetic drift.** How does genetic drift take place? **In small populations, individuals that carry a particular allele may leave more descendants than other individuals, just by chance. Over time, a series of chance occurrences of this type can cause an allele to become common in a population.**

Genetic drift may occur when a small group of individuals colonizes a new habitat. These individuals may carry alleles in different relative frequencies than did the larger population from which they came. If so, the population that they found will be genetically different from the parent population. Here, however, the cause is not natural selection but simply chance—specifically, the chance that particular alleles were in one or more of the founding individuals, as shown in **Figure 16–9.** A situation in which allele frequencies change as a result of the migration of a small subgroup of a population is known as the **founder effect.** One example of the founder effect is the evolution of several hundred species of fruit flies found on different Hawaiian Islands. All of those species descended from the same original mainland population. Those species in different habitats on different islands now have allele frequencies that are different from those of the original species.

CHECKPOINT *What is genetic drift?*

Figure 16–9 **In small populations, individuals that carry a particular allele may have more descendants than other individuals. Over time, a series of chance occurrences of this type can cause an allele to become more common in a population.** This model demonstrates how two small groups from a large, diverse population could produce new populations that differ from the original group.

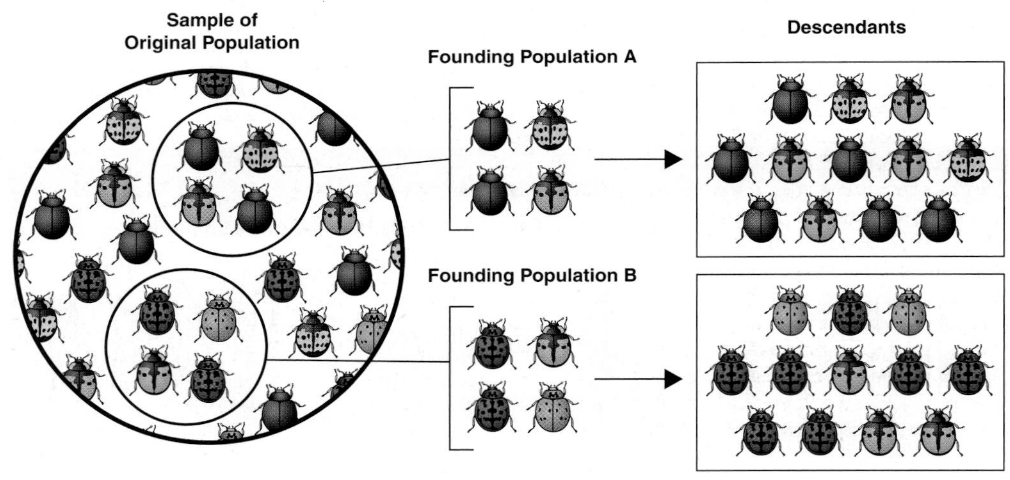

FACTS AND FIGURES

***Mutiny on the* Bounty**

A good example of founder effect in human populations is the population of Pitcairn Island in the South Pacific. The island's population today has limited genetic variability, because it was founded by only a handful of people in the late 1700s. The founders consisted of nine mutineers from the H. M. S. *Bounty*, all of whom were English, along with six Tahitian men and eight or nine Tahitian women. A few years after the population was founded, the number of people declined even more because of a disagreement between the English and Tahitian men. When Pitcairn Island was discovered by American whalers in 1808, the population consisted of just one Englishman, several Tahitian women, and some children. Because the population was geographically isolated, few new genes entered the gene pool over subsequent years, and genetic variation remained limited.

Quick Lab

Can the environment affect survival?

Materials scissors, construction paper (several colors), transparent tape, 15-cm ruler, watch with a second hand

Procedure

1. **Predicting** Predict what would happen to a population of butterflies that includes some individuals that are easy for predators to see and some that blend in with the environment.
2. Choose three different-colored sheets of construction paper. Cut out a butterfly shape from each sheet, 5 × 10 cm in size, as shown. **CAUTION:** *Be careful with scissors.*
3. Tape your butterflies to different-colored surfaces. Then, return to your seat.

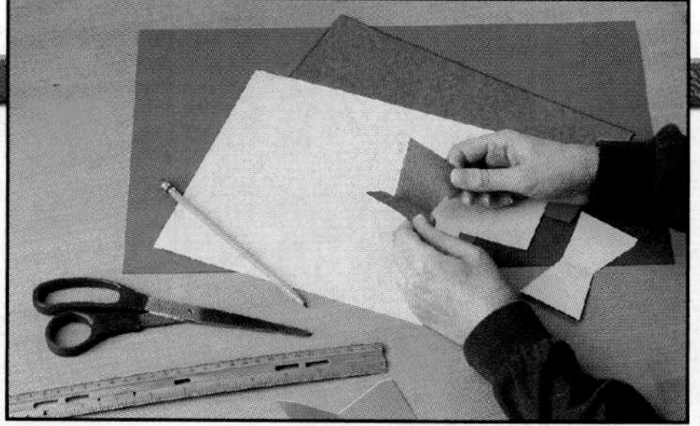

4. Record how many shapes of each color you can count from your desk in 5 seconds.
5. Exchange your observations with your classmates to determine the class total for each color.

Analyze and Conclude

1. **Analyzing Data** According to your class data, which colors of butterfly are easiest to see? Which color of butterfly would be most easily caught by a predator?
2. **Inferring** What will happen to the butterfly population after many generations if predators consume most of the easy-to-see butterflies?

Evolution Versus Genetic Equilibrium

You have just seen several of the factors that can cause a population to evolve over time. To clarify how such a set of factors operates, scientists often find it helpful to determine what happens when *no* change takes place. So biologists ask: Are there any conditions under which evolution will not occur? Is there any way to recognize when that is the case? The answers to those questions are provided by the Hardy-Weinberg principle, named after two researchers who independently proposed it in 1908.

The **Hardy-Weinberg principle** states that allele frequencies in a population will remain constant unless one or more factors cause those frequencies to change. The situation in which allele frequencies remain constant is called **genetic equilibrium** (juh-NET-ik ee-kwih-LIB-ree-um). If the allele frequencies do not change, the population will not evolve.

Under what conditions does the Hardy-Weinberg principle hold? **Five conditions are required to maintain genetic equilibrium from generation to generation: There must be random mating; the population must be very large; and there can be no movement into or out of the population, no mutations, and no natural selection.**

In some populations, these conditions may be met or nearly met for long periods of time. If, however, the conditions are not met, the genetic equilibrium will be disrupted, and the population will evolve.

KEEP CURRENT WITH . . . SCIENCE NEWS®
To find out more about the topics in this chapter, go to: www.phschool.com

TEACHER TO TEACHER

Using a series of overhead transparencies, I explain the Hardy-Weinberg principle to the entire class. Then, I distribute a problem sheet to the students and have them work in pairs. One student is the tutor, while the other is the student. While students are teaching one another, I circulate through the classroom, providing help where needed. After each pair of students has solved three problems, I have the students reverse roles with their partners. I find that students understand the Hardy-Weinberg principle much more quickly and thoroughly when they are able to explain it to one another. At the end of this activity, I have each pair write a new problem on an overhead transparency. I then use these new problems as a warm-up activity for genetics.

—*Marion LaFemina, Biology Teacher Ridgewood High School, Ridgewood, NJ*

Quick Lab

Objective Students will be able to analyze data and infer that the environment affects survival.

Skills Focus Analyzing Data, Inferring

Materials scissors, construction paper (several colors), transparent tape, 15-cm ruler, watch with a second hand

Time 20 minutes

Advance Prep Select surfaces that will not be harmed by tape. Provide students with construction paper in some colors that blend with and other colors that contrast with the selected surfaces.

Strategy Relate the lab to natural selection.

Expected Outcome Students will find that butterflies in contrasting colors are easier to see.

Analyze and Conclude

1. Butterflies in colors that contrast with the surfaces are the easiest to see. These butterflies would be the most easily caught by a predator.

2. After many generations, the population will be made up only of butterflies in colors that are difficult to see.

Evolution Versus Genetic Equilibrium

Make Connections

Mathematics Explain that in addition to allele frequencies remaining constant when a population is in Hardy-Weinberg equilibrium, genotype proportions also remain constant and can be calculated from the allele frequencies. If p is the frequency of allele *A* for a trait and q is the frequency of allele *a* for the same trait, then genotype proportions are given by $(p + q)^2 = p^2$ (*AA*) + 2pq (*Aa*) + q^2 (*aa*). Ask: **If a population is in Hardy-Weinberg equilibrium and the value of p is 0.3, what proportion of the population has each genotype?** *(The proportion of* AA *individuals is p^2, or 0.09; the proportion of* Aa *individuals is 2pq, or 0.42; and the proportion of* aa *individuals is q^2, or 0.49.)* Point out that the genotype proportions must add up to 1.00.

Answer to . . .

CHECKPOINT *Random change in allele frequencies*

16–2 (continued)

Build Science Skills

Inferring Explain that selection for heterozygotes can also lead to equilibrium in allele frequencies, and give the following example. State that, in some African populations where malaria is prevalent, heterozygotes for sickle cell hemoglobin have the highest fitness, because they are somewhat resistant to malaria and largely unaffected by sickle cell anemia. Homozygotes for sickle cell hemoglobin have the lowest fitness, because they have sickle cell anemia. Normal homozygotes have somewhat reduced fitness, because they have no resistance to malaria. As a result, the allele for sickle cell hemoglobin persists in these populations. Ask: **What do you think would happen to the sickle cell allele in these populations if malaria were eradicated?** *(The allele would be selected against and become less common.)*

3 ASSESS

Evaluate Understanding

Ask students to write a paragraph summarizing the different types of natural selection on polygenic traits.

Reteach

Using the chalkboard or a transparency, work with students to make a concept map showing the conditions required for Hardy-Weinberg equilibrium.

ALTERNATIVE ASSESSMENT

One way students can model selection is to use the different-sized squares to represent individual phenotypes in a population. They can increase the number of either small or large squares to model directional selection, of medium-sized squares to model stabilizing selection, and of both small and large squares to model disruptive selection.

Use iText to review the key concepts in Section 16–2.

▲ **Figure 16–10 One of the five conditions that are needed to maintain genetic equilibrium from one generation to the next is large population size.** The allele frequencies of large populations, such as this group of birds, are less likely to be changed through the process of genetic drift.

Random Mating All members of the population must have an equal opportunity to produce offspring. Random mating ensures that each individual has an equal chance of passing on its alleles.

In natural populations, however, mating is rarely completely random. Many species, including lions and wolves, select mates based on particular inheritable traits, such as size or strength. Such nonrandom mating means that the genes for those traits are *not* in equilibrium but are under strong selection pressure.

Large Population A large population size is also important in maintaining genetic equilibrium. That is because genetic drift has less effect on large populations, such as the population of birds shown in **Figure 16–10,** than on small ones.

No Movement Into or Out of the Population Because individuals may bring new alleles into a population, there must be no movement of individuals into or out of a population. In genetic terms, the population's gene pool must be kept together and kept separate from the gene pools of other populations.

No Mutations If genes mutate from one form into another, new alleles may be introduced into the population, and allele frequencies will change.

No Natural Selection All genotypes in the population must have equal probabilities of survival and reproduction. No phenotype can have a selective advantage over another. In other words, there can be no natural selection operating on the population.

16–2 Section Assessment

1. **Key Concept** Describe how natural selection can affect traits controlled by single genes.
2. **Key Concept** Describe three patterns of natural selection on polygenic traits. Which one leads to two distinct phenotypes?
3. **Key Concept** How does genetic drift lead to a change in a population's gene pool?
4. **Key Concept** What is the Hardy-Weinberg principle?
5. **Critical Thinking Comparing and Contrasting** How are directional selection and disruptive selection similar? How are they different?

iTEXT Assessment Use iText to review the important concepts in Section 16–2.

ALTERNATIVE ASSESSMENT

Using Models Demonstrate natural selection on polygenic traits by cutting a sheet of paper into squares of five different sizes to represent sizes in a population. Use the squares to model directional, stabilizing, and disruptive selection.

16–2 Section Assessment

1. It can lead to changes in allele frequencies and the evolution of traits.
2. Directional selection favors one extreme; stabilizing selection favors the middle of the range; disruptive selection favors both extremes and leads to two phenotypes.
3. Genetic drift causes random changes in allele frequencies in small populations.
4. Allele frequencies in a population remain constant unless one or more factors cause the frequencies to change.
5. Both are types of selection on polygenic traits in which the curve shifts away from the middle. In directional selection, the curve shifts toward one end, and in disruptive selection, toward both ends.

Should the Use of Antibiotics Be Restricted?

Natural selection is everywhere. One dramatic example may pose a threat to public health: Disease-causing bacteria are becoming resistant to antibiotics, substances intended to kill them or interfere with their growth.

Antibiotics are one of medicine's greatest weapons against bacterial diseases. When antibiotics were discovered, they were called "magic bullets" and "wonder drugs" because they were so effective. They have made diseases like pneumonia much less of a threat than they were about sixty years ago. However, people may be overusing antibiotics. Doctors sometimes prescribe them for teenagers with acne. Commercial feed for chickens and other farm animals is laced with antibiotics to prevent infection.

As a result of such wide use, many bacteria—including *Mycobacterium tuberculosis,* which causes tuberculosis—are now resistant to antibiotics. The resistance developed because the original treated populations contained a few individuals with the genetic ability to survive the antibiotic. Their descendants thrived and became one of today's dangerous strains. Once-powerful antibiotics are useless against them. Given the risks of this situation, should government agencies such as the Food and Drug Administration restrict the use of antibiotics?

The Viewpoints

Antibiotic Use Should Be Restricted

The danger of an incurable bacterial epidemic is so high that action must be taken on a national level as soon as possible. Doctors overuse antibiotics in humans because patients demand them. The livestock industry likes using antibiotics in animal feeds and will not change their practice unless forced to do so.

Antibiotic Use Should Not Be Restricted

Researchers are coming up with new drugs all the time. These drugs can be reserved for human use only. Doctors need to be able to prescribe antibiotics as they choose, and our food supply depends on the use of antibiotics in agriculture. The medical profession and the livestock industry need the freedom to find solutions that work best for them.

You Decide

1. **Defining the Issues** In your own words, explain the threat caused by overuse of antibiotics.
2. **Analyzing the Viewpoints** List the advantages and disadvantages of restricting the use of antibiotics.
3. **Forming Your Opinion** Should antibiotics be restricted? Are there some situations in which such regulations would be more appropriate than others?
4. **Persuasive Writing** Suppose you are a doctor. You want to use antibiotics to help your patients but are also concerned about the risks of antibiotic-resistant bacteria. Write an article for a newspaper explaining the issue and your position on it.

Suggest that students research the problem of antibiotic-resistant bacteria. For example, have them investigate the role patients play in the development of resistance by demanding antibiotics and then failing to take them correctly. Also, have students investigate bacterial resistance to other agents because of the widespread use of antibacterial products, ranging from disinfectant sprays to hand gels, soaps, and lotions.

You Decide

1. Overuse of antibiotics can lead to antibiotic-resistant bacteria, which could lead, in turn, to an incurable bacterial epidemic.

2. Advantages of restricting the use of antibiotics include a reduced risk of bacteria becoming resistant to antibiotics and less danger of an incurable bacterial epidemic. Disadvantages include the likelihood of more deaths and suffering from infectious diseases and a possible reduction in the food supply because of more infections in farm animals.

3. Some students might say that antibiotics should be restricted to human use or to people who have serious infectious diseases.

4. In their articles, students might write that doctors should be allowed to use antibiotics for their patients as long as they use them responsibly.

Section 16-3

1 FOCUS

Objectives

16.3.1 ***Identify*** the factors involved in the formation of new species.

16.3.2 ***Describe*** the process of speciation in the Galápagos finches.

Guide for Reading

Vocabulary Preview

Introduce students to the Vocabulary terms by explaining that speciation, or the formation of new species, comes about because of one or more types of reproductive isolation: behavioral, geographic, or temporal isolation.

Reading Strategy

Suggest that students make two graphic organizers as they read to summarize the information in the two parts of the section. For example, they might make a concept map to show the types of isolating mechanisms that lead to speciation and a flowchart to show how speciation of Darwin's finches occurred.

2 INSTRUCT

Isolating Mechanisms

Meet Diverse Needs

Help students appreciate the importance of behavior as a reproductive isolating mechanism. Suggest that interested students research the role behavior plays in reproduction in a species of their choice. Have them use an example other than mating songs in birds, which is the example used in the text. For example, they might describe courtship dances in bees. Urge students to share what they learn in a brief oral presentation. **Learning modality: verbal**

16–3 The Process of Speciation

Guide for Reading

Key Concepts
- What factors are involved in the formation of new species?
- Describe the process of speciation in the Galápagos finches.

Vocabulary
speciation
reproductive isolation
behavioral isolation
geographic isolation
temporal isolation

Reading Strategy: Using Visuals Before you read, preview **Figure 16–17.** As you read about speciation of Darwin's finches, notice what happens at each step in the process.

Factors such as natural selection and chance events can change the relative frequencies of alleles in a population. But how do these changes lead to the formation of new species, or **speciation**?

Recall that biologists define a species as a group of organisms that breed with one another and produce fertile offspring. This means that individuals in the same species share a common gene pool. Because a population of individuals has a shared gene pool, a genetic change that occurs in one individual can spread through the population as that individual and its offspring reproduce. If a genetic change increases fitness, that allele will eventually be found in many individuals of that population.

Isolating Mechanisms

You know that the gene pool of a species refers to the sum of its alleles. What happens to a gene pool as one species evolves into one or more species? **As new species evolve, populations become reproductively isolated from each other.** When the members of two populations cannot interbreed and produce fertile offspring, **reproductive isolation** has occurred. At that point, the populations have separate gene pools. They respond to natural selection or genetic drift as separate units. Reproductive isolation can develop in a variety of ways, including behavorial isolation, geographic isolation, and temporal isolation.

Behavioral Isolation One type of isolating mechanism, **behavioral isolation,** occurs when two populations are capable of interbreeding but have differences in courtship rituals or other types of behavior. For example, the eastern and western meadowlarks shown in **Figure 16–11** are very similar birds whose habitats overlap in the center of the United States. Members of the two species will not mate with each other, however, partly because they use different songs to attract mates. Eastern meadowlarks will not respond to western meadowlark songs, and vice versa.

Figure 16–11 The eastern meadowlark (left) and western meadowlark (right) have overlapping ranges. They do not interbreed, however, because they have different mating songs. **Applying Concepts** *What type of reproductive isolation does this situation illustrate?*

TIME SAVER — SECTION RESOURCES

Print:
- ***Teaching Resources,*** Section Review 16–3, Chapter 16 Exploration
- ***Guided Reading and Study Workbook,*** Section 16–3
- ***Issues and Decision Making,*** Issues and Decisions 16

Technology:
- ***iText,*** Section 16–3

Figure 16–12 **When two populations of a species become reproductively isolated, new species can develop.** The Kaibab squirrel evolved from the Abert squirrel. The Kaibab squirrels were isolated from the main population by the Colorado River.

Geographic Isolation With **geographic isolation,** two populations are separated by geographic barriers such as rivers, mountains, or bodies of water. The Abert squirrel in **Figure 16–12,** for example, lives in the Southwest. About 10,000 years ago, the Colorado River split the species into two separate populations. Two separate gene pools formed. Genetic changes that appeared in one group were not passed to the other. Natural selection worked separately on each group and led to the formation of a distinct subspecies, the Kaibab squirrel.

Geographic barriers do not guarantee the formation of new species, however. Separate lakes may be linked for a time during a flood, or a land bridge may temporarily form between islands, enabling separated populations to mix. If two formerly separated populations can still interbreed, they remain a single species. Also, any potential geographic barrier may separate certain types of organisms but not others. A large river will keep squirrels and other small rodents apart, but it does not necessarily isolate bird populations.

Temporal Isolation A third isolating mechanism is **temporal isolation,** in which two or more species reproduce at different times. For example, three similar species of orchid all live in the same rain forest. Each species releases pollen only on a single day. Because the three species release pollen on different days, they cannot pollinate one another.

How does temporal isolation prevent species from interbreeding?

Build Science Skills

Applying Concepts Divide the class into several groups, and challenge each group to brainstorm a scenario in which a small population of a species becomes geographically isolated from the remainder of the species long enough to evolve into a separate species. Urge groups to consider both natural events and human activities when they brainstorm ways that geographic isolation could come about. Have each group elect a spokesperson to describe their scenario to the class. In each case, ask: **Why did the geographically isolated population evolve into a different species?** *(Answers will vary depending on scenarios. Students might say, for example, that the isolated population was genetically different to begin with because of founder effect and that it became even more different through time due to different selective pressures.)*

Use Visuals

Figure 16–12 Have students use the key to locate the range of each type of squirrel. Point out how the Colorado River effectively isolates the two types of squirrels geographically, despite the closeness of their ranges, because the river has formed the Grand Canyon between the two ranges.

Build Science Skills

Inferring Have students infer the reproductive characteristics of species most likely to be affected by temporal isolation. Ask: **What must be true about the reproductive behavior of species that are isolated by temporal isolation?** *(Their reproductive behavior must be limited to a certain time of day or a certain season.)*

PRESENTATIONS MADE EASY!

The Presentation Assistant Plus contains the Prentice Hall Presentation Pro and the Transparencies, which provide easy-to-follow visual support for every step of this section. If you have a computer presentation station, use Prentice Hall Presentation Pro for Section 16–3, or use the transparencies listed here.

Section 16–3: **Interest Grabber**
Section Outline
Concept Map

Answers to . . .

CHECKPOINT *By reproducing at different times, they are unlikely to reproduce with each other.*

Figure 16–11 *Behavioral isolation*

Testing Natural Selection in Nature

Use Visuals

Figure 16–13 Point out that the woodpecker finch uses its beak to hold a cactus spine, which it pokes into holes in trees in order to spear insects. Ask: **What tool does its beak resemble?** *(Students might say pliers or needle-nosed pliers.)* **If another species of fruit-eating finch was discovered, what type of beak do you think it would have?** *(Students are likely to infer that it would have a beak like the vegetarian tree finch, which also eats fruit.)*

Build Science Skills

Applying Concepts Point out that the Grants used the scientific method in their research on the Galápagos Islands. Challenge students to brainstorm the steps involved in the scientific method. Assign a student to record the steps on the chalkboard. *(State problem, gather information and form hypothesis, experiment, record and analyze data, state conclusion)* Then, have students describe each step of the scientific method as it applies to the Grants' research. *(For example, the Grants' problem was to demonstrate natural selection in action. Their hypotheses were that there was enough inheritable variation in beak size and shape to provide raw material for natural selection and that variation in beak size and shape produced differences in fitness.)*

Galápagos Islands Finches

Shape of Head and Beak						
Common Name of Finch Species	Vegetarian tree finch	Large insectivorous tree finch	Woodpecker finch	Cactus ground finch	Sharp-beaked ground finch	Large ground finch
Main Food	Fruit	Insects	Insects	Cactus	Seeds	Seeds
Feeding Adaptation	Parrotlike beak	Grasping beak	Uses cactus spines	Large crushing beak	Pointed crushing beak	Large crushing beak
Habitat	Trees	Trees	Trees	Ground	Ground	Ground

▲ **Figure 16–13** Detailed genetic studies have shown that these finches evolved from a species with a more-or-less general-purpose beak. **Formulating Hypotheses** ***Suggest how one of these beaks could have resulted from natural selection.***

Testing Natural Selection in Nature

Now that you know the basic mechanisms of evolutionary change, you might wonder if these processes can be observed in nature. The answer is yes! In fact, some of the most important studies showing natural selection in action involve descendants of the finches that Darwin observed in the Galápagos Islands.

Those finch species looked so different from one another that when Darwin first saw them, he did not realize they were all finches. He thought they were blackbirds, warblers, and other kinds of birds! The species he examined differed greatly in the sizes and shapes of their beaks and in their feeding habits, as shown in **Figure 16–13**. Some species fed on small seeds, while others ate large seeds with thick shells. One species used cactus spines to pry insects from dead wood. One species, not shown here, even pecked at the tails of large sea birds and drank their blood!

Once Darwin discovered that these birds were all finches, he hypothesized that they had descended from a common ancestor. Over time, he proposed, natural selection shaped the beaks of different bird populations as they adapted to eat different foods.

That was a reasonable hypothesis. But was there any way to test it? No one thought so, until the work of Peter and Rosemary Grant from Princeton University proved otherwise. For more than twenty years, the Grants, shown in **Figure 16–14**, have been banding and measuring finches on the Galápagos Islands. They realized that Darwin's hypothesis relied on two testable assumptions. First, in order for beak size and shape to evolve, there must be enough inheritable variation in those traits to provide raw material for natural selection. Second, differences in beak size and shape must produce differences in fitness that cause natural selection to occur. The Grants tested these hypotheses on the

FACTS AND FIGURES

Fruit fly speciation
The North American fruit fly *Rhagoletis pomonella* appears to be in the process of speciation. Before the 1800s, *R. pomonella* infested only hawthorn trees. Then, when apple trees were introduced to North America, the fruit fly began infesting them as well. Today, the species exists in separate populations on each type of fruit tree. The different populations do not interbreed and have some genetic differences. Although they are still one species, they appear to be on their way to becoming separate species.

medium ground finch on Daphne Major, one of the Galápagos islands large enough to support good-sized finch populations, yet small enough to enable the Grants to catch and identify nearly every bird.

Variation The Grants' first task was to identify and measure as many individual birds as possible on a single island. They recorded which birds were still living and which had died, which had succeeded in breeding and which had not. For each individual, they also recorded wing length, leg length, beak length, beak depth, beak color, feather colors, and total bird mass. Many of these characteristics appeared in bell-shaped distributions typical of polygenic traits. From these data, the Grants concluded that there is great variation of inheritable traits among the Galápagos finches.

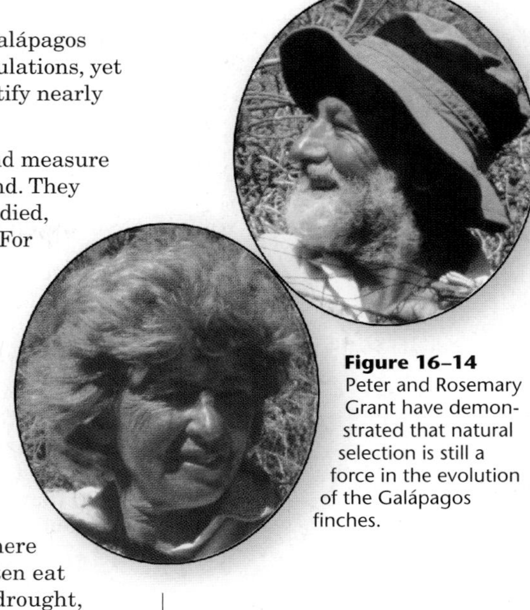

Figure 16–14 Peter and Rosemary Grant have demonstrated that natural selection is still a force in the evolution of the Galápagos finches.

Natural Selection Other researchers who had visited the Galápagos did not see the different finches competing or eating different foods. During the rainy season, when these researchers visited, there is plenty of food. Under these conditions, finches often eat the most available type of food. During dry-season drought, however, some foods become scarce, and others disappear altogether. At that time, differences in beak size can mean the difference between life and death. To survive, birds become feeding specialists. Each species selects the type of food its beak handles best. Birds with big, heavy beaks, for example, select big, thick seeds that no other species can crack open.

The Grants' most interesting discovery was that individual birds with different-sized beaks had different chances of survival during a drought. When food for the finches was scarce, individuals with the largest beaks were more likely to survive, as shown in **Figure 16–15.** Beak size also plays a role in mating behavior, because big-beaked birds tend to mate with other big-beaked birds. As a result, average beak size in that population increased dramatically. This change in beak size is an example of directional selection.

▼ **Figure 16–15** This graph shows the survival rate of one species of ground-feeding finches, the medium ground finch, or *Geospiza fortis.* **Using Tables and Graphs** *What trend does this graph show?*

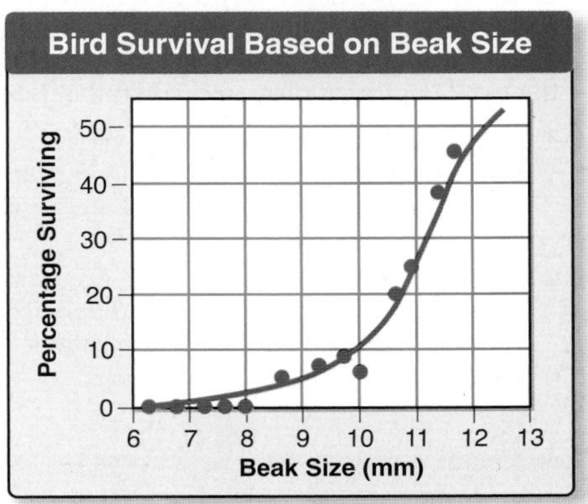

Rapid Evolution By documenting natural selection in the wild, the Grants provided evidence of the process of evolution: The next generation of finches had larger beaks than did the generation before selection had occurred. An important result of this work was their finding that natural selection takes place frequently—and sometimes very rapidly. Changes in the food supply on the Galápagos caused measurable fluctuations in the finch populations over a period of only decades. This is a markedly different picture from the slow, gradual evolution that Darwin envisioned.

What type of natural selection did the Grants observe in the Galápagos?

Meet Diverse Needs

Some students may be able to visualize the speciation process better if they draw flowcharts that summarize the Grants' research, observations, and conclusions. In their flowcharts, students should include examples of variation and the effects of drought and rainy seasons on the different bird species. **Learning modality: visual**

Build Science Skills

Inferring Challenge students to assume the role of an evolutionary biologist. First, have them choose an organism that they will study. Then, ask them to list the kinds of observations they would need to make to determine if the organism was undergoing natural selection. *(You would need to observe evidence of inheritable variation in the species and evidence that different phenotypes vary in fitness.)* Ask: **What might you observe if speciation was occurring?** *(You might observe that populations of the species had become separated so they no longer shared the same gene pool. You also might observe genetic differences between the populations.)*

BIO INSIGHTS FACTS AND FIGURES

Birds and flies in Hawaii

In the process of adaptive radiation on the Galápagos Islands, one species of finches gave rise to many species of finches. Similarly, five million years of adaptive radiation in Hawaiian birds known as honeycreepers resulted in a wide array of beak shapes and as many as 43 species. However, human actions have resulted in the extinction of most of these species.

Diverging physical traits do not cause all speciation. In Hawaii, a variety of courtship songs has separated the native *Drosophila* fruit fly into more than 500 species! Some Hawaiian *Drosophila* sound more like cicadas than flies. Others make a cricketlike noise. Still others make a sound like that of a North American fruit fly, but they create the sound by vibrating their abdomen instead of their wings.

Answers to . . .

CHECKPOINT *Directional selection*

Figure 16–13 *Sample answer: The large, heavy beak of the large ground finch evolved because it helped the bird crush seeds.*

Figure 16–15 *The larger a bird's beak, the greater its chances of survival.*

Speciation in Darwin's Finches

Encourage students to view "The Galápagos Islands: A Glimpse Into the Past" on the BioDetectives Videotape.

Build Science Skills

Applying Concepts Challenge students to apply the concept of founder effect to the example of Darwin's finches. Ask: **How did the first finches to arrive on the Galápagos compare genetically with finches on the mainland?** *(They had only a tiny fraction of the total genetic variability of the mainland finches and, through chance, may not have been genetically representative of mainland finches.)*

Analyzing Data

Explain to students that the arrows in the diagrams imply evolutionary relationships. For example, in hypothesis A, both B and G are presumed to have evolved from A.

Answers

1. Hypothesis A suggests that Lake 1 and Lake 2 brown fishes are unrelated, and the gold fishes from the two lakes are unrelated. This differs from hypothesis B, which suggests that Lake 1 gold fishes evolved from Lake 2 gold fishes and Lake 2 brown fishes evolved from Lake 1 brown fishes.
2. In hypothesis A, the brown (B) and gold (G) fish populations each evolved independently. In hypothesis B, the brown (B) fish populations in both lakes evolved from fish type A in Lake 1, and the gold (G) fish populations in both Lakes evolved from fish type A in Lake 2.
3. This evidence supports hypothesis A.
4. You would need to determine whether fishes from the two lakes can interbreed and produce fertile offspring. If not, then they are members of different species.

To find out more about ongoing research on the Galápagos, view the videotape "The Galápagos Islands: A Glimpse Into the Past."

Speciation in Darwin's Finches

The Grants' work demonstrates that finch beak size can be changed by natural selection. If we combine this information with other evolutionary concepts you have learned in this chapter, we can devise a hypothetical scenario for the evolution of all Galápagos finches from a single group of founding birds. **Speciation in the Galápagos finches occurred by founding of a new population, geographic isolation, changes in the new population's gene pool, reproductive isolation, and ecological competition.** As you read about each step, follow this process in **Figure 16–17** on page 410.

1 Founders Arrive Many years ago, a few finches from the South American mainland—species A—flew or were blown to one of the Galápagos Islands. Finches are small birds that do not usually fly far over open water. These birds may have gotten lost, or they may have been blown off course by a storm. Once they arrived on one of the islands, they managed to survive and reproduce.

2 Separation of Populations Later on, some birds from species A crossed to another island in the Galápagos group. Because these birds do not usually fly over open water, they rarely move from island to island. Thus, finch populations on the two islands were essentially isolated from each other and no longer shared a common gene pool.

Analyzing Data

How Are These Fish Related?

A research team studied two lakes in an area that sometimes experiences flooding. Each lake contained two types of similar fish: a dull brown form and an iridescent gold form. The team wondered how all the fish were related, and they considered the two hypotheses diagrammed on the right.

Hypothesis A

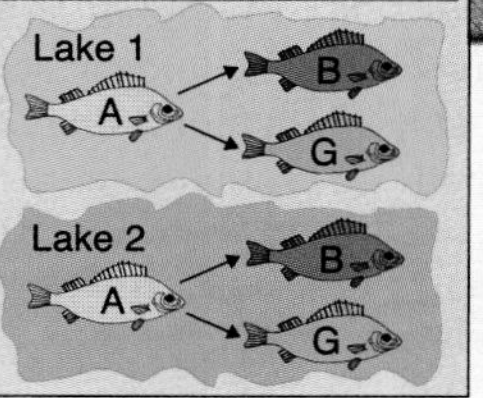

Hypothesis B

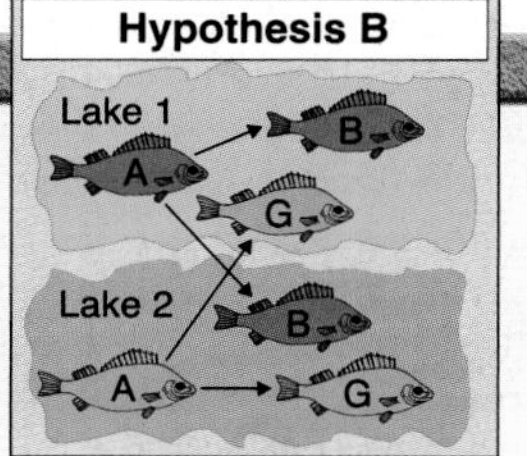

A = Possible ancestor
B = Contemporary brown form
G = Contemporary gold form
→ Shows possible line of descent

1. **Interpreting Graphics** Study the two diagrams. What does hypothesis A indicate about the ancestry of the fish in Lake 1 and Lake 2? What does hypothesis B indicate?
2. **Comparing and Contrasting** According to the two hypotheses, what is the key difference in the way the brown and gold fish populations might have formed?
3. **Drawing Conclusions** A DNA analysis showed that the brown and gold fish from Lake 1 are the most closely related. Which hypothesis does this evidence support?
4. **Going Further** What evidence could help determine whether the brown and gold fish are members of separate species?

BIO INSIGHTS — FACTS AND FIGURES

Not just finches
Among birds on the Galápagos Islands, Darwin's finches are better known than the mockingbirds, but it was the four species of mockingbirds that first drew Darwin's attention to the diversity of species on the islands. Darwin discovered that three of the mockingbird species were each confined to a single island, and it surprised him to learn that the islands were all similar and within sight of one another. Like Darwin's finches, the mockingbird species had evolved differences primarily in the size and shape of their beaks that reflected the different food sources they relied upon.

3 Changes in the Gene Pool Over time, populations on each island became adapted to their local environments. The plants growing on the first island may have produced small thin-shelled seeds, whereas the plants on the second island may have produced larger thick-shelled seeds. On the second island, directional selection would favor individuals with larger, heavier beaks. These birds could crack open and eat the large seeds more easily. Thus, birds with large beaks would be better able to survive on the second island. Over time, natural selection would have caused that population to evolve larger beaks, forming a separate population, B.

4 Reproductive Isolation Now, imagine that a few birds from the second island cross back to the first island. Will the population-A birds breed with the population-B birds? Probably not. These finches choose their mates carefully. As part of the courtship process, they inspect a potential partner's beak very closely. Finches prefer to mate with birds that have the same-sized beak as they do. In other words, big-beaked birds prefer to mate with other big-beaked birds, and smaller-beaked birds prefer to mate with other smaller-beaked birds. Because the birds on the two islands have different-sized beaks, it is likely that they would not choose to mate with each other. Thus, differences in beak size, combined with mating behavior, could lead to reproductive isolation. The gene pools of the two bird populations remain isolated from each other—even when individuals live together in the same place. The two populations have now become separate species.

5 Ecological Competition As these two new species live together in the same environment (the first island), they compete with each other for available seeds. During the dry season, individuals that are most different from each other have the highest fitness. The more specialized birds have less competition for certain kinds of seeds and other foods, and the competition among individual finches is also reduced. Over time, species evolve in a way that increases the differences between them. The species-B birds on the first island may evolve into a new species, C.

6 Continued Evolution This process of isolation on different islands, genetic change, and reproductive isolation probably repeated itself time and time again across the entire Galápagos island chain. Over many generations, it produced the 13 different finch species found there today. **Figure 16–17** on page 410 shows how two species with larger and smaller beaks might have formed. Use the steps in this illustration to explain how other Darwin finches, such as the vegetarian tree finch that feeds on fruit, might have evolved.

▲ **Figure 16–16** The Galápagos Islands are actually tips of undersea volcanoes that reach from the ocean floor to just above sea level. **Inferring** ***What can you infer about the mechanism of the Galápagos finches' evolution based on the location of these islands?***

Make Connections

Environmental Science Introduce students to the concept of adaptive radiation, which is the evolution of many diversely adapted species from a common ancestor. Explain that Darwin's finches could not have evolved into so many different species if the niches they evolved to fill had already been filled by other birds. Point out that the Galápagos are volcanic islands that at one time had many available niches for land birds. Ask: **Besides the formation of islands by volcanoes, how might an area come to have many available niches for an invading species to fill by adaptive radiation?** *(One possible answer is the occurrence of a natural disaster, such as a forest fire or flood, that destroys habitats. As the original habitats gradually return, niches open up.)*

Build Science Skills

Inferring Point out the role of ecological competition in the speciation of Darwin's finches. Ask: **How does competition increase the differences between species?** *(Individuals that are more specialized and less like the other species have less competition and higher fitness. This leads to an increase in the differences between the species.)*

Answer to . . .

Figure 16–16 *The finches evolved new species because of geographic isolation on the different Galápagos Islands and environmental differences among the islands.*

16–3 (continued)

Use Visuals

Figure 16–17 Challenge students to create new captions for the sequence of drawings to explain how another species of Darwin's finches, such as the vegetarian tree finch, might have evolved. Ask volunteers to share their captions with the class.

3 ASSESS

Evaluate Understanding

Call on students at random to name and give examples of each of the ways reproductive isolation comes about.

Reteach

Have students write on a notecard a brief summary of each step in the speciation of Darwin's finches. Then, have students shuffle the cards and try to put them back in the correct order.

Take It to the NET

Students should explain that Darwin's finches all started out as members of the same species but diverged from one another due to different selective pressures in different environments. In contrast, the Australian birds are not related to the European birds they resemble. Instead, they are a product of similar selective pressures in similar environments. For additional information, visit **www.phschool.com**

Use iText to review the key concepts in Section 16–3.

Figure 16–17 **Speciation in the Galápagos finches occurred by founding of new populations, geographic isolation, gene pool changes, reproductive isolation, and ecological competition.** Small groups of finches moved from one island to another, became reproductively isolated, and evolved into new species.

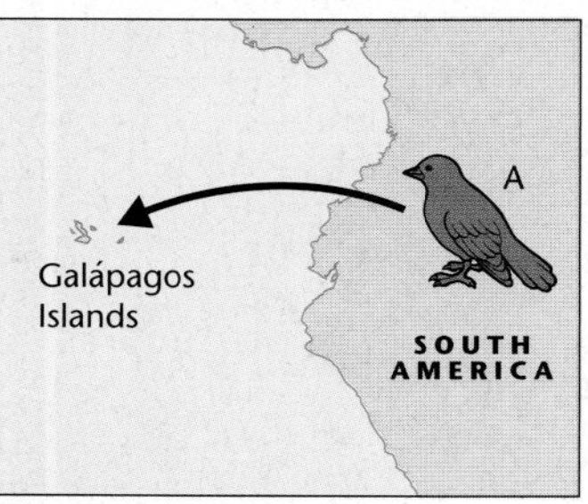

1 Founders Arrive
A few finches travel from South America to one of the islands. There, they survive and reproduce.

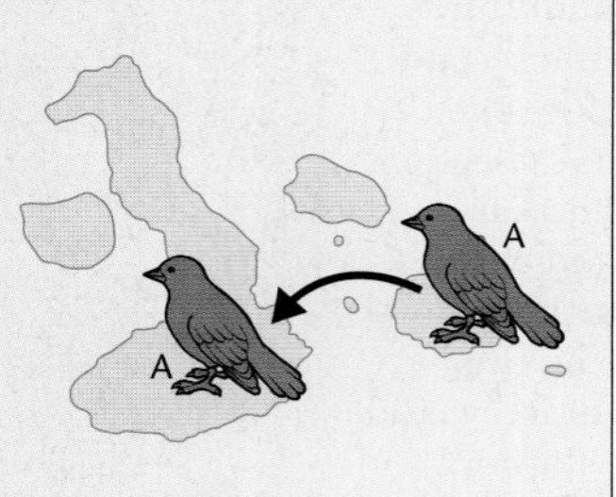

2 Separation of Populations
Some birds from species A cross to a second island. The two populations no longer share a gene pool.

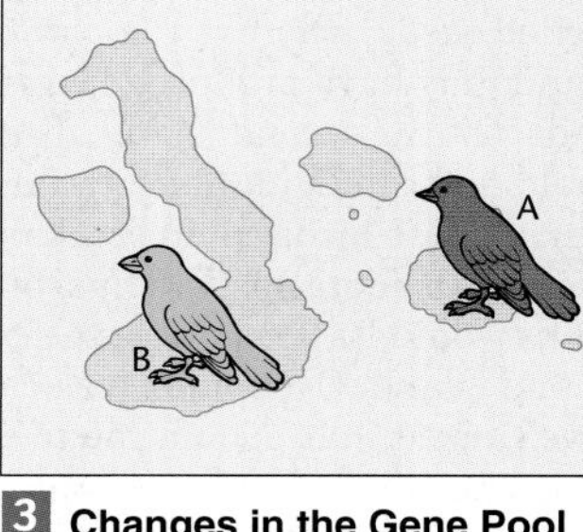

3 Changes in the Gene Pool
Seed sizes on the second island favor birds with larger beaks. The population on the second island evolves into a population, B, with larger beaks.

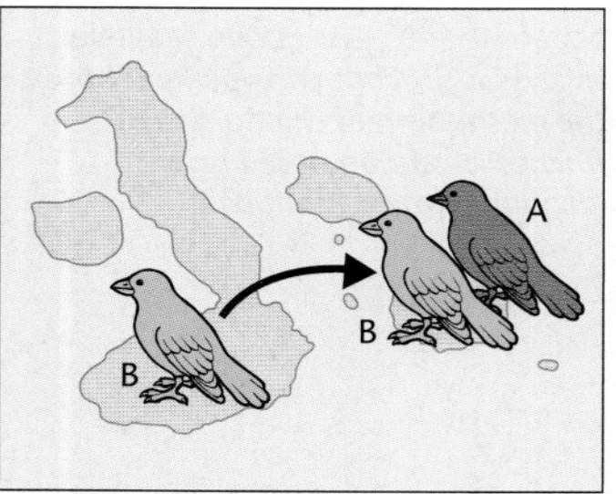

4 Reproductive Isolation
If a few population-B birds cross back to the first island, they will not mate with the birds of population A. The gene pools are now separate. Populations A and B are separate species.

5 Ecological Competition
As species A and B compete for seeds on the first island, they continue to evolve. A new species, C, may evolve. Some members of the original species B may travel to a new island.

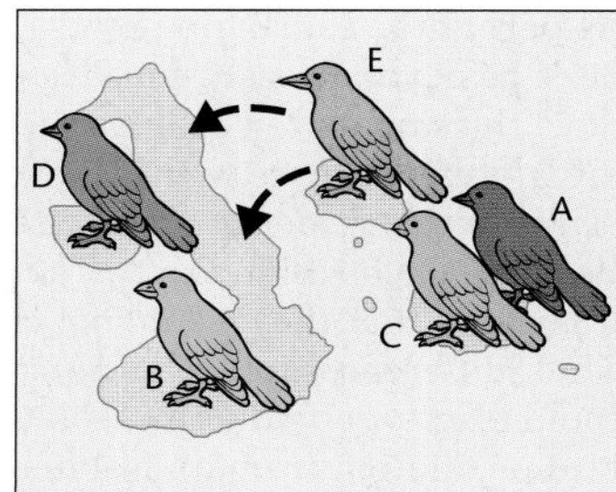

6 Continued Evolution
The process continues, leading to the formation of all 13 finch species on the Galápagos.

16–3 Section Assessment

1. **Key Concept** How is reproductive isolation related to the formation of new species?
2. **Key Concept** What type of isolating mechanism was important in the formation of different Galápagos finch species?
3. Explain how behavior can play a role in the evolution of species.
4. **Critical Thinking Applying Concepts** Leopard frogs and tree frogs share the same habitat. Leopard frogs mate in April; tree frogs mate in June. How are these species isolated from each other?

iTEXT Assessment Use iText to review the important concepts in Section 16–3.

Take It to the NET

Read how DNA data has been used to study Australian birds. Then, write a paragraph comparing the evolution of those Australian birds with that of Darwin's finches. Use the links provided in the Biology area at the Prentice Hall Web site for help in completing this activity: **www.phschool.com**

16–3 Section Assessment

1. For new species to evolve, populations must be reproductively isolated from each other.
2. Directional selection
3. Behavioral isolation can occur when two populations that could otherwise interbreed do not because of differences in behavior. This can lead to the evolution of different species.
4. The species are isolated from each other by temporal isolation.

Exploration

Investigating Genetic Diversity in Bacteria

Genetic diversity can make a population of organisms more adaptable. Some bacteria are able to survive in the presence of antibiotics that kill other bacteria. In this investigation, you will test a population of bacteria for the presence of antibiotic-resistant bacteria.

Problem **How common are antibiotic-resistant bacteria?**

Materials

- liquid bacterial culture
- sterile swabs
- sterile agar plate
- glass-marking pencil
- antibiotic paper disks
- forceps
- transparent tape
- 70% alcohol
- metric ruler

Skills Observing, Analyzing Data

Procedure   

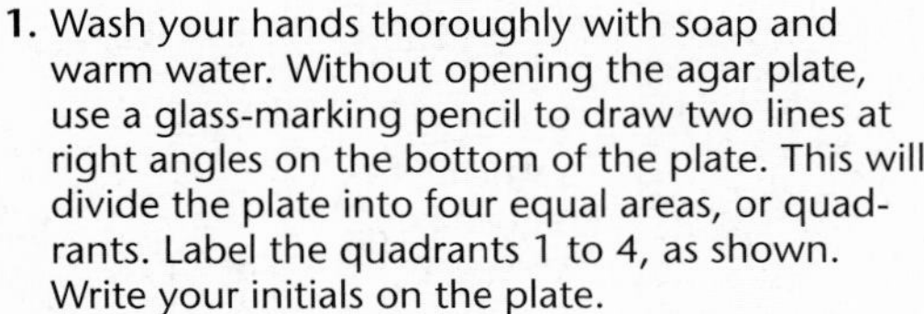

1. Wash your hands thoroughly with soap and warm water. Without opening the agar plate, use a glass-marking pencil to draw two lines at right angles on the bottom of the plate. This will divide the plate into four equal areas, or quadrants. Label the quadrants 1 to 4, as shown. Write your initials on the plate.
2. Dip a sterile swab in the bacterial culture. Remove the cover of the agar plate and rub the swab gently over the entire surface of the agar. Immediately replace the cover. Follow your teacher's directions for disposing of the swab.
3. Remove the cover of the agar plate again. Use clean forceps to place an antibiotic disk on the agar in the center of each quadrant. Replace the cover; then tape the plate closed.
4. Place the plate upside down in the area designated by your teacher.
5. Return the forceps to your teacher for disinfection. Wipe your work surface with 70% alcohol and a paper towel. Wash your hands well with soap and warm water before leaving the lab.
6. After 24 hours, observe the growth of bacteria around each antibiotic disk. Record your observations. **CAUTION:** *Do not open the plate.*
7. Use the metric ruler to measure the diameter of the zone of reduced bacterial growth, called the zone of inhibition, around each antibiotic disk. Record the diameter of each zone of inhibition.
8. Carefully observe the zones of inhibition. Do you see any evidence of bacterial growth there? Record your observations. Give the used plate to your teacher for safe disposal.

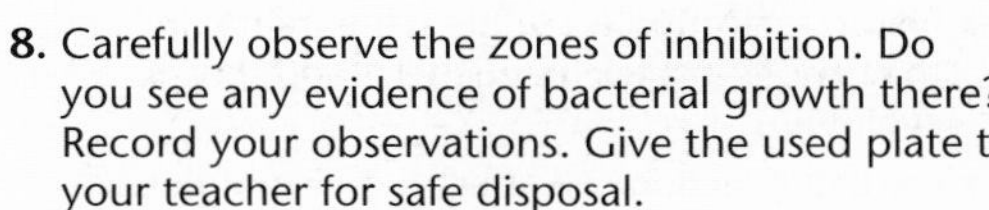

Analyze and Conclude

1. **Observing** How did the antibiotic disks affect the growth of the bacteria?
2. **Inferring** What effect, if any, did the antibiotic disks have on the gene pool of these bacteria?
3. **Classifying** What type of selection (directional, stabilizing, or disruptive) occurred in this experiment? Explain your answer.
4. **Drawing Conclusions** Did your data support the idea that antibiotic-resistant bacteria are common? Explain your answer.

Go Further

Applying Concepts Investigate genetic diversity further by using your school library and the Internet to research the use of wild relatives of food crops to increase genetic variation in plants.

Analyze and Conclude

1. The antibiotic disks reduced the growth of the bacteria nearby.

2. The antibiotic disks increased the frequency of alleles that confer resistance to the antibiotics.

3. Directional selection occurred in this experiment, because the frequency of the antibiotic-resistant phenotype increased.

4. Answers will depend on the data. In general, some bacterial growth will be observed around most or all of the antibiotic disks. This suggests that antibiotic-resistant bacteria are common enough that the swab deposited some in each zone of inhibition.

Exploration

Objective Students will be able to observe how antibiotics affect bacteria cultures.

Skills Focus **Observing, Analyzing Data**

Time 15 minutes one day; 30 minutes the next day

Advance Prep
- Obtain bacteria that are harmless to most people. Do not use *Serratia marcescens*, which is no longer thought to be safe.
- Students with weakened immunity because of HIV infection, immunosuppressive or cancer therapy, or alcohol or drug abuse should not participate in the lab. School administrators and parents or guardians should be notified of the lab and its risks to these students.

Safety Tips
- Stress the need to handle the bacteria with great care.
- Make sure that students wear disposable plastic gloves when handling the agar plate. Dispose of the gloves properly.
- Supervise the disposal of used swabs and plates in a plastic container filled with dilute bleach.
- After steps 5 and 8, wipe down all surfaces with dilute bleach and have students thoroughly wash their hands with soap and warm water.

Strategy Ask: **How do you predict the antibiotic disks will affect the bacteria?** *(Students might predict that the disks will prevent the bacteria from growing around them.)*

Procedure
4. Provide students with a warm, dark place to put their disks.

Go Further

Improvement of food crops through plant breeding requires genetic variation in traits, such as resistance to disease, that must be sought in the wild relatives of the food crops.

Chapter 16 Study Guide

Study Tip

Have pairs of students quiz each other on the Vocabulary terms. Suggest that students review the answers to the Key Concept questions in the Section Assessments.

Thinking Visually

1. Genetic drift
2. Single-gene traits
3. Stabilizing selection
4. Disruptive selection

Chapter 16 Assessment

Reviewing Content

1. a	5. c	9. a
2. a	6. b	10. b
3. b	7. b	
4. b	8. c	

Understanding Concepts

11. The relative frequency of an allele is the number of times that the allele occurs in a gene pool compared with the number of times other alleles occur. For example, there are two alleles for the gene that controls fur color in mice. If one of the alleles is present in half the members of the population, its frequency is 50 percent.

12. In sexual reproduction, alleles can recombine to produce different genotypes, resulting in different phenotypes and hence variation within a population.

13. The number of phenotypes produced for a given trait depends on how many genes control the trait.

14. A single-gene trait is a trait controlled by one gene.

15. A polygenic trait is controlled by two or more genes, and each gene often has two or more alleles. As a result, there can be many possible phenotypes, represented by a bell curve.

Chapter 16 Study Guide

16–1 Genes and Variation

Key Concepts

- Biologists have discovered that there are two main sources of genetic variation: mutations and the genetic shuffling that results from sexual reproduction.
- The number of phenotypes produced for a given trait depends on how many genes control the trait.

Vocabulary

gene pool, p. 394
relative frequency, p. 394
single-gene trait, p. 395
polygenic trait, p. 396

16–2 Evolution as Genetic Change

Key Concepts

- Natural selection on single-gene traits can lead to changes in allele frequencies and thus to evolution.
- Natural selection can affect the distributions of phenotypes in any of three ways: directional selection, stabilizing selection, or disruptive selection.
- In small populations, individuals that carry a particular allele may leave more descendants than other individuals, just by chance. Over time, a series of chance occurrences of this type can cause an allele to become common in a population.
- Five conditions are required to maintain genetic equilibrium from generation to generation: There must be random mating; the population must be very large; and there can be no movement into or out of the population, no mutations, and no natural selection.

Vocabulary

directional selection, p. 398
stabilizing selection, p. 399
disruptive selection, p. 399
genetic drift, p. 400
founder effect, p. 400
Hardy-Weinberg principle, p. 401
genetic equilibrium, p. 401

16–3 The Process of Speciation

Key Concepts

- As new species evolve, populations become reproductively isolated from each other.
- Speciation in the Galápagos finches occurred by founding of a new population, geographic isolation, changes in the new population's gene pool, reproductive isolation, and ecological competition.

Vocabulary

speciation, p. 404
reproductive isolation, p. 404
behavioral isolation, p. 404
geographic isolation, p. 405
temporal isolation, p. 405

Thinking Visually

Using the information in this chapter, complete the following concept map about evolution of populations:

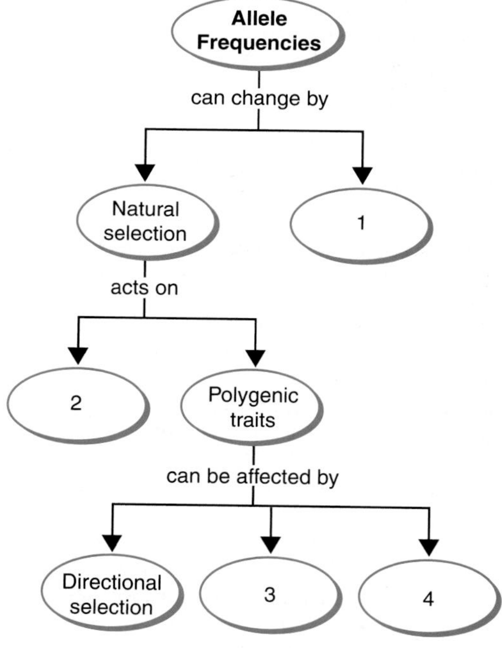

CHAPTER RESOURCES

Print:

- ***Teaching Resources,*** Chapter Vocabulary Review, Graphic Organizer
- ***Chapter Tests: Levels A and B,*** Chapter 16 Test
- ***PH Assessment System,*** Practice Test

Technology:

- ***Computer Test Bank,*** Chapter 16 Test
- ***iText,*** Chapter 16 Assessment

Chapter 16 Assessment

Reviewing Content

Choose the letter that best answers the question or completes the statement.

1. The combined genetic information of all members of a particular population forms a
   a. gene pool. c. phenotype.
   b. niche. d. population.
2. The success of an organism in surviving and reproducing is a measure of its
   a. fitness. c. speciation.
   b. adaptation. d. gene pool.
3. Traits that are controlled by more than one gene, such as human height, are known as
   a. single-gene traits. c. recessive traits.
   b. polygenic traits. d. dominant traits.
4. The type of selection in which individuals of average size have greater fitness than small or large individuals is called
   a. disruptive selection.
   b. stabilizing selection.
   c. directional selection.
   d. genetic drift.
5. The type of selection in which individuals at one end of a curve have the highest fitness is called
   a. stabilizing selection.
   b. disruptive selection.
   c. directional selection.
   d. the founder effect.
6. If coat color in a rabbit population is a polygenic trait, which process might have produced the graph below?

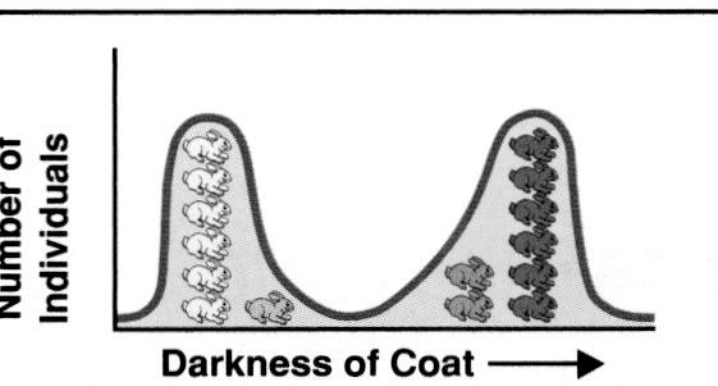

   a. stabilizing selection
   b. disruptive selection
   c. directional selection
   d. genetic equilibrium
7. A random change in a population's allele frequency is known as
   a. a gene pool.
   b. genetic drift.
   c. variation.
   d. fitness.
8. A change in allele frequency that results from the migration of a small subgroup of a population is called
   a. natural selection.
   b. the Hardy-Weinberg principle.
   c. the founder effect.
   d. genetic equilibrium.
9. Similar organisms that can breed with each other and produce fertile offspring in the natural environment make up a
   a. species. c. population.
   b. gene pool. d. genetic drift.
10. The evolution of Darwin's finches is an example of
    a. equilibrium. c. stabilizing selection.
    b. speciation. d. artificial selection.

Understanding Concepts

11. Explain what the term *relative frequency* means. Include an example in your answer.
12. Explain why sexual reproduction is a source of genetic variation.
13. Explain what determines the number of phenotypes for a given trait.
14. What is meant by the term *single-gene trait*?
15. Why are certain polygenic traits represented by a bell curve?
16. Define evolution in genetic terms.
17. How are speciation and reproductive isolation related?
18. How do stabilizing selection and disruptive selection differ?
19. What is genetic drift? In what kinds of situations is it likely to occur?
20. What is genetic equilibrium? What conditions are required to maintain genetic equilibrium?
21. Explain how isolation of groups can be involved in speciation.
22. What was the objective of the Grants' study?
23. What two testable assumptions were the basis for Darwin's hypothesis about the evolution of the Galápagos finches?
24. How did the work of Rosemary and Peter Grant reinforce Darwin's hypothesis about finch evolution in the Galápagos Islands?
25. Explain how the Galápagos finches may have evolved.

HOMEWORK GUIDE

Section:	Questions:
Section 16–1	1–3, 11–13
Section 16–2	4–8, 14–16, 18–20, 30–31
Section 16–3	9, 10, 17, 21–29, 32, 33

16. Evolution can be defined as a change in the relative frequency of alleles in the gene pool of a population.

17. Speciation occurs only when populations are reproductively isolated. Reproductively isolated populations have different gene pools and eventually form new species.

18. In stabilizing selection, individuals near the center of the curve have higher fitness than individuals at either end. In disruptive selection, individuals at both ends of the curve have higher fitness than individuals near the center.

19. Genetic drift is the random change in allele frequencies in a population. It is most likely to occur in small populations or when a small group of organisms colonizes a new habitat.

20. Genetic equilibrium occurs when the allele frequencies in a population remain constant. Five conditions are required to maintain genetic equilibrium: random mating, extremely large population size, no movement into or out of the population, no mutations, and no natural selection.

21. When two populations of a species become isolated, each group can evolve independently until they become separate species.

22. Their objective was to show that 13 species of Darwin's finches could have evolved from a single species through natural selection.

23. The assumptions were that there had to be enough inheritable variation to provide raw material for natural selection, and the variation, such as differences in beak size, must produce differences in fitness.

24. The Grants showed that beak size changed as a result of changes in food supply. This showed that the various Galápagos finches could have evolved from a common ancestor.

25. Students' answers should be consistent with the material on pages 408–410.

Critical Thinking

26. The shortest length of beak is 6 mm. About 2 percent of these birds have a beak this length.

27. Species A: 9.5 mm; Species B: 14.5 mm; Species C: 22 mm

28. The range is from 15.5 mm to 22 mm.

29. Species A probably eats small seeds. Species B can probably eat seeds larger than those eaten by species A. Species C can probably eat seeds that are larger than those eaten by either species A or species B.

30. Some students' models might consist of colored beads to represent the alleles in a gene pool. Evolution will occur, because there will be a change in the allele frequency of the new, distinct gene pool.

31. If the habitat occupied by these organisms is altered, the species may not have the ability to change and survive, and the species may become extinct.

32. Female bower birds only mate with males of their own species. As a result, the gene pools of each species remain isolated from each other.

33. One hypothesis may be that the other violets are the result of variation arising from genetic recombination between two plant species.

34. Ecology involves the study of interactions among populations of organisms and their enviroment. Changes in these interactions that occur over time result in evolution.

Chapter 16 Assessment

Critical Thinking

The graph below shows data on the lengths of the beaks of three species of Darwin's finches. The percentage of individuals in each category of beak length is given. Each of these species lives on the ground. Use this information to answer questions 26–29.

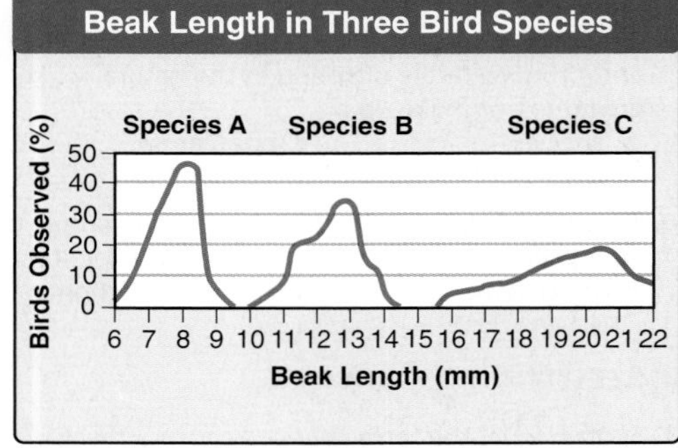

26. **Interpreting Graphics** What is the shortest beak length observed in species A? About what percentage of the birds of species A have this beak length?

27. **Interpreting Graphics** What are the longest beak lengths of each of the three species?

28. **Interpreting Graphics** What is the range of beak lengths for the birds of species C?

29. **Inferring** Based on these data, what can you infer about the sizes of the seeds eaten by each of these species of birds?

30. **Using Models** Construct a model to simulate genetic drift due to a small population's separating from a large population and establishing a new, distinct gene pool. Will evolution occur? Explain your answer.

31. **Applying Concepts** How might having a gene pool with minimal variation be dangerous for a particular species?

32. **Applying Concepts** The males of each species of bower bird build a distinctive bower, a structure of twigs, grasses, and colored objects. The females respond only to the bowers of their own species. What is the genetic effect of this behavior?

33. **Formulating Hypotheses** A botanist identifies two distinct species of violets growing in a field. Also in the field are several other types of violets that, although somewhat similar to the two known species, appear to be new species. Develop a hypothesis explaining how the new species may have originated.

34. **Making Connections** Sometimes biologists say, "Evolution is ecology over time." Use what you learned in Unit 2 to explain that statement.

Performance-Based Assessment

In Your Community Study the variations that exist in a species of tree, flowering plant, or insect in your neighborhood. Document the variations, using descriptive notes along with photographs or drawings. Present your findings in a visually interesting way. Describe how the variations may have contributed to the evolution of the species.

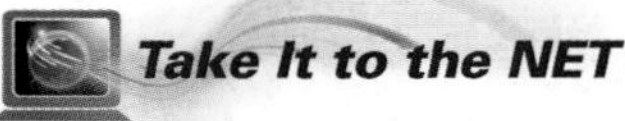

Can you identify the most genetically valuable animal in a pedigree? Visit the Prentice Hall Web site at **www.phschool.com** to play a game about the science of population management. Then, answer the following questions:

- How do population managers try to maintain variation within a population?
- Which animals in a population are considered the most genetically valuable?
- How do captive breeding programs attempt to compensate for genetic drift?

Performance-Based Assessment

Variations might include differences in size, shape, color, and form. In their responses, students should demonstrate an understanding of the factors that influence evolution.

Standardized Test Prep

Test-Taking Tip If you have trouble answering a question, make a mark beside it and go on. (Do not write in this book.) You may find information in later questions that will allow you to eliminate some answer choices in your unanswered question.

Directions: Choose the letter that best answers the question or completes the statement.

1. Which of the following conditions is likely to result in speciation?
(A) random mating
(B) small population size
(C) no migrations into or out of the population
(D) absence of natural selection
(E) lack of mutations

2. Which of the following is a source of genetic variation?
I. Mutations
II. Polygenic traits
III. Genetic shuffling that results from sexual reproduction
(A) I only
(B) II only
(C) I and III only
(D) II and III only
(E) I, II, and III

3. In a population of lizards, the smallest and largest lizards are more easily preyed upon than middle-sized lizards. What kind of natural selection is most likely to occur in this situation?
(A) size selection
(B) sexual selection
(C) stabilizing selection
(D) directional selection
(E) disruptive selection

4. When two species reproduce at different times, the situation is called
(A) temporal isolation.
(B) speciation.
(C) genetic drift.
(D) temporal selection.
(E) geographic isolation.

5. Change is to evolution as lack of change is to
(A) genetic equilibrium.
(B) polygenic traits.
(C) gene pool.
(D) fitness.
(E) genetic variation.

Questions 6–8 Each of the lettered choices below refers to the following numbered statements. Select the best lettered choice. A choice may be used once, more than once, or not at all.

(A) Fitness
(B) Single-gene trait
(C) Polygenic trait
(D) Hardy-Weinberg principle
(E) Gene pool

6. The combined genetic information of all members of a particular population

7. Survival and reproduction of individuals best suited to their environment

8. Characteristic of the traits that Mendel tracked in pea plants

Questions 9–10

The graphs show the changes in crab color at one beach.

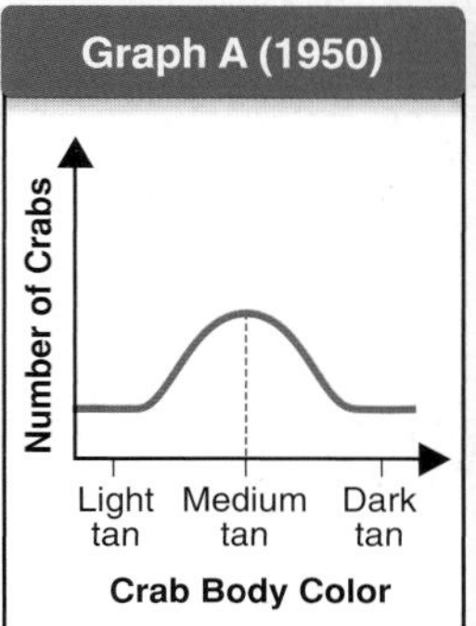

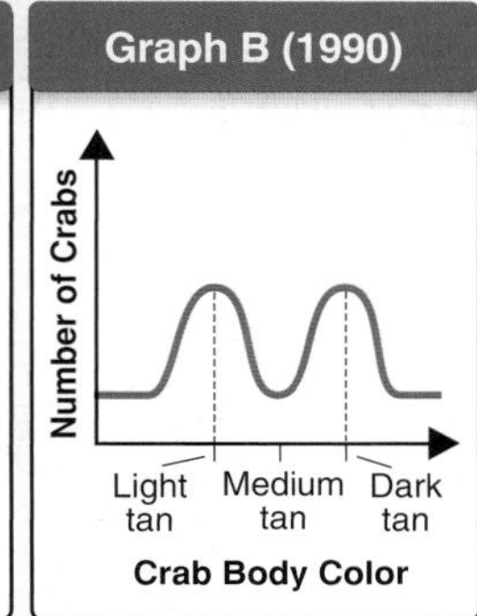

9. What process occurred over the 40-year period?
(A) artificial selection
(B) geographic selection
(C) stabilizing selection
(D) disruptive selection
(E) directional selection

10. What might have caused the change in distribution?
(A) A new predator prefers dark-tan crabs.
(B) A new predator prefers light-tan crabs.
(C) A new beach color makes medium-tan crabs the least visible to predators.
(D) A new beach color makes medium-tan crabs the most visible to predators.
(E) A food source died out.

Standardized Test Prep

1. B **2.** C **3.** C **4.** A **5.** A **6.** E **7.** A **8.** B **9.** D **10.** D

Take It to the NET

• Population managers try to maintain genetic variation in a population by giving breeding priority to animals that carry rare alleles.

• The ones whose alleles are least common in the living population

• The potential for genetic drift in captive populations is high because the populations are typically small. Captive breeding programs attempt to maximize the retention of genetic diversity. Managers use pedigree analysis to decide which animals should breed, with whom, and how often.

For additional information, visit

www.phschool.com

Chapter Planner 17 The History of Life

Section and Section Objectives	Time	Activities and Labs
17–1 The Fossil Record, pp. 417–422 **17.1.1** ***Describe*** the fossil record. **17.1.2** ***State*** the information that relative dating and radioactive dating provide about fossils. **17.1.3** ***Identify*** the divisions of the geologic time scale.	**2 periods (1 block)**	**SE:** ***Inquiry Activity,*** How can you date a rock?, p. 416 **TE:** ***Demonstration,*** p. 417 **TE:** ***Build Science Skills,*** p. 418 **TE:** ***Build Science Skills,*** p. 419 **SE:** ***Quick Lab***, What is a half-life?, p. 420
17–2 Earth's Early History, pp. 423–428 **17.2.1** ***Describe*** how conditions on early Earth were different from conditions today. **17.2.2** ***Explain*** what Miller and Urey's experiments showed. **17.2.3** ***State*** the hypotheses that have been proposed for how life first arose on Earth. **17.2.4** ***Identify*** some of the main evolutionary steps in the early evolution of life.	**2 periods (1 block)**	**TE:** ***Demonstration,*** p. 424 **SE:** ***Careers in Biology,*** Fossil Preparator, p. 433
17–3 Evolution of Multicellular Life, pp. 429–434 **17.3.1** ***Describe*** the key forms of life in the Paleozoic, Mesozoic, and Cenozoic eras.	**2 periods (1 block)**	**SE:** ***Analyzing Data,*** Changing Number of Marine Families, p. 438
17–4 Patterns of Evolution, pp. 435–440 **17.4.1** ***Identify*** important patterns of macroevolution.	**1 period (1/2 block)**	**SE:** ***Exploration,*** Modeling Coevolution, p. 441
Chapter Assessment, pp. 442–445	**1 period (1/2 block)**	

ACTIVITY PLANNER

SE: ***Inquiry Activity,*** p. 416; (10 min.); piece of shale, hand lens, transparent metric ruler

TE: ***Demonstration,*** p. 417; (5 min.); fossils or casts of fossils

TE: ***Build Science Skills,*** p. 418; (15 min.); plaster of Paris, water, flat-bottomed container, organic specimen such as a shell or leaf

TE: ***Build Science Skills,*** p. 419; (20 min.); slabs of clay, sheets of colored paper, or other suitable materials

SE: ***Quick Lab,*** p. 420; (15 min.); 100 1-cm squares of paper, plastic or paper cup

TE: ***Demonstration,*** p. 424; (5 min.); box of wooden matches

SE: ***Exploration,*** p. 441; (45 min.); long forceps, spoon, dried peas, 3 25-mL graduated cylinders, 3 100-mL beakers, watch or clock with second hand

PLANNING KEY

Ability Levels

- **B Basic** For students who need additional help
- **A Average** For all students
- **E Enriched** For students who need to be challenged

Components

SE	Student Edition	**GRSW**	Guided Reading and Study Workbook	**IDM**	Issues and Decision Making
TE	Teacher's Edition	**CT**	Chapter Tests: Levels A and B	**CTB**	Computer Test Bank
LMA	Laboratory Manual A	**PHAS**	PH Assessment System	**PA**	Presentation Assistant Plus
LMB	Laboratory Manual B	**LA**	Lab Assessment with Scoring Guide	**BD**	BioDetectives Videotape
TR	Teaching Resources	**BTM**	BioTechnology Manual	**iT**	iText
IF	Investigations in Forensics				

Program Resources	Assessment	Media and Technology
LMB: Chapter 17 Lab B A **TR:** Section Review 17–1 B A **GRSW:** Section 17–1 B A **IDM:** Issues and Decision Making 14 A E	**SE:** 17–1 Section Assessment, p. 422 **TR:** Section Review 17–1	**PA:** 17–1 Interest Grabber, Section Outline, Compare/Contrast Table, Figure 17–2, Figure 17–5 **BD:** "Mummies: Ties to the Past" **iT:** Section 17–1
LMA: Chapter 17 Lab A E **TR:** Section Review 17–2 B A **GRSW:** Section 17–2 B A	**SE:** 17–2 Section Assessment, p. 428 **TR:** Section Review 17–2	**PA:** 17–2 Interest Grabber, Section Outline, Flowchart, Figure 17–8, Figure 17–12 **iT:** Section 17–2
TR: Section Review 17–3 B A **GRSW:** Section 17–3 B A	**SE:** 17–3 Section Assessment, p. 435 **TR:** Section Review 17–3	**PA:** 17–3 Interest Grabber, Section Outline, Geological Eras and Periods **iT:** Section 17–3
TR: Section Review 17–4 B A Chapter 17 Exploration B A E **GRSW:** Section 17–4 B A **IDM:** Issues and Decisions 13	**SE:** 17–4 Section Assessment, p. 440 **TR:** Section Review 17–4	**PA:** 17–4 Interest Grabber, Section Outline, Concept Map **iT:** Section 17–4
	SE: Chapter 17 Assessment, pp. 442–445 **TR:** Chapter Vocabulary Review, Graphic Organizer **CT:** Chapter 17 Test **CTB:** Chapter 17 Test **PHAS:** Practice Text	**CTB:** Chapter 17 Test **iT:** Chapter 17 Assessment

PRESSED FOR TIME?

To Preview the Chapter

- Introduce students to the Vocabulary terms and Key Concepts in each section.
- Assign the reading strategies for each section.

To Cover the Chapter Quickly

- Have students read Fossils and Ancient Life and Geologic Time Scale in Section 17–1, the boldfaced sentences in Sections 17–2 and 17–3, and the introduction in Section 17–4.
- Assign questions 1 and 3 in Section Assessments 17–1 through 17–3, questions 1, 2, 6, 7, 9–11, 14, 18, 20, 22, and 23 in Chapter 17 Assessment, and questions 2, 3, and 6 in Chapter 17 Standardized Test Prep.

To Review the Chapter

- Assign Sections 17–1 through 17–4 in the Guided Reading and Study Workbook.
- Assign the Section Reviews for 17–1 through 17–4 and the Chapter Vocabulary Review for Chapter 17 in the Teaching Resources.

ENGAGE/EXPLORE

Inquiry Activity

Objective Students will be able to infer how long it took for a sample of shale to form.

Skills Focus **Inferring, Calculating**

Materials piece of shale, hand lens, transparent metric ruler

Time 10 minutes

Advance Prep Shale billets from the Green River formation in Colorado, Wyoming, and Utah can be obtained from mineralogy suppliers and scientific supply houses.

Strategies

- Offer students dissecting probes or toothpicks for counting layers.
- Explain that the shale samples are from an ancient lake floor and that the alternating light and dark layers formed when sediment washed into the lake in summers and winters, respectively.

Expected Outcome Sample data: 35 layers in 5 mm of rock = 7 layers (years) per mm. 600 m = 600,000 mm. 600,000 mm × 7 years/mm = 4,200,000 years that the lake existed.

Think About It

1. Students should multiply the average number of layers per millimeter from step 3 by the thickness of their specimen.
2. Students should multiply the average number of layers per millimeter by 600,000 mm.

Discrepant Event

Engage students' interest in evolutionary change by describing living fossils, which are organisms that have remained virtually unchanged for millions of years. Examples include starfishes, crocodiles, turtles, opossums, ants, and dragonflies. Ask: **What are some other examples of living fossils?** *(Sharks and cockroaches are well-known examples.)* Explain that living fossils are rare, because most organisms have undergone continuous evolutionary change since they first appeared on Earth, as students will learn in this chapter.

Chapter 17 The History of Life

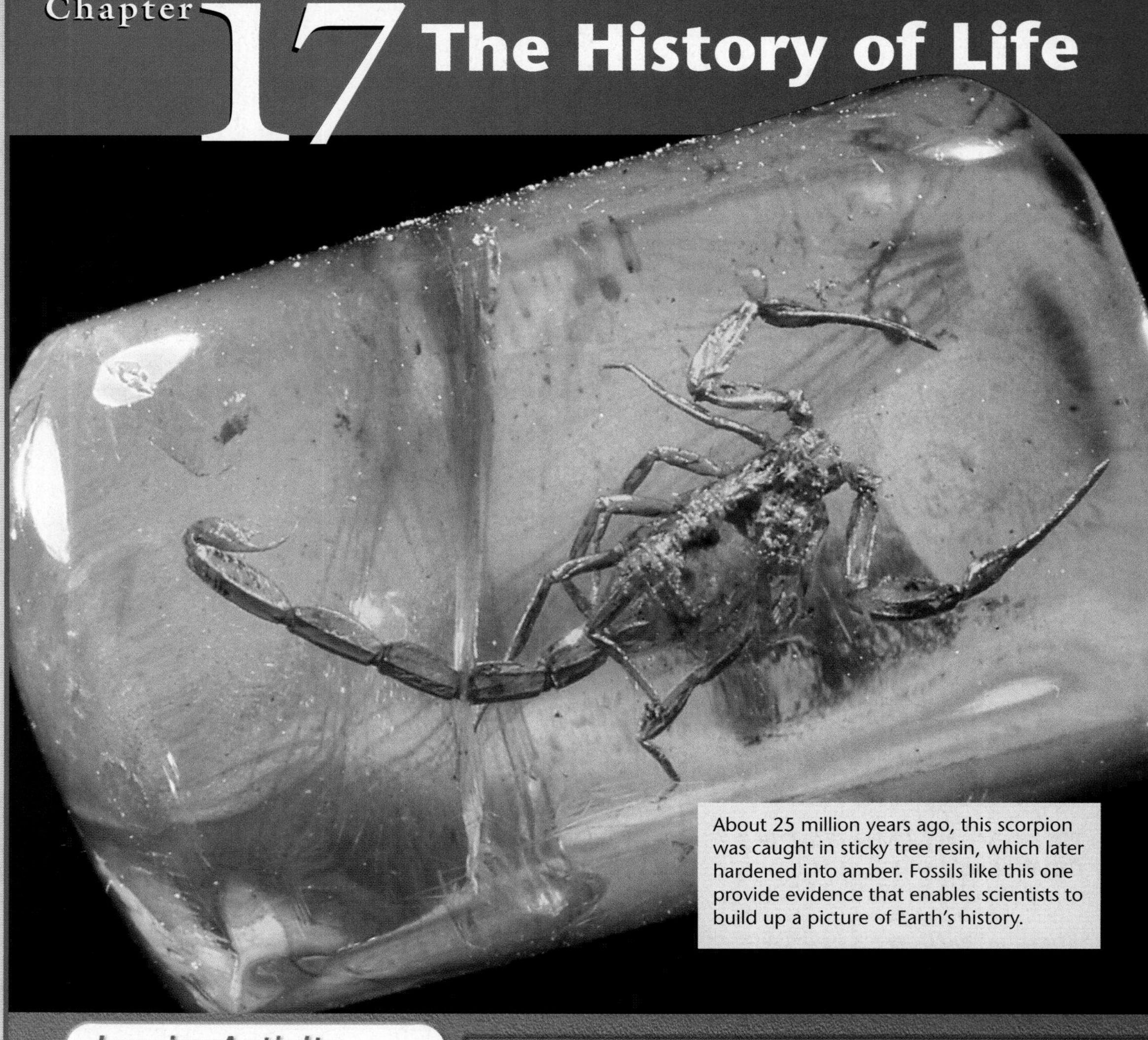

About 25 million years ago, this scorpion was caught in sticky tree resin, which later hardened into amber. Fossils like this one provide evidence that enables scientists to build up a picture of Earth's history.

Inquiry Activity

How can you date a rock?

Procedure

1. Examine a piece of shale with a hand lens. This rock formed from the sediment deposited at the bottom of an ancient lake. As the shale formed, one dark layer and one light layer were deposited each year.
2. Place a transparent metric ruler next to the shale sample. Count and record the number of dark layers in a 5-mm section of the shale.
3. Divide your result in step 2 by 5 to determine the average number of layers per millimeter.

Think About It

1. **Inferring** How many years did it take for your specimen to form?
2. **Calculating** Suppose your specimen came from a deposit of shale that is 600 meters thick. How long did it take for the complete deposit to form?

17–1 The Fossil Record

The history of life on Earth is filled with mystery, life-and-death struggles, and bizarre plants and animals as amazing as any mythological creatures. Studying life's history is one of the most fascinating and challenging parts of biology, and researchers go about it in several ways. One technique is to read the pieces of the story that are "written" in ancient rocks, in the petrified sap of ancient trees, in peat bogs and tar pits, and in polar glaciers. You may recall that these traces and preserved remains of ancient life are called fossils.

Fossils and Ancient Life

Paleontologists (pay-lee-un-TAHL-uh-jists) are scientists who study fossils. They collect fossils such as the one shown in **Figure 17–1.** From these fossils, they infer what past life forms were like—the structure of the organisms, what they ate, what ate them, and the environment in which they lived. Paleontologists also classify fossil organisms. They group similar organisms together and arrange them in the order in which they lived—from oldest to most recent. Together, all this information about past life is called the **fossil record.** **The fossil record provides evidence about the history of life on Earth. It also shows how different groups of organisms have changed over time.**

The fossil record reveals a remarkable fact: Fossils occur in a particular order. Certain fossils appear only in older rocks, and other fossils appear only in more recent rocks. In other words, the fossil record shows that life on Earth has changed over time. In fact, more than 99 percent of all species that have ever lived on Earth have become **extinct,** which means the species died out. Meanwhile, over billions of years, ancient unicellular organisms have given rise to the modern bacteria, protists, fungi, plants, and animals that you will study in later units.

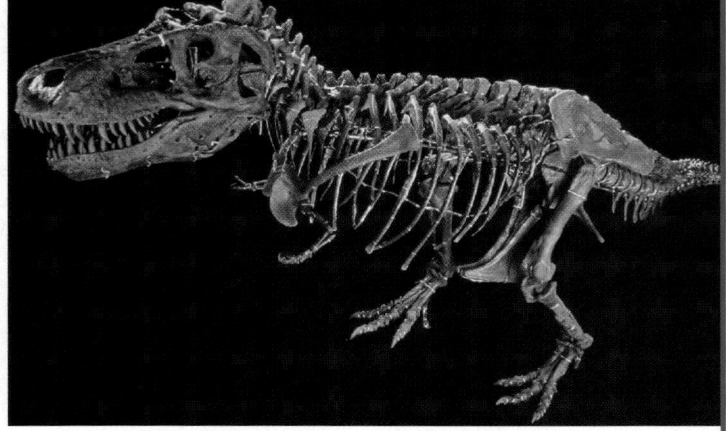

▶ **Figure 17–1** This remarkably complete dinosaur fossil reveals many characteristics of the original animal. **Inferring** *Based on this dinosaur's teeth, what type of food do you think it ate?*

Guide for Reading

Key Concepts
- What is the fossil record?
- What information do relative dating and radioactive dating provide about fossils?
- What are the main divisions of the geologic time scale?

Vocabulary
- paleontologist • fossil record
- extinct • relative dating
- index fossil • half-life
- radioactive dating
- geologic time scale • era
- period

Reading Strategy: Finding Main Ideas Before you read, write down this idea: Scientists use the fossil record to learn about the history of life on Earth. As you read, make a list of the kinds of evidence that support this main idea.

Section Resources

Print:
- ***Laboratory Manual B,*** Chapter 17 Lab
- ***Teaching Resources,*** Section Review 17–1
- ***Guided Reading and Study Workbook,*** Section 17–1
- ***Issues and Decision Making,*** Issues and Decisions 14

Technology:
- ***BioDetectives Videotape,*** "Mummies: Ties to the Past"
- ***iText,*** Section 17–1

Section 17–1

1 FOCUS

Objectives

17.1.1 ***Describe*** the fossil record.
17.1.2 ***State*** the information that relative dating and radioactive dating provide about fossils.
17.1.3 ***Identify*** the divisions of the geologic time scale.

Guide for Reading

Vocabulary Preview

Before students read about the Vocabulary terms *fossil record* and *index fossil*, ask: **What is a fossil?** *(Traces and preserved remains of ancient life)* Point out that traces are footprints, droppings, or any other type of evidence an organism might leave behind.

Reading Strategy

The kinds of evidence that students might list include the fossils themselves, as well as the types of environments and time periods in which the organisms lived.

2 INSTRUCT

Fossils and Ancient Life

Demonstration

Display fossils or casts of fossils for students to inspect. If possible, pass fossils around the room for students to examine. Ask: **Do any of these fossils resemble organisms that still exist today?** *(Answers will depend on the fossils.)* **Can you guess how these organisms might have lived, based on their fossils?** *(Students might say, for example, that an organism might have lived in water because it resembles a living aquatic organism.)* **What other fossils have you seen?** *(Students are likely to have seen fossils in a museum if not at a fossil bed or other natural site.)* Explain that, in this section, students will learn how fossils form and what they reveal about the history of life on Earth.

Answer to . . .

Figure 17–1 *The pointed teeth are those of a meat eater.*

17–1 (continued)

How Fossils Form

Build Science Skills

Using Models Help students appreciate how fossils form by giving them an opportunity to make a model fossil of a shell, leaf, fern frond, nut, or other small organic specimen. First, have students pour a plaster of Paris mixture into a small, flat-bottomed container. When the plaster just begins to harden, students should press the specimen into its surface. After the plaster hardens, they should carefully remove the specimen. Explain that the resulting imprint models a type of fossil called a mold. Add that fossils also form when minerals replace organic materials in a decaying specimen. This process, called petrification, creates a stony duplicate of the original specimen.

Interpreting Fossil Evidence

Meet Diverse Needs

Point out that because the fossil record is incomplete, fossils representing crucial evolutionary events, such as the divergence of major lineages, may be missing from the fossil record. Add that scientists now use molecular clocks to help interpret the fossil record and date important evolutionary events. Explain that molecular clocks are based on the assumption that, through time, the DNA of an organism diverges more and more from the DNA of its ancestors and that the greater the differences between the DNA of living related species, the longer the time since the species shared a common ancestor. Challenge interested students to research the results of using molecular clocks to date evolutionary events. For example, have them investigate how data from molecular clocks suggest that mammals began evolving long before dinosaurs disappeared, a conclusion that was not apparent from the fossil record alone. Urge students to share what they learn with the class in a brief oral report. **Learning modality: verbal**

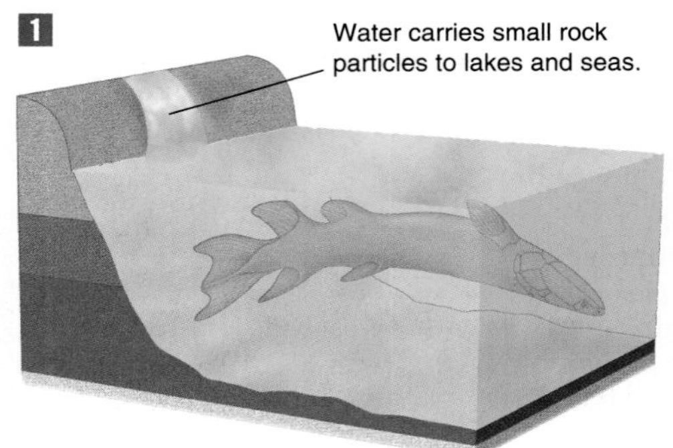

1
Water carries small rock particles to lakes and seas.

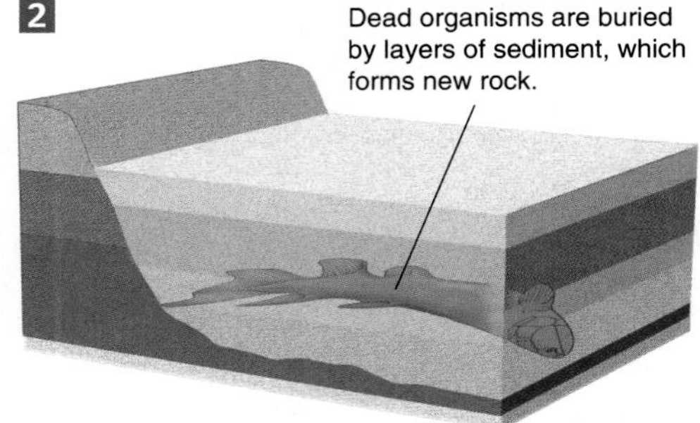

2
Dead organisms are buried by layers of sediment, which forms new rock.

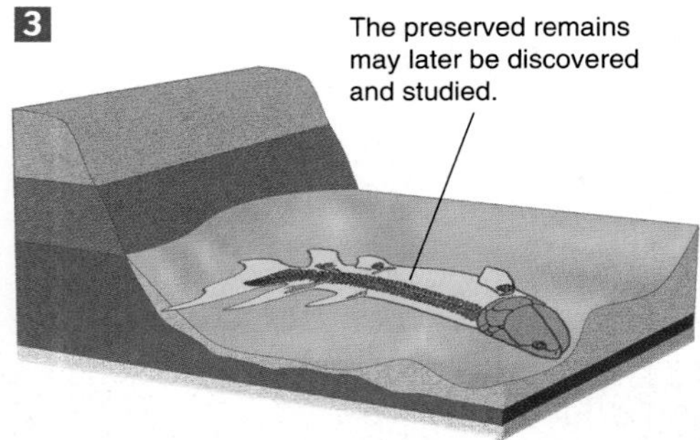

3
The preserved remains may later be discovered and studied.

▲ **Figure 17–2** **The fossil record provides evidence about the history of life on Earth.** Some fossils are formed in sedimentary rock. (1) Water carries small particles from existing rocks to lakes and seas. (2) The rock particles sink to the bottom, sometimes burying dead organisms. The weight of the upper layers compresses the lower layers into new rocks. Minerals replace all or part of the organism's body. (3) The preserved remains may later become exposed. The outline above shows the organism's original shape.

How Fossils Form

A fossil can be as large and complete as an entire, perfectly preserved animal, or as small and incomplete as a tiny fragment of a jawbone or leaf. There are fossil eggs, fossil footprints, and even fossilized animal droppings. For a fossil to form, either the remains of the organism or some trace of its presence must be preserved. The formation of any fossil depends on a precise combination of conditions. Because of this, the fossil record provides incomplete information about the history of life. For every organism that leaves a fossil, many more die without leaving a trace.

Most fossils form in sedimentary rock, as shown in **Figure 17–2.** Sedimentary rock is formed when exposure to rain, heat, wind, and cold breaks down existing rock into small particles of sand, silt, and clay. These particles are carried by streams and rivers into lakes or seas, where they eventually settle to the bottom. As layers of sediment build up over time, dead organisms may also sink to the bottom and become buried. If conditions are right, the remains may be kept intact and free from decay. The weight of layers of sediment gradually compresses the lower layers and, along with chemical activity, turns them into rock.

The quality of fossil preservation varies. In some cases, the small particles of rock surrounding the remains of an organism preserve an imprint of its soft parts. In other cases, the hard parts are preserved when wood, shells, or bones are saturated or replaced with long-lasting mineral compounds. Occasionally, organisms are buried quickly in fine-grained clay or volcanic ash before they begin to decay, so they are perfectly preserved.

✓CHECKPOINT *Why is the fossil record described as an incomplete record of life's history?*

Interpreting Fossil Evidence

The natural forces that form sedimentary rock can also reveal fossils that have been hidden deep in layers of rock for millions of years. Forces inside Earth lift rocks up into mountain ranges, where wind, rain, and running water erode the rock. Bit by bit, flowing water and wind wear away the upper, younger layers, exposing the older fossil-bearing layers beneath.

When a fossil is exposed, a fortunate (and observant) paleontologist may happen along at just the right time and remove the fossil for study.

PRESENTATIONS MADE EASY!

The Presentation Assistant Plus contains the Prentice Hall Presentation Pro and the Transparencies, which provide easy-to-follow visual support for every step of this section. If you have a computer presentation station, use Prentice Hall Presentation Pro for Section 17–1, or use the transparencies listed here.

Section 17–1: **Interest Grabber**
Section Outline
Compare/Contrast Table
Figure 17–2
Figure 17–5

Paleontologists occasionally unearth the remains of an entire organism. More often, though, they must reconstruct an extinct species from a few fossil bits—remains of bone, a shell, leaves, or pollen. Fossil reconstruction requires a thorough knowledge of the anatomy of living organisms, as well as great skill. Also, one of the most important pieces of information about a fossil is its age. Paleontologists determine the age of fossils using two techniques: relative dating and radioactive dating.

Relative Dating About two centuries ago, geologists noted that rock layers containing certain fossils consistently appeared in the same vertical order no matter where they were found. Also, a particular species of trilobite—a common fossil and an extinct relative of horseshoe crabs—might be found in one rock layer but be absent from layers above or below it. How might such a pattern be useful?

In **relative dating,** the age of a fossil is determined by comparing its placement with that of fossils in other layers of rock, as shown in **Figure 17–3.** Recall that sedimentary rock is formed from the gradual deposition of layers of sand, rock, and other types of sediment. The rock layers form in order by age—the oldest layers on the bottom, with more recent layers on top, closer to Earth's surface.

Scientists also use **index fossils** to compare the relative ages of fossils. To be used as an index fossil, a species must be easily recognized and must have existed for a short period but have had a wide geographic range. As a result, it will be found in only a few layers of rock, but these specific layers will be found in different geographic locations. **Relative dating allows paleontologists to estimate a fossil's age compared with that of other fossils.** However, it provides no information about its absolute age, or age in years.

Word Origins

The word part *paleo-* means "ancient" or "early," and *-zoic* means "life." The word part *meso-* means "middle." The word part *ceno-* means "recent." **Use this information to explain the meaning of *paleozoic, mesozoic,* and *cenozoic.***

▼ **Figure 17–3 In relative dating, a paleontologist estimates a fossil's age in comparison with that of other fossils.** Each of these fossils is an index fossil. It enables scientists to date the rock layer in which it is found. Scientists can also use index fossils to date rocks from different locations.

Word Origins

The Paleozoic Era is the era of ancient life, the Mesozoic Era the era of middle life, and the Cenozoic Era the era of recent life.

Build Science Skills

Using Models Divide the class into small groups, and have each group design and build a model showing how the fossils contained in one sequence of rock layers can be used to determine the relative ages of fossils in another sequence of rock layers. To represent the rock layers, students can use slabs of clay, stacks of paper of different colors, or other suitable materials. They should label the layers with pictures of fossils they have sketched, photocopied from books, or printed from the Internet. Give each group a chance to present its model to the class and explain how relative dating can be used to date one sequence of fossils based on the other.

Use Visuals

Figure 17–3 Have students read the figure caption. Then, ask: **What assumption do paleontologists make when they use relative dating to estimate the ages of fossils?** *(They assume that fossils found in the upper layers of sedimentary rock are younger than fossils found in the lower layers of rock.)* **What might happen to invalidate this assumption?** *(Anything that disturbs rock layers so that older layers end up on top of younger layers, including movement of rock layers at a fault or human activities such as mining.)*

Answer to . . .

CHECKPOINT *Because many organisms die without leaving fossils*

Quick Lab

Objective Students will be able to analyze data and calculate the "half-life" of a model radioactive element.

Skills Focus **Analyzing Data, Calculating**

Materials 100 1-cm squares of paper, plastic or paper cup

Time 15 minutes

Advance Prep Students can make their own paper squares in advance.

Strategy Explain to students that, on average, about half the remaining squares will be removed each time step 4 is repeated. Ask: **Why does this model radioactive decay?** *(Because half the radioactive element decays during each half-life)*

Expected Outcome Students will need to spill and remove paper squares about four or five times to reduce the number of squares to five or fewer.

Analyze and Conclude

1. In most cases, about half the squares will be removed in one spill and about three fourths of the squares will be removed in two spills.
2. One year

Encourage students to view "Mummies: Ties to the Past" on the BioDetectives Videotape.

Use Visuals

Figure 17–4 Ask: **Why does the curve fall steeply and then start to level out.** *(Because it is decreasing by half of an ever smaller amount)* **What fraction of potassium-40 will be present in five half-lives?** *(1/32)* Some students may have a better appreciation for the rate of decay if they convert the fractions into percentages.

Quick Lab

What is a half-life?

Materials 100 1-cm squares of paper, plastic or paper cup

Procedure 

1. Construct a data table with 2 columns and 5 blank rows. Label the columns "Spill number" and "Number of squares returned."
2. Place an *X* on each square of paper, and put all the squares in the cup.
3. Mix up the squares in the cup. Then, spill them out and separate all squares that overlap.
4. Remove the squares that have an *X* showing. Record the number of squares remaining and return them to the cup.
5. Repeat steps 3 and 4 until there are 5 or fewer squares remaining. Make a graph of your results with the number of spills on the *x*-axis and the number of squares remaining on the *y*-axis.

Analyze and Conclude

1. **Analyzing Data** How many spills were required to remove half of the squares? To remove three fourths?
2. **Calculating** If each spill represents one year, what is the half-life of the squares?

Radioactive Dating Scientists use radioactive decay to assign absolute ages to rocks. Some elements found in rocks are radioactive. Radioactive elements decay, or break down, into nonradioactive elements at a steady rate, which is measured in a unit called a half-life. A **half-life** is the length of time required for half of the radioactive atoms in a sample to decay. As shown in **Figure 17–4,** after one half-life, half of the original radioactive atoms in a sample have decayed. Of those remaining atoms, half again are decayed after another half-life.

Radioactive dating is the use of half-lives to determine the age of a sample. **In radioactive dating, scientists calculate the age of a sample based on the amount of remaining radioactive isotopes it contains.** Different radioactive elements have different half-lives and therefore provide natural clocks that "tick" at different rates. Carbon-14, for example, has a half-life of about 5730 years. Carbon-14 is taken up by living things while they are alive. After an organism dies, the carbon-14 in its body begins to decay to form nitrogen-14, which escapes into the air. Carbon-12, the most common isotope of carbon, is not radioactive and does not decay. By comparing the amounts of carbon-14 and carbon-12 in a fossil, researchers can determine when the organism lived. The more carbon-12 there is in a sample compared to carbon-14, the older the sample is.

Because carbon-14 has a relatively short half-life, it is useful only for dating fossils younger than about 60,000 years. To date rocks that are billions of years old, researchers use the slower clocks offered by the decay of potassium-40 and other isotopes with longer half-lives.

CHECKPOINT *What is a half-life?*

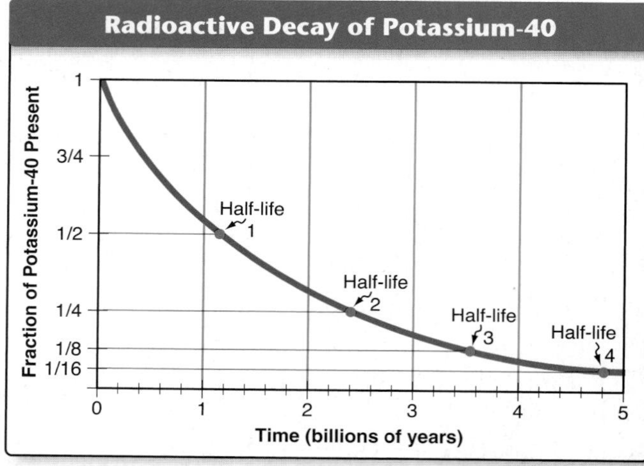

▲ **Figure 17–4** **Radioactive dating involves measuring the amounts of radioactive isotopes in a sample to determine its actual age.** Such measurements enable scientists to determine the absolute age of rocks and the fossils they contain.

To find out how radioactive dating was used to study some old human remains from South America, view the videotape "Mummies: Ties to the Past."

HISTORY OF SCIENCE

Pliny's footprints and Noah's ravens

The first dinosaur footprints ever discovered in the United States were found by a 12-year-old boy. In 1802, while plowing a field on his family's farm in western Massachusetts, Pliny Moody turned up a flat stone with footprints on it that resembled bird footprints but were much too large to have been made by any living bird. When news of Pliny's discovery spread, crowds came to view the prints. People thought that the prints must have been made by giant ravens released by Noah from the Ark. Prompted by Pliny's discovery, Edward Hitchcock, who was president of Amherst College in Massachusetts, began a 30-year search for more prints. He eventually discovered tracks of 49 different types of dinosaurs. Believing the tracks to have been made by large, ostrichlike birds, Hitchcock called the prints ornithichites, which means "stony bird tracks."

Geologic Time Scale

Paleontologists use divisions of the **geologic time scale** to represent evolutionary time. **Figure 17–5** shows the most recent version of the geologic time scale. Scientists first developed the geologic time scale by studying rock layers and index fossils worldwide. With this information, they placed Earth's rocks in order according to relative age. As geologists studied the fossil record, they found major changes in the fossil animals and plants at specific layers in the rock. These times were used to mark where one segment of geologic time ends and the next begins—long before anyone knew how long these various segments actually were.

Years later, radioactive dating techniques were used to assign specific ages to the various rock layers. Not surprisingly, the divisions of the geologic time scale did not turn out to be of standard lengths, such as 100 million years. Instead, geologic divisions vary in duration by many millions of years. Scientists use several levels of divisions for the geologic time scale. Geologic time begins with Precambrian (pree-KAM-bree-un) Time. Although few multicellular fossils exist from this time, the Precambrian actually covers about 88 percent of Earth's history, as shown in **Figure 17–6** on page 422. **After Precambrian Time, the basic divisions of the geologic time scale are eras and periods.**

Eras Geologists divide the time between the Precambrian and the present into three **eras.** They are the Paleozoic Era, the Mesozoic Era, and the Cenozoic Era. The Paleozoic (pay-lee-uh-ZOH-ik) began about 544 million years ago and lasted for almost 300 million years. Many vertebrates and invertebrates—animals with and without backbones—lived during the Paleozoic.

The Mesozoic (mez-uh-ZOH-ik) began about 245 million years ago and lasted about 180 million years. Some people call the Mesozoic the Age of Dinosaurs, yet dinosaurs were only one of many kinds of organisms that lived during this era. Mammals began to evolve during the Mesozoic.

Earth's most recent era is the Cenozoic (sen-uh-ZOH-ik). It began about 65 million years ago and continues to the present. The Cenozoic is sometimes called the Age of Mammals because mammals became common during this time.

Geologic Time Scale

Era	Period	Time (millions of years ago)
Cenozoic	Quarternary	1.8 – present
	Tertiary	65 – 1.8
Mesozoic	Cretaceous	145 – 65
	Jurassic	208 – 145
	Triassic	245 – 208
Paleozoic	Permian	290 – 245
	Carboniferous	363 – 290
	Devonian	410 – 363
	Silurian	440 – 410
	Ordovician	505 – 440
	Cambrian	544 – 505
Precambrian Time	Vendian	650 – 544

▲ **Figure 17–5** **The basic units of the geologic time scale after Precambrian Time are eras and periods.** Each era is divided into periods.

Geologic Time Scale

Meet Diverse Needs

Have students make a time line of the geologic time scale that shows the relative length of each era and period. They should use a long piece of paper from a roll or tape several sheets of paper end-to-end to create one long sheet. Before beginning their timeline, students should determine the scale they will use. For example, if their paper is at least 130 cm long, they might let 1 cm equal 5 million years. In addition to labeling the eras, periods, and years, students should label the major "ages" mentioned in the text, including the Age of Dinosaurs (Mesozoic) and the Age of Mammals (Cenozoic). As students read the rest of the chapter, suggest that they add important evolutionary events to their time lines. **Learning modality: visual**

Use Visuals

Figure 17–5 Make sure students understand the table by asking: **What is the name of the earliest era in geologic time?** *(Precambrian Time)* **What are the periods of the Paleozoic era, from oldest to youngest?** *(Cambrian, Ordovician, Silurian, Devonian, Carboniferous, and Permian)* **When did the Cretaceous Period end?** *(65 million years ago)* **Which era and period do we live in?** *(Cenozoic Era and Quaternary Period)*

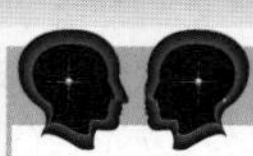

TEACHER TO TEACHER

To help students remember the geological time scale, I divide the class into four groups, assigning a geological era to each group. Then, I have each group make a poster of their era, showing the periods within the era and a drawing of at least two types of organisms that appeared in the period. I display the posters in the classroom and refer to them as we discuss the evolution of multicellular life.

—*Janice Lagatol,*
Biology Teacher
Fort Lee High School,
Fort Lee, NJ

Answer to . . .

CHECKPOINT *The length of time required for half of the radioactive atoms in a sample to decay*

17–1 (continued)

Build Science Skills

Using Analogies Students may have a better appreciation of how recently most life forms appeared in Earth's history if you compare Earth's age to a 24-hour day. Explain that if Earth was formed at 12:01 AM, then the oldest known fossils appeared at about 6 AM, the oldest nucleated cells between 4 and 5 PM, the oldest complex organisms between 8 and 9 PM, the oldest plants between 9 and 10 PM, and the oldest mammals at about 11 PM. Ask: **When do you think the first humans appeared?** *(Student might guess 11:30 or 11:45 PM. They probably will be surprised to learn that the first humans did not appear until the last 30 seconds before midnight.)*

3 ASSESS

Evaluate Understanding

Have students make a Venn diagram to compare and contrast relative and absolute dating.

Reteach

Make a copy of the geologic time scale in Figure 17–5 with several of the eras and periods left blank. Have students work in pairs to fill in the missing terms.

ALTERNATIVE ASSESSMENT

Students' time lines should be based on Figure 17–5 and the information found on pages 421 and 422 of the text.

Use iText to review the key concepts in Section 17–1.

Answer to . . .

Figure 17–6 *The first prokaryotes appeared at about 2:00 PM; the first land plants at 11:00 PM; the first humans about 12:00 AM.*

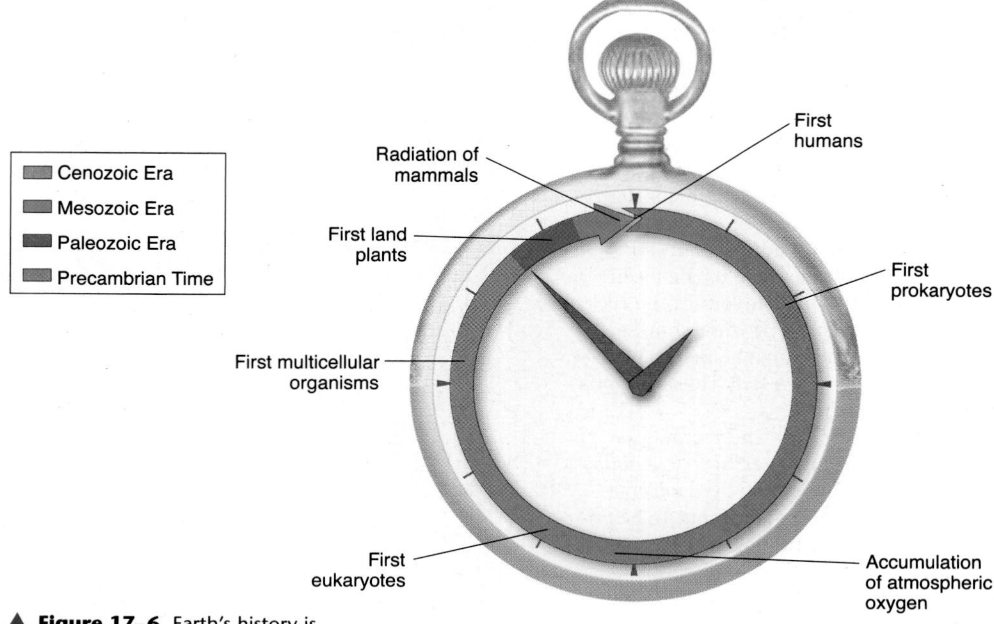

▲ **Figure 17–6** Earth's history is often compared to a familiar measurement, such as the twelve hours between noon and midnight. In such a comparison, notice that Precambrian Time lasts from noon until after 10:30 PM. **Interpreting Graphics** ***Using this model, about what time did life appear? The first plants? The first humans?***

Periods Eras are subdivided into **periods,** which range in length from tens of millions of years to less than two million years. The Mesozoic Era, for example, includes three periods: the Triassic Period, the Jurassic Period, and the Cretaceous Period. Many periods are named for places around the world where geologists first described the rocks and fossils of that period. The name Cambrian, for example, refers to Cambria, the old Roman name for Wales. Jurassic refers to the Jura Mountains in France. The Carboniferous ("carbon-bearing") Period, on the other hand, is named for the large coal deposits that formed during that period.

17–1 Section Assessment

1. **Key Concept** What can be learned from the fossil record?
2. **Key Concept** Which type of dating provides an absolute age for a given fossil? Describe how this is done.
3. **Key Concept** How are eras and periods related?
4. **Critical Thinking Drawing Conclusions** Many more fossils have been found since Darwin's day, allowing several gaps in the fossil record to be filled. How might this information make relative dating more accurate?

iTEXT **Assessment** Use iText to review the important concepts in Section 17–1.

ALTERNATIVE ASSESSMENT

Constructing a Time Line Create a time line that shows the four main divisions in the geologic time scale and the key events that occurred during those divisions.

17–1 Section Assessment

1. The fossil record provides evidence about the history of life on Earth and how different groups of organisms changed over time.
2. Radioactive dating provides an absolute age for a given fossil. Scientists calculate the age of a sample based on the amount of remaining radioactive isotopes it contains.
3. Periods are subdivisions of the eras of the geologic time scale.
4. More fossils might make relative dating more accurate because the method depends on comparisons of fossils.

17–2 Earth's Early History

In Chapter 1 you read about people's theories and experiments on the origin of life. The theory of spontaneous generation—life from nonlife—was disproved about 140 years ago. But if life comes only from life, then how did life on Earth first begin? This section presents the current scientific view of events on the early Earth. These hypotheses, however, are based on a relatively small amount of evidence. As new evidence is found, scientists' ideas about the early Earth and the origin of life may change.

Formation of Earth

Geologic evidence shows that Earth was not "born" in a single event. Instead, pieces of cosmic debris were probably attracted to one another over the course of about 100 million years. While the planet was young, it was struck by one or more objects, possibly as large as the planet Mars. This collision produced enough heat to melt the entire globe.

Once Earth melted, its elements rearranged themselves according to density. The most dense elements formed the planet's core. There, radioactive decay generated enough heat to convert Earth's interior into molten rock. Moderately dense elements floated to the surface, much as fat floats to the top of hot chicken soup. These elements ultimately cooled to form a solid crust. The least dense elements—including hydrogen and nitrogen—formed the first atmosphere.

This infant planet, shown in **Figure 17–7**, was so different from today's Earth that you would not recognize it. The sky was not blue but pinkish-orange. **Earth's early atmosphere probably contained hydrogen cyanide, carbon dioxide, carbon monoxide, nitrogen, hydrogen sulfide, and water.** Had you been there, a few deep breaths would have killed you!

Guide for Reading

Key Concepts

- What substances made up Earth's early atmosphere?
- What did Miller and Urey's experiments show?
- What occurred when oxygen was added to Earth's atmosphere?
- What hypothesis explains the origin of eukaryotic cells?

Vocabulary

proteinoid microsphere
microfossil
endosymbiotic theory

Reading Strategy: Making Comparisons
Before you read, write three sentences about Earth as it is today. As you read, write three sentences that describe how Earth was very different in the past.

▼ **Figure 17–7** The early Earth was much hotter than it is now, and there was little or no oxygen in the atmosphere. **Earth's early atmosphere was probably made up of hydrogen cyanide, carbon dioxide, carbon monoxide, nitrogen, hydrogen sulfide, and water.**

TIME SAVER — SECTION RESOURCES

Print:

- ***Laboratory Manual A,*** Chapter 17 Lab
- ***Teaching Resources,*** Section Review 17–2
- ***Guided Reading and Study Workbook,*** Section 17–2

Technology:

- ***iText,*** Section 17–2

Section 17–2

1 FOCUS

Objectives

17.2.1 ***Describe*** how conditions on early Earth were different from conditions today.
17.2.2 ***Explain*** what Miller and Urey's experiments showed.
17.2.3 ***State*** the hypotheses that have been proposed for how life first arose on Earth.

Guide for Reading

Vocabulary Preview

Break down some of the Vocabulary terms into their component parts so their meanings are easier to decipher. Explain that *-oid* means "resembling" and that *micro-* means "tiny." Then, ask: **What is a proteinoid microsphere?** *(A tiny sphere resembling a protein)* **What is a microfossil?** *(A tiny fossil)*

Reading Strategy

Because of the complexity of the material, students may benefit by creating graphic organizers as they read to summarize the information.

2 INSTRUCT

Formation of Earth

Use Visuals

Figure 17–7 Show students a recent photograph of Earth taken from a satellite in space. Have them compare the recent photograph with the drawing of early Earth shown in the figure. Ask: **What features can you see on Earth's surface in the photograph and in the drawing?** *(Features in the photograph include white clouds, blue oceans, and green and brown landmasses. Features in the drawing include erupting volcanoes, meteors, and lightning.)* Then, ask: **What are the basic requirements for human life that are found on Earth today?** *(Water, oxygen, and plants and animals for nutrients)* **Which basic requirements were present on early Earth?** *(Only water)*

17–2 (continued)

The First Organic Molecules

Demonstration

Demonstrate the importance of energy as a prerequisite for chemical reactions. Have students observe as you light a match by running it across its striker. Challenge students to identify the factors involved in lighting the match. *(Energy and a chemical reaction)* Relate the demonstration to the work done by Miller and Urey. Explain that for amino acids to form, energy was required for chemical reactions. Ask: **Where did this energy come from on early Earth?** *(Lightning)*

Build Science Skills

Inferring Explain that several years after Miller and Urey's experiment, a meteorite crashed to Earth in Australia. It was carefully split open and analyzed. Inside were found the same amino acids that had been produced in Miller and Urey's apparatus. Ask: **Why did this support Miller and Urey's experimental results?** *(Because the amino acids in the meteorite were most likely not produced by living organisms)*

Use Visuals

Figure 17–8 Ask: **Why did Miller and Urey use a mixture of nitrogen, hydrogen, methane, and ammonia in their apparatus?** *(Because this mixture of gases resembles Earth's early atmosphere)* **Why was it necessary to perform their experiment in a closed system?** *(To prevent oxygen from entering, because Earth's early atmosphere had no oxygen)* **Why did they boil water to produce water vapor?** *(Because water vapor was present in the early atmosphere)* **What was the purpose of the electric sparks?** *(To simulate lightning and provide energy for the chemical reactions)*

About 4 billion years ago, Earth cooled enough to allow the first solid rocks to form on its surface. For millions of years afterward, violent volcanic activity shook Earth's crust. Comets and asteroids bombarded its surface. Oceans did not exist because the surface was extremely hot.

About 3.8 billion years ago, Earth's surface cooled enough for water to remain a liquid. Thunderstorms drenched the planet, and oceans covered much of the surface. Those primitive oceans were brown because they contained lots of dissolved iron. The earliest sedimentary rocks, which were deposited in water, have been dated to this period. This was the Earth on which life appeared.

CHECKPOINT *Why did the early Earth not have oceans?*

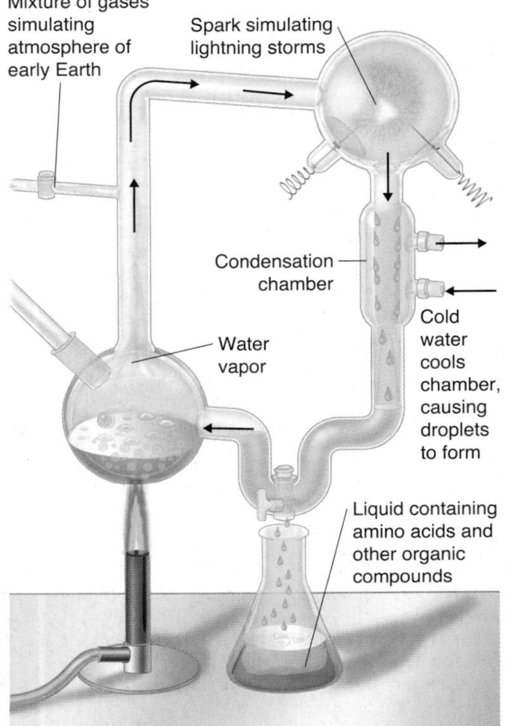

▲ **Figure 17–8** Miller and Urey produced amino acids, which are needed to make proteins, by passing sparks through a mixture of hydrogen, methane, ammonia, and water. **This and other experiments suggested how simple compounds found on the early Earth could have combined to form the organic compounds needed for life.**

The First Organic Molecules

For several reasons, atoms do not assemble themselves into complex organic molecules or living cells on Earth today. For one thing, the oxygen in the atmosphere is very reactive and would destroy any organic molecules that formed. In addition, as soon as organic molecules appeared, something—bacteria or some other life form—would probably eat them! But the early Earth was a very different place. Could organic molecules have evolved under those conditions?

In the 1950s, American chemists Stanley Miller and Harold Urey tried to answer that question by simulating conditions on the early Earth in a laboratory setting. They filled a flask with hydrogen, methane, ammonia, and water to represent the atmosphere. They made certain that no microorganisms could contaminate the results. Then, as shown in **Figure 17–8,** they passed electric sparks through the mixture to simulate lightning.

The results were spectacular. Over a few days, several amino acids—the building blocks of proteins—began to accumulate. **Miller and Urey's experiments suggested how mixtures of the organic compounds necessary for life could have arisen from simpler compounds present on a primitive Earth.** Scientists now know that Miller and Urey's original simulations of Earth's early atmosphere were not accurate. However, similar experiments based on more current knowledge of Earth's early atmosphere have also produced organic compounds. In fact, one of Miller's experiments in 1995 produced cytosine and uracil, two of the bases found in RNA.

PRESENTATIONS MADE EASY!

The Presentation Assistant Plus contains the Prentice Hall Presentation Pro and the Transparencies, which provide easy-to-follow visual support for every step of this section. If you have a computer presentation station, use Prentice Hall Presentation Pro for Section 17–2, or use the transparencies listed here.

Section 17–2:

Interest Grabber
Section Outline
Flowchart
Figure 17–8
Figure 17–12

How Did Life Begin?

A stew of organic molecules is a long way from a living cell, and the leap from nonlife to life is the greatest gap in scientific theories of Earth's early history. Scientists do know that about 200 to 300 million years after Earth cooled enough to carry liquid water, cells similar to modern bacteria were common. How might these cells have originated?

Formation of Microspheres Under certain conditions, large organic molecules can form tiny bubbles called **proteinoid microspheres,** as shown in **Figure 17–9.** Microspheres are not cells, but they have some characteristics of living systems. Like cells, they have selectively permeable membranes through which water molecules can pass. Microspheres also have a simple means of storing and releasing energy. Several hypotheses suggest that structures similar to proteinoid microspheres might have acquired more and more characteristics of living cells.

Evolution of RNA and DNA Another unanswered question in the evolution of cells is the origin of DNA and RNA. Remember that all cells are controlled by information stored in DNA, which is transcribed into RNA and then translated into proteins. How could this complex biochemical machinery have evolved?

Science cannot yet solve this puzzle, although molecular biologists have made surprising discoveries in this area. Under the right conditions, some RNA sequences can help DNA replicate. Other RNA sequences process messenger RNA after transcription. Still others catalyze chemical reactions. Some RNA molecules can even grow and duplicate themselves—suggesting that RNA might have existed before DNA. A series of experiments that simulated conditions of the early Earth have suggested that small sequences of RNA could have formed and replicated on their own. From this relatively simple RNA-based form of life, several steps could have led to the system of DNA-directed protein synthesis that exists now. This hypothesis is shown in **Figure 17–10.** Future experiments are aimed at refining and retesting this hypothesis.

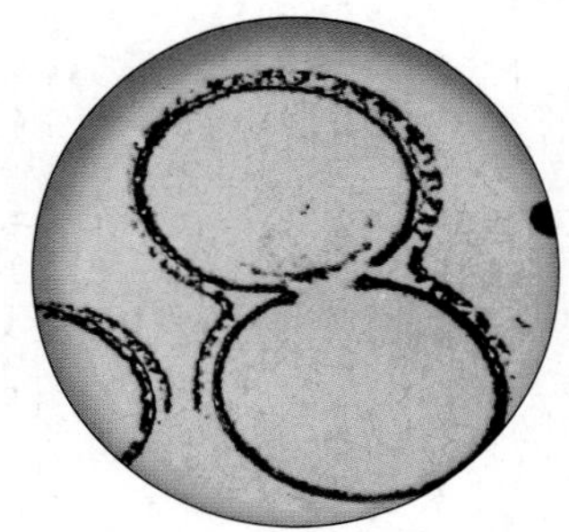

(magnification: about 10,000×)

▲ **Figure 17–9** Large organic molecules can sometimes form tiny proteinoid microspheres like the ones shown here. **Comparing and Contrasting** *How are proteinoid microspheres similar to cells? How are they different?*

▼ **Figure 17–10** One hypothesis about the origin of life, illustrated here, suggests that RNA could have evolved before DNA. Scientists have not yet demonstrated the later stages of this process in a laboratory setting. **Interpreting Graphics** *How might RNA have stored genetic information?*

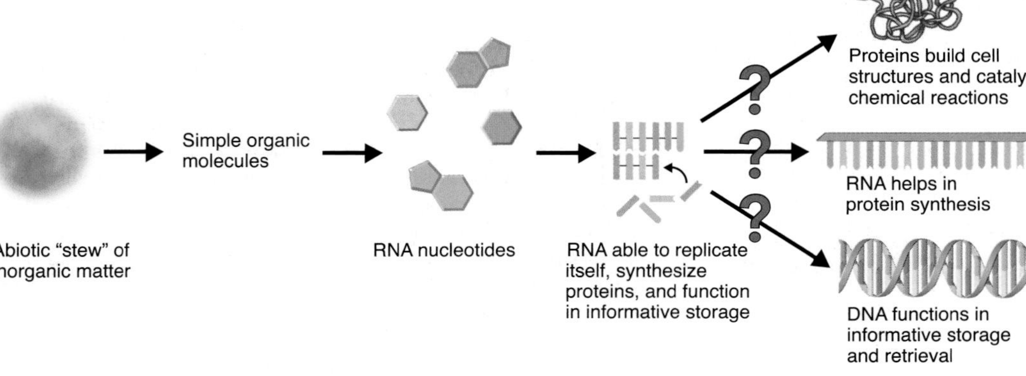
Abiotic "stew" of inorganic matter
Simple organic molecules
RNA nucleotides
RNA able to replicate itself, synthesize proteins, and function in informative storage
?
?
?
Proteins build cell structures and catalyze chemical reactions
RNA helps in protein synthesis
DNA functions in informative storage and retrieval

How Did Life Begin?

Meet Diverse Needs

Challenge students who need an extra challenge to develop a television program for young children that explains the origin of life on Earth. Have students write a script for the program and then videotape a presentation using the script. Show students' videotapes to the class. **Learning modality: verbal**

Build Science Skills

Inferring Help students understand the importance of proteinoid microspheres. Remind students that cells are the basic functional units of most living things and that cells cannot exist without semipermeable cell membranes. Ask: **Why do cells need membranes?** *(To control which substances move into and out of the cells)* Conclude by saying that the development of membranes in proteinoid microspheres was a crucial step in the evolution of living cells.

Meet Diverse Needs

At-risk students may better understand the material on the evolution of RNA and DNA if they first review the structure of RNA and DNA, how RNA and DNA replicate, and how proteins are synthesized. Suggest that students review Chapter 12 at this time. For example, they might read the boldfaced sentences or study the figures and captions. **Limited English proficiency**

Answers to . . .

CHECKPOINT *Because the surface was extremely hot*

Figure 17–9 *Like cells, proteinoid microspheres have a selectively permeable membrane and a simple means of storing and releasing energy. Unlike cells, they do not have DNA or RNA.*

Figure 17–10 *RNA may have acted much like the present DNA molecules —groups of nucleotides may have served as codes for genetic information.*

Free Oxygen

Build Science Skills

Using Tables and Graphs Tell students that Earth's early atmosphere was 92.2% carbon dioxide, 5.1% nitrogen, 0.0 % oxygen, and 2.7% other gases, whereas Earth's present-day atmosphere is 0.03% carbon dioxide, 78.1% nitrogen, and 20.9% oxygen, and 0.03% other gases. Have students display the data in a table and in a bar or line graph. Then, ask: **Where did the oxygen come from?** *(It was produced by photosynthesis.)*

Address Misconceptions

Some students might think that the first organisms must have been able to make their own food. Emphasize that the first known fossils do not represent organisms that could make their own food, or autotrophs, but instead organisms that depended on organic compounds for energy, or heterotrophs. Explain that autotrophs, such as photosynthetic bacteria, are chemically more complex organisms than the simplest heterotrophs. Therefore, it is unlikely that autotrophs evolved first.

Build Science Skills

Inferring Ask: **If photosynthetic organisms had not evolved, what do you think life would be like on Earth today?** *(Students should describe ways Earth would be different without oxygen in the oceans and atmosphere. Oxygen-based life would not have evolved, and organisms that did not depend on oxygen would no doubt have evolved further than they did.)*

▲ **Figure 17–11** **Ancient photosynthetic organisms produced a rise in oxygen in Earth's atmosphere.** These rocklike formations, called stromatolites, were made by cyanobacteria, which were among the earliest organisms to evolve on Earth. The stromatolites above are growing in the ocean near Australia.

Free Oxygen

Microscopic fossils, or **microfossils,** of single-celled prokaryotic organisms that resemble modern bacteria have been found in rocks more than 3.5 billion years old, as shown in **Figure 17–11.** Those first life forms must have evolved in the absence of oxygen, because Earth's first atmosphere contained little or none of that highly reactive gas.

Over time, as indicated by fossil evidence, photosynthetic bacteria became common in the shallow seas of the Precambrian. By 2.2 billion years ago at the latest, these organisms were steadily churning out oxygen, an end product of photosynthesis. One of the first things oxygen did was to combine with iron in the oceans. In other words, it caused the oceans to rust! When iron oxide was formed, it fell from the sea water to the ocean floor. There, it formed great bands of iron that are the source of most of the iron ore mined today. Without iron, the oceans changed color from brown to blue-green.

Next, oxygen gas started accumulating in the atmosphere. As atmospheric oxygen concentrations rose, concentrations of methane and hydrogen sulfide began to decrease, the ozone layer began to form, and the skies turned their present shade of blue. Over the course of several hundred million years, oxygen concentrations rose until they reached today's levels.

The increase in this highly reactive gas created the first global "pollution" crisis. To the first cells, oxygen was a deadly poison!  **The rise of oxygen in the atmosphere drove some life forms to extinction, while other life forms evolved new, more efficient metabolic pathways that used oxygen for respiration.** Organisms that had evolved in an oxygen-free atmosphere were forced into a few airless habitats, where their anaerobic descendants remain today. Some organisms, however, evolved ways of using oxygen for respiration and protecting themselves from oxygen's powerful reactive abilities. The stage was set for the evolution of modern life.

✓CHECKPOINT *What process added oxygen to Earth's atmosphere?*

BIO INSIGHTS — FACTS AND FIGURES

Polymers on the rocks

After small organic molecules formed on prebiotic Earth, the second major chemical step before life appeared was most likely polymerization, or the formation of organic polymers from monomers. Polymers are synthesized by dehydration reactions. In living cells, specific enzymes catalyze these reactions. However, polymerization also occurs in laboratory situations without enzymes, for example, when dilute solutions of organic monomers are dripped onto hot sand, clay, or rock. The heat vaporizes the water in the solutions and concentrates the monomers on the underlying substance. Some of the monomers then spontaneously bond together in chains, forming polymers. In a similar way on early Earth, rain or waves may have splashed dilute solutions of organic monomers onto fresh lava or other hot rocks and then rinsed proteinoids and other polymers into the sea.

Origin of Eukaryotic Cells

Several important events in the history of life have been revealed through molecular studies of cells and their organelles. One of these events is the origin of eukaryotic cells, which are cells that have nuclei. About 2 billion years ago, prokaryotic cells—cells without nuclei—began evolving internal cell membranes. The result was the ancestor of all eukaryotic cells.

Then, something radical seems to have happened. Other prokaryotic organisms entered this ancestral eukaryote. These organisms did not infect their host, as parasites would have done, and the host did not digest them, as it would have digested prey. Instead, the smaller prokaryotes began living inside the larger cell, as shown in **Figure 17–12.** Over time, a symbiotic, or interdependent, relationship evolved. According to the **endosymbiotic theory,** eukaryotic cells formed from a symbiosis among several different prokaryotic organisms. One group of prokaryotes had the ability to use oxygen to generate energy-rich molecules of ATP. These evolved into the mitochondria that are now in the cells of all multicellular organisms. Other prokaryotes that carried out photosynthesis evolved into the chloroplasts of plants and algae. **The endosymbiotic theory proposes that eukaryotic cells arose from living communities formed by prokaryotic organisms.**

This hypothesis was proposed more than a century ago, when microscopists saw that the membranes of mitochondria and chloroplasts resembled the plasma membranes of free-living prokaryotes. Yet, the endosymbiotic theory did not receive much support until the 1960s, when it was championed by Lynn Margulis of Boston University. She and her supporters built their argument on several pieces of evidence: First, mitochondria and chloroplasts contain DNA similar to bacterial DNA.

KEEP CURRENT WITH . . . SCIENCE NEWS®

To find out more about the topics in this chapter, go to: **www.phschool.com**

▼ **Figure 17–12** **The endosymbiotic theory proposes that eukaryotic cells arose from living communities formed by prokaryotic organisms.** Ancient prokaryotes may have entered primitive eukaryotic cells and remained there as organelles.

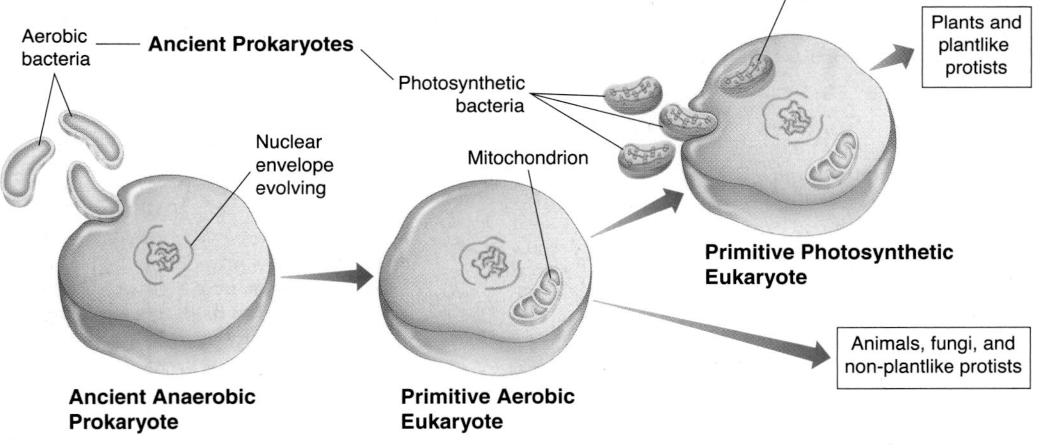

Origin of Eukaryotic Cells

SCIENCE NEWS®

Encourage students to visit **www.phschool.com** for the most current information on this topic.

Meet Diverse Needs

Have students who need an extra challenge research the infolding theory, which is another theory of the origin of eukaryotic cells. Students should investigate what the theory proposes and what evidence supports it. Encourage students to draw a diagram, similar to Figure 17–12, to illustrate the infolding theory. Ask volunteers to use their diagrams to explain the theory to the class. **Learning modality: verbal**

Use Visuals

Figure 17–12 Have students trace the path of the arrows through the figure. Check their understanding of the processes being modeled by asking: **According to the endosymbiotic theory, which organelles did aerobic bacteria become in primitive eukaryotes?** *(Mitochondria)* **Which organelles did photosynthetic bacteria become in primitive photosynthetic eukaryotes?** *(Chloroplasts)* **What did primitive eukaryotes give rise to?** *(Primitive photosynthetic eukaryotes and animals, fungi, and non-plantlike protists)* **What did primitive photosynthetic eukaryotes give rise to?** *(Plants and plantlike protists)*

Answer to . . .

✓CHECKPOINT *Photosynthesis added oxygen to Earth's atmosphere.*

17–2 (continued)

Sexual Reproduction and Multicellularity

Build Science Skills

Drawing Conclusions Ask: How do you think the evolution of life forms on Earth might have been different if sexual reproduction had not evolved? *(There would have been less genetic variation, so evolution by natural selection would have proceeded more slowly.)*

3 ASSESS

Evaluate Understanding

Have students write a concise paragraph describing the role of photosynthetic bacteria in the evolution of early life on Earth.

Reteach

Work with students to make a simple time line of Earth's early history that includes the following events: formation of Earth, first organic molecules, first prokaryotic cells, formation of free oxygen, first eukaryotic cells, first cells to reproduce sexually, and first multicellular organisms.

Take It to the NET

The cartoon or flowchart should explain the discovery made by Professor Jeon Kwang at the University of Tennessee. Kwang's work showed that it is possible for an organism to become dependent and a functional part of another organism, thus illustrating the process of Lynn Margulis's endosymbiotic theory. For additional information, visit **www.phschool.com**

Use iText to review the key concepts in Section 17–2.

Answer to . . .

Figure 17–13 *Impressions in the fossil radiate out from a central point.*

Second, mitochondria and chloroplasts have ribosomes whose size and structure closely resemble those of bacteria. Third, like bacteria, mitochondria and chloroplasts reproduce by binary fission when the cells containing them divide by mitosis. Thus, mitochondria and chloroplasts have many of the features of free-living bacteria. These similarities provide strong evidence of a common ancestry between free-living bacteria and the organelles of living eukaryotic cells.

▲ **Figure 17–13** This ancient jellyfish, an early multicellular animal from Precambrian Time, did not have bones or other hard parts, but it left behind a fossil that allowed biologists to infer its overall shape. **Observing** *What evidence shows that this organism had body parts arranged around a central point?*

Sexual Reproduction and Multicellularity

Some time after eukaryotic cells arose, those cells began to reproduce sexually. This development enabled evolution to take place at far greater speeds than ever before. How did sexual reproduction speed up the evolutionary process?

Most prokaryotes reproduce asexually. Often, they simply duplicate their genetic material and divide into two new cells. Although this process is efficient, it yields daughter cells that are exact duplicates of the parent cell. This type of reproduction restricts genetic variation to mutations in DNA. Sexual reproduction, on the other hand, shuffles and reshuffles genes in each generation, much like a person shuffling a deck of cards. The offspring of sexually reproducing organisms, therefore, never resemble their parents exactly. This increase in genetic variation greatly increases the chances of evolutionary change in a species due to natural selection.

A few hundred million years after the evolution of sexual reproduction, evolving life forms crossed another great threshold: the development of multicellular organisms from single-celled organisms. In the blink of an evolutionary eye, these first multicellular organisms, such as the one shown in **Figure 17–13**, experienced a great increase in diversity. The evolution of life was well on its way.

17–2 Section Assessment

1. **Key Concept** What substances probably made up Earth's early atmosphere?
2. **Key Concept** What molecules were the end products in Miller and Urey's experiments?
3. **Key Concept** How did the addition of oxygen to Earth's atmosphere affect life of that time?
4. **Key Concept** According to the endosymbiotic theory, how might chloroplasts and mitochondria have originated?
5. **Critical Thinking Formulating Hypotheses** In Chapter 1, you read that the hypothesis of spontaneous generation was disproved. But you just read that life arose from nonlife billions of years ago. Could life arise from nonlife today? Explain.

iTEXT Assessment Use iText to review the important concepts in Section 17–2.

Take It to the NET

Read about the supporting evidence for the endosymbiotic theory. Then, draw a cartoon or flowchart that illustrates this evidence. Use the links provided in the Biology area at the Prentice Hall Web site for help in completing this activity: **www.phschool.com**

17–2 Section Assessment

1. Hydrogen cyanide, carbon dioxide, carbon monoxide, nitrogen, hydrogen sulfide, and water
2. Amino acids, which are the building blocks of proteins
3. Oxygen drove some life forms to extinction; others evolved ways of using oxygen for respiration.
4. Ancient aerobic and photosynthetic bacteria may have entered primitive eukaryotes and evolved into mitochondria and chloroplasts.
5. This probably couldn't happen again because the same conditions no longer exist on Earth. The oxygen in the atmosphere would likely react with and destroy any new kinds of organic molecules.

17–3 Evolution of Multicellular Life

Although the fossil record has missing pieces, paleontologists have assembled good evolutionary histories for many groups of organisms. Further, the fossil record indicates that major changes occurred in Earth's climate, geography, and life forms. In this section, you will get an overview of how multicellular life evolved from its earliest forms to its present-day diversity.

Guide for Reading

Key Concept
- What were the characteristic forms of life in the Paleozoic, Mesozoic, and Cenozoic eras?

Vocabulary
mass extinction

Reading Strategy: Using Graphic Organizers
As you read, make a table of the three geologic eras described in the section. Include information about the typical organisms and main evolutionary events of each era.

Precambrian Time

Recall that almost 90 percent of Earth's history occurred during the Precambrian. During this time, simple anaerobic forms of life appeared and were followed by photosynthetic forms, which added oxygen to the atmosphere. Aerobic forms of life evolved, and eukaryotes appeared. Some of those organisms gave rise to multicellular forms that continued to increase in complexity. Few fossils exist from this time because the animals were all soft-bodied. Life existed only in the sea.

Paleozoic Era

Early in the Paleozoic Era, the fossil record became rich with evidence of many types of marine life. Scientists once thought that those different forms of life evolved rapidly at the beginning of the Paleozoic, but increasing evidence from Precambrian fossils suggests that life began to diversify much earlier. Regardless of when these forms evolved, fossil evidence shows that life was highly diverse by the first part of the Paleozoic Era, the Cambrian Period. An artist's portrayal of Cambrian life is shown in **Figure 17–14.**

▼ **Figure 17–14** **Early in the Paleozoic Era, the fossil record became rich with evidence of many types of marine life.** These and other unfamiliar organisms dwelt in the sea during the Cambrian Period, a time when animals with hard parts evolved.

TIME SAVER — SECTION RESOURCES

Print:
- ***Teaching Resources,*** Section Review 17–3
- ***Guided Reading and Study Workbook,*** Section 17–3

Technology:
- ***iText,*** Section 17–3

Section 17–3

1 FOCUS

Objectives

17.3.1 ***Describe*** the key forms of life in the Paleozoic, Mesozoic, and Cenozoic eras.

Guide for Reading

Vocabulary Preview
Read the names of the periods aloud and encourage students to repeat them after you. Knowing how to pronounce the words correctly will help students remember them.

Reading Strategy
Depending on the amount of detail you expect students to learn, you might want to suggest that they make a separate row in their table for each period.

2 INSTRUCT

Precambrian Time

Demonstration
The information in the text on Precambrian Time provides a concise summary of the detailed material in Section 17–2. Students may benefit from a review of the material. Work with the class to create a simple flowchart on the chalkboard or an overhead transparency. Call on students to identify the correct sequence of events for the flowchart.

Paleozoic Era

Meet Diverse Needs
Challenge at-risk students to make a poster of the Paleozoic Era as they read the first half of the section. Their posters should show with pictures and labels the major evolutionary events that occurred and the most important types of life forms that lived during the different periods of the era. **Limited English proficiency**

17–3 (continued)

Meet Diverse Needs

Challenge students who are gifted in writing to create a newspaper story entitled, "Cambrian Explosion Rocks the World." Using a journalistic style, students should describe the tremendous diversification of life forms that occurred during the Cambrian Period. Suggest that students use Internet or library resources to learn more about the Cambrian Period before writing their stories. Invite students to read their completed stories to the class. **Learning modality: verbal**

Build Science Skills

Inferring Point out that the first organisms with shells and outer skeletons evolved during the Cambrian Period. Then, ask: **Why would having hard parts such as shells be an advantage to organisms?** *(The hard body parts would help protect the organisms from predators.)*

Meet Diverse Needs

Divide the class into groups. Challenge each group to create a board game in which players must correctly answer questions about the periods of the Paleozoic Era in order to advance around the board. Each player should represent a type of organism that actually lived during the Paleozoic. Games also might incorporate environmental changes that occurred during the Paleozoic, such as the growth of vast swampy forests during the Carboniferous Period. Game rules might include players "going extinct" (going out of the game) if they miss a certain number of questions. Give groups an opportunity to exchange and play their games. **Learning modality: kinesthetic**

Build Science Skills

Drawing Conclusions Ask: **How did life on Earth differ after the mass extinction that occurred in the Permian Period from life on Earth before that time?** *(Most plants and animals on land and in the seas went extinct, but most fishes and many reptiles survived into the next era.)*

Cambrian Period Paleontologists call the diversification of life during the early Cambrian Period the "Cambrian Explosion." For the first time, organisms had hard parts, including shells and outer skeletons, as shown in **Figure 17–14** on page 429. During the Cambrian Period, the first known representatives of most animal phyla evolved. Invertebrates—such as jellyfishes, worms, and sponges—drifted through the water, crawled along the sandy bottom, or attached themselves to the ocean floors. Brachiopods, which were small animals with two shells, were especially common. They resembled—but were unrelated to—modern clams. Trilobites were also common.

✓CHECKPOINT ***What major evolutionary advance occurred during the Cambrian Period?***

▲ **Figure 17–15** During the Ordovician Period, aquatic arthropods like this eurypterid evolved. Eurypterids had segmented bodies and lived in water. They are now extinct. **Comparing and Contrasting** *Which of today's animals do eurypterids resemble?*

Ordovician and Silurian Periods During the Ordovician (awr-duh-VISH-un) and Silurian (sih-LOOR-ee-un) periods, the ancestors of the modern octopi and squid appeared, as did aquatic arthropods like the one in **Figure 17–15.** Some animals of this time grew to a length of almost 13 meters. Among the first vertebrates (animals with backbones) to appear were jawless fishes. These fishes, which had suckerlike mouths, soon became common in the seas. Among the invertebrates, the first insects appeared. The first plants evolved from their aquatic ancestors. These simple plants grew low to the ground in damp areas.

Devonian Period By the Devonian (dih-VOH-nee-un) Period, some plants, such as ferns, had adapted to drier areas, allowing them to invade more habitats. In the seas, both invertebrates and vertebrates thrived. Even though the invertebrates were far more numerous, the Devonian is often called the Age of Fishes because many groups of fishes were present in the oceans. Most fishes of this time had jaws, bony skeletons, and scales on their bodies. Sharks appeared in the late Devonian.

During the Devonian, animals began to invade the land. The first fishes to develop the ability to crawl awkwardly on leglike fins were still fully aquatic animals. Some of these early four-legged vertebrates evolved into the first amphibians. An amphibian (am-FIB-ee-un) is an animal that lives part of its life on land and part of its life in water.

Carboniferous and Permian Periods Throughout the rest of the Paleozoic Era, life expanded over Earth's continents. Other groups of vertebrates, such as reptiles, evolved from certain amphibians. Reptiles are animals that have scaly skin and lay eggs with tough, leathery shells. Winged insects evolved into many forms, including huge dragonflies and cockroaches. Giant ferns and other plants formed vast swampy forests, shown in **Figure 17–16.** The remains of those ancient plants formed thick deposits of sediment that changed into coal over millions of years, giving the Carboniferous its name.

TIME SAVER — PRESENTATIONS MADE EASY!

The Presentation Assistant Plus contains the Prentice Hall Presentation Pro and the Transparencies, which provide easy-to-follow visual support for every step of this section. If you have a computer presentation station, use Prentice Hall Presentation Pro for Section 17–3, or use the transparencies listed here.

Section 17–3:

Interest Grabber
Section Outline
Geological Eras and Periods

At the end of the Paleozoic, many organisms died out. This was a **mass extinction,** in which many types of living things became extinct at the same time. **The mass extinction at the end of the Paleozoic affected both plants and animals on land and in the seas. As much as 95 percent of the complex life in the oceans disappeared.** For example, trilobites, which had existed since early in the Paleozoic, suddenly became extinct. Many amphibians also became extinct. Not all organisms disappeared, however. The mass extinction did not affect many fishes. Numerous reptiles also survived.

▲ **Figure 17–16** Ancient forests like this one from the Carboniferous Period were characterized by a huge variety of life forms. **At the end of the Paleozoic Era, many types of animals and plants became extinct.**

Mesozoic Era

The Mesozoic Era lasted approximately 180 million years. **Events during the Mesozoic include the increasing dominance of dinosaurs. The Mesozoic is marked by the appearance of flowering plants.**

Triassic Period Those organisms that survived the Permian mass extinction became the main forms of life early in the Triassic (try-AS-ik) Period. Important organisms in this new ecosystem were fishes, insects, reptiles, and cone-bearing plants like the one in **Figure 17–17.** Reptiles were so successful during the Mesozoic Era that this time is often called the Age of Reptiles.

About 225 million years ago, the first dinosaurs appeared. One of the earliest dinosaurs, *Coelophysis,* was a meat-eater that had light, hollow bones and ran swiftly on its hind legs. Mammals also first appeared during the late Triassic Period, probably evolving from mammallike reptiles. Mammals of the Triassic were very small, about the size of a mouse or shrew.

▼ **Figure 17–17** Among the seed plants of the early Mesozoic Era were cone-bearing plants called cycads, which left this modern descendant. **Formulating Hypotheses** ***How might the evolution of seeds increase a plant's chances of reproducing successfully?***

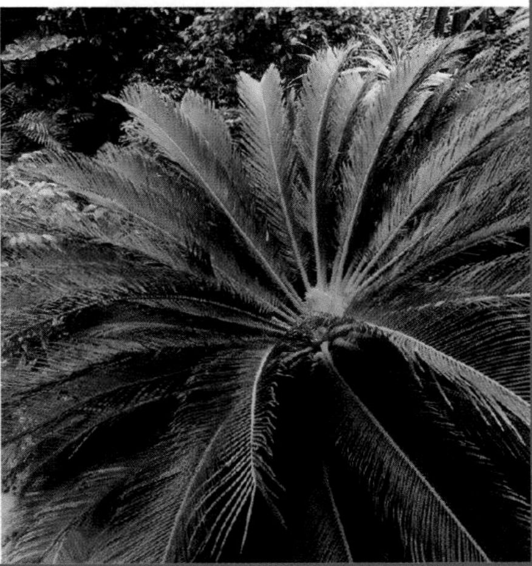

Meet Diverse Needs

Give students who are talented in art a chance to create a sketch or three-dimensional diorama of the Carboniferous Period. Their sketches or dioramas should show some of the important plants and animals that lived during the period and what the environment was like. Invite students to display their artwork in the classroom. **Learning modality: tactile**

Mesozoic Era

Make Connections

Earth Science Show students maps of the location of Earth's landmasses at various times during the Mesozoic Era. Include a map showing Earth at around 225 million years ago, when all the major landmasses were joined together in the supercontinent of Pangaea, and also around 180 million years ago, when Pangaea had split apart to form Laurasia and Gondwanaland. Have students compare these maps with the present-day locations of the continents. Ask: **Why would the drifting of continents have affected climate?** *(Because climate is determined by the distance north and south of the equator and by the position of large bodies of water)* **How might the evolution of life forms have been affected?** *(Changes in climate might have made some life forms go extinct, while favoring others. Also, the separation of land masses might have led to geographic isolation and the emergence of different species on the different landmasses.)*

Answers to . . .

✓CHECKPOINT *For the first time, organisms had hard parts, including shells and outer skeletons.*

Figure 17–15 *Possible answers include a crab and a lobster.*

Figure 17–17 *Seeds provide protection for a developing embryo and provide a means of dispersal.*

Address Misconceptions

Some students might think that dinosaurs were not very successful in evolutionary terms because they all went extinct at the end of the Cretaceous Period. Point out that dinosaurs "ruled" Earth for a total period of about 150 million years. Put this time span in perspective by comparing it with the length of time that the human family, the hominids, has been in existence, which is less than 10 million years.

Cenozoic Era

Build Science Skills

Drawing Conclusions Point out that the first mammals probably evolved during the Triassic Period but that mammals did not flourish until the Cenozoic Era. Ask: **Why did mammals not become successful for more than 100 million years after they first evolved?** *(During the Mesozoic, early mammals had to compete with dinosaurs for food and places to live. When dinosaurs went extinct at the end of the Mesozoic, it left many niches available for mammals to fill.)*

▲ **Figure 17–18** **During the Mesozoic Era, dinosaurs were dominant.** *Dicraeosaurus* (foreground) was a plant-eater that grew to about 20 meters in length.

Jurassic Period During the Jurassic (joo-RAS-ik) Period, dinosaurs became the dominant animals on land. Dinosaurs "ruled" Earth for about 150 million years, but different types lived at different times. At 20 meters long, *Dicraeosaurus*, shown in **Figure 17–18,** was one of the larger dinosaurs of the Jurassic Period.

One of the first birds, called *Archaeopteryx,* appeared during this time. Many paleontologists now think that birds are close relatives of dinosaurs. Since the 1990s, scientists working in China have found evidence for this hypothesis in other fossils that have the skulls and teeth of dinosaurs but the body structure and feathers of birds.

Cretaceous Period Reptiles were still the dominant vertebrates throughout the Cretaceous (krih-TAY-shus) Period. Dinosaurs such as the meat-eating *Tyrannosaurus rex* dominated land ecosystems, while flying reptiles and birds soared in the sky. Flying reptiles, however, became extinct during the Cretaceous. In the seas, turtles, crocodiles, and extinct reptiles such as plesiosaurs swam among fishes and marine invertebrates.

The Cretaceous also brought new forms of life, including leafy trees, shrubs, and small flowering plants like those you see today. Unlike the conifers, flowering plants produce seeds enclosed in a fruit, which protects the seed and aids in dispersing it to new locations.

At the close of the Cretaceous, another mass extinction occurred. More than half of all plant and animal groups were wiped out, including all of the dinosaurs.

CHECKPOINT *When did flowering plants evolve?*

FACTS AND FIGURES

How sweet it is

Fruits and seeds were a major evolutionary advance in the reproduction of plants. However, if animals eat unripe fruits, the immature seeds in them are not capable of sprouting and growing. As a result, plants have evolved ways to discourage animals from eating their unripe fruits. Many unripe fruits are green and contain bitter-tasting chemical compounds. The green color of the unripe fruits makes them more difficult to see among a plant's leaves, and the bitter taste helps discourage animals from eating them. As the seeds mature, the bitter-tasting chemical compounds break down, and the fruits become laden with sugars. While this process occurs, the fruits also change color from green to red, orange, purple, or whatever color indicates ripeness in that species. These colors are more easily seen by animals against the background of green leaves, and the fruits' sweet taste reinforces the eating response.

Figure 17–19 **During the Cenozoic Era, mammals evolved adaptations that allowed them to live on land, in water, and even in the air.** Two of the traits that contributed to the success of mammals were a covering of hair that provided insulation against the cold and the protection of the young before and after birth.

Cenozoic Era

During the Mesozoic, early mammals competed with dinosaurs for food and places to live. The extinction of dinosaurs at the end of the Mesozoic, however, created a different world. **During the Cenozoic, mammals evolved adaptations that allowed them to live in various environments—on land, in water, and even in the air.** One land mammal from the early Cenozoic is shown in **Figure 17–19.** Paleontologists often call the Cenozoic the Age of Mammals.

Tertiary Period During the Tertiary Period, Earth's climates were generally warm and mild. In the oceans, marine mammals such as whales and dolphins evolved. On land, flowering plants and insects flourished. Grasses evolved, providing a food source that encouraged the evolution of grazing mammals, the ancestors of today's cattle, deer, sheep, and other grass-eating mammals. Some mammals became very large, as did some birds.

Careers in Biology

Fossil Preparator

Job description: work for private industries, museums, or universities to expose fossils covered by rock or soil or to construct missing fossil parts

Education: a college degree in biology or geology, knowledge about information concerning the fossils being worked on

Skills: be knowledgeable about many areas of science, ability to use fine tools under a microscope, self-motivated, patient, ability to handle very fragile specimens for long periods

Highlights: work with fossil specimens; work with many types of people—from amateur fossil collectors to professional paleontologists

"When I receive a specimen to prepare, it looks rather drab and more like a rock," says fossil preparator Marc Behrendt. "But when preparation is complete, the fossil stands out in all its glory, and I know I made it this way. It is a great feeling and probably the biggest reason I enjoy my work."

Take It to the NET

For more career information, visit the Prentice Hall Web site: **www.phschool.com**

Meet Diverse Needs

Have students who need an extra challenge investigate the diversity of mammals that led to the Cenozoic Era being named the Age of Mammals. Students should try to find names and descriptions of some of the more common mammals that lived during the Tertiary and Quaternary periods. They should include both land and sea mammals. They should also find out which of the mammals went extinct and which gave rise to descendants that are still living today. Urge students to share their research with the class. If possible, they should show pictures of what some of the mammals of the Cenozoic looked like. **Learning modality: verbal**

Careers in Biology

- Sculpting is a good skill to have for this career because fossil preparators occasionally must fabricate missing fossil parts.
- Some fossil preparators spend months working in a field camp at a paleontological dig. They may also spend time in the field collecting fossils.

Resources Students can contact a university paleontology department, the Paleontological Association, the Paleontological Research Institute, or the personnel department of a natural history museum.

Take It to the NET

For additional information on this career, visit **www.phschool.com**

Answer to . . .

CHECKPOINT *During the Cretaceous Period*

17–3 (continued)

Make Connections

Environmental Science Provide students with background information on the ice ages. Explain that over the past two million years, there were four major ice ages, each lasting at least 100,000 years or longer and between which were long periods of warmer climate. During the peak of the most recent ice age, which ended just over 10,000 years ago, ice covered much of North America, reaching as far south as the present-day lower Midwestern states. Scientists think the ice ages were caused by variations in the position of Earth relative to the sun, changes in the sun's energy output due to sunspots, and continental movement.

3 ASSESS

Evaluate Understanding

Read each of the Key Concepts in the section, leaving the name of the era or period blank. Call on students at random to fill in the blanks.

Reteach

Have pairs of students make and quiz each other with flashcards that each have an important evolutionary event on one side and the correct era and period on the other side.

ALTERNATIVE ASSESSMENT

If students have a hard time developing ideas for their stories, suggest that they brainstorm in small groups. Stories should include information from the text as well as additional reliable sources.

Use iText to review the key concepts in Section 17–3.

Answer to . . .

Figure 17–20 *Organisms that could not migrate to a warmer climate or adapt to the change in climate would have gone extinct.*

▶ **Figure 17–20** During the Quaternary Period, Earth's climate cooled, producing a series of ice ages. Among the characteristic animals of the time were these huge mammoths. **Inferring** *How might the change to a colder climate have affected different types of organisms?*

Quaternary Period Mammals that had evolved during the Tertiary Period eventually faced a changing environment during the Quaternary Period. During this time, Earth's climate cooled, causing a series of ice ages. Repeatedly, thick continental glaciers advanced and retreated over parts of Europe and North America. So much of Earth's water was frozen in continental glaciers that the level of the oceans fell by more than 100 meters. Then, about 20,000 years ago, Earth's climate began to warm. Over the course of thousands of years, the continental glaciers melted. This caused sea levels to rise again.

In the oceans, algae, coral, mollusks, fish, and mammals thrived. Insects and birds shared the skies. On land, mammals—such as bats, cats, dogs, cattle, and the mammoths shown in **Figure 17–20**—became common. The fossil record suggests that the very earliest ancestors of our species appeared about 4.5 million years ago but that they did not look entirely human. Modern humans, called *Homo sapiens,* may have evolved as early as 100,000 years ago in Africa. From there, they began a series of migrations that ultimately colonized the world.

17–3 Section Assessment

1. **Key Concept** Where did life exist during the early Paleozoic Era?
2. **Key Concept** What evolutionary milestone involving animals occurred during the Devonian Period?
3. **Key Concept** What are two key events from the Mesozoic Era?
4. **Critical Thinking Inferring** If you were a paleontologist investigating fossils from the Cenozoic Era, what fossils might you find?

iTEXT Assessment Use iText to review the important concepts in Section 17–3.

ALTERNATIVE ASSESSMENT

Creative Writing Choose one of the periods described in this section. Then, write a story about what life was like during that time. Include information about the terrain, life forms, weather, and other characteristics of the period.

17–3 Section Assessment

1. Early life existed in the sea.
2. During the Devonian Period, animals began to invade the land.
3. Events include the first appearance of dinosaurs and the appearance of flowering plants.
4. You might find fossils of flowering plants, insects, birds, and mammals, including humans.

17–4 Patterns of Evolution

The history of life is the story of increasing complexity and diversity, but what does this history reveal about the process of evolution? Does evolution happen at a consistent pace? Do lineages evolve independently of one another, or is evolution an interactive process? Answers to these questions fall under the topic of macroevolution. **Macroevolution** refers to the large-scale evolutionary changes that take place over long periods of time. **Six important patterns of macroevolution are mass extinctions, adaptive radiation, convergent evolution, coevolution, punctuated equilibrium, and changes in developmental genes.**

Mass Extinctions

Extinction occurs all the time. More than 99 percent of all species that ever lived are now extinct. Usually, extinctions happen at a fairly constant rate. Several times, however, huge numbers of species have disappeared in mass extinctions. Recently, paleontologists have begun to reexamine mass extinctions. New fossil studies show that those mass extinctions not only extinguished species but also wiped out whole ecological systems, disrupting energy flow throughout the biosphere and causing food webs to collapse.

What could have caused such widespread destruction? Until recently, most researchers looked for a single major cause. One hypothesis suggests that a huge asteroid caused the Cretaceous extinction. Evidence does suggest that a large asteroid struck Earth at about that time, as depicted in **Figure 17–21.** Such an impact would have thrown huge amounts of dust and water vapor into the atmosphere, altering the global climate. These changes would have affected the plants that dinosaurs ate and thus probably played a role in the demise of the dinosaurs.

However, many paleontologists think that most mass extinctions were caused by multiple factors. At about the time of the Permian and Cretaceous extinctions, many large volcanoes were erupting, continents were changing positions, and sea levels were changing. Thus, it is difficult to pinpoint a single cause for the extinctions. Determining what actually happened will occupy researchers for years to come.

What effects have mass extinctions had on the history of life? As you can imagine, the disappearance of so many species left many habitats open. For the survivors, there was a new world of ecological opportunity. Often, the result was a burst of evolution that produced an abundance of new species.

Guide for Reading

Key Concept

- What are six important patterns of macroevolution?

Vocabulary

macroevolution
adaptive radiation
convergent evolution
coevolution
punctuated equilibrium

Reading Strategy: Summarizing

List the six patterns described in this section. As you read, write a statement describing each pattern.

▼ **Figure 17–21** **Mass extinctions are one pattern of macroevolution.** A huge asteroid hitting Earth may have caused the extinction of the dinosaurs at the end of the Cretaceous Period. This drawing shows an artist's conception of that event.

SECTION RESOURCES

Print:

- ***Teaching Resources,*** Section Review 17–4, Chapter 17 Exploration
- ***Guided Reading and Study Workbook,*** Section 17–4
- ***Issues and Decision Making,*** Issues and Decisions 13

Technology:

- ***iText,*** Section 17–4

Section 17–4

1 FOCUS

Objectives

17.4.1 ***Identify*** important patterns of macroevolution.

Guide for Reading

Vocabulary Preview

Explain that *co-* means "together" and that *macro-* means "large scale." Then, ask: **What do you think the terms *macroevolution* and *coevolution* mean?** *(Macroevolution means large-scale evolution, and coevolution means the evolution of two species together.)*

Reading Strategy

Suggest that students add to their summary an example of each type of macroevolutionary pattern, such as the mass extinction of dinosaurs that occurred during the Cretaceous Period or the adaptive radiation of mammals during the Cenozoic Era.

2 INSTRUCT

Mass Extinctions

Make Connections

Environmental Science Help put mass extinctions in perspective and relate them to environmental changes with which students are more familiar. Have students research the number of extinctions of plant and animal species that have occurred in the past 100 years. Students should also find out the names of several particular species that have gone extinct and the reason for their extinction. Have students share what they learn with the class. Then, ask: **Do you think extinctions are occurring at a faster rate today than they were in 1900?** *(Because most extinctions today are due to human activities destroying habitats, they are occurring more rapidly now than they were in 1900.)*

Section 17–4

Adaptive Radiation

Build Science Skills

Applying Concepts Review the evolution of Darwin's finches, which is the example of adaptive radiation mentioned in the text. Remind students that a single species of finch from mainland South America traveled to the Galápagos Islands and evolved into multiple species that used different food resources. Ask: **If mass extinction was not responsible for the adaptive radiation of Darwin's finches, what was?** *(The ancestral finch was one of the first land birds ever to reach the islands. Therefore, many niches were available.)*

Convergent Evolution

Meet Diverse Needs

Have students write the terms *Divergent Evolution* and *Convergent Evolution* at the top of a sheet of paper. Encourage the students to list terms and phrases that are associated with the appropriate process. Have them add drawings or photographs too. Then, using the terms, phrases, and drawings/photographs, tell them to prepare a visual summary of these two processes. **Limited English proficiency**

Use Visuals

Figure 17–22 Point out that the common ancestor at the bottom of the diagram is the oldest species and that present-day species are at the top of the diagram. Explain that each branching as you travel up the "tree" represents a point where speciation has occurred and the two resulting groups have gone on to evolve separately. The more recently the branching occurred, the less different two lines of evolution are.

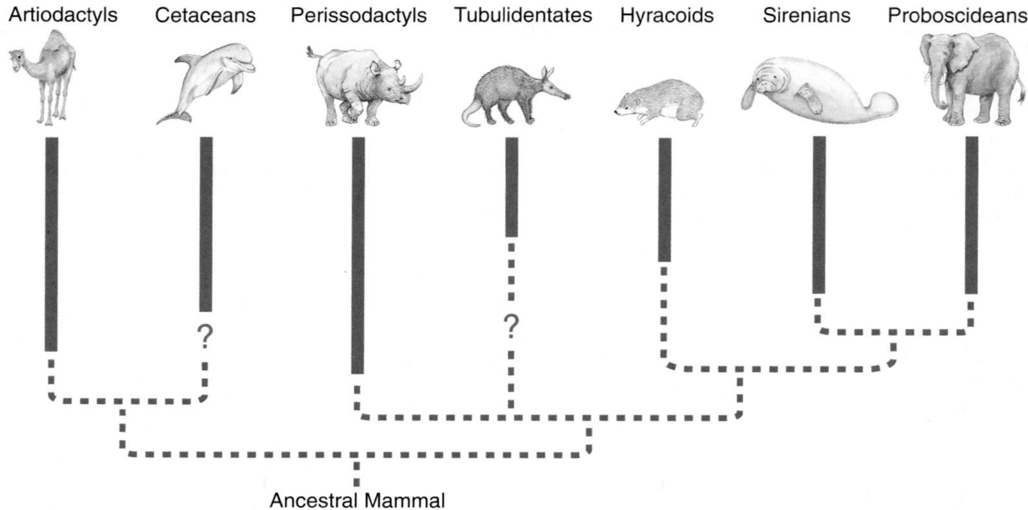

▲ **Figure 17–22** Adaptive radiation occurs when a species or group of species evolves into many new species. This drawing shows how one major group of mammals evolved. **Interpreting Graphics** ***According to this diagram, which mammal group is the most closely related to elephants?***

Adaptive Radiation

Often, studies of fossils or of living organisms show that a single species or a small group of species has evolved into several different forms that live in different ways. This process is known as **adaptive radiation.** You have already learned about the adaptive radiation of Darwin's finches. In that case, more than a dozen species evolved from a single species.

Adaptive radiations can also occur on a much larger scale. Dinosaurs, for example, were the products of a spectacular adaptive radiation among ancient reptiles. The first dinosaurs and the earliest mammals evolved at about the same time. Dinosaurs and other ancient reptiles, however, underwent an adaptive radiation first and "ruled" Earth for about 150 million years. During that time, mammals remained small and relatively scarce. But the disappearance of the dinosaurs cleared the way for the great adaptive radiation of mammals. This radiation, part of which is shown in **Figure 17–22,** produced the great diversity of mammals of the Cenozoic.

Convergent Evolution

Adaptive radiations can have an interesting evolutionary "side effect." They can produce unrelated organisms that look remarkably similar to one another. How does that happen? Sometimes, groups of different organisms, such as mammals and dinosaurs, undergo adaptive radiation in different places or at different times but in ecologically similar environments. These organisms start out with different "raw material" for natural selection to work on, but they face similar environmental demands, such as moving through air, moving through water, or eating similar foods.

Shark

Penguins

Dolphin

Figure 17–23 Each of these animals has a streamlined body and various appendages that enable it to move rapidly through water. Yet, the shark (above) is a fish, the penguin (center) is a bird, and the dolphin (bottom) is a mammal. **Applying Concepts** *How did these different animals come to resemble one another?*

In these situations, natural selection may mold different body structures, such as arms and legs, into modified forms, such as wings or flippers. The wings or flippers function in the same way and look very similar. This process, by which unrelated organisms come to resemble one another, is called **convergent evolution.** Convergent evolution has occurred time and time again in both animals and plants.

Consider swimming animals, for example. An animal can move through the water rapidly with the least amount of energy if its body is streamlined and if it has body parts that can be used like paddles. That is why convergent evolution involving fishes, two different groups of aquatic mammals, and swimming birds has resulted in sharks, dolphins, seals, and penguins whose streamlined bodies and swimming appendages look a lot alike, as shown in **Figure 17–23.** Structures such as a dolphin's flukes and a fish's tail fin, which look and function similarly but are made up of parts that do not share a common evolutionary history, are called analogous structures. There are a surprising number of animals (including one of Darwin's finches) that have evolved adaptations analogous to those of woodpeckers for feeding on insects living beneath the bark of trees and in rotted wood.

✓CHECKPOINT *How do biologists explain the similar shapes of sharks and dolphins?*

Coevolution

Sometimes organisms that are closely connected to one another by ecological interactions evolve together. Many flowering plants, for example, can reproduce only if the shape, color, and odor of their flowers attract a specific type of pollinator. Not surprisingly, these kinds of relationships can change over time. An evolutionary change in one organism may also be followed by a corresponding change in another organism. The process by which two species evolve in response to changes in each other over time is called **coevolution.**

Coevolution

Build Science Skills

Applying Concepts Point out that to coevolve, species must interact in some way over a long period of time. For example, flowering plants and the bees that pollinate them have mutualistic relationships, whereas plants and some plant-eating insects have parasitic relationships. Ask: **What other pairs of species do you think might have coevolutionary relationships?** *(Students should name pairs of species that interact in a symbiotic, predator-prey, or other type of long-term relationship. One example is humans and their intestinal bacteria, which have a mutualistic relationship.)*

TIME SAVER

PRESENTATIONS MADE EASY!

The Presentation Assistant Plus contains the Prentice Hall Presentation Pro and the Transparencies, which provide easy-to-follow visual support for every step of this section. If you have a computer presentation station, use Prentice Hall Presentation Pro for Section 17–4, or use the transparencies listed here.

Section 17–4:  

Interest Grabber
Section Outline
Concept Map

Answer to . . .

✓CHECKPOINT *The similar shapes of sharks and dolphins resulted from convergent evolution: natural selection in a water environment resulted in streamlined bodies with parts that work like paddles.*

Figure 17–22 *Sirenians*

Figure 17–23 *By the process of convergent evolution*

Analyzing Data

Help students appreciate the significance of the data in the graph. Point out that marine organisms are of special interest because they evolved long before land organisms and, therefore, have a much longer evolutionary history to study.

Answers

1. Overall, there is an increase in the number of marine families.
2. The number of marine families decreased by about 200 families at the end of the Paleozoic Era. The number decreased by about 100 families at the end of the Mesozoic.
3. The mass extinctions, or loss of so many families, might be explained by a large asteroid colliding with Earth or by a combination of factors, such as numerous large volcanoes erupting, continents changing positions, and sea levels changing.
4. Sample answer: Global warming or pollution of ocean water might lead to a decline in the number of marine families in 1000 years. In the next 10,000,000 years, there might be an increase in marine families due to natural selection. Natural selection may cause the development of different body structures that may help organisms survive in a hostile environment. Eventually, these surviving marine families would produce more organisms with similar charactersistics.

Figure 17–24 This orchid from Madagascar has an unusually long spur containing a supply of nectar in its tip. The hawk moth of Madagascar has an equally long feeding tube that enables it to feed on the nectar. The flower spur and the feeding tube are an example of coevolution. **Inferring** ***How might natural selection bring about the evolution of this orchid and the moth?***

The pattern of coevolution involving flowers and insects is so common that biologists in the field often discover additional examples. When Charles Darwin saw an orchid like the one in **Figure 17–24,** he closely examined the long structure called a spur. At the tip of that 40-centimeter spur is a supply of nectar, which serves as a food source for many insects. Darwin predicted the discovery of a pollinating insect with a 40-centimeter-long structure that could reach the orchid's nectar. About fifty years later, researchers discovered a moth that matched Darwin's prediction.

Consider another example, the relationships between plants and plant-eating insects. Insects have been feeding on flowering plants since both groups emerged during the Mesozoic. Over time, a number of plants have evolved poisonous compounds that prevent insects from feeding on them. In fact, some of the most powerful poisons known in nature are plant compounds that have evolved in response to insect attacks. But once plants began to produce poisons, natural selection in herbivorous insects began to favor any variants that could alter, inactivate, or eliminate those poisons. In a few cases, coevolutionary relationships can be traced back over millions of years.

CHECKPOINT *What happens during coevolution?*

Analyzing Data

Changing Number of Marine Families

Using fossil evidence, scientists make inferences about the kinds and number of organisms that lived at different times in the past. Further, they classify those organisms in ways that facilitate comparisons between past and present types. The graph on the right gives an estimate of the number of ocean-dwelling families over time. In biology, a family consists of several groups of related species.

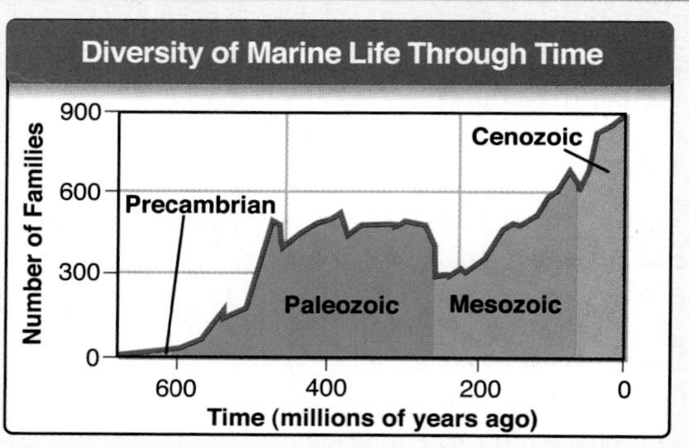

1. **Using Tables and Graphs** What overall trend does this graph show?
2. **Calculating** What was the change in the number of marine families at the end of the Paleozoic Era? At the end of the Mesozoic?
3. **Inferring** What kind of event(s) might explain the changes at the end of the Paleozoic and Mesozoic eras?
4. **Going Further** How do you expect this graph to change in the next 1000 years? The next 10,000,000 years? Explain.

BIO INSIGHTS **FACTS AND FIGURES**

The birds and the bees

One of the most unusual examples of coevolution of plants and their animal pollinators is the orchid. This tropical flowering plant is pollinated by any of several different species of insects in which the male insects emerge in the spring before the females. Orchid flowers have evolved both shapes and odors that mimic the stimuli presented by the female insects. The males, eager to mate, fly around searching for females. They happen upon the insect-mimicking orchid flowers and try to mate with one after another. In the process, they pollinate the orchids. Other plants and their pollinators are so highly adapted to each other that only one species of insect is able to pollinate them. In Hawaii, *Brighamia* flowers can be pollinated only by drepanidid birds. Because the birds have declined greatly in numbers, the plants as well as the birds are facing extinction.

Punctuated Equilibrium

How quickly does evolution operate? Does it always occur at the same speed? These are questions on which some modern biologists would disagree with Darwin. Recall that Darwin was enormously impressed by the way Hutton and Lyell discussed the slow and steady nature of geologic change. Darwin, in turn, felt that biological change also needed to be slow and steady, an idea known as gradualism. In many cases, the fossil record confirms that populations of organisms did, indeed, change gradually over time.

But there is also evidence that this pattern does not always hold. Some species, such as horseshoe crabs, have changed little from the time they first appeared in the fossil record. In other words, much of the time these species are in a state of equilibrium, which means they do not change very much. Every now and then, however, something happens to upset the equilibrium. At several points in the fossil record, changes in animals and plants occurred over relatively short periods of time. Some biologists suggest that most new species are produced by periods of rapid change. (Remember that "short" and "rapid" are relative to the geologic time scale. Short periods of time for geologists can be hundreds of thousands—even millions—of years!)

Rapid evolution after long periods of equilibrium can occur for several reasons. It may occur when a small population becomes isolated from the main part of the population. This small population can then evolve more rapidly than the larger one because genetic changes can spread more quickly among fewer individuals. Or it may occur when a small group of organisms migrates to a new environment. That's what happened with the Galápagos finches, for example. Organisms evolve rapidly to fill available niches. In addition, mass extinctions can open many ecological niches and provide new opportunities to those organisms that survive. Thus, it is not surprising that some groups of organisms have evolved rapidly following mass extinctions.

Scientists use the term **punctuated equilibrium** to describe this pattern of long, stable periods interrupted by brief periods of more rapid change. The concept of punctuated equilibrium, illustrated in **Figure 17–25,** has generated much debate and is still somewhat controversial among biologists today. It is clear, however, that evolution has often proceeded at different rates for different organisms at different times during the long history of life on Earth.

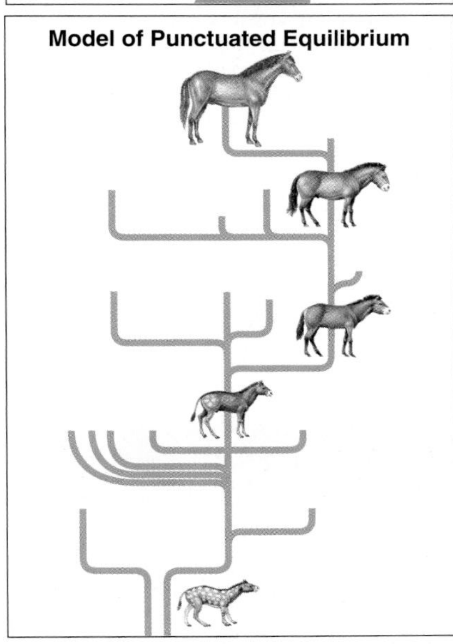

▲ **Figure 17–25** Biologists have considered two different explanations for the rate of evolution, as illustrated in these diagrams. Gradualism involves a slow, steady change in a particular line of descent. Punctuated equilibrium involves stable periods interrupted by rapid changes involving many different lines of descent. **Interpreting Graphics** *How do the diagrams illustrate these explanations?*

Punctuated Equilibrium

Build Science Skills

Inferring Challenge students to infer how the fossil record would differ if evolution is modeled by punctuated equilibrium instead of by gradualism. *(Students should infer that the fossil record would show only minor changes in fossils for long time periods and then sudden, major changes if evolution is modeled by punctuated equilibrium, whereas the fossil record would show continuous minor changes if evolution is modeled by gradualism.)* Point out that both patterns have been found in different organisms, suggesting that both models may apply in different cases.

Answers to . . .

CHECKPOINT *Over time, two species evolve in response to changes in each other.*

Figure 17–24 *The original flowers may have had moderately long spurs that only a few moths could feed on. These moths survived and reproduced more successfully than others, and also helped fertilize flowers with longer spurs. Over time, the flower spurs and the moth's feeding tubes both became longer.*

Figure 17–25 *The broad, branching effect shows the slow, steady change of gradualism. The thin branching lines show the stable periods, interrupted by rapid changes involving many lines of descent.*

Developmental Genes and Body Plans

Meet Diverse Needs

Challenge students who need an extra challenge to learn more about hox genes. They should use the Internet to find out the most recent research in this new field. Encourage students to share what they learn in an oral report. **Learning modality: verbal**

3 ASSESS

Evaluate Understanding

Have students write a paragraph explaining mass extinction and adaptive radiation and how the two are related.

Reteach

Divide the class into pairs, and have each pair create a Venn diagram showing the similarities and differences between gradualism and punctuated equilibrium. Encourage pairs to exchange and compare Venn diagrams.

ALTERNATIVE ASSESSMENT

Students' tables should have rows for each of the six patterns of macroevolution and columns for explanations and examples of the patterns. Students should fill in each row of the table with appropriate information. For example, they might explain that adaptive radiation is the evolution of several different forms from a single species and give the example of Darwin's finches. Tables should also have a title, such as "Patterns of Macroevolution."

Use iText to review the key concepts in Section 17–4.

Ancient Insects

Two Types of Modern Insects

two pairs of wings

one pair of wings

▲ **Figure 17–26** **Changes in developmental genes are one major pattern of macroevolution.** Fossil evidence shows that some ancient insects (top left) had no wings, but others (top right) had winglike structures on many body segments. In modern insects (bottom), genes may turn off wing development in all except one or two body segments.

Developmental Genes and Body Plans

Until recently, biologists could only wonder how animals evolved their diverse body plans, but breakthroughs in molecular biology are changing that. Recall from Chapter 12 that geneticists discovered "master control genes," called hox genes, that control growth as an embryo develops. Some hox genes determine which parts become front, rear, top, and bottom. Others control the growth of body parts such as arms, legs, and wings.

Hox genes can help reveal how evolution occurred. First, molecular studies show that homologous hox genes establish body plans in animals as different as insects and humans—even though these animals have not shared a common ancestor in at least 700 million years!

Second, major evolutionary changes—such as the different numbers of wings, legs, and body segments in insects—may be based on hox genes. For instance, if one gene, called "wingless," is activated in an insect body segment, that segment grows no wings. Thus, ancient insects with winglike structures on every segment, as shown in **Figure 17–26,** could have evolved into the insects of today that have two pairs or one pair of wings.

Finally, geneticists are learning that even small changes in the timing of genetic control during embryonic development can make the difference between long legs and short ones—or long, slender fingers or short, stubby toes—thus contributing to the variation involved in natural selection. This hot field of research is likely to continue revealing major news about the evolution of life.

17–4 Section Assessment

1. **Key Concept** What is macroevolution? Describe two patterns of macroevolution.
2. What role have mass extinctions played in the history of life?
3. Use an example to explain the concept of coevolution.
4. How might hox genes contribute to variation?
5. **Critical Thinking Comparing and Contrasting** Compare and contrast the theories of gradualism and punctuated equilibrium.

iTEXT Assessment Use iText to review the important concepts in Section 17–4.

ALTERNATIVE ASSESSMENT

Making a Table
Create a table that lists each of the six patterns of macroevolution, explains each pattern, and gives one example for each. Add a title to your table.

17–4 Section Assessment

1. Macroevolution is large-scale evolutionary change over long time periods. Students should describe any two of the five types of macroevolution.
2. Mass extinctions periodically wiped out huge numbers of species and made way for the rapid evolution of new species.
3. Sample answer: Plants evolved poisons to combat insects, and insects, in turn, evolved ways to resist the poisons.
4. Hox genes regulate timing of genetic control in the embryo. Even small changes in the timing can cause variation in traits such as leg length.
5. Gradualism: evolutionary change is slow and steady. Punctuated equilibrium: evolutionary change occurs in brief periods of rapid change.

Exploration

Modeling Coevolution

Flowering plants and the animals that pollinate their flowers include many examples of coevolving species. In this investigation, you will model how these plants and animals evolve in response to one another.

Problem **How do flowering plants and their pollinators coevolve?**

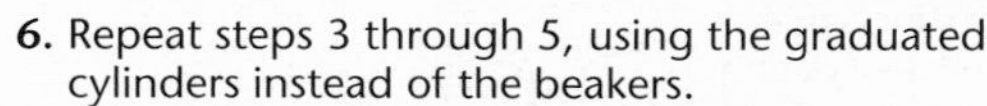

Materials

- long forceps
- spoon
- dried peas
- 3 25-mL graduated cylinders
- 3 100-mL beakers
- watch or clock with second hand

Skills Using Models, Inferring

Procedure

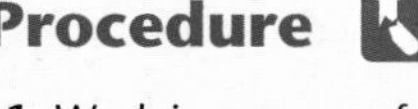

1. Work in groups of three. Each group member represents a different bird species. To represent the birds' beaks, one group member will use forceps, the second group member will use a spoon, and the third will use two fingertips.
2. On a separate sheet of paper, make a copy of the data table shown. The beakers represent short, open flowers and the graduated cylinders represent long, narrow flowers. The dried peas represent the flowers' nectar, which is the birds' food. Fill the beakers and the graduated cylinders halfway with dried peas.
3. For 1 minute, use the method you chose in step 1 to remove the peas. Remove them one at a time from your beaker. Do not move or tip the beaker as you do this.
4. Record the number of peas you removed in your data table.
5. To produce seeds, a flower must be pollinated by a member of its own species. Assume that 1 flower was pollinated for every 5 peas removed. Record the number of pollinations for each bird.
6. Repeat steps 3 through 5, using the graduated cylinders instead of the beakers.
7. **Calculating** Exchange data with your classmates and record the class averages for each bird species in your data table.

Data Table

Beak Type	Individual Data		Class Average	
	Peas	Pollinations	Peas	Pollinations
Forceps				
Spoon				
Fingers				

Analyze and Conclude

1. **Analyzing Data** Which bird species obtained the most nectar from the beakers? From the graduated cylinders?
2. **Analyzing Data** From which type of flower was each bird most successful in obtaining food?
3. **Inferring** What is the benefit to a plant of short, open flowers?
4. **Inferring** What is the benefit to a bird of a long, narrow beak?
5. **Drawing Conclusions** Which type of bird is the best pollinator for long, narrow flowers?
6. **Evaluating and Revising** How does this model represent coevolution? How could you improve this model?

Go Further

Using Models Construct a model that demonstrates coevolution between flowers of different colors and pollinating insects attracted to specific colors.

Exploration

Objectives Students will be able to
- model coevolution;
- infer how plants and animals evolve in response to one another.

Skills Focus Using Models, Inferring

Time 45 minutes

Advance Prep You can obtain dried peas from a supermarket or bulk foods store. Other small dried legumes, such as pinto beans, could be used instead.

Safety Tip Advise students who are using their fingers for beaks not to force their hands into the beakers or cylinders because they could break.

Teaching Strategies Have students read the entire procedure. Then, ask: **What type of relationship exists between the birds and the flowering plants in the model?** *(A mutualistic relationship)* **How does each type of organism benefit from the relationship?** *(The birds benefit by obtaining nectar for food. The plants benefit by being pollinated so they can reproduce.)*

Procedure

5. To obtain the number of pollinations for each bird, students should divide the number of peas removed by that bird by five.

7. Make a data table on the chalkboard for students to use in compiling data for the class. Check that all the students have correctly calculated the class average for each bird species.

Analyze and Conclude

1. Spoon beaks obtained the most nectar from the beakers. Forceps beaks obtained the most nectar from the graduated cylinders.

2. Spoon beaks and finger beaks were most successful with short, open flowers. Forceps beaks were most successful with long, narrow flowers.

3. Short, open flowers allow a plant to be pollinated by more types of birds.

4. A long, narrow beak allows a bird to feed from long, narrow flowers that other birds cannot feed from.

5. The bird with the long, narrow beak is the best pollinator for long, narrow flowers.

6. The model represents coevolution because it shows how traits in a species evolve in response to changes in another species. A better model would show how the birds and flowers change in response to one another through time.

Go Further

Students might modify the model in the Exploration by using containers of different colors to represent flowers of different colors and by having each student remove peas from only containers of one of the colors.

Chapter 17 Study Guide

Study Tip

Suggest that students review the Key Concept questions in the section assessments. Also suggest that they make flashcards for the Vocabulary terms and use them to quiz a partner.

Thinking Visually

Students' concept maps should include all four geological eras, their respective periods, and a major event from each period.

Chapter 17 Assessment

Reviewing Content

1. b **2.** d **3.** a **4.** a **5.** d **6.** d **7.** a **8.** b **9.** c **10.** a

Understanding Concepts

11. In relative dating, the age of a fossil is determined by comparing its placement in rock layers with the placement of fossils in other rock layers.

12. Radioactive elements decay at a steady rate, measured in units called half-lives. Radioactive dating uses half-lives to determine the age of a sample. Scientists can calculate the age of a rock sample based on the amount of remaining radioactive isotopes it contains.

13. The geologic time scale, which represents evolutionary time, was developed by scientists who studied rock layers and index fossils worldwide.

14. When Earth was young, a collision with a very large object produced enough heat to melt Earth. Elements then rearranged themselves by density, with the densest elements in the core. Less dense elements floated to the surface where they cooled, forming Earth's crust. The least dense elements, including hydrogen and nitrogen, formed the first atmosphere. About 3.8 billion years ago, Earth cooled enough for water to remain a liquid. Thunderstorms drenched the planet, eventually forming the oceans.

Chapter 17 Study Guide

17–1 The Fossil Record

Key Concepts

- The fossil record provides evidence about the history of life on Earth. It also shows how different groups of organisms have changed over time.
- Relative dating allows paleontologists to estimate a fossil's age compared with that of other fossils.
- In radioactive dating, scientists calculate the age of a sample based on the amount of remaining radioactive isotopes it contains.
- After Precambrian Time, the basic divisions of the geologic time scale are eras and periods.

Vocabulary

paleontologist, p. 417
fossil record, p. 417
extinct, p. 417
relative dating, p. 419
index fossil, p. 419
half-life, p. 420
radioactive dating, p. 420
geologic time scale, p. 421
era, p. 421
period, p. 422

17–2 Earth's Early History

Key Concepts

- Earth's early atmosphere probably contained hydrogen cyanide, carbon dioxide, carbon monoxide, nitrogen, hydrogen sulfide, and water.
- Miller and Urey's experiments suggested how mixtures of the organic compounds necessary for life could have arisen from simpler compounds present on a primitive Earth.
- The rise of oxygen in the atmosphere drove some life forms to extinction, while other life forms evolved new, more efficient metabolic pathways that used oxygen for respiration.
- The endosymbiotic theory proposes that eukaryotic cells arose from living communities formed by prokaryotic organisms.

Vocabulary

proteinoid microsphere, p. 425
microfossil, p. 426
endosymbiotic theory, p. 427

17–3 Evolution of Multicellular Life

Key Concepts

- Early in the Paleozoic Era, the fossil record became rich with evidence of many types of marine life.
- During the Devonian, animals began to invade the land.
- The mass extinction at the end of the Paleozoic affected both plants and animals on land and in the seas. As much as 95 percent of the complex life in the oceans disappeared.
- Events during the Mesozoic include the increasing dominance of dinosaurs. The Mesozoic is marked by the appearance of flowering plants.
- During the Cenozoic, mammals evolved adaptations that allowed them to live in various environments—on land, in water, and even in the air.

Vocabulary

mass extinction, p. 431

17–4 Patterns of Evolution

Key Concept

- Six important patterns of macroevolution are mass extinctions, adaptive radiation, convergent evolution, coevolution, punctuated equilibrium, and changes in developmental genes.

Vocabulary

macroevolution, p. 435
adaptive radiation, p. 436
convergent evolution, p. 437
coevolution, p. 437
punctuated equilibrium, p. 439

Thinking Visually

Use information from the chapter to create a concept map that shows the four major divisions of geologic time, the periods within those divisions, and an example of a major event from each period.

CHAPTER RESOURCES

Print:

- ***Teaching Resources,*** Chapter Vocabulary Review, Graphic Organizer
- ***Chapter Tests: Levels A and B,*** Chapter 17 Test
- ***PH Assessment System,*** Practice Test

Technology:

- ***Computer Test Bank,*** Chapter 17 Test
- ***iText,*** Chapter 17 Assessment

Chapter 17 Assessment

Reviewing Content

Choose the letter that best answers the question or completes the statement.

1. Scientists who specialize in the study of fossils are called
   a. biologists. c. zoologists.
   b. paleontologists. d. anthropologists.
2. Sedimentary rocks form when layers of small particles are compressed
   a. in the atmosphere. c. in mountains.
   b. in a snow field. d. under water.
3. Radioactive dating of rock samples
   a. is a method of absolute dating.
   b. is a method of relative dating.
   c. forms a geologic column.
   d. forms a geologic time scale.
4. Half-life is the length of time required for half the atoms in a radioactive sample to
   a. decay. c. expand.
   b. double. d. be created.
5. Earth's first atmosphere contained little or no
   a. hydrogen cyanide. c. nitrogen.
   b. hydrogen sulfide. d. oxygen.
6. In Miller and Urey's experiments with the origin of life forms, electric sparks were passed through a mixture of gases to
   a. simulate temperature.
   b. simulate sunlight.
   c. sterilize the gases.
   d. simulate lightning.
7. Outlines of ancient cells that are preserved well enough to identify them as prokaryotes are
   a. microfossils. c. autotrophs.
   b. heterotrophs. d. phototrophic.
8. Which event occurred at the end of the Paleozoic Era?
   a. coevolution c. punctuated equilibrium
   b. mass extinction d. convergent evolution
9. The process that produces a similar appearance among unrelated groups of organisms is
   a. adaptive radiation. c. convergent evolution.
   b. coevolution. d. changes in hox genes.
10. As a group, the large-scale evolutionary changes that take place over long periods of time are called
    a. macroevolution. c. convergent evolution.
    b. coevolution. d. geologic time.

Understanding Concepts

11. How does relative dating enable paleontologists to estimate a fossil's age?
12. Explain how radioactivity is used to date rocks.
13. What is the geologic time scale? How was it developed?
14. Discuss what scientists hypothesize about Earth's early atmosphere and the way oceans formed.
15. Use the diagram below to explain the significance of Miller and Urey's experiment.

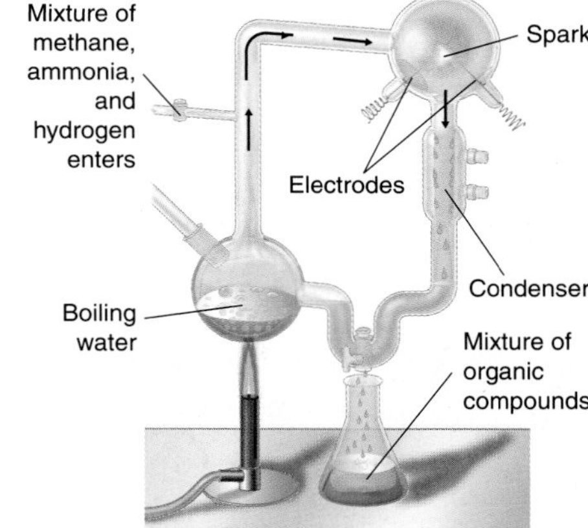

16. How are proteinoid microspheres like living cells?
17. How did the addition of oxygen to Earth's atmosphere affect the evolution of life?
18. Describe the endosymbiotic theory.
19. What effect did sexual reproduction have on evolution?
20. Describe life as it existed in Precambrian Time.
21. What significant mammalian adaptations led to their success during the Cenozoic Era?
22. What events led to the diversification of mammals?
23. Explain the process of adaptive radiation. Give an example.
24. Explain the pattern known as punctuated equilibrium.
25. How can hox genes provide evidence of evolution?

TIME SAVER HOMEWORK GUIDE

Section:	Questions:
Section 17–1	1–4, 11–13, 30, 32–34
Section 17–2	5–7, 14–19, 26–28, 31, 35
Section 17–3	8, 20–22, 29
Section 17–4	9, 10, 23–25

15. Miller and Urey first demonstrated how organic matter might have formed in Earth's primitive atmosphere. By recreating the early atmosphere (ammonia, water, hydrogen, and methane) and passing an electric spark (lightning) through the mixture, they proved that organic matter, such as amino acids, could have arisen from simpler compounds.

16. Proteinoid microspheres, like cells, have a selectively permeable membrane across which water molecules can travel and have a simple means of storing and releasing energy.

17. Some organisms began to evolve more efficient metabolic pathways that used oxygen for respiration; others became extinct.

18. The endosymbiotic theory states that the first eukaryotic cells were formed from symbiosis among several different prokaryotic cells. One type had the ability to use oxygen to generate ATP and evolved into mitochondria. Another type could carry out photosynthesis and evolved into chloroplasts. Other types took in those cells.

19. Sexual reproduction caused evolution to take place at a far greater speed, because it increased genetic variation, which increased the chances of evolution by natural selection.

20. During Precambrian Time, the history of life on Earth began. The first life forms, which included the first prokaryotes, appeared in the sea. Unicellular life evolved photosynthetic forms, and then aerobic forms of life evolved. Finally, the first eukaryotes appeared.

21. Mammalian adaptations included hair that provided insulation against the cold and the protection of young before and after birth.

22. Disappearance of the dinosaurs enabled the smaller, relatively scarce mammals to flourish and diversify.

23. In adaptive radiation, a single or a small group of species evolves into several different forms that live in different ways; examples: dinosaurs and other ancient reptiles.

24. Punctuated equilibrium is a pattern in which long, stable periods of little or no evolutionary change are interrupted by brief periods of rapid change.

25. Homologous hox genes established body plans in organisms that did not share common ancestors for millions of years.

Chapter 17 Assessment

Critical Thinking

26. Students' answers should compare the physical conditions on Earth—such as presence or absence of oceans, geological activity, and atmospheric content—and types of life forms.

27. Condensing water vapor represents rain. Rain carried many chemicals from the atmosphere into the primitive sea. The sea was also the site of the first steps in chemical evolution.

28. Mitochondria release energy, enabling the cells to use various nutrients. Chloroplasts are photosynthetic, enabling the cells to make their own food.

29. Geological changes often produce changes in Earth's atmosphere in the form of clouds, dust, and water vapor. The changes in the atmosphere directly affect the global climate, which in turn may affect plants and the life forms that eat plants. Because organisms are adapted to specific environments, they may not be able to survive in a changed environment.

30. After one half-life, half of the original radioactive atoms in a sample have decayed. It would take four half-lives for the sample to contain 1/16 of the amount of carbon-14. One half-life is 5770 years, so four half-lives are 23,080 years. Therefore, the age of the fossil would be about 23,080 years.

31. At 2.5 billion years ago, photosynthetic organisms appeared. They added oxygen to the atmosphere.

32. Problems that paleontologists face include an incomplete fossil record, variation in the quality of fossil preservation, and difficulties in dating fossils accurately.

33. Some organisms never became fossils because they did not live near water and their remains never became part of sedimentary rock. Other organisms may not have had hard body parts that could be preserved.

Chapter 17 Assessment

Critical Thinking

26. Comparing and Contrasting Compare and contrast the conditions on the early Earth with those on the modern Earth.

27. Using Models What part of Miller and Urey's apparatus represents rain? What important part would rain play in chemical evolution?

28. Applying Concepts In what way might the cells that took in the ancestors of mitochondria and chloroplasts have benefited from the relationship?

29. Inferring Geologic changes often accompany mass extinctions of life forms. Why do you think this is true?

30. Problem Solving The half-life of carbon-14 is 5730 years. What is the age of a fossil containing 1/16 the amount of carbon-14 of living organisms? Explain your reasoning.

31. Applying Concepts The graph shows an approximation of the amount of oxygen in the atmosphere since life began. What event occurred at the point indicated by the arrow?

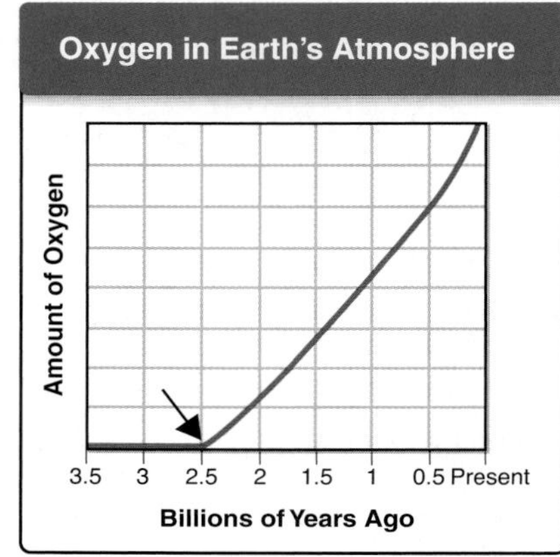

32. Applying Concepts What are some problems faced by paleontologists when reconstructing the history of Earth?

33. Applying Concepts Evolutionary biologists say that there is good reason for gaps in the fossil record. Can you explain why some extinct animals and plants were never fossilized?

34. Applying Concepts How might relative dating provide inaccurate data?

35. Making Connections Recall what you learned about chemistry in Chapter 2. When Earth's atmosphere first began to form, it did not contain oxygen (O_2), and hydrogen (H_2) was the most abundant element in the solar system. However, there is very little H_2 in the atmosphere today, and the element makes up less than 1 percent of Earth's mass. What might have happened to the H_2?

Performance-Based Assessment

Imagine you could observe the formation and early history of Earth. Write your experiences in the form of a booklet four to six pages long to be read by middle-school students. Include a table of contents, color illustrations, and an activity at the end to evaluate students' understanding of the concept. The activity could be a puzzle, a completion activity, or another similar activity.

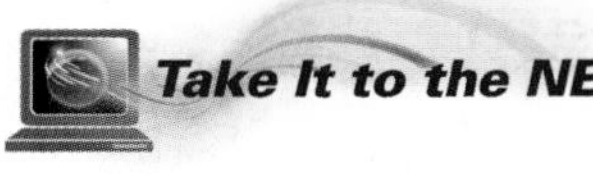

Do biologists study life only on Earth? Visit the Prentice Hall Web site at **www.phschool.com** to find out about the study of life elsewhere in the universe. Then, answer the following questions:

- What does the term *exobiology* mean?
- Describe the circumstances in which Stanley Miller came to conduct his famous electrical discharge experiment with Harold Urey.
- What advice does Dr. Miller have for a student interested in studying exobiology?

Performance-Based Assessment

Students' booklets will vary, but they should contain information about the geologic time scale, Earth's early atmosphere, how early Earth was formed, and the appearance of eukaryotes and other early forms of life.

Standardized Test Prep

1. C 5. A
2. A 6. D
3. D 7. B
4. C 8. A

Test-Taking Tip If you find particular questions difficult, put a light mark beside them and keep working. As you answer later questions, you may find information that helps you find the answers you still need. (Do not write in this book.)

Directions: Choose the letter that best answers the question or completes the statement.

1. Which of the following is characteristic of an index fossil?
  I. Distinctive species
  II. Lived in a wide geographic range
  III. Lived for a long period of time
  (A) I only
  (B) II only
  (C) I and II only
  (D) II and III only
  (E) I, II, and III

2. In which geologic era do you live?
  (A) Cenozoic
  (B) Mesozoic
  (C) Cambrian
  (D) Precambrian
  (E) Paleozoic

3. The endosymbiotic theory includes all of the following EXCEPT
  (A) Photosynthetic prokaryotes evolved into chloroplasts.
  (B) Aerobic prokaryotes evolved into mitochondria.
  (C) Eukaryotic cells arose from the merging of different prokaryotic organisms.
  (D) All organelles evolved from specialized enfoldings of the plasma membrane.
  (E) Eukaryotic cells are the result of an interdependent relationship among different organisms.

4. Which of the following is evidence for the endosymbiotic theory?
  I. Mitochondria and chloroplasts contain DNA similar to bacterial DNA.
  II. Mitochondria and chloroplasts contain ribosomes that differ from bacterial ribosomes.
  III. Mitochondria and chloroplasts reproduce by binary fission.
  (A) I only
  (B) II only
  (C) I and III only
  (D) II and III only
  (E) I, II, and III

Questions 5–6 Complete each analogy by selecting the correct letter. In analogies, A : B :: C : *means* A is to B as C is to __?__.

5. Mass extinction : adaptive radiation :: disappearance of dinosaurs : __?__
  (A) diversification of mammals
  (B) extinction of mammoths
  (C) extinction of trilobites
  (D) spread of agriculture
  (E) progression of ice ages

6. Triassic : Age of Reptiles :: Cambrian : __?__
  (A) Age of Humans
  (B) Age of Fishes
  (C) Age of Dinosaurs
  (D) Age of Invertebrates
  (E) Age of Vertebrates

Questions 7–8

The graph shows the radioactive decay of an isotope.

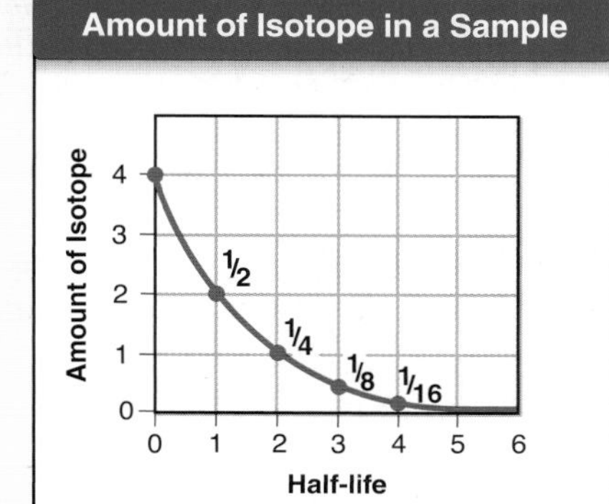

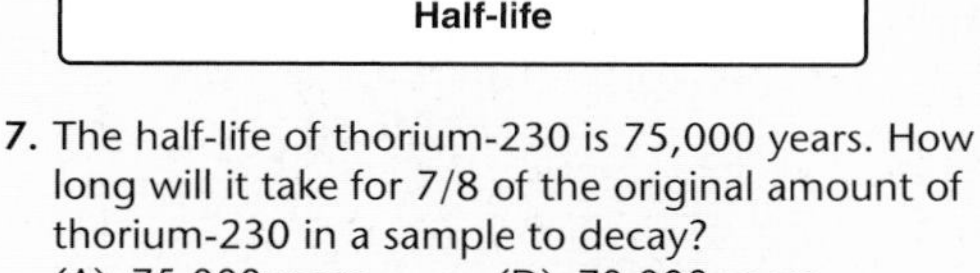

7. The half-life of thorium-230 is 75,000 years. How long will it take for 7/8 of the original amount of thorium-230 in a sample to decay?
  (A) 75,000 years
  (B) 225,000 years
  (C) 25,000 years
  (D) 70,000 years
  (E) 150,000 years

8. The half-life of potassium-40 is about 1300 million years. The age of a fossil that contains only one half of its original potassium-40 is about
  (A) 1300 million years.
  (B) 26,000 million years.
  (C) 650 million years.
  (D) 32.5 million years.
  (E) 40 million years.

Chapter 17 Assessment (continued)

34. Relative dating depends on the position of the fossil sample. Relative dating might prove inaccurate if movements in Earth push rock layers that contain older fossils above layers that contain younger fossils.

35. The hydrogen became part of compounds, especially water and organic compounds.

Take It to the NET

• The term *exobiology* refers to the search for life beyond Earth.

• The experiments were done in Urey's lab when Miller was a graduate student. Urey gave a lecture in October of 1951, when Miller first arrived at Chicago, and suggested the experiment. Urey told Miller that the experiment was risky and probably wouldn't work. They agreed to see if they could get any results in six months to a year. As it turned out, Miller got results in a matter of weeks.

• A background in basic chemistry is essential, along with knowledge of organic chemistry, geology, and physics.

For additional information, visit

www.phschool.com

Chapter Planner 18 Classification

Section and Section Objectives	Time	Activities and Labs
18–1 Finding Order in Diversity, pp. 447–450 **18.1.1** ***Explain*** how living things are organized for study. **18.1.2** ***Describe*** binomial nomenclature. **18.1.3** ***Explain*** Linnaeus's system of classification.	1 period (1/2 block)	**SE:** ***Inquiry Activity,*** How can you classify fruits?, p. 446 **TE:** ***Demonstration,*** p.449 **TE:** ***Build Science Skills,*** p. 450
18–2 Modern Evolutionary Classification, pp. 451–456 **18.2.1** ***Explain*** how evolutionary relationships are important in classification. **18.2.2** ***Identify*** the principle behind cladistic analysis. **18.2.3** ***Explain*** how we can compare very dissimilar organisms.	1 period (1/2 block)	**TE:** ***Demonstration,*** p. 451 **SE:** ***Quick Lab,*** How is a cladogram used?, p. 453 **TE:** ***Demonstration,*** p. 454 **SE:** ***Technology and Society,*** The Search for New Species, p. 456
18–3 Kingdoms and Domains, pp. 457–461 **18.3.1** ***Name*** the six kingdoms of life as they are now identified. **18.3.2** ***Describe*** the three-domain system of classification.	1 period (1/2 block)	**TE:** ***Demonstration,*** p. 460 **SE:** ***Real-World Lab,*** Using Dichotomous Keys, pp. 462–463
Chapter Assessment, pp. 464–467	1 period (1/2 block)	

ACTIVITY PLANNER

SE: ***Inquiry Activity,*** p. 446; (15 min.); 5 different fruits, scalpel

TE: ***Demonstration,*** p.449; (5 min.); pictures of domestic dog, wolf, fox, and mountain lion

TE: ***Build Science Skills,*** p. 450; (10 min.); hair clip, bobby pin, safety pin, straight pin, screw, nail, paper clip, and staple

TE: ***Demonstration,*** p. 451; (5 min.); pictures of plants, animals, and protists

SE: ***Quick Lab,*** p. 453; (15 min.); no materials needed

TE: ***Demonstration,*** p. 454; (5 min.); cytochrome-c family tree

TE: ***Demonstration,*** p. 460; (10 min.); microprojector, slides of amoeba and paramecium

TE: ***Real-World Lab,*** pp. 462–463; (45 min.); leaf specimens, second set of biological specimens

PLANNING KEY

Ability Levels

B **Basic**	For students who need additional help
A **Average**	For all students
E **Enriched**	For students who need to be challenged

Components

SE	Student Edition	**GRSW**	Guided Reading and Study Workbook	**IDM**	Issues and Decision Making
TE	Teacher's Edition	**CT**	Chapter Tests: Levels A and B	**CTB**	Computer Test Bank
LMA	Laboratory Manual A	**PHAS**	PH Assessment System	**PA**	Presentation Assistant Plus
LMB	Laboratory Manual B	**LA**	Lab Assessment with Scoring Guide	**BD**	BioDetectives Videotape
TR	Teaching Resources	**BTM**	BioTechnology Manual	**iT**	iText
IF	Investigations in Forensics				

Program Resources	Assessment	Media and Technology
TR: Section Review 18–1 B A **GRSW:** Section 18–1 B A **IF:** Investigation 4 A E	**SE:** 18–1 Section Asessment, p. 450 **TR:** Section Review 18–1	**PA:** 18–1 Interest Grabber, Section Outline, Flowchart, Figure 18–5 **iT:** Section 18–1
LMA: Chapter 18 Lab A E **TR:** Section Review 18–2 B A **GRSW:** Section 18–2 B A	**SE:** 18–2 Section Asessment, p. 455 **TR:** Section Review 18–2	**PA:** 18–2 Interest Grabber, Section Outline, Traditional Classification Versus Cladistic Analysis **iT:** Section 18–2
LMB: Chapter 18 Lab B A **TR:** Section Review 18–3 B A Chapter 18 Real-World Lab B A E **GRSW:** Section 18–3 B A	**SE:** 18–3 Section Asessment, p. 461 **TR:** Section Review 18–3	**PA:** 18–3 Interest Grabber, Section Outline, Concept Map, Figure 18–12, Figure 18–13 **iT:** Section 18–3
	SE: Chapter 18 Assessment, pp. 464–467 **TR:** Chapter Vocabulary Review, Graphic Organizer **CT:** Chapter 18 Test **CTB:** Chapter 18 Test **PHAS:** Practice Text	**CTB:** Chapter 18 Test **iT:** Chapter 18 Assessment

PRESSED FOR TIME?

To Preview the Chapter
- Have students read the boldfaced sentences in each section.
- Introduce students to the Vocabulary terms in each section.

To Cover the Chapter Quickly
- Have students read Linnaeus's System of Classification in Section 18–1, Evolutionary Classification in Section 18–2, and all of Section 18–3.
- Assign questions 2 and 3 in 18–1 Section Assessment and all of 18–3 Section Assessment, questions 2, 3, 5, 8–10, 13, 14, 21–25, 27, 28, and 30–35 in Chapter 18 Assessment, and questions 1–3, 6, and 7 in Chapter 18 Standardized Test Prep.

To Review the Chapter
- Assign Sections 18–1 through 18–3 in the Guided Reading and Study Workbook.
- Assign the Section Reviews for 18–1 through 18–3 and the Chapter Vocabulary Review for Chapter 18 in the Teaching Resources.

ENGAGE/EXPLORE

Inquiry Activity

Objective Students will be able to conclude which of five fruits are most closely related based on observable characteristics.

Skills Focus **Observing, Classifying**

Materials 5 different fruits, scalpel

Time 15 minutes

Advance Prep Choose some fruits that are similar, such as apples and pears or oranges and grapefruits, and also some fruits that are dissimilar, such as peaches and bananas or lemons and kiwis.

Safety Remind students to be careful using scalpels.

Strategy If students are having difficulty thinking of four different characteristics, mention some they may not have thought of, such as scent, firmness, and thickness of skin.

Expected Outcome Students will be able to classify a sample of fruits based on how similar the fruits are in observable characteristics.

Think About It

1. Students are likely to have selected such readily observable characteristics as size, shape, color, and presence or absence of seeds.

2. Students should conclude that the most closely related fruits are the ones that are most similar in the characteristics they included in their table.

Assess Prior Knowledge

Find out if students are familiar with Linnaeus's binomial classification system. Ask: **What is the scientific name for the human species?** *(Homo sapiens)* **What do you think are the common names for *Felis catus* and *Canis familiaris*?** *(Cat, dog)* **In each case, what does the first of the two names refer to?** *(The genus)* **What does the second of the two names refer to?** *(The species)* **Which term, *genus* or *species*, is the more inclusive group?** *(Genus)* Point out that, in this chapter, students will learn more about how organisms are classified.

Chapter 18 Classification

People everywhere are fascinated by the diversity of life around them. Here, in a forest in Myanmar, villagers are using a field guide to identify some of the local birds.

Inquiry Activity

How can you classify fruits?

Procedure

1. Obtain five different fruits. Use a paring knife to cut each fruit open and examine its structure. **CAUTION:** *Use caution with sharp instruments.*
2. Construct a table with five rows and four columns. Label each row with the name of a different fruit.
3. Observe each fruit and choose four characteristics by which you can tell the fruits apart. Label the columns in your table with these four characteristics.
4. Record a description of each fruit in your table.

Think About It

1. **Observing** What characteristics did you use to describe the fruits?
2. **Classifying** Based on your table, which fruits are most closely related? Explain.

TEACHER TO TEACHER

Near the beginning of the chapter on classification, I do a demonstration using characteristics of students' shoes to develop a dichotomous key. Each student takes off his or her left shoe and puts it on the floor in the front of the room. As a group, we identify characteristics that vary in the sample of shoes, such as white/nonwhite and tennis/nontennis, and develop a dichotomous key that identifies all the shoes and their owners. If possible, I have the principal or another teacher come into the classroom at this point and return some of the shoes to their owners by following the key. I usually let the rest of the students retrieve their own shoes once they see that the dichotomous key really works. The demonstration is fun for students and makes the concept of dichotomous key easier to understand.

—*Bob Demmink,*
Biology Teacher
East Kentwood High School,
Kentwood, MI

18–1 Finding Order in Diversity

For more than 3.5 billion years, life on Earth has been constantly changing. This process has led to a staggering variety of organisms. A tropical rain forest, for example, may support thousands of species per acre. Recall that a species is a population of organisms that share similar characteristics and can breed with one another and produce fertile offspring. Biologists have identified and named about 1.5 million species so far. They estimate that anywhere between 2 and 100 million additional species have yet to be discovered.

Why Classify?

To study this great diversity of organisms, biologists must give each organism a name. Biologists must also attempt to organize living things into groups that have biological meaning.  **To study the diversity of life, biologists use a classification system to name organisms and group them in a logical manner.**

In the discipline known as **taxonomy,** scientists classify organisms and assign each organism a universally accepted name. One example appears in **Figure 18–1.** By using a scientific name, biologists can be certain that everyone is discussing the same organism. When taxonomists classify organisms, they organize them into groups that have biological significance. When you hear the word "bird," for example, you immediately form a mental picture of the organism being discussed—a flying animal that has feathers. But science often requires smaller categories as well as larger, more general categories. In a good system of classification, organisms placed into a particular group are more similar to each other than they are to organisms in other groups.

You use classification systems also, for example, when you refer to "teachers" or "mechanics," or more specifically, "biology teachers" or "auto mechanics." Such a process, like scientific classification, uses accepted names and common criteria to group things.

▶ **Figure 18–1** Depending on where you live, you might recognize this as a mountain lion, a puma, a cougar, or a panther—all of which are common names for the same animal. The scientific name for this animal is *Felis concolor.* **To avoid the confusion caused by regional names, biologists use a classification system to group organisms in a logical manner and to assign names.**

Guide for Reading

Key Concepts
- How are living things organized for study?
- What is binomial nomenclature?
- What is Linnaeus's system of classification?

Vocabulary
taxonomy
binomial nomenclature
genus
taxon
family
order
class
phylum
kingdom

Reading Strategy: Building Vocabulary
As you read about the seven categories established by Linnaeus, list those categories in order, starting with the smallest group. Then, create a memory aid to help you remember them.

SECTION RESOURCES

Print:
- ***Teaching Resources,*** Section Review 18–1
- ***Guided Reading and Study Workbook,*** Section 18–1

Technology:
- ***iText,*** Section 18–1

Section 18–1

1 FOCUS

Objectives

18.1.1 ***Explain*** how living things are organized for study.
18.1.2 ***Describe*** binomial nomenclature.
18.1.3 ***Explain*** Linnaeus's system of classification.

Guide for Reading

Vocabulary Preview

Explain how the Vocabulary terms are related. State that the term *taxonomy* refers to the classification of organisms and that the term *binomial nomenclature* refers to the familiar system of taxonomy developed by Linnaeus. In this system, organisms are classified into categories. Ask: **Which of the Vocabulary terms refer to categories in Linnaeus's system?** *(Genus, family, order, class, phylum, and kingdom)* Add that the general term for these categories is *taxon.*

Reading Strategy

One example of a memory aid to help students remember the seven taxonomic categories is: *S*am *g*ave *F*red *o*ne *c*opper *p*adlock *k*ey.

2 INSTRUCT

Why Classify?

Meet Diverse Needs

Help students appreciate the need for classification with a quick demonstration. First, have all the students stand up. Then, as you read aloud each of the following physical characteristics, have students without the characteristic sit down: over 5 feet tall, brown eyes, female, left-handed. By the time you have named all the characteristics, all or nearly all of the students are likely to be sitting down. Point out that with each characteristic you named, the remaining group became narrower. Conclude that grouping organisms based on shared characteristics makes it easier to understand the diversity of life. **Learning modality: kinesthetic**

Assigning Scientific Names

Build Science Skills

Applying Concepts Challenge students to brainstorm other examples of species with more than one common name. *(Possible examples include the woodchuck, which is also called ground hog, and the yellow poplar tree, which is also called tulip tree.)*

Use Community Resources

Display several field guides for your region. Explain how field guides are used to help identify the species of a plant or animal based on physical characteristics similar to the ones that were used in early efforts at naming. For example, a field guide to trees identifies holly trees based on such characteristics as whether the leaf edges are scalloped and whether they are hairy on their undersides. Encourage interested students to borrow the field guides and use them to identify flora or fauna in the community. Give students a chance to share their observations with the class.

Meet Diverse Needs

At-risk students may have a better understanding of binomial nomenclature if you compare it with the use of first and last names. Ask students to find a last name in a telephone book that occurs more than once. Have them read the first names of two people with that last name. Then, ask: **Which name, the first name or the last name, is like the genus of an organism and which name is like the species?** *(The last name is like the genus, and the first name is like the species.)* **Limited English proficiency**

Word Origins

A biped has two feet.

▲ **Figure 18–2** The problem of naming organisms efficiently continues to challenge biologists as they discover new species. This barking deer was recently discovered near the border of Laos and Vietnam. Its scientific name, which is based on Latin, is *Muntiacus muntjak.* **In binomial nomenclature, each animal is assigned a two-part scientific name.**

Assigning Scientific Names

By the eighteenth century, European scientists recognized that referring to organisms by common names was confusing. Common names vary among languages and even among regions within a single country. The animal you saw in **Figure 18–1,** for example, can be called a cougar, a puma, a panther, or a mountain lion. Furthermore, different species sometimes share a single common name. In the United Kingdom, the word *buzzard* refers to a hawk, whereas in many parts of the United States, *buzzard* refers to a vulture. To eliminate such confusion, scientists agreed to use a single name for each species. Because eighteenth-century scientists understood Latin and Greek, they used those languages for scientific names. This practice is still followed today in naming newly discovered species, such as the barking deer in **Figure 18–2.**

Early Efforts at Naming Organisms The first attempts at standard scientific names often described the physical characteristics of a species in great detail. As a result, these names could be twenty words long! For example, the English translation of the scientific name of a particular tree might be "Oak with deeply divided leaves that have no hairs on their undersides and no teeth around their edges." This system of naming had another major drawback. It was difficult to standardize the names of organisms because different scientists described different characteristics.

Binomial Nomenclature A major step was taken by Carolus Linnaeus, shown in **Figure 18–3,** a Swedish botanist who lived during the eighteenth century. He developed a two-word naming system called **binomial nomenclature** (by-NOH-mee-ul NOH-mun-klay-chur). This system is still in use today. **In binomial nomenclature, each species is assigned a two-part scientific name.** The scientific name is always written in italics. The first word is capitalized, and the second word is lowercased.

For example, the grizzly bear shown in **Figure 18–4** is called *Ursus arctos.* The first part of the scientific name—in this case, *Ursus*—is the genus to which the organism belongs. A **genus** (JEE-nus; plural: genera, JEN-ur-uh) is a group of closely related species. The genus *Ursus* contains five other kinds of bears, including *Ursus maritimus,* the polar bear.

The second part of a scientific name—in this case, *arctos* or *maritimus*—is unique to each species within the genus. Often, this part of the name is a Latinized description of some important trait of the organism or an indication of where the organism lives. The Latin word *maritimus,* referring to the sea, comes from the fact that polar bears often live on pack ice that floats in the sea.

CHECKPOINT *Do* Ursus arctos *and* Ursus maritimus *belong to the same species? To the same genus?*

Word Origins

Binomial and ***nomenclature*** are built from some familiar roots. *Bi-* is Latin for "two." *Nomen-* is Latin for "name." So *binomial nomenclature* means a two-name system of assigning names. **If *pedis* is Latin for "of the foot," how many feet does a *biped* have?**

PRESENTATIONS MADE EASY!

The Presentation Assistant Plus contains the Prentice Hall Presentation Pro and the Transparencies, which provide easy-to-follow visual support for every step of this section. If you have a computer presentation station, use Prentice Hall Presentation Pro for Section 18–1, or use the transparencies listed here.

Section 18–1:

Interest Grabber
Section Outline
Flowchart
Figure 18–5

Linnaeus's System of Classification

In taxonomy, a group or level of organization is called a taxonomic category, or **taxon** (plural: taxa). **Linnaeus's system of classification uses seven taxonomic categories. They are—from smallest to largest—species, genus, family, order, class, phylum, and kingdom.** You can see these seven categories in **Figure 18–5** on the next page. The two smallest categories, genus and species, were discussed in the example of the bears. The giant panda, also shown in **Figure 18–4,** resembles the grizzly bear and the polar bear in important ways. However, it differs enough from these bears and other species in the genus *Ursus* that it is placed in its own genus, *Ailuropoda*.

Genera that share many characteristics, such as *Ursus* and *Ailuropoda,* are grouped in a larger category, the **family**—in this case, Ursidae. These bears, together with six other families of meat-eating animals, such as dogs (Canidae) and cats (Felidae), are grouped together in the order Carnivora. An **order** is a broad taxonomic category composed of similar families. The next larger category, the **class,** is composed of similar orders. For example, carnivores are placed in the class Mammalia, which includes animals that are warm-blooded, have body hair, and produce milk for their young.

Several different classes make up a **phylum** (FY-lum; plural: phyla). A phylum includes many different organisms that nevertheless share important characteristics. The class Mammalia is grouped with birds (class Aves), reptiles (class Reptilia), amphibians (class Amphibia), and all classes of fishes into the phylum Chordata. All these organisms share important features of their body plan and internal functions.

Finally, all animals are placed in the kingdom Animalia. The **kingdom** is the largest and most inclusive of Linnaeus's taxonomic categories. Linnaeus named two kingdoms, Animalia and Plantae.

▲ **Figure 18–3** Carolus Linnaeus (1707–1778) brought order to the process of naming species and classifying them into groups. **Evaluating** ***Why do biologists consider Linnaeus's system an improvement over earlier systems?***

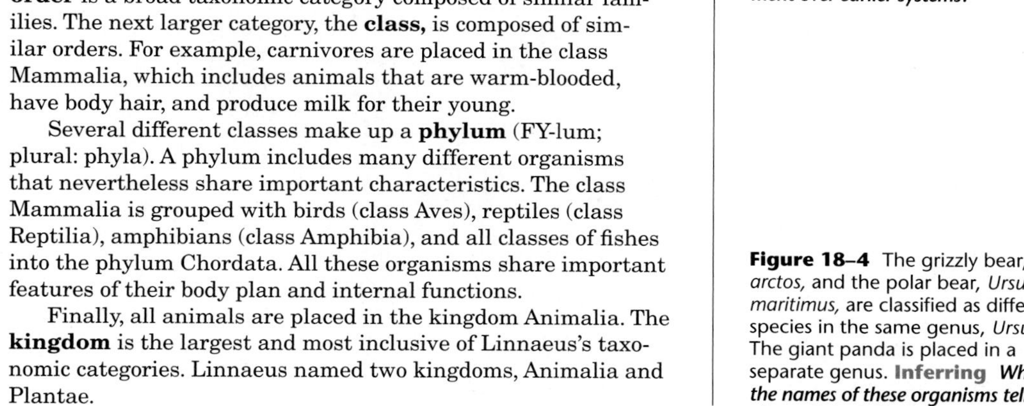

Figure 18–4 The grizzly bear, *Ursus arctos,* and the polar bear, *Ursus maritimus,* are classified as different species in the same genus, *Ursus.* The giant panda is placed in a separate genus. **Inferring** ***What do the names of these organisms tell you about their similarity to each other?***

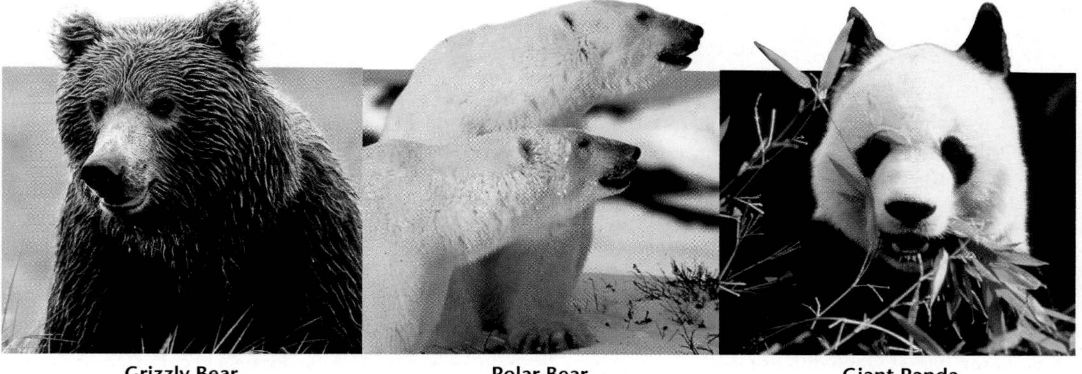

Grizzly Bear *Ursus arctos* | **Polar Bear** *Ursus maritimus* | **Giant Panda** *Ailuropoda melanoleuca*

Linnaeus's System of Classification

Address Misconceptions

Students might think that different breeds of dogs, cats, and other domesticated animals are different species. Explain that the term *breed* refers to a domesticated variety of an organism that is a subgroup of a species. For example, dogs of different breeds, no matter how dissimilar they look, all belong to the species *Canis familiaris.* Because they are members of the same species, they can mate and produce fertile offspring.

Demonstration

Demonstrate how Linnaeus's system of classification consists of organisms that are increasingly similar as you go from the level of kingdom to the level of species. Show students pictures of a domestic dog, wolf, fox, and mountain lion. Ask: **What are some ways these animals are similar, and what are some ways they are different?** *(Accept all reasonable responses.)* Then, explain that the mountain lion, fox, wolf, and dog are classified together at the level of order (*Carnivora*), the fox, wolf, and dog at the level of family (*Canidae*), and the wolf and dog together at the level of genus (*Canis*).

Answers to . . .

CHECKPOINT *They do not belong to the same species, but they do belong to the same genus.*

Figure 18–3 *Because it provides a brief and unique name for each species*

Figure 18–4 *The genus name* Ursus *indicates that two of the species are in the same genus and thus are closely related.*

18–1 (continued)

Build Science Skills

Classifying Have the class work in groups to develop a system, similar to the Linnaean system, to classify a collection that includes a hair clip, bobby pin, safety pin, straight pin, screw, nail, paper clip, and staple. *(All are fasteners, and subsets might be classified on the basis of other shared characteristics. For example, hair clips and bobby pins are fasteners of hair, screws and nails are fasteners of wood, and paper clips and staples are fasteners of paper. Other characteristics that might be used include sharpness, shape, or color.)* Have groups share their systems. Then, ask: **How is the classification affected by the characteristics selected?** *(Different objects are grouped together if different characteristics are selected.)*

3 ASSESS

Evaluate Understanding

Have students write a paragraph explaining why it is important to classify the diversity of living things.

Reteach

Call on students to name the taxa of the Linnaean classification system in order from smallest to largest. Write each term on the board. Have students brainstorm examples of each taxon, such as Chordata for phylum and Mammalia for class.

Take It to the NET

The full name of the organism (e.g., *Ursus arctos*) should be written the first time it is used in the report. Thereafter, the name of the genus may be abbreviated as part of the species name (e.g., *U. arctos*). The genus name is *always* capitalized. The species name is *never* capitalized.
www.phschool.com

Use iText to review the key concepts in Section 18–1.

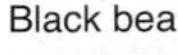

▶ **Figure 18–5 Linnaeus's system of classification uses seven taxonomic categories.** This illustration shows how a grizzly bear, *Ursus arctos,* is grouped within each taxonomic category. Only some representative species are illustrated for each category above the species level.

18–1 Section Assessment

1. **Key Concept** How are living things organized for study?
2. **Key Concept** Describe the system for naming species that Linnaeus developed.
3. **Key Concept** What are the seven taxonomic categories of Linnaeus's classification system?
4. Why do scientists avoid using common names when discussing organisms?
5. **Critical Thinking Applying Concepts** Which category has more biological meaning—all brown birds or all hawklike birds? Why?

Assessment Use iText to review the important concepts in Section 18–1.

Take It to the NET

Find out the proper way to use binomial nomenclature in scientific writing. Then, write a paragraph or two about the different species of bears, which illustrates each rule for using this naming system. Use the links provided in the Biology area at the Prentice Hall Web site for help in completing this activity: **www.phschool.com**

18–1 Section Assessment

1. Biologists use a classification system to name organisms with a universally accepted name. They also group organisms in a logical manner. Organisms placed into a particular group are more similar to one another than they are to organisms in other groups.
2. Each species is assigned a two-part scientific name.
3. Species, genus, family, order, class, phylum, and kingdom
4. Because common names vary among languages and even among regions within a single country
5. All hawklike animals, because it refers to a taxonomic category (hawk) rather than a single characteristic (color)

18–2 Modern Evolutionary Classification

Linnaeus worked to decide rationally what traits should be considered when classifying organisms. He compared the structures of different organisms as well as many details of anatomy. Based on these features, he grouped organisms into categories—some of which are still in use today.

Guide for Reading

Key Concepts
- How are evolutionary relationships important in classification?
- How can DNA and RNA help scientists determine evolutionary relationships?

Vocabulary
evolutionary classification
derived character
cladogram
molecular clock

Reading Strategy: Predicting Before you read, preview **Figure 18-7.** Predict how the field of taxonomy has changed since Linnaeus's time. As you read, note whether or not your prediction was correct.

Problems With Traditional Classification

Suppose you lived during Linnaeus's time. How might you have classified organisms such as dolphins? Would you have classified them as fishes because they live in water and have streamlined bodies with limbs that look like fins? Or would you have classified dolphins as mammals because they are warmblooded and breathe air? How might you have classified the three organisms shown in **Figure 18–6?** The barnacle and the limpet have similarly shaped shells and look quite like each other. The crab, on the other hand, has a very different body form. Based on their anatomy, then, you might classify the barnacle and limpet together, and place the crab in a different group.

Both of these examples point out the problems faced by taxonomists who relied on body structure comparisons. Sometimes, due to convergent evolution, organisms that are quite different from each other evolve similar body structures. These apparent similarities made it difficult for taxonomists to decide how many organisms should be classified.

Figure 18–6 Classifying species based on their anatomy sometimes posed problems for taxonomists. Scientists debated which of these three organisms were more closely related—crabs (top left), barnacles (bottom left), and limpets (right). **Classifying** ***Draw two simple diagrams to show two different ways of grouping these three organisms.***

SECTION RESOURCES

Print:
- ***Laboratory Manual A,*** Chapter 18 Lab
- ***Teaching Resources,*** Section Review 18–2
- ***Guided Reading and Study Workbook,*** Section 18–2

Technology:
- ***iText,*** Section 18–2

Section 18–2

1 FOCUS

Objectives

18.2.1 ***Explain*** how evolutionary relationships are important in classification.

18.2.2 ***Identify*** the principle behind cladistic analysis.

18.2.3 ***Explain*** how we can compare very dissimilar organisms.

Guide for Reading

Vocabulary Preview

Explain how some of the Vocabulary terms are related. Point out that the terms *phylogenetic tree* and *cladogram* refer to two types of evolutionary classification. Ask: **What do you think the term *evolutionary classification* refers to?** *(A type of classification of organisms that shows how the organisms are related and not just how similar or different they are)*

Reading Strategy

In comparing the phylogenetic tree and cladogram in Figure 18–7, students might conclude that both show evolutionary relationships but use different types of characteristics.

2 INSTRUCT

Problems With Traditional Classification

Demonstration

Show students pictures of a variety of plants and animals. In each case, ask them to identify the kingdom to which the organism belongs. Point out that plants and animals are the only two kingdoms in Linnaeus's system. Then, show students pictures of single-celled organisms, such as paramecia, and challenge them to identify the kingdom to which they belong. *(Students may or may not be able to identify the kingdom of paramecia as Protista.)* Explain that Linnaeus did not include such organisms in his classification system because the microscope had not yet been invented. That is one reason the Linnaean system needed to be revised.

Evolutionary Classification

Build Science Skills

Using Models Tell students that most scientists used to think that monkeys of the New and Old Worlds had diverged from a monkeylike common ancestor fairly recently. Add that now most scientists think that New and Old World monkeys diverged from a more generalized common ancestor much longer ago and later evolved similar characteristics because of similar environments. Challenge students to represent each of these theories with a phylogenetic tree. *(A phylogenetic tree for the first theory would show a recent branching. A tree for the second theory would show a much less recent branching, followed by parallel evolution in the two groups.)*

Demonstration

Show students a human family tree that includes at least three generations. Point out that both family trees and phylogenetic trees show relationships among descendants of a common ancestor. Explain how relationships among species in a phylogenetic tree are similar to relationships among relatives in a family tree. For example, species with a very recent common ancestor are like siblings in a family, whereas species with a remote common ancestor are like distant cousins in a family.

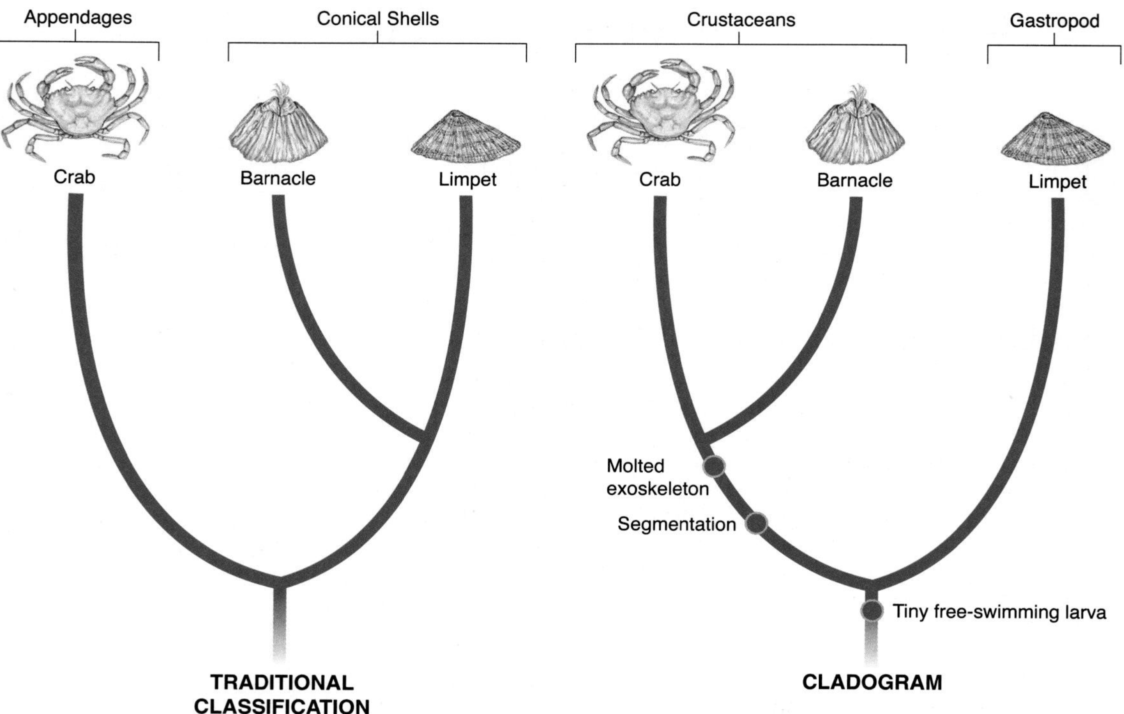

Figure 18–7 In traditional classification (left), organisms were grouped according to similarities in appearance. Until about 150 years ago, barnacles and limpets were grouped together because both had conical shells. **Biologists now group organisms based on evolutionary descent, not just physical similarities.** In the cladogram (above), crabs and barnacles are grouped together because they share important evolutionary characteristics, such as a segmented body and an exoskeleton that the organism molts. Limpets do not share these characteristics.

Evolutionary Classification

Darwin's theory of evolution changed the entire way that biologists thought about classification. Scientists began to understand that organisms share certain traits because they share an evolutionary history. This new approach to classification provided answers to many classification questions.

Biologists now group organisms into categories that represent lines of evolutionary descent, not just physical similarities. In other words, species placed within the same genus should be more closely related to one another than to species of any other genus. Genera placed within a family should be more closely related to one another than to members of any other family. The same is true of all the other taxonomic levels, including kingdoms.

This strategy of grouping organisms together based on their evolutionary history is called **evolutionary classification**. It sounds simple, but it is not easy. Constructing an evolutionary classification scheme requires nothing less than understanding the history of life. It sometimes also requires a radical rethinking of how organisms should be classified. An example of the rethinking that sometimes occurs is shown in **Figure 18–7.** By comparing the two classification schemes, you can see how information about evolutionary history led scientists to change their views of how crabs, barnacles, and limpets should be classified.

PRESENTATIONS MADE EASY!

The Presentation Assistant Plus contains the Prentice Hall Presentation Pro and the Transparencies, which provide easy-to-follow visual support for every step of this section. If you have a computer presentation station, use Prentice Hall Presentation Pro for Section 18–2, or use the transparencies listed here.

Section 18–2: **Interest Grabber**
Section Outline
Traditional Classification Versus Cladistic Analysis

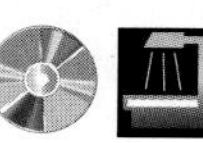

Classification Using Cladograms

To refine the process of evolutionary classification, many biologists now prefer a method called cladistic analysis. Cladistic analysis identifies and considers only those characteristics of organisms that are evolutionary innovations—new characteristics that arise as lineages evolve over time. Characteristics that appear in recent parts of a lineage but not in its older members are called **derived characters.**

Derived characters can be used to construct a **cladogram,** a diagram that shows the evolutionary relationships among a group of organisms. You can see an example of a cladogram on the right-hand side of **Figure 18–7.** Notice how derived characters, such as "free-swimming larva" and "segmentation," appear at certain locations along the branches of the cladogram. These locations are the points at which these characteristics first arose. You can see that crabs and barnacles share some derived characters that barnacles and limpets do not. One such shared derived character is a segmented body. Another is a molted exoskeleton. Thus, this cladogram groups crabs and barnacles together as crustaceans and separates them from limpets, which are classified as gastropods.

Cladograms are useful tools that help scientists understand how one lineage branched from another in the course of evolution. Just as a family tree shows the relationships among different lineages within a family, a cladogram represents a type of evolutionary tree, showing evolutionary relationships among a group of organisms.

CHECKPOINT *What is a cladogram?*

KEEP CURRENT WITH . . . SCIENCE NEWS®

To find out more about the topics in this chapter, go to: **www.phschool.com**

Quick Lab

How is a cladogram constructed?

Procedure

1. Identify the organism in the table that is least closely related to the others.
2. Use the information in the table to construct a cladogram of these animals.

Derived Characters in Organisms

Organism	Derived Character		
	Backbone	Legs	Hair
Earthworm	Absent	Absent	Absent
Trout	Present	Absent	Absent
Lizard	Present	Present	Absent
Human	Present	Present	Present

Analyze and Conclude

1. **Analyzing Data** What trait separates the least closely related organism from the other animals?
2. **Classifying** List the animals in your cladogram in order of distance from the least closely related organism.
3. **Drawing Conclusions** Does your cladogram indicate that lizards and humans share a more recent common ancestor than either does with an earthworm? Explain.
4. **Inferring** Where would you insert a frog if you added it to the cladogram? Explain your answer.

BIO INSIGHTS FACTS AND FIGURES

Homologous vs. analogous

When classifying organisms, taxonomists are careful to distinguish between homologous structures and analogous structures. Homologous structures have a similar structure and development pattern. However, the function of homologous structures may be different. The wing of a bird and the human arm are homologous structures due to their similar structure pattern of development. Analogous structures appear similar and perform similar functions; however, their structure and developmental patterns are quite different. The wing of a bird and the wing of a butterfly are analogous structures.

Classification Using Cladograms

SCIENCE NEWS®

Encourage students to visit **www.phschool.com** for the most current information on this topic.

Quick Lab

Objective Students will be able to construct a cladogram to classify a group of animals.

Skills Focus Classifying

Time 15 minutes

Strategy Explain that the outgroup in cladistic analysis is the organism that lacks at least one characteristic that all the other organisms share.

Procedure

1. Check that students have correctly identified the earthworm as the outgroup before they continue their analysis.
2. Refer students to Figure 18–7 for ideas about how to construct a cladogram.

Expected Outcome Students should draw a cladogram that shows backbones evolved first, followed by legs, and then by hair.

Analyze and Conclude

1. Backbone
2. Trout, lizard, and human
3. No; a cladogram does not necessarily show ancestral-descendant relationships.
4. A frog would occupy a branch between the trout and the lizard, because it has the derived characteristic of legs. Another derived characteristic, such as dry skin, would then have to be added for the lizard.

Answer to . . .

CHECKPOINT *A cladogram is a diagram that shows evolutionary relationships among organisms.*

Similarities in RNA and DNA

Make Connections

Chemistry Explain that the most precise method of comparing the DNA of two species is DNA sequencing, in which the researcher first prepares comparable DNA segments from two species and then determines the extent to which nucleotide sequences are the same in the two segments. (See Chapter 13, Section 2.) Another method, called DNA–DNA hybridization, measures the extent of hydrogen bonding between single strands of DNA from different species. The more hydrogen bonding that occurs, the greater the similarity between the DNA strands of the two species.

Demonstration

Obtain and display a copy of a cytochrome-c family tree, which is a phylogenetic tree based solely on mutations in the protein cytochrome-c. (Alternatively, you might want to ask students to research and locate a cytochrome-c tree.) Explain that cytochrome-c is a molecule that organisms need for cellular respiration. Point out how closely the phylogenetic tree based on this single important protein resembles traditional phylogenetic trees based on physical characteristics.

▲ **Figure 18–8 Similarities at the molecular level in the genes of organisms can be used to help determine classification.** Traditionally, African vultures (top) and American vultures (center) were classified together in the falcon family. But DNA analysis has revealed that American vultures are actually more closely related to storks (bottom).

Similarities in DNA and RNA

All of the classification methods discussed so far are based primarily on anatomical similarities and differences. But suppose you were trying to compare very diverse organisms such as humans and yeasts, which are single-celled organisms. Obviously, it is of little use to compare the anatomical features of such diverse organisms.

But even very different organisms have common traits. For example, all organisms use DNA and RNA to pass on information and to control growth and development. Hidden in the genetic code of all organisms are remarkably similar genes. Because DNA and RNA are so similar across all forms of life, these molecules provide an excellent way of comparing organisms at their most basic level—their genes.

The genes of many organisms show important similarities at the molecular level. These similarities can be used as criteria to help determine classification. Now that scientists can sequence, or "read," the information coded in DNA, they can compare the DNA of different organisms to trace the history of genes over millions of years.

Even the genes of diverse organisms such as humans and yeasts show many surprising similarities. For example, humans have a gene that codes for myosin, a protein found in our muscles. Researchers were surprised to find a gene in yeast that codes for a myosin protein. This was surprising because yeasts don't have muscles! As it turns out, myosin in yeast interacts with other proteins to enable internal cell parts to move. Myosin is just one example of similarities at the molecular level—an indicator that humans and yeasts share a common ancestry.

DNA comparisons have also shed light on classification questions regarding closely related species. For example, you can see that the bird in the top photograph of **Figure 18–8** looks a lot like the bird in the middle photograph. Both birds have traditionally been classified together as "vultures." One group of birds inhabits Africa and Asia, and the other, the Americas. But American vultures have a peculiar habit: When they get overheated, they urinate on their legs so that evaporative cooling removes some body heat. The only other birds known to behave this way are storks, which look quite different from vultures and have always been put in a separate family.

Should American vultures be classified with the other vultures in the falcon family? Or should they be put in a family with the storks? To answer these questions, scientists analyzed the DNA of these three birds. The DNA analysis revealed that American vultures are indeed more closely related to storks than they are to other vultures.

✔CHECKPOINT *What gene indicates that humans and yeast have a common ancestry?*

Molecular Clocks

Comparisons of DNA can also be used to mark the passage of evolutionary time. A model known as a **molecular clock** uses DNA comparisons to estimate the length of time that two species have been evolving independently. To understand molecular clocks, think about a pendulum clock. It marks time with a periodically swinging pendulum. A molecular clock also relies on a repeating process to mark time—mutation.

Simple mutations occur all the time, causing slight changes in the structure of DNA, as shown in **Figure 18–9.** Some mutations have a major positive or negative effect on an organism's phenotype. These mutations are under powerful pressure from natural selection. Other mutations have no effects on phenotype. These neutral mutations accumulate in the DNA of different species at about the same rate. A comparison of such DNA sequences in two species can reveal how dissimilar the genes are. The degree of dissimilarity is, in turn, an indication of how long ago the two species shared a common ancestor.

The use of molecular clocks is not simple, however, because there is not just one molecular clock in a genome. Instead, there are many, each of which "ticks" at a different rate. This is because some genes accumulate mutations faster than others. These different clocks allow researchers to time different kinds of evolutionary events. Think of a conventional clock. If you want to time a brief event, you pay attention to the second hand. To time an event that lasts longer, you use the minute hand or the hour hand. In the same way, researchers would use a different molecular clock to compare modern bird species than they would to estimate the age of the common ancestor of yeasts and humans.

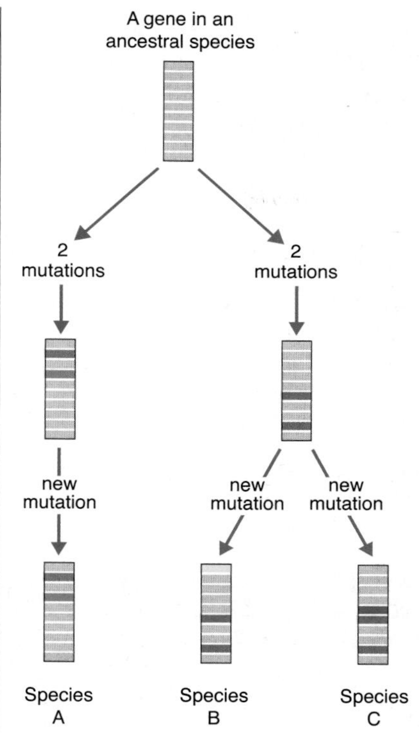

▲ **Figure 18–9** By comparing the DNA sequences of two or more species, biologists estimate how long the species have been separated. **Analyzing Data** ***What evidence indicates that species C is more closely related to species B than to species A?***

18–2 Section Assessment

1. **Key Concept** How is information about evolutionary relationships useful in classification?
2. **Key Concept** How are genes used to help scientists classify organisms?
3. What is the principle behind cladistic analysis?
4. Describe the relationship between evolutionary time and the similarity of genes in two species.
5. **Critical Thinking Applying Concepts** How have new discoveries in molecular biology affected the way in which we classify organisms compared with the system used by Linnaeus?

iTEXT Assessment Use iText to review the important concepts in Section 18–2.

ALTERNATIVE ASSESSMENT

Constructing a Chart
Draw a cladogram of a manufactured item, such as an automobile or a household item, that has changed over the years. Label derived characters that appeared as new models arose. For example, automobiles came to have electronic fuel injection and antilock brakes.

18–2 Section Assessment

1. Organisms are grouped according to evolutionary descent, not just physical similarities.
2. Scientists compare the DNA of different organisms to establish similarities between them and reconstruct possible evolutionary relationships.
3. Cladistic analysis traces the process of evolution in a group of organisms by focusing on unique features that appear in some organisms but not in others.
4. The longer it has been since two species descended from a common ancestor, the more different their genes are likely to be.
5. New ways of classifying organisms reflect evolutionary relationships based on genetic similarities, whereas Linnaeus's system of classifying organisms was based on physical similarities between organisms.

Molecular Clocks

Use Visuals

Figure 18–9 Have students read the caption of the figure. Then, ask: **Why do biologists study mutations in genes that do not code for essential proteins?** *(Those mutations occur in different species at about the same rate, and they can be used as a basis for comparison.)*

3 ASSESS

Evaluate Understanding

Have students make a Venn diagram to show similarities and differences between phylogenetic trees and cladograms.

Reteach

Call on students to explain in their own words what molecular clocks are, how they are used, and why some molecular clocks "tick" at different rates. Correct any errors or misunderstandings.

ALTERNATIVE ASSESSMENT

Students should draw a cladogram based on several derived characteristics of a type of manufactured item. Instead of the automobile, they might choose the television, video game, or camera. Their diagrams should show the order in which innovations were developed in the item they chose. For example, a cladogram for the television might show that this item first acquired colored pictures, then solid state circuitry, and then remote controls.

Use iText to review the key concepts in Section 18–2.

Answers to . . .

CHECKPOINT *A gene that codes for myosin protein*

Figure 18–9 *The DNA molecules in species B and C show two common mutations that do not appear in the DNA in species A.*

TECHNOLOGY & SOCIETY After students have read this feature, you might want to discuss one or more of the following:

- The reasons that new species are likely to live in remote, hard-to-reach places
- Why tropical forests have so many different species compared with other types of ecosystems
- How advances in technology, such as portable computers, wireless communications, and the Internet, have made research in remote locations easier and more efficient
- The ways that technological advances, such as electron microscopy and DNA analysis, are used to determine whether specimens are new species

On Your Own

Students should describe and sketch ideas for inventions that would help them search for new species high up in the tree canopy of a forest or in some other hard-to-reach place, such as a sheer rock wall, a deep cave, or the ocean floor. For example, students might describe and sketch a system of harnesses and platforms, similar to those used by window washers, to search for new species on sheer rock walls, or they might describe a pressurized compartment, like a bathysphere, to search for new species on the ocean floor.

The Search for New Species

How many kinds of living things are there on Earth? So far, scientists have identified about 1.5 million species. Yet, millions more have never been studied. Researchers continue to find new species—not just tiny organisms, but also fish, birds, and mammals.

Because new species are likely to live in remote, hard-to-reach places, scientists call on technology to help in the search, including scuba gear, helicopters, and ultralight airplanes. Remote cameras and e-mail let scientists in one spot follow the work of others continents away.

Exploring the Forest Roof

One place to search for new species is in tropical forests, which are teeming with life. Researchers especially want better ways to study the canopy—the upper layers of the forest. Scientists have used ropes to climb the tall trees, but it is hard to stay up long or collect specimens. Then, French researchers invented an unusual "raft" suspended from a hot-air balloon that floats over the tops of the trees. Scientists on the raft could work together for longer periods of time, collecting many more species.

One canopy explorer, biologist Margaret Lowman, worked with a structural engineer to design and build a canopy walkway as her "green laboratory." The walkway looks like a huge treehouse 75 feet above the forest floor, with platforms on which researchers can work.

Another new and dramatic route into the canopy is a huge construction crane like those used in building skyscrapers. Scientists on the arm of the crane get a close-up look at trees. Today there is a worldwide network of forest crane sites.

New Species or Not?

When researchers spot an unfamiliar organism, they may use simple observation to classify it. How many petals are on the flower? How many toes are on the animal? If the organism does not match known categories, the species may be new. Unusual antlers, for instance, were a major clue in identifying a new deer species in Vietnam.

External appearances can fool you, however. X-rays and electron microscopes may reveal differences that set one species apart from another. The most exciting advances have come with studies of DNA. By analyzing DNA, scientists can demonstrate how two organisms are—or are not—related.

On Your Own

Describe and sketch your own ideas for an invention that would help scientists search for new species in a forest canopy or other location that is hard to reach.

18–3 Kingdoms and Domains

In taxonomy, as in all areas of science, ideas and models change as new information arises. Some explanations have been discarded altogether, whereas others, such as Darwin's theory of evolution by natural selection, have been upheld and refined through years of research. So, it should not be surprising that early attempts at drawing life's universal tree were based on some misguided assumptions. Some of the earliest trees of life were dominated by humans. These models represented vertebrates as the most important and abundant animals. They also implied that "higher" animals evolved from "lower" animals that were identical to modern forms. Biologists now know these notions are incorrect.

The Tree of Life Evolves

The scientific view of life was simpler in Linnaeus's time. The only known differences among living things were the fundamental traits that separated animals from plants. Animals were mobile organisms that used food for energy. Plants were green, photosynthetic organisms that used energy from the sun.

As biologists learned more about the natural world, they realized that Linnaeus's two kingdoms, Animalia and Plantae, did not adequately represent the full diversity of life. First, microorganisms, such as the protist and bacterium in **Figure 18–10,** were recognized as being significantly different from plants and animals. Scientists soon agreed that microorganisms merited their own kingdom, which was named Protista. Then, the mushrooms, yeasts, and molds were separated from the plants and placed in their own kingdom, Fungi. Later still, scientists realized that bacteria lack the nuclei, mitochondria, and chloroplasts found in other forms of life. Therefore, they were placed in another new kingdom, Monera. This process produced five kingdoms—Monera, Protista, Fungi, Plantae, and Animalia.

Guide for Reading

Key Concepts
- What are the six kingdoms of life as they are now identified?
- What is the three-domain system of classification?

Vocabulary
- domain • Bacteria
- Eubacteria • Archaea
- Archaebacteria • Eukarya
- Protista • Fungi
- Plantae • Animalia

Reading Strategy: Classifying As you read, write the names of the six kingdoms recognized by biologists. Label each group as either prokaryotes or eukaryotes.

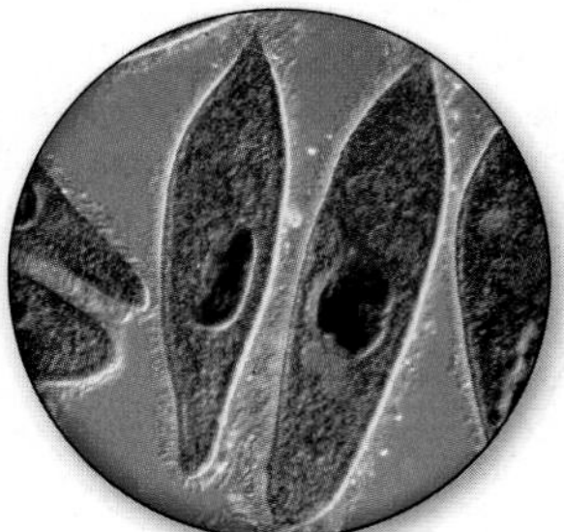

Paramecium caudatum
(magnification: about 1000×)

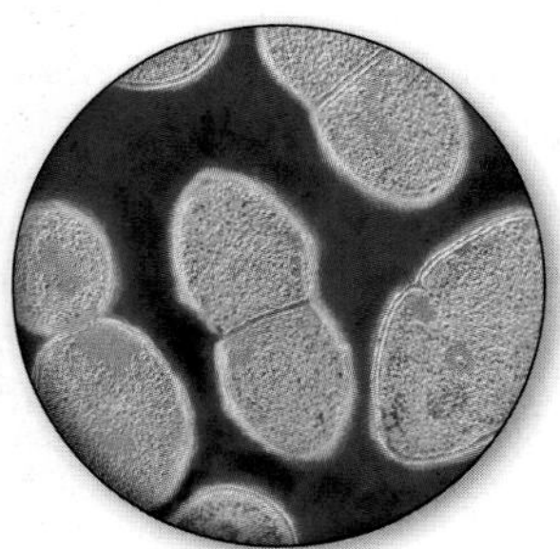

Streptococcus faecalis
(magnification: 26,000×)

Figure 18–10 The paramecium (left) is a single-celled organism that is eukaryotic, or has a nucleus. *Streptococcus faecalis* (right) is a bacterium that evolved long before eukaryotic cells. Bacteria are prokaryotes—they do not have membrane-bound organelles. The classification of these two organisms has changed greatly over the years. **Classifying** ***List reasons that these two organisms should be classified in separate kingdoms.***

SECTION RESOURCES

Print:
- ***Laboratory Manual B,*** Chapter 18 Lab
- ***Teaching Resources,*** Section Review 18–3, Chapter 18 Real-World Lab
- ***Guided Reading and Study Workbook,*** Section 18–3

Technology:
- ***iText,*** Section 18–3

Section 18–3

1 FOCUS

Objectives

18.3.1 ***Name*** the six kingdoms of life as they are now identified.

18.3.2 ***Describe*** the three-domain system of classification.

Guide for Reading

Vocabulary Preview

Introduce students to the Vocabulary terms by explaining that the term *domain,* like the term *kingdom,* refers to a very broad grouping of related organisms. Add that all of the other Vocabulary terms are the names of specific kingdoms or domains.

Reading Strategy

Students should label the Archaebacteria and Eubacteria as prokaryotes, and they should label the Protists, Plantae, Fungi, and Animalia as eukaryotes.

2 INSTRUCT

The Tree of Life Evolves

Build Science Skills

Inferring Remind students that all the kingdoms in the six-kingdom system are eukaryotes except for the two bacterial kingdoms. Ask: **As the only prokaryotic kingdoms, how do Eubacteria and Archaebacteria differ from the other four kingdoms?** *(They lack nuclei, mitochondria, and chloroplasts, and they reproduce by binary fission.)*

Answer to . . .

Figure 18–10 *Bacteria do not contain nuclei or mitochondria, as do paramecia. Bacteria are prokaryotic; paramecia are eukaryotic.*

The Three-Domain System

Address Misconceptions

Students may not understand why bacteria are put into two separate domains while all other living things are put into just one domain. Stress that organisms are grouped into domains according to how long they have been evolving independently. Remind students that bacteria have been evolving for 3.5 billion years, as compared with 2.0 billion years or less for eukaryotic organisms.

Meet Diverse Needs

Encourage students who need an extra challenge to research the proposed nine-kingdom system of classification, in which protists are divided into three separate kingdoms. Students should find the criteria for dividing the protists into kingdoms and the rationale behind selecting those particular criteria. Students should also try to assess how widely accepted the nine-kingdom classification system is. Urge students to share what they learn in an oral report. **Learning modality: verbal**

Changing Number of Kingdoms

First Introduced	Names of Kingdoms					
1700s	Plantae					Animalia
Late 1800s	Protista			Plantae		Animalia
1950s	Monera		Protista	Fungi	Plantae	Animalia
1990s	Eubacteria	Archaebacteria	Protista	Fungi	Plantae	Animalia

▲ **Figure 18–11** This diagram shows some of the ways organisms have been classified into kingdoms over the years. **The six-kingdom system includes the following kingdoms: Eubacteria, Archaebacteria, Protista, Fungi, Plantae, and Animalia.**

In recent years, as evidence about microorganisms continued to accumulate, biologists came to recognize that the Monera were composed of two distinct groups. Some biologists consider the differences between these two groups to be as great as those between animals and plants. As a result, the Monera have been separated into two kingdoms, Eubacteria and Archaebacteria, bringing the total number of kingdoms to six.

The six-kingdom system of classification includes the kingdoms Eubacteria, Archaebacteria, Protista, Fungi, Plantae, and Animalia. This system of classification is shown in the bottom row of **Figure 18–11.**

The Three-Domain System

Some of the most recent evolutionary trees have been produced using comparative studies of a small subunit of ribosomal RNA that occurs in all living things. Using a molecular clock model, scientists have grouped modern organisms according to how long they have been evolving independently.

Molecular analyses have given rise to a new taxonomic category that is now recognized by many scientists. The **domain** is a more inclusive category than any other—larger than a kingdom. **The three domains are: the domain Bacteria, which corresponds to the kingdom Eubacteria; the domain Archaea, which corresponds to the kingdom Archaebacteria; and the domain Eukarya, which is composed of protists, fungi, plants, and animals.**

Clearly, modern classification is a rapidly changing science, and we must pick a convention to classify life's diversity for the purposes of this book. In this book, we recognize the three domains and also refer frequently to the six kingdoms. The relationship between the three domains and the six kingdoms is shown in **Figure 18–12.** It also summarizes the key characteristics of each kingdom. You can see that some groups share one or more traits with other groups.

TIME SAVER — PRESENTATIONS MADE EASY!

The Presentation Assistant Plus contains the Prentice Hall Presentation Pro and the Transparencies, which provide easy-to-follow visual support for every step of this section. If you have a computer presentation station, use Prentice Hall Presentation Pro for Section 18–3, or use the transparencies listed here.

Section 18–3: **Interest Grabber**

Section Outline
Concept Map
Figure 18–12
Figure 18–13

Domain Bacteria

The members of the domain **Bacteria** are unicellular and prokaryotic. Their cells have thick, rigid cell walls that surround a cell membrane. The cell walls contain a substance known as peptidoglycan. The domain Bacteria corresponds to the kingdom **Eubacteria.** These bacteria are ecologically diverse, ranging from free-living soil organisms to deadly parasites. Some photosynthesize, while others do not. Some need oxygen to survive, while others are killed by oxygen.

Domain Archaea

Also unicellular and prokaryotic, members of the domain **Archaea** live in some of the most extreme environments you can imagine—volcanic hot springs, brine pools, and black organic mud totally devoid of oxygen. Indeed, many of these bacteria can survive only in the absence of oxygen. Their cell walls lack peptidoglycan, and their cell membranes contain unusual lipids that are not found in any other organism. The domain Archaea corresponds to the kingdom **Archaebacteria.**

CHECKPOINT ***What characteristics distinguish members of the domain Bacteria from members of the domain Archaea?***

▼ **Figure 18–12** **Organisms are grouped in three domains. There is a simple relationship between the three domains and the six kingdoms.** This table summarizes key evidence used in classifying organisms into these major taxonomic groups.

Classification of Living Things

DOMAIN	Bacteria	Archaea	Eukarya			
KINGDOM	**Eubacteria**	**Archaebacteria**	**Protista**	**Fungi**	**Plantae**	**Animalia**
CELL TYPE	Prokaryote	Prokaryote	Eukaryote	Eukaryote	Eukaryote	Eukaryote
CELL STRUCTURES	Cell walls with peptidoglycan	Cell walls without peptidoglycan	Cell walls of cellulose in some; some have chloroplasts	Cell walls of chitin	Cell walls of cellulose; chloroplasts	No cell walls or chloroplasts
NUMBER OF CELLS	Unicellular	Unicellular	Most unicellular; some colonial; some multicellular	Most multicellular; some unicellular	Multicellular	Multicellular
MODE OF NUTRITION	Autotroph or heterotroph	Autotroph or heterotroph	Autotroph or heterotroph	Heterotroph	Autotroph	Heterotroph
EXAMPLES	*Streptococcus, Escherichia coli*	Methanogens, halophiles	*Amoeba, Paramecium,* slime molds, giant kelp	Mushrooms, yeasts	Mosses, ferns, flowering plants	Sponges, worms, insects, fishes, mammals

Domain Bacteria

Build Science Skills

Classifying Have students assume that they are biologists and that they have just discovered a new species. The organism makes its own food, has no nucleus, and has peptidoglycan in its cell walls. Ask: **In which domain should you classify this species?** *(Bacteria)* **In which kingdom does it belong?** *(Eubacteria)*

Domain Archaea

Build Science Skills

Inferring Point out that Archaea are the most ancient organisms on Earth and they exist in extreme environments. Ask: **What explains the ability of Archaea to live in extreme environments?** *(The early Earth had extreme environments, and this was when Archaea first evolved.)*

Use Visuals

Figure 18–12 Check students' comprehension of the table. Ask: **How many cells do Archaea have?** *(Archaea are unicellular.)* **What makes Fungi different from Protists?** *(Fungi have cell walls of chitin.)* **What sets Animalia apart from all other kingdoms of organisms?** *(Animals do not have cell walls or chloroplasts)* **What sets Plantae apart from all other kingdoms?** *(Plants have cell walls of cellulose.)*

Answer to . . .

CHECKPOINT *Members of domain Archaea live in extreme environments, whereas members of domain Bacteria are ecologically diverse. Also, the cell walls of Bacteria contain peptidoglycan, while those of Archaea do not.*

Domain Eukarya

Meet Diverse Needs

Have students use field guides, encyclopedias, textbooks, or other sources to find examples of Eukarya in each kingdom. Suggest that they sketch or copy photographs of several species in each kingdom and use the images to create a poster illustrating the diversity of Eukarya. Display their posters in the classroom. **Learning modality: visual**

Demonstration

Use a microprojector to show students examples of unicellular protists, including amoebae and paramecia. Have students identify the characteristics—such as nuclei, cell walls, and chloroplasts—that are used to classify the organisms as protists. Suggest that students sketch the organisms and label the important structures.

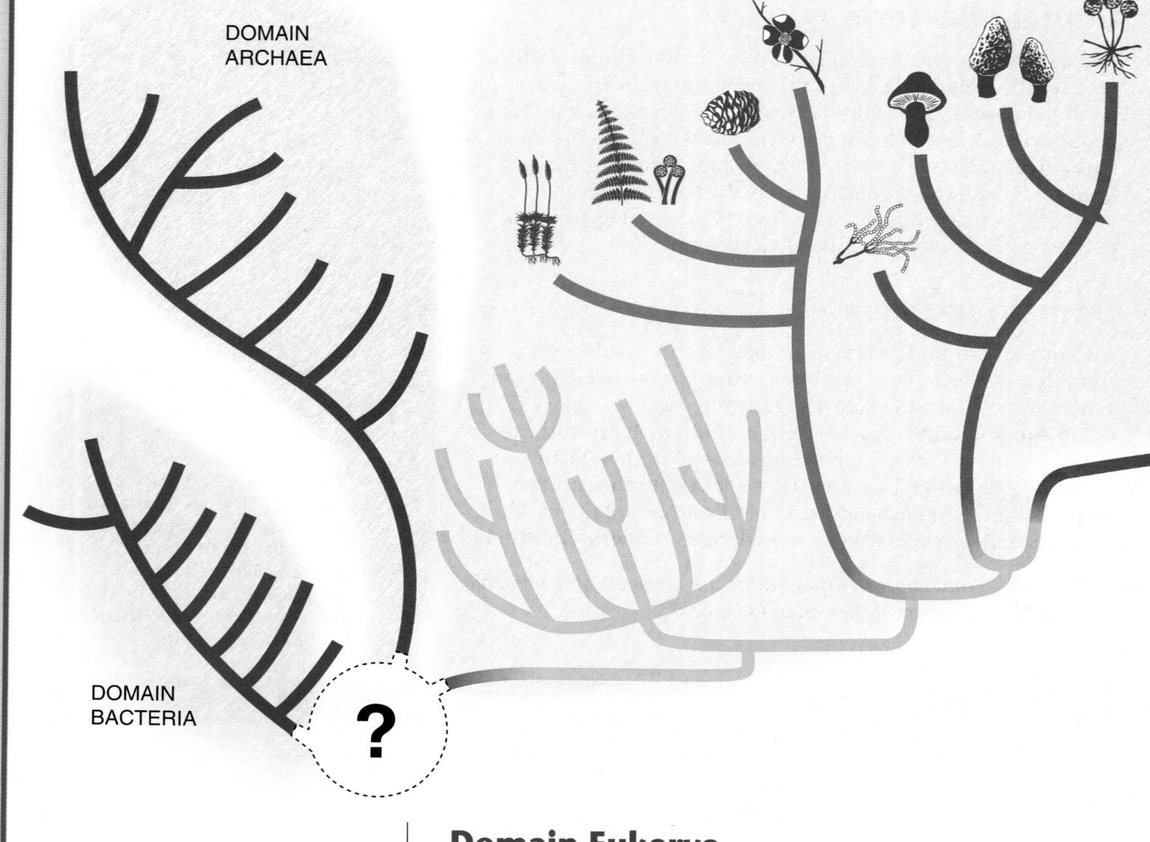

Domain Eukarya

The domain **Eukarya** consists of all organisms that have a nucleus. It is organized into the four remaining kingdoms of the six-kingdom system: Protista, Fungi, Plantae, and Animalia, as shown in **Figure 18–13.**

Protista The kingdom **Protista** is composed of eukaryotic organisms that cannot be classified as animals, plants, or fungi. Of the six kingdoms, Protista is the least satisfying classification, because its members display the greatest variety. Most protists are single-celled organisms, but some, such as the multicellular algae, are not. Some protists are photosynthetic, while others are heterotrophic. Some share characteristics with plants, others with fungi, and still others with animals.

Fungi Members of the kingdom **Fungi** are heterotrophs. Most feed on dead or decaying organic matter. Unlike other heterotrophs, these fungi secrete digestive enzymes into their food source. They then absorb the smaller food molecules into their bodies.

Most fungi are multicellular. The most recognizable fungi are mushrooms. Some fungi, such as yeasts, are unicellular.

FACTS AND FIGURES

By any other name

The term *algae* is the plural form of the Latin word *alga,* which means seaweed. However, not all algae are seaweed, and not all seaweed is algae. The term *algae* is actually used to represent a different range of organisms that may belong to any of two different kingdoms. Yellow-green algae, golden-brown algae, and certain types of brown, red, and green algae belong to the kingdom Protista. Most green algae and certain types of red and brown algae are classified as plants due to the presence of photosynthetic pigments.

▲ **Figure 18–13** The domains Bacteria and Archaea include the same organisms that are in the kingdoms Eubacteria and Archaebacteria. The domain Eukarya includes the protists, fungi, plants, and animals. Biologists continue to investigate how these three large groups originated. **Interpreting Graphics** ***Which domain includes organisms from more than one kingdom?***

Plantae Members of the kingdom **Plantae** are multicellular organisms that are photosynthetic autotrophs. In other words, they carry out photosynthesis. Plants are nonmotile—they cannot move from place to place. They also have cell walls that contain cellulose. The plant kingdom includes cone-bearing and flowering plants as well as mosses and ferns. Although older classification systems regard multicellular algae as plants, in this book we group algae with the protists.

Animalia Members of the kingdom **Animalia** are multicellular and heterotrophic. The cells of animals do not have cell walls. Most animals can move about, at least for some part of their life cycle. As you will see in later chapters, there is incredible diversity within the animal kingdom, and many species of animals exist in nearly every part of the planet.

18–3 Section Assessment

1. **Key Concept** What are the six kingdoms of life as they are now identified?
2. **Key Concept** What are the three domains of life?
3. Why was the kingdom Monera divided into two separate kingdoms?
4. Why might kingdom Protista be thought of as the "odds and ends" kingdom?
5. **Critical Thinking Classifying** Which kingdoms include only prokaryotes? Which kingdoms include only heterotrophs?

iTEXT Assessment Use iText to review the important concepts in Section 18–3.

MAKING CONNECTIONS

Cell Structures Review what you learned in Chapter 3 about how the cells of various organisms differ. Then, write a riddle describing the characteristics of members of a particular kingdom. Exchange your riddle with a classmate, and see if you can guess the kingdom being described.

18–3 Section Assessment

1. The six kingdoms are Archaebacteria, Eubacteria, Protista, Plantae, Fungi, and Animalia.
2. The three domains are Archaea, Bacteria, and Eukarya.
3. Monera was divided into two kingdoms because scientists have come to recognize profound differences among two broad groups of Monera.
4. Members of the kingdom Protista display the greatest variety, sharing characteristics with plants, fungi, or animals; protists cannot be classified in any other group.
5. Eubacteria and Archaebacteria include only prokaryotes. Fungi and Animalia contain only heterotrophs.

Use Visuals

Figure 18–13 Ask students to identify by color each of the kingdoms of Eukarya in the diagram. *(The red segment is Animalia, the brown segment is Fungi, the green segment is Plantae, and the yellow segment is Protista.)*

3 ASSESS

Evaluate Understanding

Call on students at random to name the kingdoms in the six-kingdom classification system. Call on other students to name examples of organisms in each kingdom.

Reteach

Write the name of each of the three domains on the chalkboard. Then, have students brainstorm characteristics of organisms in each domain. List the characteristics on the board under the name of the corresponding domain.

MAKING CONNECTIONS

Students' riddles should include several of the characteristics listed in Figure 18–12 on page 459—characteristics of prokaryotic, plant, or animal cells.

Use iText to review the key concepts in Section 18–3.

Answer to . . .

Figure 18–13 *Domain Eukarya*

Real-World Lab

Objective Students will be able to make and use a dichotomous key to classify organic specimens.

Skills Focus **Observing, Classifying, Forming Operational Definitions**

Time 45 minutes

Advance Prep

- For Part B, obtain graphite pencils (with and without erasers) and ballpoint and felt-tip pens. Other groups of items may include: different types of nuts and bolts or different types of nails and pens.

Teaching Strategies Have students read the entire procedure. Explain that the term *dichotomous* means "having two forms." Add that a dichotomous key uses two forms of each of several characteristics to identify a species. Then, ask: **What characteristics are used in the dichotomous key to identify leaves?** *(Whether the leaf is simple or compound, how the leaflets are arranged, how the leaf veins are arranged, the shape of the leaf edge, and the shape of the leaf)* **How many choices are you given for each characteristic?** *(Two)* **Could you use the same set of characteristics to identify leaves of species other than the ones shown in the book?** *(Yes, if they differed in these characteristics.)*

Procedure

1–3. Make sure students take time to familiarize themselves with the two forms of each characteristic so they will be less likely to make a mistake in the identification process.

Real-World Lab

Using Dichotomous Keys

What tools are available to help people identify unfamiliar organisms? One is a field guide, a book with illustrations that highlight differences between similar-looking organisms. Another tool used to identify organisms is a dichotomous key. A dichotomous key is a series of paired statements that describe physical characteristics of different organisms. In this activity, you will use a dichotomous key to identify tree leaves.

Problem How are dichotomous keys used and made?

Materials 

- 6–8 writing implements or other group of common items

Skills Observing, Classifying, Forming Operational Definitions

Procedure

Part A: Using a Dichotomous Key

1. To use the dichotomous key for leaves, begin by reading paired statements 1a and 1b. Notice that the statements are opposites.
2. Carefully observe the leaf labeled I on page 463. Decide which statement, 1a or 1b, applies to this leaf. Then, follow the direction at the end of the statement. For example, because the leaf is a simple leaf, go to step 2.
3. Continue reading the paired statements and following the direction at the end of the applicable statement until you determine the identity of leaf I.
4. Repeat steps 2 and 3 for leaves II through VII.

Part B: Constructing a Dichotomous Key

5. Examine the writing implements or other group of items your teacher gives you. List some characteristics you could use to classify these items into groups.
6. Using the dichotomous key from Part A as a model, construct a dichotomous key for your group of items. You may wish to use some of the characteristics you listed in step 5 to construct your key. Make sure that each of the paired statements in your key are opposites.
7. Once your dichotomous key is complete, test it with each item and revise your key, if necessary.
8. Exchange keys and items with a classmate. Use your classmate's key to identify his or her items. Then, suggest ways to improve that key.

Dichotomous Key for Leaves

1. Compound or simple leaf
   1a) Compound leaf (leaf divided into leaflets) ....go to step 2
   1b) Simple leaf (leaf not divided into leaflets) ....go to step 4
2. Arrangement of leaflets
   2a) Palmate arrangement of leaflets (leaflets all attached at one central point) ....*Aesculus* (buckeye)
   2b) Pinnate arrangement of leaflets (leaflets attached at several points) ....go to step 3
3. Leaflet shape
   3a) Leaflets taper to pointed tips ....*Carya* (pecan)
   3b) Oval leaflets with rounded tips ....*Robinia* (locust)
4. Arrangement of leaf veins
   4a) Veins branch out from one central point ....go to step 5
   4b) Veins branch off main vein in the middle of the leaf ....go to step 6
5. Overall shape of leaf
   5a) Leaf is heart shaped..........*Cercis* (redbud)
   5b) Leaf is star shaped ....*Liquidambar* (sweet gum)
6. Appearance of leaf edge
   6a) Leaf has toothed (jagged) edge ....*Betula* (birch)
   6b) Leaf has untoothed (smooth) edge ....*Magnolia* (magnolia)

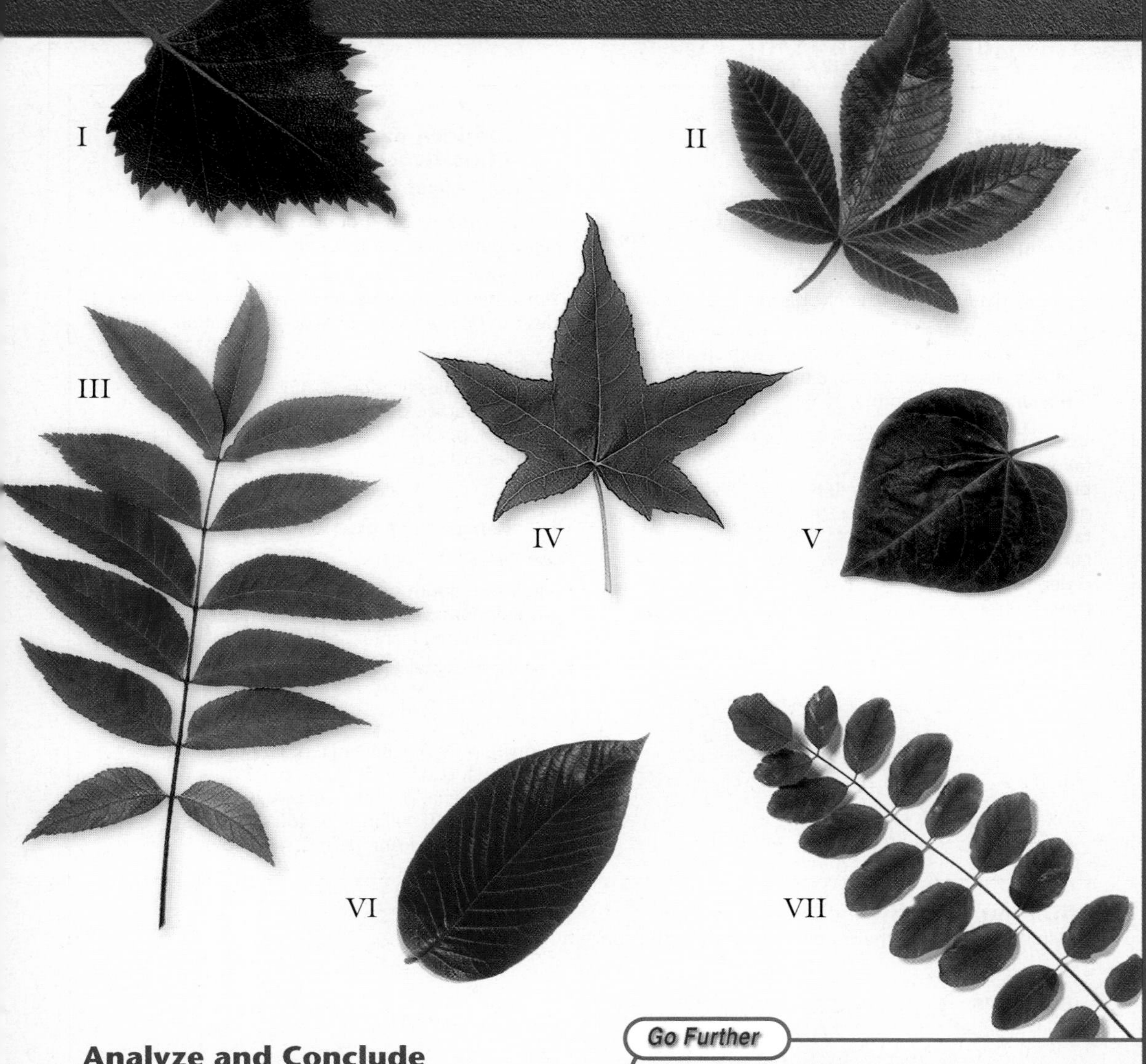

5. Characteristics students select will vary depending on the group of items. For example, if writing implements are used, they might select the characteristic ink/inkless. Each characteristic they select should vary in at least one of the items.
6. Make sure that all of the characteristics students select are dichotomous. For example, color is not a dichotomous characteristic, but black or nonblack is a dichotomous characteristic.

Go Further

Students may indicate that the descriptions and drawings of the basic leaf types and tree shapes helped to determine the identity of each tree. Field guides also provide the following characteristics of trees: types of fruits and flowers and habitats.

Analyze and Conclude

1. **Classifying** In Part A, identify leaves I through VII.
2. **Applying Concepts** In Part B, how did you choose the characteristics for your key? How did you decide on the key's order?
3. **Evaluating and Revising** Based on your classmate's feedback, does the key you developed in Part B need to be revised? If so, how?
4. **Inferring** Why is it important that the paired statements in a dichotomous key be opposites?

Go Further

Classifying Collect 3 or 4 leaves from different trees in your neighborhood. Then, use a field guide to trees in your area to determine the identity of each tree. Which characteristics of the leaves were useful in determining their identity? In addition to leaves, does the field guide use other characteristics of the trees to help identify them? If so, which ones?

Analyze and Conclude
1. I: *Betula* (birch); II: *Aesculus* (buckeye); III: *Carya* (pecan); IV: *Liquidambar* (sweetgum); V: *Cercis* (redbud); VI: *Magnolia* (magnolia); VII: *Robinia* (locust)
2. Characteristics chosen will depend on the writing implements or groups of items provided.
3. Students' answers will depend on which characteristics they chose for their classifications.
4. Paired statements must be opposites because each statement leads to either another step or identification of the species.

Chapter 18 Study Guide

Study Tip

Suggest that students review the chapter by studying the figures and their captions.

Thinking Visually

1. Classes
2. Archaebacteria
3. Protista
4. Plantae
5. Fungi
6. Animalia

Chapter 18 Assessment

Reviewing Content

1. b **2.** d **3.** c **4.** a **5.** a **6.** d **7.** d **8.** c **9.** b **10.** c

Note: There may be some confusion regarding "d" as the answer to question 2. In a scientific name such as *Rhizopus nigricans*, the first word is the name of the genus. The two words together name the species. The second word alone is not a scientific name.

Understanding Concepts

11. Biologists assign each organism a universally accepted name to provide consistency and avoid confusion.

12. Each organism is given a two-part scientific name consisting of the genus and species. The system must show evolutionary relationships as well as emphasize the structural similarities of the organisms.

13. Binomial nomenclature is useful to all scientists because it uses a single name that identifies the genus and species.

14. The seven taxonomic groups are: species, genus, family, order, class, phylum, and kingdom.

15. The goal of evolutionary classification is to group organisms based on their evolutionary history instead of grouping only according to physical similarities.

16. A derived character is a characteristic that appears in recent parts of a lineage but not in its older members; segmentation is an example.

Chapter 18 Study Guide

18–1 Finding Order in Diversity

Key Concepts

- To study the diversity of life, biologists use a classification system to name organisms and group them in a logical manner.
- In binomial nomenclature, each species is assigned a two-part scientific name.
- Linnaeus's system of classification uses seven taxonomic categories. They are—from smallest to largest—species, genus, family, order, class, phylum, and kingdom.

Vocabulary

taxonomy, p. 447
binomial nomenclature, p. 448
genus, p. 448
taxon, p. 449
family, p. 449
order, p. 449
class, p. 449
phylum, p. 449
kingdom, p. 449

18–2 Modern Evolutionary Classification

Key Concepts

- Organisms are now grouped into categories that represent lines of evolutionary descent.
- The genes of many organisms show important similarities at the molecular level. These similarities can be used as criteria for classification.

Vocabulary

evolutionary classification, p. 452
derived character, p. 453
cladogram, p. 453
molecular clock, p. 455

18–3 Kingdoms and Domains

Key Concepts

- The six-kingdom system of classification includes the kingdoms, Eubacteria, Archaebacteria, Protista, Fungi, Plantae, and Animalia.
- The three domains are Bacteria, Archaea, and Eukarya.

Vocabulary

- domain, p. 458 • Bacteria, p. 459
- Eubacteria, p. 459 • Archaea, p. 459
- Archaebacteria, p. 459 • Eukarya, p. 460
- Protista, p. 460 • Fungi, p. 460
- Plantae, p. 461 • Animalia, p. 461

Thinking Visually

Use information from the chapter to complete the concept map below.

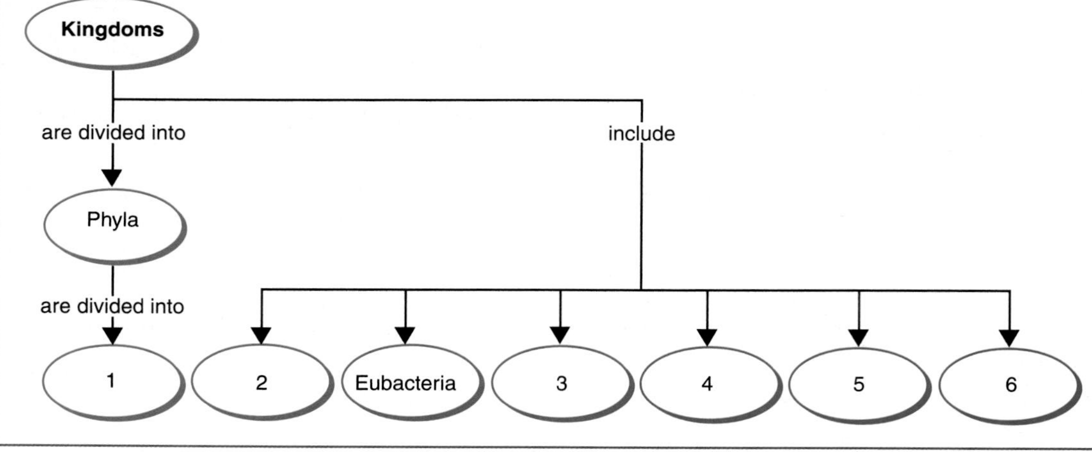

CHAPTER RESOURCES

TIME SAVER

Print:

- ***Teaching Resources,*** Chapter Vocabulary Review, Graphic Organizer
- ***Chapter Tests: Levels A and B,*** Chapter 18 Test
- ***PH Assessment System,*** Practice Test

Technology:

- ***Computer Test Bank,*** Chapter 18 Test
- ***iText,*** Chapter 18 Assessment

Chapter 18 Assessment

Reviewing Content

Choose the letter that best answers the question or completes the statement.

1. The science that specializes in the classification of organisms is
   a. anatomy. **c.** botany.
   b. taxonomy. **d.** paleontology.
2. Solely from its name, you know that *Rhizopus nigricans* must be
   a. a plant.
   b. an animal.
   c. in the genus *nigricans.*
   d. in the genus *Rhizopus.*
3. A useful classification system does NOT
   a. show relationships.
   b. reveal evolutionary trends.
   c. use different scientific names for the same organism.
   d. change the taxon of an organism based on new data.
4. In classifying organisms, orders are grouped together into
   a. classes. **c.** families.
   b. phyla. **d.** genera.
5. The largest and most inclusive of Linnaeus's taxonomic categories is the
   a. kingdom. **c.** phylum.
   b. order. **d.** species.
6. Which of the following shows the evolutionary relationships among a group of organisms?
   a. taxon
   b. molecular clock
   c. binomial nomenclature
   d. cladogram
7. A unique trait that is used to construct a cladogram is called a
   a. taxon. **c.** domain.
   b. molecular clock. **d.** derived character.
8. The three domains are
   a. Animalia, Plantae, Archaebacteria.
   b. Plantae, Fungi, Eubacteria.
   c. Bacteria, Archaea, Eukarya.
   d. Protista, Bacteria, Animalia.
9. A kingdom that includes only heterotrophs is
   a. Protista.
   b. Fungi.
   c. Plantae.
   d. Eubacteria.
10. Which organism belongs in the kingdom Animalia?

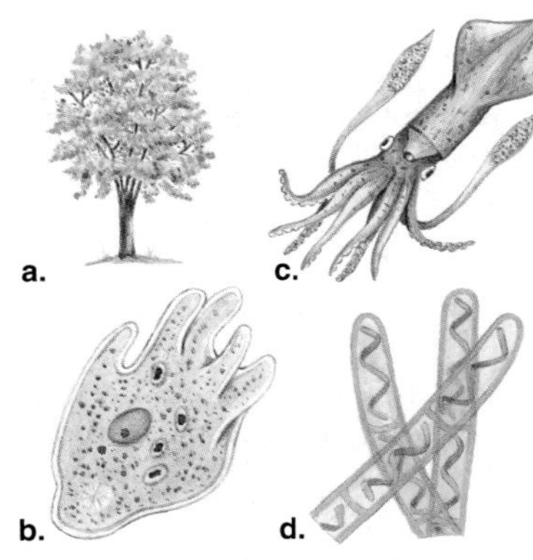

Understanding Concepts

11. Why do biologists assign each organism a universally accepted name?
12. What criteria are used to classify an organism?
13. What features of binomial nomenclature make it useful for scientists of all nations?
14. Sequence the seven taxonomic categories from smallest to largest.
15. Explain the goal of evolutionary classification.
16. What is a derived character? Give an example of a derived character.
17. How is a cladogram used in classification?
18. How do biologists use DNA and RNA to help classify organisms?
19. What do scientists conclude from the presence of myosin in both humans and yeasts?
20. Describe how a molecular clock is used to estimate the length of time that two related species have been evolving independently.
21. How do domains and kingdoms differ?
22. What characteristics are used to place an organism in the domain Bacteria?
23. In which domain are organisms from the most extreme environments placed?
24. Describe the four kingdoms that comprise the domain Eukarya.
25. What characteristic(s) differentiate the kingdom Fungi from the kingdom Plantae?

17. A cladogram traces the process of evolution in a group of organisms by focusing on unique features that appear in some organisms but not in others.

18. RNA and DNA are used to help classify organisms at the molecular level, because these molecules are so similar across all forms of life. They provide an excellent way of comparing organisms that look extremely different as well as very similar.

19. Scientists conclude that myosin is one of the proteins that carry out similar functions in very different organisms, an indication of common ancestry.

20. A molecular clock relies on a repeating process, a mutation, to estimate the length of time that two species have been evolving independently. A comparison of DNA sequences in two species indicates how alike or dissimilar the genes are. The degree of dissimilarity is, in turn, an indication of how long ago the species shared a common ancestor.

21. A domain is more inclusive and larger than a kingdom.

22. Members of domain Bacteria are all unicellular and prokaryotic. Cell walls contain peptidoglycan.

23. They are placed in the kingdom Archaea.

24. The four kingdoms making up the domain Eukarya are Protists, Fungi, Plantae, and Animalia.

25. Members of the kingdom Fungi typically obtain energy and nutrients from dead organic material. Members of the kingdom Plantae are multicellular organisms that are photosynthetic autotrophs.

HOMEWORK GUIDE

Section:	Questions:
Section 18–1	1–5, 11–14, 27, 28, 31, 33, 35
Section 18–2	6, 7, 15–20, 26, 29
Section 18–3	8–10, 21–25, 30, 32, 34

Chapter 18 Assessment

Critical Thinking

26. Biochemical tests can be used to compare the differences in the DNA of organisms either directly or indirectly. The more closely the DNA sequences match, the more closely related are the organisms.

27. Taxonomic classification emphasizes both. Similarities place organisms together in large groups, and differences separate organisms into smaller groups.

28. *Entamoeba histolytica* and *Entamoeba coli* are more closely related because they belong to the same genus.

29. Students' answers should indicate that the internal structures would have to be examined for similarities and that the organisms would have to be examined for genetic similarities and differences.

30. Mushrooms are heterotrophic, and plants are photosynthetic. The cell walls of a mushroom are composed of chitin, while the cell walls of plants are composed of cellulose.

31. A is labeled *All Animals,* B is labeled *Animals With Backbones,* C is labeled *Mammals,* and D is labeled *Insects.*

32. This organism would be placed in the kingdom Protista because it is unicellular, contains a nuclear membrane, and has chloroplasts.

33. Organisms in the same family have many characteristics in common. The fact that the organisms are in two genera indicates that they have very specific structural, genetic, biochemical, or evolutionary differences.

34. Organism A belongs in the kingdom Plantae. Organism B belongs in the kingdom Archaebacteria. Organism C belongs in the kingdom Protista.

35. Gene mutations would probably be more useful because chromosomal mutations may cause abnormalities that can be harmful. Gene mutations are more likely to be neutral, and thus suitable for use as molecular clocks.

Chapter 18 Assessment

Critical Thinking

26. Applying Concepts How did advances in scientific technology influence the classification of organisms?

27. Making Judgments Does taxonomic classification place emphasis on the similarities between organisms, the differences between organisms, or both? Explain your reasoning.

28. Inferring Which two of the following species are more closely related: *Entamoeba histolytica, Escherichia coli, Entamoeba coli*? Explain your answer.

29. Applying Concepts Both snakes and worms are tube-shaped, with no legs. How could you determine whether the similarity in shape means that they share a recent common ancestor?

30. Comparing and Contrasting Compare the characteristics of fungi with those of plants. Why are mushrooms not placed in the same kingdom as other food sources that people call "vegetables"?

31. Classifying Venn diagrams can be used to make models of classification schemes. A Venn diagram is shown below. Four groups are represented by circular regions—A, B, C, and D. Each region represents a collection of organisms or members of a taxonomic level. Regions that overlap, or intersect, share common members. Regions that do not overlap do not have members in common. Use the following terms to label the regions shown in the diagram: All Animals, Animals That Have Backbones, Insects, Mammals.

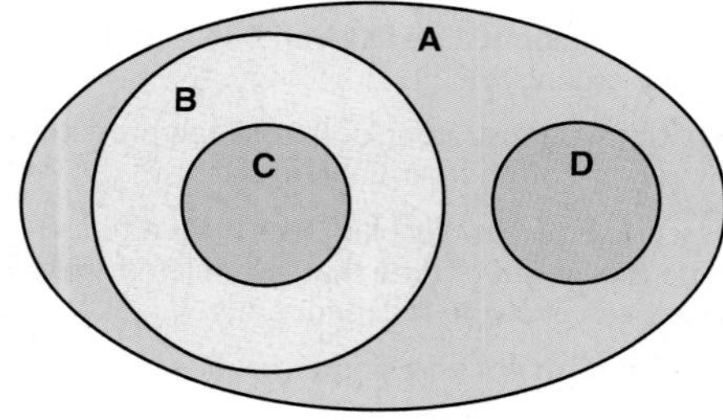

32. Classifying Suppose you discovered a new single-celled organism. This organism has a nucleus, mitochondria, and a giant chloroplast. In which kingdom would you place this organism? What are your reasons?

33. Applying Concepts Two groups of organisms are in different genera, but they are included in the same family. What does this information tell you about the two groups?

34. Classifying Study the descriptions of the following organisms and place them in the correct kingdom.

Organism A: Multicellular, photosynthetic autotrophs, with cell walls that contain cellulose.

Organism B: Their cell walls lack peptidoglycan, and their cell membranes contain certain lipids that are not found in any other organisms. Many live in some of the most extreme environments and can survive only in the absence of oxygen.

Organism C: Single-celled, eukaryotic organisms that have cholorplasts.

35. Making Connections Refer back to Chapter 12 to help you answer the following question: Which type of mutations would be more useful to scientists as molecular clocks—gene mutations or chromosomal mutations? Explain.

Performance-Based Assessment

Writing a Script It has been estimated that there are more unknown species in the tropical rain forests than there are known species in the world. Scientists are concerned that these rain forests might be destroyed before the species in them can be classified. Write a script for a television news program explaining this issue to the general public. Tape your presentation and share it with the class.

Take It to the NET

How do scientists identify and classify fossils and more recent remains of animals? Visit the Prentice Hall Web site at **www.phschool.com** to find out about how scientists at the Natural History Museum in London identified the remains of what was called the "Beast of Bodwin Moor." Then, answer the following questions:

- What was the first step undertaken in identifying the "beast"?
- What evidence indicated that the skull belonged to a cat?
- What type of cat was the "beast," and how was that determined?
- What evidence indicated that the "beast" did not die on Bodwin Moor?

Performance-Based Assessment

Some students may present ethical reasons that organisms in rain forests should be protected. Other students may focus on the potential benefits to humans of learning about and classifying organisms. Students also may mention economic benefits, medicines, or new sources of food.

Standardized Test Prep

Test-Taking Tip When you open your test booklet, reassure yourself that the question format is similar to the ones that you have seen in these practice tests. Notice that the directions and the number of choices are similar to those with which you have experience.

Directions: Choose the letter that best answers the question or completes the statement.

1. Which of the following is NOT a characteristic of Linnaeus's system for naming organisms?
(A) two-part name
(B) multi-part name describing several traits
(C) name that identifies the organism's genus
(D) name that includes the organism's species identifier
(E) name unique to a single species

2. What is true about using similarities to classify different species?
(A) Only similar species, such as two species of rabbits, can be meaningfully compared.
(B) Genetic similarities are no indication of the relationship between two species.
(C) Even dissimilar species can be compared at the level of certain genes.
(D) Species are not compared for the purpose of classification.
(E) It is impossible to compare dissimilar species because they have no traits in common.

3. In the six-kingdom system of classifying living things, the kingdom(s) that contain(s) microscopic organisms is(are)
I. Eubacteria
II. Archaebacteria
III. Protista
(A) I only
(B) II only
(C) I and II only
(D) II and III only
(E) I, II, and III

4. If species A and B have very similar genes and proteins, what is probably true?
(A) Species A and B shared a relatively recent common ancestor.
(B) Species A evolved independently of species B for a long period.
(C) Species A and species B are the same species.
(D) Species A is older than species B.
(E) Species A is younger than species B.

5. The length of time that two taxa have been evolving separately can be estimated using a model called a
(A) phylogenetic tree.
(B) cladogram.
(C) molecular clock.
(D) six-kingdom system.
(E) three-domain system.

Questions 6–7 Complete each analogy by selecting the correct letter. In analogies, A : B :: C : ___?___ *means* A is to B as C is to ___?___.

6. Animalia : kingdom :: Eukarya : ___?___
(A) order
(B) class
(C) species
(D) phylum
(E) domain

7. *Ursus maritimus* : scientific name :: polar bear : ___?___
(A) Latin name
(B) genus name
(C) species name
(D) common name
(E) phylum name

8. The figure below shows the presumed relationships between three insect taxa.

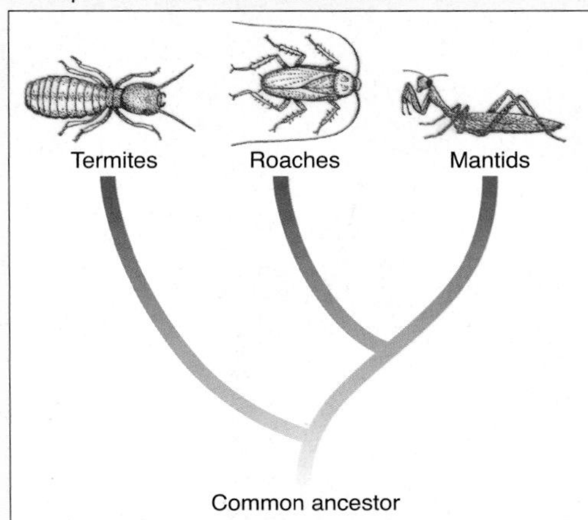

What is true about these three groups of insects?
I. Roaches and mantids share a more recent common ancestor than do roaches and termites.
II. Roaches and mantids share a more recent common ancestor than do mantids and termites.
III. Termites, roaches, and mantids share a common ancestor.
(A) I only
(B) II only
(C) I and III only
(D) II and III only
(E) I, II, and III

Standardized Test Prep

1. B
2. C
3. E
4. A
5. C
6. E
7. D
8. E

Take It to the NET

• The skull was compared with several skulls in the museum's collection to see which type of animal it resembled.

• The number, position, and type of teeth indicated that the "beast" was a cat.

• The "beast" was a leopard, *Panthera pardus.*

• The "beast" probably did not die on Bodwin Moor, because inside the skull was an egg case from a tropical roach not found in the area.

For additional information, visit

www.phschool.com

Unit 6

Dear Colleague,

To be perfectly honest, this unit is one of my favorite parts of this textbook. You might not expect this, since most of my teaching and research deals with the material in Units 3 and 4, but it's true nonetheless. Some of this comes from the challenges presented by the study of these organisms. Students don't always appreciate the importance of living things such as protists and bacteria, and it's a special challenge to open their eyes to these remarkable forms of life.

I think this is important for a number of reasons. Every time I take a walk through the woods near my house, I'm struck by the obvious ways in which decomposers such as fungi and slime molds shape the living world. Students take it for granted that dead things "rot." But why should they? Most living things, humans included, simply can't break down cork, cellulose, and other complex substances found in the forest. If this were true of all organisms, after a few years, the floors of the forests around the world would be littered with leaves and twigs and the undecayed bodies of insects.

As I pointed out in Chapter 21, fungi are different. They produce enzymes that can break down just about anything, even the chitinous exoskeletons of insects, and it's a good thing, too. Fungi's biochemical magic returns nutrients and organic matter to the soil, making it possible for new organisms to thrive in the recycled environment.

This is just one way in which these organisms shape the world around us. Even more amazing are the protists, whose various members exemplify nearly every conceivable way of making a living on this little planet. Molecular studies of these organisms have confirmed the suspicions of many biologists—this single

▶ These scarlet waxy cap mushrooms, a type of fungus, were photographed growing among the leaves and debris on a forest floor in Tennessee.

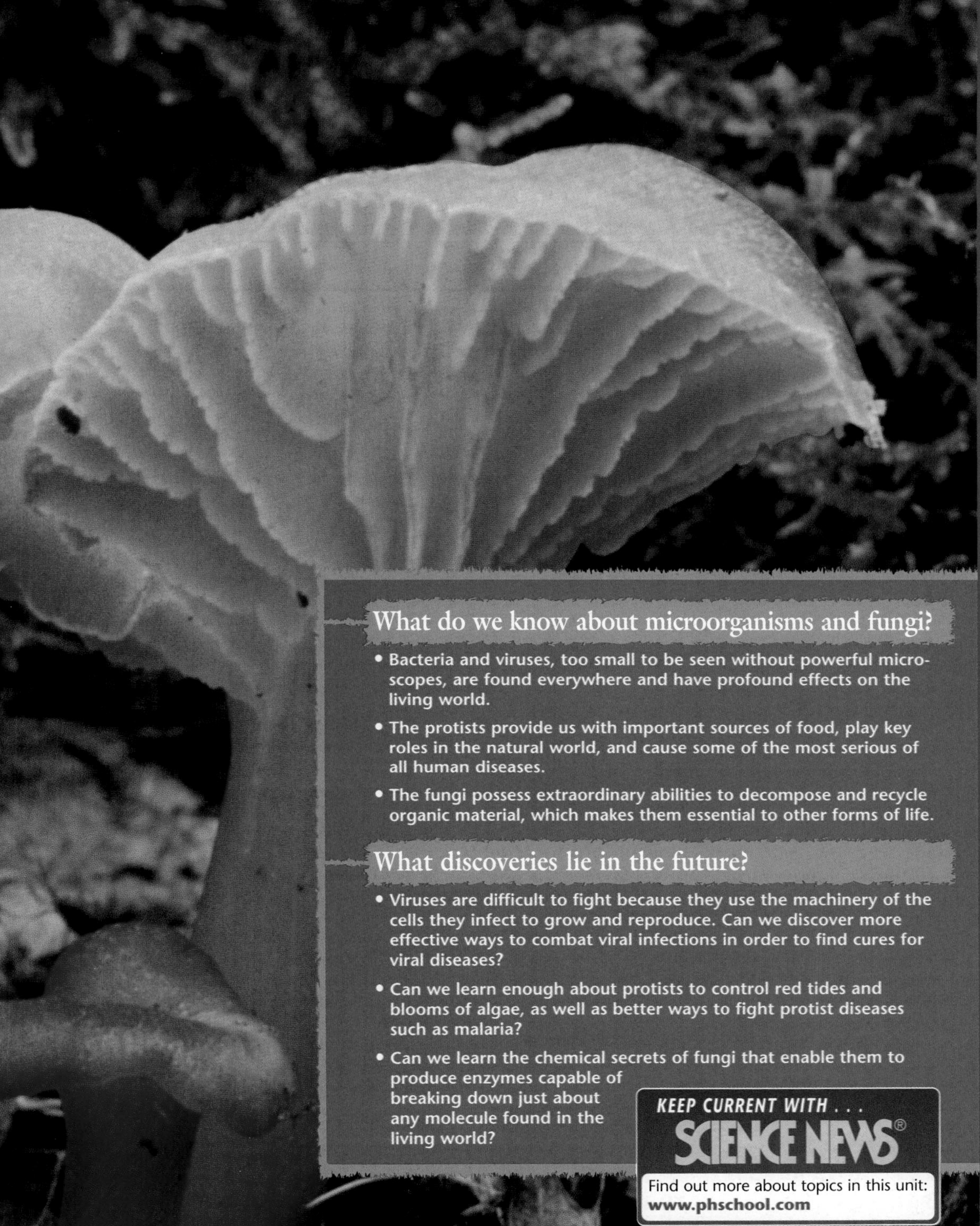

phylum contains organisms whose differences from each other are so great that the protists themselves could easily be split into several phyla of their own. At least a few taxonomists have done exactly that, although we decided to spare you and your students these complications, at least for now.

What do we know about microorganisms and fungi?
• Bacteria and viruses, too small to be seen without powerful microscopes, are found everywhere and have profound effects on the living world.
• The protists provide us with important sources of food, play key roles in the natural world, and cause some of the most serious of all human diseases.
• The fungi possess extraordinary abilities to decompose and recycle organic material, which makes them essential to other forms of life.
What discoveries lie in the future?
• Viruses are difficult to fight because they use the machinery of the cells they infect to grow and reproduce. Can we discover more effective ways to combat viral infections in order to find cures for viral diseases?
• Can we learn enough about protists to control red tides and blooms of algae, as well as better ways to fight protist diseases such as malaria?
• Can we learn the chemical secrets of fungi that enable them to produce enzymes capable of breaking down just about any molecule found in the living world?
KEEP CURRENT WITH . . .
SCIENCE NEWS®
Find out more about topics in this unit:
www.phschool.com

Knowing that bacteria and viruses cause any number of serious diseases, I'm sure your students will understand many of the reasons for studying them. On a global scale, however, there is good evidence that we are just beginning to learn the extent to which bacteria dominate life on Earth.

Drilling samples, taken hundreds of meters below the surface of Earth, have now confirmed something that bacteriologists have long suspected. Great numbers of bacteria live deep beneath the surface, thriving in darkness, often under some of the most extreme conditions imaginable. A few biologists have suggested that the abundance of underground bacteria is so great that their mass might dwarf all life found on Earth's surface.

The jury is still out as to whether such remarkable estimates are correct. One thing, however, is certain. There is no corner of this planet that does not harbor microbial life.

We humans tend to think of ourselves as the dominant forms of life on planet Earth, and, in some respects, that is true. The organisms discussed in this unit, however, may have a better claim. They were here before us, they outnumber us, and our lives depend upon their presence in ways almost too numerous to count.

As teachers, one of the greatest gifts we can give our students is to extend their vision beyond the obvious. I can think of no better way to do exactly that than to spend some time investigating these extraordinary organisms.

Sincerely,

Ken Miller

SCIENCE NEWS®

Have students visit the Prentice Hall Web site at
www.phschool.com
to find the most current information on microorganisms and fungi.

Chapter Planner 19 Bacteria and Viruses

Section and Section Objectives	Time	Activities and Labs
19–1 Prokaryotes, pp. 471–476 **19.1.1** ***Explain*** how the two groups of prokaryotes differ. **19.1.2** ***Describe*** the factors that are used to identify prokaryotes.	2 periods (1 block)	**SE:** ***Inquiry Activity,*** Where are bacteria found?, p. 470 **TE:** ***Build Science Skills,*** p. 472 **TE:** ***Demonstration,*** p. 473 **TE:** ***Build Science Skills,*** p. 473 **SE:** ***Careers in Biology,*** Epidemiologist, p. 475 **SE:** ***Demonstration,*** p. 476
19–2 Bacteria in Nature, pp. 477–481 **19.2.1** ***Describe*** the ecological roles that bacteria play in the environment. **19.2.2** ***Explain*** how bacteria cause disease. **19.2.3** ***Identify*** ways humans use bacteria. **19.2.4** ***Describe*** how bacteria are controlled.	1 period (1/2 block)	**SE:** ***Biology and History,*** Eliminating Disease, pp. 478–479 **TE:** ***Build Science Skills,*** p. 479 **TE:** ***Build Science Skills,*** p. 480 **SE:** ***Exploration,*** Identifying Limits to the Growth of Bacteria, pp. 488–489
19–3 Viruses, pp. 482–487 **19.3.1** ***Describe*** the structure of a virus. **19.3.2** ***Explain*** how viruses cause infection.	1 period (1/2 block)	**TE:** ***Build Science Skills,*** p. 483 **SE:** ***Quick Lab,*** How do viruses differ in structure?, p. 486 **TE:** ***Build Science Skills,*** p. 486
Chapter Assessment, pp. 490–493	1 period (1/2 block)	

ACTIVITY PLANNER

SE: ***Inquiry Activity,*** p. 470; (15 min. each for 3 days); 2 sterile agar plates, 2 plate covers, glass–marking pencil, transparent tape

TE: ***Build Science Skills,*** p. 472; (20 min.); variety of craft materials

TE: ***Demonstration,*** p. 473; (10 min.); marbles, beads, spheres of modeling clay or malted milk balls; unsharpened pencils, pieces of chalk, or short dowels; spring, pipe cleaner coil

TE: ***Build Science Skills,*** p. 473; (20 min.); prepared slides of various species of bacteria, microscope

SE: ***Demonstration,*** p. 476; (15 min.; 15 min.); soil, bucket, freezer, sandwich bag, 2 petri dishes of agar

TE: ***Build Science Skills,*** p. 479; (15 min.; 15 min.); 6 petri dishes of agar, dish covers, 6 sterile cotton swabs, glass–marking pencil, incubator

TE: ***Build Science Skills,*** p. 480; (20 min.); yogurt, bowl, dropper pipette, microscope slide, coverslip, methylene blue, microscope

SE: ***Exploration,*** pp. 488–489; (15 min., 15 min., 45 min.); 3 sterile agar plates, hand lens, bacterial culture, sterile cotton swabs, glass–marking pencil, transparent tape, thermometer

TE: ***Build Science Skills,*** p. 483; (10 min.); sunflower seeds

SE: ***Quick Lab,*** p. 486; (20 min.); metric ruler, scissors, tape, craft materials such as colored paper, foam ball, pipe cleaners, yarn, sandpaper

TE: ***Build Science Skills,*** p. 486; (15 min.); advertisements for and packages of cold remedies

PLANNING KEY

Ability Levels

B	**Basic**	For students who need additional help
A	**Average**	For all students
E	**Enriched**	For students who need to be challenged

Components

SE	Student Edition	**GRSW**	Guided Reading and Study Workbook	**IDM**	Issues and Decision Making
TE	Teacher's Edition	**CT**	Chapter Tests: Levels A and B	**CTB**	Computer Test Bank
LMA	Laboratory Manual A	**PHAS**	PH Assessment System	**PA**	Presentation Assistant Plus
LMB	Laboratory Manual B	**LA**	Lab Assessment With Scoring Guide	**BD**	BioDetectives Videotape
TR	Teaching Resources	**BTM**	BioTechnology Manual	**iT**	iText
IF	Investigations in Forensics				

Program Resources	Assessment	Media and Technology
TR: Section Review 19–1 B A **GRSW:** Section 19–1 B A **BTM:** Lab 5 A E	**SE:** 19–1 Section Assessment, p. 476 **TR:** Section Review 19–1	**PA:** 19–1 Interest Grabber, Section Outline, Concept Map, Figure 19–2 **iT:** Section 19–1
LMA: Chapter 19 Lab A E **LMB:** Chapter 19 Lab B A **TR:** Section Review 19–2 B A **GRSW:** Section 19–2 B A **IDM:** Issues and Decisions 35 A E **BTM:** Labs 1, 16 A E **IF:** Investigation 6 A E	**SE:** 19–2 Section Assessment, p. 481 **TR:** Section Review 19–2	**PA:** 19–2 Interest Grabber, Section Outline, Common Diseases Caused by Bacteria **iT:** Section 19–2
TR: Section Review 19–3 B A Chapter 19 Exploration B A E **GRSW:** Section 19–3 B A	**SE:** 19–3 Section Assessment, p. 487 **TR:** Section Review 19–3	**PA:** 19–3 Interest Grabber, Section Outline, Common Diseases Caused by Viruses, Figure 19–13, Figure 19–14, Figure 19–15 **iT:** Section 19–3 **BD:** "Influenza: Tracking a Virus" "Hantavirus: A Tale of Mice and People" Discovery Channel School
	SE: Chapter 19 Assessment, pp. 490–493 **TR:** Chapter Vocabulary Review, Graphic Organizer **CT:** Chapter 19 Test **CTB:** Chapter 19 Test **PHAS:** Practice Test	**CTB:** Chapter 19 Test **iT:** Chapter 19 Assessment

PRESSED FOR TIME?

To Preview the Chapter
- Introduce students to Key Concepts and Vocabulary terms in each section.
- Assign the Reading Strategies for each section.

To Cover the Chapter Quickly
- Have students read Classifying Prokaryotes and Identifying Prokaryotes in Section 19–1, Bacteria and Disease and Controlling Bacteria in Section 19–2, and all of Section 19–3.
- Assign the 19–3 Section Review and questions 1–10 in Chapter 19 Assessment and Chapter 19 Standardized Test Prep.

To Review the Chapter
- Assign Sections 19–1 through 19–3 in the Guided Reading and Study Workbook.
- Assign Section Reviews for 19–1 through 19–3 and the Chapter Vocabulary Review for Chapter 19 in the Teaching Resources.

ENGAGE/EXPLORE

Inquiry Activity

Objective Students will be able to draw a conclusion that there are bacteria in the air.

Skill Focus **Observing, Drawing Conclusions**

Materials 2 sterile agar plates, 2 plate covers, glass-marking pencil, transparent tape

Time 15 minutes each for 2 days

Safety Make sure that students wash their hands with soap and hot water after handling the plates. Rigorous application of sterile laboratory technique is a must for all microbiology labs. Soak the plates overnight in undiluted chlorine bleach, 70% isopropyl alcohol, or another disinfectant before autoclaving and disposing.

Strategies
- Emphasize to students the importance of not touching the exposed plates. Plastic gloves may be used to emphasize this safety precaution.
- Show students how to tape the plates closed.
- Sealing the plates with parafilm can help prevent agar from drying out.

Expected Outcomes On the exposed plate, there will typically be 12 colonies after 24 hours and 16 colonies after 48 hours.

Think About It

1. Students should observe many more colonies on the exposed plate and infer that it had more because it was exposed to the air.
2. Students should conclude that bacterial spores and dust-borne bacteria landed on the agar when the plate was exposed.

Assess Prior Knowledge

Display a variety of photographs of bacteria and viruses taken from old microbiology and biology texts and science journals. You could use a microprojector or videocamera to show slides of the major shapes of bacteria and several shapes of viruses. Tell students that some of these photos are of bacteria and some are of viruses. Then have small groups of students classify a pile of photos into two groups—bacteria and viruses.

Chapter 19 Bacteria and Viruses

Bacteria can survive in extreme temperatures. Some bacteria can even survive in this hot spring in Yellowstone National Park.

Inquiry Activity

Where are bacteria found?

Procedure

1. Label 2 sterile agar plates "control" and "exposed."
2. Tape closed the cover of the control plate. Remove the cover of the exposed plate. Leave both plates on the table for 5 minutes. Do not touch or breathe on the agar.
3. After 5 minutes, tape closed the lid of the exposed plate. Store both plates upside down in a warm place.
4. After 2 days, record the number of bacterial colonies on each plate. **CAUTION:** *Do not open the plates. Give them to your teacher for proper disposal.*

Think About It

1. **Observing** Which plate had more bacterial colonies? Explain your answer.
2. **Drawing Conclusions** Where did the bacteria on your plates come from? Explain your answer.

FACTS AND FIGURES

Earth's cycles depend on bacteria
Earth's environment depends on a cycling of substances through the world ecosystem. These substances include water, carbon, nitrogen, sulfur, phosphorus, sodium, potassium, and other materials. Their cycles are sometimes called biogeochemical cycles, because they involve both biological and geologic parts of the ecosystem. Bacteria are an essential part of all these cycles. For instance, the cyanobacteria are a primary component of the carbon cycle, for through their photosynthesis they contribute much of the oxygen to the atmosphere that is used in cellular respiration. The nitrogen-fixing bacteria, such as *Rhizobium,* are central to the nitrogen cycle. The many bacteria that decompose dead organisms contribute to all the cycles.

19–1 Prokaryotes

Imagine living all your life as the only family on your street. Then, one morning, you open the front door and discover houses all around you. You see neighbors tending their gardens and children walking to school. Where did all the people come from? What if the answer turned out to be that they had always been there—you just hadn't seen them? In fact, they had lived on your street for years and years before your house was even built. How would your view of the world change? What would it be like to go, almost overnight, from thinking that you were the only folks on the block to just one family in a crowded community? A bit of a shock?

Humans once had just such a shock. Suddenly, the street was very crowded! Thanks to Robert Hooke and Anton van Leeuwenhoek, the invention of the microscope opened our eyes to the world around us.

Microscopic life covers nearly every square centimeter of Earth. There are microorganisms of many different sizes and shapes, even in a drop of pond water. The smallest and most common microorganisms are **prokaryotes**—single-celled organisms that lack a nucleus.

Prokaryotes typically range in size from 1 to 5 micrometers, making them much smaller than most eukaryotic cells, which generally range from 10 to 100 micrometers in diameter. There are exceptions to this, of course. One example is *Epulopiscium fisheloni,* a gigantic prokaryote, shown in **Figure 19–1,** that is about 500 micrometers long.

Guide for Reading

Key Concepts
- How do the two groups of prokaryotes differ?
- What factors are used to identify prokaryotes?

Vocabulary
prokaryote
bacillus
coccus
spirillum
flagellum
photoautotroph
chemoautotroph
photoheterotroph
binary fission
conjugation
endospore

Reading Strategy: Finding Main Ideas Before you read this section, write down the major headings of the section. Then, as you read the section, list the important information under each heading.

Classifying Prokaryotes

For many years, most prokaryotes were simply called "bacteria" and placed in a single kingdom—Monera. The word *bacteria* is so familiar that we will continue to use it as a common term to describe prokaryotes. More recently, however, biologists have begun to appreciate that prokaryotes can be divided into two very different groups: the eubacteria (yoo-bak-TEER-ee-uh) and the archaebacteria (ahr-kee-bak-TEER-ee-uh). Each group is now considered to be a separate kingdom. Some biologists think that the split between these two groups is so ancient and so fundamental that they should be called domains, a level of classification even higher than kingdom.

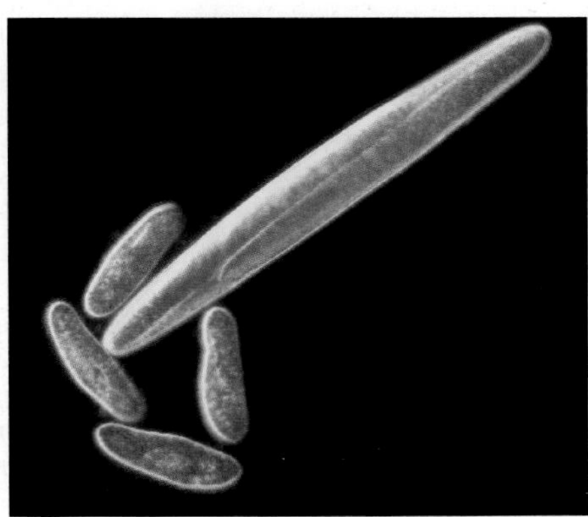

(magnification: 100×)

▶ **Figure 19–1** The large cell in this photograph is *Epulopiscium fisheloni,* one of the largest prokaryotes. Notice its size in relation to the neighboring cells, which are eukaryotic paramecia.

Section 19–1

1 FOCUS

Objectives

19.1.1 ***Explain*** how the two groups of prokaryotes differ.
19.1.2 ***Describe*** the factors that are used to identify prokaryotes.

Guide for Reading

Vocabulary Preview

Call on students at random to pronounce the Vocabulary terms in the order in which they appear. Correct any mispronunciations.

Reading Strategy

Have students make an outline of the section, using the blue headings as the first level of the outline and the green side headings as the second level. Explain that they should add third and fourth levels to their outlines by finding details in the section that support each of the headings.

2 INSTRUCT

Classifying Prokaryotes

Make Connections

Mathematics Point out that 1 micrometer equals 1/1,000,000 meter, or 1/10,000 centimeter. A typical prokaryote ranges in size from 1 to 5 micrometers. Then, ask students: **How many prokaryotic cells could be lined up across a coin that is 1 centimeter in diameter?** *(2000 to 10,000 cells)*

TIME SAVER **SECTION REVIEW**

Print:
- ***Teaching Resources,*** Section Review 19–1
- ***Guided Reading and Study Workbook,*** Section 19–1
- ***Biotechnology Manual,*** Lab 5

Technology:
- ***iText,*** Section 19–1

Use Visuals

Figure 19–2 To reinforce for students the difference between prokaryotic cells and eukaryotic cells, have them make a labeled drawing of each kind of cell. For the typical prokaryotic cell, they can use the illustration in Figure 19–2 as a model. For the typical eukaryotic cell, have them turn back to Figure 7–5 on page 174 and use the animal cell as a model.

Build Science Skills

Using Models Have students gather a variety of craft materials from school and home to make models of bacteria. These materials might include yarn, sandpaper, textured fabrics, and pipe cleaners. As a resource for this model, students may use any of the photos or illustrations of bacteria in this chapter or in another textbook or one of the drawings they made in observing bacteria with a microscope.

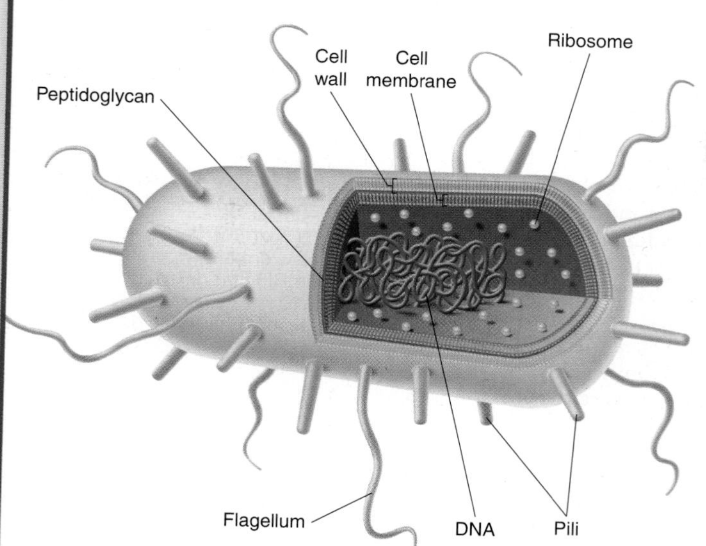

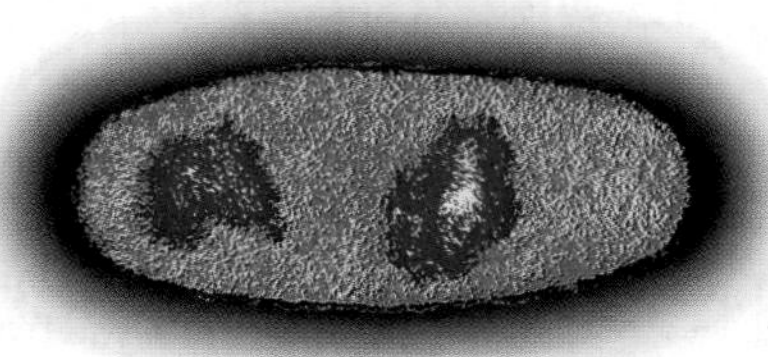

(magnification: 32,300×)

Figure 19–2 A bacterium such as *E. coli* has the basic structure typical of most prokaryotes: cell wall, cell membrane, and cytoplasm. The flagella are used by some prokaryotes for movement. The pili are involved in cell-to-cell contact. **The cell walls of eubacteria contain peptidoglycan, a type of carbohydrate that is not found in archaebacteria.**

Eubacteria The larger of the two kingdoms of prokaryotes is the eubacteria. Eubacteria include a wide range of organisms with different lifestyles. The variety is so great, in fact, that biologists do not agree on exactly how many phyla to divide the kingdom into. Eubacteria live almost everywhere. Some live in the soil, whereas others infect large organisms and cause disease. **Figure 19–2** shows a diagram of *E. coli,* a typical eubacterium that lives in human intestines.

Like other prokaryotes, eubacteria are usually surrounded by a cell wall that protects the cell from injury and determines its shape. The cell walls of eubacteria contain peptidoglycan, a carbohydrate. Within the cell wall is a cell membrane that surrounds the cytoplasm. Some eubacteria have a second, outer, membrane.

Archaebacteria Under a microscope, archaebacteria look very similar to eubacteria. They are equally small, lack nuclei, and have cell walls. **Archaebacteria lack peptidoglycan, a carbohydrate found in the cell walls of eubacteria, and their membrane lipids are quite different. Also, the DNA sequences of key archaebacterial genes are more like those of eukaryotes than those of eubacteria.** Based on this and other data, scientists reason that archaebacteria may be the ancestors of eukaryotes.

Many archaebacteria live in extremely harsh environments. One group of archaebacteria is the methanogens, prokaryotes that produce methane gas. Methanogens live in oxygen-free environments, such as thick mud and the digestive tracts of animals. Other archaebacteria live in extremely salty environments, such as Utah's Great Salt Lake, or in hot springs where temperatures approach the boiling point of water.

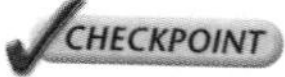

Where do many archaebacteria live?

TIME SAVER — PRESENTATIONS MADE EASY!

The Presentation Assistant Plus contains the Prentice Hall Presentation Pro and the Transparencies, which provide easy-to-follow visual support for every step of this lesson. If you have a computer presentation station, use Prentice Hall Presentation Pro Section 19–1, or use the transparencies listed here.

Section 19–1:

Interest Grabber
Section Outline
Concept Map
Figure 19–2

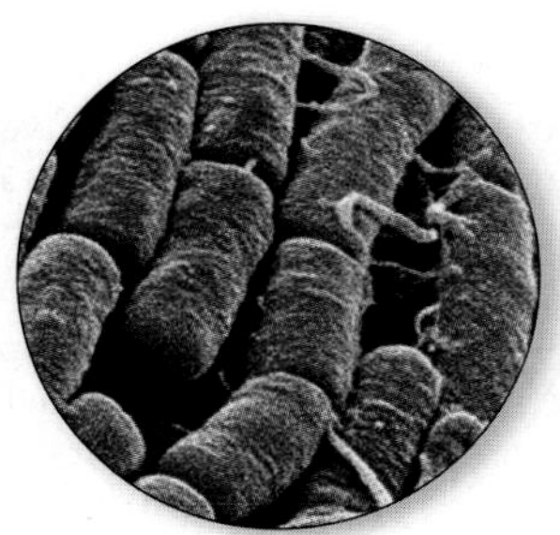

Bacilli
(magnification: 7000×)

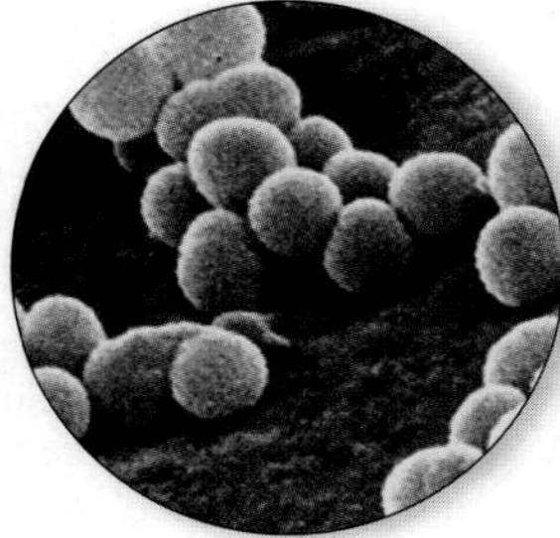

Cocci
(magnification: 137,000×)

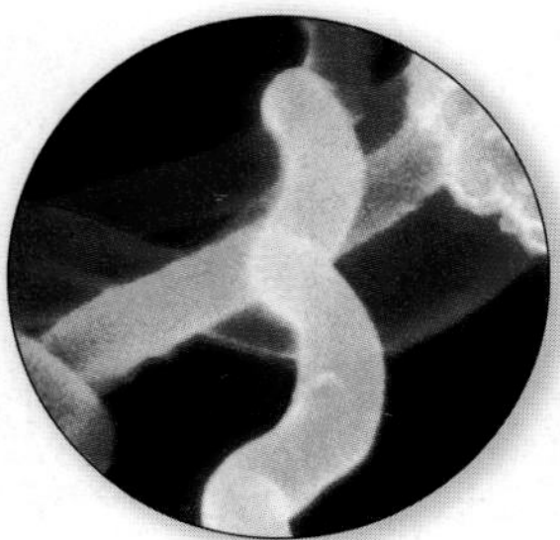

Spirilla
(magnification: about 100,000×)

Figure 19–3 **Prokaryotes can be identified by their shapes.** Prokaryotes usually have one of three basic shapes: rods (bacilli), spheres (cocci), or spirals (spirilla).

Identifying Prokaryotes

Because prokaryotes are so small, it may seem difficult to identify their characteristics. **Prokaryotes are identified by their shapes, the chemical natures of their cell walls, the ways they move, and the ways they obtain energy.**

Shapes Look at the different shapes of prokaryotes shown in **Figure 19–3.** Rod-shaped prokaryotes are called **bacilli** (buh-SIL-eye; singular: bacillus). Spherical prokaryotes are called **cocci** (KAHK-sy; singular: coccus). Spiral and corkscrew-shaped prokaryotes are called **spirilla** (spy-RIL-uh; singular: spirillum).

Prokaryotes can arrange themselves in a number of different ways. Some cocci, including the disease-causing bacteria *Streptococcus* and *Pneumococcus,* form long chains. Others, such as *Staphylococcus,* form large clumps or clusters.

Cell Walls Two different types of cell walls are found in eubacteria. A method called Gram staining is used to tell them apart. The Gram stain consists of two dyes—one violet (the primary stain) and the other red (the counterstain). Bacterial cells with a cell wall containing mainly peptidoglycan absorb only the violet dye, so they appear purple under the microscope, as shown in **Figure 19–4.** These bacteria are called Gram-positive. Other bacteria have a second, outer, layer of lipid and carbohydrate molecules. This extra layer absorbs only the red stain. These bacteria, which appear pink, are said to be Gram-negative.

Movement You can also identify prokaryotes by studying how they move. Some are propelled by **flagella** (singular: flagellum). Flagella are whiplike structures used for movement. Other prokaryotes lash, snake, or spiral forward. Still others glide slowly along a layer of slimelike material they secrete. Many prokaryotes do not move at all.

Figure 19–4 **Prokaryotes can be identified by the chemical natures of their cell walls.** When treated with Gram stain, Gram-positive bacteria appear purple. Gram-negative bacteria appear pink.

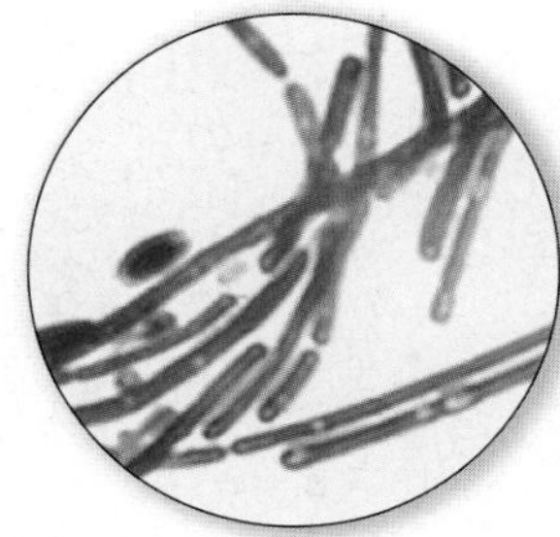

Gram-Positive Bacteria
(magnification: about 3000×)

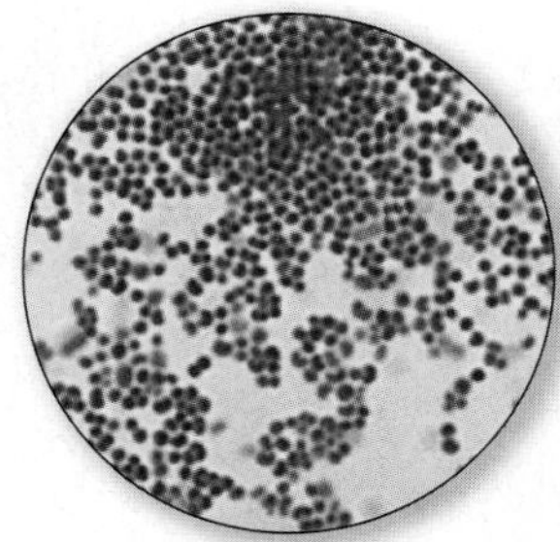

Gram-Negative Bacteria
(magnification: 150×)

Identifying Prokaryotes

Demonstration

Collect some common items that can be used to model the three basic shapes of bacteria as you discuss the shapes with students. For example, you can represent cocci with marbles, beads, spheres of modeling clay, or malted milk balls. You can represent bacilli with unsharpened pencils, pieces of chalk, or short dowels. You can represent spirilla with springs or pipe cleaners that have been shaped into spirals by wrapping them around a pencil.

Build Science Skills

Observing Set up at least one learning station with a microscope and a number of prepared slides showing various species of bacteria, each labeled with the species name. Provide opportunities for students to use the station during class periods. To guide students as they make their observations, prepare a study sheet containing the following instructions to use with each slide.

- What is the scientific name of this bacterium?
- What magnification did you use to see the bacterium clearly?
- Draw a picture of the bacterium, and label the cell wall.
- How would you classify this bacterium according to cell shape?
- Optional: Find out what this bacterium does in nature. For example, does it cause a certain disease? Does it decompose dead organic material? Does it take part in the nitrogen cycle?

FACTS AND FIGURES

Prokaryotes in a cow's gut

The kingdom Archaebacteria include exotic prokaryotes that live in such extreme environments as deep ocean vents and hot sulfur springs. Archaebacteria also include common prokaryotes that live in the digestive tracts of all animals, especially in the rumen of cows and other grazing beasts. These prokaryotes, called methanogens, use hydrogen and carbon to produce methane (CH_4), and most of the methane in the atmosphere is the result of this process. In fact, cows have been called "40-gallon methane tanks on four legs." In the atmosphere, the methane reacts with oxygen to produce CO_2. If it were not for methanogens, Earth would be a much different place. Carbon would pile up in huge deposits in the ground, and oxygen would make up a much greater percentage of the atmosphere.

Answer to . . .

CHECKPOINT *Many archaebacteria live in harsh environments, including thick mud, animal digestive tracts, salt lakes, and hot springs.*

Obtaining Energy

Use Visuals

Figure 19–5 Ask students: **What kind of prokaryotes might you find near an ocean vent?** *(Chemoautotrophs)* **How do chemoautotrophs obtain the energy they need to carry out life processes?** *(They get energy from chemical reactions involving ammonia, hydrogen sulfide, nitrites, sulfur, or iron.)* **From what chemical do chemoautotrophs obtain energy near ocean vents?** *(From hydrogen sulfide gas that flows from the vents)*

Meet Diverse Needs

Help students with limited English proficiency differentiate among the different groups of prokaryotes by reviewing the word parts that make up the terms used to describe these organisms. On the board, write the following:
- *auto* = "self"
- *chemo* = "chemical"
- *photo* = "light"
- *hetero* = "other"
- *troph* = "nourishment"

Then, have students write definitions for the terms using these equivalencies.
- *autotroph,* an organism that gets "nourishment from itself"
- *photoautotroph,* an organism that gets "nourishment from itself using light"
- *chemoautotroph,* an organism that gets "nourishment from itself using chemicals"
- *heterotroph,* an organism that gets "nourishment from others"
- *photoheterotroph,* an organism that gets "nourishment from others and from using light" **Limited English proficiency**

Obtaining Energy

Prokaryotes have diverse adaptations that allow them to live in nearly every environment imaginable. No characteristic of prokaryotes illustrates their diversity better than the ways in which they obtain energy.

Autotrophs Several groups of prokaryotes carry out photosynthesis in a manner similar to green plants, and are called **photoautotrophs** (foh-toh-AW-tuh-trohfs). As you might expect, these organisms are found where light is plentiful, near the surfaces of lakes, streams, and oceans. One group, the cyanobacteria (sy-uh-noh-bak-TEER-ee-uh), contains a bluish pigment and chlorophyll *a,* the key pigment in photosynthesis. Cyanobacteria are found throughout the world—in fresh and salt water and on land. A few species survive in extremely hot water, such as in hot springs. Others survive in the Arctic, where they can even grow on snow. In fact, cyanobacteria are often the very first species to recolonize the site of a natural disaster, such as a volcanic eruption.

Other prokaryotes, called **chemoautotrophs** (keem-oh-AW-tuh-trohfs), obtain energy directly from inorganic molecules. Chemoautotrophs get energy from chemical reactions involving ammonia, hydrogen sulfide, nitrites, sulfur, or iron. Some chemoautotrophs live deep in the darkness of the ocean. They obtain energy from hydrogen sulfide gas that flows from hydrothermal vents on the ocean floor, such as the one shown in **Figure 19–5.**

Heterotrophs Most prokaryotes are heterotrophs like us, obtaining energy by taking in organic molecules and then breaking them down. In many situations, this means that prokaryotes compete directly with us for food. If food is not handled carefully, bacteria like *Staphylococcus aureus* may get to the dinner table before you do! Once there, these bacteria may not only "eat" some of the food ahead of time, but may also release chemicals that cause food poisoning.

A small but very interesting group of prokaryotes combines the autotrophic and heterotrophic styles of life. These organisms are photosynthetic—they capture sunlight for energy. But they also need organic compounds for nutrition. These bacteria are called **photoheterotrophs** (foh-toh-HET-ur-oh-trohfs), and there is nothing quite like them in the rest of the living world.

✓CHECKPOINT *What are photoheterotrophs?*

◀ **Figure 19–5** Ocean vents, such as this one, are often home to a rich fauna of organisms, including tube worms and other exotic organisms. **Applying Concepts** *Would photoautotrophs survive in this environment? Why or why not?*

TEACHER TO TEACHER

When I teach students about bacteria and viruses, I try to give students as many examples that relate to real-life experiences as possible. With such examples, the material becomes more interesting for students and keeps their attention on the subject at hand. For example, we spend a good amount of time on the causes, symptoms, and spread of bacterial and viral diseases. I encourage students to relate their own experiences with such diseases, as well as those of family members. I also try to provide as many graphic organizers, diagrams, and charts as possible in order to help students organize what they are learning. Finally, I design experiences in which students can actively participate.

—*Brenda Waldon,*
Biology Teacher
Clayton County Public Schools,
Morrow, GA

Careers in Biology

Epidemiologist

Job Description: work for a university, health department, research or health organization, or medical corporation to identify and track diseases and develop programs that prevent or control the spread of disease

Education: Masters or Doctoral degree in epidemiology, including course work in statistics, demography, research design, and public health

Skills: good communication skills, strong computer skills, knowledge of health and medical conditions

Highlights: You get to ask lots of questions and travel. You can work on infectious diseases such as tuberculosis. Some epidemiologists work on specific issues such as tobacco addiction.

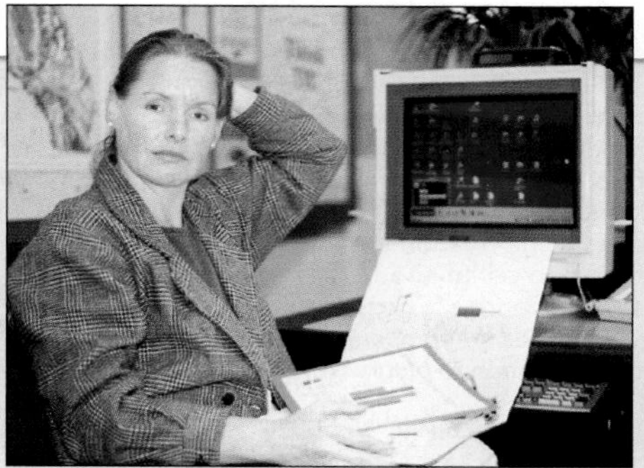

Elizabeth Lawton currently works on the infectious disease tuberculosis. She loves her job. "Because public health works at the population level, I get to help many people at one time," she says.

Take It to the NET

For more career information, visit the Prentice Hall Web site: **www.phschool.com**

Releasing Energy

Like all organisms, bacteria need a constant supply of energy. This energy is released by the processes of cellular respiration, which requires oxygen, and fermentation, which does not. Organisms that require a constant supply of oxygen in order to live are called obligate aerobes. We, and many species of bacteria, are obligate aerobes. Some bacteria, however, do not require oxygen and, in fact, may be poisoned by it! These bacteria are called obligate anaerobes because they must live in the absence of oxygen. *Clostridium botulinum*—shown in **Figure 19–6**—is an obligate anaerobe found in soil. Because of its ability to grow without oxygen, it can grow in canned food that has not been properly sterilized. The bacteria produce a potentially deadly form of food poisoning known as botulism. Gases produced by the bacteria can cause affected cans of food to bulge.

A third group of bacteria can survive with or without oxygen and are known as facultative anaerobes. Facultative anaerobes do not require oxygen, but neither are they poisoned by its presence. Their ability to switch between cellular respiration and fermentation means that facultative anaerobes are able to grow just about anywhere. These bacteria are found in freshwater lakes and ponds, at the bottom of the ocean, and at the tops of the highest mountains. They are also found in the most thoroughly disinfected hospital rooms, and even in our own digestive systems.

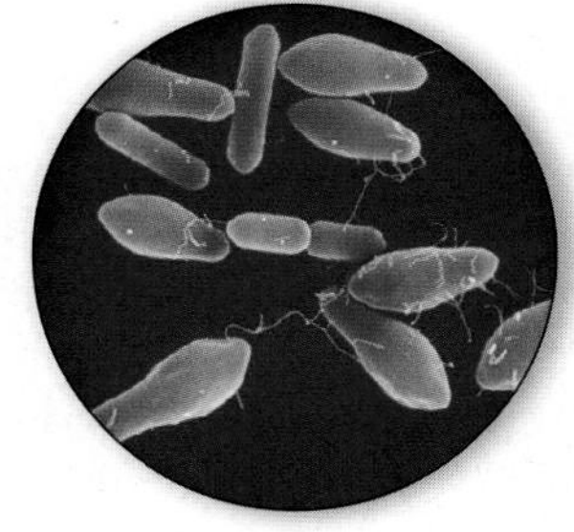

(magnification: 4000×)

▲ **Figure 19–6** Botulism, a kind of food poisoning, is caused by the bacterium *Clostridium botulinum.* This type of bacterium is often found in foods that have not been properly sterilized. **Applying Concepts** *How can you avoid botulism?*

Careers in Biology

- Epidemiology focuses on where, when, and how often diseases occur; on how diseases are transmitted; and on how diseases can be controlled.
- Epidemiologists collect and analyze data that are relevant in describing the occurrence of a disease under study and its probable cause.
- When investigating a disease epidemic, an epidemiologist may collect information about the gender, age, occupation, socioeconomic status, personal habits, and history of immunization of those who have contracted the disease.

Resources All states and many large cities employ epidemiologists in their public health departments.

Take It to the NET

For additional information about this career, visit **www.phschool.com**

Releasing Energy

Meet Diverse Needs

To help at-risk students understand fermentation in bacteria, have them turn back to Figure 9–4 on page 225. To help them understand cellular respiration in bacteria, have them turn back to Figure 9–2 on page 222 and review these processes. **Learning modality: visual**

BIO INSIGHTS — FACTS AND FIGURES

Anaerobes get energy

There are four main ways that anaerobes obtain energy. In fermentation, which is performed by many bacteria as well as by fungi such as yeasts, an energy-rich molecule such as glucose is split, releasing energy. In nitrate reduction, which occurs in a number of bacteria that are facultative anaerobes, the oxygen in the nitrate ion is used to oxidize an organic compound and so obtain energy. In carbonate reduction, which is carried out by methanogens, the oxygen in carbon dioxide or carbonate is used to oxidize hydrogen produced by other microorganisms and so obtain energy. In sulfate reduction, the oxygen in the sulfate ion is used to oxidize organic matter or hydrogen and so obtain energy. One of the products of this reaction under acidic conditions is hydrogen sulfide (H_2S), a foul-smelling gas that is poisonous to most living things.

Answers to . . .

CHECKPOINT *Photosynthetic organisms that also need organic compounds*

Figure 19–5 *No, because no sunlight reaches deep into the ocean.*

Figure 19–6 *By avoiding food from bulging cans*

Growth and Reproduction

Demonstration

To show that bacteria can survive through such harsh conditions as freezing temperatures, place a small amount of soil into a plastic container. Cover the container and place it in a freezer overnight. The next day, sprinkle some soil onto a petri dish of agar. On another dish of agar, sprinkle some of the soil from the container that was in the freezer overnight. Cover the dishes and place them in an incubator overnight. The next day, have students observe both dishes for evidence of bacterial colonies growing on the agar.

3 ASSESS

Evaluate Understanding

Call on students to explain the differences between eubacteria and archaebacteria and how prokaryotes can be identified, obtain energy, release energy, grow, and reproduce.

Reteach

Direct students' attention to the labeled illustration of a eubacterium in Figure 19–2, and review the basic structure and function of prokaryotes.

ALTERNATIVE ASSESSMENT

Students' Venn diagrams should show that both eubacteria and archaebacteria are prokaryotic, have cell walls, and contain DNA. The diagrams should also show that archaebacteria lack peptidoglycan, have different membrane lipids, and have different DNA sequences in key genes.

iTEXT

Use iText to review the key concepts in Section 19–1.

Answer to . . .

Figure 19–7 *During conjugation, a protein bridge forms between two cells, and genes move from one cell to another. In binary fission, a cell divides in half, and there is no exchange of genetic information.*

▼ **Figure 19–7** Most prokaryotes reproduce by binary fission (top), producing two identical "daughter" cells. Some prokaryotes take part in conjugation (bottom). Parts of genetic information are transferred from one cell to another by way of a hollow bridge. **Comparing and Contrasting** ***Compare the process of conjugation to binary fission.***

(magnification: 26,500×)

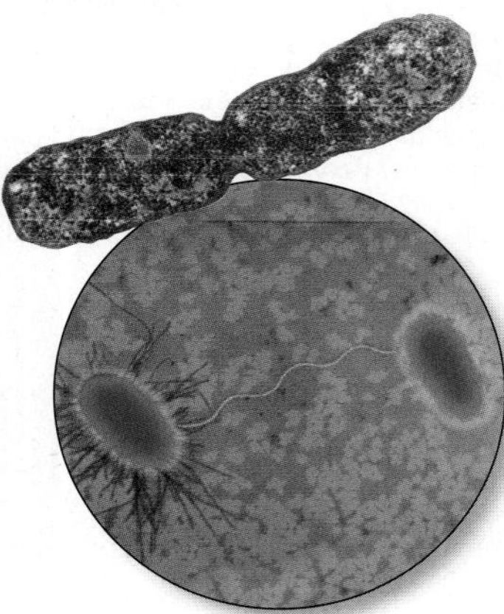

(magnification: 7000×)

Growth and Reproduction

When conditions are favorable, prokaryotes can grow and divide at astonishing rates. Some divide as often as every 20 minutes! If unlimited space and food were available to a single prokaryote and if all of its offspring divided every 20 minutes, in just 48 hours (2 days) they would reach a mass approximately 4000 times the mass of Earth! Fortunately, this does not happen. In nature, growth is held in check by the availability of food and the production of waste products.

How do prokaryotes reproduce? When a prokaryote has grown so that it has nearly doubled in size, it replicates its DNA and divides in half, producing two identical "daughter" cells. This type of reproduction is known as **binary fission.** Because binary fission does not involve the exchange or recombination of genetic information, it is an asexual form of reproduction.

Although most prokaryotes reproduce through binary fission, others can transfer genetic material from one cell to another. This exchange of genetic information is called conjugation. During **conjugation,** a hollow bridge forms between two cells, as shown in **Figure 19–7,** and genes move from one cell to the other. This transfer of genetic information increases the genetic diversity in populations of bacteria.

When growth conditions become unfavorable, many bacteria form structures called spores. One type of spore, called an **endospore,** is formed when a bacterium produces a thick internal wall that encloses its DNA and a portion of its cytoplasm. The endospore can remain dormant for months or even centuries, until more favorable growth conditions arise. The ability to form spores makes it possible for some bacteria to survive harsh conditions—such as extreme heat, dryness, or lack of nutrients—that might otherwise kill them.

19–1 Section Assessment

1. **Key Concept** Compare and contrast the two kingdoms of prokaryotes.
2. **Key Concept** What three factors can be used to identify prokaryotes?
3. What are some of the different ways that prokaryotes obtain energy?
4. Describe how prokaryotes reproduce and exchange genetic material.
5. **Critical Thinking Inferring** Why might an infection by Gram-negative bacteria be more difficult to treat than a Gram-positive bacterial infection?

ALTERNATIVE ASSESSMENT

Making a Venn Diagram Create a Venn diagram that illustrates the similarities and differences between eubacteria and archaebacteria.

iTEXT Assessment Use iText to review the important concepts in Section 19–1.

19–1 Section Assessment

1. Archaebacteria lack peptidoglycan, and their membrane lipids are quite different. Also, the DNA sequences of key archaebacterial genes are more like those of eukaryotes than eubacteria.
2. They are identified by their shapes, the chemical natures of their cell walls, the ways they move, and the ways they obtain energy.
3. Photoautotrophs carry out photosynthesis; chemoautotrophs obtain energy directly from inorganic molecules; heterotrophs obtain energy by taking in organic molecules; and photoheterotrophs carry out photosynthesis and take in molecules.
4. Some reproduce by binary fission, and others exchange genetic information by conjugation.
5. Gram-positive bacteria have only a single cell wall, making them more susceptible to antibiotics.

19–2 Bacteria in Nature

You probably remember the principal actors in the last film you saw. You might even recall some of the supporting actors. Have you ever thought that there would be no film at all without the hundreds of workers who are never seen on screen? Bacteria are just like those unseen workers.  **Bacteria are vital to maintaining the living world. Some are producers that capture energy by photosynthesis. Others help to break down the nutrients in dead matter and the atmosphere, allowing other organisms to use the nutrients.**

Decomposers

Every living thing depends on a supply of raw materials. If these materials were lost forever when an organism died, life could not continue. Before long, plants would drain the soil of minerals and die, and the animals that depend on plants for food would starve. As decomposers, bacteria help the ecosystem recycle nutrients. When a tree dies and falls to the forest floor, armies of bacteria attack and digest the dead tissue. The bacteria break down dead matter into simpler substances, which are released into the soil and taken up by the roots of plants. Bacteria, as well as some eukaryotic organisms, such as insects and fungi, play important roles in this process.

As recyclers, bacteria also perform critical steps in sewage treatment. Sewage contains human waste, discarded food, organic garbage, and even chemical waste. Bacteria break down complex compounds in the sewage into simpler ones. This process produces purified water, nitrogen and carbon dioxide gases, and leftover products that can be used as fertilizers.

Guide for Reading

Key Concepts
- What ecological roles do bacteria play in the environment?
- How do bacteria cause disease?

Vocabulary
nitrogen fixation
pathogen
antibiotic
sterilization

Reading Strategy: Using Prior Knowledge
Before you read this section, make a list of five things for which bacteria are known. Then, compare your list to the text as you read.

◀ **Figure 19–8 Bacteria help to break down the nutrients in this tree, allowing other organisms to use the nutrients.**

SECTION REVIEW

Print:
- ***Laboratory Manual A,*** Chapter 19 Lab
- ***Laboratory Manual B,*** Chapter 19 Lab
- ***Teaching Resources,*** Section Review 19–2
- ***Guided Reading and Study Workbook,*** Section 19–2
- ***Issues and Decision Making,*** Issues and Decisions 35
- ***Biotechnology Manual,*** Labs 1 and 16
- ***Investigations in Forensics,*** Investigation 6

Technology:
- ***iText,*** Section 19–2

Section 19–2

1 FOCUS

Objectives

19.2.1 ***Describe*** the ecological roles that bacteria play in the environment.
19.2.2 ***Explain*** how bacteria cause disease.
19.2.3 ***Identify*** ways humans use bacteria.
19.2.4 ***Describe*** how bacteria are controlled.

Guide for Reading

Vocabulary Preview

Have students write the vocabulary words, dividing each into its separate syllables as best they can. Remind students that each syllable usually has only one vowel sound. The correct syllabications are: ni•tro•gen fix•a•tion, path•o•gen, an•ti•bi•ot•ic, ster•il•i•za•tion.

Reading Strategy

Before they read, have students rewrite the blue headings as questions about bacteria. Then, as they read the section, they should write brief answers to those questions using the main ideas from the text.

2 INSTRUCT

Decomposers

Use Community Resources

Encourage interested students to schedule a visit to a local wastewater treatment plant to find out how bacteria are utilized in purifying wastewater. Have students who visit the treatment plant gather information and any pamphlets about the process used and then make a report to the class.

19–2 (continued)

Nitrogen Fixers

Use Visuals

Figure 19–9 Point out that the relationship between the soybean plant and the *Rhizobium* bacteria is an example of mutualism, a symbiotic relationship in which both organisms benefit. Ask students: **What process in the plant provides food for the bacteria?** *(Photosynthesis)* Then, have students take a deep breath, and emphasize that most of what they take into their lungs is nitrogen. Ask: **Can you use any of this nitrogen?** *(Some students may know that none of the nitrogen is used.)* Remind students that nitrogen is an essential element in protein and that we need proteins to survive. Ask: **How do humans and other animals get the nitrogen needed to make proteins?** *(They eat plants or animals that have eaten plants, which get nitrogen from such nitrogen-fixing bacteria as* Rhizobium *that can use nitrogen from the air.)* Tell students that soybeans are a good food source of protein, and now they know why.

Biology and History

Help place these discoveries in historical context by asking when events from other fields occurred during the period covered by this time line. For instance, in 1815 Napoleon Bonaparte was defeated at the battle of Waterloo; in 1865 President Abraham Lincoln was assassinated at Ford's Theater; in 1901 legendary trumpeter Louis Armstrong was born in New Orleans; in 1937 Pablo Picasso painted the mural *Guernica*; and in 1969 Neil Armstrong set foot on the moon. Then, discuss how each of the discoveries on the time line affected society as a whole.

Writing Activity

Students might find information about these scientists and their discoveries in books about the history of medicine. They also might look for books that contain short biographies of noted scientists.

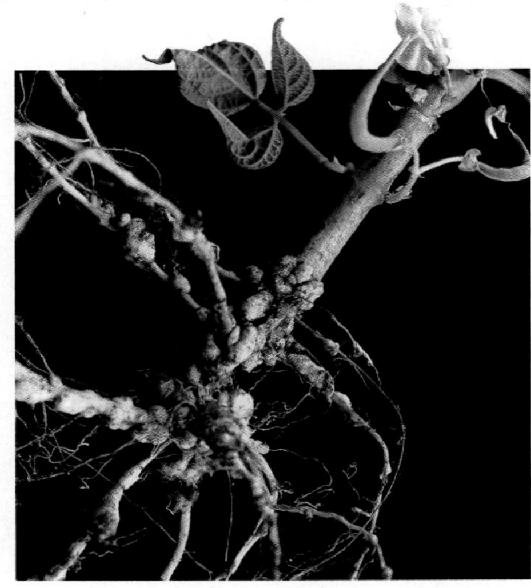

▲ **Figure 19–9** The knoblike structures on the roots of this soybean plant are called nodules. Within these nodules are the rod-shaped, nitrogen-fixing bacteria *Rhizobium*.

Nitrogen Fixers

Plants and animals depend on bacteria for nitrogen. Plants need nitrogen to make amino acids, which are the building blocks of proteins. Because animals eat plants, plant proteins supply nitrogen for animals. Although Earth's atmosphere is made up of approximately 80 percent nitrogen gas (N_2), plants cannot use that nitrogen directly. Nitrogen must first be "fixed" chemically to ammonia (NH_3) or other nitrogen compounds. Expensive synthetic fertilizers contain these nitrogen compounds, but bacteria produce them naturally. The process of converting nitrogen into a form plants can use is known as **nitrogen fixation.** Certain bacteria are the only organisms that can fix nitrogen in this way.

Many plants have symbiotic relationships with nitrogen-fixing bacteria. For example, soybeans and other legumes host the bacterium *Rhizobium. Rhizobium* grows in nodules, or knobs, that form on the roots of the soybean plant, as shown in **Figure 19–9**. The soybean plant provides a source of nutrients for *Rhizobium,* which converts nitrogen in the air into ammonia, which helps the plant. All plants benefit from nitrogen-fixing bacteria, but soybeans are a step ahead. Soybeans have their own fertilizer factories in their roots!

CHECKPOINT *What is nitrogen fixation?*

Biology and History

Eliminating Disease

Early discoveries with vaccination allowed new branches of science and medicine to develop. These new fields, such as bacteriology and immunology, would help in the crusade against diseases caused by bacteria and viruses.

1800

1820 Missouri Compromise temporarily maintains the balance of free and slave states in the United States.

1849 **John Snow** Snow proves for the first time that cholera is spread by contaminated drinking water. Cholera is a bacterial infection of the intestines that causes diarrhea.

1856 **William Budd** Budd shows that typhoid fever is a contagious disease. Typhoid is a bacterial infection that causes a high fever.

1881 **Louis Pasteur** Pasteur develops the first effective vaccine against an infectious bacterial disease, anthrax. Anthrax is one of the oldest recorded diseases of animals.

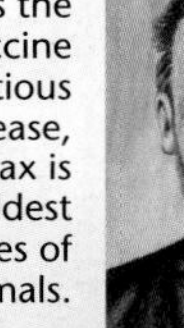

1900

PRESENTATIONS MADE EASY!

The Presentation Assistant Plus contains the Prentice Hall Presentation Pro and the Transparencies, which provide easy-to-follow visual support for every step of this lesson. If you have a computer presentation station, use Prentice Hall Presentation Pro Section 19–2, or use the transparencies listed here.

Section 19–2: **Interest Grabber**
Section Outline
Common Diseases Caused by Bacteria

Bacteria and Disease

Have you ever heard a teacher say that when a few people misbehave, they ruin it for everybody? In a way, that saying could be applied to bacteria. Bacteria are everywhere in nature, but only a few cause disease. However, these **pathogens,** or disease-causing agents, seem to get all the attention, and they give the other bacteria a bad reputation.

Bacteria cause disease in one of two general ways. Some damage the tissues of the infected organism directly by breaking them down for food. Other bacteria release toxins (poisons) that harm the body.

Heterotrophic bacteria can make you sick by damaging cells and tissues. For example, the bacteria that cause tuberculosis break down lung tissue. In contrast, many cases of food poisoning are caused by bacterial toxins. When meat, poultry, and eggs are not cooked properly, these toxins can make you sick. The symptoms of food poisoning range from an upset stomach to serious illness. Bacterial toxins can also travel throughout the body. For example, the *Streptococcus* bacteria that cause strep throat can release toxins into the bloodstream. These toxins can cause a reddish rash over the body called scarlet fever.

Many bacterial diseases can be prevented by stimulating the body's immune system with vaccines. If a bacterial infection does occur, a number of drugs and natural compounds can be used to attack and destroy the invading bacteria. These drugs include antibiotics, such as penicillin and tetracycline.

Word Origins

Pathogen comes from the Greek words *pathos,* meaning "suffering," and *-genes,* meaning "born" or "produced." So a pathogen is something that produces suffering. **The Greek word *karkinos* means "cancer." What do you think a carcinogen is?**

Writing Activity

Use the Internet or a library to find out more about one of the people in this time line. Write a summary of the person's discovery as it might appear in a newspaper story of the time.

1904

Mary Mallon
Mallon is found to be the cause of an epidemic of typhoid fever in New York. She flees authorities, but before her death 51 cases of typhoid and 3 deaths will be attributed to her, giving her the nickname "Typhoid Mary."

1928

Alexander Fleming
Fleming discovers penicillin accidentally when an experiment with bacteria is contaminated by mold. He finds that penicillin is nontoxic but inhibits the growth of many types of disease-causing bacteria.

1980

Smallpox Eradicated
The World Health Organization certifies that smallpox has been eradicated. This was the first major disease to be completely eliminated.

1989

Fall of Berlin Wall; Cold War ends

1991

Cholera Epidemic
Over 390,000 cases of cholera are reported in 11 countries throughout South and Latin America. The disease appears on the continent after being absent from it for more than 70 years.

2000

BIO INSIGHTS — FACTS AND FIGURES

Extremely poisonous exotoxins
Bacterial toxins are usually divided into two groups: exotoxins and endotoxins. Exotoxins are produced and released as part of the normal metabolism of certain bacteria. Endotoxins are typically lipopolysaccharides that were originally part of the cell wall and that are released by the lysis of the bacterium. In general, exotoxins are much more potent than endotoxins. For instance, 1 milligram of exotoxin from *Clostridium botulinum* would be fatal to 1 million guinea pigs. Just 30 grams of exotoxin from *Corynebacterium diphtheriae,* the pathogen that causes the disease diphtheria, could kill every person in New York City—about 8 million people. Diseases caused by exotoxins include botulism, cholera, diphtheria, gas gangrene, food poisoning, scarlet fever, tetanus, and toxic shock syndrome.

Bacteria and Disease

Word Origins

A carcinogen is a substance that causes cancer.

Build Science Skills

Observing Point out that bacteria are almost everywhere in nature, but only a few cause disease. Have students investigate where on the body are the most bacteria. Ask pairs of students to prepare six petri dishes of sterile nutrient agar. Have the students choose one of the pair for the investigation. The other student should use separate sterile cotton swabs to rub a 2-centimeter area at six different places on the first student's body: forehead, side of nose, cheek, back of hand, palm of hand, and ankle. For each rubbing, the student should roll the cotton swab over the agar in one of the dishes and throw the swab away. Have the students cover the dishes, label them, and place them in an incubator or a warm spot in the room for 48 hours. Then, have the student pairs observe and compare the growth on each of the dishes. Have all students report their findings to the class.

Meet Diverse Needs

Have students who need additional challenges research one of the well-known bacterial diseases. These include diphtheria, tuberculosis, syphilis, strep throat, tetanus, typhoid fever, cholera, Lyme disease, Legionnaire's disease, whooping cough, leprosy, anthrax, and food poisoning (including *Salmonella* and *E. coli*). Ask students to prepare a report on the disease, including detailed information on the type of bacterium that causes the disease, as well as the symptoms, transmission, and treatment of the disease. You may want some students to make a presentation to the class. **Learning modality: verbal**

Answer to . . .

CHECKPOINT *The process of converting nitrogen to a form plants can use*

Build Science Skills

Applying Concepts Ask students: **What are antibiotics?** *(Antibiotics are compounds that block the growth and reproduction of bacteria.)* Explain that, although antibiotics have proven amazingly effective in combating bacterial diseases, many bacteria have become increasingly resistant to most antibiotics, worrying medical authorities. Ask: **What is the process among living things that results in the appearance of such resistant bacteria?** *(Evolution)* Call on students at random to describe the process of evolution that results in antibiotic resistance. Then, have students reread the description of antibiotic resistance on page 403 in Chapter 16.

Human Uses of Bacteria

Build Science Skills

Observing Tell students that you are preparing a microscope slide to examine fresh yogurt under the microscope. As you prepare the slide, involve them by asking questions about the process. Add water to a tiny amount of plain yogurt to make a thin, cloudy mixture. The sample has to be thinned for light to pass through and for individual particles to be more visible. Place a drop of the yogurt mixture on a microscope slide. Stain the sample with a drop of methylene blue. Put on a coverslip. Then, have students observe the slide under high magnification. Ask students: **What do you see?** *(Blue ovals or cylinders)* Explain that the cylinders are *Lactobacillus* bacteria. Ask: **Why might there be bacteria in yogurt?** *(Students might suggest that the yogurt is spoiled or that the bacteria are used to make yogurt.)* Explain that *Lactobacillus* is used to make milk into yogurt. The bacteria carry out fermentation using milk sugar, or lactose. A product of that fermentation is lactic acid. The lactic acid inhibits the growth of microorganisms that would spoil the milk and also greatly lowers the pH of the product, which causes milk protein to coagulate and thicken, producing yogurt.

Common Diseases Caused by Bacteria

Disease	Pathogen	Prevention
Tooth decay	*Streptococcus mutans*	Regular dental hygiene
Lyme disease	*Borrelia burgdorferi*	Protection from tick bites
Tetanus	*Clostridium tetani*	Current tetanus vaccination
Tuberculosis	*Mycobacterium tuberculosis*	Vaccination
Salmonella food poisoning	*Salmonella enteritidis*	Proper food-handling practices
Pneumonia	*Streptococcus pneumoniae*	Maintaining good health
Cholera	*Vibrio cholerae*	Clean water supplies

▲ **Figure 19–10** **Bacteria cause disease in one of two general ways. Some damage the tissues of an infected organism directly by breaking them down for food. Other bacteria release toxins that hurt the body.** Some of the diseases caused by pathogenic bacteria are listed in the above table.

Antibiotics are compounds that block the growth and reproduction of bacteria. They can be used to cure many bacterial diseases. One of the major reasons for the dramatic increase in life expectancy during the past two centuries is an increased understanding of how to prevent and cure bacterial infections. **Figure 19–10** shows some common bacterial diseases, what pathogens cause them, and how they can be prevented.

Human Uses of Bacteria

Every day, you probably use food products that have been manufactured using bacteria. Bacteria are used in the production of a variety of foods, including cheese, yogurt, buttermilk, and sour cream. The cheeses shown in **Figure 19–11** are examples of such foods. Some bacteria are used to make pickles and sauerkraut, and some make vinegar from wine.

Bacteria are also used in industry. One type of bacterium can digest petroleum, making it very helpful in cleaning up small oil spills. Some bacteria remove waste products and poisons from water. Others can even help to mine minerals from the ground. Still others are used to synthesize drugs and chemicals through the techniques of genetic engineering.

Biotechnology companies have begun to realize that bacteria adapted to extreme environments may be a rich source of heat-stable enzymes. These enzymes can be used in medicine, food production, and industrial chemistry. Recently, a company signed a unique "bioprospecting" agreement with Yellowstone National Park, where more than half of all the hot springs and geysers on Earth are found.

◀ **Figure 19–11** Cheeses are only one kind of food made using bacteria. **Applying Concepts** *What other products are made with the help of bacteria?*

FACTS AND FIGURES

Those helpful bacteria

There are many types of bacteria that are important to humans—far more than there is space to describe them. *Streptomyces* bacteria produce tetracycline and many other antibiotics. In fact, they produce more kinds of antibiotics than any other type of microbe. One strain of *Streptomyces* changes lignin, a chemical in wood pulp, into a form that enhances antibody production when injected along with a vaccine. A number of bacteria can be used to selectively "sponge up" toxic metals such as cobalt, uranium, and zinc. These bacteria, which either bind to the metals or ingest them, are much easier to remove than the metal ions. Certain chemical companies have developed strains of bacteria that break down chemical pollutants such as cyanide, dioxin, PCBs, and phenolics. One genetically engineered stain of bacteria can even dispose of the herbicide Agent Orange.

Controlling Bacteria

Most bacteria are harmless, and many are beneficial. However, the risks of bacterial infection are great enough to warrant efforts to control bacterial growth.

Sterilization destroys bacteria by subjecting them either to great heat or to chemical action. Most bacteria cannot survive high temperatures for a long time and can be killed in boiling water. An entire hospital, of course, cannot be dropped into boiling water. But a hospital can be sterilized, one room at a time, by using disinfectants. A disinfectant is a chemical solution that kills bacteria. Disinfectants are also used in the home to clean bathrooms, kitchens, and other rooms where bacteria may cause disease.

Bacteria can cause food to spoil. One method of stopping food from spoiling is refrigeration. Bacteria, like most organisms, usually grow more slowly at low temperatures. Food that is stored at a low temperature will keep longer because the bacteria will take much longer to multiply. In addition, many kinds of food can be sterilized by boiling, frying, or steaming. Each of these cooking techniques raises the temperature of the food to a point where the bacteria are killed.

If food is to be preserved for a long time, a method called canning is sometimes used. The food is heated to a high temperature. It then must be immediately placed into sterile glass jars or metal cans and sealed. Food that has been properly canned will last almost indefinitely. Finally, a number of chemical treatments will inhibit the growth of bacteria in food. These include treating food with everyday chemicals such as salt, vinegar, or sugar. Salted meat, pickled vegetables, and jam are examples of chemically preserved foods.

KEEP CURRENT WITH . . . SCIENCE NEWS®

To find out more about the topics in this chapter, go to: **www.phschool.com**

19–2 Section Assessment

1. **Key Concept** What is the importance of bacteria in the environment?
2. **Key Concept** How do bacteria cause disease?
3. How are bacterial infections often treated?
4. Describe three methods of preventing bacterial growth in food.
5. **Critical Thinking Applying Concepts** You think you might have a bacterial infection. Would it be a good idea to ask for a vaccination against the bacteria? Why or why not?

iTEXT Assessment Use iText to review the important concepts in Section 19–2.

ALTERNATIVE ASSESSMENT

Creative Writing

In *War of the Worlds,* a book written by H. G. Wells, Earth is invaded by aliens. No weapons can kill the invaders, and civilization seems doomed. Earth is saved, however, when the invaders die from diseases they contract. Using a similar premise, write a story about people from Earth voyaging to another planet some time in the future.

19–2 Section Assessment

1. Bacteria are vital to maintaining the living world. Some are producers that capture energy by photosynthesis. Others help to break down the nutrients in dead matter and the atmosphere, allowing other organisms to use the nutrients.
2. Bacteria cause disease either by damaging the tissues of the infected organism or by releasing toxins that harm the body.
3. A number of drugs and natural compounds can be used to attack and destroy invading bacteria. These drugs include antibiotics, such as penicillin and tetracycline.
4. Students should describe three of the methods discussed in this section, including sterilization, refrigeration, canning, and chemical treatment.
5. It would not be a good idea, because a vaccine prevents bacterial disease rather than curing a bacterial infection.

Controlling Bacteria

SCIENCE NEWS®

Encourage students to visit **www.phschool.com** for the most current information on this topic.

Build Science Skills

Designing Experiments Challenge groups of students to design an experiment to test the hypothesis that washing hands with antibacterial soap reduces the number of bacteria on the hands. A typical experiment will suggest dragging a washed and an unwashed finger across agar in separate petri dishes and then comparing bacterial growth on the agar.

3 ASSESS

Evaluate Understanding

Ask students to write a paragraph that explains why bacteria are vital to maintaining the living world. In their paragraphs, students should mention the importance of decomposers and nitrogen fixers.

Reteach

Have pairs of students work together to make a small public-health pamphlet that focuses on the prevention and treatment of bacterial diseases.

ALTERNATIVE ASSESSMENT

A typical story might focus on the carrying of disease-causing bacteria by the travelers from Earth and the lack of immunity to those bacteria by the residents of another planet. The result would be an epidemic of bacterial diseases.

Use iText to review the key concepts in Section 19–2.

Answers to . . .

Figure 19–11 *Yogurt, buttermilk, sour cream, pickles, sauerkraut, vinegar, drugs, chemicals*

Section 19–3

1 FOCUS

Objectives

19.3.1 ***Describe*** the structure of a virus.

19.3.2 ***Explain*** how viruses cause infection.

Guide for Reading

Vocabulary Preview

Have students preview the vocabulary words by skimming the section for the boldfaced terms and recording the definition of each.

Reading Strategy

Before students read, have them preview the different viral structures shown in Figure 19–13 and make a list of questions about the structure and function of viruses. Students should look for answers to their questions as they read the section.

2 INSTRUCT

What Is a Virus?

Use Visuals

Figure 19–12 Before students have read the introduction to the section or the caption to the figure, have them look at the photo of the infected tobacco leaf. Then, describe the puzzle that faced scientists who were trying to determine the cause of tobacco mosaic disease. Review the experiments that led to the discovery of viruses. Have students analyze for themselves the results of each experiment and suggest to them further experiments that could be performed. Then, have students read the text. By looking into the problem for themselves, students will gain a much better understanding of the way viruses were discovered.

19–3 Viruses

Guide for Reading

Key Concepts
- What is the structure of a virus?
- How do viruses cause infection?

Vocabulary
virus
capsid
bacteriophage
lytic infection
lysogenic infection
retrovirus
prion

Reading Strategy: Using Visuals As you read about viral replication in this section, trace each step in **Figures 19–14** and **19–15.** Then, list the steps, and write a few sentences to describe each step.

Imagine that you have been presented with a great challenge. Farmers in your region have begun to lose a valuable crop to a plant disease. The disease produces large pale spots on the leaves of plants similar to those shown in **Figure 19–12.** The diseased leaves look like mosaics of yellow and green. As the disease progresses, the leaves turn yellow, wither, and fall off, killing the plant.

To determine what is causing the disease, you take leaves from a diseased plant and extract a juice. You place a few drops of the juice on the leaves of healthy plants. A few days later, the mosaic pattern is right where you put the drops. Could the source of disease be in the juice?

You use a microscope to look for a germ that might cause the disease, but none can be seen. Even when the tiniest of cells are filtered out of the juice, it still causes the disease. You infer that the juice must contain pathogens so small that they are not visible under the light microscope. Although you cannot see the disease-causing particles, you're sure they're there. You give them the name *virus,* from the Latin word for "poison."

If you think you could have come to all of these conclusions, congratulations! You're walking in the footsteps of a 28-year-old Russian biologist named Dmitri Ivanovski. In 1892, Ivanovski pinpointed the cause of tobacco mosaic disease to juice extracted from infected plants. In 1897, Dutch scientist Martinus Beijerinck determined that tiny particles in the juice caused the disease, and named these particles viruses.

What Is a Virus?

In 1935, when the American biochemist Wendell Stanley purified the tobacco mosaic virus into a crystal, it became clear that viruses were not living things. **Viruses are particles of nucleic acid, protein, and in some cases lipids that can reproduce only by infecting living cells.** Viruses differ widely in terms of size and structure. You can see examples of the diversity of viruses in **Figure 19–13.** All viruses, however, have one thing in common: They enter living cells and, once inside, use the machinery of the infected cell to produce more viruses.

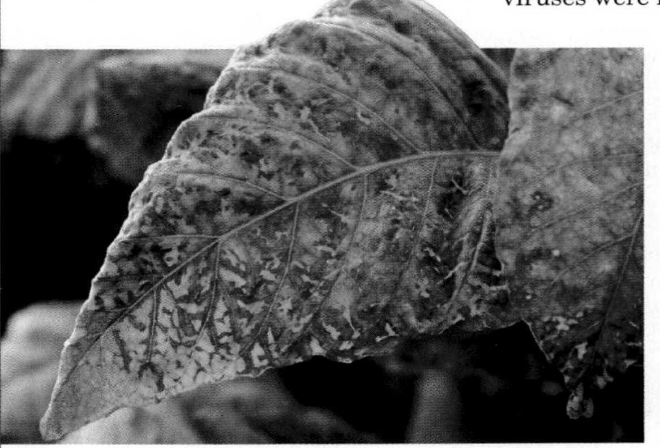

◀ **Figure 19–12** Tobacco mosaic virus causes the leaves of tobacco plants to develop a pattern of spots called a mosaic.

SECTION REVIEW

Print:
- ***Teaching Resources,*** Section Review 19–3, Chapter 19 Exploration
- ***Guided Reading and Study Workbook,*** Section 19–3

Technology:
- ***iText,*** Section 19–3
- ***BioDetectives Videotape:*** "Influenza: Tracking a Virus"; "Hantavirus: A Tale of Mice and People"

Figure 19–13 Virus Structures

Viruses come in a variety of sizes and shapes. **A typical virus is composed of a core of either DNA or RNA, surrounded by a protein coat, or capsid.**

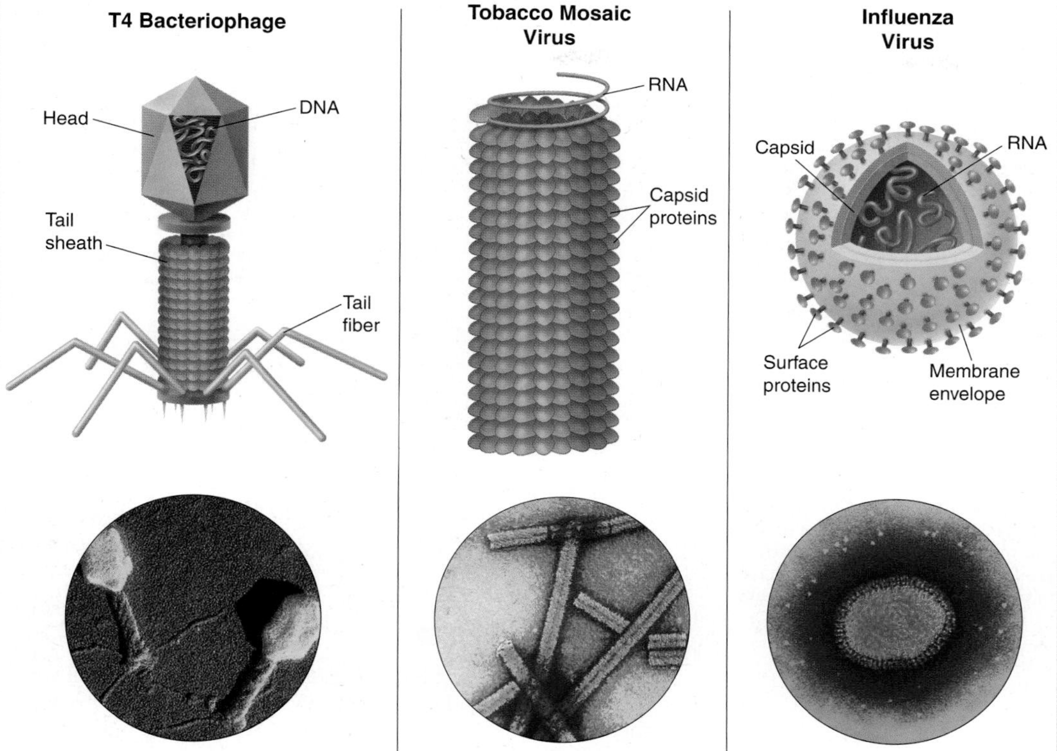

T4 Bacteriophage

Head
DNA
Tail sheath
Tail fiber

Tobacco Mosaic Virus

RNA
Capsid proteins

Influenza Virus

Capsid
RNA
Surface proteins
Membrane envelope

T4 Bacteriophage
(magnification: 82,000×)

Tobacco Mosaic Virus
(magnification: 200,000×)

Influenza Virus
(magnification: 1,000,000×)

Most viruses are so small they can be seen only with the aid of a powerful electron microscope. **A typical virus is composed of a core of either DNA or RNA surrounded by a protein coat.** The simplest viruses contain only a few genes, while the most complex may have more than a hundred genes.

A virus's outer protein coat is called its **capsid.** The capsid includes proteins that enable a virus to enter a host cell. The capsid proteins of a typical virus bind to the surface of a cell and "trick" the cell into allowing it inside. Once inside, the viral genes take over. The cell transcribes the viral genes, putting the genetic program of the virus into effect. Sometimes that genetic program may simply cause the cell to make copies of the virus, but often it destroys the host cell.

Use Visuals

Figure 19–13 Ask students: **From these three examples, can you describe the typical shape of a virus?** *(No. The shapes are so different that there is no typical shape.)* **What parts do all three kinds of viruses have in common?** *(A capsid and a core of nucleic acid, either DNA or RNA)* Point out that each of the three examples in the figure infects different kinds of organisms—bacteria, plants, and animals. Explain that viruses are often classified according to the type of organism they infect.

Build Science Skills

Using Models Give each student an unshelled sunflower seed. (Other easily shelled seeds will also work well, including peanuts, pumpkinseeds, and pistachio nuts.) Then, ask: **In what ways is the structure of a virus like the structure of a sunflower seed?** *(Students should recognize that both sunflower seeds and viruses consist of a protective outer shell that encases vital contents.)* **What does the shell of the sunflower seed represent in a virus?** *(The capsid)* **How are the functions of a sunflower seed's shell and a virus's capsid similar?** *(Both protect the contents.)* **What does the kernel of the sunflower seed represent?** *(The virus's core of DNA or RNA)* **What is the function of the virus's core?** *(To put the genetic program of the virus into effect)*

PRESENTATIONS MADE EASY!

The Presentation Assistant Plus contains the Prentice Hall Presentation Pro and the Transparencies, which provide easy-to-follow visual support for every step of this lesson. If you have a computer presentation station, use Prentice Hall Presentation Pro Section 19–3, or use the transparencies listed here.

Section 19–3:

Interest Grabber
Section Outline
Common Diseases Caused by Viruses
Figure 19–13
Figure 19–14
Figure 19–15

Viral Infection

Build Science Skills

Predicting Before students read about viral infections, show them an electron micrograph that shows a virus attaching to a cell membrane. Give a simple description of what the image shows, and then ask students what they think will happen to the virus and the cell. Have students consider this question by making a prediction about what events will occur next and how the virus will ultimately affect the cell.

Use Visuals

Figure 19–14 Ask students: **What are bacteriophages?** *(They are viruses that infect bacteria.)* **Do all viruses infect bacteria?** *(No. There are viruses that infect animal cells and viruses that infect plant cells.)* Explain that plant and animal viruses have similar replication cycles, though none is exactly like the lytic or the lysogenic cycles of bacteriophages. Then, ask: **In a lytic infection, how does the virus DNA get into a host cell?** *(The bacteriophage attaches to a bacterium's cell wall and injects its DNA into the bacterium.)* **What eventually happens to the host cell?** *(The replication of virus particles inside the host cell causes it to burst.)* Explain that bursting, or breaking open, is called *lysis,* which is why this process is called a *lytic cycle.*

Encourage students to view "Influenza: Tracking a Virus."

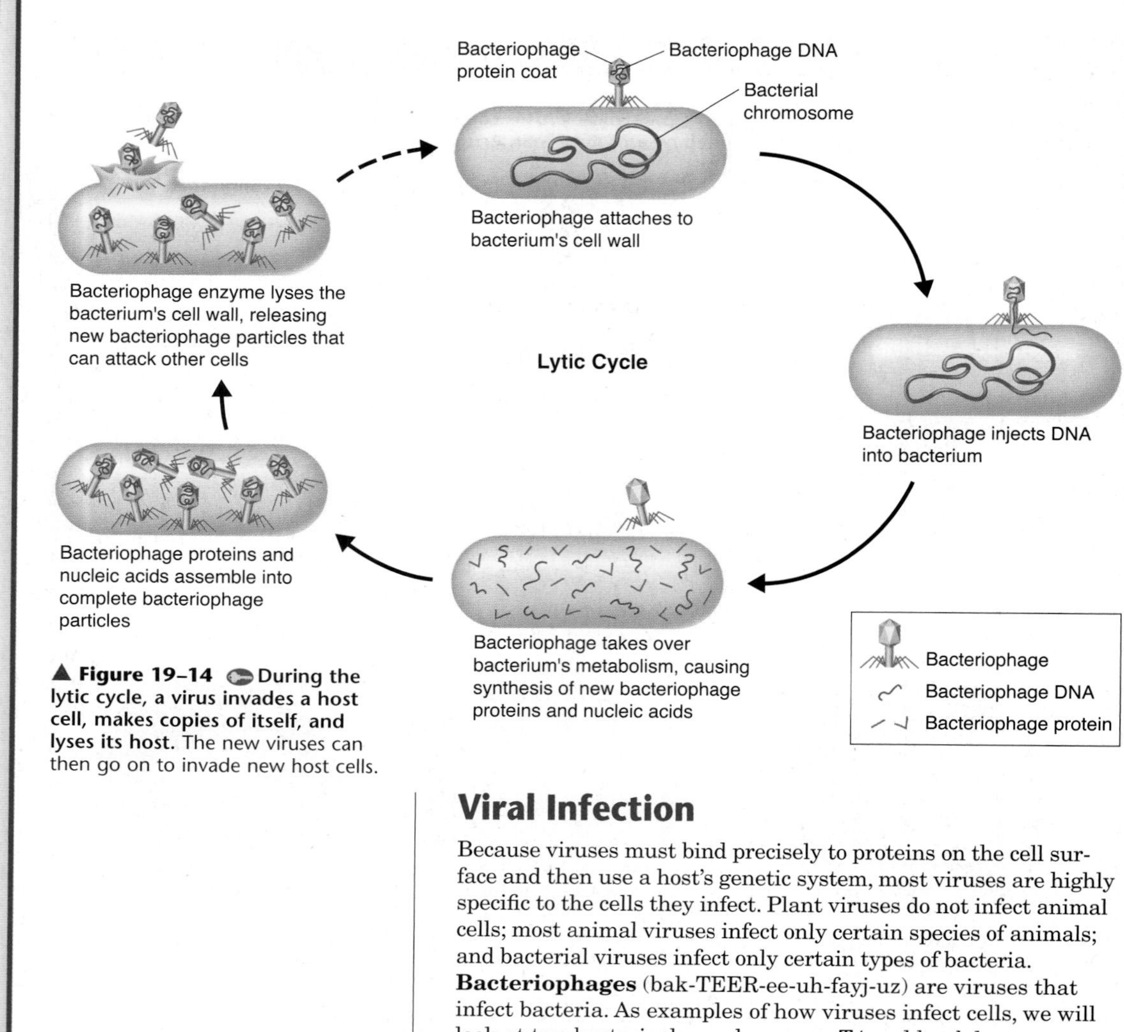

Bacteriophage protein coat
Bacteriophage DNA
Bacterial chromosome
Bacteriophage attaches to bacterium's cell wall
Bacteriophage injects DNA into bacterium
Bacteriophage takes over bacterium's metabolism, causing synthesis of new bacteriophage proteins and nucleic acids
Bacteriophage proteins and nucleic acids assemble into complete bacteriophage particles
Bacteriophage enzyme lyses the bacterium's cell wall, releasing new bacteriophage particles that can attack other cells
Lytic Cycle
Bacteriophage
Bacteriophage DNA
Bacteriophage protein

▲ **Figure 19–14** **During the lytic cycle, a virus invades a host cell, makes copies of itself, and lyses its host.** The new viruses can then go on to invade new host cells.

To find out more about the transmission of a virus, view the videotape "Influenza: Tracking a Virus."

Viral Infection

Because viruses must bind precisely to proteins on the cell surface and then use a host's genetic system, most viruses are highly specific to the cells they infect. Plant viruses do not infect animal cells; most animal viruses infect only certain species of animals; and bacterial viruses infect only certain types of bacteria. **Bacteriophages** (bak-TEER-ee-uh-fayj-uz) are viruses that infect bacteria. As examples of how viruses infect cells, we will look at two bacteriophages known as T4 and lambda.

✔ CHECKPOINT *What is a bacteriophage?*

Lytic Infection **Figure 19–14** shows the lytic cycle of bacteriophage T4. **In a lytic infection, a virus enters a cell, makes copies of itself, and causes the cell to burst.** Bacteriophage T4 has a DNA core inside an intricate capsid that is activated by contact with a host cell. T4 then injects its DNA directly into the cell. In most cases, the host cell cannot tell the difference between its own DNA and the DNA of the virus. Consequently, the cell begins to make messenger RNA from the genes of the virus. This viral mRNA acts like a molecular wrecking crew, shutting down and taking over the infected host cell. Some viral genes turn off the synthesis of molecules that are important to the infected cell.

BIO INSIGHTS **FACTS AND FIGURES**

Classifying viruses
Because viruses are not living things, they are not part of any kingdom, and they are not identified as species. Classification of viruses depends on the chemical and physical properties of the virus. The major division focuses on their genetic material; thus, there are DNA viruses and RNA viruses. Viruses are then further divided by the shape of their protein coats and their sizes. This scheme results in a major group called the picornaviruses, which are small RNA viruses with a polyhedral shape. Both poliovirus and the rhinoviruses (which cause the common cold) are subgroups of the picornaviruses. Another way of grouping viruses is by the type of host a virus infects. Thus, animal viruses infect animals, plant viruses infect plants, and bacterial viruses—or bacteriophages—infect bacteria.

The virus uses the materials of the host cell to make thousands of copies of itself. Before long, the infected cell lyses, or bursts, and releases hundreds of virus particles that may go on to infect other cells. Because the host cell is lysed and destroyed, this process is called a **lytic infection.**

In its own way, a lytic virus is similar to a desperado in the Old West. First, the outlaw eliminates the town's existing authority (host cell DNA). Then, the desperado demands to be outfitted with new weapons, horses, and riding equipment by terrorizing the local people (using the host cell to make proteins). Finally, the desperado forms a gang that leaves the town to attack new communities (the host cell bursts, releasing hundreds of virus particles).

Lysogenic Infection Other viruses cause a **lysogenic infection,** in which a host cell makes copies of the virus indefinitely. The bacteriophage lambda causes lysogenic infections, as shown in **Figure 19–15.** **In a lysogenic infection, a virus embeds its DNA into the DNA of the host cell and is replicated along with the host cell's DNA.** Unlike lytic viruses, lysogenic viruses do not lyse the host cell right away. Instead, a lysogenic virus will insert its DNA into the DNA of the host cell. The viral DNA that is embedded in the host's DNA is called a prophage.

▼ **Figure 19–15** **In a lysogenic infection, the viral DNA enters a host cell and inserts itself into the host's DNA.** Certain conditions can cause a lysogenic virus to enter the lytic cycle.

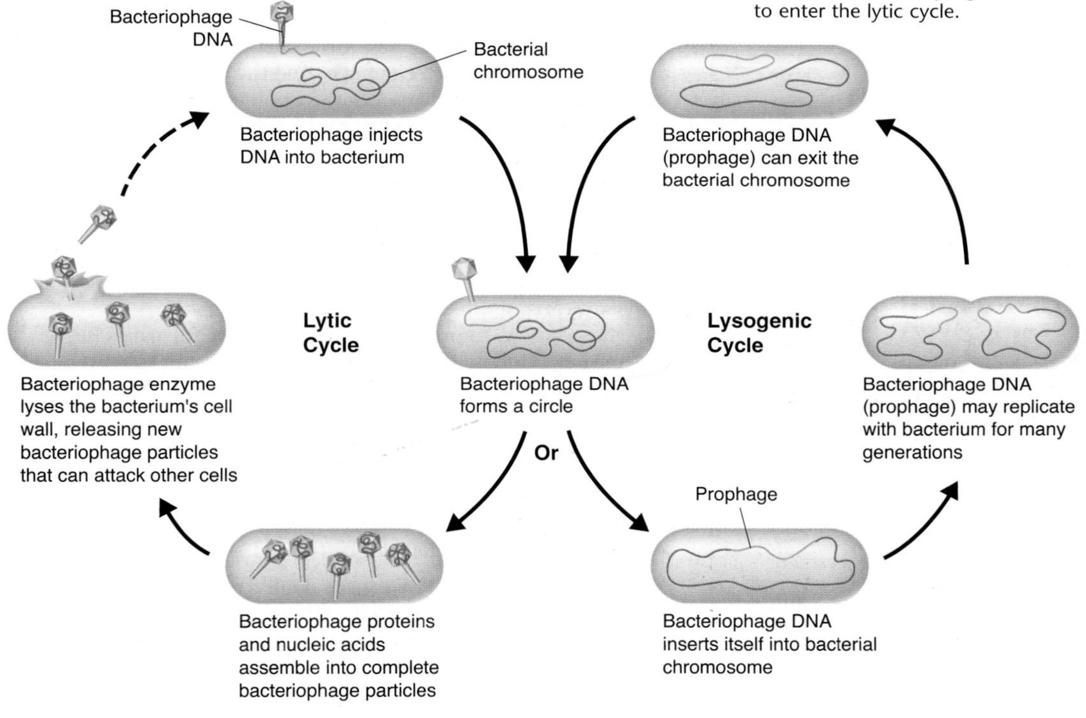
Bacteriophage DNA
Bacterial chromosome
Bacteriophage injects DNA into bacterium
Bacteriophage DNA (prophage) can exit the bacterial chromosome
Lytic Cycle
Lysogenic Cycle
Bacteriophage enzyme lyses the bacterium's cell wall, releasing new bacteriophage particles that can attack other cells
Bacteriophage DNA forms a circle
Bacteriophage DNA (prophage) may replicate with bacterium for many generations
Or
Prophage
Bacteriophage proteins and nucleic acids assemble into complete bacteriophage particles
Bacteriophage DNA inserts itself into bacterial chromosome

Use Visuals

Figure 19–15 Ask students: **In the lysogenic cycle, what happens to the virus DNA?** *(It inserts itself into the bacterial chromosome.)* **What is the viral DNA called while it is embedded in the bacterial DNA?** *(A prophage)* Explain that the bacterium can replicate for many generations with the prophage embedded in its DNA, giving rise to many host cells that contain a prophage. When conditions change, the virus can switch from the lysogenic cycle to the lytic cycle. Explain that it is usually some kind of environmental change that causes the switch, such as a chemical change or radiation. As you describe this process to students, have them trace the path with a finger. Begin at the upper left, where the bacteriophage attaches to the bacterial cell in the lytic cycle. Trace the finger down to the right and into the lysogenic cycle. Move the finger around the lysogenic cycle back to the middle, where a switch in cycles can occur. If it does, then move the finger down to the left and around the lytic cycle. Tracing through the cycles makes a figure eight. Make sure that students understand that a switch in cycles may not occur. The virus can move around the lysogenic cycle for many generations of the bacteria.

Address Misconceptions

After students have read about lytic and lysogenic infections, ask: **Do viruses have one of the important characteristics of living things—the ability to reproduce?** *(Viruses are not living, so they do not reproduce; they replicate.)* Point out that in the description of each type of infection, the virus is described as making copies of itself. In a lytic infection, though, the virus uses the materials of the host cell to make copies of itself. In a lysogenic infection, the virus uses the DNA of the host cell to make copies of itself. Explain that, for this reason, biologists often talk about viral "replication" or "multiplication" rather than "reproduction."

BIO INSIGHTS

FACTS AND FIGURES

Viruses get in

Although bacteriophages typically inject their DNA into the host cell, not all viruses invade a host cell in this manner. Many animal viruses, such as the semiliki virus, enter the host through endocytosis—the binding of the virus to the cell membrane, inducing the cell to take in the virus. Once inside the host cell, the virus sheds its protein coat and either undergoes replication or becomes part of the host's DNA. Interestingly, a few animal viruses, such as those responsible for rabies, AIDS, and influenza, leave the host cell through budding, which can be thought of as the opposite of endocytosis.

Answer to . . .

CHECKPOINT *A bacteriophage is a virus that infects bacteria.*

Quick Lab

Objective Students will make models of two different viruses and conclude that viruses differ in structure.

Skills Focus **Using Models, Drawing Conclusions, Calculating**

Materials metric ruler, scissors, tape, craft materials

Time 20 minutes

Strategy Make sure that students accurately follow steps 3 and 4. A model of T4, for example, that is 5 cm long is 50 million nm long; 50 million nm/370 nm = 135,000. The model is 135,000 times as long as the actual virus.

Expected Outcomes Students will learn that viruses differ in structure.

Analyze and Conclude

1. Both models should include a capsid and a core of either DNA or RNA.
2. A model of a T4 bacteriophage should include a head, a tail sheath, and a tail fiber. A model of an influenza virus should include surface proteins and a membrane envelope.
3. Students should measure the image of the virus they modeled in Figure 19–13 and divide this length by the magnification to determine the actual size of the virus. For example, the image of the T4 bacteriophage is 3 cm long; 3 cm = 3×10^{-2} m; 3×10^{-2} m/82,000 = 0.37×10^{-6} m = 370 nm.

Viruses and Disease

Build Science Skills

Making Judgments Prepare a display of advertisements and packages of cold remedies. Ask students: **What is the purpose of these products?** *(To relieve cold symptoms)* **How do they relieve cold symptoms?** *(Lower fever, relieve aches and pains, reduce congestion, stop cough, and so on)* **Is this a sign that you are cured?** *(No. Point out that these medications merely provide relief from symptoms. A cure would have to disable the virus that causes the cold.)*

Encourage students to view "Hantavirus: A Tale of Mice and People."

Quick Lab

How do viruses differ in structure?

Materials craft materials, metric ruler, scissors, tape

Procedure

1. Make models of two of the viruses shown in **Figure 19–13** on page 483.
2. Label the parts of each of your virus models.
3. Measure and record the length of each of your virus models in centimeters. Convert the length of each model into nanometers: 1 cm = 10 million nm.
4. Calculate the length of each virus you modeled. Divide the length of each model by the length of the actual virus to determine how many times larger each model is than the virus it represents.

Analyze and Conclude

1. **Using Models** What parts of your models are found in all viruses?
2. **Drawing Conclusions** What parts do one or both of your models include that are found in only some viruses?
3. **Calculating** How many times larger are your models than the viruses they represent?

Viral DNA may not stay in the prophage form indefinitely. Eventually, any one of a number of factors will activate the DNA of the prophage, which will then remove itself from the host cell DNA and direct the synthesis of new virus particles. There are many differences between bacteriophages and the viruses that infect eukaryotic cells. Most viruses, however, show patterns of infection similar to either the lytic or lysogenic cycles of bacteriophages.

Viruses and Disease

Viruses cause human diseases such as polio, measles, AIDS, mumps, influenza, yellow fever, rabies, and the common cold. In most viral infections, viruses attack and destroy certain cells in the body, causing the symptoms of the disease.

The best way to protect against most viral diseases lies in prevention, often by the use of vaccines. A vaccine is a preparation of weakened or killed virus or viral proteins. When injected into the body, a vaccine stimulates the immune system, sometimes producing permanent immunity to the disease.

Most vaccines provide protection only if they are used before an infection begins. Once a viral disease has been contracted, it may be too late to control the infection. However, sometimes the symptoms of the infection can be treated.

Viruses and Cancer Certain viruses called oncogenic viruses cause cancer in animals. Oncogenic viruses generally carry genes that disrupt the normal controls over cell growth and division. By studying such viruses, scientists have identified many of the genes that regulate cell growth in eukaryotes.

To find out more about how scientists study disease, view the videotape "Hantavirus: A Tale of Mice and People."

HISTORY OF SCIENCE

An end to smallpox

In 1980, the World Health Organization announced that the smallpox virus had been eradicated. This virus was the cause of many terrible epidemics throughout human history, and as recently as 1967 it caused 2 million deaths worldwide. The introduction of the virus into the Americas by Europeans caused particularly bad epidemics among Native Americans because none had immunity. In Europe and Asia, people had long recognized that someone who had contracted the less severe form of smallpox was forever immunized to the more severe form. In the late 1700s, English physician Edward Jenner noticed that milkmaids who contracted cowpox also gained immunity from smallpox. From that observation and subsequent experimentation, Jenner developed the first vaccine, a term he named from the Latin word for cow, *vacca,* because it was made from the cowpox virus.

Retroviruses Some viruses that contain RNA as their genetic information are called **retroviruses.** When retroviruses infect a cell, they produce a DNA copy of their RNA. This DNA, much like a prophage, is inserted into the DNA of the host cell. Retroviruses get their name from the fact that their genetic information is copied backward—that is, from RNA to DNA instead of from DNA to RNA. Retroviruses are responsible for some types of cancer in animals, including humans. HIV, the virus that causes AIDS, is a retrovirus.

Prions In 1972, American scientist Stanley Prusiner became interested in scrapie, an infectious disease in sheep for which the exact cause was unknown. Although he first suspected a virus, experiments suggested that the disease might actually be caused by tiny particles found in the brain. Unlike viruses, these particles contained no DNA or RNA, only protein. Prusiner called these particles **prions,** short for "protein infectious particles." There is strong evidence that mad cow disease and a similar disease in humans may also be caused by prions.

▲ **Figure 19–16** Prions may cause several infectious diseases, including mad cow disease. This cow was killed by mad cow disease. **Comparing and Contrasting** How are prions similar to viruses? How are they different?

Are Viruses Alive?

Viruses share the genetic code with living things and affect living things. But most biologists do not consider viruses to be alive because viruses do not have all the characteristics of life, which you learned about in Chapter 1. For example, viruses are not cells and are not able to reproduce independently. However, when viruses do infect living cells, they can make copies of themselves, regulate gene expression, and even evolve.

Although viruses are smaller and simpler than the smallest cells, they could not have been much like the first living things. It seems more likely that viruses developed after living cells. In fact, the first viruses may have evolved from the genetic material of living cells. Viruses have continued to evolve, along with the cells they infect, over billions of years.

19–3 Section Assessment

1. **Key Concept** What are the parts of a virus?
2. **Key Concept** Compare and contrast two ways that viruses cause infection.
3. What is the difference between a bacteriophage and a prophage?
4. What is a retrovirus?
5. **Critical Thinking Making Judgments** Do you think viruses should be considered a form of life? Describe the reasons for your opinion.

iTEXT Assessment Use iText to review the important concepts in Section 19–3.

Take It to the NET

Research a virus that is currently in the news. Then, prepare a FAQ (Frequently Asked Questions) sheet about the virus. Use the links provided in the Biology area at the Prentice Hall Web site for help in completing this activity: **www.phschool.com**

Are Viruses Alive?

Build Science Skills

Applying Concepts Have students turn back to the list of characteristics of living things on page 16 in Section 1–3. Have students assess whether viruses exhibit each characteristic. Viruses are not made of cells, they don't grow and develop, they don't obtain and use materials and energy, they don't respond to their environment, and they don't maintain an internal balance. Some students may argue that viruses reproduce, but remind students that they replicate. Viruses perhaps exhibit two of the characteristics: They are based on a universal genetic code, and they change over time.

3 ASSESS

Evaluate Understanding

Have students make two flowcharts to show two examples of the way viruses infect cells. Students should use Figure 19–14 and Figure 19–15.

Reteach

Have students compare the illustrations of virus structures in Figure 19–13 with the illustration of bacterium structure in Figure 19–2. Place emphasis on what viruses don't have.

Take It to the NET

Possible student answers may include the following: What type of virus is it? What effects does this virus have on people's health? Where was the virus found? What is being done to control the virus? Where can people go for more information on the virus? For additional information, visit **www.phschool.com**

19–3 Section Assessment

1. A typical virus is composed of a core of either DNA or RNA surrounded by a protein coat, which is called a capsid.
2. In a lytic infection, a virus enters a cell, makes copies of itself, and causes the cell to burst. In a lysogenic infection, a virus embeds its DNA into the DNA of the host cell and replicates along with the host cell's DNA.
3. A bacteriophage is a virus that infects bacteria. A prophage is the lysogenic viral DNA that is embedded in the host's DNA.
4. A retrovirus is a virus that contains genetic information copied from RNA to DNA.
5. Most students will assert that viruses should not be considered a form of life because they do not exhibit all the characteristics of life, such being made of cells and being able to reproduce independently.

iTEXT

Use iText to review the key concepts in Section 19–3.

Answer to . . .

Figure 19–16 *Like viruses, prions can cause diseases. Unlike viruses, prions contain no DNA or RNA— only protein.*

Exploration

Objective Students will be able to draw the conclusion that temperature does limit the growth and reproduction of bacteria.

Skills Focus **Analyzing Data, Drawing Conclusions**

Time 2 hours prelab preparation if you are pouring your own plates. Class time: 15 minutes on day 1, 15 minutes on day 2, and 45 minutes on day 3

Advance Prep Provide a diluted liquid culture of noninfectious bacteria for this lab. Do not use *Serratia marcescens* or *Bacillus subtilis* for this lab. Although they were once thought to be safe, they are now known to be dangerous for students with compromised immune systems. Check the dilution by culturing in advance to ensure that the colonies are not too few or too numerous to count. Then, refrigerate the diluted culture until the class begins. Plan on about 2 hours for prelab preparation if you are pouring your own plates. Make a 37°C incubator available to the class for this activity.

Alternative Materials An alternative to having students carry out this lab using bacterial cultures is to acquire a CD-ROM simulation of a similar lab.

Safety Make that sure students put on plastic, disposable gloves before beginning step 4. Don't allow students to collect wild bacteria or culture mouth swabs. Ensure that students wash their hands with soap and hot water after handling the plates. Properly dispose of plastic gloves. Rigorous application of sterile laboratory technique is a must for all microbiology labs. Use a disinfectant, such as diluted bleach, to wipe down all surfaces where bacteria might have been deposited. Students with compromised immune systems are always at risk in a microbiology lab, and it is difficult to know if such students are in your class. The best procedure is to inform parents if you are using any potentially dangerous materials. Provide a container in which students can safely dispose of used swabs and plates. For safe disposal, soak the plates and swabs overnight in undiluted chlorine bleach, 70% isopropyl alcohol, or another disinfectant. It may be possible to place the used plates and swabs in biohazard bags and dispose of them through a local hospital.

Sample Data Table

Temperature	Number of Colonies	
	24 hours	48 hours
3°C	0	1
20°C	16	209
37°C	152	383

Exploration

Identifying Limits to the Growth of Bacteria

Bacteria can be found nearly everywhere on Earth and are able to reproduce with amazing speed. So, why isn't Earth covered by huge numbers of bacteria? What prevents them from growing and reproducing in nature as quickly as they can in the laboratory? In this investigation, you will determine whether an environmental factor such as temperature can control the growth and reproduction of bacteria.

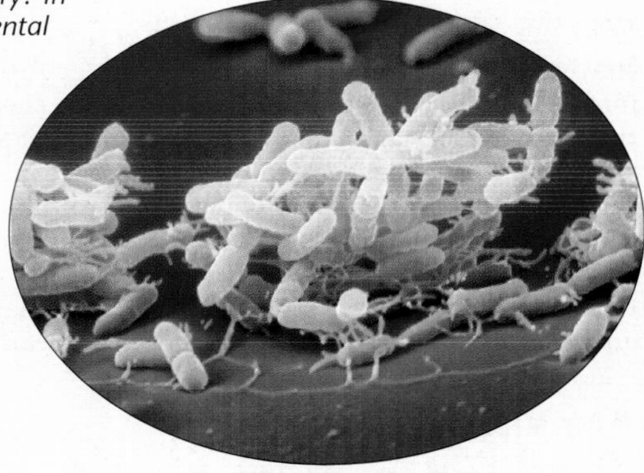

Salmonella enteritidis **bacteria** (magnification: 17,000×)

Problem **Does temperature limit the growth and reproduction of bacteria?**

Materials

- 3 sterile agar plates
- hand lens
- bacterial culture
- sterile cotton swabs
- glass-marking pencil
- transparent tape
- thermometer

Skills Analyzing Data, Drawing Conclusions

Procedure    

1. **Predicting** Predict whether temperature will affect the growth rate of bacterial colonies. Record your prediction.
2. Use the hand lens to examine the sterile agar plates. They should appear clean, with no bacterial growth. Return any plates to your teacher that appear to be contaminated by bacteria or mold. **CAUTION:** *Wash your hands with warm water and soap before and after handling the agar plates.*
3. Use a glass-marking pencil to label the agar plates "3°C," "room temperature," and "37°C." Also, mark your name on each plate.
4. Put on your plastic gloves. Dip a sterile swab in the bacterial culture and wipe it back and forth in a zigzag pattern over the entire surface of the agar on one plate. Cover the plate and seal it with transparent tape. **CAUTION:** *Do not open the plates once they have been exposed to the air.*
5. Repeat step 4 with each plate, using a new sterile swab for each plate.
6. On a separate sheet of paper, make a copy of the data table shown. Use a thermometer to measure the room temperature. Record this temperature in the blank row of your copy of the data table.
7. Place the plate labeled "3°C" in a refrigerator. Leave the plate labeled "room temperature" at room temperature in a place designated by your teacher. Place the plate labeled "37°C" in an incubator. Be sure to store each plate upside down.
8. After 24 hours, examine each plate with a hand lens. Bacterial colonies look like small white or colored dots on the surface of the agar. In your copy of the data table, record the number of bacterial colonies on each agar plate. Return each of the plates to its location described in step 7.

Data Table

Temperature	Number of Colonies	
	24 hours	48 hours
3°C		
37°C		

9. After a second period of 24 hours, record in your data table the number of bacterial colonies on each agar plate. After you have completed your data table, place all your agar plates in the container designated by your teacher for safe disposal.
10. Make a graph of the results in your data table. Plot time on the *x*-axis and number of bacterial colonies on the *y*-axis. Use a different symbol to represent data from each day. After you have plotted all your data on your graph, draw a straight line or smooth curve as close as possible to all the points that represent observations after 24 hours. Draw a second curve or line through the points that represent observations after 48 hours.

Analyze and Conclude

1. **Analyzing Data** According to the graph of your data, at what temperature were the most bacterial colonies visible after 24 hours? At what temperature were the fewest bacterial colonies visible after 24 hours?
2. **Analyzing Data** Did the same plate have the most bacteria after 48 hours? The fewest?
3. **Analyzing Data** Describe the effect of temperature on the growth of bacteria in this experiment. How do you think the results might differ if you included higher temperatures in your experiment?
4. **Evaluating** Did the results of your experiment confirm your prediction?
5. **Inferring** What other factors besides temperature would you expect to affect the rate at which bacteria grow and reproduce?
6. **Drawing Conclusions** How can the results of your experiment help explain why the world is not covered by a thick layer of bacteria?

Go Further

Formulating Hypotheses Temperature is not the only environmental factor that affects the growth of bacteria. Propose a hypothesis about the effects of another variable on the growth of bacteria. Describe an experiment that could test your hypothesis.

Teaching Tips

- Make sure that all students follow the safety procedures. You must provide adequate training, and you should document that the training has occurred.
- You should remind students each day about proper technique when dealing with bacterial cultures, as well as how to respond in the event of an accident and the nature of the materials being used.

Procedure

3. If possible, have students label the edges of the plates so that the labels will not interfere with visual counting of colonies.
4. Remind students to put on plastic gloves. Demonstrate how to dip a swab in the bacterial culture and wipe it over the surface of the agar on a plate.
7. Show students where to store their plates. Explain that plates should be stored upside down to keep condensation from splashing on the agar and scattering bacteria, thus starting new colonies.
8. Make sure that students record the number of bacterial colonies on their data tables. Check that students return the plates to their former locations.
9. Show students the container in which to dispose of used swabs and plates.

Expected Outcomes Students should find that bacteria grow more at 37°C than at 3°C. Therefore, they should draw the conclusion that a low temperature does limit the growth and reproduction of bacteria.

Analyze and Conclude

1. Students should observe that the most bacterial colonies were visible at 37°C and the fewest at 3°C after 24 hours.

2. The same plate has the most bacteria after 48 hours, though differences may be smaller than after 24 hours.

3. The higher temperature promoted the growth of bacteria. Raising the temperature more may reduce the rate, not enhance it.

4. Answers will depend on students' predictions. Most students' predictions were probably confirmed.

5. Typical responses might mention pH, amount of sunlight, presence of predators, and concentrations of toxins.

6. Temperature and other environmental factors such as food supply limit the growth rate of bacteria, keeping the rate well below the rapid growth rates observed under ideal conditions.

Go Further

A typical hypothesis might suggest that lower or higher pH will affect the growth of bacteria. Most bacteria grow best near neutral pH, though some bacteria grow well in acidic solutions. Some students might propose a hypothesis that focuses on how osmotic pressure—how wet or dry the environment is—affects bacterial growth.

Chapter 19 Study Guide

Study Tip

Divide the class into small groups, and have students quiz one another about the Vocabulary terms and the Key Concepts.

Thinking Visually

1. Archaebacteria
2. Bacilli
3. Cocci
4. Spirilla

Chapter 19 Assessment

Reviewing Content

1. a	**5.** d	**9.** c
2. c	**6.** c	**10.** b
3. b	**7.** d	
4. a	**8.** c	

Understanding Concepts

11. Prokaryotes are the smallest and most common microorganisms. They are single-celled and lack a nucleus.

12. The three shapes of prokaryotes are the rod-shaped bacilli, spherical-shaped cocci, and corkscrew-shaped spirilli.

13. Gram-positive bacteria with a single cell wall layer absorb only the violet primary stain. Gram-negative bacteria have a second outer layer of lipid and carbohydrate molecules. This layer absorbs the red stain so that the bacteria appear pink. The second layer also makes gram-negative bacteria resistant to antibacterial drugs.

14. Some prokaryotes move by flagella, some spiral forward, and some glide along on a slimelike material they secrete.

15. Both photoautotrophs and chemoautotrophs make their own food. Photoautotrophs obtain energy from photosynthesis and thus depend upon light. Chemoautotrophs obtain energy from chemical reactions involving hydrogen sulfide, nitrates, sulfur, or iron.

Chapter 19 Study Guide

19–1 Prokaryotes

Key Concepts

- Archaebacteria lack peptidoglycan, a carbohydrate found in the cell walls of eubacteria, and their membrane lipids are quite different. Also, the DNA sequences of key archaebacterial genes are more like those of eukaryotes than eubacteria.
- Prokaryotes are identified by their shapes, the chemical natures of their cell walls, the ways they move, and the ways they obtain energy.

Vocabulary

prokaryote, p. 471
bacillus, p. 473
coccus, p. 473
spirillum, p. 473
flagellum, p. 473
photoautotroph, p. 474
chemoautotroph, p. 474
photoheterotroph, p. 474
binary fission, p. 476
conjugation, p. 476
endospore, p. 476

19–2 Bacteria in Nature

Key Concepts

- Bacteria are vital to maintaining the living world. Some are producers that capture energy by photosynthesis. Others help to break down the nutrients in dead matter and the atmosphere, allowing other organisms to use the nutrients.
- Bacteria cause disease in one of two general ways. Some damage the tissues of the infected organism directly by breaking them down for food. Other bacteria release toxins (poisons) that harm the body.

Vocabulary

nitrogen fixation, p. 478
pathogen, p. 479
antibiotic, p. 480
sterilization, p. 481

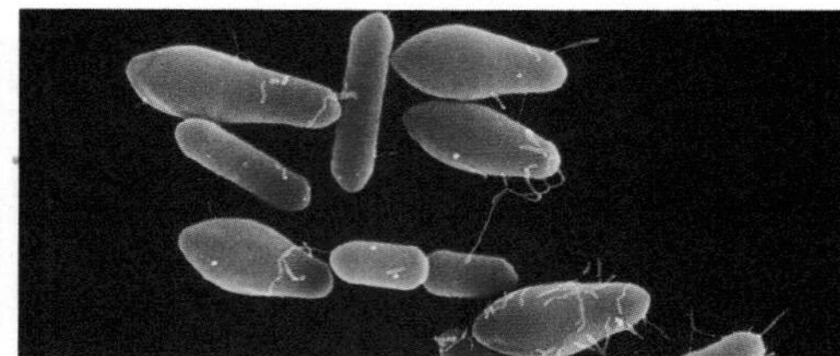

19–3 Viruses

Key Concepts

- A typical virus is composed of a core of either DNA or RNA surrounded by a protein coat.
- In a lytic infection, a virus enters a cell, makes copies of itself, and causes the cell to burst.
- In a lysogenic infection, a virus embeds its genome into the DNA of the host cell and is replicated along with the host cell's DNA.

Vocabulary

virus, p. 482
capsid, p. 483
bacteriophage, p. 484
lytic infection, p. 485
lysogenic infection, p. 485
retrovirus, p. 487
prion, p. 487

Thinking Visually

Complete this concept map, which shows the relationships among the groups of prokaryotes.

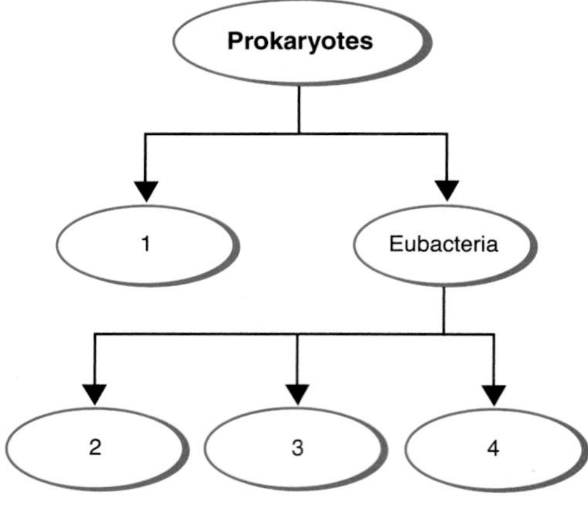

CHAPTER RESOURCES

Print:

- ***Teaching Resources,*** Chapter Vocabulary Review, Graphic Organizer
- ***Chapter Tests: Levels A and B,*** Chapter 19 Test
- ***PH Assessment System,*** Practice Test

Technology:

- ***Computer Test Bank,*** Chapter 19 Test
- ***iText,*** Chapter 19 Assessment

Chapter 19 Assessment

Reviewing Content

Choose the letter that best answers the question or completes the statement.

1. Prokaryotes are unlike all other organisms in that their cells
   a. lack nuclei. c. have cell walls.
   b. have organelles. d. lack nucleic acids.
2. Which photograph best represents bacillus bacteria?

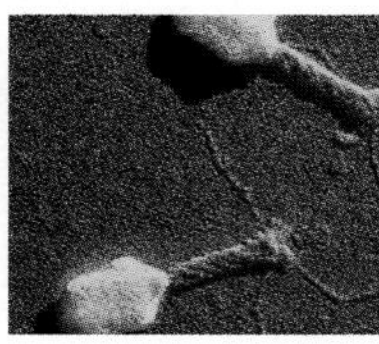
a.

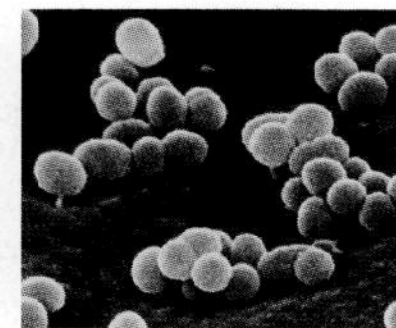
b.

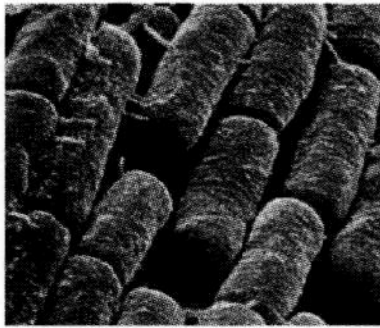
c.

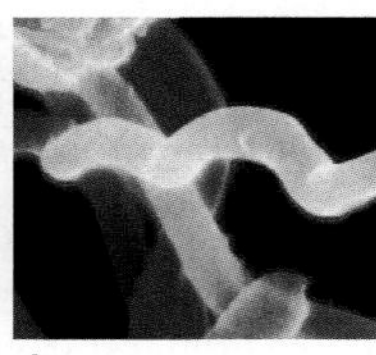
d.

3. Bacteria that contain chlorophyll *a* belong in the group
   a. archaebacteria. c. chemoautotrophs.
   b. cyanobacteria. d. pathogens.
4. Bacteria reproduce asexually by
   a. binary fission. c. conjugation.
   b. spores. d. fixation.
5. The process of converting nitrogen into a form plants can use is known as
   a. conjugation. c. decomposition.
   b. sterilization. d. nitrogen fixation.
6. Disease-causing bacteria are known as
   a. cocci. c. pathogens.
   b. bacilli. d. archaebacteria.
7. Particles made up of nucleic acids, proteins, and in some cases lipids that can reproduce only by infecting living cells are known as
   a. bacteria. c. prophages.
   b. capsids. d. viruses.
8. The outer protein coat of a virus is a
   a. core of DNA. c. capsid.
   b. core of RNA. d. membrane envelope.
9. A lytic infection occurs when a
   a. virus infects a bacterium and kills it immediately.
   b. virus embeds its genome into the DNA of the host cell.
   c. virus enters a cell, makes copies of itself, and causes the cell to burst.
   d. virus inserts its DNA into the DNA of the host cell and remains a part of the host cell for many generations.
10. One group of viruses that contain RNA as their genetic information are
    a. oncogenic viruses. c. capsids.
    b. retroviruses. d. prophages.

Understanding Concepts

11. What are the distinguishing characteristics of prokaryotes?
12. Describe the three main cell shapes of prokaryotes.
13. Distinguish between Gram-positive and Gram-negative bacteria.
14. Describe two methods by which prokaryotes move.
15. How are photoautotrophs similar to chemoautotrophs? How are they different?
16. Describe the characteristics that make photoheterotrophs unique.
17. Distinguish between an obligate aerobe and an obligate anaerobe.
18. Facultative anaerobes can survive with or without oxygen. How is this advantageous to them?
19. What is the role of certain bacteria in changing atmospheric nitrogen into a form usable by plants?
20. Viruses differ widely in terms of size and shape. What one thing do they all have in common?
21. Why is the capsid protein important?
22. Sequence the events that occur during the lytic cycle of a T4 bacteriophage.
23. Describe what happens to the host cell of a lysogenic virus.
24. What is the best way to protect against most viral diseases?
25. How are viruses highly specific to the cells they infect?

16. Photoheterotrophs are unique because they capture sunlight for energy but need organic compounds for nutrition.

17. Obligate aerobes require oxygen to survive. Obligate anaerobes are killed by oxygen.

18. Because facultative anaerobes are able to switch between cellular respiration and fermentation for their energy demands, they are able to grow anywhere.

19. Because atmospheric nitrogen cannot be used directly by plants, nitrogen must be "fixed" chemically to ammonia or other nitrogen compounds that can be used by plants.

20. One thing all viruses have in common is that they enter living cells and, once inside, use the machinery of the infected cell to replicate more viruses.

21. The capsid protein of a virus is important because it binds to the surface of a cell and tricks the cell into allowing it inside. Once inside, the viral genes take over.

22. In a lytic infection, a virus enters a cell, makes copies of itself, and causes the cell to burst.

23. During a lysogenic infection, a virus embeds its DNA into the DNA of the host cell and replicates along with the host cell's DNA.

24. The best way to protect against most viral diseases is prevention. Once a viral disease has been contracted, it might be too late to control the disease.

25. Viruses are highly specific to the cells they infect because they must bind precisely to proteins on the cell surface and then use the host's genetic system.

HOMEWORK GUIDE

Section:	Questions:
Section 19–1	1–4, 11–18, 30, 34, 35
Section 19–2	5–6, 19, 26, 28, 29, 31, 32, 36
Section 19–3	7–10, 20–25, 27, 33

Critical Thinking

26. Because other organisms depend on bacteria for converting nitrogen into nitrogen compounds, these organisms might die if bacteria lost their ability to fix nitrogen.

27. Viruses can replicate only within living things. As a result, viruses can grow on cultures of bacteria but not on synthetic media.

28. These foods are dehydrated, and bacteria need water to live.

29. Not brushing leaves particles on teeth that bacteria can use for food. This encourages bacterial growth.

30. The organism probably belongs to Eubacteria because it is unicellular, has a cell wall containing peptidoglycan, and lacks a nucleus.

31. Antibiotics B and C were the least effective. The growth of the bacteria was not retarded at all.

32. Antibiotics A and D would be good treatments because both retarded the growth of the bacteria.

33. Viruses, prokaryotes, and eukaryotes all have nucleic acids and proteins. Prokaryotes and eukaryotes have cell membranes, and eukaryotes have organelles.

34. Binary fission produces two cells from one, whereas endospore formation and conjugation do not increase the number of cells.

35. Two labeled agar plates are needed. Touch one plate with a finger. Leave both plates uncovered for 20 minutes. Then, cover the plates and store them in a protected area of the classroom. Use a hand lens and count the bacteria colonies after 24 and 48 hours.

36. Bacteria break down carbon compounds, so they can be used to make all four types of organic compounds.

Chapter 19 Assessment

Critical Thinking

26. **Predicting** Suppose that bacteria lost the ability to fix nitrogen. How would this affect other organisms?

27. **Applying Concepts** Bacteria can be grown in the laboratory on synthetic media. Can viruses be grown on cultures of bacteria? Explain your answer.

28. **Applying Concepts** Why don't foods such as uncooked rice and raisins spoil?

29. **Problem Solving** Bacteria that live on teeth produce an acid that causes decay. Why do people who do not brush regularly have more cavities than those who do?

30. **Classifying** A scientist finds a new organism but is unsure which kingdom it belongs to. The organism is unicellular, has a cell wall containing peptidoglycan, has a circular DNA molecule and ribosomes, but it lacks a nucleus. Based on those characteristics, which kingdom does it belong to?

Questions 31–32
An experiment was conducted to determine the effectiveness of different antibiotics against a certain strain of bacteria. Four disks, each soaked in a different antibiotic, were placed in a petri dish where the bacteria were growing. The results are summarized below.

Effects of Antibiotics

Antibiotic	Observation After One Week
A	Growth retarded for 6 mm diameter
B	Growth not retarded
C	Growth not retarded
D	Growth retarded for 2 mm diameter

31. **Analyzing Data** Which antibiotics were the least effective at retarding the growth of the bacteria? Explain your answer.

32. **Inferring** Which antibiotics might be good treatments for an infection caused by this strain of bacteria? Explain your answer.

33. **Comparing and Contrasting** Make a chart that compares viruses with prokaryotes and eukaryotes.

34. **Comparing and Contrasting** How does the outcome of binary fission differ from that of endospore formation and conjugation?

35. **Designing an Experiment** Develop an experiment to test the hypothesis that contact of an agar plate with a finger results in more bacterial growth than the exposure of the plate to classroom air.

36. **Making Connections** Many prokaryotes are decomposers, helping to recycle materials, including organic molecules. How are chemical reactions involved in the formation of organic molecules? (You may wish to review Chapter 2.)

Performance-Based Assessment

Creative Writing You are writing a brief essay entitled "Viruses in the Biosphere" for the local newspaper. Explain the role viruses play in the environment, and include how they are both helpful and harmful. Your essay should also have an illustration.

Take It to the NET

Can bacteria become ill? Visit the Prentice Hall Web site at **www.phschool.com** to learn more about bacteriophages, viruses that infect bacteria. Then, answer the following questions:

- How can you determine whether bacteriophages are present in bacteria?
- Can bacteriophages be used to cure humans of diseases caused by pathogenic bacteria?
- Why are bacteriophages considered to be important tools in bacteriological research?

Performance-Based Assessment

Helpful aspects that student essays might mention: Viruses can be used in the production of vaccines that could eradicate specific diseases such as measles and polio; genetic engineers can correct genetic defects by using viruses to carry desirable genes from one cell to another. Harmful aspects: Viruses are pathogens and resistant to antibiotics. Viral diseases that affect humans include the common cold, measles, chicken pox, mumps, AIDS, and polio. Viral diseases that affect animals include distemper, rabies, and pneumonia. Viral diseases that affect plants may discolor leaves, stunt growth, or even kill the plant.

Standardized Test Prep

Test-Taking Tip For questions containing the word NOT, begin by jotting down items that do fit the characteristic in question. Then, compare your notes with the answer choices and eliminate those that correspond to your list. Finally, check to see that your answer is correct by confirming that it does not fit the characteristic in question.

Directions: Choose the letter that best answers the question or completes the statement.

1. Which of the following is used to identify specific prokaryotes?
I. Size
II. Shape
III. Movement
(A) I only
(B) II only
(C) I and III only
(D) II and III only
(E) I, II, and III

2. Which of the following can be used to protect food against microorganisms?
I. Salting
II. Freezing
III. Sterilization
(A) I only
(B) II only
(C) I and III only
(D) II and III only
(E) I, II, and III

3. Which illness is NOT caused by a virus?
(A) AIDS
(B) polio
(C) botulism
(D) common cold
(E) flu

4. Which are parts of a typical virus?
I. Capsid
II. Genome
III. Retrovirus
(A) I only
(B) II only
(C) III only
(D) I and II only
(E) I, II, and III

5. All bacteria are classified as
(A) eukaryotes.
(B) protists.
(C) archaea.
(D) prokaryotes.
(E) blue-green algae.

Questions 6–10 Each of the lettered choices below refers to the following numbered statements. Select the best lettered choice. A choice may be used once, more than once, or not at all.
(A) Cocci
(B) Conjugation
(C) Binary fission
(D) Bacteriophage
(E) Methanogen

6. Type of parasite that attacks certain prokaryotes

7. Process of transferring genetic information

8. Spherical prokaryotes

9. Process of asexual reproduction

10. Member of Archaea

Question 11 Use the graph below to answer the question.

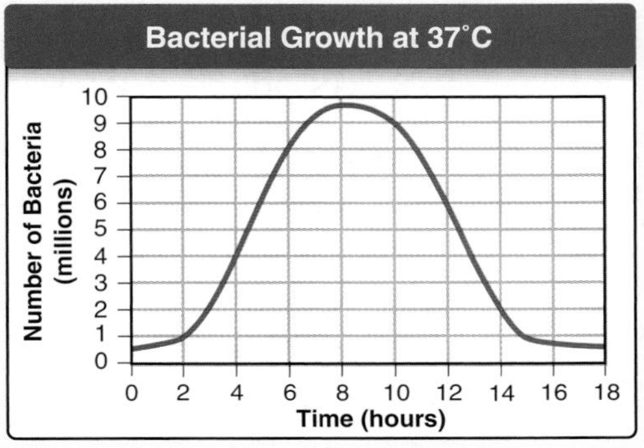

11. At which point in the graph does the number of living bacteria increase at the greatest rate?
(A) Between hours 14 and 16
(B) Between hours 4 and 6
(C) Between hours 6 and 10
(D) Between hours 10 and 12
(E) During the first 3 hours

Complete the following analogy by selecting the correct letter. In analogies, A : B :: C : __?__ *means* A is to B as C is to __?__.

12. Cell : cell membrane :: virus : __?__.
(A) cell wall
(B) capsid
(C) bacteriophage
(D) prophage
(E) DNA

Standardized Test Prep

1. D **2.** E **3.** C **4.** A **5.** D **6.** D **7.** B **8.** A **9.** C **10.** E **11.** B **12.** B

Take It to the NET

• When bacteria are cultured in the laboratory on agar plates, they can completely cover the plate with a visible layer of growth. If bacteriophages are present in the culture, they will produce a clear circular area called a plaque on the agar plate containing the visible bacteria. A liquid that has become cloudy from bacteria will become clear again when the bacteriophages destroy all the living bacterial cells.

• Bacteriophage therapy has been used in the past to cure infectious diseases, especially in Eastern Europe and Russia, and research is continuing.

• Bacteriophages can be used as vehicles to introduce DNA into a bacterial cell. Microbiologists can also use bacteriophages to study the formation of mutations in a bacterial population. For additional information, visit
www.phschool.com

Chapter Planner 20 Protists

Section and Section Objectives	Time	Activities and Labs
20–1 The Kingdom Protista, pp. 495–496 **20.1.1** ***Explain*** what a protist is.	**1 period (1/2 block)**	**SE:** ***Inquiry Activity,*** What are protists?, p. 494 **TE:** ***Build Science Skills,*** p. 495 **TE:** ***Build Science Skills,*** p. 496
20–2 Animallike Protists: Protozoans, pp. 497–503 **20.2.1** ***Describe*** the major phyla of animallike protists. **20.2.2** ***Explain*** how animallike protists harm other living things.	**2 periods (1 block)**	**TE:** ***Build Science Skills,*** pp. 498, 499 **SE:** ***Quick Lab,*** How does a paramecium eat?, p. 502 **TE:** ***Demonstration,*** p. 503 **SE:** ***Issues in Biology,*** How Should Water Be Protected Against *Cryptosporidium?*, p. 504
20–3 Plantlike Protists: Unicellular Algae, pp. 505–509 **20.3.1** ***Describe*** the function of chlorophyll and accessory pigments in algae. **20.3.2** ***Describe*** the major phyla of unicellular algae. **20.3.3** ***Summarize*** the ecological roles of unicellular algae.	**2 periods (1 block)**	**TE:** ***Demonstration,*** p. 505 **TE:** ***Build Science Skills,*** p. 506 **TE:** ***Build Science Skills,*** p. 507 **SE:** ***Analyzing Data,*** Fertilizers and Algae, p. 508 **SE:** ***Design an Experiment,*** Investigating Contractile Vacuoles, pp. 521
20–4 Plantlike Protists: Red, Brown, and Green Algae, pp. 510–515 **20.4.1** ***Describe*** the major phyla of multicellular algae. **20.4.2** ***Explain*** how multicellular algae reproduce. **20.4.3** ***Identify*** some human uses of algae.	**2 periods (1 block)**	**TE:** ***Build Science Skills,*** p. 511 **TE:** ***Build Science Skills,*** p. 512
20–5 Funguslike Protists, pp. 516–520 **20.5.1** ***Compare and Contrast*** funguslike protists and fungi. **20.5.2** ***Describe*** slime molds and water molds. **20.5.3** ***Summarize*** the ecological roles of funguslike protists.	**1 period (1/2 block)**	**TE:** ***Demonstration,*** p. 517 **TE:** ***Demonstration,*** p. 518
Chapter Assessment, pp. 522–525	**1 period (1/2 block)**	

ACTIVITY PLANNER

SE: ***Inquiry Activity,*** p. 494; (20 min.); mixed protist culture, microscope slide, methyl cellulose, coverslip, microscope

TE: ***Build Science Skills,*** p. 495; (20 min.); pond water, jars, microscope slides, coverslips, microscope

TE: ***Build Science Skills,*** p. 496; (10 min.); photographs/slides of protists, microprojector

TE: ***Build Science Skills,*** p. 498; (10 min.); grass, glass jar with lid, bottled water, dropper pipette, microscope slide, coverslip, microscope

TE: ***Build Science Skills,*** p. 499; (15 min.); slide of paramecium, microscope

SE: ***Quick Lab,*** p. 502; (20 min.); paramecium culture, 2 dropper pipettes, microscope, microscope slide, coverslip, *Chlorella* culture, toothpick, carmine dye

TE: ***Demonstration,*** p. 503; (20 min.); termite, microscope slide, coverslip, microscope

TE: ***Demonstration,*** p. 505; (15 min.); filter paper, denatured ethyl alchohol, 3 beakers, scissors, green, brown, and red algae

TE: ***Build Science Skills,*** p. 506; (15 min.); slide of euglena, microscope

TE: ***Build Science Skills,*** p. 507; (20 min.); jar, coverslip, slide, microscope

SE: ***Design an Experiment,*** pp. 521; (90 minutes); *Paramecium caudatum* cultures, dropper pipette, slides, coverslips, microscope, cotton ball, forceps, clock

TE: ***Build Science Skills,*** p. 511; (20 min.); sea lettuce, fern, mushroom, moss, flowering plant

TE: ***Build Science Skills,*** p. 512; (20 min.); living cultures of green algae, microscope slides, coverslips, dropper pipette, microscope

TE: ***Demonstration,*** p. 517; (15 min.); dead leaf or piece of bark, dry oatmeal flakes, petri dish with cover

TE: ***Demonstration,*** p. 518; (10 min.); dead fish, water, jar with lid

PLANNING KEY

Ability Levels

B	**Basic**	For students who need additional help
A	**Average**	For all students
E	**Enriched**	For students who need to be challenged

Components

SE	Student Edition	**GRSW**	Guided Reading and Study Workbook	**IDM**	Issues and Decision Making
TE	Teacher's Edition	**CT**	Chapter Tests: Levels A and B	**CTB**	Computer Test Bank
LMA	Laboratory Manual A	**PHAS**	PH Assessment System	**PA**	Presentation Assistant Plus
LMB	Laboratory Manual B	**LA**	Lab Assessment With Scoring Guide	**BD**	BioDetectives Videotape
TR	Teaching Resources	**BTM**	BioTechnology Manual	**iT**	iText
IF	Investigations in Forensics				

Program Resources	***Assessment***	***Media and Technology***
TR: Section Review 20–1 B A **GRSW:** Section 20–1 B A	**SE:** 20–1 Section Assessment, p. 496 **TR:** Section Review 20–1	**PA:** 20–1 Interest Grabber, Section Outline, Concept Map **iT:** Section 20–1
LMB: Chapter 20 Lab B A **TR:** Section Review 20–2 B A **GRSW:** Section 20–2 B A **IDM:** Issues and Decisions 19 A E	**SE:** 20–2 Section Assessment, p. 503 **TR:** Section Review 20–2	**PA:** 20–2 Interest Grabber, Section Outline, Conjugation, Figure 20–4, Figure 20–5, Figure 20–7 **iT:** Section 20–2
TR: Section Review 20–3 B A **GRSW:** Section 20–3 B A	**SE:** 20–3 Section Assessment, p. 509 **TR:** Section Review 20–3	**PA:** 20–3 Interest Grabber, Section Outline, Euglena **iT:** Section 20–3
TR: Section Review 20–4 B A **GRSW:** Section 20–4 B A	**SE:** 20–4 Section Assessment, p. 515 **TR:** Section Review 20–4	**PA:** 20–4 Interest Grabber, Section Outline, *Ulva* Life Cycle, Figure 20–17 **iT:** Section 20–4
LMA: Chapter 20 Lab A E **TR:** Section Review 20–5 B A Chapter 20 Design an Experiment B A E **GRSW:** Section 20–5 B A	**SE:** 20–5 Section Assessment, p. 520 **TR:** Section Review 20–5	**PA:** 20–5 Interest Grabber, Section Outline, The Life Cycle of a Water Mold, Figure 20–22, Figure 20–23 **iT:** Section 20–5
	SE: Chapter 20 Assessment, pp. 522–525 **TR:** Chapter Vocabulary Review, Graphic Organizer **CB:** Chapter 20 Test **CTB:** Chapter 20 Test **PHAS:** Practice Test	**CTB:** Chapter 20 Test **iT:** Chapter 20 Assessment

PRESSED FOR TIME?

To Preview the Chapter

- Introduce students to Key Concepts and Vocabulary terms in each section.
- Assign the Reading Strategies for each section.

To Cover the Chapter Quickly

- Have students read all of Section 20–1; Sarcodines and Ciliates in Section 20–2; Euglenophytes, Dinoflagellates, Chrysophytes, and Diatoms in Section 20–3; Red Algae, Brown Algae, and Green Algae in Section 20–4; and Slime Molds in Section 20–5.
- Assign the 20–3 Section Review and questions 1–10 in Chapter 20 Assessment and Chapter 20 Standardized Test Prep.

To Review the Chapter

- Assign Sections 20–1 through 20–5 in the Guided Reading and Study Workbook.
- Assign Section Reviews for 20–1 through 20–5 and the Chapter Vocabulary Review for Chapter 20 in the Teaching Resources.

ENGAGE/EXPLORE

Inquiry Activity

Objective Students will be able to form an operational definition of what a protist is.

Skill Focus **Forming Operational Definitions**

Materials mixed protist culture, microscope slide, methyl cellulose, coverslip, microscope

Time 20 minutes

Advance Prep Prepare a mixed culture that contains various protists for students to observe, including amoebas, paramecia, euglenas, and multicellular algae.

Safety Caution students to wash their hands after concluding the activity.

Strategy Remind students that they have learned about structures within cells, and that they should draw upon that knowledge in drawing and labeling what they observe in these microorganisms.

Expected Outcomes Students should observe a variety of microorganisms and be able to get a sense of what a protist is.

Think About It

1. Bacteria may be present but will not be visible at the magnification used to see most protists. Protists observed will be visibly eukaryotic (nucleated). Some students may assume incorrectly that motile organisms are animals and green, nonmotile organisms are plants.
2. A typical definition might suggest that protists are unicellular eukaryotes.

Brain Teaser

Have students compare the photo on this chapter-opening page with those in Figure 20–1 on page 495. As students observe the photographs, ask: **What similarities are there among the four types of organisms shown in these photographs?** *(Students may mention that three of the four appear to be unicellular. Many will say that these organisms share few, if any, similarities.)* Reinforce students' feeling that these organisms make up a diverse group. Develop the idea that this kingdom is a catchall, in which membership is determined mainly by exclusion from the other kingdoms.

Chapter 20 Protists

These colorful diatoms make up a small part of the diverse group of protists.

Inquiry Activity

What are protists?

Procedure

1. Place a drop of water containing a variety of microorganisms on a microscope slide. Add a drop of methyl cellulose and a coverslip. Observe the slide under the microscope at low and high magnifications.
2. Record your observations. Draw and label each type of organism.
3. Draw a chart listing each type of organism that you observed and its characteristics.

Think About It

1. **Classifying** Are any of these organisms bacteria, animals, or plants? Explain your answer.
2. **Forming Operational Definitions** The organisms you observed are members of a group called protists. Write a definition of *protist*.

HISTORY OF SCIENCE

A new kingdom

In the nineteenth century, microscopes were refined to the point where biologists began to describe many different kinds of single-celled organisms. Some scientists, including the German naturalist Ernst Haeckel (1834–1919), proposed that a new kingdom needed to be created to include all these organisms, which were not really plants or animals. But, not until the 1960s, with the advent of more powerful microscopic technology, did most biologists recognize the gross inadequacy of the two-kingdom, animal/plant system. By the 1970s, the term protist, which means "first organism," came to be used for single-celled, nucleated organisms and their derivatives. Some biologists have used another term, protoctist, to encompass the same organisms because *protist* has too often been used as a synonym for *protozoan.*

20–1 The Kingdom Protista

On a dark, quiet night you sit at the stern of a tiny sailboat as it glides through the calm waters of a coastal inlet. Suddenly, the boat's wake sparkles with its own light. As the stern cuts through the water, glimmering points of light leave a ghostly trail into the darkness. What's responsible for this eerie display? You've just had a close encounter with one group of some of the most remarkable organisms in the world—the protists.

Guide for Reading

Key Concept
- What are protists?

Vocabulary
protist

Reading Strategy: Summarizing As you read, find the main ideas for each blue heading. Write down a few key words from each main idea. Then, use the key words in your summary. Reread and revise your summary, keeping only the most important ideas.

What Is a Protist?

The kingdom Protista is a diverse group that may include more than 200,000 species. Biologists have argued for years over the best way to classify protists, and the issue may never be settled. In fact, protists are defined less by what they are and more by what they are not: A **protist** is any organism that is not a plant, an animal, a fungus, or a prokaryote. **Protists are eukaryotes that are not members of the kingdoms Plantae, Animalia, or Fungi.** Recall that a eukaryote has a nucleus and other membrane-bound organelles. Although most protists are unicellular, quite a few are not, as you can see in **Figure 20–1.** A few protists actually consist of hundreds or even thousands of cells but are still considered protists because they are so similar to others that are truly unicellular.

Evolution of Protists

Protists are members of a kingdom whose formal name, *Protista,* comes from Greek words meaning "the very first." The name is appropriate. The first eukaryotic organisms on Earth, which appeared nearly 1.5 billion years ago, were protists.

Figure 20–1 Protists are a diverse group of mainly single-celled eukaryotes. Examples of protists include freshwater ciliates, radiolarians, and *Spirogyra. Spirogyra* may form slimy floating masses in fresh water. The organism's name refers to the helical arrangement of its ribbonlike chloroplasts.

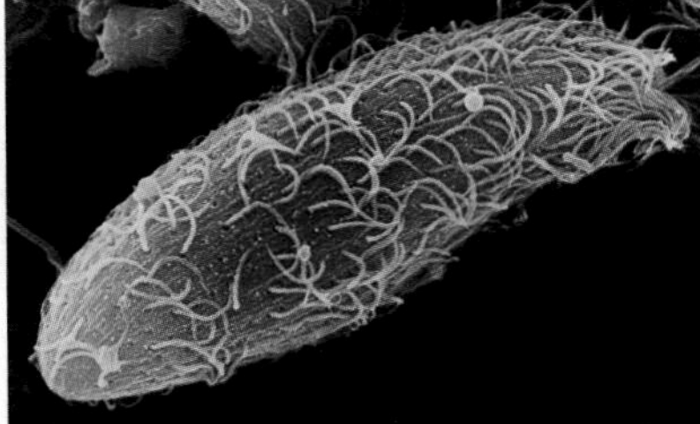

***Euplotes* (a freshwater ciliate)**
(magnification: about 140×)

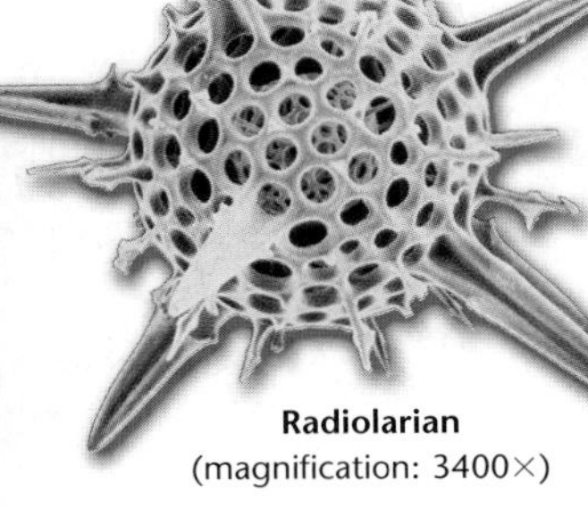

Radiolarian
(magnification: 3400×)

Spirogyra
(magnification: 400×)

SECTION RESOURCES

Print:
- ***Teaching Resources,*** Section Review 20–1
- ***Guided Reading and Study Workbook,*** Section 20–1

Technology:
- ***Presentation Assistant Plus,*** Interest Grabber, Section Outline, Concept Map
- ***iText,*** Section 20–1

Section 20–1

1 FOCUS

Objectives

20.1.1 ***Explain*** what a protist is.

Guide for Reading

Vocabulary Preview

Before students read the section, call on volunteers to propose a definition for the word *protist.*

Reading Strategy

Ask students to find evidence in the section for this statement: The kingdom Protista is a catchall grouping for organisms that don't fit into other kingdoms.

2 INSTRUCT

What Is a Protist?

Build Science Skills

Observing Collect samples of pond water in several jars. In each jar, include some mud from the pond's bottom. Show students the jars and ask whether they think they contain any living organisms. Then, have students make slides of samples from the water and observe the slides through a microscope. Ask students to make drawings of at least two of the organisms and to pay special attention to how they move.

Evolution of Protists

Make Connections

Earth Science Explain that 1.5 billion years ago, when the first protists appeared, the world was much different than it is today. Point out that the ocean covered much of Earth, and the land that was above water had no life on it—there were no plants, animals, or even microorganisms on the land. Explain that Earth itself formed about 4.6 billion years ago, so eukaryotic organisms appeared about 3 billion years after the planet formed and more than a billion years after the first prokaryotes. Yet, it was about another billion years before the Cambrian Explosion occurred at the beginning of the Paleozoic Era.

Classification of Protists

Build Science Skills

Classifying Display a variety of photographs of protists. Include some images of animallike, plantlike, and funguslike protists. Use a microprojector or videocamera to show slides of various organisms, such as an amoeba, a euglena, a paramecium, a diatom, and a cellular slime mold. Have students work in small groups to brainstorm lists of similarities and differences that exist among the protists they observe. Ask students to create a classification system. Discuss group lists and systems as a class.

3 ASSESS

Evaluate Understanding

Call on students to explain the classification of protists based on nutrition. Students should describe animallike protists, plantlike protists, and funguslike protists.

Reteach

Have students look at the organisms shown in Figure 20–1 and explain why none of the three could be classified as a fungus or an animal.

ALTERNATIVE ASSESSMENT

Students' newspaper stories should explain that early in Earth's history, different kinds of prokaryotic cells, including photosynthetic prokaryotes, probably began to live inside larger cells. This relationship began as a parasitic one, but over time the different cells came to be mutually dependent.

Use iText to review the key concepts in Section 20–1.

Answer to . . .

Figure 20–2 *Chloroplast*

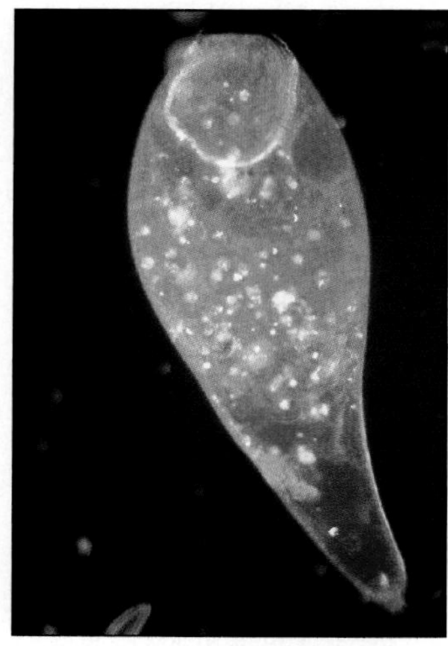

(magnification: 350×)

▲ **Figure 20–2** According to one hypothesis, some organelles in eukaryotic cells were once symbiotic prokaryotes that lived inside other cells. For example, the mitochondria found in this *Stentor* may be descended from early prokaryotes. **Formulating Hypotheses** ***What other organelle may originally have been symbiotic cells?***

Where did the first protists come from? American biologist Lynn Margulis has hypothesized that the first eukaryotic cells may have evolved from a symbiosis of several cells. Mitochondria and chloroplasts found in eukaryotic cells may be descended from aerobic and photosynthetic prokaryotes that began to live inside larger cells. **Figure 20–2** shows a typical protist.

Classification of Protists

Protists are so diverse that many biologists have suggested that they should be broken up into several kingdoms. This idea is supported by recent studies of protist DNA indicating that different groups of protists evolved independently from archaebacteria. Unfortunately, at present, biologists simply don't agree on how best to classify the protists. Therefore, in this textbook, we will take the traditional approach of considering the protists as a single kingdom.

One way to classify protists is according to the way they obtain nutrition. Thus, many protists that are heterotrophs are called animallike protists. Those that produce their own food by photosynthesis are called plantlike protists. Finally, those that obtain their food by external digestion—either as decomposers or parasites—are called funguslike protists. This is the way in which we will organize our investigation of the protists.

It is important to understand, however, that these categories are an artificial way to organize a very diverse group of organisms. Categories based on the way protists obtain food do not reflect the evolutionary history of these organisms. For example, all animallike protists did not necessarily share a relatively recent ancestor. The protistan family tree is likely to be redrawn many times as the genes of the many species of protists are analyzed and compared using the powerful tools of molecular biology.

20–1 Section Assessment

1. **Key Concept** What is a protist?
2. Describe Margulis's theory about the evolution of protists.
3. Are most protists unicellular or multicellular?
4. What are the three methods that protists use to obtain food?
5. **Critical Thinking Using Analogies** In what way is the kingdom Protista similar to a group of people who do not belong to a political party?

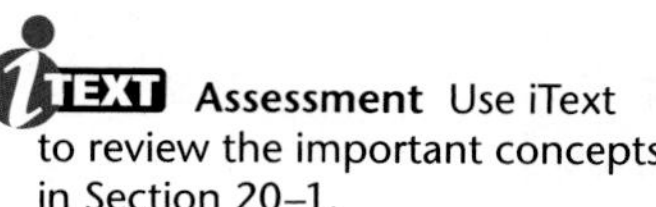

Assessment Use iText to review the important concepts in Section 20–1.

ALTERNATIVE ASSESSMENT

Creative Writing
Write and illustrate a brief newspaper story explaining the hypothesis that eukaryotic cells evolved from a symbiosis of several prokaryotes with larger cells.

20–1 Section Assessment

1. A protist is a eukaryote that is not a member of the kingdoms Plantae, Animalia, or Fungi.
2. The first eukaryotic cells may have evolved from a symbiosis of several prokaryotes with larger cells.
3. Most are unicellular.
4. Animallike protists ingest food; plantlike protists produce food by photosynthesis; and funguslike protists obtain their food by external digestion either as decomposers or as parasites.
5. Like people who do not belong to a political party, protists are defined less by what they are and more by what they are not.

20–2 Animallike Protists: Protozoans

At one time, animallike protists were called protozoa, which means "first animals," and were classified separately from more plantlike protists. Like animals, these organisms are heterotrophs. The four phyla of animallike protists are distinguished from one another by their means of movement. As you will read, zooflagellates swim with flagella, sarcodines move by extensions of their cytoplasm, ciliates move by means of cilia, and sporozoans do not move on their own at all.

Zooflagellates

Many protists easily move through their aquatic environments propelled by flagella. Flagella are long, whiplike projections that allow a cell to move.  **Animallike protists that swim using flagella are classified in the phylum Zoomastigina and are often referred to as zooflagellates.** Most zooflagellates (zoh-oh-FLAJ-uh-lits) have either one or two flagella, although a few species have many flagella. Two representative zooflagellates are shown in **Figure 20–3**.

Zooflagellates are generally able to absorb food through their cell membranes. Many live in lakes and streams, where they absorb nutrients from decaying organic material. Others live within the bodies of other organisms, taking advantage of the food that the larger organism provides.

Most zooflagellates reproduce asexually by means of binary fission, including mitotic cell division. Binary fission results in two cells that are genetically identical. Some zooflagellates, however, have a sexual life cycle as well. During sexual reproduction, gamete cells are produced by meiosis. When gametes from two organisms fuse, an organism with a new combination of genetic information is formed.

Guide for Reading

Key Concepts
- What are the distinguishing features of the major phyla of animallike protists?
- How do animallike protists harm other living things?

Vocabulary
- pseudopod
- amoeboid movement
- food vacuole • cilium
- trichocyst • macronucleus
- micronucleus • gullet
- anal pore • contractile vacuole
- conjugation

Reading Strategy: Building Vocabulary
Before you read, preview new vocabulary by skimming the section and making a list of the boldfaced terms. Leave space to make notes as you read.

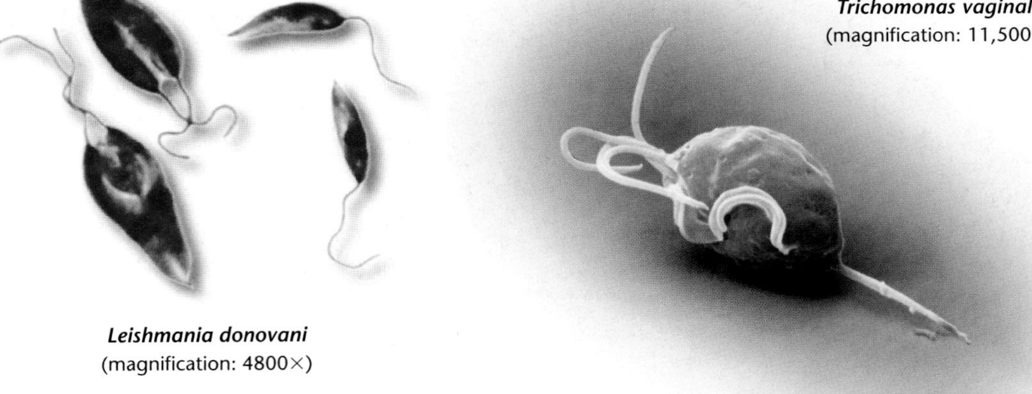

Figure 20–3 Zooflagellates are animallike protists that swim using flagella.

Trichomonas vaginalis (magnification: 11,500×)

Leishmania donovani (magnification: 4800×)

SECTION RESOURCES

TIME SAVER

Print:
- ***Laboratory Manual B,*** Chapter 20 Lab
- ***Teaching Resources,*** Section Review 20–2
- ***Guided Reading and Study Workbook,*** Section 20–2
- ***Issues and Decision Making,*** Issues and Decisions 19

Technology:
- ***iText,*** Section 20–2

Section 20–2

1 FOCUS

Objectives

20.2.1 ***Describe*** the major phyla of animallike protists.

20.2.2 ***Explain*** how animallike protists harm other living things.

Guide for Reading

Vocabulary Preview

Have students write the Vocabulary terms, dividing each into its separate syllables as best they can. Remind students that each syllable usually has only one vowel sound. The correct syllabications are: pseu•do•pod, a•moe•boid move•ment, food vac•u•ole, cil•i•um, trich•o•cyst, mac•ro•nu•cle•us, mi•cro•nu•cle•us, gul•let, a•nal pore, con•trac•tile vac•u•ole, con•ju•ga•tion

Reading Strategy

Before students read, ask them to skim the section to find the boldfaced Key Concepts. Have them copy each of the concepts onto a note card. Then, as they read they should note details and examples that support each Key Concept.

2 INSTRUCT

Zooflagellates

Make Connections

Health Science Explain that the zooflagellates include several parasitic protists that cause human diseases, such as the pathogens that cause African sleeping sickness and giardiasis. The zooflagellate *Trichomonas vaginalis* causes a common sexually transmitted disease that afflicts women, called vaginitis. Encourage interested students to find out how this disease is spread, what the symptoms are, and how it can be treated.

Sarcodines

Word Origins

The word *pseudonym* means "false name."

Use Visuals

Figure 20–4 Ask students: **Which animallike protist phylum includes *Amoeba proteus?*** *(Sarcodina)* **Why do you think an amoeba is often described as "shape-shifting?** *(It has no permanent shape. It changes its shape as it pushes out projections called pseudopods.)* **What is the function of the food vacuole?** *(It temporarily stores food.)*

Build Science Skills

Observing Have each student gather a handful of grass from a field near the school. The grass should then be dried on a flat tray for at least one day. After the grass is dried, have students place the grass in a clean glass jar, add water until the jar is about three-quarters full, and seal it tightly with a lid. After three days, students should open the jar in a well-ventilated area and gently stir the contents. Have students then use a dropper pipette to make slides from the water in the jar and observe the slides under a microscope. Typically, students will observe several different types of protists, such as paramecia and amoebas. Ask students to make drawings and try to identify the organisms they see.

Word Origins

Pseudopod comes from the Greek words *pseudes,* meaning "false" and *-pous,* meaning "foot." So *pseudopod* means "false foot." The suffix *-onym* comes from the Greek word *onama,* meaning "name." **What do you think the word *pseudonym* means?**

Sarcodines

Members of the phylum Sarcodina, or sarcodines, move by means of temporary projections of cytoplasm known as **pseudopods** (SOO-doh-pahdz). **Sarcodines are animallike protists that use pseudopods for feeding and movement.** The best-known sarcodines are the amoebas, shown in **Figure 20–4.** Amoebas are flexible, active cells with thick pseudopods that extend out of the central mass of the cell. The cytoplasm of the cell streams into the pseudopod, and the rest of the cell follows. This type of locomotion is known as **amoeboid movement.**

Amoebas can capture and digest particles of food and even other cells. They do this by surrounding their meal, then taking it inside themselves to form a food vacuole. A **food vacuole** is a small cavity in the cytoplasm that temporarily stores food. Once inside the cell, the material is digested rapidly and the nutrients are passed along to the rest of the cell. Amoebas reproduce by means of binary fission.

Foraminiferans, another member of Sarcodina, are abundant in the warmer regions of the oceans. Foraminiferans secrete shells of calcium carbonate ($CaCO_3$). As they die, the calcium carbonate from their shells accumulates on the bottom of the ocean. In some regions, thick deposits of foraminiferan shells have formed on the ocean floor. The white chalk cliffs of Dover, England, are huge deposits of foraminiferan skeletons that were raised above sea level by geological processes.

The sarcodines also include a group of organisms known as the heliozoans. The name *Heliozoan* means "sun animal." Heliozoans produce shells of silica (SiO_2). Thin spikes of cytoplasm, supported by microtubules, project from the shells, making heliozoans look like the sun's rays.

▼ **Figure 20–4** **Sarcodines use pseudopods for feeding and movement.** *Amoeba proteus,* a common sarcodine, moves by first extending a pseudopod away from its body. The organism's cytoplasm then streams into the pseudopod. This shifting of the mass of the cell away from where it originated is a slow but effective way to move from place to place. Amoebas also use pseudopods to surround and ingest prey.

(magnification: 330×)

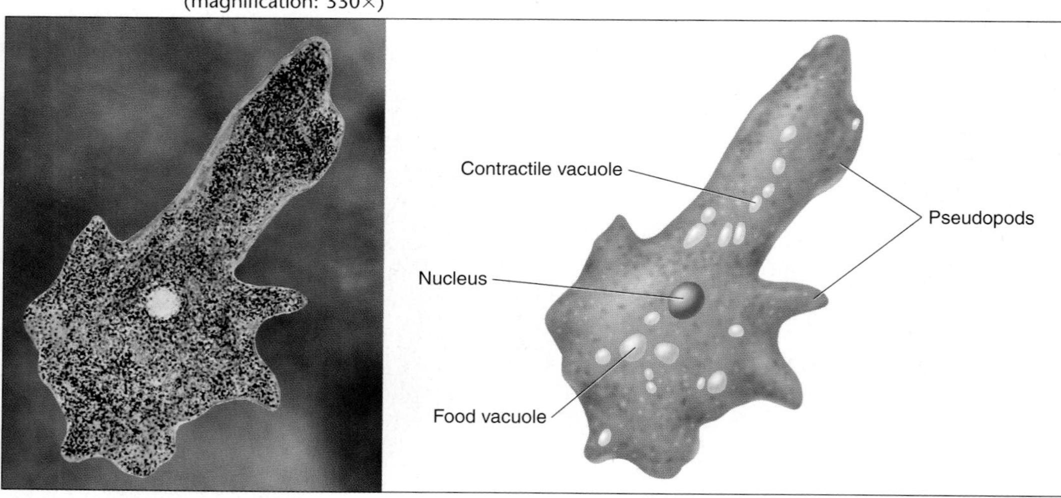

PRESENTATIONS MADE EASY!

The Presentation Assistant Plus contains the Prentice Hall Presentation Pro and the Transparencies, which provide easy-to-follow visual support for every step of this lesson. If you have a computer presentation station, use Prentice Hall Presentation Pro Section 20–2, or use the transparencies listed here.

Section 20–2:

Interest Grabber
Section Outline
Conjugation
Figure 20–4
Figure 20–5
Figure 20–7

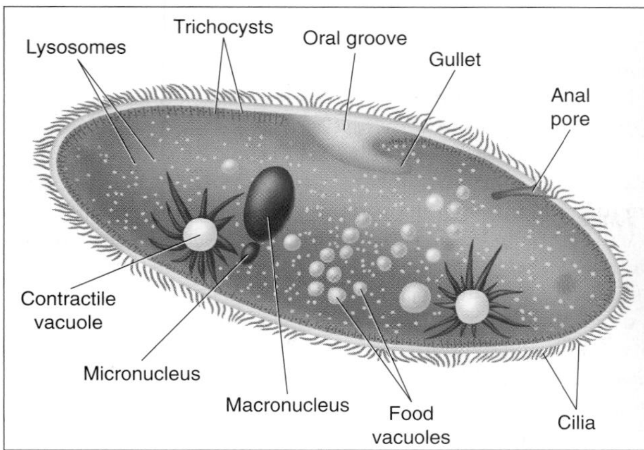

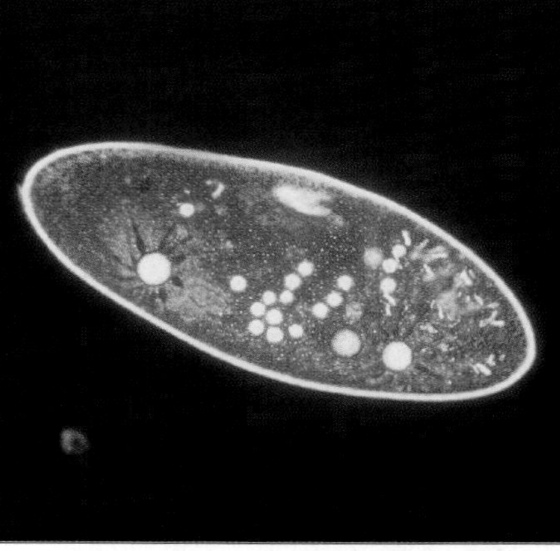

(magnification: 2500×)

▲ **Figure 20–5 Ciliates use hairlike projections called cilia for feeding and movement.** Ciliates, including this paramecium, are covered with short hairlike cilia that propel them through the water. Cilia also line the organism's gullet and move its food—usually bacteria—to the organism's interior. There, the food particles are engulfed, forming food vacuoles. The contractile vacuoles collect and remove excess water.

Ciliates

The phylum Ciliophora is named for **cilia** (singular: cilium), short hairlike projections similar to flagella. **Members of the phylum Ciliophora, known as ciliates, use cilia for feeding and movement.** The internal structure of cilia and flagella are identical. The beating of cilia, like the pull of hundreds of oars in an ancient ship, propels a cell rapidly through water.

Ciliates are found in both fresh and salt water. In fact, a lake or stream near your home might contain many different ciliates. Most ciliates are free living, which means that they do not exist as parasites or symbionts.

CHECKPOINT *What are cilia, and how do ciliates use them?*

Internal Anatomy Some of the best known ciliates belong to the genus *Paramecium.* A paramecium can be as long as 350 micrometers. Its cilia, which are organized into evenly spaced rows and bundles, beat in a regular, efficient pattern. The cell membrane of a paramecium is highly structured and has trichocysts just below its surface. **Trichocysts** (TRY-koh-sists) are very small, bottle-shaped structures used for defense. When a paramecium is confronted by danger, such as a predator, the trichocysts release stiff projections that protect the cell.

A paramecium's internal anatomy is shown in **Figure 20–5.** Like most ciliates, a paramecium possesses two types of nuclei: a macronucleus and one or more smaller micronuclei. Why does a ciliate need two types of nuclei? The **macronucleus** is a "working library" of genetic information—a site for keeping multiple copies of most of the genes that the cell needs in its day-to-day existence. The **micronucleus,** by contrast, contains a "reserve copy" of all of the cell's genes.

Ciliates

Use Visuals

Figure 20–5 Ask students: **Which animallike protist phylum includes paramecia?** *(Ciliophora)* **What structures do paramecia use for movement?** *(Cilia)* **What are some other structures in a paramecium cell?** *(An oral groove, a gullet, an anal pore, a contractile vacuole, a micronucleus, a macronucleus, and food vacuoles)*

Build Science Skills

Observing Provide students with a prepared slide of a paramecium. Have them use a microscope to observe the slide and make a labeled drawing of what they see.

FACTS AND FIGURES

No difference

Students often wonder what the real difference is between a cilium and a flagellum. Some might suspect that there must be a subtle difference in internal structure about which their textbook or teacher is not telling them. The truth is that there is no difference—a cilium and a flagellum are the same organelle. The difference in terminology is derived from the days of the light microscope, when biologists thought that the many fine hairs surrounding some cells might well turn out to be different from the few long whips that move other cells. With the advent of the electron microscope, however, it became clear that the structure and biochemistry of both organelles are identical, at least in protists. There is a real difference, however, between the flagella of prokaryotes and those of protists.

Answer to . . .

CHECKPOINT *Cilia are short hairlike projections similar to flagella. Ciliates use cilia for feeding and movement.*

Use Visuals

Figure 20–6 After students have studied the figure, ask: **What is conjugation?** *(Conjugation is the process that allows paramecia to exchange genetic material with other individuals in times of stress.)* **What is the advantage of conjugation for a paramecium species?** *(Conjugation provides new combinations of genes, which help create and maintain genetic diversity.)*

Sporozoans

Meet Diverse Needs

At-risk students may have difficulty understanding the concept of *sporozoite.* Explain that the word is derived from a Greek word for "seed." Point out that sporozoites are similar to seeds but different in that most sporozoites are haploid, while most seeds are diploid. **Learning modality: verbal**

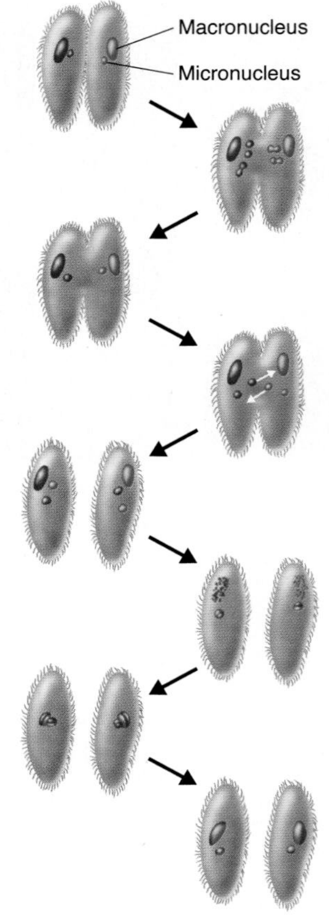

▲ **Figure 20–6** During conjugation, two paramecia attach themselves to each other and exchange genetic information. Conjugation increases genetic diversity. **Interpreting Graphics** ***What structures do paramecia exchange during conjugation?***

Many ciliates obtain food by using cilia to sweep food particles into the **gullet,** an indentation in one side of the organism. The particles are trapped in the gullet and forced into food vacuoles that form at its base. The food vacuoles pinch off into the cytoplasm and eventually fuse with lysosomes, which contain digestive enzymes. The material in the food vacuoles is digested, and the organism obtains nourishment. Waste materials are emptied into the environment when the food vacuole fuses with a region of the cell membrane called the **anal pore.**

In fresh water, water may move into the paramecium by osmosis. This excess water is collected in vacuoles. These vacuoles empty into canals that are arranged in a star-shaped pattern around contractile vacuoles. **Contractile vacuoles** are cavities in the cytoplasm that are specialized to collect water. When a contractile vacuole is full, it contracts abruptly, pumping water out of the organism.

Conjugation Under most conditions, ciliates reproduce asexually by mitosis and binary fission. When placed under stress, however, paramecia may engage in a process known as **conjugation** that allows them to exchange genetic material with other individuals. The process of conjugation is shown in **Figure 20–6.**

As conjugation begins, two paramecia attach themselves to each other. After meiosis of their diploid micronuclei, each organism is left with four haploid micronuclei. Three of these micronuclei disintegrate. The remaining micronucleus in each organism divides, forming a pair of identical micronuclei. The two organisms then exchange one micronucleus from their pair. The macronuclei disintegrate, and new macronuclei form from micronuclei. The two paramecia that participated in conjugation are both genetically changed from their former state. By the end of the process, they are genetically identical to each other.

Strictly speaking, conjugation is not reproduction because no new individuals are formed. It is, however, a sexual process because new combinations of genetic information are produced. Within a large population, the process of conjugation helps to create and maintain genetic diversity.

Sporozoans

While many animallike protists are free living, some are parasites of animals. **Members of the phylum Sporozoa do not move on their own and are parasitic.** Sporozoans are parasites of a wide variety of organisms, including worms, fish, birds, and humans. Many sporozoans have complex life cycles that involve more than one host. Sporozoans reproduce by means of sporozoites. Under the right conditions, a sporozoite can attach itself to a host cell, penetrate it, and then live within it as a parasite.

CHECKPOINT *How do sporozoans reproduce?*

FACTS AND FIGURES

Why conjugation?
Conjugation is an interesting aspect of ciliate reproduction, but many students find it confusing. During the process, the two cells exchange part of their micronuclear "libraries" and form new combinations of genetic information. Once these new combinations are formed, the cell destroys its old macronucleus and makes a new one from the new set of information. Each cell leaves the conjugation event with a genetic makeup that is different from the one with which it entered. The macronuclei seem to contain the genes that must function on a daily basis to keep the cell alive. For the sake of efficiency, those genes have been copied hundreds of times. The existence of two kinds of nuclei seems to help the cell to express the genes required all the time. It also allows the cell to keep a repository of genetic information that may be passed on to future generations.

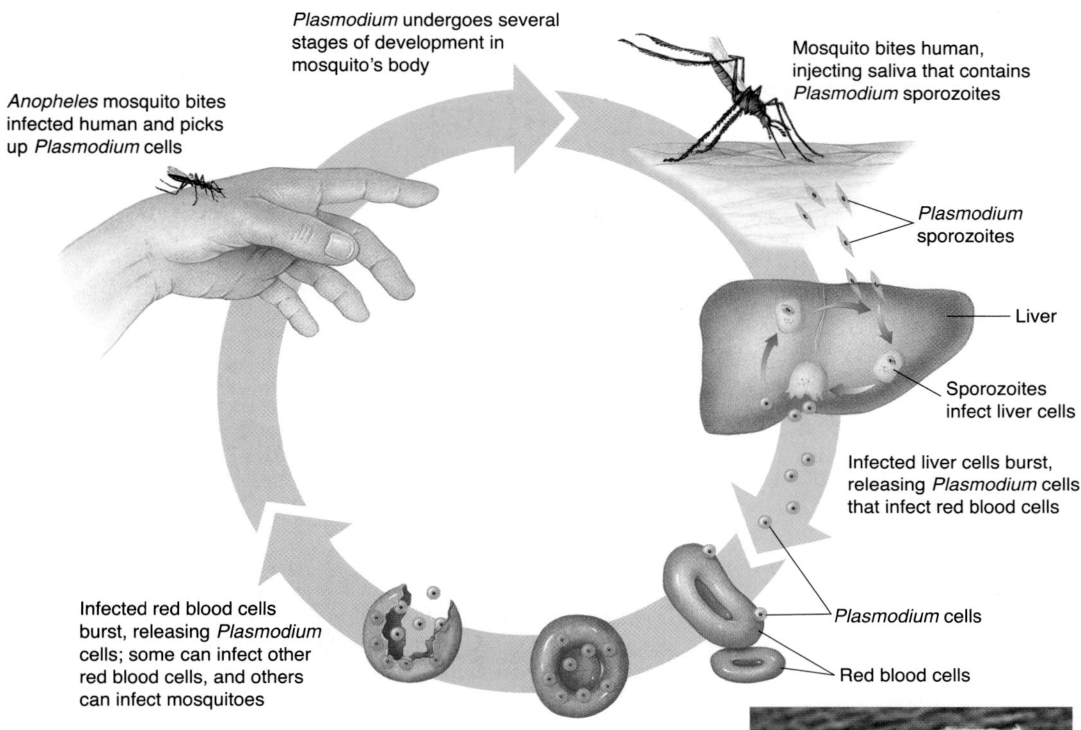
Plasmodium undergoes several stages of development in mosquito's body
Mosquito bites human, injecting saliva that contains Plasmodium sporozoites
Anopheles mosquito bites infected human and picks up Plasmodium cells
Plasmodium sporozoites
Liver
Sporozoites infect liver cells
Infected liver cells burst, releasing Plasmodium cells that infect red blood cells
Plasmodium cells
Red blood cells
Infected red blood cells burst, releasing Plasmodium cells; some can infect other red blood cells, and others can infect mosquitoes

Animallike Protists and Disease

Animallike protists are found throughout the world. They are some of the most common organisms in the oceans. They are also abundant in fresh water, on land, and in the bodies of larger organisms. Unfortunately for humans and for other organisms, many protists are disease-causing parasites. **Some animallike protists cause serious diseases, including malaria and African sleeping sickness.**

Malaria Malaria is one of the world's most serious infectious diseases. Between 300 and 500 million people suffer from malaria, and as many as 2 million people die from it every year. The sporozoan *Plasmodium,* which causes malaria, is carried by the female *Anopheles* mosquito.

The cycle of malarial infection is illustrated in **Figure 20–7.** When an infected mosquito bites a human, its saliva, which contains sporozoites of the parasite, enters the bloodstream. Once inside the body, *Plasmodium* infects liver cells and then red blood cells. *Plasmodium* multiplies rapidly within the infected cells. When red blood cells burst, they dump large amounts of toxins, or poisons, into the bloodstream. The toxins produce the chills and fever that are symptoms of malaria.

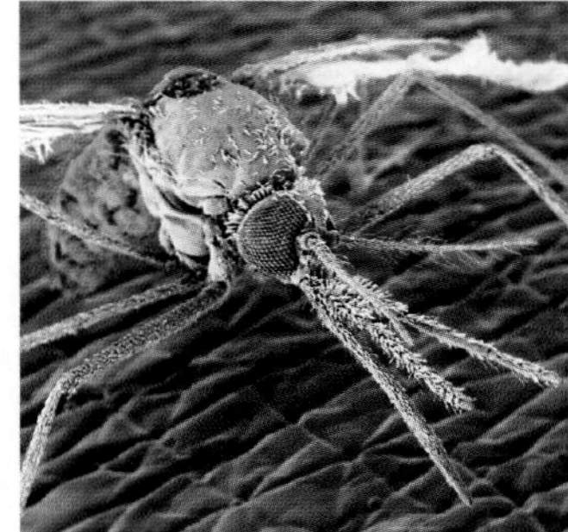

Figure 20–7 **Animallike protists can cause serious diseases, including malaria.** The bite of an *Anopheles* mosquito can transmit *Plasmodium* sporozoites. Once in the human body, *Plasmodium* infects liver cells and red blood cells and multiplies.

Animallike Protists and Disease

Make Connections

Health Science Ask students: **Where is malaria most common?** *(Some students may know that malaria is common in tropical and subtropical regions of the world, including Africa, Southeast Asia, and Central and South America.)* Explain that the classic treatment of malaria was with quinine, a medicine derived from the bark of the cinchona tree. Stronger, synthetic forms of that drug are used today. Eradicating the mosquito carriers and their breeding areas is an important preventative measure against malaria.

Use Community Resources

Invite a health professional or malaria victim to give a brief talk about this disease that still affects so many people around the world. There are many forms of malaria, so it makes an interesting discussion topic.

BIO INSIGHTS

FACTS AND FIGURES

The malarial life cycle

In Figure 20–7, there is a slight oversimplification in the life cycle of *Plasmodium,* which was done to make the material clearer. The form of the parasite that enters the human body is known as a sporozoite. Sporozoites infect the cells of the liver, penetrating and growing within the liver cells until they burst, releasing large amounts of the merozoite stage into the bloodstream. These are the cells that infect red blood cells. Finally, a fraction of the merozoites develop into gametes, which may be taken up by a mosquito when it bites an infected person. Fertilization of the gametes takes place in the digestive system of the mosquito and sporozoites migrate from there to the salivary glands, and the cycle continues.

Answers to . . .

CHECKPOINT *Sporozoans reproduce by means of sporozoites that live within host cells as parasites.*

Figure 20–6 *Two paramecia exchange one micronucleus from a pair of identical micronuclei in each.*

Quick Lab

Objective Students will be able to formulate a hypothesis about how paramecia feed.

Skill Focus **Observing, Formulating Hypotheses**

Materials paramecium culture, 2 dropper pipettes, microscope, microscope slide, coverslip, *Chlorella* culture, toothpick, carmine dye

Time 20 minutes

Advance Prep Order cultures of *Paramecium* and *Chlorella*, as well as carmine dye, from a biological supply house.

Safety Make sure that students wash their hands at the conclusion of the lab.

Strategies

- Demonstrate the use of a toothpick in transferring granules of carmine dye to the drops on the slide.
- You may choose to have students observe the organisms through the microscope before adding carmine red.

Expected Outcomes Students should observe the paramecia feeding on the *Chlorella* cells by trapping the cells in the gullet and then moving the cells into the cytoplasm in food vacuoles.

Analyze and Conclude

1. Students should observe that the *Chlorella* cells and the carmine dye accumulate inside the paramecia.
2. Students should infer from their observations that the paramecia trapped the *Chlorella* cells and dye granules in the gullet and then forced the particles into food vacuoles.
3. Students should hypothesize that the paramecia took in the *Chlorella* cells and the dye granules by endocytosis.

SCIENCE NEWS®

Encourage students to visit **www.phschool.com** for the most current information on this topic.

Quick Lab

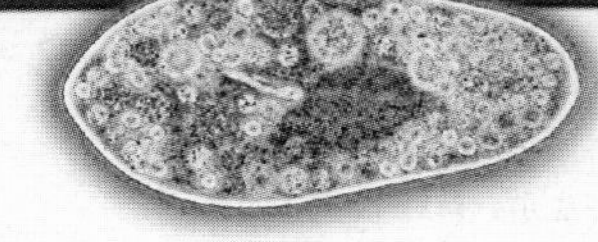

How does a paramecium eat?

Materials paramecium culture, 2 dropper pipettes, microscope, microscope slide, coverslip, *Chlorella* culture, toothpick, carmine dye

Procedure 

1. Use separate dropper pipettes to place a drop of paramecium culture and a drop of *Chlorella* (green alga) culture next to each other on a microscope slide.
2. Use a toothpick to transfer a few granules of carmine dye to the drops on the slide. Add a coverslip so that the two drops mix.
3. Place the slide on the stage of a microscope. Use the low-power objective to locate several paramecia.
4. Use the high-power objective to observe the contents and behavior of the paramecia.

Analyze and Conclude

1. **Observing** Where did the *Chlorella* cells and carmine dye granules accumulate?
2. **Inferring** How do you think this happened to the *Chlorella* cells and carmine dye granules?
3. **Formulating Hypotheses** What process in the paramecia do you think resulted in this change?

Although drugs such as chloroquinine are effective against some forms of the disease, many strains of *Plasmodium* are resistant to these drugs. Medical scientists have developed a number of vaccines against malaria, but to date most are only partially effective. Therefore, for the immediate future, the best means of controlling malaria involve controlling the mosquitoes that carry it.

Other Protistan Diseases Zooflagellates of the genus *Trypanosoma* are responsible for African sleeping sickness. The trypanosomes that cause African sleeping sickness are spread by the bite of an insect known as the tsetse fly. Trypanosomes cause chills and rashes, and they can also infect nerve cells. Severe damage to the nervous system causes individuals to lose consciousness, lapsing into the deep and often fatal coma from which the disease gets its name. The control of the tsetse fly and the protist pathogens that it spreads is a major goal of health workers in Africa.

Amebic dysentery, which is characterized by severe diarrhea, is caused by an organism that looks like the harmless amoebas that you may find in a nearby pond. *Entamoeba,* a parasite spread by contaminated drinking water, can attack the wall of the intestine, causing extensive bleeding.

Amebic dysentery is most common in areas with poor sanitation, but even crystal-clear mountain streams may be contaminated with another flagellated pathogen, *Giardia. Giardia* produces tough microscopic cysts that can be killed only by boiling water thoroughly or by adding iodine to the water. Infection by *Giardia* can cause severe diarrhea and digestive system problems.

KEEP CURRENT WITH . . .

To find out more about the topics in this chapter, go to: **www.phschool.com**

BIO INSIGHTS

FACTS AND FIGURES

Trypanosomes in disguise

African sleeping sickness is one of the worst infectious diseases known, and it has had a devastating effect across central Africa. About 20,000 new cases of the disease are diagnosed each year, and without treatment it is almost always fatal. There is no good treatment for the disease because the protist that causes it, *Trypanosoma,* has a remarkable ability to thwart the human immune system. Normally, when a pathogen invades the body, the immune system makes antibodies that can destroy the invader and end the infection. When trypanosomes infect a person, the immune system produces antibodies that destroy almost all of the invading cells. But about 1 percent of the trypanosomes react by changing the proteins on the surfaces of their cells, and the antibodies made to destroy trypanosomes no longer recognize the cells as enemies.

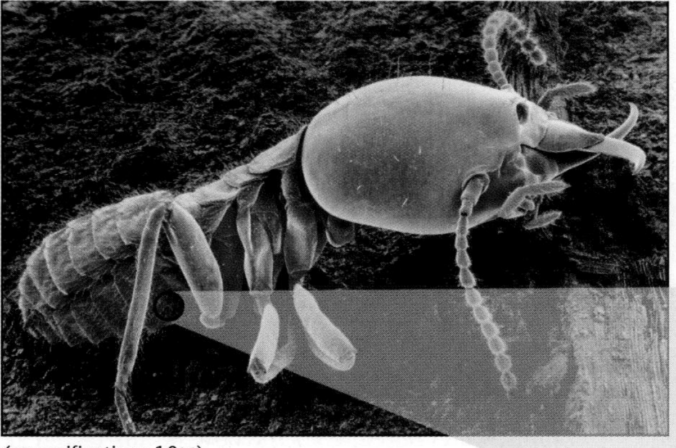
(magnification: 10×)

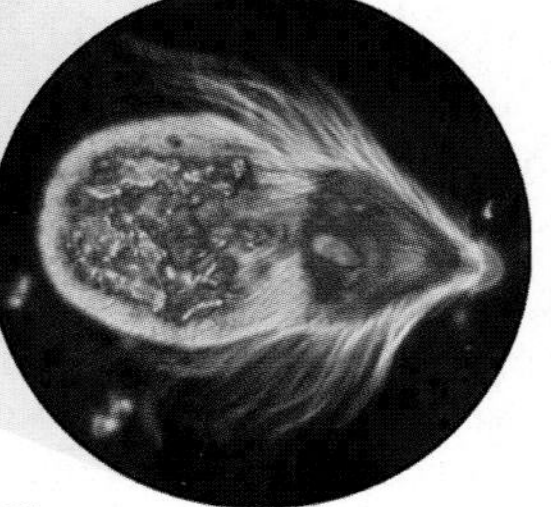
(magnification: about 250×)

Figure 20–8 You can see particles of wood inside the body of *Trichonympha*, a wood-digesting protist (below). *Trichonympha* lives in the digestive systems of insects such as termites (left), allowing them to obtain nutrients from the wood they eat. **Predicting** *What would happen if a termite's* Trichonympha *colony died?*

Ecology of Animallike Protists

Many animallike protists play essential roles in the living world. Some live symbiotically within other organisms. Others recycle nutrients by breaking down dead organic matter. Many animallike protists live in seas and lakes, where they are eaten by tiny animals, which in turn serve as food for larger animals.

Some animallike protists are beneficial to other organisms. *Trichonympha,* shown in **Figure 20–8,** is a zooflagellate that lives within the digestive systems of termites. This protist makes it possible for the termites to eat wood. Termites do not have enzymes to break down the cellulose in wood. (Incidentally, neither do humans, so it does us little good to nibble on a piece of wood.) How, then, does a termite digest cellulose? In a sense, it doesn't. *Trichonympha* does.

Trichonympha and other organisms in the termites' gut manufacture cellulase. Cellulase is an enzyme that breaks the chemical bonds in cellulose and makes it possible for termites to digest wood. Thus, with the help of their protist partners, termites can munch away, busily digesting all the wood they can eat.

20–2 Section Assessment

1. **Key Concept** What are the four major phyla of animallike protists? How do members of each of these groups move?
2. **Key Concept** What animallike protists cause disease?
3. How does a macronucleus differ in function from a micronucleus?
4. Describe the role of animallike protists in the environment.
5. **Critical Thinking Comparing and Contrasting** Compare animallike protists that have flagella to those that have cilia.

iTEXT Assessment Use iText to review the important concepts in Section 20–2.

ALTERNATIVE ASSESSMENT

Creating a Pamphlet
Write and illustrate a public health pamphlet that features two types of waterborne protists that cause disease in humans. Your pamphlet should list symptoms associated with infection and present information on how to avoid waterborne diseases.

Ecology of Animallike Protists

Demonstration

Trichonympha lives in the gut of the termite. It is relatively easy to make a squash slide of a termite. Pull the head off the termite, bringing the intestinal tract with it. Squash the digestive tract in a drop of distilled water, and look for the movement of the protists. Once you have located the protists, either project them on a screen or allow students to look into the microscope. Point out that these protozoans are ciliates. Without them, termites could not digest the wood they eat.

3 ASSESS

Evaluate Understanding

Ask students to write a paragraph that compares an amoeba to a paramecium. In this comparison, students should emphasize differences in the way the two protists move and feed.

Reteach

Have students make a compare/contrast table that organizes the information they have learned about animallike protists. Column headings for this table might include Phylum, Characteristics, and Examples.

ALTERNATIVE ASSESSMENT

Students' pamphlets should feature two common waterborne parasites such as *Entamoeba, Giardia, Balatidium,* or *Leishmania.* Brochures should note that drinking water is to be taken only from approved sources (such as a public water supply) and that even clear stream water may be contaminated with protist parasites.

20–2 Section Assessment

1. Zooflagellates swim with flagella; sarcodines move by extensions of their cytoplasm; ciliates move by means of cilia; and sporozoans do not move at all.
2. *Plasmodium* causes malaria; zooflagellates of the genus *Trypanosoma* are responsible for African sleeping sickness; *Entamoeba* causes amebic dysentery; and *Giardia* can cause diarrhea and digestive problems.
3. A macronucleus is a "working library" of genetic information; a micronucleus contains a "reserve" copy of all the genes.
4. Some live symbiotically within other organisms. Others recycle nutrients by breaking down dead organic matter. Many live in seas and lakes, where they are eaten by tiny animals.
5. Zooflagellates have flagella; some live within other organisms. Ciliates have cilia; most are free living.

Use iText to review the key concepts in Section 20–2.

Answer to . . .

Figure 20–8 *The termite would have no food and would also die.*

Have students answer the You Decide questions, in which each takes a position about how a major city should address this issue. Then, ask student volunteers to interview a manager who has the responsibility of protecting your local water supply. Have the students ask if anything has been done to protect the drinking water from *Cryptosporidium* contamination and what the cost is or would be for such protection. After students have reported to the class about what they learned, discuss whether this new information has changed any opinions.

You Decide

1. The protist *Cryptosporidium* is so small that it can pass through filters in public water purification systems, and the protist is also resistant to chlorine. The major public policy issue is how to protect the public from contaminated water.
2. One option is to advise consumers to purify the water within their household; the other option is for public systems to install better filters. The benefit of better purifying the public supply is that it would be more effective. But that option would cost taxpayers more than point-of-use protection.
3. Some students may think responsibility should fall on individual householders. Others may argue that protection of the water supply is a government responsibility.
4. Whichever position a student takes, the opinion should be supported by logical arguments.

How Should Water Be Protected Against *Cryptosporidium*?

In April of 1993, more than 403,000 people in Milwaukee were infected, and 47 died, in an outbreak of severe intestinal diarrhea spread by public drinking water. The cause was a parasitic protist known as *Cryptosporidium* that attaches itself to the lining of the intestines. The epidemic was brought under control only by requiring the boiling of drinking water.

How did the water become contaminated with *Cryptosporidium*? No one knows for sure, but it's possible that runoff from an animal slaughterhouse had contaminated streams that flow into the city's water supply. Milwaukee's water was purified by filtration and chlorination and met the highest government standards. Unfortunately, *Cryptosporidium* is so small—only 4 to 7 µm in diameter—that it can pass through the high-volume filters used in public water purification systems. *Cryptosporidium* is also resistant to chlorine. What is the best way to protect the public against future outbreaks?

The Viewpoints

Purify at Point of Use

Because public water purification systems cannot control *Cryptosporidium,* public policy should focus on the individual. Consumers everywhere should be advised to purchase and install household filters. The best of these filters can remove 99.9 percent of particles larger than 1 µm, which should effectively eliminate *Cryptosporidium* from the drinking water of most users. In addition, people with weakened immune systems should be advised to boil all of their drinking water.

Purify and Protect the Supply

Point-of-use purification will never provide effective public protection against a Milwaukee-like outbreak. It is unrealistic to expect every houshold to install and maintain high-tech filtering systems. The best strategy is, therefore, to focus on the water supply itself. Water from streams that feed into public water supplies should be carefully tested for *Cryptosporidium* and vigorously protected against contaminant runoff. Even though absolute removal of all *Cryptosporidium* may not be possible, filters should be installed that reduce contamination to levels low enough to protect the public health.

You Decide

1. **Defining the Issue** What are the major public issues regarding water supply protection from the protist *Cryptosporidium*?
2. **Analyzing the Viewpoints** What are the options for the protection of drinking water? What are the benefits of each option? What are the costs? Who is affected by each option?
3. **Forming Your Opinion** Should public policy focus on the water supply or on point-of-use protection for individuals?
4. **Role-Playing** Suppose you were the head of the water supply board of a major American city that had a small amount of extra money in its annual budget. How would you advise the city council to allocate the money: to public education about *Cryptosporidium* or to research on better ways to lower the level of *Cryptosporidium* in the water supply?

BACKGROUND

A parasitic protozoan

Cryptosporidium, like *Plasmodium,* is a sporozoan, and sporozoans are all obligate intracellular parasites with complex life cycles that may include more than one host. The life cycle of *Cryptosporidium* involves the production of a protective capsule called a cyst, by which the parasite can survive outside a host. The cyst form is important, since the transmission of the parasite occurs when cysts in feces contaminate water supplies. The normal chemical treatment of the water supply does not affect these cysts. When a person drinks the contaminated water, the cysts break open in the stomach, releasing *Cryptosporidium* cells that cause diarrhea and other intestinal problems. In most people, the infection is short-lived. But in people with compromised immune systems, including those with AIDS, an infection can be life threatening.

20–3 Plantlike Protists: Unicellular Algae

Many protists contain the green pigment chlorophyll and carry out photosynthesis. Many of these organisms are highly motile, or able to move about. Despite this, the fact that they perform photosynthesis is so important that we group these protists in a separate category, the plantlike protists. Plantlike protists are commonly called "algae."

Some scientists place those algae that are more closely related to plants in the kingdom Plantae. In this textbook, we will consider all forms of algae, including those most closely related to plants, to be protists. There are seven major phyla of algae classified according to a variety of cellular characteristics. The first four phyla, which contain unicellular organisms, are discussed in this section. These four phyla are the euglenophytes, the dinoflagellates, the chrysophytes, and the diatoms. The last three phyla include many multicellular organisms and will be discussed in the next section.

Guide for Reading

Key Concepts
- What is the function of chlorophyll and accessory pigments in algae?
- What are the distinguishing features of the major phyla of unicellular algae?

Vocabulary
accessory pigment
eyespot
pellicle
phytoplankton

Reading Strategy: Summarizing As you read, make a list of the types of unicellular algae. Write a sentence about each type.

Chlorophyll and Accessory Pigments

One of the key characteristics used to classify algae is the type of photosynthetic pigments they contain. As you will remember, light is necessary for photosynthesis, and it is chlorophyll and the accessory pigments that trap the energy of sunlight.

Life in deep water poses a major difficulty for algae: a shortage of light. As sunlight passes through water, much of the light's energy is absorbed by the water. In particular, sea water absorbs large amounts of the red and violet wavelengths. Therefore, the light becomes dimmer and bluer as the depth of the water increases. Because chlorophyll *a* is most efficient at capturing red and violet light, the dim blue light that penetrates into deep water contains very little light energy that chlorophyll *a* can use.

In adapting to conditions of limited light, various groups of algae have evolved different forms of chlorophyll. Each form of chlorophyll—chlorophyll *a*, chlorophyll *b*, and chlorophyll *c*—absorbs different wavelengths of light. The result of this evolution is that algae can use more of the energy of sunlight than just the red and violet wavelengths.

▶ **Figure 20–9** **Chlorophyll and other pigments allow algae to collect and use energy from sunlight.** These green algae of the species *Acetabularia calyculus* live on the roots of mangrove trees in Florida.

TIME SAVER — SECTION RESOURCES

Print:
- ***Teaching Resources,*** Section Review 20–3
- ***Guided Reading and Study Workbook,*** Section 20–3

Technology:
- ***iText,*** Section 20–3

Section 20–3

1 FOCUS

Objectives

20.3.1 ***Describe*** the function of chlorophyll and accessory pigments in algae.
20.3.2 ***Describe*** the major phyla of unicellular algae.
20.3.3 ***Summarize*** the ecological roles of unicellular algae.

Guide for Reading

Vocabulary Preview

Have students preview the Vocabulary terms by skimming the section for these boldfaced terms and writing down their definitions.

Reading Strategy

Point out that in several of the sections, the phrases or sentence students should write after each heading would be the Key Concept highlighted in boldface type.

2 INSTRUCT

Chlorophyll and Accessory Pigments

Demonstration

Before class, under a vent hood, use a water bath to boil some samples of green, brown, and red algae in separate beakers of alcohol to dissolve their pigments. Take 3 disks of filter paper large enough to cover the tops of the beakers, and in each, cut two parallel slits 1/2 cm apart. Bend each paper strip so that it extends into the liquid and acts as a wick. Within a class period, the streaks of the different pigments can be seen. Have students observe and compare the pigments on the filter paper. Then, ask: **What pigment(s) seem to be present in every type of alga?** *(Chlorophylls)* **Why aren't all algae green?** *(The other pigments—the accessory pigments—mask the color of the chlorophyll.)* **Why do algae have pigments other than chlorophyll?** *(The accessory pigments are capable of absorbing wavelengths of light that chlorophyll cannot, making photosynthesis more efficient.)*

20–3 (continued)

Euglenophytes

Use Visuals

Figure 20–10 Ask students: **Which phylum of plantlike protists includes members of the genus *Euglena*?** *(Euglenophyta)* **Why are euglenas classified as plantlike protists and not animallike protists?** *(They contain chloroplasts that carry out photosynthesis.)* **What does the eyespot on a euglena give it the ability to do?** *(It gives it the ability to sense light.)* **How is a euglena like a paramecium?** *(They are both unicellular organisms, and they both expel excess water through a contractile vacuole.)*

Build Science Skills

Observing Provide students with a prepared slide of a euglena. Ask them to use a microscope to observe the slide and make a labeled drawing of what they see.

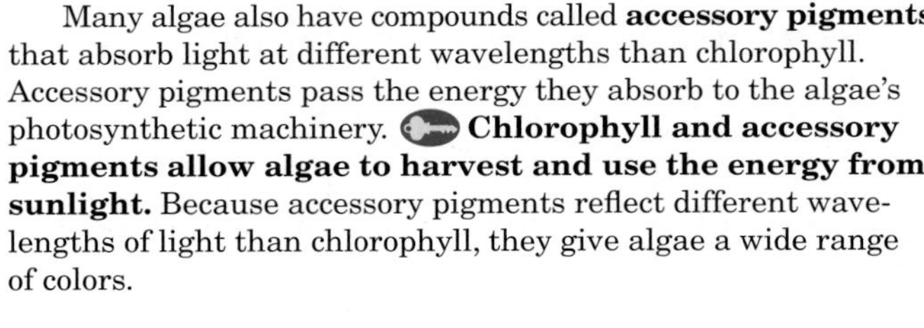

Many algae also have compounds called **accessory pigments** that absorb light at different wavelengths than chlorophyll. Accessory pigments pass the energy they absorb to the algae's photosynthetic machinery. **Chlorophyll and accessory pigments allow algae to harvest and use the energy from sunlight.** Because accessory pigments reflect different wavelengths of light than chlorophyll, they give algae a wide range of colors.

Euglenophytes

Members of the phylum Euglenophyta (yoo-glee-nuh-FYT-uh), or euglenophytes, are closely related to the animallike flagellates. **Euglenophytes are plantlike protists that have two flagella but no cell wall.** Although euglenophytes possess chloroplasts, in most other respects they are remarkably similar to zooflagellates.

The phylum takes its name from the genus *Euglena*. Euglenas are found in ponds and lakes throughout the world. A typical euglena, such as the one shown in **Figure 20–10,** is about 50 micrometers in length. Euglenas are excellent swimmers. Two flagella emerge from a gullet at one end of the cell, and the longer of these two flagella spins in a pattern that pulls the organism rapidly through the water. Near the gullet end of the cell is a cluster of reddish pigment known as the **eyespot,** which helps the organism find sunlight to power photosynthesis. If sunlight is not available, euglenas can also live as heterotrophs, absorbing the nutrients available in decayed organic material. Euglenas store carbohydrates in small storage bodies.

Euglenas do not have cell walls, but they do have an intricate cell membrane called a **pellicle.** The pellicle is folded into a series of ribbonlike ridges, each ridge supported by microtubules. The pellicle is tough and flexible, allowing euglenas to squirm and crawl through mud when there is not enough water to allow them to swim. Euglenas reproduce asexually by means of binary fission.

CHECKPOINT *What are eyespots, and why are they important to euglenas?*

▼ **Figure 20–10 Euglenophytes are plantlike protists that have two flagella but no cell wall.** The green structures inside the euglena shown are chloroplasts, which allow the organism to carry on photosynthesis when light is available. Euglenas are covered by a ridged pellicle. A pigmented eyespot helps the organism find the light that powers photosynthesis, while movement is produced by the flagella that protrude from one end of the organism. Like paramecia, euglenas expel excess water through a contractile vacuole.

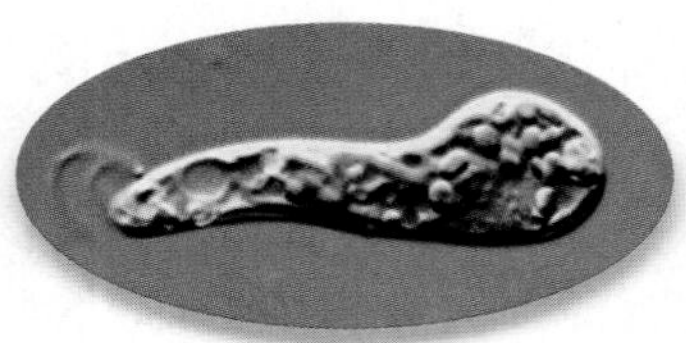

(magnification: 540×)

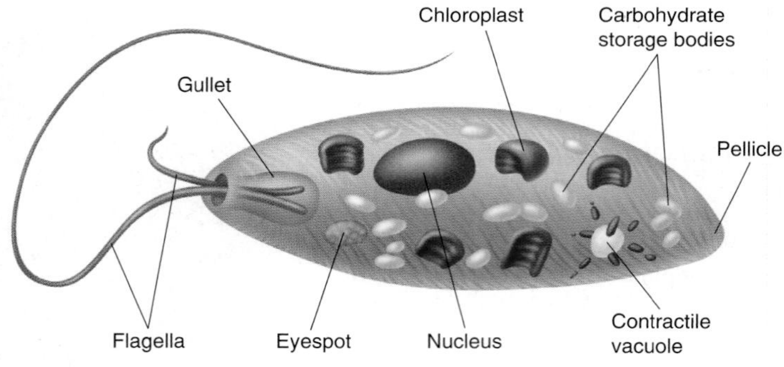

PRESENTATIONS MADE EASY!

The Presentation Assistant Plus contains the Prentice Hall Presentation Pro and the Transparencies, which provide easy-to-follow visual support for every step of this lesson. If you have a computer presentation station, use Prentice Hall Presentation Pro Section 20–3, or use the transparencies listed here.

Section 20–3: **Interest Grabber**
Section Outline
Euglena

Dinoflagellates

Dinoflagellates are members of the phylum Pyrrophyta (pir-uh-FYT-uh). **About half of dinoflagellates are photosynthetic; the other half live as heterotrophs.** Dinoflagellates generally have two flagella, and these often wrap around the organism in grooves between two thick plates of cellulose that protect the cell, as shown in **Figure 20–11.** Most dinoflagellates reproduce asexually by binary fission.

Many dinoflagellate species are luminescent. When agitated by sudden movement in the water, many dinoflagellates give off light. Some areas of the ocean are so filled with dinoflagellates that the movement of an oar or the hull of a boat will cause the dark water to shimmer with a ghostly blue light. This luminescent property gives the phylum its name, *Pyrrophyta*, which means "fire plants."

Another interesting property of the dinoflagellates has to do with their genetic material. Like other organisms, dinoflagellates store genetic information in the form of DNA. In all other eukaryotic cells, however, that DNA is tightly bound with proteins known as histones. Dinoflagellates do not have histones; in fact, they are the only eukaryotes that do not. The reason for this difference, as well as an explanation of how the functions of histone proteins are carried out when none are present in dinoflagellates, remains a mystery.

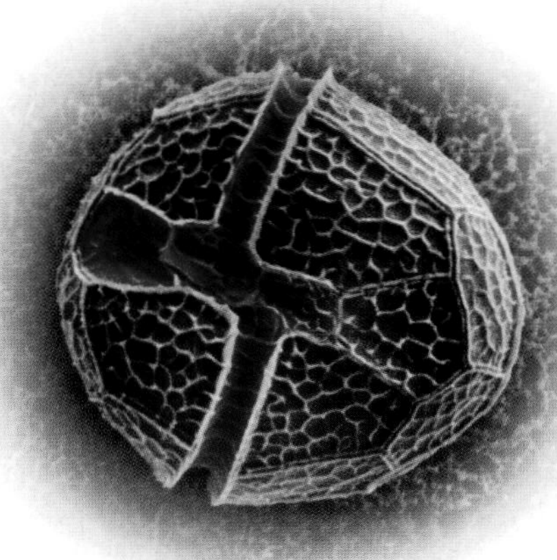

(magnification: 1600×)

▲ **Figure 20–11** **Some dinoflagellates are photosynthetic, while others are heterotrophs.** The paired flagella of a dinoflagellate lie in grooves around its circumference, shown here in red. The flagella propel the organism, spinning, through the water.

Chrysophytes

The phylum Chrysophyta (kris-uh-FYT-uh) includes the yellow-green algae and the golden-brown algae. The chloroplasts of these organisms contain bright yellow pigments that give the phylum its name. *Chrysophyta* means "golden plants." **Members of the phylum Chrysophyta are a diverse group of plantlike protists that have gold-colored chloroplasts.**

The cell walls of some chrysophytes contain the carbohydrate pectin rather than cellulose, while others contain both pectin and cellulose. Chrysophytes generally store food in the form of oil rather than starch. They reproduce both asexually and sexually. Most are solitary, but some form threadlike colonies.

Diatoms

Members of the phylum Bacillariophyta (bas-uh-lehr-ee-uh-FYT-uh), or diatoms, are among the most abundant organisms on Earth. They are also some of the most beautiful. **Diatoms produce thin, delicate cell walls rich in silicon (Si)—the main ingredient in glass.** These walls are shaped like the two sides of a petri dish or flat pillbox, with one side fitted snugly into the other. The cell walls have fine lines and patterns that almost seem to be etched, or carved, into their glasslike brilliance, as shown in **Figure 20–12.**

▼ **Figure 20–12** **Tiny jewellike diatoms such as this centric diatom have cell walls rich in silicon.**

(magnification: 2200×)

FACTS AND FIGURES

Diatoms

Diatoms constitute an important part of the phytoplankton. Diatoms can be found floating on the ocean and on fresh water. They occur primarily as single cells, but some form colonies. The shells of diatoms are called frustules and consist of two halves, called valves, that fit together like parts of a pillbox. These shells are formed as the organism absorbs silicates from the water. The shells consist of minute passageways that connect the internal cytoplasm with the external environment. The remains of these shells, so-called diatomaceous earth, are used in filters, commercial abrasives, the manufacture of dynamite, and rubber and plastic products.

Dinoflagellates

Use Visuals

Figure 20–11 Have students examine the figure and read the caption. Then, ask: **Which protist phylum includes the dinoflagellates?** *(Pyrrophyta)* **What is a luminescent organism?** *(An organism that produces light.)* **Which group of animallike protists are dinoflagellates most like? Explain why.** *(They are most like the zooflagellates, because both groups of protists use flagella for movement.)*

Chrysophytes

Make Connections

Chemistry Ask students: **What is unusual about the way chrysophytes store food?** *(They generally store food in the form of oils rather than starch.)* **How do the energy-storing abilities of oils compare to those of starch?** *(Oils, which are lipids, can store more than twice as much energy per gram as starches, which are carbohydrates.)*

Diatoms

Build Science Skills

Observing Ask students how they think they could collect diatoms to observe. Suggest that they look for brownish-yellow, crusty coatings on rocks, twigs, or shells in shallow ocean, lake, or pond water. Have students follow these steps to collect and observe diatoms.

1. Place a coated rock, twig, or shell and some of the water in a jar.

2. In the lab, drain off most of the water, and then float a clean glass coverslip in the remaining water. If left for 1–2 days, diatoms will attach to the coverslip.

3. Scrape the coverslip with a scalpel, spread the material on a slide, and observe with a microscope.

Have students make drawings and try to identify the diatoms they observe.

Answer to . . .

CHECKPOINT *An eyespot is a cluster of reddish pigment that helps the organism find sunlight to power photosynthesis. Eyespots are important to euglenas because they can carry out photosynthesis when sunlight is available.*

Ecology of Unicellular Algae

Analyzing Data

Fertilizer in runoff from agricultural fields as well as from lawns in suburban areas can cause algal blooms in lakes and other bodies of water. The experiment described in this Analyzing Data is typical of those investigating such pollution problems.

Answers

1. The responding variable in the students' experiment is the amount of undiluted liquid plant fertilizer added to a container of pond water.

2. The container to which no fertilizer was added serves as the control.

3. The algae grew the most in the container in which 2 mL of fertilizer were added.

4. Students should draw the conclusion that fertilizers increase the growth of algae.

Analyzing Data

Fertilizers and Algae

The growth of algae in bodies of water is affected by the addition of plant fertilizers—a pollutant. A group of students collected three large, clear containers of pond water. They used a turbidity meter to measure the cloudiness of the water. The cloudiness, or turbidity, is a rough indicator of the amount of algae present.

The students did not add anything to the first container. To the second container, they added 1 mL of undiluted liquid plant fertilizer. To the third container, they added 2 mL of fertilizer. They then left the containers in a window for 1 week and measured the turbidity again on the eighth day. Their data are summarized in the table.

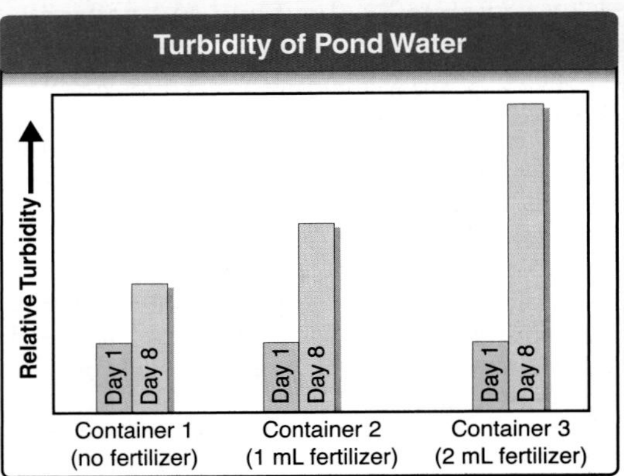

1. **Controlling Variables** What is the responding variable in the students' experiment?
2. **Designing Experiments** What is the role of the first container of water, to which no fertilizer was added?
3. **Using Tables and Graphs** In which container did the algae grow the most?
4. **Drawing Conclusions** What can you conclude about the effect of fertilizers on the growth of algae?

Ecology of Unicellular Algae

Plantlike protists are common in both fresh and salt water, and thus are an important part of freshwater and marine ecosystems. A few species of algae, however, can cause serious problems.

Plantlike protists play a major ecological role on Earth. Plantlike protists are important organisms whose position at the base of the food chain makes much of the diversity of aquatic life possible. They make up a considerable part of the **phytoplankton** (fy-toh-PLANK-tun), the population of small, photosynthetic organisms found near the surface of the ocean. About half of the photosynthesis that occurs on Earth is carried out by phytoplankton. Phytoplankton provide a direct source of nourishment for organisms as diverse as shrimp and whales. Even land animals such as humans obtain nourishment indirectly from the phytoplankton. When you eat a tuna fish sandwich, you are eating fish that fed on smaller fish that fed on still smaller animals that fed on plantlike protists.

Symbiotic Algae Unicellular algae form some spectacular symbiotic relationships with other organisms. For example, many types of coral contain intercellular dinoflagellates. These dinoflagellates allow the tiny coral animals to use the food products of photosynthesis. This food allows coral to grow in areas where nutrients are scarce. In turn, the dinoflagellates can feed on the waste products of the coral animals.

FACTS AND FIGURES

The base of the ocean's food web

Oceans cover about three fourths of Earth. In the deep ocean, relatively few species live much below a few meters. But much life can be found at and near the ocean's surface in a collection of floating organisms known as plankton. In fact, most of Earth's biomass can be found drifting with ocean currents. The zooplankton include various protozoa, larvae and eggs, and tiny invertebrates. The phytoplankton, the photosynthesizing portion of the plankton, consists of plantlike algae, including dinoflagellates, diatoms, and many other forms. These producers capture the energy of sunlight and, in so doing, provide the basis of the food web in the marine ecosystem. The zooplankton depend on the phytoplankton for food, and the other organisms in the sea gain their sustenance from the zooplankton.

Other dinoflagellates make their homes within other organisms. In the giant clam *Tridacna gigas*, an organ called the mantle contains large numbers of symbiotic photosynthetic protists. These dinoflagellates are positioned so that they gather as much sunlight as possible, thereby increasing the nutrient benefit to the clam.

Algal Blooms Because many protists, including euglenophytes, absorb organic material directly and use it for food, they grow rapidly in regions where sewage is discharged. These protists play a vital role in recycling sewage and other waste materials. When the amount of waste is excessive, however, populations of euglenophytes and other algae may grow into enormous masses known as blooms. While not harmful in themselves, these algal blooms quickly deplete the water of nutrients, and the cells begin to die in great numbers. The decomposition of these dead algae can rob water of its oxygen, choking its resident fish and invertebrate life.

Great blooms of the dinoflagellates *Gonyaulax* and *Gymnodinium* have occurred in recent years on the east coast of the United States, although scientists are not sure of the reason. These blooms, such as the one shown in **Figure 20–13,** are known as "red tides." These species produce a potentially dangerous toxin. Filter-feeding shellfish such as clams can trap *Gonyaulax* and *Gymnodinium* for food and become filled with the toxin. Eating shellfish from water infected with red tide can cause serious illness, paralysis, and even death.

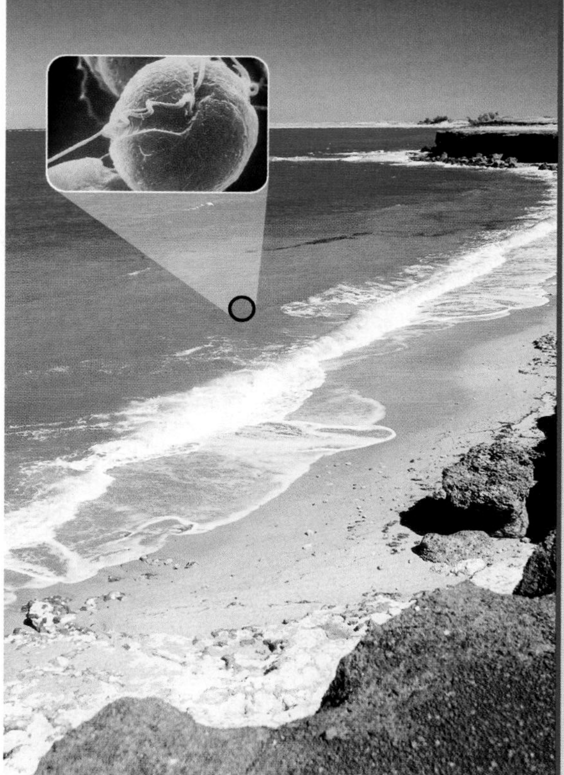

Figure 20–13 Blooms of the dinoflagellate *Gymnodinium* (inset) can produce red tides. *Gymnodinium* contains a toxin that becomes concentrated in the tissue of filter feeders such as clams and oysters. **Inferring** *How can red tides be harmful to humans?*

20–3 Section Assessment

1. **Key Concept** What do chlorophyll and accessory pigments do in algae?
2. **Key Concept** What are the four phyla of unicellular plantlike protists?
3. What is the role of unicellular algae in the environment?
4. How do most unicellular algae get food? How does this differ from the way most animallike protists get food?
5. **Critical Thinking Problem Solving** Identify two ways to reduce the problem of algal blooms in fresh water.

iTEXT Assessment Use iText to review the important concepts in Section 20–3.

Take It to the NET

Read about a group of algae called choanoflagellates. Then, write a brief report on the structure and evolutionary significance of these protists. Use the links provided in the Biology area at the Prentice Hall Web site for help in completing this activity: **www.phschool.com**

Meet Diverse Needs

Help students with limited English proficiency understand the term *bloom* by comparing an algal bloom to a flower's bloom. Point out that in both cases, the organism shows growth and vigor and increases in size. Have students use a dictionary to compare the meanings of *bloom* in different contexts. **Limited English proficiency**

3 ASSESS

Evaluate Understanding

Call on students at random to name the phylum, describe the characteristics, and provide examples for each of the groups of plantlike protists discussed in this section: the euglenophytes, the dinoflagellates, the chrysophytes, and the diatoms.

Reteach

Call on students to compare the labeled illustration of a euglena in Figure 20–10 with the labeled illustration of a paramecium in Figure 20–5. Help students see the similarities and differences between these two organisms. Place emphasis on the chloroplast within the euglena, which explains why euglenas are considered plantlike and not animallike protists.

Take It to the NET

Students' reports should describe the structure of choanoflagellates and discuss their evolutionary significance. For additional information, visit **www.phschool.com**

Use iText to review the key concepts in Section 20–3.

20–3 Section Assessment

1. They allow algae to harvest and use the energy from sunlight.
2. Euglenophyta, Pyrrophyta, Chrysophyta, Bacillariophyta
3. They are at the base of aquatic food chains, and they make up a considerable part of the phytoplankton. Unicellular algae also form symbiotic relationships with other organisms.
4. Most unicellular algae use the energy of sunlight to produce food. Animallike protists, by contrast, get food by absorbing food through their cell membranes, capturing and digesting food, or trapping food in the gullet.
5. Sample answer: Eliminate sewage discharge into fresh water and reduce the amount of plant fertilizers that move into fresh water.

Answer to . . .

Figure 20–13 *Toxins from the algae that produce red tides can get into clams and cause illness, paralysis, and death in humans who eat the clams.*

Section 20–4

1 FOCUS

Objectives

20.4.1 ***Describe*** the major phyla of multicellular algae.
20.4.2 ***Explain*** how multicellular algae reproduce.
20.4.3 ***Identify*** some human uses of algae.

Guide for Reading

Vocabulary Preview

Pronounce each of the vocabulary words out loud, and ask students to pronounce the terms back in unison.

Reading Strategy

Explain that an outline should include several levels of entries, with each of the entries providing support for the level above. To make an outline of this section, students should use the blue headings as their first level of entries. The green headings, such as those under Reproduction in Green Algae, should form the second level of entries. Third and fourth levels should include supporting details, concepts, and examples.

2 INSTRUCT

Red Algae

Make Connections

Physics Some students may not know that the color of an object depends on which colors of the visible spectrum of light are absorbed and which are reflected. Point to a pair of blue pants and ask students: **Are these pants blue because they absorb blue light or reflect blue light?** *(The pants are blue because they reflect blue light.)* Point out that the pants not only reflect blue light but also absorb the other colors in the visible light spectrum. Explain that the different pigments in the different kinds of algae absorb some colors and reflect others. The pigments in red algae, for example, reflect red light and absorb other colors.

20–4 Plantlike Protists: Red, Brown, and Green Algae

Guide for Reading

Key Concepts
- What are the distinguishing features of the major phyla of multicellular algae?
- How do multicellular algae reproduce?

Vocabulary
phycobilin
filament
alternation of generations
gametophyte
spore
sporophyte

Reading Strategy: Outlining Before you read, use the blue and green headings to make an outline about multicellular algae. As you read, add phrases or a sentence after each heading to provide key information.

Have you ever taken a walk along a rocky beach at low tide? As the water recedes, in many places it reveals a damp forest of green and brown "plants" clinging to the rocks. These seaweeds, as they are generally called, have the size, color, and appearance of plants, but technically they are not plants. They are actually algae. Unlike the algae you studied in the last section, however, most of these algae are multicellular, like plants. They also have reproductive cycles that are sometimes very similar to those of plants. Many of them have cell walls and photosynthetic pigments that are identical to those of plants. Many of these algae also possess highly specialized tissues.

The three phyla of algae that are largely multicellular are commonly known as red algae, brown algae, and green algae. Although there are many differences among these phyla, the most important ones, for which the groups are named, involve their photosynthetic pigments.

Red Algae

Red algae are members of the phylum Rhodophyta (roh-duh-FYT-uh), meaning "red plants." **Red algae are able to live at great depths due to their efficiency in harvesting light energy. Red algae contain chlorophyll *a* and reddish accessory pigments called phycobilins. Phycobilins** (fy-koh-BIL-inz) are especially good at absorbing blue light, enabling red algae to live deeper in the ocean than many other photosynthetic algae. Many red algae are actually green, purple, or reddish black, depending upon the other pigments they contain. Red algae are an important group of marine algae that can be found in waters from the polar regions to the tropics. The highly efficient light-harvesting pigments in these algae enable them to grow anywhere from the ocean's surface to depths of up to 260 meters.

Most species of red algae are multicellular, and all species have complex life cycles. Red algae lack flagella and centrioles.

One common red alga is *Chondrus crispus*, or Irish moss. It grows in tide pools and on rocky coastlines. Other red algae, known as the coralline algae and shown in **Figure 20–14,** play an important role in the formation of coral reefs by helping to stabilize them.

Figure 20–14 **Red algae contain chlorophyll *a* and reddish pigments called phycobilins.** Coralline algae, a type of red alga, collect calcium carbonate in their cell walls, giving them a tough, stony texture.

SECTION RESOURCES

Print:
- ***Teaching Resources,*** Section Review 20–4
- ***Guided Reading and Study Workbook,*** Section 20–4

Technology:
- ***iText,*** Section 20–4

Brown Algae

Brown algae belong to the phylum Phaeophyta (fay-uh-FYT-uh), meaning "dusky plants." **Brown algae contain chlorophyll *a* and *c*, as well as a brown accessory pigment, fucoxanthin.** The combination of fucoxanthin (fyoo-koh-ZAN-thin) and chlorophyll *c* gives most of these algae a dark, yellow-brown color. Brown algae are the largest and most complex of the algae. All brown algae are multicellular and most are marine, commonly found in cool, shallow coastal waters of temperate or arctic areas.

The largest known alga is giant kelp, a brown alga that can grow to more than 60 meters in length. Another brown alga called *Sargassum* forms huge floating mats many kilometers long in an area of the Atlantic Ocean near Bermuda known as the Sargasso Sea. Bunches of *Sargassum* often drift on currents to beaches in the Caribbean and southern United States.

One of the most common brown alga is *Fucus*, or rockweed, found along the rocky coast of the eastern United States. Each *Fucus* plant has a holdfast, a structure that attaches the alga to the bottom. The body of the alga consists of flattened stemlike structures called stipes, leaflike structures called blades, and gas-filled swellings called bladders, which float and keep the algae upright in the water. **Figure 20–15** shows the structures of a brown alga.

CHECKPOINT *What does a holdfast do?*

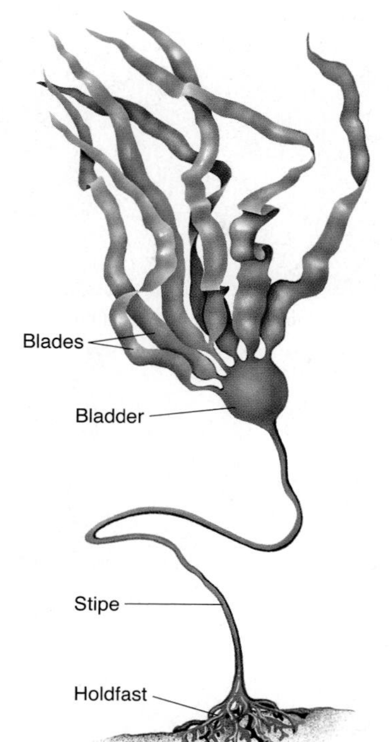

▲ **Figure 20–15** **Brown algae contain chlorophyll *a* and *c*, plus fucoxanthin, a brown pigment.**

Green Algae

Green algae are members of the phylum Chlorophyta (klawr-uh-FYT-uh), which means "green plants" in Greek. **Green algae share many characteristics with plants, including their photosynthetic pigments and cell wall composition.** Green algae have cellulose in their cell walls, contain chlorophyll *a* and *b*, and store food in the form of starch, just like land plants. One stage in the life cycle of mosses—small land plants you will learn about in the next unit—looks remarkably like a tangled mass of green algae strands. All these characteristics lead scientists to hypothesize that the ancestors of modern land plants looked a lot like certain species of living green algae. Unfortunately, algae rarely form fossils, so there is no single specific fossil that scientists can call an ancestor of both living algae and mosses. However, scientists think that mosses and green algae shared such a common algaelike ancestor millions of years ago.

Green algae are found in fresh and salt water, and even in moist areas on land. Many species live most of their lives as single cells. Others form colonies, groups of similar cells that are joined together but show few specialized structures. A few green algae are multicellular and have well-developed specialized structures.

Brown Algae

Demonstration

Display a large map of North America or the Western Hemisphere for students to see. Point out the area of ocean called the Sargasso Sea, which is southeast of Bermuda. Explain that some brown algae, such as kelp, have a holdfast that attaches the seaweed to rocks or other surfaces. The *Sargassum* in the Sargasso Sea, by contrast, has no holdfast. Instead, this form of brown algae has gas-filled bladders—floats—at the base of the seaweed's blades that keep the algae afloat in the Sargasso Sea. Explain that some students may have seen this brown alga on the Florida shores of the Gulf of Mexico. After tropical storms, large quantities of *Sargassum* are washed up along the beaches there.

Green Algae

Build Science Skills

Classifying Before students read about green algae, divide the class into small groups and give each group several samples to observe, including a sample of "sea lettuce" or another kind of multicellular green alga, a fern, a mushroom, a flowering plant, and some kind of moss. Ask students to examine these organisms and speculate about the environment to which each organism is adapted. Have each group consider which of the samples could be considered a plant and which could not be. Then, have several groups present their findings to the class. Challenge groups to give reasons why they classified some organisms as plants but not others.

PRESENTATIONS MADE EASY!

The Presentation Assistant Plus contains the Prentice Hall Presentation Pro and the Transparencies, which provide easy-to-follow visual support for every step of this lesson. If you have a computer presentation station, use Prentice Hall Presentation Pro Section 20–4, or use the transparencies listed here.

Section 20–4:

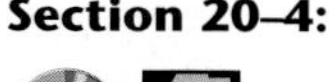

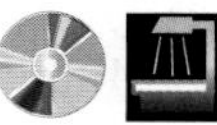

Interest Grabber
Section Outline
***Ulva* Life Cycle**
Figure 20–17

Answer to . . .

CHECKPOINT *A holdfast is a structure that attaches the alga to the bottom of the ocean.*

20–4 (continued)

Build Science Skills

Comparing and Contrasting Provide students with access to living cultures of different forms of green algae, such as *Chlamydomonas, Spirogyra,* and *Ulva*, and have them make slides from these cultures. (To make a slide from the *Chlamydomonas* culture, they can use a dropper pipette to place one drop of the culture on a slide and cover with a coverslip. To make a slide from the *Spirogyra* culture, they can separate a strand into a 2-centimeter segment using a dissecting needle, add a drop of water, and cover with a coverslip. To make a slide from the *Ulva* culture, they can separate a small piece of the alga from the sample, add a drop of water, and cover with a coverslip.) Ask students to observe the slides under a microscope and make labeled drawings of what they see. After students have concluded their observations, have them compare the different kinds of green algae in a class discussion.

Reproduction in Green Algae

Address Misconceptions

The idea of alternation of generations may confuse some students. They might conclude that every other generation of an organism is radically different than the previous generation. Point out that this use of the term *generation* has a different meaning from what it might have in another context, such as the generations in a person's family. Synonyms for *generation* in this context include *phase* and *stage.*

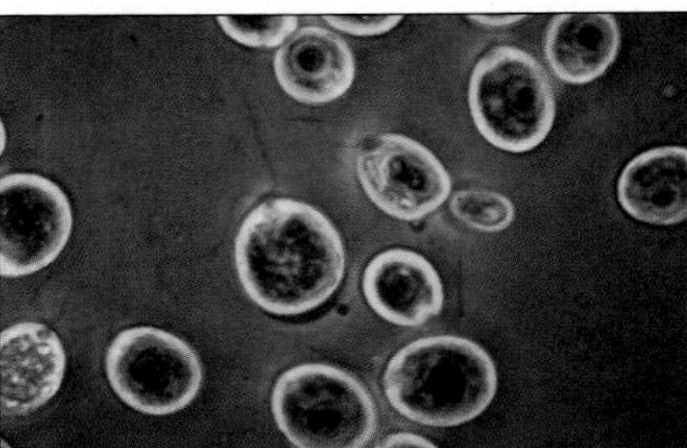

Chlamydomonas (magnification: 1000×)

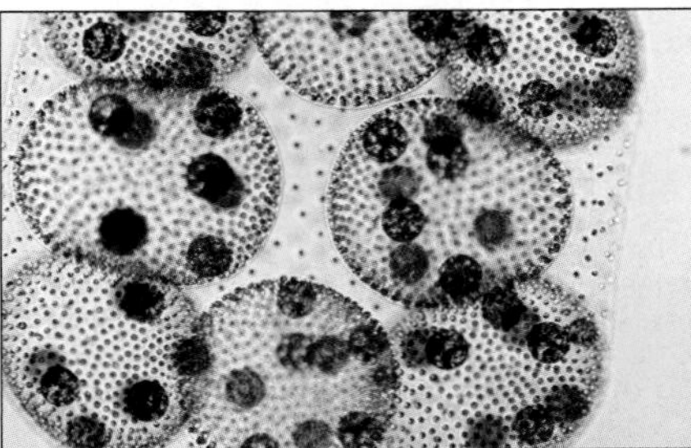

Volvox (magnification: 450×)

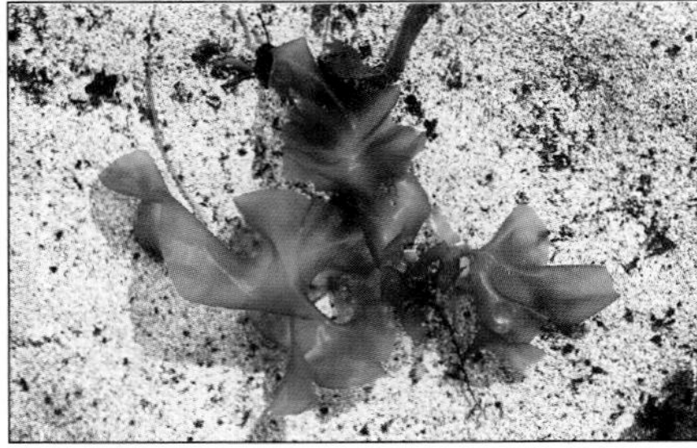

Ulva

Figure 20–16 **Green algae have the same photosynthetic pigments and cell wall compositions as plants.** *Chlamydomonas* is a unicellular green alga that lives in ponds. Delicate spherical colonies of the green alga *Volvox* live in fresh water. New colonies can develop within existing colonies and are released when the older colony ruptures. *Ulva* is a multicellular green alga that lives along seacoasts.

Unicellular Green Algae *Chlamydomonas* (kluh-mid-uh-MOHN-uz), a typical single-celled green alga, grows in ponds, ditches, and wet soil. *Chlamydomonas* is a small egg-shaped cell with two flagella and a single large, cup-shaped chloroplast. Within the base of the chloroplast is a region that synthesizes and stores starch. *Chlamydomonas* lacks the large vacuoles found in the cells of land plants. Instead, it has two small contractile vacuoles. *Chlamydomonas* and two other green algae are shown in **Figure 20–16.**

Colonial Green Algae Several species of green algae live in multicellular colonies. The freshwater alga *Spirogyra* forms long threadlike colonies called **filaments,** in which the cells are stacked almost like soda cans placed end to end.

Volvox colonies are more elaborate, consisting of as few as 500 to as many as 50,000 cells arranged to form hollow spheres. The cells in a *Volvox* colony are connected to one another by strands of cytoplasm, enabling them to coordinate movement. When the colony moves, cells on one side of the colony "pull" with their flagella, and the cells on the other side of the colony have to "push." Although most cells in a *Volvox* colony are identical, a few gamete-producing cells are specialized for reproduction. Because it shows some cell specialization, *Volvox* straddles the fence between colonial and multicellular life.

Multicellular Green Algae *Ulva*, or "sea lettuce," is a bright-green marine alga that is commonly found along rocky seacoasts. *Ulva* is a true multicellular organism, containing several specialized cell types. Although the body of *Ulva* is only two cells thick, it is tough enough to survive the pounding of waves on the shores where it lives. A group of cells at its base forms holdfasts that attach *Ulva* to the rocks.

Reproduction in Green Algae

The life cycles of many algae include both a diploid and a haploid generation. Recall from Chapter 11 that diploid cells have two sets of chromosomes, whereas haploid cells have a single set. Many algae switch back and forth between haploid and diploid stages during their life cycles, in a process known as **alternation of generations.** Many species also shift back and forth between sexual and asexual forms of reproduction.

Reproduction in *Chlamydomonas* The single-celled *Chlamydomonas* spends most of its life in the haploid stage. As long as its living conditions are suitable, this haploid cell reproduces asexually, producing cells called zoospores by mitosis. As you learned in Chapter 10, reproduction by mitosis is asexual. The two haploid daughter cells produced by mitosis are genetically identical to the single haploid cell that entered mitosis.

FACTS AND FIGURES

Ancestors of land plants
It is generally believed that the chlorophytes, or green algae, are the group from which land plants evolved. Among the algae, only the chlorophytes have cellulose in their cell walls, contain chlorophylls *a* and *b,* and store their food in the form of starch, all of which are also characteristics of land plants. Because algae ordinarily do not form fossils, we do not have direct evidence of an evolutionary relationship. But one stage in the life cycle of mosses looks remarkably like a tangle of green algal filaments. Perhaps both mosses and the modern multicellular green algae descended from a common algaelike ancestor.

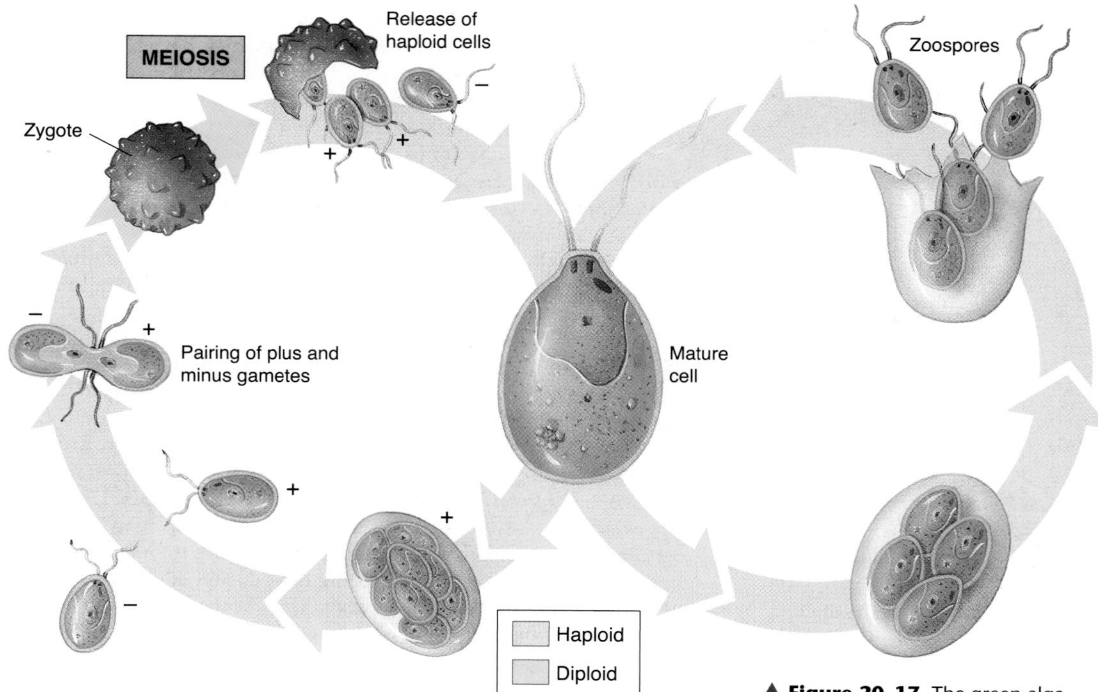

▲ **Figure 20–17** The green alga *Chlamydomonas* reproduces asexually by producing zoospores and sexually by producing zygotes. **Interpreting Graphics** ***Which form of reproduction includes a diploid organism that can survive adverse conditions?***

If conditions become unfavorable, *Chlamydomonas* can also reproduce sexually. The life cycle of *Chlamydomonas* is shown in **Figure 20–17.** The haploid cells continue to undergo mitosis, but instead of releasing zoospores, the cells release gametes. The gametes, which look identical, are of two opposite mating types, + (plus) and − (minus). During sexual reproduction, the gametes gather in large groups. Then + and − gametes form pairs that soon move away from the group. The paired gametes join flagella and spin around in the water. Both members of the pair then shed their cell walls and fuse, forming a diploid zygote.

The zygote sinks to the bottom of the pond and grows a thick protective wall. Within this protective wall, *Chlamydomonas* can survive freezing or drying conditions that would ordinarily kill it. When conditions once again become favorable, the zygote begins to grow. It divides by meiosis to produce four flagellated haploid cells. These haploid cells can swim away, mature, and reproduce asexually. Thus, during its life cycle, *Chlamydomonas* alternates between a haploid stage, in which it spends most of its life, and a brief diploid stage, represented by the zygote cell.

 CHECKPOINT ***What two types of gametes does*** **Chlamydomonas** ***produce?***

Meet Diverse Needs

To understand the life cycle of *Chlamydomonas,* at-risk students may need to review what they have learned about reproduction. Ask students: **What is the difference between asexual and sexual reproduction?** *(Asexual reproduction involves the division of a single parent cell. Sexual reproduction involves the joining of two parent cells, or gametes.)* **What is the difference between cells with a diploid number of chromosomes and cells with a haploid number?** *(Diploid cells have the full complement of chromosomes for a particular species; haploid cells have half the complement.)* **What is meant by alternation of generations?** *(Shifting back and forth between haploid and diploid stages during the life cycle)* **Learning modality: verbal**

BIO INSIGHTS FACTS AND FIGURES

Alternating phases

The basic plan of alternation of generations is a life cycle in which diploid (2N) and haploid (N) phases alternate. Use of the term *generation* can be confusing, since these are phases in one complete life cycle of an organism rather than the production of offspring. The following are generalizations that apply to an alternation of generations in any organism, from algae to vascular plants.

- Any cell of the sporophyte generation is usually diploid (2N).
- Any cell of the gametophyte generation is usually haploid (N).
- The change from sporophyte to gametophyte occurs as the result of meiosis.
- The change from gametophyte to sporophyte occurs as a result of fertilization, or the fusion of gametes.

Answers to . . .

CHECKPOINT Chlamydomonas *produces two gametes of opposite mating types, + (plus) and − (minus).*

Figure 20–17 *Sexual reproduction*

20–4 (continued)

Use Visuals

Figure 20–18 Ask students: **What is the pattern called by which *Ulva* reproduces?** *(Alternation of generations)* **Which generation, or phase, produces haploid spores?** *(The sporophyte generation)* **What cellular process is involved in producing these spores?** *(Meiosis)* **Which generation produces gametes?** *(The gametophyte generation)* **What does the fusion of the gametes produce?** *(A zygote)* **What does the zygote grow to become?** *(The sporophyte generation)*

Reproduction in *Ulva* The life cycle of the green alga *Ulva* involves an alternation of generations in which both the diploid and haploid phases are large, multicellular organisms. In fact, the haploid and diploid phases of *Ulva* are so similar that only an expert can tell them apart!

The haploid phase of *Ulva* produces two forms of gametes—male and female. Because they produce gametes, the haploid forms of *Ulva* are known as **gametophytes** (guh-MEET-uh-fyts), or gamete-producing plants.

When male and female gametes fuse, they produce a diploid zygote cell, which then grows into a large, diploid multicellular *Ulva*. The diploid *Ulva* undergoes meiosis to produce haploid reproductive cells called **spores**. Each of these spores is able to grow into a new individual without fusing with another cell. Because the diploid *Ulva* produces spores, it is known as a **sporophyte** (SPOH-ruh-fyt), or spore-producing organism.

Take a close look at the life cycle of *Ulva* in **Figure 20–18,** because the alternation of generations it displays is a pattern you will see repeated over and over again in the plants. *Ulva*'s life cycle includes two separate phases that alternate in a regular pattern: sporophyte, then gametophyte, then sporophyte again. Complex life cycles involving alternation of generations are characteristic of the members of the plant kingdom. This is one of the reasons some biologists favor classifying multicellular algae such as *Ulva* as plants.

▼ **Figure 20–18** **The life cycles of most algae include both diploid and haploid generations.** The multicellular green alga *Ulva* exhibits alternation of generations. The haploid generation produces a diploid generation, then the diploid generation produces a haploid generation. The two generations are multicellular and virtually indistinguishable from each other.

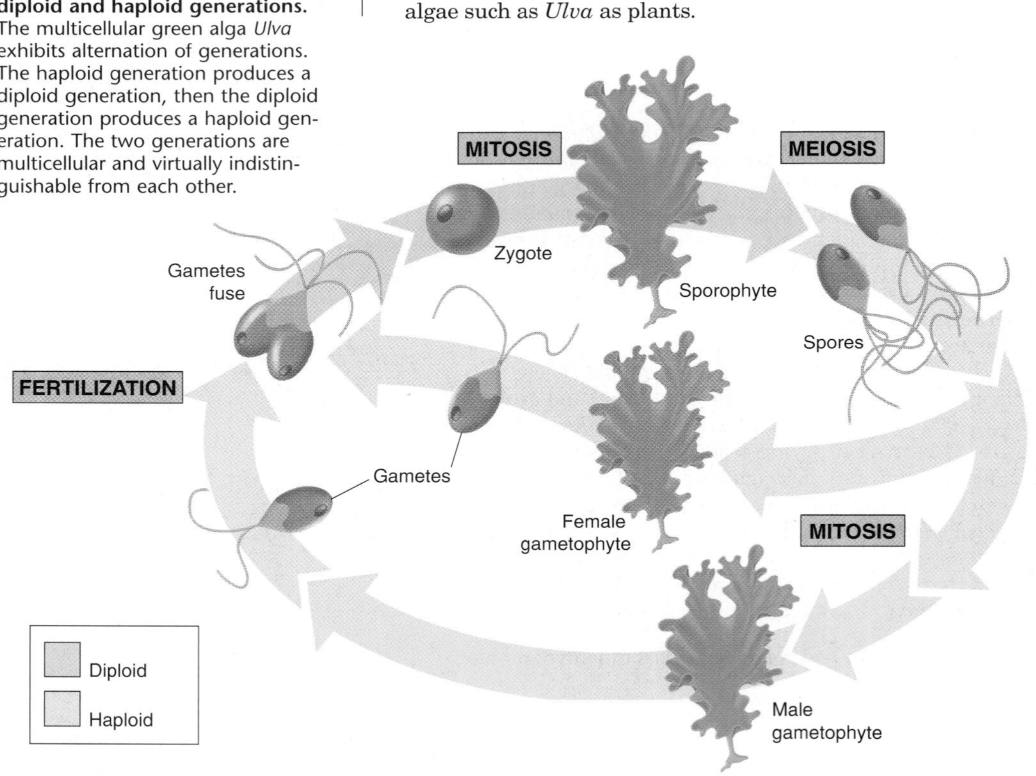

BIO INSIGHTS — FACTS AND FIGURES

An evolutionary link

The characteristics of the green alga *Ulva*—often called sea lettuce—demonstrate an evolutionary link between simpler green algae and more complex land plants. Although only two cells thick, *Ulva* is truly multicellular, forming such specialized structures as holdfasts. While *Ulva* exhibits alternation of generations like the algae and simpler land plants, it exhibits heterogamy; that is, it has one nonmotile gamete—the "egg"—that is slightly larger than the motile gamete—the "sperm."

Human Uses of Algae

Algae are a major food source for life in the oceans. Algae have even been called the "grasses" of the seas, because they make up much of the base of the food chain upon which sea animals "graze." The enormous brown kelp forests off the coasts of North America are home to many animal species.

Algae produce much of Earth's oxygen through photosynthesis. Scientists calculate that about half of all the photosynthesis that occurs on Earth is performed by algae. This fact alone makes algae one of the most important groups of organisms on the entire planet.

Over the years, people have learned to use algae—and the chemicals produced by algae—in many different ways. Many species of algae are rich in vitamin C and iron. Chemicals in algae are used to treat stomach ulcers, high blood pressure, arthritis, and other health problems.

Have you ever eaten algae? Almost certainly, your answer should be yes. In Japan, the red alga *Porphyra* is grown on special marine farms. Dried *Porphyra*—called *nori* in Japanese—is dark green and paper-thin. Nori is used to wrap portions of rice, fish, and vegetables to make sushi, as shown in **Figure 20–19.** You say you've never had sushi? Well, you've probably eaten ice cream, salad dressing, pudding, or a candy bar. Other products from algae are used in pancake syrups and eggnog.

Industry has even more uses for algae. Chemicals from algae are used to make plastics, waxes, transistors, deodorants, paints, lubricants, and even artificial wood. Algae even have an important use in scientific laboratories. The compound agar, derived from certain seaweeds, thickens the nutrient mixtures scientists use to grow bacteria and other microorganisms.

▲ **Figure 20–19** People have found many different uses for algae. The red alga *Porphyra* is used as a wrapper in Japanese sushi rolls. Ice cream often contains algin, a thickener made from brown algae. **Predicting** ***How would your life be different without products made from algae?***

20–4 Section Assessment

1. **Key Concept** Describe the main features of the major phyla of multicellular algae.
2. **Key Concept** What is alternation of generations?
3. How are multicellular algae important at a global level?
4. Why can red algae live in deeper water than green algae?
5. **Critical Thinking Classifying** Do you think green algae should be classified as plants? Give reasons for your answer.

iTEXT **Assessment** Use iText to review the important concepts in Section 20–4.

ALTERNATIVE ASSESSMENT

Organizing Information
Make a poster illustrating three types of multicellular algae. Your poster should have detailed drawings or photographs of each group. Each illustration must show the correct classification and have two written characteristics of each group.

Human Uses of Algae

Use Community Resources

Seaweed, or multicellular algae, is edible and part of the cuisine of Japan and other countries. Have students look for seaweed foods at a specialty market and report to the class about the products they found. Also encourage students interested in cooking to make an appointment to interview a chef at a local Japanese restaurant about how seaweed is used in Japanese recipes. You might ask these students to prepare a seaweed dish for the class.

3 ASSESS

Evaluate Understanding

Ask students to make a table that contains information about the three phyla of multicellular plantlike protists. This table should include the phylum names, the common names, characteristics, and examples of each.

Reteach

Ask students to make their own drawings of the life cycle of the multicellular green alga *Ulva,* using Figure 20–18 as a model. Then, call on students to define the terms *alternation of generations, gametophyte,* and *sporophyte.*

ALTERNATIVE ASSESSMENT

A student's poster should show several drawings or photographs of multicellular algae, including at least one example each of red algae, brown algae, and green algae. Each illustration should be clearly labeled with the phylum the alga is in as well as the alga's scientific name.

20–4 Section Assessment

1. Students should describe the main features of algae in the phyla Rhodophyta, Phaeophyta, and Chlorophyta.
2. A process in which algae switch back and forth between haploid and diploid during their life cycles.
3. Algae perform about half of all photosynthesis on Earth, thus providing much of Earth's oxygen.
4. Red algae contain the reddish accessory pigments known as phycobilins, which are especially good at absorbing blue light, enabling red algae to live deeper in the ocean than other algae.
5. Some students may suggest that green algae should be classified as plants because they have the same photosynthetic pigments and cell wall composition, and they store food in the form of starch.

Use iText to review the key concepts in Section 20–4.

Answer to . . .

Figure 20–19 *Many products might be different, including ice cream, salad dressing, and pudding.*

Section 20–5

1 FOCUS

Objectives

20.5.1 ***Compare and Contrast*** funguslike protists and fungi.
20.5.2 ***Describe*** slime molds and water molds.
20.5.3 ***Summarize*** the ecological roles of funguslike protists.

Guide for Reading

Vocabulary Preview

Call on students at random to pronounce the vocabulary words in the order in which they appear. Correct any mispronunciations.

Reading Strategy

Before students read, have them rewrite the blue headings in the section as *how, why,* or *what* questions about funguslike protists. Then, as they read, they can write down answers to the heading questions.

2 INSTRUCT

Slime Molds

Address Misconceptions

Because of the terminology involved in the two groups of slime molds, students may infer that cellular slime molds are the rule and acellular slime molds the exception. Explain that the majority of slime mold species are acellular and form plasmodia.

20–5 Funguslike Protists

Guide for Reading

Key Concepts
- What are the similarities and differences between funguslike protists and fungi?
- What are the defining characteristics of the slime molds and water molds?

Vocabulary
cellular slime mold
acellular slime mold
plasmodium
hypha
zoosporangium
antheridium
oogonium

Reading Strategy: Predicting Before you read, preview the life cycles in **Figures 20–22** and **20–23.** Predict how these life cycles are similar and how they are different.

If you look closely at the debris-laden floor of a forest after several days of rain, you may see glistening patches of what looks like brightly colored mold. Funguslike protists grow in damp, nutrient-rich environments and absorb food through their cell membranes, much like fungi. In fact, these organisms have sometimes been classified as fungi, even though their cellular structure more closely resembles that of the protists. **Like fungi, the funguslike protists are heterotrophs that absorb nutrients from dead or decaying organic matter. But unlike most true fungi, funguslike protists have centrioles. They also lack the chitin cell walls of true fungi.** The funguslike protists include the cellular slime molds, the acellular slime molds, and the water molds.

Slime Molds

Slime molds are found in places that are damp and rich in organic matter, such as the floor of a forest or a backyard compost pile. **Slime molds are funguslike protists that play key roles in recycling organic material.** At one stage of their life cycle, slime molds look just like amoebas. At other stages, they form moldlike clumps that produce spores, almost like fungi.

Two broad groups of slime molds are recognized. The individual cells of **cellular slime molds** remain distinct—separated by cell membranes—during every phase of the mold's life cycle. Slime molds that pass through a stage in which their cells fuse to form large cells with many nuclei are called **acellular slime molds.**

▼ **Figure 20–20** **Funguslike protists lack chlorophyll and absorb nutrients from dead organic matter.** Slime molds like this red raspberry slime mold are often found in the damp, shaded environments preferred by many fungi.

Cellular Slime Molds Cellular slime molds belong to the phylum Acrasiomycota (ak-ruh-see-oh-my-KOH-tuh). They spend most of their lives as free-living cells that are not easily distinguishable from soil amoebas. In nutrient-rich soils, these amoeboid cells reproduce rapidly. When their food supply is exhausted, they send out chemical signals that attract other cells of the same species. Within a few days, thousands of cells aggregate into a large sluglike colony that begins to function like a single organism. The colony migrates for several centimeters, then stops and produces a fruiting body, a slender reproductive structure that produces spores. Eventually, the spores are scattered from the fruiting body. Each spore gives rise to a single amoeba-like cell that starts the cycle all over again, as shown in **Figure 20–22.**

SECTION RESOURCES

Print:
- ***Laboratory Manual A,*** Chapter 20 Lab
- ***Teaching Resources,*** Section Review 20–5, Chapter 20 Design an Experiment
- ***Guided Reading and Study Workbook,*** Section 20–5

Technology:
- ***iText,*** Section 20–5

◀ **Figure 20–21** **Slime molds help recycle organic matter.** The two main groups of slime molds are cellular slime molds and acellular slime molds.

In many ways, these remarkable organisms challenge our understanding of what it means to be multicellular. During much of their life cycle, cellular slime molds are unicellular organisms that look and behave like animallike protists. When they aggregate, however, they act very much like multicellular organisms. Slime molds have been especially interesting to biologists who study how cells send signals and regulate development. They have kept biologists busy for decades, but their secrets are still not fully understood.

CHECKPOINT ***Why is it difficult to classify cellular slime molds as unicellular or multicellular?***

▼ **Figure 20–22** Cellular slime molds reproduce asexually. **Interpreting Graphics** ***Is most of the cellular slime mold life cycle haploid or diploid?***

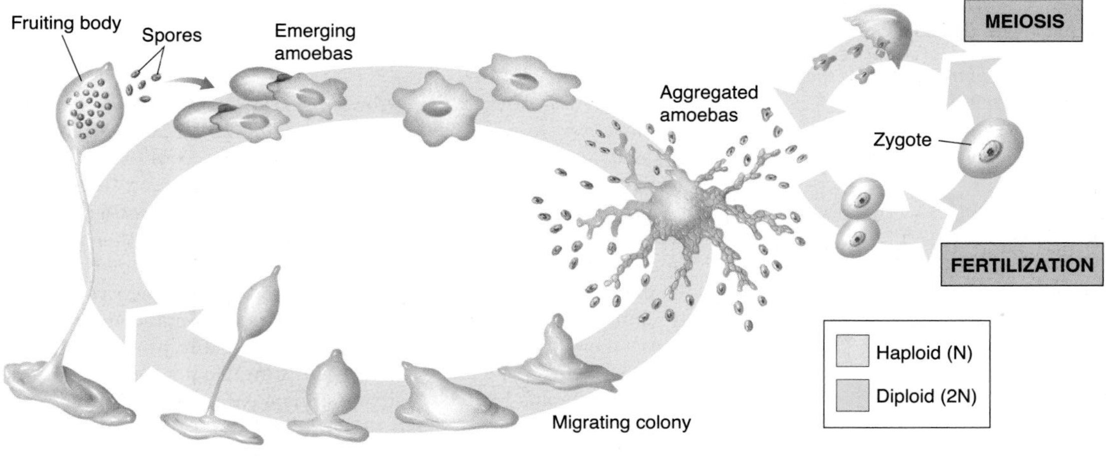

Use Visuals

Figure 20–22 Have students study the life cycle of cellular slime molds, and ask: **What are slime molds?** *(Funguslike protists that play key roles in recycling organic material)* **How are cellular slime molds different from acellular slime molds?** *(The individual cells of cellular slime molds remain distinct, while the cells of acellular slime molds fuse to form large cells with many nuclei.)* **How do the individual cells of cellular slime molds reproduce?** *(They reproduce by cell division.)* Emphasize that most of the life cycle is haploid.

Demonstration

The spores of slime molds are abundant in airborne dusts. To demonstrate, place a dead leaf or piece of bark on a few dry oatmeal flakes in a petri dish. Sprinkle some water over the flakes, and cover the dish. If you put the dish aside for a few days, an acellular slime mold plasmodium will likely grow on food. Have students observe the funguslike protist and make drawings.

PRESENTATIONS MADE EASY!

The Presentation Assistant Plus contains the Prentice Hall Presentation Pro and the Transparencies, which provide easy-to-follow visual support for every step of this lesson. If you have a computer presentation station, use Prentice Hall Presentation Pro Section 20–5, or use the transparencies listed here.

Section 20–5:

Interest Grabber
Section Outline
The Life Cycle of a Water Mold
Figure 20–22
Figure 20–23

Answers to . . .

CHECKPOINT *During most of their life cycle, cellular slime molds are unicellular organisms that look and behave like animallike protists. When they aggregate, however, they act very much like a multicellular organism.*

Figure 20–22 *Haploid*

20–5 (continued)

Use Visuals

Figure 20–23 Ask students: **What forms when cells of acellular slime molds aggregate?** *(A plasmodium forms.)* **What contains the many nuclei within the plasmodium?** *(A single cell membrane)* Explain that when environmental conditions change, a plasmodium will break up and produce fruiting bodies, which are reproductive structures. Ask: **What are produced within the fruiting bodies?** *(Spores)* **Are the spores haploid or diploid?** *(Haploid)*

Water Molds

Demonstration

Several days before students read about water molds, ask a local pet store to provide you with a dead tropical fish. Put the dead fish in a jar of water, place a top on the jar, and set it aside for a few days. Have students observe the fuzzy water mold that grows on the dead fish. Explain that the "fuzziness" is actually a mass of hyphae, which students will learn more about when they study fungi. Ask students: **What is the food source for this water mold?** *(The decaying body of the dead fish)* Point out that the water mold is providing a necessary environmental service in recycling this dead organic matter.

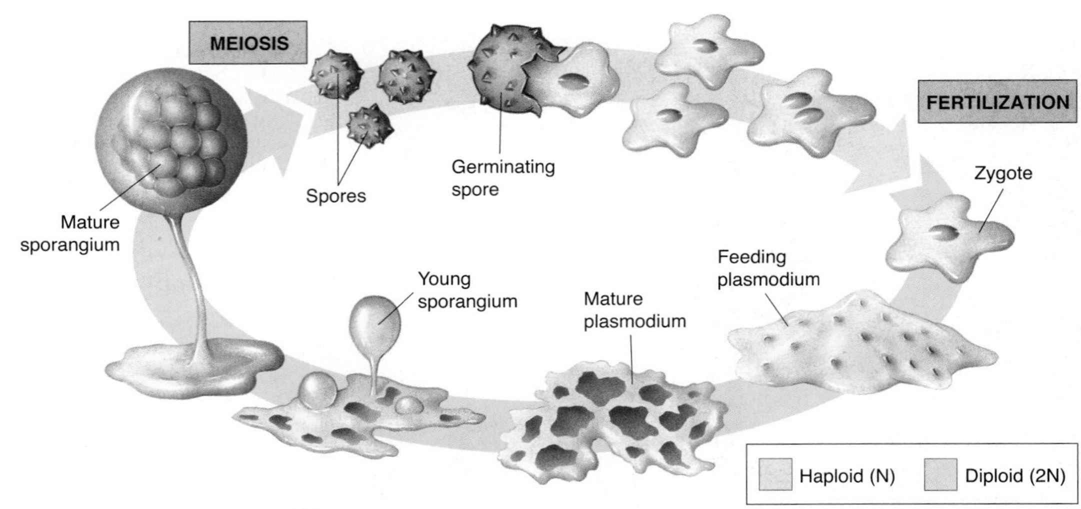

Figure 20–23 The plasmodium of an acellular slime mold is the collection of many amoeba-like organisms, but their separateness is not preserved. The plasmodium is a multinucleate structure contained in a single cell membrane. The plasmodium will eventually produce sporangia, which in turn will produce haploid spores. Upon pairing up and fusing, these result in new diploid amoeba-like cells. **Interpreting Graphics** ***What stage of the life cycle is shown in the photograph?***

Acellular Slime Molds Acellular slime molds belong to the phylum Myxomycota (myk-suh-my-KOH-tuh). Like cellular slime molds, acellular slime molds begin their life cycles as amoeba-like cells. However, when they aggregate, their cells fuse to produce structures with many nuclei.

These structures are known as **plasmodia** (singular: plasmodium). The large plasmodium of an acellular slime mold, such as the one shown in **Figure 20–23,** is actually a single structure with many nuclei. A plasmodium may grow as large as several meters in diameter!

Eventually, small fruiting bodies, or sporangia, spring up from the plasmodium. The sporangia produce haploid spores by meiosis. These spores scatter to the ground where they germinate into flagellated cells. The flagellated cells then fuse to produce diploid zygotes that repeat the cycle.

Water Molds

If you have seen white fuzz growing on the surface of a dead fish in the water, you have seen a water mold in action. Water molds, or oomycetes, are members of the phylum Oomycota (oh-oh-my-KOH-tuh). **Oomycetes thrive on dead or decaying organic matter in water and are plant parasites on land.** Oomycetes are commonly known as water molds, but they are not true fungi. Water molds produce thin filaments known as **hyphae.** These hyphae do not have walls between their cells; as a result, water mold hyphae are multinucleate. In addition, water molds have cell walls made of cellulose and produce motile spores, two characteristics that fungi do not have.

Water molds have both sexual and asexual phases in their life cycle, as shown in **Figure 20–24.** In asexual reproduction, portions of the hyphae develop into **zoosporangia** (singular: zoosporangium), which are spore cases. Each zoosporangium

FACTS AND FIGURES

The attack of the giant amoeba

An acellular slime mold begins its life as an amoebalike cell. When their cells aggregate to form a plasmodium, it becomes more like a giant amoeba. Plasmodia are usually white, but they may also be colorless, orange, yellow, violet, blue, or black. In a favorable environment, a plasmodium may increase 25 times its original size in just one week, and it can grow to become 45 centimeters in length. A plasmodium tends to creep in one direction at a rate of 2.5 centimeters per hour. If the environment suddenly becomes unfavorable—if, for example, the food supply suddenly diminishes—a plasmodium will usually change into many separate, small sporangia, each of which contains thousands of spores. In some species, the plasmodium forms a single spore-bearing body.

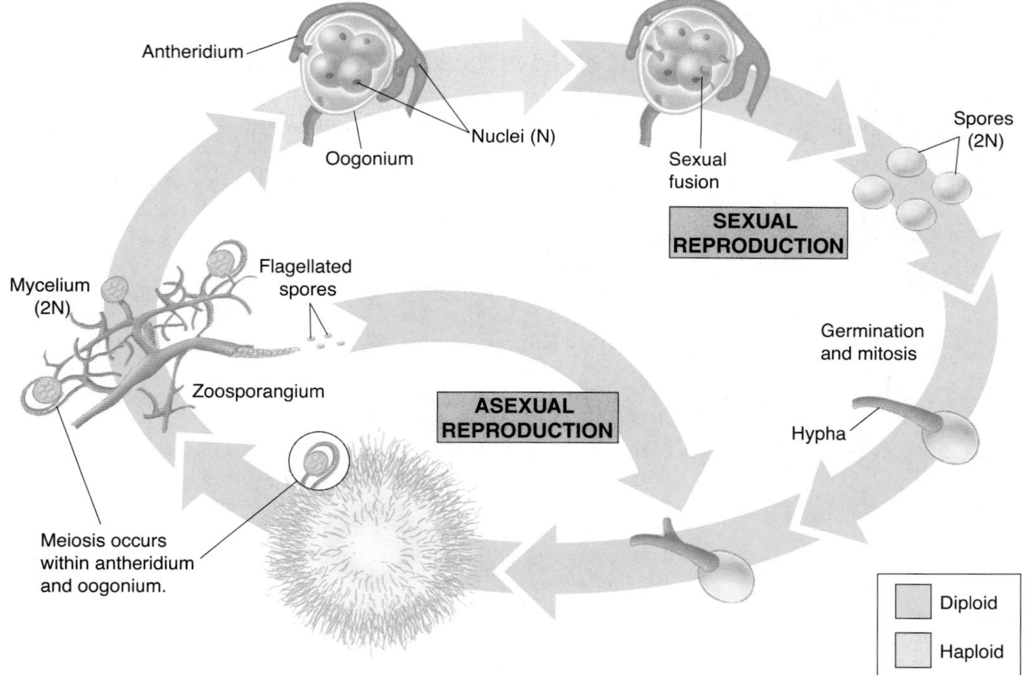

▲ **Figure 20–24** **Water molds live on decaying organic matter in water.** Water molds reproduce both asexually and sexually. During asexual reproduction, flagellated spores are produced by the diploid (2N) mycelium. These spores grow into new mycelia. During sexual reproduction, a male nucleus fuses with a female nucleus.

produces flagellated spores that swim away from the zoosporangium in search of food. When they find food, the spores develop into hyphae, which then grow into new organisms.

Sexual reproduction takes place in specialized structures that are formed by the hyphae. One structure, the **antheridium** (an-thur-ID-ee-um), produces male nuclei. The other structure, the **oogonium** (oh-oh-GOH-nee-um), produces female nuclei. Fertilization, or sexual fusion, occurs within the oogonium, and the spores that form develop into new organisms.

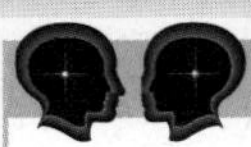
Where does sexual reproduction in water molds take place?

Ecology of Funguslike Protists

Slime molds and water molds are most important as recyclers of organic material. In plain language, that means that they help things rot. How important is that? A walk through woods or grassland will quickly show that the ground is not littered with the bodies of dead animals and plants. Why not? After these organisms die, their tissues are quickly broken down by slime molds, water molds, mushrooms, and other decomposers. The dark, rich topsoil that provides plants with nutrients is the product of all of this activity.

Some funguslike protists can harm living things. In addition to their beneficial function as decomposers, land-dwelling water molds cause a number of important plant diseases. These diseases include mildews and blights of grapes and tomatoes.

Use Visuals

Figure 20–24 Ask students: **What is the cellular process that produces male and female nuclei in water molds?** *(Meiosis)* **Where are these nuclei produced?** *(The male nuclei are produced in the antheridium, and the female nuclei are produced in the oogonium.)* **Are the spores produced by the mycelia haploid or diploid?** *(Diploid)* Explain that a mycelium is a mass of hyphae, as shown in the bottom left of the figure. Ask: **How are oomycetes different from true fungi?** *(Oomycetes have cell walls made of cellulose and produce motile spores.)*

Ecology of Funguslike Protists

Make Connections

Environmental Science Focus students' attention on the role that funguslike protists play in the environment. Ask: **What do funguslike protists feed on?** *(Dead or decaying organic matter)* **What are organisms called that feed on dead material?** *(Decomposers)* **How is the role played by decomposers like that of the recyclers who collect the glass and paper you put in recycle bins?** *(Like the recyclers of glass and paper, the decomposers use the material accumulated in dead organisms for new purposes instead of letting that material go to waste.)*

TEACHER TO TEACHER

As a review of the many different organisms included in the Kingdom Protista, I use a game with a format like Bingo. The game uses a card or grid with either the written name or a picture of each organism being reviewed. I develop several different cards and copy them onto card stock. Plastic pieces cut from colored transparencies can be used as game pieces. In this game, the teacher draws out a description of an organism from a container and reads it to the class. The students match the description with the name or picture of the organism, and in doing so, try to get Bingo. The degree of difficulty depends on the descriptions you write for the protists.

—*Lynne M. McElhaney*
Special Services Teacher
Leflore High School,
Mobile, AL

Answers to . . .

CHECKPOINT *Sexual reproduction takes place within the oogonium.*

Figure 20–23 *The photograph shows a mature sporangium.*

20–5 (continued)

Water Molds and the Potato Famine

Meet Diverse Needs

Encourage students who need an extra challenge to research the Great Potato Famine in Ireland in the 1800s. Have them investigate the ramifications of that human crisis and find out how such a plant disease would be treated today. Ask students to report what they learned to the class. **Learning modality: verbal**

3 ASSESS

Evaluate Understanding

Call on students at random to compare and contrast cellular slime molds with acellular slime molds. Students should mention that both types are funguslike heterotrophs, and they should distinguish between the "slug" of the cellular slime mold and the plasmodium of the acellular slime mold.

Reteach

Use Figure 20–23 to reteach the basics of funguslike protists. Make sure students understand the formation of fruiting bodies and the production of haploid spores. This knowledge will set the stage for the next chapter, which focuses on fungi.

ALTERNATIVE ASSESSMENT

The steps in the students' flowcharts should reflect an understanding of the life cycles illustrated in Figure 20–22 for cellular slime molds and Figure 20–23 for acellular slime molds.

Use iText to review the key concepts in Section 20–5.

Answer to . . .

Figure 20–25 *About 1.5 million Irish people migrated to the United States, where they changed the ethnic and political character of many American cities.*

Figure 20–25 *Phytophthora infestans* is an oomycete that attacks potatoes (bottom right). In the summer of 1846, *Phytophthora infestans* destroyed nearly the entire potato crop of Ireland in days, leading to the Great Potato Famine. **Applying Concepts** ***How did the famine affect the United States?***

Water Molds and the Potato Famine

One water mold helped to permanently change the character of the United States. Roughly 40 million Americans can trace at least some part of their ancestry to Ireland. If you are one of those people, the chances are very good that your life and the lives of your ancestors were changed by the combination of a plant and a protist.

The plant was the potato. Potatoes are native to South America, where they were cultivated by the Incas. Spanish explorers were so impressed with this plant that they introduced it to Europe. By the 1840s, potatoes had become the major food crop of Ireland.

The protist was *Phytophthora infestans*, an oomycete that produces airborne spores that destroy all parts of the potato plant. Potatoes that are infected with *Phytophthora infestans* may appear normal at harvest time. Within a few weeks, however, the protist makes its way into the potato, reducing it to a spongy sac of spores and dust. The summer of 1845 was unusually wet and cool, ideal conditions for the growth of *Phytophthora infestans*. By the end of the growing season, the potato blight caused by this pathogen had destroyed as much as 60 percent of the Irish potato crop. The photographs in **Figure 20–25** show how *Phytophthora infestans* attacks potatoes. The art shows a woman digging for potatoes in a field.

Because the poorest farmers depended upon potatoes for their food, the effects were tragic. The loss of much of the crop in 1845 and an even greater loss in 1846 led to the starvation of more than a million people.

The Great Potato Famine, or the Great Hunger, as the event is also known, led to the immediate migration of about 1.5 million Irish people to the United States. There, they quickly changed the ethnic and political character of many American cities.

20–5 Section Assessment

1. **Key Concept** How are funguslike protists and fungi similar? How are they different?
2. **Key Concept** Compare acellular slime molds, cellular slime molds, and water molds.
3. What is the role of slime molds in the environment?
4. How can water molds affect other living things?
5. **Critical Thinking Comparing and Contrasting** How is the sluglike mass of cellular slime molds similar to the plasmodium of acellular slime molds? How do they differ?

iTEXT Assessment Use iText to review the important concepts in Section 20–5.

ALTERNATIVE ASSESSMENT

Constructing a Flowchart Draw two flowcharts—one showing the steps from unicellular existence through multicellular existence and reproduction in cellular slime molds and one showing those steps in acellular slime molds.

20–5 Section Assessment

1. Like fungi, funguslike protists are heterotrophs that absorb nutrients from dead or decaying organic matter. Unlike most true fungi, funguslike protists have centrioles and lack the chitin cell walls of true fungi.
2. The individual cells of cellular slime molds remain distinct throughout the life cycle. Acellular slime molds pass through a stage in which their cells fuse to form large cells with many nuclei. Water molds have both sexual and asexual phases in the life cycle.
3. They recycle organic material.
4. Water molds can cause plant diseases, such as potato blight.
5. Both the cellular slime mold mass and the plasmodium function like a single organism, and both produce a fruiting body. They differ in that the cells of a plasmodium fuse, while cells in a slime mold mass preserve their separate cellular identities.

Design an Experiment

Investigating Contractile Vacuoles

Most freshwater protists have contractile vacuoles. These organelles regulate the concentration of water in the cytoplasm. In this investigation, you will observe how this structure works under various conditions.

Problem **How do the salt concentration and temperature of the environment affect the action of contractile vacuoles?**

Materials

- 3 *Paramecium caudatum* cultures at room temperature, 25°C (fresh water, 0.5% salt solution, 1.0% salt solution)
- *Paramecium caudatum* culture at 2°C in fresh water
- dropper pipette
- 4 microscope slides
- coverslips
- microscope
- cotton ball
- forceps
- clock with second hand

Skills Designing Experiments, Observing

Design Your Experiment  

1. Use a dropper pipette to put one drop of *Paramecium caudatum* culture in fresh water at 25°C on a microscope slide.
2. Use forceps to pull apart a cotton ball and put a few threads in the drop of water. Cover the drop with a coverslip.
3. Use the low-power objective of the microscope to locate and focus on one paramecium. If necessary, increase the magnification to observe the alternating contractions of the two contractile vacuoles.
4. Record how long a contractile vacuole takes to contract and refill.
5. **Formulating Hypotheses** Record a hypothesis about how salt concentration and temperature will affect the rate at which the contractile vacuole contracts and expands.
6. **Designing Experiments** Design an experiment to test your hypothesis. Construct a data table to record your observations. With your teacher's approval, carry out your experiment.

Analyze and Conclude

1. **Observing** How did an increase in the concentration of salt in its environment affect the paramecium's contractile vacuoles?
2. **Inferring** What can you infer from this result about the rate at which water enters the paramecium in salt solutions? Explain your answer.
3. **Observing** How did temperature affect the contractile vacuoles?
4. **Drawing Conclusions** What can you conclude about the paramecium's use of energy from the effect of temperature on the contractile vacuoles?

Go Further

Designing Experiments Does temperature affect paramecia in other ways? Design an experiment to investigate the effects of temperature on movement or feeding. With your teacher's approval, carry out your experiment.

Analyze and Conclude

1. Increasing the salt concentration slowed down the contractions of the contractile vacuoles.

2. The higher the salt concentration outside the organism, the less water that diffuses into the paramecium, because water will diffuse from an area of high concentration to an area of low concentration.

3. Students should observe that the action of the contractile vacuoles slowed down at a lower temperature.

4. The greater activity of the contractile vacuoles at higher temperatures implies that the paramecium uses energy in contracting its contractile vacuoles.

Design an Experiment

Objective Students will conclude that salt concentration and temperature affect the action of contractile vacuoles.

Skills Focus **Designing Experiments, Observing**

Time 90 minutes

Advance Prep
- Order cultures of *Paramecium* from a biological supply house; one culture is usually adequate for a class of 24.
- To prepare a 0.5% salt solution, add 0.5 grams of table salt to 100 milliliters of water and mix well.
- Prepare a 1.0% salt solution by adding 1 gram of table salt to 100 milliliters of water.

Teaching Tips Notice that as water evaporates from the slide, the coverslip presses down on the paramecia, making the contraction of the contractile vacuoles easier to see.

Procedure

1. Demonstrate how to use a dropper pipette to put one drop of culture on a slide.

2. Demonstrate how to pull apart the cotton ball and put a few threads in the drop of water.

5. Make sure that students record a hypothesis that predicts for both salt concentration and temperature.

6. Check each experimental design to make sure that it tests the students' hypotheses and is feasible.

Expected Outcomes Students should observe that higher salt concentrations and lower temperatures reduce the rate at which the contractile vacuole contracts.

Go Further

A typical experiment might investigate whether paramecia feed more or less at a higher temperature. Such an experiment might involve observing paramecia feeding on *Chlorella* or yeast at two temperatures. Students should clearly designate the variable they are testing.

Chapter 20 Study Guide

Study Tip

Divide the class into small groups, and have students quiz each other about the Vocabulary terms and the Key Concepts.

Thinking Visually

In their tables, students should include information about animallike protists, unicellular plantlike protists, multicellular plantlike protists, and funguslike protists. Students should indicate that animallike protists and funguslike protists are heterotrophic, while plantlike protists are autotrophic. Movement varies among protists. Three of the four groups of animallike protists are motile, as are most of the unicellular plantlike protists.

Chapter 20 Assessment

Reviewing Content

1. c **2.** c **3.** c **4.** b **5.** d **6.** c **7.** a **8.** d **9.** b **10.** d

Understanding Concepts

11. Possible answer: Yes, the terms are useful because many protists have similar characteristics to plants, animals, or fungi.

12. In fresh water, the water may move into a protozoan by osmosis. The excess water is collected by contractile vacuoles.

13. Ciliates use short, hairlike projections called cilia to move. The cilia beat, propelling the ciliate through water. Sarcodines use pseudopods for movement. These pseudopods extend out of the central mass of the cell. Cytoplasm streams into the pseudopod, and the rest of the cell follows.

Chapter 20 Study Guide

20–1 The Kingdom Protista

Key Concept

- Protists are eukaryotes that are not members of the kingdoms Plantae, Animalia, or Fungi.

Vocabulary
protist, p. 495

20–2 Animallike Protists: Protozoans

Key Concepts

- Animallike protists that swim using flagella are classified in the phylum Zoomastigina and are often referred to as zooflagellates.
- Sarcodines are animallike protists that use pseudopods for feeding and movement.
- Members of the phylum Ciliophora, known as ciliates, use cilia for feeding and movement.
- Members of the phylum Sporozoa do not move on their own and are parasitic.
- Some animallike protists cause serious diseases, including malaria and African sleeping sickness.

Vocabulary
- pseudopod, p. 498
- amoeboid movement, p. 498
- food vacuole, p. 498 • cilium, p. 499
- trichocyst, p. 499 • macronucleus, p. 499
- micronucleus, p. 499 • gullet, p. 500
- anal pore, p. 500 • contractile vacuole, p. 500
- conjugation, p. 500

20–3 Plantlike Protists: Unicellular Algae

Key Concepts

- Chlorophyll and accessory pigments allow algae to harvest and use the energy from sunlight.
- Euglenophytes are plantlike protists that have two flagella but no cell wall.
- About half of dinoflagellates are photosynthetic; the other half live as heterotrophs.
- Members of the phylum Chrysophyta are a diverse group of plantlike protists that have gold-colored chloroplasts.
- Diatoms produce thin, delicate cell walls rich in silicon (Si)—the main ingredient in glass.

Vocabulary
- accessory pigment, p. 506 • eyespot, p. 506
- pellicle, p. 506 • phytoplankton, p. 508

20–4 Plantlike Protists: Red, Brown, and Green Algae

Key Concepts

- Red algae are able to live at great depths due to their efficiency in harvesting light energy. Red algae contain chlorophyll *a* and reddish accessory pigments called phycobilins.
- Brown algae contain chlorophyll *a* and *c*, as well as a brown accessory pigment, fucoxanthin.
- Green algae share many characteristics with plants, including their photosynthetic pigments and cell wall composition.
- The life cycles of most algae include both a diploid and a haploid generation.

Vocabulary
phycobilin, p. 510
filament, p. 512
alternation of generations, p. 512
gametophyte, p. 514
spore, p. 514
sporophyte, p. 514

20–5 Funguslike Protists

Key Concepts

- Funguslike protists lack chlorophyll and absorb nutrients from dead or decaying organic matter. But unlike most true fungi, funguslike protists have centrioles. They also lack the chitin cell walls of true fungi.
- Slime molds are funguslike protists that play key roles in recycling organic material.
- Oomycetes thrive on dead or decaying organic matter in water and are plant parasites on land.

Vocabulary
cellular slime mold, p. 516
acellular slime mold, p. 516
plasmodium, p. 518
hypha, p. 518
zoosporangium, p. 518
antheridium, p. 519
oogonium, p. 519

Thinking Visually

Make a table that compares the means of feeding and movement of the four main groups of protists.

TIME SAVER

CHAPTER RESOURCES

Print:
- ***Teaching Resources,*** Chapter Vocabulary Review, Graphic Organizer
- ***Chapter Tests: Levels A and B,*** Chapter 20 Test
- ***PH Assessment System,*** Practice Test

Technology:
- ***Computer Test Bank,*** Chapter 20 Test
- ***iText,*** Chapter 20 Assessment

Chapter 20 Assessment

Reviewing Content

Choose the letter that best answers the question or completes the statement.

1. Which of the following descriptions applies to most protists?
   a. unicellular prokaryotes
   b. multicellular prokaryotes
   c. unicellular eukaryotes
   d. multicellular eukaryotes
2. Which of the following is NOT true of amoebas?
   a. They reproduce by binary fission.
   b. They move by pseudopodia.
   c. They have a definite shape.
   d. They form temporary food vacuoles.
3. For defense, a paramecium uses small, bottle-shaped structures known as
   a. cilia.
   b. pseudopodia.
   c. trichocysts.
   d. micronuclei.
4. Which of the diagrams below shows the process of conjugation?

a. 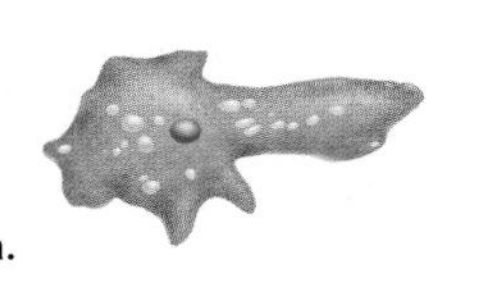

c. 

b. 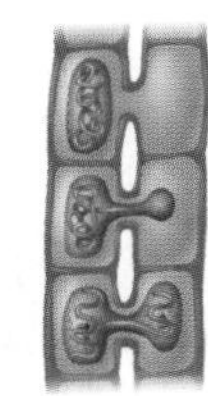

d. 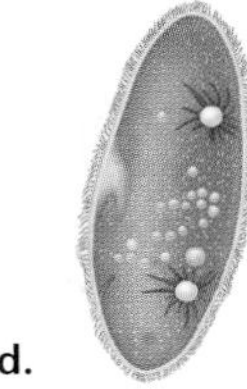

5. The wide range of colors in algae depends upon the presence of
   a. chlorophyll *a* and *b*.
   b. chlorophyll *a* and *c*.
   c. chlorophyll *a* and *d*.
   d. accessory pigments.
6. The population of small, photosynthetic organisms found near the surface of the ocean is called
   a. euglenophytes.
   b. chrysophytes.
   c. phytoplankton.
   d. dinoflagellates.
7. What characteristics do green algae share with plants?
   a. photosynthetic pigments and cell wall composition
   b. photosynthetic and accessory pigment composition
   c. accessory pigments and cell wall composition
   d. accessory pigments and cell membrane composition
8. Alternation of generations is defined as the switching back and forth between the production of
   a. cells by mitosis and meiosis.
   b. asexual and sexual reproductive cells.
   c. gametophytes and sporophytes.
   d. diploid and haploid cells.
9. Slime molds are found primarily in
   a. oceans.
   b. rotting wood or compost piles.
   c. fast-moving streams.
   d. deserts.
10. The thin filaments produced by water molds are known as
    a. oogonia.
    b. antheridia.
    c. zoosporangia.
    d. hyphae.

Understanding Concepts

11. Are the categories animallike, plantlike, or funguslike useful in classifying protists? Explain your answer.
12. All freshwater protozoans have contractile vacuoles to get rid of excess water. Describe the process responsible for this excess water.
13. Compare the structures used for movement in the ciliates and sarcodines.
14. Describe the process of conjugation. Is conjugation a form of reproduction? Explain your answer.
15. What characteristics distinguish algae from other protists?
16. Describe the two methods euglenophytes can use to obtain energy.
17. Explain why plantlike protists are so important to aquatic food chains.
18. List the three phyla of multicellular plantlike protists. Give an example of an organism in each phylum.
19. Describe the process of alternation of generations. Explain its significance.

TIME SAVER HOMEWORK GUIDE

Section:	Questions:
Section 20–1	1, 11, 26
Section 20–2	2–4, 12–14, 20, 22, 28
Section 20–3	5, 6, 15–17, 21, 22, 24, 27, 28, 29
Section 20–4	7, 8, 18, 19, 29
Section 20–5	9, 10, 23–25

14. Conjugation allows ciliates to exchange genetic material. Two paramecia join together. After meiosis of their diploid nuclei, each organism is left with four haploid nuclei. Three of the nuclei disintegrate, leaving one nucleus in each organism to divide, forming a pair of identical nuclei. The two paramecia then exchange one nucleus from their pairs. Conjugation is not a form of reproduction, because no new offspring are formed. The two paramecia are genetically changed from their former state, but they are identical to each other.

15. Algae contain the green pigment chlorophyll and carry out photosynthesis, unlike other protists.

16. Euglenophytes obtain energy by photosynthesis. If sunlight is not available, euglenophytes can obtain energy by absorbing nutrients available in decayed organic material.

17. Their position at the bottom of the food chain makes much of the diversity of aquatic life possible. Photoplankton provide a direct source of energy for organisms as diverse as shrimp and whales.

18. The phlya of plantlike protists are: 1) Rhodophyta or red algae; example: *Chondros crispus*, or Irish moss; 2) Phaeophyta or brown algae; example: *Sargassum*; and 3) Chlorophyta or green algae; example: *Volvox*.

19. Many algae switch back and forth between haploid and diploid stages during their life cycles, enabling them to survive unfavorable conditions. Under adverse conditions, a single-celled organism will produce haploid gametes by mitosis. These gametes, which are of two opposing mating types, bind to each other, shed their cell walls, and fuse to from a diploid zygote. The zygote can form a protective wall enabling it to survive freezing or drying conditions that would normally kill it. When conditions are favorable, the zygote begins to grow.

Chapter 20 Assessment

Critical Thinking

20. The antibiotic kills wood-digesting symbiotic bacteria that live inside the cytoplasm of the protists. Because the termites can no longer digest wood, they will die of starvation.

21. Water pollution involving an excess of nutrients might cause a bloom of dinoflagellates which results in a red tide.

22. Sexual reproduction allows for an exchange of genes. New combinations of genes can enable species to adapt to changes in the environment.

23. Possible answer: Small organisms are important in life because they are on the bottom of the food chain, which many larger organisms depend on for food. In history, they are important because they caused events such as the Irish potato famine.

24. Protist A belongs to the phylum Sarcodina; protist B belongs to the phylum Euglenophyta; protist C belongs to the phylum Myxomycota.

25. Slime molds produce sporangia when subjected to environmental stress for two reasons: greater mobility and increased genetic diversity. Greater spore mobility increases the organism's chances of finding another source of food. Greater diversity helps the slime mold adapt to changes in environmental conditions.

26. Protists that belong to the phylum Euglenophyta have characteristics of animallike protists in the way they move and ingest food. However, they also have characteristics of plantlike protists in that they contain chloroplasts. These organisms cannot be classified as either an animal or a plant.

27. If the radiation slows the growth of phytoplankton or kills it, the amount of oxygen in the air might decrease and the amount of carbon dioxide might increase. If the radiation speeds up the growth of phytoplankton, the amount of oxygen in the air might increase and the amount of carbon dioxide decrease.

28. If red blood cells are infected with *Plasmodium* cells and are present in blood, they could be passed along by a transfusion. Once inside the recipient, the infected red blood cells could burst, releasing *Plasmodium* cells, which would then infect other red blood cells.

Chapter 20 Assessment

Critical Thinking

20. Formulating Hypotheses A scientist observes that termites that are fed a certain antibiotic die of starvation after a few days. The scientist also notices that the antibiotic affects certain protists that live inside the termite's gut in a peculiar way. Although the protists continue to thrive, they lose a certain kind of structure in their cytoplasm. Develop a hypothesis to explain these observations.

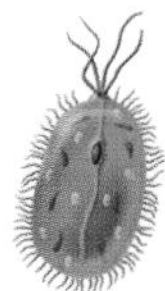
Protist before exposure to antibiotic

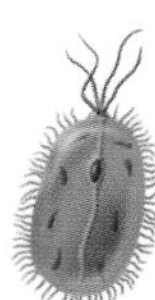
Protist after exposure to antibiotic

21. Applying Concepts How might water pollution result in a red tide?

22. Inferring During its lifetime, a paramecium can reproduce asexually about 700 times. However, it can reproduce many more times if it conjugates as well. How could the capability for sexual reproduction affect the evolution of paramecia?

23. Making Judgments Some people would argue that small organisms are not important in life and in history. Considering the information in this chapter, would you agree or disagree with this point of view? Explain your answer.

24. Classifying Your teacher asks you to observe and classify into the correct phylum the following protists:
Protist A: Organism has no cell wall, lacks chlorophyll, and moves using pseudopodia.
Protist B: Organism has no cell wall, contains chlorophyll, and has two flagella.
Protist C: Cells appear amoeba-like and appear to fuse to produce structures with many nuclei, lack chlorophyll, and have sporangia that produce spores that germinate into flagellated cells.

25. Inferring Slime molds produce sporangia and spores only when food is scarce. Why do you think this is so? What advantages do slime molds gain from this?

26. Applying Concepts At one time, living things were classified as animals if they moved or ingested food, and as plants if they did not move or ingest food. What difficulties would arise in trying to classify the protists according to these criteria?

27. Predicting Growing "holes" in Earth's ozone layer may increase the amount of radiation that reaches the surface of the ocean. If this radiation were to affect the growth of phytoplankton, what long-term consequences might this have on Earth's atmosphere?

28. Inferring Examine the life cycle of *Plasmodium* illustrated in **Figure 20–7** on page 501. Based on the illustration, do you think malaria could be transmitted by a blood transfusion?

29. Making Connections What are the reactants and products of photosynthesis? Where might algae get the raw materials they need to carry out photosynthesis? (*Hint:* You may wish to refer back to Chapter 8 for help answering this question.)

Performance-Based Assessment

Making Models Select a representative protist from each of the four animallike protist groups. Make a model of each organism. Describe the characteristics that place it in that group.

Take It to the NET

Which protists live in a pond environment? Visit the Prentice Hall Web site at **www.phschool.com** to find out about the residents of a typical pond. Then, answer the following questions:

- What major groups of protists are found in ponds?
- How can you create an image of an algal protist using fluorescence? Which parts will be visible?
- What are mummy-shaped diatoms?
- What is the approximate width of an amoeba?

Performance-Based Assessment

Students should make models of any of the animallike protists described in Section 20–2. Typically, students will make a model of *Trichomonas,* an amoeba, and a paramecium. You might want to provide illustrations from college biology books for an example of a sporozoan; *Plasmodium* would be a good choice. Provide craft materials for students to use in making their models, including some kind of commercial gelatin for cytoplasm. You might have students label their models with toothpick-and-paper flags. Students should describe each of the organisms they model, especially the means of movement of each organism.

Standardized Test Prep

Test-Taking Tip As you briefly scan the questions, mark those that may be pure guesswork on your part and save them for last. (Do not write in this book.) Use your time on those questions that you can reason through and for which you can eliminate answers.

Directions: Choose the letter that best answers the question or completes the statement.

1. Which of the following is NOT a characteristic of protists?
(A) cell wall containing peptidoglycan
(B) membrane-bound nucleus
(C) flagella
(D) cilia
(E) chlorophyll

2. In amoebas, what structure helps the organism move and feed?
(A) flagellum
(B) cilia
(C) food vacuole
(D) pseudopod
(E) contractile vacuole

3. Which of the following is true of the process of conjugation in protists?
(A) It occurs only in photosynthetic protists.
(B) It results in the trading of some genetic material with another organism.
(C) It produces offspring that are genetically identical to the parent.
(D) Four new individuals are formed from each single organism.
(E) It decreases the genetic diversity of a population of organisms.

4. Which of the following is NOT a characteristic of funguslike protists such as slime molds?
(A) eukaryotic
(B) lack cell walls of chitin
(C) multicellular at some time in life cycle
(D) photosynthetic
(E) have centrioles

5. Which of the following is characteristic of some types of algae?
I. Alternation of generations
II. Multicellularity
III. Parasitism
(A) I only
(B) II only
(C) I and II only
(D) II and III only
(E) I, II, and III

Questions 6–9 Each of the lettered choices below refers to the following numbered statements. Select the best lettered choice. A choice may be used once, more than once, or not at all.

(A) Contractile vacuole
(B) Trichocyst
(C) Anal pore
(D) Gullet
(E) Food vacuole

6. Contains food particles in organism's body
7. Indentation leading to organism's mouth
8. Collects and gets rid of excess water
9. Site where waste is released to the environment

Questions 10–11 Use the graph below to answer the following questions.

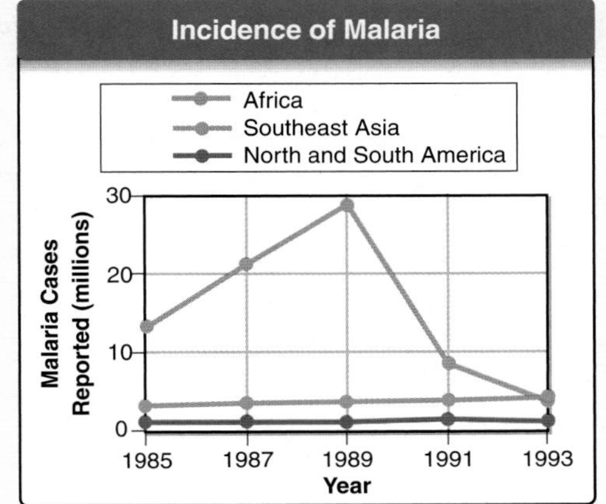

10. It is estimated that there are at least ten actual cases of malaria for every one reported and shown in the graph. Based on this estimate, how many millions of cases of malaria were there in Africa in 1991?
(A) 9
(B) 5
(C) 20
(D) 50
(E) 90

11. Based on the data in the graph, the incidence of malaria is
I. declining in Africa.
II. increasing in Southeast Asia.
III. increasing in North and South America.
(A) I only
(B) II and III only
(C) I and II only
(D) III only
(E) I, II, and III

Take It to the NET

• Algae (plantlike protists) and heterotrophs (animallike protists) such as actinopods and amoeba.

• The algae can be illuminated with light of a relatively short wavelength—one at which chlorophyll absorbs light. The chlorophyll will reemit, or fluoresce, the light energy at a longer wavelength when photographed. Because the chlorophyll in an alga is gathered in its chloroplasts, it is the chloroplasts inside the algal cells that will show up in the image.

• There are two basic types of diatoms: round and elongated. The silica shells of elongated diatoms resemble mummy cases and are thus called mummy-shaped diatoms. These diatoms can move themselves about; round diatoms cannot.

• Less than 30 microns

For additional information, visit

www.phschool.com

Standardized Test Prep

1. A
2. D
3. B
4. D
5. C
6. E
7. D
8. A
9. C
10. E
11. C

Chapter 20 Assessment (continued)
29. The reactants of photosynthesis are carbon dioxide and water. The products are glucose and oxygen. Algae would get water from the water they live in and carbon dioxide from the air.

Chapter Planner 21 Fungi

Section and Section Objectives	Time	Activities and Labs
21–1 The Kingdom Fungi, pp. 527–529 **21.1.1** ***Identify*** the defining characteristics of fungi. **21.1.2** ***Describe*** the main structures of a fungus. **21.1.3** ***Explain*** how fungi reproduce.	1 period (1/2 block)	**SE:** ***Inquiry Activity,*** What are mushrooms made of?, p. 526 **TE:** ***Build Science Skills,*** Observing, p. 529 **TE:** ***Build Science Skills,*** Observing, p. 530 **SE:** ***Quick Lab,*** What is the structure of bread mold?, p. 531 **TE:** ***Build Science Skills,*** Observing, p. 533 **TE:** ***Demonstration,*** p. 535 **TE:** ***Build Science Skills,*** Using Models, p. 535
21–2 Classification of Fungi, pp. 530–536 **21.2.1** ***Identify*** the characteristics of the four main groups of fungi.	2 periods (1 block)	**SE:** ***Problem Solving,*** Repotting Orchids, p. 541 **SE:** ***Real-World Lab,*** Examining Seeds for Fungi, p. 543
21–3 Ecology of Fungi, pp. 537–542 **21.3.1** ***Explain*** what the ecological role of fungi is. **21.3.2** ***Describe*** problems that parasitic fungi cause. **21.3.3** ***Describe*** what kinds of mutualistic relationships fungi form with other organisms.	2 periods (1 block)	**TE:** ***Build Science Skills,*** Observing, p. 540
Chapter Assessment, pp. 544–547	1 period (1/2 block)	

ACTIVITY PLANNER

SE: ***Inquiry Activity***, p. 526; (10 min.); mushroom

TE: ***Build Science Skills,*** p. 529; (15 min.); mature mushroom cap, paper, microscope slide, microscope

TE: ***Build Science Skills,*** p. 530; (10 min. for setup; 15 min. 2–3 days later); various foods, plastic container, dampened paper

SE: ***Quick Lab,*** p. 531; (15 min.); transparent tape, moldy bread, microscope slide, microscope

TE: ***Build Science Skills,*** p. 533; (45 min.); package of dry yeast, beaker, molasses, aluminum foil, dropper pipette, microscope, microscope slide, coverslip, and methylene blue

TE: ***Demonstration,*** p. 535; (15 min.); samples of wild basidiomycetes, field guides

TE: ***Build Science Skills,*** p. 535; (20 min.); modeling compound, paper, paints, paint brushes

TE: ***Build Science Skills,*** p. 540; (10 min.); photos of lichens

SE: ***Real-World Lab,*** p. 543; (45 min.); seeds stored in cold and dry conditions, seeds stored in warm and moist conditions, forceps microscope slide, coverslip, microscope, aniline blue stain, scalpel, dropper pipette, small beaker, paper towels

PLANNING KEY

Ability Levels

B Basic	For students who need additional help
A Average	For all students
E Enriched	For students who need to be challenged

Components

SE	Student Edition	**GRSW**	Guided Reading and Study Workbook	**IDM**	Issues and Decision Making
TE	Teacher's Edition	**CT**	Chapter Tests: Levels A and B	**CTB**	Computer Test Bank
LMA	Laboratory Manual A	**PHAS**	PH Assessment System	**PAP**	Presentation Assistant Plus
LMB	Laboratory Manual B	**LA**	Lab Assessment With Scoring Guide	**BD**	BioDetectives Videotape
TR	Teaching Resources	**BTM**	BioTechnology Manual	**iT**	iText
IF	Investigations in Forensics				

Program Resources	Assessment	Media and Technology
TR: Section Review 21–1 B A **GRSW:** Section 21–1 B A	**SE:** 21–1 Section Assessment, p. 529 **TR:** Section Review 21–1	**PAP:** 21–1 Interest Grabber, Section Outline, Hyphae Structure, Figure 21–2 **iT:** Section 21–1
LMA: Chapter 21 Lab A E **LMB:** Chapter 21 Lab B A **TR:** Section Review 21–2 B A **GRSW:** Section 21–2 B A **IDM:** Issues and Decisions 20 A E	**SE:** 21–2 Section Assessment, p. 536 **TR:** Section Review 21–2	**PAP:** 21–2 Interest Grabber, Section Outline, Concept Map, Figure 21–5, Figure 21–7, Figure 21–8 **iT:** Section 21–2
TR: Section Review 21–3 B A Chapter 21 Real-World Lab B A E **GRSW:** Section 21–3 B A	**SE:** 21–3 Section Assessment, p. 542 **TR:** Section Review 21–3	**PAP:** 21–3 Interest Grabber, Section Outline, Lichen Structure **iT:** Section 21–3
	SE: Chapter 21 Assessment, pp. 544–547 **TR:** Chapter Vocabulary Review, Graphic Organizer **CT:** Chapter 21 Test **CTB:** Chapter 21 Test **PHAS:** Practice Test	**CTB:** Chapter 21 Test **iT:** Chapter 21 Assessment

PRESSED FOR TIME?

To Preview the Chapter
- Introduce students to Key Concepts and Vocabulary terms in each section.
- Assign the Reading Strategies for each section.

To Cover the Chapter Quickly
- Have students read all of Section 21–1, the introductory paragraph and Figures 21–5, 21–7, and 21–8 of Section 21–2, and all of Section 21–3.
- Assign the 21–1 Section Review and 21–3 Section Review, as well as questions 1–10 in Chapter 21 Assessment and questions 1–10 in Chapter 21 Standardized Test Prep.

To Review the Chapter
- Assign Sections 21–1 through 21–3 in the Guided Reading and Study Workbook.
- Assign Section Reviews for 21–1 through 21–3 and the Chapter Vocabulary Review for Chapter 21 in the Teaching Resources.

Chapter 21

ENGAGE/EXPLORE

Inquiry Activity

Objective Students will be able to distinguish a mushroom from a plant and describe the structure of a mushroom.

Skill Focus Comparing and Contrasting

Materials mushroom

Time 10 minutes

Advance Prep Buy common mushrooms from a grocery store.

Safety Use only store-bought edible mushrooms. Make certain students do not have allergies to mushrooms.

Strategies Ask students whether they think mushrooms should be classified as plants, as they once were.

Expected Outcomes
Students will observe that mushrooms are different from plants and are composed of compressed filaments.

Think About It

1. Students should observe that mushrooms are composed of thread-like parts, or filaments.
2. They are similar in that both have a stalk or a stem. They are different in that plants have green leaves, stems, roots, flowers, fruits, and seeds, none of which mushrooms have. Mushrooms, in contrast, have a cap with gills.

Assess Prior Knowledge

Ask students: **What are all the different kinds of fungi you can think of?** *(Many students will mention molds, yeasts, morels, and mushrooms sold in groceries. Some might also mention rusts, mildew, and lichens.)* **How do you think fungi reproduce?** *(Accept all reasonable responses. Some students might correctly suggest that fungi reproduce through the broadcast of spores.)*

Chapter 21 Fungi

These morels are a type of fungus prized by many people for their distinctive flavor. Unlike the violets, fungi are not plants and do not produce their own food.

Inquiry Activity

What are mushrooms made of?

Procedure

1. Examine a mushroom without damaging it. Record your observations, and include a sketch.
2. Carefully separate the stalk and cap of the mushroom. Try to break the stalk across and lengthwise.
3. Crumble a piece of the stalk. Describe the shape of the parts that make up the stalk.
4. Break the cap in two and examine the thin sheets on the underside of the cap. Record your observations.

Think About It

1. **Observing** Was the stalk made up of parts with specific shapes? If so, what are the shapes of those parts?
2. **Comparing and Contrasting** Compare a mushroom to a plant. How are they similar? Different?

FACTS AND FIGURES

The oldest and biggest
The kingdom Fungi is known in some sources as the kingdom Mycota, from the Greek word *mykes,* which means "fungus." The branch of botany that focuses on fungi is mycology, and biologists who specialize in the study of fungi are called mycologists. Fungi include a wide variety of organisms, from unicellular yeasts to perhaps the largest multicellular organisms on Earth. In the 1990s, researchers in Michigan discovered an example of the fungus *Armillaria bulbosa,* the "honey mushroom," that spread through more than 15 hectares of forest soil—the size of more than 33 football fields. Biologists estimated that it was over 1500 years old. Researchers also documented an individual of *Armillaria ostoyae* in Washington state that was even larger. A claim has been made that these are the largest and oldest organisms on Earth.

21–1 The Kingdom Fungi

In spring, if you know where to look, you can find one of the most prized of all foods—the common morel—growing wild in woodlands throughout the United States. Its ridged cap is often camouflaged by dead leaves that collect in abandoned orchards or underneath old oaks or tulip poplars. Some morels grow alone, but others grow in groups. They appear suddenly, often overnight, and live for only a few days. What are these mysterious organisms? How do they grow so quickly?

Guide for Reading

 **Key Concepts**

- What are the defining characteristics of fungi?
- What is the internal structure of a fungus?
- How do fungi reproduce?

Vocabulary

chitin
hypha
mycelium
fruiting body
sporangium
sporangiophore
gametangium

Reading Strategy: Asking Questions
Before you read, preview **Figures 21–1** and **21–2.** Make a list of questions you have about the structure of fungi. As you read, look for answers to your questions.

What Are Fungi?

Like mushrooms and molds, morels are fungi. The way in which many fungi grow from the ground once led scientists to classify them as nonphotosynthetic plants. But they aren't plants at all. In fact, fungi are very different from plants.

Fungi are eukaryotic heterotrophs that have cell walls. The cell walls of fungi are made up of **chitin,** a complex carbohydrate that is also found in the external skeletons of insects. Recall that heterotrophs depend on other organisms for food. Unlike animals, fungi do not ingest their food. Instead, they digest food outside of their bodies and then absorb it. Many fungi feed by absorbing nutrients from decaying matter in the soil. Others live as parasites, absorbing nutrients from the bodies of their hosts.

Structure and Function of Fungi

Except for yeasts, all fungi are multicellular. Multicellular fungi are composed of tiny filaments called **hyphae** (HY-fee; singular: hypha). Each hypha is only one cell thick. In some fungi, cross walls divide the hyphae into cells containing one or two nuclei, as shown in **Figure 21–1.** In the cross walls, there are tiny openings through which the cytoplasm and nuclei can move. Other hyphae lack cross walls and contain many nuclei.

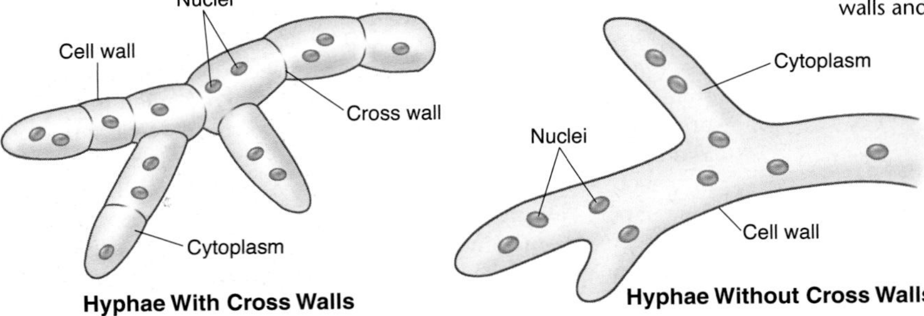

Figure 21–1 Fungi are eukaryotes that have cell walls made of chitin. Most fungi are made up of filaments called hyphae. In some fungi, the hyphae are divided by cross walls. These cells may contain one or two nuclei. In other fungi, the hyphae lack cross walls and contain many nuclei.

SECTION RESOURCES

Print:

- ***Teaching Resources,*** Section Review 21–1
- ***Guided Reading and Study Workbook,*** Section 21–1

Technology:

- ***iText,*** Section 21–1

Section 21–1

1 FOCUS

Objectives

21.1.1 ***Identify*** the defining characteristics of fungi.
21.1.2 ***Describe*** the main structures of a fungus.
21.1.3 ***Explain*** how fungi reproduce.

Guide for Reading

Vocabulary Preview

Ask volunteers to pronounce each vocabulary word. Correct any mispronunciations. Survey students for their ideas of what the words mean.

Reading Strategy

Have students copy the Key Concepts into their notebooks. As they read the section, have students write supporting details for each Key Concept.

2 INSTRUCT

What Are Fungi?

Build Science Skills

Comparing and Contrasting
Have students make a compare/contrast table that compares characteristics of bacteria, protists, fungi, plants, and animals. Column headings should include Prokaryotes/Eukaryotes, Autotrophs/Heterotrophs, and Method of Obtaining Nutrition. To complete this table, students can draw on the knowledge gained from previous chapters in this unit, as well as their common knowledge about plants and animals.

Structure and Function of Fungi

Meet Diverse Needs

For students with limited English proficiency, pronounce the terms *filament* and *hypha.* Explain that *filament* is derived from a Latin word meaning "to spin," and *hypha* is derived from a Greek word meaning "web." Point out that you "spin" a "web" with thread; both words should call to mind a threadlike structure. In the case of hyphae, the threads are tubular. **Limited English proficiency**

21–1 (continued)

Use Visuals

Figure 21–2 Point out that fungi have a great variety of shapes and sizes, and the fungus illustrated here is only a representative that is helpful as an introduction to fungus structure. Ask: **What is the function of the mushroom you see above ground?** *(The mushroom, or fruiting body, is the reproductive structure of the fungus.)* **What are both the mushroom and the mycelium made of?** *(Tiny filaments called hyphae)* **What are the cell walls of these hyphae made of?** *(Chitin, a complex carbohydrate)*

Build Science Skills

Inferring Have students recall that in Chapter 10, they learned about cell size and ratio of surface area to volume ratio. Ask: **As cell volume increases, what happens to the ratio of surface area to volume?** *(It decreases.)* **Why is such a decrease a disadvantage to a cell?** *(With a smaller ratio, it becomes more difficult for a cell to bring materials into the cell and send waste materials out.)* **With this concept in mind, how does the structure of the mycelium correlate with its function for the organism?** *(The structure of the mycelium provides a large ratio of surface area to volume for the organism's cells. This large ratio correlates with the structure's function, which is absorbing nutrients from decaying matter in the soil or from the body of the host.)*

Reproduction in Fungi

Meet Diverse Needs

Ask students who need an additional challenge to investigate what causes an organism to reproduce either sexually or asexually. Students should discover that asexual reproduction occurs when conditions are stable and favorable to growth. Sexual reproduction, by contrast, occurs when environmental conditions are changing. Have students make a report to the class of their findings. **Learning modality: verbal**

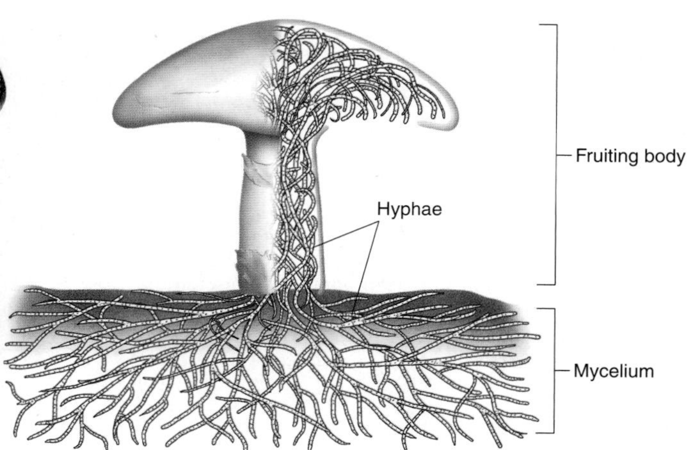

Figure 21–2 **The body of a mushroom is part of a mycelium formed from many tangled hyphae.** The major portion of the mycelium grows below ground. The visible portion of the mycelium is the reproductive structure, or fruiting body, of the mushroom.

Figure 21–2 shows the structure of a multicellular fungus. **The bodies of multicellular fungi are composed of many hyphae tangled together into a thick mass called a mycelium.** The **mycelium** (my-SEE-lee-um; plural: mycelia) is well suited to absorb food because it permits a large surface area to come in contact with the food source through which it grows.

What you recognize as a mushroom is actually the fruiting body of a fungus. A **fruiting body** is a reproductive structure that develops from a mycelium that grows below the surface of the ground. Clusters of mushrooms are often part of the same mycelium, which means that they are part of a single organism.

Some mycelia can live for many years. As time goes by, soil nutrients near the center of the mycelium become depleted. As a result, new mushrooms sprout only at the edges of the mycelium, producing a ring like the one in **Figure 21–3.** People once thought fairies dancing in circles during warm nights produced these rings, so they were called "fairy rings." Over many years, fairy rings can become enormous—from 10 to 30 meters in diameter.

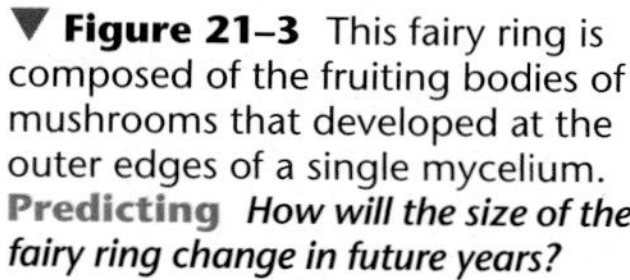

▼ **Figure 21–3** This fairy ring is composed of the fruiting bodies of mushrooms that developed at the outer edges of a single mycelium. **Predicting** *How will the size of the fairy ring change in future years?*

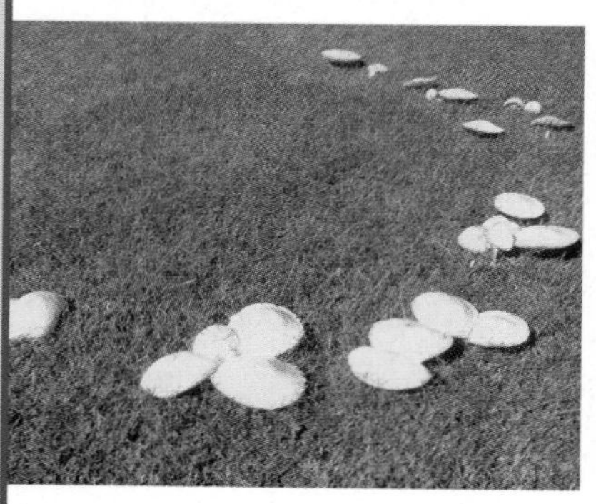

CHECKPOINT *What is a fruiting body?*

Reproduction in Fungi

Most fungi reproduce both asexually and sexually. Asexual reproduction takes place when cells or hyphae break off from a fungus and begin to grow on their own. Some fungi also produce spores, which can scatter and grow into new organisms. You may recall that a spore is a reproductive cell formed by mitosis that is capable of growing into a new organism. In some fungi, spores are produced in structures called **sporangia** (spoh-RAN-jee-uh; singular: sporangium). Sporangia are found at the tips of specialized hyphae called **sporangiophores** (spoh-RAN-jee-oh-fawrz).

PRESENTATIONS MADE EASY!

The Presentation Assistant Plus contains the Prentice Hall Presentation Pro and the Transparencies, which provide easy-to-follow visual support for every step of this lesson. If you have a computer presentation station, use Prentice Hall Presentation Pro Section 21–1, or use the transparencies listed here.

Section 21–1: **Interest Grabber**
Section Outline
Hyphae Structure
Figure 21–2

Sexual reproduction in fungi usually involves two different mating types. Because gametes of both mating types are about the same size, they are not called male and female. Rather, one mating type is referred to as "+" (plus), and the other is referred to as "–" (minus). When the hyphae of opposite mating types meet, each hypha forms a **gametangium** (gam-uh-TAN-jee-um; plural: gametangia), or structure that forms gametes. Then, the two gametangia join, and the haploid nuclei contained in them fuse to form a diploid nucleus, or zygote. After the zygote forms, meiosis takes place, producing haploid nuclei that dominate the remainder of the life cycle. In most fungi, the zygote is the only cell in the entire life cycle that is diploid.

How Fungi Spread

Fungal spores are found in almost every environment. This is why molds seem to spring up in any location that has the right combination of moisture and food. Many fungi produce dry, almost weightless spores, as shown in **Figure 21–4.** These spores scatter easily in the wind. On a clear day, a few liters of fresh air may contain hundreds of spores from many species of fungi.

If these spores are to germinate, they must land in a favorable environment. There must be the proper combination of temperature, moisture, and food so that the spores can grow. Even under the best of circumstances, the probability that a spore will produce a mature organism can be less than one in a billion.

Other fungi are specialized to lure animals, which disperse fungal spores over long distances. Stinkhorns smell like rotting meat, which attracts flies. When they land on the stinkhorn, the flies ingest the sticky, smelly fluid on the surface of the fungus. The spore-containing fluid will pass unharmed out of the flies' digestive systems, depositing spores over many kilometers.

▲ **Figure 21–4 Most fungi reproduce both sexually and asexually.** One form of asexual reproduction is spore formation. Here, an earthstar puffball *(Geastrum saccatum)* that has been struck by a raindrop expels a cloud of spores.

21–1 Section Assessment

1. **Key Concept** What characteristics do all fungi have in common?
2. **Key Concept** Describe the structure of the body of a typical fungus.
3. **Key Concept** Briefly describe asexual and sexual reproduction in fungi.
4. By what means are fungal spores spread to new locations?
5. **Critical Thinking Applying Concepts** Tissue from several mushrooms gathered near the base of a tree were tested and found to be genetically identical. How might you explain this?

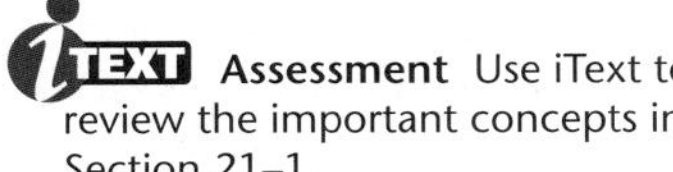

Assessment Use iText to review the important concepts in Section 21–1.

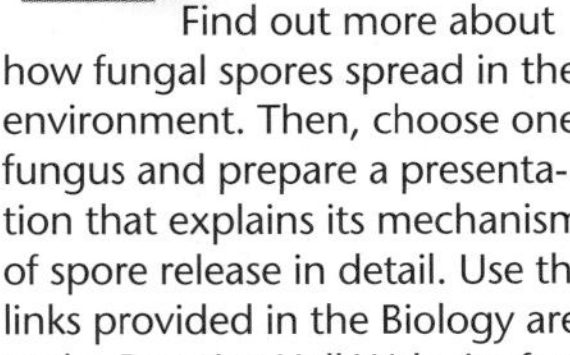

Take It to the NET

Find out more about how fungal spores spread in the environment. Then, choose one fungus and prepare a presentation that explains its mechanism of spore release in detail. Use the links provided in the Biology area at the Prentice Hall Web site for help in completing this activity: **www.phschool.com**

How Fungi Spread

Build Science Skills

Observing Shake or scrape spores from the underside of a mature mushroom cap onto a sheet of paper. Invite students to observe the spores with the naked eye, and then, transfer some of the spores to slides. Have each student observe spores under a microscope. Ask: **How would you describe these spores?** *(The spores are tiny, dry structures. The shape varies with the variety of mushroom.)*

3 ASSESS

Evaluate Understanding

Have volunteers explain different parts of Figure 21–2. Ask about the structures of a typical fungus, its asexual and sexual reproductive parts, and how its spores are spread.

Reteach

Have students draw and label a typical fungus, as in Figure 21–2. Students may add other drawings to this page as they learn about the main groups of fungi in the next section.

Take It to the NET

Students may select examples from among a variety of spore-releasing mechanisms, including wind dispersal (most common), water dispersal, raindrop forcing (e.g., bird's nest fungi), active ejection (e.g., puffballs, *Pilobilus*), and animal dispersal (e.g., stinkhorns). The above-average presentation will include drawings or photographs of the fungus and its method of spore release. For additional information, visit **www.phschool.com**

21–1 Section Assessment

1. Fungi are eukaryotic heterotrophs that have cell walls. Fungi do not ingest food; they digest food outside their cells and absorb it.
2. The bodies of multicellular fungi are composed of many hyphae tangled together into a thick mass called a mycelium. The visible portion of the mycelium is the reproductive structure, or fruiting body.
3. Asexual reproduction takes place when cells or hyphae break off from a fungus and begin to grow on their own. Some fungi also produce spores. Sexual reproduction in fungi usually involves two different mating types, which mate to form zygote nuclei.
4. Some spores are scattered by the wind; some by animals.
5. The genetically identical mushrooms were part of the same mycelium, which means they were part of the same organism.

Use iText to review the key concepts in Section 21–1.

Answers to . . .

CHECKPOINT *A reproductive structure that develops from a mycelium that grows below the surface of the ground*

Figure 21–3 *The fairy ring will become larger as the mycelium grows.*

21–2 Classification of Fungi

1 FOCUS

Objective

21.2.1 ***Identify*** the characteristics of the four main groups of fungi.

Guide for Reading

Vocabulary Preview

Help students remember the meanings of the second and third vocabulary words by explaining that *rhizoid* is derived from a Greek word meaning "root" and *stolon* is derived from a Latin word meaning "branch."

Reading Strategy

Students' main topics should be the four groups of fungi. For each, students should note details about structure and function and list examples.

2 INSTRUCT

The Common Molds

Build Science Skills

Observing Divide the class into small groups, and give each group a different food sample in an open plastic container with a dampened paper towel lining the bottom. Foods might include bread (without preservatives), fruit, vegetable, fruit juice, or potato chips. Have students dampen the food with water and expose it to the air for the rest of the day. Then, place all samples in a warm, dark place for two or three days. Have students observe and make drawings of any mold that grows on their samples. Ask students to compare their observations.

Guide for Reading

Key Concept

- What are the characteristics of the four main phyla of fungi?

Vocabulary

zygospore
rhizoid
stolon
conidium
ascus
ascospore
basidium
basidiospore

Reading Strategy: Finding Main Ideas Before you read, skim the section to identify the four main groups of fungi. Write the name of each group on a note card. As you read, make note of the characteristics of each group.

The kingdom Fungi is a large one, with over 100,000 species. Fungi are classified according to their structure and method of reproduction. As you will read, the methods by which fungi reproduce are unlike those of any other kingdom. The four main groups of fungi are the common molds (Zygomycota), the sac fungi (Ascomycota), the club fungi (Basidiomycota), and the imperfect fungi (Deuteromycota).

The Common Molds

The familiar molds that grow on meat, cheese, and bread are members of the phylum Zygomycota, also called zygomycetes. **Zygomycetes have life cycles that include a zygospore.** A **zygospore** (ZY-goh-spawr) is a resting spore that contains zygotes formed during the sexual phase of the mold's life cycle. The hyphae of zygomycetes generally lack cross walls, although the cells of their reproductive structures do have cross walls.

Structure and Function of Molds One of the best-known zygomycetes is the black bread mold, *Rhizopus stolonifer.* You can grow bread mold by exposing a slice of bread that does not contain preservatives to airborne dust. If you keep the bread warm and moist in a covered container, in a few days a layer of dark fuzz will appear.

Look closely at the moldy bread with a magnifying glass, and you will see tangles of delicate hyphae. Actually, you will be looking at more than one kind of hypha. The rootlike hyphae that penetrate the surface of the bread are called **rhizoids** (RY-zoydz). Rhizoids anchor the fungus to the bread, release digestive enzymes, and absorb digested organic material. The stemlike hyphae that run along the surface of the bread are called **stolons.** The hyphae that push up into the air are the sporangiophores, which form sporangia at their tips. A single sporangium may contain as many as 40,000 spores, each of which can grow into a new fungus.

CHECKPOINT *What is a zygospore?*

Life Cycle of Molds The life cycle of black bread mold is shown in **Figure 21–5.** Sexual reproduction in bread molds and other zygomycetes occurs when two hyphae from different mating types come together, forming gametangia. Haploid (N) gametes produced in the gametangia fuse with gametes of the opposite mating type to form diploid (2N) nuclei, or zygotes, which make up a single zygospore. A thick wall develops around the zygospore, which may remain dormant for months. When conditions become favorable, the zygospore germinates, then undergoes meiosis, and new haploid spores are released.

SECTION RESOURCES

Print:

- ***Laboratory Manual A,*** Chapter 21 Lab
- ***Laboratory Manual B,*** Chapter 21 Lab
- ***Teaching Resources,*** Section Review 21–2
- ***Guided Reading and Study Workbook,*** Section 21–2
- ***Issues and Decision Making,*** Issues and Decisions 20

Technology:

- ***iText,*** Section 21–2

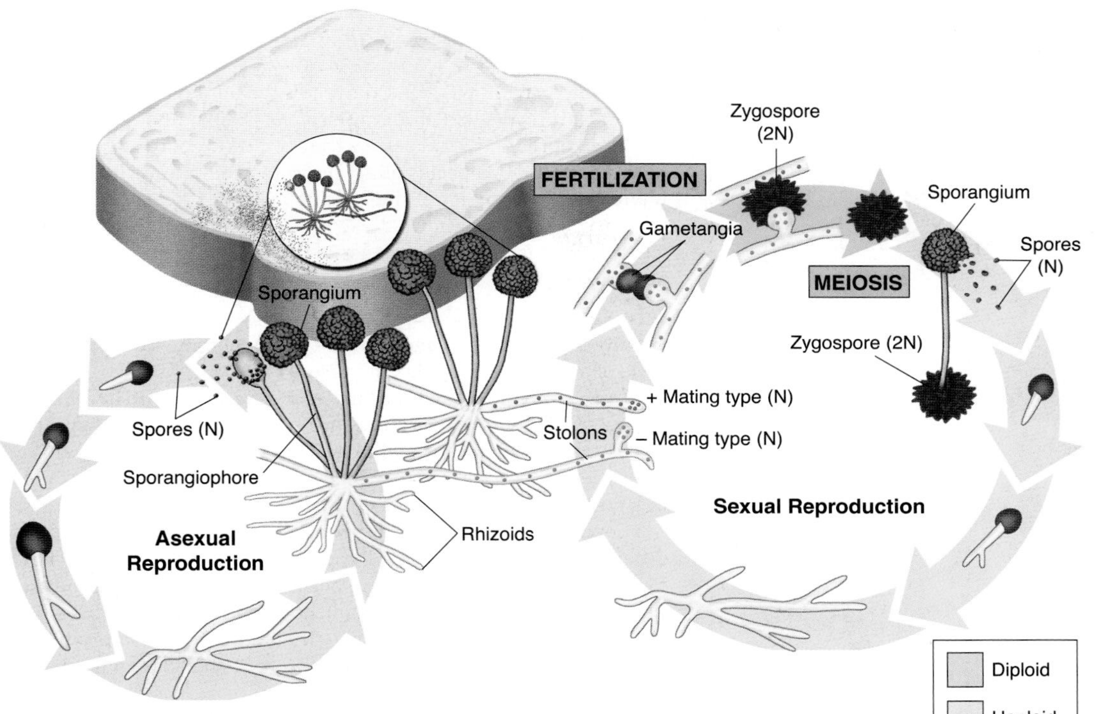

▲ **Figure 21–5** **Zygomycetes have life cycles that include a zygospore.** During sexual reproduction in the bread mold *Rhizopus stolonifer,* hyphae from two different mating types form gametangia. The gametangia fuse, and zygotes form within a zygospore. The zygospore develops a thick wall and can remain dormant for long periods. The zygospore eventually germinates, and a sporangium emerges. The sporangium reproduces asexually by releasing haploid spores produced by meiosis.

Quick Lab

What is the structure of bread mold?

Materials transparent tape, moldy bread, microscope slide, microscope

Procedure

1. Touch the sticky side of a 2-cm piece of transparent tape to the black "fuzzy" area of a bread mold.
2. Gently stick the tape to a glass slide. Observe the slide under the compound microscope. Make a sketch of your observations.
3. Return all slides to your teacher for proper disposal. Wash your hands before leaving the laboratory.

Analyze and Conclude

1. **Observing** Describe the structures you observed in the bread mold.
2. **Formulating Hypotheses** What do you think the function of the round structures is? Why do you think a single mass of bread mold produces so many of the round structures?
3. **Inferring** How can your observations help explain the ability of molds to appear on foods even in very clean kitchens?

PRESENTATIONS MADE EASY!

The Presentation Assistant Plus contains the Prentice Hall Presentation Pro and the Transparencies, which provide easy-to-follow visual support for every step of this lesson. If you have a computer presentation station, use Prentice Hall Presentation Pro Section 21–2, or use the transparencies listed here.

Section 21–2:

Interest Grabber
Section Outline
Concept Map
Figure 21–5
Figure 21–7
Figure 21–8

Quick Lab

Objective Students will be able to observe the major structures of a mold and hypothesize why bread mold produces so many sporangia.

Skill Focus Formulating Hypotheses

Materials transparent tape, moldy bread, microscope slide, microscope

Time 15 minutes

Advance Prep Prepare moldy bread by moistening slices of bread and placing them in a warm, dark place several days in advance of the activity.

Safety Students who have allergies to molds should avoid any exposure to the bread mold. Make sure students wash their hands.

Strategies Suggest that students look at the slide near the edge of the tape, where it may be easier for them to see the hyphae and spores. If students are unable to identify the sporangia, encourage them to review the subsection, "Structure and Function of Molds," and Figure 21–5.

Expected Outcomes Students should observe hyphae and reproductive structures in bread mold.

Analyze and Conclude

1. The tangled filaments are hyphae, including rhizoids, stolons, and sporangiophores. The round structures are sporangia.
2. Sporangia produce and release spores. The production of such a large number of sporangia increases the number of spores released, thus increasing the chances of the mold's reproduction.
3. Molds produce large numbers of very tiny spores that are easily spread by wind and animals. Keeping all spores out of a kitchen is impossible.

Answer to . . .

CHECKPOINT *A zygospore is a resting spore that contains zygotes formed during the sexual phase of the mold's life cycle.*

21–2 (continued)

The Sac Fungi

Word Origins

A mycologist studies fungi.

Address Misconceptions

Make sure students understand that ascomycetes produce two different kinds of spores. Which kind they produce depends on the environmental conditions. Ask: **Which kind of spores do sac fungi produce in asexual reproduction?** *(Conidia)* **Which kind of spores do they produce in sexual reproduction?** *(Ascospores)* Point out that bread yeasts, which are ascomycetes, reproduce asexually by budding, not by the production of conidia. Yet, when yeasts reproduce sexually, they produce ascospores.

Use Visuals

Figure 21–7 Have students study the life cycle. Then, ask: **Are the conidia produced in asexual reproduction haploid or diploid?** *(Haploid)* **Which type of reproduction involves development of a fruiting body?** *(Sexual reproduction)* **What cellular process results in haploid ascospores?** *(Meiosis)* **After mitosis occurs, how many ascospores are there per ascus?** *(Eight)*

Word Origins

The name of each phylum of fungi ends in *-mycota.* This suffix is derived from *mukes,* the Greek word for "fungi." The term *mycelium* is also derived from this root. **What organisms do you think a mycologist studies?**

The Sac Fungi

Sac fungi, also known as ascomycetes, belong to the phylum Ascomycota. The phylum Ascomycota is named for the ascus, a reproductive structure that contains spores. There are more than 30,000 species of ascomycetes, making it the largest phylum of the kingdom Fungi. Some ascomycetes, such as the cup fungi shown in Figure 21–6, are large enough to be visible when they grow above the ground. Others, such as yeasts, are microscopic.

Life Cycle of Sac Fungi The life cycle of an ascomycete usually includes both asexual and sexual reproduction. The life cycle of a cup fungus is shown in **Figure 21–7.**

In asexual reproduction, tiny spores called **conidia** (koh-NID-ee-uh; singular: conidium) are formed at the tips of specialized hyphae called conidiophores. These spores get their name from the Greek word *konis,* which means "dust." If conidia land in a suitable environment, they grow into a haploid mycelium.

Sexual reproduction occurs when the haploid hyphae of two different mating types (+ and –) grow close together. The N + N hyphae then produce a fruiting body in which sexual reproduction continues. Gametangia from the two mating types fuse, but the haploid (N) nuclei do not fuse. Instead, this fusion produces hyphae that contain haploid nuclei from each of the mating types (N + N).

The **ascus** (plural: asci) forms within the fruiting body. Within the ascus, two nuclei of different mating types fuse to form a diploid zygote (2N). The zygote soon divides by meiosis, producing four haploid cells. In most ascomycetes, meiosis is followed by a cycle of mitosis, so that eight cells known as **ascospores** are produced. In a favorable environment, an ascopore can germinate and grow into a haploid mycelium.

CHECKPOINT *Where are ascospores formed? Are they haploid or diploid?*

▼ **Figure 21–6** These cup fungi are members of the phylum Ascomycota. In cup fungi, asci lie on the interior surface of the cup. At maturity, the spore-filled asci burst, releasing the spores into the air. **Applying Concepts** *What type of spores are formed by the cup fungi?*

FACTS AND FIGURES

The sport of mushroom hunting

In springtime across northern United States, scores of intrepid souls tramp over fields and through woods hunting for a highly prized "mushroom." Actually, they are searching for morels, which are ascomycetes, rather than basidiomycetes, the true mushrooms. Morels, most commonly *Morchella esculenta,* are small and tan and have a wrinkled, conelike top, as shown in this chapter's opening photograph. Each of the cup-shaped depressions on the morel's surface contains thousands of asci. Some morels produce mycorrhizae. Mushroom hunters find morels growing in a wide range of habitats, though they are often found in orchards. Another ascomycete found in southern Europe is even more prized—the delicious black truffle, *Tuber melanosporum.*

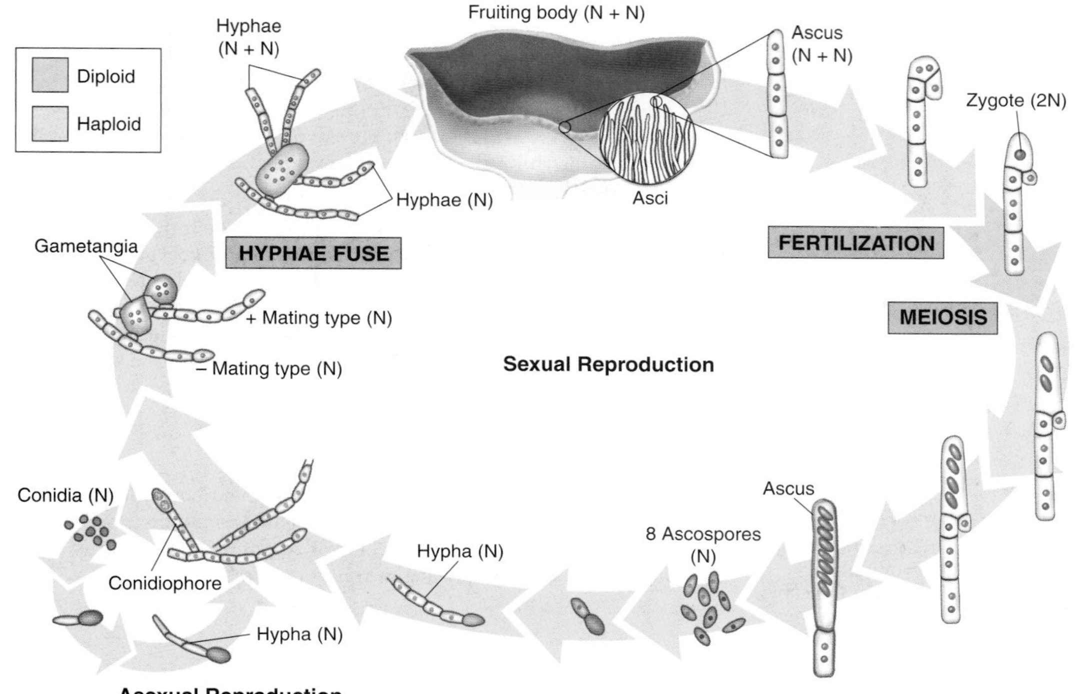

▲ **Figure 21–7** The life cycle of ascomycetes includes both asexual and sexual reproduction. During asexual reproduction, spores called conidia are formed at the tips of specialized hyphae called conidiophores. During sexual reproduction, hyphae of two mating types fuse to form hyphae with two haploid nuclei (N + N). The N + N hyphae then form a fruiting body, which eventually releases ascospores. **Ascomycetes are named for the ascus, the reproductive structure that contains ascospores.**

Yeasts Yeasts are unicellular fungi. The yeasts used by humans for baking and brewing are classified as ascomycetes because they form asci with ascospores during the sexual phase of their life cycle.

You might think of yeast as a lifeless, dry powder that is used to make bread. Actually, the dry granules contain ascospores, which become active in a moist environment. To see this for yourself, add a spoonful of dry yeast to half a cup of warm water that contains some sugar. In about 20 minutes, when you examine a drop of this mixture under a microscope, you will be able to see cell division in the rapidly growing yeast cells. The asexual process by which yeasts increase is called budding.

The common yeasts used for baking and brewing are members of the genus *Saccharomyces,* which means "sugar fungi." These yeasts are grown in a rich nutrient mixture containing very little oxygen. Prior to baking, the nutrient mixture is a mound of thick dough. Lacking oxygen, the yeasts within the mixture use the process of alcoholic fermentation to obtain energy. The byproducts of alcoholic fermentation are carbon dioxide and alcohol. The carbon dioxide gas makes beverages bubble and bread rise (by producing bubbles within the dough). The alcohol in bread dough evaporates during baking. In brewing, alcohol remains in the resulting alcoholic beverages.

Build Science Skills

Observing Allow students to carry out the activity described on page 533. Divide the class into small groups, and provide each group with a package of dry yeast, beaker, molasses, aluminum foil, dropper pipette, microscope, slide, coverslip, and methylene blue. Have students mix 5 mL of molasses and 500 mL of warm water in the beaker, and then stir in half the package of dry yeast. They should cover the top of the beaker and place it in a warm spot for 20–30 minutes. Then, students should make slides of the yeast cells that have grown in the beaker and observe them under a microscope at low and high power. Adding a drop of methylene blue under the coverslip will ensure that the cells can be clearly observed. Have students make drawings of the yeast cells and share their observations in a class discussion.

Build Science Skills

Designing Experiments Explain to students that bromthymol blue solution turns green to yellow in the presence of carbon dioxide, which is one of the byproducts of alcoholic fermentation. Then, divide the class into small groups and ask each group to design an experiment that investigates at what temperature yeast is most active. A typical experiment will involve adding bromthymol blue solution to a yeast-molasses mixture at various temperatures and observing how fast the color changes.

BIO INSIGHTS — FACTS AND FIGURES

Yeast on the shower curtain!

Yeasts are unicellular fungi that reproduce both asexually and sexually. When yeasts reproduce asexually, it is mostly by budding. A parent cell forms a bud on its outer surface that eventually breaks off. Yeasts also reproduce by fission. Sexual reproduction occurs when two haploid yeasts fuse to form a diploid zygote. The zygote then undergoes meiosis, which results in haploid spores. These haploid spores remain for some period within the diploid cell wall—the ascospores and ascus of these ascomycetes. Yeasts are found widely in nature, mostly in liquid or moist environments. Yeasts are often seen as a white powder on leaves and fruits. One yeast, *Rhodotorula,* is seen in the home as a pink coating on shower curtains. *Saccharomyces* is not only used in baking and brewing but also often in research, because it is so easily cultured.

Answers to . . .

CHECKPOINT *Ascospores are formed in the ascus. They are haploid.*

Figure 21–6 *Conidia*

21–2 (continued)

The Club Fungi

Use Visuals

Figure 21–8 After students have studied the figure, ask: **What occurs that produces a secondary mycelium?** *(Mycelia of different mating types fuse.)* Explain that each cell of the secondary mycelium has two nuclei. **What is a button?** *(A thick bulge of growing hyphae at the soil's surface)* The common mushrooms found in the produce section at the grocery are buttons of the basidiomycete *Agaricus bisporus.* Ask: **Where are the basidia found on the fruiting body?** *(Lining the gills on the underside of the cap)* **What cellular process results in haploid basidiospores?** *(Meiosis)* Point out that the basidiospores are forcibly discharged from the gills, as shown in one of the bottom illustrations. **What force distributes these basidiospores far from the mushroom cap?** *(The wind)*

Address Misconceptions

Show students a photo of a mushroom growing in the wild, and ask: **Is there a difference between this mushroom and a toadstool?** *(Some students may suggest that a toadstool is a kind of poisonous mushroom.)* Explain that folklore in some places makes distinctions between mushrooms and toadstools; however, botanists make no such distinctions. A toadstool is a folk term—not a scientific term—for some kinds of mushrooms.

The Club Fungi

The phylum Basidiomycota, or club fungi, gets its name from a specialized reproductive structure that resembles a club. The spore-bearing structure is called the **basidium** (buh-SID-ee-um; plural: basidia). Basidia are found on the gills that grow on the underside of mushroom caps.

Life Cycle of Club Fungi Basidiomycetes undergo what is probably the most elaborate life cycle of all the fungi. As shown in **Figure 21–8**, a basidiospore germinates to produce a haploid primary mycelium, which begins to grow. Before long, the mycelia of different mating types fuse to produce a secondary mycelium. The cells of the secondary mycelium contain haploid nuclei of each mating type. Secondary mycelia may grow in the soil for years, reaching an enormous size. A few mycelia have been found to be hundreds of meters across, making them perhaps the largest organisms in the world.

When the right combination of moisture and nutrients occurs, spore-producing fruiting bodies push above the ground. You would recognize these fruiting bodies as mushrooms. Each mushroom begins as a mass of growing hyphae that forms a button, or thick bulge, at the soil's surface.

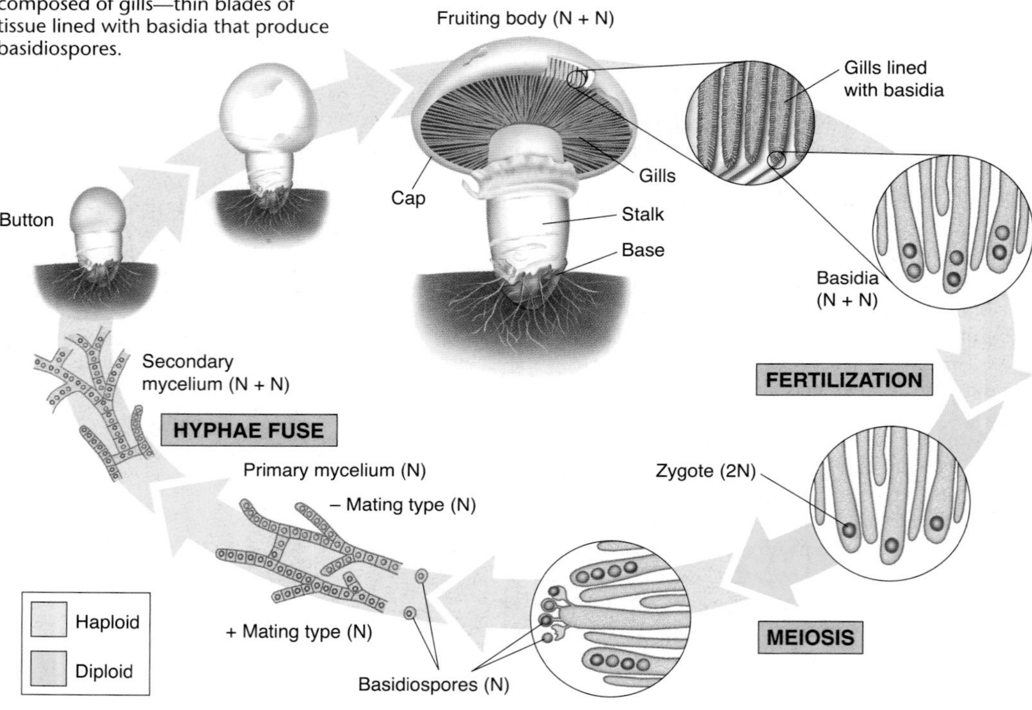

▼ **Figure 21–8** **The club fungi are named after the club shape of their reproductive structure, the basidium.** The cap of a basidiomycete such as a mushroom is composed of tightly packed hyphae. The lower side of the cap is composed of gills—thin blades of tissue lined with basidia that produce basidiospores.

FACTS AND FIGURES

Cultivated mushrooms

The common "white button" mushrooms sold in grocery stores are the buttons of *Agaricus bisporus.* This mushroom was probably first cultivated in and around Paris, France, in the mid-1600s. In the United States, one of the main centers for commercial cultivation of white buttons is Kennett Square, a small town in southeastern Pennsylvania. Large-scale mushroom growing is generally done in long, windowless warehouses, or "mushroom houses." The mushrooms are cultivated on compost made from straw and manure, first pasteurized to destroy harmful microorganisms. The compost is germinated with compact mycelium and watered regularly. The temperature is kept cool (9–13°C) to cut down on disease and insect attacks. For taste reasons, mushrooms are harvested as immature buttons, before spores are produced in great numbers.

Figure 21–9 Diversity of Club Fungi

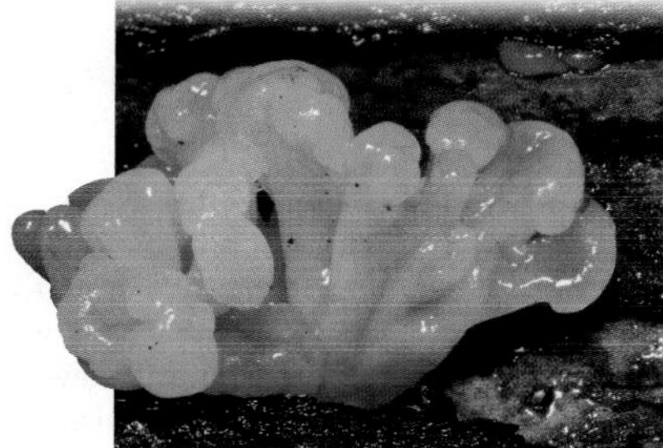

Orange Jelly

Pigskin Poison Puffball

Fly Agaric

Star Stinkhorn Fungi

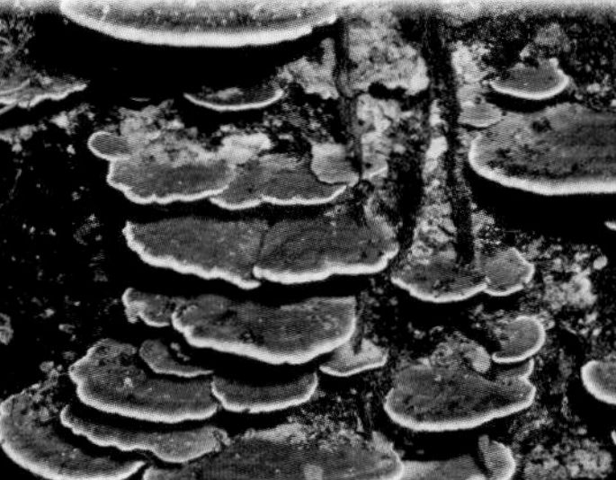

Shelf Fungus

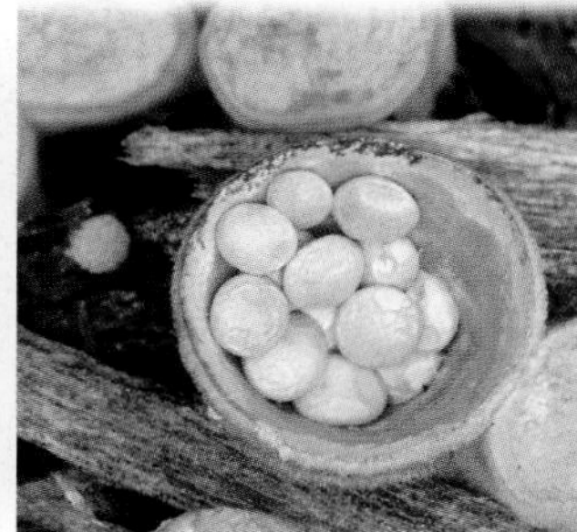

Bird's Nest Fungus

Fruiting bodies expand with astonishing speed, sometimes producing fully developed mushrooms overnight. This remarkable growth rate is caused by cell enlargement, not cell division. The cells of the hyphae enlarge by rapidly taking in water.

When the mushroom cap opens, it exposes hundreds of tiny gills on its underside. Each gill is lined with basidia. The two nuclei in each basidium fuse to form a diploid (2N) zygote cell, which then undergoes meiosis, forming clusters of haploid **basidiospores.** The basidiospores form at the edge of each basidium and, within a few hours, are ready to be scattered. Mushrooms are truly amazing reproductive structures—a single mushroom can produce billions of spores, and giant puffballs can produce trillions.

Diversity of Club Fungi In addition to mushrooms, basidiomycetes include shelf fungi, which grow near the surfaces of dead or decaying trees. The visible bracketlike structure that forms is a reproductive structure, and it, too, is a prolific producer of spores. Puffballs, earthstars, jelly fungi, and plant parasites known as rusts are other examples of basidiomycetes. **Figure 21–9** shows some examples of basidiomycetes.

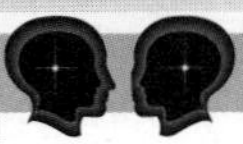

On which part of a mushroom would you find basidia?

Figure 21–9 As you can see, the club fungi are a very diverse group. These fungi are all decomposers, but other kinds of club fungi are parasites of plants and animals. At least two of these fungi, the pigskin poison puffball and the fly agaric, are poisonous. **Inferring** *Can you tell by looking at a fungus whether or not it is poisonous?*

Demonstration

Collect samples of basidiomycetes from local wild areas and bring them to class. (To collect a sample, use a self-sealing plastic sandwich bag. Turn it inside out, place it over a hand like a glove, pick the fungus, and invert the bag over the sample. You can use a plastic fork or similar tool to pry up the sample. If collecting proves impractical, obtain samples from a biological supply house or use photographs.) Display your collection for students to examine. Challenge students to identify the fruiting body, the hyphae, and the mycelium of each sample. Provide field guides, and encourage students to identify the different samples displayed.

Build Science Skills

Using Models Provide modeling compound, and challenge students to make a simple model of a basidiomycete. For an example of what to make, students can use illustrations in their textbook, photos in other books, or samples collected by teacher or students. Have students also make labels for the parts they include in their model. When the modeling compound dries, encourage students to use paints to simulate the colors of real basidiomycetes.

TEACHER TO TEACHER

To help students understand how fungal spores spread, I have them make "mushroom prints." Give each student a mature mushroom and have them remove the stalk from the cap with a knife. Place the cap on a piece of white paper, with the gills down. Place a glass, cup, or bowl over the cap to make sure it is undisturbed, and leave it overnight. When the cover and mushroom are removed, there will be a radiating pattern on the paper, caused by basidiospores falling to the paper from the gills. Students can transfer some of the basidiospores onto a slide and examine them with a microscope. They can preserve their print by lightly spraying it with an artist's fixative or varnish.

—*Audra Williams,*
Biology Teacher
Sprayberry High School,
Marietta, GA

Answers to . . .

CHECKPOINT *Basidia are found on the gills in the caps of mushrooms.*

Figure 21–9 *You cannot tell by looking, because many species of poisonous mushrooms look very similar to edible mushrooms.*

21–2 (continued)

The Imperfect Fungi

Meet Diverse Needs

Encourage students who need a challenge to research and prepare a report on the discovery of the "wonder drug" penicillin. Direct students to books about famous scientists to read about Alexander Fleming, who won a Nobel Prize for his work. Make sure students focus on the initial experiment that showed how a culture of *Penicillium notatum* killed bacteria. **Learning modality: verbal**

3 ASSESS

Evaluate Understanding

Have students write a paragraph that compares and contrasts the life cycles of a sac fungus and a club fungus.

Reteach

Ask students to make a compare/contrast table entitled The Four Main Groups of Fungi. Column heads could include Name, Phylum Name, Characteristic Structures, Life Cycle, and Examples. Students should include as many important details about each of the four main groups as possible.

ALTERNATIVE ASSESSMENT

Encourage students to talk to the produce manager at a local supermarket. Students might also talk with the chef of a local restaurant, including Asian restaurants. Suggest that they investigate foods using portobello mushrooms (*Agaricus bisporus*), oyster mushrooms (*Pleurotus ostratus*), shiitake mushrooms (*Lentinus edodes*), or enoki mushrooms (*Flammulina velutipes*). Blue cheese is made using a *Penicillium* mold. *Aspergillus* fungi are used to produce soy sauce, as well as the Japanese food called *miso.*

Use iText to review the key concepts in Section 21–2.

Figure 21–10 **The phylum Deuteromycota is made up of fungi that cannot be classified in any other phylum.** Under the microscope, the brushlike clusters of many small, spherical conidia characterize *Penicillium notatum.* This organism was the first of the *Penicillium* fungi used to produce the antibiotic penicillin.

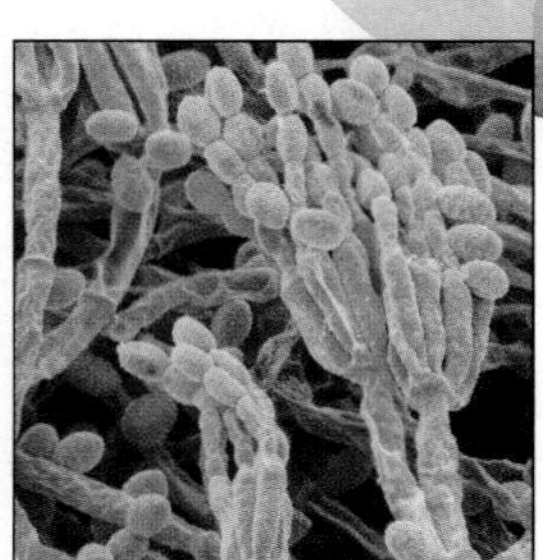

(magnification: 930×)

Edible and Inedible Mushrooms Many types of fungi have long been considered delicacies, and several different species of mushrooms are cultivated for food. You may have already tasted sliced mushrooms on pizza, feasted on delicious sautéed portobello mushrooms, or eaten shiitake mushrooms. When properly cooked and prepared, domestic mushrooms are tasty and nutritious.

Wild mushrooms are a different story: Although some are edible, many are poisonous. Because many species of poisonous mushrooms look almost identical to edible mushrooms, you should never pick or eat any mushrooms found in the wild. Instead, mushroom gathering should be left to experts who can positively identify each mushroom they collect. The result of eating a poisonous mushroom can be severe illness, or even death.

The Imperfect Fungi

Deuteromycota is the phylum of imperfect fungi, which are called deuteromycetes. **Deuteromycota is an extremely varied phylum. It is composed of those fungi that are not placed in other phyla because researchers have never been able to observe a sexual phase in their life cycles.** A majority of the imperfect fungi closely resemble ascomycetes. Others are similar to basidiomycetes, and a few resemble zygomycetes. The term *imperfect*, by the way, does not mean that the deuteromycetes are defective or less successful than other fungi. The term is just used to refer to fungi that do not appear to have sexual reproduction.

One of the best-known genera of the imperfect fungi is *Penicillium.* The species *Penicillium notatum,* shown in **Figure 21–10,** is a mold that frequently grows on fruit and is the source of the antibiotic penicillin. Like the ascomycetes, *Penicillium* reproduces asexually by means of conidia, leading many biologists to conclude that *Penicillium* evolved from an ascomycete that lost the sexual phase of its life cycle.

21–2 Section Assessment

1. **Key Concept** List the four phyla of fungi and the main features that can be used to identify members of each phylum.
2. How do conidia form? What is their function?
3. Which fungal phylum contains the largest number of species?
4. **Critical Thinking Comparing and Contrasting** Compare the structure and function of an ascus and a basidium.

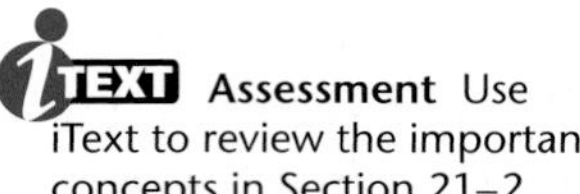

Assessment Use iText to review the important concepts in Section 21–2.

ALTERNATIVE ASSESSMENT

In Your Community

Visit a local supermarket to find out how fungi are used in the cuisine of different cultures. Consider fresh and dried mushrooms, blue cheeses, and truffles. Present your findings as a written report or as recipe cards.

21–2 Section Assessment

1. Zygomycetes have life cycles that include a zygospore. Ascomycetes have tough sacs, called asci, that contain spores. Basidiomycetes have a specialized reproductive structure that resembles a club. Deuteromycetes do not have an observed sexual phase in their life cycles.
2. In asexual reproduction of some ascomycetes, tiny spores called conidia are formed at the tip of specialized hyphae.
3. Phylum Ascomycota
4. The ascus, a tough sac that contains spores, forms within the fruiting body of an ascomycete. Within the ascus, two nuclei of different mating types fuse to form a diploid zygote. The spore-bearing structure of a basidiomycete is called the basidium, which is found on the gills in the cap of mushrooms. A basidiospore within a basidium germinates to produce a haploid primary mycelium.

21–3 Ecology of Fungi

Fungi have been around since life first moved onto land. In fact, the oldest known fossils of fungi, shown in **Figure 21–11**, were formed about 460 million years ago. At that time, the largest land plants were small organisms similar to mosses. Paleontologists think that fungi helped early plants to obtain nutrients from the ground. Their early appearance suggests that fungi may have been essential to plants' successful colonization of the land, one of the key events in the history of life.

Over time, fungi have become an important part of virtually all ecosystems, adapting to conditions in every corner of Earth. Because most fungi live their lives out of our sight, people often overlook them. But without fungi, the world would be a very different place.

Guide for Reading

Key Concepts

- What is the main role of fungi in natural ecosystems?
- What problems do parasitic fungi cause?
- What kinds of symbiotic relationships do fungi form with other organisms?

Vocabulary

saprobe
lichen
mycorrhiza

Reading Strategy: Using Prior Knowledge Before you read this section, write down all the different ways that you think fungi interact in the environment. As you read, add to or revise your list as necessary.

All Fungi Are Heterotrophs

As heterotrophs, fungi cannot manufacture their own food. Instead, they must rely on other organisms for their energy. Unlike animals, fungi cannot move to capture food, but their mycelia can grow very rapidly into the tissues and cells of plants and other organisms. Many fungi are **saprobes,** organisms that obtain food from decaying organic matter. Others are parasites, which harm other organisms while living directly on or within them. Still other fungi are symbionts that live in close and mutually beneficial association with other species.

Although most fungi feed on decaying matter, a few feed by capturing live animals. *Pleurotus ostreatus* is a carnivorous fungus that lives on the sides of trees. As roundworms crawl into the fungus to feed, they are exposed to a fungal chemical that makes them become sluggish. As the worms slow to a stop, fungal hyphae penetrate their bodies, trapping them in place and then digesting them.

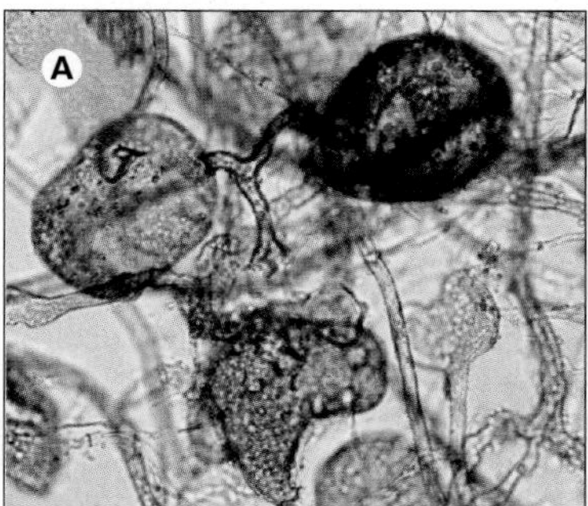

(magnification: 280×)

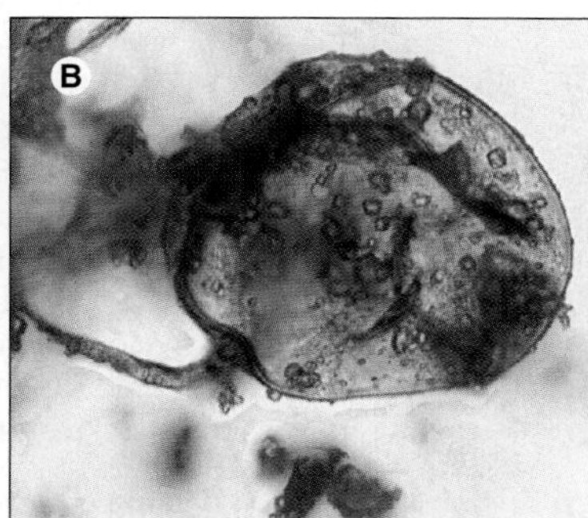

(magnification: 560×)

Figure 21–11 These microscopic images show fossils of the earliest known fungi, zygomycetes that lived about 460 million years ago. **A** shows an overview of fossilized hyphae with spores. **B** is a close-up of hyphae growing out of a spore. **Observing** ***Can you identify structures similar to those of modern molds?***

SECTION RESOURCES

Print:

- ***Teaching Resources,*** Section Review 21–3
- ***Guided Reading and Study Workbook,*** Section 21–3

Technology:

- ***iText,*** Section 21–3

Section 21–3

1 FOCUS

Objectives

21.3.4 ***Explain*** what the ecological role of fungi is.
21.3.5 ***Describe*** problems that parasitic fungi cause.
21.3.6 ***Describe*** what kinds of mutualistic relationships fungi form with other organisms.

Guide for Reading

Vocabulary Preview

Have students write the vocabulary words, dividing each into its separate syllables as best they can. Remind students that each syllable usually has only one vowel sound. The correct syllabications are: sap•robe, li•chen, my•cor•rhi•za.

Reading Strategy

Have students rewrite each of the section's blue headings in the form of a question and then find details within each subsection to answer their questions.

2 INSTRUCT

Build Science Skills

Formulating Hypotheses Point out the statement on page 537 that fungi may have been essential to plants' successful colonization of the land. Also review the definitions of the three kinds of fungi: saprobes, parasites, and mutualists. Then, ask each student to write a hypothesis about how fungi helped in plants' colonization of the land. Their hypotheses should be in the form of a brief statement. Also ask students to write a paragraph that more fully develops their concept of what they think occurred. Tell students that they will learn whether their hypotheses are correct later in the section.

Answer to . . .

Figure 21–11 *Modern molds have hyphae and spores, just as the fossil fungi had.*

Fungi as Decomposers

Meet Diverse Needs

Help at-risk students understand the importance of recycling nutrients by having them recall what they learned about organic molecules in Chapter 2. Ask: **What are the four groups of compounds found in living things?** *(Carbohydrates, lipids, proteins, and nucleic acids)* **Which of these compounds do living things use to store energy?** *(Carbohydrates and lipids)* Carbohydrates and lipids are the energy-rich compounds that decomposers help recycle. Point out that fungi also recycle all the other compounds accumulated by living things. **Learning modality: verbal**

Make Connections

Earth Science To help students understand how fungi aid in soil formation, explain that soil is a combination of mineral and organic matter, water, and air. Soil forms through the weathering, or breaking down, of rock at the surface of the earth. Although rock and mineral fragments form the major part of soil, it also contains a significant amount of organic matter, called humus. Display a pile of sand and a mound of potting soil, and have students examine and compare both materials. Then, ask: **Which of these materials will best support plant life, and why?** *(Students should know that the potting soil will best support plant life. Some may know that it does so because it contains humus.)* Explain that geologists don't classify a material as soil unless it contains humus. The humus is the result of decomposers, including bacteria and fungi.

Fungi as Parasites

Build Science Skills

Posing Questions Divide the class into small groups, and ask each group to brainstorm a list of questions about parasitic fungi. Typical questions might include: How do parasitic fungi harm plants? Are any human diseases caused by parasitic fungi serious or fatal? How can human diseases caused by parasitic

▲ **Figure 21–12 Many fungi are decomposers that recycle nutrients by breaking down the bodies of other organisms.** The mycelia of these mushrooms have released enzymes that are breaking down the wood tissues of the decaying tree stump.

Fungi as Decomposers

Fungi are found in every ecosystem, where they recycle nutrients by breaking down the bodies and wastes of other organisms. Like the fungi in **Figure 21–12,** many fungi feed by releasing digestive enzymes that break down leaves, fruit, and other organic material into simple molecules. These molecules then diffuse into the fungus. The mycelia of fungi produce digestive enzymes that speed the breakdown of dead organisms, thereby helping to recycle nutrients and essential chemicals.

Imagine a world without fungi and other decomposers. Without decay, the energy-rich compounds that organisms accumulate during their lifetimes would be lost forever. Many organisms, especially plants, remove important trace elements and nutrients from the soil. If these materials were not eventually returned, the soil would quickly be depleted, and Earth would become lifeless and barren.

Fungi as Parasites

As useful as many fungi are, others cause tremendous losses of food and crops. **Parasitic fungi cause serious plant and animal diseases. A few fungi cause diseases in humans.**

Plant Diseases Fungi cause diseases such as corn smut, which destroys the corn kernels, as shown in **Figure 21–13.** Mildews, which infect a wide variety of fruits, are also fungi. Fungal diseases are responsible for the loss of approximately 15 percent of the crops grown in temperate regions of the world. In tropical areas, where high humidity favors fungal growth, the loss of crops is sometimes as high as 50 percent. Fungi are in direct competition with humans for food. Unfortunately for us, sometimes fungi win that competition.

One fungal disease—wheat rust—affects one of the most important crops grown in North America. Rusts are caused by a type of basidiomycete that needs two different plants to complete its life cycle. Spores produced by rust in barberry plants are carried by the wind into wheat fields. There, the spores germinate and infect wheat plants. The patches of rust produce a second type of spore that infects other wheat plants, allowing the disease to spread through the field like wildfire.

Later in the growing season, a new variety of spore is produced by the rust. These tough black spores easily survive through the winter. In spring, they go through a sexual phase and produce spores that infect barberry plants. Once on the barberry leaves, the rust produces the spores that infect wheat plants, and the cycle continues. Fortunately, once agricultural scientists understood the life cycle of the rust, they were able to slow its spread by destroying barberry plants.

CHECKPOINT *What are two examples of plant diseases caused by fungi?*

TIME SAVER **PRESENTATIONS MADE EASY!**

The Presentation Assistant Plus contains the Prentice Hall Presentation Pro and the Transparencies, which provide easy-to-follow visual support for every step of this lesson. If you have a computer presentation station, use Prentice Hall Presentation Pro Section 21–3, or use the transparencies listed here.

Section 21–3: **Interest Grabber**
Section Outline
Lichen Structure

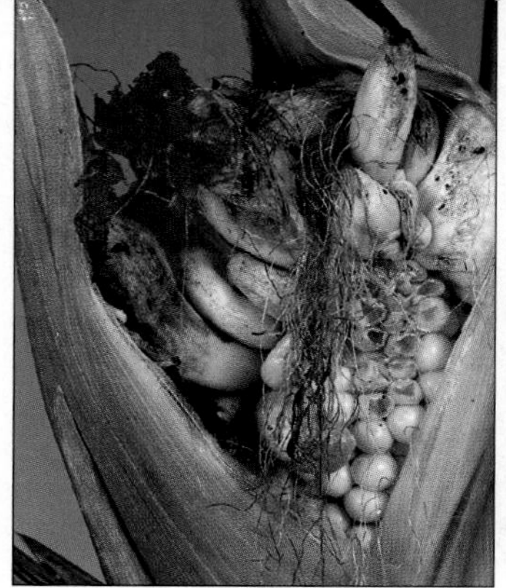

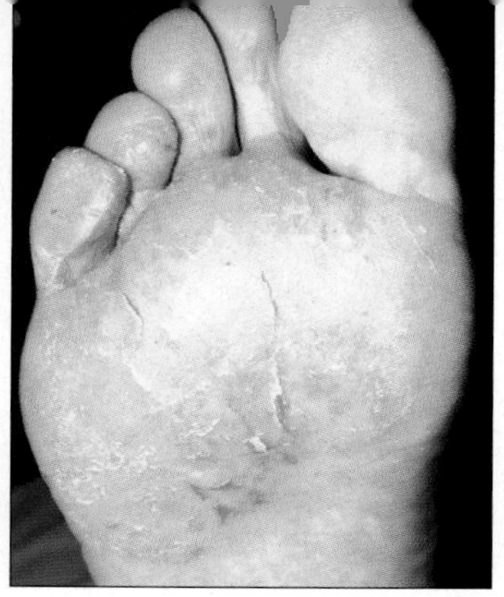

Figure 21–13 **Parasitic fungi cause serious diseases in plants and animals.** Corn smut (left) grows on the ears, stalks, and leaves of a corn plant, damaging it. The fungus then releases millions of spores that survive in the soil during the winter and begin their life cycle again in the spring. Wheat rust (center) is a basidiomycete that infects both wheat and barberry plants. Athlete's foot (right) infects the outer layers of human skin.

Human Diseases Fungal parasites can also infect humans. One deuteromycete can infect the areas between the toes, causing the infection known as athlete's foot. The fungus forms a mycelium directly within the outer layers of the skin. This produces a red, inflamed sore from which the spores can easily spread from person to person. When the same fungus infects other areas, such as the skin of the scalp, it produces a red scaling sore known as ringworm, which is not a worm at all.

A different type of fungal disease is caused by the yeast *Candida albicans,* which grows in moist regions of the body. Usually its growth is kept in check by competition from bacteria that grow in the body and by the body's immune system. This normal balance can be upset by many factors, including the use of antibiotics, which kill bacteria, or by damage to the immune system. When this happens, *Candida* may produce thrush, a painful mouth infection. Yeast infections of the female reproductive tract usually are due to overgrowth of *Candida.*

Other Animal Diseases As problematic as human fungal diseases can be, few are as deadly as the infection by one fungus from the genus *Cordyceps.* This fungus infects grasshoppers in rain forests in Costa Rica. Microscopic spores become lodged in the grasshopper, where they germinate and produce enzymes that slowly penetrate the insect's tough external skeleton. The spores multiply in the insect's body, digesting all its cells and tissues until the insect dies. To complete the process of digestion, hyphae develop, cloaking the decaying exoskeleton in a web of fungal material. Reproductive structures, which will produce more spores that will spread the infection, then emerge from the grasshopper's remains, as shown in **Figure 21–14.**

▲ **Figure 21–14** This grasshopper is the victim of a fungus of the genus *Cordyceps.* Once the fungus's tiny spore enters the insect's body, it multiplies rapidly and digests body tissues. Within days, all that is left of the insect is its hard outer shell. The structures growing out of the grasshopper's body are the fungus's fruiting bodies. **Comparing and Contrasting** ***Some pathogens rely on their host to spread them to other potential hosts. How does this fungus spread?***

fungi be prevented? Are pets susceptible to fungal diseases? Once groups have made their lists, discuss as a class which questions would be most productive to investigate. Then, encourage interested students to find the answers to some of the questions.

Meet Diverse Needs

Encourage students who need a challenge to further investigate the problem of wheat rust. Explain that the fungus that causes the plant disease is *Puccinia graminis,* which is often known as black stem rust of wheat. Ask the students to prepare a presentation to the class about wheat rust, including an illustration of the organism's life cycle. Students should discover that the wheat-rust problem persists because as scientists have developed rust-resistant strains of wheat, the fungus has evolved many races that are able to attack the resistant strains. **Learning modality: verbal**

Make Connections

Health Science After students have read about the fungal parasite that causes athlete's foot, ask: **In what kind of location are you most likely to "catch" this disease?** *(Many students will know that athlete's foot is spread in locker rooms.)* Point out that the disease is spread from person to person by spores. Ask: **What is it about locker rooms that enhances the spread of these fungal spores?** *(Locker rooms are warm and damp and people walk around barefoot, especially from the shower to lockers. Spores in a sore on one person's foot can easily spread to other people's feet.)*

FACTS AND FIGURES

The fungus among us
Fungal infections in humans are called mycoses. Fungi that cause superficial skin, or cutaneous, infections are known as dermatophytes. These pathogens are generally classified as deuteromycetes, and they include members of the fungi genera *Trichophyton, Epidermophyton,* and *Microsporum.* The medical names of cutaneous mycoses look like genus and species names, but they really identify the infected part of the body. For example, the common "athlete's foot" is known as tinea pedis. *Tinea* means "worm," and *pedis* means "foot." Other cutaneous mycoses are tinea capitis (ringworm of the scalp), tinea cruris (ringworm of the groin, or "jock itch"), and tinea unguium (ringworm of the nails). Usually, these cutaneous infections occur when there are cuts and other breaks in the skin that become infected with fungal spores.

Answers to . . .

CHECKPOINT *Corn smut, wheat rust*

Figure 21-14 *The spores of* Cordyceps *are spread by fruiting bodies that grow out of the grasshopper's body.*

21–3 (continued)

Symbiotic Relationships

Make Connections

Earth Science Explain that lichens are able to break down rocks through both mechanical and chemical weathering. Mechanical weathering includes processes that break rock into smaller pieces. Chemical weathering actually changes the chemical makeup of rocks. The fungus part of a lichen sends its hyphae into cracks in a rock, eventually wedging the rock apart. This is mechanical weathering. More important, the fungus produces acids that seep into rock and break it apart. This is chemical weathering. In addition to these weathering processes, lichens that grow on bare rock trap soil particles. As soil builds up, plants are able to grow. Thus, lichens are often the most important part of the so-called pioneer community on bare rock.

Use Visuals

Figure 21–16 Call students' attention to the lichen's layers. Then, ask: **Which of the organisms in this mutualistic association provides a protective upper layer?** *(The fungus)* **How would you describe the photosynthetic component of a lichen?** *(The algal or cyanobacterial cells are scattered among strands of fungal hyphae in the second layer of the lichen.)* **What attaches the lichen to a rock or tree?** *(Small projections)* Explain that these lichen anchors are fungal hyphae called rhizines.

Build Science Skills

Observing Provide students with photos of different species of lichens. Explain that lichens are found on trees and rocks, as well as on the sides of buildings, gravestones, and other rocklike structures. Encourage students to find one or two examples of lichens near their homes. For each example, they should make a drawing and write a description.

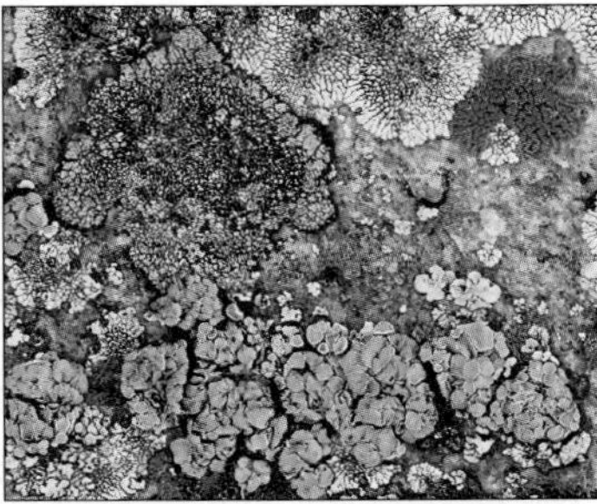

▲ **Figure 21–15** Lichens often grow on rocks and in other environments where few organisms can survive. Lichens grow in one of three forms. Crustose lichens (top) are flat, foliose lichens (middle) resemble leaves, and fruticose lichens (bottom) grow upright. **Classifying** ***What forms of lichens are visible in these pictures?***

Symbiotic Relationships

Fungi often grow in close association with members of other species in symbiotic relationships. Although fungi are parasites in many of these relationships, that is not always the case. **Some fungi form symbiotic relationships in which both partners benefit. Two such mutualistic associations, lichens and mycorrhizae, are essential to many ecosystems.**

Lichens **Lichens** (LY-kunz) are not single organisms. Rather, they are symbiotic associations between a fungus and a photosynthetic organism. The fungi in lichens are usually ascomycetes, although a few are basidiomycetes. The photosynthetic organism is either a green alga or a cyanobacterium, or both. **Figure 21–16** shows the structure of a lichen.

Lichens are extremely resistant to drought and cold. Therefore, they can grow in places where few other organisms can survive—on dry, bare rock in deserts and on the tops of mountains. Lichens are able to survive in these harsh environments because of the relationship between the two partner organisms. The algae or cyanobacteria carry out photosynthesis, providing the fungus with a source of energy. The fungus, in turn, provides the algae or bacteria with water and minerals that it collects and protects the delicate green cells from intense sunlight.

Lichens are often the first organisms to enter barren environments, gradually breaking down the rocks on which they grow. In this way, lichens help in the early stages of soil formation. Lichens are also remarkably sensitive to air pollution, and they are among the first organisms to be affected when air quality deteriorates.

CHECKPOINT *What two groups of organisms grow together in lichens?*

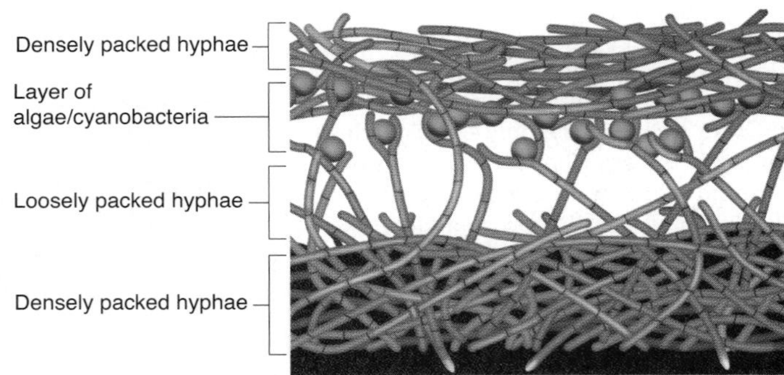

▲ **Figure 21–16** **Lichens are a mutualistic relationship between a fungus and an alga or a cyanobacterium, or both.** The protective upper surface of a lichen is composed of fungal hyphae. Below this is the layer of cyanobacteria or algae with loosely woven hyphae. The third layer consists of loosely packed hyphae. The bottom layer is a protective surface covered by small projections that attach the lichen to a rock or tree.

FACTS AND FIGURES

A merger makes a "dual organism"
The mutualistic association between a fungus and a photoautotroph is so complete that biologists give lichens genus and species names. Over 25,000 species of lichens have been identified. It is the fungus that usually gives the lichen its characteristic shape, and the fungus hyphae make up most of a lichen's mass. The spongy body of a lichen is called a thallus. The fungus protects the alga and provides it with water and minerals. The alga provides the fungus with food. Although lichens vary in color and shape, most can be classified into one of three growth forms. Foliose lichens are flat with leaflike lobes. Fruticose lichens look like small shrubs, with branchlike extensions. Crustose lichens are flat and often look like paint smears. One well-known lichen is the so-called reindeer moss, which can cover kilometers of land in arctic regions.

Problem Solving

Repotting Orchids

You are working in a greenhouse that has just begun to grow orchids. The plants arrive in small pots from a nursery. When they outgrow the pots, your supervisor asks you to place them in larger pots with fresh soil, just as you have done with other plants. However, every time you follow the greenhouse procedure for repotting, which includes carefully washing off the "old" soil and placing the roots into a sterilized soil mix, the plants soon wither and die.

Defining the Problem In your own words, what is the problem the greenhouse faces?

Organizing Information What problems could sterile, microbe-free soil present to a plant? Are there microorganisms in soil that might be essential to orchids? Might the loss of such organisms cause problems for the plants? What kinds of problems?

Creating a Solution Describe an experiment that you could use to find out if the use of sterile soil is causing the problems with repotting. Be sure to devise controls that might determine whether the mechanical stress of repotting is causing the problems, rather than the soil mixture.

Presenting Your Plan Make a poster showing the steps and procedures in your proposed experiment and explain it to the class.

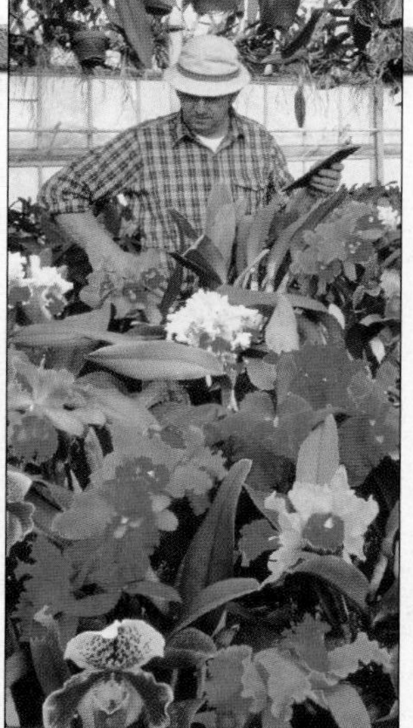

Mycorrhizae Fungi also form mutualistic relationships with plants. Almost half of the tissues of trees are hidden beneath the ground in masses of tangled roots. These roots are woven into a partnership with an even larger web of fungal mycelia. These associations of plant roots and fungi are **mycorrhizae** (my-koh-RY-zee; singular: mycorrhiza).

Scientists have known about this partnership for years, but recent research shows that it is more common and more important than was previously thought. Researchers now estimate that 80 percent of all plant species form mycorrhizae with fungi.

How do plants and fungi benefit from each other? The tiny hyphae of the fungi aid plants in absorbing water and minerals. They do this by producing a network that covers the roots of the plants and increases the effective surface area of the root system. This allows the roots to absorb more water and minerals from the soil. In addition, the fungi release enzymes that free nutrients in the soil. The plants, in turn, provide the fungi with the products of photosynthesis.

The presence of mycorrhizae is essential for the growth of many plants. The seeds of some plants, such as orchids, cannot germinate in the absence of mycorrhizal fungi. Many trees are unable to survive without fungal symbionts. Mycorrhizal associations have even been cited as an adaptation that was critical in the evolution of land plants from more-aquatic ancestors.

KEEP CURRENT WITH . . . SCIENCE NEWS®

To find out more about the topics in this chapter, go to: **www.phschool.com**

BIO INSIGHTS FACTS AND FIGURES

Fungus roots

The term *mycorrhizae* means "fungus roots," and the name aptly describes the association that develops between plant roots and fungi. The hyphae of some fungi form a sheath around the root, and hyphae also penetrate a short way into the root, growing between the root cells. These are called ectomycorrhizae. Other fungi have hyphae that penetrate root cells, through which materials are exchanged. These are called endomycorrhizae. Many plants have difficulty absorbing such elements as phosphorus from the soil, and the hyphae provide these elements to the plant. In return, the plant provides the fungus with sugars and amino acids. About half of all basidiomycetes that form mushrooms live in mycorrhizae with trees such as oaks and pines. The mushrooms that pop up at the base of these trees are evidence of the "fungus roots" underground.

Problem Solving

Explain that the problem described is a common one experienced by greenhouse workers. Although many plants can be repotted into fresh, sterile soil, those that depend on mycorrhizae cannot. The fungi that form mycorrhizae with orchids are zygomycetes that live in soil.

Defining the Problem Students' definitions of the problem will differ, though all should mention that repotting plants in a sterilized soil mix causes the plants to die.

Organizing Information Students should suggest that sterilized soil would not contain the fungi for the mycorrhizal relationships with orchids that the plants need to absorb necessary minerals.

Creating a Solution A typical experiment might retain some of the old soil attached to the roots when repotting a plant. To determine whether mechanical stress is part of the problem, students might suggest adding fungicide to soil instead of replacing it.

Presenting Your Plan Students' plans should show the steps necessary to carry out the proposed experiment. Each plan should designate a control, a variable, and a means to collect the data needed to evaluate the results.

Use Community Resources

Invite a manager of a local greenhouse to speak to the class about repotting plants and whether and why sterilized soil is ever used. Have students write questions ahead of time both about mycorrhizal associations and about fungal diseases that affect greenhouse plants.

SCIENCE NEWS®

Encourage students to visit **www.phschool.com** for the most current information on this topic.

Answers to . . .

CHECKPOINT *A lichen is a symbiotic association between a fungus and a photosynthetic organism.*

Figure 21–15 *Crustose, foliose, and fruticose*

21–3 (continued)

Use Visuals

Figure 21–17 Ask students: **What did the seedlings on the left, grown without mycorrhizae, have less of in comparison with the seedlings on the right?** *(They had less water and nutrients, which fungal symbionts aid plants in absorbing in mycorrhizae.)* **If the plants on the right benefited from a mycorrhizal association, how did the fungi in that association benefit?** *(The fungi were provided with the products of photosynthesis by the plants.)*

3 ASSESS

Evaluate Understanding

Call on students at random to compare and contrast the relationship between the fungus that causes corn smut and a corn plant and the relationship between a mycorrhizal fungus and a Douglas fir. Students should contrast a parasitic relationship with a symbiotic relationship.

Reteach

Have students make a chart listing the beneficial roles and the harmful roles of fungi in the environment.

MAKING CONNECTIONS

Both bacteria and fungi are decomposers that feed by releasing digestive enzymes that break down organic matter into simple molecules. Thus, they share the characteristics of digesting food outside their bodies and of recycling nutrients and essential chemicals, which are released into the soil and taken up by the roots of plants.

Use the iText to review the key concepts in Section 21–3.

Answer to . . .

Figure 21–17 *Mutualism*

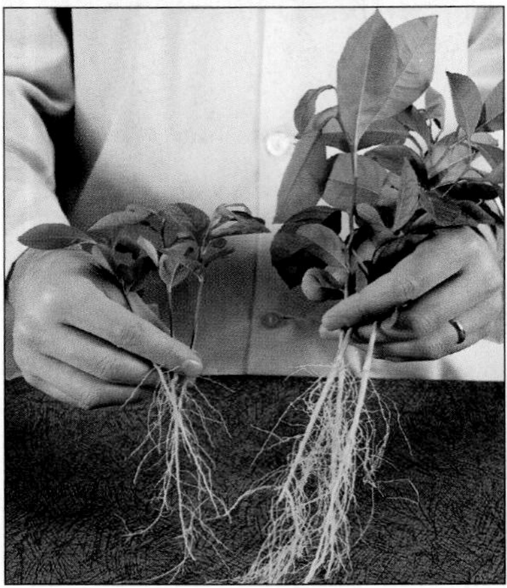

Figure 21–17 Plants and fungi often form associations called mycorrhizae (shown in the top photograph). The fungi in the mycorrhizae enable the host plant to absorb more water and nutrients. In the bottom photograph, the lemon seedlings on the left were grown without mycorrhizae. The ones on the right, which are the same age, were grown with mycorrhizae. **Applying Concepts** *What type of symbiotic relationship is illustrated by mycorrhizae?*

Mycorrhizal relationships are often very specialized. For example, the Douglas fir forests of the Pacific Northwest are dependent on the presence of a particular species of white truffle. In Europe, black truffles are found growing with oak and beech trees. The fly agaric grows mostly with birch and pine trees. **Figure 21–17** shows how mycorrhizae affect the growth of young lemon trees.

Why is this networking relationship so important? The partnership between plant and fungus does not end with a single plant. The roots of each plant are plugged into mycorrhizal networks that connect many plants. What's more astounding is that these networks appear to connect plants of different species.

A recent experiment showed that carbon atoms from one tree often end up in another nearby tree. In an experiment using carbon isotopes to track the movement of carbon, ecologist Suzanne Simard found that mycorrhizal fungi transferred carbon from paper birch trees growing in the sun to Douglas fir trees growing in the shade. As a result, the sun-starved fir trees thrived, basically by being "fed" carbon from the birches.

Simard's findings suggest that plants are far from being isolated individuals, as was previously thought. Instead, plants—and their associated fungi—may be evolving as part of an ecological partnership.

21–3 Section Assessment

1. **Key Concept** What is the major role of fungi in an ecosystem?
2. **Key Concept** How can fungi harm humans and other living things?
3. **Key Concept** Describe two mutualistic relationships that fungi form with other organisms.
4. Describe the life cycle of wheat rust.
5. **Critical Thinking Applying Concepts** What might happen to a garden if it were sprayed with a long-acting fungicide?

iTEXT Assessment Use iText to review the important concepts in Section 21–3.

MAKING CONNECTIONS

Structure and Function Both bacteria and fungi are decomposers. What characteristics do these two groups share that allow them to function in this ecological role? Use the information in Chapter 19 to help answer this question.

21–3 Section Assessment

1. To recycle nutrient material by breaking down the bodies of other organisms
2. Parasitic fungi cause serious plant and animal diseases, including in humans.
3. A lichen is a symbiotic association between a fungus and a photosynthetic organism. Mycorrhizae are mutualistic relationships between plant roots and fungi.
4. Spores produced by the rust in barberry plants are carried by wind into wheat fields, where they infect wheat plants and produce a second type of spore that infects other wheat plants. Another type of spore survives through the winter and produces yet another type of spore in spring that infects barberry plants, continuing the cycle.
5. The garden plants would not flourish, because the mycorrhizae between plants and fungi benefit both plants and fungi.

Real-World Lab

Examining Seeds for Fungi

The fungi that you are probably most familiar with are mushrooms and the molds that attack stored foods. In this investigation, you will examine how storage conditions affect the growth of fungi on seeds.

Problem **What storage conditions best protect seeds from fungi?**

Materials

- seeds stored in cold, dry conditions
- seeds stored in warm, moist conditions
- forceps
- microscope slide
- coverslip
- microscope
- aniline blue stain
- scalpel
- dropper pipette
- paper towels

Skills Formulating Hypotheses

Procedure

1. **Formulating Hypotheses** Develop a hypothesis about the effect of temperature and moisture on the growth of a seed-destroying fungus. Predict whether you will find more hyphae in seeds stored in cold, dry conditions or in seeds stored in warm, moist conditions.
2. Use a dropper pipette to place a drop of aniline blue stain on a microscope slide. **CAUTION:** *Avoid getting the stain on your hands or clothing.*
3. Use forceps to carefully remove the outer seed coat from a seed stored in cool, dry conditions. Place the seed in the drop of aniline blue stain.
4. Use the flat side of a scalpel or forceps to gently mash and flatten the seed in the drop of stain. Place a coverslip on top of the mashed seed. Leave the seed in the stain for 1 minute.
5. Use a dropper pipette to place a drop of water on the slide, touching one edge of the coverslip.
6. Touch a paper towel to the edge of the coverslip opposite the drop of water to draw the water under the coverslip. Repeat steps 4 and 5 until you have removed the drop of stain.
7. Use the high-power objective of the microscope to examine the stained seed. Any hyphae that are present will be stained blue. Record your observations as notes and sketches.
8. Repeat steps 1 to 6 with a seed stored in warm, moist conditions.

Analyze and Conclude

1. **Observing** Which seeds had more hyphae?
2. **Analyzing Data** What conditions favor the growth of fungi? What conditions are better for storing seeds?
3. **Drawing Conclusions** Did your observations support your hypothesis? Are the environmental requirements of this fungus typical of most fungi?
4. **Inferring** Aniline blue stains the cell walls of fungi more easily than plant cell walls. What substance in fungi do you think aniline blue binds to? Explain your answer.

Go Further

Designing Experiments Plan an experiment to compare the growth of plants from both healthy and fungus-infected seeds. What are your controlled and manipulated variables? Obtain your teacher's permission before carrying out your experiment.

Analyze and Conclude

1. Seeds stored in warm, moist conditions have more hyphae.

2. Warm, moist conditions favor the growth of fungi, and thus, cool, dry conditions are better for storing seeds.

3. Answer will depend on a student's hypothesis. Observations should support the hypothesis that fungal growth is greater in seeds stored in warm, moist conditions. This is typical of the environmental requirements of most fungi.

4. Aniline blue stain binds to chitin, which is common in fungal cells but lacking in plant cell walls.

Real-World Lab

Objectives Students will be able to
- formulate and test a hypothesis about the effects of temperature and moisture on a fungus;
- draw a conclusion about what storage conditions best protect seeds from fungi.

Skills Focus **Formulating Hypotheses**

Time 45 minutes

Advance Prep At least ten days in advance, put one batch of dry seeds—such as corn, wheat, or beans—in a sealed, airtight container in a refrigerator. Put a second batch in a dark, warm, moist place. Don't use seeds that are stained pink, which indicates treatment with a fungicide. The day before the activity, soak the seeds in 1 M sodium hydroxide (40 g/L NaOH) overnight to soften them. Wear safety goggles and rubber gloves when working with the liquid. The next day, drain the seeds and rinse them with several changes of tap water until the water is neutral pH.

Safety Make sure all students wear gloves and safety goggles.

Procedure

1. Ask students what their hypotheses and predictions are. If a prediction does not follow from a hypothesis, ask the student to explain how he or she arrived at the prediction.

3. Demonstrate how to remove the outer seed coat from a seed.

6. Demonstrate how to touch a paper towel to the edge of a coverslip to draw water under the coverslip.

Expected Outcomes Students should conclude that fungal infestation is more severe in seeds stored in warm, moist conditions than in cool, dry conditions.

Go Further

Have students develop a detailed plan for how to go about carrying out such an experiment. Then, provide a sunny space in the classroom for the plants to grow. Make sure students collect growth data every two days or so for several weeks.

Chapter 21 Study Guide

Study Tip

Divide the class into small groups, and ask each group to write a list of review questions that address all the vocabulary words and Key Concepts. Then, have groups exchange lists and answer each other's questions.

Thinking Visually

1. Life cycle includes zygospore; have rhizoids and stolons; reproduce both sexually and asexually
2. Hyphae form a gametangium
3. Cup fungi, some yeasts
4. Conidia on conidiophores
5. Hyphae form a gametangium
6. Mycelia form a secondary mycelium
7. No observed sexual phase of life cycle
8. Unknown

Chapter 21 Assessment

Reviewing Content

1. a **2.** b **3.** c **4.** a **5.** b **6.** c **7.** d **8.** c **9.** d **10.** c

Understanding Concepts

11. The cells of fungi are similar to the exoskeletons of insects in that both contain chitin.

12. Hyphae are tiny filaments that are only one cell thick, whereas a mycelium is a thick mass composed of many hyphae tangled together.

13. Spores are produced in sporangia, which are found at the tops of specialized hyphae called sporangiophores. Spores can grow into new organisms.

14. Many fungi produce dry, almost weightless spores, which scatter easily in the wind. Other fungi are specialized to lure animals, which disperse fungal spores.

15. Spores must land in a favorable environment. There must be a proper combination of temperature, moisture, and food.

16. Fungi are classified according to their structure and method of reproduction.

Chapter 21 Study Guide

21–1 The Kingdom Fungi

Key Concepts

- Fungi are eukaryotic heterotrophs that have cell walls made of chitin.
- The bodies of multicellular fungi are composed of many hyphae tangled together into a thick mass called a mycelium.
- Most fungi reproduce both asexually and sexually.

Vocabulary
chitin, p. 527 • hypha, p. 527
mycelium, p. 528 • fruiting body, p. 528
sporangium, p. 528 • sporangiophore, p. 528
gametangium, p. 529

21–2 Classification of Fungi

Key Concepts

- Zygomycetes have life cycles that include a zygospore.
- The phylum Ascomycota is named for the ascus, a reproductive structure that contains spores.
- The phylum Basidiomycota, or club fungi, gets its name from the basidium, a specialized reproductive structure that resembles a club.
- Deuteromycota is an extremely varied phylum. It is composed of those fungi that are not placed in other phyla because researchers have never been able to observe a sexual phase in their life cycles.

Vocabulary
zygospore, p. 530 • rhizoid, p. 530
stolon, p. 530 • conidium, p. 532
ascus, p. 532 • ascospore, p. 532
basidium, p. 534 • basidiospore, p. 535

21–3 Ecology of Fungi

Key Concepts

- Fungi are found in every ecosystem, where they recycle nutrients by breaking down the bodies of other organisms.
- Parasitic fungi cause serious plant and animal diseases. A few fungi cause diseases in humans.
- Some fungi form symbiotic relationships in which both partners benefit. Two such mutualistic associations, lichens and mycorrhizae, are essential to many ecosystems.

Vocabulary
saprobe, p. 537
lichen, p. 540
mycorrhiza, p. 541

Thinking Visually

Use the information in Section 21–2 to complete the following compare-and-contrast table about the different phyla of Fungi:

Four Phyla of Fungi

Phylum	Examples	Characteristics	Reproduction	
			Asexual	Sexual
Zygomycota (common molds)	*Rhizopus stolonifer* (black bread mold)	1	Spores in sporangiophores	2
Ascomycota (sac fungi)	3	Long stage in which cells have two nuclei; yeasts are unicellular	4	5
Basidiomycota (club fungi)	Mushrooms, puffballs, earthstars, shelf fungi, jelly fungi, rusts	Extremely variable; long stage in which cells have two nuclei	None or conidia on conidiophores	6
Deuteromycota (imperfect fungi)	*Penicillium*, ringworm, and athlete's foot fungus	7	Conidia on conidiophores	8

TIME SAVER — CHAPTER RESOURCES

Print:
- ***Teaching Resources,*** Chapter Vocabulary Review, Graphic Organizer
- ***Chapter Tests: Levels A and B,*** Chapter 21 Test
- ***PH Assessment System,*** Practice Test

Technology:
- ***Computer Test Bank,*** Chapter 21 Test
- ***iText,*** Chapter 21 Assessment

Chapter 21 Assessment

Reviewing Content

Choose the letter that best answers the question or completes the statement.

1. Which of the following is NOT a characteristic of the kingdom Fungi?
   a. All are unicellular. c. All are eukaryotic.
   b. All have cell walls. d. All are heterotrophs.
2. The body of a typical fungus consists of a tangled mass of filaments called a(an)
   a. basidium. c. hypha.
   b. mycelium. d. antheridium.
3. When hyhae of opposite mating types of fungi meet, each hypha forms a
   a. sporangium. c. gametangium.
   b. zygospore. d. zoospore.
4. In the diagram of bread mold shown below, X is pointing to what structure?

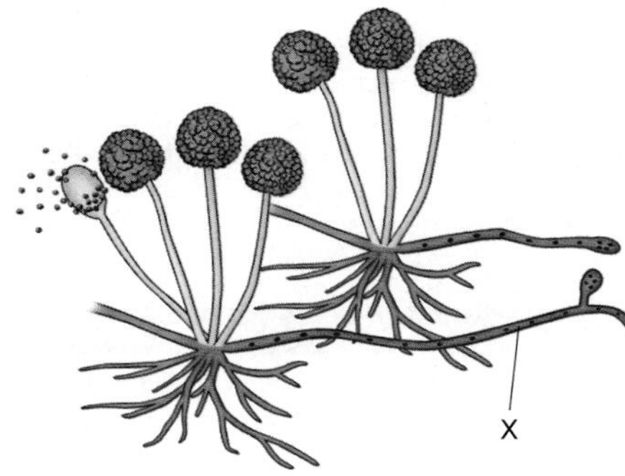

   a. stolon c. basidium
   b. rhizoid d. ascus
5. The asexual spores of ascomycetes are called
   a. zygospores. c. ascospores.
   b. conidia. d. zoospores.
6. In baking, yeast cells bud and carry out the process of
   a. lactic acid fermentation.
   b. aerobic respiration.
   c. alcoholic fermentation.
   d. digestion.
7. A mushroom that you see above the ground is actually a
   a. basidiospore. c. fruiting body.
   b. gametangium. d. basidium.
8. Sexual reproduction has never been observed in
   a. zygomycetes. c. basidiomycetes.
   b. ascomycetes. d. deuteromycetes.
9. Organisms that obtain food from decaying organic matter are called
   a. mutualists.
   b. autotrophs.
   c. parasites.
   d. saprobes.
10. A symbiotic association between a fungus and an alga or a cyanobacterium is a
    a. mycorrhiza.
    b. fruiting body.
    c. lichen.
    d. mushroom.

Understanding Concepts

11. How are the cell walls of fungi similar to those of insects?
12. Distinguish between the terms *hyphae* and *mycelium.*
13. How does a sporangiophore function in the reproduction of fungi?
14. Describe one way in which fungi are adapted to disperse spores.
15. What conditions are necessary for fungal spores to germinate?
16. Explain the basis for the classification of fungi.
17. Describe the reproductive cycle of bread mold.
18. Compare the structure and function of rhizoids and stolons.
19. Yeasts are unicellular fungi. In which phylum are most yeasts classified? What is the basis of this classification?
20. Why is it dangerous to eat wild mushrooms?
21. Why do many biologists think that *Penicillium* evolved from an ascomycete?
22. Distinguish between a saprobe and a parasite. Give an example of each.
23. How does the method by which fungi obtain nutrients help in recycling nutrients and essential chemicals?
24. Describe two symbiotic relationships involving fungi and members of another kingdom.
25. What is the evolutionary significance of mycorrhizae?

HOMEWORK GUIDE (TIME SAVER)

Section:	Questions:
Section 21–1	1–3, 11–15, 26, 27, 29, 31, 33
Section 21–2	4–8, 16–20, 28, 34
Section 21–3	9, 10, 21–25, 30, 32, 35, 36

17. Two hyphae from different mating types come together, forming gametangia. Haploid gametes produced in the gametangia fuse with gametes of the opposite mating type to form diploid nuclei. A thick wall develops around the nuclei, producing a zygospore that may remain dormant for months. When conditions become favorable, the zygospore germinates, undergoes meiosis, and develops into a new individual.

18. Rhizoids are rootlike hyphae that penetrate surfaces, anchor fungi, release digestive enzymes, and absorb digested organic material. Stolons are stemlike hyphae that run along surfaces and are involved in reproduction.

19. Most yeasts are classified in the phylum Ascomycota because they form asci with ascospores during the sexual phase of their life cycle.

20. Many species of poisonous mushrooms look almost identical to edible mushrooms.

21. Like ascomycetes, *Penicillium* reproduces asexually by means of conidia.

22. A saprobe, such as mushrooms, obtains food from decaying organic matter. A parasite, such as wheat rust, harms other organisms while living directly on or within them.

23. The mycelia of fungi produce digestive enzymes that speed the breakdown of dead organisms, thereby helping to recycle nutrients and essential chemicals.

24. A lichen is a symbiotic association between a fungus and a photosynthetic organism. The alga or cyanobacterium provide the fungus with a source of energy; the fungus provides the alga or cyanobacterium with water and minerals. Mycorrhizae are mutualistic relationships between plant roots and fungi. The hyphae of the fungi aid plants in absorbing water and minerals; the plants provide the fungi with the products of photosynthesis.

25. Mycorrhizal associations have been cited as an adaptation that was critical in the evolution of land plants from more aquatic ancestors.

Chapter 21 Assessment

Critical Thinking

26. All of the structures listed are used in sexual reproduction except conidia and yeast buds.

27. Fungi obtain food by absorbing nutrients from decaying matter in the soil or by absorbing nutrients from the bodies of their hosts. Humans obtain food by ingesting plants and animals.

28. The division to which an unknown fungus belongs can be determined by examining its structures for sexual production. Common molds produce zygospores. Club fungi have basidia, and sac fungi have asci. Imperfect fungi do not have known structures for sexual reproduction.

29. Tropical regions are warmer and have more moisture, which are conditions that favor fungal growth.

30. Answers may vary. A typical answer might suggest that bacteria and fungi compete for the same food source, and as a result fungi evolved a mechanism for killing bacteria.

31. The trees with mycorrhizae grew taller. Plants with mycorrhizae have a faster rate of growth than those without mycorrhizae.

32. With both methods of reproduction, fungi increase their chance of reproducing in different environmental conditions.

33. Students might suggest that the soil in the area where the mushrooms grow must contain a lot of nutrients. Some students may mention the possibility that the mushrooms are evidence of mycorrhizae in that area.

34. A principal role of fungi in the environment is to decompose dead organisms and recycle nutrients. If a lake contains few fungi, little decomposition and recycling will occur, and the water will become a less hospitable place for other organisms to survive.

Chapter 21 Assessment

Critical Thinking

26. Classifying Fungi can reproduce both sexually and asexually. Identify which of the following structures can be involved in a process of asexual reproduction: hyphae, fruiting bodies, sporangia, gametangia, zygospores, conidia, ascospores, basidiospores, yeast buds.

27. Comparing and Contrasting Both humans and fungi are heterotrophs. Compare the way fungi obtain food with the way humans do.

28. Classifying Suppose someone gave you an unknown fungus to classify. What criteria would you use to determine the phylum to which the fungus belongs?

29. Applying Concepts Why are fungi a more serious problem to agriculture in tropical regions of the world than they are in temperate regions?

30. Developing Hypotheses The antibiotic penicillin is a natural secretion of a certain kind of fungus—a green mold called *Penicillium.* Penicillin kills bacteria. Why might a mold species have evolved a way of killing bacteria?

31. Interpreting Graphics The graph below illustrates the growth rates of three species of trees—two individuals of each. One tree of each species grew with mycorrhizae and one grew without mycorrhizae. For each species, how does the growth of the two plants compare? Make a generalization about the growth rate of plants with mycorrhizae.

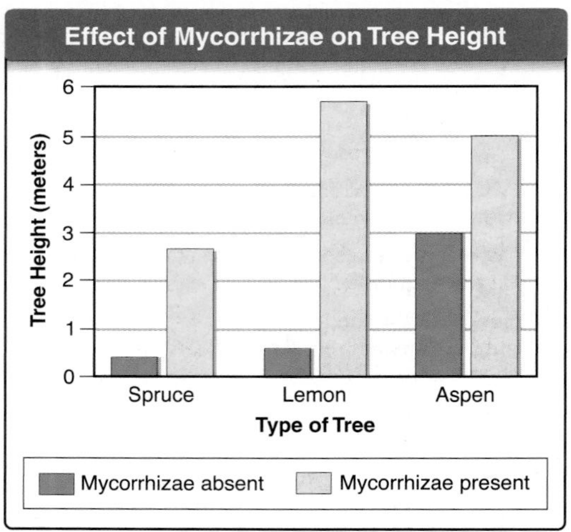

32. Inferring Most fungi have evolved the ability to produce spores through both sexual and asexual reproduction. How is this an advantage to fungi?

33. Inferring Suppose mushrooms appeared repeatedly in only one small part of your yard. What would this indicate about the soil in that area?

34. Predicting Heavily polluted fresh water contains few fungi. How might this affect life in a lake?

35. Creative Writing A debate is raging in your classroom. Some students argue that because fungi cause human diseases and damage crops, they should be eradicated from Earth. Their case seems compelling. You, however, are responsible for defending the opposing viewpoint. Let the fungi be, you maintain. Write the script of an argument you would present in this debate.

36. Making Connections How do fungal cells differ from the cells of plants or animals? Draw a diagram or make a chart that compares the cells of multicellular organisms in these three kingdoms: Animalia, Plantae, and Fungi. Use the information in Chapters 7 and 18 to help in answering this question.

Performance-Based Assessment

In Your Community Use a field guide to find and identify fungi growing near your home. Sketch what you find, but do not touch or collect them. Note the environment in which each fungus is growing. What do you think is their source of nutrition? Share your field notebook with your class.

Visit the Prentice Hall Web site at **www.phschool.com** to find out about fungal gardens that are cultivated by ants. Then, answer the following:

- Describe the nest of a leaf-cutting ant.
- On what material does the fungus grow in the ant nest?
- How do the ants keep unwanted species of fungi out of their garden?
- What part of the fungus do the ants eat?

Performance-Based Assessment

Students can use field guides for fungi or mushroom hunters' guides. If there is a limited supply of field guides, divide the class into pairs or small groups. Before students attempt to find fungi, lead a brainstorming session with the class about where there are nearby wild areas, especially city, state, or national parks. The fungi students find will depend on the season and the area they search. For each example found, students should attempt an identification and note details of the environment in their field notebooks.

Test-Taking Tip Before you begin answering questions, determine the total number of questions on the test and how much time, on average, you have to answer each question. Try to partition your time accordingly.

Directions: Choose the letter that best answers the question or completes the statement.

1. Which of the following organisms is NOT a fungus?
(A) mushroom
(B) morel
(C) water mold
(D) bread mold
(E) yeast

2. Which of the following is characteristic of some types of fungi?
I. Decomposition
II. Parasitism
III. Mutualism
(A) I only
(B) II only
(C) I and II only
(D) II and III only
(E) I, II, and III

Questions 3–5 Each of the lettered choices below refers to the following numbered statements. Select the best lettered choice. A choice may be used once, more than once, or not at all.

(A) Lichen
(B) Mycorrhiza
(C) *Penicillium*
(D) Mycelium
(E) Chitin

3. Cell wall carbohydrate

4. Tangled mass of hyphae

5. Fungal source of antibiotic

Questions 6–7 Complete each analogy by selecting the correct letter. In analogies, A : B :: C : ___?___ *means* A is to B as C is to ___?___.

6. Sac fungus : morel :: club fungus : ___?___
(A) mushroom
(B) yeast
(C) bread mold
(D) *Penicillium*
(E) lichen

7. Plant : root :: mold : ___?___
(A) gametangium
(B) zygospore
(C) rhizoid
(D) stolon
(E) sporangiophore

Questions 8–10

Ripe grapes are covered with a grayish film called "bloom," which contains yeasts and sometimes other microorganisms. A group of students prepared three test tubes of fresh, mashed grapes. They heated two of the test tubes to the boiling point, then cooled them. They inoculated one of these test tubes with live yeast. They incubated all three test tubes at 30°C for 48 hours and then examined the test tubes for signs of fermentation—the presence of bubbles and alcohol. Their data are summarized in the table below.

Evidence of Fermentation

Test-Tube Contents	Alcohol Odor (yes or no)	Bubbles (yes or no)
Unheated grape mash	yes	yes
Boiled grape mash	no	no
Boiled grape mash inoculated with yeast	yes	yes

8. What is the independent variable in the students' investigation?
(A) presence of live yeast or other microorganisms
(B) light
(C) bubbles
(D) odor of alcohol
(E) time

9. What is the dependent variable in the students' investigation?
I. Boiling
II. Odor of alcohol
III. Presence of bubbles
(A) I only
(B) II only
(C) I and III only
(D) II and III only
(E) I, II, and III

10. What can you conclude, based on the students' results?
I. Uninoculated, boiled grape mash does not seem to ferment over a 48-hour period.
II. Boiled grape mash that contains live yeast undergoes fermentation.
III. Grape mash does not ferment unless live yeast is added.
(A) I only
(B) II only
(C) I and II only
(D) II and III only
(E) I, II, and III

Standardized Test Prep

1. C
2. E
3. E
4. D
5. A
6. A
7. C
8. A
9. D
10. C

(Continued from page 546)

35. Many students will suggest that eliminating the fungi might have unforeseen harmful effects on the environment, since fungi play an important role in decomposing and recycling nutrients. Students' scripts should be well reasoned and accurate.

36. Animal cells have no cell walls or chloroplasts. Plant cells have chloroplasts and cell walls of cellulose. Fungal cells have cell walls of chitin and do not have chloroplasts.

Take It to the NET

• The nests of leaf-cutting ants can extend nearly a meter into the ground. They are composed of distinct chambers. There may be as many as 2,000 chambers in a typical nest.

• The fungi grow on a pastelike substance that consists of crushed leaves and saliva from the ants.

• Worker ants eat unwanted foreign fungi. Secretions from the ants' bodies contain chemicals that help kill species of fungi other than the one they are cultivating.

• The ants eat the fungal hyphae and their swollen tips.

For additional information, visit **www.phschool.com**

Unit 7

Dear Colleague,

Each spring, I teach a large freshman course in general biology at my university. At the beginning of the class, students ask all sorts of questions about what I intend to cover during the semester, and, every now and then, one of them asks whether or not I intend to teach any botany. When I say "yes," they aren't always pleased. They've got an image of plant science as dull, pointless, and old-fashioned. But they are wrong.

As I do my best to explain, plant biology today is one of the most exciting and interesting areas of biology. Think of it this way: Imagine that you had to find a way to survive with your feet permanently anchored in cement. You couldn't move, couldn't hide, couldn't seek food, couldn't even walk to water. Doesn't sound like much of a life, does it? Let's suppose, however, that you managed not only to survive under such conditions but to prosper. Let's suppose that you and your descendants became the dominant form of life on land, transforming the landscape and making life possible for thousands of other organisms. Would you find this remarkable? Would you wonder how you managed to pull it off? I'll bet you would.

Well, that's exactly what plants have done. They stand there for all to see, surrounded by potential predators, and they prevail. They inhabit a landscape where water and nutrients are often hidden from view, and yet they find them. They have no way to search for mates; nonetheless they manage to bring their reproductive cells together, often over great distances. Plants are, in many ways, the ultimate survivors, the ultimate winners in the battle for control of life on land.

▶ These colorful poppies, found growing on the Kenai Peninsula in Alaska, are only one example of the thousands of species of flowering plants that inhabit the Earth.

What do we know about plants?
• Plants are the most adaptable, versatile, and successful form of multicellular life on this planet.
• Plants came to dominate life on land because of two great evolutionary innovations—vascular tissue, which enabled them to draw water from the soil, and seeds, which increased their chances of success at reproduction.
• Plants aren't the passive life forms we often take them to be. Plants can respond to changes in their environments and to stress, and they can even fight off attackers.
What discoveries lie in the future?
• Will studies of plant genetics and molecular biology enable us to learn how the different plant groups are related to one another?
• Can we use plant genome data and genetic engineering to design better, more productive crop plants that will place less stress on the environment?
• Will the study of plants reveal chemicals or medicines that can be effective in treating human diseases?
KEEP CURRENT WITH . . .
SCIENCE NEWS®
Find out more about topics in this unit:
www.phschool.com

I don't know how your students will approach the study of plants, but we have done our best to make sure that they'll understand just how remarkable these organisms really are. In New England, plants mark the coming of spring and the passage of summer; they celebrate autumn with colors so vibrant that they draw tourists from across the country to enjoy the spectacle. In the great American Midwest, plants produce a harvest that sustains our nation's growing population and millions of others around the world. Plants shape the landscape of the desert, cover the freshwater marshes of the Everglades, and produce forests that are homes to an endless variety of wildlife.

When the first complete DNA sequence for a plant (*Arabadopsis*) was determined in the year 2000, many people were surprised that it contained nearly 25,500 genes, almost double that of the fruit fly, *Drosophila*. They shouldn't have been surprised. Plants may not be able to move, but in their own way, they have figured out ways to do many things better than animals. Far from being "simple" organisms, plants survive and succeed because they are complex and sophisticated. Perhaps the best way to think of this is to tell students that plants have evolved a survival strategy so different from that of animals that organisms like us have a hard time even noticing it.

The next time students are in doubt about whether plants are anything more than passive spectators in the game of life, ask them what an animal is *really* doing when it eats an apple. The answer, as we try to make clear in Chapter 24, is that an act of deception is going on. The plant is "bribing" the unsuspecting creature into spreading its seeds over great distances. The apple, of course, still tastes great, and the animal never knows it's been taken advantage of. Now, that's clever!

Sincerely,

Ken Miller

SCIENCE NEWS®

Have students visit the Prentice Hall Web site at
www.phschool.com
to find the most current information on plants.

Chapter Planner 22 Plant Diversity

Section and Section Objectives	Time	Activities and Labs
22–1 Introduction to Plants, pp. 551–555 **22.1.1** ***Explain*** what a plant is. **22.1.2** ***Describe*** what plants need to survive. **22.1.3** ***Describe*** how the first plants evolved.	**2 periods (1 block)**	**SE:** ***Inquiry Activity,*** Are all plants the same?, p. 550 **TE:** ***Build Science Skills,*** p. 552 **SE:** ***Problem Solving,*** "Plantastic" Voyage, p. 553 **TE:** ***Make Connections,*** p. 554
22–2 Bryophytes, pp. 556–559 **22.2.1** ***Describe*** the adaptations of bryophytes. **22.2.2** ***Identify*** the three groups of bryophytes. **22.2.3** ***Explain*** how bryophytes reproduce.	**1 period (1/2 block)**	**TE:** ***Build Science Skills,*** p. 556 **TE:** ***Demonstration,*** p. 558 **TE:** ***Build Science Skills,*** p. 559
22–3 Spore-Bearing Vascular Plants, pp. 560–563 **22.3.1** ***Explain*** how vascular tissue is important to ferns and their relatives. **22.3.2** ***Describe*** the three phyla of spore-bearing plants. **22.3.3** ***Identify*** the stages in the life cycle of ferns.	**1 period (1/2 block)**	**TE:** ***Build Science Skills,*** p. 561 **TE:** ***Build Science Skills,*** p. 562
22–4 Seed Plants, pp. 564–568 **22.4.1** ***Describe*** the reproductive adaptations of seed plants. **22.4.2** ***Describe*** the evolution of seed plants. **22.4.3** ***Identify*** the four groups of gymnosperms.	**2 periods (1 block)**	**SE:** ***Quick Lab,*** How do seeds differ from spores?, p. 565
22–5 Angiosperms—Flowering Plants, pp. 569–572 **22.5.1** ***Identify*** the characteristics of angiosperms. **22.5.2** ***Explain*** what monocots and dicots are. **22.5.3** ***Describe*** the three different life spans of angiosperms.	**1 period (1/2 block)**	**TE:** ***Build Science Skills,*** p. 569 **SE:** ***Careers in Biology,*** Botanical Illustrator, p. 571 **TE:** ***Meet Diverse Needs,*** p. 572 **SE:** ***Exploration,*** Comparing Mosses and Ferns, p. 573
Chapter Assessment, pp. 574–577	**1 period (1/2 block)**	

ACTIVITY PLANNER

SE: ***Inquiry Activity,*** p. 550; (15 min.); hand lens, specimens of mosses, mature ferns with sori, flowering plants with flowers

TE: ***Build Science Skills,*** p. 552; (15 min.); potting soil, small pot, seeds

TE: ***Make Connections,*** p. 554; (15 min.); fossil specimens of mosses and ferns

TE: ***Build Science Skills,*** p. 556; (15 min.); samples of bryophytes

TE: ***Demonstration,*** p. 558; (15 min.); moss plant

TE: ***Build Science Skills,*** p. 559; (20 min.); peat moss, soil, beakers

TE: ***Build Science Skills,*** p. 561; (15 min.); fern frond, metric ruler, scissors, microscope slides, microscope

TE: ***Build Science Skills,*** p. 562; (20 min.); 2-L soda bottle, scissors, peat moss, fern spores

SE: ***Quick Lab,*** p. 565; (20 min.); fern frond with sori, microscope, scalpel, slide, coverslip, dropper pipette, peanuts, paper bag, hand lens

TE: ***Build Science Skills,*** p. 569; (15 min.); ripe apple, knife or scalpel

TE: ***Meet Diverse Needs,*** p. 572; (10 min.); packet of flower seeds

SE: ***Exploration,*** p. 573; (45 min.); fern plant, moss plants, hand lens, forceps, slide, dropper pipette, coverslip, microscope

PLANNING KEY

Ability Levels

(B) **Basic**	For students who need additional help
(A) **Average**	For all students
(E) **Enriched**	For students who need to be challenged

Components

SE	Student Edition	**GRSW**	Guided Reading and Study Workbook	**IDM**	Issues and Decision Making
TE	Teacher's Edition	**CT**	Chapter Tests: Levels A and B	**CTB**	Computer Test Bank
LMA	Laboratory Manual A	**PHAS**	PH Assessment System	**PA**	Presentation Assistant Plus
LMB	Laboratory Manual B	**LA**	Lab Assessment with Scoring Guide	**BD**	BioDetectives Videotape
TR	Teaching Resources	**BTM**	BioTechnology Manual	**iT**	iText

Program Resources	*Assessment*	*Media and Technology*
TR: Section Review 22–1 (B) (A) **GRSW:** Section 22–1 (B) (A)	**SE:** 22–1 Section Assessment, p. 555 **TR:** Section Review 22–1	**PA:** 22–1 Interest Grabber, Section Outline, Generalized Plant Life Cycle, Figure 22–2, Figure 22–6, Figure 22–7 **iT:** Section 22–1
LMA: Chapter 22 Lab (A) (E) **LMB:** Chapter 22 Lab (B) (A) **TR:** Section Review 22–2 (B) (A) **GRSW:** Section 22–2 (B) (A)	**SE:** 22–2 Section Assessment, p. 559 **TR:** Section Review 22–2	**PA:** 22–2 Interest Grabber, Section Outline, Compare/Contrast Table, Figure 22–11 **iT:** Section 22–2
TR: Section Review 22–3 (B) (A) **GRSW:** Section 22–3 (B) (A)	**SE:** 22–3 Section Assessment, p. 563 **TR:** Section Review 22–3	**PA:** 22–3 Interest Grabber, Section Outline, Compare/Contrast Table, Figure 22–17 **iT:** Section 22–3
TR: Section Review 22–4 (B) (A) **GRSW:** Section 22–4 (B) (A)	**SE:** 22–4 Section Assessment, p. 568 **TR:** Section Review 22–4	**PA:** 22–4 Interest Grabber, Section Outline, Features of Seed Plants, Figure 22–19 **iT:** Section 22–4
TR: Section Review 22–5 (B) (A) Chapter 22 Exploration (B) (A) (E) **GRSW:** Section 22–5 (B) (A) **IDM:** 22–1 (A) (E)	**SE:** 22–5 Section Assessment, p. 572 **TR:** Section Review 22–5	**PA:** 22–5 Interest Grabber, Section Outline, Concept Map, Figure 22–25 **iT:** Section 22–5
	SE: Chapter 22 Assessment, pp. 574–577 **TR:** Chapter Vocabulary Review, Graphic Organizer **CB:** Chapter 22 Test **CTB:** Chapter 22 Test **PHAS:** Practice Test	**CTB:** Chapter 22 Test **iT:** Chapter 22 Assessment

PRESSED FOR TIME?

To Preview the Chapter
- Introduce students to Key Concepts and Vocabulary terms in each section.
- Assign the Reading Strategies for each section.

To Cover the Chapter Quickly
- Have students read all of Section 22–1; Life Cycle of Bryophytes in Section 22–2; Evolution of Vascular Tissue and Life Cycle of Ferns in Section 22–3; Reproduction Free From Water in Section 22–4; and Flowers and Fruits in Section 22–5.
- Assign the 22–1 Section Review, questions 1–10 in Chapter 22 Assessment, and Chapter 22 Standardized Test Prep.

To Review the Chapter
- Assign Sections 22–1 through 22–5 in the Guided Reading and Study Workbook.
- Assign Section Reviews for 22–1 through 22–5 and the Chapter Vocabulary Review for Chapter 22 in the Teaching Resources.

ENGAGE/EXPLORE

Inquiry Activity

Objective Students will be able to compare and contrast the structures of three different plants.

Skill Focus **Comparing and Contrasting**

Materials hand lens, plants such as mosses, mature ferns with sori, and flowering plants with flowers

Time 15 minutes

Advance Prep Obtain moss plants in damp, shady areas or through a biological supply house. Obtain mature ferns and potted plants from a garden store or florist.

Strategy You could divide the class into small groups and provide each group with a set of specimens.

Expected Outcomes Students will observe that there are similarities among the plants, but differences as well.

Think About It

1. Answers will vary, depending on the plants. All the plants will contain chlorophyll. The plants will differ in the structure of their leaves, stems, and roots (or the analogous structures in bryophytes and ferns) and of their reproductive structures.
2. Students should be able to infer the functions of roots, stems, leaves, and reproductive structures.
3. Accept all reasonable answers. Students should be able to justify their classifications based on specific aspects of plant structure that they observed.

Assess Prior Knowledge

Have students brainstorm a list of plants that are common to their area. Then ask them whether they know any logical way to classify the plants they have named into a few large groups, or phyla. Typically, students will divide plants into "evergreens" and leafy plants. Some students might also place mosses and ferns in separate phyla.

Chapter 22 Plant Diversity

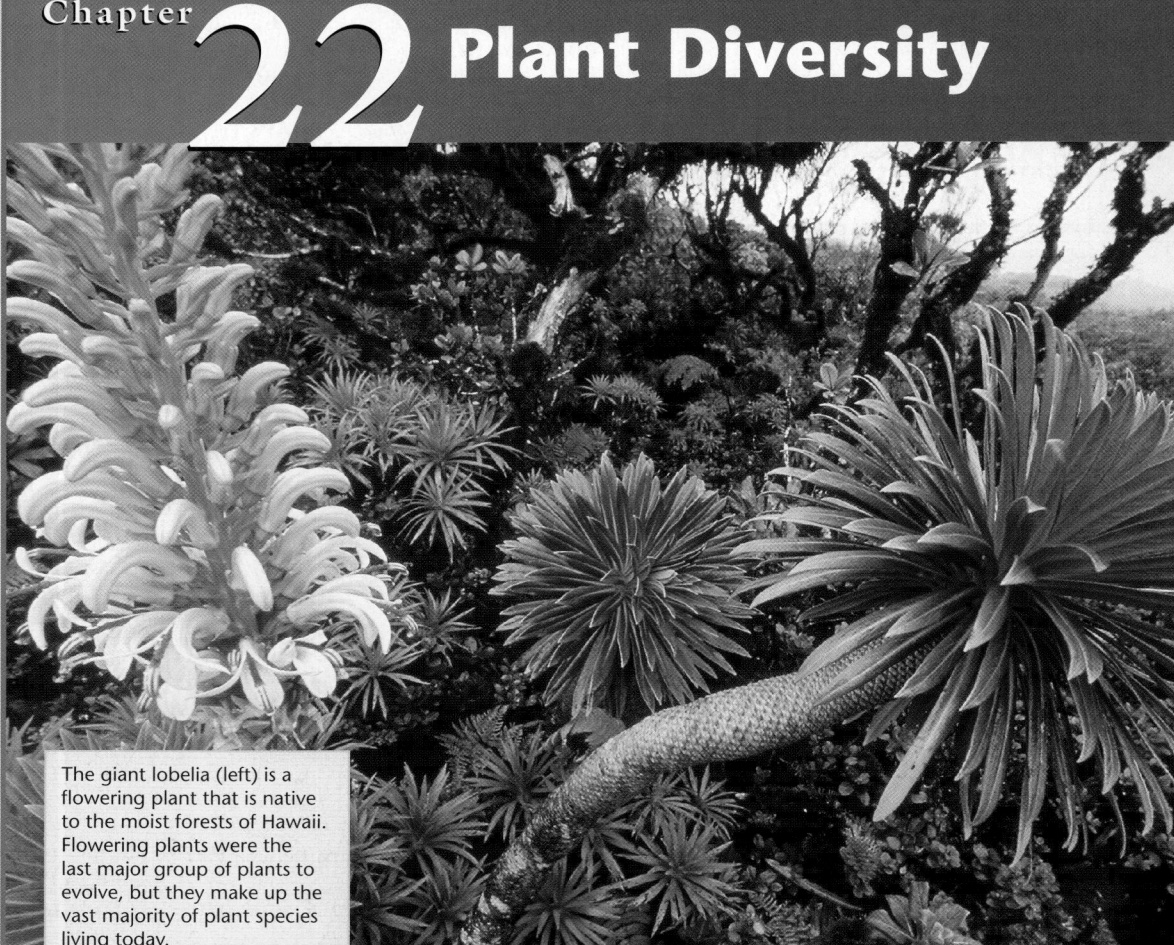

The giant lobelia (left) is a flowering plant that is native to the moist forests of Hawaii. Flowering plants were the last major group of plants to evolve, but they make up the vast majority of plant species living today.

Inquiry Activity

Are all plants the same?

Procedure

1. Obtain three plants, a metric ruler, and a hand lens.
2. Construct a table for recording your data.
3. Identify the major parts of each plant. Measure the heights of the plants and the sizes of their parts.
4. Use the hand lens to examine the plants. Record any other observations you make.

Think About It

1. **Comparing and Contrasting** How are the three plants alike? How do they differ?
2. **Inferring** What are the functions of the major parts of each plant?
3. **Classifying** Use your observations to classify the three plants into two groups. Explain your reasons for classifying them in these groups.

FACTS AND FIGURES

The success of flowering plants

Angiosperms, such as the plants in the photograph of flowering plants in Hawaii, have enjoyed remarkable success. The pea family (Leguminosae) alone has around 14,000 living species. This single family of angiosperms outnumbers all the surviving ferns, which number only about 9000 species. That is adaptive radiation in a big way!

22–1 Introduction to Plants

What color is life? That's a silly question, of course, because living things can be just about any color. But consider it in a different way. Imagine yourself in a place on Earth where the sounds and scents of life are all around you. The place is so abundant with life that when you stand on the ground, living things blot out the sun. Now, what color do you see? If you have imagined a thick forest or a teeming jungle, then one color will fill the landscape of your mind—green—the color of plants.

Plants dominate the landscape. Where plants are plentiful, other organisms, such as animals, fungi, and microorganisms, take hold and thrive. Plants provide the base for food chains on land. They also provide shade, shelter, and oxygen for animals of every size and kind. The oldest fossil evidence of plants dates from about 470 million years ago. Since then, plants have colonized and transformed nearly every corner of Earth.

What Is a Plant?

Plants are members of the kingdom Plantae.  **Plants are multicellular eukaryotes that have cell walls made of cellulose. They develop from multicellular embryos and carry out photosynthesis using the green pigments chlorophyll *a* and *b*.** Plants include trees, shrubs, and grasses as well as other organisms such as mosses and ferns. Most plants, including the one in **Figure 22–1,** are autotrophs, although a few are parasites or saprobes that live on decaying materials.

Plants are so different from animals that sometimes there is a tendency to think of them as not being alive. With few exceptions, plants do not gather food, nor do they move about or struggle directly with their predators. Plants can neither run away from danger nor strike blows against an adversary. But as different as they are from animals, plants are everywhere. How have they managed to be so successful?

That question has many answers. In the next few chapters, we will explore some of them. For now, it might help to think of plants as a well-known botanist once described them—as "stationary animals that eat sunlight"!

Guide for Reading

Key Concepts
- What is a plant?
- What do plants need to survive?
- How did the first plants evolve?

Vocabulary
gametophyte
sporophyte

Reading Strategy: Using Prior Knowledge
Before you read the chapter, make a list of the different groups of plants that you know. As you read, revise your list to include new information about plant groups.

▶ **Figure 22–1** **All plants are multicellular eukaryotes that have cell walls made of cellulose.** Their leaves appear green because of the photosynthetic pigments chlorophyll *a* and *b*, which are located in chloroplasts.

SECTION RESOURCES

Print:
- ***Teaching Resources,*** Section Review 22–1
- ***Guided Reading and Study Workbook,*** Section 22–1

Technology:
- ***iText,*** Section 22–1

Section 22–1

1 FOCUS

Objectives

22.1.1 ***Explain*** what a plant is.
22.1.2 ***Describe*** what plants need to survive.
22.1.3 ***Describe*** how the first plants evolved.

Guide for Reading

Vocabulary Preview

Explain to students that the suffix *-phyte* means "plant." Thus, *gametophyte* means "gamete plant," and *sporophyte* means "spore plant."

Reading Strategy

Before students read, ask them to skim the section to find the three boldfaced Key Concepts. Have them copy each onto a note card. Then, as they read, they should make notes of supporting details.

2 INSTRUCT

What Is a Plant?

Build Science Skills

Observing Take students on a guided tour of the exterior of your school building. Look for the many places that terrestrial plants can grow. You might begin by looking in some of the obvious locations first, such as the lawn or garden of the school. Then, look in some of the less obvious places—in pavement cracks, on the shady sides of the building or walls, on rocks, on trees, or near a source of standing water. Examine each plant and have the students note the following:
- Does it have leaves?
- Does it have veins?
- Where was the plant growing?
- What is the approximate size of the plant?
- Is the plant mosslike or does it have a green or woody stem?

22–1 (continued)

The Plant Life Cycle

Use Visuals

Figure 22–2 Ask students: **Which generation of a plant is diploid and which is haploid?** *(The sporophyte generation is diploid, and the gametophyte generation is haploid.)* **Which generation produces gametes?** *(The gametophyte)* **What does the sporophyte produce?** *(Spores)*

What Plants Need to Survive

Build Science Skills

Applying Concepts Perhaps the best way to help students understand what plants need to survive is to allow them to grow their own seedlings. This is a simple activity that every child has probably done in school at one time or another. You may be surprised at the excitement that it will generate among older students. Provide potting soil, small containers, and seeds. Any seeds will do, but those that germinate quickly are more fun—small flowers, beans, corn, and so on. Put these in a warm, light area and allow students brief opportunities to observe and care for them every day. You can make this as basic or elaborate as you wish. The seedlings can be used in subsequent chapters to study plant structure, although some students may want to take them home.

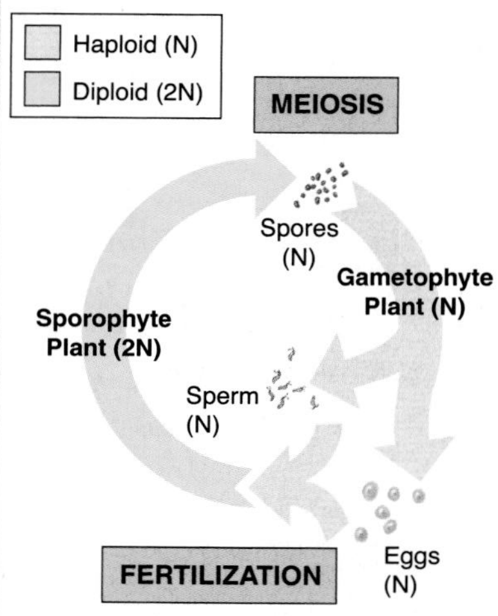

▲ **Figure 22–2** All plants have a life cycle with alternation of generations, in which the haploid gametophyte phase alternates with the diploid sporophyte phase. **Interpreting Graphics** *What stage in the life cycle is produced by fertilization?*

The Plant Life Cycle

Plants have life cycles that are characterized by alternation of generations, as shown in **Figure 22–2.** As you learned in Chapter 20, the two generations are the haploid (N) **gametophyte,** or gamete-producing plant, and the diploid (2N) **sporophyte,** or spore-producing plant. Recall that gametes—eggs and sperm—are haploid cells that fuse together to produce a new diploid individual. Spores are reproductive cells that produce a new individual by mitosis. Although all plants have a gametophyte stage and a sporophyte stage, their forms differ dramatically from phylum to phylum.

To be fully terrestrial, plants must be able to reproduce in dry environments where there is no water through which gametes can move from plant to plant. Seed plants have evolved reproductive cycles that are carried out independently of water. Many plants also have forms of vegetative, or asexual, reproduction.

What Plants Need to Survive

Surviving as stationary organisms on land is a difficult task, and plants have developed a number of adaptations that make them successful. **The lives of plants revolve around the need for sunlight, water and minerals, gas exchange, and the movement of water and nutrients throughout the plant body.**

Sunlight Plants use the energy from sunlight to carry out photosynthesis. As a result, every plant displays adaptations shaped by the need to gather sunlight. Photosynthetic organs such as leaves are typically broad and flat and are arranged on the stem so as to maximize light absorption.

Water and Minerals All cells require a constant supply of water. For this reason, plants must obtain and deliver water to all their cells—even those that grow above ground in the dry air. Water is one of the raw materials of photosynthesis, so it is used up quickly when the sun is shining. Sunny conditions, such as those in the desert shown in **Figure 22–3,** can cause living tissues to dry out. Thus, plants have developed structures that limit water loss.

As they absorb water, plants also absorb minerals. Minerals are nutrients in the soil that are needed for plant growth.

Gas Exchange Plants require oxygen to support respiration as well as carbon dioxide to carry out photosynthesis. They must exchange these gases with the atmosphere without losing excessive amounts of water through evaporation.

Movement of Water and Nutrients Plants take up water and minerals through their roots but make food in their leaves. Most plants have specialized tissues that carry water and nutrients upward from the soil and distribute the products of photosynthesis throughout the plant body. Simpler types of plants carry out these functions by diffusion.

▼ **Figure 22–3** **All plants need sunlight, water, minerals, oxygen, carbon dioxide, and a way to move water and nutrients to all their cells.** Adaptations allow them to live in even the driest locations, such as this desert.

PRESENTATIONS MADE EASY!

The Presentation Assistant Plus contains the Prentice Hall Presentation Pro and the Transparencies, which provide easy-to-follow visual support for every step of this lesson. If you have a computer presentation station, use Prentice Hall Presentation Pro Section 22–2, or use the transparencies listed here.

Section 22–2:

Interest Grabber
Section Outline
Generalized Plant Life Cycle
Figure 22–2
Figure 22–6
Figure 22–7

Problem Solving

"Plantastic" Voyage

You are part of a team that is planning a space mission that will send astronauts into space for two years. As part of their food, the astronauts will be growing yam plants, *Dioscorea composita*. Your job is to develop a plan to help plants grow on the spacecraft.

Defining the Problem In your own words, state the problem at hand.

Organizing Information Research the types of conditions these plants would need. What requirements would the plants have for moisture? Soil conditions? Light intensity? Day length?

Creating a Solution Make a detailed scale drawing of a container for growing 10 of these plants. (*Dioscorea* plants are vines; assume that each is 10 cm long and 0.5 cm wide.) Determine what material(s) you will use for your container. As you devise your plan, be sure to keep a journal in which you record your team's ideas, drawings, data, and other information.

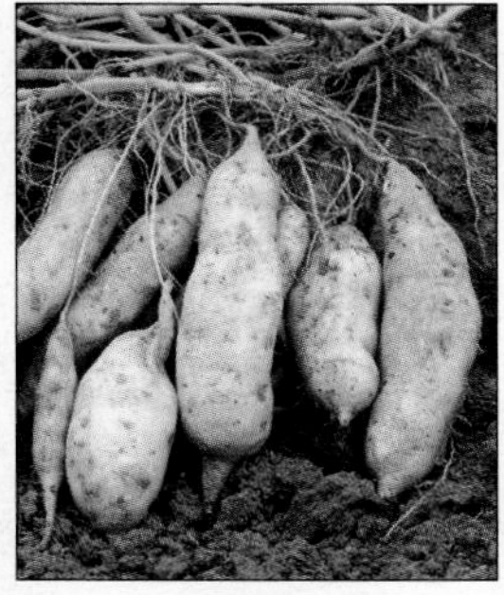

Presenting Your Plan Prepare a multimedia presentation for your classmates as if they were the managers of the space mission. Describe how your team solved the problem, the sources of information you used, the design itself, and what you learned during the project.

Early Plants

For most of Earth's history, plants did not exist. Life was concentrated in oceans, lakes, and streams. Algae and photosynthetic prokaryotes added the oxygen to our planet's atmosphere and provided food for animals and microorganisms.

When plants appeared, much of the existing life on Earth changed. As these new photosynthetic organisms colonized the land, they changed the environment in ways that made it possible for other organisms to develop. New ecosystems emerged, and organic matter began to form soil. How did plants adapt to the conditions of life on land? How plants evolved structures that acquire, transport, and conserve water is the key to answering this question.

Origins in the Water You may recall from Chapter 20 that green algae, shown in **Figure 22–4**, are photosynthetic, plantlike protists. Many of these algae are multicellular. **The first plants evolved from an organism much like the multicellular green algae living today.** Multicellular green algae have the size, color, and appearance of plants. But the resemblance of many green algae to plants is more than superficial. They have reproductive cycles that are similar to those of plants. In addition, green algae have cell walls and photosynthetic pigments that are identical to those of plants.

CHECKPOINT What was the greatest "challenge" to plants as they began to live on land?

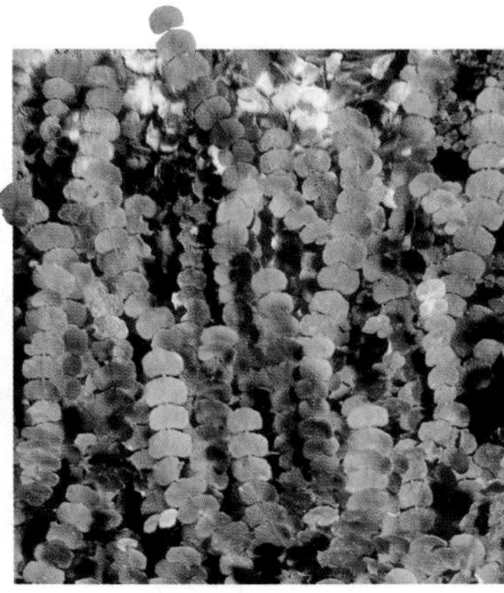

▲ **Figure 22–4 The first plants evolved from an organism much like the modern multicellular green algae.** The alga *Halimeda* is found in Honduras in Central America. It has many cellular features in common with plants.

Problem Solving

A yam is a plant, similar to a sweet potato, in which the branch roots swell and provide storage for large quantities of carbohydrates. The yam plant is thought to have originated in or near India, and these food-storage roots are a staple in some tropical regions of the world.

Defining the Problem The problem is to grow yams successfully under artificial conditions aboard a spacecraft.

Organizing Information To determine the optimal conditions a yam plant needs, students might use the reference section of their public library or contact an expert, either at a garden store or the botany department of a local university.

Creating a Solution Teams should make detailed drawings of the proposed container. For 10 plants, the bottom of this container needs to be at least 50 square centimeters. Students might suggest using a container with a solid bottom with tops and sides that have openings, so that gas exchange is adequate.

Presenting Your Plan Budget class time for each team to make its multimedia presentation. All plans should take into account what plants need to survive, including light, water, gas exchange, and nutrients.

Early Plants

Use Visuals

Figure 22–4 As students study the algae in the photograph, ask: **How are green algae like plants?** *(Green algae have the size, color, and appearance of plants, a similar reproductive cycle, and cell walls and photosynthetic pigments identical to those of plants.)*

FACTS AND FIGURES

Arriving on land first

When students think of life first emerging from the sea, they invariably envision an amphibian-like creature skulking around the shore. In truth, much smaller animals—such as insects—were the first to colonize dry land. But plants arrived on land before any animal species. Without plants, land animals would have had nothing to eat. Some biologists believe that plants did not make the transition to land by themselves. Their theory is that plants coevolved with fungi, developing the very first mycorrhizae. The term mycorrhiza (plural: mycorrhizae) refers to the symbiotic relationship between certain fungi and the root cells of some vascular plants, such as orchids. This plant–fungi partnership allowed necessary minerals to be extracted from sterile, inorganic soils.

Answers to . . .

CHECKPOINT *Acquiring, transporting, and conserving water*

Figure 22–2 *Sporophyte or spore-producing plant*

22–1 (continued)

Make Connections

Earth Science Display specimens, pictures, or slides of early plant fossils, including mosses and ferns. Review with students the process by which fossils form. For example, these are the steps that occur in the formation of a mold fossil: (1) a plant is buried in sediment; (2) the sediment hardens into rock; (3) the organic material of the plant decays, leaving an empty space in the rock. After reviewing fossil formation, discuss how geologists and paleontologists determine the age of fossils. Explain relative age to students, including the law of superposition. Also explain the basics of radioactive dating, in which the decay of radioactive elements is used to date certain rock formations.

Use Visuals

Figure 22–6 After students have studied the cladogram, ask: **What are the four main groups of plants?** *(Mosses and their relatives, ferns and their relatives, cone-bearing plants (gymnosperms), and flowering plants (angiosperms))* **What do mosses and their relatives lack that all other plants have?** *(Vascular tissue)* **Which groups of plants don't have seeds?** *(Mosses and their relatives and ferns and their relatives)*

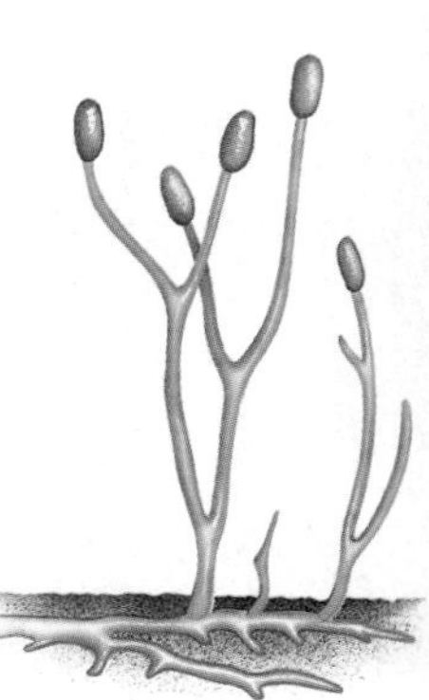

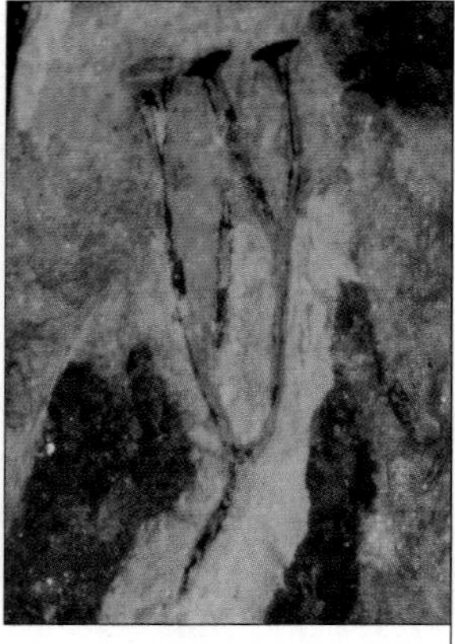

▲ **Figure 22–5** One of the earliest fossil plants was *Cooksonia,* which looked similar to mosses living today. *Cooksonia* had simple branched stalks that bore reproductive structures at their tips. **Inferring** ***Which structures of this early plant seem to be adapted to carry out photosynthesis? To obtain water and minerals?***

The First Plants The first true plants were still dependent on water to complete their life cycles. But before long, the demands of life on land favored the evolution of plants that were more resistant to the drying rays of the sun, more capable of conserving water, and more capable of reproducing on dry land. Early plants were similar to today's mosses in that they were simple in structure and grew close to the ground. **Figure 22–5** shows how these plants may have looked. Soon these early plants were common in damp and swampy regions, just as most mosses are today.

From these plant pioneers, several major groups of plants evolved. One group developed into mosses and their relatives. Another lineage gave rise to all the other plants on Earth today—ferns, cone-bearing plants, and flowering plants. All of these groups of plants are now successful in living on dry land, but they have evolved very different adaptations for a wide range of terrestrial environments.

CHECKPOINT *To what group of living plants were early plants most similar?*

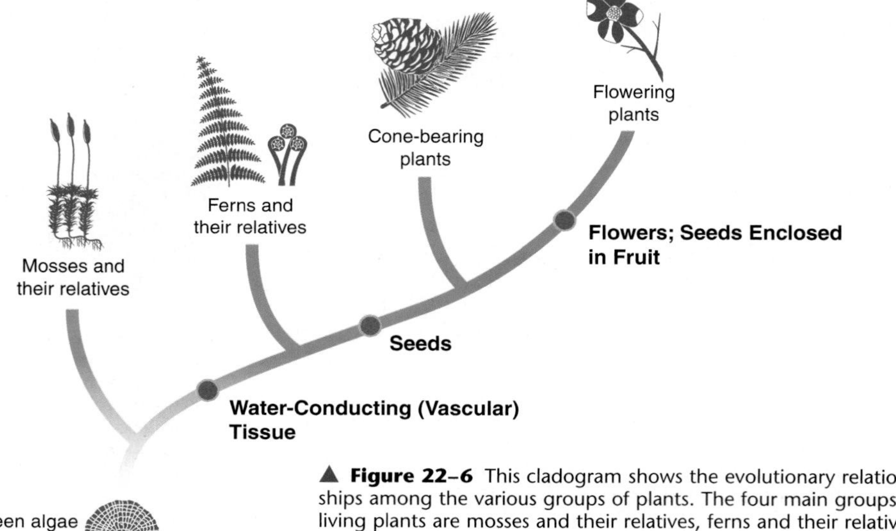

▲ **Figure 22–6** This cladogram shows the evolutionary relationships among the various groups of plants. The four main groups of living plants are mosses and their relatives, ferns and their relatives, cone-bearing plants, and flowering plants. **Interpreting Graphics** ***Which two groups of plants contain seeds?***

FACTS AND FIGURES

Living large on land

The development of vascular tissue was essential for plants to live on land. But the real keys to plant success on land were those involving reproduction. Three simultaneous developments in the reproductive habits of the seed plants, in particular, enabled them to live on dry land: the reduction of the gametophyte generation, the evolution of pollination, and the evolution of the seed. As the gametophyte shrank into little more than a parasite of the sporophyte, that stage of the life cycle was protected from the vicissitudes of the environment. Similarly, pollination made it possible for different plants to exchange genetic material in a truly terrestrial environment. Finally, the tidy drought-resistant package called the seed protected the fragile embryo during inclement weather and provided food for early growth.

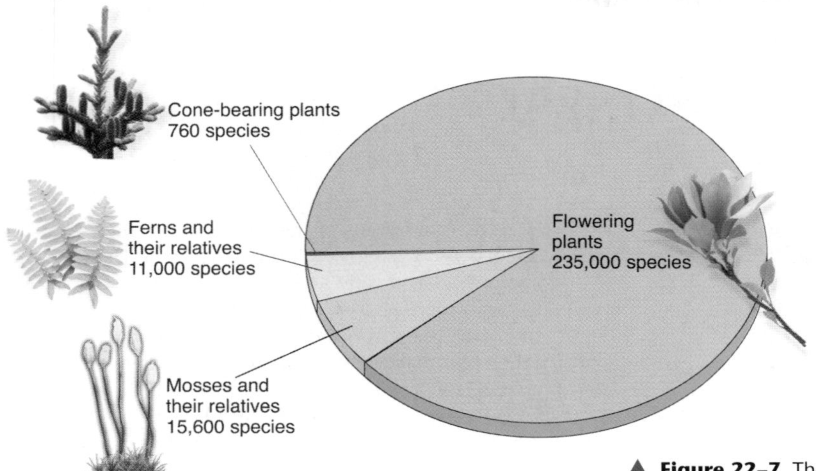

▲ **Figure 22–7** The great majority of plants alive today are angiosperms, which are also known as flowering plants. **Interpreting Graphics** *What is the second largest group of plants?*

Overview of the Plant Kingdom

Botanists divide the plant kingdom into four groups based on three important features: water-conducting tissues, seeds, and flowers. The relationship of these groups is shown in **Figure 22–6.** There are, of course, many other features by which plants are classified, including reproductive structures and body plan.

Today, plant scientists can classify plants more precisely by comparing the DNA sequences of various species. Since 1994, a team of biologists from twelve nations has begun to change our view of plant relationships. Their project, known as Deep Green, has provided strong evidence that the first plants evolved from green algae that lived in fresh water, not in the sea as had been thought.

In the rest of this chapter, we will explore how important plant traits evolved over the course of millions of years. In particular, we will examine the success of the flowering plants. As shown in **Figure 22–7,** flowering plants consist of 235,000 species—almost 90 percent of all living species of plants.

KEEP CURRENT WITH . . . SCIENCE NEWS®

To find out more about the topics in this chapter, go to: **www.phschool.com**

22–1 Section Assessment

1. **Key Concept** What features distinguish plants from other organisms?
2. **Key Concept** To live successfully on land, what substances must plants obtain from their environment?
3. **Key Concept** From which group of protists did the first plants evolve? How are plants similar to these protists?
4. **Critical Thinking Comparing and Contrasting** Compare the gametophyte and sporophyte stages of the plant life cycle. Which is haploid? Which is diploid?

iTEXT Assessment Use iText to review the important concepts in Section 22–1.

MAKING CONNECTIONS

Cell Structure How do the cells of plants differ from those of animals? How are they different from those of fungi? Refer to Chapters 7 and 21 for help in answering this question.

22–1 Section Assessment

1. Plants are multicellular eukaryotes that have cell walls made of cellulose. They develop from multicellular embryos and carry out photosynthesis using the green pigments chlorophyll *a* and *b*.
2. Students should describe how plants meet the basic needs of sunlight, water, gas exchange, and the movement of water and nutrients throughout the plant body.
3. Land plants evolved from an organism much like multicellular green algae. Multicellular green algae have the size, color, and appearance of plants, similar reproductive cycles, and identical cell walls and photosynthetic pigments.
4. The haploid gametophyte produces eggs and sperm that fuse together to form a new individual—a haploid sporophyte. The sporophyte produces spores by meiosis that develop into the gametophyte.

Overview of the Plant Kingdom

Use Visuals

Figure 22–7 Ask: **What are the three most important features of plants that botanists use to classify them into four groups?** *(Water-conducting tissue, seeds, and flowers)* **From what kind of organism did all plants evolve?** *(Freshwater green algae)*

SCIENCE NEWS®

Encourage students to visit **www.phschool.com** for the most current information on this topic.

3 ASSESS

Evaluate Understanding

Call on students at random to list the main groups of the plant kingdom, explain which plant characteristics were important in the evolution of the different groups, and describe the generalized plant life cycle.

Reteach

Have students list the characteristics that define a living thing as a plant. Then, review the characteristics that divide plants into major groups.

MAKING CONNECTIONS

Plant cells contain cell walls made of cellulose, large vacuoles, and chloroplasts. Animal cells do not have cell walls or chloroplasts. The cells of fungi have no chloroplasts and have cell walls made of chitin rather than cellulose.

Use iText to review the key concepts in Section 22–1.

Answers to . . .

 *Mosses*

Figure 22–5 *The green, stemlike structures; the rootlike structures*

Figure 22–6 *Cone-bearing plants and flowering plants*

Figure 22–7 *Mosses and their relatives*

Section 22–2

1 FOCUS

Objectives

22.2.1 ***Describe*** the adaptations of bryophytes.
22.2.2 ***Identify*** the three groups of bryophytes.
22.2.3 ***Explain*** how bryophytes reproduce.

Guide for Reading

Vocabulary Preview

Call on students at random to pronounce the Vocabulary words in the order they appear. Correct any mispronunciations.

Reading Strategy

Ask students to write a paragraph that explains the life cycle of a moss, using the information in Figure 22–11. After they have read the section, have them revise their paragraphs.

2 INSTRUCT

Groups of Bryophytes

Build Science Skills

Observing Display samples of bryophytes—including mosses, liverworts, and hornworts—for students to examine. If you are unable to find samples locally, living or preserved specimens can be ordered from a biological supply house. Ask students to observe and record the color, size, and appearance of the bryophytes.

22–2 Bryophytes

Guide for Reading

Key Concepts
- What adaptations of bryophytes enable them to live on land?
- What are the three groups of bryophytes?
- How do bryophytes reproduce?

Vocabulary
bryophyte
rhizoid
gemma
protonema
antheridium
archegonium

Reading Strategy: Using Visuals
Before you read, preview **Figure 22–11,** which shows the life cycle of a moss. In your own words, describe the basic process of reproduction shown. As you read the section, add information that you learn about reproduction in bryophytes.

In the cool forests of the northern woods, the moist ground is carpeted with green. When you walk, this soft carpet feels spongy. Look closely and you will see the structure of this carpet—mosses. Mosses and their relatives are generally called **bryophytes** (BRY-oh-fyts), or nonvascular plants. Unlike all other plants, these organisms do not have vascular tissues, or specialized tissues that conduct water and nutrients. **Bryophytes have life cycles that depend on water for reproduction. Lacking vascular tissue, these plants can draw up water by osmosis only a few centimeters above the ground.** This arrangement keeps them relatively small.

During at least one stage of their life cycle, bryophytes produce sperm that must swim through water to reach the eggs of other individuals. Therefore, they must live in places where there is rainfall or dew for at least part of the year.

Groups of Bryophytes

The most recognizable feature of bryophytes is that they are low-growing plants that can be found in moist, shaded areas. Where water is in regular supply—in habitats from the polar regions to the tropics—these plants thrive. **Bryophytes include mosses, liverworts, and hornworts.** Today, most botanists classify these groups of plants in three separate phyla.

Mosses The most common bryophytes are mosses, which are members of the phylum Bryophyta (bry-OH-fy-tuh). Mosses grow most abundantly in areas with water—in swamps and bogs, near streams, and in rain forests. Bryophytes are well adapted to life in wet habitats and nutrient-poor soils. Many mosses can tolerate low temperatures, allowing them to grow in harsh environments where other plants cannot. In fact, mosses are the most abundant plants in the polar regions.

Mosses vary in appearance from miniature evergreen trees to small, filamentous plants that together form a threadlike carpet of green, as shown in **Figure 22–8.** The moss plants that you might have observed on a walk through the woods are actually clumps of gametophytes growing close together. When mosses reproduce, they produce thin stalks, each containing a capsule. This is the sporophyte stage, as shown in **Figure 22–9.** Each moss plant has a thin, upright shoot that looks like a stem with tiny leaves. These are not true stems or leaves, however, because they do not contain vascular tissue.

◀ **Figure 22–8** Mosses grow best in moist environments, such as on the rocks by this waterfall. **Like all bryophytes, mosses have life cycles that depend on water for reproduction.**

SECTION RESOURCES

Print:
- ***Laboratory Manual A,*** Chapter 22 Lab
- ***Laboratory Manual B,*** Chapter 22 Lab
- ***Teaching Resources,*** Section Review 22–2
- ***Guided Reading and Study Workbook,*** Section 22–2

Technology:
- ***iText,*** Section 22–2

Because the "leaves" of mosses are only one cell thick, these plants lose water quickly if the surrounding air is dry. The lack of vascular tissues also means that mosses do not have true roots. Instead, they have **rhizoids,** which are long, thin cells that anchor them in the ground and absorb water and minerals from the surrounding soil. Water moves from cell to cell through the rhizoids and into the rest of the plant.

Liverworts If you have come across odd little plants that look almost like flat leaves attached to the ground, you have probably seen a liverwort, shown in **Figure 22–10.** These plants belong to the phylum Hepaticophyta (hih-pat-ik-OH-fy-tuh) and get their name from the fact that some species resemble the shape of a liver. Liverworts in their gametophyte stage are broad and thin structures that draw up moisture directly from the surface of the soil. When the plants mature, the gametophytes produce structures that look like tiny green umbrellas. These "umbrellas" carry the structures that produce eggs and sperm.

Liverworts can also reproduce asexually by means of gemmae. **Gemmae** (JEM-ee; singular: gemma) are small multicellular spheres that contain many haploid cells. In some species of liverworts, gemmae are produced in cuplike structures called gemma cups. When washed out of the gemma, these cells can divide by mitosis to produce a new individual.

Hornworts Hornworts are members of the phylum Anthocerophyta (an-thoh-sehr-UH-fy-tuh). Like the liverworts, hornworts are generally found only in soil that is damp nearly year-round. Their gametophytes look very much like those of liverworts. The hornwort sporophyte, however, looks like a tiny green horn.

CHECKPOINT *How do bryophytes reproduce asexually?*

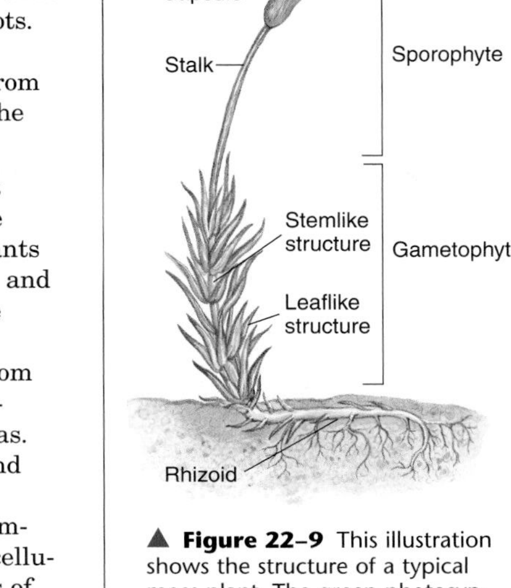

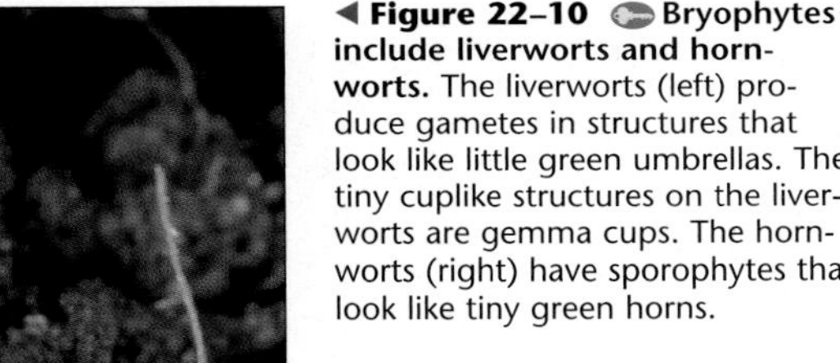

▲ **Figure 22–9** This illustration shows the structure of a typical moss plant. The green photosynthetic portion is the gametophyte. The brown structure on the tip of the gametophyte is the sporophyte. **Applying Concepts** ***Which stage of the moss plant provides nutrients for the other stage?***

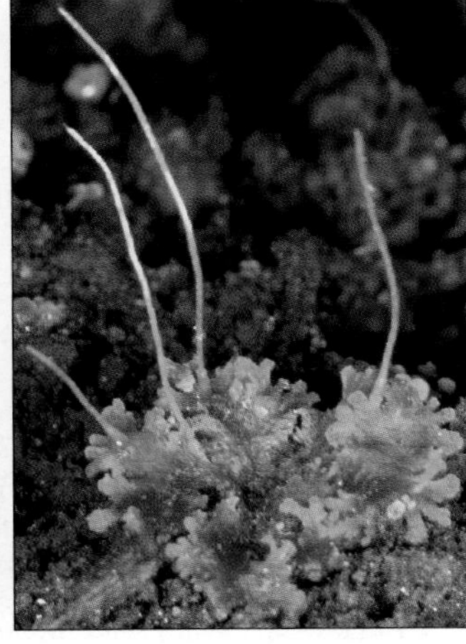

◀ **Figure 22–10** **Bryophytes include liverworts and hornworts.** The liverworts (left) produce gametes in structures that look like little green umbrellas. The tiny cuplike structures on the liverworts are gemma cups. The hornworts (right) have sporophytes that look like tiny green horns.

Meet Diverse Needs

For students with limited English proficiency, explain that the common English names of many plants end in the suffix *–wort.* Examples are liverwort, hornwort, milkwort, and spiderwort. The ending *–wort* means "plant." It can be traced to Old English, the ancestor of our modern language. More than 800 years ago our predecessors referred to plants, particularly herbs, as *wyrt,* and the name is only slightly altered today. **Limited English proficiency**

Use Visuals

Figure 22–10 As students study the photos of liverworts and hornworts, discuss the characteristics of each and ask if any students can remember seeing these plants in the area. Then, ask students who need an extra challenge to investigate hornworts and liverworts and make a presentation to the class. Help them find visual aids that would enhance their presentation, such as pictures or slides that could be used in a microprojector. Ask that as part of their investigation, they find out where in the local area students can observe these bryophytes, such as in a park or woodland.

PRESENTATIONS MADE EASY!

The Presentation Assistant Plus contains the Prentice Hall Presentation Pro and the Transparencies, which provide easy-to-follow visual support for every step of this lesson. If you have a computer presentation station, use Prentice Hall Presentation Pro Section 22–2, or use the transparencies listed here.

Section 22–2: **Interest Grabber**
Section Outline
Compare/Contrast Table
Figure 22–11

Answers to . . .

CHECKPOINT *Liverworts, for example, reproduce asexually by producing gemmae or gemma cups made up of haploid cells. These cells can divide by mitosis to produce a new individual.*

Figure 22–9 *The gametophyte*

22–2 (continued)

Life Cycle of Bryophytes

Use Visuals

Figure 22–11 Have students examine the life cycle and read the caption. Then, ask: **Which generation of moss is the form of the plant with which you are most familiar?** *(Gametophyte)* **Is the gametophyte haploid or diploid?** *(Haploid)* **Where does the sporophyte develop?** *(It develops within the gametophyte.)* **Is the sporophyte haploid or diploid?** *(Diploid)* **What does the sporophyte produce?** *(Spores)* **When a spore germinates, what does it produce?** *(Protonema)*

Demonstration

Take students outside the school building, and take along a moss plant that includes a mature sporophyte. As students observe, compress the capsule—the sporangium—of the sporophyte between your fingers, which will release the spores contained within. Ask students: **In what sort of environment do you suppose these spores must land for them to germinate?** *(They must land in a moist environment.)* **If one of these spores does germinate, what will it first grow into?** *(A protonema)* **What will the protonema become?** *(A gametophyte)*

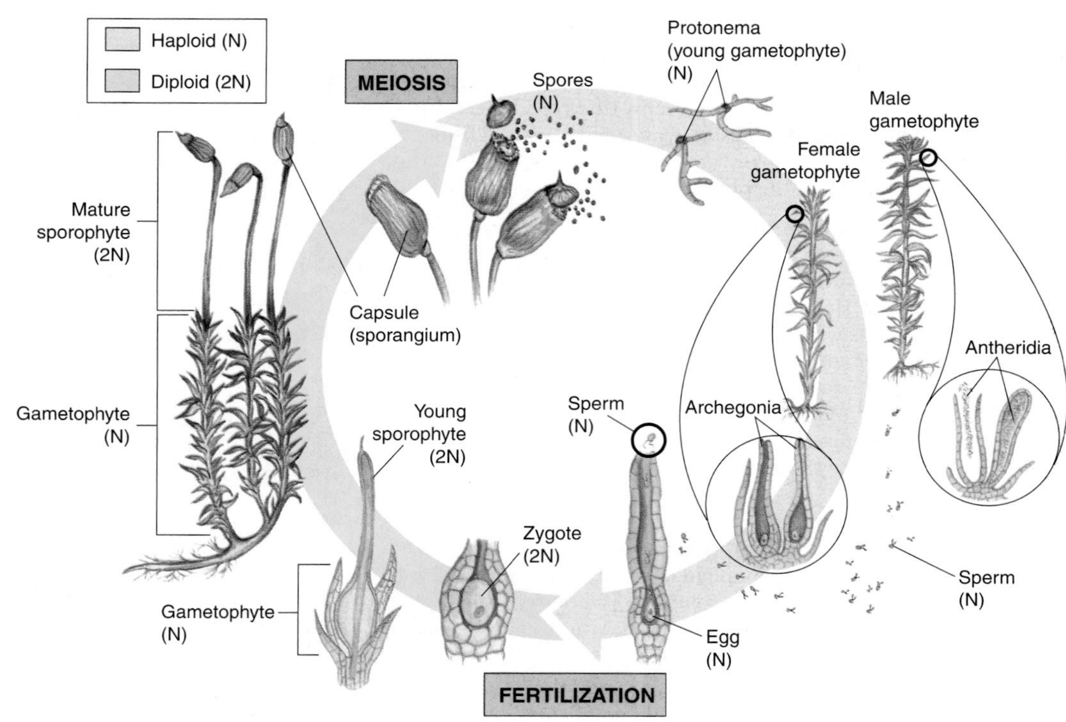

▲ **Figure 22–11**  **In bryophytes, the gametophyte is the dominant, recognizable stage of the life cycle and is the form that carries out photosynthesis.** Sporophytes, which produce haploid spores, grow at the top of the gametophyte plant. When the spores are ripe, they are shed from the capsule like pepper from a shaker. In some species, gametes (sperm and eggs) are produced on separate male and female gametophyte plants.

Life Cycle of Bryophytes

Like all plants, bryophytes reproduce with alternation of generations. 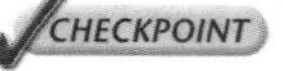 **In bryophytes, the gametophyte is the dominant, recognizable stage of the life cycle and is the stage that carries out most of the plant's photosynthesis.** The sporophyte is dependent on the gametophyte for supplying water and nutrients.

Dependence on Water For fertilization to occur, the sperm of a bryophyte must swim to an egg. The sperm may swim through standing water or through a coating of water left by dew. Sometimes raindrops can splash sperm from one plant to another. Because of this limit to reproduction, bryophytes must live in habitats where water is available.

Life Cycle of a Moss The life cycle of a moss, shown in **Figure 22–11,** helps illustrate how bryophytes reproduce. When a moss spore lands in a moist place, it germinates and grows into a mass of tangled green filaments called a **protonema** (proh-toh-NEE-muh). As the protonema grows, it forms rhizoids that grow into the ground and shoots that grow into the air. These shoots grow into the familiar green moss plants, which are the gametophyte stage of its life cycle.

✓CHECKPOINT *What is a protonema?*

BIO INSIGHTS **FACTS AND FIGURES**

Mosses in surprising places

As the text emphasizes, mosses need abundant water to grow and reproduce. Yet many mosses are found in areas with seasonal droughts. Even more surprising, some mosses live in tundras and other frigid climates, where liquid water may be unavailable for months at a time. Mosses survive such habitats by entering a state similar to suspended animation. Their tissues virtually dehydrate when water is not available, and they neither grow nor reproduce. But, though they may not prosper without water, mosses have adapted to periods without it, and that has let them live in some surprising places.

Gametes are formed in reproductive structures at the tips of the gametophytes. Sperm with whiplike tails are produced in **antheridia** (an-thur-ID-ee-uh; singular: antheridium), and egg cells are produced in **archegonia** (ahr-kuh-GOH-nee-uh; singular: archegonium). Some species produce both sperm and eggs on the same plant, whereas other species produce sperm and eggs on separate plants. Once sperm are released and reach egg cells, fertilization produces a diploid zygote. This zygote is the beginning of the sporophyte stage of the life cycle. It grows directly out of the body of the gametophyte and actually depends on it for water and nutrients. The mature sporophyte is a long stalk ending in a capsule that looks like a saltshaker. Inside the capsule, haploid spores are produced by meiosis. When the capsule ripens, it opens and haploid spores are scattered to the wind to start the cycle again.

▼ **Figure 22–12** The compacted remains of sphagnum moss may eventually form thick deposits of peat. When it is cut and dried, it can be burned to produce heat. Peat has been used as a form of fuel in Ireland for many centuries. **Inferring** *What can you infer about the climate of an area where sphagnum moss grows abundantly in peat bogs?*

Human Use of Mosses

Sphagnum (SFAG-num) mosses are a group of mosses that thrive in the acidic water of bogs. Dried sphagnum moss absorbs many times its own weight in water and thus acts as a sort of natural sponge. In certain environments the dead remains of sphagnum accumulate to form thick deposits of peat. Peat can be cut from the ground, as shown in **Figure 22–12,** and then burned as a fuel.

Peat moss is also used in gardening. Gardeners add peat moss to the soil because it improves the soil's ability to retain water. Peat moss also has a low pH, so when added to the soil it increases the soil's acidity. Some plants, such as azaleas, grow well only if they are planted in acidic soil.

22–2 Section Assessment

1. **Key Concept** How is water essential in the life cycle of a bryophyte?
2. **Key Concept** List the three groups of bryophytes. In what type of habitat do they live?
3. **Key Concept** What is the relationship between the gametophyte and the sporophyte in mosses and other bryophytes?
4. What is an archegonium? An antheridium? How are these structures important in the life cycle of a moss?
5. **Critical Thinking Inferring** What characteristic of bryophytes is responsible for their small size? Explain.

iTEXT Assessment Use iText to review the important concepts in Section 22–2.

Take It to the NET

Find out more about sphagnum moss. Then, write a paragraph about the growth, harvesting, and use of sphagnum moss. Use the links provided in the Biology area at the Prentice Hall Web site for help in completing this activity: **www.phschool.com**

Human Use of Mosses

Build Science Skills

Designing Experiments Ask students why they think people use peat moss for growing plants. Then provide groups of students with peat moss (*Sphagnum* spp.), soil, beakers, and water. Challenge each group to design an experiment that will demonstrate a characteristic of peat moss that would be useful to a gardener. *(Most students will design an experiment to show the superior water-absorbing ability of peat moss when compared with soil.)*

3 ASSESS

Evaluate Understanding

Call on students at random to describe the life cycle of a moss. Make sure students know that in bryophytes, the gametophyte is the dominant stage of the life cycle.

Reteach

Point out the differences in structure among the three kinds of bryophytes shown in Figures 22–9 and 22–10. Ask students to point to the gametophyte and the sporophyte in each.

Take It to the NET

Students will discover that sphagnum, commonly called peat moss, is any species of moss in the genus *Sphagnum.* Peat mosses are widespread and can sometimes be seen in the form of floating mats over water. For additional information, visit **www.phschool.com**

22–2 Section Assessment

1. Bryophytes produce gametes that must swim through water to reach other individuals.
2. The three groups are mosses, liverworts, and hornworts. They live in moist, shaded areas where water is in regular supply.
3. The gametophyte is the dominant, recognizable stage and is the form that carries out most of the plant's photosynthesis. The sporophyte depends on the gametophyte for water and nutrients.
4. An archegonium is the reproductive structure that produces egg cells; an antheridium is the reproductive structure that produces flagellated sperm. These gametes are necessary to complete the life cycle.
5. Bryophytes are limited in size because they lack vascular tissue and therefore can draw water up from the ground by osmosis only a few centimeters.

Use iText to review the key concepts in Section 22–2.

Answers to . . .

CHECKPOINT *The young gametophyte that develops into a moss plant*

Figure 22–12 *The climate is probably wet.*

Section 22–3

1 FOCUS

Objectives

22.3.1 ***Explain*** how vascular tissue is important to ferns and their relatives.
22.3.2 ***Describe*** the three phyla of seedless plants.
22.3.3 ***Identify*** the stages in the life cycle of ferns.

Guide for Reading

Vocabulary Preview

Have students write the vocabulary words, dividing each into its separate syllables as best they can. Remind students that each syllable usually has only one vowel sound. The correct syllabications are: vas•cu•lar tis•sue, tra•che•id, xy•lem, phlo•em, root, leaf, vein, stem, rhi•zome, frond, spor•an•gi•um, so•rus.

Reading Strategy

Have students preview the life cycle of a typical fern, shown in Figure 22–17. Ask them to write a paragraph describing the life cycle. Then, ask them to make any necessary revisions to their paragraphs after reading the section.

2 INSTRUCT

Evolution of Vascular Tissue

Use Visuals

Figure 22–13 Ask students: **What kind of cells are the two cells shown in the middle of the cross section of a club moss?** *(Tracheids)* **Tracheids are key cells in what kind of plant tissue?** *(Xylem)* **What is the function of xylem?** *(Xylem carries water upward from roots to every part of a plant.)* **What is the other kind of vascular tissue plants possess?** *(Phloem)* **Why were tracheids one of the great evolutionary innovations of the plant kingdom?** *(Tracheids provided for the movement of water and plant fluids over great distances, even against gravity. This allowed plants to grow large and tall.)*

22–3 Seedless Vascular Plants

Guide for Reading

Key Concepts

- How is vascular tissue important to ferns and their relatives?
- What are the characteristics of the three phyla of seedless vascular plants?
- What are the stages in the life cycle of ferns?

Vocabulary

- vascular tissue • tracheid
- xylem • phloem • lignin
- root • vein • leaf • stem
- rhizome • frond
- sporangium • sorus

Reading Strategy: Building Vocabulary Before you read, preview new vocabulary by skimming the section and making a list of the boldfaced terms. Leave space to make notes about each term as you read.

As you have read, bryophytes have only one way of transporting water—from cell to cell by osmosis. This fact limits them to just a few centimeters in height. About 420 million years ago, something remarkable happened. In just a few million years, plants grew to a whole new scale on the landscape. The small, mosslike plants were still around, of course, just as they are today. But now, they were joined by plants that were more than a meter in height, and others that were as large as small trees. What had happened? Fossil evidence shows that these plants contained **vascular tissue,** a type of tissue that is specialized to conduct water and nutrients through the body of the plant.

Evolution of Vascular Tissue

The first vascular plants had a new type of cell that was specialized to conduct water. **Tracheids** (TRAY-kee-idz), shown in **Figure 22–13,** were one of the great evolutionary innovations of the plant kingdom. They are the key cells in **xylem** (ZY-lum), a form of vascular tissue that carries water upward from the roots to every part of a plant. Tracheids are hollow cells with thick cell walls that resist pressure. Within a plant, they are connected end to end like a series of drinking straws. Tracheids allow water to move through a plant much more efficiently than by diffusion alone.

Vascular plants also possess a second type of vascular tissue called phloem. **Phloem** (FLOH-um) transports solutions of nutrients and carbohydrates produced by photosynthesis. Like xylem, the main cells of phloem are long and specialized to move fluids throughout the plant body. **Both forms of vascular tissue—xylem and phloem—can move fluids throughout the plant body, even against the force of gravity.**

Vascular plants also evolved the ability to produce **lignin,** a substance that makes cell walls rigid. The presence of lignin allows vascular plants to grow upright and to reach great heights.

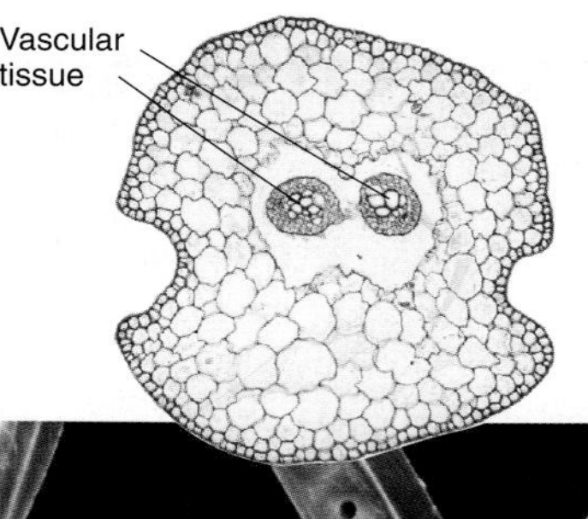

◀ **Figure 22–13 Vascular tissue conducts water and nutrients throughout the plant body.** It also provides support for the leaves and other organs of the plant. The two types of vascular tissue are xylem, which conducts water, and phloem, which conducts solutions of nutrients. The cross section (top) shows the vascular tissue in a club moss. The bottom photo shows a much-magnified view of tracheids from the xylem of a white pine.

SECTION RESOURCES

Print:

- ***Teaching Resources,*** Section Review 22–3
- ***Guided Reading and Study Workbook,*** Section 22–3

Technology:

- ***iText,*** Section 22–3

Ferns and Their Relatives

Seedless vascular plants include club mosses, horsetails, and ferns. The most numerous phylum of these is the ferns.

Like other vascular plants, ferns and their relatives have true roots, leaves, and stems. **Roots** are underground organs that absorb water and minerals. Water-conducting tissues are located in the center of the root. **Leaves** are photosynthetic organs that contain one or more bundles of vascular tissue. This vascular tissue is gathered into **veins** made of xylem and phloem. **Stems** are supporting structures that connect roots and leaves, carrying water and nutrients between them.

Club Mosses What was once a large and ancient group of land plants—phylum Lycophyta (ly-KOH-fy-tuh)—exists now as a much smaller group that includes the club mosses. Once, ancient club mosses grew into huge trees—up to 35 meters tall—and some produced Earth's first forests. The fossilized remains of these forests exist today as huge beds of coal.

Today, club mosses are small plants that live in moist woodlands and near streambeds and marshes. *Lycopodium,* the common club moss shown in **Figure 22–14,** looks like a miniature pine tree. For this reason it is also called "ground pine."

Horsetails The only living genus of Arthrophyta (ahr-THROH-fy-tuh) is *Equisetum,* which is a plant that grows about a meter tall. Like the club mosses, *Equisetum* has true leaves, stems, and roots. Its leaves are arranged in distinctive whorls at joints along the stem. *Equisetum* is called horsetail, or scouring rush, because its stems look similar to horses' tails and contain crystals of abrasive silica. During Colonial times, horsetails were commonly used to scour pots and pans.

CHECKPOINT *What chemical makes the stems of* Equisetum *abrasive?*

Figure 22–14 Club mosses and horsetails are seedless vascular plants. The club moss *Lycopodium* (left) looks like a tiny pine tree growing on the forest floor. The only living genus of Arthrophyta is *Equisetum,* or horsetail (above).

Ferns and Their Relatives

Build Science Skills

Observing Most students probably have never closely examined a fern frond. Give each student a frond from a fern plant. Also provide metric rulers, scissors, slides, and microscopes. Ask students to write the best description of the frond that they can, including such characteristics as size, color, structure, and so on. Make sure they look for sporangia on the underside of the fronds. Have students make diagrams of what they see, both with the unaided eye and with the microscope. Once everyone has completed the activity, have volunteers present their findings.

Meet Diverse Needs

Ask students who are interested in careers in forestry to find out what kinds of club mosses and ferns are indigenous to your area and whether horsetails can be found in the area. Explain that most libraries have books in the reference section on local flora, and these can be used to identify ferns that students might find in a local park or woodland. Ask that students report to the class about what they have learned.
Learning modality: verbal

TIME SAVER **PRESENTATIONS MADE EASY!**

The Presentation Assistant Plus contains the Prentice Hall Presentation Pro and the Transparencies, which provide easy-to-follow visual support for every step of this lesson. If you have a computer presentation station, use Prentice Hall Presentation Pro Section 22–3, or use the transparencies listed here.

Section 22–3: **Interest Grabber**
Section Outline
Compare/Contrast Table
Figure 22–17

Answer to . . .

CHECKPOINT *Silica*

22–3 (continued)

Life Cycle of Ferns

Build Science Skills

Observing The best way for students to learn about ferns is to try to grow their own in a homemade terrarium. Have students follow these steps.

- Obtain an empty 2-liter soda bottle that is made of colorless plastic and has an opaque plastic base.
- Remove the base from the bottom of the bottle. Fill the base with peat moss to within 2 centimeters of the top and moisten thoroughly with water.
- Cut the transparent portion of the bottle in half along its horizontal axis. Discard the top portion containing the cap. The bottom half will become the dome of the terrarium.
- Collect fern spores from a frond of an actively growing fern plant. Sprinkle the spores over the moistened peat moss.
- Cover the dome of the terrarium. In about three weeks, prothallia, the fern gametophytes, should be visible.

The terrarium should not be kept in direct sunlight. It should be monitored periodically to correct for improper water balance. There should always be some moisture clinging to the dome of the terrarium. If the terrarium is completely fogged and the contents are not visible, the top should be removed for a few minutes. If the dome appears to be dry, water should be added to the peat moss using a spray bottle and the dome replaced immediately. As the plants grow, make sure students identify the gametophyte and sporophyte generations.

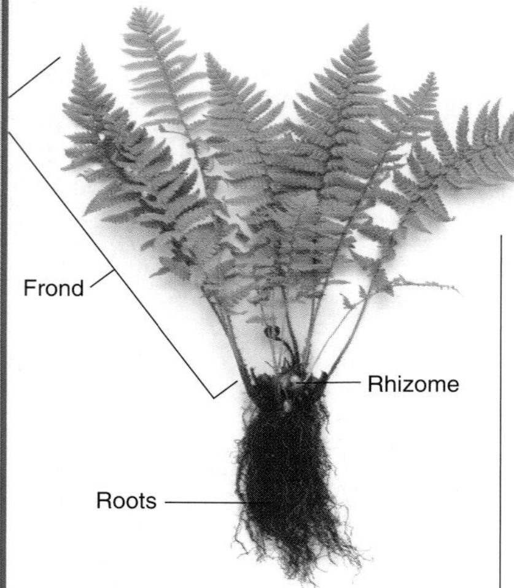

▲ **Figure 22–15** Ferns are easily recognized because of their delicate leaves, which are called fronds. Fronds grow from a rhizome, which grows horizontally through the soil. **Applying Concepts** *Is the plant shown a sporophyte or a gametophyte?*

Ferns Ferns, members of phylum Pterophyta (tehr-OH-fy-tuh), probably evolved about 350 million years ago, when great club moss forests covered the ancient Earth. Ferns have survived during the Earth's long history in numbers greater than any other group of spore-bearing vascular plants. More than 11,000 species of ferns are living today.

Ferns have true vascular tissues, strong roots, creeping or underground stems called **rhizomes,** and large leaves called **fronds,** shown in **Figure 22–15.** Ferns can thrive in areas with little light. They are most abundant in wet, or at least seasonally wet, habitats around the world. They are often found living in the shadows of forest trees, where direct sunlight hardly penetrates the forest's leafy umbrella. Ferns are found in great numbers in the rain forests of the Pacific Northwest. In tropical forests, some species grow as large as small trees.

Life Cycle of Ferns

The large plants we recognize as ferns are actually diploid sporophytes. **Ferns and other vascular plants have a life cycle in which the diploid sporophyte is the dominant stage.** Fern sporophytes produce haploid spores on the underside of their fronds in tiny containers called **sporangia** (spoh-RAN-jee-uh; singular: sporangium). Sporangia are grouped into clusters called **sori** (SOH-ry; singular: sorus), shown in **Figure 22–16.** Spores released from sporangia may be carried by wind and water over long distances.

When the spores germinate, they develop into haploid gametophytes. The small gametophyte first grows a set of rootlike rhizoids. It then flattens into a thin, heart-shaped, green structure that is the mature gametophyte. Although it is tiny, the gametophyte grows independently of the sporophyte.

The antheridia and archegonia are found on the underside of the gametophyte. As in bryophytes, fertilization requires at least a thin film of water, allowing the sperm to swim to the eggs. The diploid zygote produced by fertilization immediately begins to grow into a new sporophyte plant. As the sporophyte grows, the gametophyte withers away. Fern sporophytes often live for many years. In some species, the fronds produced in the spring die in the fall, but the rhizomes live through the winter and sprout again the following spring.

▶ **Figure 22–16** Many clusters of sporangia—each called a sorus—form on the underside of fern leaves. In each sporangium, cells undergo meiosis to produce spores. **Inferring** *Are these spores haploid or diploid?*

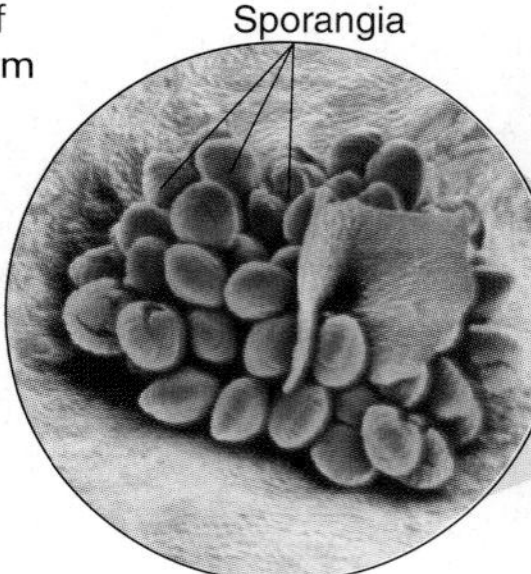

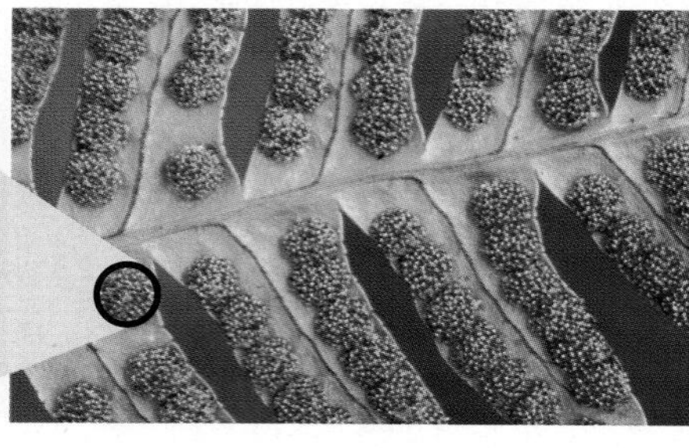

TEACHER TO TEACHER

To introduce students to the great diversity of plants, I give each team of students a set of 10 related plants and have them devise a classification system for that set. For example, one team might be given 10 different gymnosperms. Students classify the plants according to length of needle, number of needles in a whorl, or any other characteristic they consider significant. Other teams are given 10 angiosperms, 10 ferns, or 10 bryophytes, and each team devises a system based on a significant characteristic of their choosing. After 20 minutes, I have the teams present their systems to the class. This activity dramatically demonstrates the diversity of plants.

—*John E. Gonzales,*
Biology Teacher,
Temescal Canyon High School,
Lake Elsinore, CA

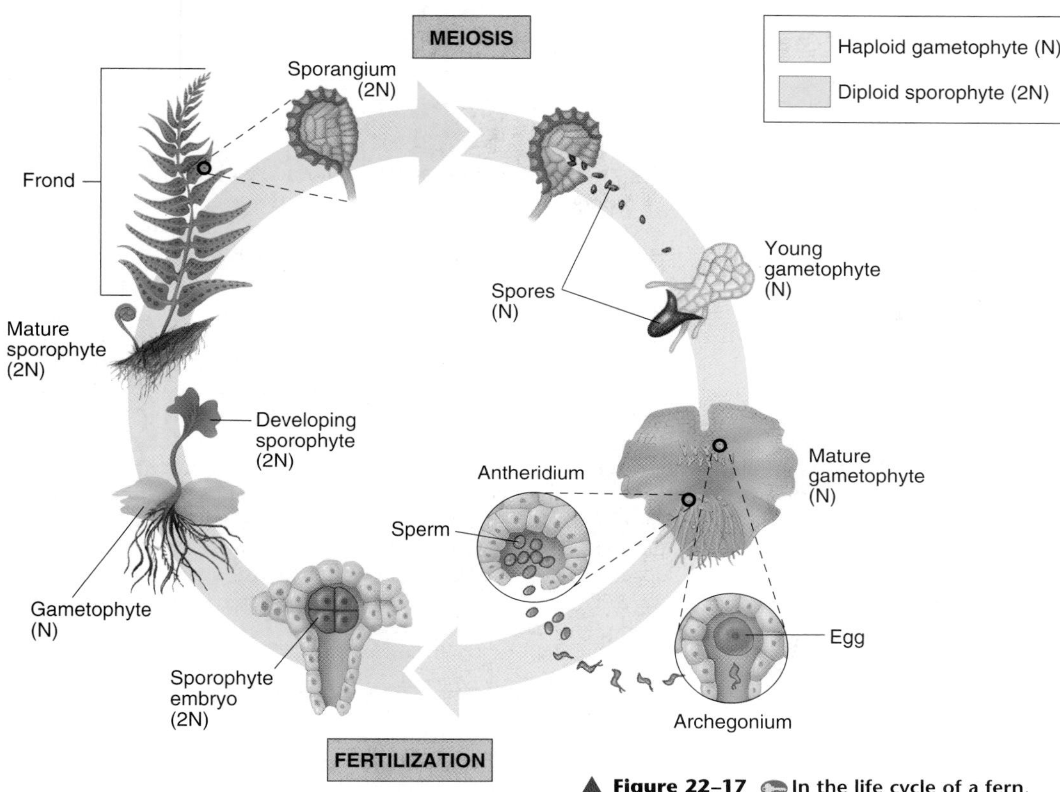

▲ **Figure 22–17** **In the life cycle of a fern, the dominant and recognizable stage is the diploid sporophyte.** The tiny, heart-shaped gametophyte grows close to the ground and relies on dampness for the sperm it produces to fertilize an egg. The young sporophyte grows from the gametophyte.

22–3 Section Assessment

1. **Key Concept** What are the two types of vascular tissue? Describe the function of each.
2. **Key Concept** What are the three phyla of seedless vascular plants? Give an example of each.
3. **Key Concept** What is the dominant stage of the fern life cycle? What is the relationship of the fern gametophyte and sporophyte?
4. **Critical Thinking Inferring** The size of plants increased dramatically with the evolution of vascular tissue. How might these two events be related?

iTEXT Assessment Use iText to review the important concepts in Section 22–3.

ALTERNATIVE ASSESSMENT

Making a Photo Essay
Find out more about club mosses, horsetails, and ferns. Use this information along with photographs of these plants to put together a two-page photo essay about seedless vascular plants.

22–3 Section Assessment

1. Xylem is the form of vascular tissue that transports water from the roots throughout the plant. Phloem transports nutrients and the products of photosynthesis.
2. Lycophyta: club mosses; Arthrophyta: horsetails; and Pterophyta: ferns
3. Ferns and other seedless vascular plants have a life cycle in which the diploid sporophyte is the dominant stage. The tiny gametophyte grows independently of the sporophyte.
4. Plants that lack vascular tissue can draw up water by osmosis only a few centimeters above the ground. The evolution of vascular tissue allowed plants to increase dramatically in size.

Use Visuals

Figure 22–17 Have students examine the life cycle and read the caption. Then, ask: **Which generation in the life cycle of the fern is the large, leafy plant we all know?** *(The sporophyte)* **How is the gametophyte produced?** *(The sporophyte produces spores. A spore will grow into a gametophyte.)* **What does the gametophyte produce?** *(Sperm and eggs, or gametes)* **Is the gametophyte diploid or haploid?** *(Haploid)* **Is the sporophyte diploid or haploid?** *(Diploid)*

3 ASSESS

Evaluate Understanding

Ask students to make a flowchart that describes the steps in the life cycle of a fern using information from the text and from Figure 22–17.

Reteach

Ask students to write a paragraph that explains what vascular tissue is and why it was important in the evolution of ferns and their relatives.

ALTERNATIVE ASSESSMENT

Students could use a camera to take their own photos of club mosses, horsetails, and ferns. A good place to take pictures is a local botanical garden. Students might also copy photographs from botany textbooks or library books about plants. As an alternative, students could make drawings of these plants from the photos they find. For each illustration in the photo essay, students should include the common name of the plant, the scientific name, where the photo was taken or obtained, and the habitat where the plant might be found.

Use iText to review the key concepts in Section 22–3.

Answers to . . .

Figure 22–15 *Sporophyte*

Figure 22–16 *Haploid*

Section 22–4

1 FOCUS

Objectives

22.4.1 ***Describe*** the reproductive adaptations of seed plants.

22.4.2 ***Describe*** the evolution of seed plants.

22.4.3 ***Identify*** the four groups of gymnosperms.

Guide for Reading

Vocabulary Preview

Pronounce each term in the list of Vocabulary words, and ask that students repeat the correct pronunciation back to you in unison.

Reading Strategy

Before students read, ask them to draw a line down the center of a piece of paper. Then, as they read, they should write the main topics of the section on the left side of the line and supporting details on the right side of the line.

2 INSTRUCT

Reproduction Free From Water

Build Science Skills

Designing Experiments Ask students how long they think a seed for a common garden plant could be kept out of soil and still grow if planted in proper conditions. Then, have pairs of students work together to design an experiment that would test the survivability of a certain kind of seed kept away from soil under a variety of conditions.

Address Misconceptions

Many students have trouble differentiating between pollen grains and gametes. Remind students that a gamete is a cell that must fuse with another gamete to form a new individual. Point out that pollen grains, therefore, are not gametes; they are spores, because they grow by mitosis into a new individual—the gametophyte.

22–4 Seed Plants

Guide for Reading

Key Concepts
- What adaptations allow seed plants to reproduce without standing water?
- What are the four groups of gymnosperms?

Vocabulary
gymnosperm
angiosperm
cone
flower
pollen grain
pollination
seed
embryo
seed coat

Reading Strategy: Building Vocabulary As you read, make notes about the meaning of each term listed above. After you have read the section, draw a concept map to show the relationship among these terms.

Whether they are acorns, pine nuts, dandelion seeds, or kernels of corn, seeds can be found everywhere. Seeds are so common, in fact, that their importance may be overlooked. Over millions of years, plants with a single trait—the ability to form seeds—became the most dominant group of photosynthetic organisms on land.

Seed plants are divided into two groups: gymnosperms and angiosperms. **Gymnosperms** (JIM-noh-spurmz) bear their seeds directly on the surfaces of cones, whereas **angiosperms** (AN-jee-oh-spurmz), which are also called flowering plants, bear their seeds within a layer of tissue that protects the seed. Gymnosperms include the conifers, such as pines and spruces, as well as palmlike plants called cycads, ancient ginkgoes, and the very weird gnetophytes. Angiosperms include grasses, flowering trees and shrubs, and all wildflowers and cultivated species of flowers. The angiosperms are discussed in Section 22–5. This section begins by exploring some of the reasons that seed plants became so successful.

Reproduction Free From Water

Like all plants, seed plants have a life cycle that alternates between a gametophyte stage and a sporophyte stage. Unlike mosses and ferns, however, seed plants do not require water for fertilization of gametes. As a result, seed plants can live just about anywhere—from moist habitats that are often dominated by seedless plants, to dry and cold habitats where most seedless plants cannot survive. **Adaptations that allow seed plants to reproduce without water include flowers or cones, the transfer of sperm by pollination, and the protection of embryos in seeds.**

Cones and Flowers The gametophytes of seed plants grow and mature within sporophyte structures called **cones,** which are the seed-bearing structures of gymnosperms, and **flowers,** which are the seed-bearing structures of angiosperms. The cones of a common gymnosperm are shown in **Figure 22–18.** The gametophyte generations of seed plants live inside these reproductive structures.

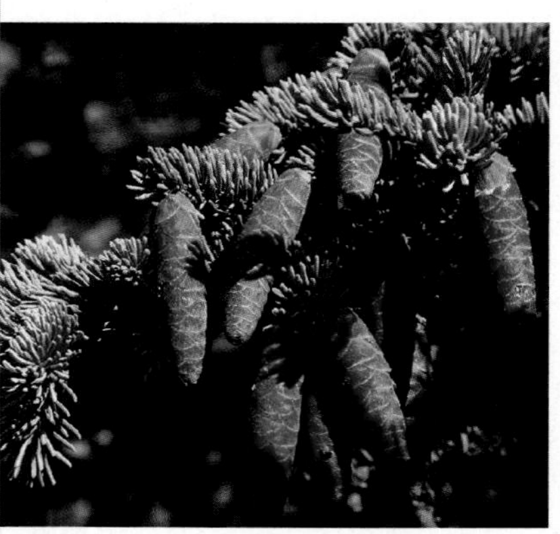

◀ **Figure 22–18** **Adaptations that allow seed plants to reproduce without water include reproduction in flowers or cones, the transfer of sperm by pollination, and the protection of embryos in a seed.** Gymnosperms, such as this spruce tree, bear their seeds on the scales of cones.

SECTION RESOURCES

Print:
- ***Teaching Resources,*** Section Review 22–4
- ***Guided Reading and Study Workbook,*** Section 22–4

Technology:
- ***iText,*** Section 22–4

Pollen In seed plants, the entire male gametophyte is contained in a tiny structure called a **pollen grain.** Sperm produced by this gametophyte do not swim through water to fertilize the eggs. Instead, the pollen grain is carried to the female gametophyte by wind, insects, birds, small animals, or sometimes even bats. The transfer of pollen from the male gametophyte to the female gametophyte is called **pollination.**

Seeds A **seed** is an embryo of a plant that is encased in a protective covering and surrounded by a food supply. An **embryo** is the early developmental stage of the sporophyte plant. The seed's food supply provides nutrients to the embryo as it grows. The **seed coat** surrounds and protects the embryo and keeps the contents of the seed from drying out. Seeds may also have special tissues or structures that aid in their dispersal to other habitats. Some seed coats are textured so that they stick to the fur or feathers of animals. Other seeds are contained in fleshy tissues that are eaten and dispersed by animals.

After fertilization, the zygote contained within a seed grows into a tiny plant—the embryo. The embryo often stops growing while it is still small and contained within the seed. The embryo can remain in this condition for weeks, months, or even years. When the embryo begins to grow again, it uses nutrients from the stored food supply. As a result of this strategy, seeds can survive long periods of bitter cold, extreme heat, or drought—beginning to grow only when conditions are once again right.

What is a pollen grain?

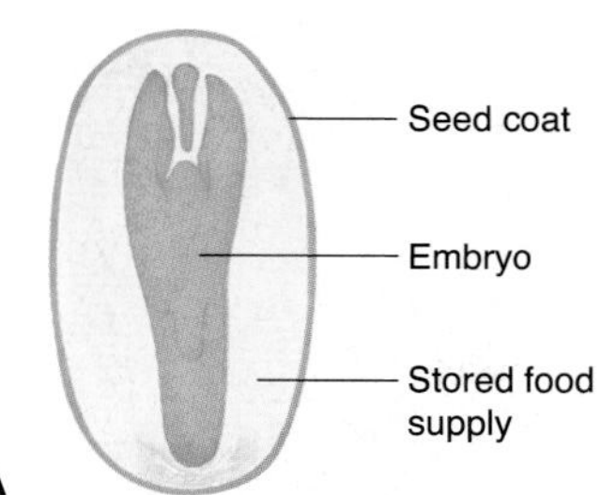

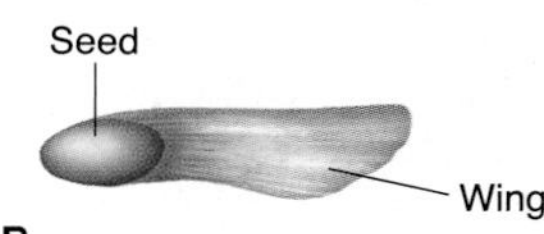

▲ **Figure 22–19** This cross section shows the internal structure of the seed of a pine tree. **Predicting** *How might the food stored in the seed affect the reproductive success of the pine tree?*

Quick Lab

How do seeds differ from spores?

Materials Fern frond with sori, microscope, scalpel, microscope slide, coverslip, dropper pipette, peanuts in the shell, brown paper bag, hand lens

Procedure

1. Use a scalpel to scrape sori from the underside of a fern frond onto a microscope slide. Add a drop of water and a coverslip and examine the slide under the low power objective of a microscope. Sketch a few spores. **CAUTION:** *Use care with the scalpel.*
2. Open a peanut shell. Separate the two halves, or cotyledons of a seed. Examine both halves with a hand lens and sketch the embryo.
3. Rub the peanut on a piece of a brown paper bag. Then, hold the paper up to the light. A bright spot indicates the presence of lipids.

Analyze and Conclude

1. **Observing** What evidence did you observe that nutrients are stored in peanut seeds?
2. **Predicting** A spore and a seed are deposited in an area where the soil is poor in nutrients. Based on your observations in this activity, which is more likely to survive in a nutrient-poor environment—the spore or the seed? Explain.
3. **Formulating Hypotheses** What are the advantages of a plant disseminating millions of tiny spores as it reproduces? What are the advantages of a plant disseminating a relatively few seeds?

Quick Lab

Objective Students should be able to observe how seeds differ from spores.

Skill Focus **Observing, Predicting**

Materials fern frond with sori, microscope, scalpel, microscope slide, coverslip, dropper pipette, peanuts in the shell, brown paper bag, hand lens

Time 20 minutes

Advance Prep Obtain mature fern fronds from a garden store, florist, or a damp wooded area. Obtain a bag of peanuts in the shell from a grocery store.

Safety Make sure students are careful with the scalpel.

Strategies

- Demonstrate how to scrape the sori from the underside of the frond onto a microscope slide.
- Demonstrate how to separate the cotyledons of the peanut.

Expected Outcomes Students should observe that seeds contain an embryo plant and stored food while spores do not, and they should infer that seed-bearing plants are more likely to survive in less fertile environments.

Analyze and Conclude

1. The brown spot on the paper bag where the peanut was rubbed indicates the presence of lipid.
2. The seed. A seed can store nutrients that allow the young plant to survive in poor soil until it is able to support itself by photosynthesis.
3. Disseminating millions of spores increases the chances that some of them will land in an environment suitable for seedless plants. A plant that produces relatively few seeds can store food in the seed to improve its chances of survival.

PRESENTATIONS MADE EASY!

The Presentation Assistant Plus contains the Prentice Hall Presentation Pro and the Transparencies, which provide easy-to-follow visual support for every step of this lesson. If you have a computer presentation station, use Prentice Hall Presentation Pro Section 22–4, or use the transparencies listed here.

Section 22–4: **Interest Grabber**
Section Outline
Features of Seed Plants
Figure 22–19

Answers to . . .

CHECKPOINT *The structure that contains the male gametophyte*

Figure 22–19 *The stored food supply might improve the pine's reproductive success by providing nutrients for the seed in the early stages of its growth.*

Evolution of Seed Plants

Use Visuals

Figure 22–20 Ask students: **Do ferns today reproduce using seeds?** *(No. Ferns are spore-bearing vascular plants.)* **Why did the evolution of seeds allow plants to live in places where mosses and ferns could not?** *(Seeds provide protection and a food supply for the embryo. With seeds, plants can reproduce free from water.)*

Gymnosperms—Cone Bearers

Build Science Skills

Forming Operational Definitions Before students read about gymnosperms, display a variety of photographs of examples of gymnosperms taken from old botany books, nature magazines, or personal photographs. You might also show commercial slides of conifers and other gymnosperms on a slide projector. Then, divide the class into groups to brainstorm a list of characteristics they think all gymnosperms exhibit.

▲ **Figure 22–20** Seed ferns are part of the fossil record. They represent a link between ferns that do not form seeds and seed plants. This ancient plant had leaves that resemble the leaves of modern ferns. **Comparing and Contrasting** ***If this plant were alive, what structures would distinguish it from a fern?***

Evolution of Seed Plants

The ancestors of seed plants evolved a variety of new adaptations that enabled them to survive in many places in which most mosses and ferns could not—from frigid mountains to scorching deserts. The most important of these adaptations was the seed.

Mosses and ferns underwent major adaptive radiations during the Carboniferous and Devonian periods, 300 to 400 million years ago. During these periods, land environments were much wetter than they are today. Tree ferns and other seedless plants grew into lush forests that covered much of Earth. Over a period of millions of years, however, continents became much drier, making it harder for seedless plants to survive and reproduce. For that reason, many moss and fern species became extinct. They were replaced by seed plants with adaptations that equipped them to deal with drier conditions.

Fossils of seed-bearing plants exist from almost 360 million years ago. As shown in **Figure 22–20,** some of these early seed plants outwardly resembled ferns. Seed fern fossils document several evolutionary stages in the development of the seed.

The early seed plants reached every landmass on Earth. Together with now-extinct seed ferns and other seedless vascular plants, seed plants formed dense forests and swamps that spread over much of what is now the eastern United States. Their remains now exist in the form of coal deposits.

Gymnosperms—Cone Bearers

The most ancient surviving seed plants are the gymnosperms. **Gymnosperms include gnetophytes, cycads, ginkgoes, and conifers.** These plants all reproduce with seeds that are exposed—gymnosperm means "naked seed."

Gnetophytes About 70 present-day species of the phylum Gnetophyta (nee-TOH-fy-tuh) are known, placed in just three genera. The reproductive scales of these plants are clustered into cones. *Welwitschia,* an inhabitant of the Namibian desert in southwestern Africa, is one of the most remarkable gnetophytes. It has only two huge leathery leaves, shown in **Figure 22–21,** which grow continuously and spread across the ground. The genus *Ephedra* grows in the American southwest and is sometimes known as Mormon tea.

Figure 22–21 The *Welwitschia* plant (below), a type of gnetophyte, is an odd desert plant that produces only two leaves during its entire life. Cones are produced at the bases of the two leaves. **Classifying** ***In what phylum is this plant classified?***

HISTORY OF SCIENCE

They just keep on keeping on

In 1879, a botany professor at Michigan Agricultural College (now Michigan State University) designed a long-term experiment to investigate the survivability of common weed seeds. Dr. W. J. Beal gathered 50 freshly grown seeds from each of 23 different types of plants, including common mallow and common mullein. He then prepared 20 sets of seeds by mixing each set in moist sand that filled a pint bottle. He buried those bottles in a row on a sandy knoll, with the tops left uncovered and the bottles slanting down so that they would not fill with water. Since then, one of Beal's bottles has been dug up every five or ten years to see if any of the seeds in it would germinate. Some of the seeds of the three species in the bottle dug up in 1980—after 100 years—still germinated when placed in good growing conditions.

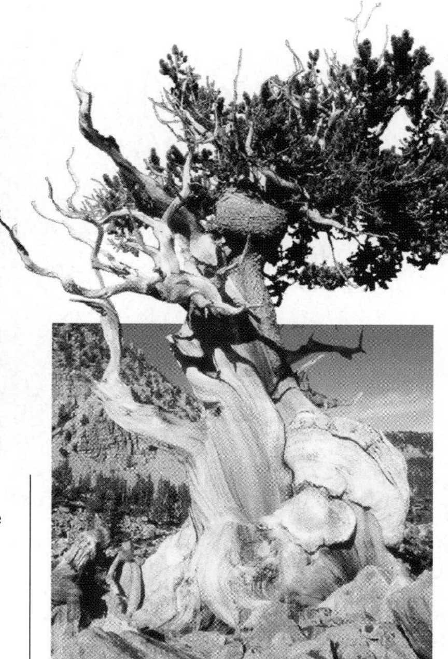

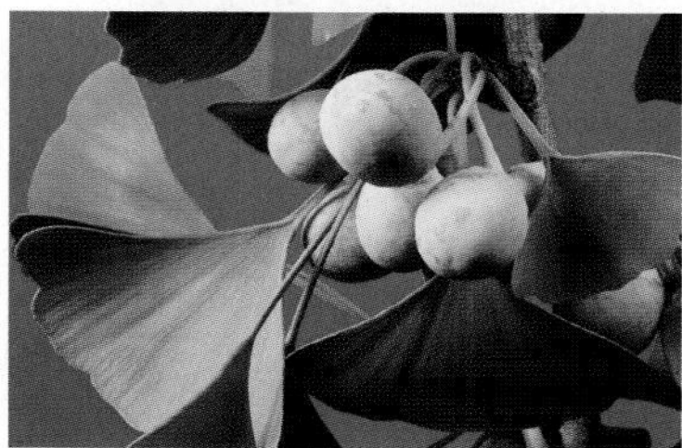

Figure 22–22 **Cycads, ginkgoes, and conifers are gymosperms.** Cycads (top left) produce seeds in reproductive structures that look like giant pinecones. The bristlecone pine (top right) is a conifer that can live for thousands of years. The ginkgo tree (bottom) is sometimes called a "living fossil" because it has changed little over millions of years.

Cycads Cycads, members of the phylum Cycadophyta (si-kad-OH-fy-tuh), are beautiful palmlike plants that reproduce with large cones, as shown in **Figure 22–22.** Cycads first appeared in the fossil record during the Triassic Period, 225 million years ago. Huge forests of cycads thrived when dinosaurs roamed Earth. Today, only nine genera of cycads exist. Cycads can be found growing naturally in tropical and subtropical places such as Mexico, the West Indies, Florida, and parts of Asia, Africa, and Australia.

Ginkgoes Ginkgoes were common when dinosaurs were alive, but today the phylum Ginkgophyta (ging-KOH-fy-tuh) contains only one species, *Ginkgo biloba.* The living ginkgo species looks similar to its fossil ancestors, so it is truly a living fossil. In fact, *Ginkgo biloba,* also shown in **Figure 22–22,** may be one of the oldest seed plant species alive today. Ginkgo trees were carefully cultivated in China, where they were often planted around temples. Ginkgoes are now often planted in urban settings in the United States, where their toughness and resistance to air pollution make them popular shade trees.

CHECKPOINT *How many different species of ginkgoes exist?*

Conifers By far the most common gymnosperms, with more than 500 known species, are the conifers. The phylum Coniferophyta (koh-nif-er-OH-fy-tuh) includes pines, spruces, firs, cedars, sequoias, redwoods, and yews. Some conifers, such as the bristlecone pine tree at right, can live for more than 4000 years. Other species, such as giant redwoods, can grow to more than 100 meters in height.

Meet Diverse Needs

To help students with limited English proficiency, give special attention to pronouncing the names of the four groups of gymnosperms. Point out that the initial letter in *cycad* and *conifer* is the same but stands for different sounds because of the vowel that follows each. Make sure students understand that the *g* in *gnetophyte* is silent. **Limited English proficiency**

Address Misconceptions

As you talk about reproduction in gymnosperms, emphasize that they produce pollen and seeds just like flowering plants. Sometimes students fail to understand the similarity.

Build Science Skills

Comparing and Contrasting Initiate a discussion of students' knowledge and experience with gymnosperms, including common shrubs such as taxus and junipers and common pine and spruce trees. Ask students to compare "evergreens" with leafy trees—angiosperms—such as maples and oaks. In this comparison, students should mention needles and pine cones, as well as gymnosperms staying green throughout the year.

FACTS AND FIGURES

In the pines

The conifers make up the largest phylum of gymnosperms, and the largest genus of conifers is *Pinus,* which includes 100 species of pine trees. Pines make up much of the coniferous forests, or taiga, of the Northern Hemisphere. Only one species of pine occurs naturally in the Southern Hemisphere. The pines also claim the oldest living organisms, the bristlecone pines. A bristlecone pine cut down in 1964 was estimated to be 4900 years old. The wood of the eastern white pine, *Pinus strobus,* has long been used in furniture making and flooring. It was valued so greatly for use in the masts of sailing ships that in colonial days large trees were marked for use by the English navy.

Answers to . . .

CHECKPOINT *Only one species,* Ginkgo biloba

Figure 22–20 *Its seeds*

Figure 22–21 *Gnetophyta*

Build Science Skills

Observing Divide the class into small groups, and have each group make a survey of gymnosperms in a specific area near the school, such as a park, a small neighborhood, or a farm. Ask groups to find a field guide in a library that will help them identify specific trees and shrubs. Their product should be a table that lists observed gymnosperms, cites locations, provides descriptions of habitat, and identifies characteristics.

3 ASSESS

Evaluate Understanding

Call on students at random to describe the features that allow seed plants to reproduce without water. Ask students to explain why such reproduction is significant in the evolution of plants.

Reteach

Direct students' attention to Figure 22–19 and ask them to point out the seed, the embryo, the stored food supply, and the seed coat. Then, ask students to explain how the evolution of seeds helped allow plants to reproduce free from water.

ALTERNATIVE ASSESSMENT

In their stories, students should be both creative and scientifically accurate. Whether in passing or in detail, a typical story should mention a forest landscape that includes gnetophytes, ginkgoes, cycads, and conifers.

Use the iText to review the key concepts in Section 22–4.

Answer to . . .

Figure 22–23 *Large, flat leaves might lose water rapidly by evaporation, causing the tree to dry out.*

Figure 22–23 These longleaf pines in North Carolina grow in an area that receives abundant rainfall. Yet water sinks quickly through the sandy soil, limiting the availability of water to tree roots. In this environment, the pines' water-conserving needles (inset) are an adaptation that contributes to the trees' survival. **Predicting** ***What might happen to a tree with large, flat leaves planted in this environment? Explain.***

Ecology of Conifers Today, conifers thrive in a wide variety of habitats: on mountains, in sandy soil, and in cool, moist areas such as the temperate rain forest of the Pacific Northwest. Surprisingly, conifer leaves have specific adaptations to dry conditions. How did these adaptations develop? Scientists have hypothesized that more than 250 million years ago, when conifers evolved, climate conditions were dry and cool. In response to these conditions, most conifers developed leaves that are long and thin, like the pine needles in **Figure 22–23.** This shape reduces the surface area from which water can be lost by evaporation. Another water-conserving adaptation is the thick, waxy layer that covers conifer leaves. In addition, the openings of leaves that allow for gas exchange are located in cavities below the surface of the leaves, also reducing water loss.

Most conifers are "evergreens"—that is, they retain their leaves throughout the year. The needles of most conifer species remain on the plant for 2 to 14 years. Older needles are gradually replaced by new needles, so the trees never become bare. However, not all species are evergreen. Larches and bald cypresses, for example, lose their needles every fall.

22–4 Section Assessment

1. **Key Concept** What are the main characteristics of seed plants?
2. **Key Concept** What are the different groups of gymnosperms?
3. What major change in Earth's climate favored the evolution of seed plants?
4. **Critical Thinking Applying Concepts** Pollination is a process that occurs only in seed plants. What process in seedless plants is analogous to pollination?

iTEXT Assessment Use iText to review the important concepts in Section 22–4.

ALTERNATIVE ASSESSMENT

Creative Writing Suppose you could visit Earth as it was about 300 million years ago, when gymnosperms were the dominant plants and angiosperms had not yet developed. Write a story that describes a forest landscape of this period.

22–4 Section Assessment

1. The main characteristics of seed plants include a life cycle that alternates between a dominant sporophyte stage and a much-reduced gametophyte stage; the ability to reproduce without water; the formation of cones or flowers; the transfer of sperm by pollination; and the protection of embryos in seeds.
2. Conifers, cycads, ginkgoes, and gnetophytes
3. Earth's climate became cooler and drier.
4. Pollination is analogous to the male gametes, or sperm, of seedless plants swimming to the female gametes, or eggs.

22–5 Angiosperms—Flowering Plants

Flowering plants, or angiosperms, are members of the phylum Anthophyta (an-THOH-fy-tuh). Flowering plants first appeared during the Cretaceous Period, about 135 million years ago, making their origin the most recent of all plant phyla. Flowering plants originated on land and quickly came to dominate Earth's plant life. The vast majority of living plant species reproduce with flowers.

Flowers and Fruits

Angiosperms have unique reproductive organs known as flowers. In general, flowers are an evolutionary advantage to plants because they attract animals such as bees, moths, or hummingbirds, which then transport pollen from flower to flower. This means of pollination is much more efficient than the wind pollination of most gymnosperms.

Flowers contain ovaries, which surround and protect the seeds. The presence of an ovary gives angiosperms their name: Angiosperm means "enclosed seed." After pollination, the ovary develops into a fruit, which protects the seed and aids in its dispersal.

The unique angiosperm **fruit**—a thick wall of tissue surrounding the seed—is another reason for the success of these plants. When an animal eats a fruit, seeds from the core of the fruit generally enter the animal's digestive system. By the time these seeds leave the digestive system—ready to sprout—the animal may have traveled many kilometers. By using fruit to attract animals, flowering plants increase the ranges they inhabit, spreading seeds over hundreds of square kilometers.

Guide for Reading

Key Concepts
- What are the characteristics of angiosperms?
- What are monocots and dicots?
- What are the three categories of plant life spans?

Vocabulary
fruit
monocot
dicot
cotyledon
annual
biennial
perennial

Reading Strategy: Finding Main Ideas
Angiosperms are the most diverse group of plants. As you read, make notes of the ways by which their diversity can be organized.

◀ **Figure 22–24** **Angiosperms have unique reproductive structures known as flowers, which contain ovaries that surround and protect the seeds.** Apple flowers (left) produce seeds inside ovaries, which mature into fruits (right).

SECTION RESOURCES

Print:
- ***Teaching Resources,*** Section Review 22–5, Chapter 22 Exploration
- ***Guided Reading and Study Workbook,*** Section 22–5
- ***Issues and Decision Making,*** 22–1

Technology:
- ***iText,*** Section 22–5

Section 22–5

1 FOCUS

Objectives

22.5.1 ***Identify*** the characteristics of angiosperms.
22.5.2 ***Explain*** what monocots and dicots are.
22.5.3 ***Describe*** the three different life spans of angiosperms.

Guide for Reading

Vocabulary Preview

Before students read, have them write definitions of what they think each of the Vocabulary terms means. Then, have them skim the section to find the boldfaced terms, read the definitions, and revise what they have written.

Reading Strategy

Before students read, ask them to preview the photographs of angiosperms shown in the section and make a list of questions they have about the diversity of flowering plants. Then, as they read, they can write down the answers to their questions.

2 INSTRUCT

Flowers and Fruits

Build Science Skills

Formulating Hypotheses Before students read about fruits, give each pair of students a ripe apple and a scalpel or paring knife. Ask students to write a description of the outside of the apple before cutting into it. Then, instruct them to cut the apple in half and closely examine the inside. (Caution students to be careful when handling the scalpel or knife.) Ask students to write descriptions of the inside of the apple and make drawings of the apple's core. Also, ask them to count whatever objects are inside the apple. As a final task, have students formulate a hypothesis about the role the apple plays in the life cycle of an apple tree.

Diversity of Angiosperms

Build Science Skills

Forming Operational Definitions Before students read about angiosperms, display a variety of photographs of examples of angiosperms taken from old botany books, nature magazines, or personal photographs. You might also show commercial slides of angiosperms on a slide projector. Make sure many of the photographs or slides show plants in bloom. Then, have students brainstorm a list of characteristics that they think all angiosperms exhibit.

Use Visuals

Figure 22–25 Ask students: **If the veins in the leaves of an unknown plant are parallel, what do you know about that plant?** *(It is a monocot.)* **What is a main characteristic of dicot seeds?** *(They have two cotyledons.)* **What is the difference in stem structure between monocots and dicots?** *(Monocots have vascular bundles scattered throughout the stem; dicots have vascular bundles arranged in a ring.)*

Diversity of Angiosperms

The angiosperms are an incredibly diverse group. Not surprisingly, there are many different ways of categorizing these plants. These include monocots and dicots; woody and herbaceous plants; and annuals, biennials, and perennials. As you read about each category, keep in mind that the categories can overlap. An iris, for example, is a monocot plant that is also an herbaceous perennial. These categories simply provide a way of appreciating and organizing the diversity of angiosperms.

Monocots and Dicots There are two classes within the angiosperms: the Monocotyledonae, or **monocots,** and the Dicotyledonae, or **dicots.** The general characteristics of both groups are shown in **Figure 22–25. Monocots and dicots are named for the number of seed leaves, or cotyledons, in the plant embryo. Monocots have one seed leaf, and dicots have two.** Other differences include the distribution of vascular tissue in stems, roots, and leaves, and the number of petals per flower. Monocots include corn, wheat, lilies, orchids, and palms. Dicots include roses, clover, tomatoes, oaks, and daisies.

CHECKPOINT *What is a cotyledon?*

Figure 22–25 Monocots and dicots are named for the number of seed leaves, or cotyledons, in the plant embroyo. The table compares the characteristics of monocots and dicots.

Characteristics of Monocots and Dicots

	Monocots	Dicots
Seeds	Single cotyledon 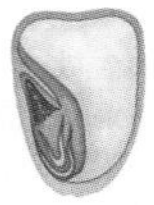	Two cotyledons 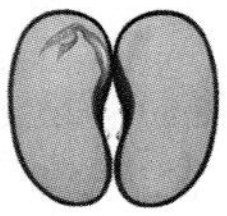
Leaves	Parallel veins 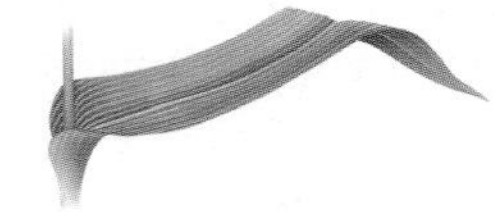	Branched veins 
Flowers	Floral parts often in multiples of 3 	Floral parts often in multiples of 4 or 5 
Stems	Vascular bundles scattered throughout stem 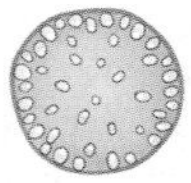	Vascular bundles arranged in a ring 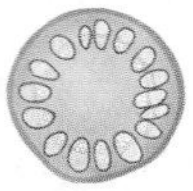
Roots	Fibrous roots 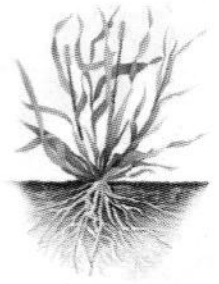	Taproot 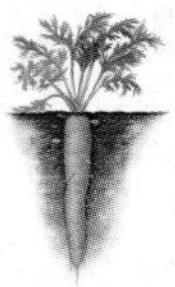

TIME SAVER PRESENTATIONS MADE EASY!

The Presentation Assistant Plus contains the Prentice Hall Presentation Pro and the Transparencies, which provide easy-to-follow visual support for every step of this lesson. If you have a computer presentation station, use Prentice Hall Presentation Pro Section 22–5, or use the transparencies listed here.

Section 22–5:  **Interest Grabber**
Section Outline
Concept Map
Figure 22–25

Careers in Biology

Botanical Illustrator

Job Description: work in a museum, outdoors, in a botanical garden, or at home to illustrate plants and organisms related to the plants

Education: two- or four-year college degree in an art school or other school noted for its art and design department

Skills: ability to observe nature; artistic talent; knowledge of biology; detail oriented; knowledge of the Internet, library, and museum research sources

Highlights: You provide illustrations that help people understand and appreciate biology. You have the pleasure of taking people of all ages on exciting visual adventures into the world of plants.

Linda Seabrooks Campbell is a professional botanical and science illustrator who finds great satisfaction in passing on her knowledge to students. "I take kids on nature hikes," she says, "and show them how to identify and make illustrations of plants."

Take It to the NET

For more career information visit the Prentice Hall Web site: **www.phschool.com**

Woody and Herbaceous Plants The flowering plants can be subdivided into various groups according to the characteristics of their stems. One of the most important and noticeable stem characteristics is woodiness. Woody plants are made primarily of cells with thick cell walls that support the plant body. Woody plants include trees, shrubs, and vines. Shrubs are typically smaller than trees, and vines have stems that are long and flexible. Examples of woody vines are grapes and ivy. Examples of shrubs include blueberries, rhododendrons, and roses.

Plant stems that are smooth and nonwoody are characteristic of herbaceous plants. Herbaceous plants do not produce wood as they grow. Examples of herbaceous plants include dandelions, zinnias, petunias, and sunflowers.

Annuals, Biennials, and Perennials If you've ever planted a garden, you know that many flowering plants grow, flower, and die in a single year. Other types of plants continue to grow from year to year. The lifespan of plants is determined by a combination of genetic and environmental factors. Many long-lived plants continue growing despite yearly environmental fluctuations. However, harsh environmental conditions can shorten the life of other plants. **There are three categories of plant life spans: annual, biennial, and perennial.**

Word Origins

Annual comes from the Latin word *annus,* which means "year." The Latin prefix *bi-* means "two." **Based on the characteristics of perennials, what do you think the Latin prefix *per-* means?**

Careers in Biology

- Botanical illustrators, also called botanical artists, combine artistic skills with detailed knowledge of botany. Those who follow this career path try to communicate their scientific knowledge and appreciation of plants and flowers in an artistically pleasing way.
- Some botanical illustrators work for museums or similar institutions. Many also work at home as freelance commercial artists. Their skills are utilized by book publishers, magazines, and organizations that publish pamphlets and brochures.
- A botanical illustrator usually markets his or her work with an artist's portfolio, which is a collection of samples of the artist's best work.

Take It to the NET

The American Society of Botanical Artists (ASBA), established in 1995, is a nonprofit organization that promotes awareness of botanical art. The ASBA maintains a Web site with links to the work of numerous botanical artists. To contact local botanical illustrators, you can call the art department of a local magazine or a publishing company and ask for a reference to a local freelancer. For more information about this career, visit **www.phschool.com**

Word Origins

Students might infer from the description of perennials that the Latin word *per* means "through." Thus, a perennial lives "through the years."

FACTS AND FIGURES

Evolution of angiosperms

The oldest angiosperm fossils are fossils of grains of pollen found in southern England that date from the early Cretaceous Period. By the middle of that geologic period, flowering plants had spread and diversified and become very successful. There are a number of reasons for their success, including protecting their seeds inside ovaries. Some biologists also point to the relative quickness with which angiosperms set their seed and grow. During this same period, the giant dinosaurs that had ruled Earth during the Jurassic Period were disappearing. They were replaced by much smaller, low-feeding species. If a plant could not gain a foothold and grow quickly, it would be eaten up by the smaller dinosaurs. In this respect, the slow-growing gymnosperms were at a disadvantage compared to the quick-growing angiosperms.

Answer to . . .

CHECKPOINT *A cotyledon is a seed leaf in the embryo of an angiosperm.*

22–5 (continued)

Meet Diverse Needs

To help at-risk students distinguish among annuals, biennials, and perennials, show the class a packet of common annual flower or garden seeds, with a picture of the plant on the cover of the packet. Then, call attention to any trees or shrubs that can be viewed from classroom windows. Ask students: **Nurseries and garden stores feature seeds for gardeners to plant every spring and summer. Why do they usually not sell seeds for shrubs and trees?** *(Many common garden plants are annuals that must be replaced every year. Trees do not need to be replaced each year—they are perennials.)* Point out that trees and shrubs are usually too slow-growing for most gardeners to start them from seed. **Learning modality: visual**

3 ASSESS

Evaluate Understanding

Ask students to write a paragraph that explains why flowers and fruit aid in the reproduction of angiosperms.

Reteach

Have students study the table in Figure 22–25. Then, call on students to describe the differences between monocots and dicots.

ALTERNATIVE ASSESSMENT

Have students use reference sources such as encyclopedias, field guides, gardening magazines, or seed catalogs to research specific plants. Students' displays should show how the plants they selected have the characteristics of monocots or dicots listed in Figure 22–25.

Use iText to review the key concepts in Section 22–5.

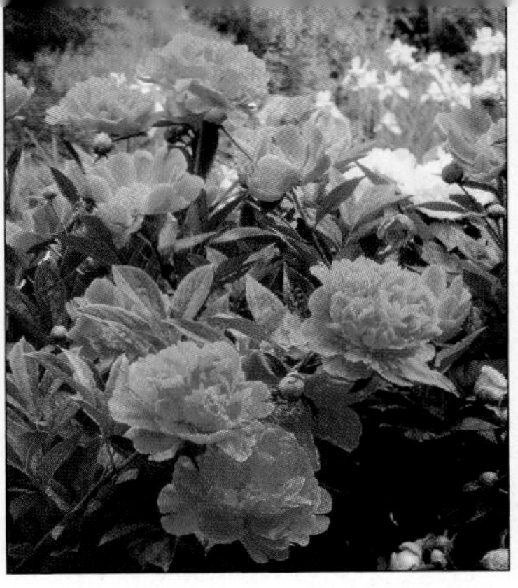

Figure 22–26 Categories of plant life spans include annuals, biennials, and perennials. Zinnias (left) are annual plants, which germinate, grow to maturity, set seed, and die in one growing season. Biennials such as the evening primrose (middle) grow roots, stems, and seeds in their first year, then produce flowers and seeds in their second year. Perennials such as peonies (right) live through many years.

Some plants grow from seed to maturity, flower, produce seeds, and die all in the course of one growing season. Flowering plants that complete a life cycle within one growing season are called **annuals.** Annuals include many garden plants, such as marigolds, petunias, pansies, and the zinnias in **Figure 22–26.** Wheat and cucumbers are also annuals.

Angiosperms that complete their life cycle in two years are called **biennials** (by-EN-ee-ulz). In the first year, biennials germinate and grow roots, very short stems, and sometimes leaves. During their second year, biennials grow new stems and leaves and then produce flowers and seeds. Once the flowers produce seeds, the plant dies. Evening primrose, parsley, celery, and foxglove are biennials.

Flowering plants that live for more than two years are called **perennials.** Perennials usually live through many years. Some perennials, such as peonies, asparagus, and many grasses, have herbaceous stems that die each winter and are replaced in the spring. Most perennials, however, have woody stems. Palm trees, sagebrush, maple trees, and honeysuckle are examples of woody perennials.

22–5 Section Assessment

1. **Key Concept** What reproductive structures are unique to angiosperms? Briefly describe the function of each.
2. **Key Concept** What are monocots and dicots?
3. **Key Concept** How do annuals, biennials, and perennials differ?
4. Compare the growth forms of plants with woody stems and those with herbaceous stems.
5. **Critical Thinking Forming Hypotheses** Which are more likely to be dispersed by animals—the seeds of an angiosperm or the spores of a fern? Explain your reasoning.

iTEXT Assessment Use iText to review the important concepts in Section 22–5.

ALTERNATIVE ASSESSMENT

Classifying

Prepare a display comparing two specific plants, one monocot and one dicot. On this display, write a brief summary of the basic differences between these two types of angiosperms.

22–5 Section Assessment

1. Flowers and fruits. In a flower, seeds develop within a protective structure called an ovary. The ovary matures into a fruit, which is a thick wall of tissue surrounding the seed.
2. Angiosperms are classified as either monocots or dicots. Monocots have one seed leaf, or cotyledon, in the plant embryo, and dicots have two.
3. Annuals are flowering plants that complete a life cycle within one growing season. Biennials complete their life cycle in two years. Perennials live for more than two years, usually many years.
4. Plants with woody stems are trees, shrubs, or vines. Plants with herbaceous, or nonwoody, stems include flowers such as zinnias and petunias.
5. The seeds of angiosperms are more likely to be dispersed by animals, because the seeds are enclosed in fruit, which animals eat.

Exploration

Comparing Mosses and Ferns

As plants evolved from their aquatic ancestors, they adapted to increasingly drier environments. In this investigation, you will compare a moss and a fern to determine which plant is better adapted for life in a dry environment.

Problem
Are ferns or mosses better adapted for life in a dry environment?

Materials
- fern plant
- clump of moss plants
- hand lens
- forceps
- microscope slide
- dropper pipette
- coverslip
- compound microscope

Skills
Observing, Comparing and Contrasting

Procedure  

1. Carefully examine a fern frond. Record whether the surface of the frond is shiny or dull.
2. Gently bend the fern frond back and forth. Record whether the frond bends easily.
3. Remove a few moss plants from the clump of moss. Gently bend one plant back and forth. Record whether the moss bends easily.
4. Use a hand lens to examine a fern leaf. Note whether there are veins in the leaf. Draw and label a diagram of what you observe.
5. Use a forceps to gently transfer a single moss plant from the clump of moss to the center of a clean microscope slide. Use a dropper pipette to place a drop of water on top of the moss plant. Cover the moss with a coverslip.
6. Examine the leafy top of the moss plant under the low-power objective of your microscope. Note whether there are veins in the moss. Draw and label a diagram of what you observe.

Analyze and Conclude

1. **Inferring** Was the surface of the fern frond shiny? What substance on the surface of the fern accounts for this observation? How does this substance help ferns to live on dry land?

2. **Observing** Did you observe veins in the fern? In the moss?
3. **Comparing and Contrasting** Which plant was firmer—the fern or the moss? How can you explain this difference?
4. **Formulating Hypotheses** Why do you think the fern is able to grow larger than the moss?
5. **Drawing Conclusions** Which of the plants shows adaptations that make it better able to survive in a dry environment? Explain your answer.

Go Further

Observing Use a microscope to examine prepared slides of cross sections of mosses and ferns. Draw and label what you see. Where do you see vascular tissue?

Exploration

Objective Students will be able to draw the conclusion that ferns are better adapted than mosses for life on land.

Skills Focus Observing, Comparing and Contrasting

Time 45 minutes

Advance Prep Obtain fern plants from a garden store or florist. Ferns can also be found in damp, wooded areas. Obtain moss plants in damp, shady areas or through a biological supply house.

Teaching Tips
- Remind students to use only the low-power objective in examining their slides.
- Station yourself by the plant material from time to time. Students usually take too large a sample for microscope observation and may attempt to fit a clump of moss under a coverslip, instead of a single moss plant.

Procedure

2. Ask students to think about what the purpose is of bending the fronds back and forth. Students should infer that this is a way of seeing if the fern has supporting tissue to hold its fronds upright.

5. Demonstrate how to transfer a single moss plant to a slide, add a drop of water, and cover with a coverslip.

Expected Outcomes Students should observe a waxy cuticle and vascular tissue in the fern that help them draw the conclusion that ferns are better adapted than mosses for life on land.

Analyze and Conclude

1. Students should observe that the fern frond was shiny, especially on its upper surface, because of the waxy cuticle there. This layer of wax helps ferns live on dry land by preventing them from drying out.

2. The fern has veins in its fronds; the moss does not have veins.

3. The fern should be firmer. Students might correctly suggest that the fern is firmer because it has vascular tissue.

4. Students should hypothesize that the fern can grow larger because it contains vascular tissue that provides support and supplies water to the plant's top. The moss has no vascular tissue.

5. Both the waxy cuticle and the vascular tissue help prevent the fern from drying out, and the vascular tissue also provides support. Therefore, the fern is better adapted for life on land.

Go Further

Provide prepared slides of cross sections of mosses and ferns for students to observe. Students should observe vascular tissue in the cross sections of ferns, not in those of mosses.

Chapter 22 Study Guide

Study Tip

Divide the class into small groups, and ask each group to make a list of questions that would cover all the Key Concepts in the chapter. Then, have groups exchange lists and answer the questions they receive from another group.

Chapter 22 Assessment

Reviewing Content

1. b **2.** b **3.** d **4.** c **5.** d **6.** b **7.** a **8.** d **9.** c **10.** c

Understanding Concepts

11. In alternation of generations, the plant's life cycle has two stages: the gametophyte and the sporophyte, one of which is the dominant stage.

12. The theory that the first land plants evolved from multicellular green algae is supported by the fact that most green algae have the size, color, and appearance of plants; cell walls; and photosynthetic pigments identical to those in plants.

13. Botanists divide the plant kingdom into four groups based on water-conducting tissue, seeds, and flowers.

14. Because they lack vascular tissue, bryophytes draw water up by osmosis.

15. Bryophytes depend upon the presence of water to complete their life cycle, because the only way the sperm can reach the egg is to swim through rainwater or dew.

16. In bryophytes, a protonema is the tangled mass of green filaments that forms the young gametophyte. The haploid protonema grows into the male or female gametophyte.

17. Tracheids are hollow, tubelike cells that make up xylem. The function of tracheids is to transport water through a plant.

18. The evolution of lignin made the cell walls of plants rigid. This enabled plants to grow upright and reach great heights.

Chapter 22 Study Guide

22–1 Introduction to Plants

Key Concepts

- Plants are multicellular eukaryotes that have cell walls made of cellulose. They develop from multicellular embryos and carry out photosynthesis using the green pigments chlorophyll *a* and *b*.
- The lives of plants revolve around the need for sunlight, water and minerals, gas exchange, and the movement of water and nutrients throughout the plant body.
- The first plants evolved from an organism much like the multicellular green algae living today.

Vocabulary

gametophyte, p. 552
sporophyte, p. 552

22–2 Bryophytes

Key Concepts

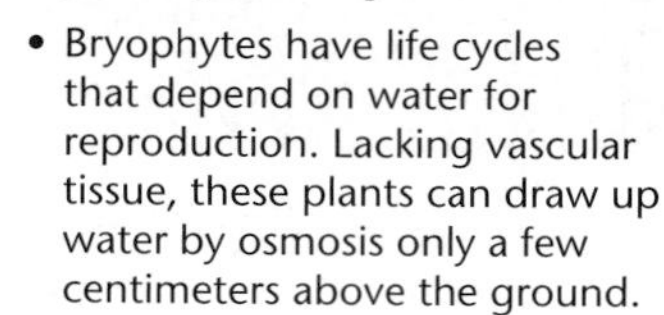

- Bryophytes have life cycles that depend on water for reproduction. Lacking vascular tissue, these plants can draw up water by osmosis only a few centimeters above the ground.
- Bryophytes include mosses, liverworts, and hornworts.

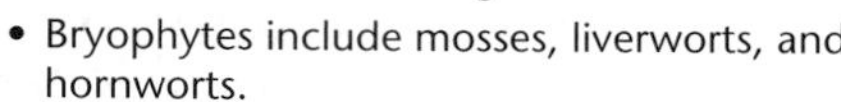

- In bryophytes, the gametophyte is the dominant, recognizable stage of the life cycle and is the stage that carries out most of the plant's photosynthesis.

Vocabulary

- bryophyte, p. 556 • rhizoid, p. 557
- gemma, p. 557 • protonema, p. 558
- antheridium, p. 559 • archegonium, p. 559

22–3 Seedless Vascular Plants

Key Concepts

- Both forms of vascular tissue—xylem and phloem—can move fluids throughout the plant body, even against the force of gravity.
- Seedless vascular plants include club mosses, horsetails, and ferns.
- Ferns and other vascular plants have a life cycle in which the diploid sporophyte is the dominant stage.

Vocabulary

- vascular tissue, p. 560 • tracheid, p. 560
- xylem, p. 560 • phloem, p. 560
- lignin, p. 560 • root, p. 561
- leaf, p. 561 • vein, p. 561 • stem, p. 561
- rhizome, p. 562 • frond, p. 562
- sporangium, p. 562 • sorus, p. 562

22–4 Seed Plants

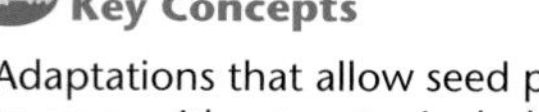

Key Concepts

- Adaptations that allow seed plants to reproduce in areas without water include flowers or cones, the transfer of sperm by pollination, and the protection of embryos in seeds.
- Gymnosperms include gnetophytes, cycads, ginkgoes, and conifers.

Vocabulary

- gymnosperm, p. 564 • angiosperm, p. 564
- cone, p. 564 • flower, p. 564
- pollen grain, p. 565 • pollination, p. 565
- seed, p. 565 • embryo, p. 565
- seed coat, p. 565

22–5 Angiosperms—Flowering Plants

Key Concepts

- Angiosperms have unique reproductive organs known as flowers. Flowers contain ovaries, which surround and protect the seeds.
- Monocots and dicots are named for the number of seed leaves, or cotyledons, in the plant embryo. Monocots have one seed leaf, and dicots have two.
- There are three categories of plant life spans: annual, biennial, and perennial.

Vocabulary

- fruit, p. 569 • monocot, p. 570 • dicot, p. 570
- cotyledon, p 570 • annual, p. 572
- biennial, p. 572 • perennial, p. 572

Thinking Visually

Using the information in this chapter, make a compare-and-contrast table comparing bryophytes, ferns, gymnosperms, and angiosperms. Compare these groups of plants in terms of reproduction (seeds or seedless), tissues (vascular or nonvascular), typical size, and type of habitat.

TIME SAVER CHAPTER RESOURCES

Print:

- ***Teaching Resources,*** Chapter Vocabulary Review, Graphic Organizer
- ***Chapter Tests: Levels A and B,*** Chapter 22 Test
- ***PH Assessment System*** Practice Test

Technology:

- ***Computer Test Bank,*** Chapter 22 Test
- ***iText,*** Chapter 22 Assessment

Chapter 22 Assessment

Reviewing Content

Choose the letter that best answers the question or completes the statement.

1. Which of the following is NOT a characteristic of plants?
   a. eukaryotic
   b. cell walls contain chitin
   c. multicellular
   d. contain chlorophyll
2. The first plants evolved from
   a. brown algae.
   b. green algae.
   c. red algae.
   d. golden algae.
3. The most recognizable stage of a moss is the
   a. sporophyte.
   b. protonema.
   c. archegonium.
   d. gametophyte.
4. The small, multicellular spheres by which liverworts reproduce asexually are
   a. protonemas. c. gemmae.
   b. rhizoids. d. archegonia.
5. Water is carried upward from the roots to every part of a plant by
   a. cell walls. c. cuticle.
   b. phloem. d. xylem.
6. The leaves of ferns are called
   a. sori. c. rhizomes.
   b. fronds. d. spores.

7. To which group does the plant shown above belong?
   a. bryophytes c. gymosperms
   b. ferns d. angiosperms
8. The reproductive structures of cycads are called
   a. flowers.
   b. sporangia.
   c. sori.
   d. cones.
9. In angiosperms, the mature seed is surrounded by a
   a. cone.
   b. flower.
   c. fruit.
   d. cotyledon.
10. A plant that has a life cycle that lasts two years is a
    a. dicot
    b. monocot
    c. biennial
    d. perennial

Understanding Concepts

11. What is alternation of generations?
12. What evidence supports the theory that plants evolved from multicellular green algae?
13. Describe the three important features used by botanists to divide the plant kingdom into four groups.
14. By what process does water move through the body of a bryophyte?
15. During the life cycle of a moss, what environmental conditions are necessary for fertilization to occur?
16. What is a protonema? Is it haploid or diploid?
17. What are tracheids? What is their function in a vascular plant?
18. How was the ability to produce lignin significant to the evolution of plants?
19. Describe the dominant stage in the life cycle of a fern.
20. Compare the structure and function of rhizomes, rhizoids, and roots.
21. Describe the male gametophyte of a seed plant.
22. What adaptations allow conifers to live in dry habitats?
23. Which group of plants contains the most species?
24. How do fruits aid in the dispersal of angiosperms?
25. How does the pattern of veins differ in a monocot and a dicot leaf? Draw an example of each.

19. The dominant stage in the life cycle of a fern is the sporophyte, which when mature consists of roots, underground stems called rhizomes, and fronds, which are large leaves. On the undersides of the fronds grow small containers called sporangia which grow in clusters called sori and which release spores.

20. Rhizoids are long, thin cells that anchor bryophytes in the ground and absorb water and minerals. The water moves from cell to cell through the rhizoids to the rest of the plant. Rhizomes are creeping or underground stems that conduct materials between the roots and leaves of a fern. Roots are underground organs that anchor vascular plants and absorb water and minerals from the soil.

21. In seed plants, the male gametophyte is contained in pollen grains.

22. Features of conifers that suggest they evolved to live in dry habitats include long, thin needles to reduce the surface area of their leaves; the leaves' waxy outer covering; and the placement of leaf openings in cavities in the surface of the leaves to reduce water loss by evaporation.

23. Angiosperms contain the most living species.

24. Fruits attract and are eaten by animals that spread the seeds enclosed in the fruits widely, increasing the ranges that the angiosperms inhabit.

25. Monocots have leaves with parallel veins. Dicots have leaves with branched veins.

TIME SAVER

HOMEWORK GUIDE

Section:	Questions:
Section 22–1	1, 2, 11, 12, 26, 30
Section 22–2	3, 4, 7, 13–16, 28, 31
Section 22–3	5, 6, 17–20, 27, 35
Section 22–4	8, 9, 21, 22, 32
Section 22–5	10, 23–25, 29, 33, 34

Chapter 22 Assessment

Critical Thinking

26. Unlike plants, brown algae do not develop from multicellular embryos, nor do they have roots, stems, and leaves.

27. Vascular tissue is necessary to support a tall plant and carry water and nutrients from the soil to its upper regions. Thus, ferns and trees, which have vascular tissue, grow tall, whereas moss plants cannot grow tall, because they lack vascular tissue.

28. A desert area is too dry to support the natural growth of bryophytes, which require a moist environment. The garden would need to be designed to create a microclimate in which there would be constant moisture for the mosses and liverworts and protection from too much sun.

29. Student answers should reflect the concept that angiosperms have protected seeds and many ways in which the seeds can be dispersed, which increases the chances of survival.

30. Both *Cooksonia* and a geranium are green and have branching stems. Differences include that the geranium has roots, stems, leaves, and flowers that produce seeds, while *Cooksonia* was similar to a moss in that it was simple in structure, grew close to the ground, and bore reproductive structures at its tips.

31. The British army used peat moss as bandages because of its high rate of absorbency and its acidity (low pH), which helped prevent infection.

32. The function of the gametophyte is the same in all three groups, but there is an evolutionary trend toward smaller gametophytes. In bryophytes, the gametophyte is the dominant stage. In ferns, the gametophyte is much smaller than the sporophyte and lives independently. In seed plants, the gametophytes are further reduced to tissues that develop inside cones or flowers.

33. The plant makes the voyage as the embryo within the seed. The endosperm provides the food supply needed to colonize the new land. The seed coat protects the contents of the seed during the voyage and may have a structure that aids in the seed's dispersal.

34. The plant is a monocot, since monocots can have floral parts in multiples of three.

Chapter 22 Assessment

Critical Thinking

26. **Classifying** Many brown algae are multicellular, photosynthetic organisms. Why are they not classified as plants? Refer to Chapter 19 for help in answering this question.

27. **Comparing and Contrasting** Moss plants are small. Ferns can grow as tall as a small tree. Explain why this is so.

28. **Predicting** A friend of yours lives in a desert area of New Mexico. She wants to grow a garden of mosses and liverworts. What environmental conditions would she need to maintain in her garden for it to be successful?

29. **Formulating Hypotheses** Propose a hypothesis to explain why angiosperms have become the dominant type of plant on Earth.

30. **Interpreting Graphics** The plant below is called *Cooksonia*. At one time, scientists thought that it was the ancestor of all land plants. Suggest how this plant may have been similar to, yet different from, a modern flowering plant such as a geranium.

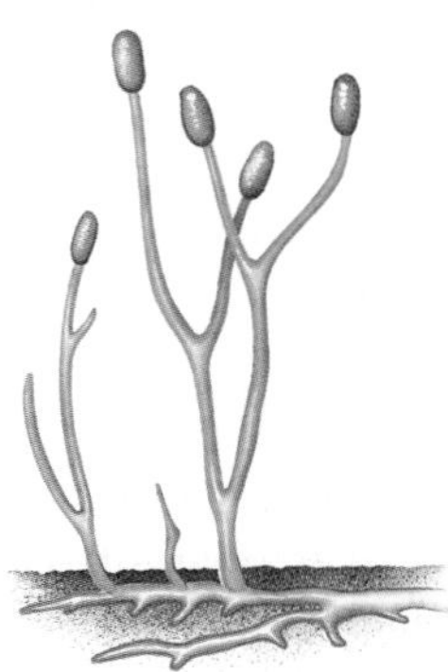

31. **Applying Concepts** During World War I, the British army used sterilized sphagnum moss to bandage millions of wounds. What properties of sphagnum moss make it suitable for use in bandages?

32. **Comparing and Contrasting** Compare the size and function of the gametophyte in bryophytes, ferns, and seed plants. Then describe a general trend in the size of the gametophyte in plant evolution.

33. **Using Analogies** One botanist described a seed as "a ship that carries a plant on a voyage to colonize a new land." Describe the role of each part of the seed in this voyage.

34. **Classifying** Study the photograph of the orchid below. Is this plant a monocot or dicot? Explain your answer.

35. **Making Connections** Use what you know about natural selection to explain how the first nonvascular land plants might have evolved into vascular plants. Refer to Chapter 15 for help in answering this question.

Performance-Based Assessment

Making a Time Line Make a time line to show the major milestones in the evolution of plants. Include a representative plant to show major evolutionary changes in the development of plants. Use the geologic time scale and other information in Chapter 17 for help in drawing your time line.

Take It to the NET

How many kinds of bryophytes are there? Visit the Prentice Hall Web site at **www.phschool.com** to find out about bryophytes in North America. Then, answer the following questions:

- Describe the project undertaken by the New York Botanical Garden.
- How many bryophyte specimens does the New York Botanical Garden have from the United States and Canada?
- How many species of bryophytes have been identified so far?
- What organizations are working on this project with the New York Botanical Garden? List at least five organizations.

Performance-Based Assessment

Student time lines should include a multicellular green alga, a moss, a fern, a gymnosperm such as a conifer, and an angiosperm such as a geranium.

Standardized Test Prep

Test-Taking Tip If you find particular questions difficult, put a light pencil mark beside them and keep working. (Do not write in this book.) As you answer later questions, you may find information that helps you answer the difficult questions.

Directions: Choose the letter that best answers the question or completes the statement.

1. Which of the following is a basic requirement of plants?
I. Sunlight
II. Carbon dioxide
III. Water
(A) I only
(B) II only
(C) I and II only
(D) II and III only
(E) I, II, and III

2. What stage is represented by cones?
I. Sporophytes
II. Gametophytes
III. Pollen grains
(A) I only
(B) II only
(C) I and II only
(D) II and III only
(E) I, II, and III

Questions 3–4 Complete each analogy by selecting the correct letter. In analogies, A : B :: C : D means A is to B as C is to ___?___.

3. Gymnosperm : cones :: angiosperm : ___?___
(A) roots
(B) seeds
(C) stems
(D) leaves
(E) flowers

4. Monocots : grasses :: dicots : ___?___
(A) day lilies
(B) two seed leaves
(C) netlike veins
(D) oak trees
(E) flowers

Questions 5–8 Each of the lettered choices below refers to the following numbered statements. Select the best lettered choice. A choice may be used once, more than once, or not at all.

(A) Gymnosperm
(B) Pollen grain
(C) Fruit
(D) Cotyledon
(E) Protonema

5. Male gametophyte

6. Cone-bearing plant

7. Seed leaf

8. Plant ovary

Questions 9–11

A group of students placed a sprig of a conifer in a beaker of water. They measured the amount of oxygen given off during a set period of time to determine the rate of photosynthesis. They changed the temperature of the beaker using an ice bucket and a hot plate. Their data are summarized in the graph below.

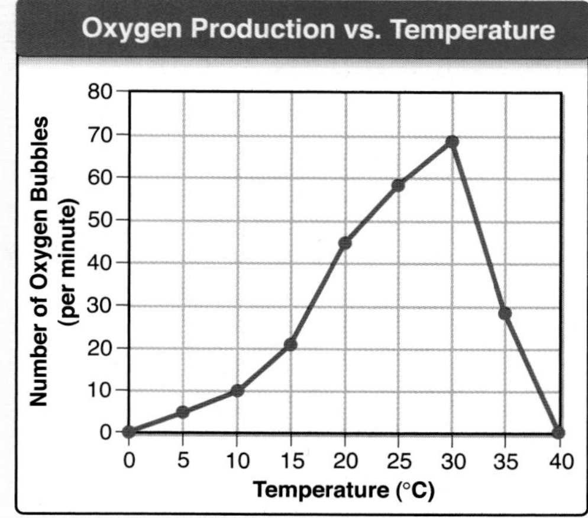

9. What is the independent variable in the students' investigation?
(A) light intensity
(B) temperature
(C) plant growth
(D) oxygen bubbles
(E) photosynthesis rate

10. Which variables should the students have held constant?
I. Plant type
II. Temperature
III. Light intensity
(A) I only
(B) II only
(C) I and III only
(D) II and III only
(E) I, II, and III

11. What can you conclude based on the graph?
I. The higher the temperature, the more oxygen bubbles are released.
II. There is an optimum temperature for photosynthesis in this species of conifer.
III. All plants are most efficient at 30°C.
(A) I only
(B) II only
(C) I and II only
(D) II and III only
(E) I, II, and III

Standardized Test Prep

1. E
2. D
3. E
4. A
5. B
6. A
7. D
8. C
9. B
10. C
11. B

35. Accept all reasonable hypotheses. Answers should include the idea that vascular tissue evolved as a result of variations in plant structure due to mutations. The evolution of vascular tissue improved the transport of water and nutrients within the plant and the absorption of water and minerals from the soil. This development, along with the evolution of lignin, also allowed plants to grow taller. Thus vascular plants were able to colonize drier habitats and compete for sunlight by raising leaves above surrounding plants.

Take It to the NET

• The New York Botanical Garden is cataloging its specimens of mosses, liverworts, and hornworts as part of a project to catalog its entire herbarium—more than 6 million specimens.

• It has more than 200,000 bryophyte specimens from North America north of Mexico.

• About 25,000 living species of bryophytes are recognized. Bryophytes make up one of the largest groups of land plants.

• Among the great number listed are Acadia University, the University of Illinois, the University of Oklahoma, the University of Alaska Museum, and the Ohio State University.

For more information, visit

www.phschool.com

Chapter Planner 23 Roots, Stems, and Leaves

Section and Section Objectives	Time	Activities and Labs
23–1 Specialized Tissues in Plants, pp. 579–583 **23.1.1** ***Describe*** the organs and tissues of vascular plants. **23.1.2** ***Contrast*** meristematic tissue with other plant tissues. **23.1.3** ***Identify*** the specialized cells of vascular tissue.	1 period (1/2 block)	**SE: *Inquiry Activity,*** What parts of plants do we eat?, p. 578 **TE: *Build Science Skills,*** p. 579 **TE: *Build Science Skills,*** p. 583
23–2 Roots, pp. 584–588 **23.2.1** ***Describe*** the two main types of roots. **23.2.2** ***Identify*** the tissues and structures in a mature root. **23.2.3** ***Describe*** the different functions of roots.	1 period (1/2 block)	**TE: *Build Science Skills,*** pp. 584, 585, 588 **TE: *Make Connections,*** p. 586 **TE: *Demonstration,*** p. 586
23–3 Stems, pp. 589–594 **23.3.1** ***Describe*** the two main functions of stems. **23.3.2** ***Contrast*** monocot and dicot stems. **23.3.3** ***Explain*** how primary growth and secondary growth occur in stems.	1 period (1/2 block)	**TE: *Build Science Skills,*** p. 589 **SE: *Analyzing Data,*** Reading a Tree's History, p. 592 **TE: *Demonstration,*** p. 593
23–4 Leaves, pp. 595–598 **23.4.1** ***Describe*** how the structure of a leaf enables it to carry out photosynthesis. **23.4.2** ***Describe*** how gas exchange takes place in a leaf.	1 period (1/2 block)	**TE: *Build Science Skills,*** p. 595 **TE: *Build Science Skills,*** p. 597
23–5 Transport in Plants, pp. 599–602 **23.5.1** ***Explain*** how water is transported throughout a plant. **23.5.2** ***Describe*** how the products of photosynthesis are transported throughout a plant.	1 period (1/2 block)	**TE: *Demonstration,*** p. 599 **TE: *Build Science Skill,*** p. 600 **SE: *Quick Lab,*** What is the role of leaves in transpiration?, p. 601 **SE: *Exploration,*** Identifying the Growth Zones in a Plant, p. 603
Chapter Assessment, pp. 604–607	1 period (1/2 block)	

ACTIVITY PLANNER

SE: *Inquiry Activity,* p. 578; (15 min.); onion, potato, artichoke

TE: *Build Science Skills,* p. 579; (20 min.); plant, tools, dissecting microscope, petri dish

TE: *Build Science Skills,* p. 583; (20 min.); prepared slides, microscope

TE: *Build Science Skills,* p. 584; (15 min.); photos of plants with roots

TE: *Build Science Skills,* p. 585; (15 min.); microscope, prepared slides

TE: *Make Connections,* p. 586; (10 min.); soil samples, beaker

TE: *Demonstration,* p. 586; (5 min.); various fertilizer bags and cartons

TE: *Build Science Skills,* p. 588; (5 min.); water, balloon, water dropper

TE: *Build Science Skills,* p. 589; (15 min.); stems, tools, and microscope

TE: *Demonstration,* p. 593; (10 min.); bark samples from several trees

TE: *Build Science Skills,* p. 595; (15 min.); several plant leaves, dissecting microscope, dissecting tools, microscope, slides, coverslips, stain

TE: *Build Science Skills,* p. 597; (10 min.); 2 elongated balloons, water

TE: *Demonstration,* p. 599; (10 min.); colored water; glass tubes, pan

TE: *Build Science Skills,* p. 600; (5 min.); potted plant, clear plastic bag

SE: *Quick Lab,* p. 601; (10 min. each on 2 days); celery, beaker, food coloring, petroleum jelly, cotton swab, scalpel, metric ruler

SE: *Exploration,* p. 603; (35 min. to set up); 150–mL beaker, metric ruler, paper towels, India ink, 4 large seeds, toothpick, petri dish

PLANNING KEY

Ability Levels

B	**Basic**	For students who need additional help
A	**Average**	For all students
E	**Enriched**	For students who need to be challenged

Components

SE	Student Edition	**GRSW**	Guided Reading and Study Workbook	**IDM**	Issues and Decision Making
TE	Teacher's Edition	**CT**	Chapter Tests: Levels A and B	**CTB**	Computer Test Bank
LMA	Laboratory Manual A	**PHAS**	PH Assessment System	**PA**	Presentation Assistant Plus
LMB	Laboratory Manual B	**LA**	Lab Assessment with Scoring Guide	**BD**	BioDetectives Videotape
TR	Teaching Resources	**BTM**	BioTechnology Manual	**iT**	iText

Program Resources	Assessment	Media and Technology
TR: Section Review 23–1 B A **GRSW:** Section 23–1 B A	**SE:** 23–1 Section Assessment, p. 583 **TR:** Section Review 23–1	**PA:** 23–1 Interest Grabber, Section Outline, Four Types of Plant Tissues, Figure 23–1 **iT:** Section 23–1
LMB: Chapter 23 Lab B A **TR:** Section Review 23–2 B A **GRSW:** Section 23–2 B A	**SE:** 23–2 Section Assessment, p. 588 **TR:** Section Review 23–2	**PA:** 23–2 Interest Grabber, Section Outline, Essential Plant Nutrients, Figure 23–7, Figure 23–9 **iT:** Section 23–2
LMA: Chapter 23 Lab A E **TR:** Section Review 23–3 B A **GRSW:** Section 23–3 B A	**SE:** 23–3 Section Assessment, p. 594 **TR:** Section Review 23–3	**PA:** 23–3 Interest Grabber, Section Outline, Compare/Contrast Table, Figure 23–14, Figure 23–15 **iT:** Section 23–3
TR: Section Review 23–4 B A **GRSW:** Section 23–4 B A	**SE:** 23–4 Section Assessment, p. 598 **TR:** Section Review 23–4	**PA:** 23–4 Interest Grabber, Section Outline, Function of Guard Cells, Figure 23–18 **iT:** Section 23–4
TR: Section Review 23–5 B A Chapter 23 Exploration B A E **GRSW:** Section 23–5 B A	**SE:** 23–5 Section Assessment, p. 602 **TR:** Section Review 23–5	**PA:** 23–5 Interest Grabber, Section Outline, Transpiration, Figure 23–24 **iT:** Section 23–5
	SE: Chapter 23 Assessment, pp. 604–607 **TR:** Chapter Vocabulary Review, Graphic Organizer **CT:** Chapter 23 Test **CTB:** Chapter 23 Test **PHAS:** Practice Test	**CTB:** Chapter 23 Test **iT:** Chapter 23 Assessment

PRESSED FOR TIME?

To Preview the Chapter
- Instruct students to find all of the Vocabulary terms in the chapter and write a definition for each.
- Have students look at the figures in the chapter and read the captions.

To Cover the Chapter Quickly
- Have students read all of Sections 23–1, 23–2, 23–3, 23–4, and 23–5. This entire chapter is required to understand structure and function in plants.
- Assign all Section Reviews and all questions in the Section Assessment.

To Review the Chapter
- Assign Sections 23–1 through 23–5 in the Guided Reading and Study Workbook.
- Assign the Chapter Vocabulary Review for Chapter 23 in the Teaching Resources.

Chapter 23

ENGAGE/EXPLORE

Inquiry Activity

Objective Students will be able to infer what parts of plants they eat.

Skills Focus **Classifying, Inferring**

Materials onion, potato, artichoke

Time 40 minutes

Advance Prep Trim the stems off the artichoke to avoid having students confuse the leaf bud with the stem. You can substitute Brussels sprouts. Obtain onions that have visible roots.

Strategies
- Suggest that students label on their sketches the stems, roots, and leaves of each vegetable.
- Many students will assume incorrectly that onions and potatoes are roots because they grow underground.

Expected Outcomes Students will classify each vegetable as a root, stem, leaf, or other plant part based on their own knowledge of plants.

Think About It

1. Some students might correctly classify the onion as a small stem surrounded by leaves. The leaves are thin and flat, and are attached to the stem at the base. The stem is the part of the onion that joins the leaves to the roots.
2. Some students might correctly identify the potato as a stem. The "eyes" are buds that grow into branches.
3. Some students might correctly identify the artichoke as a floral bud surrounded by modified leaves. The leaves are green because they contain chloroplasts, indicating that they are active in photosynthesis.

Assess Prior Knowledge

Write the words *Roots, Stems,* and *Leaves* on the board. Encourage students to tell what they know about each plant structure. Record their responses under the appropriate heading. Throughout the chapter, correct and add to the information under each heading as students learn about that plant structure.

Chapter 23 Roots, Stems, and Leaves

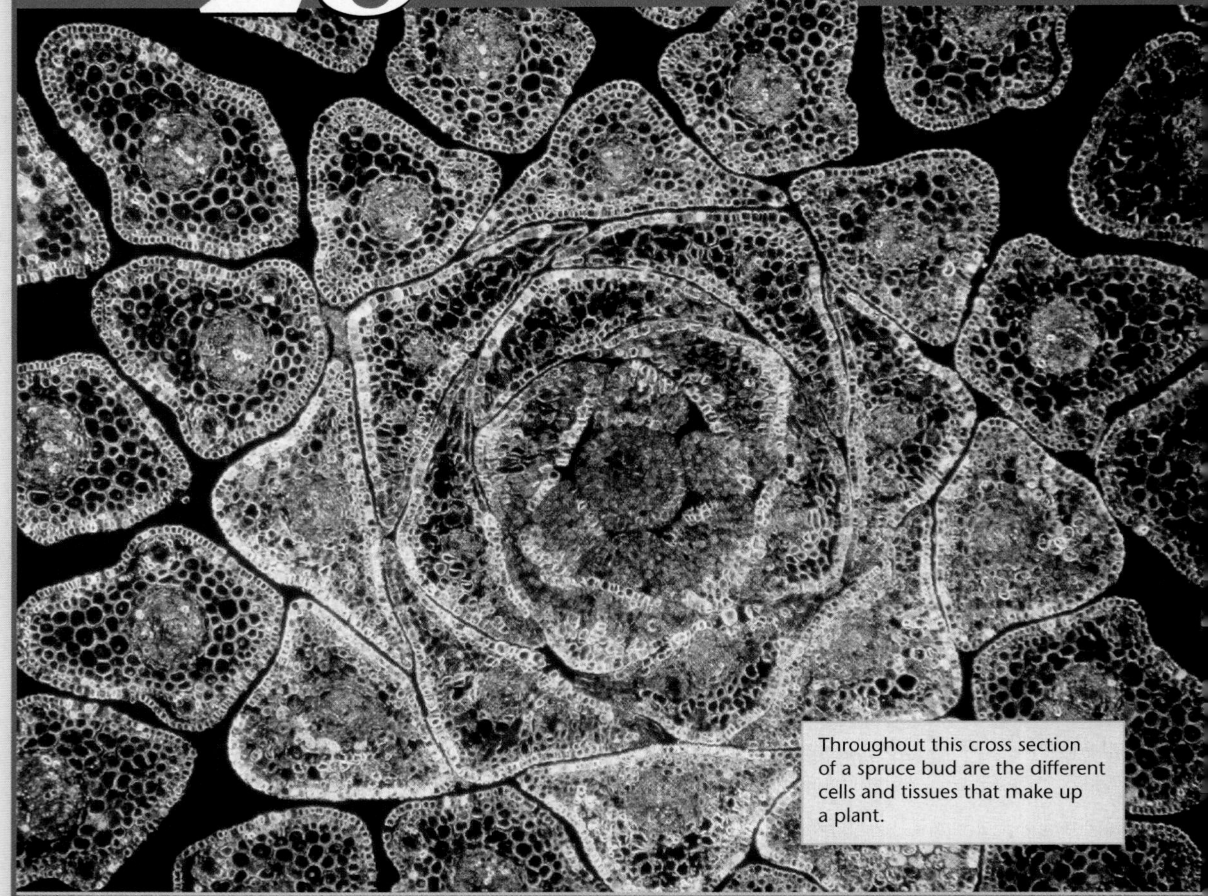

Throughout this cross section of a spruce bud are the different cells and tissues that make up a plant.

Inquiry Activity

What parts of plants do we eat?

Procedure

1. Examine an onion, a potato, and an artichoke. Record your observations as notes and labeled sketches.
2. Use your observations to classify each vegetable as a root, stem, leaf, or other plant part.

Think About It

1. **Classifying** How did you classify the onion? Explain what characteristics you used to make this decision.
2. **Inferring** How did you classify the potato? How is its structure related to its function?
3. **Inferring** How did you classify the artichoke? What does its inner structure tell you about its function?

FACTS AND FIGURES

Soil and plants

Soil, climate, and plants interact in ways that affect the response of ecosystems to disturbance. Across the American Midwest, for example, deep, sandy soil was covered for many years by native grasses whose leaves and roots decayed to produce thick, humus-laden soil. That soil is superbly suited to production of crops that can be sustained for decades with proper management. In most tropical rain forests, on the other hand, heavy rainfall, high temperatures, and high humidity cause organic matter to break down so quickly that humus is restricted to a thin surface layer. When vegetation is removed for farming, humus quickly vanishes. The remaining soil is exhausted of nutrients, and compacts into clay so hard that it can break a plow. Such land turns to wasteland in about five years after clearing.

23–1 Specialized Tissues in Plants

Have you ever wondered if plants were really alive? Day after day, they just seem to sit there, quiet and unmoving. Compared to animals, plants don't seem to do much. Yet, in one sense, plants have been more successful than animals. Individual plants outnumber animals and also make up far more of Earth's biomass. So, it's only fair to admit that plants must be doing something right. And so they are.

If you look deep inside a living plant, that first impression of inactivity vanishes. Instead, you will find a busy and complex organism packed with specialized cells and tissues. Materials are moving throughout the plant, and growth and repair are taking place continually. Plants may act at a pace that you consider slow, but the ways in which their cells act together are remarkably effective in ensuring the survival of plants.

Guide for Reading

Key Concepts
- What are the principal organs and tissues of vascular plants?
- How is meristematic tissue different from other plant tissues?
- What specialized cells make up vascular tissue?

Vocabulary
meristematic tissue
apical meristem
epidermal cell
cuticle
trichome
vessel element
sieve tube element
companion cell
parenchyma
collenchyma
sclerenchyma

Reading Strategy: Building Vocabulary Before you read, preview new vocabulary by skimming the section and making a list of the boldfaced terms. Leave space to make notes of definitions as you read.

Structure of Seed Plants

The cells of a seed plant are organized into different tissues and organs, as shown in **Figure 23–1** on page 580.  **The three principal organs of seed plants are roots, stems, and leaves.**

Roots Roots perform several important functions. They absorb water and dissolved nutrients from moist soil. They anchor plants in the ground. Roots also hold plants upright and prevent them from being knocked over by wind and rain. Roots are able to do all these jobs because as they grow, they develop complex branching networks that penetrate the soil and grow between soil particles.

Stems The stem is the part of the plant that supports the plant body and transports nutrients among different parts of the plant. To compete with other plants for sunlight, many plants have very tall stems that hold a plant's leaves up to the sun. The leaves of a tree can be as high as 100 meters above the ground. To support this weight, the stems of tall plants are sturdy and contain great amounts of vascular tissue that supplies the plant with water and nutrients. The vascular tissue of stems lifts water from roots up to the leaves and sends the products of photosynthesis from the leaves down to the roots.

Leaves Leaves are the principal organs in which plants carry out photosynthesis. The broad, flat surfaces of leaves help increase the amount of sunlight absorbed by plants. Leaves also expose a great deal of tissue to the dryness of the air and must, therefore, be protected against water loss. Adjustable pores in leaves help conserve water while allowing oxygen and carbon dioxide to enter and leave the leaf.

SECTION RESOURCES

Print:
- ***Teaching Resources,*** Section Review 23–1
- ***Guided Reading and Study Workbook,*** Section 23–1

Technology:
- ***iText,*** Section 23–1

Section 23–1

1 FOCUS

Objectives

23.1.1 ***Describe*** the organs and tissues of vascular plants.
23.1.2 ***Contrast*** meristematic tissue with other plant tissues.
23.1.3 ***Identify*** the specialized cells of vascular tissue.

Guide for Reading

Vocabulary Preview

Read aloud the Vocabulary terms to students. Then, instruct students to copy the words from their textbook and divide them into syllables. *(mer•i•ste•mat•ic tis•sue, ap•i•cal mer•i•stem, ep•i•der•mal cell, cu•ti•cle, trich•ome, ves•sel el•e•ment, sieve tube el•e•ment, com•pan•ion cell, pa•ren•chy•ma, col•len•chy•ma, scle•ren•chy•ma)*

Reading Strategy

Encourage students to practice saying the Vocabulary terms aloud as they read the chapter. They should use the phonetic spellings to help them with correct pronunciation.

2 INSTRUCT

Structure of Seed Plants

Build Science Skills

Observing Have students examine small, bare-root plants. Instruct them to locate and observe the three major organs of the plant. Have them diagram the plant and label the leaves, stems, and roots. Then, have students examine the roots, stems, and leaves under a dissecting microscope. Encourage them to use dissecting tools to tease apart the plant tissue to observe the cells inside. Instruct students to record and illustrate their observations.

23–1 (continued)

Tissue Systems

Meet Diverse Needs

Have at-risk students and students with limited English proficiency create a concept map in which they show the levels of organization in plants. In their concept maps they should include the three types of plant organs and the three tissue systems. **Learning modality: visual**

Meristematic Tissue

Use Visuals

Figure 23–2 Have students study the diagram in the figure. Ask: **How is meristematic tissue different from other plant tissue?** *(It's the only tissue that produces new cells by mitosis.)* **Where are the apical meristems on this plant?** *(At the tips of shoots and roots)* **What occurs at the apical meristem?** *(Growth; it is the area where many actively dividing cells are located.)* **What group of larger cells is located at the tip of a root?** *(Cells that form the root cap, which protects the apical meristem by pushing through the soil during growth)*

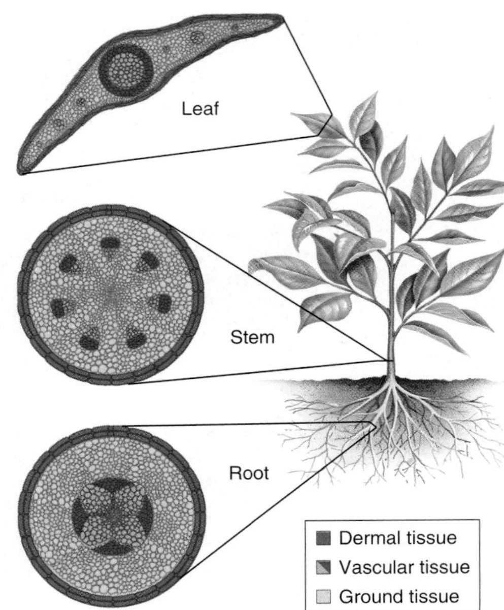

◀ **Figure 23–1** **Vascular plants consist of roots, stems, and leaves.** Each of these organs contains dermal tissue, vascular tissue, and ground tissue, as shown by the cross sections of the leaf, stem, and root. **Interpreting Visuals** ***Which tissue is found in the center of a plant stem?***

Tissue Systems

Within the roots, stems, and leaves of plants are specialized tissue systems. **Plants consist of three tissue systems: dermal tissue, vascular tissue, and ground tissue.** In a sense, dermal tissue forms the "skin" of a plant in that it is the outermost layer of cells. Vascular tissue is like the plant's "bloodstream," transporting water and nutrients throughout the plant, and ground tissue is everything else. A fourth type of tissue, **meristematic tissue** (mehr-uh-stuh-MAT-ik), is found only in the tips of shoots and roots. **Figure 23–2** shows two examples of meristematic tissue, which is responsible for the growth that takes place throughout the life of a plant. It is described first because it is the source of all other tissues in a plant.

Meristematic Tissue

A distinguishing feature of plants is that they have an open, or indeterminate, type of growth. They grow and produce new, undifferentiated cells at their tips for as long as they live. Even a tree that is many years old and that has mature tissues throughout most of its body continually increases in height above ground and in length below ground.

Most mature plant cells do not divide to form new cells. New growth is instead produced in cells that make up meristematic tissue. **Meristematic tissue is the only plant tissue that produces new cells by mitosis.** All the cells of a plant originate in meristems and at first look alike: They divide rapidly and have thin cell walls. As meristematic cells mature, they differentiate into one of the three main tissues of a plant.

Meristematic tissue is found in several places in a plant. At the end, or tip, of each growing stem and root is an apical meristem. An **apical meristem** is a group of undifferentiated cells that divide to produce increased length of stems and roots. **Figure 23–2** shows the location and structure of a shoot apical meristem and a root apical meristem.

TIME SAVER — PRESENTATIONS MADE EASY!

The Presentation Assistant Plus contains the Prentice Hall Presentation Pro and the Transparencies, which provide easy-to-follow visual support for every step of this section. If you have a computer presentation station, use Prentice Hall Presentation Pro for Section 23–1, or use the following transparencies.

Section 23–1:

Interest Grabber
Section Outline
Four Types of Plant Tissues
Figure 23–1

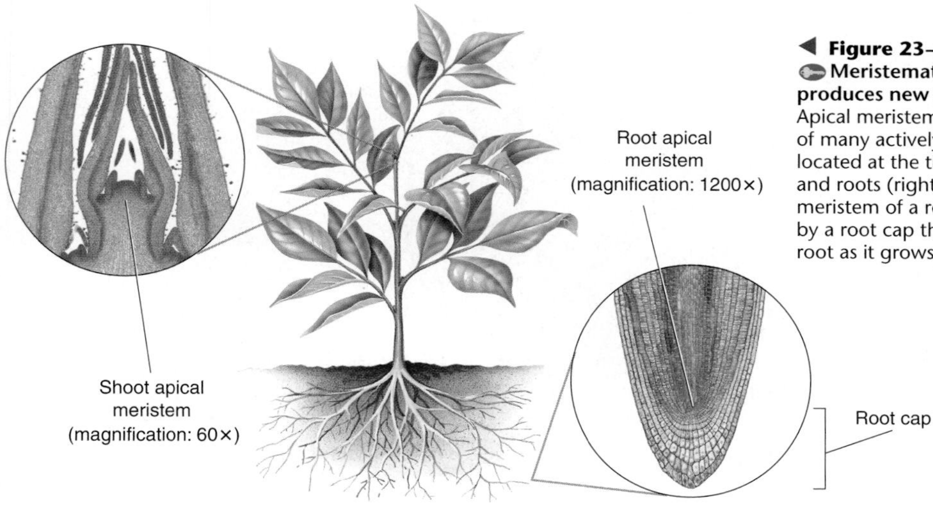

◀ **Figure 23–2** **Meristematic tissue produces new cells by mitosis.** Apical meristems, which consist of many actively dividing cells, are located at the tips of shoots (left) and roots (right). The apical meristem of a root is surrounded by a root cap that protects the root as it grows through the soil.

Immediately behind each apical meristem, cells increase in size and length. Farther from the meristem, cells take on the structures and functions of mature cells. This ongoing process of cell division, maturation, elongation, and development causes the youngest, least mature cells in any plant to be closest to the meristems.

Many plants also grow in width as a result of meristematic tissue that lines the stems and roots of a plant. Later in the chapter, you will learn how this type of growth takes place.

Dermal Tissue

The outer covering of a plant consists of dermal tissue. Dermal tissue typically consists of a single layer of **epidermal cells,** shown in **Figure 23–3.** The exposed outer surfaces of these cells are often covered with a thick, waxy layer, or **cuticle,** that protects against water loss and injury. The surfaces of some leaves also have tiny cellular projections known as **trichomes** (TRY-kohmz), which help protect the leaf and also give it a fuzzy appearance. In roots, dermal tissue includes root hair cells that provide a large amount of surface area and aid in water absorption. On the underside of leaves, dermal tissue contains guard cells, which regulate water loss and gas exchange.

CHECKPOINT *What is the cuticle?*

▼ **Figure 23–3** The photo shows the epidermis of the outer covering of a rosebud. The epidermis is covered with thin, unicellular trichomes as well as large, bulbous trichomes that secrete chemicals that protect the plant against insect attack (magnification: 150×). **Formulating Hypotheses** ***Develop a hypothesis to explain how natural selection might have led to the development of plants with large trichomes.***

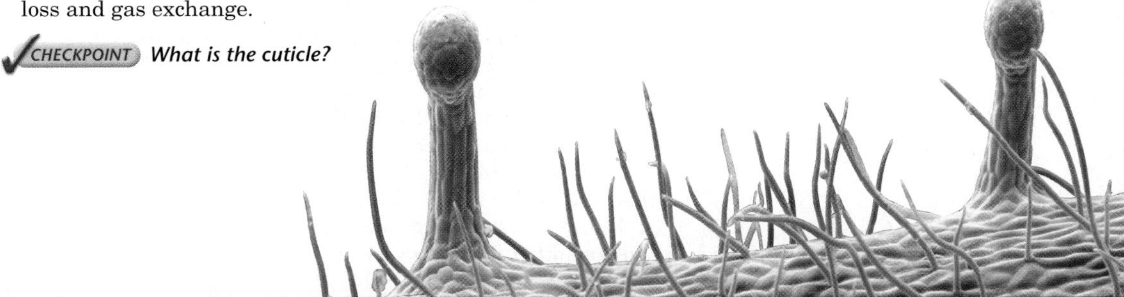

Meet Diverse Needs

The vocabulary in this section might be particularly troublesome for at-risk students and students with limited English proficiency. Help these students develop a glossary system, either in a notebook or with spiral-bound index cards, for the Vocabulary terms. In their glossaries, students should include phonetic spellings for each term and formalized definitions, as well as definitions using their own words. Encourage students to also include the meanings of prefixes and suffixes, diagrams, and mnemonics. Students with limited English proficiency may also include phrases in their native language. **Limited English proficiency**

Dermal Tissue

Meet Diverse Needs

Have students who would like an additional challenge learn more about trichomes. They should discover what their function is and which plants have them. Students can create a poster to help them present their findings to the class. **Learning modality: verbal**

Answers to . . .

CHECKPOINT *A thick, waxy layer on the outer surfaces of epidermal cells that protects against water loss and injury*

Figure 23–1 *Ground tissue*

Figure 23–3 *Plants with larger trichomes might have been better able to protect themselves against insects, which allowed them to survive and reproduce better than plants with smaller trichomes.*

Vascular Tissue

Use Visuals

Figure 23–4 Have student volunteers identify the xylem tissue and the phloem tissue. Ask: **What does xylem transport?** *(Water)* **What does phloem transport?** *(Food)* Then, have students identify the cell types that make up xylem *(tracheids and vessel elements)* and phloem *(companion cells and sieve tube elements)*. Challenge students to infer which plant organ is used in the illustration. *(Stem)* Have them refer to Figure 23–1 to help them identify it.

Meet Diverse Needs

Have at-risk students write a "parts list" for vascular tissue to help them review its structure and function. Students should describe the types of cells that make up vascular tissue and the characteristics of these cells. Encourage students to include an "assembly diagram" in their parts list that shows the structure of the tissue. **Learning modality: logical/mathematical**

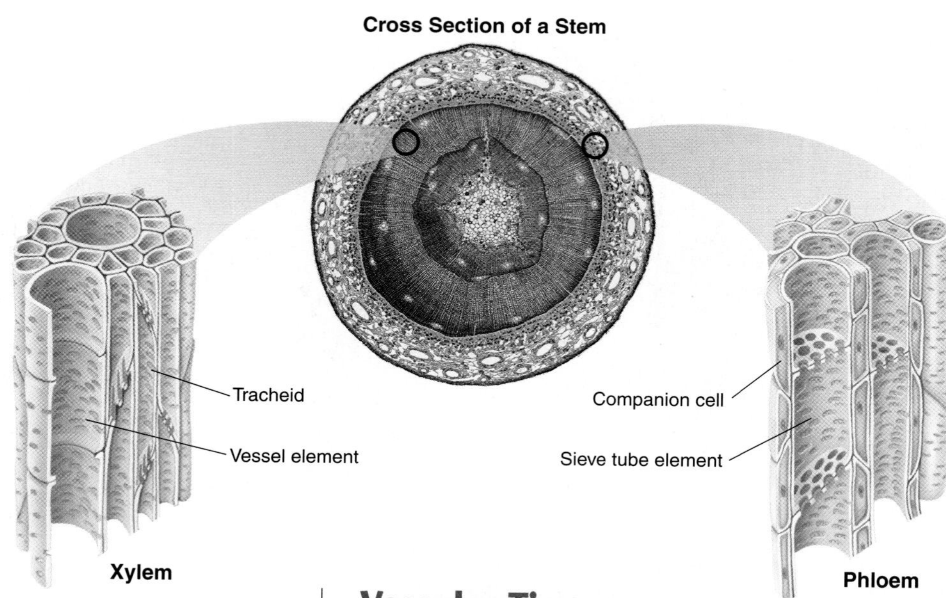

▲ **Figure 23–4** **Vascular tissue is made up of several different types of cells. Xylem consists of tracheids and vessel elements. Phloem consists of sieve tube elements and companion cells.** Xylem tissue (left) conducts water from the roots to the rest of the plant. Phloem tissue (right) conducts a variety of materials, mostly carbohydrates, throughout a plant.

Vascular Tissue

Recall from the last chapter that vascular tissue transports water and nutrients throughout the plant. The principal types of vascular tissue are xylem, a water-conducting tissue, and phloem, a food-conducting tissue. **Vascular tissue contains several different cell types. Xylem consists of tracheids and vessel elements. Phloem consists of sieve tube elements and companion cells.** As you can see in **Figure 23–4,** xylem and phloem are made up of networks of hollow connected cells.

Xylem All seed plants have a type of xylem cell called a tracheid. Tracheids are long, narrow cells with walls that are impermeable to water. These walls, however, are pierced by openings that connect neighboring cells to one another. When tracheids mature, they die, and their cytoplasm disintegrates.

Angiosperms have another kind of xylem cell that is called a **vessel element.** Vessel elements are much wider than tracheids. Like tracheids, they mature and die before they conduct water. Vessel elements are arranged end to end on top of one another like a stack of tin cans. The cell walls at both ends are lost when the cells die, transforming the stack of vessel elements into a continuous tube through which water can move freely.

Phloem The main phloem cells are **sieve tube elements.** These cells are arranged end to end, like vessel elements, to form sieve tubes. The end walls of sieve tube elements have many small holes in them. Materials can move through these holes from one adjacent cell to another. As sieve tube elements mature, they lose their nuclei and most of the other organelles in their cytoplasm. The remaining organelles hug the inside of the cell wall. The rest of the space is a pipeline through which sugars and other foods are carried in a watery stream.

FACTS AND FIGURES

Characteristics of specialized plant cells
Parenchyma cells are found in all the major parts of plants. Although these cells are usually spherical when first produced, their thin walls are easily flattened as they are packed against each other. The majority end up having a shape with 14 sides. The main function of parenchyma cells with chloroplasts is photosynthesis; those without chloroplasts store water or food.

Companion cells are phloem cells that surround sieve tube elements. Companion cells keep their nuclei and other organelles throughout their lifetime. Companion cells support the phloem cells and aid in the movement of substances in and out of the phloem stream.

Ground Tissue

The cells that lie between dermal and vascular tissues make up the ground tissues shown in **Figure 23–5.** In most plants, ground tissue consists mainly of parenchyma. **Parenchyma** (puh-RENG-kih-muh) cells have thin cell walls and large central vacuoles surrounded by a thin layer of cytoplasm. In leaves, these cells are packed with chloroplasts and are the site of most of a plant's photosynthesis. Ground tissue may also contain two types of cells with thicker cell walls. **Collenchyma** (kuh-LENG-kih-muh) cells have strong, flexible cell walls that help support larger plants. Collenchyma cells make up the familiar "strings" of a stalk of celery. **Sclerenchyma** (sklih-RENG-kih-muh) cells have extremely thick, rigid cell walls that make ground tissue tough and strong.

Figure 23–5 Ground tissue is made of cells whose cell walls have different thicknesses. Parenchyma cells have thin walls and function mainly in storage and photosynthesis. The root cells shown are filled with purple-staining starch grains. Collenchyma and sclerenchyma cells both function in support. Collenchyma cells have irregularly shaped walls, but the walls of sclerenchyma cells are much thicker and harder. **Predicting** ***Where would you expect to find more sclerenchyma—in the leaves or the stem of a plant?***

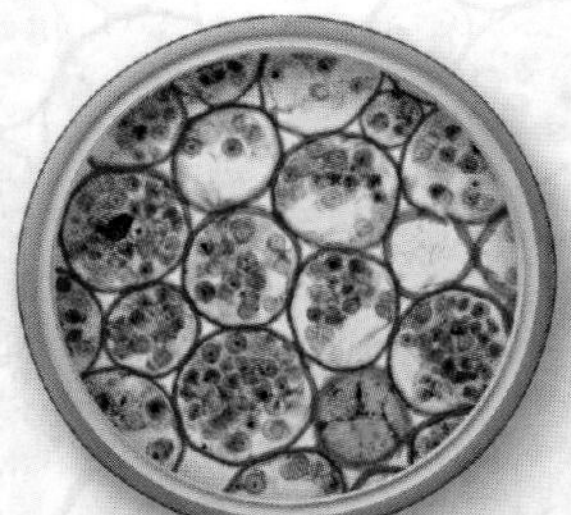

Parenchyma
(magnification: about 50×)

Collenchyma
(magnification: about 150×)

Sclerenchyma
(magnification: about 200×)

23–1 Section Assessment

1. **Key Concept** List the three tissue systems of plants. Describe how each tissue is distributed in stems, tissues, and leaves.
2. **Key Concept** What is the function of meristematic tissue in a plant?
3. **Key Concept** What two cell types make up xylem? Phloem?
4. In a stem that needs to support heavy leaves, what type of ground tissue might you expect to find?
5. **Critical Thinking Comparing and Contrasting** The vascular system of a plant has been compared to the circulatory system of a human. How are these two systems similar? How are they different?

iTEXT Assessment Use iText to review the important concepts in Section 23–1.

Take It to the NET

Choose one of the tissue systems in plants and make a concept map to show the different structures and types of cells formed by that system. Use the links provided in the Biology area of the Prentice Hall Web site for help in completing this activity: **www.phschool.com**

23–1 Section Assessment

1. Dermal tissue: outermost layer of cells; vascular tissue: cells that transport water and nutrients throughout the plant; ground tissue: all other cells making up the plant
2. Produces new cells by mitosis
3. Tracheids and vessel elements; sieve tube elements and companion cells
4. Collenchyma cells because they have strong, flexible cell walls that support larger plants
5. Both are a system of tubes that transports materials through the body. The vascular system is composed of plant cells and the circulatory system is composed of animal cells.

Ground Tissue

Build Science Skills

Observing Have students examine prepared microscope slides of parenchyma cells, collenchyma cells, and sclerenchyma cells. Instruct students to draw labeled diagrams of the cells they observe. Encourage them to label as many parts of a plant cell as they can, such as nucleus, cell wall, cytoplasm, chloroplast, nuclear membrane, and vacuoles.

3 ASSESS

Evaluate Understanding

Play a word association game in which you name a type of plant cell and a student volunteer names the tissue from which it comes.

Reteach

Have students create a table in which they organize and describe the three types of plant tissue (dermal, vascular, and ground) and the types of cells that make them up. Students might also wish to include sketches of the cells in their tables.

Take It to the NET

Students should choose meristematic, dermal, vascular, or ground tissue and construct a graphic organizer to show the different characteristics of the tissue. For example, if students choose ground tissue, they should include information about parenchyma, collenchyma, and sclerenchyma. For additional information, visit **www.phschool.com**

Use iText to review the key concepts in Section 23–1.

Answer to . . .

Figure 23–5 *Stem*

Section 23–2

1 FOCUS

Objectives

23.2.1 ***Describe*** the two main types of roots.
23.2.2 ***Identify*** the tissues and structures in a mature root.
23.2.3 ***Describe*** the different functions of roots.

Guide for Reading

Vocabulary Preview

As you read aloud the Vocabulary terms that refer to root structure, point out their location in Figure 23–7. Contrast the words *endodermis* and *epidermis.* Explain that the suffix *-dermis* means "skin." Challenge students to infer what the prefixes *endo-* (inside) and *epi-* (upon) mean based on the location of these structures in the root.

Reading Strategy

Encourage students to include diagrams of types of roots and root structures in their outlines. Also suggest that they include all Vocabulary terms and Key Concepts in their outlines.

2 INSTRUCT

Types of Roots

Build Science Skills

Classifying Give students ten to fifteen pictures of different plants with their root structures. Instruct students to classify the roots as being taproots or fibrous roots. Then, have students determine what other characteristics the members of each group share. Challenge students to write a general statement to describe the types of plants in each group.

23–2 Roots

Guide for Reading

Key Concepts
- What are the two main types of roots?
- What are the main tissues in a mature root?
- What are the different functions of roots?

Vocabulary
taproot
fibrous root
root hair
cortex
endodermis
vascular cylinder
root cap
Casparian strip

Reading Strategy: Outlining Before you read, use the headings of the section to make an outline about plant roots. As you read, fill in phrases or a sentence after each heading to provide key information.

As soon as a seed begins to grow, it puts out its first root to draw water and nutrients from the soil. Other roots soon branch out from this first root, adding length and surface area to the root system. With continued growth, the overall size of a plant's root system can be astonishing: The total surface area of the root system of a rye plant was measured at more than 600 square meters—130 times greater than the combined surface areas of stems and leaves.

Types of Roots

The two main types of roots are taproots, which are found mainly in dicots, and fibrous roots, which are found mainly in monocots. In some plants, the primary root grows long and thick while the secondary roots remain small. This type of primary root is called a **taproot,** shown in **Figure 23–6.** Taproots of oak and hickory trees grow so long that they can reach water far below the Earth's surface. Carrots, dandelions, beets, and radishes have short, thick taproots that store sugars or starches.

In other plants, such as grasses, **fibrous roots** branch to such an extent that no single root grows larger than the rest. The extensive fibrous root systems produced by many plants help prevent topsoil from being washed away by heavy rain.

CHECKPOINT *How do roots help prevent erosion?*

▼ **Figure 23–6** **Plants have taproots, fibrous roots, or both.** Taproots have a central primary root and generally grow deep into the soil. Fibrous roots are usually shallow and consist of many thin roots.

SECTION RESOURCES

Print:
- ***Laboratory Manual B,*** Chapter 23 Lab
- ***Teaching Resources,*** Section Review 23–2
- ***Guided Reading and Study Workbook,*** Section 23–2

Technology:
- ***iText,*** Section 23–2

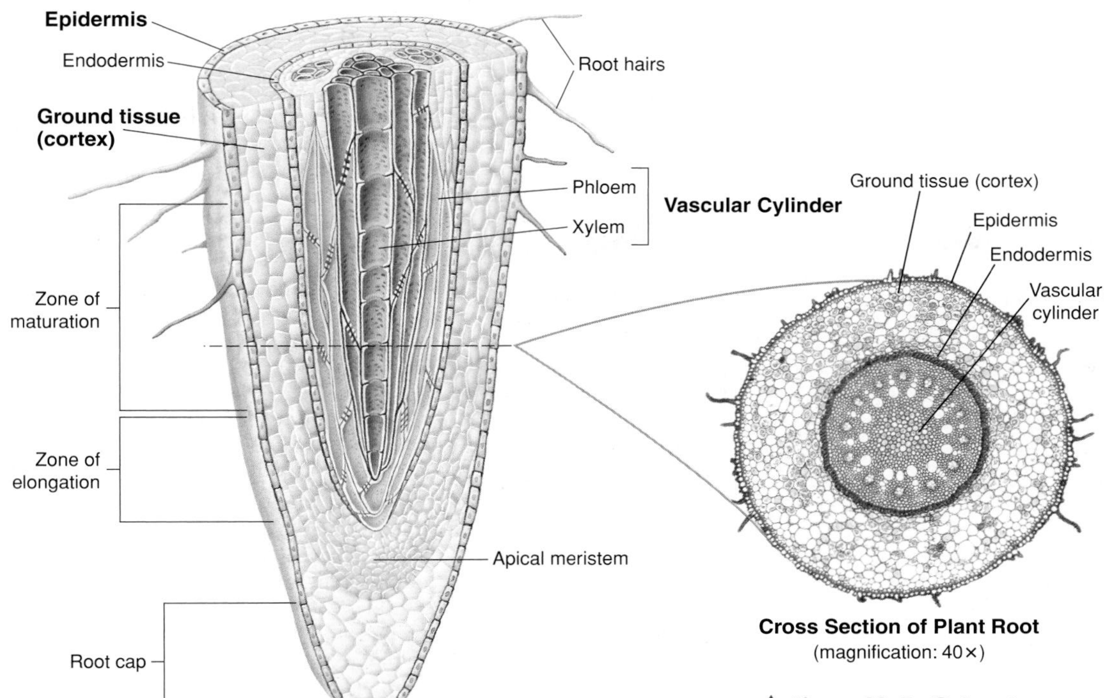

Cross Section of Plant Root
(magnification: 40×)

▲ **Figure 23–7** **A root consists of a central vascular cylinder surrounded by ground tissue and the epidermis.** Root hairs along the surface of the root aid in water absorption. Only the cells in the root tip divide. In the area just behind the root tip, the newly divided cells increase in length, pushing the root tip farther into the soil. The root cap, located just ahead of the root tip, protects the dividing cells as they are pushed forward. Dicot roots, such as the one shown in the cross section, have a central column of xylem cells arranged in a radiating pattern.

Root Structure and Growth

You have already learned that roots contain cells from the three tissue systems. **A mature root has an outside layer, the epidermis, and a central cylinder of vascular tissue. Between these two tissues lies a large area of ground tissue.** Refer to **Figure 23–7** as you read about the structure of a root. The epidermis of a root is covered with tiny projections called **root hairs.** These hairs penetrate the spaces between soil particles and produce a large surface area through which water can enter the plant. Just inside the epidermis is a spongy layer of ground tissue known as the **cortex.** This layer extends to another layer of cells called the **endodermis.** The endodermis completely encloses vascular tissue in a central region called the **vascular cylinder.**

Roots grow in length as their apical meristem produces new cells near the root tip. These fragile new cells are covered by a tough **root cap** that protects the root as it forces its way through the soil. As the root grows, the root cap secretes a slippery substance that lubricates the progress of the root through the soil. Cells at the very tip of the root cap are constantly being scraped away, and new root cap cells are continually added by the meristem. Most of the increase in root length occurs immediately behind the meristem, where cells are growing longer. At a later stage, these cells mature and take on specialized functions.

Root Structure and Growth

Use Visuals

Figure 23–7 Relate the four plant tissues to the diagram of the root in the figure. Make sure students can identify the location of meristematic tissue, dermal tissue, vascular tissue, and ground tissue. Help students identify the different cell types within each tissue. Ask: **Would you expect to observe chlorophyll in the parenchyma cells of a root?** *(No, roots do not receive sunlight and have no need for chlorophyll.)* Then, discuss where new growth originates from. Ask: **As roots grow, which portion of the root actually elongates?** *(The portion located just behind the root cap)*

Build Science Skills

Observing Set up microscope stations at which students can observe prepared slides of longitudinal and cross sections of plant roots. Include both monocot and dicot plant roots to give students the opportunity to compare and contrast their structures. Students should draw labeled diagrams of their observations. They can use Figure 23–7 to help them identify the root structures.

TIME SAVER — PRESENTATIONS MADE EASY!

The Presentation Assistant Plus contains the Prentice Hall Presentation Pro and the Transparencies, which provide easy-to-follow visual support for every step of this section. If you have a computer presentation station, use Prentice Hall Presentation Pro for Section 23–2, or use the following transparencies.

Section 23–2:

Interest Grabber
Section Outline
Essential Plant Nutrients
Figure 23–7
Figure 23–9

Answer to . . .

CHECKPOINT *Extensive, branching fibrous roots hold soil in place.*

Root Functions

Make Connections

Earth Science Display samples of sand, silt, clay, and various soils that are combinations of each. Demonstrate how the pore size of sand enables water to quickly filter through it, while the small pore size of clay causes water to seep through it slowly. Explain that this pore size directly relates to the amount of nutrients held in a soil. Ask: **Why can't sandy soils hold as many nutrients as silt and clay soils?** *(Water washes the nutrients out of sandy soils more quickly and carries them away.)* **Why do you think clay soils are difficult for many plants to grow in?** *(They tend to be water-logged due to poor drainage.)*

Demonstration

Display different types of plant fertilizers to the class. Show students how to read the nutrient analysis information on the bag or carton, especially the Nitrogen-Phosphorus-Potassium number. Discuss when and why fertilizers are used for plants, as well as the dangers of overfertilizing and the potential for harming lakes and ponds from fertilizer runoff (increased phosphates in the pond stimulate algae growth).

Root Functions

Roots anchor a plant in the ground and absorb water and dissolved nutrients from the soil. How does a root go about the job of absorbing water and minerals from the soil? Although it might seem to, water does not just "soak" into the root from soil. It takes energy on the part of the plant to absorb water. Our explanation of this process begins with a description of soil and plant nutrients.

Uptake of Plant Nutrients An understanding of soil helps explain how plants function. Soil is a complex mixture of sand, silt, clay, air, and bits of decaying animal and plant tissue. Soil in different places and at different depths contains varying amounts of these ingredients. Sandy soil, for example, is made of large particles that retain few nutrients, whereas the finely textured silt and clay soils of the Midwest and southeastern United States are high in nutrients. The ingredients define the soil and determine, to a large extent, the kinds of plants that can grow in it.

To grow, flower, and produce seeds, plants require a variety of inorganic nutrients in addition to carbon dioxide and water. The most important of these nutrients are nitrogen, phosphorus, potassium, magnesium, and calcium. The functions of these essential nutrients within a plant are described in **Figure 23–8.** These nutrients are located in varying amounts in the soil and are drawn up by the roots of a plant. In addition to these essential nutrients, trace elements are required in small quantities to maintain proper plant growth. Trace elements include sulfur, iron, zinc, molybdenum, boron, copper, manganese, and chlorine. Large amounts of trace elements in the soil can be poisonous.

CHECKPOINT *What are essential nutrients and trace nutrients?*

▼ **Figure 23–8** Soil contains several nutrients that are essential for plant growth. Each nutrient plays a different role in plant functioning and development, and produces distinct effects when deficient in the soil. **Interpreting Graphics** *If you notice that a plant is becoming paler and more yellow, what nutrient might need to be added?*

Essential Plant Nutrients

Nutrient	Role in Plant	Result of Deficiency
Nitrogen	Proper leaf growth and color; synthesis of amino acids, proteins, nucleic acids, and chlorophyll	Stunted plant growth; pale yellow leaves
Phosphorus	Synthesis of DNA; development of roots, stems, flowers, and seeds	Poor flowering; stunted growth
Potassium	Synthesis of proteins and carbohydrates; development of roots, stems, and flowers; resistance to cold and disease	Weak stems and stunted roots; edges of leaves turn brown
Magnesium	Synthesis of chlorophyll	Thin stems; mottled, pale leaves
Calcium	Cell growth and division; cell wall structure; cellular transport; enzyme action	Stunted growth; curled leaves

FACTS AND FIGURES

Roots and the underground

Many plants produce roots above ground as well as below. Corn plants, for example, form roots that emerge from the stems and grow toward the ground. Orchids frequently grow perched high on tree trunks and branches. They attach themselves to the tree with roots that secrete a kind of cement. Orchids actually grow on other plants. They gain no nourishment from their unintended hosts. They get nutrients from leaves that fall and decompose near their roots.

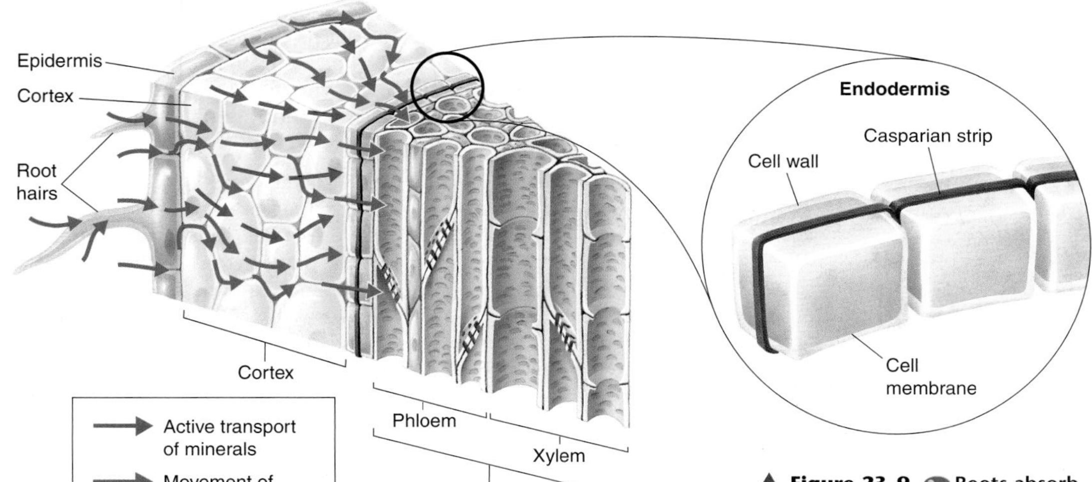

▲ **Figure 23–9** **Roots absorb water and dissolved nutrients from the soil.** Most water and minerals enter a plant through the tiny hairs on plant roots. Water moves from the outside of the roots into the cortex, then passes through the cells of the endodermis into the vascular cylinder. Finally, water reaches the xylem, where it is transported throughout the plant. Cells in the endodermis are made waterproof by the Casparian strip, which prevents water molecules from seeping back between the cells.

Active Transport of Minerals The cell membranes of root hairs and other cells in the root epidermis contain active transport proteins. These proteins use ATP (an energy source) to pump mineral ions from the soil into the plant. The high concentration of mineral ions in the plant cells causes water molecules to move into the plant by osmosis, as shown in **Figure 23–9.**

You may recall that osmosis is the movement of water across a membrane toward an area where the concentration of dissolved material is higher. By using active transport to accumulate ions from the soil, cells of the root epidermis create conditions under which osmosis causes water to "follow" those ions and flow into the root. Note that the root does not actually pump water. But by pumping dissolved minerals into its own cells, it does almost the same thing.

Movement Into the Vascular Cylinder Active transport in the cells of the root epidermis causes water and minerals to move into the cortex. From there, the water and dissolved minerals pass the inner boundary of the cortex and enter the endodermis. This process is shown in **Figure 23–9.**

The endodermis encloses the vascular cylinder and stretches up and down the entire length of the root, like a cylinder. It is composed of many individual cells, each shaped a bit like a brick. Each of these cells is surrounded on four sides by a waterproof strip called a **Casparian strip.** To imagine what the Casparian strip looks like, think of a brick with a thick, sticky rubber band stretched around four sides. The rubber bands stick together like mortar between the bricks. Now imagine many of these bricks placed edge to edge to build a cylinder. When a root is viewed in cross section, the endodermis looks like a circle.

Meet Diverse Needs

You might need to review the processes of active transport and osmosis with at-risk students. Have students apply the diagrams describing the process of active transport and osmosis from Chapter 7 to the movement of minerals and water in a root. Encourage students to create a graphic organizer to summarize these processes in plants. **Learning modality: visual**

Use Visuals

Figure 23–9 As students study how water and minerals move through the epidermis, through the cortex, and into the vascular cylinder, point out that water moves through the cortex cells, as well as around them in the spaces between. Make sure students understand that the Casparian strips only prevent water and nutrients from moving around the endodermal cells—not through them. Ask: **What stops dissolved minerals from moving back through the endodermal cells into the cortex?** *(These cells use active transport to force the nutrients into the vascular cylinder.)* **What stops water from diffusing backward through endodermal cells?** *(If water moved backward, it would be moving from an area of low water concentration to one of high water concentration.)*

FACTS AND FIGURES

Nutrients and active transport

Active transport is required to move nutrients into roots, because nutrient ions are present in soil water in lower concentrations than they are in epidermal cells. In fact, these ions would tend to move out of root hairs by diffusion if active transport did not pull them inside. Active transport requires ATP and oxygen. Thus, roots need a constant supply of oxygen. Roots normally obtain oxygen from the air in soil spaces. But, if the soil spaces are filled with water, the roots of most land plants cannot obtain the oxygen they need. This is why overwatering houseplants can kill them. However, if the concentration of water in soil spaces is too low, water may even move out of root hairs and back into the soil. This is called root burn. It often affects plants that have been overfertilized.

Answers to . . .

CHECKPOINT *Organic nutrients required by plants to grow, flower, and produce seeds*

Figure 23–8 *Nitrogen*

Build Science Skills

Using Models Students can model the effect of the Casparian strip by filling a balloon with water, then filling a water dropper. Encourage students to describe which model is more similar to what occurs in roots and explain how the Casparian strip contributes to root pressure.

3 ASSESS

Evaluate Understanding

Play a game in which students must draw a picture of the word they have on a card. Make up word cards that include all Vocabulary terms from the section, as well as some of the Key Concepts. While drawing, students may not speak, or give clues using body language.

Reteach

Have students make a chart with the headings Water Absorption and Nutrient Uptake. Under each heading, have them describe how each process occurs in the root. Then, have them list in order the root tissues that are involved in the process.

ALTERNATIVE ASSESSMENT

Encourage students to base their diagrams on either actual plants or photographs from gardening magazines and books or botany books. They should also describe how roots work, based on the information from this section.

Recall that water moves into the vascular cylinder by osmosis. Because water and minerals cannot pass through the waxy Casparian strip, once they pass through the endodermis, they are trapped in the vascular cylinder. As a result, there is a one-way passage of materials into the vascular cylinder in plant roots.

Root Pressure Why do plants "need" a system that ensures the one-way movement of water and minerals? That system is how the plant generates enough pressure to move water out of the soil and up into the body of the plant. As minerals are pumped into the vascular cylinder, more and more water follows by osmosis, producing a strong pressure. If the pressure were not contained, roots would expand as they filled with water.

Instead, contained within the Casparian strip, the water has just one place to go—up. Root pressure, produced within the cylinder by active transport, forces water through the vascular cylinder and into the xylem. As more water moves from the cortex into the vascular cylinder, more water in the xylem is forced upward through the root into the stem. In **Figure 23–10,** you can see a demonstration of root pressure in a carrot root. Root pressure is the starting point for the movement of water through the vascular system of the entire plant. But it is just the beginning. Once you have learned about stems and leaves, you will see how water and other materials are transported within an entire plant.

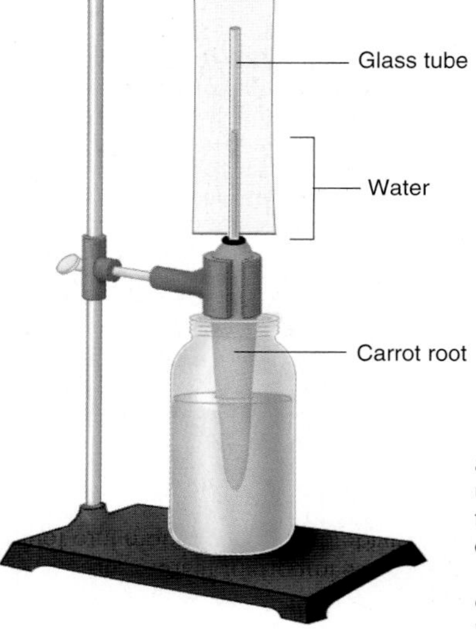

◀ **Figure 23–10** As a carrot root absorbs water, root pressure forces water upward into the glass tube, which takes the place of the carrot plant in this demonstration. **Applying Concepts** ***Would you expect root pressure to increase or decrease as you go up a plant? Explain your answer.***

23–2 Section Assessment

1. **Key Concept** Compare a taproot and a fibrous root.
2. **Key Concept** How are tissues distributed in a plant root?
3. **Key Concept** Describe the two main functions of roots.
4. How is osmosis involved in the absorption of water and nutrients?
5. **Critical Thinking Inferring** Why is it important that the root endodermis permit only a one-way passage of materials?

iTEXT Assessment Use iText to review the important concepts in Section 23–2.

ALTERNATIVE ASSESSMENT

Making a Diagram Make two diagrams, one showing a root's structure and growth, the other showing how roots absorb water and nutrients. Label the diagrams and write brief descriptions of the processes shown in each.

Use iText to review the key concepts in Section 23–2.

23–2 Section Assessment

1. Taproots have a central primary root and generally grow deep into the soil. Fibrous roots are shallow and consist of many thin roots.
2. Roots have an outside layer of epidermal cells and a central cylinder of vascular tissue; between these lies a large area of ground tissue.
3. Anchor a plant in the ground and absorb water and dissolved nutrients from the soil
4. Active transport through the root epidermis results in a high concentration of mineral ions in the root cells that causes water molecules to move into the root by osmosis.
5. The one-way passage of materials creates the root pressure that moves water up into the stem and leaves.

Answer to . . .

Figure 23–10 *Decrease; moving farther away from the place the pressure is created*

23–3 Stems

What do a barrel cactus, a tree trunk, a dandelion stem, and a potato have in common? They are all types of stems. Stems vary greatly in size and shape. Some grow entirely underground; others reach far into the air. Stems also vary in their structure and internal arrangement of cells.

Stem Structure and Function

In general, stems have three important functions: They produce leaves, branches and flowers; they hold leaves up in the sunlight; and they transport substances between roots and leaves. The vascular tissue in stems conducts water, nutrients, and other compounds up and down the plant. Xylem and phloem tissues form continuous tubes from the roots through the stems to the leaves. These vascular tissues link all parts of the plant, allowing water and nutrients to be carried throughout the plant. Stems can also function in storage and photosynthesis.

Like the rest of the plant, the stem is composed of three tissue systems: dermal, vascular, and ground tissue. Stems are surrounded by a layer of epidermal cells that have thick cell walls and a waxy protective coating.

In most plants, stems contain distinct **nodes,** where leaves are attached, and **internode** regions between the nodes, as shown in **Figure 23–11.** Small buds are found where leaves attach to the nodes. **Buds** contain undeveloped tissue that can produce new stems and leaves. In larger plants, stems develop woody tissue that helps support leaves and flowers.

Guide for Reading

Key Concepts
- What are the three main functions of stems?
- How do monocot and dicot stems differ?
- How do primary growth and secondary growth occur in stems?

Vocabulary
- node • internode • bud
- vascular bundle • pith
- primary growth
- secondary growth
- vascular cambium
- cork cambium • heartwood
- sapwood • bark

Reading Strategy: Using Visuals Before you read, preview the art in **Figure 23–15.** As you read the section, refer to this art to learn about the structure of mature woody stems.

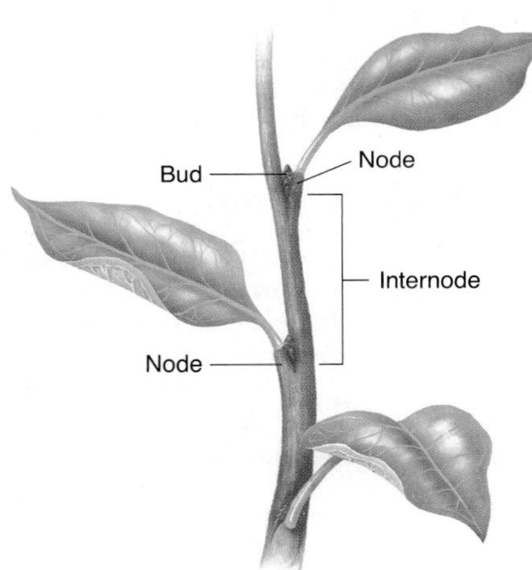

◀ **Figure 23–11** **Stems produce leaves and branches and hold leaves up to the sunlight, where they carry out photosynthesis.** Leaves are attached to a stem at structures called nodes. These nodes are separated by regions of the stem called internodes.

SECTION RESOURCES

Print:
- ***Laboratory Manual A,*** Chapter 23 Lab
- ***Teaching Resources,*** Section Review 23–3
- ***Guided Reading and Study Workbook,*** Section 23–3

Technology:
- ***iText,*** Section 23–3

Section 23–3

1 FOCUS

Objectives

23.3.1 ***Describe*** the three main functions of stems.
23.3.2 ***Contrast*** monocot and dicot stems.
23.3.3 ***Explain*** how primary growth and secondary growth occur in stems.

Guide for Reading

Vocabulary Preview

List the Vocabulary terms on the board. Invite students to identify terms they already know and give definitions for them. Then, challenge students to infer the meanings of the remaining terms. Review the definitions throughout the section and correct definitions as needed.

Reading Strategy

As students preview the figure, encourage them to identify the Vocabulary terms used as labels in the diagram. Have students find their meanings as they read the section.

2 INSTRUCT

Stem Structure and Function

Build Science Skills

Observing Provide students with examples of various stems, such as woody tree branches, flower stems, ivy, sprouted tulip or daffodil bulbs, and sprouted potatoes. Challenge students to find the nodes, internodes, and buds on these stems. Suggest that they use dissecting tools to tease apart stem tissue and examine it under a dissecting microscope. Also encourage students to examine cross sections of stems. Students should draw labeled diagrams of their observations. Make sure they observe the differences between underground stems and more "traditional" stems.

Monocot and Dicot Stems

Use Visuals

Figure 23–12 Use the stem cross-sections in the figure to compare and contrast stem structure in monocots and dicots. Discuss characteristics of the stem structures that are different. Also discuss their similarities. Make sure students can correctly identify all parts of the stem, including the locations of the three types of plant tissue.

Meet Diverse Needs

Have at-risk students and students with limited English proficiency construct a table to compare and contrast the structure of monocot and dicot stems. Encourage students to include illustrations in their tables, as well as definitions of terms they have difficulty with. **Learning modality: verbal**

Primary Growth of Stems

Build Science Skills

Designing Experiments Challenge students to design an experiment to determine if all plants have the same rate of primary growth. Students should decide how they will measure primary growth and determine what plants they will study. They should write a complete procedure and estimate the time it will take to complete the study.

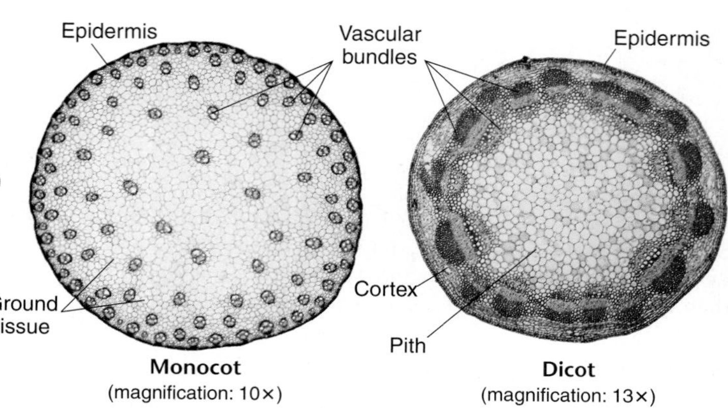

▶ **Figure 23–12** The arrangement of vascular bundles in the stem of a monocot differs from that in the stem of a dicot. **In a monocot, vascular bundles are scattered throughout the stem. In a dicot, vascular bundles are arranged in a ring.**

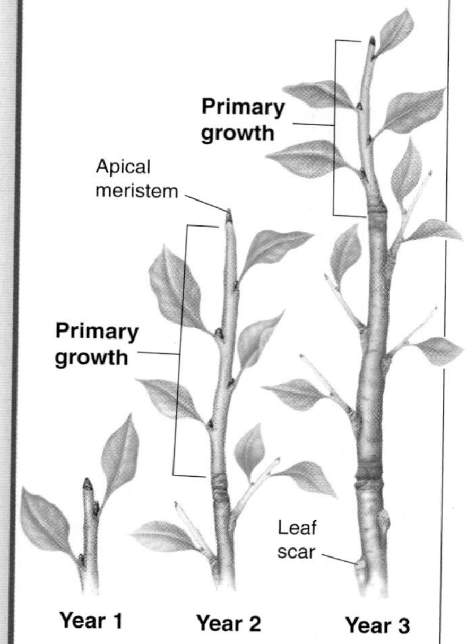

▲ **Figure 23–13 All seed plants undergo primary growth, which is an increase in length.** Every year, apical meristems, shown in red, divide to produce new growth. The primary growth for one season consists of a stem and several leaves.

Monocot and Dicot Stems

The arrangement of tissues in a stem differs among seed plants. **In monocots, vascular bundles are scattered throughout the stem. In dicots and most gymnosperms, vascular bundles are arranged in a cylinder.** Recall that monocots and dicots are two types of flowering plants, or angiosperms. For a comparison of monocot and dicot stems, look at **Figure 23–12.**

Monocot Stems The cross section of a young monocot stem shows all three tissue systems clearly. The stem has a distinct epidermis, which encloses a series of **vascular bundles,** each of which contains xylem and phloem tissue. Phloem faces the outside of the stem, and xylem faces the center. In monocots, these bundles are scattered throughout the ground tissue. The ground tissue is fairly uniform, consisting mainly of parenchyma cells.

Dicot Stems Young dicot stems have vascular bundles, but they are generally arranged in an organized, ringlike pattern. The parenchyma cells inside the ring of vascular tissue are known as **pith,** while those outside form the cortex of the stem. In dicots these relatively simple tissue patterns become more complex as the plant grows larger and the stem increases in diameter.

Primary Growth of Stems

Plants grow in ways that are distinctly different from other organisms. For their entire life, new cells are produced at the tips of roots and shoots. This type of growth, occurring only at the ends of a plant, is called **primary growth.** The increase in length produced by primary growth from year to year is shown in **Figure 23–13. Primary growth of stems is produced by cell divisions in the apical meristem. It takes place in all seed plants.**

PRESENTATIONS MADE EASY!

The Presentation Assistant Plus contains the Prentice Hall Presentation Pro and the Transparencies, which provide easy-to-follow visual support for every step of this section. If you have a computer presentation station, use Prentice Hall Presentation Pro for Section 23–3, or use the following transparencies.

Section 23–3:

Interest Grabber
Section Outline
Compare/Contrast Table
Figure 23–14
Figure 23–15

Secondary Growth of Stems

If a plant is to grow larger year after year, its stems must increase in thickness as well as in length. They have more weight to support and more fluid to move through their vascular tissues. Yet, only meristematic tissue can produce new cells for growth. Some monocots, such as palm trees, produce thick stems from a meristem that becomes wider as the plant grows. However, most monocots, such as grasses, produce only fleshy growth and do not grow very tall. Many dicots grow extremely tall and also grow in width to support this extra weight. This growth occurs as a result of meristems other than the apical meristem.

The pattern of growth in which stems increase in width is called **secondary growth.** In **Figure 23–14** you can see the pattern of secondary growth in a dicot stem. **In conifers and dicots, secondary growth takes place in lateral meristematic tissues called the vascular cambium and cork cambium.** The type of lateral meristematic tissue called **vascular cambium** produces vascular tissues and increases the thickness of stems over time. **Cork cambium** produces the outer covering of stems. Another kind of cambium enables roots to grow thicker and branch. The addition of new tissue in these cambium layers increases the thickness of the stem.

Formation of the Vascular Cambium In a young dicot stem produced by primary growth, bundles of xylem and phloem are arranged in a ring. Once secondary growth begins, the vascular cambium appears as a thin layer situated between clusters of vascular tissue. This new meristematic tissue forms between the xylem and phloem of each vascular bundle. Divisions in the vascular cambium give rise to new layers of xylem and phloem. As a result, the stem becomes wider. The cambium continues to produce new layers of vascular tissue, causing the stem to become thicker and thicker.

CHECKPOINT *What tissue divides to produce secondary growth in dicots?*

▼ **Figure 23–14** **Dicots produce secondary growth from meristematic tissue called vascular cambium.** This tissue forms between the xylem and phloem of the individual vascular bundles, as shown in A. Once the tissue forms, as shown in B, it divides to produce xylem cells toward the center of the stem and phloem cells toward the outside. These different tissues form the bark and wood of a mature stem, shown in C.

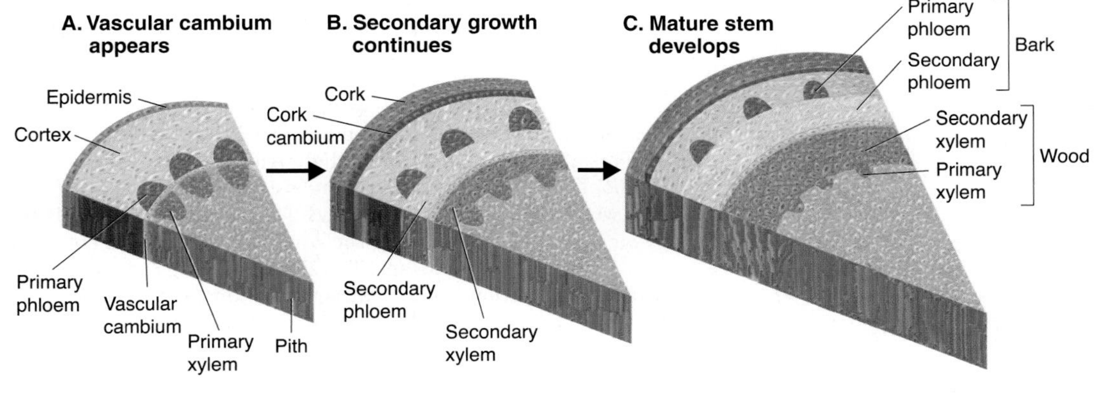

Secondary Growth of Stems

Meet Diverse Needs

If students have made a concept map that shows the levels of organization of plant cells, tissues, and organs, then have them add vascular cambium and cork cambium to it. Students should also note that primary growth occurs from the apical meristem and secondary growth occurs from the cambium. **Learning modality: visual**

Use Visuals

Figure 23–14 Use the diagram to review the formation of vascular cambium and secondary growth. Ask: **Where does the vascular cambium appear when secondary growth begins?** *(Between the xylem and phloem of primary vascular tissue)* **What causes the stem to become wider?** *(Divisions of vascular cambium give rise to new layers of xylem and phloem, widening the stem)* **Where do new phloem cells form?** *(Toward the outside of the stem)* **Where do new xylem cells form?** *(Toward the center of the stem)*

Analyzing Data

Thick growth rings indicate that the growing season had adequate moisture. Narrow growth rings form during dry years.

Answers

1. About 25 years old
2. Rainfall and temperature
3. The tree laid down more new wood on the side away from the fire than on the side of the fire.
4. Area D is the xylem (or wood). Area E is the phloem. The xylem carries water and nutrients up the stem (trunk), whereas the phloem carries sugars down the stem to all parts of the tree.
5. Diagrams should show a cross section of the tree trunk with the youngest xylem cells next to the vascular cambium toward the center of the stem. The youngest phloem cells are next to the vascular cambium toward the outside of the stem. These tissues are produced by the vascular cambium. See Figure 23–15 for reference.

Analyzing Data

Reading a Tree's History

The field of dendrochronology (*dendron* means "tree;" *chronos* means "time") analyzes tree rings to determine information about a tree and the environment in which it grew. A tree's age, for example, can be measured by counting its growth rings—each produced by a year of growth. The specific environmental conditions can be inferred for each year of its growth by examining the relative width and color of each ring. Use the photograph below to answer each question.

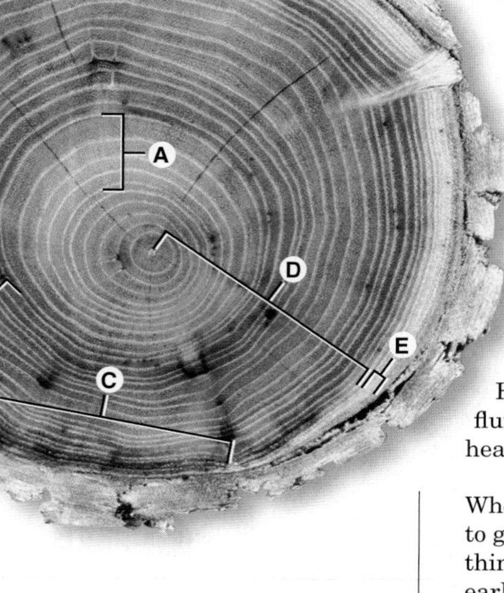

1. **Interpreting Graphics** Approximately how old was this tree when it was cut down?
2. **Inferring** Areas A and B were both produced by four years of growth, yet they are different widths. What climatic conditions might account for this difference?
3. **Interpreting Graphics** The area at C is blackened from a fire that apparently affected only one side of the tree. Describe how the tree grew after this fire.
4. **Comparing and Contrasting** Areas D and E are two types of wood. Give their names, and explain how they differ.
5. **Applying Concepts** On a separate sheet of paper, draw a simple sketch of the tree, indicating where the xylem and phloem are located. Where are the youngest xylem cells located? The youngest phloem cells? What tissue produces both of these cells?

Formation of Wood Most of what we call "wood" is actually layers of xylem. These cells build up year after year, layer on layer. As woody stems grow thicker, the older xylem near the center of the stem no longer conducts water and instead becomes what is known as **heartwood.** Heartwood usually darkens with age because it accumulates impurities that cannot be removed. Heartwood is surrounded by **sapwood,** which is active in fluid transport and therefore usually lighter in color. Both heartwood and sapwood are shown in **Figure 23–15.**

In most of the temperate zone, tree growth is seasonal. When growth begins in the spring, the vascular cambium begins to grow rapidly, producing large, light-colored xylem cells with thin cell walls. The result is a light-colored layer of wood called early wood. As the growing season continues, the cells become smaller and have thicker cell walls, forming a layer of dark wood. This darker wood is called late wood.

This alternation of dark and light wood produces what we commonly call tree rings. Each ring is composed of a band of light wood and a band of dark wood. Thus, a ring corresponds to a year of growth. By counting the rings in a cross section of a tree, you can estimate its age. The size of the rings may even provide information about weather conditions, such as wet or dry years. Thick rings indicate that weather conditions were favorable for tree growth, whereas thin rings indicate less favorable conditions.

BIO INSIGHTS

FACTS AND FIGURES

Dating archaeological sites with annual rings Some tropical trees produce a uniform wood without annual rings because the cambium makes xylem throughout the year. But most wood shows seasonal variations. For instance, the trees of the American Southwest grow for only a few months a year, when water is available, and thus show distinct rings. In that region, archaeologists have studied the rings of ancient wooden beams found in Native American pueblos. Through careful correlation, they have established an accurate chronology for the region going back to 59 BC. That is, they can now date a specific site by matching the rings of beams at that site with beams at other sites. In Europe, similar efforts have been made throughout the continent, using old trees and beams in German cathedrals and Roman ruins.

Formation of Bark On most trees, **bark** includes all of the tissues outside the vascular cambium, as shown in **Figure 23–15.** These tissues include phloem, the cork cambium, and cork. How does bark form? Picture a tree as new xylem is being laid down. It is expanding in width, or girth. Recall that the phloem tissue lies to the outside of this xylem. Phloem must grow to accommodate the larger size of the tree. As the vascular cambium increases in diameter, it forces the phloem tissue outward. This expansion causes the oldest tissues to split and fragment as they are stretched by the expanding stem. Were this expansion left unchecked, the outer covering of the stem might eventually split and break.

Another layer of growing tissue, the cork cambium, solves this potential problem. The cork cambium surrounds the cortex and produces a thick protective layer of cork. Cork consists of cells that have thick walls and usually contain fats, oils, or waxes. These waterproof substances help prevent the loss of water from the stem. The outermost cork cells are usually dead. As the stem increases in size, this dead bark often cracks and flakes off in strips or patches.

CHECKPOINT *What is heartwood?*

KEEP CURRENT WITH . . . SCIENCE NEWS®

To find out more about the topics in this chapter, go to: **www.phschool.com**

▼ **Figure 23–15** In a mature tree that has undergone several years of secondary growth, the vascular cambium lies between layers of xylem to the inside, and layers of phloem to the outside. The youngest xylem, called sapwood, transports water and minerals. **Classifying** *Which layer contains meristematic cells?*

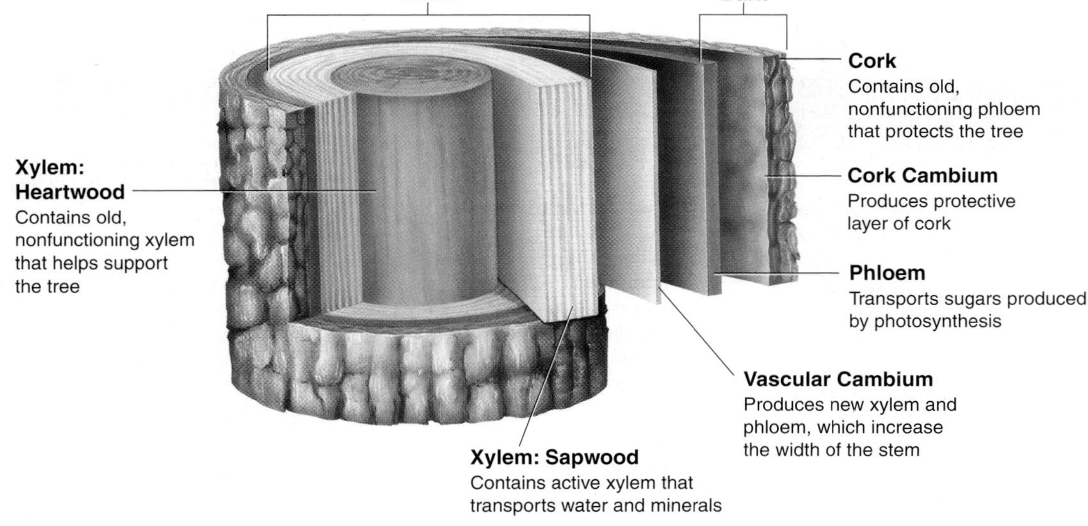
Wood
Bark
Cork
Contains old, nonfunctioning phloem that protects the tree
Cork Cambium
Produces protective layer of cork
Phloem
Transports sugars produced by photosynthesis
Vascular Cambium
Produces new xylem and phloem, which increase the width of the stem
Xylem: Sapwood
Contains active xylem that transports water and minerals
Xylem: Heartwood
Contains old, nonfunctioning xylem that helps support the tree

Meet Diverse Needs

Encourage students who would like an additional challenge to learn about and demonstrate maple tree tapping to the class. Students should explain how to tap the tree, what is actually being collected, and why it can be done only in the spring. **Learning modality: verbal**

Demonstration

Display samples of bark from several species of trees. Explain that because the appearance of bark differs among species of trees, bark appearance is used to identify trees. Ask: **What type of cells make up the bark?** *(Secondary phloem, cork, and cork cambium)* **Why does bark split?** *(As the vascular cambium increases in diameter, it forces the phloem tissue outward. This expansion causes the oldest tissues to split and fragment as they are stretched by the expanding stem.)*

SCIENCE NEWS®

Encourage students to visit **www.phschool.com** for the most current information on this topic.

Answers to . . .

CHECKPOINT *Older xylem near the center of a woody stem that no longer conducts water*

Figure 23–15 *Vascular cambium*

23–3 (continued)

Use Visuals

Figure 23–16 Have students identify which stem is adapted for storage *(potato, cactus)*, which is adapted for photosynthesis *(cactus)*, and which is adapted for dormancy *(ginger)*. Discuss how each of these stems helps the plant survive during periods of poor growing conditions. Ask: **When do plants use the food that was stored in the stems?** *(When the plant begins to grow after dormancy, until its new growth can make enough food)*

3 ASSESS

Evaluate Understanding

Have students write three review questions for the section. Invite students to take turns asking one question of the class. Continue until everyone has had a turn, or until unique questions have been answered.

Reteach

Have students use Figure 23–14 and Figure 23–15 to describe the structure of a mature stem and how secondary growth occurs in stems. Students can describe this process to you or to another student.

ALTERNATIVE ASSESSMENT

Travelogues should trace the path of water and nutrients into a plant's roots from the soil and up into the stem. Travelogues should include a description of the plant's root structures, type of root system, and the process of absorbing materials from the soil and transporting them up through the plant's stem. You might consider having students continue their travelogues to include leaf structure and transpiration in the next section.

Use iText to review the key concepts in Section 23–3.

FIGURE 23–16 STEMS ADAPTED FOR STORAGE AND DORMANCY

Many kinds of plants have modified stems that store food. Tubers, rhizomes, bulbs, and corms can remain dormant during cold or dry periods until favorable conditions for growth return.

Tuber A tuber is a stem, usually growing underground, that stores food. In potato plants grown from cuttings (shown here), the tubers form at the end of underground stems. In potato plants grown from seed, tubers form at the tips of stems that grow along the ground surface.

Potato

Bulb A bulb is made up of a central stem surrounded by short, thick leaves. As in the amaryllis bulb shown here, the leaves wrap around and protect the stem and also store food. A bulb may remain dormant for a long time, yet still grow into a plant.

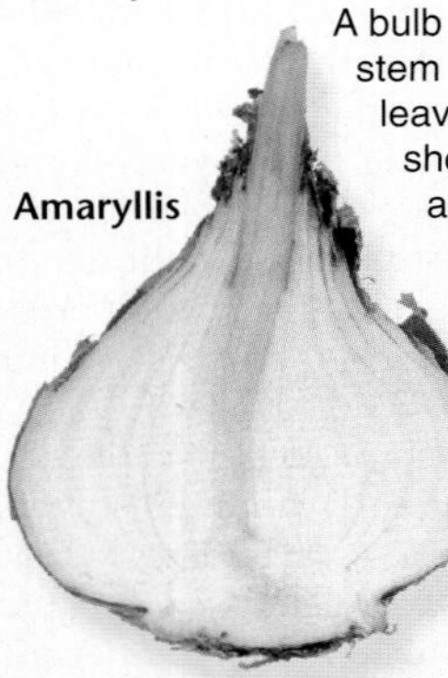

Amaryllis

Corm A corm looks similar to a bulb, but is a thickened stem that stores food. A corm has an outer covering that consists of layers of thin leaves. Plants such as the gladiolus (shown here) and the crocus form corms.

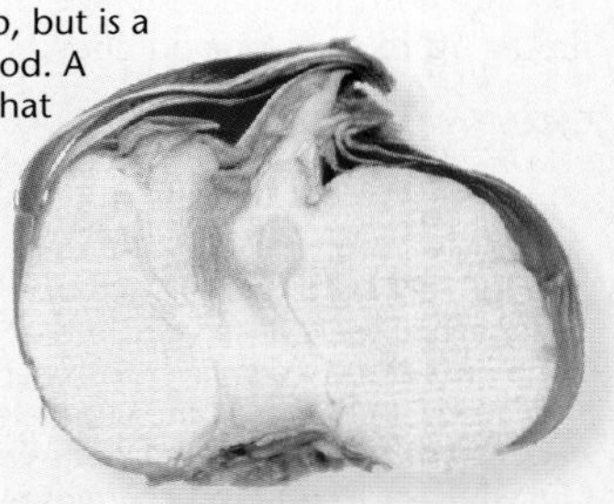

Gladiolus

Rhizome The stem of a ginger is a rhizome, which is a horizontal, underground stem. As shown in the ginger, new shoots can form from a rhizome, allowing plants to undergo periods of dormancy.

Ginger

23–3 Section Assessment

1. **Key Concept** How do the functions of a stem relate to the roots and leaves of a plant?
2. **Key Concept** Describe how the arrangement of vascular bundles differs between monocot and dicot stems.
3. **Key Concept** Define primary and secondary growth. Which involves divisions of the apical meristem?
4. How do heartwood and sapwood differ?
5. **Critical Thinking Formulating Hypotheses** When European settlers were struggling to clear heavily wooded land in North America, they often "girdled" large trees by removing a strip of bark all the way around the base of the tree. Why would this cause the tree to die?

iTEXT Assessment Use iText to review the important concepts in Section 23–3.

ALTERNATIVE ASSESSMENT

Creative Writing
Pretend that you are small enough to enter a plant through its root system. Describe what you would see as you traveled into a plant and through one of its stems. Include illustrations.

23–3 Section Assessment

1. Stems transport substances between roots and leaves.
2. Monocots: scattered throughout stem; dicots: arranged in a cylinder
3. Primary growth occurs only at the end of plants. Secondary growth is a pattern in which stems increase in width. Primary growth involves the apical meristem.
4. Heartwood contains old, nonfunctioning xylem. Sapwood contains active xylem.
5. Girdling removes the phloem from the entire circumference of the tree, preventing the tree from transporting sugars to the roots. Without sugar, active transport cannot occur and the roots will not take up nutrients and water.

23–4 Leaves

The leaves of a plant are its main organs of photosynthesis. In a sense, plant leaves are the world's most important manufacturers of food. Sugars, starches, and oils manufactured by plants in their leaves are sources of food for virtually all land animals.

Recall from Chapter 8 that photosynthesis uses carbon dioxide and water to produce sugars and oxygen. Leaves, therefore, must have a way of obtaining the materials needed for photosynthesis as well as distributing its end products. Much of the internal structure of leaves can be understood in terms of their functions in carrying out photosynthesis.

Guide for Reading

Key Concepts
- How does the structure of a leaf enable it to carry out photosynthesis?
- How does gas exchange take place in a leaf?

Vocabulary
blade
petiole
mesophyll
palisade mesophyll
spongy mesophyll
stoma
guard cell
transpiration

Reading Strategy: Monitoring Your Understanding Make a table with three columns, labeled K, W, and L. Before you read, write what you already know about leaves in the first column (K). Under the next heading, write down what you want to learn about leaves (W). After you read, write down what you learned about leaves in the last column (L).

Leaf Structure

The structure of a leaf is optimized for absorbing light and carrying out photosynthesis. As you can see in **Figure 23–17,** leaves may differ greatly in shape, yet share certain structural features. To collect sunlight, most leaves have thin, flattened sections called **blades.** The blade is attached to the stem by a thin stalk called a **petiole.** Like roots and stems, leaves have an outer covering of dermal tissue and inner regions of ground and vascular tissues. As shown in **Figure 23–18,** leaves are covered on the top and bottom by epidermis made of a layer of tough, irregularly shaped cells. The epidermis of many leaves is also covered by the cuticle. Together, the cuticle and epidermal cells form a waterproof barrier that protects tissues and limits the loss of water through evaporation.

The vascular tissues of leaves are connected directly to the vascular tissues of stems. In leaves, xylem and phloem tissues are gathered together into bundles that run from the stem into the petiole. Once they are in the leaf blade, the vascular bundles are surrounded by parenchyma and sclerenchyma cells.

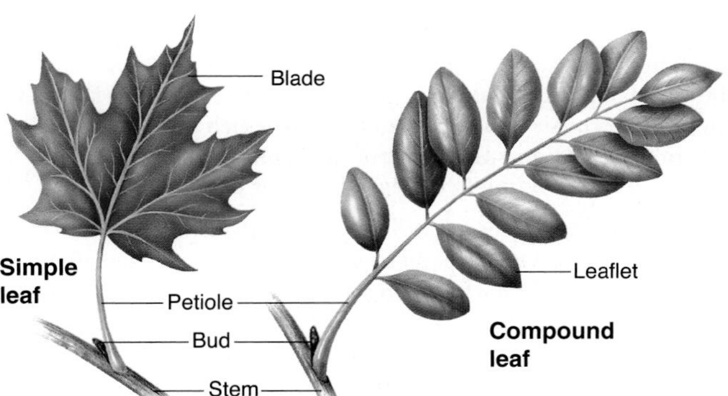

◀ **Figure 23–17** Most of a leaf consists of a blade attached to the stem by a petiole. The blade of a simple leaf (left) can be different shapes. In a compound leaf (right), the blade is divided into many separate leaflets.

SECTION RESOURCES

Print:
- ***Teaching Resources,*** Section Review 23–4
- ***Guided Reading and Study Workbook,*** Section 23–4

Technology:
- ***iText,*** Section 23–4

Section 23–4

1 FOCUS

Objectives

23.4.1 ***Describe*** how the structure of a leaf enables it to carry out photosynthesis.
23.4.2 ***Describe*** how gas exchange takes place in a leaf.

Guide for Reading

Vocabulary Preview

Explain that the prefix *meso-* means "middle," and the suffix *-phyll* means "leaf." Challenge students to infer what mesophyll is. *(Specialized ground tissue that makes up a leaf)* Then, explain that a palisade is a tall wooden fence. Have students infer how palisade mesophyll might differ from spongy mesophyll. *(Palisade mesophyll has tall, column-shaped cells. Spongy mesophyll is loose with many air spaces between cells.)*

Reading Strategy

As students read the section, encourage them to sketch diagrams of leaf structures in their table. Also encourage students to write the Vocabulary terms and their definitions in the table.

2 INSTRUCT

Leaf Structure

Build Science Skills

Observing Provide leaves from several species of plants for students to observe. Choose leaves that represent a wide range of shapes and sizes. Encourage students to examine the leaves under a dissecting microscope and draw labeled diagrams of their observations. Also have students use a light microscope to examine leaf cross sections, either those that they prepare themselves or prepared slides.

Leaf Functions

Use Visuals

Figure 23–18 Review the structure of a leaf as diagrammed in the figure. If students diagrammed leaf structure from their observations of leaves, encourage them to compare their diagrams to the diagram in the figure. Discuss the function of each leaf part labeled in the diagram. For each part, have students describe how it works to help the leaf produce carbohydrates in the process of photosynthesis.

Meet Diverse Needs

Some students might need to review the process of photosynthesis and where and how it occurs in a leaf. Have students create a comic strip in which they show and tell where photosynthesis occurs in the plant. They should describe how the raw materials required for photosynthesis get into the leaf and its cells and how the products move from the leaf cells to the rest of the plant. Help students plan and set up their comic strip to mirror the step-by-step process of photosynthesis as it relates to leaf structure. **Learning modality: visual**

Word Origins

Chlorophyll means "green leaf"

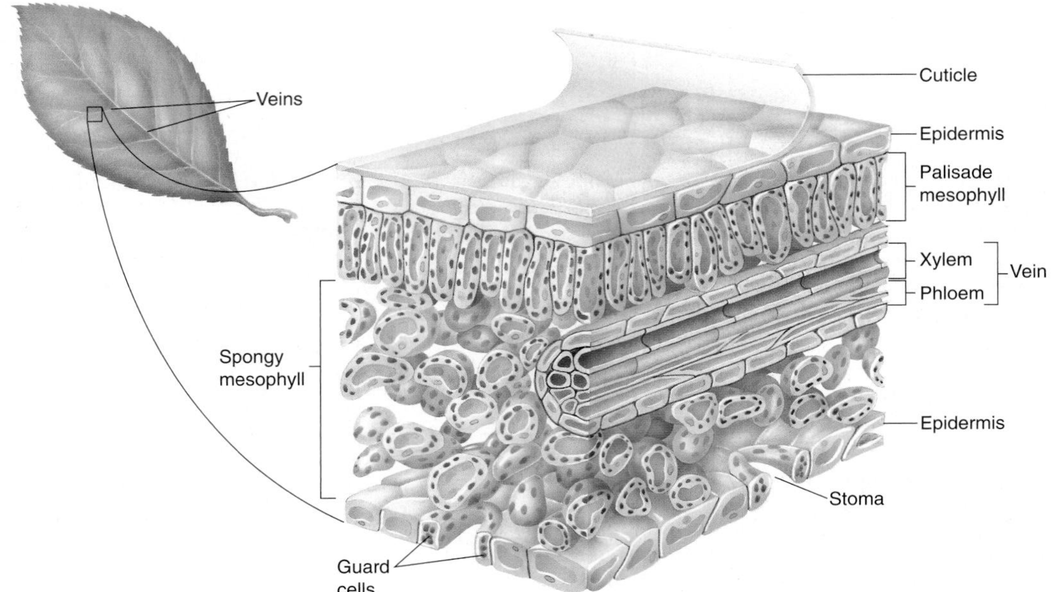

▲ **Figure 23–18** **Leaves absorb light and carry out most of the photosynthesis in a plant.** Some of the most important manufacturing sites on Earth are found in the leaves of plants. The cells in plant leaves are able to use light energy to make carbohydrates.

Word Origins

Mesophyll comes from two Greek words: *meso,* meaning "middle," and *phyllon,* meaning "leaf." **If the Greek word *chloro* means "green," what does the term *chlorophyll* mean?**

Leaf Functions

Plants must take in all the materials needed for photosynthesis. Specialized cells on the underside of the leaf regulate this process.

Photosynthesis The bulk of most leaves is composed of a specialized ground tissue known as **mesophyll,** shown in **Figure 23–18.** Mesophyll cells are packed with chloroplasts and carry out nearly all the photosynthetic activity of most plants. Carbohydrates produced in photosynthesis move from mesophyll cells into phloem vessels, which carry them to the rest of the plant.

Just under the upper epidermis is a layer of tall, column-shaped mesophyll cells called the **palisade mesophyll.** These closely packed cells absorb much of the light that enters the leaf. Beneath the palisade layer is the **spongy mesophyll,** a loose tissue with many air spaces between its cells. These air spaces connect with the exterior through **stomata** (singular: stoma), which are pore-like openings in the underside of the leaf that allow carbon dioxide and oxygen to diffuse in and out of the leaf. Each stoma consists of two **guard cells,** which are specialized cells in the epidermis that control the opening and closing of stomata by responding to changes in water pressure.

Transpiration The surfaces of spongy mesophyll cells are kept moist so that gases can enter and leave the cells easily. This also means that water evaporates from these surfaces and is lost to the atmosphere. Water is lost from leaves in a process called transpiration. **Transpiration** is the loss of water from a plant through its leaves. It is replaced by water drawn into the leaf through xylem vessels in the vascular tissue.

PRESENTATIONS MADE EASY!

The Presentation Assistant Plus contains the Prentice Hall Presentation Pro and the Transparencies, which provide easy-to-follow visual support for every step of this section. If you have a computer presentation station, use Prentice Hall Presentation Pro for Section 23–4, or use the following transparencies.

Section 23–4:

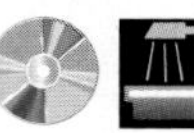

Interest Grabber
Section Outline
Function of Guard Cells
Figure 23–18

Gas Exchange No leaf could survive completely sealed off from the atmosphere that surrounds it. Leaves take in carbon dioxide and give off oxygen during photosynthesis. When plant cells use the food they make, the cells respire, taking in oxygen and giving off carbon dioxide (just as animals do). Plant leaves allow gas exchange between air spaces in the spongy mesophyll and the exterior by opening their stomata.

You might think that plants would keep their stomata open all the time, allowing gas exchange to take place as quickly as possible—especially when the sun is shining brightly and photosynthesis is running at top speed. However, when stomata are wide open, water evaporates from the damp surfaces of mesophyll cells and is lost through the stomata to the atmosphere. If stomata were kept open all the time, water loss due to transpiration would be so great that few plants would be able to take in enough water to survive. Therefore, plants maintain a kind of balance. **Plants keep their stomata open just enough to allow photosynthesis to take place, but not so much that they lose an excessive amount of water.**

Guard cells control the stomata and thus regulate the movement of gases, especially water vapor, into and out of leaf tissues. The stomata open and close in response to changes in water pressure within the guard cells, as shown in **Figure 23–19.** When water pressure within the guard cells is high, the thin outer walls of the cells are forced into a curved shape. This pulls the thick inner walls of the guard cells away from each other, opening the stoma. When water pressure within the guard cells decreases, the inner walls pull together and the stoma closes.

In general, stomata are open during the daytime when photosynthesis is active, and then closed at night, when open stomata would only lead to water loss. However, stomata may be closed even in bright sunlight under hot, dry conditions in which water conservation is a matter of life and death.

CHECKPOINT *What factor regulates the opening and closing of stomata?*

Figure 23–19 Plants regulate opening and closing of their stomata to balance water loss with rates of photosynthesis. A stoma opens or closes in response to the changes in pressure within the guard cells that surround the opening. When the guard cells are swollen with water (bottom, left), the stoma is open. When the guard cells lose water, the opening closes, limiting further water loss from the leaf.

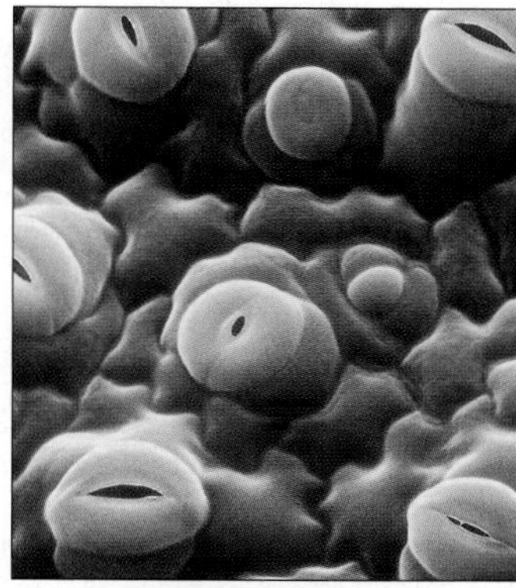

(magnification: 420×)

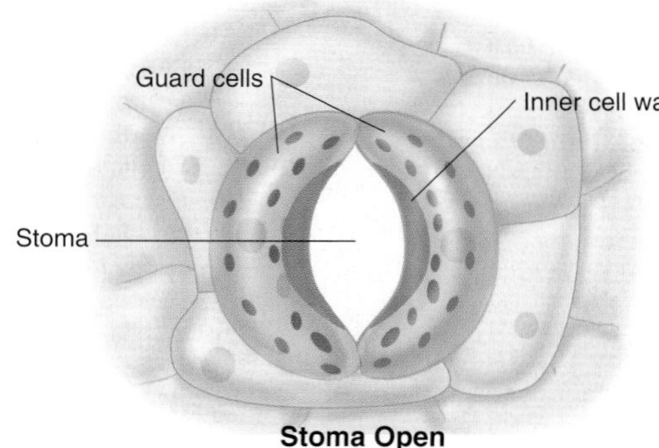

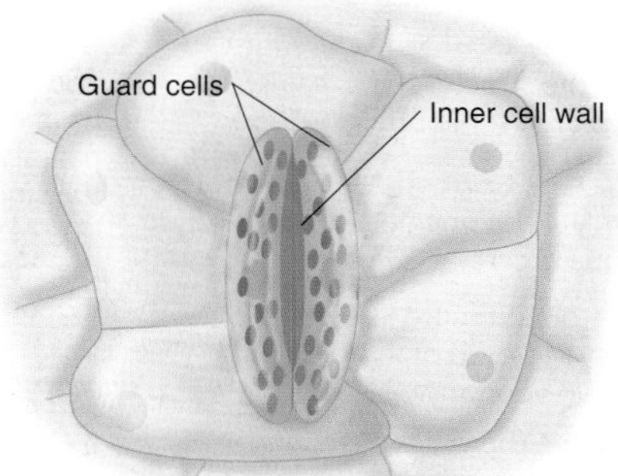

Build Science Skills

Using Models Give student pairs two elongated balloons and challenge them to use the balloons to model the action of stomata. Point out to the class how stomata are a plant adaptation that helps to protect plants in their environment. Have students draw diagrams showing how their balloon model is similar to the action of guard cells. They should describe the conditions under which the stomata are open and when they are closed.

Address Misconceptions

Some students might think that plants have no use for oxygen, because they focus only on the process of photosynthesis as a way for plants to manufacture carbohydrates. Make sure students realize that plants also use the carbohydrates they manufacture for growth, repair, and the active transport required to take up nutrients and water through roots. Identify for students the locations of plant cells that require oxygen and what the oxygen is used for. If needed, review the process of cellular respiration and plant cell structure.

TEACHER TO TEACHER

I like to provide as many opportunities as possible for students to observe actual plant structures. In a simple strategy to examine stomata, I have students coat the underside of a leaf with clear fingernail polish. After the polish has dried, I instruct students to carefully peel it off and place it on a slide. I have them add a coverslip and examine it under a microscope.

To observe transpiration, I have students fill plastic tubing with colored water and place a bean stem with leaves into the tubing. The stem must fit tightly. Tape the apparatus to a white board and mark the water level. Have students measure the change in water level due to transpiration by measuring every ten minutes.

—John E. Gonzales,
Biology Teacher
Temeseal Canyon High School,
Lake Elsinore, CA

Answer to . . .

CHECKPOINT *Changes in water pressure within guard cells and rate of photosynthesis*

Use Visuals

Figure 23–20 Have students compare and contrast the leaf adaptations of the rock plant, cactus, and pine. Discuss how these plants are adapted to living in dry conditions. Ask: **How is the pine leaf adapted to reduce water loss?** *(Waxy epidermis and stomata sunken below surface of the leaf both act to keep water in the leaf.)* **How are the adaptations of the cactus leaf similar to the pine leaf?** *(Actually, cactus leaves are very different from pine leaves; cactus leaves do not carry out photosynthesis. However, both are structured to reduce water loss.)*

3 ASSESS

Evaluate Understanding

Have students write a paragraph in which they describe how a leaf functions to produce energy for a plant. Students can include diagrams to help describe the process if they wish. Stipulate that students use all Vocabulary terms in their paragraphs.

Reteach

Have students construct a concept map that relates the structure of a leaf with its functions. Help students first identify the functions of the leaf, then identify the structures that enable the leaf to carry out those functions.

MAKING CONNECTIONS

Photosynthesis takes place in the chloroplasts contained in a leaf's mesophyll cells. The light-dependent reactions occur in the thylakoid membranes, which are arranged in stacks called grana. The light-independent reactions (or Calvin cycle) take place in the stroma, the region in the chloroplast that is outside the thylakoid membrane. The leaf obtains water for photosynthesis through the xylem and carbon dioxide through the stomata in the leaf's lower surface.

Use iText to review the key concepts in Section 23–4.

FIGURE 23–20 ADAPTATIONS OF LEAVES

The leaves of many plant species show specific adaptations to dry or low nutrient conditions.

Pitcher plant
The leaf of a pitcher plant is modified to attract and then digest insects and other small prey. Carnivorous plants typically live in nutrient-poor soils and rely on insects as their source of nitrogen.

Cactus
Cactus leaves are actually nonphotosynthetic thorns that protect against herbivores. Most of the plant's photosynthesis is carried out in its stem.

Pine
The narrow leaves of a pine tree contain a waxy epidermis as well as stomata that are sunken below the surface of the leaf. This arrangement reduces water loss from the leaf.

Rock plant
The leaves of a rock plant are adapted for hot, dry conditions. They are round, with few stomata, and often have clear tissue that allows light to penetrate into the leaf.

23–4 Section Assessment

1. **Key Concept** Describe how the structure of a leaf is optimized for light absorption.
2. **Key Concept** What factors regulate the opening and closing of guard cells?
3. Are stomata more likely to be open or closed on a hot day? Explain your answer.
4. Describe the cell types found within a typical leaf.
5. **Critical Thinking Inferring** The leaves of desert plants often have two or more layers of palisade mesophyll, rather than the single layer that is characteristic of most leaves. How might this modified structure be advantageous to a desert plant?

iTEXT Assessment Use iText to review the important concepts in Section 23–4.

MAKING CONNECTIONS

Leaf Structure Where within the structure of a leaf does each stage of photosynthesis occur? How does the structure of a leaf allow it to obtain energy and materials for photosynthesis? Refer to Chapter 8, pp. 208–213, for details on photosynthesis. Then draw and label a diagram that answers these questions.

23–4 Section Assessment

1. Most leaves have thin, flattened sections, called blades, to collect sunlight.
2. Rate of photosynthesis and to balance water loss
3. Closed; to prevent the loss of too much water from the plant
4. Leaves are covered on the top and bottom with tough, cube-shaped epidermal cells. Xylem and phloem tissues are gathered together in bundles that run from the stem into the petiole. In the leaf blade, the vascular bundles are surrounded by parenchyma and sclerenchyma cells.
5. To help reduce the loss of water from the plant

23–5 Transport in Plants

The pressure created by water entering the tissues of a root can push water upward in a plant stem. This creates more than enough pressure to force water into the vascular system and out of the root. However, root pressure does not exert enough pressure to lift water up into trees, such as the topmost needles of a redwood tree 90 meters above the ground. To draw water to such great heights, plants take advantage of some of water's most interesting physical properties.

Guide for Reading

Key Concepts

- How is water transported throughout a plant?
- How are the products of photosynthesis transported throughout a plant?

Vocabulary

adhesion
capillary action
pressure-flow hypothesis

Reading Strategy: Making Comparisons This section describes how xylem and phloem function in transport. As you read, write down statements about similarities and differences between the functions of these two tissues.

Water Transport

Recall that xylem tissue forms a continuous set of tubes that stretch from roots through stems and out into the spongy mesophyll of leaves. Active transport and root pressure cause water to move from soil into plant roots. Root pressure alone, however, cannot account for the movement of water and dissolved materials throughout an entire plant. Obviously, other forces are at work. These include capillary action and transpiration.  **The combination of root pressure, capillary action, and transpiration provides enough force to move water through the xylem tissue of even the largest plant.** As you will learn, transpiration is the most powerful of these forces.

Capillary Action Water molecules are attracted to one another by a force called cohesion. Recall from Chapter 2 that cohesion is the attraction of molecules of the same substance to each other. Because of cohesion, water molecules have a tendency to form hydrogen bonds with each other. Water molecules can also form hydrogen bonds with other substances.This results from a force called **adhesion,** which is attraction between unlike molecules. Place empty glass tubes of various widths into a dish of water, as shown in **Figure 23–21,** and you will see both forces at work. The tendency of water to rise in a thin tube is called **capillary action.** Water is attracted to the walls of the tube, and water molecules are attracted to each other. The thinner the tube, the higher the water will rise inside it.

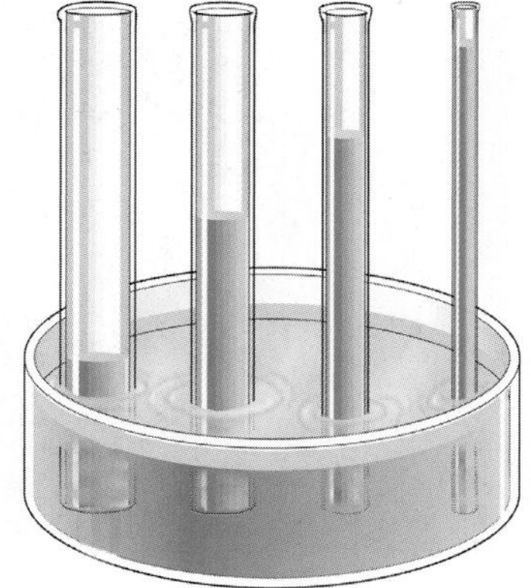

▶ **Figure 23–21** Capillary action—the result of water molecules' ability to stick to one another and to the walls of a tube—contributes to the movement of water up the cells of xylem tissue. As shown here, capillary action causes water to move much higher in a narrow tube than in a wide tube. **Applying Concepts** ***Which force—adhesion or cohesion—causes the water to stick to the walls of the glass tube?***

SECTION RESOURCES

Print:

- ***Teaching Resources,*** Section Review 23–5, Chapter 23 Exploration
- ***Guided Reading and Study Workbook,*** Section 23–5

Technology:

- ***iText,*** Section 23–5

Section 23–5

1 FOCUS

Objectives

23.5.1 ***Explain*** how water is transported throughout a plant.
23.5.2 ***Describe*** how the products of photosynthesis are transported throughout a plant.

Guide for Reading

Vocabulary Preview

Have students study Figure 23–21 and read the caption to learn what is meant by capillary action. Then, have them do the same for Figure 23–24 to learn about pressure-flow hypothesis.

Reading Strategy

After students read the section, encourage them to use their notes about the similarities and differences of xylem and phloem to construct a graphic organizer, such as a table or a concept map.

2 INSTRUCT

Water Transport

Demonstration

Demonstrate capillary action by placing empty glass tubes of various sizes in a dish of colored water, as shown in Figure 23–21. As students observe the water moving, ask: **What causes the water to move up the tubes?** *(Water molecules are attracted to the walls of the tube and to each other.)* **Do you expect water to move highest up the thinnest tube or the thickest tube?** *(Thinnest tube)* **Why doesn't gravity pull the water down?** *(It does. However, the forces of adhesion and cohesion are greater and work together to pull the water molecules up inside the tube.)*

Answer to . . .

Figure 23–21 *Adhesion*

23–5 (continued)

Build Science Skills

Observing Students can easily observe transpiration by covering a potted plant with a plastic bag. The plant should have been watered normally and placed in a well-lighted area. After a few days, have students describe any changes. *(Moisture accumulated inside the bag.)* Discuss where the water came from. Make sure students understand that as each molecule of water evaporates, it pulls up the next molecule of water to take its place.

Meet Diverse Needs

Have at-risk students and students with limited English proficiency describe how water moves through xylem, starting from the roots and ending at the leaves. Encourage students to talk through the process in a "play-by-play" manner, similar to the way a radio announcer describes a sporting event. You might have one student describe all three means by which water moves at the same time. Or, you might have a student focus on only one of the three methods—capillary action, transpiration, and root pressure—at a time. **Learning modality: verbal**

▶ **Figure 23–22 Root pressure, capillary action, and transpiration contribute to the movement of water within a plant.** Transpiration is the movement of water molecules out of leaves. The faster water evaporates from a plant, shown in A, the stronger the pull of water upward from the roots, shown in B.

▼ **Figure 23–23** In hot, dry conditions, transpiration can lead to water loss that is severe enough to cause wilting, shown here in a coleus plant. High transpiration rates can cause a loss of osmotic pressure in a plant's cells. In leaves, this loss of pressure causes guard cells to close, thereby slowing down the rate of transpiration. **Inferring** ***Why do hot, dry conditions cause transpiration rates to increase?***

What does capillary action have to do with water movement through xylem? Recall that there are two main types of xylem tissue in flowering plants: tracheids and vessel elements. Recall that both tracheids and vessel elements form hollow connected tubes similar to a thin, glass capillary tube. Capillary action in the tubelike structures formed by both types of cells causes water to rise well above the level of the ground.

Transpiration For trees and other large plants, the combination of root pressure and capillary action does not provide enough force to lift water to the topmost branches and leaves. The major force in water transport is provided by the evaporation of water from leaves during transpiration. When water is lost through transpiration, osmotic pressure moves water out of the vascular tissue of the leaf, as shown in **Figure 23–22.** Then, like a locomotive pulling a train with hundreds of cars, the movement of water out of the leaf "pulls" water upward through the vascular system all the way from the roots. This process is known as transpiration pull.

How important is transpiration pull? On a hot day, even a small tree may lose as much as 100 liters of water to transpiration. The hotter and drier the air, and the windier the day, the greater the amount of water lost. As a result of this water loss, the plant draws up even more water from the roots.

Controlling Transpiration To understand what regulates the rate of transpiration, it helps to follow the path water takes through a leaf. Water enters the leaf through the xylem and moves into the spongy mesophyll. This movement of water into the leaf raises the water pressure in the guard cells, opening the stomata. The rate of transpiration increases as water vapor escapes through the open stomata. Falling water pressure in the leaf also affects the guard cells, which then close the stomata. This limits further water loss from the leaf and helps the plant to maintain homeostasis.

PRESENTATIONS MADE EASY!

The Presentation Assistant Plus contains the Prentice Hall Presentation Pro and the Transparencies, which provide easy-to-follow visual support for every step of this section. If you have a computer presentation station, use Prentice Hall Presentation Pro for Section 23–5, or use the following transparencies.

Section 23–5:

Interest Grabber
Section Outline
Transpiration
Figure 23–24

Quick Lab

What is the role of leaves in transpiration?

Materials 3 stalks of celery with leaves, 250-mL beaker, food coloring, petroleum jelly, cotton swab, scalpel, metric ruler

Procedure

1. Cut 1 cm off the bottoms of the celery stalks. **CAUTION:** *Use the scalpel with care.*
2. Remove the leaves from one stalk. Use a cotton swab to apply petroleum jelly to both sides of all the leaves on another stalk. Place all three stalks into a beaker containing 5 cm of water and food coloring.
3. Place the beaker in a sunny location. Observe the celery at the end of the class and the next day. Record your observations each day.

Analyze and Conclude

1. **Observing** In which stalk did the colored water rise the most? The least?
2. **Inferring** What effect did the petroleum jelly have on transpiration? What part of the leaf did the petroleum jelly affect?
3. **Drawing Conclusions** How are leaves involved in transpiration?

Transpiration and Wilting Osmotic pressure keeps a plant's leaves and stems rigid, or stiff. High transpiration rates can lead to wilting, shown in **Figure 23–23.** Wilting results from the loss of water—and therefore of the pressure in a plant's cells. Without this internal pressure to support them, the plant's cell walls bend inward, and the plant's leaves and stems wilt. When a leaf wilts, its stomata close. As a result, transpiration slows down significantly. Thus, wilting helps a plant to conserve water.

CHECKPOINT *What happens when a plant wilts?*

Nutrient Transport

You have learned how transpiration *pulls* water upward through a plant. But most plant nutrients, including sugars, minerals, and complex organic compounds, are *pushed* through phloem.

Functions of Phloem Many plants pump sugars into their fruits. This action often requires moving sugars out of leaves or roots into stems, and then through stems to the fruits. All of this movement takes place in the phloem. In cold climates, many plants pump food down into their roots for winter storage. This stored food must be moved back into the trunk and branches of the plant before growth begins again in the spring. Phloem carries out this seasonal movement of sugars within a plant.

FACTS AND FIGURES

The nutrient highway
The exact mechanism by which phloem transport occurs is not fully known. It is difficult to investigate, because phloem is extremely delicate. One technique for the study of phloem is the use of aphids. An aphid's mouthpart forms a long tube that it can insert into a plant so that the end of the tube enters a single sieve element. The contents of the element are under pressure. The fluid in the phloem goes into the mouthpart tube and on through the aphid's gut with such force that the feeding aphids often have a drop of "honeydew" on their posterior ends. The fluid that comes from the phloem can be collected and analyzed. By using several aphids on different parts of the plant, a scientist can introduce substances into the phloem at certain points and study their speed and direction of flow.

Quick Lab

Objective Students will be able to observe the role of leaves in transpiration.

Skills Focus Drawing Conclusions

Materials 3 stalks of celery with leaves, 250-mL beaker, food coloring, petroleum jelly, cotton swab, scalpel, metric ruler

Time Day 1: 10 minutes; Day 2: 20 minutes

Advance Prep Purchase celery, and separate the individual stalks. You can substitute one leafless stalk for one of the three leafy stalks listed in the materials.

Strategies

- Discuss the purpose of each celery stalk. Ask: **Which celery stalk is the control?** *(The leafy stalk without petroleum jelly)*
- Have students place the celery stalks on a paper towel or a cutting board to help keep the stalks from slipping.
- Students should cut the stalks to the same length.

Expected Outcomes The water will rise the most in the leafy stalk without petroleum jelly. It will rise the least in the stalk without leaves.

Analyze and Conclude

1. Leafy stalk not coated with petroleum jelly; stalk without leaves
2. The petroleum jelly reduces transpiration by plugging up the stomata.
3. Transpiration occurs through leaf stomata.

Nutrient Transport

Meet Diverse Needs

Have at-risk students and students with limited English proficiency diagram the movement of plant nutrients through phloem tissue in a fruit tree. Students should show seasonal movements, as well as the movement of sugars to the developing fruit. Students might differentiate between the different types of movement by using different colors to represent the nutrient flow. **Learning modality: visual**

Answer to . . .

Figure 23–23 *More water evaporates into the air during hot, dry conditions.*

23–5 (continued)

Using Visuals

Figure 23–24 Use the diagram in the figure to make sure students understand the pressure-flow hypothesis. Ask: **Where is the pressure in the phloem the highest?** *(At the source, where nutrients enter and water follows, as it moves from areas of high concentration to low concentration)* **How does low pressure at the sink help move nutrients through the phloem?** *(Low pressure pulls the nutrients toward it, much like a straw or vacuum cleaner)*

3 ASSESS

Evaluate Understanding

Randomly ask students to describe how capillary action and transpiration work to move water through xylem tissue. Base your questions on the diagrams in Figures 23–21 and 23–22. Do the same for Figure 23–24 and the pressure-flow hypothesis for the movement of nutrients through phloem tissue.

Reteach

Have students create a concept map to show the ways in which water and nutrients are transported through a plant. Students need to include the Vocabulary terms from the section, as well as the words *xylem* and *phloem*.

ALTERNATIVE ASSESSMENT

Experimental designs can be similar to that of the Quick Lab on page 601. However, students should design the experiment to test the effects of changes in temperature, humidity, and light on the rate of transpiration.

Use iText to review the key concepts in Section 23–5.

Answer to . . .

Figure 23–24 *Water from the soil follows the movement of nutrients by osmosis.*

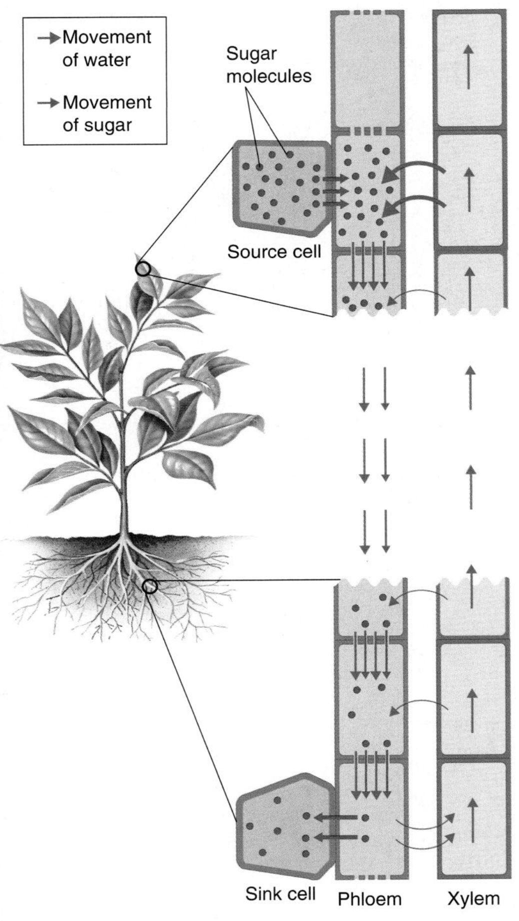

Movement From Source to Sink A process of phloem transport moves sugars through a plant from a source to a sink. The source can be any cell in which sugars are produced by photosynthesis. The sink is a cell where the sugars are used or stored. How does phloem transport take place?

One idea put forward by many plant scientists is called the **pressure-flow hypothesis.** As you can see in **Figure 23–24,** sugars are pumped into the phloem at one point, called the source. For example, sugars produced by photosynthesis may move from a leaf. As concentrations of sugar increase in the phloem, water from the xylem moves in by osmosis. This movement causes an increase in pressure at that point, forcing nutrient-rich fluid to move through the phloem away from nutrient-producing regions and toward a region that uses these nutrients, called the sink.

Conversely, if part of a plant actively absorbs nutrients from the phloem, osmosis causes water to follow. This movement of water decreases pressure and causes a movement of fluid in the phloem toward the sink. **When nutrients are pumped into or removed from the phloem system, the change in concentration causes a movement of fluid in that same direction. As a result, phloem is able to move nutrients in either direction to meet the nutritional needs of the plant.**

◀ **Figure 23–24** The diagram shows the movement of sugars and water throughout the phloem and xylem as explained by the pressure-flow hypothesis. Materials move from a source cell, where photosynthesis produces a high concentration of sugars, to a sink cell, where sugars are lower in concentration. **Interpreting Diagrams** *What is the source of the water that forces nutrients through phloem tissue?*

23–5 Section Assessment

1. **Key Concept** What three processes work together to cause water to flow upward through a plant?
2. **Key Concept** How does the pressure-flow hypothesis explain the function of phloem?
3. Why is capillary action insufficient to move water through a plant?
4. **Critical Thinking Predicting** If a plant's stomata close on a hot, dry day, how could this affect the plant's rate of photosynthesis?

iTEXT Assessment Use iText to review the important concepts in Section 23–5.

ALTERNATIVE ASSESSMENT

Designing Experiments Devise an experiment to measure the rate of transpiration from a plant cutting. Describe results you would expect with changes in temperature, humidity, and light.

23–5 Section Assessment

1. Root pressure, capillary action, and transpiration
2. The change in concentration of nutrients in the phloem system causes a movement of nutrients in either direction to meet the nutritional needs of the plant.
3. It does not provide enough force to lift water to the topmost parts of large plants.
4. With their stomata closed, leaves would not be able to take in carbon dioxide, thus slowing the plant's rate of photosynthesis.

Exploration

Identifying the Growth Zones in a Plant

Do roots grow at the tips or do existing root tissues grow longer? In this investigation, you will answer this question by examining root growth.

Problem **In which part of a root does most growth occur?**

Materials

- 150-mL beaker
- metric ruler
- paper towels
- India ink
- 4 large seeds
- toothpick
- petri dish

Skills Measuring, Analyzing Data

Procedure

1. Fill a 150-mL beaker loosely with crumpled paper towels. Wet the towels with water.
2. Place 4 seeds between the towels and the sides of the beaker. Cover the beaker with a petri dish. Keep the paper towels damp. On a separate sheet of paper, make a copy of the data table shown.
3. When the roots appear, gently place one seedling on a wet paper towel. Use a ruler to measure the length of the root. Record this length in your copy of the data table. Use another sprout if this one becomes damaged.
4. Pick up a very small drop of India ink on the tip of a toothpick. Use the toothpick to mark the root with small dots of ink 3, 10, 15, and 20 mm from the root tip. **CAUTION:** *India ink stains skin and clothing.*
5. Allow the ink dots to dry. Return the sprout to the beaker and replace the cover. Keep the paper towels in the beaker moist.
6. **Predicting** Record your prediction of which part of the root will grow the most over the next 3 days.
7. **Measuring** Record the length of the root and the positions of the dots in your data table each day for 3 days.

Data Table

Days	Position of Mark (mm from root tip)				Root Length (mm)
	3	10	15	20	
1					
2					
3					

Analyze and Conclude

1. **Observing** Did most of the growth occur at the tip of the root (0–3 mm) or farther up?
2. **Analyzing Data** Which part of the root grew the most?
3. **Drawing Conclusions** Do your data support the idea that roots grow mostly at their tips or that growth farther up the root pushes the root tip through the soil?

Go Further

Designing Experiments Design a similar experiment to determine where most stem growth occurs. With your teacher's permission, perform your experiment.

Take It to the NET Log on to the the Prentice Hall Web site at **www.phschool.com** to enter your data for this lab. Compare your results to the data entered by other students around the country.

Analyze and Conclude

1. At the tip
2. In most cases, growth is concentrated in the area that was initially within 0–3 mm of the tip.
3. Roots grow mostly at their tips.

Take It to the NET Encourage students to pool and compare their data with other students nationwide by visiting **www.phschool.com**

Exploration

Objective Students will be able to analyze data to determine in which part of a root the most growth occurs.

Skills Focus **Measuring, Analyzing Data**

Time 35 minutes to set up; 10 minutes every day for 3 days to record measurements

Advance Prep Obtain seeds such as bean, corn, or pea.

Alternative Materials You can use a fine-tipped permanent marker instead of India ink.

Safety Caution students about India ink stains. Students should wear lab aprons and gloves.

Teaching Tips

- Have students use forceps to handle the seeds.
- Instruct students to measure and mark all sprouts in their beakers in case one is damaged. They should have separate data tables for each.
- Water should not puddle at the bottom of the beakers. Have students use water droppers to remoisten the toweling.

Procedure

6. Some will predict that the root tip grows the most. Others might predict the part closest to the seed grows the most.

7. Typically, a root might grow to a length of 43 mm in 3 days, with 19 mm of the 23 mm increase occurring near the root tip.

Expected Outcome Nearly all root growth occurs at the tip of the root (within the region that was initially 3 mm from the tip).

Go Further

Students should set up their experiments in the same way described in this laboratory, except they measure stem length.

Chapter 23 Study Guide

Study Tip

Write each Vocabulary term on a separate card. Divide the class into two teams. Draw a vocabulary card, and have one member from each team draw diagrams or use pantomime to convey the meaning of the term to their team members. The first team to guess the term correctly wins a point. Continue until all the cards have been used.

Chapter 23 Assessment

Reviewing Content

1. b **2.** a **3.** c **4.** c **5.** c **6.** a **7.** b **8.** c **9.** b **10.** d

Understanding Concepts

11. The two kinds of vascular tissue in plants are xylem and phloem. Xylem consists of tracheids and vessel elements, and phloem consists of sieve tube elements and companion cells.

12. Parenchyma cells function mainly in storage and photosynthesis. Collenchyma cells help support large plants, and sclerenchyma cells make tissue tough and strong.

13. A root has a vascular cylinder at its center, surrounded by a cortex of ground tissue. A dicot stem has ground tissue in the center, surrounded by a ring of vascular tissue.

Chapter 23 Study Guide

23–1 Specialized Tissues in Plants

Key Concepts

- The three principal organs in seed plants are roots, stems, and leaves.
- Plants consist of three tissue systems: dermal tissue, vascular tissue, and ground tissue.
- Meristematic tissue is the only plant tissue that produces new cells by mitosis.
- Vascular tissue contains several different cell types. Xylem consists of tracheids and vessel elements, and phloem consists of sieve tube elements and companion cells.

Vocabulary

- meristematic tissue, p. 580
- apical meristem, p. 580 • epidermal cell, p. 581
- cuticle, p. 581 • trichome, p. 581
- vessel element, p. 582
- sieve tube element, p. 582
- companion cell, p. 583 • parenchyma, p. 583
- collenchyma, p. 583 • sclerenchyma, p. 583

23–2 Roots

Key Concepts

- The two main types of roots are taproots, found mainly in dicots, and fibrous roots, found mainly in monocots.
- A mature root has an outside layer of epidermal cells and a central cylinder of vascular tissue separated by a large area of ground tissue called the cortex.
- Roots anchor a plant in the ground and absorb water and dissolved nutrients from the soil.

Vocabulary

- taproot, p. 584 • fibrous root, p. 584
- root hair, p. 585 • cortex, p. 585
- endodermis, p. 585 • vascular cylinder, p. 585
- root cap, p. 585 • Casparian strip, p. 587

23–3 Stems

Key Concepts

- Stems have three important functions: They produce leaves, branches, and flowers; they hold leaves up in the sunlight; and they transport various substances between roots and leaves.
- In monocots, vascular bundles are scattered throughout the stem. In dicots and most gymnosperms, vascular bundles are arranged in a cylinder.
- In all seed plants, primary growth of stems is produced by cell divisions in the apical meristem.
- In conifers and dicots, secondary growth takes place in lateral meristematic tissues called the vascular cambium and cork cambium.

Vocabulary

- node, p. 589 • internode, p. 589
- bud, p. 589 • vascular bundle, p. 590
- pith, p. 590 • primary growth, p. 590
- secondary growth, p. 591
- vascular cambium, p. 591 • cork cambium, p. 591
- heartwood, p. 592 • sapwood, p. 592
- bark, p. 593

23–4 Leaves

Key Concepts

- The structure of a leaf is optimized for absorbing light and carrying out photosynthesis.
- Plants keep their stomata open just enough to allow photosynthesis to take place, but not so much that they lose an excessive amount of water.

Vocabulary

- blade, p. 595 • petiole, p. 595
- mesophyll, p. 596 • palisade mesophyll, p. 596
- spongy mesophyll, p. 596 • stoma, p. 596
- guard cell, p. 596 • transpiration, p. 596

23–5 Transport in Plants

Key Concepts

- Root pressure, capillary action, and transpiration work together to move water through the xylem tissue of even the largest plant.
- When nutrients are pumped into or removed from the phloem system, the change in concentration causes a movement of water in that same direction. As a result, phloem is able to move nutrients in either direction to meet the nutritional needs of the plant.

Vocabulary

- adhesion, p. 599 • capillary action, p. 599
- pressure-flow hypothesis, p. 602

Thinking Visually

Make a flowchart of the tissues through which water passes, from when it enters a plant at the root until it escapes from the plant through the leaves. Use the following terms in your flowchart: *spongy mesophyll, root epidermis, stomata, cortex, endodermis, xylem.*

TIME SAVER

CHAPTER RESOURCES

Print:

- ***Teaching Resources,*** Chapter Vocabulary Review, Graphic Organizer
- ***Chapter Tests: Levels A and B,*** Chapter 23 Test
- ***PH Assessment System,*** Practice Test

Technology:

- ***Computer Test Bank,*** Chapter 23 Test
- ***iText,*** Chapter 23 Assessment

Chapter 23 Assessment

Reviewing Content

Choose the letter that best answers the question or completes the statement.

1. The plant structure that is responsible for support of the plant body and for carrying nutrients between different parts of the plant is the
   a. root. c. leaf.
   b. stem. d. flower.
2. Which type of plant tissue would be found only in the circled areas of the plant shown below?
   a. meristematic tissue c. dermal tissue
   b. vascular tissue d. ground tissue

3. Phloem functions primarily in
   a. transport of water.
   b. growth of the root.
   c. transport of products of photosynthesis.
   d. increasing stem diameter.
4. Tracheids and vessel elements make up
   a. phloem. c. xylem.
   b. trichomes. d. meristem.
5. The waterproof strip that surrounds cells of the endodermis is the
   a. vascular cambium. c. Casparian strip.
   b. vascular cylinder. d. cortex.
6. Increases in the thickness of stems over time result from the production of vascular tissue by the
   a. vascular cambium.
   b. cork cambium.
   c. apical meristem.
   d. ground tissue.
7. Within a leaf, there are many air spaces between the cells of the
   a. palisade layer. c. meristem.
   b. spongy mesophyll. d. cuticle.
8. Stomata open and close in response to pressure within
   a. root cells. c. guard cells.
   b. cell walls. d. xylem.
9. The tissue that conducts the products of photosynthesis through a plant's stem is
   a. xylem.
   b. phloem.
   c. mesophyll.
   d. ground tissue.
10. The rise of water in a tall plant depends on root pressure and
    a. osmosis.
    b. evaporation.
    c. capillary action.
    d. transpiration pull.

Understanding Concepts

11. What are the two different kinds of vascular tissue in plants? Briefly describe each kind.
12. Explain the functions of these cells: parenchyma, collenchyma, and sclerenchyma.
13. If your classmate gave you a cross section of a dicot, how would you know whether the section was from a root or a stem?
14. How are root hairs important to plants?
15. What is the function of the vascular cambium in the secondary growth of stems?
16. From what type of plant tissue does bark develop?
17. What are the three main functions of leaves?
18. What is the function of the epidermis and cuticle layers in a leaf? What is the function of the pore-like openings in these layers?
19. What properties of water are important in its movement up a plant?
20. What is the function of guard cells in regulating transpiration and wilting?
21. What are the functions of phloem?
22. What are source cells and sink cells? Explain.

HOMEWORK GUIDE

Section:	Questions:
Section 23–1	1–3, 11, 12
Section 23–2	4, 13–14
Section 23–3	5, 6, 15, 16, 25, 27, 30
Section 23–4	7, 8, 17, 18, 20, 23, 24, 26, 28, 31
Section 23–5	9, 10, 19, 21, 22, 29, 32–34

14. The cell membranes of root hairs contain active transport proteins, which pump mineral ions from the soil into the plant, a process that leads to the movement of water into the plant by osmosis.

15. In the secondary growth of a stem, the vascular cambium produces vascular tissue and increases the thickness of stems over time.

16. Bark develops from the cork cambium.

17. The three main functions of leaves are photosynthesis, transpiration, and gas exchange.

18. The epidermis and cuticle layers of dermal tissue that form the outer covering of a plant have a protective function. The function of pore-like openings in these layers is to allow gas exchange between the plant and the environment.

19. The properties of water that are important in its movement up a plant are cohesion, or the attraction of water molecules to one another, and adhesion, or the attraction of water molecules to the walls of a tube. As a result of this combination of forces, water is able to rise in tubes by capillary action.

20. When the guard cells are filled with water, the pressure within them increases, and they swell. This causes the stomata to open and transpiration to occur. When the guard cells lose water, the stomata close, preventing water from leaving the leaf. This in turn prevents wilting due to excessive loss of water by the leaf.

21. The function of phloem is to pump food down from the leaves into the stems and roots for storage and back again from the roots to other parts of the plant when the food is needed.

22. Source cells are located where sugars are pumped into the phloem, and sink cells are located where there is a low concentration of sugars. The pressure-flow hypothesis explains how phloem moves sugars and water from source cells to sink cells.

Chapter 23 Assessment

Critical Thinking

23. The person training the miniature tree trims off the apical meristems at the tips of shoots and roots. This keeps the tree short. However, the person does not touch the vascular cambium in the stem, so the stem continues to increase in thickness.

24. Companion cell: vascular tissue; sclerenchyma: ground tissue; tracheid: vascular tissue; cuticle: dermal tissue. Students' sentences should reflect an understanding of the definitions of these terms.

25. A dicot would have just one taproot, while a monocot has multiple fibrous roots. The advantage of a taproot is that it can reach water far beneath the surface and can also be used for storage. Disadvantages might include less surface area than a network of fibrous roots. The advantages of fibrous roots include stabilizing the soil in which the plant grows. Fibrous roots are also shallow, however, limiting the plant to water that is available in the top layer of soil.

26. Without the Casparian strip, water could flow out of the xylem and phloem and back into the cortex of the root. The Casparian strip seals and waterproofs the cells of the endodermis around their edges so that water can only move through them in one direction.

27. Wood is made up of sapwood, or active xylem, and heartwood, or old, nonfunctioning xylem. Both types of wood lie inside the vascular cambium. Bark is made up of tissues outside the vascular cambium: phloem, the cork cambium, and cork, the inactive outer covering that protects the tree.

28. To avoid killing the tree, the cork must be removed so as not to damage the cork cambium that will produce a new layer of cork or the phloem that conducts nutrients throughout the tree.

29. Student's experimental design should include a reasonable hypothesis and a control.

30. Students' definitions should reflect an understanding of how leaf structures catch light and take in carbon dioxide and water for photosynthesis, and how they move the products of photosynthesis to the rest of the plant.

Chapter 23 Assessment

Critical Thinking

23. Inferring In Japan, the art of growing miniature trees is highly valued. By cutting the roots and tips of the branches, gardeners can keep the tree small. The trunk of the tree, however, continues to increase in diameter. How do you explain the ever-increasing growth of the diameter of the trunk?

24. Classifying Write a sentence about each of the following, explaining whether it should be classified as dermal tissue, vascular tissue, or ground tissue: companion cell, sclerenchyma, tracheid, cuticle.

25. Comparing and Contrasting Compare taproots with fibrous roots. What are the advantages and disadvantages of each type of root?

26. Predicting How would the function of a plant root be affected if the endodermis cells did not have Casparian strips? Explain.

27. Applying Concepts What is the difference between bark and wood in terms of their functions and in terms of the tissues that give rise to these layers?

28. Applying Concepts Cork is a lightweight, spongy material made from the outer bark of a type of oak tree. How must cork be removed to avoid killing the tree?

29. Designing Experiments What relationship would you expect between the length of a plant's life and its ability to undergo secondary growth? What data could you collect and compare to test your hypothesis? Describe an experiment to collect the data.

30. Forming Operational Definitions Review the structure and functions of a leaf and use this information to write an operational definition that explains in your own words what a leaf is.

31. Inferring During the nineteenth century, people often raised ferns and other delicate plants, which normally required a great deal of water, in enclosed glass containers called Wardian cases. Plants in Wardian cases did not have to be watered for years. What is the most logical explanation for this?

32. Using Analogies Someone has said, "A tree is like a skyscraper." In what ways would you agree or disagree with this statement? In your answer, refer to the processes responsible for the transport of water and nutrients in trees and other plants.

33. Applying Concepts Why are maple trees tapped for their sugar in the early spring rather than in the summer or autumn?

34. Interpreting Graphics During transpiration, water evaporates from the leaves of plants into the air. Examine the graph that follows and answer the following questions.

a. What does the graph show?

b. During which span of time is the greatest amount of water lost through transpiration?

c. About how many grams of water are lost every 2 hours when the transpiration curve is at its highest peak?

d. What can you conclude about the relationship between transpiration and water intake?

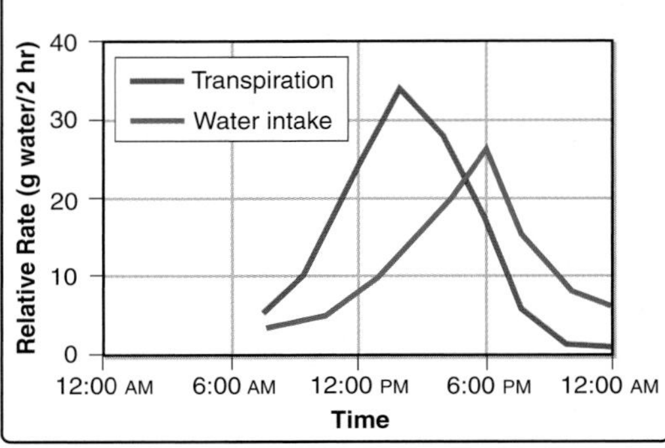

35. Making Connections Recall from Chapter 22 four things that plants need to survive. Describe how roots, stems, and leaves each contribute to meeting at least two of those needs.

Performance-Based Assessment

Making Models Make a three-dimensional model of one of the following: the layers in a plant leaf, the structure of a plant root, or the structure of a woody stem with secondary growth. Label the major structures in your model. On a separate sheet of paper, describe the function of each structure.

Take It to the NET

Can you tell how old a tree is? Visit the Prentice Hall Web site at **www.phschool.com** to find out how to count tree rings. Then, answer the following questions:

- What is dendrochronology?
- How can you use tree rings from different trees to date events that are older than one tree?
- What factors affect the ring growth patterns in bristlecone pines?

Performance-Based Assessment

Students' models and descriptions should reflect an understanding of the structure and function of leaves, stems, or roots.

Standardized Test Prep

Test-Taking Tip When presented with questions that are related to data in a table, study each column and row of the table for the information you need to answer the questions.

Directions: Choose the letter that best answers the question or completes the statement.

1. Which of the following cell types is NOT found in a plant's vascular tissue?
   (A) tracheid
   (B) vessel element
   (C) guard cell
   (D) companion cell
   (E) sieve tube element
2. Where in a plant does mitosis produce new cells?
   I. Meristematic tissue
   II. Shoots
   III. Roots
   (A) I only
   (B) III only
   (C) I and III only
   (D) II and III only
   (E) I, II, and III
3. Tree bark is made of which of the following tissues?
   I. Phloem
   II. Cork
   III. Cork cambium
   (A) I only
   (B) III only
   (C) I and III only
   (D) II and III only
   (E) I, II, and III
4. Which is NOT a factor in the movement of water through a plant's vascular tissues?
   (A) transpiration
   (B) capillary action
   (C) osmotic pressure
   (D) meristems
   (E) water evaporation from leaves
5. All of the following conduct fluids in a plant EXCEPT
   (A) heartwood.
   (B) sapwood.
   (C) vascular tissue.
   (D) phloem.
   (E) xylem.
6. Where does most of the photosynthesis occur in a plant?
   (A) stomata
   (B) guard cells
   (C) bark
   (D) vascular cambium
   (E) mesophyll tissue

Questions 7–8

A student compared the average number of stomata on the top side and the underside of different plants. Her data are summarized in the table.

Average Number of Stomata (per square mm)

Plant	Top Surfaces of Leaves	Bottom Surfaces of Leaves
Pumpkin	29	275
Tomato	12	122
Bean	40	288

7. What generalization can be made based on the data?
   (A) All plants have more stomata on the top side of their leaves than on the bottom side.
   (B) Plants have fewer stomata on the top side of their leaves than on the bottom side.
   (C) Some plants have more stomata on the top side of their leaves than on the bottom side.
   (D) The number of stomata varies greatly from plant to plant.
   (E) Most plants have about the same number of stomata.
8. Pumpkins, tomatoes, and beans all grow in direct sunlight. Assuming the plants receive plenty of water, stomata on the lower surface of their leaves
   (A) are always closed.
   (B) are usually clogged with dust.
   (C) are unlikely to close at night.
   (D) stay open during daylight hours.
   (E) attract insects.

Questions 9–10 Complete each analogy by selecting the correct letter. In analogies, A : B :: C : _?_ means A is to B as C is to _?_.

9. Ground tissue : sclerenchyma :: vascular tissue : _?_
   (A) apical meristem
   (B) cuticle
   (C) xylem
   (D) collenchyma
   (E) trichomes
10. Taproot : carrot :: fibrous root : _?_
   (A) dandelion
   (B) potato
   (C) radish
   (D) grass
   (E) beet

Take It to the NET

• Dendrochronology is the dating of past events by studying tree ring growth.

• By comparing the ring patterns of living and dead trees of differing ages, you can find identical growth patterns. Matching these growth patterns up will allow you to carry the chronology further into the past.

• Rainfall, slope gradient, sun, wind, soil properties, temperature, and snow accumulation all affect ring growth patterns.

For additional information, visit

www.phschool.com

Standardized Test Prep

1. C **2.** E **3.** E **4.** D **5.** A **6.** E **7.** B **8.** D **9.** C **10.** D

31. The water that evaporated from the plant leaves was contained in the Wardian case, fell back to the soil, and could be used again by the plants.

32. Sample answers: Like a skyscraper, a tree has structures that transport materials from its lowest level to its highest. Unlike a skyscraper, a tree is an organism that functions without human intervention.

33. In early spring, the daily rise and fall of temperature causes the sap to start flowing up from the maple tree's roots. During the summer and autumn, the flow would be in the opposite direction and the sap would not be as concentrated.

34. a. How the rates of water intake and transpiration vary with the time of day **b.** Between about 11:00 AM and 2:00 PM **c.** About 35 grams of water **d.** As transpiration increases or decreases, water intake also increases or decreases.

35. Students' answers should discuss how roots, stems, and leaves contribute to meeting a plant's needs for two of the following: sunlight, water, gas exchange, and the movement of water and nutrients.

Chapter Planner 24 Reproduction of Seed Plants

Section and Section Objectives	Time	Activities and Labs
24–1 Reproduction With Cones and Flowers, pp. 609–616 **24.1.1** ***Identify*** the reproductive structures of gymnosperms and angiosperms. **24.1.2** ***Explain*** how pollination and fertilization differ between angiosperms and gymnosperms.	2 periods (1 block)	**SE: *Inquiry Activity,*** How do seeds and fruits vary?, p. 608 **TE: *Demonstrations,*** pp. 608, 610 **TE: *Build Science Skills,*** pp. 610, 611 **SE: *Quick Lab,*** What is the structure of a flower?, p. 613 **SE: *Technology and Society,*** Flowers by Design, p. 617 **SE: *Design an Experiment,*** Investigating Pollination, p. 627
24–2 Seed Development and Germination, pp. 618–621 **24.2.1** ***Describe*** the development of seeds and fruits. **24.2.2** ***Explain*** how seeds are dispersed. **24.2.3** ***List*** the factors that influence the dormancy and germination of seeds.	1 period (1/2 block)	**TE: *Demonstration,*** p. 618 **SE: *Analyzing Data,*** Temperature and Seed Germination, p. 620 **TE: *Demonstration,*** p. 621
24–3 Plant Propagation and Agriculture, pp. 622–626 **24.3.1** ***Identify*** the forms of plant vegetative reproduction. **24.3.2** ***Describe*** plant propagation. **24.3.3** ***Identify*** the major-food-supply crops for humans.	1 period (1/2 block)	**TE: *Demonstrations,*** pp. 622, 623 **TE: *Build Science Skills,*** pp. 623, 624 **SE: *Biology and History,*** The Evolution of Agriculture, pp. 624–625
Chapter Assessment, pp. 628–631	1 period (1/2 block)	

ACTIVITY PLANNER

SE: *Inquiry Activity,* p. 608; (15 min.); hand lens, seeds, fruits, petri dish, scalpel

TE: *Demonstration,* p. 608; (5 min.); pine cone, apple, knife

TE: *Build Science Skills,* p. 610; (5 min.); small pine branch with pollen cones and seed cones

TE: *Demonstration,* p. 610; (10 min.); pollen cone, slide, coverslip

TE: *Build Science Skills,* p. 611; (5 min.); pine seed, knife, hand lens

SE: *Quick Lab,* p. 613; (20 min.); flower, forceps, scalpel, microscope slide, dropper pipette, coverslips, microscope

TE: *Demonstration,* p. 618; (5 min.); variety of fruits, knife

TE: *Demonstration,* p. 621; (5 min.); variety of monocot and dicot seeds, 2 paper towels, plate, plastic wrap

TE: *Demonstration,* p. 622; (5 min.); spider plant, crab grass, bulb

TE: *Build Science Skills,* p. 623; (5 min., 5 min.); raw sweet potato, 4 toothpicks, small container of water

TE: *Demonstration,* p. 623; (5 min.); tree branch sections, knife, cloth tape

TE: *Build Science Skills,* p. 624; (5 min.); oranges with and without seeds, knife

SE: *Design an Experiment,* p. 627; (45 min.); flowering plants, hand lens, small paintbrush, forceps, pollen nutrient solution, pollen nutrient solution without calcium, conc. calcium chloride solution, dissecting probe, microscope slides, coverslips, dropper pipette, microscope

PLANNING KEY

Ability Levels

- Ⓑ **Basic** — For students who need additional help
- Ⓐ **Average** — For all students
- Ⓔ **Enriched** — For students who need to be challenged

Components

SE	Student Edition	**GRSW**	Guided Reading and Study Workbook	**IDM**	Issues and Decision Making
TE	Teacher's Edition	**CT**	Chapter Tests: Levels A and B	**CTB**	Computer Test Bank
LMA	Laboratory Manual A	**PHAS**	PH Assessment System	**PA**	Presentation Assistant Plus
LMB	Laboratory Manual B	**LA**	Lab Assessment with Scoring Guide	**BD**	BioDetectives Videotape
TR	Teaching Resources	**BTM**	BioTechnology Manual	**iT**	iText
IF	Investigations in Forensics				

Program Resources	Assessment	Media and Technology
TR: Section Review 24–1 Ⓑ Ⓐ **GRSW:** Section 24–1 Ⓑ Ⓐ **IF:** Investigation 4 Ⓐ Ⓔ	**SE:** 24–1 Section Assessment, p. 616 **TR:** Section Review 24–1	**PA:** 24–1 Interest Grabber, Section Outline, Compare/Contrast Table, Figure 24–1, Figure 24–4, Figure 24–5, Figure 24–7 **iT:** Section 24–1
LMA: Chapter 24 Lab Ⓐ Ⓔ **LMB:** Chapter 24 Lab Ⓑ Ⓐ **TR:** Section Review 24–2 Ⓑ Ⓐ **GRSW:** Section 24–2 Ⓑ Ⓐ	**SE:** 24–2 Section Assessment, p. 621 **TR:** Section Review 24–2	**PA:** 24–2 Interest Grabber, Section Outline, Concept Map **iT:** Section 24–2
TR: Section Review 24–3 Ⓑ Ⓐ **GRSW:** Section 24–3 Ⓑ Ⓐ	**SE:** 24–3 Section Assessment, p. 626 **TR:** Section Review 24–3	**PA:** 24–3 Interest Grabber, Section Outline, Compare/Contrast Table **iT:** Section 24–3
	SE: Chapter 24 Assessment, pp. 628–631 **TR:** Chapter Vocabulary Review, Graphic Organizer **CT:** Chapter 24 Test **CTB:** Chapter 24 Test **PHAS:** Practice Text	**CTB:** Chapter 24 Test **iT:** Chapter 24 Assessment

PRESSED FOR TIME?

To Preview the Chapter

- Have students read the Key Concepts in each section.
- Introduce students to the Vocabulary terms in each section.

To Cover the Chapter Quickly

- Have students read Gymnosperms, Angiosperms, Pollination, and Fertilization in Section 24–1, all of Section 24–2, and the Biology and History time line in Section 24–3.
- Assign Section Assessments 24–1 and 24–2, questions 1–9, 11–13, 15, 16, and 20–25 in Chapter 24 Assessment, and questions 1–5 and 7–11 in Chapter 24 Standardized Test Prep.

To Review the Chapter

- Assign Sections 24–1 and 24–2 in the Guided Reading and Study Workbook.
- Assign the Section Reviews for 24–1 and 24–2 and the Chapter Vocabulary Review for Chapter 24 in the Teaching Resources.

ENGAGE/EXPLORE

Inquiry Activity

Objective Students will be able to observe structures in seeds and predict which structures are involved in reproduction.

Skills Focus **Observing, Formulating Hypotheses, Predicting**

Materials hand lens, variety of seeds and fruits, petri dish, scalpel

Time 15 minutes

Advance Prep If you soak the seeds in water overnight before the lab, they will be easier to cut open.

Strategy Make sure students cut the seeds lengthwise, or they may not be able to see all the structures.

Expected Outcome Students should observe the embryo and other structures inside the seeds.

Think About It

1. All seeds have an embryo, seed coat, stored food, and one or two cotyledons.
2. The cotyledons and endosperm contain stored nutrients.
3. Depending on the type of seeds, students might have observed burrs, "wings," or other structures that enable the seeds to attach to fur or clothing or to glide on the wind.

Demonstration

Display a pine cone and an apple. Cut the apple in half to expose the seeds and shake some of the seeds out of the pine cone. Then, ask: **What do the pine cone and apple have in common?** *(Both contain the plant's seeds.)* Explain that cone-bearing plants such as pine trees and fruit-bearing plants such as apple trees produce seeds in different ways. Add that students will learn more about the reproduction of both types of plants in this chapter.

Chapter 24 Reproduction of Seed Plants

Red nodding thistle flowers show a dramatic change as they undergo fertilization and seed development. At maturity, the seeds—each attached to long, white threads—detach from the flowers and are dispersed by wind.

Inquiry Activity

How do seeds and fruits vary?

Procedure

1. Use a hand lens to examine a variety of seeds and fruits. (*Hint:* Review the material on seeds in Chapter 22, page 565). Record your observations.
2. Place each seed in a petri dish and use a scalpel to cut the seed lengthwise. **CAUTION:** *Use care with sharp instruments.* Use a hand lens to examine the inside of each seed. Draw and label the structures you observe. Label the embryo of each seed.

Think About It

1. **Observing** What types of structures did you observe in all the seeds?
2. **Formulating Hypotheses** A seed contains stored nutrients that nourish the new plant until it becomes autotrophic. Which part of the seed might contain these nutrients?
3. **Predicting** What structures did you observe that could help spread the offspring of a plant over a larger area? Explain your answer.

HISTORY OF SCIENCE

In 1879, a botany professor at Michigan Agricultural College (now Michigan State University) designed a long-term experiment to investigate the survivability of common weed seeds. Dr. W. J. Beal gathered 50 freshly grown seeds from each of 23 different types of plants, including common mallow and common mullein. He then prepared 20 sets of seeds by mixing each set in moist sand that filled a pint bottle. He buried those bottles in a row on a sandy knoll, with the tops left uncovered and the bottles slanting down so that they would not fill with water. Since then, one of Beal's bottles has been dug up every five or ten years to see if any of the seeds in it would germinate. Some of the seeds of three species in the bottle dug up in 1980—after 100 years—still germinated when placed in good growing conditions.

24–1 Reproduction With Cones and Flowers

Seed plants are well adapted to the demands of life on land, especially in the way that they reproduce. As you may recall, the gametes of seedless plants, such as ferns and mosses, need water for fertilization to be successful. Water allows gametes to move from plant to plant. The gametes of seed plants, however, can achieve fertilization even when the plants are not wet from rain or dew. As a result, they can reproduce just about anywhere. The way in which seed plants reproduce has allowed them to survive the dry conditions of life on land.

Alternation of Generations

All plants have a life cycle in which a diploid sporophyte generation alternates with a haploid gametophyte generation. Gametophyte plants produce male and female gametes—sperm and eggs. When the gametes join, they form a zygote that begins the next sporophyte generation. In some plants, the two stages of the life cycle are distinct, independent plants. In most ferns, for instance, the gametophyte is a small, heart-shaped plant that grows close to the ground. The sporophyte is the familiar fern plant itself made up of graceful fronds.

Where are these two generations in seed plants? Recall from Mendel's work on peas that seed-bearing plants are diploid. Therefore, the recognizable part of seed-bearing plants must be the diploid sporophyte.

If the sporophyte is what we recognize as the plant, then where is the gametophyte? The answer may surprise you. As shown in **Figure 24–1,** the gametophytes of seed plants are actually hidden deep within tissues of the sporophyte plant. In gymnosperms they are found inside cones, and in angiosperms they are found inside flowers.

Guide for Reading

Key Concepts
- What are the reproductive structures of gymnosperms and angiosperms?
- How does pollination differ between angiosperms and gymnosperms?

Vocabulary
- pollen cone • seed cone
- ovule • pollen tube
- sepal • petal • stamen
- filament • anther • carpel
- ovary • style • stigma
- embryo sac • endosperm
- double fertilization

Reading Strategy: Making Comparisons
Before you read, preview **Figure 24–4** and **Figure 24–7.** As you read, compare the life cycles of gymnosperms and angiosperms.

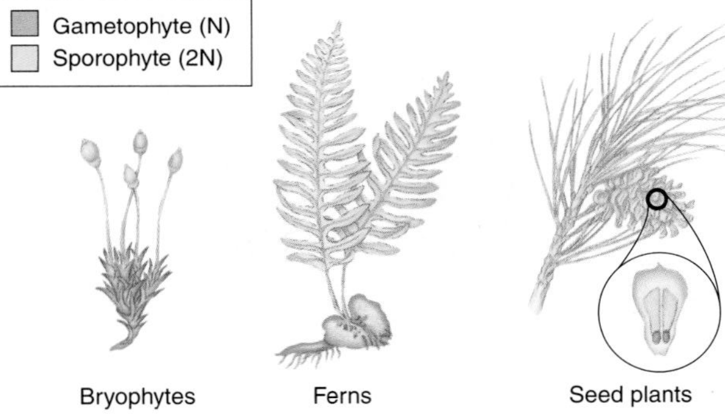

◀ **Figure 24–1** An important trend in plant evolution is the reduction of the gametophyte and the increasing size of the sporophyte. Bryophytes consist of a relatively large gametophyte and smaller sporophytes that are located on stalks. Seedless vascular plants, such as ferns, have a small gametophyte and a larger sporophyte. Seed plants have an even smaller gametophyte that is contained within sporophyte tissues. **Interpreting Graphics** ***How does the relative size of the haploid and diploid stages of plants differ between bryophytes and seed plants?***

TIME SAVER — SECTION RESOURCES

Print:
- ***Teaching Resources,*** Section Review 24–1
- ***Guided Reading and Study Workbook,*** Section 24–1
- ***Investigations in Forensics,*** Investigation 7

Technology:
- ***iText,*** Section 24–1

Section 24–1

1 FOCUS

Objectives

24.1.1 ***Identify*** the reproductive structures of gymnosperms and angiosperms.

24.1.2 ***Explain*** how pollination and fertilization differ between angiosperms and gymnosperms.

Guide for Reading

Vocabulary Preview

Ask students to predict which Vocabulary terms refer to the reproductive parts of gymnosperms, or cone-bearing plants, and which terms refer to the reproductive parts of angiosperms, or flowering plants. *(Pollen cone and seed cone are parts of gymnosperms. Sepal, petal, stamen, anther, carpel, ovary, style, and stigma are parts of angiosperms. Both types of plants have pollen grains, pollen tubes, and ovules.)* Students should check to see if their predictions were correct after they read the section.

Reading Strategy

Suggest that students find each boldfaced term in the text, read its definition, and then locate it in Figure 24–4 or Figure 24–7.

2 INSTRUCT

Alternation of Generations

Meet Diverse Needs

On the chalkboard or an overhead transparency, create a graphic organizer, such as a concept map or Venn diagram, to review basic differences and similarities between gymnosperms and angiosperms. The graphic organizer should show that both types of plants are seed plants but that angiosperms produce flowers and seeds within the ovaries (fruits), whereas gymnosperms produce cones and "naked" seeds outside the ovaries. **Learning modality: visual**

Answer to . . .

Figure 24–1 *Seed plants have smaller haploid stages and larger diploid stages.*

Life Cycle of Gymnosperms

Build Science Skills

Observing Obtain a small pine branch that has both pollen cones and seed cones. Point out how the two types of cones are arranged on the branch so that pollen from a pollen cone is likely to fall on a seed cone. Call students' attention to the scales on a seed cone and how they are arranged. Remove some of the scales, and let students examine the base of the scales. *(Even if the seeds have been shed, an impression of the seeds still remains.)* Also, have students examine the scales of a seed cone that has been soaked in water. *(The scales are closed.)* Ask: **What is the function of the scales of a seed cone?** *(To protect the seeds)*

Demonstration

Dust some pollen grains from a cone on a microscope slide. Prepare a wet-mount slide and focus on low power. Use a microprojector or have students take turns observing the pollen. Suggest that students sketch what they see. Ask: **How is the structure of the pollen grain related to its function?** *(A pollen grain has two tiny wings on either side of its rounded center that aid in its dispersal by wind.)*

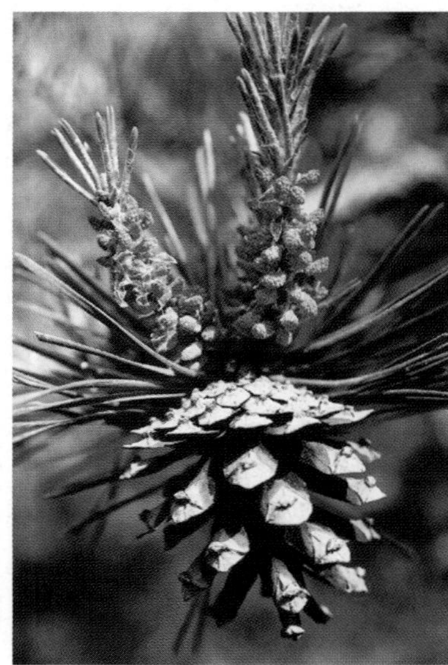

▲ **Figure 24–2** **Reproduction in gymnosperms takes place in structures called cones.** Pollen cones, shown on the top in this pine tree, produce male gametophytes, which are pollen grains. Seed cones, shown on the bottom, produce female gametophytes that develop into a new embryo following fertilization.

Life Cycle of Gymnosperms

Pine trees and other gymnosperms are diploid sporophytes. As you will see, this sporophyte develops from a zygote that is contained within a seed. How and where is this seed produced? **Reproduction in gymnosperms takes place in cones, which are produced by a mature sporophyte plant.** Gymnosperms produce two types of cones: pollen cones and seed cones.

Pollen Cones and Seed Cones **Pollen cones,** shown in **Figure 24–2,** are also called male cones. Pollen cones produce the male gametophytes, which are called pollen grains. As tiny as it is, the pollen grain makes up the entire male gametophyte stage of the gymnosperm life cycle. One of the haploid nuclei in the pollen grain will divide later to produce two sperm nuclei.

The more familiar **seed cones,** which produce female gametophytes, are generally much larger than pollen cones. Near the base of each scale are two **ovules** in which the female gametophytes develop. Within the ovules, meiosis produces haploid cells that grow and divide to produce female gametophytes. These gametophytes may contain hundreds or thousands of cells. When mature, each gametophyte contains a few large egg cells, each ready for fertilization by sperm nuclei.

Pollination The gymnosperm life cycle typically takes two years to complete. The cycle begins in the spring as male cones release enormous numbers of pollen grains. This pollen is carried by the wind, as shown in **Figure 24–3.** Some of these pollen grains reach female cones. There, some pollen grains are caught in a sticky secretion on one of the scales of the female cone. This sticky material, known as a pollination drop, ensures that pollen grains stay on the female cone.

CHECKPOINT *What are pollen cones and seed cones?*

Figure 24–3 Pollen grains are male gametophytes. Pollen is carried by the wind until it reaches a female cone. **Inferring** *Male and female cones are distributed on a plant such that pollen usually lands on a different plant from where it started. Why might this strategy have evolved?*

Pollen Grains
(magnification: 750×)

PRESENTATIONS MADE EASY!

The Presentation Assistant Plus contains the Prentice Hall Presentation Pro and the Transparencies, which provide easy-to-follow visual support for every step of this section. If you have a computer presentation station, use Prentice Hall Presentation Pro for Section 24–1, or use the transparencies listed here.

Section 24–1:

Interest Grabber
Section Outline
Compare/Contrast Table
Figure 24–1
Figure 24–4
Figure 24–5
Figure 24–7

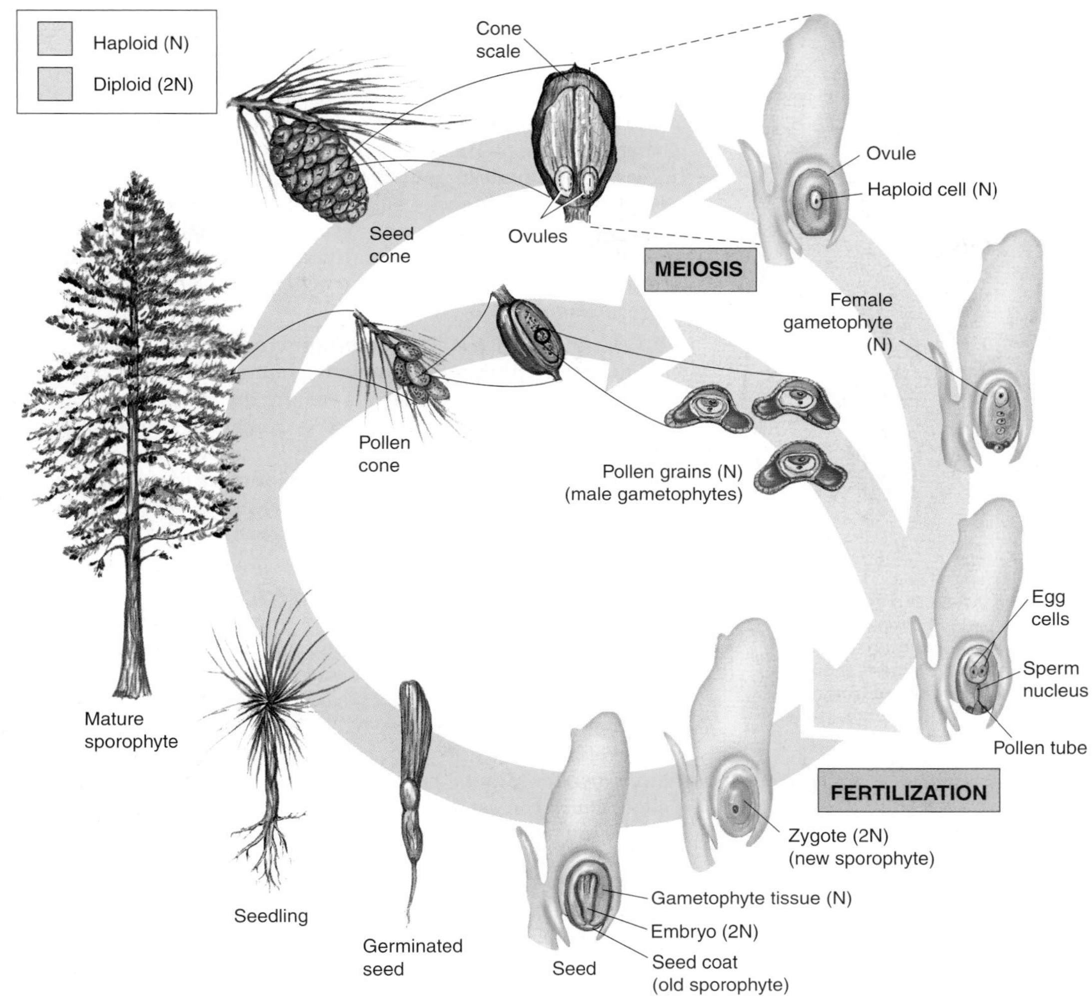

▲ **Figure 24–4** This illustration shows the life cycle of a typical gymnosperm. A pine tree—the mature sporophyte—produces male and female cones. Male cones produce pollen, and female cones produce ovules located on cone scales. If an egg is fertilized by the sperm, it becomes a zygote that is nourished by the female cone. In time, the zygote develops into a new sporophyte plant. **Classifying** ***Classify each of the following terms as to whether they belong to the haploid or diploid stage of the pine tree's life cycle: pollen tube, seed cone, embryo, ovule, seedling.***

Fertilization and Development If a pollen grain lands near an ovule, the grain splits open and begins to grow a structure called a **pollen tube,** which contains two haploid sperm nuclei. Once the pollen tube reaches the female gametophyte, one sperm nucleus disintegrates, and the other fertilizes the egg contained within the female gametophyte. If sperm from another pollen tube reaches the female gametophyte, both egg cells may be fertilized, but just one embryo grows. As shown in **Figure 24–4,** fertilization produces a diploid zygote—the new sporophyte plant. This zygote grows into a small embryo. During this time, it is encased within what will soon develop into a seed. The seed consists of three generations of the life cycle. The outer seed coat is part of the old sporophyte generation, the haploid cells surrounding the embryo are part of the female gametophyte, and the embryo is the new sporophyte plant.

Use Visuals

Figure 24–4 Make sure students understand the diagram. Point out all the steps where the next drawing in the sequence is an enlargement of the previous drawing. For example, explain how the single cone scale at the top of the diagram is just one of many cone scales on the seed cone in the previous drawing. Similarly, the drawing that shows the haploid cell in the cone scale is an enlargement of the previous drawing of the cone scale. Add that the same holds true for the male pollen cone and its pollen grains. Then, review the entire life cycle of a pine tree and have students follow along in the diagram. As you identify the structures involved in each stage, students should locate them in the diagram. Check students' comprehension of the life cycle by asking: **Which parts of the plant are haploid?** *(The haploid cell in the ovule, the female gametophyte, and the male gametophytes in the pollen grains)* **Why is the zygote diploid?** *(Because fertilization has occurred)*

Build Science Skills

Applying Concepts As students watch, cut a pine seed in half. Point out the three layers of the seed: the outer seed coat, the gametophyte, and the embryo. You may want to provide students with a hand lens to examine the three layers. Explain that the seed consists of three generations of the pine tree. Ask: **Which generation of the pine tree is represented by each layer of the seed?** *(The outer seed coat is part of the old sporophyte plant, the cells surrounding the embryo are part of the female gametophyte, and the embryo is the new sporophyte plant.)*

BIO INSIGHTS — BACKGROUND

In an attempt to simplify, pollen grains often are referred to as gametes. It is important, though, to be clear about exactly what is a gamete and what is a spore. Recall that a gamete is a cell that must fuse with another gamete to form a new organism. Pollen grains, therefore, are not gametes; they are spores because they grow by mitosis into a new organism—the gametophyte. In angiosperms, the true male gametes are the two sperm nuclei that appear in the pollen tube. The true female gametes are the egg cell and the polar nuclei that fuse with the sperm nuclei to form the embryo and endosperm, respectively.

Answers to . . .

✓CHECKPOINT *Pollen cones produce the male gametophytes. Seed cones produce the female gametophytes.*

Figure 24–3 *Because it increases genetic variation*

Figure 24–4 *Haploid stage: pollen tube; diploid stage: seed cone, ovule, seedling, embryo*

Structure of Flowers

Build Science Skills

Classifying Display pictures of a wide variety of angiosperms. Include trees, shrubs, perennial and annual herbaceous plants, ground covers, grasses, and water plants. Give students a chance to view the pictures, and then have them brainstorm a list of characteristics that they think all angiosperms share. *(Students might identify green leaves, flowers, and fruits, among other possible shared characteristics.)* Then, ask: **How do angiosperms differ from gymnosperms?** *(Students might say that angiosperms have broad leaves instead of needles and that they produce flowers and fruits instead of cones.)*

Meet Diverse Needs

Because flowers vary greatly in structure, it can be difficult to identify flower parts. Give students who are gifted in art a chance to use their talents to create a poster illustrating several very different types of flowers, such as orchids, magnolias, and daisies. Students should label each flower with the following structures: sepals, petals, stamen, anthers, ovary, style, and stigma. Display their posters in the classroom. **Learning modality: visual**

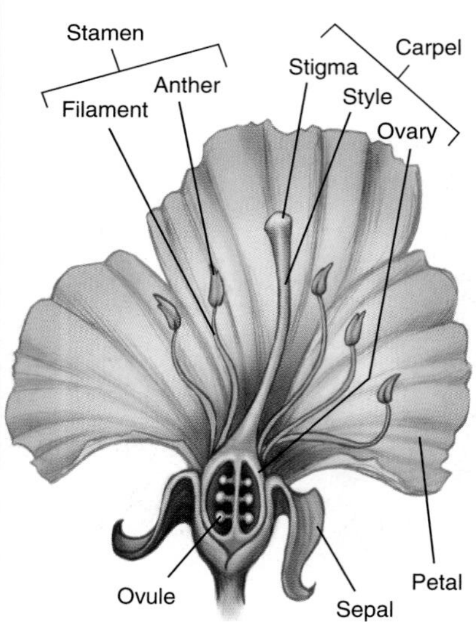

▲ **Figure 24–5** This cross section shows the parts of a typical flower. The flowers of some species, however, may not have all the parts shown here. **Flowers are reproductive organs that include sepals, petals, stamens, and carpels.**

Structure of Flowers

You may think of flowers as decorative objects that brighten the world. However, the presence of so many flowers in the world is visible evidence of something else—the stunning evolutionary success of the angiosperms, or flowering plants. Flowers are the key to understanding why angiosperms have been so successful.

Flowers are reproductive organs that are composed of four kinds of specialized leaves: sepals, petals, stamens, and carpels. These structures are shown in the flower in **Figure 24–5.**

Sepals and Petals The outermost circle of floral parts contains the **sepals,** which in many plants are green and closely resemble ordinary leaves. Sepals enclose the bud before it opens, and they protect the flower while it is developing. **Petals,** which are often brightly colored, are found just inside the sepals. The petals attract insects and other pollinators to the flower. Because they do not produce reproductive cells, the sepals and petals of a flower are sometimes called sterile leaves.

Stamens and Carpels Within the ring of petals are the structures that produce male and female gametophytes. The male parts consist of an anther and a filament, which together make up the **stamen.** The **filament** is a long, thin stalk that supports an anther. At the tip of each filament is an **anther,** an oval sac where meiosis takes place, producing haploid male gametophytes—pollen grains. In most angiosperms, each flower has several stamens. If you rub your hand on the anthers of a flower, a yellow-orange dust may stick to your skin. This is pollen, which consists of thousands of individual pollen grains.

The innermost floral parts are **carpels,** also called pistils, which produce the female gametophytes. Each carpel has a broad base forming an **ovary,** which contains one or more ovules where female gametophytes are produced. The diameter of the carpel narrows into a stalk called the **style.** At the top of the style is a sticky portion known as the **stigma,** where pollen grains frequently land. Some flowers have several carpels fused together to form a single reproductive structure called a compound carpel.

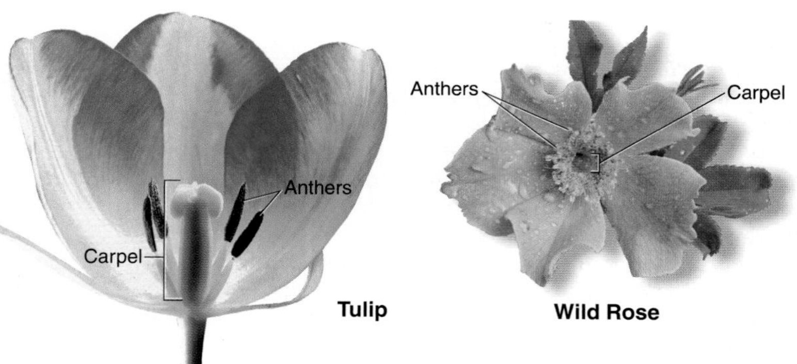

Figure 24–6 Flowers vary enormously in structure. The tulip (left) has only a single carpel, whereas the rose flower (right) has many carpels, each of which develops into the fleshy part of a rose fruit. Some flowerlike structures are actually clusters of many individual flowers. In the sunflower (facing page), disk flowers toward the inside of the cluster are reproductive, whereas ray flowers toward the outside are nonreproductive and form what look like petals. **Formulating Hypotheses** ***How might it be an advantage for a plant to have many flowers together in a single structure?***

FACTS AND FIGURES

Flowery facts

In many flowers, both sepals and petals are brightly colored and help attract pollinators. In other plants, sepals are smaller and thicker than petals and green in color. In these plants, the sepals' function is to protect the more fragile flower bud from damage.

Some angiosperm plants have evolved unique ways to attract pollinators. For example, an African plant, *Anchomanes difformis*, does the botanical equivalent of burning incense. The flower has a foot-tall structure called a spadix. The plant's tissues generate heat and warm the spadix to about 40°C, so it produces a sweet aroma that attracts the beetles that pollinate the flower. Most angiosperm flowers contain both pistils and stamens. However, some species, including date palms, willows, and poplars, produce unisexual flowers that have only stamens (staminate flowers) or pistils (pistillate flowers).

Quick Lab

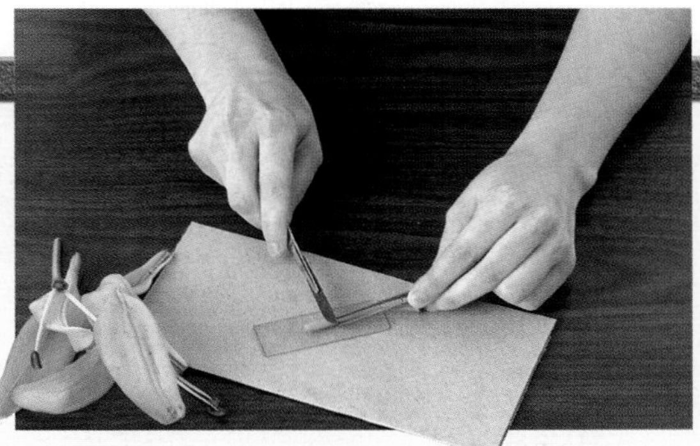

What is the structure of a flower?

Materials flower, forceps, scalpel, microscope slide, dropper pipette, coverslips, microscope

Procedure

1. Examine a flower carefully. Make a detailed drawing of the flower and label as many parts as you can. Note whether the anthers are above or below the stigma.
2. Remove an anther and place it on a slide. While holding the anther with forceps, use the scalpel to cut one or more thin slices across the anther. **CAUTION:** *Be careful with sharp tools.*
3. Lay the slices flat on the microscope slide and add a drop of water and a coverslip. Observe the slices with the microscope at low power. Make a labeled drawing of your observations.
4. Repeat steps 2 and 3 with the ovary.

Analyze and Conclude

1. **Observing** Are the anthers in this flower located above or below the stigma? How could this affect what happens to the pollen produced by the anthers? Explain your answer.
2. **Applying Concepts** What structures did you identify in the anther? What is the function of these structures?
3. **Applying Concepts** What structures did you identify in the ovary? What is the function of these structures?
4. **Drawing Conclusions** Which parts of the flower will become the seeds? The fruit?

Flowers vary greatly in shape, color, and size, as shown in **Figure 24–6.** A typical flower produces both male and female gametophytes. In some plants, however, male and female gametophytes are produced in separate flowers on the same individual. Corn, for example, has separate male and female flowers on the same plant. The tassel is a flower that produces male gametophytes, and the silk is the style of a flower that contains the female gametophyte. In other cases, many flowers grow together to form a composite structure that looks like a single flower, as shown in the sunflower.

CHECKPOINT *What are the male structures in a typical flower? The female structures?*

Quick Lab

Objective Students will be able to observe the structures of a flower and conclude which structures become seeds and which structures become the fruit.

Skills Focus Observing, Applying Concepts, Drawing Conclusions

Materials flower, forceps, scalpel, microscope slide, dropper pipette, coverslips, microscope

Time 20 minutes

Strategy Before students cut their flower, make sure they have noted whether the anthers are above or below the stigma.

Analyze and Conclude

1. Self-pollinated flowers typically have anthers higher than the stigma, and pollen falls directly from the anthers onto the stigma. Many cross-pollinated plants have taller stigmas that receive windblown or animal-borne pollen from other flowers.
2. Students may be able to observe mature or immature pollen in the anthers.
3. Students may be able to observe mature or immature ovules in the ovary.
4. The ovules will become the seeds. Generally, the ovary becomes the fruit, although other parts of the flower may also contribute to fruit formation.

Meet Diverse Needs

Give hands-on learners a chance to create a model of a flower using whatever materials they find around the classroom or at home. For example, they might use colored construction paper for sepals and petals; toothpicks for filaments; modeling clay for anthers, stigma, and ovary; cornmeal for pollen; a drinking straw for the style; and dry peas for ovules. Invite students to share their models with the class and identify each of its parts. **Learning modality: tactile**

Answers to . . .

CHECKPOINT *The male structures are the stamen and anthers; the female structures are the carpels, ovary, style, and stigma.*

Figure 24–6 *Many flowers together in a single structure might attract more insects, so chances of pollination are increased.*

24–1 **(continued)**

Life Cycle of Angiosperms

Use Visuals

Figure 24–7 Some students might be confused by the figure. Check their comprehension by asking: **Where does fertilization take place?** *(Inside the ovary)* **How do pollen grains reach the ovary?** *(By growing pollen tubes down through the style)* **How many sets of chromosomes are contained within the endosperm?** *(Three)* **How many sets of chromosomes does the embryo have?** *(Two)* **From which part of the plant does the seed coat develop?** *(The outer part of the ovule)*

Meet Diverse Needs

Encourage students who need an extra challenge to write a "biography" of a mature seed plant of their choice. Their biographies should incorporate all of the important events in the plant's life cycle, including formation as a seed, germination, transportation away from the parent plant, and growth to maturity. Encourage students to be creative but accurate in describing the life cycles of their plants. Urge students to share their completed work with the class. **Learning modality: verbal**

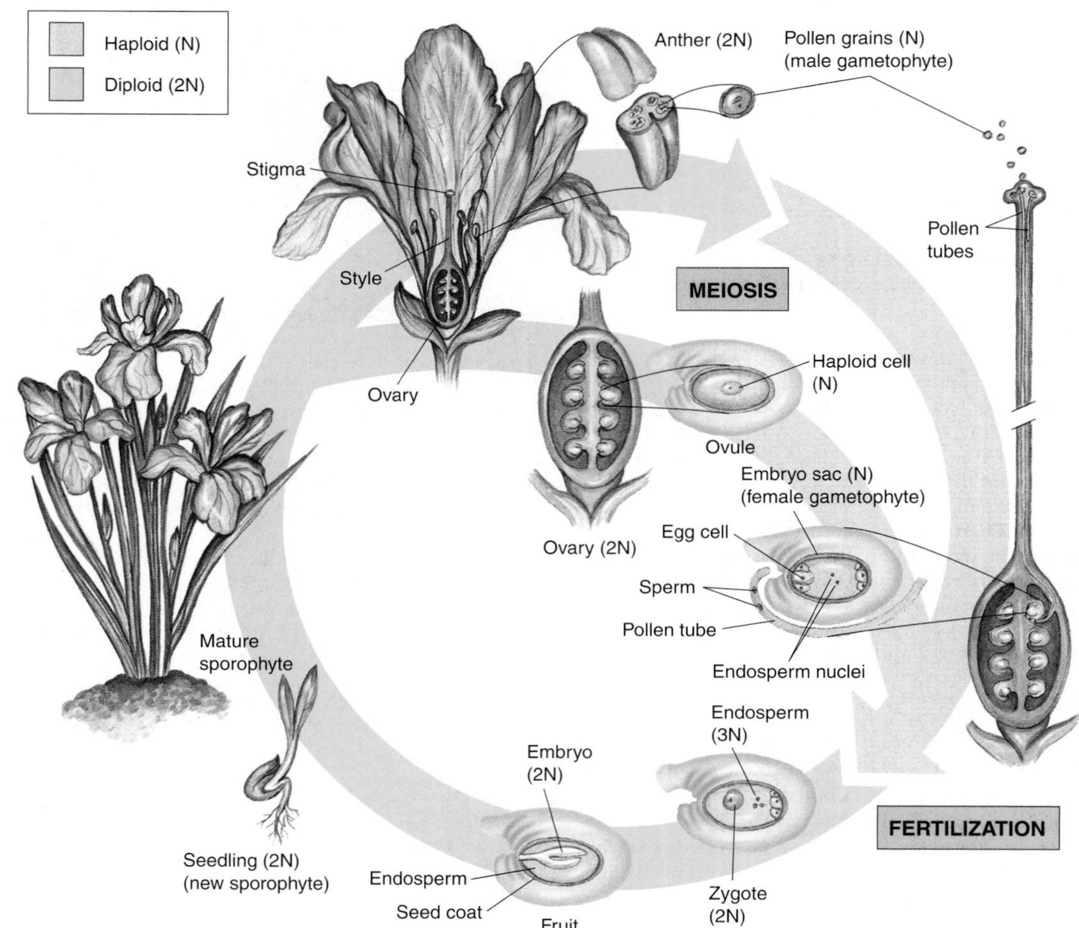

▲ **Figure 24–7** This illustration shows the life cycle of a typical angiosperm—an iris. The developing seeds of a flowering plant are protected and nourished inside the ovary, which is located at the base of the flower.  **Reproduction in angiosperms takes place within the flower. After pollination, the seeds of angiosperms develop inside protective structures.**

Life Cycle of Angiosperms

Reproduction in angiosperms takes place within the flower. Following pollination and fertilization, the seeds develop inside protective structures. The life cycle of angiosperms is shown in **Figure 24–7.** You can think of the angiosperm life cycle as beginning when the mature sporophyte produces flowers. Each flower contains anthers and an ovary. Inside the anthers—the male part of the flower—each cell undergoes meiosis and produces four haploid spore cells. Each of these cells becomes a single pollen grain. The wall of each pollen grain thickens, protecting the contents of the pollen grain from dryness and physical damage when it is released from the anther.

The nucleus of each pollen grain undergoes one mitotic division to produce two haploid nuclei. The pollen grain, which is the entire male gametophyte, usually stops growing until it is released from the anther and deposited on a stigma.

BIO INSIGHTS **FACTS AND FIGURES**

All about angiosperms

There are about 250,000 known species of angiosperms. Given their numbers, it is not surprising that they show great variability. For example, the length of time for completion of the angiosperm life cycle ranges from less than a month to as long as 150 years. Pollen tubes also show great variation. In corn, the pollen tube may be as long as 50 cm, but in most plants the pollen tube is much shorter. In addition, a pollen tube may complete its growth in less than 24 hours, but in some plants it takes over a year. The size of flowers varies greatly as well. The smallest flowers are those of the tiny duckweed *Wolffia columbiana*. Its flowers are only about 0.1 mm long. The largest flowers are those of the *Rafflesia* plant, which is indigenous to Indonesia. Its huge blooms can grow to 1 m in diameter and attain a mass of 9 kg.

The ovary of the flower contains the ovules, in which the female gametophyte develops. A single diploid cell goes through meiosis to produce four haploid cells, three of which disintegrate. The remaining cell undergoes mitosis to produce eight nuclei. These eight nuclei and the surrounding membrane are called the **embryo sac**. The embryo sac, contained within the ovule, is the female gametophyte of a flowering plant. One of the eight nuclei, near the base of the gametophyte, is the egg nucleus—the female gamete. If fertilization takes place, this cell will become the zygote that grows into a new sporophyte plant.

CHECKPOINT *Where does the female gametophyte develop?*

Pollination

Once the gametophytes have developed inside the flower, pollination takes place. **Most gymnosperms and some angiosperms are wind pollinated, whereas most angiosperms are pollinated by animals.** These animals, mainly insects, birds, and bats, carry pollen from one flower to another. Because wind pollination is less efficient than animal pollination, wind-pollinated plants, such as the oak tree in **Figure 24–8,** rely on favorable weather and sheer numbers to get pollen from one plant to another. Animal-pollinated plants have a variety of adaptations, such as bright colors and sweet nectar, to attract animals. Animals have developed behaviors to help them find flowers. They have also evolved body shapes that enable them to reach nectar deep within certain flowers.

Insect pollination is adaptive because it increases the fitness of both organisms. It is beneficial to insects and other animals because it provides a dependable source of food. The food may take the form of pollen itself or the sugar-rich liquid called nectar. Plants also benefit because the insects take their pollen directly from flower to flower. Insect pollination is much more efficient than wind pollination, giving insect-pollinated plants a higher probability of reproductive success. In fact, many plant biologists suggest that the angiosperms displaced the gymnosperms so thoroughly during the past 100 million years in part because of insect pollination.

Figure 24–8 **Most angiosperms are pollinated by animals, although some are pollinated by wind.** The shape of a flower often indicates how it is pollinated. The flowers of an oak tree (A) are typical of wind-pollinated flowers in that they are small, are not brightly colored, and produce vast amounts of pollen. To attract insects and other animals, many animal-pollinated flowers are large and brightly colored. The rose flower (B) is pollinated by a variety of insects, whereas the trumpet creeper flower (C) has a tube shape that is adapted specifically to the long beak of a hummingbird.

Pollination

Build Science Skills

Applying Concepts Have students assume that they are botanists who have just discovered a new plant that has not yet been identified. They note that the plant has tiny green flowers that are difficult to see against the background of green leaves. Ask: **How do you think this plant is pollinated?** *(By the wind, because it does not have large colorful flowers to attract animal pollinators)*

Make Connections

Health Science Point out that many people are allergic to the pollen of flowers. Explain that allergies to pollen are actually reactions to proteins in the coat of the pollen grain and that people are allergic to different pollens because each type has a different protein coat. One of the most common pollen allergies is the allergic reaction known as "hay fever." You might want to take a poll of students to see how many have this type of allergy. Explain that hay fever is not an allergy to hay but to ragweed, which is a widespread wind-pollinated wild plant. Ask: **Why might wind-pollinated plants create more problems for allergy sufferers than animal-pollinated plants?** *(Wind-pollinated plants usually produce more pollen because pollination by wind is less efficient than pollination by animals.)*

Answer to . . .

CHECKPOINT *The female gametophyte develops in the ovules, which are contained in the ovary of the flower.*

Fertilization in Angiosperms Meet Diverse Needs

Because the double fertilization process is complicated, encourage students to draw a flowchart. In their flowcharts, they should indicate which cells are haploid, diploid, and triploid. **Learning modality: visual**

3 ASSESS

Evaluate Understanding

Trace Figure 24–5 and give students a copy without the labels. Then, have students label the parts of the flower shown in the diagram.

Reteach

Review the life cycle of gymnosperms and angiosperms as students follow the stages shown in Figure 24–4 and Figure 24–7.

ALTERNATIVE ASSESSMENT

Seed plants: Dominant stage—Diploid (2N); Zygote formation—Two sperm nuclei reach female gametopyhte in pollen tube, one sperm nucleus disintegrates and the other fertilizes the egg, forming a diploid zygote; Occurrence of meiosis—In gymnosperms, meiosis occurs in the pollen grains and in the ovules. In angiosperms, meiosis occurs in anthers and in ovules. *Chlamydomonas*: Dominant stage—Haploid (N); Zygote formation—gametes gather in large groups, and then – and + gametes form pairs, which join flagella and shed their cell walls and fuse, forming a diploid zygote; Occurrence of meiosis—The thick-walled zygote divides and produces four flagellated haploid cells.

Use iText to review the key concepts in Section 24–1.

Answer to . . .

Figure 24–9 *As the seed develops, the food stored in the endosperm is absorbed by the cotyledon and then used by the growing embryo.*

Fertilization in Angiosperms

If a pollen grain lands on the stigma of an appropriate flower, it begins to grow a pollen tube. The generative nucleus within the pollen grain divides and forms two sperm nuclei. The pollen tube now contains a tube nucleus and two sperm nuclei. The pollen tube grows into the style. There, it eventually reaches the ovary and enters the ovule.

Inside the embryo sac, two distinct fertilizations take place. First, one of the sperm nuclei fuses with the egg nucleus to produce a diploid zygote. The zygote will grow into the new plant embryo. Second, the other sperm nucleus does something truly remarkable—it fuses with two endosperm nuclei in the embryo sac to form a triploid (3N) cell. This cell will grow into a food-rich tissue known as **endosperm,** which nourishes the seedling as it grows.

As shown in **Figure 24–9,** a seed of corn, a monocot, contains a rich supply of endosperm. In many dicots, including garden beans, the cotyledons absorb the endosperm as the seed develops. The cotyledons then serve as the stored food supply for the embryo when it begins to grow.

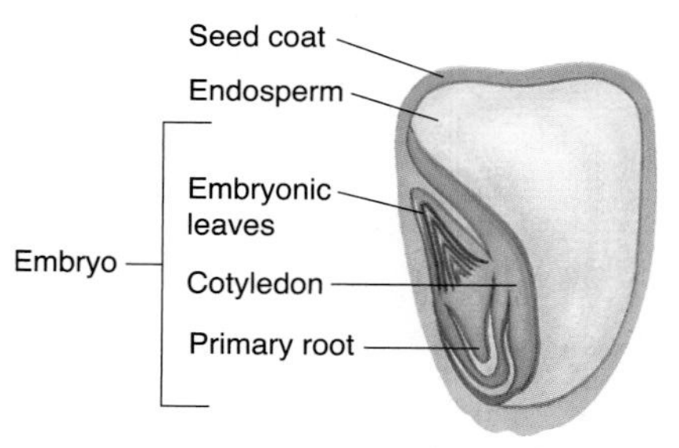

▲ **Figure 24–9** The endosperm of a corn seed develops through the process of double fertilization. After one sperm nucleus fertilizes the egg cell, the zygote forms. Then, the other sperm nucleus fuses with the two endosperm nuclei to form a triploid cell, which develops into the endosperm. **Predicting** ***What will happen to the endosperm when the seed begins to grow?***

Because two fertilization events take place between the male and female gametophytes, this process is known as **double fertilization.** Double fertilization may be one of the reasons why the angiosperms have been so successful. Recall that in gymnosperms, the food reserve built up in seeds is produced before fertilization takes place. As a result, if an ovule is not fertilized, those resources are wasted. In angiosperms, if an ovule is not fertilized, the endosperm does not form, and food is not wasted by preparing for a nonexistent zygote.

24–1 Section Assessment

1. **Key Concept** What are the reproductive structures of gymnosperms?
2. **Key Concept** Describe the flower and how it is involved in reproduction.
3. **Key Concept** Are angiosperms typically wind pollinated or animal pollinated? How does this process take place?
4. What is endosperm? Where does it form in a flowering plant?
5. **Critical Thinking Inferring** Many flowers have bright patterns of coloration that directly surround the reproductive structures. How might this type of coloration be advantageous to the plant?

iTEXT **Assessment** Use iText to review the important concepts in Section 24–1.

MAKING CONNECTIONS

Alternation of Generations Review the life cycle of the green alga *Chlamydomonas* in Chapter 20, p. 513. Make a compare-and-contrast table comparing alternation of generations in seed plants and *Chlamydomonas.* Include in the table which stage of each organism's life cycle is dominant (haploid or diploid), the process by which zygotes form, and when meiosis occurs.

24–1 Section Assessment

1. The reproductive structures of gymnosperms are pollen cones, pollen grains, seed cones, ovules, and pollen tubes.
2. Flowers are reproductive organs that are composed of four kinds of specialized leaves: sepals, petals, stamens, and carpels. The stamens produce male gametophytes, and the carpels produce female gametophytes.
3. Angiosperms are typically pollinated by animals. Insects, birds, and mammals carry pollen from one flower to another as they gather nectar.
4. A food-rich tissue that nourishes a seedling as it grows; inside the embryo sac
5. Bright patterns of coloration might attract insects and other animals to the reproductive structures of the flower and increase the chances of pollination.

Flowers by Design

What's your favorite flower? Like many people, you might have said "the rose." Roses are the world's most popular ornamental flowers, prized for their beauty and fragrance. They come in many colors. Chances are you've seen red, white, pink, or even yellow roses. But have you ever seen a blue rose? Probably not! Roses do not have the enzymes to produce blue pigments, so even the best efforts of plant breeders have not produced a blue rose.

What Makes a Flower?

Plant biologists have discovered that flower development is controlled by a series of genes. By manipulating these genes, scientists have produced plants that will flower earlier and much more quickly than normal. Even young seedlings have been induced to flower.

Changing the color of a flower, however, has proved a little more difficult. Knowing that petunias often produce blue flowers, in 1991 Australian researchers isolated the gene for the enzyme that produces blue pigment. Then, they transferred this "blue gene" to a rose. To their disappointment, however, the new roses were just as red as ever. Apparently, flower color is a tricky and unpredictable business—particularly in roses—that involves complex interactions with other genes and pigments.

A White Sportcoat and a Violet Carnation?

When the Australian scientists turned from roses to carnations, they succeeded in producing a carnation with unique violet flowers. Again, they inserted the gene from the blue petunias into a carnation plant. The result, shown in the photos, was a deep violet carnation unlike any ever seen in nature. In 1999, these genetically modified carnation plants were introduced for sale in Europe and the United States. A number of biotech companies are now rushing to master the intricacies of color genetics in flowers. Before long, one of these companies may have what they've all been seeking—a blue rose.

On Your Own

1. In addition to new varieties of flowers, plant breeders have developed genetically modified fruits, vegetables, and grains. Pick a common food crop and research how plant breeders have modified it to give it specific characteristics.
2. Suppose you are a plant geneticist and you want to create a new color of lily. Select the flower color you would like to produce. Then, write down the scientific steps that you would take to produce the new flower color.

After students have read this feature, you might want to discuss one or more of the following:

- Genetic engineering methods, such as the use of restriction enzymes and DNA insertion, that are used to isolate a gene from one plant or insert it into another plant
- Other traits of flowers, besides color, that breeders might try to modify, such as season of bloom, length of bloom period, size of flowers, number of petals, and number of flowers
- Examples of plants produced by breeders that have unusual characteristics, such as plants that have black or nearly black flowers (for example, columbine, hollyhock, viola, and sweet pea)
- Reasons why varieties of plants bred for certain traits, such as color, may not be as hardy as the standard varieties

On Your Own

1. Students should visit the Florigene Web site and learn about their recent achievements in plant breeding, including whether they have produced a blue rose.

2. Calla lilies are white. Students should select any color they would like to produce, such as yellow, pink, red, or orange. The steps they would take might include first isolating a gene from another plant that codes for the color of their choice and then inserting the gene into a calla lily plant.

Section 24–2

1 FOCUS

Objectives

24.2.1 ***Describe*** the development of seeds and fruits.

24.2.2 ***Explain*** how seeds are dispersed.

24.2.3 ***List*** the factors that influence the dormancy and germination of seeds.

Guide for Reading

Vocabulary Preview

Ask: **What are some examples of fruits?** *(Examples might include apples, oranges, bananas, and grapes.)* Explain that the common meaning of the term *fruit* is not the same as its scientific meaning. In biological terms, *fruit* means a ripened ovary that contains angiosperm seeds. Add that many foods not commonly thought of as fruits fit this definition, including tomatoes and cucumbers.

Reading Strategy

Suggest that students include the boldfaced terms and sentences in their summaries.

2 INSTRUCT

Seed and Fruit Development

Demonstration

Display an apple, peach, tomato, bean pod, and acorn. Ask: **How are these specimens similar?** *(They are all fruits, although students may not realize that the tomato, bean, and acorn are fruits.)* Explain that each specimen is actually an enlarged and ripened ovary, which, by definition, is a fruit. Ask: **Which fruits have soft, fleshy outer walls?** *(Apple, peach, and tomato)* Point out that these fruits are classified as fleshy fruits, whereas the bean pod and acorn are classified as dry fruits. Cut the fruits in half and ask students to describe what they see inside. *(Mature, fertilized seeds)*

24–2 Seed Development and Germination

Guide for Reading

Key Concepts
- How do fruits form?
- How are seeds dispersed?
- What factors influence the dormancy and germination of seeds?

Vocabulary
dormancy
germination

Reading Strategy: Summarizing As you read, take notes on the development, dispersal, dormancy, and germination of seeds. Write a few sentences summarizing each of these processes.

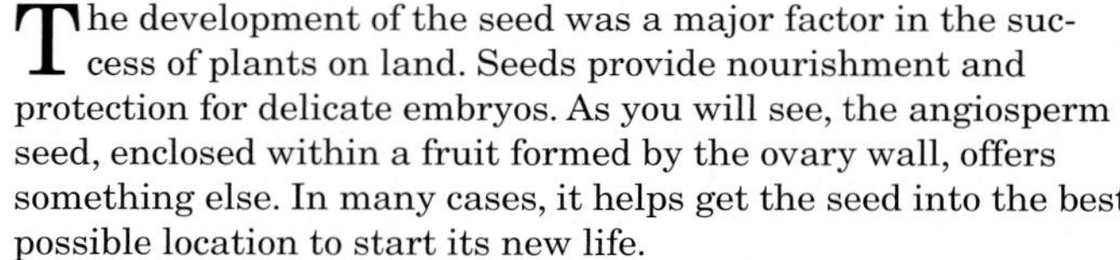

The development of the seed was a major factor in the success of plants on land. Seeds provide nourishment and protection for delicate embryos. As you will see, the angiosperm seed, enclosed within a fruit formed by the ovary wall, offers something else. In many cases, it helps get the seed into the best possible location to start its new life.

Seed and Fruit Development

Once fertilization is complete, nutrients flow into the flower tissue and support the development of the growing embryo within the seed. **As angiosperm seeds mature, the ovary walls thicken to form a fruit that encloses the developing seeds.** A fruit is a ripened ovary that contains angiosperm seeds. Examples of fruits are shown in **Figure 24–10**. Parts of the ovule toughen to form a seed coat, which is the outer layer that protects the delicate embryo and its tiny food supply. The ovary wall then thickens and joins with other parts of the flower stem. These structures together form a fruit that encloses the seeds.

The term *fruit,* biologically speaking, applies to any seed that is enclosed within its embryo wall. The term applies to the things we usually think of as fruits, such as apples, grapes, and strawberries. However, foods such as peas, corn, beans, rice, cucumbers, and tomatoes, which we commonly call vegetables, are also fruits. Whether it tastes sweet or not, if it contains a seed enclosed inside the ovary wall, it is a fruit.

The ovary wall surrounding a simple fruit may be fleshy, as it is in grapes and tomatoes, or tough, like the pod of a bean. In some fruits, such as peaches and cherries, the inner wall of the ovary is attached rigidly to the surface of the seed. In others, such as the maple, the dry fruit forms an aerodynamic shape that helps the seed whirl gracefully down when it is released from the parent plant.

CHECKPOINT *What is a fruit?*

Figure 24–10 **As seeds mature, the ovary walls thicken to form a fruit that encloses the developing seeds.** Like the flowers from which they develop, fruits vary in structure. They can contain one seed, as in the lychee nut, or several, as in the apple. Fruits also have different amounts of tissue, which often relates to the mode of seed dispersal.

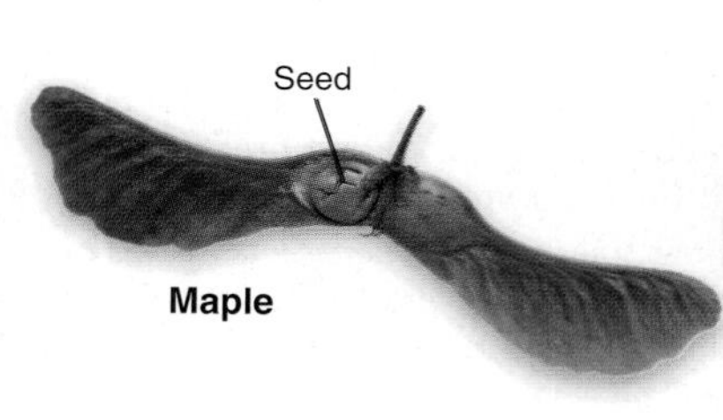

SECTION RESOURCES

Print:
- ***Laboratory Manual A,*** Chapter 24 Lab
- ***Laboratory Manual B,*** Chapter 24 Lab
- ***Teaching Resources,*** Section Review 24–2
- ***Guided Reading and Study Workbook,*** Section 24–2

Technology:
- ***iText,*** Section 24–2

Seed Dispersal

What are fruits for? They are certainly not there to nourish the seedling—the endosperm does that. Why should an entire phylum of plants have seeds that are wrapped in an additional layer of tissue—tissue that is often packed with nutrients and is later discarded when the fruit is released from the plant? It seems to make no sense.

Think of the blackberries that grow wild in the forests of North America. Each seed is enclosed in a sweet, juicy fruit, making it a tasty treat for all kinds of birds and mammals. What good does all that sweetness do the fruit? All it does is get the seed eaten! Well, believe it or not, that's exactly the point.

Dispersal by Animals The seeds of many plants, especially those with sweet, fleshy fruits, are eaten by animals, as shown in **Figure 24–11.** The seeds are covered with tough coatings that protect them from digestive chemicals, enabling them to pass through an animal's digestive system unharmed. The seeds then sprout in the feces eliminated from the animal. **Seeds dispersed by animals are typically contained in fleshy, nutritious fruits.** These fruits provide nutrition for the animal and also help the plant disperse its seeds—often to areas where there is less competition with the parent plants.

Dispersal by Wind and Water Animals are not the only means by which plants can scatter their seeds. Seeds are also adapted for dispersal by wind and water. **Seeds dispersed by wind or water are typically lightweight, allowing them to be carried in the air or to float on the surface of the water.** The seeds of ash and maple trees are encased in winglike structures that spin and twirl as they are released, helping them glide considerable distances from their parent plants. Westerners are familiar with tumbleweed plants, shown in **Figure 24–12.** These plants break off at their roots and tumble along the dry plains, scattering their seeds as they are blown by the wind. An example of a seed that is dispersed by water is the coconut. This seed contains a liquid endosperm layer (the "milk" of the coconut). A coconut is buoyant enough to float in sea water within its protective coating for many weeks. Water dispersal is one reason for the success of this species in reaching remote islands.

▲ **Figure 24–11** **Seeds that are dispersed by animals typically contain fleshy, sweet tissue.** A cedar waxwing feasts on mountain ash berries. Berries are enclosed in sugary tissue that is eaten by birds or other animals. Berries contain seeds that pass through the animal and are dispersed away from the parent plant.

▶ **Figure 24–12** **Wind-dispersed seeds are typically lightweight.** Tumbleweed plants release small seeds as the plants are blown along open stretches of land.

Seed Dispersal

Build Science Skills

Inferring Explain that the seeds of some plants, such as clover, do not germinate well unless their seed coat has been scarified, or scratched. Add that clover is eaten by grazing animals. Then, ask: **How does the need to be scarified before germination ensure that clover seeds sprout in the right place and at the right time?** *(The scarification of the seeds signals that they have been eaten, passed through the digestive system of an animal, and deposited in a suitable place for germination.)*

Meet Diverse Needs

Challenge students to write and illustrate a short story for children about the dispersal of a seed by wind, water, or an animal. Encourage students to be creative but accurate in their description of how the seed is dispersed to a suitable location for germination to take place. **Learning modality: verbal**

Build Science Skills

Designing Experiments Divide the class into groups, and have each group brainstorm a way of determining whether fruit-eating animals are attracted to the color of fruit or to its scent. Each group should formulate a hypothesis and design an experiment to test the hypothesis. Remind students to include a control in their experimental design. Give groups a chance to share their ideas. *(Students should hypothesize that animals are attracted either more by scent or more by color. They might design an experiment to see if animals are attracted to fruit when they cannot see it, for example, because it is in a darkened room or when they cannot detect its scent, for example, because the fruit is wrapped in plastic.)*

TIME SAVER **PRESENTATIONS MADE EASY!**

The Presentation Assistant Plus contains the Prentice Hall Presentation Pro and the Transparencies, which provide easy-to-follow visual support for every step of this section. If you have a computer presentation station, use Prentice Hall Presentation Pro for Section 24–2, or use the transparencies listed here.

Section 24–2: **Interest Grabber**
Section Outline
Concept Map

Answer to . . .

CHECKPOINT *A fruit is a ripened ovary that contains angiosperm seeds.*

Seed Dormancy

Analyzing Data

Help students put the data in an experimental context. Ask: **What variables do the data represent?** *(Climate of origin, temperature during dormancy, and whether or not germination occurred)* **What other variables do you think the plant biologists had to control?** *(Possible answers include the amount of water the seeds received and the temperature at which germination took place.)*

Answers

1. Chilling increases the percentage of seeds that germinate, especially for seeds from Ontario.

2. The increase of the percentage of seeds that germinate at lower temperatures might indicate an adaptation to lower temperatures.

Build Science Skills

Applying Concepts Explain that arctic lupines are plants whose seeds can remain dormant for thousands of years. Ask: **Why might this be an advantage for a plant living in an arctic environment?** *(For much of the year, the arctic is extremely cold and dark. Lupine seeds might have to wait many years until a suitable combination of soil, moisture, light, and temperature allow for successful germination.)*

Analyzing Data

Temperature and Seed Germination

Arisaema dracontium—"green dragon"—is a plant that grows from the southern United States to Canada. The graph shows germination properties of *Arisaema* seeds gathered from Clinton, Ontario, and from Baton Rouge, Louisiana. Seeds from both locations were stored at two different temperatures: 3°C and 24°C. The graph indicates the rate of seed germination following storage at these different temperatures.

1. **Interpreting Graphics** What effect does chilling have on germination of seeds from Ontario? How does chilling affect the seeds from Louisiana?
2. **Forming Hypotheses** Keeping in mind that annual temperatures are much lower in Ontario than in Louisiana, describe how the different rates of seed germination might be explained in terms of adaptation to the local climate.

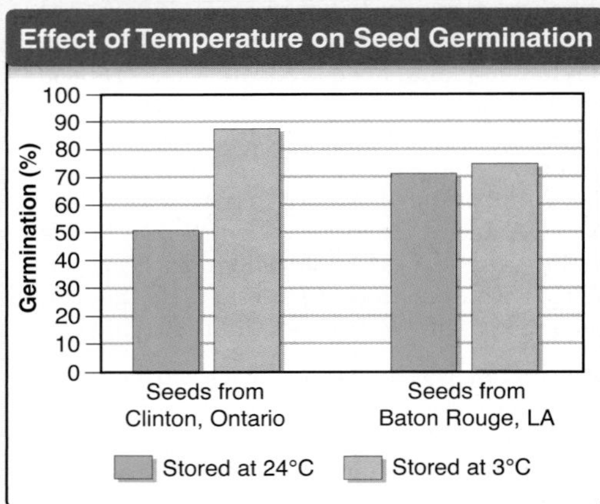

Seed Dormancy

Some seeds sprout so rapidly that they are practically instant plants. Bean seeds are a good example. With proper amounts of water and warmth, a newly planted mature bean seed rapidly develops into a bean plant. But many seeds will not grow when they first mature. Instead, these seeds enter a period of **dormancy,** during which the embryo is alive but not growing. The length of dormancy varies in different plant species. **Environmental factors such as temperature and moisture can cause a seed to end dormancy and germinate.**

Seed dormancy can be adaptive in several ways. It can allow for long-distance dispersal, as in a coconut that floats across the sea for weeks or even months until it washes ashore. It may also allow seeds to germinate under ideal growth conditions. The seeds of many temperate plants do not germinate during the summer or winter, since the extremes of temperature would make it impossible for seedlings to survive. Instead, most seeds germinate in the spring, when conditions are best for growth. The long period of cold temperatures during which the seeds are dormant is required before growth can begin.

Other environmental conditions can end seed dormancy. Some pine trees, for example, produce seeds in sealed cones. These seeds remain dormant until the high temperatures generated by forest fires cause the cones to open, as shown in **Figure 24–13.** This process activates the seeds, allowing the plants to reclaim the forest floor quickly after a fire.

▼ **Figure 24–13** **Environmental factors such as temperature and moisture can end dormancy.** The cones of this bishop pine open and release seeds only after being exposed to the heat of a forest fire.

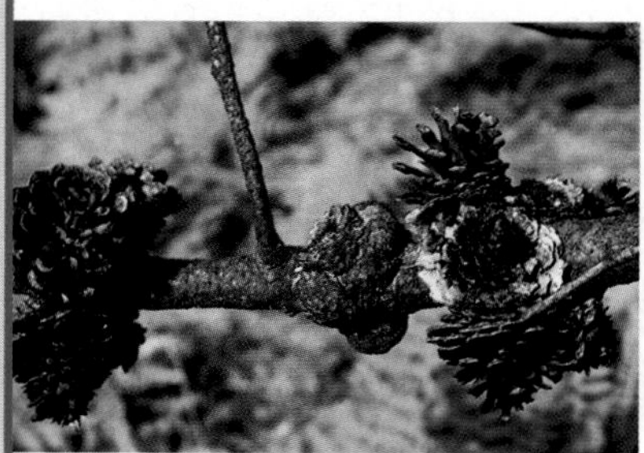

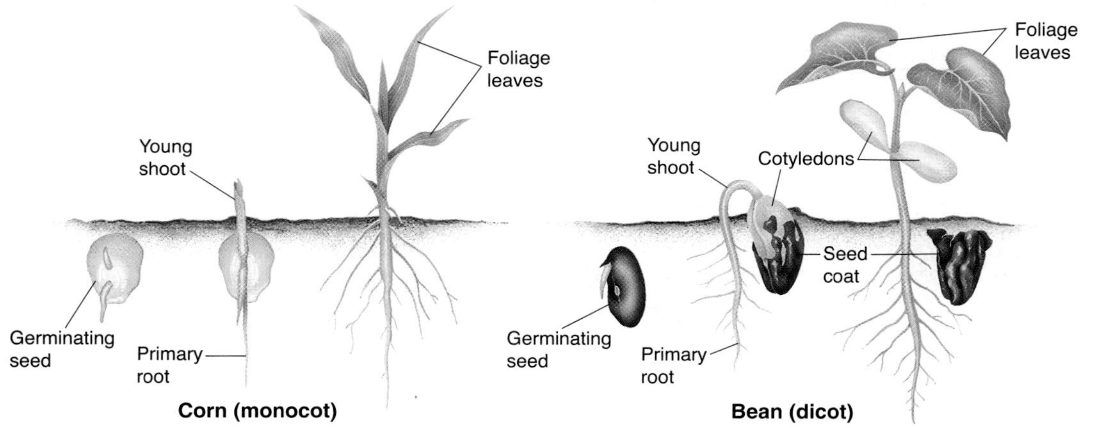

▲ **Figure 24–14** The corn seedling (left) is a monocot in which the shoot grows directly upward, protected by its sheath. The garden bean (right) is a dicot in which the cotyledons emerge above ground. **Applying Concepts** *How does germination differ between monocots and dicots?*

Seed Germination

Seed **germination** is the early growth stage of the plant embryo. **Figure 24–14** shows germination in monocots and dicots. When seeds germinate, they absorb water. The absorbed water causes the endosperm to swell, cracking open the seed coat. Through the cracked seed coat, the young root emerges and begins to grow.

Recall that monocots have a single cotyledon, or seed leaf. In most monocots, the single cotyledon remains underground. The growing shoot emerges while protected by a sheath. In dicots, which have two cotyledons, germination takes place in one of two ways. In some species, the cotyledons emerge above ground and protect the first foliage leaves. They then wither and drop off the plant. In other species, such as the bean plant in **Figure 24–14,** the cotyledons remain below the soil and provide a food source for the growing seedling. In this case, the young shoot grows longer and forms an arch that protects the delicate shoot tip. As the arch lengthens, it pulls the cotyledons and the shoot tip above the surface.

24–2 Section Assessment

1. **Key Concept** Describe what happens as fertilized angiosperm seeds mature.
2. **Key Concept** Compare the typical structure of seeds that are dispersed by animals to those dispersed by wind and water.
3. **Key Concept** Why is it adaptive for some seeds to remain dormant before they germinate?
4. **Critical Thinking Applying Concepts** Many environmentalists state that controlling fires in the western United States will change the structure of the ecosystem. How might the example of seed dormancy in certain types of pines support their case?

iTEXT Assessment Use iText to review the important concepts in Section 24–2.

Take It to the NET

Read about different ways that seeds can travel. Then, make a concept map to summarize the different ways in which seeds are dispersed. Use the links provided in the Biology area at the Prentice Hall Web site for help in completing this activity: **www.phschool.com**

24–2 Section Assessment

1. Nutrients flow into the flower tissue and support the development of the embryo within the seed. Parts of the ovule toughen to form a seed coat, and the ovary wall thickens and joins with other flower parts to form a fruit that encloses and protects the seed.
2. Seeds dispersed by animals typically have a tough coat and are contained in fleshy fruits. Seeds dispersed by wind and water typically are lightweight and may be encased in winglike structures.
3. It allows for long-distance dispersal and for germination under ideal conditions.
4. Certain types of pine seeds remain dormant until the high temperatures generated by forest fires cause the cones to open.

Seed Germination

Demonstration

Place a variety of seeds, including both monocots such as corn and dicots such as beans, between two wet paper towels on a plate. Place plastic wrap over the plate to keep the towels moist, and put the plate in a warm place where it will not be disturbed. After a few days, remove the plastic and the top paper towel and call students' attention to the germinated seeds. Have students locate the root and shoot of each seed and determine whether it is a monocot or dicot.

3 ASSESS

Evaluate Understanding

Read the boldfaced sentences and the sentences defining the Vocabulary terms, in each case leaving blank the most significant term in the sentence. Call on students at random to fill in the blanks.

Reteach

Using the chalkboard or an overhead transparency, work with students to create flowcharts summarizing the steps of seed germination. Create one flowchart for monocots and another for dicots.

Take It to the NET

Concept maps should include seed dispersal by means of wind, water, and animals. They should also include at least one example of each method of dispersal. For additional information, visit **www.phschool.com**

Use iText to review the key concepts in Section 24–2.

Answer to . . .

Figure 24–14 *In monocots, the single cotyledon remains within the seed and the growing shoot emerges while protected by a sheath. In dicots, the cotyledons emerge above ground and protect the first foliage leaves or else they remain below ground and provide a food source for the seedling.*

Section 24–3

1 FOCUS

Objectives

24.3.1 ***Identify*** the forms of plant vegetative reproduction.
24.3.2 ***Describe*** plant propagation.
24.3.3 ***Identify*** the major food-supply crops for humans.

Guide for Reading

Vocabulary Preview

Point out that the word *vegetative* in the term *vegetative reproduction* means "growing" and not "having to do with vegetables," as students might assume. Explain that the term *vegetative reproduction* refers to any type of reproduction in plants that involves vegetative, or growing, tissues instead of reproductive tissues and seeds.

Reading Strategy

Students should list the following methods of growing food plants: seeds, cuttings, grafting, and budding.

2 INSTRUCT

Vegetative Reproduction

Demonstration

Bring to class several different plants or plant parts that grow by vegetative reproduction. You might include a spider plant, a clump of crab grass, and a daffodil bulb. As you display each plant or plant part in turn, ask: **How do you think this plant or part reproduces asexually?** *(A spider plant produces plantlets that can take root to form new plants. Crab grass produces horizontal stems or stolons that can put down roots to form new plants. A daffodil bulb produces roots and shoots when placed underground and given warmth and moisture.)*

24–3 Plant Propagation and Agriculture

Guide for Reading

Key Concepts
- What forms of vegetative reproduction occur in plants?
- What is plant propagation?
- Which crops are the major food supply for humans?

Vocabulary
vegetative reproduction
stolon
grafting
budding

Reading Strategy: Using Prior Knowledge
Before you read the section, make a list of methods that humans use to grow food plants such as fruit trees and grains. As you read, add new information to your list.

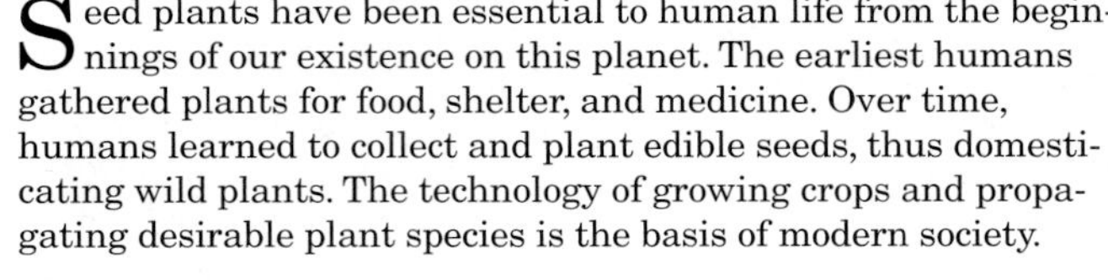

Seed plants have been essential to human life from the beginnings of our existence on this planet. The earliest humans gathered plants for food, shelter, and medicine. Over time, humans learned to collect and plant edible seeds, thus domesticating wild plants. The technology of growing crops and propagating desirable plant species is the basis of modern society.

Vegetative Reproduction

Although we have concentrated on patterns of sexual reproduction, many kinds of flowering plants also reproduce asexually by **vegetative reproduction.** Vegetative reproduction enables a single plant that is well adapted to a particular environment to produce many offspring genetically identical to itself. This process takes place naturally in many plants, and it is also used as a technique by horticulturalists who want to produce many copies of an individual plant.

Vegetative reproduction includes the production of new plants from horizontal stems, from plantlets, and from underground roots.

Because vegetative reproduction does not involve pollination or seed formation, it can enable plants to reproduce very quickly. Several species of angiosperms, such as the spider plant shown in **Figure 24–15,** produce tiny plants, or plantlets, along their leaves or stems. If the parent plant is knocked over or if plantlets fall to the soil, they can take root and grow into new plants. New plants can also grow from the leaves of a parent plant if the leaves fall to the ground under conditions that allow them to root.

Another way in which plants reproduce vegetatively is by growing horizontal stems. Strawberry plants, shown in **Figure 24–16,** send out long trailing stems called **stolons** that produce roots when they touch the ground. Once the roots are well established, each stolon may be broken, forming a new plant that is truly independent of its parent. Bamboo plants grow long underground stems that can send up new shoots in several places. In fact, bamboo forests that cover huge areas are often the descendants of a single bamboo plant that reproduced asexually.

◀ **Figure 24–15** **The production of plantlets is a form of asexual reproduction.** The spider plant produces plantlets at the tips of its leaves. When a plantlet reaches the soil, it can develop roots and grow into a new spider plant.

TIME SAVER — SECTION RESOURCES

Print:
- ***Teaching Resources,*** Section Review 24–3, Chapter 24, Design an Experiment
- ***Guided Reading and Study Workbook,*** Section 24–3

Technology:
- ***iText,*** Section 24–3

◀ **Figure 24–16** The strawberry plant reproduces vegetatively by producing thin, horizontal stems called stolons. Each node along the stolon produces roots that anchor the plant into the ground. **Applying Concepts** *Describe how asexual reproduction might allow a plant to become established rapidly in a new area.*

Plant Propagation

Sometimes the characteristics of a particular plant are so attractive or beneficial that horticulturists want to make many exact copies of the plant. But the growers also want to avoid the variation that would result if the plant reproduced sexually by seeds. In addition, new varieties of some plants, such as grapefruits and navel oranges, do not produce seeds. **In plant propagation, horticulturists use cuttings, grafting, or budding to make many identical copies of a plant or to produce offspring from seedless plants.**

Cuttings One of the simplest ways to reproduce plants vegetatively is by cuttings. A grower "cuts" from the plant a length of stem that includes a number of buds containing meristematic tissue. That stem is then partially buried in soil or in a special rooting mixture. Some common plants, such as coleus, root so easily that no other treatment is necessary. The cuttings of many woody plants, however, do not develop roots easily. To help cuttings of these plants form roots, growers use mixtures of plant hormones called rooting powders.

Grafting and Budding Grafting and budding are used to reproduce seedless plants and varieties of woody plants that do not produce strong root systems. In both of these techniques, new plants are grown on plants that have strong root systems. To do this, a piece of stem or a lateral bud is cut from the parent plant and attached to another plant. The cut piece is called the scion, and the plant to which it is attached is called the stock. When stems are used as scions, the process is called **grafting,** shown in **Figure 24–17.** When buds are used as scions, the process is called **budding.**

Grafting usually works best when plants are dormant because the wounds created can heal before new growth starts. In all cases, grafts are successful only if the vascular cambiums of scion and stock are firmly connected to each other.

CHECKPOINT *What are the different techniques used to propagate woody plants?*

▼ **Figure 24–17 Plant propagation uses a variety of techniques to make identical copies of a single plant.** Here, a scion of a commercial orange tree is being grafted to a larger, established tree.

Build Science Skills

Observing Provide each student with a raw sweet potato. Show students how to insert four toothpicks into the sweet potato around the middle so that the bottom half of it can be suspended in a container of water. Have students keep the water level above the bottom of the sweet potato and observe it each day until it starts to grow roots and shoots. Ask: **What type of reproduction is represented by the growth of the sweet potato?** *(Vegetative reproduction)*

Plant Propagation

Demonstration

Obtain two small sections of a tree branch and use them to demonstrate grafting. Using a sharp knife, make a deep notch in the end of one section (the stock) and cut the end of the other section (the scion) into a V-shaped point. Insert the pointed end of the scion into the deeply notched end of the stock. Wrap the two pieces tightly together with cloth tape, making sure that the cambium layers are properly aligned. Explain that the two pieces must be held tightly together until they start to grow together. Ask: **If the stock came from a red delicious apple tree and the scion came from a yellow delicious apple tree, what color fruit would the scion produce?** *(Yellow)*

PRESENTATIONS MADE EASY!

The Presentation Assistant Plus contains the Prentice Hall Presentation Pro and the Transparencies, which provide easy-to-follow visual support for every step of this section. If you have a computer presentation station, use Prentice Hall Presentation Pro for Section 24–3, or use the transparencies listed here.

Section 24–3: **Interest Grabber**
Section Outline
Compare/Contrast Table

Answers to . . .

CHECKPOINT *Cuttings, grafting, and budding*

Figure 24–16 *It might put out stolons that take root to form new plants all around the original plant.*

Build Science Skills

Inferring Bring two oranges to class, one with seeds and one without. Cut the oranges in half, and ask students to explain how they differ. Challenge students to explain how offspring could be produced from each type of orange. *(The orange with seeds can be grown from seed. The orange without seeds must be grown by grafting or budding.)*

Agriculture

Use Community Resources

Ask a local farmer or the owner of a greenhouse in the community to visit the class and describe advances in agricultural or horticultural methods that are used in his or her type of business. Possible methods might include plant propagation techniques, the use of pesticides or herbicides, soil-conservation practices such as crop rotation or contour plowing, the use of irrigation, or the introduction of genetically engineered plants. Ask the speaker to address how the methods have increased production, led to the production of better plants, or otherwise improved the business. Encourage students to ask any questions they might have.

Biology and History

Provide interested students with the challenge of continuing the time line to the present. They should add more recent changes in agriculture, such as the invention of the iron plow and the development of genetically engineered food crops.

Writing Activity

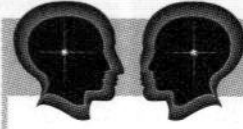

Arrange to have students share their research so they can compare the effect of climate and other factors on the type of crop that was important in each region. Students should give examples of ways the cultivation of crops in the region they selected affected the human population and its culture.

▲ **Figure 24–18** **Most of the world's food supply comes from a few crop plants.** Rice, here being planted by hand, is a staple crop in China and many nations of Southeast Asia.

Agriculture

The importance of agriculture—the systematic cultivation of plants—should be obvious, even to those of us who live in urban areas and seldom visit a farm. Modern farming is the foundation on which human society is built. North America has some of the richest, most productive cropland in the world. As a result, farmers in the United States and Canada produce so much food that they are able to feed millions of people around the world as well as their own citizens.

Worldwide Patterns of Agriculture Many scholars now trace the beginnings of human civilization to the cultivation of crop plants. Evidence suggests that agriculture developed separately in many parts of the world about 10,000 to 12,000 years ago. Once people discovered how to grow plants for food, the planting and harvesting of crops tended to keep them in one place for much of the year, leading directly to the establishment of social institutions. Even today, agriculture, shown in **Figure 24–18,** is the principal occupation of more human beings than any other activity.

Thousands of different plants—nearly all of which are angiosperms—are raised for food in various parts of the world. **Most of the people of the world depend on a few crop plants, such as wheat, rice, and corn, for the bulk of their food supply.** The same crops are also used to feed livestock.

Biology and History

The Evolution of Agriculture

More than 10,000 years ago, humans began a gradual transition from hunter-gatherer societies to civilizations that were reliant on cultivated crops—many of which are still cultivated today. Because of regional differences in climate, soil type, and naturally occurring plant life, the crops planted today arose in different parts of the world.

8000 BC

Inhabitants of the Middle East begin to cultivate wheat. The change from gathering a crop in the wild to farming it eventually contributes to the rise of one of the earliest Middle Eastern civilizations.

7000 BC

Chilies and avocados are cultivated as important additions to the diets of Mesoamerican people. Chilies are used for flavoring foods, and avocados provide vitamins and oils.

5500 BC

Barley is cultivated in the Nile Valley of Egypt. About 2000 years later, farming settlements are united throughout the Nile Valley, and Egyptian culture flourishes.

TEACHER TO TEACHER

To introduce students to the concept of vegetative reproduction, I ask them to bring a small jar to class. I have the students fill the jars almost to the top with water. After carefully removing stems from either coleus plants or impatiens plants, I have the students place the stems into the water. Using a permanent marker, I instruct students to write the date the cutting was inserted into the water on the jar. For the next two weeks, I have the students observe their cuttings every day, recording any changes they see. Hairlike roots should begin to appear in about one to two weeks. Then, I plant the rooted cuttings in soil so that students see how the plants continue to grow. This also gives me a new supply of plants that I can use for this activity next year.

—Janice Lagatol,
Biology Teacher
Fort Lee High School,
Fort Lee, NJ

You may not have thought of it this way, but the food we take from crop plants is stored in their seeds. Recall that the food stored within the seeds of all angiosperms is a tissue known as endosperm. Worldwide, then, most of humanity depends for food on the endosperm of only a few carefully cultivated species of grass. The pattern in the United States is similar. Roughly 80 percent of all U.S. cropland is used to grow just four crops: wheat, corn, soybeans, and hay. Of these crops, three—wheat, corn, and hay—are derived from grasses.

CHECKPOINT *How is endosperm related to the world's food supply?*

Changes in Agriculture The discovery and introduction of new plants has changed human history. Before they were discovered in the Americas, many important crops—including corn, peanuts, beans, and potatoes—were unknown in Europe. The introduction of these plants changed European agriculture rapidly. Within a century, many of these foods had become important parts of the European diet. We think of boiled potatoes, for example, as traditional staples of German and Irish cooking, but 400 years ago they were new items in the diets of Europeans.

The efficiency of agriculture has been improved through the selective breeding of crop plants and improvements in farming techniques. The corn grown by Native Americans, for example, was developed more than 8000 years ago from teosinte, a wild grass found in Mexico.

KEEP CURRENT WITH . . .

To find out more about the topics in this chapter, go to: **www.phschool.com**

Writing Activity

The domestication of all major crops had a major impact on the growth of civilizations. Choose one of the crops discussed below and research how that crop contributed to the rise of civilization and culture in that region.

5000 BC

People in central Mexico domesticate corn, also called maize. Early corncobs are only about an inch long and have a few dozen kernels. The ancestor of corn was probably a wild grass called *teosinte.*

4500 BC

Rice cultivation becomes well established in southern China, southeast Asia, and northern India. Rice farming spreads widely from these regions, and rice later becomes a major Chinese export.

3500 BC

The potato is domesticated in the Andes Mountains of South America. Early Andean farmers eventually produce 700 varieties of potatoes by cultivating them on irrigated terraces built on mountain slopes.

HISTORY OF SCIENCE

Grafting in history

There is evidence that the Chinese understood grafting as early as 1000 B.C. The Greek botanist Theophrastus, who is sometimes called the founder of botany, wrote about grafting and other forms of vegetative reproduction in the second century B.C. in his book *Causes of Plants.* The history of the navel orange provides an example of the benefits of careful grafting. Around 1820, a farmer near Bahia, Brazil, noticed that the fruit on one branch of one of his orange trees—probably a natural mutant—was superior to all his other fruit. Through grafting, he multiplied that form of the fruit. Some 50 years later, a missionary sent a dozen of the orange trees to Washington, D.C., and two of those were sent to a farm near Riverside, California. From those two trees sprang almost the entire navel orange industry the world over.

SCIENCE NEWS®

Encourage students to visit **www.phschool.com** for the most current information on this topic.

Make Connections

Health Science Have students compare the nutrient content of unbleached wheat flour, brown rice, and cornmeal. Students should display their findings in a compare/contrast table that lists the amount of nutrients contained in one serving of each of the three foods. Also, have students compare the nutrients in their table with recommended daily allowances. Ask: **Which major nutrient are these foods high in?** *(Carbohydrates)* **Which major nutrient are these foods low in?** *(Protein)* Point out how each food is also high in some vitamins and minerals but low in others. Explain that people in many countries often have little to eat besides one of these staple crops. Ask: **If you ate almost nothing except one of these foods, how healthy do you think you would be?** *(You probably would not be very healthy, because you would be deficient in protein and other important nutrients.)*

Answer to . . .

CHECKPOINT *Endosperm of only a few species of grasses provides most of humanity with the majority of its food.*

24–3 (continued)

Use Visuals

Figure 24–19 Check students' understanding of the graph. Ask: **What was the corn yield in the United States in 1974?** *(About 71 bushels per acre)* **In which year was the corn yield the highest?** *(1994)* **What do you think explains the ups and down from year to year in the graph?** *(Variations in the weather from year to year)*

3 ASSESS

Evaluate Understanding

Ask students to write a paragraph summarizing worldwide patterns of agriculture.

Reteach

Have pairs of students work together to create graphic organizers comparing and contrasting vegetative reproduction and plant propagation. Call on several pairs of students to share their graphic organizers with the class.

ALTERNATIVE ASSESSMENT

Students should choose a plant, such as geranium or coleus, that grows well from cuttings. Have students create a pamphlet for gardeners that describes the process of growing cuttings from plants.

Use iText to review the key concepts in Section 24–3.

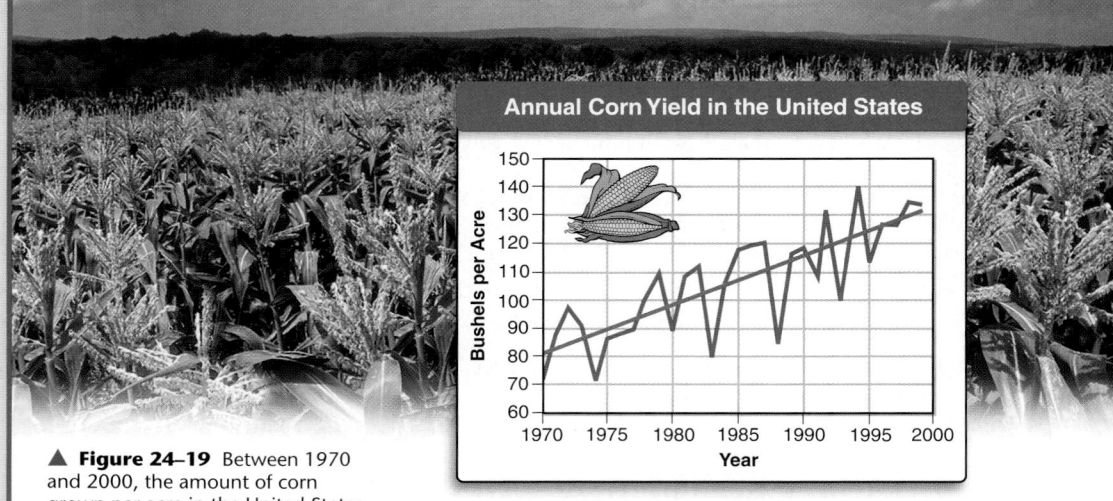

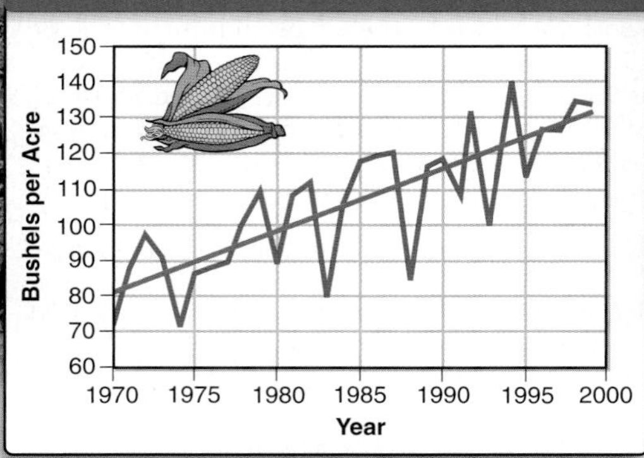

▲ **Figure 24–19** Between 1970 and 2000, the amount of corn grown per acre in the United States increased more than 60 percent. A field of corn, also called *Zea mays,* is shown in the photograph. **Interpreting Graphics** *Describe the trend shown in the graph for the years 1983 and 1988.*

In more recent times, other familiar crops have been the product of selective breeding. Sugar beets, the source of most refined sugar from the United States, were produced from the ordinary garden beet using selective breeding. Plants as different as cabbage, broccoli, and brussel sprouts have been developed from a single species of wild mustard.

Improvements in farming techniques have been responsible for dramatic improvements in crop yields, as shown in **Figure 24–19.** Some of the most important techniques have been the use of pesticides and fertilizers. These improvements have lowered the price of food and enabled farmers to feed many more people without any expansion of the amount of land under cultivation.

24–3 Section Assessment

1. **Key Concept** Define vegetative reproduction. How do the offspring produced compare to the parent plant?
2. **Key Concept** What is the purpose of plant propagation?
3. **Key Concept** What are the main food crops? What techniques have improved crop yields during the past several decades?
4. Compare grafting and budding. Why are these techniques preferable to sexual propagation of woody plants?
5. **Critical Thinking Inferring** Dandelions employ an unusual form of reproduction that produces seeds but does not involve meiosis and the production of haploid gametes. The pollen produced within flowers is sterile and produces seeds without fertilization. What advantages might this system have over sexual reproduction of viable seeds?

iTEXT **Assessment** Use iText to review the important concepts in Section 24–3.

ALTERNATIVE ASSESSMENT

Creative Writing
Write a short story describing how a new plant could form by vegetative reproduction or plant propagation. Your story should include the part played by tissues in stems in the process. (*Hint:* Review the blue heading on stem structure and function on page 589 in Chapter 23.)

24–3 Section Assessment

1. Vegetative reproduction is the production of new plants from horizontal stems, plantlets, or underground roots. The offspring are genetically identical to the parent plant.
2. To make identical copies of a plant or to produce offspring from seedless plants
3. The main crops are wheat, rice, and corn. Selective breeding, pesticides, and fertilizers have improved crop yields.
4. In grafting, a stem is attached. In budding, a bud is attached. Both involve growing a new plant by cutting a piece from a parent plant with desirable traits and attaching it to another plant that has a strong root system.
5. This system might have the advantages of not requiring other plants nearby in order for pollination and fertilization to occur and of producing new plants that are genetically identical to the parent plant.

Answer to . . .

Figure 24–19 *Both 1983 and 1988 showed a significant drop in the annual corn yield.*

Investigating Pollination

In this investigation, you will design an experiment to test a hypothesis about the chemical signals that steer the growth of pollen tubes toward the ovary.

Problem

What controls the direction of pollen tube growth?

Materials

- flowering plants, such as beans or *Brassicas*
- hand lens
- small paintbrush
- forceps
- pollen nutrient solution
- pollen nutrient solution without calcium
- concentrated calcium chloride solution
- dissecting probe
- microscope slides
- coverslips
- dropper pipette

Skills

Designing Experiments, Controlling Variables

Design Your Experiment

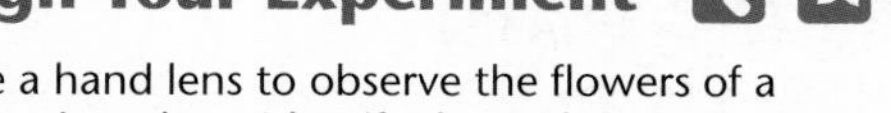

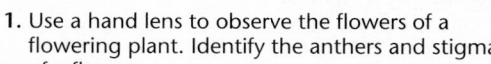

1. Use a hand lens to observe the flowers of a flowering plant. Identify the anthers and stigma of a flower.
2. Use a small paintbrush to transfer pollen from several flowers to the stigmas of other flowers.
3. Use forceps to transfer several anthers to a microscope slide. Add a drop of pollen nutrient solution. Gently tap the anthers with the tip of a dissecting probe to release pollen.
4. Discard the anthers and add a coverslip. Observe the pollen with the microscope at low power. Make a labeled drawing of your observations.
5. Your teacher will provide slides containing pollen that has been in pollen nutrient solution for several hours. Observe these slides with the microscope. Record your observations.
6. Pollen tubes have been found to grow toward calcium or pieces of ovaries. Design an experiment to test the hypothesis that calcium is the chemical signal that guides the growing pollen tube toward the ovary.
7. As you plan your experiment, be sure to control all important variables. If observing pollen tube growth in a flower directly is too difficult, you will need to choose some other method to test the hypothesis. Have your teacher check your plan before you begin your experiment.

Analyze and Conclude

1. **Applying Concepts** The pollen of most plants will not germinate in pure water. What function of the stigma and style did the pollen nutrient solution replace?
2. **Observing** Did the pollen tubes grow toward a source of calcium? Toward ovary tissue?
3. **Drawing Conclusions** In many experiments, pollen tubes grow toward either calcium or ovary tissue. From these results, could you conclude that calcium directs pollen tube growth toward the ovary in flowers? Explain.

Go Further

Designing Experiments Plan an experiment to test the effect of light on the rate and direction of pollen tube growth.

Design an Experiment

Objective Students will be able to design an experiment to determine what controls the direction of pollen tube growth.

Skills Focus **Designing Experiments, Controlling Variables**

Time 45 minutes

Advance Prep

- Prepare the pollen nutrient solution with 30% sucrose, 0.01% boric acid, and 0.02% calcium chloride.
- Prepare the pollen nutrient solution without calcium in the same way but omit the calcium chloride.
- Prepare a 1% solution of calcium chloride for the concentrated calcium chloride solution.
- Prepare slides with several grains of pollen in a drop of nutrient solution, cover the slides with a coverslip, and let them stand for several hours before students use them in step 5 of the lab.

Teaching Strategies Have students read the entire procedure. Point out how the procedure models the pollination of flowers by insects. Then, ask: **What role does the paintbrush play?** *(The role of the insect pollinator)* **What role is played by the pollen nutrient solution on the slide?** *(The role of the stigma and style)*

Procedure

7. The most likely experimental design is to observe if pollen tubes grow when pollen is placed in a drop of pollen nutrient solution without calcium.

Go Further

Students might design an experiment in which pollen grains in pollen nutrient solution are placed in the dark or in bright light for several hours and then inspected microscopically to observe the rate and direction of pollen tube growth.

Analyze and Conclude

1. It replaced the nutrients provided by the stigma and style.

2. In general, pollen tubes grow toward calcium and toward ovary tissue.

3. The results would support but not prove the hypothesis. Proof would require demonstrating a biochemical mechanism by which calcium directs pollen tube growth.

Chapter 24 Study Guide

Study Tip

Have students rewrite the boldfaced sentences as questions and answer them. They should look up the answers to any questions they are unsure of.

Thinking Visually

1. Mature sporophyte; **2.** Pollen cone; **3.** Seed cone; **4.** Pollen grains; **5.** Female gametophyte; **6.** Zygote; **7.** Seed

Chapter 24 Assessment

Reviewing Content

1. a	**5.** b	**9.** c
2. a	**6.** a	**10.** c
3. a	**7.** d	**11.** d
4. a	**8.** a	

Understanding Concepts

12. A gametophyte plant produces male and female gametes (sperm and eggs). A sporophyte plant produces spores.

13. An ovule is a structure in which the female gametophyte develops. When a pollen grain lands near an ovule, the grain splits open and grows a pollen tube, which contains two haploid cells. Once the pollen tube reaches the female gametophyte, one sperm cell disintegrates and the other fertilizes the egg within the female gametophyte.

14. Male pollen cones produce male gametophytes called pollen grains, which are four-celled organisms that contain haploid cells. Later, one of the cells of the gametophyte divides to produce sperm cells.

15. Check students' diagrams against Figure 24–4 for accuracy.

16. The carpel, which produces the female gametophytes, is the innermost part of the flower. Each carpel has a broad base that contains an ovary. The diameter narrows into a stalk called the style. At the top of the style is the stigma.

17. Pollen may be transferred from plant to plant by wind, insects, birds, or bats.

Chapter 24 Study Guide

24–1 Reproduction With Cones and Flowers

Key Concepts

- Reproduction in gymnosperms takes place in cones, which are produced by a mature sporophyte plant.
- Flowers are reproductive organs that are composed of four kinds of specialized leaves: sepals, petals, stamens, and carpels.
- Reproduction in angiosperms takes place within the flower. Following pollination and fertilization, the seeds develop inside protective structures called fruits.
- Most gymnosperms are wind pollinated, whereas most flowering plants are pollinated by animals.

Vocabulary

- pollen cone, p. 610 • seed cone, p. 610
- ovule, p. 610 • pollen tube, p. 611
- sepal, p. 612 • petal, p. 612 • stamen, p. 612
- filament, p. 612 • anther, p. 612 • carpel, p. 612
- ovary, p. 612 • style, p. 612 • stigma, p. 612
- embryo sac, p. 615 • endosperm, p. 616
- double fertilization, p. 616

24–2 Seed Development and Germination

Key Concepts

- As angiosperm seeds mature, the ovary walls thicken to form a fruit that encloses the developing seeds.
- Seeds dispersed by animals are typically contained in fleshy, nutritious fruits.
- Seeds dispersed by wind or water are typically lightweight, allowing them to be carried in the air or to float on the surface of the water.
- Environmental factors such as temperature and moisture can cause a seed to end dormancy and germinate.

Vocabulary

dormancy, p. 620
germination, p. 621

24–3 Plant Propagation and Agriculture

Key Concepts

- Vegetative reproduction includes the production of new plants from horizontal stems, cuttings, leaves, plantlets, and underground roots.
- Horticulturists use plant propagation to make many identical copies of a plant or to produce offspring from seedless plants.
- Most of the people of the world depend on a few crop plants, such as wheat, rice, and corn, for the bulk of their food supply.

Vocabulary

- vegetative reproduction, p. 622
- stolon, p. 622 • grafting, p. 623
- budding, p. 623

Thinking Visually

Use the following terms to complete the flowchart about reproduction in gymnosperms: *female gametophyte, seed, pollen cone, mature sporophyte, seed cone, zygote, pollen grains.*

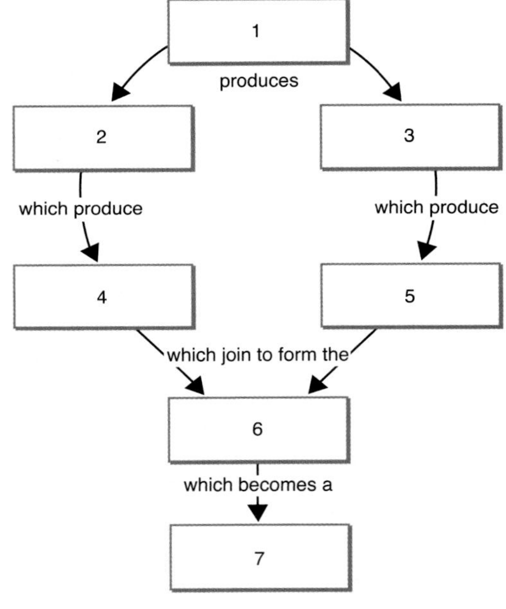

CHAPTER RESOURCES

Print:

- ***Teaching Resources,*** Chapter Vocabulary Review, Graphic Organizer
- ***Chapter Tests: Levels A and B,*** Chapter 24 Test
- ***PH Assessment System,*** Practice Test

Technology:

- ***Computer Test Bank,*** Chapter 24 Test
- ***iText,*** Chapter 24 Assessment

Chapter 24 Assessment

Reviewing Content

Choose the letter that best answers the question or completes the statement.

1. Two structures specialized for reproduction in seed plants are
   a. cones and flowers.
   b. cones and lateral buds.
   c. lateral and terminal buds.
   d. meristems and flowers.
2. Which of the following is NOT true of reproduction in a pine tree?
   a. The pollen tube contains two diploid sperm.
   b. One sperm fertilizes the egg.
   c. One sperm disintegrates.
   d. The zygote grows into an embryo.
3. In angiosperms, the structures that produce the male gametophyte are called the
   a. anthers.
   b. sepals.
   c. pollen tubes.
   d. stigmas.
4. The outermost circle of flower parts consists of several
   a. sepals. c. carpels.
   b. petals. d. corollas.
5. Pollination occurs when pollen lands on the
   a. style. c. filament.
   b. stigma. d. anther.
6. The thickened ovary wall of a plant joins with other parts of the flower stem to become the
   a. fruit. c. endosperm.
   b. seed. d. cotyledon.
7. The seed leaves of a flowering plant are known as
   a. endosperm.
   b. carpels.
   c. radicles.
   d. cotyledons.
8. In seed plants, the structure that encloses the male gametophyte and transports it to another plant is called a
   a. pollen grain.
   b. seed.
   c. flower.
   d. pollinator.
9. The period during which the embryo is alive but not growing is called
   a. fertilization.
   b. vegetative growth.
   c. dormancy.
   d. germination.

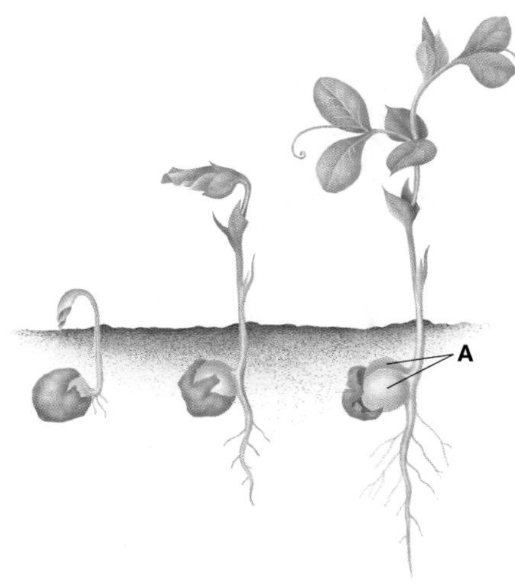

10. The illustration shows the germination of a pea plant. The feature labeled *A* is a(n)
    a. anther. c. cotyledon.
    b. seed coat. d. root.
11. The process in which a single plant produces many offspring genetically identical to itself is called
    a. sexual reproduction.
    b. agriculture.
    c. dormancy.
    d. vegetative reproduction.

Understanding Concepts

12. What is a gametophyte plant? How is it different from a sporophyte plant?
13. What is an ovule? Describe what happens to an ovule of a pine cone if it is fertilized by the male gametophyte.
14. What role do male pine cones play in reproduction?
15. Draw and label a diagram showing the stages in the life cycle of a typical gymnosperm.
16. What is a carpel? Where is it located in a typical flower?
17. Describe at least two ways in which pollen is transferred from one plant to another.
18. Briefly describe each stage in the life cycle of an angiosperm, starting with germination of the seed.
19. What purposes are served by seed dormancy?
20. What is vegetative reproduction?
21. Describe three ways in which plants can be propagated artificially.
22. What is the function of endosperm?

HOMEWORK GUIDE

Section:	Questions:
Section 24–1	1–6, 8, 12–16, 18, 22–24, 28, 33
Section 24–2	7, 9, 10, 17, 19, 25–27, 29–31
Section 24–3	11, 20, 21, 32

18. Germination is followed by growth of the sporophyte. In anthers, cells undergo meiosis, reproducing haploid spore cells that develop into pollen grains. In ovules, cells undergo meiosis, producing eggs. Pollen grains are released from the anther and deposited on a stigma. After pollination and fertilization, eggs develop into zygotes, ovules develop into seeds, and ovaries develop into fruits. Seeds are disbursed, and the cycle repeats.

19. Seed dormancy can allow for long-distance dispersal, and it may allow seeds to germinate under ideal conditions.

20. Vegetative reproduction is asexual reproduction in which new plants are produced from horizontal stems, plantlets, or underground roots.

21. Plants can be propagated asexually by cuttings, grafting, and budding. In cuttings, a length of stem is cut and placed in a rooting mixture. In grafting and budding, a piece of a parent plant is attached to another plant.

22. Endosperm is the stored food supply in angiosperm seeds that nourishes the embryo plant.

Critical Thinking

23. Female cones secrete a pollination drop that provides a sticky landing site for pollen grains. Without it, pollen grains would not stick to the cones and fertilization would not occur.

24. Fruit could not form on flowers that lack carpels because fruit develops from the ovary, which is part of the carpel.

25. If pollen grains of wind-pollinated flowers were sticky, they might stick to anything, not just the female flowers.

26. One possible answer is that, in such harsh environments, a seed might have to wait many years before suitable conditions for germination and growth occur.

27. Students' experimental designs will vary. One possible answer is to choose seeds with large cotyledons and remove the cotyledons before planting. Leave the cotyledons on some seeds as a control.

28. Pollen is produced inside the anthers, labeled C. The stigma is labeled A; it is where pollen grains land. Seeds develop in the ovary, labeled F. A sepal is labeled G and a petal is labeled H.

29. In monocots, the single cotyledon remains within the seed. The growing shoot emerges while protected by a sheath. In some species of dicots, the cotyledons emerge above the ground and protect the first foliage leaves. In other species, the cotyledons remain below the ground, providing a food source for the developing seedling.

30. The seed needs water from the soil for germination. The root emerges first to obtain water and nutrients from the soil.

31. When seeds germinate, they absorb water. The absorbed water causes the endosperm and cotyledons to swell, cracking open the seed coat. The primary root begins to grow. A leaky ceiling could result in the seed package becoming wet, which could lead to premature seed germination.

Chapter 24 Assessment

Critical Thinking

23. **Inferring** What is the function of the pollination drop (sticky substance) secreted by female pine cones? What would happen if it were not present?

24. **Predicting** Some plants form flowers that produce stamens but no carpels. Could fruit form on one of these flowers? Explain your answer.

25. **Formulating Hypotheses** Would you expect pollen grains of wind-pollinated flowers to be sticky? How would you test the accuracy of your answer?

26. **Inferring** The seeds of lupines, an arctic plant, can remain dormant for thousands of years. Why might this trait be important to a plant in an arctic environment?

27. **Designing an Experiment** A friend suggests that seeds do not need cotyledons to grow. You argue that cotyledons are important to seeds. Design an experiment that shows the effect that removing cotyledons has on seed growth.

28. **Interpreting Graphics** The diagram below shows the parts of a typical flower.
    a. Inside which structure is pollen produced? What is the name of this structure?
    b. What structure is represented by A? What is its function?
    c. In which structure do seeds develop?
    d. What are the names of structures G and H?

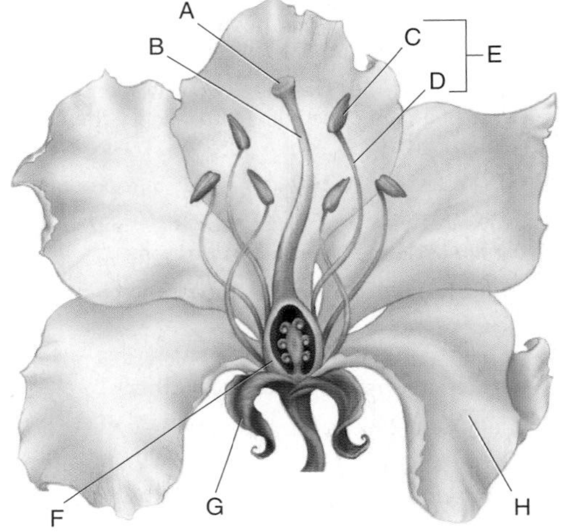

29. **Comparing and Contrasting** How is seed germination similar in monocots and dicots? How is it different?

30. **Inferring** What does a plant need that makes it necessary for seed germination to start with the emergence of a root rather than a shoot?

31. **Predicting** It is important to store seeds in a dry, dark place. Predict what might happen if water from a leaky ceiling were to drip onto packages of seeds on a store shelf.

32. **Applying Concepts** Suppose that you want to produce an apple tree that will bear two different kinds of apples. Which method of artificial propagation would you choose? Why would the other method of artificial propagation not be suitable?

33. **Making Connections** Review the blue heading on coevolution on page 438 of Chapter 17. Discuss how the coevolution of plants and the animals that pollinate them might have taken place. (*Hint:* What are several characteristics of plants that represent adaptations to animal pollinators? What characteristics of these animals are the result of coevolution with plants?)

Performance-Based Assessment

Create a video presentation in which you demonstrate different types of artificial propagation. If possible, prepare the video over a long period so that you can show the growth of propagated plants. Include in your documentary a discussion of the advantages and disadvantages of artificial propagation.

Take It to the NET

Do all flowers smell sweet? Visit the Prentice Hall Web site at **www.phschool.com** to find out about flowers that smell unpleasant. Then, answer the following questions:

- What is a carrion flower? Why do some smell like rotting flesh?
- What happens to the maggots that are laid in a carrion flower?
- Describe five other flowers that have unusual or unpleasant odors. How are they pollinated?

Take It to the NET

- A carrion flower is one that smells like a rotting dead animal. The petals are typically flesh-colored and covered with hair. The smell attracts insects that feed on feces, rotting flesh, and other decaying organic matter. The insects lay their eggs in the flower, and this helps the plant get pollinated.
- The maggots die from lack of food.
- Students may describe any five flowers that have unusual or unpleasant odors: stinking corpse lily (*Rafflesia arnoldii*), Indian almond (*Sterculia foetida*), dragon arum (*Dracunculus vulgaris*), "Tiffy Titan" or titan arum (*Amorphophallus titanum*), yellow skunk cabbage.

Standardized Test Prep

Test-Taking Tip When answering questions pertaining to experimental situations, read all of the questions first. Then, read the passage carefully and examine any accompanying data, looking for the specific information required to answer the questions.

Directions: Choose the letter that best answers the question or completes the statement.

1. Which of the following are NOT part of a flower?
   (A) sepals
   (B) petals
   (C) stamens
   (D) stems
   (E) carpels
2. Where in a flower are pollen grains produced?
   (A) sepals
   (B) carpels
   (C) anthers
   (D) ovary
   (E) stigma
3. Which part of a flower develops into a fruit?
   (A) pollen tube
   (B) sepals
   (C) anthers
   (D) ovary
   (E) stigma
4. Which flower structure includes all the others listed below?
   (A) style
   (B) carpel
   (C) stigma
   (D) ovary
   (E) ovule
5. All of the following are fruits EXCEPT
   (A) tomato.
   (B) corn.
   (C) beet.
   (D) cucumber.
   (E) pumpkin.
6. Which is an example of vegetative reproduction?
   I. Grafting
   II. Budding
   III. Flowering
   (A) I only
   (B) II only
   (C) I and II only
   (D) II and III only
   (E) I, II, and III
7. What is endosperm?
   I. A 3N cell
   II. Food-rich tissue
   III. Tissue formed from the second stage of double fertilization
   (A) I only
   (B) II only
   (C) I and II only
   (D) II and III only
   (E) I, II, and III

Questions 8–9 Complete each analogy by selecting the correct letter. In analogies, A : B :: C : ___?___ *means* A is to B as C is to ___?___.

8. Male gametophyte : pollen grain :: female gametophyte : ___?___
   (A) embryo sac
   (B) ovule
   (C) egg
   (D) ovary
   (E) endosperm
9. Gymnosperm : pines :: angiosperm : ___?___
   (A) irises
   (B) two seed leaves
   (C) pollination
   (D) cones
   (E) flowers

Questions 10–11

A scientist measured the average time it took different fruits to fall 1 meter (m) from the parent tree. Assume that for every second a fruit falls, it is carried 1.5 m away from the parent tree.

Relationship Between Fruit Type and Dispersal Time

Type of Tree	Average Time (sec) for Seed to Fall 1 m
Norway maple	0.98
Silver maple	0.64
White ash	0.30
Shagbark hickory	0.16
Red oak	0.16

Norway maple Silver maple White ash Shagbark hickory Red oak

10. Which fruit was carried the farthest from the parent tree?
    (A) silver maple
    (B) Norway maple
    (C) white ash
    (D) red oak
    (E) shagbark hickory
11. According to these data, what benefit does a winged fruit have over an acorn?
    I. It is lighter.
    II. It is heavier.
    III. It will travel farther.
    (A) I only
    (B) II only
    (C) III only
    (D) I and III
    (E) I, II, and III

Standardized Test Prep

1. D **2.** C **3.** D **4.** B **5.** C **6.** C **7.** E **8.** C **9.** A **10.** B **11.** C

Chapter 24 Assessment (continued)

32. Grafting is the method of artificial propagation that fuses together pieces of two different plants, so it would be an appropriate method for producing an apple tree that will bear two different kinds of apples. Cuttings, however, generate clones of a plant but do not combine two different plants.

33. Coevolution is the process by which two organisms evolve in response to changes in each other. A relationship exists between the evolution of angiosperms and the evolution of modern insects, mammals, and birds.

Performance-Based Assessment

Students' videos should demonstrate an understanding of cuttings, grafting, and budding.

(Lysichiton americanum), "lords-and-ladies" *(Arum maculatum),* lantern stinkhorn *(Lysurus mokusin),* and starfish flower *(Stapelia gigantea),* among others.

For additional information, visit **www.phschool.com**

Chapter Planner 25 Plant Responses and Adaptations

Section and Section Objectives	Time	Activities and Labs
25–1 Hormones and Plant Growth, pp. 633–638 **25.1.1** ***Describe*** patterns of plant growth. **25.1.2** ***Explain*** what plant hormones are. **25.1.3** ***Describe*** how auxins, cytokinins, gibberellins, and ethylene affect plant growth.	**2 periods (1 block)**	**SE:** ***Inquiry Activity,*** How are plants adapted to their environment?, p. 632 **TE:** ***Demonstrations,*** pp. 633, 637 **TE:** ***Meet Diverse Needs,*** p. 635 **TE:** ***Build Science Skills,*** pp. 635, 636 **SE:** ***Analyzing Data,*** Auxins and Plant Growth, p. 637 **TE:** ***Make Connections,*** p. 638 **SE:** ***Real-World Lab,*** Using Hormones to Control Plant Development, pp. 648–649
25–2 Plant Responses, pp. 639–642 **25.2.1** ***Explain*** what plant tropisms are. **25.2.2** ***Explain*** what photoperiodism is. **25.2.3** ***Describe*** how temperate plants prepare for winter.	**1 period (1/2 block)**	**TE:** ***Demonstration,*** p. 640 **SE:** ***Quick Lab,*** Can a plant find its way through a maze?, p. 640 **TE:** ***Building Science Skills,*** p. 642
25–3 Plant Adaptations, pp. 643–646 **25.3.1** ***Summarize*** how plants are adapted to different environments. **25.3.2** ***Describe*** how plants obtain nutrients. **25.3.3** ***Explain*** how plants use chemical defenses.	**1 period (1/2 block)**	**TE:** ***Build Science Skills,*** pp. 643, 644 **SE:** ***Issues in Biology,*** Are Herbal Drugs Safe?, p. 647
Chapter Assessment, pp. 650–653	**1 period (1/2 block)**	

ACTIVITY PLANNER

SE: ***Inquiry Activity,*** p. 632; (15 min.); desert and rain forest plants

TE: ***Demonstration,*** p.633; (10 min.); plant such as geranium

TE: ***Meet Diverse Needs,*** p. 635; (10 min.); balloon, transparent tape

TE: ***Build Science Skills,*** p. 635; (5 min. set up; 5 min. observation); plant such as coleus in four-sided plastic pot

TE: ***Build Science Skills,*** p. 636; (15 min.); twigs with terminal and lateral buds

TE: ***Demonstration,*** p. 637; (20 min. for set up; 10 min. for observations); wheat seeds, potting soil, 2 small flats, gibberellic acid, ethyl alcohol, distilled water, spray bottle

TE: ***Make Connections,*** p. 638; (10 min.); artificially ripened fruit

TE: ***Demonstration,*** p. 640; (5 min.); *Mimosa pudica*

SE: ***Quick Lab,*** p. 640; (20 min. for set up; 5 min./day for 2 weeks for observation); scissors, masking tape, cardboard dividers, bean seeds, small flower pots containing soil

TE: ***Building Science Skills,*** p. 642; (10 min.); dormant tree branches

TE: ***Building Science Skills,*** p. 643; (15 min.); aquatic plants

TE: ***Building Science Skills,*** p. 644; (15 min.); various desert plants

SE: ***Real-World Lab,*** pp. 648–649; (45 min. for setup; 10 min. for observation few times over 3 weeks); coleus plants, scalpels, metric rulers, rooting compounds, potting soils, paper cups, flat wooden toothpicks

PLANNING KEY

Ability Levels

B **Basic**	For students who need additional help
A **Average**	For all students
E **Enriched**	For students who need to be challenged

Components

SE	Student Edition	**GRSW**	Guided Reading and Study Workbook	**IDM**	Issues and Decision Making
TE	Teacher's Edition	**CT**	Chapter Tests: Levels A and B	**CTB**	Computer Test Bank
LMA	Laboratory Manual A	**PHAS**	PH Assessment System	**PA**	Presentation Assistant Plus
LMB	Laboratory Manual B	**LA**	Lab Assessment with Scoring Guide	**BD**	BioDetectives Videotape
TR	Teaching Resources	**BTM**	BioTechnology Manual	**iT**	iText
IF	Investigations in Forensics				

Program Resources	Assessment	Media and Technology
LMA: Chapter 25 Lab A E **TR:** Section Review 25–1 B A **GRSW:** Section 25–1 B A **BTM:** Concept 7 A E	**SE:** 25–1 Section Assessment, p. 638 **TR:** Section Review 25–1	**PA:** 25–1 Interest Grabber, Section Outline, Hormone Action in Plants, Figure 25–3, Figure 25–5 **iT:** Section 25–1
LMB: Chapter 25 Lab B A **TR:** Section Review 25–2 B A **GRSW:** Section 25–2 B A	**SE:** 25–2 Section Assessment, p. 642 **TR:** Section Review 25–2	**PA:** 25–2 Interest Grabber, Section Outline, Photoperiodism and Flowering **iT:** Section 25–2
TR: Section Review 25–3 B A Chapter 25 Real-World Lab B A E **GRSW:** Section 25–3 B A	**SE:** 25–3 Section Assessment, p. 646 **TR:** Section Review 25–3	**PA:** 25–3 Interest Grabber, Section Outline, Compare/Contrast Table **iT:** Section 25–3
	SE: Chapter 25 Assessment, pp. 650–653 **TR:** Chapter Vocabulary Review, Graphic Organizer **CT:** Chapter 25 Test **CTB:** Chapter 25 Test **PHAS:** Practice Text	**CTB:** Chapter 25 Test **iT:** Chapter 25 Assessment

PRESSED FOR TIME?

To Preview the Chapter
- Have students read the Key Concepts and Vocabulary terms in each section.
- Have students examine all the figures and read their captions.

To Cover the Chapter Quickly
- Have students read Patterns of Plant Growth and Hormones and the Control of Plant Growth in Section 25–1 and Tropisms in Section 25–2.
- Assign questions 1–2 in 25–1 Section Assessment and questions 1 and 5 in 25–2 Section Assessment.

To Review the Chapter
- Assign Sections 25–1 through 25–3 in the Guided Reading and Study Workbook.
- Assign the Section Review for 25–1 through 25–3 and the Chapter Vocabulary Review for Chapter 25 in the Teaching Resources.

Chapter 25

ENGAGE/EXPLORE

Inquiry Activity

Objective Students will be able to identify characteristics that make plants adapted to their environments.

Skills Focus **Classifying, Formulating Hypotheses, Predicting**

Materials Two groups of plants: desert plants, such as cactus and crown-of-thorns, and rain forest plants, such as philodendron, ferns, and African violet

Time 15 minutes

Safety Check for students with allergies to plants. Warn students to avoid cactus spines and to not crush the leaves of plants.

Strategy You can place the plants at stations around the classroom and have students observe the plants at each station.

Expected Outcome Students should observe that some desert plants have thick leaves and cuticles while others have few, small leaves or no leaves at all; spines or thorns; and thick, fleshy stems. Rain forest plants have large, broad leaves with thinner cuticles and may be vines with aerial roots. Both types of plants have chlorophyll, stems, roots, and some type of leaves.

Think About It

1. Characteristics of desert plants that students might identify include reduced surface area and leaf size; thick leaves and cuticles; spines or thorns; and thick, fleshy stems. Rain forest plants have larger, thinner leaves and thinner cuticles, and fewer of them have thorns or spines. Vines are also common rain forest plants.

2. The reduced leaf surface area and thick cuticle of desert plants help conserve water. The thick, green, fleshy stems of cacti perform photosynthesis and store water. Tropical rain forest plants have large, broad leaves that capture the dim light available below the tree canopy and provide a large surface area for evaporation that helps to keep the plants cool. Climbing vines are also common in the rain forest, where they grow up around trees toward the brighter light high in the leaf canopy.

3. Student drawings and descriptions should include both adaptations to dry conditions (such as deep roots or thick cuticles) and to cold conditions (such as seeds, bulbs, or woody perennial stems that can survive through winter dormancy).

Chapter 25 Plant Responses and Adaptations

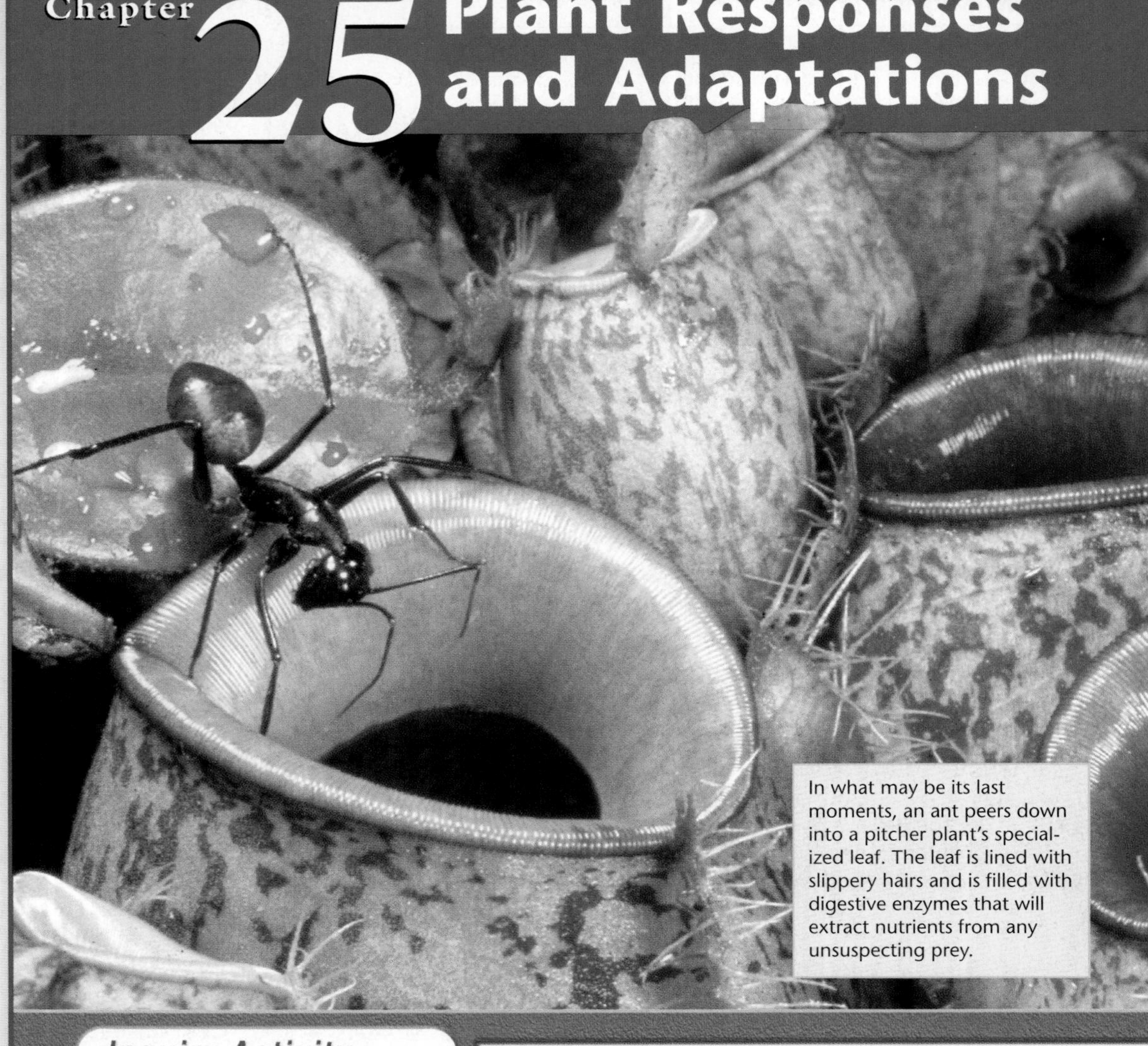

In what may be its last moments, an ant peers down into a pitcher plant's specialized leaf. The leaf is lined with slippery hairs and is filled with digestive enzymes that will extract nutrients from any unsuspecting prey.

Inquiry Activity

How are plants adapted to their environments?

Procedure

1. Examine several desert plants and several rain forest plants. Note any differences between these two groups of plants. Record your observations.
2. List the characteristics that distinguish desert plants and rain forest plants. List any characteristics that you observed in both types of plants.

Think About It

1. **Classifying** What characteristics did you identify that distinguish desert plants and rain forest plants?
2. **Formulating Hypotheses** How could these characteristics help desert and rain forest plants survive in their environments?
3. **Predicting** Draw a real or an imaginary plant that is adapted for warm, dry summers and rainy, cold winters. Write a paragraph describing the adaptations of your plant.

25–1 Hormones and Plant Growth

Unlike most animals, plants do not have a rigidly set organization to their bodies. Cows have four legs, ants have six, and spiders have eight; but tomato plants do not have a predetermined number of leaves or branches. However, plants such as the baobab tree in **Figure 25–1** show distinct patterns of growth. As a result, you can easily tell the difference between a tomato plant and a corn plant, between an oak tree and a pine tree.

Patterns of Plant Growth

Although plant growth is not determined precisely, it still follows general patterns that differ among species. What controls these patterns of development? Biologists have discovered that plant cells send signals to one another that indicate when to divide and when not to divide, and when to develop into a new kind of cell.

There is another difference between growth in plants and animals. Once most animals reach adulthood, they stop growing. In contrast, even plants that are thousands of years old continue to grow new needles, add new wood, and produce cones or new flowers, almost as if parts of their bodies remained "forever young." As you have learned, the secrets of plant growth are found in meristems, regions of tissue that can produce cells that later develop into specialized tissues. Meristems are found at places where plants grow rapidly—the tips of growing stems and roots, and along the outer edges of woody tissues that produce new growth every year.

If meristems are the source of plant growth, how is that growth controlled and regulated? Plants grow in response to environmental factors such as light, moisture, temperature, and gravity. But how do roots "know" to grow down, and how do stems "know" to grow up toward light? How do the tissues of a plant determine the right time of year to produce flowers? How do plants ensure that their growth is evenly balanced—that the trunk of a tree grows large enough to support the weight of its leaves and branches? The answers to these questions involve the actions of chemicals that direct, control, and regulate plant growth.

Guide for Reading

Key Concepts
- What are plant hormones?
- How do auxins, cytokinins, gibberellins, and ethylene affect plant growth?

Vocabulary
hormone
target cell
phototropism
auxin
gravitropism
lateral bud
apical dominance
herbicide
cytokinin
gibberellin
ethylene

Reading Strategy: Finding Main Ideas
Before you read, skim the section to identify the key ideas about plant hormones. Then, read the section carefully, making a list of supporting details for each main idea.

▶ **Figure 25–1** All plants follow a highly regulated pattern of growth that continues throughout the life of the plant. This pattern of growth leads to distinct shapes, such as the thick trunk and widely spaced branches of this baobab tree. **Applying Concepts** *In which plant tissue does growth occur?*

SECTION RESOURCES

Print:
- ***Laboratory Manual A,*** Chapter 25 Lab
- ***Teaching Resources,*** Section Review 25–1
- ***Guided Reading and Study Workbook,*** Section 25–1
- ***Biotechnology Manual,*** Concept 7

Technology:
- ***iText,*** Section 25–1

Section 25–1

1 FOCUS

Objectives

25.1.1 ***Describe*** patterns of plant growth.
25.1.2 ***Explain*** what plant hormones are.
25.1.3 ***Describe*** how auxins, cytokinins, gibberellins, and ethylene affect plant growth.

Guide for Reading

Vocabulary Preview

Call students' attention to the Vocabulary terms *phototropism* and *gravitropism.* Explain that the root word *tropism* is from a Greek word meaning "turning." Challenge students to infer the meaning of the two terms. (*Phototropism: turning due to light; gravitropism: turning due to gravity*)

Reading Strategy

Have students read the Key Concepts in the text to find the main ideas about plant hormones. Students can organize the main ideas and supporting details under the heads Auxins, Cytokinins, Gibberellins, and Ethylene.

2 INSTRUCT

Patterns of Plant Growth

Demonstration

Display a common houseplant, such as a geranium, from which the soil has been removed from the roots. Also be sure the stem can be plainly seen. Ask: **How does growth occur in this plant?** (*Growth is the result of cell division and cell enlargement.*) **Where do these kinds of cell activities take place in this plant?** (*In the meristematic regions at the tips of the roots and stems*) Next, show a small woody twig and a tree branch. Ask: **In what other way does this kind of plant stem grow?** (*Some plants grow in thickness as well as in length.*)

Answer to . . .

Figure 25–1 *In meristems*

25–1 (continued)

Plant Hormones

Use Visuals

Figure 25–2 Ask: **Where are hormone-producing cells in a plant?** (*In apical meristems, young leaves, roots, and growing flowers and fruits*) **What are target cells?** (*Cells that contain a hormone receptor and are affected by particular hormones*) **How do hormones affect target cells?** (*By changing their metabolism, affecting their growth rate, or activating the transcription of certain* genes) **In the figure, how do you think the hormones produced in the flower will affect the target cells in the flower bud?** (*They will probably affect their growth rate so the flower opens and activate the transcription of certain genes so the reproductive organs in the flower mature.*)

Auxins

Meet Diverse Needs

Students who need an extra challenge might enjoy trying to duplicate Charles and Francis Darwin's experiment with phototropism, described in the text and illustrated in Figure 25–3. Like the Darwins, they can use oat seedlings, which are fast growing. They can use aluminum foil for the opaque caps and bands on the oat shoots and clear plastic wrap for the clear caps. Have students share their results with the class. **Learning modality: logical/mathematical**

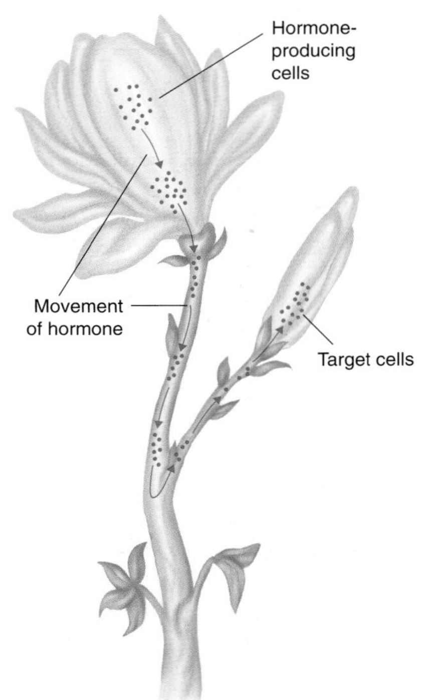

▲ **Figure 25–2** **Plant hormones are chemical substances that control patterns of development as well as plant responses to the environment.** Hormones are produced in apical meristems, in young leaves, in roots, and in growing flowers and fruits. From their place of origin, hormones move to other parts of the plant, where target cells respond in a way that is specific to the hormone.

Plant Hormones

In plants, the division, growth, maturation, and development of cells are controlled by a group of chemicals called hormones. A **hormone** is a substance that is produced in one part of an organism and affects another part of the same individual. **Plant hormones are chemical substances that control a plant's patterns of growth and development, and the plant's responses to environmental conditions.**

The general mechanism of hormone action in plants is shown in **Figure 25–2.** As you can see, the hormone moves through the plant from the place where it is produced to the place where it triggers its response. The portion of an organism affected by a particular hormone is known as its **target cell** or target tissue. To respond to a hormone, the target cell must contain a hormone receptor—usually a protein—to which the hormone binds. If the appropriate receptor is present, the hormone can exert an influence on the target cell by changing its metabolism, affecting its growth rate, or activating the transcription of certain genes. Cells that do not contain receptors are generally unaffected by hormones.

Different kinds of cells may have different receptors for the same hormone. As a result, a single hormone may affect two different tissues in different ways. For example, a particular hormone may stimulate growth in stem tissues but inhibit growth in root tissues.

CHECKPOINT *In which cells do hormones carry out their functions?*

Auxins

The experiment that led to the discovery of the first plant hormone was carried out by Charles Darwin. In 1880, Darwin and his son Francis published a book called *The Power of Movement in Plants.* In this book, they described an experiment in which oat seedlings demonstrated a response known as phototropism. **Phototropism** is the tendency of a plant to grow toward a source of light.

Figure 25–3 shows an experiment similar to the one carried out by the Darwins. Notice that the tip of one of the oat seedlings was covered with an opaque cap. This plant did not bend toward the light, even though the rest of the plant was uncovered. However, if an opaque shield was placed a few centimeters below the tip, the plant would bend toward the light as if the shield were not there. Clearly, something was taking place at the tip of the seedling.

PRESENTATIONS MADE EASY!

The Presentation Assistant Plus contains the Prentice Hall Presentation Pro and the Transparencies, which provide easy-to-follow visual support for every step of this section. If you have a computer presentation station, use Prentice Hall Presentation Pro for Section 25–1, or use the transparencies listed here.

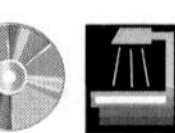

Section 25–1: **Interest Grabber**
Section Outline
Hormone Action in Plants
Figure 25–3
Figure 25–5

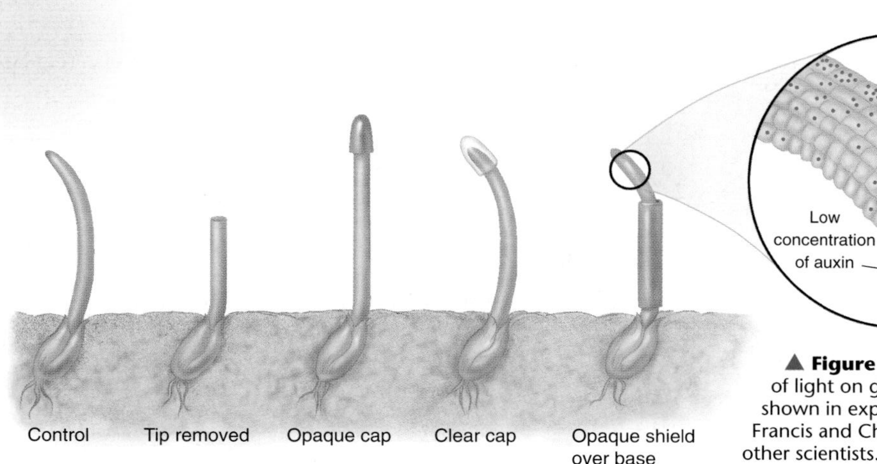

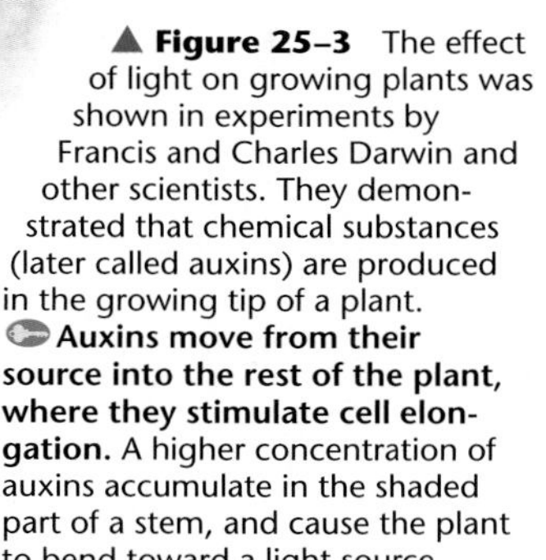

▲ **Figure 25–3** The effect of light on growing plants was shown in experiments by Francis and Charles Darwin and other scientists. They demonstrated that chemical substances (later called auxins) are produced in the growing tip of a plant. **Auxins move from their source into the rest of the plant, where they stimulate cell elongation.** A higher concentration of auxins accumulate in the shaded part of a stem, and cause the plant to bend toward a light source.

Auxins and Phototropism The Darwins suspected that the tip of each seedling produced substances that regulated cell growth. Forty years later, these substances were identified and named **auxins.** **Auxins are produced in the apical meristem and are transported downward into the rest of the plant. They stimulate cell elongation.** When light hits one side of the stem, a higher concentration of auxins develops in the shaded part of the stem. This change in concentration stimulates cells on the dark side to elongate. As a result, the stem bends away from the shaded side and toward the light. Recent experiments have shown that auxins migrate toward the shaded side of the stem, possibly due to changes in membrane permeability in response to light.

Auxins and Gravitropism Auxins are also responsible for **gravitropism,** which is the tendency of a plant to grow in a direction in response to the force of gravity. By mechanisms that are still not understood, auxins build up on the lower sides of roots and stems. In stems, auxins stimulate cell elongation, helping turn the plant upright, as shown in **Figure 25–4.** In roots, however, the effects of auxins are exactly the opposite. There, auxins inhibit cell growth and elongation, causing the roots to grow downward.

Auxins are also involved in the way roots grow around objects in the soil. If a growing root is forced sideways by an obstacle such as a rock, auxins accumulate on the lower side of the root. Once again, high concentrations of auxins inhibit the elongation of root cells. The uninhibited cells on the top elongate more than the auxin-inhibited cells on the bottom of the root. As a result, the root grows downward.

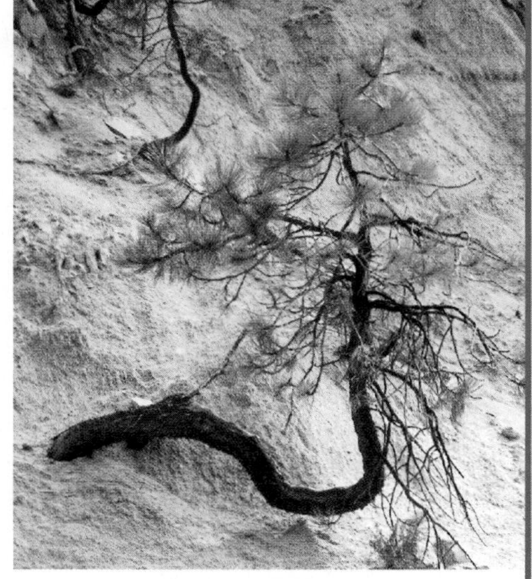

▶ **Figure 25–4** Auxins are responsible for the plant response called gravitropism. Auxins caused the tip of this tree stem to grow upright. **Comparing and Contrasting** *Compare how auxins affect the growth of stems and roots.*

Meet Diverse Needs

For students who learn best through visual presentation of material, use a long balloon and transparent tape to model the elongation of one side of a stem versus the other side of the stem. To represent a stem growing straight, blow the balloon up part way and hold the end closed. Then, ask a volunteer to apply a long piece of transparent tape lengthwise to one side of the balloon. Point out that the tape represents an area of low auxin concentration. Ask: **What do you predict will happen as the stem continues to grow?** (*It will curve inward relative to the low auxin concentration.*) Blow up the balloon so students can confirm their predictions. Ask: **Where is the concentration of auxins higher?** (*On the outside curve of the stem*) **What causes the stem to curve in this fashion?** (*High concentrations of auxin stimulate cells to elongate, so the cells on the outside of the curve are longer than the cells on the inside of the curve.*) **Learning modality: visual**

Build Science Skills

Predicting Divide the class into small groups, and give each group a small, fast-growing potted plant, such as a coleus plant. The activity works best if the plant is in a four-sided plastic pot. Ask each group to write a prediction of how the plant will react if the pot is placed on its side. Once the predictions are made, ask each group to find a location in the classroom to turn the pot on its side. (If the plant is in a round pot, students can prop the pot with books or other objects.) After a day or two, students should observe that all the plant stems have turned upward.

HISTORY OF SCIENCE

Charles Darwin is hailed as one of the greatest scientists in history. It is less well known, however, that he had an inauspicious beginning to his career. He failed both at medical school and in an attempt to become a minister. It was at Cambridge University that Darwin found his calling, under the tutelage of the botanist John Stevens Henslow. Around school, Darwin became known as "the man who walks with Henslow" because he spent many days in the field learning about plants from the professor. Darwin never lost his interest in plants, and late in his life he made great strides in understanding what he called heliotropism.

Answers to . . .

CHECKPOINT *In target cells or target tissue*

Figure 25–4 *Auxins cause stems to grow upward and roots to grow downward.*

25–1 (continued)

Build Science Skills

Applying Concepts Gather a few twigs with terminal buds and lateral buds that can be easily seen. Distribute the twigs for examination by small groups. Direct students' observations by asking: **Where will this stem grow in length?** (*It will lengthen at the tip.*) **What name is given to the region of rapidly dividing cells at the tip?** (*It is called the apical meristem.*) Point out that the meristematic cells are located in the bud. The bud itself is made up of newly formed, unopened leaves. If the bud is dormant, it will be covered by a ring of bud scales. Direct students to look for bud scales covering the bud. Explain that woody stems produce bud scales to protect the bud at the end of a growing season. The bud scales fall away in the spring when new growth begins. Ask: **When bud scales fall off, a set of rings called bud scale scars are left on the stem. Can bud scale scars be seen on your stem?** (*Answers will vary.*) **How can you determine the amount of growth that occurred during a year?** (*Because bud scale scars mark the location of former terminal buds, the distance between them indicates one year's growth.*) Next, call attention to the lateral buds on the side of the stem. Ask: **What do you think develops from the lateral buds?** (*New branches, leaves, and sometimes flowers develop from lateral buds.*)

Cytokinins

Meet Diverse Needs

The first cytokinin to be discovered was zeatin, which was isolated from corn kernels in 1964. Since then, three other cytokinins have been identified, including kinetin. Kinetin is the cytokinin that has been most used in research. Encourage students who need an extra challenge to learn more about cytokinins and their roles in plant growth and aging. Ask students to present their findings to the class in an oral report or poster display. **Learning modality: verbal**

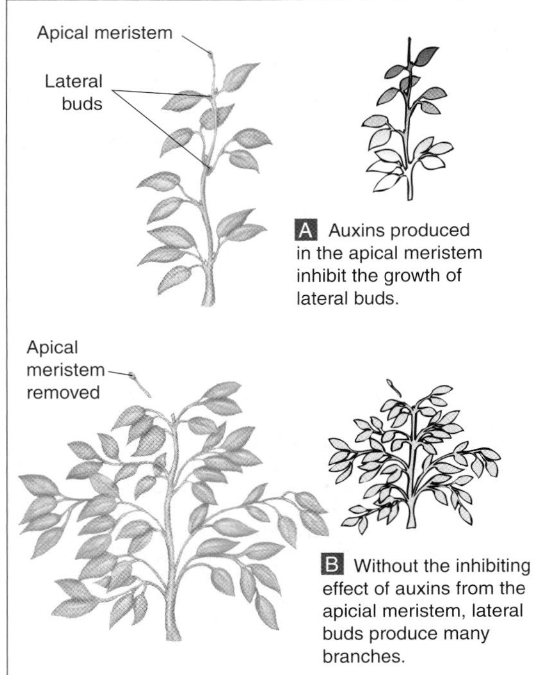

Apical meristem
Lateral buds
A Auxins produced in the apical meristem inhibit the growth of lateral buds.
Apical meristem removed
B Without the inhibiting effect of auxins from the apicial meristem, lateral buds produce many branches.

▲ **Figure 25–5** Apical dominance, shown here, is controlled by the relative amounts of auxins and cytokinins. During normal growth (A), lateral buds are kept dormant because of the production of auxins in the apical meristem. If the apical meristem is removed (B), the concentration of auxins drops. **Cytokinins then stimulate cell division and the growth of lateral buds.**

Auxins and Branching Auxins also regulate cell division in meristems. As a stem grows in length, it produces lateral buds, as shown in **Figure 25–5.** A **lateral bud** is a meristematic area on the side of a stem that gives rise to side branches. Most lateral buds do not start growing right away. The reason for this delay is that growth at the lateral buds is inhibited by auxins. Because auxins move out from the apical meristem, the closer a bud is to the stem's tip, the more it is inhibited. This phenomenon is called **apical dominance.**

Although not all gardeners have heard of auxins, most of them know how to overcome apical dominance. If you snip off the tip of a plant, the side branches begin to grow more quickly, resulting in a rounder, fuller plant. Why does this happen? When the tip is removed, the apical meristem—the source of the growth-inhibiting auxins—goes with it. Without the influence of auxins, meristems in the side branches grow more rapidly, changing the overall shape of the plant.

Auxinlike Weed Killers Chemists have produced many compounds that mimic the effects of auxins. Because high concentrations of auxins inhibit growth, many of these compounds are used as **herbicides,** which are compounds that are toxic to plants. Herbicides include a chemical known as 2,4-D (2,4-dichlorophenoxyacetic acid), which is used to kill weeds. A mixture containing 2,4-D was used as Agent Orange, a chemical defoliant sprayed during the Vietnam War.

CHECKPOINT *What role do auxins play in apical dominance?*

Cytokinins

Cytokinins are plant hormones that are produced in growing roots and in developing fruits and seeds. **In plants, cytokinins stimulate cell division and the growth of lateral buds, and cause dormant seeds to sprout.** Cytokinins also delay the aging of leaves and play important roles in the early stages of plant growth.

Cytokinins often produce effects opposite to those of auxins. For example, auxins stimulate cell elongation, whereas cytokinins inhibit elongation and cause cells to grow thicker. Auxins inhibit the growth of lateral buds, whereas cytokinins stimulate lateral bud growth. Recent experiments show that the rate of cell growth in most plants is determined by the ratio of the concentration of auxins to cytokinins. In growing plants, therefore, the relative concentrations of auxins, cytokinins, and other hormones determine how the plant grows.

FACTS AND FIGURES

Hanging tight
Growers of apples and citrus fruits used to lose considerable amounts of their crop when fruits fell from trees before harvest time. Now, orchards are often sprayed with synthetic auxins, such as 2-4-D, to induce fruits to remain on trees longer. The auxins apparently retard the formation of the abscission layer that forms between the fruit petiole and the stem.

Analyzing Data

Auxins and Plant Growth

Auxins affect plant growth in a variety of ways. This graph shows the results of experiments in which carrot cells were grown in the presence of varying concentrations of auxins. The orange line on the graph shows the growth pattern of the carrot plants' roots. The green line shows the growth pattern of the carrot plants' stems.

1. **Analyzing Data** At what auxin concentration are the stems stimulated to grow the most?
2. **Analyzing Data** How is the growth of the roots affected by the auxin concentration at which stems grow the most?
3. **Drawing Conclusions** Use the data in the graph to describe the relationship between the concentration of auxins and the growth of carrot plant stems.
4. **Inferring** If you were a carrot farmer, what concentration of auxin should you apply to your fields to produce the largest-sized carrots?

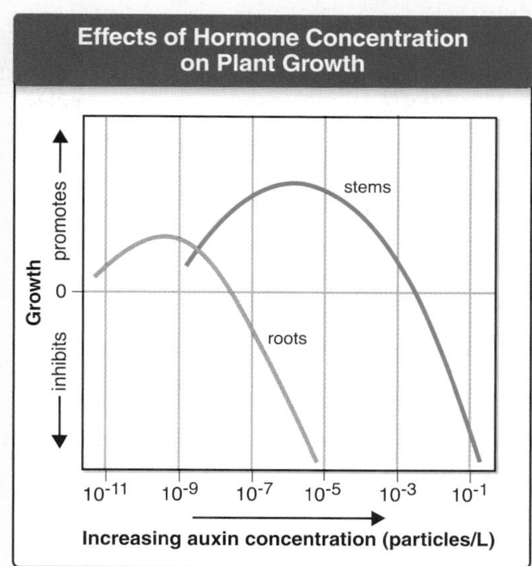

Analyzing Data

The graph shows how carrot cells respond to varying concentrations of auxins. Review with students how data are shown on the graph: increasing auxin concentration is shown on the *x*-axis and plant growth is shown on the *y*-axis. The effects on stem and root cells are shown using green and orange lines, respectively.

Answers

1. Maximum stem growth occurs at about 10^{-6} particles/L.
2. That concentration inhibits the growth of roots.
3. Concentrations between approximately 10^{-9} and 10^{-3} particles/L promote stem growth. Concentrations above about 10^{-2} particles/L inhibit stem growth.
4. Because carrots are roots, a concentration of approximately 10^{-10} to 10^{-9} particles/L would produce the largest-sized carrots.

Gibberellins

For years, farmers in Japan knew of a disease that weakened rice plants by causing them to grow unusually tall. They called the disease the "foolish seedling" disease. In 1926, Japanese biologist Eiichi Kurosawa discovered that this extraordinary growth was caused by a fungus: *Gibberella fujikuroi*. His experiments showed that the fungus produced a growth-promoting substance that was named **gibberellin.**

Before long, other researchers had learned that plants themselves produce more than 60 similar compounds, all of which are now known as gibberellins. **Gibberellins produce dramatic increases in size, particularly in stems and fruit.** Their effects on a flower are shown in **Figure 25–6.** Gibberellins are also produced by seed tissue and are responsible for the rapid early growth of many plants.

How were gibberellins discovered?

▼ **Figure 25–6 Gibberellins cause an increase in the overall size of plants and individual plant structures.** Their effect can be seen in the difference between an untreated geranium flower (left) and a geranium flower treated with gibberellin (right).

Gibberellins

Demonstration

Use this simple experiment to demonstrate the effect of gibberellins on plant growth. First, plant wheat seeds in soil in two flats or other small containers, such as cutoff plastic milk jugs. After the seedlings grow to about 3 centimeters high, water one container with a gibberellin solution and the other with plain water. (Gibberellic acid is available from biological supply companies. To use it, dissolve about 25 milligrams in a few milliliters of 70% ethyl alcohol, then mix with 1 liter of distilled water. Spray solutions of gibberellic acid may also be available at nurseries or garden stores.) Students should see a marked difference in the growth of the treated and untreated seedlings.

TEACHER TO TEACHER

To illustrate the effects of ethylene on the ripening of fruit, I set up a simple experiment for students to participate in and observe. I bring to class several pears, apples, and bananas in different stages of ripeness—none, though, that are overly ripe. I ask students to predict which would ripen first: a combination of the fruits left out in the classroom exposed to light or a similar combination of fruits enclosed in a paper bag. I encourage students to formulate a hypothesis and identify the variables in the experiment. Then, we set up the experiment and observe the fruit each day. After a few days, students conclude that the fruit in the paper bag ripen first, because the bag holds the ethylene around the fruit more than the fruit left in the open.

–Mary Colvard
Biology Teacher
Cobleskill-Richmondville High School
Cobleskill, NY

Answers to . . .

CHECKPOINT *Auxins produced in the apical meristem inhibit the growth of lateral buds. The closer a bud is to a stem's tip, the more it is inhibited, a phenomenon called apical dominance.*

CHECKPOINT *Eiichi Kurosawa, a Japanese biologist, discovered that a fungus,* Gibberella fujikuroi, *caused rice plants to grow unusually tall.*

25–1 (continued)

Ethylene

Make Connections

Health Science Show students a fruit from the supermarket that has the color of a ripe fruit, but feels hard and unripened. Ask: **Does this fruit look good enough to eat?** (*Most students will probably say yes.*) Hand the fruit to a student, and ask: **Does this fruit feel good enough to eat?** (*Probably not*) Encourage students to share their experiences with fruit that looked good but didn't taste ripe. Challenge interested students to find out about the nutritional value of unripened fruits treated with synthetic ethylene compared to fruits that ripen naturally.

SCIENCE NEWS®

Encourage students to visit **www.phschool.com** for current information on this topic.

3 ASSESS

Evaluate Understanding

Call on students at random to identify the four types of plant hormones and explain their roles in the control of plant growth.

Reteach

Have students make a table that lists and describes the effects of the four types of plant hormones.

ALTERNATIVE ASSESSMENT

Check that the clues and answers in the students' puzzles accurately reflect the information in the section.

Use iText to review the key concepts in Section 25–1.

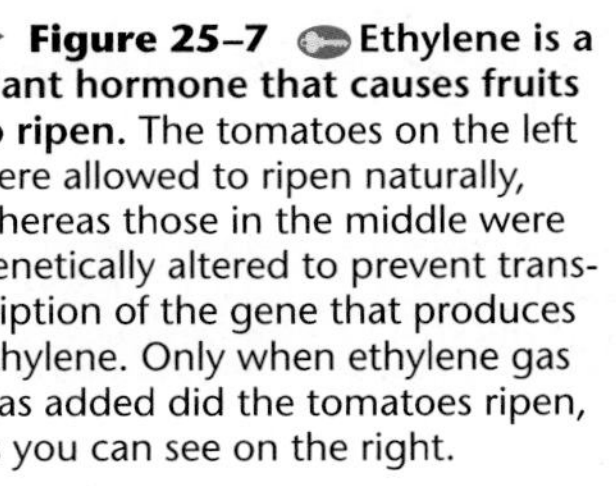

▶ **Figure 25–7** **Ethylene is a plant hormone that causes fruits to ripen.** The tomatoes on the left were allowed to ripen naturally, whereas those in the middle were genetically altered to prevent transcription of the gene that produces ethylene. Only when ethylene gas was added did the tomatoes ripen, as you can see on the right.

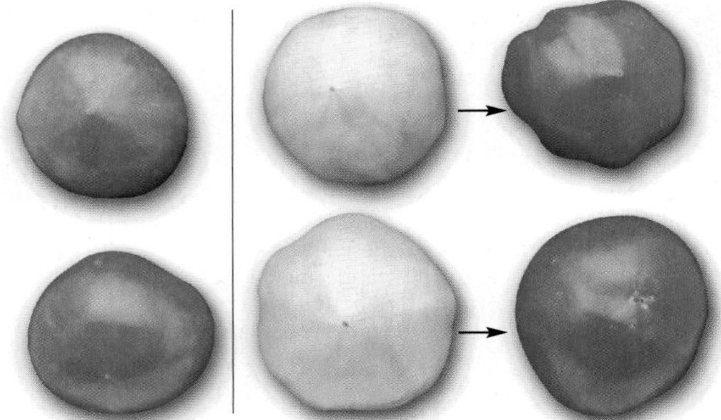

Ethylene

When natural gas was used in city street lamps in the nineteenth century, people noticed that trees along the street suffered leaf loss and stunted growth. This effect was eventually traced to **ethylene,** one of the minor components of natural gas.

Today, scientists know that plants produce their own ethylene, and that it affects plants in a number of ways. **In response to auxins, fruit tissues release small amounts of the hormone ethylene. Ethylene then stimulates fruits to ripen.**

Commercial producers of fruit sometimes use this hormone to control the ripening process. Many crops, including lemons and tomatoes, shown in **Figure 25–7,** are picked before they ripen so that they can be handled without damage to the fruit. Just before they are delivered to market, the fruits are treated with synthetic ethylene to produce a ripe color quickly. This trick does not always produce a ripe flavor, which is one reason why naturally ripened fruits often taste much better.

KEEP CURRENT WITH . . . **SCIENCE NEWS®**

To find out more about the topics in this chapter, go to: **www.phschool.com**

25–1 Section Assessment

1. **Key Concept** What effects do hormones have within a growing plant?
2. **Key Concept** List the four main types of hormones. What parts of the plant does each hormone affect?
3. Compare the effects of auxins and cytokinins on plant growth.
4. **Critical Thinking Inferring** A person who trims trees for a living must know the effect of apical dominance on the shape of trees. Explain.

iTEXT Assessment Use iText to review the important concepts in Section 25–1.

ALTERNATIVE ASSESSMENT

Crossword Puzzle Create a crossword puzzle that reviews some of the information you learned in this section. Then, exchange puzzles with a classmate to complete.

25–1 Section Assessment

1. They control a plant's branching pattern, the rate at which its stems elongate, and the plant's responses to environmental conditions.
2. Auxins: stems, roots, lateral buds; cytokinins: lateral buds, seeds, leaves; gibberellins: stems, fruits, flowers; ethylene: fruits
3. Auxins stimulate cell elongation; cytokinins inhibit elongation and cause cells to grow thicker. Auxins inhibit lateral bud growth; cytokinins stimulate lateral bud growth.
4. The person will know to remove the apical meristem to make the tree grow rounder and fuller or leave it to make the tree grow taller and narrower.

25–2 Plant Responses

Like all living things, plants respond to changes in their environments. Some biologists call these responses "plant behavior," which is a useful way of thinking about them. Plants generally do not respond as quickly as animals do, but that does not make their responses any less effective. Some plant responses are so fast that even animals cannot keep up with them!

Guide for Reading

Key Concepts
- What are plant tropisms?
- What is photoperiodism?
- How do deciduous plants prepare for winter?

Vocabulary
tropism
thigmotropism
short-day plant
long-day plant
photoperiodism
phytochrome
dormancy
abscission layer

Reading Strategy: Using Visuals Before you read, preview **Figure 25–10.** From this figure, what can you conclude about the topic of photoperiodism?

Tropisms

Plants change their patterns and directions of growth in response to a multitude of cues. The responses of plants to environmental stimuli are called **tropisms,** from a Greek word that means "turning."  **Plant tropisms include gravitropism, phototropism, and thigmotropism. Each of these responses demonstrates the ability of plants to respond effectively to conditions in which they live.**

Gravitropism and Phototropism You have already read about gravitropism, the response of a plant to gravity, and phototropism, the response of a plant to light. Both of these responses are controlled by the hormone auxin. Gravitropism causes the shoot of a germinating seed to grow out of the soil—against the force of gravity. It also causes the roots of a plant to grow with the force of gravity and into the soil.

Phototropism causes a plant to grow toward a light source. This response can be so quick that young seedlings reorient themselves in a matter of hours.

Thigmotropism The response of plants to touch is called **thigmotropism** (thig-MAH-troh-piz-um). A plant that is touched regularly, for example, may be stunted in its growth—sometimes quite dramatically. Another example of thigmotropism is the growth of vines and climbing plants. The stems of these plants do not grow straight up. Rather, the growing tip of each stem points sideways and twists in circles as the shoot grows. When the tip encounters an object, it quickly wraps around it. Some climbing plants have long, twisting leaf tips or petioles that wrap tightly around small objects. Other plants, such as the grapes in **Figure 25–8,** have extra growths called tendrils that emerge near the base of the leaf and wrap tightly around any object they encounter.

▶ **Figure 25–8** **Plant tropisms include gravitropism, phototropism, and thigmotropism.** One effect of thigmotropism—growth in response to touch—is that plants curl and twist around objects, as shown by the stems of this grapevine.

Section 25–2

1 FOCUS

Objectives

25.2.1 ***Explain*** what plant tropisms are.
25.2.2 ***Explain*** what photoperiodism is.
25.2.3 ***Describe*** how temperate plants prepare for winter.

Guide for Reading

Vocabulary Preview

Ask students to review the meaning of the term *phototropism* from Section 25–1. (*The tendency of a plant to grow toward a source of light*) Then, call students' attention to the Vocabulary term *photoperiodism* and challenge them to infer its meaning. Have students skim the text to find the term and verify their predictions.

Reading Strategy

As students read the section, have them use the blue heads and the green heads to create an outline. They should include relevant details under each heading.

2 INSTRUCT

Tropisms

Building Science Skills

Inferring Point out that in environments such as tropical rain forests where there is dense growth, there are many varieties of vining plants. Ask: **How are vines an adaptation to that kind of environment?** (*Vines can compete with larger plants, such as trees, for sunlight by climbing on the tree trunks to reach the tops of trees where more light is available.*)

SECTION RESOURCES

Print:
- ***Laboratory Manual B,*** Chapter 25 Lab
- ***Teaching Resources,*** Section Review 25–2
- ***Guided Reading and Study Workbook,*** Section 25–2

Technology:
- ***iText,*** Section 25–2

25–2 (continued)

Rapid Responses

Demonstration

Obtain a *Mimosa pudica.* Ask a volunteer to touch the plant at the end of its leaves so the other students can watch as the leaves fold closed. Challenge students to infer how this response is an adaptative advantage for this plant. (*Students might infer that the delicate leaves are less prone to damage by insects and other animals when they are folded closed.*) Have a volunteer time how long it takes for the leaves to reopen.

Quick Lab

Objective Students will be able to observe the effects of phototropism on plants.

Skills Focus **Observing, Inferring**

Materials scissors, masking tape, cardboard box, cardboard dividers, 4 bean seeds, small flower pot containing soil

Time 20 minutes for set up; 5 minutes every 2 to 3 days for 2 weeks for observations

Advanced Prep Collect copy-paper boxes from an office or copy center. To save time, cut the holes in the boxes before class.

Strategies

- Have students work in small groups to reduce the space needed for the box mazes.
- After placing the boxes next to a light source and covering them, students should secure the covers with weights or easily removable tape to prevent the seedlings from pushing the box lids up and growing over the walls of the maze.
- Emphasize that the lids should be opened only briefly to water and observe the plants.

Expected Outcome The seedlings will grow around the barriers toward the source of light at the opening of the box.

Analyze and Conclude

1. The seedlings grew horizontally and around the barriers to reach the source of light at the opening of the box.
2. Phototropism caused the plants to grow toward the source of light.

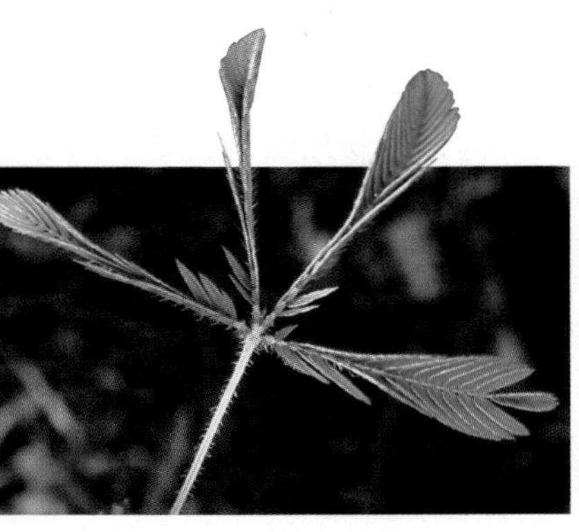

Figure 25–9 The mimosa plant responds to touch by folding in its leaves quickly. This response is produced by decreased osmotic pressure in cells near the base of each leaflet. **Inferring** ***What adaptive value might rapid responses have for a plant?***

Rapid Responses

Some plant responses do not involve growth. In fact, they are so rapid that it would be a mistake to call them tropisms. **Figure 25–9** shows what happens if you touch a leaf of *Mimosa pudica,* appropriately called the "sensitive plant." Within only two or three seconds, its two leaflets fold together completely. The secret to this movement is changes in osmotic pressure. Recall that osmotic pressure is caused by the diffusion of water into cells. The leaves are held apart due to osmotic pressure where the two leaflets join. When the leaf is touched, cells near the center of the leaflet pump out ions and lose water due to osmosis. Pressure from cells on the underside of the leaf, which do not lose water, force the leaflets together.

The carnivorous Venus' flytrap also demonstrates rapid responses. When a fly triggers sensory cells on the inside of the flytrap's leaf, electrical signals are sent from cell to cell. A combination of changes in osmotic pressure and cell wall expansion causes the leaf to snap shut, trapping the insect inside.

Quick Lab

Can a plant find its way through a maze?

Materials scissors, masking tape, cardboard box, cardboard dividers, 4 bean seeds, small flower pot containing soil

Procedure 

1. Make a maze by taping cardboard dividers upright inside a cardboard box as shown. Cut a hole in the side of the box at the end of the maze. **CAUTION:** *Use care when handling scissors.*
2. Plant 4 bean seeds in a small flowerpot of soil. Water the flowerpot.
3. Place the flowerpot in the box at the beginning of the maze. Close the box so that the only light in the box comes from the hole that you cut. **CAUTION:** *Wash your hands with soap and warm water after handling soil or plants.*

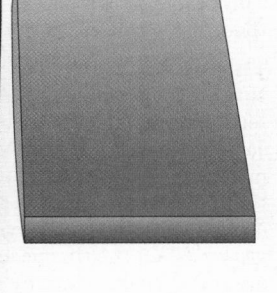

4. Over the next 2 weeks, open the box every 2 to 3 days to water the seeds and observe the seedlings. Record your observations each day.

Analyze and Conclude

1. **Observing** Summarize what happened to the seedlings.
2. **Inferring** What caused the plants to grow the way they did?

PRESENTATIONS MADE EASY!

The Presentation Assistant Plus contains the Prentice Hall Presentation Pro and the Transparencies, which provide easy-to-follow visual support for every step of this section. If you have a computer presentation station, use Prentice Hall Presentation Pro for Section 25–2, or use the transparencies listed here.

Section 25–2: **Interest Grabber**
Section Outline
Photoperiodism and Flowering

Photoperiodism

"To everything there is a season." Nowhere is this more evident than in the regular cycles of plant growth. Year after year, some plants flower in the spring, others in summer, and still others in the fall. Plants such as chrysanthemums and poinsettias flower when days are short and are therefore called **short-day plants.** Plants such as spinach and irises flower when days are long and are therefore known as **long-day plants.**

How do all these plants manage to time their flowering so precisely? In the early 1920s, scientists discovered that tobacco plants flower according to the number of hours of light and darkness they receive. Additional research showed that many other plants also respond to periods of light and darkness, a response called **photoperiodism.** This type of response is summarized in **Figure 25–10.** **Photoperiodism in plants is responsible for the timing of seasonal activities such as flowering and growth.**

It was later discovered that a plant pigment called **phytochrome** (FYT-uh-krohm) is responsible for photoperiodism. Phytochrome absorbs red light and activates a number of signaling pathways within plant cells. By mechanisms that are still not understood completely, plants respond to regular changes in these pathways. These changes determine the patterns of a variety of plant responses.

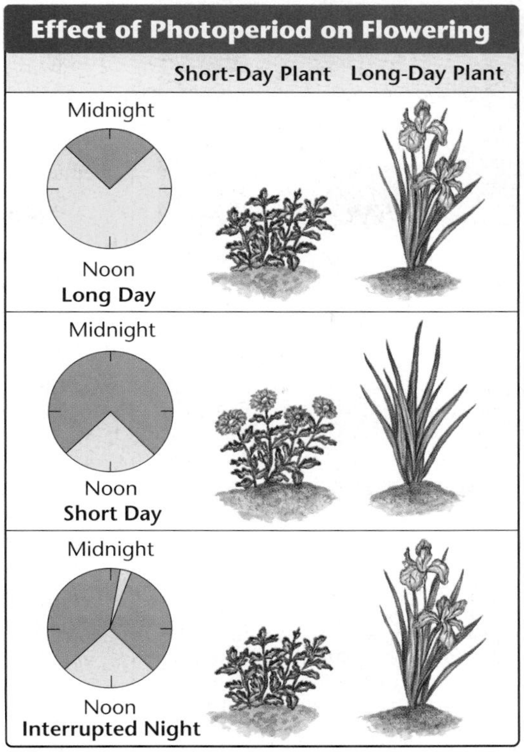

Effect of Photoperiod on Flowering

▲ **Figure 25–10** **Photoperiodism controls the timing of flowering and seasonal growth.** The response of flowering, shown here, is controlled by the amount of darkness plants receive. Short-day plants, such as chrysanthemums, flower only when exposed to an extended period of darkness every night—and thus a short period of light during the day. Long-day plants, such as irises, flower when exposed to a short period of darkness or to a long period of darkness interrupted by a brief period of light.

Winter Dormancy

Phytochrome also regulates the changes in activity that prepare many plants for dormancy as winter approaches. **Dormancy** is the period during which an organism's growth and activity decrease or stop.

The changes that prepare a plant for dormancy are important adaptations that protect plants over the cold winter months. **As cold weather approaches, deciduous plants turn off photosynthetic pathways, transport materials from leaves to roots, and seal leaves off from the rest of the plant.** In early autumn, the shorter days and lower temperatures gradually reduce the efficiency of photosynthesis. With these changing conditions, the plant gains very little by keeping its leaves alive. In fact, the thin, delicate leaves produced by most flowering plants would have little chance of surviving a tough winter, and their continued presence would be costly in terms of water loss.

CHECKPOINT *What is dormancy? What changes do plants undergo as colder weather approaches?*

Photoperiodism

Use Community Resources

Invite a floriculturist or a manager of a greenhouse to speak to the class about photoperiodism and how plants are brought to bloom for specific seasons. For example, ask how poinsettias are grown so that they are in bloom for the winter. Before the speaker arrives, have students develop a list of other questions to ask.

Winter Dormancy

Address Misconceptions

Some students might think that dormancy is induced only by low temperatures. Ask: **What is dormancy?** (*The period during which an organism's growth and activity decrease or stop*) **What, other than low temperatures, do you think could cause a plant to become dormant?** (*Students might suggest hot, dry conditions*) Point out that many plants in environments with seasonal dry periods go through a time of dormancy. The plants may lose their leaves and form drought-resistant buds, in a similar way to how plants respond in winter dormancy. Many seeds also have dormancy periods and will not germinate immediately after they are released from the parent plant. Some seeds remain dormant until they have the right temperature and moisture conditions for growth. Other seeds require a period of low temperatures or intense heat, such as from a forest fire, before they will germinate. Challenge students to infer the adaptative advantages of these different types of dormancy.

Answers to . . .

CHECKPOINT *Dormancy is the period during which an organism's growth and activity decrease or stop. Deciduous plants lose their leaves, form scales over buds, and produce ions and organic compounds.*

Figure 25–9 *Rapid responses might help reduce damage to leaves or, in the case of carnivorous plants, help the plant to capture prey.*

Building Science Skills

Observing Provide dormant tree branches for students to observe. (If dormant branches are not available, nondormant branches can be used.) Have students find an abscission layer. Ask: **What grew from this area?** (*A leaf*) Challenge students to find the small holes where the vascular bundles passed from the leaf into the branch. Ask: **Why is it important that the vascular system be sealed before the leaf drops off?** (*So that nutrients and water are not lost*) Have students locate a terminal bud. Ask: **How is this bud prepared to survive winter?** (*Thick, waxy scales form a protective layer around the new leaf buds, and ions and organic compounds are pumped into the vascular tissue to prevent the tree's sap from freezing.*)

3 ASSESS

Evaluate Understanding

Have students use the Vocabulary terms to create a concept map that summarizes the Key Concepts of the section.

Reteach

Ask students to create a table to compare and contrast the various plant responses discussed in the section.

MAKING CONNECTIONS

Check that students' proposed mechanisms agree with the process of natural selection as described in Chapter 15.

Use iText to review the key concepts in Section 25–2.

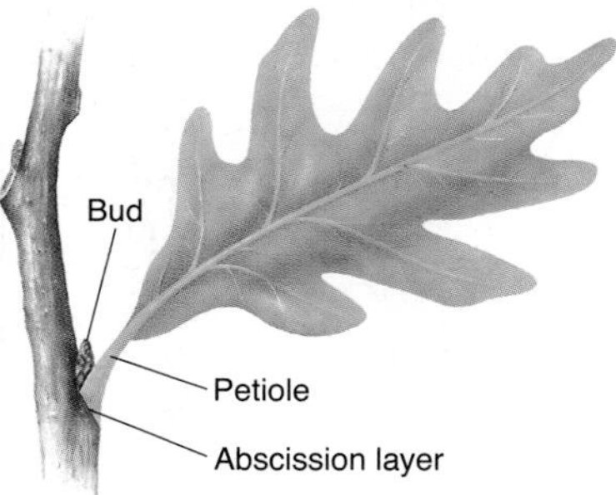

Figure 25–11 **Deciduous plants undergo changes in preparation for winter dormancy.** Photosynthetic pathways in leaves shut down (top). An abscission layer of cells forms at the petiole to seal the leaf off from the rest of the plant (bottom). Eventually, the leaf falls off.

Leaf Abscission In temperate regions, most flowering plants lose their leaves during the colder months. During the warm growing season, auxins are produced in leaves. At summer's end, the phytochrome in leaves absorbs less light as days shorten and nights become longer. Auxin production drops, but the production of ethylene increases. The change in the relative amounts of these two hormones starts a series of events that gradually shut down the leaf.

The chemical pathways for chlorophyll synthesis stop first. When light destroys the remaining green pigment, other pigments that have been present all along—including yellow and orange carotenoids—become visible for the first time. Production of new plant pigments—the reddish anthocyanins—begins in the autumn. The brilliant colors of autumn leaves are a direct result of these processes.

Behind the scenes, enzymes extract nutrients from the broken-down chlorophyll. These nutrients are then transported to other parts of the plant, where they are stored until spring. Every available carbohydrate is transported out of the leaf, and much of the leaf's water is extracted. Finally, an **abscission layer** of cells at the petiole seals the leaf off from the plant's vascular system. The location of the abscission layer is shown in **Figure 25–11.** Before long, the leaf falls to the ground, a sign that the tree is fully prepared for winter.

Overwintering of Meristems Hormones also produce important changes in apical meristems. Instead of continuing to produce leaves, meristems produce thick, waxy scales that form a protective layer around new leaf buds. Enclosed in its coat of scales, a terminal bud can survive the coldest winter days. At the onset of winter, xylem and phloem tissues pump themselves full of ions and organic compounds. These molecules act like antifreeze in a car, preventing the tree's sap from freezing, thus making it possible to survive the bitter cold.

25–2 Section Assessment

1. **Key Concept** Describe three types of plant tropisms.
2. **Key Concept** Compare short-day and long-day plants. Which type of plant is likely to bloom in the summer?
3. **Key Concept** What changes occur in plants before winter? How do these changes help the plant to survive?
4. Describe the process of leaf abscission.
5. **Critical Thinking Designing Experiments** How could a garden store owner determine what light conditions are needed for a particular flowering plant to bloom? Design a controlled experiment to find out.

iTEXT **Assessment** Use iText to review the important concepts in Section 25–2.

MAKING CONNECTIONS

Evolution Review what you learned about evolution by natural selection in Chapter 15. Then, using what you know about natural selection, describe how plant adaptations for dormancy may have developed over time.

25–2 Section Assessment

1. Gravitropism: response to gravity; phototropism: response to light; thigmotropism: response to touch
2. Short-day plants: flower when days are short; long-day plants: flower when days are long. Long-day plants.
3. Deciduous plants lose their leaves, form scales over buds, and produce ions and organic compounds. Losing leaves reduces water loss, formation of scales protects buds from cold, and the production of ions and organic compounds acts as an antifreeze.
4. Auxin production drops and production of ethylene increases; chlorophyll synthesis stops; enzymes extract nutrients from chlorophyll; carbohydrates and water are transported out of leaf; abscission layer seals off vascular system; leaf falls.
5. Students' experiments should involve exposing the plant to light patterns.

25–3 Plant Adaptations

Flowering plants grow in a variety of places—in deserts, in ponds, on mountaintops, in salt water, in polar regions, and in the tropics. Angiosperms can survive in these areas because they have evolved features through natural selection that allow them to live in each location. In this section, we explore how plants have become adapted to various environments through evolutionary change.

Aquatic Plants

Aquatic plants typically grow in mud that is saturated with water and nearly devoid of oxygen.  **To take in sufficient oxygen, many aquatic plants have tissues with large air-filled spaces through which oxygen can diffuse.** In waterlilies, shown in **Figure 25–12,** there are large open spaces in the long petioles that reach from the leaves down to the roots at the bottom. Oxygen diffuses from these open spaces into the roots.

Many other plants show similar adaptations. Several species of mangrove trees grow in shallow water along tropical seacoasts. Mangroves survive because they have specialized air roots with air spaces in them, just like waterlily stems. These spaces conduct air down to the buried roots, allowing the root tissues to respire normally. Stately bald cypress trees thrive in freshwater swamps in the southern United States. These trees grow structures called knees, which protrude above the water. The knees bring oxygen-rich air down to the roots.

The reproductive adaptations of aquatic plants include seeds that can float in water and delay germination until after long periods of flooding. Many aquatic plants grow quickly after germination, thereby extending the growing shoot above the surface of the water.

Guide for Reading

Key Concepts
- How are plants adapted to different environments?
- How do plants obtain nutrients from sources other than photosynthesis?
- How do plants defend themselves from insects?

Vocabulary
xerophyte
epiphyte

Reading Strategy: Using Prior Knowledge Before you read, list the different environments in which plants grow. Next to each environment listed, describe adaptations you might expect to find in plants. As you read, compare your predictions with information about different plant adaptations.

▼ **Figure 25–12 Aquatic plants have air-filled spaces in their tissues that allow for the uptake and diffusion of oxygen.** These waterlilies transport oxygen from the air to their roots through large spaces in their petioles.

SECTION RESOURCES

Print:
- ***Teaching Resources,*** Section Review 25–3, Chapter 25 Real-World Lab
- ***Guided Reading and Study Workbook,*** Section 25–3

Technology:
- ***iText,*** Section 25–3

Section 25–3

1 FOCUS

Objectives

25.3.1 ***Summarize*** how plants are adapted to different environments.
25.3.2 ***Describe*** how plants obtain nutrients.
25.3.3 ***Explain*** how plants use chemical defenses.

Guide for Reading

Vocabulary Preview

Explain the root word *phyte* comes from a Greek word meaning "plant." Have students skim the text to find out what kind of plants xerophytes and epiphytes are.

Reading Strategy

To help students get started making their list of different environments, have them look at the figures and read the captions in the section.

2 INSTRUCT

Aquatic Plants

Build Science Skills

Inferring Provide specimens of waterlily leaves, water hyacinth plants, and any other aquatic plants that you can obtain. Invite students to observe the plants and look for special adaptations that the plants have for aquatic environments. You might cut open the long petiole of a waterlily leaf so students can observe the large air spaces through which oxygen diffuses. Also point out the stomata on the upper surface of the waterlily leaf. Ask: **How are these stomata an adaptation to an aquatic environment?** (*They allow the plant to take in carbon dioxide directly from the air.*) **Why do you think there are no stomata on the bottom of the leaf?** (*They would be useless for exchanging gases because they are under the water level.*) Challenge students to make inferences about other adaptations they observe.

25–3 (continued)

Salt-Tolerant Plants

Meet Diverse Needs

Some students might need to review the process of osmosis, which was discussed in Chapter 7. Ask: **What is osmosis?** (*The diffusion of water through a selectively permeable membrane*) Remind students that a selectively permeable membrane allows some substances to pass through, but not others. Then, have students turn back to page 186 and look at Figure 7–17. Ask: **Where is the concentration of water molecules higher, inside the cell or outside the cell?** (*Outside the cell*) **In which direction will the water move?** (*From outside to inside*) **Learning modality: visual**

Desert Plants

Word Origins

Hydrophytes live in water.

Build Science Skills

Inferring Display various cactuses, a crown-of-thorns plant, and any other desert plants that you can obtain. Invite students to observe the plants and look for special adaptations that the plants have for a desert environment. Point to a cactus and ask: **Where are the leaves on this plant?** (*The spines are modified leaves.*) **What function do the spines serve?** (*They provide defense against predators that might try to eat the plant.*) **Where do you think photosynthesis is carried out in this cactus?** (*In the green stem*) **What other function does the stem serve?** (*It stores water.*) Challenge students to make inferences about other adaptations they observe.

Word Origins

Xerophyte comes from the Greek words *xeros,* meaning "dry," and *phyton,* meaning "plant." **Where do you think hydrophytes live?**

Salt-Tolerant Plants

When plant roots take in dissolved minerals, a difference in the concentration of water molecules is created between the root cells and the surrounding soil. This concentration difference causes water to enter the root cells by osmosis. For plants that grow in salt water, such as mangroves, this means taking in much more salt than the plant can use. The roots of salt-tolerant plants are adapted to salt concentrations that would quickly destroy the root hairs on most plants. The leaves of these plants have specialized cells that pump salt out of the plant tissues and onto the leaf surfaces, where it is washed off by rain.

Desert Plants

Desert plants, also called **xerophytes,** must survive where strong sun and daytime heat combine with sandy soil and infrequent rainfall. Instead of staying near the surface, rainwater sinks rapidly through desert soils. The hot, dry air quickly removes moisture from any wet surface, making life difficult for plants. **Plant adaptations to a desert climate include extensive roots, reduced leaves, and thick stems that can store water.**

One familiar group of desert plants is the cactuses (family Cactaceae), shown in **Figure 25–13.** Cactuses have root systems that either spread out for long distances just beneath the soil surface or that reach deep down into the soil. In addition, the roots have many hairs that quickly absorb water after a rainstorm, before the water sinks too deeply into the soil.

To reduce water loss due to transpiration, cactus leaves have been reduced to thin, sharp spines. Cactuses also have thick green stems that carry out photosynthesis and are adapted to store water. The stems of cactuses swell during rainy periods and shrivel during dry spells, when the plants are forced to use up their water reserves.

▼ **Figure 25–13** **Desert plants typically have deep roots; reduced leaves; and thick, photosynthetic stems.** Spines, which are visible on many of these plants, are actually reduced leaves that carry out little or no photosynthesis and, as a result, lose little water. Most of the plant's photosynthesis is carried out in its fleshy stem.

TIME SAVER **PRESENTATIONS MADE EASY!**

The Presentation Assistant Plus contains the Prentice Hall Presentation Pro and the Transparencies, which provide easy-to-follow visual support for every step of this section. If you have a computer presentation station, use Prentice Hall Presentation Pro for Section 25–3, or use the transparencies listed here.

Section 25–3: **Interest Grabber**
Section Outline
Compare/Contrast Table

Seeds of many desert plants can remain dormant for years, germinating only when sufficient moisture guarantees them a chance for survival. Other desert plants have bulbs, tubers, or other specialized stems that can remain dormant for years. When rain does come, the plants mature, flower, and set seed in a matter of weeks or even days, before the water disappears.

CHECKPOINT *How are the roots and leaves of desert plants specialized for the environment in which they live?*

Nutritional Specialists

Some plants grow in environments that have low concentrations of nutrients in the soil. **Plants that have specialized features for obtaining nutrients include carnivorous plants and parasites.**

Carnivorous Plants Some plants live in bogs, wet and acidic environments where there is very little or no nitrogen present. Because conditions are too wet and too acidic, bacteria that cause decay cannot survive. Without these bacteria, neither plant nor animal material is broken down into the nutrients plants can use.

A number of plants that live in these habitats obtain nutrients using specialized leaves that trap and digest insects. Pitcher plants drown their prey in pitcher-shaped leaves that hold rainwater and digestive enzymes. Sundews trap insects on leaf hairs tipped with sticky secretions. The best known of the carnivorous plants is the Venus' flytrap, shown in **Figure 25–14.** This plant has leaf blades that are hinged at the middle. If an insect touches the trigger hairs on the leaf, the leaf folds up suddenly, trapping the animal inside. Over a period of several days, the leaf secretes enzymes that digest the insect and release nitrogen for the plant to use.

Parasites Some plants extract water and nutrients directly from a host plant. Like all parasites, these plants harm their host organisms and sometimes even pose a serious threat to other species. The dodder plant *Cuscuta* is a parasitic plant that has no chlorophyll and thus does not produce its own food. The plant grows directly into the vascular tisue of its host. There, it extracts nutrients and water. Mistletoe grows as a parasite on many plants, including conifers in the western United States.

Epiphytes

Plants that grow directly on the bodies of other plants are known as **epiphytes**. Epiphytes are attached to the plants they grow on, but, unlike parasites, they gather their own moisture, generally from rainfall, and produce their own food. One of the most common epiphytes found in warm, moist regions is Spanish moss. This plant is actually not a moss at all but a member of the bromeliad family. Many orchids are epiphytes as well, growing on the surfaces of other plants.

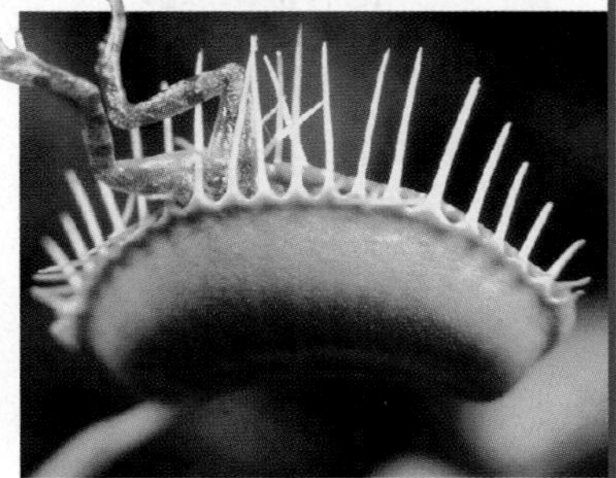

Carnivorous Plant: Venus' flytrap

Parasite: Mistletoe

Figure 25–14 **Plants that have specialized features for obtaining nutrients include carnivorous plants and parasites.** Carnivorous plants, such as the Venus' flytrap, digest insects—and occasionally frogs—as a source of nutrients. Parasites grow into the tissues of their host plant and extract water and nutrients, causing harm to the host.

Nutritional Specialists

Meet Diverse Needs

Scientists speculate that carnivorous plants evolved as plants in nitrogen-poor soil collected rainwater in depressions on their leaves. Insects landing in the water drowned and decomposed, providing the plants with needed nutrients. Thus, plants in nitrogen-poor environments with certain shaped leaves had a reproductive advantage. Eventually, the leaves became more specialized for capturing insects and other small animals. Encourage students who need a challenge to find out about the different types of carnivorous plants. Have students make an oral report to the class that includes pictures of various carnivorous plants. **Learning modality: verbal**

Epiphytes

Use Community Resources

Visit a local public conservatory or botanical garden so students can observe examples of epiphytes, including orchids and bromeliads. Some commercial greenhouses grow epiphytes and may be willing to offer a tour. Point out the aerial roots of these plants, and explain that they are modified with a spongy outer layer that absorbs moisture in the air. Ask: **In what type of environment do you think epiphytes naturally live?** (*In a humid environment such as tropical rain forest*) Point out how bromeliads trap water in the spaces around the base of their leaves. Ask: **How do you think this helps bromeliads survive in their environment?** (*Because bromeliads do not have roots in the ground, this is a way for these plants to store water for times when there is less water available.*) Challenge students to identify other adaptations of epiphytes.

FACTS AND FIGURES

Plant carnivores

Carnivorous plants have adaptations in their lives that provide the plants with needed nutrients. The tentacle-covered leaves of the sundew are one of four kinds of insect-trapping mechanisms. Another is found in the Venus' flytrap. Its leaves are fashioned like a steel trap, with two halves of the blade hinged along a middle rib. Stiff projections along the leaf margins trap an insect when it touches trigger hairs on the leaf surface. Still another mechanism is found in bladderworts, which float in shallow water. These plants have stomach-shaped bladders at the base of their leaves. When an insect touches a trigger hair, a "trapdoor" springs open and water rushes into the bladder, taking the insect in with it. Finally, the leaves of pitcher plants are formed like vases. When an insect ventures to the bottom of the "vase," a pool of liquid and a slippery inner surface make it difficult for the insect to climb out.

Answer to . . .

CHECKPOINT *Desert plants have extensive root systems that spread out for long distances just beneath the surface or grow down deep into the soil. The roots have many root hairs to absorb water. To reduce water loss, the leaves are often reduced to spines.*

Chemical Defenses

Make Connections

Health Science Point out that many common plants are poisonous to humans. Even some familiar food plants have poisonous parts. For example, the seeds of peaches, apricots, and cherries are poisonous, as are the leaves of potatoes and tomatoes. Emphasize to students that they should never put any part of a plant in their mouth unless they are sure that it is harmless. Explain that some poisonous plants, such as poison ivy, cause irritation to the skin. Encourage interested students to create a chart for a bulletin board of local poisonous plants.

3 ASSESS

Evaluate Understanding

Ask students to compare and contrast the adaptations that aquatic plants have with the adaptations that desert plants have.

Reteach

List the different environments discussed in the section. Then, randomly call on students to identify adaptations that plants have to live in that environment.

ALTERNATIVE ASSESSMENT

This activity can be completed individually or in small groups. Provide students with a variety of materials to choose from, including basic art supplies, paint, water colors, charcoal, fabric, and construction paper. You might also allow students to bring materials from home to include in their artwork or coordinate this activity with an art class at your school. Students should depict a plant in its natural environment. Encourage students to be creative, yet accurate, in their artwork.

Use iText to review the key concepts in Section 25–3.

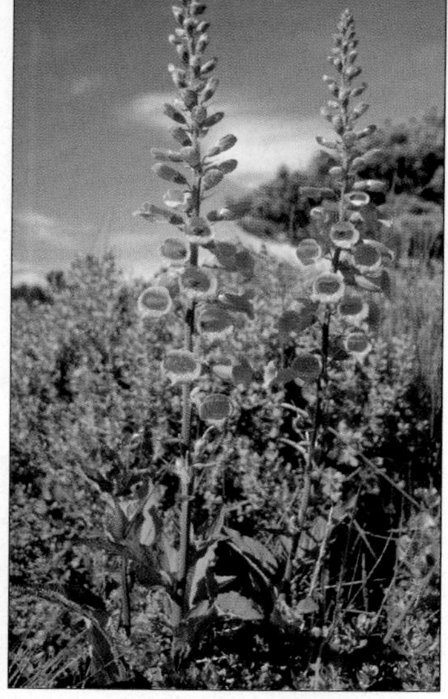

Figure 25–15 Many plants produce chemical compounds that ward off potential predators. *Digitalis* (left), which is also called foxglove, is poisonous when eaten. The monarch caterpillar (right) is able to eat milkweed—which is toxic to most animals—because it can store the toxic compounds in its body.

Chemical Defenses

Seed plants and insects have had such a long relationship that each has had plenty of time to adapt to the other. The beginnings of the relationship are obvious—plants represent an important source of food for insects, as shown in **Figure 25–15.** Plants, therefore, fall prey to a host of plant-eating insects. Because plants cannot run away, you might think that they are defenseless against insects that are armed with biting and sucking structures. But plants have their own defenses.

Many plants defend themselves against insect attack by manufacturing compounds that have powerful effects on animals. Some of these chemicals are poisons that can be lethal when eaten. Other chemicals act as insect hormones, disrupting normal growth and development and preventing insects from reproducing. These chemicals include those used in aspirin, codeine, and scores of other drugs that humans use as medicines.

As you may know, nicotine is a chemical that is found in tobacco plants. When a person smokes tobacco in the form of cigarettes, the nicotine in the tobacco affects the human nervous system. Biologists hypothesize that nicotine is a natural insecticide that disrupts the nervous system of many insects, protecting tobacco plants from potential predators.

25–3 Section Assessment

1. **Key Concept** Compare the adaptations of aquatic plants and desert plants. Which plants have adaptations for obtaining sufficient oxygen?
2. **Key Concept** Describe how carnivorous plants and parasites obtain their nutrients.
3. **Key Concept** How do some plants defend themselves from insect predators?
4. How are salt-tolerant plants adapted to their environment?
5. **Critical Thinking Drawing Conclusions** Why might the production of poisonous compounds be higher in plants that live in areas with dense insect populations?

iTEXT Assessment Use iText to review the important concepts in Section 25–3.

ALTERNATIVE ASSESSMENT

Creating Artwork
Choose one of the plants discussed in this section. Then, create a piece of artwork that shows how the plant is adapted to live in its natural environment.

25–3 Section Assessment

1. Aquatic plants have adaptations to take in sufficient oxygen while desert plants have adaptations to take in and conserve water.
2. Carnivorous plants obtain nutrients by trapping and digesting insects. Parasitic plants obtain nutrients from the tissues of other plants.
3. Some plants make compounds that are poisonous to animals or disrupt their growth and development.
4. Salt-tolerant plants are able to pump excess salt out of tissues.
5. Because of many potential predators, more plants may have evolved this defense.

Are Herbal Drugs Safe?

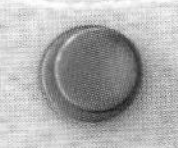

A Chinese herb that damaged the kidneys of dozens of dieters in the 1990s appears to pack a second punch—cancer and precancerous lesions, according to a report in the *New England Journal of Medicine*. These findings draw one of the strongest links yet between the use of an herbal product and cancer.

Natural herbal medicines and dietary supplements can be found in the medicine cabinets of millions of Americans. Last year, Americans spent more than $6 billion on dietary supplements—a third of which was spent on herbal remedies. These remedies include products such as St. John's wort, for treatment of depression; *Echinacea* for cold and flu; and *Ephedra* for weight loss.

Because these preparations are made from plants and plant extracts, they are considered to be foods and food supplements, not drugs. As a result, the Food and Drug Administration (FDA) cannot require studies to determine the safety and effectiveness of herbal substances. Advocates for herbal products say that additional regulations are not needed. Critics worry that many of these products are as powerful and as dangerous as drugs.

The Viewpoints

Herbal Remedies Are Safe

Natural herbal products have been used for thousands of years by people of every culture. *Ephedra,* for example, comes from the Chinese herb *ma huang* and has been used to treat asthma and nasal congestion for centuries. Remedies using *Echinacea* were developed long ago by Native Americans. Such substances should continue to be exempt from new FDA regulations and available without a prescription. Herbal substances present consumers with increased health benefits combined with low risks.

Herbal Remedies Are Potentially Dangerous Drugs

Just because a product is "natural" does not mean it is safe. Plants produce many substances more powerful and dangerous than synthetic drugs. In 1992, more than 50 people in Belgium suffered kidney problems due to a diet remedy containing the herb *Aristolochia*. *Ephedra* itself is a powerful stimulant that can cause hypertension and stroke. St. John's wort interferes with the functions of many drugs, including medications for AIDS, epilepsy, and heart disease. As with other drugs, the FDA should regulate and test herbal substances for safety and effectiveness.

You Decide

1. **Defining the Issue** Explain the major issue being debated about herbal substances.
2. **Analyzing the Viewpoints** Why do some people prefer herbal remedies to drugs? Why do others feel that herbal remedies should be better regulated?
3. **Forming Your Opinion** If an extract of an herb such as *Echinacea,* shown below, produces effects as powerful as those of synthetic drugs, should it be regulated in the same way? What principles should shape government policies regarding these substances?
4. **Role-Playing** You are the owner of a natural foods store for which herbal products make up a growing percentage of annual sales. How would you react to a proposal requiring that new herbal products be tested for several years before they could be sold in your store?

Ask student volunteers to look through popular magazines to find advertisements for herbal medicines and dietary supplements. Other students can look for articles supporting or opposing the sale of herbal drugs. Have students bring the advertisements and articles, or copies of them, to class so other students may also read them. Challenge students to find any claims the manufacturers make about the products and any verification of the products' efficacy.

You Decide

1. The major issue is whether herbal drugs are safe.

2. Some people prefer herbal remedies because they believe these products are "natural" as opposed to synthetic. Others think that herbal remedies are potentially dangerous because they have not undergone rigorous testing.

3. Students' opinions may vary. Some students might believe that if the effects of an herbal extract are as powerful as those of synthetic drugs, the herbal substance should be regulated in the same way, because the misuse or abuse of the herbal substance could be harmful to people's health. Students might suggest that the principles that should shape public policy regarding herbal substances are freedom of choice versus public safety.

4. Have student volunteers role-play this situation, with one volunteer playing the role of a government agent informing the owner of the natural foods store that many of the herbal medicines and dietary supplements in the store cannot be sold until they have been tested and approved by the FDA. Have one or two additional students play the role of customers in the natural foods store. After the rest of the class has observed the role-play, have students comment on the different positions portrayed.

Real-World Lab

Objective Students will be able to identify the locations of meristems that can be forced to form roots on leaf and stem cuttings through the use of rooting hormone.

Skills Focus **Observing, Formulating Hypotheses, Comparing and Contrasting**

Time 45 minutes for setup; 10 minutes for observation several times over 3 weeks

Advance Prep Assemble materials ahead of time. Coleus plants are readily available either by purchase or on loan from a house plant grower. They must routinely be cut back, so taking cuttings should not be a problem. To avoid confounding variables, all cuttings should come from the same cultivar. Rooting hormone and potting soil are available at most lawn and garden centers.

Safety
- Students should use caution with scalpels. Keep the potting soil moist and provide dust masks to any students who may be allergic to dust or mold.
- Make sure that students wear plastic gloves when applying rooting compound. Properly dispose of gloves.

Teaching Tips
- Rooting hormone belongs to a class of chemical messengers called auxins. Their general effect is to control cell size and shape, but they often act in concert with cytokinins to initiate cell proliferation and differentiation.
- Before students take their cuttings, you may need to remind them that each branch is a stem segment; they do not need to take "stem tip" cuttings from only the central stem of each plant.
- Compare and contrast the nervous system and the chemical system of hormones in animals and plants. Point out that animals have both, but plants must rely on only a chemical system. Thus, plants are dependent on hormones for sophisticated developmental control as seen in the effects of auxins on both root and leaf development.

Real-World Lab

Using Hormones to Control Plant Development

Plant hormones have many practical uses. Growers spray gibberellins on sugar cane and fruits to promote their growth. Orchid growers use cytokinins when they clone orchids. Auxins are used to keep potatoes from sprouting and apples from falling from trees before they are ripe. Auxins are also used to stimulate pineapples to flower and develop fruits. Some synthetic auxins are used as weed killers. In this investigation, you will use auxins to identify the locations of meristems that can be forced to form roots on leaf and stem cuttings.

Problem How do auxins affect plant development?

Materials
- large coleus plants (total of at least 4 branches)
- scalpel
- metric ruler
- rooting compound (auxin powder)
- potting soil
- 12 paper cups
- flat, wooden toothpick

Skills Observing, Formulating Hypotheses, Comparing and Contrasting

Procedure

Part A: Observing the Effects of Auxins on Root and Leaf Development

1. Use a scalpel to cut a piece containing a stem tip from a coleus plant as shown. The stem-tip cutting should include a stem tip and 2 nodes that are at least 1 cm from the tip of the stem. Cut the stem tip 3 mm below these 2 nodes. Cut 3 more stem-tip cuttings. **CAUTION:** *Be careful with sharp instruments.*
2. Cut off the petioles growing from the bottom node of each stem-tip cutting. Make sure the cut is 3 mm from the stem. See the illustration.
3. Cut the top from each stem-tip cutting, 3 mm above the top node. Using a toothpick, apply only enough rooting compound to coat the cut surfaces on the tops of 2 stem-tip cuttings.
4. Cut 8 pieces from the lower stems of each plant as shown. As in step 1, each stem cutting should contain at least 2 nodes and be cut 3 mm below the lower node.
5. Dip the stem-tip cuttings and 6 of the lower stem cuttings into powdered rooting hormone (an auxin) so that the bottom node is covered with powder. Leave 2 stem cuttings untreated.
6. Use a scalpel to punch several small drainage holes in the bottoms of the paper cups. Fill each paper cup with potting soil. Push the bottom of each cutting into the potting soil in a paper cup so that the bottom nodes are buried. Keep the soil moist but not wet. Label the paper cups to indicate what type of cutting each cup contains.
7. After 1 week, carefully pull 1 treated and 1 untreated stem cutting from the potting soil. Gently wash the soil off the roots and observe the differences. Record your observations and discard the cuttings you removed. Repeat this procedure after 2 weeks.
8. Allow the stem-tip cuttings to grow for 3 weeks. Observe and record any differences in leaf growth between the treated and untreated plants.

Stem-Tip Cutting

At least 1 cm
Nodes
Petioles
3 mm
Cut here
Step 1

Cut here
Cut here
3 mm
Step 2

Cut here
3 mm
Step 3

Stem Cutting

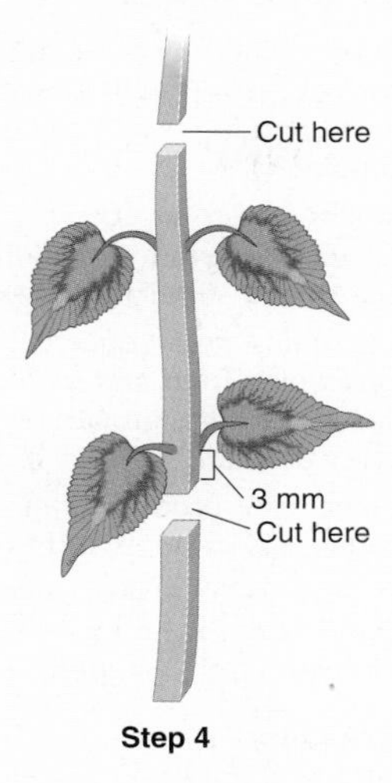

Part B: Using the Effects of Auxins

9. **Formulating Hypotheses** Because auxins stimulate meristems to produce new roots and other plant parts, auxins can be used to locate meristems. Record a hypothesis about whether there are meristems in stems between nodes and in the veins on the bottoms of leaves.
10. **Designing Experiments** Design an experiment to test your hypothesis. You may need to nick the leaf veins slightly with a scalpel to expose any meristems in the veins to the rooting compound and moist soil. With your teacher's approval, carry out your experiment.

Analyze and Conclude

1. **Comparing and Contrasting** What differences did you see between the roots of the auxin-treated and untreated cuttings after 1 week? How can you explain these differences?
2. **Comparing and Contrasting** Was there more difference between roots of treated cuttings and untreated cuttings after 1 week or 2 weeks? How can you explain this result?
3. **Inferring** In step 8, what differences did you observe between the leaves of the treated and untreated stem-tip cuttings? Explain your observations.
4. **Drawing Conclusions** Did the results of your experiment in step 10 show that there are meristem cells in the stem between nodes? Explain your conclusion.
5. **Drawing Conclusions** Did the results of your experiment in step 10 show that there are meristem cells in the veins on the underside of the leaves? Explain your conclusion.

Go Further

Designing Experiments Grow your coleus plants until they develop small blue flowers. Design an experiment to determine how ethylene gas affects the development of flowers and leaves. You can use an apple that has been bruised and left to sit for 4 days as a source of ethylene gas.

Expected Outcomes

- In Part A, all plants should develop roots. The greatest difference in root development should be seen in the week one plants. By 2 weeks, the natural proliferation of roots should begin to overshadow the "jump start" effect of using rooting hormone. The tip cuttings in Part A that are treated at the tops should show apical dominance, while the untreated ones will show lateral dominance.
- In Part B, no roots should develop in the internodal segments. It is possible that treating only an internode will cause roots to develop from an adjacent node as the rooting hormone is transported to the node. Roots will develop from the vascular tissue on the undersides of leaves, but the veins must be nicked before treating in order to expose the terminal meristem inside the outer layer of cells. Students must make sure the leaves are firmly in contact with moist soil for this procedure to work.

Go Further

The first effects of ethylene gas should be withered flowers followed by leaves dying.

Analyze and Conclude

1. The treated plants have more roots than untreated ones. The effect of the rooting hormone initiating root development accounts for this.

2. There is relatively greater difference between treated and untreated plants in the first week. Rooting hormone is effective only to start the rooting process. After it is initiated, normal proliferation of roots controls development.

3. Treated plants should show signs of apical dominance, such as longer internodes and smaller leaves. Untreated plants should show a general uniformity of leaf size.

4. No roots should develop in the internodal regions. Meristematic tissue is very scarce in that area.

5. Meristematic tissue is present in the leaf veins. Roots can be reliably developed from the undersides of leaves if the veins are nicked and the leaves are kept in contact with moist soil.

Chapter 25 Study Guide

Study Tip

Write each Vocabulary term on a separate card, as well as a question for each Key Concept. Place the cards into a box. Have students draw a card and give the definition of the Vocabulary term or the answer to the Key Concept question. Continue until all cards have been selected.

Thinking Visually

1. Ethylene production increases.
2. Chlorophyll is destroyed.
3. An abscission layer forms.

Chapter 25 Assessment

Reviewing Content

1. a	5. b	9. b
2. a	6. d	10. a
3. d	7. b	
4. c	8. b	

Understanding Concepts

11. Auxins cause growth in plants by stimulating cell elongation. These substances are produced in the growing tip of a plant.

12. Auxins diffuse to the side of a stem away from light. High concentrations of auxin on the shady side of a stem cause these cells to increase in length. Thus, the stem bends toward the light.

13. Apical dominance is delay in growth at the lateral bud because auxins diffuse out from the apical meristem. The closer the bud to the apex, the more it is inhibited. Example: If you remove the tip of a branch, more side branches will grow, changing the shape of the plant.

14. The responses of plants to environmental stimuli are called tropisms. Stems show a positive tropism when they grow toward light and a negative tropism when they grow away from gravity. Roots show a positive tropism when they grow toward gravity and a negative tropism when they grow away from light.

Chapter 25 Study Guide

25–1 Hormones and Plant Growth

Key Concepts

- Plant hormones are chemical substances that control a plant's patterns of growth and development, and the plant's responses to environmental conditions.
- Auxins are produced in the apical meristem and are transported downward into the rest of the plant. They stimulate cell elongation.
- Cytokinins are produced in growing roots and in developing fruits and seeds. They stimulate cell division and the growth of lateral buds, and cause dormant seeds to sprout.
- Gibberellins produce dramatic increases in size, particularly in stems and fruit.
- In response to auxins, fruit tissues release small amounts of the hormone ethylene. Ethylene then stimulates fruits to ripen.

Vocabulary

hormone, p. 634 • target cell, p. 634
phototropism, p. 634 • auxin, p. 635
gravitropism, p. 635 • lateral bud, p. 636
apical dominance, p. 636 • herbicide, p. 636
cytokinin, p. 636 • gibberellin, p. 637
ethylene, p. 638

25–2 Plant Responses

Key Concepts

- Plant tropisms include gravitropism, phototropism, and thigmotropism. Each of these responses demonstrates the ability of plants to respond effectively to conditions in which they live.
- Photoperiodism in plants is responsible for the timing of seasonal activities such as flowering and growth.
- As cold weather approaches, deciduous plants turn off photosynthetic pathways, transport materials from leaves to roots, and seal leaves off from the rest of the plant.

Vocabulary

tropism, p. 639 • thigmotropism, p. 639
short-day plant, p. 641 • long-day plant, p. 641
photoperiodism, p. 641 • phytochrome, p. 641
dormancy, p. 641 • abscission layer, p. 642

25–3 Plant Adaptations

Key Concepts

- To take in sufficient oxygen, many aquatic plants have tissues with large air-filled spaces through which oxygen can diffuse.
- Plant adaptations to a desert climate include extensive roots, reduced leaves, and thick stems that can store water.
- Plants that have specialized features for obtaining nutrients include carnivorous plants and parasites.
- Many plants defend themselves against insect attack by manufacturing compounds that have powerful effects on animals.

Vocabulary

xerophyte, p. 644
epiphyte, p. 645

Thinking Visually

Using the information in this chapter, complete the following flowchart about leaf abscission.

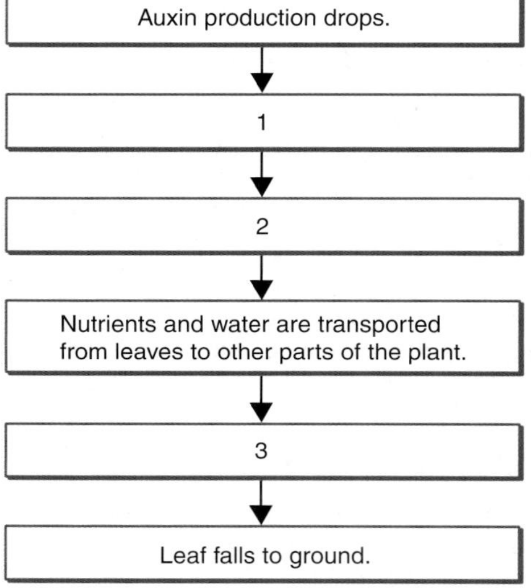
Auxin production drops.
1
2
Nutrients and water are transported from leaves to other parts of the plant.
3
Leaf falls to ground.

CHAPTER RESOURCES

Print:

- ***Teaching Resources,*** Chapter Vocabulary Review, Graphic Organizer
- ***Chapter Tests: Levels A and B,*** Chapter 25 Test
- ***PH Assessment System,*** Practice Test

Technology:

- ***Computer Test Bank,*** Chapter 25 Test
- ***iText,*** Chapter 25 Assessment

Chapter 25 Assessment

Reviewing Content

Choose the letter that best answers the question or completes the statement.

1. A substance produced in one part of a plant that affects another part is a(an)
   a. hormone.
   b. enzyme.
   c. auxin.
   d. phytochrome.
2. A high concentration of auxins can inhibit plant growth. Many of these compounds are used as
   a. herbicides.
   b. pesticides.
   c. fruit ripeners.
   d. growth stimulants.
3. In the illustration below, what phenomenon is responsible for the shape of the plant on the left?
   a. gravitropism
   b. dormancy
   c. phytochromes
   d. apical dominance

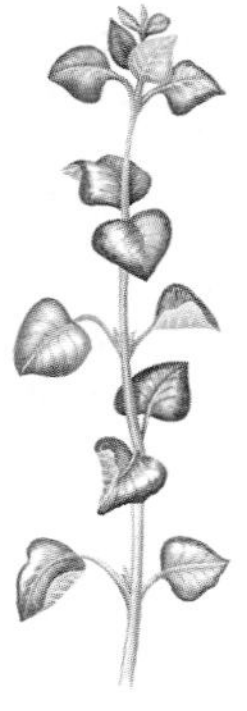

4. Substances that stimulate cell division and cause dormant seeds to sprout are
   a. gibberellins.
   b. auxins.
   c. cytokinins.
   d. phytochromes.
5. Japanese scientists found that the extraordinary growth of a certain rice plant was caused by
   a. auxin.
   b. gibberellin.
   c. cytokinin.
   d. ethylene.
6. The response of a plant to touch is
   a. gravitropism. **c.** photoperiodism.
   b. phototropism. **d.** thigmotropism.
7. Photoperiodism is the response of plants to
   a. water and dryness.
   b. light and darkness.
   c. gravity.
   d. nutrients.
8. The period during which an organism's growth and activity decreases or stops is called
   a. abscission.
   b. dormancy.
   c. thigmotropism.
   d. gravitropism.
9. Plants that have air-filled spaces in their tissues are likely to be
   a. desert plants.
   b. aquatic plants.
   c. epiphytes.
   d. parasites.
10. Plants that grow directly on the bodies of other plants but manufacture their own food are
    a. epiphytes.
    b. aquatic plants.
    c. carnivorous plants.
    d. parasites.

Understanding Concepts

11. What is the role of auxins in a plant? Where are these substances produced?
12. How do auxins cause a plant to grow toward a light source?
13. Explain and give an example of apical dominance.
14. What is a tropism? Give an example of a tropism that affects plant stems and one that affects roots.
15. What is photoperiodism?
16. Describe two different ways in which a plant may respond to changes in day length.
17. Many Arctic plants flower in the early spring when the days are still very short. Are these plants more likely to be long-day plants or short-day plants? Explain.
18. What roles does phytochrome play in plants?
19. Describe what happens to deciduous plants during winter dormancy.
20. What are two adaptations found in many desert plants?

HOMEWORK GUIDE

Section:	Questions:
Section 25–1	1–5, 11–13, 23–25
Section 25–2	6–8, 14–19, 21, 22, 26–30
Section 25–3	9, 10, 20

15. Photoperiodism is responsible for the timing of seasonal activities such as flowering and growth.

16. Many plants time their flowering by day length. Plants that flower in the late spring or early summer when days are longer are called long-day plants. Plants that flower in late summer, autumn, or winter when days are short are called short-day plants.

17. They are short-day plants because they flower when days are short.

18. Phytochrome is responsible for photoperiodism. Phytochrome absorbs red light and activates a number of signaling pathways within plant cells. Plants respond to regular changes in these pathways. The changes determine the patterns of a variety of plant responses.

19. Deciduous plants begin to shut their leaves down. This process includes turning off the pathways of photosynthesis, transporting materials to the roots, and sealing the leaf off from the rest of the plant.

20. Adaptations of desert plants include extensive roots, reduced leaves, and thick stems that can store water.

Chapter 25 Assessment

Critical Thinking

21. Window light comes from one direction only. A plant growing in a window will grow toward the light. Turning the plant will keep exposing a new part of the stem to light. The stem will continue to grow straight.

22. Flowers of a species need to open at the same time to ensure pollination.

23. Positive geotropism will force the root to grow down, while negative geotropism will force the stem to grow up.

24. a) A probable hypothesis is that the plant's growth is affected by gravity. Stems will grow away from gravity, which is negative tropism and roots will grow toward gravity, which is positive tropism. b) No, the light might affect the plant's growth. c) Student answers will vary, but should show an understanding of tropisms and the environmental factors that affect plant growth.

25. Trees continue to grow taller because the top of each shoot has an apical meristem that contains cells that are actively dividing. Thus, tree branches continue to increase in length as long as the tree is alive.

26. The number of night hours in the northern United States is less than ten hours.

27. Carnivorous plants grow in nitrogen-poor soil. They get their nitrogen from capturing and digesting animals.

28. Loss of leaves allows light to reach the new leaves of trees in spring.

29. Being able to climb allows the plants to grow high enough to expose their leaves to light.

30. One of the defining characteristics of plants is that they produce their own food by photosynthesis. Because some parasitic plants do not do this, students may argue that they should not be considered to be plants.

Chapter 25 Assessment

Critical Thinking

21. **Applying Concepts** People grow houseplants on windowsills. Many books advise giving houseplants a one-quarter turn every week. Why is this good advice to follow if you want to grow attractive plants?

22. **Inferring** Why is it important that the flowers of a particular species open at about the same time?

23. **Predicting** What would happen if you accidentally planted a seed wrong side up?

24. **Interpreting Graphics** The responses of plants to stimuli are called tropisms. The response is called positive if the plant part grows toward the stimulus. The response is called negative if the plant part grows away from the stimulus. Different parts of the same plant may respond differently to the same stimulus. The experiment shown below was intended to test the effect of gravitropism on plant growth. The conclusion drawn from the experiment was that the plant stems grow upward due to negative gravitropism.

a. What was the probable hypothesis for this experiment?

b. From the experimental setup shown, was the hypothesis successfully tested? Explain.

c. Indicate what kinds of changes you would make to improve this experimental design.

25. **Applying Concepts** The tallest humans stop growing eventually, yet a tall tree increases its height year after year. Why are plants able to continue to grow taller as long as they live?

26. **Inferring** Spinach is a long-day plant that grows best with a night length of 10 hours. Why is spinach not usually grown in the northern United States?

27. **Applying Concepts** How is trapping and digesting insects an adaptation that contributes to the survival of the Venus' flytrap?

28. **Problem Solving** Many plants and trees exhibit a seasonal loss of leaves as a means of conserving nutrients. Can you think of another advantage that the loss of leaves would provide?

29. **Inferring** Why might climbing plants have a survival advantage over some nonclimbing plants in tropical rain forests and other densely grown areas?

30. **Making Connections** Review the characteristics shared by members of the kingdom Plantae that you learned about in Chapter 18 and Chapter 22. Can you make a case for not including some parasitic plants in this kingdom?

Performance-Based Assessment

Bulletin Board Display Create a bulletin board display that shows the effects that auxins, cytokinins, gibberellins, and ethylene have on plant growth and development. You can use photos from gardening catalogs or magazines. Include information on how gardeners can use this knowledge to achieve desired effects.

Take It to the NET

Do plants grow differently in the absence of gravity? Visit the Prentice Hall Web site at **www.phschool.com** to find out about plant responses in space. Then answer the following questions:

- What happens when plants are grown in space?
- What is graviperception?
- What is graviresponse?
- Describe the work being done on gravitropism in two different scientific labs.

Performance-Based Assessment

Review the information that students will use in their bulletin board displays for accuracy. The illustrations and examples they cite should show an understanding of the role each hormone plays in plant development. For example, students can illustrate and explain how auxin and cytokinin levels control the shape of some plants.

Standardized Test Prep

1. E
2. C
3. B
4. E
5. C
6. A
7. E
8. C
9. D
10. A

Test-Taking Tip Take the time to read each question completely, including all the answer choices. Consider each possible choice before determining which answer is correct.

Directions: Choose the letter that best answers the question or completes the statement.

1. Which of the following are caused by auxins?
I. Apical dominance
II. Cell elongation
III. Phototropism
(A) I only
(B) II only
(C) I and II only
(D) II and III only
(E) I, II, and III

2. Which of the following cause fruit to ripen?
(A) auxins
(B) cytokinins
(C) ethylene
(D) 2,4-D chemicals
(E) gibberellins

3. Which of the following is an example of thigmotropism?
(A) leaf abscission
(B) climbing vines
(C) blooming
(D) photoperiodism
(E) rapid leaf movements

4. All of the following are plant adaptations to a desert climate EXCEPT
(A) thick stems.
(B) small leaves.
(C) deep root system.
(D) many root hairs.
(E) salt tolerance.

5. What causes a short-day plant to flower?
I. Continuous darkness for a certain length of time
II. Phytochromes
III. At least 10 hours of continuous red light
(A) I only
(B) II only
(C) I and II only
(D) II and III only
(E) I, II, and III

Questions 6–8 Each of the lettered choices below refers to the following numbered statements. Select the best lettered choice. A choice may be used once, more than once, or not at all.

(A) Lateral bud
(B) Apical dominance
(C) Gibberellin
(D) Cytokinin
(E) Dormancy

6. Meristematic area on the side of a stem that gives rise to side branches

7. Includes turning off photosynthesis and sealing the leaf off from the rest of the plant

8. Increases growth in plant stems and fruits

Questions 9–10 The results of an experiment are summarized in the art below. Use information from the art to answer the questions that follow.

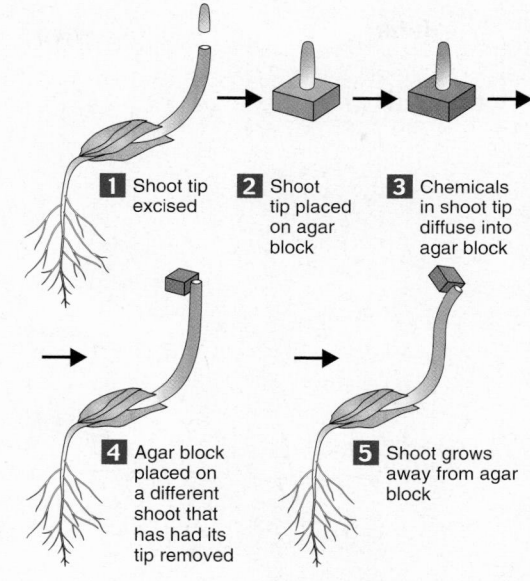

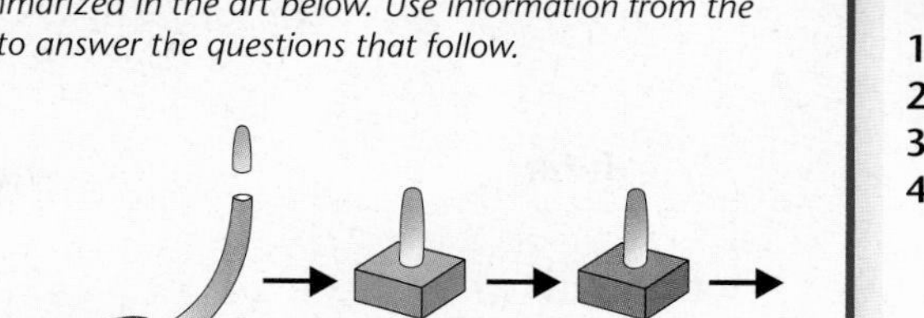
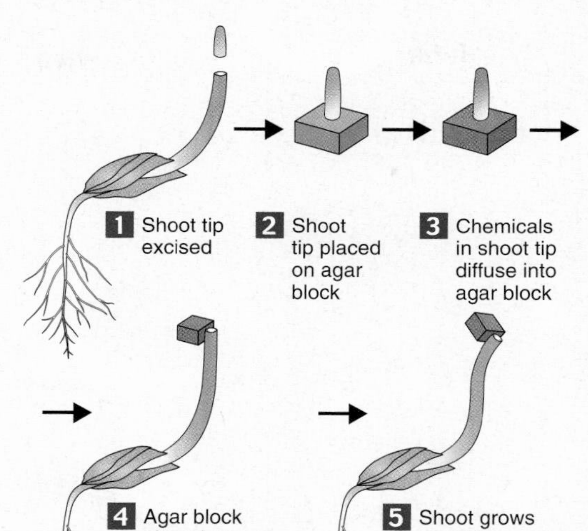
1 Shoot tip excised
2 Shoot tip placed on agar block
3 Chemicals in shoot tip diffuse into agar block
4 Agar block placed on a different shoot that has had its tip removed
5 Shoot grows away from agar block

9. Which of the following can be concluded from the results of this experiment alone?
(A) Hormones are produced in the growing tips of plants.
(B) Plants grow toward the sun because of compounds produced in their stems.
(C) Agar blocks contain a variety of plant compounds.
(D) Compounds produced in shoot tips can cause stems to bend.
(E) Chemicals produced in plant stems stimulate plant growth.

10. Based on your knowledge of plant hormones, which of the following best explains the results of this experiment?
I. Auxins produced in the shoot tip caused cell enlargement in the growing stem.
II. Cytokinins produced in the shoot tip caused cell enlargement in the growing stem.
III. Auxins produced in the shoot tip caused lateral bud growth.
(A) I only
(B) II only
(C) III only
(D) I and III only
(E) none of the above

Take It to the NET

- Space experiments show that some plant species germinate, grow, and reproduce in a weightless environment. Plants adapt to life without gravity. Shoots grow toward light only.
- Graviperception is the immediate response of a plant's statocytes to the change in gravity when a plant is turned on its side.
- Graviresponse involves all the signals that cause regions of actively elongating cells to change their rate of growth. As a result, shoots turn upward and roots turn downward.
- The work of several different labs is described on hyperlinks to this Web site.

For additional information, visit

www.phschool.com

Unit 8

Dear Colleague,

There's no doubt about it. Those of us who live mostly indoors in urban areas usually see invertebrates as nuisances—if we even see them at all. There are cockroaches that ensure that life will persist on Earth, even if we humans eradicate one another. There are ants that, sooner or later, infest nearly any structure we build. There are Japanese beetles that devour our gardens. And there are mosquitos that seem determined to devour us whenever we try to enjoy the outdoor life.

You don't need to go far outside many cities, though, to come across invertebrates more like these remarkable thorn bugs. I moved to a woodsy place outside Boston last year, and was immediately dazzled by—of all things—dragonflies! I had almost forgotten them, but here they were—red ones, blue ones, small ones, huge ones—darting about and settling on every plant in sight. So it seemed especially fitting to me that a dragonfly would grace the cover of this book!

But what really took me aback, once I settled in, were the odd and unusual (to me, anyway) hymenopterans. I was accustomed to run-of-the-mill honeybees, bumblebees, and yellow jackets. I was not prepared for some of their relatives and look-alikes that swarmed over our yard. Several were just hymenopteran species I hadn't seen before, and which I still haven't identified. Others were hymenopteran mimics; stingless, harmless insects that mimic the body forms and colors of their less palatable cousins. "Yes Joe," they seemed to be buzzing, "all that evolution and natural history stuff you write about us in these books *is* real after all—and not just in tropical rain forests!"

UNIT 8 Invertebrates

Chapters

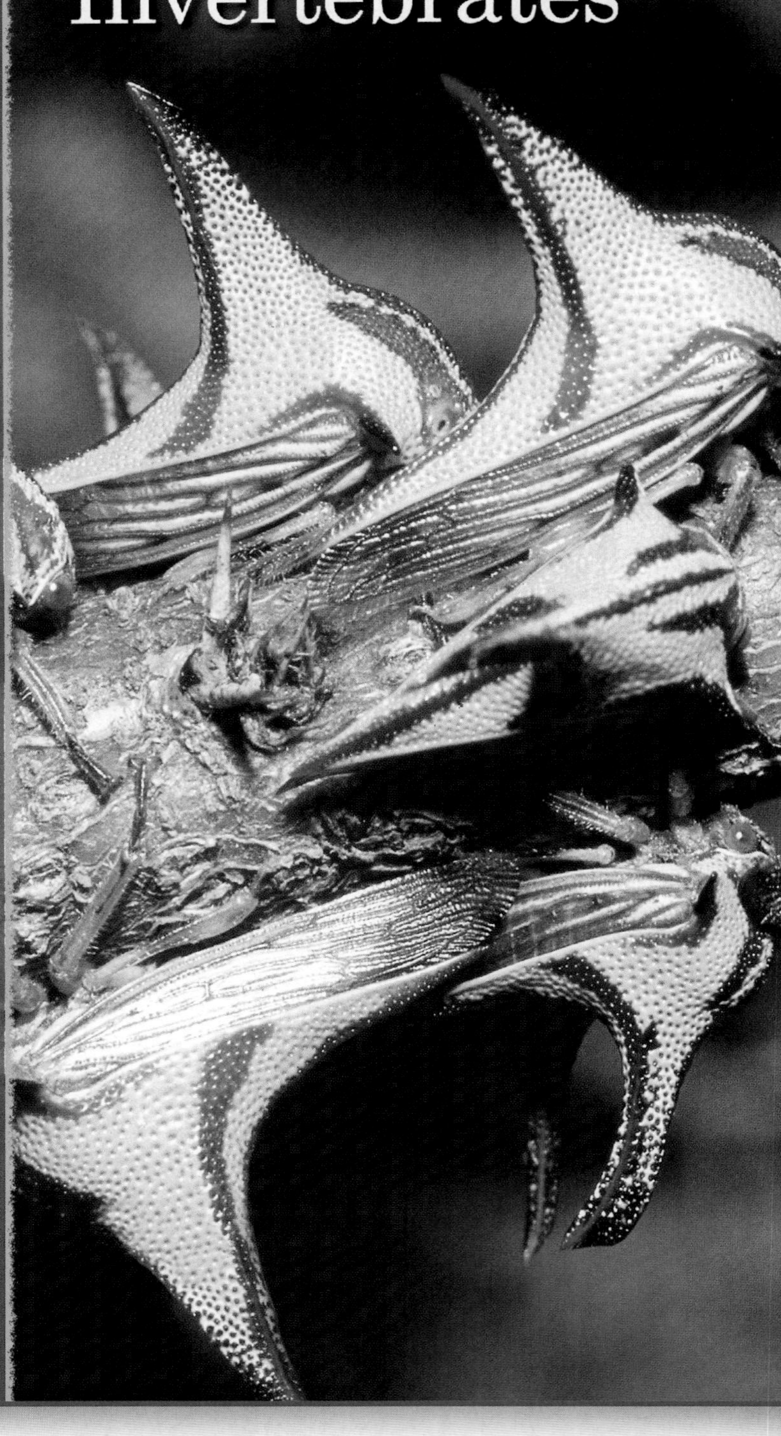

▶ Thorn bugs got their name from the fact that they look like thorns, thus scaring away any predators. The close resemblance of an organism such as these thorn bugs to an object in its environment—in this case thorns—is known as mimicry.

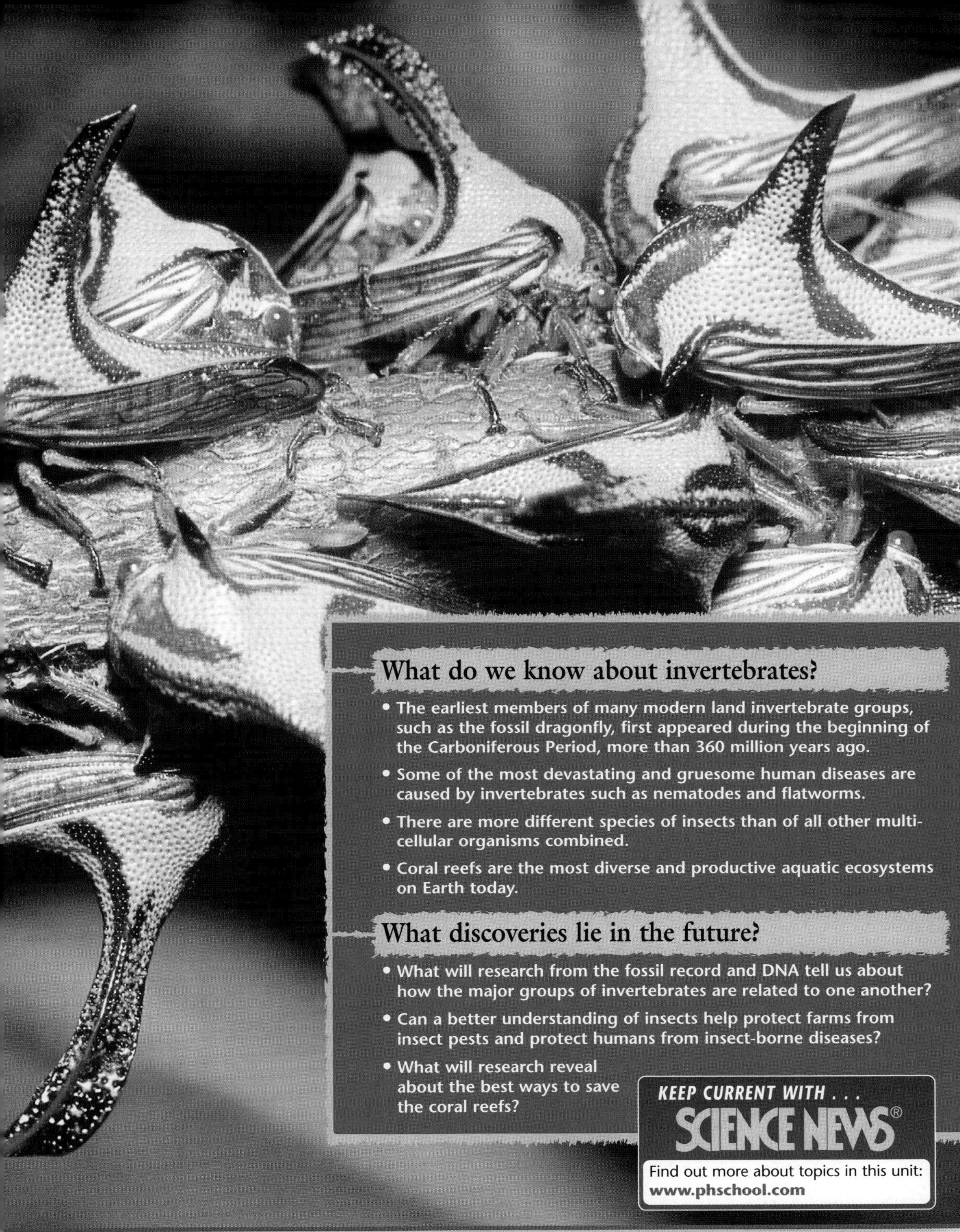

What do we know about invertebrates?
• The earliest members of many modern land invertebrate groups, such as the fossil dragonfly, first appeared during the beginning of the Carboniferous Period, more than 360 million years ago.
• Some of the most devastating and gruesome human diseases are caused by invertebrates such as nematodes and flatworms.
• There are more different species of insects than of all other multi-cellular organisms combined.
• Coral reefs are the most diverse and productive aquatic ecosystems on Earth today.
What discoveries lie in the future?
• What will research from the fossil record and DNA tell us about how the major groups of invertebrates are related to one another?
• Can a better understanding of insects help protect farms from insect pests and protect humans from insect-borne diseases?
• What will research reveal about the best ways to save the coral reefs?
KEEP CURRENT WITH . . .
SCIENCE NEWS®
Find out more about topics in this unit:
www.phschool.com

I can imagine, though, that—personal fascination with inverts aside—more than a few of you look at this unit with mixed feelings. How can you cover all this stuff? Should you even try? The answers depend on your own likes and dislikes (and local standards), but here's my take: Invertebrates have profound effects on our lives in scores of ways—depending, in large part, on where we live. To my mind, the best way to approach this material is to zero in on cases that you can make relevant to your particular collection of students.

If you live in Florida, focus on coral reefs—their otherworldly collection of creatures and their major ecological importance to southern Florida and to the tropics beyond. If you live in the South or Southwest, consider insects and arachnids that carry diseases of humans and livestock. Some of these "bugs" might become more important to our lives than we might like; global warming seems to be encouraging disease-carrying tropical mosquitos to move north and settle on our side of the Rio Grande and along the Gulf Coast. Wherever you live, the story of plant-pollinator coevolution is as vibrant and important today as it has ever been; if we lose our pollinating bees (and several species are in trouble), many crops across the country could face a pollination crisis.

There is also the sobering reality that if we think about "success" on Earth in terms of total numbers of species and individuals, invertebrates win the prize hands down over the piddling few of us with backbones. Their phenomenal diversity of body forms and ways of making a living are endlessly fascinating—and instructive—to those of us with open minds. And if you need some comic relief, there is always Jonathan Swift's perceptive ditty:

So, naturalists observe, a flea
Hath smaller fleas that on him
prey;
And those have smaller still to bite
'em;
And so proceed *ad infinitum*

Joe Levine

SCIENCE NEWS®

Have students visit the Prentice Hall Web site at **www.phschool.com** to find the most current information on invertebrates.

Chapter Planner 26 Sponges and Cnidarians

Section and Section Objectives	Time	Activities and Labs
26–1 Introduction to the Animal Kingdom, pp. 657–663 **26.1.1** ***List*** the characteristics that all animals share. **26.1.2** ***Describe*** the essential functions that animals carry out. **26.1.3** ***Identify*** the important trends in animal evolution.	1 period (1/2 block)	**SE:** ***Inquiry Activity,*** What makes an animal an animal?, p. 656 **TE:** ***Build Science Skills,*** p. 661 **SE:** ***Quick Lab,*** How can body symmetry affect adaptation?, p. 662
26–2 Sponges, pp. 664–667 **26.2.1** ***Explain*** what a sponge is. **26.2.2** ***Describe*** how sponges carry out essential functions. **26.2.3** ***Describe*** the ecology of sponges.	1 period (1/2 block)	**TE:** ***Build Science Skills,*** p. 664 **TE:** ***Build Science Skills,*** p. 665 **TE:** ***Demonstration,*** p. 666 **SE:** ***Technology & Society,*** Sunscreen From the Sea, p. 668
26–3 Cnidarians, pp. 669–675 **26.3.1** ***Explain*** what a cnidarian is. **26.3.2** ***Describe*** the two body plans that exist in the cnidarian life cycle. **26.3.3** ***Describe*** how cnidarians carry out essential functions. **26.3.4** ***Identify*** the three groups of cnidarians. **26.3.5** ***Describe*** the ecology of cnidarians.	1 period (1/2 block)	**TE:** ***Demonstration,*** p. 670 **TE:** ***Demonstration,*** p. 671 **SE:** ***Analyzing Data,*** Coral Vanishing Act, p. 674 **SE:** ***Exploration,*** Examining the Responses of Hydras, pp. 676–677
Study Guide, pp. 678–681	1 period (1/2 block)	

ACTIVITY PLANNER

SE: ***Inquiry Activity,*** p. 656; (15 min.); specimens or photos of a variety of organisms, including animals, plants, protists, fungi, and bacteria

TE: ***Build Science Skills,*** p. 661; (20 min.); 3 different-colored blocks of modeling compound, plastic knife

SE: ***Quick Lab,*** p. 662; (15 min.); modeling clay, plastic knife

TE: ***Build Science Skills,*** p. 664; (15 min.); natural sponge, hand lens, microscope slide and coverslip, microscope

TE: ***Build Science Skills,*** p. 665; (15 min.); natural sponge, coffee filter, paper towel, large basin, container of muddy water

TE: ***Demonstration,*** p. 666; (5 min.); natural sponge, artificial sponge, balance scale, water

TE: ***Demonstration,*** p. 670; (5 min.); clear plastic cup, colored plastic cup

TE: ***Demonstration,*** p. 671; (5 min.); oblong balloon, umbrella

SE: ***Exploration,*** pp. 676–677; (45 minutes, 10 minutes the following day); 6 test tubes with screw caps, test-tube rack, green hydras, brown hydras, aluminum foil, pond or spring water, glass-marking pencil, dropper pipette, cellophane tape

PLANNING KEY

Ability Levels

B Basic	For students who need additional help
A Average	For all students
E Enriched	For students who need to be challenged

Components

SE	Student Edition	**GRSW**	Guided Reading and Study Workbook	**IDM**	Issues and Decision Making
TE	Teacher's Edition	**CT**	Chapter Tests: Levels A and B	**CTB**	Computer Test Bank
LMA	Laboratory Manual A	**PHAS**	PH Assessment Plus	**PAP**	Presentation Assistant Plus
LMB	Laboratory Manual B	**LA**	Lab Assessment with Scoring Guide	**BD**	BioDetectives Videotape
TR	Teaching Resources	**BTM**	BioTechnology Manual	**iT**	iText

Program Resources	Assessment	Media and Technology
TR: Section Review 26–1 B A **GRSW:** Section 26–1 B A **IDM:** 26–1 A E	**SE:** 26–1 Section Assessment, p. 663 **TR:** Section Review 26–1	**PAP:** 26–1 Interest Grabber, Section Outline, Body Symmetry, Figure 26–5, Figure 26–4 **iT:** Section 26–1
TR: Section Review 26–2 B A **GRSW:** Section 26–2 B A	**SE:** 26–2 Section Assessment, p. 667 **TR:** Section Review 26–2	**PAP:** 26–2 Interest Grabber, Section Outline, Sponge Life Cycle, Figure 26–8 **iT:** Section 26–2
LMA: Chapter 26 Lab A E **LMB:** Chapter 26 Lab B A **TR:** Section Review 26–3 B A **GRSW:** Section 26–3 B A **IDM:** 26–2 A E	**SE:** 26–3 Section Assessment, p. 675 **TR:** Section Review 26–3	**PAP:** 26–3 Interest Grabber, Section Outline, Jelly Fish Life Cycle, Figure 26–12 **iT:** Section 26–3
	SE: Chapter 26 Assessment, pp. 678–681 **TR:** Chapter Vocabulary Review, Graphic Organizer **CT:** Chapter 26 Test **CTB:** Chapter 26 Test **PHAS:** Practice Test	**CTB:** Chapter 26 Test **iT:** Chapter 26 Assessment

PRESSED FOR TIME?

To Preview the Chapter

- Introduce students to Key Concepts and Vocabulary terms in each section.
- Assign the Reading Strategies for each section.

To Cover the Chapter Quickly

- Have students read all of Section 26–1, read What Is a Sponge? in Section 26–2, and read What Is a Cnidarian? and Groups of Cnidarians in Section 26–3.
- Assign the 26–1 Section Review and questions 1–10 in Chapter 26 Assessment and questions 1–10 in Chapter 26 Standardized Test Prep.

To Review the Chapter

- Assign the Sections 26–1 through 26–3 in the Guided Reading and Study Workbook.
- Assign Section Reviews for 26–1 through 26–3 and the Chapter Vocabulary Review for Chapter 26 in the Teaching Resources.

Chapter 26

ENGAGE/EXPLORE

Inquiry Activity

Objective Students should form an operational definition of an animal.

Skill Focus **Forming Operational Definitions**

Materials specimens or photos of a variety of organisms, including animals, plants, protists, fungi, and bacteria

Time 15 minutes

Safety Avoid exposing students to noxious preservatives and to potential allergens such as animal hair or pollen.

Strategies

- Include a plant that responds to touch, such as a Venus' flytrap (*Dionaea muscipula).*
- You may want to set up the specimens and photos at stations around the room and have students move from station to station.

Expected Outcomes Students should easily classify most of the organisms into categories, though they may have difficulty classifying sponges and motile protists.

Think About It

1. Students should give at least one reason for how they classified each organism.

2. Students might list such characteristics as multicellular structure, movement, response to stimuli, and lack of chlorophyll.

Assess Prior Knowledge

Remind students that the classification system used in this text includes six kingdoms. Ask a volunteer to list the kingdoms. *(Archaebacteria, Eubacteria, Protista, Fungi, Plantae, Animalia)* Then, ask: **What characteristics distinguish animals from organisms of the other kingdoms?** *(Animals are multicellular heterotrophs that have the ability to move.)* **Are there any animals that don't move during their lives?** *(Some students may know that sponges, for instance, are sessile animals.)* Have students speculate about what functions animals must carry out to survive.

Chapter 26 Sponges and Cnidarians

A worker washes soft sponges recently harvested along the coast of Florida. Sponges are simple animals that live in either marine or freshwater habitats.

Inquiry Activity

What makes an animal an animal?

Procedure

1. Observe the specimens or photographs of organisms provided by your teacher. Some of the organisms are animals, whereas others are not. Examine each organism carefully.
2. Make a list of each organism's characteristics.

Think About It

1. **Classifying** Classify the organisms into two groups: animals and nonanimals. Give your reasons for putting each organism into a particular group.
2. **Forming Operational Definitions** List at least three characteristics shared by each of the organisms you classified as animals. Describe how these characteristics separate them from the nonanimals.

FACTS AND FIGURES

Why so many kinds of animals?

Animals are tremendously diverse. Animals can be found in almost all habitats, though most animal phyla inhabit Earth's seas. There are about 35 animal phyla, encompassing more than 1.5 million recognized species. Some biologists estimate that there may actually be 30 million extant species. Plant species aren't nearly as numerous, and the reasons for that have to do with how plants and animals live. Plants are generally nonmotile, and they obtain the energy they need to carry out cellular functions through photosynthesis. Animals, by contrast, obtain their energy by ingesting other organisms, and they generally must move about and expend energy to acquire the foods they need to live. The great variety of animal shapes and sizes is in large part a consequence of the adaptations made to the great variety of foods that animals eat.

26–1 Introduction to the Animal Kingdom

Of all the kingdoms of organisms, the animal kingdom is the most diverse in appearance. Some animals look familiar to us, whereas others resemble creatures from a nightmare or a horror movie. Some animals are so small that they live on or inside the bodies of other animals. Others are many meters long and live in the depths of the sea. Animals can be black, white, brightly colored, or transparent. They may walk, swim, crawl, burrow, or fly—or not move at all. As you will see, each major group, or phylum, has its own typical body plan.

What Is an Animal?

As different as they are, all animals share certain characteristics. Animals, including those in **Figure 26–1**, are all heterotrophs, meaning that they obtain nutrients and energy by feeding on organic compounds from other organisms. Animals are multicellular, or composed of many cells. The cells that make up animal bodies share certain characteristics as well. All animal cells are eukaryotic, meaning that they contain a nucleus and membrane-bound organelles. Unlike the cells of algae, fungi, and plants, animal cells do not have cell walls.  **Animals, members of the kingdom Animalia, are multicellular, eukaryotic heterotrophs whose cells lack cell walls.**

Over 95 percent of all animal species are often grouped in a single, informal category: invertebrates. This group is defined in an odd way—by describing a characteristic that its members do *not* have. **Invertebrates** are animals that have no backbone, or vertebral column. They range in size from microscopic dust mites to the giant squid, which is more than 20 meters in length. They include groups as diverse as sea stars, worms, jellyfish, and insects. The other 5 percent of animals, including fishes, amphibians, reptiles, birds, and mammals, are called **vertebrates,** because they have a backbone.

Guide for Reading

Key Concepts
- What characteristics do all animals share?
- What essential functions do animals carry out?
- What are the important trends in animal evolution?

Vocabulary
- invertebrate • vertebrate
- parasite • host
- blastula • protostome
- deuterostome • anus
- endoderm • mesoderm
- ectoderm • radial symmetry
- bilateral symmetry
- cephalization

Reading Strategy: Monitoring Your Understanding Before you read, write down what you already know about animals. After you have read this section, write down what you learned about animals.

▶ **Figure 26–1** The animal kingdom includes an incredible diversity of forms and lifestyles. **Despite their differences in appearance, both the collared lizard and the grasshopper are eukaryotic heterotrophs whose cells lack cell walls.**

SECTION RESOURCES

Print:
- ***Teaching Resources,*** Section Review 26–1
- ***Guided Reading and Study Workbook,*** Section 26–1
- ***Issues and Decision Making,*** 26–1

Technology:
- ***iText,*** Section 26–1

Section 26–1

1 FOCUS

Objectives

26.1.1 ***List*** the characteristics that all animals share.
26.1.2 ***Describe*** the essential functions that animals carry out.
26.1.3 ***Identify*** the important trends in animal evolution.

Guide for Reading

Vocabulary Preview

Call on volunteers to pronounce each of the Vocabulary words aloud. Correct any mispronunciations, and note any words that students with limited English proficiency have special trouble pronouncing.

Reading Strategy

Consider conducting a class brainstorming activity in which students together identify everything they know about animals. Write their answers on the board or chart paper that can be saved. At this point, accept all ideas uncritically. After students have read the section, have them check the characteristics they listed earlier, revising them or adding to them as necessary.

2 INSTRUCT

What Is an Animal?

Build Science Skills

Classifying Have the class brainstorm a list of animals they commonly see in their environment, including birds, insects, mammals, worms, fishes, and so on. Then divide the class into groups and have each group classify each animal as either a chordate or an invertebrate. Then ask a member of one group to read aloud its classification. The list will likely be favored toward chordates. Ask students to speculate why more chordates were mentioned when 97 percent of all animal species are invertebrates.

26–1 (continued)

What Animals Do to Survive

Build Science Skills

Comparing and Contrasting Divide the class into small groups, and ask each group to make a large compare/contrast table on posterboard that shows how a variety of different animals carry out the seven essential functions. Encourage students to add drawings to their tables where appropriate. Check to make sure no two groups are doing the same animals. Display the tables on the classroom wall when the groups have finished. You may want groups to leave space on their posters for the addition of other animals they learn about in this and subsequent chapters.

Meet Diverse Needs

To reinforce at-risk students' understanding of the seven essential functions, display a picture of an animal with which students are very familiar, such as a dog. Then, call on students at random to explain how a dog carries out each of the seven essential functions. Next, display a picture of a more unfamiliar animal, such as a clam or a jellyfish. Have students speculate on how that animal carries out the essential functions. **Learning modality: verbal**

Build Science Skills

Applying Concepts Challenge students to create an animal that has never lived before. Each new animal should meet the definition of *animal* learned in this section, and it must have specializations to enable it to carry out the seven essential animal functions. Tell students they can be as creative as they want in the form of their animals, as long as form meets function in the seven essential ways.

What Animals Do to Survive

All animals survive and respond to the environment in different ways. **Animals carry out the following essential functions: feeding, respiration, circulation, excretion, response, movement, and reproduction.** Over millions of years, animals with different body plans have evolved an extraordinary variety of ways to carry out these functions. Some of these are shown in **Figure 26–2.** For each animal group you read about in the next several chapters, you will examine these functions and learn about the cells, tissues, organs, and organ systems that perform them.

Feeding Animals have evolved a variety of ways to feed. Herbivores are animals that eat plants, including roots, stems, leaves, flowers, and fruits. Carnivores feed on other animals. Filter feeders are aquatic animals that strain tiny floating plants and animals from the water around them. Detritivores (dee-TRYT-uh-vawrz) are animals that feed on pieces of decaying plant and animal material called detritus (dee-TRYT-us).

Animals can also form symbiotic relationships, in which two species live in close association with each other. A **parasite,** for example, is a type of symbiont that lives within or on another organism, the **host.** The parasite feeds on the host, harming it.

Respiration Whether they live in water or on land, all animals respire, which means that they take in oxygen and give off carbon dioxide. Because of their very simple, thin-walled bodies, some animals can rely on the diffusion of these substances through their skin. Most other animals, however, have evolved complex tissues and organ systems for respiration.

Circulation Many small aquatic animals, such as some aquatic worms, rely solely on diffusion to transport oxygen, nutrients, and waste products among all their cells. Diffusion is sufficient because these animals are only a few cell layers thick. Larger animals, however, have some kind of circulatory system to move materials around within their bodies.

Feeding

Respiration

Circulation

Excretion

PRESENTATIONS MADE EASY!

The Presentation Assistant Plus contains the Prentice Hall Presentation Pro and the Transparencies, which provide easy-to-follow visual support for every step of this lesson. If you have a computer presentation station, use Prentice Hall Presentation Pro Section 26–1, or use the transparencies listed here.

Section 26–1: **Interest Grabber**
Section Outline
Body Symmetry
Figure 26–4

Excretion A primary waste product of cellular metabolism is ammonia, a poisonous substance that contains nitrogen. A buildup of ammonia and other waste products would kill an animal. Therefore, excretion is critical to life. Most animals have an excretory system that either eliminates ammonia quickly or converts it into a less toxic substance that is removed from the body. Excretory systems vary from groups of cells that pump water out of the body to complex organs such as kidneys.

Response Animals respond to events in their environment using specialized cells called nerve cells. In most animals, nerve cells hook up together to form a nervous system. Some cells, called receptors, respond to sound, light, and other stimuli. Other nerve cells process information and determine how the animal responds. The arrangement of nerve cells in the body changes dramatically from phylum to phylum.

Movement Some animals live their entire adult lives attached to a single spot. Most animals, however, are motile, meaning they can move. But both stick-in-the-muds and jet-setters usually have either muscles or musclelike tissues that generate force by becoming shorter when stimulated. Muscle contraction enables motile animals to move around, usually by working in combination with a support structure called a skeleton. Muscles also help even sedentary animals feed and pump water and fluids through their bodies.

Reproduction Most animals reproduce sexually by producing haploid gametes. Sexual reproduction helps create and maintain genetic diversity in populations. It therefore helps improve species' abilities to evolve when the environment changes. Many animals, especially invertebrates, can also reproduce asexually. Asexual reproduction produces offspring that are genetically identical to the parent. It allows animals to increase their numbers rapidly.

CHECKPOINT *How do sexual and asexual reproduction differ?*

Figure 26–2 Animals carry out seven essential functions: feeding, respiration, circulation, excretion, response, movement, and reproduction. Snakes feed by constricting, or squeezing, their prey. Humans respire by breathing oxygenated air into lungs. A rabbit's circulatory system pumps blood through closed vessels, which are visible in its ears. Crabs rid their bodies of metabolic wastes by excreting fluid. Like many insects, moths respond to stimuli that they detect from the environment using specialized sense organs such as antennae. Herons move using a system of muscles attached to a low-density skeleton. Animals reproduce either sexually or asexually; lions reproduce sexually and have only a few offspring per litter.

Response

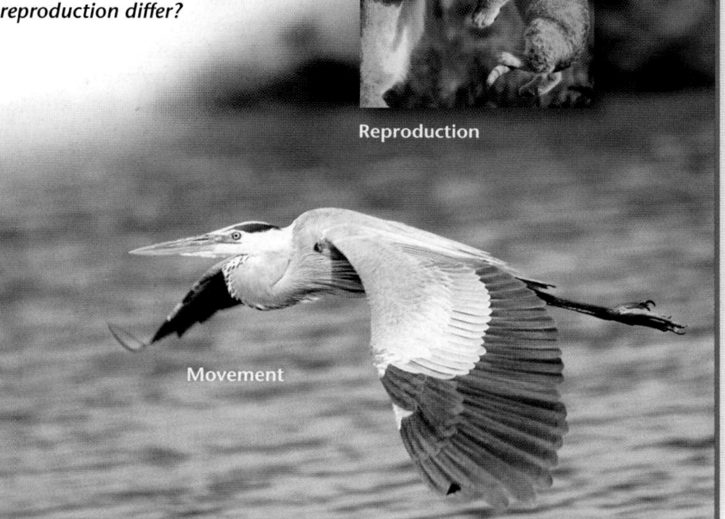

Reproduction

Movement

Meet Diverse Needs

Have students who need an extra challenge choose one of the seven essential functions and do an in-depth study of the way several animals carry out that function. These animals should be a diverse group of specific animals from various phyla. For example, a student might study how circulation is accomplished in a jellyfish, a worm, a spider, and a dog. Students could prepare a brief presentation about each animal, to be delivered when the class is studying the phylum in which the animal is included.
Learning modality: verbal

Use Community Resources

Contact a local zoo for a speaker to address the class about how modern zoos try to create environments in which animals can carry out essential functions in the most natural ways possible. Have students prepare questions ahead of time related to the seven functions discussed in their text and dealing with animals from phyla they will learn about in the next several chapters.

BIO INSIGHTS

FACTS AND FIGURES

Taking advantage of good times
An animal that can reproduce asexually has the perfect response to good conditions—a rapid increase in population. For instance, the food supply in an area may suddenly become abundant or the living space for a species may suddenly expand. By reproducing asexually in great numbers, some animals can gain a competitive edge by taking advantage of the favorable environment. If conditions become unfavorable for some reason, organisms reproduce sexually. Methods of asexual reproduction include not only fission and budding but also fragmentation. Some organisms—including sponges as well as certain cnidarians, echinoderms, and annelids—exploit an ability to regrow lost parts (regeneration) to produce new individuals (fragmentation). A sea star, for example, can produce a new individual from a single arm.

Answer to . . .

CHECKPOINT *Sexual reproduction, which involves the joining of two haploid gametes, helps create and maintain genetic diversity in populations, while asexual reproduction produces offspring that are genetically identical to the parent.*

Trends in Animal Evolution

Use Visuals

Figure 26–3 Explain that a cladogram is a diagram in the form of a branching tree that shows the evolution of groups of organisms. A cladogram branches where characteristics, or traits, can distinguish between the different phyla. Then, ask: **Which group of animals is more closely related to annelids: flatworms or arthropods?** *(Arthropods)* **How should you interpret this cladogram in that it shows chordates farther away from mollusks than from echinoderms?** *(Chordates are more closely related to echinoderms than to mollusks.)*

Meet Diverse Needs

To help at-risk students understand levels of organization, display an illustration of a human figure that shows internal structures, such as digestive organs, bones, muscles, and nerves. Explain that animals have four types of tissues: epithelial, connective, muscle, and nervous. Then, call on students to describe the tissues and organs that make up the digestive system, the skeletal system, the nervous system, and so on. **Learning modality: visual**

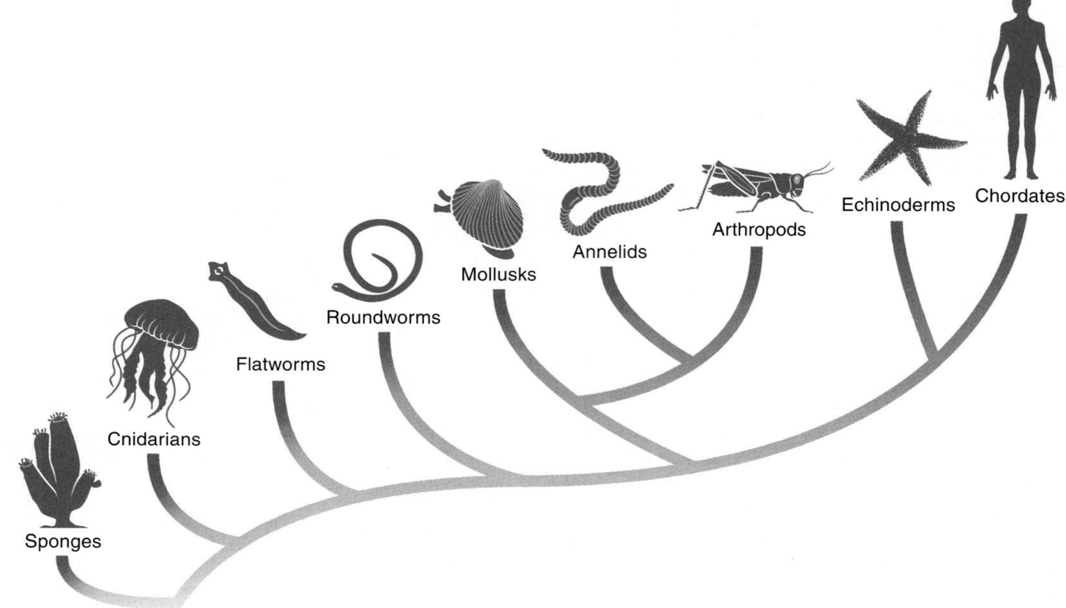

▲ **Figure 26–3** This cladogram indicates evolutionary relationships among major groups of animals. Groups shown close together, such as echinoderms and chordates, are more closely related than groups that are shown farther apart, such as echinoderms and cnidarians. During the course of evolution that produced these different groups, important traits evolved.  **Animals that are more complex typically have specialized cells, bilateral body symmetry, cephalization, and a body cavity.**

Trends in Animal Evolution

Your survey of the animal kingdom will begin with simple forms and move through more complicated ones. These different phyla are related to one another by a common evolutionary heritage. The cladogram in **Figure 26–3** shows our most current understanding of evolutionary relationships among groups of living animals. A comparison of the groups in the cladogram shows important trends in animal evolution. **Complex animals tend to have high levels of cell specialization and internal body organization, bilateral body symmetry, a front end or head with sense organs, and a body cavity.** In addition, the embryos of complex animals develop in layers.

Cell Specialization and Levels of Organization As animals have evolved, their cells have become specialized to carry out different functions, such as movement and response. Large animals need greater efficiency in body processes than do very small animals. Single-celled organisms, such as amoebas, move nutrients and waste products directly across their cell membranes. In multicellular organisms such as animals, however, each cell type has a structure and chemical composition that enable it to perform a specialized function. Groups of specialized cells form tissues. Tissues join together to form organs and organ systems—all of which work together to carry out a variety of complex functions.

BIO INSIGHTS

FACTS AND FIGURES

The basic types of tissues

A tissue is a group of specialized cells that have a common structure and a common function. Despite the great diversity of kinds of animals that have evolved, there are only four basic types of animal tissues: epithelial, connective, muscle, and nervous. Epithelial tissue, which consists of tightly packed cells, lines the cavities inside the body and covers the body's outside. A primary function of epithelial tissue is protection against injury, invaders, and fluid loss. Connective tissue connects and supports other tissues. It includes threadlike fibers, bone, cartilage, and blood. Muscle tissue consists of long cells that can contract. It is the most abundant kind of tissue in most animals, which makes sense for an organism that needs to move to survive. Nervous tissue includes cells that are specialized to sense stimuli and transmit signals from one place to another.

Early Development Animals that reproduce sexually begin life as a zygote, or fertilized egg. **Figure 26–4** shows development after fertilization. The zygote undergoes a series of divisions to form a **blastula** (BLAS-tyoo-luh), which is a hollow ball of cells. The blastula becomes flattened on one side and folds in on itself, forming a single opening called a blastopore. The process of blastopore formation changes a simple ball of cells—similar to an inflated balloon—into an elongated structure with a tube inside, as if you were holding the balloon and pushing your thumbs toward the center.

The blastopore leads into a central tube that runs the length of the developing embryo. This tube becomes the digestive tract and is formed in one of two ways. A **protostome** (PROH-tuh-stohm) is an animal whose mouth is formed from the blastopore. Most invertebrate animals are protostomes. A **deuterostome** (DOO-tur-uh-stohm) is an animal whose anus is formed from the blastopore. The **anus** is the opening through which wastes leave the digestive tract. The mouth is formed second, after the anus (*deuterostome* means "second mouth"). Echinoderms and all vertebrates are deuterostomes.

During early development, the cells of most animal embryos differentiate into three layers called germ layers. The **endoderm,** or innermost germ layer, develops into the linings of the digestive tract and much of the respiratory system. The **mesoderm,** or middle layer, gives rise to muscles and much of the circulatory, reproductive, and excretory organ systems. The **ectoderm,** or outermost layer, gives rise to sense organs, nerves, and the outer layer of the skin.

CHECKPOINT *Which layer develops into the muscles and the circulatory, reproductive, and excretory systems?*

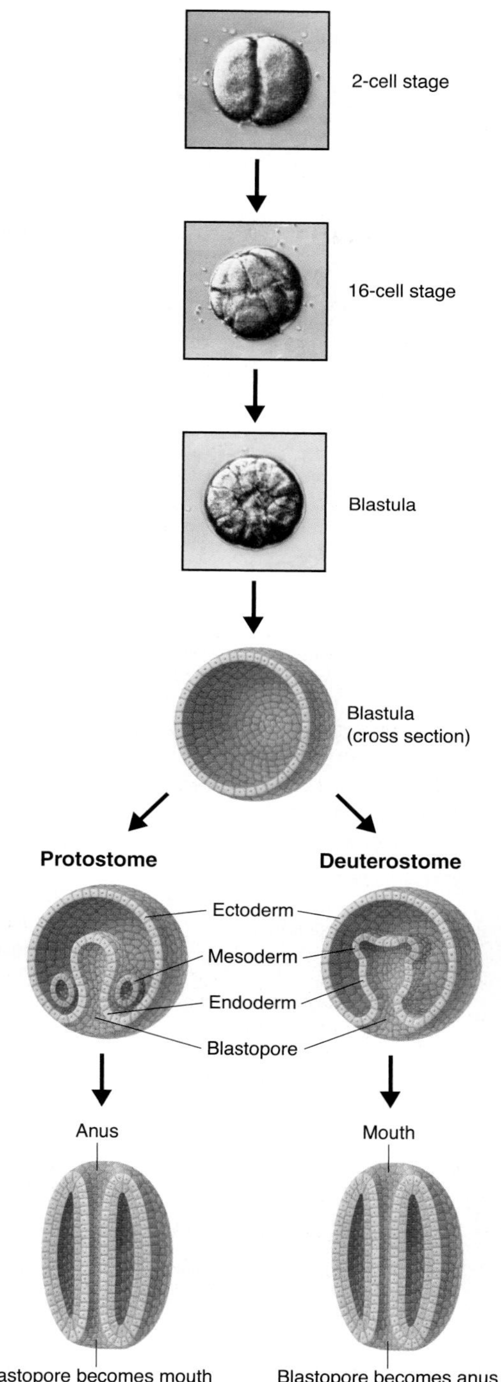

▶ **Figure 26–4** During the early development of animal embryos, cells divide to produce a hollow ball of cells called a blastula. A tube called a blastopore forms in the center of this ball. In protostomes, the blastopore develops into the mouth. In deuterostomes, the blastopore forms an anus, and the mouth forms later. **Interpreting Diagrams** *Which cell layer lines the digestive tract in both protostomes and deuterostomes?*

Use Visuals

Figure 26–4 Ask: **What does the illustrated process show about the differences among kinds of animals?** *(In protostomes, the blastopore develops into a mouth; in deuterostomes, the blastopore develops into an anus.)* Call on volunteers to identify the three tissue layers by color and to explain what each layer develops into in the adult organism. *(Endoderm—lining of the digestive tract, much of the respiratory system; mesoderm—muscles and much of the circulatory, reproductive, and excretory systems; ectoderm—sense organs, nerves, and outer layer of the skin)*

Build Science Skills

Using Models Divide the class into pairs, and give each pair three colors of modeling compound. Challenge students to work with their partners to create a series of models showing the process of early animal development from zygote to protostome and deuterostome, including how cells differentiate into three tissues. Students can use Figure 26–4 for reference.

Meet Diverse Needs

Help students with limited English proficiency understand the meaning of the section's vocabulary terms by having them use a dictionary to find the meaning of the following prefixes: *endo-* ("inside"), *meso-* ("middle"), and *ecto-* ("outside"). Explain that the word part *derm* derives from a Latin word for "skin," which can be interpreted as "tissue." Then, have students use what they've learned to write the meaning of the words *endoderm, mesoderm,* and *ectoderm.* **Limited English proficiency**

BIO INSIGHTS — HISTORY OF SCIENCE

Following the path of stained cells

During early animal development, the cells of the blastula are rearranged to become an embryo called the gastrula, usually with three tissue layers. This process, called gastrulation, involves dramatic movements of cells from the surface of the blastula to interior locations. How do biologists know exactly what happens during this process? In the 1920s, German embryologist W. Vogt carried out classic studies of frog blastulas that showed where cells ended up. His method involved staining blastula cells with different colors of nontoxic dyes. After allowing the process to proceed for different intervals, he would slice open embryos to see where the stained cells had moved. Through this method, he charted "fate maps" for the various cells in the blastula and, thus, mapped out gastrulation. Today, similar studies are done using fluorescent substances.

Answers to . . .

 *The mesoderm*

Figure 26–4 *The endoderm*

Quick Lab

Objective Students will be able to describe some advantages of a bilaterally symmetrical body plan over a radially symmetrical body plan.

Skill Focus **Using models**

Materials modeling clay, plastic knife

Time 15 minutes

Advance Prep Provide each student with two paper towels—one for each model—to prevent staining their desks with the modeling compound.

Strategy After students have completed the activity, point out that in addition to the direct benefits of bilateral symmetry, such a body plan makes possible such additional benefits as cephalization and segments that carry specialized structures such as legs.

Expected Outcomes Students will find it much easier to devise a plausible model of a bilaterally symmetrical walking animal than a radially symmetrical one.

Analyze and Conclude

1. Bilateral symmetry
2. Most are bilaterally symmetrical, because it is difficult to coordinate walking unless legs are paired and parallel.

Meet Diverse Needs

To give students practice with the terms *ventral, dorsal, anterior,* and *posterior,* have them complete the following sentences: (1) The belly is on the [*ventral*] surface of a fish. (2) The back of a wasp is on its [*dorsal*] surface. (3) The head is on the [*anterior*] end of a snail. (4) The tail is on the [*posterior*] end of a lizard. (5) A turtle carries its shell on its [*dorsal*] surface. (6) A coral attaches to the substrate on its [*ventral*] surface. **Learning modality: verbal**

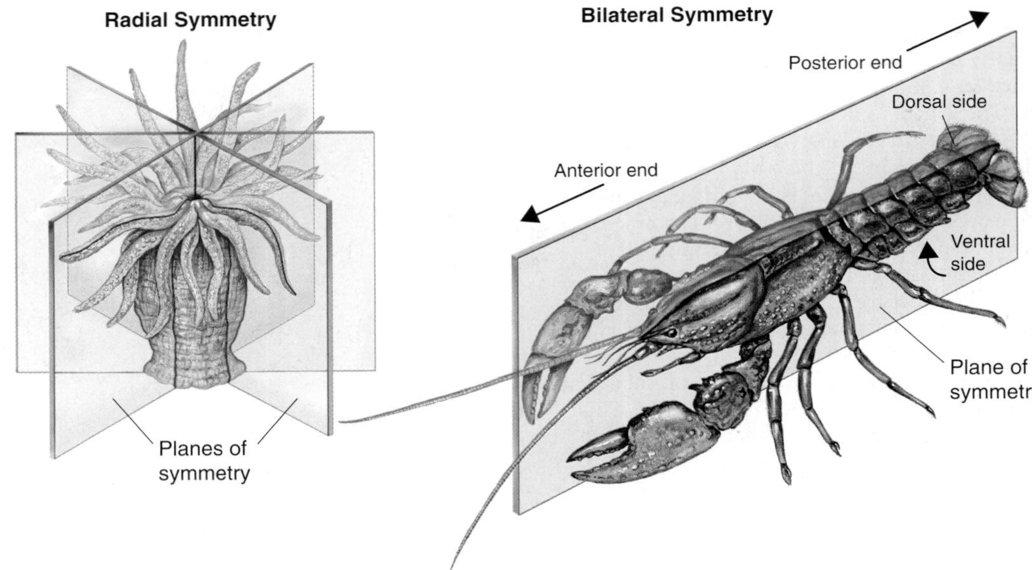

▲ **Figure 26–5** Animals with radial symmetry, such as the sea anemone, have body parts that extend from a central point. Animals with bilateral symmetry, such as the crayfish, have distinct anterior and posterior ends and right and left sides. **Interpreting Graphics** *How many planes of symmetry does the crayfish have?*

Quick Lab

How can body symmetry affect movement?

Material modeling clay

Procedure

1. Use modeling clay to make models of two animals. Make one model radially symmetrical and the other long, narrow, and bilaterally symmetrical.
2. Make grooves to divide each model into similar segments.
3. Add legs to some segments of your models.

Analyze and Conclude

1. **Inferring** Which type of body symmetry is more suited to walking forward?
2. **Using Models** Are most walking animals bilaterally symmetrical? Why do you think this is?

Body Symmetry With the exception of sponges, all animals exhibit some type of body symmetry. Many simple animals, such as the sea anemone shown on the left in **Figure 26–5,** have body parts that repeat around the center of the body. These animals exhibit **radial symmetry,** similar to that of a bicycle wheel, in which any number of imaginary planes can be drawn through the center, each dividing the body into equal halves.

In animals with **bilateral symmetry,** such as the crayfish in **Figure 26–5,** only a single imaginary plane can divide the body into two equal halves. Animals with bilateral symmetry have left and right sides. They also usually have front and back ends and upper and lower sides. The anterior is the front end, and the posterior is the back end. The dorsal is the upper side, and the ventral is the lower side.

A body plan with bilateral symmetry allows for segmentation, in which the body is constructed of many repeated and similar parts, or segments. Animals with bilateral symmetry, such as worms, insects, and vertebrates, typically have external body parts that repeat on either side of the body. The combination of bilateral symmetry and segmentation is found in two of the most successful animal groups—arthropods and vertebrates. Geneticists are now beginning to learn how gene interactions during development control the growth and form of segments and appendages. Amazingly, the same controls are found in humans and insects!

CHECKPOINT *How do radial symmetry and bilateral symmetry differ?*

BIO INSIGHTS **FACTS AND FIGURES**

Variations on a theme
Most animals that have radial symmetry have a body like a cylinder, with a main axis around which the body parts are arranged. This main axis runs from the oral end—where the mouth is—to the aboral end—the end opposite the mouth. Any plane passing through that axis splits the animal into mirror images. For animals that are sessile, such as coral, or drifting, such as jellyfishes, this arrangement is adaptive because the animal can meet the environment equally in all directions. Perfect radial symmetry is rare, occurring only in some sponges and coral polyps. Other radially symmetrical animals have variations on the theme. Sea anemones, for example, have biradial symmetry, since parts of the body are specialized and only two planes through the central axis will produce a mirror image. Many jellyfishes have quadriradial symmetry, and many sea stars have pentaradial symmetry.

◀ **Figure 26–6** Animals with cephalization, such as this dragonfly, have the brain and other sense organs toward the front of the body. This end of the body comes into contact with the environment first, allowing animals to respond effectively to stimuli. **Inferring** *How might cephalization help animals to move quickly?*

Cephalization Animals with bilateral symmetry usually exhibit what is called cephalization (sef-uh-lih-ZAY-shun). **Cephalization** is the concentration of sense organs and nerve cells at the anterior, or front, end of the body. Animals with cephalization, such as the dragonfly in **Figure 26–6,** respond to the environment more quickly and in more sophisticated ways than simpler animals can. Animals with bilateral symmetry usually move with the anterior end forward, so this end comes in contact with new parts of the environment first. As sense organs such as eyes and ears have evolved, they have tended to gather at the anterior end, as have nerve cells that process information and "decide" what the animal should do. In general, the more complex animals become, the more pronounced their degree of cephalization. The anterior end is often different enough from the rest of the body that it is called a head.

Body Cavity Formation Most animals have a body cavity, which is a fluid-filled space that lies between the digestive tract and the body wall. A body cavity is important because it provides a space in which internal organs can be suspended so that they are not pressed on by muscles or twisted out of shape by body movements. Body cavities also allow for specialized regions to develop, and they provide room for internal organs to grow and expand. In some animals, body cavities contain fluids that are involved in circulation, feeding, and excretion.

26–1 Section Assessment

1. **Key Concept** What is an animal?
2. **Key Concept** Describe the seven essential functions performed by all animals.
3. **Key Concept** In what ways are complex animals different from simple animals?
4. How are body symmetry and cephalization related?
5. **Critical Thinking Applying Concepts** How might having specialized cells increase efficiency in multicellular animals?

iTEXT Assessment Use iText to review the important concepts in Section 26–1.

ALTERNATIVE ASSESSMENT

Constructing a Chart
Make a two-column chart of the different functions that enable animals to survive and respond to the environment. In the first column, list each function. In the second column, include a drawing, photograph, or magazine clipping that illustrates an example of that function.

26–1 Section Assessment

1. An animal is a multicellular, eukaryotic heterotroph whose cells lack cell walls.
2. Students should describe the seven essential functions: feeding, respiration, circulation, excretion, response, movement, and reproduction.
3. Complex animals tend to have high levels of cell specialization and internal organization, bilateral symmetry, cephalization, and a body cavity.
4. Animals with bilateral symmetry usually exhibit cephalization. They usually move with their anterior end forward. As a result, their sense organs have tended to gather at the anterior end.
5. Each specialized cell type performs different tasks for the organism. Multicellular animals with specialized cells can carry out different functions using only those cells specialized for each task.

3 ASSESS

Evaluate Understanding

Make a list on the board of some common animals, including a worm, an ant, a snail, a fish, and a jellyfish. Then, call on students at random to describe how one of the animals listed carries out the seven essential functions. Accept any reasonable speculation as long as students demonstrate an understanding of the seven essential functions.

Reteach

Ask each student to create a flowchart that explains the process involved in an animal's early development, as shown in Figure 26–4. Students' flowcharts should begin with a zygote and show a split among animals as the blastopore becomes either a mouth or an anus.

ALTERNATIVE ASSESSMENT

Provide students with an assortment of nature magazines from which they can cut photographs. Students' charts should include the functions of feeding, respiration, circulation, excretion, response to the environment, movement, and reproduction.

Use iText to review the key concepts in Section 26–1.

Answers to . . .

CHECKPOINT *With radial symmetry, any number of imaginary lines can be drawn through the center, each dividing the body into equal halves. With bilateral symmetry, only a single imaginary line can be drawn to divide the body into two equal halves.*

Figure 26–5 *One*

Figure 26–6 *The concentration of nerve cells and sense organs in the anterior end enables quick detection of stimuli and processing the response. Many animals with cephalization have limbs or fins that move efficiently and quickly.*

Section 26–2

1 FOCUS

Objectives

26.2.1 ***Explain*** what a sponge is.
26.2.2 ***Describe*** how sponges carry out essential functions.
26.2.3 ***Describe*** the ecology of sponges.

Guide for Reading

Vocabulary Preview

Have students write the Vocabulary terms, dividing each into its separate syllables as best they can. Remind students that each syllable usually has only one vowel sound. The correct syllabications are: cho•a•no•cyte, os•cu•lum, spi•cule, a•moe•bo•cyte, spong•in, in•ter•nal fer•til•i•za•tion, lar•va, gem•mule.

Reading Strategy

Before students read the section, have them draw a line down the center of a piece of paper. Explain that as they read through the section, they should write down the main topics of the section on the left side of the line. On the right side, they should make notes of supporting details and examples.

2 INSTRUCT

What Is a Sponge?

Build Science Skills

Observing Divide the class into small groups, and give each group a natural sponge and a hand lens. Ask students to observe the sponge with the hand lens and make drawings of what they see. Then, provide groups with glass microscope slides and coverslips. To prepare a slide, students should tear off a tiny piece of the sponge, place it on a slide, and observe it under a microscope. Have them make drawings of what they observe.

26–2 Sponges

Guide for Reading

Key Concepts

- Why are sponges classified as animals?
- How do sponges carry out essential functions?

Vocabulary

choanocyte
osculum
spicule
archaeocyte
internal fertilization
larva
gemmule

Reading Strategy: Using Visuals Before you read, preview **Figure 26–8** and **Figure 26–9.** For each figure, write a brief statement that summarizes the content of the illustration. Once you have read the section, explain how each illustration reinforces or enhances the content of the section.

Sponges are the simplest and probably the most unusual animals. Living on Earth for at least 540 million years, sponges are also the most ancient animals. Today, most sponges live in the ocean, from the Arctic and Antarctic regions to the tropics, and from shallow water to depths of several hundred meters. To humans, however, they are probably best known in their dried form—the natural sponges used for bathing.

What Is a Sponge?

Sponges are placed in the phylum Porifera (poh-RIF-ur-uh), which means "pore-bearers." This name is appropriate because sponges have tiny openings, or pores, all over their bodies, as shown in **Figure 26–7.** Sponges are sessile, meaning that they live their entire adult life attached to a single spot.

Given these unusual features, why are sponges considered animals? **Sponges are classified as animals because they are multicellular, heterotrophic, have no cell walls, and contain a few specialized cells.** Because sponges are so different from other animals, some scientists think that they evolved independently from all other animals. Other evidence suggests that sponges share a common ancestor with other animals, but that they separated from this ancestor long before the other groups did.

CHECKPOINT *Why is the phylum name Porifera appropriate for sponges?*

Form and Function in Sponges

Sponges have nothing resembling a mouth or gut, and they have no tissues or organ systems. Simple functions are carried out by a few specialized cells.

▼ **Figure 26–7** **Sponges are animals because they are heterotrophic and have specialized cells.** Sponges are probably the least typical of what we think of as animals. They grow in irregular shapes and live attached to the floor of oceans and freshwater bodies. Water enters the body of a sponge through small holes called pores (inset photo).

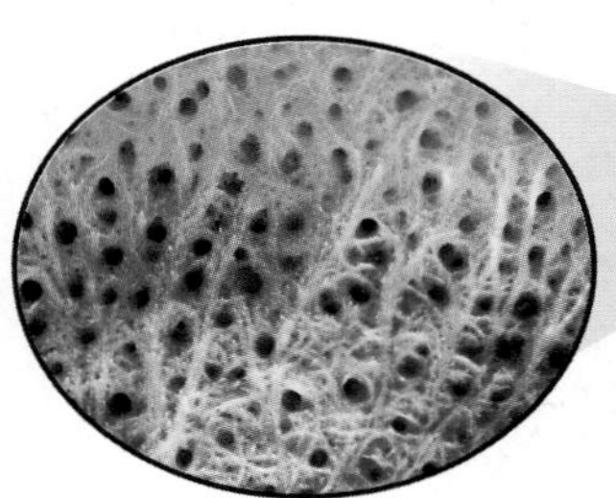

SECTION RESOURCES

Print:

- ***Teaching Resources,*** Section Review 26–2
- ***Guided Reading and Study Workbook,*** Section 26–2

Technology:

- ***iText,*** Section 26–2

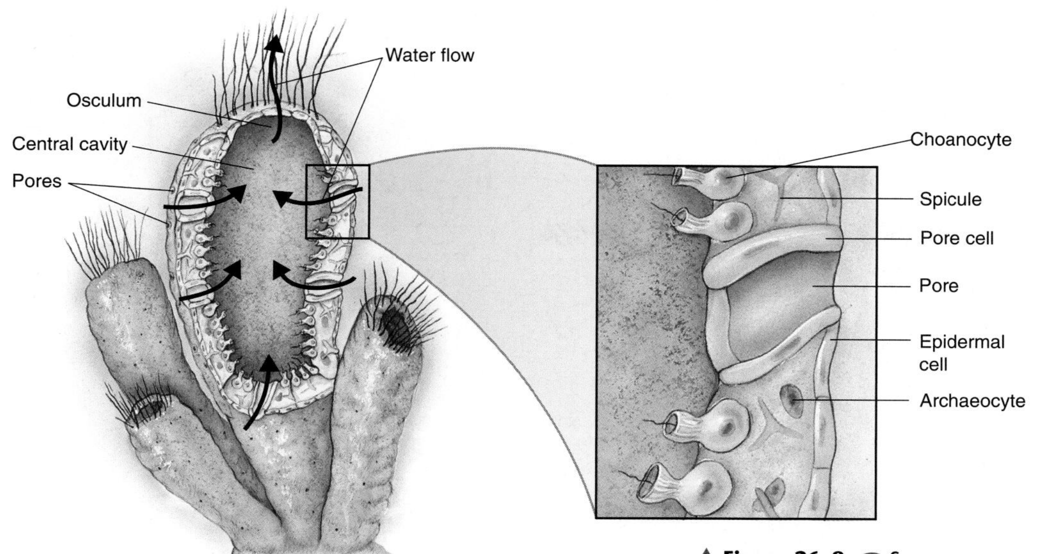

▲ **Figure 26–8** **Sponges carry out basic functions, such as feeding and circulation, by moving water through their bodies.** Choanocytes use flagella to move water through pores in the wall of the sponge and out through the osculum. As water moves through the sponge, food particles are filtered from the water, and wastes are removed from the sponge.

Body Plan Sponges are asymmetrical; they have no front or back ends, and no left or right sides. A sponge can be thought of as a large, cylindrical water pump. The body of a sponge, shown in **Figure 26–8**, forms a wall around a large central cavity through which water is circulated continually. **Choanocytes** (koh-AN-uh-sytz) are specialized cells that use flagella to move a steady current of water through the sponge. This water—in some cases, several thousand liters per day—enters through pores located in the body wall. Water then leaves through the **osculum** (AHS-kyoo-lum), a large hole at the top of the sponge. **The movement of water through the sponge provides a simple mechanism for feeding, respiration, circulation, and excretion.**

Sponges have a simple skeleton. In harder sponges, the skeleton is made of spiny spicules. A **spicule** is a spike-shaped structure made of chalklike calcium carbonate or glasslike silica. Spicules are made by **archaeocytes** (ARK-ee-uh-sytz), which are specialized cells that move around within the walls of the sponge. Softer sponges have an internal skeleton made of spongin, a network of flexible protein fibers. These are the sponges that are harvested and used as natural bath sponges.

Feeding Sponges are filter feeders that sift microscopic food particles from the water. Digestion is intracellular, meaning that it takes place inside cells. As water moves through the sponge, food particles are trapped and engulfed by choanocytes that line the body cavity. These particles are then digested or passed on to archaeocytes. The archaeocytes complete the digestive process and transport digested food throughout the sponge.

Form and Function in Sponges

Address Misconceptions

Students may have the misconception that a simple or primitive body plan is inferior or less than optimal. Point out that sponges and other so-called primitive animals evolved hundreds of millions of years ago and have persisted through cataclysmic environmental changes until today. Ask: **What does the longevity of the sponge say about its body plan in terms of adaptability to its environment?** *(The longevity of the sponge is evidence that it is extremely well-adapted to its environment.)*

Use Visuals

Figure 26–8 Ask: **Does this sponge exhibit symmetry?** *(It doesn't exhibit symmetry; sponges are asymmetrical.)* **Through what structures does water enter a sponge?** *(Pores)* **What do choanocytes use to move a current of water through a sponge?** *(Flagella)* **Through what structure does water leave the sponge?** *(The osculum)* **Is this sponge a harder or softer sponge?** *(It is a harder sponge, because it has spicules.)*

Build Science Skills

Comparing and Contrasting Divide the class into small groups. Give each group a natural sponge, a coffee filter, a heavy paper towel, a large basin, and a container of muddy or sandy water. Instruct students to pour the muddy water through the sponge and the two common filters and compare the cleanliness of the water that falls into the basin after filtering. Students should observe that the sponge does the best job of filtering impurities from the water.

PRESENTATIONS MADE EASY!

The Presentation Assistant Plus contains the Prentice Hall Presentation Pro and the Transparencies, which provide easy-to-follow visual support for every step of this lesson. If you have a computer presentation station, use Prentice Hall Presentation Pro Section 26–2, or use the transparencies listed here.

Section 26–2: **Interest Grabber**
Section Outline
Sponge Life Cycle
Figure 26–8

Answer to . . .

CHECKPOINT Porifera *means "pore bearers," and sponges have pores all over their bodies.*

26–2 (continued)

Demonstration

Emphasize that sponges rely on the movement of water through their bodies for the essential functions of feeding, respiration, circulation, and excretion. Demonstrate how much water a sponge can hold by comparing the water-holding capacity of a natural sponge and a synthetic sponge of about the same size. Measure the mass of each sponge on a scale, and record the masses on the board. Then, soak each sponge in water, and measure and record their masses again. Students should observe that the natural sponge holds more water than the synthetic sponge.

Meet Diverse Needs

Help at-risk students understand respiration and excretion in sponges by reviewing what they have learned about diffusion. Ask: **What is diffusion?** *(It is a process by which molecules spread through a liquid from regions of high concentration to regions of low concentration.)* Reinforce the idea that diffusion occurs across cell membranes. Then, ask: **How would you describe the process of diffusion in sponge respiration?** *(Oxygen diffuses into a cell through the cell membrane from the water circulating through the sponge, because the concentration of oxygen in the water is greater than that inside the cell.)* Explain that the opposite occurs with wastes in the process of excretion.

Use Visuals

Figure 26–9 After students have studied the illustration of sexual reproduction in a sponge, ask: **Is a mature sponge haploid or diploid?** *(Diploid)* **What cellular process produces sperm and egg cells?** *(Meiosis)* **How do sperm reach eggs, and where does fertilization occur?** *(Sperm are released into the water, and currents carry them into the pores of other sponges. Fertilization occurs in the wall of a sponge.)* **What is the immature stage of a sponge called?** *(A larva)*

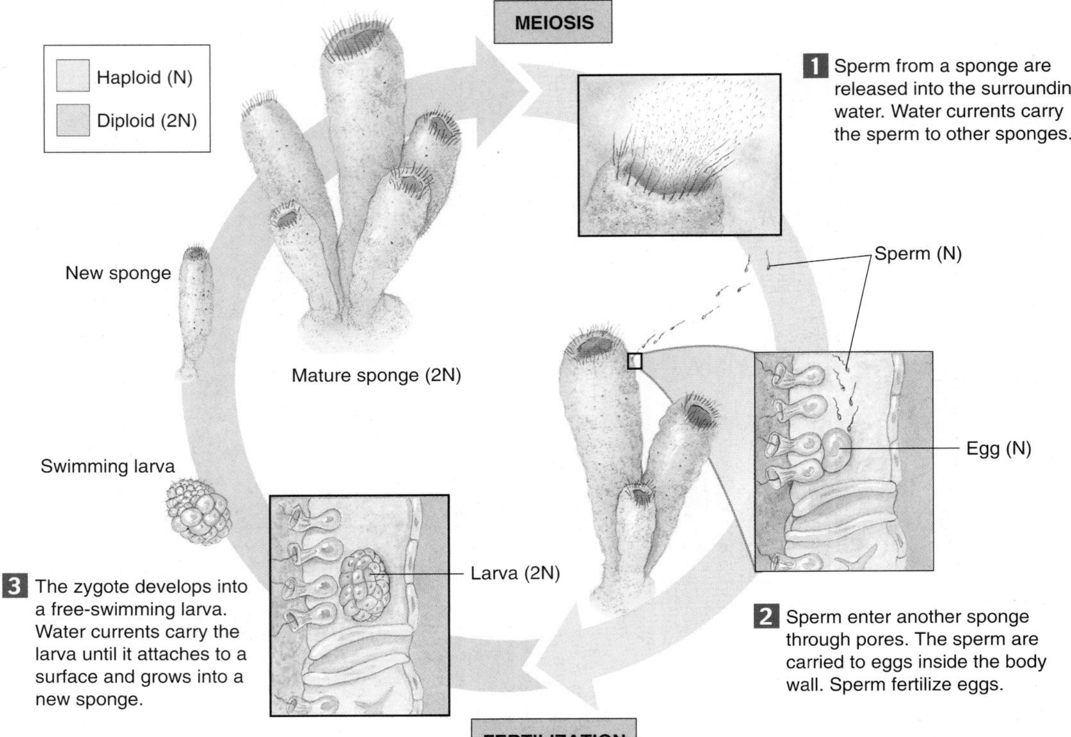
MEIOSIS
Haploid (N)
Diploid (2N)
1 Sperm from a sponge are released into the surrounding water. Water currents carry the sperm to other sponges.
Sperm (N)
New sponge
Mature sponge (2N)
Egg (N)
Swimming larva
Larva (2N)
3 The zygote develops into a free-swimming larva. Water currents carry the larva until it attaches to a surface and grows into a new sponge.
2 Sperm enter another sponge through pores. The sperm are carried to eggs inside the body wall. Sperm fertilize eggs.
FERTILIZATION

▲ **Figure 26–9** Most sponges reproduce sexually, and many have internal fertilization. **Interpreting Graphics** *Is an adult sponge haploid or diploid?*

Respiration, Circulation, and Excretion Sponges rely on the movement of water through their bodies to carry out body functions. As water moves through the body cavity, oxygen dissolved in the water diffuses into the surrounding cells. At the same time, carbon dioxide and other wastes, such as ammonia, diffuse into the water and are carried away.

Response Sponges do not have nervous systems that would allow them to respond to changes in their environment. However, many sponges protect themselves by producing toxins that make them unpalatable or poisonous to potential predators.

Reproduction Sponges can reproduce either sexually or asexually. The steps in sexual reproduction are diagrammed in **Figure 26–9.** In most sponge species, a single sponge forms both eggs and sperm. A sponge usually produces its eggs and sperm at different times. In sponges, eggs are fertilized inside the sponge's body, a process called **internal fertilization.** Sperm are released from one sponge and are carried by water currents until they enter the pores of another sponge. Archaeocytes carry the sperm to an egg, which is located in the wall of the sponge. After fertilization, the zygote develops into a larva. A **larva** is an immature stage of an organism that looks different from the adult form. The larvae of sponges are motile and are usually carried by currents before they settle to the sea floor.

BIO INSIGHTS

HISTORY OF SCIENCE

Plant or animal?
Because sponges are sessile and asymmetric, most common observers might think that a living sponge is some kind of a plant. In fact, sponges have traditionally been thought of as plants, which is how the ancient Greeks classified them. It wasn't until naturalists in the late 1700s described the flow of water through sponges that these organisms were recognized as some kind of animal.

Throughout the 1800s, most naturalists thought sponges were related to corals and other members of the cnidarian class Anthozoa. It was thought that sponges, like anthozoans, had only a polyp stage in their life cycle. Early in the twentieth century, sponges became generally accepted as constituting a phylum of their own, separate from all other animals. Phylum Porifera now includes about 9,000 recognized species in three classes.

Sponges can reproduce asexually by budding or by producing gemmules. In budding, part of a sponge breaks off of the parent sponge, settles to the sea floor, and grows into a new sponge. When faced with difficult environmental conditions, some sponges produce **gemmules** (JEM-yoolz), which are groups of archaeocytes surrounded by a tough layer of spicules. Gemmules can survive freezing temperatures and drought conditions that would kill adult sponges. When conditions become favorable, a gemmule grows into a new sponge.

Ecology of Sponges

Sponges play an important part in the ecology and survival of numerous aquatic organisms. Sponges have an irregular shape and many are large. These characteristics make sponges ideal habitats for marine animals such as snails, sea stars, sea cucumbers, and shrimp, such as the shrimp in **Figure 26–10.** More important to the sponges are their mutually beneficial relationships with bacteria, algae, and plantlike protists. In fact, many sponges are colored green because these organisms are living in their tissues. These photosynthetic organisms provide food and oxygen to the sponge, while the sponge provides a protected area where these organisms can thrive. Because of this relationship, sponges containing photosynthetic organisms play an important role in the ecology and primary productivity of coral reefs.

Sponges usually live attached to the sea floor, where they are often many meters from the water surface and receive only low levels of filtered sunlight. Recently, scientists have found clues to the mystery of how organisms within the sponge get enough light to carry out photosynthesis. The spicules of some sponges look like cross-shaped antennae. Like a lens or magnifying glass, they focus and direct incoming sunlight to cells lying below the surface of the sponge—where symbiotic organisms carry out photosynthesis. This adaptation may allow sponges to survive in a wider range of habitats.

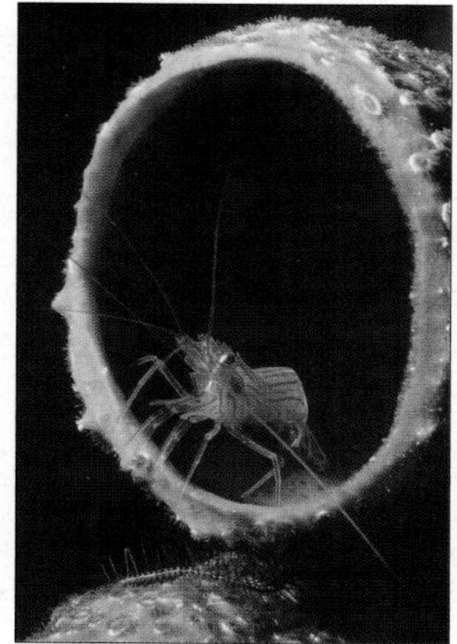

▲ **Figure 26–10** Sponges often provide habitats for other organisms. Observe how the sponge provides shelter for this snapping shrimp. **Inferring** *How might the sponge protect the shrimp from predators?*

26–2 Section Assessment

1. **Key Concept** What features do sponges share with all other animals?
2. **Key Concept** How do sponges use water to carry out essential functions?
3. Describe the different types of sponge skeletons.
4. Why are symbiotic relationships critical to the ecology of sponges?
5. **Critical Thinking Drawing Conclusions** Why would sponges be unable to live on land?

iTEXT **Assessment** Use iText to review the important concepts in Section 26–2.

ALTERNATIVE ASSESSMENT

Creating an Exhibit

Use posterboard to make an exhibit about sponges. Illustrate the characteristics that sponges share with other animals as well as the differences between sponges and other animals.

Ecology of Sponges

Meet Diverse Needs

Ask students who need extra challenges to prepare a report on symbiotic relationships between sponges and other animals, called commensalism, in which one member benefits and the other is not harmed. Explain that a variety of animals, including worms, shrimp, snails, and crabs, use sponges for protection and even for the food particles suspended in the water flowing through a sponge. Have students present what they learned to the class. **Learning modality: verbal**

3 ASSESS

Evaluate Understanding

Ask students to turn back to the chapter-opening photo of the sponger on the boat washing newly harvested sponges. Then, call on students at random to explain why the sponges shown are considered animals and how sponges carry out the seven essential animal functions.

Reteach

Have students make their own drawing of Figure 26–8, and then define each term in the labels and explain how each part of the sponge aids the organism in one of the seven essential functions.

ALTERNATIVE ASSESSMENT

Students' posters should demonstrate that sponges, unlike other animals, are asymmetrical and lack true tissues and nerve cells. Like other animals, sponges are heterotrophs, contain no cell walls, have specialized cells and a skeleton, and can reproduce sexually.

26–2 Section Assessment

1. Sponges are heterotrophic, have no cell walls, and contain specialized cells.
2. The movement of water through the sponge carries needed materials, such as food and oxygen, and carries wastes away. Water also carries sperm to eggs.
3. The skeleton of many sponges is made of spiny spicules. Softer sponges have a skeleton made of flexible spongin.
4. Bacteria, cyanobacteria, and plantlike protists provide food and oxygen to many sponges, while the sponges provide a protected area where these organisms can thrive.
5. Sponges depend on the movement of water for most functions, including feeding, respiration, circulation, excretion, and reproduction.

Use iText to review the key concepts in Section 26–2.

Answers to . . .

Figure 26–9 *Diploid*

Figure 26–10 *By providing a place of concealment*

After students have read this feature, you might want to discuss one or more of the following:

- Ask students to think about how corals evolved in a way that they contain a chemical that protects them from the sun. Students should apply their knowledge of natural selection to this example.
- Have students explain why it is important that a way to produce Sunscreen 855 in the laboratory was developed. Students should infer that biologists don't want to harvest corals to extract the chemical, because coral reefs are already under high threat worldwide.
- Discuss with students the importance of bioprospecting, as well as how the prospect of products from plants and animals argues for the continued maintenance of biodiversity. Students could brainstorm a list of products they think could be derived from other animals in the wild. Suggest that they think about adaptations animals have evolved that could be exploited for helpful products.

On Your Own

For things that the product should do, students might mention protecting against a severe sunburn and preventing skin cancer. For things that the product should not do, students might mention that the sunscreen should not cause a skin rash and should not cause some kind of systemic allergic reaction or long-term disease. For testing the different claims, students might suggest first carrying out experiments in which animals are tested with the sunscreen and then, if there are no evident harmful effects, devising controlled studies with human volunteers.

Sunscreen From the Sea

When it comes to inventing new gadgets, high technology cannot be beat. But when it comes to searching for new compounds that affect living organisms, sometimes the best approach is "low tech." One way of generating new medicines and drugs, for example, is to look for them in nature. Organisms of all kinds have been battling each other and their physical environment since life began. So, researchers can take 100-million-year shortcuts by searching for molecules that have been assembled and tested by the oldest process for generating new compounds on Earth—natural selection.

Natural UV Protection in Corals

One of these "new" molecules may be the world's first naturally produced sunscreen. Known as Sunscreen 855, this compound was discovered by researchers at the Australian Institute of Marine Science. These researchers were studying corals that live in shallow waters along Australia's Great Barrier Reef. During the low tide, these corals are exposed to the air and full sunlight. Investigators reasoned that these corals might have evolved some sort of protection against the damaging ultraviolet (UV) radiation of intense sunlight. Sure enough, their search turned up a UV-blocking compound in the tissues of these corals.

From Natural to Synthetic

After isolating and analyzing the compound in Sunscreen 855, the researchers learned that it was structurally different from the compounds used in synthetic sunscreens. They devised a way to produce it in the laboratory so that corals would not need to be harvested to make the sunscreen. Preliminary tests have shown that the sunscreen is highly efficient in absorbing radiation in the damaging UV-B region of the spectrum.

But Sunscreen 855 is not sold in any drugstore—nor will it be for several years. Researchers are working with investors, lawyers, and businesspeople to test the new product for effectiveness and safety. If it passes final tests, Sunscreen 855 could be the best—and most natural—protection yet against the harmful effects of the sun.

On Your Own

Suppose that Sunscreen 855 were made into a product that people could buy. Make a list of things that the product should do. Make another list of things it should not do (such as harmful side effects it might cause). Describe how you would test these different claims.

FACTS AND FIGURES

Sunscreens and UV-B radiation

UV radiation makes up that part of the electromagnetic spectrum with wavelengths just shorter than those of visible light. People need some exposure to UV radiation for the production of vitamin D, which promotes healthy bones and teeth. But, excessive exposure causes skin damage and even cancer. UV radiation is divided into two regions: UV-A radiation has longer wavelengths than UV-B radiation. UV-B radiation is much more harmful, and most commercial suntan and sunscreen products absorb UV-B radiation. Sunscreen 855 has proven to be very efficient in absorbing and dissipating UV-B radiation. The development of this product is an example of bioprospecting, or biodiversity prospecting, which is the exploration of wild plants and animals for commercially valuable genetic and biochemical resources.

26–3 Cnidarians

Imagine that you are swimming in warm, tropical waters. Far away, delicate jellyfishes float in the ocean currents. Within arm's reach, sea fans sway in the shallow currents. Brightly colored sea anemones cling to rocks, looking more like underwater flowers than animals. All these creatures are animals in the phylum Cnidaria (ny-DAYR-ee-uh), a group that includes hydras, jellyfishes, sea anemones, and corals. These fascinating animals are found in waters all over the world. Some cnidarians live as individuals. Others live in colonies composed of dozens or even thousands of connected individuals.

Guide for Reading

Key Concepts
- What is a cnidarian?
- What two body plans exist in the cnidarian life cycle?
- What are the three groups of cnidarians?

Vocabulary
cnidocyte
nematocyst
polyp
medusa
gastrovascular cavity
nerve net
hydrostatic skeleton
external fertilization

Reading Strategy: Finding Main Ideas Before you read, skim the section to identify the key concepts. Read the section carefully, then write down the information that supports each key concept.

What Is a Cnidarian?

A few important features unite the cnidarians as a group. **Cnidarians are soft-bodied, carnivorous animals that have stinging tentacles arranged in circles around their mouths. They are the simplest animals to have body symmetry and specialized tissues.** Cnidarians get their name from the **cnidocytes** (NY-duh-syts), or stinging cells, that are located along their tentacles. **Figure 26–11** shows the structure of cnidocytes. Cnidarians use these cells for defense and to capture prey. Within each cnidocyte is a nematocyst (NEM-uh-toh-sist). A **nematocyst** is a poison-filled, stinging structure that contains a tightly coiled dart. When an unsuspecting shrimp or small fish brushes up against the tentacles, thousands of nematocysts explode into the animal, releasing enough poison to paralyze or kill the prey.

CHECKPOINT *What is the function of cnidocytes?*

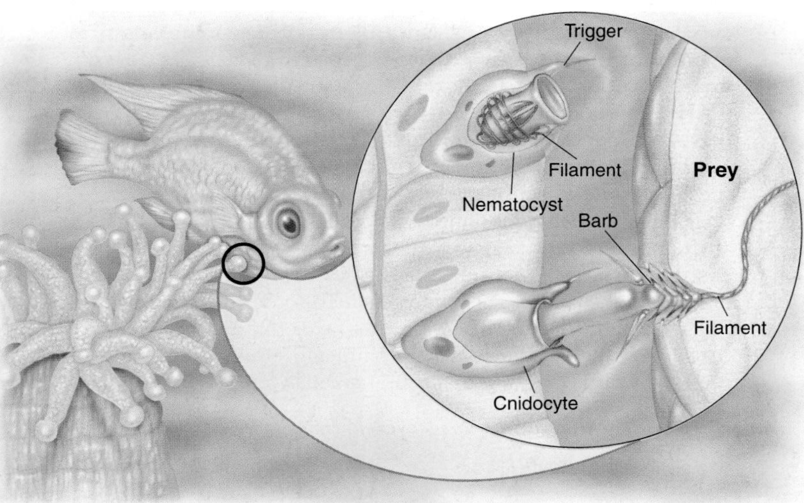

◀ Figure 26–11 Cnidarians are carnivorous animals that have stinging tentacles arranged around their mouths. Stinging cells called cnidocytes are used to capture and paralyze prey. Within each cnidocyte is a stinging structure called a nematocyst. Here, a sea anemone captures a fish that has brushed the trigger of the nematocyst. When an animal touches the trigger of a nematocyst, the filament inside uncoils and shoots a barb into the animal.

TIME SAVER — SECTION RESOURCES

Print:
- ***Laboratory Manual A,*** Chapter 26 Lab
- ***Laboratory Manual B,*** Chapter 26 Lab
- ***Teaching Resources,*** Section Review 26–3
- ***Guided Reading and Study Workbook,*** Section 26–3
- ***Issues and Decision Making,*** 26–3

Technology:
- ***iText,*** Section 26–3

Section 26–3

1 FOCUS

Objectives

26.3.1 ***Explain*** what a cnidarian is.
26.3.2 ***Describe*** the two body plans that exist in the cnidarian life cycle.
26.3.3 ***Describe*** how cnidarians carry out essential functions.
26.3.4 ***Identify*** the three groups of cnidarians.
26.3.5 ***Describe*** the ecology of cnidarians.

Guide for Reading

Vocabulary Preview

Explain that the name *cnidarian* is derived from Greek *knide,* which means "nettle." A nettle is a common plant with toothed leaves and stinging hairs. Point out that the first Vocabulary term, cnidocyte, is derived from the same Greek word.

Reading Strategy

Point out that the section's Key Concepts are highlighted in boldface type. Have students write the boldface sentences in their notebooks and find information that supports each.

2 INSTRUCT

What Is a Cnidarian?

Use Visuals

Figure 26–11 Ask: **In this figure, what part of a cnidarian is enlarged in the inset?** *(The end of a tentacle)* Point out that the inset shows two specialized cells. Ask: **What are these cells called?** *(Cnidocytes)* **What is the stinging structure called inside each cnidocyte?** *(A nematocyst)* **What is released from the nematocyst that kills or paralyzes prey?** *(A poison)*

Answer to . . .

CHECKPOINT *Cnidocytes function in defense and capturing prey.*

Form and Function in Cidarians

Use Visuals

Figure 26–12 As students study the figure, point out that a cnidarian has only two tissue layers, an endoderm and an ectoderm. Then, ask: **What is the third layer in cnidarians?** *(The mesoglea, which varies from a thin, noncellular layer to a thick jellylike material)* **In which form is the mesoglea most prominent?** *(The medusa)* Emphasize that the mesoglea is not a tissue layer made of cells.

Build Science Skills

Using Models To reinforce the body plan of cnidarians, have students search for objects around the school that exhibit radial symmetry. Ask students to make a list of such objects, which might include an electric fan, a petri dish, a bicycle wheel, a trashcan, a basketball, a showerhead, a bowl, and a flowerpot.

Demonstration

Use two plastic cups, one clear and one colored, to demonstrate the difference between a cnidarian polyp and a medusa. Place the colored cup inside the clear cup, and explain that these two cups represent the two tissue layers of a cnidarian, the inside gastroderm and the outside epidermis. Then, display the double cup right side up and explain that this represents the polyp form of a cnidarian, with the mouth facing upward. Turn the double cup upside down, and explain that this represents the medusa form of a cnidarian, with mouth facing downward.

Word Origins

Cnidarian medusas have long tentacles that are something like Medusa's snakes.

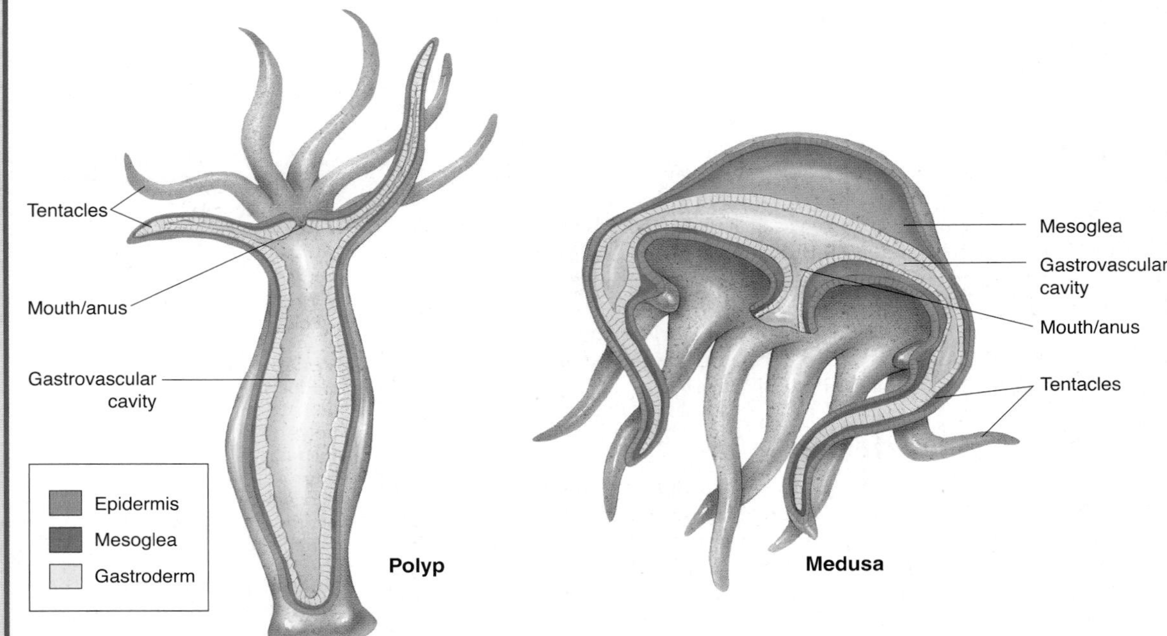

▲ **Figure 26–12** **Many cnidarians have both a polyp stage (left) and a medusa stage (right).** Both stages have an outer epidermal tissue; a gastroderm tissue, which lines the gastrovascular cavity; and a mesoglea layer, which lies between the two tissues. (Note that a medusa's tentacles are much narrower than in the illustration.)

Word Origins

Medusa is the name of a monster in Greek mythology. In the myth, Medusa was once a beautiful woman, but she bragged about her beauty, and so a jealous goddess changed her into a hideous monster. Medusa had long, twisting snakes for hair. **In what way are cnidarian medusas similar to the monster named Medusa?**

Form and Function in Cnidarians

Cnidarians are only a few cells thick and have simple body systems. Most of their responses to the environment are carried out by specialized cells and tissues. These tissues function in processes such as feeding and movement.

Body Plan Cnidarians are radially symmetrical. They have a central mouth surrounded by numerous tentacles that extend outward from the body. **Cnidarians typically have a life cycle that includes two different-looking stages: a polyp and a medusa.** Both forms are shown in **Figure 26–12.** A **polyp** (PAHL-ip) is a cylindrical body with armlike tentacles. In a polyp, the mouth points upward. Polyps are usually sessile. A **medusa** (muh-DOO-suh) has a motile, bell-shaped body with the mouth on the bottom.

Cnidarian polyps and medusas each have a body wall that surrounds an internal space called a gastrovascular cavity. The gastroderm is the inner lining of the gastrovascular cavity, where digestion takes place. The epidermis is the outer layer of cells. The mesoglea (mez-uh-GLEE-uh) is a layer that lies between these two tissues. It varies from a thin, noncellular membrane to a thick, jellylike material that contains cells.

CHECKPOINT *What are the three layers in cnidarians?*

PRESENTATIONS MADE EASY!

The Presentation Assistant Plus contains the Prentice Hall Presentation Pro and the Transparencies, which provide easy-to-follow visual support for every step of this lesson. If you have a computer presentation station, use Prentice Hall Presentation Pro Section 26–3, or use the transparencies listed here.

Section 26–3: **Interest Grabber**
Section Outline
Jellyfish Life Cycle
Figure 26–12

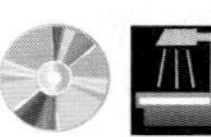

Before

After

Figure 26–13 Cnidarians have nerve nets that consist of many individual nerve cells, as shown in the hydra below. Many cnidarians respond to touch by pulling their tentacles inside their bodies. This response, shown at left in cup corals, is cued by nerve cells located in the tentacles. **Formulating Hypotheses** *How might a nerve net differ between motile and sessile cnidarians?*

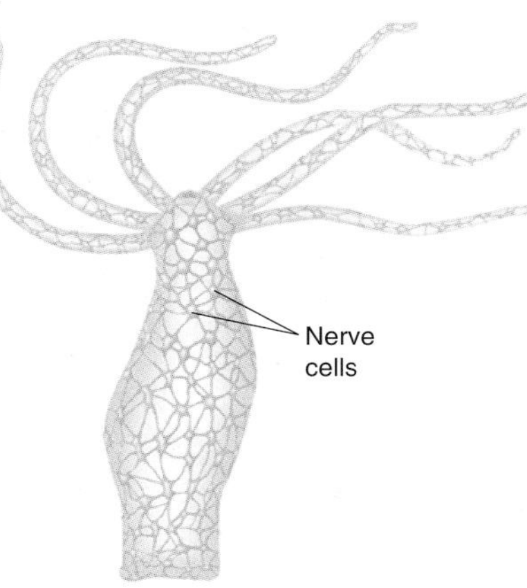

Feeding After paralyzing its prey, a cnidarian pulls the prey through its mouth and into its **gastrovascular cavity,** a digestive chamber with one opening. Food enters and wastes leave the body through that opening. Digestion—the breakdown of food—begins in the gastrovascular cavity. The digestion that occurs in the gastrovascular cavity is extracellular, meaning that it takes place outside of cells. Partially digested food is absorbed by the gastroderm. Digestion is completed intracellularly, within cells in the gastroderm. Any materials that cannot be digested are passed out of the body through the mouth.

Respiration, Circulation, and Excretion Following digestion, nutrients are usually transported throughout the body by diffusion. Cnidarians respire and eliminate the wastes of cellular metabolism by diffusion through their body walls.

Response Cnidarians gather information from their environment using specialized sensory cells. Both polyps and medusas have a nerve net, shown in **Figure 26–13.** A **nerve net** is a loosely organized network of nerve cells that together allow cnidarians to detect stimuli such as the touch of a foreign object. The nerve net is usually distributed uniformly throughout the body, although in some species it is concentrated around the mouth or in rings around the body. Cnidarians also have statocysts, which are groups of sensory cells that help determine the direction of gravity. Ocelli (oh-SEL-eye; singular: ocellus) are eyespots made of cells that detect light.

Movement Different cnidarians move in different ways. Some cnidarians, such as sea anemones, have a hydrostatic skeleton. The **hydrostatic skeleton** consists of a layer of circular muscles and a layer of longitudinal muscles that, together with the water in the gastrovascular cavity, enable the cnidarian to move. For example, if the anemone's circular muscles contract when the anemone's mouth is closed, the water inside the cavity can't escape. The pressure of the water makes the body become taller. In contrast, medusas move by jet propulsion. Muscle contractions cause the bell-shaped body to close like a folding umbrella. This action pushes water out of the bell, moving the medusa forward, as shown in **Figure 26–14**.

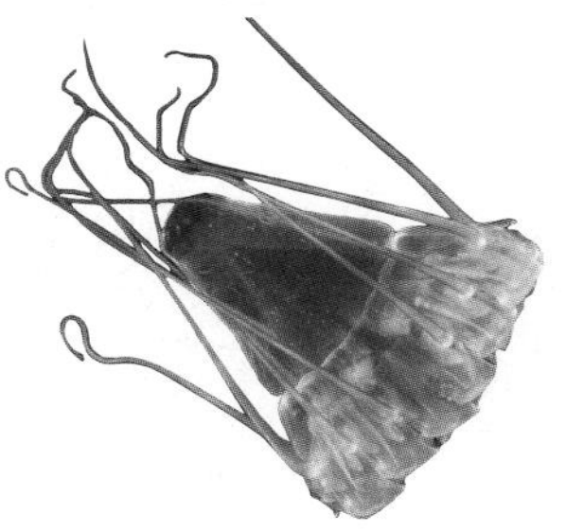

▲ **Figure 26–14** Jellyfishes move by means of jet propulsion. The body contracts to force water out, moving the jellyfish in the opposite direction. **Applying Concepts** *Is the body plan of this jellyfish a medusa or a polyp?*

Build Science Skills

Comparing and Contrasting Ask students to write a paragraph that compares and contrasts sponges and cnidarians in how they carry out the seven essential functions. Students should suggest that there is great similarity between the two groups in respiration, circulation, and excretion. They should point to significant differences in feeding, response, movement, and reproduction.

Demonstration

Use familiar objects to demonstrate the difference in the ways cnidarian polyps and medusas move. For the polyp, partially fill an oblong balloon with water and tie the opening closed. Tell students that the balloon represents a cnidarian gastrovascular cavity. Then, show by squeezing parts of the balloon how it can change shape, with one part growing larger while the other shrinks. Ask: **What kind of skeleton does this represent?** *(A hydrostatic skeleton)* Next, pick up an umbrella, and tell students that it represents the bell-shaped body of a medusa. Rapidly open and close the umbrella, and explain that medusas have muscles to contract and expand their bells in a similar way. Just as the umbrella pushes air backward, a medusa's bell pushes water backward, and the organism moves in the opposite direction.

BIO INSIGHTS — FACTS AND FIGURES

Feeding with the help of nematocysts
Nematocysts, also called cnidae, are the characteristic structures of cnidarians. These cells are used for a number of functions, including for movement, defense, attachment, and capturing prey. Biologists aren't exactly sure how nematocysts are produced, but there is evidence that they are secretions of the Golgi apparatus of cnidocytes. Nematocysts are perhaps the largest and most complex cellular structures found in all cells. A fully formed nematocyst is a cigar-shaped, fluid-filled capsule that encloses a coiled, hollow filament—the "dart." At the end of each nematocyst is a modified cilium—the "trigger." When the cilium is stimulated, a "lid" opens, and the coiled tube springs out, similar to a spring uncoiling from a can. Nematocysts used in feeding have barbs that can penetrate flesh, and then a paralyzing toxin is injected into the prey.

Answers to . . .

✓CHECKPOINT *The gastroderm is the inner lining of the gastrovascular cavity. The epidermis is the outer layer of cells. The mesoglea is a layer that lies between these two tissues.*

Figure 26–13 *Students might correctly infer that the nerve net is more extensive in a motile cnidarian. In many medusas, nerve cells are complex and concentrated around the margin of the bell, which is more likely to come into contact with objects and other organisms than other parts of the medusa.*

Figure 26–14 *A medusa*

26–3 (continued)

Use Visuals

Figure 26–15 Have students study the figure. Then, ask: **Is the jellyfish polyp haploid or diploid?** *(Diploid)* **Is the medusa haploid or diploid?** *(It also is diploid.)* **What process occurs that ensures both are diploid organisms?** *(The polyp is diploid because it grows from a zygote produced by the joining of haploid egg and sperm. The medusa is diploid because it is produced through the process of budding by a polyp.)* **How are polyps produced?** *(Male medusas release sperm, and female medusas release eggs. Fertilization occurs in open water. The resulting zygote grows into a larva, which becomes a polyp.)*

Groups of Cnidarians

Meet Diverse Needs

Help at-risk students understand how cnidarians are classified by emphasizing which form, polyp or medusa, predominates in the life of the organism. Ask students: **In which form do hydrozoans live most of their lives?** *(They live most of their lives as polyps.)* **In which form do scyphozoans live most of their lives?** *(They live most of their lives as medusas.)* **In which form do anthozoans spend their lives?** *(They have only a polyp stage in their life cycle.)*

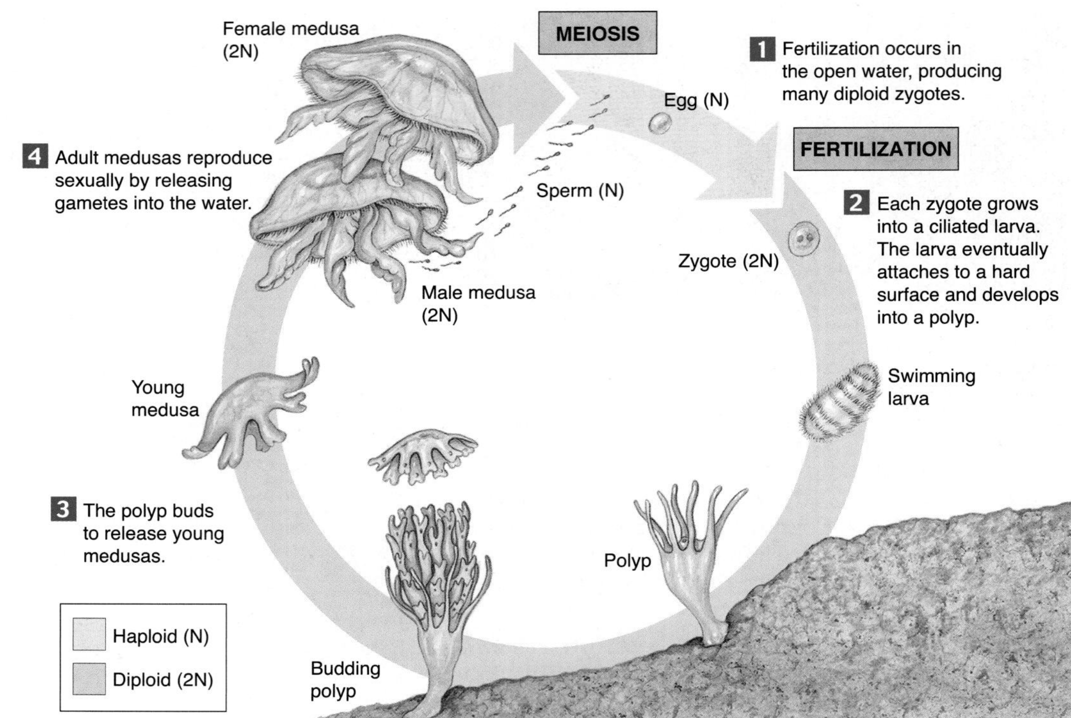

▲ **Figure 26–15** Jellyfishes reproduce sexually by producing eggs and sperm. Depending on the species, fertilization is either internal or external. In *Aurelia,* shown here, fertilization is external, occurring after eggs and sperm are released into the water. **Interpreting Graphics** *What cells are formed by the process of meiosis?*

Reproduction Most cnidarians reproduce both sexually and asexually. Polyps can reproduce asexually by budding. The new animal is genetically identical to the parent animal. One type of budding begins with a swelling on the side of an existing polyp. This swelling grows into a new polyp. In another type of budding, polyps produce tiny medusas that separate and become new individuals.

In most cnidarians, sexual reproduction takes place with external fertilization in water. **External fertilization** takes place outside the female's body. The sexes are usually separate—each individual is either male or female. The female releases eggs into the water, and the male releases sperm. The life cycle of *Aurelia,* a common jellyfish, is shown in **Figure 26–15.** Observe that the zygote grows into a free-swimming larva. The larva eventually attaches to a hard surface and develops into a polyp. Then, the polyp buds and releases a medusa that begins the cycle again.

Groups of Cnidarians

All cnidarians live under water, and nearly all live in the ocean.  **Cnidarians include jellyfishes, hydras and their relatives, and sea anemones and corals.** Some of the most familiar cnidarians are the jellyfishes.

TEACHER TO TEACHER

When introducing the invertebrate phyla described in this chapter, I provide specimens of sponges and cnidarians as well as pictures, videos, or laser-disk examples. I also divide students into groups of four, and ask each group to develop questions about the various organisms. I then display these questions on the classroom walls. As students progress through the chapter, they answer the displayed questions, keeping a record of both questions and answers in their notebooks. In addition, I have the student groups make charts comparing the characteristics of sponges and cnidarians.

—*Keith Orgeron,*
Teacher
Caiencro High School,
Lafayette, LA

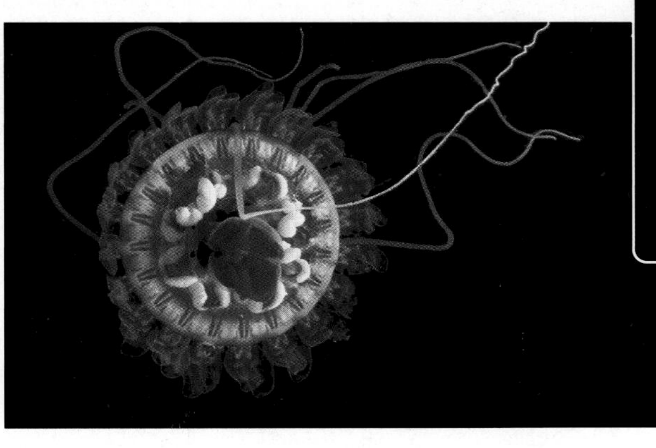

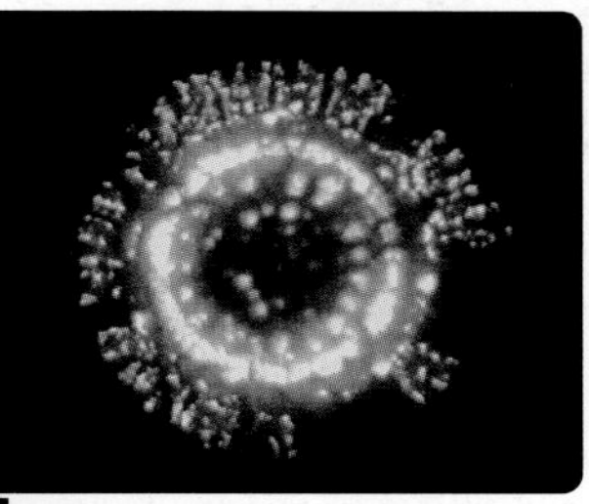

Figure 26–16 Like many marine organisms, jellyfishes use bioluminescence, or the production of light by an organism, to ward off predators. The entire body of this jellyfish becomes bioluminescent when it is threatened (inset). **Hypothesizing** *How might bioluminescence discourage potential predators?*

Jellyfishes The class Scyphozoa (sy-fuh-ZOH-uh) contains the jellyfishes, such as the jellyfish shown in **Figure 26–16.** Scyphozoans, which means "cup animals," live their lives primarily as medusas. The polyp form of jellyfishes is restricted to a small larval stage, and no elaborate colonies ever form. Jellyfishes can be quite large—the largest jellyfish ever found was almost 4 meters in diameter and had tentacles more than 30 meters long. Jellyfishes reproduce sexually.

Hydras and Their Relatives The class Hydrozoa (hy-druh-ZOH-uh) contains hydras and other related animals. The polyps of most hydrozoans grow in branching colonies that sometimes extend more than a meter. Within the colony, polyps are specialized to perform different functions. In the Portuguese man-of-war, shown in **Figure 26–17,** one polyp forms a balloonlike float that keeps the entire colony afloat. Other polyps in the colony produce long tentacles that hang several meters under water and sting prey (and humans!) using nematocysts. Some polyps digest food held by the tentacles, while others make eggs and sperm.

The most common freshwater hydrozoans are hydras. Hydras differ from other cnidarians in this class because they lack a medusa stage. Instead, they live only as solitary polyps. Hydras reproduce asexually, by budding, or sexually, by producing eggs and sperm in the body wall. Many hydras get their nutrition from capturing, stinging, and digesting small prey. Some hydras, however, get their nutrition from symbiotic photosynthetic protists that live in their tissues.

How do hydras reproduce?

▶ **Figure 26–17** **Jellyfishes, hydrozoans, sea anemones, and corals are all cnidarians.** The Portuguese man-of-war, shown here, is a colonial hydrozoan that is composed of many specialized polyps. A single polyp that is enlarged and full of air helps keep the animal afloat, while other specialized polyps below water function in feeding and reproduction.

Use Visuals

Figure 26–17 Ask: **What cnidarian class does this Portuguese man-of-war represent?** *(The class Hydrozoa)* Emphasize that hydrozoans spend most of their lives as polyps. Then, ask: **Are you looking at one individual polyp or many?** *(Many, since a Portuguese man-of-war is a colonial hydrozoan)* Explain that the enlarged polyp at the top is called a float, and the colony has mechanisms that can regulate the gas in the float, which keeps the colony at a particular depth. The feeding tentacles at the bottom can be as long as 13 meters in some Atlantic species.

Build Science Skills

Comparing and Contrasting
Have students make a compare/contrast table that organizes the information they learn about the three classes of cnidarians. Column heads might include Cnidarian Class, Description, Reproduction, and Examples. After students have completed the task, divide the class into small groups, and encourage students to compare information included in their tables, revising where they think they have left out important information.

BIO INSIGHTS

FACTS AND FIGURES

Animals with no middle tissue layer
Cnidarians only have two embryonic tissue, or germ, layers. The endoderm develops into the inner layer of the body wall, which is called the gastrodermis. The ectoderm develops into an outer layer of the body wall, called the epidermis. There is no middle germ layer, and as such cnidarians are said to possess a diploblastic body plan, in contrast to the triploblastic body plan of more complex animals with three germ layers.

The middle layer in cnidarians is a thick, jellylike mixture called mesoglea, which usually contains some cells and fibers. In the hydrozoans, the middle layer has virtually no cells. This jellylike middle layer is more abundant in the medusa form than in the polyp form, which explains the name *jellyfish* for scyphozoan medusas. Without a middle germ layer, cnidarians never possess the complex organs of triploblastic animals.

Answers to . . .

CHECKPOINT *Hydras reproduce asexually by budding or sexually by producing sperm and eggs.*

Figure 26–15 *Sperm and egg cells*

Figure 26–16 *Bioluminescence makes the jellyfish seem larger and more threatening.*

Ecology of Corals

Analyzing Data

Coral reefs are the "rain forests" of the ocean, a place where life is most varied and abundant. If the reefs are lost, then life on Earth will be changed dramatically. Overexploitation of marine resources includes everything from overfishing to even more destructive practices. For instance, fisheries in Indonesia sometimes use dynamite to stun reef-dwelling fish, making the take easier. Perhaps more troubling is the threat of global warming, which may eventually destroy almost all coral reefs.

Answers

1. The order, from greatest to least high threat, is exploitation of marine resources, inland pollution, coastal development, and marine pollution.
2. The high threat of overexploitation is almost four times greater than the high threat of coastal development.
3. A typical generalization will suggest that human activities threaten the destruction of the world's coral reefs.
4. A typical response might propose limits on the exploitation of marine resources, either by amount of catch or by restrictions on where fisheries can harvest resources.

Make Connections

Chemistry Explain that the "stony" substance associated with stony corals is limestone, or calcium carbonate. To help explain the formation of a coral reef, write the formula of calcium carbonate on the board: $CaCO_3$. Point out that this compound contains the elements calcium, carbon, and oxygen. Explain that a coral animal derives the calcium from seawater that flows into its gastrovascular cavity. The carbon and oxygen are from carbon dioxide, a product of the photosynthesis carried out by the algae symbionts. One of the products of a chemical reaction at the base of a coral is calcium carbonate, which precipitates downward. The result is a buildup of a stony exoskeleton, the coral reef.

Analyzing Data

Coral Vanishing Act

The World Resources Institute, an organization that examines global environmental problems, recently announced that 58 percent of the world's coral reefs are in danger of dying. Threats to coral reefs fall into four broad categories shown in the graph. The graph indicates the percentage of reefs that are threatened by each of these categories. It also rates the threat as medium or high, based on the distance between the coral reef and the source of the threat.

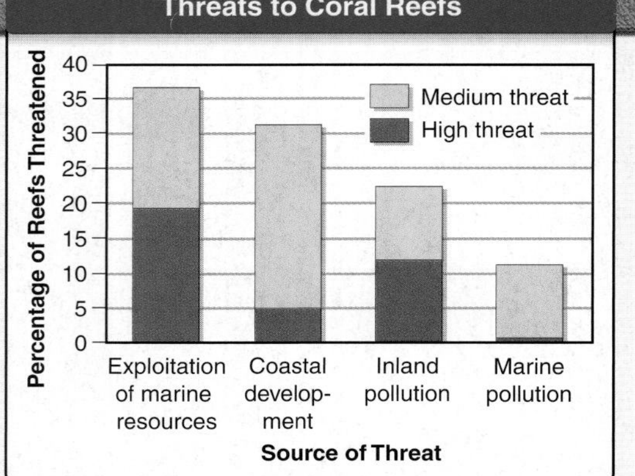

1. **Classifying** Place the four categories of risk in order from greatest high threat to least high threat.
2. **Using Tables and Graphs** Approximately how much greater is the high threat of overexploitation than the high threat of coastal development?
3. **Inferring** Based on the graph, write a generalization about the effect of human activities on the destruction of coral reefs.
4. **Going Further** Assume that you are a legislator drafting a law to protect coral reefs. Choose one of the threats shown in the graph, and outline a law that you would propose to counter the threat.

▼ **Figure 26–18** Coral reefs are home to many types of organisms and are rivaled only by rain forests in their biological diversity. Each flowerlike form shown in this photograph is an entire colony made of thousands of individual coral polyps. **Drawing Conclusions** *How would you describe the symmetry of individual coral polyps?*

Sea Anemones and Corals The class Anthozoa (an-thuh-ZOH-uh) contains sea anemones and corals, animals that have only the polyp stage in their life cycle. Anthozoans all have a central body surrounded by tentacles—a form that gave them their name, *anthozoa,* which means "flower animal." Many species are colonial, or composed of many individual polyps. The appearance of an entire reef can include varied forms, as shown in **Figure 26–18.**

Sea anemones are solitary polyps that live at all depths of the ocean. Using nematocysts, they catch a variety of marine organisms. Many shallow-water species also depend on nutrition from photosynthetic symbionts.

Individual coral polyps look like miniature sea anemones. But most corals are colonial, and their polyps grow together in large numbers. Hard coral colonies are usually founded when a motile larva settles onto a hard surface and develops into a single polyp. New polyps are produced by budding, and as the colonies grow, they secrete an underlying skeleton of calcium carbonate, or limestone. These colonies grow slowly and may live for hundreds or even thousands of years. Many coral colonies growing near one another produce the magnificent structures known as coral reefs.

Anthozoans reproduce sexually by producing eggs and sperm that are released into the water. The zygote grows into a ciliated larva that becomes a new polyp. Some species can also reproduce asexually by budding or splitting into two halves.

BIO INSIGHTS

BIOLOGY UPDATE

Too late to save the world's coral reefs?
At the International Coral Reef Symposium in 2000, scientists reported that over 25 percent of the world's coral reefs have already been destroyed and warned that in the coming decades the rest might perish. Experts cited a number of causes of the destruction, including pollution, overfishing, and, most significantly, global warming, which causes bleaching. As the sea temperature rises, the algae produce more oxygen. The corals begin to suffer from oxygen poisoning, and so expel the algae. With the loss of algae, the corals lose their primary source of energy. In response to grave concerns about reef destruction, in 2000 President Clinton created the Northwestern Hawaiian Islands Coral Reef Reserve, the country's largest nature preserve. The preserve encompasses almost 70 percent of coral reefs within U.S. boundary waters.

Ecology of Corals

The worldwide distribution of corals is determined by a few variables: temperature, water depth, and light intensity. The "stony" or "hard" corals that build coral reefs require high levels of light. Why should light be a requirement for an animal? Light is necessary because these corals rely on symbioses with algae that capture solar energy, recycle nutrients, and help corals lay down their calcium carbonate skeletons. Symbionts provide as much as 60 percent of the energy that corals need. This arrangement allows coral reefs to live in water that carries few nutrients.

Many coral reefs are now suffering from human activity. For example, recreational divers sometimes damage coral reefs. Silt and other sediments from logging, farming, mining, and construction can wash onto reefs and smother corals. Chemical fertilizers, insecticides, and industrial pollutants can poison the corals. Overfishing can upset the ecological balance of coral reefs. Even when human-caused problems do not kill corals, they can cause stress that makes reefs susceptible to other threats.

Meanwhile, a problem called coral bleaching has become common. High temperatures can kill the algae that usually live in the tissues of corals, leaving behind only transparent cells atop ghostly white skeletons. The results of coral bleaching are shown in **Figure 26–19.** In the past, bleaching was a rare and short-term event from which many corals recovered. Over the last 20 years, however, bleaching has become more common and more severe, causing many corals to die. Researchers fear that rising ocean temperatures, produced by global warming, may be contributing to this problem. If this is the case, many reefs around the world could soon be in serious danger.

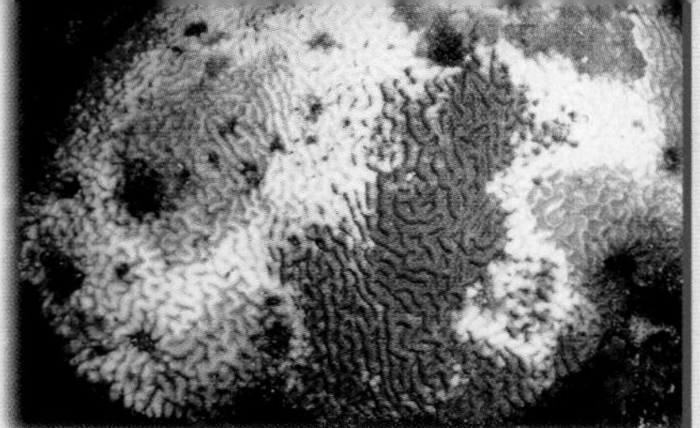

▲ **Figure 26–19** Under normal conditions, algae live within coral tissues, carrying out photosynthesis and giving the coral its green appearance. However, when stressed by pollutants or increasing temperatures, these algae can die, so only the clear cells of the coral remain. **Inferring** *What effect might the loss of symbiotic algae have on the coral?*

KEEP CURRENT WITH . . . SCIENCE NEWS®

To find out more about the topics in this chapter, go to: **www.phschool.com**

26–3 Section Assessment

1. **Key Concept** Describe three characteristics that all cnidarians share.
2. **Key Concept** How do the two body plans of cnidarians differ?
3. **Key Concept** Describe the three groups of cnidarians and give an example from each.
4. Describe how the digestion and absorption of food take place in cnidarians.
5. **Critical Thinking Inferring** A medusa typically has more specialized organs for movement and response than a polyp does. Why might this be the case? (*Hint:* How does the lifestyle of a medusa differ from that of most polyps?)

iTEXT Assessment Use iText to review the important concepts in Section 26–3.

Take It to the NET

View photographs of animals from one of the three groups of cnidarians. Then, prepare a 3-minute presentation on the diversity of that group.Use the links provided in the Biology area at the Prentice Hall Web site for help in completing this activity: **www.phschool.com**

SCIENCE NEWS®

Encourage students to visit **www.phschool.com** for the most current information on this topic.

3 ASSESS

Evaluate Understanding

Display a picture of an organism from each of the three classes of cnidarians. Ask students to identify the class of each and explain how it carries out the seven essential functions of animals.

Reteach

Ask students to write a story of a year in the life of a jellyfish in which they use these terms: *polyp, medusa, nerve net, nematocyst, gastrovascular cavity, and hydrostatic skeleton.* Students should strive to be both creative and scientifically accurate.

Take It to the NET

Good sources of photography on the Internet include the Waikiki Aquarium Marine Life Profiles and the cnidarian photo album at the University of Ottawa. Students' photo essays should illustrate organisms from one of the three cnidarian classes: Hydrozoa, Scyphozoa, or Anthozoa. For additional information, visit **www.phschool.com**

iTEXT

Use the iText to review the key concepts in Section 26–3.

26–3 Section Assessment

1. All cnidarians are soft-bodied, carnivorous, and have stinging tentacles arranged in circles around the mouth.
2. A polyp has a cylindrical body with armlike tentacles; the mouth points upward. A medusa has a bell-shaped body with the mouth pointing downward.
3. Hydrozoans, such as hydras, spend most of their lives as polyps. Scyphozoans, such as jellyfishes, live their lives primarily as medusas. Anthozoans, such as corals, have only the polyp stage in their life cycle.
4. Extracellular digestion takes place in the gastrovascular cavity. Cells in the gastroderm absorb partially digested materials. Digestion is completed intracellularly.
5. A polyp is sessile and, thus, does not move around. A medusa is motile and, thus, needs a more complex nervous system to detect stimuli in different environments.

Answers to . . .

Figure 26–18 *Individual coral polyps exhibit radial symmetry.*

Figure 26–19 *The loss of the algae might cause the corals to die.*

Exploration

Objectives Students will be able to
- Observe how two different kinds of hydras respond to light.
- Infer why green hydras move toward light.
- Compare and contrast the behavior of hydras with that of more complex animals.

Skill Focus **Inferring, Drawing Conclusions**

Time 45 minutes; 10 minutes the following day

Advance Prep Order green hydras (*Chlorohydra viridissima)* and brown hydras (*Hydra littoralis* or another non-green species) well in advance. Small *Daphnia, Cyclops,* brine shrimp (*Artemia),* or other small invertebrates can be fed to both green and brown hydras. Feed only small *Daphnia* to hydras, because large *Daphnia* may attack the hydras. Keep the green hydras in a well-lit environment. You can collect local clean pond or spring water or purchase spring water.

Pre-Lab Discussion Have students brainstorm a list of behaviors exhibited by large-brained animals such as mammals and small-brained animals such as insects. Have students try to explain how each behavior contributes to an animal's survival or reproduction. Have volunteers describe the cnidarian nerve net and speculate about the behavior such a simple nervous system might produce. Then, have students read the Exploration. Ask: **What are hydras?** *(Hydras are cnidarians of the class Hydrozoa.)* **From what kind of symbionts do some hydras get their nutrition?** *(Photosynthetic protists living within their tissues)* **Why do you think part of the procedure of this lab is to leave the hydras in the test tubes overnight and observe them the next day?** *(Students might infer that the purpose is to give time for the hydras to orient themselves to their environment. Students might suggest that hydras lack the complex nervous system required for direct movement toward or away from the light.)*

Safety Caution students not to drink the spring water. Advise them to handle the hydras carefully.

Exploration

Examining the Responses of Hydras

Hydras, a type of cnidarian, are some of the simplest known animals to have a nervous system. What kinds of behavior can their simple nerve nets produce? Can they detect food and move toward it? Can they detect predators and move away from them? How do they respond to light, temperature, and other physical factors? How do these responses help them to survive? In this investigation, you will observe and try to explain the behavior of hydras.

Problem

How do hydras respond to light?

Materials

- 6 test tubes with screw caps
- test-tube rack
- green hydras
- brown hydras
- aluminum foil
- pond or spring water
- glass-marking pencil
- dropper pipette
- transparent tape

Skills

Inferring, Drawing Conclusions

Procedure

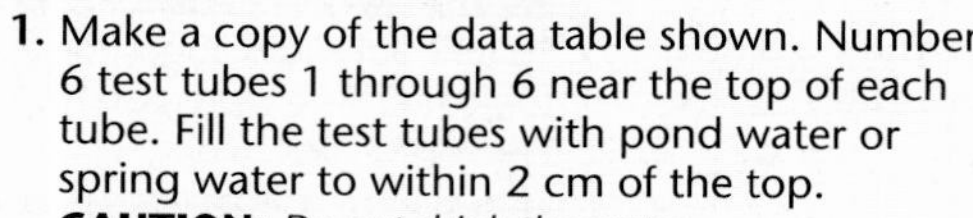

1. Make a copy of the data table shown. Number 6 test tubes 1 through 6 near the top of each tube. Fill the test tubes with pond water or spring water to within 2 cm of the top. **CAUTION:** *Do not drink the water.*
2. Use a dropper pipette to gently place 3 brown hydras in the bottoms of the test tubes labeled 1 through 3, and place 3 green hydras in the bottoms of the test tubes labeled 4 through 6.
3. Wrap the bottom half of each test tube in aluminum foil.
4. Tightly cap all 6 test tubes. Place test tubes 1 and 4 right side up in the test-tube rack and test tubes 2 and 5 upside down.
5. Label the test-tube rack with your name and place it in a brightly lit place.
6. Lay test tubes 3 and 6 on their sides next to the test-tube rack so that all 6 test tubes are equally well lit. Tape test tubes 3 and 6 in place. Place the tape over the foil and caps so that it does not block the light.
7. **Predicting** Record the time that you completed step 6. Make a prediction of where the hydras will move—either away from or toward the light. Record your prediction of any other behavior that you expect to see, along with the reasons for your predictions.
8. Observe the test tubes. Record a description of any hydra behavior you observe. Include such information as when the behavior occurred, how many hydras you saw, what they did, and any other observations you made. Leave the test tubes overnight. Be sure to wash your hands before leaving the lab.
9. The next day, observe the test tubes and again record any hydra behavior you observe. Count the number of hydras in the light and in the dark in each test tube. Record these observations in your data table.
10. Share your observations with the class to complete the Class Total columns of your data table.

Sample Data Table

Tube	Hydras	Source of Light	Number of Hydras		Class Total	
			In light	In dark	In light	In dark
1	brown	above	1	2	20	40
2	brown	below	1	2	20	40
3	brown	side	1	3	20	40
4	green	above	3	0	60	0
5	green	below	3	0	60	0
6	green	side	3	0	60	0

Data Table						
Tube	Hydras	Source of Light	Number of Hydras		Class Total	
			In light	In dark	In light	In dark
1	brown	above				
2	brown	below				
3	brown	side				
4	green	above				
5	green	below				
6	green	side				

Analyze and Conclude

1. **Observing** Which type of hydra moved toward the light? Which type avoided light?
2. **Observing** How did the hydras move? Were their movements random or in a specific direction?
3. **Observing** What differences between the behavior of green and brown hydras did you observe?
4. **Inferring** Green hydras are green because of the presence of green algae in their bodies. What seems to be the relationship between the presence of algae and the behavior of green hydras?
5. **Drawing Conclusions** How might their response to light help green hydras survive?
6. **Comparing and Contrasting** The nervous system directs animal behavior. Compare the behavior of hydras to the behavior of animals with more complex nervous systems that you have observed, such as dogs and insects.

Go Further

Design an Experiment What are some other behaviors that hydras exhibit? Do they react to changes in temperature, differences in prey behavior, or the presence of predators? Do they wander at random, or do they benefit from moving in specific ways and directions? Can they learn? Design an experiment to investigate a specific question about hydra behavior. Have your teacher approve your plan before you perform your experiment.

Take It to the NET Visit the Prentice Hall Web site at **www.phschool.com** and enter your results from this investigation. Compare your results with those that other students have posted on this Web site. Hydras do not always behave in predictable ways. Did some students observe behaviors that you did not? Does this larger set of data support your conclusions from your own experiment?

Teaching Tips

- Because hydra behavior is somewhat unpredictable, some students may observe more activity than others. Encourage students to share observations with others.
- To simplify data sharing, set up a data table on the board or overhead projector in which each student or group can enter data.
- You may want to add prey to the test tubes to allow students to observe how hydras feed. If you do, tell students that some of the prey, such as *Artemia* brine shrimp, are attracted to light. Ask students how this might affect hydra behavior and how they might design an experiment to distinguish the direct effect of light on hydra behavior from any possible tendency to migrate toward light-seeking prey.

Procedure

2. Demonstrate how to use a dropper pipette to gently place hydras in the bottom of a test tube.

3. Make sure students do not wrap more than half a test tube in foil.

7. Have students record the time they completed step 6, as well as their predictions for each of the test tubes, on a separate piece of paper.

8. Provide a well-lit place for students to leave their test tubes overnight.

Expected Outcomes

Students should observe that green hydras tend to migrate toward light, while brown hydras do not.

Go Further

Check students' experimental plans for sound design, safety, and the potential to test a clearly defined hypothesis before giving approval. A typical experiment might involve setting up a temperature differential within an environment and observing how hydras respond.

Analyze and Conclude

1. Green hydras moved toward the light. Brown hydras avoided light.

2. Movement can occur in several ways, and may or may not be fast enough to see. Hydras can creep, tumble, float, or sink. Green hydras move toward light. The movement of brown hydras, if it occurs, is random.

3. Students should observe that green hydras moved toward the light, while brown hydras moved little, apparently at random.

4. When algae are present in hydras, the hydras move toward light. This behavior provides the light the green algae need for photosynthesis. The behavior of the green hydras implies that they benefit from the algae.

5. Students should conclude that the algae provide the hydras with the oxygen or carbohydrates produced through photosynthesis.

6. Like more complex animals, hydras can respond to the environment in ways that help them to survive, though this behavior is much simpler and less direct than that of more complex animals.

Take It to the NET

Have students visit to pool and analyze data with students nationwide.
www.phschool.com

Chapter 26 Study Guide

Study Tip

Divide the class into small groups, and ask each group to write a review question for each Key Concept and each Vocabulary term in one of the sections. When students have completed writing their questions, have the groups place their lists in a central location. Then, ask that each group pick up a list of questions for one of the other two sections. After groups have had a chance to collaborate on answering the questions, repeat the process, with groups answering the questions for a third section.

Thinking Visually

1. Bilateral symmetry
2. Many planes of symmetry

Chapter 26 Assessment

Reviewing Content

1. c
2. c
3. a
4. b
5. c
6. c
7. c
8. b
9. a
10. b

Understanding Concepts

11. All animals are multicellular, eukaryotic heterotrophs whose cells lack cell walls. Animals are specialized to carry out the functions of feeding, respiration, circulation, excretion, response, movement, and reproduction.

12. The terms *anterior, posterior, dorsal, lateral, bilateral symmetry,* and *motile* should be used on the drawings of a fish. The terms *radial symmetry* and *motile* should be used as titles on the drawing of a jellyfish. The term *sessile* should be used to label the sponge.

13. Because cephalization involves the location of sense organs and nerve cells that process information at its anterior end, the animal can respond to the environment more quickly and in more sophisticated ways than simpler animals can.

Chapter 26 Study Guide

26–1 Introduction to the Animal Kingdom

Key Concepts

- An animal is a multicellular, eukaryotic heterotroph whose cells lack cell walls.
- Animals are specialized to carry out the following essential functions: feeding, respiration, circulation, excretion, response, movement, and reproduction.
- In general, complex animals tend to have high levels of cell specialization and internal organization, bilateral body symmetry, cephalization, and a body cavity.

Vocabulary

invertebrate, p. 657
vertebrate, p. 657
parasite, p. 658
host, p. 658
blastula, p. 661
protostome, p. 661
deuterostome, p. 661
anus, p. 661
endoderm, p. 661
mesoderm, p. 661
ectoderm, p. 661
radial symmetry, p. 662
bilateral symmetry, p. 662
cephalization, p. 663

26–2 Sponges

Key Concepts

- Sponges are classified as animals because they are multicellular, heterotrophic, have no cell walls, and contain a few specialized cells.
- The movement of water through a sponge provides a simple mechanism for feeding, respiration, circulation, and excretion.

Vocabulary

choanocyte, p. 665
osculum, p. 665
spicule, p. 665
archaeocyte, p. 665
internal fertilization, p. 666
larva, p. 666
gemmule, p. 667

26–3 Cnidarians

Key Concepts

- Cnidarians are soft-bodied, carnivorous animals that have stinging tentacles arranged in circles around their mouth. They are the simplest animals to have body symmetry and specialized tissues.
- Cnidarians typically have a life cycle that includes two different-looking stages, a polyp and a medusa.
- Cnidarians include jellyfishes, hydras and their relatives, sea anemones, and corals.

Vocabulary

cnidocyte, p. 669
nematocyst, p. 669
polyp, p. 670
medusa, p. 670
gastrovascular cavity, p. 671
nerve net, p. 671
hydrostatic skeleton, p. 671
external fertilization, p. 672

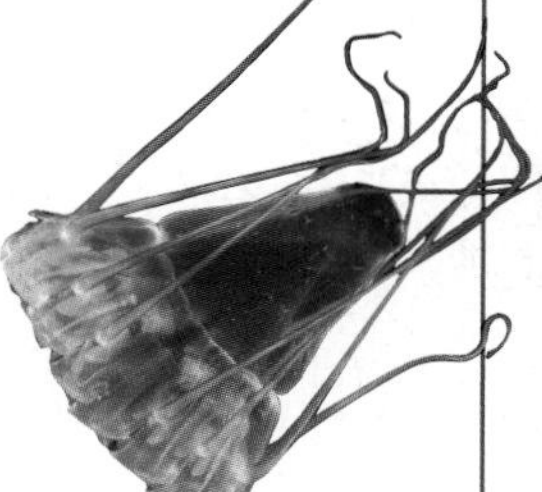

Thinking Visually

Complete the following concept map using information from the chapter:

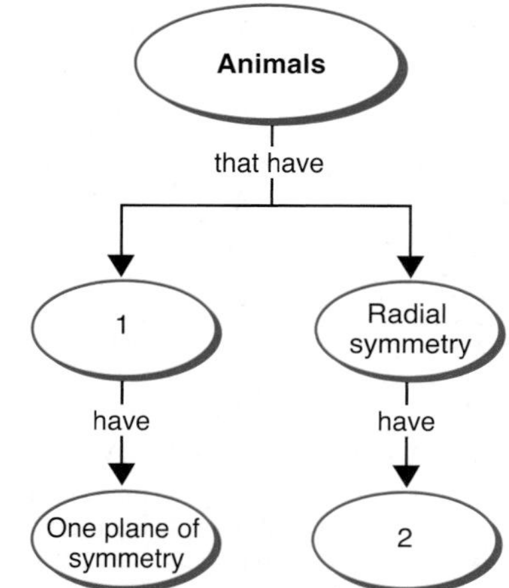

CHAPTER RESOURCES

Print:

- ***Teaching Resources,*** Chapter Vocabulary Review, Graphic Organizer
- ***Chapter Tests: Levels A and B,*** Chapter 26 Test
- ***PH Assessment System,*** Practice Test

Technology:

- ***Computer Test Bank,*** Chapter 26 Test
- ***iText,*** Chapter 26 Assessment

Chapter 26 Assessment

Reviewing Content

Choose the letter that best answers the question or completes the statement.

1. A multicellular eukaryotic heterotroph whose cells lack cell walls is a(an)
   a. protist. c. animal.
   b. virus. d. plant.

2. The process by which animals take in oxygen and give off carbon dioxide is known as
   a. circulation. c. respiration.
   b. reproduction. d. response.

3. Animals that have a backbone, also called a vertebral column, are known as
   a. vertebrates. c. deuterostomes.
   b. prokaryotes. d. invertebrates.

4. Many animals have body symmetry with distinct front and back ends. This type of symmetry is
   a. radial. c. circular.
   b. bilateral. d. dorsal.

5. The developing embryo shown below is a __?__, a group that includes __?__.
   a. protostome; simple invertebrates
   b. protostome; vertebrates
   c. deuterostome; echinoderms and chordates
   d. deuterostome; invertebrates

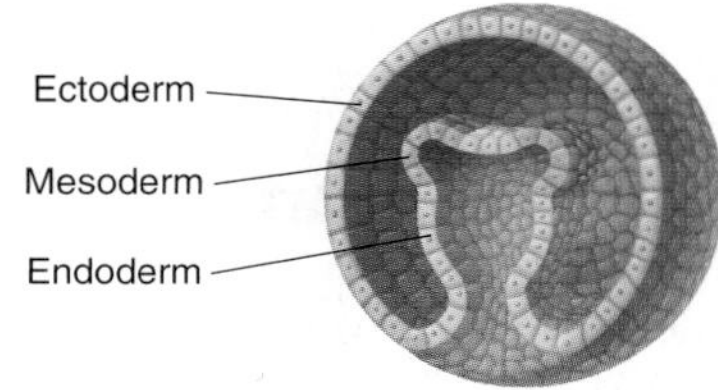

6. An animal whose mouth is formed from the blastopore is a
   a. deuterostome. c. protostome.
   b. detritivore. d. carnivore.

7. Animals in the phylum Porifera include
   a. chordates. c. sponges.
   b. sea stars. d. sea anemones.

8. A concentration of sense organs and nerve cells in the anterior end of the body is known as
   a. fertilization. c. symmetry.
   b. cephalization. d. anteriorization.

9. The sessile body form of a cnidarian is a
   a. polyp. c. planula.
   b. medusa. d. nematocyst.

10. A soft-bodied animal with stinging tentacles arranged around its mouth is a
    a. spicule. c. vertebrate.
    b. cnidarian. d. choanocyte.

Understanding Concepts

11. Describe the characteristics that all animals share.
12. Draw a fish, a jellyfish, and a sponge. Label each drawing, using as many of the following terms as appropriate: radial symmetry, bilateral symmetry, anterior, posterior, dorsal, lateral, ventral, sessile, motile.
13. Explain the advantages that cephalization confers on an animal.
14. Distinguish between a protostome and a deuterostome.
15. During the early development of many animals, cells differentiate into three germ layers. Name these layers and give an example of a body structure that develops from each layer.
16. What are archaeocytes?
17. Briefly describe nutrition, respiration, and excretion in a sponge.
18. Describe the mutually beneficial relationships that exist between many sponges and certain photosynthetic organisms.
19. What is the function of statocysts?
20. Describe the process of feeding in cnidarians.
21. Describe two ways in which budding occurs in polyps.
22. Describe the life cycle of *Aurelia*, a common jellyfish. Be sure to include how the polyp form alternates with the medusa form.

HOMEWORK GUIDE (TIME SAVER)

Section:	Questions:
Section 26–1	1–6, 8, 11–15, 23
Section 26–2	7, 16, 17, 22, 24–26
Section 26–3	9, 10, 18–21, 27–31

Chapter 26 Assessment (continued)

14. A protostome is an animal whose mouth is formed from the blastopore, and a deuterostome is an animal whose anus is formed from the blastopore.

15. The endoderm is the innermost layer of tissue, which develops into the lining of the digestive tract and much of the respiratory system. The mesoderm is the middle layer of tissue, which develops into the muscular system and much of the circulatory, reproductive, and excretory systems. The ectoderm is the outermost layer of tissue, which develops into sense organs, nerves, and the outer layer of the skin.

16. Specialized cells that move around within the walls of sponges

17. Choanocytes trap and engulf food particles sifted from water that flows into the pores, and digestion is completed by archaeocytes. From water that flows inside the body cavity, oxygen diffuses into the cells and wastes are carried away.

18. Many sponges have photosynthetic organisms in their tissues. These photosynthetic organisms provide food and oxygen for the sponge, and the sponge provides a protected area for the photosynthetic organisms.

19. Statocysts in cnidarians help determine the direction of gravity.

20. The cnidarian paralyzes its prey and pulls it into its gastrovascular cavity.

21. In one type, a bud grows from the side of an existing polyp. In another type, polyps produce tiny medusas that become new individuals.

22. Male and female medusas produce eggs and sperm. After external fertilization, the zygote grows into a larva that eventually becomes a polyp. The polyp buds to release young medusas.

Chapter 26 Assessment

Critical Thinking

23. Like other animals, sponges are multicellular, heterotrophic, have some specialized cells, and lack cell walls. Unlike most other animals, sponges have pores all over their bodies and are sessile.

24. Sample answers: How long can the gemmules survive without water? How long can the gemmules survive being kept in a freezer at 0°C? How long does it take gemmules that have survived drought or freezing to grow when moved to a favorable environment?

25. The particles mixed with water that moved through the pores into the central cavity and out through the osculum. Choanocytes, using flagella, caused the movement.

26. Cnidarians have radial symmetry. Since radially symmetrical animals lack a front end, they do not usually move forward in one direction.

27. Many of the comb jelly's characteristics are similar to those of cnidarians, but the latter do not have an anal opening. Therefore, the comb jelly should not be classified as a cnidarian.

28. Sample answer: Governments might pass laws that restrict the use of fertilizers and insecticides in coastal areas with coral reefs in the ocean nearby. These laws might make it difficult for farmers to make a living.

29. Sample answer: The life cycle is more complex in a cnidarian. In the latter, larvae that form as a result of fertilization develop into polyps. The polyps then reproduce asexually, forming medusas that reproduce sexually to complete the life cycle. In a sponge, there is no asexual stage in a complete life cycle, although pieces of adult sponges can reproduce asexually.

30. The nerve net enables cnidarians to detect external stimuli. Cnidocytes are activated by an external stimulus—a brush against the cnidarian's tentacles.

Chapter 26 Assessment

Critical Thinking

23. Comparing and Contrasting Explain how sponges are similar to most other animals. How are they different?

24. Posing Questions The gemmules of some sponges can survive periods of severe drought or freezing. Suppose you have the opportunity to study gemmules. Write three different questions you could investigate.

25. Drawing Conclusions Suppose you place harmless tiny particles in water surrounding a vase-shaped sponge. After a while, you notice these particles coming out of the top of the sponge. Describe the path the particles took through the sponge. What cells were responsible for the movement of the particles?

26. Inferring Most cnidarians do not swim toward their prey. Instead, they capture prey carried by water currents. How is this behavior related to their body plan?

27. Classifying The comb jelly below has a body made of two layers separated by mesoglea. Its digestive system includes an anal opening through which wastes can pass. Radiating around its body are eight "combs" of cilia, which produce movement. A pair of tentacles enable it to capture food. Should this animal be classified as a cnidarian? Explain.

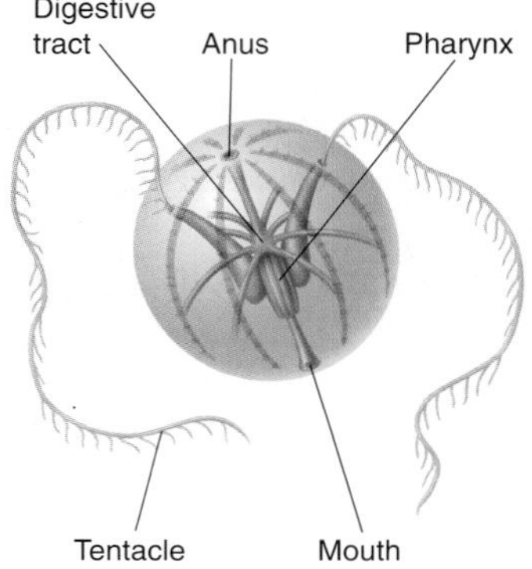

28. Making Judgments Choose one human activity that can harm coral reefs. Describe measures that people might take to reduce the damage. Then evaluate the impact the measures might have on human society.

29. Applying Concepts Would you say that the life cycle of most cnidarians is more or less complex than the life cycle of sponges? Give details to justify your answer.

30. Inferring How might the nerve net of a cnidarian be related to the functioning of the cnidarian's cnidocytes?

31. Making Connections What are some of the differences in the ways that large animals and amoebas carry out their life processes? Give two examples to support your answer. See Chapter 20 for more information on amoebas.

Performance-Based Assessment

Making Models Construct a two- or three-dimensional model of a sponge or cnidarian. Label the organism's important structures. Explain how the organism obtains food and responds to the environment.

Take It to the NET

Coral reefs are an important part of the Earth's marine ecosystems. Visit the Prentice Hall Web site at **www.phschool.com** to find out more about coral reefs. Then, answer the following questions:

- What are the four main types of coral reefs?
- How are mangrove forests, sandy beaches, and sea grass beds important for coral reefs' health?
- In what parts of the world can coral reefs be found? Where is it impossible for corals to grow?

Take It to the NET

- The four main types of coral reefs are atolls, fringing reefs, patch reefs, and barrier reefs.
- Sandy beaches help coral reefs by filtering sediment from the water. Sea grass helps coral reefs by filtering sediment and by providing a breeding ground for many of the fish that are important to the coral reef ecosystem.
- Coral reefs are mostly found in the tropics and in areas where warm water flows from the tropics. Fresh water can kill corals, so corals are not found near river openings or coastal areas with excessive runoff.

For additional information, visit **www.phschool.com**

Standardized Test Prep

Test-Taking Tip When evaluating multiple-choice answers, read all the answer choices, even if the first choice seems to be the correct one. By doing so, you can make sure that the answer you choose is the best one.

Directions: Choose the letter that best answers the question or completes the statement.

The graph below shows the growth rate of a hypothetical coral species under different conditions. Use this information to answer questions 1 and 2.

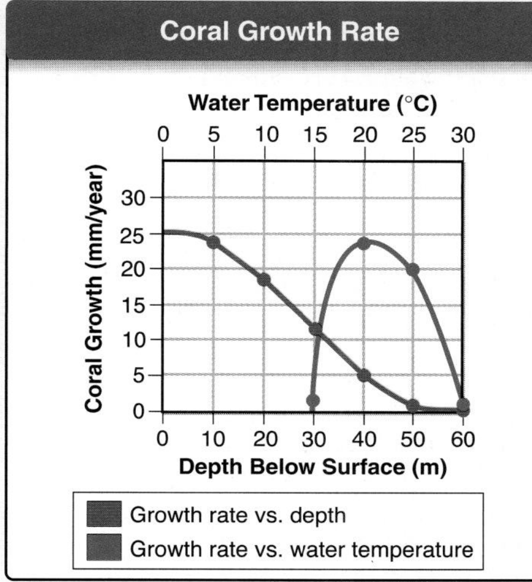

1. This coral grows best at depths of __?__ and a temperature of __?__.
(A) 0–10 m; 20°C
(B) less than 10 m; 15°C
(C) less than 10 m; 28°C
(D) more than 10 m; 21°C
(E) all depths, if water temperature is correct

2. Which of the following statements best explains the trend shown in the graph?
(A) The growth rate of the coral increases as the depth below the water surface increases.
(B) At temperatures of 15°C or above, the growth rate depends only on temperature.
(C) Corals cannot grow below 30 m.
(D) This coral grows best from 18° to 23°C.
(E) Water temperatures depend on the depth of the coral below the surface.

3. Which of the following is a type of tissue that arises in most animals during development?
I. Endoderm
II. Mesoderm
III. Ectoderm
(A) I only
(B) II only
(C) I and II only
(D) II and III only
(E) I, II, and III

4. An adult sponge has all of the characteristics below EXCEPT
I. Body symmetry
II. Ability to move from place to place
III. Cells without cell walls
(A) I only
(B) II only
(C) I and II only
(D) II and III only
(E) I, II, and III

Questions 5–7 Complete each analogy by selecting the correct letter. In analogies, A : B :: C : __?__ *means* A is to B as C is to __?__.

5. Porifera : sponge :: Cnidaria : __?__
(A) hydra
(B) osculum
(C) nematocyst
(D) blastula
(E) gemmule

6. Radial symmetry : jellyfish :: asymmetry : __?__
(A) medusa
(B) polyp
(C) sea anemone
(D) coral
(E) sponge

7. Hard sponge : spicule :: soft sponge : __?__
(A) hydrostatic skeleton
(B) vertebrae
(C) body cavity
(D) spongin
(E) blastula

Questions 8–11 Each of the lettered choices below refers to the following numbered statements. Select the best lettered choice. A choice may be used once, more than once, or not at all.

(A) Osculum
(B) Protostome
(C) Archaeocyte
(D) Deuterostome
(E) Blastula

8. A hollow ball of cells, formed after the zygote undergoes division

9. An animal whose mouth is formed from the blastopore

10. A large hole through which water leaves a sponge

11. A specialized cell that moves around within the wall of a sponge

Standardized Test Prep

1. A	**6.** E	**11.** C
2. D	**7.** D	
3. E	**8.** E	
4. C	**9.** B	
5. A	**10.** A	

(continued from p. 680)

31. Sample answer: Large animals have cells that are specialized for life functions, and amoebas carry on all these functions within a single cell. Two examples are feeding and respiration, for which most large animals have organ systems made up of complex tissues containing many cells. In an amoeba, respiration and feeding take place entirely within a single cell, moving nutrients, oxygen, and waste products directly across its cell membrane.

Performance-Based Assessment

Labeled parts of a model of a sponge should include the osculum, central cavity, choanocytes, and flagella. Labeled parts of a model of a cnidarian should include tentacles, mouth/anus, gastrovascular cavity, and mesoglea layer. The sponge obtains food by filter feeding, and may produce toxins that protect it from potential predators. To feed, a cnidarian polyp paralyzes its prey with its stinging cells and uses its tentacles to push the prey into its gastrovascular cavity. A cnidarian has a nerve net and specialized sensory cells to detect environmental stimuli. Responses include movement and capturing prey.

Chapter Planner 27 Worms and Mollusks

Section and Section Objectives	Time	Activities and Labs
27–1 Flatworms, pp. 683–688 **27.1.1** ***Describe*** the defining features of flatworms. **27.1.2** ***Identify*** the characteristics of the groups of flatworms.	1 period (1/2 block)	**SE:** ***Inquiry Activity,*** Does a planarian have a head?, p. 682 **TE:** ***Build Science Skills,*** p. 686
27–2 Roundworms, pp. 689–693 **27.2.1** ***Describe*** the defining features of roundworms. **27.2.2** ***Explain*** how digestion takes place in roundworms. **27.2.3** ***Identify*** roundworms that are important in human disease.	1 period (1/2 block)	**TE:** ***Build Science Skills,*** p. 690 **SE:** ***Careers in Biology,*** Meat Inspector, p. 691
27–3 Annelids, pp. 694–699 **27.3.1** ***Describe*** the defining features of annelids. **27.3.2** ***Identify*** the characteristics of the classes of annelids. **27.3.3** ***Describe*** the ecology of annelids.	1 period (1/2 block)	**TE:** ***Use Visuals,*** p. 694 **TE:** ***Build Science Skills,*** p. 694, p. 696, p. 697 **SE:** ***Quick Lab,*** Does an earthworm have a heartbeat?, p. 695
27–4 Mollusks, pp. 701–708 **27.4.1** ***Describe*** the defining features of mollusks. **27.4.2** ***Describe*** the basic body plan of mollusks. **27.4.3** ***Identify*** the characteristics of the three main classes of mollusks. **27.4.4** ***Describe*** the ecology of mollusks.	2 periods (1 block)	**SE:** ***Issues in Biology,*** What Can Be Done About the Zebra Mussel?, p. 700 **TE:** ***Demonstration,*** p. 702, p. 706 **TE:** ***Build Science Skills,*** p. 703, p. 705, p. 706 **TE:** ***Make Connections,*** p. 704 **TE:** ***Meet Diverse Needs,*** p. 705 **SE:** ***Analyzing Data,*** Raising Clams, p. 707 **SE:** ***Exploration,*** Investigating Land Snails, p. 709
Chapter Assessment, pp. 710–713	1 period (1/2 block)	

ACTIVITY PLANNER

SE: ***Inquiry Activity,*** p. 682; (10 min.); black and white paper, petri dish, planarian, spring water, rubber band

TE: ***Build Science Skills,*** p. 686; (20 min.); 3 planarians, microscope slide, ice cube, scalpel or razor blade, 9 petri dishes, pond water

TE: ***Build Science Skills,*** p. 690; (15 min.); planarians, vinegar eels, pond water, petri dish, hand lens, stereo microscope, depression slide

TE: ***Use Visuals,*** p. 694; (15 min.); modeling compound, toothpicks

TE: ***Build Science Skills,*** p. 694; (5 min.); long sock with toe cut off

SE: ***Quick Lab,*** p. 695; (15 min.); earthworm, dropper pipette, nonchlorinated water, large and clear plastic straw, dissecting microscope

TE: ***Build Science Skills,*** p. 696; (20 min.); plastic box, sand, topsoil, pond water, 6–12 earthworms, clear plastic wrap

TE: ***Build Science Skills,*** p. 697; (15 min.); earthworm, hand lens, dish

TE: ***Demonstration,*** p. 702; (5 min.); rasp, scrap of wood

TE: ***Build Science Skills,*** p. 703; (15 min.); variety of mollusk shells

TE: ***Make Connections,*** p. 704; (5 min.); balloon

TE: ***Build Science Skills,*** p. 705; (20 min.); 20–40 liter aquarium and cover, sand, pond water, aquatic plants, pond snails

TE: ***Meet Diverse Needs,*** p. 705; (10 min.); land snail

TE: ***Build Science Skills,*** p. 706; (15 min.); pond water, 4 containers, 4 beakers, sieve, coffee filter, piece of screen or wire mesh, cheesecloth

TE: ***Demonstration,*** p. 706; (5 min.); cuttlebone

SE: ***Exploration,*** p. 709; (45 min.); snail, slide, dropper pipette, dissecting tray, black paper, lamp, ruler, microscope, petri dish, clock

PLANNING KEY

Ability Levels

B	**Basic**	For students who need additional help
A	**Average**	For all students
E	**Enriched**	For students who need to be challenged

Components

SE	Student Edition	**GRSW**	Guided Reading and Study Workbook	**IDM**	Issues and Decision Making
TE	Teacher's Edition	**CT**	Chapter Tests: Levels A and B	**CTB**	Computer Test Bank
LMA	Laboratory Manual A	**PHAS**	PH Assessment System	**PA**	Presentation Assistant Plus
LMB	Laboratory Manual B	**LA**	Lab Assessment With Scoring Guide	**BD**	BioDetectives Videotape
TR	Teaching Resources	**BTM**	BioTechnology Manual	**iT**	iText

Program Resources	Assessment	Media and Technology
TR: Section Review 27–1 B A **GRSW:** Section 27–1 B A	**SE:** 27–1 Section Assessment, p. 688 **TR:** Section Review 27–1	**PA:** 27–1 Interest Grabber, Section Outline, Schistosome Life Cycle, Figure 27–3 **iT:** Section 27–1
TR: Section Review 27–2 B A **GRSW:** Section 27–2 B A	**SE:** 27–2 Section Assessment, p. 693 **TR:** Section Review 27–2	**PA:** 27–2 Interest Grabber, Section Outline, Diseases Caused by Roundworms **iT:** Section 27–2
TR: Section Review 27–3 B A **GRSW:** Section 27–3 B A **IDM:** 27–1 A E	**SE:** 27–3 Section Assessment, p. 699 **TR:** Section Review 27–3	**PA:** 27–3 Interest Grabber, Section Outline, Compare/Contrast Matrix, Figure 27–16 **iT:** Section 27–3
LMA: Chapter 27 Lab A E **LMB:** Chapter 27 Lab B A **TR:** Section Review 27–4 B A Chapter 27 Exploration B A E **GRSW:** Section 27–4 B A	**SE:** 27–4 Section Assessment, p. 708 **TR:** Section Review 27–4	**PA:** 27–4 Interest Grabber, Section Outline, Three Major Groups of Mollusks, Figure 27–21, Figure 27–23 **iT:** Section 27–4
	SE: Chapter 27 Assessment, pp. 710–713 **TR:** Chapter Vocabulary Review, Graphic Organizer **CB:** Chapter 27 Test **PHAS:** Practice Test	**CTB:** Chapter 27 Test **iT:** Chapter 27 Assessment

PRESSED FOR TIME?

To Preview the Chapter

- Introduce students to all Key Concepts and Vocabulary terms.
- Assign the Reading Strategies for each section.

To Cover the Chapter Quickly

- Have students read What Is a Flatworm? and Form and Function in Flatworms in Section 27–1; What Is a Roundworm? and Form and Function in Roundworms in Section 27–2; all of Section 27–3; and What Is a Mollusk? and Form and Function in Mollusks in Section 27–4.
- Assign 27–3 Section Review; questions 1–14, 18–22, and 27–29 in Chapter 27 Assessment; and Chapter 27 Standardized Test Prep.

To Review the Chapter

- Assign Sections 27–1 through 27–4 in the Guided Reading and Study Workbook.
- Assign Section Reviews for 27–1 through 27–4 and the Vocabulary Review for Chapter 27 in the Teaching Resources.

ENGAGE/EXPLORE

Inquiry Activity

Objective Students will be able to draw conclusions about the structure and function of a planarian.

Skill Focus **Drawing Conclusions**

Materials black construction paper, petri dish, white sheet of paper, planarian, spring water, 4-cm piece of rubber band, pencil

Time 10 minutes

Advance Prep Cut the rubber bands into 4-cm pieces ahead of time.

Safety Have students wear disposable plastic gloves. After the activity, dispose of the gloves.

Strategies
- You may want to place the planarians in the petri dishes for the students.
- Caution students to be gentle with the planarians, and make sure they are always covered with water.

Expected Outcomes Students should observe that the planarian's head leads as the flatworm responds to stimuli, and that the planarian avoids both contact and bright light.

Think About It
1. Yes, the head end leads the planarian's movements.
2. Sample answer: A planarian's avoidance of contact and light aids in defense against predators, and thus is beneficial to the organism's survival.

Assess Prior Knowledge

Call on a volunteer to list the seven essential functions of an animal. *(Feeding, respiration, circulation, excretion, response, movement, and reproduction)* Then, show students a photo of a jellyfish and another of an octopus. Ask: **In what ways is the octopus different from the jellyfish in the seven essential functions?** *(Students might suggest that an octopus has a much more complex nervous system and much greater abilities in movement.)*

Chapter 27 Worms and Mollusks

The tips of the beautiful, tentacle-like structures of this nudibranch, *Flavella affinis,* release venom for defense against predators. A nudibranch is a kind of mollusk.

Inquiry Activity

Does a planarian have a head?

Procedure
1. Using black construction paper, cover half of the outside of a petri dish. Place a white sheet of paper under the other half. Place a planarian in the center of the dish, and add spring water to keep it moist. Observe the planarian for 2 minutes. Record how long it stays on each side of the petri dish.
2. Where did the planarian spend more time? Hypothesize why the planarian preferred this side.
3. Tape a 4-cm piece of rubber band to a pencil so that 1 cm of the rubber band hangs freely. Use the tip of the rubber band to gently prod each end of the planarian. Observe its behavior.

Think About It
1. **Observing** When the planarian moved, did one end always go first?
2. **Drawing Conclusions** How might the behaviors that you observed help the planarian survive?

FACTS AND FIGURES

More complexity than cnidarians

The bodies of flatworms, such as planarians, have clearly defined upper and lower surfaces, as well as clearly defined front and rear ends. These four areas of the body are most evident in more complex animals. Another important characteristic of flatworms is that they have three tissue, or germ, layers—endoderm, mesoderm, and ectoderm. All three germ tissue layers form in the flatworm embryo. This indicates that flatworms are more complex than cnidarians, which have only two tissue layers. The ectoderm is the outer tissue layer in the flatworm, and the endoderm is the inner layer. Between the two is the mesoderm, which enables cells to develop independently of the ectoderm and the endoderm. In more complex animals, the mesoderm gives rise to muscles, reproductive structures, bones, kidneys, and other internal organs and tissues.

27–1 Flatworms

When most people think of worms, they think of long, squiggly earthworms. But there are many other kinds of worms. Some are the length of your body or as thick as your arm. Others look like glowing, furry blobs. Worms can flutter and glide, or climb around with paddlelike bristles. Still others are very small and live in tubes cemented to rocks.

How is their body shape beneficial to worms? A long, slender body allows an animal to move about more rapidly than a radially symmetrical body, like that of a cnidarian. Worms can move forward in a single direction rather than remaining stationary or drifting in currents. In addition, the mouth, sense organs, and brain (if there is one) are usually located at the anterior end, or head, of the body. This arrangement allows worms to locate food and respond to stimuli as they move. Many groups of organisms have worm-shaped bodies. The familiar earthworm is a segmented worm, which you will read about later in this chapter. The unsegmented worms include flatworms and roundworms. The simplest of these are the flatworms.

Guide for Reading

Key Concepts
- What are the defining features of flatworms?
- What are the characteristics of the three groups of flatworms?

Vocabulary
- acoelomate • coelom
- pharynx • flame cell
- ganglion • eyespot
- hermaphrodite
- fission • scolex
- proglottid • testis

Reading Strategy: Outlining Before you read, use the headings of the section to make an outline about the characteristics of flatworms. As you read, fill in subtopics where they apply in the outline. Add phrases after each subtopic to provide key information.

What Is a Flatworm?

The phylum Platyhelminthes (plat-ih-hel-MIN-theez) consists of the flatworms. Most flatworms are no more than a few millimeters thick. **Flatworms are soft, flattened worms that have tissues and internal organ systems. They are the simplest animals to have three embryonic germ layers, bilateral symmetry, and cephalization.**

Flatworms are known as **acoelomates** (ay-SEE-luh-mayts), meaning "without coelom." A **coelom** (SEE-lum) is a fluid-filled body cavity that is lined with mesoderm. No coelom forms between the tissues of flatworms. **Figure 27–1** shows that the digestive cavity, which is lined with endoderm, is the only body cavity. Flatworms also have bilateral symmetry. Bilateral symmetry means that the animal has two well-formed sides that can be identified as left and right. Most flatworms exhibit enough cephalization to have what is called a head.

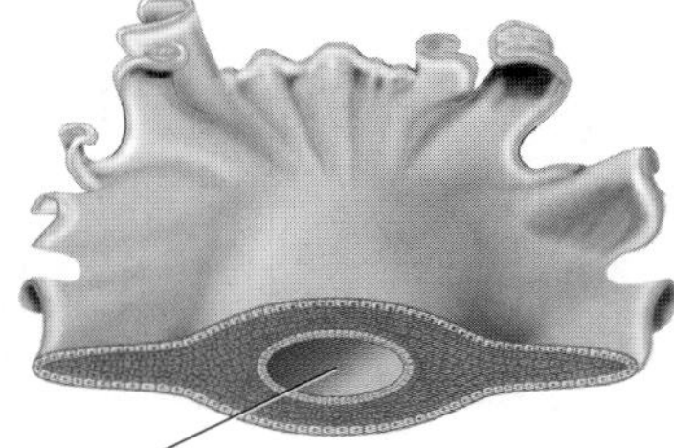

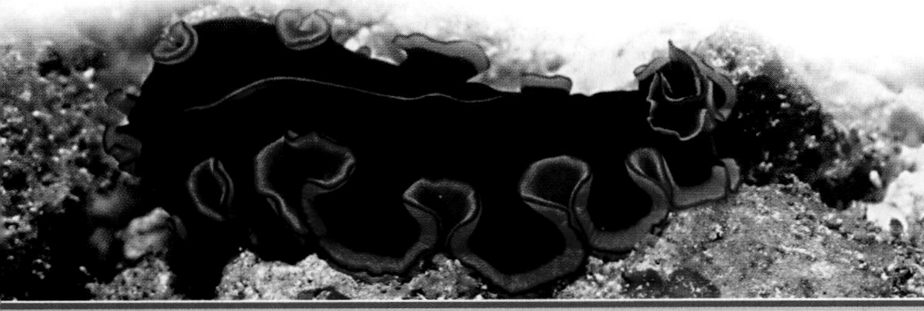

Figure 27–1 **Flatworms are the simplest animals to have three embryonic germ layers—ectoderm, endoderm, and mesoderm.** Shown here is the tropical, free-living flatworm *Pseudobiceros gloriosus.*

SECTION RESOURCES

Print:
- ***Teaching Resources,*** Section Review 27–1
- ***Guided Reading and Study Workbook,*** Section 27–1

Technology:
- ***iText,*** Section 27–1

Section 27–1

1 FOCUS

Objectives

27.1.1 ***Describe*** the defining features of flatworms.

27.1.2 ***Identify*** the characteristics of the three groups of flatworms.

Guide for Reading

Vocabulary Preview

Direct students' attention to the words *acoelomate* and *coelom.* Explain that *coelom* is pronounced with a long *e* and that such is often the case when a word contains the letter combination *oe.* Then, explain that *coelom* is derived from a Greek word meaning "cavity" or "hollow." A *coelomate* is an organism that has a body cavity. An *acoelomate* is an organism that lacks a body cavity, because the prefix *a-* means "without" or "not."

Reading Strategy

Advise students to use the blue headings for the first level of heads in their outlines. For the second level, they should use the green subheads, found in the longer subsections.

2 INSTRUCT

What Is a Flatworm?

Use Visuals

Figure 27–1 Review the three tissue, or germ, layers that develop in an animal embryo: the inner endoderm, the middle mesoderm, and the outer ectoderm. Then, direct students' attention to the cross-section of a flatworm body. Ask: **Is there space between the three layers?** *(There is no space between the layers.)* **What is a coelom?** *(A coelom is a fluid-filled body cavity lined with mesoderm.)* Emphasize that there is no body cavity in a flatworm that is lined with mesoderm, since the mesoderm touches the endoderm and the ectoderm. Ask: **What is an animal called that lacks a coelom?** *(An acoelomate)*

Form and Function in Flatworms

Build Science Skills

Applying concepts Flatworms are the simplest animals that exhibit bilateral symmetry. Challenge students to find objects in and around the school that also exhibit bilateral symmetry. Examples include clocks, vases, and chairs.

Address Misconceptions

When many students think of a "worm," they automatically think of an earthworm. Point out that the familiar earthworm is actually a much more advanced animal than the worms students will study in this and the next section. Emphasize that flatworms and roundworms are unsegmented worms, meaning that their bodies are not divided into parts, or segments. Also, point out that many organisms commonly referred to as worms are not worms at all, but rather the larval stage of insects.

Meet Diverse Needs

For students of limited English proficiency, explain that the cells that filter and remove excess water from the body have the name "flame cells" because their action is reminiscent of the flame of a fire. Within the flame cells, tufts of cilia "flicker." When the excess tissue fluid moves into the flame cells, the flickering of the cilia drives the fluid down the tubule system to the outside of the organism. **Limited English proficiency**

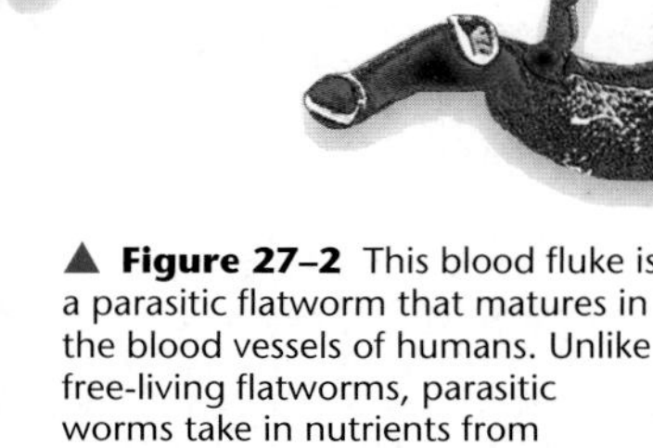

▲ **Figure 27–2** This blood fluke is a parasitic flatworm that matures in the blood vessels of humans. Unlike free-living flatworms, parasitic worms take in nutrients from another organism. **Comparing and Contrasting** ***How do the internal structures of parasitic flatworms compare to those of free-living flatworms?***

Form and Function in Flatworms

Because flatworms are thin and most of their cells are close to the external environment, materials can pass easily into and out of their bodies. All flatworms rely on diffusion for some essential body functions, such as respiration and circulation. Other processes are carried out in different ways in different species. Free-living flatworms have organ systems for digestion, excretion, response, and reproduction.

Parasitic species of flatworms, such as the fluke in **Figure 27–2,** probably evolved from free-living ancestors. As the worms evolved into parasites, internal organs and other structures were modified or even lost. As a result, parasitic species are typically simpler in structure than their free-living relatives.

Feeding Free-living flatworms can be carnivores that feed on tiny aquatic animals, or they can be scavengers that feed on recently dead animals. **Figure 27–3** shows the internal structures of a planarian, a typical flatworm. Like cnidarians, flatworms have a gastrovascular cavity with a single opening, or mouth, through which food and wastes pass. Near the mouth is a muscular tube called a **pharynx** (FAR-inks). Flatworms extend the pharynx out of the mouth. The pharynx then pumps food into the cavity. Once inside, food is digested by cells of the gut, or digestive cavity, where digestion and nutrient absorption take place. Digested food diffuses from the gastrovascular cavity into all other body tissues.

Parasitic worms feed on blood, tissue fluids, or pieces of cells within the host's body. Many parasitic worms obtain nutrients from foods that have already been digested by their host. Therefore, most parasitic worms do not need a complex digestive system. Many parasitic species have a digestive tract that is simpler than that of free-living forms. Some species have a pharynx that pumps food into a pair of dead-end intestinal sacs for digestion. Tapeworms, on the other hand, have no digestive tract at all. They live within the intestine of their host, such as a cow or a human, and simply absorb digested nutrients that are in their host's intestine.

Respiration, Circulation, and Excretion Because their bodies are so flat and thin, many flatworms do not need a circulatory system to transport materials. Instead, flatworms rely on diffusion to transport oxygen and nutrients to their internal tissues, and to remove carbon dioxide and other wastes from their bodies. Flatworms have no gills or other respiratory organs, and no heart, blood vessels, or blood.

Some flatworms have flame cells that function in excretion. **Flame cells** are specialized cells that filter and remove excess water from the body. They also remove metabolic wastes such as ammonia and urea. Many flame cells are joined together to form a network of tubes that empties into the outside environment through tiny pores in the animal's skin.

✓CHECKPOINT *What is the function of flame cells?*

PRESENTATIONS MADE EASY!

The Presentation Assistant Plus contains the Prentice Hall Presentation Pro and the Transparencies, which provide easy-to-follow visual support for every step of this section. If you have a computer presentation station, use Prentice Hall Presentation Pro Section 27–1, or use the transparencies listed here.

Section 27–1:

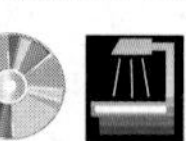

Interest Grabber
Section Outline
Schistosome Life Cycle
Figure 27–3

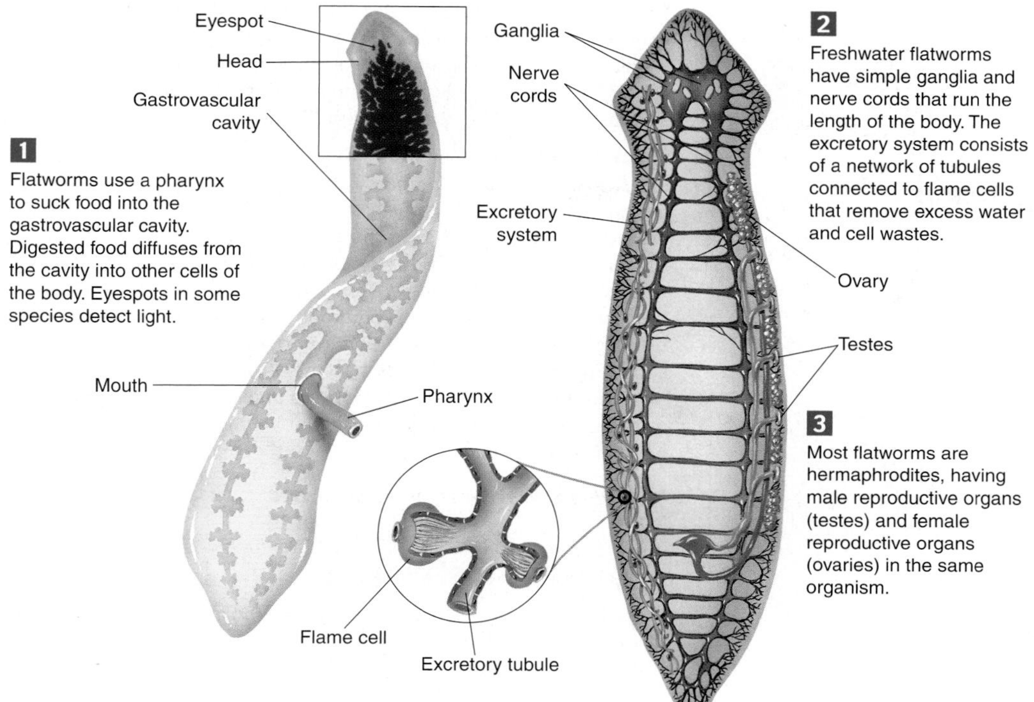
Eyespot
Head
Gastrovascular cavity
1
Flatworms use a pharynx to suck food into the gastrovascular cavity. Digested food diffuses from the cavity into other cells of the body. Eyespots in some species detect light.
Mouth
Pharynx
Flame cell
Excretory tubule
Ganglia
Nerve cords
Excretory system
2
Freshwater flatworms have simple ganglia and nerve cords that run the length of the body. The excretory system consists of a network of tubules connected to flame cells that remove excess water and cell wastes.
Ovary
Testes
3
Most flatworms are hermaphrodites, having male reproductive organs (testes) and female reproductive organs (ovaries) in the same organism.

Response Most flatworms have more complex structures for detecting and responding to their enviroment than those of cnidarians or sponges. In free-living flatworms, a head encloses several **ganglia** (singular: ganglion), or groups of nerve cells, that control the nervous system. These ganglia are not complex enough to be called a brain. Two long nerve cords run from the ganglia along both sides of the body. Locate these nerve cords in **Figure 27–3.** Observe that shorter nerve cords run across the body, like the rungs of a ladder. Parasitic flatworms interact little with their external environment and typically have a less complex nervous system.

Many free-living flatworms have what look like eyes near the anterior end of their body. Each "eye" is actually an **eyespot,** or group of cells that can detect changes in the amount of light in their environment. In addition to having eyespots, most flatworms have specialized cells that detect stimuli, such as chemicals found in food or the direction in which water is flowing. These cells are usually scattered throughout the body.

The nervous systems of free-living flatworms allow them to gather information from their environment. They use this information to locate food and to find dark hiding places beneath stones and logs during the day.

▲ **Figure 27–3** All flatworms, including this planarian, have organ systems that perform essential life functions. The gastrovascular cavity (left) is branched throughout the body and opens to the outside through the pharynx. The diagram on the right shows the excretory system, nervous system, and reproductive system. The excretory system (in purple) consists of many flame cells (in red) that remove waste. The nervous system (in dark gray) consists of ganglia and two nerve cords that run the length of the body. The reproductive system (in green) has testes and ovaries, or male and female reproductive organs, along both sides of the body. **Inferring** ***How is a branched gastrovascular cavity advantageous to a flatworm?***

Use Visuals

Figure 27–3 Have students list some of the important organs present in flatworms. For example, students might mention the pharynx, brain, and nerve cord. Point out that although the flatworm does not have a respiratory system or circulatory system, it does have a digestive system and a nervous system.

Build Science Skills

Designing Experiments Divide the class into small groups, and ask each group to design an experiment that would investigate how sensitive a free-living flatworm's eyespot is. Advise students that they should first write a hypothesis that can be tested. A group's experiment should designate a manipulated variable and a control, as well as a plan to collect and evaluate data.

BIO INSIGHTS

FACTS AND FIGURES

Getting rid of wastes with flame cells
Freshwater turbellaria have an organ system that regulates the volume and salt concentration of their body fluid. This system depends on one or more units called protonephridia. Each unit of protonephridia consists of branched tubules that extend from a pore at the body surface to many cup-shaped flame cells in the body tissues. Within the flame cells, tufts of cilia flicker—thus the name flame cells. When excess tissue fluid moves into the flame cells, the flickering of the cilia drives the fluid down the tubule system to the outside of the organism.

Answers to . . .

CHECKPOINT *Flame cells are specialized cells that filter and remove excess water from the body. They also function in the removal of metabolic wastes such as ammonia, urea, and amino acids. Many flame cells are joined together to form a network of tubes that empties through tiny pores in the animal's skin.*

Figure 27–2 *The internal structures of parasitic flatworms are generally simpler than those of free-living flatworms.*

Figure 27–3 *The branched cavity aids in more efficient digestion because branches reduce the distance that nutrients must diffuse.*

27–1 (continued)

Build Science Skills

Predicting Ask students: **Suppose that we cut a flatworm into three pieces. Assuming that we put each piece in a suitable environment, what do you think will happen?** *(The correct answer is that each part will regenerate.)* Then, take three specimens of live planarians and cut them into three pieces. This can be done by placing each planarian on a flat microscope slide, holding the slide over an ice cube to chill the worm, and using a scalpel or razor blade to cut the worm into pieces. Put each section in a separate petri dish labeled head, middle, or tail. Fill each petri dish half full with pond water; cover the dishes and place them in a dark place. Have students observe the sections three times a week for three weeks and record what they see. Students can compare their observations with their predictions.

Groups of Flatworms

Build Science Skills

Using Tables and Graphs Have students make a compare/contrast table to organize the information they learn about groups of flatworms. The table title should be Groups of Flatworms, and column heads could include Class, Description, Environment, and Examples. Encourage students to include as many details as possible in their table.

Movement Free-living flatworms typically move in two ways. Cilia on their epidermal cells help them glide through the water and over the bottom of a stream or pond. Muscle cells controlled by the nervous system allow them to twist and turn so that they are able to react rapidly to environmental stimuli.

Reproduction Most free-living flatworms are hermaphrodites that reproduce sexually. A **hermaphrodite** (hur-MAF-roh-dyt) is an individual that has both male and female reproductive organs. During sexual reproduction, two worms join in a pair. The worms in the pair deliver sperm to each other. The eggs are laid in clusters and hatch within a few weeks.

Asexual reproduction is common in free-living flatworms. It takes place by **fission,** in which an organism splits in two, and each half grows new parts to become a complete organism. In some species, a worm simply "falls to pieces," and each piece grows into a new worm. Parasitic flatworms often have complex life cycles that involve both sexual and asexual reproduction.

CHECKPOINT *What does an eyespot detect?*

Groups of Flatworms

Flatworms are an enormously diverse group with many different forms. The three main groups of flatworms are turbellarians, flukes, and tapeworms. Most turbellarians are free-living. Most other flatworm species are parasites that depend on hosts such as snails, dogs, cattle, and humans.

Turbellarians Free-living flatworms belong to the class Turbellaria (tur-buh-LAYR-ee-uh). **Turbellarians are free-living flatworms. Most live in marine or fresh water.** Most species are bottom dwellers, living in the sand or mud under stones and shells. In fact, if you put a piece of liver in a freshwater stream, it will probably soon attract many turbellarians. The most familiar flatworms of this group are the planarians, the "cross-eyed" freshwater worms. Turbellarians can vary greatly in color, form, and size, as shown in **Figure 27–4.**

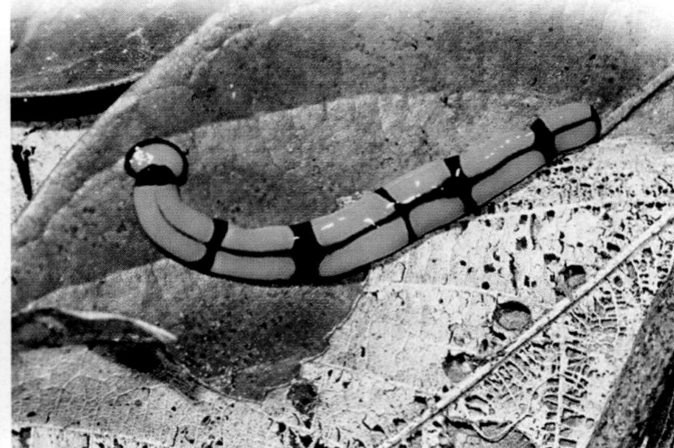

Figure 27–4 Free-living flatworms are called turbellarians. Turbellarians vary immensely in size, shape, coloration, and habitat. The species at left is feeding on a coral reef, and the species at right lives in the leaf litter in a tropical forest.

BIO INSIGHTS **FACTS AND FIGURES**

Did flatworms evolve from cnidarians?
Scientists have discovered that the simplest turbellaria and the larval stages of flukes and tapeworms resemble the planula of the cnidarian life cycle. Planulae are formed from zygotes as part of the cnidarian reproductive process; eventually they grow into polyps. This similarity between flatworms and planulae has led some scientists to hypothesize that ancient bilateral animals evolved from ancestors that were much like planulae. This may have occurred through increased cephalization and the emergence of tissues derived from the mesoderm. If this theory is accurate, then planula-like organisms may have given rise to most groups of complex animals. So far, this theory has not been proven, but there is much evidence to support it.

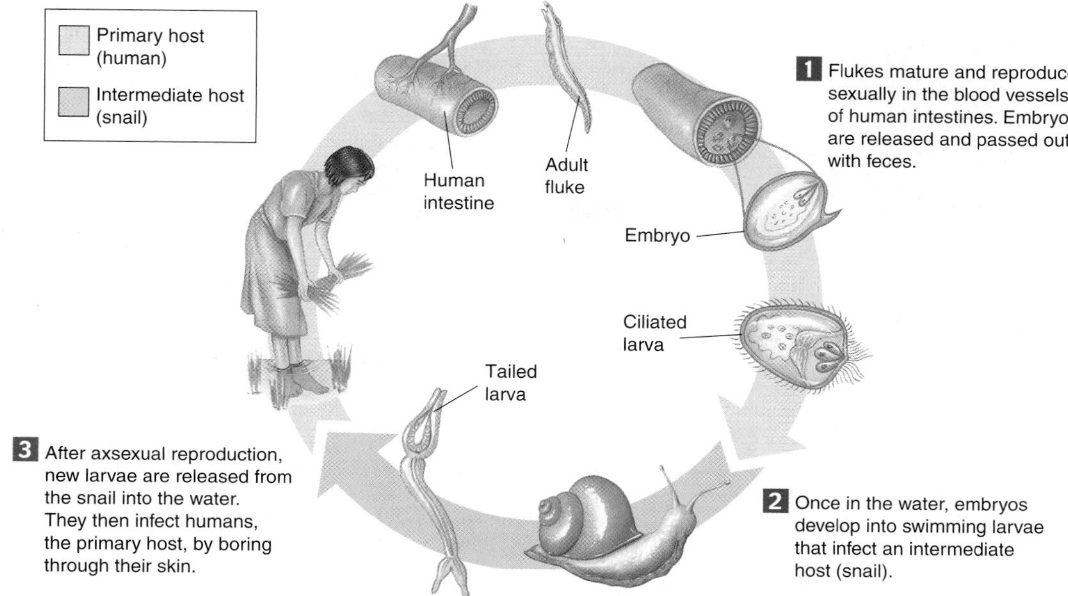
Primary host (human)
Intermediate host (snail)
Human intestine
Adult fluke
1 Flukes mature and reproduce sexually in the blood vessels of human intestines. Embryos are released and passed out with feces.
Embryo
Ciliated larva
Tailed larva
3 After axsexual reproduction, new larvae are released from the snail into the water. They then infect humans, the primary host, by boring through their skin.
2 Once in the water, embryos develop into swimming larvae that infect an intermediate host (snail).

▲ **Figure 27–5** **Flukes usually infect the internal organs of their host.** The life cycle of the blood fluke *Schistosoma mansoni* involves two hosts: humans and snails. In humans, it matures in blood vessels. After *Schistosoma* eggs are fertilized, embryos pass out of the body in feces. If the embryos reach water, they develop into larvae that can infect freshwater snails. The larvae multiply asexually and then exit the snail, searching for a human host.

Flukes Members of the class Trematoda (trem-uh-TOH-duh) are known as flukes. **Flukes are parasitic flatworms. Most flukes infect the internal organs of their host.** They can infect the blood or virtually any internal organ of the host. Some flukes are external parasites that live on the skin, mouth, gills, or other outside parts of a host.

The blood fluke *Schistosoma mansoni* has a life cycle that is typical of parasitic flukes and of many parasites in general. As shown in **Figure 27–5,** the fluke lives in multiple hosts. Its primary host, the organism in which it reproduces sexually, is a human. Blood flukes infect humans by burrowing through exposed skin. Once inside, they are carried to the tiny blood vessels of the intestine. There, the flukes mature into adults, reproduce sexually, and release embryos into the intestine. The embryos are passed out of the body in feces.

If the embryos reach water, they develop into swimming larvae and infect freshwater snails, the intermediate host. An intermediate host is an organism in which a parasite reproduces asexually. Larvae that result from asexual reproduction are eventually released to begin the cycle again.

The *Schistosoma* fluke causes schistosomiasis (shis-tuh-soh-MY-uh-sis) in humans. Schistosomiasis is a serious disease in which the *Schistosoma* eggs clog blood vessels, causing swelling and tissue decay in the lungs, liver, spleen, or intestines. Schistosomiasis affects millions of people worldwide. It is particularly widespread in tropical areas that lack proper sewage systems, where human wastes are tossed into streams or used as fertilizer. There, the parasites are transmitted to intermediate hosts and back to humans with deadly efficiency.

FACTS AND FIGURES

Flukes and planarians

As parasites, flukes exhibit many differences and some similarities when compared with free-living planarians. Unique to the fluke is the thick outer layer of cells called the tegument. The tegument protects flukes from being digested by their hosts. Unlike free-living worms, flukes don't have muscles or cilia for movement. Instead, they have suckers that they use to attach themselves to their hosts. Flukes also lack specialized sense organs. Flukes are similar to planarians in that they have similar excretory systems. They are also like planarians in that they are hermaphrodites.

Use Visuals

Figure 27–5 Ask students: **What disease is caused by the blood fluke?** *(Schistosomiasis)* **How does the life cycle of the blood fluke point to the need for effective sewage treatment?** *(Because the eggs are released in the feces of infected humans, proper treatment of sewage destroys eggs before they hatch into swimming larvae and infect an intermediate host.)* **What is the difference between an intermediate host and a primary host?** *(A primary host is an organism in which the parasite reproduces sexually. An intermediate host is an organism in which the parasite reproduces asexually.)*

Meet Diverse Needs

Reinforce at-risk students' understanding of the life cycle of a flatworm by having them sequence the following events. Write the events on the board, and ask students to rewrite them in the proper sequence.

1. Human becomes infected while standing in shallow water.
2. Fluke eggs hatch into swimming larvae.
3. Adult flukes produce eggs.
4. Snail releases tailed larvae.
5. Flukes mature in blood vessels of human intestine.
6. Human eliminates solid wastes containing fluke eggs.
7. Swimming larvae infect an intermediate host (snail).

(Proper sequence: 1, 5, 3, 6, 2, 7, 4)
Learning modality: verbal

Answer to . . .

CHECKPOINT *An eyespot detects changes in the amount of light in the environment.*

27–1 (continued)

Use Visuals

Figure 27–6 Ask students: **What are proglottids?** *(The segments that make up most of a tapeworm's body)* **When a mature proglottid breaks off, what is the result?** *(Eggs are released that pass out of the host in feces.)* **In a tapeworm's life cycle, what is the primary host, and what is the secondary host?** *(The primary host is the human. The secondary host is another animal, such as a cow or fish.)* **How does a human become infected with a tapeworm?** *(A human eats incompletely cooked meat that contains a tapeworm cyst.)*

3 ASSESS

Evaluate Understanding

Call on students at random to explain feeding, respiration, circulation, excretion, response, movement, and reproduction in flatworms.

Reteach

Have students review the life cycle of a fluke in Figure 27–5. Then, point out that the life cycle of a tapeworm is described in the text on page 688. Challenge students to use this description to illustrate the life cycle of a tapeworm in a way similar to that in Figure 27–5.

ALTERNATIVE ASSESSMENT

Exhibits could include information about feeding, organ systems, and reproduction. Encourage students to create an interesting and accurate exhibit that shows both the similarities and the differences between the two types of flatworms. You may want to have students display their work for another class.

Use iText to review the key concepts in Section 27–1.

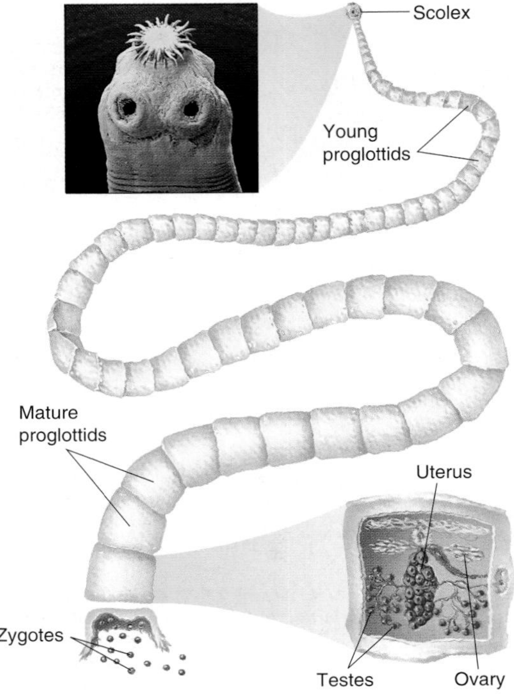

▲ **Figure 27–6 Tapeworms are parasitic flatworms that live in the intestine of their host.** A tapeworm attaches to the host using hooks or suckers on its scolex. A single tapeworm is made of many proglottids. The youngest proglottids are at the anterior (head) end, and the largest and most mature proglottids are at the posterior (tail) end. When mature, proglottids break off and release eggs that are then fertilized and passed out of the host in feces.

Tapeworms Members of the class Cestoda (ses-TOHD-uh) are called tapeworms. **Tapeworms are long, flat, parasitic worms that are adapted to life inside the intestines of their hosts.** There, they are surrounded by food that has already been digested, so it can be absorbed directly through their body walls. They have no digestive tract.

Figure 27–6 shows the structure of a tapeworm. The head of an adult tapeworm is called a **scolex** (SKOH-leks), a structure that can contain suckers or hooks. The tapeworm uses its scolex to attach to the intestinal wall of its host, where it absorbs nutrients from the host's intestine. Behind the scolex is a narrow neck region that divides to produce many **proglottids** (proh-GLAHT-idz), which are the segments that make up most of the worm's body. Mature proglottids contain both male and female reproductive organs. Sperm produced by the **testes,** or male reproductive organs, can fertilize eggs of other tapeworms or of the same individual. Mature proglottids break off and burst to release fertilized eggs, or zygotes. These zygotes are passed out of the host in feces.

If food or water contaminated with tapeworm zygotes is consumed by cows, fishes, or other intermediate hosts, the eggs enter the host and hatch into larvae. These larvae grow and then burrow into the muscle tissue of the intermediate host. There they form a dormant protective stage called a cyst. If a human eats incompletely cooked meat containing these cysts, the larvae become active and grow into adult worms within the human's intestines, beginning the cycle again.

27–1 Section Assessment

1. **Key Concept** What is a flatworm?
2. **Key Concept** List the three groups of flatworms and give an example of each.
3. How do the feeding methods of parasitic and free-living flatworms relate to their specific environments?
4. Describe the life cycle of the blood fluke, *Schistosoma mansoni.*
5. **Critical Thinking Applying Concepts** Explain why you should cook meat and fish thoroughly, especially in areas that have parasitic worms.

ALTERNATIVE ASSESSMENT

Organizing Information Create an exhibit that compares free-living and parasitic flatworms. You may want to include photographs, drawings, or models in your exhibit.

iTEXT **Assessment** Use iText to review the important concepts in Section 27–1.

27–1 Section Assessment

1. A flatworm is a soft, flattened worm with tissues, organ systems, three germ layers, bilateral symmetry, and cephalization.
2. Turbellaria: planarian; Trematoda: fluke; Cestoda: tapeworm
3. Many parasitic flatworms obtain nutrients directly from their host's body; they lack digestive systems. Free-living flatworms actively capture and digest food; they have organs and a digestive system to do this.
4. *S. mansoni* matures in the blood vessels of human intestines. Embryos are released and passed out with feces. Embryos hatch into swimming larvae that infect an intermediate host (a snail). Larvae released from the intermediate host into water can infect humans by boring through the skin.
5. High temperatures destroy worm cysts, which can cause disease in humans.

27–2 Roundworms

Members of the phylum Nematoda (nee-muh-TOHD-uh), also known as roundworms, are among the most numerous of all animals. It is difficult to imagine how many live around us. A single rotting apple can contain as many as 90,000 roundworms. A cubic meter of garden soil can be home to more than a million!

What Is a Roundworm?

Roundworms are slender, unsegmented worms with tapering ends. They range in size from microscopic to a meter in length. Most species of roundworms are free-living, inhabiting soil, salt flats, aquatic sediments, and water, from polar regions to the tropics. Many others are parasitic and live in hosts that include almost every kind of plant and animal.

Like the flatworms, all roundworms develop from three germ layers. However, roundworms have a body cavity between the endoderm and mesoderm tissues. Because this cavity is lined only partially with mesoderm tissue, it is called a **pseudocoelom** (soo-doh-SEE-lum), which means "false coelom." Observe the pseudocoelom in **Figure 27–7.**

Also, unlike the flatworms, roundworms have a digestive tract with two openings. This body plan is often called a tube-within-a-tube. The inner tube is the digestive tract, and the outer tube is the body wall. This arrangement makes digestion in roundworms very different from that in flatworms because food moves in one direction through the digestive tract. Any material in the food that cannot be digested leaves through the anus. The **anus** is the posterior opening of the digestive tract. **Roundworms are unsegmented worms that have pseudocoeloms and digestive systems with two openings—a mouth and an anus.**

Guide for Reading

Key Concepts
- What are the defining features of roundworms?
- What roundworms are important in human disease?

Vocabulary
pseudocoelom
anus

Reading Strategy: Using Visuals As you read, write a statement explaining how each illustration or photograph reinforces or enhances the content of the section.

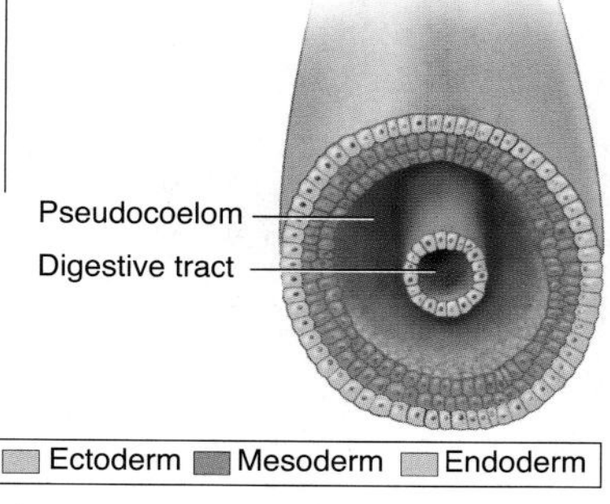

Figure 27–7 Roundworms such as the hookworms are unsegmented worms that have a pseudocoelom and a digestive system with a mouth and an anus. Roundworms develop from three germ layers, and a pseudocoelom forms between the endoderm and mesoderm layers. The pseudocoelom allows for greater specialization and movement of internal organs.

TIME SAVER — SECTION RESOURCES

Print:
- ***Teaching Resources,*** Section Review 27–2
- ***Guided Reading and Study Workbook,*** Section 27–2

Technology:
- ***iText,*** Section 27–2

Section 27–2

1 FOCUS

Objectives

27.2.1 ***Describe*** the defining features of roundworms.
27.2.2 ***Explain*** how digestion takes place in roundworms.
27.2.3 ***Identify*** roundworms that are important in human disease.

Guide for Reading

Vocabulary Preview

Have students write the vocabulary words, dividing each into its separate syllables as best they can. Remind students that each syllable usually has only one vowel sound. The correct syllabications are: pseu•do•coe•lom, a•nus.

Reading Strategy

Before students read, have them skim the section to find the boldfaced Key Concepts. Ask students to copy the sentences onto separate sheets of paper. Then, as they read, they should make notes of details that support each Key Concept.

2 INSTRUCT

What Is a Roundworm?

Meet Diverse Needs

Explain to students with limited English proficiency that the prefix *pseudo-* is used in a word they might come across in a literature class: *pseudonym,* or "false name." Explain that authors sometimes publish under a pseudonym to protect their real identities. Then, ask: **What is "false" about a pseudocoelom?** *(A coelom is a body cavity that is completely lined with mesoderm tissue. A pseudocoelom is "false" because it is only partially lined with mesoderm tissue.)*

Form and Function in Roundworms

Build Science Skills

Comparing and Contrasting Set up a classroom display of live flatworms and roundworms so that students can observe and compare the two groups of animals. An appropriate flatworm is a planarian; vinegar eels are roundworms that make excellent subjects for observation. Place several planarians in a small amount of pond water or aquarium water in a petri dish. Have students use a hand lens or a stereo microscope to observe these animals move. Place a few drops of vinegar eel culture in a depression slide or on a plain microscope slide. Do not use a coverslip. Have students observe the slide under low power. Then, ask: **How would you describe the movement of the planarians?** *(They glide through the water or along the surface of the petri dish.)* **How would you describe the movement of the roundworms?** *(They move with a rapid, jerky motion.)*

Roundworms and Human Disease

Build Science Skills

Comparing and Contrasting
Have students make a compare-and-contrast table to organize the information they learn about roundworms and human disease. Column heads should include Parasite, Disease, and Characteristics.

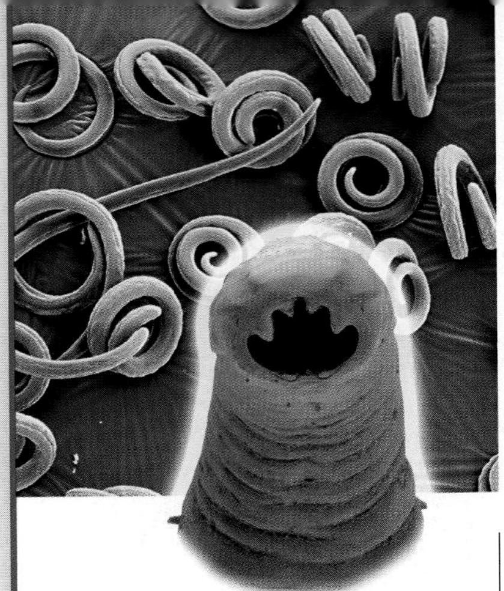

Figure 27–8 **Parasitic roundworms include trichinosis-causing *Trichinella* worms (top) and hookworms (inset).** *Trichinella* worms reproduce in the intestines of their host—including pigs and other vertebrates—and then form cysts in the muscle tissue. Hookworms affect as many as one quarter of the world's population. They suck the host's blood from inside the intestines, weakening the host.

Form and Function in Roundworms

Roundworms have specialized tissues and organ systems that carry out essential body functions. In general, the body systems of free-living roundworms tend to be more complex than those of parasitic forms, shown in **Figure 27–8.**

Feeding Many free-living roundworms are carnivores that use grasping mouthparts and spines to catch and eat other small animals. Some soil-dwelling and aquatic forms eat algae, fungi, or pieces of decaying organic matter. Others digest the bacteria and fungi that break down dead animals and plants.

Respiration, Circulation, and Excretion Like flatworms, roundworms exchange gases and excrete metabolic waste through their body walls. They have no internal transport system. Therefore, they depend on diffusion to carry nutrients and waste through their bodies.

Response Roundworms have simple nervous systems, consisting of several ganglia. Several nerves extend from ganglia in the head and run the length of the body. These nerves transmit sensory information and control movement. Roundworms have several types of sense organs, simple structures that detect chemicals given off by prey or hosts.

Movement The muscles of roundworms extend the length of their bodies. Together with the fluid in the pseudocoelom, these muscles function as a hydrostatic skeleton. Aquatic roundworms contract these muscles to move like snakes through the water. Soil-dwelling roundworms simply push their way through the soil by thrashing around.

Reproduction Roundworms reproduce sexually, and most species of roundworms have separate males and females. Roundworms reproduce using internal fertilization. Usually, the male deposits sperm inside the female's reproductive tract. Parasitic roundworms, such as hookworms or ascarid worms, often have complex life cycles that involve two or three different hosts or several organs within a single host.

CHECKPOINT *How do free-living roundworms that are carnivores obtain their food?*

Roundworms and Human Disease

Although most roundworms are free-living, the phylum is better known for species that parasitize their hosts, including humans. Parasitic roundworms, such as those in **Figure 27–8,** have been evolving relationships with other organisms for hundreds of millions of years. Unfortunately, this process has produced worms that cause a great deal of pain and suffering in humans. **Parasitic roundworms include trichinosis-causing worms, filarial worms, ascarid worms, and hookworms.**

PRESENTATIONS MADE EASY!

The Presentation Assistant Plus contains the Prentice Hall Presentation Pro and the Transparencies, which provide easy-to-follow visual support for every step of this section. If you have a computer presentation station, use Prentice Hall Presentation Pro Section 27–2, or use the transparencies listed here.

Section 27–2: **Interest Grabber**
Section Outline
Diseases Caused by Roundworms

Careers in Biology

Meat Inspector

Job description: work with farms and meat-processing plants to ensure that all meat and poultry products use healthy animals, are processed in a sanitary manner, and are labeled truthfully with no harmful ingredients added; enforce government regulations to ensure that proper safety, sanitation, preservation, disposal, and packaging procedures are followed

Education: college courses in sanitation and public health; USDA certification

Skills: knowledge of food-borne illnesses, proper sanitation practices, and regulations; public relations skills for dealing with different people in the industry; patience and communication skills for educating the public; ability to work independently and with a team

Highlights: You help protect the safety of the public by working to eliminate food-borne illnesses. You inspect farms to make sure that sanitary procedures are followed.

"We are basically 'silent guardians' of the public's health. When you buy meat or order it at a restaurant, you can rest assured that the food is safe because meat inspectors have done their job."

Take It to the NET For more information about this career, visit the Prentice Hall Web site: **www.phschool.com**

Trichinosis-Causing Worms Trichinosis (trik-ih-NOH-sis) is a terrible disease caused by the roundworm *Trichinella*. Adult worms live and mate in the intestines of their hosts, which include humans, pigs, and other mammals. Females carrying fertilized eggs burrow into the intestinal wall and then release larvae. These larvae travel through the bloodstream and burrow into organs and tissues, causing terrible pain for the host. The larvae form cysts and become inactive in the host's muscle tissue. *Trichinella* completes its life cycle only when another animal eats muscle tissue containing these cysts.

Filarial Worms Filarial worms, which are found primarily in tropical regions of Asia, are threadlike worms that live in the blood and lymph vessels of birds and mammals, including humans. They are transmitted from one primary host to another through biting insects, especially mosquitoes. In severe infections, large numbers of filarial worms may block the passage of fluids within the lymph vessels. This causes elephantiasis, shown in **Figure 27–9**, a condition in which the affected part of the body swells enormously.

CHECKPOINT *Describe the cause of elephantiasis.*

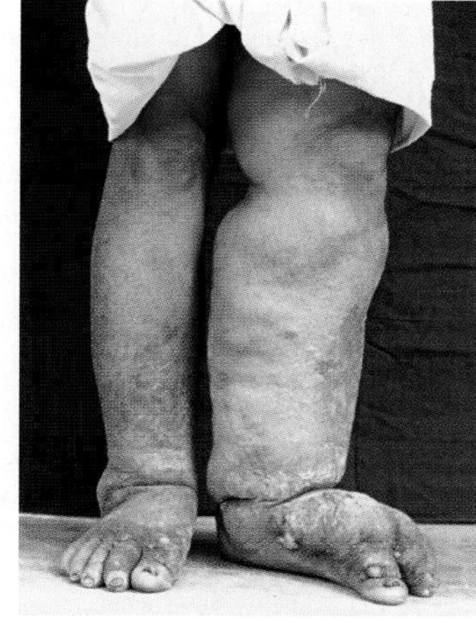

▲ **Figure 27–9** **Filarial worms are one kind of parasitic roundworm.** Elephantiasis, shown here in an advanced stage, is a disease caused by filarial worms.

Careers in Biology

- The meat inspector pictured at the top right of the feature is Evangelina Martinez, the program manager over Meat Safety Assurance in south Texas. She has 15 hours of college courses in sanitation and a two-course U.S. Department of Agriculture (USDA) certificate.
- The occupational outlook handbook for a meat inspector suggests a BA/BS in agricultural science.
- Inspections of meat and enforcement of regulations help prevent trichinosis and other diseases caused by roundworms and other organisms.

Resources Have students who want additional information on this career contact the U.S. Department of Agriculture's (USDA) Food Safety and Inspection Service (FSIS), which has the responsibility for ensuring that meat, poultry, and egg products are safe, wholesome, and accurately labeled. For more information about this career, visit **www.phschool.com**

BIO INSIGHTS — FACTS AND FIGURES

Roundworms on the farm

The importance of nematodes as plant parasites was not understood until fairly recently, partly because they are smaller and less visibly destructive than well-recognized pests such as insects, snails, and slugs. Every year, nematodes reduce crop yields by an estimated 10 percent in the United States and prompt the use of more than 50 million kilograms of pesticides. Practices such as crop rotation, cultivation, addition of organic matter, and control of soil moisture and acidity help control nematode populations. Ironically, nematodes also benefit agriculture because they are parasites of many insect pests. For example, one nematode species attacks both the larvae and adults of the woodwasp that damages pine trees. Other parasitic nematodes enter the body cavity of insect hosts and introduce species-specific bacteria.

Answers to . . .

CHECKPOINT *Carnivorous free-living flatworms use grasping mouthparts and spines to catch and eat small animals.*

CHECKPOINT *Elephantiasis occurs when large numbers of filarial worms block the passage of fluids within the lymph vessels of a part of the body.*

27–2 (continued)

Use Visuals

Figure 27–10 Direct students' attention to the life cycle of the ascarid worm, and ask a student to read the annotations aloud. Then, ask: **Why is this worm classified as a parasite?** *(It takes nourishment and lives at the expense of its host, such as a human. The host gains nothing from the relationship.)* **In what part of the body does the parasite do the most damage?** *(In the small intestine)*

Meet Diverse Needs

Have students who need an extra challenge find out how some of the diseases caused by parasitic roundworms are treated medically. Students may also wish to contact a veterinarian to find out which diseases caused by roundworms are likely to infect animals in your area. Ask students to make a report to the class about what they learned. **Learning modality: verbal**

Research on *C. elegans*

Meet Diverse Needs

Encourage students who need an extra challenge to prepare a report about the investigation of genomes other than the well-publicized Human Genome Project. Students can use library resources and periodicals to find out what scientists determined about the sequence of base pairs in *C. elegans* DNA and how they accomplished that task. Students could also find out which other organisms have been similarly investigated. **Learning modality: verbal**

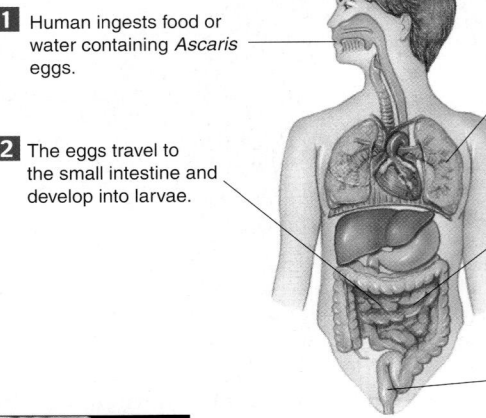

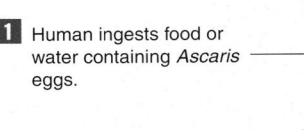

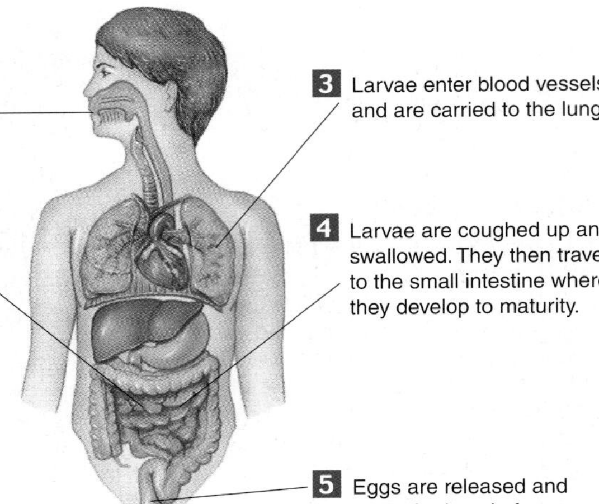

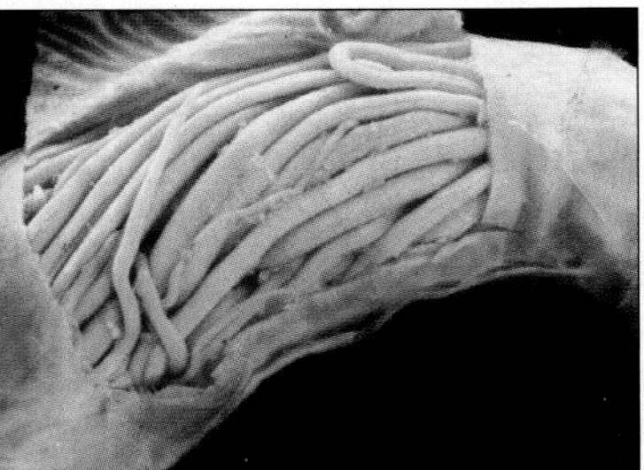

5 Eggs are released and leave the host in feces.

Figure 27–10 *Ascaris lumbricoides* fill the host's intestine. These worms absorb the host's digested food and can cause severe malnutrition. Blockage of the intestine can be severe enough, as shown in a pig intestine in the photograph, that it causes death. **Interpreting Graphics** *What is the sequence of organs that* Ascaris *travels through in humans?*

Ascarid Worms *Ascaris lumbricoides* is a serious parasite of humans and many other vertebrate animals. It causes malnutrition in more than 1 billion people worldwide, including many people living in the southeastern United States. It is commonly spread by eating vegetables or other foods that are not washed properly.

The life cycle of *Ascaris* is summarized in **Figure 27–10** above. *Ascaris* matures in the intestines of its host, such as a human, and can reach a length of almost 50 cm. In the intestine, the ascarid worms produce a large number of fertilized eggs, which leave the body in the feces. If food or water contaminated with these feces is eaten by another host, then the eggs hatch in the small intestine of the new host. The young worms burrow into the walls of the intestines and enter the surrounding blood vessels. The worms are carried in the blood until they reach the lungs. There, they spread into air passages and into the throat, where they are swallowed. Carried back into the intestines, they mature, and the cycle repeats itself.

Species that are closely related to *Ascaris* affect horses, cattle, pigs, chickens, dogs, cats, and many other animals. *Ascaris* and its relatives, which are collectively known as ascarids, have life cycles that are similar to one another. One of the reasons puppies are wormed while they are young is to rid them of the ascarid worms that affect dogs.

CHECKPOINT *How are* Ascaris *eggs spread?*

Hookworms Today, as many as one quarter of the people in the world are infected with hookworms. Hookworm eggs hatch outside the body of the host and develop in the soil. If they find an unprotected foot, they use sharp toothlike plates and hooks to burrow into the skin and enter the bloodstream. Hookworms travel through the blood of their host to the lungs and down to the intestines. There, they suck the host's blood, causing weakness and poor growth.

FACTS AND FIGURES

A great lab animal
Caenorhabditis elegans has become such a well-established laboratory animal that more is known about its biology than that of almost any other organisms. Because it is only 1 mm long when mature, *C. elegans* can be raised in small laboratory dishes. It takes only 12 hours from fertilization of the egg to hatching of the juvenile worm. In that time, successive cell divisions produce 671 cells, of which 113 are programmed to die, leaving 558 in the worm that hatches. This "programmed-to-die" characteristic is valuable to researchers studying the aging process. The precise number of 959 cells in the mature worm is adequate for studying the development of complex organ systems, but not so many that it is impossible to track the divisions of each cell. The pattern and number of cell divisions in *C. elegans* are unvarying, making it possible to study the effects of a single genetic mutation.

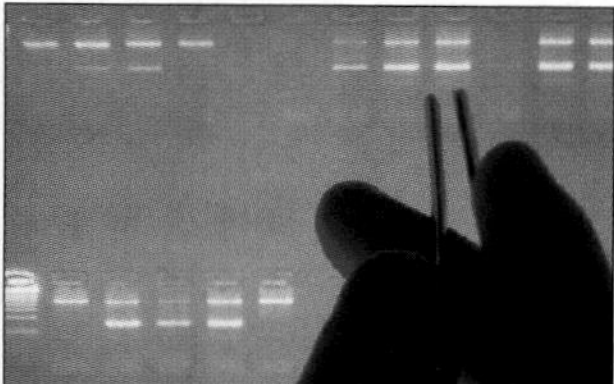

Figure 27–11 The DNA of *C. elegans,* a free-living roundworm, was the first genome of any multicellular animal to be sequenced completely. Biologists used techniques such as gel electrophoresis, shown at right, to determine the exact sequence of base pairs in each chromosome. **Predicting** *How might these results be important to our understanding of human development?*

Research on C. *elegans*

Roundworms have recently been making headlines in scientific research. The free-living roundworm *Caenorhabditis elegans*, or *C. elegans*, is shown in **Figure 27–11,** above left. This worm lives a modest existence feeding on rotting vegetation. However, this species is extraordinary because its DNA was the first of any multicellular animal's to be sequenced completely.

Scientists now have the sequence of all 97 million base pairs of *C. elegans* DNA. This is roughly one thirtieth the number of base pairs in human DNA. They have also traced the development of each body cell of *C. elegans*, starting from a single fertilized egg. Researchers are still learning how this development is controlled by the animal's DNA. This research will lead to a better understanding of how eukaryotes became multicellular. Information from *C. elegans* may also shed light on how genes make multicellular organisms both similar to and different from one another.

KEEP CURRENT WITH . . . SCIENCE NEWS®

To find out more about the topics in this chapter, go to: **www.phschool.com**

27–2 Section Assessment

1. **Key Concept** What is a roundworm?
2. **Key Concept** What are the parasitic roundworms?
3. Describe how humans become infected with the parasitic roundworm *Ascaris*.
4. How do hookworms enter the human body?
5. **Critical Thinking Problem Solving** How might the spread of elephantiasis be reduced?

iTEXT Assessment Use iText to review the important concepts in Section 27–2.

ALTERNATIVE ASSESSMENT

Creating a Poster
Choose a type of roundworm that can cause disease in humans. Design an educational poster that promotes prevention of the disease. Be sure to include information about how the roundworm infects humans.

27–2 Section Assessment

1. A roundworm is an unsegmented worm that has a pseudocoelom and a digestive system with two openings—a mouth and an anus.
2. Parasitic roundworms include trichinosis-causing worms, filarial worms, ascarid worms, and hookworms.
3. A human becomes infected by ingesting food or water containing *Ascaris* eggs.
4. Hookworms enter the human body by burrowing into the skin of a foot.
5. The spread of elephantiasis could be reduced by reducing numbers of biting insects and by encouraging people to wear protective clothing and use insect repellent.

3 ASSESS

Evaluate Understanding

Ask students to write a comparison of flatworms and roundworms. Tell them that they should compare both form and function, beginning with whether or not each type of invertebrate has a coelom.

Reteach

Have students write an article that might be published in the local newspaper about a person who has contracted trichinosis. Explain that they should describe the disease and how it was contracted, as well as the organism that causes the disease.

ALTERNATIVE ASSESSMENT

Discuss what makes an effective poster, and have students determine who their audience is as well as the poster's objective. Posters should explain how one type of roundworm spreads to humans and how infection can be prevented.

SCIENCE NEWS®

Encourage students to visit **www.phschool.com** for the most current information on this topic.

Use iText to review the key concepts in Section 27–2.

Answers to . . .

CHECKPOINT *Ascaris eggs leave the host's body in feces. If food or water contaminated with the feces is eaten by another host, then the eggs hatch in the small intestine of the new host.*

Figure 27–10 *Mouth, small intestine, blood vessels, lungs, throat, small intestine*

Figure 27–11 *Information from* C. elegans *may shed light on how an animal's DNA controls the animal's development from a single fertilized egg to a complex multicellular organism.*

Section 27–3

1 FOCUS

Objectives

27.3.1 ***Describe*** the defining features of annelids.
27.3.2 ***Identify*** the characteristics of the three classes of annelids.
27.3.3 ***Describe*** the ecology of annelids.

Guide for Reading

Vocabulary Preview

Call on volunteers to pronounce each of the vocabulary words aloud. Correct any mispronunciations, and note any words that students with limited English proficiency have special trouble pronouncing.

Reading Strategy

Advise students to compare the labeled diagram in Figure 27–16 with that in Figure 27–3 in Section 27–1.

2 INSTRUCT

What Is an Annelid?

Use Visuals

Figure 27–12 Divide the class into pairs, and give each pair three different-colored blocks of clay. Then, ask students to make three models, beginning with one that matches the cross-section of the annelid shown in this figure. After that is completed, students should make similar models of the cross-sections shown in Figures 27–1 and 27–7. Also provide toothpicks for students to make labels for their models.

Build Science Skills

Using Models To help students visualize a digestive tract inside a body wall, give each student or group a long sock with the toe cut off. Tell students to turn the sock halfway inside out to form a tube-within-a-tube. Explain that the inner layer of the sock represents the digestive tract, and the outer layer represents the body wall.

27–3 Annelids

Guide for Reading

Key Concepts
- What are the defining features of annelids?
- What are the characteristics of the three classes of annelids?

Vocabulary
- septum • seta
- crop • gizzard
- closed circulatory system
- gill • nephridium
- clitellum

Reading Strategy: Using Visuals Before you read, preview **Figure 27–16.** How does this animal seem to differ from the other worms you have already studied? Briefly summarize any differences you notice.

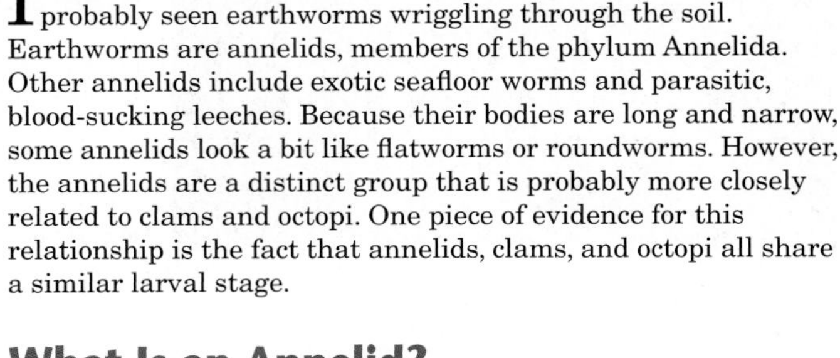

If you have ever dug in a garden in the spring, you have probably seen earthworms wriggling through the soil. Earthworms are annelids, members of the phylum Annelida. Other annelids include exotic seafloor worms and parasitic, blood-sucking leeches. Because their bodies are long and narrow, some annelids look a bit like flatworms or roundworms. However, the annelids are a distinct group that is probably more closely related to clams and octopi. One piece of evidence for this relationship is the fact that annelids, clams, and octopi all share a similar larval stage.

What Is an Annelid?

The name Annelida (uh-NEL-ih-duh) is derived from the Latin word *annellus*, which means "little ring." The name refers to the ringlike appearance of annelids' body segments. The body of an annelid is divided into segments that are separated by **septa** (singular: septum), which are internal walls between each segment. Most segments are similar to one another, although they may be modified to perform special functions. Some body segments may carry one or more pairs of eyes, several pairs of antennae, and other sense organs. Other segments may be specialized for functions such as respiration. In many annelids, bristles called **setae** (SEE tee; singular: seta) are attached to each segment.

Annelids are worms with segmented bodies. They have a true coelom that is lined with mesoderm. These structures are shown in **Figure 27–12.** Recall that flatworms have no coelom, whereas roundworms have a pseudocoelom that forms between the endoderm and the mesoderm. Like the roundworms, annelids have a tube-within-a-tube digestive tract that food passes through from the mouth to the anus.

CHECKPOINT *What are some functions performed by specialized segments?*

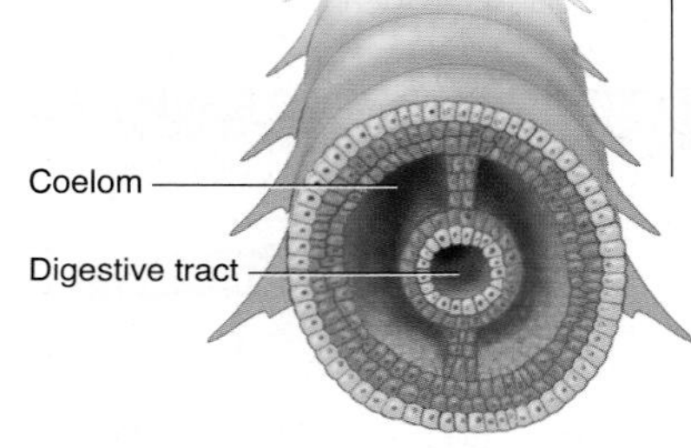

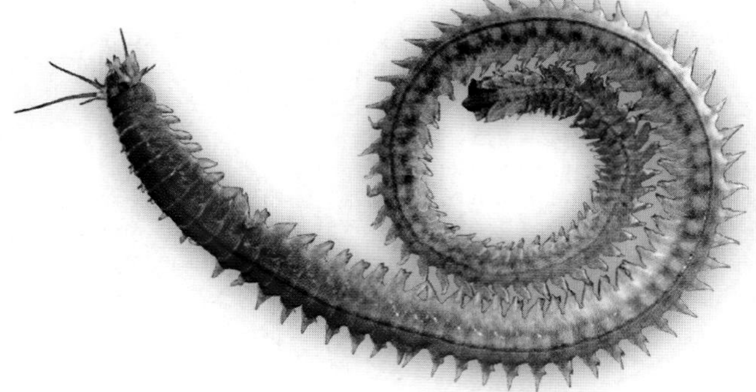

Figure 27–12 **Annelids are among the simplest animals to have a true coelom that is lined with mesoderm.** Annelids are also called segmented worms because the body is divided into many similar segments. The photo shows a marine annelid.

SECTION RESOURCES

Print:
- ***Teaching Resources,*** Section Review 27–3
- ***Guided Reading and Study Workbook,*** Section 27–3
- ***Issues and Decision Making,*** 27–1

Technology:
- ***iText,*** Section 27–3

Quick Lab

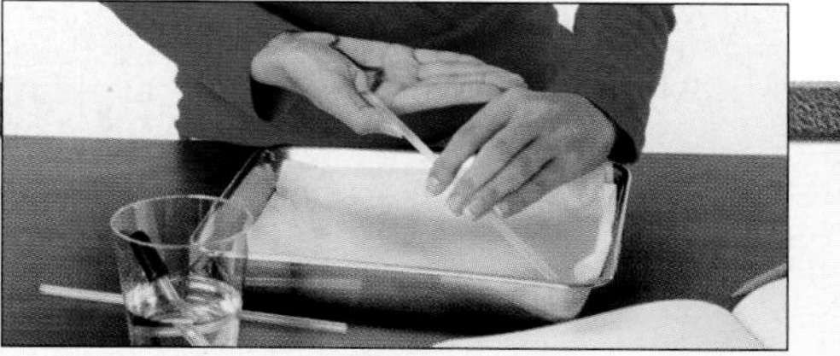

Does an earthworm have a heartbeat?

Materials earthworm; dropper pipette; nonchlorinated water; large, clear plastic soda straw; dissecting microscope

Procedure

1. Carefully insert an earthworm into a clear plastic straw. Do not force the worm into the straw. **CAUTION:** *Handle the earthworm carefully to avoid harming it. Wash your hands after handling the worm.*
2. Use a dropper pipette to add a drop or two of nonchlorinated water into the straw.
3. Examine the straw using a microscope. Direct light through the straw from below. Look near the front of the worm for the large ring blood vessels. Count how often these organs beat. Observe the rest of the circulatory system.

Analyze and Conclude

1. **Inferring** Did you see the worm breathing? Explain your answer. Why must the earthworm's skin be kept moist? How do your answers relate to how earthworms live in their environment?
2. **Observing** Is an earthworm's circulatory system open or closed? Explain your answer.

Form and Function in Annelids

Annelids have complex organ systems. Many of these systems are unique because of the segmented body plan of this group.

Feeding and Digestion Annelids range from filter feeders to predators that are fearsome—at least for their size. Many annelids get their food using a pharynx. In carnivorous species, such as the *Nereis* in **Figure 27–13,** the pharynx usually holds two or more sharp jaws that are used to attack prey. In annelids that feed on decaying vegetation, the pharynx is covered with sticky mucus. The worm collects food particles by extending its pharynx and pressing it against the surrounding sediments. Other annelids obtain nutrients by filter feeding. They fan water through tubelike burrows and catch food particles in a mucus bag.

In earthworms, the pharynx pumps food and soil into a tube called the esophagus. The food then moves through the **crop,** where it can be stored, and through the **gizzard,** where it is ground into smaller pieces. The food is absorbed farther along in the digestive tract, in an organ called the intestine.

Circulation Annelids typically have a **closed circulatory system,** in which blood is contained within a network of blood vessels. An earthworm's blood circulates through two major blood vessels that run from head to tail. Blood in the dorsal (top) vessel moves toward the head of the worm. Blood in the ventral (bottom) vessel runs from head to tail. In each body segment, a pair of smaller blood vessels called ring vessels connect the dorsal and ventral blood vessels and supply blood to the internal organs. The dorsal blood vessel functions like a heart because it contracts rhythmically and helps pump blood.

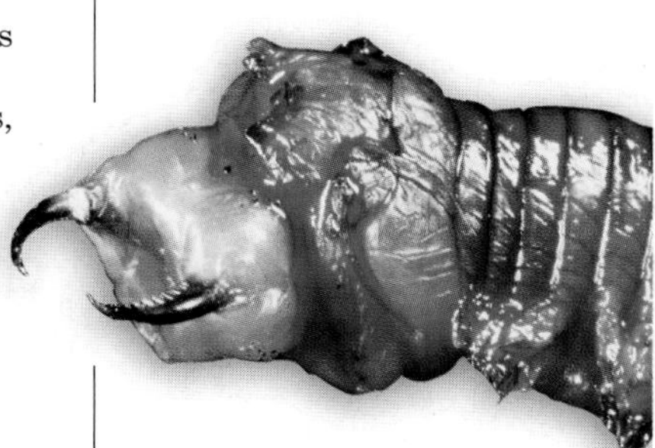

▲ **Figure 27–13** The annelid *Nereis* uses jaws to capture prey. When prey approaches, the worm lunges forward, rapidly extends its pharynx, and grabs the prey using its jaws. **Inferring** *How is the structure of a* Nereis*'s jaws related to their function?*

PRESENTATIONS MADE EASY!

The Presentation Assistant Plus contains the Prentice Hall Presentation Pro and the Transparencies, which provide easy-to-follow visual support for every step of this section. If you have a computer presentation station, use Prentice Hall Presentation Pro Section 27–3, or use the transparencies listed here.

Section 27–3: **Interest Grabber**
Section Outline
Compare/Contrast Matrix
Figure 27–16

 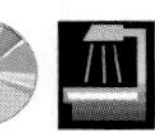

Form and Function in Annelids

Quick Lab

Objective Students will be able to describe the structure and function of an earthworm's circulatory system.

Skill Focus Observing

Materials earthworm, dropper pipette, nonchlorinated water, large and clear plastic straw, dissecting microscope

Time 15 minutes

Advance Prep Collect earthworms outdoors, or buy them from a bait shop. Pond water, aquarium water, and bottles of spring water are all acceptable forms of nonchlorinated water. Tap water can be dechlorinated by boiling and cooling overnight in an open container.

Safety Make sure students wash their hands after handling the earthworms.

Strategies

- If students have trouble inserting the worm in a straw, try slitting the straw lengthwise.
- Students can also put the earthworm and a few drops of water in a petri dish cover, with the bottom of the petri dish inverted on top to hold the worm in place. Do not allow the worms to dry out.

Expected Outcomes Students should see the earthworm's heart beating and that an earthworm has a closed circulatory system.

Analyze and Conclude

1. An earthworm has no breathing movements, because it exchanges gases through its skin. The earthworm's skin must be kept moist, because otherwise it will not be able to exchange gases. Earthworms live in moist soil.
2. The earthworm has a closed circulatory system, because blood never leaves the blood vessels.

Answers to . . .

CHECKPOINT *Sample answer: sense organs, respiration*

Figure 27–13 *Hooks with sharp points are adapted to catch prey.*

27–3 (continued)

Build Science Skills

Observing Earthworms are among the most familiar of organisms, yet probably few students have taken the time to observe earthworms closely. To give students this opportunity, fill a plastic box with about 2 centimeters of sand. Place about 7 centimeters of loosely packed topsoil over the sand. Use pond water to slightly moisten the soil. (Add more water whenever the soil appears dry.) Place 6 to 12 earthworms on top of the soil. Cover the box with clear plastic wrap, and put a few air holes in the plastic wrap. Have students observe the earthworms for several days. Ask them to make labeled diagrams of the animals. Advise them to note especially how earthworms move through the soil.

Use Community Resources

Contact a local environmental group for a reference to a person in your area who uses earthworms to compost household organic garbage. Ask this person to speak to the class about how to set up such a system and what foods can and cannot be added to the earthworm habitat. Students might be surprised to learn that such a system can be clean and without unpleasant odors. It can not only dispose of organic wastes responsibly, but also provide great soil for a garden.

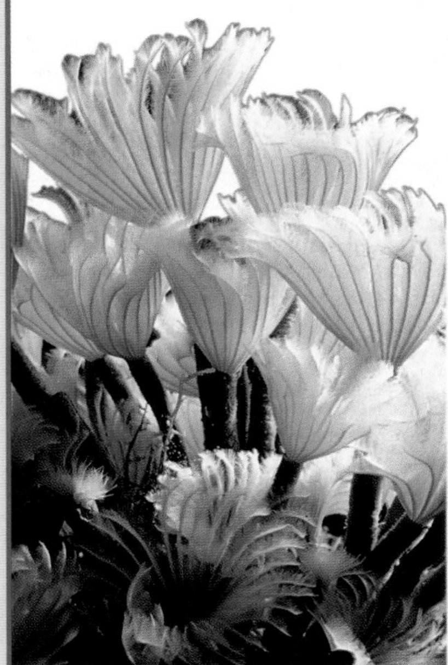

▲ **Figure 27–14** These feather-duster worms exchange gases underwater using feathery gills. **Applying Concepts** *How do land-dwelling annelids exchange gases?*

Respiration Aquatic annelids often breathe through gills. A **gill** is a filamentous organ specialized for the exchange of gases underwater. In feather-duster worms, shown in **Figure 27–14,** feathery gills protrude from the opening of the worm's burrow or tube. Land-dwelling annelids, such as earthworms, take in oxygen and give off carbon dioxide through their moist skin. These annelids secrete a thin protective coating of mucus, which keeps their skins moist.

Excretion Like other animals, annelids produce two kinds of waste. Digestive waste passes out through the anus at the end of the digestive tract. Cellular waste containing nitrogen is eliminated by **nephridia** (nee-FRID-ee-uh; singular: nephridium), which are excretory organs that filter fluid in the coelom.

Response Most annelids have a well-developed nervous system consisting of a brain and several nerve cords. However, the sense organs are best developed in free-living marine annelids. Many of these species have a variety of adaptations for detecting stimuli: sensory tentacles, chemical receptors, statocysts that help detect gravity, and two or more pairs of eyes.

Movement Annelids have two major groups of body muscles that function as part of a hydrostatic skeleton. Longitudinal muscles run from the front of the worm to the rear and can contract to make the worm shorter and fatter. Circular muscles wrap around each body segment and can contract to make the worm longer and thinner. The earthworm moves by alternately contracting these two sets of muscles. Burrowing annelids use their muscles to force their way through heavy sediment. Marine annelids also have paddlelike appendages, or parapodia (singular: parapodium), on each segment, which they use for swimming and crawling.

Reproduction Most annelids reproduce sexually. Some species use external fertilization and have separate sexes—each individual is either male or female. Other annelids, such as earthworms and leeches, are hermaphrodites: each worm produces both sperm and eggs. Individuals rarely fertilize their own eggs. Instead, two worms attach to each other, as shown in **Figure 27–15,** exchange sperm, and then store the sperm in special sacs. When eggs are ready for fertilization, a **clitellum** (kly-TEL-um), or band of thickened, specialized segments, secretes a mucus ring into which eggs and sperm are released. Fertilization takes place within this ring. The ring then slips off the worm's body and forms a protective cocoon. Young worms hatch weeks later.

▶ **Figure 27–15** Some annelids, including these earthworms, are hermaphrodites. Each worm produces both eggs and sperm. During mating, the worms exchange sperm, which will eventually be used to fertilize egg cells. **Applying Concepts** *When are the eggs fertilized?*

FACTS AND FIGURES

Slithering through the soil

Annelids move through soil and sediment by using the power of their muscles and the liquid inside their body segments—their hydrostatic skeleton. Each body segment is sealed off from the segment next to it, which means body fluids can't move from one segment to another. When the longitudinal muscles contract and make the worm shorter, each segment has to become wider. In a similar manner, when the circular muscles contract and make the worm longer, each segment must become narrower. When the earthworm moves forward, its first few body segments elongate while the segments just behind them hold their position. Then, the first few segments shorten and widen. Alternating contractions and elongations continue along the length of the worm's body, enabling it to move through soil or sediment.

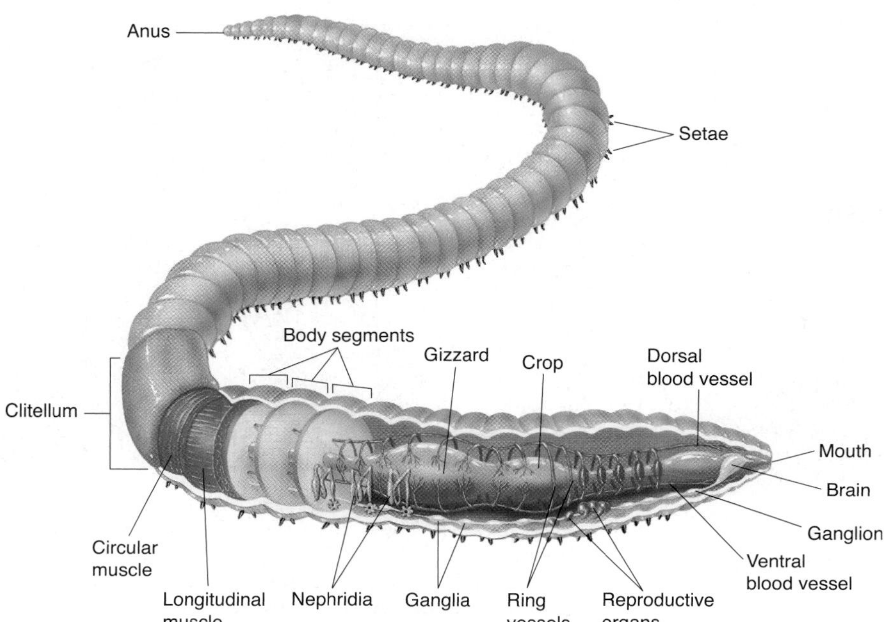

▲ **Figure 27–16 Earthworms are oligochaetes that live in soil.** Earthworms carry out essential functions using digestive, circulatory, excretory, nervous, and reproductive systems. Many organs, including nephridia and blood vessels, repeat in nearly every body segment.

Groups of Annelids

Because of their visible segmentation, all annelids show a basic similarity. Annelids are divided into three classes—oligochaetes, leeches, and polychaetes.

Oligochaetes The class Oligochaeta, or oligochaetes (AHL-ih-goh-keets), contains earthworms and their relatives. **Oligochaetes are annelids that typically have only a few setae. Most oligochaetes live in soil or fresh water.** Earthworms, such as the one diagrammed in **Figure 27–16,** are long, pinkish-brown worms that are common in woods, fields, and gardens. Tubifex worms—another common oligochaete—are red, threadlike aquatic worms that are sold in pet stores as food for tropical fish.

Although earthworms spend most of their lives hidden underground, you may find evidence of their presence above ground in the form of squiggles of mud known as castings. Recall that an earthworm—which swallows just about anything it can get into its mouth—uses its pharynx to suck a mixture of detritus and soil particles into its mouth. As the mixture of food and soil passes through the intestine, part of it is digested and absorbed. Sand grains, clay particles, and indigestible organic matter pass out through the anus in large quantities, producing castings. Some tropical earthworms produce enormous castings—as large as 18 centimeters long and 2 centimeters in diameter!

CHECKPOINT *What are earthworm castings?*

Word Origins

Oligochaete comes from the Greek words *oligos*, meaning "few" or "small," and *chaite*, meaning "hair." **If *poly-* means "many," what is a characteristic of the group of annelids known as polychaetes?**

Groups of Annelids

Use Visuals

Figure 27–16 Have students study the diagram of the oligochaete. Point out that this worm has body segments—annelids are worms with segmented bodies. Then, as you point out different labeled parts, call on students to describe the feeding, circulation, respiration, and response of an oligochaete. Ask: **Where does fertilization take place in an oligochaete?** *(In the clitellum)*

Build Science Skills

Inferring Divide the class into small groups, and provide each group with an earthworm, a type of oligochaete. Encourage students to rub a finger lightly along the earthworm's sides and write a description of what they feel. Next, students should examine the worm with a hand lens and describe what they see. Have groups formulate a hypothesis to explain the function of the structures students felt and saw. Then, have students place the earthworm on a smooth surface, such as a glass dish or the shiny side of a piece of aluminum foil, as well as on a rough surface, such as a damp paper towel. Students should compare the worm's movements on the two surfaces and infer what the function is of the structures they observed. *(Students should infer that these structures—setae—enable an earthworm to grip a surface as it moves.)*

Word Origins

The annelids of the class Polychaeta have "many hairs."

TEACHER TO TEACHER

Have students in groups of four observe live earthworm movements under different conditions, such as dry, wet, cold, or warm, and on different surfaces, such as felt, sandpaper, glass, wood, plastic wrap, or gauze. Students record their observations, and each group reports to the class.

Students can use different tuning forks to see how earthworms react to different vibrations. Have groups decide how this information could be used to "hunt" for earthworms.

—Keith Orgeron,
Biology Teacher
Carenero High School
Lafayette, Louisiana

Answers to . . .

CHECKPOINT *Earthworm castings are a mixture of sand, clay, and undigested food that an earthworm expels from its anus.*

Figure 27–14 *Land-dwelling annelids exchange gases through their moist skin.*

Figure 27–15 *Eggs are fertilized after eggs and sperm are released into the mucus ring secreted by the clitellum.*

Meet Diverse Needs

Ask students with limited English proficiency whether they have ever heard a person called a "leech" or been asked to "leech" something from somebody else. Explain that the meaning of *leech* in common speech derives from the parasitic feeding of members of the annelid class Hirudinea—the leeches. Point out that a "leech" is a person who borrows often and never seems to pay back or seems always to be asking for a favor from friends. Thus, the word *leech* has a bad connotation. Someone called a leech is being called a parasite, and is being compared to these invertebrates.
Learning modality: verbal

Build Science Skills

Classifying Divide the class into small groups, and ask each group to make up 10 to 20 questions for a game called Annelid Worms—Which Class? The idea of the game is for the question to be a statement about one group of annelids. The question is answered by classifying the statement according to which annelid class it applies. For example: "These worms spend most of their lives underground—which class?" The answer is Oligochaeta. When all groups have finished writing, pool the questions and eliminate any duplicates. Place the remaining questions in a box for students to draw at random.

Figure 27–17 **Most leeches are external parasites.** Medicinal leeches, such as the one below, were once used routinely to attempt to treat conditions ranging from headaches to mental illness to obesity. Doctors believed that diseases were caused by an excess of blood, so they applied leeches to the patient's skin to remove blood from the body. Here, a man who lived in the Middle Ages has become so fat that he has been confined to a room and covered with leeches.

Leeches The class Hirudinea (hir-yoo-DIN-ee-uh) contains the leeches, most of which live in moist habitats in tropical countries. **Leeches are typically external parasites that suck the blood and body fluids of their host.** Roughly one fourth of all leeches are carnivores that feed on soft-bodied invertebrates such as snails, worms, and insect larvae.

Leeches have powerful suckers at both ends of their bodies that help them cling to their hosts. The posterior sucker can also anchor a leech to rocks or leaves as it waits for a host to pass. Some leeches force a muscular extension called a proboscis (proh-BAHS-is) into the tissue of their host. Others slice into the skin with a razor-sharp pair of jaws. Once a wound has been made, the leech uses its pharynx to suck blood from the area. Some leeches also release a substance that anesthetizes the wound—keeping the host from knowing it has been bitten!

Leeches were once commonly used to treat medical conditions, as shown in **Figure 27–17.** Today the use of medicinal leeches is undergoing a revival of sorts. Doctors are finding that leeches can reduce swelling after surgery. After surgeries in which a body part is reattached, hungry leeches are applied to the area. These leeches can suck several milliliters of blood at a time—up to five times their own weight! They also secrete a fluid that prevents blood from clotting. This anti-clotting mechanism helps relieve pressure and congestion in the healing tissues.

▼ **Figure 27–18** **Polychaetes are marine annelids.** The bearded fireworm is a polychaete that lives in coral reefs. It is best known for its method of defense—its setae, or bristles, break off when touched and cause irritation and burning.

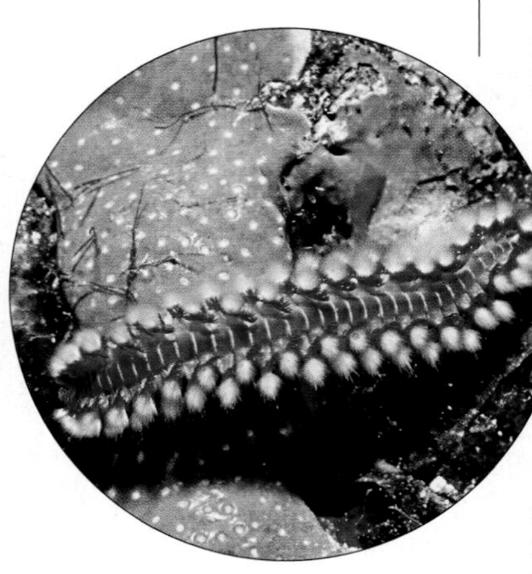

Polychaetes The class Polychaeta, or polychaetes (PAHL-ih-keets), contains sandworms, bloodworms, and their relatives. **Polychaetes are marine annelids that have paired, paddlelike appendages tipped with setae.** The setae are the brushlike structures on the worm shown in **Figure 27–18.** Polychaetes live in cracks and crevices in coral reefs; in sand, mud, and piles of rocks; or even out in the open water. Some burrow through or crawl over sediment.

HISTORY OF SCIENCE

Leeching to health
For centuries, the medicinal leech *Hirudo medicinalis* was used for bloodletting—a treatment thought to cure a wide range of illnesses. Shortly after the Civil War, more than 1.5 million leeches per year were used in the United States alone. When in contact with a host, the leech attaches itself and draws out blood by a pumping action. At the same time, the leech's salivary glands secrete hirudin, a substance that dilutes the host's blood, prevents blood from clotting, and acts as an anesthetic. A leech may eat up to five times its own body mass in blood before it drops off, and it may not need to feed again for 30 weeks. Once common throughout Europe, the leech is now scarce due to overcollecting and habitat destruction. It is still in demand, though, for hirudin, which is used as an anticoagulant for some heart patients and in some surgical procedures.

Ecology of Annelids

▲ **Figure 27–19** Some annelids, including this earthworm, burrow through soil, mixing it as they go. **Applying Concepts** ***What is the role of an annelid in the ecology of the sea?***

The importance of earthworms in nature was noted as far back as ancient Greece, when Aristotle called them "the intestines of the earth." Charles Darwin was impressed enough with earthworms that he devoted years—and an entire book—to their study. Earthworms, like the one shown in **Figure 27–19,** and many other annelids spend their lives burrowing through soil, aerating it, and mixing it to depths of 2 meters or more. Their tunnels provide passageways for plant roots and water and allow the growth of beneficial, oxygen-requiring soil bacteria. Earthworms pull plant matter down into the soil and pass it through the gut. There, they grind it, partially digest it, and mix it with bacteria that help the plant matter decompose. Worms also "mine" minerals from deeper soil layers, bringing them up to the surface. Earthworm feces (castings) are rich in nitrogen, phosphorus, potassium, micronutrients, and beneficial bacteria.

You've probably seen a bird struggling to pull an earthworm out of the ground. Earthworms are an important part of the diet of many birds, such as robins. Moles, skunks, toads, and snakes also feed on earthworms.

In the sea, annelids participate in a wide range of food chains. Many marine annelids have free-swimming larvae that are part of the animal plankton that is consumed by fishes and other plankton feeders. As adults, some marine annelids are mud-dwelling filter feeders that are common in areas where sediment is disturbed or large amounts of organic material are present. These worms are especially numerous where pollution from sewage promotes the growth of bacteria and algae. As any fisher knows, many bottom-dwelling polychaetes are important in the diets of fishes as well as crustaceans, such as crabs and lobsters.

27–3 Section Assessment

1. **Key Concept** What features distinguish annelids from roundworms?
2. **Key Concept** List the defining characteristics for each class of annelid.
3. Describe the feeding strategies of earthworms and leeches.
4. **Critical Thinking Inferring** An earthworm has more light-sensitive cells in its anterior and posterior segments than in other parts of its body. Explain how this is advantageous for the worm.

iTEXT Assessment Use iText to review the important concepts in Section 27–3.

ALTERNATIVE ASSESSMENT

Creative Writing
Write a story about a gardener who is trying to rid her garden of pesky earthworms. Be sure your story ends with the gardener's discovering that her actions proved to be a mistake.

27–3 Section Assessment

1. Unlike roundworms, annelids have segmented bodies and a true coelom that is lined with mesoderm.
2. Oligochaetes typically have only a few setae and live in soil or fresh water. Leeches are typically external parasites that suck the blood and body fluids of their host. Polychaetes are marine annelids that have paired, paddlelike appendages tipped with setae.
3. Earthworms use their pharynxes to suck soil and detritus into their mouths. Leeches suck the blood and body fluids of their host.
4. Having more light-sensitive cells in the front and back ends is advantageous, because the animal moves forward and may be attacked by a predator from the rear.

Ecology of Annelids

Make Connections

Earth Science Explain that good soil contains sediment particles, humus (organic matter), water, and air. The air is especially important, because if the soil is too compact, plants have a difficult time growing. Ask students: **How do earthworms help to mix air into soil?** *(By moving through the soil, they break up particles and make tunnels. These actions provide space for air to move throughout the soil. The movement of earthworms aerates the soil.)*

3 ASSESS

Evaluate Understanding

Call on students at random to provide characteristics and examples of the three classes of annelids: oligochaetes, leeches, and polychaetes.

Reteach

Have students revise the summary they wrote when they previewed Figure 27–15. Students should display that they now have a better understanding of the differences between annelids and the other worms they have studied.

ALTERNATIVE ASSESSMENT

Encourage students to be creative yet factual in their stories. Although stories will vary, each should culminate in the gardener's learning about the beneficial role that earthworms play in loosening and enriching soil.

Use the iText to review the key concepts in Section 27–3.

Answer to . . .

Figure 27–19 *Annelids are part of many marine food chains.*

After students have read the feature, lead a class discussion of the problems caused by zebra mussels and other exotic species. Then, encourage students to further investigate the zebra mussel problem and prepare a report to the class. You might divide the class into small groups, and assign each group one aspect of the problem, including zebra mussels' life cycle and feeding habits, problems caused by zebra mussels to power plants and other facilities, the threat to native mussel populations and other species, and methods previously tried to eradicate the zebra mussels. After groups have reported their findings, have students discuss what they think should be done to address this problem.

You Decide

1. A typical response will suggest that major issues include (1) the damage done by zebra mussels to power plants and other facilities, (2) the threat to the ecology of aquatic communities by the invasion of zebra mussels, (3) what can be done to control zebra mussels and other exotic species, and (4) how to prevent new exotic species from arriving.
2. Most students will suggest that the advantage of eradication would be that the zebra mussels would no longer cause problems. The disadvantage would include cost and possible harmful effects on other species. An advantage of control and prevention would be a lower cost. A disadvantage might be a lack of effectiveness and continued damage caused by zebra mussels.
3. A thoughtful response will reflect a realistic assessment of the problem and the difficulty in finding a solution.

What Can Be Done About the Zebra Mussel?

Zebra mussels *(Dreissena polymorpha)* were introduced into the United States from Eastern Europe and Asia when ships from the areas emptied their ballast tanks. They were first spotted in the Great Lakes in the mid-1980s. Zebra mussels have few natural enemies here and reproduce very rapidly. Carried mainly by the normal flow of water and boat traffic, zebra mussels have already colonized the entire Great Lakes region and have spread to rivers in more than ten states, including Mississippi and Arkansas. The map shows the distribution of zebra mussels in the United States.

Zebra mussels live attached to almost any surface—from metal pipes to fiberglass boats—and can form layers up to 20 centimeters thick. As a result, they have caused serious structural damage and have clogged water supply lines to power plants and water treatment facilities. One paper company along Lake Michigan, for example, spent over a million dollars to remove zebra mussels that were clogging its cooling pipes.

Zebra mussels also threaten the ecology of aquatic communities. They can tolerate a wide range of temperatures and light intensities. In some habitats, they have displaced native mollusks, almost making them extinct. Because they feed largely on phytoplankton, zebra mussels have also depleted a critical food source for many fish species.

What can be done to control zebra mussels and other exotic (non-native) species and prevent new ones from arriving?

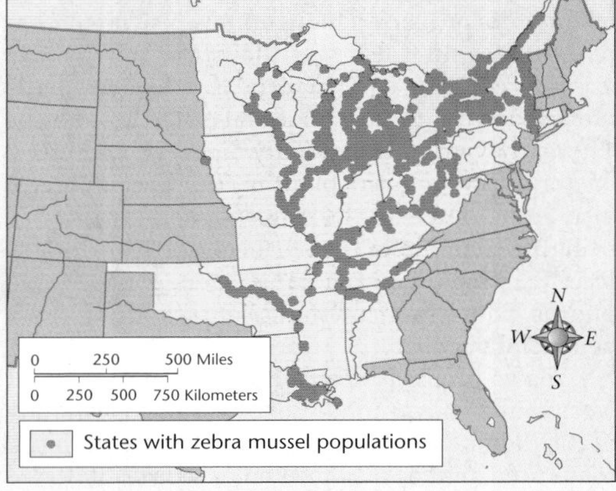

The Viewpoints

Control and Prevention

Many scientists believe that there is no way to remove zebra mussels and many other established exotic species. Instead, these scientists attempt to control the growth of populations and prevent the transfer of exotic species to new areas. One regulation, for example, could require boaters to filter and chemically clean all ballast water. Another approach would be to find beneficial uses for zebra mussels. Scientists are already exploring the ability of zebra mussels to filter large volumes of waste water.

Eradication

Other groups contend that zebra mussels should be eradicated. Engineers, for example, are developing robotic submarines that can remove mussels from pipelines. Chemists are testing chemicals for the potential to destroy or disrupt the life cycle of zebra mussels. Other scientists are adding chemicals to paints and plastics to prevent mussels from attaching to new surfaces.

You Decide

1. **Defining the Issue** In your own words, explain the major issues surrounding the problem of dealing with zebra mussels.
2. **Analyzing the Viewpoints** What are the advantages and disadvantages of each proposed solution to the problems caused by zebra mussels?
3. **Forming Your Opinion** What measures do you think would be most effective in dealing with exotic species?

BACKGROUND

Clogged pipes cause problems

A mussel is a bivalve that permanently attaches itself to an underwater surface by means of anchor lines called byssal threads. These threads are secreted as a liquid by the byssal gland in the animal's foot. The liquid flows down a groove in the foot, sticks to the rock or other surface, and hardens. Then, the foot is withdrawn, with the thread permanently in place. In this way, zebra mussels attach themselves to the inside of water-intake pipes. A zebra mussel is only about 2 centimeters in length, and a few of them in a pipe doesn't cause concern. But, Detroit Edison reported that on a single water-intake screen, there were 700,000 mussels per square meter. In the winter of 1988, ice combined with mussels blocked water intake to Detroit Edison, resulting in power outages. During the 1990s, billions of dollars were spent around the Great Lakes cleaning and refitting pipes.

27–4 Mollusks

They climb trees in tropical rain forests and float over coral reefs. They crawl into garbage cans, eat their way through farm crops, and speed through the deep ocean. Some are so small that you can hardly see them with the unaided eye, while others are 20 meters long! They are the mollusks—one of the oldest and most diverse phyla. Mollusks come in so many sizes, shapes, and forms that you might wonder why they are classified in the same phylum. To learn the answer, read on.

What Is a Mollusk?

Members of the phylum Mollusca, known as mollusks, are named from the Latin word *molluscus*, which means "soft." **Mollusks are soft-bodied animals that usually have an internal or external shell.** Mollusks include snails, slugs, clams, squids, and octopi. But a snail looks very different from a squid, which looks very different from a clam. So why are they all placed in the same phylum? One reason is that many mollusks share similar developmental stages. Many aquatic mollusks have a free-swimming larval stage called a **trochophore** (TRAHK-oh-fawr). The trochophore larva, shown in **Figure 27–20,** is also characteristic of annelids, indicating that these two groups are probably closely related. Molecular studies suggest that a common ancestor of annelids and mollusks lived more than 550 million years ago.

Guide for Reading

Key Concepts
- What are the defining features of mollusks?
- What is the basic body plan of mollusks?
- What are the characteristics of the three main classes of mollusks?

Vocabulary
- trochophore • foot
- mantle • shell • visceral mass
- radula • siphon
- open circulatory system

Reading Strategy: Building Vocabulary
As you read, make notes about the meaning of each term in the list above. After you read the section, make a table listing the different types of mollusks on the left and the vocabulary words that apply on the right.

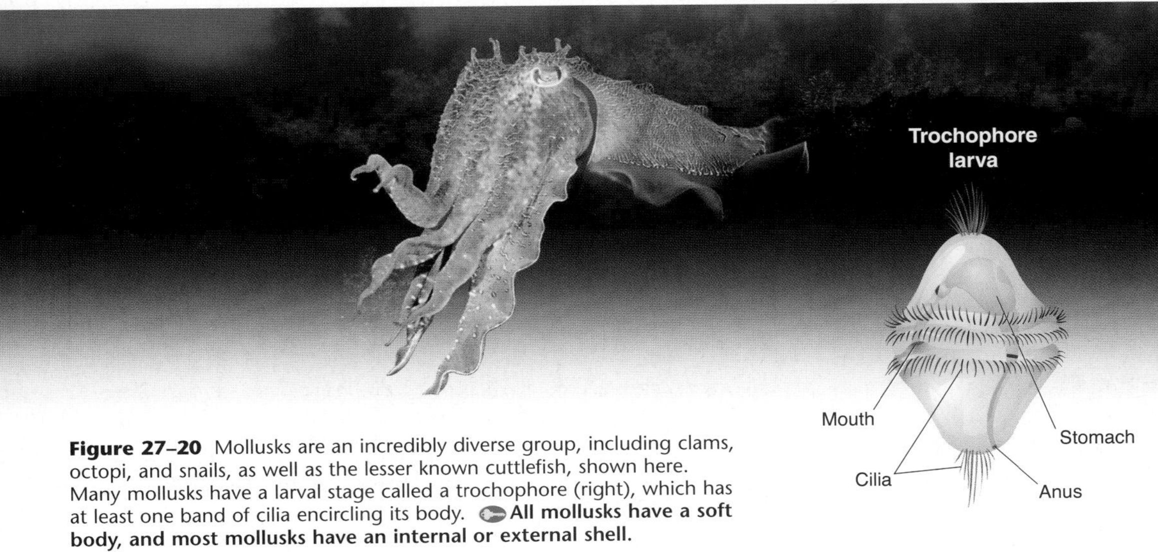

Figure 27–20 Mollusks are an incredibly diverse group, including clams, octopi, and snails, as well as the lesser known cuttlefish, shown here. Many mollusks have a larval stage called a trochophore (right), which has at least one band of cilia encircling its body. **All mollusks have a soft body, and most mollusks have an internal or external shell.**

SECTION REVIEW

Print:
- ***Laboratory Manual A,*** Chapter 27 Lab
- ***Laboratory Manual B,*** Chapter 27 Lab
- ***Teaching Resources,*** Section Review 27–4, Chapter 27 Exploration
- ***Guided Reading and Study Workbook,*** Section 27–4

Technology:
- ***iText,*** Section 27–4

Section 27–4

1 FOCUS

Objectives

27.4.1 ***Describe*** the defining features of mollusks.
27.4.2 ***Describe*** the basic body plan of mollusks.
27.4.3 ***Identify*** the characteristics of the three main classes of mollusks.
27.4.4 ***Describe*** the ecology of mollusks.

Guide for Reading

Vocabulary Preview

Explain that students may use a few of the vocabulary words in everyday speech, including *foot, mantle,* and *sinus.* Caution students, especially students with limited English proficiency, that they shouldn't allow the common meanings of these words to influence their understanding of the terms in the context of mollusk anatomy.

Reading Strategy

The terms *trochophore, foot, mantle, shell, visceral mass, open circulatory system,* and *sinus* apply to all mollusk groups. The term *radula* applies only to gastropods, and the term *siphon* applies only to bivalves and cephalopods.

2 INSTRUCT

What Is a Mollusk?

Use Visuals

Figure 27–20 Ask students: **How are the two organisms shown in the figure related?** *(The organism on the left is a mature cuttlefish, a type of mollusk. The labeled organism to the right is a trochophore, which is a free-swimming larval stage of a mollusk.)*

27–4 (continued)

Form and Function in Mollusks

Use Visuals

Figure 27–21 Point out that the three living mollusks all descended from an early mollusk, shown in the lower left. Explain that the snail, clam, and squid each represent one of the three major classes of mollusks. Then, ask: **How is the shell different in the squid than in the other two mollusks shown?** *(The shell in the squid is much less prominent than the shells of the snail and the clam, and it is internal.)* Explain that a squid is a cephalopod, and most modern cephalopods have only small internal shells.

Demonstration

Show students a rasp, a common tool used by woodworkers. Then, use the rasp to scrape a piece of scrap wood, making a mark and producing some sawdust. Ask: **How is a snail's radula like this rasp?** *(Like the surface of a rasp, a radula has hundreds of tiny teeth that can scrape and tear up a surface.)* **Why do you think that clams and similar mollusks do not have a radula?** *(Because they are filter feeders that obtain food by straining particles from water)*

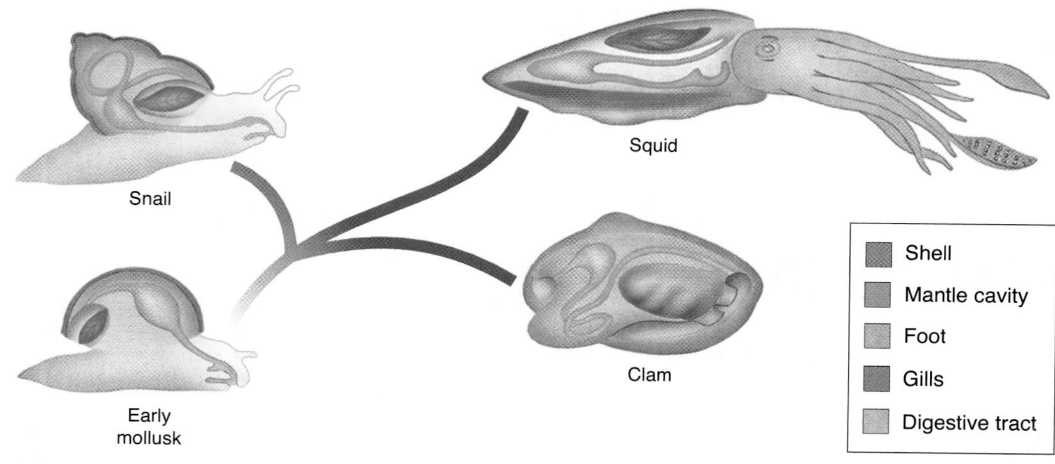

▲ **Figure 27–21** **The body plan of most mollusks includes a foot, mantle, shell, and visceral mass.** Early mollusks may have looked like the animal shown at the bottom. As they evolved, their body parts became adapted for different functions.

Form and Function in Mollusks

Like the annelids, mollusks have true coeloms surrounded by mesoderm tissue. They also have complex organ systems that carry out processes such as respiration and excretion.

Body Plan The different body shapes of mollusks are variations on a single body plan, shown in **Figure 27–21.** **The body plan of most mollusks has four parts: foot, mantle, shell, and visceral mass.** The muscular **foot** takes many forms, including flat structures for crawling, spade-shaped structures for burrowing, and tentacles for capturing prey. The **mantle** is a thin layer of tissue that covers most of the mollusk's body, much like a cloak. The **shell** is made by glands in the mantle that secrete calcium carbonate. The shell has been reduced or lost in slugs and some other mollusk groups. Just beneath the mantle is the **visceral mass,** which consists of the internal organs.

Feeding Mollusks can be herbivores, carnivores, filter feeders, detritivores, or parasites. Snails and slugs feed using a flexible, tongue-shaped structure known as a **radula** (RAJ-oo-luh; plural: radulae), shown in **Figure 27–22,** to which hundreds of tiny teeth are attached. Herbivorous mollusks use their radula to scrape algae off rocks or to eat the soft tissues of plants. Carnivorous mollusks use their radula to drill through shells of other animals and to tear up and swallow the prey's soft tissue.

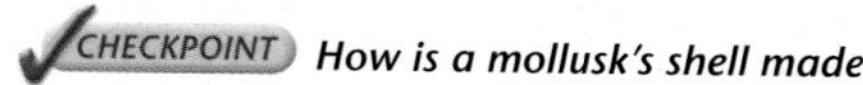

How is a mollusk's shell made?

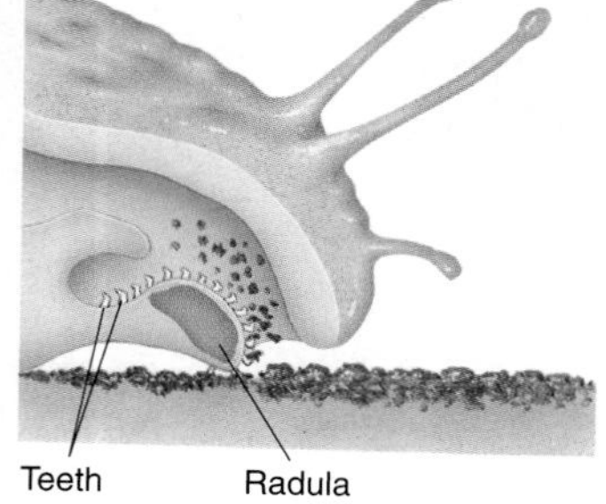

Figure 27–22 Snails use a radula for feeding. The teeth of a radula give it the look and feel of sandpaper. Beneath the radula is a stiff supporting rod of cartilage. When the mollusk feeds, it places the tip of the radula on its food and pulls the sandpapery layer back and forth. **Formulating Hypotheses** *How might radulae with different structures allow snails to inhabit different environments?*

TIME SAVER — PRESENTATIONS MADE EASY!

The Presentation Assistant Plus contains the Prentice Hall Presentation Pro and the Transparencies, which provide easy-to-follow visual support for every step of this section. If you have a computer presentation station, use Prentice Hall Presentation Pro Section 27–4, or use the transparencies listed here.

Section 27–4:

Interest Grabber
Section Outline
Three Major Groups of Mollusks
Figure 27–21
Figure 27–23

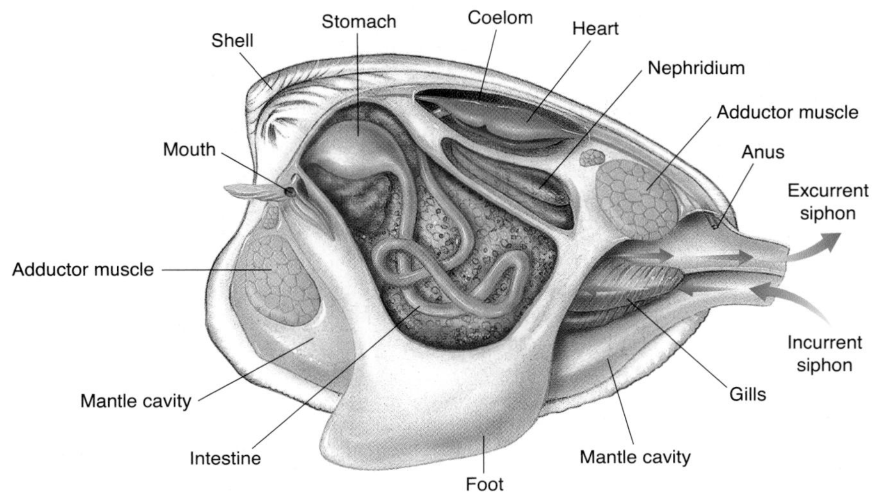

▲ **Figure 27–23** The anatomy of a clam, shown here, is typical of bivalves, or two-shelled mollusks. The mantle and part of the foot have been cut away to show internal organs. The adductor muscles are used to open and shut the two exterior shells. The gills exchange oxygen and carbon dioxide between the body and the surrounding water. The arrows show the path of water over the gills. **Predicting** ***What might happen if a clam's incurrent siphon became blocked?***

Octopi and certain sea slugs use their sharp jaws to eat their prey. To subdue their prey, some octopi also produce poisons. Some of these poisons are strong enough to harm humans! Clams, oysters, and scallops lead a quieter existence by filter feeding using feathery gills. Food is carried by water, which enters through the incurrent siphon, shown on the right in **Figure 27–23.** A **siphon** is a tubelike structure through which water enters and leaves the body. The water flows over the gills and then leaves by the excurrent siphon. As water passes over the gills, plankton become trapped in sticky mucus. Cilia on the gills move the mixture of mucus and food into the mouth.

Respiration Aquatic mollusks such as snails, clams, and octopi typically breathe using gills inside their mantle cavity. As water passes through the mantle cavity, oxygen and carbon dioxide diffuse over the surface of the animal's gills. Land snails and slugs do not have gills. Instead, they respire using a mantle cavity that has a large surface area lined with blood vessels. Because this lining must be kept moist so that oxygen can diffuse across its surface, land snails and slugs typically live only in moist places.

Circulation Oxygen and nutrients are carried to all parts of a mollusk's body by a circulatory system. The circulatory system of mollusks is either open or closed. "Open" does not mean that blood can spill to the outside of the animal! In an **open circulatory system,** blood is pumped through vessels by a simple heart. Blood eventually leaves the vessels and works its way through different sinuses. A sinus is a large saclike space. The blood passes from the sinuses to the gills, where oxygen and carbon dioxide are exchanged, and then back to the heart.

Build Science Skills

Classifying Display a variety of mollusk shells. These might include clam, oyster, nautilus, and snail shells. Explain that biologists think the color of shells is primarily the result of the food the mollusk has eaten. Provide students with several shell guides or other resources that they can use to identify the shells. Then, challenge students to classify each shell as to which organism it belongs. When students have completed classification, discuss their findings as a class. Have volunteers then write a caption for each shell and create a classroom display.

Address Misconceptions

Many students associate mollusks with the term *shellfish.* Explain that *shellfish* is a common term for any marine animal with an external shell, which includes a variety of invertebrates. Point out that fish are vertebrates. Ask students: **Is a mollusk a vertebrate or an invertebrate?** *(A mollusk is an invertebrate.)* Emphasize that mollusks cannot be classified as any kind of fish, despite the common label of *shellfish.*

FACTS AND FIGURES

Shells of all shapes and sizes

Mollusk shells occur in such a variety of shapes and sizes that they serve as the main means of identification for many mollusk species. The obvious advantage of a hard exterior shell is the protection it provides for the animal's soft body. Like the exoskeletons of arthropods, exterior shells have one major disadvantage: Because shells do not consist of living, dividing cells, mollusks outgrow them as they develop. Many mollusks, however, have evolved shell designs that allow them to build onto the shell to accommodate their increased body size. The shell is not continuously added to but is expanded periodically as needed. Another disadvantage of shells is that they reduce mobility. Most mollusks, such as snails, lumber along under the load of their heavy shells or, such as clams, are fairly stationary throughout their adult lives.

Answers to . . .

CHECKPOINT *Glands in the mantle secrete the calcium carbonate of which the shell is made.*

Figure 27–22 *Depending on its structure, a radula can be used for different purposes, including scraping the algae off of rocks, eating the soft tissues of plants, drilling through shells of other animals, and tearing up a prey's soft tissue. These feeding adaptations enable snails to inhabit diverse habitats, including ponds, land, and so forth.*

Figure 27–23 *Since water carries food and oxygen to the clam, the clam could not obtain food or oxygen if its incurrent siphon was blocked.*

27–4 (continued)

Build Science Skills

Designing Experiments Divide the class into small groups, and challenge each group to design an experiment that would test how intelligent octopi are. Students should first write a hypothesis that they can test. Then, they should describe an experiment that has a control and a manipulated variable. Students should also indicate what sort of data they expect the experiment would yield that could prove or disprove their hypothesis.

Make Connections

Physics After students have read about the jet propulsion of an octopus, explain that this is an example of Sir Isaac Newton's third law of motion. The third law says that for every action, there is an equal and opposite reaction. Ask: **In this case, what is the action, and what is the reaction?** *(The action is the movement of water expelled through the siphon. The reaction is the movement of the octopus forward.)* As students watch, blow up a balloon, and then release it. Students should observe the balloon rapidly moving in the opposite direction of the air moving out of its nozzle. Ask: **How is what you have just observed similar to and different from the jet propulsion used by an octopus?** *(It is similar in that there is an action and a reaction. It is different in that there is a movement of air from the balloon, while there is a movement of water from the octopus.)*

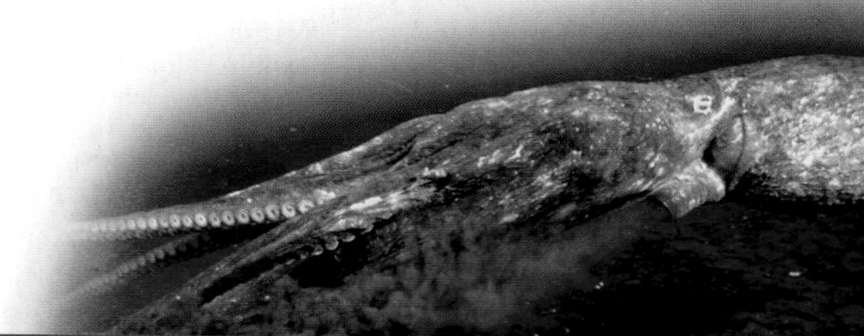

Figure 27–24 Mollusks have evolved a variety of ways of responding to potential danger. Snails (above) protect themselves by withdrawing into their shells in a matter of seconds. A hard plate blocks the entrance to the shell, protecting the snail inside. Once the danger has passed, the snail re-emerges and moves forward on its muscular foot. Octopi (right) and squids squirt ink from inside their digestive tracts. The ink startles predators and may also cause temporary numbness. **Predicting** ***How might the hard plate protect snails during a period of drought?***

Open circulatory systems work well for slow-moving mollusks such as snails and clams, in which the demand for oxygen is relatively low. Faster-moving mollusks such as octopi and squid have a closed circulatory system. A closed circulatory system can transport blood through an animal's body much more quickly than an open circulatory system.

Excretion Cells of the body release nitrogen-containing waste into the blood in the form of ammonia. Tube-shaped nephridia remove ammonia from the blood and release it outside the body.

Response The complexity of the nervous system and the ability to respond to environmental conditions vary greatly among mollusks. Clams and other two-shelled mollusks typically lead inactive lives, burrowing in the mud or sand. They have a simple nervous system consisting of small ganglia near the mouth, a few nerve cords, and simple sense organs, such as chemical receptors and eyespots.

In contrast, octopi and their relatives, such as the octopus in **Figure 27–24,** are active and intelligent predators that have the most highly developed nervous system of all invertebrates. Because of their well-developed brains, these animals can remember things for long periods and may be more intelligent than some vertebrates. Octopi are capable of complex behavior, such as opening a jar to get food inside, and they have been trained to perform different tasks for a reward or to avoid punishment.

Movement Mollusks move in many different ways. Snails—which are legendary for their lack of speed—secrete mucus along the base of the foot, and then move over surfaces using a rippling motion of the foot. The fast-moving octopus uses a form of jet propulsion. It draws water into the mantle cavity and then forces the water out through a siphon. Water leaving the body propels the octopus in the opposite direction.

Reproduction Mollusks reproduce in a variety of ways. Many snails and two-shelled mollusks reproduce sexually by external fertilization. They release enormous numbers of eggs and sperm into the open water. The eggs are fertilized in the water and then develop into free-swimming larvae. In tentacled mollusks and certain snails, fertilization takes place inside the body of the female. Some mollusks are hermaphrodites, having both male and female reproductive organs. Individuals of these species usually fertilize eggs from another individual.

BIO INSIGHTS — FACTS AND FIGURES

A chiton is a marine mollusk that has an elongated body, a large, broad foot, and a radula. Chitons eat algae, hydrozoans, and other low-growing organisms.

The dorsal shells of chitons display beautiful variations of pattern and color. The dorsal shells, which are divided into a series of eight plates, are also very practical. These plates make the shell flexible enough so that the chiton can roll up into a smaller ball when it is dislodged from its attachment. Thus, it can protect itself until it can safely unroll and reattach elsewhere.

Another defense mechanism of the chiton is its ability to anchor itself to its substrate when it is disturbed or when it is exposed by a receding tide. The muscles in its foot pull the animal down tightly so that the edge of the mantle, which partly or completely covers the shell plates, can function like the rim of a suction cup. In this way, it becomes extremely difficult to dislodge the chiton.

Figure 27–25 Gastropods move by using a large, muscular foot located on the ventral side. They can be shell-less, such as the nudibranch or sea slug (top left), or have a single shell, such as the tree snail (top right). Many sea hares (bottom) have a reduced shell covered by the mantle. The sea hare defends itself by "inking"—squirting ink at potential predators.

Groups of Mollusks

Mollusks are divided into several classes according to characteristics of the foot and the shell. The three major classes of mollusks are gastropods, bivalves, and cephalopods.

Gastropods Members of the class Gastropoda, or gastropods (GAS-truh-pahdz), include pond snails, land slugs, sea butterflies, sea hares, limpets, and nudibranchs (NOO-duh-branks). **Gastropods are shell-less or single-shelled mollusks that move by using a muscular foot located on the ventral side.**

Many gastropods, such as the snails shown on the top right in **Figure 27–25**, have a single shell that protects their bodies. When threatened, they can pull completely into their shells. Some snails are also protected by a hard disk on the foot that forms a solid "door" when they withdraw.

Land slugs and nudibranchs have no shell but protect themselves in other ways. Most land slugs spend daylight hours hiding under rocks and logs, hidden from birds and other potential predators. Some sea hares, when threatened, can squirt ink into the surrounding water, producing a "smoke screen" that confuses predators.

Some nudibranchs have chemicals in their bodies that taste bad or are poisonous. Many nudibranchs are able to recycle the nematocysts from cnidarians they eat, using them to sting predators. These "booby-trapped" nudibranchs are usually brightly colored. The bright coloring serves as a warning to potential predators.

CHECKPOINT *How do shell-less gastropods protect themselves?*

Groups of Mollusks

Build Science Skills

Observing Set up a 20 to 40 liter freshwater aquarium in the classroom. Have students add 3 to 4 centimeters of sand on the bottom. Then, have students fill the container with pond water to about 10 centimeters from the top. Add aquatic plants and several pond snails. Also, place a top over the aquarium so that the snails won't escape. Have students observe the snails, with the unaided eye and with a hand lens. They should study the shell, head, foot, and any other feature of snail anatomy they can see. Have students make drawings and write a description of what they see.

Meet Diverse Needs

To help visually impaired students understand gastropod form and function, place a land snail in a student's hand. Once the animal acclimates itself to the surface, it will move across the hand. Tell the student to feel for the action of the snail's radula. Then, have the student use his or her other hand to feel the snail's shell. Because the snail's shell can be quite fragile, caution the student to touch the animal gently. **Learning modality: tactile**

FACTS AND FIGURES

How the gastropod got its twist
The coiled shell of the snail and other gastropods is the result of an internal realignment process called torsion. During a gastropod's development, the animal's visceral mass begins to grow upward. This growth is uneven on the right and left sides. The uneven growth, coupled with the contraction of certain muscles, causes the posterior mantle cavity to twist around to the right. At a critical moment, the body rotates a full 180° so that the back end of the body comes to rest just behind the head. The result is that the gastropod balances its internal organs above the rest of the body much as a human would carry a backpack. The coiled shell provides a retreat for the animal's head in times of danger. The twisted body arrangement has its drawbacks, though. The gastropod has its anus and kidney openings above the head, creating somewhat of a sanitation problem.

Answers to . . .

CHECKPOINT *Most land slugs spend the daylight hours hiding under rocks and logs. Some sea hares squirt ink into the surrounding water, confusing predators. Some nudibranchs have chemicals in their bodies that taste bad or are poisonous. Many nudibranchs recycle cnidarian nematocysts, moving the stinging cells to their own exterior.*

Figure 27–24 *By blocking the opening in the shell, the hard plate helps keep moisture inside the shell.*

Build Science Skills

Observing Help students understand how bivalves obtain nutrients by filter feeding through a demonstration of filtering particles from water. Divide a sample of water from a pond, lake, or ocean into several parts, pouring each in a separate container. Then, filter the water in each container into a beaker using one of these filter devices: a sieve, a coffee filter, a piece of screen or wire mesh, and a piece of cheesecloth. Have students observe the materials that remain after the water has been filtered, first with the unaided eye and then with a microscope. Ask: **Do you think any of these materials might be useful to an organism as food?** *(Answers may vary. In many cases, the correct answer is yes.)* Have students relate what they have observed to the filter-feeding mechanism of a bivalve. Point out that the gills of a bivalve are able to trap particles of exactly the right size so that the animal can obtain the type of food it needs.

Demonstration

Show students a cuttlebone, which can be purchased in many pet stores. Explain that cuttlebones are used by bird owners to condition and sharpen birds' beaks. After students have had a chance to examine the cuttlebone, ask: **What mollusk class includes the cuttlefish?** *(Cephalopoda)* Explain that a cuttlefish, like a nautilus, can regulate its buoyancy—and therefore its depth in the water—by altering the amount of fluid and gas in the chambers of its shell.

Word Origins

Pseudopod means "false foot."

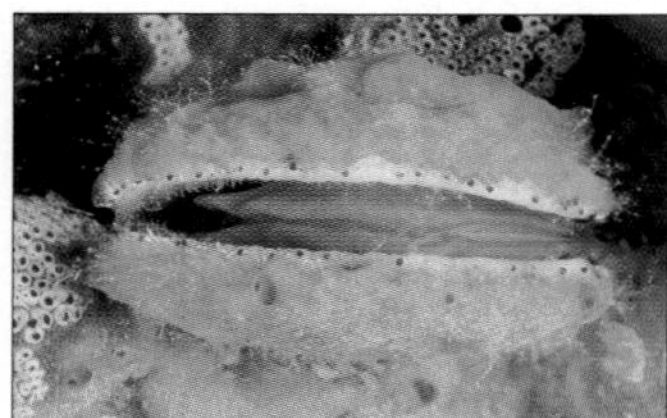

▲ **Figure 27–26 Bivalves are two-shelled mollusks that include clams, mussels, oysters, and scallops like the one above.** Observe the tiny blue eyespots along the open edges of the shell.

Bivalves

Members of the class Bivalvia have two shells that are held together by one or two powerful muscles. Common bivalves include clams, oysters, mussels, and scallops. Most bivalves stay in one place for much of the time. Clams, shown in **Figure 27–26**, burrow in mud or sand, whereas mussels use sticky threads to attach themselves to rocks. Scallops are the least sedentary bivalves and can move around rapidly by flapping their shells when threatened.

Currents created by cilia on the gills circulate water through the body cavities of bivalves. Once water is inside the body, filter-feeding bivalves use mucus and cilia on their gills to trap food particles in the water. Some bivalves feed on material deposited in sand or mud. They use long, muscular extensions of tissue that surround the mouth to collect food particles from the surrounding sediments. The indigestible sand or mud particles are expelled from the mantle cavity.

Word Origins

Cephalopod comes from the Greek *kephale*, meaning "head," and *podos*, meaning "foot." **Pseudopods** are structures found in some single-celled organisms. **If *pseudo-* means "false," what does *pseudopod* mean?**

Cephalopods

Cephalopods (SEF-uh-luh-pahdz)—members of the class Cephalopoda—are the most active of the mollusks. This class includes octopi, squids, cuttlefishes, and nautiluses. **Cephalopods are typically soft-bodied mollusks in which the head is attached to a single foot. The foot is divided into tentacles or arms.** Cephalopods have eight or more tentacles equipped with sucking disks that grab and hold prey. Nautiluses have many more tentacles than other cephalopods—in some cases up to 90! Their tentacles lack suckers but have a sticky, mucuslike covering.

As with some of the gastropods, most modern cephalopods have only small internal shells or no shells at all. The only present-day cephalopods with external shells are nautiluses, such as the one shown in **Figure 27–27.** These animals can control their depth in the water by regulating the amount of gas in their shells. Nautiluses look much like ammonites, an extinct group of cephalopods that dominated the seas more than 500 million years ago.

CHECKPOINT *Where is a cephalopod's foot located?*

Figure 27–27 Nautiluses like the one shown here are the most primitive group of cephalopods. **Comparing and Contrasting** *How does this nautilus differ from most cephalopods?*

FACTS AND FIGURES

A coiled shell with many chambers

The chambered nautilus is so named because of its coiled shell of many chambers. By taking in and releasing gas from chambers in its shell, a nautilus can change its buoyancy. This means that it can live at any level of the ocean, from the surface down to 600 meters. The body of the chambered nautilus is divided into two sections. The first section is the head, which is covered by a tough tissue called the hood. The hood acts as a shield. Tentacles—of which a nautilus may have more than 90—are located in the head. Unlike tentacles of other cephalopods, the tentacles of the nautilus do not have suckers. Instead, they are covered with a sticky substance that helps to hold prey. The second section of the body consists primarily of a large sac that contains the nautilus's organs. This sac is enclosed by the mantle. Between the mantle and the sac are four large gills.

Analyzing Data

Raising Clams

Aquaculture is the growth of aquatic animals and plants for use by humans. In one example of aquaculture, hard clams are first grown in commercial hatcheries under very favorable conditions. The young clams are then removed from the hatcheries and placed into the mud beds of creeks, where they develop into adults. At that time, the size of the young clams is around 40 millimeters.

Because Georgian clams grow so quickly, they are ideal for aquaculture. Unlike the hard clams in the northeastern United States that grow only during the warm months, Georgian hard clams grow year-round. As a result, the Georgian clams grow to market size in less than half the time that the northeastern clams need to grow. The graph shows how clam shells grow over a period of 10 years.

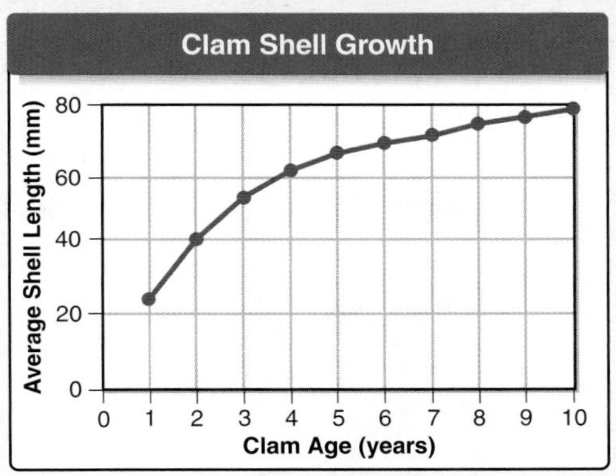

1. **Interpreting Graphics** Approximately how many years does it take clams to reach a size at which they can be removed from hatcheries and put in creeks?
2. **Applying Concepts** How does climate affect the growth of most clams?
3. **Interpreting Graphics** How much did the clams grow during the first 5 years? The next 5 years?
4. **Formulating Hypotheses** Formulate a hypothesis to explain the slower growth rate from years 5–10.
5. **Drawing Conclusions** What general trends do you observe about growth from the graph?

Cuttlefishes have small shells inside their bodies. These are the cuttlebones given to pet birds to condition their beaks. A squid's internal shell has evolved into a thin supporting rod known as a pen. Octopi have lost their shells completely.

Cephalopods also have numerous complex sense organs that help them distinguish shapes by sight and texture by touch. The eyes of many cephalopods, such as the squid shown in **Figure 27–28,** are as complex as those of some vertebrates, such as fishes and humans. Cephalopod eyes can be large—the size of a dinner plate in some species—and can distinguish objects as small as 0.5 centimeters from a meter away, allowing squids to locate a wide variety of prey. Though cephalopod eyes may look something like vertebrate eyes from the outside, their internal structures are quite different.

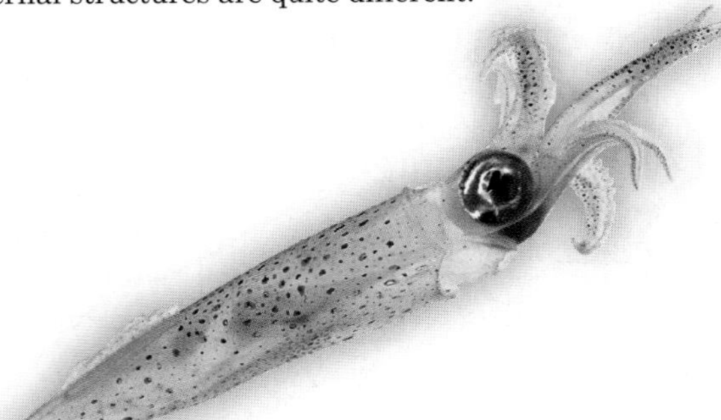

◀ **Figure 27–28** **Most cephalopods are mollusks in which the head is attached to a single foot that is divided into tentacles or arms.** They have the most complex nervous system of all the mollusks, with a highly developed brain and sense organs, such as the eye of this common squid.

BIO INSIGHTS — FACTS AND FIGURES

There are some giant mollusks

Biologists have described about 50,000 living mollusk species, and another 60,000 are known by their fossils. Some mollusks are quite small; the shells of some freshwater bivalves are almost never over 2 millimeters across. Yet, there are some really large mollusks. For example, the largest bivalve is the giant tropical clam, *Tridacna,* whose shells can measure more than 1.2 meters across. One species, *T. gigas,* can have a mass of over 400 kilograms. The largest octopus is the common Pacific octopus, *Octopus hongkongensis,* which can measure up to 9.7 meters from the tip of one tentacle to the tip of the opposite tentacle. The largest squid is the giant squid, *Architeuthis,* which can have a body 4 meters long with tentacles over 9 meters long.

Analyzing Data

Aquaculture is the cultivation of fish or other marine animals for food. It is a growing industry.

Answers

1. Approximately 2 years
2. Most clams grow only during warm months.
3. The clams grew to about 68 mm during the first five years. They grew an additional 12 mm, to 80 mm, during the next 5 years.
4. Sample hypothesis: The older the clam, the less frequently its cells divide.
5. Clam growth is greatest in the first four or five years. Then, it levels off to a slow but steady growth.

Meet Diverse Needs

Explain to students that the cephalopod eye is similar in many ways to the eye of vertebrates, though they are not exactly the same. The two types of eyes are often cited by biologists as a good example of convergent evolution, the process by which unrelated species independently evolve similar adaptations. Encourage interested students who need a challenge to investigate the structure and function of the cephalopod eye and draw a comparison with the human eye. Suggest that they find out how the cephalopod eye works and whether it forms images and sees colors. **Learning modality: verbal**

Answers to . . .

CHECKPOINT *A cephalopod's foot is attached to its head.*

Figure 27–27 *Unlike most cephalopods, the nautilus has an external shell.*

Ecology of Mollusks

Use Community Resources

Students can call the state environmental protection agency and find out whether it has a program to test bivalves for pollutants. Have the students report to the class about their findings.

3 ASSESS

Evaluate Understanding

Have students make drawings of a snail, a squid, and a clam similar to those in Figure 27–21. Then, direct their attention to the labeled drawing in Figure 27–22. Challenge students to use as many of the labels on the second figure as they can to label their drawings of the three mollusks.

Reteach

Have students make a compare/contrast table of the three major classes of mollusks. In this table, they should include the names of the classes, important characteristics of each class, and examples of each.

Take It to the NET

Students' collages should include photographs of their chosen mollusk as well as its habitat. For information about a specific species, students can use library resources. Each student can draw a labeled diagram of the chosen mollusk, with important anatomical details noted. For additional information, visit **www.phschool.com**

iTEXT

Use iText to review the key concepts in Section 27–4.

Answer to . . .

Figure 27–29 *Mollusks feed on—and provide food for—other organisms; they filter water; they are hosts and parasites.*

▲ **Figure 27–29** These clams will find their way to many people's dinner tables. **Applying Concepts** *Besides providing food for humans and other animals, what are some other roles that mollusks play in ecosystems?*

Ecology of Mollusks

Mollusks play many different roles in living systems. For example, they feed on plants, prey on animals, and "clean up" their surroundings by filtering algae out of the water or by eating detritus. Some of them are hosts to symbiotic algae or to parasites; others are themselves parasites. In addition, mollusks are an important source of food for many organisms, including humans.

Biologists' understanding of molluskan diversity and ecology is growing all the time. Recent explorations around deep-sea volcanic vents called "black smokers" have revealed a fascinating community that includes several bivalves. Researchers have discovered symbiotic bacteria within the foot-long bivalves clustered around these vents. These bacteria extract chemical energy from simple compounds released in the superheated water. From this energy, the bacteria produce food molecules that the mollusks can use. Without such a relationship, these mollusks would be unable to inhabit this extreme environment. Other research has discovered a similar symbiosis between related bacteria and bivalves that live in the mud of salt marshes and mangrove swamps.

Scientists have found some new uses for mollusks. Because filter-feeding bivalves concentrate dangerous pollutants and microorganisms in their tissues, they can be used to monitor water quality. Careful checks of bivalves can warn biologists and public health officials of health problems long before scientists can detect these dangers in the open water. Besides acting as environmental monitors, mollusks also serve as subjects in biological research. Some current investigations are based on the observation that snails and other mollusks never seem to develop any form of cancer. If scientists can determine what protects the cells of these animals from cancer, they will gain valuable insights into how to fight cancer in humans.

27–4 Section Assessment

1. **Key Concept** What is a mollusk?
2. **Key Concept** List and describe the four parts of the mollusk body plan.
3. **Key Concept** Describe the main characteristics of the three major classes of mollusks.
4. Why are land snails restricted to moist environments?
5. **Critical Thinking Comparing and Contrasting** Compare open and closed circulatory systems. Why are open circulatory systems found mostly in small animals that move slowly?

iTEXT Assessment Use iText to review the important concepts in Section 27–4.

Take It to the NET

Choose one species of mollusk and create a collage about it. Include a detailed diagram of the mollusk. Use the links provided in the Biology area at the Prentice Hall Web site for help in completing this activity: **www.phschool.com**

27–4 Section Assessment

1. A mollusk is a soft-bodied animal that usually has an internal or external shell.
2. Foot, mantle, shell, visceral mass. The muscular foot can have different forms, e.g., spade-shaped; mantle is thin tissue layer covering most of the mollusk's body; shell, when present, made of calcium carbonate; visceral mass is internal organs.
3. Gastropods—shell-less or one shell, ventral foot; bivalves—two shells; cephalopods—head attached to foot.
4. Land snails respire using a mantle cavity that has a large surface lined with blood vessels. Because this lining must be kept moist, it confines land snails to moist places.
5. In an open system, blood is pumped through vessels by a simple heart and works its way through different sinuses. In a closed system, blood is circulated through a network of blood vessels. A closed system can be more efficient because blood moves more quickly through the body.

Exploration

Investigating Land Snails

Although most mollusks are aquatic, some snails live on land. In this investigation, you will explore how land snails are adapted to survive in this environment.

Problem **How do land snails move and react to various stimuli?**

Materials

- land snail
- glass slides
- dropper pipette
- dissecting tray
- black construction paper
- paper towels
- 40-watt desk lamp
- metric ruler
- dissecting microscope
- petri dish
- clock with second hand

Skills Observing, Calculating, Using Tables and Graphs

Procedure

1. Using a clean pipette, put a drop of water in the center of a glass slide. Gently place the snail in the water drop. Look for the mucus trail as the snail begins to move.
2. Gently turn the slide over and place it on top of a petri dish. Place the petri dish under the dissecting microscope and observe the movement of the muscular foot under low power. Look for the radula as it scrapes the slide.
3. Copy the data table onto a separate sheet of paper. Line each half of a dissecting tray with a separate piece of paper towel. Place a sheet of black construction paper above one half of the tray. Shine the desk lamp on the other half of the tray from a distance of 30 cm. **CAUTION:** *Do not touch the lamp, because it may be hot.*
4. Place the snail in the center of the tray and observe its behavior. Record the number of seconds in each minute that the snail spends in the dark.
5. Exchange data with the class and determine class averages.
6. Return the snail to its habitat, clean up your materials, and wash your hands.

Data Table

Time (minutes)	Time in Dark (seconds)	
	Group	Class Average
0-1		
1-2		
2-3		
3-4		
4-5		

Analyze and Conclude

1. **Drawing Conclusions** Describe the movement of the snail across the glass slide. Name one advantage and one limitation of this type of movement.
2. **Using Tables and Graphs** Make a bar graph of the class average data that shows the time the snails spent in the dark for each of the five minutes. What trend do you see in your graph? How can you explain this result?
3. **Drawing Conclusions** Do snails prefer dark places or bright places? How does this behavior help snails survive?

Go Further

Take It to the NET

Visit the Prentice Hall Web site at **www.phschool.com** and follow the links to this lab. Add your data to the combined data of students across the country. Compare your class averages to those of other classes. Why might they be different?

Exploration

Objective Students will be able to draw conclusions about how land snails move and react to light.

Skills Focus **Using Tables and Graphs, Observing, Calculating,**

Time 45 minutes

Advance Prep Obtain live snails from a biological supply company. If specimens are to be observed for a period of time, keep them in a terrarium with moist soil and moss.

Alternative Materials Depending on the size of the snails and the range through which the microscope focuses, students may need to substitute a small beaker or finger bowl for the petri dish in step 2.

Safety Caution students that the lamps can become quite hot.

Teaching Tips

- Remind students that snails are living things and should be handled gently.
- Put a data table on an overhead transparency or the board for students to record their results for the class.
- Remind students to return the snails to the proper habitat upon completion of the lab.

Procedure

1. Demonstrate how to place the snail on the glass slide so that it stays on the slide long enough to be seen under the microscope.
2. As students turn the slide over, ask them how they think the snail stays attached to the slide when it is upside down.
3. Demonstrate how to place the black construction paper over half of the tray and where to position the lamp.

Expected Outcomes Students should observe that the snail leaves a mucus trail behind it when it moves and that the snail moves away from the light to the darkness under the black construction paper.

Analyze and Conclude

1. The snail moves forward with its anterior end in front; the snail's foot moves in wavelike muscular contractions and leaves a mucus trail behind. Advantages: The snail moves with its head and sense organs in front; the mucus helps the snail slide over the surface. A disadvantage is that the snail moves very slowly.
2. The bar graph should reflect the class averages. Although specific times will vary, the trend should be that the snail spends more time in the dark with each increasing minute. Snails will usually move into the dark, moist area within the first two minutes and remain there the rest of the time. The explanation for this is that a snail prefers dark places to lighted places.
3. A snail prefers dark, damp places over warm, bright places. This behavior enables the snail to avoid being seen by predators and to avoid dehydration.

Take It to the NET

Have students visit **www.phschool.com** to pool and analyze data with students nationwide.

Chapter 27 Study Guide

Study Tip

Have students work in pairs to write questions tied to Vocabulary terms and Key Concepts and then trade questions with other pairs to answer them.

Thinking Visually

Students' concept maps should include gastropods, bivalves, and cephalopods and the characteristics of each as described in the text. Examples may include any of those mentioned in the section on mollusks.

Chapter 27 Assessment

Reviewing Content

1. d	**4.** b	**7.** c	**10.** c
2. b	**5.** b	**8.** b	
3. b	**6.** b	**9.** b	

Understanding Concepts

11. A coelomate has a body cavity, and an acoelomate has no body cavity.

12. Oxygen and nutrients are taken in through the skin and diffuse to internal cells; wastes are removed by diffusion or excreted by flame cells through pores in the skin.

13. The muscular pharynx takes food into the gastrovascular cavity. Inside the gut, digestion and absorption occur.

14. Flatworms have a simple brain, one or more long nerve cords, and short cords across the body; some have eyespots and other cells that detect and respond to stimuli. Cnidarians lack a brain or nerve cord but have a network of nerve cells that can respond to stimuli such as touch.

15. It causes the disease schistosomiasis, characterized by clogged blood vessels and damage to lungs, liver, spleen, or intestines. To limit outbreaks, proper sewage systems should be provided.

16. A tapeworm uses its scolex to attach to its host's intestine wall; it absorbs nutriens from the intestine.

17. Segments called proglottids contain male and female reproductive organs. Proglottids release zygotes, which leave the host's body in feces.

Chapter 27 Study Guide

27–1 Flatworms

Key Concepts

- Flatworms are soft, flattened worms that have tissues and internal organ systems. They are the simplest animals to have three embryonic germ layers, bilateral symmetry, and cephalization.
- Turbellarians are free-living marine or freshwater flatworms.
- Flukes are parasitic flatworms that usually infect the internal organs of their hosts.
- Tapeworms are long, flat, parasitic worms that are adapted to life inside the intestines of their hosts.

Vocabulary
- acoelomate, p. 683 • coelom, p. 683
- pharynx, p. 684 • flame cell, p. 684
- ganglion, p. 685 • eyespot, p. 685
- hermaphrodite, p. 686 • fission, p. 686
- scolex, p. 688 • proglottid, p. 688
- testis, p. 688

27–2 Roundworms

Key Concepts

- Roundworms are unsegmented worms that have pseudocoeloms and digestive systems with two openings—a mouth and an anus.
- Parasitic roundworms include trichinosis-causing worms, filarial worms, ascarid worms, and hookworms.

Vocabulary
- pseudocoelom, p. 689 • anus, p. 689

27–3 Annelids

Key Concepts

- Annelids are worms with segmented bodies. They have a true coelom that is completely lined with mesoderm.
- Oligochaetes are annelids that typically have only a few setae and live in soil or fresh water.
- Leeches are typically external parasites that suck the blood and body fluids of their host.
- Polychaetes are marine annelids that have paired, paddlelike appendages tipped with setae.

Vocabulary
- septum, p. 694 • seta, p. 694 • crop, p. 695
- gizzard, p. 695 • closed circulatory system, p. 695
- gill, p. 696 • nephridium, p. 696
- clitellum, p. 696

27–4 Mollusks

Key Concepts

- Mollusks are soft-bodied animals that usually have an internal or external shell.
- The typical mollusk body plan has four parts: foot, mantle, shell, and visceral mass.
- Gastropods are shell-less or single-shelled mollusks that move by using a muscular foot located on the ventral side.
- Bivalves have two shells that are held together by one or two powerful muscles.
- Cephalopods are typically soft-bodied mollusks in which the head is attached to a single foot. The foot is divided into tentacles or arms.

Vocabulary
- trochophore, p. 701 • foot, p. 702
- mantle, p. 702 • shell, p. 702
- visceral mass, p. 702 • radula, p. 702
- siphon, p. 703 • open circulatory system, p. 703

Thinking Visually

Create a concept map that shows the classes and main characteristics of mollusks. Include at least two examples of types of mollusks within each class.

CHAPTER RESOURCES

Print:
- ***Teaching Resources,*** Chapter Vocabulary Review, Graphic Organizer
- ***Chapter Tests: Levels A and B,*** Chapter 27 Test
- ***Assessment Plus,*** Practice Test

Technology:
- ***Computer Test Bank,*** Chapter 27 Test
- ***iText,*** Chapter 27 Assessment

Chapter 27 Assessment

Reviewing Content

Choose the letter that best answers the question or completes the statement.

1. The muscular tube found near the mouth of the gastrovascular cavity in flatworms is called a(an)
a. proglottid. **c.** anus.
b. scolex. **d.** pharynx.

2. The head of an adult tapeworm is called a
a. flame cell. **c.** cuticle.
b. scolex. **d.** mantle.

3. The body cavity of a roundworm is called a
a. coelom. **c.** gizzard.
b. pseudocoelom. **d.** crop.

4. What are the clusters of nerve cells in roundworms called?
a. flame cells **c.** proglottids
b. ganglia **d.** radulae

5. In the earthworm, waste created by cellular metabolism is eliminated by the
a. crop. **c.** gizzard.
b. nephridia. **d.** flame cell.

6. The digestive organ in which an earthworm stores food is number
a. 1. **c.** 3.
b. 2. **d.** 4.

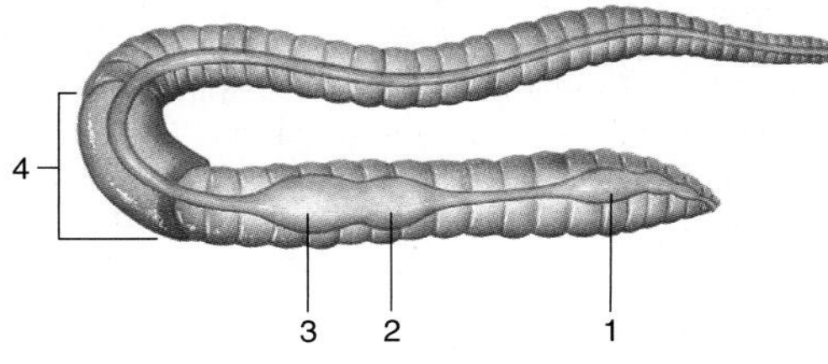

7. In earthworms, the clitellum is used in
a. digestion. **c.** reproduction.
b. excretion. **d.** respiration.

8. The tongue-shaped structure that some mollusks use for feeding is the
a. sinus. **c.** mantle.
b. radula. **d.** proglottid.

9. Mollusks eliminate nitrogen-containing wastes through simple tube-shaped organs called
a. gills. **c.** radulae.
b. nephridia. **d.** nephrons.

10. A mollusk with a shell consisting of two parts is a member of the class
a. Cephalopoda. **c.** Bivalvia.
b. Annelida. **d.** Gastropoda.

Understanding Concepts

11. Distinguish between coelomates and acoelomates.

12. Describe how respiration, circulation, and excretion are accomplished in the flatworm.

13. Explain how feeding and digestion occur in planarians.

14. How is the nervous system of a flatworm more complex than the sensory cells and nerve net of a cnidarian?

15. How does the *Schistosoma* fluke affect humans? What step can be taken to limit the number of outbreaks of schistosomiasis?

16. What adaptations do tapeworms have for their parasitic life cycle?

17. How do tapeworms reproduce?

18. Describe how respiration, circulation, and excretion are accomplished in roundworms.

19. Outline the life cycle of the *Trichinella* roundworm.

20. How does the roundworm *Ascaris* cause malnutrition?

21. List three adaptations for feeding in annelids.

22. Explain the process by which earthworms move.

23. What is a hermaphrodite? Give an example.

24. Compare respiration in aquatic and land-dwelling annelids.

25. What evidence exists to indicate that annelids and mollusks are probably closely related?

26. Compare the various feeding behaviors exhibited by the three classes of mollusks.

27. Describe the path of blood in an open circulatory system.

28. Distinguish between respiration in aquatic mollusks and that in land-dwelling mollusks.

29. Explain how many two-shelled mollusks reproduce.

30. Why can mollusks be used to measure water quality?

TIME SAVER

HOMEWORK GUIDE

Section:	Questions:
Section 27–1	1, 2, 11–17
Section 27–2	3, 4, 18–20
Section 27–3	5–7, 21–25, 34, 39, 40
Section 27–4	8–10, 26–33, 35–38, 41

18. Roundworms respire and excrete metabolic wastes through their body walls. Nutrients and wastes are transported through their bodies by diffusion.

19. Adult *Trichinella* worms live and mate in the intestines of their host. Females burrow into the intestinal wall, where they release larvae, which travel through the bloodstream and burrow into organs and tissues. There, they form cysts. When another animal eats meat from these tissues containing cysts, they enter the animal's intestine, and the life cycle is completed.

20. By absorbing the host's digested food

21. Sample answer: sharp jaws; pharynx covered with mucus to which food particles stick; mucus bag for catching food particles

22. Annelids have longitudinal muscles and circular muscles. By contracting these sets of muscles alternately, the worm can move forward, swim, or burrow. Marine annelids also have parapodia, used for swimming or crawling, on each segment.

23. A hermaphrodite such as an earthworm is an animal that produces both sperm and eggs.

24. Aquatic annelids respire through gills. Land-dwelling annelids take in oxygen and give off carbon dioxide through their moist skin.

25. A free-swimming larval phase called a trochophore is characteristic of both mollusks and annelids.

26. Gastropods use a radula to eat algae and soft plant tissues or bore through the shells of prey. Cephalopods have tentacles that grab and hold prey. Bivalves are passive filter feeders.

27. In an open circulatory system, blood is pumped by a simple heart through vessels and moves through saclike sinuses, where gas exchange occurs, and back to the heart.

28. Aquatic mollusks respire with gills inside their mantle cavity, and land-dwelling mollusks respire using a mantle cavity that is lined with blood vessels and kept moist.

29. Many bivalves reproduce sexually, by external fertilization; eggs develop into free-swimming larvae.

30. Filter-feeding bivalves concentrate pollutants in their tissues; this concentration can be measured.

Chapter 27 Assessment

Critical Thinking

31. Planarians move with cilia and use muscle cells to twist and turn; earthworms move by alternately contracting longitudinal and circular muscles; and scallops move rapidly by flapping their shells. They are similar in that they all have muscle cells for movement, and different in the specific ways that they move.

32. The snail would be unable to move.

33. They both take in material—soil in the case of the earthworm and water in the case of the clam—that contains both food and substances that are not food. A clam is a filter-feeder; an earthworm is not. Food enters an earthworm's body through the mouth; it enters a clam's body through the incurrent siphon.

34. Earthworms aerate soil with their tunnels and enrich soil with their castings.

35. The siphon must remain above the surface for respiration and feeding.

36. When an irritating grain of sand is converted into a pearl, the sand is no longer an irritant.

37. Sample hypothesis: The glands secrete a substance that promotes brooding behavior. If the surgically altered octopi are treated with chemicals from the glands, they will resume brooding and then die after brooding is finished.

38. Sample answer: most annelids feed on either decaying vegetation or materials they filter from water; these food sources are virtually inexhaustible. Also, annelids have adpated to a variety of habitats.

39. The earthworm would die from a lack of oxygen, which it must take in through moist skin.

40. Leeches feed by sucking blood from their hosts. The chemical keeps the blood flowing freely while a leech feeds.

41. Cross-fertilization is more likely to produce new, and possibly beneficial, combinations of genes.

Chapter 27 Assessment

Critical Thinking

31. **Comparing and Contrasting** Which structures are used for locomotion in the planarian, earthworm, and scallop? How are they similar? How are they different?

32. **Predicting** What would happen to a land snail if its foot stopped producing mucus?

33. **Comparing and Contrasting** In what ways are the feeding habits of the earthworm and the clam similar? In what ways are they different?

34. **Applying Concepts** Why do people purchase earthworms to put in their gardens?

35. **Inferring** Although many bivalves live buried in sand or mud, the openings to their siphons remain above the surface. Why is this important for a bivalve?

36. **Predicting** In order for an oyster to produce a pearl, a grain of sand or other irritant must get inside its shell. The mantle then secretes a substance that forms a protective covering over the irritant. Why is this an advantage for the oyster?

37. **Formulating Hypotheses** Female octopi usually die after brooding their eggs (tending and protecting eggs until they hatch). However, if certain glands near the brooding octopus's eyes are surgically removed, the octopus stops brooding, resumes feeding, and has a lifespan longer than the normal three to four years. Develop a hypothesis to explain what might happen if the surgically altered octopi were treated with chemicals from the glands.

38. **Applying Concepts** Annelids are, as a group, considered quite successful. How do you account for the success of this phylum?

39. **Predicting** During heavy rains, earthworms often emerge from their burrows. What might happen to an earthworm if it did not return to its burrow when the ground dried out?

40. **Inferring** Researchers have identified a chemical in leeches that suppresses blood clotting. Why is this chemical important in leeches?

41. **Making Connections** The nudibranch shown below is a hermaphrodite. Hermaphrodites rarely fertilize their own eggs. Explain why fertilization of another individual is more advantageous than self-fertilization. (*Hint:* See Section 1 in Chapter 26.)

Performance-Based Assessment

Worm Autobiography You are a reporter for a local newspaper and are working on the children's activity section. You decide to feature different animals as if each one were writing its autobiography. The first feature is entitled "A Day in the Life of an Earthworm." Include in your autobiography how the worm performs each of the life functions, its habitat, its importance, and illustrations. The reading level of the article should be fourth or fifth grade.

Trichinosis infection occurs worldwide. Visit the Prentice Hall Web site at **www.phschool.com** to find out more about the disease. Then, answer the following questions:

- How can people get trichinosis?
- What are the first symptoms of trichinosis? How soon after infection will those symptoms appear?
- What are five ways to prevent trichinosis?

Performance-Based Assessment

Student features should include simple descriptions and drawings derived from the text.

Standardized Test Prep

Test-Taking Tip For questions containing the words NOT, EXCEPT, and so on, begin by eliminating each answer choice that *does* fit the characteristic in question. After eliminating four choices, check to see that your answer is correct by confirming that it does not fit the characteristic in question.

Directions: Choose the letter that best answers the question or completes the statement.

1. All of the following are mollusks EXCEPT
(A) leeches. (D) clams.
(B) squids. (E) snails.
(C) octopi.

2. Which invertebrates have segmented bodies?
(A) flatworms (D) annelids
(B) roundworms (E) flukes
(C) mollusks

3. Which are NOT parasitic roundworms?
(A) hookworms
(B) filarial worms
(C) ascarid worms
(D) tapeworms
(E) trichinosis-causing worms

4. The body cavity in annelids is called a(n)
(A) coelom. (D) trochophore.
(B) pseudocoelom. (E) acoelom.
(C) scolex.

5. A scientist conducts an experiment to test the hypothesis that earthworms aid in the growth of plant roots. She grows two identical plants in pots A and B but adds earthworms only to pot B. Which of the following is true about the experiment?
(A) There is no control.
(B) There is no difference between pots A and B.
(C) Either pot could serve as the control.
(D) Pot A is the control.
(E) Pot B is the control.

6. The simplest animal to develop from three germ layers belongs in the phylum
(A) Mollusca. (D) Nematoda.
(B) Annelida. (E) Gastropoda.
(C) Platyhelminthes.

7. Waste products are excreted from the body of a planarian by
(A) nephridia. (D) scolex.
(B) flame cells. (E) cilia.
(C) proglottids.

8. Which characteristics apply to flatworms?
I. Cephalization
II. Bilateral symmetry
III. Segmented bodies
(A) I only
(B) II only
(C) I and II only
(D) II and III only
(E) I, II, and III

Questions 9–13 Use the lettered choices below to answer questions 9–13. Select the best lettered choice. A choice may be used once, more than once, or not at all.

(A) Flatworms (D) Snails
(B) Roundworms (E) Mollusks
(C) Annelids

9. Includes gastropods, bivalves, and cephalopods

10. Has internal walls, or septa, between body segments

11. Usually has an internal or external shell

12. Has a pseudocoelom

13. Includes turbellarians, flukes, and tapeworms

Questions 14–15

This two-headed planarian was created by cutting a planarian's head in half lengthwise. Use your knowledge about flatworms to answer the questions that follow.

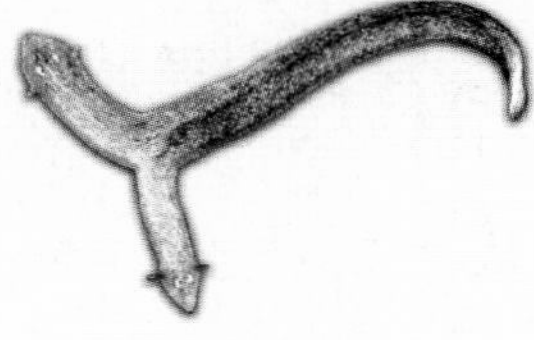

14. The process illustrated in the diagram is known as
(A) fission.
(B) sexual reproduction.
(C) regeneration.
(D) hermaphroditism.
(E) metabolism.

15. Two spots on the head of the planarian are sensitive to
(A) heat. (D) chemicals.
(B) light. (E) touch.
(C) sound.

Standardized Test Prep

1. A	**5.** D	**9.** E	**13.** A
2. D	**6.** C	**10.** C	**14.** A
3. D	**7.** B	**11.** E	**15.** B
4. A	**8.** C	**12.** B	

Take It to the NET

• Eating raw or undercooked meat that contains roundworms causes trichinosis.
• Nausea, diarrhea, vomiting, fatigue, fever, and abdominal discomfort are the first symptoms of trichinosis. Abdominal symptoms can occur 1–2 days after infection. Other symptoms usually start 2–8 weeks after eating contaminated meat.

• Answers may include the following: (1) Cook meat products until the juices run clear or to an internal temperature of at least 170°F. (2) Freeze pork less than 6 inches thick for 20 days at 5°F to kill any worms. (3) Cook wild game meat thoroughly. (4) Cook all meat fed to pigs or other wild animals. (5) Do not allow hogs to eat uncooked carcassses of other animals, including rats. (6) Clean meat grinders thoroughly if you prepare your own ground meats.

For additional information visit

www.phschool.com

Chapter Planner 28 Arthropods and Echinoderms

Section and Section Objectives	Time	Activities and Labs
28–1 Introduction to the Arthropods, pp. 715–719 **28.1.1** ***Identify*** the defining features of arthropods. **28.1.2** ***Describe*** the important trends in arthropod evolution. **28.1.3** ***Explain*** growth and development in arthropods.	1 period (1/2 block)	**SE: *Inquiry Activity,*** What is an arthropod?, p. 714 **TE: *Make Connections,*** p. 716 **TE: *Build Science Skills,*** p. 717 **SE: *Quick Lab,*** Do crickets respond to odors?, p. 718
28–2 Groups of Arthropods, pp. 720–725 **28.2.1** ***Explain*** how arthropods are classified. **28.2.2** ***Identify*** the distinguishing features of the three major groups of arthropods.	2 periods (1 block)	**TE: *Build Science Skills,*** p. 720 **TE: *Meet Diverse Needs,*** p. 722 **SE: *Analyzing Data,*** Ticks and Lyme Disease, p. 724
28–3 Insects, pp. 726–733 **28.3.1** ***Identify*** the distinguishing features of insects. **28.3.2** ***Describe*** two types of development in insects. **28.3.3** ***Explain*** what types of insects form societies.	2 periods (1 block)	**TE: *Build Science Skills,*** p. 727 **TE: *Build Science Skills,*** p. 728 **SE: *Biology and History,*** Insect-Borne Diseases, pp. 730–731 **TE: *Demonstration,*** p. 733
28–4 Echinoderms, pp. 734–738 **28.4.1** ***Identify*** the distinguishing features of echinoderms. **28.4.2** ***Describe*** the functions carried out by the water vascular system of echinoderms. **28.4.3** ***Compare*** the different classes of echinoderms.	1 period (1/2 block)	**TE: *Demonstration,*** p. 735 **TE: *Build Science Skills,*** p. 736 **TE: *Build Science Skills,*** p. 736 **SE: *Design an Experiment,*** Observing Ant Behavior, p. 739
Chapter Assessment, pp. 740–743	1 period (1/2 block)	

ACTIVITY PLANNER

SE: *Inquiry Activity,* p. 714; (10 min.); specimens or photos of arthropods, specimens or photos of other animals, lenses

TE: *Make Connections,* p. 716; (10 min.); fossils of trilobites

TE: Build Science Skills, p. 716; (20 min.); grasshopper in a small container, crayfish in a water basin, lettuce, small piece of bologna, hand lens

TE: Build Science Skills, p. 717; (10 min.); book, large paper clips, ruler

SE: *Quick Lab,* p. 718; (15 min.); live crickets in terrarium, wooden blocks

TE: *Build Science Skills,* p. 719; (30 min.); shovel or spade, gloves, shoebox

TE: *Build Science Skills,* p. 720; (15 min.); live lobster in a clear container

TE: *Build Science Skills,* p. 721; (15 min.); raw shrimp, hand lens

TE: *Meet Diverse Needs,* p. 722; (15 min.); photos of chelicerates

TE: *Meet Diverse Needs,* p. 725; (15 min.); specimens of uniramians

TE: *Build Science Skills,* p. 727; (30 min.); fruit flies, light source, meter stick

TE: *Build Science Skills,* p. 728; (15 min.); preserved grasshopper, hand lens

TE: *Demonstration,* p. 733; (20 min.); honey, spoon, sheet of paper

TE: *Demonstration,* p. 735; (15 min.); preserved sea star

TE: *Build Science Skills,* p. 736; (10 min.); small suction cup

TE: *Build Science Skills,* p. 736; (15 min.); sea star, dissecting tray, hand lens

SE: *Design an Experiment,* p. 739; (45 min.); ants of the same species from two colonies, ants of a second species, petri dishes with covers, hand lens, field guide, watch or clock with a second hand

PLANNING KEY

Ability Levels

B	**Basic**	For students who need additional help
A	**Average**	For all students
E	**Enriched**	For students who need to be challenged

Components

SE	Student Edition	**GRSW**	Guided Reading and Study Workbook	**IDM**	Issues and Decision Making
TE	Teacher's Edition	**CT**	Chapter Tests: Levels A and B	**CTB**	Computer Test Bank
LMA	Laboratory Manual A	**PHAS**	PH Assessment System	**PA**	Presentation Assistant Plus
LMB	Laboratory Manual B	**LA**	Lab Assessment with Scoring Guide	**BD**	BioDetectives Videotape
TR	Teaching Resources	**BTM**	BioTechnology Manual	**iT**	iText

Program Resources	*Assessment*	*Media and Technology*
TR: Section Review 28–1 B A **GRSW:** Section 28–1 B A	**SE:** 28–1 Section Assessment, p. 719 **TR:** Section Review 28–1	**PA:** 28–1 Interest Grabber, Section Outline, Compare/Contrast Table, Figure 28–4 **iT:** Section 28–1
TR: Section Review 28–2 **GRSW:** Section 28–2	**SE:** 28–2 Section Assessment, p. 725 **TR:** Section Review 28–2	**PA:** 28–2 Interest Grabber, Section Outline, Anatomy of a Crayfish, Figure 28–10 **iT:** Section 28–2
LMA: Chapter 28 Lab A E **LMB:** Chapter 28 Lab B A **TR:** Section Review 28–3 B A **GRSW:** Section 28–3 B A **IDM:** 28–1 A E	**SE:** 28–3 Section Assessment, p. 733 **TR:** Section Review 28–3	**PA:** 28–3 Interest Grabber, Section Outline, Insect Diversity, Figure 28–18 **BD:** "Insect Clues: The Smallest Witness" **iT:** Section 28–3 Discovery CHANNEL SCHOOL
TR: Section Review 28–4 B A Chapter 28 Design an Experiment B A E **GRSW:** Section 28–4 B A **IDM:** 28–2 A E	**SE:** 28–4 Section Assessment, p. 738 **TR:** Section Review 28–4	**PA:** 28–4 Interest Grabber, Section Outline, Compare/Contrast Table, Figure 28–23 **iT:** Section 28–4
	SE: Chapter 28 Assessment, pp. 740–743 **TR:** Chapter Vocabulary Review, Graphic Organizer **CB:** Chapter 28 Test **CTB:** Chapter 28 Test **PHAS:** Practice Test	**CTB:** Chapter 28 Test **iT:** Chapter 28 Assessment

PRESSED FOR TIME?

To Preview the Chapter

- Introduce students to Key Concepts and Vocabulary terms in each section.
- Assign the Reading Strategies for each section.

To Cover the Chapter Quickly

- Have students read all of Section 28–1, the introduction to Section 28–2, What Is an Insect? in Section 28–3, and all of Section 28–4.
- Assign Section Review 28–1 and Section Review 28–4, as well as questions 1–15 in Chapter 28 Assessment and questions 1–10 in Chapter 28 Standardized Test Prep.

To Review the Chapter

- Assign Sections 28–1 through 28–4 in the Guided Reading and Study Workbook.
- Assign Section Reviews for 28–1 through 28–4 and the Chapter Vocabulary Review for Chapter 28 in the Teaching Resources.

ENGAGE/EXPLORE

Inquiry Activity

Objective Students will be able to write an operational definition of *arthropod* in their own words.

Skill Focus **Forming Operational Definitions**

Materials variety of specimens or photographs of arthropods, several specimens or photographs of animals that are not arthropods, hand lenses

Time 10 minutes

Advance Prep Collect a variety of specimens, such as an ant, grasshopper, spider, millipede, centipede, and crayfish. Also collect other kinds of animals, such as an earthworm, planarian, snail, and starfish. Try to supply as many actual specimens as possible.

Safety If you use live organisms, students should wear disposable plastic gloves. Make sure that students do not harm the animals and that they wash their hands after handling them. Dispose of the plastic gloves after the activity.

Strategy
Have students use hand lenses to examine the specimens.

Expected Outcomes Students will observe the characteristics of arthropods.

Think About It

1. Accept any reasonable definition at this point. After students have read Section 1, have them revise their definitions on the basis of what they have learned.
2. Accept all reasonable classifications based on observable characteristics.

Assess Prior Knowledge

Ask students to spend a few minutes writing down the names of all the arthropods that come to mind. Compile the list on a transparency or the chalkboard. Then, ask: **What characteristics can you use to divide this long list of animals into smaller groups?** *(Students may mention habitat, food sources, and body structures.)* Explain that arthropods are divided into groups largely on the basis of structure and function.

Chapter 28 Arthropods and Echinoderms

Papilio maacki, a butterfly native to Japan and China, is one of more than 750,000 species of arthropods—the largest phylum of animals.

Inquiry Activity

What is an arthropod?

Procedure

1. Examine a variety of specimens or photographs of arthropods. Make a list of features that all of these organisms have in common.
2. Look at some organisms that are not arthropods. Make a list of features that all of these organisms have in common.
3. Compare the two lists.

Think About It

1. **Formulating Operational Definitions** Write a definition of the term *arthropod.* Include in your definition at least two characteristics that all arthropods share but most other organisms do not.
2. **Classifying** Classify the arthropods you observed into two or more groups. Which characteristics did you use to distinguish the groups?

FACTS AND FIGURES

A flexible exoskeleton
The chitin that forms arthropod exoskeletons is more flexible than the calcium carbonate of which mollusk shells are made. Chitin can be molded into a variety of shapes and is less cumbersome to carry around. The chitinous exoskeleton provides the same support as a mollusk shell but does not restrict the animal's mobility. To get these advantages, however, arthropods have had to sacrifice a measure of safety. While mollusks are able to add on to their existing shells, arthropods can retain their flexibility only by molting and growing a new exoskeleton. They must do this several times during their growth, and are vulnerable each time as the new exoskeleton hardens. Insect wings, such as those of the butterfly *Papilio maacki,* are also made of chitin. These appendages, which are not adaptations of legs, are composed of thin sheets of chitin over a framework of hollow veins.

28–1 Introduction to the Arthropods

If you have ever admired a spider's web, watched the flight of a butterfly, or eaten shrimp, you have had close encounters with members of the phylum Arthropoda (ahr-THRAHP-oh-duh). In terms of evolutionary success, which is measured as the number of living species, arthropods are the most successful animals of all time. At least three quarters of a million species have been identified—more than three times the number of all other animal species combined!

What Is an Arthropod?

Arthropods include animals such as insects, crabs, centipedes, and spiders. **Arthropods have a segmented body, a tough exoskeleton, and jointed appendages. Figure 28–1** shows these features in a millipede. Like annelids, arthropods have bodies that are divided into segments. The number of these segments varies among groups of arthropods.

Arthropods are also surrounded by a tough external covering, or **exoskeleton.** The exoskeleton is like a suit of armor that protects and supports the body. It is made from protein and a carbohydrate called **chitin** (KY-tun). Exoskeletons vary greatly in size, shape, and toughness. The exoskeletons of caterpillars are firm and leathery, whereas those of crabs and lobsters are so tough and hard that they are almost impossible to crush by hand. The exoskeletons of many terrestrial, or land-dwelling, species have a waxy covering that helps prevent the loss of body water. Terrestrial arthropods, like all animals that live entirely on land, need adaptations that hold water inside their bodies.

All arthropods have jointed appendages. **Appendages** are structures such as legs and antennae that extend from the body wall. Jointed appendages are so distinctive of arthropods that the phylum is named for them: *arthron* means "joint" in Greek, and *podos* means "foot."

Guide for Reading

Key Concepts
- What are the main features of arthropods?
- What are the important trends in arthropod evolution?
- What happens when an arthropod outgrows its exoskeleton?

Vocabulary
exoskeleton
chitin
appendage
tracheal tube
spiracle
book lung
Malpighian tubule
molting

Reading Strategy: Finding Main Ideas Before you read, skim the section to find the three boldfaced sentences. Copy each sentence onto a note card. As you read, make notes of supporting details.

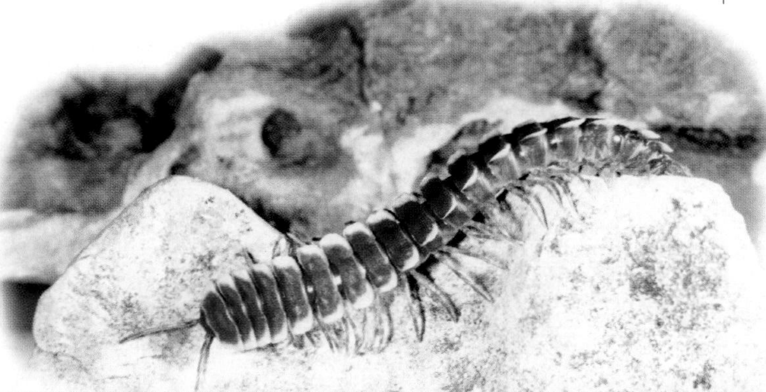

◀ **Figure 28–1 Arthropods such as the cave millipede have a body usually composed of segments, a tough exoskeleton, and jointed appendages.** Observe the millipede's legs, which are adapted for walking.

SECTION RESOURCES

Print:
- ***Teaching Resources,*** Section Review 28–1
- ***Guided Reading and Study Workbook,*** Section 28–1

Technology:
- ***iText,*** Section 28–1

Section 28–1

1 FOCUS

Objectives

28.1.1 ***Identify*** the defining features of arthropods.
28.1.2 ***Describe*** the important trends in arthropod evolution.
28.1.3 ***Explain*** what happens when an arthropod outgrows its exoskeleton.

Guide for Reading

Vocabulary Preview

Explain that the prefix *ex-* derives from a Latin word meaning "out of." Thus, an *exoskeleton* is a skeleton that is "out of" the body, or on the outside of the body. The word *exit,* meaning a way "out of" a room, derives from the same Latin word.

Reading Strategy

Have students make an outline of the section, using the blue heads as the first level of the outline and the green heads as the second level.

2 INSTRUCT

What Is an Arthropod?

Use Visuals

Figure 28–1 Make sure students understand the meaning of the term *appendage* at this point. Explain that, basically, an appendage is an "attachment" to a body segment of an arthropod. Refer students to the photo, and point out that each pair of the millipede's legs is a pair of appendages attached to a segment. In the case of a millipede, each segment has two pairs of appendages. Explain that in other arthropods, segments have fused and appendages have become modified to perform many functions other than locomotion. In a crayfish, the first two appendages are antennae. Another pair of appendages, the first pair of legs, bear large claws used to catch, pick up, crush, and cut food.

28–1 (continued)

Evolution of Arthropods

Make Connections

Earth Science Show students one or more fossils of trilobites, and have them observe the structure of these early arthropods. Review the process by which fossils are formed. Then, explain that trilobites became extinct at the end of the Permian Period, about 245 million years ago. Geologists and paleontologists use trilobite fossils to date rocks and correlate rock formations in different locations. Fossils that can be used in dating are called index fossils. An index fossil is a fossil that is associated with a particular span of geologic time. If a rock formation contains a trilobite fossil, it can be dated as having formed before 245 million years ago.

Form and Function in Arthropods

Build Science Skills

Comparing and Contrasting Divide the class into small groups, and give each group a grasshopper in a small container, a crayfish in water in a basin, lettuce, and a small piece of bologna. Have students place the lettuce in the grasshopper's container and use a hand lens to observe the grasshopper's mouthparts as it eats. Then, have students place the bologna into the basin and observe the crayfish's mouthparts with a hand lens as it eats. Ask students to make drawings of what they observe and write a comparison of the structures of these arthropods' mouthparts.

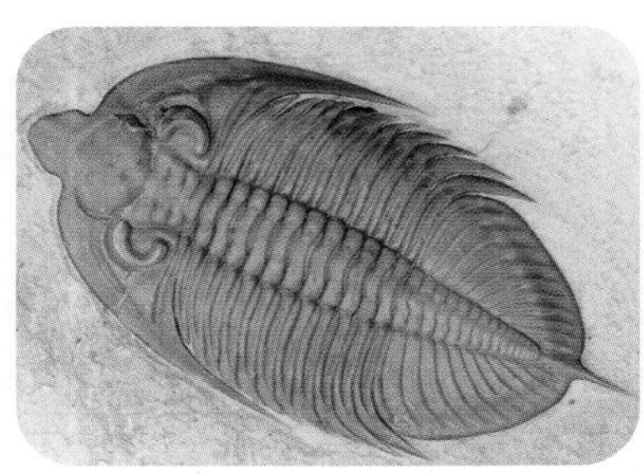

▲ **Figure 28–2** Trilobites, such as the fossilized one shown above, were marine arthropods that were abundant more than 500 million years ago. They were divided into many body segments, each with a walking leg. Trilobites became extinct some 200 million years ago. **Living arthropods generally have fewer body segments and more specialized appendages than ancestral arthropods.**

Evolution of Arthropods

The first arthropods appeared in the sea more than 600 million years ago. Since then, arthropods have moved into all parts of the sea, most freshwater habitats, the land, and the air. **The evolution of arthropods has led to fewer body segments and highly specialized appendages for feeding, movement, and other functions.**

A typical primitive arthropod was composed of many identical segments, each carrying a pair of appendages. Its body probably closely resembled that of a trilobite (TRY-loh-byt), shown in **Figure 28–2.** This early body plan was modified gradually. Body segments were lost or fused over time. Most living arthropods, such as spiders and insects, have only two or three body segments. Arthropod appendages also evolved into different forms that have different functions. These appendages include antennae, claws, walking legs, wings, flippers, mouthparts, tails, and other specialized structures.

These gradual changes in arthropods are similar to the changes in modern cars since the Model T, the first mass-produced automobile. The Model T had all the basic components, such as an internal combustion engine, wheels, and a frame. Over time, the design and style of each component changed, producing cars as different as off-road vehicles, sedans, and sports cars. Similarly, modifications to the arthropod body plan have produced creatures as different as a tick and a lobster.

CHECKPOINT *What are the differences between modern arthropods and primitive arthropods?*

Form and Function in Arthropods

Arthropods use complex organ systems to carry out different essential functions. Some of these organs are found only in this phylum. Most arthropods use tracheal tubes or other specialized organs for respiration, have an open circulatory system, and excrete wastes through saclike tubules.

Feeding Arthropods include herbivores, carnivores, and omnivores. There are arthropod bloodsuckers, filter feeders, detritivores, and parasites. Arthropod mouthparts have evolved in ways that enable different species to eat almost any food you can imagine. Their mouthparts range from pincers or fangs to sickle-shaped jaws that can cut through the tissues of captured prey. The mouthparts of a nut weevil are shown in **Figure 28–3.**

◀ **Figure 28–3** This nut weevil uses its mouthparts to bore into and eat nuts. **Applying Concepts** *Do you think a nut weevil would be able to capture and eat other arthropods? Explain your answer.*

TIME SAVER **PRESENTATIONS MADE EASY!**

The Presentation Assistant Plus contains the Prentice Hall Presentation Pro and the Transparencies, which provide easy-to-follow visual support for every step of this lesson. If you have a computer presentation station, use Prentice Hall Presentation Pro Section 28–1, or use the transparencies listed here.

Section 28–1:

Interest Grabber
Section Outline
Compare/Contrast Table
Figure 28–4

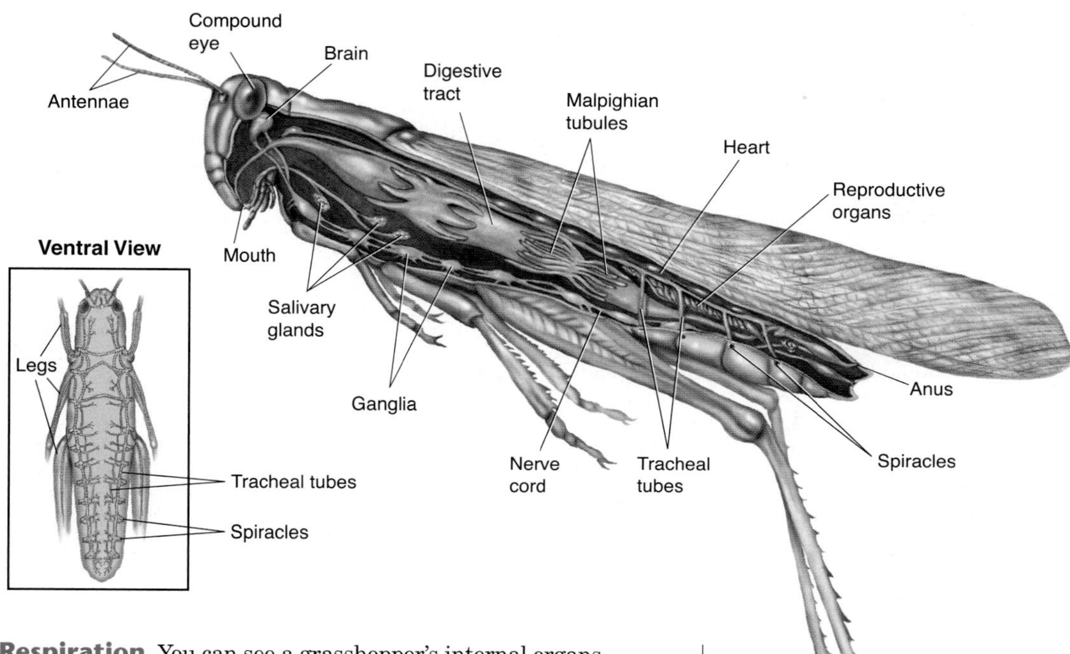

Respiration You can see a grasshopper's internal organs, including those used for respiration, in **Figure 28–4.** Like all terrestrial animals, grasshoppers need a way of obtaining oxygen from air rather than from water. Most terrestrial arthropods breathe through a network of branching **tracheal** (TRAY-kee-ul) **tubes** that extend throughout the body. Air enters and leaves the tracheal tubes through **spiracles** (SPEER-uh-kulz), which are small openings located along the side of the body. Other terrestrial arthropods, such as spiders, respire using book lungs. **Book lungs** are organs that have layers of respiratory tissue stacked like the pages of a book. Most aquatic arthropods, such as lobsters and crabs, respire through featherlike gills. The horseshoe crabs, however, respire through organs called book gills.

Circulation Arthropods have an open circulatory system. A well-developed heart pumps blood through arteries that branch and enter the tissues. Blood leaves the blood vessels and moves through sinuses, or cavities. The blood then collects in a large sinus surrounding the heart. From there, it re-enters the heart and is again pumped through the body.

Excretion Most terrestrial arthropods, such as insects and spiders, dispose of nitrogenous wastes using Malpighian (mal-PIG-ee-un) tubules. **Malpighian tubules** are saclike organs that extract wastes from the blood and then add them to feces, or digestive wastes, that move through the gut. In aquatic arthropods, diffusion moves cellular wastes from the arthropod's body into the surrounding water.

CHECKPOINT *What is the function of Malpighian tubules?*

▲ **Figure 28–4** The grasshopper has organ systems typical of most arthropods. These organ systems carry out functions such as circulation, excretion, response, and movement. Arthropods have several different types of respiratory organs. In insects, tracheal tubes (inset) move air throughout the tissues of the body. **Interpreting Graphics** ***Where is the grasshopper's nerve cord located?***

Use Visuals

Figure 28–4 Point out that this grasshopper is a representative arthropod and that other members of the phylum have somewhat different structures. Explain that a grasshopper, which is an insect, has three body sections. From front to back, the sections are called the head, thorax, and abdomen. Point out that all three pairs of legs, as well as the pair of wings, are attached to the grasshopper's abdomen, as in all insects. Then, call on volunteers to explain the function of each of the labeled parts of this arthropod.

Build Science Skills

Using Models Help students understand that book lungs provide a large surface area for gas exchange by having them compare the surface areas of an open book and a closed book. First, ask students to calculate the total surface area of the front and back covers of a book. Then, have them divide that book into 10 sections, holding the pages together with large paper clips. Ask students to calculate the total surface area of the book with the page surfaces exposed. Students will find that the total surface area of the divided book is 10 times that of the closed book.

FACTS AND FIGURES

Regulating airflow with valves

Insects' spiracles are guarded by fine, hairlike bristles that keep out dirt and have valves that can be opened or closed to regulate airflow. A grasshopper has ten pairs of spiracles. The first four pairs open only at inspiration, and the remaining six pairs open only at expiration. Closing the valves also helps to decrease the evaporation of water. For the system of main longitudinal and transverse tracheal tubes, smaller branches connect to all parts of the insect's body, eventually becoming so small that groups of the smallest ones, called tracheoles, are formed by single cells. In some places, large tubes widen to form air sacs. Muscular breathing movements aid in air circulation by alternately compressing the air sacs and then allowing them to expand. In the smallest branches, oxygen moves by diffusion alone.

Answers to . . .

CHECKPOINT *Modern arthropods have fewer body segments and more specialized appendages for feeding, movement, and other functions.*

CHECKPOINT *Malpighian tubules extract wastes from the blood.*

Figure 28–3 *No, because the structure of a weevil's mouthparts is adapted to a diet of nuts, not other arthropods.*

Figure 28–4 *The nerve cord is located in the ventral part of the grasshopper's body.*

Quick Lab

Objective Students will be able to draw a conclusion about how responses to odor help crickets survive.

Skill Focus Drawing Conclusions

Materials live crickets in terrarium, wooden blocks

Time 15 minutes

Advance Prep Crickets can be purchased inexpensively at a pet shop or bait shop. Place the crickets in a screen-covered aquarium or other transparent container. Rub one wooden block with fresh grass clippings or freshly chopped leaves. Rub a second block with moist soil. Soak a third block overnight in water with hair from a barbershop or with feathers. Leave the fourth block unscented. Label each block with the name of its odor.

Safety Students should wear disposable plastic gloves. Dispose of the gloves properly after the activity. Caution students to be careful not to injure the crickets. Some students may have allergies; check before selecting leaves and other materials for their odor.

Strategies You may want to make a data table on the chalkboard or an overhead projector so that students or groups can record data for the whole class.

Expected Outcomes Crickets will avoid blocks scented with hair or feathers and climb mostly on the one rubbed with grass clippings.

Analyze and Conclude

1. Students should observe that crickets prefer the block rubbed with grass clippings.
2. The crickets' preference for a particular block and avoidance of others indicates that they can respond to odors.
3. Odors provide clues to where foods such as grass and predators such as insect-eating mammals or birds are located. Crickets can respond to these cues by following them toward food and away from predators.

Quick Lab

Do crickets respond to odors?

Materials live crickets in terrarium, wooden blocks

Procedure

1. **Predicting** Crickets are common in grassy areas. They eat leaves and are eaten by mice, some birds, and other animals. Record a prediction of how they will respond to the odors of grass, soil, and hair.
2. On a separate sheet of paper, copy the data table shown. Your teacher will provide a set of blocks labeled with the odors they carry. Place the blocks in the container with the crickets so that the blocks do not touch each other. **CAUTION:** *Place the blocks in the container gently to avoid injuring the crickets.*
3. In your data table, record the number of crickets on each block every minute for 10 minutes.

Data Table

Time (min)	Number of crickets			
	Grass	Soil	Hair	Control
1				
2				

Analyze and Conclude

1. **Observing** Did the crickets tend to climb on some blocks more than others? If so, which blocks did they prefer?
2. **Inferring** What can you infer from these results about the ability of crickets to respond to odors?
3. **Drawing Conclusions** How could the behavior you observed help crickets survive? Explain your answer.

Response Most arthropods have a well-developed nervous system. All arthropods have a brain. The brain serves as a central switchboard that receives incoming information and then sends outgoing instructions to muscles. Two nerves that encircle the esophagus connect the brain to a ventral nerve cord. Along this nerve cord are several ganglia, or groups of nerve cells. These ganglia coordinate the movements of individual legs and wings. Most arthropods have sophisticated sense organs, such as eyes and taste receptors, for gathering information from the environment.

Movement Arthropods move using well-developed groups of muscles that are coordinated and controlled by the nervous system. These muscles generate force by contracting and then pulling on the exoskeleton. At each body joint, different muscles either flex (bend) or extend (straighten) the joint. This process is diagrammed in **Figure 28–5.** The pull of muscles against the exoskeleton allows arthropods to beat their wings against the air to fly, push their legs against the ground to walk, or beat their flippers against the water to swim.

CHECKPOINT *How do arthropods move?*

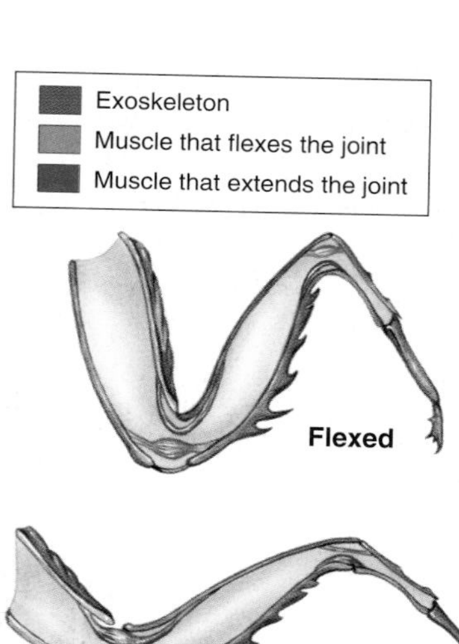

◀ **Figure 28–5** This diagrammatic representation shows how muscles attached to the exoskeleton bend and straighten the joints. (Actual muscles are much larger than those shown here.) **Applying Concepts** *How are muscles controlled and coordinated?*

BIO INSIGHTS — FACTS AND FIGURES

For arthropods, every decision is a no-brainer One of the great differences between animals such as arthropods and "higher" animals is the fact that the responses of arthropods depend only on the various stimuli received by their nerves. Although arthropods have a well-developed nervous system and a simple brain, it is a mistake to attribute "thought" to these animals. Unlike higher animals, arthropods are not capable of "thought" or "decision making," and so their reactions in a particular situation are almost totally predictable. Aristotle, the great observational scientist, was the first to notice that wasps can remain alive and at almost normal activity levels even when their heads have been removed.

Reproduction Terrestrial arthropods have internal fertilization. In some species, males have a reproductive organ that places sperm inside females. In other species, the males deposit a sperm packet that is picked up by the females. Aquatic arthropods may have internal or external fertilization. External fertilization takes place outside the female's body. It occurs when females release eggs into the external environment and males shed sperm around the eggs.

▲ **Figure 28–6 When they become too large for their exoskeletons, arthropods undergo periods of molting.** This cicada has just molted and is climbing out of its old exoskeleton.

Growth and Development in Arthropods

An exoskeleton does not grow as the animal grows. Imagine that you are wearing a suit of armor fitted exactly to your measurements. Think of it not only as skintight but as part of your skin. What would happen when you grew taller and wider? Arthropods have this same difficulty. **When they outgrow their exoskeletons, arthropods undergo periods of molting.** During **molting,** an arthropod sheds its entire exoskeleton and manufactures a larger one to take its place.

As the time for molting approaches, skin glands digest the inner part of the exoskeleton, and other glands secrete a new skeleton. When the new exoskeleton is ready, the animal pulls itself out of what remains of the original skeleton, as shown in **Figure 28–6.** This process can take several hours. While the new exoskeleton is still soft, the animal fills with air or fluids to allow room for growth before the next molting. Most arthropods molt several times between hatching and adulthood. This process is dangerous because the animal is vulnerable to predators while its shell is soft. To protect themselves, arthropods typically hide during the molting period.

28–1 Section Assessment

1. **Key Concept** What are the main features of arthropods?
2. **Key Concept** What is the evolutionary trend for segmentation in arthropods?
3. **Key Concept** How is the process of molting related to growth in arthropods?
4. What organs are used in arthropod respiration? Which are found in terrestrial arthropods? Aquatic arthropods?
5. **Critical Thinking Inferring** Terrestrial arthropods often have valves that can open and close their spiracles. How are these valves an adaptation to life on land?

iTEXT Assessment Use iText to review the important concepts in Section 28–1.

ALTERNATIVE ASSESSMENT

Creative Writing
Use information from the section to write a one-page short story about a day in the life of an arthropod. Write the story from the point of view of the arthropod.

28–1 Section Assessment

1. Arthropods have a segmented body, a tough exoskeleton, and jointed appendages.
2. The evolution of arthropods has led to fewer body segments.
3. In order to grow, arthropods undergo periods of molting, during which an arthropod sheds its entire exoskeleton and manufactures a larger one to take its place.
4. Most terrestrial arthropods breathe through tracheal tubes. Other terrestrial arthropods respire using book lungs. Most aquatic arthropods respire through featherlike gills. The horseshoe crab respires through organs called book gills.
5. The valves that open and close the spiracles help terrestrial arthropods conserve water by limiting evaporation.

Growth and Development in Arthropods

Build Science Skills

Observing Have students investigate what types of arthropods live in soil. Take the class outdoors to a field, vacant lot, or wooded area. Divide the class into small groups, and have each group mark a 0.5-m^2 area on the ground. Let students dig up the soil to a depth of 8–10 centimeters and examine it for living arthropods and molted exoskeletons. Challenge students to identify as many arthropods as they can on their own and by using field guides.

3 ASSESS

Evaluate Understanding

Call on students to explain how arthropods carry out the seven essential functions: feeding, respiration, circulation, excretion, response, movement, and reproduction.

Reteach

Have students make their own drawing of the grasshopper shown in Figure 28–4. Then, ask them to classify each label in the drawing according to which of the seven essential functions it is related to.

ALTERNATIVE ASSESSMENT

Students' stories should be both creative and based on information in the chapter. They should include reference to the seven essential functions.

Use iText to review the key concepts in Section 28–1.

Answers to . . .

CHECKPOINT They use well-developed groups of muscles that generate force by pulling on the exoskeleton.

Figure 28–5 *The nervous system controls and coordinates the action of muscles.*

Section 28–2

1 FOCUS

Objectives

28.2.1 ***Explain*** how arthropods are classified.

28.2.2 ***Identify*** the distinguishing features of the three major groups of arthropods.

Guide for Reading

Vocabulary Preview

Pronounce each vocabulary word, and have students repeat the pronunciation as a class. Pay special attention to words that are difficult for students with limited English proficiency.

Reading Strategy

Have students preview Figures 28–8 and 28–9 and write down questions about any differences they observe. Then, as they read, they should try to answer their questions from the information in the section.

2 INSTRUCT

Crustaceans

Build Science Skills

Observing Display a live lobster. Encourage students to examine the lobster closely and make labeled sketches of what they see. Ask: **What structures does this lobster have that mark it as a crustacean?** *(It has two pairs of branched antennae, two body sections, and chewing mouthparts called mandibles.)* Explain that lobsters are members of the crustacean order Decapoda ("ten feet"), so named because members of this order have five pairs of walking legs.

28–2 Groups of Arthropods

Guide for Reading

Key Concepts
- How are arthropods classified?
- What are the distinguishing features of the three major groups of arthropods?

Vocabulary
cephalothorax
thorax
abdomen
carapace
mandible
cheliped
swimmeret
chelicera
pedipalp
spinneret

Reading Strategy: Building Vocabulary
Before you read, preview new vocabulary by skimming the section and making a list of the boldfaced terms. Leave space to make notes as you read.

You are a naturalist sent to the rain forests of Brazil to bring back a representative sample of arthropods from the region. You have nets, collection jars, and a good knowledge of arthropods. As you search the forest, your collection grows to include an astonishing array of arthropods—butterflies several centimeters across, armored wormlike animals that move about using dozens of legs, and beetles that defend themselves by shooting out a stream of poisonous liquid. You must organize your collection before you return home, but you know that there are hundreds of thousands of arthropod species. Where to begin?

This is the challenge that has faced biologists for many decades—how to catalogue all the world's arthropods. The diversity of arthropods is daunting to any biologist interested in classification. As you will see, however, arthropod classification is based on a few characteristics. **Arthropods are classified based on the number and structure of their body segments and appendages—particularly their mouthparts.** The three major groups of arthropods are crustaceans, spiders and their relatives, and insects and their relatives.

Crustaceans

The crustaceans (krus-TAY-shunz) are primarily aquatic and include organisms such as crabs, shrimps, lobsters, crayfishes, and barnacles. Crustaceans range in size from small terrestrial pill bugs to spider crabs that have masses around 20 kilograms. **Crustaceans typically have two pairs of branched antennae, two or three body sections, and chewing mouthparts called mandibles.** An example of a crustacean is shown in **Figure 28–7.**

▶ **Figure 28–7** **Arthropods are classified based on the number and structure of their body segments and appendages.** The fiddler crab shown here is an example of a crustacean.

SECTION RESOURCES

TIME SAVER

Print:
- ***Teaching Resources,*** Section Review 28–2
- ***Guided Reading and Study Workbook,*** Section 28–2

Technology:
- ***iText,*** Section 28–2

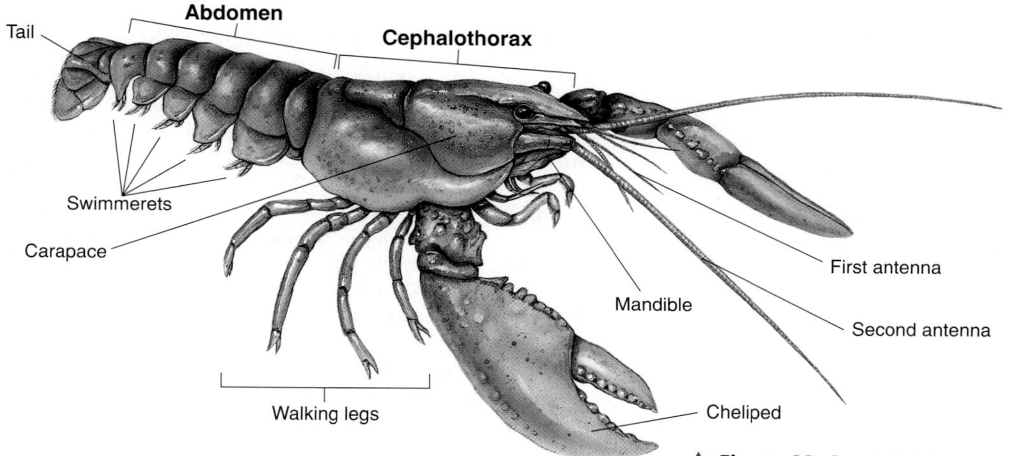

▲ **Figure 28–8** **Crustaceans typically have two pairs of antennae, two or three body sections, and chewing mouthparts called mandibles.** Notice these structures in this illustration of a crayfish, an aquatic crustacean.

The crayfish has a body plan, shown in **Figure 28-8,** that is typical of many crustaceans. Its body is divided into a cephalothorax (sef-uh-loh-THAWR-aks) and an abdomen. The anterior **cephalothorax** is formed by fusion of the head with the **thorax,** which lies just behind the head and houses most of the internal organs. The **abdomen** is the posterior part of the body. The **carapace** is the part of the exoskeleton that covers the cephalothorax.

Crustacean appendages vary in form and function. The first two pairs of appendages are antennae, which bear many sensory hairs. In crayfish, antennae are primarily sense organs. In other crustaceans, they are used for filter feeding or swimming. The third pair of appendages are the mandibles. A **mandible** is a mouthpart adapted for biting and grinding food. Gills are attached to the appendages associated with the cephalothorax.

Crayfishes, lobsters, and crabs are members of the largest group of crustaceans: the decapods. The decapods have five pairs of legs. In crayfishes, the first pair of legs, called **chelipeds,** bear large claws that are modified to catch, pick up, crush, and cut food. Behind these legs are four pairs of walking legs. Along the abdomen are several pairs of **swimmerets,** which are flipperlike appendages used for swimming. The final abdominal segment is fused with a pair of paddlelike appendages to form a large, flat tail. When the abdominal muscles contract, the crayfish's tail snaps beneath its body. This pushes the animal backward.

The barnacles are another group of crustaceans. Unlike the decapods, barnacles are sessile, or attached to a single spot. Barnacles are crustaceans that have lost their abdominal segments and no longer use mandibles. Because of their outer shell-like coverings, barnacles were once classified as mollusks. Barnacles attach themselves to rocks along the shore and in tide pools. They even attach to the surface of marine animals such as whales. Barnacles use their appendages to capture and draw food particles into their mouths.

✓CHECKPOINT *What are the body sections of a crustacean?*

Word Origins

Decapod comes from the Greek word *deka* meaning "ten" and the Greek word *podos* meaning "foot." So, *decapod* means "ten-footed." **If *cephalo* means "head," what do you think the term *cephalopod* means?**

Use Visuals

Figure 28–8 Ask students: **What appendages does this crayfish have?** *(Antennae, chelipeds, mandibles, walking legs, and swimmerets)* Emphasize that all crustaceans have two pairs of branched antennae, as shown in the figure. **How does this aquatic arthropod respire?** *(Through featherlike gills)* **Does a crayfish have two or three body sections?** *(Two. The cephalothorax is a fusion of the head and the thorax, and the abdomen is the posterior part of the body.)*

Build Science Skills

Observing Provide each student or pair of students with a whole unshelled, raw shrimp. (Caution students not to place their hands near their face or mouth after handling the shrimp and to wash their hands when they have completed their observations.) Have each student use a hand lens to observe the crustacean. Then, students should sketch the shrimp's body, note any appendages, and label all parts that can be identified. Once students have finished their sketches, ask: **From your observations, what can you infer about a shrimp's range of motion and the way it moves from place to place?** *(Students might correctly infer that a shrimp contracts its ventral muscles and spreads its fanlike sections, so that it jerks backward in the water. It also walks and swims with its legs.)*

Word Origins

The term *cephalopod* means "head footed."

TIME SAVER PRESENTATIONS MADE EASY!

The Presentation Assistant Plus contains the Prentice Hall Presentation Pro and the Transparencies, which provide easy-to-follow visual support for every step of this lesson. If you have a computer presentation station, use Prentice Hall Presentation Pro Section 28–2, or use the transparencies listed here.

Section 28–2: **Interest Grabber**
Section Outline
Anatomy of a Crayfish
Figure 28–10

Answer to . . .

✓CHECKPOINT *Crustaceans have two or three body sections. The cephalothorax and the abdomen are the body sections of a crayfish.*

28–2 (continued)

Spiders and Their Relatives

Meet Diverse Needs

Show students photographs or slides that illustrate some of the representative kinds of chelicerates, including various spiders, ticks, scorpions, and horseshoe crabs. As you show each example, ask students to identify the organism, or tell them the names if they cannot. Then, ask: **What characteristics do all chelicerates have in common?** *(They have two pairs of appendages attached near the mouth, called chelicerae and pedipalps. Chelicerates also have two body sections and four or five pairs of legs.)* Call on volunteers to point out these characteristics in the photos or slides of chelicerates. **Learning modality: visual**

Use Visuals

Figure 28–9 Ask students: **What structures does the spider share with some other arthropods?** *(Nervous system, well-developed head with brain and sense organs such as eyes, Malpighian tubules for excretion, heart, open circulatory system, spiracles)* **What structures are unique to this spider and some other chelicerates?** *(Book lungs, poison gland, pedipalps and chelicerae, silk gland, four pairs of legs)*

Spiders and Their Relatives

Horseshoe crabs, spiders, ticks, and scorpions are chelicerates. **Chelicerates have mouthparts called chelicerae and two body sections, and nearly all have four pairs of walking legs.** Locate these structures in the spider in **Figure 28–9.** Note that chelicerates lack the antennae found on most other arthropods. As in crustaceans, the bodies of chelicerates are divided into a cephalothorax and an abdomen. The cephalothorax contains the brain, eyes, mouth, and walking legs. The abdomen contains most of the internal organs.

Chelicerates have two pairs of appendages attached near the mouth that are adapted as mouthparts. One pair, called **chelicerae** (kuh-LIS-ur-ee; singular: chelicera), contain fangs and are used to stab and paralyze prey. The other pair, called **pedipalps** (PED-ih-palps), are longer than the chelicerae and are usually modified to grab prey. Chelicerates respire using either book gills or book lungs. Horseshoe crabs, which are aquatic, move water across the membranes of book gills. In spiders, which are terrestrial, air enters through spiracles and then circulates across the surfaces of the book lung.

Chelicerates are divided into two main groups: horseshoe crabs and arachnids. The arachnids include spiders, mites, ticks, and scorpions.

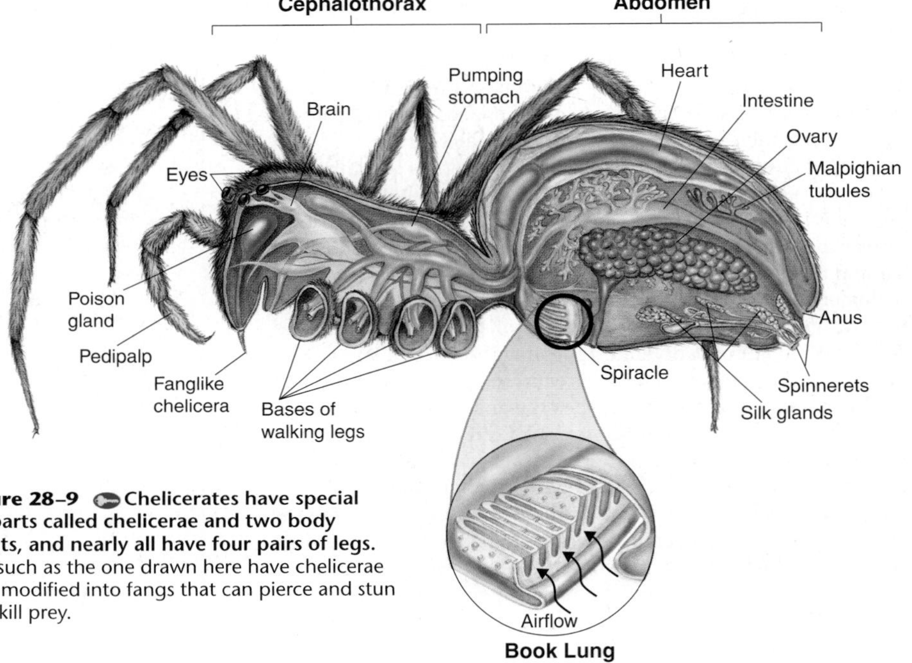

▶ **Figure 28–9 Chelicerates have special mouthparts called chelicerae and two body segments, and nearly all have four pairs of legs.** Spiders such as the one drawn here have chelicerae that are modified into fangs that can pierce and stun or even kill prey.

FACTS AND FIGURES

Ballooning off to new territory

Female spiders usually lay eggs in a small cocoon spun from silk. In some, such as members of the genus *Theridion,* the young live on the mother's web for a month or so after hatching. When the mother captures prey, she signals to the young by strumming the web with her legs. When danger threatens, she rubs the web a different way, and the young scurry for the shelter of their cocoon.

Once they are a few weeks old, most spiders live alone. Some baby spiders leave the nest by climbing onto a tall plant and releasing a long silk thread. When a strong breeze picks up the thread, the spider lets go of its perch and sails off in the wind. This behavior, called ballooning, can carry the baby spider for hundreds of kilometers to a new, possibly less crowded, territory.

▲ **Figure 28–10** Horseshoe crabs look a bit like true crabs, but their bodies more closely resemble those of spiders and other chelicerates. The abdomen and cephalothorax of these animals are encased in a hard shell. **Inferring** *From this photograph, what can you infer about the habitat of horseshoe crabs?*

Horseshoe Crabs Horseshoe crabs, shown in **Figure 28–10,** are among the oldest living arthropods. They first appeared more than 500 million years ago and have changed little since that time. Despite their name, horseshoe crabs are not true crabs at all. They are heavily armor-plated, like crabs, but have an anatomy closer to that of spiders. They have chelicerae, five pairs of walking legs, and a long spikelike tail that is used for movement. Horseshoe crabs grow to about the size—and shape—of a large frying pan. They are common along the marshes and shallow bays of the eastern United States seacoast.

Spiders Spiders, the largest group of arachnids, capture and feed on animals ranging from other arthropods to small birds. They catch their prey in a variety of ways. Some spin webs of a strong, flexible protein called silk, which they use to catch flying prey. Others, including the tarantula shown in **Figure 28–11,** stalk and then pounce on their prey. Others lie in wait beneath a camouflaged burrow, leaping out to grab insects that venture too near.

Because spiders do not have jaws for chewing, they must liquefy their food to swallow it. Once a spider captures its prey, it uses fanglike chelicerae to inject paralyzing venom into it. When the prey is paralyzed, the spider injects digestive enzymes into the wounds. These enzymes break down the prey's tissues, enabling the spider to suck the tissues into a specialized pumping stomach. The stomach forces the liquefied food through the rest of the spider's digestive system.

Whether or not they spin webs, all spiders produce silk. Spider silk is much stronger than steel! Spiders spin silk into webs, cocoons for eggs, and wrappings for prey. They do this by forcing liquid silk through **spinnerets,** which are organs that contain silk glands. As the silk is pulled out of the spinnerets, it hardens into a single strand. Web-spinning spiders use that strand to make a web. Spiders can spin webs almost as soon as they hatch; the complicated procedure of spinning webs seems to be preprogrammed behavior.

How do chelicerates respire?

▲ **Figure 28–11** The tarantula shown here is an example of a chelicerate. The chelicerae, or specialized mouthparts, can inject poison by way of a painful bite. **Applying Concepts** *How might this action be useful to tarantulas?*

Build Science Skills

Using Models Divide the class into pairs, and ask each pair to make a simple two- or three-dimensional model of a chelicerate's body plan. Explain that they can use materials of their choice and also choose the chelicerate they want to model. Students should use written labels or tags to name the chelicerate's body sections and major appendages.

BIO INSIGHTS — FACTS AND FIGURES

A great research animal

The horseshoe crab, *Limulus polyphemus*, can survive great changes in temperature and salinity and does not seem to be affected by doses of radiation high enough to kill humans. They can also live for almost a year without eating. For these reasons, *Limulus* has interested biologists for many years. This chelicerate is found only in the eastern part of North America, from Nova Scotia to Mexico. In the spring and summer, great numbers of *Limulus* can be seen in the shallow water of protected bays and estuaries as they prepare for mating. Biologists have studied *Limulus* reproduction extensively. The *Limulus* eye has also been invaluable to researchers who investigate vision. Because it has a relatively simple structure, it provides an excellent model for studies of the way that vision works.

Answers to . . .

CHECKPOINT *Chelicerates respire using book gills or book lungs.*

Figure 28–10 *Horseshoe crabs live on the seacoast.*

Figure 28–11 *The ability to inject poison enables the tarantula to capture prey and defend itself against predators.*

Analyzing Data

The name for the disease is derived from a location—Lyme, Connecticut—near where a cluster of cases was first reported in 1975. Lyme disease is caused by the bacterial spirochete *Borrelia burgdorferi.* For the bacterium to be transferred from tick to human, the tick must remain on the human for days, and therefore prompt removal of the tick will prevent the disease. But the deer tick that carries the bacterium in the East, *Ixodus dammini,* is so small that a person bitten by the tick may not notice it at all. A deer tick feeds three times during its life: usually on field mice as a larva and as a nymph, and then usually on a deer as an adult tick. Deer and other wild animals show no signs of being affected by the disease. In humans, antibiotics are usually effective in treating Lyme disease.

Answers

1. The areas where the incidence of Lyme disease is greatest are where conditions are best for ticks to feed on humans—humid, wooded areas.
2. One hypothesis is that the ticks are less abundant in the dry areas of the Southwest than in the more humid areas of the West Coast. Another hypothesis is that in the warm Southwest, the ticks prefer to feed on reptiles rather than humans.

Insects and Their Relatives

Meet Diverse Needs

To reinforce arthropod classification for at-risk students, show the class photographs or specimens of a variety of uniramians, including centipedes, millipedes, and a number of different insects. Ask: **What do all these uniramians have in common?** *(All have jaws, one pair of antennae, and unbranched appendages.)* **What is the difference between a centipede and a millipede?** *(Most body segments of a centipede bear one pair of legs each. Each millipede segment bears two pairs of legs.)*

Analyzing Data

Ticks and Lyme Disease

Lyme disease is caused by a bacterium found in two species of small ticks, the deer tick (*Ixodes scapularis*) and the western black-legged tick (*Ixodes pacificus*). Both species are most common in humid, wooded areas. They feed by sucking blood from deer, mice, birds, or humans. In warmer climates where reptiles such as lizards and snakes are most common, deer ticks prefer to feed on reptiles. The disease-causing bacteria are transmitted to the host by the bite of an infected tick. In humans the bacteria can cause a rash, fever, fatigue, joint and muscle pain, and damage to the nervous system. The bacteria do not survive well in reptiles.

The map shows the distribution of the two tick species and reported cases of Lyme disease. Use the map to help you answer the following questions:

High incidence of Lyme disease
Range of *Ixodes pacificus*
Range of *Ixodes scapularis*

1. **Interpreting Graphics** How can you explain the differences in the incidence of Lyme disease within the range of deer ticks?
2. **Formulating Hypotheses** What are two possible reasons that Lyme disease is not common in the parts of the dry southwest where western black-legged ticks are found?

▼ **Figure 28–12** Scorpions are easily recognized by their clawlike pedipalps and curved abdomen that bears a stinger at its tip. Although scorpions inflict stings on humans—usually causing as much pain as a wasp sting—they typically prey on other invertebrates, such as insects. **Comparing and Contrasting** *How do scorpions and spiders capture their prey?*

Mites and Ticks Mites and ticks are small arachnids that are usually parasitic. Their chelicerae and pedipalps are specialized for digging into a host's tissues and sucking out blood or plant fluids. In many species, the chelicerae are needlelike structures that are used to pierce the skin of the host. The pedipalps are often equipped with claws for attaching to the host. These mouthparts are so strong that if a tick begins to feed on you and you try to pull it off, its cephalothorax may separate from its abdomen and remain in your skin!

Mites and ticks parasitize a variety of organisms. Spider mites damage houseplants and are major agricultural pests on crops such as cotton. Others—including chiggers, mange, and scabies mites—cause itching or painful rashes in humans and other mammals. Ticks can transmit bacteria that cause serious diseases, such as Rocky Mountain spotted fever and Lyme disease.

Scorpions Scorpions are widespread in warm areas around the world, including the southern United States. Scorpions have pedipalps that are enlarged into claws, as shown in **Figure 28–12.** The long, segmented abdomen of a scorpion carries a venomous stinger that can kill or paralyze prey. Unlike spiders, scorpions chew their prey, using their chelicerae.

✓CHECKPOINT *Where are scorpions usually found?*

BIO INSIGHTS **FACTS AND FIGURES**

The sting of a scorpion

Many biologists think that scorpions are the most ancient of land-dwelling arthropods. They probably moved onto land more than 300 million years ago during the Carboniferous Period. Scorpions usually spend most of the day hidden under rocks or logs. All scorpions are predators, and a scorpion first catches prey with its large front claws, or pedipalps. At the tip of a scorpion's abdomen is a stinging apparatus called the aculeus, which has a sharp, barbed point. At the base of the aculeus are venom-producing glands. When a scorpion catches prey, it stings it with the aculeus and ejects venom through the point, paralyzing the catch. Although scorpions are widely feared by people, only a few have venom that is extremely toxic to humans. *Centuroides,* which is native to the Southwest, is one scorpion whose venom can be deadly to humans.

Insects and Their Relatives

Centipedes, millipedes, and insects are all uniramians (yoo-nuh-RAY-mee-unz), a group that contains more species than all other groups of animals alive today. **Uniramians have jaws, one pair of antennae, and unbranched appendages.** Although they all have unbranched appendages, uniramians have widely varying forms and lifestyles. Centipedes and millipedes have long, wormlike bodies composed of many leg-bearing segments, as shown in **Figure 28–13.** Insects have compact, three-part bodies, and most are adapted for flight. The insects are so diverse and important as a group that they are discussed separately, in the next section.

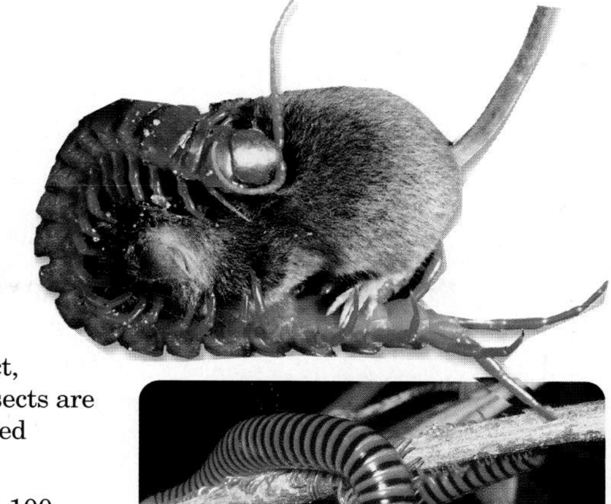

Centipedes Centipedes have from a few to more than 100 pairs of legs, depending on the species. Most body segments bear one pair of legs each. Centipedes are carnivores whose mouthparts include a pair of venomous claws. They use these claws to catch and stun or kill their prey—including other arthropods, earthworms, toads, small snakes, and even mice. Centipedes usually live beneath rocks or in the soil. Their spiracles cannot close, and they lack a waterproof coating on their exoskeleton. As a result, their bodies lose water easily. This characteristic restricts centipedes to moist or humid areas.

Millipedes Like the centipedes, millipedes have a highly segmented body. However, each millipede segment bears two, not one, pairs of legs. These two pairs of legs per segment develop from the fusion of two segments in the millipede embryo. Millipedes live under rocks and in decaying logs. They feed on dead and decaying plant material. Unlike centipedes, they are timid creatures. When disturbed, many millipedes roll up into a ball to protect their softer undersides. They may also defend themselves by secreting unpleasant or toxic chemicals.

Figure 28–13 **Uniramians such as centipedes and millipedes have jaws, one pair of antennae, and unbranched appendages.** A centipede (top) is a carnivore that feeds on earthworms and other small animals. A millipede (bottom) is a herbivore that feeds on rotting vegetation.

28–2 Section Assessment

1. **Key Concept** What characteristics are used to classify arthropods?
2. **Key Concept** How do the three largest groups of arthropods differ?
3. Describe the process of digestion in spiders.
4. Compare and contrast the body plans and feeding habits of millipedes and centipedes.
5. **Critical Thinking Applying Concepts** Suppose you want to catch a crayfish with a net. Should you try to scoop it up head first or tail first? Explain.

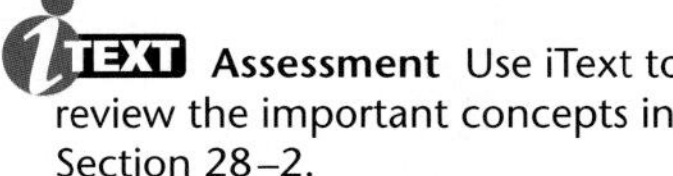

Assessment Use iText to review the important concepts in Section 28–2.

ALTERNATIVE ASSESSMENT

Designing an Arthropod
Use information from this section to design a new type of arthropod. Make sure that the arthropod has all the characteristics described in this section. Draw the arthropod and give it a name. Include a brief description of what it eats and where it lives.

3 ASSESS

Evaluate Understanding

Call on students at random to explain the differences in structure among the three major groups of arthropods.

Reteach

Have students make a compare/contrast table to organize the information about the three major groups of arthropods. Headings might include Group, Characteristics, and Examples. Students could continue adding to this table with information from Section 28–3.

ALTERNATIVE ASSESSMENT

Consider working with an art teacher at your school in order to provide students with more options for their drawings. Drawings should be accompanied by a name and a brief description of the fantasy arthropod, including feeding and habitat. All organisms should have a segmented body, an exoskeleton, and jointed appendages. In their drawings, students should pay special attention to the structure of the arthropod's mouthparts.

Use iText to review the key concepts in Section 28–2.

28–2 Section Assessment

1. Arthropods are classified based on the number and structure of their body segments and appendages—particularly their mouthparts.
2. Students should describe characteristics of crustaceans, chelicerates, and uniramians.
3. Spiders first liquefy their food, and then suck the tissues into a specialized pumping stomach, which forces the liquid through the rest of the digestive system.
4. Most centipede body segments bear one pair of legs each; each millipede segment bears two pairs of legs. Centipedes use claws to stun or kill prey; millipedes feed on dead or decaying plant material.
5. Tail first, because the tail can provide a powerful swimming stroke to help the crayfish escape

Answers to . . .

CHECKPOINT *Scorpions are widespread in warm areas around the world.*

Figure 28–12 *Some spiders catch prey in webs. Others stalk, then pounce on their prey. Others lie in wait beneath a camouflaged burrow, leaping out to grab insects that venture too near. Scorpions use a venomous stinger that can kill or paralyze prey.*

Section 28–3

1 FOCUS

Objectives

28.3.1 ***Identify*** the distinguishing features of insects.
28.3.2 ***Describe*** two types of development in insects.
28.3.3 ***Explain*** what types of insects form societies.

Guide for Reading

Vocabulary Preview

Help students organize the section's vocabulary words by pointing out that they fall into two general categories. The first four apply to the life cycle of insects; the last three apply to the formation by some kinds of insects of complex arrangements called societies.

Reading Strategy

Point out that in looking for the important concepts in each paragraph, students should pay attention to the headings of the section. The important concepts usually relate to the headings.

2 INSTRUCT

Use Visuals

Figure 28–14 Have students study the information contained on the pie chart. Then, ask: **What percentage of animals are insects?** *(73%)* **What percentage are vertebrates?** *(4%)*

28–3 Insects

Guide for Reading

Key Concepts
- What are the distinguishing features of insects?
- What two types of development can insects undergo?
- What types of insects form societies?

Vocabulary
incomplete metamorphosis
nymph
complete metamorphosis
pupa
pheromone
society
caste

Reading Strategy: Summarizing As you read, find the most important concepts in each paragraph. Then, use the important concepts to write a summary of what you have read.

What animals other than humans have the greatest impact on the activities of this planet? If you said "insects," you would be correct. From bees that flit from flower to flower to weevils that feed on crops, insects seem to be everywhere. As **Figure 28–14** shows, this single class of animals contains more species than any other group of animals. Ants and termites alone account for nearly one third of all the animal biomass in the Amazon basin.

Many characteristics of insects have contributed to their evolutionary success. These include different ways of responding to stimuli; the evolution of flight, which allowed insects to disperse long distances and colonize new habitats; and a life cycle in which the young differ from adults in appearance and feeding methods. These features have allowed insects to thrive in almost every terrestrial habitat on Earth, as well as in many freshwater and some marine environments.

The insects cover an incredible variety of life forms—from stunning, iridescent beetles and butterflies to the less attractive fleas, weevils, cockroaches, and termites. Biologists sometimes disagree on how to classify insects, and the number of living orders ranges from 26 to more than 30.

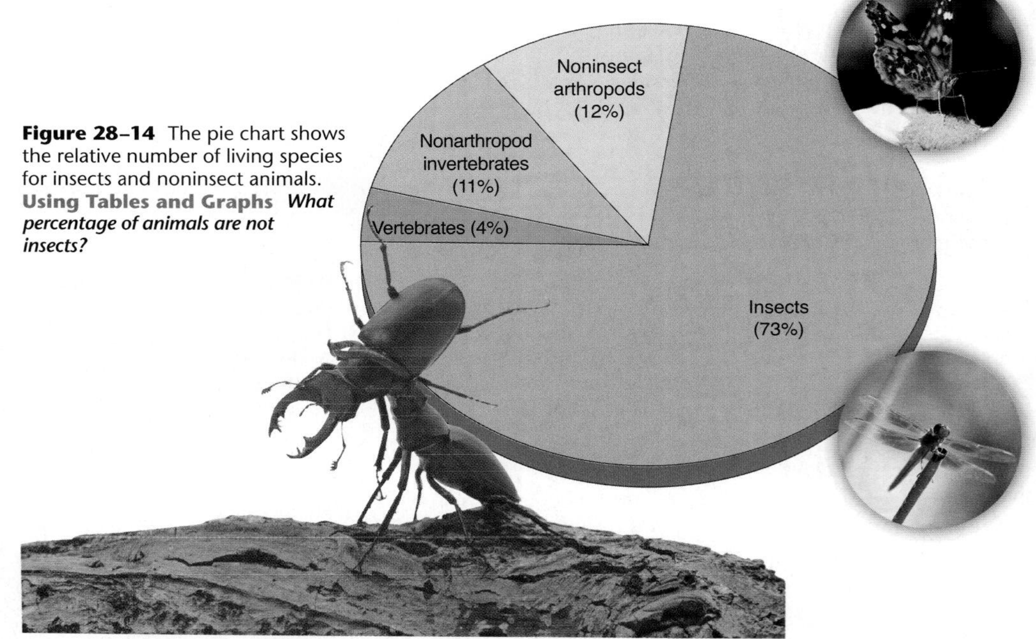

Figure 28–14 The pie chart shows the relative number of living species for insects and noninsect animals. **Using Tables and Graphs** ***What percentage of animals are not insects?***

SECTION REVIEW

Print:
- ***Laboratory Manual A,*** Chapter 28 Lab
- ***Laboratory Manual B,*** Chapter 28 Lab
- ***Teaching Resources,*** Section Review 28–3, Chapter 28 Design an Experiment
- ***Guided Reading and Study Workbook,*** Section 28–3
- ***Issues and Decision Making,*** 28–1

Technology:
- ***BioDetectives Videotape,*** "Insect Clues"
- ***iText,*** Section 28–3

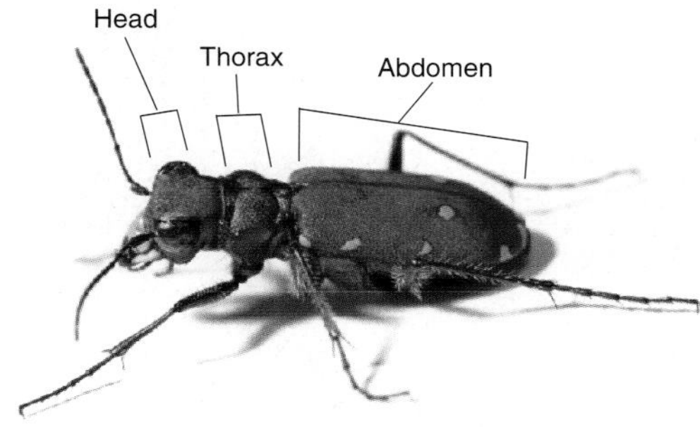

◀ **Figure 28–15** **Insects have a body divided into three parts—head, thorax, and abdomen. Three pairs of legs are attached to the thorax.** In addition to these features, this green tiger beetle has other characteristics of a typical insect—wings, antennae, compound eyes, and tracheal tubes for respiration.

What Is an Insect?

Like all arthropods, insects have a segmented body, an exoskeleton, and jointed appendages. They also have several features that are specific to insects. **Insects have a body divided into three parts—head, thorax, and abdomen. Three pairs of legs are attached to the thorax.** The beetle in **Figure 28–15** exhibits these characteristics. In many insects such as ants, the body parts are clearly separated from each other by narrow connections. In other insects, such as grasshoppers, the divisions between the three body parts are not as sharply defined. A typical insect also has a pair of antennae and a pair of compound eyes on the head, two pairs of wings on the thorax, and tracheal tubes that are used for respiration.

The essential life functions in insects are carried out in basically the same ways as they are in other arthropods. However, insects have a variety of interesting adaptations that deserve a closer look.

CHECKPOINT *What are the names of the three parts of an insect's body?*

Responses to Stimuli Insects use a multitude of sense organs to respond to stimuli. Compound eyes are made of many lenses that detect minute changes in color and movement. The brain assembles this information into a single, detailed image. Compound eyes produce an image that is less detailed than what we see. However, eyes with multiple lenses are far better at detecting movement—one reason it is so hard to swat a fly!

Insects have chemical receptors for taste and smell on their mouthparts, as might be expected, and also on their antennae and legs. When a fly steps in a drop of water, it knows immediately whether the water contains salt or sugar. Insects also have sensory hairs that detect slight movements in the surrounding air or water. As objects move toward insects, the insects can feel the movement of the displaced air or water and respond appropriately. Many insects also have well-developed ears that hear sounds far above the human range. These organs are located in what we would consider odd places—behind the legs in grasshoppers, for example.

What Is an Insect?

Build Science Skills

Designing Experiments Divide the class into small groups, and give each group these materials: a vial containing 10 fruit flies, a light source, and a meter stick. One culture tube of fruit flies should provide enough flies for an entire class. Transfer 10 adult flies to a separate vial for each group. Challenge each group to formulate a hypothesis and design an experiment to investigate how fruit flies respond to light. (*In a typical experiment, students might vary the distance of the light from the flies and observe any differences in behavior.*) Have groups review their experiments with you before proceeding with the activity.

PRESENTATIONS MADE EASY!

The Presentation Assistant Plus contains the Prentice Hall Presentation Pro and the Transparencies, which provide easy-to-follow visual support for every step of this lesson. If you have a computer presentation station, use Prentice Hall Presentation Pro Section 28–3, or use the transparencies listed here.

Section 28–3: **Interest Grabber**
Section Outline
Insect Diversity
Figure 28–18

Answers to . . .

CHECKPOINT *Head, thorax, and abdomen*

Figure 28–14 *27 percent*

Build Science Skills

Observing Have specimens of large grasshoppers serve as a representative insect for students to examine with both the unaided eye and with a hand lens. You may also want to provide students with diagrams on which they can label the various structures and their functions. If possible, have preserved specimens of other insects so that students can examine the variety of mouthparts that enable insects to obtain food from many different sources.

Use Community Resources

Invite a local lepidopterist to address the class about collecting and preserving butterflies. You might be able to find such a collector through the biology department of a local college or by contacting an entomologist. Ask the lepidopterist to present his or her collection, explain how the insects are caught, and demonstrate how butterflies are preserved and mounted. Have students prepare for the presentation by brainstorming a list of questions to ask. Make sure that students look for specific insect structures as they examine the mounted butterflies.

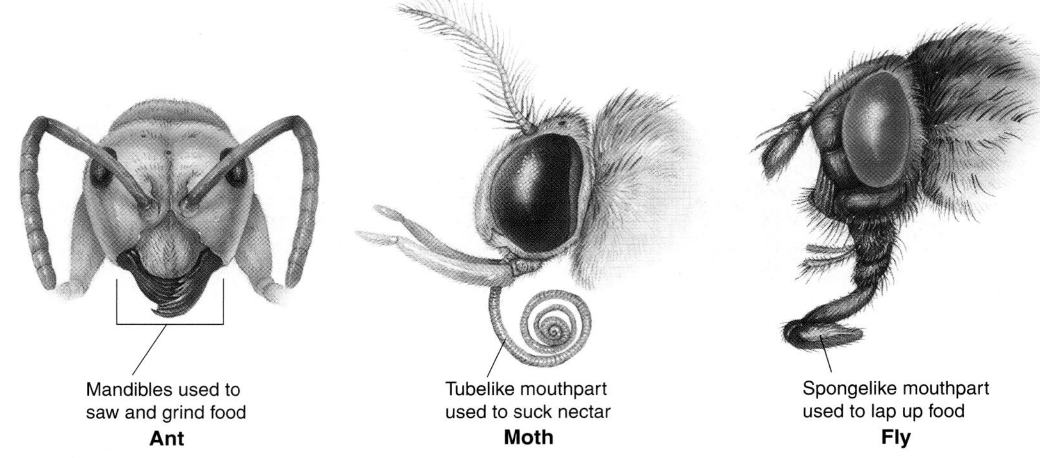

▲ **Figure 28–16** Insect mouthparts are specialized for a variety of functions. An ant's mouthparts can saw through and then grind food into a fine pulp. The mouthpart of a moth consists of a long tube that can be uncoiled to sip nectar from a flower. Flies have a spongy mouthpart that is used to stir saliva into food and then lap up the food. **Applying Concepts** *What is the function of saliva?*

Adaptations for Feeding Insects have three pairs of appendages that are used as mouthparts, including a pair of mandibles. These mouthparts can take on a variety of shapes, as shown in **Figure 28–16.**

Insect adaptations for feeding are not restricted to their mouthparts. Many insects produce saliva containing digestive enzymes that help break down food. The chemicals in bee saliva, for example, help change nectar into a more digestible form—honey. Glands on the abdomen of bees secrete wax, which is used to build storage chambers for food and other structures within a beehive.

Movement and Flight Insects have three pairs of legs, which in different species are used for walking, jumping, or capturing and holding prey. In many insects, the legs have spines and hooks that are used for grasping and defense.

Many insects can fly, as shown in **Figure 28–17.** Flying insects typically have two pairs of wings made of chitin—the same substance that makes up an insect's exoskeleton.

The evolution of flight has allowed insects to disperse long distances and to colonize a wide variety of habitats. Flying abilities and styles vary greatly among the insects. Butterflies usually fly slowly. Flies, bees, and moths, however, can hover, change direction rapidly, and dart off at great speed. Dragonflies can reach speeds of 50 kilometers per hour.

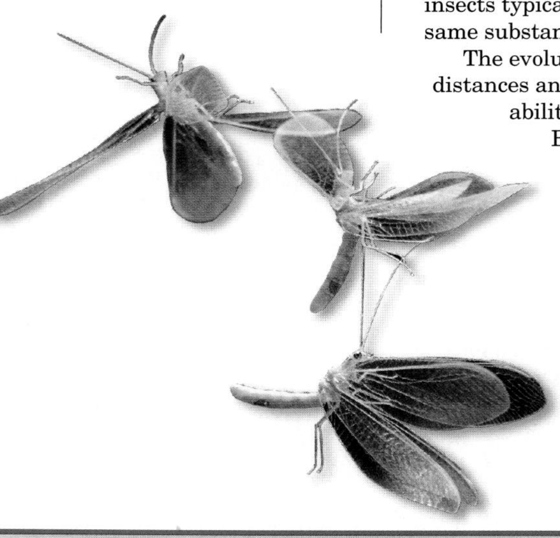

◀ **Figure 28–17** Flying insects, such as this lacewing, move their wings using two sets of muscles. The muscles contract to change the shape of the thorax, alternately pushing the wings down and lifting them up and back. In some small insects, these muscles can produce wing speeds of up to 1000 beats per second! **Drawing Conclusions** *How might the evolution of flight change an animal's habitat?*

BIO INSIGHTS — FACTS AND FIGURES

Survivability through the senses
A large measure of insects' survival ability is due to the development of their senses. The hairs that cover most insects are sensitive to touch and can detect chemicals as well. These hairs are concentrated on the head and lower legs, where they are most likely to come in contact with objects and materials in the environment. The compound eyes of insects consist of many lenses—up to 30,000 in some dragonflies. These large, multilensed eyes give insects the ability to scan a wide area at one time, allowing them to detect the motion of predators or prey. Some insects rely heavily on hearing. Mosquitoes, for example, can detect sounds with their antennae. Crickets, grasshoppers, and other insects have a membrane called a tympanum on the abdomen or legs. These structures function much like the human eardrum in sensing sound vibrations.

Metamorphosis **The growth and development of insects usually involve metamorphosis, which is a process of changing shape and form. Insects undergo either incomplete metamorphosis or complete metamorphosis.** Both complete and incomplete metamorphosis are shown in **Figure 28–18**. The immature forms of insects that undergo gradual or **incomplete metamorphosis,** such as the chinch bug, look very much like the adults. These immature forms are called **nymphs** (NIMFS). Nymphs lack functional sexual organs and other adult structures, such as wings. As they molt several times and grow, the nymphs gradually acquire adult structures. This type of development is characterized by a similar appearance throughout all stages of the life cycle.

Many insects, such as bees, moths, and beetles, undergo a more dramatic change in body form during a process called **complete metamorphosis.** These animals hatch into larvae that look and act nothing like their parents. They also feed in completely different ways from adult insects. The larvae typically feed voraciously and grow rapidly. They molt a few times and grow larger but change little in appearance. Then they undergo a final molt and change into a **pupa** (PYOO-puh; plural: pupae)—the stage in which an insect changes from larva to adult. During the pupal stage, the body is completely remodeled inside and out. The adult that emerges seems like a completely different animal. Unlike the larva, the adult typically can fly and is specialized for reproduction. **Figure 28–18** shows the complete metamorphosis of a ladybug beetle.

To find out how insect metamorphosis plays a part in forensic science, view the videotape "Insect Clues: The Smallest Witnesses."

Figure 28–18 **The growth and development of insects usually involve metamorphosis, which is a process of changing shape and form. Insects undergo incomplete metamorphosis or complete metamorphosis.** The chinch bug (left) undergoes incomplete metamorphosis, and the developing nymphs look similar to the adult. The ladybug (right) undergoes complete metamorphosis, and during the early stages the developing larva and pupa look completely different from the adult.

CHECKPOINT *What is a pupa?*

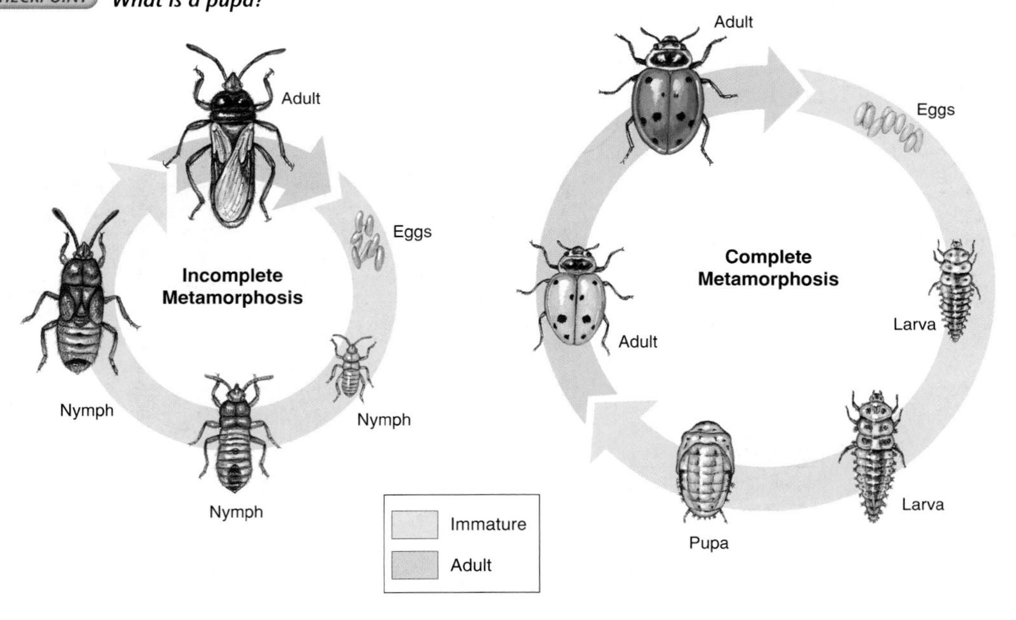

Use Visuals

Figure 28–18 Point out that the insects in the two life cycles shown are in different orders. The chinch bug is a plant bug, Order Homoptera, and it feeds on grasses. The ladybug is a type of beetle, Order Coleoptera. Then, ask: **Which type of metamorphosis includes larva and pupa stages?** *(Complete metamorphosis)* **In incomplete metamorphosis, what are the differences between the nymph and the adult?** *(Nymphs lack functional sexual organs, wings, and other adult structures.)* **In which type of metamorphosis is there a dramatic change in shape?** *(Complete metamorphosis)*

Meet Diverse Needs

Reinforce the idea of metamorphosis for students with limited English proficiency by explaining the meaning of the word parts in the term. On the board, write *meta* = *change* and *morph* = *form.* Then, ask: **How would you define *metamorphosis* now that you know the meaning of these word parts?** *(Metamorphosis means "change in form.")*

Encourage students to view "Insect Clues: The Smallest Witnesses" on the BioDetectives Videotape.

BIO INSIGHTS: FACTS AND FIGURES

Studying insects from murder scenes

Insects and their larvae provide clues to forensic scientists about the circumstances of crimes—especially murders. Forensic entomologists examine the species of insects in a piece of evidence—a package of marijuana or a corpse, for example—to determine where the crime was committed. Since the larvae of many insects, such as blowflies, develop at an extremely regular rate, larvae removed from a corpse can be raised in carefully controlled conditions. The length of time it takes the larvae to develop into adults gives investigators a fairly accurate indication of when the parent fly laid her eggs on the corpse. And because the time it takes for a corpse to attract insects is also a known constant, the investigators can pinpoint the time of death.

Answers to . . .

CHECKPOINT *A pupa is the stage in which an insect changes from larva to adult.*

Figure 28–16 *Saliva contains enzymes that help break down food.*

Figure 28–17 *The habitat would change from mostly on the ground to include the air and the high places previously difficult to reach.*

Insects and Humans

Use Community Resources

Invite a local farmer to speak to the class about insect pest problems common to farms in your area. Have the farmer talk about kinds of damage insects can do to crops, specific insects that are a threat in your area, and methods commonly used to prevent insect damage. If possible, have the farmer bring to class examples of insect damage caused to crops.

Biology and History

After students have examined the time line, discuss the ethics of using insecticides to eliminate disease-causing organisms. DDT, for example, proved invaluable in controlling outbreaks of malaria. But the chemical did so much damage to the environment that its use was banned in the United States. Yet, DDT is still used in other countries for disease control. Elicit students' opinions about whether the benefits of DDT use outweigh the harmful effects.

Writing Activity

Students might use encyclopedias, microbiology textbooks, or medical reference books on diseases to complete their research. Bubonic plague is a serious disease caused by the bacterium *Yersinia pestis.* Plague is normally a disease of rats, and the intermediate host is the rat flea, *Xenopsylla cheopis.* In the late 1800s, physicians in various parts of the world began to observe that plague outbreaks in humans were associated with large populations of rats, and that diseased rats were infested with fleas that left the rats' bodies after the rats died of plague. The rat flea transmits the pathogen when it jumps from rat to rat, or rat to human. This disease is known as *bubonic* plague after the swollen lymph nodes, called buboes, it causes. The spread of the disease can be controlled by reducing rat and flea populations.

Insects and Humans

Many insects are known for their negative effects. Termites destroy wood structures, moths eat their way through wool clothing and carpets, and bees and wasps produce painful stings. Insects such as desert locusts cause billions of dollars in damage each year to livestock and crops. Boll weevils are notorious for the trouble they cause cotton farmers in the South. Mosquitoes are annoying and have been known to spoil many a leisurely outdoor activity. Only female mosquitoes bite humans and other animals to get a blood meal for their developing eggs. Male mosquitoes, on the other hand, do not bite; they feed on nectar. Many insects, including mosquitoes, cause far more serious damage than itchy bites. Their bites can infect humans with microorganisms that cause devastating diseases such as malaria, yellow fever, and bubonic plague.

Despite their association with destruction and disease, insects also contribute enormously to the richness of human life. Agriculture would be very different without the bees, butterflies, wasps, moths, and flies that pollinate many crops. One third of the food you eat depends on plants pollinated by animals, including insects. Insects also produce commercially valuable products such as silk, wax, and honey. They are even considered a food delicacy in certain countries of Africa and Asia.

CHECKPOINT *How do insects affect humans negatively? Positively?*

Biology and History

Insect-Borne Diseases

For as long as humans and insects have shared planet Earth, humans have been victims of diseases carried by insects. Researchers have discovered which insects transmit specific diseases. Such discoveries have often shed light on how the diseases can be controlled.

1900

1906
Robert Koch discovers that fleas transmit the bubonic-plague bacterium. The plague killed 25% of Europe's population between 1347 and 1351.

1909
Charles Nicolle discovers that one form of typhus, which is caused by a bacterium, is transmitted by the body louse.

1920
Nineteenth amendment to U.S. Constitution gives women the right to vote.

1924
African sleeping sickness is discovered in inhabitants of central Africa. The disease is caused by a protist transmitted by tsetse flies that live in forests and areas near water.

1943
DDT, a powerful insecticide, is used for the first time during World War II to control the spread of typhus. It is also used to control outbreaks of malaria.

FACTS AND FIGURES

Yikes—that bite itches!
Although almost everyone has been bitten by a mosquito, most people may not be aware that it is only the female that bites. Male mosquitoes cause no trouble at all, flying around and collecting pollen from flowers. The biting females use the nutrients in blood to help them produce large numbers of eggs. To prevent blood from clotting as they drink it, mosquitoes inject their saliva when they first pierce the skin. It is this saliva that can carry disease-causing organisms such as the malaria-causing protozoan, *Plasmodium falciparum.* And it is the human body's allergic reaction to this saliva that causes the itching and swelling that comes with mosquito bites.

Insect Communication

Insects communicate using sound, visual, chemical, and other types of signals. Much of their communication involves finding a mate. To attract females, male crickets chirp by rubbing their forewings together, and male cicadas buzz by vibrating special membranes on the abdomen. Some insects use sound waves to locate prey.

Male fireflies use visual cues to communicate with potential mates. As shown in **Figure 28–19,** a light-producing organ in the abdomen is used to produce a distinct series of flashes. When female fireflies see the signal, they flash back a signal of their own, inducing the males to fly to them. This interaction is sometimes more complicated, however, because the carnivorous females of one genus of fireflies can mimic the signal of another genus—and then lure unsuspecting males to their death!

Many insects communicate using chemical signals. Female moths, for example, attract distant males to them by releasing chemicals. These chemicals are called **pheromones** (FER-uh-mohnz), which are specific chemical messengers that affect the behavior or development of other individuals of the same species. Some pheromones function to signal alarm or alert other insects to the death of a member of the colony. Other pheromones enable males and females to communicate during courtship and mating.

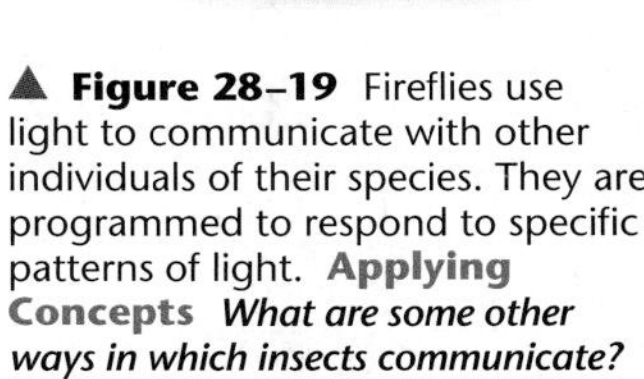

▲ **Figure 28–19** Fireflies use light to communicate with other individuals of their species. They are programmed to respond to specific patterns of light. **Applying Concepts** ***What are some other ways in which insects communicate?***

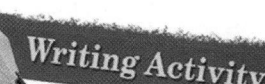

Writing Activity

Some insect-borne diseases have an intermediate host in which the parasite reproduces asexually. Conduct research on the bubonic plague to identify its intermediate host. Write a report on how this host was discovered and how the discovery affected control of the disease.

1957 First satellite launched into orbit

1972 Use of DDT is severely restricted in the United States because it is found to be toxic to fishes, birds, and possibly humans.

1974 The World Health Organization begins to get rid of the black fly population of West Africa. Black flies transmit river blindness, which is caused by a roundworm.

1999 An outbreak of West Nile virus occurs in New York City and its suburbs—the first sighting of this disease in the Western Hemisphere. The disease is carried by mosquitoes and can affect humans as well as birds and livestock. Officials order spraying of insecticides near bodies of water in which mosquitoes might breed.

2000

TEACHER TO TEACHER

When I teach students about arthropods, I try to present issues and ideas that they can relate to in their own, everyday lives. A teacher should always remember that with very few exceptions the students taking high school biology will become neither biologists nor doctors. We as teachers, then, should strive to give students a handle upon which to grab life—the biology of life. For instance, I try to spend class time on spiders and their webs, as well as on the process of silk production. I also try to help students understand how and why common insects function as they do. I make a daily effort to capitalize on students' interests in order to make the study of living things relevant to their lives.

—*Dr. Chuck Campbell,*
Biology Teacher
Burbank High School,
Burbank, CA

Insect Communication

Build Science Skills

Observing If the season is right, ask volunteers to use a jar to collect fireflies one evening. Explain that the lid of the jar must be pierced to allow airflow so that the insects can breathe. Have the students bring the jar of fireflies to class the next day, and encourage students to examine the organisms with a hand lens. Explain that fireflies are a type of beetle. People in primitive societies around the world have long trapped fireflies to use for light at night. Instruct students to release the insects when they have concluded their observations.

Answers to . . .

CHECKPOINT *Insects affect humans negatively by destroying structures, wool clothing, and carpets; by producing painful stings; by causing billions of dollars of damage each year to crops; and by transmitting devastating diseases. Insects affect humans positively by pollinating crops; by producing commercially valuable products such as silk, wax, and honey; and by serving as food.*

Figure 28–19 *Other ways in which insects communicate include sounds, chemicals, and other types of signals.*

28–3 (continued)

Insect Societies

Use Visuals

Figure 28–20 Ask students: **What is the role of the queen in a tropical leaf-cutter society?** *(The queen's sole purpose is to lay eggs.)* **Which kind of ants would you likely observe outside the nest?** *(Major workers would likely be seen outside the nest, because they forage for food.)* **What kinds of insects form societies?** *(Ants, bees, termites, and some of their relatives)*

Use Community Resources

Invite a local beekeeper to speak to the class. You might find a beekeeper by contacting an entomologist at a local university or by asking at a local store that sells beekeeping supplies. Ask the beekeeper to talk about how to start a hive, what supplies and implements are needed, how the bees behave, and what purpose the bees serve in the community. Before the speaker arrives, encourage students to make a list of questions to ask about beekeeping.

Demonstration

Ask students to help locate an active anthill outdoors. Then, put a spoonful of honey on the ground about 1 meter away from it. Put a sheet of paper between the honey and the anthill, and have students observe the ants. The ant scouts will find the honey and establish a pheromone trail directly back to the anthill. While the ants are traveling back and forth on the trail regularly, quickly turn the paper one-quarter turn. The ants will seem confused as they search for the old trail, but eventually, they will establish a new trail to the honey.

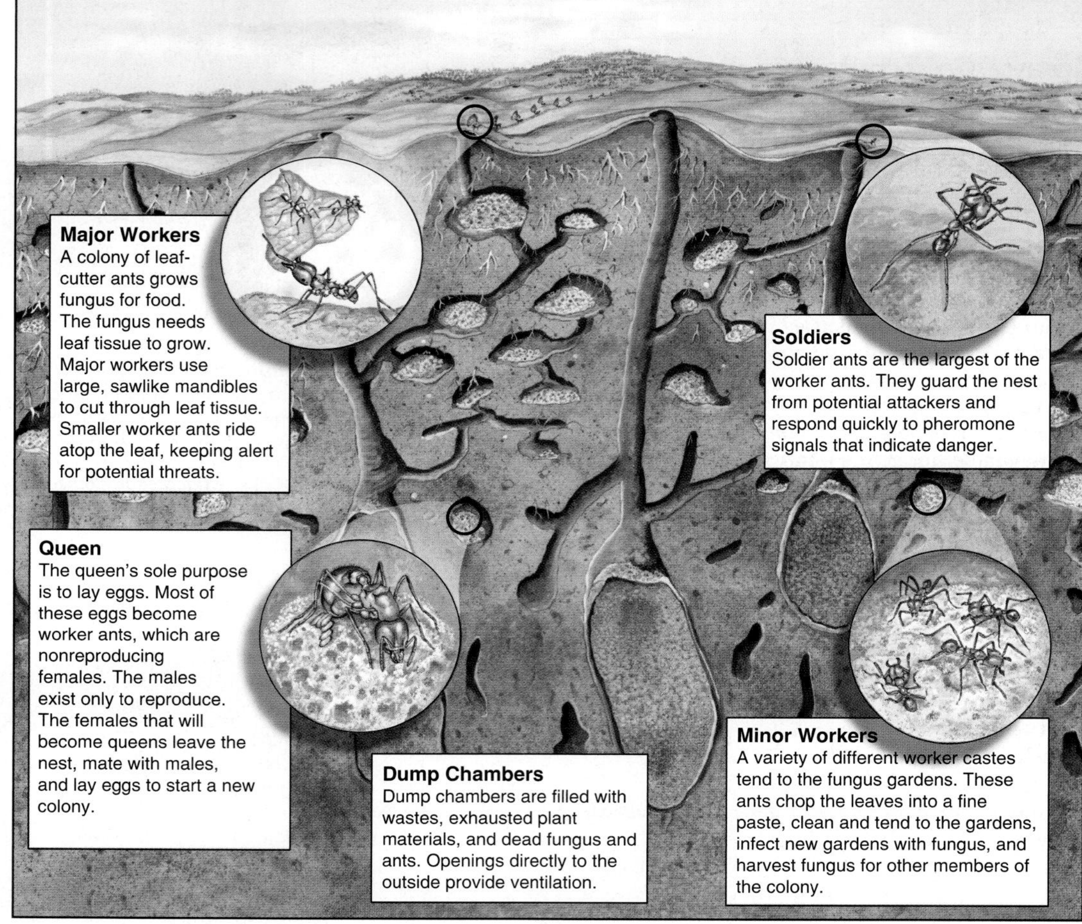

Major Workers
A colony of leaf-cutter ants grows fungus for food. The fungus needs leaf tissue to grow. Major workers use large, sawlike mandibles to cut through leaf tissue. Smaller worker ants ride atop the leaf, keeping alert for potential threats.
Soldiers
Soldier ants are the largest of the worker ants. They guard the nest from potential attackers and respond quickly to pheromone signals that indicate danger.
Queen
The queen's sole purpose is to lay eggs. Most of these eggs become worker ants, which are nonreproducing females. The males exist only to reproduce. The females that will become queens leave the nest, mate with males, and lay eggs to start a new colony.
Dump Chambers
Dump chambers are filled with wastes, exhausted plant materials, and dead fungus and ants. Openings directly to the outside provide ventilation.
Minor Workers
A variety of different worker castes tend to the fungus gardens. These ants chop the leaves into a fine paste, clean and tend to the gardens, infect new gardens with fungus, and harvest fungus for other members of the colony.

▲ **Figure 28–20**  **Some insects, such as these tropical leaf-cutter ants, form societies.** In a tropical leaf-cutter society, only a single queen reproduces. The queen can produce thousands of eggs in a single day. Several different castes of leaf-cutter ants perform all other tasks within the colony. They care for the queen and her eggs and young; they grow fungus for food; and they build, maintain, and defend the colony's home. One group of workers even cultivates bacteria that produce antibiotics! These antibiotics prevent the growth of parasitic molds on the fungus that the ants use for food.

Insect Societies

Just as people form teams that work together toward a common goal, some insects live and work together in groups. Unlike people, however, insects act instinctively rather than voluntarily. **Ants, bees, termites, and some of their relatives form complex associations called societies.** A **society** is a group of closely related animals of the same species that work together for the benefit of the whole group. Insect societies may consist of more than 7 million individuals. A tropical leaf-cutter ant colony is shown in **Figure 28–20.**

Castes Within a society, individuals may be specialized to perform particular tasks, or roles. These are performed by groups of individuals called **castes.** Each caste has a body form specialized for its role. The basic castes are reproductive females called queens (which lay eggs), reproductive males, and workers. Most insect societies have only one queen, which is typically the largest individual in the colony.

BIO INSIGHTS

FACTS AND FIGURES

Life in a honeybee colony

In a honeybee colony, the queen bee most of the time does little more than eat honey and lay eggs that will develop into workers. In the spring, workers build two kinds of enlarged brood cells in the honeycomb. Into one set of the cells, the queen deposits unfertilized eggs that develop into male drones. Into the other set of enlarged cells, workers place special salivary-gland secretions that turn their honey into "royal jelly." The fertilized eggs that the queen deposits in these cells develop rapidly into large pupae that emerge as new queens. In the meantime, the workers lose interest in the old queen. Eventually, she leaves the hive with a few thousand of her daughters and a number of drones in a swarming flight to found a new colony.

Communication in Societies A sophisticated system of communication is necessary for the functioning of a society. Each species of social insect has its own "language" of visual, touch, sound, and chemical signals that convey information among members of the colony. When a worker ant finds food, for example, she leaves behind a trail of a special pheromone as she heads back to the nest. Her nest mates can then detect her trail to the food by using sensory hairs on their antennae.

Honeybees communicate with complex movements as well as with pheromones. Worker bees are able to convey information about the type, quality, direction, and distance of a food source by "dancing." As shown in **Figure 28–21,** bees have two basic dances: a round dance and a waggle dance. In the round dance, the bee that has found food circles first one way and then the other, over and over again. This dance tells the other bees that there is food within a relatively short distance from the hive. The frequency with which the dancing bee changes direction indicates the quality of the food source: The more frequent the changes in direction, the greater the energy value of the food.

In the waggle dance, the bee that has found food runs forward in a straight line while waggling her abdomen. She circles around one way, runs in a straight line again, and circles around the other way. The waggle dance tells the other bees that the food is a longer distance away. The longer the bee takes to perform the straight run and the more she waggles, the farther away the food. The direction of the straight run indicates in which direction the food is to be found. The angle of the bee indicates the direction of the food in relation to the sun. For example, if the dancer runs straight up the vertical part of the honeycomb, the food is in the same direction as the sun.

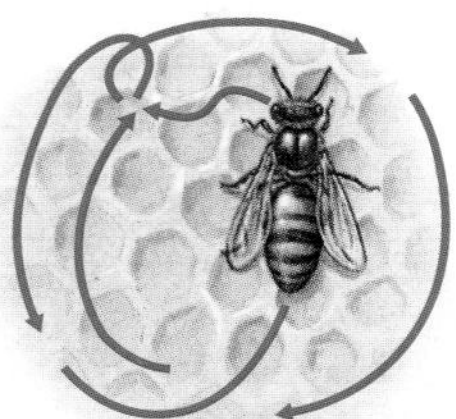

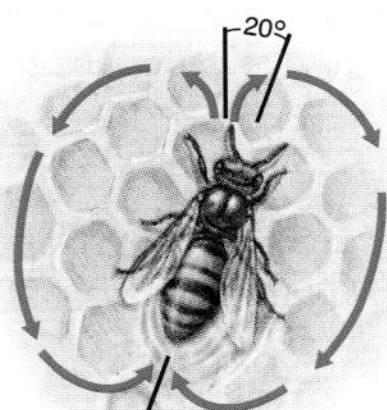

▲ **Figure 28–21** Bees use dances to communicate information about food sources. The round dance indicates that food is fairly close to the hive. The waggle dance indicates that food is farther away. **Interpreting Graphics** ***In what direction does the food lie, according to this bee's waggle dance?***

28–3 Section Assessment

1. **Key Concept** Describe the basic body plan of an insect.
2. **Key Concept** Compare the processes of incomplete and complete metamorphosis. Which involves a dramatic change in form?
3. **Key Concept** Describe the organization of a leaf-cutter ant society. What are the roles of the different castes?
4. What information is passed on by the dances of honeybees? Compare the messages of both types of dances.
5. **Critical Thinking Drawing Conclusions** The compound eyes of insects are better at detecting movement than the fine details of an image. Why might the ability to detect movement be more important in insects than in some other animals, such as humans?

iTEXT **Assessment** Use iText to review the important concepts in Section 28–3.

MAKING CONNECTIONS

Cells and Societies

Recall from Chapter 7 that the cells in multicellular organisms are specialized to perform specific functions. Compare the individual cells in an organism with the individual members of an insect society.

28–3 Section Assessment

1. Insects have a body divided into three parts—head, thorax, and abdomen. Three pairs of legs are attached to the thorax.
2. Incomplete metamorphosis: the immature forms, called nymphs, gradually acquire adult structures; appearance is similar in nymphs and adults. Complete metamorphosis: larvae change into adults, and the body is completely remodeled, a dramatic change in form.
3. The society consists of the queen, who reproduces; males, who mate with the queen; and various castes of female workers, who perform tasks such as growing fungus.
4. The dances communicate the quality, distance, and direction of food. A round dance indicates that food is closer than a waggle dance.
5. Sample answer: Most insects are small. An ability to detect motion helps them escape from larger predators.

3 ASSESS

Evaluate Understanding

Have students turn back to the labeled drawing of a grasshopper in Figure 28–4. Ask them to explain what characteristics the grasshopper has that make it an insect and not a crustacean or a chelicerate.

Reteach

Ask students to look at one of the ants shown in Figure 28–20. Then, call on volunteers to explain the structures that make up that insect and how those structures help the organism carry out the essential functions.

MAKING CONNECTIONS

Students may say that both cells and members of an insect society may be specialized to perform specific functions. Cells are often part of an organism, whereas members of an insect society are each individual organisms.

Use the iText to review the key concepts in Section 28–3.

Answer to . . .

Figure 28–21 *The food lies in the direction that is 20° from the position of the sun.*

Section 28–4

1 FOCUS

Objectives

28.4.1 ***Identify*** the distinguishing features of echinoderms.
28.4.2 ***Describe*** the functions carried out by the water vascular system of echinoderms.
28.4.3 ***Compare*** the different classes of echinoderms.

Guide for Reading

Vocabulary Preview

Suggest that students preview the meaning of the Vocabulary terms in the section by skimming the text to find the boldfaced words and their meanings.

Reading Strategy

Have students preview the photographs of the echinoderms shown in the section and make a list of questions they have about the form, function, and diversity of these animals. Then, as they read, they should write down the answers to their questions.

2 INSTRUCT

What Is an Echinoderm?

Meet Diverse Needs

To help students with limited English proficiency, write the word *oral* on the chalkboard. Then, ask: **What does this word mean?** *(Having to do with the mouth)* **Which surface of an echinoderm is the oral surface?** *(The side with the mouth)* Write *ab-* = *away from* on the board. **Which side is the aboral surface?** *(The side opposite the mouth)* You may want to have a volunteer point out the oral and aboral surfaces on an actual specimen. **Learning modality: verbal**

28–4 Echinoderms

Guide for Reading

 **Key Concepts**
- What are the distinguishing features of echinoderms?
- What functions are carried out by the water vascular system of echinoderms?
- What are the different classes of echinoderms?

Vocabulary
endoskeleton
water vascular system
madreporite
tube foot

Reading Strategy: Using Visuals Before you read, preview **Figure 28–23.** As you read, notice where in the sea star each function occurs.

One of the most unusual sights along the seashore might be the sea stars, sea urchins, and sand dollars that have washed up on the beach. These animals look like stars, pincushions, and coins. They are all echinoderms (ee-KY-noh-durmz), members of the phylum Echinodermata. *Echino-* means "spiny," and *dermis* means "skin." If you have ever touched a sea star, you will know why this name is appropriate. The skin of echinoderms is stretched over an internal skeleton, or **endoskeleton,** that is formed of hardened plates of calcium carbonate. These plates give the animal a bumpy and irregular texture. Echinoderms live only in the sea. Some are delicate, brightly colored, feathery-armed creatures. Others look like mud-brown half-rotten cucumbers!

What Is an Echinoderm?

The body plan of echinoderms is like no other in the animal kingdom. Adult echinoderms typically have no anterior or posterior end and lack cephalization. However, the bodies of most echinoderms are two-sided. The side in which the mouth is located is called the oral surface, and the opposite side is called the aboral surface.

Echinoderms are characterized by spiny skin, an internal skeleton, a water vascular system, and suction-cuplike structures called tube feet. Most adult echinoderms exhibit five-part radial symmetry. The body parts, which usually occur in multiples of five, are arranged around the central body like the spokes of a wheel. The brittle star in **Figure 28–22** exhibits this kind of symmetry. Although radial symmetry is characteristic of simpler animals such as cnidarians, echinoderms are actually more closely related to humans and other vertebrates. The larvae of echinoderms are bilaterally symmetrical, indicating that body symmetry evolved differently in this group than in simpler animals. Also, echinoderms are deuterostomes, animals in which the blastopore develops into an anus. This type of development is found in echinoderms and vertebrates, indicating that these groups are closely related.

◀ **Figure 28–22** **Echinoderms such as this brittle star have spiny skin, five-part radial symmetry, an internal skeleton, a water vascular system, and suction-cuplike structures called tube feet.** Observe that the brittle star has five arms. The bodies of most echinoderms are divided into parts that are multiples of five.

TIME SAVER — SECTION REVIEW

Print:
- ***Teaching Resources,*** Section Review 28–4, Chapter 28 Design an Experiment
- ***Guided Reading and Study Workbook,*** Section 28–4
- ***Issues and Decision Making,*** 28–2

Technology:
- ***iText,*** Section 28–4

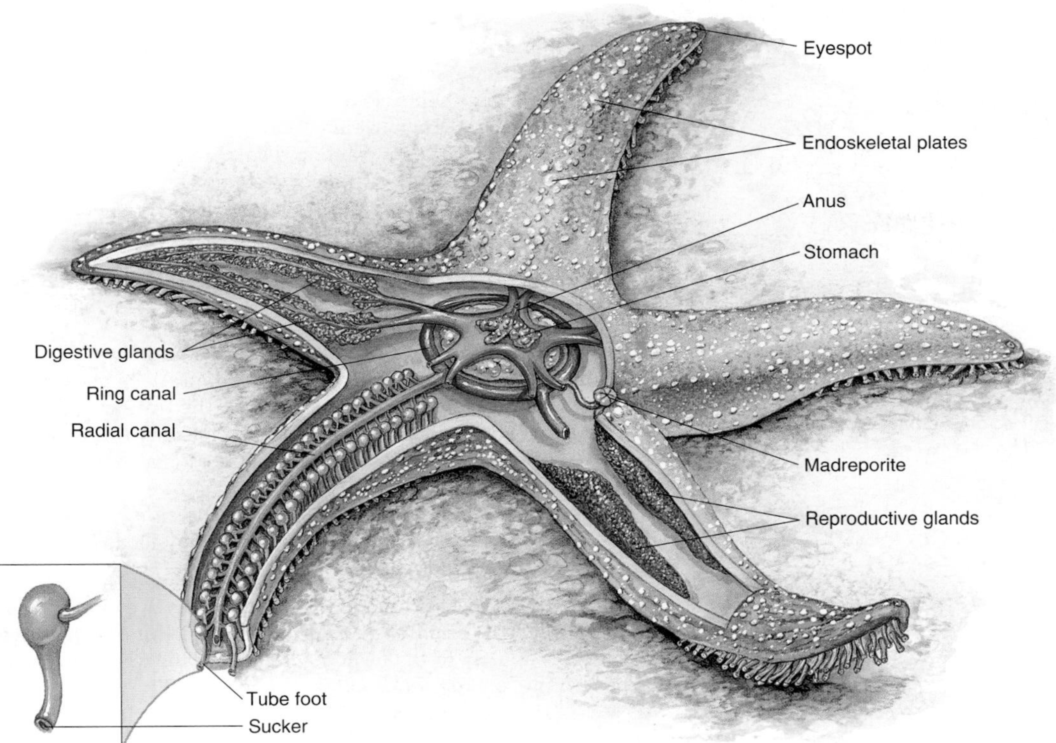

▲ **Figure 28–23** The most distinctive system of echinoderms is the water vascular system, shown here in a sea star. **The water vascular system, which extends throughout the body, functions in respiration, circulation, and movement.**

Form and Function in Echinoderms

A unique feature of echinoderms is a system of internal tubes called a **water vascular system,** which is shown in **Figure 28–23.** **The water vascular system, which is filled with fluid, carries out many essential body functions in echinoderms, including respiration, circulation, and movement.** It opens to the outside through a sievelike structure called a **madreporite** (MAD-ruh-pawr-yt). In sea stars, the madreporite connects to a ring canal that forms a circle around the animal's mouth. From the ring canal, five radial canals extend along body segments.

Attached to each radial canal are hundreds of tube feet. A **tube foot** is a structure that operates much like a suction cup. Each tube foot has a sucker on the end. Muscles pull the center of the sucker upwards, forming a cup shape. This action creates suction on the surface to which the foot is attached, so the tube foot pulls on the surface. Hundreds of tube feet acting together create enormous force, allowing echinoderms to "walk" and even to pull open shelled prey such as clams.

CHECKPOINT *What is the system of internal tubes in echinoderms?*

Form and Function in Echinoderms

Use Visuals

Figure 28–23 Ask students: **What body systems does a sea star have?** *(Digestive system, reproductive system, water vascular system, and nervous system)* **What structures are part of the water vascular system?** *(The madreporite, ring canal, radial canal, and tube feet)* **What essential body functions does the water vascular system carry out in an echinoderm?** *(Respiration, circulation, and movement)*

Demonstration

Display a preserved sea star. (Rinse excess preservative from the specimen, and place it in a dissecting pan.) Invite students to examine the sea star. After students have examined the sea star, ask: **What are some typical animal traits that a sea star appears not to have?** *(Answers will vary. Students might notice the absence of a head and sense organs.)* **Does the body appear to be segmented?** *(No)* Point out that the absence of segmentation is one indication that echinoderms are not close relatives of annelids and arthropods. Then, ask: **What type of symmetry does a sea star have?** *(A sea star exhibits radial symmetry.)* Review the difference between bilateral and radial symmetry, if necessary.

PRESENTATIONS MADE EASY!

The Presentation Assistant Plus contains the Prentice Hall Presentation Pro and the Transparencies, which provide easy-to-follow visual support for every step of this lesson. If you have a computer presentation station, use Prentice Hall Presentation Pro Section 28–4, or use the transparencies listed here.

Section 28–4: **Interest Grabber**
Section Outline
Compare/Contrast Table
Figure 28–23

Answer to . . .

CHECKPOINT *The water vascular system*

Build Science Skills

Using Models Divide the class into small groups, and give each group a small suction cup. Challenge students to make the suction cup adhere to a vertical surface for at least one minute. (*Through trial and error, students will discover that the surface must be smooth and that the cup will stay in place longer if it is first moistened.*) Ask groups to share their findings. Discuss how an echinoderm's tube feet are like suction cups.

Build Science Skills

Observing Divide the class into pairs, and give each pair a preserved or live sea star and a dissecting tray. Make sure students wear goggles, disposable gloves, and lab aprons for this activity. (Caution students to keep their hands away from their faces throughout this activity and to wash their hands afterward, because the preservative used to preserve the organism may cause skin and eye irritation.) Students should observe the sea star, make a sketch of what they see, and label all structures they can identify. Advise students to compare the two sides of the sea star and look especially for its tube feet. Once they have finished their sketches, ask students to explain in writing the purpose of each part they labeled in their drawings.

SCIENCE NEWS®

Encourage students to visit **www.phschool.com** for the most current information on this topic.

▲ **Figure 28–24** Echinoderms use all types of feeding methods. Sea stars, like the one shown above, are carnivores that typically feed on mussels and other bivalves. **Comparing and Contrasting** *How do other groups of echinoderms feed?*

Feeding Echinoderms have several methods of feeding. Sea urchins use five-part jawlike structures to scrape algae from rocks. Sea lilies use tube feet along their arms to capture floating plankton. Sea cucumbers move like bulldozers across the ocean floor, taking in sand and detritus. Sea stars usually feed on mollusks such as clams and mussels, as shown in **Figure 28–24.** Once the prey's shell is open, the sea star pushes its stomach out through its mouth, pours out enzymes, and digests the mollusk in its own shell. Then the sea star pulls its stomach and the partially digested prey into its mouth.

Respiration and Circulation Other than the water vascular system, echinoderms have few adaptations to carry out respiration or circulation. In most species, the thin-walled tissue of the tube feet provides the main surface for respiration. In some species, small outgrowths called skin gills also function in gas exchange.

Circulation of needed materials and wastes takes place throughout the water vascular system. Oxygen, food, and wastes are carried by the water vascular system.

Excretion In most echinoderms, solid wastes are released as feces through the anus. Nitrogen-containing cellular wastes are excreted primarily in the form of ammonia. This waste product is passed into surrounding water through the thin-walled tissues of tube feet and skin gills.

Response As you might expect in animals that have no head, echinoderms do not have a highly developed nervous system. Most have a nerve ring that surrounds the mouth, and radial nerves that connect the ring with the body sections. Most echinoderms also have scattered sensory cells that detect light, gravity, and chemicals released by potential prey.

Movement Most echinoderms move using tube feet and thin layers of muscle fibers attached to their endoskeleton. An echinoderm's mobility is determined in part by the structure of its endoskeleton. Sand dollars and sea urchins have movable spines attached to the endoskeleton. Sea stars and brittle stars have flexible joints that enable them to use their arms for locomotion. In sea cucumbers, the plates of the endoskeleton are reduced and contained inside a soft, muscular body wall. These echinoderms crawl along the ocean floor by the combined action of tube feet and the muscles of the body wall.

Reproduction Echinoderms reproduce by external fertilization. In most sea star species, the sexes are separate. Sperm are produced in testes, and eggs are produced in ovaries. Both types of gametes are shed into open water, where fertilization takes place. The larvae, which have bilateral symmetry, swim around for some time and then swim to the ocean bottom, where they develop into adults that have radial symmetry.

CHECKPOINT *How do echinoderms move?*

KEEP CURRENT WITH . . . SCIENCE NEWS®

To find out more about the topics in this chapter, go to: **www.phschool.com**

BIO INSIGHTS

FACTS AND FIGURES

Are echinoderms really invertebrates?
Although the basic nervous system and lack of a brain appear to place echinoderms among the very simple animals, they have some structures more typical of complex animals, including a unique internal skeleton. Hard nodules of calcium carbonate called ossicles are embedded in the body walls and surrounded by living tissues, providing the strength and protection of a mollusk shell. Many scientists wonder if these animals should really be classified with the invertebrates. Although echinoderms do not have backbones, their larvae appear to have much in common with a wormlike ancestor of the vertebrates. Also, the ossicles of the brittle star fit together much like the vertebrae of a backbone. There are far fewer echinoderm species living today than exist in the fossil record, which may indicate that this phylum is left over from a branch of animal evolution that did not prove to be particularly successful.

Groups of Echinoderms

There are roughly 7000 species of echinoderms—all of which live in the world's oceans. **Classes of echinoderms include sea urchins and sand dollars; brittle stars; sea cucumbers; sea stars; sea lilies and feather stars.** Some of these echinoderms are shown in **Figure 28–25.**

Sea Urchins and Sand Dollars This class includes sea urchins and disk-shaped sand dollars. These echinoderms are unique in having large, solid plates that form a box around their internal organs. Many are detritivores or grazers that eat large quantities of algae. They defend themselves in different ways. Sand dollars often burrow under layers of sand or mud. Some sea urchins wedge themselves in rock crevices during the day, whereas others defend themselves using long, sharp spines.

Brittle Stars Brittle stars are common in many parts of the sea, especially on coral reefs. They have slender, flexible arms and can scuttle around quite rapidly to escape predators. In addition to using speed for protection, brittle stars shed one or more arms when attacked. The detached arm keeps moving, distracting the predator while the brittle star escapes. Brittle stars are filter feeders and detritivores that hide by day and wander around under cover of darkness.

Sea Cucumbers Sea cucumbers look like warty, moving pickles. Most sea cucumbers are detritus feeders that move along the sea floor while sucking up organic matter and the remains of other animals and plants. Herds containing hundreds of thousands of sea cucumbers roam across the deep-sea floor.

Sea Stars Sea stars are probably the best-known group of echinoderms. They move by creeping slowly along the ocean floor. Most are carnivorous, preying on bivalves that they encounter. Many sea stars have incredible abilities to repair themselves when damaged. If a sea star is pulled into pieces, each piece will grow into a new animal, as long as it contains a portion of the central part of the body.

Figure 28–25 **Sea urchins, brittle stars, sea cucumbers, and sea stars represent different classes of echinoderms.** Observe the characteristics of these representatives of each class.

Long-Spined Sea Urchin

Brittle Star

Red-Lined Sea Cucumber

Sun Star

Groups of Echinoderms

Address Misconceptions

Explain that sea stars and starfish are different names for the same kind of echinoderm. Many students, who may have seen starfish on a beach or in a coastal souvenir shop, may think that a starfish is some kind of fish. Point out that echinoderms are invertebrates and fishes are vertebrates, and thus a starfish cannot be classified as a fish. Similarly, some students may be misled by the echinoderm names *sea cucumber* and *sea lily.* Discuss how these animals may have gotten their names, and emphasize that they are animals, not plants.

Meet Diverse Needs

To reinforce at-risk students' understanding of echinoderm classification, show students photos or slides of a variety of different echinoderms, making sure that all classes of echinoderms are represented by at least one example. Ask volunteers to classify each echinoderm as it is shown according to the class to which it belongs. As each echinoderm class is mentioned, call on students at random to review the characteristics of members of that class, such as how it feeds or moves. **Learning modality: visual**

BIO INSIGHTS

FACTS AND FIGURES

Millions of brittle stars

Brittle stars are the most abundant echinoderms, both in terms of numbers of species and of individuals. About 2000 species are found worldwide, from the seashore to depths as great as 6000 meters. In some places, millions of individuals live in clusters on the ocean floor. Brittle stars move by crawling or clinging with their flexible arms. The arms are quite flexible moving back and forth—that is, on a plane perpendicular to the line from the oral surface to the aboral surface. But the arms of a brittle star are not at all flexible moving up and down—that is, on a plane parallel to the same line. For that reason, the arms are "brittle" and break off easily.

Answers to . . .

CHECKPOINT *Most echinoderms move using tube feet and thin layers of muscle fibers attached to their endoskeleton.*

Figure 28–24 *Sea urchins use five-part jaws to scrape algae from rocks. Sea lilies use tube feet along their arms to capture floating plankton. Sea cucumbers move like bulldozers across the ocean floor, taking in sand and detritus.*

Ecology of Echinoderms

Meet Diverse Needs

Encourage students who need extra challenges to investigate further the threat that the crown-of-thorns poses to coral reefs. Suggest that students write a report on the threat using library and Internet resources and share their findings with the class. **Learning modality: verbal**

3 ASSESS

Evaluate Understanding

Ask students to write a description of an echinoderm's water vascular system and what functions it serves.

Reteach

Have students make their own drawing of the labeled sea star in Figure 28–23. Have students also define each of the terms shown as labels.

Take It to the NET

Most sea stars spread their stomachs over a food source and suck in partially digested nutrients; asexual reproduction occurs in some sea stars. Many sea cucumbers use tentacles to take in organic detritus; sea cucumbers usually carry their embryos on the exterior of their bodies. Many sea urchins feed using a complex apparatus called Aristotle's lantern; sea urchins possess multiple sex organs. For additional information, visit **www.phschool.com**

Use iText to review the key concepts in Section 28–4.

Answer to . . .

Figure 28–26 *Sea lilies live attached to the ocean floor by a long stalk.*

Figure 28–26 Sea lilies belong to the most ancient class of echinoderms, known as crinoids. The red crinoid (top) is one of the few species of this class that are alive today. This stalked crinoid fossil (bottom) is an example of the types of crinoids that dominated Earth during the Paleozoic Era. **Comparing and Contrasting** *How are sea lilies different from other echinoderms?*

Sea Lilies and Feather Stars These filter feeders, which have long, feathery arms, make up the oldest class of echinoderms. Sea lilies and feather stars are common in tropical oceans today, and a rich fossil record shows that they were distributed widely throughout ancient seas. Like modern sea lilies, their fossilized ancestors lived attached to the ocean bottom by a long, stemlike stalk, as seen in **Figure 28–26.** Many modern feather stars live on coral reefs, where they perch on top of rocks and use their tube feet to catch floating plankton.

Ecology of Echinoderms

Echinoderms are common in a variety of marine habitats. In many areas, a sudden rise or fall in the number of echinoderms can cause major changes to populations of other marine organisms. Sea urchins help control the distribution of algae and other forms of marine life. Sea stars are important carnivores that help control the numbers of other organisms such as clams and corals.

A major threat to coral reefs is the sea star called the crown-of-thorns. This echinoderm is named for the rows of poisonous spines located along its arms. It feeds almost exclusively on coral. In the Great Barrier Reef of Australia—one of the largest reef systems in the world—this organism has destroyed extensive areas of coral.

28–4 Section Assessment

1. **Key Concept** What is an echinoderm?
2. **Key Concept** What is the water vascular system? How is it important to echinoderms?
3. **Key Concept** List the major classes of echinoderms and describe their characteristics.
4. Echinoderms are deuterostomes. What does this indicate about their relationship to other animals?
5. **Critical Thinking Inferring** Why is tearing a sea star apart and throwing it back into the water an ineffective way of trying to reduce sea star populations?

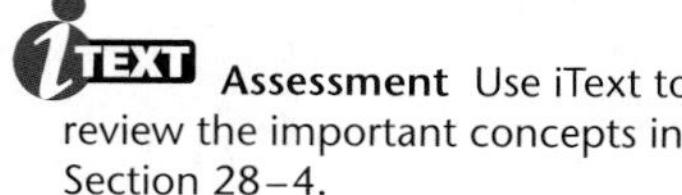

Assessment Use iText to review the important concepts in Section 28–4.

Take It to the NET

Describe how sea stars, sea cucumbers, and sea urchins eat and reproduce. Share this information with your class in the form of a report. Be sure to include drawings or photographs. Use the links provided in the Biology area at the Prentice Hall Web site for help in completing this activity: **www.phschool.com**

28–4 Section Assessment

1. An echinoderm has a spiny skin, an internal skeleton, a water vascular system, and tube feet. Most have five-part radial symmetry.
2. The water vascular system is a system of internal tubes. The system carries out respiration, circulation, and movement.
3. Sea urchins and sand dollars have plates that form a box around their internal organs. Brittle stars have long, flexible arms and can move quickly. Sea cucumbers look like cucumbers. Sea stars move by creeping slowly and can repair themselves when damaged. Sea lilies and feather stars have a stalk by which they attach to the ocean floor.
4. Echinoderms are more closely related to chordates than to other invertebrates, most of which are protostomes.
5. If a sea star is pulled into pieces, each piece will usually grow into a new animal.

Design an Experiment

Observing Ant Behavior

Unlike most insects, many ant species live in large, social groups. The ants within each group work together to support the group. In this investigation, you will design an experiment to determine how ants respond to members of other colonies and other species.

Problem **How do ants respond to members of other colonies and other species?**

Materials

- covered petri dish containing 10 ants of species A from the same colony (**CAUTION:** *Do not use fire ants.*)
- hand lens or dissecting microscope
- field guide
- watch or clock with a second hand
- 3 covered petri dishes, each containing 5 ants of species A from different colonies
- covered petri dish containing 5 ants from species B (**CAUTION:** *Do not use fire ants.*)

Skills Predicting, Drawing Conclusions

Design Your Experiment 

Part A: Observing Ants That Are Related

1. Obtain a petri dish containing 10 ants from the same colony. Look at the ants under a hand lens or dissecting microscope. Use a field guide to identify the species to which they belong.
2. For 30 seconds, count the number of ants that are fighting with one another. Record this number on a sheet of paper. If the ants are not fighting, write "0."
3. **Predicting** Record your prediction of whether ants from separate colonies of the same species will fight, and whether ants of two different species will fight.

Part B: Observing Ants That Are Not Related

4. **Designing Experiments** Design experiments to test your predictions. Write a hypothesis for each experiment and control all variables except the one you are testing. **CAUTION:** *Ants are delicate, and some have stinging bites. Do not try to pick them up with your hands.* Have your teacher check your plan before you begin to perform your experiment.

Analyze and Conclude

1. **Observing** Did most of the ants fight in step 2? How would you explain the behavior you observed?
2. **Observing** What happened when you put ants from two different colonies of the same species together? When you put ants from two different species together? Were your predictions correct?
3. **Drawing Conclusions** How do you think the behavior you observed helps the ants survive?

Go Further

Posing Questions Think of some other aspects of ants and their behavior that you would like to learn about. For example, you might be curious about how different environmental conditions affect an ant colony, or which foods individual ants prefer. Write your ideas as a series of questions. Choose one of your questions and find an answer to it, either by finding information in reference materials or designing an experiment. Before performing any experiments, obtain your teacher's approval.

Analyze and Conclude

1. Most of the ants did not fight. Ants from the same colony almost never fight one another. Because they are part of the same colony, they need to cooperate, not compete, to survive.

2. Ants of the same species, but from different colonies, will usually fight. (However, Pharaoh ants from different colonies will not fight.) Ants from different species will almost always fight. Students should explain why their predictions were or were not correct.

3. Ants must compete for resources such as food. By attacking ants from other colonies or species, they reduce the number of ant colonies that compete for the same resources.

Design an Experiment

Objective Students will observe how ants respond to members of the same colony, other colonies, and other species.

Skills Focus **Observing, Predicting, Drawing Conclusions**

Time 45 minutes

Advance Prep Collect or order ants in advance. Freshly collected wild ants are preferable. Those from supply houses have been separated from the queen and colony for so long that they have lost their identifying odors. Attract ants by putting a piece of a sugary food near cracks in a sidewalk. The pavement ant, *Tetramorium caespitum,* is a good choice for species A. It is common in the eastern United States, California, and Washington. Collect ants from two widely separated areas to ensure that they are from different colonies. Pharaoh ants, *Monomorium pharaonis,* are a good choice for species B.

Safety Students should not touch the ants. Make sure not to use biting species such as fire ants or harvester ants, or destructive species such as carpenter ants. Check state and local regulations before ordering ants.

Teaching Tips
- Explain that ants often communicate and identify one another by touch. Fights involve grasping with the mandibles.
- Remind students to record the number of ants fighting, not the number of fights. One fight may involve several ants.

Expected Outcomes Students should observe that ants won't fight members of their own colony but will fight members of other colonies.

Go Further

Students doing library research might look for information under the following topics: ants, insects, insect societies, animal behavior. Supervise all Internet research. If students choose to perform experiments, check and approve their plans before allowing them to begin.

Chapter 28 Study Guide

Study Tip

Divide the class into pairs, and have students quiz each other about the Vocabulary and the Key Concepts.

Thinking Visually

The concept map for arthropods should include three major groups: crustaceans, chelicerates, and uniramians. Under each of the groups students should include the groups of organisms discussed in Section 28–2. For example, uniramians include centipedes, millipedes, and insects. The concept map for echinoderms should include five classes: sea urchins and sand dollars, brittle stars, sea cucumbers, and sea lilies and feather stars.

Chapter 28 Assessment

Reviewing Content

1. b **2.** a **3.** b **4.** b **5.** b **6.** d **7.** d **8.** d **9.** c **10.** b

Understanding Concepts

11. The variety of respiratory organs among arthropods enables arthropods to live in both terrestrial and aquatic environments. Terrestrial arthropods obtain oxygen through tracheal tubes or book lungs. Aquatic arthropods use gills or book gills to remove oxygen from water.

12. Most terrestrial arthropods dispose of nitrogen-containing waste by using Malpighian tubes, which remove wastes from the blood, concentrate them, and then add them to undigested food before it leaves via the anus. In aquatic arthropods cellular wastes diffuse from the body into the water.

13. All have a brain. Two nerves that run around the esophagus connect the brain to a ventral nerve cord. Ganglia along the cord coordinate movements of the legs and wings.

14. The part of the exoskeleton that covers the cephalothorax

15. Decapods are motile, whereas barnacles are sessile. Barnacles have no abdominal segments and do not use mandibles.

16. A mouthpart that is adapted for biting and grinding food

Chapter 28 Study Guide

28–1 Introduction to the Arthropods

Key Concepts

- Arthropods have a segmented body, a tough exoskeleton, and jointed appendages.
- In many groups of arthropods, continuing evolution has led to fewer body segments and highly specialized appendages for feeding, movement, and other functions.
- When they outgrow their exoskeletons, arthropods undergo periods of molting.

Vocabulary

exoskeleton, p. 715
chitin, p. 715
appendage, p. 715
tracheal tube, p. 717
spiracle, p. 717
book lung, p. 717
Malpighian tubule, p. 717
molting, p. 719

28–2 Groups of Arthropods

Key Concepts

- Arthropods are classified based on the number and structure of their body segments and appendages, particularly their mouthparts.
- Crustaceans typically have two pairs of branched antennae, two or three body sections, and chewing mouthparts called mandibles.
- Chelicerates have mouthparts called chelicerae and two body sections, and most have four pairs of walking legs.
- Uniramians have jaws, one pair of antennae, and unbranched appendages.

Vocabulary

cephalothorax, p. 721
thorax, p. 721
abdomen, p. 721
carapace, p. 721
mandible, p. 721
cheliped, p. 721
swimmeret, p. 721
chelicera, p. 722
pedipalp, p. 722
spinneret, p. 723

28–3 Insects

Key Concepts

- Insects have a body divided into three parts—head, thorax, and abdomen. Three pairs of legs are attached to the thorax.
- The growth and development of insects usually involve metamorphosis, which is a process of changing shape and form. Insects undergo either incomplete metamorphosis or complete metamorphosis.
- Ants, bees, termites, and some of their relatives form complex associations called societies.

Vocabulary

incomplete metamorphosis, p. 729
nymph, p. 729
complete metamorphosis, p. 729
pupa, p. 729
pheromone, p. 731
society, p. 732
caste, p. 732

28–4 Echinoderms

Key Concepts

- Echinoderms are characterized by spiny skin, five-part radial symmetry, an internal skeleton, a water vascular system, and suction-cuplike structures called tube feet.
- The water vascular system carries out many essential body functions in echinoderms, including respiration, circulation, and movement.
- Classes of echinoderms include sea lilies and feather stars, sea stars, brittle stars, sea urchins and sand dollars, and sea cucumbers.

Vocabulary

endoskeleton, p. 734
water vascular system, p. 735
madreporite, p. 735
tube foot, p. 735

Thinking Visually

Construct two concept maps—one for arthropods and the other for echinoderms. Each concept map should show how the members of each phylum are classified. Include specific examples for each group.

TIME SAVER CHAPTER RESOURCES

Print:

- ***Teaching Resources,*** Chapter Vocabulary Review, Graphic Organizer
- ***Chapter Tests: Levels A and B,*** Chapter 28 Test
- ***PH Assessment,*** Practice Test

Technology:

- ***Computer Test Bank,*** Chapter 28 Test
- ***iText,*** Chapter 28 Assessment

Chapter 28 Assessment

Reviewing Content

Choose the letter that best answers the question or completes the statement.

1. All arthropods have
   a. gills.
   b. jointed appendages.
   c. antennae.
   d. chelicerae.

2. An arthropod's exoskeleton performs all of the following functions except
   a. production of gametes.
   b. protection of internal organs.
   c. support of the animal's body.
   d. preventing loss of body water.

3. Most terrestrial arthropods breathe using branched, air-filled structures called
   a. gills. c. book gills.
   b. tracheal tubes. d. book lungs.

4. Most arthropods have
   a. no circulatory system.
   b. an open circulatory system.
   c. a closed circulatory system.
   d. skin gills.

5. Crustaceans are the only arthropods that have
   a. three pairs of legs.
   b. two pairs of antennae.
   c. chitin in their exoskeleton.
   d. chelicerae.

6. Which of the organisms below belongs in the subphylum Chelicerata?

a.

c.

b.

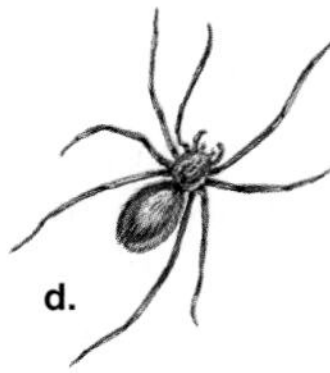
d.

7. Unlike spiders, horseshoe crabs have
   a. antennae. c. mandibles.
   b. a madreporite. d. ten legs.

8. All insects have
   a. two pairs of legs.
   b. two pairs of antennae.
   c. two pairs of wings.
   d. three body sections.

9. Most adult echinoderms show
   a. bilateral symmetry.
   b. top and bottom symmetry.
   c. radial symmetry.
   d. no symmetry.

10. Oxygen is moved around the body of a sea star in its
    a. stemlike stalk. c. madreporite.
    b. water vascular system. d. bony plates.

Understanding Concepts

11. How have the various respiratory structures found in arthropods contributed to their overall success?
12. Compare the process of excretion in terrestrial arthropods with that in aquatic arthropods.
13. Describe the structure of arthropods' nervous system.
14. What is the function of a crustacean's carapace?
15. How are barnacles different from decapods?
16. What is the function of a mandible?
17. Distinguish between chelicerae and pedipalps.
18. How are the mouthparts of mites and ticks adapted to a specific lifestyle?
19. Compare and contrast the body structure of the different groups of uniramians.
20. How have the characteristics of insects contributed to their evolutionary success?
21. Describe some of the special feeding adaptations found in insects.
22. How does the term *society* relate to ants, bees, and termites?
23. Describe the various methods of locomotion found in the echinoderms.
24. Briefly describe the process of sexual reproduction in sea stars.
25. How has the sea star called the crown-of-thorns affected coral reefs?

TIME SAVER HOMEWORK GUIDE

Section:	Questions:
Section 28–1	1–5, 11–14, 35
Section 28–2	6, 7, 15–19, 28, 30, 31
Section 28–3	8, 20–22, 26, 27, 29, 34
Section 28–4	9, 10, 23–25, 32, 33

17. Both chelicerae and pedipalps are appendages adapted as mouthparts. Chelicerae contain fangs used to capture and paralyze prey, and pedipalps are usually modified to handle prey.

18. Ticks and mites are parasites. Their mouthparts are adapted to dig into a host's tissues and suck out fluids.

19. Centipedes have many segments, each with one pair of legs. Millipedes have many segments, each with two pairs of legs. The bodies of insects are divided into three sections—head, thorax, and abdomen—with three pairs of legs attached to the thorax.

20. Some of the characteristics of insects that have contributed to their evolutionary success include the different ways of responding to stimuli, the evolution of flight, and a life cycle in which the young differ from adults in appearance and feeding methods.

21. Insect adaptations for feeding include: mouthparts adapted to specific feeding functions, e.g., grinding or sucking; saliva containing digestive enzymes; in bees, chambers for the storage of food.

22. Ants, bees, and termites form societies in which individuals work together for the benefit of the whole group. Individuals specialize in performing specific roles or tasks.

23. Most echinoderms move using tube feet and thin layers of muscle fibers attached to the endoskeleton. Sand dollars and sea urchins have movable spines attached to the endoskeleton. Sea stars and brittle stars have flexible joints that allow them to use their arms for locomotion. Sea cucumbers use the muscles of the body wall in combination with tube feet to crawl along the ocean floor.

24. The eggs and sperm of sea stars are released into open water, where fertilization occurs. Eventually the larvae, which have bilateral symmetry, swim to the ocean bottom, where they mature into adults that have radial symmetry.

25. The crown-of-thorns feeds on coral and has destroyed extensive areas of the Great Barrier Reef.

Chapter 28 Assessment

Critical Thinking

26. The adaptation enables honeybees to carry pollen from one flower to another, thus pollinating the flowers in the process. The adaptation also enables honeybees to collect food and carry it back to the hive.

27. Crabs have soft shells soon after they molt because the new exoskeleton has not had time to become hardened.

28. The animal is not an insect, because insects have three distinct body regions, one pair of antennae, one pair of compound eyes, three pairs of mouthparts, and three pairs of walking legs.

29. As the temperature decreases, the time for the eggs to hatch increases. It would take about 62 hours for the eggs to hatch at 18°C, 40 hours for them to hatch at 25°C, and 88 hours for them to hatch at 10°C.

30. The movement of the crayfish's legs can increase the amount of oxygen dissolved in the stagnant pool and create a flow of this oxygenated water over the gills, where respiration occurs.

31. Adults and larvae do not compete with one another for food. Also, different types of food may be abundant at different times of the year, and these differences may correlate to stages in the insect's life cycle.

32. Unlike arthropods, echinoderms have spiny skin, radial symmetry, an internal skeleton, a water vascular system, and suction-cuplike structures called tube feet.

33. Pheromones warn of danger and enable males and females to communicate during courtship and mating, thus helping to ensure survival of individuals and species.

34. Proteins are organic compounds needed for the growth and repair of cells. Polysaccharides are complex carbohydrates.

Chapter 28 Assessment

Critical Thinking

26. Applying Concepts The legs and bodies of honeybees are covered with hair that collects pollen and other materials. How is this adaptation helpful to flowering plants and honeybees?

27. Applying Concepts Blue crabs usually have hard shells. During certain times of the year some of the blue crabs have thin, papery shells. In terms of the life processes of arthropods, explain why these blue crabs have soft shells.

28. Classifying An animal is discovered that has an exoskeleton, sucking mouthparts, head fused with thorax, no wings, and four pairs of walking legs. Would you classify the animal as an insect? Explain your answer.

29. Analyzing Data Brine shrimp are small crustaceans found in salty lakes and ponds. The graph shows the effect of water temperature on the time it takes for brine shrimp eggs to hatch. Based on the graph, what can you conclude about the relationship between water temperature and hatching time? How many hours would it take for eggs to hatch at 18°C and at 25°C? Can you predict the amount of time it would take for eggs to hatch at 10°C?

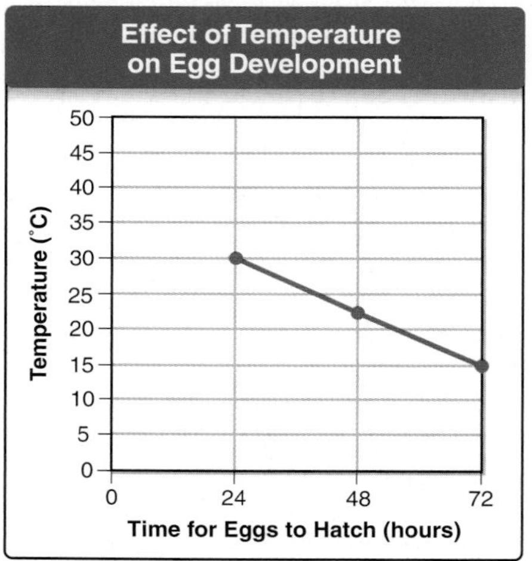

30. Inferring In a stagnant pool of water, a crayfish may spend much of its time lying with one side of its carapace near the surface of the water. In this position, it will move the walking legs on that side in a back-and-forth motion. Explain the value of this behavior.

31. Inferring In many insect species, insect adults and larvae feed on different substances. How might this characteristic help members of those species survive?

32. Comparing and Contrasting How are echinoderms structurally different from arthropods?

33. Applying Concepts What role do pheromones play in insect survival?

34. Making Connections Chitin is made of protein and polysaccharides. What are these two substances? You might want to review relevant concepts in Chapter 2.

Performance-Based Assessment

Around the Neighborhood Make a photograph collection of arthropods in your neighborhood. Use field guides to identify the arthropods in your photographs. Mount the photographs in a display that indicates the major characteristics of arthropods and the various groups of arthropods.

Take It to the NET

What insects do we find in art? What insects affect us psychologically? Visit the Prentice Hall Web site at **www.phschool.com** to learn about a subject called cultural entomology. Then, answer the following questions:

- Which insects are frequently found in Native American myths, and why?
- How did the ancient Chinese regard cicadas?
- What is entomophobia?
- What was the most important use of insects to Australian Aborigines? Give three examples.

Performance-Based Assessment

Student displays should reflect an understanding of the diversity of arthropods as well as the ability to identify the characteristics that place the different groups in the same phylum.

Standardized Test Prep

1. C
2. B
3. B
4. C
5. D
6. C
7. E
8. A
9. B
10. B

Test-Taking Tip If you are taking a long time to answer a question, consider coming back to it later. As you answer the other questions, you may remember the information you needed to answer the skipped question.

Directions: Choose the letter that best answers the question or completes the statement.

1. Mites and ticks are examples of
(A) crustaceans.
(B) swimmerets.
(C) arachnids.
(D) chelicerae.
(E) uniramians.

2. In spiders, the organs that contain the silk glands are called
(A) carapaces.
(B) spinnerets.
(C) swimmerets.
(D) madreporites.
(E) tube feet.

3. Which of these is NOT a characteristic of an echinoderm?
(A) five-part radial symmetry
(B) a pair of antennae
(C) tube feet
(D) a water vascular system
(E) an internal skeleton

Questions 4–8 Each of the lettered choices below refers to the following numbered statements. Select the best lettered choice. A choice may be used once, more than once, or not at all.

(A) Trilobites
(B) Pedipalps
(C) Arachnids
(D) Pheromones
(E) Sea stars

4. Types of animals that have four pairs of walking legs

5. Chemical messengers that affect the behavior or development of other individuals of the same species

6. Group containing spiders, scorpions, ticks, and mites

7. Carnivorous echinoderms that move by creeping slowly along the ocean floor

8. Extinct group of marine arthropods that were abundant more than 500 million years ago

Questions 9–10

A biology student is investigating the relationship between cricket chirps and temperature. She catches a cricket and places it in a jar. She leaves the jar outside, and each day she measures the number of chirps during a 15-second period. At the same time, she records the outside temperature near the cricket. Her data for a 5-day period are shown below.

Relationship Between Temperature and Cricket Chirping

Day	Number of Chirps in 15 Seconds	Outside Temperature (°C)
Monday	31	23
Tuesday	20	16
Wednesday	12	11
Thursday	29	21
Friday	25	19

9. What can the student conclude from this experiment?
(A) Crickets cannot chirp more than 31 times in 15 seconds.
(B) The number of chirps decreases when the temperature decreases.
(C) Crickets never chirp more than 31 times every 15 seconds.
(D) The number of chirps increases when the temperature decreases.
(E) There is no relationship between the number of cricket chirps and temperature.

10. At which of the following temperatures would a cricket be most likely to chirp 9 times in 15 seconds?
(A) 2°C
(B) 10°C
(C) 18°C
(D) 0°C
(E) 25°C

Take It to the NET

• Butterflies and moths are frequently found in Native American myths, because of their beauty, power of flight, and complete metamorphosis.

• The ancient Chinese regarded cicadas as symbols of rebirth or immortality.

• Entomophobia is the fear of insects.

• Insects were an important food for the Australian Aborigines. Examples: moths in New South Wales; witchety grubs (larvae) found in desert *Acacia* bushes; both honeypot ants and the "honeybag" (hive) of stingless native bees as a source of dietary sugar.

For additional information, visit

www.phschool.com

Chapter Planner 29 Comparing Invertebrates

Section and Section Objectives	Time	Activities and Labs
29–1 Invertebrate Evolution, pp. 745–750 **29.1.1** ***Explain*** what the Cambrian Explosion was. **29.1.2** ***Identify*** the modern evolutionary relationships among major groups of living invertebrates. **29.1.3** ***Describe*** the major trends in invertebrate evolution.	**2 period (1 block)**	**SE:** ***Inquiry Activity,*** Which protective covering is best?, p. 744 **TE:** ***Build Science Skills,*** p. 747 **SE:** ***Problem Solving,*** Creating an Imaginary Invertebrate, p. 750
29–2 Form and Function in Invertebrates, pp. 751–758 **29.2.1** ***Describe*** how the different invertebrate phyla carry out their essential life functions.	**3 periods (1 1/2 blocks)**	**TE:** ***Build Science Skills,*** p. 751 **SE:** ***Quick Lab,*** How do clams and crayfish breathe?, p. 753 **TE:** ***Demonstration,*** p. 756 **SE:** ***Design an Experiment,*** Comparing Invertebrate Responses to Stimuli, p. 759
Chapter Assessment, pp. 760–763	**1 period (1/2 block)**	

ACTIVITY PLANNER

SE: ***Inquiry Activity***, p. 744; (15 min.); mollusk shells, arthropod exoskeletons

TE: ***Build Science Skills***, p. 747; (20 min.); live and preserved invertebrates, photos of invertebrates

TE: ***Build Science Skills***, p. 751; (30 min. set up); aquarium; pond water, sediments, plants, and invertebrates

SE: ***Quick Lab***, p. 753; (20 min.); live clam, food coloring, crayfish, small container of water

TE: ***Demonstration***, p. 756; (10 min.); planarians, petri dish, water, flashlight

SE: ***Design an Experiment***, p. 759; (45 min.); dropper pipette, hydra culture, watch glass, dissecting microscope, blunt metal probe, planarian, petri dish, crayfish, brine shrimp, cooked egg yolk, slice of bologna

PLANNING KEY

Ability Levels	
B Basic	For students who need additional help
A Average	For all students
E Enriched	For students who need to be challenged

Components

SE	Student Edition	**GRSW**	Guided Reading and Study Workbook	**IDM**	Issues and Decision Making
TE	Teacher's Edition	**CT**	Chapter Tests: Levels A and B	**CTB**	Computer Test Bank
LMA	Laboratory Manual A	**PHAS**	PH Assessment System	**PA**	Presentation Assistant Plus
LMB	Laboratory Manual B	**LA**	Lab Assessment with Scoring Guide	**BD**	BioDetectives Videotape
TR	Teaching Resources	**BTM**	BioTechnology Manual	**iT**	iText

Program Resources	Assessment	Media and Technology
TR: 29–1, Graphic Organizer B A Enrichment E **GRSW:** 29–1 B A	**SE:** 29–1 Section Assessment, p. 754 **TR:** 29–1, Section Review	**PA:** 29–1 Interest Grabber, Section Outline, Compare/Contrast Table, Figure 9–4 **iT:** Section 29–1
TR: 29–2, Graphic Organizer B A Chapter 29 Design an Experiment B A E **GRSW:** 29–2 B A	**SE:** 29–2 Section Assessment, p. 762 **TR:** 29–2, Section Review	**PA:** 29–2 Interest Grabber, Section Outline, Types of Invertebrate Skeletons, Figure 29–8, Figure 29–9, Figure 29–10, Figure 29–11, Figure 29–12 **iT:** Section 29–2
	SE: Chapter 29 Assessment, pp. 760–763 **TR:** Chapter Vocabulary Review **TB:** Chapter 29 Test **CTB:** Chapter 29 Test **PHAS:** Practice Test	**CTB:** Chapter 29 Test **iT:** Chapter 29 Assessment

PRESSED FOR TIME?

To Preview the Chapter

- Introduce students to Key Concepts and Vocabulary terms in each section.
- Assign the Reading Strategies for each section.

To Cover the Chapter Quickly

- Have students read The Origin of the Invertebrates, Figure 29–4, and Figure 29–5 in Section 29–1, and read all of Section 29–2.
- Assign the Section Review 29–2 and questions 1–10 in Chapter 29 Assessment and questions 1–10 in Chapter 29 Standardized Test Preparation.

To Review the Chapter

- Assign Sections 29–1 and 29–2 in the Guided Reading and Study Workbook.
- Assign Section Reviews for 29–1 and 29–2 and the Chapter Vocabulary Review for Chapter 29 in the Teaching Resources.

ENGAGE/EXPLORE

Inquiry Activity

Objective Students will be able to draw conclusions about the biological costs and benefits of similar adaptations.

Skill Focus **Drawing conclusions**

Materials mollusk shells, arthropod exoskeletons

Time 15 minutes

Advance Prep Among the examples of arthropod exoskeletons you might collect are crab or lobster "shells" and preserved, dried insects from insect collections.

Strategies Check to see that students consider the costs and benefits of a number of characteristics when comparing the protective coverings. These include weight, thickness, and ability to penetrate.

Expected Outcome Students should conclude that mollusk shells provide more protection than arthropod exoskeletons but are more difficult to move around. They should infer that this helps explain why many more arthropods are highly active and more successful out of water, where weight is more important.

Think About It

1. Mollusk shells are more difficult to penetrate because they are thicker.
2. Arthropod exoskeletons are more useful to active, motile animals because they are lighter and therefore easier to carry around.
3. A typical response might suggest that the heavier mollusk shell is better suited to the needs of slow-moving animals because fast-moving animals would have to expend too much energy to carry it around. The speed of many arthropods can make up for their thinner, weaker coverings. The heaviness of the shell makes less difference submerged than on land because of the buoyant force of water, which makes objects feel lighter.

Chapter 29 Comparing Invertebrates

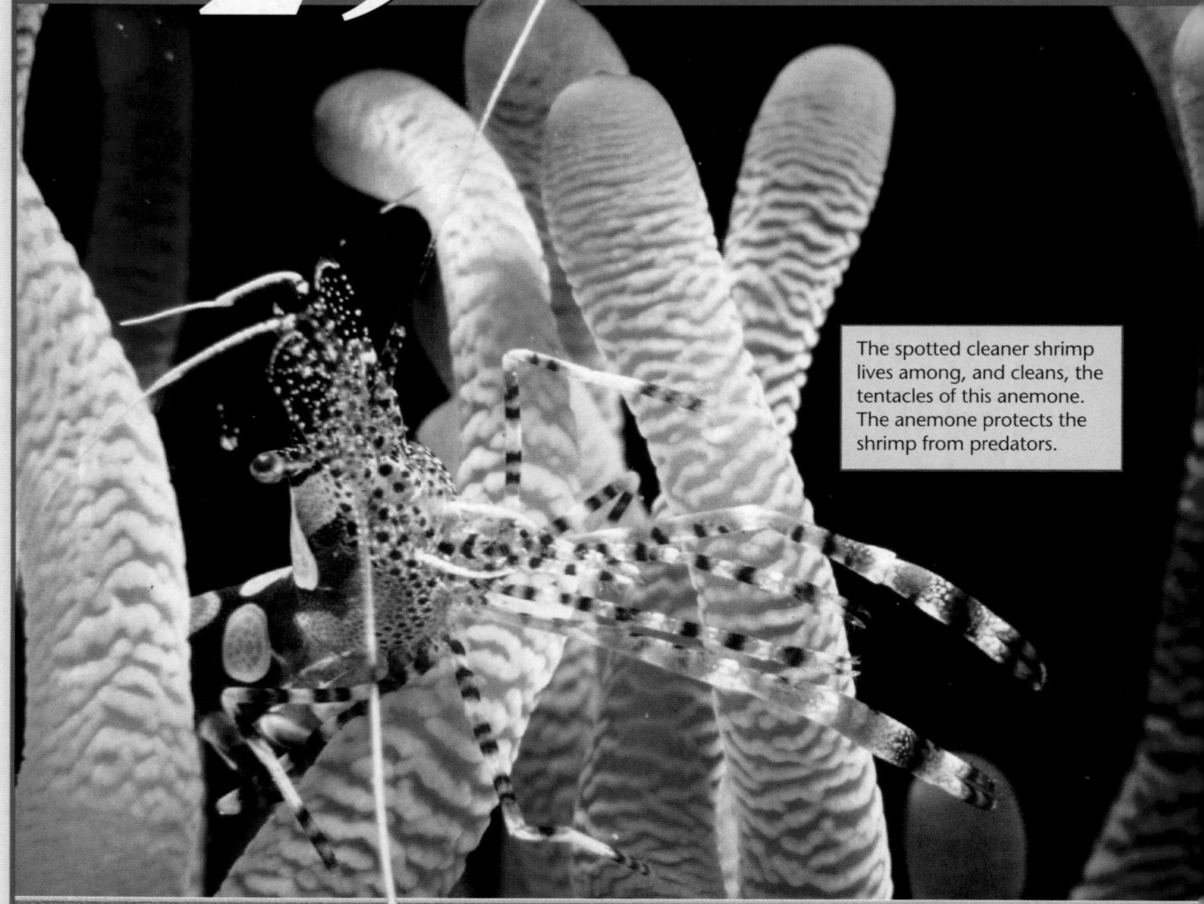

The spotted cleaner shrimp lives among, and cleans, the tentacles of this anemone. The anemone protects the shrimp from predators.

Inquiry Activity

Which protective covering is best?

Procedure

1. Examine some arthropod exoskeletons and mollusk shells. Observe as many differences as you can between these two types of protective coverings.
2. List the differences you observed. Next to each item, note how that difference in protective covering is adaptive to the organism in its own particular niche and habitat.

Think About It

1. **Drawing Conclusions** Which covering is more difficult for a predator to penetrate? Explain.
2. **Predicting** Animals must use energy to move. Which type of covering is more useful to an active, motile animal? Explain your answer.
3. **Drawing Conclusions** How can your observations help explain the fact that most mollusks are slow-moving animals, whereas many arthropods are more active?

FACTS AND FIGURES

The first animals

The fossils of the earliest animals appear in Precambrian rocks from about 650 to 540 million years ago. A few sites around the world contain these organisms, but the first discovered and still the most important is an area in South Australia called the Ediacara Hills. As a result, these animals are often called Ediacarans. They vary in length from less than 1 cm to more than 1 m. Most of these soft-bodied animals were either disc-shaped or leaf-shaped, much like the modern sea pen, a cnidarian. Some resemble jellyfishes, and others are like primitive arthropods. *Dickinsonia,* shown in Figure 29–1, resembles an annelid worm, though some paleontologists think it is more like a cnidarian polyp. These organisms did have some specialized cells, and one even had a primitive skeleton. Whether there is a direct link between these animals and those of the Cambrian Explosion is a matter of debate.

29–1 Invertebrate Evolution

Until recently, the origins of invertebrates were shrouded in mystery. This was because few fossils old enough to shed light on this period in Earth's history had been found. But ongoing discoveries around the world are shedding new light on the origins of invertebrates. Treasure troves of beautifully preserved invertebrate fossils, dating between 575 and 543 million years ago, have been discovered in the Ediacara Hills of Australia and in Chengjiang, China. These fossils join those known from the Burgess Shale deposits in the Canadian Rockies to show a fascinating history of early multicellular life.

Guide for Reading

Key Concept
- What are the major trends in invertebrate evolution?

Vocabulary
radial symmetry
bilateral symmetry
cephalization
coelom

Reading Strategy: Using Visuals Before you read, preview **Figure 29–4.** As you read, notice how the evolutionary trends in the cladogram are discussed in the text.

Origin of the Invertebrates

The Ediacaran fossils brought to light a strange group of ancient invertebrates. These peculiar fossils puzzled paleontologists for years because they seemed quite different from any modern invertebrates. More recently, paleontologists have identified beautifully preserved, microscopic fossils, between 610 and 570 million years old, that seem to be the developing embryos of early multicellular animals. From the same time period, they also identified what are called trace fossils. Trace fossils are tracks and burrows made by soft-bodied animals whose bodies were not fossilized.

Molecular biologists and paleontologists have also created a new field called molecular paleontology. This research uses cutting-edge studies in genetics to understand how different animal body plans evolved. DNA comparisons among living invertebrates help determine which phyla are most closely related. In addition, geneticists are studying how small changes in certain genes can cause major changes in body structures.

The First Multicellular Animals The Ediacaran fossils include some of the earliest and most primitive animals known. Most, like the animal shown in **Figure 29–1,** were flat and plate-shaped and lived on the bottom of shallow seas. They were made of soft tissues that absorbed nutrients from the surrounding water. Some may have had photosynthetic algae living within their tissues. These animals were segmented and had bilateral symmetry. However, they show little evidence of cell specialization or organization into a front and back end. Some of these early animals may have been related to soft-bodied invertebrates such as jellyfishes and worms. Their body plan, however, is distinct from anything alive today. Regardless of their relationships to other organisms, these animals were probably simple and had little internal specialization.

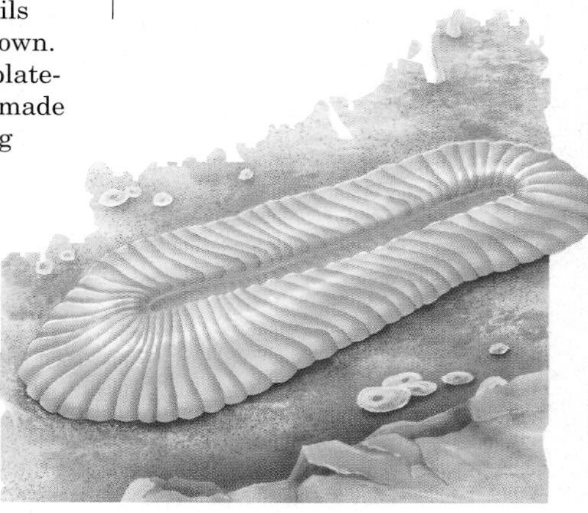

▼ **Figure 29–1** The drawing is an artist's conception of what an early invertebrate might have looked like. **Applying Concepts** *In what environment did most early invertebrates live?*

SECTION RESOURCES (Time Saver)

Print:
- ***Teaching Resources,*** 29–1 Section Review
- ***Guided Reading and Study Workbook,*** Section 29–1

Technology:
- ***iText,*** Section 29–1

Section 29–1

1 FOCUS

Objectives

29.1.1 ***Explain*** what the Cambrian Explosion was.

29.1.2 ***Identify*** the modern evolutionary relationships among major groups of living invertebrates.

29.1.3 ***Describe*** the major trends in invertebrate evolution.

Guide for Reading

Reading Strategy

Students have already learned about specific invertebrate phyla and should remember the basics of the history of life from Chapter 17. Ask students to write a paragraph describing what they already know about the origin and evolution of invertebrates. Then, as they read the chapter, they should revise these paragraphs as needed.

2 INSTRUCT

Origin of the Invertebrates

Make Connections

Earth Science Explain that the fossil shown in Figure 29–1 was probably found in a rock formation. Ask: **How would you describe the process by which this fossil might have formed?** *(Some students might correctly describe a process in which the organism died and was buried in sediments, which hardened into sedimentary rock, leaving a mold, cast, or imprint of the original organism.)* Point out that this organism had no hard body parts. **Why is it remarkable that such an organism left fossil remains?** *(Most soft tissue deteriorates more quickly than sediment hardens into rock, leaving no fossil evidence behind.)* Explain that relatively few of these earliest multicellular animals have been found because of their lack of hard parts.

Answer to . . .

Figure 29–1 *They lived on the bottom of shallow seas.*

Use Visuals

Figure 29–3 Have students examine the illustration of Burgess Shale animals, and then direct their attention to the trilobite shown, *Olenoides.* Point out that this organism is the earliest known example of a trilobite, which students know from Chapter 28 is an ancient form of marine arthropod. Have students turn back to the subsection Evolution of Arthropods in Section 28–1 and review what they read about trilobites. Then, ask: **What can you say about this Burgess Shale trilobite in terms of body symmetry, skeleton, segmentation, cephalization, and appendages?** *(This trilobite had bilateral symmetry, an exoskeleton, three lobes lengthwise, a head with compound eyes, and appendages.)* Point out that these features, or similar ones, are characteristic of living arthropods. Then, ask: **In what ways is this organism different from the animal shown in Figure 29–1?** *(Although the animal was segmented, it had no front and back end, no skeleton, and no appendages.)* Emphasize that the animals of the Burgess Shale represent the first appearance of almost all the major groups of modern animals. The illustration shows an early sponge, early arthropods, and an early annelid.

Meet Diverse Needs

Encourage two or three gifted students to investigate further the remarkable fossils of the Burgess Shale and prepare a presentation to the class. For resources, suggest they look for library books on prehistoric animals, the evolution of life, and paleontology. Perhaps the best book on these fossils is by Stephen Jay Gould, *Wonderful Life: The Burgess Shale and the Nature of History* (New York: Norton, 1989). **Learning modality: verbal**

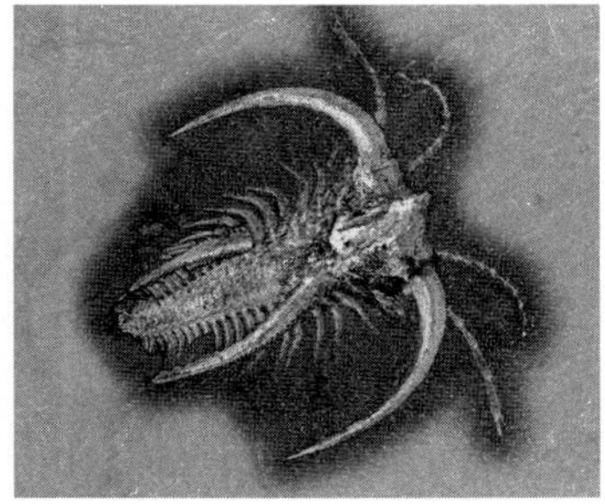

▲ **Figure 29–2** The fossilized arthropod *Marrella splendens,* like most Burgess Shale animals, had body symmetry, segmentation, a skeleton, a front and a back end, and appendages adapted for many functions. **Comparing and Contrasting** *How is this fossil similar to modern arthropods?*

▼ **Figure 29–3** This illustration shows what some of the Cambrian organisms found in the Burgess Shale may have looked like. Note the wide variety of body shapes and appendages. **Observing** *What body features of these animals are similar to those of modern invertebrates?*

Beginnings of Invertebrate Diversity Fossils from a few million years later—a short period in geological time—paint a radically different picture of invertebrate life. The Cambrian Period, which began 544 million years ago, is marked by an abundance of different fossils. Why the difference from earlier periods? By the Cambrian period, some animals had evolved shells, skeletons, and other hard body parts—all of which are readily preserved in fossils. Suddenly, the fossil record provided a wealth of information about animal diversity, body plans, and adaptations to life. One of the best-known sites of Cambrian fossils is the Burgess Shale of Canada. A fossil from the Burgess Shale is shown in **Figure 29–2.**

You can see what some of the Burgess Shale animals may have looked like in **Figure 29–3.** Trilobites such as *Olenoides* moved along the ocean floor. *Wiwaxia* had two rows of long, pointed spikes. The annelid *Canadia,* like many annelids today, had prominent setae. *Anomalocaris,* the largest Burgess Shale fossil, had fearsome-looking forelimbs that were probably used to grasp prey. The animals of the Burgess Shale are far more numerous and diverse than anything that lived earlier.

In just a few million years, animals had evolved complex body plans. They acquired specialized cells, tissues, and organs. Because of the extraordinary growth in animal diversity, events of the early Cambrian Period are called the Cambrian Explosion. During that time, the ancestors of most modern animal phyla first appear in the fossil record.

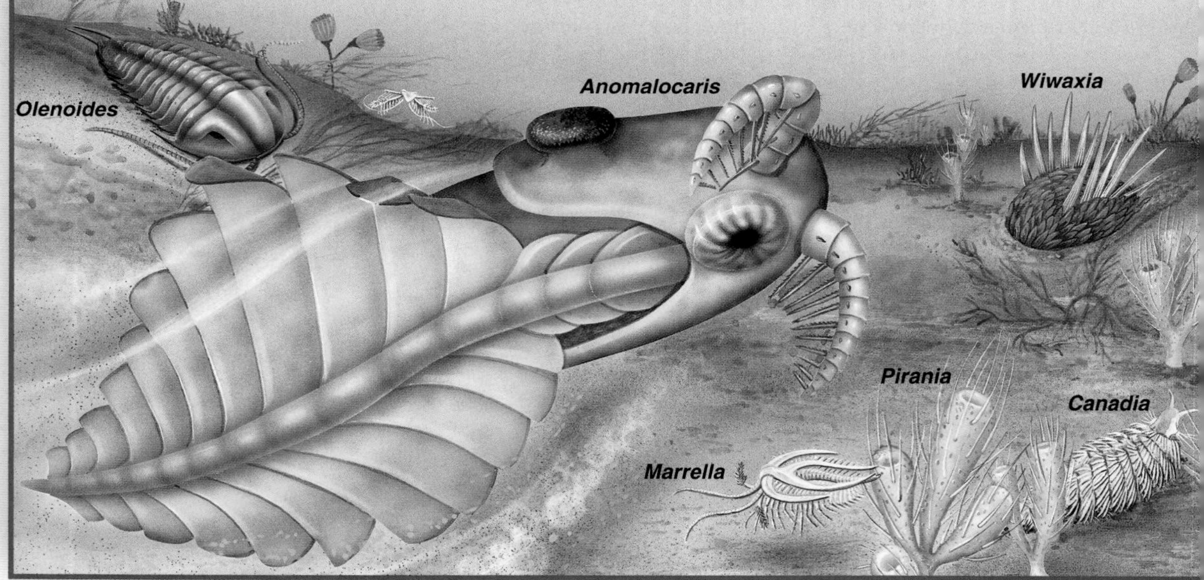

HISTORY OF SCIENCE

Creatures of the Burgess Shale

In 1909, Charles Doolittle Walcott, then secretary of the Smithsonian Institution, discovered a section of rock on the side of Mt. Stephen in British Columbia, Canada, that is possibly the most important fossil find ever. From this rock unit, about 60 m long and 2.5 m thick, Walcott collected more than 65,000 fossils. *Marrella,* a 2.5-cm-long swimming arthropod with long antennae and at least 24 pairs of legs and gills, is the most common Burgess shale organism. *Wiwaxia,* 2–5 cm long, is a bottom feeder covered by hard plates and two rows of upright spines. *Olenoides,* a bottom predator as large as 10 cm long, is the earliest example of a trilobite. *Canadia,* 2.5–5 cm long, is an annelid with two slender tentacles and a body covered with short bristles. *Pirania* is an early sponge.

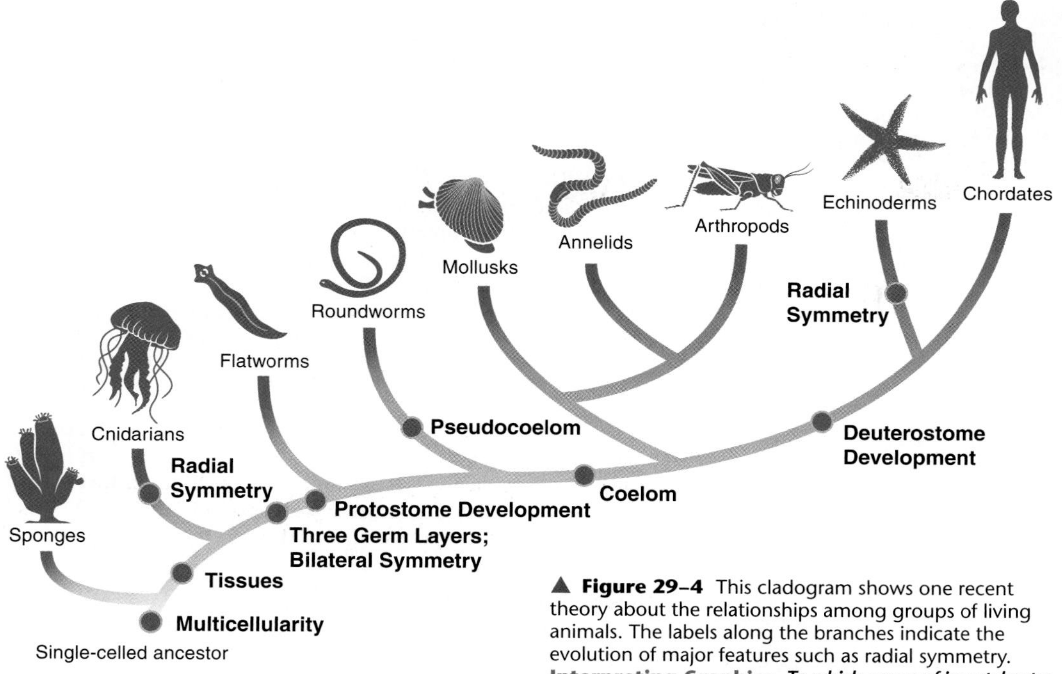

▲ **Figure 29–4** This cladogram shows one recent theory about the relationships among groups of living animals. The labels along the branches indicate the evolution of major features such as radial symmetry. **Interpreting Graphics** ***To which group of invertebrates are echinoderms least closely related?***

What features of the Cambrian animals made them so successful? One way of determining this is to find their common features—especially those that are present in animals today. Burgess Shale animals typically had body symmetry, segmentation, some type of skeleton, a front and a back end, and appendages adapted for a multitude of functions. These features are characteristic of most invertebrates living today.

Modern Evolutionary Relationships

The cladogram in **Figure 29–4** shows the evolutionary relationships among major groups of living invertebrates. It also indicates the sequence in which some important features evolved. These features include tissues and organs, patterns of early development, body symmetry, cephalization, segmentation, and the formation of three germ layers and a coelom. Many of these features, which have persisted up to modern times, evolved in animals of the Cambrian Period. As you review the major trends in invertebrate evolution, consider how each feature might have contributed to the evolutionary success of animals.

CHECKPOINT *What groups of animals are deuterostomes?*

Word Origins

The word *germ* in the term *germ layers* comes from the Latin word *germen,* which means "embryo" or "sprout." **If the suffix *-ate* means "to become," what happens to a seed when it germinates?**

Modern Evolutionary Relationships

Build Science Skills

Inferring Construct a classroom display of as many invertebrates as possible, using photos as well as live and preserved invertebrates. Try to provide a diverse assemblage, including at least one from each of the groups studied in previous chapters. Label each animal with its common or species name. Then, ask students: **Which of these invertebrates do you think are closely related to one another?** *(Accept all reasonable responses, but challenge students to think about relationships across phylum lines.)* **What further information would you need to be sure about how closely these invertebrates are related to one another?** *(Anatomical, behavioral, and molecular information about these animals.)*

Use Visuals

Figure 29–4 Ask: **What does the cladogram show as the ancestor of all invertebrates?** *(A single-celled organism)* **What is the first important feature that developed in animal evolution?** *(Multicellularity)* **What important feature do all invertebrate groups except the sponges have?** *(Tissues)*

Word Origins

When a seed germinates, it sprouts and begins growing.

TIME SAVER PRESENTATIONS MADE EASY!

The Presentation Assistant Plus contains the Prentice Hall Presentation Pro and the Transparencies, which provide easy-to-follow visual support for every step of this section. If you have a computer presentation station, use Prentice Hall Presentation Pro for Section 29–1, or use the transparencies listed here.

Section 29–1: **Interest Grabber**
Section Outline
Compare/Contrast Table
Figure 9–4

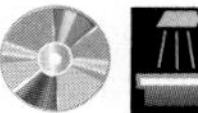

Answers to . . .

CHECKPOINT *Echinoderms and chordates*

Figure 29–2 *Like modern arthropods, the fossil has an exoskeleton, bilateral symmetry, cephalization, segmentation, and jointed appendages.*

Figure 29–3 *Asymmetry in the spongelike animals; bilateral symmetry in the other animals; segmentation; cephalization; appendages, including antennae; pores in the spongelike animals.*

Figure 29–4 *Sponges*

Evolutionary Trends

SCIENCE NEWS®

Encourage students to visit **www.phschool.com** to find the most current information on this topic.

Address Misconceptions

Many students believe that the more-complex animals evolved from simpler animals, and thus are somehow "better" in an evolutionary sense than simpler animals. Point out that each phylum evolved as animals changed through adaptation to changing environmental conditions. Simpler animals have shown that they are quite well adapted to many environments and have persisted in much the same forms for millions and millions of years.

Use Visuals

Figure 29–5 Have students study the table of major characteristics, and also have them compare the table with the cladogram in Figure 29–4. Then, ask: **From the information in the table, what can you say about the difference between sponges and cnidarians?** *(They are the same except for two features. Cnidarians have germ layers and body symmetry, whereas sponges have neither.)* Have students look back to the cladogram and confirm that those differences are reflected on that arrangement of phyla. Continue this strategy of providing connections between the information presented in the two figures.

KEEP CURRENT WITH . . . SCIENCE NEWS®

To find out more about the topics in this chapter, go to: **www.phschool.com**

Evolutionary Trends

The appearance of each phylum in the fossil record represents the evolution of a successful and unique body plan. Features of this body plan typically change over time, leading to the formation of many new traits. The major trends of invertebrate evolution are summarized in **Figure 29–5.**

Specialized Cells, Tissues, and Organs Modern sponges and cnidarians have little internal specialization. They carry out essential functions using individual cells or simple tissues. As larger and more complex animals evolved, specialized cells joined together to form tissues, organs, and organ systems that work together to carry out complex functions. Flatworms have simple organs for digestion, excretion, response, and reproduction. More complex animals, such as mollusks and arthropods, have organ systems.

Body Symmetry Sponges lack body symmetry. **All invertebrates except sponges exhibit some type of body symmetry.** Cnidarians and echinoderms exhibit **radial symmetry**—body parts extend from the center of the body. Worms, mollusks, and arthropods exhibit **bilateral symmetry,** or have mirror-image left and right sides.

Cephalization Most invertebrates with bilateral symmetry rely on movement for feeding, defense, and other important functions. The evolution of this body plan and lifestyle was accompanied by the trend toward **cephalization,** which is the concentration of sense organs and nerve cells in the front of the body. **Invertebrates with cephalization can respond to the environment in more sophisticated ways than can simpler invertebrates.** In most worms and arthropods, nerve cells are arranged in structures called ganglia. In more complex invertebrates, such as certain mollusks, nerve cells form an organ called a brain.

CHECKPOINT *How does cephalization benefit an animal?*

▶ **Figure 29–5** This table shows the major characteristics of the main groups of invertebrates. **Germ layers, body symmetry, cephalization, and development of a coelom are more common in complex invertebrates than in simple ones.** Mollusks, for example, have all of these features, but sponges have none of them.

Comparing Invertebrates

	Sponges 	Cnidarians 	Flatworms 
Germ Layers	Absent	Two	Three
Body Symmetry	Absent	Radial	Bilateral
Cephalization	Absent	Absent	Present
Coelom	Absent	Absent	Absent
Early Development	———	———	Protostome

FACTS AND FIGURES

Which came first?

There is disagreement among zoologists about which came first, radial symmetry or bilateral symmetry. Some theorize that the first multicellular organisms had radial symmetry. Then, some animals began living on the ocean floor, and creeping forward along the floor favors organisms with a front end and a back end. Hence, they evolved into bilateral animals with a concentration of sensory organs at the front, that is, with cephalization. Other zoologists think that bilateral animals evolved first, with the first multicellular organism being much like a flatworm. Then, the radial stage of the life cycle of an ancestral organism did well as a weak swimmer (such as plankton) and eventually evolved into a separate group. Alternatively, radial symmetry may have evolved as some bilateral animals adapted to a more sedentary way of life.

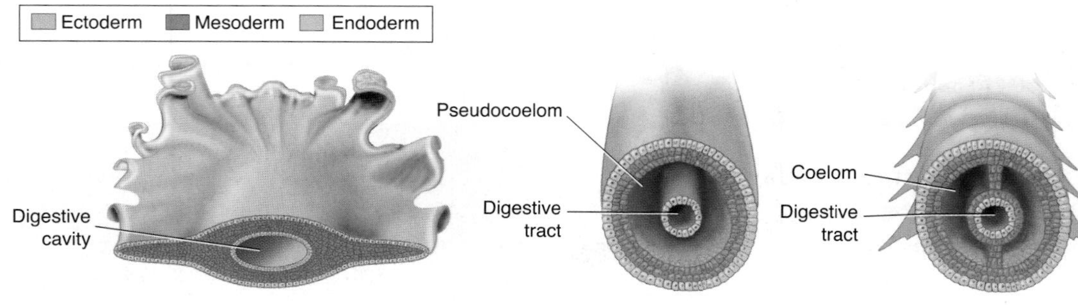

▲ **Figure 29–6** Acoelomates do not have a coelom, or body cavity, between their germ layers. Pseudocoelomates have body cavities that are partially lined with mesoderm. **Most complex animal phyla are coelomates, meaning that they have a true coelom that is lined completely with mesoderm.**

Segmentation Most invertebrates with bilateral symmetry also have segmented bodies. Over the course of evolution, different segments have often become specialized for specific functions. Because the same structures are repeated in each body segment, segmentation also allows an animal to increase in body size with a minimum of new genetic material.

Coelom Formation Jellyfishes have a simple construction in which a jellylike layer lies between ectoderm and endoderm tissues. Other invertebrates develop from three germ layers, the endoderm, mesoderm, and ectoderm, as shown in **Figure 29–6.** Invertebrate phyla differ in the arrangement of these layers. Flatworms are acoelomates, meaning that no **coelom,** or body cavity, forms between the germ layers. Pseudocoelomates, such as roundworms, have a body cavity lined partially with mesoderm. **Most complex animal phyla have a true coelom that is lined completely with mesoderm.**

Early Development In most invertebrates, the zygote divides repeatedly to form a blastula—a hollow ball of cells. In protostomes, the blastopore, or the opening of the blastula, develops into a mouth. In deuterostomes, the blastopore forms an anus. Worms, arthropods, and mollusks are protostomes, and echinoderms are deuterostomes.

Roundworms	Annelids	Mollusks	Arthropods	Echinoderms
Three	Three	Three	Three	Three
Bilateral	Bilateral	Bilateral	Bilateral	Radial (adults)
Present	Present	Present	Present	Absent (adults)
Pseudocoelom	True coelom	True coelom	True coelom	True coelom
Protostome	Protostome	Protostome	Protostome	Deuterostome

Use Visuals

Figure 29–6 Review with students the names of the three germ layers, as discussed in Section 26–1. Then, ask: **What difference can you see between an acoelomate and a pseudocoelomate?** *(In the pseudocoelomate, there is a cavity between the endoderm and the mesoderm, while in the acoelomate there is no cavity—there is no space at all between the endoderm and the mesoderm.)* **What difference can you see between the pseudocoelomate and the coelomate?** *(The cavity in the coelomate is lined completely with mesoderm, while the cavity in the pseudocoelomate is only partially lined with mesoderm.)*

Build Science Skills

Using Models Divide the class into small groups and give each group three colors of modeling compound. Then, ask each group to make models of an acoelomate, a pseudocoelomate, and a coelomate, using the illustrations in Figure 29–6 as examples of each kind of organism.

Use Community Resources

Invite an expert to visit the classroom and speak about how scientists determine the relationships among invertebrate phyla. A university professor who has done research in molecular biology will be able to explain modern methods of biological investigation and answer questions about how molecular data can be used to confirm phylogenetic relationships.

FACTS AND FIGURES

Advantages of a coelom

The coelom is a fluid-filled cavity between the gut or digestive tube and the outer body wall, creating a tube-within-a-tube construction. The coelom has a number of functions. This cavity serves as a buffer between the outer wall and the inner organs, cushioning them against harm. It allows for the growth of internal organs without distorting the body's outer wall. It serves as a storage place. For invertebrates with an open circulatory system, it provides a place for circulation to occur. Also, the fluid in the cavity serves as a hydrostatic skeleton for many animals. There are several theories about when and how the coelom evolved. Some zoologists think that it evolved twice, once in protostomes and again in deuterostomes. One thing is certain—there is great adaptive advantage for a crawling or burrowing organism to have a coelom.

Answer to . . .

CHECKPOINT *Because sense organs and nerve cells are concentrated in the head end, animals with cephalization can respond to the environment in more complex ways than can animals that lack cephalization.*

Problem Solving

Defining the Problem Have students write a detailed description of the habitat they have chosen.

Organizing Information Make sure students consider all relevant features as they pick the body systems that would work best in the chosen environment.

Creating a Solution Advise students to write a general description of the invertebrate they create and then describe as many body systems as they can in detail.

Presenting Your Plan Have students present their "perfect invertebrates" to the class or provide bulletin board space for students to display their plans.

3 ASSESS

Evaluate Understanding

Call on students at random to explain the major trends of invertebrate evolution.

Reteach

Have students look at Figure 29–4. Ask each student to write a paragraph that explains how the groups of invertebrates are related to one another, giving a reason for each time the cladogram branches.

ALTERNATIVE ASSESSMENT

Students should compare animals such as those in Figure 29–3 with animals described under the subheading The First Multicellular Animals. Students should emphasize that the Burgess Shale animals had hard body parts, complex body plans, segmentation, and organ systems, whereas the earlier animals did not.

Use iText to review the key concepts in Section 29–1.

Problem Solving

Creating an Imaginary Invertebrate

The moth in the photo is a real animal, but you may think that it looks like a science-fiction monster. Several of the most frightening "monsters" dreamed up for the science-fiction films of the past 20 years have actually been based on bits and pieces of anatomy and behavior of real invertebrates. Now that you have studied all the invertebrate phyla, you can take a turn at devising the "perfect invertebrate" for a habitat of your choice.

Defining the Problem First, choose a habitat: a temperate zone desert, a tropical coral reef, or inside the body of a mammal. Depending on which habitat you chose, define the environmental challenges (such as heat, cold, or lack of water) and the biological needs (such as food and oxygen) that your organism must meet.

Organizing Information Once you have defined the problem, look back over the characteristics of all the invertebrate groups you have studied, and pick the kind of body systems that you think would work best in your chosen habitat.

Creating a Solution Assemble the body systems you have chosen into an imaginary animal. Make sure that the systems you use can work in harmony. You could not, for example, expect an animal to breathe through its skin if it had an impermeable exoskeleton covering its entire body! Make sure that you have considered all the organism's needs. Give your animal an appropriate name.

Presenting Your Plan Create external and cutaway diagrams of your animal, including any larval stages. Label the diagrams, including the name of the real-life invertebrate system that fulfills each essential function. Conclude by describing the complete life cycle of your organism.

29–1 Section Assessment

1. **Key Concept** Describe three major trends in the evolution of invertebrates.
2. Compare the first multicellular animals with those of the Burgess Shale.
3. How was the evolution of internal specialization important to invertebrate form and function?
4. Compare the body structures and other characteristics of cnidarians and arthropods.
5. **Critical Thinking Inferring** Evolutionary relationships are inferred from both molecular and body-structure data. Why might this approach be more accurate than only studying body structure?

iTEXT Assessment Use iText to review the important concepts in Section 29–1.

ALTERNATIVE ASSESSMENT

Creative Writing

Imagine that you are one of the first paleontologists to find fossils in the Burgess Shale. Suppose that you have studied the fossils and compared them with earlier animal fossils such as the one in **Figure 29–1.** Write a report for a scientific journal about your discovery and its significance.

29–1 Section Assessment

1. Three of the following trends: specialized cells, tissues, and organs; body symmetry; cephalization; segmentation; coelom formation; and patterns of early development.
2. The first multicellular animals were soft-bodied and show little evidence of cell specialization or cephalization. Animals of the Burgess Shale had hard parts as well as cephalization and specialized cells, tissues, and organ systems.
3. Specialized cells, tissues, organs, and organ systems work together to carry out complex functions.
4. Cnidarians have two germ layers and radial symmetry. Arthropods have three germ layers, bilateral symmetry, cephalization, a coelom, and the protostome development pattern.
5. Molecular data might point to connections that are not obvious from comparing anatomy.

29–2 Form and Function in Invertebrates

To survive, all animals perform the same essential tasks: feeding and digestion, respiration, circulation, excretion, response, movement, and reproduction. In many ways, each animal phylum represents an "experiment" in the adaptation of body structures to carry out these tasks. The appearance of each phylum in the fossil record, therefore, represents the evolutionary development of a unique body plan. The continued history of each phylum is the story of further evolutionary changes to that plan.

Biologists can learn a great deal about the nature of life by comparing body systems among groups of living invertebrates. Body systems that perform the essential tasks of life have taken many different forms in different phyla. Each phylum has a particular type of breathing device, a certain type of body support system, and numerous variations on other body functions. More complicated systems are not necessarily better than simpler systems. The fact that any system is found in living animals testifies to its success in performing functions adequately. This section reviews the basic evolutionary trends in each body system, using examples from a variety of invertebrate groups.

Guide for Reading

Key Concept
- How do different invertebrate phyla carry out their essential life functions?

Vocabulary
intracellular digestion
extracellular digestion
open circulatory system
closed circulatory system
hydrostatic skeleton
exoskeleton
endoskeleton
external fertilization
internal fertilization

Reading Strategy: Finding Main Ideas Before you read, skim the section to identify the key ideas. Then, carefully read the section, making a list of supporting details for each main idea.

Feeding and Digestion

Invertebrates have evolved many different ways of obtaining food. The spider in **Figure 29–7**, for example, is feeding on a caterpillar after killing it with venom. Before food can be used for energy, the food must be broken down, or digested. The digested food must then be absorbed into the animal's body. Complex animals accomplish these processes in different ways than simpler ones.

Intracellular and Extracellular Digestion Invertebrates have evolved different ways of digesting food. **The simplest animals break down food primarily through intracellular digestion, but more complex animals use extracellular digestion.** Sponges digest their food inside archaeocytes, which pass nutrients to other cells by diffusion. Because food is digested inside cells, this process is known as **intracellular digestion.** In contrast, mollusks, annelids, arthropods, and echinoderms rely almost entirely on extracellular digestion. In **extracellular digestion,** food is broken down outside the cells in a digestive cavity or tract and then absorbed into the body. Flatworms and cnidarians use both intracellular and extracellular digestion.

▶ **Figure 29–7** **Complex animals break down food using extracellular digestion.** The spider's venom is breaking down the tissues of the caterpillar. Later, the broken-down food molecules will be absorbed into the spider's digestive tract.

SECTION RESOURCES

Print:
- ***Teaching Resources,*** Section Review 29–2
- ***Guided Reading and Study Workbook,*** Section 29–2

Technology:
- ***iText,*** Section 29–2

Section 29–2

1 FOCUS

Objective

29.2.1 ***Describe*** how the different invertebrate phyla carry out their essential life functions.

Guide for Reading

Vocabulary Preview

Before students read the section, have them locate each vocabulary term and read its definition.

Reading Strategy

Suggest that students copy key ideas in their notebooks, leaving enough space for supporting details. Then, as they read the section, they should look for support for each key idea.

2 INSTRUCT

Feeding and Digestion

Build Science Skills

Observing Set up an aquarium in the classroom and encourage volunteers to collect water, gravel and other sediment, plants, and invertebrates from a local freshwater pond. In the pond, students should be able to find planaria, snails, leeches, insect larvae, and hydras, which can often be found attached to rocks and stems of water plants. Ask students to make multiple trips to the pond, first building the habitat in the aquarium and then adding any invertebrates they can find. Once the aquarium contains invertebrates, encourage students keep a daily record of what they observe about how the animals move about, feed, respond to stimuli, and defend themselves.

Meet Diverse Needs

Some at-risk students and students with limited English proficiency may have difficulty understanding the difference between the terms *intracellular* and *extracellular*. Have students use a dictionary to find out that the prefix *intra-* means "within" and the prefix *extra-* means "outside or beyond." Thus, intracellular digestion occurs within cells, while extracellular digestion occurs outside of cells. **Limited English proficiency**

Use Visuals

Figure 29–8 After students have examined the figure, ask: **Which of the four invertebrates shown ingest food and expel waste through a single opening?** *(The cnidarian and the flatworm)* **What specialized regions can you see in the digestive tracts of any of the invertebrates?** *(The digestive tract of the cnidarian has no specialized regions, and the tract of the flatworm has only a pharynx. The one-way digestive tract of the annelid has a pharynx, crop, gizzard, intestine, and anus. The one-way digestive tract of the arthropod has a pharynx, crop, stomach and digestive glands, intestine, rectum, and anus.)* Point out that the digestive tracts shown represent the great variety of digestive systems in the invertebrate phyla.

Respiration

Demonstration

Thoroughly wet a cotton handkerchief or some other piece of cotton cloth. Gather the ends of the cloth, form it into a pouch, and then blow into it so that it expands. Finally, squeeze the air out of the pouch through the cloth. Point out that many invertebrates respire through their skin, including aquatic invertebrates and terrestrial annelids. Just as the expelled breath easily moved through the cloth, gas exchange can take place through an invertebrate's skin.

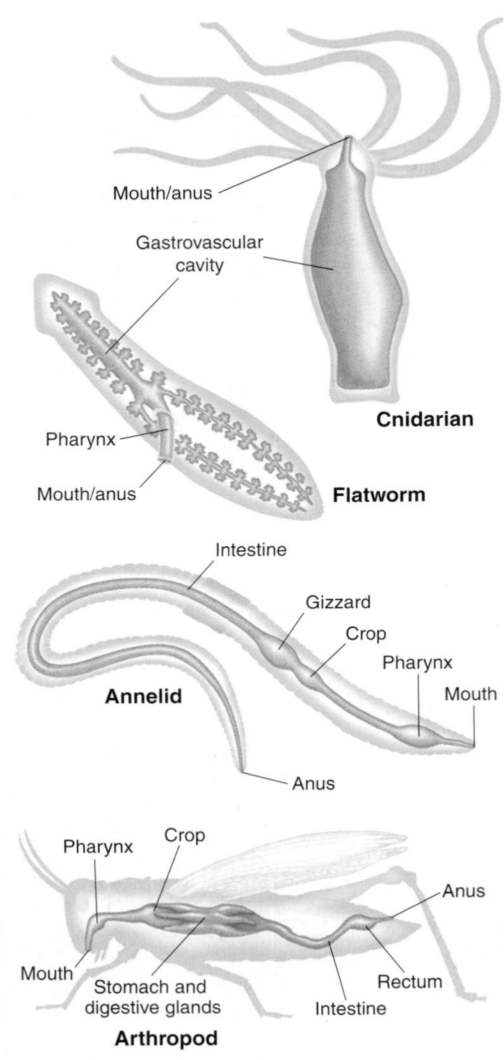

▲ **Figure 29–8** Cnidarians and flatworms have a digestive system with only one opening. In more complex animals, the digestive system has two openings. In addition, the digestive organs have become more specialized. **Interpreting Graphics** *Which of these animals has the least specialized digestive system?*

Patterns of Extracellular Digestion

Invertebrates have a variety of digestive systems, as shown in **Figure 29–8.** Simple animals such as cnidarians and flatworms ingest food and expel wastes through a single opening. Food is digested in the gastrovascular cavity through both extracellular and intracellular means. Some cells of the gastrovascular cavity secrete enzymes and absorb the digested food. Other cells surround food particles and digest them in vacuoles. Digested food then diffuses throughout the body.

More-complex animals digest food in a tube called the digestive tract. Food enters the body through the mouth, and wastes leave through the anus. A one-way digestive tract (which is characteristic of roundworms, annelids, mollusks, arthropods, and echinoderms) often has specialized regions, such as a stomach and intestines. Specialization of the digestive tract allows food to be processed more efficiently, because each step in the process takes place in order, at a specific place along the digestive tract.

Respiration

All animals must exchange oxygen and carbon dioxide with the environment. The more surface area that is exposed to the environment, the greater the amount of gas exchange that can occur. In addition, gases diffuse most efficiently across a thin, moist membrane. Given these principles, all respiratory systems share two basic features. **Respiratory organs have large surface areas that are in contact with the air or water. Also, for diffusion to occur the respiratory surfaces must be moist.**

Aquatic Invertebrates Aquatic animals, such as cnidarians and some flatworms, naturally have moist respiratory surfaces. Many animals even respire through their skins. However, for most active animals larger than worms, skin respiration alone is not sufficient. Aquatic mollusks, arthropods, and many annelids exchange gases through gills. Gills are feathery structures that expose a large surface area to the water. Gills are rich in blood vessels that bring blood close to the surface for gas exchange.

TIME SAVER — PRESENTATIONS MADE EASY!

The Presentation Assistant Plus contains the Prentice Hall Presentation Pro and the Transparencies, which provide easy-to-follow visual support for every step of this section. If you have a computer presentation station, use Prentice Hall Presentation Pro for Section 29–2, or use the transparencies listed here.

Section 29–2:

Interest Grabber
Section Outline
Invertebrate Skeletons
Figure 29–8
Figure 29–9
Figure 29–10
Figure 29–11
Figure 29–12

Quick Lab

How do clams and crayfishes breathe?

Materials live clam, food coloring, crayfish, small container of water

Procedure 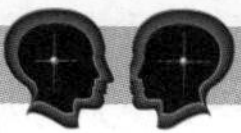

1. Put a drop of food coloring in the water near a clam's siphons. Observe what happens to the coloring.
2. Put a drop of food coloring in the water near the middle of a crayfish's carapace. **CAUTION:** *Keep your fingers away from the crayfish's pincers.* Observe what happens to the coloring.

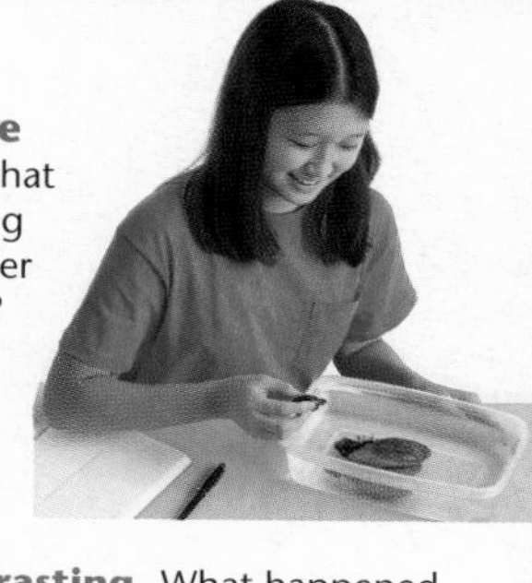

Analyze and Conclude

1. **Observing** Describe what happened to the coloring in step 1. How does water move past a clam's gills?
2. **Inferring** What is the clam's main defense? How is the location of the clam's siphons related to this defense?
3. **Comparing and Contrasting** What happened in step 2? Compare the flow of water past the gills of clams and crayfish.
4. **Inferring** Why do you think the crayfish has gills rather than spiracles, as some other arthropods do?

Terrestrial Invertebrates In terrestrial animals, respiratory surfaces are covered with water or mucus, thereby minimizing water loss. In addition, air is moistened as it travels through the body to the respiratory surface.

Terrestrial invertebrates have several types of respiratory surfaces. The mantle cavity of a land snail is a moist tissue that has an extensive surface area lined with blood vessels. Spiders respire using organs called book lungs, such as the one shown in **Figure 29–9.** Book lungs are made of parallel, sheetlike layers of thin tissues that contain blood vessels. In insects, air enters the body through openings called spiracles. It then enters a network of tracheal tubes, where gases diffuse in and out of surrounding body fluids.

CHECKPOINT *How does respiration in aquatic invertebrates differ from respiration in terrestrial invertebrates?*

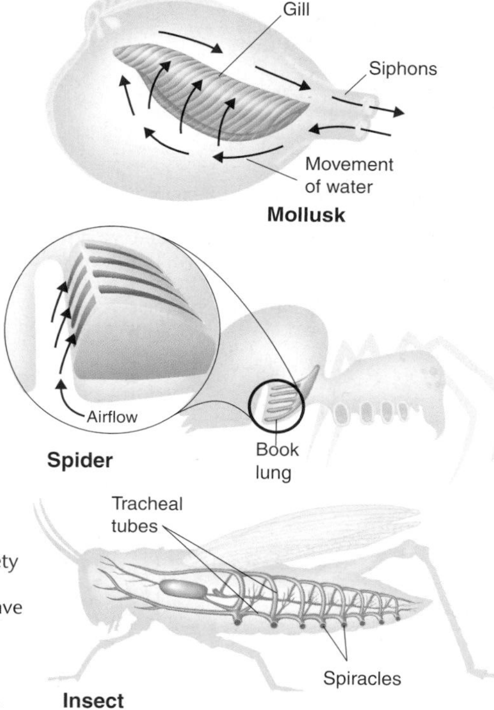

▶ **Figure 29–9** Invertebrates have a variety of respiratory structures. Clams and other aquatic mollusks have gills. Many spiders have book lungs. Grasshoppers and other insects have spiracles and tracheal tubes. **All respiratory organs have large, moist surface areas in contact with air or water.**

Quick Lab

Objective Students will be able to relate differences in the mechanism of gas exchange to overall adaptation in a clam and a crayfish.

Skill Focus **Observing, Inferring**

Materials live clam, food coloring, crayfish, small container of water

Time 20 minutes

Advance Prep You can keep marine clams alive for a few days in a 4% solution of sodium chloride.

Safety Make sure students are careful when handling the crayfish.

Strategy

- Have students compile a list of differences they observe between the clam and the crayfish. Have them relate these differences to the behavioral differences between the two.

Expected Outcome Students should observe that the food coloring enters one of the clam's siphons and exits through the other. They should also observe the turbulence around the middle of the crayfish's ventral surface, revealing the location of its gills.

Analyze and Conclude

1. The coloring entered one siphon and left through the other. Inside the clam, it flowed through the gills.
2. Its main defense is the shell. The location of the siphons allows the clam to pump water through its gills without opening its shell very wide.
3. Students should observe that the coloring was drawn up under the crayfish's carapace. Both clams and crayfish draw water into the body, pass it over the gills, and then release it. A clam must open its shell to do this, whereas a crayfish has openings through which water passes in and out.
4. Spiracles do not work under water, where crayfish live.

TEACHER TO TEACHER

When I introduce topics related to invertebrate form and function, I find that my students are almost always fascinated with the diversity of structure and process in both digestion and reproduction. To respond to this interest, I try to provide students with a great variety of examples in both areas. Then, I challenge students to explain the reasons for the success of each adaptation presented. This teaching strategy not only helps students gain some appreciation of the great diversity among invertebrates, but it also gives them an opportunity to apply their understanding of the processes involved in evolution.

—*Chuck Campbell,*
Biology Teacher
Burbank High School,
Burbank, CA

Answers to . . .

CHECKPOINT *Most aquatic animals have gills for removing oxygen from water and releasing carbon dioxide. Terrestrial animals get oxygen from air; respiratory surfaces are moist.*

Figure 29–8 *The cnidarian, because its digestive system consists only of a gastrovascular cavity and one opening that serves as both mouth and anus*

Circulation

Use Visuals

Figure 29–10 Have students use the figure to compare and contrast the two circulatory systems. Ask: **How does each type of system get blood to tissues and organs?** *(In the open circulatory system, blood is pumped to a cavity or sinus, where it comes in direct contact with tissues and organs. In a closed circulatory system, blood is pumped through vessels to tissues and organs.)* Explain that the blood in an open system aids many invertebrates in movement, acting as part of the animal's hydrostatic skeleton. Point out that although an open system may not be as efficient as a closed system, it works well for the invertebrates that have it.

Excretion

Making Connections

Chemistry Explain that every amino acid contains an amino group, —NH_2. The first step in the breakdown of an amino acid, called deamination, is the removal of the amino group. With the addition of a proton, an amino group becomes ammonia, NH_3. Use a clear glass beaker to show students some household ammonia. Be sure the room is well ventilated and that students don't come close to the beaker. Explain that this commercial product contains ammonia in solution with water and a detergent. Most students will know that even in this dilute solution, the ammonia can be harmful. Emphasize that both urea and uric acid are much less toxic than ammonia, which is why those compounds can be held for long periods of time and excreted by land animals without doing harm to themselves or the environment.

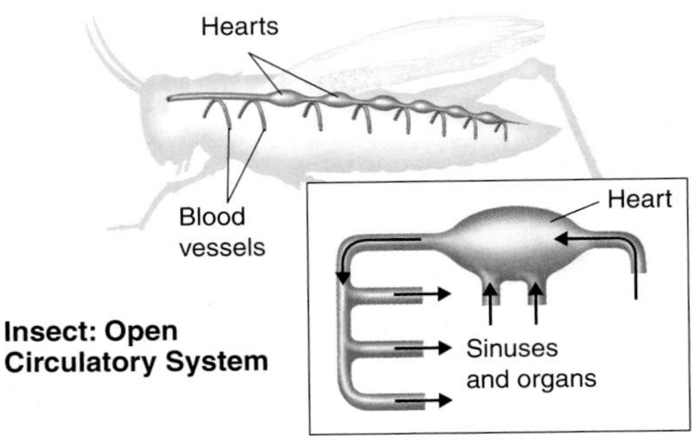

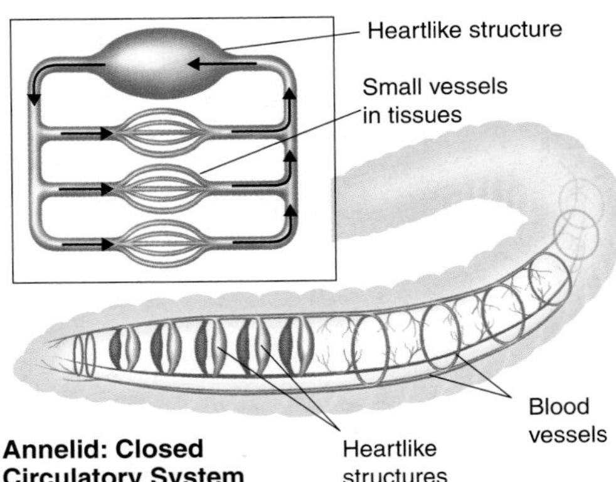

▲ **Figure 29–10 Most complex animals have one or more hearts to move fluid through their bodies in either an open or closed circulatory system.** An insect has an open circulatory system in which blood leaves blood vessels and then moves through sinuses, or body cavities. An annelid has a closed circulatory system in which blood stays in blood vessels as it moves through the body.

Circulation

All cells require a constant supply of oxygen and nutrients, and the cells must also remove metabolic wastes. The smallest and thinnest animals meet this requirement by simple diffusion between their body surface and the environment. But this system is usually insufficient for larger animals. **Most complex animals move blood through their bodies using one or more hearts and either an open or closed circulatory system.** Both types of circulatory systems are shown in **Figure 29–10.**

Open Circulatory Systems In an **open circulatory system,** blood is only partially contained within a system of blood vessels. Instead, one or more hearts or heartlike organs pump blood through blood vessels into a system of sinuses, or spongy cavities. The blood comes in direct contact with the tissues and eventually makes its way back to the heart. Open circulatory systems are characteristic of arthropods and most mollusks.

Closed Circulatory Systems In a **closed circulatory system,** a heart or heartlike organ forces blood through vessels that extend throughout the body. The blood stays within these blood vessels. Materials reach body tissues by diffusing across the walls of the blood vessels. Closed circulatory systems are characteristic of larger, more active animals. Because blood trapped within the blood vessels is kept at high pressure, it can be circulated more efficiently than in an open circulatory system. Among the invertebrates, closed circulatory systems are found in annelids and some mollusks.

CHECKPOINT *Why are closed circulatory systems more efficient than open circulatory systems?*

Excretion

Multicellular animals, whether they are aquatic or terrestrial, must control the amount of water in their tissues. At the same time, all animals must get rid of ammonia, a toxic nitrogenous (nitrogen-containing) waste produced as a result of metabolism. Ammonia (NH_3) results from the breakdown of amino acids. **Most animals have an excretory system that rids the body of metabolic wastes while controlling the amount of water in the tissues.** The excretory systems of invertebrates carry out these functions in a variety of ways, as shown in **Figure 29–11.**

FACTS AND FIGURES

Benefits of an open circulatory system
In arthropods with an open circulatory system, the blood empties from blood vessels directly into the body cavity, where it bathes the organs. It might seem that this type of system is extremely sloppy and inefficient. Yet, the open circulatory system often has uses to the organism beyond circulation. For example, for many clams and snails, the blood in the body cavities functions as a hydrostatic skeleton, helping the animal in movement and burrowing. The blood also functions as a hydrostatic skeleton in aquatic arthropods when they molt. Many spiders are able to extend their legs by forcing the blood in the open system into the limbs. In addition, for large terrestrial insects, the open circulatory system functions as the body's thermal regulator, maintaining the body temperature within the range that cells can function.

Aquatic Invertebrates In aquatic invertebrates such as sponges, cnidarians, and some roundworms, ammonia diffuses from their body tissues into the surrounding water. The water immediately dilutes the ammonia and carries it away.

If freshwater invertebrates did not continually rid their bodies of excess water, they would swell up like water balloons. Flatworms use a network of flame cells to eliminate excess water. Fluid travels through execretory tubules and leaves the body through tiny pores in the animal's skin.

Terrestrial Invertebrates Terrestrial invertebrates must conserve body water while removing nitrogenous wastes from the body. To do this, many animals convert ammonia into a compound called urea, which is much less toxic than ammonia. Urea is eliminated from the body in urine. Urine is highly concentrated, so little water is lost. In annelids and mollusks, urine forms in tubelike structures called nephridia. Fluid enters the nephridia through openings called nephrostomes. Urine leaves the body through excretory pores.

Some insects and arachnids have Malpighian tubules, saclike organs that convert ammonia into uric acid. Uric acid is much less toxic than ammonia. Both uric acid and digestive wastes combine to form a thick paste that leaves the body through a structure called the rectum. Because the paste contains little water, this process also reduces water loss.

▼ **Figure 29–11 Most animals dispose of wastes through excretory systems. Excretory systems also control an organism's water levels.** Flatworms excrete ammonia directly into the water and use flame cells to remove excess water. Annelids use nephridia to convert ammonia into urea and to concentrate it in urine. Some arthropods have Malpighian tubules, which convert ammonia into uric acid. Uric acid is eliminated from the body in a paste.

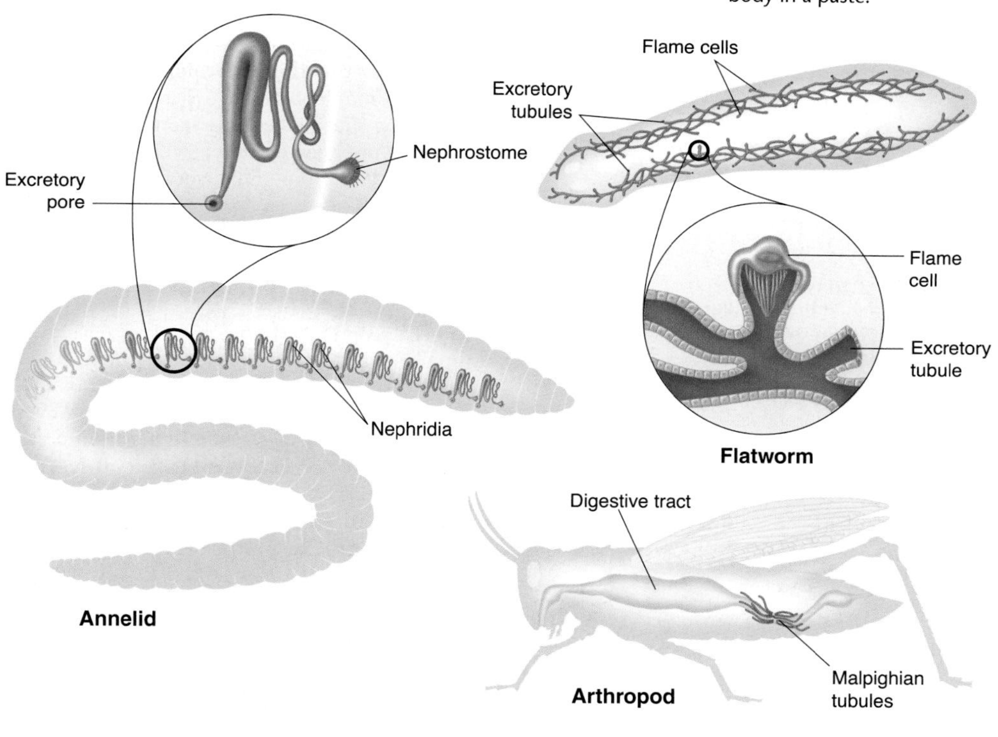

Use Visuals

Figure 29–11 Have students study the examples of the three different methods for disposing of wastes. Then, ask: **How would you compare the environments in which these three invertebrates live?** *(The flatworm lives in an aquatic environment, while the annelid and the arthropod live on land.)* **Why can the flatworm excrete ammonia directly into its environment, while the annelid and arthropod cannot?** *(When the ammonia diffuses from the flatworm's body, it is immediately diluted by the surrounding water. If the land invertebrates excreted ammonia, the ammonia would not be diluted.)* Emphasize that all land organisms must conserve water, and excreting uric acid in solid or semisolid form, as most invertebrates do, conserves water.

Build Science Skills

Comparing and Contrasting Divide the class into small groups, and assign each group one of the invertebrate phyla studied in this unit. Have the members of each group work together to make a large chart on poster board that includes labeled drawings of the digestive and excretory systems used by organisms in their phylum. Once all groups have finished, have each group present its work and then display its charts on the classroom wall.

FACTS AND FIGURES

Getting rid of ammonia

Protein is an essential part of an animal's diet, and the digestion of protein in foods produces amino acids. An organism uses some of these amino acids to produce the proteins and other compounds it needs for a variety of functions. But the chemical reactions involved in these processes produce nitrogen in the form of ammonia, which is highly poisonous to the organism. The aquatic invertebrates that allow ammonia to diffuse out of their bodies are for that reason limited to aquatic environments, because water is necessary to dilute the ammonia, which would be harmful to all organisms if not diluted. Therefore, the ability to produce the relatively harmless uric acid is an important reason why invertebrates have been so successful on land. Also, because uric acid is excreted in a solid or semisolid form, a land animal is able to conserve precious water.

Answer to . . .

CHECKPOINT *Because blood is kept at high pressure, it can be circulated more quickly than in an open circulatory system. Also, the flow of blood can be directed more precisely.*

Response

Use Visuals

Figure 29–12 After students have compared the four examples in the figure, ask: **Which is the simplest nervous system shown, and what is it called?** *(The simplest is that shown in the cnidarian, and it is called a nerve net.)* **What controls and coordinates the nervous system in the arthropod and the mollusk?** *(The brain)* **Which of the four invertebrates exhibits cephalization?** *(The flatworm, the arthropod, and the mollusk)*

Demonstration

Place live planarians in a petri dish, and cover half the dish with a piece of dark paper. Then, shine a flashlight on the uncovered area. Have students observe that the planarians avoid the light by moving under the paper. Have students hypothesize about the selective advantage of planarians' ability to detect light and tendency to move away from light into a dark area.

Movement and Support

Make Connections

Physics Show students a hydraulic pump, such as a hydraulic car jack. Explain that when pressure is applied to a fluid in a confined area, an increase in pressure is transmitted uniformly to all parts of the fluid. This is known as Pascal's principle after the French physicist Blaise Pascal, who first described this idea. The principle is used in hydraulic pumps, as well as by various invertebrates. With a hydraulic jack, a person applies pressure by pushing down on the handle, and when the pressure is uniformly distributed, it pushes up on a piston, which raises the car. Similarly, an invertebrate applies pressure on internal fluid by contracting muscles in one part of its body and relaxing muscles in another part. As the pressure is uniformly distributed, the animal can move forward (worm), extend tube feet (echinoderm), or make any number of other movements.

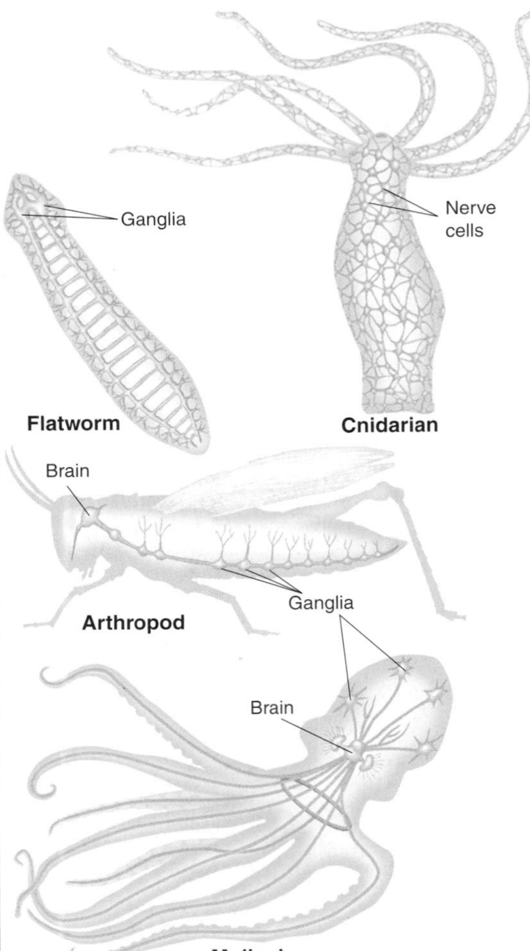

▲ **Figure 29–12** **Invertebrate nervous systems have different degrees of centralization, cephalization, and specialization.** Cnidarians have a simple nerve net. Flatworms, whose nervous systems are more centralized, have small ganglia in their heads. Arthropods and cephalopod mollusks have a centralized brain and specialized sensory organs.

Response

Nervous systems gather and process information from the environment and allow animals to respond appropriately. **Figure 29–12** shows the nervous system of four invertebrates. **Invertebrates show three trends in the evolution of the nervous system: centralization, cephalization, and specialization.** Different nervous systems have various degrees of each of these characteristics.

Centralization and Cephalization The simplest nervous systems, found in cnidarians, are called nerve nets. Nerve nets consist of individual nerve cells that form a netlike arrangement throughout the animal's body. In flatworms and roundworms, the nerve cells are more concentrated, or centralized. There are a few small clumps of nerve tissue, or ganglia, in the head. In cephalopod mollusks and arthropods, ganglia are organized into a brain that controls and coordinates the nervous system. This concentration of nerve tissue and organs in one end of the body is called cephalization.

Specialization The more complex an animal's nervous system is, the more developed its sense organs tend to be. Flatworms, for example, have simple eyespots that detect only the presence of light. More complex animals, such as insects, have eyes that detect motion and color and form images. Complex animals may have a variety of specialized sense organs that detect light, sound, chemicals, movement, and even electricity to help them discover what is happening around them.

CHECKPOINT *What is a nerve net?*

Movement and Support

Most animals use specialized tissues called muscles to move, breathe, pump blood, and perform other life functions. Muscles work by contracting, or becoming shorter. This is the only way that muscle tissue can generate force. When they are not stimulated, muscles relax. In most animals, muscles work together with some sort of skeletal system that provides firm support. **Invertebrates have one of three main kinds of skeletal systems: hydrostatic skeletons, exoskeletons, or endoskeletons.**

Hydrostatic Skeletons Some invertebrates, such as annelids and certain cnidarians, have **hydrostatic skeletons,** shown in **Figure 29–13.** In these animals, muscles surround a fluid-filled body cavity that supports the muscles. When the muscles contract, they push against fluid in the body cavity, causing the body to change shape.

FACTS AND FIGURES

Invertebrate eyes

Almost all invertebrates have some kind of sense organ that responds to light, though light-sensing ability varies greatly. The eyespots, or ocelli, of flatworms and some other invertebrates are composed of light-sensitive cells that give the organism much information about both the intensity and the direction of light. Many arthropods, some annelids, and some mollusks have compound eyes, which are composed of many units, each with a separate nerve track that leads to a large optic nerve. The fields of vision of each unit overlap somewhat with neighboring units, giving the organism great ability for detecting movement. Some cephalopods, including squids and octopuses, have complex, or camera, eyes. These eyes, which are much like vertebrate eyes, form the best images among all invertebrate eyes.

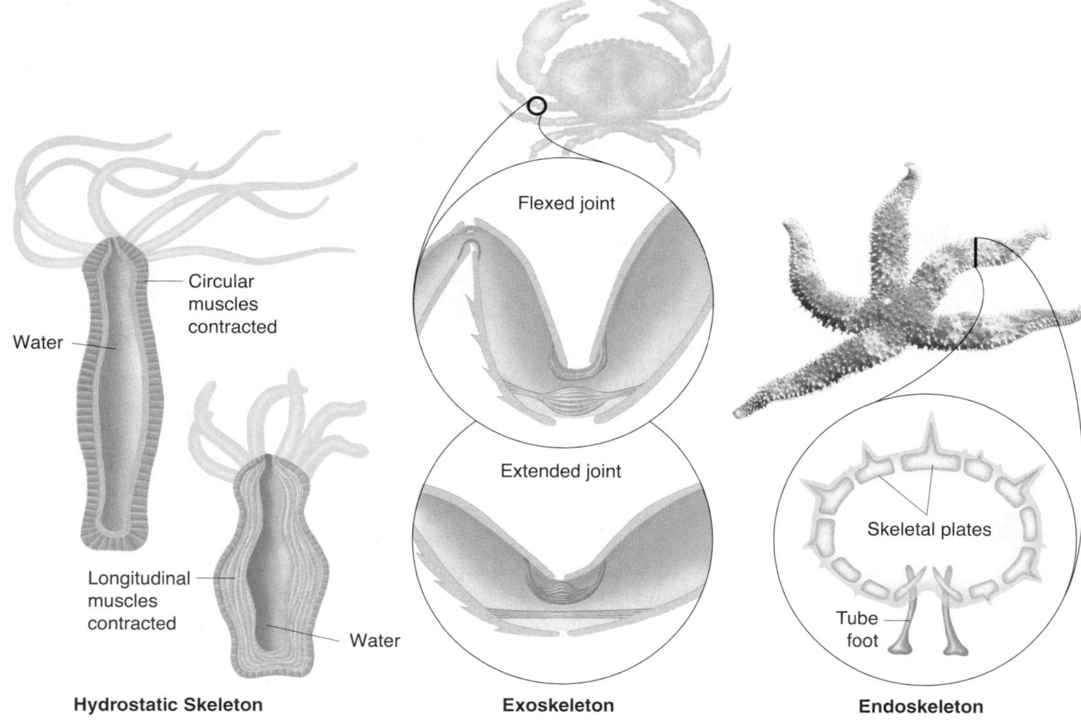

▲ **Figure 29–13** **The three main types of invertebrate skeletons are hydrostatic skeletons, exoskeletons, and endoskeletons.** In animals with hydrostatic skeletons, muscles contract against a fluid-filled body cavity. In animals with exoskeletons, the muscles pull against the insides of the exoskeleton. Echinoderms and some sponges have endoskeletons.

Exoskeletons In arthropods, the **exoskeleton,** or external skeleton, is a hard body covering made of chitin. Arthropods move by using muscles that are attached to the inside of the exoskeleton. These muscles bend and straighten different joints. The shells of some mollusks can also be considered exoskeletons. Muscles attached to the shell make it possible for snails to withdraw into their shells and for bivalves to close.

Endoskeletons An **endoskeleton** is a structural support located inside the body. Sea stars and other echinoderms have an endoskeleton made of calcified plates. These plates function in support and protection, and also give these animals a bumpy and irregular texture. Vertebrates' bones are also endoskeletons.

Reproduction

Most invertebrates reproduce sexually during at least part of their life cycle. Depending on environmental conditions, however, many invertebrates may also reproduce asexually. Each form of reproduction has advantages and disadvantages. Asexual reproduction allows animals to reproduce rapidly and take advantage of favorable conditions in the environment. Sexual reproduction, however, maintains genetic diversity in a population by creating individuals with new combinations of genes.

Use Visuals

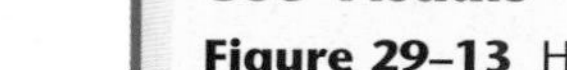

Figure 29–13 Have students examine the three types of skeletons. Then, ask: **How does a hydra change its shape?** *(It contracts muscles that surround a fluid-filled body cavity.)* **Describe how an invertebrate with an exoskeleton bends and extends a limb.** *(When bending a limb, the animal contracts one muscle and relaxes another. When extending the limb, the animal contracts and relaxes the opposite muscles.)* Point out that muscles can pull but cannot push. Vertebrates, which have endoskeletons, use muscles in the same way to flex and extend limbs.

Reproduction

Build Science Skills

Designing Experiments Divide the class into small groups, and ask each group to design an experiment to investigate what conditions are best for the reproduction of a specific kind of invertebrate. Tell students to imagine that they have the resources of any university biology department and an unlimited amount of time. Instruct students to write a hypothesis, identify manipulated and controlled variables, describe how they would collect data, and predict the results of the experiment.

FACTS AND FIGURES

Invertebrate hermaphrodites

In Greek myth, Hermaphroditus, the son of Hermes and Aphrodite, caught the eye of a nymph of the spring in which he was bathing. She fell in love with and clung to him, and they melded into one being—half male and half female. Likewise, a hermaphroditic animal contains both male and female organs and thus can produce both eggs and sperm. Hermaphroditism is common in invertebrates such as flatworms, some worms, some gastropods, some leeches, and some arthropods. During sexual reproduction, different animals pass sperm from one to the other. As a result, eggs in both organisms become fertilized. That result is an advantage of hermaphroditism, because two organisms, not one, are impregnated by each encounter. Such an event is called mutual cross-fertilization.

Answer to . . .

CHECKPOINT *A nerve net is the simplest type of nervous system. It consists of individual nerve cells that form a netlike arrangement throughout the animal's body.*

29–2 (continued)

Meet Diverse Needs

Provide students with limited English proficiency groupings of related terms used in discussing invertebrate structure and function. Ask them to write short paragraphs using the terms in each group in context, comparing and contrasting kinds of invertebrates. Here are some possible groups:

- gastrovascular cavity, digestive tract
- mantle cavity, book lungs, spiracles, tracheal tubes
- open circulatory system, closed circulatory system
- ammonia, urea, uric acid
- nerve net, ganglia, brain
- hydrostatic skeleton, exoskeleton, endoskeleton
- asexual reproduction, sexual reproduction

Limited English proficiency

3 ASSESS

Evaluate Understanding

Read aloud each of the boldface sentences in the section. For each, call on a volunteer to provide a supporting detail for that key idea. Then, ask others in the class for additional supporting details. After students have provided support for the idea, ask for a volunteer to explain the importance of that idea in understanding form and function in invertebrates.

Reteach

Ask each student to choose any two organisms from two different invertebrate phyla and write a paragraph comparing the animals in terms of their feeding and digestion, respiration, circulation, excretion, response, movement and support, and reproduction.

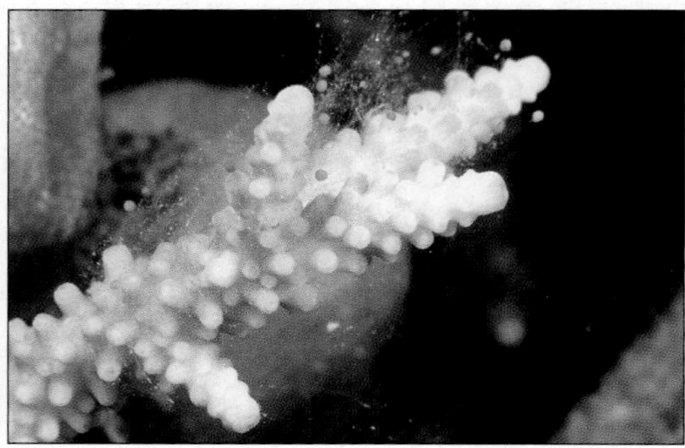

Figure 29–14 Invertebrates may reproduce asexually or sexually. Note that the largest sea anemone in this group is undergoing asexual reproduction by splitting into two parts (left). The *Acorpora* coral (right) is releasing brown eggs into the water. The eggs will be fertilized externally. This is an example of sexual reproduction.

In asexual reproduction, all offspring produced are genetically identical to the parent. Asexual reproduction may occur by fragmentation, in which an organism breaks into pieces that grow into new individuals. It may also occur by budding, in which new individuals are produced from outgrowths of the parent's body wall. Some animals, such as the sea anemone on the left in **Figure 29–14,** reproduce asexually by dividing in two.

Most multicellular animals reproduce sexually. Sexual reproduction is the production of offspring from the fusion of male and female gametes. Most animals have separate sexes, meaning that an individual produces either sperm or eggs. But some animals, including certain mollusks and annelids, are hermaphrodites, or individual animals that can produce both sperm and eggs.

Sperm and eggs may meet in two different ways. In **external fertilization,** eggs are fertilized outside the female's body. Adults may release sperm and eggs into the surrounding water, and the sperm swim to the eggs and fertilize them. In **internal fertilization,** eggs are fertilized inside the female's body. Males typically use specialized organs to deposit sperm inside the female's reproductive tract.

29–2 Section Assessment

1. **Key Concept** In your own words, describe the evolution of three different body systems of invertebrates.
2. Compare circulation in annelids and arthropods.
3. What are the three main kinds of skeleton systems in invertebrates?
4. Compare asexual and sexual reproduction. What are the advantages and disadvantages of each?
5. **Critical Thinking Applying Concepts** List the three forms of nitrogenous wastes excreted by animals. How are the ways in which animals dispose of these wastes related to each animal's environment?

iTEXT Assessment Use iText to review the important concepts in Section 29–2.

Take It to the NET

Many invertebrates live in marine ecosystems. Choose one species of marine invertebrate to research. Then present your findings. Include a description and photograph of the animal, its species and common name, phylum, and habitat. Use the links provided in the Biology area at the Prentice Hall Web site for help in completing this activity: **www.phschool.com**

29–2 Section Assessment

1. Students should describe the evolution of three body systems discussed in the section.
2. Annelids have a closed circulatory system; arthropods have an open circulatory system.
3. Hydrostatic skeletons, exoskeletons, endoskeletons
4. Asexual reproduction allows animals to reproduce rapidly and take advantage of favorable environments, though it does not maintain genetic diversity. Sexual reproduction maintains genetic diversity in a population, but it is not rapid.
5. Ammonia, urea, and uric acid. The method largely depends on environment: aquatic animals generally need to get rid of excess water; terrestrial animals must conserve it.

Design an Experiment

Comparing Invertebrate Responses to Stimuli

The responses of animals to stimuli depend on their nervous systems. In this investigation, you will design experiments to test the responses of three invertebrates to touch and food.

Problem

How do the responses of invertebrates relate to the structures of their nervous systems?

Materials

- dropper pipette
- hydra culture
- watch glass
- dissecting microscope
- blunt metal probe
- planarian
- petri dish
- crayfish
- brine shrimp
- cooked egg yolk
- slice of bologna

Skills Formulating Hypotheses, Observing

Design Your Experiment

1. Use a dropper pipette to transfer a hydra and some water to the center of a watch glass or petri dish.
2. Place the watch glass or petri dish on the stage of a dissecting microscope and observe the hydra's movements for a few minutes.
3. With a blunt metal probe, gently touch one of the hydra's tentacles from several directions. Observe and record the hydra's responses. Return the hydra to its culture.
4. Design similar experiments to determine how a planarian and a crayfish respond to touch. Include touching both ends of each animal in your experimental plan.
5. Now design another set of experiments to determine how each animal will respond to food. Hydras will consume brine shrimp, planarians will eat cooked egg yolk, and crayfish will eat small pieces of bologna.
6. **Predicting** For each experiment you plan, write your prediction of the result. After your teacher approves your plan, carry out the experiments you have designed. Handle and touch the animals gently at all times. Record your observations. **CAUTION:** *Wash your hands before leaving the lab.*

Analyze and Conclude

1. **Comparing and Contrasting** Describe how each animal responded to touch. How were the responses of the animals related to the direction from which they were touched? What, if any, were the differences among the animals?
2. **Drawing Conclusions** Which animal displayed the most specific response to touch? Explain your answer in terms of the animals' nervous systems.
3. **Comparing and Contrasting** Describe how each animal responded to its food. Did your results support your hypothesis? How do each animal's responses relate to the structure of its nervous system?
4. **Drawing Conclusions** Which of these animals shows cephalization? Explain how your answer relates to each animal's behavior.

Go Further

Designing Experiments Design similar experiments using other invertebrates such as sponges, or earthworms. Obtain your teacher's permission before carrying out the experiments.

Analyze and Conclude

1. Students should observe that when a hydra is touched, the entire hydra contracts into a ball, whereas when a planarian or crayfish is touched, it moves away from the stimulus. The crayfish may also try to grasp the object that touches it with its pincers.
2. The crayfish demonstrated the most specific response by moving away and grasping. This can be explained by its more complex nervous system.
3. The hydra responded by waving its tentacles until one or more contacted the brine shrimp. The planarian moved toward the food. The crayfish grasped the food with its pincers and bit off small pieces. The crayfish, whose response was most complex, has the most complex nervous system.
4. The crayfish and planarian show cephalization, as reflected in their response toward or away from stimuli.

Design an Experiment

Objectives
Students will be able to:
- observe how different invertebrates respond to touch and food.
- draw conclusions about how the responses of invertebrates relate to the structures of their nervous systems.

Time 45 minutes

Advance Prep Obtain invertebrates from scientific supply houses. Planarians and hydras can also be obtained from pond water. Live brine shrimp are available at many pet stores. Don't feed animals for 24 hours before the activity. About an hour before the lab, add a suspension of carmine red powder to the shrimp culture to color them. Also, hard-boil eggs and cut up the yolks in advance.

Safety Make sure students are careful when handling the crayfish. Students should wear disposable plastic gloves and then dispose of them properly after the activity.

Teaching Tips If the planarian eats the egg yolk, students may be able to observe the egg yolk inside the digestive tract by looking at the planarian under a microscope. The yellow color will reveal the shape of the digestive system.

Expected Outcome Students should observe that different invertebrates respond differently to touch and food. They should draw the conclusion that these different responses relate to the structure of the nervous system of each kind of invertebrate.

Go Further

Students' designs will vary, though most will be similar to the experiments carried out in this activity. From these further experiments, students should conclude that invertebrates with more complex nervous systems have more complex responses to stimuli than do organisms with simpler nervous systems.

Chapter 29 Study Guide

Study Tip

Divide the class into small groups, and ask each group to brainstorm a list of challenging questions that cover all the chapter concepts. Then, have the members of each group work together to answer the questions devised by another group.

Thinking Visually

The hydra flowchart might include: food enters gastrovascular cavity through mouth; digested and absorbed in gastrovascular cavity; wastes expelled through mouth. Earthworm: food enters mouth; moves through pharynx, crop, gizzard, and intestines; wastes leave through anus.

Chapter 29 Assessment

Reviewing Content

Multiple Choice

1. b	**4.** a	**7.** b	**10.** b
2. a	**5.** d	**8.** c	
3. d	**6.** d	**9.** c	

Understanding Concepts

11. Specialized cells, tissues, and organ systems; body symmetry; segmentation; some type of skeleton; a front and back end; and appendages

12. Specialized cells led to the development of tissues and organ systems.

13. Radial: body parts extend from center; sea star. Bilateral: animals have mirror-image right and left halves; earthworm.

14. With cephalization, animals can respond to the environment more quickly and in more sophisticated ways. This is an advantage for feeding and defense.

15. Ectoderm, endoderm, mesoderm

16. Acoelomates have no body cavity; pseudocoelomates have a body cavity partially lined with mesoderm; coelomates have a true body cavity lined completely with mesoderm.

Chapter 29 Study Guide

29–1 Invertebrate Evolution

 **Key Concepts**

- As animals became larger and more complex, specialized cells joined together to form tissues, organs, and organ systems that work together to carry out complex functions.
- All invertebrates except sponges exhibit some type of body symmetry—either radial symmetry or bilateral symmetry.
- Invertebrates with cephalization can respond to the environment more quickly and in more sophisticated ways than can simpler invertebrates.
- Most invertebrates with bilateral symmetry also have segmented bodies. Over the course of evolution, different segments have often become specialized for specific functions.
- Most animal phyla have a true coelom that is lined completely with mesoderm.
- Worms, arthropods, and mollusks are protostomes, and echinoderms are deuterostomes.

Vocabulary

radial symmetry, p. 748
bilateral symmetry, p. 748
cephalization, p. 748
coelom, p. 749

29–2 Form and Function in Invertebrates

Key Concepts

- The simplest animals break down food primarily through intracellular digestion, whereas more complex animals use extracellular digestion.
- Respiratory organs have large surface areas that are in contact with the air or water. In order for diffusion to occur, these respiratory surfaces must be kept moist.
- Most complex animals move fluid through their bodies using one or more hearts and an open or closed circulatory system.
- Most animals have an excretory system that rids the body of metabolic wastes and controls the amount of water in their tissues.
- Invertebrates show three trends in the evolution of the nervous system: centralization, cephalization, and specialization.
- Invertebrates have one of three main kinds of skeletal systems: hydrostatic skeletons, exoskeletons, and endoskeletons.
- Most invertebrates reproduce sexually during at least part of their life cycle. Depending on environmental conditions, however, many invertebrates may also reproduce asexually.

Vocabulary

intracellular digestion, p. 751
extracellular digestion, p. 751
open circulatory system, p. 754
closed circulatory system, p. 754
hydrostatic skeleton, p. 756
exoskeleton, p. 757
endoskeleton, p. 757
external fertilization, p. 758
internal fertilization, p. 758

Thinking Visually

Create two flowcharts describing the steps in the digestion of food. One flowchart should describe digestion in a hydra. The second flowchart should describe digestion in an earthworm.

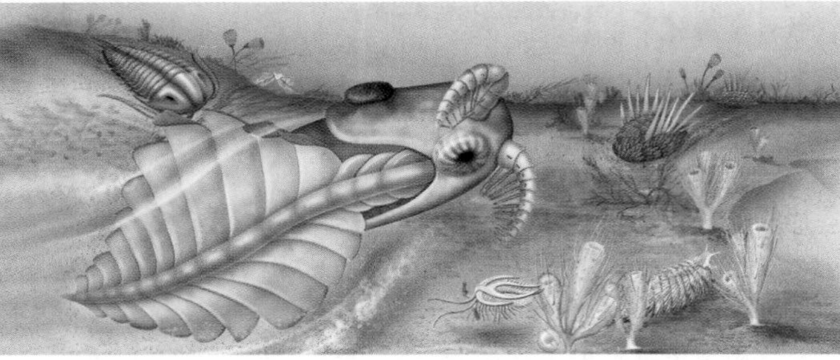

CHAPTER RESOURCES

Print:

- ***Teaching Resources,*** Chapter 29 Vocabulary Review
- ***Test Book,*** Chapter 29 Test

Technology:

- ***Computer Test Bank,*** Chapter 29 Test

Chapter 29 Assessment

Reviewing Content

Choose the letter that best answers the question or completes the statement.

1. The ancestors of most modern animal phyla first appeared during the
   a. Burgess Period.
   b. Cambrian Period.
   c. Precambrian Era.
   d. Ediacaran Period.
2. A cladogram shows
   a. evolutionary relationships.
   b. size relationships.
   c. symbiotic relationships.
   d. functional relationships.
3. Roundworms, which have body cavities that are partially lined with mesoderm, are classified as
   a. acoelomates.
   b. coelomates.
   c. deuterostomes.
   d. pseudocoelomates.
4. An animal that relies primarily on intracellular digestion is the
   a. sponge. c. dragonfly.
   b. clam. d. earthworm.
5. Which organ system does the diagram below illustrate?

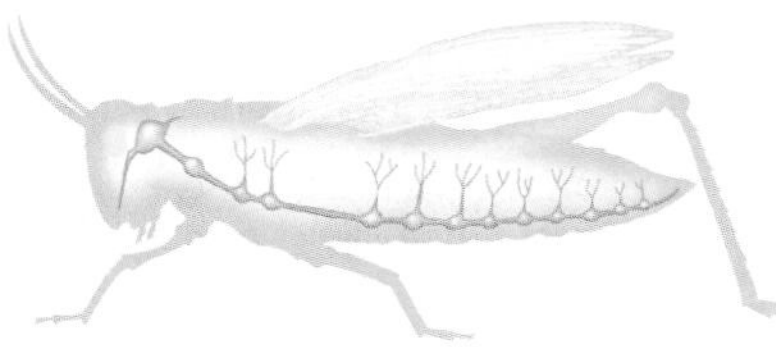

   a. digestive system c. excretory system
   b. circulatory system d. nervous system
6. In order for the exchange of oxygen and carbon dioxide to take place, an animal's respiratory surfaces must be kept
   a. cold. c. hot.
   b. dry. d. moist.
7. In a closed circulatory system, blood
   a. comes in direct contact with tissues.
   b. remains within blood vessels.
   c. empties into sinuses.
   d. does not transport oxygen.
8. Malpighian tubules convert nitrogenous wastes into
   a. urine. c. uric acid.
   b. ammonia. d. urea.
9. The simplest nervous systems are called
   a. ganglia. c. nerve nets.
   b. motor neurons. d. sensory neurons.
10. Individual animals that produce both sperm and eggs are called
    a. gametes. c. buds.
    b. hermaphrodites. d. fragments.

Understanding Concepts

11. What features of Burgess Shale animals are found in most invertebrates living today?
12. What effect did the development of specialized cells have on evolution?
13. Describe the major forms of body symmetry. Give an example for each type of symmetry.
14. What is one major advantage of cephalization?
15. List the three germ layers.
16. Distinguish among the following terms: *acoelomate, pseudocoelomate,* and *coelomate.*
17. Compare the processes of intracellular digestion and extracellular digestion.
18. Why is the development of a one-way digestive system important to the evolution of animals?
19. Describe two types of respiratory structures found in terrestrial invertebrates.
20. Describe the two types of circulatory systems. Give an example of an animal that has each type.
21. What are the three forms of nitrogenous wastes excreted by animals?
22. What three major trends in the evolution of the nervous system do invertebrates exhibit?
23. Describe the three main types of skeletal systems found in invertebrates. Give an example of an animal that has each type.
24. Compare and contrast the processes of asexual reproduction and sexual reproduction.
25. Compare and contrast internal and external fertilization.

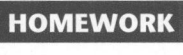

HOMEWORK GUIDE

Section:	**Questions:**
Section 29-1	1–3, 11–16, 28, 31, 33, 35
Section 29-2	4–10, 17–27, 29, 30, 32, 34

17. Intracellular digestion is the process in which food is broken down inside the cell and occurs in simpler organisms. In extracellular digestion, food is broken down outside the cell in specialized structures and occurs in more complex organisms.

18. A one-way digestive system often has specialized regions that allow food to be processed more efficiently.

19. Sample answer: the mantle cavity is moist tissue that has an extensive surface area lined with blood vessels. Book lungs are made of parallel, sheetlike layers of thin tissue that contain blood vessels. Students might also mention spiracles and tracheal tubes.

20. Open circulatory system: found in arthropods and most mollusks; does not keep blood contained within blood vessels; blood comes in direct contact with the tissues, collects in body sinuses, and makes its way back to the heart. Closed circulatory system: found in annelids and chordates; keeps the blood completely contained within blood vessels; materials diffuse from the blood to the tissue, and vice versa through the walls of the blood vessels; blood kept at high pressure.

21. Ammonia, urea, uric acid

22. Centralization, cephalization, and specialization

23. Hydrostatic skeleton: muscles surround a fluid-filled body cavity that supports the muscles. Exoskeleton: system of rigid, nonliving supporting structures that enclose the living tissue of the organism. Endoskeleton: system of rigid support structures embedded within the living tissue of the organism.

24. Asexual reproduction: one parent; offspring are genetically identical. Sexual reproduction: two parents of different sexes; internal or external fertilization; offspring have genetic diversity.

25. In internal fertilization, eggs are fertilized inside the female's body; males deposit sperm in the female's reproductive tract. In external fertilization, eggs are fertilized outside the female's body after sperm and eggs have been released into the water.

Chapter 29 Assessment

Critical Thinking

26. In small aquatic invertebrates, the toxic ammonia diffuses from the animal's body into the water as soon as it is produced, and before it can harm the animal.

27. The slimy mucus coating of slugs helps prevent their bodies from drying out. The mucus coating also aids in the absorption of oxygen and allows slugs to move across surfaces.

28. Animals with bilateral symmetry usually have specialized front and back ends as well as upper and lower sides. Animals with bilateral symmetry usually move with anterior end first, so this end encounters new parts of the environment first. Sense organs tend to gather at the anterior end into a head region; this gathering is cephalization, which is advantageous for feeding and defense.

29. Many terrestrial invertebrates convert ammonia into urea, a less toxic compound that can be concentrated to produce urine. Some terrestrial invertebrates convert ammonia into uric acid, which is concentrated into solid crystals. Both processes concentrate the waste product and therefore reduce water loss.

30. Most respiratory structures found in invertebrates are thin, moist, and have a large surface area. In aquatic invertebrates, respiratory structures are usually exposed directly to the water. The respiratory surfaces of terrestrial animals tend to be located inside the body, where they are protected from drying out.

31. Over the course of evolution, segments often became specialized for specific functions. Therefore, without segmentation, the process of specialization might have been impeded.

32. The diagrams show a hydrostatic skeleton, which consists of longitudinal and circular muscles that surround a fluid-filled cavity. When the muscles contract, they push against the fluid, causing the body to change shape.

33. If a flatworm's flame cells were damaged, its ability to remove excess water would be impaired.

Chapter 29 Assessment

Critical Thinking

26. Inferring The excretory systems of terrestrial invertebrates, such as earthworms, convert ammonia to less toxic components. Why is this change unnecessary in small aquatic invertebrates, such as planarians?

27. Applying Concepts The external surface of slugs is slimy. What might the adaptive advantage of this characteristic be?

28. Applying Concepts Why is bilateral symmetry an important development in the evolution of animals?

29. Problem Solving No matter where they live, all animals need to control the amount of water within their bodies as well as get rid of ammonia—a toxic nitrogenous waste. How were invertebrates able to perform these functions, especially as they moved to terrestrial environments?

30. Comparing and Contrasting Invertebrates use a variety of structures for respiration. How are these structures similar? How are they different?

31. Inferring What might have happened to the evolution of animals if segmentation had not occurred?

32. Applying Concepts The diagrams below show a type of skeletal system found in invertebrates. What is the name for this type of skeleton? Describe how it functions.

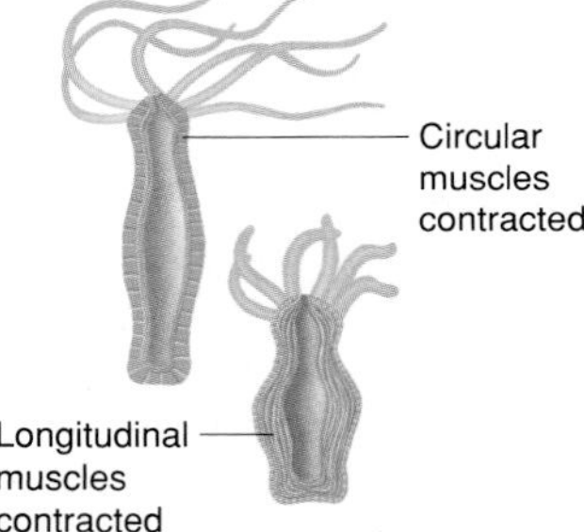

33. Predicting Predict what might happen if a flatworm's flame cells were damaged.

34. Applying Concepts Animals with cephalization have sense organs concentrated in the anterior end. What kinds of things can these animals do that would be difficult or impossible for animals that lack cephalization?

35. Comparing and Contrasting Compare the structures of a hydrostatic skeleton and an exoskeleton. Also compare the way both of these types of skeletons enable movement.

36. Making Connections In Chapter 15, you learned about Charles Darwin's theory of natural selection. How could this theory account for the wide variety of organisms in the Burgess Shale, and the fact that most of those organisms are now extinct?

Performance-Based Assessment

Using the Writing Process Choose a kind of invertebrate, such as a cnidarian or annelid. Imagine that you are that invertebrate and are in the process of looking for employment. Prepare a resume that will inform a potential employer of your specialized skills.

What kinds of organisms lived in the area of the Burgess Shale over 500 million years ago? Visit the Prentice Hall Web site at **www.phschool.com** to see artists' recreations of some Burgess Shale creatures, along with photographs of the fossils. Then, answer the following questions:

- Who discovered the Burgess Shale fossils, and when did the discovery occur?
- How do the Burgess Shale fossils differ from most other Cambrian deposits?
- What unique and unusual characteristics are attributed to the organism called *Opabinia?*

Performance-Based Assessment

Students should identify the type of invertebrate they are and the kind of employment they are seeking. Then, they should match the invertebrate's special functions to the job.

Standardized Test Prep

Test-Taking Tip Before taking a standardized test, it helps to become familiar with the format of the test, including the different question types. One method for this is to complete practice tests, such as this one. Even if you have practiced for a standardized test, be sure to read direction lines carefully before you begin.

Directions: Choose the letter that best answers the question or completes the statement.

1. In protostomes, the blastopore develops into the
(A) ectoderm.
(B) mouth.
(C) anus.
(D) deuterostome.
(E) spiracles.

2. Which trend did NOT occur during invertebrate evolution?
(A) specialization of cells
(B) loss of a true coelom
(C) segmentation of bodies
(D) bilateral symmetry
(E) cephalization

3. All animals have some form of body symmetry EXCEPT
(A) sponges.
(B) jellyfishes.
(C) worms.
(D) arthropods.
(E) echinoderms.

4. What is a function of the excretory system?
(A) to supply cells with oxygen and nutrients
(B) to rid the body of metabolic wastes
(C) to exchange oxygen and carbon dioxide with the environment
(D) to gather information from the environment
(E) to break down food

5. Specialized tissues used to move, breathe, and pump blood are called
(A) germ layers.
(B) excretory systems.
(C) endoderms.
(D) muscles.
(E) ectoderms.

6. Which invertebrates have an open circulatory system?
(A) most mollusks only
(B) arthropods only
(C) annelids only
(D) arthropods and most mollusks only
(E) arthropods and annelids only

7. The concentration of nerve tissue and organs in one end of the body is called
(A) cephalization.
(B) segmentation.
(C) diffusion.
(D) body symmetry.
(E) nerve nets.

8. Which of the following do NOT have a mesoderm?
(A) jellyfishes
(B) earthworms
(C) flatworms
(D) octopi
(E) snails

Questions 9–10

A biology student has two samples of earthworms, as shown below. The student knows that because the worms' body temperature changes with the environment, the worms in Sample A have a higher body temperature than those in Sample B. The student uses a stereomicroscope to count the number of heartbeats per minute for three worms from each sample.

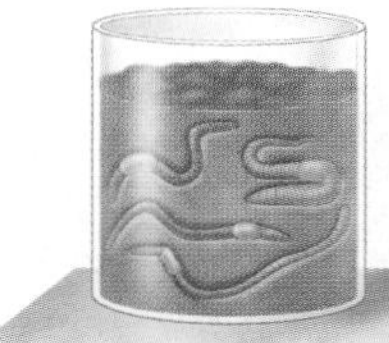

Sample A: At temperature of worms' soil environment

Sample B: In ice water

9. Look at the student's two samples. What can you conclude?
(A) Sample A is the control.
(B) Sample B is the control.
(C) Either sample can serve as the control.
(D) This is not a controlled experiment.
(E) Controlled experiments do not work with living organisms.

10. The student finds that the worms from Sample A have a faster heart rate than the worms from Sample B. What conclusion can be drawn?
(A) The worms in Sample A are healthier than the worms in Sample B.
(B) A decrease in body temperature corresponds to an increase in heart rate.
(C) There is no relationship between body temperature and heart rate.
(D) A decrease in body temperature corresponds to a decrease in heart rate.
(E) The worms in Sample A will not live as long as the worms in Sample B.

Standardized Test Prep

1. B	**5.** D	**9.** A
2. B	**6.** D	**10.** D
3. A	**7.** A	
4. B	**8.** A	

34. Without cephalization, an animal would have difficulty moving forward to catch prey or escape danger. Also, without a concentration of sense organs in one region, the animal could not sense and respond to its environment as efficiently as could an animal with cephalization.

35. A hydrostatic skeleton consists of two layers of muscles, longitudinal and circular, that surround a fluid-filled cavity. An exoskeleton is a hard external skeleton to which muscles attach. In both types of skeletons, the contraction of muscles causes body movement. In the hydrostatic skeleton, the muscles push against the fluid in the body cavity; muscles pull on an exoskeleton, bending and straightening joints.

36. According to Darwin's theory, environmental conditions favorable to many organisms would account for the wide variety of animals in the Burgess Shale. They probably became extinct because of a combination of environmental change and competition with other organisms.

Take It to the NET

- Charles D. Walcott discovered the Burgess Shale fossils in 1909.
- The original organisms were buried in underwater mud that preserved intricate details of their soft parts. In most other Cambrian fossil deposits, only hard parts were preserved.
- *Opabinia* had five eyes and a 2.5 cm proboscis.

For more information visit

www.phschool.com

Unit 9

Dear Colleague,

Most biologists I know have a particular group of critters of which they are especially—some would say inordinately—fond. Some of us establish that fondness early in life, and it becomes one of the reasons we choose to become professional biologists. In other cases, one or another group of critters just happens to grow on us, say sometime between freshman year in college and graduate school.

For me, the process involved both of the above. I grew up in an apartment building whose management prohibited dogs and cats. Birds were out of the question, too, because my brother and I were allergic to feathers. So, when I won a goldfish at a county fair by tossing a coin into its bowl, I started keeping fishes as pets by default. (Incidentally, it wasn't until graduate school that I learned the correct way to use the words *fish* and *fishes*. *Fish* properly refers to a single fish or to a group of individuals of the same species. *Fishes* is used when talking about several individuals of more than one species.)

My early infatuation with fishes stuck. Years later, when professors steered me away from medical school by spiriting me off to a marine biological station in the Caribbean (in January!), fishes were on my mind. Years of home aquarium keeping turned out to be useful professionally; because I could build sophisticated aquaria and maintain delicate specimens, I was able to study a number of odd and unusual species during my graduate research on the evolution of color vision.

A special familiarity with animals is part of the fun of being a biologist. I could tell stories about fishes for days without running out of material. I could also tell stories about other "fish people" who used their expertise in intriguing ways; several

▶ The greater bulldog bat (*Noctilio leporinus*), which is found in Mexico, Argentina, Brazil, and the Bahamas, is one of only a few bat species that catch and eat fish.

ichthyologists I know employed their understanding of fish behavior to become master anglers!

What do we know about chordates?
• There are more species of fishes than all other groups of chordates combined.
• The earliest mammals evolved at about the same time as the early dinosaurs but remained in the shadows until those great reptiles disappeared.
• The arms, legs, wings, and flippers of all four-limbed vertebrates are supported by different versions of the same bones.
What discoveries lie in the future?
• What, exactly, killed the dinosaurs?
• What combination of factors enabled the first vertebrates to leave the water for the land?
• What environmental factors are causing a decline in the populations of amphibians, reptiles, and birds? How can these organisms be protected?
• How do so many fishes, birds, and reptiles navigate thousands of kilometers in their migrations?
KEEP CURRENT WITH . . .
SCIENCE NEWS®
Find out more about topics in this unit:
www.phschool.com

Developing my own expertise was fun, but I got even more of a kick from my fellow graduate students and their "special" knowledge. If I had a question about mammals, I ran up a flight of stairs in our lab building to ask Christine or Kathleen. (Both are now professors; one of them kept a hyrax as a pet back then.) I had two other friends I could ask almost anything about amphibians or reptiles ("herps" we affectionately called them), and a whole floor of folks to bug for information on insects. (Sorry!)

But the most fun came as we compared notes about our pets and experimental subjects. Time and time again, we found useful and fascinating comparisons across the diverse animals we studied. We discussed similarities and differences in the relationship between form and function. We compared animals' sense organs, feeding habits, parental care, and adaptive radiations—in much the same way as Chapter 33 does in this unit. The more we learned, the more we realized that we had lots more yet to learn. Our subject was endless—and endlessly fascinating. To my mind, there is no better remedy for bored and blasé students than a good dose of substantive education in natural history. I'm in good company; no less a thinker than Thomas Henry Huxley agreed:

To a person uninstructed in natural history, his country or seaside stroll is a walk through a gallery filled with wonderful works of art, nine tenths of which have their faces turned to the wall.

Sincerely,

Joe Levine

SCIENCE NEWS®

Have students visit the Prentice Hall Web site at **www.phschool.com** to find the most current information on chordates.

Chapter Planner 30 Nonvertebrate Chordates, Fishes, and Amphibians

Section and Section Objectives	Time	Activities and Labs
30–1 The Chordates, pp. 767–770 **30.1.1** ***Identify*** the characteristics that all chordates share. **30.1.2** ***Explain*** what vertebrates are. **30.1.3** ***Describe*** the two groups of nonvertebrate chordates.	1 period (1/2 block)	**SE:** ***Inquiry Activity,*** Is a lancelet a fish?, p. 766 **TE:** ***Build Science Skills,*** p. 768 **TE:** ***Meet Diverse Needs,*** p. 770
30–2 Fishes, pp. 771–781 **30.2.1** ***Identify*** the basic characteristics of a fish. **30.2.2** ***Summarize*** the evolution of fishes. **30.2.3** ***Explain*** how fishes are adapted for life in water. **30.2.4** ***Describe*** the three main groups of fishes. **30.2.5** ***Describe*** the relationship of fishes to their environment.	2 periods (1 block)	**TE:** ***Demonstration,*** p. 773 **TE:** ***Make Connections,*** p. 773 **SE:** ***Quick Lab,*** How do fishes use gills?, p. 775 **TE:** ***Make Connections,*** p. 776 **TE:** ***Demonstration,*** p. 777 **TE:** ***Build Science Skills,*** p. 778, p. 780
30–3 Amphibians, pp. 782–789 **30.3.1** ***Describe*** what an amphibian is. **30.3.2** ***Summarize*** events in the evolution of amphibians. **30.3.3** ***Explain*** how amphibians are adapted for life on land. **30.3.4** ***Describe*** essential life functions in amphibians. **30.3.5** ***Name*** the main groups of living amphibians. **30.3.6** ***Explain*** the ecology of amphibians.	2 periods (1 block)	**TE:** ***Build Science Skills,*** p. 782, p. 787 **TE:** ***Demonstration,*** p. 784 **TE:** ***Make Connections,*** p. 785 **SE:** ***Analyzing Data,*** Amphibian Population Trends, p. 787 **SE:** ***Exploration,*** Investigating Homeostasis in Fishes and Amphibians, pp. 790–791
Chapter Assessment, pp. 792–795	1 period (1/2 block)	

ACTIVITY PLANNER

SE: ***Inquiry Activity,*** p. 766; (10 min.); bony fish, hand lens, lancelet

TE: ***Build Science Skills,*** p. 768; (10 min.); skeletons of vertebrates

TE: ***Meet Diverse Needs,*** p. 770; (15 min.); preserved lancelet

TE: ***Demonstration,*** p. 773; (10 min.); straw, various objects

TE: ***Make Connections,*** p. 773; (15 min.); clear tub of water, round object, square object, streamlined (spindle-shaped) object

SE: ***Quick Lab,*** p. 775; (10 min.); fish food, food coloring, plastic cup, dropper pipette, live fish in an aquarium

TE: ***Make Connections,*** p. 776; (30 min.); cucumber slices, saltwater solution, distilled water, 2 beakers or jars

TE: ***Demonstration,*** p. 777; (10 min.); balloon, string, screw, tub

TE: ***Build Science Skills,*** p. 778; (20 min.); 10–15 pictures of fishes

TE: ***Build Science Skills,*** p. 780; (30 min); fish, dissecting tools

TE: ***Build Science Skills,*** p. 782; (15 min.); variety of live amphibians

TE: ***Demonstration,*** p. 784; (20 min.); preserved frog or frog model

TE: ***Make Connections,*** p. 785; (5 min.); balloon

TE: ***Build Science Skills,*** p. 787; (30 min.); materials for models

SE: ***Exploration,*** pp. 790–791; (45 min.); 5 g saltwater fish, 5 g freshwater fish, balance, 4 test tubes, paper towels, 2 glass rods, 10-mL graduated cylinder, 2 funnels, 2 filter-paper circles, silver nitrate solution, 1000-mL beaker, vinegar, distilled water, string, scissors, transparent tape, blue litmus paper, sodium bicarbonate (baking soda), glass-marking pencil

PLANNING KEY

Ability Levels

B Basic	For students who need additional help
A Average	For all students
E Enriched	For students who need to be challenged

Components

SE	Student Edition	**GRSW**	Guided Reading and Study Workbook	**IDM**	Issues and Decision Making
TE	Teacher's Edition	**CT**	Chapter Tests: Levels A and B	**CTB**	Computer Test Bank
LMA	Laboratory Manual A	**PHAS**	PH Assessment System	**PA**	Presentation Assistant Plus
LMB	Laboratory Manual B	**LA**	Lab Assessment with Scoring Guide	**BD**	BioDetectives Videotape
TR	Teaching Resources	**BTM**	BioTechnology Manual	**iT**	iText

Program Resources	Assessment	Media and Technology
TR: Section Review 30–1 B A **GRSW:** Section 30–1 B A	**SE:** 30–1 Section Assessment, p. 770 **TR:** Section Review 30–1	**PA:** 30–1 Interest Grabber, Section Outline, Chordate Cladogram, Figure 30–1 **iT:** Section 30–1
TR: Section Review 30–2 B A **GRSW:** Section 30–2 B A **IDM:** 30–1, 30–2 A E	**SE:** 30–2 Section Assessment, p. 781 **TR:** Section Review 30–2	**PA:** 30–2 Interest Grabber, Section Outline, Fish and Frog Circulation, Figure 30–11 **iT:** Section 30–2
LMA: Chapter 30 Lab A E **LMB:** Chapter 30 Lab B A **TR:** Section Review 30–3 B A Chapter 30 Exploration B A E **GRSW:** Section 30–3 B A **IDM:** 30–3 A E	**SE:** 30–3 Section Assessment, p. 789 **TR:** Section Review 30–3	**PA:** 30–3 Interest Grabber, Section Outline, Concept Map, Figure 30–26 **iT:** Section 30–3
	SE: Chapter 30 Assessment, pp. 792–795 **TR:** Chapter Vocabulary Review, Graphic Organizer **CT:** Chapter 30 Test **CTB:** Chapter 30 Test **PHAS:** Practice Test	**CTB:** Chapter 30 Test **iT:** Chapter 30 Assessment

PRESSED FOR TIME?

To Preview the Chapter

- Introduce students to Key Concepts and Vocabulary terms in each section.
- Assign the reading strategy for each section.

To Cover the Chapter Quickly

- Have students read all of Section 30–1, read Form and Function in Fishes and Figures 30–17, 30–18, and 30–19 in Section 30–2, and read Form and Function in Amphibians and Figure 30–28 in Section 30–3.
- Assign the Section Review 30–1; questions 1, 2, 4–12, 15–19, 21–26, and 28–33 in Chapter 30 Assessment; and the Chapter 30 Standardized Test Prep.

To Review the Chapter

- Assign Sections 30–1 through 30–3 in the Guided Reading and Study Workbook.
- Assign Section Reviews for 30–1 through 30–3 and the Chapter Vocabulary Review for Chapter 30 in the Teaching Resources.

ENGAGE/EXPLORE

Inquiry Activity

Objective Students will be able to explain why a lancelet is not a fish.

Skills Focus **Classifying**

Materials bony fish, hand lens, preserved lancelet

Time 10 minutes

Advance Prep Purchase bony fish from a grocery store, fish market, or scientific supply house. Purchase preserved lancelets from a scientific supply house.

Safety Students should wear disposible plastic gloves. Make sure students dispose of the gloves properly and then wash their hands thoroughly after the activity.

Strategy Partially dissect one fish and one lancelet so students can observe muscle structure and the absence of bones in the lancelet. Set this up as a demonstration or have students work in groups.

Expected Outcomes From their comparisons, students should not classify lancelets as fishes.

Think About It

1. Accept all valid comparisons. Similar: Both have a mouth, tail, gill-like structures. Different: Fishes have eyes, jaws, scales, and fins.

2. Accept all reasonably supported answers. Lancelets are not fishes; they lack a backbone.

Brain Teaser

Challenge students to compare a fish, amphibian, reptile, bird, and mammal. Name specific animals to help students focus on what they are comparing. Ask: **How are all of these animals similar?** *(Accept all logical responses, but the best answer is that all have backbones.)*

Chapter 30 Nonvertebrate Chordates, Fishes, and Amphibians

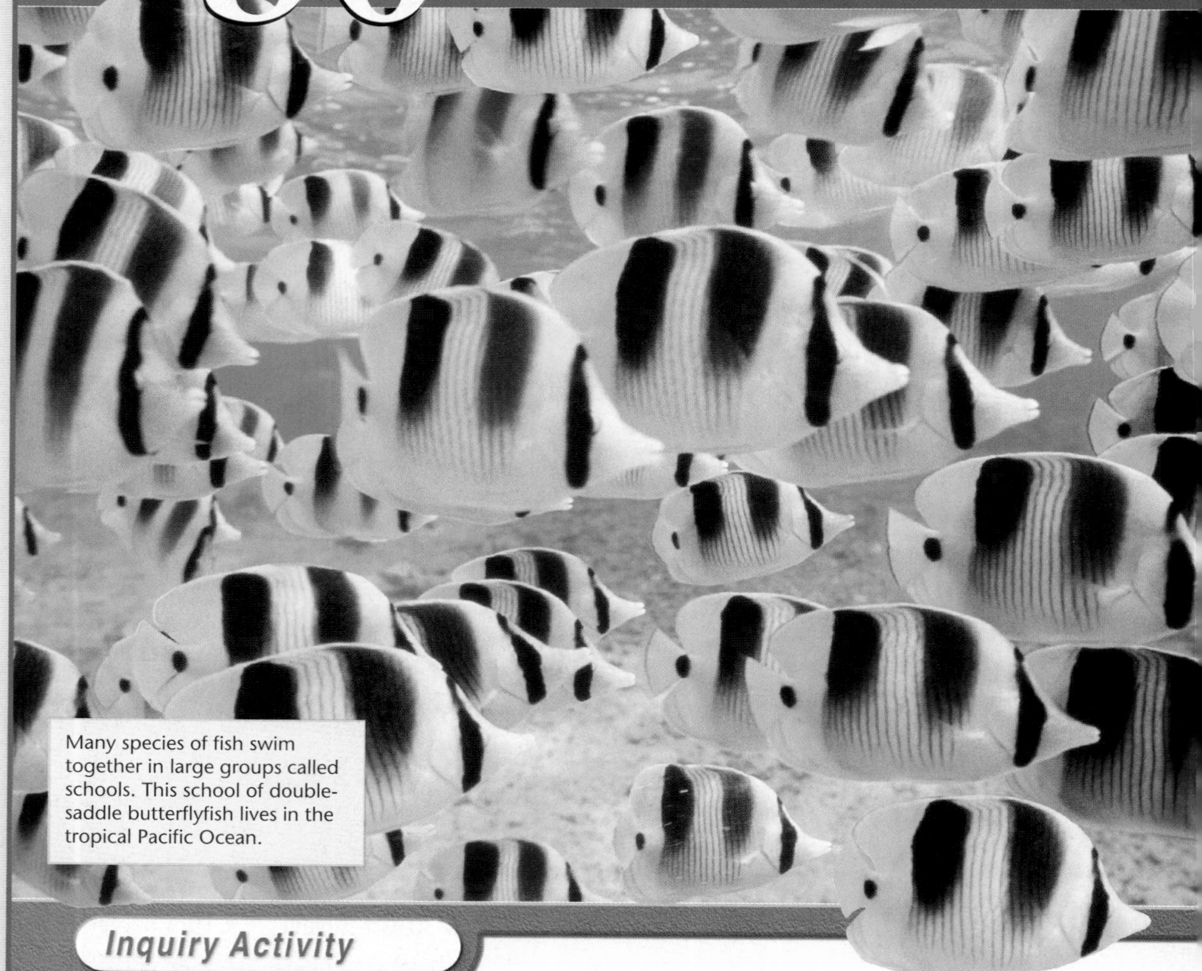

Many species of fish swim together in large groups called schools. This school of double-saddle butterflyfish lives in the tropical Pacific Ocean.

Inquiry Activity

Is a lancelet a fish?

Procedure

1. Closely examine a fish, using a hand lens if you like. Also look at a dissected fish. Record your observations. Make a list of what you think are the main characteristics of fishes.
2. Now, closely examine a preserved lancelet and a dissected lancelet. Make a list of the characteristics of lancelets.

Think About It

1. **Comparing and Contrasting** How are the fish and the lancelet similar? How are they different from each other?
2. **Classifying** Not all fishes have jaws or scales. Given this information, do you think the lancelet is a type of fish? Explain your answer.

FACTS AND FIGURES

Chordates related to echinoderms

Even though it seems that a huge gulf of evolutionary distance separates echinoderms and chordates, the distance is actually not that great. Wormlike marine vertebrates called hemichordates bridge that gulf. Hemichordate larvae look surprisingly similar to echinoderm larvae, suggesting that hemichordates and echinoderms share a common ancestor. Hemichordates also have pharyngeal gill clefts and the suggestion of a dorsal nerve cord that relate them to chordates. And, even more compelling, all three phyla have a common pattern of early embryological development. They are all deuterostome coelomates, meaning that during early embryonic development the mouth forms separately from the anus and internal organs are held within a body cavity.

30–1 The Chordates

At first glance, fishes, amphibians, reptiles, birds, and mammals appear to be very different from one another. Some have feathers; others have fins. Some fly; others swim or crawl. These variations are some of the characteristics that biologists use to separate these animals into different classes, yet all are members of the phylum Chordata (kawr-DAHT-uh).

What Is a Chordate?

Members of the phylum Chordata are called **chordates** (KAWR-dayts). To be classified as a chordate, an animal must have four key characteristics, although these characteristics need not be present during the entire life cycle. **A chordate is an animal that has, for at least some stage of its life, a dorsal, hollow nerve cord; a notochord; pharyngeal (fuh-RIN-jee-ul) pouches; and a tail that extends beyond the anus.** Refer to **Figure 30–1** as you read about each of these characteristics.

The hollow nerve cord runs along the dorsal (back) part of the body. Nerves branch from this cord at regular intervals and connect to internal organs, muscles, and sense organs.

The **notochord** is a long supporting rod that runs through the body just below the nerve cord. Most chordates have a notochord only when they are embryos.

Pharyngeal pouches are paired structures in the throat (pharynx) region. In some chordates—such as fishes and amphibians—slits develop that connect the pharyngeal pouches to the outside of the body. These slits may then develop into gills that are used for gas exchange.

At some point in their lives, all chordates have a tail that extends beyond the anus. The tail can contain bone and muscle and is used in swimming by many aquatic species.

CHECKPOINT *What is a notochord?*

Guide for Reading

Key Concepts
- What characteristics do all chordates share?
- What are the two groups of nonvertebrate chordates?

Vocabulary
chordate
notochord
pharyngeal pouch
vertebra

Reading Strategy: Building Vocabulary
Before you read, preview new vocabulary by skimming the section and making a list of the boldfaced terms. As you read, make notes next to each term.

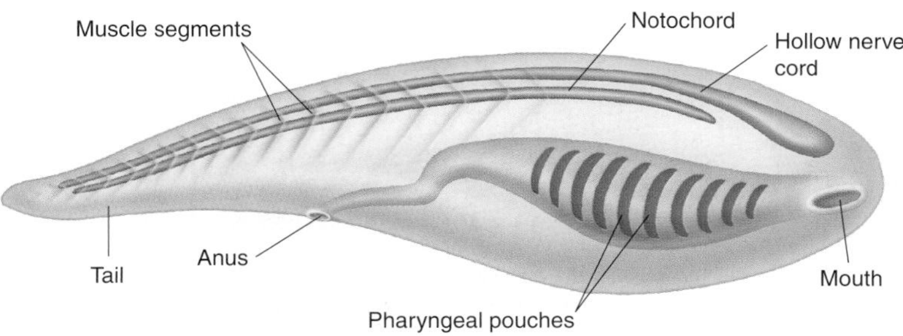

◀ **Figure 30–1 All chordates share four characteristics: a dorsal, hollow nerve cord; a notochord; pharyngeal pouches; and a tail that extends beyond the anus.** Some chordates possess all these characteristics as adults; others, only as embryos.

SECTION RESOURCES

Print:
- ***Teaching Resources,*** Section Review 30–1
- ***Guided Reading and Study Workbook,*** Section 30–1

Technology:
- ***iText,*** Section 30–1

Section 30–1

1 FOCUS

Objectives

30.1.1 ***Identify*** the characteristics that all chordates share.
30.1.2 ***Explain*** what vertebrates are.
30.1.3 ***Describe*** the two groups of nonvertebrate chordates.

Guide for Reading

Vocabulary Preview

Explain that *notochord* comes from the Greek words *noto,* meaning "back," and *chord,* meaning "string." The notochord is the structure for which chordates are named. Also explain that *pharyngeal* is an adjective used to describe objects located in the pharynx, or throat. Ask: **Where would pharyngeal pouches be located?** *(In the pharynx, or throat)*

Reading Strategy

Before students read the section, have them preview Figures 30–1, 30–3, and 30–5. Challenge them to predict how tunicates and lancelets are related. Then, as students read the section, ask them to reassess their predictions.

2 INSTRUCT

What Is a Chordate?

Build Science Skills

Applying Concepts Show students pictures of the embryos of various animals, such as humans, birds, frogs, snakes, and fish. Invite students to identify chordate structures in each embryonic picture. Emphasize that these characteristics need not be present during the entire life cycle of a chordate. In fact, most chordates have these characteristics for only a short time during the embryonic stage.

Answers to . . .

CHECKPOINT *A notochord is a long supporting rod located just below the nerve cord.*

Most Chordates Are Vertebrates

Use Visuals

Figure 30–2 As students study the cladogram, remind them that chordates located on the same branch are more closely related to each other than to other chordates. Also tell them that the points of branching represent common ancestors. Ask: **Which of these chordate groups are more closely related—birds, fishes, reptiles?** *(Birds and reptiles)* Explain that scientists determine the relationships among organisms by their similarities in structure, embryological development, and DNA sequences. Ask: **What structures do all vertebrate chordates have in common?** *(Vertebral column)*

Build Science Skills

Observing Display skeletons of various vertebrates for students to observe. If skeletons are not available, substitute pictures or diagrams. Encourage students to observe the skeletons and locate the vertebral column for each. Make sure they can also identify the vertebrae. Have students describe similarities and differences. Ask: **How are these vertebrates similar?** *(All have backbones and internal skeletons.)* Briefly discuss their differences, explaining that students will learn more about these differences in later chapters.

Make Connections

Physics Explain to students that the pull of the muscles against the vertebral column is responsible for all movement in vertebrates. Muscles and bones work together as levers to produce movement. A lever is a rigid object that moves around a pivot point. The fulcrum is the pivot point of a lever. The input force is the force used to move the lever. Tell students to lift their heads. Explain that the fulcrum is the joint between the topmost vertebrae and the skull. Ask: **What provided the input force?** *(The muscles at the back of the neck)*

Most Chordates Are Vertebrates

The diagram in **Figure 30–2** shows the current understanding of how chordates are related. More than 99 percent of all chordates are placed in the subphylum Vertebrata and are called vertebrates. A vertebrate is a chordate that has a strong supporting structure known as the vertebral column, or backbone. In vertebrates, the dorsal, hollow nerve cord is called the spinal cord. As a vertebrate embryo develops, the front end of the spinal cord grows into a brain. The backbone, which replaces the notochord in most developing vertebrates, is made of individual segments called **vertebrae** (singular: vertebra) that enclose and protect the spinal cord.

A vertebrate's backbone is part of an endoskeleton, or internal skeleton. Like an arthropod's exoskeleton, a vertebrate's endoskeleton supports and protects the animal's body and gives muscles a place to attach. However, unlike an arthropod's exoskeleton, a vertebrate's skeleton grows as the animal grows and does not need to be shed periodically. In addition, whereas an arthropod's skeleton is made entirely of nonliving material, a vertebrate's skeleton contains living cells as well as nonliving material. The cells produce the nonliving material in the skeleton.

CHECKPOINT *What is the function of the vertebral column?*

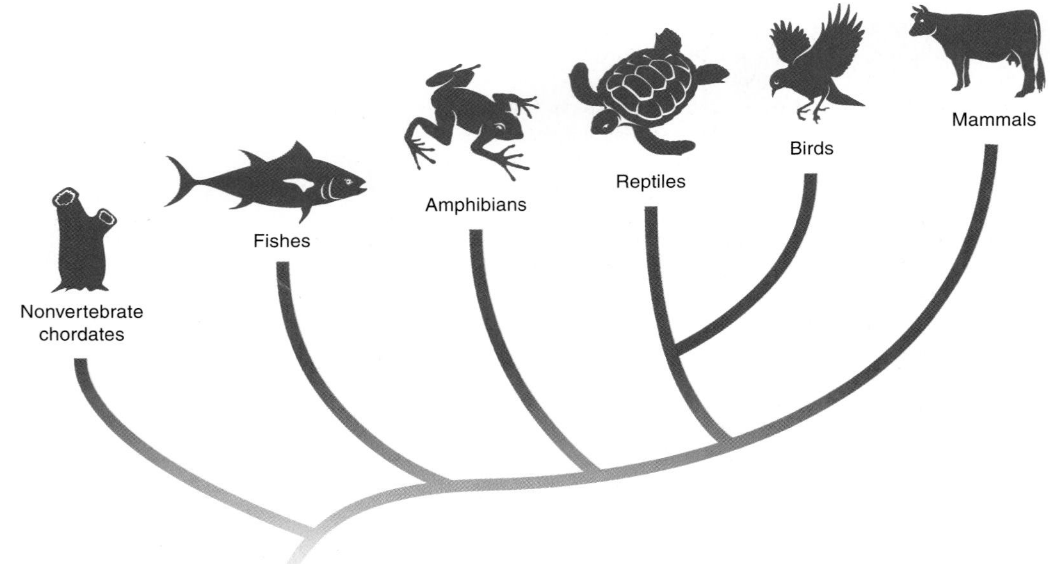

▲ **Figure 30–2** Although nonvertebrate chordates lack a vertebral column, they share a common ancestor with vertebrates. **Interpreting Graphics** *To which other vertebrate group are birds most closely related?*

TIME SAVER **PRESENTATIONS MADE EASY!**

The Presentation Assistant Plus contains the Prentice Hall Presentation Pro and the Transparencies, which provide easy-to-follow visual support for every step of this section. If you have a computer presentation station, use Prentice Hall Presentation Pro for Section 30–1, or use the transparencies listed here.

Section 30–1: 
Interest Grabber
Section Outline
Chordate Cladogram
Figure 30–1

▼ **Figure 30–3** **Tunicates are one of two groups of nonvertebrate chordates.** The tadpole-shaped tunicate larva (left) has all four chordate characteristics. When most tunicate larvae grow into adults, they lose their tails and attach to a solid surface. Adult tunicates (right) look nothing like the larvae, or even like other adult chordates. Both larvae and adults are filter feeders. The blue arrows show where water enters and leaves the tunicate's body.

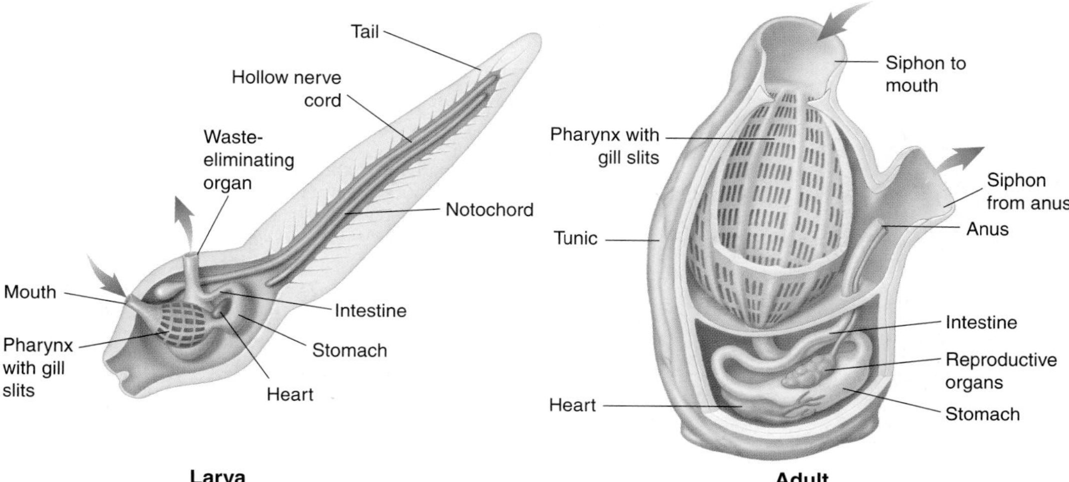

Nonvertebrate Chordates

There are two subphyla of chordates that do not have backbones. **The two groups of nonvertebrate chordates are tunicates and lancelets.** Both are soft-bodied marine organisms. Like all chordates, these animals have a hollow nerve cord, a notochord, pharyngeal pouches, and a tail at some stage of their life cycle.

In some ways, studying nonvertebrate chordates is like using a time machine to investigate the ancestors of our own subphylum, Vertebrata. Similarities in structure and embryological development indicate that vertebrates and nonvertebrate chordates evolved from a common ancestor. Fossil evidence from the Cambrian Period places this divergence at more than 550 million years ago. Although they seem to be simple animals, tunicates and lancelets are relatives of ours—very distant ones.

Tunicates Filter-feeding tunicates (subphylum Urochordata) certainly do not look as if they are related to us. **Figure 30–3** shows the body structure of a tunicate larva and an adult. Observe that the larval form has all of the chordate characteristics. In contrast, adult tunicates, like the ones in **Figure 30–4**, have neither a notochord nor a tail.

▲ **Figure 30–4** Tunicates get their name from the adult's body covering—the tough, nonliving tunic. They are more commonly known as sea squirts, because of the stream of water they sometimes eject. **Inferring** *In what kind of ecosystem are you likely to find tunicates?*

Nonvertebrate Chordates

Build Science Skills

Drawing Conclusions Explain that scientists have two theories that describe the chordate ancestor. In one theory, the ancestor was like a lancelet from which a sessile line evolved to become the tunicates. Another line remained motile and evolved into vertebrates. A second theory describes the ancestor as a tunicate from which lancelets and vertebrates arose from adaptations of the tadpole-shaped tunicate larva. Challenge students to conclude whether the chordate ancestor was like a tunicate or a lancelet. They should give reasons for their choice.

Use Visuals

Figure 30–3 Ask volunteers to point out the chordate structures in the illustration of the tunicate larva. Ask: **What chordate structure is found in the adult?** *(Pharynx with gill slits)* **In what ways do tunicates differ from vertebrates?** *(The notochord does not develop into a vertebral column.)*

Meet Diverse Needs

Encourage at-risk students to construct a Venn diagram that compares and contrasts tunicates and lancelets. Venn diagrams should show the characteristics specific to tunicates, those specific to lancelets, and those shared by both. Ask: **Why are lancelets and tunicates classified as chordates?** *(Both have a notochord, hollow nerve cord, pharyngeal pouches, and a tail at some stage in their life cycle.)* **Learning modality: visual**

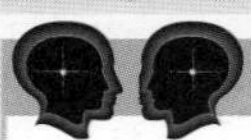

TEACHER TO TEACHER

To help my students actually see the relationship between the spinal cord and the vertebrae, I have them examine chicken necks. These are easy to obtain from the local grocery store or butcher, and I boil them prior to students handling them. First, I encourage students to locate the vertebrae and observe how they are shaped and how they allow movement. Then, I instruct students to use dissecting probes to locate the spinal cord. I also point out that the vertebrae developed from the notochord and the spinal cord came from the dorsal, hollow nerve cord in the embryo. When they have finished examining the chicken necks, I instruct my students to draw labeled diagrams of their observations.

—*Heidi Busa,*
Biology Teacher
Marcellus High School,
Marcellus, NY

Answers to . . .

CHECKPOINT *To enclose and protect the spinal cord and give support*

Figure 30–2 *Birds are most closely related to reptiles.*

Figure 30–4 *In the ocean*

30–1 (continued)

Meet Diverse Needs

All students will benefit from re-examining the preserved lancelet used in the Chapter Inquiry Activity. Encourage students to draw diagrams of the lancelet anatomy and label the four chordate characteristics. Remind students that the lancelet is one of the few chordates that have all four chordate characteristics present in the adult. **Learning modality: visual**

3 ASSESS

Evaluate Understanding

Invite student volunteers to name the four chordate characteristics. Make a table on the board entitled *Nonvertebrate Chordates* with the headings *Tunicates* and *Lancelets*. Call on students to complete the table by describing their key characteristics.

Reteach

Use Figure 30–1 to reinforce the vocabulary words from this section. You might have students write down the definitions of the words on a chordate diagram that they draw themselves. Ask: **Which chordates have vertebrae?** *(Vertebrates)*

ALTERNATIVE ASSESSMENT

Students' articles should be written in the style of the typical newspaper article. Their articles should describe one of the nonvertebrate chordates discussed in this section. You might provide students with copies of *Science News* or *The New York Times* science section as examples of the style and format to use for their articles.

Use iText to review the key concepts in Section 30–1.

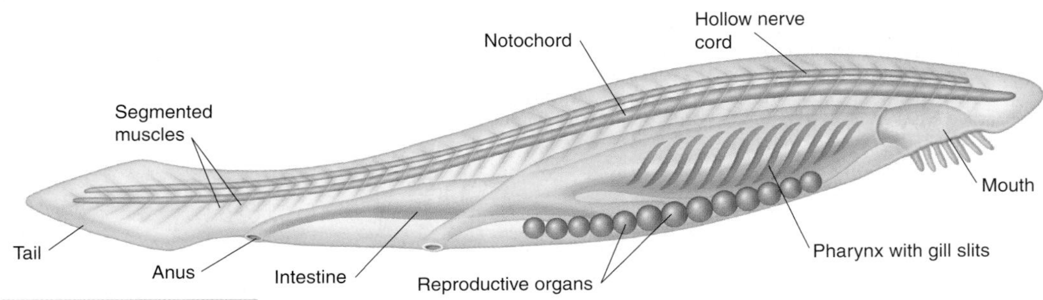

Figure 30–5 Lancelets are small nonvertebrate chordates that often live with their bodies half-buried in sand. Because lancelets do not have fins or legs, they can move only by contracting the paired muscles on their bodies. **Interpreting Graphics** *Which chordate characteristics do lancelets have?*

Lancelets The small, fishlike creatures called lancelets form the subphylum Cephalochordata. Lancelets live on the sandy ocean bottom. You can see a lancelet's body structure in **Figure 30–5.** Observe that, unlike an adult tunicate, an adult lancelet has a definite head region that contains a mouth. The mouth opens into a long pharynx with up to 100 pairs of gill slits. As water passes through the pharynx, a sticky mucus catches food particles. The lancelet then swallows the mucus into the digestive tract. Unlike adult tunicates, lancelets use the pharynx only for feeding, not gas exchange. Lancelets are thin enough to exchange gases through their body surface.

Lancelets have a closed circulatory system. They do not have a true heart. Instead, the walls of the major blood vessels contract to push blood through the body. The fishlike motion of lancelets results from contracting muscles that are organized into V-shaped units. The muscle units are paired on either side of the body.

30–1 Section Assessment

1. **Key Concept** Describe four characteristics of chordates.
2. **Key Concept** How do lancelets and tunicates differ?
3. What one characteristic distinguishes vertebrates from the other chordates?
4. Which characteristics of nonvertebrate chordates suggest that they developed from the same ancestor as vertebrates?
5. **Critical Thinking Inferring** How would a free-swimming larval stage be an advantage for tunicates?

iTEXT Assessment Use iText to review the important concepts in Section 30–1.

ALTERNATIVE ASSESSMENT

Creative Writing
Imagine that a scientist has just discovered the existence of one of the nonvertebrate chordate groups. Write a short newspaper article describing what the scientist has discovered.

30–1 Section Assessment

1. Hollow nerve cord: runs along back, nerves branch from it to rest of body; notochord: long supporting rod located just below nerve cord; pharyngeal pouches: paired structures in the throat region; tail that extends beyond anus
2. Unlike adult tunicates, adult lancelets have a definite head region containing a mouth and use the pharynx only for feeding.
3. The vertebral column, or backbone
4. Similarities in embryological development and structure, i.e., the typical chordate structures of notochord, dorsal nerve cord, etc.
5. Adult tunicates are immobile. Free-swimming larvae disperse the young throughout a wide area. This reduces competition for food and space.

30–2 Fishes

If you think of Earth as land, then the name "Earth" is not particularly appropriate for the planet on which you live, for more than two thirds of its surface is water. And almost anywhere there is water—fresh or salt—there are fishes. At the edge of the ocean, blennies jump from rock to rock and occasionally dunk themselves in tide pools. Beneath the Arctic ice live fishes whose bodies contain a biological antifreeze that keeps them from freezing solid. In some shallow desert streams, pupfishes tolerate temperatures that would cook almost any other animal.

What Is a Fish?

You might think that with such extreme variations in habitat, fishes would be difficult to characterize. However, describing a fish is a rather simple task.  **Fishes are aquatic vertebrates that are characterized by paired fins, scales, and gills.** Fins are used for movement, scales for protection, and gills for exchanging gases. You can observe most of those characteristics in **Figure 30–6.**

Fishes are so varied, however, that for almost every general statement there are exceptions. For example, some fishes, such as catfish, do not have scales. One reason for the enormous diversity among living fishes is that these chordates belong to very different classes. Thus, many fishes—sharks, lampreys, and perch, for example—are no more similar to one another than humans are to frogs!

CHECKPOINT *What are the basic functions of fins, scales, and gills?*

Guide for Reading

Key Concepts
- What are the basic characteristics of a fish?
- What were the important developments during the evolution of fishes?
- How are fishes adapted for life in water?
- What are the three main groups of fishes?

Vocabulary
- cartilage • atrium • ventricle
- cerebrum • cerebellum
- medulla oblongata
- lateral line system
- swim bladder • oviparous
- ovoviviparous • viviparous

Reading Strategy: Using Prior Knowledge
Before you read, make a list of the things you already know about fishes. After you have finished reading, check the list. Correct any errors and add new facts.

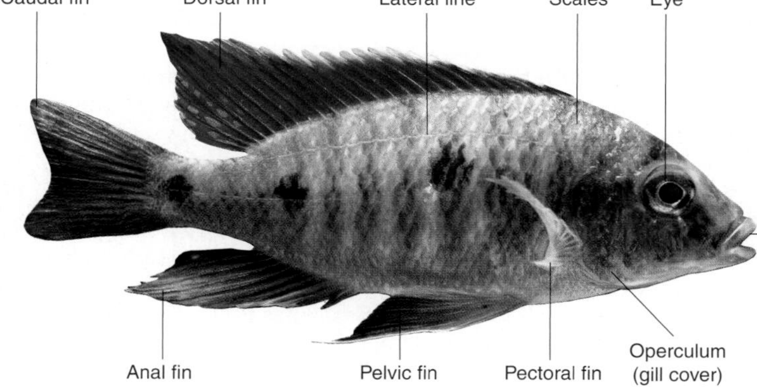

◀ **Figure 30–6** Fishes come in many shapes and sizes. **Like most fishes, this African cichlid has paired fins, scales, and gills.**

SECTION RESOURCES

Print:
- ***Teaching Resources,*** Section Review 30–2
- ***Guided Reading and Study Workbook,*** Section 30–2
- ***Issues and Decision Making,*** 30–1, 30–2

Technology:
- ***iText,*** Section 30–2

Section 30–2

1 FOCUS

Objectives

30.2.1 ***Identify*** the basic characteristics of a fish.
30.2.2 ***Summarize*** the evolution of fishes.
30.2.3 ***Explain*** how fishes are adapted for life in water.
30.2.4 ***Describe*** the three main groups of fishes.
30.2.5 ***Describe*** the relationship of fishes to their environment.

Guide for Reading

Vocabulary Preview

Read aloud the Vocabulary terms so that students can hear the correct pronunciation of each word. Encourage students to use the phonetic spellings in the text to practice saying the words aloud.

Reading Strategy

Encourage students to write down the Vocabulary terms and their meanings as they read. Also encourage them to sketch some of the diagrams to help them visualize some of the body systems in fishes.

2 INSTRUCT

What Is a Fish?

Build Science Skills

Using Models Challenge students to create a model of a fish based on the defining characteristics of fishes: aquatic vertebrate with fins, scales, and gills. Encourage students to design their model fish to have specific adaptations to survive in its particular environment. Students can simply illustrate their fish models or create a three-dimensional model. Have students present their models to the class.

Answers to . . .

CHECKPOINT *Fins: movement, scales: protection, gills: gas exchange*

Figure 30–5 *All four chordate characteristics*

Evolution of Fishes

Meet Diverse Needs

Have at-risk students make a time line to show the sequence of events in the evolution of fishes. Students should list the major stages of fish evolution as they read this subsection. Refer them to the Geologic Time Scale in Figure 17–5 on page 421 of this textbook to help them put the evolution of fishes in perspective with the evolution of other species in Earth's history. **Learning modality: logical/mathematical**

Address Misconceptions

Some students might be under the impression that the fossil record for fishes is complete. Ask: **What parts of an organism fossilize well?** *(Hard parts, such as bone and teeth)* **Which parts do not?** *(Soft tissue)* Explain that many early fishes had few hard body parts (bones) and scientists make many inferences about the gaps in the fossil record based on the structures of living organisms and fossils.

Use Visuals

Figure 30–7 Challenge students to infer how the various adaptations of the fishes in the illustration made them better suited to their environment. Explain that after the adaptive radiation during the Ordovician and Silurian periods, fishes inhabited every kind of environment in the oceans. Ask: **Why do you think some of these early fishes eventually became extinct at the end of the Devonian Period?** *(They were not as efficient at moving, getting food, and protecting themselves against predators as fishes with jaws and paired fins.)*

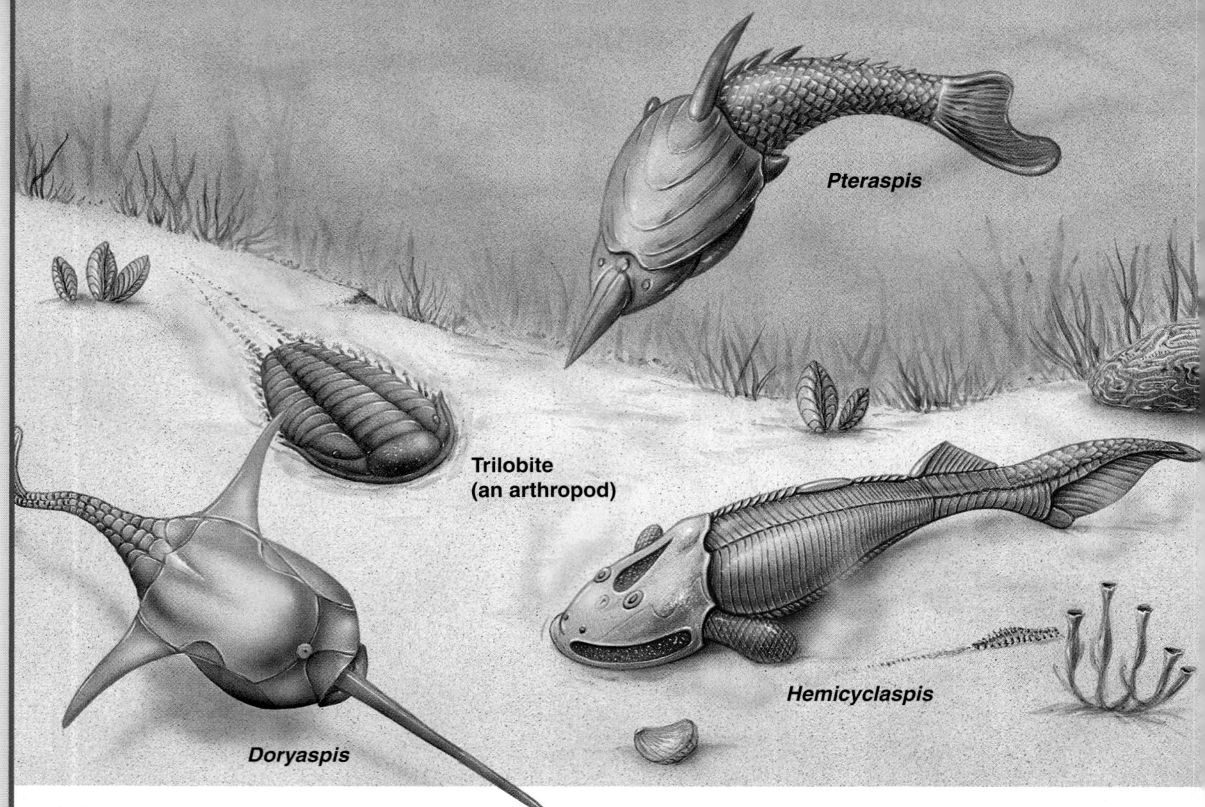

▲ **Figure 30–7** Ancient jawless fishes swam in shallow seas during the early Devonian Period, about 400 million years ago. Lacking jaws, early jawless fishes were limited in their ability to feed and to defend themselves against predators. **The evolution of paired fins, however, gave these fishes more control over their movement in the water.**

Evolution of Fishes

Fishes were the first vertebrates to evolve. They did not arise directly from tunicates or lancelets, but fishes and nonvertebrate chordates probably did evolve from common invertebrate ancestors. During the course of their evolution, fishes underwent several important changes. **The evolution of jaws and the evolution of paired fins were important developments during the rise of fishes.**

The First Fishes The earliest fishes to appear in the fossil record were odd-looking, jawless creatures whose bodies were armored with bony plates. They lived in the oceans during the late Cambrian Period, about 510 million years ago. Fishes kept this armored, jawless body plan for 100 million years.

The Age of Fishes During the Ordovician and Silurian Periods, about 505 to 410 million years ago, fishes underwent a major adaptive radiation. The species to emerge from the radiation ruled the seas during the Devonian Period, which is often called the Age of Fishes. Some of these fishes were jawless species that had very little armor. These jawless fishes were the ancestors of modern hagfishes and lampreys. Others, such as those in **Figure 30–7,** were armored and ultimately became extinct at the end of the Devonian Period, about 360 million years ago.

TIME SAVER — PRESENTATIONS MADE EASY!

The Presentation Assistant Plus contains the Prentice Hall Presentation Pro and the Transparencies, which provide easy-to-follow visual support for every step of this section. If you have a computer presentation station, use Prentice Hall Presentation Pro for Section 30–2, or use the transparencies listed here.

Section 30–2:

Interest Grabber
Section Outline
Fish and Frog Circulation
Figure 30–11

The Arrival of Jaws and Paired Fins Still other ancient fishes kept their bony armor and possessed a feeding adaptation that would revolutionize vertebrate evolution: These fishes had jaws. Observe the powerful jaws of the ancient fish in **Figure 30–8.** Jaws are an extremely useful adaptation. Jawless fishes are limited to eating small particles of food that they filter out of the water or suck up like a vacuum cleaner. Because jaws can hold teeth and muscles, jaws make it possible for vertebrates to nibble on plants and munch on other animals. Thus, animals with jaws can eat a much wider variety of food. They can also defend themselves by biting.

The evolution of jaws in early fishes accompanied the evolution of paired pectoral (anterior) and pelvic (posterior) fins. These fins were attached to girdles—structures of cartilage (KAHR-tl-ij) or bone that support the fins. **Cartilage** is a strong tissue that supports the body and is softer and more flexible than bone. **Figure 30–9** shows the fins and fin girdles in one ancient fish species.

Paired fins gave fishes more control of body movement. In addition, tail fins and powerful muscles gave fishes greater thrust when swimming. The combination of accuracy and speed enabled fishes to move in new and varied patterns. This ability, in turn, helped fishes use their jaws in complex ways.

The Rise of Modern Fishes Although the early jawed fishes soon disappeared, they left behind two major groups that continued to evolve and still survive today. One group—the ancestors of modern sharks and rays—evolved a skeleton made of strong, resilient cartilage. The other group evolved skeletons made of true bone. A subgroup of bony fishes, called lobe-finned fishes, had fleshy fins from which the limbs of chordates would later evolve.

CHECKPOINT *Which two groups of early jawed fishes still survive today?*

▲ **Figure 30–8** This photograph shows a reconstruction of an ancient armored fish called *Dunkleosteus,* an enormous predator that lived in the inland seas of North America during the late Devonian Period. **Drawing Conclusions** *What feature made this fish a successful predator in its time?*

▼ **Figure 30–9** This ancient Devonian fish is called *Eusthenopteron.* Although its skeleton differs from those of most modern fishes, its basic features—vertebral column, fins, and fin girdles—have been retained in many species. **Comparing and Contrasting** *How does this fish differ from the fishes in* **Figure 30–7***?*

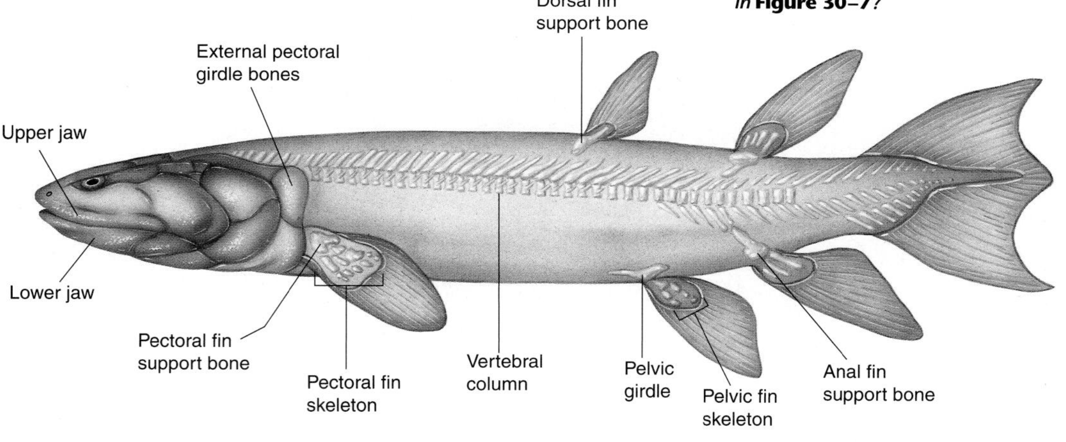

Demonstration

Show students how jaws enabled fishes to eat a larger variety of food by comparing a drinking straw to your hand mimicking the action of a jaw. Use the straw to try to pick up a variety of objects that represent food. Then, use your hand acting as a jaw to pick up those same objects. Ask: **What advantage did a jaw give to fishes?** *(Jaws enabled fishes to open up their mouths and close them with force in order to bite larger pieces of food from a larger variety of food sources. They also provided a means for defense—biting.)*

Make Connections

Physics Explain that a fish must overcome inertia, or the resistance to motion, to move through water. Most of this resistance is in the form of drag, which is caused by the friction of water as it flows over the body of the fish. Drag is also caused by the backward pull of the eddies of water that form behind the fish's tail. If the fish is streamlined, the water flowing past both sides of the fish meet and blend together, producing less turbulence and, hence, less drag. Students can experiment with different body shapes moving through water to observe this phenomena. They might compare the eddies of a round object, a square object, and a streamlined (spindle-shaped) object as they move them through water.

FACTS AND FIGURES

New tail design makes fish faster
Primitive fishes had asymmetrical tails in which the vertebral column either pointed upward or downward as it extended from the body. When the fins pushed against the water to propel the fish forward, the movement was inefficient. The forward push was unevenly distributed along the body of the fish.

Modern fishes have tails in which two symmetrical lobes extend from the end of the vertebral column. The forward thrust provided by this tail is greater and more evenly distributed along the length of the body. Fishes with symmetrical tails swim faster and more efficiently. Most of the back and forth motion that propels the fish forward comes from the posterior end of the fish, keeping the anterior end still and better streamlined.

Answers to . . .

CHECKPOINT *Sharks and rays and lobe-finned fishes*

Figure 30–8 *Powerful jaws*

Figure 30–9 *It has jaws.*

30–2 (continued)

Form and Function in Fishes

Meet Diverse Needs

Preview this subsection with students with limited English proficiency by writing the key words on the board and reading them aloud. Help students find synonyms for the words as you discuss their meanings. Reinforce the meanings of these words by locating the structures on a fish diagram or by drawing diagrams to illustrate the meaning of the words. **Limited English proficiency**

Use Visuals

Figure 30–11 Have students trace the path of food through the digestive system in the illustration. Ask: **Where does digestion occur?** *(Stomach, pyloric secum, intestine)* **Where does nutrient absorption occur?** *(Pyloric secum, intestine)* Explain that the size of the stomach and intestines varies among fishes, depending on their mode of feeding. Ask: **Would you expect herbivores or carnivores to have a longer digestive tract?** *(Herbivores; plant matter is more difficult to digest because of the cellulose in the cell walls of plant cells.)*

Use Community Resources

Take students to a local aquarium, zoo, or fish store to give them the opportunity to observe many different fishes and their adaptations. Before going, make a class list of adaptations to look for, such as specific adaptations for getting food, attracting mates, defending against predators, and moving. When viewing the fishes, discuss their specific adaptations and how they help the fishes to survive.

▲ **Figure 30–10** **Adaptations to aquatic life include various modes of feeding.** This deep-sea anglerfish has a built-in "fishing pole" that it uses to attract prey.

Form and Function in Fishes

Over time, fishes have evolved to survive in a tremendous range of aquatic environments. **Adaptations to aquatic life include various modes of feeding, specialized structures for gas exchange, and paired fins for locomotion.** Fishes have other types of adaptations, too, as you will learn.

Feeding Every mode of feeding is seen in fishes. There are herbivores, carnivores, parasites, filter feeders, and detritus feeders. In fact, a single fish may exhibit several modes of feeding, depending on what type of food happens to be available. Certain carp, for example, eat algae, aquatic plants, worms, mollusks, arthropods, dead fish, and detritus. Other fishes, such as barracuda, are highly specialized carnivores. A few fishes, such as some lampreys, are parasites. **Figure 30–10** shows a fish that even uses a fleshy bait to catch its meals!

Use **Figure 30–11** to locate the internal organs that are important during the fish's digestion of its food. From the fish's mouth, food passes through a short tube called the esophagus to the stomach, where it is partially broken down. In many fishes, the food is further processed in fingerlike pouches called pyloric ceca (py-LAWR-ik SEE-kuh; singular: cecum). The pyloric ceca secrete digestive enzymes and absorb nutrients from the digested food. Other organs, including the liver and pancreas, add enzymes and other digestive chemicals to the food as it moves through the digestive tract. The intestine completes the process of digestion and nutrient absorption. Any undigested material is eliminated through the anus.

▼ **Figure 30–11** The internal organs of a typical bony fish are shown here. **Applying Concepts** ***What is the function of the pyloric cecum?***

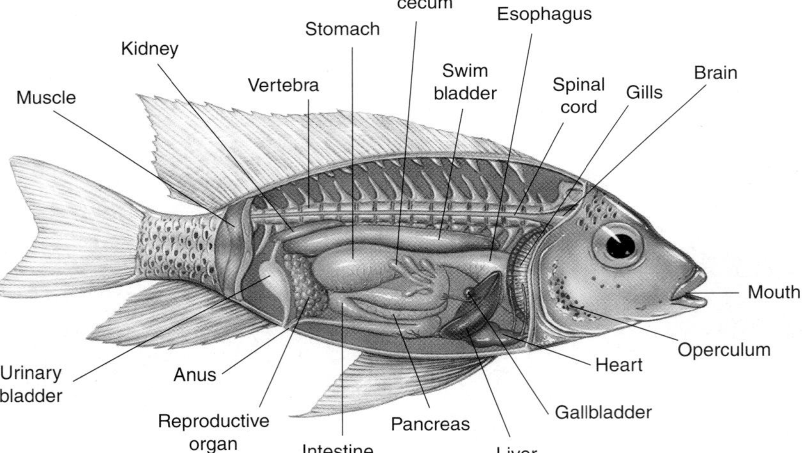

FACTS AND FIGURES

Getting a hold on food

Scientists observe as many different mouth and teeth adaptations in fishes as there are modes of feeding. Most carnivores have simple, cone-shaped teeth on the jaws, roof of the mouth, and gill arches in the pharynx. The teeth in the pharynx region are commonly called throat teeth. In many carnivores, the teeth hold prey and orient it for swallowing. Such fishes have a flexible esophagus to accommodate the size of the food. Some carnivores have cutting teeth for biting chunks off their prey.

Many fishes have only throat teeth, which are used to crush or grind food. Others have no teeth at all. These fishes, often those that eat plankton, have many long, stiff rods, called gill rakers, attached to the gill bars. These rakers strain food from the water as it passes over the gills.

Quick Lab

How do fishes use gills?

Materials fish food, food coloring, plastic cup, dropper pipette, live fish in an aquarium

Procedure

1. Mix some fish food and food coloring in a small volume of aquarium water in a plastic cup.
2. Use a dropper pipette to release the mixture near a fish in an aquarium. Release the mixture gently so that it does not scatter.
3. Observe what happens when the fish approaches the mixture. Watch the fish's gills especially closely.

Analyze and Conclude

1. **Drawing Conclusions** Describe what happened to the food coloring. What does this tell you about how water moves through a fish's body?
2. **Inferring** Why do most fishes seem to move or swallow continuously? What might happen if a fish were not able to move or stopped "swallowing"?

Respiration Most fishes exchange gases using gills located on either side of the pharynx. The gills are made up of feathery, threadlike structures called filaments. Each filament contains a network of fine capillaries that provides a large surface area for the exchange of oxygen and carbon dioxide. Fishes that exchange gases using gills do so by pulling oxygen-rich water in through their mouths, pumping it over their gill filaments, and then pushing oxygen-poor water out through openings in the sides of the pharynx.

Some fishes, such as lampreys and sharks, have several gill openings. Most fishes, however, have a single gill opening on each side of the body through which water is pumped out. This opening is hidden beneath a protective bony cover called the operculum.

A number of fishes—such as the lungfish in **Figure 30–12**—have an adaptation that allows them to survive in oxygen-poor water or in areas where bodies of water often dry up. These fishes have specialized organs that serve as lungs. A tube brings oxygen from the air to this organ through the fish's mouth. Some lungfishes are so dependent on getting oxygen from the air that they will suffocate if prevented from reaching the surface of the water.

CHECKPOINT *What structures do fishes use for gas exchange?*

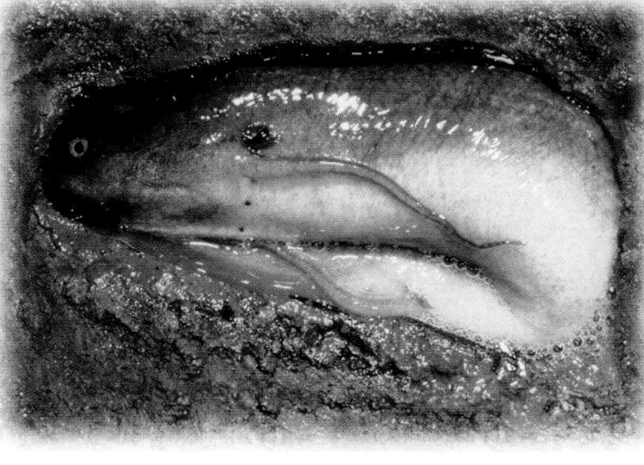

▶ **Figure 30–12** This African lungfish has a breathing adaptation that allows it to survive in shallow waters that are subject to drought. It burrows into mud, covers itself with mucus, and becomes dormant. For several months until the rains fall, the lungfish breathes through its mouth and lungs. **Drawing Conclusions** ***How is it an advantage for this lungfish to cover itself with mucus?***

FACTS AND FIGURES

Sharks don't stop to breathe

Sharks have five to seven gill slits on both sides of their heads. In order to breathe, water must continually flow across these gill slits. Sharks do not open and close their mouth to pump water across their gills as bony fish do. To keep water flowing across the gill slits, a shark must swim constantly. They can stop swimming if they stop in a current. Nurse sharks will fan water across the gills with their fins.

Some sharks have spiracles, which are an extra pair of gill slits located behind the eyes. These gill slits enable sharks to breathe while their mouth is full. Spiracles are also commonly found on bottom-dwelling sharks to help them breathe while they are resting on the ocean floor. Most fast-swimming sharks do not have spiracles.

Quick Lab

Objective Students will be able to infer how fishes use gills.

Skills Focus **Drawing Conclusions, Inferring**

Materials fish food, food coloring, plastic cup, dropper pipette, live fish in an aquarium

Time 10 minutes

Advance Prep Do not feed the fish for 2–3 days before the activity.

Strategies

- For optimum visibility of the flow of food coloring, transfer the fish to any clear container with water about 4 cm deep and place these containers on a white background.
- Do not operate air pumps during the activity.

Expected Outcomes Students should observe the food coloring move into the fish's mouth and out through its gills.

Analyze and Conclude

1. The food coloring moved into the fish's mouth and out through its gills. This shows the path of water through a fish's body.
2. To keep water moving over the gills; it could die from lack of oxygen.

Build Science Skills

Applying Concepts Ask: **What structures increase the surface area of gills?** *(Feathery filaments)* **What advantage does this give fishes?** *(Take in more oxygen and remove more carbon dioxide in less time)* Challenge students to consider other biological processes, organisms, or objects in which an increased surface area is advantageous. *(Examples include wide leaves—getting energy from sunlight; wide fan blades—moving air; ramps—moving objects.)*

Answers to . . .

CHECKPOINT *Gills or lunglike organs*

Figure 30–11 *The pyloric cecum secretes digestive enzymes and absorbs nutrients.*

Figure 30–12 *Mucus prevents the fish from drying out as water evaporates.*

Use Visuals

Figure 30–13 Ask: **What makes the circulatory system in fishes a closed system?** *(The blood is enclosed in vessels.)* As students study the direction of blood flow in the diagram, point out that the blood travels in one loop and that the fish heart has only one atrium and one ventricle. Ask: **Does the heart pump oxygenated blood?** *(No)* **Why not?** *(The heart pumps deoxygenated blood from the body directly to the gills; from the gills, the oxygenated blood goes directly to the body tissues.)*

Make Connections

Chemistry To review osmosis, soak cucumber slices in a saltwater solution and in distilled water for about 30 minutes. Discuss the results of the experiment, focusing on where water had the higher and lower concentrations. *(Salt water: lower concentration of water, cucumber shriveled; distilled water: higher concentration of water, cucumber swelled)* Ask: **What could happen to saltwater fishes if they did not have kidneys?** *(Shrivel up because the water concentration is less outside their body.)* **To freshwater fishes?** *(Bloat because the water concentration is greater outside their body.)*

Address Misconceptions

Students might get the mistaken idea that fishes moving from salt water to fresh water can consciously adjust their kidneys to function one way or another. Relate the involuntary control fishes have over their internal organs to the involuntary control that students have over some of their own body functions, such as digesting food.

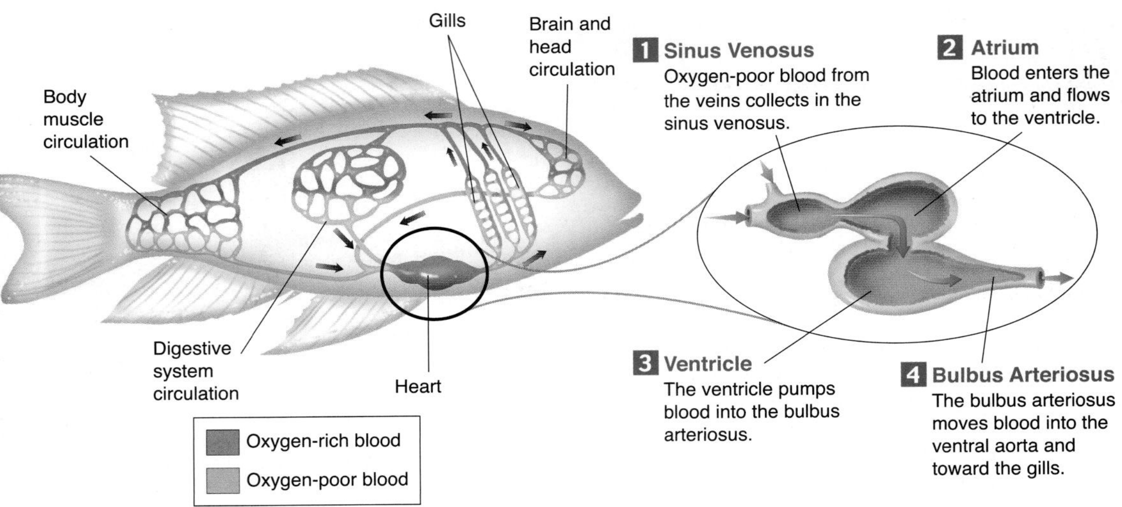
Gills
Brain and head circulation
Body muscle circulation
1 Sinus Venosus
Oxygen-poor blood from the veins collects in the sinus venosus.
2 Atrium
Blood enters the atrium and flows to the ventricle.
Digestive system circulation
Heart
3 Ventricle
The ventricle pumps blood into the bulbus arteriosus.
4 Bulbus Arteriosus
The bulbus arteriosus moves blood into the ventral aorta and toward the gills.
Oxygen-rich blood
Oxygen-poor blood

▲ **Figure 30–13** Blood circulates through a fish's body in a single loop—from the heart to the gills to the rest of the body, and then back to the heart again. **Interpreting Graphics** ***Is the blood that flows from the heart to the gills rich in oxygen or does it lack oxygen?***

Circulation Fishes have closed circulatory systems with a heart that pumps blood around the body in a single loop—from the heart to the gills, from the gills to the rest of the body, and back to the heart. **Figure 30–13** shows the path of blood and the structure of the heart.

In most fishes, the heart consists of four parts: the sinus venosus (SYN-us vuh-NOH-sus), atrium (AY-tree-um), ventricle, and bulbus arteriosus (BUL-bus ahr-teer-ee-OH-sus). The sinus venosus is a thin-walled sac that collects blood from the fish's veins before it flows to the **atrium,** a large muscular chamber that serves as a one-way compartment for blood that is about to enter the ventricle. The **ventricle,** a thick-walled, muscular chamber, is the actual pumping portion of the heart. It pumps blood to a large, muscular tube called the bulbus arteriosus. At its front end, the bulbus arteriosus connects to a large blood vessel called the aorta, through which blood moves to the fish's gills.

Excretion Like many other aquatic animals, most fishes rid themselves of nitrogenous wastes in the form of ammonia. Some wastes diffuse through the gills into the surrounding water. Others are removed by kidneys, which are excretory organs that filter wastes from the blood.

Kidneys help fishes control the amount of water in their bodies. Fishes in salt water tend to lose water by osmosis. To solve this problem, the kidneys of marine fishes concentrate wastes and return as much water as possible to the body. In contrast, a great deal of water continually enters the bodies of freshwater fishes. The kidneys of freshwater fishes pump out plenty of dilute urine. Some fishes are able to move from fresh to salt water by adjusting their kidney function.

BIO INSIGHTS

FACTS AND FIGURES

Salty fish

Both saltwater fishes and freshwater fishes have an internal salt content of about one percent. With the concentration of salt in ocean water at about 3.5 percent, the body systems of saltwater fishes must work to conserve water. Most saltwater fishes drink ocean water and secrete excess salt from the gills. Sharks and rays, however, maintain a high concentration of salt within their body by storing urea in the blood. These fishes do not lose water by osmosis and do not need to drink water.

Freshwater fishes live in environments with a very low concentration of salt. To keep from taking up too much water, freshwater fishes do not drink water and their kidneys serve to pump water out of their bodies in very dilute urine. Freshwater fishes still lose salt, however, and take in the dilute salts in the water with the gills.

Response Fishes have well-developed nervous systems organized around a brain, which has several parts, as shown in **Figure 30–14.** The most anterior parts of a fish's brain are the olfactory bulbs, which are involved with the sense of smell, or olfaction. They are connected to the two lobes of the cerebrum (SEHR-uh-brum). In most vertebrates, the **cerebrum** is responsible for all voluntary activities of the body. However, in fishes, the cerebrum primarily processes the sense of smell. The optic lobes process information from the eyes. The **cerebellum** (sehr-uh-BEL-um) coordinates body movements. The **medulla oblongata** (mih-DUH-luh ahb-lahn-GAHT-uh) controls the functioning of many internal organs.

Most fishes have highly developed sense organs. Almost all fishes that are active in daylight have well-developed eyes and color vision that is at least as good as yours. Many fishes have specialized cells called chemoreceptors that are responsible for their extraordinary senses of taste and smell. Although most fishes have ears inside their head, they may not hear sounds well. Most fishes can, however, detect gentle currents and vibrations in the water with a sensitive receptor called the **lateral line system.** Fishes use this system to sense the motion of other fishes or prey swimming nearby. In addition to detecting motion, some fishes, such as catfish and sharks, have evolved sense organs that can detect low levels of electric current. Some fishes, such as the electric eel shown in **Figure 30–15,** can even generate their own electricity!

CHECKPOINT *What are the parts of a fish's brain?*

Movement Most fishes move by alternately contracting paired sets of muscles on either side of the backbone. This creates a series of S-shaped curves that move down the fish's body. As each curve travels from the head toward the tail fin, it creates backward force on the surrounding water. This force, along with the action of the fins, propels the fish forward. The fins of fishes are also used in much the same way that airplanes use stabilizers, flaps, and rudders—to keep on course and adjust direction. Fins also increase the surface area of the tail, providing an extra boost of speed. The streamlined body shapes of most fishes help reduce the amount of drag (friction) as they move through the water.

Because their body tissues are more dense than the water they swim in, sinking is an issue for fishes. Many bony fishes have an internal, gas-filled organ called a **swim bladder** that adjusts their buoyancy. The swim bladder lies just beneath the backbone.

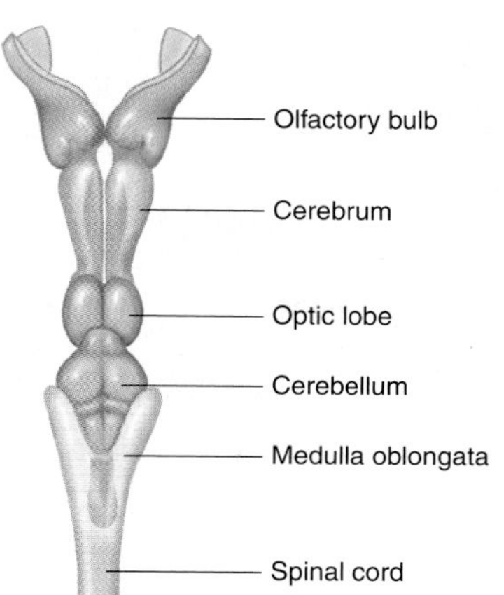

▲ **Figure 30–14** The brain of a fish, like all vertebrate brains, is situated at the anterior end of the spinal cord and has several different parts. **Inferring** *How might the size of the various parts of the brain differ in a blind cave fish that relies primarily on its sense of smell?*

▶ **Figure 30–15** The electric eel, *Electrophorus electricus,* can produce several hundred volts of electricity in brief bursts. **Formulating Hypotheses** *What function might such powerful electric bursts serve?*

Build Science Skills

Posing Questions Challenge students to consider a fish's senses and the environment in which it lives. For example, have students consider the different environments of fishes living near the water's surface and those living along the bottom. Have small student groups work together to develop a scientific question about the senses of these two groups of fishes and how they might be similar or different. Remind students that a scientific question is very specific so that it can be answered through observation and experimentation. Discuss each group's question and possible methods of finding its answer.

Demonstration

Show students how a swim bladder works by tying a small screw to the neck of a deflated balloon. Ask: **Why did the "fish" sink?** *(The "fish" weighed more than the force of the water pushing up on it.)* Then blow up the balloon, reattach the screw, and place it into the water. Ask: **Why did the "fish" float?** *(The buoyant force of the water was greater than the weight of the "fish.")* Explain that this is similar to how a submarine works, except internal tanks are filled with water to make the submarine sink. They are emptied to make the submarine float.

FACTS AND FIGURES

Some fishes all "charged up"

By detecting low levels of electric current, sharks and other fishes can detect the presence of nearby fishes or other animals. Every time an animal moves, even slightly, its muscles create a small electric current. Even a camouflaged animal that is hiding from a shark or other predator with the ability to sense electricity can be detected by the predator because the hiding animal is producing an electric current by moving the muscles required for breathing.

Fishes, such as eels, that produce their own electric current are able to detect animals as well as nonliving objects that might be in their path. The electric field that they create around their bodies helps them to find prey or to navigate. As an added benefit, eels use their electricity to stun or kill prey and to repel predators.

Answers to . . .

CHECKPOINT *Olfactory bulbs, cerebrum, optic lobe, cerebellum, medulla oblongata*

Figure 30–13 *It lacks oxygen.*

Figure 30–14 *The brain of the cave fish might have a smaller optic lobe and a larger cerebrum and olfactory bulbs because the fish probably relies on its sense of smell.*

Figure 30–15 *To stun prey and deter enemies*

30–2 (continued)

Meet Diverse Needs

Some at-risk students and students with limited English proficiency might need extra practice with the words that describe the types of embryonic development in fishes. Help these students develop a method for remembering the definitions of the words. Some students might draw pictures to illustrate the definitions. Others might set up a table. In any case, say the words aloud several times for students to hear their correct pronunciation. Encourage them to repeat the words after you. **Limited English proficiency**

Groups of Fishes

Build Science Skills

Classifying Give student groups 10 to 15 pictures of different kinds of fishes. Challenge students to develop criteria for dividing the fishes into groups. Have students share their method of classification with the class. They should explain the criteria they used to categorize the fishes. Discuss the similarities and differences in the classification systems among the student groups.

Make Connections

Environmental Science Explain that lampreys once lived only in Lake Ontario. They could not enter the other Great Lakes because of the natural barrier formed by Niagara Falls. In the early nineteenth century, the Welland Ship Canal was built as a shipping lane around Niagara Falls. Not long after this, the fish population in the inland Great Lakes began to decrease. In fact, lake trout were almost eliminated. Ask: **What might have caused the decrease in fish population?** *(Invasion of lampreys)* **How could lampreys devastate the fish population so rapidly?** *(Lampreys are not indigenous to the inland Great Lakes and have few natural predators.)* Scientists have developed a chemical that kills only lamprey larvae to help reinstate the fish population. Ask: **Why is this important?** *(A nonspecific chemical could kill beneficial organisms.)*

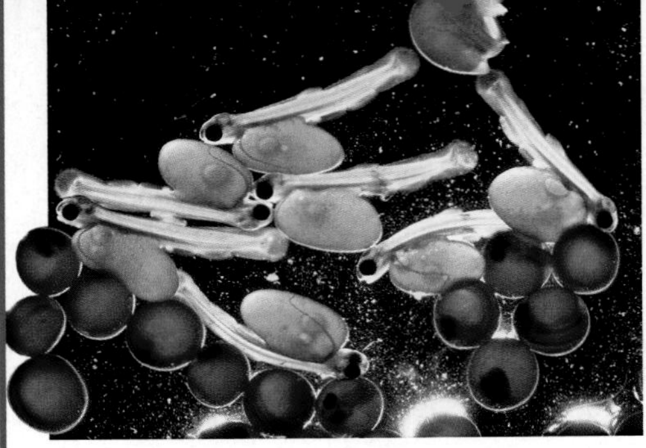

▲ **Figure 30–16** Some newly hatched fishes, such as these coho salmon, are nourished by yolk sacs on their bellies. **Inferring** *What are the orange spheres at the bottom of the photograph?*

Reproduction The eggs of fishes are fertilized either externally or internally, depending on the species. In many fish species, the female lays the eggs and the embryos in the eggs develop and hatch outside her body. Fishes whose eggs hatch outside the mother's body are **oviparous** (oh-VIP-uh-rus). As the embryos of oviparous fishes develop, they obtain food from the yolk in the egg. The salmon in **Figure 30–16** are oviparous. In contrast, in **ovoviviparous** (oh-voh-vy-VIP-uh-rus) species, such as guppies, the eggs stay in the mother's body after internal fertilization. Each embryo develops inside its egg, using the yolk for nourishment. The young are then "born alive," the way the young of most mammals are. A few fish species, including several sharks, are viviparous. In **viviparous** (vy-VIP-uh-rus) animals, the embryos stay in the mother's body, as they do in ovoviviparous species. However, these embryos obtain the substances they need directly from the mother's body, not from material stored within an egg. The young of viviparous species are also born alive.

CHECKPOINT *What are the three different modes of fish reproduction?*

Groups of Fishes

With over 24,000 living species, fishes are an extremely diverse group of chordates. These diverse species can be grouped according to body structure. **When you consider their basic internal structure, all living fishes can be classified into three groups: jawless fishes, cartilaginous fishes, and bony fishes.**

Figure 30–17 **Jawless fishes make up one of three major groups of living fishes.** Modern jawless fishes are divided into two classes: lampreys (top) and hagfishes (bottom).

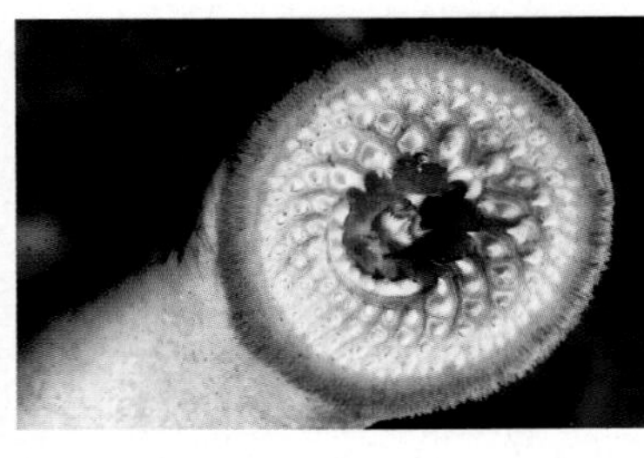

Jawless Fishes As their name implies, jawless fishes have no true teeth or jaws. Their skeletons are made of fibers and cartilage. They lack vertebrae, and instead keep their notochords as adults. Modern jawless fishes are divided into two classes: lampreys and hagfishes.

Lampreys are typically filter feeders as larvae and parasites as adults. An adult lamprey's head is taken up almost completely by a circular sucking disk with a round mouth in the center, which you can see in **Figure 30–17.** Adult lampreys attach themselves to fishes, and occasionally to whales and dolphins. There, they scrape away at the skin with small toothlike structures that surround the mouth and with a strong, rasping tongue. The lamprey then sucks up the tissues and body fluids of its host.

Hagfishes have pinkish gray, wormlike bodies and four or six short tentacles around their mouths. Hagfishes lack eyes, although they do have light-detecting sensors scattered around their bodies. They feed on dead and dying fish by using a toothed tongue to scrape a hole into the fish's side. Hagfishes have other peculiar traits: They secrete incredible amounts of slime, have six hearts, possess an open circulatory system, and regularly tie themselves into knots!

FACTS AND FIGURES

Fish mothers and fathers

Most oviparous fishes do not provide any care for their young; they simply produce hundreds, or even millions, of fertilized eggs and "let nature take its course." Most eggs do not even form into young fish; they are often eaten or damaged.

Some oviparous fishes, however, do care for their young. Some fishes build nests to protect the fertilized eggs. Siamese fighting fishes build nests of bubbles, and sticklebacks use twigs. Some cichlids hold their eggs and young in their mouths. Seahorses hold fertilized eggs in a pouch until the eggs are ready to hatch. Fishes that care for their young usually do not produce as many eggs as those that simply lay the eggs and leave.

Sharks and Their Relatives The class Chondrichthyes (kahn-DRIK-theez) contains sharks, rays, skates, and a few uncommon fishes such as sawfishes and chimaeras. Some chondrichthyes are shown in **Figure 30–18.** *Chondros* is the Greek word for cartilage, so the name of this class tells you that the skeletons of these fishes are built entirely of cartilage, not bone. The cartilage of these animals is similar to the flexible tissue that supports your nose and your external ears. Most cartilaginous fishes also have toothlike scales covering their skin. These scales make shark skin so rough that it can be used as sandpaper.

Most of the 350 or so living shark species have large curved tails, torpedo-shaped bodies, and pointed snouts with the mouth underneath. One of the most noticeable characteristics of sharks is their enormous number of teeth. Many sharks have thousands of teeth arranged in several rows. As teeth in the front rows are worn out or lost, new teeth are continually replacing them. A shark goes through about 20,000 teeth in its lifetime!

Not all sharks have such fierce-looking teeth, however. Some, like the basking shark, are filter feeders with specialized feeding structures and teeth that are so small they are virtually useless. Other sharks have flat teeth adapted for crushing the shells of mollusks and crustaceans. Although there are a number of carnivorous sharks large enough to prey on humans, most sharks do not attack people.

Skates and rays are even more diverse in their feeding habits than their shark relatives. Some feed on bottom-dwelling invertebrates by using their mouths as powerful vacuums. However, the largest rays, like the largest sharks, are filter feeders that eat floating plankton. Skates and rays often glide through the sea with flapping motions of their large, winglike pectoral fins. When they are not feeding or swimming, many skates and rays cover themselves with a thin layer of sand and spend hours resting on the ocean floor.

▼ **Figure 30–18** Sharks and rays have skeletons that are made of cartilage. The large jaws and teeth of many sharks make them top predators in the world's oceans. **Applying Concepts** *How is the structure of a basking shark's mouth related to its diet?*

Use Visuals

Figure 30–18 Explain that shark teeth are made from bonelike material. Scientists infer that they are specialized scales. Ask: **Why is it advantageous for sharks to have teeth that are continually replaced?** *(If teeth are damaged or lost, sharks could not get food.)* Explain that most sharks are very fast swimmers. Ask: **What characteristics of the shark's body make it a fast swimmer?** *(Torpedo body shape, paired fins, strong tail)*

Address Misconceptions

Many students might think that sharks are very dangerous animals and should be killed on sight. Remind students that shark attacks are infrequent, but their publicity makes these attacks appear more frequent. Ask: **What role do sharks have in the environment?** *(Most are predators.)* **What would happen if sharks were hunted to the point of extinction?** *(The prey populations would increase to the point where the environment could not support them, or they would become a nuisance.)*

BIO INSIGHTS **BIOLOGY UPDATE**

Where is the great white shark?

In March, 2000, scientists in Australia tagged a young female great white shark with a satellite tag. This was the first shark to ever be tagged in this way. The satellite tag is an electronic tag that transmits its position by satellite to a computer at the research station. From this data, researchers will learn where a great white shark travels and how it interacts with other great white sharks. This information will contribute to the knowledge of the great white's behavior and its role in the ecosystem. This knowledge will help contribute to the National Recovery Plan being developed in Australia for the great white shark.

Answers to . . .

CHECKPOINT *Oviparous, ovoviviparous, and viviparous*

Figure 30–16 *Salmon eggs that are ready to hatch*

Figure 30–18 *It's a filter feeder and has specialized structures for filtering plankton.*

Build Science Skills

Observing Allow student groups to dissect a fish obtained from a fish market or scientific supply house. Encourage students to carefully remove muscle tissue to observe the skeleton. As they examine the fish, instruct them to diagram and label the structures that are characteristic of bony fishes, such as the fin rays, swim bladder, and bony skeleton.

Use Visuals

Figure 30–19 Ask: **How are all the fishes shown here similar?** (*They are all bony fishes belonging to the group called ray-finned fishes. They all have ray fins.*) **What is the other group of bony fishes called?** (*Lobe-finned fishes*) **How are they different from ray-finned fishes?** (*The fleshy fins of lobe-finned fishes have more substantial support bones than the rays of ray-finned fishes. Some of these bones are jointed.*)

FIGURE 30–19 DIVERSITY OF RAY-FINNED FISHES

Combtooth Blenny

Emperor Angelfish

Flying Fish

Peacock Flounder

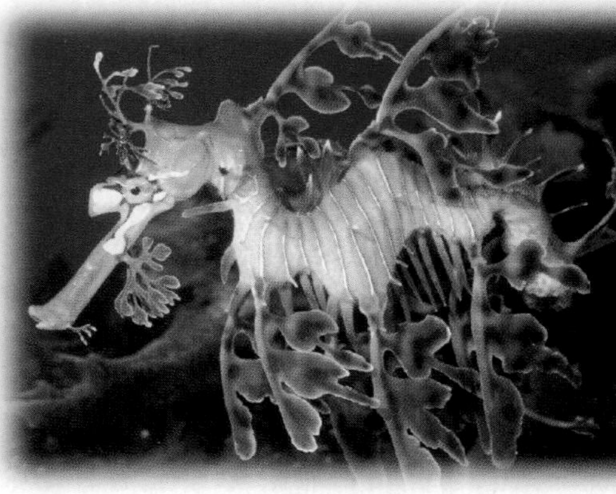

Leafy Sea Dragon

Nearly all bony fishes belong to an enormous and diverse group called ray-finned fishes. These fishes have thin, bony spines that form the fins. **Observing** *What unusual adaptations do you see in each of these fishes?*

▲ **Figure 30–20** The coelacanth (genus *Latimeria*) is a lobe-finned fish that was thought to be extinct until one was caught in the Indian Ocean in 1938. Since then, many more specimens have been found. **Classifying** *Which group of living fishes is most closely related to the coelacanth?*

Bony Fishes Bony fishes make up the class Osteichthyes (ahs-tee-IK-theez). The skeletons of these fishes are made of hard, calcified tissue called bone. Almost all living bony fishes belong to a huge group called ray-finned fishes, some of which are shown in **Figure 30–19.** The name "ray-finned" refers to the slender bony spines, or rays, that are connected by a thin layer of skin to form the fins. The fin rays support the skin much as the thin rods in a handheld folding fan hold together the webbing of the fan.

Only seven living species of bony fishes are not classified as ray-finned fishes. These are the lobe-finned fishes, a subclass that includes lungfishes and the coelacanth (SEE-luh-kanth). Lungfishes live in fresh water, but the coelacanth, shown in **Figure 30–20,** lives in salt water. The fleshy fins of lobe-finned fishes have support bones that are more substantial than the rays of ray-finned fishes. Some of these bones are jointed, like the arms and legs of land vertebrates.

HISTORY OF SCIENCE

Fish tale

Perhaps the greatest American naturalist of the nineteenth century was Louis Agassiz (1807–1837), who from 1848 until his death was a professor of zoology at Harvard University. Agassiz was born in Switzerland, and his earliest scientific work was the classification of fish specimens brought to Europe from Brazil. He won worldwide attention in the 1830s for his study of fossil fishes. That fame led to a course of lectures in the United States in the 1840s. Agassiz made many contributions to science, perhaps the greatest being his revelation that Earth had Ice Ages in the past. But fishes remained an interest throughout his life. According to legend, he would lock a new student in a room for a day with one object, a dead fish. At day's end, the student faced an unenviable task: reporting to the professor all that he had learned by looking at that fish.

▶ **Figure 30–21** Adult salmon return from the sea to spawn in the stream or river in which they were born. Their journey is often long and strenuous. The salmon must swim upstream against the current and may even leap up waterfalls! **Applying Concepts** *What sense do the salmon use to find their home stream?*

Ecology of Fishes

Some fishes—such as lampreys, sturgeons, and salmon—spend most of their lives in the ocean but migrate to fresh water to breed. Fishes with this type of behavior are called anadromous (uh-NAH-druh-mus). Salmon, for example, begin their lives in rivers or streams but soon migrate to the sea. After one to four years at sea, mature salmon return to the place of their birth to spawn. This trip can take several months, covering as much as 3200 kilometers, and can involve incredible feats of strength, as shown in **Figure 30–21.** The adult salmon recognize their home stream using their sense of smell.

In contrast to anadromous fishes, some fishes live their lives in fresh water but migrate to the ocean to breed. These fishes are said to be catadromous (kuh-TAD-ruh-mus). European eels, for instance, live and feed in the rivers of North America and Europe. They travel up to 4800 kilometers to lay their eggs in the Sargasso Sea, in the North Atlantic Ocean. The eggs are carried by currents to shallow coastal waters. As they grow into young fish, the eels find their way to fresh water and migrate upstream.

30–2 Section Assessment

1. **Key Concept** Identify the main characteristics of fishes.
2. **Key Concept** What advantages do jaws and fins provide for fishes?
3. **Key Concept** List four specific ways in which fishes are adapted for aquatic life.
4. **Key Concept** Name the three main groups of fishes and give an example for each group.
5. Why might a scientist investigating evolutionary relationships study a coelacanth?
6. **Critical Thinking Applying Concepts** For fishes to survive in an aquarium, the water must be kept clean and well oxygenated. Explain why water quality is so important to a fish's survival.

MAKING CONNECTIONS

Comparing and Contrasting In Chapter 27, you learned about the circulatory system of annelids. Create a Venn diagram comparing the circulatory system of an annelid with that of a fish. How are the two circulatory systems similar and different?

iTEXT **Assessment** Use iText to review the important concepts in Section 30–2.

Ecology of Fishes

Make Connections

Environmental Science Explain that the construction of dams across many rivers in the northwestern U.S. has affected the population of salmon. Ask: **Why would dams cause a reduction in the population of salmon?** *(Dams prevent the salmon from swimming upriver to spawn.)* Explain that some dams have "fish ladders" to help salmon swim upstream of the dams.

3 ASSESS

Evaluate Understanding

Have students write a sentence that describes the characteristics used to classify fishes. Then, instruct them to make a table in which they list the three main groups of fishes, examples of each, and the key characteristics of each group.

Reteach

Have students create a concept map that shows at least four different ways in which fishes are adapted to live in water.

MAKING CONNECTIONS

Students' diagrams should note that the circulatory systems of an annelid and fish are similar in that both are closed and consist of a single loop. The fish has a true heart; the annelid does not. The fish's blood picks up oxygen from gills; the annelid's does not.

Use iText to review the key concepts in Section 30–2.

30–2 Section Assessment

1. Aquatic vertebrates with fins, scales, and gills.
2. Jaws: defense, can eat a wider variety of food; fins: more controlled movements, move faster
3. Answers include various modes of feeding; gills; paired fins; kidneys that control water balance; lateral line system; and swim bladder.
4. Jawless fishes: lampreys or hagfishes; cartilaginous fishes: sharks, rays, skates, sawfishes; bony fishes: guppies, groupers, salmon, eels, lungfishes, coelacanth
5. A coelacanth, with its fleshy, limblike fins, is similar to the ancestors of land vertebrates.
6. Fish get oxygen from the water. Water that is unclean and not ventilated is low in oxygen, causing the fish to suffocate.

Answers to . . .

Figure 30–19 *Answers include color, body shape, and structure of fins and mouths.*

Figure 30–20 *Lungfishes*

Figure 30–21 *Sense of smell*

Section 30–3

1 FOCUS

Objectives

30.3.1 ***Describe*** what an amphibian is.
30.3.2 ***Summarize*** events in the evolution of amphibians.
30.3.3 ***Explain*** how amphibians are adapted for life on land.
30.3.4 ***Describe*** essential life functions in amphibians.
30.3.5 ***Name*** the main groups of living amphibians.
30.3.6 ***Explain*** the ecology of amphibians.

Guide for Reading

Vocabulary Preview

Explain that *nictitating* comes from the Latin word *nictare,* meaning "to wink." *Tympanic* comes from the Latin word *tympanum,* meaning "drum." Ask: **Where do you think the nictitating and tympanic membranes are located in an amphibian?** *(Nictitating membrane is in the eye and tympanic membrane is in the ear.)*

Reading Strategy

Suggest to students that while reading the section, they also list ways in which amphibians are adapted to live on land.

2 INSTRUCT

What Is an Amphibian?

Build Science Skills

Observing Display a variety of live amphibians for students to observe, or take students to a zoo, aquarium, or pet store. As students observe the amphibians, instruct them to specifically look for ways in which the amphibians are adapted for life on land. Remind students that adaptations are not only structural but behavioral as well. Students should record all of their observations.

30–3 Amphibians

Guide for Reading

Key Concepts
- What is an amphibian?
- How are amphibians adapted for life on land?
- What are the main groups of living amphibians?

Vocabulary
cloaca
nictitating membrane
tympanic membrane

Reading Strategy: Making Comparisons
As you read, write down similarities and differences between fishes and amphibians. Consider such characteristics as body structure, habitat, and method of reproduction.

Amphibians have survived for hundreds of millions of years, typically living in places where fresh water is plentiful. With over 4000 living species, amphibians are the only modern descendants of an ancient group that gave rise to all other land vertebrates.

What Is an Amphibian?

The word *amphibian* means "double life," emphasizing that these animals live both in water and on land. The larvae are fishlike aquatic animals that respire using gills. In contrast, the adults of most species of amphibians are terrestrial animals that respire using lungs and skin.

An amphibian is a vertebrate that, with some exceptions, lives in water as a larva and on land as an adult, breathes with lungs as an adult, has moist skin that contains mucus glands, and lacks scales and claws. In a sense, amphibians are to the animal kingdom what mosses and ferns are to the plant kingdom: They are descendants of ancestral organisms that evolved some—but not all—of the adaptations necessary for living entirely on land.

Evolution of Amphibians

The first amphibians to climb onto land probably resembled lobe-finned fishes similar to the modern coelacanth. However, the amphibians had legs, as shown in **Figure 30–22.** They appeared in the late Devonian Period, about 360 million years ago.

The transition from water to land involved more than just having legs and clambering out of the water. Vertebrates colonizing land habitats faced the same challenges that had to be overcome by invertebrates. Terrestrial vertebrates have to breathe air, protect themselves and their eggs from drying out, and support themselves against the pull of gravity.

◀ **Figure 30–22** Evolving in the swamplike tropical ecosystems of the Devonian Period, amphibians were the first chordates to live at least part of their lives on land. **Most amphibians live in water as larvae and on land as adults.**

TIME SAVER — SECTION RESOURCES

Print:
- ***Laboratory Manual A,*** Chapter 30 Lab
- ***Laboratory Manual B,*** Chapter 30 Lab
- ***Teaching Resources,*** Section Review 30–3, Chapter 30 Exploration
- ***Guided Reading and Study Workbook,*** Section 30–3
- ***Issues and Decision Making,*** 30–3

Technology:
- ***iText,*** Section 30–3

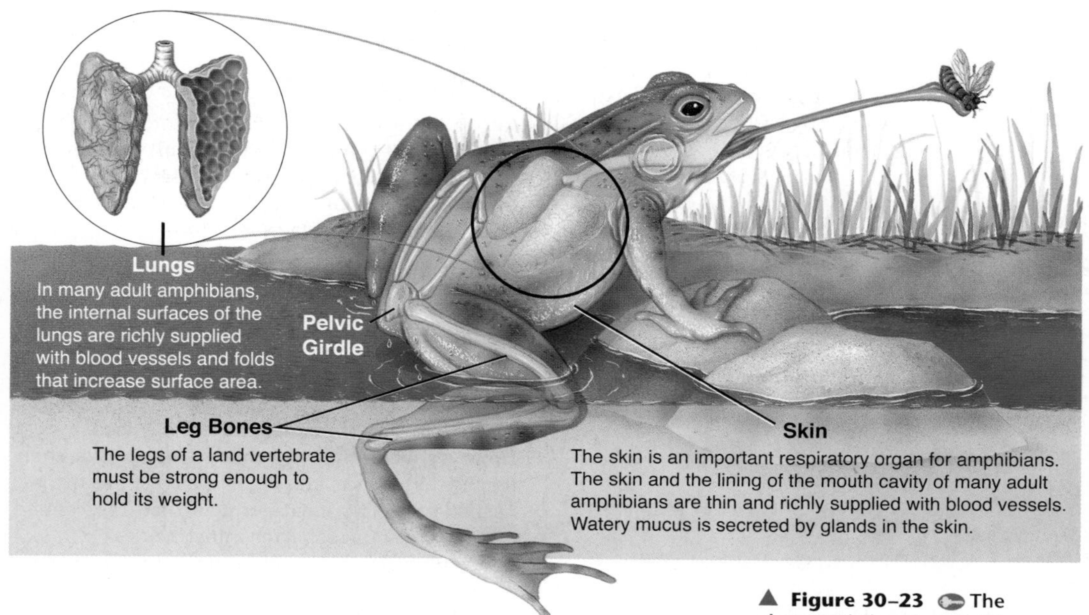

Lungs
In many adult amphibians, the internal surfaces of the lungs are richly supplied with blood vessels and folds that increase surface area.
Pelvic Girdle
Leg Bones
The legs of a land vertebrate must be strong enough to hold its weight.
Skin
The skin is an important respiratory organ for amphibians. The skin and the lining of the mouth cavity of many adult amphibians are thin and richly supplied with blood vessels. Watery mucus is secreted by glands in the skin.

▲ **Figure 30–23** **The characteristics of amphibians include adaptations for living partially on land.** For example, lungs enable adult amphibians to obtain oxygen from air.

Early amphibians evolved several adaptations that helped them live at least part of their lives out of water. Bones in the limbs and limb girdles of amphibians became stronger, permitting more-efficient movement. Lungs and breathing tubes enabled amphibians to breathe air. The sternum, or breastbone, formed a bony shield to support and protect internal organs, especially the lungs. Some of these adaptations are shown in **Figure 30–23.**

Soon after they first appeared, amphibians underwent a major adaptive radiation. Some of these ancient amphibians were huge. One early amphibian, *Eogyrinus,* is thought to have been about 5 meters long. Amphibians became the dominant form of animal life in the warm, swampy fern forests of the Carboniferous Period, about 360 to 286 million years ago. In fact, they were so numerous that the Carboniferous Period is sometimes called the Age of Amphibians. These animals gave rise to the ancestors of living amphibians and of vertebrates that live completely on land.

The great success of amphibians didn't last, however. Climate changes caused many of their low, swampy habitats to disappear. Most amphibian groups became extinct by the end of the Permian Period, about 245 million years ago. Only three orders of small amphibians survive today—frogs and toads, salamanders, and caecilians (see-SIL-ee-unz).

CHECKPOINT *Which geological period is called the Age of Amphibians?*

Word Origins

Carboniferous is a combination of two root words—*carbone* and *fer. Carbone* is a French word for coal; *fer* is a Latin suffix meaning "bearing or producing." *Carboniferous* is an adjective describing the coal-making period of the Paleozoic Era. **If *cone* refers to a reproductive structure of a tree, what do you think the word *coniferous* means?**

Evolution of Amphibians

Word Origins

Coniferous is an adjective that describes trees that bear or produce cones.

Meet Diverse Needs

Gifted students might enjoy the challenge of writing an instruction manual that describes how to live successfully on land. They should include step-by-step instructions that explain how to overcome the special challenges of living on land, such as movement, reproduction without water, breathing air, supporting themselves against gravity, and protecting themselves from drying out. Students can present their manuals to the class to reinforce the difficulties that vertebrates faced when they moved to land. **Learning modality: logical/mathematical**

Use Visuals

Figure 30–23 Have students describe how the adaptations shown in the illustration make it possible for amphibians to live successfully on land. Ask: **What is the advantage of moist skin?** *(It protects the amphibian from drying out.)* Continue in the same manner for the other adaptations shown. Then, ask: **How did these adaptations help amphibians become the dominant land animal during the Carboniferous Period?** *(They were the only vertebrates adapted to live on land. They had few predators, favorable climate conditions, and plenty of food and shelter.)*

TIME SAVER PRESENTATIONS MADE EASY!

The Presentation Assistant Plus contains the Prentice Hall Presentation Pro and the Transparencies, which provide easy-to-follow visual support for every step of this section. If you have a computer presentation station, use Prentice Hall Presentation Pro for Section 30–3 or use the transparencies listed here.

Section 30–3:

Interest Grabber
Section Outline
Concept Map
Figure 30–26

Answer to . . .

 *Carboniferous Period*

Form and Function in Amphibians

Build Science Skills

Comparing and Contrasting As students study this subsection, encourage them to compare the form and function of amphibians with that of fishes. They might wish to organize their ideas in a Venn diagram or create a table. Challenge students to identify differences that are specific adaptations to a terrestrial environment and to an aquatic environment. *(Lungs vs. gills, nictitating membrane vs. no eyelids)* Ask: **Do you think amphibians are more highly evolved vertebrates than fishes?** *(Accept any reasonable answers. Some students might think so because the internal systems are more complicated. Others might think not because fishes are so well adapted to their aquatic environments.)*

Demonstration

You might wish to dissect a frog so that the class can observe its internal anatomy. Point out the parts of the digestive system, the lungs, and the heart. Encourage students to draw labeled diagrams of the internal structures that they observe. As an alternative, provide a three-dimensional frog model or diagrams of frog anatomy.

Use Visuals

Figure 30–24 Have students trace the path of food as it travels through the frog's digestive system. Begin with the frog catching a fly with its tongue. Then, call randomly on students to tell where the food will travel next and what will happen to it there. After completing the path, ask: **How does the digestive system in a tadpole differ from an adult frog?** *(Tadpoles have longer intestines to help digest plant material.)*

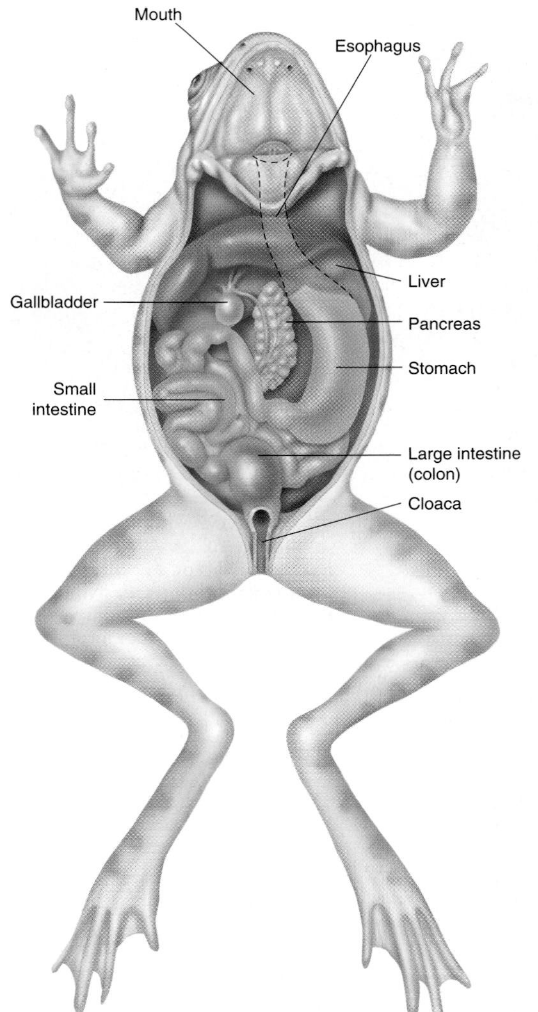

▲ **Figure 30–24** This illustration shows the organs of a frog's digestive system. **Comparing and Contrasting** ***Which digestive organs are found in both frogs and fishes?***

Form and Function in Amphibians

Although the class Amphibia is relatively small, it is diverse enough to make it difficult to identify a typical species. As you examine essential life functions in amphibians, you will focus on the structures found in frogs.

Feeding The double lives of amphibians are reflected in the feeding habits of frogs. Tadpoles are typically filter feeders or herbivores that graze on algae. Like other herbivores, the tadpoles eat almost constantly. Their intestines, whose long, coiled structure helps break down hard-to-digest plant material, are usually filled with food. However, when tadpoles change into adults, their feeding apparatus and digestive tract are transformed to strictly meat-eating structures, complete with a much shorter intestine.

Adult amphibians are almost entirely carnivorous. They will eat practically anything they can catch and swallow. Legless amphibians can only snap their jaws open and shut to catch prey. In contrast, many salamanders and frogs have long, sticky tongues specialized to capture insects.

Trace the path of food in a frog's digestive system in **Figure 30–24.** From the mouth, food slides down the esophagus into the stomach. The breakdown of food begins in the stomach and continues in the small intestine, where digestive enzymes are manufactured and food is absorbed. Tubes connect the intestine with organs such as the liver, pancreas, and gallbladder that secrete substances that aid in digestion. The small intestine leads to the large intestine, or colon. At the end of the large intestine is a muscular cavity called the **cloaca** (kloh-AY-kuh), through which digestive wastes, urine, and eggs or sperm leave the body.

Respiration In most larval amphibians, gas exchange occurs through the skin as well as the gills. Lungs typically replace gills when an amphibian becomes an adult, although some gas exchange continues through the skin and the lining of the mouth cavity. In frogs, toads, and many other adult amphibians, the lungs are reasonably well developed. In other amphibians, such as salamanders, the lungs are not as well developed. In fact, many terrestrial salamanders have no lungs at all! Lungless salamanders exchange gases through the thin lining of the mouth cavity as well as through the skin.

FACTS AND FIGURES

Amphibians not completely adapted to land Although amphibians do live successfully on land, they also depend on an aquatic environment. One reason for this is that they have aquatic larvae. Even more importantly, their eggs do not have a shell. Without shells, the eggs will dry out unless they are laid in water or another moist environment. Another reason for the amphibian's dependence on water is that amphibians do not have scales, fur, or any other protective covering to keep their skin from drying out. However, the skin does have mucous glands whose secretions help keep the skin moist. This adaptation is especially important because many amphibian adults use their skin for respiration. Oxygen and carbon dioxide must be dissolved in water before they can diffuse through tissue.

Circulation In frogs and other adult amphibians, the circulatory system forms what is known as a double loop. The first loop carries oxygen-poor blood from the heart to the lungs and skin, and takes oxygen-rich blood from the lungs and skin back to the heart. The second loop transports oxygen-rich blood from the heart to the rest of the body and oxygen-poor blood from the body back to the heart.

The amphibian heart, shown in **Figure 30–25,** has three separate chambers: left atrium, right atrium, and ventricle. Oxygen-poor blood circulates from the body into the right atrium. At the same time, oxygen-rich blood from the lungs and skin enters the left atrium. When the atria contract, they empty their blood into the ventricle. The ventricle then contracts, pumping blood out to a single, large blood vessel that divides and branches off into smaller blood vessels. Because of the pattern in which the blood vessels branch, most oxygen-poor blood goes to the lungs, and most oxygen-rich blood goes to the rest of the body. However, there is some mixing of oxygen-rich and oxygen-poor blood.

CHECKPOINT *How many chambers are in an amphibian's heart?*

Excretion Amphibians have kidneys that filter wastes from the blood. The excretory product of the kidneys—urine—travels through tubes called ureters into the cloaca. From there, urine can be passed directly to the outside, or it may be temporarily stored in a small urinary bladder just above the cloaca.

▼ **Figure 30–25** Like all vertebrates, amphibians have a circulatory system and an excretory system. An amphibian's heart has three chambers—two atria and one ventricle. Although some wastes diffuse across the skin, kidneys remove most wastes from the bloodstream. **Applying Concepts** ***What excretory product do the kidneys produce?***

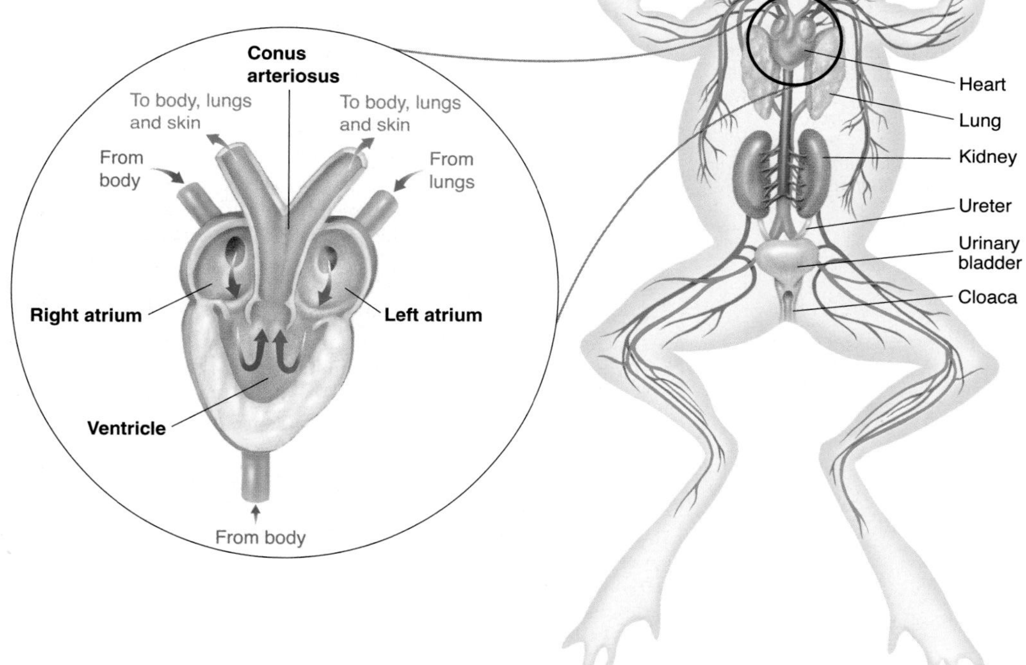

Make Connections

Physics Explain to students that changes in air pressure help to force air from the frog's mouth into the lungs. Air is a fluid and readily moves from areas of high pressure to areas of lower pressure. You can demonstrate this by blowing up a balloon. Explain that the air you push into the balloon is at a higher pressure than the air inside the balloon, causing the balloon to expand. Then, let the air out of the balloon. Ask: **Why did the air escape from the balloon?** *(The air inside the balloon was at greater pressure because the sides of the balloon were pushing it, so the air moved out.)*

Use Visuals

Figure 30–25 Have students trace the path of blood through the frog's heart. Ask: **How many loops are in the frog's circulatory system?** *(Two; one from the heart to the lungs and back, another from the heart to the body and back)* Then, have students review the fish heart in Figure 30–13 on page 776 and compare it to the frog heart. Ask: **How many loops does the fish have?** *(One)* Explain that the tadpole heart is similar in structure and function to the fish heart. In fact, the fish heart is similar to most vertebrate embryos. The double-loop system is linked to the development of the lungs. Ask: **Why might the double-loop system be a better adaptation for terrestrial animals?** *(Tissues are supplied with oxygen-rich blood more efficiently because there is no loss of blood pressure. This occurs in fishes when blood goes through the gills, then to body tissues.)*

FACTS AND FIGURES

Frogs "drink" air

Frogs are unable to inhale and exhale as we do because they do not have the musculature for it. Instead, they fill their mouth cavity with air, close their mouth, and force air back through the open glottis into the lungs. The glottis closes to keep the air inside the lungs. When its lungs are full, the frog keeps expanding and contracting the floor of its mouth. This action brings air into and out of the mouth through the nostrils. Some gas exchange occurs in the mouth tissues at this time. The continual movement of air in and out also clears any "stale" air remaining from the last breath. When the glottis and the mouth open, the lungs empty with a rush. Then, the process begins again.

Answers to . . .

CHECKPOINT *Three*

Figure 30–24 *Esophagus, liver, gallbladder, pancreas, stomach, intestine*

Figure 30–25 *Urine*

30–3 (continued)

Use Visuals

Figure 30–26 Go through the steps in the metamorphosis of a tadpole to a frog. Ask: **In what ways are tadpoles similar to fishes?** *(Both have gills, tails, lateral line systems, and live in water.)* **In what ways do tadpoles change to live on land?** *(Develop legs, lungs, carnivorous digestive system)* Tell students that tadpoles also have a heart and circulatory system similar to a fish's, but it changes to a double-loop system during metamorphosis.

Address Misconceptions

Some students might think that they could get warts from touching a toad. Ask: **Has anyone ever caught a toad? Did you get warts?** *(No)* Explain that although toads have bumpy skin, they do not have warts and cannot pass warts to humans. Remind students that warts are caused by viruses.

Meet Diverse Needs

Both at-risk students and students with limited English proficiency can use flashcards to review amphibian form and function and Vocabulary terms. Have students write the body structure on one side of the flashcard, such as nictitating membrane. On the other side of the flashcard, students should write its function and where it is located. You might also want students to explain how it helps the amphibian survive on land. Student pairs can take turns holding the cards and describing the form or function. **Learning modality: verbal**

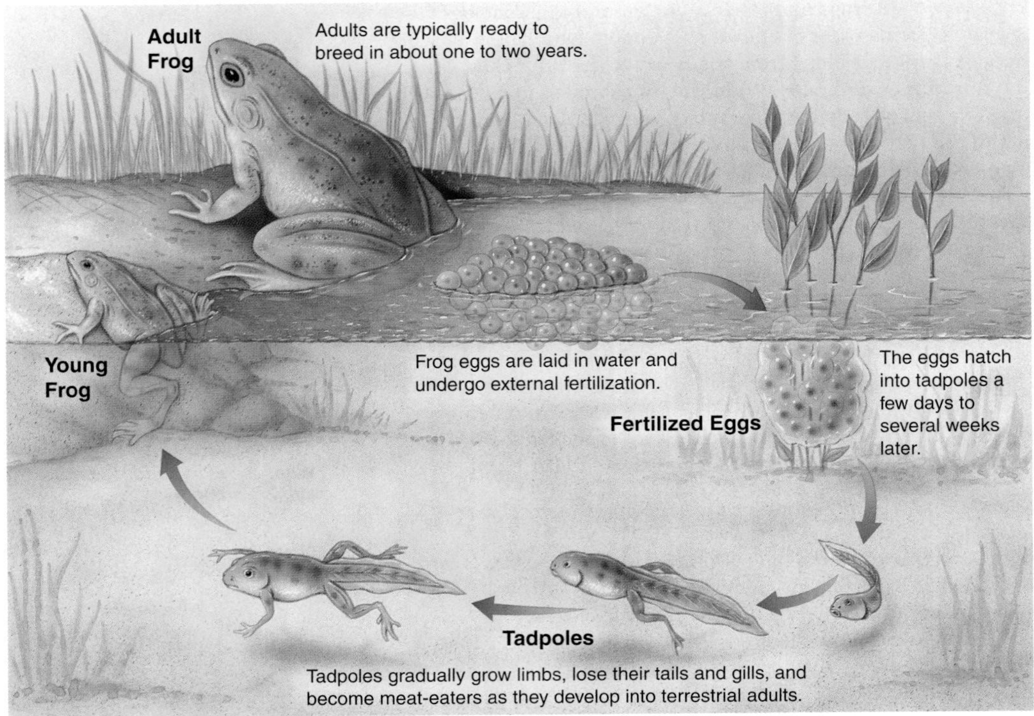

Adult Frog
Adults are typically ready to breed in about one to two years.
Young Frog
Frog eggs are laid in water and undergo external fertilization.
Fertilized Eggs
The eggs hatch into tadpoles a few days to several weeks later.
Tadpoles
Tadpoles gradually grow limbs, lose their tails and gills, and become meat-eaters as they develop into terrestrial adults.

▲ **Figure 30–26** An amphibian typically begins its life in the water, then moves onto land as an adult. This diagram shows the process of metamorphosis in a frog. **Comparing and Contrasting** ***How are tadpoles similar to fish? How are they different?***

Reproduction Amphibian eggs do not have shells and tend to dry out if they are not kept moist. Thus, in most species of amphibians, the female lays eggs in water, then the male fertilizes them externally. In a few species, including most salamanders, eggs are fertilized internally.

When frogs reproduce, the male climbs onto the female's back and squeezes. In response to this stimulus, the female releases as many as 200 eggs that the male then fertilizes. Frog eggs are encased in a sticky, transparent jelly that attaches the egg mass to underwater plants and makes the eggs difficult for predators to grasp. The jelly nourishes the developing embryos until they hatch into larvae that are commonly called tadpoles. **Figure 30–26** shows the metamorphosis of tadpoles into frogs.

Most amphibians, including common frogs, abandon their eggs after they lay them. A few take great care of both eggs and young. Some amphibians incubate their young in highly unusual places, such as in the mouth, on the back, or even in the stomach! Male midwife toads wrap sticky strings of fertilized eggs around their hind legs and carry them about until the eggs are ready to hatch.

CHECKPOINT *What are the functions of the jelly surrounding frog eggs?*

BIO INSIGHTS

FACTS AND FIGURES

Male or female?

By looking at a frog, it is difficult to tell whether it's a male or a female. Sex differences in frogs are almost completely internal. Female frogs have a pair of large ovaries that produce and release eggs. The eggs pass down the oviducts into a storage area near the cloaca. Before the eggs are released, the oviduct walls surround them with a jellylike yolk.

Male frogs have a pair of testes that produce sperm. Sperm passes from the testes through a series of ducts into the cloaca. Some frogs have a seminal vesicle in which sperm is stored.

Movement Amphibian larvae often move very much like fishes, by wiggling their bodies and using a flattened tail for propulsion. Most adult amphibians, like other four-limbed vertebrates, use their front and back legs to move in a variety of ways. Adult salamanders have legs that stick out sideways. These animals walk—or, in some cases, run—by throwing their bodies into S-shaped curves and using their legs to push backward against the ground. Other amphibians, including frogs and toads, have well-developed hind limbs that enable them to jump long distances. Some amphibians, such as tree frogs, have disks on their toes that serve as suction cups for climbing.

Response The brain of an amphibian has the same basic parts as that of a fish. Like fishes, amphibians have well-developed nervous and sensory systems. **Figure 30–27** points out some of these systems in a typical frog. An amphibian's eyes are large and can move around in their sockets. The surface of the eye is protected from damage under water and kept moist on land by a transparent **nictitating membrane** (NIK-tuh-tayt-ing). This movable membrane is located inside the regular eyelid, which can also be closed over the eye. Frogs have keen vision for spotting moving insects, but they probably do not see color as well as fishes do.

Amphibians hear through **tympanic membranes** (tim-PAN-ik), or eardrums, located on each side of the head. In response to sound, a tympanic membrane vibrates, sending sound waves deeper within the skull to the middle and inner ear. Many amphibian larvae and adults also have lateral line systems, like those of fishes, that detect water movement.

▼ **Figure 30–27** A frog's eyes and ears are among its most important sensory organs. Transparent eyelids called nictitating membranes protect the eyes underwater and keep them moist in air. Tympanic membranes receive sound vibrations from air as well as water. **Inferring** *What functions does hearing serve in frogs?*

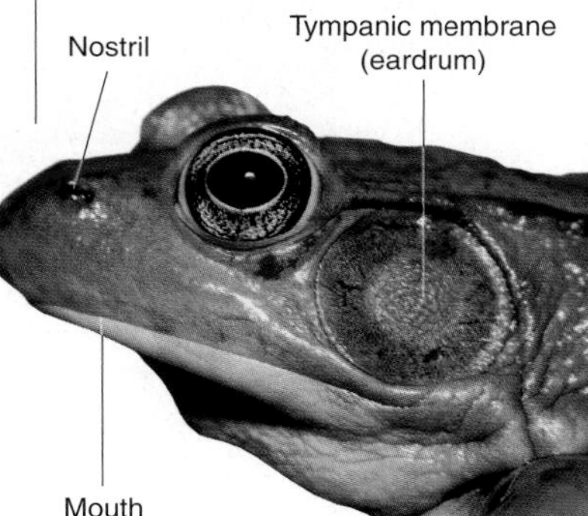

Analyzing Data

Amphibian Population Trends

Over the past several decades, scientists have reported changes in amphibian populations worldwide. In 2000, a team of researchers analyzed data sets contributed by various amphibian population studies conducted in 37 different countries. The results of this analysis are shown in the table. Study the data table and answer the questions.

Numbers of Amphibian Populations

Region	Declining	Increasing	No Trend
Western Europe	309	248	29
North America	130	96	14
South America	31	19	1
Australia/NZ	17	6	1
Asia	10	10	1
Eastern Europe	4	5	0
Africa/Middle East	2	2	1

1. **Using Tables and Graphs** How many amphibian populations were studied?
2. **Predicting** If the trends presented in the data table continue, how do you expect amphibian populations in North America to change in the next two decades?
3. **Calculating** What percentage of worldwide amphibian populations is decreasing?
4. **Making Judgments** Do you think that regional population studies can be used to predict global population trends? Explain your answer.

Build Science Skills

Using Models Challenge student groups to choose one type of amphibian and model its movement. Students can use materials such as pipe cleaners, rubber bands, paper clips, straws, craft sticks, suction cups, or toothpicks to construct their models. Encourage students to do extra research to learn exactly how their amphibian moves. Groups can present their models to the class.

Build Science Skills

Applying Concepts Challenge students to consider how a frog's senses help to protect it from predators. Ask: **How would a frog sense a predator?** *(By sight or sound)* **How would a frog defend itself from predators?** *(By jumping or swimming away, by camouflage, or by being poisonous)*

Analyzing Data

Make sure students understand how to interpret information in the table.

Answers

1. 936 populations
2. Amphibian populations will decline.
3. 53.7 percent
4. Students might agree or disagree, but must give reasons for their answers. Some might think that if population studies from many different regions are combined, then predictions could be made about global populations. However, others might think that regions have site-specific conditions, making them unsuitable for global predictions.

FACTS AND FIGURES

Amphibians adapt to temperature extremes
Like fishes, amphibians are ectothermic animals. Unlike fishes, whose body temperature is very close to that of the water in which they live, amphibians absorb solar radiation, which causes their body temperature to be higher than the air temperature.

Amphibians living in areas that freeze during winter enter a dormant state called hibernation. Animals store fat in their bodies to use as energy. Then, they bury themselves in the mud in stream banks or at the bottom of ponds. Their metabolism slows until warmer temperatures arrive. Amphibians living in areas with hot, dry summers enter a dormant state called estivation to keep from drying out. During estivation, amphibians burrow into the mud and coat the inside of the burrow with mucus and dead skin. They remain in this state until the rains come.

Answers to . . .

✓CHECKPOINT *The jelly protects the eggs from predators and nourishes the embryos.*

Figure 30–26 *Both have tails and gills, but tadpoles lack true fins. Also, tadpoles grow limbs and lungs as they become adults.*

Figure 30–27 *To find mates, locate prey, and escape predators*

30–3 (continued)

Groups of Amphibians

Build Science Skills

Comparing and Contrasting Have students compare and contrast the characteristics of each of the three groups of amphibians. You might ask students to construct a table or other graphic organizer, or you might discuss this orally as a class. Students should focus on the characteristics that make each group an amphibian, as well as the characteristics that define each group.

Meet Diverse Needs

Ask students who need an additional challenge to find out what amphibian species are common to their region and to identify specific local habitats where amphibians can be found. They might use library resources, check with local or state agencies that oversee wildlife, interview naturalists, or call the biology department at a local college. Students can then key a map of the area to where various amphibians are found. **Learning modality: visual**

Ecology of Amphibians

Make Connections

Environmental Science Explain that amphibians are good indicators of changes in the environment. Challenge students to identify amphibian characteristics that would make them susceptible to environmental changes. *(Moist skin, small body, unshelled eggs, reliance on both land and water)*

FIGURE 30–28 DIVERSITY OF AMPHIBIANS

Living amphibians are classified into three groups: salamanders, frogs and toads, and caecilians. Salamanders, such as this brightly colored red salamander, usually have long bodies, legs, and tails. Frogs and toads, including this Chilean red-spotted toad, lack tails and can jump. Caecilians, such as this bright blue one, have no legs.

Groups of Amphibians

Modern amphibians can be classified into three categories. **The three groups of amphibians alive today are salamanders, frogs and toads, and caecilians.** Representative members are shown in **Figure 30–28.**

Salamanders Members of the order Urodela (yoor-oh-DEE-luh), including salamanders and newts, have long bodies and tails. Most also have four legs. Both adults and larvae are carnivores. The adults usually live in moist woods, where they tunnel under rocks and rotting logs. Some salamanders, such as the mud puppy, keep their gills and live in water all their lives.

Frogs and Toads The most obvious feature that members of the order Anura (uh-NOOR-uh) share is their ability to jump. Frogs tend to have long legs and make lengthy jumps, whereas the relatively short legs of toads limit them to short hops. Frogs are generally more closely tied to water—including ponds and streams—than toads, which often live in moist woods and even in deserts. Adult frogs and toads lack tails.

Caecilians The least known of the amphibians are the caecilians, members of the order Apoda (ay-POH-duh). Caecilians are legless animals that live in water or burrow in moist soil or sediment, feeding on small invertebrates such as termites. Many have fishlike scales embedded in their skin—which demonstrates that some amphibians don't fit the general definition.

BIOLOGY UPDATE

Incidence of deformed frogs rising
Since 1995, when middle-school students found many deformed frogs in a Minnesota pond, the reported number of deformed frogs has been increasing. While it is normal for about 1 percent of a population of frogs to have some deformities, these increasing numbers are alarming because frogs are bioindicators of the environment. They are more susceptible to subtle changes in the environment than many other species.

Researchers have been working to find the cause of these deformities. Several hypotheses include chemical contamination, infection with a parasitic worm, exposure to the sun's ultraviolet rays, and physical trauma. Some researchers think that the deformities are caused by the interaction of more than one factor at the same time in a specific place.

Ecology of Amphibians

Because amphibians have no feathers, fur, or scales, many of them make an ideal meal for predators such as birds and mammals. However, amphibians have adaptations that protect them from predators. For example, many species have skin colors and markings that enable them to blend in with their surroundings. Most adult amphibians have skin glands that ooze an unpleasant-tasting and poisonous substance, or toxin.

Some amphibians that release toxins, like the toad in **Figure 30–29,** have bodies that are brightly colored and have bold patterns. The colors and patterns serve as a warning to potential predators. Other amphibian species that are nontoxic may have bodies that mimic, or resemble, those of the toxic amphibians. The mimicry protects the nontoxic species, because predators confuse them with the toxic species and avoid them.

Recently, scientists have noticed an alarming trend in amphibian populations worldwide. For the past several decades, the numbers of living species have been decreasing. The golden toad of Costa Rica, for example, seems to be extinct. In North America, the numbers of boreal toads have dwindled. Even the leopard frog—which is present throughout the world—is getting harder to find.

Scientists do not yet know what is causing the global amphibian population to decline. It is possible that amphibians are susceptible to a wide variety of environmental threats, such as decreasing habitat, depletion of the ozone layer, acid rain, water pollution, fungal infections, introduced aquatic predators, and an increasing human population.

To better understand this phenomenon, biologists worldwide have been focusing their efforts and sharing data about amphibian populations. In the late 1990s, a group of scientists set up monitoring programs that cover the entire area of North America. One such program relies mostly on the efforts of volunteers, who are trained to recognize the specific call of various species such as cricket frogs, bullfrogs, or spring peepers.

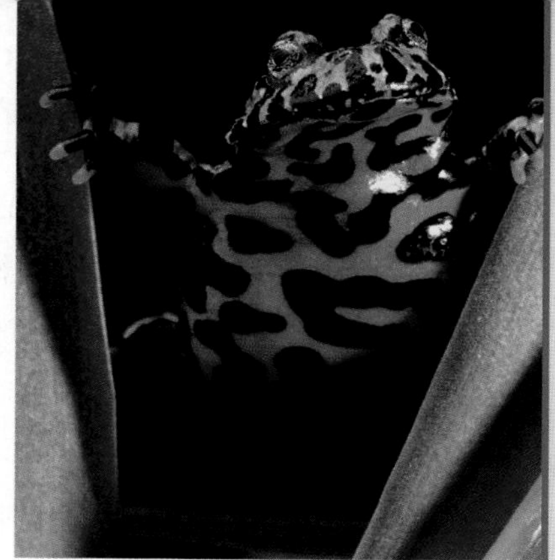

▲ **Figure 30–29** A European fire-bellied toad displays its brightly colored underside, which warns of a toxic and bad-tasting skin secretion. **Using Analogies** *How is the underside of this frog comparable to a dog showing its teeth?*

KEEP CURRENT WITH . . . SCIENCE NEWS®

To find out more about the topics in this chapter, go to: **www.phschool.com**

30–3 Section Assessment

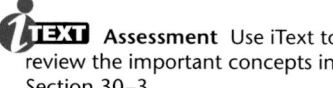

1. **Key Concept** List the characteristics of amphibians.
2. **Key Concept** What adaptations helped amphibians evolve into land animals?
3. **Key Concept** List the three groups of amphibians.
4. What characteristics usually restrict amphibian reproduction to moist environments?
5. **Critical Thinking Formulating Hypotheses** Most caecilian species are totally blind as adults. How do you think this characteristic has evolved?

iTEXT Assessment Use iText to review the important concepts in Section 30–3.

Take It to the NET

Find out more about the different types of amphibian-monitoring programs that exist today. List the programs and indicate which, if any, are seeking volunteers in your area. Use the links provided in the Biology area at the Prentice Hall Web site for help in completing this activity: **www.phschool.com**

SCIENCE NEWS®

Encourage students to visit **www.phschool.com** for the most current information on this topic.

3 ASSESS

Evaluate Understanding

Call on students to give amphibian characteristics that are adaptations to life on land and describe how amphibians are still dependent on water.

Reteach

Give students a frog diagram and instruct them to label the adaptations that enable the frog to live on land.

Take It to the NET

The North American Amphibian Monitoring Program (NAAMP) comprises the nations of Canada, the U.S., and Mexico. There are five prongs to its strategy: calling surveys, terrestrial salamander monitoring, aquatic surveys, atlassing, and western surveys. Monitoring programs for calling surveys and terrestrial salamanders use volunteers. Students can contact the NAAMP regional coordinator to determine whether volunteers are being sought. For more information, visit the Teacher's area of the Biology Web site at **www.phschool.com**

iTEXT

Use iText to review the key concepts in Section 30–3.

30–3 Section Assessment

1. Vertebrate that lives in water as a larva and on land as an adult, breathes with lungs as an adult, has moist skin with mucus glands, and lacks scales and claws
2. Strong limb bones; sternum that supports and protects internal organs; and lungs
3. Salamanders, frogs and toads, caecilians
4. Shell-less eggs and aquatic larvae
5. As burrowers, caecilians do not need keen vision to survive.

Answer to . . .

Figure 30–29 *Both are warnings to potential predators.*

Exploration

Objective Students will be able to use models to determine how fishes and amphibians maintain homeostasis.

Skills Focus Evaluating and Revising, Using Models

Time 45 minutes

Advance Prep
• Obtain samples of freshwater fish (perch, walleye, catfish) and saltwater fish (cod, halibut, mackerel) from a grocery store or fish market. Fresh fish is better than frozen.
• Precut 5-g samples of fish for students, or provide scalpels for students to cut their own.
• Prepare a 0.1 M silver nitrate solution by adding 1.7 g $AgNO_3$ to 100 mL of distilled water. **CAUTION:** *Wear safety goggles and latex or nitrile gloves when preparing this solution.*

Alternative Materials Use clear, plastic one-quart wide-mouthed beverage jugs instead of 1000-mL beakers. Use rubber stoppers instead of folded paper towels to act as cushions in step 3.

Safety Silver nitrate is toxic and can be hazardous if used improperly. It will stain the skin, but will wear off in about 4–7 days. Students should wear disposable plastic gloves during the activity and appropriately dispose of the gloves afterward.

Pre-Lab Discussion Review homeostasis with students. Ask: **What is homeostasis?** *(The maintenance of constant conditions in an organism)* Discuss the adaptations that saltwater fishes and freshwater fishes have for keeping the amount of water constant in their bodies. *(Kidneys remove extra water or keep water in the body, as needed.)* Review how amphibians get oxygen through skin.

Teaching Tip Use qualitative filter paper. The fine pores of quantitative filter paper are easily clogged.

Procedure
1. Some students might predict that there is no difference. Some might predict that saltwater fishes have saltier flesh.

Exploration

Investigating Homeostasis in Fishes and Amphibians

All living organisms must maintain homeostasis, or a controlled internal environment. Fishes are adapted to avoid gaining or losing excessive amounts of water or salts due to osmosis. Amphibians need to maintain a surface that can absorb oxygen from air and release carbon dioxide. In this investigation, you will examine these adaptations.

Green Frog

Warty Frog Fish

Problem How do fishes and amphibians maintain homeostasis?

Materials
• 5 g saltwater fish
• 5 g freshwater fish
• balance
• 4 test tubes
• test tube rack
• paper towels
• 2 glass rods
• 10-mL graduated cylinder
• 2 funnels
• 2 filter-paper circles
• silver nitrate solution
• 1000-mL beaker
• vinegar
• distilled water
• string
• scissors
• transparent tape
• blue litmus paper
• sodium bicarbonate (baking soda)
• glass-marking pencil

Skills Evaluating and Revising, Using Models

Procedure   

Part A: Osmotic Homeostasis in Fishes

1. **Predicting** Predict whether saltwater fishes or freshwater fishes will have saltier flesh.
2. Obtain 5-g samples of freshwater fish and saltwater fish. Label 2 test tubes "salt" and "fresh" with a glass-marking pencil. Place each sample into the corresponding test tube and add 10 mL of distilled water. Put the test tubes in the rack.
3. Fold 2 paper towels in half 3 times to make 2 cushions. Place a paper towel cushion under each test tube. To make an extract of each fish sample, gently mash the sample with a glass rod until it becomes pasty. Use a separate glass rod for each sample. **CAUTION:** *Be careful not to break the rods or the test tubes.*
4. Label 2 more test tubes "salt filtered" and "fresh filtered." Put the test tube in a rack and place a funnel in each of these test tubes. Fold 2 filter-paper circles in half, and then in half again. Open one layer of each folded filter paper to form a cone as shown. Insert a paper cone into each funnel.

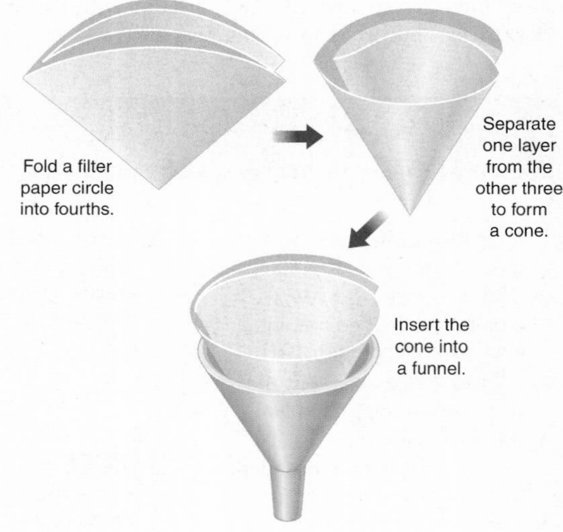
Fold a filter paper circle into fourths.
Separate one layer from the other three to form a cone.
Insert the cone into a funnel.

5. Pour the contents of the saltwater fish test tube into the funnel in the "salt filtered" test tube. Pour the contents of the freshwater fish test tube into the funnel in the "fresh filtered" test tube. Allow the liquid to filter through, and then remove the funnels.
6. Put on your safety goggles, plastic gloves, and lab apron. Silver nitrate is a chemical that is used to detect salt. A drop of silver nitrate turns cloudy when it is added to a solution that contains salt. **CAUTION:** *Silver nitrate is toxic and can stain skin.* Observe each filtered sample as you add 1 drop of silver nitrate solution. Record your observations.

Part B: Gas Exchange in Air

7. **Predicting** Amphibians need to exchange oxygen and carbon dioxide with the air around them. Record your prediction of whether gases will enter a dry surface or a moist one more quickly.
8. Place 100 mL of vinegar in a 1000-mL beaker. Cut a piece of paper large enough to cover the beaker and extend approximately 3 cm beyond the sides of the beaker.
9. Near the center of the paper, tape two 5-cm pieces of string approximately 3 cm apart. Then, tape a piece of blue litmus paper to the end of each string.
10. Use a drop of distilled water to moisten one of the strips of litmus paper, being sure to keep the other strip dry. The color of the litmus paper will change to red in the presence of carbon dioxide gas, which acts as an acid. The reaction between vinegar and sodium bicarbonate produces this gas.
11. Add 5 g of sodium bicarbonate to the beaker of vinegar. Quickly cover the beaker with the paper lid so that the filter strips hang down into the beaker as shown in the photograph. Record the time required for each strip of litmus paper to change color.

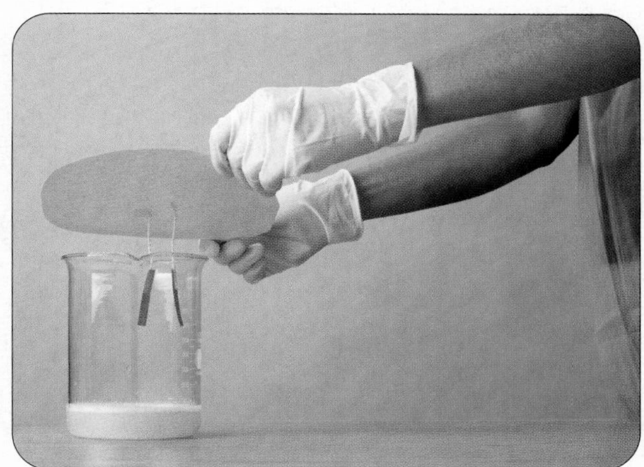

Analyze and Conclude

1. **Comparing and Contrasting** Compare the appearance of the saltwater and freshwater fish extracts after adding the silver nitrate.
2. **Inferring** What can you infer from this result about the ability of freshwater and saltwater fishes to maintain homeostasis?
3. **Drawing Conclusions** What must a freshwater fish do to maintain homeostasis? How would these activities differ in a saltwater fish?
4. **Inferring** What do your results in Part B indicate about the ability of gases to enter moist and dry surfaces?
5. **Inferring** Explain why it is important for amphibians to maintain a moist surface for gas exchange.

Go Further

Researching Salmon are fish that live their adult lives in the ocean but breed in freshwater rivers and streams. Do research in the library to find out how salmon regulate the water and salt content of their bodies as they move between fresh and salt water. Give an oral report to your class.

7. Some students might predict that gases enter a wet surface more quickly. Others might predict that gases enter a dry surface faster.

11. Wet litmus paper turns pink in about 10 seconds. Dry litmus paper turns pink in about 60 seconds.

Expected Outcomes

Students should find the salt content in freshwater fishes to be the same as in saltwater fishes. The wet litmus paper should turn pink much faster than the dry litmus paper.

Go Further

Student research should discuss osmotic regulation in fresh and salt water, and how salmon adjust to the change of conditions as they move between the two environments. In addition to consulting library materials, students might contact the U.S. Fish and Wildlife Service for information, or similar agencies in the states of Alaska or Washington. Students should learn that as salmon move from fresh to salt water, their kidneys must work harder to remove excess salt from their body fluids. When they return to fresh water for spawning, the salt content of the water decreases, and their bodies must use active-transport mechanisms to retain electrolytes.

Analyze and Conclude

1. Both extracts appear similar.

2. Both saltwater and freshwater fishes are able to maintain osmotic homeostasis.

3. A freshwater fish excretes excess water in dilute urine because its body cells contain more salt than the water in which it lives. It also absorbs salts from the water. A saltwater fish excretes concentrated urine because its cells lose water to the salty water in which it lives. It also drinks large quantities of water and excretes the excess salt.

4. The faster reaction of the moist litmus paper indicates that gases enter moist surfaces more quickly than dry surfaces.

5. Gases are exchanged more efficiently through a moist surface. If an amphibian dries out, it could suffocate.

Chapter 30 Study Guide

Study Tip

Students can review the chapter by rereading each section and taking notes about the Key Concepts. Students should also write definitions for each Vocabulary term.

Thinking Visually

1. Jawless fishes
2. Cartilaginous fishes
3. Bony fishes
4. Sharks and their relatives
5. Lobe-finned fishes

Chapter 30 Assessment

Reviewing Content

1. c	**5.** d	**9.** c
2. b	**6.** a	**10.** d
3. c	**7.** c	
4. a	**8.** a	

Understanding Concepts

11. The backbone replaces the notochord in most developing vertebrates.

12. As water passes through the lancelet's pharynx, mucus catches food particles. The lancelet swallows the mucus into the digestive tract.

13. Cartilaginous fishes, which include sharks and rays, and bony fishes

14. Every mode of feeding is seen in fishes. They are herbivores, carnivores, parasites, filter feeders, and detritus feeders. A single fish may exhibit more than one mode of feeding, depending upon what is available.

15. Oxygen-poor blood is pumped from the body into the sinus venosus. Blood then flows into the atrium, then into the ventricle. The ventricle pumps blood into the bulbus arteriosus, which connects to the aorta, through which blood moves to the gills.

16. In the form of ammonia

Chapter 30 Study Guide

30–1 The Chordates

Key Concepts

- A chordate is an animal that has, for at least some stage of its life, a dorsal, hollow nerve cord; a notochord; pharyngeal pouches; and a tail that extends beyond the anus.
- The two groups of nonvertebrate chordates are tunicates and lancelets.

Vocabulary
chordate, p. 767
notochord, p. 767
pharyngeal pouch, p. 767
vertebra, p. 768

30–2 Fishes

Key Concepts

- Fishes are aquatic vertebrates that are characterized by paired fins, scales, and gills.
- The evolution of jaws and the evolution of paired fins were important developments during the rise of fishes.
- Fishes' adaptations to aquatic life include various modes of feeding, specialized structures for gas exchange, and paired fins for locomotion.
- On the basis of their basic internal structure, all living fishes can be classified into three groups: jawless fishes, cartilaginous fishes, and bony fishes.

Vocabulary
cartilage, p. 773
atrium, p. 776
ventricle, p. 776
cerebrum, p. 777
cerebellum, p. 777
medulla oblongata, p. 777
lateral line system, p. 777
swim bladder, p. 777
oviparous, p. 778
ovoviviparous, p. 778
viviparous, p. 778

30–3 Amphibians

Key Concepts

- An amphibian is a vertebrate that, with some exceptions, lays eggs in water, lives in water as a larva and on land as an adult, breathes with lungs as an adult, has moist skin that contains mucus glands, and lacks scales and claws.
- Early amphibians evolved several adaptations that helped them live at least part of their lives out of water. Bones in the limbs and limb girdles of amphibians became stronger, permitting more-efficient movement. A set of lungs and breathing tubes enabled them to breathe air. Their sternum formed a bony shield that supports and protects the internal organs, especially the lungs.
- The three groups of living amphibians are salamanders, frogs and toads, and caecilians.

Vocabulary
cloaca, p. 784
nictitating membrane, p. 787
tympanic membrane, p. 787

Thinking Visually

Using information from this chapter, complete the following concept map:

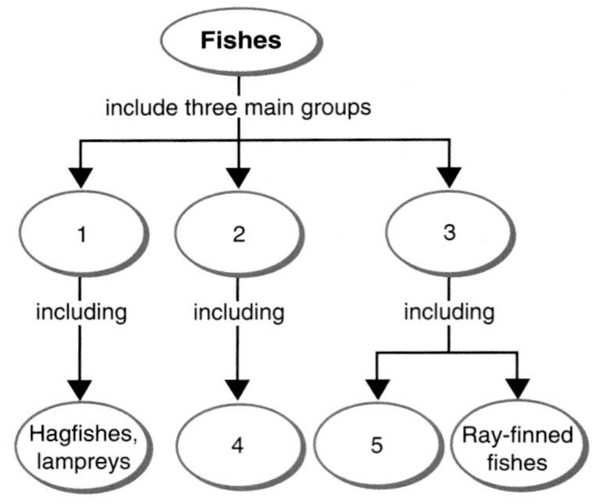

CHAPTER RESOURCES

Print:
- ***Teaching Resources,*** Chapter Vocabulary Review, Graphic Organizer
- ***Chapter Tests: Levels A and B,*** Chapter 30 Test
- ***PH Assessment System,*** Practice Test

Technology:
- ***Computer Test Bank,*** Chapter 30 Test
- ***iText,*** Chapter 30 Assessment

Chapter 30 Assessment

Reviewing Content

Choose the letter that best answers the question or completes the statement.

1. Which of the following is NOT characteristic of all chordates?
 a. hollow nerve cord **c.** fins
 b. pharyngeal pouches **d.** notochord

2. The term that is least closely related to the others is
 a. chordate. **c.** invertebrate.
 b. cerebrum. **d.** lancelet.

3. The evolution of jaws and paired fins was an important development during the rise of
 a. tunicates. **c.** fishes.
 b. lancelets. **d.** amphibians.

4. Most fishes exchange gases by pumping water from their mouths
 a. over the gill filaments.
 b. through the pyloric ceca.
 c. over the atrium.
 d. through the esophagus.

5. In fishes, the part of the brain that coordinates body movements is the
 a. olfactory lobe. **c.** cerebrum.
 b. optic lobe. **d.** cerebellum.

6. A species that lays eggs that develop outside of the mother's body is
 a. oviparous. **c.** ovoviviparous.
 b. viviparous. **d.** nonviparous.

7. Examine the diagrams below. Which of these is a jawed cartilaginous fish?

a.

b.
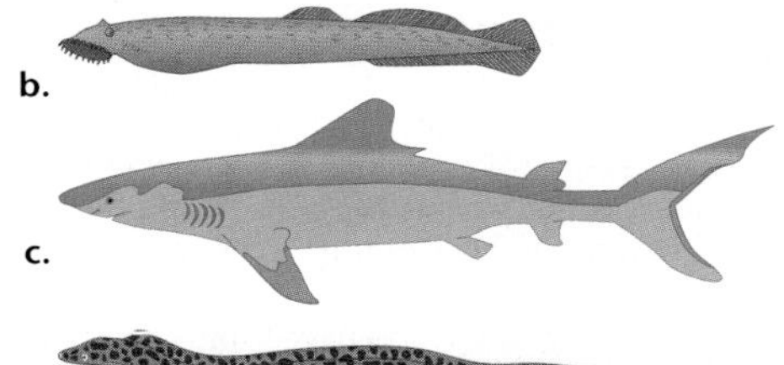
c.

d.

8. At the end of the large intestine of a frog is a muscular cavity called the
 a. cloaca. **c.** gallbladder.
 b. pancreas. **d.** esophagus.

9. An adult amphibian's heart typically has
 a. one chamber.
 b. two chambers.
 c. three chambers.
 d. four chambers.

10. Each of the following serves as an organ of gas exchange in frogs, toads, and many salamanders EXCEPT the
 a. skin. **c.** lungs.
 b. mouth cavity. **d.** nictitating membrane.

Understanding Concepts

11. Describe what happens to the notocord in most developing vertebrates.

12. How does a lancelet obtain food?

13. Which two major groups of fishes evolved from the early jawed fishes and still survive today?

14. Identify three feeding modes that are observed in fishes.

15. Describe the flow of blood through the heart of a typical fish, naming the four structures.

16. In what form is nitrogenous waste excreted from the bodies of most fishes?

17. What is a lateral line system? What does it enable a fish to do?

18. What is the function of a fish's swim bladder?

19. How are lampreys and sharks similar? How are they different?

20. List some of the challenges that early vertebrates faced as they moved from water to land habitats during the course of evolution.

21. Why is the name *amphibian* particularly appropriate for the group of animals that includes frogs, toads, salamanders, and caecilians?

22. How are tadpoles and adult frogs adapted for their specific feeding behaviors?

23. What adaptation do many adult amphibians have to carry out respiration?

24. Discuss how blood flows through the heart of an adult frog.

25. Many amphibians have specialized structures that aid in movement. Describe two of these structures.

17. The lateral line system is a motion-sensing organ. Fishes use the system to sense motion of other fishes, potential predators, and potential prey.

18. Many bony fishes have a gas-filled organ called a swim bladder that adjusts their buoyancy and keeps them from sinking.

19. Lampreys and sharks are similar in that both are fishes with skeletons that are at least partially made of cartilage. Unlike lampreys, sharks have jaws, true teeth, and scales.

20. Breathing air, protecting themselves and their eggs from drying out, and supporting their bodies against the pull of gravity

21. *Amphibian* means "double life." Most amphibians live the first part of their lives in water, exchanging gases through gills. In the second part, they move to land and breathe through lungs.

22. Tadpoles are filter feeders or herbivores that feed on algae. Their long, coiled intestines help them break down hard-to-digest plant materials. Adult amphibians are mostly carnivorous. Their feeding apparatus and digestive tract are transformed to a meat-eating structure with a much shorter intestine.

23. Lungs

24. Oxygen-poor blood circulates from the body into the right atrium. At the same time, oxygen-rich blood from the lungs and skin enters the left atrium. The atria contract and blood is pumped into the ventricle. When the ventricle contracts, blood is pumped into a single vessel, which divides and distributes blood to the lungs and body. Most oxygen-poor blood goes to the lungs, and most oxygen-rich blood goes to the rest of the body.

25. Examples of structures used by amphibians for movement include tails in larvae; four legs; well-developed hind limbs for jumping long distances; and disks on their toes that serve as suction cups.

HOMEWORK GUIDE

Section:	Questions:
Section 30–1	1, 2, 11, 12, 29
Section 30–2	3–7, 13–19, 26, 27, 33
Section 30–3	8–10, 20–25, 28, 30–32

Critical Thinking

26. A saltwater fish could probably not survive in fresh water unless its kidneys could switch to a freshwater mode by excreting excess water and conserving salts.

27. Since dams would be an obstacle in the upstream swim of salmon, the dams would prevent some salmon from reproducing.

28. Pollutants and radiation can travel through thin, moist skin more easily than dry skin. Shell-less eggs are more vulnerable to pollutants than eggs with shells.

29. a. Devonian Period **b.** Osteichthyes; the line for amphibians originates in Osteichthyes. **c.** Jawless fishes and Osteichthyes **d.** Placoderms

30. a. The caecilian would most likely live in an environment where sight is not essential, e.g., burrowed in soil or sediment. **b.** The spadelike head would help the caecilian burrow, the thick skull would protect it as it burrowed, and the needle-like teeth would help it obtain food.

31. The animal is probably a lungfish. It is not an amphibian because its heart has only two chambers.

32. Students need to find out what tadpoles normally eat and then alter that diet in their experiment. They would need to control the temperature, pH, and oxygen content of the water. They would have to decide whether to use increases in mass, length, or time required for metamorphosis as a measurement of development.

33. The arthropod mandible, which is designed for biting and grinding food, is similar to a fish's mouth. Mandibles are also used as filter feeders in some arthropods. A mandible differs from a fish's mouth in structure; an insect has no jaws or teeth.

Performance-Based Assessment

Student models will vary, but should reflect the structure of the organism and how these structures are adapted to the habitat and behavior of the animal selected.

Chapter 30 Assessment

Critical Thinking

26. **Applying Concepts** The kidneys of saltwater fishes are adapted to meet the needs of a marine environment. Would it be possible for a saltwater fish to survive in fresh water? Explain your answer.

27. **Inferring** How might dams across rivers affect the reproduction of salmon?

28. **Inferring** The skin of amphibians is thin and moist. Amphibian eggs have no shell and must be kept moist. How might the worldwide decline of amphibian populations be related to these two characteristics?

29. **Interpreting Graphics** The chart below shows changes in five groups of vertebrates over the past 500 million years. The thickness of each band indicates changes in the relative number of species over geologic time. Use this chart to answer the questions.
    a. During which period did amphibians evolve?
    b. Did the amphibians evolve from early jawless fishes or from early bony fishes (Osteichthyes)? Explain your answer.
    c. In which groups of fishes have the number of species increased during recent times?
    d. Which group of fishes is extinct?

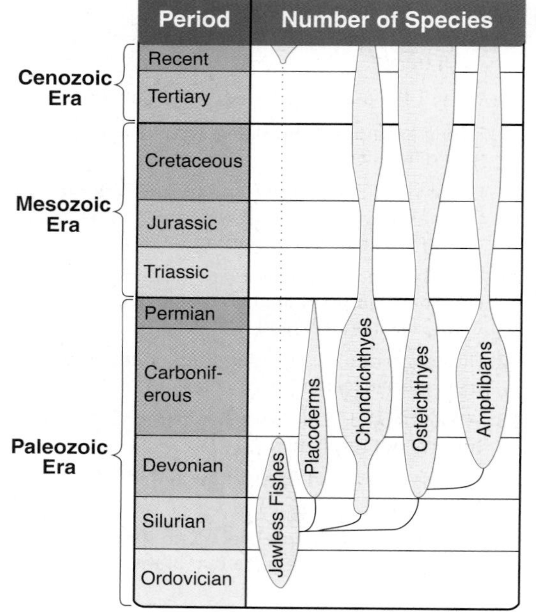

30. **Classifying** On an expedition, you have found a caecilian. This caecilian is blind and has two rows of needlelike teeth on the upper and lower jaws. It has no gills. The caecilian's head is shaped like a spade. The skull is thick and sturdy.
    a. Based on this information, in what kind of environment would this caecilian most likely live?
    b. How might the structures of the head and skull be adaptations for moving and obtaining food in this environment?

31. **Formulating Operational Definitions** Suppose you were visiting South America and you discovered an organism that reproduces by laying eggs. The organism has a backbone, lungs, kidneys, and a two-chambered heart. Is the organism a fish, an amphibian, or something else? Explain.

32. **Designing Experiments** Design an experiment to determine the effect of diet on the development of tadpoles. What variables would you need to control?

33. **Making Connections** In Chapter 28, you learned about structure and function in arthropods. Which structure of a typical bony fish is similar to the mandible of an arthropod? How are the two structures different?

Performance-Based Assessment

Modeling Structure and Function Using modeling clay, paper, or other suitable materials, make a three-dimensional model of a fish or an amphibian. Identify each of the external structures described in the chapter. Attach flags or markers that describe how each of these structures is adapted to the habitat and behavior of the animal you have modeled.

Take It to the NET

The 1938 discovery of the first living coelacanth was a significant event in fish biology. Visit the Prentice Hall Web site at **www.phschool.com** to find out more about this rare and ancient fish. Then, answer the following questions:

- In what areas of the world have living coelacanths been sighted?
- What methods do scientists use to learn about the behavior of coelacanths?
- What is Project Splashback?

Take It to the NET

- South Africa (Comoros, Mozambique, Madagascar, and Sodwana) and Indonesia
- Interviews with local fishermen, studies of fossils, and direct observations using submersibles
- Project Splashback is a coelacanth conservation project. The project distributes a device called the Deep Release Kit to fishermen in the Comoros Islands. This device helps fishermen release an accidentally caught coelacanth back to the ocean floor without further stressing the fish.

Test-Taking Tip If a test question seems confusing, try rephrasing it in your own words. Often, rephrasing a question will allow you to better understand it.

Directions: Choose the letter that best answers the question or completes the statement.

1. Which of the following is NEVER true of oviparous fishes?
(A) Their eggs are fertilized externally.
(B) Their eggs hatch outside the mother's body.
(C) They have paired fins.
(D) The embryos receive nourishment directly from the mother's body.
(E) Their skeletons are made of bone.

2. Which of the following indicates how amphibian larvae typically feed?
I. Filter feeders
II. Carnivores
III. Herbivores
(A) I only
(B) III only
(C) I and II only
(D) I and III only
(E) I, II, and III

3. Into which of the following groups can nonvertebrate chordates be classified?
I. Lancelets
II. Tunicates
III. Fishes
(A) I only
(B) I and II only
(C) I and III only
(D) II and III only
(E) I, II, and III

Questions 4–6 Each of the lettered choices below refers to the following numbered statements. Select the best lettered choice. A choice may be used once, more than once, or not at all.

(A) Tunicates
(B) Lancelets
(C) Fishes
(D) Salamanders
(E) Caecilians

4. Legless amphibians

5. Organisms that feed through a mouth with no jaws, are thin enough to breathe through their body surface, and do not have a true heart

6. Members of the subphylum Cephalochordata

Questions 7–8 Complete each analogy by selecting the correct letter. In analogies, A : B :: C : _?_ *means* A is to B as C is to _?_.

7. tadpole : gills :: frog : _____?_____
(A) atrium
(B) lungs
(C) scales
(D) eggs
(E) stomach

8. Urodela : salamander :: Apoda : _____?_____
(A) shark
(B) frog
(C) snake
(D) caecilian
(E) lancelet

Questions 9–10

An ecologist collected data about the number of frogs that inhabit a certain pond each year. In addition, he collected data about the total amount of rainfall in that area each spring. The data are shown in the table.

Rainfall and Frog Population in Pond

Year	Amount of Rainfall (centimeters)	Number of Frogs
1995	13	45
1996	20	61
1997	8	33
1998	5	20
1999	23	63

9. In what year were the most frogs observed?
(A) 1995
(B) 1996
(C) 1997
(D) 1998
(E) 1999

10. Which statement is best supported by the data?
(A) The number of frogs increased each year.
(B) The number of frogs decreased each year.
(C) The number of frogs increases or decreases based on whether it is an odd or even numbered year.
(D) The number of frogs in the pond increased as the amount of rainfall increased.
(E) The number of frogs in the pond decreased as the amount of rainfall increased.

Standardized Test Prep

1. D
2. D
3. B
4. E
5. B
6. B
7. B
8. D
9. E
10. D

Chapter Planner 31 Reptiles and Birds

Section and Section Objectives	Time	Activities and Labs
31–1 Reptiles, pp. 797–805 **31.1.1** ***Describe*** the characteristics of reptiles. **31.1.2** ***Summarize*** the evolution of reptiles. **31.1.3** ***Explain*** how reptiles are adapted to life on land. **31.1.4** ***Identify*** the four living orders of reptiles. **31.1.5** ***Explain*** why many reptiles are dwindling in number.	**2 periods (1 block)**	**SE:** ***Inquiry Activity,*** How are bird eggs adapted for life on land?, p. 796 **SE:** ***Problem Solving,*** A Massive Controversy, p. 799 **TE:** ***Demonstration,*** p. 800 **TE:** ***Make Connections,*** p.801 **TE:** ***Build Science Skills,*** p. 804
31–2 Birds, pp. 806–814 **31.2.1** ***Describe*** the characteristics that all birds have in common. **31.2.2** ***Summarize*** the evolution of birds. **31.2.3** ***Explain*** how birds are adapted for flight. **31.2.4** ***Describe*** the diversity of birds. **31.2.5** ***Identify*** ways in which birds interact with the environment and with humans.	**2 periods (1 block)**	**TE:** ***Build Science Skills,*** p. 808 **TE:** ***Make Connections,*** p. 808 **SE:** ***Quick Lab,*** How do birds breathe?, p. 811 **TE:** ***Make Connections,*** p. 812 **SE:** ***Exploration,*** Examining Bird Bones, p. 815
Chapter Assessment, pp. 816–819	**1 periods (1/2 block)**	

ACTIVITY PLANNER

SE: ***Inquiry Activity,*** p. 796; (15 min.); plastic gloves, frog eggs, chicken eggs, disposable plastic or paper plates

TE: ***Demonstration,*** p. 800; (15 min.); 3 rocks, heat lamp, container of cool water, shady spot, 3 thermometers, tape

TE: ***Make Connections,*** p. 801; (10 min.); 2 beakers, 50 mL tap water, 1 spoonful of sugar, 1 small ball of clay

TE: ***Build Science Skills,*** p. 804; (10 min.); pictures of a snapping turtle, a sea turtle, a tortoise, and a painted turtle.

TE: ***Build Science Skills,*** p. 808; (15 min.); 10–15 pictures of various birds, including flightless birds and excellent fliers

TE: ***Make Connections,*** p. 808; (20 min.); various insulating materials chosen by students, water, thermometer, jar or beaker, tape

SE: ***Quick Lab,*** p. 811; (15 min.); 6 round balloons, hand-powered balloon pump, measuring tape, clock with second hand

TE: ***Make Connections,*** p. 812; (20 min.); toy gliders or paper to make airplanes

SE: ***Exploration,*** p. 815; (45 min.); cut sections of bird and mammal bones, bird breastbone, hand lens, mammal bone, bird wing bone, balance, 250-mL graduated cylinder, dissecting probe, calculator

PLANNING KEY

Ability Levels

- B **Basic** — For students who need additional help
- A **Average** — For all students
- E **Enriched** — For students who need to be challenged

Components

SE	Student Edition	**GRSW**	Guided Reading and Study Workbook	**IDM**	Issues and Decision Making
TE	Teacher's Edition	**CT**	Chapter Tests: Levels A and B	**CTB**	Computer Test Bank
LMA	Laboratory Manual A	**PHAS**	PH Assessment System	**PA**	Presentation Assistant Plus
LMB	Laboratory Manual B	**LA**	Lab Assessment with Scoring Guide	**BD**	BioDetectives Videotape
TR	Teaching Resources	**BTM**	BioTechnology Manual	**iT**	iText

Program Resources	***Assessment***	***Media and Technology***
LMA: Chapter 31 Lab A E **TR:** Section Review 31–1 B A **GRSW:** Section 31–1 B A **IDM:** 31–1 A E	**SE:** 31–1 Section Assessment, p. 805 **TR:** Section Review 31–1	**PA:** 31–1 Interest Grabber, Section Outline, Structure of a Turtle's Heart, Figure 31–4 **iT:** Section 31–1
LMB: Chapter 31 Lab B A **TR:** Section Review 31–2 B A Chapter 31 Exploration B A E **GRSW:** Section 31–2 B A **IDM:** 31–2 A E	**SE:** 31–2 Section Assessment, p. 814 **TR:** Section Review 31–2	**PA:** 31–2 Interest Grabber, Section Outline, Concept Map, Figure 31–16, Figure 31–18 **iT:** Section 31–2
	SE: Chapter 31 Assessment, pp. 816–819 **TR:** Chapter Vocabulary Review, Graphic Organizer **CT:** Chapter 31 Test **CTB:** Chapter 31 Test **PHAS:** Practice Test	**CTB:** Chapter 31 Test **iT:** Chapter 31 Assessment

TIME SAVER

PRESSED FOR TIME?

To Preview the Chapter

- Introduce students to the Key Concepts and Vocabulary terms in each section.
- Have students examine Figures 31–4, 31–8, 31–9, 31–14, 31–16, and 31–18 and read their captions.

To Cover the Chapter Quickly

- Have students read What Is a Reptile? and Form and Function in Reptiles in Section 31–1 and What Is a Bird? and Form and Function in Birds in Section 31–2.
- Assign the Key Concept questions from 31–1 and 31–2 Section Assessments.

To Review the Chapter

- Assign Sections 31–1 and 31–2 in the Guided Reading and Study Workbook.
- Assign Section Reviews for 31–1 and 31–2 and the Chapter Vocabulary Review for Chapter 31 in the Teaching Resources.

ENGAGE/EXPLORE

Inquiry Activity

Objective Students will be able to hypothesize how bird eggs are adapted for life on land.

Skill Focus **Formulating Hypotheses**

Materials plastic gloves, frog eggs (or other amphibian or fish eggs), chicken eggs, disposable plastic or paper plates

Time 15 minutes

Safety To prevent possible exposure to *Salmonella* in raw eggs, stress the importance of keeping raw egg away from the face, wearing gloves, and washing hands well after the activity.

Strategies

- Review the environment in which frogs live and where they lay their eggs.
- Encourage students to identify parallels between their observations of frog and bird eggs. For example, the albumen of a bird's egg replicates the aquatic environment of a frog's egg.

Expected Outcomes Students should describe the frog egg as small, moist, and unprotected and the bird egg as large, hard-shelled, and containing large amounts of yellow and white liquids.

Think About It

1. Moist conditions; frogs must live near water or other moist places so they have a place to lay their eggs.
2. Because bird eggs have hard protective shells to prevent the egg from drying out, birds are not restricted to living near water.

Brain Teaser

Ask students: **Which came first, the chicken or the egg?** Before accepting any answers, challenge students to think of the question in an evolutionary sense. In other words, encourage students to think of animal adaptations that enabled animals to live successfully on land without being dependent on water for part of their life cycle. Accept all reasonable, thoughtful answers.

Chapter 31 Reptiles and Birds

A spur-thighed tortoise hatches from its egg, ready to face life as a young reptile.

Inquiry Activity

How are bird eggs adapted for life on land?

Procedure

1. Put on plastic gloves. Examine a frog egg. Describe the characteristics of the egg.
2. Examine a chicken egg. Open the egg on a disposable plate. Describe the structures inside. **CAUTION:** *Do not eat raw egg. Wash your hands after completing this activity.*

Think About It

1. **Inferring** What conditions do frog eggs require to develop? How does this affect which types of habitats these animals can live in?
2. **Formulating Hypotheses** How do the characteristics of bird eggs affect which types of habitats birds can live in?

FACTS AND FIGURES

Egg makes life on land possible

Reptiles evolved from a branch of amphibians that were already living on land. However, as the climate became drier at the end of the Carboniferous Period, the amphibians began dying out, because the nature of their life cycle required their dependence on water for fertilization and embryonic development. Reptiles began to diversify and occupy the niches once held by amphibians. Reptiles were more suited to living in drier areas because of internal fertilization and an amniotic egg protected by a shell. The amniotic egg is most important, because it provides the gas exchange, nourishment, and watery environment for the developing embryo. When the young reptile hatches, it looks like a small adult; it does not require an aquatic larval stage.

31–1 Reptiles

Humans have always been fascinated by—and sometimes frightened of—reptiles. Some people fear snakes because of their venomous bites or the way they crawl. Explorers' encounters with lizards and crocodiles inspired images of dragons in European folk tales. Turtles, too, are the subject of many a fable. The truth about reptiles is that they are as astonishing as any creatures of human imagination.

Guide for Reading

Key Concepts

- What are the characteristics of reptiles?
- How are reptiles adapted to life on land?
- What are the four living orders of reptiles?

Vocabulary

ectotherm
amniotic egg
carapace
plastron

Reading Strategy: Outlining Before you read, use the headings in this section to make an outline about reptiles. As you read, add phrases or a sentence about each topic and subtopic in your outline.

What Is a Reptile?

The basic body plan of a reptile is typical of land vertebrates: a well-developed skull, a backbone and tail, two limb girdles, and four limbs. The iguana in **Figure 31–1** exhibits this body plan. Two types of reptiles have slightly different body plans. Snakes are mostly limbless, while turtles have hard shells that are fused to their vertebrae.

What characteristics do snakes, turtles, and other reptiles share? **A reptile is a vertebrate that has dry, scaly skin, lungs, and terrestrial eggs with several membranes.** These characteristics enable reptiles to live their entire lives out of water, unlike their amphibious relatives.

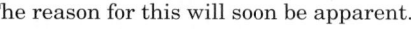

Reptilian skin is dry and often covered with thick, protective scales. These scales may be smooth or rough. A reptile's body covering helps prevent the loss of body water in dry environments. But dry, waterproof skin can also be a disadvantage to reptiles. Because the tough, scaly layer of skin does not grow when the rest of a reptile grows, it must be shed periodically as the reptile increases in size.

Today, reptiles are widely distributed on Earth. Temperate and tropical areas contain populations of reptiles that are remarkably diverse in appearance and lifestyle. The only places on Earth that most reptiles cannot live in are very cold areas. The reason for this will soon be apparent.

CHECKPOINT *What are the advantages of dry, scaly skin for reptiles?*

▶ **Figure 31–1** **Like all reptiles, this green iguana has lungs and dry, scaly skin.** These characteristics help the iguana live on land.

SECTION RESOURCES

Print:

- ***Laboratory Manual A,*** Chapter 31 Lab
- ***Teaching Resources,*** Section Review 31–1
- ***Guided Reading and Study Workbook,*** Section 31–1
- ***Issues and Decision Making,*** 31–1

Technology:

- ***iText,*** Section 31–1

Section 31–1

1 FOCUS

Objectives

31.1.1 ***Describe*** the characteristics of reptiles.
31.1.2 ***Summarize*** the evolution of reptiles.
31.1.3 ***Explain*** how reptiles are adapted to life on land.
31.1.4 ***Identify*** the four living orders of reptiles.
31.1.5 ***Explain*** why many reptiles are dwindling in number.

Guide for Reading

Vocabulary Preview

Explain that the term *ectotherm* comes from the Greek words *ecto,* meaning "external," and *therm* meaning "heat." Ask: **How do you think ectothermic animals maintain their body temperature?** *(By interacting with the environment; for example, moving into shade or into sunlight)*

Reading Strategy

Remind students to include Vocabulary terms and Key Concepts in their outlines. Also, encourage them to include information from figure captions.

2 INSTRUCT

What Is a Reptile?

Build Science Skills

Comparing and Contrasting Students can make a Venn diagram to compare the characteristics of amphibians and reptiles. Ask: **Do reptiles and amphibians have any characteristics in common?** *(Answers include lungs, backbone, limbs.)* **In what ways are reptiles better suited to live on land?** *(Scaly skin keeps them from drying out; eggs that hatch on land do not need water.)* Encourage students to continue making comparisons between amphibians and reptiles throughout the section.

Answer to . . .

CHECKPOINT *The skin protects the body and prevents loss of body water in dry environments.*

Evolution of Reptiles

Word Origins

Saurian describes an animal that has the characteristics of a lizard.

Meet Diverse Needs

Students can organize the sequence of events in the evolution of reptiles by making a time line. Encourage students to customize their timelines to help them organize particular facts or events. For example, students with limited English proficiency might wish to include phrases in their native languages. Gifted students might add additional details about the time periods or the evolutionary steps that are not described in the section. Other students might illustrate their time lines with plants and animals living during the time periods. Students can use their time lines as study guides. **Learning modality: logical/mathematical**

Make Connections

Environmental Science Explain to students that climate changes always affect plants and animals. Ask: **Why would a change in climate cause some animal populations to decline and others to grow?** *(Animals that cannot adapt to the changes will die out. Those that are more adaptable or that can better survive in the new climate will increase in number.)* Discuss the ways in which people have changed many environments in the world. Ask: **How do these changes in the environment affect the plants and animals there?** *(Some cannot adapt to changes and become endangered or extinct. Others are able to thrive in the changes, sometimes even becoming a nuisance.)* You might wish to lead the discussion into a debate about the pros and cons of changing the environment for the benefit of people or for preserving natural habitats for other organisms.

Word Origins

Dinosaur is a combination of two Greek words: *deinos,* meaning "terrible" and *sauros,* meaning "lizard." The suffix *-ian* is used to turn a noun into an adjective. The adjective *dinosaurian,* for example, describes a dinosaur-like animal. **What do you think the adjective *saurian* describes?**

Evolution of Reptiles

To colonize permanently dry habitats, animals needed a way to reproduce that did not require depositing eggs into water. Reptiles were the first animals to evolve this adaptation. The fossil of the first known reptile dates back to the early Carboniferous Period, some 350 million years ago. However, reptiles did not become common until 40 or 50 million years later. As the Carboniferous Period came to a close and the Permian Period began, Earth's climate became cooler and less humid. Many lakes and swamps dried up, reducing the available habitat for water-dependent amphibians. Under these drier conditions, the first great adaptive radiation of reptiles began.

Mammal-like Reptiles By the end of the Permian Period, about 245 million years ago, a great variety of reptiles roamed Earth. One early group was the mammal-like reptiles, which displayed a mix of reptilian and mammalian characteristics. These chordates eventually came to dominate many land habitats. However, the mammal-like reptiles went extinct in just a few million years. Toward the end of the Triassic Period, about 215 million years ago, they were replaced in the fossil record by another group of reptiles that had remained in the background for millions of years—the dinosaurs.

Enter the Dinosaurs During the late Triassic and Jurassic periods, a great adaptive radiation of reptiles took place. The vast diversity and abundance of reptiles during that time are the main reasons why the Mesozoic Era is often called the Age of Reptiles. Two separate groups of large aquatic reptiles swam in the seas. Ancestors of modern turtles, crocodiles, lizards, and snakes populated many land habitats. And dinosaurs were everywhere. **Figure 31–2** shows two dinosaurs, *Plateosauras* and *Coelophysis.* The illustration also shows another kind of reptile, *Teratosaurus.*

▼ **Figure 31–2** In the Triassic Period, reptiles such as these lived in the forests. The herbivorous *Plateosaurus* (left), nibbling on leaves, was a dinosaur, as were the group of carnivorous *Coelophysis* (center). The large carnivorous *Teratosaurus* (right) was a reptile but not a dinosaur. **Observing** ***What characteristics did these reptiles have in common with modern reptiles?***

TIME SAVER — PRESENTATIONS MADE EASY!

The Presentation Assistant Plus contains the Prentice Hall Presentation Pro and the Transparencies, which provide easy-to-follow visual support for every step of this section. If you have a computer presentation station, use Prentice Hall Presentation Pro for Section 31–1, or use the transparencies listed here.

Section 31–1: **Interest Grabber**
Section Outline
Structure of a Turtle's Heart
Figure 31–8

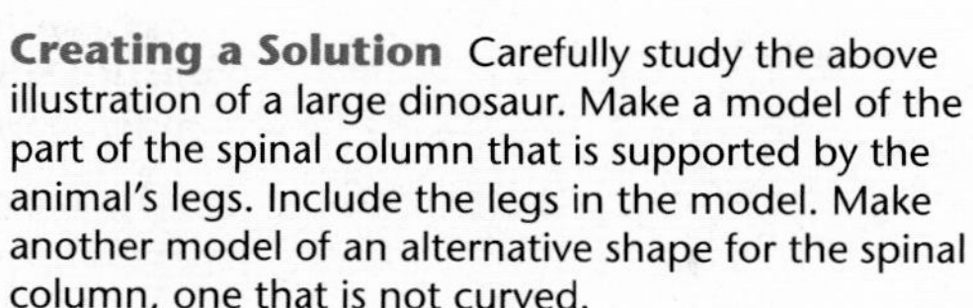

Problem Solving

A Massive Controversy

Dinosaurs were the largest animals ever to walk on Earth. The plant-eating dinosaur *Brachiosaurus* reached lengths greater than 22 meters and had a mass of about 50,000 kilograms. It would take about 10 elephants to match the mass of one *Brachiosaurus*. How could the skeleton of such an animal support its immense mass? Imagine that you are a paleontologist searching for an answer to this question. Your job is to examine fossil skeletons of large dinosaurs for clues.

Defining the Problem Use your own words to describe the problem you face.

Organizing Information List the kinds of skeletal adaptations that would help a dinosaur support its mass.

Creating a Solution Carefully study the above illustration of a large dinosaur. Make a model of the part of the spinal column that is supported by the animal's legs. Include the legs in the model. Make another model of an alternative shape for the spinal column, one that is not curved.

Presenting Your Plan Describe what you might do to each model to discover which would support a greater mass. Show how you would test the models. Next to the models, place a card describing the steps in your test.

Dinosaurs ranged in size from small to enormous. They ran on two legs or lumbered along on four. Some, like *Plateosaurus,* ate leafy plants. *Coelophysis* and other hunters traveled in herds. Others, such as duckbilled *Maiasaura,* lived in small family groups, caring for their eggs and young in carefully constructed nests. Certain dinosaurs may even have had feathers, which may have evolved as a means of regulating body temperature. All of the dinosaurs, however, belonged to one of two major groups: the Ornithischia (awr-nuh-THISH-ee-uh), or "bird-hipped" dinosaurs, and the Saurischia (saw-RISH-ee-uh), or "lizard-hipped" dinosaurs. From one of these two branches of dinosaurs, probably the Saurischia, came the earliest members of evolutionary lines that would lead to modern birds.

Exit the Dinosaurs At the end of the Cretaceous Period, about 65 million years ago, a mass extinction occurred worldwide. This extinction was caused by a dramatic series of natural disasters. These disasters probably included a string of massive volcanic eruptions and lava flows, the dropping of sea level, and a huge asteroid or comet smashing into what is now the Yucatan Peninsula in Mexico. The asteroid or comet collision produced major forest fires and enormous dust clouds. After these events, dinosaurs, along with many other animal and plant groups, became extinct. The disappearance of these organisms during the late Cretaceous Period opened up niches on land and in the sea, providing opportunities for other kinds of organisms to evolve.

CHECKPOINT *How did the extinction of the dinosaurs pave the way for modern reptiles?*

KEEP CURRENT WITH . . . SCIENCE NEWS®

To find out more about the topics in this chapter, go to: **www.phschool.com**

Problem Solving

Scientists used to think that *Brachiosaurus* stayed submerged in water to help support its body weight. However, now scientists know that water pressure at the depths required to cover the body would prevent the lungs from filling with air. *Brachiosaurus* had a strong, lightweight skeleton with broad, columnar legs that were probably strong enough to support its full weight.

Defining the Problem Sample answer: Determine the features of the *Brachiosaurus* skeleton that enable it to support its mass.

Organizing Information Accept all reasonable responses. These include thick leg bones, legs placed directly under body, quadruped, lightweight vertebral column, large hip bones, and curved backbone.

Creating a Solution Display diagrams of various sauropod skeletons for students to observe. You might also display skeletons of smaller dinosaurs for the sake of comparison. Provide students with materials, such as modeling clay or toothpicks and glue, to make their models. They might also draw sketches of the skeletons instead of building a three-dimensional model.

Presenting Your Plan Most students will describe a test in which they add weight to the top of their skeleton models. Assess the testing plans for logic, clarity, comprehensiveness, and creativity.

SCIENCE NEWS®

Encourage students to visit **www.phschool.com** for the most current information on this topic.

BIOLOGY UPDATE

Evidence for extinction

The Chicxulub crater in the Yucatan Peninsula is thought to have caused the mass extinction at the K-T boundary. Studies have shown that it was created at about the same time by an extraterrestrial object. Recently, a planetary geoscientist, Peter Schultz, analyzed the Chicxulub crater and compared it to craters on the moon, Venus, and Mercury. He concluded that the asteroid hit Earth at an angle pointing toward the northwest. He theorizes that a huge cloud of hot vapor continued northwest, instantly setting fire to most of North America. This scenario helps explain why the extinction rate of plants in North America was at least triple that in the rest of the world. It also explains why land species living in North America were nine times more likely to go extinct than aquatic species.

Answers to . . .

CHECKPOINT *New niches on land and sea became available.*

Figure 31–2 *Backbone; lungs; dry, scaly skin*

Form and Function in Reptiles

Demonstration

Demonstrate how ectothermic animals control their body temperature by placing a rock under a heat lamp, a rock in cool water, and a rock in a shady spot. Have students predict the relative temperatures of the tops of the rocks in each location. Then, read the temperature of each location on a thermometer. *(The rock under the heat lamp will be warmest.)* Discuss different ways in which students keep themselves warm or cool. Then, relate their behaviors to the behaviors of ectotherms in controlling their body temperature.

Meet Diverse Needs

Pair at-risk students and students with limited English proficiency with other students in the class. Instruct students to take turns asking each other questions about form and function in reptiles. Encourage students to ask questions about ideas that they do not fully understand. Monitor students to make sure they are giving correct answers. **Learning modality: verbal**

Form and Function in Reptiles

Most reptiles have adapted to a fully terrestrial life. Tough, scaly skin is one adaptation to this type of life. **Well-developed lungs; a double-loop circulatory system; a water-conserving excretory system; strong limbs; internal fertilization; and shelled, terrestrial eggs are the other adaptations that have contributed to the success of reptiles on land.** In addition, reptiles can control their body temperature by changing their environments.

Body Temperature Control The ability to control their body temperature is an enormous asset for active animals. All the animals that you have read about so far are ectotherms (EK-toh-thurmz). **Ectotherms** rely on behavior to help control body temperature. Turtles, snakes, and other modern reptiles are all ectotherms. To warm up, they bask in the sun during the day or stay under water at night. To cool down, they move to the shade, go for a swim, or take shelter in underground burrows.

▲ **Figure 31–3** The gaboon viper, like all snakes, is entirely carnivorous. It eats mice and other small mammals by stretching its jaws wide and swallowing its prey whole. **Inferring** ***Besides feeding, what other function might fangs serve in snakes?***

Feeding Reptiles eat a wide range of foods. Iguanas, which are herbivores, tear plants into shreds and swallow the tough, fibrous chunks. Their long digestive systems enable them to break down plant material. Many other reptiles are carnivores. Snakes, for example, prey on small animals, bird eggs, or even other snakes, grabbing them with their jaws and swallowing them whole as shown in **Figure 31–3.** Crocodiles and alligators eat fish and even land animals when they can catch them. Chameleons have sticky tongues as long as their bodies that flip out to catch insects.

Respiration The lungs of reptiles are spongy, providing more gas-exchange area than those of amphibians. This isn't surprising, because most reptiles cannot exchange gases through their skin the way many moist-skinned amphibians do. Many reptiles have muscles around their ribs that expand the chest cavity to inhale and collapse the cavity to force air out. Several species of crocodiles also have flaps of skin that can separate the mouth from the nasal passages, allowing these crocodiles to breathe through their nostrils while their mouth remains open. To exchange gases with the environment, reptiles have two efficient lungs or, in the case of certain species of snakes, one lung.

Circulation Reptiles have an efficient double-loop circulatory system. One of the loops brings blood to and from the lungs, and the other loop brings blood to and from the rest of the body. The heart diagram in **Figure 31–4** shows how blood flows through a turtle's heart. Reptile hearts contain two atria and either one or two ventricles. Most reptiles have a single ventricle with a partial septum, or wall, that helps separate oxygen-rich and oxygen-poor blood during the pumping cycle. Crocodiles and alligators, however, have the most developed hearts of living reptiles. The heart consists of two atria and two ventricles—an arrangement that is also found in birds and mammals.

BIO INSIGHTS — FACTS AND FIGURES

Maintaining body temperature
All animals have a specific internal temperature at which their muscles respond best. If body temperature becomes too high, muscles tire easily and other body systems are stressed. Ectothermic animals generally have relatively low metabolic rates when they are resting. Because of this, they do not generate much internal heat and much of this heat is lost because they don't have insulation, like hair or feathers. In order to control their body temperature, they must get heat from their environment. So, for example, a lizard might bask in the sun to warm up. Once its body reaches a certain temperature, it will move around, going about its business. The action of its muscles generates more heat. If the lizard becomes too warm, it will find a shady place to lose heat.

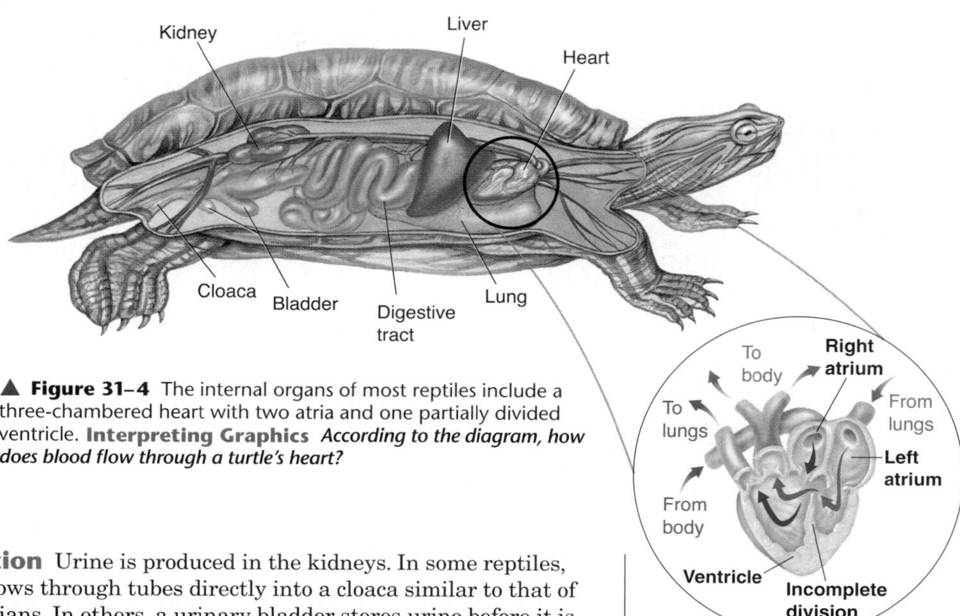

▲ **Figure 31–4** The internal organs of most reptiles include a three-chambered heart with two atria and one partially divided ventricle. **Interpreting Graphics** *According to the diagram, how does blood flow through a turtle's heart?*

Excretion Urine is produced in the kidneys. In some reptiles, urine flows through tubes directly into a cloaca similar to that of amphibians. In others, a urinary bladder stores urine before it is expelled from the cloaca.

Reptiles' urine contains either ammonia or uric acid. Reptiles that live mainly in water, such as crocodiles and alligators, excrete most of their nitrogenous wastes in the form of ammonia, a toxic compound. Crocodiles and alligators drink a large amount of water, which dilutes the ammonia in the urine and helps carry it away. In contrast, many other reptiles—especially those that live entirely on land—do not excrete ammonia directly. Instead, they convert ammonia into a compound called uric acid. Uric acid is much less toxic than ammonia, so it does not have to be diluted as much. In these reptiles, excess water is absorbed in the cloaca, reducing urine to crystals of uric acid that form a pasty white solid. By eliminating wastes that contain little water, a reptile can conserve water.

Response The basic pattern of a reptile's brain is similar to that of an amphibian, although the cerebrum and cerebellum are considerably larger compared to the rest of the brain. Reptiles that are active during the day tend to have complex eyes and can see color well. Many snakes also have an extremely good sense of smell. In addition to a pair of nostrils, most reptiles have a pair of sensory organs in the roof of the mouth that can detect chemicals. Reptiles have simple ears with an external eardrum and a single bone that conducts sound to the inner ear. Snakes can also pick up vibrations in the ground through bones in their skulls. Some snakes, such as the viper in **Figure 31–5**, have the extraordinary ability to detect the body heat of their prey.

▼ **Figure 31–5** The heat-sensitive pits above this eyelash viper's mouth enable it to locate prey, even in total darkness. Snakes that have these pits are commonly called pit vipers. **Inferring** *How would these organs give pit vipers an advantage over other reptiles?*

CHECKPOINT *How does a reptile's brain compare to an amphibian's?*

Use Visuals

Figure 31–4 Have students trace the path of blood through the heart. Make sure they understand that the circulatory system has two loops, just as the amphibian circulatory system has. Point out that oxygenated blood from the lungs and deoxygenated blood from the body go through the single ventricle at the same time. Ask: **What structure in the ventricle helps separate oxygen-rich and oxygen-poor blood?** *(Partial internal walls in the ventricle)* **Which reptiles have two ventricles instead of one?** *(Crocodiles and alligators)*

Make Connections

Chemistry Demonstrate how uric acid helps conserve water by mixing a spoonful of sugar in about 25 mL of water. Explain that the sugar represents ammonia. Have students compare this to a ball of clay (which represents uric acid) in 25 mL of water. Ask: **Where has the sugar gone?** *(It has dissolved in the water.)* **Why hasn't the clay disappeared?** *(It cannot dissolve in water.)* **Will an animal lose more water or less water when it excretes uric acid?** *(Less; the excess water is reabsorbed into the body, and the solid waste is eliminated.)* Make sure students understand that the ammonia must remain dissolved in water, otherwise it will poison the body cells. The body must excrete the ammonia with all of the water in which it is dissolved. There is no extra for the body to reabsorb.

FACTS AND FIGURES

Excreting nitrogenous wastes

Excess amino acids cannot be stored or excreted. They are broken down and used as fuel for the body. Ammonia is produced when amino acids are broken down. Cells cannot survive high concentrations of ammonia. To be transported without harming cells, 1 gram of ammonia must be dissolved in 300 to 500 mL of water. In many small aquatic animals, ammonia simply diffuses from their body tissues directly into the water. Terrestrial animals, however, must conserve water. Most reptiles convert ammonia to uric acid. Uric acid is less toxic than ammonia and less soluble. One gram of uric acid needs only 10 mL of water to be transported. In the excretory system, most of the water is returned to the body, and solid crystals of uric acid are removed as a thick paste.

Answers to . . .

CHECKPOINT *It is similar, although the cerebrum and cerebellum are larger.*

Figure 31–3 *Protection from predators*

Figure 31–4 *From body to right atrium to ventricle to lungs to left atrium to ventricle to body*

Figure 31–5 *They are able to find food without relying on sight.*

Build Science Skills

Inferring Challenge students to make inferences about the relative survival rates of oviparous and ovoviviparous reptilian embryos. Ask: **Which embryos are more likely to survive: turtle eggs abandoned in nests or lizard eggs inside the mother's body?** *(Lizard eggs; better protected from predators)* **What adaptive advantage does an ovoviviparous reptile have over an oviparous one?** *(Greater chance of eggs hatching, so it can produce fewer eggs)* **Why aren't all reptiles ovoviviparous?** *(Accept all answers. It might require less energy to lay more eggs and hope for the best than to carry the eggs until they hatch. It might depend on the environment.)*

Meet Diverse Needs

Have at-risk students construct a concept map that shows how reptiles are adapted for life on land. Students should start the concept map with "Adaptations for Living on Land." They should write the different adaptations in circles that branch from the beginning. Make sure students include adaptations such as internal fertilization, amniotic egg, stronger limbs, and uric acid wastes. **Learning modality: visual**

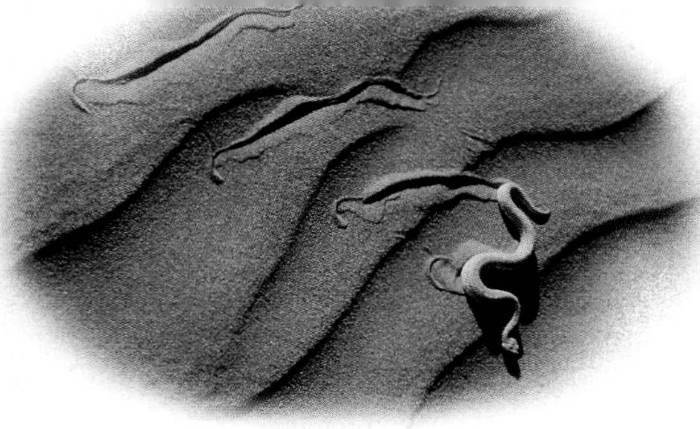

Figure 31–6 The shovel-snouted lizard (left) is not moving forward; rather, it lifts its feet to limit contact with the hot desert sand. The sidewinding adder propels itself forward by digging its ventral scales against the dunes while pushing its body into long curving waves. **Comparing and Contrasting** ***How are the lizard's legs different from those of an amphibian?***

▼ **Figure 31–7** After a female box turtle digs a hole in the ground for her nest, she lays her eggs, dropping them one by one and gently lowering them into the hole with her hind feet. When she finishes, she will cover up her nest and leave without a backward glance. **Inferring** ***Why would it be an advantage for turtles to lay a large number of eggs?***

Movement Compared with most amphibians, reptiles with legs tend to have larger, stronger limbs that enable them to walk, run, burrow, swim, or climb. The legs of some reptiles are also rotated further under the body than those of amphibians, enabling reptiles to carry more body weight. The legs and feet of many aquatic turtles have developed into flippers. **Figure 31–6** shows some ways that reptiles can move. As with amphibians, the backbones of reptiles help accomplish much of their movement.

Reproduction All reptiles reproduce by internal fertilization, in which the male deposits sperm inside the body of the female. Most male reptiles have a penis that allows them to deliver sperm into the female's cloaca. After fertilization has occurred, the female's reproductive system covers the embryos with several membranes and a leathery shell.

Most reptiles are oviparous, laying eggs that develop outside the mother's body. Some species, such as the box turtle in **Figure 31–7,** lay their eggs in carefully prepared nests, then abandon them. Alligators also lay their eggs in nests, but they guard the eggs until they hatch, and provide some care after hatching. Some snakes and lizards are ovoviviparous, and the young are born alive. By carrying her eggs within her body, the female can protect the eggs and keep them warm.

Unlike an amphibian egg, which almost always needs to develop in water, the shell and membranes of a reptilian egg create a protected environment in which the embryo can develop without drying out. This type of egg is called an **amniotic egg** (am-nee-AHT-ihk), named after the amnion, one of the four membranes that surrounds the developing embryo. The other three membranes are the yolk sac, the chorion, and the allantois. Find each of these membranes in **Figure 31–8** and learn about their functions. The amniotic egg, also seen in birds, is one of the most important adaptations to life on land.

✓CHECKPOINT ***What are the four parts of an amniotic egg?***

FACTS AND FIGURES

Reptilian mothers

Surprisingly, alligators and crocodiles are very motherly reptiles. They build a nest with mud, sticks, and vegetation. This "compost pile" incubates the eggs as the vegetation breaks down. The mother stays near the nest, protecting it from predators. A large percentage of eggs hatch because of this protection. When the mother hears the babies squeaking after hatching, she uncovers the nest and picks up the babies in her mouth. Sometimes she carries the babies to water for food and protection. Baby alligators and crocodiles often stay together in groups, called pods, for their first year. During that year, they are highly susceptible to predators, but their mothers often stay nearby to provide protection.

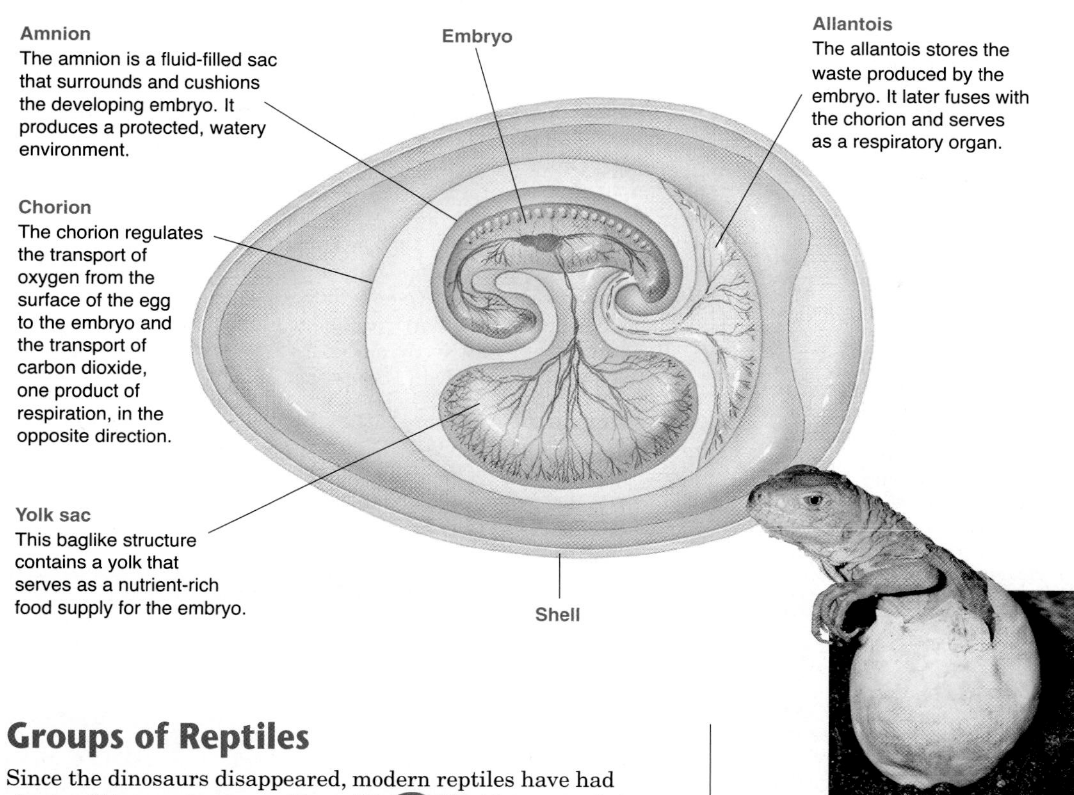

Amnion
The amnion is a fluid-filled sac that surrounds and cushions the developing embryo. It produces a protected, watery environment.
Embryo
Allantois
The allantois stores the waste produced by the embryo. It later fuses with the chorion and serves as a respiratory organ.
Chorion
The chorion regulates the transport of oxygen from the surface of the egg to the embryo and the transport of carbon dioxide, one product of respiration, in the opposite direction.
Yolk sac
This baglike structure contains a yolk that serves as a nutrient-rich food supply for the embryo.
Shell

▲ **Figure 31–8** An amniotic egg contains several membranes and an external shell. Although it is waterproof, the egg shell is porous, allowing gases to pass through. The shell of reptile eggs is usually soft and leathery. The photograph shows a hatching iguana leaving the broken shell of its amniotic egg. **The amniotic egg is one of the most important adaptations to life on dry land.**

Groups of Reptiles

Since the dinosaurs disappeared, modern reptiles have had plenty of time and space to diversify. **The four surviving groups of reptiles are lizards and snakes, crocodilians, turtles and tortoises, and the tuatara (too-uh-TAH-ruh).**

Lizards and Snakes Modern lizards and snakes belong to the order Squamata (skwah-MAH-tuh), or scaly reptiles. Most lizards have legs, clawed toes, external ears, and movable eyelids. Some lizards have evolved into highly specialized forms. For example, Gila (HEE-luh) monsters—large, stocky lizards that live in the southwestern United States and Mexico—have glands in the lower jaw that produce venom for defense against predators.

Snakes have lost both pairs of legs during the course of their evolution. Although they are legless, snakes are highly efficient predators, even in the ocean. Some snakes are so small that they resemble earthworms. Others, such as some species of python, can grow to more than 8 meters in length. The ability of certain snakes to produce venom has caused some people to harbor an unjustified fear of all snakes. More people in the United States die from bee stings than from snakebites. In fact, most snakes tend to avoid people, not to confront them!

Use Visuals

Figure 31–8 Review the structure and function of the amniotic egg. Then, compare the amphibian egg to the reptilian amniotic egg. Ask: **How do the parts of the amniotic egg enable it to survive on land?** *(Shell: protects from drying out; allantois and chorion: gas exchange and waste storage; yolk sac: food for embryo; amnion: water environment to cushion embryo)* **Why are reptiles completely independent of water for reproduction?** *(Internal fertilization and amniotic egg)*

Groups of Reptiles

Build Science Skills

Using Models When students have learned about the four groups of reptiles, challenge them to choose one reptilian order and create a model of their own reptile based on the characteristics of the group. Students can illustrate their models, or they can create models from clay or other materials. Have students present their models to the class. Challenge other students to classify each model into a group based on its characteristics.

Address Misconceptions

Many students might think that snakes have slimy skin. Help dispel this misconception by giving students the opportunity to touch snakes, either in the classroom or while on a field trip to a zoo or pet shop.

FACTS AND FIGURES

Color, shape, and regeneration
Lizards have many adaptations to help them survive. Geckos, for example, have pads on their toes to help them cling to trees and move across diverse terrain speedily to escape predators. Geckos can also cast off their tails if grabbed by a predator. The tailless gecko escapes, and its tail will quickly regenerate. Some lizards blend into the environment to escape predators. Anoles and chameleons change their skin color when frightened or alarmed. The change in skin color can startle a predator or enable the lizard to better blend into its environment. The frilled dragon is a lizard with a frill of skin around its neck. When startled, it extends and opens up the frill, making itself appear much larger and fearsome than it really is.

Answers to . . .

CHECKPOINT *Amnion, yolk sac, chorion, and allantois*

Figure 31–6 *The lizard's legs are stronger and larger than those of an amphibian.*

Figure 31–7 *To increase the chance that some will survive predation, because turtles do not protect their young from predators*

Meet Diverse Needs

Encourage at-risk students to devise a way to organize the information given about the four groups of reptiles. Students might choose to make a chart, a concept map, or an outline. Encourage students to illustrate their organizers to help them visualize the differences among the four groups. **Learning modality: visual**

Using Visuals

Figure 31–9 Have student volunteers match each reptile pictured to its order. Ask: **How do snakes differ from lizards?** *(Snakes are legless.)* **Why are tuataras in a separate order from snakes and lizards?** *(Tuataras lack external ears, have primitive scales, and have a "third" eye.)* **Is the member of the order Testudines in Figure 31–9 a turtle or a tortoise?** *(Tortoise)* **How do you know?** *(It doesn't have flipperlike feet.)*

Build Science Skills

Classifying Display pictures of a snapping turtle, a sea turtle, a tortoise, and a painted turtle. Challenge students to identify which live on land *(tortoise)*, which live in water *(snapping turtle, painted turtle, sea turtle)*, and which cannot pull back into their shell *(snapping turtle)*. Make sure students give reasons for their classifications by identifying the adaptations or characteristics that they used for classification.

Build Science Skills

Inferring Challenge students to infer why tuataras still exist. Discuss the causes of the mass extinction at the K-T boundary and the location of New Zealand. Ask: **How might an island location contribute to the survival of the tuatara?** *(Answers include tuataras were isolated from predators and from competition for resources by better adapted animals.)*

▼ **Figure 31–9** The four orders of living reptiles are the Squamata, Crocodilia, Testudines, and Sphenodonta. **The common names of these modern reptile groups are lizards and snakes, crocodilians, turtles and tortoises, and the tuatara.**

Crocodilians Examples of crocodilians and other reptile groups are shown in **Figure 31–9.** Any member of the order Crocodilia—including alligators, crocodiles, caimans, and gavials—can easily be recognized by its long and typically broad snout and its squat appearance. Crocodilians are fierce carnivores that prey on animals such as fishes, deer, and even humans. Crocodilians are very protective of their young. The females guard their eggs from predators. After the eggs are hatched, the mother gently carries her young to a nursery area and watches over them.

Crocodilians live only in the tropics and subtropics, where the climate remains warm year-round. Alligators, and their relatives the caimans, live only in fresh water and are found almost exclusively in North and South America. Crocodiles, on the other hand, may live in either fresh or salt water and are native to Africa, India, and Southeast Asia.

Turtles and Tortoises Turtles and tortoises are members of the order Testudines (tes-TOO-duh-neez). The name *turtle* usually refers to members of this order that live in water; the name *tortoise* refers to those that live on land. A terrapin is a turtle that is found in water that is somewhat salty.

FIGURE 31–9 DIVERSITY OF REPTILES

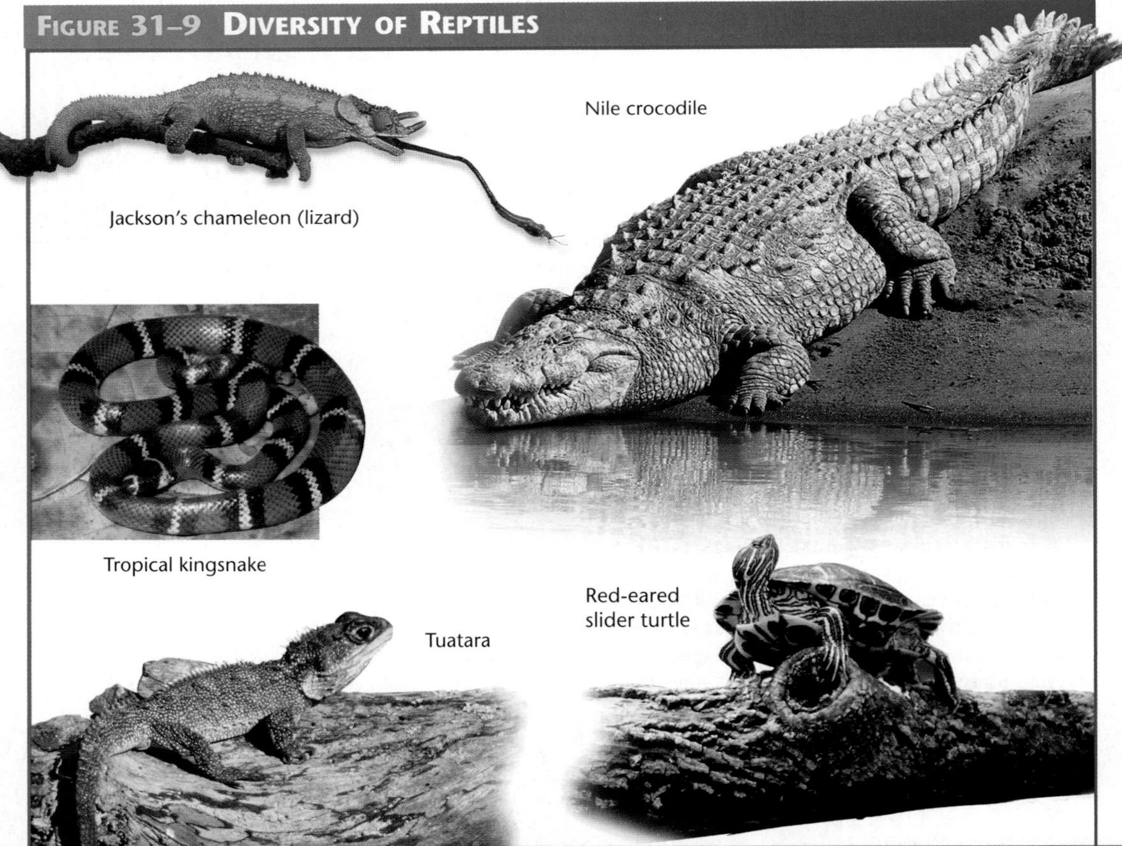

BIOLOGY UPDATE

Saving sea turtles

Sea turtles have inhabited Earth's oceans for millions of years. However, their existence on Earth is threatened. Their demise has been caused by many different factors, but all of them are the result of human activity. Sea turtles are hunted directly for their meat, eggs, leather, and shells. They are harmed indirectly by their accidental capture in fishing nets, by ingestion of trash, by polluted ocean water, and by the loss of nesting sites. Many laws have been enacted to help protect sea turtles. Recently, eight nations from North and South America ratified a treaty to protect sea turtles. A multinational treaty is necessary, because sea turtles have large migratory routes. Identifying these migratory routes has been made easier by tagging turtles with satellite global positioning transmitters.

Turtles and tortoises have a shell built into the skeleton, although in a few species the shell is not very hard. The shell consists of two parts: a dorsal part, or **carapace,** and a ventral part, or **plastron.** The animal's backbone forms the center of the carapace. The head, legs, and tail stick out through holes where the carapace and plastron join. Tortoises and most turtles pull into their shells to protect themselves.

Several other adaptations allow turtles and tortoises to live in a wide range of habitats—dry, wet, and in-between. Lacking teeth, these reptiles have horny ridges that cover the upper and lower jaws. The jaws are often powerful enough to deliver a damaging bite. All possess strong limbs to lift their body off the ground when walking or, in the case of sea turtles, to drag themselves across a sandy shore to lay eggs.

Tuataras The tuatara is the only surviving member of the order Sphenodonta (sfe-nuh-DON-tuh). It is found only on a few small islands off the coast of New Zealand. Tuatara resemble lizards, but they differ from lizards in many ways. For example, they lack external ears and retain primitive scales. Tuatara also have a legendary "third eye," which is part of a complex organ located on top of the brain. The function of this organ, if any, is still unknown.

Ecology of Reptiles

Many reptiles are in danger because their habitats have been, and are being, destroyed. In addition, humans hunt reptiles for food, to sell as pets, and for their skins, from which bags, boots, and combs are made. Laws now protect some species, such as sea turtles, which were once numerous in both the Atlantic and Pacific oceans. Sea turtle recovery programs, such as the one shown in **Figure 31–10,** give many young turtles a head start on survival. Although there are many other programs in place that protect reptiles, more conservation efforts are needed worldwide to counteract their dwindling numbers.

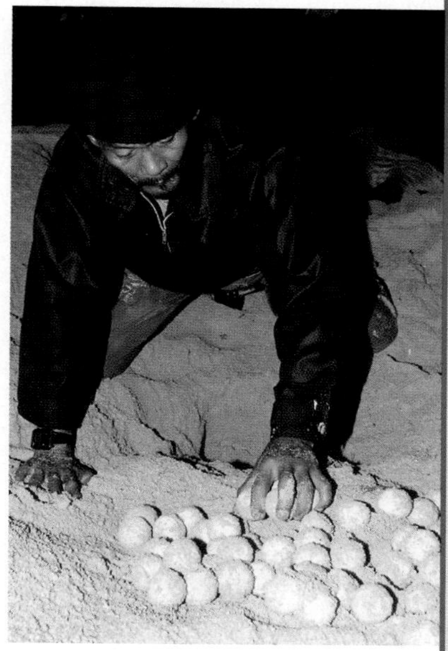

▲ **Figure 31–10** This wildlife ranger is retrieving green sea turtle eggs on Turtle Island National Park in Borneo. He will bring the eggs to an incubation station, where they can hatch safe from harm. After hatching, the young turtles will be released to the sea. **Inferring** ***What might harm sea turtle eggs that are left on a beach to hatch?***

Ecology of Reptiles

Make Connections

Environmental Science Make sure students realize how human activity can change the environment to make it unfavorable for species living there. Ask: **How might sea turtles be affected if the beaches on which they lay their eggs become popular tourist beaches?** *(Eggs have a greater chance of being destroyed; fewer sea turtles will hatch and grow to adulthood.)*

3 ASSESS

Evaluate Understanding

Play a quiz game in which you give students the answers and they give you the questions. Focus on adaptations that enable reptiles to live on land and the features of the four reptile groups.

Reteach

Instruct students to draw a diagram of a typical reptile that shows the main characteristics of reptiles. They should also show how reptiles are adapted to live on land.

MAKING CONNECTIONS

Some endangered reptiles that the brochures might feature are the American crocodile, the blue racer snake, the Komodo dragon, and the Indian python. Brochures should clearly indicate the threats to the reptiles and explain protective measures.

iTEXT

Use iText to review the key concepts in Section 31–1.

31–1 Section Assessment

1. **Key Concept** List the main characteristics of reptiles.
2. **Key Concept** List five ways that reptiles are adapted to life on dry land.
3. **Key Concept** Name the four orders of modern reptiles and give an example of each.
4. How is excretion carried out in reptiles that live on land?
5. How does a lizard control its body temperature?
6. **Critical Thinking Predicting** What might happen to reptiles if conditions on Earth became permanently warmer and much damper?

Assessment Use iText to review the important concepts in Section 31–1.

MAKING CONNECTIONS

Biodiversity
In Chapter 6, you learned about threats to biodiversity. Do research to find out what factors threaten a reptile such as the sea turtle, and what steps are taken to protect this reptile. Make a brochure that shows what you have learned.

31–1 Section Assessment

1. Vertebrate, scaly skin, lungs, amniotic egg
2. Any five: lungs, double-loop circulatory system, strong limbs, efficient excretory system, shelled eggs, internal fertilization
3. Squamata: lizard, snake; Crocodilia: alligator, crocodile, caiman, gavial; Testudines: turtle, tortoise; Sphenodonta: tuatara
4. They convert ammonia to uric acid.
5. By basking in the sun, moving to shade, resting under water, or moving to burrows
6. Some reptiles might colonize areas that are now too cold for them. Others might die out if they cannot successfully compete with damp-loving competitors, such as amphibians.

Answer to . . .

Figure 31–10 *Predators, storms*

Section 31–2

1 FOCUS

Objectives

31.2.1 ***Describe*** the characteristics that all birds have in common.

31.2.2 ***Summarize*** the evolution of birds.

31.2.3 ***Explain*** how birds are adapted for flight.

31.2.4 ***Describe*** the diversity of birds.

31.2.5 ***Identify*** ways in which birds interact with the environment and with humans.

Guide for Reading

Vocabulary Preview

Have students compare *endotherm* to *ectotherm.* Ask: **If *endo-* means "within," how does an endotherm control its body temperature?** *(Endotherms generate their own body heat; they control body temperature from within.)*

Reading Strategy

Before students read this section, have them preview Figure 31–14. Instruct them to list characteristics common to all birds. As students read, encourage them to add or subtract characteristics to complete their list.

2 INSTRUCT

What Is a Bird?

Use Visuals

Figure 31–11 Have students compare and contrast the structure and function of contour and down feathers. Ask: **Which feathers insulate a bird's body?** *(Down)* **Which feathers help the bird to fly?** *(Contour)* Discuss how the structure of down feathers makes them good for insulation. Ask: **Would you expect a bird with only down feathers to fly?** *(No; down feathers do not give the stability needed for flight.)*

31–2 Birds

Guide for Reading

Key Concepts
- What characteristics do birds have in common?
- How are birds adapted for flight?

Vocabulary
feather
endotherm
crop
gizzard
air sac

Reading Strategy: Monitoring Your Understanding
As you read, make sure that you understand what you read. If you have difficulty, think of a strategy that might make the text clearer. For example, you might read the paragraph again, slowly; see whether an illustration helps you understand the printed text; or ask another student or your teacher for help.

Whether they are greeting the dawn with song or coloring the air with brilliant feathers, birds are among the most obvious and welcome of all animals. From common robins to the spectacular and rare quetzal of Central America, the nearly 10,000 modern bird species seem to live everywhere.

What Is a Bird?

In a group this diverse, it is difficult to find many characteristics that are shared by all members. But we can identify the features that most birds have in common. **Birds are reptilelike animals that maintain a constant internal body temperature. They have an outer covering of feathers; two legs that are covered with scales and are used for walking or perching; and front limbs modified into wings.** Most of these features are adaptations for flight.

The single most important characteristic that separates birds from living reptiles, and from all other living animals, is feathers. **Feathers** are made mostly of protein and develop from pits in the birds' skin. Feathers help birds fly and also keep them warm. **Figure 31–11** shows the two main types of feathers: contour feathers and down. Herons and some other birds that live on or in water also have powder down, which releases a fine powder that repels water.

▼ **Figure 31–11** Birds have different types of feathers that vary in structure and function. **An outer covering of feathers is the main characteristic that sets birds apart from other animals.**

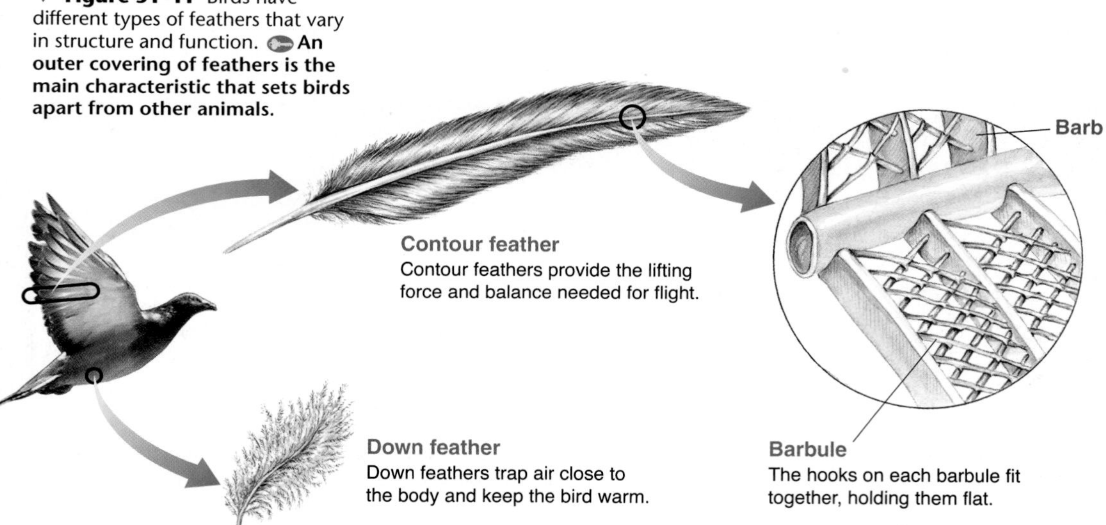
Barb
Contour feather
Contour feathers provide the lifting force and balance needed for flight.
Down feather
Down feathers trap air close to the body and keep the bird warm.
Barbule
The hooks on each barbule fit together, holding them flat.

SECTION RESOURCES

Print:
- ***Laboratory Manual B,*** Chapter 31 Lab
- ***Teaching Resources,*** Section Review 31–2, Chapter 31 Exploration
- ***Guided Reading and Study Workbook,*** Section 31–2
- ***Issues and Decision Making,*** 31–2

Technology:
- ***iText,*** Section 31–2

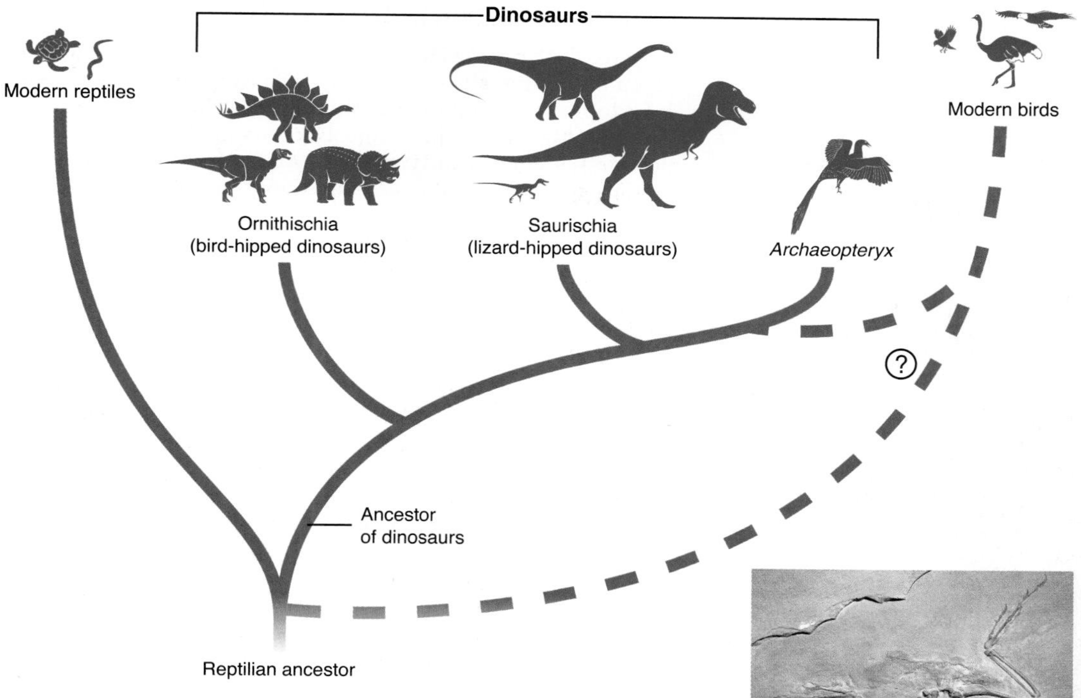

Evolution of Birds

To many paleontologists a bird is a dinosaur with feathers. That definition may sound odd, but it makes sense. The first fossil ever found of an early birdlike animal is in the genus *Archaeopteryx* (ahr-kee-AHP-tur-iks) and dates from the late Jurassic Period, about 150 million years ago. *Archaeopteryx* looked like a small, running dinosaur. In fact, *Archaeopteryx* would be classified as a dinosaur except for one important feature: It had well-developed feathers covering most of its body. Because of this, the crow-sized *Archaeopteryx* is considered an early bird. Unlike modern birds, however, this creature had teeth in its beak, a bony tail, and toes and claws on its wings. Thus, *Archaeopteryx* is a transitional species with a combination of dinosaurlike and birdlike characteristics.

Scientists debate whether birds evolved directly from dinosaurs or both dinosaurs and birds evolved from a common ancestor. Today, most evidence suggests that birds and dinosaurs are close relatives. Although this relationship is shown in **Figure 31–12**, the evolutionary origin of birds is still not completely resolved.

CHECKPOINT *What is* Archaeopteryx*?*

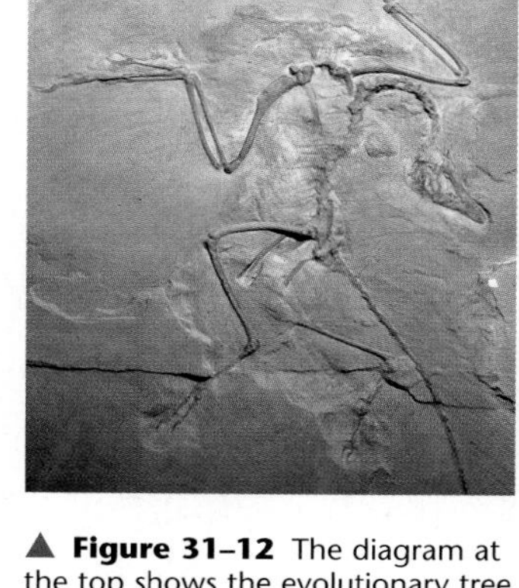

▲ **Figure 31–12** The diagram at the top shows the evolutionary tree of modern birds. None of the animals shown are direct ancestors of modern birds. But fossils such as *Archaeopteryx* (above) do show a mixture of characteristics of birds and dinosaurs. **Interpreting Graphics** ***Based on the cladogram, what are the two alternative explanations for the evolution of modern birds?***

Evolution of Birds

Use Visuals

Figure 31–12 Have students examine Figure 31–12. Ask: **In what ways was *Archaeopteryx* similar to birds?** *(It had feathers.)* **How was it similar to dinosaurs?** *(Its skeleton looked similar to a two-legged dinosaur with teeth, heavy skull, and a jointed tail.)* **Why do you think many scientists infer that birds evolved from dinosaurs?** *(Discoveries of fossilized intermediate species show characteristics of both dinosaurs and birds.)*

Meet Diverse Needs

Remind students that many researchers believe birds evolved directly from dinosaurs, based on the evidence found in fossilized species. Challenge gifted students to infer what kind of fossilized evidence researchers would expect to find if birds and dinosaurs had instead evolved from a common ancestor. *(If birds and dinosaurs each evolved from a common ancestor, you would not expect to find any fossilized species that have characteristics of both birds and dinosaurs or any species that are intermediate between birds and dinosaurs.)* Students can write a short report that describes their inference and the evidence or background information on which they based their inference. **Learning modality: logical/mathematical**

TIME SAVER — PRESENTATIONS MADE EASY!

The Presentation Assistant Plus contains the Prentice Hall Presentation Pro and the Transparencies, which provide easy-to-follow visual support for every step of this section. If you have a computer presentation station, use Prentice Hall Presentation Pro for Section 31–2, or use the transparencies listed here.

Section 31–2:

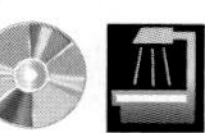

Interest Grabber
Section Outline
Concept Map
Figure 31–13
Figure 31–16

Answers to . . .

CHECKPOINT *Extinct species with bird-like and dinosaur-like features*

Figure 31–12 *Either evolved from dinosaurs or from a reptile ancestor common to dinosaurs and birds*

Form, Function, and Flight

Build Science Skills

Predicting Give student groups 10 to 15 pictures of various birds. Instruct groups to predict which birds fly and which do not. Next, have students predict which of the flying birds are the best fliers. After making their predictions, have groups list the characteristics they used for making their predictions. Then, tell students the answers. Encourage them to review their predictions and the criteria they used to make them. Ask groups if they would change any of the criteria they used to make their predictions and why.

Make Connections

Physics Let students experiment to discover how insulation helps conserve heat. Allow student groups to brainstorm a list of materials that would be good insulators. Then, have students test these materials by observing how well they can keep a warm object warm. Students might devise a plan as simple as wrapping a jar of hot water with the material and measuring the water temperature over time to determine how much heat is lost. The better the insulator, the less heat is lost. Ask: **What quality determines the best insulators?** *(Often the best insulators trap the most air around an object.)*

Use Community Resources

Arrange a field trip to a bird aviary or a display of stuffed birds at a natural history museum. Challenge students to identify the type of food each bird eats based on the shape of its bill.

Form, Function, and Flight

One reason for the evolutionary success of birds is found in the adaptations that allow them to fly. **Birds have a number of adaptations that enable them to fly. These adaptations include highly efficient digestive, respiratory, and circulatory systems; aerodynamic feathers and wings; and strong chest muscles.** Most birds have these characteristics, even though some birds cannot fly.

The ways in which birds carry out their life functions, such as obtaining food and oxygen, contribute to their ability to fly. For example, flight requires an enormous amount of energy, which birds obtain from the food they eat. Birds also require energy to maintain their body temperature.

Body Temperature Control Unlike reptiles, which must draw body warmth from their environment, birds can generate their own body heat. Animals that can generate their own body heat are called **endotherms.** Endotherms, which include birds, mammals, and some other animals, have a high rate of metabolism compared to ectotherms such as reptiles. Recall that metabolism is the sum of chemical and physical processes that go on inside the body. Metabolism produces heat. A bird's feathers insulate its body enough to conserve most of its metabolic energy, allowing the bird to warm its body more efficiently. The body temperature of most birds is about 41°C even on cold winter days.

CHECKPOINT *What is an endotherm?*

Feeding Any body heat that a bird loses must be regained by eating food. The more food a bird eats, the more heat energy its metabolism can generate. Because small birds lose heat relatively faster than large ones, small birds must eat more, relative to their body size. In fact, the phrase "eats like a bird" is quite misleading, because most birds are voracious eaters!

As you can see in **Figure 31–13,** birds' beaks, or bills, are adapted to the type of food they eat. Insect-eating birds have short, fine bills that can pick ants and other insects off leaves and branches, or can catch flying insects. Seed-eaters have short, thick bills. Carnivorous birds, such as eagles, shred their prey with strong hooked bills. Long, thin bills can be used for gathering nectar from flowers or probing soft mud for worms and shellfish. Large, long bills help birds to pick fruit from branches, while long, flat bills are used to grasp fish.

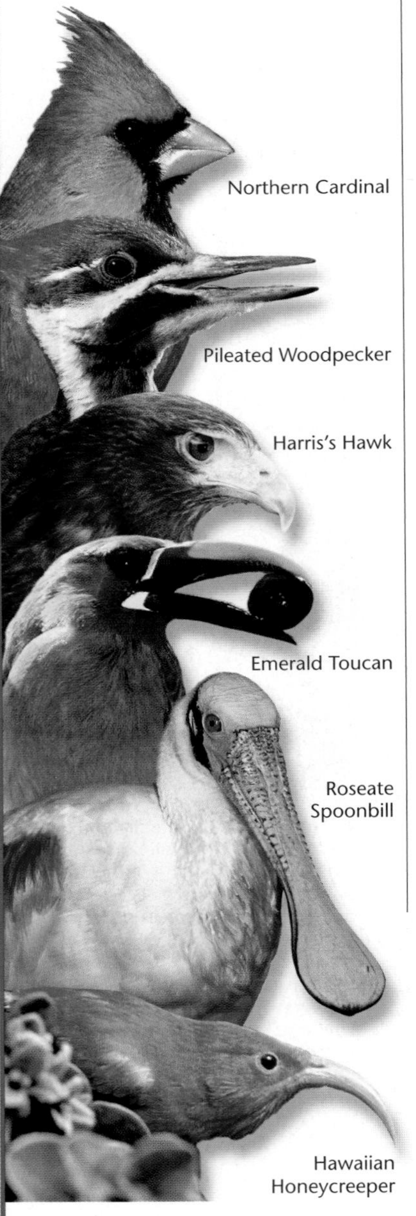

Figure 31–13 Bird bills come in a variety of shapes and sizes. You can tell a good deal about a bird's feeding habits from its bill. **Drawing Conclusions** *Based on the size and shape of its bill, what does a roseate spoonbill feed on?*

FACTS AND FIGURES

Bird beaks and feeding habits
Not only do birds eat insects and small animals, but birds also feed on plant materials, such as seeds, fruit, and nectar. Some birds eat only one kind of food, while others eat a wide variety of foods. When birds first evolved, they were probably insect-eaters. Woodpeckers are insect eaters that are specially adapted to drill or "peck" holes into wood and pull out the insects living there.

Pollen and nectar feeders such as hummingbirds have long, probing bills to reach deep into flowers. Their long, brushlike tongues lick up nectar and fruit juices. Birds that eat seeds and fruits have either short, stout bills or long, sharp bills, depending on the type of seed or fruit they eat. Filter feeders such as ducks and flamingoes have broad beaks with strainers built into the upper and side parts of the bill.

▼ **Figure 31–14** **Birds have a number of adaptations that enable them to fly, including an efficient digestive system.** Trace the path of food through the digestive system.

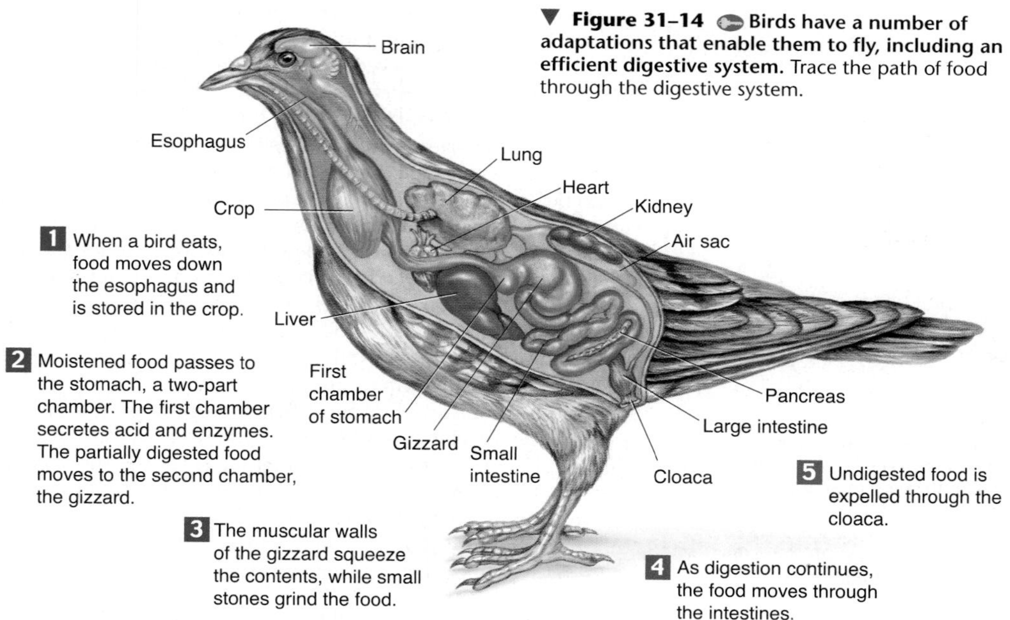

Brain
Esophagus
Lung
Heart
Kidney
Crop
Air sac
1 When a bird eats, food moves down the esophagus and is stored in the crop.
Liver
2 Moistened food passes to the stomach, a two-part chamber. The first chamber secretes acid and enzymes. The partially digested food moves to the second chamber, the gizzard.
First chamber of stomach
Gizzard
Small intestine
Pancreas
Large intestine
Cloaca
5 Undigested food is expelled through the cloaca.
3 The muscular walls of the gizzard squeeze the contents, while small stones grind the food.
4 As digestion continues, the food moves through the intestines.

The digestive system of a bird is shown in **Figure 31–14.** Birds lack teeth, and therefore they cannot break down food by chewing it. However, many birds have specialized structures to help digest food. One such structure is the **crop,** which is located at the lower end of the esophagus. Food is stored and moistened in the crop before it moves further in the digestive tract.

In some birds, such as pigeons, the crop has a second function. During nesting season, the breakdown of cells in the crop produces a substance that is rich in protein and fat. Parent birds regurgitate this substance and feed their newly hatched young with it. This substance provides the young birds with materials they need to grow.

From the crop, moistened food moves into the stomach. The form that a bird's stomach takes depends on the bird's feeding habits. Birds that eat meat or fish have an expandable area in which large amounts of soft food can be stored. Birds that eat insects or seeds, however, have a muscular organ called the **gizzard** that helps in the mechanical breakdown of food by grinding it. The gizzard forms part of the stomach. In many species of bird, the gizzard contains small pieces of stone and gravel that the bird has swallowed. The thick, muscular walls of the gizzard grind the gravel and food together, crushing food particles and making them easier to digest.

Food moves from the stomach to the small intestine, where the breakdown of food is completed and food is absorbed into the body. Digestive wastes leave the body through the cloaca.

Address Misconceptions

Students might think birds do not eat large amounts of food. Many have heard the phrase "eats like a bird" in reference to someone who doesn't eat much food. Emphasize that because birds have a very high metabolic rate, they burn many Calories to generate body heat. They also require a lot of energy for movement. To fill their energy needs, birds eat almost constantly.

Use Visuals

Figure 31–14 Have students trace the path of food through the bird's digestive system. Ask: **What happens to food in the crop?** *(It's stored and moistened.)* **What is the function of the gizzard?** *(It grinds and crushes food.)* Remind students that not all birds have gizzards. Ask: **Would insect-eating birds or fish-eating birds have a gizzard?** *(Insect-eating birds)* **Why do birds need the gizzard and the crop?** *(They don't have teeth. These organs help prepare food for digestion.)*

Meet Diverse Needs

At-risk students can review the process of digestion in birds by making a flowchart. Students should include every part of the digestion system in which something happens to food. They should start with the mouth and end with the cloaca. Students with limited English proficiency can label their flowcharts in their native language. **Learning modality: visual**

BIO INSIGHTS — FACTS AND FIGURES

Specialized digestive systems
Like other vertebrates, a bird's digestive system is slightly different depending on its diet. Birds do not have teeth and cannot chew their food into smaller pieces. Birds that eat small animals either tear off small pieces with their bills or swallow their food whole. These birds usually do not have a crop at the end of the esophagus, because the food does not have to be softened. Their stomachs usually have only one compartment. They do not have a gizzard. Birds that primarily eat seeds usually have a crop. The crop is required to soften the hard seeds, making them susceptible to digestive enzymes. These birds often have a two-part stomach that includes a gizzard.

Answers to . . .

CHECKPOINT *Animal that generates its own body heat*

Figure 31–13 *Fish*

Meet Diverse Needs

To help all students visualize the flow of air through bird lungs, have the students act as air molecules moving through the respiratory system. Use masking tape to delineate the anterior air sacs, lungs, posterior air sacs, and trachea. Students carrying red paper circles (O_2) enter the trachea upon inhalation 1 and move into posterior air sac. During exhalation 1, students move into lungs and exchange red circles for blue circles (CO_2). During inhalation 2, new "red" students enter posterior air sac. The "blue" students move to anterior air sac. During exhalation 2, the "blue" students move out into the air and the "red" students move into the lungs and exchange "gases." Continue in this manner until all students have moved through the respiratory system. **Learning modality: kinesthetic**

Meet Diverse Needs

Divide the class into small groups that represent a mixture of academic abilities. Groups should discuss what they know about the form and function of birds. Have one group member take notes during the discussion. Then, instruct groups to summarize how specific body structures and systems make birds adapted for flight. Suggest that groups also discuss what makes some birds able to fly while others cannot. Groups should summarize their conclusions and present them to the class. Compile the groups' conclusions into a table that you can update as you complete the section. **Learning modality: verbal**

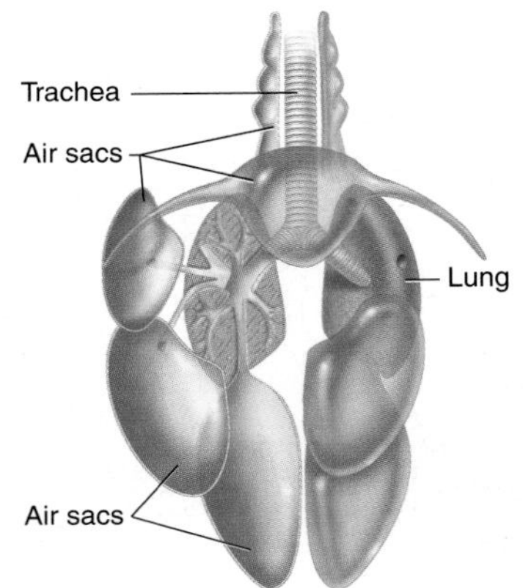

▲ **Figure 31–15** Birds have a unique respiratory system. Air sacs direct air through the lungs in an efficient, one-way flow. **Comparing and Contrasting** *How does this system differ from that of most land vertebrates?*

Respiration Birds have a unique and highly efficient way of taking in oxygen and eliminating carbon dioxide. When a bird inhales, most air first enters large posterior **air sacs** in the body cavity and bones. Observe the air sacs in **Figure 31–15.** The inhaled air then flows through the lungs. Air travels through the lungs in a series of small tubes. These tubes are lined with specialized tissue, where gas exchange takes place.

The complex system of air sacs and breathing tubes ensures that air flows into the air sacs and out through the lungs in a single direction. The one-way flow constantly exposes the lungs to oxygen-rich air. Contrast this to the system found in most land vertebrates, in which oxygen-rich air is inhaled, and oxygen-poor air is exhaled. The air travels in two directions, in and out. In an in-out system, the lungs are exposed to oxygen-rich air only during inhalation.

What advantage does the efficient respiratory system of birds provide? The constant, one-way flow of oxygen-rich air helps birds maintain their high metabolic rate. Birds need a high metabolism to maintain body temperature and provide the large amounts of energy required for flight. In addition, the abundant supply of oxygen enables birds to fly at high altitudes where there is little oxygen in the atmosphere.

✓CHECKPOINT *How is their respiratory system advantageous to birds?*

Circulation Birds have four-chambered hearts and two separate circulatory loops. Notice in **Figure 31–16** that a bird's heart, unlike that of amphibians and most reptiles, has two separate ventricles, the right ventricle and the left ventricle. There is complete separation of oxygen-rich and oxygen-poor blood. One half of the heart receives oxygen-poor blood from the body and pumps this blood to the lungs. Oxygen-rich blood returns to the other side of the heart to be pumped to the rest of the body. This double-loop system ensures that oxygen collected by the lungs is distributed to the body tissue with maximum efficiency.

▼ **Figure 31–16** To keep blood moving rapidly, a bird's heart beats quickly—from 150 to more than 1000 beats per minute! **Applying Concepts** *Why is it important for a bird's heart to move blood so rapidly?*

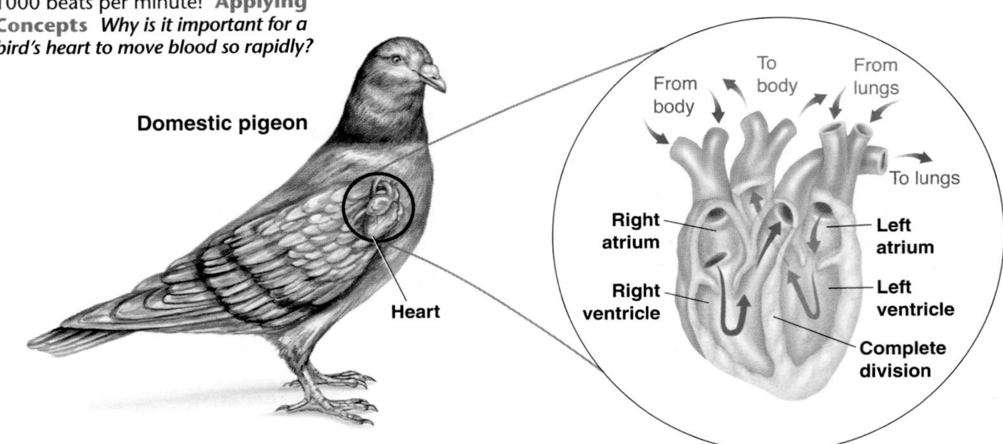

FACTS AND FIGURES

Bird sighted flying above the clouds

Some of the highest flying birds are bar-headed geese. These geese have been observed flying over the Himalayas, which reach altitudes of over 7600 meters. Birds are able to fly at such high altitudes because of the efficiency of their lungs. In contrast, humans have difficulty climbing Mount Everest because they inhale less oxygen due to the lower air pressure.

Not only do bird lungs function efficiently at gas exchange, but the air sacs in lungs also help birds to lose heat. The air sacs are located among the bird's internal organs, and they are connected to the bones. Bird bones have hollow spaces to reduce mass, but also function to hold air. As air moves across the organs and through the bones during the process of respiration, it works to cool the bird's body.

Quick Lab

How do birds breathe?

Materials 6 round balloons, hand-powered balloon pump, measuring tape, clock with second hand

Procedure

1. Work in groups of three. Make a copy of the data table at right on a blank sheet of paper. One person will inflate a balloon by mouth, while a second person inflates a balloon with a hand-powered pump. The third person is the timekeeper.
2. Begin inflating both balloons at the same time. After 10 seconds, the timer will say "stop." Stop inflating the balloons and pinch the necks of the balloons to keep the air inside. **CAUTION:** *Do not try to inflate balloons if you have a condition that would make this dangerous for you.*
3. Measure and record the circumference of each balloon in your data table. **CAUTION:** *Discard all balloons that have been inflated.*

Data Table

Name	Balloon circumference (cm)		Difference
	Mouth	Pump	

Average difference ___________

4. Repeat Steps 1–3 until each member of your group has inflated two balloons. In your data table, record the difference in balloon diameter for each person and the average difference for the group.

Analyze and Conclude

1. **Analyzing Data** Which method was faster? Which method required more effort?
2. **Using Models** Which method worked like reptile lungs? Which method worked like bird lungs? Explain your answers.
3. **Formulating Hypotheses** How is efficient respiration especially valuable to birds?

Excretion The excretory systems of many birds are similar to those of some reptiles. Nitrogenous wastes are removed from the blood by the kidneys, converted to uric acid, and deposited in the cloaca. There, most of the water is reabsorbed, leaving uric acid crystals in a white, pasty form that you may recognize as bird droppings.

Response To coordinate the movements required for flight, birds have well-developed sense organs. They also have a brain that can quickly interpret and respond to a lot of incoming signals. A bird's brain, shown in **Figure 31–17**, is relatively large for its body size. The cerebrum, which controls such behaviors as flying, nest building, care of young, courtship, and mating, is quite large. The cerebellum is also well developed, as you might expect in an animal that uses precise, coordinated movements. The medulla oblongata coordinates basic body processes, such as the heartbeat.

Birds have extraordinarily well-developed eyes and sizable optic lobes in the brain. Birds see color very well—in many cases, better than humans. Most bird species can also hear quite well. The senses of taste and smell, however, are not well developed in most birds, and the olfactory bulbs in a bird's brain are small.

▼ **Figure 31–17** Compared to reptiles, birds have an enlarged cerebellum that coordinates the movements of wings and legs. **Formulating Hypotheses** *Why would the cerebrum also be larger in birds than in reptiles?*

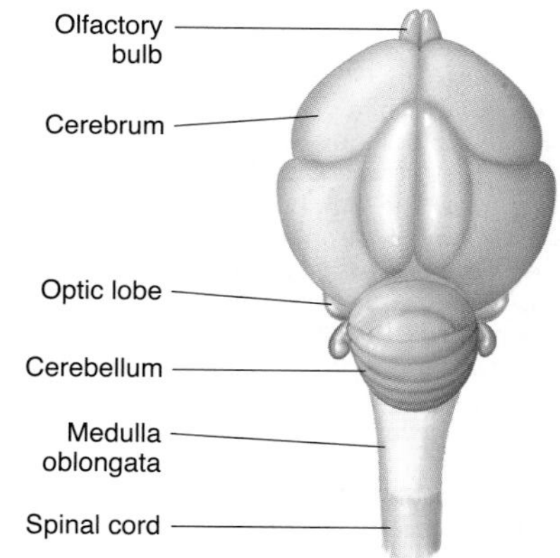

Quick Lab

Objective Students will be able to use models to explain how birds breathe.

Skills Focus **Using Models**

Materials 6 round balloons, hand-powered balloon pump, measuring tape, clock with second hand

Time 15 minutes

Advance Prep Inexpensive balloon pumps are available at party supply stores.

Strategies

- Diagram on the board the flow of air that occurs when a balloon is inflated by mouth and when it is pumped.
- Discuss why birds need a more efficient way to get oxygen than reptiles. *(Muscles require oxygen to burn food for energy; there is little oxygen at high altitudes.)* Have students rate the movements of reptiles and birds. Ask: **What do muscles need to keep working efficiently?** *(Oxygen)*

Expected Outcomes Balloons are more highly inflated with a hand pump than by mouth.

Analyze and Conclude

1. Using the pump is faster. Mouth inflation requires more effort.
2. Mouth inflation simulates the flow of air in and out of the same opening, as in reptile lungs. Air flows in one end of the pump and out the other, as in bird lungs.
3. Flight requires a high level of cellular respiration in the muscles. Also, high-altitude flight requires extra oxygen. Therefore, birds need a large oxygen supply.

BIO INSIGHTS — FACTS AND FIGURES

Birds sing to communicate

Birds use sound to communicate with each other. Ornithologists differentiate between two kinds of bird sounds. Calls are short sounds used to warn others of danger and to communicate between members of the same species. These calls are innate. Songs are longer vocalizations that involve many different notes. Songs are also learned from adult to offspring. Some songbirds even learn new songs each year. Birds raised in soundproof environments do not learn songs. In most cases, only males learn songs to establish and defend territories and to attract mates.

As in humans, vibrating membranes in birds produce sound. These membranes are located in the syrinx at the posterior end of the trachea. Muscles in the syrinx cause the different pitches in the calls and songs.

Answers to . . .

CHECKPOINT *It maintains a high metabolic rate and supplies the extra oxygen required for high-altitude flight.*

Figure 31–15 *Air travels in one direction only, rather than in and out.*

Figure 31–16 *To maintain high levels of oxygen in muscles*

Figure 31–17 *To control precise movements and complex behaviors*

Make Connections

Physics Challenge student groups to experiment with different wing shapes to produce flight. Give groups toy gliders made from foam or balsam, or have them construct gliders from paper. Encourage students to change the shape of the wings and nose to improve lift. You might need to explain how air moving faster over the tops of the wing and the nose of the plane provides lift, the upward force. Have groups race their planes to see which fly fastest and which fly farthest.

Address Misconceptions

Some students might think that birds simply move their wings up and down during flight. Explain that birds move their wings in a circular motion, similar to the movement of oars when rowing. On the downstroke, feathers are held together, and the wings move down and rotate forward. This motion pushes air down and back, providing lift and propelling the bird through the air. On the upstroke, feathers are opened up to allow air to move through them, making it easier to move the wings upward. The wings bend up, moving closer to the body, and rotate backward.

Groups of Birds

Build Science Skills

Classifying Have students devise their own criteria for grouping the bird orders pictured in Figure 31–19. You might also give students pictures of birds from other orders that are not pictured in the figure. For their classification systems, students should describe what features they are using to define the characteristics of each order.

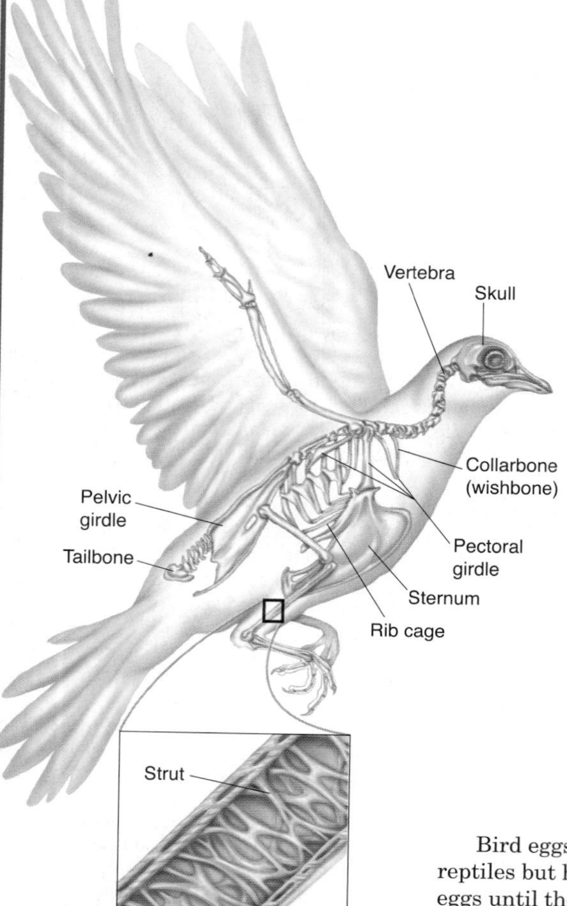

▲ **Figure 31–18** Like most of its anatomy, a bird's skeleton is well adapted for flight, providing a sturdy attachment point for muscles. The long bones are exceptionally strong and light because of cross-bracing and air spaces. In strong flying birds, such as pigeons, the chest muscles may account for as much as 30 percent of the animal's mass. **Calculating** *If this pigeon has a mass of 200 grams, and 30 percent of its mass is chest muscles, what is the mass of its chest muscles?*

Movement Some birds cannot fly. Instead, they get around mainly by walking or running, like ostriches, or by swimming, like penguins. However, the vast majority of birds can fly.

Observe a bird's skeletal system in **Figure 31–18.** Although the bones in a bird's wings are homologous to the bones in the front limbs of other vertebrates, they have very different shapes and structures. In flying birds, many large bones, such as the collarbone, are fused together, making a bird's skeleton more rigid than a reptile's. These bones form a sturdy frame that anchors the muscles used for flight. The bones are strengthened by internal struts similar to those used in the framework of tall buildings and bridges. Birds also have large chest muscles that power the upward and downward wing strokes necessary for flight. The muscles attach to a long keel that runs down the front of an enlarged breastbone, or sternum.

Reproduction In birds, both male and female reproductive tracts open into the cloaca. The sex organs—which are internal in both sexes—often shrink in size when the birds are not breeding. As birds prepare to mate, the ovaries and testes grow larger until they reach functioning size. Mating birds press their cloacas together to transfer sperm from the male to the female. Some male birds have a penis that transfers sperm to the female's cloaca.

Bird eggs are amniotic eggs. They are similar to the eggs of reptiles but have hard outer shells. Most birds incubate their eggs until the eggs hatch. When a chick is ready to hatch, it uses a small tooth on its bill to make a hole in the shell. After much pushing, poking, and prodding by the chick, the eggshell breaks open. Once the exhausted bird has hatched, it collapses for a while and allows its feathers to dry. Both parents may be kept busy providing food for their hungry offspring.

Do birds have external or internal fertilization?

Groups of Birds

Birds fill the woods and fields with song. Flocks of birds are drawn to backyard feeders. Imagine how dull the world would be without the color, song, and variety of birds.

With nearly 30 different orders, it is impossible to present each type of bird here. Instead, **Figure 31–19** provides an overview of some of the better-known groups and their specific adaptations. By far, the largest order of birds is the passerines (pass-uh-REENZ), or perching birds. This group includes songbirds such as larks, sparrows, and finches. There are over 5000 species of perching birds.

BIO INSIGHTS

FACTS AND FIGURES

Air pressure "lifts" birds

Birds are able to fly because of lift. Lift is the difference in air pressure above the wing and below the wing. As birds fly, air moves across both sides of the wings. Air pressure below the wing is greater than air pressure above the wing. In effect, the air is "lifting" the wing. Moving air exerts less pressure than air that is not moving. The faster air moves, the less pressure it exerts.

Bird wings are shaped so that air moving across the top of the wings is moving faster. The top of a bird's wing is rounded, forcing the air to travel a greater distance in the same amount of time as the air moving under the wing. Because the air moving across the top of the wing has to go a greater distance in the same time span, it must move faster.

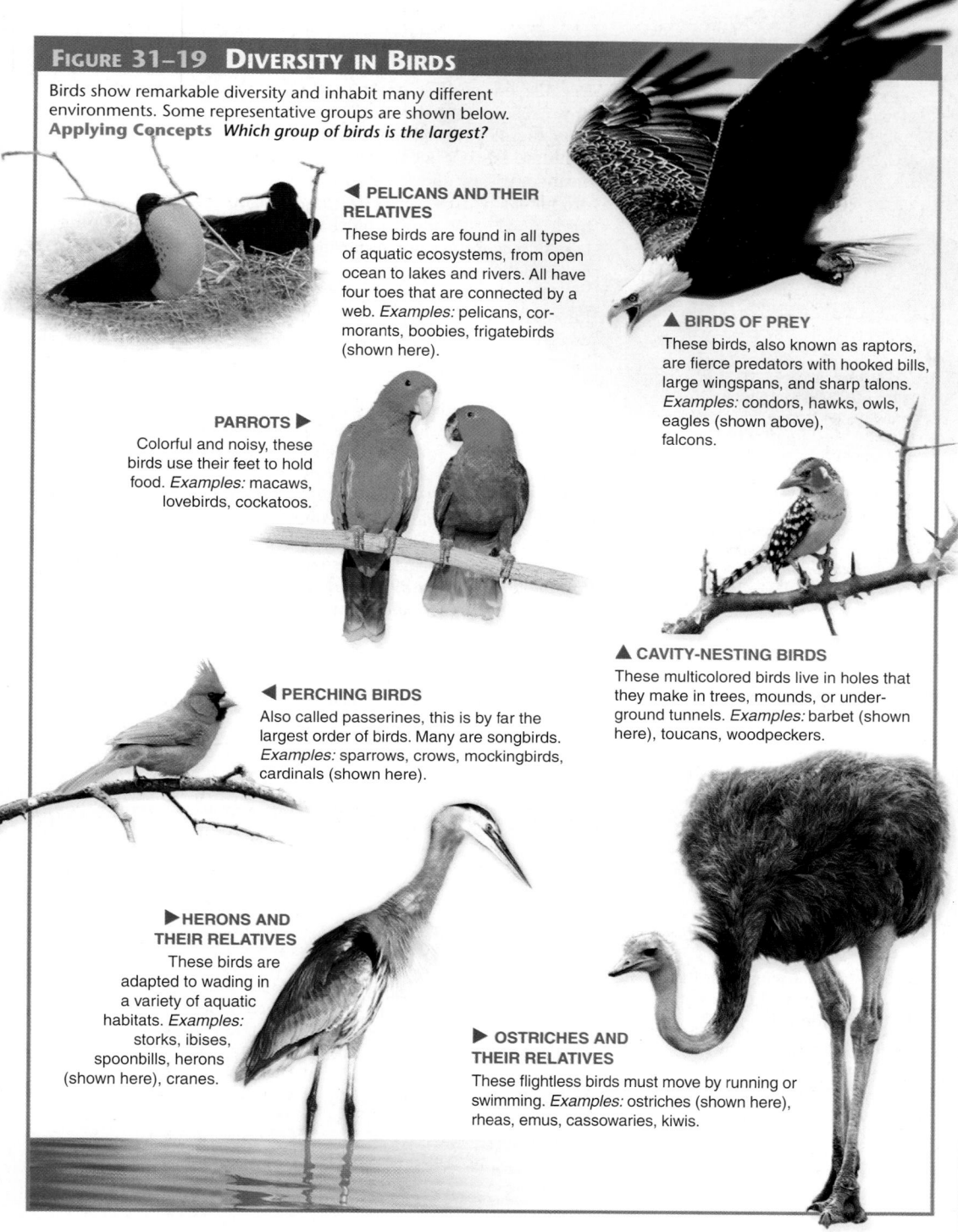

FIGURE 31–19 DIVERSITY IN BIRDS

Birds show remarkable diversity and inhabit many different environments. Some representative groups are shown below. **Applying Concepts** *Which group of birds is the largest?*

◀ **PELICANS AND THEIR RELATIVES**
These birds are found in all types of aquatic ecosystems, from open ocean to lakes and rivers. All have four toes that are connected by a web. *Examples:* pelicans, cormorants, boobies, frigatebirds (shown here).

▲ **BIRDS OF PREY**
These birds, also known as raptors, are fierce predators with hooked bills, large wingspans, and sharp talons. *Examples:* condors, hawks, owls, eagles (shown above), falcons.

PARROTS ▶
Colorful and noisy, these birds use their feet to hold food. *Examples:* macaws, lovebirds, cockatoos.

▲ **CAVITY-NESTING BIRDS**
These multicolored birds live in holes that they make in trees, mounds, or underground tunnels. *Examples:* barbet (shown here), toucans, woodpeckers.

◀ **PERCHING BIRDS**
Also called passerines, this is by far the largest order of birds. Many are songbirds. *Examples:* sparrows, crows, mockingbirds, cardinals (shown here).

▶ **HERONS AND THEIR RELATIVES**
These birds are adapted to wading in a variety of aquatic habitats. *Examples:* storks, ibises, spoonbills, herons (shown here), cranes.

▶ **OSTRICHES AND THEIR RELATIVES**
These flightless birds must move by running or swimming. *Examples:* ostriches (shown here), rheas, emus, cassowaries, kiwis.

Use Visuals

Figure 31–19 Encourage students to compare and contrast the features of birds from different orders. Ask: **How are game birds different from ostriches?** *(Game birds are smaller and can fly.)* **How are parrots different from perching birds?** *(Parrots use their feet to hold up food.)* **What features are common to birds of prey?** *(Hooked bills, large wingspans, and sharp talons)* **How do pelicans differ from herons?** *(Pelicans have webbed feet; herons do not.)* **How are pelicans and herons similar?** *(Both live in aquatic habitats.)*

FACTS AND FIGURES

Classifying birds
Scientists group birds into 23 different orders. To classify birds, scientists use characteristics such as bills, wings, tails, and feet. These specialized characteristics enable birds to inhabit different types of environments, move in different manners, or get different types of food. Birds with similar specialized characteristics often inhabit similar environments or have similar niches. Peacocks, for example, belong to the order Galliformes. These ground-dwelling birds have short, stout bills. Their heavy feet have short, strong claws adapted for running and scratching the ground. They have short wings and are poor fliers. Herons, as well as flamingoes and storks belong to the order Ciconiiformes. These wading birds have long legs and necks and broad feet that are not usually webbed.

Answers to . . .

CHECKPOINT *Birds have internal fertilization.*

Figure 31–18 *60 grams*

Figure 31–19 *Perching birds (passerines)*

31–2 (continued)

Ecology of Birds

Make Connections

Environmental Science Have interested students read Rachel Carson's book, *Silent Spring*. Then, invite the students to lead a class discussion about the book in which they explain why they think Ms. Carson wrote the book and how effective her message was. Point out that at the time, the Department of Agriculture was advocating the use of many different types of dangerous chemicals to combat insect pests. Discuss whether or not students think that Ms. Carson's book is relevant today.

3 ASSESS

Evaluate Understanding

Call on students at random to describe the characteristics of birds. Then, call on other students to describe ways in which birds are adapted for flight.

Reteach

Have students use Figure 31–11 and Figure 31–19 to review the characteristics of birds and the adaptations for flight.

Take It to the NET

In their posters, students can use either scientific or common names for the birds they choose. Students can use either photographs or illustrations to depict a bird from each order. For additional information, visit **www.phschool.com**

iTEXT

Use iText to review the key concepts in Section 31–2.

Answer to . . .

Figure 31–20 *Mutualism*

▲ **Figure 31–20** This hummingbird uses its long, thin beak to draw nectar from a flower. While feeding, the bird may pick up pollen on its beak and carry it to the next flower it visits, thereby helping the flower to pollinate. **Applying Concepts** *Which type of ecological relationship is represented by the hummingbird and the flower: parasitism, mutualism, or commensalism?*

Ecology of Birds

Because birds are so numerous and diverse, they interact with natural ecosystems and human society in many different ways. For example, hummingbirds, like the one in **Figure 31–20**, pollinate flowers in both tropical and temperate zones. Fruit-eating birds swallow seeds but may not digest them, so their droppings disperse seeds over great distances. Insect-eating birds, such as swallows and chimney swifts, catch great numbers of mosquitoes and other insects, and therefore help control insect populations.

Many birds migrate long distances—often over hundreds of kilometers of open sea. Such migrations are usually seasonal. It can be startling during a winter visit to a tropical country to see Northern orioles or bright red cardinals flitting around banana trees with parrots and toucans! How do migrating birds find their way? Some species use stars and other celestial bodies as guides. Other species may use a combination of landmarks and cues from Earth's magnetic field.

Because birds are highly visible and are an important part of the biosphere, they can serve as indicators of environmental health. It is no accident that conservationist Rachel Carson chose songbirds for the focus of her pioneering campaign in the 1960s against the careless use of DDT and other pesticides. In her book *Silent Spring,* Carson described to the public for the first time how pesticides that stay in the environment can accumulate in food chains and cause harm to animals they were never intended to affect. Thanks to the efforts of Carson and other conservationists, many birds—especially predators such as eagles and ospreys—have returned from the brink of extinction.

31–2 Section Assessment

1. **Key Concept** Describe the characteristics of a bird.
2. **Key Concept** List three ways in which birds are well adapted for flight.
3. What is the evolutionary relationship between birds and dinosaurs?
4. How does a chick get out of its eggshell?
5. **Critical Thinking Applying Concepts** Explain why crops and gizzards are especially common and well developed in seed-eating birds but less common in carnivorous birds.

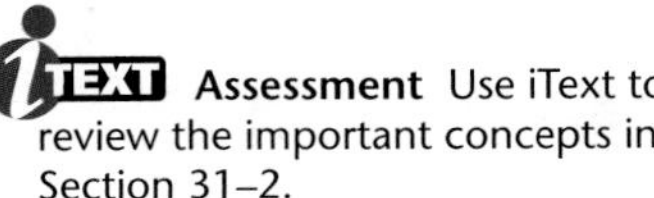

Assessment Use iText to review the important concepts in Section 31–2.

Take It to the NET

Find out more about the orders of birds. Then, create a poster that shows one representative from each order. Use the links provided in the Biology area at the Prentice Hall Web site for help in completing this activity: **www.phschool.com**

31–2 Section Assessment

1. Reptilelike animal, endothermic, hollow bones, feathers, two legs, wings
2. Highly efficient respiratory, digestive, and circulatory systems; aerodynamic feathers and wings; strong chest muscles; strong, lightweight skeleton
3. Birds descended either directly from dinosaurs or from a common ancestor of modern birds and dinosaurs.
4. The chick uses a small tooth on its bill to poke a hole in the shell.
5. Seeds, with their tough outer coverings, are much more difficult to digest than meat. Crops and gizzards are not advantageous to carnivorous birds, because animal tissue does not require extra softening and grinding to digest.

Examining Bird Bones

Birds have many adaptations that enable them to fly, including the structure and properties of their skeletons. In this investigation, you will compare bones from birds and mammals to determine how bird bones are adapted for flight.

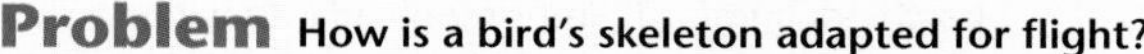

Problem How is a bird's skeleton adapted for flight?

Materials

- cut sections of bird and mammal bones
- bird breastbone
- hand lens
- mammal bone
- bird wing bone
- balance
- 250-mL graduated cylinder
- dissecting probe
- calculator

Skills Observing, Measuring, Calculating

Procedure   

Part A: Bone Structure

1. Use a hand lens to examine cut sections of bird and mammal bones. Look at the interiors of the bones and record your observations.
2. Look at a bird breastbone (sternum). Carefully observe its structure.

Part B: Bone Density

3. Make a copy of the data table on a separate sheet of paper. Use a balance to measure the mass of a bird wing bone.
4. Put 180 mL of water in the graduated cylinder. **CAUTION:** *Handle the graduated cylinder carefully. If it breaks, tell your teacher immediately.*
5. Use a dissecting probe to hold the bird wing bone under water in the graduated cylinder. In your data table, record the water level in the cylinder. Subtract the original water volume from this value to find the volume of the bone.
6. The density of an object is equal to its mass divided by its volume (D = M/V). Calculate the density of the bone by dividing its mass by its volume. Record the density of the bird bone in your data table.
7. Repeat steps 3 to 6 to find the density of the mammal bone.

Data Table

Source of bone	Mass (g)	Volume (mL)			Density of bone (g/cm^3)
		Water	Water + bone	Bone	
Bird					
Mammal					

Analyze and Conclude

1. **Comparing and Contrasting** How are the bird and mammal bones similar? Different? How is the bird bone adapted for flight?
2. **Inferring** What might be the function of the muscles that attach to a bird's sternum? How is the protruding bird sternum an adaptation for flight?
3. **Drawing Conclusions** How are the densities of bird and mammal bones related to the lives of these animals?

Go Further

Applying Concepts In addition to specialized bones, birds' adaptations to flight include several types of feathers. Use reference materials to find out how each type of feather contributes to birds' adaptations.

Analyze and Conclude

1. Both are hard on the outside and partly hollow inside. Bird bones have a thinner outer covering, are more hollow, and have internal struts. These features make bird bones less dense, making flight easier.

2. Muscles attached to a bird's sternum pull the wings downward during flight. The protruding bird sternum anchors the large flight muscles.

3. The low-density bones of birds reflect their adaptation to flight. The denser bones of mammals reflect the mammals' greater need for strong, weight-bearing bones, to support the body in response to the pull of gravity.

Exploration

Objective Students will be able to observe how a bird's skeleton is adapted for flight.

Skills Focus **Observing, Measuring, Calculating**

Time 45 minutes

Advance Prep

- Use a hacksaw or ask a butcher to cut chicken or turkey leg bones and beef or pork ribs into sections so the interior structure is visible.
- Obtain a chicken or turkey sternum. Boil bones thoroughly to remove any meat and kill bacteria. Allow them to dry before using.
- Students should wear disposable plastic gloves. Dispose of the gloves after the activity.

Pre-Lab Discussion Begin a class discussion about a bird's adaptations for flight. Discuss how the density of bones might affect flight. Then, have students read the procedure. Answer any questions students have.

Teaching Tips

- Be prepared to review the concept of density and how it is calculated.
- If possible, use bones from a mammal and a bird of similar size, such as a squirrel and a chicken.

Procedure

1. Bird bones have more hollow spaces within them.

2. Birds have a protruding sternum, humans do not.

6. Students might need to adjust the water level or use a larger graduated cylinder if the bone is too large to be completely submerged.

7. Typical adult mammal bones have densities of about 1.7–2.0 g/mL. The densities of bird bones are less than that of mammals.

Expected Outcome Students should find that bird bones are less dense than mammal bones.

Go Further

Contour feathers give birds the strength and stability for flight. Light, fluffy down feathers insulate birds. Filoplumes sense the positions other feathers.

Chapter 31 Study Guide

Study Tip

Students can construct a Venn diagram to show characteristics and adaptations that birds and reptiles have in common, and those that are specific to each.

Thinking Visually

1. Ectotherms

2. Uric acid

3, 4. Crocodilians; Turtles and Tortoises

Chapter 31 Assessment

Reviewing Content

1. c	**5.** b	**9.** c
2. a	**6.** b	**10.** c
3. b	**7.** d	
4. c	**8.** b	

Understanding Concepts

11. The skin is shed periodically as a reptile increases in size.

12. Earth's climate became cooler and less humid. Since reptiles were better adapted than amphibians to survive in this drier climate, a great adaptive radiation of reptiles began.

13. At the end of the Cretaceous Period, a string of massive volcanic eruptions, lava flows, the dropping of sea level, and a huge asteroid or comet colliding into the Yucatan Peninsula in Mexico occurred. The asteroid or comet collision produced enormous dust clouds and major forest fires. Within a few million years of these events, dinosaurs, along with many other animal and plant groups, disappeared.

14. Interactions with the environment help the animal control its body temperature. To warm up, reptiles seek a warm environment, such as sunlight. To cool down, reptiles move to a cooler environment, such as shade.

Chapter 31 Study Guide

31–1 Reptiles

Key Concepts

- A reptile is a vertebrate that has scaly skin, lungs, and eggs with several membranes.
- Well-developed lungs; a double-loop circulatory system; an efficient excretory system; strong limbs; internal fertilization; and shelled, terrestrial eggs are the main adaptations that have contributed to the success of reptiles on land.
- The four surviving groups of reptiles are lizards and snakes, crocodilians, turtles and tortoises, and the tuatara.

Vocabulary

ectotherm, p. 800
amniotic egg, p. 802
carapace, p. 805
plastron, p. 805

31–2 Birds

Key Concepts

- Birds are reptilelike animals that maintain a constant internal body temperature. They have an outer covering of feathers; two legs that are covered with scales and are used for walking or perching; and front limbs modified into wings.
- Birds have a number of adaptations that enable them to fly. These adaptations include highly efficient digestive, respiratory, and circulatory systems; aerodynamic feathers and wings; and strong chest muscles.

Vocabulary

feather, p. 806
endotherm, p. 808
crop, p. 809
gizzard, p. 809
air sac, p. 810

Thinking Visually

Using information from this chapter, complete the following concept map:

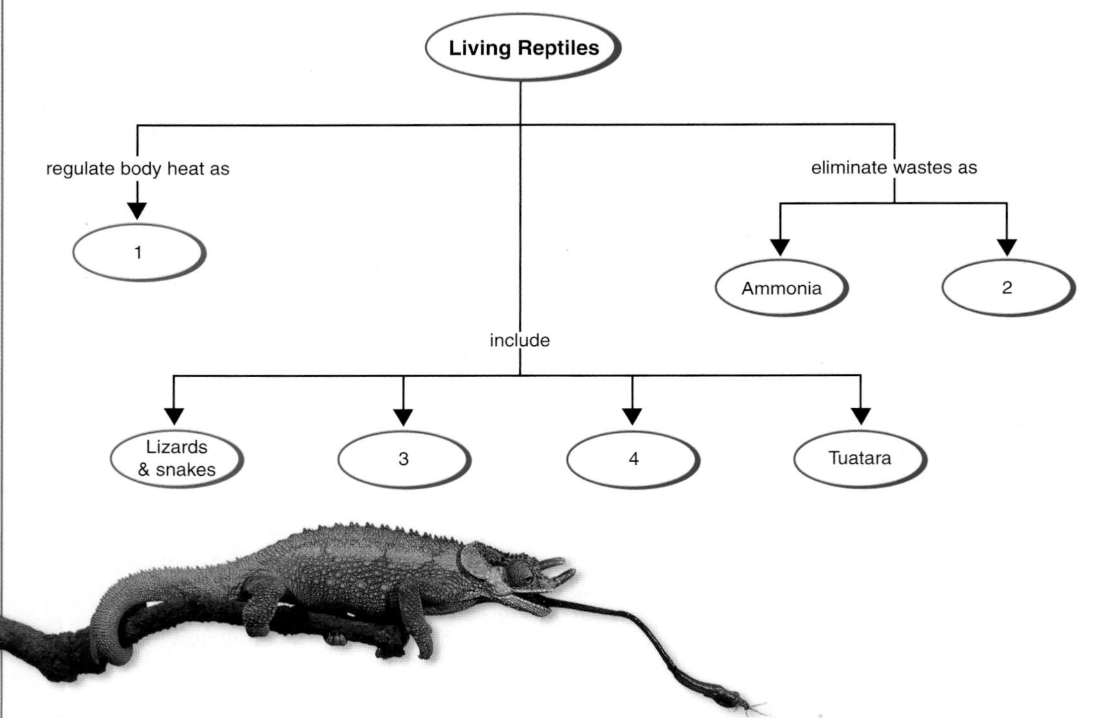

TIME SAVER — CHAPTER RESOURCES

Print:

- ***Teaching Resources,*** Chapter Vocabulary Review, Graphic Organizers
- ***Chapter Tests: Levels A and B,*** Chapter 31 Test
- ***PH Assessment System,*** Practice Test

Technology:

- ***Computer Test Bank,*** Chapter 31 Test
- ***iText,*** Chapter 31 Assessment

Chapter 31 Assessment

Reviewing Content

Choose the letter that best answers the question or completes the statement.

1. Which adaptation is NOT characteristic of reptiles?
   a. scaly skin c. gills
   b. amniotic egg d. lungs
2. Dinosaurs became extinct at the end of the
   a. Cretaceous Period. c. Carboniferous Period.
   b. Triassic Period. d. Permian Period.
3. An animal that relies on interaction with the environment to help it control body temperature is known as a(an)
   a. endotherm. c. flightless bird.
   b. ectotherm. d. endoderm.
4. Which reptiles have some type of shell covering their bodies?
   a. lizards and snakes c. turtles and tortoises
   b. crocodilians d. tuatara
5. In the diagram below, the membrane labeled *Y* represents what part of the amniotic egg?

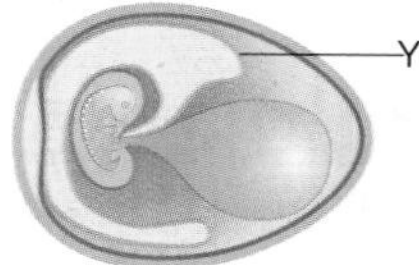

   a. amnion c. allantois
   b. chorion d. yolk sac
6. The single most important characteristic that separates birds from other animals is the presence of
   a. hollow bones. c. two legs.
   b. feathers. d. wings.
7. Which of the following bird structures are especially adapted to support flight?
   a. cloacas c. bills
   b. legs d. chest muscles
8. The muscular part of a bird's stomach that contains gravel, which crushes food, is the
   a. cloaca. c. crop.
   b. gizzard. d. air sac.
9. Birds excrete nitrogenous wastes mostly in the form of
   a. urine. c. uric acid.
   b. ammonia. d. urea.
10. Unlike other vertebrates, birds have respiratory systems that
   a. take in oxygen and release carbon dioxide.
   b. excrete nitrogenous wastes.
   c. maintain a one-way flow of air.
   d. have modified scales.

Understanding Concepts

11. As a reptile grows, what happens to its skin?
12. What climate conditions prevailed at the end of the Carboniferous Period? How did these conditions affect the evolution of reptiles?
13. What conditions may have caused the mass extinction of the dinosaurs?
14. In what way do interactions with the environment affect the body temperatures of reptiles?
15. How is the process of respiration in reptiles adapted to life on land?
16. Why is the amniotic egg considered to be one of the most important adaptations to life on land?
17. Describe the structure of a turtle's shell.
18. How do crocodilians care for their young?
19. If a bird has a short, thick bill, what does it probably feed on?
20. How does a pigeon's crop help enable it to care for young?
21. Describe the structure of bird eggs and explain what usually happens to the eggs after they are laid.
22. What adaptation enables birds to live in environments that are colder than those typically supporting reptiles?
23. What functions do the cerebrum and cerebellum control in birds?
24. Name three groups of birds, and describe some of their characteristics.
25. How do migrating birds find their way?

HOMEWORK GUIDE

Section:	Questions:
Section 31–1	1–5, 11–17, 28, 29, 33–35
Section 31–2	6–10, 18–27, 29–32

Chapter 31 Assessment (continued)

15. Many reptiles have muscles around their ribs to help expand the chest cavity to inhale and collapse the cavity to force air out. Others have flaps of skin that separate the mouth from the nasal passages, allowing them to breathe through their nostrils while their mouths remain open. Most reptiles have two lungs.

16. The shells and membranes of reptilian eggs create a protected environment in which the embryos can develop without drying out.

17. A turtle's shell is built into the skeleton. The carapace is the dorsal part and the plastron is the ventral part.

18. Mothers guard their eggs from predators. They carry hatchlings to a nursery area and watch over them.

19. A bird with a short, thick bill probably feeds on seeds.

20. During nesting season, the crop produces a substance high in protein and fat. Parent birds regurgitate this substance and feed it to their young.

21. Bird eggs are amniotic eggs, with membranes that include the amnion, chorion, allantois, and yolk sac. They have hard outer shells. Most birds incubate their eggs until the eggs are ready to hatch.

22. Unlike reptiles, birds are endothermic. They also have feathers, which insulate the body to conserve heat.

23. The cerebrum controls such behaviors as flying, nest building, caring for young, courtship, and mating. The cerebellum controls movement.

24. Possible answers include bird groups described in Figure 31–19.

25. Migrating birds navigate by using one or more of the following guides: stars and other celestial bodies; landmarks; Earth's magnetic field.

Chapter 31 Assessment

Critical Thinking

26. Sample hypothesis: *Archaeopteryx* used its clawed wings to glide down from trees to catch insects.

27. Sample questions: Which birds use more energy for flight? What foods are most available in each bird's habitat? Which birds are more active?

28. The snake might have moved from a cooler location to a warmer one, or the air temperature might have increased during the course of the day in a single location.

29. You would expect to find more reptiles on the tropical island, because ectotherms are more common in warmer climates.

30. The long legs of wetland birds enable the birds to wade out into the water in search of food.

31. The description closely fits that of a bird. Unlike reptiles, amphibians, and fish, birds are endothermic. The presence of modified front limbs, or wings, is a characteristic of birds.

32. The presence of a great amount of myoglobin in the chest muscles of ducks would indicate that they use these muscles for a great deal of flying. Less myoglobin in the chest muscles of chickens would indicate that these chest muscles are not used as much as those of ducks.

33. Endothermy requires a high metabolic rate, which means that oxygen must be delivered to cells efficiently. A circulatory system with a four-chambered heart accomplishes this by preventing oxygenated and deoxygenated blood from mixing.

34. The long, thin shape and interlocking barbules of contour feathers provide a lightweight, solid surface for lift. The "fuzzy" structure of down feathers traps air and provides insulation.

35. Each student should choose a scale and use the scale to construct the diagrams. Diagrams should also include a title and a key.

36. Answers should reflect an understanding of the differences in form and function of reptiles and amphibians. These may include differences in feeding, respiration, circulation, excretion, response, and movement.

Chapter 31 Assessment

Critical Thinking

26. Formulating Hypotheses From the small size of its sternum, or breastbone, scientists infer that *Archaeopteryx* was a poor flier. Propose a hypothesis to explain how *Archaeopteryx* might have used its wings.

27. Posing Questions Hummingbirds eat high-energy foods, such as nectar and fruit. Ducks eat foods that store less energy, such as grass and leaves. What are some related questions you could investigate to discover more about the birds' diets and energy needs?

28. Drawing Conclusions The body temperature of a snake was monitored every half hour for two hours. The temperature readings were 30°C, 32°C, 38°C, 39°C, 39°C. Suggest possible conditions that might explain these changes.

29. Predicting Imagine that you plan a visit to a warm tropical island followed by a visit to a much cooler island. In which of these places would you expect to find more reptiles? Explain your prediction.

30. Inferring Most wetland birds, such as storks and flamingos, have long legs. How might this adaptation help these birds obtain food?

31. Drawing Conclusions You are told that an animal is endothermic, has two legs, and modified front limbs. It also has a four-chambered heart and two separate circulatory loops. What kind of an animal is it? Explain.

32. Inferring The muscles that a bird uses most often contain the greatest amount of a protein called myoglobin. The chest muscles of ducks contain more myoglobin than the chest muscles of chickens. What can you infer about the flight of these two birds?

33. Applying Concepts Animals that are endotherms also have four-chambered hearts. Explain why these characteristics go together.

34. Comparing and Contrasting Compare the structure of down feathers to the structure of contour feathers. Explain how the structure of each type of feather is related to its function.

35. Using Tables and Graphs Look at the information in the chart that follows. Using the length of each snake, construct scaled diagrams on graph paper. Develop a measurement scale (for example, 1 grid square = 2 cm). Include a key to your scale. Color each snake according to its markings.

Snake Descriptions

Snake	Length (cm)	Markings
Western coral snake	45	Black, yellow, and red rings successively from head to tail
Patch-nosed snake	92	Yellow and brown stripe down the back

36. Making Connections Recall what you learned about amphibians in the previous chapter. Make a table that shows how amphibians and reptiles are adapted for life in different environments.

Performance-Based Assessment

In Your Community Take time to look at some birds that live in your area. If necessary, use a field guide to identify them. Write descriptions of traits you observe, such as different kinds of feathers, bills, and feet. Based on your observations, what do the birds eat? What types of habitats do they prefer?

Take It to the NET

One of the most interesting aspects of birds is their ability to migrate over long distances. Visit the Prentice Hall Web site at **www.phschool.com** to find out more about bird migration. Then, answer the following questions:

- How are migratory birds threatened by human activities?
- What are the four major migration routes in North America?
- What is bird-banding, and why is it done?

Take It to the NET

- One of the biggest human threats comes from destruction of habitats, such as wetlands. Migratory birds depend on wetlands for rest, food gathering, and protection.
- The Pacific, Central, Mississippi, and Atlantic flyways
- Scientist attach bands to the legs of birds to gather data about migration. Each band carries a unique serial number and other tracking information.

For additional information, visit

www.phschool.com

Standardized Test Prep

Test-Taking Tip When presented with questions that are related to data in a table, study each column and row of the table for information you need to answer the questions.

Directions: Choose the letter that best answers the question or completes the statement.

1. In general, reptiles can carry more body mass than amphibians because
(A) they have a higher body temperature.
(B) they do not live any portion of their lives in water.
(C) their limb bones are stronger than those of amphibians.
(D) their embryos can develop outside water.
(E) their skin is dry and scaly.

2. Birds probably evolved from
(A) mammal-like reptiles.
(B) amphibians.
(C) mammals.
(D) snakes.
(E) dinosaurs.

3. The following animals are all reptiles EXCEPT
(A) the tuatara.
(B) lizards and snakes.
(C) crocodilians.
(D) turtles and tortoises.
(E) passerines.

4. Amniotic eggs are a characteristic of
I. Amphibians
II. Reptiles
III. Birds
(A) I only
(B) II only
(C) I and II only
(D) II and III only
(E) I, II, and III

5. Which of these is a characteristic of reptiles?
I. Scaly skin
II. Eggs that have several membranes
III. Lungs
(A) I only
(B) II only
(C) I and II only
(D) II and III only
(E) I, II, and III

6. When birds breathe, most of the inhaled air first enters the
(A) lungs.
(B) gizzard.
(C) crop.
(D) air sacs.
(E) heart.

7. Feathers that provide lifting force and balance needed for flight are known as
(A) down feathers.
(B) powder feathers.
(C) barbules.
(D) contour feathers.
(E) barbs.

8. Which of the following is NOT a characteristic of birds' bones?
(A) Many are hollow.
(B) They are strengthened by struts.
(C) Many are fused together.
(D) The breastbone is small.
(E) The wing bones are homologous to other vertebrates' forelimb bones.

Questions 9–10

An experiment was conducted to see how air temperature affects a snake's ability to move. The experimenter placed the snake a fixed distance away from a piece of food and recorded the air temperature. Then, she recorded the time it took for the snake to reach the food. She repeated the experiment four times. Each time, the experimenter changed the air temperature. The data are shown below.

The Effect of Temperature on Snake Movement

Temperature (°C)	Time (seconds)
4	51
10	50
15	43
21	37
27	35

9. At what air temperature did the snake reach the food the fastest?
(A) 4°C
(B) 10°C
(C) 15°C
(D) 21°C
(E) 27°C

10. What conclusion can be drawn from the data?
(A) As the air temperature increased, the time it took for the snake to reach the food increased.
(B) As the air temperature decreased, the time it took for the snake to reach the food increased.
(C) Air temperature had no effect on the time it took the snake to reach the food.
(D) Snakes are ectotherms.
(E) Most snakes are carnivorous.

Standardized Test Prep

1. C **2.** E **3.** E **4.** D **5.** E **6.** D **7.** D **8.** D **9.** E **10.** B

Performance-Based Assessment

Student answers should include descriptions of the birds' various traits and behaviors.

Chapter Planner 32 Mammals

Section and Section Objectives	Time	Activities and Labs
32–1 Introduction to the Mammals, pp. 821–827 **32.1.1** ***List*** the characteristics of mammals. **32.1.2** ***Tell*** when mammals evolved. **32.1.3** ***Describe*** how mammals perform essential life functions.	2 periods (1 block)	**SE:** ***Inquiry Activity,*** How are teeth adapted to processing different foods?, p. 820 **TE:** ***Build Science Skills,*** p. 822 **TE:** ***Build Science Skills,*** p. 823 **TE:** ***Meet Diverse Needs,*** p. 824 **SE:** ***Problem Solving,*** Breathless Divers, p. 825 **TE:** ***Build Science Skills,*** p. 826
32–2 Diversity of Mammals, pp. 828–832 **32.2.1** ***Explain*** how the three groups of living mammals differ from one another. **32.2.2** ***Name*** the major orders of placental mammals. **32.2.3** ***Describe*** how convergent evolution caused mammals on different continents to be similar in form and function.	1 period (1/2 block)	**TE:** ***Build Science Skills,*** p. 829 **TE:** ***Build Science Skills,*** p. 830 **SE:** ***Issues in Biology,*** Should Marine Mammals Be Kept in Captivity?, p. 833
32–3 Primates and Human Origins, pp. 834–841 **32.3.1** ***Identify*** the characteristics that all primates share. **32.3.2** ***Describe*** the major evolutionary groups of primates. **32.3.3** ***Describe*** the various ancestors of humans.	2 periods (1 block)	**SE:** ***Quick Lab,*** How is binocular vision useful?, p. 835 **TE:** ***Meet Diverse Needs,*** p. 835 **TE:** ***Build Science Skills,*** p. 836 **SE:** ***Biology and History,*** Human Fossil Seekers, pp. 838–839 **SE:** ***Real-World Lab,*** Using Fibers as Forensic Evidence, pp. 842–843
Chapter 32 Assessment, pp. 844–847	1 period (1/2 block)	

ACTIVITY PLANNER

SE: ***Inquiry Activity,*** p. 820; (15 min.); variety of mammal teeth, including incisors and canines from carnivores and molars from herbivores

TE: ***Build Science Skills,*** p. 822; (15 min.); various animal hides

TE: ***Build Science Skills,*** p. 823; (15 min.); celery stick, hand mirror

TE: ***Meet Diverse Needs,*** p. 824; (30 min.); sheep, cow, or pig heart, dissecting tools, dissecting tray, protective gloves, lab apron

TE: ***Build Science Skills,*** p. 826; (15 min.); skeletons or pictures of skeletons of various mammals

TE: ***Build Science Skills,*** p. 829; (30 min.); modeling clay, pipe cleaners, yarn, netting, tape, glue, photographs or diagrams of developing placental embryos

TE: ***Build Science Skills,*** p. 830; (15 min.); ten pictures of different mammals

SE: ***Quick Lab,*** p. 835; (10 min.); sheet of paper

TE: ***Meet Diverse Needs,*** p. 835; (10 min.); bulky mittens, small objects

TE: ***Build Science Skills,*** p. 836; (15 min.); pictures of different primates

SE: ***Real-World Lab,*** pp. 842–843; (45 min.); reference fibers, unknown fibers, microscope slides, coverslips, dropper pipette, microscope, glass-marking pencil, facial tissues, isopropyl alcohol, rubber cement, forceps, test-tube rack, 4 test tubes of biuret reagent, 4 glass stirring rods, hot water bath

PLANNING KEY

Ability Levels

- **B Basic** — For students who need additional help
- **A Average** — For all students
- **E Enriched** — For students who need to be challenged

Components

SE	Student Edition	**GRSW**	Guided Reading and Study Workbook	**IDM**	Issues and Decision Making
TE	Teacher's Edition	**CT**	Chapter Tests: Levels A and B	**CTB**	Computer Test Bank
LMA	Laboratory Manual A	**PHAS**	PH Assessment System	**PA**	Presentation Assistant Plus
LMB	Laboratory Manual B	**LA**	Lab Assessment with Scoring Guide	**BD**	BioDetectives Videotape
TR	Teaching Resources	**BTM**	BioTechnology Manual	**iT**	iText

Program Resources	Assessment	Media and Technology
TR: Section Review 32–1 B A **GRSW:** Section 32–1 B A	**SE:** 32–1 Section Assessment, p. 827 **TR:** Section Review 32–1	**PA:** 32–1 Interest Grabber, Section Outline, Structure of a Bear's Heart, Figure 32–4 **iT:** Section 32–1
TR: Section Review 32–2 B A **GRSW:** Section 32–2 B A **IDM:** 32–1 A E	**SE:** 32–2 Section Assessment, p. 832 **TR:** Section Review 32–2	**PA:** 32–2 Interest Grabber, Section Outline, Concept Map, Figure 32–13 **iT:** Section 32–2
LMA: Chapter 32 Lab A E **LMB:** Chapter 32 Lab B A **TE:** Section 32–3 B A Chapter 32 Real-World Lab B A E **GRSW:** Section 32–3 B B A	**SE:** 32–3 Section Assessment, p. 841 **TR:** Section Review 32–3	**PA:** 32–3 Interest Grabber, Section Outline, Comparison of Skulls of Human Ancestors, Figure 32–16 **BD:** "Mummies," "Wrongly Accused" **iT:** Section 32–3 Discovery Channel School
	SE: Chapter 32 Assessment, pp. 844–847 **TR:** Chapter Vocabulary Review, Graphic Organizer **CT:** Chapter 32 Test **CTB:** Chapter 32 Test **PHAS:** Practice Test	**CTB:** Chapter 32 Test **iT:** Chapter 32 Assessment

PRESSED FOR TIME?

To Preview the Chapter
- Introduce students to Key Concepts and Vocabulary terms in each section.
- Have students study the illustrations and read the captions in Figures 32–12, 32–15, and 32–16.

To Cover the Chapter Quickly
- Have students read all of Sections 32–1 and 32–2.
- Assign Section Reviews 32–1 and 32–2, questions 1–8, 11–22, 27–32, and 35 in the Chapter 32 Assessment, and questions 1, 3, 4, 6–10 in Chapter 32 Standardized Test Prep.

To Review the Chapter
- Review the Chapter 32 Study Guide and assign the concept map.
- Assign Section Reviews 32–1 through 32–3 in the Guided Reading and Study Workbook.

ENGAGE/EXPLORE

Inquiry Activity

Objectives Students will be able to infer how teeth are adapted to process different foods.

Skills Focus **Classifying, Inferring**

Materials variety of mammal teeth, including incisors and canines from carnivores and molars from herbivores, or pictures of mammal teeth

Time 15 minutes

Strategies

- Discuss why different types of teeth are required to break off and chew different types of food.
- Relate teeth to different tools that are used for similar tasks, such as scissors and incisors for cutting off grass or animal tissue.
- Give students hand mirrors to examine the shapes of their own teeth.

Expected Outcome Students should infer that sharp, tearing teeth belong to mammals that eat other animals and flat, grinding teeth belong to mammals that eat plants.

Think About It

1. Students might sort the teeth into narrow, sharp teeth and wide, flat teeth. They might also distinguish flat, slicing incisors from pointed canine (cuspid) teeth. Students should explain how they classified the teeth.
2. Accept all reasonable answers. Narrow, sharp teeth are adapted for cutting and tearing meat. Wide, flat teeth are adapted for grinding plant material.

Assess Prior Knowledge

Find out what students already know about mammals by inviting them to name as many mammals as possible. If humans have not been mentioned, ask: **Are humans mammals?** *(Yes)* Then, have students give as many characteristics of mammals as they can. List these characteristics on the board and update them as you study the chapter.

Chapter 32 Mammals

A black bear nurses her two cubs in the Smoky Mountains of North Carolina. **Like all mammals, black bears have hair, breathe air, and nurse their young with milk.**

Inquiry Activity

How are teeth adapted to processing different foods?

Procedure

1. Examine a mammal tooth. Describe the shape of the tooth.
2. Based on the tooth's structure, try to infer whether the mammal ate mainly plants or other animals.
3. Repeat steps 1 and 2 for other mammal teeth.

Think About It

1. **Classifying** Sort the teeth into different groups based on their structure. Explain how you classified the teeth.
2. **Inferring** Describe what type of food you think each type of tooth is adapted to processing. Explain your reasoning.

FACTS AND FIGURES

Hair to hold in heat

Early mammals were probably nocturnal. Because they were active at night, they could not rely on their environment to help regulate their body temperature. External hair and body fat evolved as insulation to conserve body heat. Paleontologists have yet to determine exactly how hair evolved. Long hair would have been of little advantage to an ectothermic reptile, but without long hair an endothermic mammal seems impossible. One theory is that hairs first evolved as sensory projections that gave organisms tactile information about the environment. This is especially helpful at night. As hairs multiplied, they provided insulation, and that property of hair eventually became the focus of adaptation.

32–1 Introduction to the Mammals

It is late January in the Appalachian Mountains. In a rocky den beneath the snowdrifts, a black bear has just given birth. Two tiny cubs are nursing on their mother's rich milk. It is bitterly cold outside, but the mother's dense fur and thick layer of body fat keep her and her cubs comfortably warm. The mother and cubs will stay in the den for several more months. When spring arrives, the hungry bears will emerge from the den. For the next two years, the cubs will follow their mother as she teaches them to search for food and defend themselves.

Bears are mammals, members of the class Mammalia. All mammals are characterized by two notable features: hair and mammary glands. In female mammals, **mammary glands**—the feature for which mammals are named—produce milk to nourish the young. **In addition to having hair and the ability to nourish their young with milk, all mammals breathe air, have four-chambered hearts, and are endotherms that generate their body heat internally.**

Guide for Reading

Key Concepts

- What are the characteristics of mammals?
- When did mammals evolve?
- How do mammals maintain homeostasis?

Vocabulary

mammary gland
subcutaneous fat
rumen
diaphragm
cerebral cortex

Reading Strategy: Asking Questions Before you read, rewrite the headings in the section as *how, why,* or *what* questions about mammals. As you read, write brief answers to these heading questions.

Evolution of Mammals

Neither mammary glands nor hair are preserved in the fossil record. But mammals have several other characteristics that help scientists to identify mammalian fossils. These characteristics include a jaw joint that allows sideways movement, complex teeth that are replaced just once in a lifetime, and several distinctive features of the limbs and the backbone.

According to the fossil record, the first ancestors of mammals diverged from ancient reptiles during the Permian Period, from 290 to 250 million years ago. For millions of years, various mammal-like reptiles lived alongside dinosaurs.

The first true mammals appeared during the late Triassic Period, about 220 million years ago. These mammals were very small and probably resembled modern tree shrews, like the one in **Figure 32–1.** While dinosaurs ruled the Cretaceous Period, from about 145 to 65 million years ago, mammals were generally small and remained out of sight. These mammals were probably nocturnal, or active at night.

After the disappearance of the dinosaurs at the end of the Cretaceous Period, mammals underwent a burst of adaptive radiation. They increased in size and established many new niches. In fact, the Cenozoic Era, which followed the Cretaceous Period, is usually called the Age of Mammals. During the process of continental drift, three groups of mammals became isolated from one another around 60 million years ago. Surviving members of these groups, which include the monotremes, the marsupials, and the placental mammals, continue to inhabit Earth today.

▼ **Figure 32–1** **The first mammals appeared on Earth about 220 million years ago.** They may have resembled this tree shrew from Madagascar, shown here clutching a beetle. Like this tree shrew, early mammals probably ate insects.

SECTION RESOURCES

Print:

- ***Teaching Resources,*** Section Review 32–1
- ***Guided Reading and Study Workbook,*** Section 32–1

Technology:

- ***iText,*** Section 32–1

Section 32–1

1 FOCUS

Objectives

32.1.1 ***List*** the characteristics of mammals.
32.1.2 ***Tell*** when mammals evolved.
32.1.3 ***Describe*** how mammals maintain homeostasis and perform essential life functions.

Guide for Reading

Vocabulary Preview

Explain that the prefix *sub-* means "under," and *cutaneous* means "having to do with the skin." Then, ask: **Where do you think subcutaneous fat is located?** *(Under the skin)*

Reading Strategy

Have students also write *how, why,* or *what* questions for the subheadings in the section. Remind students to leave room under each question to write its answer as they read the section.

2 INSTRUCT

Evolution of Mammals

Meet Diverse Needs

Students who need an extra challenge might enjoy learning about early mammals, such as cynodonts (mammallike reptiles), pantotheres (gave rise to marsupials and placentals), or *Eohippus* (early horse), *Protylopus* (early camel), *Miacis* (early dog), *Moeritherium* (early elephant), or *Megatherium* (giant land sloth). Encourage students to find out the characteristics of these animals that made them mammalian. Students can develop a class presentation to share what they have learned. **Learning modality: verbal**

Form and Function in Mammals

Build Science Skills

Inferring Borrow various animal hides from a zoo or natural history museum. Challenge students to make inferences about the animals' habitat based on the type of hairs in their coats. *(In general, animals in cold climates have heavy coats with two layers of hairs. Animals in warm environments have thinner coats or no hair at all. Exceptions are seals, whales, and walruses, which are protected by layers of blubber.)*

Meet Diverse Needs

At-risk students might find it helpful to review homeostasis. Preview this subsection, pointing out that it follows the same format as the other form and function subsections in previous chordate chapters. During the preview, discuss how each body function works to help maintain homeostasis in a mammal's body. Write these ideas on the board in an outline form for students to copy. **Limited English proficiency**

Make Connections

Environmental Science Relate the diversity of mammalian modes of feeding to the adaptive radiation of mammals in the Cenozoic Era. Ask: **Why do you think the first mammals were insectivores?** *(Possible answers: insects provided a lot of energy to an endothermic mammal; mammals' small size prevented them from being predators during the age of dinosaurs.)* **How did it become possible for mammals to evolve to eat different types of food?** *(The extinction of dinosaurs left many niches open; mammals were equipped to live successfully in the changing climate, and lack of competition and predation allowed them to evolve to fill empty niches.)* Point out that the changing climate also affected plant life, and many mammals coevolved with plants. One example is grasses evolving along with mammalian herbivores in grassland ecosystems.

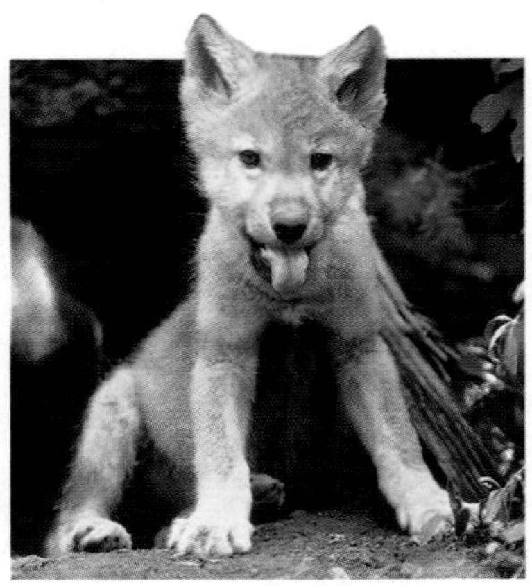

▲ **Figure 32–2 As endotherms, mammals are capable of adjusting their body heat internally.** When they get too warm, some mammals, such as this gray wolf puppy, pant to rid their bodies of excess heat.

Form and Function in Mammals

The mammalian body has adapted in varied ways to a great many habitats. As a member of this class of chordates, you may be familiar with some of these adaptations.

Body Temperature Control Like birds, mammals are endotherms. Because their bodies can generate heat internally, mammals do not rely on the sun to keep warm. Mammals—especially small ones—have a much higher metabolic rate than most other chordates. The high rate of metabolism helps mammals generate body heat. Mammals also have external body hair and subcutaneous (sub-kyoo-TAYN-ee-us) fat that help conserve body heat. **Subcutaneous fat** is a layer of fat cells located under the skin. Many mammals also have sweat glands that help cool the body. When the sweat produced by these glands evaporates from the skin, body temperature is lowered. Mammals that lack sweat glands, like the wolf in **Figure 32–2**, often pant to rid themselves of excess heat. **The ability of mammals to regulate their body heat from within is an example of homeostasis.** This ability also allows mammals to move about after dark and in the cold, while most other animals would seek shelter.

CHECKPOINT *What is the function of subcutaneous fat?*

Feeding Because of its high metabolic rate, a mammal must eat nearly ten times as much food as a reptile of the same size! Some mammals, such as rabbits and giraffes, eat only plants. Others, including cats and weasels, are meat-eaters. Bears and humans are omnivores, consuming all types of food. Certain whales, like the one in **Figure 32–3**, are filter feeders that eat plankton and small animals that they strain from the sea.

Early mammals ate insects. **As mammals evolved, the form and function of their jaws and teeth became adapted to eat foods other than insects.** The joint between the skull and lower jaw became stronger than that of reptiles. This joint allowed mammals to evolve larger, more powerful jaw muscles and different ways of chewing.

▶ **Figure 32–3** The teeth of certain whales, such as this humpback, have been replaced by huge, stiffened plates called baleen. The fringed baleen acts like a filter to strain out small animals from the mouthfuls of water that the whale takes in. **Applying Concepts** *What kind of animals do humpback whales eat?*

PRESENTATIONS MADE EASY!

The Presentation Assistant Plus contains the Prentice Hall Presentation Pro and the Transparencies, which provide easy-to-follow visual support for every step of this section. If you have a computer presentation station, use Prentice Hall Presentation Pro for Section 32–1, or use the transparencies listed here.

Section 32–1: **Interest Grabber**
Section Outline
Structure of a Bear's Heart
Figure 32–4

FIGURE 32–4 JAWS AND TEETH OF MAMMALS

The specialized jaws and teeth of mammals are adapted for different diets. Carnivorous mammals use sharp canines and incisors to grip and slice flesh from their prey. Their jaws usually move up and down as they chew. Herbivorous mammals use flat-edged incisors to grasp and tear vegetation, and flattened molars to grind the food. Their jaws generally move from side to side. Researchers often use tooth shape and structure to classify mammals.

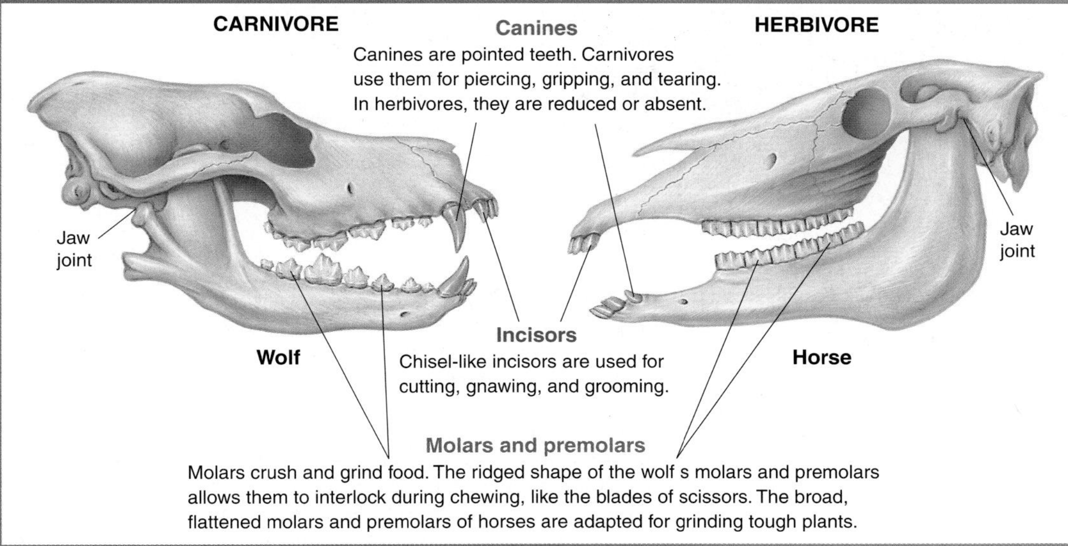

CARNIVORE
HERBIVORE
Canines
Canines are pointed teeth. Carnivores use them for piercing, gripping, and tearing. In herbivores, they are reduced or absent.
Jaw joint
Jaw joint
Incisors
Chisel-like incisors are used for cutting, gnawing, and grooming.
Wolf
Horse
Molars and premolars
Molars crush and grind food. The ridged shape of the wolf s molars and premolars allows them to interlock during chewing, like the blades of scissors. The broad, flattened molars and premolars of horses are adapted for grinding tough plants.

Modern mammals have specialized teeth—canines, incisors, molars, and premolars—which you can see in **Figure 32–4.** Observe that the structure of carnivores' teeth is different from that of herbivores' teeth. Mammals' teeth enable food to be processed efficiently. The more efficiently an animal can obtain and process its food, the more energy it can obtain.

A mammal's digestive tract is adapted to break down and absorb the type of food that it eats. Because digestive enzymes can quickly break down meat, carnivores have a relatively short intestine. Tough, fibrous plant tissues take much more time to digest, so most herbivores have a much longer intestine.

Many herbivores also have specialized digestive organs to break down plant matter. Cows and their relatives have a stomach chamber called the **rumen,** in which newly swallowed plant food is stored and processed. The rumen contains symbiotic bacteria that digest the cellulose of most plant tissues. After some time, the grazer regurgitates the food from the rumen into its mouth. The partially digested food is again chewed and mixed with saliva. The second time the food is swallowed, it moves through the rest of the stomach and into the intestines.

Word Origins

The word **incisor** comes from the Latin word *incisus,* meaning "to cut." **In surgery, what is an incision?**

Use Visuals

Figure 32–4 Have students compare and contrast the herbivore and carnivore teeth in the illustration. Make a Venn diagram on the board to note the similarities and differences. Ask: **Why do you think it is advantageous for herbivores to have flat molars?** *(The grinding motion of the teeth and jaws helps break apart tough plant fibers.)* **Could a dog successfully live on a diet of grass?** *(No)* **Why?** *(Dogs have the teeth of a carnivore; although the teeth are sharp, they could not effectively grind plant material to break it apart. The dog's digestive system is also not long enough to remove all the nutrients from plant tissue.)* Point out how carnivores use their jaws differently from herbivores. Carnivores use mostly up and down motion to chew food. Herbivores use side-to-side motion to make the plant matter (usually long fibrous stems) small enough to be swallowed.

Build Science Skills

Observing Give students a celery stick. Have them chew and swallow the celery. While they chew, challenge students to observe in a mirror how their teeth and jaws work to chew the food. Discuss students' observations, focusing on the characteristics of their teeth that enabled them to chew the food. Remind students that they are omnivores with teeth adapted for eating both plants and animals.

Word Origins

An incision is a cut made into a tissue or organ.

FACTS AND FIGURES

Digestion is "ruminentery"

While grazing, ruminants quickly chew grass just until it's small enough to swallow. It moves to the first chamber of the stomach, the rumen, which stores large amounts of food. It is here that simple carbohydrates, proteins, and cellulose are broken down. While resting, the ruminant regurgitates food from the rumen and rechews it. After reswallowing, the food moves into the reticulum, which screens out larger food particles, allowing smaller particles to move into the omasum. There, excess water is removed from the food by squeezing and grinding action. Then, food moves into the abomasum, where acids and digestive enzymes break down protein, as in a carnivore's stomach. From there, the food enters the intestines, where nutrients and water are absorbed; then wastes are excreted.

Answers to . . .

CHECKPOINT *Subcutaneous fat helps conserve body heat.*

Figure 32–3 *Plankton and very small fishes*

32–1 (continued)

Use Visuals

Figure 32–5 Have students trace the path of blood through the heart. They can compare the mammalian heart in Figure 32–5 to the reptilian heart in Figure 31–4 on p. 801. Remind students that mammals evolved from reptiles. Ask: **How does the mammalian heart differ from the reptilian heart?** *(The mammalian heart has two separate ventricles; most reptiles have a single ventricle.)* **Why is it advantageous to have two separate ventricles?** *(The unoxygenated blood never mixes with the oxygenated blood, so the blood going to the body has the highest possible level of oxygen.)*

Meet Diverse Needs

Students who would like an additional challenge might enjoy dissecting a mammalian heart. Obtain a cow, pig, or sheep heart from a butcher. Students also need dissecting tools and a dissecting tray. Students should wear protective gloves while dissecting the heart and wash their hands thoroughly when finished. Have students diagram the structure of the heart and label its parts. You can display the dissected hearts and the diagrams for the class to observe. **Learning modality: kinesthetic**

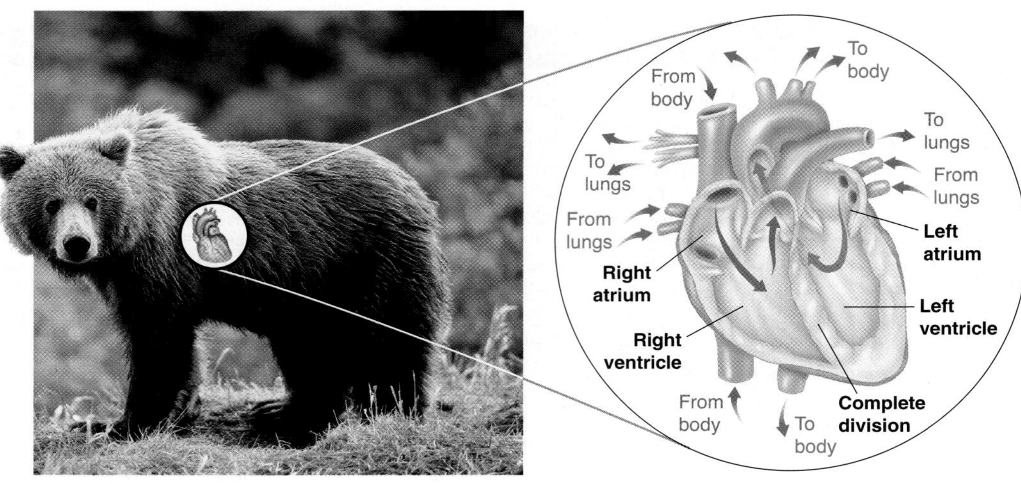

Figure 32–5 All mammals, including this brown bear, have a four-chambered heart that pumps blood in two separate circuits around the body. **Interpreting Graphics** ***According to the diagram, which chamber receives blood that is low in oxygen?***

Respiration All mammals, even those that live in water, use lungs to breathe. These lungs are controlled by two sets of muscles. Mammals inhale when muscles in the chest lift the rib cage up and outward, increasing the volume of the chest cavity. At the same time, a powerful muscle called the **diaphragm** (DY-uh-fram) pulls the bottom of the chest cavity downward, which further increases its volume. As a result, air is pulled into the lungs. When the chest muscles lower the rib cage, and the diaphragm relaxes, the volume of the chest cavity decreases. This action pushes air out of the lungs.

Circulation The mammalian circulatory system is divided into two completely separate loops with a four-chambered heart, shown in **Figure 32–5.** The right side of the heart receives oxygen-poor blood from all over the body and pumps it to the lungs. After picking up oxygen in the lungs, blood returns to the left side of the heart. This oxygen-rich blood is then pumped through blood vessels to the rest of the body. The two separate circuits—one to and from the lungs, and the other to and from the rest of the body—efficiently transport materials throughout the body.

Excretion Mammals have highly developed kidneys that help control the composition of body fluids. Mammalian kidneys extract nitrogenous wastes from the blood in the form of urea. Urea, other wastes, and water combine to form urine. From the kidneys, urine flows to a urinary bladder, where it is stored until it is eliminated.  **The kidneys of mammals help maintain homeostasis by filtering urea from the blood and by excreting or retaining excess liquid.** They also retain salts, sugars, and other compounds the body cannot afford to lose. Because they are so efficient at controlling and stabilizing the amount of water in the body, the kidneys enable mammals to live in many habitats, such as deserts, in which they could not otherwise survive.

BIO INSIGHTS — FACTS AND FIGURES

Respiratory system makes noise
Mammals make vocalizations for various reasons. Some vocalizations warn other species members of danger. Others are used to find mates or to defend territories. To make these vocalizations, mammals use the respiratory system. As air moves into the pharynx and through the trachea to the lungs, it passes through the larynx. The larynx is the location of the vocal cords. The vocal cords are a pair of folds in the cartilaginous walls of the larynx. The space between these folds is the glottis. When air is expelled from the lungs, it vibrates the vocal cords to produce a sound. The cartilage in the larynx can be highly specialized from one species to another to produce distinct sounds. Speech is produced by shaping vocal sounds into patterns using the mouth, tongue, and lips.

Response Mammals have the most highly developed brains of any animals. As you can see in **Figure 32–6,** the brain consists of three main parts: the cerebrum, the cerebellum, and the medulla oblongata. The cerebrum makes possible such complicated behaviors as thinking and learning. The cerebellum controls muscular coordination. The medulla oblongata regulates involuntary body functions, or those that are not under conscious control, such as breathing and heart rate.

A mammal's cerebrum contains a well-developed outer layer called the **cerebral cortex**, which is the center of thinking and other complex behaviors. Some activities, such as reading this textbook, are possible only with the human cerebral cortex. However, mammals other than humans also exhibit complex behaviors, such as storing food for later use.

Mammals rely on highly developed senses to provide information about their external environment. Many mammals have well-developed senses of smell and hearing. You probably know, for example, that dogs can easily identify people by their particular scent. Although mammalian ears all have the same basic parts, they differ in their ability to detect sound. For example, dogs, bats, and dolphins can detect sounds at much higher frequencies than humans can. In fact, bats and dolphins can find objects in their environment using the echo of their own high-frequency sounds. Other mammals, such as elephants, can detect sounds at much lower frequencies.

Many mammals have some color-sensing structures in their eyes, yet the ability to distinguish colors may vary among different species. Color vision is most useful to diurnal animals—those that are active during daylight. Although mammals such as cats can detect color, they may not see the full range of colors that humans and some other primates can.

CHECKPOINT *What is the function of the cerebral cortex?*

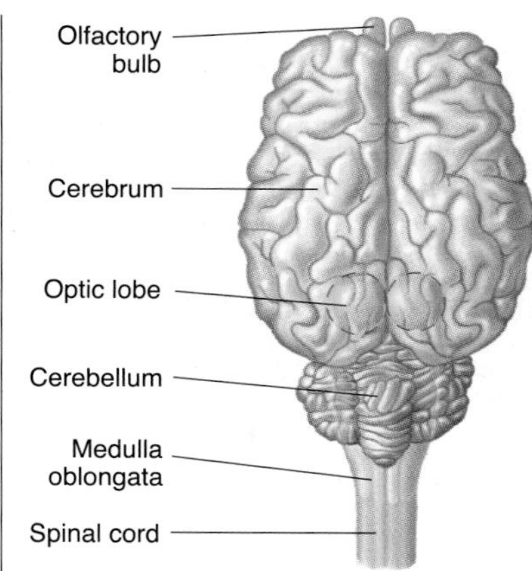

▲ **Figure 32–6** Mammals have large brains in proportion to their body size. Most of the brain is taken up by an enlarged cerebrum, which contains a well-developed cerebral cortex. **Inferring** *How would a large cerebrum be advantageous to a mammal?*

Problem Solving

Breathless Divers

Many marine mammals have adaptations that allow them to do what no land mammal can do—live under water. A sperm whale, for example, can dive deeper than 1.5 km below the surface, holding its breath for more than an hour at a time. How can it go so long without inhaling? One clue lies in the amount of oxygen that whales can store in their bodies. During a dive, whales store, on average, 9 percent of oxygen in their lungs, 41 percent in their blood, 41 percent in muscles, and 9 percent in tissues. In contrast, human beings store an average of 34 percent of oxygen in their lungs, 41 percent in blood, 13 percent in muscles, and 12 percent in tissues.

Defining the Problem On the basis of what you have read, identify a question you would like answered.

Organizing Information Create a table that allows you to easily compare the percentages of oxygen stored in different parts of whales' and humans' bodies.

Creating a Solution Compare and contrast the data in your table. Then, formulate a hypothesis that might identify a characteristic shared by mammals that can hold their breath for a long time.

Presenting Your Plan Formulate a plan for evaluting your hypothesis. Identify the kinds of information you would need.

BIO INSIGHTS FACTS AND FIGURES

Why a larger mammalian brain?
Some scientists think the mammalian brain evolved as a result of the needs of a nocturnal animal. Reptiles and birds are active during the day and depend primarily on eyesight to find food. Visual information, especially the three-dimensional impressions that result from binocular vision, needs little analysis and thus relatively less brain matter. A nocturnal animal, however, must also depend on information from scent and sound. As the animal moves, it must compare and integrate perceptions from three senses, a process that requires a relatively more complex brain. Furthermore, an animal that could associate such information with past events—compare past to present—would have a selective advantage.

Problem Solving

Besides storing oxygen in muscles, whales have other adaptations that enable them to stay underwater for long periods of time. When whales dive, the body reduces the blood flow to the muscles, but maintains a normal flow rate to the heart and brain. The heartbeat also slows, which conserves oxygen. When a whale returns to the surface, it must take several breaths to recharge its tissues with oxygen.

Defining the Problem Sample question: What characteristics are shared by mammals that can hold their breath for a long time?

Organizing Information Students should create a table similar to the one below.

Amount of Oxygen Stored in Body

Body Part	Whale	Human
Lungs	9%	34%
Blood	41%	41%
Muscles	41%	13%
Tissues	9%	12%

Creating a Solution Sample hypothesis: Mammals that can hold their breath for a long time store more oxygen in their muscles than in their lungs.

Presenting Your Plan Students' plans might involve experiments and / or library and Internet research. Students will probably try to learn whether other marine mammals, such as dolphins, store more oxygen in their muscles than in their lungs.

Answers to . . .

CHECKPOINT *Center of thinking and other complex behaviors*

Figure 32–5 *The right atrium*

Figure 32–6 *The increased ability for complex thinking increases a mammal's adaptability.*

32–1 (continued)

Use Visuals

Figure 32–7 Have students compare the mammalian limbs in Figure 32–7. Ask: **What limb characteristics are common to mammals that run?** *(Longer, less flexible, no side digits)* **How do the limbs of digging mammals differ from climbing mammals?** *(Climbing mammals have longer, more slender digits and limbs. Digging mammals have shorter, thicker digits and stocky limbs.)* **How are the limbs of swimming mammals similar to those of flying mammals?** *(Both have limbs and digits that are modified to support either the flipper or flaps of skin that form the wings.)*

Build Science Skills

Classifying Provide skeletons of different mammals for students to examine. You can also use diagrams if skeletons are not available. Challenge students to divide the skeletons into groups based on how the mammals move. Students should identify the characteristics of the skeletons that helped them make their classifications. Share with students the identity of each skeleton. Point out the features of the skeleton that could be used to make the correct classification.

Meet Diverse Needs

Review the terms *oviparous* and *viviparous* with at-risk students. Encourage students to devise a mnemonic for each term to help them remember its meaning. Looking for similarities between the term and its meaning can help students develop a mnemonic.
Learning modality: logical/mathematical

Figure 32–7 The limbs and digits (fingers and toes) of many mammals are adapted to their particular way of life. Note the variety of lengths and shapes of the limb bones that different mammals use for movement. Homologous bones are the same color in all the drawings. **Applying Concepts** ***Which structure shown in this figure would most closely resemble the limbs and digits of a whale?***

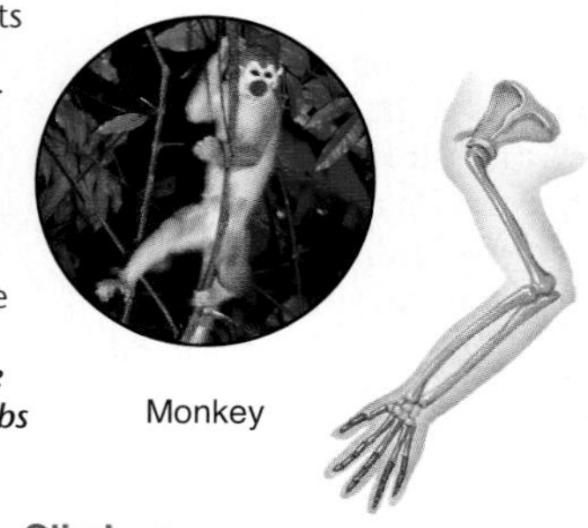

Monkey

Climbers
Climbing mammals have long, flexible fingers and toes that can grasp vines and branches. They also have a flexible wrist joint.

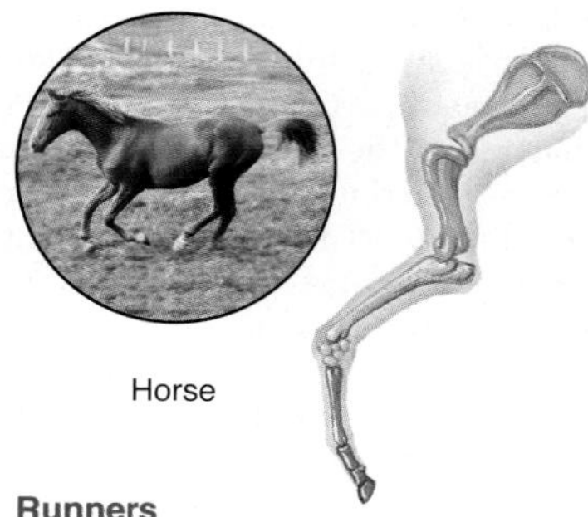

Horse

Runners
Running mammals need long limbs that can absorb shock. These animals have lost the side digits on their front and back feet. They stand on the tips of their remaining toes, which are called hooves.

Movement Mammals have evolved a variety of adaptations that aid in movement, including a backbone that flexes both vertically and side to side. This flexibility allows mammals to move with a bouncing, leaping stride. Shoulder and pelvic girdles have become more streamlined and flexible, permitting both front and hind limbs to move in a variety of ways.

Compare the adaptations of mammalian limbs shown in **Figure 32–7.** Variations in the limb bones and muscles allow mammals to run, walk, climb, burrow, hop, pounce, swing, fly, leap, and swim. Depending on their lifestyle, mammals may use any number of these methods to move about.

▼ **Figure 32–8** Still wobbly, a newborn wildebeest rises to its feet minutes after birth. Its mother will nurse and protect the calf until it is able to live on its own. **Classifying** ***Is the wildebeest an oviparous or viviparous mammal?***

Reproduction Mammals reproduce by internal fertilization. When mammals mate, the male deposits sperm inside the reproductive tract of the female, where fertilization occurs.

As you will learn in the next section, mammals are classified into three groups, based on their modes of development and birth. One group retains the reptilian characteristic of being oviparous, or egg-laying. The other two mammal groups are viviparous, or live-bearing. Their embryos develop within the mother for a time, and then are born alive. Most viviparous mammals nourish their embryos inside the mother's body before giving birth. Others deliver young that develop in a pouch on the outside of the mother's body. But, regardless of the mode of development, all newborn mammals feed on their mother's milk.

Many newborn mammals can stand up and move around on their own a short time after birth. The newborn wildebeest in **Figure 32–8** is awkward and barely able to stand. Within a few hours, however, it will be able to see and walk around on its own. On the other hand, the young of mammals such as mice and monkeys are helpless at birth and remain that way for some time. Such young depend on their mother for food and protection.

BIO INSIGHTS

FACTS AND FIGURES

Elephants care about their young
Elephants have complex social interactions and behaviors associated with raising their young. The gestation period for elephants is about 22 months. Females first start mating around the age of 20 years. They will continue to have calves every two to four years until they reach about 50 years of age. Calves are highly dependent on their mothers for food for their first two years. These calves are not only cared for by their mothers, but also by the other females in the herd. Older females help new mothers. Younger females play with the babies to help them prepare to become mothers. When a baby has finished weaning from its mother, it reaches an age of adolescence. Young males leave the herd, often joining bachelor herds. Young females stay with the herd, but help care for other newborns.

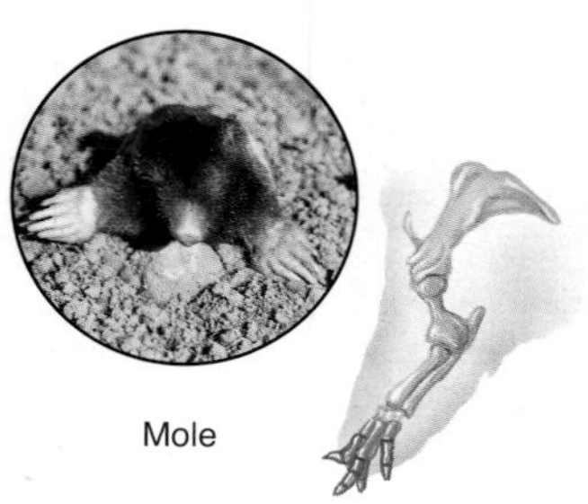

Diggers
Digging mammals have strong, thick claws, especially on their front feet. Their limbs are short and stocky, with large projections that anchor powerful muscles.

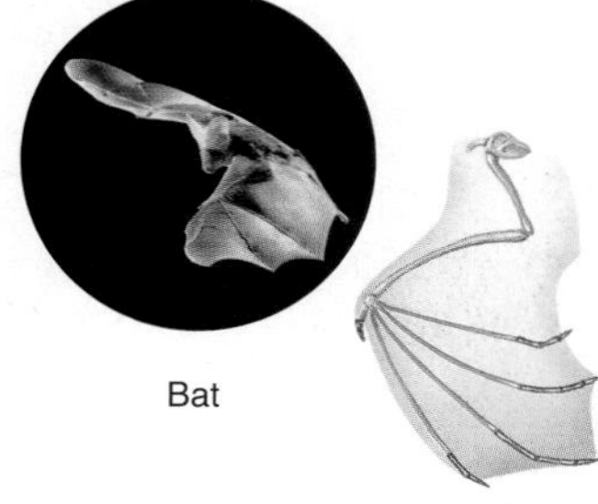

Flyers
The arms and hands of bats are modified to support flaps of skin that form wings.

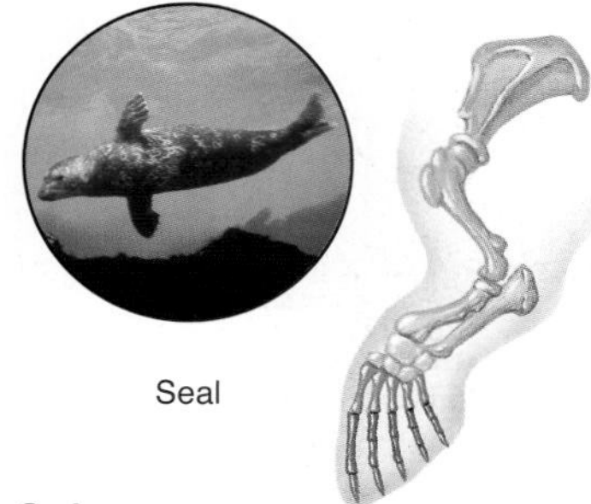

Swimmers
Swimming mammals concentrate most of their movement between the arm and shoulder girdle. Their limbs are modified into broad, flat paddles, with the bones of their hands or feet extended to make a flipper, or fin.

Young mammals are generally helpless when they are born and for a long time afterward. During this period, they are cared for by one or both parents. Maternal care is an important mammalian characteristic, and the bond between mother and young is very close. Males of many species also play a role in caring for the young.

The duration and intensity of parental care varies among different species. Some mammals have a prolonged period when the young and the mother live together. The young may spend several years developing before they are able to live on their own. During that period, the juvenile learns from its caregiver the behaviors it needs to survive in its particular environment. Some mammal species, such as lions and elephants, live in groups in which the young may be cared for by adults other than the parents. Group living provides young mammals with the opportunity for complex social interaction among adults and juveniles.

32–1 Section Assessment

1. **Key Concept** Name the characteristics that are common to all mammals.
2. **Key Concept** When did mammalian ancestors diverge from the reptiles?
3. **Key Concept** List two ways in which mammals maintain homeostasis.
4. How are the teeth of mammals adapted to their different diets?
5. **Critical Thinking Inferring** Many humans have their wisdom teeth removed because their jaws are too small to accommodate those teeth. What might this suggest about the evolution of the human jaw?

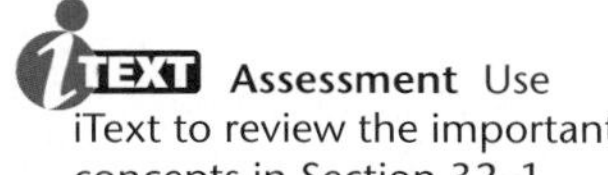
Assessment Use iText to review the important concepts in Section 32–1.

MAKING CONNECTIONS

Comparing and Contrasting Compare the structure of a mammal's brain to that of a fish, as shown in **Figure 30–14,** on page 777. What structures are more prominent in each animal's brain? How might these differences relate to the way the animals live?

Use Community Resources

Invite a zookeeper or zoologist to the class to describe the adaptive significance of maternal care in mammals. Ask the speaker to contrast the number of offspring produced by mammals with that of other vertebrates and to explain the current thinking that describes why mammals expend so much energy for maternal care.

3 ASSESS

Evaluate Understanding

Invite student volunteers to write on the board one characteristic of mammals. When students have exhausted all their ideas, add to the list, if necessary, to make it complete. Then, ask students to match the characteristics to the life functions that mammals perform.

Reteach

Have student pairs study the mammals pictured in this section and make a list of characteristics that mammals have in common. Students can compare their list with the description of mammals given at the beginning of the section.

MAKING CONNECTIONS

In mammals, the cerebrum is much larger, relative to the rest of the brain, than in fishes. In contrast, fishes have much larger olfactory bulbs. Mammals depend heavily on behaviors such as learning that are regulated by the cerebral cortex. Fishes are highly dependent on the sense of smell to capture prey.

Use iText to review the key concepts in Section 32–1.

32–1 Section Assessment

1. Hair, mammary glands, breathe air, have four-chambered hearts, endotherms
2. During the Permian Period, between 290 and 250 million years ago
3. Any two: regulating body heat from within, excreting or retaining excess liquid with the kidneys, eating a variety of foods
4. Carnivores have sharp canines and incisors. Herbivores have flat-edged incisors and flattened molars.
5. During the course of evolution, humans' jaws became smaller. However, the number of teeth did not decrease.

Answers to . . .

Figure 32–7 *The limbs of a seal, a swimming mammal*

Figure 32–8 *Viviparous*

Section 32–2

1 FOCUS

Objectives

32.2.1 ***Explain*** how the three groups of living mammals differ from one another.
32.2.2 ***Name*** the major orders of placental mammals.
32.2.3 ***Describe*** how convergent evolution caused mammals on different continents to be similar in form and function.

Guide for Reading

Vocabulary Preview

Say each Vocabulary word aloud and have students divide the word into syllables as best they can. Remind students that each syllable usually has only one vowel sound. *(mon•o•treme, mar•su•pi•al, and pla•cen•ta)*

Reading Strategy

Have students make a table with the headings *Monotreme, Marsupial,* and *Placental.* Before they read, tell students to write what they know about these mammal groups. After they read, students should add additional information and correct any misconceptions they had.

2 INSTRUCT

Monotremes and Marsupials

Build Science Skills

Comparing and Contrasting Have students make a Venn diagram to compare and contrast the characteristics of monotremes and reptiles. In the overlap area, students should list features that monotremes and reptiles share *(cloaca, females lay soft-shelled eggs that incubate outside body).* In the separate areas of the circles, students should write characteristics specific to reptiles *(do not care for young, ectothermic, have scales)* and those specific to monotremes *(nourish young with milk from body, endothermic, have hair).*

32–2 Diversity of Mammals

Guide for Reading

Key Concepts
- How do the three groups of living mammals differ from one another?
- How did convergent evolution cause mammals on different continents to be similar in form and function?

Vocabulary
monotreme
marsupial
placenta

Reading Strategy: Summarizing As you read, make a list of the major groups of mammals. Write several sentences describing the characteristics of each group. Then, give an example for each.

The class Mammalia contains about 4500 species, and the diversity of these species is astonishing. From a tiny mouse nibbling its way along a corncob to an African elephant uprooting a gigantic tree with its tusks and trunk, mammals have the greatest range of size of any group of vertebrates.

As you have read, tooth structure is one characteristic that scientists use to classify mammals. Mammals are also classified by the number and kinds of bones in the head. But the most important way to categorize living mammals is by the way they reproduce and develop.

The three groups of living mammals are the monotremes (MAHN-oh-treemz), the marsupials (mahr-SOO-pee-ulz), and the placentals. These three groups differ greatly in their means of reproduction and development.

Monotremes and Marsupials

Monotremes lay eggs. Marsupials bear live young that complete their development in a pouch. All monotremes are grouped in a single order, while marsupials are split into several different orders.

Monotremes Members of the **monotremes,** or egg-laying mammals, share two notable characteristics with reptiles. In monotremes, both the reproductive system and the urinary system open into a cloaca that is similar to the cloaca of reptiles. In fact, the name *monotreme* means "single opening." Reproduction in monotremes also resembles reproduction in reptiles more than other mammals. As in reptiles, a female monotreme lays soft-shelled eggs that are incubated outside her body. The eggs hatch into young animals in about ten days. Unlike young reptiles, however, young monotremes are nourished by their mother's milk, which they lick from pores on the surface of her abdomen.

Only three species of monotremes exist today: the duckbill platypus, shown in **Figure 32–9,** and two species of spiny anteaters, or echidnas. These animals are found in Australia and New Guinea.

Figure 32–9 Like all monotremes, the platypus lays eggs that hatch outside the body but nourishes its young with milk produced in mammary glands. The unusual snout of this duckbill platypus can sense electromagnetic signals put out by the muscles of other animals. The platypus uses its sensitive snout to locate prey, such as worms and mollusks, that burrow in the sediments.

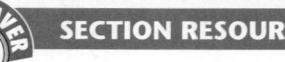

SECTION RESOURCES

Print:
- ***Teaching Resources,*** Section Review 32–2
- ***Guided Reading and Study Workbook,*** Section 32–2
- ***Issues and Decision Making,*** 32–1

Technology:
- ***iText,*** Section 32–2

Marsupials Kangaroos, koalas, and wombats are examples of **marsupials**—mammals bearing live young that complete their development in an external pouch. When marsupials reproduce, the fertilized egg develops into an embryo inside the mother's reproductive tract. There, it is nourished by a small yolk sac. When the food in the yolk sac is used up, the embryo leaves its mother's body. The tiny embryo crawls across its mother's fur into a pouch called the marsupium (mahr-SOO-pee-um) on the outside of her body. Marsupials are named after this structure. Once inside the marsupium, the embryo, looking much like the one in **Figure 32–10,** locates a nipple, attaches to it, and spends several months there. It will continue to drink milk in its mother's pouch until it grows large enough to survive on its own.

CHECKPOINT *How does a marsupial differ from a monotreme?*

Figure 32–10 Most marsupials, including this wallaby, are originally from Australia and New Guinea. **Marsupials bear live young that complete their development in a pouch.** The pink, newborn wallaby (inset) is still an embryo but will soon grow into a "joey" that resembles a small adult.

Placental Mammals

Placental mammals are the mammals with which you are most familiar. Mice, cats, dogs, whales, elephants, humans, and the sea lions in **Figure 32–11** all fall within this category. This group gets its name from an internal structure called the **placenta,** which is formed when the embryo's tissues join with tissues from within the mother's body.

In placental mammals, nutrients, oxygen, carbon dioxide, and wastes are exchanged between embryo and mother through the placenta. The placenta allows the embryo to develop for a much longer time inside the mother—from a few weeks in mice and rats to as long as two years in elephants. After birth, most placental mammals care for their young and provide them with nourishment by nursing. **Figure 32–12,** on the following pages, describes the main orders of placental mammals.

◀ **Figure 32–11** The California sea lion is an example of a placental mammal. **In placental mammals, nutrients, oxygen, carbon dioxide, and wastes are exchanged between embryo and mother through the placenta.**

Make Connections

Environmental Science Explain to students that populations of marsupials in Australia and New Guinea are declining. This decline is caused in part by the introduction of rats, sheep, and rabbits to the continent. Ask: **These placental mammals that have been introduced are not predators. How could they cause a decline in the population of native marsupials?** *(These mammals fill many of the same niches and compete for the same resources as the native marsupials, so there are fewer resources available for the native marsupials.)* **Why do you think there are not many marsupials in other parts of the world?** *(The placental mammals outcompeted the marsupials for resources in the environment. The marsupials might also have been easier prey for predators.)*

Placental Mammals

Build Science Skills

Using Models Challenge student groups to construct a model of a placenta with materials such as modeling clay, pipe cleaners, yarn, netting, tape, or glue. Display photographs or diagrams of a developing placental embryo as a guide. Have groups describe how the placenta works to protect the developing embryo and transfer nutrients to and wastes away from it. Ask: **Why does the placenta allow an embryo to develop longer than embryos that develop inside eggs?** *(The egg has finite sources of energy for growth and a finite space for storing the wastes produced. The placenta provides an unlimited supply of energy—from the mother's food intake—and the ability to continually remove wastes via the mother's body.)*

TIME SAVER **PRESENTATIONS MADE EASY!**

The Presentation Assistant Plus contains the Prentice Hall Presentation Pro and the Transparencies, which provide easy-to-follow visual support for every step of this section. If you have a computer presentation station, use Prentice Hall Presentation Pro for Section 32–2, or use the transparencies listed here.

Section 32–2: **Interest Grabber**
Section Outline
Concept Map
Figure 32–13

Answer to . . .

CHECKPOINT *Monotremes lay eggs; marsupials bear live young.*

Use Visuals

Figure 32–12 Have students examine the photographs and read the caption for each mammalian order. Ask: **What characteristics are used to classify placental mammals?** *(Feeding habits, teeth, limbs)* **Which orders of mammals have hooves?** *(Artiodactyls and Perissodactyls)* **Which order has a single pair of long, curved incisor teeth in the upper and lower jaws?** *(Rodents)* **What mammal belongs to the order Chiropteran?** *(Bats)* **To which order do you belong?** *(Primates)*

Build Science Skills

Classifying Give students ten pictures of different mammals. If possible, include mammals that students are not familiar with. Challenge students to use the information in Figure 32–12 to identify the order to which each mammal belongs. Students should list the characteristics of each mammal on which they based their classification.

Use Community Resources

Take the class to the zoo. Before going, have students use the information in Figure 32–12 to create a field guide for placental mammals. Students should use their field guide at the zoo to identify the mammalian order to which each mammal belongs.

FIGURE 32–12 ORDERS OF PLACENTAL MAMMALS

The 12 orders of mammals shown on these pages contain the vast majority of living placental species. **Classifying** ***How are perissodactyls similar to artiodactyls? How are the two orders different?***

◀ **INSECTIVORES**
These insect eaters have long, narrow snouts and sharp claws that are well suited for digging. *Examples:* shrews, hedgehogs (shown here), moles.

▼ **SIRENIANS**
Sirenians are herbivores that live in rivers, bays, and warm coastal waters scattered throughout most of the world. These large, slow-moving mammals lead fully aquatic lives. *Examples:* manatees, dugongs (shown here).

▼ **CETACEANS**
Like sirenians, cetaceans—the order that includes whales and dolphins—are adapted to underwater life yet must come to the surface to breathe. Most cetaceans live and breed in the ocean. *Examples:* humpback whales (shown here), narwhals, sperm whales, beluga whales, river dolphins.

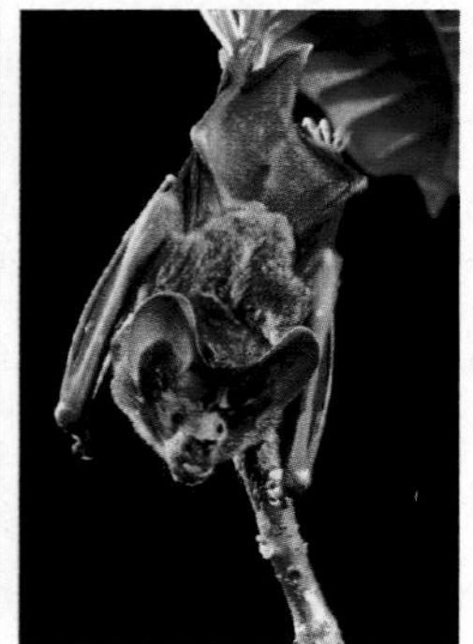

◀ **CHIROPTERANS**
Winged mammals—or bats—are the only mammals capable of true flight. Bats account for about one fifth of all mammalian species. They eat mostly insects or fruit and nectar, although three species feed on the blood of other vertebrates.

RODENTS ▶
Rodents have a single pair of long, curved incisor teeth in both their upper and lower jaws, which they use for gnawing wood and other tough plant material. *Examples:* mice, rats (shown here), voles, squirrels, beavers, porcupines, gophers, chipmunks, gerbils, prairie dogs, chinchillas.

▲ **PERISSODACTYLS**
This order contains hoofed animals with an odd number of toes on each foot. *Examples:* horses, tapirs, rhinoceroses, and zebras (shown here).

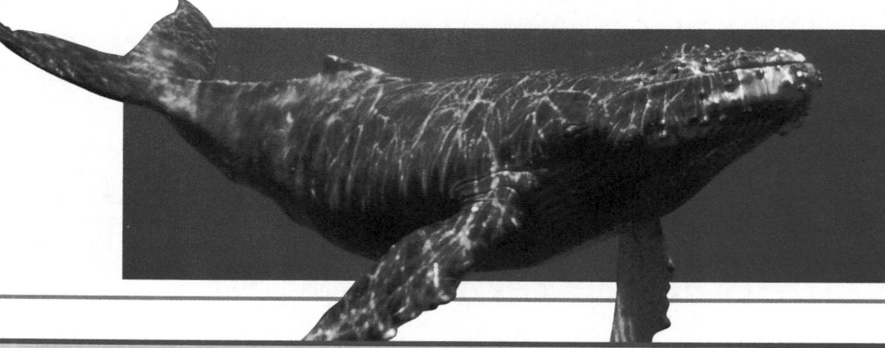

TEACHER TO TEACHER

To help my students realize how diverse mammals are, I break them into small groups and give each group a picture of a mammal that represents a particular mammalian order. First, I instruct the groups to list the characteristics of their animal that identifies it as a mammal. Then, I have the groups list the characteristics that make their animal different from other mammals. Each group creates a poster of their mammalian order that describes the characteristics of mammals belonging to that order. Groups present their posters to the class. The visualization of the many mammalian orders around the room really impresses upon the students the diversity of mammals.

—Heidi Busa,
Biology Teacher
Marcellus High School,
Marcellus, NY

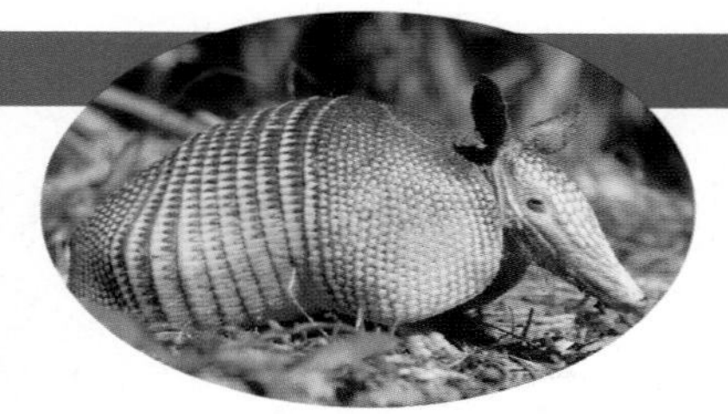

▲ **XENARTHRANS**
Most of the mammals in this order have no teeth. Some have very small teeth that are usually found in the back of the jaw. *Examples:* sloths, anteaters, armadillos (shown here).

▲ **CARNIVORES**
Many carnivores, or meat-eaters, such as tigers and hyenas, stalk and chase their prey by running and pouncing, then kill the prey with sharp teeth and claws. Some animals in this group eat plants as well as meat. Marine carnivores feed in the ocean but bear their young on land. *Examples:* dogs, foxes, bears, raccoons, walruses (shown here).

◀ **ARTIODACTYLS**
These hoofed mammals have an even number of digits on each foot. Like perissodactyls, this order contains mostly large, grazing animals. *Examples:* cattle, sheep, goats, pigs, ibex (shown here), giraffes, hippopotami, camels, antelope, deer, gazelles.

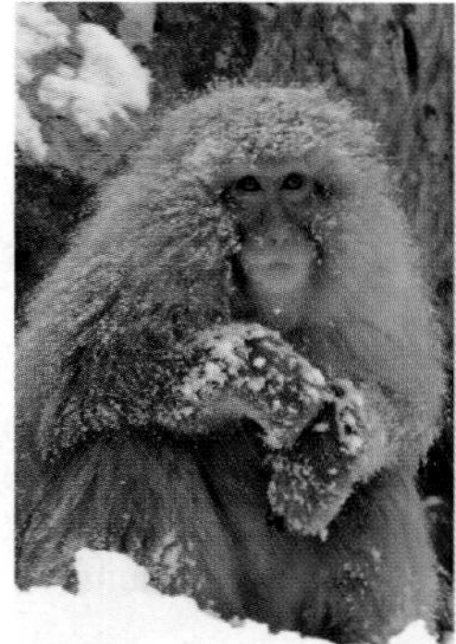

◀ **PRIMATES**
Members of this order are closely related to the ancient insectivores but have a highly developed cerebrum and complex behaviors. *Examples:* lemurs, tarsiers, apes, gibbons, macaques (shown here), humans.

▼ **PROBOSCIDEANS**
These are the mammals with trunks. Some time ago, this order went through an extensive adaptive radiation that produced many species, including mastodons and mammoths, which are now extinct. Only two species, the Asian elephant and this African elephant, survive today.

▲ **LAGOMORPHS**
Like rodents, members of this order are entirely herbivorous. They differ from rodents by having two pairs of incisors in the upper jaw. Most lagomorphs have hind legs that are adapted for leaping. *Examples:* Snowshoe hares (shown here), rabbits.

Address Misconceptions

Some students might think that whales are fishes, not mammals. Review the characteristics of fishes. *(Scales, gills, ectotherms, lay eggs)* Ask: **How do whales breathe?** *(They breathe air with lungs by coming to the surface of the water.)* **Do whales lay eggs or give birth to live young?** *(Give birth to live young that they nourish with their own milk)* If students do not know the answers to these questions, show them pictures of whales illustrating these behaviors, or show them a video about whales.

Meet Diverse Needs

Students with limited English proficiency might wish to make a glossary for the mammalian orders. In their glossaries, they can illustrate common members of each order and write the descriptions of the mammals in English and their native language. Under the name of the order, students can also write in English and their native language the names of animals belonging to the order. **Limited English proficiency**

Make Connections

Environmental Science Show students pictures of various endangered mammals, such as kangaroos, gorillas, cheetahs, rhinoceroses, and manatees. Discuss why the populations of these mammals are declining. Some reasons include loss of habitat, poaching, competition for resources with nonnative mammals, and accidental injury caused by increased boat traffic. Ask: **What is the ultimate cause for the decline in these mammal populations?** *(The activities of people)*

BIO INSIGHTS

HISTORY OF SCIENCE

Aristotle classifies animals

During the fourth century BC, the Greek philosopher Aristotle was the first to classify animals based on their own characteristics rather than whether they were helpful or harmful to people. He published very detailed observations of the animals (and plants) that he knew. These observations led him to divide animals into two groups: those with blood and those without blood. Animals without blood were invertebrates, including insects, cephalopods, and crustaceans. Animals containing blood are now grouped as vertebrates. He recognized that some animals have lungs, breathe air, are warm-blooded, and nourish their young with milk. Although he recognized that whales, dolphins, and porpoises had mammalian characteristics, he placed them in a group separate from mammals and fishes.

Answer to . . .

Figure 32–12 *Both perissodactyls and artiodactyls have feet with hoofs. Perissodactyls have an odd number of toes; artiodactyls have an even number.*

32–2 (continued)

Biogeography of Mammals

Use Visuals

Figure 32–13 Remind students that in convergent evolution, species that live in similar environments in different locations evolve similar adaptations. Ask: **What food do these mammals eat?** *(Ants and termites)* **What adaptations to eating ants do these mammals have in common?** *(Long, hairless snouts; long, sticky tongues; strong, sturdy claws for digging)* **What other adaptations are common to these mammals?** *(Scales or spines for protection against predators)*

3 ASSESS

Evaluate Understanding

Call on students at random to describe the differences between monotremes, marsupials, and placental mammals. Challenge students to name the orders of placental mammals and give an example of each.

Reteach

Encourage students to use Figure 32–12 to help them construct a table that lists the name of each mammalian order, its distinguishing characteristics, and an example.

MAKING CONNECTIONS

Monotremes lay eggs; marsupials bear tiny live young that complete their development in the mother's pouch; the young of placental mammals develop for a long time before birth. Similarities include all the mammalian characteristics: fur or hair, feeding young with milk, endothermy, four-chambered heart, and breathing air.

Use iText to review the key concepts in Section 32–2.

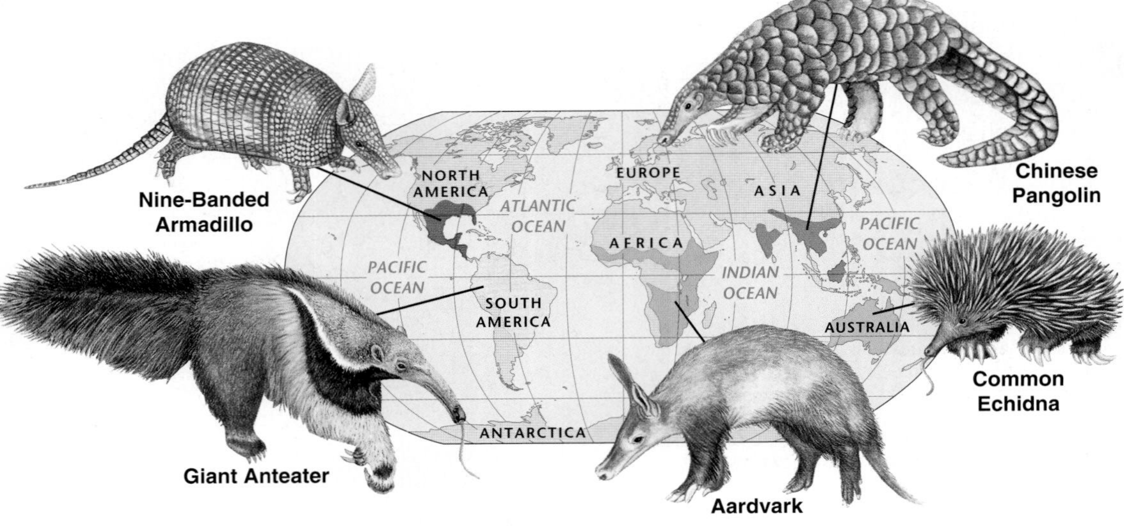

▲ **Figure 32–13** **Similar ecological opportunities on different continents have resulted in convergent evolution among these and other mammals.** Mammals that feed on ants and termites evolved not once but five times in different regions. Powerful front claws; a long, hairless snout; and a tongue covered with sticky saliva are common adaptations in these insect-eating animals.

Biogeography of Mammals

The history of Earth's geography has helped shape today's mammals. During the Paleozoic Era, the continents were one large landmass, and mammals could migrate freely across it. But when the continents drifted apart early in the Cenozoic Era, ancestors of different mammal groups were isolated from one another. Each landmass took with it a unique array of species.

Similar ecological opportunities on the different continents have produced some striking examples of convergent evolution in mammals. Thousands of kilometers apart, mammals such as those in **Figure 32–13** evolved similar adaptations in form and function. When some of the landmasses merged again in the late Cenozoic Era, mammals dispersed and intermingled in new habitats. Living mammals reflect the diversity that resulted from these events.

32–2 Section Assessment

1. **Key Concept** Name the three groups of living mammals and describe the ways each develops.
2. **Key Concept** With regard to mammals, what was the result of continental drift during the Cenozoic Era?
3. What is the function of the placenta?
4. List the major orders of placental mammals.
5. **Critical Thinking Inferring** How are powerful front claws and sticky tongues useful adaptations in mammals that feed on ants?

iTEXT Assessment Use iText to review the important concepts in Section 32–2.

MAKING CONNECTIONS

Comparing and Contrasting Create a compare/contrast table that describes the characteristics of monotremes, marsupials, and placental mammals. Include characteristics that they share as well as ways in which they differ.

32–2 Section Assessment

1. Monotremes: lay eggs; marsupials: immature young finish developing in marsupium; placental mammals: embryo in placenta develops completely inside the mother.
2. Convergent evolution led to mammals with similar adaptations in form and function.
3. Nutrients and oxygen pass from the mother to the embryo through the placenta. Carbon dioxide and other wastes pass from the embryo to the mother through the placenta.
4. Insectivores, sirenians, cetaceans, chiropterans, rodents, perissodactyls, artiodactyls, carnivores, lagomorphs, xenarthrans, primates, proboscideans
5. Powerful front claws help the animals dig into ant colonies. The ants adhere to the sticky tongues.

32–3 Primates and Human Origins

Our own species, *Homo sapiens,* belongs to the order that also includes lemurs, monkeys, and apes. Carolus Linnaeus named our order Primates, which means "first" in Latin.

What Is a Primate?

Just what are primates "first" in? When the first primates appeared, there was little to distinguish them from other mammals besides an increased ability to use their eyes and front limbs together to perform certain tasks. As primates evolved, however, several other characteristics became distinctive.

Primates share several important adaptations, many of which are extremely useful for a life spent mainly in trees. **In general, primates have binocular vision, a well-developed cerebrum, fingers and toes, and arms that can rotate around their shoulder joints.** The gibbon in **Figure 32–14** shows many of these primate characteristics.

Fingers, Toes, and Shoulders Primates normally have five flexible fingers that can curl around objects. Most also have flexible toes. Flexible digits enable many primates to run along tree limbs and swing from branch to branch with ease. Primates' arms are well adapted to climbing because they can rotate in broad circles around a strong shoulder joint. In most primates, the thumb and big toe can move against, or oppose, the other digits. The presence of opposable digits allows many primates to hold objects firmly in their hands or feet.

Well-Developed Cerebrum The large and intricate cerebrum of primates—including a well-developed cerebral cortex—enables them to display more complex behaviors than many other mammals. For example, many primate species have elaborate social behaviors that include adoption of orphans and even warfare between rival primate troops.

Guide for Reading

Key Concepts
- What characteristics do all primates share?
- What are the major evolutionary groups of primates?
- What hominids does the fossil record include?

Vocabulary
binocular vision
prosimian
anthropoid
prehensile
hominoid
hominid
bipedal
opposable thumb

Reading Strategy: Finding Main Ideas Before you read, draw a line down the center of a sheet of paper. On the left side, write down the main topics about primates and human origins. On the right side, note supporting details and examples.

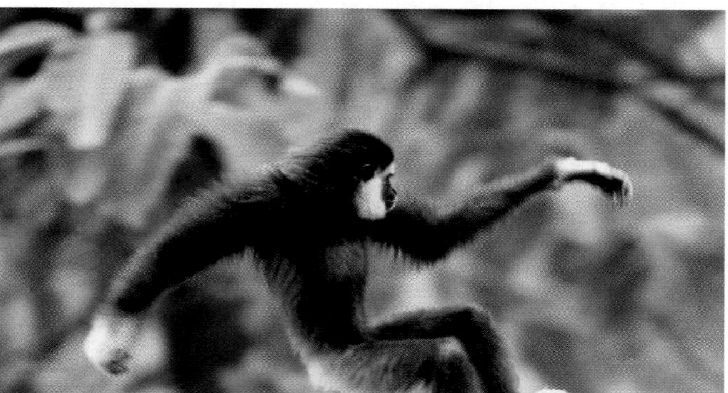

◀ **Figure 32–14** A white-handed gibbon displays several primate characteristics as it swings from tree to tree. **Like all primates, the gibbon has flexible fingers and toes and has arms that can rotate in broad circles around the shoulder joint.**

SECTION RESOURCES

Print:
- ***Laboratory Manual A,*** Chapter 32 Lab
- ***Laboratory Manual B,*** Chapter 32 Lab
- ***Teaching Resources,*** Section Review 32–3, Chapter 32 Real-World Lab
- ***Guided Reading and Study Workbook,*** Section 32–3

Technology:
- ***BioDetective Videotape,*** "Mummies," "Wrongly Accused"
- ***iText,*** Section 32–3

Section 32–3

1 FOCUS

Objectives

32.3.1 ***Identify*** the characteristics that all primates share.
32.3.2 ***Describe*** the major evolutionary groups of primates.
32.3.3 ***Describe*** the various ancestors of humans.

Guide for Reading

Vocabulary Preview

Help students differentiate between the words *hominoid* and *hominid.* First, say each word aloud. Then, write them on the board. Point out that the words differ only by their suffixes, *-oid* and *-id.* Explain that the suffix *-oid* comes from the Greek word *eidos,* meaning "a form or shape." Then, explain that *homo-* means "human being." Ask: **If hominid is the name of the family that includes only humans, what does the word *hominoid* describe?** *(It describes the family of primates that look like humans. It includes humans as well as apes.)*

Reading Strategy

While students read the section, they can write down the main topics on their sheet of paper. Remind them that they can find main ideas in boldfaced type, in topic sentences of paragraphs, and in headings and subheadings within the section.

2 INSTRUCT

What is a Primate?

Meet Diverse Needs

Students probably take for granted their ability to pick up small objects. To help them sense the importance of flexible digits, challenge students to pick up small objects while wearing bulky mittens. Then, discuss how flexible digits not only help primates grasp tree branches, but also enable them to express additional behaviors, such as using tools, eating certain foods, and grooming. **Learning modality: kinesthetic**

Quick Lab

Objective Students will be able to infer how binocular vision is useful.

Skills Focus Inferring

Material sheet of paper

Time 10 min.

Safety Make sure students have enough room to move so they don't trip over things while catching.

Strategy Have students name animals with eyes on the front of their head and those with eyes on the side. Challenge students to identify what the animals in each list have in common. *(Generally, predators have binocular vision and herbivores don't.)* Discuss how these vision patterns are beneficial to predators and herbivores.

Expected Outcome
Students will find the ball more difficult to catch when they have one eye closed.

Analyze and Conclude
1. Graphs should show that more students are able to catch the ball with both eyes open. The combination of two perspectives with both eyes open provides depth perception.
2. Many primates move by swinging through trees. The ability to judge distances enables them to grasp branches and fruit quickly.

Evolution of Primates

Build Science Skills

Classifying Give student groups pictures of several different primates. Challenge groups to classify the primate in each picture as a prosimian or an anthropoid. Students should list characteristics of the primate that caused them to classify it as they did.

Quick Lab

Is Binocular Vision Useful?

Material paper crumpled into a ball

Procedure
1. Throw the paper ball to your partner, who should try to catch the ball with one hand. Record whether your partner caught the ball.
2. Now have your partner close one eye. Repeat step 1.

Analyze and Conclude
1. **Using Graphs** Exchange results with other groups. Make a bar graph for the class data comparing the results with both eyes open and one eye shut.
2. **Drawing Conclusions** How is binocular vision useful to primates?

Binocular Vision Many primates have a flat face, so both eyes face forward with overlapping fields of view. This facial structure gives primates excellent binocular vision. **Binocular vision** is the ability to merge visual images from both eyes, thereby providing depth perception and a three-dimensional view of the world. This is a handy adaptation for judging the locations of tree branches, from which many primates swing.

Evolution of Primates

Humans and other primates evolved from a common ancestor that lived more than 65 million years ago. Very early in their history, primates split off into several groups. **Primates that evolved from two of the earliest branches look very little like typical monkeys and are called prosimians (proh-SIM-ee-unz). Members of the more familiar primate group that includes monkeys, apes, and humans are called anthropoids (AN-thruh-poydz).** Refer to **Figure 32–15** as you read about the relationships among these groups.

Prosimians With few exceptions, **prosimians** alive today are small, nocturnal primates with large eyes that are adapted to seeing in the dark. Many have doglike snouts. Living prosimians include the bush babies of Africa, the lemurs of Madagascar, and the lorises and tarsiers of Asia.

CHECKPOINT *What is a prosimian?*

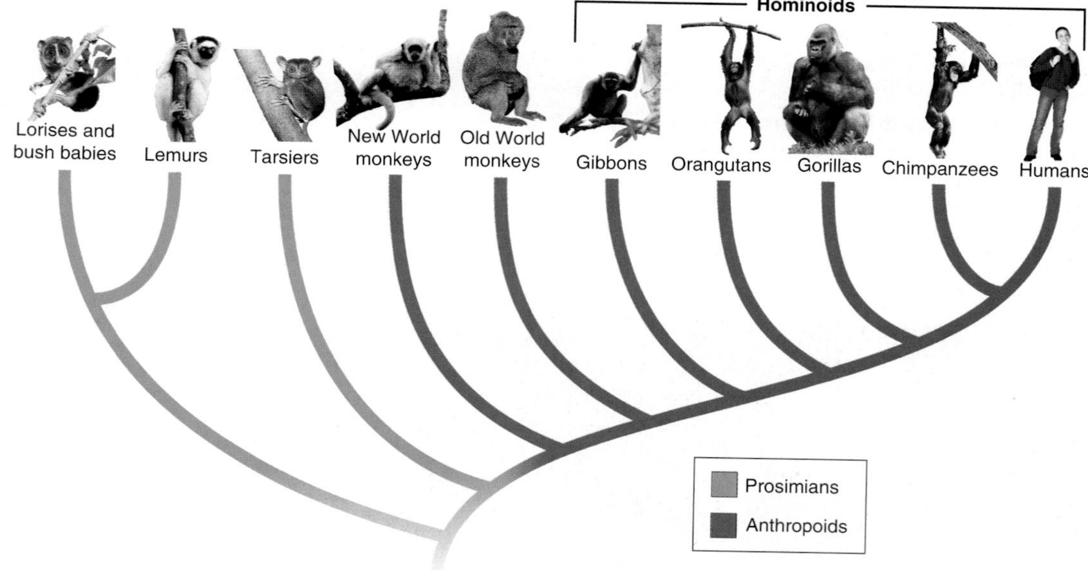

▲ **Figure 32–15** Modern primates evolved from a common ancestor that lived more than 65 million years ago. **The two main groups of primates are prosimians and anthropoids.**

TIME SAVER — PRESENTATIONS MADE EASY!

The Presentation Assistant Plus contains the Prentice Hall Presentation Pro and the Transparencies, which provide easy-to-follow visual support for every step of this section. If you have a computer presentation station, use Prentice Hall Presentation Pro for Section 32–3, or use the transparencies listed here.

Section 32–3:

Interest Grabber
Section Outline
Comparison of Skulls of Human Ancestors
Figure 32–16

Anthropoids Humans, apes, and most monkeys belong to a group called **anthropoids,** which means humanlike primates. This group split very early in its evolutionary history into two major branches. These branches became separated from each other as drifting continents moved apart. One branch, found today in Central and South America, is called the New World monkeys. (After Columbus's voyage to America, Europeans began to use the term *New World* to refer to North and South America.) New World monkeys, which include squirrel monkeys and spider monkeys, live almost entirely in trees. They have long, flexible arms that enable them to swing from branch to branch. New World monkeys also have a long, prehensile tail. A **prehensile** tail is a tail that can coil tightly enough around a branch to serve as a "fifth hand."

The other anthropoid group, which evolved in Africa and Asia, includes the Old World monkeys and great apes. Old World monkeys, such as baboons and macaques (muh-KAHKS), spend time in trees but lack prehensile tails. Great apes, also called **hominoids,** include gibbons, orangutans, gorillas, chimpanzees, and humans. Recent molecular studies confirm that chimpanzees are humans' closest relatives among the great apes. Humans and chimps share an astonishing 98 percent of their DNA!

What Is a Hominid?

Around 6 million years ago, the hominoid line gave rise to a branch that ultimately led to the ancestors and closest relatives of modern humans. The **hominid** family, which includes modern humans, displayed several distinct evolutionary trends. Fossil evidence shows that as hominids evolved over millions of years, they became able to walk upright and developed thumbs adapted for grasping. They also developed large brains.

The skull, neck, spinal column, hipbones, and leg bones of early hominid species changed shape in ways that enabled later species to walk upright. **Figure 32–16** shows some ways in which the skeletons of modern humans differ from those of gorillas. The evolution of this **bipedal,** or two-foot, locomotion was very important, because it freed both hands to use tools. Meanwhile, the hominid hand evolved an **opposable thumb** that enabled grasping objects and using tools.

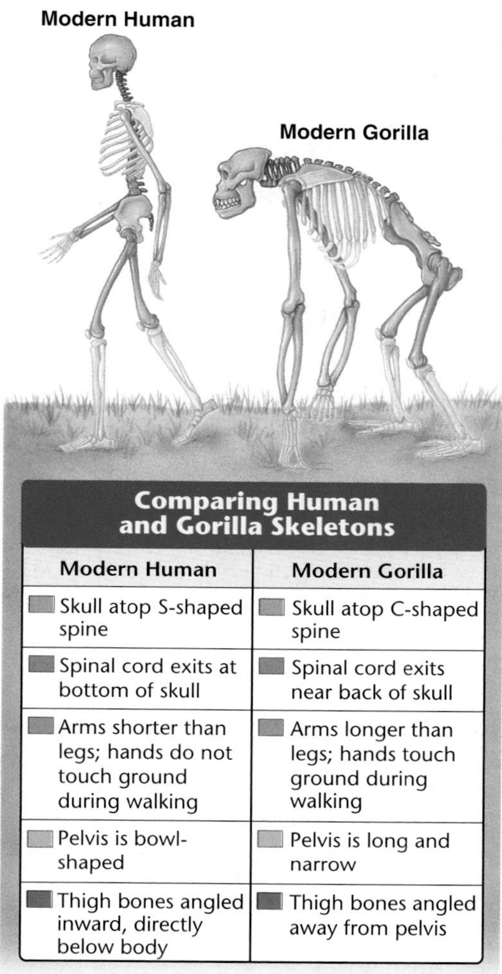

Comparing Human and Gorilla Skeletons

Modern Human	Modern Gorilla
Skull atop S-shaped spine	Skull atop C-shaped spine
Spinal cord exits at bottom of skull	Spinal cord exits near back of skull
Arms shorter than legs; hands do not touch ground during walking	Arms longer than legs; hands touch ground during walking
Pelvis is bowl-shaped	Pelvis is long and narrow
Thigh bones angled inward, directly below body	Thigh bones angled away from pelvis

▲ **Figure 32–16** Modern hominids walk upright on two legs; gorillas use all four limbs. **Comparing and Contrasting** ***According to the chart and illustration, what are the other differences between humans and gorillas?***

Make Connections

Earth Science On a map, show students how the eastern coast of South America fits into the western coast of Africa. Explain that primates first evolved when these two continents were connected. As the continents drifted apart, primate species were separated. Ask: **Why do you think New World and Old World monkeys are so different?** *(As the two groups became separated, they responded to different selection pressures—climate, food sources, environment—and evolved differently.)* Discuss the kinds of environmental changes that helped make the Old World monkeys different from New World monkeys. *(Old World monkeys adapted to an environment with fewer trees. They lost their prehensile tail, tend to sit upright, and have an opposable thumb. New World monkeys remain completely adapted to living in trees. They have a prehensile tail and a grasping hind foot, but no opposable thumb.)*

What Is a Hominid?

Meet Diverse Needs

To help them remember the main ideas, at-risk students or students with limited English proficiency can create a concept map to show the relationships and characteristics of prosimians, anthropoids, hominoids, and hominids. **Learning modality: visual**

Use Visuals

Figure 32–16 Explain that the S-shaped spine of the human skeleton places the center of gravity directly over the pelvis. Ask: **Why can't the gorilla walk on two legs?** *(It needs its arms to balance its body because the body leans forward.)* Have students compare the size of the human and the gorilla skulls. Ask: **Why do gorillas have larger jaws and teeth?** *(They are herbivores; humans are omnivores.)*

BIO INSIGHTS **FACTS AND FIGURES**

Prosimians live here

Prosimians are considered to be more primitive primates because they retain some characteristics of early mammals, such as being nocturnal. Primate features in prosimians are usually less developed than those of higher primates. For example, some prosimians have long snouts because their sense of smell is still very important to their survival. Others have very large eyes for a nocturnal life. Prosimians are found only in the tropical forests of Africa, Southeast Asia, Madagascar, and the West Indies. The lemurs found on Madagascar are probably most similar to the common primate ancestor, possibly because they have been isolated from other primates. Many prosimians are in danger of extinction because of habitat destruction.

Answers to . . .

✓CHECKPOINT *A small, nocturnal primate with large eyes*

Figure 32–16 *Spine shape, site where spinal cord exits skull, length of arms, position of hands during walking, shape of pelvis, angle of thigh bones*

Address Misconceptions

Some students might think that humans evolved directly from modern apes or chimpanzees. Explain that humans and apes shared a common ancestor, but humans did not directly evolve from modern apes. You can illustrate this idea by drawing a phylogenetic tree showing apes and humans diverging from a common ancestor.

Biology and History

Discuss how theories about human ancestors have changed over time. Explain that DNA evidence, used in conjunction with fossil evidence, is also changing the way human history is interpreted. Point out the different scientific disciplines that have been involved in the study of human ancestry. Make sure students know the specialty of each scientist and understand what that specialty entails. Discuss how the knowledge of these scientists has contributed to the study of human origins.

Writing Activity

Remind students that there is no single correct answer. Challenge them to put themselves into Mary Leakey's shoes. Give them as much background information about Mary Leakey and her work as possible. As they write their journal entry, students should feel and convey the excitement that Mary Leakey felt upon making her discovery. Remind students that the journal entry should be written in the first person. Encourage them to imagine and develop any details about the day and the discovery.

▲ **Figure 32–17** Between 8 and 3.6 million years ago, members of a species of *Australopithecus* made these footprints. The footprints show that hominids walked upright millions of years ago. ***Australopithecus* is one of the five known genera of hominids.**

Hominids also displayed a remarkable increase in brain size. Chimpanzees, our closest living relatives among the apes, have a brain size of 280 to 450 cubic centimeters. The brain of *Homo sapiens,* on the other hand, ranges in size from 1200 to 1600 cubic centimeters! Most of the difference in brain size results from an enormously expanded cerebrum—the "thinking" area of the brain.

Early Hominids For years, paleontologists searched for a single fossil species that would link humans with their nonhuman primate ancestors. Recent discoveries have unearthed much more: a treasure trove of hominid species. **Today most paleontologists agree that the hominid fossil record includes 5 genera—*Ardipithecus, Australopithecus, Paranthropus, Kenyanthropus,* and *Homo*—and as many as 16 separate hominid species. This diverse group of fossils covers roughly 4.5 million years.** All of these species are relatives of modern humans, but they are not all human ancestors. To understand the distinction between relatives and ancestors, think of your own family. Your relatives may include aunts, uncles, cousins, grandparents, and great-grandparents. Of those, only your grandparents and great-grandparents are your ancestors.

Many questions remain about how hominid fossil species are related to one another and to humans. What once seemed to be a relatively simple pattern now looks like a dense, branching tree with many twigs. Let us examine some of those twigs.

Biology and History

Human-Fossil Seekers

The study of human origins is an exciting search for our past. To piece together this complicated story requires the skills of many scientists.

1800

1812
Georges Cuvier
Cuvier, a French zoologist, rejects the idea of evolution based on a lack of evidence in the fossil record. He is noted for saying "Fossil man does not exist!" He believed species were static and unchanging.

1836
Siege of the Alamo

1843
Wagons first leave on the Oregon Trail

1868
Edouard Lartet
Henry Christy
French geologist Lartet and English banker Christy unearth several ancient human skeletons in a rock shelter called Cro-Magnon in France. These hominid fossils are the first to be classified as *Homo sapiens.*

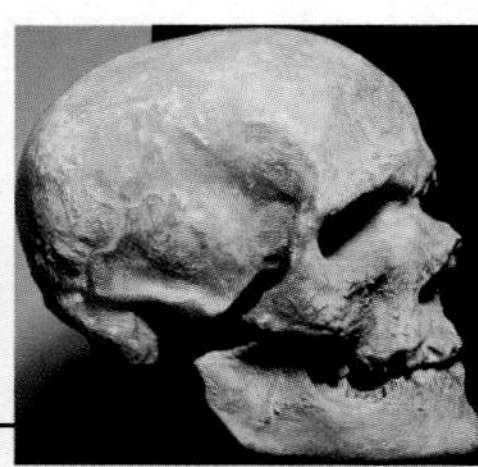

1886
Marcel de Puydt
Max Lohest
De Puydt and Lohest, archaeologist and geologist, describe two Neanderthal skeletons found in a cave in Belgium. Their detailed description of the skeleton shows that Neanderthals were an extinct human form, not an abnormal form of modern human.

HISTORY OF SCIENCE

Edouard Lartet—Founder of Paleontology
Although Edouard Lartet was trained as a lawyer, his discovery of fossil remains at the age of 33 changed his life forever. From then on, he devoted his time to excavating caves in France. He found many examples of early tools made from bone, flint, and antlers. Many caves had colorful drawings of animals. In 1863, the English banker Henry Christy teamed up with Lartet, giving him funding to support his research. Working together, they found a mammoth bone with an image of an extinct animal carved in it. Their discoveries showed that Ice Age mammals lived at the same time as ancient humans. This idea was under great debate at the time. They also showed that the Stone Age was made up of different phases of human culture.

Australopithecus The earliest well-known group of hominids, members of the genus *Australopithecus,* lived from about 4 million to a million years ago. These hominids were bipedal apes that spent at least some time in trees. The structure of their teeth suggests a diet rich in fruit. Some *Australopithecus* species seem to have been human ancestors, while others formed separate branches off the main hominid line.

The best known species is *Australopithecus afarensis*—described from a remarkably complete female skeleton, nicknamed Lucy, who stood only about 1 meter tall. The humanlike footprints shown in **Figure 32–17,** which are between 3.6 and 8 million years old, were probably made by members of the same species as Lucy. Since *Australopithecus* fossils have small brains, the Laetoli footprints show that hominids walked bipedally long before large brains evolved.

Paranthropus Three later species, which grew to the size of well-fed football linebackers, were originally placed in the genus *Australopithecus*. However, they are now usually placed in their own genus, *Paranthropus.* The known *Paranthropus* species had huge, grinding back teeth. Their diets probably included coarse and fibrous plant foods like those eaten by modern gorillas. Most paleontologists now place *Paranthropus* on a separate, dead-end branch of our family tree.

CHECKPOINT *What are the characteristics of* Australopithecus*?*

To find out more about human history, view the videotape "Mummies: Ties to the Past."

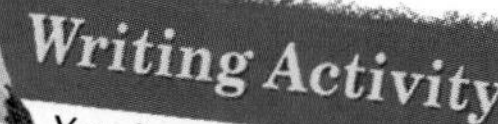

You have found Mary Leakey's journal and noticed that the entry for her discovery of the footprints at Laetoli is missing. Write an entry for the journal as she would have, describing the events of the day and her initial reaction to the find.

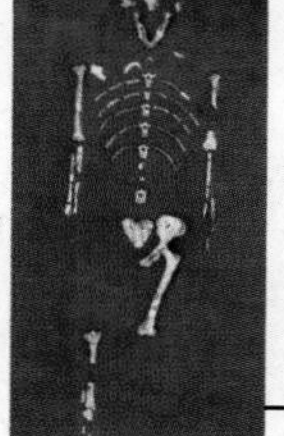

1974

Donald Johanson
An American paleontologist and his team find a nearly complete skeleton of *Australopithecus,* which they call Lucy, in the Afar region of Ethiopia. The skeleton is about 3.2 million years old.

1999

Douglas Wallace
Wallace and fellow geneticists create a family tree of human evolution based on their studies of mitochondrial DNA, which is passed only from mother to child.

00

2000

1924

Raymond Dart
Dart, an Australian anatomist, finds the first hominid fossil—a nearly complete skull of a young child—in South Africa. This specimen was placed in a new genus called *Australopithecus.*

1951

First color-television broadcast in the United States

1978

Mary Leakey
Leakey, a British anthropologist, discovers a set of 3.5 million-year-old fossil hominid footprints at Laetoli in Tanzania. The footprints provide evidence that early hominids walked erect on two legs.

Encourage students to view the "Mummies" segment of the BioDetectives Videotape.

Meet Diverse Needs

Students will benefit from constructing a time line that marks the time period that each hominid species lived. Students should realize that some hominid species lived during the same time. Help students put into perspective the large expanse of time over which these hominid ancestors lived and died. **Learning modality: visual**

Meet Diverse Needs

Students who would like an extra challenge can read Mary Leakey's autobiography entitled *Disclosing the Past.* Students who have read the book can discuss what they think about Mary Leakey's life and how they felt after reading her story. Or, you might have these students work together to prepare a class presentation about Mary Leakey's life. **Learning modality: verbal**

BIO INSIGHTS

HISTORY OF SCIENCE

The Leakey family of anthropologists
Mary Nicol Leakey was born in London in 1913, but she spent much of her life moving around Europe with her family. During her early twenties, she began working at archaeological sites, where she learned to be methodical and careful. She also became known for her abilities in illustration. She married the anthropologist Louis Leakey in 1936, after meeting him at a dinner party after a lecture. She went with him to Africa, where he was working to prove that humans originated there rather than in Asia, as was popularly thought at the time. She spent over twenty years excavating sites in the Serengeti Plains in northern Tanzania. She and her husband collected many tools and fossilized skulls of early hominids. Her greatest find, the fossilized footprints at Laetoli, came after her husband's death.

Answer to . . .

CHECKPOINT Australopithecus *was a bipedal ape that probably ate a diet rich in fruit.*

32–3 (continued)

Use Visuals

Figure 32–18 Point out that the skulls are arranged in order according to the age of the fossil species, with the oldest, *Kenyanthropus platyops,* at the top, and the most recent, *Homo erectus,* at the bottom. Have students compare and contrast the structure of the skulls. Ask: **In what ways are the skulls of *Kenyanthropus platyops* and *Homo erectus* similar? In what ways are they different?** (Both have eye sockets facing forward, indicating that they have binocular vision, as do all primates. Both have relatively large brain cases. However, *H. erectus* has the larger brain. *K. platyops* has a flat face.)

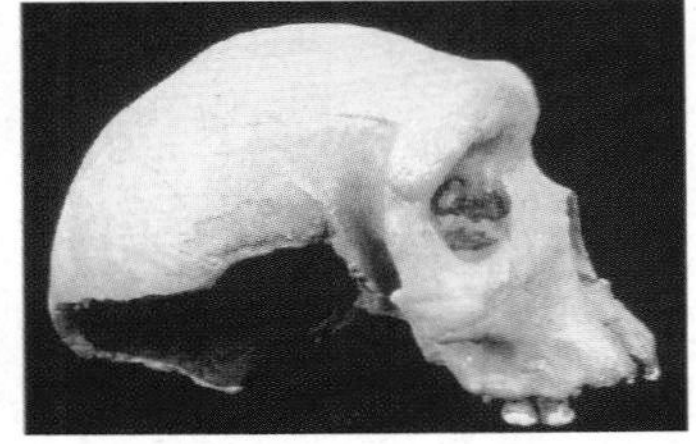

▲ **Figure 32–18** Paleontologists' interpretations of hominid evolution are based on the study of fossils such as these skulls—*Kenyanthropus platyops* (top), *Paranthropus robustus* (middle), and *Homo erectus* (bottom). **Observing** *Which of these skulls most closely resembles the skull of a modern human?*

Kenyanthropus Early in the year 2001, a team led by Meave Leakey announced a spectacular and puzzling discovery. On the western side of Lake Turkana in northern Kenya, they uncovered a well-preserved skull that has a confusing combination of characteristics. Its ear structures resemble those of chimpanzees, and its brain is rather small. Yet some of its facial features resemble those of fossils usually placed in the genus *Homo*.

The researchers decided that this skull should be placed in a new genus, *Kenyanthropus*, whose name comes from the country in which the fossil was found. Since the skull has a flat face, the researchers gave it the species name *Kenyanthropus platyops.* The word *platyops* comes from Greek words meaning "flat" and "face." *Kenyanthropus platyops* is one of the fossil skulls in **Figure 32–18.** Evidence indicates that *Kenyanthropus platyops* existed at the same time as *A. afarensis.*

The researchers further proposed that a specimen previously named *Homo rudolfensis* was similar enough to *Kenyanthropus platyops* that it should be renamed *Kenyanthropus rudolfensis.* This discovery raised many questions, not only about the two *Kenyanthropus* species, but about the evolutionary relationships of hominid species in general.

How Do the Branches Connect? *Kenyanthropus* is the most recent hominid species to be described. It most certainly will not be the last. In the years between 1985 and the present time, paleontologists have more than doubled the number of recognized hominid species. It now seems clear that hominid evolution, like the evolution of other mammalian groups, did not involve the simple, straight-line transformation of one species into another. Rather, a series of complex adaptive radiations produced a large number of species whose relationships are tough to determine. Which species are true ancestors? Which are just relatives? And precisely how are those relatives related to each other and to us?

At the present time no one knows the answers to any of those questions for certain. **Figure 32–19** shows one recent attempt to chart the evolutionary relationships of known hominid species. The chart begins with the hominid descendants of a common ancestor shared by hominids and chimpanzees some time around 6 million years ago. The question mark indicates that this common ancestor has not yet been discovered. Note the many other question marks, each indicating *possible* lines of descent. It will probably take many years of work to more fully understand the fascinating and complex story of hominid evolution.

✓CHECKPOINT *What is* **Kenyanthropus platyops***?*

FACTS AND FIGURES

Changing African climate and evolution
The climate of Africa began changing about 10 million years ago. The air became drier, and forests gave way to grasslands. Many primates remained in the forests. But, as the environment became more diverse, different primates evolved to fill these new niches. These primates had characteristics that enabled them to live more successfully in open grassland. Their diet changed from being completely herbivorous to omnivorous. They began walking upright on two feet. Bipedalism enabled primates to see over the tops of grass and bushes. It enabled them to carry food or offspring in their arms. It also kept them cooler, because they received less of the sun's direct rays and could catch cool breezes above the ground. The gradual loss of body hair also helped to keep them cooler.

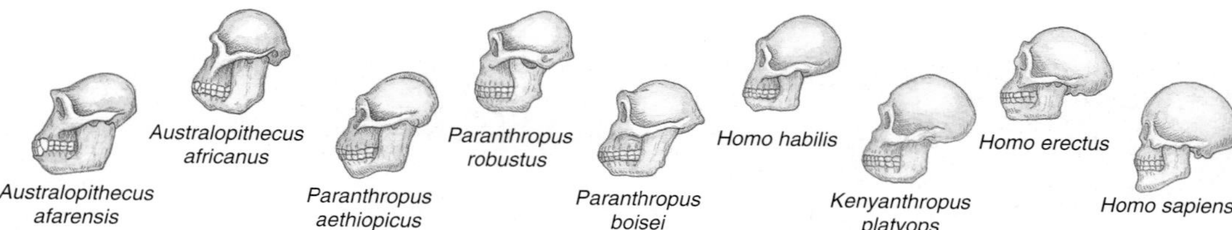

The Road to Modern Humans

Modern humans belong to the species *Homo sapiens*. As you can see from **Figure 32–19**, other species in the genus *Homo* existed before *Homo sapiens* appeared. The history and interrelationships of these species, and the path by which they led to modern humans, are fascinating and still not completely understood.

The Genus *Homo* About 2.5 million years ago, a new hominid appeared in Africa. Its fossils show that it resembled modern humans enough to be classified as a member of our own genus, *Homo*. Because this species was found with tools made of stone and bone, researchers called it *Homo habilis* (HAB-ih-lis), which means "handy man."

Homo habilis was the first of several members of our genus to arise in Africa. About 2 million years ago, a larger species appeared with bigger brains and downward-facing nostrils that resembled those of modern humans. Today, most researchers call the African fossils of this species *Homo ergaster*. Either *H. ergaster* or a closely related species, *Homo erectus,* soon began migrating out of Africa. By about 1.8 million years ago, these migrants had crossed Asia and reached China and Java. By a million years ago, populations of *Homo erectus* were living in several places across Asia.

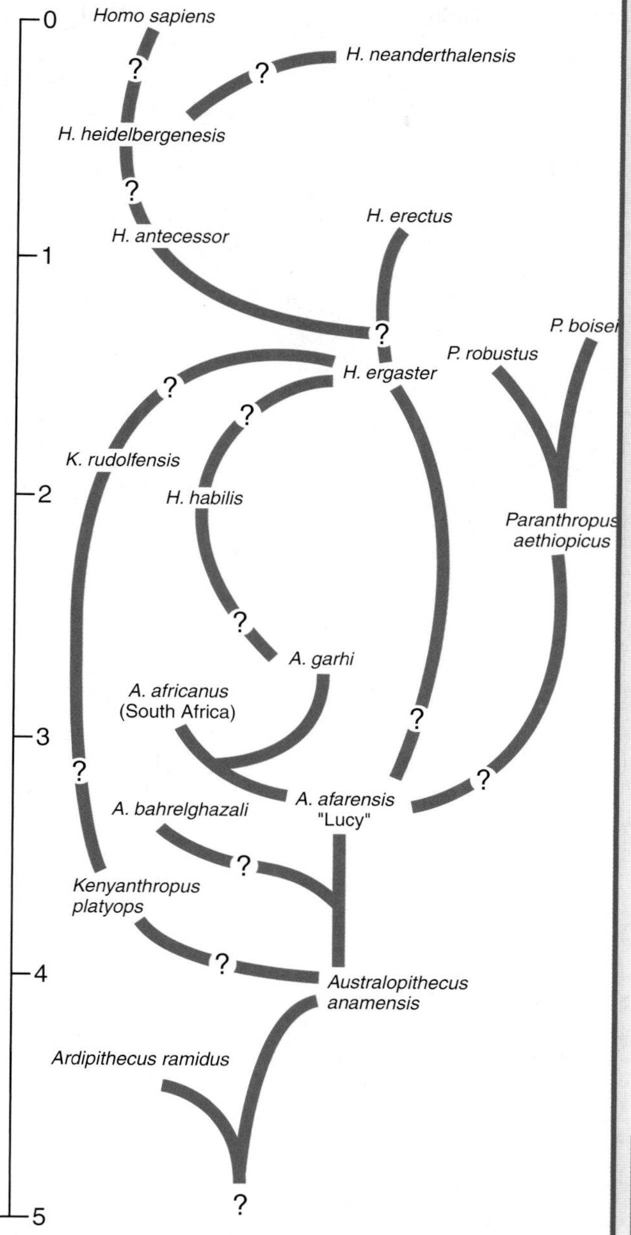

Homo sapiens
H. neanderthalensis
H. heidelbergenesis
H. antecessor
H. erectus
H. ergaster
P. robustus
P. boisei
K. rudolfensis
H. habilis
Paranthropus aethiopicus
A. garhi
A. africanus (South Africa)
A. bahrelghazali
A. afarensis "Lucy"
Kenyanthropus platyops
Australopithecus anamensis
Ardipithecus ramidus
?
0 1 2 3 4 5
Millions of years ago

Figure 32–19 The hominid fossil record includes five genera and several species. Only *Homo sapiens* survives today. However, several earlier hominid species lived at the same time as one another. The existence of these fossils is well established, but the diagram shows that paleontologists are debating just how they are related to one another and to modern humans. **Interpreting Graphics** ***Trace two possible lines of descent from*** **A. anamensis** ***to*** **H. sapiens.**

The Road to Modern Humans

Address Misconceptions

Some students might have the misconception that human ancestors were "dumb cave men." Address this by explaining that a large part of human evolution was developing the ability to learn and to teach. Point out that our knowledge base is large because it continues to be built on what is already known. This base of knowledge will continue to grow as more is learned about our past and new discoveries are made. If you wish, you can illustrate this concept with interlocking building blocks. Starting at the base with blocks representing simple tools made from sticks, bones, and stones, students can build a wall or other structure. Each block they add to the structure should represent some innovation or discovery that expands the knowledge base of humans.

Answers to . . .

CHECKPOINT Kenyanthropus platyops *is the species name given to a fossil skull discovered in Kenya by Meave Leakey's team. The skull has a flat face. It has some characteristics of chimpanzees and some characteristics of the genus* Homo.

Figure 32–18 Homo erectus

Figure 32–19 *(1)* A. anamensis *to* A. afarensis *to* H. ergaster *to* H. antecessor *to* H. heidelbergensis *to* H. sapiens. *(2)* A. anamensis *to* A. afarensis *to* A. garhi *to* H. habilis *to* H. ergaster *to* H. antecessor *to* H. heidelbergensis *to* H. sapiens.

32–3 (continued)

Out of Africa—But Who and When?

Use Visuals

Figure 32–20 Ask: **At which sites did hominids live more than 2 million years ago?** *(Olduvai, Kanapoi, and Hadar)* **How many times might hominids have left Africa for the Middle East?** *(Four times)* **When?** *(1.5 to 2.0 million years ago, 0.5 to 1.0 million years ago, 0.1 to 0.5 million years ago, and less than 0.1 million years ago)* **When were hominids first in what is now Beijing?** *(0.5 to 1.0 million years ago)* **How have scientists learned the history of human ancestors?** *(By studying the fossil record and testing the mitochondrial DNA of fossilized human ancestors)*

Build Science Skills

Making Judgments Challenge students to make a list of objects that they would include in a time capsule. Students should choose no more than ten items and give reasons for each choice. They should choose items with the idea that the time capsule will be opened 100,000 years from now. These items should give anthropologists information about what students' lives were like and how they lived.

Build Science Skills

Applying Concepts Challenge students to make comparisons of their lifestyle to that of ancient humans. Discuss how different our lives are now, as well as how some aspects of our lives might be similar. Encourage students to make predictions about what life will be like in the future. You could have students write an essay describing their thoughts and predictions.

SCIENCE NEWS®

Encourage students to visit **www.phschool.com** for the most current information on this topic.

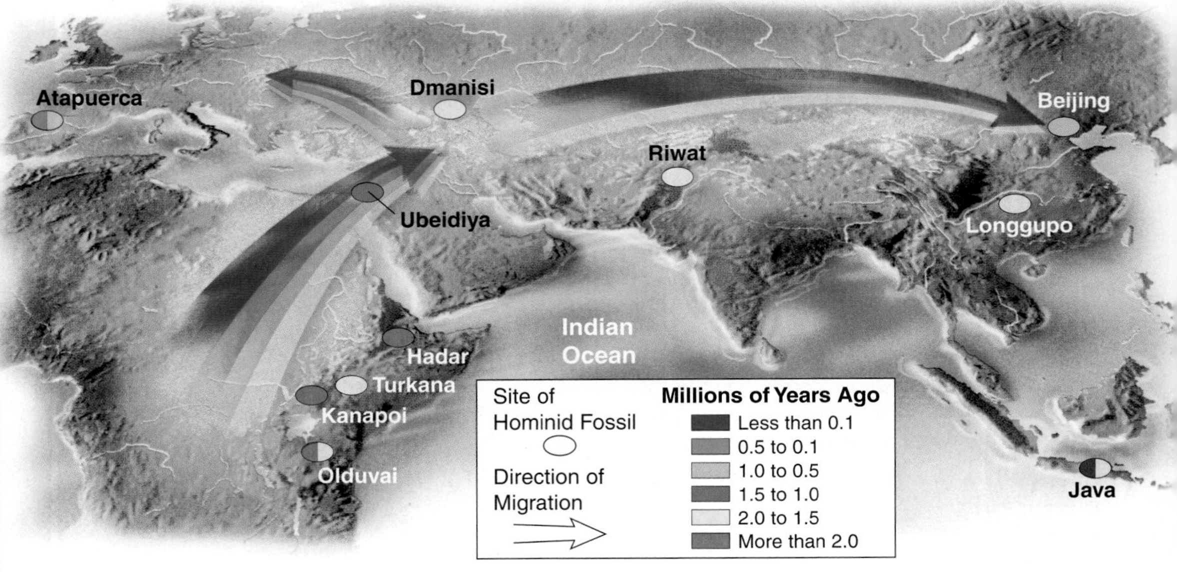

▲ **Figure 32–20** Data show that relatives and ancestors of modern humans left Africa several different times. But when did early hominids leave Africa, and how far did they travel? By testing the mitochondrial DNA of fossilized human ancestors and continuing to study the fossil record, scientists hope to improve our understanding of the complex history of *Homo sapiens.*

KEEP CURRENT WITH . . . SCIENCE NEWS®

To find out more about the topics in this chapter go to; **www.phschool.com**

Out of Africa—But Who and When?

Precisely what happened next has been the subject of much scientific debate. How did modern *Homo sapiens* evolve from earlier members of the genus *Homo*? Two hypotheses describe two very different possible histories. One hypothesis, known as the multi-regional model, suggests that *Homo sapiens* could have evolved independently in several places around the world. This hypothesis proposes that modern humans descended directly from the far-flung populations of *H. erectus* that were already living outside of Africa more than a million years ago.

A second hypothesis, known as the out-of-Africa model, argues that the first true *Homo sapiens* evolved in Africa, probably between 200,000 and 150,000 years ago. This model further proposes that members of this species left Africa in one or more recent waves of migration, as shown in **Figure 32–20.** These migrants then replaced the descendants of *H. erectus* around the globe to found local populations of modern humans. This hypothesis has received powerful support from genetic analysis based on DNA found in the mitochondria of cells. The molecular data argue powerfully for a single African origin for all modern humans. For that reason, the out-of-Africa hypothesis is accepted by most researchers today.

Modern *Homo sapiens*

▲ **Figure 32–21** This ancient cave painting from France shows the remarkable artistic abilities of Cro-Magnons. **Inferring** ***How might these painted images be related to the lifestyle of these early humans?***

The story of modern humans over the past 500,000 years involves two main groups. The earliest of these species is now called *Homo neanderthalensis,* named after the Neander Valley in Germany where their remains were first found. Neanderthals, as they are commonly called, flourished from Europe through western Asia between about 200,000 and 30,000 years ago. Evidence from Neanderthal sites in Europe and the Middle East suggests that they not only made stone tools but also lived in organized social groups.

The other group is anatomically modern *Homo sapiens*—in other words, people whose skeletons look like those of modern humans. These *H. sapiens,* who probably arose in Africa, appeared in the Middle East around 100,000 years ago. They joined Neanderthals who had been living in that region for at least 100,000 years. As far as anyone can tell, Neanderthals and *Homo sapiens* lived side by side in what is now Israel, Lebanon, Syria, and Turkey for around 50,000 years, using similar tools and living in remarkably similar ways.

That situation changed dramatically around 50,000–40,000 years ago. That's when some populations of *H. sapiens* seem to have fundamentally changed their way of life. They used new technology to make more sophisticated stone blades, and made elaborately worked tools from bones and antlers. They produced spectacular cave paintings, such as the one in **Figure 32–21.** These *Homo sapiens* buried their dead with elaborate rituals. In other words, these people began to behave like modern humans. About 40,000 years ago, one such group, known as Cro-Magnons (kroh-MAG-nunz) appeared in Europe.

By 30,000 years ago, Neanderthals had disappeared from Europe—and from the Middle East as well. How and why they disappeared is not yet known. But since that time, our species has been Earth's only hominid.

32–3 Section Assessment

1. **Key Concept** List five characteristics that all primates share.
2. **Key Concept** Describe the major primate groups and explain how they are related.
3. **Key Concept** Name the genera that currently make up the hominid fossil record.
4. Compare and contrast hominids and hominoids. How are they similar? Different?
5. **Critical Thinking Applying Concepts** How did the separation of the continents contribute to the development of New World and Old World monkeys?

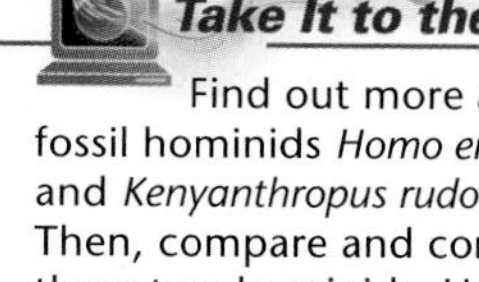

iTEXT Assessment Use iText to review the important concepts in Section 32–3.

Take It to the NET

Find out more about fossil hominids *Homo ergaster* and *Kenyanthropus rudolfensis.* Then, compare and contrast these two hominids. Use the links provided in the Biology area at the Prentice Hall Web site for help in completing this activity: **www.phschool.com**

32–3 Section Assessment

1. Flattened faces, binocular vision, flexible digits, arms developed for swinging and climbing, well-developed cerebrum
2. Two major groups descended from a common primate ancestor. Prosimians: small, nocturnal primates; anthropoids: humanlike primates, split into two groups: New World monkeys and Old World monkeys and hominoids
3. *Ardipithecus, Australopithecus, Paranthropus, Kenyanthropus,* and *Homo*
4. Both groups are similar in that they are anthropoids. For differences, see the chart in Figure 32–16, p. 835.
5. The two groups responded to different environmental pressures and evolved differently.

Modern *Homo sapiens*

Build Science Skills

Formulating Hypotheses
Challenge students to develop a hypothesis to explain why *Homo neanderthalensis* died out but *Homo sapiens* did not. Have students describe the type of fossilized evidence they must find that would support their hypothesis. Also have them describe what type of fossilized evidence would refute their hypothesis.

3 ASSESS

Evaluate Understanding

Have students make a "family tree" that shows how the primate groups (prosimians, anthropoids, hominoids, and hominids) evolved from a common ancestor. Instruct students to list the characteristics of each group.

Reteach

Have students copy the vocabulary words from this section. For each word, students should write its meaning in their own words. For those words that describe primate groups, students should include the characteristics of primates belonging to that group.

Take It to the NET

Both fossil species are extinct hominids. Students will learn that, *Kenyanthropus rudolfensis* was formerly classified in the genus *Homo,* but it is more similar to *Kenyanthropus platyops;* therefore it is now in the genus *Kenyanthropus. Homo erectus* had a larger brain than *K. rudolfensis.*

For additional information, visit

www.phschool.com

Use iText to review the key concepts in Section 32–3.

Answer to . . .

Figure 32–21 *The paintings might show how these early humans hunted large animals.*

Real-World Lab

Objective Students will be able to infer how forensic scientists identify unknown hairs and fibers.

Skills Focus **Observing, Inferring, Analyzing Data**

Time 45 minutes

Advance Prep

- Collect six reference fibers: two from people, two from animals, and two nonanimal fibers such as cotton and synthetic fibers. The four unknown fibers should include one of the human reference samples and three nonhuman fibers. Collect animal fibers directly from pets or by removing them from clothes. Collect nonanimal fibers from clothes, carpeting, or thread.
- Prepare fresh biuret reagent no more than one day in advance, and store it out of light. Make a 0.1 M solution of sodium hydroxide (NaOH) by dissolving 4 g in 1 L of water. Add 1.4 g $CuSo_4$ or 2.2 g $CuSO_4{\bullet}5\,H_2O$. To reduce the risk to students in handling this solution, dispense small test tubes containing 10 mL of biuret reagent for use in Part 2.

Safety Wear plastic gloves, safety goggles, and a lab apron when handling NaOH or biuret reagent. Dispose of the gloves properly after the lab.

Pre-Lab Discussion After students read the procedure, ask: **What is hair composed of?** *(Protein)* **How could you tell whether a fiber is hair or something else?** *(By examining it with a microscope and testing it for protein)* **Can mammals be identified by their hairs?** *(Yes, although students might not know this yet.)*

Teaching Tips
When cleaning up after the lab, place a screen over the sink drain and have students empty their test tubes carefully into a stream of running cold water, avoiding splashing. The screen will keep hair from clogging the drain.

Procedure

2. Students should record the color, shape, texture, and any other observations they make about the fiber.

Real-World Lab

Using Fibers as Forensic Evidence

Hair and other fibers are often used by police as evidence that a suspect was at the scene of a crime such as a burglary. In this investigation, you will examine a variety of hairs and other fibers to match unknown fibers to known reference fibers. The two human hairs represent hairs from two people who are suspected of having been at the crime scene. The unknown fibers represent fibers found at the crime scene.

Discovery Channel SCHOOL — To find out more about how scientists use forensic evidence, view the videotape "Wrongly Accused: Science and Justice."

Problem

How do forensic scientists identify unknown hairs and fibers?

Materials

- reference fibers
- unknown fibers
- microscope slides
- coverslips
- dropper pipette
- microscope
- glass-marking pencil
- facial tissues
- isopropyl alcohol
- rubber cement
- forceps
- test-tube rack
- 4 test tubes of biuret reagent
- 4 glass stirring rods
- hot water bath

Skills

Observing, Inferring, Analyzing Data

Procedure

Part A: Observing Fibers

1. Place one of the reference fibers on a microscope slide. **CAUTION:** *Microscopes and slides are fragile. Handle them carefully. If you break any glass, inform your teacher immediately.* Add a drop of water and a coverslip. Label the slide with the name of the fiber. On a separate sheet of paper, make a copy of the data table shown with 10 blank lines.
2. Place the slide on the stage of a microscope and look at it under 100× magnification. Examine the fiber carefully, looking for features such as color, shape, texture, and whether or not a hair root is attached. Record your observations in your data table. Draw and label a sketch of the fiber.
3. Repeat steps 1 and 2 for each of the reference and unknown fibers.
4. Clean one of the reference fibers by pulling it through a folded tissue moistened with a small amount of alcohol. **CAUTION:** *Alcohol is flammable. Do not use it in the presence of an open flame or sparks.*
5. Smear a thin layer of rubber cement on the middle of a glass slide. Quickly place the fiber on the surface of the rubber cement.
6. Before the cement dries, lift the fiber off the slide with forceps. You should see an imprint of the fiber on the cement. Put the slide under a microscope and observe the surface texture of the fiber. Record your observations.
7. Repeat steps 4 to 6 for each of the other fibers.

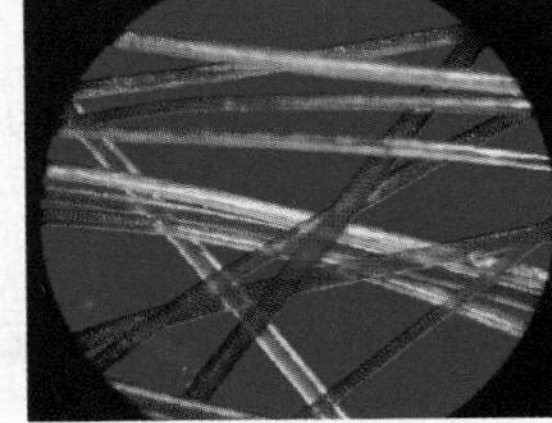

Human Hairs
(magnification: 22×)

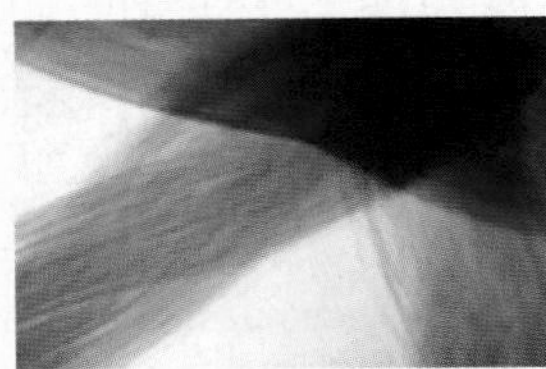

Polyester Threads
(magnification: 70×)

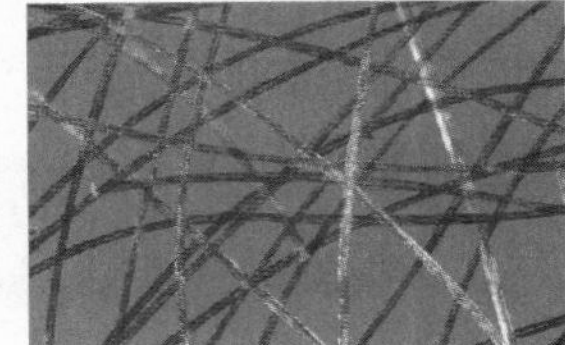

Silk Fibers
(magnification: about 50×)

Data Table			
Fiber	General Observations	Surface Texture	Biuret Test Result

Part B: Testing for Protein

8. **Making Predictions** On the basis of the observations you have recorded in your data table and your knowledge of hair from this chapter, write a prediction of which unknown fibers contain protein. Synthetic and plant fibers do not contain protein. Include the reasons for your prediction, explaining what evidence supports your prediction about each fiber.
9. Label 4 test tubes of biuret reagent solution 1 through 4. **CAUTION:** *Wear safety goggles, a lab apron, and plastic gloves when working with biuret reagent solution. If any of the solution gets on your skin or clothing, wash it off immediately and inform your teacher.* Use forceps to place several strands of each unknown fiber in the test tube with the same number. Record the time.
10. Place a glass stirring rod in each test tube. Place the test tubes in the hot water bath. Stir each test tube occasionally. **CAUTION:** *Leave the stirring rods in the test tubes. Do not place the wet stirring rods on the table.*
11. Observe the color of each test tube. A change from blue to purple or reddish-brown within 5 minutes indicates the presence of protein. Add your observations to your data table. Follow your teacher's instructions for safe disposal of the biuret reagent.

Analyze and Conclude

1. **Comparing and Contrasting** How are hairs and synthetic fibers different?
2. **Observing** Did you observe any differences between human hair and other hair? If you did, describe the differences.
3. **Drawing Conclusions** Did your observations support the idea that one or both of the suspects may have been at the crime scene? Explain your answer.
4. **Making Judgments** Did your observations leave room for doubt about this conclusion? If so, what other evidence would provide a stronger test of your conclusion? Explain your answer.

Go Further

Additional Research Forensic science is the application of scientific knowledge to questions involving law. Do research to learn more about forensic science. Some topics you might investigate include the following:

- DNA evidence
- Evidence of poisoning
- Forensic dentistry
- Forensic anthropology
- Forensic pathology
- Ballistics

Analyze and Conclude

1. Hairs have a root at one end and a scaly surface. Synthetic fibers are uniformly smooth and featureless. Hairs contain protein; synthetic fibers do not.

2. Human hair is not very different from other hair. The scales of human hair are more regular than those of other hair, but the basic structure of hair is the same for all mammals.

3. Yes, one of the unknown hairs found at the crime scene matched one suspect's reference hairs.

4. Yes, the suspect's hair was similar to one found at the crime scene, but this similarity does not prove that only this person has hair that would match the hair found at the scene. Other evidence, such as matching fingerprints or DNA sequences, would make a stronger case.

6. Students should record the texture and pattern made by the fiber in the rubber cement.

8. Student predictions will vary. They might correctly predict that unknown fibers they believe to be hairs contain protein.

11. Test tubes with hair should change color from blue to purple or reddish-brown within five minutes.

Expected Outcome Students will distinguish hairs from nonanimal fibers on the basis of microscopic appearance and a positive biuret reaction (color change from blue to purple or reddish-brown).

A local police laboratory or state crime laboratory might be able to provide information or direct students to useful resources on this subject.

Encourage students to view "Wrongly Accused" from the BioDetectives Videotape.

Chapter 32 Study Guide

Study Tip

Have a "Biology Bee" and ask students questions about the Vocabulary terms and Key Concepts. When a student misses a question, he or she is out. However, allow the students who are "out" to answer a missed question so they can get back "in."

Thinking Visually

1. Marsupials
2. Placental mammals
3. Platypuses and echidnas

Chapter 32 Assessment

Reviewing Content

1. c	5. b	9. d
2. c	6. c	10. a
3. a	7. a	
4. a	8. b	

Understanding Concepts

11. Hair and subcutaneous fat conserve heat; a high metabolic rate generates heat.

12. Sharp teeth, such as canines and incisors, are used for biting and ripping flesh from prey. Most carnivores also have sharp molars that are used to slice meat into small pieces. Herbivores have flattened molars to grind plant food.

13. Chest muscles lift the rib cage, and the diaphragm pulls the bottom of the chest cavity downward, increasing the volume of the chest cavity. Air enters the lungs. Chest muscles then lower the rib cage, the diaphragm relaxes, and air is pushed out of the lungs.

14. The kidney excretes nitrogenous waste, helps maintain homeostasis by excreting or retaining excess liquid, and retains salts, sugars, and other important molecules the body needs.

Chapter 32 Study Guide

32–1 Introduction to the Mammals

Key Concepts

- In addition to having hair and the ability to nourish their young with milk, all mammals breathe air and are endotherms that generate their body heat internally.
- The first true mammals appeared during the late Triassic Period, about 220 million years ago.
- The ability of mammals to regulate their body heat from within is an example of homeostasis.
- As mammals evolved to eat foods other than insects, the form and function of their jaws and teeth became adapted to their diets.
- The kidneys of mammals help maintain homeostasis by excreting or retaining excess liquid.

Vocabulary

mammary gland, p. 821
subcutaneous fat, p. 822
rumen, p. 823
diaphragm, p. 824
cerebral cortex, p. 825

32–2 Diversity of Mammals

Key Concepts

- The three groups of living mammals are the monotremes, the marsupials, and the placentals. Marsupials bear live young that complete their development in a pouch. Monotremes lay eggs. In placental mammals, nutrients, oxygen, carbon dioxide, and wastes are exchanged between embryo and mother through the placenta.
- Similar ecological opportunities on the different continents have produced some striking examples of convergent evolution in mammals.

Vocabulary

monotreme, p. 828
marsupial, p. 829
placenta, p. 829

32–3 Primates and Human Origins

Key Concepts

- In general, primates have binocular vision, a well-developed cerebrum, fingers and toes, and arms that rotate in their joints.
- Primates that evolved from two of the earliest ancestral branches look very little like typical monkeys and are called prosimians. Members of the more familiar primate group that includes monkeys, apes, and humans are called anthropoids.
- Today most paleontologists agree that the hominid fossil record includes at least five genera—*Ardipithecus, Australopithecus, Paranthropus, Kenyanthropus,* and *Homo*—and as many as 16 separate hominid species. This diverse group of fossils covers roughly 4.5 million years.

Vocabulary

binocular vision, p. 834
prosimian, p. 834
anthropoid, p. 835
prehensile, p. 835
hominoid, p. 835
hominid, p. 835
bipedal, p. 835
opposable thumb, p. 835

Thinking Visually

Using information from this chapter, complete the following concept map:

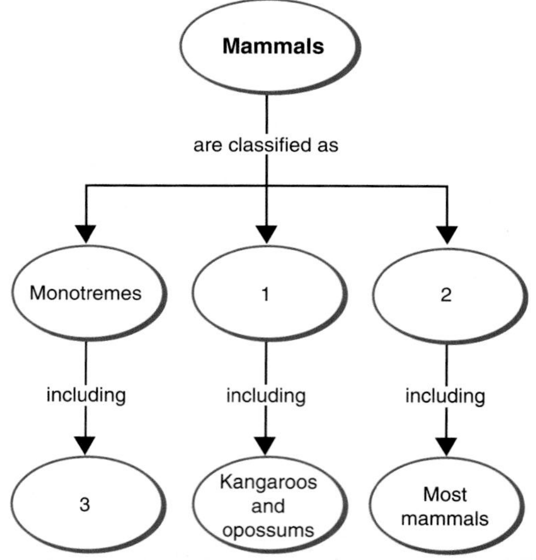

CHAPTER RESOURCES

Print:

- ***Teaching Resources,*** Chapter Vocabulary Review, Graphic Organizer
- ***Chapter Tests: Levels A and B,*** Chapter 32 Test
- ***PH Assessment System,*** Practice Test

Technology:

- ***Computer Test Bank,*** Chapter 32 Test
- ***iText,*** Chapter 32 Assessment

Chapter 32 Assessment

Reviewing Content

Choose the letter that best answers the question or completes the statement.

1. Which structure in female mammals produces milk to nourish young?
   a. kidney
   b. cloaca
   c. mammary gland
   d. placenta

2. The first true mammals appeared during the early
   a. Permian Period.
   b. Cretaceous Period.
   c. Triassic Period.
   d. Jurassic Period.

3. Which of the animals shown below is a mammal?

a. 

c. 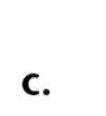 

b. 

d. 

4. In mammals, the powerful muscle that aids in breathing is the
   a. diaphragm.
   b. placenta.
   c. cerebrum.
   d. kidney.

5. The composition and levels of body fluids in mammals are controlled by the
   a. lungs.
   b. kidneys.
   c. intestine.
   d. heart.

6. The reproductive system of a monotreme empties into the
   a. placenta.
   b. testes.
   c. cloaca.
   d. urinary bladder.

7. The pouch in which the young of kangaroos develop is called a
   a. marsupium.
   b. placenta.
   c. diaphragm.
   d. lagomorph.

8. Which of the following are NOT examples of placental mammals?
   a. cetaceans
   b. marsupials
   c. carnivores
   d. primates

9. Primates consist of two groups, anthropoids and
   a. monotremes.
   b. apes.
   c. hominids.
   d. prosimians.

10. How many hominid species exist today?
    a. one
    b. two
    c. nine
    d. twelve

Understanding Concepts

11. Describe three adaptations mammals have to conserve body heat.
12. Describe how the teeth of mammals are adapted for different types of food.
13. Sequence the events that occur during mammalian breathing.
14. What functions do the kidneys of mammals carry out?
15. In general, how do the brains of mammals compare with the brains of other vertebrates? What is the significance of that difference?
16. Describe an example of a mammalian adaptation for movement.
17. Describe how the young of monotremes, marsupials, and placental mammals obtain nourishment.
18. What survival advantage does the placenta confer on mammals?
19. Describe an example of convergent evolution in mammals.
20. What structural characteristic allows for the binocular vision that occurs in primates?
21. Describe how various adaptations make primates successful tree dwellers.
22. List the unique characteristics of the family known as Hominidae. Give an example of a hominid.
23. What are the Laetoli footprints? What is their significance?
24. What was probably the earliest species in the genus *Homo*? What does its species name mean, and why was it given that name?
25. What is the hypothesis known as the out-of-Africa model? What evidence supports this hypothesis?

TIME SAVER HOMEWORK GUIDE

Section:	Questions:
Section 32–1:	1–6, 11–18, 28, 30, 32
Section 32–2:	7, 8, 19–22, 27, 29, 31, 35
Section 32–3:	9, 10, 23–26, 33, 34

Chapter 32 Assessment (continued)

15. Mammals have larger brains than other animals in proportion to their body size. As a result, mammals are capable of complicated behaviors such as learning and social conduct.

16. Sample answers: a flexible backbone; limb bones and muscles that enable mammals to run, walk, burrow, fly, hop, swim, swing, and pounce.

17. The young of all three groups feed on milk. Monotremes lick milk from their mothers' abdomens; marsupials attach to nipples in the mother's marsupium; placental mammals obtain milk by nursing.

18. Compared to young that are hatched from eggs, the young of placental mammals are given a longer period of development during which they receive regular nourishment.

19. Mammals that feed on ants and termites evolved in different groups in different regions. These include the giant anteater, the aardvark, the common echidna, the Chinese pangolin, and the nine-banded armadillo.

20. A flat facial structure allows both eyes to face forward, with overlapping fields of view.

21. Primates have hands, and usually feet, with opposable thumbs. The position of the thumbs enables primates to grasp branches and other objects.

22. Hominids are omnivores that have bipedal locomotion, opposable thumbs, and well-developed cerebrums. Humans are an example.

23. The Laetoli footprints are fossil footprints that were probably made by a species of *Australopithecus* between 8 and 3.6 million years ago. They show that hominids were bipedal millions of years ago.

24. *Homo habilis,* which means "handy man." *H. habilis* was given this name because it apparently made and used tools.

25. The out-of-Africa hypothesis proposes that the first *Homo sapiens* evolved in Africa and then left Africa in one or more waves of migration. The hypothesis is supported by analysis of mitochondrial DNA.

Chapter 32 Assessment

Critical Thinking

26. The first diagram has *A. africanus* as the only descendant of *Australopithecus*, whereas the second diagram has both *A. africanus* and *Homo habilis* as descendants.

27. The embryo of a placental mammal develops in the mother's uterus for a longer period of time than does the embryo of a marsupial. Therefore, a marsupial is born sooner and is less well developed than a placental mammal. A newborn marsupial must develop further in the mother's pouch.

28. Well-developed senses enable mammals to be aware of dangers and to find food. Well-developed brains enable mammals to react much more quickly to dangers. For example, dolphins can detect location of objects by sound, so they can find food even in poor light. Dogs can track prey by scent, so their chance of finding food is increased.

29. Monotremes have two reptile characteristics: they have a cloaca, and they lay eggs that are incubated outside the body.

30. Mammals have hair and produce milk to nourish the young, characteristics that bats share. Birds lay eggs and have feathers and do not nourish their young with milk, so bats are not birds, even though they fly.

31. Mammal A is a chiropteran, or member of the bat order, because it can fly. Mammal B is a rodent such as a rabbit or chipmunk, because of its diet and tooth structure. Mammal C is a cetacean, such as a whale or dolphin, because it is a filter feeder and lives its entire life in water.

32. Advantage: Parents protect developing young and may teach them ways to survive. Disadvantage: If the parents die before the young are mature, the young may also die before mating and reproducing.

33. Humans are omnivores because they eat both plant and animal foods.

Chapter 32 Assessment

Critical Thinking

26. **Interpreting Graphics** The following flowcharts show two alternative lines of descent from *Australopithecus afarensis*. Describe how the two lines of descent differ.

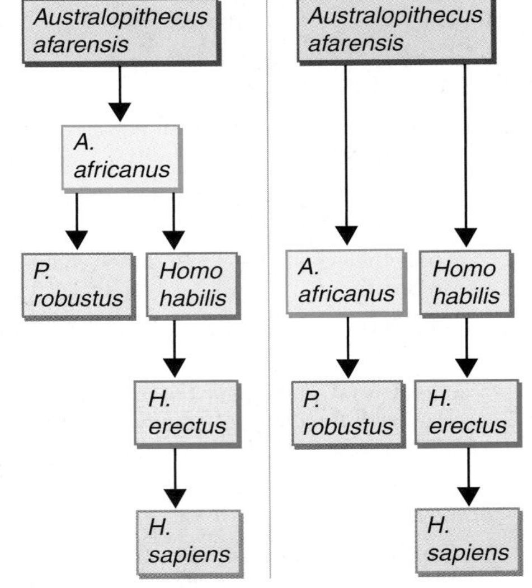

27. **Comparing and Contrasting** Describe the differences between a newborn placental mammal and a newborn marsupial.

28. **Inferring** In what ways have well-developed senses contributed to the success of specific mammals?

29. **Inferring** What evidence suggests that monotremes may have been the first mammals to evolve from reptiles?

30. **Forming Operational Definitions** Write definitions of "mammal" and "bird" that would help you explain why bats are classified as mammals even though they can fly.

31. **Classifying** You are given the following descriptions of three placental mammals: Mammal A can fly, has sharp teeth, and consumes a liquid diet. Mammal B has a single pair of sharp, curved incisor teeth and eats only plant material. Mammal C is a filter feeder, mates and bears its young in water, but comes to the surface to breathe. Place each mammal in its proper order, and explain your decision.

32. **Comparing and Contrasting** Some species of mammals care for their young for many years. How might this adaptation be advantageous compared to patterns shown by other chordates? How might it be disadvantageous?

33. **Drawing Conclusions** Are humans carnivores, herbivores, or omnivores? Give evidence to support your answer.

34. **Inferring** Why is it important for paleontologists to estimate the age of a hominid fossil as well as analyze its structural characteristics?

35. **Making Connections** In Chapter 15, you learned how adaptations contribute to the survival of a species. Name three orders of mammals. Identify two adaptations of each order, and describe the survival value of each adaptation for species in that order.

Performance-Based Assessment

Persuasive Writing Producers of a new television series want to create interesting episodes about the characteristics and diversity of mammals. They ask you whether viewers will enjoy the show more if it focuses on mammals alone or shows mammals along with other chordates. Write a memo giving your opinion. Include at least three specific examples to prove your point.

The National Museum of Natural History houses one of the most important collections of mammals in the world. Visit the Prentice Hall Web site at **www.phschool.com** to find out more about this collection. Then, answer the following questions:

- How many voucher specimens are preserved at the National Museum of Natural History?
- During which two periods in history did the NMNH mammal collection grow the most? Why?
- What are the specialties of the mammal curators who work in the Department of Vertebrate Zoology?

Standardized Test Prep

Test-Taking Tip Take the time to read each question completely on a standardized test, including all of the answer choices. Consider each possible choice before determining which answer is correct.

Directions: Choose the letter that best answers the question or completes the statement.

1. Which of the following is NOT a characteristic of all mammals?
   (A) the ability to nourish young with milk
   (B) giving birth to live young
   (C) having hair
   (D) the ability to breathe air
   (E) the ability to generate body heat internally
2. Humans belong to the order
   (A) Chiroptera.
   (B) Carnivora.
   (C) Sirenia.
   (D) Hominidae.
   (E) Primates.
3. When did the first true mammals appear?
   (A) Cretaceous Period
   (B) Triassic Period
   (C) Cenozoic Era
   (D) Permian Period
   (E) Carboniferous Period
4. Which mammal is an example of a monotreme?
   (A) elephant
   (B) kangaroo
   (C) duckbill platypus
   (D) bat
   (E) armadillo
5. All of the following characteristics belong to primates EXCEPT
   (A) a well-developed cerebrum.
   (B) binocular vision.
   (C) flexible digits.
   (D) arms adapted to swinging and climbing.
   (E) a small brain in proportion to body size.
6. How are living mammals classified into groups?
   (A) method of development
   (B) structure of kidneys
   (C) method of respiration
   (D) method of regulating body temperature
   (E) type of circulatory system
7. Which is NOT an example of a placental mammal?
   (A) whale
   (B) rat
   (C) kangaroo
   (D) bat
   (E) elephant

Questions 8–10

Radioactive substances found in living things decay at a specific rate over time. The rate at which a substance decays is measured by its half-life. A half-life is the amount of time it takes for half a radioactive sample to decay. For example, the half-life of carbon-14 is 5770 years. Use the bar graph to answer the following questions.

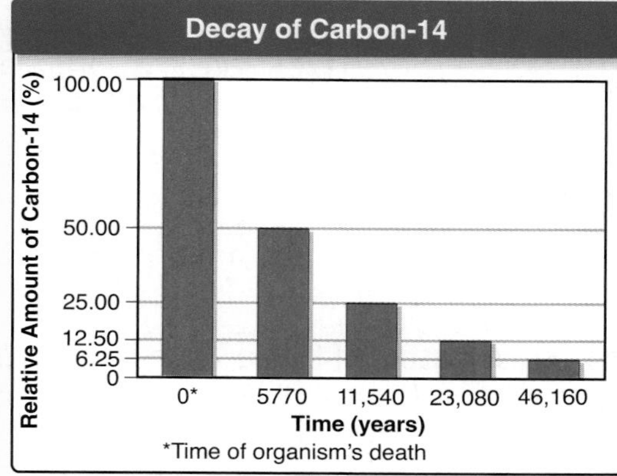

8. How much carbon-14 would remain in an 11,540-year-old fossil?
   (A) 25 percent
   (B) 35 percent
   (C) 50 percent
   (D) 60 percent
   (E) 75 percent
9. A paleontologist determines that a particular fossil has 1/8 of the amount of carbon-14 that was present at the time the organism died. How old is the fossil estimated to be?
   (A) 5770 years
   (B) 11,540 years
   (C) 23,080 years
   (D) 34,620 years
   (E) 46,160 years
10. Scientists cannot accurately detect the amount of carbon-14 in a fossil when more than 1/16 of the carbon-14 has decayed. Which of these fossils could NOT be dated accurately using carbon-14?
    (A) a 2500-year-old fossil
    (B) a 5000-year-old fossil
    (C) a 10,000-year-old fossil
    (D) a 25,000-year-old fossil
    (E) a 75,000-year-old fossil

Standardized Test Prep

1. B	**5.** E	**9.** C
2. E	**6.** A	**10.** E
3. B	**7.** C	
4. C	**8.** A	

(continued from p. 846)

34. By estimating a fossil's age, paleontologists can infer when it was alive relative to other hominid species. Paleontologists can then put fossil species on a time line, which helps them infer descent lines.

35. Sample adaptations: carnivores have sharp teeth that make them very efficient at capturing and eating prey; insectivores have long, narrow snouts and sharp claws that enable them to dig for food.

Performance-Based Assessment

Students should describe key mammal characteristics and examples of mammal diversity as sample topics. Some students may say that mammal diversity is so rich, it's not necessary to show other chordates; others may argue that showing how mammals compare with other chordates helps explain mammal evolution and show distinctive mammalian characteristics.

Take It to the NET

• There are roughly 570,000 voucher specimens, by far the world's largest and nearly twice the size of the next largest mammal collections.

• According to the average yearly growth chart, the two most important times for the USNM mammal collection were (1) the U.S. Biological Survey and Smithsonian Institute's African Expedition from about 1890 to 1930, and (2) the African Mammal Project and Smithsonian Institute's Venezuelan Project around 1970.

• Rodents and Old World Mammals, Bats and New World Mammals, Marine Mammals, and Primates/Squirrels. (Note: these may change with time; teachers should check the Web site for updates.)

For additional information, visit

www.phschool.com

Chapter Planner 33 Comparing Chordates

Section and Section Objectives	Time	Activities and Labs
33–1 Chordate Evolution, pp. 849–853 **33.1.1** ***Identify*** the origins of chordates. **33.1.2** ***Explain*** how the different chordate groups are related. **33.1.3** ***Summarize*** a main trend in the evolution of chordates. **33.1.4** ***Describe*** the diversity of chordates.	**1 period (1/2 block)**	**SE:** ***Inquiry Activity,*** What are some adaptations of vertebrae?, p. 848 **TE:** ***Address Misconceptions,*** p. 851
33–2 Controlling Body Temperature, pp. 854–856 **33.2.1** ***Describe*** how the control of body temperature is an important aspect of vertebrate life. **33.2.2** ***Contrast*** ectotherms and endotherms. **33.2.3** ***Evaluate*** the several hypotheses describing the evolution of temperature control.	**1 period (1/2 block)**	**SE:** ***Analyzing Data,*** Comparing Ectotherms and Endotherms, p. 855
33–3 Form and Function in Chordates, pp. 857–864 **33.3.1** ***Describe*** how the organ systems of the different groups of chordates carry out essential life functions.	**2 periods (1 block)**	**TE:** ***Build Science Skills,*** p. 857 **TE:** ***Demonstration,*** p. 858 **TE:** ***Build Science Skills,*** p. 859 **TE:** ***Demonstration,*** p. 859 **SE:** ***Quick Lab,*** How does water affect nitrogen excretion?, p. 861 **SE:** ***Exploration,*** Comparing Chordate Family Trees, p. 865
Chapter Assessment, pp. 866–869	**1 period (1/2 block)**	

ACTIVITY PLANNER

SE: ***Inquiry Activity,*** p. 848; (15 min.); plastic gloves, chicken neck, dissecting probe, hand lens

TE: ***Address Misconceptions,*** p. 852; (10 min.); blocks or beads that differ only in color

TE: ***Build Science Skills,*** p. 857; (15 min.); ten pictures, models, or skulls of different vertebrates whose teeth are clearly visible

TE: ***Demonstration,*** p. 858; (15 min.); 2 mortar and pestles; cooked piece of meat; green grass, leaves, or twigs

TE: ***Build Science Skills,*** p. 859; (60 min.); balloons, tubing, string, fabric, pipe cleaners, screening

TE: ***Demonstration,*** p. 859; (15 min.); sheet of paper, large piece of fabric or flat bed sheet

SE: ***Quick Lab,*** p. 861; (15 min.); disposable plastic gloves, 2 test tubes, 2 stoppers, test-tube rack, graduated cylinder, balance, closed glass container of ammonia, urea, uric acid, glass-marking pencil

SE: ***Exploration,*** p. 865; (45 min.); scissors, modeling clay, drinking straws, toothpicks, masking tape

PLANNING KEY

Ability Levels	
(B) **Basic**	For students who need additional help
(A) **Average**	For all students
(E) **Enriched**	For students who need to be challenged

Components

SE	Student Edition	**GRSW**	Guided Reading and Study Workbook	**IDM**	Issues and Decision Making
TE	Teacher's Edition	**CT**	Chapter Tests: Levels A and B	**CTB**	Computer Test Bank
LMA	Laboratory Manual A	**PHAS**	PH Assessment System	**PA**	Presentation Assistant Plus
LMB	Laboratory Manual B	**LA**	Lab Assessment with Scoring Guide	**BD**	BioDetectives Videotape
TR	Teaching Resources	**BTM**	BioTechnology Manual	**iT**	iText

Program Resources	*Assessment*	*Media and Technology*
TR: Section Review 33–1 (B) (A) **GRSW:** Section 33–1 (B) (A)	**SE:** 33–1 Section Assessment, p. 853 **TR:** Section Review 33–1	**PA:** 33–1 Interest Grabber, Section Outline, Concept Map, Figure 33–2, Figure 33–4, Figure 33–5 **iT:** Section 33–1
TR: Section Review 33–2 (B) (A) **GRSW:** Section 33–2 (B) (A)	**SE:** 33–2 Section Assessment, p. 856 **TR:** Section Review 33–2	**PA:** 33–2 Interest Grabber, Section Outline, Temperature Control in Vertebrates **iT:** Section 33–2
LMA: Chapter 33 Lab (A) (E) **LMB:** Chapter 33 Lab (B) (A) **TR:** Section Review 33–3 (A) (B) Chapter 33 Exploration (B) (A) (E) **GRSW:** Section 33–3 (A) (B)	**SE:** 33–3 Section Assessment, p. 864 **TR:** Section Review 33–3	**PA:** 33–3 Interest Grabber, Section Outline, Compare/Contrast Matrix, Figure 33–9, Figure 33–10, Figure 33–11, Figure 33–12, Figure 33–13 **iT:** Section 33–3
	SE: Chapter 33 Assessment, pp. 866–869 **TR:** Chapter Vocabulary Review, Graphic Organizer **CT:** Chapter 33 Test **CTB:** Chapter 33 Test **PHAS:** Practice Test	**CTB:** Chapter 33 Test **iT:** Chapter 33 Assessment

PRESSED FOR TIME?

To Preview the Chapter
- Have students read the Key Concepts in each section.
- Assign the Reading Strategies for each section.

To Cover the Chapter Quickly
- Have students read Figure 33–2 in Section 33–1, Body Temperature and Homeostasis in Section 33–2, and all of Section 33–3.
- Assign the Section Review 33–3, questions 5–7, 9, 10, 15–27, 29, 30, 32, and 35 in Chapter 33 Assessment, and questions 3–5, and 7 in Chapter 33 Standardized Test Prep.

To Review the Chapter
- Have students study Figure 33–2 in Section 33–1, and Figure 33–9 and Figures 33–11 through 33–13 in Section 33–3.
- Assign the Section Reviews for 33–1 through 33–3 and the Chapter Vocabulary Review for Chapter 33 in the Teaching Resources.

Chapter 33

ENGAGE/EXPLORE

Inquiry Activity

Objective Students will be able to infer how the structure of vertebrae is related to their function.

Skill Focus Inferring

Materials chicken neck, dissecting probe, hand lens, plastic gloves

Time 15 minutes

Advance Prep Obtain fresh chicken necks from a butcher. Soak chicken necks in bleach, then rinse thoroughly.

Safety Make sure students wash their hands carefully after handling the chicken necks. As they observe the chicken necks, remind them to not to put their hands to their faces to prevent potential infections.

Strategies
- Make sure students try to insert the dissecting probe into the hole for the spinal cord.
- Students can use scissors to cut away the skin from the neck to better view the vertebrae.

Expected Outcome Students should infer that the structure of the vertebrae allows for a wide range of motion, as well as protection for the spinal cord.

Think About It

1. The many bones of the neck allow for a wide range of motion. The opening in the vertebrae houses and protects the spinal cord.
2. The chicken would have a rigid, inflexible body, and its spinal cord would not have any protection.
3. Larger, to support a larger skull and body

Assess Prior Knowledge

Review the characteristics of chordates. Ask: **What is a chordate?** *(An animal that has, for at least some stage of its life, a dorsal, hollow nerve cord; a notochord; pharyngeal pouches; and a muscular tail)* **Are all chordates vertebrates?** *(No; tunicates and lancelets do not have vertebral columns.)* **Which chordates are vertebrates?** *(Fishes, amphibians, reptiles, birds, and mammals)*

Chapter 33 Comparing Chordates

A cat-eyed snake is devouring some leaf frog eggs. Both the snake and the developing frogs are members of the chordate phylum.

Inquiry Activity

What are some adaptations of vertebrae?

Procedure

1. Put on plastic gloves. Use a hand lens to examine a chicken neck.
2. Bend the neck back and forth and from side to side.
3. Insert a dissecting probe into the opening at the top of the neck. What do you observe? **CAUTION:** *Use care with sharp instruments.*

Think About It

1. **Inferring** How is the structure of the chicken's neck related to its function?
2. **Predicting** What would happen if the chicken's neck vertebrae were one bone with no central opening?
3. **Drawing Conclusions** How would you expect the vertebrae to be different in an elephant's neck? Explain your answer.

FACTS AND FIGURES

Why compare chordates?
Comparing the structure and function of various chordates ultimately leads scientists to divide them into groups based on their similarities and differences. As more and more chordate species have been identified, their classification has been changed to reflect the new knowledge. Classification systems have also been affected by the discovery of fossilized chordate species. But what is to be gained scientifically by comparing chordates? First, it increases the knowledge of how things work, for the pure sake of biology. Second, it gives scientists a sense of how organisms, chordates in particular, have evolved over time. This is especially important when paleontologists try to identify fossilized species. Third, it gives scientists an idea about how chordates are related to other animal phyla.

33–1 Chordate Evolution

Ever since the first chordates appeared more than 500 million years ago, they have been evolving. During this continual process, chordates developed an incredible variety of adaptations. Some of these traits—scales or hair, for example—are relatively simple. Others—such as a four-chambered heart or an amniotic egg—are far more complex. All these adaptations were tested and shaped by natural selection.

Chordate Origins

Much of what scientists know about the origins of chordates comes from studying the embryos of living organisms. Such studies suggest that the most ancient chordates were closely related to echinoderms. Do scientists know what these early chordates looked like? Surprisingly, the answer is yes.

The variety of fossilized organisms preserved in the rich Cambrian deposits of Canada's Burgess Shale includes a peculiar organism called *Pikaia* (pih-KAY-uh), shown in **Figure 33–1.** When *Pikaia* was first discovered, it was thought to be a worm. On closer inspection, scientists determined that *Pikaia* had a **notochord**—a flexible, supporting structure that is found only in chordates. *Pikaia* also had paired serial muscles that were arranged in a manner similar to those of nonvertebrate chordates, such as lancelets. Scientists now consider *Pikaia* an early chordate.

To better understand the early evolution of chordates, biologists study a nonvertebrate chordate that is alive today—the tunicate. The tadpolelike larvae of tunicates are the simplest living animals to have a notochord, a dorsal hollow nerve cord, a tail that extends posterior to the anus, and pharyngeal pouches—key features common to all chordates. Today, biologists are studying the genes that control the development of these features.

Guide for Reading

Key Concepts
- How are the different chordate groups related?
- What is a main trend in the evolution of chordates?

Vocabulary
notochord
adaptive radiation

Reading Strategy: Asking Questions Before you read, study the cladogram in **Figure 33–2.** Make a list of questions about the cladogram. As you read, write down the answers to your questions.

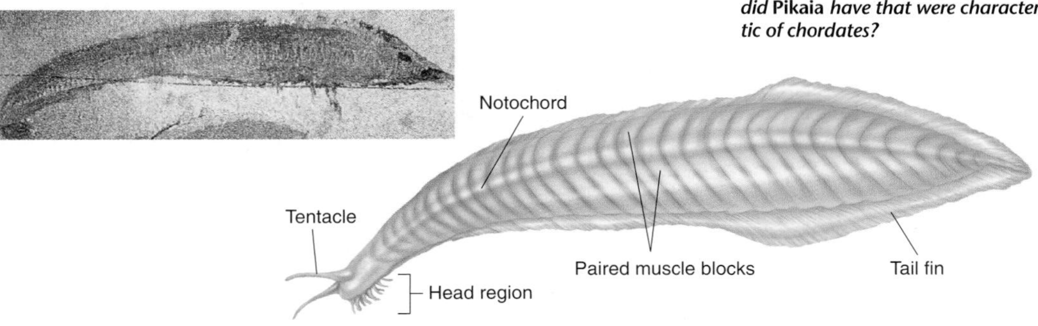

Figure 33–1 This is a reconstruction of *Pikaia,* a soft-bodied animal that lived during the Cambrian Period. **Classifying** ***Which features did* Pikaia *have that were characteristic of chordates?***

TIME SAVER — SECTION RESOURCES

Print:
- ***Teaching Resources,*** Section Review 33–1
- ***Guided Reading and Study Workbook,*** Section 33–1

Technology:
- ***iText,*** Section 33–1

Section 33–1

1 FOCUS

Objectives

33.1.1 ***Identify*** the origins of chordates.
33.1.2 ***Explain*** how the different chordate groups are related.
33.1.3 ***Summarize*** a main trend in the evolution of chordates.
33.1.4 ***Describe*** the diversity of chordates.

Guide for Reading

Vocabulary Preview

Review the meanings of the terms *adaptive radiation* and *convergent evolution.* Encourage students to draw diagrams to illustrate the meanings of these two terms.

Reading Strategy

When students study the cladogram in Figure 33–2, challenge them to consider what the characteristics of the chordate ancestor might be.

2 INSTRUCT

Chordate Origins

Make Connections

Earth Science Ask: **What part of an organism is most commonly fossilized?** *(Hard parts, such as bones, teeth, and shells)* **Why don't soft tissues fossilize?** *(They usually decay before the fossilization process is complete.)* Explain that Canada's Burgess Shale contains many fossilized organisms from the middle Cambrian age, about 530 million years ago. These specimens are well-preserved fossils of soft-bodied organisms. Scientists think a mudslide buried the organisms, and the absence of oxygen in the mud preserved the organisms until the mud hardened to rock, fossilizing them.

Answer to . . .

Figure 33–1 *Notochord and paired muscles*

33–1 (continued)

The Chordate Family Tree

Use Visuals

Figure 33–2 Help students interpret the information illustrated in this cladogram. Be sure they realize that the chordate groups shown are only those that exist today. Extinct groups are not shown. Ask: **Which chordate group is most closely related to birds?** *(Crocodiles; they share a more recent common ancestor.)* **Why are hagfishes considered to be an older group than lungfishes?** *(They evolved earlier.)* Discuss how the appearance of certain adaptations led to the adaptive radiation of different chordate groups. Ask: **What group evolved after the appearance of four limbs?** *(Amphibians)* Point out that the cladogram shows the uncertainty about when endothermy appeared. **What evidence do scientists need to be more certain of its appearance?** *(Finding more evidence of the appearance of endothermy in the fossil record, such as a common ancestor of birds and mammals that was endothermic.)* **Why is this evidence difficult to find?** *(The characteristics of endothermy are generally soft tissue adaptations or behavioral adaptations that do not fossilize well.)* Discuss whether or not endothermy could have evolved separately in two different evolutionary lines.

Meet Diverse Needs

Students who need extra review can develop a time line based on the cladogram in Figure 33–2. In their time lines, have them chart the time in the geologic time scale when each vertebrate group first emerged. Encourage students to also note when vertebrate features, such as jaws and limbs, emerged. **Learning modality: visual**

The Chordate Family Tree

The chordate family tree has its roots in ancestors that vertebrates share with tunicates and lancelets. The cladogram in **Figure 33–2** shows how the different groups of living chordates are related to one another and to their invertebrate ancestors. It also shows the evolution of distinctly vertebrate features, such as jaws and limbs. As you study this cladogram, notice that the fishes—from hagfishes to lungfishes—include six different groups with long and separate evolutionary histories. On the other hand, modern amphibians, reptiles, birds, and mammals share much more recent common ancestors. Where do extinct groups, such as dinosaurs, fit into the chordate phylum? The answer may be found in the fossil record.

CHECKPOINT *How many groups of fishes are alive today?*

Figure 33–2 The phylum Chordata includes both vertebrates and nonvertebrate chordates. All of these subphyla share a common invertebrate ancestor. This cladogram shows the relationship of modern chordate groups to that common ancestor. The different colored lines represent the traditional groupings of these animals, as listed in the key. The red circles indicate some of the important chordate adaptations.

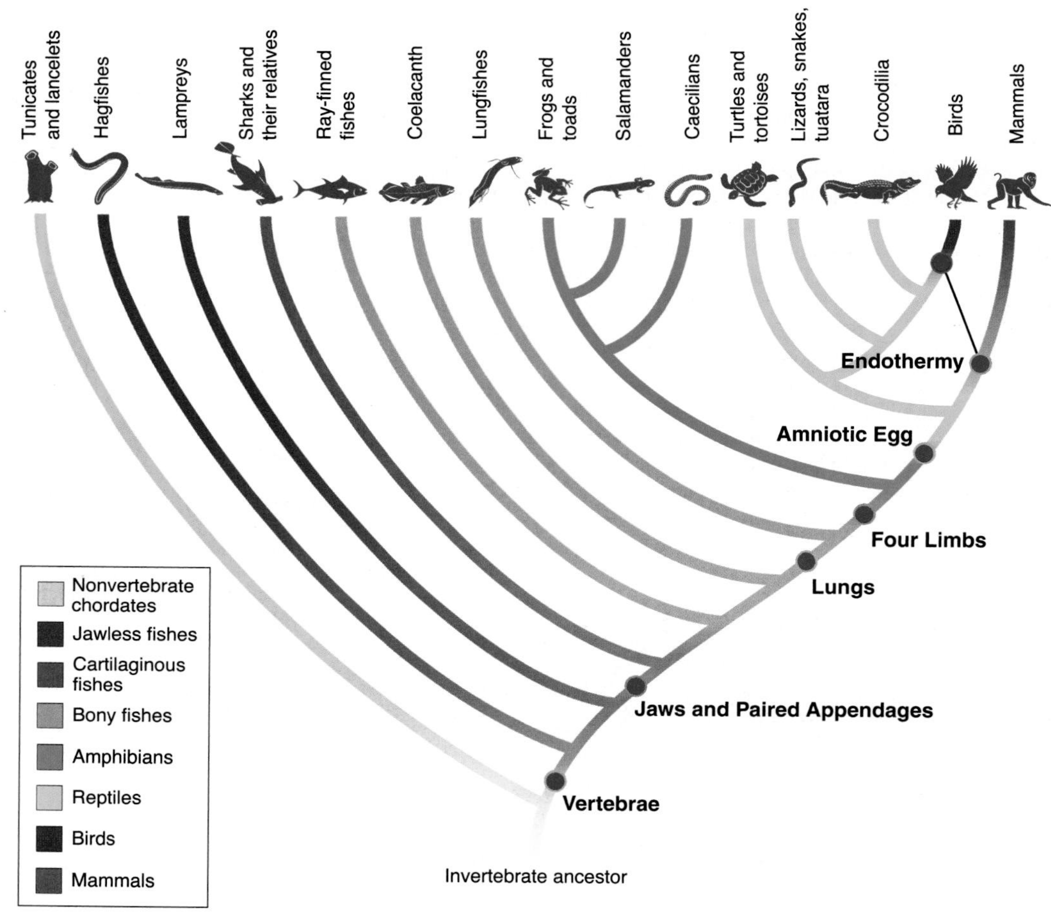

PRESENTATIONS MADE EASY!

The Presentation Assistant Plus contains the Prentice Hall Presentation Pro and the Transparencies, which provide easy-to-follow visual support for every step of this section. If you have a computer presentation station, use Prentice Hall Presentation Pro for Section 33–1, or use the transparencies listed here.

Section 33–1: **Interest Grabber**
Section Outline
Concept Map
Figure 33–2
Figure 33–4
Figure 33–5

Evolutionary Trends in Vertebrates

The hard body structures of many vertebrates have left behind an excellent fossil record. As a result, scientists know a great deal about vertebrates' evolutionary history. In addition, scientists infer evolutionary trends by studying the characteristics of chordates living today.

Adaptive Radiations The number of species within each chordate group has changed over geologic time. Look at the cladogram in **Figure 33–2** again. The red circles in that figure represent the origin of certain adaptive features. For example, one notable event in chordate evolution was the development of jaws. Another event was the development of paired appendages, including pectoral and pelvic fin or limb girdles. Paired appendages allowed chordates, such as the salamander in **Figure 33–3**, to move more efficiently. **Over the course of evolution, the appearance of new adaptations—such as jaws and paired appendages—has launched adaptive radiations in chordate groups.** An **adaptive radiation** is the rapid diversification of species as they adapt to new conditions.

Convergent Evolution Adaptive radiations sometimes produce species that are similar in appearance and behavior, even though they are not closely related. This trend is called convergent evolution. Convergent evolution occurred many times during chordate evolution when unrelated species encountered similar ecological conditions and evolved similar adaptations. For example, convergent evolution has produced flying vertebrates as different as birds and bats.

Chordate Diversity

Living chordates are extremely diverse, as shown in **Figure 33–4** on page 852. Yet, the species of chordates that are alive today are a small fraction of the total number of chordate species that have existed over time. Today, vertebrates make up about 96 percent of all living chordates and account for more than 50,000 species throughout the world. The six living groups of chordates are the nonvertebrate chordates, fishes, amphibians, reptiles, birds, and mammals. Of these, the largest group by far is the fishes.

KEEP CURRENT WITH . . . SCIENCE NEWS®

To find out more about the topics in this chapter, go to: **www.phschool.com**

Figure 33–3 Amphibians were the first chordates to have four limbs. Limbs allowed animals like this modern tiger salamander to crawl on land. **A rapid increase in the number and diversity of land vertebrates followed the evolution of four limbs.**

BIO INSIGHTS — FACTS AND FIGURES

Convergent mammals

There are many examples of convergent evolution between marsupials and placental mammals. The ocelot, a placental mammal, and the quoll, a marsupial, are both catlike predators that hunt at night. Both inhabit forests or grasslands, and both can easily climb trees.

Wombats and woodchucks are both burrowing herbivores. Wombats are marsupials that make their nests in underground burrows. They are primarily nocturnal and feed on grasses, tree bark, and roots. They have continuously growing front teeth, small eyes and ears, stocky bodies, and virtually no tail. Woodchucks are placental mammals that also live in complex underground burrows. Although they are active during the day, they also feed on grasses and have continuously growing front teeth.

SCIENCE NEWS®

Encourage students to visit **www.phschool.com** for the most current information on this topic.

Evolutionary Trends in Vertebrates

Build Science Skills

Using Models Divide the class into two groups. Challenge one group to develop and perform a skit that models adaptive radiation. The other group can develop and perform a skit to model convergent evolution. Work with groups as they develop their skits to make sure their models are correct. Encourage students to use props and even scenery as space and time allows. Each group can perform their skit for the other. Afterwards, discuss how the skits model the evolutionary trends.

Build Science Skills

Applying Concepts Challenge students to identify other examples of convergent evolution in the chordate family tree. One example is aquatic vertebrates. Have students illustrate the vertebrates, showing their similar adaptations. Students should also note the features that separate the vertebrates into different groups.

Chordate Diversity

Address Misconceptions

Some students might confuse diversity with numbers in a population. Demonstrate the difference in meaning with groups of colored blocks or other objects such as beads. The blocks should be similar in every way, except color. Use only blocks of one color to make up the first group. Use many different colored blocks in the second group. The first group should have more blocks than the second group. Discuss with students which group has more diversity and why. *(The second group has more diversity; it has more blocks that are different from each other.)*

Answer to . . .

CHECKPOINT *Six*

33–1 (continued)

Use Visuals

Figure 33–4 Help students interpret the pie chart by asking the following questions. **Which chordate group has the most living species?** *(Fishes)* **Which group has the least?** *(Nonvertebrate chordates)* **Which group of amphibians has the most living species?** *(Frogs and toads)* **Which group of reptiles has the fewest living species?** *(Crocodilians)* **Of the living chordates, what percentage are birds?** *(18%)*

3 ASSESS

Evaluate Understanding

Instruct students to draw a family tree to show the relationships among the different chordate groups. Students should show which chordates share common ancestors and where various vertebrate features, such as limbs, lungs, and jaws, arose.

Reteach

Have students develop a concept map that shows the major trends in chordate evolution. In their concept maps, students should include a definition and an example for each trend.

MAKING CONNECTIONS

Students may note that to live on land, both plants and chordates needed adaptations to conserve water and to reproduce on dry land. Students might mention the following adaptations: chordates—amniotic egg, kidneys, thick skin; plants—vascular tissue, flowers, pollination, seeds.

Use iText to review the key concepts in Section 33–1.

Answer to . . .

Figure 33–4 *96 %*

Figure 33–4 This pie chart shows the diversity of chordates. The area of each slice represents the relative number of living species in each group of chordates. The inner circle shows the six major chordate groups and gives the percentage of species contained in each. The outer circle breaks down each major group and shows the number of known species. **Calculating** ***Of the total number of fish species, what percentage is represented by the ray-finned fishes?***

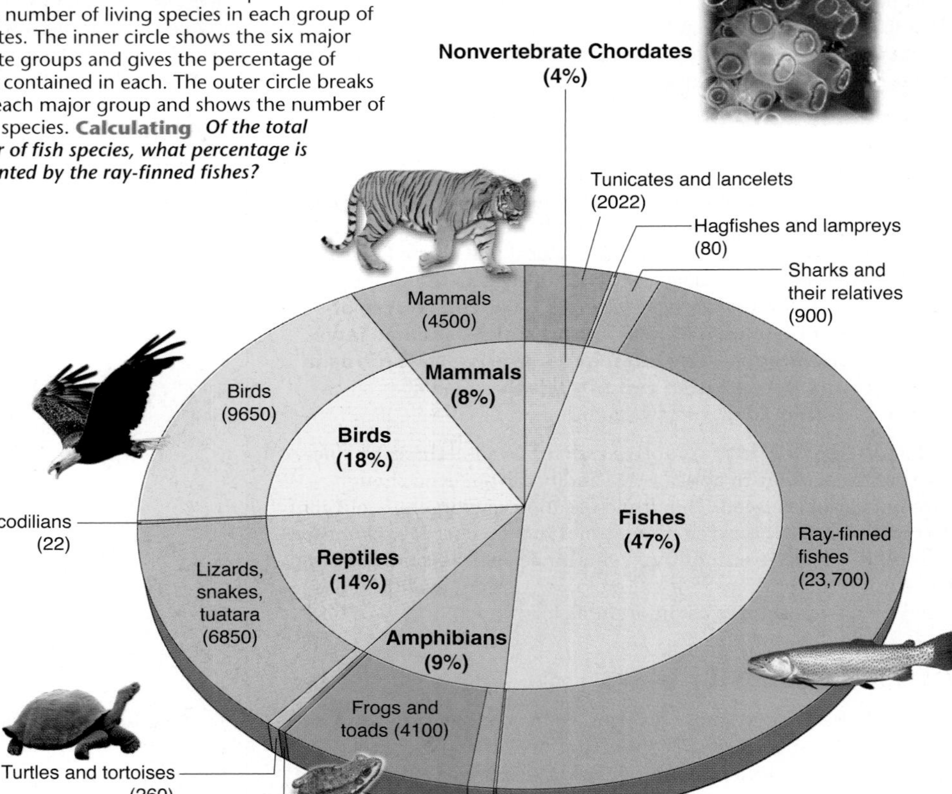

33–1 Section Assessment

1. **Key Concept** To which groups of animals are vertebrates most closely related?
2. **Key Concept** Describe a major trend in chordate evolution.
3. Which characteristic appeared first: four limbs or jaws?
4. What is meant by adaptive radiation?
5. **Critical Thinking Inferring** Both frogs and ducks have webbed feet. However, ducks are more closely related to perching birds than to frogs. Explain the process that has resulted in both frogs and ducks having webbed feet.

iTEXT Assessment Use iText to review the important concepts in Section 33–1.

MAKING CONNECTIONS

Comparing and Contrasting
Recall what you learned about plant evolution in Chapter 22. In what ways are chordate adaptations to life on land similar to plant adaptations to life on land?

33–1 Section Assessment

1. Tunicates and lancelets
2. Accept either: adaptive radiation—the rapid growth in the diversity of a group of organisms; convergent evolution—unrelated animals evolve similar body forms and habits independently
3. Jaws
4. Adaptive radiation is the rapid diversification of species as they adapt to new conditions.
5. The webbed feet are the result of convergent evolution. The adaptation helps both frogs and ducks survive in a similar environment—one that includes water.

Should Marine Mammals Be Kept in Captivity?

December 26. A female beluga whale died today at a marine park in Canada. Two months ago, the park purchased nine beluga whales for a new exhibit. The whales had been caught in Russia's Sea of Okhotsk. Marine mammal experts attributed today's death to the stress of capture, transport, and confinement.

Many types of marine mammals, including dolphins, killer whales, and seals, are kept in captive display for educational, entertainment, and research purposes. Yet, there is strong debate about whether public display of such animals is ethical. Should we prohibit the capture of marine mammals for public display?

The Viewpoints

Pro: Captivity Should Be Allowed

Some people believe that we have an obligation to convey knowledge of the natural world to the public by displaying animals and educating ourselves about them. Information obtained by observing captive animals may be helpful in managing their populations in the wild. Many people argue that the adverse effects of captivity are outweighed by the benefits of conservation, an enhanced human appreciation for animals, and the advancement of scientific knowledge. There is also evidence that human interactions with captive dolphins may help people with disabilities, such as autism.

Con: Captivity Should Be Prohibited

Other people believe that because marine mammals are naturally social, with strong family bonds, they are not suited to capture or confinement. These people are concerned that the process of capture disrupts social groups.

Those opposed to the captivity of marine mammals also argue that confinement places the animals in an unnatural situation—one that is monotonous, limited, and unhealthy. In the wild, whales and dolphins travel long distances and dive much deeper than is possible in a shallow display tank. There is also a concern that human interaction with captive marine mammals increases the risk of transmitting diseases to the animals.

You Decide

1. **Defining the Issue** In your own words, explain the major issues surrounding public display of marine mammals.
2. **Analyzing the Viewpoints** List the options for education, entertainment, and research involving marine mammals. What are the benefits? The costs? Who is affected by each option?
3. **Forming Your Opinion** Should marine mammals be kept in captivity? Are there some instances when captivity is a good solution and other instances when it is not? Explain.
4. **Role-Playing** Suppose you are a wildlife biologist. Your job is to help manage a declining population of wild bottlenose dolphins living off the Florida coast. You need to learn about the lifestyle of this dolphin before you can recommend any solutions. You also want to increase public awareness to help protect the population. Write a proposal on how you will do all this.

BACKGROUND

Should Willy be freed?

The killer whale Keiko is at the heart of the debate about captive marine mammals. Keiko, caught at the age of 2 near Iceland, was sold to an amusement park in Mexico City. When Keiko's poor health and living conditions became public in the 1993 movie *Free Willy,* the public demanded that he be freed. After millions of dollars in fund-raising, Keiko was returned to his native waters in Iceland. However, he is still not free. He lives in a bay closed off with a net. He is not interested in hunting live salmon, preferring to be fed herring. In the summer of 2000, he went on many ocean walks and even interacted with other wild orcas, but he always returned to his enclosure. His caretakers remain committed to helping him return to the wild. However, some think he will never return.

After students have read the feature, invite them to learn more about this issue. Students might wish to interview a zookeeper, a marine biologist, or an animal caregiver at a local marine park. After students have gathered more information, organize a class debate about this issue.

You Decide

1. Possible answers: Observing captive marine mammals will teach us about marine mammals in the wild. Keeping marine mammals captive is cruel to them and inhibits their lifestyle.
2. Possible answers include the following. Captivity: General public is educated about and entertained by marine mammals. It is profitable to the companies owning the marine parks. Research is easier to conduct; however, living conditions are not natural. Captivity prohibited: General public would not be easily entertained and educated unless they go out to sea on a tour boat. Research would be more difficult to conduct, because of the difficult environment and the extreme distances and depths traveled by these mammals. However, the results would be based on observations of animals behaving in their natural environment rather than in captivity. Research would be more costly, but marine mammals would not be adversely affected.
3. Some students will think that captivity should be allowed; others will think it shouldn't be. Still others might think captivity is a good solution sometimes, but not always. In all cases, students must explain the reasoning behind their opinions.
4. Student proposals should include a plan to get the public involved in the plight of the dolphins, as well as a plan for learning about the dolphins' lifestyle.

Section 33–2

1 FOCUS

Objectives

33.2.1 ***Explain*** how the control of body temperature is an important aspect of vertebrate life.

33.2.2 ***Contrast*** ectotherms and endotherms.

33.2.3 ***Evaluate*** hypotheses describing the evolution of temperature control.

Guide for Reading

Vocabulary Preview

Review the terms *endotherm* and *ectotherm* with students. On the board, create a list of what students already know about these terms.

Reading Strategy

As students read the section, encourage them to take notes in a compare/contrast table to help them differentiate between endothermy and ectothermy.

2 INSTRUCT

Body Temperature and Homeostasis

Use Visuals

Figure 33–5 Invite a student volunteer to identify a penguin as an endotherm or ectotherm. (*Endotherm*) Ask: **How is a penguin able to maintain homeostasis in a cold climate?** *(Generates own body heat; feathers act as insulation)* **Why is it important for a penguin to be able to maintain a constant internal temperature?** *(Essential life functions are carried out most efficiently when an animal's internal temperature stays within a certain range.)*

33–2 Controlling Body Temperature

Guide for Reading

Key Concepts
- How is the control of body temperature an important aspect of vertebrate life?
- What is the difference between ectotherms and endotherms?

Vocabulary
ectotherm
endotherm

Reading Strategy: Finding Main Ideas Before you read, skim the section to identify the key-idea sentences about body temperature control. Then, carefully read the section, making a list of supporting details for each main idea.

On a spring morning, after a cold night, a tortoise lies on a rock basking in the sun. Nearby, a snake slides out of its burrow beneath a rotting stump. In a tree overhead, a young robin puffs up its downy feathers. As you walk out of the water after an early swim, your skin gets goose bumps and you shiver. All these activities are examples of the different ways that vertebrates control their body temperature.

Body Temperature and Homeostasis

Recall from Chapter 2 that many of the chemical reactions that are important in metabolism are influenced by temperature. For this reason, essential life functions can be carried out most efficiently when an animal's internal body temperature is within a particular "operating range." For muscles to operate quickly and efficiently, for example, their temperature can neither be too low nor too high. If muscles are too cold, they may contract slowly, making it difficult for the animal to respond quickly to events around it. If an animal gets too hot, on the other hand, its muscles may tire easily and other body systems may not function properly.

Because most chordates are vertebrates, and mechanisms for controlling body temperature are well developed among vertebrates, this section will focus exclusively on that group. **The control of body temperature is important for maintaining homeostasis in vertebrates, particularly in habitats where temperature varies widely with time of day and with season.** Vertebrates, such as the penguins in **Figure 33–5,** have a variety of ways to control their body temperature. All of these ways incorporate three important features: a source of heat for the body, a way to conserve that heat, and a method of eliminating excess heat when necessary. In terms of how they generate and control their body heat, vertebrates can be classified into two basic groups: ectotherms and endotherms.

◀ **Figure 33–5** Birds and other endotherms are able to generate their own body heat. **The internal control of body temperature allows these emperor penguins to live in cold Antarctic climates, where their feathers act as insulation.**

SECTION RESOURCES

Print:
- ***Teaching Resources,*** Section Review 33–2
- ***Guided Reading and Study Workbook,*** Section 33–2

Technology:
- ***iText,*** Section 33–2

Analyzing Data

Comparing Ectotherms and Endotherms

Endotherms, such as humans, depend on their metabolism to maintain high body temperatures. Ectotherms, on the other hand, depend primarily on heat from the environment to regulate their body temperatures. The accompanying graph shows the internal body temperatures maintained by several ectotherms and endotherms at different environmental temperatures.

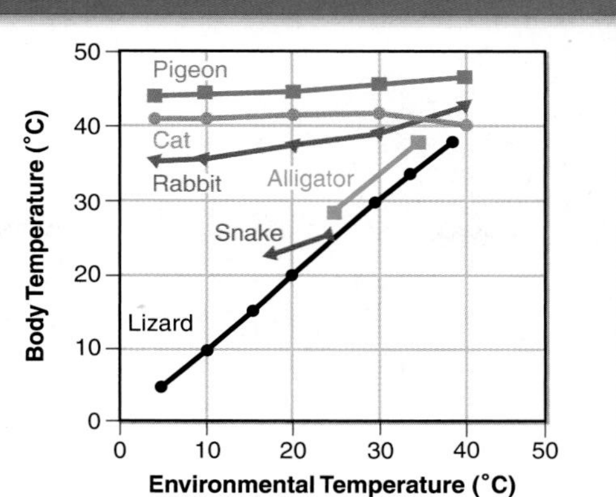

1. **Using Tables and Graphs** Which chordate has the highest body temperature when the environmental temperature is between 0° and 10°C? Which chordate has the lowest body temperature under those same conditions?
2. **Inferring** Which animals shown in the graph are ectotherms? Which are endotherms? Explain your answers.
3. **Predicting** Describe the patterns of activity you would expect for the animals shown in this graph if they lived in your local environment. Would you expect all of the animals to be equally active year-round? If not, why not?

Ectothermy On cool, sunny mornings, lizards often bask in the sun. This doesn't mean that they are lazy! A lizard is an **ectotherm,** which means that its body temperature is mainly determined by the temperature of its environment. **Most reptiles, fishes, and amphibians are ectotherms—animals whose body temperatures are controlled primarily by picking up heat from, or losing heat to, their environment.** Ectotherms often warm up by basking in the sun, and may cool down by seeking shelter in underground burrows.

Ectotherms have relatively low rates of metabolism when they are resting. Thus, their bodies do not generate much heat. When active, an ectotherm's muscles generate heat, just as your muscles do. However, because its body lacks effective insulation, the heat is lost to the environment fairly easily.

Endothermy An **endotherm** is an animal that is able to control its body temperature from within. **Birds and mammals are endotherms, which means they can generate and retain heat inside their bodies.** Endotherms have relatively high metabolic rates that generate a significant amount of heat, even when they are resting. Birds conserve body heat primarily through insulating feathers, such as down. Mammals have body fat and hair for insulation. Mammals can get rid of excess heat by panting, as dogs do, or by sweating, as humans do.

CHECKPOINT *Give an example of an ectotherm and an endotherm.*

Word Origins

Ectothermy and **endothermy** share the same suffix, which is derived from the Greek word *therme*, meaning "heat." The prefix *endo-* is a Greek word meaning "within." Therefore, the word *endotherm* literally means "heat from within." **What do you think the prefix *ecto-* means?**

TIME SAVER — PRESENTATIONS MADE EASY!

The Presentation Assistant Plus contains the Prentice Hall Presentation Pro and the Transparencies, which provide easy-to-follow visual support for every step of this section. If you have a computer presentation station, use Prentice Hall Presentation Pro for Section 33–2, or use the transparencies listed here.

Section 33–2: **Interest Grabber**
Section Outline
Temperature Control in Vertebrates

Analyzing Data

Have student volunteers describe the line on the graph for each of the animals. Elicit descriptions in which they explain the animal's body temperature as a function of environmental temperature. For example, the body temperature of the alligator is about 3°C higher than the environmental temperature.

1. Highest: pigeon; lowest: lizard

2. The lizard, snake, and alligator are ectotherms. Their body temperature fluctuates based on the environmental temperature. The rabbit, cat, and pigeon are endotherms. Their body temperature remains relatively the same as the environmental temperature changes.

3. In areas with cold winters, the ectotherms would not be active during the winter. They would be active during warm months. The endotherms might be active all year, regardless of temperature changes.

Word Origins

Ecto- means "outer," "outside," or "external."

Build Science Skills

Applying Concepts Invite students to identify human behaviors that help to control body temperature. List student responses on the board. When all ideas have been exhausted, have students evaluate the behaviors and classify them as either a method of conserving body heat or a method of eliminating excess heat. Then, ask: **Do people have behaviors to control body temperature that are similar to those used by ectotherms?** *(Yes, behaviors such as sitting in the shade or the sun, swimming on a hot day, or covering up with blankets at night)*

Answer to . . .

CHECKPOINT *Ectotherms: fishes, amphibians, and reptiles; endotherms: birds and mammals*

Comparing Ectotherms and Endotherms

Meet Diverse Needs

Have the class debate the pros and cons of ectothermy. You can either stage an entire class debate or have small groups debate each other. You might also want students to switch sides so that they have the opportunity to argue for both types of temperature control. **Learning modality: verbal**

Evolution of Temperature Control

Build Science Skills

Formulating Hypotheses Challenge students to use their own ideas about evolution and the control of body temperature to devise a hypothesis to explain when endothermy first evolved. Encourage students to refer to additional resources to increase their knowledge. Students should note the evidence on which their hypothesis is based.

3 ASSESS

Evaluate Understanding

Ask students to name the three features of body temperature control. Then, have students give examples of each feature for both endotherms and ectotherms.

Reteach

Students can create a Venn diagram to compare and contrast endothermy and ectothermy.

ALTERNATIVE ASSESSMENT

Ideally, flashcards should show five endotherms and five ectotherms, and a diversity of vertebrates.

Use iText to review the key concepts in Section 33–2.

▲ **Figure 33–6** **Unlike birds and mammals, which can regulate their body temperature from within, lizards and other ectotherms rely on their surroundings to gain or lose body heat.** The venomous gila monster, for example, makes its home in arid regions of the southwestern United States and Mexico, most often in desert and grassland biomes. To cool down, it burrows below the ground.

Comparing Ectotherms and Endotherms

In an absolute sense, neither endothermy nor ectothermy is superior. Each strategy has advantages and disadvantages in different environments. For example, endotherms move around easily during cool nights or in cold weather because they generate and conserve their own body heat. That's how musk ox live in the tundra and killer whales swim through polar seas. But the high metabolic rate that generates that heat requires a lot of fuel. The amount of food needed to keep a single cow alive would be enough to feed ten cow-sized lizards!

In environments where temperatures stay warm and fairly constant most of the time, ectothermy is a more energy-efficient strategy. Ectothermic animals, like the gila monster shown in **Figure 33-6,** need much less food than similarly-sized endotherms. But large ectotherms run into trouble in habitats where temperatures get cold at night or for long periods. It takes a long time for a large animal to warm up in the sun after a cold night. Most large lizards and amphibians live in the tropics and subtropics, and in sunny deserts.

Evolution of Temperature Control

There is little doubt that the first land vertebrates were ectotherms. But there is some doubt as to when endothermy evolved. Although modern reptiles are ectotherms, some biologists hypothesize that dinosaurs were endotherms. Others hypothesize that endothermy evolved a long time after the appearance of the dinosaurs, so that at least some of the dinosaurs were ectotherms. Evidence suggests that endothermy has evolved more than one time—once along the evolutionary line of reptiles that led to birds and once along the evolutionary line of reptiles that led to mammals.

33–2 Section Assessment

1. **Key Concept** What important function does the control of body temperature serve in chordates?
2. **Key Concept** Compare and contrast ectotherms and endotherms.
3. What three features are needed to control an animal's body temperature?
4. How does endothermy affect an animal's need for food?
5. **Critical Thinking Inferring** Why is it unlikely that you would find a giant lizard living in the wild in North Dakota?

iTEXT Assessment Use iText to review the important concepts in Section 33–2.

ALTERNATIVE ASSESSMENT

Using Flashcards Construct a set of 10 flashcards showing a variety of endothermic and ectothermic chordates. Draw an illustration of each animal on one side of the flashcard. On the other side of the flashcard, identify the animal as an endotherm or an ectotherm.

33–2 Section Assessment

1. Helps maintain homeostasis
2. Ectotherms obtain heat from outside the body and have a low metabolic rate. Endotherms can generate heat inside the body and have a high metabolic rate.
3. A source of heat for the body, a way to conserve heat, and a method of eliminating excess heat
4. Endotherms need more food in order to burn enough energy to generate body heat.
5. Winters in North Dakota are too cold for a giant lizard to maintain enough warmth for activity.

33–3 Form and Function in Chordates

The nonvertebrate chordates that are alive today represent a simple and ancient stage in the development of chordate body systems. However, the fact that the organ systems are simple does not mean they are inferior. After all, lancelets and tunicates have survived to the present day, so their body systems are well equipped to perform the essential functions of life.

Among vertebrates, organ systems exhibit a wider range of complexity than those of nonvertebrate chordates. In the hundreds of millions of years since chordates first appeared, the phylum has experienced many adaptive radiations. Each radiation produced a variety of specialized organ systems. The complexity of vertebrate organ systems can be seen in the different ways that vertebrates feed, breathe, respond, move, and reproduce.

Guide for Reading

Key Concept
- How do the organ systems of the different groups of chordates carry out essential life functions?

Vocabulary
alveolus

Reading Strategy: Using Graphic Organizers
As you read, create a table that compares and contrasts the different life functions in nonvertebrate chordates, fishes, amphibians, reptiles, birds, and mammals.

Feeding

Most tunicates, and all lancelets, are filter feeders. These chordates remove small organisms called plankton from the water that passes through their pharynx. A few adult tunicates feed on deposited material from the surface of the sediments on which they dwell.

The skulls and teeth of vertebrates are adapted for feeding on a much wider assortment of foods, ranging from insects to large mammals, and from leaves to fruits and seeds. Some vertebrates—such as baleen whales, flamingoes, and manta rays—are filter feeders with sievelike mouth structures that enable them to strain small crustaceans and fish from the water. The long bill of the hummingbird and the narrow snout of the honey possum are both adaptations that enable them to feed on nectar. Other vertebrates, such as the crocodile in **Figure 33–7**, are adapted to eating meat. Many mammals have sharp canine teeth and incisors that they use to tear and slice their food.

▶ **Figure 33–7** The blunt, broad jaws and numerous peglike teeth of this crocodile help it catch large prey—such as zebra—even in thick vegetation. **Comparing and Contrasting** *How do the mouth structures of a filter-feeding vertebrate differ from those of a carnivore like this reptile?*

TIME SAVER — SECTION RESOURCES

Print:
- ***Laboratory Manual A,*** Chapter 33 Lab
- ***Laboratory Manual B,*** Chapter 33 Lab
- ***Teaching Resources,*** Section Review 33–3, Chapter 33 Exploration
- ***Guided Reading and Study Workbook,*** Section 33–3

Technology:
- ***iText,*** Section 33–3

Section 33–3

1 FOCUS

Objectives

33.3.1 ***Describe*** how the organ systems of the different groups of chordates carry out essential life functions.

Guide for Reading

Vocabulary Preview

Write the words *alveolus* and *alveoli* on the board, then pronounce them for students. Ask: **Which word is singular and which is plural?** *(Singular: alveolus, plural: alveoli)* Explain that many words in science are from Latin. Latin words that end in *-us* are the singular version of the word. The word is made plural by removing *-us* and adding *-i*. Have students make these singular words into plural: *stimulus, nucleus, bronchus, ascus, villus,* and *radius.*

Reading Strategy

Before students read the section, they can set up their table using the main heads in the section as the titles for the columns. They can use the chordate groups as titles for the rows.

2 INSTRUCT

Feeding

Build Science Skills

Inferring Give students at least ten pictures of different vertebrates whose teeth are clearly visible. Challenge students to infer what kinds of foods each vertebrate eats, based on the shape of the teeth, mouth, and skull. Ask: **What would happen to a vertebrate if its food source was unavailable, but other food sources were?** *(The vertebrate might die because its teeth and digestive system are not equipped to use the other food sources.)*

Answers to . . .

Figure 33–7 *Filter feeders have sievelike mouth structures. Carnivores have sharp teeth.*

Use Visuals

Figure 33–8 As students study the digestive systems illustrated, point out that the organs are actually arranged much more compactly in live animals. Ask: **Why are structures such as the gallbladder, liver, and pancreas included as part of the digestive system?** *(These organs secrete enzymes that help to digest food.)* Help students compare and contrast the vertebrate digestive systems by asking questions like the following: **Which vertebrate has the shortest intestine?** *(Shark)* **Is a shark a herbivore or a carnivore?** *(Carnivore)* **How can you tell that a cow is a herbivore?** *(Long intestine)* **What is the purpose of the crop and gizzard in the pigeon?** *(The crop stores food, and the gizzard acts like teeth to break food down.)* **Why do birds need these organs?** *(They don't have teeth.)*

Demonstration

Show students the difficulty of digesting plant material by using a mortar and pestle to grind a piece of cooked meat and some green grass, leaves, or stems. You might also add a little water to make a paste. First, have student volunteers make analogies of your process to the vertebrate digestive system. Then, discuss why it took longer to grind the plant material into a mush (if at all) than it did the meat. Ask: **What characteristic of plant cells makes it more difficult to break them down?** *(Cellulose, which makes up the cell wall, gives a plant support and stability, acting as its "skeleton.")*

Respiration

Meet Diverse Needs

Have student pairs quiz each other on the structures that a particular vertebrate uses for respiration. You can provide flashcards for students to use, or give each student in a pair a different chart of animals. **Learning modality: verbal**

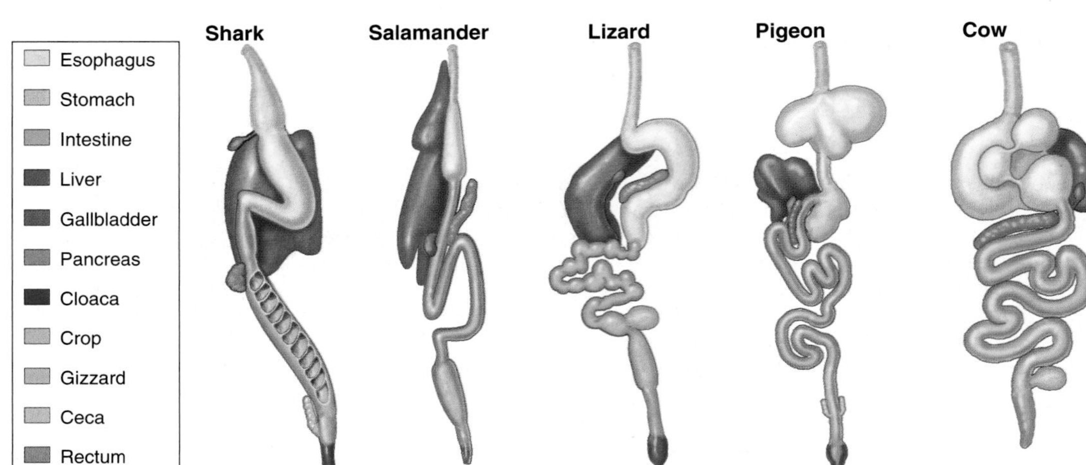

▲ **Figure 33–8** **The digestive systems of vertebrates are adapted for a variety of feeding modes.** As you can see, these systems differ in their degree of complexity.

The digestive systems of vertebrates have organs that are well adapted for different feeding habits. Such variety is shown in **Figure 33–8.** Carnivores such as sharks typically have short digestive tracts that produce fast-acting, meat-digesting enzymes. Herbivores such as cows, on the other hand, often have long intestines that harbor colonies of bacteria. These bacteria are helpful in digesting the tough cellulose fibers in plant tissues.

CHECKPOINT *Compare the digestive tracts of herbivores and carnivores.*

Respiration

Chordates typically have one of two basic structures for respiration, or gas exchange. **As a general rule, aquatic chordates—such as tunicates, fishes, and amphibian larvae—use gills for respiration. Land vertebrates, including adult amphibians, reptiles, birds, and mammals, use lungs.** However, some animals "break the rules." For example, several fishes, such as lungfishes, have both gills and lungs.

Some chordates have respiratory structures in addition to gills and lungs. Many bony fishes, for example, have accessory organs for respiration, such as simple air sacs, that are derived from the gut. All lancelets and some sea snakes respire by the diffusion of oxygen across their body surfaces. (Recall that diffusion is the process by which molecules move from an area of higher concentration to an area of lower concentration.) Many adult amphibians use their moist skins and the linings of their mouths and pharynxes to respire by diffusion.

Gills The diagram in **Figure 33–9** shows how gills function in chordates. As water passes over the gill filaments, oxygen molecules diffuse into blood in the capillaries. At the same time, carbon dioxide diffuses from blood into the water.

PRESENTATIONS MADE EASY!

The Presentation Assistant Plus contains the Prentice Hall Presentation Pro and the Transparencies, which provide easy-to-follow visual support for every step of this section. If you have a computer presentation station, use Prentice Hall Presentation Pro for Section 33–3, or use the transparencies listed here.

Section 33–3:

Interest Grabber
Section Outline
Compare/Contrast Table
Figure 33–9
Figure 33–10
Figure 33–11
Figure 33–12
Figure 33–13

Lungs Although the structure of the lungs varies, the basic process of breathing is the same among land vertebrates. Inhaling brings oxygen-rich air from outside the body through the trachea (TRAY-kee-uh) and into the lungs. The oxygen diffuses into the blood inside the lung capillaries. At the same time, carbon dioxide diffuses out of the capillaries into the air within the lungs. Oxygen-poor air is then exhaled.

As you move from amphibians to mammals, the surface area of the lungs increases. Observe this trend in **Figure 33–10.** The typical amphibian lung is little more than a sac with ridges. Reptilian lungs are often divided into a series of large and small chambers that increase the surface area available for gas exchange. In mammals, the lungs branch extensively, and their entire volume is filled with thousands of bubblelike structures called **alveoli** (al-VEE-uh-ly; singular: alveolus). Alveoli provide an enormous surface area for gas exchange. This lung structure enables mammals to take in the large amounts of oxygen required by their endothermic metabolism. However, because air must move in and out through the same passageways, there is always stale, oxygen-poor air trapped in the lungs of mammals.

In contrast, in the lungs of birds, air flows in only one direction. A system of tubes in a bird's lungs, plus air sacs, enables this one-way air flow. Thus, gas exchange surfaces are constantly in contact with fresh air that contains a lot of oxygen. This supply of oxygen enables birds to fly at high altitudes, where there is less oxygen in the atmosphere than at lower altitudes.

▼ **Figure 33–9** Fishes and many other aquatic chordates use gills for respiration. **Interpreting Graphics** ***Describe the path of water as it flows into and out of the fish.***

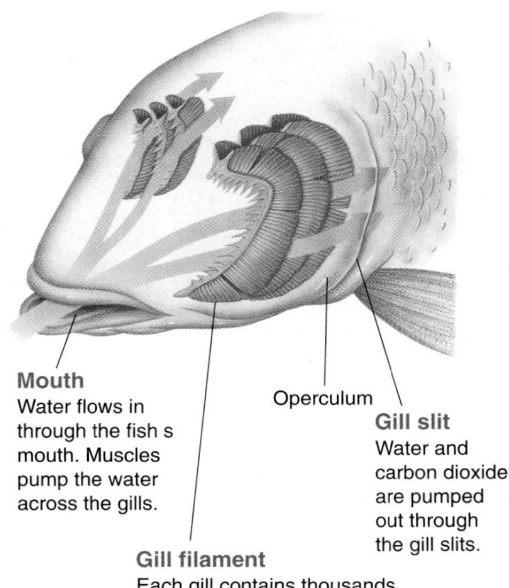

Mouth
Water flows in through the fish s mouth. Muscles pump the water across the gills.
Operculum
Gill slit
Water and carbon dioxide are pumped out through the gill slits.
Gill filament
Each gill contains thousands of filaments that absorb oxygen from the water.

▼ **Figure 33–10** **Unlike most aquatic chordates, land vertebrates—like salamanders, lizards, birds, and primates—use lungs to breathe.** A few aquatic chordates, such as sea turtles and marine mammals, use lungs as well.

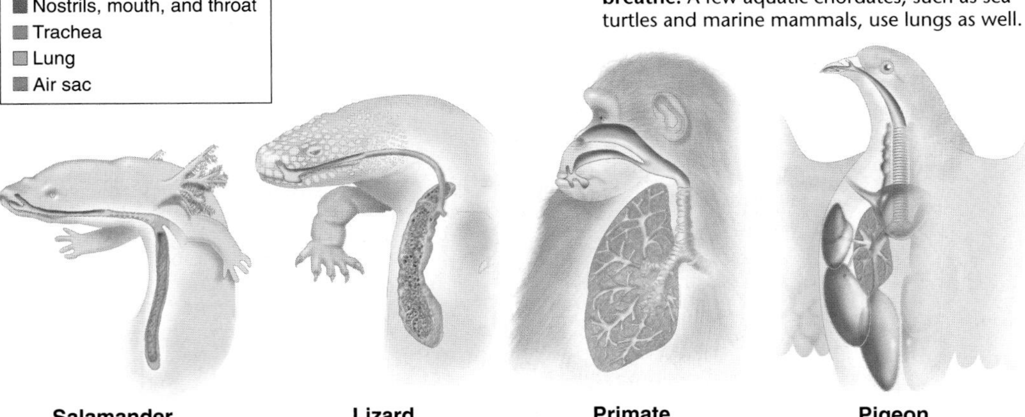

Nostrils, mouth, and throat
Trachea
Lung
Air sac
Salamander
Lizard
Primate
Pigeon

Build Science Skills

Using Models Challenge groups of students to model the respiratory structures (lungs, gills, air sacs, and skin) of one vertebrate group. Students can use materials such as balloons, tubing, string, fabric, pipe cleaners, and screening to construct their models. Each group should present its model to the class, describing how the respiratory structures work to efficiently exchange gases.

Demonstration

Show students how ridges and folds increase surface area by comparing the surface area of a sheet of paper (22 cm by 28 cm) to that of a large piece of fabric that is folded up to be the same size as the paper. Have students calculate the area of the paper. Then, unfold the cloth and measure it. Have students calculate the area of the fabric. Ask: **Which has more surface area?** *(The fabric)* **Why is it advantageous to have folds, ridges, and chambers in the lungs?** *(They increase the surface area so that more gas exchange can occur without taking up more space.)* **Would you expect an endotherm or an ectotherm to have more ridges and chambers in its lungs? Explain.** *(Endotherms require more oxygen to maintain their higher metabolic rate.)*

FACTS AND FIGURES

Complexity of lungs related to oxygen need
Amphibians have small, simple lungs. This is because they are small ectotherms and require less oxygen than endotherms. In addition, amphibians rely on the skin for gas exchange, mainly to remove carbon dioxide from the body. In fact, some amphibians have no lungs at all. However, amphibians are also dependent on the moisture in the environment to dissolve oxygen before it can diffuse through the skin.

In contrast, larger vertebrates that are completely terrestrial require larger lungs with more surface area because the skin is not available for gas exchange. The skin is thicker and covered with scales, feathers, or hair to help prevent water loss. These vertebrates also require more oxygen than amphibians because of their size or because they are endothermic.

Answers to . . .

CHECKPOINT *The digestive tracts of herbivores are longer than those of carnivores and often contain bacteria that aid in digesting cellulose.*

Figure 33–9 *Into mouth, across gills, out gill slit*

Circulation

Build Science Skills

Forming Operational Definitions Challenge students to develop two or three basic rules that relate the structural complexity of the circulatory system to its function in all the chordate groups. Encourage students to think about how the structure of the circulatory system changes from lancelets and tunicates to birds and mammals. Some questions you can ask students to help them get started include: Why don't lancelets have a heart? Why do only endotherms have double-loop systems with two ventricles that are completely divided? Why do terrestrial vertebrates require a double-loop system?

Meet Diverse Needs

At-risk students might need to review the differences between a single-loop and a double-loop circulatory system. Encourage students to draw diagrams of these systems, using Figure 33–11 as a guide. Students can write detailed notes on their diagrams and label the location of the heart, lungs or gills, and body tissues. **Learning modality: visual**

Use Visuals

Figure 33–11 Encourage students to compare and contrast the three circulatory systems by using a finger to trace the movement of blood. Ask: **Why does oxygenated blood and deoxygenated blood mix together in the amphibian heart?** *(The heart has only one ventricle.)* **Why is it more important in mammals and birds that unoxygenated blood and oxygenated blood do not mix?** *(Endothermic mammals and birds have a higher metabolic rate and require more oxygen for cellular respiration. These vertebrates are also more active, which requires more energy, and more oxygen.)*

Circulation

Like modern tunicates and lancelets, the first chordates probably had simple circulatory systems. Tunicates, for example, have short, tubelike hearts with a simple pump. There are no true chambers in the heart. Lancelets have a fairly well-developed circulatory system but no specialized heart.

Single- and Double-Loop Circulation As chordates evolved, more complex organ systems and more efficient channels for internal transport developed. **Figure 33–11** shows the main transport systems in vertebrates. Those that use gills for respiration have a single-loop circulatory system. In this system, blood travels from the heart to the gills, then to the rest of the body, and back to the heart in one circuit.

Vertebrates that use lungs for respiration have a double-loop circulatory system. The first loop carries blood between the heart and lungs. Oxygen-poor blood from the heart is pumped to the lungs, while oxygen-rich blood from the lungs returns to the heart. The second loop carries blood between the heart and the body. Oxygen-rich blood from the heart is pumped to the body, while oxygen-poor blood from the body returns to the heart.

CHECKPOINT *What is a single-loop circulatory system?*

▼ **Figure 33–11** Most vertebrates that use gills for respiration have a single-loop circulatory system that forces blood around the body in one direction. Vertebrates that use lungs have a double-loop system. **The hearts of fishes have two chambers. Amphibians and most reptiles have three-chambered hearts. Crocodilians, birds, and mammals have hearts with four separate chambers.**

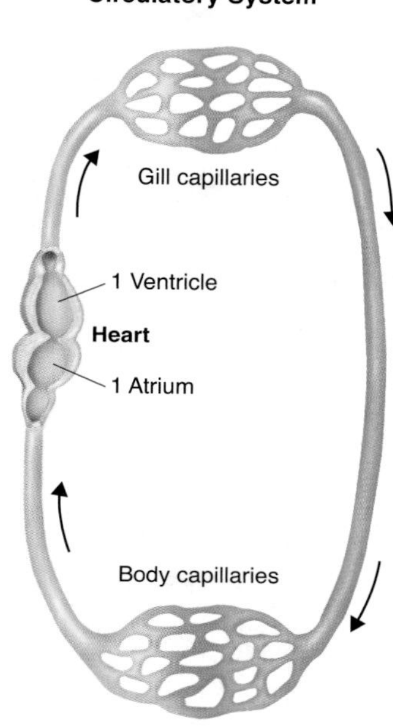

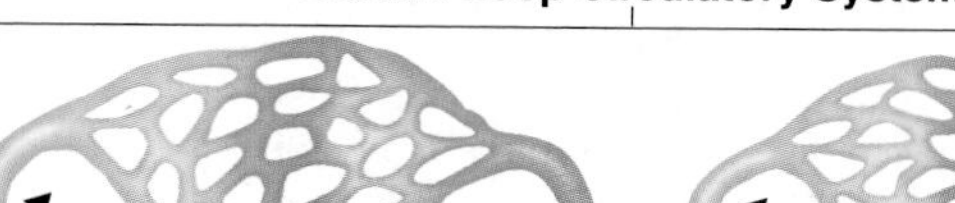

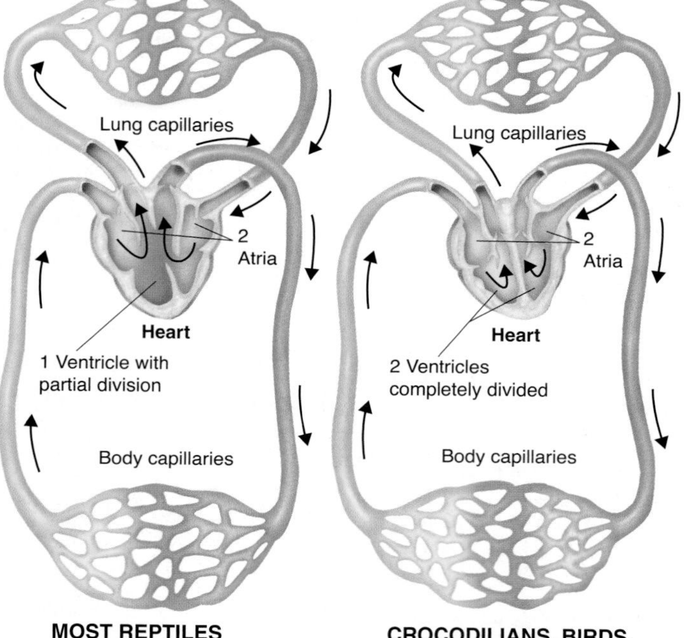

BIO INSIGHTS — FACTS AND FIGURES

Embryonic development echoes evolution The development of the human heart during the growth of a fetus echoes the evolutionary development of the heart from cephalochordates to mammals. In a three-week old human embryo, the heart is similar to the specialized blood vessel that serves as a heart in cephalochordates. Later, the embryo's heart develops into a line of four chambers similar to the sinus venosus, atrium, ventricle, and conus arteriosus in fishes. As in fishes, the sinus venosus of the human embryo serves as the pacemaker. As the human embryo continues to develop, the sinus venosus and conus arteriosus become incorporated into the heart and disappear. Eventually, the partitions that separate the right and left atria and the right and left ventricles grow into place.

Heart Chambers Chordate hearts are adapted to the complexity of internal transport for each of the different groups. **During the course of chordate evolution, the heart developed chambers and partitions that help separate oxygenated and deoxygenated blood traveling in the circulatory system.** In vertebrates that use gills for respiration, such as fishes and larval amphibians, the heart consists of two chambers: an atrium that receives blood from the body, and a ventricle that pumps blood to the gills and then on to the rest of the body.

The hearts of most amphibians have three chambers: two atria and one ventricle. The left atrium receives oxygen-rich blood from the lungs. The right atrium receives oxygen-poor blood from the body. Both atria empty into the ventricle. There is some mixing of oxygen-rich and oxygen-poor blood in the ventricle. However, the internal structure of the ventricle directs the flow of blood so that most oxygen-poor blood goes to the lungs, and most oxygen-rich blood goes to the rest of the body.

Most reptiles have a three-chambered heart. However, unlike amphibians, most reptiles have a partial partition in their ventricle. Because of this partition, there is even less mixing of oxygen-rich and oxygen-poor blood than there is in amphibian hearts.

Birds, mammals, and crocodilians have hearts that are completely partitioned into four chambers. This type of heart is sometimes described as a double pump. One pump moves blood through the lung loop and the other moves blood through the body loop. The two loops of the circulatory system are completely separated. There is no mixing of oxygen-rich and oxygen-poor blood.

Excretion

Excretory systems eliminate nitrogenous wastes from the body. In nonvertebrate chordates and fishes, gills and gill slits play an important role in excretion. However, most vertebrates rely on kidneys—excretory organs composed of small filtering tubes that remove wastes from the blood.

Nitrogenous wastes—formed from the breakdown of proteins—are first produced in the form of ammonia. Ammonia is a highly toxic compound that must quickly be eliminated from the body or changed into a less poisonous form. In tunicates, ammonia leaves the body through the outflow siphons. Other waste byproducts, such as uric acid, are stored within the tunicate's body and released only when the animal dies.

In vertebrates, excretion is carried out mostly by the kidneys. Aquatic amphibians and most fishes also excrete ammonia directly from the gills into the surrounding water through simple diffusion. In mammals, land amphibians, and cartilaginous fishes, ammonia is changed into urea, a less-toxic compound, before it is excreted. In most reptiles and birds, ammonia is changed into uric acid. Besides filtering wastes, vertebrate kidneys help maintain homeostasis by regulating the amounts of water, salt, and other substances dissolved in body fluids.

Quick Lab

How does water affect nitrogen excretion?

Materials 2 test tubes, 2 stoppers, test-tube rack, graduated cylinder, balance, container of ammonia, urea, uric acid, glass-marking pencil

Procedure  

1. Label one test tube "urea" and the other "uric acid." Place 2 grams of uric acid in the test tube labeled "uric acid." Place 2 grams of urea in the test tube labeled "urea."
2. Add 15 mL of water to each test tube. Stopper and shake the test tubes for 3 minutes.
3. Observe each test tube and the ammonia. Record your observations. **CAUTION:** *Do not open the container of ammonia.*

Analyze and Conclude

1. **Observing** Which substance—uric acid or urea—is most soluble? Least soluble?
2. **Inferring** Reptiles excrete nitrogenous wastes in the form of uric acid. How does this adaptation help reptiles survive on land?

BIO INSIGHTS FACTS AND FIGURES

Embryonic excretion and evolution
Uric acid is thought to be an adaptation for the development of the terrestrial egg. Nitrogenous wastes produced by the embryo are safely stored inside the egg as uric acid. Because uric acid is an insoluble paste, it does not require any of the limited supply of water within the egg. Mammalian embryos are not under the same constraints as reptilian and avian embryos. A mammalian mother's body safely removes wastes produced by an embryo because of the exchange of blood through the umbilical cord. For amphibian embryos, urea moves easily across the egg membrane and into the surrounding water.

Excretion

Use Community Resources

Invite a veterinarian to class to discuss comparative anatomy and physiology of vertebrates. Request that he or she bring preserved organs for students to observe. Before the visit, have students prepare questions about vertebrate form and function.

Quick Lab

Objective Students will be able to analyze data to determine how water affects nitrogen excretion.

Skills Focus Inferring

Materials disposable plastic gloves, 2 test tubes, 2 stoppers, test-tube rack, graduated cylinder, balance, container of ammonia, urea, uric acid, glass-marking pencil

Time 15 minutes

Advance Prep Premeasure the uric acid and urea.

Safety Students should wear disposable gloves. Dispose of the gloves after the activity.

Strategies

- Before the lab, discuss why it is important for terrestrial animals to conserve water.
- Diagram on the board the chemical structures of urea (CH_4ON_2), uric acid ($C_5H_4O_3N_4$), and ammonia (NH_3). Explain that polar substances, which have a net charge, attract and separate molecules of water and effectively disperse between the water molecules to become dissolved.

Expected Outcomes Urea is more soluble than uric acid. The solution of urea should be clear, like ammonia.

Analyze and Conclude

1. Urea is most soluble; uric acid is least soluble.

2. To live successfully on land, reptiles must conserve water. Because uric acid crystallizes as a solid precipitate in water, it does not carry water with it when excreted from the body.

Answer to . . .

CHECKPOINT *A single-loop circulatory system is one in which blood travels through only one circuit: from the heart to the gills, then to the rest of the body, and finally back to the heart.*

Response

Meet Diverse Needs

Encourage at-risk students to develop a parts manual for the vertebrate brain and nervous system. Students should use illustrations and words to describe the structure and function of the individual parts of the brain and nervous system. They should also show how the individual parts are assembled to form the nervous system. **Learning modality: logical/ mathematical**

Use Visuals

Figure 33–12 Have students compare and contrast the brain sizes of the different chordate groups. Ask: **How do folds in the cerebrum affect its size?** *(Increase it by increasing the surface area)* Also discuss the importance of the relative sizes of the parts of the brain and their functions in the different vertebrate groups. Ask: **Why do you think the cerebellum is best-developed in birds and mammals?** *(Accept all reasonable answers. One possibility is that these more active endotherms move more quickly than ectotherms and require more brain function to coordinate the greater movement.)*

Address Misconceptions

Students might assume that because human brains are the most highly developed, humans also have the best-developed senses of all animals. Remind students of the superior senses of hearing and smell in dogs and cats. Also point out that fishes, some turtles, and many birds can see colors and patterns much better than humans. Encourage students to find other examples of animals with superior senses or that have senses that humans don't even have, such as the "third eye" in tuataras, electrical sense of some fishes, and lateral lines in fishes.

Response

Compared with invertebrates, most chordates have elaborate systems that allow them to respond to stimuli in their environment. **Nonvertebrate chordates have a relatively simple nervous system with a mass of nerve cells that form a brain. Vertebrates have a more complex brain with distinct regions, each with a different function.**

Nonvertebrate chordates do not have specialized sensory organs. In tunicates, however, sensory cells in and on the siphons and other internal surfaces may help control the amount of water passing through the pharynx. Lancelets—which have a more defined head region—have a small, hollow brain with a pair of eyespots that detect light.

Vertebrates display a high degree of cephalization, or concentration of sense organs and nerve cells at the front of the body. The head contains a well-developed brain, which is situated on the end of the spinal cord. The vertebrate brain is divided into several parts, including the cerebrum, cerebellum, medulla oblongata, optic lobes, and olfactory bulbs. The medulla oblongata controls the functioning of many internal organs. The optic lobes are involved in vision and the olfactory bulbs in the sense of smell.

Figure 33–12 shows how the size and complexity of the cerebrum and cerebellum increase from fishes to mammals. The cerebrum is the "thinking" region of the brain. It receives, interprets, and determines the response to sensory information. The cerebrum is also involved in learning, memory, and conscious thought. In fishes, amphibians, and reptiles, the cerebrum is relatively small. In birds and mammals, especially primates, the cerebrum is greatly enlarged and may contain folds that increase its surface area. The cerebellum, which coordinates movement and controls balance, is also most developed in birds and mammals.

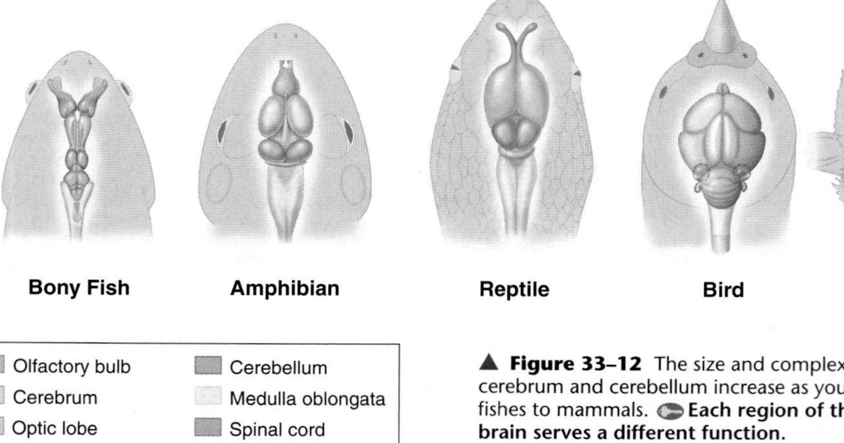

▲ **Figure 33–12** The size and complexity of the cerebrum and cerebellum increase as you move from fishes to mammals. **Each region of the vertebrate brain serves a different function.**

FACTS AND FIGURES

Brainy evolution

The vertebrate brain evolved from a set of three bulges at the anterior end of the spinal cord. These regions—the forebrain, midbrain, and hindbrain—are present during embryonic development. As the brain evolved, three major trends changed these regions. First, brain size increased relative to body size. Birds and mammals have larger brains relative to body size than do fishes, amphibians, and reptiles. Second, the original three regions became divided into subregions that assumed specific control and sensory functions. Third, the cerebrum became more powerful in its ability to process information. The larger cerebrum is directly correlated with the more sophisticated behavior of birds and mammals.

Careers in Biology

Veterinary Technician

Job Description: work in a kennel, veterinary hospital or clinic, zoo, or other setting to provide basic medical care for animals. May specialize in X-ray technology, anesthesiology, or other areas.

Education: a two-year associate or four-year bachelor's degree in Animal Health Technology. Each state has its own licensing requirements.

Skills: patient; enjoy working with animals; a good team member; effective communicator; quick thinker; excellent observer.

Highlights: You help take care of all kinds of animals in different settings. Your work can lead to medical advances that apply to humans.

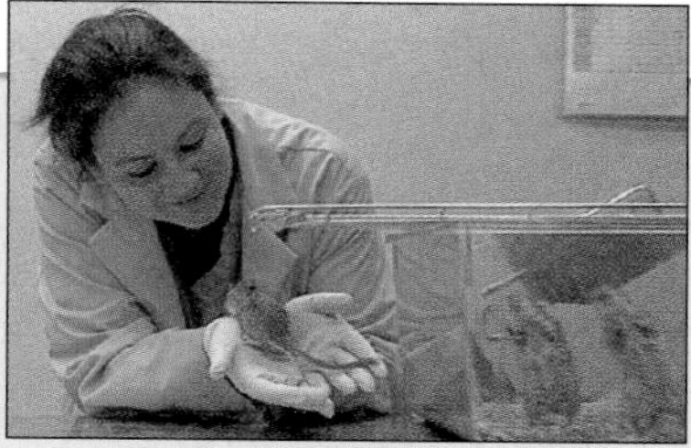

"I like the challenge of veterinary medicine, because the animals cannot tell you what is wrong, or where it hurts. I enjoy having to solve the puzzle," says Verda Davis. "It is also one of the most rewarding feelings to be involved in saving an animal's life."

Take It to the NET

For more career information, visit the Prentice Hall Web site at **www.phschool.com.**

Careers in Biology

- Not all veterinary technicians work in animal hospitals or zoos. Many work in biomedical research facilities, diagnostic labs, and veterinary supply companies.
- Typical duties include administering medications and vaccines, diagnostic laboratory procedures, hospital management, and surgical assistance.
- To prepare for this career, high school students should take college prep courses in science, math, and English.

Take It to the NET

For more information, visit **www.phschool.com**

Movement

Unlike most other chordates, nonvertebrate chordates lack bones. They do, however, have muscles. Lancelets and larval tunicates swim with a fishlike movement of their muscular tails. Some adult tunicates use their siphons to swim by jet propulsion. However, most adult tunicates lose their tails and attach to a hard surface on the ocean floor for life.

The skeletal and muscular systems support a vertebrate's body and make it possible to control movement. Vertebrates are much more mobile than nonvertebrate chordates. With the exception of hagfishes, all vertebrates have an internal skeleton of bone—as shown in **Figure 33–13**—or, in the case of certain fishes, cartilage. The skeleton includes a backbone made up of individual bones called vertebrae. In most vertebrates, tough yet flexible tissues called ligaments connect the vertebrae and allow the backbone to bend without falling apart. Most vertebrates have fin girdles or limb girdles that attach two pairs of appendages to the backbone.

In many fishes and snakes, the main body muscles are arranged in blocks on either side of the backbone. These muscle blocks contract in waves that make the body bend back and forth, generating forward thrust. In many amphibians and reptiles, the limbs stick out sideways from the body in a position resembling a push-up. Most mammals stand with their legs straight under them, whether they walk on two legs or on four. In this position, the legs can support the body weight efficiently.

CHECKPOINT *What three structures support a vertebrate's body and allow it to move?*

▼ **Figure 33–13** Like the skeletons of most vertebrates, this lizard's skeleton has two pairs of appendages. **Muscles and ligaments attach the appendages to the backbone and help control movement.**

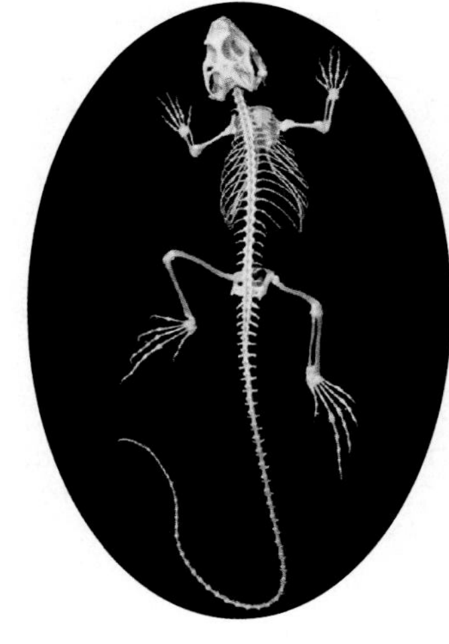

Movement

Make Connections

Physics Diagram on the board the two types of vertebrate stances and draw in the lines of force. The lines of force for the animal's body mass point straight down, due to the force of gravity. The lines of force for the limbs point up at the angle they attach to the "hips." In amphibians with almost horizontal limbs, the lines of force are almost horizontal. In reptiles and mammals with vertical limbs, the lines of force point nearly straight up, almost directly opposite to the lines of force of the mass. Ask: **By looking at these lines of force, which stance can hold more mass?** *(The stance with vertical limbs)* **Why?** *(The limbs push directly upward.)*

FACTS AND FIGURES

Take a stand

As vertebrates adapted to terrestrial life, the position of both pairs of limbs changed. Two trends can be seen in the evolution from amphibians to mammals. First, the position of the limbs relative to the body shifts toward the center. Second, the movement of the vertebral column when the animal runs changes from a side-to-side motion to an up-and-down motion.

The positions of the pectoral and pelvic girdles and the limb bones differ among vertebrates. More primitive vertebrates, such as salamanders, have limbs that stick out from the sides of the body. The limbs of reptiles allow the body to be lifted higher off the ground. In mammals, the limbs are positioned directly beneath the body.

Answer to . . .

CHECKPOINT *Muscles, skeleton, and ligaments*

33–3 (continued)

Reproduction

Build Science Skills

Comparing and Contrasting Have students compare and contrast the amount of energy required, the number of eggs produced, and the chances of the offspring's survival for the three modes of development in vertebrates. Then, discuss the advantages and disadvantages of each mode of development. *(Viviparous development requires the most energy from the parent, fewer eggs are produced, and the chances of the offspring's survival are the highest. Oviparous requires the least amount of energy, more eggs are produced, and the survival of the offspring is lowest. Ovoviviparous development is in between.)*

3 ASSESS

Evaluate Understanding

Play a game of Jeopardy™ in which you give students the answers to questions about the seven organ systems in the six living chordate groups. Students can play as teams or individually to give the questions.

Reteach

Instruct student pairs to take turns interviewing each other about the structures and functions of the various organ systems that perform the seven essential life functions in chordates.

Take It to the NET Students might work collaboratively on this activity. Use the information in the Biology area of the Prentice Hall Web site to check the accuracy of students' charts.

Use iText to review the key concepts in Section 33–3.

Answer to . . .

Figure 33–14 *The mountain lion*

▲ **Figure 33–14** Chordates differ enormously in the way they reproduce and develop. The male band-tailed cardinalfish (left) carries externally fertilized eggs in his mouth while the eggs incubate. Like most birds, the female emperor goose (center) actively defends her nest, which contains eggs that were internally fertilized. After bearing live young, this female mountain lion (right) nurses her cubs with milk. **Applying Concepts** *Which of these animals is viviparous?*

Reproduction

You can see in **Figure 33–14** that chordates show tremendous diversity in the ways they reproduce and develop. Almost all chordates reproduce sexually.

Vertebrate evolution shows a general trend from external to internal fertilization. The eggs of most nonvertebrate chordates are fertilized externally. Many fishes and amphibians also have external fertilization, while the eggs of reptiles, birds, and mammals are fertilized internally.

After fertilization, the development of chordates can be oviparous, ovoviviparous, or viviparous. In oviparous species, which include most fishes and amphibians and all birds, the eggs develop outside the mother's body. In ovoviviparous animals, such as sharks, the eggs develop within the mother's body and the embryos receive nutrients from the yolk in the egg. The young of ovoviviparous species are born alive. The developing embryos of viviparous species—including most mammals—obtain nutrients directly from the mother's body. As with ovoviviparous species, the young of viviparous animals are born alive.

33–3 Section Assessment

1. **Key Concept** List the various organ systems that chordates use to perform essential life functions. How does each system vary between nonvertebrate chordates and vertebrates?
2. Compare and contrast the respiratory systems of a frog, a gorilla, and a sparrow.
3. Describe the parts of the body that most vertebrates use in movement.
4. Explain the difference between oviparous, ovoviviparous, and viviparous modes of development. Give an example of each.
5. **Critical Thinking Applying Concepts** What advantage does a double-loop circulatory system with a three-chambered heart provide that a single-loop system with a two-chambered heart does not?

iTEXT Assessment Use iText to review the important concepts in Section 33–3.

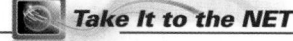

Take It to the NET Read about the chordates that lived during the Permian, Jurassic, Cretaceous, and Eocene Periods. Then, construct a table that shows the time period and environment in which each group of chordates lived. Use the links provided in the Biology area at the Prentice Hall Web site for help in completing this activity: **www.phschool.com**

33–3 Section Assessment

1. Digestive, respiratory, circulatory, excretory, nervous, skeletal, and reproductive. Each organ system becomes more complex.
2. Frog lungs: small sacs with some ridges; gorilla lungs: extensively branched and filled with thousands of alveoli; sparrow: efficient system of tubes and air sacs to ensure that oxygen-poor air is never in the lungs
3. Muscles and ligaments attach the appendages to the fin or limb girdles and help control movement.
4. Oviparous: eggs develop outside body, most fishes, most amphibians, and all reptiles; ovoviviparous: eggs develop internally, birds; viviparous: embryo receives nutrition from mother's body, mammals
5. In a single-loop circulatory system, during one circuit, the ventricle has to pump blood with enough force to travel the entire loop through the body. In a double-loop system, the heart pumps blood through two relatively shorter loops.

Exploration

Comparing Chordate Family Trees

Differences in the amino acid sequence of a protein can indicate how long ago two or more species diverged from a common ancestor. In this investigation, you will compare the family trees of several chordate species based on their anatomy and amino acid sequences.

Problem **How can you use anatomical and molecular evidence to determine the evolutionary relationships among chordates?**

Species	Amino Acid Sequence of Cytochrome C											
Human	GDVEK	GKKIF	IMKCS	QCHTV	EKGGK	HKTGP	NLHGL	FGRKT	GQAPG	YSYTA	ANKNK	GIIWG
Donkey	GDVEK	GKKIF	VQKCA	QCHTV	EKGGK	HKTGP	NLHGL	FGRKT	GQAPG	FSYTD	ANKNK	GITWK
Horse	GDVEK	GKKIF	VQKCA	QCHTV	EKGGK	HKTGP	NLHGL	FGRKT	GQAPG	FTYTD	ANKNK	GITWK
Chicken	GDIED	GKKIF	VQKCS	QCHTV	EKGGK	HKTGP	NLHGL	FGRKT	GQAEG	FSYTD	ANKNK	GITWG
Turkey	GDIEK	GKKIF	VQKCS	QCHTV	EKGGK	HKTGP	NLHGL	FGRKT	GQAEG	FSYTD	ANKNK	GITWG
Rattlesnake	GDVEK	GKKIF	TMKCS	QCHTV	EKGGK	HKTGP	NLHGL	FGRKT	GQAVG	YSYTA	ANKNK	GITWG

G=glycine, A=alanine, V=valine, L=leucine, I=isoleucine, M=methionine, F=phenylalanine, W=tryptophan, P=proline, S=serine, T=threonine, C=cysteine, Y=tyrosine, N=asparagine, Q=glutamine, D=aspartate, E=glutamate, K=lysine, R=arginine, H=histidine

Materials 

- scissors
- toothpicks
- modeling clay
- masking tape
- drinking straws

Skills Using Models, Analyzing Data

Procedure

1. Use your knowledge of chordate anatomy to decide how to arrange humans, donkeys, horses, chickens, turkeys, and rattlesnakes on a cladogram. The more closely two species are related, the shorter you should make the branches that connect them.
2. Cut pieces of soda straws to form the main branches of the family tree. Use balls of modeling clay to connect the straws.
3. Break toothpicks into appropriate lengths to represent branches within the main groups. Use clay to attach the toothpicks to your model.
4. Write the name of each species on a piece of masking tape. Attach these labels to your model to represent the position of each species.
5. Cytochrome c is a protein found in most eukaryotic cells. The table above the Materials list shows the first 60 amino acids that make up this protein in each species listed in step 1.
6. Construct a data table with the headings "Donkey," "Horse," and "Chicken." Count the number of amino acids that differ in the sequences of chicken and horse cytochrome c. Record this number in your data table.
7. Complete your data table by comparing the amino acid sequences of each pair of species.
8. Make a family tree based on differences among species in cytochrome c.

Analyze and Conclude

1. **Comparing and Contrasting** Did your two cladograms agree? Explain your answer.
2. **Using Models** With which species do horses share the most recent ancestor? Explain.
3. **Evaluating** Could a cladogram based on anatomy differ from one based on amino acid sequences? Why or why not?

Go Further

Comparing and Contrasting What advantages would comparing the nucleotide sequences of DNA have over comparing amino acid sequences?

Exploration

Objective Students will be able to model the evolutionary relatedness among chordates by comparing and contrasting anatomical and molecular evidence.

Skills Focus **Using Models, Analyzing Data**

Time 45 minutes

Teaching Tips

- If you are pressed for time, students can draw the cladograms on paper.
- Point out that students need to complete only half of the table, because each pair of species appears twice.

Procedure

4. Most students will show that animals that look similar are closely related.

6. Horse and chicken differ by 6 amino acids.

7. Human-donkey: 6, human-horse: 8, human-chicken: 8, human-turkey: 7, human-rattlesnake: 3, donkey-horse: 1, donkey-chicken: 5, donkey-turkey: 4, donkey-rattlesnake: 7, horse-turkey 5, horse-rattlesnake: 7, chicken-turkey: 1, chicken-rattlesnake: 6, turkey-rattlesnake: 7

Expected Outcomes The anatomical and molecular data do not agree. The greatest anatomical difference is between humans and rattlesnakes. However, the cytochrome C sequences of these two species are very similar. Chickens and turkeys are more closely related to rattlesnakes than to mammals.

Go Further

There can be differences in the DNA sequence that do not cause differences in amino acids. Examining the DNA sequence gives a finer percentage of similarity.

Analyze and Conclude

1. In most cases, cladograms will differ. Molecular data and anatomical data do not always lead to similar conclusions.

2. Donkeys. Horses and donkeys differ by only one amino acid in the sequence of cytochrome c.

3. Yes. Similar anatomical traits may be the result of convergent evolution rather than a close relationship.

Chapter 33 Study Guide

Study Tip

Challenge students to write a set of generalizations that describe how the form and function of the seven organ systems changed over the course of evolution from nonvertebrate chordates to mammals.

Thinking Visually

1. The animal's body
2. Ectotherms
3. Endotherms

Chapter 33 Assessment

Reviewing Content

1. d	5. b	9. b
2. a	6. c	10. b
3. b	7. c	
4. b	8. a	

Understanding Concepts

11. Notochord, dorsal hollow nerve cord, a postanal tail, and pharyngeal pouches
12. Unrelated species from different evolutionary lines evolve similar adaptations when encountering similar ecological conditions.
13. Endotherms do not need to rely on the environment for body heat, but they need to eat a lot of food to fuel a high metabolic rate. Ectotherms depend on the environment for body heat, but they eat relatively little compared to endotherms.
14. Some scientists think that endothermy evolved once along the line of reptiles that led to birds, and once along the line of reptiles that led to mammals. Some think that endothermy evolved long after the appearance of dinosaurs; others think that dinosaurs were endotherms.
15. By removing small organisms from the water that passes through their pharynx
16. As water flows over gill filaments, oxygen diffuses into blood in the capillaries and carbon dioxide leaves the blood.

Chapter 33 Study Guide

33–1 Chordate Evolution

 **Key Concepts**

- The chordate family tree has its roots in ancestors that vertebrates share with tunicates and lancelets.
- Over the course of evolution, the appearance of new adaptations—such as jaws and paired appendages—has launched adaptive radiation in chordate groups.

Vocabulary
notochord, p. 849
adaptive radiation, p. 851

33–2 Controlling Body Temperature

 **Key Concepts**

- The control of body temperature is important for maintaining homeostasis in many vertebrates, particularly in habitats where temperature varies widely with time of day and with season.
- Most fishes, amphibians, and reptiles are ectotherms—organisms that obtain heat from outside their bodies. Birds and mammals are endotherms, which means they can generate heat inside their bodies.

Vocabulary
ectotherm, p. 855
endotherm, p. 855

33–3 Form and Function in Chordates

Key Concepts

- The digestive systems of vertebrates have organs that are well adapted for different feeding habits.
- Aquatic chordates—such as tunicates, fishes, and amphibian larvae—use gills for respiration. Land vertebrates, including adult amphibians, reptiles, birds, and mammals, use lungs.
- During the course of chordate evolution, the heart developed chambers and partitions that help separate the blood traveling in the circulatory system.
- Nonvertebrate chordates have a relatively simple nervous system with a mass of nerve cells that form a brain. Vertebrates have a more complex brain with distinct regions, each with a different function.
- Muscular and skeletal systems support a vertebrate's body and make it possible to control movement.

Vocabulary
alveolus, p. 859

Thinking Visually

Using information from this chapter, fill in the following concept map:

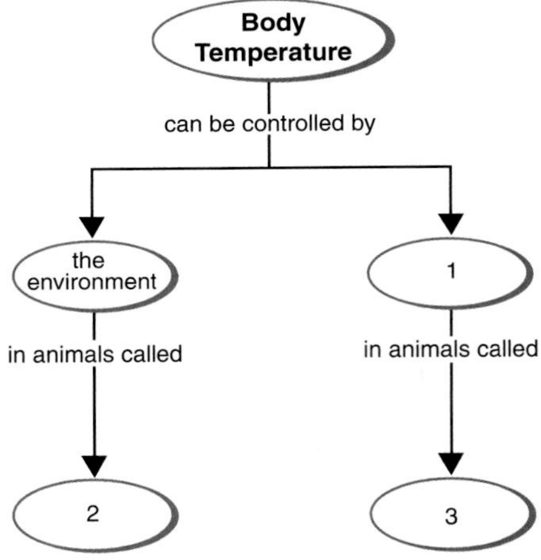

CHAPTER RESOURCES

Print:
- ***Teaching Resources,*** Chapter Vocabulary Review, Graphic Organizer
- ***Chapter Tests: Levels A and B,*** Chapter 33 Test
- ***PH Assessment System,*** Practice Test

Technology:
- ***Computer Test Bank,*** Chapter 15 Test
- ***iText,*** Chapter 15 Assessment

Chapter 33 Assessment

Reviewing Content

Choose the letter that best answers the question or completes the statement.

1. Which characteristic is unique to chordates?
   a. ectothermy
   b. diffusion
   c. response to light
   d. a notochord
2. Which of the following has an amniotic egg?
   a. birds
   b. tunicates
   c. fishes
   d. amphibians
3. Which of the following animals does not belong with the others?

a. b. c. d.

4. The main source of heat in ectotherms is
   a. their high metabolism.
   b. the environment.
   c. their own bodies.
   d. their food.
5. A characteristic of endotherms is that they
   a. control body temperature through behavior.
   b. control body temperature from within.
   c. obtain heat from outside their bodies.
   d. have relatively low rates of metabolism.
6. Aquatic chordates such as tunicates, fishes, and amphibian larvae typically respire using
   a. lungs. c. gills.
   b. skin. d. air sacs.
7. Most chordates that use gills for respiration have a(an)
   a. double-loop circulatory system.
   b. accessory lung.
   c. single-loop circulatory system.
   d. four-chambered heart.
8. An excretory organ composed of small tubes that filter wastes from the blood is the
   a. kidney. c. cloaca.
   b. ureter. d. gill.
9. The "thinking" region of the chordate brain is the
   a. medulla.
   b. cerebrum.
   c. cerebellum.
   d. spinal cord.
10. Most vertebrates have
    a. an inflexible backbone.
    b. a flexible backbone.
    c. a backbone made of cartilage.
    d. no backbone.

Understanding Concepts

11. What characteristics do tunicates have in common with other chordates?
12. What happens during convergent evolution?
13. Explain the advantages and disadvantages of ectothermy and endothermy.
14. Describe what scientists currently infer about the evolution of endothermy.
15. How do vertebrate filter feeders obtain food?
16. Describe how gills function.
17. How does the structure of the alveoli affect the process of gas exchange?
18. Compare single-loop circulation and double-loop circulation.
19. How do the number of heart chambers compare in a frog, a typical reptile, and a bird?
20. How do tunicates eliminate nitrogenous wastes from their bodies?
21. What are the major excretory organs in vertebrates?
22. In what way(s) do vertebrates display a high degree of cephalization?
23. Name the main parts of the vertebrate brain and describe the function of each part.
24. Describe the vertebrate backbone and explain how it enables an animal to move in complex ways.
25. What type of fertilization is characteristic of birds and mammals?

HOMEWORK GUIDE

Section:	Questions:
Section 33–1	1, 2, 8, 11, 12, 28, 34
Section 33–2	3, 4, 13, 14, 31, 33,
Section 33–3	5–7, 9, 10, 15–27, 29, 30, 32, 35

Chapter 33 Assessment (continued)

17. Alveoli provide an enormous surface area for gas exchange.

18. Single-loop circulation is found in vertebrates with gills. Blood travels in one direction, from heart to gills to body to heart. Double-loop circulation is found in vertebrates with lungs. The first loop carries blood between the lungs and the heart. The second loop carries blood between the heart and the body.

19. Frogs have two atria and one ventricle. Most reptiles have two atria and one ventricle with a partial partition. A bird has two atria and two ventricles.

20. In tunicates, ammonia leaves the body through the outflow siphons.

21. Gills, gill slits, and kidneys

22. There is a concentration of sense organs and nerve cells at the front of the body.

23. The cerebrum receives, interprets, and determines the response to sensory information, and is also involved in learning, memory, and conscious thought; the cerebellum coordinates movement and controls balance; the medulla oblongata controls many internal organs; the optic lobes are involved in vision; and the olfactory bulbs are involved in smell.

24. The backbone is made of individual bones called vertebrae. Since the backbone consists of many small bones rather than a single bone, it is flexible and therefore enables complex movements.

25. Internal fertilization is characteristic of birds and mammals.

Critical Thinking

26. Students should give reasons and examples to support their position.

27. a. B **b.** A **c.** C

28. The similarities between fishes and whales are the result of convergent evolution; similar selective pressures result in similar body shape.

29. The legs of mammals, unlike those of amphibians and most reptiles, are positioned directly under the body. This enables them to support the weight of the body more efficiently.

30. Terrestrial animals must conserve water because of the evaporative effects of air.

31. These behaviors help the duck maintain a constant body temperature by conserving body heat (sitting in the sun with wings outspread) or getting rid of excess body heat (sitting in the shade with bill open).

32. Endotherms have four-chambered hearts. Endothermy requires a lot of energy, which is supplied by reactions in cells. These reactions require oxygen. A four-chambered heart, with its complete separation of oxygenated and deoxygenated blood, is an efficient way of delivering oxygen to cells.

33. Sample experiment: fill two identical containers with hot water at the same temperature. Cover one with a piece of fur or a down comforter; leave the other exposed to air. After a time, measure the water temperature in both containers.

34. a. Bony fishes (Amphibians acceptable if student refers to tadpoles.)

b. Reptiles (specifically crocodiles)

c. Tunicates

35. Students should recognize that if the similarities are due to convergent evolution, then the birds descended from different evolutionary lines. They could examine DNA sequences of the birds to determine how close they are.

Performance-Based Assessment

Student models should show the correct circulatory systems and hearts with the correct number of chambers, as shown in Figure 33–11 and discussed on page 860.

Chapter 33 Assessment

Critical Thinking

26. Making Judgments Groups of animals that have evolved more recently are sometimes called "advanced," whereas earlier groups are called "primitive." Do you agree with these descriptions? Use examples from the chordates to explain your position.

27. Interpreting Graphics The diagrams below show three kinds of circulatory systems.
   a. Which diagram illustrates a heart with blood containing carbon dioxide but little oxygen?
   b. Which diagram shows a circulatory system with a four-chambered heart?
   c. Which diagram illustrates a heart that has oxygen-rich and oxygen-poor blood in the same ventricle?

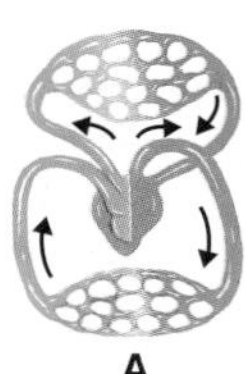
A

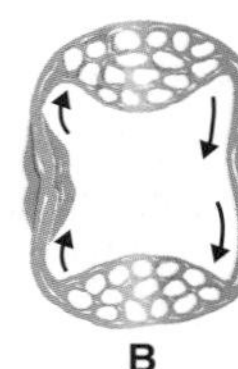
B

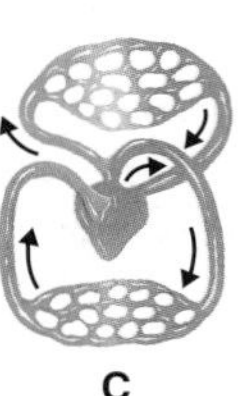
C

28. Comparing and Contrasting Fishes and whales are not closely related, but they share a number of similarities, such as overall body shape and the absence of legs. How can their similarities be explained?

29. Comparing and Contrasting How is the position of the legs of mammals different from those of amphibians and most reptiles? In what way is this characteristic an adaptive advantage?

30. Inferring Of all the nitrogenous wastes eliminated by animals, uric acid requires the least water to excrete. Why is the production of uric acid an advantage to animals that live on land?

31. Formulating Hypotheses On cool days, a student notices that a duck sits on a sunny lawn with its wings outspread. On hot days, she sees the same duck sitting in the shade of a tree with its bill open. How might each of these behaviors help maintain the duck's body temperature?

32. Classifying What is the general relationship between whether an animal is an endotherm and whether it has a four-chambered heart? Relate this to the animal's need for energy.

33. Designing Experiments Design an experiment to determine how fur and feathers affect the ability of animals to retain heat in their bodies.

34. Classifying Read the following descriptions of animals and identify the vertebrate group to which each animal belongs.
   a. Two-chambered heart; single-loop circulatory system; excretes ammonia; vertebral column
   b. Four-chambered heart; feet not directly beneath the body when standing; ectotherm
   c. Muscles but no bones; sensory cells on siphons

35. Making Connections North American hummingbirds and Hawaiian honeycreepers have long, thin bills adapted for drinking nectar from flowers. Recall from Chapter 18 that organisms' DNA can be used to infer evoutionary relationships. How could you determine whether the similarities between these two birds are the result of convergent evolution or adaptive radiation?

Performance-Based Assessment

Making Models Using materials such as modeling clay, wires, or pipe cleaners, construct models of the circulatory systems of a fish, an amphibian, and a mammal. Describe whether each vertebrate has single- or double-loop circulation, and whether or not the blood flowing through the heart is rich in oxygen.

Take It to the NET

An ongoing controversy in the area of paleontology is whether dinosaurs were endotherms or ectotherms. Visit the Prentice Hall Web site at **www.phschool.com** to find out more about this debate. Then, answer the following questions:

- What are three lines of evidence that support the hypothesis that dinosaurs were endotherms?
- What are three lines of evidence that support the hypothesis that dinosaurs were ectotherms?
- What are the main current hypotheses concerning temperature control in dinosaurs? Do you agree with any of them? Explain your answer.

Take It to the NET

• Dinosaur fossils have been found at high latitudes where ectotherms generally don't live. Dinosaurs were ancestors of birds, so dinosaurs must have been endotherms. Dinosaur bone is more similar to mammalian and avian bone than to reptilian bone.

• Some dinosaur bones have lines of arrested growth, which are found only in modern ectotherms. The Mesozoic climate was mild and warm, so dinosaurs didn't need to be endothermic. Fossilized skin impressions show that dinosaurs had scaly skin like modern ectotherms.

• (1) Dinosaurs, like their probable descendants, birds, were endotherms. (2) Dinosaurs were ectotherms and thrived in the warm climate of the Mesozoic era. Students should use the lines of evidence gathered to support their agreement with either hypothesis.

For additional information, visit **www.phschool.com**

Standardized Test Prep

Test-Taking Tip Before you answer questions about a diagram, study the diagram and ask yourself what the diagram is about and what it tells you.

Directions: Choose the letter that best answers the question or completes the statement.

1. Which of the following are features common to all chordates?
   I. A series of connected vertebrae
   II. A notochord
   III. Pharyngeal pouches
   (A) I only
   (B) II only
   (C) I and II
   (D) II and III
   (E) I, II, and III
2. Which of the following helps vertebrates control their body temperature?
   I. A source of heat in the environment
   II. Feathers
   III. Panting
   (A) I only
   (B) II only
   (C) I and II
   (D) II and III
   (E) I, II, and III
3. Which is NOT a characteristic of breathing?
   (A) inhalation of oxygen-rich air into the lungs
   (B) diffusion of oxygen into the blood within the lung capillaries
   (C) diffusion of carbon dioxide out of the blood within the lung capillaries
   (D) exhalation of oxygen-rich air
   (E) passage of air through the trachea
4. In chordates with four-chambered hearts, there is
   (A) a total mixing of oxygen-rich and oxygen-poor blood.
   (B) a partial mixing of oxygen-rich and oxygen-poor blood.
   (C) a partial partition in the ventricle.
   (D) a partial partition in the atrium.
   (E) no mixing of oxygen-rich and oxygen-poor blood.
5. In oviparous species, the eggs
   (A) develop internally.
   (B) obtain nutrients directly from the mother's body.
   (C) obtain nutrients from the external environment.
   (D) develop outside the body.
   (E) develop in the absence of fertilization.

Questions 6–7 Complete each analogy by selecting the correct letter. In analogies, A : B :: C : ___?___ means A is to B as C is to ___?___.

6. Snake : ectotherm :: mouse : ___?___
   (A) chordate
   (B) endotherm
   (C) vertebrate
   (D) convergent evolution
   (E) mesotherm
7. Tunicates : ammonia :: reptiles : ___?___
   (A) urea
   (B) ammonia
   (C) uric acid
   (D) salt
   (E) toxins

Questions 8–10 Refer to the following diagram:

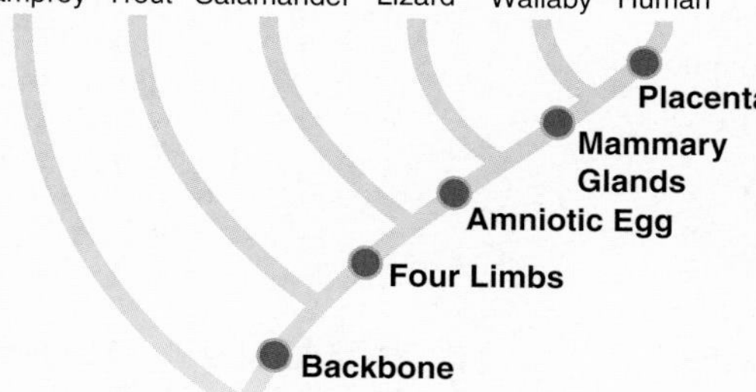

8. Which characteristic is shared by humans, wallabies, and trout?
   (A) placenta
   (B) notochord
   (C) amniotic egg
   (D) four limbs
   (E) mammary glands
9. Which have the closest evolutionary relationship?
   (A) humans and wallabies
   (B) humans and lizards
   (C) humans and lampreys
   (D) humans and salamanders
   (E) humans and trout
10. A valid conclusion from this cladogram is that
   (A) salamanders, trout, and lampreys all have a backbone.
   (B) four limbs appeared in vertebrate evolution before the notochord.
   (C) humans and lampreys share a common ancestor.
   (D) salamanders have amniotic eggs.
   (E) mammary glands appeared in vertebrate evolution after the placenta.

Standardized Test Prep

1. D **2.** E **3.** D **4.** E **5.** D **6.** B **7.** C **8.** B **9.** A **10.** C

Chapter Planner 34 Animal Behavior

Section and Section Objectives	Time	Activities and Labs
34–1 Elements of Behavior, pp. 871–876 **34.1.1** ***Identify*** what produces behavior in animals. **34.1.2** ***Summarize*** how behavior is related to evolution. **34.1.3** ***Explain*** what an innate behavior is. **34.1.4** ***Describe*** the major types of learning. **34.1.5** ***Describe*** behaviors that result from a combination of instinct and learning.	**2 periods (1 block)**	**SE:** ***Inquiry Activity,*** What is learning?, p. 870 **TE:** ***Demonstration,*** p. 872 **TE:** ***Build Science Skills,*** p. 873 **SE:** ***Quick Lab,*** What kind of learning is practice?, p. 875 **SE:** ***Technology & Society,*** Using Remote Sensing to Study Animal Behavior, p. 877
34–2 Patterns of Behavior, pp. 878–882 **34.2.1** ***Explain*** how environmental changes affect animal behavior. **34.2.2** ***Describe*** how courtship and social behavior increase an animal's evolutionary fitness. **34.2.3** ***Identify*** behavioral patterns used to claim and defend territories. **34.2.4** ***Summarize*** how animals communicate.	**2 periods (1 block)**	**SE:** ***Analyzing Data,*** Caring for Eggs, p. 879 **TE:** ***Build Science Skills,*** p. 880 **SE:** ***Design an Experiment,*** Observing Behavior in Fish, p. 883
Chapter Assessment, pp. 884–887	**1 period (1/2 block)**	

ACTIVITY PLANNER

SE: ***Inquiry Activity***, p. 870; (10 min.); coffee cans, rings and ring stands, or wooden blocks can be used as noisemakers

TE: ***Demonstration,*** p. 872; (15 min.); earthworms, mealworms, or sow bugs; shoebox with lid; bright desk lamp

TE: ***Build Science Skills,*** p. 873; (10 min.); crumpled paper ball, safety goggles

SE: ***Quick Lab,*** p. 875; (15 min.); rectangular paper, ruler, scissors, clock with second hand

TE: ***Build Science Skills***, p. 880; (15 min.) ant farm

SE: ***Design an Experiment,*** p. 883; (45 min.); male betta fish, aquarium net, clear plastic box of aquarium water, small mirror, construction paper, colored pencils or markers, transparent tape, popsicle sticks, watch with a second hand

PLANNING KEY

Ability Levels

B **Basic**	For students who need additional help
A **Average**	For all students
E **Enriched**	For students who need to be challenged

Components

SE	Student Edition	**GRSW**	Guided Reading and Study Workbook	**IDM**	Issues and Decision Making
TE	Teacher's Edition	**CT**	Chapter Tests: Levels A and B	**CTB**	Computer Test Bank
LMA	Laboratory Manual A	**PHAS**	PH Assessment System	**PA**	Presentation Assistant Plus
LMB	Laboratory Manual B	**LA**	Lab Assessment with Scoring Guide	**BD**	BioDetectives Videotape
TR	Teaching Resources	**BTM**	BioTechnology Manual	**iT**	iText

Program Resources	Assessment	Media and Technology
LMA: Chapter 34 Lab A E **LMB:** Chapter 34 Lab B A **TR:** Section Review 34–1 B A **GRSW:** Section 34–1 B A	**SE:** 34–1 Section Assessment, p. 876 **TR:** Section Review 34–1	**PA:** 34–1 Interest Grabber, Section Outline, Inheritance of Behavior, Figure 34–5 **iT:** Section 34–1
TR: Section Review 34–2 Chapter 34 Design an Experiment B A E **GRSW:** Section 34–2 **IDM:** 34–1 B A	**SE:** 34–2 Section Assessment, p. 882 **TR:** Section Review 34–2	**PA:** 34–2 Interest Grabber, Section Outline, Concept Map, Figure 34–8 **iT:** Section 34–2
	SE: Chapter 34 Assessment, pp. 884–887 **TR:** Chapter Vocabulary Review, Graphic Organizer **CT:** Chapter 34 Test **CTB:** Chapter 34 Test **PHAS:** Practice Test	**CTB:** Chapter 34 Test **iT:** Chapter 34 Assessment

TIME SAVER

PRESSED FOR TIME?

To Preview the Chapter
- Instruct students to read the Key Concepts and Vocabulary terms in each section.
- Assign the Reading Strategies for each section.

To Cover the Chapter Quickly
- Have students read all of Section 34–1 and only the captions for Figures 34–8, 34–9, 34–10, and 34–12 in Section 34–2.
- Assign the Section 34–1 Review questions and questions 1–6, 11–15, and 21–24 in Chapter 34 Assessment and questions 1–10 in the Standardized Test Prep.

To Review the Chapter
- Review the concept map in the Chapter 34 Study Guide.
- Assign Section Review 34–1 in the Guided Reading and Study Workbook.

Chapter 34

ENGAGE/EXPLORE

Inquiry Activity

Objective Students will be able to explain how learning occurs in response to a stimulus.

Skill Focus Formulating Hypotheses

Materials coffee cans, rings and ring stands, or wooden blocks can be used as noisemakers

Time 10 minutes

Advance Prep Write or select a paragraph in which the word *and* appears often and the word *an* appears at least once near the end of the paragraph.

Strategies
- Behavior during this activity may be more manageable at the end of the class period than at the beginning.
- As you read the paragraph aloud, strike the table or make a gesture such as sweeping your arm, each time you read the word *and.* Also do this when you read the word *an* near the end of the paragraph.

Expected Outcomes Students will observe that many will also respond to the word *an* when it is paired with the same gesture that accompanies the word *and.*

Think About It
1. Some students will sound their noisemakers in response to the word *an*. Some may not respond to some of the *and*s at the beginning of the paragraph.
2. Students learned that the teacher made a gesture or struck the table while reading the word *and*. Some students also sounded their noisemakers to this gesture when it was paired with the word *an*.

Discrepant Event

Show students a picture of ducklings or goslings following a person. (You might find pictures of Konrad Lorenz, who studied imprinting in geese, or use Figure 34–7 on page 876.) Ask: **Why are these birds following a human?** *(Accept reasonable answers. The birds have imprinted on the human.)* Discuss how this behavior might affect how these birds are able to survive in their environment.

Chapter 34 Animal Behavior

Two elk bulls lock antlers in a battle for access to a female elk.

Inquiry Activity

What is learning?

Procedure
1. Your teacher will give you a noisemaker and read a paragraph out loud. Each time your teacher reads the word "and," sound your noisemaker once. Record a mark on a piece of paper each time you sound your noisemaker.
2. Observe when other students are sounding their noisemakers.
3. Compare the number of times that you and other students sounded the noisemakers.

Think About It
1. **Observing** Did all students sound their noisemakers the same number of times? Explain any differences.
2. **Drawing Conclusions** What did you and your classmates learn as you performed the activity? How do you think this learning affected the number of times students sounded their noisemakers?

FACTS AND FIGURES

Animal behavior under analysis
People have always observed how animals behave. In early times, these observations simply allowed people to survive. Only recently have scientists begun to systematically study animal behavior. Scientists approach this systematic study in different ways. Some scientists directly analyze the function of the brain and nerves. These neurophysiologists might stimulate neurons with electrodes and observe the response. Comparative psychologists concentrate on establishing the laws of animal behavior based on observing how animals react to specific stimuli. Teaching a rat to move through a maze is one experiment they might conduct. Ethologists observe the behavior of animals in their natural environments. They are interested in the biological significance of behavior patterns and how these behaviors might have evolved.

34–1 Elements of Behavior

Do you wash your vegetables before you eat them? If so, you have something in common with a troop of Japanese macaque (muh-KAHK) monkeys that live on the Pacific island of Koshima. Many years ago, biologists in Koshima began leaving sweet potatoes on a sandy beach to entice the resident monkeys into the open. The monkeys ate their potatoes with sand still stuck to them. One day, a young female member of the troop dunked her potato into a nearby pool and scrubbed the sand off it with her hand. The young monkey, apparently preferring the taste of a washed potato, repeated this technique each day. Soon, another monkey in the troop started to imitate her. Months later, her mother began to copy her, too. Eventually, all troop members came to wash their potatoes in the pool. To this day, the descendants of the monkeys on the island of Koshima wash their sweet potatoes before eating them.

Guide for Reading

Key Concepts
- What produces behavior in animals?
- What is an innate behavior?
- What are the major types of learning?

Vocabulary
behavior
stimulus
response
innate behavior
learning
habituation
classical conditioning
operant conditioning
insight learning
imprinting

Reading Strategy: Using Prior Knowledge Before you read, write a definition of behavior based on what you already know. After reading this section, use what you have learned to revise your definition and give examples to support it.

Stimulus and Response

The macaque monkey in **Figure 34–1** is exhibiting a learned behavior. Biologists define **behavior** as the way an organism reacts to changes in its internal condition or external environment. A behavior can be simple, such as turning your head in the direction of a noise, or complex, such as washing food. Usually, behaviors are performed when an animal reacts to a stimulus. A **stimulus** (plural: stimuli) is any kind of signal that carries information and can be detected. If you are hungry, your body is providing you with an internal stimulus that might prompt you to eat. The sound of your phone ringing on a Friday night is an external stimulus that might result in your running to answer it!

A single, specific reaction to a stimulus—such as waking up when you hear an alarm—is called a **response.** A behavior may consist of more than one response. For example, a tiger shark might respond to the movements of a potential prey by swimming toward the stimulus, attacking the source of the movement, and swallowing the prey. What stimuli are you responding to right now?

▶ **Figure 34–1** On the island of Koshima, Japanese macaques like this one rinse their sweet potatoes in water. **Inferring** *How did this monkey acquire this behavior?*

SECTION RESOURCES

Print:
- ***Laboratory Manual A,*** Chapter 34 Lab
- ***Laboratory Manual B,*** Chapter 34 Lab
- ***Teaching Resources,*** Section Review 34–1
- ***Guided Reading and Study Workbook,*** Section 34–1

Technology:
- ***iText,*** Section 34–1

Section 34–1

1 FOCUS

Objectives

34.1.1 ***Identify*** what produces behavior in animals.
34.1.2 ***Summarize*** how behavior is related to evolution.
34.1.3 ***Explain*** what an innate behavior is.
34.1.4 ***Describe*** the major types of learning.
34.1.5 ***Describe*** behaviors that result from a combination of instinct and learning.

Guide for Reading

Vocabulary Preview

Read aloud the vocabulary words to students. Then, instruct students to copy the words from their textbook and divide them into syllables. *(be•hav•ior, stim•u•lus, re•sponse, in•nate, learn•ing, ha•bit•u•a•tion, clas•si•cal con•di•tion•ing, op•er•ant, in•sight, im•print•ing)*

Reading Strategy

As they read, students might draw concept maps that show the relationships among the vocabulary words. For example, four types of learning are habituation, classical conditioning, operant conditioning, and insight learning.

2 INSTRUCT

Stimulus and Response

Build Science Skills

Observing Instruct students to observe a group of people or animals for about an hour. As students observe their behaviors, they should record the stimuli and the responses that define the behaviors. Invite students to share their observations with the class.

Answer to . . .

Figure 34–1 *By imitating the behavior of other monkeys*

34–1 (continued)

Demonstration

Demonstrate how simple animals, such as earthworms, mealworms, or sow bugs, respond to light. Place the animals in the center of a shoebox or dissecting tray, and cover half of the box or tray. Shine a bright light over the uncovered half. The animals should move away from the light. Ask: **What is the stimulus?** *(Light)* **What is the response?** *(Movement away from the light)* **What body systems were involved in this response?** *(Nervous system and muscles)* **How do you think this response helps the animal to survive?** *(Accept all responses. These animals live in dark environments. Therefore, moving away from light moves them into an environment in which they have the best chance to survive.)*

Meet Diverse Needs

Pair at-risk students with other students and instruct these pairs to devise a flowchart to show how an animal responds to a particular stimulus. You can assign a specific animal and stimulus or allow pairs to chose their own. Students should include in their flowcharts the appropriate sense organs, the nervous system, the muscles, and any other body system that is involved in the response. **Learning modality: visual**

Behavior and Evolution

Use Visuals

Figure 34–3 Discuss how the circular pattern on the wings of the *Automeris* moth helps to protect it from predators. *(The circles look like owl eyes and scare off predators.)* Ask: **How did the wing-flipping behavior evolve in these moths?** *(Moths that did not lift their wings did not scare off predators and had a greater chance of being eaten; they did not reproduce. Those that lifted their wings had a greater chance of scaring away predators and were able to reproduce. They passed on the genes that influenced this behavior to their offspring.)*

▲ **Figure 34–2 Behavior is produced by the interaction of body systems.** This frog detected a noise with its ears and is now using its brain and muscles to leap out of the water.

Types of Stimuli Animals respond to many types of stimuli, such as light, sound, odors, and heat. However, not every animal can detect all of these stimuli. Humans perceive the world through many senses—including sight, smell, touch, taste, and hearing. Other animals have different senses and may, therefore, respond to stimuli that you are not equipped to sense. The Mexican bulldog bat, for instance, uses high-pitched sounds, which humans cannot hear, to detect the ripples made by a fish breaking the surface of a lake. Some birds can detect Earth's magnetic field and use it to navigate over complex terrain.

How Animals Respond Because of the differences in animals' sensory abilities, responses can vary greatly. **When an animal responds to a stimulus, body systems—including the sense organs, nervous system, and muscles—interact to produce the resultant behavior.** Once an animal's senses have detected a stimulus, that information is passed along nerve cells to the brain. The brain and other parts of the nervous system process the information and direct the body's response. Animals with very simple nervous systems are capable of only very simple behaviors, such as moving toward a stimulus or away from it. For example, an earthworm will move away from bright light. Animals with more complex nervous systems, such as the frog in **Figure 34–2**, are better equipped to respond with more complicated and precise behaviors.

Behavior and Evolution

Animal behavior is as important to survival and reproduction as any physical characteristic, such as teeth or claws. Recall that physical traits develop according to a specific set of genetic instructions. Many behaviors are also influenced by genes. Therefore, some behaviors can be inherited by an animal's offspring. Behaviors, like physical characteristics, may evolve under the influence of natural selection. A behavior that is directed by genes may help an individual to survive and reproduce. For example, the genes that code for behavior of the moth in **Figure 34–3** may help the moth escape predators. Organisms with an adaptive behavior will survive and reproduce better than organisms that lack the behavior. After natural selection has operated for many generations, most individuals in the population will exhibit the adaptive behavior.

Figure 34–3 Moths of the genus *Automeris* normally rest with their front wings over their hind wings (left). If disturbed, the moth will lift its front wings and hold them up to expose a striking circular pattern on its hind wings (right). As one scientist has suggested, this behavior may scare off predators when they mistake the moth's hind-wing pattern for the eyes of predatory owls. **Inferring** ***If the scientist's hypothesis is correct, how might you explain the evolution of wing-lifting behavior in this moth?***

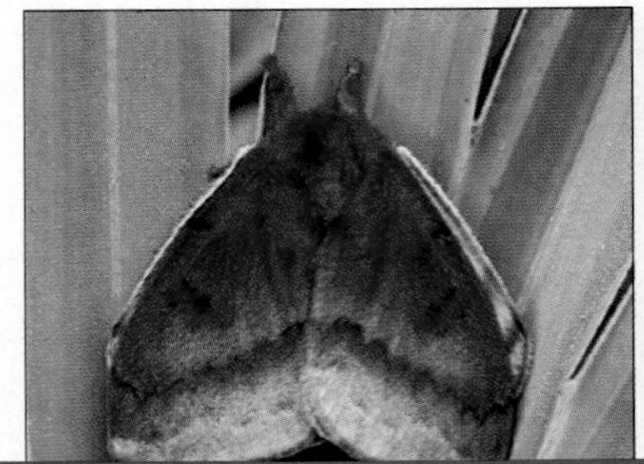

TIME SAVER — PRESENTATIONS MADE EASY!

The Presentation Assistant Plus contains the Prentice Hall Presentation Pro and the Transparencies, which provide easy-to-follow visual support for every step of this section. If you have a computer presentation station, use Prentice Hall Presentation Pro for Section 34–1, or use the transparencies listed here.

Section 8–1: **Interest Grabber**
Section Outline
Inheritance of Behavior
Figure 34–5

Innate Behavior

Why do newly hatched birds beg for food within moments after hatching? How do spiders know how to build their first web? These animals are exhibiting an **innate behavior,** also called an instinct, or inborn behavior. **Innate behaviors appear in fully functional form the first time they are performed, even though the animal may have had no previous experience with the stimuli to which it responds.** One of the simplest innate behaviors is the suckling of a newborn mammal. Other innate behaviors, such as the weaving of a spider web like the one in **Figure 34–4**, or the building of hanging nests by weaver birds, can be quite complex. All innate behaviors depend on internal mechanisms that develop as a result of complex interactions between an animal's genes and its environment. Biologists do not yet fully understand just how these kinds of interactions occur.

CHECKPOINT *What is innate behavior?*

▲ **Figure 34–4 Innate behaviors appear in fully functional form the first time they are performed.** Because web building is an innate behavior, a spider weaves a web correctly the first time it performs the behavior.

Learned Behavior

Animals often live in unpredictable environments, so their behavior must be flexible enough to deal with uncertainty and change. Many animals can alter their behavior as a result of experience. Such changes are called **learning.** Acquired behavior is another name for learning, because these behaviors develop over time.

Many animals have the ability to learn. Organisms with simple nervous systems, such as most invertebrates, may learn only rarely. Among a few invertebrates, and many chordates, learning is common and occurs under a wide range of circumstances. In organisms that care for their young, for example, offspring can learn behaviors from their parents or other caretakers. Scientists have identified several different ways of learning. **The four major types of learning are habituation, classical conditioning, operant conditioning, and insight learning.**

KEEP CURRENT WITH . . .
SCIENCE NEWS®
To find out more about the topics in this chapter, go to: **www.phschool.com**

Innate Behavior

Build Science Skills

Applying Concepts Have student pairs take turns gently tossing a paper ball at each other's face. Students should wear safety goggles to protect their eyes. When students toss the paper ball, they should watch for their partner's response. *(Blink their eyes)* Explain that blinking is a reflex action—a simple innate behavior. Ask: **What is the importance of the blinking reflex?** *(Protects the eyes)*

Learned Behavior

Address Misconceptions

Students might attribute human feelings and motivations to animals while discussing animal behavior. Explain to students that this tendency, called anthropomorphism, is a common mistake that biologists and behaviorists must be careful not to make. Remind students that most animals behave innately to stimuli in their environment without premeditation. Some animals can also learn to change their innate behaviors as their environment changes. However, these behaviors cannot be applied to human behaviors, nor can humans judge how or why animals behave in certain ways.

SCIENCE NEWS®
Encourage students to visit **www.phschool.com** for the most current information on this topic.

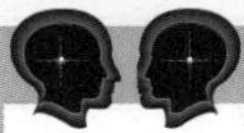

TEACHER TO TEACHER

I like to introduce animal behavior with a dramatic event. I invite a coworker to rush in and excitedly share some good news with me. My response is equally dramatic. We display as many behaviors, visual signals, sound signals, and language cues as we can. We also pretend to be completely oblivious to the class.

After my coworker leaves, I ask students to identify the stimulus, then identify the response behaviors that they observed. I list these on the board, and help students categorize these behaviors into Innate Behaviors and Learned Behaviors. Also, I have students identify the types of communication. I keep the list on the board and change it as needed while studying the chapter.

Susan Madden,
Biology Teacher
Chippewa Valley High School,
Clinton Township, MI

Answers to . . .

CHECKPOINT *A behavior that appears in fully functional form the first time it is performed*

Figure 34–3 *Since the eyelike pattern probably discourages predators, the behavior may give these moths a greater chance of surviving and passing the trait to offspring.*

34–1 (continued)

Build Science Skills

Using Analogies Remind students of Aesop's fable about the boy who cried wolf. Ask: **What kind of learning did the villagers engage in?** *(Habituation)* Discuss why this is an example of habituation. *(The villagers stopped responding to the boy's cry of wolf because they learned to associate it with a nonthreatening, unrewarding stimulus.)* Encourage students to think of other analogies of habituation. Emphasize that habituation is the loss of a response to a stimulus, not the acquisition of a new response to a stimulus.

Use Visuals

Figure 34–5 Ask students: **What type of learning does Pavlov's experiment model?** *(Classical conditioning)* **What is the stimulus in Pavlov's experiment?** *(The ringing bell)* **What is the reward?** *(Food)* **Why did the dogs salivate when hearing the bell, even if no food was present?** *(The dogs associated the ringing bell with food, so they salivated when they heard the bell, even in the absence of food.)* Emphasize that in classical conditioning, an animal's reflexes, or innate behaviors, are trained to respond to a stimulus.

Meet Diverse Needs

At-risk students can review the methods of classical conditioning by posing as a newspaper reporter interviewing a student who is posing as Ivan Pavlov. Encourage the "newspaper reporter" to ask "Pavlov" *who, what, where, when,* and *why* questions about the classical conditioning experiment with dogs. **Learning modality: verbal**

1 Before Conditioning
When a dog sees or smells food, it produces saliva. Food is the stimulus and the dog's response is salivation. Dogs do not usually salivate in response to nonfood stimuli.

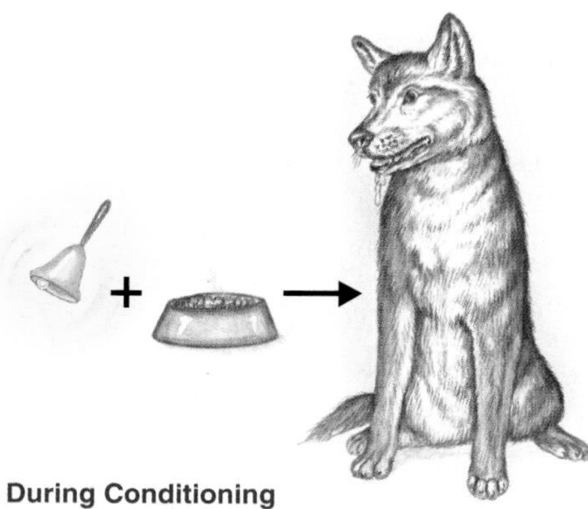

2 During Conditioning
By ringing a bell every time he fed the dog, Pavlov trained the dog to associate the sight and smell of food with the ringing bell.

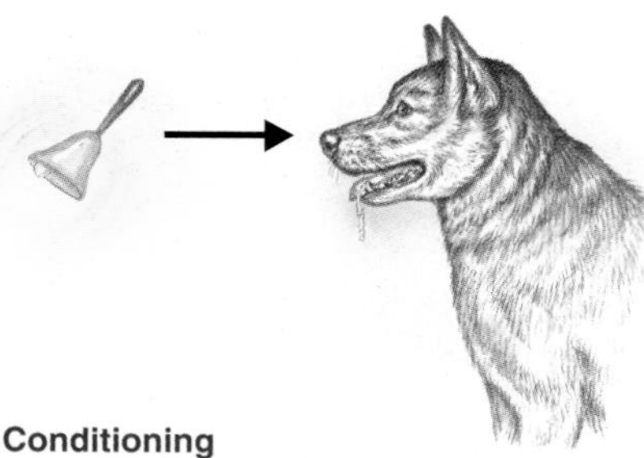

3 After Conditioning
When Pavlov rang a bell in the absence of food, the dog still salivated. The dog was conditioned to salivate in response to a stimulus that it did not normally associate with food.

Habituation The simplest type of learning is habituation. **Habituation** is a process by which an animal decreases or stops its response to a repetitive stimulus that neither rewards nor harms the animal. By ignoring a nonthreatening or unrewarding stimulus, animals can spend their time and energy more efficiently.

Consider the common shore ragworm. This animal lives in a sandy tube that it leaves only to feed. If a shadow passes overhead, the worm will instantly retreat to the safety of its burrow. Yet, if repeated shadows pass within a short time span, this response quickly subsides. When the worm has learned that the shadow is neither food nor threat, it will stop responding. At this point the worm has habituated to the stimulus.

Classical Conditioning When a dog sees its owner approaching with a leash, it may wag its tail and bark, eager to go for a walk. The dog has learned to associate the sight of the leash with a walk. Any time an animal makes a mental connection between a stimulus and some kind of reward or punishment, it has learned by **classical conditioning.** In the case of the dog and its owner, the stimulus of the leash is associated with a pleasant reward—a brisk walk. Now, think of what happens if a dog tries to attack a skunk. The skunk sprays the dog with a substance that stings and smells awful. In the future, that dog is likely to avoid skunks, because it associates the stimulus of the sight and scent of the skunk with the punishment of its foul spray.

The most famous example of classical conditioning is the work of the Russian physiologist Ivan Pavlov, around 1900. Pavlov was studying salivation—an innate behavior—in dogs. He discovered that if he always rang a bell at the same time he fed his dog, the dog would eventually begin to salivate whenever it heard a bell, even if no food was present. **Figure 34–5** shows how the dog in Pavlov's experiment learned to associate the bell (stimulus) with the arrival of food (reward).

◀ **Figure 34–5** Ivan Pavlov taught his dog to expect food whenever a bell was rung. **Pavlov's experiment is an example of classical conditioning, one of the four major types of learning.**

HISTORY OF SCIENCE

Pavlov's incidental discovery
Ivan Pavlov (1849–1936) was a Russian physiologist working in St. Petersburg. He pioneered studies of the digestive system, and even won the Nobel Prize for Medicine in 1904 for his work on the physiology of the circulatory, digestive, and nervous systems. In his research, he measured the saliva produced when dogs, secured in harnesses, were fed. But after the dogs had been in the laboratory for a while, they would salivate as soon as they were put in a harness. This infuriated Pavlov, since it invalidated his measurements. So, he began his studies of this behavior in an attempt to eliminate it. These studies proved fascinating, though, when he discovered that he could cause dogs to salivate simply by ringing a bell or turning on a light.

Operant Conditioning Conditioning is often used to train animals. **Operant conditioning** occurs when an animal learns to behave in a certain way through repeated practice, in order to receive a reward or avoid punishment. Operant conditioning is also called trial-and-error learning because it begins with a random behavior that is rewarded in an event called a trial. Most trials result in errors, but occasionally a trial will lead to a reward or punishment.

Operant conditioning was first described in the 1940s by the American psychologist B. F. Skinner. Skinner invented a testing procedure that used a certain type of box—the "Skinner box" shown in **Figure 34–6.** A Skinner box contains a colored button or lever that, when pressed, delivers a food reward. After an animal is rewarded several times, it learns that it gets food whenever it presses the button or lever. At this point, the animal has learned by operant conditioning how to obtain food.

CHECKPOINT *What is operant conditioning?*

▲ **Figure 34–6** Notice the pigeon in the Skinner box. Sooner or later, a laboratory animal placed in a Skinner box will accidentally press a button or lever that delivers a food reward. In time, this pigeon will learn how to obtain food whenever it wants. **Applying Concepts** *Which type of learning occurs in a Skinner box?*

Insight Learning The most complicated form of learning is **insight learning,** or reasoning. Insight learning occurs when an animal applies something it has already learned to a new situation, without a period of trial and error. For instance, if you are given a new math problem on an exam, you may apply principles you have already learned in the class in order to solve the problem. Insight learning is common among humans and other primates. In one experiment, a hungry chimpanzee used insight learning to figure out how to reach a bunch of bananas hanging overhead: it stacked some boxes on top of one another and climbed to the top of the stack. In contrast, if a dog accidentally wraps its leash around a tree, the dog is usually unable to free itself.

Quick Lab

What kind of learning is practice?

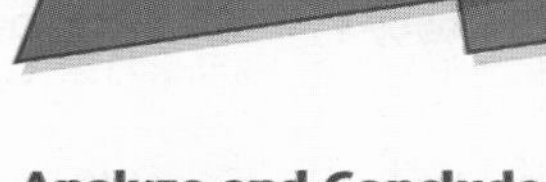

Materials paper, ruler, scissors

Procedure

1. Draw straight lines on a piece of paper to divide it into several sections of different sizes and shapes. Then cut the paper into sections along those lines.
2. Shuffle the pieces and then have another student time you as you try to reassemble the pieces. Record how long it takes you to do this task.
3. Repeat step 2 three times. Construct a graph showing how the time you needed to assemble the puzzle changed with repeated practice.

Analyze and Conclude

1. **Analyzing Data** Explain the shape of your graph. How did the time you needed to reassemble the pieces change as you repeated the task?
2. **Drawing Conclusions** What kind of learning did you display in this activity? Was it classical conditioning, operant conditioning, habituation, or some other kind of learning? Explain your answer.

FACTS AND FIGURES

Nature vs. nurture
The ability to learn is inherited because animals inherit their brain structures, making them capable of learning. However, knowing exactly how large an impact heredity has on learning is difficult because the environment plays such a large role in determining an animal's behavior. Most scientists agree that learned behaviors are based on innate behaviors that have been changed by experiences in the environment.

Learning is valuable to an animal because it can improve the animal's chance for survival, thus increasing its chance of passing its genes to its offspring. Young animals learn from their parents. However, learning occurs only in animals that have the time and opportunity to learn. For example, a fawn learns many things from its mother, but a frog must rely on instinct.

Meet Diverse Needs

To review the four major types of learning, have at-risk students and students with limited English proficiency create a table in which they compare and contrast habituation, classical conditioning, operant conditioning, and insight learning. Encourage students to illustrate their tables and add notes in their native languages. **Limited English proficiency**

Quick Lab

Objective Students will be able to draw conclusions to classify practice as a kind of learning.

Materials rectangular paper, ruler, scissors, clock with second hand

Time 15 minutes

Strategy
Students will get straighter cuts if they use the ruler to draw the cutting lines.

Expected Outcome The time required to assemble the puzzle will decrease with each try.

Sample Data Table

Trial	Student 1	Student 2
1	60 sec.	12 sec.
2	15 sec.	12 sec.
3	14 sec.	9 sec.

Analyze and Conclude

1. Graphs should show that the time required to assemble the puzzle decreased as students repeated the task.
2. The learning in this activity, practicing, is different from habituation, classical conditioning, and operant conditioning. Practicing requires conscious insight, an ability not involved in the other types of learning.

Answers to . . .

CHECKPOINT *Learning in which an animal learns a behavior through practice, in order to receive a reward or avoid punishment*

Figure 34–6 *Operant conditioning*

Instinct and Learning Combined

Make Connections

Environmental Science Show the movie, *Fly Away Home,* Columbia Pictures, 1996. Discuss the large responsibility this family accepted when they allowed the goslings to imprint on them. Help students understand the impact they have on their environment and why it's important that they take responsibility for their actions.

3 ASSESS

Evaluate Understanding

Ask students: **What causes behavior?** *(Stimuli in the environment)* **How do innate behaviors and learned behaviors differ?** *(Innate—fully functional the first time it is performed; learned—developed over time in response to environmental changes)* **Name five kinds of learning.** *(Habituation, classical conditioning, operant conditioning, insight learning, and imprinting)*

Reteach

Have students study each figure in the section and identify the type of behavior—innate or learned—that is exemplified by the figure. Students should also explain why they think it represents that behavior.

ALTERNATIVE ASSESSMENT

Students might construct a Venn diagram, a hierarchical map, or a concept map. The organizer should include innate behavior, learned behavior, and examples of each, including, habituation, classical conditioning, operant conditioning, insight learning, and imprinting.

Use iText to review the key concepts in Section 34–1.

Answer to . . .

Figure 34–7 *They have imprinted on the aircraft.*

▲ **Figure 34–7** These young Canada geese were trained to migrate behind this ultralight aircraft in an experiment called Operation Migration. The geese followed the craft as closely as they would their own parents. This type of conditioning is now being used to help endangered species, such as whooping cranes, learn a migration route. **Inferring** ***Why would these birds follow this aircraft?***

Instinct and Learning Combined

Most behaviors result from a combination of innate ability and learning. Young white-crowned sparrows, for example, have an innate ability to recognize their own species' song. To sing the complete version, however, the young birds must first hear it sung by the adults.

Some very young animals, such as ducks and geese, learn to recognize and follow the first moving object that they see during a critical time early in their lives. Usually, this object is their mother. This process is called **imprinting.** Imprinting keeps young animals close to their mother, who protects them and leads them to food sources. Once imprinting has occurred, the behavior cannot be changed.

Imprinting involves both innate and learned behavior. The young animals have an innate urge to follow the first moving object they see, but they are not born knowing what that object will look like. The young animal must learn from experience what object to follow. In fact, the object on which the young animal imprints does not have to be its mother, or even a living organism. The birds in **Figure 34–7** have imprinted on an aircraft!

Imprinting can occur through scent as well as sight. Newly hatched salmon, for example, imprint on the odor of the stream in which they hatch. Young salmon then head out to sea. Years later, when they mature, the salmon remember the odor of their home stream and return there to spawn.

34–1 Section Assessment

1. **Key Concept** Which body systems interact to produce a behavioral response?
2. **Key Concept** Compare and contrast innate and learned behavior.
3. **Key Concept** Define the four major types of learning.
4. Explain the difference between a stimulus and a response.
5. How does natural selection affect animal behavior?
6. **Critical Thinking Applying Concepts** Give an example of how humans learn through classical conditioning.

iTEXT Assessment Use iText to review the important concepts in Section 34–1.

ALTERNATIVE ASSESSMENT

Creating a Graphic Organizer

Create a graphic organizer to compare innate behavior with the different forms of learned behavior discussed in this section. Include at least one example of each kind of behavior in your graphic organizer.

34–1 Section Assessment

1. Sense organs, nervous system, muscles
2. Innate—performed perfectly the first time; learned—changed as a result of experience
3. Habituation—decreased response to repetitive stimulus; classical conditioning—connecting a stimulus to a reward; operant conditioning—learning a behavior through practice, in order to receive reward or escape punishment; insight learning—applying knowledge to new situation
4. Stimulus—signal that carries information; response—a specific reaction to a stimulus
5. Organisms with an adaptive behavior are better able to survive and reproduce.
6. Sample answer: A baby learns to associate the sight of a juice bottle with the treat of a sweet drink.

Using Remote Sensing to Study Animal Behavior

Studying any animal in the wild is difficult. But following elephants as they travel through a jungle or blue whales as they swim through the open ocean is almost impossible. Or is it? The first efforts at such studies involved hands-on techniques that required the capture, banding, release, and recapture of individual animals. Researchers would mark or band an animal with a tag that included a unique way of identifying the individual. If that animal was seen again or recaptured, the identification tag would be recorded and compared to the original field notes. Using this method, scientists could get an idea of the places their subjects visited. But they had few clues to the routes that animals traveled or where they went between capture points.

Remote Sensing

Today, small radio tags or transmitters, whose signals can be located by orbiting satellites, are used to track the positions of some animals as they travel in the wild. As with banding, the lightweight transmitters are attached to individual animals. Satellites that orbit Earth are programmed to locate the transmitter signal and record the position—latitude, longitude, and even depth—of the animal as it moves. Some transmitters even contain computer chips that can record the animal's body temperature, rate of breathing, and other physiological characteristics. These data can be made available to researchers over periods of days, weeks, or even months. This method, called satellite telemetry (tehl-EHM-uh-tree), can be expensive, but the data it provides are extremely valuable.

In the Jungle

Scientists are using remote sensing techniques to track elephants through the dense jungles of Thailand and Malaysia. Preliminary data suggest that elephants can move across long distances within a home range of almost 7000 square kilometers. Such a large area would have been impossible for researchers to cover from the ground, or even by airplane or helicopter.

In the Ocean

Researchers also use remote sensing to study marine animals—particularly sea turtles. Because sea turtles spend most of their lives at sea and come ashore only during breeding season, little is known about their daily habits or migration routes. To get that information, scientists are using satellite telemetry to track the behavior of sea turtles. A transmitter about the size of a portable CD player is glued to the back of the turtle's carapace, where it remains for up to 8 to 10 months. Over time, the information that scientists gain from this technology will help in efforts to protect turtles, elephants, and other endangered species.

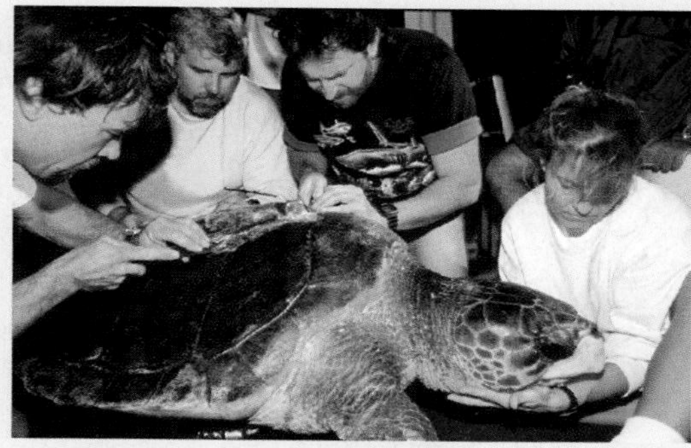

On Your Own

Find out more about the use of remote sensing in studies of animal behavior. Log on to the Prentice Hall Web site at **www.phschool.com**.

After students have read this feature, you might want to discuss one or more of the following:

- What kinds of behaviors are scientists studying—innate or learned or both?
- Are the actions of the scientists affecting the behaviors of the animals they are observing? What might happen if they are?
- How do these kinds of studies help scientists protect endangered animals? What kinds of information can help save an endangered species?
- Does remote sensing tell scientists everything about the behavior of an animal? What other information does a scientist need to get the complete picture of an animal's behavior?

On Your Own

Encourage students to visit **www.phschool.com** to get updated information about the locations and behaviors of various animals being studied with remote sensing.

Section 34–2

1 FOCUS

Objectives

34.2.1 ***Explain*** how environmental changes affect animal behavior.

34.2.2 ***Describe*** how courtship and social behavior increase an animal's evolutionary fitness.

34.2.3 ***Identify*** behavioral patterns used to claim and defend territories.

34.2.4 ***Summarize*** how animals communicate.

Guide for Reading

Vocabulary Preview

Explain that the term *circadian* comes from the Latin words *circa*, meaning "about," and *dies*, meaning "day." Therefore, *circadian* means "a period of about one day." Ask: **What is a circadian rhythm?** *(A cycle of behaviors that occur in daily, or 24-hour, patterns)*

Reading Strategy

Before students read this section, have them preview the figures and read their captions. Then, as students read the section, remind them to write a sentence that explains how the figure relates to what they are reading.

2 INSTRUCT

Behavioral Cycles

Use Visuals

Figure 34–8 As students examine the map of the sea turtle migration, ask: **What behavioral cycle are the sea turtles engaged in?** *(Migration, an annual cycle)* **How do these sea turtles know when to leave Brazil to go to Ascension Island?** *(Accept all reasonable answers. Changes in the length of day might cause green sea turtles to migrate.)* **How is migration an adaptive advantage to green sea turtles?** *(Accept all reasonable answers. Migration has improved the fitness of green sea turtles because they feed in areas with plenty of food and lay their eggs where the young have the best chance of survival.)*

34–2 Patterns of Behavior

Guide for Reading

Key Concepts
- How do environmental changes affect animal behavior?
- How do courtship and social behavior increase an animal's evolutionary fitness?
- How do animals communicate?

Vocabulary
migration
circadian rhythm
courtship
territory
aggression
communication
language

Reading Strategy: Using Visuals As you read, write a sentence explaining how each diagram or photograph reinforces or enhances the content of this section.

At this very moment, somewhere in an African grassland, elephants are calling to one another. Elephants communicate with sounds that they use to locate each other across distances more than 2 kilometers away. When they are not calling long-distance, elephants may spar with each other to test their strength or greet each other by wrapping their trunks together. These behaviors are patterns that have evolved in elephants. In this section, you will investigate some common patterns of animal behavior.

Behavioral Cycles

The environment is full of natural cycles. Night follows day, seasons change, the moon has phases, the tides rise and fall. **Many animals respond to periodic changes in the environment with daily or seasonal cycles of behavior.** For example, several species of reptiles and mammals are active during warm seasons but enter into a sleeplike state, or dormancy, during cold seasons. Dormancy allows an animal to survive periods when food and other resources may not be available.

Another type of behavior that is influenced by changing seasons is **migration,** the periodic movement from one place to another and then back again. Animals that migrate include species of birds, butterflies, and whales. **Figure 34–8** shows the migratory pattern of green sea turtles. Migration usually allows animals to take advantage of favorable environmental conditions. For example, when birds fly south for the winter, they go to regions where food is more plentiful than in northern areas.

Behavioral cycles that occur in daily patterns are called **circadian rhythms** (sur-KAY-dee-un). The fact that you sleep at night and attend school during the day is an example of a circadian rhythm.

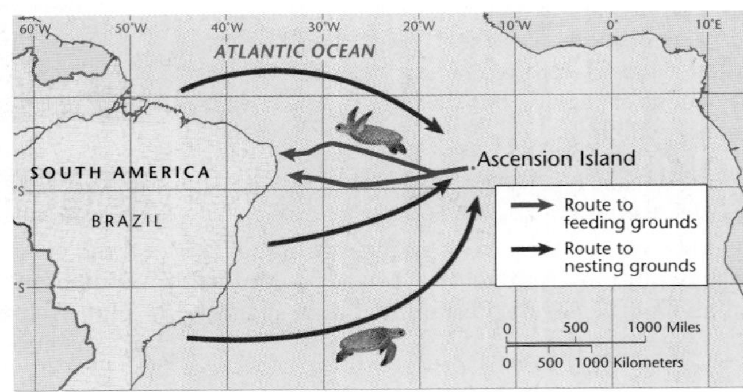

▶ **Figure 34–8** Each year, between December and June, green sea turtles migrate from their feeding grounds along the coast of Brazil to mate and nest on Ascension, a tiny island more than 2000 kilometers away. **Like many animals, sea turtles migrate in response to seasonal changes in their environment.**

TIME SAVER — SECTION RESOURCES

Print:
- ***Teaching Resources,*** Section Review 34–2, Chapter 34 Design an Experiment
- ***Guided Reading and Study Workbook,*** Section 34–2
- ***Issues and Decision Making,*** 34–1

Technology:
- ***iText,*** Section 34–2

Analyzing Data

Caring for Eggs

Reproduction is vital to animal survival. Humans can learn child-rearing skills. Is there evidence that other animals learn to care for their young?

The data at right are from field studies of the short-tailed shearwater, *Puffinus tenuirostris.* Each pair of parents produces only one egg a year. If that egg breaks or if the chick dies, the egg is not replaced. The graph shows the percentage of eggs that hatch and develop into free-flying young, in relation to the number of years that the parents have been breeding. This variable is referred to as reproductive success. The purple line indicates the success rate of female parents. The green line indicates the success rate of male parents.

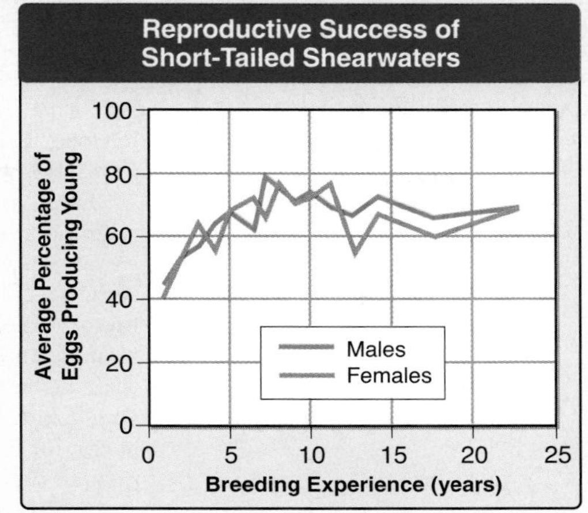

1. **Using Tables and Graphs** What is the approximate success rate of a female shearwater with 5 years of breeding experience?
2. **Using Tables and Graphs** Are there obvious differences in reproductive success between male and female shearwaters?
3. **Drawing Conclusions** Do older shearwaters have better reproductive success than younger birds? Explain your answer.
4. **Formulating Hypotheses** Do you think these birds learn to raise young more successfully over time? Is there an alternative hypothesis that could explain these data?

Analyzing Data

Have student volunteers explain what is measured on the vertical axis and the horizontal axis of this graph. Ask: **What does a reading of 60% at 4 years indicate?** *(That 60% of the four-year-old parents kept their chick alive until it was able to fly)*

Answers

1. Almost 70%
2. No
3. In general, yes. This is indicated by the rise in the graph line up until about 11 years. After 11 years, there is a slight decrease in reproductive success.
4. Most students will infer that over time, shearwaters learn to raise young more successfully. Alternative hypothesis: the fertility of shearwaters is highest between 7 and 11 years.

Courtship

Animal behavior is geared toward reproduction as well as survival. **To pass along its genes to the next generation, any animal that reproduces sexually needs to locate and mate with another member of its species at least once. Courtship behavior helps many animals identify healthy mates.**

In **courtship,** an individual sends out stimuli—such as sounds, visual displays, or chemicals—in order to attract a member of the opposite sex. For example, fireflies flash a distinct series of light signals to indicate their readiness to mate. The musical trill of a tree frog and the sheeplike bleat of a narrowmouth toad are among the many distinctive breeding calls of amphibians.

In some species, courtship involves an elaborate series of behaviors called rituals. A ritual is a series of behaviors performed the same way by all members of a population for the purpose of communicating. Most rituals consist of specific signals and individual responses that continue until mating occurs. For example, newly paired cranes, such as those in **Figure 34–9,** engage in intense periods of dancing before they mate.

CHECKPOINT *What is the function of courtship behavior?*

▼ **Figure 34–9 Courtship behavior helps many animals identify healthy mates.** The courtship ritual of this pair of Japanese cranes consists of head bobbing, deep bows, leaps, grasping and tossing objects, short flights, and several other moves. If a potential mate does not perform the parts of this dance in the proper sequence, it will be rejected and must locate a different mate.

Courtship

Build Science Skills

Applying Concepts Invite students to identify human courtship rituals. List their responses on the board. Then, categorize these rituals according to the kind of signal—sound, visual, or chemical. Discuss how these behaviors and rituals work to help a person find a mate. Also, have students rate how successful each behavior is.

TIME SAVER PRESENTATIONS MADE EASY!

The Presentation Assistant Plus contains the Prentice Hall Presentation Pro and the Transparencies, which provide easy-to-follow visual support for every step of this section. If you have a computer presentation station, use Prentice Hall Presentation Pro for Section 34–2, or use the transparencies listed here.

Section 8–1: **Interest Grabber**
Section Outline
Concept Map
Figure 34–8

Answer to . . .

CHECKPOINT *Courtship behavior helps many animals identify healthy mates.*

Social Behavior

Word Origins

A sociobiologist studies the behavior of animals as they interact with other members of their group.

Build Science Skills

Observing Allow students to observe the interaction of ants in an ant farm. You can purchase one ready-made or make one from two plexiglass sheets in a wooden frame. Challenge students to identify the role that each ant, or group of ants, has in the colony.

Meet Diverse Needs

Challenge small groups of students to develop and perform a skit in which they show how social behaviors help an animal society increase its evolutionary success. Students can choose any animal and any behavior. Students must use accurate information and include a bibliography with their skit. Have students perform their skits for the class. Volunteers from the class should identify how the behaviors contribute to the evolutionary success of the animals in the society. **Learning modality: kinesthetic**

Word Origins

The origin of the adjective **social** is the Latin word *socialis,* meaning "companionship." Animals that are social spend most of their time in a group. **What does a sociobiologist do?**

Social Behavior

Whenever animals interact with members of their own species, as in courtship, they are exhibiting social behavior. For some species, social behavior offers great survival advantages. Zebras and other grazers, for example, band together when searching for food. They are safer from predators when they are part of a group than when alone.

Some animals—including ants, certain shrimps, and some mammals—go a step further in their social behavior and form societies. A society is a group of closely related animals of the same species that work together for the benefit of the group. It takes millions of termites, for example, to build a single termite mound. Animal societies also use strength in numbers to improve their ability to hunt, to protect their territory, to guard their young, and to fight with rivals if necessary. In wild African dog packs, for instance, adult females take turns guarding all the pups in the pack, while the other adults hunt together for prey.

Usually, members of a society are related to one another. Related individuals share a large proportion of each other's genes. Therefore, helping a relative survive increases the chance that the genes an individual shares with that relative will be passed along to offspring. Thus, social behavior that helps a relative survive and reproduce improves an individual's evolutionary fitness.

Primates form some of the most complex animal societies known. Macaque, baboon, and other primate societies hunt together, travel in search of new territory, and interact with neighboring societies. A great deal of what we know about primate societies comes from the work of Jane Goodall, the animal behaviorist pictured in **Figure 34–10,** who spent thousands of hours observing chimps in their natural habitat.

CHECKPOINT *What is an animal society?*

▶ **Figure 34–10** **Animal societies enhance the reproductive success of individual members.** The work of the British behaviorist Jane Goodall, at right, laid the foundation for modern primate studies. Goodall observed chimpanzees in their natural habitat, as shown here. Goodall's methodology and profound scientific discoveries revolutionized the field of animal behavior.

FACTS AND FIGURES

Jane in the company of chimps

Jane Goodall began her studies of chimpanzees in 1960, under the direction of anthropologist Louis Leakey. Goodall took a noninvasive approach to her studies. She quietly observed chimpanzees from a distance until they accepted her presence. Then she quietly followed them around.

Her observations of social behavior in chimpanzees corrected many misconceptions of the time. She observed that chimpanzees have more complex social interactions and more behaviors similar to humans than scientists had ever imagined. For example, she learned that chimpanzees are skilled at making and using tools. Instead of vegetarians, they are omnivores and hunt and eat large animals. She also witnessed a group of chimpanzees kill off another group for no obvious survival reason.

Competition and Aggression

Some animals have behaviors that help prevent others from using limited resources. Often, such patterns involve a specific area, or **territory,** that is occupied and protected by an animal or group of animals. Territories contain resources, such as food, water, nesting sites, shelter, and potential mates, that are necessary for an animal's survival and reproduction. By claiming a territory, an animal keeps others at a distance. If a rival enters a territory, the "owner" of the territory may attack the rival and drive it away. Algae-eating damselfish are notorious for such attacks. An algae-eating damselfish can distinguish other algae-feeding species from species that do not eat algae. The damselfish chases the other algae-eaters away, but ignores the fish that do not eat algae.

When two or more animals try to claim limited resources, such as a territory or food, competition occurs. Many animals, such as the giraffes in **Figure 34–11,** use rituals and displays when they compete. During competition, animals may also show **aggression,** a threatening behavior that one animal uses to gain control over another. For instance, before a pride of lions settles down to eat, individuals may snap, claw, and snarl at one another. The most aggressive members will get to eat their fill of prey. The less aggressive lions will have to wait for their chance to feed.

▲ **Figure 34–11** By intertwining their long necks, these two giraffes compete for resources on an African savanna. **Inferring** *What resources might these giraffes compete for?*

Communication

Often, when animal behavior involves more than one individual, some form of **communication**—the passing of information from one organism to another—is involved. **Animals may use visual, sound, touch, or chemical signals to communicate with one another.** The specific techniques that animals use depend on the types of stimuli their senses can detect.

Visual Signals Animals with good eyesight often use visual signals involving movement and color. Cuttlefish, for example, have large eyes that are as sophisticated as those of vertebrates. In a matter of seconds, a single cuttlefish, like the one in **Figure 34–12,** can undergo changes in the colors and patterns on its body. Its skin will pucker into bumps and spines, then suddenly become smooth as stone. These visual displays—as fascinating as any computer screen saver—function in defense, hunting, mating, warning, and perhaps other forms of communication that are not yet known.

▶ **Figure 34–12** **Animals use visual, sound, touch, and chemical signals to communicate.** Like many animals with good eyesight, this Pacific giant cuttlefish uses visual signals in displaying a variety of bright colors and patterns on its body.

Competition and Aggression

Build Science Skills

Formulating Hypotheses Explain that many behaviorists have observed that animals that do not face many dangers in their environment are less aggressive and lead a relatively relaxed life. However, animals that face many dangers in their environment are very aggressive, even among themselves. Challenge students to develop a hypothesis to explain these observations.

Communication

Meet Diverse Needs

Encourage students with limited English proficiency to make sketches that illustrate each of the behaviors described in this section. Then, have students label their sketches with the appropriate vocabulary words. Also, allow students to label the sketches in their native language. **Limited English proficiency**

Demonstration

Communicate with the class without using any language. Try to get the class to perform a specific task, such as preparing to take notes or opening their books to a certain page. After students successfully complete the task, have them identify the types of signals you used to communicate with them.

FACTS AND FIGURES

Animal talk

Animals communicate with each other for many different reasons, such as finding a mate, establishing a territory, finding the location of food, and warning against danger. The behaviors associated with finding a mate are some of the most complicated types of communication. Choosing the correct mate is essential to the survival of a species. Animals have developed a complicated system of signals between males and females of a species to make certain that the choice is correct. Signals that animals use to communicate with other members of their species usually correlate with the senses that these animals use best to detect stimuli. For example, many male bird and fish species use brightly colored body parts to attract females and to warn potential rivals.

Answers to . . .

CHECKPOINT *An animal society is a group of closely related animals of the same species that work together for the benefit of the whole group.*

Figure 34–11 *Food, water, mates*

Make Connections

Chemistry Explain that pheromones are usually organic acids or alcohols that are highly volatile and can be detected in very small quantities. These chemicals work like hormones, except pheromones travel from one organism to another, rather than from one tissue to another. Like hormones, pheromones are chemical messengers that can directly or indirectly activate an enzyme. The enzyme, in turn, causes a biochemical reaction that helps to produce a response to the pheromone stimulus. Ask: **Are responses to pheromones learned behaviors or innate behaviors?** *(Innate)*

3 ASSESS

Evaluate Understanding

Have students write a paragraph in which they explain how animals communicate with each other in various social interactions, such as courtship or competition.

Reteach

Student pairs can develop a graphic organizer that shows the relationships among the vocabulary words for this section.

Take It to the NET

In their presentations, students should describe various bear behaviors, including how they communicate with one another. Encourage students to record the bear sounds or allow them to play the sounds directly from the Internet links while giving their presentations. For additional information, visit **www.phschool.com**

Use iText to review the key concepts in Section 34–2.

Answer to . . .

Figure 34–13 *Frequency in kiloHertz and time in seconds*

Chemical Signals Animals with well-developed senses of smell, including insects, fishes, and many mammals, may communicate with chemicals. For example, some animals release pheromones (FEHR-uh-mohnz), chemical messengers that affect the behavior of other individuals of the same species, to mark a territory or to signal their readiness to mate.

Sound Signals Animals with strong vocal abilities, including crickets, toads, and birds, communicate with sound. Some animals that use sound have evolved elaborate communication systems. Dolphins, for example, rely mainly on sound signals in the dark and often murky ocean depths where vision is not very useful. Scientists have discovered that bottlenose dolphins each have their own unique "signature" whistle that is used for recognition, like the ones whose patterns are shown on the graph in **Figure 34–13.** The dolphins' whistles function something like your signature on a letter, letting others know who is sending the communication.

Language The most complicated form of communication is language. **Language** is a system of communication that combines sounds, symbols, or gestures according to sets of rules about word order and meaning, such as grammar and syntax. Many animals, like dolphins, elephants, and gorillas, have fairly complex ways of communicating. However, outside of experiments in which they were trained by humans, none of those animals have been shown to use language. Only humans are known to use language.

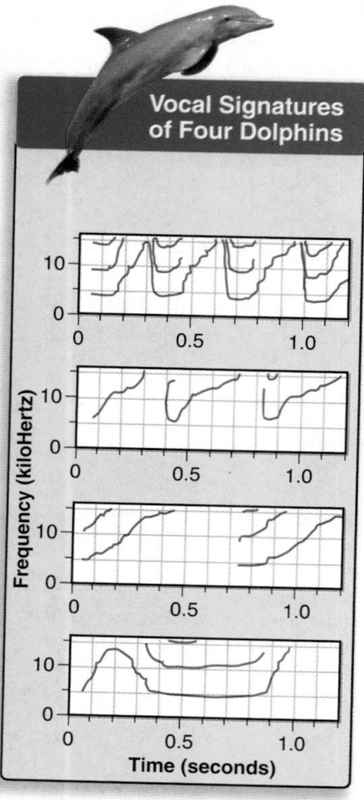

◀ **Figure 34–13** Individual bottlenose dolphins use vocal "signatures" during communication. The spectrograms at left show the signature signals of four different dolphins. **Interpreting Graphics** ***What two variables are plotted in a spectrogram?***

34–2 Section Assessment

1. **Key Concept** Name two ways in which animal behavior is related to environmental cycles.
2. **Key Concept** Explain how an animal society can contribute to the survival of an individual animal.
3. **Key Concept** What are the main ways in which animals communicate with each other?
4. Define "courtship ritual," and give an example of an animal's courtship ritual.
5. **Critical Thinking Inferring** Suppose you discover a new type of animal that is very different in appearance from other animals you have seen. How could observing the sense organs of this animal help you to understand if and how it communicates?

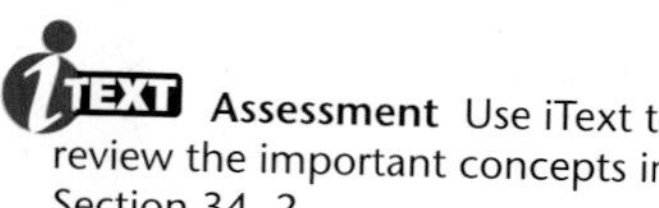

Assessment Use iText to review the important concepts in Section 34–2.

Take It to the NET

Read about the behavior of bears. Then, prepare a multimedia presentation that includes photographs or drawings showing the behavior and habitat of bears, along with any sounds that they make. Use the links provided in the Biology area at the Prentice Hall Web site for help in completing this activity.
www.phschool.com

34–2 Section Assessment

1. Migration and circadian rhythms
2. Animals within a society help each other to survive by cooperatively performing such tasks as hunting, defense, and guarding the young.
3. By visual, sound, touch, or chemical signals
4. An elaborate series of behaviors consisting of specific signals and responses that are performed to attract a mate; example: dancing of Japanese cranes
5. By observing how well the animal's sense organs are developed, one can infer how it communicates. For example, if an animal has well-developed ears, it can be inferred that the animal communicates with sounds.

Observing Behavior in Fish

Animals of the same species often use aggressive behavior to signal others to retreat, but rarely do they hurt each other. In this investigation, you will examine some stimuli that provoke aggressive behavior.

Problem **What triggers the aggressive behavior of male betta fish?**

Materials

- male betta fish
- aquarium net
- clear plastic box of aquarium water
- small mirror
- construction paper
- colored pencils or markers
- transparent tape
- popsicle sticks
- watch with a second hand

Skills Posing Questions, Designing Experiments

Design Your Experiment 

Part A: Observing Aggressive Displays

1. Use an aquarium net to transfer a male betta from the aquarium to a clear plastic box of aquarium water. **CAUTION:** *Do not touch the fish with your hands. Fish are easily injured.*
2. Observe the betta's behavior.
3. Place a mirror against the side of the box so that the fish can see its reflection. Observe and record the betta's behavior. Remove the mirror within 1 minute so that the fish does not habituate to its reflection.

Part B: Identifying the Stimulus for Aggression

4. **Predicting** What feature of a betta provokes aggressive behavior in other bettas? Is it color, size, movement, or something else? Record a prediction of what provokes aggressive displays by bettas.
5. Design an experiment that will use paper models of bettas to test your prediction. You can tape the models to popsicle sticks and use colored pencils or markers to add details. Have your teacher check your plan before you begin your experiment.
6. Carry out your experiment. Record your observations of the betta's behavior. **CAUTION:** *To avoid exhausting the betta, always allow it at least 1 minute of rest between stimuli.*

Analyze and Conclude

1. **Observing** Did the male betta exhibit aggressive behavior? If so, how did it show aggression?
2. **Evaluating** What stimuli provoked the most aggression? Did your observations support your prediction?
3. **Inferring** Male bettas are more aggressive toward other males when a female betta is present. How can such behavior be an advantage to the male? How does it help the species survive?

Go Further

Designing Experiments Male bettas use aggression to defend their territory against invasion from other male bettas. Design an experiment to investigate what traits determine which male bettas will be successful in conflicts with other males.

Analyze and Conclude

1. Bettas show aggression by behaviors such as swimming quickly toward the mirror or model, presenting the side of the body, arching the back, lowering the head, raising the fins—especially the dorsal fin, spreading and beating the tail, extending the gill covers, or intensifying in color.

2. Bright colors and movement usually provoke the most aggression.

3. The more aggressive male is more likely to be accepted as a mate by the nearby female. The competition between the males increases the chance that only the strongest and healthiest males find mates and pass on their genes to the next generation. This increases the fitness of the entire species.

Design an Experiment

Objective Students will be able to design an experiment to determine what triggers the aggressive behavior of fish.

Time 45 minutes

Advance Prep
- Betta fish are sold in aquarium shops as Siamese fighting fish. Do not keep male bettas together in the same tank.
- Provide white, blue, red, and green construction paper.
- Put fish in the containers a few hours in advance of the class to allow the fish to acclimate to the environment.

Alternative Materials Instead of clear boxes, you can use clear 2-L bottles with the tops cut off.

Safety Touching the fish can remove their protective mucus layer, leading to infection in the fish.

Pre-Lab Discussion Discuss how aggression helps an animal to survive. Ask: **When can aggression be harmful to a species?** *(When individuals injure or kill each other)* **How does a species benefit when individuals use only symbolic threats of aggression?** *(Individuals participate in confrontations without risking injuries that might result from aggressive physical interaction.)*

Teaching Tips
- Mirrors and paper fish, and so on, should only be put up to the container from the outside.
- If the mirror is left in place for too long in step 3, the fish might become habituated to the image and fail to respond to stimuli later.
- Make sure students test only one variable in their experiment, such as color, size, or movement, and keep the other variables constant.

Expected Outcomes Fish should respond to bright color and to movement.

Go Further

Before approving proposed experiments, review them for sound design and hazards to students and fish.

Chapter 34 Study Guide

Study Tip

Have students make flashcards for each of the Vocabulary words and for the Key Concepts. Encourage student pairs to take turns quizzing each other with their flashcards.

Thinking Visually

1. Classical Conditioning
2. Operant Conditioning
3. Insight Learning

Chapter 34 Assessment

Reviewing Content

1. a	**5.** b	**9.** a
2. d	**6.** b	**10.** b
3. b	**7.** b	
4. c	**8.** a	

Understanding Concepts

11. Sample answer: stimulus—seeing a peach; response—reaching for the peach.

12. Senses detect the stimulus and pass that information to the brain. The brain interprets the information and directs the body's reponse.

13. Habituation enables animals to react properly to dangerous stimuli and to ignore harmless ones.

14. Pavlov rang a bell every time he fed a dog. After a while, he rang the bell without feeding the dog. The dog salivated in response to the bell, despite the fact that dogs normally salivate only in response to food.

Chapter 34 Study Guide

34–1 Elements of Behavior

Key Concepts

- When an animal responds to a stimulus, body systems—including the sense organs, nervous system, and muscles—interact to produce the resultant behavior.
- Innate behaviors appear in fully functional form the first time they are performed, even though the animal may have had no previous experience with the stimuli to which it responds.
- The four major types of learning are habituation, classical conditioning, operant conditioning, and insight learning.

Vocabulary

behavior, p. 871
stimulus, p. 871
response, p. 871
innate behavior, p. 873
learning, p. 873
habituation, p. 874
classical conditioning, p. 874
operant conditioning, p. 875
insight learning, p. 875
imprinting, p. 876

34–2 Patterns of Behavior

Key Concepts

- Many animals respond to periodic changes in the environment with daily or seasonal cycles of behavior.
- To pass along its genes to the next generation, any animal that reproduces sexually needs to locate and mate with another member of its species at least once. Courtship behavior helps many animals identify healthy mates.
- Usually, members of a society are related to one another. Related individuals share a large proportion of each other's genes. Therefore, helping a relative survive increases the chance that the genes an individual shares with that relative will be passed along to the next generation of offspring.
- Animals may use visual, sound, touch, or chemical signals to communicate with one another.

Vocabulary

migration, p. 878
circadian rhythm, p. 878
courtship, p. 879
territory, p. 881
aggression, p. 881
communication, p. 881
language, p. 882

Thinking Visually

Using information from this chapter, complete the following concept map:

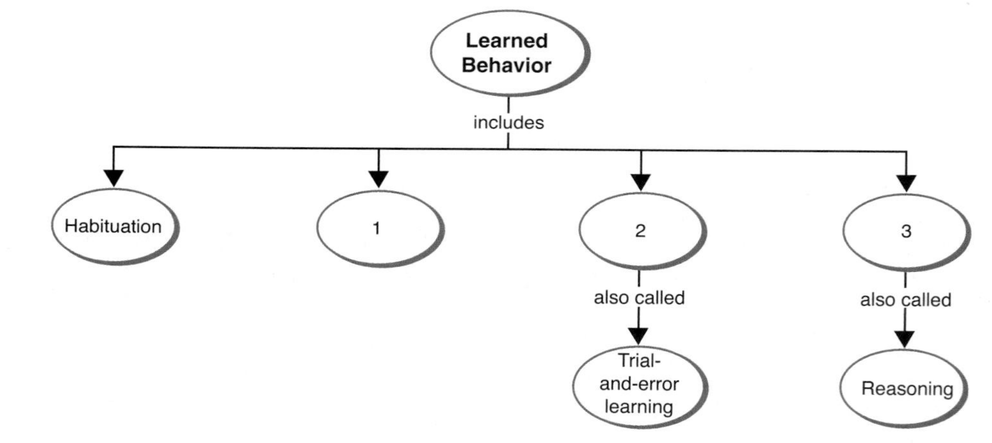

CHAPTER RESOURCES

Print:

- ***Teaching Resources,*** Chapter Vocabulary Review, Graphic Organizer
- ***Chapter Tests: Levels A and B,*** Chapter 34 Test
- ***PH Assessment System,*** Practice Test

Technology:

- ***Computer Test Bank,*** Chapter 34 Test
- ***iText,*** Chapter 34 Assessment

Chapter 34 Assessment

Reviewing Content

Choose the letter that best answers the question or completes the statement.

1. The set of reactions of an organism to changes in its internal condition or external environment is called
   a. behavior. c. conditioning.
   b. learning. d. stimuli.
2. Light, sound, and temperature are examples of
   a. responses. c. circadian rhythms.
   b. behaviors. d. stimuli.
3. A dog learns to expect food whenever a bell is rung. This is an example of
   a. insight learning.
   b. classical conditioning.
   c. migration.
   d. instinct.
4. A decrease in response to a stimulus that neither rewards nor harms an animal is called
   a. instinct.
   b. operant conditioning.
   c. habituation.
   d. classical conditioning.
5. Insight learning is common among
   a. dogs.
   b. primates.
   c. birds and insects.
   d. birds only.
6. Study the diagram below. What type of learning is occurring?

   a. insight learning
   b. imprinting
   c. classical conditioning
   d. operant conditioning
7. The fact that you sleep at night and attend school during the day is an example of a(an)
   a. migration.
   b. circadian rhythm.
   c. aggressive behavior.
   d. social behavior.
8. Each year, a bird called the American redstart travels from its winter home in South America to its nesting area in New York. This behavior is called
   a. migration.
   b. competition.
   c. imprinting.
   d. courtship.
9. Which of the following is NOT a type of social behavior?
   a. migration
   b. communication
   c. hunting in a pack
   d. courtship
10. A system of communication that uses meaningful sounds, symbols, or gestures according to specific rules is called
   a. behavior.
   b. language.
   c. competition.
   d. a signature.

Understanding Concepts

11. Describe an example of a stimulus and a corresponding response in animal behavior.
12. What is the brain's role in an animal's response to a stimulus?
13. How can habituation contribute to an animal's survival?
14. Describe Pavlov's experiment.
15. Explain why imprinting is a combination of innate ability and learning.
16. Because a highway has been constructed through a forest, many of the animals that once lived there have had to move to a different wooded area. Is their move an example of migration? Explain.
17. Identify two ways in which social behavior can benefit an animal.
18. What is the significance of Jane Goodall's work?
19. Explain how aggression and territorial behavior are related.
20. What are pheromones? Give an example of how they are used.
21. What animals are known to use language?

15. An animal is born with the innate ability to follow the first moving object it sees. Learning is involved because the animal must learn to recognize that object.
16. No. Migration is a periodic movement from one place to another and then back again that is related to changing seasons. The movement of these animals had nothing to do with changing seasons.
17. Sample answer: if a group searches for food, they are more likely to find it than if an individual searched; a large group is safer from predators than an individual is.
18. Goodall spent a long time observing animals in their natural habitat. She recorded detailed observations of their behavior.
19. Animals often use aggression or threatening behaviors to establish a territory and defend it when a rival tries to claim it.
20. Pheromones are chemical messengers that are released by an animal and affect the behavior of other animals of the same species. Sample use: marking a territory.
21. Only humans are known to use language.

HOMEWORK GUIDE

Section:	Questions:
Section 34–1:	1–6, 11–15, 21–24
Section 34–2:	7–10, 16–20, 25–31

Chapter 35 Assessment

Critical Thinking

22. Accept all reasonable experimental designs. The only variable in students' designs should be the frequency of giving treats. Studies have shown that an occasional treat is a more effective way to train a dog than giving a treat each time a trick is completed.

23. Operant conditioning; smiling is reinforced by the reward of cuddling.

24. Horses are bred for desirable characteristics, but can be conditioned, or trained, over time.

25. If industrial wastes were to pollute the stream, the odor of the water would change and the returning salmon might not recognize it as its home stream.

26. Stimuli include thirst, cold air, the baseball, and light. Responses include a sneeze, eating, flying, and laughter.

27. Its body temperature fluctuates during winter months and is stable in warmer months. In winter, it is in a state of dormancy.

28. Killing the cubs sired by the previous male removes a threat to the new lion's future offspring. If allowed to live, the old cubs would compete with the new cubs for food and other resources.

29. Less competition for resources

30. Sample answer: When cooks try new recipes, they use their ability to read the recipe plus their experience in cooking similar foods.

31. Plant growth and the bloom time of flowers, for example, occur at particular times of the year. The environmental conditions at these times may favor the growth of the plant as well as the activity of pollinators.

Chapter 34 Assessment

Critical Thinking

22. **Designing Experiments** Some people train a dog by giving the animal a treat every single time it performs a behavior successfully. Other people reward the correct behavior on a more random schedule. Design an experiment to determine which method of training is more effective.

23. **Inferring** A baby smiles when her mother comes near. Often, the baby is picked up and cuddled as a result of smiling. Explain what type of learning the baby is showing.

24. **Applying Concepts** Explain how a racehorse's ability to win races is a combination of inherited and learned behaviors.

25. **Predicting** A young salmon imprints on the odor of the stream in which it hatches. Years later, the mature salmon returns to that stream to spawn. Suppose that over the course of the salmon's development, the stream becomes polluted with industrial wastes. Predict what effects the pollution might have on the salmon as it returns to the stream.

26. **Classifying** Classify each of the following as a stimulus or a behavior: thirst, cold air, a baseball being thrown at you, a sneeze, light, eating, flying, laughter.

27. **Interpreting Graphics** When temperatures are low and food is scarce, some mammals enter into a state of dormancy. Dormancy is an energy-saving adaptation in which metabolism decreases and, therefore, body temperature declines. The graph below tracks a ground squirrel's body temperature over the course of a year. Describe the pattern that you observe. What can you infer about the squirrel's behavior at different times of the year?

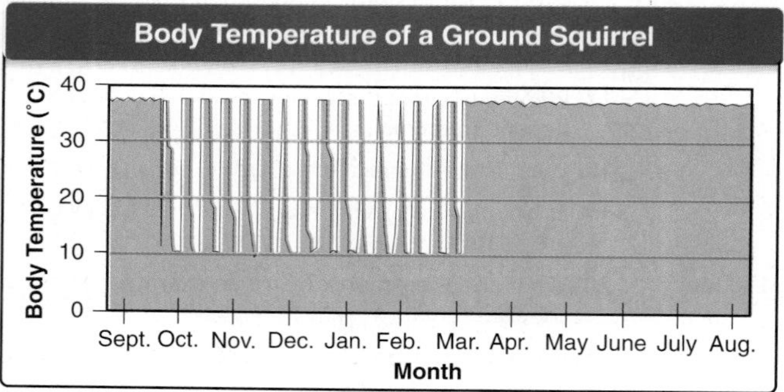

28. **Inferring** A pride of lions consists of several males, many females, and their offspring. About every two years, a group of new male lions drives the resident males from the pride. Often, one of the first acts of the new males is to try to kill all the young lion cubs.Explain how this behavior might give an evolutionary advantage to the new male lions.

29. **Formulating Hypotheses** Although the members of many animal species derive benefits from living in social groups, members of other species live alone. What might be the adaptive advantage of solitary living?

30. **Applying Concepts** Give an example of something you have learned by insight learning. Explain how you used past knowledge and experience in learning it.

31. **Making Connections** Review what you learned about plant responses in Chapter 25. Describe how some of these responses, like some animal behaviors, are related to cycles in the environment.

Performance-Based Assessment

Being Social In daily life, humans demonstrate a wide variety of behaviors. Make a list of ten social behaviors that you observe in your classmates and other people with whom you interact. Identify each type of behavior and describe how it might or might not be adaptive to the survival of humans.

Take It to the NET

What kinds of animal behavior studies are currently being conducted? Visit the Prentice Hall Web site at **www.phschool.com** to find out about current projects. Then, answer the following questions:

- What are three scientific projects that are currently underway in animal behavior?
- Who is working on these projects?
- Where is the research conducted?
- What do scientists hope to learn from the projects?

Performance-Based Assessment

Behaviors that students describe will vary. All students should include ten different social behaviors. Examples include specific hand gestures, mannerly behaviors, flirting behaviors, aggressive behaviors, and so on. Students should identify each behavior as being learned or innate, as well as being a particular pattern of behavior, such as a behavioral cycle, courtship behavior, social behavior, competition or aggression, and communication. Students should also describe why the behavior is or is not an adaptation for human survival.

Standardized Test Prep

Test-Taking Tip When you are asked to analyze a graph showing experimental data, first look at the shape of the line. Identify the variables and try to determine how they are related.

Directions: Choose the letter that best answers the question or completes the statement.

1. Which kind of behavior does NOT involve learning?
(A) habituation
(B) trial and error
(C) imprinting
(D) instinct
(E) insight

2. A male three-spined stickleback fish will attack male red-bellied sticklebacks and models of fishes that have a red underside. It will not attack males or models lacking a red underside. What can you conclude from the three-spined stickleback's behavior?
(A) The stimulus for an attack is a red underside.
(B) The stimulus for an attack is aggression.
(C) The stimulus for an attack is the presence of a fish with red fins.
(D) The stimulus for an attack is the presence of a fish model.
(E) There is no predictable stimulus for an attack.

Questions 3–4 Complete each analogy by selecting the correct letter. In analogies, A : B :: C : __?__ *means* A is to B as C is to __?__.

3. Stimulus : taunting a dog :: response : __?__.
(A) a dog growling
(B) running away from a dog
(C) running toward a dog
(D) yelling loudly
(E) a dog yelping in pain

4. Courtship behavior : finding a mate :: __?__ : protecting a territory
(A) feeding
(B) aggression
(C) migration
(D) animal society
(E) habituation

Questions 5–8 Each of the lettered choices below refers to the following numbered statements. Select the best lettered choice. A choice may be used once, more than once, or not at all.

(A) Insight learning
(B) Operant conditioning
(C) Classical conditioning
(D) Habituation

5. A rat learns to press a button to get food.

6. A dog always salivates at the ringing of a bell.

7. A chimpanzee stacks boxes in order to reach a banana hanging from the ceiling.

8. A bird stops responding to a repeated warning call when it is not followed by an attack.

Questions 9–10

A researcher observed sedge warblers during breeding season. She charted the number of different songs a male bird sang compared to the time it took him to pair with a mate. The graph shows her data.

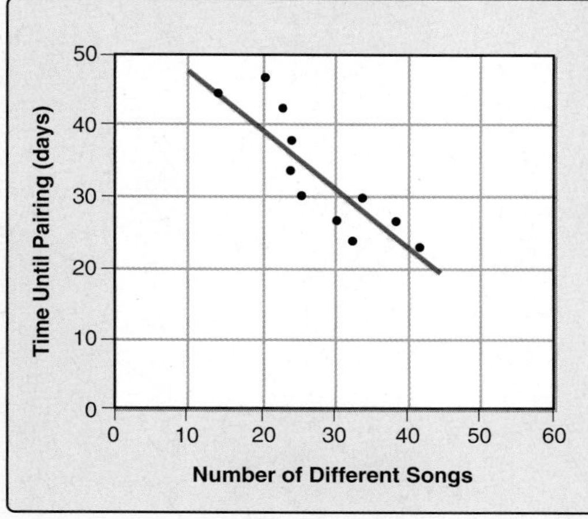

9. The researcher was trying to find out whether there is a correlation between
(A) the number of a male bird's songs and the number of offspring.
(B) the number of a male bird's songs and his attractiveness to females.
(C) a male's age and the number of songs he sings.
(D) a male's age and when he mates.
(E) a female's age and when she mates.

10. What can you conclude based on the graph?
(A) Males prefer females that do not sing.
(B) Females prefer males that do not sing.
(C) Males prefer females with a large number of songs.
(D) Females prefer males with a large number of songs.
(E) Songs are not related to mate selection in sedge warblers.

Standardized Test Prep

1. D	**5.** B	**9.** B
2. A	**6.** C	**10.** D
3. A	**7.** A	
4. B	**8.** D	

Take It to the NET

• Students should describe three projects underway. Projects might include those on different species of primates or bears.

• Research teams typically include student research assistants, college students, volunteers, zoo staff, and research scientists.

• Answers will depend on the research projects described. Projects are carried out at zoos, primate reserves, and other areas.

• Answers will depend on the research projects described. Possible objectives include studying the adjustment of newly introduced animals as they adjust to their new surroundings and answering questions about the cognitive capacity and problem-solving abilities of different animals. For additional information, visit

www.phschool.com

Unit 10

Dear Colleague,

"You never appreciate what you have until it's gone." The wisdom of that old saying came back to me a couple of years ago in the midst of a very busy semester. In the spring, I teach a freshman biology class with hundreds of students, and I struggle with the challenges of keeping up with so many names and faces.

This day, however, was different. I didn't feel very hungry in the morning, so I skipped breakfast. As I prepared for my morning lecture, getting my slides and notes in order, I knew something was wrong. I felt nervous and jumpy, maybe even feverish. Perhaps I was getting a cold or a touch of the flu?

One of my teaching assistants remarked that I looked a little pale. I smiled and assured her that I was just fine. But when I bent down to pick up a notebook, I felt a pain deep in the right side of my abdomen, an unusual pain. Indigestion? No, I hadn't eaten anything at all.

I managed to sweat my way through the lecture, but when I walked back to my lab, I felt weak and very sick. Just before I called my doctor, I tried to put everything together: fever, weakness, lack of appetite, and a sharp, growing pain just below the stomach in my right side. I tried to be jovial when I spoke to my physician. "Hugh," I grinned, "I think I need a white cell count."

I had *never* felt a pain like this before, and there was only one thing I could think of: appendicitis. All the symptoms fit together, and a count of the white cells in my blood would confirm my amateur diagnosis. If my appendix was swollen and infected with bacteria, my body's immune system would have sprung into action days ago, sending millions of white blood cells into my bloodstream to fight the infection. If an

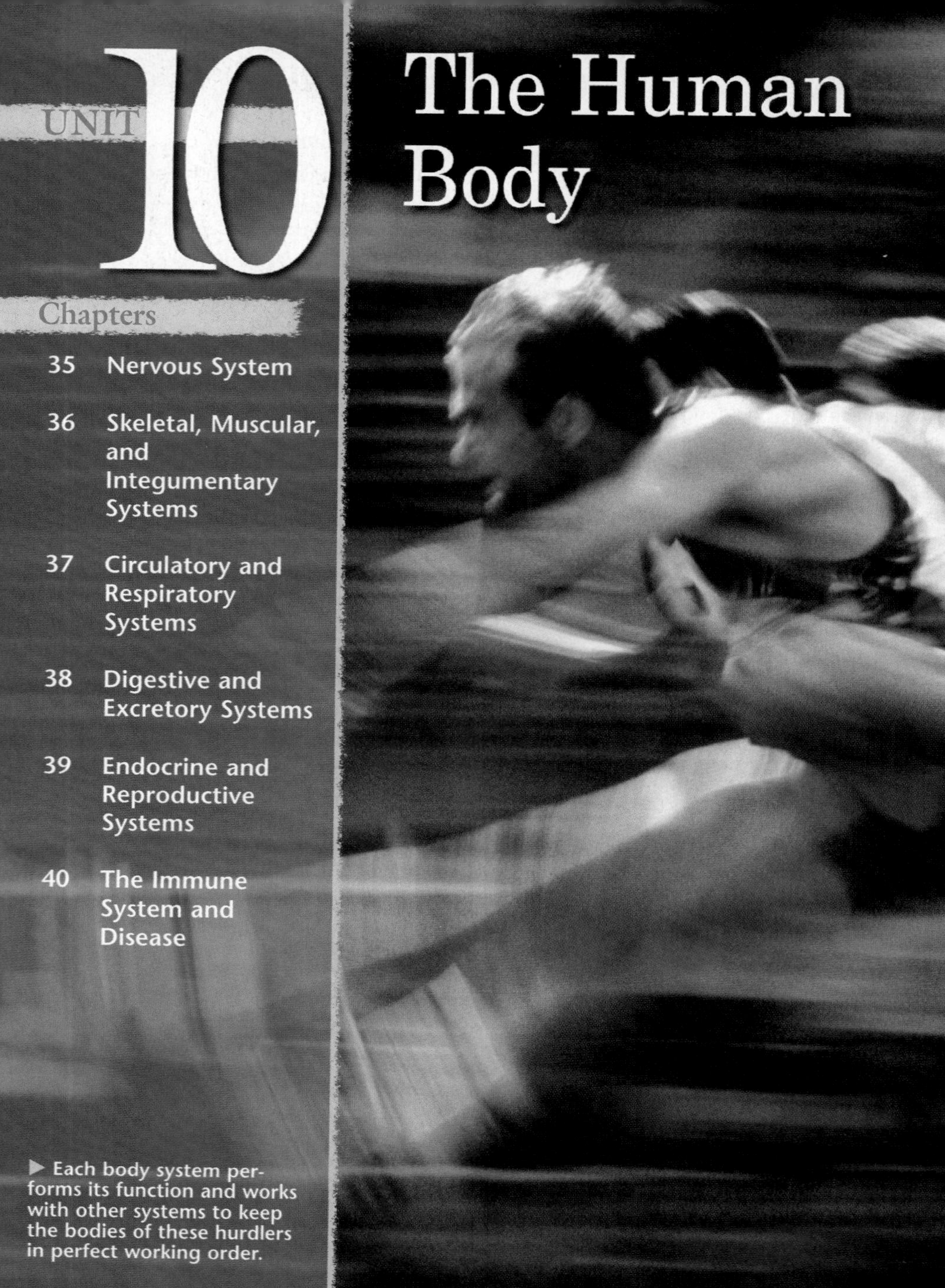

UNIT 10

The Human Body

Chapters

▶ Each body system performs its function and works with other systems to keep the bodies of these hurdlers in perfect working order.

888

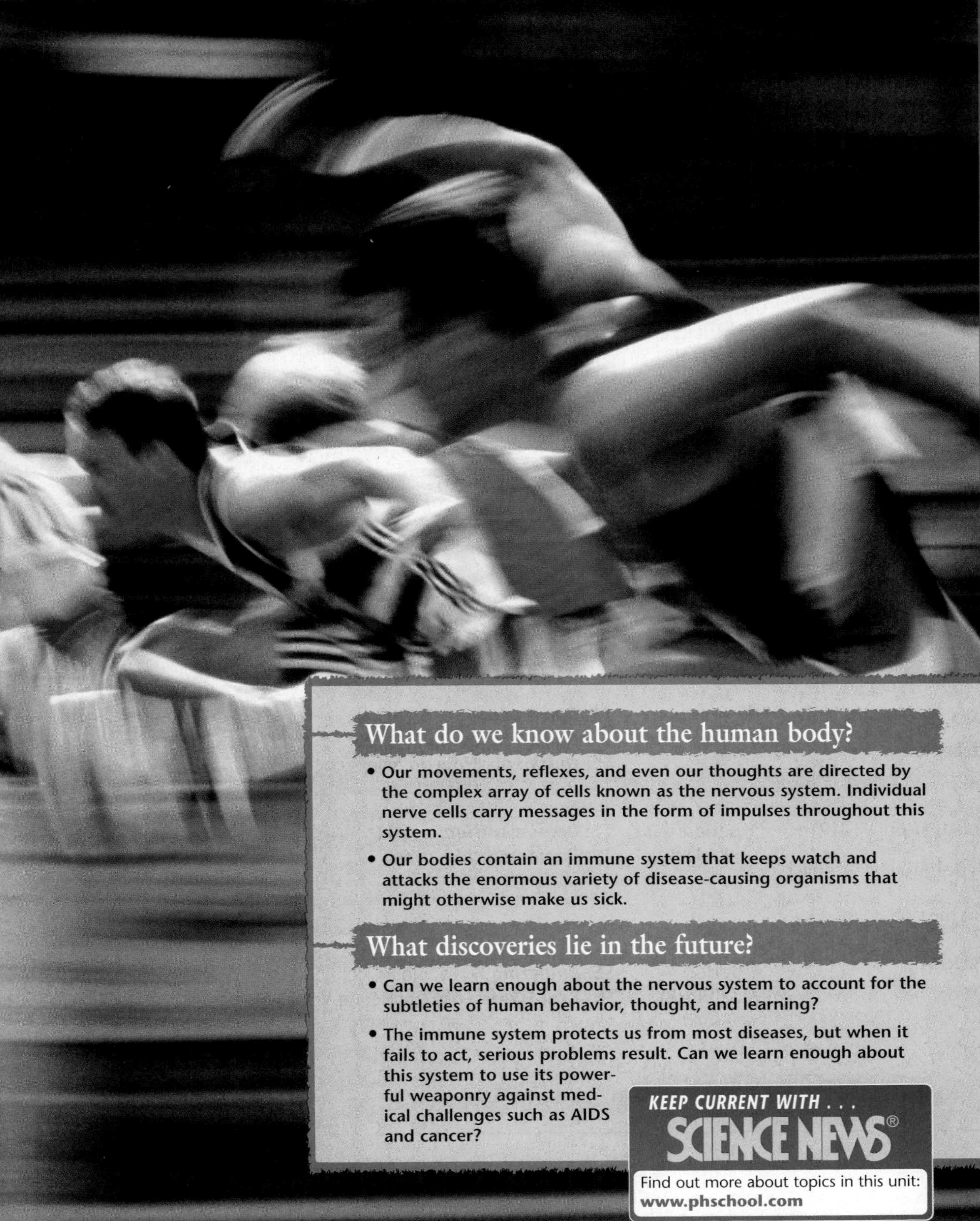

What do we know about the human body?

- Our movements, reflexes, and even our thoughts are directed by the complex array of cells known as the nervous system. Individual nerve cells carry messages in the form of impulses throughout this system.
- Our bodies contain an immune system that keeps watch and attacks the enormous variety of disease-causing organisms that might otherwise make us sick.

What discoveries lie in the future?

- Can we learn enough about the nervous system to account for the subtleties of human behavior, thought, and learning?
- The immune system protects us from most diseases, but when it fails to act, serious problems result. Can we learn enough about this system to use its powerful weaponry against medical challenges such as AIDS and cancer?

KEEP CURRENT WITH . . .
SCIENCE NEWS®
Find out more about topics in this unit:
www.phschool.com

analysis of the cells in my bloodstream showed more than the usual number of white cells, it meant that I was fighting a serious infection. And the pain in my side left no doubt about where that infection was.

My physician laughed at my attempt to play doctor, but he agreed that a blood test was indicated. An hour later, I found out that my white cell count was nearly five times normal, and I was on my way to the hospital for an emergency appendectomy.

Recovery was quick, and I was back in the classroom and the lab in just a couple of days. Quite frankly, I was happy to be rid of that appendix. What most impressed me, however, was the number of ways in which my body reacted to that infection.

I got my first clues that something was wrong from elevated temperature and blood pressure—the body's coordinated effort to step up activity to fight infection. Unknown to me, white blood cells were being rushed into service from deep within my bones, and blood vessels were swelling around the infection, making it easier for the white blood cells to attack and subdue the bacteria.

My digestive system stopped functioning, and the hunger reflex was suppressed. My nervous system made me feel weak as more resources were directed to the site of infection, and, finally, nerves carried a sensation of pain to pinpoint the problem spot.

The separate systems of the body, which we will explore in this unit, are marvelous things in their own right. Working together, however, they are truly amazing. In my case, I was thankful that they got the message to me as quickly as they did—and even more thankful to be living in an age when modern medicine can save a life like mine as a matter of routine.

Sincerely,

Ken Miller

SCIENCE NEWS®

Have students visit the Prentice Hall Web site at
www.phschool.com
to find the most current information on the human body.

Chapter Planner 35 Nervous System

Section and Section Objectives	Time	Activities and Labs
35–1 Human Body Systems, pp. 891–896 **35.1.1** ***Describe*** how the human body is organized. **35.1.2** ***Explain*** homeostasis.	**2 periods (1 block)**	**SE:** ***Inquiry Activity,*** What are the organ systems?, p. 890 **TE:** ***Demonstrations,*** p. 890, p. 894
35–2 The Nervous System, pp. 897–900 **35.2.1** ***Identify*** the function of the nervous system. **35.2.2** ***Describe*** how a nerve impulse is transmitted.	**1 period (1/2 block)**	**TE:** ***Meet Diverse Needs,*** p. 898 **TE:** ***Meet Diverse Needs,*** p. 899 **TE:** ***Demonstration,*** p. 899
35–3 Divisions of the Nervous System, pp. 901–905 **35.3.1** ***Identify*** the functions of the central nervous system. **35.3.2** ***Describe*** the two divisions of the peripheral nervous system.	**1 period (1/2 block)**	**TE:** ***Build Science Skills,*** p. 902
35–4 The Senses, pp. 906–909 **35.4.1** ***Name*** the five types of sensory receptors. **35.4.2** ***Identify*** the five senses.	**1 period (1/2 block)**	**TE:** ***Demonstration,*** p. 903 **TE:** ***Build Science Skills,*** p. 905 **SE:** ***Quick Lab,*** How do reflexes occur?, p. 905
35–5 Drugs and the Nervous System, pp. 910–914 **35.5.1** ***Name*** the different classes of drugs that directly affect the nervous system. **35.5.2** ***Describe*** the effects of alcohol on the body.	**1 period (1/2 block)**	**TE:** ***Demonstration,*** p. 908 **TE:** ***Demonstration,*** p. 909
Chapter Assessment, pp. 916–919	**1 period (1/2 block)**	**SE:** ***Analyzing Data,*** Blood Alcohol Concentration, p. 913 **SE:** ***Real-World Lab,*** Correcting Vision With Lenses, p. 915

ACTIVITY PLANNER

SE: ***Inquiry Activity***, p. 890; (10 min.); sheets of paper, colored pencils

TE: ***Demonstration***, p. 890; (5 min.); 30-cm pieces of electrical cord

TE: ***Demonstration***, p. 894; (5 min.); plastic wrap, electrical wire, roll of packaging tape

TE: ***Meet Diverse Needs***, p. 898; (15 min.); string, beads, dry pasta, modeling clay

TE: ***Meet Diverse Needs***, p. 899; (5 min.); spring

TE: ***Demonstration***, p. 899; (5 min.); dominoes

TE: ***Build Science Skills***, p. 902; (10 min.); small box, newspapers, ruler

TE: ***Demonstration***, p. 903; (5 min.); sheet of stiff plastic, paper ball

TE: ***Build Science Skills***, p. 905; (5 min.); blindfold

SE: ***Quick Lab***, p. 905; (20 min.); string, packing tape, scissors, 30-cm ruler, plastic mousetraps

TE: ***Demonstration***, p. 908; (5 min.); glass container, water

TE: ***Demonstration***, p. 909; (10 min.); paper cups, blindfold, fruit juices

SE: ***Real-World Lab***, p. 915; (45 min.); tape, cardboard photo easels, black construction paper, unruled white index card, 6-V light bulb and socket, 6-V battery and wires with alligator clips, convex lenses, modeling clay, meter sticks, concave lens

PLANNING KEY

Ability Levels

B **Basic**	For students who need additional help
A **Average**	For all students
E **Enriched**	For students who need to be challenged

Components

SE	Student Edition	**GRSW**	Guided Reading and Study Workbook	**IDM**	Issues and Decision Making
TE	Teacher's Edition	**CT**	Chapter Tests: Levels A and B	**CTB**	Computer Test Bank
LMA	Laboratory Manual A	**PHAS**	PH Assessment System	**PA**	Presentation Assistant Plus
LMB	Laboratory Manual B	**LA**	Lab Assessment with Scoring Guide	**BD**	BioDetectives Videotape
TR	Teaching Resources	**BTM**	BioTechnology Manual	**iT**	iText

Program Resources	Assessment	Media and Technology
TR: Section Review 35–1 B A **GRSW:** Section 35–1 B A **IDM:** Issues and Decisions 4	**SE:** 35–1 Section Assessment, p. 896 **TR:** Section Review 35–1	**PA:** 35–1 Interest Grabber, Section Outline, Example of Feedback Inhibition, Figure 35–2 **iT:** Section 35–1
TR: Section Review 35–2 B A **GRSW:** Section 35–2 B A	**SE:** 35–2 Section Assessment, p. 900 **TR:** Section Review 35–2	**PA:** 35–2 Interest Grabber, Section Outline, A Neuron, Figure 35–6, Figure 35–7, Figure 35–8 **iT:** Section 35–2
LMA: Chapter 35 Lab A E **LMB:** Chapter 35 Lab B A **TR:** Section Review 35–3 B A **GRSW:** Section 35–3 B A **IDM:** Issues and Decisions 44 A E	**SE:** 35–3 Section Assessment, p. 905 **TR:** Section Review 35–3	**PA:** 35–3 Interest Grabber, Section Outline, Concept Map, Figures 35–9 and 35–11, Figure 35–12 **iT:** Section 35–3
TR: Section Review 35–4 B A **GRSW:** Section 35–4 B A	**SE:** 35–4 Section Assessment, p. 909 **TR:** Section Review 35–4	**PA:** 35–4 Interest Grabber, Section Outline, Smell and Taste, Figure 35–14, Figure 35–15 **iT:** Section 35–4
TR: Section Review 35–5 B A Chapter 35 Real-World Lab B A E **GRSW:** Section 35–5 B A **IDM:** Issues and Decisions 41, 42 A E	**SE:** 35–5 Section Assessment, p. 914 **TR:** Section Review 35–5	**PA:** 35–5 Interest Grabber, Section Outline, Commonly Abused Drugs **iT:** Section 35–5
	SE: Chapter 35 Assessment, pp. 916–919 **TR:** Chapter Vocabulary Review, Graphic Organizer **CT:** Chapter 35 Test **CTB:** Chapter 35 Test **PHAS:** Practice Test	**CTB:** Chapter 35 Test **iT:** Chapter 35 Assessment

PRESSED FOR TIME?

To Preview the Chapter
- Have students read the Key Concepts for each section.
- Have students find definitions in the text for the Vocabulary terms.

To Cover the Chapter Quickly
- Have students read all of Section 35–1; the introduction to Sections 35–2, 35–3, and 35–4; and all of Section 35–5.
- Assign the Section Assessments for 35–1 and 35–5, questions 1, 2, 10–12, and 23–25 in Chapter 35 Assessment, and questions 4–7 in Chapter 35 Standardized Test Prep.

To Review the Chapter
- Assign Sections 35–1 and 35–5 in the Guided Reading and Study Workbook.
- Assign the Section Reviews for 35–1 and 35–5 and the Chapter Vocabulary Review for Chapter 35 in the Teaching Resources.

Chapter 35

ENGAGE/EXPLORE

Inquiry Activity

Objectives Students will be able to
- identify misconceptions about the size, shape, and location of organs;
- conclude that organs can belong to more than one organ system.

Skill Focus Interpreting Graphics

Materials large sheets of paper, colored pencils or markers

Time 10 minutes

Strategy You might want to supply outlines of the human body and have students work in groups to pool their knowledge.

Expected Outcome Students are likely to find that their knowledge of human organs is incomplete.

Think About It

1. Yes; skin is part of the excretory system and integumentary system.

2. Answers will vary. Students may be surprised at the locations of some organs, such as the stomach and kidneys or the size of the heart in relation to the lungs.

Demonstration

Obtain two approximately 30-cm pieces of electrical cord. Remove insulation and fray one end of each cord by spreading out the wires to resemble dendrites. Touch the cut end of one cord to the frayed end of the other. Ask: **With the cords arranged in this way, could an electrical impulse travel from one cord to the other?** *(Yes)* **Why?** *(Because the ends are touching.)* Then, move the two cords so they are about a centimeter apart. Ask: **Now could an electrical impulse travel from one cord to the other?** *(No)* **Why?** *(The ends are no longer touching.)* **What could serve as a link between the two cords when they are in this position?** *(Accept all reasonable answers.)* Finally, explain that nervous impulses must travel across a gap between nerve cells much like the gap between the two cords, and in this chapter students will find out how this happens.

Chapter 35 Nervous System

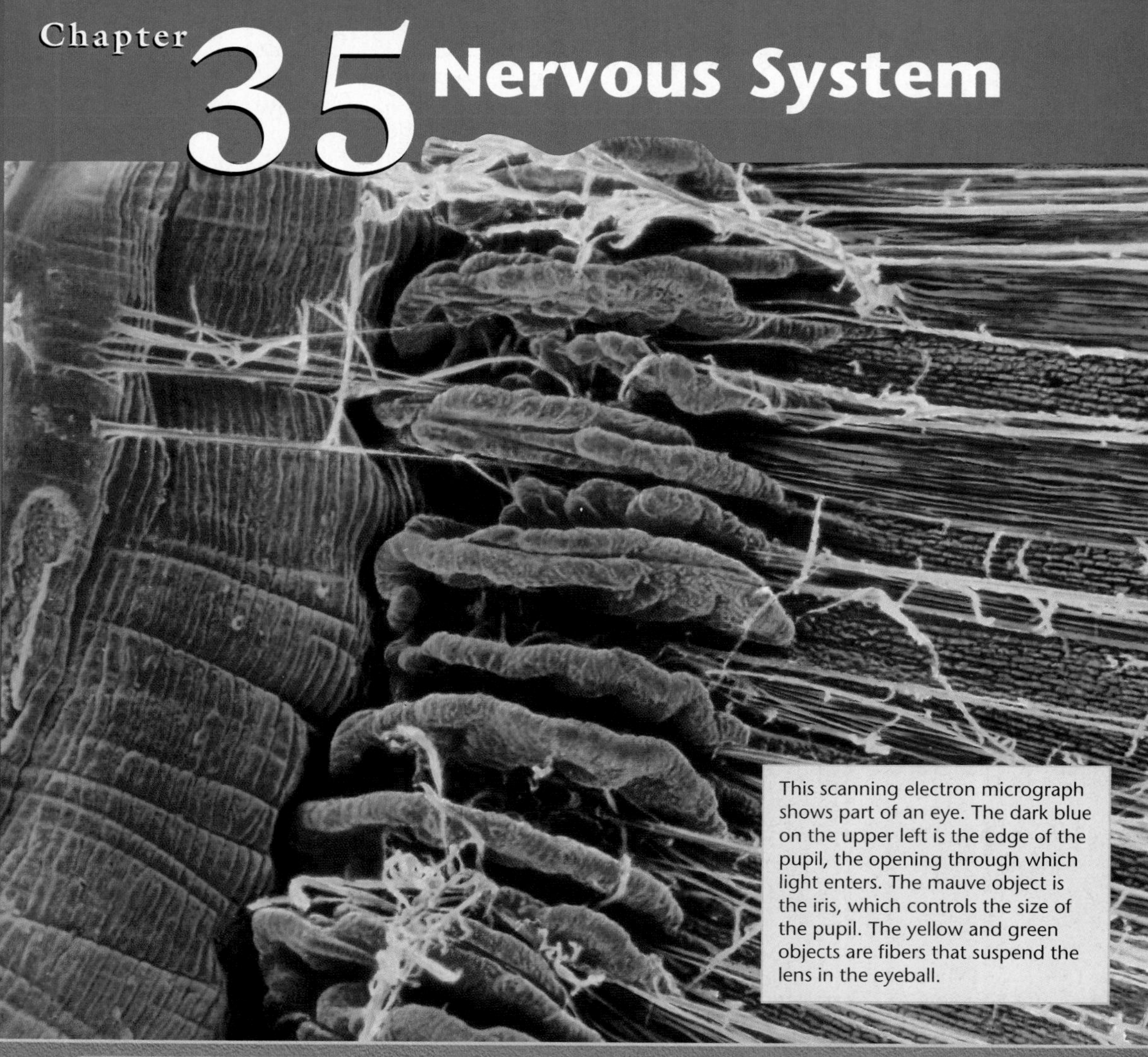

This scanning electron micrograph shows part of an eye. The dark blue on the upper left is the edge of the pupil, the opening through which light enters. The mauve object is the iris, which controls the size of the pupil. The yellow and green objects are fibers that suspend the lens in the eyeball.

Inquiry Activity

What are the organ systems?

Procedure

1. Draw an outline of the human body on a sheet of paper. Without referring to any illustrations, do your best to locate the following organs on your outline: brain, stomach, kidneys, heart, and lungs. Pay attention to the shapes of the organs and their relative sizes.
2. Make a second drawing using **Figure 35–2** on pages 892 and 893 as a reference. Indicate which organs belong to which organ systems.

Think About It

1. **Predicting** Can an organ belong to more than one organ system? Explain.
2. **Evaluating and Revising** Compare your two drawings. Describe any misconceptions you had about the size, shape, or location of the organs.

35–1 Human Body Systems

As the missed shot bounces high in the air, one of the defenders decides to take a chance. She breaks for the other end of the court. Another defender grabs the rebound, glances upcourt, and throws a long, arching pass toward the basket. Wide open, her teammate grabs the pass, dribbles, and leaps into the air, laying the basketball carefully off the backboard and into the unguarded basket. The buzzer goes off, and the game is over.

Guide for Reading

Key Concepts
- How does the human body maintain homeostasis?

Vocabulary
muscle tissue
epithelial tissue
connective tissue
nervous tissue
feedback inhibition

Reading Strategy: Predicting Before you read, use **Figure 35–2** to predict how many organ systems help to regulate body temperature. As you read, look for evidence to support your prediction.

Organization of the Body

Teamwork is a wonderful thing! Anyone watching the end of this game would be impressed at the way these two players worked together to make the winning play. But the real teamwork on this play involved a much larger number of players—nearly a hundred trillion cells that make up the human body.

Every cell in the human body is both an independent unit and an interdependent part of a larger community—the entire organism. To make a winning basket, a basketball player has to use her eyes to watch the play and her brain to figure out how to score. With the support of her bones, her muscles propel her body up the court. As she sprints for a pass, her lungs absorb oxygen, which her blood carries to her cells. Her brain monitors the sensation of the ball on her fingertips and sends signals that guide her body into the air for the final play.

Levels of Organization How does the body get so many individual cells to work together so beautifully? You can begin to answer this question by studying the organization of the human body. Recall the levels of organization in a multicellular organism—cells, tissues, organs, and organ systems. Tissues are groups of similar cells that perform a single function, such as connecting a muscle to a bone. An organ is a group of tissues that work together to perform a complex function, such as sight. An organ system is a group of organs that perform closely related functions.

The eleven organ systems of the human body work together to maintain homeostasis. The organ systems are shown in **Figure 35–2** on pages 892 and 893.

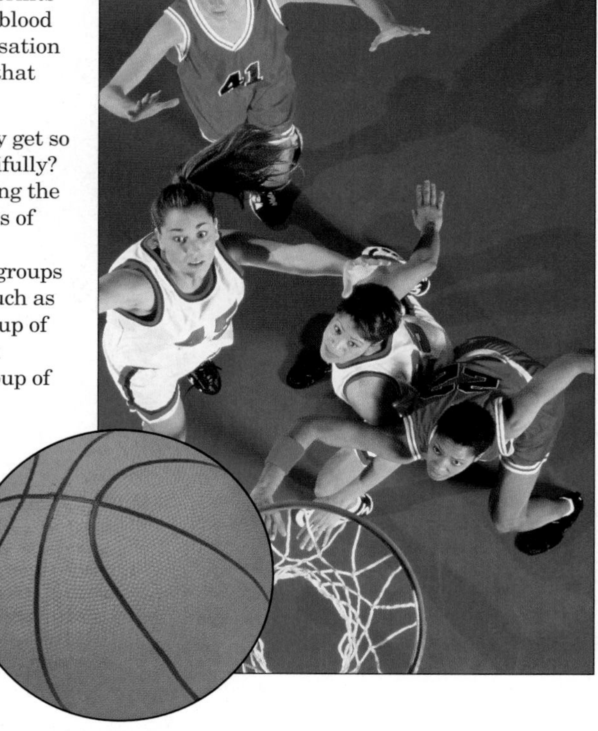

▶ **Figure 35–1** Each player on a basketball team has a different role, but together the team works toward a common goal—winning the game.

Section 35–1

1 FOCUS

Objectives

35.1.1 ***Describe*** how the human body is organized.
35.1.2 ***Explain*** homeostasis.

Guide for Reading

Vocabulary Preview
Emphasize the word *tissue,* which occurs in four of the Vocabulary terms. Remind students that a tissue is a group of similar cells that work together to perform the same function.

Reading Strategy
Point out that Figure 35–2 is a useful reference for all the chapters in this unit. Suggest that students insert a book marker on page 892 so they can refer to the figure more easily as they study this chapter and the other chapters on the body systems.

2 INSTRUCT

Organization of the Body

Build Science Skills

Inferring Challenge students to name the organ systems they think are involved in the basketball player's actions that are described on this page. *(Students might say, for example, that the eyes and brain are used to watch the play and figure out how to score, and that they are part of the nervous system. Students also might say that muscles and bones support the body and allow movement around the basketball court, and that they are part of the muscular system and skeletal system, respectively.)*

SECTION RESOURCES

Print:
- ***Teaching Resources,*** Section Review 35–1
- ***Guided Reading and Study Workbook,*** Section 35–1
- ***Issues and Decision Making,*** Issues and Decisions 4

Technology:
- ***iText,*** Section 35–1

Use Visuals

Figure 35–2 Review the organ systems in the figure by asking questions such as: **What is the function of the nervous system?** *(Coordinates the body's response to external and internal changes)* **What are the structures of the integumentary system?** *(Skin, hair, nails, sweat glands, and oil glands)* **Which system supports the body, allows movement, and stores mineral reserves?** *(Skeletal system)* **Which systems differ in males and females?** *(Endocrine and reproductive systems)*

Meet Diverse Needs

Challenge gifted students to write a poem, song, or rap that identifies the structures and functions of the human organ systems. Advise students to be accurate but creative in their descriptions. Urge students to read, sing, or rap their completed works for the class. **Learning modality: verbal**

Figure 35–2 Human Organ Systems

Each of the eleven organ systems shown here has a different set of functions. **The organ systems work together to maintain a stable internal environment.**

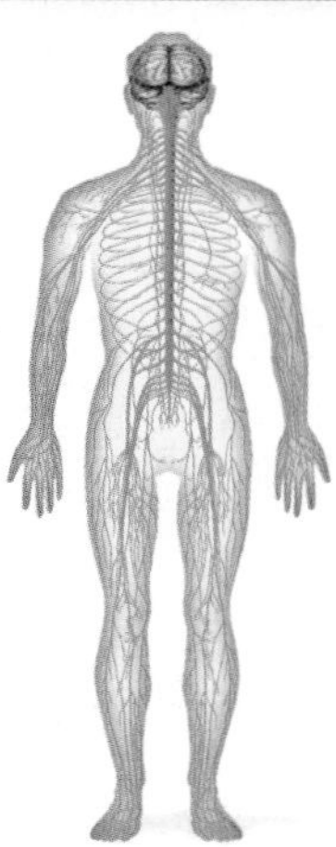

Nervous System
Structures: Brain, spinal cord, peripheral nerves
Function: Coordinates the body's response to changes in its internal and external environments

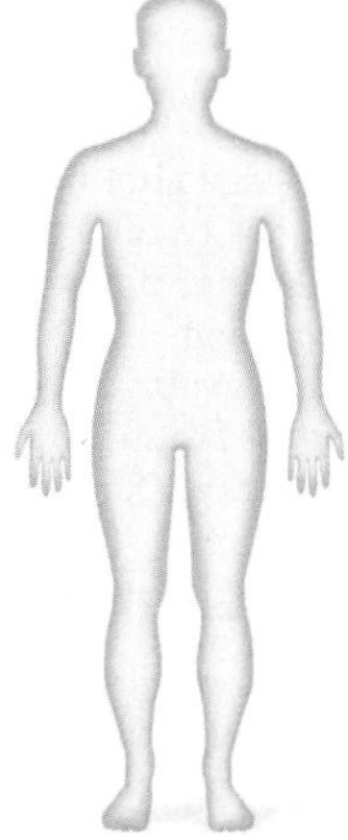

Integumentary System
Structures: Skin, hair, nails, sweat and oil glands
Function: Serves as a barrier against infection and injury; helps to regulate body temperature; provides protection against ultraviolet radiation from the sun

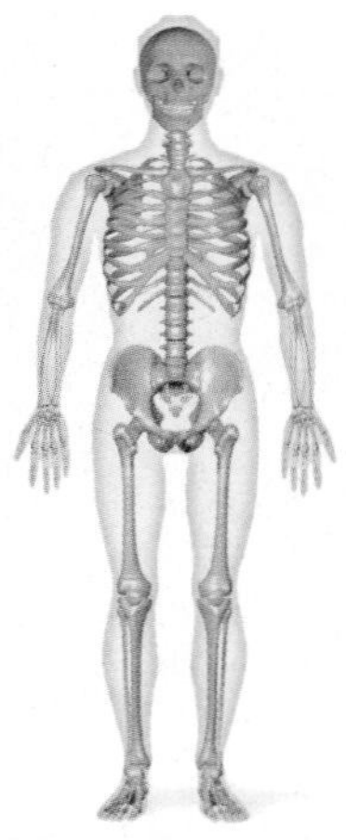

Skeletal System
Structures: Bones, cartilage, ligaments, tendons
Function: Supports the body; protects internal organs; allows movement; stores mineral reserves; provides a site for blood cell formation

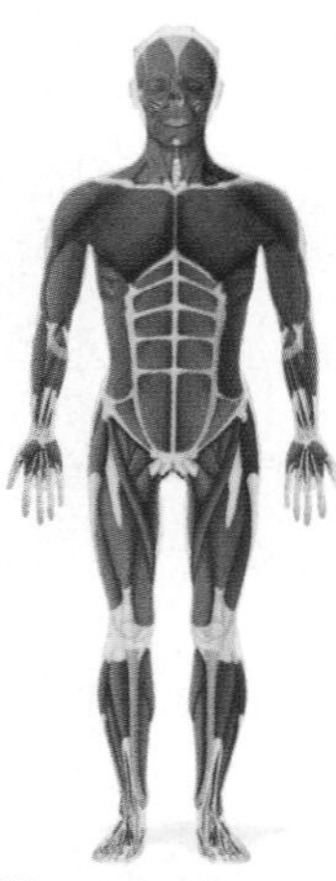

Muscular System
Structures: Skeletal muscle, smooth muscle, cardiac muscle
Function: Works with skeletal system to produce voluntary movement; helps to circulate blood and move food through the digestive system

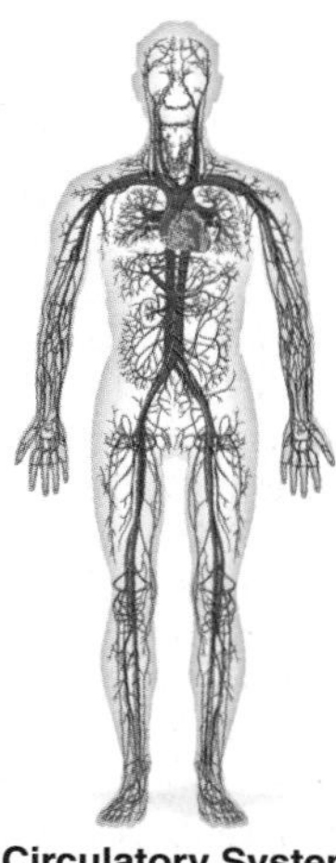

Circulatory System
Structures: Heart, blood vessels, blood
Function: Brings oxygen, nutrients, and hormones to cells; fights infection; regulates body temperature

PRESENTATIONS MADE EASY!

The Presentation Assistant Plus contains the Prentice Hall Presentation Pro and the Transparencies, which provide easy-to-follow visual support for every step of this section. If you have a computer presentation station, use Prentice Hall Presentation Pro for Section 35–1, or use the transparencies listed here.

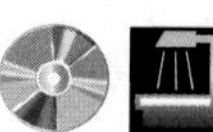

Section 35–1: **Interest Grabber**
Section Outline
Example of Feedback Inhibition
Figure 35–2

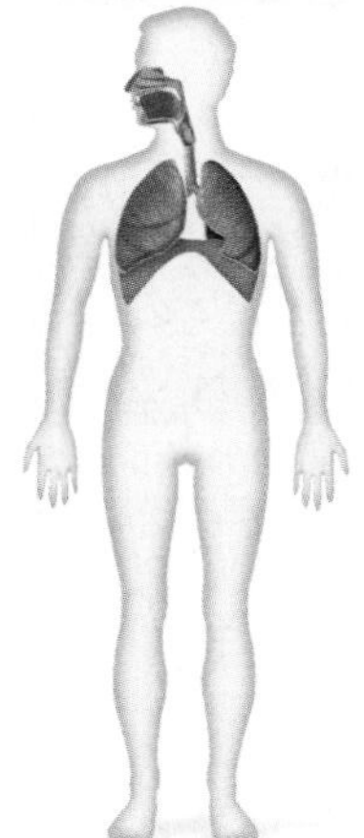

Respiratory System
Structures: Nose, pharynx, larynx, trachea, bronchi, bronchioles, lungs
Function: Provides oxygen needed for cellular respiration and removes excess carbon dioxide from the body

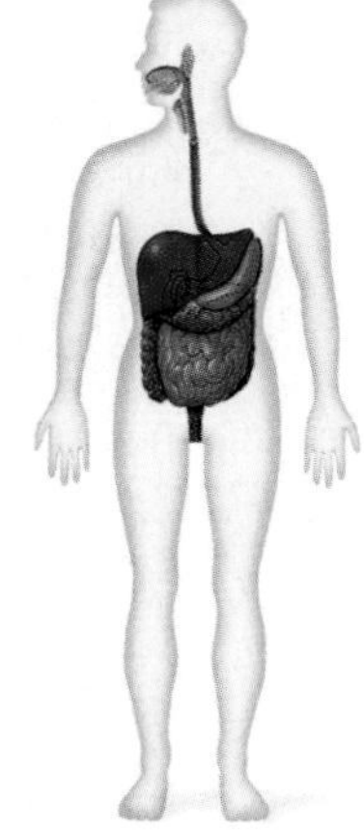

Digestive System
Structures: Mouth, pharynx, esophagus, stomach, small and large intestines
Function: Converts foods into simpler molecules that can be used by the cells of the body; absorbs food

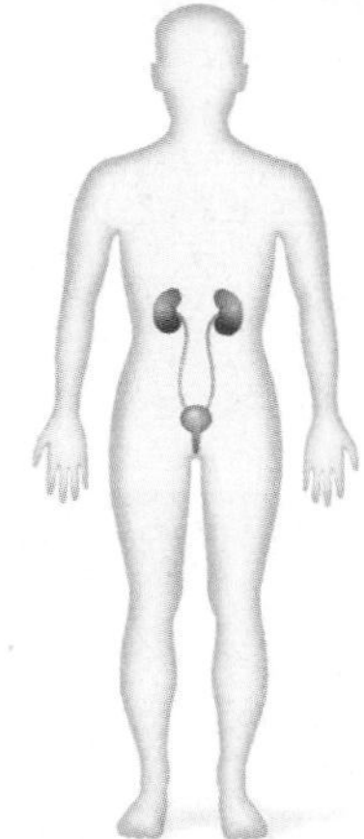

Excretory System
Structures: Skin, lungs, kidneys, ureters, urinary bladder, urethra
Function: Eliminates waste products of metabolism from the body; maintains homeostasis

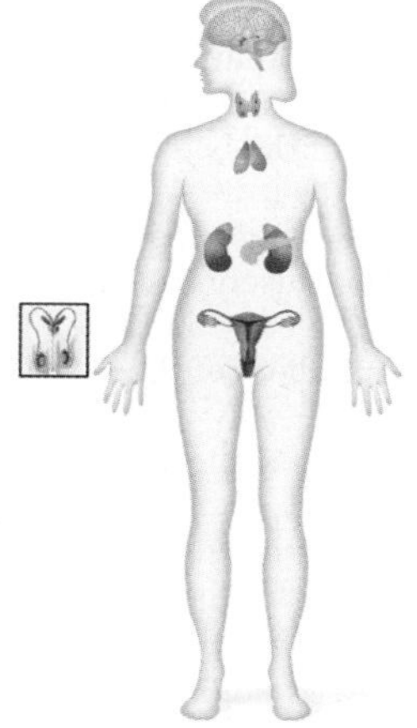

Endocrine System
Structures: Hypothalamus, pituitary, thyroid, parathyroids, adrenals, pancreas, ovaries (in females), testes (in males)
Function: Controls growth, development, metabolism, and reproduction

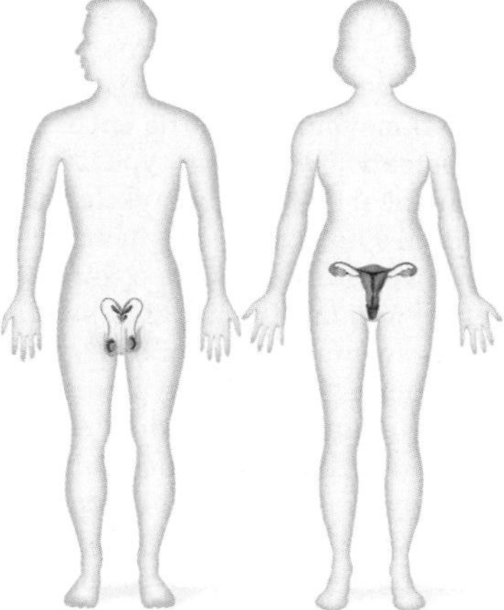

Reproductive System
Structures: Testes, epididymis, vas deferens, urethra, and penis (in males); ovaries, Fallopian tubes, uterus, vagina (in females)
Function: Produces reproductive cells; in females, nurtures and protects developing embryo

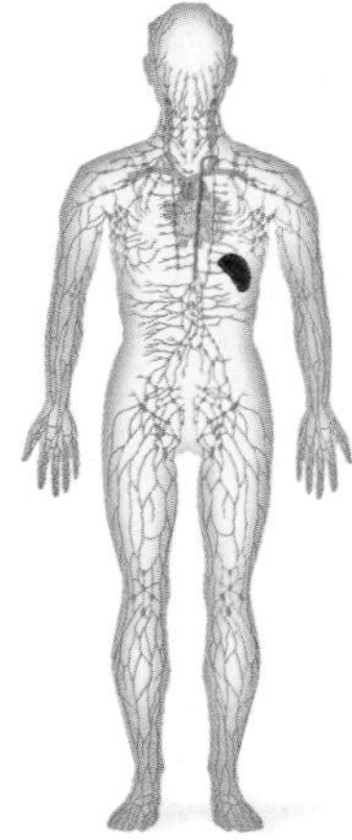

Lymphatic System
Structures: White blood cells, thymus, spleen, lymph nodes, lymph vessels
Function: Helps protect the body from disease; collects fluid lost from blood vessels and returns the fluid to the circulatory system

Demonstration

Use an analogy to demonstrate the importance of communication among human organ systems. Assign several students to two small groups. Have each group work to achieve the same simple goal, such as rearranging the books in a bookcase. Instruct one group to avoid any form of communication, including gestures, facial expressions, and eye contact, and to work independently toward the goal. Instruct the other group to communicate freely and to work together as a team toward the goal. Students will find that communication and teamwork make it much easier to get the job done. Point out that this also applies to organ systems.

Meet Diverse Needs

Encourage interested students to create an overlapping display of the human organ systems. First, students should trace or draw an outline of the human body. Next, they should trace the outline on 11 sheets of tracing paper or transparent film. Then, they should add the structures of one organ system to each sheet. Advise students to use colored pencils or markers for the different organ systems and to label the structures in each system. Allow class time for other students to examine the overlapping displays so they can see how the different organ systems are positioned in the body relative to one another. **Learning modality: tactile**

BIO INSIGHTS

FACTS AND FIGURES

Organization of animal body plans
The general organization of animal body plans is usually taught in terms of organ systems. Students might be under the impression that all animals, or at least all vertebrates, have the same major organ systems. Although this is roughly true in most cases, there are some interesting exceptions that demonstrate that the major organ systems are not all indispensable to animal life. For example, the tube worms found at deep-sea hydrothermal vents include species in which the digestive system has virtually disappeared. These worms do not eat. Instead, their digestive tracts have been reduced to a specialized organ that houses symbiotic chemosynthetic bacteria that produce organic nutrients by reducing bicarbonate ions (HCO_3^-).

35–1 (continued)

Demonstration

Display the following items: plastic wrap, electrical wire, and packaging tape. For each item, ask: **What is the purpose of this item?** *(Students might say that plastic wrap covers and protects, electrical wire transmits signals, and packaging tape binds and supports.)* Explain that three of the four types of tissues in the human body carry out similar functions. Ask: **Which type of tissue is represented by each item?** *(Epithelial tissue is represented by plastic wrap, nervous tissue by electrical wire, and connective tissue by packaging tape.)* **What could you use to represent muscle tissue?** *(Possible answers might include rubber bands or bungee cords.)*

Build Science Skills

Applying Concepts Tell students that organs and organ systems often consist of all four types of tissues. Challenge students to identify the types of tissues found in a particular organ, such as the stomach. *(The walls of the stomach consist of muscle tissue; the lining of the stomach consists of epithelial tissue; both muscle and epithelial tissues also contain nerve tissue.)*

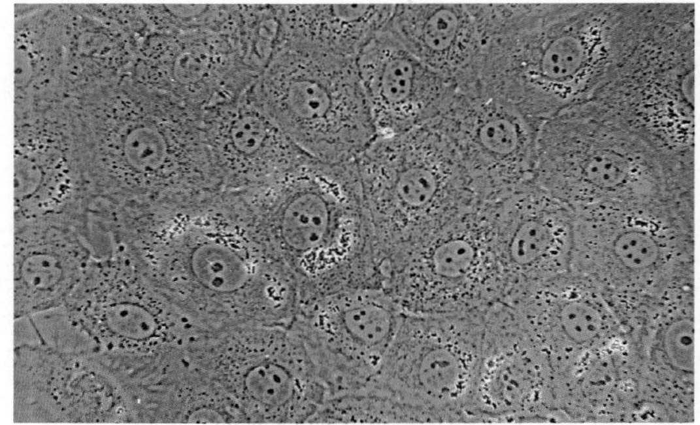

Epithelial Tissue (magnification: 6000×)

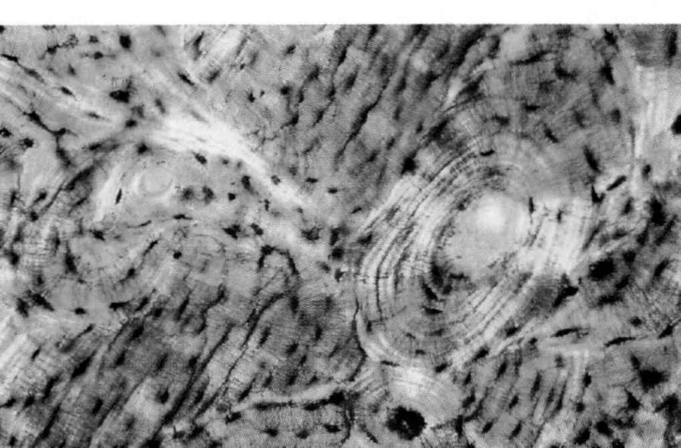

Connective Tissue (magnification: about 50×)

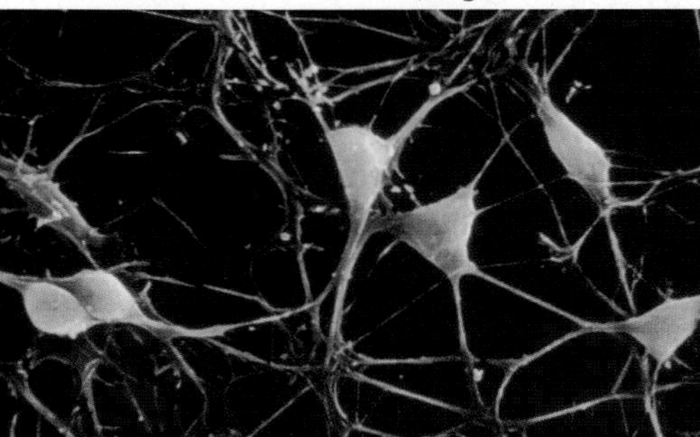

Nervous Tissue (magnification: 1100×)

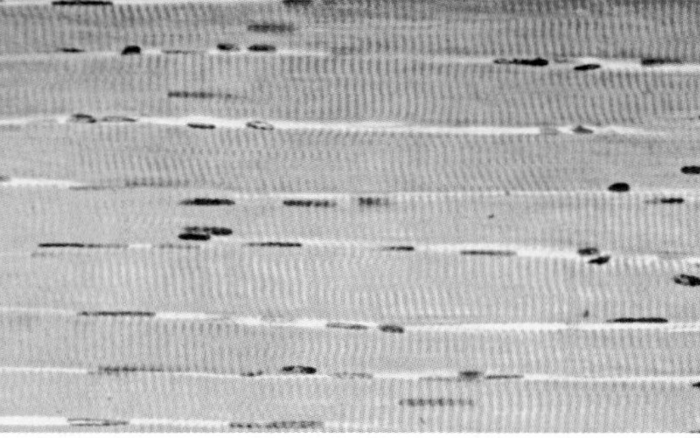

Muscle Tissue (magnification: 150×)

▲ **Figure 35–3** The four major types of tissues in the human body are epithelial tissue, connective tissue, nervous tissue, and muscle tissue. **Inferring** *What kind of tissue is bone?*

Types of Tissues Different tissue types work together within organs. **Muscle tissue** is the most abundant tissue in most animals. Muscle tissue controls the internal movement of materials such as blood through the circulatory system and food through the digestive system. Muscle tissue also controls the external movements of the entire body or parts of the body, such as your hands when you type on a computer keyboard.

The heart is mainly muscle tissue, but three other types of tissues are needed for the heart to function. The closely packed cells in **epithelial tissue** cover the surface of the body and line internal organs. Epithelial tissue lining the chambers of the heart prevents leakage of blood. Glands are made from epithelial tissue. A gland is a structure that makes and secretes, or releases, a particular product such as saliva, sweat, or milk.

Connective tissue does more than its name implies. It holds organs in place and binds different parts of the body together. The tendons that connect bones to muscles and the ligaments that join bones to bones are examples of connective tissue. This type of tissue also provides support for the body. Connective tissue keeps the walls of the heart flexible, but strong. Some connective tissue pads and insulates the body.

Nervous tissue receives messages from the body's external and internal environments, analyzes the data, and directs the response. Nervous tissue in the heart controls the rate at which the heart beats.

CHECKPOINT *What is the role of nervous tissue?*

FACTS AND FIGURES

On more than one team

Many organs can be classified as belonging to more than one system. The pancreas is part of the digestive system and the endocrine system. The heart is now known to release hormones, making it an endocrine gland as well as the key organ of the circulatory system. Bones contain tissue important to the immune system as well as to the skeletal system.

Maintaining Homeostasis

You can get a glimpse of the functions of your organ systems when you breathe deeply after climbing a steep hill or your blood clots to seal a cut. Behind the scenes, your organ systems are working constantly to do something that few people appreciate—maintain a controlled, stable internal environment. Recall from Chapter 1 that this process is called homeostasis. The cells of the body must be kept at a temperature within a certain narrow range, supplied with energy through cellular respiration, bathed in fluid, and cleansed of their waste products. Failure at any of these tasks, even for a few minutes, could lead to permanent injury or death of the entire organism.

A Nonliving Example One way to understand homeostasis is to look at a nonliving system that also keeps environmental conditions within a certain range. The heating system of a house is a perfect example. In most houses, heat is supplied by a furnance that burns oil or natural gas. When the temperature within the house drops below a set point, a sensor in a device called a thermostat switches the furnace on. Heat produced by the furnace warms the house. When the temperature rises above the set point, the thermostat switches the furnace off. Because the furnace runs only when it is needed, the temperature of the house is kept within a narrow range.

A heating system like the one described is said to be controlled by feedback inhibition. **Feedback inhibition** is the process by which the product of a system shuts down the system or limits its operation. **Figure 35–4** summarizes the feedback inhibition process in a home heating system. When the furnace is switched on, it produces a product (heat) that changes the environment of the house (by raising the air temperature). This environmental change then "feeds back" to "inhibit" the operation of the furnace. In other words, heat from the furnace eventually raises the temperature enough to send a feedback signal to switch the furnace off. Systems controlled by feedback inhibition are generally fully automated and very stable. That is why a house with a good heating system is a comfortable place to be, even on the coldest of days.

▼ **Figure 35–4** A home heating system uses feedback inhibition to maintain a stable, comfortable environment within a house. **Predicting** *In which organ system is the thermostat for the human body located?*

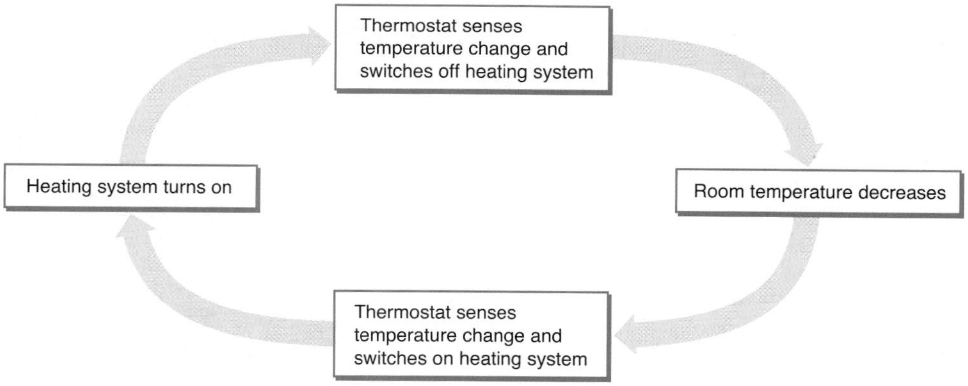

Thermostat senses temperature change and switches off heating system

Room temperature decreases

Thermostat senses temperature change and switches on heating system

Heating system turns on

FACTS AND FIGURES

Body talk

To maintain homeostasis, the body must have good internal communications. Both endocrine and nervous systems fulfill this role in humans and other animals. Endocrine communication depends on the release of chemicals, which can travel in the blood throughout the entire body. Hours or even days may elapse between the release of a chemical by the endocrine system and the response by the cells that are sensitive to the chemical. Nervous system communication, in contrast, depends on the transmission of nerve impulses along nerve pathways, which is extremely rapid. In fact, nerve impulses can typically relay information about events in one part of the body to another in less than a second.

Maintaining Homeostasis

Make Connections

Chemistry Point out that chemistry is the reason we must maintain homeostasis in body temperature. Explain that most of the biochemical processes vital to life will only occur within a very limited range of temperatures. Temperatures above or below these limits inhibit chemical reactions, denature enzymes, destroy other molecules, and otherwise wreak havoc on the body's internal biochemistry.

Answers to . . .

CHECKPOINT *The role of nervous tissue is to receive messages from the external and internal environments, analyze the data, and direct the response.*

Figure 35–3 *Bone is connective tissue.*

Figure 35–4 *Endocrine system*

35–1 (continued)

Build Science Skills

Using Models Have students compare the regulation of body temperature in humans with the regulation of air temperature in a house. Ask: **Which structure in the human body has the same role as the thermostat in a house?** *(The hypothalamus)* You could extend the model by noting that the temperature in a house can vary with location just as body temperature varies from the core to the surface.

Word Origins

Hypothermia means a below-normal body temperature.

SCIENCE NEWS®

Encourage students to visit **www.phschool.com** for the most recent information on this topic.

3 ASSESS

Evaluate Understanding

Have students draw a simple diagram to show how the body regulates temperature.

Reteach

State the function of each human organ system, and challenge students to identify the system and name its structures.

ALTERNATIVE ASSESSMENT

Students' Venn diagrams should have a nesting structure, with concentric circles representing the four levels of organization, from smallest and simplest (cells) to largest and most complex (organ systems). Examples might include neurons for cells, nervous tissue for tissues, brain for organs, and nervous system for organ systems.

Use iText to review the key concepts in Section 35–1.

KEEP CURRENT WITH . . . SCIENCE NEWS®

To find out more about the topics in this chapter, go to: **www.phschool.com**

Word Origins

Thermometer comes from the Greek words *therme,* meaning "heat," and *metron,* meaning "measure." So, thermometer means an instrument used to measure heat. **If *hypo-* is Greek for "under," what does *hypothermia* mean?**

In the Body Could biological systems achieve homeostasis through feedback inhibition? Absolutely. All that is needed is a system that regulates some aspect of the cellular environment and that can respond to feedback from its own activities by switching on or off as needed.

For the body to maintain a stable temperature, there must be a balance between heat production and heat loss. The body regulates temperature by a mechanism that is remarkably similar to that of a household heating system. A part of the brain called the hypothalamus contains nerve cells that monitor both the temperature of the skin at the surface of the body and the temperature of organs in the body's core. The temperature of the core is generally higher than the temperature of the skin.

If the nerve cells sense that the core temperature has dropped much below 37°C, the hypothalamus produces chemicals that signal cells throughout the body to speed up their activities. Heat produced by this increase in cellular activity causes a gradual rise in body temperature, which is detected by nerve cells in the hypothalamus. This feedback inhibits the production of the chemicals that speed up cellular activity and keeps body temperature from rising to a dangerous level.

Have you ever been so cold that you began to shiver? If your body temperature drops well below its normal range, the hypothalamus releases chemicals that signal muscles just below the surface of the skin to contract involuntarily—to "shiver." These muscle contractions release heat, which helps the body temperature to rise back toward the normal range.

If body temperature rises too far above 37°C, the hypothalamus slows down cellular activities, minimizing the production of heat. This is one of the main reasons you may feel tired and sluggish on a hot day. The body also responds to high temperatures by producing sweat, which helps to cool the body surface by evaporation. Because heat from the body's core is carried by the blood to the skin, evaporation at the body surface also helps to lower the temperature of the core. When this temperature returns to its set point, the body stops producing sweat.

35–1 Section Assessment

1. **Key Concept** Explain the role the nervous system plays in maintaining homeostasis.
2. What are the four types of tissue?
3. Which organ systems help to maintain body temperature?
4. Explain why the hypothalamus can be compared to a thermostat.
5. **Critical Thinking Classifying** Would you classify blood as a cell, a tissue, or an organ? Explain your answer.

iTEXT Assessment Use iText to review the important concepts in Section 35–1.

ALTERNATIVE ASSESSMENT

Making a Venn Diagram Draw a Venn diagram to link the four basic levels of organization in the human body. Provide at least three examples for each level included in your diagram.

35–1 Section Assessment

1. Nerve cells in the hypothalamus control the temperature of the body. They collect data from the skin and from organs in the body's core. In response to this data, chemicals are released that control the rate of cellular activity.
2. Epithelial, connective, nervous, muscle
3. Students are likely to say nervous, muscular, integumentary, and circulatory systems based on the text, and the endocrine system based on data in Figure 35–2.
4. Both the hypothalamus and the thermostat help to regulate temperature.
5. A tissue, because it performs a single function—the transport of materials to all parts of the body.

35–2 The Nervous System

Play any team sport—basketball, softball, soccer—and you will discover that communication is one of the keys to success. Coaches call plays, players signal to one another, and the very best teams communicate in a way that enables them to play as a single unit. Communication can make the difference between winning and losing.

The same is true for living organisms. Nearly all multicellular organisms have communication systems. Specialized cells carry messages from one cell to another so that communication among all body parts is smooth and efficient. In humans, these cells are in the nervous system. **The nervous system controls and coordinates functions throughout the body and responds to internal and external stimuli.**

Guide for Reading

Key Concepts
- What is the function of the nervous system?
- How is a nerve impulse transmitted?

Vocabulary
neuron • cell body
dendrite • axon
myelin sheath
resting potential
action potential
threshold • synapse
neurotransmitter

Reading Strategy: Summarizing As you read, find the key ideas for each paragraph. Write down a few key words from each main idea. Then, use the key words in your summary.

Neurons

The messages carried by the nervous system are electrical signals called impulses. The cells that transmit these impulses are called **neurons**. Neurons can be classified into three types according to the direction in which an impulse travels. Sensory neurons carry impulses from the sense organs to the spinal cord and brain. Motor neurons carry impulses from the brain and the spinal cord to muscles and glands. Interneurons connect sensory and motor neurons and carry impulses between them. Although neurons come in all shapes and sizes, they have certain features in common. **Figure 35–5** shows a typical neuron. The largest part of a typical neuron is the **cell body.** The cell body contains the nucleus and much of the cytoplasm. Most of the metabolic activity of the cell takes place in the cell body.

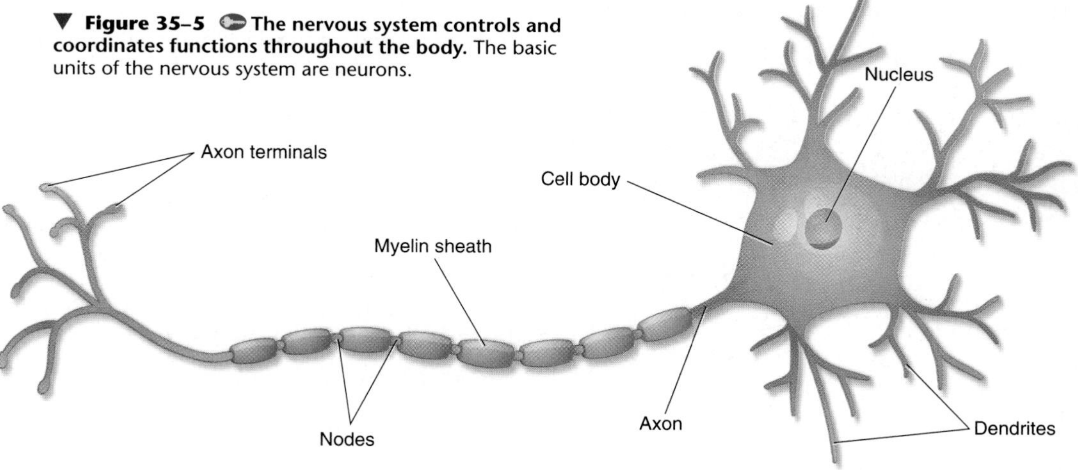

▼ **Figure 35–5 The nervous system controls and coordinates functions throughout the body.** The basic units of the nervous system are neurons.

SECTION RESOURCES

Print:
- ***Teaching Resources,*** Section Review 35–2
- ***Guided Reading and Study Workbook,*** Section 35–2

Technology:
- ***iText,*** Section 35–2

Section 35–2

1 FOCUS

Objectives

35.2.1 ***Identify*** the function of the nervous system.
35.2.2 ***Describe*** how a nerve impulse is transmitted.

Guide for Reading

Vocabulary Preview

Tell students that the prefix *neuro-* comes from the Greek word for nerve. Ask: **What do you think the Vocabulary terms *neuron* and *neurotransmitter* mean?** *(A neuron is a nerve cell; a neurotransmitter is a chemical that transmits messages from a neuron to another cell.)*

Reading Strategy

As students read, they should look for key words and key concepts in the captions and the text. Suggest that students include boldface words and sentences in their summary.

2 INSTRUCT

Demonstration

Help students appreciate how quickly the cells of the nervous system communicate. Have a volunteer repeat a movement, such as nodding the head, at irregular intervals. Have another volunteer respond to the first movement with a different movement, such as raising a finger. Challenge the class to measure the time it takes for the second volunteer's nervous system to sense, interpret, and respond to the movement made by the first volunteer. *(Students probably will find that the response time is too short to measure.)*

Neurons

Use Visuals

Figure 35–5 Point out the nucleus in the cell body. Name each of the other parts of the neuron, and have students locate them in the figure. Urge students to refer back to the figure as they read about the parts of a neuron and how they are involved in the transmission of nerve impulses.

Meet Diverse Needs

Give interested students a chance to make a three-dimensional model of a neuron. Provide them with materials, such as string, beads, dry pasta, and modeling clay. Remind students to provide a key for the parts of their model. Allow them to display their models in the classroom. **Learning modality: tactile**

The Nerve Impulse

Use Visuals

Figure 35–6 Have students look at the distribution of potassium and sodium ions. Then have them answer the question in the caption. Ask: **Why do you think the drawing has two potassium ions outside the cell but only one sodium ion inside the cell?** *(To indicate that potassium ions diffuse across the cell membrane more easily than do sodium ions)* This difference in the ability of the positive ions to diffuse creates the difference in electrical charge across the cell membrane.

Spreading out from the cell body are short, branched extensions called **dendrites.** Dendrites carry impulses from the environment or from other neurons toward the cell body. The long fiber that carries impulses away from the cell body is called the **axon.** The axon ends in a series of small swellings called axon terminals, located some distance from the cell body. Neurons may have dozens of dendrites but usually have only one axon. In most animals, axons and dendrites are clustered into bundles of fibers called nerves. Some nerves contain only a few neurons, but many others have hundreds or even thousands of neurons.

In some neurons, the axon is surrounded by an insulating membrane known as the **myelin sheath** (MY-uh-lin). The myelin sheath that surrounds a single long axon leaves many gaps, called nodes, where the axon membrane is exposed. As an impulse moves along the axon, it jumps from one node to the next, which increases the speed at which the impulse can travel.

The Nerve Impulse

The production of a nerve impulse can be compared to the flow of electricity through a wire. The transmission of electricity depends on the movement of negatively charged electrons. The production of a nerve impulse depends on the movement of positively charged ions across a cell membrane.

▼ **Figure 35–6** At rest, the inside of the neuron's membrane has a negative charge. **Predicting** *Is the distribution of positive ions shown the result of diffusion or of active transport?*

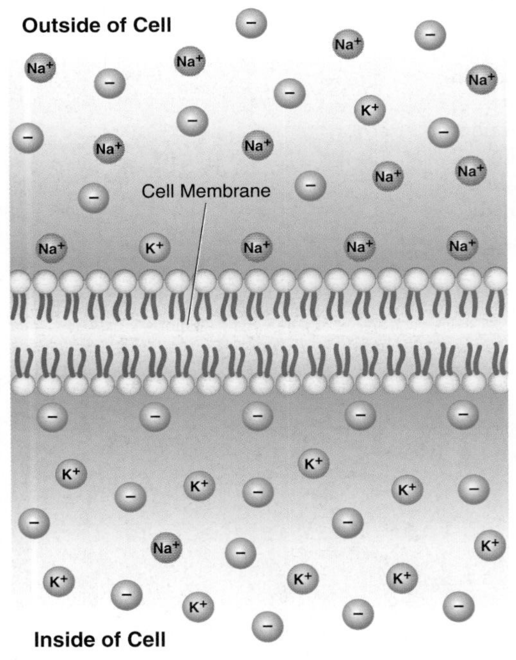

Resting Potential The distribution of sodium ions (Na^+) and potassium ions (K^+) inside and outside a neuron is shown in **Figure 35–6.** There are more potassium ions (K^+) in the cytoplasm than in the fluid outside the cell and more sodium ions in the fluid outside the cell than in the cytoplasm. Because both potassium and sodium ions can diffuse across the cell membrane, the unequal distribution of these ions must be maintained by active transport. Proteins in the cell membrane pump sodium ions out of the neuron and potassium ions into the neuron.

Potassium and sodium ions continue to diffuse across the membrane, but potassium ions diffuse out of the cell more easily than sodium ions diffuse in. As a result, a negative charge builds up on the inside of the membrane and a positive charge builds up on the outside of the membrane. This difference in electrical charge across the cell membrane of a resting neuron is its **resting potential.** A neuron has a resting potential of about –70 millivolts (mV). Thus, the magnitude of the voltage across a tiny neuron's membrane is roughly one twentieth the voltage of a flashlight battery (1.5 volts).

CHECKPOINT *What is resting potential?*

PRESENTATIONS MADE EASY!

The Presentation Assistant Plus contains the Prentice Hall Presentation Pro and the Transparencies, which provide easy-to-follow visual support for every step of this section. If you have a computer presentation station, use Prentice Hall Presentation Pro for Section 35–2, or use the transparencies listed here.

Section 35–2:

Interest Grabber
Section Outline
A Neuron
Figure 35–6
Figure 35–7
Figure 35–8

The Moving Impulse A nerve impulse is similar to the ripple caused when a rock is dropped into a pond. The ripple is caused by the up-and-down movement of water. The impulse is caused by the movement of ions across the cell membrane. **A nerve impulse begins when a neuron is stimulated by another neuron or by its environment.** The impulse travels along the axon, away from the cell body and toward the axon terminals. **Figure 35–7** summarizes the transmission of a nerve impulse along an axon.

The cell membrane of a neuron contains thousands of protein channels that allow ions to pass through when the gates to these channels are open. Generally, the gates are closed. At the leading edge of an impulse, however, the sodium gates open, allowing sodium ions to flow into the cell. This flow of positive ions causes a temporary change in the charges on the cell membrane. The inside of the membrane gains a positive charge and the outside gains a negative charge. This reversal of charges is called an **action potential.** A neuron has an action potential of about +30 mV. As the impulse passes, the potassium gates open, allowing positively charged potassium ions to flow out of the cell. The resting potential of the membrane is re-established. The membrane is once again negatively charged on the inside and positively charged on the outside.

A nerve impulse is self-propagating. That is, an impulse at any point on the membrane causes an impulse at the next point along the membrane. You can compare the flow of an impulse to the fall of a row of dominoes. As each domino falls, it causes its neighbor to fall.

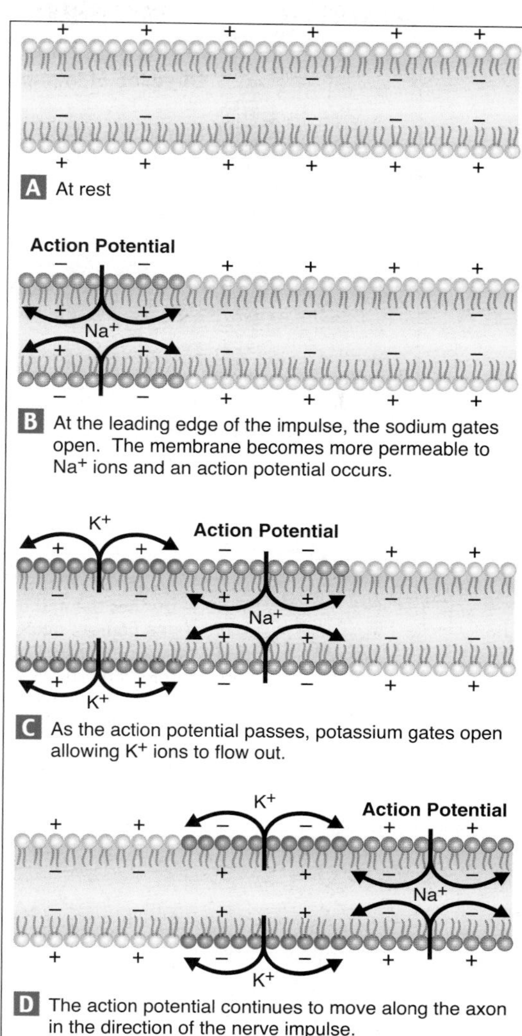

A At rest
Action Potential
Na+
B At the leading edge of the impulse, the sodium gates open. The membrane becomes more permeable to Na+ ions and an action potential occurs.
K+
Action Potential
Na+
K+
C As the action potential passes, potassium gates open allowing K+ ions to flow out.
K+
Action Potential
Na+
K+
D The action potential continues to move along the axon in the direction of the nerve impulse.

▲ **Figure 35–7** **A nerve impulse is self-propagating.** Sodium ions flowing into the neuron reverse the charges on the membrane. As the impulse passes, potassium ions flow out of the neuron and the resting potential is restored.

Threshold The strength of an impulse is always the same—either there is an impulse in response to a stimulus or there is not. In other words, a stimulus must be of adequate strength to cause a neuron to transmit an impulse. The minimum level of a stimulus that is required to activate a neuron is called the **threshold.** Any stimulus that is stronger than the threshold will produce an impulse. Any stimulus that is weaker than the threshold will produce no impulse. Thus, a nerve impulse follows the all-or-none principle: either the stimulus will produce an impulse, or it won't produce an impulse.

The all-or-none principle can be illustrated by using a row of dominoes. If you were to gently press the first domino in a row, it might not move at all. A slightly harder push might make the domino teeter back and forth but not fall. A slightly stronger push would cause the first domino to fall into the second. You have reached the threshold at which the row of dominoes would fall.

Meet Diverse Needs

Help visual learners understand the concept of electrical potential with another type of energy potential that can be demonstrated in the classroom. Use a spring to demonstrate kinetic potential. Depress the spring, and ask: **What will happen when the spring is released?** *(A burst of energy will move the spring back to its resting state.)* Illustrate this by letting go of the spring. Then, ask: **What are some other examples of kinetic potential?** *(Possible answers include a child sitting at the top of a slide and a diver poised to dive off the high board.)*

Demonstration

Use the domino analogy mentioned in the text to simulate the movement of an action potential down an axon. Arrange dominoes on end in a row, and then knock them down by giving the first one a gentle push. Ask: **Why did all the dominoes fall when only the first domino was pushed?** *(Because kinetic energy was passed from domino to domino)* **What was the source of the kinetic energy that was transmitted down the line of dominoes?** *(Some was provided by the push on the first domino, some by the position of the dominoes—standing on end, they were easily toppled by gravity when gently bumped.)* **What would you have to do in order to get the dominoes to topple again?** *(Return them to the starting position)*

BACKGROUND

All or nothing

A nerve impulse usually is described as an all-or-nothing phenomenon. This means that there is a threshold level below which a stimulus cannot trigger an action potential. Any stimulus at or above the threshold level triggers exactly the same response. However, if a neuron has just fired, this picture changes. There is a period of a few milliseconds, called the absolute refractory period, during which no stimulus can produce a response, even a stimulus above the threshold level. Then, for a slightly longer period, the relative refractory period, an intense stimulus well above the threshold level is needed to provoke a response. The closer the neuron is to complete recovery, the less intense the stimulus must be to provoke a response. When the neuron is completely recovered, it responds in the all-or-nothing way once again.

Answers to . . .

CHECKPOINT *The difference in electrical charge across the cell membrane of a resting neuron*

Figure 35–6 *Active transport must maintain the unequal distribution of positive ions.*

35–2 (continued)

The Synapse

Make Connections

Health Science Explain that many mental illnesses appear to be caused, at least in part, by abnormal levels of neurotransmitters. For example, depression is associated with lower-than-normal levels of serotonin and norepinephrine, and schizophrenia is associated with higher-than-normal levels of dopamine. Ask: **How do you think abnormal levels of neurotransmitters affect the functioning of the nervous system.** *(Students might say they would either decrease or increase the transmission of nerve impulses.)*

3 ASSESS

Evaluate Understanding

Call on students at random to define each of the Vocabulary terms. Call on other students to correct any errors.

Reteach

Provide students with copies of Figure 35–5 without the labels, and have them label each part of the neuron.

ALTERNATIVE ASSESSMENT

Students' flowcharts should include the following events: arrival of the nerve impulse at an axon terminal; release of neurotransmitters into the synaptic cleft; diffusion of neurotransmitters across the gap and attachment to receptors on a neighboring cell membrane; movement of positive ions across the cell membrane; and stimulation of the neighboring cell.

Use iText to review the key concepts in Section 35–2.

Answer to . . .

Figure 35–8 *No; a motor neuron passes an impulse to a muscle cell.*

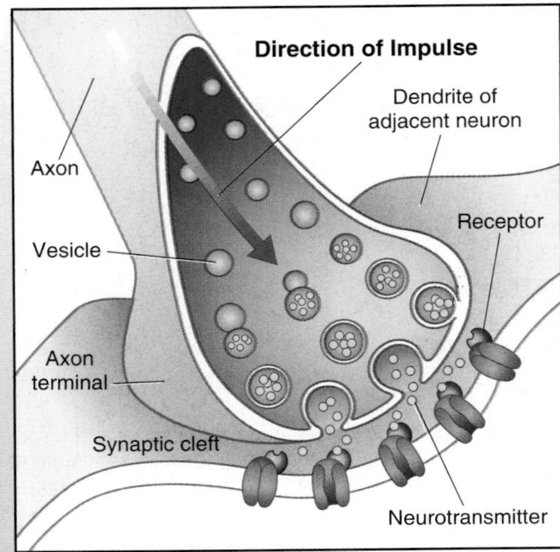

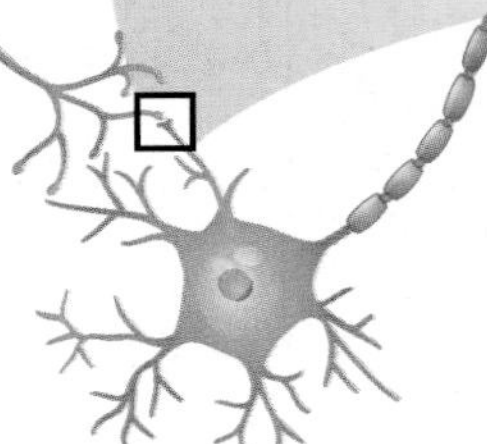

▲ **Figure 35–8** When an impulse reaches the end of the axon of one neuron, neurotransmitters are released into the synaptic cleft. The neurotransmitters bind to receptors on the membrane of an adjacent neuron. **Predicting** ***Is the adjacent cell always another neuron?***

The Synapse

At the end of the neuron, the impulse reaches an axon terminal. Usually the neuron makes contact with another cell at this location. The neuron may pass the impulse along to the second cell. Motor neurons, for example, pass their impulses to muscle cells.

The location at which a neuron can transfer an impulse to another cell is called a **synapse** (SIN-aps). As shown in **Figure 35–8,** a small cleft, or gap, separates the axon terminal from the dendrites of the adjacent cell, in this case a neuron. The terminals contain tiny sacs, or vesicles, filled with neurotransmitters (noo-roh-TRANZ-mit-urs). **Neurotransmitters** are chemicals used by a neuron to transmit an impulse across a synapse to another cell.

When an action potential arrives at an axon terminal, the sacs release the neurotransmitters into the small gap between the two cells. The neurotransmitter molecules diffuse across the gap and attach themselves to receptors on the membrane of the neighboring cell. This stimulus causes positive sodium ions to rush across the cell membrane, stimulating the second cell. If the stimulation exceeds the cell's threshold, a new impulse begins.

Only a fraction of a second after binding to their receptors, the neurotransmitter molecules are released from the cell surface. They may then be broken down by enzymes, or taken up and recycled by the axon terminal.

35–2 Section Assessment

1. **Key Concept** Describe the functions of the nervous system.
2. **Key Concept** What happens when a neuron is stimulated by another neuron?
3. What are the three types of neurons?
4. Describe the role of the myelin sheath.
5. **Critical Thinking Applying Concepts** How can the level of pain you feel vary if a stimulus causes an all-or-none response?

iTEXT Assessment Use iText to review the important concepts in Section 35–2.

ALTERNATIVE ASSESSMENT

Creating a Flowchart Create a flowchart to show the events that occur as a nerve impulse travels from one neuron to the next. Include as much detail as you can. Use your flowchart to explain the process to a classmate.

35–2 Section Assessment

1. The human nervous system controls and coordinates functions throughout the body and responds to internal and external stimuli.
2. It begins an impulse that travels rapidly along the axon toward the axon terminals, where the impulse is passed on to another cell.
3. Sensory neurons, motor neurons, and interneurons
4. The myelin sheath insulates the axon and greatly increases the speed of transmission of nerve impulses.
5. There are two possible factors: the number of sensory neurons activated by a stimulus and the frequency of the stimulation.

35–3 Divisions of the Nervous System

Neurons do not act alone. Instead, they are joined together to form a complex network—the nervous system. The human nervous system is separated into two major divisions: the central nervous system and the peripheral nervous system.

The central nervous system is the control center of the body. The functions of the central nervous system are similar to those of the central processing unit of a computer. **The central nervous system relays messages, processes information, and analyzes information.** The peripheral nervous system receives information from the environment and relays commands from the central nervous system to organs and glands.

Guide for Reading

Key Concepts
- What are the functions of the central nervous system?
- What are the two divisions of the peripheral nervous system?

Vocabulary
central nervous system
meninges • cerebrospinal fluid
cerebrum • cerebellum
brain stem • thalamus
hypothalamus • reflex

Reading Strategy: Asking Questions Before you read, rewrite the headings in the section as *how, why,* or *what* questions about the nervous system. As you read, write down the answers to your questions.

The Central Nervous System

The **central nervous system** consists of the brain, shown in **Figure 35–9,** and the spinal cord. The skull and vertebrae in the spinal column protect the brain and spinal cord. Both the brain and spinal cord are wrapped in three layers of connective tissue known as **meninges** (muh-NIN-jeez). Between two of these layers is a space filled with cerebrospinal fluid. **Cerebrospinal fluid** (sehr-uh-broh-SPY-nul) bathes the brain and spinal cord and acts as a shock absorber that protects the central nervous system. The fluid also allows for the exchange of nutrients and waste products between blood and nervous tissue.

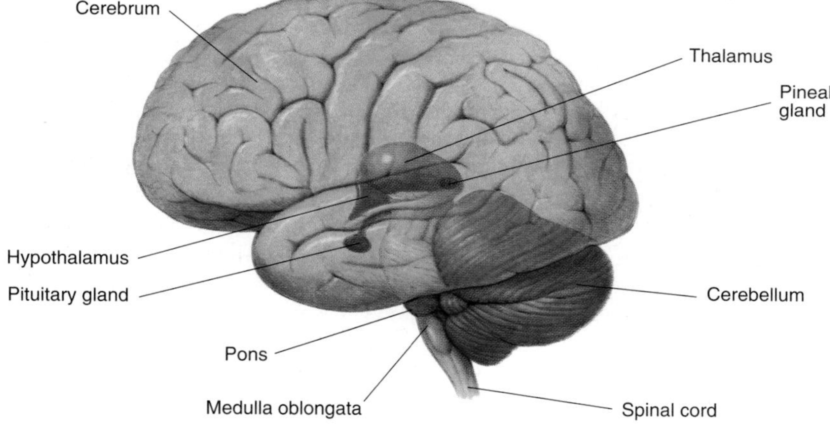

▼ **Figure 35–9** **The brain—the main switching area of the central nervous system—helps to relay messages, process information, and analyze information.** The brain consists of the cerebrum, cerebellum, and brain stem.

SECTION RESOURCES

Print:
- ***Laboratory Manual A,*** Chapter 35 Lab
- ***Laboratory Manual B,*** Chapter 35 Lab
- ***Teaching Resources,*** Section Review 35–3
- ***Guided Reading and Study Workbook,*** Section 35–3
- ***Issues and Decision Making,*** Issues and Decisions 44

Technology:
- ***iText,*** Section 35–3

Section 35–3

1 FOCUS

Objectives

35.3.1 ***Identify*** the functions of the central nervous system.

35.3.2 ***Describe*** the two divisions of the peripheral nervous system.

Guide for Reading

Vocabulary Preview

Point out that all of the Vocabulary terms refer to structures in the brain except for two terms. Ask: **Which two terms do not refer to structures in the brain?** *(Reflex and central nervous system)* Challenge students to predict what these two terms might mean, and then have them check to see if they were correct as they read the section.

Reading Strategy

Possible questions students might write include: What are the parts of the central nervous system? *(The brain and the spinal cord)* What is the role of the brain? *(It is the main switching unit of the central nervous system.)* What is the function of the spinal cord? *(It is the main communications link between the brain and the rest of the body.)* What structures make up the peripheral nervous system? *(All the nerves and associated cells that are not part of the brain and the spinal cord.)*

2 INSTRUCT

The Central Nervous System

Use Visuals

Figure 35–9 Point out the location of the cerebrum and cerebellum. Explain that the brain stem is the region just below the cerebellum that contains the pons and medulla oblongata. Ask: **Which part of the human brain is the largest part?** *(Cerebrum)* **Where in the brain are the endocrine glands located?** *(Above the brain stem)*

The Brain

Build Science Skills

Calculating Help students appreciate how greatly the creases in the brain increase its surface area. First, have students measure the sides of a small box, such as a cereal box or shoe box, and use the measurements to calculate its surface area. Next, have students stuff the box with folded sheets of newspaper until the box is full. Then, have students count the number of sheets of newspaper and find their total area (by multiplying the number of sheets by the area of one sheet). Students should add this number to the surface area of the box. Ask: **How much was the surface area increased by the folded sheets?** *(Exact answers will vary. Students will find that the surface area was increased greatly by the addition of the folded sheets.)*

Use Community Resources

Invite a diagnostic imaging technician to visit the class and explain how brain injuries, tumors, and other abnormalities of the brain are diagnosed. Ask the visitor to describe MRIs and CT scans and what they reveal about the brain. If possible, have the visitor bring sample images or scans to share with students. Urge students to take notes during the talk and later use the notes to write a summary of what they learned.

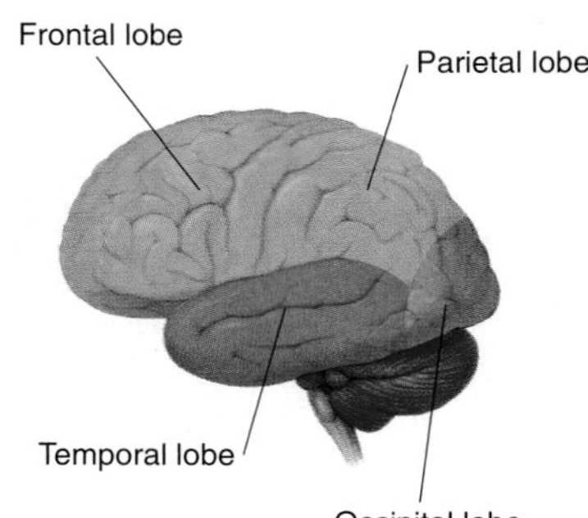

▲ **Figure 35–10** Each hemisphere of the cerebrum is divided into four lobes. Different functions of the body are controlled by different lobes of the brain. **Drawing Conclusions** ***The frontal lobe controls voluntary muscle movements. What might happen if this part of the brain became injured?***

The Brain

The brain contains approximately 100 billion neurons. The neurons in the brain are mainly interneurons. The brain has a mass of about 1.4 kilograms. It is the main switching unit of the central nervous system.

The Cerebrum The largest and most prominent region of the human brain is the **cerebrum.** The cerebrum is responsible for the voluntary, or conscious, activities of the body. It is the site of intelligence, learning, and judgment. A deep groove divides the cerebrum into right and left hemispheres. The hemispheres are connected by a band of tissue called the corpus callosum.

Folds and grooves on the surface of each hemisphere greatly increase the surface area of the cerebrum. Each hemisphere of the cerebrum is divided into regions called lobes. The lobes are named for the skull bones that cover them. The locations of four lobes of the brain are shown in **Figure 35–10.**

Remarkably, each half of the cerebrum deals mainly with the opposite side of the body. Sensations from the left side of the body go to the right hemisphere of the cerebrum, and those from the right side of the body go to the left hemisphere. Commands to move muscles are generated in the same way. The left hemisphere controls the body's right side and the right hemisphere controls the body's left side.

There is more than a simple left-right division of labor between the hemispheres. For example, some studies have suggested that the right hemisphere may be associated with creativity and artistic ability, whereas the left hemisphere may be associated with analytical and mathematical ability.

The cerebrum consists of two surfaces. The outer surface of the cerebrum is called the cerebral cortex and consists of gray matter. Gray matter consists mainly of densely packed nerve cell bodies. The cerebral cortex processes information from the sense organs and controls body movements. The inner surface of the cerebrum consists of white matter, which is made up of bundles of axons with myelin sheaths. The myelin sheaths give the white matter its characteristic color.

The Cerebellum The second largest region of the brain is the **cerebellum.** The cerebellum is located at the back of the skull. Although the commands to move muscles come from the cerebral cortex, the cerebellum coordinates and balances the actions of the muscles so that the body can move gracefully and efficiently.

The Brain Stem The **brain stem** connects the brain and spinal cord. Located just below the cerebellum, the brain stem includes two regions known as the pons and the medulla oblongata (ahb-lahn-GAHT-uh). Each of these regions acts as a neural "switchboard," regulating the flow of information between the brain and the rest of the body. Some of the body's most important functions—including blood pressure, heart rate, breathing, and swallowing—are controlled in the brain stem.

PRESENTATIONS MADE EASY!

The Presentation Assistant Plus contains the Prentice Hall Presentation Pro and the Transparencies, which provide easy-to-follow visual support for every step of this section. If you have a computer presentation station, use Prentice Hall Presentation Pro for Section 35–3, or use the transparencies listed here.

Section 35–3:

Interest Grabber
Section Outline
Concept Map
Figures 35–9 and 35–11
Figure 35–12

The Thalamus and Hypothalamus The thalamus and hypothalamus are found between the brain stem and the cerebrum. The **thalamus** receives messages from the sense organs. It relays the information to the proper region of the cerebrum for further processing. The hypothalamus is just below the thalamus. The **hypothalamus** is the control center for recognition and analysis of hunger, thirst, fatigue, anger, and body temperature.

The Spinal Cord

Like a major telephone line that carries thousands of calls at once, the spinal cord is the main communications link between the brain and the rest of the body. Thirty-one pairs of spinal nerves branch out from the spinal cord, connecting the brain to the body. **Figure 35–11** shows a cross section of the spinal cord.

Certain kinds of information, such as reflexes, are processed directly in the spinal cord. A **reflex** is a quick, automatic response to a stimulus. Sneezing and blinking are two examples of reflexes. A reflex allows your body to respond to danger immediately, without spending time thinking about a response. Animals rely heavily on reflex behaviors for survival.

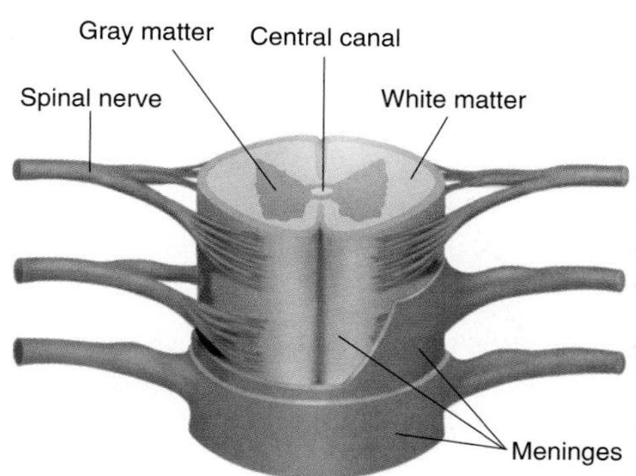

▲ **Figure 35–11** The spinal cord—the major nerve pathway to and from the brain—is protected by the vertebral column and meninges. **Comparing and Contrasting** *What is the difference between the white and gray matter?*

CHECKPOINT *What is a reflex?*

The Peripheral Nervous System

The peripheral nervous system lies outside of the central nervous system. It consists of all of the nerves and associated cells that are not part of the brain and the spinal cord. Included here are cranial nerves that pass through holes in the skull and stimulate regions of the head and neck, spinal nerves, and ganglia. Ganglia are collections of nerve cell bodies.

The peripheral nervous system can be divided into the sensory division and the motor division. **The sensory division of the peripheral nervous system transmits impulses from sense organs to the central nervous system. The motor division transmits impulses from the central nervous system to the muscles or glands.** The motor division is further divided into the somatic nervous system and the autonomic nervous system.

The Somatic Nervous System The somatic nervous system regulates activities that are under conscious control, such as the movement of the skeletal muscles. Every time you lift your finger or wiggle your toes, you are using the motor neurons of the somatic nervous system. Some somatic nerves are also involved with reflexes and can act with or without conscious control.

The Spinal Cord

Demonstration

Demonstrate a reflex by having one student stand with a sheet of stiff plastic in front of his or her face while another student tosses a ball of crumpled paper at the plastic sheet. Encourage the rest of the class to watch the face of the student holding the plastic. (*The student will involuntarily blink each time the paper ball is tossed toward his or her face.*) Point out that blinking is an automatic response to a stimulus, which allows the body to respond immediately to danger. Ask: **How does blinking protect you?** *(It helps protect the eyes from injury.)*

The Peripheral Nervous System

Meet Diverse Needs

Help at-risk students appreciate the difference between the somatic and autonomic divisions of the peripheral nervous system. First, turn to look out a window and pretend to wave at someone outside. Explain that these behaviors are voluntary and controlled by the somatic nervous system. Then, pretend to wake up from sleep and sneeze. Explain that these behaviors are involuntary and controlled by the autonomic nervous system. Finally, ask: **What are some other examples of behaviors controlled by the somatic and autonomic nervous systems?** *(Other examples include writing and chewing for the somatic nervous system and breathing and digesting food for the autonomic nervous system.)* **Learning modality: visual**

BIO INSIGHTS — **HISTORY OF SCIENCE**

Broca's area

In the middle of the nineteenth century, Paul Broca, a French neurologist, discovered that a small region in the third convolution of the left frontal lobe of the cerebral cortex controls speech. This area is now called Broca's area. Broca made his discovery by studying people with brain damage who had lost the ability to speak. He also studied split-brain patients—people whose hemispheres were no longer connected because they had suffered damage to the corpus callosum. Broca's discovery of the speech area of the brain was important for two reasons. It provided some of the first evidence that the left and right hemispheres of the brain have separate functions, and it was one of the first indicators that particular brain functions are localized in specific regions of the brain.

Answers to . . .

CHECKPOINT *A quick, automatic response to a stimulus*

Figure 35–10 *There might be less control over voluntary muscle movements, such as walking and writing.*

Figure 35–11 *White matter is made up of bundles of myelinated axons. Gray matter is made up of densely packed nerve cell bodies.*

35–3 (continued)

Quick Lab

Objective Students will be able to conclude that a stronger stimulus does not produce a stronger nerve impulse.

Skills Focus **Drawing Conclusions**

Materials string, packaging tape, scissors, 30-cm ruler, 3 plastic mouse-traps

Time 20 minutes

Safety Show students how to hold the traps open safely with one hand while using the other hand to insert a string through the bait platform.

Expected Outcome Students should find that only a tug greater than a certain threshold triggers the mousetraps.

Analyze and Conclude

1. A sufficiently strong tug is required. This level of force can be compared to the threshold level of stimulus required to activate a neuron.
2. A stronger stimulus does not produce a stronger impulse because the response of a neuron is an all-or-nothing response.
3. The "sensory neuron" mousetrap triggered the "motor neuron" mousetrap independently of the "brain" mousetrap. In the hand, sensory neurons signal motor neurons to stimulate the muscles that withdraw the hand before the impulse caused by the pain stimulus reaches the brain.

Use Visuals

Figure 35–12 Have students trace the path of the nerve impulse from the toe up the leg to the spinal cord and back down the leg to the muscle that lifts the leg. Ask: **What are the components of the reflex arc that is represented by the drawing?** *(The reflex arc is composed of a sensory receptor, sensory neuron, motor neuron, and an effector—the muscle.)*

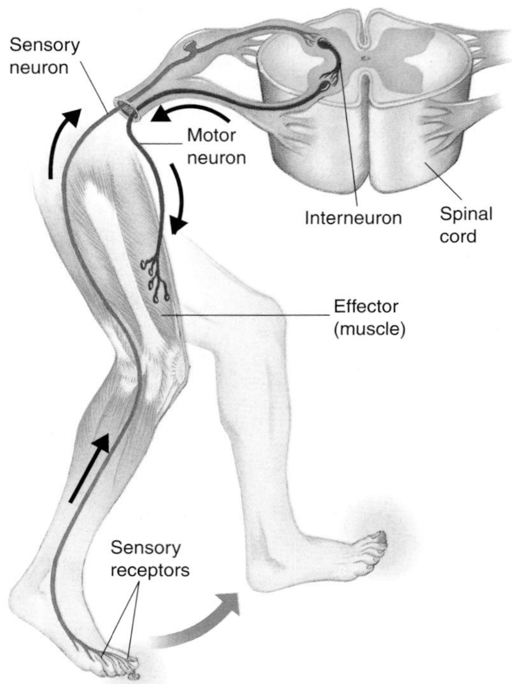

▲ **Figure 35–12** **The peripheral nervous system transmits impulses from sense organs to the central nervous system and back to muscles or glands.** When you step on a tack, sensory receptors stimulate a sensory neuron, which relays the signal to an interneuron within the spinal cord. The signal is then sent to a motor neuron, which in turn stimulates a muscle in your leg to lift your leg.

If you accidentally step on a tack with your bare foot, your leg may recoil before you are aware of the pain. This rapid response is possible because receptors in your skin stimulate sensory neurons, which carry the impulse to your spinal cord. Even before the information is relayed to your brain, a group of neurons in your spinal cord automatically activates the appropriate motor neurons. These motor neurons cause the muscles in your leg to contract, pulling your foot away from the tack.

The pathway that an impulse travels from your foot back to your leg is known as a reflex arc. As shown in **Figure 35–12,** a reflex arc includes a sensory receptor (in this case, a receptor in your toe), sensory neuron, motor neuron, and effector (leg muscle). Some reflex arcs include interneurons. In other reflex arcs, a sensory neuron communicates directly with a motor neuron.

CHECKPOINT *What is a reflex arc?*

The Autonomic Nervous System The autonomic nervous system regulates activities that are automatic, or involuntary. The nerves of the autonomic nervous system control functions of the body that are not under conscious control. For example, the autonomic nervous system regulates the heartbeat and controls the contraction of smooth muscles in the digestive system and in blood vessels.

The autonomic nervous system is further subdivided into two parts that have opposite effects on the organs they control. The two parts are known as the sympathetic nervous system and the parasympathetic nervous system. Most organs controlled by the autonomic nervous system are under the control of both sympathetic and parasympathetic neurons.

Why is it important to have two systems that control the same organs? The sympathetic and parasympathetic nervous systems have opposite effects on the same organ system. For example, heart rate is increased by the sympathetic nervous system, but decreased by the parasympathetic nervous system. The process can be compared to the process of controlling the speed of a car. One system is like the gas pedal and the other is like the brake. Because there are two different sets of neurons, the autonomic nervous system can quickly speed up the activities of major organs in response to a stimulus, or slam on the brakes if necessary.

FACTS AND FIGURES

Reflexes

Reflex responses are highly visible examples of the operation of the autonomic nervous system. The knee-jerk reflex, which activates skeletal muscles that are usually under voluntary control, provides an especially dramatic classroom illustration. However, vital autonomic reflexes constantly adjust the activities of the internal organs. The vagus nerve, for example, relays signals from the central nervous system that stimulate or reduce the rate at which the heart beats and the diaphragm draws air in and out of the lungs. Nervous regulation of the activity of the digestive organs, such as the peristaltic contraction of the small intestine, is so sophisticated that this portion of the autonomic nervous system has been called a "second brain."

Quick Lab

How do reflexes occur?

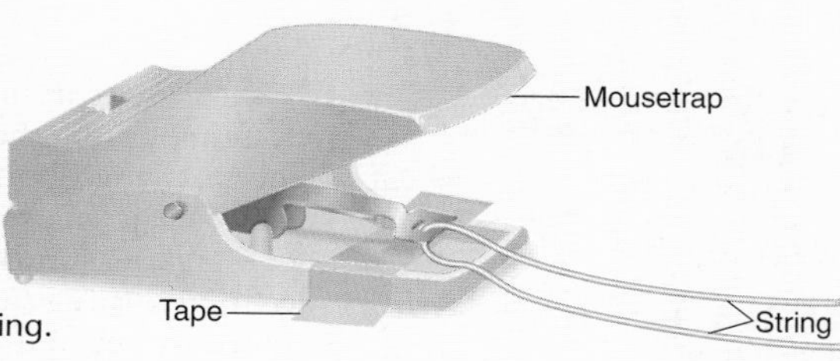

Materials string, scissors, 3 plastic mousetraps, packing tape, 30-cm ruler

Procedure 

1. To model a synapse, cut a 30-cm piece of string. **CAUTION:** *Handle scissors carefully.*
2. Hold a mousetrap open. Pull the string through the bait platform as shown. **CAUTION:** *Do not let the mousetrap snap on your fingers.* Slide a piece of tape under the bait platform and tape the trap to the table as shown. Label the trap "sensory neuron."
3. Hold one end of the string in each hand. Gently pull one end without setting off the trap. Now gradually pull harder.
4. To model a reflex arc, cut two more 30-cm pieces of string. Tie one end of each piece of string to the bait platform of a separate trap.
5. Tape the 2 new traps to the table, 20 cm from the first trap. Label one new trap "motor neuron," and the other "brain."
6. Reset the first trap, then set the new ones. Tape both ends of the strings attached to the new traps to the top of the first trap. Leave these strings slightly slack.
7. Pull the strings attached to the bait platform of the "sensory neuron."

Analyze and Conclude

1. **Drawing Conclusions** What was required for the trap to close in step 3? How does this behavior compare to the transmission of a nerve impulse?
2. **Applying Concepts** Does a stronger stimulus produce a stronger nerve impulse? Explain your answer.
3. **Using Analogies** Use your observations from step 7 to explain how your hand withdraws from a hot stove before you feel pain.

35–3 Section Assessment

1. **Key Concept** Discuss the overall function of the central nervous system.
2. **Key Concept** What are the functions of the two divisions of the peripheral nervous system?
3. Compare the central nervous system to the central processing unit of a computer.
4. Is a reflex part of the central nervous system, the peripheral nervous system, or both? Explain your answer.
5. **Critical Thinking Inferring** Why do you think the cerebrum is larger and more developed in humans than it is in other vertebrates?

MAKING CONNECTIONS

Animal Behavior

Using Section 34–1, decide which parts of the nervous system are most likely to be involved with innate behaviors. Which parts are likely to be involved with learned behaviors? Explain your reasoning.

iTEXT **Assessment** Use iText to review the important concepts in Section 35–3.

Build Science Skills

Observing Demonstrate the pupillary reflex, which is the automatic widening or narrowing of the pupil of the eye when the amount of light falling on it changes. Ask several volunteers to cover their eyes with a blindfold and keep their eyes closed. After a few minutes, have the volunteers uncover and open their eyes while the other students observe what happens to the size of the volunteers' pupils. Ask: **How did the size of their pupils change?** *(They were wide at first and gradually narrowed.)* **How long did the change take?** *(Several seconds)*

3 ASSESS

Evaluate Understanding

Ask students to make a concept map of the divisions and subdivisions of the nervous system.

Reteach

Have each student create a crossword puzzle using the Vocabulary terms. Then, have students exchange and solve the puzzles.

MAKING CONNECTIONS

Reflex arcs are most likely to be involved with innate behaviors, which are functional the first time they are performed. The brain plays a major role in learned behaviors, which depend on data collected through experience being processed and analyzed.

Use iText to review the key concepts in Section 35–3.

35–3 Section Assessment

1. To relay messages and to process and analyze information
2. The sensory division transmits impulses from sense organs to the central nervous system. The motor division transmits impulses from the central nervous system to muscles.
3. Like the central processing unit of a computer, the central nervous system is the control center of the body.
4. A reflex involves both, because it is processed in the spinal cord, which is part of the central nervous system, but the sensory neuron and motor neuron are part of the peripheral nervous system.
5. Because humans depend more on intelligence and learning than other vertebrates

Answer to . . .

CHECKPOINT *A reflex arc is the pathway that an impulse travels from a stimulus to a response. It usually includes a sensory receptor; a sensory neuron; a motor neuron; and an effector, such as a muscle.*

Section 35–4

1 FOCUS

Objectives

35.4.1 ***Name*** the five types of sensory receptors.
35.4.2 ***Identify*** the five senses.

Guide for Reading

Vocabulary Preview

Ask: **Which Vocabulary terms refer to parts of the eye?** *(Pupil, lens, retina, rod, and cone)* **Which terms refer to parts of the ear?** *(Cochlea, semicircular canal)*

Reading Strategy

Have students preview the section by studying the figures and reading the captions.

2 INSTRUCT

Build Science Skills

Applying Concepts Ask students to imagine they are at a picnic on a beautiful summer day with a picnic basket full of their favorite foods. Then, ask: **How might the different categories of your sensory receptors be stimulated at the picnic?** *(Students may say, for example, that their thermoreceptors might be stimulated by holding a cold drink and their chemoreceptors by smelling and tasting food.)*

Vision

Make Connections

Physics Explain that light is part of the electromagnetic spectrum, which includes electromagnetic waves of all different wavelengths. Add that humans can see only light that falls within a very limited range of wavelengths and that light in this range is called visible light.

35–4 The Senses

Guide for Reading

Key Concept
- What are the five types of sensory receptors?

Vocabulary
sensory receptor
pupil
lens
retina
rod
cone
cochlea
semicircular canal
taste bud

Reading Strategy: Outlining Before you read, use the headings of the section to make an outline about the five senses. As you read, fill in the subtopics and smaller topics. Then, add phrases or a sentence after each to provide key information.

The body contains millions of neurons that react directly to stimuli from the environment, including light, sound, motion, chemicals, pressure, or changes in temperature. These neurons, known as **sensory receptors,** react to light, sound, or other specific stimuli by sending impulses to other neurons, and eventually to the central nervous system. Sensory receptors are located throughout the body but are concentrated in the sense organs. These sense organs include the eyes, the inner ears, the nose, the mouth, and the skin. Sensory receptors within each organ enable it to respond to a particular stimulus.

There are five general categories of sensory receptors: pain receptors, thermoreceptors, mechanoreceptors, chemoreceptors, and photoreceptors. Pain receptors are located throughout the body except in the brain. Pain receptors respond to chemicals released by damaged cells. Pain is important to recognize because it usually indicates danger, injury, or disease. Thermoreceptors are located in the skin, body core, and hypothalamus. Thermoreceptors detect variations in temperature. Mechanoreceptors are found in the skin, skeletal muscles, and inner ears. They are sensitive to touch, pressure, stretching of muscles, sound, and motion. Chemoreceptors, located in the nose and taste buds, are sensitive to chemicals in the external environment. Photoreceptors, found in the eyes, are sensitive to light. **Figure 35–13** shows the type of photoreceptor that distinguishes the color of objects.

Vision

The world around us is bathed in light. The sense organs that we use to sense light are the eyes. The structures of the eye are shown in **Figure 35–14.** Light enters the eye through the cornea, a tough transparent layer of cells. The cornea helps to focus the light, which then passes through a small chamber called the anterior chamber. This chamber is filled with a fluid called aqueous (AY-kwee-uhs) humor. At the back of the chamber is a disklike structure called the iris. The iris is the colored part of the eye. In the middle of the iris is a small opening called the **pupil.** Tiny muscles in the iris adjust the size of the pupil to regulate the amount of light that enters the eye. In dim light, the pupil becomes larger so that more light can enter the eye. In bright light, the pupil becomes smaller so that less light enters the eye.

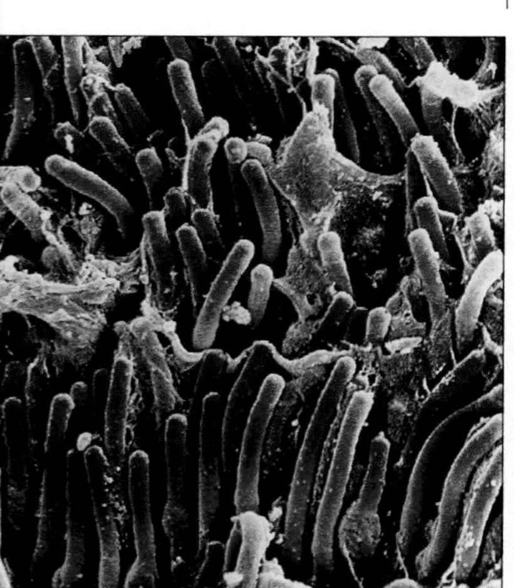

(magnification: 2000×)

◀ **Figure 35–13** **There are two types of light-sensitive photoreceptor cells in the retina—rods and cones.** This color-enhanced scanning electron micrograph shows the rod cells of an eye.

SECTION RESOURCES

Print:
- ***Teaching Resources,*** Section Review 35–4
- ***Guided Reading and Study Workbook,*** Section 35–4

Technology:
- ***iText,*** Section 35–4

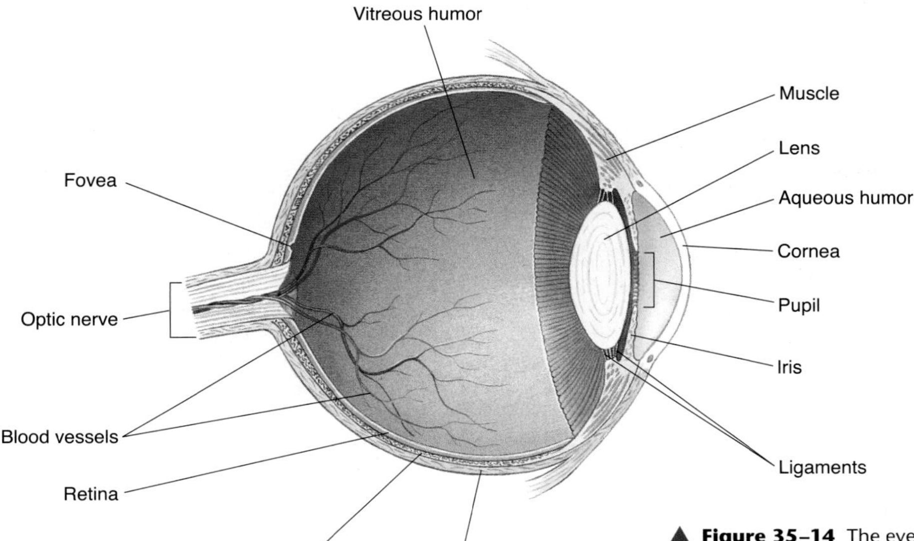

▲ **Figure 35–14** The eye is a complicated sense organ. The sclera, choroid, and retina are three layers of tissue that form the inner wall of the eyeball. **Inferring** ***Why do you think the area in the retina that contains no rods or cones is called the blind spot?***

Just behind the iris is the **lens.** Small muscles attached to the lens change its shape to help you adjust your eyes' focus to see near or distant objects. Behind the lens is a large chamber filled with a transparent, jellylike fluid called vitreous (VIH-tree-uhs) humor.

The lens focuses light onto the **retina.** Photoreceptors are arranged in a layer in the retina. The photoreceptors convert light into nerve impulses that are carried to the central nervous system. There are two types of photoreceptors: rods and cones. **Rods** are extremely sensitive to light, but they do not distinguish different colors. **Cones** are less sensitive than rods, but they do respond to light of different colors, producing color vision. Cones are concentrated in the fovea. The fovea is the site of sharpest vision.

The impulses assembled by this complicated layer of interconnected cells leave each eye by way of an optic nerve. The optic nerves then carry the impulses to the appropriate regions of the brain. The brain interprets them as visual images and provides information about the external world.

CHECKPOINT *Where are the photoreceptors located in the eye?*

Use Visuals

Figure 35–14 Ask students to locate the three layers of tissue (*sclera, choroid, and retina*) that form the inner wall of the eyeball. Then, have students trace the path of light through the eye. Call on students to identify each of the structures the light passes through. Finally, ask: **What purpose do the muscles around the lens serve?** *(They change the shape of the lens to help the eye focus to see near or distant objects.)* **Where does the lens focus the light?** *(On the retina)* **What happens to the impulses after they leave the eye by way of the optic nerve?** *(They go to the appropriate regions of the brain, where the visual images are interpreted.)*

Build Science Skills

Using Analogies Ask: **If the lens of the eye is analogous to a projector, what part of the eye is analogous to the screen?** *(The retina)* **How is the image projected on the screen different from the image projected on the retina?** *(There are no receptors on the screen to convert the image into electrical impulses.)*

Meet Diverse Needs

Give students who need extra challenges an opportunity to investigate surgical methods for correcting vision problems, including photorefractive keratectomy (PRK) and laser in situ keratomileusis (LASIK). Encourage students to present their findings to the class in an oral report illustrated with diagrams to show how the procedures correct specific vision problems. **Learning modality: verbal**

PRESENTATIONS MADE EASY!

The Presentation Assistant Plus contains the Prentice Hall Presentation Pro and the Transparencies, which provide easy-to-follow visual support for every step of this section. If you have a computer presentation station, use Prentice Hall Presentation Pro for Section 35–4, or use the transparencies listed here.

Section 35–4:

Interest Grabber
Section Outline
Smell and Taste
Figure 35–14
Figure 35–15

Answers to . . .

CHECKPOINT *The retina*

Figure 35–14 *Because without rods and cones, the light is not converted into impulses that are carried to the brain*

Hearing and Balance

Use Visuals

Figure 35–15 Name the structures that sound waves pass through after they enter the ear. As you name each structure, ask: **What role does this structure play in hearing?** *(Students might say, for example, that the auditory canal channels the sound waves to the tympanum and that the tympanum vibrates in response to the sound waves.)*

Make Connections

Health Science Explain that the region of the ear called the middle ear, which is the area between the tympanum and the semicircular canals, is prone to infections. This is because of the close connection between the middle ear and the eustachian tube, which originates in the throat. Viruses and bacteria in the throat can easily travel to the middle ear through the eustachian tube and cause infections, inflammation, and pain.

Build Science Skills

Inferring Tell students that middle ear infections often block the transmission of sounds from the outside world but not sounds, such as chewing sounds, that originate within the head. Ask: **Why can people hear "head" sounds even when their ears are blocked because of an infection?** *(Because the sound waves are transmitted directly to the inner ear through the bones of the head)*

Demonstration

Half fill a glass container with water and, as students watch, slowly tilt the container from side to side. Because the water always stays parallel to the floor due to gravity, students will observe it move up and down the sides of the glass as the glass tilts. Explain that this is also how the fluid inside the semicircular canals moves as the head changes position.

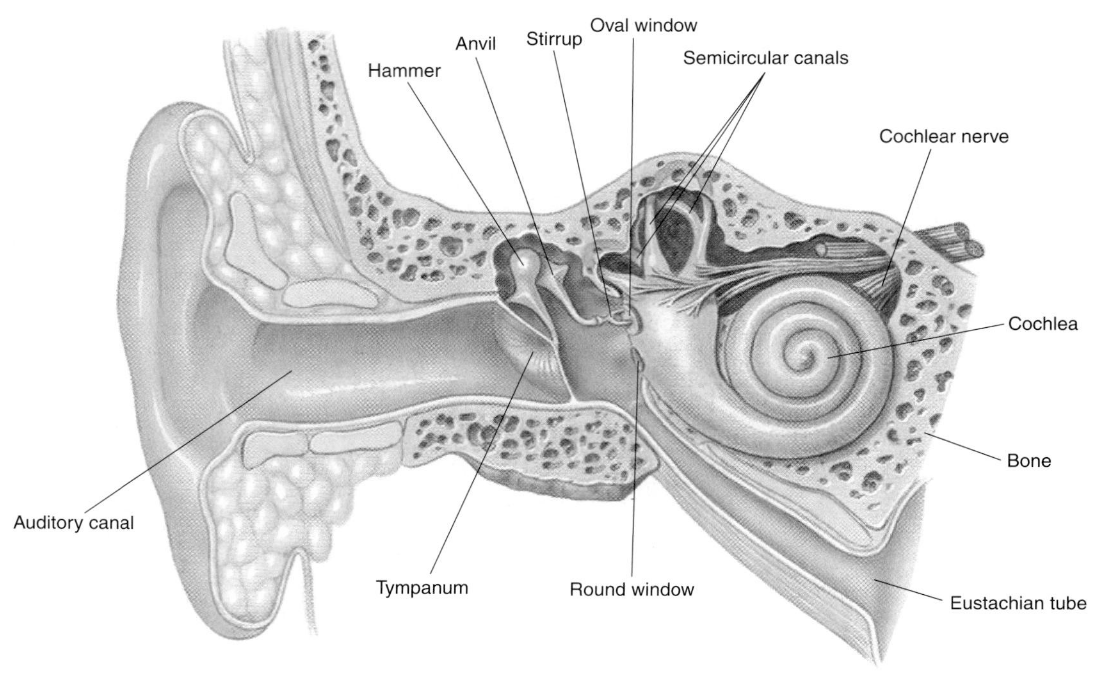

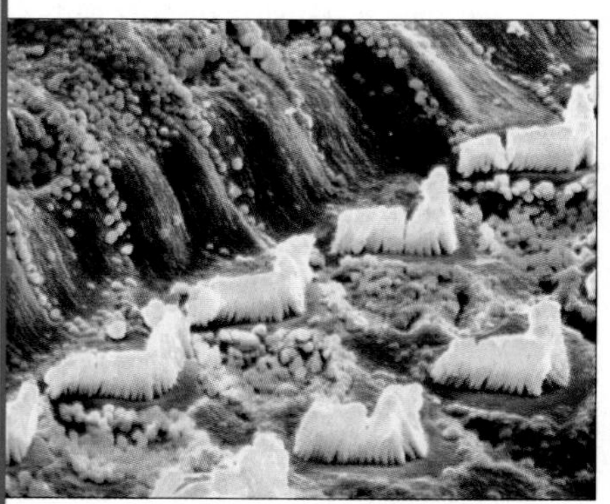

(magnification: about 3500×)

▲ **Figure 35–15** The diagram shows structures in the ear that transmit sounds. The scanning electron micrograph shows hair cells (yellow) in the inner ear. The motion of these hairs produces a nerve impulse that travels to the brain through the cochlear nerve. **Predicting** ***How would frequent exposure to loud noise affect a person's threshold for detecting sound?***

Hearing and Balance

The human ear has two sensory functions. One of these functions is hearing. The other function is maintaining balance.

Hearing Sound is nothing more than vibrations in the air around us. The ears are the sensory organs that can distinguish both the pitch and loudness of those vibrations. The structure of the ear is shown in **Figure 35–15.**

Vibrations enter the ear through the auditory canal. The vibrations cause the tympanum (TIM-puh-num), or eardrum, to vibrate. These vibrations are picked up by three tiny bones, commonly called the hammer, anvil, and stirrup. The last of these bones, the stirrup, transmits the vibrations to the oval window. Vibrations of the oval window create pressure waves in the fluid-filled **cochlea** (KAHK-lee-uh) of the inner ear.

The cochlea is lined with tiny hair cells that are pushed back and forth by these pressure waves. In response to these movements, the hair cells produce nerve impulses that are sent to the brain through the cochlear nerve.

Balance Your ears contain structures that help your central nervous system maintain your balance, or equilibrium. Within the inner ear just above the cochlea are three tiny canals at right angles to each other. They are called **semicircular canals** because each forms a half circle. The semicircular canals and the two tiny sacs located behind them monitor the position of your body, especially your head, in relation to gravity.

TEACHER TO TEACHER

When I teach about the senses, I give students a chance to experience sensory "fatigue." I have students rest a penny on the inside of their forearm against the skin and measure how long it takes until they can no longer sense the presence of the coin. When everyone is finished, we discuss why sensory fatigue occurs and when it is useful (for example, when you are wearing clothing). I also demonstrate sensory fatigue with the sense of smell. I ask a volunteer to come to the front of the room and hold one nostril closed while I hold a bottle of oil of wintergreen (available at pharmacies) under the other nostril. The class measures the time it takes until the volunteer can no longer distinguish the smell of wintergreen.

—Duane Nichols
Biology Teacher
Alhambra High School
Alhambra, CA

The semicircular canals and the sacs are filled with fluid and lined with hair cells. As the head changes position, the fluid in the canals also changes position. This causes the hair on the hair cells to bend. This action, in turn, sends impulses to the brain that enable it to determine body motion and position.

Smell and Taste

You may never have thought of it this way, but your sense of smell is actually an ability to detect chemicals. Chemoreceptors in the lining of the nasal passageway respond to specific chemicals and send impulses to the brain through sensory nerves.

Your sense of smell is capable of producing thousands of different sensations. In fact, much of what we commonly call the "taste" of food and drink is actually smell. To prove this to yourself, eat a few bites of food while holding your nose. You'll discover that much of the taste of food disappears until you open your nose and breathe freely.

Like the sense of smell, the sense of taste is a chemical sense. The sense organs that detect taste are the **taste buds.** Most of the taste buds are on the tongue, but a few are found at other locations in the mouth. The surface of the tongue is shown in **Figure 35–16.** The tastes detected by the taste buds are classified as salty, bitter, sweet, and sour. Sensitivity to these different categories varies on different parts of the tongue.

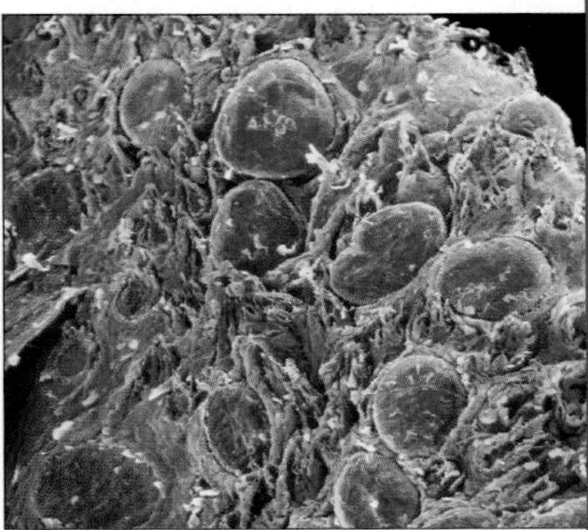

(magnification: 86×)

▲ **Figure 35–16** This color-enhanced scanning electron micrograph shows the surface of the tongue. The large pink objects are the taste buds. **Chemoreceptors found in the taste buds are sensitive to chemicals in food.**

Touch and Related Senses

The sense of touch, unlike the other senses you have just read about, is not found in one particular place. All of the regions of the skin are sensitive to touch. In this respect, your largest sense organ is your skin. Skin contains sensory receptors that respond to temperature, touch, and pain. Not all parts of the body are equally sensitive to touch, because not all parts have the same number of receptors. The greatest density of touch receptors is found on your fingers, toes, and face.

35–4 Section Assessment

1. **Key Concept** Name the five types of sensory receptors and list where they are found in the body.
2. Identify the parts of the eye and the function of each part.
3. What parts of the ear are responsible for hearing? For balance?
4. Explain why you can't "taste" food when you have a bad cold.
5. **Critical Thinking Applying Concepts** Why do you feel dizzy after spinning around? How can a dancer or ice skater do lengthy spins?

iTEXT **Assessment** Use iText to review the important concepts in Section 35–4.

ALTERNATIVE ASSESSMENT

Creative Writing
Imagine that you have to do without one of your sense organs for one day. Which one would you choose to give up? In your journal describe how the absence of this sense organ would affect your life.

35–4 Section Assessment

1. Pain receptors: everywhere except the brain; thermoreceptors: skin, body core, hypothalamus; mechanoreceptors: skin, skeletal muscles, inner ears; chemoreceptors: nose, taste buds; photoreceptors: eyes
2. Cornea: helps to focus light; pupil: controls the amount of light that enters the eye; lens: adjusts focus for near or far distances; retina: rod and cone photoreceptors convert light into electrical impulses
3. Hearing: auditory canal, tympanum, hammer, anvil, stirrup, oval window, cochlea; balance: semicircular canals and sacs
4. Because much of the sense of taste is actually the sense of smell
5. Sensory receptors lag behind the rapid changes in position. Focusing on a distant point while spinning provides a visual clue for the processing center.

Smell and Taste

Demonstration

Have volunteers taste and try to identify a variety of different fruit juices while wearing a blindfold and pinching their nose shut. *(Without sight cues and the sense of smell, students will find it difficult to distinguish the tastes.)*

Touch and Related Senses

Build Science Skills

Designing Experiments Challenge students to design an experiment to determine the distribution of heat and cold receptors in a small area of skin on the back of the hand.

3 ASSESS

Evaluate Understanding

Provide students with copies of Figure 35–14 without the labels. Have student label each part of the eye shown in the figure.

Reteach

On the chalkboard or an overhead transparency, list five general categories of sensory receptors. Have students give examples of each category of receptors at work. *(For chemoreceptors, for example, students might say smelling a flower or tasting food.)*

ALTERNATIVE ASSESSMENT

Answers will depend on which sense organ students choose. For example, if they choose the sense of smell, they might describe how their sense of taste is affected and how this, in turn, affects their enjoyment of food and their appetite.

Use iText to review the key concepts in Section 35–4.

Answer to . . .

Figure 35–15 *Loud noises can damage tiny hair cells and raise the threshold for detecting sounds.*

Section 35–5

1 FOCUS

Objectives

35.5.1 ***Name*** the different classes of drugs that directly affect the nervous system.

35.5.2 ***Describe*** the effects of alcohol on the body.

Guide for Reading

Vocabulary Preview

Challenge students to predict how the Vocabulary terms *addiction* and *drug abuse* differ. As they read, they should check to see if their predictions were correct.

Reading Strategy

In their tables, students should list stimulants, depressants, cocaine, opiates, marijuana, and alcohol. They should read the Key Concepts for the effects that each drug has on the body.

2 INSTRUCT

Address Misconceptions

Many people do not think of alcohol and nicotine as drugs because both can be used legally. Address this misconception by pointing out that alcohol and nicotine are potentially addictive drugs that can have extremely harmful effects on the body, ranging from liver damage to lung cancer. Alcohol and nicotine are also among the most widely used drugs, making their harmful effects more devastating.

Drugs That Affect the Synapse

Meet Diverse Needs

Simplify the discussion of how drugs affect the synapse. Explain that most of the drugs mentioned in the text either increase or decrease the transmission of nerve impulses across synapses and, thereby, either speed up or slow down the nervous system. Drugs that speed up the nervous system include stimulants, cocaine, and nicotine. Drugs that slow down the nervous system include depressants, opiates, and alcohol. **Limited English proficiency**

35–5 Drugs and the Nervous System

Guide for Reading

Key Concepts
- What are the different classes of drugs that directly affect the central nervous system?
- What is the effect of alcohol on the body?

Vocabulary
drug
stimulant
depressant
addiction
fetal alcohol syndrome
drug abuse

Reading Strategy: Using Graphic Organizers
As you read, create a table that lists each of the drugs in this section and the effects that each drug has on the body.

By definition, a **drug** is any substance, other than food, that changes the structure or function of the body. Some drugs, such as cocaine and heroin, are so powerful and dangerous that their possession is illegal. Other drugs, including penicillin and codeine, are prescription drugs and can be used only under the supervision of a doctor. Still other drugs, including cough and cold medicines, are sold over the counter. All drugs, both legal and illegal, have the potential to do harm if they are used improperly or abused.

Drugs differ in the ways in which they affect the body. Some drugs kill bacteria and are useful in treating disease. Other drugs affect a particular system of the body, such as the digestive or circulatory systems. Among the most powerful drugs, however, are the ones that cause changes in the nervous system, especially to the brain and the synapses between neurons.

Drugs That Affect the Synapse

The nervous system performs its regulatory functions through the transmission of information along pathways from one part of the body to another. Synapses are key relay stations along the way. The nervous system depends on neurotransmitters to bridge the gap between neurons or between a neuron and an effector. A drug that interferes with the action of neurotransmitters can disrupt the functioning of the nervous system.

Stimulants A number of drugs, called **stimulants,** increase the actions regulated by the nervous system. **Stimulants increase heart rate, blood pressure, and breathing rate. In addition, stimulants increase the release of neurotransmitters at some synapses in the brain.** This release leads to a feeling of energy and well-being. When the effects of stimulants wear off, however, the brain's supply of neurotransmitters has been depleted. The user quickly falls into fatigue and depression. Long-term use can cause circulatory problems, hallucinations, and psychological depression.

Figure 35–17 Common stimulant drugs include amphetamines, cocaine, nicotine (found in cigarettes), and caffeine (found in coffee, tea, chocolate, and cola products). **Stimulants increase heart rate, blood pressure, and breathing rate.**

SECTION RESOURCES

Print:
- ***Teaching Resources,*** Section Review 35–5, Chapter 35 Real-World Lab
- ***Guided Reading and Study Workbook,*** Section 35–5
- ***Issues and Decision Making,*** Issues and Decisions 41, 42

Technology:
- ***iText,*** Section 35–5

Depressants Some drugs, called **depressants,** decrease the rate of functions regulated by the brain. **Depressants slow down heart rate and breathing rate, lower blood pressure, relax muscles, and relieve tension.** Some depressants enhance the effects of neurotransmitters that prevent some nerve cells from starting action potentials. This calms parts of the brain that sense fear and relaxes the individual. As a result, the user comes to depend on the drug to relieve the anxieties of everyday life, which may seem unbearable without the drug. When depressants are used in combination with alcohol, the results are often fatal because the central nervous system can become so depressed that breathing stops.

CHECKPOINT *What is the general function of a depressant?*

Cocaine Even stronger effects are produced by drugs that act on neurons in what are known as the pleasure centers of the brain. The effects of cocaine and opiate drugs are so strong that they produce **addiction**—an uncontrollable craving for more of the drug. Cocaine is obtained from the leaves of coca plants like the one shown in **Figure 35–18.** **Cocaine causes the sudden release in the brain of a neurotransmitter called dopamine.** Normally, this compound is released when a basic need, such as hunger or thirst, is fulfilled. By fooling the brain into releasing dopamine, cocaine produces intense feelings of pleasure and satisfaction. So much dopamine is released when the drug is used that the supply of dopamine is depleted when the drug wears off. Users quickly discover that they feel sad and depressed without the drug. The psychological dependence that cocaine produces is difficult to break.

Cocaine also acts as a powerful stimulant, increasing heart rate and blood pressure. The stimulation can be so powerful that the heart is damaged. Sometimes, even a first-time user may experience a heart attack after using cocaine.

Crack is a particularly potent and dangerous form of cocaine. Crack becomes addictive after only a few doses. The intense "high" produced by crack wears off quickly and leaves the brain with too little dopamine. As a result, the user suddenly feels sad and depressed, and quickly seeks another dose of the drug. In time, the urge to seek this drug can be so strong that it leads users to commit serious crimes and to abandon their families and children.

Opiates The opium poppy produces a powerful class of pain-killing drugs called opiates. **Opiates mimic natural chemicals in the brain known as endorphins, which normally help to overcome sensations of pain.** The first doses of these drugs produce strong feelings of pleasure and security, but the body quickly adjusts to the higher levels of endorphins. Once this happens, the body cannot do without the drug. A user who tries to stop taking these drugs will suffer from uncontrollable pain and sickness because the body cannot produce enough of the natural endorphins.

Figure 35–18 Many illegal drugs are found in nature. Cocaine comes from the South American *Erythroxylum coca* plant (top). The centers of opium poppies (below) contain pods from which opiate drugs are derived. **Opiates mimic endorphins, which help overcome pain.** For this reason, opiates are often used medically as painkillers.

Build Science Skills

Drawing Conclusions Point out that many prescription drugs—including tranquilizers, sedatives, sleep medications, cough suppressants, and pain relievers—come with labels warning consumers to avoid the use of alcohol while taking the medications. If possible, show students examples of prescription drug bottles with alcohol-warning labels. Then, ask: **Why is it dangerous to combine such drugs with alcohol?** *(Because both alcohol and the drugs are nervous system depressants, and their combined effects can so depress the nervous system that breathing stops)*

Address Misconceptions

Students may believe that using a drug only once or a few times cannot hurt them. Explain that some drugs, such as heroin and crack cocaine, are extremely addictive and may produce a craving for the drug after only one use. In addition, illegal drugs can contain other harmful substances that may cause death.

TIME SAVER **PRESENTATIONS MADE EASY!**

The Presentation Assistant Plus contains the Prentice Hall Presentation Pro and the Transparencies, which provide easy-to-follow visual support for every step of this section. If you have a computer presentation station, use Prentice Hall Presentation Pro for Section 35–5, or use the transparencies listed here.

Section 35–5: **Interest Grabber**
Section Outline
Commonly Abused Drugs

Answer to . . .

CHECKPOINT *Depressants decrease the rate of functions regulated by the brain.*

35–5 (continued)

Use Visuals

Figure 35–19 Ask students to read about the effects on the body of the different types of commonly abused drugs. Then, guide them in applying the information by asking: **How might someone behave who is taking stimulant drugs?** *(The person might be fidgety and restless and eat very little.)* **How might someone behave who is taking depressant drugs?** *(The person might be slow moving and sleepy and speak indistinctly.)* **What particular abilities might be impaired by the two different types of drugs?** *(Stimulants might impair the ability to relax and sleep, and depressants might impair the ability to concentrate and drive.)*

Build Science Skills

Making Judgments Have students find and read five newspaper articles that relate to alcohol in some way. For example, they might find articles that report on a new alcohol treatment program, a teen killed by a drunk driver, or an increase in underage drinking. Challenge students to use the information provided in the articles to write a brief report summarizing some of the effects of alcohol abuse on society.

Address Misconceptions

Many people think that black coffee or a cold shower can sober up someone who is intoxicated by alcohol. Explain that the body breaks down alcohol at a rate that depends on the person's weight and metabolism. Black coffee and a cold shower cannot increase this rate or sober up an intoxicated person more quickly.

Commonly Abused Drugs

Drug Type	Medical Use	Examples	Effects on the Body
Stimulants	Used to increase alertness, relieve fatigue	Amphetamines	Increases heart and respiratory rates, elevates blood pressure, dilates pupils, and decreases appetite
Depressants	Used to relieve anxiety, irritability, tension	Barbiturates Tranquilizers	Slows down the actions of the central nervous system; small amounts cause calmness and relaxation; larger amounts cause slurred speech and impaired judgment
Opiates	Used to relieve pain	Morphine Codeine	Acts as a depressant; causes drowsiness, restlessness, nausea

▲ **Figure 35–19** Many abused drugs are legal and used for medical purposes. **Applying Concepts** *Do you think a person can become addicted to a legal drug?*

Because many users inject drugs for maximum effect, there is another important consequence of drug use—the increased transmission of the HIV virus that causes AIDS. The virus can be spread rapidly from person to person when drug users share contaminated needles. Many of the new AIDS cases reported in the United States can be traced back to the use of injected drugs.

Marijuana Statistically, the most widely abused illegal drug is marijuana. Marijuana comes from *Cannabis sativa,* a species of hemp plant. Marijuana is commonly called grass or pot. Hashish, or hash, is a potent form of marijuana made from the flowering parts of the plant. The active ingredient in all forms of marijuana is tetrahydrocannabinol (THC). Smoking or ingesting THC can produce a temporary feeling of euphoria and disorientation. Smoking marijuana is bad for the lungs. In fact, smoking marijuana is even more destructive to the lungs than smoking tobacco. Long-term use of marijuana can also result in loss of memory, inability to concentrate, and reduced levels of the hormone testosterone in males.

✓CHECKPOINT *What are the long-term effects of marijuana use?*

Alcohol One of the most dangerous and abused depressant drugs is alcohol. The most immediate effects of alcohol are on the central nervous system. **Alcohol is a depressant, and even small amounts of alcohol slow down the rate at which the central nervous system functions.** Alcohol slows down reflexes, disrupts coordination, and impairs judgment. Heavy drinking fills the blood with so much alcohol that the central nervous system cannot function properly. People who have two or three drinks in the span of an hour may feel relaxed and confident, but their blood contains as much as 0.10 percent alcohol, making them legally drunk in most states. They usually cannot walk or talk properly, and they are certainly not able to safely control an automobile, as shown in **Figure 35–20.**

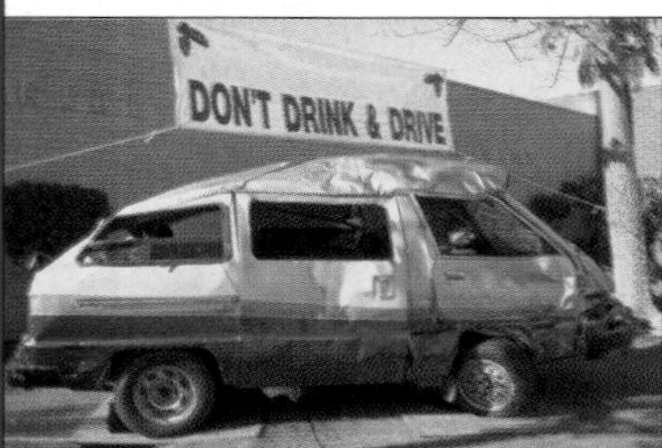

▲ **Figure 35–20** **Alcohol is a depressant that slows down the rate at which the nervous system functions.** It slows down reflexes, disrupts coordination, and impairs judgment. For this reason, you should never get into a car with a driver who has been drinking.

BIO INSIGHTS — FACTS AND FIGURES

Drugs and membrane permeability

Some drugs such as anesthetics and certain environmental toxins, including chlorinated hydrocarbons that are found in pesticides, can make neurons more or less likely to respond to electrical impulses. This is because the drugs affect the permeability of cell membranes to calcium ions. When permeability is decreased so that there is a lower-than-normal concentration of calcium ions, sodium channels may not close completely between action potentials, allowing sodium ions to cross the cell membrane. This makes the neurons fire more readily. When membrane permeability is increased and the calcium ion concentration is higher than normal, the opposite result occurs. Neurons become less excitable and more difficult to fire.

Alcohol is the drug most commonly abused by teenagers. The abuse of alcohol has a frightening social price. About 40 percent of the 50,000 people who die on American highways in a typical year are victims of accidents in which at least one driver had been drinking. One third of all homicides can be attributed to the effects of alcohol. When health care, property damage, and lost productivity are considered, alcohol abuse costs the U.S. economy at least $150 billion per year.

But the toll of alcohol abuse does not stop there! Women who are pregnant and drink on a regular basis run the risk of having a child with fetal alcohol syndrome. **Fetal alcohol syndrome** (FAS) is a group of birth defects caused by the effects of alcohol on the fetus. Babies born with FAS can suffer from heart defects, malformed faces, delayed growth, and poor motor development. More than 50,000 babies are born in this country every year with alcohol-related birth defects, many of which are irreversible.

Alcohol and Disease People who have become addicted to alcohol suffer from a disease called alcoholism. Some alcoholics feel the need to have a drink before work or school—every day! They may drink so heavily that they black out and cannot remember what they have done while drinking. Some alcoholics, however, do not drink to the point where it is obvious that they have an alcohol-abuse problem. If a person cannot function properly without satisfying the need or craving for alcohol, that person is considered to have an alcohol-abuse problem.

Analyzing Data

Blood Alcohol Concentration

Blood alcohol concentration (BAC) is a measure of the amount of alcohol in the bloodstream per 100 mL of blood. A BAC of 0.1 percent means that one tenth of 1.0 percent of the fluid in the blood is alcohol. In some states, if a driver has a BAC of 0.08 percent, he or she is considered legally drunk. In other states, drivers with a BAC of 0.10 percent are considered drunk. The graph shows the relative risk of being involved in a fatal accident as a result of the blood alcohol concentration of the driver.

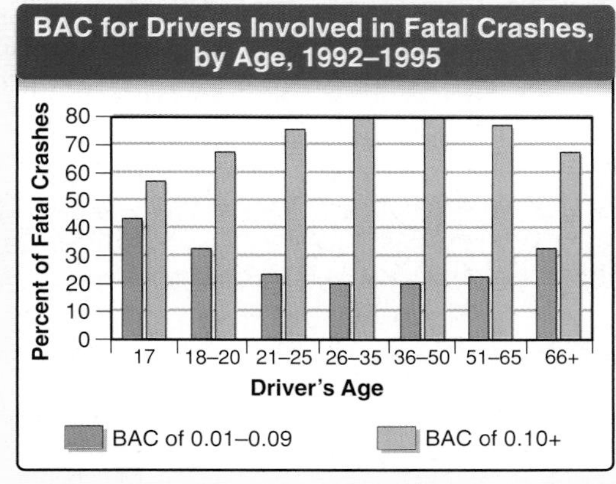

1. **Interpreting Data** What trends do you see in the number of fatal crashes from age 17 to age 66+ based on the two ranges of BAC?
2. **Interpreting Data** How does the consumption of alcohol affect driving risk for the average driver?
3. **Drawing Conclusions** Is the effect of alcohol consumption on driving independent of the age of the driver? Are young drivers more affected by alcohol or less affected by it than older drivers?
4. **Making Judgments** All levels of alcohol consumption affect driving skills, although the effect increases dramatically as more drinks are consumed. To minimize accidents and fatalities due to drunk driving, what should be the legal limit of blood alcohol for drivers?

Meet Diverse Needs

Challenge gifted students to find out more about fetal alcohol syndrome. For example, students might research the incidence of fetal alcohol syndrome and how the risk of having a baby with fetal alcohol syndrome rises with the amount of alcohol that a pregnant woman consumes. Encourage students to share the results of their research with the class by writing a brochure or public service announcement warning pregnant women of the dangers of alcohol consumption. **Learning modality: verbal**

Analyzing Data

Have students find out the BAC for the legal limit of blood alcohol for drivers in their state. Check students' understanding of what BAC means by asking: **If a person has a BAC of 0.1, how much alcohol is present in all 5 liters of his or her blood?** *(5 mL of alcohol)*

Answers

1. At the higher BAC range, the percent of fatal car crashes increases from ages 17 to 35, levels off until age 50, and then starts to decline. At the lower BAC range, the percent of fatal car crashes decreases from ages 17 to 35, levels off until age 50, and then starts to rise.
2. For the average driver, there is a greater risk of fatal crashes at the higher BAC range.
3. No, the effect is not independent of the age of the driver. Young drivers are more affected by lower levels of alcohol and less affected by higher levels than older drivers are.
4. Students probably will say that the legal limit of blood alcohol should be less than 0.08 percent.

BIO INSIGHTS — BACKGROUND

Effects of some drugs

Some drugs such as anesthetics and certain environmental toxins, including chlorinated hydrocarbons that are found in pesticides, can make neurons more or less likely to respond to electrical impulses. Often this is because the substance affects the permeability of membranes to calcium ions. When permeability is decreased so that there is a lower-than-normal concentration of calcium ions, sodium channels may not close completely between action potentials, allowing sodium ions to cross the membrane. This makes the neurons fire more readily, and muscle spasms may result. When membrane permeability is increased and the calcium ion concentration is higher than normal, the opposite result occurs; neurons become less excitable and more difficult to fire.

Answers to . . .

CHECKPOINT *Lung damage, loss of memory, inability to concentrate, and reduced testosterone levels*

Figure 35–19 *Yes, a person can become addicted to legal drugs, including amphetamines, barbiturates, tranquilizers, morphine, and codeine.*

35–5 (continued)

Drug Abuse

Use Community Resources

Encourage interested students to investigate drug abuse treatment options available in their community. Suggest that they start by looking in the Yellow Pages under *Drug Abuse and Addiction Information and Treatment Centers. (Students are likely to find numbers for government programs, self-help groups such as Narcotics Anonymous, and medical practices and clinics that specialize in the treatment of drug abuse and addiction.)* Urge students to share what they learn by creating a poster called "Help for Drug Abuse and Addiction." Display their posters in the classroom.

3 ASSESS

Evaluate Understanding

Have students create a flowchart to show how a stimulant or depressant drug affects the synapse.

Reteach

Name each type of drug described in the text, including stimulants, depressants, cocaine, opiates, marijuana, and alcohol. Challenge students to identify one or more harmful effects of each type of drug.

Take It to the NET

Students' charts should include three main headings: Drug Name, Short-Term Effects, and Long-Term Effects. Students should choose any five drugs from the list on the Web site and complete the table accordingly. They might include alcohol, tobacco, cocaine/crack, heroin, and LSD. The Web site also includes other information, such as descriptions of the drugs and slang terms for them. For additional information, visit **www.phschool.com**

Use iText to review the key concepts in Section 35–5.

Long-term alcohol use also destroys cells in the liver, where alcohol is broken down. As liver cells die, the liver becomes less able to handle large amounts of alcohol. The formation of scar tissue, known as cirrhosis of the liver, occurs next. The scar tissue blocks the flow of blood through the liver and interferes with its other important functions. Eventually, a heavy drinker may die from liver failure.

As with other drugs, dealing with alcohol abuse is not simply a matter of willpower. Alcoholics often need special help and support to quit their drinking habit. Organizations such as Alcoholics Anonymous are available in most communities to help individuals and families deal with the problems created by alcohol abuse.

Drug Abuse

Each of the drugs discussed so far presents a danger to users. The misuse of either a legal or an illegal drug is a serious problem in modern society. **Drug abuse** can be defined as using any drug in a way that most doctors could not approve. With some drugs, such as cocaine, drug abuse causes serious physical damage to the body. With other drugs, such as marijuana, drug abuse produces psychological dependence that can be strong enough to disrupt family life and schoolwork.

An uncontrollable dependence on a drug is known as a drug addiction. Some drugs cause a strong psychological dependence. People who are psychologically dependent on a drug have a mental craving, or need, for the drug. Other drugs cause a strong physical dependence. Physical dependence occurs when the body cannot function without a constant supply of the drug.

The best way to avoid the effects of drugs is to avoid drugs. The decision not to use drugs can be difficult when you are faced with pressure to take them. By deciding not to take drugs, you are acting to take control of your life.

35–5 Section Assessment

1. **Key Concept** Describe the effects of stimulants, cocaine, depressants, and opiates on the central nervous system.
2. **Key Concept** Explain the effects of alcohol on the body.
3. What is a drug?
4. Based on alcohol's effects on the central nervous system, why is drinking and driving an extremely dangerous behavior?
5. **Critical Thinking Inferring** Which do you think is a more difficult addiction to break: one in which a person is physically dependent on a drug, or one in which a person is psychologically dependent on a drug? Explain your answer.

iTEXT Assessment Use iText to review the important concepts in Section 35–5.

Take It to the NET

Read about the effects of different drugs. Then, create a chart listing five different drugs and their short-term and long-term effects on the body. Use the links provided in the Biology area at the Prentice Hall Web site for help in completing this activity: **www.phschool.com**

35–5 Section Assessment

1. Stimulants increase the release of neurotransmitters, cocaine causes the sudden release of dopamine, depressants enhance the effects of certain neurotransmitters, and opiates mimic endorphins.
2. As a depressant, alcohol slows down the rate at which the central nervous system functions.
3. Any substance other than food that causes a change in the body
4. Because alcohol slows down reflexes, disrupts coordination, and impairs judgment
5. Some students might say a psychological dependence is more difficult to break. Others might say a physical dependence is more difficult to break. Students should support their predictions with sound reasoning.

Real-World Lab

Correcting Vision With Lenses

The lenses of your eyes focus light on the retina. The lenses of people who are nearsighted focus images in front of the retina, making distant objects appear blurry. The lenses of people who are farsighted focus behind the retina, making nearby objects difficult to see. To see more clearly, these people wear glasses or contact lenses. The shapes of these artificial lenses depend on the type of correction needed.

Problem **What types of corrective lenses are needed by nearsighted individuals and by farsighted individuals?**

Materials

- tape
- 2 cardboard photo easels
- black construction paper
- unruled white index card
- 6-V light bulb and socket
- 6-V battery and wires with alligator clips
- 2 convex lenses
- modeling clay
- meter stick
- concave lens

Skills Analyzing Data, Using Models

Procedure  

1. Set up your equipment as shown. Place the white index card about 50 to 60 cm in front of the bulb.
2. Place a convex lens in front of the bulb and move the lens until an image of the bulb focuses clearly on the index card. Secure the lens in this position with modeling clay or tape. The distance between the fixed lens and the index card is the focal length of the lens.
3. Move the index card about 5 to 8 cm away from the fixed lens to simulate the formation of an image in front of the retina. Observe the image and record your observations.
4. Hold the concave lens between the light bulb and the fixed lens. Try to focus the image by moving the concave lens between the light bulb and the fixed lens.
5. Repeat step 4, but this time use the second convex lens. Record your observations.
6. Move the index card about 10 to 16 cm closer to the fixed lens to simulate image formation behind the retina. Record your observations.
7. Repeat steps 4 and 5.

Analyze and Conclude

1. **Drawing Conclusions** Does the lens in your eye focus an image right side up or upside down on your retina? Why does an image appear right side up when you look at objects?
2. **Drawing Conclusions** Which lens sharpened the image that formed in front of the retina? Behind the retina?
3. **Using Models** Which condition—long-focal length or short-focal length—do you think models the problem of nearsightedness? Which condition models farsightedness? Explain your answers.

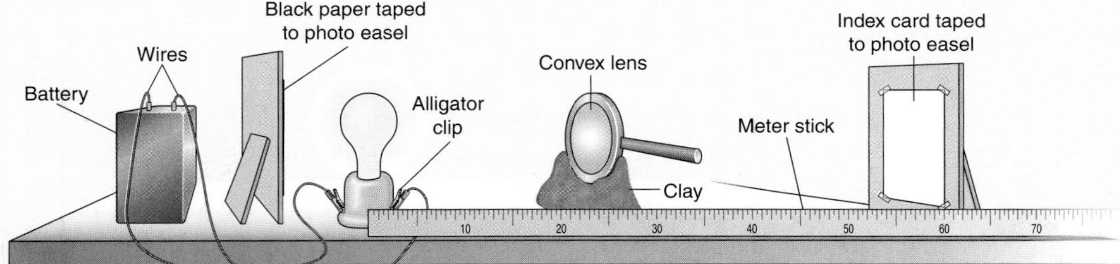

Analyze and Conclude

1. The lens in your eye focuses an image upside down on your retina. It appears right side up when you look at objects because the brain interprets the image right side up.

2. The concave lens sharpened the image that formed in front of the retina. The convex lens sharpened the image that formed behind the retina.

3. Short-focal length models the problem of nearsightedness because the image focuses in front of the "retina." Long-focal length models the problem of farsightedness because the image focuses behind the "retina."

Real-World Lab

Objective Students will be able to use a model to determine which types of corrective lenses are needed by nearsighted and farsighted individuals.

Skills Focus **Drawing Conclusions, Using Models**

Time 45 minutes

Advance Prep
- You may need to attach a piece of cardboard to the supports on the backs of the photo easels to make them stand vertically.
- An optical bench, often used in physics classes, may be used in place of the meter stick and cardboard photo easels.
- A candle can be used in place of the electric light, and may give a sharper image.

Teaching Strategies Have students read the entire procedure. Before they begin the procedure, point out that light rays change direction when they pass from one medium (such as air) into another (such as water). You may want to put a pencil in a glass of water to illustrate this point. Explain that the water bends the light as a lens does. Then, ask: **What does the fixed lens in the setup represent?** *(The lens of the eye)* **What does the index card in front of the fixed lens represent?** *(The retina of the eye)*

Procedure

2. Remind students to record the focal length before they move the index card in step 3.

3. Students should describe how the image becomes blurry or out of focus.

Expected Outcome Students should find that a concave lens sharpens the image when it forms in front of the retina and a convex lens sharpens the image when it forms behind the retina.

Chapter 35 Study Guide

Study Tip

Suggest that students review the chapter contents by using each of the Vocabulary terms correctly in a sentence. Check their sentences for errors. Then, have them rewrite their sentences as fill-in-the-blank questions by leaving out the Vocabulary terms. They can use the questions to quiz a classmate.

Thinking Visually

Graphic organizers should show that the nervous system consists of the central nervous system (brain and spinal cord) and the peripheral nervous system, which has sensory and motor divisions. The nervous system can also be divided into the somatic nervous system and the autonomic nervous system with its sympathetic and parasympathetic divisions.

Chapter 35 Assessment

Reviewing Content

1. c **2.** b **3.** a **4.** d **5.** a **6.** c **7.** b **8.** d **9.** b **10.** a

Understanding Concepts

11. Cell, tissue, organ, organ system, organism

12. Unless cells of the body are kept at a temperature within a certain range, supplied with energy, bathed in fluid, and cleansed of waste—in short, unless homeostasis is maintained—permanent injury or death can occur.

13. The largest part of a typical neuron is the cell body, which contains the cell nucleus and much of the cytoplasm. The cell body is where most of the cell's metabolic activity occurs. Short, branched extensions called dendrites carry impulses from the environment or other neurons toward the cell body. The long fiber that carries impulses away from the cell body is called the axon, which ends in small swellings called axon terminals.

14. During a resting potential, potassium ions (K^+) diffuse across a neuron's cell membrane more easily than do sodium ions (Na^+), resulting in a negative charge inside the cell membrane. During an action potential, the cell membrane becomes more permeable to Na^+ ions, resulting in a reversal of charges.

Chapter 35 Study Guide

35–1 Human Body Systems

Key Concepts

- The eleven organ systems of the human body work together to maintain homeostasis.

Vocabulary

muscle tissue, p. 894
epithelial tissue, p. 894
connective tissue, p. 894
nervous tissue, p. 894
feedback inhibition, p. 895

35–2 The Nervous System

Key Concepts

- The nervous system controls and coordinates functions throughout the body and responds to internal and external stimuli.
- A nerve impulse begins when a neuron is stimulated by another neuron or by its environment.

Vocabulary

neuron, p. 897 • cell body, p. 897
dendrite, p. 898 • axon, p. 898
myelin sheath, p. 898 • resting potential, p. 898
action potential, p. 899 • threshold, p. 899
synapse, p. 900 • neurotransmitter, p. 900

35–3 Divisions of the Nervous System

Key Concepts

- The central nervous system relays messages, processes information, and analyzes information.
- The sensory division of the peripheral nervous system transmits impulses from sense organs to the central nervous system. The motor division transmits impulses from the central nervous system to the muscles or glands.

Vocabulary

central nervous system, p. 901
meninges, p. 901 • cerebrospinal fluid, p. 901
cerebrum, p. 902 • cerebellum, p. 902
brain stem, p. 902 • thalamus, p. 903
hypothalamus, p. 903 • reflex, p. 903

35–4 The Senses

Key Concept

- There are five general categories of sensory receptors: pain receptors, thermoreceptors, mechanoreceptors, chemoreceptors, and photoreceptors.

Vocabulary

sensory receptor, p. 906 • pupil, p. 906
lens, p. 907 • retina, p. 907 • rod, p. 907
cone, p. 907 • cochlea, p. 908
semicircular canal, p. 908 • taste bud, p. 909

35–5 Drugs and the Nervous System

Key Concepts

- Stimulants increase heart rate, blood pressure, and breathing rate. In addition, stimulants increase the release of neurotransmitters at some synapses in the brain.
- Depressants slow down heart rate and breathing rate, lower blood pressure, relax muscles, and relieve tension.
- Cocaine causes the sudden release of a neurotransmitter in the brain called dopamine.
- Opiates mimic natural chemicals in the brain known as endorphins, which normally help to overcome sensations of pain.
- Alcohol is a depressant, and even small amounts of alcohol slow down the rate at which the nervous system functions.

Vocabulary

drug, p. 910 • stimulant, p. 910
depressant, p. 911 • addiction, p. 911
fetal alcohol syndrome, p. 913
drug abuse, p. 914

Thinking Visually

Develop a graphic organizer to show the relationship between the different divisions of the nervous system.

TIME SAVER CHAPTER RESOURCES

Print:

- ***Teaching Resources,*** Chapter Vocabulary Review, Graphic Organizer
- ***Chapter Tests: Levels A and B,*** Chapter 35 Test
- ***PH Assessment System,*** Practice Test

Technology:

- ***Computer Test Bank,*** Chapter 35 Test
- ***iText,*** Chapter 35 Assessment

Chapter 35 Assessment

Reviewing Content

Choose the letter that best answers the question or completes the statement.

1. Glands and tissues that cover internal and external body surfaces are
   a. muscle tissue.
   b. connective tissue.
   c. epithelial tissue.
   d. nervous tissue.

2. The process of maintaining a relatively constant internal environment despite changes in the external environment is called
   a. regulation. c. synapse.
   b. homeostasis. d. stimulation.

3. Cells that carry messages throughout the nervous system are called
   a. neurons.
   b. axons.
   c. dendrites.
   d. neurotransmitters.

4. In the diagram below, letter *A* is pointing to the
   a. myelin sheath. c. dendrite.
   b. axon. d. cell body.

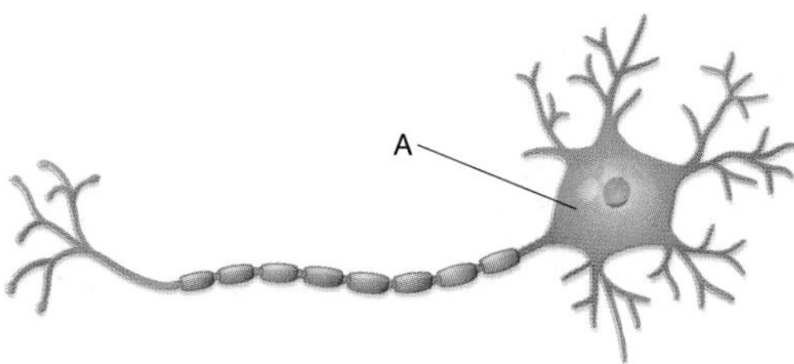

5. The place at which a neuron can transfer an impulse to another cell is known as a
   a. synapse. c. myelin sheath.
   b. dendrite. d. receptor.

6. The central nervous system consists of the
   a. sense organs.
   b. reflexes.
   c. brain and spinal cord.
   d. sensory and motor neurons.

7. Voluntary or conscious activities of the body are controlled by the
   a. medulla oblongata. c. cerebellum.
   b. cerebrum. d. brain stem.

8. The sympathetic nervous system and the parasympathetic nervous system are divisions of the
   a. peripheral nervous system.
   b. central nervous system.
   c. somatic nervous system.
   d. autonomic nervous system.

9. The semicircular canals and the two tiny sacs located behind them help maintain
   a. night vision. c. respiratory rate.
   b. equilibrium. d. temperature.

10. Drugs that increase heart rate, blood pressure, and breathing rate are
    a. stimulants. c. opiates.
    b. depressants. d. barbiturates.

Understanding Concepts

11. Sequence the following terms from simplest to most complex: *organ system, tissue, organ, organism, cell.*
12. Why is homeostasis important to an organism?
13. Describe the structure and function of a neuron.
14. What changes occur in the neuron during the resting potential? During an action potential?
15. How does the all-or-none principle relate to the transmission of a nerve impulse?
16. How is the central nervous system protected?
17. Describe the structure and function of the cerebrum.
18. Describe the advantage of a reflex response.
19. List the divisions of the autonomic nervous system and give the function of each.
20. Trace the path of light through the eye.
21. What are the functions of rods and cones?
22. Trace the path of sound through the ear.
23. Explain why a pregnant woman should avoid drinking alcohol.
24. Define drug abuse in your own words.
25. It has been said that no one can be cured of a drug dependence. Explain why.

TIME SAVER

HOMEWORK GUIDE

Section:	Questions:
Section 35–1	1, 2, 11, 12, 35
Section 35–2	3–5, 13–15, 26, 28, 29, 31, 33
Section 35–3	6–8, 16–19, 35
Section 35–4	9, 20–22, 27, 30, 32
Section 35–5	10, 23–25, 34

Chapter 35 Assessment (continued)

15. According to the all-or-none principle, any stimulus that is stronger than the threshold will produce an impulse and any stimulus below the threshold will not produce an impulse.

16. The central nervous system is protected by the skull and vertebrae in the spinal column. The central nervous system is wrapped in layers of connective tissue called meninges. Between two of these layers is a space filled with cerebrospinal fluid, which acts as a shock absorber.

17. The cerebrum consists of two hemispheres, each divided into regions called lobes. A band of tissue known as the corpus callosum connects the two hemispheres. The cerebrum is responsible for the voluntary, or conscious, activities of the body. It is the site of intelligence, learning, and judgment.

18. Reflexes allow an organism to respond to danger quickly, which is an advantage for survival.

19. The autonomic nervous system is divided into the sympathetic and parasympathetic nervous systems. The symphathetic and parasympathetic nervous systems have opposite effects on the same organ system.

20. Light enters the eye through the cornea and passes through the anterior chamber, which is filled with aqueous humor. The light then goes through the pupil, which is an opening in the iris, and through the lens into a large chamber filled with vitreous humor. The lens focuses the light on the retina, where photoreceptors convert light into impulses that are sent via the optic nerve to the brain.

21. Rods, which are extremely sensitive to light, and cones, which are less sensitive to light but can distinguish different colors, are photoreceptors in the retina. Their function is to convert light into impulses that are carried through the optic nerve to the central nervous system.

Chapter 35 Assessment

22. Sound waves, which are vibrations in the air, enter the auditory canal and cause the tympanum to vibrate. Three tiny bones, the hammer, anvil, and stirrup, pick up the vibrations, and the stirrup transmits them to the oval window. The oval window vibrates and creates pressure waves in the fluid-filled cochlea. The pressure waves push back and forth against tiny hair cells, which respond by producing nerve impulses that are sent to the brain through the cochlear nerve.

23. She risks having a child with fetal alcohol syndrome—a set of birth defects. A child with FAS can have heart defects, a malformed face, delayed growth, and poor motor development.

24. Students may state that drug abuse is the misuse of a drug, whether legal or illegal, or its use in a way that most doctors could not approve.

25. One possible answer is: Drug dependence means that the only way a person can stop using the drug is by complete abstinence. This might be called a way to control the dependence but not a cure.

Critical Thinking

26. Students' experimental designs should include variables, controls, reasonable hypotheses, and feasible procedures. The focus should be on a simple, repetitive task.

27. The advantage relates to the thermoregulatory function of the tongue in some mammals. Mammals lose excess body heat by sweating, and for many mammals, including the domestic dog, the primary organ for sweating is the tongue.

28. If an axon is disconnected from a nerve cell body, the pathway of an incoming nerve impulse will be disrupted.

29. The purpose of the knee-jerk test is to determine whether the person's reflexes are normal. The absence of a response could indicate a disorder of one of the components of the reflex arc.

Chapter 35 Assessment

Critical Thinking

26. **Designing Experiments** Design an experiment to determine the effects of fatigue on reaction time. Formulate a hypothesis and write up a procedure. Have your teacher check your experimental plan before you begin.

27. **Applying Concepts** Heat receptors of mammals are particularly concentrated on the tongue. These receptors keep humans from burning the mouth with hot food. What advantage is it for a wild mammal that doesn't cook its food to have so many heat receptors in its tongue?

28. **Inferring** Suppose a portion of an axon is cut so that it is no longer connected to its nerve cell body. What effect would that have on the transmission of impulses?

29. **Applying Concepts** A routine examination by a doctor usually includes a knee-jerk test. What is the purpose of this test? What could the absence of a response indicate?

30. **Analyzing Data** The graph below compares age to the nearest distance in centimeters that many people can see an object clearly. Describe the general trend of the graph. At what age does the slope of the graph begin to change rapidly? What do you think might explain this change?

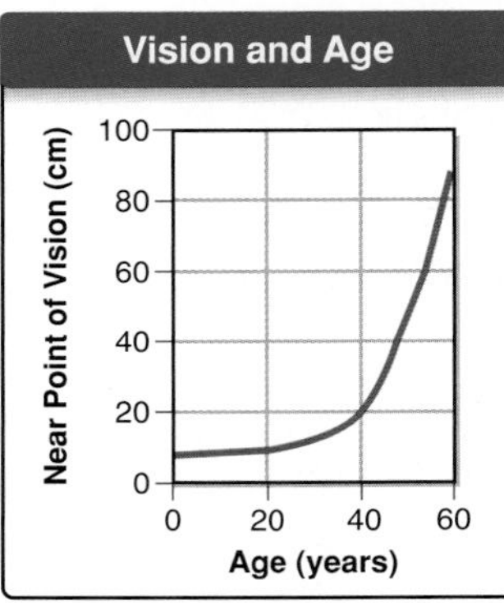

31. **Predicting** Multiple sclerosis (MS) is a disease characterized by the patchy destruction of myelin. Predict the symptoms that might be produced.

32. **Applying Concepts** Constant exposure to loud noises may cause loss of hearing. What parts of the ear may be damaged? Can the loss of hearing be reversed?

33. **Using Analogies** How are a neuron and an electrical extension cord similar? How are they different?

34. **Applying Concepts** Why are depressant drugs and alcohol a life-threatening combination?

35. **Making Connections** What functions of the body could be affected if the liver were damaged by cirrhosis?

Performance-Based Assessment

Making a Collage The left and right sides of the brain are responsible for different activities. Make a collage that shows examples of some right-brain activities and some left-brain activities. Attach to your collage a paragraph outlining what learning strategies would be useful for left-brain dominant individuals and for right-brain dominant individuals.

You can visit the Prentice Hall Web site at **www.phschool.com** to explore the many facts and figures about the human nervous system. Then, answer the following questions:

- How many synapses does a typical neuron have?
- What is the average weight of the human brain? Which species have average brain weights greater than the average weight of the human brain?
- How many taste buds does a typical human have? How many of these are on the tongue?
- Compare the number of olfactory (smell) receptors in a human with the number found in a dog.

Performance-Based Assessment

Student projects should reflect the theory that the right hemisphere of the brain is associated with creativity and artistic ability and the left hemisphere with analytical and mathematical ability.

Standardized Test Prep

Test-Taking Tip Questions that begin with a list of lettered choices (A–E) followed by numbered statements are essentially multiple-choice questions. To solve these questions, use the same process that you use to solve standard multiple-choice questions.

Questions 1–3 Each of the lettered choices below refers to the following numbered statements. Select the best lettered choice. A choice may be used once, more than once, or not at all.

(A) Synapse
(B) Myelin sheath
(C) Cerebrum
(D) Cerebellum
(E) Somatic nervous system

1. The largest and most prominent part of the human brain

2. Regulates activities that are under conscious control

3. Gap between two neurons

Questions 4–6

A student surveyed 200 students who each had an overall grade point average of A or B. The results of the survey are summarized in the graph below.

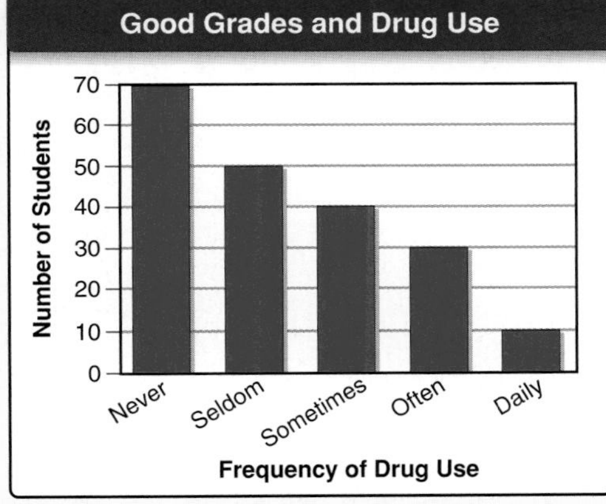

4. What is the responding variable in the study?
(A) good grades
(B) age
(C) popularity at school
(D) frequency of drug use
(E) intelligence

5. What percentage of students with good grades say they never use drugs?
(A) 70%
(B) 50%
(C) 35%
(D) 25%
(E) 10%

6. The student concluded that students with good grades use drugs less frequently than students with poor grades. What's wrong with her conclusion?
(A) She doesn't have any data on students with poor grades.
(B) Students with good grades use drugs 70% of the time.
(C) She didn't survey enough students.
(D) She surveyed students only in her school.
(E) Her graph isn't supported by her data.

Directions: Choose the letter that best answers the question or completes the statement.

7. The process by which organisms keep internal conditions relatively constant is called
(A) resting potential.
(B) positive feedback.
(C) feedback inhibition.
(D) the all-or-none principle.
(E) homeostasis.

8. Which of the following is NOT a kind of tissue in the human body?
(A) epithelial
(B) connective
(C) neuron
(D) nervous
(E) muscle

9. The part of a neuron that carries impulses away from the cell body is called a(an)
(A) axon.
(B) dendrite.
(C) node.
(D) vesicle.
(E) synapse.

10. Which of the following sensory receptors is found in the skin?
I. pain receptors
II. mechanoreceptors
III. photoreceptors
(A) I only
(B) II only
(C) I and II only
(D) II and III only
(E) I, II, and III

11. Which of the following is NOT a structure of the human ear?
(A) tympanum
(B) cochlea
(C) stirrup bone
(D) vitreous humor
(E) semicircular canals

Standardized Test Prep

1. C **2.** E **3.** A **4.** D **5.** A **6.** A **7.** E **8.** C **9.** A **10.** C **11.** D

(continued from page 918)

30. The slope of the graph starts to change rapidly at the age of 40 as the distance at which the person can focus clearly on nearby objects increases. Students may infer that the shape of the cornea or of the lens changes with age, affecting the focus of light entering the eyes.

31. With less myelin, nerve impulses in people with MS will travel more slowly. This will result in loss of control over motor functions, leading to paralysis, poor coordination, slurred speech, blurred vision, and tremor.

32. Constant exposure to loud noises would damage the delicate structure of the inner ear, the cochlea and the membrane covering the oval window. Hearing loss caused by damage to these structures is irreversible.

33. Both a neuron and an extension cord carry electrical impulses. A neuron is a living cell whereas an extension cord is nonliving.

34. Alcohol is itself a depressant drug and in combination with other depressants can slow down breathing until breathing stops.

35. Digestion of fats and destruction of worn-out red blood cells

Take It to the NET

• A typical neuron has between 1,000 and 10,000 synapses.

• The weight of the average human brain is 1,300 to 1,400 g. The sperm whale, bottle-nosed dolphin, and elephant all have average brain weights greater than this.

• A typical human has about 10,000 taste buds, 9,000 of which are on the tongue.

• A human has about 40 million olfactory receptors, whereas a dog has about 1 billion.

For additional information, visit

www.phschool.com

Chapter Planner 36 Skeletal, Muscular, and Integumentary Systems

Section and Section Objectives	Time	Activities and Labs
36–1 The Skeletal System, pp. 921–925 **36.1.1** ***State*** the functions of the skeletal system. **36.1.2** ***Describe*** the structure of a typical bone. **36.1.3** ***Explain*** how bones develop. **36.1.4** ***Identify*** the three different kinds of joints.	**2 periods (1 block)**	**SE:** ***Inquiry Activity,*** How do your joints move?, p. 920 **TE:** ***Meet Diverse Needs,*** p. 921 **TE:** ***Demonstration,*** p. 923 **TE:** ***Build Science Skills,*** p. 924
36–2 The Muscular System, pp. 926–931 **36.2.1** ***Describe*** the three types of muscle tissue. **36.2.2** ***Explain*** how muscles contract. **36.2.3** ***Explain*** how muscles and bones interact.	**2 periods (1 block)**	**SE:** ***Quick Lab,*** What do tendons do?, p. 930 **TE:** ***Build Science Skills,*** p. 931
36–3 The Integumentary System, pp. 933–936 **36.3.1** ***State*** the functions of the integumentary system. **36.3.2** ***Describe*** the structure of hair and nails.	**1 period (1/2 block)**	**SE:** ***Technology & Society,*** Artificial Skin, p. 932 **TE:** ***Demonstration,*** p. 933 **TE:** ***Meet Diverse Needs,*** p. 934 **SE:** ***Analyzing Data,*** The UV Index and Sunburn, p. 935 **SE:** ***Real-World Lab,*** Making a Model of a Transdermal Patch, p. 937
Chapter Assessment, pp. 938–941	**1 period (1/2 block)**	

ACTIVITY PLANNER

SE: ***Inquiry Activity,*** p. 920; (10 min.); hinge, ball-and-socket joint

TE: ***Meet Diverse Needs,*** p. 921; (10 min.); human skeletal model

TE: ***Demonstration,*** p. 923; (5 min.); clean chicken bone, beaker, vinegar

TE: ***Build Science Skills,*** p. 924; (15 min.); craft sticks, toothpicks, pipe cleaners, modeling clay, glue, tacks

SE: ***Quick Lab,*** p. 930; (20 min.); plastic gloves, lab apron, raw chicken wing treated with bleach, paper towels, forceps, scissors, scalpel

TE: ***Build Science Skills,*** p. 931; (10 min.); ruler, eraser, tape

TE: ***Demonstration,*** p. 933; (5 min.); apple, knife, plastic wrap

TE: ***Meet Diverse Needs,*** p. 934; (5 min.); chalkboard eraser, pencil, heating pad, ice cube

SE: ***Real-World Lab,*** p. 937; (30 min.); 15-cm dialysis tubing, plastic cup, phenolphthalein solution, 30-mL graduated cylinder, paper towels, scissors, metric ruler, filter paper, dropper pipette, sodium bicarbonate solution

PLANNING KEY

Ability Levels

B **Basic**	For students who need additional help
A **Average**	For all students
E **Enriched**	For students who need to be challenged

Components

SE	Student Edition	**GRSW**	Guided Reading and Study Workbook	**IDM**	Issues and Decision Making
TE	Teacher's Edition	**CT**	Chapter Tests: Levels A and B	**CTB**	Computer Test Bank
LMA	Laboratory Manual A	**PHAS**	PH Assessment System	**PA**	Presentation Assistant Plus
LMB	Laboratory Manual B	**LA**	Lab Assessment with Scoring Guide	**BD**	BioDetectives Videotape
TR	Teaching Resources	**BTM**	BioTechnology Manual	**iT**	iText

Program Resources	Assessment	Media and Technology
LMA: Chapter 36 Lab A E **TR:** Section Review 36–1 B A **GRSW:** Section 36–1 B A **IDM:** Issues and Decisions 38 A E	**SE:** 36–1 Section Assessment, p. 925 **TR:** Section Review 36–1	**PA:** 36–1 Interest Grabber, Section Outline, Skeletal System Figure 36–3, Figure 36–4, Figure 36–5 **iT:** Section 36–1
LMB: Chapter 36 Lab B A **TR:** Section Review 36–2 B A **GRSW:** Section 36–2 B A	**SE:** 36–2 Section Assessment, p. 931 **TR:** Section Review 36–2	**PA:** 36–2 Interest Grabber, Section Outline, Flowchart, Figure 36–7, Figure 36–8, Figure 36–11 **iT:** Section 36–2
TR: Section Review 36–3 B A **GRSW:** Chapter 36 Real-World Lab B A E	**SE:** 36–3 Section Assessment, p. 936 **TR:** Section Review 36–3	**PA:** 36–3 Interest Grabber, Section Outline, Concept Map, Figure 36–13 **iT:** Section 36–3
	SE: Chapter 36 Assessment, pp. 938–941 **TR:** Chapter Vocabulary Review, Graphic Organizer **CT:** Chapter 36 Test **CTB:** Chapter 36 Test **PHAS:** Practice Test	**CTB:** Chapter 36 Test **iT:** Chapter 36 Assessment

PRESSED FOR TIME?

To Preview the Chapter

- Have students skim each section of Chapter 36 for highlighted sentences and vocabulary terms.
- Assign the Reading Strategies for each section.

To Cover the Chapter Quickly

- Have students read The Skeleton and Types of Joints in Section 36–1, Types of Muscle Tissue and How Muscles and Bones Interact in Section 36–2, and all of Section 36–3.
- Assign questions 1 and 3 in Section Reviews 36–1 and 36–2 and all of the questions in Section Review 36–3. Also assign questions 6, 7, 10–11, 16, 20–25, 30, 33–35, and the performance-based assessment in Chapter 36 Assessment and questions 1–3 and 7–9 in Chapter 36 Standardized Test Prep.

To Review the Chapter

- Assign the Section Reviews 36–1 through 36–3 in the Guided Reading and Study Workbook.
- Assign Section Reviews for 36–1 through 36–3 and the Chapter Vocabulary Review for Chapter 36 in the Teaching Resources.

ENGAGE/EXPLORE

Inquiry Activity

Objective Students will be able to classify joints based on how they move.

Skill Focus **Classifying, Inferring**

Materials hinge and ball-and-socket joint examples

Time 10 minutes

Advance Prep Lay out hinges and ball-and-socket joints where students can examine them. Objects with ball-and-socket joints include joysticks from computers or video games, shower-head arm mounts, and single-lever faucets.

Strategies

- Give students room to stand and move freely.
- Point out examples of other common objects that have joints, such as book covers (hinges) and ball-point pens (ball-and-socket joints).

Expected Outcome Students should be able to classify hinge and ball-and-socket joints based on their range of motion.

Think About It

1. Hinge joints, including the knee and elbow, allow back-and-forth movement.
2. Ball-and-socket joints, including the hip and shoulder, allow circular movement.
3. Pivot joints allow one bone to rotate around another. Saddle joints permit one bone to slide in two directions.

Assess Prior Knowledge

Guide students in organizing their prior knowledge of the three systems covered in the chapter. Have them complete the following sentences, and then call on students at random to read their completed sentences to the class. "The skeletal system consists of . . ." *(bones, cartilage, ligaments, and tendons)* "The forces that put the skeleton into motion come from the . . ." *(muscles)* "The major function of the skin is . . ." *(to protect the body)*

Chapter 36 Skeletal, Muscular, and Integumentary Systems

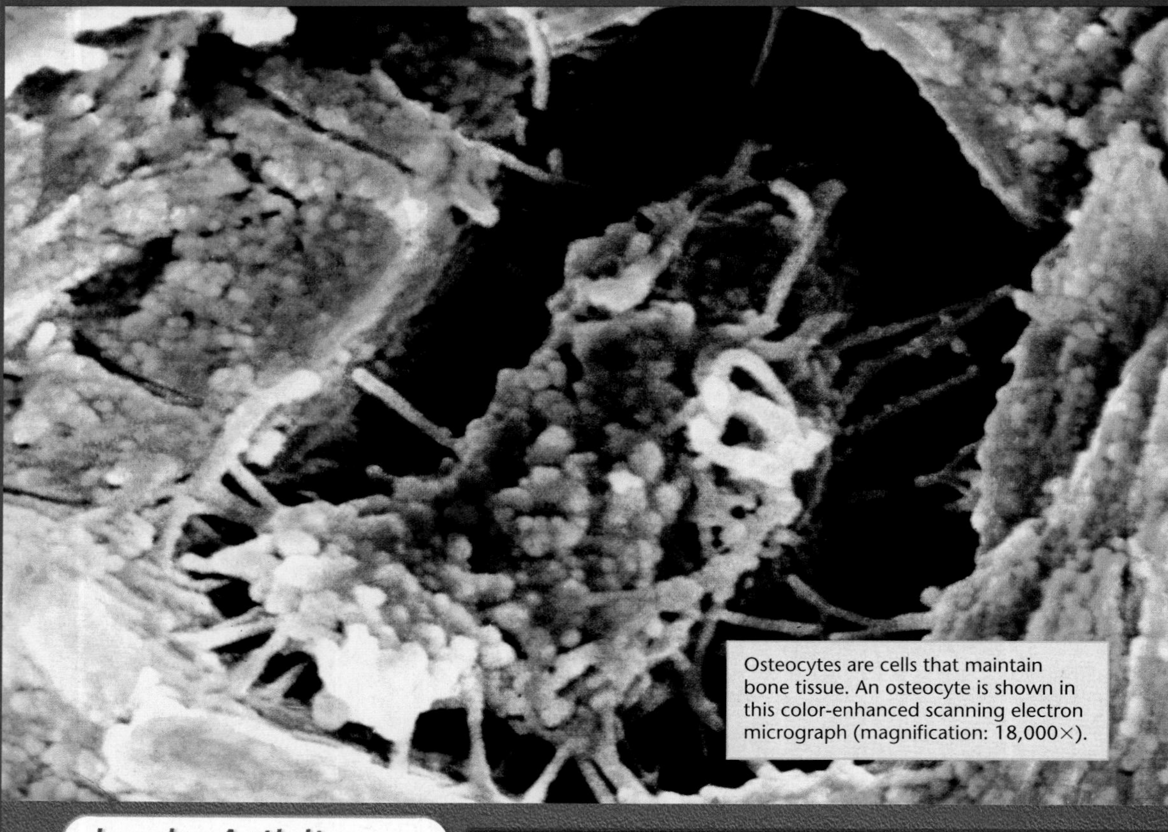

Osteocytes are cells that maintain bone tissue. An osteocyte is shown in this color-enhanced scanning electron micrograph (magnification: 18,000×).

Inquiry Activity

How do your joints move?

Procedure

1. Look at the examples of a hinge and a ball-and-socket joint provided by your teacher. Determine how each moves.
2. Based on your observations, identify joints in your body that are hinge joints and joints that are ball-and-socket joints.

Think About It

1. **Classifying** What type of movement does a hinge joint allow?
2. **Inferring** What type of movement does a ball-and-socket joint allow?
3. **Inferring** Your body also has joints called pivot joints and saddle joints. Based on their names, what type of movement might these joints allow? *Hint:* Consider how a rider might move in a saddle.

FACTS AND FIGURES

Bones from the past

Bones are one of the most important tools paleontologists have for studying the evolution of vertebrates, including humans. Because bones are made of hard, dense material, they are more likely than other tissues, such as muscle and skin, to be preserved after an animal dies. Bones are preserved as fossils, which form when water in the ground gradually leaches away the organic material in the bones and replaces it with minerals. Paleontologists study fossils and compare them with the bones of living animals to learn more about the anatomy and way of life of extinct animals. This is much more difficult than it sounds, because complete skeletons of extinct organisms are rarely found. Instead, most fossils consist only of fragments of bone.

36–1 The Skeletal System

To retain their shape, all organisms need some type of support. Thickened cell membranes provide the support for single-celled organisms. In multicellular animals, support is provided by some form of skeleton, including the external exoskeletons of arthropods and the internal endoskeletons of vertebrates. The human skeleton is composed of a type of connective tissue called bone. Bones and other connective tissues, such as cartilage and ligaments, form the skeletal system.

Scientists can infer a lot about the behavior of extinct species by studying their fossil bones and reconstructing their skeletons. The human skeleton also contains important clues. The shape of your hip bones shows that you walk upright on two legs. The structure of the bones in your hands, especially your opposable thumbs, indicates that you have the ability to grasp objects. The size and shape of your skull is a clue that you have a well-developed brain.

Guide for Reading

 **Key Concepts**
- What are the functions of the skeletal system?
- What is the structure of a typical bone?
- What are the three different kinds of joints?

Vocabulary
periosteum
Haversian canal
bone marrow
cartilage
ossification
joint
ligament

Reading Strategy: Asking Questions Before you read, rewrite the headings in this section as *how, why,* or *what* questions about the skeletal system. As you read, write brief answers to those heading questions.

The Skeleton

The skeletal system has many important functions. **The skeleton supports the body, protects internal organs, provides for movement, stores mineral reserves, and provides a site for blood cell formation.** The bones that make up the skeletal system support and shape the body much like an internal wooden frame supports a house. Just as a house could not stand without its wooden frame, the human body would collapse without its bony skeleton. Bones protect the delicate internal organs of the body. For example, the skull forms a protective shell around the brain, and the ribs form a basketlike cage that protects the heart and lungs.

Bones provide a system of levers on which muscles act to produce movement. Levers are rigid rods that can be moved about a fixed point. In addition, bones contain reserves of minerals, mainly calcium salts, that are important to many body processes. Finally, bones are the site of blood cell formation. Blood cells are produced in the soft marrow tissue that fills the internal cavities in some bones.

There are 206 bones in the adult human skeleton. As shown in **Figure 36–2** on page 922, these bones can be divided into two parts—the axial skeleton and the appendicular skeleton. The axial skeleton supports the central axis of the body. It consists of the skull, the vertebral column, and the rib cage. The bones of the arms and legs, along with the bones of the pelvis and shoulder area, form the appendicular skeleton.

▼ **Figure 36–1 Bones provide a system of levers on which muscles act to produce movement.** Without this coordination, movement would not be possible.

TIME SAVER — SECTION RESOURCES

Print:
- ***Laboratory Manual A,*** Chapter 36 Lab
- ***Teaching Resources,*** Section Review 36–1
- ***Guided Reading and Study Workbook,*** Section 36–1
- ***Issues and Decision Making,*** Issues and Decisions 38

Technology:
- ***iText,*** Section 36–1

Section 36–1

1 FOCUS

Objectives

36.1.1 ***State*** the functions of the skeletal system.
36.1.2 ***Describe*** the structure of a typical bone.
36.1.3 ***Explain*** how bones develop.
36.1.4 ***Identify*** the three different kinds of joints.

Guide for Reading

Vocabulary Preview

Tell students that words beginning with *os,* the Latin word for bone, have something to do with bone. For example, the word *ossification* means "the process of bone formation." Challenge students to find other words beginning with *os,* such as osteoarthritis and osteocyte, and explain each word's connection with bone.

Reading Strategy

Have students preview the material in the section by studying the figures and reading the captions. They should make note of any words they do not know and find the definitions as they read the section.

2 INSTRUCT

The Skeleton

Meet Diverse Needs

Invite students to examine a three-dimensional model of the human skeleton. Challenge them to identify the bones of the axial skeleton (skull, vertebral column, rib cage) and the appendicular skeleton (arms, legs, pelvis, and shoulders). Urge students to manipulate the bones so they have a better understanding of how the axial skeleton supports the body and the appendicular skeleton allows movement. **Learning modality: tactile**

36–1 (continued)

Structure of Bones

Address Misconceptions

Students may have difficulty conceiving of bone as living tissue. Ask: **Which do you think is a better model of a bone, a stick of chalk or a piece of sponge?** *(Some students may say that a stick of chalk is a better model.)* Point out that a stick of chalk may look more like a bone, but a piece of sponge is more like a bone in its structure. Both the sponge and the bone contain a network of tubes or spaces through which things can pass. Ask: **What passes through the tubes and spaces inside bone?** *(Blood vessels and nerves)*

Use Visuals

Figure 36–3 Make sure students understand how the two parts of the figure are related. Point out how the drawing on the right shows a cross-section of a tiny piece of the bone on the left. Guide students in using the figure to distinguish between compact and spongy bone. Ask: **What structures are found in compact bone?** *(Haversian canals, veins, arteries, and osteocytes)* **Where is spongy bone found?** *(Inside compact bone at the ends of long bones and in the middle of short, flat bones)*

Development of Bones

Meet Diverse Needs

Work with the class to create a table comparing and contrasting bone and cartilage. Have a volunteer record the information in a chart on the chalkboard as the class brainstorms the similarities and differences between the two types of tissue. **Learning modality: visual**

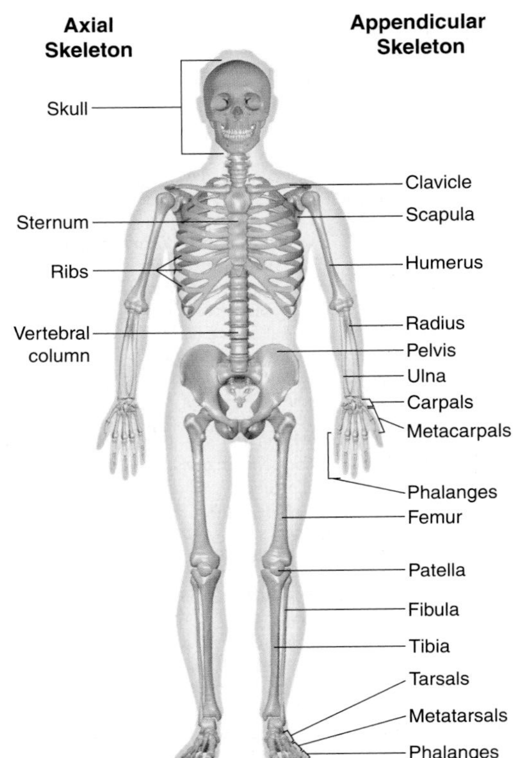

▲ **Figure 36–2** **The skeleton supports the body.** The human skeleton is divided into two parts: the axial skeleton and the appendicular skeleton.

Structure of Bones

It is easy to think of bones as nonliving. After all, most of the mass of bone is mineral salts—mainly calcium and phosphorus. However, bones are living tissue. **Bones are a solid network of living cells and protein fibers that are surrounded by deposits of calcium salts.**

Figure 36–3 shows a typical bone. The bone is surrounded by a tough layer of connective tissue called the **periosteum** (pehr-ee-AHS-tee-um). Blood vessels that pass through the periosteum carry oxygen and nutrients to the bone. Beneath the periosteum is a thick layer of compact bone. Although compact bone is dense, it is far from being solid. Running through compact bone is a network of tubes called **Haversian canals** (huh-VUR-zhun) that contain blood vessels and nerves.

A less dense tissue known as spongy bone is found inside the outer layer of compact bone. It is found in the ends of long bones and in the middle part of short, flat bones. Despite its name, spongy bone is not soft and spongy; it is actually quite strong. Near the ends of bones where force is applied, spongy bone is organized into structures that resemble the supporting girders in a bridge. This latticework structure of spongy bone helps to add strength to bone without adding mass.

Within bones are cavities that contain a soft tissue called **bone marrow.** There are two types of bone marrow: yellow and red. Yellow marrow is made up primarily of fat cells. Red marrow produces red blood cells, some kinds of white blood cells, and cell fragments called platelets.

Development of Bones

The skeleton of a newborn baby is composed almost entirely of a type of connective tissue called **cartilage.** Cartilage cells are scattered in a network of protein fibers—tough collagen and flexible elastin. Unlike bone, cartilage does not contain blood vessels. Cartilage cells must rely on nutrients from the tiny blood vessels in surrounding tissues. Because cartilage is dense and fibrous, it can support weight, despite its extreme flexibility.

Cartilage is replaced by bone during the process of bone formation called **ossification** (ahs-uh-fih-KAY-shun). The cells involved have names that begin with *osteo-* (AHS-tee-oh), meaning "bone." Osteoblasts create bone. Osteocytes maintain the cellular activities of bone. Osteoclasts break down bone.

TIME SAVER — PRESENTATIONS MADE EASY!

The Presentation Assistant Plus contains the Prentice Hall Presentation Pro and the Transparencies, which provide easy-to-follow visual support for every step of this section. If you have a computer presentation station, use Prentice Hall Presentation Pro for Section 36–1, or use the transparencies listed here.

Section 36–1:

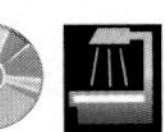

Interest Grabber
Section Outline
Skeletal System
Figure 36–3
Figure 36–4
Figure 36–5

Figure 36–3 Structure of a Bone

Bones are a solid network of living cells and protein fibers that are supported by deposits of calcium salts. A typical bone such as the femur contains spongy bone and compact bone tissues. Running through compact bone is a network of tubes called Haversian canals, which contain blood vessels and nerves.

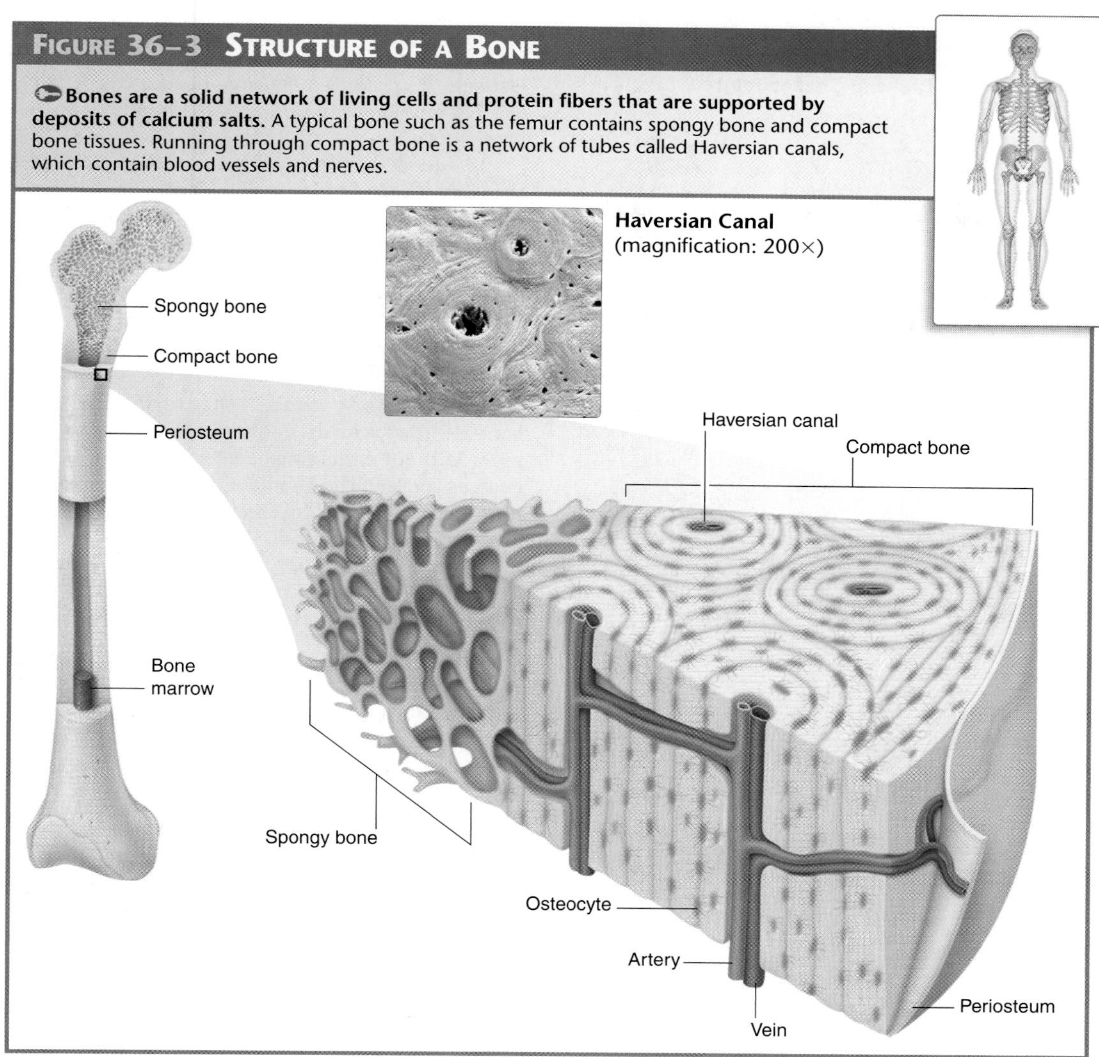

Ossification begins to take place up to seven months before birth. Bone tissue forms as osteoblasts secrete mineral deposits that replace the cartilage in developing bones. When the osteoblasts become surrounded by bone tissue, they mature into osteocytes. Many long bones, including those of the arms and legs, have growth plates at either end. The growth of cartilage at these plates causes the bones to lengthen. Gradually, this new growth of cartilage is replaced by bone tissue, and the bones become larger and stronger. During late adolescence or early adulthood, the cartilage in the growth plates is replaced by bone, the bones become completely ossified, and the person "stops growing."

Make Connections

Health Science Inform students that force must be placed on bone for ossification to occur, because it is force that stimulates the osteoblasts to secrete the minerals that replace cartilage. Ask: **What effect do you think an exercise such as walking would have on the bones of the legs?** *(It would stimulate ossification, so the bones would contain more minerals and be stronger.)* Ask: **What do you think might happen to bones that are not exposed to force, such as the bones of astronauts in zero gravity?** *(The bones would lose minerals because of lack of force exerted on them, so they would become weaker.)*

Demonstration

Demonstrate to students that even ossified bones contain a framework of collagen. Bring a clean chicken bone to class and, after pointing out how relatively hard and inflexible it is, place it in vinegar to soak. After a few days, remove the bone from the vinegar and invite students to inspect it. They will observe that the bone has become rubbery and flexible. Explain that the vinegar dissolved the calcium in the bone, leaving behind the collagen. Ask: **What role does collagen play in an ossified bone?** *(It provides a framework for the minerals in the bone and gives the bone some flexibility.)*

Meet Diverse Needs

Challenge gifted students to learn more about how bones lengthen and change in shape as they ossify, a process that is called remodeling. Then, have them create diagrams to illustrate the process and explain it to the rest of the class. **Learning modality: visual**

BIO INSIGHTS — FACTS AND FIGURES

Broken bones splint themselves

As tough as bones are, they still occasionally break if enough force is applied to them. In order for a broken bone to heal, the broken edges must be held in contact with one another. This is accomplished by a splintlike structure called a callus, which naturally forms around the site of the break. The callus is formed by osteoblasts, which are produced by the periosteum. Like a splint that a doctor puts on a minor fracture, the callus holds the broken ends of the bones together while osteoblasts fill in and strengthen the broken area. The callus itself is eventually reabsorbed by the bone. As a result, once the break is completely healed, only a medical expert can tell that the bone was ever broken.

36–1 (continued)

Types of Joints

Meet Diverse Needs

Pair limited English proficiency or other at-risk students with students who excel academically. Have the members of each pair work together to create a concept map or Venn diagram to organize the information on types of joints. For example, a concept map would show that types of joints include immovable, slightly movable, and freely movable and that movable joints include hinge, ball-and-socket, pivot, and saddle. Advise students to save their graphic organizers to use as study guides. **Limited English proficiency**

Build Science Skills

Using Models Provide students with materials such as craft sticks, toothpicks, pipe cleaners, modeling clay, tacks, and glue. Then, challenge them to create models of one or more types of joints shown in Figure 36–4. Invite students to demonstrate their completed models to the class. Ask: **What type of joint and what range of motion does your model illustrate?** *(Models should illustrate the range of motion of one of the four types of joints shown in the figure.)* Call on other students to name examples of that type of joint.

Demonstration

Ask a volunteer to model the movement of several different joints. As you name each joint, have the student demonstrate the range of motion permitted by the joint. In each case, challenge the rest of the class to name other joints that have the same range of motion.

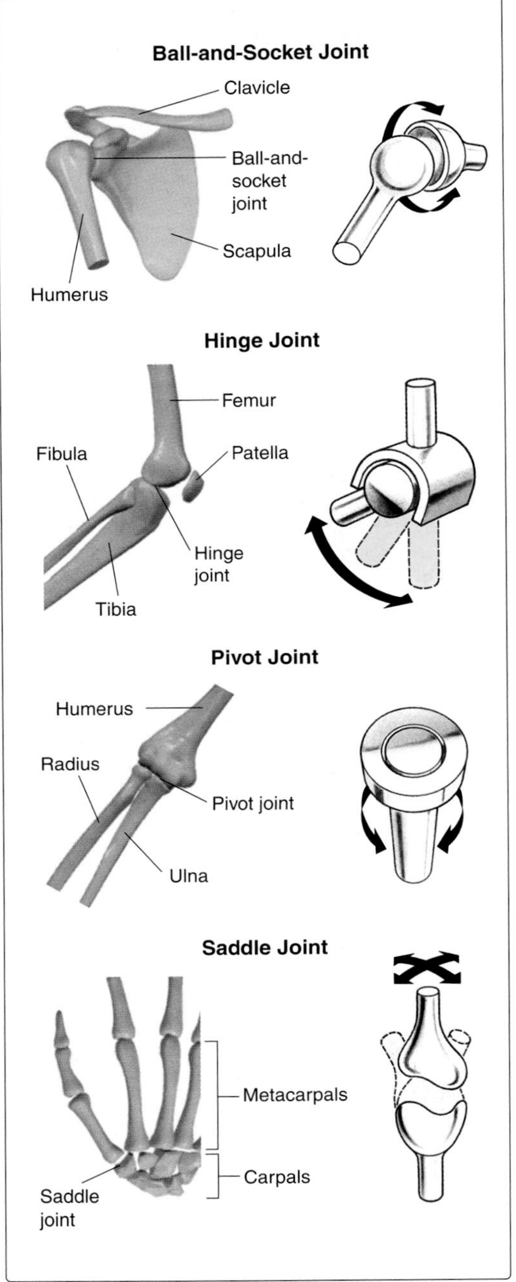

▲ **Figure 36–4**  **Freely movable joints are classified by the type of movement they permit.** The joints illustrated are in the hip, knee, elbow, and hand.

Bone formation also occurs when a bone is broken. Osteoclasts remove damaged bone tissue. Osteoblasts produce new bone tissue. The repair of a broken bone can take months because the process is slow and gradual.

In adults, cartilage is found in those parts of the body where flexibility is needed, such as the tip of the nose and the external ears. Cartilage also is found where the ribs are attached to the sternum, which allows the rib cage to move during breathing.

Types of Joints

A place where one bone attaches to another bone is called a **joint.** Joints permit bones to move without damaging each other. Some joints, such as those of the shoulder, allow extensive movement. Others, like the joints of the fully developed skull, allow no movement at all. **Depending on its type of movement, a joint is classified as immovable, slightly movable, or freely movable.**

Immovable Joints Immovable joints, often called fixed joints, allow no movement. The bones at an immovable joint are interlocked and held together by connective tissue, or they are fused. The places where the bones in the skull meet are examples of immovable joints.

Slightly Movable Joints Slightly movable joints permit a small amount of restricted movement. The bones of slightly movable joints are separated from each other. The joints between the two bones of the lower leg and the joints between adjacent vertebrae are examples of slightly movable joints.

Freely Movable Joints Freely movable joints permit movement in one or more directions. Freely movable joints are grouped according to the shapes of the surfaces of the adjacent bones. The most common types of freely movable joints are shown in **Figure 36–4.**

Ball-and-socket joints permit circular movement—the widest range of movement. Hinge joints permit back-and-forth motion, like the opening and closing of a door. Pivot joints allow one bone to rotate around another. Saddle joints permit one bone to slide in two directions.

✓CHECKPOINT *What are the four common types of freely movable joints?*

BIO INSIGHTS **BIOLOGY UPDATE**

Bionic joints

Osteoarthritis plagues many older adults, causing them to have stiff, aching joints and keeping them from being as active as they would like. Replacing arthritic joints, especially of the hip and knee, with artificial joints made of metal and plastic is a common solution to this problem. The major drawback has been that artificial joints tend to wear out in just 10 to 15 years. Now, a new type of polyethylene is being used to make artificial joints that last much longer. Machines that test artificial joints by putting them through a million movements a week have confirmed that the polyethylene joints should last for at least 27 years. Scientists are also researching ways to rebuild aging joints so they will not need to be replaced. For example, they are testing a type of cell that replaces damaged cartilage and a protein paste that helps repair damaged joints.

Structure of Joints

In freely movable joints, the ends of the bones are covered with a smooth surface layer of cartilage that protects the bones as they move against each other. The joints are also surrounded by a fibrous joint capsule that helps hold the bones together while still allowing them to move.

The joint capsule consists of two layers. One layer forms strips of tough connective tissue called **ligaments.** Ligaments are attached to the membranes that surround bones and hold the bones together. Cells in the other layer of the joint capsule produce a substance called synovial (sin-OH-vee-ul) fluid, which forms a thin film within the bone surfaces of a joint. This lubricating film enables the ends of the bones to slip past each other smoothly.

In some freely movable joints, such as the knee in **Figure 36–5,** small sacs of synovial fluid called bursae (BUR-see; singular: bursa) form. A bursa reduces the friction between the bones of a joint and also acts as a tiny shock absorber.

When a tissue is damaged, the body's response is called inflammation. Symptoms include swelling, redness, heat, and pain. Inflammation of a bursa is called bursitis. Too much fluid fills the bursa, resulting in a painful swelling. A more serious disorder is arthritis, which involves inflammation of one or more joints. There are over 100 different types of arthritis, which as a group affect approximately 10 percent of the world's population.

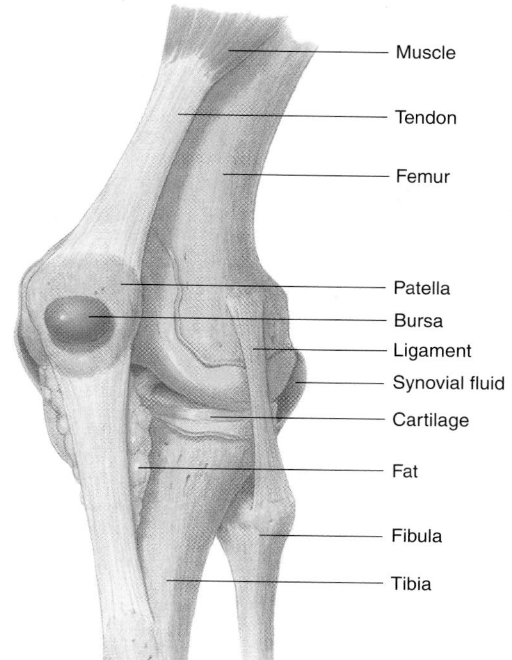

▲ **Figure 36–5** The knee joint is protected by cartilage and bursae. The ligaments hold the bones associated with the knee joint—femur, patella, tibia, and fibula—together. **Inferring** *How do the cartilage and bursae help reduce friction?*

36–1 Section Assessment

1. **Key Concept** List the different functions of the skeletal system.
2. **Key Concept** Describe the structure of a typical bone.
3. **Key Concept** What is a joint? List the three types of joints.
4. How does compact bone differ from spongy bone?
5. **Critical Thinking Inferring** Why do you think the amount of cartilage decreases and the amount of bone increases as a person develops?

iTEXT Assessment Use iText to review the important concepts in Section 36–1.

Take It to the NET

Read about the wrist joint. Then, draw the wrist joint, labeling the adjacent bones and ligaments. Describe what kind of movement the wrist joint permits. Use the links provided in the Biology area at the Prentice Hall Web site for help in completing this activity:
www.phschool.com

36–1 Section Assessment

1. The skeletal system supports the body, protects internal organs, allows movement, stores mineral reserves, and provides a site for blood cell formation.
2. A typical bone has a thick layer of compact bone covered by the periosteum. Haversian canals contain the blood vessels and nerves. At the ends of long bones, there is a layer of spongy bone inside the compact bone.
3. A joint is a place where one bone attaches to another. Three types of joints are immovable, slightly movable, and freely movable.
4. Compact bone is denser than spongy bone. Spongy bone is found in the ends of long bones and in the middle of short, flat bones.
5. The cartilage decreases because minerals replace cartilage during ossification.

Structure of Joints

Use Community Resources

Invite a professional from the medical community to speak to the class about joints and joint problems. Possible speakers might include a radiology technician, physical therapist, chiropractor, or physician's assistant in sports medicine, rheumatology, or orthopedics. Encourage students to prepare questions for the speaker in advance. Afterward, have them write a summary of what they learned.

3 ASSESS

Evaluate Understanding

Read each of the highlighted vocabulary words in the section. As you read, call on students at random to define the terms without referring to their books.

Reteach

Work with students to make a table summarizing the similarities and differences among the different types of joints. Label the columns: Type of Joint, Range of Motion, Examples.

Take It to the NET

Students' drawings should include the ulna and radius in the lower arm and the eight carpal bones in the wrist, with the carpals arranged in two rows of four bones each. Students should state that the wrist joint permits back-and-forth and side-to-side movement of the hand. For additional information, visit
www.phschool.com

Use iText to review the key concepts in Section 36–1.

Answers to . . .

CHECKPOINT *The four types of freely movable joints are the ball-and-socket, hinge, pivot, and saddle.*

Figure 36–5 *The cartilage and bursae help reduce friction by providing a smooth, flexible surface between bones in joints.*

1 FOCUS

Objectives

36.2.1 ***Describe*** the three types of muscle tissue.
36.2.2 ***Explain*** how muscles contract.
36.2.3 ***Explain*** how muscles and bones interact.

Guide for Reading

Vocabulary Preview

Call students' attention to the term *neuromuscular*. Point out that the term is made up of two parts, *neuro-*, which means "of or relating to the nervous system," and *muscular*, which means "of or relating to the muscular system." Ask: **What do you think the term *neuromuscular* means?** *(Of or relating to the nervous and muscular systems together)*

Reading Strategy

Before students read the section, suggest that they rewrite the headings as how, why, or what questions about the muscular system. As they read, they should write brief answers to their questions.

2 INSTRUCT

Types of Muscle Tissue

Build Science Skills

Inferring Show students a picture of a person with larger-than-average muscles, such as a wrestler or weight lifter, and then show them a picture of a person with average-sized muscles. Ask: **Would you infer that the person with larger muscles has more skeletal muscle cells?** *(Students are likely to say yes, even though the inference is incorrect.)* Explain that most people have about the same number of muscle cells, and then, ask: **In what other way could muscles become larger?** *(By increasing the size of existing cells)*

36–2 The Muscular System

Guide for Reading

Key Concepts
- What are the three types of muscle tissue?
- How do muscles contract?

Vocabulary
myosin
actin
neuromuscular junction
acetylcholine
tendon

Reading Strategy: Summarizing As you read, find the main ideas for each paragraph. Write down a few key words from each main idea. Then, use the key words in your summary. Reread your summary, keeping only the most important ideas.

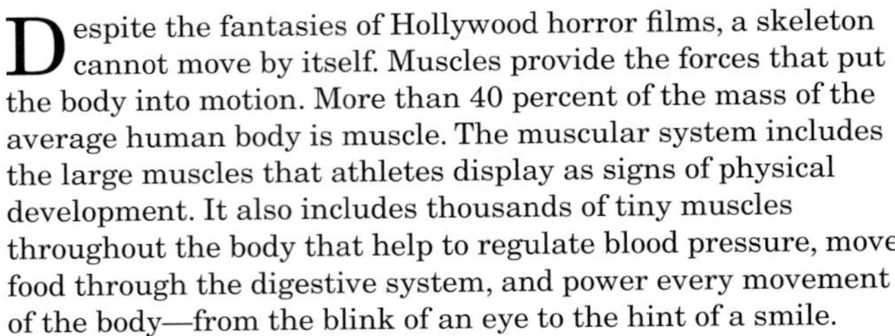

Despite the fantasies of Hollywood horror films, a skeleton cannot move by itself. Muscles provide the forces that put the body into motion. More than 40 percent of the mass of the average human body is muscle. The muscular system includes the large muscles that athletes display as signs of physical development. It also includes thousands of tiny muscles throughout the body that help to regulate blood pressure, move food through the digestive system, and power every movement of the body—from the blink of an eye to the hint of a smile.

Types of Muscle Tissue

Muscle tissue is found everywhere in the body—not only just beneath the skin but also deep within the body. **There are three different types of muscle tissue: skeletal, smooth, and cardiac.** Each type of muscle has a different structure and plays a different role in the body. Refer to **Figure 36–6** as you read about the different types of muscles.

Skeletal Muscles Skeletal muscles are usually attached to bones. Skeletal muscles are responsible for such voluntary movements as typing on a computer keyboard, dancing, or winking an eye. When viewed under a microscope at high magnification, skeletal muscle appears to have alternating light and dark bands or stripes called striations. For this reason, skeletal muscle is sometimes called striated muscle. Most skeletal muscles are controlled by the central nervous system.

Skeletal muscle cells are large, have many nuclei, and vary in length from 1 millimeter to about 30 centimeters. Because skeletal muscle cells are long and slender, they are often called muscle fibers. Complete skeletal muscles consist of muscle fibers, connective tissues, blood vessels, and nerves. **Figure 36–7** shows the structure of a skeletal muscle in the leg.

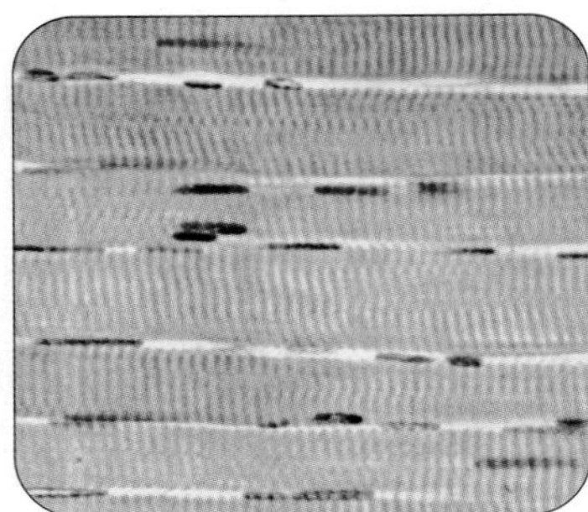
Skeletal Muscle (150×)

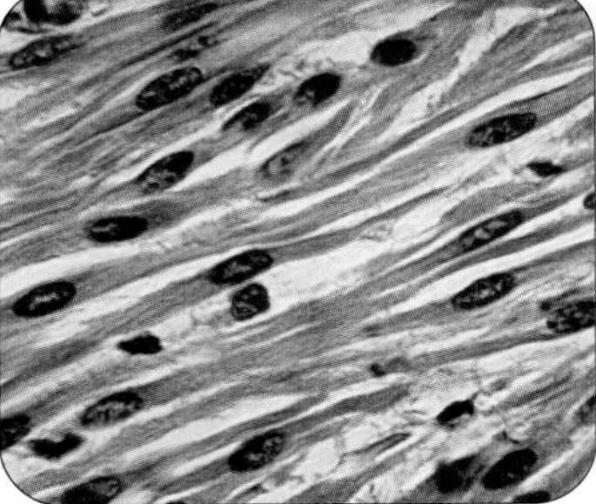
Smooth Muscle (400×)

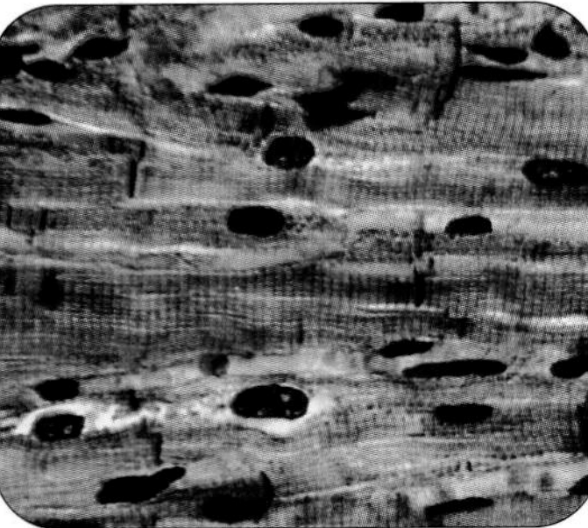
Cardiac Muscle (500×)

Figure 36–6 **There are three types of muscle tissue: skeletal, smooth, and cardiac.** Skeletal muscle cells have striations, or stripes, and many nuclei. Smooth muscle cells are spindle-shaped, and have one nucleus and no striations. Cardiac muscle cells have striations and usually only one nucleus.

SECTION RESOURCES

Print:
- ***Laboratory Manual B,*** Chapter 36 Lab
- ***Teaching Resources,*** Section Review 36–2
- ***Guided Reading and Study Workbook,*** Section 36–2

Technology:
- ***iText,*** Section 36–2

FIGURE 36–7 SKELETAL MUSCLE STRUCTURE

Skeletal muscles are made up of bundles of muscle fibers, which in turn are composed of myofibrils. Each myofibril contains thin filaments made of actin and thick filaments made of myosin. Muscle fibers are divided into functional units called sarcomeres. **Applying Concepts** ***What nervous system structures carry messages to skeletal muscles?***

Skeletal muscle
Bundle of muscle fibers
Actin
Myosin
Sarcomere
Z disc
Myofibril
Muscle fiber (cell)

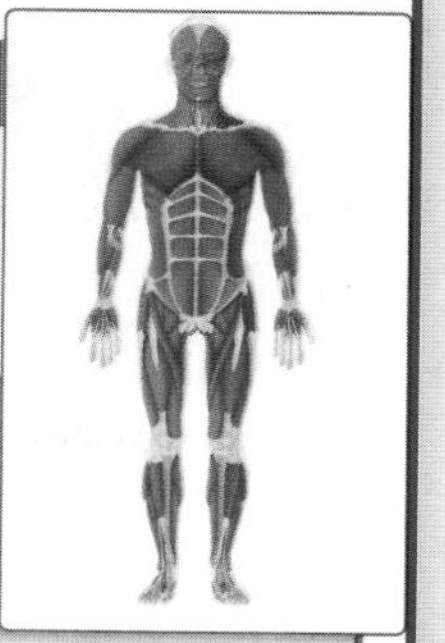

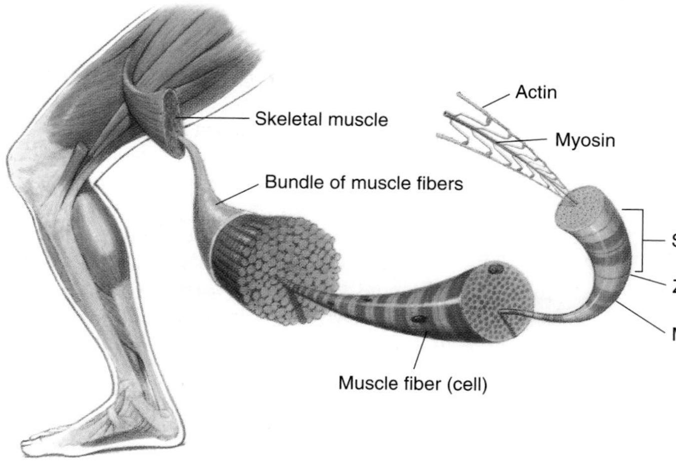

Smooth Muscles Smooth muscles are usually not under voluntary control. A smooth muscle cell is spindle-shaped, has one nucleus, and is not striated. Smooth muscles are found in hollow structures such as the stomach, blood vessels, and the small and large intestines. Smooth muscles move food through your digestive tract, control the way blood flows through your circulatory system, and decrease the size of the pupils of your eyes in bright light. Most smooth muscle cells can function without nervous stimulation. They are connected to one another by gap junctions that allow electrical impulses to travel directly from one muscle cell to a neighboring muscle cell.

Cardiac Muscle Cardiac muscle is found in just one place in the body—the heart. The prefix *cardio-* comes from a Greek word meaning "heart." Cardiac muscle shares features with both skeletal muscle and smooth muscle. Cardiac muscle is striated like skeletal muscle, although its cells are smaller. Cardiac muscle cells usually have one nucleus, but they may have two. Cardiac muscle is similar to smooth muscle because it is usually not under the direct control of the central nervous system and cardiac cells are connected to their neighbors by gap junctions. You will learn more about cardiac muscle in Chapter 37.

CHECKPOINT *What kind of muscle tissue lines the blood vessels?*

Use Visuals

Figure 36–7 Call students' attention to the figure, which they might find confusing. Check their understanding by having them put the following terms in order from largest to smallest: myosin, muscle fiber, skeletal muscle, myofibril. *(Skeletal muscle, muscle fiber, myofibril, myosin)* Help students integrate the figure with the text by asking: **Which part of the drawing represents a single muscle cell?** *(The muscle fiber)*

Meet Diverse Needs

Urge at-risk students to organize the information on types of muscle tissue in a compare/contrast matrix. Their matrices should have columns for type of tissue, how it is controlled, where it is found, whether or not it is striated, whether its cells are small or large, and whether it has just one nucleus or many nuclei. Check students' completed matrices for accuracy, and advise them to save their matrices for review.
Learning modality: visual

Address Misconceptions

When students think of exercising their muscles, they are likely to think of exercising only their skeletal muscles, for example, by lifting barbells or doing push-ups. Point out that cardiac muscle also benefits from exercise. Like muscles of the skeleton, the heart increases in strength and fitness with regular exercise. However, to exercise the heart, aerobic exercise is needed. Aerobic exercise is exercise that speeds up the heart rate and works large skeletal muscles for at least 20 minutes. Ask: **What are some examples of aerobic exercise?** *(Examples include brisk walking, jogging, bicycling, racquetball, basketball, and swimming.)*

TIME SAVER — PRESENTATIONS MADE EASY!

The Presentation Assistant Plus contains the Prentice Hall Presentation Pro and the Transparencies, which provide easy-to-follow visual support for every step of this section. If you have a computer presentation station, use Prentice Hall Presentation Pro for Section 36–2, or use the transparencies listed here.

Section 36–2:

Interest Grabber
Section Outline
Flowchart
Figure 36–7
Figure 36–8
Figure 36–11

Answers to . . .

CHECKPOINT *Smooth muscle tissue lines the blood vessels.*

Figure 36–7 *Motor neurons carry messages to skeletal muscles.*

Muscle Contraction

Build Science Skills

Inferring Point out to students that the description of muscle contraction in the text applies specifically to skeletal muscles, which are easy to study. Guide students in inferring whether other muscles are likely to contract in a similar way. First ask: **Do you think that cardiac muscle or smooth muscles have alternating bands of thick and thin filaments as skeletal muscles do?** *(Students should infer that cardiac muscle has the filaments because it is striated like skeletal muscle, whereas smooth muscle lacks the filaments because it is not striated.)* Then, ask: **Do you think that smooth muscles or cardiac muscle contracts in a way that is similar to skeletal muscle contractions?** *(Students should infer that cardiac muscle may contract in a similar way but that smooth muscles probably do not.)*

Meet Diverse Needs

Some students may be better able to understand the process of muscle contraction if they can see the steps summarized in a diagram. Challenge students to make a cycle diagram of muscle contraction based on the Key Concepts in the text. They should use boxes and arrows connected in a circular arrangement to show the correct sequence of steps in a muscle contraction. After students have completed their diagrams, ask: **Why is a cycle diagram the best type of diagram to represent this process?** *(Because it is a cyclical process that is repeated many times in each muscle contraction.)* **Learning modality: visual**

Muscle Contraction

The muscle fibers in skeletal muscles are composed of smaller structures called myofibrils. Each myofibril is made up of even smaller structures called filaments. The striations in skeletal muscle cells are formed by an alternating pattern of thick and thin filaments. The thick filaments contain a protein called **myosin** (MY-uh-sin). The thin filaments are made up mainly of a protein called **actin.** The filaments are arranged along the muscle fiber in units called sarcomeres, which are separated from each other by regions called Z discs. As **Figure 36–8** shows, when a muscle is relaxed, there are no thin filaments in the center of a sarcomere.

The tiny myosin and actin filaments are the force-producing engines that cause a muscle to contract. **A muscle contracts when the thin filaments in the muscle fiber slide over the thick filaments.** This process is called the sliding-filament model of muscle contraction. For a muscle to contract, the thick myosin filament must form a cross-bridge with the thin actin filament. As the cross-bridge changes shape, it pulls on the actin filament, which slides toward the center of the sarcomere. The distance between the Z discs decreases. The cross-bridge detaches from the actin filament. The cycle is repeated when the myosin binds to another site on the actin filament.

When hundreds of thousands of myosin cross-bridges change shape in a fraction of a second, the muscle fiber shortens with considerable force. **The energy for muscle contraction is supplied by ATP.** Because one molecule of ATP supplies the energy for one interaction between a myosin cross-bridge and an actin filament, the cell needs plenty of ATP molecules for a strong contraction. Recall that the cell can produce ATP in two ways—by cellular respiration and by fermentation.

CHECKPOINT *What is actin? What is myosin?*

Relaxed Muscle
Z disc
Myosin
Actin
Z disc
Sarcomere
Contracted Muscle
Cross-bridges
Z disc

Figure 36–8 During muscle contraction, the actin filaments slide over the myosin filaments, decreasing the distance between the Z discs.

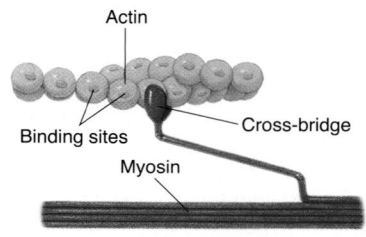

Movement of Actin Filament

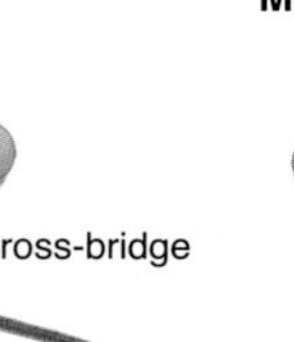

During muscle contraction, the knoblike head of a myosin filament attaches to a binding site on actin, forming a cross-bridge.

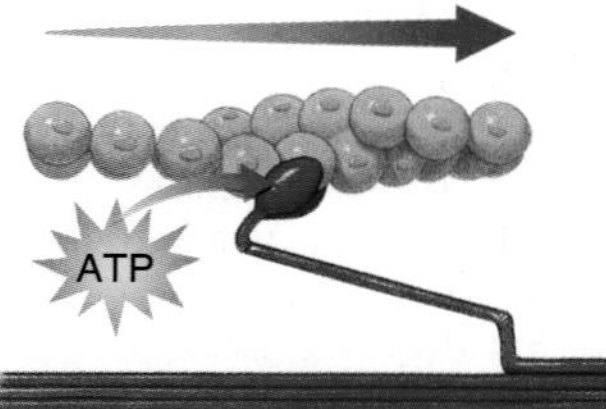

Powered by ATP, the myosin cross-bridge changes shape and pulls the actin filament toward the center of the sarcomere.

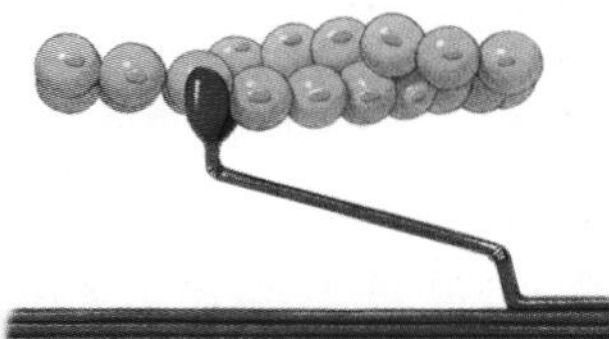

The cross-bridge is broken, the myosin binds to another site on the actin filament, and the cycle begins again.

TEACHER TO TEACHER

After teaching about muscle contraction, I challenge students to defend one of two positions regarding the best way to prepare for a workout: first warm up and then stretch or first stretch and then warm up. I guide the class in concluding that warming up should precede stretching, because a cold muscle cannot be adequately stretched. I also point out that a stretched muscle can contract with greater force than a muscle that has not been stretched.

After teaching about the synapse and the enzyme cholinesterase, I ask students to predict what would happen if the enzyme were somehow inactivated. This facilitates student understanding of muscle paralysis and the actions of insecticides and nerve gases.

—*Thomas P. Rooney, Ph.D.*
Science Department Chair
Father Judge High School,
Philadelphia, PA

Control of Muscle Contraction

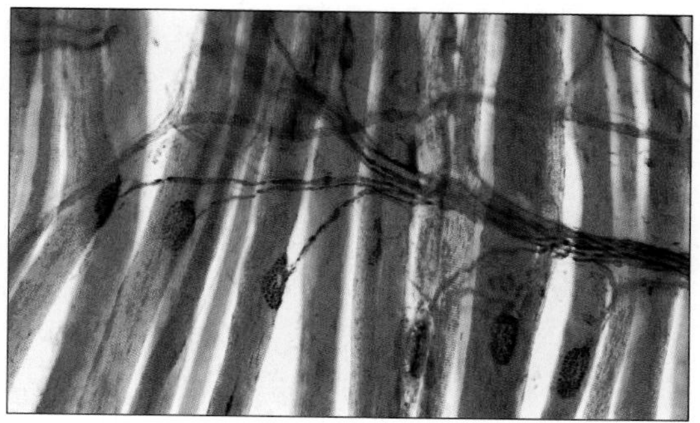

▲ **Figure 36–9** This photograph shows a neuromuscular junction—the point of contact between a motor neuron and a skeletal muscle. The threadlike structure is a motor neuron with its knoblike axon terminals. **Applying Concepts** ***How does the neurotransmitter produced by the motor neuron cause the skeletal muscle to contract?***

Skeletal muscles are useful only if they contract in a controlled fashion. Remember that motor neurons connect the central nervous system to skeletal muscle cells. Impulses from motor neurons control the contraction of skeletal muscle fibers.

Figure 36–9 is a photo of a **neuromuscular junction** (noo-roh-MUS-kyoo-lur), which is the point of contact between a motor neuron and a skeletal muscle cell. Vesicles, or pockets, in the axon terminals of the motor neuron release a neurotransmitter called **acetylcholine** (as-ih-til-KOH-leen). Acetylcholine molecules diffuse across the synapse, producing an impulse in the cell membrane of the muscle fiber. The impulse causes the release of calcium ions (Ca^{2+}) within the fiber. The calcium ions affect regulatory proteins that allow actin and myosin filaments to interact. From the time a nerve impulse reaches a muscle cell, it is only a few milliseconds before these events occur and the muscle cell contracts.

A muscle cell remains contracted until the release of acetylcholine stops and an enzyme produced at the axon terminal destroys any remaining acetylcholine. Then, the cell pumps calcium ions back into storage, the cross-bridges stop forming, and contraction ends.

The contraction of a single muscle fiber is an all-or-none process. A stimulated fiber will contract to its full extent. So how can there be strong and weak contractions? Each muscle contains hundreds of cells. A single motor neuron may form synapses with more than one muscle fiber.

▼ **Figure 36–10** Because this rock climber exercises regularly, her muscles have remained firm and also have increased in size. **Predicting** ***What do you think would happen to this rock climber's muscles if she stopped exercising regularly?***

HISTORY OF SCIENCE

A painter and a poison

One of the earliest scientists to study and correctly portray the human muscular system was the Italian artist Leonardo da Vinci, who lived between 1452 and 1519. Up until da Vinci's time, knowledge of the muscular system was based as much on myth as on fact. Da Vinci's knowledge of the muscular system, in contrast, was based on dissections, and his drawings of the muscles were accurate as well as beautiful. In the mid-1800s, the role of nerves in the contraction of skeletal muscles was established by a scientist named Claude Bernard, who did experiments using a drug called curare. Curare blocks the transmission of nerve impulses, and it was used by some Amazonian Native Americans to poison the tips of their hunting arrows. Bernard injected curare into muscles and found that the muscles became paralyzed when nerve impulses were blocked by the poison.

Control of Muscle Contraction

Make Connections

Health Science Help students relate nervous control of muscles to health issues. Point out that many cases of paralysis occur as a result of spinal cord injuries. Remind students that the spinal cord carries nerve impulses from the brain to other parts of the body. Ask: **How does a spinal cord injury cause paralysis of the legs?** *(The injury interrupts the pathway of impulses from the brain to the nerves that control muscles in the legs. Without impulses from the nerves, the muscles cannot contract, and paralysis results.)*

Meet Diverse Needs

Some students may find it difficult to follow the detailed description of control of muscle contraction. Using the chalkboard or an overhead transparency, work with the class to develop a flow chart that shows the steps involved in the contraction of a muscle due to a nerve impulse. *(Release of acetylcholine; diffusion across synapse; production of impulse in muscle cell membrane; release of calcium ions; interaction of actin and myosin)* Ask: **What causes the muscle to stop contracting?** *(The release of acetylcholine stops, an enzyme produced at the axon terminal destroys any remaining acetylcholine, calcium ions are pumped back into storage, cross-bridges stop forming, and contraction ends.)* **Learning modality: visual**

Answers to . . .

✓CHECKPOINT *Actin is the protein in the thin filaments of skeletal muscles. Myosin is the protein that makes up the thick filaments of skeletal muscles.*

Figure 36–9 *The neurotransmitter produces an impulse in the cell membrane of the muscle cell. This causes a release of calcium ions, which affect regulatory proteins that allow actin and myosin filaments to interact.*

Figure 36–10 *Her muscles would decrease in size.*

How Muscles and Bones Interact

SCIENCE NEWS®

Encourage students to visit **www.phschool.com** for the most current information on this topic.

Quick Lab

Objective Students will be able to compare and contrast movements of the tendons that control chicken wings and their own fingers.

Skill Focus **Comparing and Contrasting**

Materials plastic gloves, raw chicken wing treated with bleach, paper towels, forceps, scissors, scalpel

Time 20 minutes

Safety All work surfaces should be disinfected at the end of the lab.

Advance Prep Briefly soak the wings in bleach to kill any surface bacteria. Then, rinse them thoroughly in water and dry them. If you do not use the wings immediately, refrigerate them until you do.

Strategies

- If necessary, help students find the biceps muscle in the chicken wing.
- Students can observe the tendons that control their fingers by watching the backs of their hands as they drum their fingers on their desks.

Expected Outcome Students should observe that pulling on the tendon in the wing causes the wing to bend and that bending their fingers causes the tendons in their hands to move.

Analyze and Conclude

1. The wing bent at the joint. In a live chicken, the biceps muscle would pull on the tendon.
2. Like the chicken's biceps muscle, muscles controlling the fingers cause the fingers to bend by pulling on tendons.

KEEP CURRENT WITH . . . SCIENCE NEWS®

To find out more about the topics in this chapter, go to: **www.phschool.com**

How Muscles and Bones Interact

Skeletal muscles generate force and produce movement by contracting, or pulling on body parts. Individual muscles can only pull in one direction. Yet, you know from experience that your legs bend when you sit and extend when you stand up. How is this possible?

Skeletal muscles are joined to bones by tough connective tissues called **tendons.** Tendons are attached in such a way that they pull on the bones and make them work like levers. The joint functions as a fulcrum—the fixed point around which the lever moves. The muscles provide the force to move the lever. Usually, there are several muscles surrounding each joint that pull in different directions.

Most skeletal muscles work in opposing pairs. When one muscle contracts, the other relaxes. The muscles of the upper arm shown in **Figure 36–11** are a good example of this dual action. When the biceps muscle contracts, it bends, or flexes, the elbow joint. When the triceps muscle contracts, it opens, or extends, the elbow joint. A controlled movement, however, requires contraction by both muscles. To hold a tennis racket or a violin, both the biceps and triceps must contract in balance. This is why the training of athletes and musicians is so difficult. The brain must learn how to work opposing muscle groups in just the right ways to make the joint move precisely.

Quick Lab

What do tendons do?

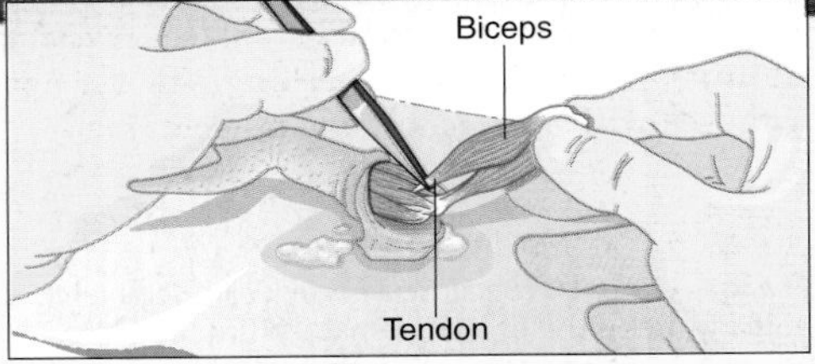

Materials plastic gloves, raw chicken wing treated with bleach, paper towels, forceps, scissors, scalpel

Procedure

1. Put on the plastic gloves. **CAUTION:** *Do not touch your face with your hands during the lab. Be careful with the scissors and scalpel.*
2. Put a chicken wing on a paper towel. Peel back or cut away the skin and fat of the largest wing segment to expose the large muscle. This muscle is called the biceps. Find the tendon that attaches the biceps to the bones of the middle segment of the wing. Tendons are the tough, shiny white cords that join the muscles to the bones.
3. Use forceps to pull on the tendon of the biceps and observe what happens to the chicken wing.
4. Clean your tools and dispose of the chicken wing and gloves according to your teacher's instructions. Wash your hands with soap and warm water.
5. Observe the back of your hand as you move each of your fingers in turn. Compare what you see to how the chicken wing moved.

Analyze and Conclude

1. **Applying Concepts** What happened when you pulled on the tendon? In a live chicken, what structure would pull on the tendon to move the wing?
2. **Comparing and Contrasting** How is the way the wing moves similar to the way your fingers move?

FACTS AND FIGURES

All about muscles

There are about 600 different muscles in the human body and an astounding 6 trillion individual muscle fibers. The largest muscle is the gluteus maximus, covering the buttocks. The smallest is the stapedius, located in the middle ear. Contrary to popular belief, muscles are not made up mostly of protein. Protein makes up only about 20 percent of muscle. Water makes up most of the rest. Muscles are surprisingly inefficient. Even under ideal conditions, more than half the total chemical energy used by muscles is lost in the form of heat. After playing squash for just 7 minutes, a 62-kilogram person produces enough heat to raise the temperature of 91 liters of water by 1°C. Although most people complete their growth in body size by age 20, muscular strength keeps increasing, usually peaking sometime between the ages of 20 and 30.

▼ **Figure 36–11** By contracting and relaxing, the triceps and biceps in the upper arm enable you to bend or straighten your elbow. **Applying Concepts** ***Which skeletal muscle must contract in order for you to straighten your elbow?***

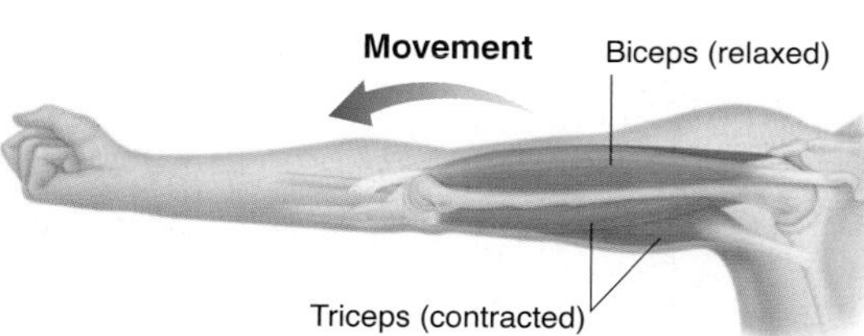

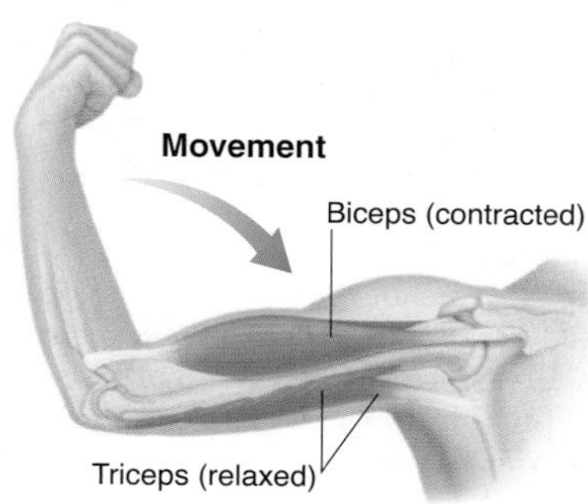

Skeletal muscles generally remain in a state of partial contraction. At any given time, a few muscle cells are being stimulated while others are not. This limited stimulation causes a tightening of some muscles called resting muscle tone. Muscle tone is responsible for keeping the back and legs straight and the head upright, even when you are relaxed. Regular exercise is good for your body because it increases muscle tone. Muscles that are exercised regularly stay firm and increase in size by adding more material to the inside of the muscle cells. Regular exercise also helps your body systems become more efficient. For example, some types of exercise increase the efficiency of your heart and lungs. Muscles that are not used at all become weak and can visibly decrease in size.

36–2 Section Assessment

1. **Key Concept** List the three types of muscle tissue and explain the function of each.
2. **Key Concept** Explain how a muscle contracts.
3. How do bones and muscles work together to move the body?
4. What is acetylcholine, and what is its role in muscle contraction?
5. **Critical Thinking Predicting** If a muscle cell receives a second stimulus while it is contracting, will it respond to the second stimulus? Explain.

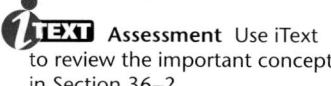

iText **Assessment** Use iText to review the important concepts in Section 36–2.

ALTERNATIVE ASSESSMENT

Making a Model
Create your own model to show how actin filaments slide over myosin filaments during a muscle contraction. Include as much detail in your model as possible.

36–2 Section Assessment

1. Skeletal, which controls voluntary movements; smooth, which controls involuntary movements; and cardiac, which controls contractions of the heart
2. Myosin cross-bridges cause the thin filaments to slide over the thick filaments, shortening the muscle.
3. Tendons connect muscles to bones across joints. When a muscle contracts, a tendon pulls on a bone, which moves at the joint.
4. Acetylcholine is a neurotransmitter. It diffuses across nerve synapses to produce impulses in muscle cell membranes.
5. No, because a stimulated muscle cell contracts to its full extent and must relax before it can respond to a second impulse.

Build Science Skills

Using Models Instruct students to hang a strip of tape off each end of a ruler. Have them make a lever by balancing the ruler on an eraser and then pull down on one tape strip. Ask: **If your lever was a model showing how a bone moves, what would each part of the model represent?** *(The ruler represents a bone, the eraser represents a joint, the tape represents a tendon, and the pull represents a muscle contraction.)* Ask: **How could you return the "bone" to its original position?** *(Pull on the other "tendon.")*

Meet Diverse Needs

Challenge gifted students to research the names, locations, and ranges of motion of other pairs of opposing muscles in the human body. Suggest that they create a diagram or other visual way to share what they learn with the rest of the class. **Learning modality: visual**

3 ASSESS

Evaluate Understanding

Have students make Venn diagrams comparing and contrasting skeletal muscle tissue, smooth muscle tissue, and cardiac muscle tissue.

Reteach

Using the chalkboard or a transparency, work with the class to make a flow chart showing how a motor neuron stimulates a muscle cell.

ALTERNATIVE ASSESSMENT

The models should illustrate the following: a cross-bridge forms between the actin and myosin filaments. When the cross-bridge bends, the actin slides over the myosin. Then, the cross-bridge detaches, unbends, and reattaches to a new site on the actin.

Use iText to review the key concepts in Section 36–2.

Answer to . . .

Figure 36–11 *The triceps muscle must contract to straighten your elbow.*

Students will get more out of the feature if they first read Section 36–3. After students have read the feature, you might want to discuss one or more of the following:

- How burns are classified based on the degree of skin damage they cause, as first-degree, second-degree, or third-degree burns, with third-degree burns being the most serious.
- How burns that affect the dermis differ from burns that affect only the epidermis.
- What causes burns, including matches, flammable liquids, hot water, and steam.
- How students can prevent burns, for example, by following package precautions when using flammable liquids and testing bathwater before getting in.

On Your Own

1. Students will find that first aid for burns depends on how serious the burns are. For third-degree burns, first aid includes keeping the burns covered, elevating the hands and feet, treating possible shock, and getting the victim to a hospital as soon as possible. It is important that the burned skin be replaced with a new barrier against infection, either skin grafts or some type of artificial skin.

2. If a local hospital does not have a burn clinic that uses artificial skin, you could research hospitals that do. Point out that research in the treatment of burns is ongoing. Challenge students to investigate other recent advances that have been made in treating badly burned skin.

Manufacturing Artificial Skin

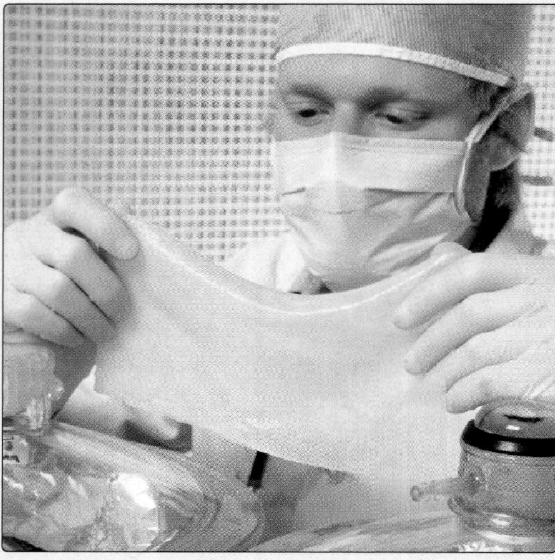

The skin is not only the largest organ in the body, it is also one of the most easily injured, especially by fire. More than 2 million Americans suffer burn injuries every year, and more than 10,000 die from such injuries. The skin is the body's most important barrier against infection, but burns can destroy that barrier, leaving tissues exposed and vulnerable.

The best way to protect badly burned tissue is to cover it with a layer of fresh skin. If the burned region is small, this can be done with skin grafts taken from other parts of the body. For larger burns, however, this isn't possible. Scientists have now developed a way to help many victims of serious burns—they have developed artificial skin.

Constructing a Scaffold

Skin is a complex organ. For this reason, researchers realized that the best way to replace skin would be with an artificial skin that the body's own cells could grow into. After the outer layer of burned tissue is removed from a severely burned patient, surgeons can apply artificial skin made from a biodegradable meshwork of protein fibers similar to those in human skin. Cells from the dermis migrate upward and gradually "take over" the artificial layer, replacing the meshwork with human proteins. Thus, a new layer of dermis is produced. A very thin layer of the patient's own epidermal cells, grown in culture, is then applied to the surface of the artificial skin.

Perfecting the Technique

Artificial skin is used only in the treatment of burns so severe that normal healing is not possible. One of its main drawbacks is that the migration of cells into the artificial layer may take as long as three weeks, enough time for infection and other complications to develop. Researchers are trying to speed up the process by placing cell-growth signal chemicals in the artificial layer. If they succeed, the successful treatment of even serious burns may become routine.

On Your Own

1. Use reference materials to find information on the treatment of serious burns. Design a brochure that explains and illustrates the steps in the treatment of third-degree burns.
2. Visit or telephone your local hospital to see if it has a burn clinic that uses artificial skin. If it does, arrange to either visit the hospital or have information sent to you. Write a brief summary of what you find out.

36–3 The Integumentary System

"Good fences make good neighbors," wrote the American poet Robert Frost as he explained the importance of property boundaries. Living things have their own "fences," and none is as important as the skin—the boundary that separates the human body from the outside world.

The skin, the single largest organ of the body, is part of the integumentary (in-teg-yoo-MEN-tuh-ree) system. The word *integument* comes from a Latin word that means "to cover," reflecting the fact that the skin and its related structures form a covering over the entire body. Skin and its related structures—the hair, nails, and a variety of glands—make up the integumentary system.

The Skin

The skin has many different functions, but its most important function is protection. **The integumentary system serves as a barrier against infection and injury, helps to regulate body temperature, removes waste products from the body, and provides protection against ultraviolet radiation from the sun.** Because the largest component of the integumentary system—the skin—contains several types of sensory receptors, it serves as the gateway through which sensations such as pressure, heat, cold, and pain are transmitted to the nervous system.

The skin is made up of two main layers—the epidermis and the dermis. Beneath the dermis is a subcutaneous layer of fat and loose connective tissue that helps to insulate the body.

Guide for Reading

Key Concept
- What are the functions of the integumentary system?

Vocabulary
epidermis
keratin
melanin
dermis
hair follicle

Reading Strategy: Building Vocabulary
Before you read, preview **Figure 36–13** to identify vocabulary with which you are unfamiliar. As you read, look for the meaning of these terms.

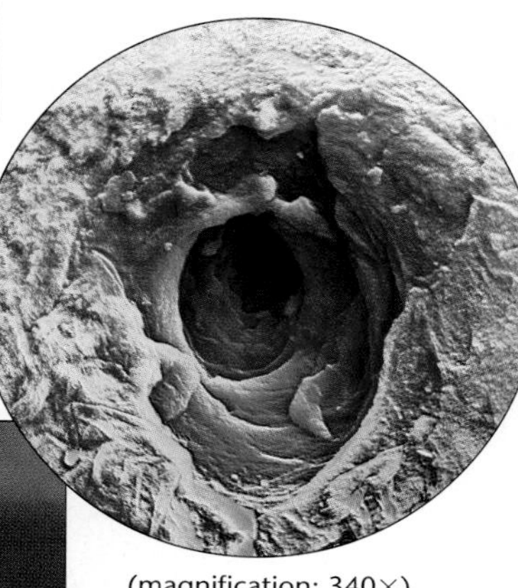

(magnification: 340×)

Figure 36–12 **After strenuous exercise, the skin produces sweat, which decreases the temperature of the body and rids the body of wastes.** Sweat is secreted by sweat glands and leaves the body through sweat pores.

SECTION RESOURCES

Print:
- ***Teaching Resources,*** Section Review 36–3, Chapter 36 Real-World Lab
- ***Guided Reading and Study Workbook,*** Section 36–3

Technology:
- ***iText,*** Section 36–3

Section 36–3

1 FOCUS

Objectives

36.3.1 ***State*** the functions of the integumentary system.
36.3.2 ***Describe*** the structure of hair and nails.

Guide for Reading

Vocabulary Preview

Before students read the section, suggest that they preview new vocabulary by finding each vocabulary word in the section and reading its definition.

Reading Strategy

Call students' attention to the Key Concepts on this page that state the functions of the skin. Then, when they preview Figure 36–13, have students predict which structures are involved in each function. As students read the section, they should note whether or not their predictions were correct.

2 INSTRUCT

The Skin

Demonstration

Before class begins, cut an apple in half. Tightly cover one half of the apple with plastic wrap and leave the other half exposed to the air. During class, pass the two apple halves around the room so students can inspect them. Then, ask: **How do the two apple halves differ?** *(The cut surface of the unwrapped half has started to turn brown and dry out. The cut surface of the wrapped half is still white and moist.)* **Based on your observations, what role do you think the skin of the apple plays?** *(It protects the inside of the apple from drying out and turning brown.)* **How is the skin of an apple like human skin?** *(Both protect what is inside.)*

Word Origins

Epiphyte means "on the outside of a plant." It is a plant that grows on another plant.

Meet Diverse Needs

Have students close their eyes and try to identify a familiar object, such as a chalkboard eraser, by touch alone. Then, have students experience pressure by pushing the eraser end of a pencil against the palm of their hand. Finally, have students touch a warm object such as a heating pad and a cold object such as an ice cube. After students have experienced each of these sensory abilities, ask: **How could these sensory abilities of the skin protect the body?** *(Answers will vary. Students might say, for example, that the ability to sense heat could prevent a burn because it lets you know when you are about to touch something hot.)* **Learning modality: tactile**

Use Visuals

Figure 36–13 Have students use the information in the figure to make a chart comparing and contrasting the dermis and epidermis in terms of their location and thickness and the structures they contain. *(Student charts should show that the epidermis is the thinner, outer layer of skin containing hairs and pores, and the dermis is the thicker, inner layer of skin containing blood vessels, nerve endings, muscles, hair follicles, and sweat and sebaceous glands.)*

Build Science Skills

Using Models Have students sketch three simple cross-sectional models of the epidermis. Then, have them use their models to show how cells in the epidermis are replaced. They should modify the first sketch to show skin cells dividing, the second sketch to show skin cells moving upward to the skin's surface, and the third sketch to show skin cells being shed. Ask volunteers to share their completed models with the class.

▼ **Figure 36–13** The skin has an outer layer called the epidermis and an inner layer called the dermis. **Predicting** *What is the function of the dermis?*

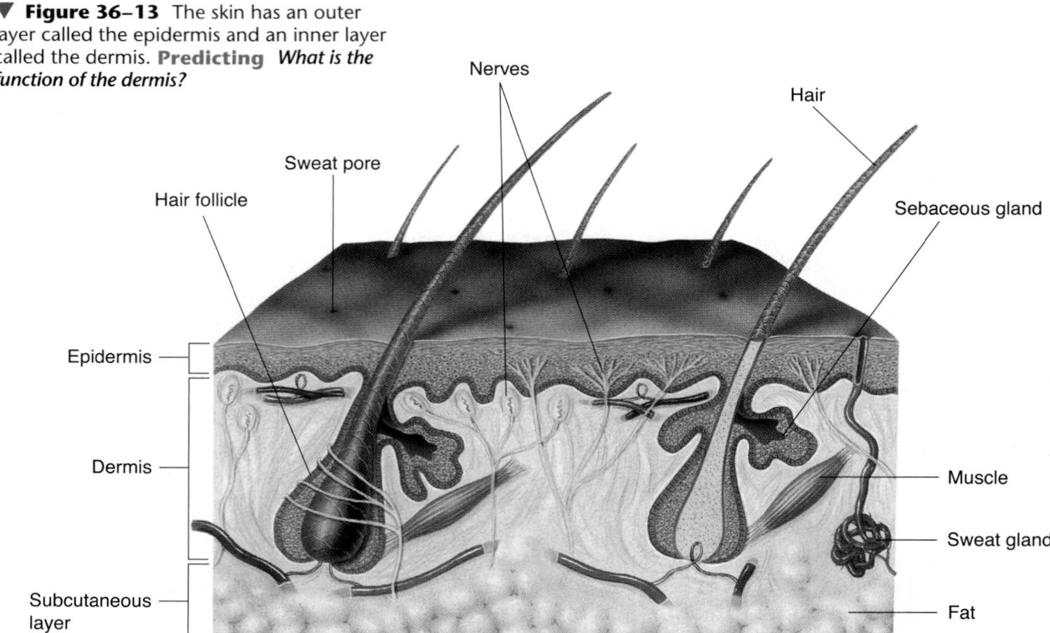

Word Origins

Epidermis comes from two Greek words: *epi,* meaning "on the outside," and *derma,* meaning "skin." **If the Greek word *phyton* means "plant," what does the term *epiphyte* mean?**

Epidermis The outer layer of the skin is the **epidermis.** The epidermis itself has two layers. The outside of the epidermis—the part that comes in contact with the environment—is made up of dead cells. The inner layer of the epidermis is made up of living cells.

Cells in the inner layer of the epidermis undergo rapid cell division, producing new cells that push older cells to the surface of the skin. As they move upward, the older cells become flattened and their organelles disintegrate. They also begin making **keratin,** a tough, fibrous protein.

Eventually, the keratin-producing cells die and form a tough, flexible, waterproof covering on the surface of the skin. This outer layer of dead cells is shed or washed away at a surprising rate—once every four to five weeks.

The epidermis also contains melanocytes (MEL-uh-noh-syts). Melanocytes are cells that produce **melanin,** a dark brown pigment. Although most people have roughly the same number of melanocytes in their skin, differences in skin color are caused by the different amount of melanin the melanocytes produce and where these cells are distributed.

Look closely at **Figure 36–13** and you will see that there are no blood vessels in the epidermis. This explains why a slight scratch will not cause bleeding.

✓CHECKPOINT *What is melanin?*

PRESENTATIONS MADE EASY!

The Presentation Assistant Plus contains the Prentice Hall Presentation Pro and the Transparencies, which provide easy-to-follow visual support for every step of this section. If you have a computer presentation station, use Prentice Hall Presentation Pro for Section 36–3, or use the transparencies listed here.

Section 36–3: **Interest Grabber**
Section Outline
Concept Map
Figure 36–13

Dermis The inner layer of the skin is the **dermis.** It lies beneath the epidermis and contains collagen fibers, blood vessels, nerve endings, glands, sense organs, smooth muscles, and hair follicles. When the body needs to conserve heat on a cold day, the blood vessels in the dermis narrow, helping to limit heat loss. On hot days, the blood vessels widen, bringing heat from the body's core to the skin and increasing heat loss.

The dermis contains two major types of glands: sweat glands and sebaceous (suh-BAY-shus), or oil, glands. These glands have openings in the epidermis at the surface of the skin through which they release their products. If your body gets too hot, sweat glands produce perspiration, or sweat. When sweat evaporates, it takes heat away from your body. Perspiration contains water, salts, and other compounds. The release of these secretions is stimulated by nerve impulses when the temperature of the body rises above the normal range.

Sebaceous glands produce an oily secretion called sebum that spreads out along the surface of the skin and helps to keep the keratin-rich epidermis flexible and waterproof.

Analyzing Data

The UV Index and Sunburn

Ultraviolet (UV) radiation is one type of energy from the sun. UV rays cause sunburn, some cataracts, and skin cancer. There are many factors that affect the amount of UV radiation to which you are exposed. These include the time of day, the season, the weather conditions, and your location. Recently, the National Weather Service, the Environmental Protection Agency, and the Centers for Disease Control agreed upon a national UV index. The UV index is issued daily to advise you of conditions in your region of the country. Use the information in the chart to answer the questions that follow.

Protection From Sunburn

UV Index Level	How to Protect Yourself	Minutes to Burn
Minimal (0–2)	Apply sunscreen Wear sunglasses near snow and water	60
Low (3–4)	Apply sunscreen Wear sunglasses and hat	45
Moderate (5–6)	Apply sunscreen Wear sunglasses and hat Apply lip balm	30
High (7–9)	Apply sunscreen Wear sunglasses and hat Seek shade from 10 AM to 4 PM	15
Very High (10+)	Apply sunscreen Wear sunglasses and hat Avoid sun from 10 AM to 4 PM	10

1. **Interpreting Graphics** Describe the trend in the amount of time it takes to sunburn, from a minimal UV index level to a very high UV index level.
2. **Applying Concepts** Why do you think applying sunscreen is always recommended?
3. **Drawing Conclusions** Why should a hat worn as protection against UV rays have a brim?
4. **Predicting** The minutes to burn data apply to most people. What variable could cause the time for a particular person to burn to be shorter or longer?
5. **Making a Graph** Use the data in the table to construct a bar graph. Place the UV index levels on the *x*-axis and the minutes to burn on the *y*-axis.

Address Misconceptions

Some students may think that people with dark skin do not need to protect their skin from the sun or that people who tan without burning are not damaging their skin when they get darker in the summer. Correct these misconceptions by explaining that any skin can be damaged by exposure to sunlight. Although melanin helps protect the skin from sunlight, even people with a lot of melanin in their skin can suffer sun damage.

Analyzing Data

Call on students to give a definition of the term *UV index. (An indicator of the strength of UV radiation based on how long it takes skin to burn)* Suggest to students that they watch a televised weather report on a sunny day and note how the UV index is reported and what its value is.

Answers

1. The amount of time it takes to burn decreases.
2. Because even low levels of UV radiation can damage the skin
3. To protect the face and eyes
4. Amount of melanin in the skin
5. Graphs should have five bars of decreasing height.

BIO INSIGHTS FACTS AND FIGURES

Evolution of human skin color

Human skin color shows a gradual geographic trend in Africa and Europe: populations increasingly far from the equator tend to have less and less melanin in their skin. Virtually all the theories that have been proposed to account for this trend assume that variation in the amount of sunlight is the ultimate cause. One widely held theory hypothesizes that darker skin is selected for at lower latitudes because its higher melanin content helps protect it from serious sunburn and skin cancer, which can threaten survival. Another theory proposes that lighter skin is selected for at higher latitudes because it can be penetrated by sunlight, which is needed to produce vitamin D in deep layers of the skin. According to this theory, the extra vitamin D produced in the skin of lighter-skinned people helps prevent rickets, which can jeopardize female fertility by causing pelvic deformities.

Answers to . . .

CHECKPOINT *Melanin is a dark brown pigment produced by melanocytes in the epidermis.*

Figure 36–13 *Based on structures located in the dermis, students may predict that the dermis produces sweat and oil, controls growth of hair, and senses stimuli such as touch.*

Hair and Nails

Build Science Skills

Designing Experiments Point out to students that many different factors—such as age, gender, general health status, genetic background, some diseases, and certain medications—can affect the pattern and rate of hair growth. Challenge students to design an experiment to measure the effects of one particular factor on hair growth. Call on students to give a brief description of their experimental design, including the hypothesis they would test. Ask: **Which variable would you investigate and which variables would you control?** *(Students should investigate one variable, such as age or gender, and control, or hold constant, any other variables believed to affect hair growth, such as certain illnesses or medications.)*

3 ASSESS

Evaluate Understanding

Call on several students at random to name the functions of the skin.

Reteach

Have students define or describe the function of each of the structures of the skin that are shown in Figure 36–13.

MAKING CONNECTIONS

Some of the topics students might address are the outer waterproof coverings; the roles of the guard cells and sweat and oil glands; trichomes and nails; and the roles of root hair cells and human hair.

Use iText to review the key concepts in Section 36–3.

Answer to . . .

Figure 36–14 *The dermis contains the hair follicle.*

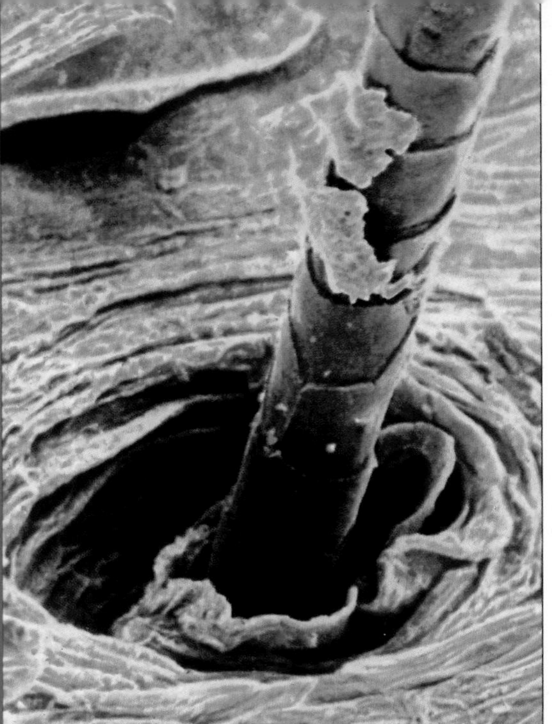

▲ **Figure 36–14** In this color-enhanced scanning electron micrograph of a hair shaft, the scalelike structures are layers of skin cells. The part of the hair that is above the skin is made up of dead cells that become filled with keratin. **Observing** ***What layer of the skin contains the hair follicle?***

Hair and Nails

The basic structure of human hair and nails is keratin. In other animals, keratin forms a variety of structures, including bull horns, reptile scales, bird feathers, and porcupine quills.

Hair Hair covers almost every exposed surface of the body and has important functions. Hair on the head protects the scalp from ultraviolet light from the sun and provides insulation from the cold. Hairs in the nostrils, external ear canals, and around the eyes (eyelashes) prevent dirt and other particles from entering the body.

Hair is produced by cells at the base of structures called hair follicles. **Hair follicles** are tubelike pockets of epidermal cells that extend into the dermis. The individual hair shown in **Figure 36–14** is actually a large column of cells that have filled with keratin and then died. Rapid cell growth at the base of the hair follicle causes the hair to grow longer. Hair follicles are in close contact with sebaceous glands. The oily secretions of these glands help maintain the condition of each individual hair. Hair follicles also contain clusters of stem cells that give rise to epidermal cells.

Nails Nails protect the tips of the fingers and toes. Nails grow from an area of rapidly dividing cells known as the nail root. The nail root is located near the tips of the fingers and toes. During cell division, the cells of the nail root fill with keratin and produce a tough, platelike nail that covers and protects the tips of the fingers and toes. Nails grow at an average rate of 3 millimeters per month, with fingernails growing more rapidly than toenails—about four times as fast.

36–3 Section Assessment

1. **Key Concept** List the functions of the integumentary system.
2. What organs and tissues make up the integumentary system?
3. Compare the structures of the epidermis and dermis.
4. In what way is the growth of hair and nails similar?
5. **Critical Thinking Applying Concepts** Why does cutting your skin hurt, while cutting your hair or nails does not?

iTEXT **Assessment** Use iText to review the important concepts in Section 36–3.

MAKING CONNECTIONS

Plant Structure
Compare the structure and function of the dermal tissue in plants discussed in Section 23–1 with the structures in human skin.

36–3 Section Assessment

1. Serves as a barrier against infection and injury, helps regulate body temperature, removes waste products from the body, protects against UV radiation, and allows sensory input
2. Skin, hair, nails, and glands
3. The epidermis is the outer, thinner layer of skin. It contains melanin and has a surface layer of dead cells. The dermis is the inner, thicker layer of skin. It contains blood vessels, nerves, glands, sense organs, muscles, and hair follicles.
4. Both grow from an area of rapidly dividing cells at the base of the hair or nail.
5. Cutting your skin hurts because the dermis contains nerves. Cutting your hair or nails does not hurt because hair and nails are composed of dead cells and have no nerves.

Real-World Lab

Making a Model of a Transdermal Patch

Some medications are introduced into the body using a patch attached to the skin, rather than by mouth or by injection. This is especially useful for medications that need to be continuously released in very small quantities over an extended period of time. In this investigation, you will model how these patches, called transdermal patches, work.

Problem **How can some medications be given through the skin?**

Materials

- dialysis tubing
- plastic cup
- phenolphthalein solution
- 50-mL graduated cylinder
- paper towels
- scissors
- metric ruler
- filter paper
- dropper pipette
- sodium bicarbonate solution

Skills Using Models, Observing

Procedure   

1. Soak a piece of dialysis tubing in a cup of water until it is soft (about 1 minute).
2. Tie a knot in one end of the dialysis tubing. Use a graduated cylinder to fill the tubing with phenolphthalein solution. **CAUTION:** *Phenolphthalein is toxic. Do not rub your eyes during this investigation.*
3. Squeeze as much air out of the tubing as you can, then tie a knot in the open end of the tubing to seal it off. The tubing represents the cell membrane of a skin cell.
4. Lay the model skin cell down on a paper towel. Use another paper towel to wipe dry the outside of the tubing.
5. Carefully cut out four 1-cm squares of filter paper. **CAUTION:** *Scissors are sharp. Handle them carefully.* Stack the filter-paper squares on top of the model skin cell. The filter paper represents a patch that will be saturated with the medication to be delivered.
6. Using a dropper pipette, carefully soak the filter paper, 1 drop at a time, with sodium bicarbonate solution. Try not to let the solution run down the sides of the tubing. The sodium bicarbonate solution represents the medication.
7. Observe the model cell for 10 to 15 minutes and record your observations.

Analyze and Conclude

1. **Observing** What happened when you added the sodium bicarbonate solution to the filter paper?
2. **Inferring** What property did the "cell membrane" (dialysis tubing) need to possess for you to observe these changes?
3. **Drawing Conclusions** What kinds of substances would be absorbed most easily in this way? Explain your answer.

Go Further

Additional Reasearch Research transdermal patches in the library or on the Internet. Write a brief report describing at least two uses of transdermal patches. Describe the advantages and disadvantages of transdermal patches compared with injections and oral medications.

Real-World Lab

Objective Students will be able to draw conclusions about how some medications can be given through the skin.

Skills Focus **Using Models, Observing**

Time 45 minutes

Advance Prep
- Make the sodium bicarbonate solution by stirring baking soda into water until the solution has a pH between 8.0 and 9.0.
- You can save time by precutting the filter paper squares.

Safety Remind students to use extra caution when handling the toxic phenolphthalein solution.

Teaching Tips
Have students read the entire procedure for this investigation. Then, ask students the following questions:
- **How does a nicotine patch work?** *(By delivering a steady supply of nicotine that reduces the person's cravings for a cigarette)*
- **What kinds of substances can pass easily through cell membranes?** *(Water, alcohol, and small lipid molecules)*

Procedure
7. Explain that phenophthalein solution turns red when exposed to alkaline substances such as sodium bicarbonate.

Go Further

Students should describe at least two uses of transdermal patches, such as the gradual delivery of heart medications to people with angina. An advantage of transdermal patches is that medications can be given continuously in very small quantities over an extended time. A disadvantage is that transdermal patches must be attached to the skin for extended periods.

Analyze and Conclude

1. The phenolphthalein solution near the filter paper squares turned red.
2. Permeability
3. Substances with small, nonpolar molecules that are soluble in lipids because small lipid molecules can diffuse directly across cell membranes

Chapter 36 Study Guide

Study Tip

Suggest that students review their answers to the Key Concept questions in the section assessments. Divide the class into pairs and have students quiz each other on definitions of the vocabulary words.

Thinking Visually

1. Ligaments
2. Protection
3. Storage of minerals
4. Flexibility
5. Connect muscle to bone

Chapter 36 Assessment

Reviewing Content

1. c **2.** c **3.** a **4.** d **5.** a **6.** b **7.** c **8.** b **9.** d **10.** c

Understanding Concepts

11. Connective tissues including compact bone, spongy bone, cartilage, ligaments, periosteum; yellow and red bone marrow

12. Bones are a solid network of living cells and protein fibers that are surrounded by deposits of calcium salts.

13. Students' drawings should include spongy bone, compact bone, the periosteum, bone marrow, a Haversian canal, an artery, and a vein. Arteries carry oxygen and nutrients, and Haversian canals carry blood vessels and nerves.

14. Spongy bone adds strength, but not mass at the point on the bone at which force is applied.

15. Red blood cells and some types of white blood cells

16. Skeletal muscles control voluntary movements; smooth muscles move food through the digestive tract, control blood flow, and decrease the size of the pupils; cardiac muscle causes the heart to contract and pump blood.

Chapter 36 Study Guide

36–1 The Skeletal System

Key Concepts

- The human skeleton supports the body, protects internal organs, provides for movement, stores mineral reserves, and provides a site for blood cell formation.
- Bones are a solid network of living cells and protein fibers that are surrounded by deposits of calcium salts.
- Depending on its type of movement, a joint is classified as immovable, slightly movable, or freely movable.

Vocabulary

periosteum, p. 922
Haversian canal, p. 922
bone marrow, p. 922
cartilage, p. 922
ossification, p. 922
joint, p. 924
ligament, p. 925

36–2 The Muscular System

Key Concepts

- There are three different types of muscle tissue: skeletal muscle, smooth muscle, and cardiac muscle.
- A muscle fiber contracts when the thin filaments in the muscle fiber slide over the thick filaments.
- The energy for muscle contraction is supplied by ATP.

Vocabulary

myosin, p. 928
actin, p. 928
neuromuscular junction, p. 929
acetylcholine, p. 929
tendon, p. 930

36–3 The Integumentary System

Key Concept

- The integumentary system serves as a barrier against infection and injury, helps to regulate body temperature, removes waste products from the body, and provides protection against ultraviolet radiation from the sun.

Vocabulary

epidermis, p. 934
keratin, p. 934
melanin, p. 934
dermis, p. 935
hair follicle, p. 936

Thinking Visually

Using the information in this chapter, complete the following concept map:

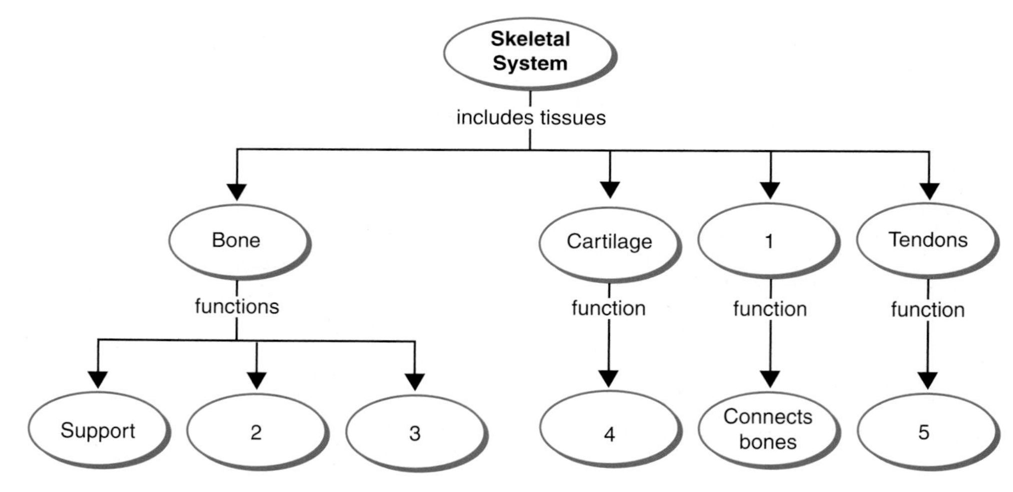

CHAPTER RESOURCES

Print:

- ***Teaching Resources***, Chapter Vocabulary Review, Graphic Organizer
- ***Chapter Tests: Levels A and B***, Chapter 36 Test
- ***PH Assessment System***, Practice Test

Technology:

- ***Computer Test Bank***, Chapter 36 Test
- ***iText***, Chapter 36 Assessment

Chapter 36 Assessment

Reviewing Content

Choose the letter that best answers the question or completes the statement.

1. The tough connective tissue layer surrounding each bone is called
   a. tendon. **c.** periosteum.
   b. ligament. **d.** cartilage.
2. The network of tubes that runs through compact bone is called the
   a. periosteum. **c.** Haversian canals.
   b. joint. **d.** marrow.
3. Cartilage is replaced by bone during the process known as
   a. ossification. **c.** photosynthesis.
   b. calcification. **d.** marrow replacement.
4. The tough connective tissue that holds bones together is the
   a. tendon. **c.** striated muscle.
   b. smooth muscle. **d.** ligament.
5. Small pouches of synovial fluid, which help to reduce friction between structures, are called
   a. bursae. **c.** tendons.
   b. ligaments. **d.** striations.
6. Joints that allow for circular movement are
   a. gliding joints.
   b. ball-and-socket joints.
   c. hinge joints.
   d. pivot joints.
7. Which of the following figures shows smooth muscle tissue?

a. 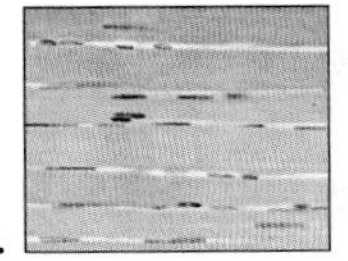 **c.** 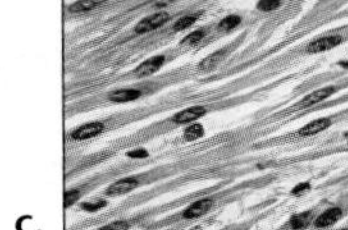

b. 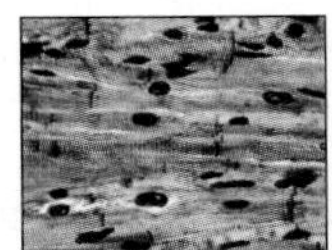 **d.** 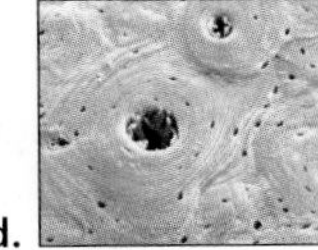

8. Two proteins that are involved in the contraction of muscle are
   a. cytosine and guanine.
   b. actin and myosin.
   c. adenine and thymine.
   d. uracil and actin.
9. The point of contact between a motor neuron and a skeletal muscle cell is called a(an)
   a. enzyme.
   b. periosteum.
   c. tendon.
   d. neuromuscular junction.
10. The outermost layer of the skin is called the
   a. dermis.
   b. keratin.
   c. epidermis.
   d. melanin.

Understanding Concepts

11. What types of tissues make up the skeletal system?
12. What are bones?
13. Draw a diagram of a long bone and label the structures. Identify which structures carry oxygen and nutrients, and identify which carry blood vessels and nerves.
14. Explain why spongy bone tissue is found in the ends of long bones.
15. Which cells are produced in red bone marrow?
16. Describe the primary function of the three types of muscle.
17. Use the sliding filament model to describe how skeletal muscles work.
18. Describe how the release of acetylcholine from a motor neuron affects a muscle cell.
19. Compare a ligament with a tendon.
20. Explain the statement: "Most skeletal muscles work in opposing pairs."
21. What is the most important function of the integumentary system? Describe three ways it performs that function.
22. Compare the outer and inner layers of the skin.
23. How does melanin affect the color of skin?
24. How does the skin help control body temperature?
25. How do fingernails and toenails grow?

HOMEWORK GUIDE

Section:	Questions:
Section 36–1	1–6, 11–15, 26, 28–32, 35, 36
Section 36–2	7–9, 16–20, 27, 33
Section 36–3	10, 21–25, 34

Chapter 36 Assessment (continued)

17. One end of the myosin filament forms a cross-bridge with the actin filament. Using energy supplied by ATP, the cross-bridge changes shape, pulling the actin filament along. The cross-bridge then detaches from the actin filament, snaps back to its original shape, and binds to another site on the actin filament.

18. It produces an impulse in the cell membrane of the muscle cell, which causes the release of calcium ions that affect regulatory proteins and allow actin and myosin to interact.

19. A ligament is connective tissue that holds bones together. A tendon is connective tissue that attaches skeletal muscles to bones.

20. Individual muscles can only pull bones in one direction by contracting. By working in opposing pairs, muscles allow movement in more than one direction around a joint.

21. The most important function is protection. It performs this function by serving as a barrier against infection and injury, helping to regulate body temperature, removing waste products from the body, and providing protection against ultraviolet radiation from the sun.

22. The outer layer serves as a barrier against injury and infection. It contains sweat pores and cells that produce melanin. The inner layer contains hair follicles, blood vessels, sensory receptors, sweat glands, and oil glands.

23. Melanin, a brown pigment, gives color to the skin. The color produced depends on the amount of melanin present and the way it is distributed.

24. Blood vessels in the skin widen or narrow so that heat can be lost from the surface of the body or conserved, as needed. Sweat produced by the skin evaporates, which cools the body when it is overheated.

25. Nails grow from a nail root, an area of rapidly dividing cells. Cells of the nail root fill with keratin and produce tough, platelike nails at the tips of fingers and toes.

Chapter 36 Assessment

Critical Thinking

26. These disks serve to protect and cushion the bones.

27. Because without acetylcholine from motor neurons, muscles cannot contract, including muscles that control swallowing and breathing

28. The hand on the left, which has the largest clear areas between the shaft and the knobs of the individual bones, belongs to the youngest person because bones are less ossified in younger people.

29. Eating calcium-rich foods can help prevent osteoporosis because it provides the body with a supply of calcium to replace calcium that is lost from bones.

30. Student answers might include the fact that the elbow is where the humerus, radius, and ulna meet, and that it is both a pivot joint and a hinge joint.

31. Students might explain that the repeated pressure on the elbow caused the bursa in the joint to swell in order to protect the joint from injury.

32. Injured ligaments might heal more slowly because they have less oxygen and fewer nutrients available to them.

33. Adverse effects of overexercising include too little body fat, joint injuries, and cessation of menstruation in females.

34. Experimental designs may vary. One possible design is to have volunteers expose small patches of protected and unprotected skin to sunlight for measured periods of time to determine how well the sunscreens work.

35. People often get calluses on their feet because the skin is repeatedly rubbed by their shoes.

36. One possible example is to compare the forelimbs of animals that climb, such as monkeys, with the forelimbs of animals that walk on four legs, such as horses. The forelimbs of monkeys have joints that allow a wider range of movement.

Chapter 36 Assessment

Critical Thinking

26. **Inferring** Disks of rubbery cartilage are found between the individual bones in the spinal column. What function do you think these disks serve?

27. **Formulating Hypotheses** Certain bacteria produce a toxin that prevents the release of acetylcholine from the motor neurons. Why can this poison result in a fatal loss of muscle movement?

28. **Interpreting Graphics** Because cartilage does not appear on X-ray film, it is seen as a clear area between the shaft and the knobs of the individual bones. Examine the X-rays below. Which hand belongs to the youngest person? How do you know?

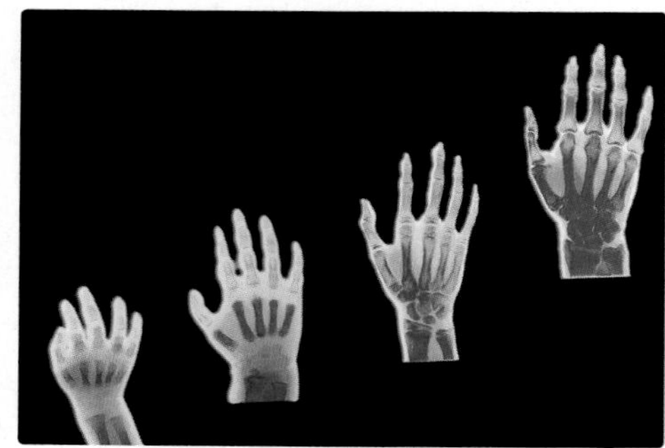

29. **Applying Concepts** Osteoporosis is a disease that usually occurs in older women. It involves a loss and weakening of bone tissue. Doctors recommend that all women eat more calcium-rich foods. How might this be helpful in preventing osteoporosis?

30. **Using Models** Suppose that you want to build a robotic arm that works the way the human elbow works. Describe or sketch three facts about the elbow that you could use in your planning.

31. **Formulating Hypotheses** You have a habit of leaning on your elbow while reading. One day, you develop a noticeable swelling at your elbow. Explain what might have happened.

32. **Predicting** Blood vessels bring oxygen and nutrients to all parts of the body. Ligaments contain fewer blood vessels than some other kinds of tissues. How might this situation affect the rate of healing in injured ligaments? Explain.

33. **Applying Concepts** Although exercising can increase your strength and endurance, overexercising can have some adverse effects on the body. Use resources in the library or on the Internet to find out what these adverse effects are. Summarize your findings in a brief report.

34. **Designing Experiments** Ultraviolet rays from the sun can cause sunburn. Sunscreens have been advertised as effective protection against sunburns. Design an experiment to determine whether the advertising claims are accurate.

35. **Inferring** A skin callus is a thickening of the epidermis caused by repeated rubbing. Why do people often get calluses on their feet?

36. **Making Connections** Recall what you learned about the bones of fishes, amphibians, reptiles, birds, and mammals. Compare examples of specific skeletal parts, such as backbones or forelimbs. Relate the bones to the way the animal moves.

Performance-Based Assessment

Demonstrating Bone Movement With one or more partners, prepare a safe demonstration showing the location of some immovable, slightly movable, and freely movable joints. Show examples of different types of movable joints.

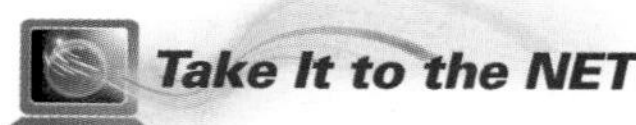

One common bone disorder among adolescents is scoliosis, or curvature of the spine. Visit the Prentice Hall Web site at **www.phschool.com** to find out more about scoliosis. Then, answer the following questions:

- What is idiopathic scoliosis?
- How does nonstructural scoliosis differ from structural scoliosis?
- What treatments are available for scoliosis?

Performance-Based Assessment

Examples of immovable joints are the joints of the skull; slightly movable joints include the joints of the vertebrae; freely movable joints include ball-and-socket joints such as the shoulder, hinge joints such as the knee and elbow, pivot joints such as the elbow, and saddle joints such as the wrist.

Standardized Test Prep

1. B
2. A
3. E
4. B
5. D
6. A
7. E
8. A
9. D

Test-Taking Tip When evaluating multiple-choice answers, be sure to read all the choices, even if the first choice seems to be correct. When you consider all the choices, you are more likely to choose the best one.

Directions: Choose the letter that best answers the question or completes the statement.

1. What determines differences in skin color between individuals?
   (A) number of melanocytes in the skin
   (B) amount of melanin produced by each melanocyte
   (C) amount of keratin in the skin
   (D) amount of sebum produced
   (E) distribution of keratin in the skin
2. In which of the following place(s) in the body is smooth muscle found?
   (A) walls of blood vessels
   (B) heart
   (C) appendicular skeleton
   (D) skeletal muscles
   (E) joints
3. All of the following are important roles of the skeletal system EXCEPT
   (A) protection of internal organs.
   (B) facilitation of movement.
   (C) storage of mineral reserves.
   (D) production of red blood cells.
   (E) regulation of body temperature.

Questions 4–6 Each of the lettered choices below refers to the following numbered statements. Select the best lettered choice. A choice may be used once, more than once, or not at all.

(A) Myosin
(B) ATP
(C) Actin
(D) Acetylcholine
(E) ADP

4. Supplies the energy required for muscle contraction
5. Is released by the motor neuron at the neuromuscular junction
6. Composes the thick filaments

Questions 7–8

Osteoporosis is a disease characterized by the loss and weakening of bone tissue. One possible explanation for this condition is that as people age, the mineral content of their bones decreases. To assess this hypothesis, the bone mineral content of 250 men and 250 women was measured. The data are shown below.

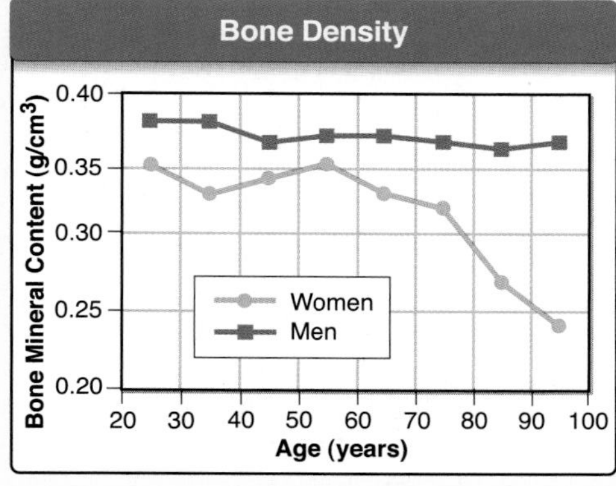

7. At which of the following ages do women show the lowest bone mineral content?
   (A) 50–59 years
   (B) 60–69 years
   (C) 70–79 years
   (D) 80–89 years
   (E) 90–95 years
8. A valid conclusion that can be drawn from this graph is that, on average,
   (A) women lose more bone mineral content as they age than men do.
   (B) men lose more bone mineral content as they age than women do.
   (C) women and men lose the same bone mineral content as they age.
   (D) women gain bone mineral content as they age.
   (E) men gain bone mineral content as they age.

Question 9 Complete the analogy by selecting the correct letter. In analogies, A : B :: C : ___?___ *means* A is to B as C is to ___?___.

9. Lever : bone :: fulcrum : ___?___.
   (A) muscle
   (B) ligament
   (C) tendon
   (D) joint
   (E) skin

Take It to the NET

- Idiopathic scoliosis is scoliosis for which the cause is unknown.
- In structural scoliosis, the vertebrae are rotated as well as curved to the side. This kind of scoliosis tends to become worse with time.
- Treatments available for scoliosis include: physical therapy to improve posture and tone spinal muscles; braces or plaster casts to hold the spine straight until growth is completed; and surgery in which a metal rod may be inserted to keep the spine straight.

For additional information, visit

www.phschool.com

Chapter Planner 37 Circulatory and Respiratory Systems

Section and Section Objectives	Time	Activities and Labs
37–1 The Circulatory System, pp. 943–950 **37.1.1** ***Identify*** the functions of the human circulatory system. **37.1.2** ***Describe*** the structures of the circulatory system. **37.1.3** ***Name*** the three types of blood vessels in the circulatory system. **37.1.4** ***Describe*** blood pressure. **37.1.5** ***Identify*** disorders of the circulatory system.	2 periods (1 block)	**SE:** ***Inquiry Activity,*** What factors affect your heart rate?, p. 942 **TE:** ***Demonstration,*** p. 944 **TE:** ***Meet Diverse Needs,*** p. 946 **SE:** ***Biology and History,*** Cardiovascular Advances, pp. 948–949 **TE:** ***Demonstration,*** p, 949
37–2 Blood and the Lymphatic System, pp. 951–955 **37.2.1** ***Describe*** blood plasma. **37.2.2** ***Explain*** the functions of red blood cells, white blood cells, and platelets. **37.2.3** ***Describe*** the role of the lymphatic system.	1 period (1/2 block)	**TE:** ***Demonstration,*** p. 953 **SE:** ***Analyzing Data,*** Predicting the Success of Blood Transfusions, p. 954
37–3 The Respiratory System, pp. 956–963 **37.3.1** ***Describe*** respiration. **37.3.2** ***Identify*** the structures of the respiratory system. **37.3.3** ***Describe*** gas exchange and breathing. **37.3.4** ***Explain*** how smoking affects the respiratory system.	2 periods (1 block)	**TE:** ***Meet Diverse Needs,*** p. 957 **TE:** ***Demonstration,*** p, 958 **SE:** ***Careers in Biology,*** Respiratory Care Practitioner, p. 959 **TE:** ***Build Science Skills,*** p. 959 **SE:** ***Quick Lab,*** Does oxygen or carbon dioxide regulate breathing?, p. 960 **TE:** ***Demonstration,*** p. 961 **SE:** ***Design an Experiment,*** Modeling Breathing, pp. 964–965
Chapter Assessment, pp. 966–969	1 period (1/2 block)	

ACTIVITY PLANNER

SE: ***Inquiry Activity,*** p. 942; (10 min.); stopwatch or watch with second hand

TE: ***Demonstration,*** p. 944; (5 min.); three-dimensional model of the heart

TE: ***Meet Diverse Needs,*** p. 946; (5 min.); tennis ball

TE: ***Demonstration,*** p. 949; (5 min.); bicycle pump, rubber tubing

TE: ***Demonstration,*** p. 953; (10 min.); microprojector, prepared slides of red and white blood cells and platelets

TE: ***Meet Diverse Needs,*** p. 957; (15 min.); modeling clay, string, dry pasta and beans, craft items

TE: ***Demonstration,*** p. 958; (10 min.); clear glass container, calcium hydroxide, water, straw

TE: ***Build Science Skills,*** p. 959; (10 min.); large round balloon, tape measure

SE: ***Quick Lab,*** p. 960; (10 min.); seltzer tablet, plastic cup or 250-mL beaker, water

TE: ***Demonstration,*** p. 961; (5 min.); tobacco, water, hot plate, paper towel, beaker, spray bottle, plant with aphids

SE: ***Design an Experiment,*** pp. 964–965; (45 min.); small clear plastic bottle, large round balloon, small round balloon, one-hole rubber stopper, scissors

PLANNING KEY

Ability Levels

B	**Basic**	For students who need additional help
A	**Average**	For all students
E	**Enriched**	For students who need to be challenged

Components

SE	Student Edition	**GRSW**	Guided Reading and Study Workbook	**IDM**	Issues and Decision Making
TE	Teacher's Edition	**CT**	Chapter Tests: Levels A and B	**CTB**	Computer Test Bank
LMA	Laboratory Manual A	**PHAS**	PH Assessment System	**PA**	Presentation Assistant Plus
LMB	Laboratory Manual B	**LA**	Lab Assessment with Scoring Guide	**BD**	BioDetectives Videotape
TR	Teaching Resources	**BTM**	BioTechnology Manual	**iT**	iText

Program Resources	Assessment	Media and Technology
LMB: Chapter 37 Lab B A **TR:** Section Review 37–1 B A **GRSW:** Section 37–1 B A	**SE:** 37–1 Section Assessment, p. 950 **TR:** Section Review 37–1	**PA:** 37–1 Interest Grabber, Section Outline, The Sinoatrial Node, Figure 37–2, Figure 37–3, Figure 37–5 **iT:** Section 37–1
TR: Section Review 37–2 B A **GRSW:** Section 37–2 B A	**SE:** 37–2 Section Assessment, p. 955 **TR:** Section Review 37–2	**PA:** 37–2 Interest Grabber, Section Outline, Blood Transfusions, Figure 37–7, Figure 37–9, Figure 37–10, Figure 37–12 **iT:** Section 37–2
LMA: Chapter 37 Lab A E **TR:** Section Review 37–3 B A Chapter 37 Design an Experiment B A E **GRSW:** Section 37–3 B A **IDM:** 37–1 A E	**SE:** 37–3 Section Assessment, p. 963 **TR:** Section Review 37–3	**PA:** 37–3 Interest Grabber, Section Outline, Flowchart, Figure 37–14, Figure 37–15, Figure 37–16 **iT:** Section 37–3
	SE: Chapter 37 Assessment, pp. 966–969 **TR:** Chapter Vocabulary Review, Graphic Organizer **CT:** Chapter 37 Test **CTB:** Chapter 37 Test **PHAS:** Practice Test	**CTB:** Chapter 37 Test **iT:** Chapter 37 Assessment

PRESSED FOR TIME?

To Preview the Chapter

- Have students read the highlighted Key Concept statements in each section.
- Have students find the highlighted Vocabulary terms in the text and read their definitions.

To Cover the Chapter Quickly

- In Section 37–1, have students read Functions of the Circulatory System; in Section 37–2, have them read the introduction; and in Section 37–3, have them read The Human Respiratory System and Tobacco and the Respiratory System.
- Assign the Key Concept questions in Section Assessment 37–3, questions 1, 8, 9, 11, 24, and 25 in Chapter 37 Assessment, and questions 2, 5, and 7–10 in Chapter 37 Standardized Test Preparation.

To Review the Chapter

- Assign the Sections for 37–1 through 37–3 in the Guided Reading and Study Workbook.
- Assign the Section Reviews for 37–1 through 37–3 and the Chapter Vocabulary Review for Chapter 37 in the Teaching Resources.

ENGAGE/EXPLORE

Inquiry Activity

Objective Students will be able to formulate hypotheses to explain the difference between sitting and standing heart rates.

Skill Focus **Formulating Hypotheses**

Materials stopwatch or watch with second hand

Time 10 minutes

Strategies

- If students cannot find a pulse in their wrist, suggest that they try to find a pulse in their neck under the jaw, where the pulse is usually stronger.
- You may want to have students predict and test how their heart rate is affected by other factors, for example, by lying down or running in place before taking their pulse.

Expected Outcome Students should find that their heart rate is faster when they are standing than when they are sitting.

Think About It One possible hypothesis to explain the faster heart rate while standing is that the heart has to do more work to supply the muscles of the legs with the extra oxygen needed to support the body in an upright position.

Brain Teaser

Point out that Chapter 37 covers both the circulatory and respiratory systems. Ask: **How are these two systems related?** *(The respiratory system brings oxygen into the body and expels carbon dioxide from the body. The circulatory system transports these two gases throughout the body.)*

Chapter 37 Circulatory and Respiratory Systems

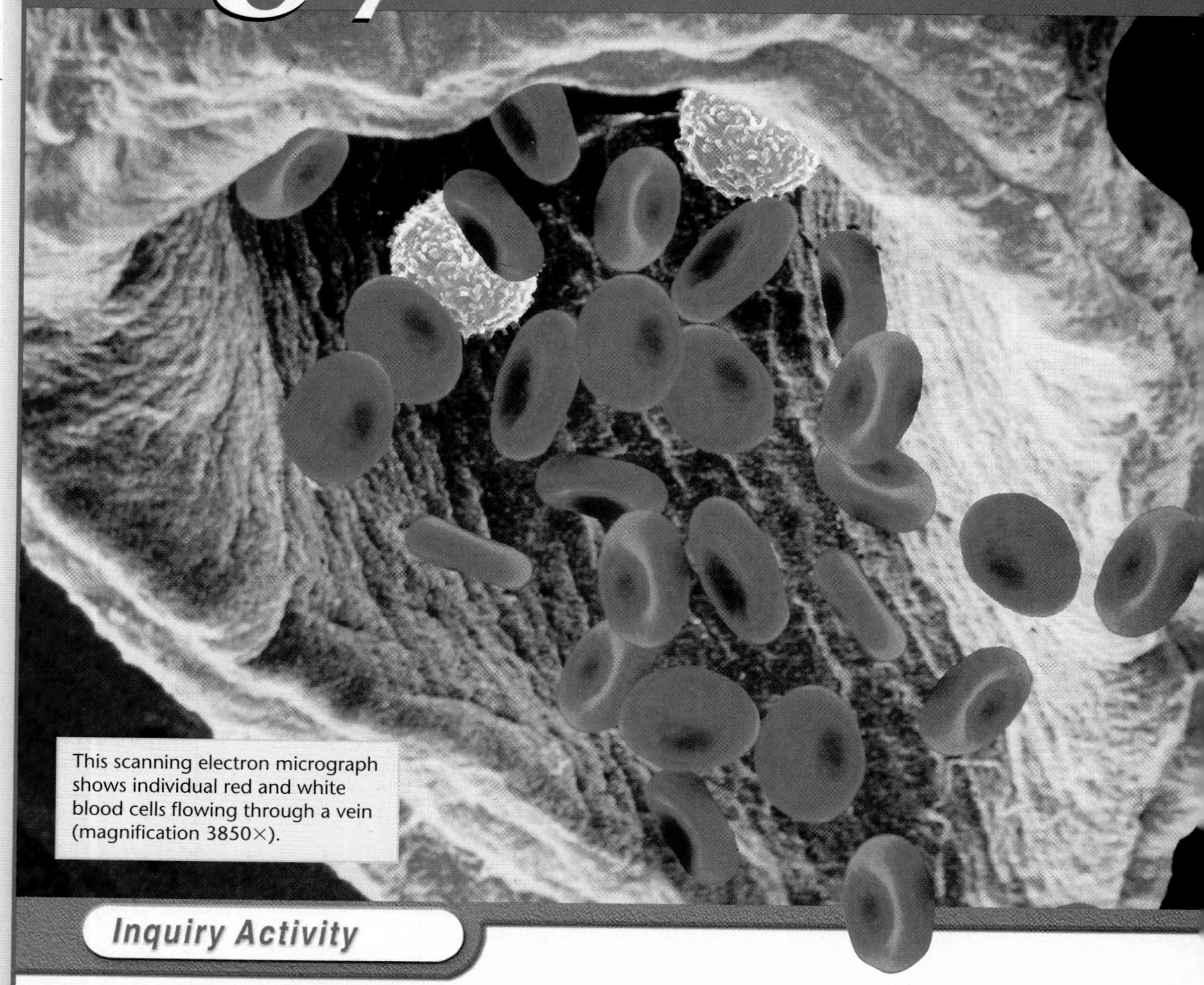

This scanning electron micrograph shows individual red and white blood cells flowing through a vein (magnification 3850×).

Inquiry Activity

What factors affect your heart rate?

Procedure

1. While sitting still, measure your heart rate. To do this, find the pulse in one of your wrists using the first two fingers of your other hand.
2. Count the number of beats you feel in 15 seconds and multiply this number by 4. This will give you the number of beats per minute.
3. What do you think would happen if you stood up? Would your heart rate decrease, increase, or stay the same? Stand up and measure your heart rate to find out.

Think About It

Formulating Hypotheses Propose an explanation for any difference between your sitting heart rate and your standing heart rate.

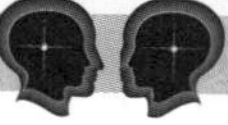

TEACHER TO TEACHER

When I teach about the circulatory system, I give students a chance to see how various drugs affect the heart rate by having them observe *Daphnia*. I have students compare the resting heart rate with the heart rate after the application of drugs in products such as tobacco, coffee, tea, soft drinks, alcohol, sleeping pills, and antihistamines. When I teach about blood, I challenge students to use their knowledge of blood groups to solve a simulated crime. Students must type simulated blood in order to solve the crime.

—*Sheila Smith*
Biology Teacher
Terry High School,
Terry, MS

37–1 The Circulatory System

Your heartbeat is a sign of life itself. Even when you drift off to sleep, your heart continues to beat at a steady rhythm. Why is this process so important that it must keep going even when you sleep?

Each breath you take brings air into your respiratory system. The oxygen in that air is needed by the trillions of cells in your body. Your heart is essential in delivering that oxygen. Its beating produces the force to move oxygen-rich blood through the circulatory system. Working together, your circulatory and respiratory systems supply cells throughout the body with the nutrients and oxygen that they need to stay alive.

Functions of the Circulatory System

Organisms composed of a small number of cells don't need a circulatory system. Most cells in such organisms are in direct contact with the environment. Oxygen, nutrients, and waste products can easily diffuse back and forth across cell membranes.

Larger organisms, however, cannot rely on diffusion. Most of their cells are not in direct contact with the environment, and substances made in one part of the organism may be needed in another part. In a way, this same problem is faced by the millions of people living in a large city. Cities have transportation systems that move people, goods, and waste material from one place to another. The transportation system of a city is its streets, highways, and rail lines. The transportation system of a living organism is its circulatory system.

Humans and other vertebrates have closed circulatory systems. This means that a circulating fluid called blood is pumped through a system of vessels. **The human circulatory system consists of the heart, a series of blood vessels, and the blood that flows through them.**

Guide for Reading

Key Concepts

- What are the structures of the circulatory system?
- What are the three types of blood vessels in the circulatory system?

Vocabulary

myocardium
atrium
ventricle
pulmonary circulation
systemic circulation
valve
pacemaker
aorta
artery
capillary
vein
atherosclerosis

Reading Strategy: Using Visuals Before you read, preview **Figure 37–3.** Make a list of questions about the illustration. As you read, write down the answers to the questions.

◀ **Figure 37–1** These roads form a transportation system. **Using Analogies** *How is the human circulatory system like the streets and highways of a large city?*

SECTION RESOURCES

Print:

- ***Laboratory Manual B,*** Chapter 37 Lab
- ***Teaching Resources,*** Section Review 37–1
- ***Guided Reading and Study Workbook,*** Section 37–1

Technology:

- ***iText,*** Section 37–1

Section 37–1

1 FOCUS

Objectives

37.1.1 ***Identify*** the functions of the human circulatory system.
37.1.2 ***Describe*** the structures of the circulatory system.
37.1.3 ***Name*** the three types of blood vessels in the circulatory system.
37.1.4 ***Describe*** blood pressure.
37.1.5 ***Identify*** disorders of the circulatory system.

Guide for Reading

Vocabulary Preview

Explain that the circulatory system consists of the heart and blood vessels. Then, call students' attention to the vocabulary words and ask: **Which words refer to structures of the heart, and which words refer to types of blood vessels?** *(Myocardium, atrium, ventricle, valve, and pacemaker refer to structures of the heart. Aorta, artery, capillary, and vein refer to types of blood vessels.)*

Reading Strategy

Have students write the headings and subheadings in outline form. As they read, have them fill in the outline with enough details to make each topic clear and informative.

2 INSTRUCT

Functions of the Circulatory System

Meet Diverse Needs

Help students appreciate how much blood is pumped through the circulatory system. Tell them that the heart pumps an average of about 5 L of blood per minute. Ask: **How many liters of blood are pumped through the circulatory system in an average lifespan of 75 years?** *(Almost 200,000,000 L)* **Learning modality: mathematical/logical**

Answer to . . .

Figure 37–1 *Blood vessels are like the streets and highways that carry materials to each part of a city.*

The Heart

Word Origins

Myocarditis means inflammation of the heart muscle.

Demonstration

Display a three-dimensional model of the heart that can be taken apart to show the inside. Call on students to identify each part of the heart described in the text, including the septum, atria, and ventricles. Have students trace the route of blood through the heart. Point out the valves, and explain how they let blood flow in only one direction.

Use Visuals

Figure 37–2 Explain that the red-colored blood vessels carry oxygen-rich blood and the blue-colored blood vessels carry oxygen-poor blood. Add that most of the oxygen-rich blood is carried in the arteries and most of the oxygen-poor blood is carried in the veins. The only exceptions are the pulmonary artery and vein. Ask: **Why are the pulmonary artery and vein exceptions in this way?** *(Because they carry blood to and from the lungs, where the blood picks up oxygen.)* Remind students that the red and blue color scheme is a convention that makes it easier to follow the flow of blood through the circulatory system, but the blue does not represent the actual color of oxygen-poor blood.

Build Science Skills

Using Models Point out that a good model of a heart valve is an automatic door that opens in only one direction, like the doors typically found in supermarkets. Ask: **How is a heart valve like a one-way door?** *(Like a one-way door, the heart valve allows only one-way flow through an opening.)*

Word Origins

The word **myocardium** comes from two Greek words: *myo,* meaning "muscle," and *kardia,* meaning "heart." **If *itis* means an "inflammation," what does *myocarditis* mean?**

▼ **Figure 37–2** The circulatory system is divided into two pathways. The pulmonary circulation carries blood between the heart and the lungs. The systemic circulation carries blood between the heart and the rest of the body. **Observing** ***What kind of blood—oxygen-rich or oxygen-poor—leaves the lungs and returns to the heart?***

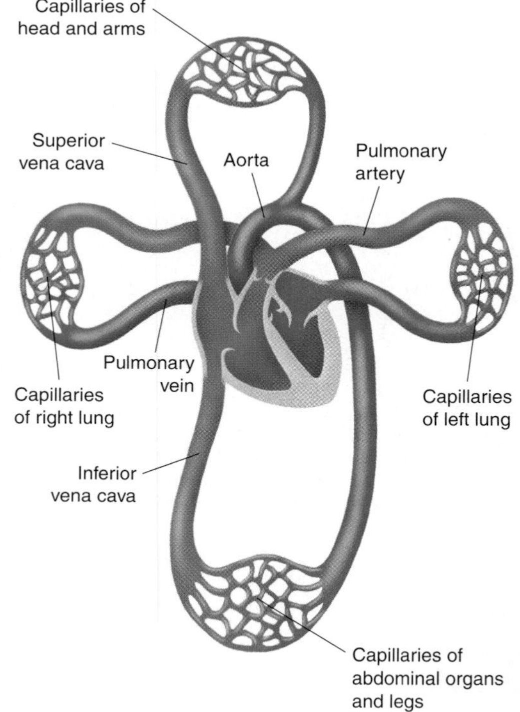

The Heart

As you can feel with your hand, your heart is located near the center of your chest. The heart, which is composed almost entirely of muscle, is a hollow organ that is about the size of your clenched fist. The heart is enclosed in a protective sac of tissue called the pericardium (pehr-ih-KAHR-dee-um). In the walls of the heart, there are two thin layers of epithelial and connective tissue that form a sandwich around a thick layer of muscle called the **myocardium**. The powerful contractions of the myocardium pump blood through the circulatory system.

The heart contracts roughly 72 times a minute, pumping about 70 milliliters of blood with each contraction. This means that during one year, an average person's heart pumps more than enough blood to fill an Olympic-sized swimming pool. (An Olympic-sized swimming pool is about 2,000,000 liters: 0.07 liters × 4320 beats per hour × 24 hours × 365 days = 2,649,024 liters.)

Dividing the right side of the heart from the left side of the heart is a septum, or wall. The septum prevents the mixing of oxygen-poor and oxygen-rich blood. On each side of the septum are two chambers. The upper chamber, which receives the blood, is the **atrium** (plural: atria). The lower chamber, which pumps blood out of the heart, is the **ventricle.** The heart has a total of four chambers—two atria and two ventricles.

Circulation Through the Body The heart functions as two separate pumps. **Figure 37–2** shows that the right side of the heart pumps blood from the heart to the lungs. This pathway is known as **pulmonary circulation.** In the lungs, carbon dioxide leaves the blood while oxygen is absorbed. The oxygen-rich blood flows into the left side of the heart and is pumped to the rest of the body. This pathway is called **systemic circulation.** Blood that returns to the right side of the heart is oxygen-poor because cells have absorbed much of the oxygen and loaded the blood with carbon dioxide. At this point, it is ready for another trip to the lungs.

Oxygen-rich and oxygen-poor blood are both shades of red. Often, oxygen-poor blood is shown as blue in art to make it easier to tell where each type of blood is found in the circulatory system.

Blood Flow Through the Heart Blood enters the heart through the right and left atria, as shown in **Figure 37–3.** As the heart contracts, blood flows into the ventricles and then out from the ventricles.

TIME SAVER

PRESENTATIONS MADE EASY!

The Presentation Assistant Plus contains the Prentice Hall Presentation Pro and the Transparencies, which provide easy-to-follow visual support for every step of this section. If you have a computer presentation station, use Prentice Hall Presentation Pro for Section 37–1, or use the transparencies listed here.

Section 37–1:

Interest Grabber
Section Outline
The Sinoatrial Node
Figure 37–2
Figure 37–3
Figure 37–5

FIGURE 37–3 STRUCTURES OF THE HEART

The circulatory system consists of the heart, a series of blood vessels, and the blood that flows through them. Notice the valves between the atria and ventricles and those between the ventricles and the blood vessels leaving the heart. The valves prevent blood from flowing backward.

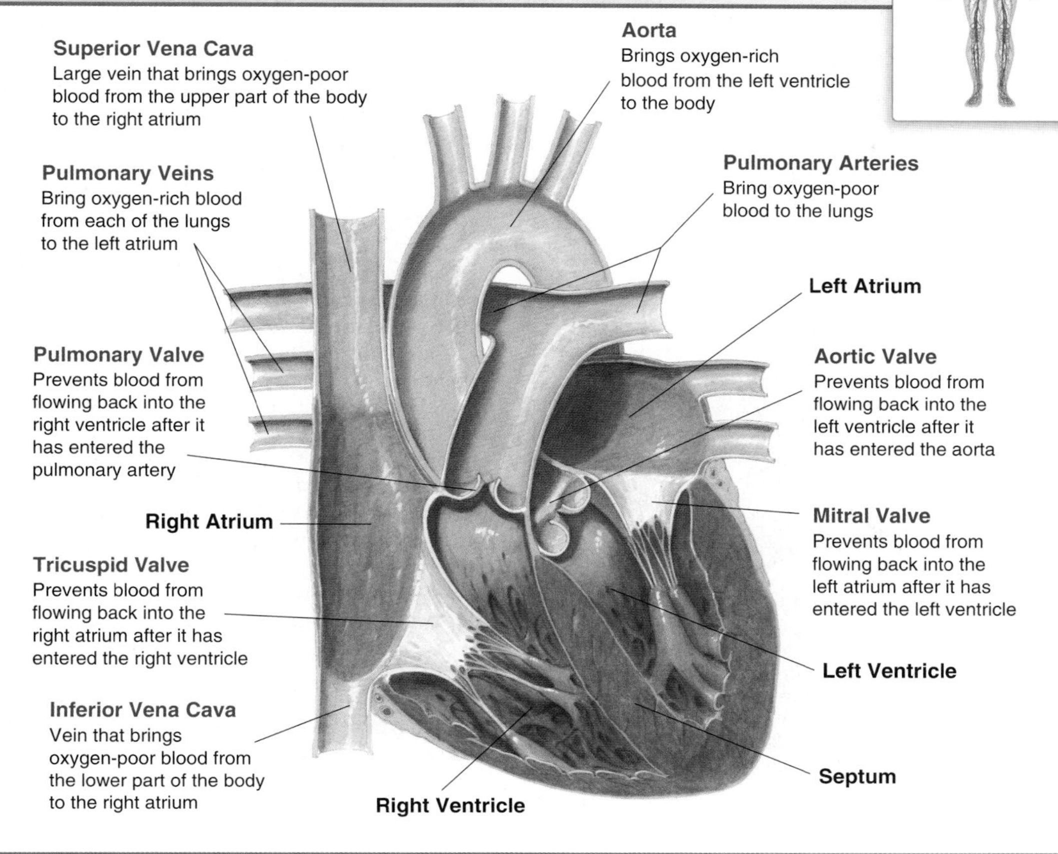

Superior Vena Cava
Large vein that brings oxygen-poor blood from the upper part of the body to the right atrium
Aorta
Brings oxygen-rich blood from the left ventricle to the body
Pulmonary Veins
Bring oxygen-rich blood from each of the lungs to the left atrium
Pulmonary Arteries
Bring oxygen-poor blood to the lungs
Left Atrium
Pulmonary Valve
Prevents blood from flowing back into the right ventricle after it has entered the pulmonary artery
Aortic Valve
Prevents blood from flowing back into the left ventricle after it has entered the aorta
Right Atrium
Mitral Valve
Prevents blood from flowing back into the left atrium after it has entered the left ventricle
Tricuspid Valve
Prevents blood from flowing back into the right atrium after it has entered the right ventricle
Left Ventricle
Inferior Vena Cava
Vein that brings oxygen-poor blood from the lower part of the body to the right atrium
Septum
Right Ventricle

There are flaps of connective tissue called **valves** between the atria and the ventricles. Blood moving from the atria holds the valves open. When the ventricles contract, the valves close, which prevents blood from flowing back into the atria.

At the exits from the right and left ventricles, there are valves that prevent blood that flows out of the heart from flowing back in. This system of valves keeps blood moving through the heart in one direction, like traffic on a one-way street. The one-way flow increases the pumping efficiency of the heart. The valves are so important to heart function that surgeons often attempt to repair or replace a damaged valve.

CHECKPOINT *What is the function of the heart valves?*

Use Visuals

Figure 37–3 Help students understand how blood flows through the heart. Explain that blood always leaves the heart through arteries and always returns to the heart through veins. Check students' understanding of how the heart pumps blood by asking: **Where is blood pumped by the atria?** *(To the ventricles)* **Where is blood pumped by the ventricles?** *(To the lungs and the rest of the body)*

Meet Diverse Needs

Have students who need an extra challenge learn about heart valve defects. They should investigate types of defects and their causes, how they affect health, and whether they can be repaired surgically. Urge students to share what they learn in an oral report. **Learning modality: verbal**

Use Community Resources

Invite a nurse or technician who administers electrocardiograms, or ECGs, to speak to the class. Suggest that the speaker explain how ECGs are performed and what they measure. If possible, have the speaker bring a sample ECG printout to class and use it to explain to students how ECGs are interpreted. Have students write a paragraph summarizing what they learn.

BIO INSIGHTS — HISTORY OF SCIENCE

William Harvey's contributions

One scientist is known above all others for his contributions to our understanding of the human circulatory system. That scientist is William Harvey, the English physician whose 1628 book on the circulation of blood was a landmark publication. Until Harvey's time, there were many misconceptions about the blood and circulation. For example, it was believed that blood formed in the liver, that it moved very sluggishly if at all, and that pulmonary and systemic blood were not connected. Harvey dissected cadavers and studied living patients to prove many of the misconceptions wrong. He determined that blood is forced by the pumping of the heart in a circular pathway throughout the body, leaving the heart in the arteries and returning to the heart in the veins. Harvey also explained how the valves in the heart and veins keep blood flowing in just one direction.

Answers to . . .

CHECKPOINT *The function of the valves is to prevent any backflow of blood from the ventricles to the atria and from the aorta and pulmonary artery to the ventricles.*

Figure 37–2 *Oxygen-rich blood leaves the lungs and returns to the heart.*

Meet Diverse Needs

Help students appreciate how much work is performed by the heart. Give several students a tennis ball, and have them squeeze the ball in their fist at a rate of about once a second. As students continue to squeeze the ball, tell them that they are simulating the work of the heart. Point out that their fist is about as large as the heart and that the force needed to squeeze the tennis ball is similar to the force needed to squeeze blood from the heart. Have students continue to squeeze the ball until their hand gets tired, say, for a couple of minutes. Conclude by reminding students that the heart contracts at about the same rate as their fist, but it continues nonstop for life. **Learning modality: tactile**

Make Connections

Health Science Point out that artificial pacemakers are implanted in people whose hearts need help maintaining a normal rate of contractions. The battery-operated pacemaker sends electrical impulses to the heart whenever it starts to beat abnormally. For example, if the heart starts to beat too slowly, the pacemaker sends electrical impulses that stimulate the heart to beat faster. Ask: **Based on how the artificial pacemaker works, how do you think the heart's natural pacemaker works to control the heart?** *(By sending out electrical impulses)*

Blood Vessels

Meet Diverse Needs

Work with at-risk students to make a graphic organizer, such as a compare/contrast table or Venn diagram, to summarize the similarities and differences among the three types of blood vessels. **Limited English proficiency**

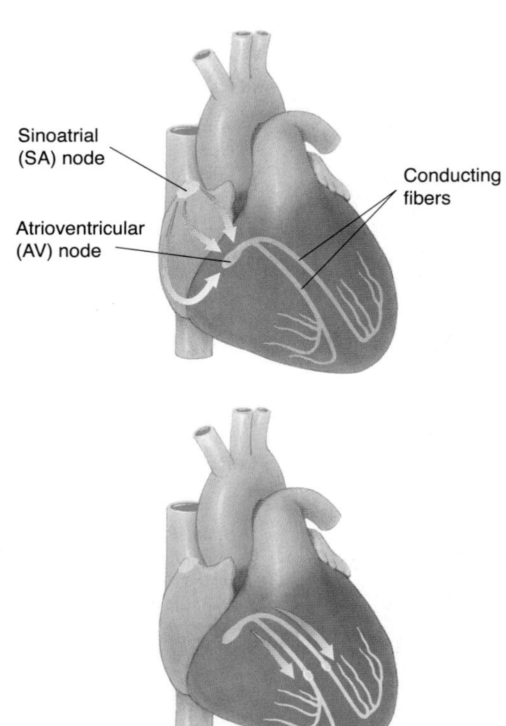

▲ **Figure 37–4** The signal to contract spreads from the sinoatrial node to the cardiac muscle cells of the atria, causing the atria to contract. The impulse is picked up by the atrioventricular node, which transmits the impulse to muscle fibers in the ventricles, causing the ventricles to contract. **Predicting** ***In times of stress, does the heart beat faster or slower?***

Heartbeat There are two networks of muscle fibers in the heart, one in the atria and one in the ventricles. When a single fiber in either network is stimulated, all the fibers are stimulated and the network contracts as a unit. Each contraction begins in a small group of cardiac muscle cells located in the right atrium—the sinoatrial node. Because these cells "set the pace" for the heart as a whole, they are also called the **pacemaker.**

As shown in **Figure 37–4,** the impulse spreads from the pacemaker to the network of fibers in the atria. It is picked up by a bundle of fibers called the atrioventricular node and carried to the network of fibers in the ventricles. When the network in the atria contracts, blood flows into the ventricles. When the network in the ventricles contracts, blood flows out of the heart. This two-step pattern of contraction makes the heart a more efficient pump.

Your heart can beat faster or more slowly, depending on your body's need for oxygen-rich blood. During vigorous exercise, your heart rate may increase to about 200 beats per minute. Although the heartbeat is not directly controlled by the nervous system, the autonomic nervous system does influence heart rate. Neurotransmitters released by neurons in the sympathetic nervous system can increase heart rate. Those released by neurons in the parasympathetic nervous system can decrease heart rate.

Blood Vessels

Blood leaving the left side of the heart is loaded with oxygen from the lungs. When it leaves the left ventricle, the blood passes into a large blood vessel known as the **aorta.** The aorta is the first of a series of blood vessels that carry the blood on its round trip through the body and back to the heart. **As blood flows through the circulatory system, it moves through three types of blood vessels—arteries, capillaries, and veins.**

Arteries Large vessels that carry blood from the heart to the tissues of the body are called **arteries.** Arteries are the superhighways of the circulatory system. Except for the pulmonary arteries, all arteries carry oxygen-rich blood. Arteries have thick walls that help them withstand the powerful pressure produced when the heart contracts and pushes blood into the arteries.

FACTS AND FIGURES

All about the heart

The nervous system influences the heart rate, but does not directly control contractions of cardiac muscle. In fact, the heart may keep beating for several minutes after it is removed from the body. The "lub-dub" sound of the heartbeat is produced by vibrations in the walls of the heart when the heart valves snap shut. The heart of a newborn beats about twice as fast as the heart of an adult, at about 140 beats per minute compared with about 70 beats per minute. Throughout a lifetime, the average person's heart beats about 3 billion times. To do all this work, cardiac muscle requires a lot of oxygen. Not surprisingly, heart tissue is supplied with more capillaries than any other tissue. Heart tissue also uses about 80 percent of the oxygen supplied to it, as compared with about 25 percent used by most other tissues.

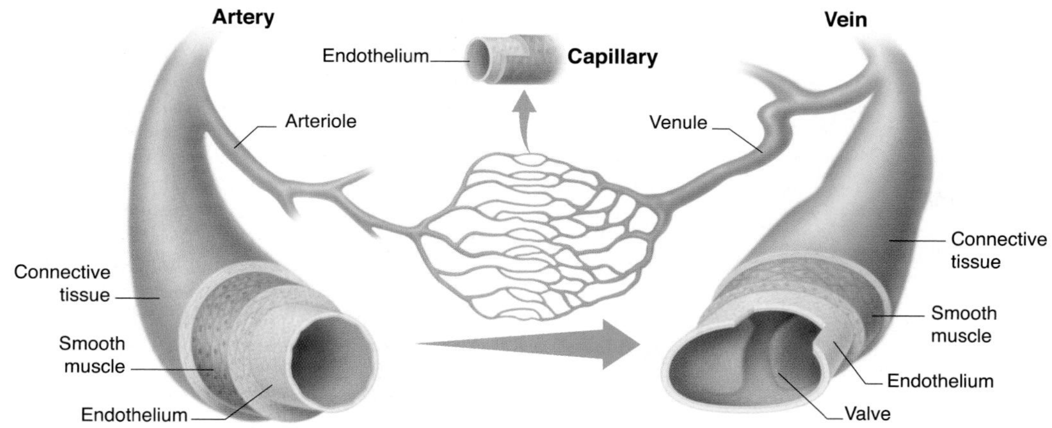

▲ **Figure 37–5** **In the circulatory system, there are three types of blood vessels—arteries, capillaries, and veins.** The walls of these vessels contain connective, muscle, and epithelial tissue.

Figure 37–5 shows that the walls contain connective tissue, smooth muscle, and epithelial cells. The elastic connective tissue allows an artery to expand under pressure. Contractions of the smooth muscle regulate the diameter of an artery.

Capillaries The smallest of the blood vessels are the **capillaries.** Capillaries are the side streets and alleys of the circulatory system. The walls of capillaries are only one cell thick, and most are so narrow that blood cells must pass through them in single file. The real work of the circulatory system—bringing nutrients and oxygen to the tissues and absorbing carbon dioxide and other waste products—is done in the capillaries.

Veins Once blood has passed through the capillary system, it must be returned to the heart. This is the job of the **veins.** As with arteries, the walls of veins contain connective tissue and smooth muscle. As shown in **Figure 37–6,** the largest veins contain one-way valves that keep blood flowing toward the heart. Many veins are located near skeletal muscles. When these muscles contract, they help to force blood through the veins. Blood flow through the veins of the arms and legs often occurs against the force of gravity. Exercise helps to keep blood from accumulating in the limbs and stretching the veins out of shape.

CHECKPOINT *What happens in the capillaries?*

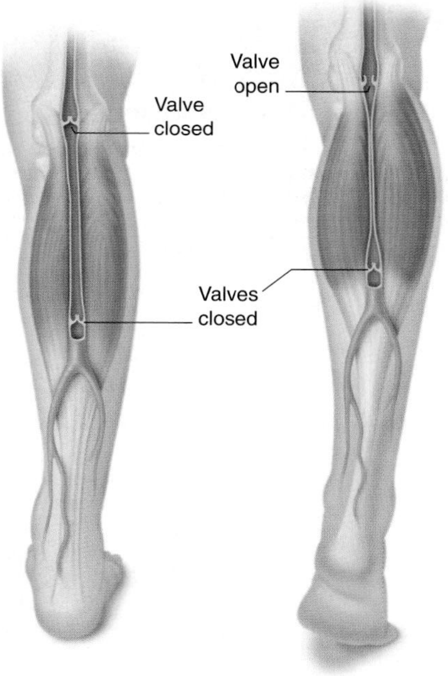

▶ **Figure 37–6** Contraction of skeletal muscles helps move blood in veins toward the heart. **Drawing Conclusions** *What role do valves play in large veins?*

Demonstration

Show students the direction in which blood travels in veins, using a demonstration originally designed by William Harvey. Select a student volunteer who has obvious veins in the forearms. Press down with your fingers on one of the more prominent veins near the wrist. While continuing to press down on the vein, run a fingertip along the same vein toward the elbow. The vein will disappear and blood will not flow back into the vein until you release the pressure near the wrist. Ask: **In which direction is blood flowing in the vein?** (*From the wrist to the elbow*) **What prevented the blood from flowing back into the vein after it was pushed toward the elbow?** *(One-way valves in the vein)*

Use Visuals

Figure 37–5 Point out the horizontal arrow in the figure, and explain that it shows the direction of blood flow through the blood vessels. Check students' understanding of the different types of blood vessels by having them complete the analogy: arterioles are to arteries as venules are to ________. *(veins)* Challenge students to identify how the drawings of the vein and artery differ. *(The vein has a valve; the artery does not. The drawings also differ in color, the red indicating oxygen-rich arterial blood and the blue indicating oxygen-poor venous blood.)*

Build Science Skills

Inferring Students are likely to be aware that they can monitor the beating of their heart by feeling a pulse in their wrist. Ask: **Why can you feel a pulse in your wrist every time your heart beats?** *(Arteries are somewhat elastic, so they expand slightly each time the heart pumps blood into the aorta. This expansion can be felt as a pulse in arteries that are close to the surface of the body, such as in the wrist.)*

FACTS AND FIGURES

Aorta, CEO of arteries

The aorta has been called the CEO of the arterial blood circulation system. It is the principal artery in the body, from which almost all other arteries divide and subdivide, down to the tiniest arteriole. At its maximum diameter, where it begins at the left ventricle, the aorta is almost 3 cm in diameter. From there, it arches back and down through the chest and diaphragm to the abdomen. Some of the major branches of the aorta as it travels through the body are the coronary arteries, which supply blood to the heart; the innominate, subclavian, and carotid arteries, which supply blood to the head, neck, and arms; and the right and left iliac arteries, which supply blood to the legs. The aorta can develop atherosclerosis, or fat deposits on the walls. Without treatment, this can contribute to high blood pressure and potentially fatal bulges in the aortic wall called aneurysms.

Answers to . . .

CHECKPOINT *Food and oxygen are brought to the tissues, and carbon dioxide and waste products are absorbed by the blood.*

Figure 37–4 *It beats faster.*

Figure 37–6 *They keep blood flowing toward the heart.*

37–1 (continued)

Blood Pressure

Address Misconceptions

Many people think that it is natural for blood pressure to increase with age. Explain that this is a myth. It is based on the tendency of older people to have high blood pressure because of years of high-fat diets and other behaviors that increase the chances of developing high blood pressure. Emphasize that high blood pressure, which is blood pressure above 120/80, is unhealthy at any age. Also, point out that young people can develop high blood pressure, especially if they are overweight and do not exercise.

Use Community Resources

Invite a school nurse or other health professional to bring a sphygmomanometer to class and show students how it is used to measure blood pressure. Encourage the health professional to explain how both systolic and diastolic pressures are read and what each measures. If possible, after the demonstration give interested students a chance to use the sphygmomanometer to take each other's blood pressure while being supervised.

Meet Diverse Needs

Some students may better understand how the body regulates blood pressure if they see the processes summarized in graphic organizers, such as cycle diagrams or flowcharts. Using the chalkboard or an overhead transparency, work with students to create a graphic organizer to show how neurotransmitters regulate blood pressure by controlling blood vessels and another graphic organizer to show how the kidneys regulate blood pressure by controlling blood volume. **Learning modality: visual**

Blood Pressure

Like any pump, the heart produces pressure. When the heart contracts, it produces a wave of fluid pressure in the arteries. The force of the blood on the arteries' walls is known as blood pressure. Blood pressure decreases when the heart relaxes, but the system still remains under pressure. It's a good thing, too. Without that pressure, blood would stop flowing through the body.

Medical workers can measure blood pressure with a device called a sphygmomanometer (sfig-moh-muh-NAHM-uh-tur). A cuff is wrapped around the upper arm. Air is pumped into the cuff until blood flow through an artery is blocked. As the pressure is released, the worker listens to the pulse and records two numbers from a pressure gauge. The first number is the systolic pressure—the force felt in the arteries when the ventricles contract. The second number is the diastolic pressure—the force of the blood felt in the arteries when the ventricles relax. An average adult's blood pressure is 120/80.

The body normally regulates blood pressure in two ways. Sensory neurons at several places in the body detect the level of blood pressure, sending impulses to the medulla oblongata region of the brain stem. When blood pressure is too high, the autonomic nervous system releases neurotransmitters that cause the smooth muscles around blood vessels to relax, lowering blood pressure. When blood pressure is too low, neurotransmitters are released that elevate blood pressure by causing these smooth muscles to contract.

Biology and History

Cardiovascular Advances

William Harvey, the father of cardiovascular medicine, correctly described the role of the heart in the circulation of blood more than three centuries ago. Since then, modern advances in this area have improved the lives of many people with heart disease.

1900

1902 **Alexis Carrel** Carrel paves the way for organ transplantation by developing techniques for rejoining severed blood vessels.

1912 The *Titanic* sinks

1924 **Willem Einthoven** Einthoven wins a Nobel Prize for his invention of the electrocardiograph (EKG), a device used to measure tiny electric currents produced by the heart.

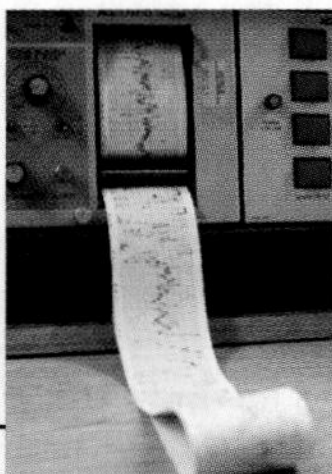

1929 Worldwide economic depression begins

FACTS AND FIGURES

Blood pressure's ups and downs
Blood pressure rises and falls throughout life and even throughout the day. Babies and children usually have much lower blood pressure than adults, and blood pressure is generally lowest at night during sleep and highest during the morning. Blood pressure also rises during exercise and periods of emotional excitement. Weight gain is usually associated with an increase in blood pressure as well. Regulation of blood pressure's ups and downs is complex.

When blood pressure falls, it causes the release of the kidney enzyme renin. Renin, in turn, activates the hormone angiotensin, which causes the arterioles to constrict. Constriction of the arterioles leads to an increase in blood pressure. Angiotensin also stimulates the adrenal gland to release aldosterone, which causes the kidney to retain salt. This leads to an increase in water in the blood, and the greater blood volume causes an increase in blood pressure.

The kidneys, which remove water from the blood, also help to regulate blood pressure. Hormones produced by the heart and other organs cause the kidneys to remove more water from the blood when blood pressure is high. This action reduces blood volume, thereby lowering the blood pressure.

CHECKPOINT *What instrument measures blood pressure?*

Disorders of the Circulatory System

Unfortunately, disorders of the circulatory system are all too common. Many of them stem from a condition known as **atherosclerosis** (ath-ur-oh-skluh-ROH-sis), in which fatty deposits called plaque build up on the walls of arteries. If these deposits get too large, they obstruct the flow of blood and may cause an increase in blood pressure. The plaque buildup also increases the risk of blood clots. If a clot breaks free, it can get stuck in an artery and obstruct blood flow to tissues beyond the clot.

High Blood Pressure If blood pressure is too high, medical problems may result. High blood pressure, or hypertension, forces the heart to work harder, which may weaken or damage the heart muscle and blood vessels. People with high blood pressure are more likely to develop heart disease and to suffer from other diseases of the circulatory system. Hypertension increases the risk of heart attack and stroke.

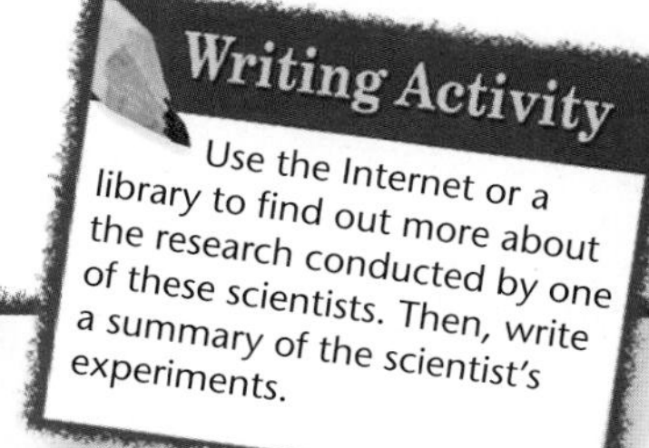

Writing Activity
Use the Internet or a library to find out more about the research conducted by one of these scientists. Then, write a summary of the scientist's experiments.

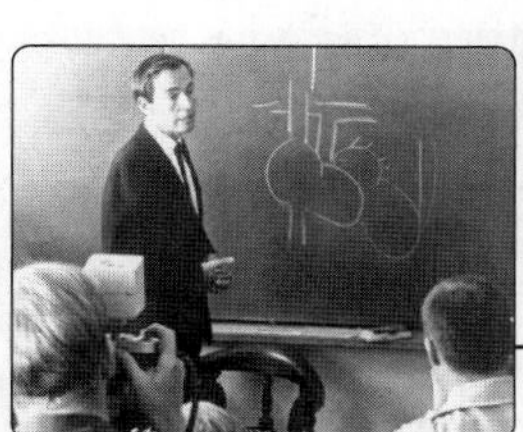

1967
Christiaan Barnard
Barnard performs the first partially successful human heart transplant. The patient lived for 18 days.

1977
Andreas Gruentzig
Gruentzig performs the first angioplasty by inserting a hollow tube containing a tiny uninflated balloon into a patient's coronary artery. The balloon is inflated, opening up the blocked area and restoring blood flow to the heart.

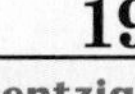

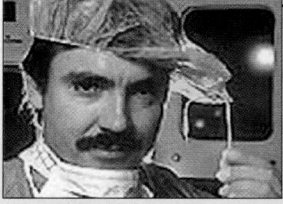

1982
William DeVries
DeVries leads a team of doctors to implant the Jarvik-7 artificial heart in a patient, who lives for 112 days.

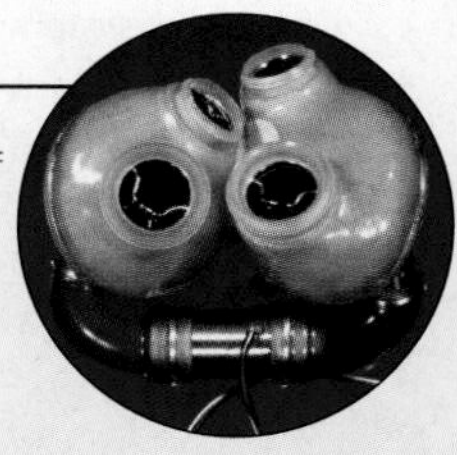

1996
Wilson Greatbatch
Greatbatch wins a Lifetime Achievement Award for his invention, the implantable pacemaker. The mechanical device emits electrical signals that keep the heart beating normally.

2000

HISTORY OF SCIENCE

Other cardiovascular advances

The first American surgeon to perform a human heart transplant was Dr. Norman E. Shumway. In 1968, just one year after the first human heart transplant was performed by Christiaan Barnard, Shumway transplanted a heart in a 54-year-old man whose own heart had been injured by a viral infection. Although this patient survived for only 15 days following transplant surgery, Shumway went on to perform many successful heart transplant surgeries. Shumway also made other achievements in heart surgery, including the transplantation of heart valves. One of the reasons early heart transplants failed was because the donor heart was rejected by the patient's immune system. The development of effective immunosuppressant drugs greatly increased the success rate of transplantation.

Disorders of the Circulatory System

Demonstration

Give students a hands-on demonstration of how atherosclerosis increases blood pressure and the work the heart has to do to pump blood. Obtain a bicycle pump and a piece of rubber tubing that fits over the air nozzle of the pump. Give several volunteers a chance first to pump air through the open tube, and then to pump air through the tube when you squeeze it almost closed. Urge students to describe to the class the difference in the amount of work required when the tube was open and when it was almost closed. Conclude by saying that this is similar to the way atherosclerosis narrows the arteries, causing the heart to work harder and blood pressure to increase.

Biology and History

Explain to students that thousands of heart transplants have been performed since the first heart transplant was performed by Christiaan Barnard in 1967. By 1995, heart transplants had a 90 percent success rate. However, heart transplants are still usually reserved for patients who have the most serious types of heart disease that cannot be treated with drugs or other types of surgery. Also explain that similar progress has not been made in developing an artificial heart, although research continues in this area.

Writing Activity

You can use the writing activity to expand students' knowledge of the scientists in the time line. For example, students might write about the many heart transplants Dr. Barnard performed after the first one in 1967. You can also use the writing activity to expand students' knowledge of others who have made important advances in cardiovascular research, such as Norman Shumway, the American surgeon who performed the first heart transplant in the United States.

Answer to . . .

CHECKPOINT *A sphygmomanometer measures blood pressure.*

SCIENCE NEWS®

Encourage students to visit
www.phschool.com
for the most current information on this topic.

Build Science Skills

Using Tables and Graphs
Challenge students to use library sources to find data tables and graphs that relate behavioral variables such as smoking, sedentary lifestyle, and high-fat diet to the risk of circulatory disorders such as high blood pressure, heart attack, and stroke. Call on volunteers to explain their tables and graphs to the class by summarizing in words what the data show in numbers.

3 ASSESS

Evaluate Understanding

Call on students at random to define each of the Vocabulary terms. Call on other students to correct any errors.

Reteach

Have students trace the path of blood through the heart in Figure 37–3 and name each of the structures through which the blood passes.

Take It to the NET

Students' brochures should stress a low-fat diet based on the Food Guide Pyramid and also a program of regular aerobic exercise such as brisk walking or swimming. For additional information, visit
www.phschool.com

Use iText to review the key concepts in Section 37–1.

KEEP CURRENT WITH . . . SCIENCE NEWS®

To find out more about the topics in this chapter, go to:
www.phschool.com

Heart Attack Atherosclerosis is particularly dangerous in the coronary arteries, the set of small arteries that bring oxygen and nutrients to the heart muscle itself. If one of these arteries becomes blocked, part of the heart muscle may begin to die for lack of oxygen—a condition known as a heart attack.

The symptoms of a heart attack include nausea, shortness of breath, and severe, crushing chest pain. People who show these symptoms need immediate medical attention. New drugs are available that can increase blood flow enough to save heart cells. These drugs must be given in the early stages of a heart attack to save the heart muscle and prevent cell death.

Stroke Blood clots formed as a result of atherosclerosis may break free and get stuck in one of the blood vessels leading to a part of the brain. This event is known as a stroke. Brain cells served by that blood vessel gradually die from a lack of oxygen, and brain function in that region may be lost. A stroke can also occur when a weakened artery in the brain bursts, flooding the area with blood. Depending on what part of the brain they affect, strokes may cause paralysis, loss of the ability to speak, and even death.

Prevention of Circulatory System Disorders Like most other disorders, cardiovascular disorders are easier to prevent than to cure. Exercise, weight control, sensible diet, and not smoking seem to be the keys to avoiding cardiovascular disorders. Exercise increases your respiratory system's efficiency. It helps control your weight, reduces body fat, and reduces stress. It also strengthens your muscles, including your heart. A diet low in saturated fat can reduce your risk of developing heart disease.

37–1 Section Assessment

1. **Key Concept** List the structures of the circulatory system.
2. **Key Concept** Compare the functions of the three types of blood vessels in the circulatory system.
3. Describe the path of blood circulation through the body.
4. How is heartbeat controlled?
5. **Critical Thinking Relating Concepts** Explain how regular exercise can promote good circulation.

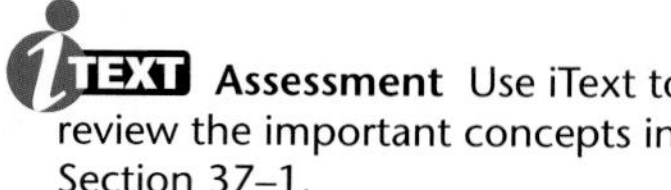

Assessment Use iText to review the important concepts in Section 37–1.

Take It to the NET

Exercise and weight control are important factors in heart disease prevention. Research current recommendations for diet and exercise and develop a brochure stressing healthy behaviors. Use the links provided in the Biology area at the Prentice Hall Web site for help in completing this activity:
www.phschool.com

37–1 Section Assessment

1. Heart, blood vessels, and blood
2. The three types are arteries, capillaries, and veins. Arteries carry oxygen-rich blood from the heart to the tissues; capillaries bring food and oxygen to the tissues and absorb carbon dioxide and waste products; veins carry oxygen-poor blood back to the heart from the rest of the body.
3. The right side of the heart pumps blood from the heart to the lungs. Oxygen-rich blood from the lungs returns to the left side of the heart, where it is pumped to the rest of the body. Veins return oxygen-poor blood to the heart to begin the path of circulation again.
4. It is controlled by the pacemaker and neurotransmitters.
5. Exercise strengthens the heart muscle and the muscles of the limbs that help force blood through the veins.

37–2 Blood and the Lymphatic System

Just as a plumbing system carries water through a series of pipes to different parts of a house, the circulatory system carries blood through a series of blood vessels to different parts of the body. Blood is a type of connective tissue containing both dissolved substances and specialized cells. Blood collects oxygen from the lungs, nutrients from the digestive tract, and waste products from tissues. Blood helps to regulate factors in the body's internal environment, such as body temperature. In addition, components in blood help to fight infections. Blood can even form clots to repair damaged blood vessels.

Guide for Reading

Key Concepts
- What is the function of each type of blood cell?
- What is the role of the lymphatic system?

Vocabulary
plasma
hemoglobin
phagocyte
platelet
lymph

Reading Strategy: Asking Questions Before you read, rewrite the headings in the sections as *how, why,* or *what* questions about blood and the lymphatic system. As you read, write brief answers to the heading questions.

Blood Plasma

The human body contains 4 to 6 liters of blood, which is about 8 percent of the total mass of the body. As **Figure 37–7** shows, about 45 percent of the volume of blood consists of cells, which are suspended in the other 55 percent—a straw-colored fluid called **plasma.** Plasma is about 90 percent water and 10 percent dissolved gases, salts, nutrients, enzymes, hormones, waste products, and proteins called plasma proteins.

Plasma proteins, which perform a variety of functions, are divided into three groups: albumins, globulins, and fibrinogen. Albumins and globulins transport substances such as fatty acids, hormones, and vitamins. Albumins also help to regulate osmotic pressure and blood volume. Some globulins fight viral and bacterial infections. Fibrinogen is the protein responsible for the ability of blood to clot.

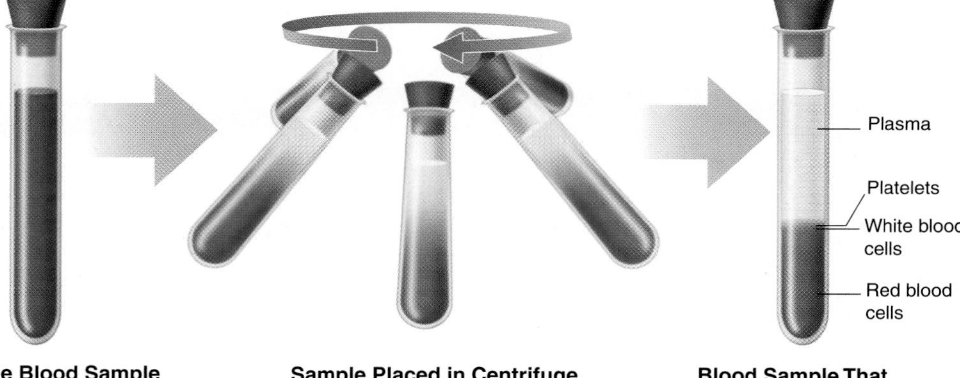

▼ **Figure 37–7** Blood consists of plasma, blood cells, nutrients, hormones, waste products, and plasma proteins. **Interpreting Graphics** ***What happens when a whole blood sample is placed in a centrifuge?***

SECTION RESOURCES

Print:
- ***Teaching Resources,*** Section Review 37–2
- ***Guided Reading and Study Workbook,*** Section 37–2

Technology:
- ***iText,*** Section 37–2

Section 37–2

1 FOCUS

Objectives

37.2.1 ***Describe*** blood plasma.
37.2.2 ***Explain*** the functions of red blood cells, white blood cells, and platelets.
37.2.3 ***Describe*** the role of the lymphatic system.

Guide for Reading

Vocabulary Preview

Have students preview new vocabulary by skimming the section and listing the boldfaced terms. They should leave space to make notes as they read the section.

Reading Strategy

Suggest that students preview section content by studying the figures and reading the captions. They should write down any unfamiliar terms and try to find the meanings as they read.

2 INSTRUCT

Blood Plasma

Meet Diverse Needs

Help at-risk students understand the composition of plasma by working with them to make a concept map that shows its components: water; salts; nutrients; enzymes; hormones; dissolved gases; waste products; and the plasma proteins, which include albumins, globulins, and fibrinogens. Suggest that students save their concept maps for study guides.
Limited English proficiency

Use Community Resources

Have students contact their local chapter of the American Red Cross to learn about blood banks and blood drives in their community. Suggest that they try to find out who can and cannot donate blood, how donations are made, and what happens to the donated blood. Urge students to share what they learn with the class.

Answer to . . .

Figure 37–7 *The cellular portion and plasma portion of blood separate.*

Blood Cells

Meet Diverse Needs

Help students appreciate the relative proportions of red and white cells in blood. Point out that a milliliter of blood contains about 5 million red blood cells (about 5.2 million cells in males and about 4.7 million cells in females) and that red blood cells outnumber white blood cells about 700 to 1. Ask: **How many white blood cells are there in a milliliter of blood?** *(About 7,000)* **If a milliliter of blood was found to have 20,000 white blood cells, what might explain this increase?** *(An infection)* **Learning modality: logical/mathematical**

Use Community Resources

Arrange for interested students to visit a clinic or hospital laboratory where they can observe blood counts being performed. If possible, have a lab technician or supervisor explain why blood counts are performed and what can be learned from them. Other topics the technician or supervisor might address include the importance of accuracy in blood counts and the safety precautions that must be taken when handling blood samples. Have students report to the class on what they learn.

Meet Diverse Needs

Guide students in organizing the material in the text on blood cells in a compare/contrast table. Suggest that students use headings for type of blood cell, number, size, shape, function(s), presence/absence of nucleus, source, and lifespan. Then, challenge students to fill in the table with a row for red blood cells and a row for white blood cells. Check their completed tables for accuracy. Advise students to save their tables for study guides. **Limited English proficiency**

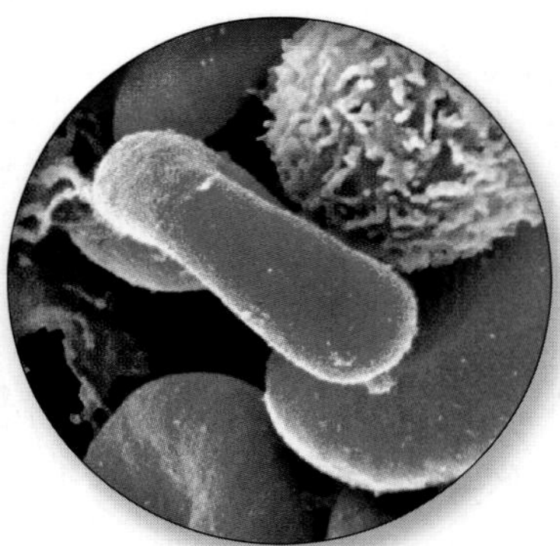

(magnification: 6000×)

▲ **Figure 37–8** **Red blood cells transport oxygen. White blood cells fight invasions of foreign substances, cells, and organisms.** Red blood cells and a single white blood cell are shown in this scanning electron micrograph.

Blood Cells

The cellular portion of blood consists of red blood cells, white blood cells, and platelets. Red blood cells transport oxygen, white blood cells perform a variety of protective functions, and platelets help in the clotting process.

Red Blood Cells The most numerous cells in the blood are the red blood cells, or erythrocytes (eh-RITH-roh-syts). One milliliter of blood contains about 5 million red blood cells. **Red blood cells transport oxygen.** They get their color from hemoglobin. **Hemoglobin** is the iron-containing protein that binds to oxygen in the lungs and transports it to tissues throughout the body where the oxygen is released.

Red blood cells, like those shown in **Figure 37–8,** are shaped like disks that are thinner in the center than along the edges. These cells are produced from cells in red bone marrow. As these cells gradually become filled with hemoglobin, their nuclei and other organelles are forced out. Thus, mature red blood cells do not have nuclei. Red blood cells circulate for an average of 120 days before they are worn out from squeezing through narrow capillaries. They are destroyed in the liver and spleen.

White Blood Cells White blood cells, or leukocytes (LOO-koh-syts), are much less abundant than red blood cells, which outnumber them about 700 to 1. White blood cells also are produced in red bone marrow, but they are released into blood with nuclei and do not contain hemoglobin. Some white blood cells live for months, but most live for just a few days.

White blood cells are the "army" of the circulatory system. **White blood cells attack foreign substances or organisms.** These include cancer cells, substances that cause allergic reactions, and transplanted organs. White blood cells called **phagocytes,** or "eating cells," engulf and digest foreign cells. Other white blood cells can slip across capillary walls and attack invading organisms in body tissues. Still others release chemicals that help the body fight disease and resist infection. **Figure 37–9** lists different types of white blood cells.

▼ **Figure 37–9** This table shows five types of white blood cells and their functions. **Interpreting Graphics** ***Which white blood cells produce antibodies?***

White Blood Cells

Cell Type	Function
Neutrophils	Engulf and destroy small bacteria and foreign substances
Eosinophils	Attack parasites; limit inflammation associated with allergic reactions
Basophils	Release histamines that cause inflammation; release anticoagulants, which prevent blood clots
Monocytes	Give rise to leukocytes that engulf and destroy large bacteria and substances
Lymphocytes	Some destroy foreign cells by causing their membranes to rupture; some develop into cells that produce antibodies, which target specific foreign substances

TIME SAVER **PRESENTATIONS MADE EASY!**

The Presentation Assistant Plus contains the Prentice Hall Presentation Pro and the Transparencies, which provide easy-to-follow visual support for every step of this section. If you have a computer presentation station, use Prentice Hall Presentation Pro for Section 37–2, or use the transparencies listed here.

Section 37–2:

Interest Grabber
Section Outline
Blood Transfusions
Figure 37–7
Figure 37–9
Figure 37–10
Figure 37–12

Like an army with units in reserve, the body is able to increase the number of white blood cells dramatically when a "battle" is underway. A sudden increase in the number of white cells is one of the ways by which physicians can tell that the body is fighting a serious infection.

Platelets and Blood Clotting Blood is essential to life. An injury can cause the body to lose this essential fluid. Fortunately, blood has an internal mechanism to slow bleeding and begin healing. A minor cut or scrape may bleed for a few seconds or minutes, but then it stops. Clean it up with soap and water, cover it with a bandage, and it begins to heal. Have you ever wondered why the bleeding stops?

The answer is that blood has the ability to form a clot. **Figure 37–10** summarizes the process. **Blood clotting is made possible by plasma proteins and cell fragments called platelets.** There are certain large cells in bone marrow that can break into thousands of small pieces. Each fragment of cytoplasm is enclosed in a piece of cell membrane and released into the bloodstream as a **platelet**.

When platelets come into contact with the edges of a broken blood vessel, their surfaces become very sticky, and a cluster of platelets develops around the wound. These platelets then release proteins called clotting factors. The clotting factors start a series of chemical reactions that are quite complicated. In one reaction, a clotting factor called thromboplastin (thrahm-boh-PLAS-tin) converts prothrombin, which is found in blood plasma, into thrombin. Thrombin is an enzyme that helps convert the soluble plasma protein fibrinogen into a sticky mesh of fibrin filaments. These filaments stop the bleeding by producing a clot. **Figure 37–11** shows the tangle of microscopic fibers in an actual blood clot.

What are platelets?

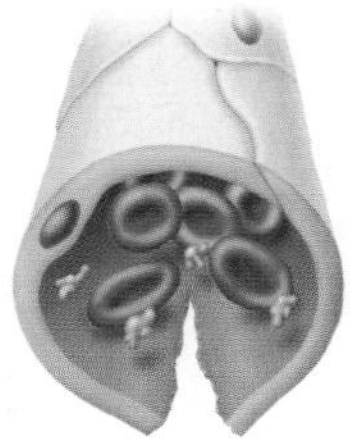

Break in Capillary Wall

Blood vessels injured.

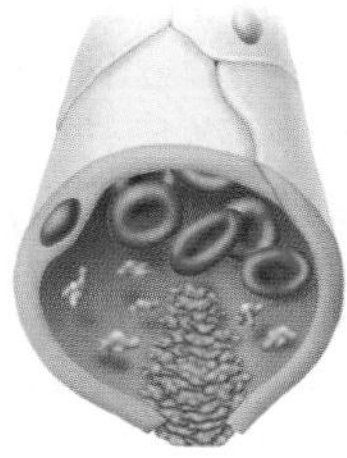

Clumping of Platelets

Platelets clump at the site and release thromboplastin. Thromboplastin converts prothrombin into thrombin.

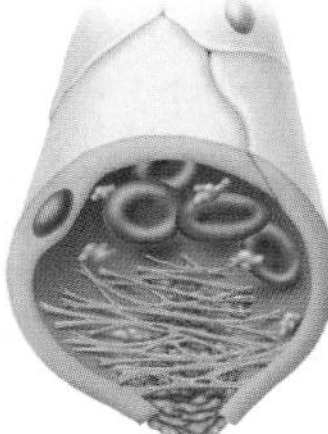

Clot Forms

Thrombin converts fibrinogen into fibrin, which causes a clot. The clot prevents further loss of blood.

▲ **Figure 37–10** **Blood clotting is made possible by a number of plasma proteins and cell fragments called platelets.** Calcium and vitamin K aid in converting prothrombin into thrombin.

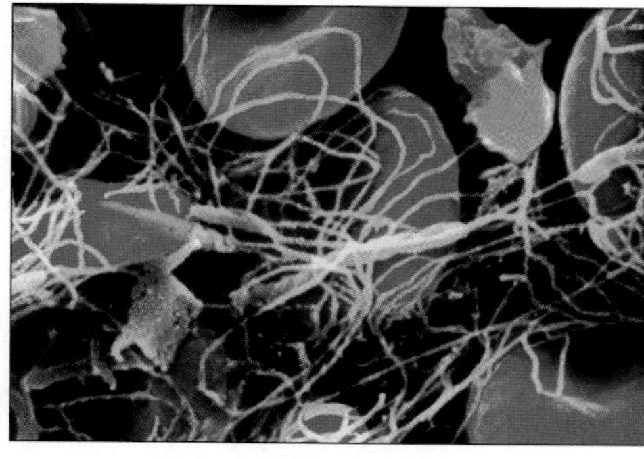

(magnification: 3000×)

▶ **Figure 37–11** Strands of fibrin trap blood cells, forming a net that prevents blood from leaving a damaged blood vessel. **Using Analogies** ***How is a blood clot similar to a screened-in porch?***

Demonstration

Use a microprojector to display prepared slides of red blood cells, white blood cells, and platelets. Have students make a sketch of each structure. Then, call on students to describe the size, shape, and general appearance of each structure.

Meet Diverse Needs

Challenge gifted students to find out how hemophilia is inherited and why it occurs almost solely in males. Suggest that they focus on the example of hemophilia in the family of Queen Victoria of England. They should find a family tree showing which of Victoria's descendants had the disease or carried the gene for it. Ask volunteers to explain to the class how hemophilia is inherited and use the family tree to illustrate their explanation. **Learning modality: verbal**

Use Visuals

Figure 37–10 Check students' comprehension of the figure by having them identify each of the following in the drawings: red blood cells (red), platelets (pink), and fibrin filaments (blue). Then, ask: **What is the main role of platelets in blood clotting?** *(The production of clotting factors such as thromboplastin)* **What role do calcium and vitamin K play in blood clotting?** *(They help convert prothrombin to thrombin.)*

BIO INSIGHTS — FACTS AND FIGURES

Red cell shapes

Normal red blood cells are disk-shaped, but some people have red blood cells with abnormal shapes, such as spherical, oval, or sickle shapes. People with spherical red blood cells have an inherited disorder called spherocytosis. Because of their shape, the red cells become trapped and destroyed by the spleen, leading to anemia. Treatment may include removal of the spleen, which corrects the anemia but not the abnormal shape of the red cells. People with oval red blood cells have the inherited disorder elliptocytosis. This sometimes causes mild anemia but usually requires no treatment. People with sickle shaped red blood cells have sickle cell disease, another inherited disorder and the most serious of the three disorders. Sickle cell disease can cause severe anemia, organ damage, deformities, and even death.

Answers to . . .

CHECKPOINT *Platelets are cell fragments that form a cluster around a wound and release clotting factors.*

Figure 37–9 *Lymphocytes*

Figure 37–11 *It is similar in forming a mesh barrier that prevents blood from leaving a damaged vessel.*

Analyzing Data

Provide students with background on the ABO blood type. Explain that it is determined by antigens on the surfaces of red blood cells: type A red cells have the A antigen, type B the B antigen, type AB both A and B antigens, and type O no antigens. Challenge students to identify which types of blood can be transfused safely into people of each blood type. *(Type A can receive types A and O; type B can receive types B and O; type AB can receive types A, B, AB, and O; and type O blood can receive only type O.)*

Answers

1. Type O is sometimes referred to as the "universal donor," because it can be successfully transfused into people of any blood type. Type AB is sometimes referred to as the "universal recipient," because people with this blood type can be transfused safely with any type of blood.

2. Yes, because people with type A blood can safely receive type O blood, but people with type O blood cannot safely receive type A blood

3. Students might hypothesize that the recipient's immune system attacks transfused blood if it is of a different type than the recipient's own blood, but not if it is of the same type.

The Lymphatic System

Meet Diverse Needs

Pair at-risk students with students who are doing well in the class, and have each pair create a graphic organizer showing similarities and differences between the lymphatic and circulatory systems. *(For example, a Venn diagram might show that both contain a network of vessels with one-way valves, but the lymphatic system contains lymph and the circulatory system contains blood.)* Encourage pairs of students to exchange graphic organizers for comparison. **Limited English proficiency**

Analyzing Data

Predicting the Success of Blood Transfusions

The first successful transfusions of human blood were performed by the British physician James Blundell between 1825 and 1830. Blundell's records indicated that at least half of his patients benefited from the transfusions, but many others had severe reactions to the transfused blood, and several of these patients died. In 1900, Karl Landsteiner, an Austrian physician, discovered why some of Blundell's patients had such severe reactions and why others died.

Landsteiner discovered the ABO blood group, which has four blood types: A, B, AB, and O. When the blood type of a donor and recipient matched, the transfusion was almost always successful. Sometimes, transfusions were successful even when the blood types of donor and recipient did not match. Use the table showing successful and unsuccessful blood transfusions to answer the following questions.

Blood Transfusions

Blood Type of Donor	Blood Type of Recipient			
	A	B	AB	O
A	✓	X	✓	X
B	X	✓	✓	X
AB	X	X	✓	X
O	✓	✓	✓	✓

X = Unsuccessful transfusion ✓ = Successful transfusion

1. **Drawing Conclusions** One blood type is sometimes referred to as the "universal donor." Which blood type is it and why? Another blood type is known as the "universal recipient." Which blood type is it and why?
2. **Drawing Conclusions** In a transfusion involving the A and O blood types, does it make a difference which blood type belongs to the recipient and which to the donor?
3. **Formulating Hypotheses** Propose a hypothesis about the effect of differences in blood type on the success of transfusions.

If the wound is small, within a few minutes the mesh of platelets and fibrin seals the wound, and bleeding stops. Most of the time, this clotting reaction works so well that we take it for granted. However, if one of the clotting factors is missing or defective, the clotting process does not work well. Hemophilia is a genetic disorder that results from a defective protein in the clotting pathway. People with hemophilia cannot produce blood clots that are firm enough to stop even minor bleeding. They must take great care to avoid injury. Fortunately, hemophilia can be treated by injecting extracts containing the missing clotting factor.

The Lymphatic System

As blood circulates, some fluid leaks from the blood into the surrounding tissues. This isn't an altogether bad thing. A steady flow of fluid helps to maintain an efficient movement of nutrients and salts from the blood into the tissues. However, more than 3 liters of fluid leak from the circulatory system into surrounding tissues every day! If this leakage continued unchecked, the body would begin to swell with fluid—not a very pleasant prospect.

Fortunately, this does not happen. **A network of vessels called the lymphatic system (lim-FAT-ik) collects the fluid that is lost by the blood and returns it to the circulatory system.** The fluid is known as **lymph** (LIMF).

FACTS AND FIGURES

Lymphatic facts

Other lymphatic tissues include the thymus, spleen, and tonsils. The thymus is located in the chest underneath the sternum. It attains its full size by age two, and then decreases in size until puberty, by which time it has almost disappeared, although it continues to function in adulthood. Its role is to secrete hormones that help T lymphocytes mature and function. The fist-sized spleen is located in the left side of the abdominal cavity under the diaphragm. Its chief role is to filter bacteria and aging red blood cells from the blood. The tonsils consist of three sets of lymphatic tissue located in the throat. Their primary role is to trap and destroy bacteria that enter the upper respiratory tract. One set of tonsils protrudes from each side of the pharynx behind the mouth. This is the set that is removed in a tonsillectomy. Another set is located higher up in the pharynx behind the nose. These tonsils are commonly called adenoids.

It collects in lymphatic capillaries and slowly flows into larger and larger lymph vessels. Like large veins, lymph vessels contain valves that prevent lymph from flowing backward. Ducts collect the lymph and return it to the circulatory system through two openings in the superior vena cava. The openings are under the left and right clavicle bones just below the shoulders. **Figure 37–12** shows the lymphatic system.

Along the length of the lymph vessels are small bean-shaped enlargements called lymph nodes. Lymph nodes act as filters, trapping bacteria and other microorganisms that cause disease. When large numbers of microorganisms are trapped in the lymph nodes, the nodes become enlarged. If you have ever had "swollen glands," you actually had swollen lymph nodes. The lymph nodes also house specialized white blood cells called lymphocytes, which protect the body from infection.

Lymph vessels do not merely return excess fluid to the circulation. They also play a very important role in nutrient absorption. Lymph vessels lie near the cells that line the intestines, where they absorb fats and fat-soluble vitamins (A, D, E, and K) from the digestive tract and carry them to the blood. Lymph moves through the lymphatic system under osmotic pressure from the blood and is pushed along by the contractions of nearby skeletal muscles. It is important that there is a steady flow of lymph. Edema, a swelling of the tissues due to the accumulation of excess fluid, can occur when lymphatic vessels are blocked due to injury or disease.

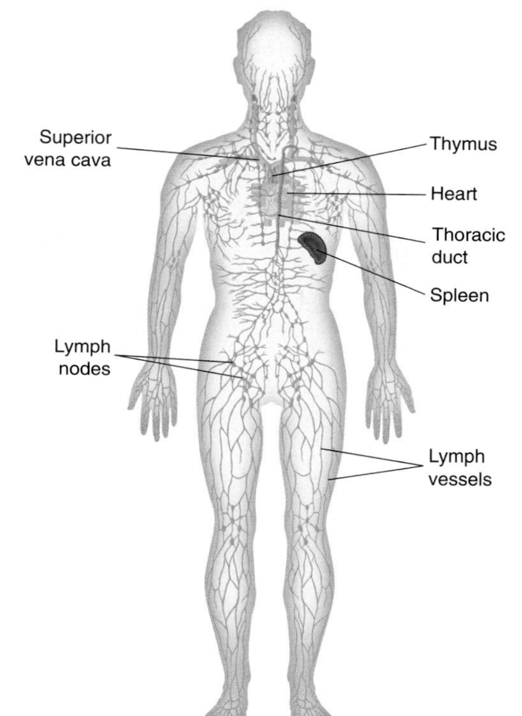

▲ **Figure 37–12** **The lymphatic system collects and returns fluid that leaks from blood vessels.** The spleen is a mass of lymphatic tissue whose main function is to destroy damaged red blood cells and platelets. Certain white blood cells called T cells mature in the thymus gland, which produces hormones that promote their development.

37–2 Section Assessment

1. **Key Concept** List the main function of red blood cells, white blood cells, and platelets.
2. **Key Concept** Describe the role of the lymphatic system.
3. What types of materials are dissolved in plasma?
4. Explain how blood clots.
5. **Critical Thinking Relating Cause and Effect** Infections sometimes cause severe swelling in the tissues. Explain why this happens.

iTEXT Assessment Use iText to review the important concepts in Section 37–2.

ALTERNATIVE ASSESSMENT

Constructing a Concept Map

Construct a concept map that shows the components of blood. Be sure to include the different types of white blood cells.

Use Visuals

Figure 37–12 Have students compare the distribution of lymphatic vessels with the distribution of blood vessels, shown in Figure 37–3. Then, ask: **How are the lymphatic and circulatory systems related?** *(The lymphatic system collects fluid that seeps into the tissues from blood and returns it to the circulatory system.)* Point out that the vein where this fluid is returned to the blood is called the superior vena cava. Have students find the superior vena cava in the figure. Also have them locate the clusters of lymph nodes. Ask: **If you had a sore throat because of an infection, which lymph nodes might become swollen?** *(The lymph nodes in the neck)*

3 ASSESS

Evaluate Understanding

Call on students at random to name each component of the blood. Call on other students to describe the function of each component.

Reteach

Using the chalkboard or a transparency, work with students to create a concept map of the functions of blood based on information in the opening paragraph of the section. Then, have students identify the parts of the blood involved in each function.

ALTERNATIVE ASSESSMENT

Students' concept maps should show that blood consists of plasma, platelets, red blood cells, and white blood cells, of which there are five main types: neutrophils, eosinophils, basophils, monocytes, and lymphoctyes.

37–2 Section Assessment

1. Red blood cells carry oxygen; white blood cells fight infection; platelets help blood to clot.
2. Its role is to collect fluid lost by blood and return it to the circulatory system.
3. Gases, salts, nutrients, enzymes, hormones, waste products, and plasma proteins
4. When platelets come in contact with the broken edges of a blood vessel, their surfaces become sticky. A cluster of platelets develops around the wound. The platelets release clotting factors, which start reactions that produce a blood clot.
5. When microorganisms that cause disease are trapped in lymph nodes, the nodes become enlarged, blocking the lymph vessels. This blockage allows fluids to accumulate in the tissues, which causes the tissues to swell.

Use iText to review the key concepts in Section 37–2.

Section 37–3

1 FOCUS

Objectives

37.3.1 ***Describe*** respiration.
37.3.2 ***Identify*** the structures of the respiratory system.
37.3.3 ***Describe*** gas exchange and breathing.
37.3.4 ***Explain*** how smoking affects the respiratory system.

Guide for Reading

Vocabulary Preview

Call students' attention to the Vocabulary terms. Ask: **Which term refers to a respiratory disease?** *(Emphysema)* **Which term refers to a toxic chemical in tobacco smoke?** *(Nicotine)* Point out that all the rest of the words are structures of the respiratory system.

Reading Strategy

Before students read the section, have them predict how respiration, gas exchange, and breathing are related. As they read, they should check to see if their predictions were correct.

2 INSTRUCT

What Is Respiration?

Address Misconceptions

Students may have the misconception that breathing is the same as respiration. Remind students that respiration is the exchange of gases that takes place in the alveoli of the lungs. Breathing is the movement of air into and out of the lungs. Ask: **How is breathing related to respiration?** *(Inhaling provides a fresh supply of oxygen to the lungs; exhaling removes excess carbon dioxide from the lungs.)*

37–3 The Respiratory System

Guide for Reading

Key Concepts
- What are the structures of the respiratory system?
- How does smoking affect the respiratory system?

Vocabulary
- pharynx • trachea
- larynx • bronchus
- alveolus • diaphragm
- nicotine • emphysema

Reading Strategy: Monitoring Your Understanding Make a table with three columns labeled *K, W,* and *L.* Before you read, write what you know about respiration in Column K and what you want to learn in Column W. After you read, write what you have learned in Column L.

When paramedics rush to the aid of an injured person, they check to see if the person is breathing. If the person's chest is not rising and falling and they cannot feel or hear air being exhaled from the mouth or nose, the person is not breathing. Paramedics will ignore broken bones or burns to focus on breathing because there is no time to lose! If breathing stops for more than a few minutes, a life may be lost.

Paramedics can do mouth-to-mouth rescue breathing to force air into the lungs. They can do chest compressions to keep the blood circulating. Cardiopulmonary resuscitation, or CPR, is rescue breathing combined with chest compressions.

What Is Respiration?

In biology, the word *respiration* is used in two slightly different ways. At the cellular level, respiration is defined as the release of energy from the breakdown of molecules in food in the presence of oxygen. Without oxygen, cells lose much of their ability to produce ATP. Without ATP, cells cannot synthesize new molecules, pump ions, and carry nerve impulses.

The blood carries oxygen and carbon dioxide—a waste product of cellular respiration—between the lungs and the trillions of cells throughout the body. The process by which oxygen and carbon dioxide are exchanged between cells, the blood, and air in the lungs is also known as respiration.

The Human Respiratory System

The basic job performed by the human respiratory system is remarkably simple—to bring about the exchange of oxygen and carbon dioxide. With each breath, air enters the body through the air passageways and fills the lungs, where gas exchange takes place. **The respiratory system consists of the nose, pharynx, larynx, trachea, bronchi, and lungs.**

Figure 37–14 shows the structures of the respiratory system. Air moves through the nose to a tube at the back of the mouth called the pharynx, or throat. The **pharynx** serves as a passageway for both air and food. Air moves from the pharynx into the **trachea**, or windpipe. A piece of cartilage called the epiglottis covers the entrance to the trachea when you swallow.

(magnification: 5600×)

◀ **Figure 37–13** In this cross section of the trachea, the cilia have been colored green. **Inferring** *What is the role of cilia in the respiratory system?*

SECTION RESOURCES

Print:
- ***Laboratory Manual A,*** Chapter 37 Lab
- ***Teaching Resources,*** Section Review 37–3
- ***Guided Reading and Study Workbook,*** Section 37–3
- ***Issues and Decision Making,*** 37–1

Technology:
- ***iText,*** Section 37–3

Figure 37–14 The Respiratory System

The respiratory system consists of the nose, pharynx, larynx, trachea, a series of smaller passageways, and lungs. Bronchi branch into smaller and smaller tubes called bronchioles, which end in alveoli, or air sacs.

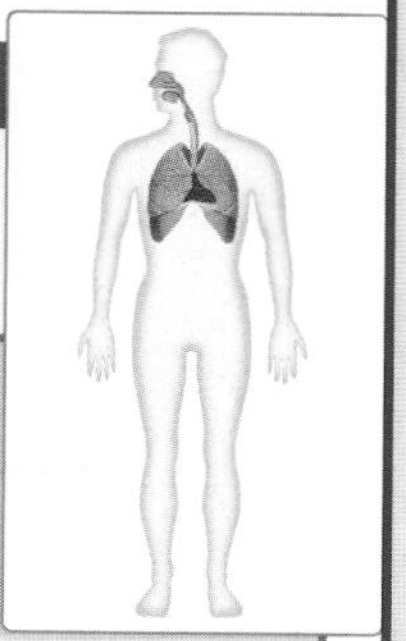

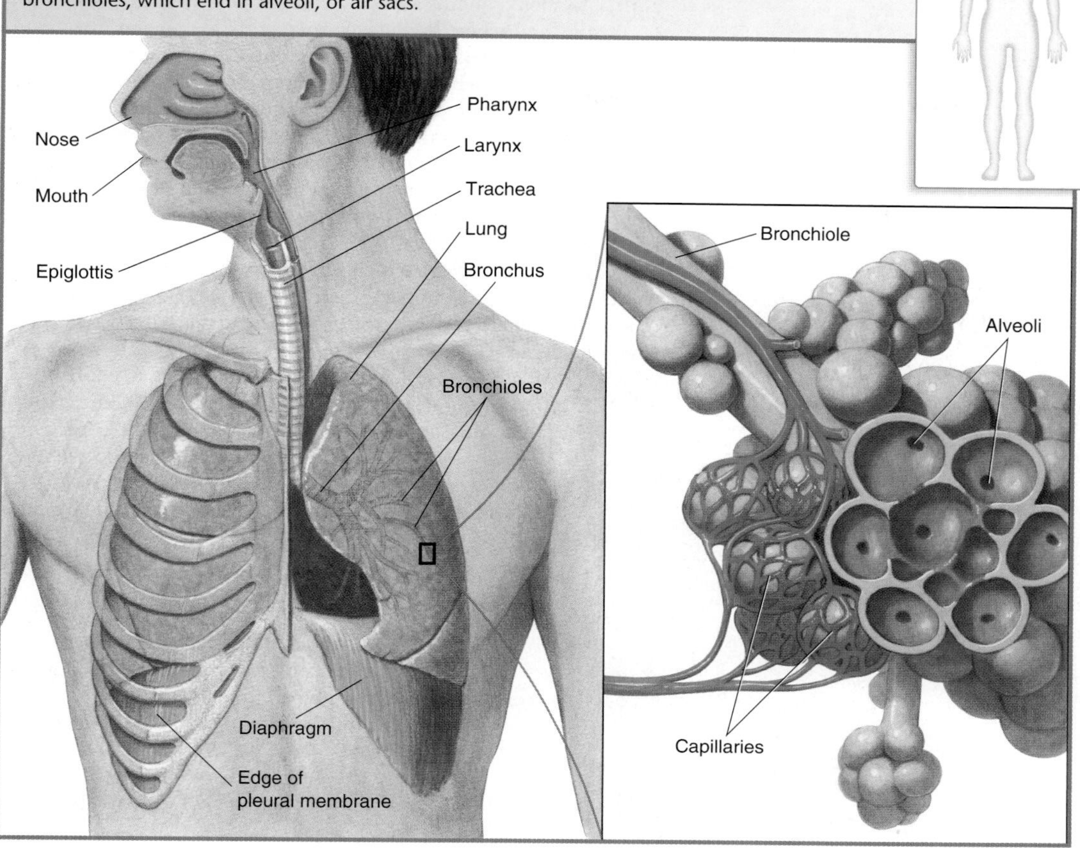

The respiratory passageways allow air to pass directly into some of the most delicate tissues in the body. To keep the lung tissue healthy, air entering the respiratory system must be warmed, moistened, and filtered. Large dust particles get trapped by the hairs lining the entrance to the nasal cavity. Some of the cells that line the respiratory system produce a thin layer of mucus. The mucus moistens the air and traps inhaled particles of dust or smoke. Cilia sweep the trapped particles and mucus away from the lungs toward the pharynx. The mucus and trapped particles are either swallowed or spit out. These protective measures help keep the lungs clean and open for the important work of gas exchange.

CHECKPOINT *What is the pharynx?*

The Human Respiratory System

Use Visuals

Figure 37–14 Make sure students understand how the drawing on the right relates to the drawing on the left. Have students use the drawings to trace the pathway of air through the respiratory system as they read about it in the text. They should identify each of the structures through which the air passes, starting with the nose and ending with the alveoli.

Meet Diverse Needs

Give students a chance to create three-dimensional models of the respiratory system using such materials as modeling clay, string, dry pasta and beans, and craft items. Students' models should show the relative size, shape, and position of each of the following structures: nose, pharynx, larynx, trachea, bronchi, and lungs. Urge students to share their models with the class. **Learning modality: tactile**

Use Community Resources

Invite a paramedic to demonstrate to the class artificial respiration and the Heimlich maneuver. Before the paramedic arrives, tell students that people sometimes stop breathing in cases of drowning, electric shock, or smoke inhalation and that artificial breathing helps keep them alive until they begin breathing again on their own. Also explain how choking occurs because of the dual role of the pharynx in the digestive and respiratory systems. Suggest that students prepare questions in advance for the paramedic to address.

Time Saver — Presentations Made Easy!

The Presentation Assistant Plus contains the Prentice Hall Presentation Pro and the Transparencies, which provide easy-to-follow visual support for every step of this section. If you have a computer presentation station, use Prentice Hall Presentation Pro for Section 37–3, or use the transparencies listed here.

Section 37–3:

Interest Grabber
Section Outline
Flowchart
Figure 37–14
Figure 37–15
Figure 37–16

Answers to . . .

CHECKPOINT *The pharynx is a tube at the back of the mouth that serves as a passageway for both air and food.*

Figure 37–13 *Cilia sweep mucus and trapped particles away from the lungs toward the pharynx.*

Meet Diverse Needs

Help at-risk students develop a memory aid for remembering the correct sequence of structures in the respiratory system: nose, pharynx, larynx, trachea, bronchus, bronchiole, alveolus. Give them an example, such as "nine people lost their book bags already." Suggest to students with limited English proficiency that they write the names of the structures both in English and in their own language and then develop a similar memory aid in their own language to remember the correct sequence. **Limited English proficiency**

Gas Exchange

Build Science Skills

Inferring Explain how exhaled air is used in artificial respiration. Point out that exhaled air has already gone through the gas exchange process in the lungs. Ask: **How can artificial respiration provide the person receiving the "second-hand" air with enough oxygen to survive?** *(Exhaled air contains less oxygen than inhaled air but enough to keep a person alive.)*

Demonstration

Make limewater in a clear glass container by adding calcium hydroxide to water until the solution is saturated. Tell students that when carbon dioxide reacts with limewater, it causes the limewater to turn cloudy. Have a student volunteer exhale through a straw into the limewater. (Caution the student not to suck any of the limewater through the straw.) While the student exhales, have other students observe what happens. (The limewater turns cloudy.) Ask: **Why did the limewater turn cloudy?** *(Because the exhaled breath contained carbon dioxide)*

At the top of the trachea is the larynx. The **larynx** contains two highly elastic folds of tissue known as the vocal cords. When muscles pull the vocal cords together, the air moving between them causes the cords to vibrate and produce sounds. Your ability to speak, shout, and sing comes from these tissues.

From the larynx, air passes through the trachea into two large passageways in the chest cavity called **bronchi** (singular: bronchus). Each bronchus leads to one of the lungs. Within each lung, the large bronchi subdivides into smaller bronchi, which lead to even smaller passageways called bronchioles. Air moving along this path can be compared to a motorist who takes an exit off an eight-lane highway onto a four-lane highway, makes a turn onto a two-lane road, and ends up on a narrow country lane.

The bronchi and bronchioles are surrounded by smooth muscle that helps to support them and enables the autonomic nervous system to regulate the size of the air passageways. The bronchioles continue to subdivide until they reach a series of dead ends—millions of tiny air sacs called **alveoli** (al-VEE-uh-ly; singular: alveolus). Alveoli are grouped in little clusters, like bunches of grapes. A delicate network of thin-walled capillaries surrounds each alveolus. The real work of the respiratory system takes place here, where blood and air are side by side.

▼ **Figure 37–15** Gas exchange occurs by diffusion across the membrane of an alveolus and a capillary. **Drawing Conclusions** ***Where is oxygen more concentrated, in an alveolus or in a capillary?***

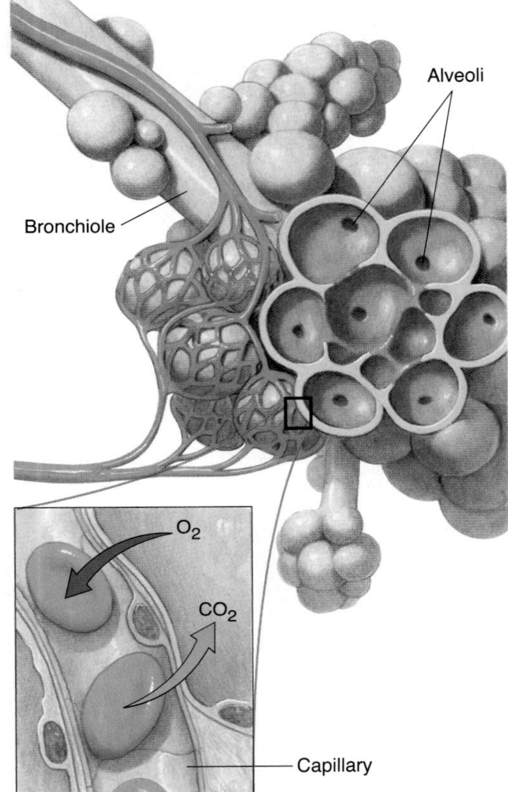

Gas Exchange

There are about 350 million alveoli in a healthy lung, providing an enormous surface area for gas exchange. Oxygen dissolves in the moisture on the inner surface of the alveoli and then diffuses across the thin-walled capillaries into the blood. Carbon dioxide in the bloodstream diffuses in the opposite direction, across the membrane of an alveolus and into the air within it. This process is illustrated in **Figure 37–15.**

The process of gas exchange in the lungs is very efficient. The air that you inhale usually contains 21 percent oxygen and 0.04 percent carbon dioxide. Exhaled air usually contains less than 15 percent oxygen and 4 percent carbon dioxide. The lungs remove about one third of the oxygen in the air that you inhale and increase the carbon dioxide content of that air by a factor of 100.

Because oxygen dissolves easily, you may wonder why hemoglobin, the oxygen-carrying protein in blood, is needed at all. The reason is efficiency. Hemoglobin binds with so much oxygen that it increases the oxygen-carrying capacity of the blood more than 60 times. Without hemoglobin to carry the oxygen that it uses, your body might need as much as 300 liters of blood to get the same result!

FACTS AND FIGURES

Breathing ins and outs

Breathing is one of the most fundamental of all bodily functions. We can go several days without eating, a few days without drinking, but only a few minutes without breathing. The average person takes in about 16 kg of air each day, compared with only about 3 kg of solid food and liquids combined. During just one day, the average adult breathes in and out a total of some 16,000 L of air. However, because air moves into and out of the lungs through the same passageways, only about 10 percent of the air in the lungs is replaced with each breath. The alveoli's job of moving gases from air to blood and blood to air requires a huge network of capillaries. At any given time, about one fourth of the body's total blood supply is concentrated in the capillaries around the alveoli of the lungs.

Careers in Biology

Respiratory Care Practitioner

Job Description: provide care for patients with respiratory problems in hospitals, clinics, nursing homes, schools, and at home

Education: a two-year or four-year training program; certification exams; individual states have additional licensing requirements

Skills: good communication skills; enjoy working with people; capable of working independently; good decision-making skills; knowledge of anatomy, physiology, microbiology

Highlights: You provide quick responses in emergency situations. You work as a member of a team.

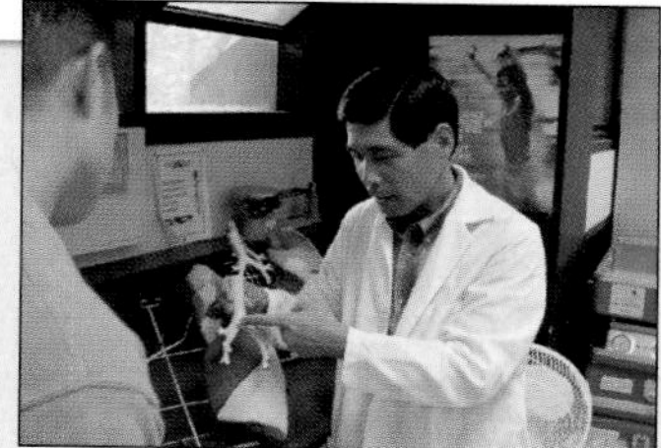

Aaron Koseki left his career as an Asian philosophy professor to start all over as a Respiratory Care Practitioner (RCP). "My oldest son received the help of Respiratory Care Practitioners at birth . . . . The work fascinated me so much that I just had to find out more about breathing . . . in a more scientific sense. That's why I became an RCP."

Take It to the NET For more career information, visit the Prentice Hall Web site at **www.phschool.com.**

Careers in Biology

- Explain that most respiratory care practitioners work in hospitals and that most hospitals have separate respiratory care departments.
- Describe some of the specific job duties of respiratory care practitioners, including maintaining and operating various kinds of breathing equipment, leading aerobic exercise classes, and conducting smoking cessation programs.

Resources For additional information on this career, students can contact the National Board for Respiratory Care or the American Association for Respiratory Care, or they can contact the respiratory care department of a local hospital.

Breathing

Breathing is the movement of air into and out of the lungs. Surprisingly, there are no muscles connected to the lungs. The force that drives air into the lungs comes from ordinary air pressure. How does the body use this force to inflate the lungs? The lungs are sealed in two sacs, called the pleural membranes, inside the chest cavity. At the bottom of the cavity is a large, flat muscle known as the **diaphragm** (DY-uh-fram).

As **Figure 37–16** shows, when you breathe in, or inhale, the diaphragm contracts and expands the volume of the chest cavity. Because the chest cavity is tightly sealed, this creates a partial vacuum inside the cavity. Atmospheric pressure does the rest, filling the lungs as air rushes into the breathing passages.

The system works only because the chest cavity is sealed. A puncture wound to the chest—even if it does not touch the lungs—may allow air to leak into the chest cavity and make breathing impossible. This is one of the reasons chest wounds are always serious.

CHECKPOINT *Why are chest wounds so serious?*

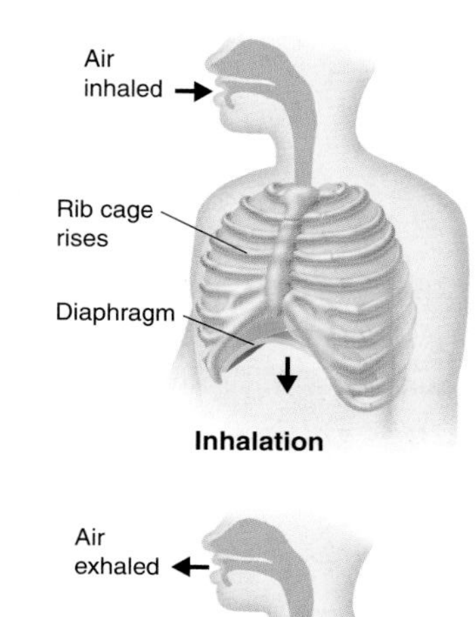

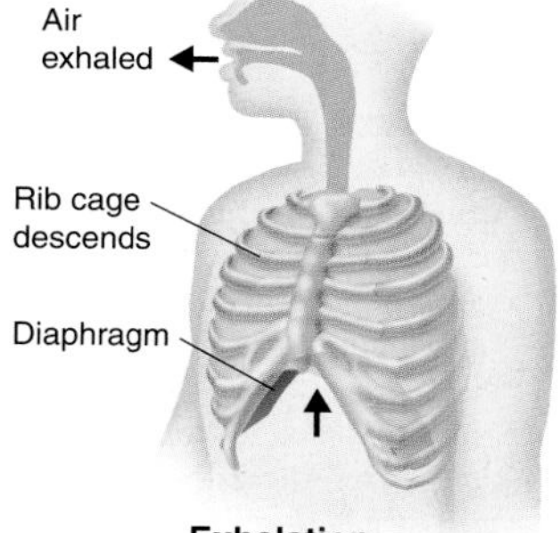

▶ **Figure 37–16** During inhalation, the diaphragm contracts, increasing the size of the chest cavity. This causes the pressure inside the lungs to decrease, and air enters. **Interpreting Graphics** *What happens as the diaphragm relaxes?*

Take It to the NET For additional information, visit **www.phschool.com**

Breathing

Build Science Skills

Measuring Students can measure their lung capacity. (Advise any with respiratory illnesses, such as asthma or bronchitis, to avoid participating.) Give each student a large round balloon and, with students working in pairs, tell students to inhale as large a breath as they can and then to exhale it as completely as possible into the balloon. Students should hold the balloon shut until their partner measures its circumference with a tape measure. Students can calculate their lung capacity by finding the volume of the inflated balloon, using the formula $V = 4/3\pi r^3$, where r is the radius of the inflated balloon. The radius can be found from the circumference, using the formula $c = 2\pi r$.

BIO INSIGHTS — FACTS AND FIGURES

High altitude hypoxia

Hypoxia, or insufficient oxygen reaching the tissues, is a problem at high altitudes. Although air at high altitudes contains the same percentage of oxygen as air at sea level, the air is less dense at higher altitudes, so the amount of oxygen in a given volume is lower. An additional problem is the lower air pressure at high altitudes, which reduces the amount of air that enters the lungs with each breath. At 5,500 meters above sea level, only about half as much air can be taken in with each breath as at sea level. This is why humans cannot live permanently above this altitude. Although theoretically people can compensate for the reduced amount of oxygen in each breath by voluntarily increasing their rate of breathing, this is hard on the cardiovascular system. It is also difficult to maintain voluntary control over breathing if hypoxia has caused mental confusion, as it typically does.

Answers to . . .

CHECKPOINT *Chest wounds are so serious because they may allow air to leak into the chest cavity and make breathing impossible.*

Figure 37–15 *In an alveolus*

Figure 37–16 *As the diaphragm relaxes, the pressure in the chest cavity becomes greater than atmospheric pressure, so air rushes out to the lungs.*

How Breathing Is Controlled

Quick Lab

Objective Students will be able to formulate a hypothesis to explain how breathing is regulated and conclude that the level of carbon dioxide regulates breathing.

Skills Focus **Formulating Hypotheses, Drawing Conclusions**

Materials seltzer tablet, plastic cup or 250-mL beaker, water.

Time 10 minutes

Safety Students who have breathing problems should not perform this lab. Students should remain seated while doing this lab.

Strategies
- For best results use straight-sided plastic cups or beakers.
- If the water is at room temperature, it will produce more carbon dioxide.

Expected Outcome Students should observe that inhaling carbon dioxide makes them feel short of breath and in need of more air.

Analyze and Conclude
1. Students may say they felt short of breath or as if they needed more air.
2. Carbon dioxide
3. If students hypothesized that carbon dioxide regulates breathing, their results supported their hypothesis, because when they inhaled air with greater-than-normal levels of carbon dioxide, they felt the need to breathe more rapidly.

Build Science Skills

Inferring Explain that extremely rapid or deep breathing, which is called hyperventilation, is caused by lower-than-normal levels of carbon dioxide in the blood. Point out that breathing into a paper bag for a few minutes can stop hyperventilation. Ask: **Why does breathing into a paper bag stop hyperventilation?** *(Because it leads to a higher-than-normal level of carbon dioxide in the air that is breathed in, and this slows down the rate of breathing)*

Most of the time, exhaling is a passive event. When the diaphragm muscle relaxes, the pressure in the chest cavity becomes greater than atmospheric pressure. Air rushes back out of the lungs. To blow out a candle, you need a greater force. Muscles surrounding the chest cavity provide that extra force, contracting vigorously just as the diaphragm relaxes.

How Breathing Is Controlled

You can control your breathing almost anytime you want, whether it's to blow up a balloon or to play a musical instrument. But this doesn't mean that breathing is purely voluntary. If you hold your breath for a minute or so, you'll see what happens. Your chest begins to feel tight, your throat begins to burn, and the muscles in your mouth and throat struggle to keep from breathing. Eventually your body takes over. It "forces" you to breathe!

Breathing is such an important function that your nervous system will not let you have complete control over it. The brain controls breathing in a center located in the medulla oblongata. Autonomic nerves from the medulla oblongata to the diaphragm and chest muscles produce the cycles of contraction that bring air into the lungs. How does the medulla oblongata "know" when it's time to breathe? Cells in its breathing center monitor the amount of carbon dioxide in the blood. As the carbon dioxide level rises, nerve impulses from the breathing center cause the diaphragm to contract, bringing air into the lungs. The higher the carbon dioxide level, the stronger the impulses. If the carbon dioxide level reaches a critical point, the impulses become so powerful that you cannot keep from breathing.

Quick Lab

Does oxygen or carbon dioxide regulate breathing?

Materials seltzer tablet, plastic cup

Procedure
1. **Formulating Hypotheses** Which do you think is more important in regulating breathing, the level of oxygen in the air or the level of carbon dioxide? Write a hypothesis about how your breathing will be affected if the level of carbon dioxide increases.
2. Place approximately 100 mL of water in the cup and add a seltzer tablet. The bubbles in the water are carbon dioxide. Bring the cup up to your face and inhale deeply.

Analyze and Conclude
1. **Drawing Conclusions** Describe what happened when you inhaled the carbon dioxide.
2. **Drawing Conclusions** Air is about 21 percent oxygen and about 0.04 percent carbon dioxide. Did your oxygen intake or your carbon dioxide intake change more during step 2?
3. **Drawing Conclusions** Did your results support your hypothesis or not? Explain your answer.

BIOLOGY UPDATE

Asthma on the rise
Asthma is a potentially fatal respiratory illness characterized by repeated asthmatic attacks, during which muscles surrounding the air passages that lead to the lungs contract. Constriction of the air passages makes it difficult to get enough air. It can also cause death in severe attacks. An estimated 5 to 10 percent of high school students suffer from asthma. That number is higher than ever before and still on the rise. Scientists believe that the increase in asthma is partly due to a worsening of air pollution. Laws regulating smokestack emissions and the use of coal have led to a reduction in industrial air pollution. However, there is more air pollution from motor vehicle exhaust, which contains many substances that are harmful to the respiratory system, including carbon monoxide, carbon dioxide, nitrogen oxides, sulfur oxides, lead, and hydrocarbons.

▲ **Figure 37–17** This pilot must use an oxygen mask because there is not enough oxygen available in the air at high altitudes. **Applying Concepts** *How would a mountain climber decide when to carry a supply of oxygen?*

That the breathing center responds primarily to carbon dioxide can have dangerous consequences. Consider a plane flying at high altitude. Although the amount of oxygen in the air decreases as the altitude increases, the passengers do not need oxygen masks because the cabin is pressurized. Oxygen is available for use in an emergency, but the passengers often have to be told to begin breathing the oxygen. Although their bodies may be starving for oxygen, they have no more carbon dioxide in their blood than usual, so the breathing center does not sense a problem. The pilot in **Figure 37–17** is not in a pressurized cabin and must use an oxygen mask at high altitudes.

CHECKPOINT *What does the breathing center do?*

Tobacco and the Respiratory System

The upper part of the respiratory system is generally able to filter out dust and foreign particles that could damage the lungs. Millions of people engage in an activity—smoking tobacco—that damages and eventually destroys this protective system.

Substances in Tobacco Tobacco smoke contains many substances that affect the body. Three of the most dangerous substances are nicotine, carbon monoxide, and tar. **Nicotine** is a stimulant drug that increases the heart rate and blood pressure. Carbon monoxide is a poisonous gas that blocks the transport of oxygen by hemoglobin in the blood. It decreases the blood's ability to supply oxygen to its tissues, depriving the heart and other organs of the oxygen they need to function. Tar contains a number of compounds that have been shown to cause cancer.

Tobacco and the Respiratory System

Demonstration

Demonstrate to students how toxic tobacco is. Before class, make a tobacco solution by boiling tobacco in water for 15 minutes and then straining the solution through a paper towel. Allow the solution to cool. During class, spray the solution on a plant that is infested with aphids, and have students observe what happens. (The aphids will die.) Ask: **What do you think killed the aphids?** *(Something in the tobacco)* Conclude by telling students that the nicotine in tobacco is so toxic that it is actually used as a pesticide.

Meet Diverse Needs

Pair at-risk students with students who excel in science. Have members of each pair work together to create a concept map showing three of the most dangerous substances in tobacco and the detrimental effects of each of the substances on the respiratory system. *(Concept maps should show that nicotine and carbon monoxide paralyze cilia so they cannot keep the lungs clear and that tar causes lung and other cancers of the respiratory system.)* Urge pairs of students to exchange and compare their completed concept maps. **Learning modality: visual**

FACTS AND FIGURES

Smoking, cancer, and death

A person who smokes cigarettes is 10 to 15 times more likely to develop lung cancer than a nonsmoker. The more cigarettes one smokes, the greater the chances of developing lung cancer and the more likely one is to die from lung cancer. If a person smokes two or more packs of cigarettes a day, he or she is 20 to 25 times more likely to die from lung cancer than a nonsmoker. Three of every four deaths from lung cancer in women are caused by smoking. Cancer is not the only risk that smokers face. Smokers are also three times more likely to die from a heart attack than nonsmokers. Men in their thirties who smoke can expect to lose about eight years of life if they do not quit smoking.

Answers to . . .

CHECKPOINT *The breathing center monitors the amount of carbon dioxide in the blood. As the level rises, nerve impulses from the breathing center cause the diaphragm to contract.*

Figure 37–17 *The mountain climber would base the decision on the altitude of the mountain.*

Use Community Resources

Invite a respiratory care practitioner or other knowledgeable health professional to address the class on diseases of the respiratory system caused by smoking. Ask the speaker to describe symptoms of such diseases as chronic bronchitis and emphysema and how the diseases limit the activity and quality of life of people who have them. Also ask the speaker to describe how respiratory therapy is used to help treat the diseases.

Make Connections

Health Science Explain that lung cancer is often fatal because there is no easy way to detect it at an early stage before it has spread. New X-ray techniques now allow doctors to detect very small lung tumors, but determining whether they are cancerous—and most are not—requires a lung biopsy. This is a major surgical procedure with potentially serious risks that is not undertaken lightly. Ask: **If a simple, nonsurgical technique were discovered to detect lung cancer at an early stage, how would this affect treatment of the disease?** *(Being able to detect lung cancer early would allow doctors to treat the cancer or remove the tumor surgically before cancer cells spread to other parts of the body.)*

Build Science Skills

Designing Experiments Challenge small groups of students to design an experiment to determine the effects of a smoking education class on teen smoking attitudes and habits. Students should describe the subject content of the class and how teen smoking attitudes and habits would be measured, both before and after the subjects attended the class. Ask groups to share their experimental designs with the class.

Smoking tobacco brings nicotine and carbon monoxide into the upper respiratory system. These compounds paralyze the cilia. With the cilia out of action, the inhaled particles stick to the walls of the respiratory tract or enter the lungs.

Without cilia to sweep it along, smoke-laden mucus becomes trapped along the airways. This explains why smokers often cough. Irritation from the accumulated mucus triggers a cough that helps to clear the airways. Smoking also causes the lining of the respiratory tract to swell, which reduces the air flow to the alveoli.

Diseases Caused by Smoking Only 30 percent of male smokers live to age 80, but 55 percent of male nonsmokers live to that age. Clearly, smoking reduces life expectancy. **Smoking can cause such respiratory diseases as chronic bronchitis, emphysema, and lung cancer.** In chronic bronchitis, the bronchi become swollen and clogged with mucus. Even smoking a moderate number of cigarettes on a regular basis can produce bronchitis. People with this disease often find simple activities, such as climbing stairs, difficult.

Long-term smoking can also cause a respiratory disease called emphysema (em-fuh-SEE-muh). **Emphysema** is the loss of elasticity in the tissues of the lungs. This condition makes breathing very difficult. People who have emphysema cannot get enough oxygen to the body tissues or rid the body of excess carbon dioxide.

Smoking is an important, but preventable, cause of lung cancer. **Figure 37–18** shows the effects of smoking on the lungs. Lung cancer is particularly deadly because its cells can spread to other locations. By the time lung cancer is detected, it usually has spread to dozens of other places. About 160,000 people in the United States are diagnosed with lung cancer each year. Few will survive for five years after the diagnosis.

▶ **Figure 37–18 Smoking can cause respiratory diseases such as chronic bronchitis, emphysema, and lung cancer.** The lung on the left is from a smoker. The lung on the right is from a nonsmoker.

HISTORY OF SCIENCE

Doll's doctors

It is common knowledge today that cigarette smoking is the major cause of lung cancer and a contributing factor to a number of other serious health problems. However, as recently as 1950, doctors were unaware of the health risks of tobacco use. All that changed in the 1950s with the innovative research of Sir Richard Doll. Doll used epidemiological methods to establish a link between cigarette smoking and many serious illnesses, including lung cancer and heart disease. His approach was to follow a large sample of people over many years to establish correlations between suspected risk factors and the development of disease. Ironically, the sample Doll followed to establish the link between smoking and lung cancer was a group of British doctors. Doll later used the same method to study the effects of other risk factors on cancer development, including the effects of asbestos on the development of lung cancer.

Smoking is also a major cause of heart disease. Smoking constricts, or narrows, the blood vessels. This causes blood pressure to rise and makes the heart work harder. The effects of smoking on the circulatory system can be seen in **Figure 37–19.** There is a drastic change in body temperature and in circulation immediately after smoking a cigarette. Smoking doubles the risk of death from heart disease for men between 45 and 65. Moreover, for men and women of all ages, the risk of death from heart disease is greater among smokers than among nonsmokers.

Smoking and the Nonsmoker In recent years, evidence has shown that tobacco smoke is damaging to anyone who inhales it, not just the smoker. For this reason, many states have restricted smoking in restaurants and other public places.

Passive smoking, or inhaling the smoke of others, is particularly damaging to young children because their lungs are still developing. Studies now indicate that the children of smokers are twice as likely as children of nonsmokers to develop respiratory problems, such as asthma.

Dealing With Tobacco Whatever the age of a smoker, and no matter how long that person has smoked, his or her health can be improved by quitting. Nicotine is a powerful drug with strong addictive qualities that make it very difficult to quit smoking. Thus, considering the cost, the medical dangers, and the powerful addiction, the best solution is not to begin smoking.

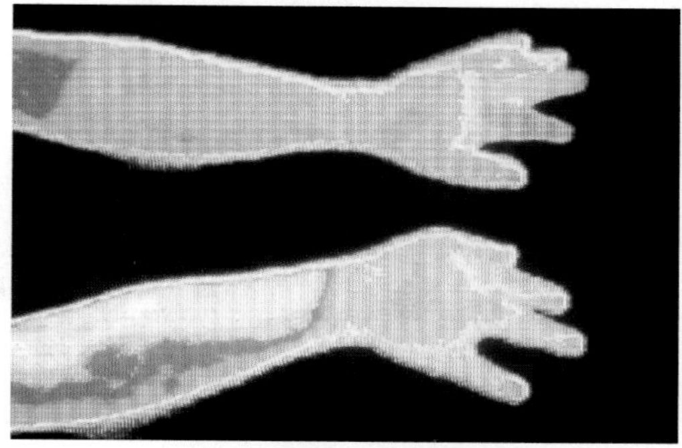

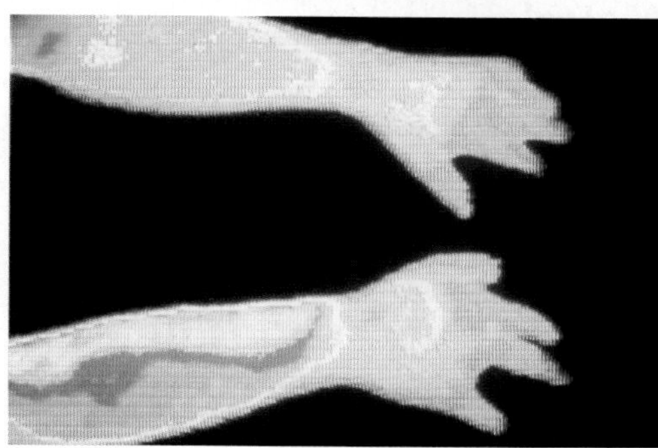

▲ **Figure 37–19** These thermograms provide a color-coded map of temperature distribution over the body surface, with blue = cold and white = hot. The top thermogram shows the forearm and hand area prior to smoking a cigarette. The bottom thermogram shows the same area after smoking. **Interpreting Graphics** ***Do you think circulation is increased or decreased after smoking?***

37–3 Section Assessment

1. **Key Concept** List in order the structures of the respiratory system through which air passes from the outside to the alveoli.
2. **Key Concept** Describe some of the health problems caused by smoking tobacco.
3. Explain the process of gas exchange in the lungs.
4. Describe how breathing is controlled.
5. **Critical Thinking Inferring** As you have read, the breathing center in the brain responds to the level of carbon dioxide in the blood—not the level of oxygen. What consequences does this have for people at high altitudes?

iText Assessment Use iText to review the important concepts in Section 37–3.

MAKING CONNECTIONS

Comparative Anatomy Compare what you learned in Unit 9 about respiration in terrestrial arthropods, fish, and flatworms, with human respiration. What do these methods have in common? How do they differ?

37–3 Section Assessment

1. Nose, pharynx, larynx, trachea, bronchi, bronchioles, alveoli
2. Chronic bronchitis: bronchi become swollen and clogged with mucus; emphysema: loss of elasticity in lungs; lung cancer: deadly disease that spreads to other parts of body
3. Oxygen diffuses from alveoli into the blood across capillary walls and carbon dioxide diffuses from blood into air in the alveoli.
4. When the level of carbon dioxide rises in the blood, the breathing center sends out nerve impulses that cause the diaphragm to contract and bring air into the lungs.
5. The level of carbon dioxide in their blood is normal, so their breathing center does not increase the rate of breathing. As a result, they do not get enough oxygen.

Use Community Resources

Have interested students contact their local chapter of the American Lung Association to find out about programs available to people who want to quit smoking, such as the Great American Smokeout. Students should request copies of pamphlets, brochures, and other written materials that are available free of charge from the association. Ask students to share these materials with the class.

3 ASSESS

Evaluate Understanding

Write the following words on the chalkboard: *nose, larynx, pharynx, trachea, lung, bronchus, alveolus.* Call on students at random to describe the function of each structure.

Reteach

Work with students to create a simple schematic diagram showing what occurs during the process of gas exchange in the alveoli.

MAKING CONNECTIONS

Students might note that flatworms, which do not have respiratory organs, use diffusion to transport and excrete materials. Students can compare tracheal tubes and book lungs of terrestrial arthropods with human respiratory structures, or the removal of oxygen from water in gills with the removal of oxygen from air in alveoli.

Use iText to review the key concepts in Section 37–3.

Answer to . . .

Figure 37–19 *Circulation is decreased after smoking. This explains why the hand in the figure is colder after smoking.*

Design an Experiment

Objective Students will be able to use a model to determine how muscle contractions move air in and out of the lungs.

Skills Focus **Using Models, Drawing Conclusions**

Time 45 minutes

Advance Prep

- You may want to have each student bring in a plastic bottle, such as a 16-oz drink bottle, to use for the lab.
- Make sure the bottles are clean before students use them.
- You can save time and reduce risk of injury by cutting off the bottoms of the plastic bottles before class.
- A number 2 rubber stopper will fit a 16-oz plastic drink bottle.

Safety Advise students to be careful when they use the scissors to puncture the plastic bottle, because the plastic is tough and may cause the scissors to slip.

Teaching Strategies Have students read the entire procedure. Then, ask:

- **What do the different parts of the model represent?** *(The bottle represents the chest or chest wall, the large balloon represents the diaphragm, the small balloon represents a lung, and the hole in the stopper represents the air passages leading to the lung.)*
- **What do you predict will happen when you pull down on the large balloon?** (Students may or may not correctly predict that the small balloon will fill with air and expand when they pull down on the large balloon.)

Procedure

9. Caution students to pull gently on the large balloon so that it does not slip off the plastic bottle.

11. If students have difficulty deciding how to modify the model to represent a punctured chest, review what each part of the model represents. Students should describe puncturing the plastic bottle to model a punctured chest. Students may or may not predict correctly that puncturing the bottle will cause the small balloon to no longer be affected by the pulling down or pressing up on the large balloon.

Design an Experiment

Modeling Breathing

As you breathe, your body moves air into and out of your lungs. All body movements depend on muscles, which work only by contracting. How does your body use muscles to cause air to flow into and out of your lungs? In this investigation, you will make a working model of human lungs that will help you answer this question.

Problem **How do muscle contractions move air into and out of the lungs?**

Materials

- small, clear plastic bottle
- large round balloon
- small round balloon
- one-hole rubber stopper
- scissors

Skills Using Models

Design Your Experiment 

Part A: A Model of Normal Lungs

1. Place a clear plastic bottle on its side. Press one point of a pair of scissors through the side of the bottle about 1 cm from the bottom.
2. Using the scissors, cut off the bottom of the bottle by cutting all the way around. Trim off any rough spots from the edge.
3. Stretch a small balloon, and blow it up several times to make it pliable.
4. Pull the opening of the small balloon over the bottom of a one-hole rubber stopper.
5. Insert the balloon through the mouth of the bottle. Press the stopper tightly into the bottle so that it holds the lip of the balloon in place.
6. Stretch a large balloon, and blow it up several times to make it pliable.
7. Using the scissors, cut off about 1 cm from the rounded, closed end of the large balloon. Tie the other end closed.
8. Stretch the large balloon far enough over the cut end of the bottle to keep the balloon from slipping off, as shown.
9. As you watch the small balloon, pull down on the knot of the large balloon. Then, still watching the small balloon, press up on the large balloon.

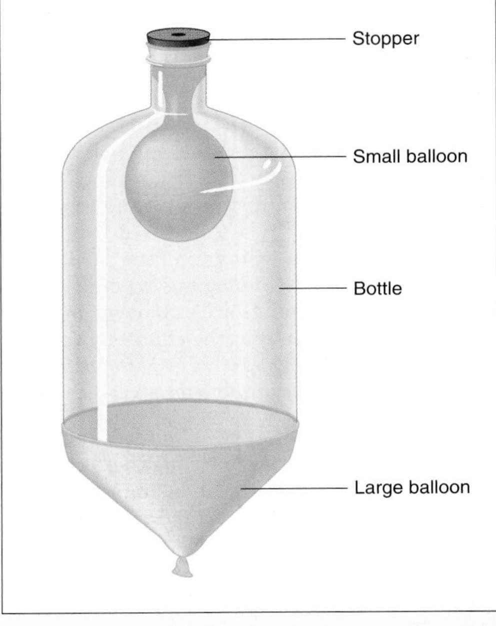

Part B: A Model of a Chest Injury

10. **Formulating Hypotheses** If a person receives an injury that punctures the skin and muscles of the chest, outside air can come into direct contact with the outer surfaces of the lungs. How would such an event affect a person's ability to breathe? Record your hypothesis.
11. Think of a way you could modify your model of human lungs to represent the lungs in a person with a punctured chest. Write a description of your plan, including your prediction of how the model will behave and how the model will test your hypothesis.
12. Show your plan to your teacher. If your teacher approves, make a model of a punctured chest. Use your model to test your hypothesis.

Analyze and Conclude

1. **Observing** What happened to the small balloon in your first model when you pulled down on the large balloon?
2. **Observing** What happened to the small balloon when you pressed up on the large balloon?
3. **Inferring** What happened to the pressure inside the bottle when you moved the large balloon up and down?
4. **Formulating Hypotheses** What caused the small balloon to expand and contract?
5. **Using Models** How is the first model you constructed similar to the human respiratory system? How is it different from the human respiratory system?
6. **Evaluating** Was your prediction in Part B correct? Did the behavior of your second model support your hypothesis? Explain your answer.
7. **Drawing Conclusions** How do muscles cause air to flow into and out of human lungs?
8. **Drawing Conclusions** What did your second model demonstrate about the importance of the chest wall in breathing? Give reasons for your answer.

Go Further

Making Models Obtain information from a hospital, doctor's office, or county health department about the mechanics of breathing and diseases such as asthma and emphysema that make breathing difficult. Find out what causes these diseases, how they affect breathing, and how they are prevented and treated. Then, make a new model that demonstrates the effects of one of these diseases.

Expected Outcomes

- In Part A, students should observe that pulling down on the large balloon causes the small balloon to inflate and that pressing up on the large balloon causes the small balloon to deflate.
- In Part B, students should puncture the bottle and then observe that the small balloon no longer inflates or deflates as the large balloon is pulled down or pressed up.

Go Further

Students will learn that asthma is caused by the narrowing of air passageways leading to the lungs, often due to allergic reactions. They will also learn that emphysema is caused by loss of elasticity in the lungs, often due to cigarette smoking. Students might model asthma by narrowing the hole in the stopper with modeling clay, tape, or some other material so that air movement into and out of the small balloon is restricted. Students might model emphysema by replacing the small balloon with a new balloon that has not been blown up or stretched out to make it pliable. In each case, there would be less inflation or deflation of the small balloon as the large balloon is pulled down or pressed up.

Analyze and Conclude

1. The small balloon inflated.
2. The small balloon deflated.
3. When the large balloon was pulled down, the pressure decreased. When the large balloon was pressed up, the pressure increased.
4. Decreased pressure in the bottle allowed air to fill the small balloon. Increased pressure in the bottle pushed the air out of the small balloon.
5. It is similar in the way changes in pressure inside the bottle cause the small balloon to expand and contract. It differs in having only one "lung" and in the way it moves the "diaphragm."
6. Movement of the large balloon does not cause the small balloon to inflate or deflate if the bottle is punctured.
7. When the diaphragm contracts, it pulls down, allowing air to enter the lungs. When the diaphragm relaxes, it pushes up, forcing air out of the lungs.
8. If the chest wall is punctured, changes in pressure needed for breathing cannot occur.

Chapter 37 Study Guide

Study Tip

Have students choose partners and quiz each other on the Key Concept questions in the section assessments. Also, have students make flashcards for the Vocabulary terms and use them to quiz each other.

Thinking Visually

1. Pharynx
2. Larynx/trachea
3. Bronchi/bronchioles

Chapter 37 Assessment

Reviewing Content

1. c	5. b	9. a
2. d	6. a	10. c
3. a	7. c	
4. b	8. a	

Understanding Concepts

11. In a closed circulatory system, a fluid is pumped through a series of connected vessels.

12. Pulmonary circulation carries blood between the heart and the lungs. Systemic circulation carries blood between the heart and the rest of the body.

13. Blood enters the heart through the atria. As the heart contracts, blood is forced first into the ventricles and then out from the ventricles into the circulation.

14. A valve in the heart prevents any backflow of blood. Valves are also found in veins.

15. The function of the pacemaker is to control the heart rate.

16. From the sinoatrial node to a network of fibers in the atria, to the atrioventricular node, to muscle fibers in the ventricles

17. Arteries are large vessels with thick walls. Capillaries are narrow vessels with thin walls. Blood cells must often travel single file through capillaries. The walls of veins and arteries contain smooth muscle and connective tissue. Large veins have one-way valves that keep blood moving toward the heart.

Chapter 37 Study Guide

37–1 The Circulatory System

Key Concepts

- The human circulatory system consists of the heart, a series of blood vessels, and the blood that flows through them.
- As the blood flows through the circulatory system, it moves through three types of blood vessels—arteries, capillaries, and veins.

Vocabulary

myocardium, p. 944
atrium, p. 944
ventricle, p. 944
pulmonary circulation, p. 944
systemic circulation, p. 944
valve, p. 945
pacemaker, p. 946
aorta, p. 946
artery, p. 946
capillary, p. 947
vein, p. 947
atherosclerosis, p. 949

37–2 Blood and the Lymphatic System

Key Concepts

- Red blood cells transport oxygen.
- White blood cells attack foreign substances or organisms.
- Blood clotting is made possible by plasma proteins and cell fragments called platelets.
- A network of vessels called the lymphatic system collects the fluid that is lost by the blood and returns it to the circulatory system.

Vocabulary

plasma, p. 951
hemoglobin, p. 952
phagocyte, p. 952
platelet, p. 953
lymph, p. 954

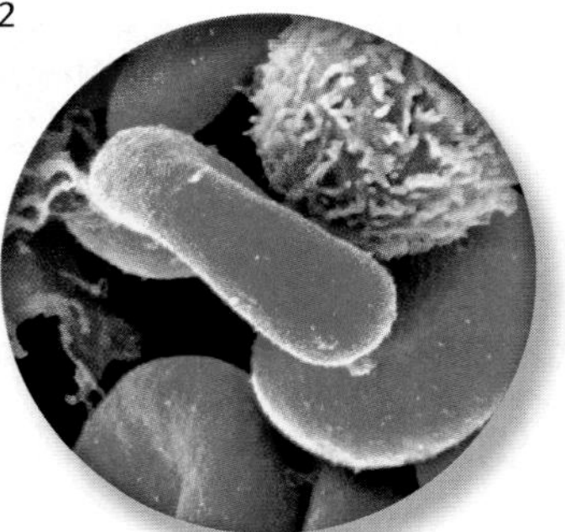

37–3 The Respiratory System

Key Concepts

- The respiratory system consists of the nose, pharynx, larynx, trachea, bronchi, and lungs.
- Smoking can cause such respiratory diseases as chronic bronchitis, emphysema, and lung cancer.

Vocabulary

pharynx, p. 956
trachea, p. 956
larynx, p. 958
bronchus, p. 958
alveolus, p. 958
diaphragm, p. 959
nicotine, p. 961
emphysema, p. 962

Thinking Visually

On a separate sheet of paper, complete the following flowchart tracing the flow of air through the respiratory system.

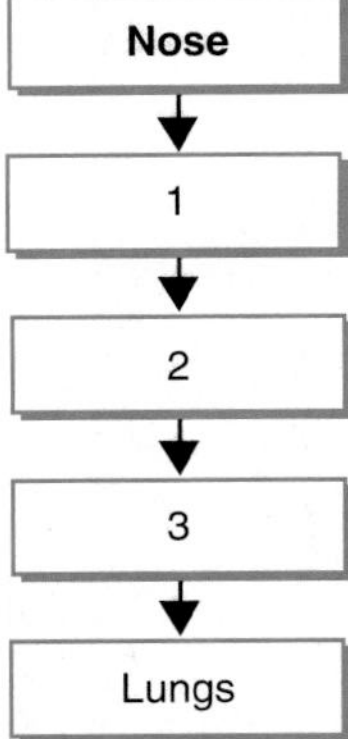

CHAPTER RESOURCES

Print:

- ***Teaching Resources,*** Chapter Vocabulary Review, Graphic Organizer
- ***Chapter Tests: Levels A and B,*** Chapter 37 Test
- ***PH Assessment System,*** Practice Test

Technology:

- ***Computer Test Bank,*** Chapter 37 Test
- ***iText,*** Chapter 37 Assessment

Chapter 37 Assessment

Reviewing Content

Choose the letter that best answers the question or completes the statement.

1. The circulatory system is composed of the
   a. lung, heart, and brain.
   b. lung, blood vessels, and heart.
   c. heart, blood, and blood vessels.
   d. heart, arteries, and veins.
2. The upper chambers of the heart are the
   a. ventricles. c. myocardia.
   b. septa. d. atria.
3. When blood leaves the left ventricle, it passes into a large blood vessel known as the
   a. aorta. c. pulmonary vein.
   b. vena cava. d. pulmonary artery.
4. The smallest of the blood vessels are the
   a. veins. c. arteries.
   b. capillaries. d. atria.
5. The straw-colored fluid that is 90 percent water and 10 percent dissolved substances is called
   a. lymph. c. hemoglobin.
   b. plasma. d. blood.
6. The iron-containing protein that carries oxygen from the lungs to the tissues of the body is
   a. hemoglobin. c. prothrombin.
   b. blood. d. chlorophyll.
7. The process shown below is made possible by a number of plasma proteins and cell fragments called
   a. fibrins. c. platelets.
   b. thrombins. d. lymphocytes.

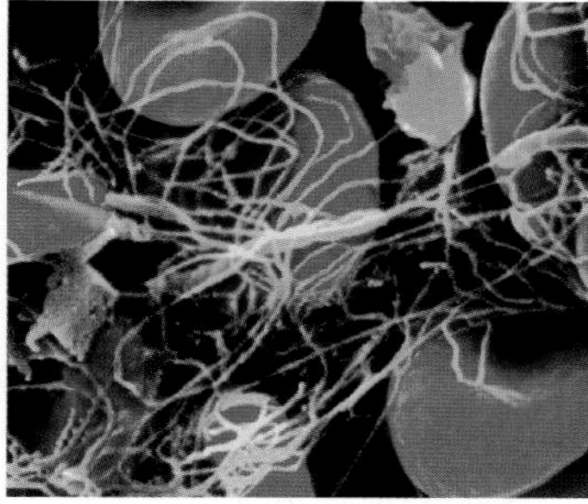

8. The tiny hollow air sacs where oxygen exchange takes place are the
   a. alveoli.
   b. lymph nodes.
   c. capillaries.
   d. bronchioles.
9. Two highly elastic folds of tissue known as the vocal cords can be found in the
   a. larynx.
   b. pharynx.
   c. trachea.
   d. bronchi.
10. The large, flat muscle that aids in breathing is the
    a. trachea.
    b. epiglottis.
    c. diaphragm.
    d. larynx.

Understanding Concepts

11. What is a closed circulatory system?
12. Compare pulmonary circulation and systemic circulation.
13. Trace the flow of blood through the heart.
14. What is the major function of a valve in the heart? Where else in the circulatory system are valves found?
15. Describe the function of the pacemaker.
16. How are impulses transmitted through the heart?
17. Compare the structures of the three types of blood vessels.
18. Distinguish between systolic pressure and diastolic pressure.
19. How does exercise help to prevent circulatory system disorders?
20. What are the major components of blood? List the functions of each component.
21. Explain why people with hemophilia need to avoid injury.
22. What are the primary functions of the lymphatic system?
23. What part of the brain controls involuntary breathing?
24. What are three of the most dangerous substances in tobacco smoke? Describe how each affects the body.
25. How does emphysema affect the respiratory system?

TIME SAVER HOMEWORK GUIDE

Section:	Questions:
Section 37–1	1–4, 11–19, 26, 27, 30, 31
Section 37–2	5–7, 20–22, 28, 29, 32, 33
Section 37–3	8–10, 23–25, 34

Chapter 37 Assessment (continued)

18. Systolic pressure is the force of the blood felt in the arteries when the ventricles contract. Diastolic pressure is the force of the blood felt in the arteries when the ventricles relax.

19. Exercise helps to prevent circulatory system disorders by increasing the respiratory system's efficiency, controlling weight, reducing body fat, reducing stress, and strengthening the heart muscle.

20. The major components of blood are plasma, platelets, white blood cells, and red blood cells. Plasma provides the fluid that carries the other blood components. It also contains proteins that are involved in several important functions, including immune reactions and blood clotting. Platelets cluster around a wound and release proteins that start a series of chemical reactions resulting in a clot. White blood cells attack foreign substances and organisms. Red blood cells transport oxygen.

21. Because people with hemophilia have a defective protein, they cannot produce blood clots that are firm enough to stop even minor bleeding.

22. The primary functions of the lymphatic system are to: collect fluid lost by the blood and return it to the circulatory system; filter bacteria and other microorganisms from the fluid; house white blood cells, called lymphocytes, that help fight infection; and absorb fat and fat-soluble vitamins from the digestive tract and carry them to the circulatory system.

23. Involuntary breathing is controlled by a center in the medulla oblongata, which is a part of the brain located just above the spinal cord.

24. Three of the most dangerous substances in tobacco smoke are nicotine, carbon monoxide, and tar. Nicotine increases the heart rate and blood pressure. Carbon monoxide blocks the transport of oxygen by hemoglobin in the blood. Tar contains compounds that cause cancer.

25. Emphysema is a loss of elasticity in lung tissues. It makes breathing difficult and prevents the tissues from getting the oxygen they need or eliminating excess carbon dioxide.

Chapter 37 Assessment

Critical Thinking

26. The most likely experimental design is to measure each subject's heart rate at rest to determine the normal heart rate and then again at frequent timed intervals after the subject has exercised, until the heart rate returns to the normal rate.

27. If a blood clot became lodged in a major blood vessel, it might block the flow of blood, deprive tissues of needed oxygen, and cause damage to the tissues.

28. A person with a low red blood cell count has fewer red blood cells to transport oxygen to cells. Without adequate oxygen, the production of energy from cellular respiration is reduced.

29. A stroke can be caused by a blood clot cutting off the flow of blood to the brain. Patients who have had a stroke can reduce their risk of more clots by taking aspirin.

30. The powerful pressure produced when the heart contracts pushes blood into and through arteries.

31. All the blood flows through the lungs to pick up oxygen. During exercise, much more blood flows through the skeletal muscles to fuel the production of energy needed for muscle contraction. So much blood flows through the kidneys because the kidneys filter the blood.

32. Removal of the lymph nodes would lessen the body's ability to fight disease. The lymph nodes filter bacteria and other disease-causing microorganisms from the lymph before it is returned to the circulatory system. The lymph nodes also house white blood cells, called lymphocytes, that help fight infection.

33. Injections of normal clotting proteins would help a hemophiliac by providing missing proteins needed for normal blood clotting. With the injections, the hemophiliac's blood would clot in case of an injury.

34. In a cell, respiration is a chemical process with oxygen as a reactant and carbon dioxide as a product. In the lungs, respiration is a physical process—the exchange of oxygen and carbon dioxide across capillary walls in the lungs.

Chapter 37 Assessment

Critical Thinking

26. Designing Experiments Design an experiment that determines the amount of time needed for a person's heart rate to return to normal after exercise.

27. Predicting What might happen if a blood clot formed inside the body and became lodged in a major blood vessel?

28. Applying Concepts If a person's red blood cell count is low, that person may complain that he or she has no energy. Explain why this person may be experiencing fatigue.

29. Inferring Aspirin reduces the clot-forming ability of the blood. Why do you think some doctors prescribe aspirin for patients who have had a stroke?

30. Drawing Conclusions Large veins contain one-way valves, which keep the blood flowing in the right direction. Why don't large arteries need similar valves?

31. Analyzing Data The following table shows the relative blood flow through various organs in the human body—that is, the fraction of blood that flows through a given human organ. Through which organ(s) does all of the blood flow? Describe and explain the change in blood flow to skeletal muscles during exercise. The kidneys consume only 6 percent of the oxygen used in the body. Why would 22 percent of blood flow though the kidneys?

Blood Flow Through Human Organs

Organ	Percentage of Total Flow
Brain	14%
Heart	5%
Kidneys	22%
Liver	13%
Lungs	100%
Skeletal muscles	18%
Skeletal muscles during exercise	75%

32. Predicting How would the removal of a person's lymph nodes affect the body's ability to fight disease?

33. Applying Concepts Hemophilia is a genetic disorder in which a defective gene for blood clotting is present. How would injections of normal clotting proteins help a hemophiliac?

34. Making Connections As you may remember from Chapter 9, the term *respiration* may be used to describe two different biological processes. How are these two processes similar? How are they different?

Performance-Based Assessment

Making a Model Construct a simple stethoscope out of rubber tubing and a metal funnel. Listen for the sounds of air rushing into and out of your lungs as you inhale and exhale. Record a description of the sounds while you are inhaling and exhaling. How does the sound change when you cough? What do you think it would sound like if you had a cold? Bronchitis? Prepare a brief report of your findings and present it to the class.

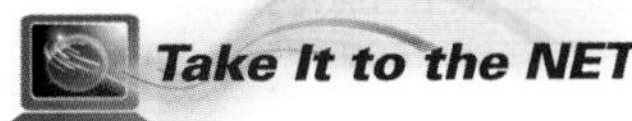

Lung disease is the number three cause of death in the United States. Visit the Prentice Hall Web site at **www.phschool.com** to find out more about lung disease. Then, answer the following questions:

- List five different chronic lung diseases.
- How much does smoking cost Americans each year in terms of health care and loss of productivity?
- How many people die from smoking-related illnesses each year in the United States?
- How does air quality affect lung health?

Performance-Based Assessment

Students might say that normal breathing sounds like a muffled roar, which changes to a loud, sharp rushing sound when they cough. With a cold, they would be likely to hear normal breathing sounds because a cold causes symptoms primarily in the upper part of the respiratory tract, such as the nose and larynx. With bronchitis, students might expect to hear wheezing sounds because of mucus in the large air passages in the chest.

Standardized Test Prep

Test-Taking Tip When you are asked questions about structures in a diagram, first identify each structure. Then, try to answer the questions.

Directions: Choose the letter that best answers the question or completes the statement.

1. Which of the following protect the human body against invading microorganisms?
   I. Red blood cells
   II. Platelets
   III. White blood cells
   (A) I only
   (B) II only
   (C) III only
   (D) II and III only
   (E) I, II, and III
2. Which structure is NOT part of the human circulatory system?
   I. Heart
   II. Veins
   III. Lymph nodes
   (A) I only
   (B) III only
   (C) I and II only
   (D) II and III only
   (E) I, II, and III
3. Where does gas exchange occur in the human respiratory system?
   I. Vocal cords
   II. Bronchi
   III. Alveoli
   (A) I only
   (B) II only
   (C) III only
   (D) I and III only
   (E) I, II, and III
4. Human blood is composed of all of the following EXCEPT
   (A) plasma.
   (B) mucus.
   (C) phagocytes.
   (D) hemoglobin.
   (E) platelets.
5. Nicotine in tobacco
   (A) is not addictive.
   (B) decreases blood pressure.
   (C) blocks the transport of oxygen.
   (D) decreases the heart rate.
   (E) paralyzes cilia.

Questions 6–7 Complete each analogy by selecting the correct letter. In analogies, A : B :: C : ___?___ means A is to B as C is to ___?___.

6. Platelets : clotting :: red blood cells : ___?___
   (A) inhalation
   (B) exhalation
   (C) oxygen transport
   (D) gas exchange
   (E) cellular respiration
7. Bronchus : tree trunk :: ___?___ : leaf
   (A) pharynx
   (B) alveolus
   (C) diaphragm
   (D) trachea
   (E) lymphatic system

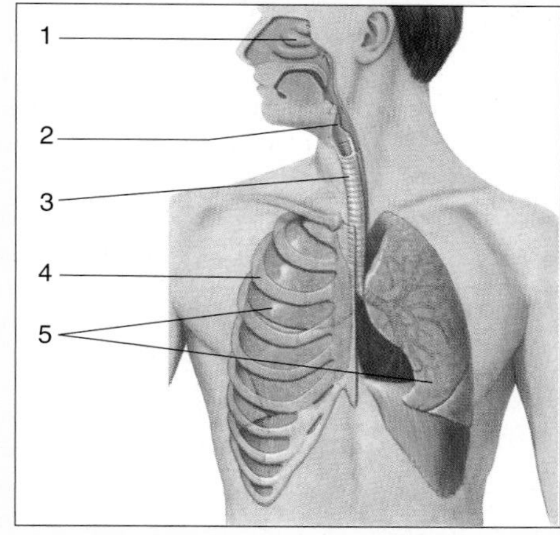

Questions 8–10 Use the diagram to answer the following questions.

8. In which structure is air warmed and moistened?
   (A) 2
   (B) 3
   (C) 4
   (D) 5
   (E) 1
9. Which structure contains the vocal cords?
   (A) 1
   (B) 2
   (C) 3
   (D) 4
   (E) 5
10. Which structure is affected by emphysema?
    (A) 2
    (B) 3
    (C) 4
    (D) 5
    (E) 1

Standardized Test Prep

1. C
2. B
3. C
4. B
5. E
6. C
7. B
8. E
9. C
10. D

Take It to the NET

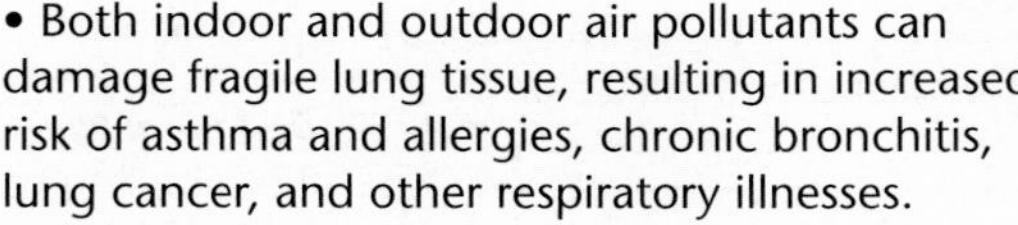

- Chronic lung diseases include asthma, chronic bronchitis, pneumonia, tuberculosis, lung cancer, and emphysema.
- Smoking costs Americans about $97 billion each year in health-care and lost productivity.
- Smoking-related diseases claim about 430,700 lives in the United States each year.
- Both indoor and outdoor air pollutants can damage fragile lung tissue, resulting in increased risk of asthma and allergies, chronic bronchitis, lung cancer, and other respiratory illnesses.

For additional information, visit

www.phschool.com

Chapter Planner 38 Digestive and Excretory Systems

Section and Section Objectives	Time	Activities and Labs
38–1 Food and Nutrition, pp. 971–977 **38.1.1 *Explain*** how food provides energy. **38.1.2 *Describe*** the nutrients your body needs. **38.1.3 *State*** why water is such an important nutrient. **38.1.4 *Explain*** how to use the Food Guide Pyramid.	**2 periods (1 block)**	**SE: *Inquiry Activity,*** What's in a chip?, p. 970 **TE: *Demonstration,*** p. 972 **SE: *Analyzing Data,*** Reading Food Labels, p. 977
38–2 The Process of Digestion, pp. 978–984 **38.2.1 *Identify*** the organs of the digestive system. **38.2.2 *Describe*** the function of the digestive system.	**2 periods (1 block)**	**TE: *Meet Diverse Needs,*** p. 978 **TE: *Demonstration,*** p. 979 **TE: *Demonstration,*** p. 980 **TE: *Make Connections,*** p. 982 **SE: *Quick Lab,*** How do villi help the small intestine absorb nutrients?, p. 982 **TE: *Meet Diverse Needs,*** p. 983
38–3 The Excretory System, pp. 985–989 **38.3.1 *Name*** the organs of the excretory system. **38.3.2 *Explain*** how the kidneys maintain homeostasis. **38.3.3 *Describe*** how homeostasis is maintained by machine.	**1 period (1/2 block)**	**TE: *Demonstration,*** p. 985 **TE: *Meet Diverse Needs,*** p. 986 **TE: *Build Science Skills,*** p. 986 **TE: *Demonstration,*** p. 987 **SE: *Design an Experiment,*** Testing the Specificity of Digestive Enzymes, pp. 990–991
Chapter Assessment, pp. 992–995	**1 period (1/2 block)**	

ACTIVITY PLANNER

SE: *Inquiry Activity,* p. 970; (10 min.); regular potato chips, baked potato chips, brown paper towels, shallow metal or glass container, matches, potato chip package labels

TE: *Demonstration,* p. 972; (5 min.; 5 min.); apple slice, potato slice, slice of bread, cracker, balance, paper plates

TE: *Meet Diverse Needs,* p. 978; (10 min.); raw egg, bowl, fork, pan of boiling water

TE: *Demonstration,* p. 979; (10 min.); soda cracker

TE: *Demonstration,* p. 980; (5 min.); 25- to 30-cm length of plastic or rubber tubing, marble

TE: *Make Connections,* p. 982; (5 min.); 100 mL 0.5% hydrochloric acid, beaker, pH paper, 2 mL sodium bicarbonate solution

SE: *Quick Lab,* p. 982; (20 min.); paper towels, scissors, cardboard tubes, metric rulers, 30-mL graduated cylinders, plastic cups

TE: *Meet Diverse Needs,* p. 983; (5 min.); piece of velvet fabric

TE: *Demonstration,* p. 985; (5 min.); balloon, water

TE: *Meet Diverse Needs,* p. 986; (15 min.); dry pasta, cereal, dried beans, clay, string, glue

TE: *Build Science Skills,* p. 986; (5 min.); water, food coloring, sand, silt, paper coffee filter

TE: *Demonstration,* p. 987; (10 min.); beef or lamb kidney, scalpel or sharp knife

SE: *Design an Experiment,* pp. 990–991; (45 min.; 15 min.); Benedict's solution, boiling water bath, cooked egg white, scalpel or single-edged razor blade, metric ruler, 6 large test tubes with stoppers, glass-marking pencil, test-tube rack, 10-mL graduated cylinder, 1% pepsin solution, 0.2% hydrochloric acid, cooked potato, 1% amylase solution, test-tube holder

PLANNING KEY

Ability Levels

B	**Basic**	For students who need additional help
A	**Average**	For all students
E	**Enriched**	For students who need to be challenged

Components

SE	Student Edition	**GRSW**	Guided Reading and Study Workbook	**IDM**	Issues and Decision Making
TE	Teacher's Edition	**CT**	Chapter Tests: Levels A and B	**CTB**	Computer Test Bank
LMA	Laboratory Manual A	**PHAS**	PH Assessment System	**PA**	Presentation Assistant Plus
LMB	Laboratory Manual B	**LA**	Lab Assessment with Scoring Guide	**BD**	BioDetectives Videotape
TR	Teaching Resources	**BTM**	BioTechnology Manual	**iT**	iText
IF	Investigations in Forensics				

Program Resources	Assessment	Media and Technology
TR: Section Review 38–1 B A **GRSW:** Section 38–1 B A **IDM:** Issues and Decisions 5, 35, 39, 49 A E	**SE:** 38–1 Section Assessment, p. 977 **TR:** Section Review 38–1	**PA:** 38–1 Interest Grabber, Section Outline, Food Guide, Figure 38–6, Figure 38–7, Figure 38–8 **iT:** Section 38–1
LMB: Chapter 38 Lab B A **TR:** Section Review 38–2 B A **GRSW:** Section 38–2 B A	**SE:** 38–2 Section Assessment, p. 984 **TR:** Section Review 38–2	**PA:** 38–2 Interest Grabber, Section Outline, Digestive Enzymes, Figure 38–10, Figure 38–13, Figure 38–14 **iT:** Section 38–2
LMA: Chapter 38 Lab A E **TR:** Section Review 38–3 B A Chapter 38 Design an Experiment B A E **GRSW:** Section 38–3 B A	**SE:** 38–3 Section Assessment, p. 989 **TR:** Section Review 38–3	**PA:** 38–3 Interest Grabber, Section Outline, Urinary System, Figure 38–17, Figure 38–18, Figure 38–19 **iT:** Section 38–3
	SE: Chapter 38 Assessment, pp. 992–995 **TR:** Chapter Vocabulary Review, Graphic Organizer **CT:** Chapter 38 Test **CTB:** Chapter 38 Test **PHAS:** Practice Test	**CTB:** Chapter 38 Test **iT:** Chapter 38 Assessment

PRESSED FOR TIME?

To Preview the Chapter

- Introduce students to the Vocabulary terms in Section 38–1 and to the organs of the digestive and excretory systems in Sections 38–2 and 38–3.
- Have students read the highlighted sentences in each section.

To Cover the Chapter Quickly

- Have students read Section 38–1, the introduction to Section 38–2, Figures 38–10 and 38–17, and Control of Kidney Function in Section 38–3.
- Assign the Section Review 38–1; question 2 in Section Reviews 38–2 and 38–3; questions 1–3, 11–14, 27, 30, and 34 in Chapter 38 Assessment; and questions 5, 6 in Chapter 38 PH Assessment System

To Review the Chapter

- Assign the Section Reviews 38–1 through 38–3 in the Guided Reading and Study Workbook.
- Assign the Section Review for 38–1 through 38–3 and the Chapter Vocabulary Review for Chapter 38 in the Teaching Resources.

ENGAGE/EXPLORE

Inquiry Activity

Objective Students will be able to infer which of two potato chips has more stored chemical energy based on the fat content of the chips.

Skills Focus **Inferring, Drawing Conclusions**

Materials 1 regular potato chip, 1 baked potato chip, 2 brown paper towels, shallow metal or glass container, matches, potato chip package labels

Time 10 minutes

Advance Prep Make copies for each student of the nutrition facts labels from the two packages of potato chips.

Strategy Suggest that students label each paper towel with the type of potato chip that was crushed in it.

Expected Outcome Students should find that the regular potato chip contains more fat and Calories, leaves a larger grease spot, and burns longer.

Think About It

1. The regular potato chip
2. The regular potato chip
3. The regular chip leaves a larger grease spot and burns longer because it has more fat and more stored chemical energy.

Brain Teaser

Ask students whether each of the following commonly believed statements is true or false: **Only foods containing sugar give you energy.** *(False, because any kind of food that contains Calories can be broken down by the body and converted into energy)* **Fats have no place in a healthy diet.** *(False, because small quantities of fats are essential for good health)*

Chapter 38 Digestive and Excretory Systems

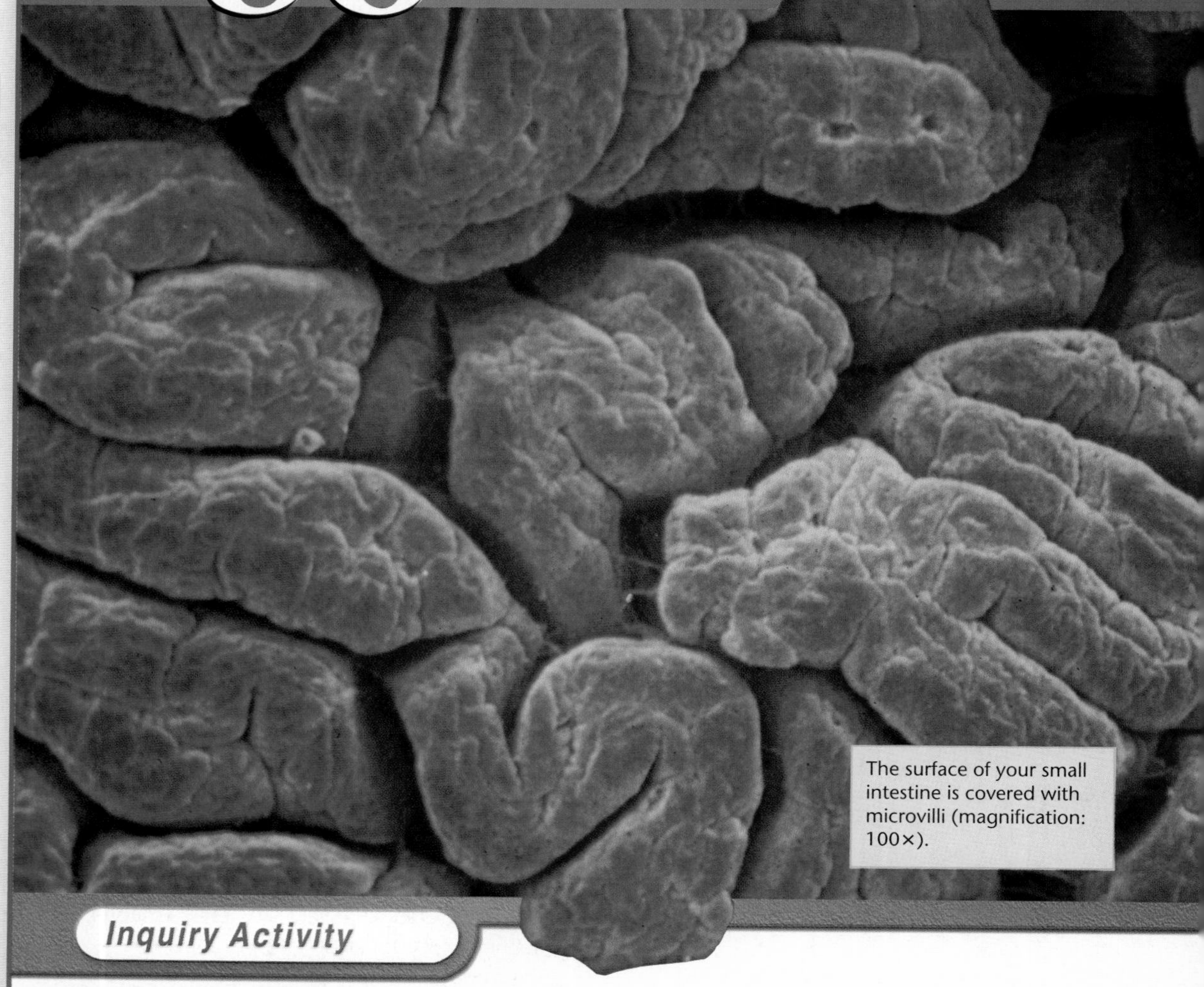

The surface of your small intestine is covered with microvilli (magnification: 100×).

Inquiry Activity

What's in a chip?

Procedure

1. Place a regular potato chip on a brown paper towel and fold the towel over the chip. Repeat using a similarly sized, baked potato chip and another towel. **CAUTION:** *Do not eat the potato chips.*
2. Press down on the towels for 1 minute, then unfold them. Hold the towels up to the light. A bright spot indicates the presence of fat.
3. Observe as your teacher burns the potato chips.

Think About It

1. **Observing** Which type of potato chip contains more fat?
2. **Inferring** Which potato chip has more stored chemical energy?
3. **Drawing Conclusions** How are the results from burning the potato chips related to the fat and Calorie contents listed on the package labels?

TEACHER TO TEACHER

When I teach nutrition, I have each student bring in 10 labels from food packages. The labels should contain the name of the product, the ingredients list, and the nutrition facts table. I have students attach each label to a sheet of paper and beside the label write the serving size and the amount of Calories, fat, and sodium one serving of the food contains. When we discuss the labels, students usually say they are surprised to learn how small serving sizes are and how much fat many foods contain. We discuss how the ingredients are always listed in order from most to least common. Students are surprised to learn that what they thought they purchased is not always the first-listed ingredient.

—Duane Nichols,
Biology Teacher
Alhambra High School,
Alhambra, CA

38–1 Food and Nutrition

How important is food in your life? Before you answer, think of two uniquely American holidays: Independence Day and Thanksgiving Day. What comes to mind? No matter where you live, chances are that a meal is the centerpiece of that special day. To most of us, food is more than just nourishment—it is an important part of our culture. Human societies throughout the world organize meetings and family gatherings around food.

Guide for Reading

Key Concepts
- What are the nutrients your body needs?
- Why is water such an important nutrient?

Vocabulary
Calorie
carbohydrate
fat
protein
vitamin
mineral

Reading Strategy: Finding Main Ideas Before you read, skim the section to identify the key ideas. Then, carefully read the section, making a list of supporting details for each main idea.

Food and Energy

Have you ever wondered why you need to eat food? The most obvious answer is to obtain energy—the ability to do work. You need energy to climb stairs, lift books, run, and even to think. Just as a car needs gasoline, your body needs fuel for all that work, and food is your fuel. Cells convert the chemical energy stored in the sugar glucose and other molecules into ATP.

The energy available in food can be measured in a surprisingly simple way—by burning the food! The amount of heat given off is measured and expressed in terms of calories. One calorie is the amount of heat needed to raise the temperature of one gram of water by one Celsius degree. Scientists refer to the energy stored in food as dietary Calories with a capital *C*. One **Calorie** is equal to 1000 calories, or 1 kilocalorie (kcal).

The energy needs of an average-sized teenager are about 2200 Calories per day for females and about 2800 Calories per day for males. If you engage in vigorous physical activity, however, your energy needs may be higher.

Chemical pathways in your body's cells can extract energy from almost any type of food. Why then does it matter which foods you eat? Although most of the food you eat is used as fuel, a certain amount of the food you eat has other important functions. Food supplies the raw materials used to build and repair body tissues. Some of these raw materials are used to manufacture new macromolecules. These include the proteins that regulate cellular reactions, the phospholipids in cell membranes, and DNA—your genetic material. Food also contains at least 45 substances that the body needs but cannot manufacture.

The science of nutrition—the study of food and its effects on the body—tries to determine how food helps the body meet all of its various needs. Based on their research, nutritionists recommend balanced diets that include many different types of food. They also plan diets for people with particular needs, such as diabetics.

▼ **Figure 38–1** Holidays and other celebrations often center around food.

SECTION RESOURCES

Print:
- ***Teaching Resources,*** Section Review 38–1
- ***Guided Reading and Study Workbook,*** Section 38–1
- ***Issues and Decision Making,*** Issues and Decisions 5, 35, 39, 49

Technology:
- ***iText,*** Section 38–1

Section 38–1

1 FOCUS

Objectives

38.1.1 ***Explain*** how food provides energy.
38.1.2 ***Describe*** the nutrients your body needs.
38.1.3 ***State*** why water is such an important nutrient.
38.1.4 ***Explain*** how to use the Food Guide Pyramid.

Guide for Reading

Vocabulary Preview

Point out that five of the vocabulary terms are nutrients, or substances in food that the body needs, and that the other term is a measure of the amount of energy in food. Ask: **Which term refers to the amount of energy in food?** *(Calorie)*

Reading Strategy

Suggest that students create a table as they read to compare and contrast the nutrients that the body needs. Possible column headings might include: Type of Nutrient, Foods in Which It Is Found, and Role It Plays in the Body. Advise students to save their tables for study guides.

2 INSTRUCT

Food and Energy

Make Connections

Chemistry Remind students that ATP stands for adenosine triphosphate and that each molecule of ATP contains one glucose molecule and three phosphate molecules. Ask: **How is the energy in ATP released so that cells can use it?** *(Energy is released when chemical bonds are broken and ATP loses phosphate groups to become, first, ADP, or adenosine diphosphate, and then AMP, or adenosine monophosphate.)*

Meet Diverse Needs

Suggest that students who need extra challenges investigate the number of Calories used in various activities, such as watching television, driving a car, riding a bike, and running. Have students create a visual representation, such as a table or graph, to summarize what they learn. Display their work in the classroom. **Learning modality: visual**

Nutrients

Demonstration

Ask: **What are the sources of water in our diets?** *(Students are likely to mention drinking water and other beverages, but they might not mention the water contained in food.)* Explain that some foods are mostly water whereas other foods contain almost no water. Demonstrate how much water is contained in a variety of foods, such as a slice of apple, a slice of potato, a slice of bread, and a cracker. Measure the masses of the foods when they are fresh. Then, leave the foods out to dry on paper plates for a few days and measure their masses again. Have students compare the dry masses with the fresh masses and infer which food contained the most water and which contained the least.

Meet Diverse Needs

Guide at-risk students in making concept maps on large pieces of poster board relating the terms *carbohydrates, sugars, starches,* and *fiber.* Show students how to find the amount of sugar and fiber on a nutrition label. As a homework assignment, have them read the labels of a variety of packaged foods and find at least one food high in sugar and one food high in fiber. Finally, have students cut pictures of foods from old magazines and use them to illustrate their concept maps. **Limited English proficiency**

▲ **Figure 38–2** **Every cell in the body needs water because many of the body's processes take place in water.** On hot days, or when you exercise, you need to drink more water to replace the water that is lost in sweat.

Nutrients

Nutrients are substances in food that supply the energy and raw materials your body uses for growth, repair, and maintenance. **The nutrients that the body needs are water, carbohydrates, fats, proteins, vitamins, and minerals.**

Water The most important of all nutrients is water. **Every cell in the human body needs water because many of the body's processes, including chemical reactions, take place in water.** Water makes up the bulk of blood, lymph, and other bodily fluids. On hot days, or when you take part in strenuous exercise, sweat glands remove water from your tissues and release it as sweat on the surface of your body. As the water in sweat evaporates, it cools the body. Water vapor is also lost from the body with every breath you exhale and in urine.

Humans need to drink at least a liter of water a day. If enough water is not taken in to replace what is lost, dehydration can result. This condition leads to problems with the circulatory, respiratory, and nervous systems. Drinking plenty of clean water, as the woman is doing in **Figure 38–2,** is one of the best things you can do to help keep your body healthy.

CHECKPOINT *What does sweat do?*

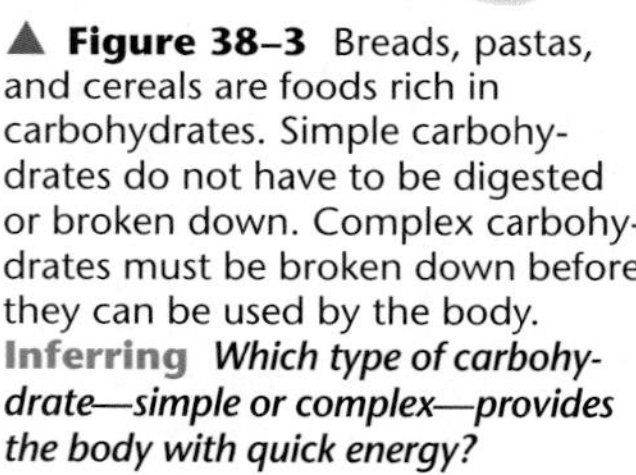

▲ **Figure 38–3** Breads, pastas, and cereals are foods rich in carbohydrates. Simple carbohydrates do not have to be digested or broken down. Complex carbohydrates must be broken down before they can be used by the body. **Inferring** *Which type of carbohydrate—simple or complex—provides the body with quick energy?*

Carbohydrates Simple and complex **carbohydrates** are the main source of energy for the body. The sugars found in fruits, honey, and sugar cane are simple carbohydrates, or mono- and disaccharides. The starches found in grains, potatoes, and vegetables are complex carbohydrates, or polysaccharides. Starches are broken down by the digestive system into simple sugars. These molecules are absorbed into the bloodstream and carried to cells throughout the body. Sugars that are not immediately used to supply energy are converted into the complex carbohydrate glycogen, which is stored in the liver and skeletal muscles.

Many foods contain the complex carbohydrate cellulose, often called fiber. Although the human digestive system cannot break down cellulose, you need fiber in your diet. The bulk supplied by fiber helps muscles to keep food and wastes moving through your digestive and excretory systems. Foods like the breads, pasta, and cereals in **Figure 38–3** are rich in fiber. So are many fruits and vegetables.

Fats Fats, or lipids, are an important part of a healthy diet. **Fats** are formed from fatty acids and glycerol. Your body cannot manufacture all of the fatty acids it needs. These fatty acids, which are known as essential fatty acids, are found in vegetable oils. Deposits of fats protect body organs, insulate the body, and store energy. Fats are used to produce cell membranes, myelin sheaths, and certain hormones. They also help the body absorb fat-soluble vitamins.

PRESENTATIONS MADE EASY!

The Presentation Assistant Plus contains the Prentice Hall Presentation Pro and the Transparencies, which provide easy-to-follow visual support for every step of this lesson. If you have a computer presentation station, use Prentice Hall Presentation Pro for Section 38–1, or use the transparencies listed here.

Section 38–1: **Interest Grabber**
Section Outline
Food Guide
Figure 38–6
Figure 38–7
Figure 38–8

Figure 38–4 **Fats and proteins are two of the six nutrients the body needs.** The foods on the left contain essential fatty acids. The foods below are good sources of proteins.

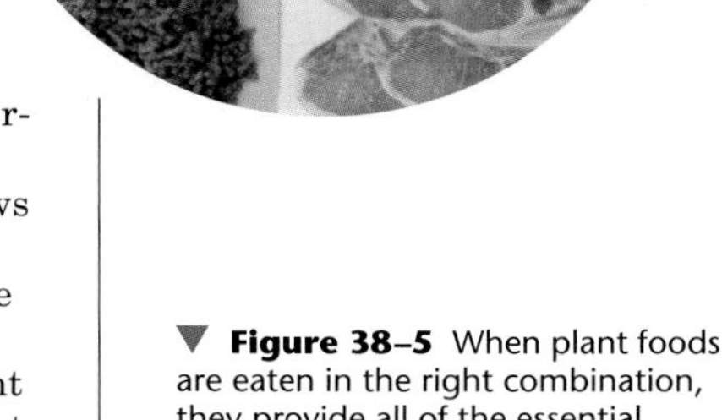

Based on the structure of their fatty acid chains, fats are classified as saturated or unsaturated. When there are only single bonds between the carbon atoms in the fatty acids, they have the maximum number of hydrogen atoms per carbon atom and the fat is said to be saturated. Most saturated fats are solids at room temperature—including butter and other animal fats.

Unsaturated fats have at least one double bond in a fatty acid chain. Unsaturated fats are usually liquids at room temperature. Because many vegetable oils contain more than one double bond, they are called polyunsaturated. **Figure 38–4** shows foods containing both saturated and unsaturated fats.

People often consume more fat than they actually need. The American Heart Association recommends a diet with a maximum of 30 percent of Calories from fat, of which only 10 percent should be from saturated fats. The health consequences of a diet high in fat are serious. They include an increased risk of high blood pressure, heart disease, obesity, and diabetes.

Proteins Proteins have a wide variety of roles. **Proteins** supply raw materials for growth and repair of structures such as skin and muscle. Proteins have regulatory and transport functions. For example, insulin controls the level of sugar in the blood. Hemoglobin transports oxygen. The enzymes that make biochemical reactions possible are proteins.

Proteins are polymers of amino acids. The body is able to produce only 12 of the 20 amino acids used to make proteins. The other 8, which are listed in **Figure 38–5**, are called essential amino acids because it is essential that they are included in the foods that you eat. Meat, fish, eggs, and milk generally contain all 8 essential amino acids. Plant foods do not. People who don't eat animal products must eat a combination of plant foods, such as beans and rice, to obtain all of the essential amino acids.

▼ **Figure 38–5** When plant foods are eaten in the right combination, they provide all of the essential amino acids. **Interpreting Graphics** ***Which amino acids are found in both grains and legumes?***

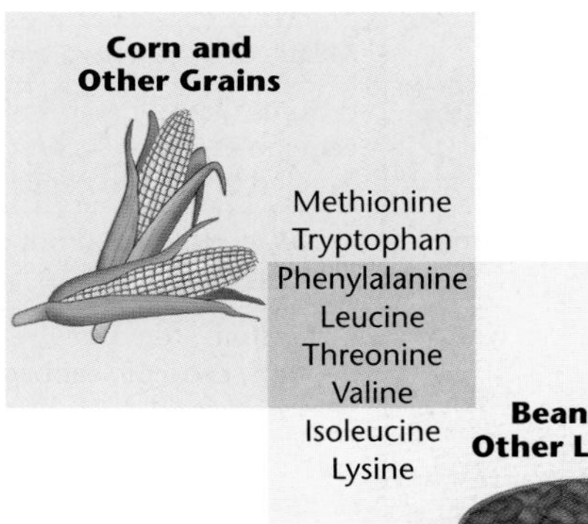

Build Science Skills

Designing Experiments Relate that populations with high-fiber diets have been found to have low rates of colon cancer. Add that people who eat high-fiber diets usually also have low-fat diets, which are known to lower colon cancer rates. Thus, it is not clear if fiber alone lowers colon cancer rates. Challenge students to design an experiment to help resolve this issue. *(Students should say they would compare colon cancer rates in people on high-fiber, low-fat diets with the rates in people on low-fiber, low-fat diets.)*

Make Connections

Mathematics Point out that no more than 30 percent of the Calories in the diet should come from fat. Ask: **If you eat 2,000 Calories a day, what is the maximum number of Calories that should come from fat?** *(600 Calories)* Urge students to read nutrition labels to find the total fat content of foods they might eat in a typical day.

Build Science Skills

Applying Concepts Explain the concept of complementary proteins, that is, proteins that individually lack one or more essential amino acids but together contain all eight. Point out that the amino acids in grains, such as corn, rice and wheat, complement the amino acids in legumes, such as beans, peas, and peanuts. Challenge students to apply the concept of complimentary proteins by planning a meatless meal that contains all eight essential amino acids. *(Possible meals might include beans with rice or peanut butter with bread.)*

FACTS AND FIGURES

How sweet it is

Because milk does not taste sweet, some people are surprised to learn that it contains sugar. In fact, 8 oz of milk contain 11 g of sugar, or more than half the sugar in the same amount of orange juice. Most of the sugar in milk is in the form of lactose, which is broken down into simpler sugars in the digestive tract by the enzyme lactase. Human infants, like the young of most other mammals, produce lactase and can digest lactose. Most adult mammals and many adult humans, on the other hand, no longer produce lactase. Therefore, they cannot digest lactose. When they drink milk, the lactose ferments in their intestines and causes gas, cramps, and diarrhea. Fortunately, there are special milk products available that lactose-intolerant people can digest because they contain lactase-producing bacteria.

Answers to . . .

CHECKPOINT *It cools the body when it evaporates from the surface.*

Figure 38–3 *Simple carbohydrates provide the body with quick energy.*

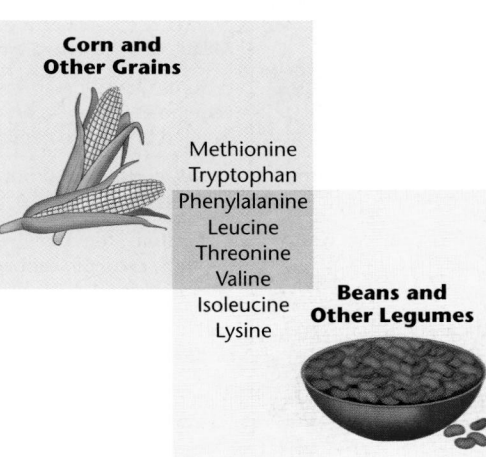

Figure 38–5 *Phenylalanine, leucine, threonine, and valine*

38–1 (continued)

Build Science Skills

Inferring Review the basic roles in the body that are played by carbohydrates, fats, and proteins. Ask: **What do you think would happen if you did not eat enough carbohydrates?** *(You might feel tired because you would not have enough immediate energy, and you would lose weight because your body would need to use stored reserves of energy. Your digestive and excretory systems might not function properly for lack of fiber.)* **What do you think would happen if you did not eat enough fat?** *(Your supply of fat-soluble vitamins might be depleted, which would affect functions such as blood clotting, vision, or bone growth. Because fats are needed for myelin sheaths, the function of the nervous system could be impaired.)* **What do you think would happen if you did not eat enough proteins?** *(Almost every body function could be affected because protein enzymes make biochemical reactions possible. You might feel tired because the body could not produce the hemoglobin needed to carry the oxygen that cells use for cellular respiration.)*

Use Visuals

Figure 38–6 Point out the column for sources of vitamins and ask: **Which types of food seem to be rich in many different vitamins?** *(Vegetables, whole grains, and dairy products)* Next, call students' attention to the column for function of vitamins and ask: **Which body systems need vitamins to function properly?** *(Virtually all body systems)* Have students compare the functions of the B vitamins in particular. Then, ask: **What general function do all the B vitamins have in common?** *(Metabolism)* Remind students that metabolism refers to all the chemical reactions that build up or break down substances in the body.

Vitamins If you think of carbohydrates, fats, and proteins as the fuel and parts of an automobile engine, then vitamins are the ignition. **Vitamins** are organic molecules that help regulate body processes, often working with enzymes. Some are made by bacteria that live in the digestive tract. Most vitamins must be obtained from food. Vitamin deficiencies, or the absence of certain vitamins, can have serious, even fatal, consequences.

The 14 vitamins listed in **Figure 38–6** are generally recognized as essential to human health. There are two types of vitamins: fat-soluble and water-soluble. The fat-soluble vitamins—vitamins A, D, E, and K—can be stored in the fatty tissues of the body. The body can build up small stores of

▼ **Figure 38–6** This table lists the food sources and functions of 14 essential vitamins. The fat-soluble vitamins are listed in the blue rows, and the water-soluble vitamins in the white rows. **Interpreting Graphics** *What is the function of vitamin K?*

Vitamins

Vitamin	Sources	Function
A (retinol)	Yellow, orange, and dark green vegetables; dairy products	Important for growth of skin cells; important for night vision
D (calciferol) 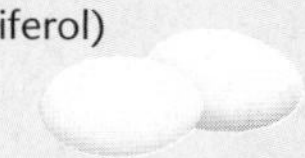	Fish oils, eggs; made by skin when exposed to sunlight; added to dairy products	Promotes bone growth; increases calcium and phosphorus absorption
E (tocopherol)	Green leafy vegetables, seeds, vegetable oils	Antioxidant; prevents cellular damage
K	Green leafy vegetables; made by bacteria that live in human intestine	Needed for normal blood clotting
B_1 (thiamine)	Whole grains, pork, legumes, milk	Normal metabolism of carbohydrates
B_2 (riboflavin) 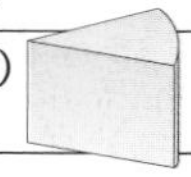	Dairy products, meats, vegetables, whole-grain cereal	Normal growth; part of electron transport chain; energy metabolism
Niacin	Liver, milk, whole grains, nuts, meats, legumes	Important in energy metabolism
B_6 (pyridoxine)	Whole grains, meats, vegetables	Important for amino acid metabolism
Pantothenic acid	Meats, dairy, whole grains	Needed for energy metabolism
Folic acid 	Legumes, nuts, green leafy vegetables, oranges, broccoli, peas, fortified bread and cereal	Coenzyme involved in nucleic acid metabolism; prevents neural-tube defects in developing fetuses
B_{12} (cyanocobalamin)	Meats, eggs, dairy products, enriched cereals	Coenzyme in nucleic acid metabolism; maturation of red blood cells
C (ascorbic acid) 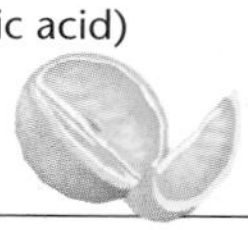	Citrus fruits, tomatoes, red or green peppers, broccoli, cabbage, strawberries	Maintenance of cartilage and bone; antioxidant; improves iron absorption; important for healthy gums, tissue repair, and wound healing
Biotin	Legumes, vegetables, meat	Coenzyme in synthesis of fat; glycogen formation; amino acid metabolism
Choline 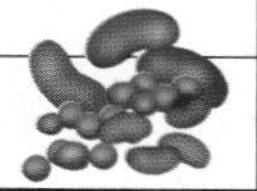	Egg yolk, liver, grains, legumes	Required for phospholipids and neurotransmitters

HISTORY OF SCIENCE

How vitamins were named

In the 1800s, sailors in the Japanese navy developed a nervous disorder named beriberi when they were fed a mostly white-rice diet. The sailors became extremely weak and suffered uncontrollable muscle spasms. Toward the end of the 1800s, a Dutch doctor noticed that prisoners who were fed mostly white rice also developed beriberi, whereas prisoners who were fed ordinary brown rice did not. The doctor inferred that some factor in the hull of the rice, which was removed when brown rice was converted to white, was needed by the body to prevent beriberi. A short time later, a Polish chemist isolated the factor and named it "vital amine," because it was so important to life and because he thought its chemical structure was that of an amine compound. He was incorrect with regard to the latter, but the name stuck and gave birth to the term *vitamin*.

Important Minerals		
Mineral	**Sources**	**Function**
Calcium	Dairy products; salmon; sardines; kale; tofu; collard greens; legumes	Bone and tooth formation; blood clotting; nerve and muscle function
Phosphorus	Dairy products; meats; poultry; grains	Bone and tooth formation; acid-base balance
Potassium	Meats; dairy products; many fruits and vegetables; grains	Acid-base balance; body water balance; nerve function
Chlorine	Table salt; processed foods	Acid-base balance; formation of gastric juice
Sodium	Table salt; processed foods	Acid-base balance; body water balance; nerve function
Magnesium	Whole grains; green leafy vegetables	Activation of enzymes in protein synthesis
Iron	Meats; eggs; legumes; whole grains; green leafy vegetables; dried fruit	Component of hemoglobin and of electron carriers used in energy metabolism
Fluorine	Fluoridated drinking water; tea; seafood	Maintenance of tooth structure; maintenance of bone structure
Iodine	Seafood; dairy products; iodized salt	Component of thyroid hormones
Zinc	Meats; seafood; grains	Component of certain digestive enzymes

▲ **Figure 38–7** Minerals are often called trace elements because they are needed by the body in such small amounts. **Inferring** ***Why do you think some cities and towns add fluoride to their water supply?***

these vitamins for future use. The water-soluble vitamins, which include vitamin C and the B vitamins, dissolve in water and cannot be stored. Therefore, they should be included in the foods you eat each day. Eating a diet containing a variety of foods will supply the daily vitamin needs of nearly everyone.

As you probably are aware, food stores and pharmacies sell vitamin supplements. Taking extra-large doses of vitamin supplements does not benefit the body, and in some cases, it may cause harm. Excessive amounts of vitamins A, D, E, and K can be toxic.

CHECKPOINT ***Why is it important to not take more than the recommended amount of fat-soluble vitamins?***

Minerals Inorganic nutrients that the body needs, usually in small amounts, are called **minerals.** Some examples of minerals are calcium, iron, and magnesium. Calcium is a major component of bones and teeth, and iron is needed to make hemoglobin, the oxygen-carrying protein in red blood cells. Magnesium is required for normal functioning of nerves and muscle tissue. **Figure 38–7** lists some of the minerals needed by the body.

Although the body does not digest the minerals it takes in, it does lose many of them in sweat, urine, and other waste products. How are these important chemicals replaced? Many of these elements are found in the living tissues of plants and other animals. By eating a variety of foods, you can meet your daily requirement of minerals.

Address Misconceptions

Ask: **Can taking a daily vitamin pill make up for a lack of vegetables, whole grains, dairy products, or other vitamin-rich foods in the diet?** *(Some students might say "Yes.")* Explain that foods such as these are rich not only in vitamins but in other nutrients as well. Ask: **What other nutrients do whole grains, vegetables, and dairy products provide?** *(Vegetables and whole grains provide carbohydrates, vitamins, and minerals. Dairy products provide proteins, fats, and minerals.)*

Use Visuals

Figure 38–7 Guide students in analyzing the information presented in the table by asking: **Which minerals are needed for healthy bones and teeth?** *(Calcium, phosphorus, and fluorine)* **Which mineral is needed for normal blood clotting?** *(Calcium)* **Which minerals are found in meats?** *(Phosphorus, potassium, iron, and zinc)* **Which minerals are found in grains?** *(Phosphorus, potassium, magnesium, iron, and zinc)* **What one food could you eat to increase the amount of iron, magnesium, and calcium in your diet?** *(Collard greens)*

BIOLOGY UPDATE

Please pass the selenium

Scientists continue to discover new substances in food that play important roles in the body. For example, in 1996 researchers at the Arizona Cancer Center found that patients who received 200 μg per day of the trace mineral selenium had a 50 to 60 percent lower risk of dying from lung, prostate, or colorectal cancer. Scientists still do not understand why selenium seems to protect against cancer, and not all scientists are convinced of its cancer-fighting abilities. Nonetheless, the results of the Arizona study have sparked further research to test selenium for its effect on specific cancers. Selenium is found in foods such as grain, meat, and fish, and most people in the United States eat enough of these foods to receive the recommended dietary allowance of 55 to 70 μg per day. However, this may not be enough selenium for an anti-cancer effect.

Answers to . . .

CHECKPOINT *They can be stored in the fatty tissues of the body and reach toxic levels.*

Figure 38–6 *Needed for normal blood clotting*

Figure 38–7 *To prevent cavities in children's teeth*

Balancing the Diet

Use Visuals

Figure 38–8 Call students' attention to the range of servings given for each food group in the Food Guide Pyramid. Challenge students to plan one day of meals and snacks that altogether contain the correct number of servings from each food group. Call on a few students to share their meal plans with the class. Ask: **How does eating according to the Food Guide Pyramid differ, if at all, from how you usually eat?** *(Most students probably will say that they do not usually eat as many servings of foods from the bottom of the pyramid and that they usually eat more servings of fats, oils, and sweets.)* **What foods could you add to your diet so it would be more balanced?** *(Students might say they could add more bread, cereal, fruits, and vegetables.)*

Make Connections

Environmental Science Point out that if you follow the Food Guide Pyramid, most of the food you eat will come from the bottom three food groups in the pyramid. Ask: **What types of foods are in the bottom three groups of the Food Guide Pyramid?** *(Plant foods)* **Where are plants always found in a food chain and what role do they fill?** *(They are always found on the bottom, and they fill the role of producer.)* Explain that only 10 percent of the energy at one level of a food chain is passed on to the next level. Conclude by saying that people can get far more energy from plants by eating plants directly than by eating animals that eat plants.

Balancing the Diet

It's no easy task to figure out the best balance of nutrients for the human diet, but nutritionists have tried to do exactly that. The result is the Food Guide Pyramid shown in **Figure 38–8.**

The Food Guide Pyramid classifies foods into six groups. It also indicates how many servings from each group should be eaten every day to maintain a healthy diet. Carbohydrate-rich foods such as bread, cereal, rice, and grains are at the base of the pyramid. At the top of the pyramid are foods such as fats and sweets, which should be used sparingly. Foods in the other groups already contain fats and sugars, so you should limit your intake of additional fats and sugars. The basic idea behind the pyramid is sound and simple—you should eat a variety of foods each day, and limit your intake of fatty, sugary foods.

▼ **Figure 38–8** The Food Guide Pyramid illustrates the main characteristics of a balanced diet. Carbohydrate-rich foods should make up the major portion of the diet, whereas foods containing fats and sugars should be eaten sparingly. **Interpreting Graphics** ***Why do you think nutritionists recommend that you limit your intake of fats, oils, and sweets?***

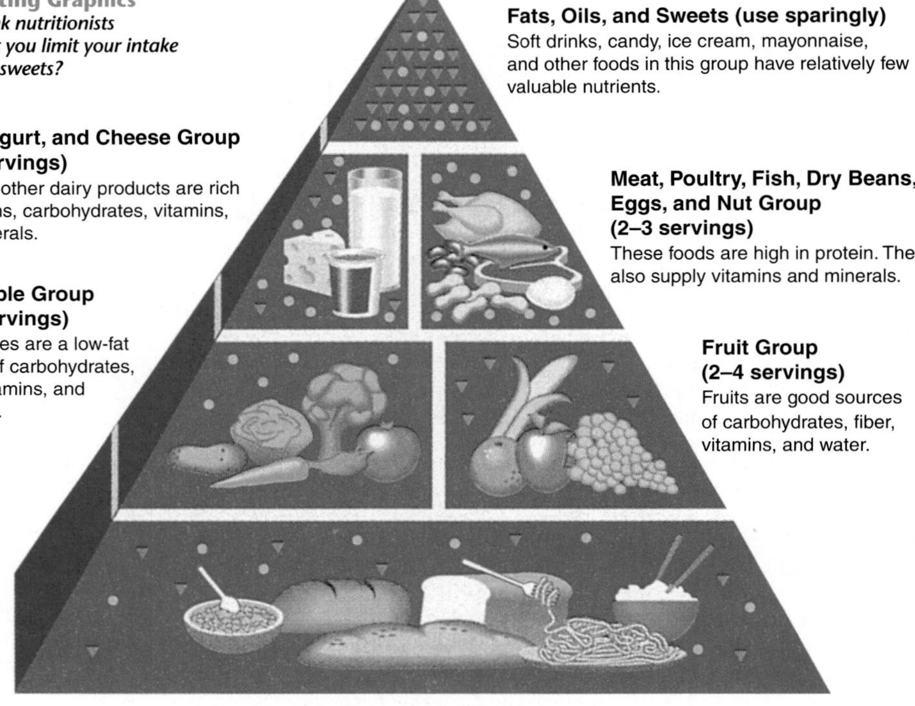
Fats, Oils, and Sweets (use sparingly)
Soft drinks, candy, ice cream, mayonnaise, and other foods in this group have relatively few valuable nutrients.
Milk, Yogurt, and Cheese Group (2–3 servings)
Milk and other dairy products are rich in proteins, carbohydrates, vitamins, and minerals.
Meat, Poultry, Fish, Dry Beans, Eggs, and Nut Group (2–3 servings)
These foods are high in protein. They also supply vitamins and minerals.
Vegetable Group (3–5 servings)
Vegetables are a low-fat source of carbohydrates, fiber, vitamins, and minerals.
Fruit Group (2–4 servings)
Fruits are good sources of carbohydrates, fiber, vitamins, and water.
Bread, Cereal, Rice, and Pasta Group (6–11 servings)
The foods at the base of the pyramid are rich in complex carbohydrates and also provide proteins, fiber, vitamins, and some minerals.

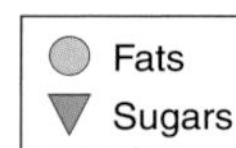
Fats
Sugars

BIO INSIGHTS

FACTS AND FIGURES

Eating bugs

Although eating bugs sounds disgusting to most Americans, in many other cultures bugs are considered to be an excellent food source. For example, in Mexico worms are served on tortillas, and in Colombia ground-up ants are spread on bread. Hundreds of other examples could be given. Why are bugs so appealing? Most insects are not only cheap sources of complete protein, but they are far cleaner and much lower in fat than other sources. Insects can also be very tasty. Deep-fried larvae and grubs, for example, are said to be delicious. Although most Americans do not deliberately eat bugs, they still get a lot of bugs in their diet—in fact, a whopping pound or two per person a year. Microscopic pieces of insects are found in many processed foods, including jam, peanut butter, tomato sauce, and frozen vegetables. In some foods, the addition of insects actually increases the nutritional content.

Analyzing Data

Reading Food Labels

Nutrients are substances your body needs for energy, growth, repair, and maintenance. Federal regulations require that labels on packaged foods display the nutrients each food contains, the percentage of daily value each nutrient represents for a person, as well as serving size, number of servings per container, and Calories per serving.

Carefully examine the nutritional information on the food label shown. Based on the information on the label, answer the questions that follow.

1. **Calculating** Calculate the daily value in grams for total carbohydrate and dietary fiber.
2. **Calculating** If you ate 2 cups of this product, how many grams of fat would you eat? How many grams of protein?
3. **Drawing Conclusions** Based on the data, which food do you think has more Calories: one with 8 g of fat or one with 8 g of carbohydrate? Explain your answer.
4. **Going Further** People with hypertension, or high blood pressure, often are advised to restrict their intake of sodium. Those who also are overweight are advised to lose excess pounds by following a diet lower in fat and in total Calories. Visit a local food store and look at the labels on 10 types of packaged foods. From this information, recommend which of the foods would be healthful for people who are overweight and have hypertension.

Nutrition Facts

Serving Size	1 cup (30g)
Servings Per Container	About 10
Amount Per Serving	
Calories 110	Calories from Fat 15
	% Daily Value*
Total Fat 2g	**3%**
Saturated Fat 0g	**0%**
Cholesterol 0mg	**0%**
Sodium 280mg	**12%**
Total Carbohydrate 22g	**7%**
Dietary Fiber 3g	**12%**
Sugars 1g	
Protein 3g	

Vitamin A 10%	• Vitamin C 20%
Calcium 4%	• Iron 45%

* Percent Daily Values are based on a 2,000 Calorie diet. Your daily values may be higher or lower depending on your caloric needs:

	Calories	2,000	2,500
Total Fat	Less than	65g	80g
Sat. Fat	Less than	20g	25g
Cholesterol	Less than	300mg	300mg
Sodium	Less than	2,400mg	2,400mg
Total Carbohydrate		300g	375g
Fiber		25g	30g

Calories per gram:
Fat 9 • Carbohydrate 4 • Protein 4

Ingredients: Whole grain oats, sugar, salt, milled corn, oat fiber, dried whey, hon... almonds, d...

Analyzing Data

Make sure students understand that the daily values on the nutrition label depend on the total Calories in the diet. Active teens may need 2,500 Calories a day instead of the 2,000 Calories that are used for calculating the percent daily values.

Answers

1. The daily value is 314 g for total carbohydrate and 25 g for dietary fiber in a 2000-Calorie diet.
2. You would eat 4 g of fat and 6 g of protein.
3. One with 8 g of fat, because there are more Calories per gram of fat.
4. Students should recommend foods such as low-fat dairy products that are relatively low in sodium, fats, and total Calories.

38–1 Section Assessment

1. **Key Concept** List the six nutrients needed by the body.
2. **Key Concept** What is the importance of water in the body?
3. Why is fiber an important part of your diet?
4. How are vitamins and minerals similar? How are they different?
5. **Critical Thinking Interpreting Graphics** Which vitamins and minerals promote healthy bones? (See **Figures 38–6** and **38–7.**)

iTEXT **Assessment** Use iText to review the important concepts in Section 38–1.

ALTERNATIVE ASSESSMENT

Designing a Brochure Design and create a brochure that explains how the body uses the six nutrients necessary for normal function. Use images from magazines or from the Internet to illustrate your brochure.

3 ASSESS

Evaluate Understanding

Call on students at random to name the six types of nutrients. Call on other students to describe their roles in the body.

Reteach

Have students review the Food Guide Pyramid. Then, have them name the nutrients that foods in each group are rich in. *(For example, the vegetable food group is rich in carbohydrates, vitamins, and minerals.)*

ALTERNATIVE ASSESSMENT

Have students begin with an outline. Many word processing programs include a brochure feature, which you may want students to explore before they begin designing their brochures. Brochures should demonstrate an understanding of the most important functions of each of the six types of nutrients.

38–1 Section Assessment

1. Water, carbohydrates, fats, proteins, vitamins, and minerals
2. Some body tissues, such as blood, are mostly water, and water is needed for many body processes, including chemical reactions, elimination of wastes, and keeping the body cool through evaporation.
3. Fiber adds bulk to the material moving through the digestive system, helping it to process food more effectively.
4. Both vitamins and minerals are nutrients that are needed in small amounts for good health, but vitamins are organic molecules, whereas minerals are inorganic.
5. Vitamins C and D; calcium, phosphorus, and fluorine

Use iText to review the key concepts in Section 38–1.

Answer to . . .

Figure 38–8 *They have few valuable nutrients and are high in Calories.*

Section 38–2

1 FOCUS

Objectives

38.2.1 ***Identify*** the organs of the digestive system.

38.2.2 ***Describe*** the function of the digestive system.

Guide for Reading

Vocabulary Preview

If students have difficulty pronouncing any of the vocabulary words, it may interfere with their comprehension. Read each of the words to the class and have students repeat them after you. Point out that *villus* is singular and the plural is *villi*.

Reading Strategy

Before they read, have students draw a line down the center of a piece of paper. On the left side they should write down the organs of the digestive system. Then, as they read the section, they should record important details about each organ on the right side of the paper, including the organ's location, structure, and function.

2 INSTRUCT

The Mouth

Meet Diverse Needs

Help students understand the difference between the mechanical and chemical digestion that take place in the mouth by allowing them to experience mechanical and chemical processes. Have one student break a raw egg into a bowl and scramble it with a fork. Have another student pour the scrambled raw egg into a pan of boiling water. Have students watch as the egg solidifies in the boiling water. Ask: **Which process was mechanical, and which was chemical?** *(Breaking and scrambling the raw egg was mechanical. Cooking the raw egg was chemical.)* **Learning modality: kinesthetic**

38–2 The Process of Digestion

Guide for Reading

Key Concepts
- What are the organs of the digestive system?
- What is the function of the digestive system?

Vocabulary
amylase
esophagus
peristalsis
stomach
peptic ulcer
chyme
small intestine
pancreas
liver
villus
large intestine

Reading Strategy: Asking Questions Before you read, rewrite the headings in the section as *how, why,* or *what* questions. As you read, write brief answers to the heading questions.

Food presents every animal with at least two challenges. The first is how to obtain it. Once an animal has caught, gathered, or engulfed its food, it faces a new challenge—how to break that food down into small molecules that can be passed to the cells that need them. This is the job of the digestive system. As food passes through the digestive system, it gets disassembled, distributing its nutrient value to the body along the way.

The human digestive system, like those of other chordates, is built around an alimentary canal—a one-way tube that passes through the body. **The digestive system includes the mouth, pharynx, esophagus, stomach, small intestine, and large intestine. Several major accessory structures, including the salivary glands, the pancreas, and the liver, add secretions to the digestive system.**

The Mouth

As you take a forkful of food into your mouth, the work of the digestive system begins. The teeth tear and crush the moistened food into a fine paste until it is ready to be swallowed. Chewing begins the process of mechanical digestion—the physical breakdown of large pieces of food into smaller pieces. But there is a great deal more to it than that. As you chew your food, digestive enzymes begin to break food molecules down into smaller molecules. This process is called chemical digestion. During chemical digestion, large food molecules are broken down into smaller food molecules. **The function of each organ of the digestive system is to help convert foods into simpler molecules that can be absorbed and used by the cells of the body.**

Teeth The teeth shown in **Figure 38–9** are anchored in the bones of the jaw. The surfaces of the teeth, which are much tougher than ordinary bone, are protected by a coating of mineralized enamel. Teeth do much of the mechanical work of digestion by cutting, tearing, and crushing food into small fragments.

What do the teeth do?

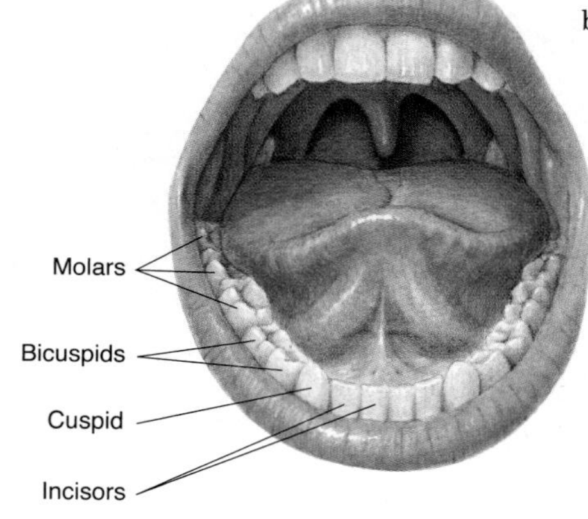

◀ **Figure 38–9** Human teeth include sharp incisors; cuspids and bicuspids, which grasp and tear food; and large, flat molars. **Inferring** *How do human teeth reflect an omnivorous diet?*

SECTION RESOURCES

Print:
- ***Laboratory Manual B,*** Chapter 38 Lab
- ***Teaching Resources,*** Section Review 38–2
- ***Guided Reading and Study Workbook,*** Section 38–2

Technology:
- ***iText,*** Section 38–2

FIGURE 38–10 THE DIGESTIVE SYSTEM

The digestive system includes the mouth, pharynx, esophagus, stomach, small intestine, and large intestine.

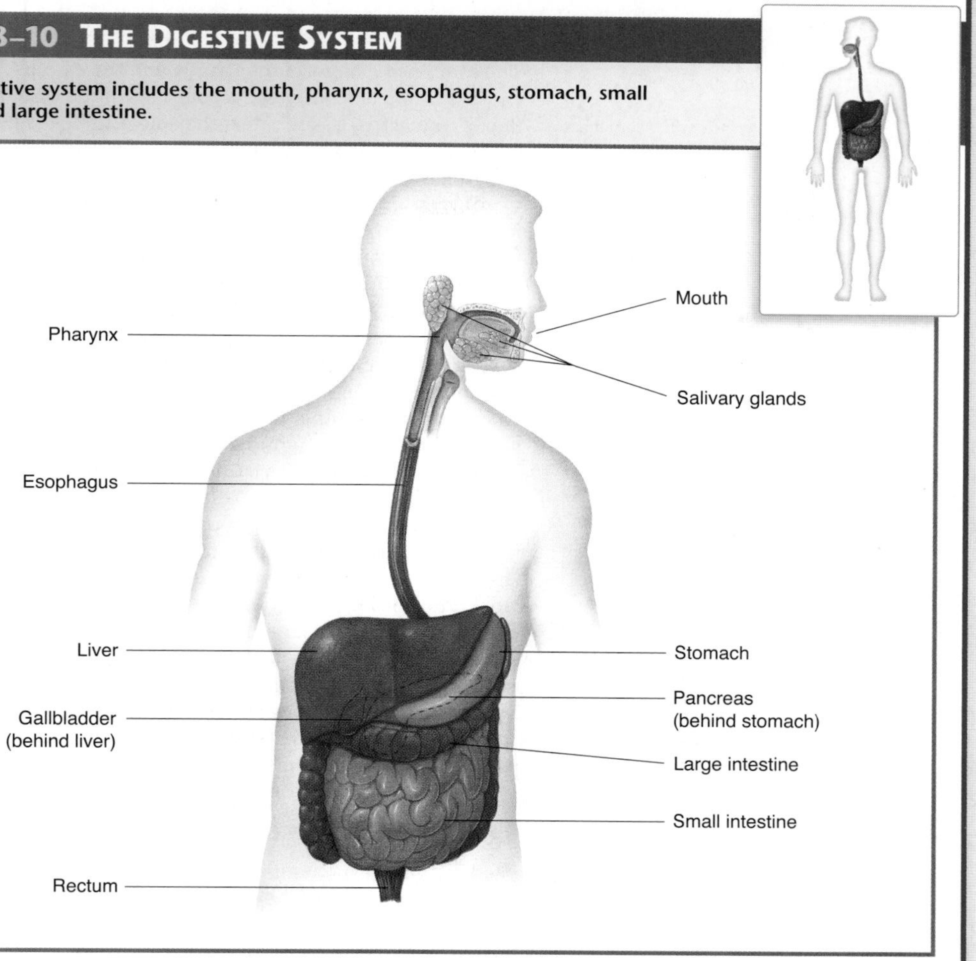

Mouth
Pharynx
Salivary glands
Esophagus
Liver
Stomach
Pancreas (behind stomach)
Gallbladder (behind liver)
Large intestine
Small intestine
Rectum

Saliva As the teeth cut and grind the food, the salivary glands secrete saliva, which helps to moisten the food and make it easier to chew. The release of saliva is under the control of the nervous system, and can be triggered by the scent of food—especially when you are hungry!

Saliva not only helps ease the passage of food through the digestive system. It begins the process of chemical digestion. Saliva contains an enzyme called **amylase** that breaks chemical bonds between the sugar monomers in starches. If you chew on a starchy food like crackers long enough, it will begin to taste sweet. This sweet taste is a sign that sugar has been released from starch by the action of amylase. Saliva also contains lysozyme, an enzyme that fights infection by digesting the cell walls of many bacteria that may enter the mouth with food.

Build Science Skills

Using Models Point out that different types of teeth have different mechanical functions: incisors cut, canines tear, and molars crush. Ask: **Can you think of tools that perform similar mechanical functions?** *(Scissors cut like incisors, tweezers tear like canines, and mallets crush like molars.)*

Demonstration

Demonstrate how the amylase in saliva chemically breaks down food. Give each student a soda cracker. Have students chew their cracker for five seconds and record how it tastes. Have them continue chewing their cracker for five minutes and again record how it tastes. Ask: **How and why did the taste of the cracker change?** *(The cracker became sweeter as amylase broke down some of the starches into sugars.)*

Use Visuals

Figure 38–10 Name each of the digestive organs, starting with the mouth and ending with the large intestine. As you name each organ, have students locate it in the figure and trace the route that food follows to reach it. Tell students that the liver and pancreas secrete substances that help break down food but that food does not actually pass through them. Ask: **Into which structure do you think the liver and pancreas release their secretions?** *(Into the small intestine)* Point out the cardiac sphincter between the esophagus and stomach and the pyloric sphincter between the stomach and small intestine. Explain that they prevent food from moving backward in the system.

PRESENTATIONS MADE EASY!

The Presentation Assistant Plus contains the Prentice Hall Presentation Pro and the Transparencies, which provide easy-to-follow visual support for every step of this section. If you have a computer presentation station, use Prentice Hall Presentation Pro for Section 38–2, or use the transparencies listed here.

Section 38–2:

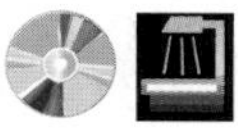

Interest Grabber
Section Outline
Digestive Enzymes
Figure 38–10
Figure 38–13
Figure 38–14

Answers to . . .

CHECKPOINT *The teeth do much of the mechanical work of digestion by cutting, tearing, and crushing food into smaller fragments.*

Figure 38–9 *The different types and functions of human teeth make them well suited for eating the variety of foods in an omnivorous diet.*

The Esophagus

Demonstration

Demonstrate with a simple model how peristalsis pushes food through the esophagus. Place a marble inside one end of a 25- to 30-cm length of flexible plastic or rubber tubing. With a squeezing motion of your hands, move the marble down and out the other end of the tube. Ask: **If this is a model of the esophagus, what does the tube represent and what does the marble represent?** *(The tube represents the esophagus, and the marble represents the bolus of food that is being swallowed.)* **How is peristalsis modeled?** *(By the squeezing of your hand along the tube from one end to the other.)*

The Stomach

Build Science Skills

Inferring Ask: **How do you know when you are hungry?** *(Students probably will say that their stomach growls or hurts.)* Explain that these feelings of hunger are controlled by a center in the hypothalamus at the base of the brain, called the hunger center. The hunger center senses when blood levels of nutrients are low, and sends out nerve impulses that lead to stomach contractions. Ask: **What do you think causes the feelings of hunger to stop once you have eaten?** *(Students should infer that increasing levels of nutrients in the blood stimulate the hunger center to send out nerve impulses that stop the stomach contractions.)*

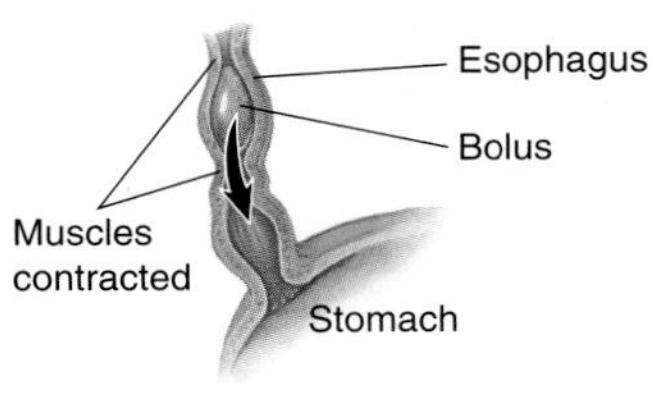

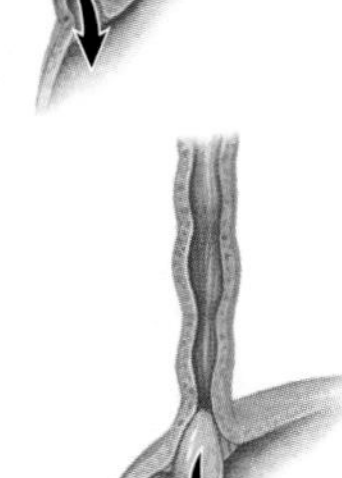

▲ **Figure 38–11** Muscles in the walls of the esophagus contract in waves. Each wave pushes the bolus in front of it. Eventually, the bolus is pushed into the stomach. **Applying Concepts** ***What kind of muscle surrounds the esophagus?***

The Esophagus

The combined actions of the tongue and throat muscles push the chewed clump of food, called a bolus, down the throat. Recall that a flap of connective tissue called the epiglottis closes over the opening to the trachea as you swallow. This action prevents food from clogging the air passageways to the lungs.

From the throat, the bolus passes through the **esophagus,** or food tube, into the stomach. You might think that gravity draws food down through the esophagus, but this is not correct. You are able to swallow food just fine while lying down or standing on your head. Astronauts are even able to swallow food in the weightless environment of space! The reason food travels through the esophagus into the stomach is that it is moved along by contractions of smooth muscle surrounding the esophagus. Known as **peristalsis** (pehr-uh-STAL-sis), these contractions squeeze the food through the 25-centimeter length of the esophagus into the stomach. Peristalsis is illustrated in **Figure 38–11.**

A thick ring of muscle, called the cardiac sphincter, closes the esophagus after food has passed into the stomach, and prevents the contents of the stomach from moving back up into the esophagus. Have you ever suffered from "heartburn"? Heartburn is a painful, burning sensation that feels as if it is coming from the center of the chest, just above the stomach. The sensation is usually caused by stomach acid that moves past the cardiac sphincter and splashes against the lining of the esophagus. Overeating or an excess of caffeinated drinks can cause the cardiac sphincter muscles to open, allowing stomach acid to back up into the esophagus.

The Stomach

Food from the esophagus empties into a large muscular sac called the **stomach.** The size of the stomach enables you to eat a few large meals a day, rather than having to nibble all the time. The stomach continues the mechanical digestion of food. Contractions of its smooth muscles thoroughly churn and mix the food you swallow.

Chemical Digestion The lining of the stomach contains millions of microscopic gastric glands that release a number of substances into the stomach. Some of these glands produce mucus, a fluid that lubricates and protects the stomach wall. Other glands produce hydrochloric acid, which makes the contents of the stomach very acidic. The acid activates an enzyme called pepsin, which is secreted by a third set of glands. Pepsin works best under the acidic conditions present in the stomach. The combination of pepsin and hydrochloric acid begins the complex process of protein digestion. Pepsin breaks proteins into smaller polypeptide fragments. Some other enzymes that help in digestion are shown in **Figure 38–12.**

✓CHECKPOINT ***What is the role of pepsin?***

FACTS AND FIGURES

Not just heartburn

Most people have experienced heartburn, the burning sensation in the chest that is caused by stomach acids entering the esophagus. In about 25 to 35 percent of people, heartburn becomes chronic and signals a more serious disorder, called gastroesophageal reflux disease, or GERD. In addition to heartburn, symptoms of GERD may include regurgitation and difficulty swallowing. There is no single cause of GERD, but factors such as defects in the lower esophageal sphincter, slower-than-normal emptying of the stomach, and decreased secretion of bicarbonate by the esophagus may all play a role. Complications of GERD include esophagitis, or inflammation of the esophagus, and Barrett's esophagus, a precancerous condition in which abnormal cells replace normal cells in the esophagus. Treatment of GERD includes lifestyle changes, medications to control stomach acids, and, in severe cases, surgery.

Ulcers The powerful acids released into the stomach sometimes damage the organ's own lining, producing a hole in the stomach wall known as a **peptic ulcer.** For years, physicians assumed that the primary cause of ulcers was too much stomach acid. They prescribed drugs that suppressed acid production, and recommended bland, easily digested diets.

Scientists have discovered that peptic ulcers are usually caused by the bacterium *Helicobacter pylori.* Doctors around the world now know that many peptic ulcers are caused by an infectious disease that can be cured. Thanks to powerful antibiotics, cure rates for peptic ulcers are as high as 90 percent.

Mechanical Digestion As digestion proceeds, stomach muscles contract to churn and mix stomach fluids and food, gradually producing a mixture known as **chyme** (KYM). After an hour or two, the pyloric valve, which is located between the stomach and small intestine, opens and chyme begins to flow into the small intestine.

Digestive Enzymes

Site	Enzyme	Role in Digestion
Mouth	Salivary amylase	Breaks down starches into disaccharides
Stomach	Pepsin	Breaks down proteins into large peptides
Small intestine (from pancreas)	Amylase	Continues the breakdown of starch
	Trypsin	Continues the breakdown of protein
	Lipase	Breaks down fat
Small intestine	Maltase, sucrase, lactase	Breaks down remaining disaccharides into monosaccharides
	Peptidase	Breaks down dipeptides into amino acids

▲ **Figure 38–12** Digestive enzymes break down foods and make nutrients available to the body. **Interpreting Graphics** ***Where in the body does the digestion of carbohydrates begin?***

The Pancreas and Liver

As chyme is pushed through the pyloric valve, it enters the duodenum (doo-oh-DEE-num). The duodenum is the first of three parts of the small intestine. The **small intestine** is the location where most of chemical digestion takes place. As chyme enters the duodenum from the stomach, it mixes with enzymes and digestive fluids from the pancreas, the liver, and even the lining of the duodenum itself. The pancreas and liver are shown in **Figure 38–13.**

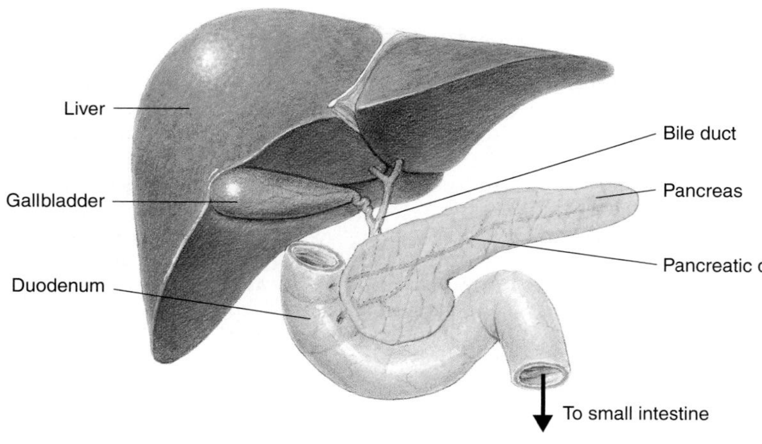

◀ **Figure 38–13** **Accessory structures, including the liver and pancreas, add secretions to the digestive system.** The pancreas secretes enzymes that help break down carbohydrates, proteins, and fats.

Use Visuals

Figure 38–12 Guide students in interpreting the information in the table. Remind them that food passes through each of the organs listed in the table and that the pancreas is a gland that secretes digestive enzymes into the small intestine. Ask: **Which enzymes break down proteins?** *(Pepsin, trypsin, and peptidase)* **Where are these enzymes found?** *(Pepsin is found in the stomach; trypsin and peptidase are found in the small intestine.)* **Where does the breakdown of starch into simpler carbohydrates take place?** *(The mouth and small intestine)* **Which nutrients do enzymes secreted by the pancreas help digest?** *(Starch, protein, and fat)*

The Pancreas and Liver

Address Misconceptions

Students may know that the pancreas produces insulin and confuse its role in the production of insulin with its role in digestion. Explain that the insulin and digestive enzymes that are secreted into the small intestine are produced by different parts of the pancreas.

Use Visuals

Figure 38–13 Point out in Figure 38–10 where the liver and pancreas are located. Explain that the role of the gallbladder is to store bile produced in the liver. Ask: **Where does the bile go after it leaves the gallbladder?** *(To the small intestine)*

BIO INSIGHTS — HISTORY OF SCIENCE

Watching as the stomach churns
In 1822, a U.S. army surgeon named William Beaumont was called upon to treat a gunshot wound in the stomach of a Canadian fur trapper. The wound eventually healed, but it left a permanent hole to the outside in the man's stomach. Beaumont saw this as a rare opportunity to study the role of the stomach in digestion. With his patient's reluctant permission, Beaumont inserted bits of food tied to strings into the stomach through the hole. Then, he withdrew them periodically to see the extent of digestion. Beaumont also siphoned off gastric secretions and had their chemical composition analyzed. He learned that digestion is primarily a chemical process and that gastric secretions consist mostly of hydrochloric acid. These and other results of Beaumont's innovative research still remain valid today.

Answers to . . .

CHECKPOINT *To break proteins into smaller polypeptide fragments*

Figure 38–11 *Smooth muscle*

Figure 38–12 *In the mouth*

Make Connections

Chemistry Pour 100 mL of 0.5 percent hydrochloric acid into a beaker and measure its acidity with pH paper. Then, stir 2 mL of sodium bicarbonate solution into the acid and test the pH again. Continue adding small amounts of sodium bicarbonate as needed until the solution has a neutral pH of 7. Ask: **Where in the digestive system is sodium bicarbonate produced?** *(In the pancreas)* **Why is it produced there?** *(To neutralize hydrochloric acid so it will not break down pancreatic digestive enzymes)*

Quick Lab

Objective Students will be able to apply the concept that folding increases surface area.

Skills Focus Applying Concepts, Inferring

Materials 2 paper towels, scissors, 2 cardboard tubes, metric ruler, 30-mL graduated cylinder, 2 plastic cups

Time 20 minutes

Advance Prep Ask students to bring in cardboard tubes from rolls of paper towels, aluminum foil, or plastic wrap to use for the lab.

Strategy You may wish to calculate class averages for the data before students answer the questions so that all the students are working with the same numbers.

Expected Outcome Students should observe that the tubes containing folded paper towels retain more water.

Analyze and Conclude

1. The folded paper towel has more surface area, which enables it to absorb more water. Students may have predicted correctly that the folded towel would absorb more water.
2. Folds and projections increase the area of the surface and its ability to absorb substances. Villi increase the surface area of the small intestine, which increases its ability to absorb nutrients.
3. Dividing the flow of blood among many small structures increases the surface area through which wastes can be removed.

Just below the stomach is the **pancreas.** The pancreas is a gland that serves three important functions. One function is to produce hormones that regulate blood sugar levels. Within the digestive system, the pancreas plays two key roles. It produces enzymes that break down carbohydrates, proteins, lipids, and nucleic acids. The pancreas also produces sodium bicarbonate, a base that neutralizes stomach acid so that these enzymes can be effective. Why is this neutralization necessary? Stomach acid can change the shapes of protein molecules and enzymes are proteins. If the shape of an enzyme's active site does not match the shape of its substrate, the enzyme will not be effective.

Assisting the pancreas is the **liver,** a large organ located just above the stomach. The liver produces bile, a fluid loaded with lipids and salts. Bile acts like a detergent, dissolving and dispersing the droplets of fat found in fatty foods. This action makes it possible for enzymes to reach the fat molecules and break them down. Bile is stored in a small, pouchlike organ called the gallbladder.

✓CHECKPOINT *What is bile?*

Quick Lab

How do villi help the small intestine absorb nutrients?

Materials 2 paper towels, scissors, 2 cardboard tubes, metric ruler, 30-mL graduated cylinder, 2 plastic cups

Procedure

1. Cut and roll up a single sheet of paper towel so that it fits in a cardboard tube without overlapping itself. **CAUTION:** *Scissors are sharp.* The tube represents the small intestine and the paper towel represents an intestinal lining without villi.
2. Spread the paper towel out flat and use the ruler to determine the area of the towel (area = width × length). Put the paper towel back in the tube.
3. Fold the second paper towel back and forth on itself in a zigzag pattern as if you are making a fan. Then, roll up the crinkled paper to fit in the second tube without overlapping itself. Cut off any excess. The folds represent an intestinal lining with villi.
4. **Predicting** Repeat step 2 for the second towel. Predict which model will absorb more water.
5. Stand each tube in a plastic cup. Slowly pour 30 mL of water down the inside of each tube. Remove the tubes. Then, measure and record the quantity of water in each cup.

Analyze and Conclude

1. **Observing** Which model had more surface area? How does surface area affect the ability to absorb substances? Was your prediction in step 4 correct?
2. **Applying Concepts** How do folds and finger-like projections affect the area of an absorbing surface? How do villi help the intestine absorb nutrients?
3. **Inferring** Your kidneys contain about 1 million microscopic structures that filter waste products from your blood. What advantage does this arrangement have over filtering the waste products out of one large blood vessel?

FACTS AND FIGURES

The gallbladder examined
Located just beneath the liver, the gallbladder is a pear-shaped sack about 9 cm long that concentrates and stores liver bile until it is needed to help digest fats. The gallbladder can store up to 50 mL of concentrated bile. When the bile is needed for digestion, it travels from the gallbladder to the small intestine through the bile duct, which also transports digestive enzymes from the pancreas to the small intestine. In some people, mineral salts in the gallbladder harden to form gallstones. Some of these may lodge in the bile duct and block it, causing pain as well as preventing the bile duct from transporting bile and pancreatic enzymes to the small intestine. Ultrasound usually is used to break up the stones so they can pass out of the body, although in severe cases removal of the gallbladder may be necessary.

FIGURE 38–14 THE SMALL INTESTINE

The lining of the small intestine consists of folds that are covered with tiny projections called villi. Within each villus there is a network of blood capillaries and lymph vessels that absorb and carry away nutrients. **Applying Concepts** *How do the folds in the small intestine help in absorption?*

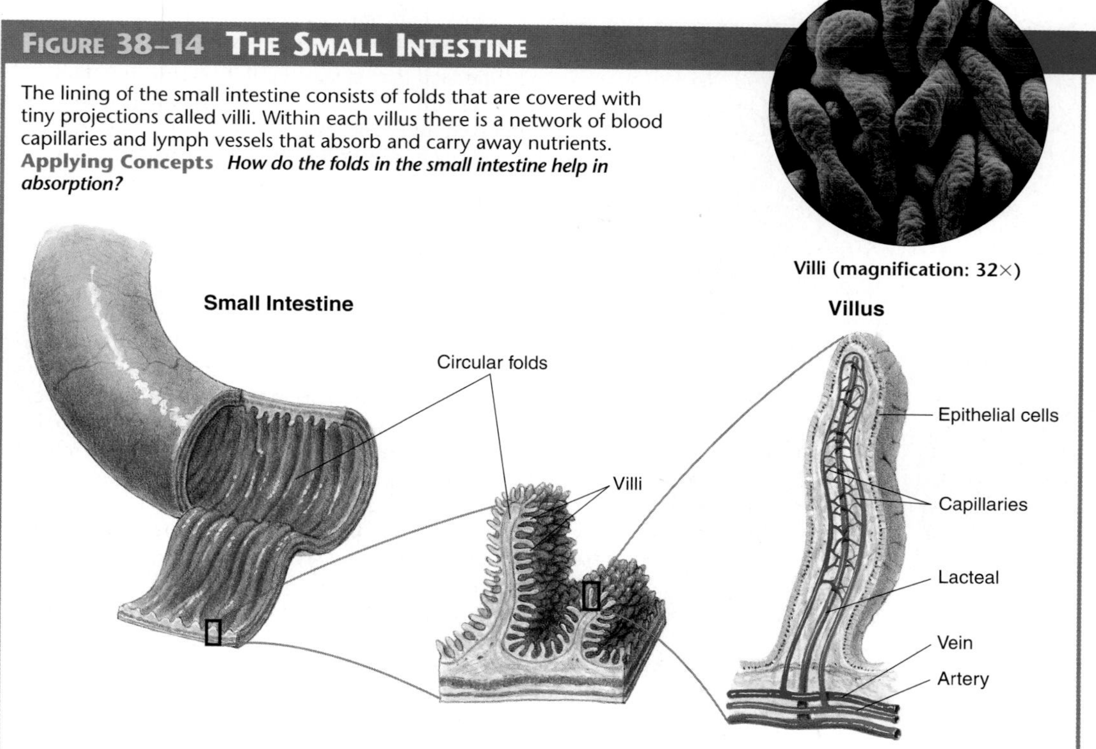

The Small Intestine

The duodenum is much shorter than the remaining parts of the small intestine—the jejunum and the ileum, which are about three meters long. By the time chyme enters these parts of the small intestine, much of the chemical digestion has been completed. The chyme is now a rich mixture of medium and small nutrient molecules.

The small intestine is specially adapted to absorb nutrients. The folded surfaces of the small intestine are covered with projections called **villi** (VIL-eye; singular: villus). The villi are illustrated in **Figure 38–14.** The surfaces of the cells of the villi are covered with thousands of fingerlike projections known as microvilli. These folds and projections mean that the small intestine has an enormous surface area available to absorb nutrient molecules. Slow, wavelike contractions of smooth muscles move the chyme along this surface.

Nutrient molecules are rapidly absorbed into the cells lining the small intestine. Most of the products of carbohydrate and protein digestion are absorbed into the capillaries in the villi. Molecules of undigested fat and some fatty acids are absorbed by lymph vessels called lacteals.

The Small Intestine

Address Misconceptions

Students may have the mistaken impression that the duodenum is the most important part of the small intestine because the bulk of chemical digestion takes place there. Point out that about 3 meters of the small intestine is devoted to absorption, whereas only about 25 centimeters are involved in digestion. Ask: **What percent of the small intestine is involved in absorbing nutrients?** *(About 92 percent)* **Why is this part of the small intestine so long?** *(Most nutrients are absorbed across the surface of capillaries, so a lot of surface area is needed.)*

Use Visuals

Figure 38–14 Make sure students understand how the different parts of the figure are related. Call attention to the many capillaries in each villus and describe their role in the absorption of nutrients. Also, help students relate the figure to the information in the text by asking them to complete the following analogy: **Villi are to the small intestine as ______ are to villi.** *(Microvilli)*

Meet Diverse Needs

Give students an opportunity to feel how small and densely distributed villi are. Pass a piece of velvet fabric around the room, and have students run their hands over the napped surface. Tell them that the tiny projections on the surface of the cloth are similar in size and density to the villi lining the small intestine. **Learning modality: tactile**

FACTS AND FIGURES

Beneficial bacteria

There are enough bacteria in your large intestine to fill a soup can. The relationship between you and the bacteria is mutualistic because both of you benefit: the bacteria provide you with vitamins and help your digestion, while you provide the bacteria with a warm, moist environment and plenty of nutrients. The environment is also a safe one for the bacteria—unless you take antibiotics for an infection. Antibiotics kill beneficial as well as harmful bacteria. If too many beneficial bacteria are killed, you may develop diarrhea because loss of beneficial bacteria impairs the removal of water from the large intestine. Other bacteria are beneficial to humans because they help in food processing. Such foods as yogurt, cheese, sour cream, buttermilk, pickles, sauerkraut, and vinegar would not exist without these beneficial bacteria.

Answers to . . .

CHECKPOINT *Bile is a fluid produced by the liver that dissolves and disperses the droplets of fat found in fatty foods.*

Figure 38–14 *The folds increase the surface area for the absorption of nutrients.*

The Large Intestine

Meet Diverse Needs

Challenge students to estimate the surface areas of the small and large intestines based on their diameters and lengths (2.5 cm by 325 cm for the small intestine and 6 cm by 150 cm for the large intestine). Students should use the formula for the area of a cylinder: $2\pi r(r+h)$. *(Surface area is about 2500 cm² for the small intestine and 2800 cm² for the large intestine.)* Because of villi, the surface area of the small intestine is actually about 8,000,000 cm^2. Ask: **Why does the large intestine need so much less surface area than the small intestine?** *(There are no nutrients absorbed in the large intestine.)* **Learning modality: logical/mathematical**

3 ASSESS

Evaluate Understanding

Have students make a table with the headings: Mouth, Stomach, Small Intestine, Pancreas. Have them list the enzymes found in or produced by each organ and the nutrients that the enzymes help break down.

Reteach

Describe the functions of the digestive organs, and have students identify them from their functions.

Take It to the NET

The table could include ulcers (*Helicobacter pylori,* pain medications, anti-inflammatory drugs); cirrhosis (alcohol); heartburn (cigarettes); diverticulosis (low-fiber diet); inflammatory bowel disease (unknown). For additional information, visit **www.phschool.com**

Use iText to review the key concepts in Section 38–2.

Answer to . . .

Figure 38–15 *To remove water from undigested material*

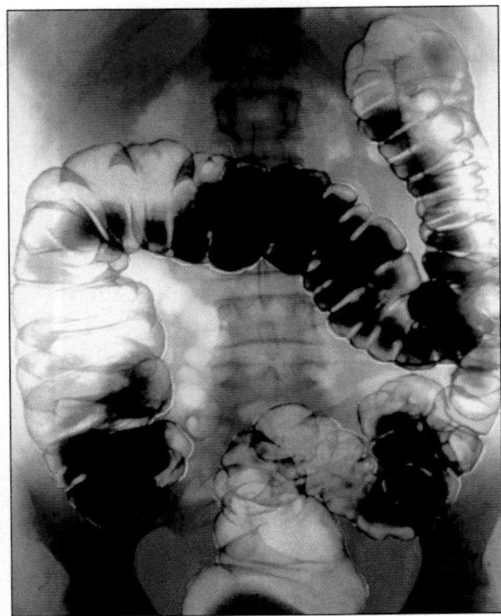

▲ **Figure 38–15** This barium X-ray shows the large intestine. **Applying Concepts** *What is the role of the large intestine?*

The Large Intestine

By the time food leaves the small intestine, it is basically nutrient-free. The complex organic molecules have been digested and absorbed, leaving only water, cellulose, and other undigestible substances behind. The chyme enters the large intestine, or colon. The primary job of the **large intestine** is to remove water from the undigested material that is left. The large intestine is shown in **Figure 38–15.**

Just below the entry to the colon is a small organ called the appendix. Some animals have appendixes in which cellulose is digested by bacteria. In humans, the appendix appears to do little to promote digestion. The only time people pay attention to the appendix is when it becomes inflamed, causing appendicitis. The remedy for acute appendicitis is to surgically remove the infected organ as quickly as possible.

Water is moved quickly across the large intestine wall. Rich colonies of bacteria grow on the undigested material left in the colon. These intestinal bacterial help the digestive process. Some of the bacteria produce compounds that the body can use, such as vitamin K. The concentrated waste material that remains after the water has been removed passes through the rectum and is eliminated from the body. When something happens that interferes with the removal of water by the large intestine, you usually become aware of it right away. The condition that is produced is known as diarrhea. The loss of salts and water due to diarrhea can be life threatening, especially for an infant. Diarrhea resulting from bacterial infections and contaminated drinking water is the leading cause of childhood death in many developing countries around the world.

38–2 Section Assessment

1. **Key Concept** List the organs of the digestive system and give the function of each.
2. **Key Concept** Explain the role of the digestive system.
3. How do mechanical and chemical digestion work together to break down foods?
4. How does bile help in the digestion of fats?
5. **Critical Thinking Inferring** What can you infer about the diet of an animal that has a large appendix?

iText Assessment Use iText to review the important concepts in Section 38–2.

Take It to the NET Read about diseases of the digestive system. Then, create a table that lists the cause or contributing factors for five digestive diseases. Use the links provided in the Biology area at the Prentice Hall Web site for help: **www.phschool.com**

38–2 Section Assessment

1. Mouth: begins mechanical digestion, begins chemical digestion of starch; esophagus: moves food to stomach; stomach: continues mechanical digestion, begins chemical digestion of protein; small intestine: completes chemical digestion of starch and protein, chemical digestion of fats; large intestine: removes water from undigested food.
2. To convert foods into simple molecules that can be absorbed and used by cells
3. Mechanical digestion physically breaks down food into smaller pieces, which makes it easier for enzymes to chemically break down large food molecules into smaller molecules.
4. The action of bile makes it possible for enzymes to reach and break down fats.
5. The diet contains a lot of cellulose.

38–3 The Excretory System

The chemistry of the human body is a marvelous thing. An intricate system of checks and balances controls everything from your blood pressure to your body temperature. Nutrients are absorbed, stored, and carefully released when they are needed. However, every living system, including the human body, produces chemical waste products that are not useful to the body. Some waste products are even so toxic that the body needs a system to eliminate them.

Guide for Reading

Key Concepts
- What are the organs of the excretory system?
- How do the kidneys maintain homeostasis?

Vocabulary
- kidney • ureter
- urinary bladder
- nephron • glomerulus
- Bowman's capsule
- filtration • reabsorption
- loop of Henle • urethra

Reading Strategy: Building Vocabulary Before you read, preview **Figure 38–17** to identify vocabulary with which you are unfamiliar. Look for the meanings of these terms as you read.

Excretion

You might think that homeostasis involves the body's efforts to respond only to changes in the external environment. Homeostasis, however, also requires the body to deal with internal processes that might upset the internal cellular environment. For example, as a normal consequence of being alive, every cell in the body produces metabolic wastes, such as excess salts, carbon dioxide, and urea. Urea is a toxic compound that is produced when amino acids are used for energy. The process by which these metabolic wastes are eliminated is called excretion. Excretion is one part of the many processes that maintain homeostasis.

You have already learned about two organs of excretion—the skin and the lungs. The skin excretes excess water and salts, as well as a small amount of urea, in the form of sweat. The lungs excrete carbon dioxide, a gas produced when energy is captured from compounds in foods. The remaining organs of excretion are the kidneys. **Together, the skin, lungs, and kidneys—along with their associated organs—make up the excretory system.**

▼ **Figure 38–16** **The skin is an organ of the excretory system.** The skin excretes water, salts, and urea in sweat.

The Kidneys

The main organs of the excretory system are the two kidneys. The **kidneys** are located on either side of the spinal column near the lower back. Each kidney is about the size of a clenched fist. A tube, called the **ureter** yoo-REET-ur), leaves each kidney, carrying urine to the urinary bladder. The **urinary bladder** is a saclike organ where urine is stored before being excreted.

What does a kidney do? Waste-laden blood enters the kidney through the renal artery. As blood travels through the kidney, urea, excess water, and other waste products are removed and collected as urine. The clean, filtered blood is returned to circulation through the renal vein.

SECTION RESOURCES

Print:
- ***Laboratory Manual A,*** Chapter 38 Lab
- ***Teaching Resources,*** Section Review 38–3, Chapter 38 Design an Experiment
- ***Guided Reading and Study Workbook,*** Section 38–3

Technology:
- ***iText,*** Section 38–3

Section 38–3

1 FOCUS

Objectives

38.3.1 ***Name*** the organs of the excretory system.
38.3.2 ***Explain*** how the kidneys maintain homeostasis.
38.3.3 ***Describe*** how homeostasis is maintained by machine.

Guide for Reading

Vocabulary Preview

Point out that all but two of the vocabulary terms are parts of the excretory system. The other two terms refer to processes of the excretory system. Ask: **Which two terms refer to processes?** *(Filtration and reabsorption)* Have students predict what these two terms mean and check to see if they were correct after they read the section.

Reading Strategy

Suggest that students outline the section by first writing the headings and subheadings on a separate sheet of paper and then filling in important details as they read.

2 INSTRUCT

Excretion

Demonstration

Before chemical wastes are excreted from the body, they must be removed from individual cells. Demonstrate the importance of this process by modeling a cell with a balloon. Attach the balloon to a faucet and gradually add water. As the balloon fills up, explain that this is what would happen to a cell if it could not eliminate its waste products. Ask: **What would happen to the cell if the amount of waste products continued to increase?** *(The cell would swell until it burst.)*

The Kidneys

Use Visuals

Figure 38–17 Explain that each nephron is about 3 cm long and only 0.03 mm in diameter, so it is too thin to be seen with the unaided eye. Also, explain that each kidney is about 10 cm long and 6 cm in diameter and contains about a million nephrons. Ask: **How do the sizes of the kidney and nephron in the figure compare with their actual sizes?** *(The kidney in the drawing is somewhat smaller than its actual size. The nephron in the drawing is much larger than its actual size.)* Suggest that students locate each part of the kidney and nephron in the figure as they read about it in the text.

Meet Diverse Needs

Have students construct a three-dimensional model of the excretory system, including the kidneys, renal blood vessels, ureter, and urinary bladder. They can use dry pasta, cereal, dried beans, clay, string, or other suitable materials to represent the different parts of the system. Ask students to explain what each part of their completed model represents. **Learning modality: tactile**

Build Science Skills

Using Models Explain that the function of the kidney is to filter out wastes and other substances from the blood. Model how the kidney works by pouring water mixed with food coloring, sand, and silt through a paper coffee filter. Invite students to examine the contents of the coffee filter and the colored water that emerges from it. Ask: **How are kidneys and coffee filters similar?** *(Both filter out substances from a fluid.)* **How are they different?** *(The kidneys filter out water and dissolved materials, whereas the coffee filter filters out only solids. The kidneys also return some of the filtered materials to the fluid.)*

FIGURE 38–17 STRUCTURE OF THE KIDNEYS

The two kidneys are the main organs of the excretory system. Each nephron has a network of capillaries called a glomerulus, which is enclosed in a cup-shaped capsule. The fluid filtered from the blood flows through a long tubule into a collecting duct.

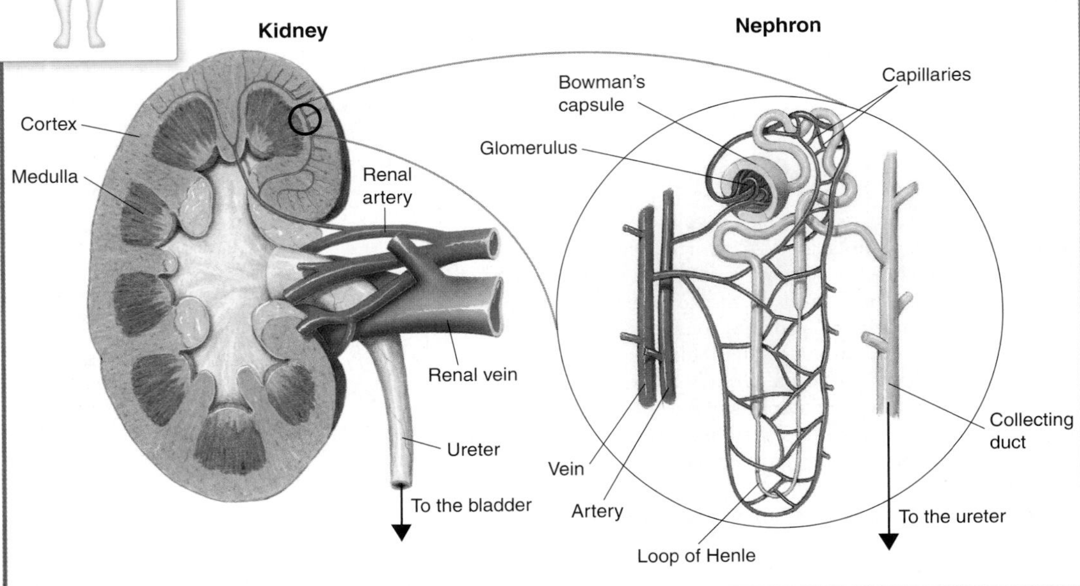

Kidney Structure If a kidney is cut in half, two distinct regions can be seen. The inner part is called the renal medulla. The outer part is called the renal cortex. The functional units of the kidney are called nephrons (NEF-rahnz). Each **nephron** is a small, independent processing unit. There are about 1 million nephrons in each kidney. The parts of a nephron are shown in **Figure 38–17.** Nephrons are in the renal cortex, except for their loops of Henle, which descend into the renal medulla.

Each nephron has its own blood supply: an arteriole, a venule, and a network of capillaries connecting them. Blood enters the nephron through the arteriole. As the blood passes through the capillaries, it is filtered. Waste products removed from the blood end up in the collecting duct, which leads to the ureter. The purified blood exits the nephron through the venule. The mechanism of blood purification is extremely complex. It involves three distinct processes: filtration, reabsorption, and secretion. These processes are summarized in **Figure 38–18.**

CHECKPOINT *What are the two parts of the kidney?*

TIME SAVER — PRESENTATIONS MADE EASY!

The Presentation Assistant Plus contains the Prentice Hall Presentation Pro and the Transparencies, which provide easy-to-follow visual support for every step of this lesson. If you have a computer presentation station, use Prentice Hall Presentation Pro for Section 38–3, or use the transparencies listed here:

Section 38–3:

Interest Grabber
Section Outline
Urinary System
Figure 38–17
Figure 38–18
Figure 38–19

Filtration As the blood enters a nephron, it flows into the glomerulus (gloh-MUR-yoo-lus). The **glomerulus** is a small network of capillaries encased in the upper end of the nephron by a cup-shaped structure called **Bowman's capsule.**

Because the blood is under pressure and the walls of the capillaries and Bowman's capsule are permeable, fluid flows from the blood into Bowman's capsule. This process is known as **filtration.** The materials that are filtered from the blood are collectively called the filtrate. The filtrate contains water, urea, glucose, salts, amino acids, and some vitamins. Because plasma proteins, cells, and platelets are too large to pass through the capillary walls, they remain in the blood.

Reabsorption and Secretion The kidneys filter the entire volume of blood approximately every 45 minutes. Needless to say, not all of the filtrate is excreted. Most of the material removed from the blood at Bowman's capsule makes its way back into the blood by a process known as **reabsorption.** Nutrients, such as amino acids and glucose, are removed from the filtrate by active transport and reabsorbed by the capillaries. Because water follows these materials by osmosis, almost 99 percent of the water that enters Bowman's capsule is reabsorbed into the blood.

While water and nutrients are being returned to the blood from the renal tubules, other materials are being secreted into the filtrate from the capillaries. The secreted materials include hydrogen ions. Remember that the concentration of hydrogen ions affects the pH of a solution such as blood plasma.

▼ **Figure 38–18** **The kidneys play an important part in maintaining homeostasis.** Nephrons control the composition, volume, and pH of blood through the processes of filtration, reabsorption, and secretion.

Filtration
Most filtration occurs in the glomerulus. Blood pressure forces water, salt, glucose, amino acids, and urea into Bowman's capsule. Proteins and blood cells are too large to cross the membrane; they remain in the blood. The fluid that enters the renal tubule is called the filtrate.

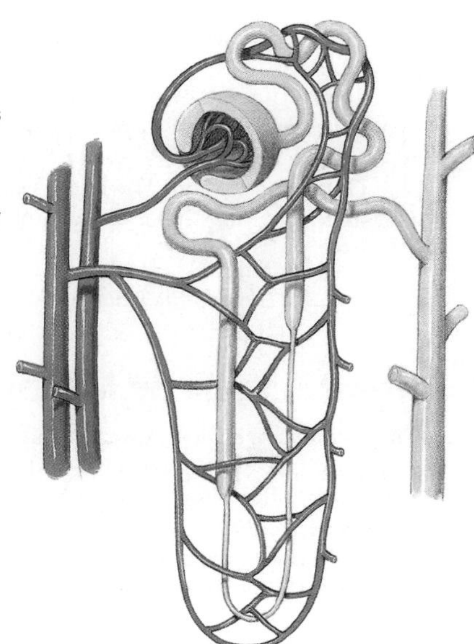

Reabsorption
As the filtrate flows through the renal tubule, most of the water and nutrients are reabsorbed into the blood. The concentrated fluid that remains is called urine.

Secretion
Substances such as hydrogen ions are transferred from the blood to the filtrate.

Demonstration

Obtain a beef or lamb kidney from a butcher and display it to the class. Ask: **How might this mammalian kidney be different from a human kidney?** *(It might be different in size, depending on the animal it came from, but its structure and function should be similar to a human kidney.)* Point out the renal artery, renal vein, and ureter. Ask: **What roles do these structures play?** *(The renal artery carries blood with impurities to the kidney, the renal vein carries purified blood away from the kidney, and the ureter carries urine from the kidney to the bladder.)* Cut the kidney lengthwise and point out the renal medulla and renal cortex. Ask: **Where are the nephrons located?** *(In the renal cortex, except for their loops of Henle)*

Use Visuals

Figure 38–18 Students may be confused by the figure because of all the similar-looking structures. Explain that the red and blue structures are arteries and veins, respectively, and the tan structures are the Bowman's capsule, the renal tubule, and the collecting duct. Point out the glomerulus, and tell students that most filtration occurs there. Ask: **Where does the filtrate go after it leaves the glomerulus?** *(Into the renal tubule)* Have students trace the path of the filtrate from the glomerulus through the renal tubule. Then, ask: **What processes take place in the renal tubule?** *(Reabsorption and secretion)*

BIO INSIGHTS

FACTS AND FIGURES

Maple syrup urine and other diseases
Some people have urine that smells like maple syrup. Others have urine that turns black when it is exposed to air. The reason? They have disorders of protein metabolism—maple syrup urine disease or alkaptonuria, respectively—that result in the kidneys excreting substances that are not normally found in the urine. Diagnosing diseases by analyzing urine is called urinalysis. It involves examination of the urine chemically, physically, and microscopically. Urinalysis is one of the most commonly performed medical laboratory procedures because the composition of the urine reflects the status of many different body functions. For example, in diabetes mellitus there is sugar in the urine, because the excess sugar in the blood is filtered out by the kidneys and excreted in the urine.

Answer to . . .

CHECKPOINT *The renal medulla, which is the inner part, and the renal cortex, which is the outer part*

SCIENCE NEWS®

Encourage students to visit **www.phschool.com** for the most current information on this topic.

Control of Kidney Function

Build Science Skills

Inferring Help students build inferring skills and increase their understanding of how the kidneys maintain homeostasis. Ask: **Why is your urine lighter in color after you drink a lot of fluids?** *(The kidneys remove the excess water from the blood and excrete it in the urine, making the urine less concentrated and lighter in color.)* **Why might your urine be darker in color after you have been sweating a lot?** *(The kidneys remove less water from the blood to compensate for the water lost in sweat, making the urine more concentrated and darker in color.)*

Make Connections

Health Science Relate the kidneys' ability to maintain homeostasis to health issues. Tell students that the role of the kidneys is essential to life, yet people can live long, healthy lives with just one kidney. Ask: **Why can someone function normally with just one kidney?** *(Students should infer that the one kidney can adapt to the greater workload placed on it by filtering out more substances from the blood.)*

Word Origins

Abrade means to scrape away.

KEEP CURRENT WITH . . . SCIENCE NEWS®

To find out more about the topics in this chapter, go to: **www.phschool.com**

Word Origins

Absorb comes from the Latin *ab-* meaning "from" or "away," and *sorbere,* meaning "to draw in." **If the Latin word *radere* means "to scrape," what does the word *abrade* mean?**

The material that remains after reabsorption, called urine, is emptied into a collecting duct. Urine, which contains urea, excess salts, and water, among other substances, is primarily concentrated in the loop of Henle. The **loop of Henle** is a section of the nephron tubule in which water is conserved and the volume of urine minimized.

As the kidney works, purified blood is returned to circulation while urine is collected in the urinary bladder. Urine is stored in the urinary bladder until it can be released from the body through a tube called the **urethra** (yoo-REE-thruh).

Control of Kidney Function

The kidneys play an important role in maintaining homeostasis. They regulate the water content of the blood and, therefore, blood volume, maintain blood pH, and remove waste products from the blood. How are these activities controlled?

To a large extent, the activity of the kidneys is controlled by the composition of blood itself. In addition, regulatory hormones are released in response to the composition of blood. These mechanisms combine to ensure that the kidneys will maintain the proper composition of blood.

When you drink glass after glass of liquid, the liquid is quickly absorbed into the blood through the digestive system. As a result, the concentration of water in the blood increases. If it were not for your kidneys, this increased concentration of water in the blood would force water into cells and tissues by osmosis, causing your body to swell.

As the amount of water in the blood increases, the rate of water reabsorption in the kidneys decreases. Less water is returned to the blood, and the excess water is sent to the urinary bladder to be excreted as urine.

If you eat salty food, your kidneys will respond to the increased level of salt in your blood. When your kidneys detect an increase in salt, they respond by returning less salt to the blood by reabsorption. The excess salt the kidneys retain is excreted in urine, thus maintaining the composition of the blood.

CHECKPOINT *How do the kidneys respond to salty foods?*

Homeostasis by Machine

The kidneys are the master chemists of the blood supply. If anything goes wrong with the kidneys, serious medical problems soon follow. Fortunately, humans have two kidneys and can survive with only one. If both kidneys are damaged by disease or injury, there are only two ways to keep an individual alive. The first way is to transplant a kidney from a healthy and compatible donor to the person in need of the kidney.

HISTORY OF SCIENCE

Bright's disease and Bowman's capsule
The first person to use urinalysis to diagnose disease was an English physician named Richard Bright. In 1829, Bright discovered that people who suffer from "dropsy," or what we now call edema, have a substance in their urine that coagulates, just as egg white does, when the urine is boiled. The substance is now known to be serum albumin, and it does not normally appear in the urine. When it does, it is a sign that the patient has nephritis, or inflammation of the kidneys. Because of Bright's hallmark work, nephritis is still sometimes referred to as Bright's disease. Another 19th-century English physician, Sir William Bowman, discovered the capsules in the kidney that are named after him. Bowman also discovered how urine is produced by filtration.

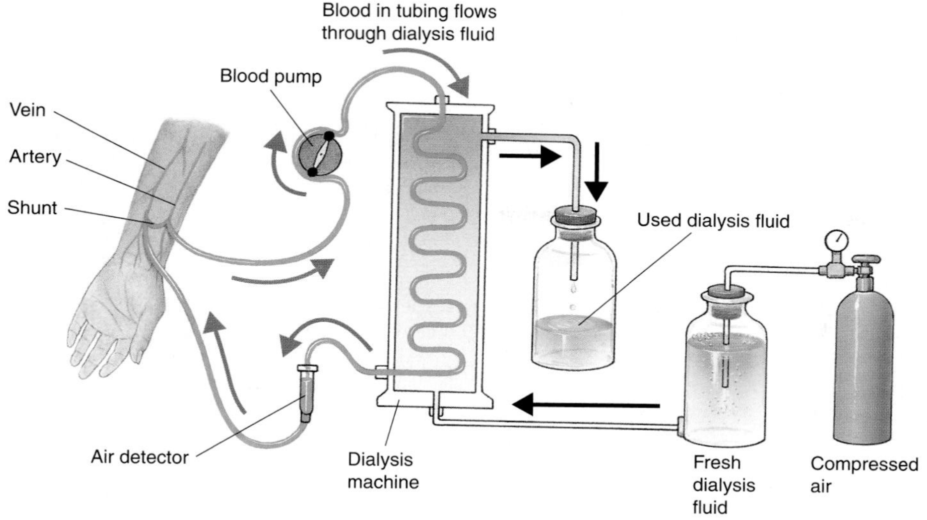

▲ **Figure 38–19** For people with damaged kidneys, dialysis machines can perform many of the functions of the kidneys. **Applying Concepts** *Why is dialysis such an important lifesaving technique?*

In many cases, a donor is not available or surgery is not advisable. In these instances, a kidney dialysis machine becomes a lifesaver. In one type of dialysis, blood is removed from the body through a tube inserted in the arm and pumped through special tubing that acts like nephrons. Tiny pores in the tubing allow salts and small molecules, including nitrogen wastes, to pass through. Wastes—urea and excess salts—diffuse out of the blood into the fluid-filled chamber, allowing purified blood to be returned to the body. This process of dialysis is shown in **Figure 38–19.** Dialysis is not only expensive, but it also is time-consuming, occupying several hours a day as often as three times a week. The ideal solution, assuming a kidney transplant is not possible, would be the implantation of an artificial kidney. Medical science is working toward developing such an artificial kidney.

38–3 Section Assessment

1. **Key Concept** What are the parts of the excretory system?
2. **Key Concept** What is the kidney's role in maintaining homeostasis?
3. Describe the structures of the kidney.
4. Describe the processes of filtration and reabsorption.
5. **Critical Thinking Drawing Conclusions** Explain why a person may temporarily lose weight after changing to a low-salt diet even without reducing Caloric intake.

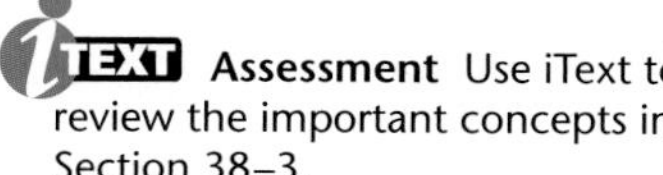

Assessment Use iText to review the important concepts in Section 38–3.

ALTERNATIVE ASSESSMENT

Constructing a Flowchart
Construct a flowchart that illustrates how wastes are removed by the kidneys.

Homeostasis by Machine

Use Community Resources

Invite a dialysis technician or nurse to speak to the class about dialysis. Suggest that the speaker address such issues as how effective dialysis is compared with normal kidney function, who needs dialysis and why, and what it is like to receive dialysis treatments. Have students take notes during the presentation and later use them to write a summary of what they learned.

3 ASSESS

Evaluate Understanding

Call on students at random to state the function of the parts of the kidney and nephron that are highlighted in the text. Call on other students to correct any errors.

Reteach

Have students use Figure 38–17 to trace the path of blood into and out of the kidney and to trace the path of urine from the kidney to the urethra.

ALTERNATIVE ASSESSMENT

Provide students with large sheets of paper and colored pens or markers. Flowcharts should demonstrate an understanding of how the kidney removes wastes such as urea from blood.

Use iText to review the key concepts in Section 38–3.

38–3 Section Assessment

1. The skin, lungs, and kidneys, along with their associated organs
2. Regulating water content of the blood, maintaining blood pH, and removing cellular waste products from the blood
3. Renal medulla: inner part of kidney; renal cortex: outer part of kidney; nephrons: functional units of kidney; renal artery and vein: blood vessels entering and leaving kidney; ureter: tube from kidney to urinary bladder; urinary bladder: saclike organ for storing urine
4. In filtration, materials are filtered from the blood. In reabsorption, most of the filtered materials re-enter the blood.
5. The kidneys respond to lowered salt intake by returning less water to the blood and excreting it as urine. This causes a temporary weight loss.

Answers to . . .

CHECKPOINT *By returning less salt to the blood through reabsorption and excreting the excess salt in the urine*

Figure 38–19 *Without dialysis, wastes in the blood would soon reach toxic levels.*

Design an Experiment

Objective Students will be able to design experiments to test their predictions about the specificity of digestive enzymes.

Skills Focus **Formulating Hypotheses, Controlling Variables, Forming Operational Definitions**

Time 45 minutes one day; 15 minutes two days later

Advance Prep
- Cook the eggs and potatoes in advance. The potatoes need only to be boiled or microwaved for a few minutes. Eggs can be microwaved in a container of water.
- To prepare 1 L of 0.2 percent hydrochloric acid, add 2 mL of concentrated hydrochloric acid to 998 mL of water.

Safety Tips
- Remind students to add the acid to the water, not the water to the acid. Remind them that the concentrated acid is extremely corrosive.
- Caution students to be careful handling the boiling water.

Teaching Strategies Have students read the entire procedure. Before they begin the procedure, you might want to have them test the egg white and potato for starch and protein. Then, ask:

- **What is the purpose of this investigation?** *(To determine whether digestive enzymes act only on specific compounds)*
- **What is the purpose of test tubes 1 and 2?** *(They are controls; they show that nothing happens to the egg white without pepsin.)*
- **What do you think would happen to egg white in a test tube of pepsin and water?** *(Students should infer that the pepsin would not be able to break down the egg white because it needs an acidic environment to work effectively.)*

Design an Experiment

Testing the Specificity of Digestive Enzymes

In this investigation, you will test the ability of the digestive enzyme pepsin to break down egg white, which is mostly protein. You will also design your own experiments to test the effect of pepsin on starch, and the effects of amylase on proteins and starch.

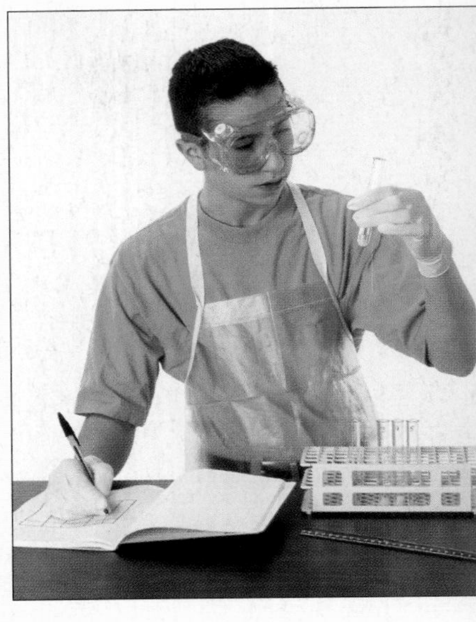

Problem **Do different digestive enzymes act only on specific types of compounds?**

Materials

- heat-resistant gloves
- Benedict's solution
- boiling water bath
- cooked egg white
- scalpel or single-edged razor blade
- metric ruler
- 6 large test tubes
- 6 stoppers for test tubes
- glass-marking pencil
- test-tube rack
- 10-mL graduated cylinder
- 1% pepsin solution
- 0.2% hydrochloric acid
- cooked potato
- 1% amylase solution
- test-tube holder

Skills Formulating Hypotheses, Controlling Variables, Forming Operational Definitions

Design Your Experiment

Part A: The Basic Procedure

1. **Predicting** Predict whether pepsin can break down protein.
2. Put on an apron and safety goggles. Label three test tubes 1, 2, and 3 and put them in a test-tube rack. Cut three 5-mm cubes of cooked egg white and add one to each test tube.
3. Put on plastic gloves. Use a graduated cylinder to add 6 mL of water to test tube 1, and 3 mL of water and 3 mL 0.2% hydrochloric acid to test tube 2. **CAUTION:** *Hydrochloric acid can damage skin and clothing. If hydrochloric acid spills, notify your teacher. Wash the affected area with large amounts of cool water.* Carefully rinse the graduated cylinder.
4. To test tube 3, add 3 mL 1% pepsin solution and 3 mL 0.2% hydrochloric acid. Carefully rinse the graduated cylinder.
5. Put a stopper in each test tube and gently turn the tubes upside down several times to mix the contents. Put the tubes back in the test-tube rack. Make a copy of the data table. Set your test-tube rack where it will not be disturbed.
6. After 2 days, examine the contents of each test tube. Record your observations in your copy of the data table.

Part B: Design Your Own Experiments

7. **Predicting** Do you think pepsin will digest potato, which is rich in starch? Write down your prediction. Now, design an experiment to test your prediction. You can use the test for sugars described in Part C to determine whether starch has been broken down. Write down your procedure. What is your manipulated variable? Your responding variable? Make sure to control all other variables. **CAUTION:** *Before you perform your experiment, have your teacher approve your procedure.*
8. Design two experiments to test whether amylase can digest protein or starch. Make sure you control your variables. Record in your copy of the data table what you put in each test tube. **CAUTION:** *Before you perform your experiments, have your teacher approve your procedures.*

Procedure

1. Students should predict that pepsin can break down protein in the presence of an acid.

6. Students should observe that the egg white broke down in test tube 3 (pepsin and hydrochloric acid) but not in the other two test tubes.

7. Students should predict that pepsin will not digest potato. They can test it by following steps 2 through 6, but using potato instead of egg white, and then following steps 11 to 13 to test for the presence of sugar.

Data Table			
Test Tube	Compound Tested	Liquid(s) Added	Observations
1	protein (egg white)	6 mL water	
2	protein (egg white)	3 mL water, 3 mL hydrochloric acid	
3	protein (egg white)	3 mL pepsin, 3 mL hydrochloric acid	

9. Set your test-tube rack aside where it will not be disturbed for 2 days.
10. After 2 days, examine each test tube. Record your observations in your data table.

Part C: Testing for Sugar

11. To test for the presence of sugar in the liquid in the tubes that contained potato: Put 1 mL of the liquid in a test tube. Add 2 mL of water and mix.
12. Add 3 mL Benedict's solution to the same tube.
13. Your teacher will provide a boiling water bath. Put on the heat-resistant gloves and use a test-tube holder to put the test tubes from step 12 in the boiling water bath. **CAUTION:** *Be careful when working with boiling water.* Observe the test tube for about 5 minutes. A change in color from blue to yellow (or green, or orange, or red) is a positive test for sugar. Record your observations in your data table.

Analyze and Conclude

1. **Applying Concepts** Why was hydrochloric acid included with the pepsin in step 4? Did you add hydrochloric acid to the amylase solution? Why or why not?
2. **Observing** What effect did pepsin have on the egg white? Was your prediction correct? Explain your answer.
3. **Observing** What effect did water, and water with hydrochloric acid, have on the egg white? What was the purpose of including these tests?
4. **Drawing Conclusions** Describe the results of the experiments you designed. Do the enzymes you tested act only on specific compounds? Explain your answer.

Go Further

Designing Experiments What factors affect the rates of the reactions you tested? How could you increase these rates? Design one or more experiments to test the effects of changing one of these factors. Remember to write a prediction and to control variables. After obtaining approval from your teacher, carry out your experiment(s).

8. Students should design an experiment based on Part A of the procedure, but they should test amylase instead of pepsin and omit the hydrochloric acid. They should test egg white in one experiment and potato in the other experiment. A test tube of water should be used as a control.

10. Students should observe that the amylase broke down the starch but not the protein.

Go Further

Possible factors to test include temperature, pH, and surface area. Increasing the temperature to 37°C, decreasing the pH (for pepsin), and chopping the foods more finely to increase surface area all will increase the reaction rate.

Analyze and Conclude

1. Pepsin works in the acidic environment of the stomach. Students should not have added hydrochloric acid to the amylase solution, because amylase works in the more neutral environment of the mouth.

2. Pepsin breaks down the egg white in the presence of hydrochloric acid because it needs an acidic environment to work effectively.

3. They had no effect. They were included as controls.

4. Students should find that amylase can digest starch but not protein.

Chapter 38 Study Guide

Study Tip

Divide the class into pairs and have members of each pair quiz each other by making up questions on the Vocabulary terms and Key Concepts. Have students make flashcards for any questions they cannot answer correctly.

Thinking Visually

Flowcharts should include all the digestive organs in sequence, including the mouth, esophagus, stomach, small intestine, and large intestine. Organs should be correctly labeled and arrows should indicate the direction of food through the system.

Chapter 38 Assessment

Reviewing Content

1. c **2.** c **3.** b **4.** c **5.** c **6.** b **7.** c **8.** d **9.** a **10.** c

Understanding Concepts

11. The body uses food for energy and to build or repair body tissues.

12. Carbohydrates and fats provide the body with energy.

13. Proteins provide the raw materials for growth and repair. They have regulatory and transport functions. The enzymes that make biochemical reactions possible are proteins.

14. The Food Guide Pyramid gives the number of servings of different types of food that should be included each day in a balanced diet.

15. A flap of tissue known as the epiglottis is forced over the opening to the air passageways as swallowing occurs.

16. Enzymes chemically break down large food molecules into smaller molecules that can be absorbed and used by the cells of the body.

17. Mechanical digestion is a physical process. Chemical digestion involves the breaking of bonds.

Chapter 38 Study Guide

38–1 Food and Nutrition

Key Concepts

- The nutrients that the body needs are water, carbohydrates, fats, proteins, vitamins, and minerals.
- Every cell in the human body needs water because many of the body's processes, including chemical reactions, take place in water.

Vocabulary
Calorie, p. 971
carbohydrate, p. 972
fat, p. 972
protein, p. 973
vitamin, p. 974
mineral, p. 975

38–2 The Process of Digestion

Key Concepts

- The digestive system includes the mouth, pharynx, esophagus, stomach, small intestine, and large intestine. Several accessory structures, including the salivary glands, the pancreas, and the liver, add secretions to the digestive system.
- The function of each organ of the digestive system is to help convert foods into simpler molecules that can be absorbed and used by the cells of the body.

Vocabulary
amylase, p. 979
esophagus, p. 980
peristalsis, p. 980
stomach, p. 980
peptic ulcer, p. 981
chyme, p. 981
small intestine, p. 981
pancreas, p. 982
liver, p. 982
villus, p. 983
large intestine, p. 984

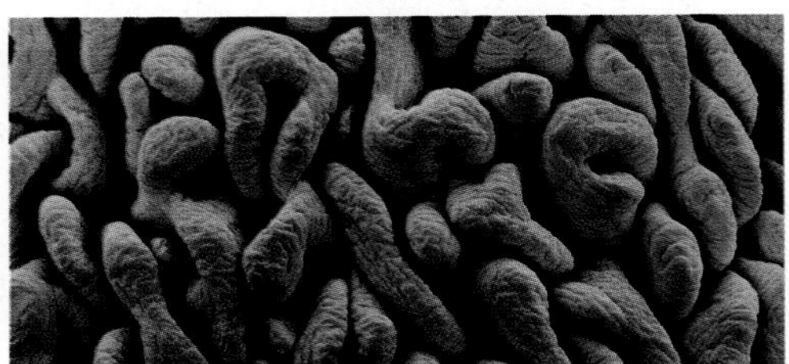

38–3 The Excretory System

Key Concepts

- Together, the skin, lungs, and kidneys—along with their associated organs—make up the excretory system.
- The kidneys play an important role in maintaining homeostasis. They regulate the water content of the blood and, therefore, blood volume, maintain blood pH, and remove waste products from the blood.

Vocabulary
kidney, p. 985
ureter, p. 985
urinary bladder, p. 985
nephron, p. 986
glomerulus, p. 987
Bowman's capsule, p. 987
filtration, p. 987
reabsorption, p. 987
loop of Henle, p. 988
urethra, p. 988

Thinking Visually

Create a flowchart that shows the path of food through the organs of the digestive system.

CHAPTER RESOURCES

Print:

- ***Teaching Resources,*** Chapter Vocabulary Review, Graphic Organizer
- ***Chapter Tests: Levels A and B,*** Chapter 38 Test
- ***PH Assessment System,*** Practice Test

Technology:

- ***Computer Test Bank,*** Chapter 38 Test
- ***iText,*** Chapter 38 Assessment

Chapter 38 Assessment

Reviewing Content

Choose the letter that best answers the question or completes the statement.

1. The amount of energy in foods is measured in
   a. ATP. c. Calories.
   b. carbohydrates. d. disaccharides.
2. The nutrients that are the main source of energy for the body are
   a. proteins. c. carbohydrates.
   b. fats. d. vitamins.
3. Inorganic nutrients that your body needs, usually in small amounts, are called
   a. vitamins. c. proteins.
   b. minerals. d. amino acids.
4. Much of mechanical digestion takes place in the
   a. esophagus. c. mouth.
   b. large intestine. d. small intestine.
5. An enzyme that breaks the chemical bonds in starch, releasing sugar, is
   a. pepsin. c. amylase.
   b. bile. d. chyme.
6. Muscle contractions that help to squeeze food through the esophagus are known as
   a. chemical digestion. c. chyme.
   b. peristalsis. d. microvilli.
7. Going without food affects the amount of urea in the urine. The graph shows that the amount of nitrogen in the urea excreted
   a. increases steadily during 14 days of fasting.
   b. decreases steadily during 14 days of fasting.
   c. increases for the first few days of fasting.
   d. will be 6 grams after 16 days of fasting.

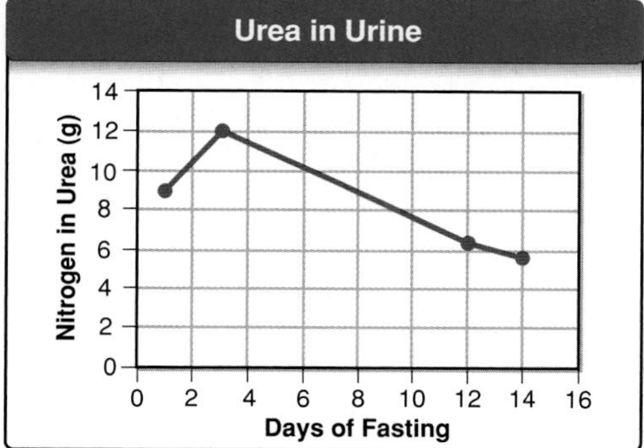

8. Digested materials are absorbed in which part of the digestive system?
   a. mouth
   b. esophagus
   c. stomach
   d. small intestine
9. The basic functional unit of the kidney is the
   a. nephron.
   b. Bowman's capsule.
   c. glomerulus.
   d. loop of Henle.
10. Urine is excreted from the body through the
   a. ureter.
   b. urinary bladder.
   c. urethra.
   d. renal vein.

Understanding Concepts

11. What are the two overall ways that the body uses food?
12. Which nutrients provide the body with energy?
13. Why are proteins important to the body?
14. What information is given in the Food Guide Pyramid?
15. Explain why swallowed food does not usually enter the airway leading to the lungs.
16. What role do enzymes play during digestion?
17. How do mechanical digestion and chemical digestion differ?
18. Describe the functions of hydrochloric acid and pepsin in the stomach.
19. How has the scientific understanding of the cause of peptic ulcers changed in recent years?
20. Describe the functions of the pancreas.
21. How is the structure of the villi adapted to their function?
22. What is the primary function of the large intestine?
23. What materials are filtered from the blood in the kidney? What materials remain in the blood?
24. What kinds of filtered materials are reabsorbed by the blood in the kidney?
25. How is the activity of the kidney controlled?

Chapter 38 Assessment (continued)

18. Hydrochloric acid activates the enzyme pepsin, which begins the complex process of protein digestion by breaking proteins into smaller polypeptide fragments.

19. Prior to 1980, doctors thought peptic ulcers were caused by too much stomach acid. Since 1980, doctors have known that most peptic ulcers are caused by bacterial infections.

20. The pancreas produces hormones that regulate blood sugar; enzymes that break down carbohydrates, proteins, lipids, and nucleic acids; and sodium bicarbonate, a base that neutralizes stomach acid so these enzymes can work effectively.

21. The villi contain a network of capillaries and lymph vessels that absorb nutrients from the small intestine. Each villus is covered with fingerlike projections called microvilli. These projections greatly increase the surface area available for absorption of nutrients.

22. The primary function of the large intestine is to remove water from undigested food before this material is excreted from the body.

23. Water, urea, glucose, salts, amino acids, and some vitamins are filtered from the blood in the kidney. Plasma proteins, cells, and platelets remain in the blood.

24. Most of the water and nutrients are reabsorbed by the blood in the kidney.

25. The activity of the kidney is controlled by the composition of blood itself and by the action of hormones that are released in response to the composition of blood.

HOMEWORK GUIDE

Section:	Questions:
Section 38–1	1–3, 11–14, 27, 30
Section 38–2	4–6, 8, 15–22, 26, 28, 29, 31, 32
Section 38–3	7, 9, 10, 23–25, 33, 34

Chapter 38 Assessment

Critical Thinking

26. Individuals can survive without a stomach if they are given predigested foods. However, they could not survive without a small intestine, which is adapted to absorb nutrients.

27. Diets with a limited variety of foods may be unhealthy because they may not provide all the vitamins, minerals, and other nutrients needed for good health.

28. a. Bicarbonate, digestive enzymes **b.** Hydrochloric acid, protein, and fat **c.** More bicarbonate is secreted. **d.** The amounts of bicarbonate and digestive enzymes secreted are equal. **e.** The amount of bicarbonate secreted decreases and the amount of digestive enzymes secreted increases.

29. One experimental design is to have subjects chew soda crackers until they start to taste sweet. Because starches are broken down into sugars when they are digested, the sweet taste is an indication that starch digestion begins in the mouth.

30. These people might be healthier because their high-carbohydrate, low-protein, low-fat diets are closer to the balanced diet represented by the Food Guide Pyramid.

31. An antibiotic that killed all the bacteria in your body would destroy the beneficial bacteria in the large intestine that normally help remove water from waste. As result, you probably would develop diarrhea.

32. Prolonged chewing would result in more chemical digestion of starches in the mouth. It would also aid in the mechanical digestion of both carbohydrates and proteins, which in turn would promote chemical digestion of these nutrients.

33. Kidney failure can be fatal because, without the kidneys to filter wastes and excess water from the blood, these substances would accumulate to dangerous levels.

34. The kidneys play a role in homeostasis by regulating the water content of blood, volume of blood, and blood pH, and by removing cellular waste products from blood.

Chapter 38 Assessment

Critical Thinking

26. Inferring Individuals who have had part, or even all, of their stomachs removed can survive. Do you think the same individuals could survive without a small intestine? Explain your answer.

27. Applying Concepts Fad diets that boast of rapid weight loss often become popular. Many of those diets involve eating only a limited variety of foods. Explain why these diets are an unhealthy way to lose weight.

28. Interpreting Graphics Pancreatic juice contains sodium bicarbonate and digestive enzymes. The juice is secreted by the pancreas in response to the specific composition of chyme in the upper portion of the small intestine. The graph below shows the secretions of the pancreas in response to the presence of three different substances.

a. Which substance is represented by the blue bars on the graph? By the green bars?

b. Each pair of bar graphs represents the response of the pancreas to a different variable. What are the three variables?

c. How does hydrochloric acid affect the amount of bicarbonate in pancreatic juice?

d. How do proteins affect the amounts of bicarbonate and digestive enzymes secreted?

e. How do fats affect the composition of pancreatic juice?

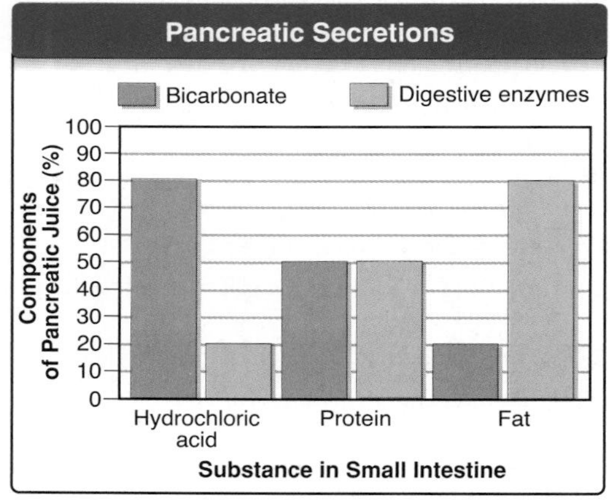
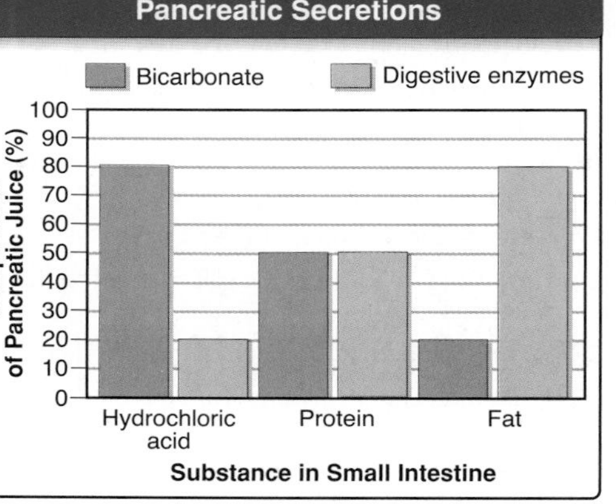

29. Designing Experiments Your friend tells you that the digestion of starches begins in the stomach. You suggest that starch digestion begins in the mouth. Design an experiment to show that your hypothesis is correct.

30. Applying Concepts In some countries, people have diets that contain more complex carbohydrates and fewer fats and proteins than the typical American diet. Why might these people be healthier than the average American?

31. Inferring Suppose your doctor prescribed an antibiotic that killed all the bacteria in your body. What effect would this have on your digestive system?

32. Formulating Hypotheses How would prolonged chewing affect the digestion of carbohydrates and proteins?

33. Applying Concepts Explain why kidney failure can be a fatal condition.

34. Making Connections In Chapter 1, you learned that an organism maintains an internal stability called homeostasis. Explain how the kidneys play a role in this process.

Performance-Based Assessment

Creative Writing A children's television workshop wants to explain the process of digestion to young viewers. You are asked to write a script that describes the travels of a hamburger and hamburger bun through the digestive system. Write an outline of your script, including information about what happens to the different nutrients in each part of the digestive system.

Take It to the NET

How can you tell which snack foods are healthy? Visit the Prentice Hall Web site at **www.phschool.com** to find out what you can learn by reading the labels on food packages. Then, answer the following questions:

- Suppose you read the label "low fat" on a carton of ice cream. What does this label tell you?
- How are "low fat" crackers different from crackers with "reduced" fat?
- Why is it important to limit the amount of fat in your diet?

Performance-Based Assessment

Students might write a script that describes a trip through the digestive system for nutrients in the hamburger (fats and proteins) and in the bun (carbohydrates). The script should show that students understand how and where each nutrient is digested, as summarized in Figure 38–12.

Standardized Test Prep

Test-Taking Tip To complete an analogy, write a sentence that clearly describes the relationship between the first pair of terms. Then, rewrite the sentence with the third term and fill in the blank with the answer choice that best completes the analogy.

Directions: Choose the letter that best answers the question or completes the statement.

1. Each of the following aids in the process of digestion EXCEPT
(A) teeth.
(B) saliva.
(C) stomach.
(D) small intestine.
(E) kidney.

2. What moves food through the esophagus?
(A) gravity
(B) the cardiac sphincter
(C) muscle contractions
(D) the epiglottis
(E) enzymes

3. In the human body, hydrochloric acid is responsible for the low pH of the contents of the
(A) kidney.
(B) gallbladder.
(C) liver.
(D) stomach.
(E) lungs.

4. Which is NOT a role of the kidneys?
(A) removal of waste products from the blood
(B) maintenance of blood pH
(C) regulation of water content of the blood
(D) maintenance of homeostasis
(E) excretion of carbon dioxide

Questions 5–6 Complete each analogy by selecting the correct letter. In analogies, A : B :: C : __?__ *means* A is to B as C is to __?__.

5. Energy : carbohydrates :: raw materials : __?__
(A) protein
(B) mineral
(C) vitamin
(D) water
(E) fats

6. Lung : carbon dioxide :: kidney : __?__
(A) oxygen
(B) nutrients
(C) urea
(D) cellulose
(E) sweat

Questions 7–9 Use the diagram below to answer the questions that follow.

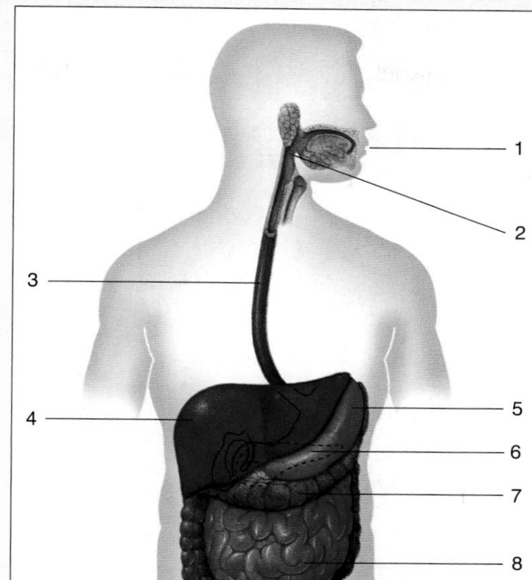

7. Where does MOST of the work of chemical digestion take place?
(A) 1
(B) 2
(C) 3
(D) 4
(E) 8

8. If stomach acid moves past the cardiac sphincter, it ends up in which organ?
(A) 1
(B) 2
(C) 3
(D) 4
(E) 5

9. Which organ removes water from undigested material?
(A) 1
(B) 2
(C) 3
(D) 7
(E) 5

Standardized Test Prep

1. E
2. C
3. D
4. E
5. A
6. C
7. E
8. C
9. D

Take It to the NET

• The low-fat ice cream cannot have more than 3 g of fat per serving.

• Low-fat crackers cannot have more than 3 g of fat per serving. Reduced-fat crackers must have at least 25 percent less fat than the regular crackers of the same brand. Reduced-fat crackers are lower in fat than regular crackers, but they are not necessarily low-fat.

• It is important to limit the amount of fat in your diet to avoid serious health problems, such as high blood pressure, heart disease, obesity, and diabetes.

For additional information, visit

www.phschool.com

Chapter Planner 39 Endocrine and Reproductive Systems

Section and Section Objectives	Time	Activities and Labs
39–1 The Endocrine System, pp. 997–1002 **39.1.1** ***State*** the function of the endocrine system. **39.1.2** ***Describe*** hormones and glands. **39.1.3** ***Explain*** how the endocrine system maintains homeostasis.	**2 periods (1 block)**	**SE:** ***Inquiry Activity,*** Where in cells do hormones go?, p. 996 **TE:** ***Demonstration,*** p. 998
39–2 Human Endocrine Glands, pp. 1003–1008 **39.2.1** ***Identify*** the functions of the major endocrine glands.	**2 periods (1 block)**	**TE:** ***Demonstration,*** p. 1007
39–3 The Reproductive System, pp. 1009–1015 **39.3.1** ***Describe*** sexual development. **39.3.2** ***Explain*** the role of the male and female reproductive systems. **39.3.3** ***Identify*** the four phases of the menstrual cycle.	**2 periods (1 block)**	**TE:** ***Demonstration,*** p. 1010 **TE:** ***Meet Diverse Needs,*** p. 1011
39–4 Fertilization and Development, pp. 1016–1022 **39.4.1** ***Describe*** fertilization. **39.4.2** ***State*** what happens during gastrulation. **39.4.3** ***Describe*** the function of the placenta. **39.4.4** ***Outline*** the life cycle after birth.	**1 period (1/2 block)**	**TE:** ***Build Science Skills,*** p. 1017 **TE:** ***Demonstration,*** p. 1018 **SE:** ***Quick Lab,*** How do embryos develop?, p. 1020 **SE:** ***Exploration,*** Modeling Blood Glucose Regulation, p. 1023
Chapter Assessment, pp. 1024–1027	**1 period (1/2 block)**	

ACTIVITY PLANNER

SE: ***Inquiry Activity,*** p. 996; (10 min.); 2 test tubes with stoppers, 2 droppers, water, vegetable oil, food coloring, annatto coloring

TE: ***Demonstration,*** p. 998; (10 min.); empty egg carton, scissors, water

TE: ***Demonstration,*** p. 1007; (5 min.); glucose test strip, paper cup, water, yellow food coloring, sugar

TE: ***Demonstration,*** p. 1010; (10 min.); prepared slide of sperm cell, microscope

TE: ***Meet Diverse Needs,*** p. 1011; (10 min.); unlabeled drawing and large anatomical model or chart of the male reproductive system

TE: ***Build Science Skills,*** p. 1017; (15 min.); modeling clay

TE: ***Demonstration,*** p. 1018; (5 min.); raw egg; resealable, gallon-size storage bag, water

SE: ***Quick Lab,*** p. 1020; (20 min.); dropper pipette, early-stage frog embryos, depression slide, dissecting microscope, prepared slides of frog embryos

SE: ***Exploration,*** p. 1023; (40 min.); 3 pieces of construction paper of different colors, scissors

PLANNING KEY

Ability Levels

B Basic	For students who need additional help
A Average	For all students
E Enriched	For students who need to be challenged

Components

SE	Student Edition	**GRSW**	Guided Reading and Study Workbook	**IDM**	Issues and Decision Making
TE	Teacher's Edition	**CT**	Chapter Tests: Levels A and B	**CTB**	Computer Test Bank
LMA	Laboratory Manual A	**PHAS**	PH Assessment System	**PA**	Presentation Assistant Plus
LMB	Laboratory Manual B	**LA**	Lab Assessment with Scoring Guide	**BD**	BioDetectives Videotape
TR	Teaching Resources	**BTM**	BioTechnology Manual	**iT**	iText

Program Resources	Assessment	Media and Technology
TR: Section Review 39–1 B A **GRSW:** Section 39–1 B A	**SE:** 39–1 Section Assessment, p. 1002 **TR:** Section Review 39–1	**PA:** 39–1 Interest Grabber, Section Outline, Hormone Action, Figure 39–2 **iT:** Section 39–1
TR: Section Review 39–2 B A **GRSW:** Section 39–2 B A **IDM:** 39–1 A E	**SE:** 39–2 Section Assessment, p. 1008 **TR:** Section Review 39–2	**PA:** 39–2 Interest Grabber, Section Outline, Concept Map, Figure 39–10 **iT:** Section 39–2
LMA: Chapter 39 Lab A E **LMB:** Chapter 39 Lab B A **TR:** Section Review 39–3 B A **GRSW:** Section 39–3 B A	**SE:** 39–3 Section Assessment, p. 1015 **TR:** Section Review 39–3	**PA:** 39–3 Interest Grabber, Section Outline, Menstrual Cycle, Figure 39–14, Figure 39–15 **iT:** Section 39–3
TR: Section Review 39–4 B A Chapter 39 Exploration B A E **GRSW:** Section 39–4 B A	**SE:** 39–4 Section Assessment, p. 1022 **TR:** Section Review 39–4	**PA:** 39–4 Interest Grabber, Section Outline, Fertilization and Implantation of Egg, Figure 39–20 **iT:** Section 39–4
	SE: Chapter 39 Assessment, pp. 1024–1027 **TR:** Chapter Vocabulary Review, Graphic Organizer **CT:** Chapter 39 Test **CTB:** Chapter 39 Test **PHAS:** Practice Test	**CTB:** Chapter 39 Test **iT:** Chapter 39 Assessment

PRESSED FOR TIME?

To Preview the Chapter
- Introduce students to key concepts and vocabulary terms in each section.
- Assign the Reading Strategies for each section.

To Cover the Chapter Quickly
- Have students read all of Section 39–1 and in Section 39–3 have them read Sexual Development and Figures 39–14 and 39–15.
- Assign the Section Review 39–1 and questions 1–7, 11–14, 18, 30, 31, and 37 in Chapter 39 Assessment and questions 3 and 9–11 in the Chapter 39 Standardized Test Prep.

To Review the Chapter
- Assign the Section Reviews 39–1 and 39–3 in the Guided Reading and Study Workbook.
- Assign the Section Reviews for 39–1 and 39–3 and the Chapter Vocabulary Review for Chapter 39 in the Teaching Resources.

ENGAGE/EXPLORE

Inquiry Activity

Objective Students will be able to infer that substances can pass through cell membranes if they are soluble in oil.

Skill Focus Observing

Materials 2 test tubes with stoppers, 2 droppers, water, vegetable oil, food coloring, annatto coloring (Annatto coloring is used to color butter and cheese. It comes from the pulp around the seeds of a tropical dicotyledonous tree.)

Time 10 minutes

Safety Remind students to handle the test tubes carefully.

Advance Prep You can substitute turmeric for annatto.

Strategy Relate the activity to hormone action. Tell students that some hormones can cross the cell membrane and work inside the cell, whereas other hormones cannot cross the cell membrane and must work instead at the cell surface.

Expected Outcome Students should observe that food coloring dissolves in water and annatto coloring dissolves in oil.

Think About It

1. The food coloring dissolves in water. Food coloring cannot pass through cell membranes.
2. The annatto coloring dissolves in oil. Annatto coloring can pass through cell membranes.

Assess Prior Knowledge

Have students recall a time when they were startled by something frightening, such as someone jumping unexpectedly out of the shadows. Ask: **What did it feel like to be startled?** *(Students are likely to mention such physiological reactions to fear as rapid heart rate, shortness of breath, and sweaty palms.)* Explain to students that these physical changes are due to hormones, which they will learn about in this chapter.

Chapter 39 Endocrine and Reproductive Systems

This photomicrograph, which was artificially colored, shows sperm (yellow objects) trying to break through the outer membrane of an egg.

Inquiry Activity

Where in cells do hormones go?

Procedure

1. Fill 2 test tubes one third full of water. Add the same amount of vegetable oil (a lipid) to each test tube.
2. Add a few drops of food coloring to one of the test tubes. Stopper the test tube and turn it upside down to mix the contents.
3. Repeat step 2 using a drop of annatto coloring and the second test tube.

Think About It

1. **Observing** Did the food coloring dissolve in water or oil? Do you think food coloring can pass through cell membranes? (*Hint:* Cell membranes are composed of lipids.)
2. **Observing** Did the annatto coloring dissolve in water or oil? Do you think this dye can pass through cell membranes?

FACTS AND FIGURES

Plants have hormones, too

Humans and other animals are not the only organisms that depend on hormones to regulate functions within the organism. Plants have hormones, too. In fact, plants depend on hormones even more than animals do. Unlike animals, plants do not have a nervous system to communicate messages from one part of the organism to another. As a result, plants must depend solely on hormones for such internal communication. Specific plant hormones regulate many important life cycle functions, including rates of growth, flowering, and seed production. Even the structure of plant leaves is controlled by hormones.

39–1 The Endocrine System

If you had to get a message to just one or two of your friends, what would you do? You might use the telephone. Wires running from your house to theirs would carry the message almost instantaneously. The telephone is a good way to reach a small number of people, but what if you wanted to get that same message to thousands of people? You might decide to broadcast it on the radio, sending the message in a way that made it possible to contact thousands of people at once.

Your nervous system works much like the telephone: Many impulses move swiftly over a system of wirelike neurons that carry specific messages from one cell to another. But another system, the endocrine system, does what the nervous system generally cannot. **The endocrine system is made up of glands that release their products into the bloodstream. These products broadcast messages throughout the body.** In the same way that a radio broadcast can reach thousands or even millions of people in a large city, the chemicals released by the endocrine system can affect almost every cell in the body.

Hormones

The chemicals that "broadcast" messages from the endocrine system are called hormones. **Hormones** are chemicals that travel through the bloodstream and affect the activities of other cells. Hormones do this by binding to specific chemical receptors on those cells. Cells that have receptors for a particular hormone are called **target cells.** If a cell does not have receptors or the receptors do not respond to a particular hormone, the hormone has no effect on it.

In general, the body's responses to hormones are slower and longer-lasting than the responses to nerve impulses. It may take several minutes, several hours, or even several days for a hormone to have its full effect on its target cells. A nerve impulse, on the other hand, may take only a fraction of a second to reach and affect its target cells.

Guide for Reading

Key Concepts
- What is the function of the endocrine system?
- How does the endocrine system maintain homeostasis?

Vocabulary
hormone
target cell
exocrine gland
endocrine gland
prostaglandin

Reading Strategy: Making Comparisons
As you read, list the differences and similarities between types of glands, and between types of hormones.

▶ **Figure 39–1** **The endocrine system releases hormones that affect the activities of other cells.** Much of the increase in heart rate and breathing that the people are experiencing on this ride is due to the actions of hormones.

SECTION RESOURCES

Print:
- ***Teaching Resources,*** Section Review 39–1
- ***Guided Reading and Study Workbook,*** Section 39–1

Technology:
- ***iText,*** Section 39–1

Section 39–1

1 FOCUS

Objectives

39.1.1 ***State*** the function of the endocrine system.
39.1.2 ***Describe*** hormones and glands.
39.1.3 ***Explain*** how the endocrine system maintains homeostasis.

Guide for Reading

Reading Strategy

Explain to students that the prefix *endo-* means "within" and that endocrine glands are glands that secrete substances within the body. Ask: **If *exo-* means "outside," what do you think exocrine glands are?** *(Glands that secrete substances to the outside)* These substances pass out of the glands into ducts, which either lead directly to the outside of the body (sweat or milk ducts) or into internal structures (saliva and digestive enzymes).

Reading Strategy

Have students study the figures and read the captions to preview the material in the section. Suggest that they write down any questions they have about the material based on the figures and then try to find the answers as they read the section.

2 INSTRUCT

Hormones

Build Science Skills

Using Analogies Help students understand the endocrine system by comparing it with familiar human relationships in which one person directs the actions of others—such as coach and team, conductor and orchestra members, traffic officer and motorists, and movie director and actors. Ask: **How are these relationships similar to the endocrine system?** *(An endocrine gland is like a director, the hormones are like verbal or visual directions, and cells are like the people being directed.)*

Demonstration

Demonstrate hormone–target cell interactions with a model. Have students use an empty egg carton to model a tissue. First, they should create "target cells" by cutting small holes in the top of the carton over a few of the sections. Then, they should pour water over the egg carton to model a circulating hormone. Ask: **Which cells in your model contain hormone?** *(Just the target cells)* **What effect did the hormone have on the other cells?** *(none)*

Glands

Build Science Skills

Inferring Call on students at random to compare and contrast endocrine and exocrine glands. *(Endocrine glands release their hormones into the bloodstream; exocrine glands release their hormones through ducts.)* Then, ask: **Based on how they release their hormones, what can you infer about the effects on the body of hormones released by endocrine and exocrine glands?** *(Hormones released by endocrine glands can affect cells throughout the body, whereas hormones released by exocrine glands can affect only nearby cells.)*

Use Visuals

Figure 39–2 Call students' attention to the figure. Make sure they understand that the ovaries are found only in females and the testes only in males. Name several different glands and have students locate them in the figure. As students locate each gland, ask: **What hormones does the gland produce, and what roles do the hormones play in the body?** *(Students should identify the hormones and roles of the glands by reading the appropriate labels in the figure.)*

Glands

A gland is an organ that produces and releases a substance, or a secretion. **Exocrine glands** release their secretions through tubelike structures called ducts. Exocrine glands include those that release sweat, tears, and digestive juices. Unlike exocrine glands, **endocrine glands** release their secretions (hormones) directly into the bloodstream. **Figure 39–2** shows the location of the major endocrine glands in the human body.

✓CHECKPOINT *What are exocrine glands?*

▼ **Figure 39–2** Endocrine glands produce hormones that affect many parts of the body. **Interpreting Graphics** *What is the function of the pituitary gland?*

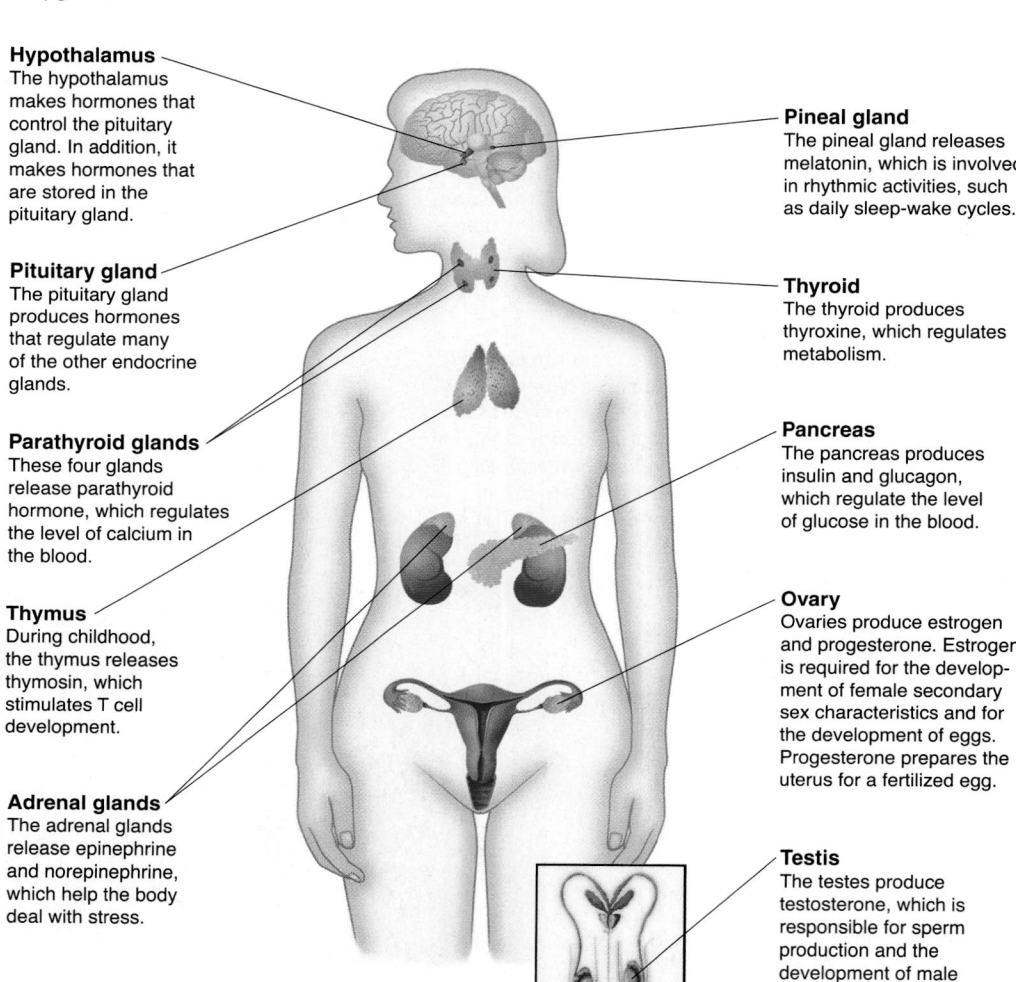

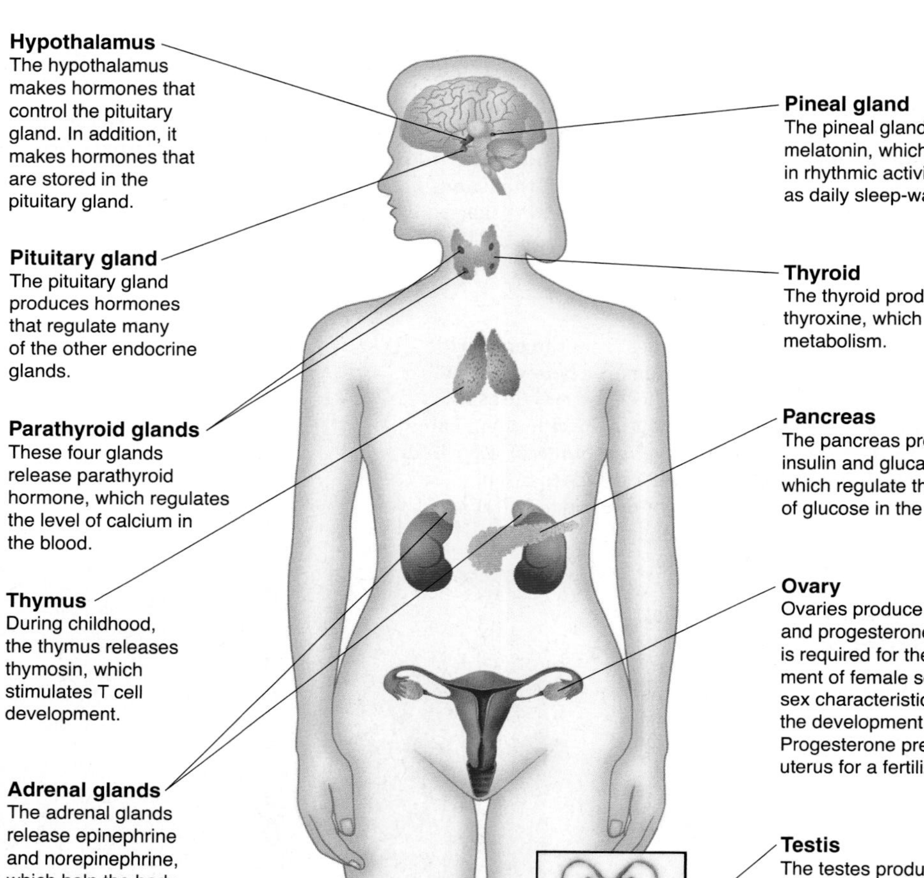
Hypothalamus
The hypothalamus makes hormones that control the pituitary gland. In addition, it makes hormones that are stored in the pituitary gland.
Pituitary gland
The pituitary gland produces hormones that regulate many of the other endocrine glands.
Parathyroid glands
These four glands release parathyroid hormone, which regulates the level of calcium in the blood.
Thymus
During childhood, the thymus releases thymosin, which stimulates T cell development.
Adrenal glands
The adrenal glands release epinephrine and norepinephrine, which help the body deal with stress.
Pineal gland
The pineal gland releases melatonin, which is involved in rhythmic activities, such as daily sleep-wake cycles.
Thyroid
The thyroid produces thyroxine, which regulates metabolism.
Pancreas
The pancreas produces insulin and glucagon, which regulate the level of glucose in the blood.
Ovary
Ovaries produce estrogen and progesterone. Estrogen is required for the development of female secondary sex characteristics and for the development of eggs. Progesterone prepares the uterus for a fertilized egg.
Testis
The testes produce testosterone, which is responsible for sperm production and the development of male secondary sex characteristics.

TIME SAVER

PRESENTATIONS MADE EASY!

The Presentation Assistant Plus contains the Prentice Hall Presentation Pro and the Transparencies, which provide easy-to-follow visual support for every step of this section. If you have a computer presentation station, use Prentice Hall Presentation Pro for Section 39–1, or use the transparencies listed here.

Section 39–1:

Interest Grabber
Section Outline
Hormone Action
Figure 39–2

Hormone Action

Hormones fall into two general groups—steroid hormones and nonsteroid hormones. Steroid hormones are produced from a lipid called cholesterol. Nonsteroid hormones include proteins, small peptides, and modified amino acids. The two basic patterns of hormone action are shown in **Figure 39–3.**

Steroid Hormones Because they are lipids, steroid hormones can cross cell membranes easily, passing directly into the cytoplasm and even into the nuclei of target cells.

1. A steroid hormone enters a cell by passing directly across its cell membrane.
2. Once inside, it binds to a steroid receptor protein (found only in its target cells) to form a hormone-receptor complex.
3. The hormone-receptor complex enters the nucleus of the cell, where it binds to a DNA control sequence.
4. This binding initiates the transcription of specific genes to messenger RNA (mRNA).
5. The mRNA moves into the cytoplasm and directs protein synthesis.

Hormone-receptor complexes work as regulators of gene expression—they can turn on or turn off whole sets of genes. Because steroid hormones affect gene expression directly, they can produce dramatic changes in cell and organism activity.

Nonsteroid Hormones Nonsteroid hormones generally cannot pass through the cell membrane of their target cells.

1. A nonsteroid hormone binds to receptors on the cell membrane.
2. The binding of the hormone activates an enzyme on the inner surface of the cell membrane.
3. This enzyme activates secondary messengers that carry the message of the hormone inside the cell. Calcium ions, cAMP (cyclic adenosine monophosphate), nucleotides, and even fatty acids can serve as second messengers.
4. Once released, these second messengers can activate or inhibit a wide range of other cell activities.

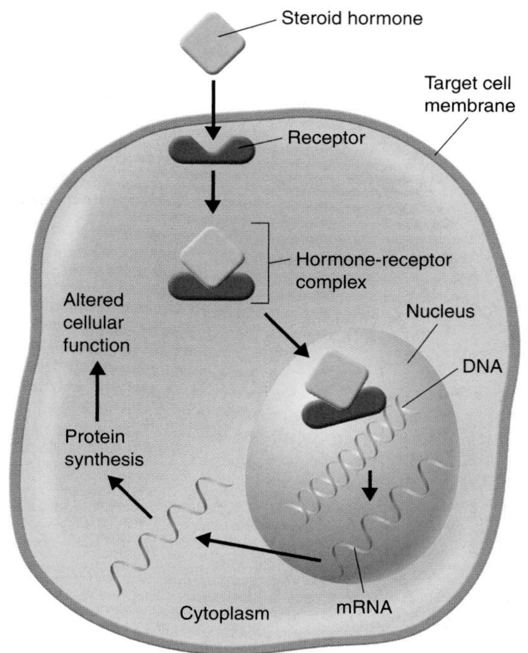

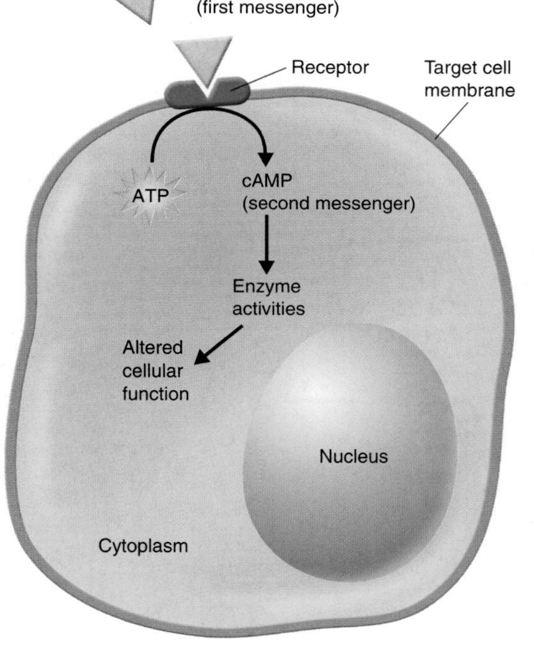

Figure 39–3 The two main types of hormones are steroid hormones and nonsteroid hormones. **Comparing and Contrasting** *How are steroid hormones different from nonsteroid hormones?*

Hormone Action

Meet Diverse Needs

Have at-risk students make a table contrasting steroid and nonsteroid hormones. Tables should have columns for the type of hormone, its composition, whether it can cross cell membranes, and how it affects target cells. Correct any errors in the tables and advise students to save the tables for study guides. **Limited English proficiency**

Use Visuals

Figure 39–3 Ask: **Why does the green hormone enter the top cell but the yellow hormone stays outside the bottom cell?** *(The green hormone is a steroid hormone, so it can cross cell membranes. The yellow hormone is a nonsteroid hormone, so it cannot cross cell membranes.)* **Why does the steroid hormone exert a greater influence on cell activity?** *(It enters the nucleus of the cell, where it regulates gene expression.)*

Meet Diverse Needs

Have students create two parallel flowcharts, one showing how a steroid hormone interacts with a target cell and the other showing how a nonsteroid hormone interacts with a target cell. Ask students to compare the two flowcharts and identify similarities and differences between the two types of hormone action. **Learning modality: visual**

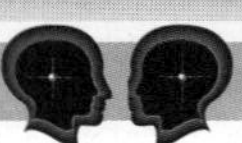

TEACHER TO TEACHER

To demonstrate the second messenger mechanism, I use a model. Prior to class, I arrange for another teacher to send a student from his or her class to my class with a message, such as "turn out the lights." The message is placed in an envelope with my name on it and the name of a student in my class. The student from the other class enters my classroom and hands the envelope to me. I hand the envelope to my student whose name is also on the envelope. This student opens the envelope and responds to the message. Then, I challenge students to tell me who represented the first messenger *(the student from the other class)*, the receptor *(me)*, and the second messenger *(my student)*.

—*Sheila Smith*
Biology Teacher
Terry High School,
Terry, MS

Answers to . . .

CHECKPOINT *Glands that release their secretions through ducts*

Figure 39–2 *It produces hormones that regulate many other endocrine glands.*

Figure 39–3 *Steroid hormones can cross cell membranes. Nonsteroid hormones cannot cross cell membranes.*

Prostaglandins

Build Science Skills

Inferring Point out that prostaglandins are called "local hormones" because they affect only nearby cells and tissues. Ask: **What advantage might this give prostaglandins over endocrine hormones?** *(Prostaglandins might work more quickly because they do not have to travel to another part of the body.)*

Meet Diverse Needs

Challenge gifted students to research more about prostaglandins. Ask them to find out how prostaglandins were discovered, how they differ from other hormones, and the roles played by specific prostaglandins, such as those in the uterus, blood vessels, or bronchioles. Urge students to share what they learn with the class in an oral report. **Learning modality: verbal**

Control of the Endocrine System

Build Science Skills

Using Analogies Help students better understand the feedback mechanisms that control the endocrine system by extending the thermostat analogy in the text. Ask: **How does a thermostat control a furnace?** *(When the temperature falls below a set point, a sensor in the thermostat signals the furnace to switch on; when the temperature rises above a set point, the sensor signals the furnace to switch off.)* Tell students that the thyroid gland is like a furnace because it can increase or decrease its output of the hormone thyroxine, which changes the rate of metabolism and, consequently, core body temperature. Ask: **If the thyroid is a furnace, what is the thermostat?** *(The hypothalamus, because it senses changes in the level of thyroxine or changes in internal body temperature and signals the anterior pituitary to release TSH.)*

▼ **Figure 39–4** **Like most body systems, the endocrine system is regulated by feedback controls that function to maintain homeostasis.** Notice how an increase in TSH causes the release of thyroxine. As the level of thyroxine increases in the blood, the level of TSH decreases. This action causes a decrease in thyroxine, which causes an increase in TSH, and the cycle begins again.

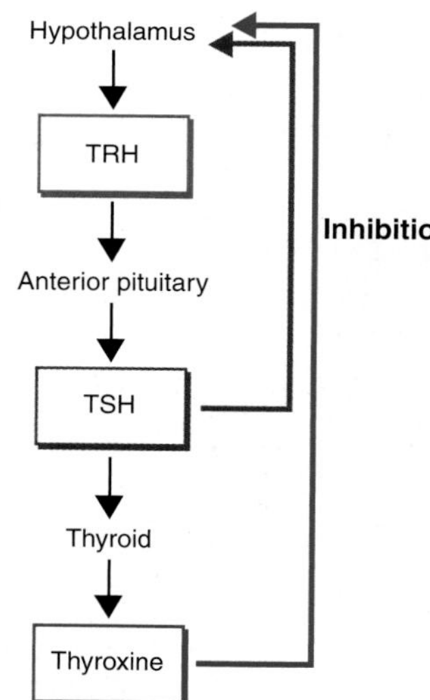

Prostaglandins

Until recently, the glands of the endocrine system were thought to be the only organs that produced hormones. However, except for red blood cells, all cells have been shown to produce small amounts of hormonelike substances called **prostaglandins** (prahs-tuh-GLAN-dinz). Prostaglandins get their name from a gland in the male reproductive system, the prostate, in which they were first discovered. Prostaglandins are modified fatty acids that are produced by a wide range of cells. They generally affect only nearby cells and tissues, and thus are known as "local hormones."

Some prostaglandins cause smooth muscles, such as those in the uterus, bronchioles, and blood vessels, to contract. One group of prostaglandins causes the sensation of pain in most headaches. Aspirin helps to stop the pain of a headache because it inhibits the synthesis of these prostaglandins.

Control of the Endocrine System

As powerful as they are, hormones must be closely monitored in order to keep the functions of different organs in balance. Even though the endocrine system is one of the master regulators of the body, it too must be controlled. **Like most systems of the body, the endocrine system is regulated by feedback mechanisms that function to maintain homeostasis.**

Recall that feedback inhibition occurs when an increase in any substance "feeds back" to inhibit the process that produced the substance in the first place. Heating and cooling systems, controlled by thermostats, are examples of mechanical feedback systems. The hormones of the endocrine system are biological examples of the same process.

Controlling Metabolism To see how a feedback mechanism regulates the activity of the endocrine system, let's look at one of the body's most important endocrine glands, the thyroid gland. Thyroxine, the gland's principal hormone, affects the activity of cells throughout the body. Increased levels of thyroxine in the blood stimulate cells to become more active. A drop in thyroxine decreases the metabolic activity of cells.

Does the thyroid gland determine how much thyroxine to release on its own? Not at all. The activity of the thyroid gland is controlled by the hypothalamus and the anterior pituitary gland. When the hypothalamus senses that the thyroxine level in the blood is low, it secretes a hormone known as thyroid-releasing hormone (TRH), which stimulates the anterior pituitary to secrete thyroid-stimulating hormone (TSH). TSH stimulates the release of thyroxine by the thyroid gland, which sets up the feedback loop shown in **Figure 39–4.** This feedback mechanism keeps the level of thyroxine in the blood relatively constant.

FACTS AND FIGURES

Fast-acting hormones

In humans and most other animals, endocrine hormones bring about relatively slow changes, sometimes taking hours or even days to achieve their full effects. In some animals, however, certain hormones produce a more immediate change. Examples are the hormones that cause vertebrates such as chameleons to change their color and pattern so they are camouflaged in their environment. The hormones that lead to such color changes usually produce their full effects in a matter of seconds. The effects are brought about by special color-containing cells in the skin, which change in size to produce a different color pattern. The color-containing cells are controlled by endocrine hormones that are produced in response to light patterns entering the eye of the animal.

Recall that the hypothalamus is also sensitive to temperature. When core body temperature begins to drop, even if the level of thyroxine is normal, the hypothalamus produces extra TRH. The release of TRH stimulates the release of TSH, which stimulates the release of additional thyroxine. The increase in metabolic activity that results helps the body maintain its core temperature despite colder air temperatures.

Maintaining Water Balance Homeostatic mechanisms regulate the levels of a wide variety of materials dissolved in the blood and in extracellular fluids. These include minerals such as sodium, potassium, and calcium, and soluble proteins such as serum albumin, which is found in blood plasma. Most of the time, homeostatic systems operate so smoothly that we are scarcely aware of their existence. However, that is not the case with one of the most important homeostatic processes, the one that regulates the amount of water in the body.

When you exercise strenuously, you lose water as you sweat. If this water loss continued, your body would soon become dehydrated. Generally, that doesn't happen because your body's homeostatic mechanisms swing into action.

The hypothalamus contains cells that are sensitive to the concentration of water in the blood. As you lose water, the concentration of dissolved materials in the blood rises. The hypothalamus responds in two ways. First, the hypothalamus signals the pituitary gland to release a hormone called antidiuretic hormone (ADH). ADH molecules are carried by the bloodstream to the kidneys, where the removal of water from the blood is quickly slowed down. Later, you experience a sensation of thirst, a signal that you should take a drink to restore lost water.

When you finally get around to taking that drink, you might take in as much as 1 or 2 liters of fluid. Most of that water is quickly absorbed across the walls of the digestive system into the bloodstream. But this volume of water added to the blood would dilute it so much that the equilibrium between the blood and the cells of the body would be disturbed. Large amounts of water would diffuse across blood vessel walls into the tissues. The cells of the body would swell with the excess water.

Needless to say, this doesn't happen, because the same homeostatic mechanism intervenes. When the water content of the blood rises, the pituitary releases less ADH. In response to lower ADH levels, the kidneys remove water from the bloodstream, restoring the blood to its original concentration. The water homeostatic system sets both upper and lower limits for blood water content: A water deficit stimulates the release of ADH, causing the kidneys to conserve water; an oversupply of water causes the kidneys to eliminate the excess.

✓CHECKPOINT *What process does thyroxine control?*

▼ **Figure 39–5** When exercising on a hot day, it is important to replenish lost liquid. **Applying Concepts** *Explain why people who are exercising should drink fluids before they are thirsty.*

Demonstration

Remind students of the discussion of feedback inhibition in Section 35–1. Explain that the endocrine system is regulated by feedback inhibition mechanisms and that feedback inhibition is sometimes referred to as negative feedback. Demonstrate the difference between a positive- and a negative-feedback mechanism by dividing the class into two groups. Tell members of one group to take turns saying the word *positive*, with each student saying it louder than the previous person. Then, instruct members of the other group to take turns saying the word *negative*, with students alternating between saying it louder and saying it softer than the previous person. Conclude by asking: **How did negative feedback affect the volume?** *(It kept the volume more or less constant.)* **How did positive feedback affect the volume?** *(It steadily increased the volume.)* **When would a positive-feedback mechanism be useful?** *(Positive feedback intensifies a response until the condition that stimulated the response is under control. For example, the signal for formation of a blood clot will be amplified until the bleeding is under control.)*

Meet Diverse Needs

To help visual learners understand how the body maintains water balance, create two flowcharts on the chalkboard, one illustrating a water deficit and one illustrating an oversupply of water. Call on students to fill in the steps for each flowchart. (*Deficit: hypothalamus signals pituitary → pituitary releases ADH → blood carries ADH to kidneys → kidneys slow removal of water. Oversupply: water content of blood rises → pituitary releases less ADH → kidneys speed removal of water from blood.*) **Learning modality: visual**

BIO INSIGHTS — FACTS AND FIGURES

The power of hormones

The endocrine glands, despite their tremendous importance in the body, are amazingly small. The pituitary gland, which produces nine different hormones and controls most of the other endocrine glands, is only as large as a pea. All of the body's endocrine tissues combined would fit in the palm of one hand. The quantity of hormones produced by this small amount of glandular tissue is also slight. For example, the average woman produces only about 5 mL, or a teaspoonful, of the steroid hormone estrogen in her entire lifetime. Obviously, to have the far-reaching effects on the body that they do, hormones must be very powerful. In fact, most hormones are so potent that they are effective at concentrations as low as one part per million.

Answers to . . .

✓CHECKPOINT *Thyroxine controls the level of activity in cells.*

Figure 39–5 *They could become dehydrated before they experience a sensation of thirst.*

SCIENCE NEWS®

Encourage students to visit **www.phschool.com** for the most current information on this topic.

Complementary Hormone Action

Meet Diverse Needs

Help students see how hormones regulate calcium concentration. Ask: **What causes the parathyroid glands to produce PTH?** *(A decrease in the level of calcium in the blood)* **How does PTH increase the concentration of calcium in the blood?** *(Stimulates the intestines to absorb more calcium, the kidneys to retain more calcium, and the bones to release calcium)* **What causes the thyroid gland to produce calcitonin?** *(An increase in the level of calcium in the blood)* **How does calcitonin decrease the concentration of calcium in the blood?** *(By stimulating the bones and kidneys to take up calcium and the intestines not to take up calcium)* **Learning modality: verbal**

3 ASSESS

Evaluate Understanding

Have some students compare steroid and nonsteroid hormones, and have others name examples of each.

Reteach

Guide students in making two Venn diagrams, comparing and contrasting *(1)* exocrine and endocrine glands and *(2)* hormones and prostaglandins.

MAKING CONNECTIONS

Students should use the structure of the cell membrane to explain why only steroid hormones can pass easily across the cell membrane.

Use iText to review the concepts in Section 39–1.

KEEP CURRENT WITH . . . SCIENCE NEWS®

To find out more about the topics in this chapter, go to: **www.phschool.com**

Complementary Hormone Action

Sometimes two hormones with opposite effects act to regulate part of the body's internal environment. Why are two hormones necessary? Think about driving a car. A good driver might be able to control a car on an open highway by using only the accelerator pedal. But driving around town, even a good driver would get into trouble using just the accelerator. There are too many situations in which the brake is needed to slow the car down.

In the same way, many endocrine functions depend on the complementary effects of two opposing hormones. Such a system regulates the level of calcium ions in the bloodstream.

The level of calcium dissolved in the bloodstream is kept within a narrow range. Two hormones regulate calcium concentration: calcitonin from the thyroid gland and parathyroid hormone (PTH) from the parathyroid glands. When blood calcium levels are too high, calcitonin helps to reduce the level. Calcitonin signals the kidneys to retain less calcium in the bloodstream. The release of calcitonin also reduces the amount of calcium absorbed in the intestine and stimulates calcium deposition in the bones.

If calcium levels drop too low, PTH is released by the parathyroids. PTH, together with vitamin D, stimulates the intestine to absorb more calcium from food. PTH also causes the kidneys to retain more calcium, and it stimulates bone cells to release some of the calcium stored in bone tissue into the bloodstream.

You may be surprised that the body regulates calcium levels so carefully. This careful regulation is necessary because calcium is one of the most important minerals in the body. If calcium levels drop below their normal range, blood cannot clot, muscles cannot contract, and the transport of materials across cell membranes may fail.

39–1 Section Assessment

1. **Key Concept** Describe the role of the endocrine system in the body.
2. **Key Concept** Explain how the endocrine system helps maintain homeostasis.
3. Compare endocrine glands and exocrine glands.
4. What are prostaglandins and why are they called "local hormones"?
5. **Critical Thinking Applying Concepts** What are the advantages of having both a nervous system and an endocrine system?

iTEXT Assessment Use iText to review the important concepts in Section 39–1.

MAKING CONNECTIONS

Cell Structure

Use what you learned in Chapter 7 about cell membranes to explain the actions of steroid hormones and nonsteroid hormones.

39–1 Section Assessment

1. To produce hormones that affect the activities of cells throughout the body
2. Through feedback mechanisms that inhibit the production of a substance
3. Endocrine glands, such as the thyroid, secrete hormones directly into the bloodstream. Exocrine glands release their secretions through ducts.
4. All cells produce hormonelike substances called prostaglandins, which are called "local hormones" because they affect only nearby cells or tissues.
5. The nervous system broadcasts specific messages quickly to a limited number of cells, whereas the endocrine system broadcasts messages slowly to target cells throughout the body.

39–2 Human Endocrine Glands

The endocrine glands are scattered throughout the body. Generally, they do not have direct connections to one another. Like signals that are beamed throughout the country from a broadcast station, the hormones released from the endocrine glands travel throughout the body, reaching almost every cell.

The human endocrine system regulates a wide variety of activities. Any improper functioning of an endocrine gland may result in a disease or a disorder. The major glands of the endocrine system include the pituitary gland, the hypothalamus, the thyroid gland, the parathyroid glands, the adrenal glands, the pancreas, and the reproductive glands.

Pituitary Gland

The **pituitary gland** is a bean-sized structure that dangles on a slender stalk of tissue at the base of the skull. As you can see in **Figure 39–6,** the gland is divided into two parts: the anterior pituitary and the posterior pituitary. **The pituitary gland secretes nine hormones that directly regulate many body functions and controls the actions of several other endocrine glands.**

Normal function of the pituitary gland is essential to good health. For example, if the pituitary gland produces too much growth hormone (GH), the body grows too quickly and a condition called gigantism results. Too little GH during childhood causes a condition known as pituitary dwarfism, which can be treated by administering growth hormone.

Guide for Reading

Key Concept
- What are the functions of the major endocrine glands?

Vocabulary
pituitary gland
diabetes mellitus
ovary
testis

Reading Strategy: Finding Main Ideas Before you read, skim the text paragraphs in this section to find the seven boldfaced sentences. Copy each sentence onto a note card. As you read, note supporting details on the cards.

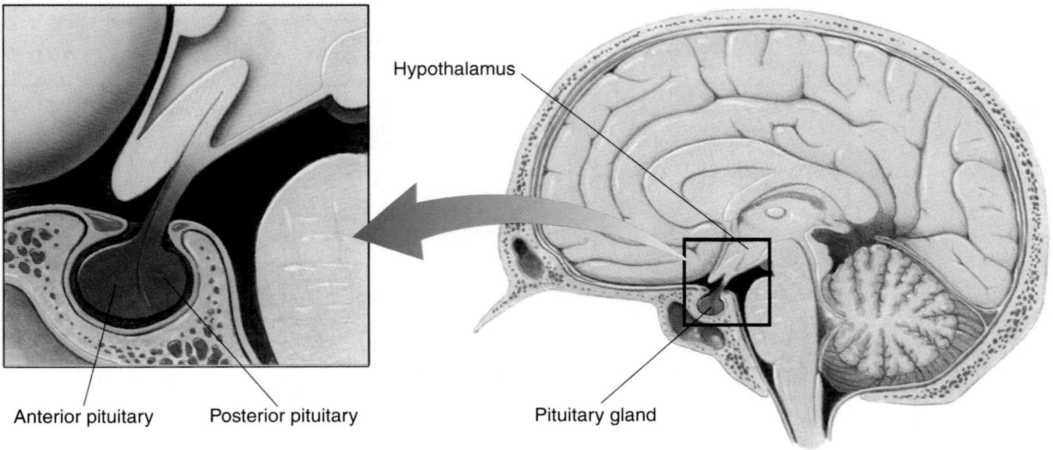

▼ **Figure 39–6** **The pituitary gland, which controls many other endocrine glands, is located below the hypothalamus in the brain.** The pituitary gland has two lobes: an anterior lobe and a posterior lobe.

SECTION RESOURCES

Print:
- ***Teaching Resources,*** Section Review 39–2
- ***Guided Reading and Study Workbook,*** Section 39–2
- ***Issues and Decision Making,*** 39–2

Technology:
- ***iText,*** Section 39–2

Section 39–2

1 FOCUS

Objective

39.2.1 ***Identify*** the functions of the major endocrine glands.

Guide for Reading

Vocabulary Preview

Before students read the section, have them preview new vocabulary by skimming the section and making a list of the boldfaced terms. They should leave spaces after the terms to write the definitions as they read the section.

Reading Strategy

Have students make a table with the headings Endocrine Gland, Location, Hormones, and Functions. As students read the section, they should fill in the table for each of the endocrine glands.

2 INSTRUCT

Pituitary Gland

Use Visuals

Figure 39–6 Explain to students that the close-up drawing on the left is greatly enlarged and that the pituitary gland is actually smaller than the tip of their little finger. Point out the close spatial relationship between the hypothalamus and pituitary and relate it to control of the pituitary by the hypothalamus. Have students locate the anterior and posterior pituitary in the drawing on the left. Tell them that the word *anterior* means "toward the front." Ask: **What do you think the word *posterior* means?** *(Toward the back)* Relate Figure 39–6 to Figure 39–7 by asking: **Which pituitary hormones are produced by the anterior pituitary, and which are produced by the posterior pituitary?** *(FSH, LH, TSH, ACTH, GH, prolactin, and MSH are produced by the anterior pituitary. ADH and oxytocin are produced by the posterior pituitary.)*

Meet Diverse Needs

Have students make an outline of the human body using Figure 39–2 as a model. Have students add the glands and organs that are targets of the pituitary gland to the sketch. These targets are identified in Figure 39–7. Finally, have students add arrows and labels to the sketch to show which pituitary hormone controls which gland or organ. **Learning modality: tactile**

Hypothalamus

Address Misconceptions

Students may have heard the pituitary gland referred to as the body's "master gland," because the pituitary's hormones control so many other glands and organs. Explain that scientists no longer refer to the pituitary gland in this way, because it is now known that the hypothalamus controls the pituitary. Ask: **What are the two mechanisms by which the hypothalamus controls the pituitary gland?** *(The hypothalamus directly stimulates cells of the posterior pituitary to secrete hormones. The hypothalamus also produces releasing hormones that stimulate cells of the anterior pituitary to secrete hormones.)*

Build Science Skills

Applying Concepts Point out that the hypothalamus responds to stress as well as to sensory input, providing one route by which stress can affect health. Ask: **How could stress, by affecting the hypothalamus, indirectly affect health?** *(Stress could cause the hypothalamus to stimulate the pituitary to produce more or less of its hormones and, indirectly, stimulate the thyroid and other glands controlled by the pituitary to produce more or less of their hormones. These hormonal imbalances, in turn, could cause health problems.)*

Hypothalamus

The hypothalamus is the part of the brain above and attached to the posterior pituitary. **The hypothalamus controls the secretions of the pituitary gland.** The activity of the hypothalamus is influenced by the levels of hormones in the blood and by sensory information collected by other parts of the central nervous system. Interactions between the nervous system and the endocrine system take place at the hypothalamus.

The posterior pituitary is made up of axons belonging to cells called neurosecretory cells, whose cell bodies are in the hypothalamus. When these cell bodies are stimulated, the axons in the posterior pituitary release their hormones into the bloodstream. In a way, the posterior pituitary is an extension of the hypothalamus.

In contrast, the hypothalamus has indirect control of the anterior pituitary. The hypothalamus produces small amounts of chemicals called releasing hormones, which are secreted directly into blood vessels. The releasing hormones are carried by the circulatory system to the anterior pituitary, where they control the production and release of hormones.

The close connection between the hypothalamus and the pituitary gland means that the nervous and endocrine systems can act together to help coordinate body activities. Hormones released by the pituitary gland are listed in **Figure 39–7.**

CHECKPOINT *What is the role of releasing hormones?*

▼ **Figure 39–7** **The hypothalamus controls the secretions of the pituitary gland.** Notice the effect that each hormone produced by the pituitary gland has on the body.

Pituitary Gland Hormones

Pituitary Gland	Hormone	Action
Posterior pituitary	Antidiuretic hormone (ADH)	Stimulates the kidneys to reabsorb water from the collecting tubules
	Oxytocin	Stimulates contractions of uterus during childbirth; releases milk in nursing mothers
Anterior pituitary	Follicle-stimulating hormone (FSH)	Stimulates production of eggs and sperm
	Luteinizing hormone (LH)	Stimulates ovaries and testes; prepares uterus for implantation of fertilized egg
	Thyroid-stimulating hormone (TSH)	Stimulates the synthesis and release of thyroxine from the thyroid gland
	Adreno-corticotropic hormone (ACTH)	Stimulates release of some hormones from the adrenal cortex
	Growth hormone (GH)	Stimulates protein synthesis and growth in cells
	Prolactin	Stimulates milk production in nursing mothers
	Melanocyte-stimulating hormone (MSH)	Stimulates the melanocytes of the skin, increasing their production of the skin pigment melanin

TIME SAVER

PRESENTATIONS MADE EASY!

The Presentation Assistant Plus contains the Prentice Hall Presentation Pro and the Transparencies, which provide easy-to-follow visual support for very step of this section. If you have a computer presentation station, use Prentice Hall Presentation Pro for Section 39–2, or use the transparencies listed here.

Section 39–2: Interest Grabber
Section Outline
Concept Map
Figure 39–10

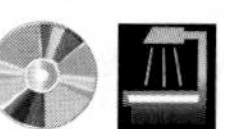

Thyroid Gland

If you look at **Figure 39–8,** you can see that the thyroid gland is located at the base of the neck and wraps around the upper part of the trachea. **The thyroid gland has the major role in regulating the body's metabolism.** Cells in the thyroid gland produce thyroxine, which is made up of the amino acid tyrosine and the mineral iodine. Remember that thyroxine affects nearly all of the cells of the body by regulating their metabolic rates. Increased levels of thyroxine can increase the cellular respiration rate, which means that the cells release more energy. Decreased levels of thyroxine can decrease the cellular respiration rate and the amount of energy released. Other cells in the thyroid gland secrete calcitonin—the hormone that decreases the level of calcium in the blood.

The homeostatic activities of the thyroid gland are so well controlled that you may never become aware of them. However, if the thyroid gland produces too much thyroxine, a condition called hyperthyroidism occurs. Hyperthyroidism results in nervousness, elevated body temperature, increased heart and metabolic rates, increased blood pressure, and weight loss. Too little thyroxine causes a condition called hypothyroidism. Lower metabolic rates and body temperature, lack of energy, and weight gain are characteristics of this condition. In some cases, hypothyroidism is associated with goiter, an enlargement of the thyroid gland.

The importance of proper thyroid activity can be seen in parts of the world where food lacks enough iodine for the thyroid to produce normal amounts of thyroxine. Unable to produce the thyroxine needed for normal development, iodine-deficient infants suffer from a condition called cretinism (KREE-tuh-niz-um) in which neither the skeletal system nor the nervous system develops properly. Two effects of cretinism are dwarfism and severe mental retardation. Cretinism usually can be prevented by the addition of small amounts of iodine to table salt or other items in the food supply.

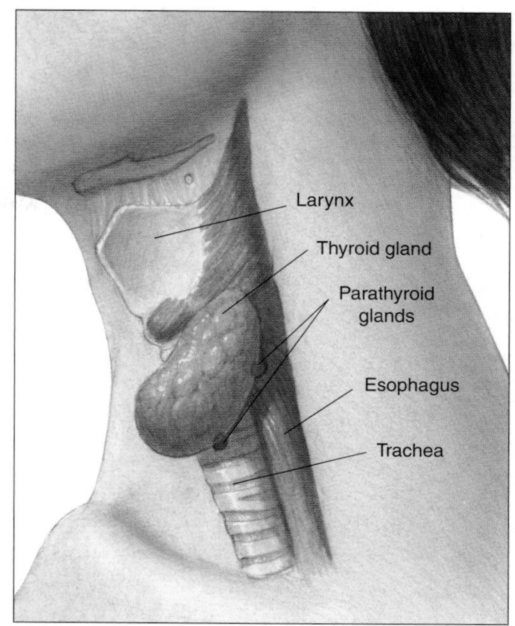

▲ **Figure 39–8 Hormones produced by the thyroid gland and the parathyroid glands maintain the level of calcium in the blood.** The thyroid gland wraps around the trachea.

Parathyroid Glands

The four parathyroid glands are found on the back surface of the thyroid gland. **Hormones from the thyroid gland and the parathyroid glands maintain homeostasis in blood calcium levels.** Parathyroid glands secrete parathyroid hormone (PTH). PTH regulates the calcium levels in the blood by increasing the reabsorption of calcium in the kidneys and by increasing the uptake of calcium from the digestive system. Parathyroid hormone is also important for promoting proper nerve and muscle function and bone structure.

BIO INSIGHTS — FACTS AND FIGURES

Effects of a faulty thyroid

Iodine deficiencies severe enough to cause thyroid problems usually occur in mountainous inland regions, such as the Alps or Andes. However, iodine deficiency is not the only cause of thyroid problems. Two different autoimmune diseases, both more common in females than in males, also cause thyroid problems. One disease is Hashimoto's disease, which, after iodine deficiency, is the second most common cause of hypothyroidism, or underproduction of thyroid hormones. Some of the signs and symptoms of hypothyroidism are enlarged thyroid gland, slow heart rate, dry skin, fatigue, and weight gain. The other disease is Graves' disease. It causes hyperthyroidism, or overproduction of thyroid hormone. Symptoms of hyperthyroidism include enlarged thyroid gland, rapid heart rate, bulging eyes, hand tremor, and weight loss.

Thyroid Gland

Meet Diverse Needs

At-risk students may have difficulty understanding the role of thyroxine unless they first review the concepts of metabolism and cellular respiration. Have students find these concepts in the glossary and copy the definitions on a sheet of paper. If students feel they still do not understand the concepts, have them find the concepts in the index and read more about them on the other pages where they occur, adding any notes to their definitions that will help them understand the concepts. Urge students to refer to their annotated definitions as they read about how thyroxine regulates body metabolism. **Limited English proficiency**

Make Connections

Health Science Explain that low levels of iodine in the diet may cause the thyroid gland to compensate by increasing in size and producing a noticeable swelling in the throat called a goiter. If possible, show students pictures of people with goiters. Also explain that lack of thyroxine in adults does not produce cretinism but a condition called myxedema, which is characterized by lethargy, puffiness, and mental dullness. Point out that people with myxedema can recover from the condition with no lasting effects. Ask: **Why are the effects of iodine deficiency permanent in children but not in adults?** *(The effects are permanent in children because they are still growing and developing.)* GH and insulin are also important regulators of metabolism, especially in young children.

Parathyroid Glands

Meet Diverse Needs

Advise at-risk students to turn back to the text under the heading "Complementary Hormone Action" in Section 39–1 to review how parathyroid hormone helps maintain homeostasis in blood calcium levels. **Limited English proficiency**

Answer to . . .

✓CHECKPOINT *Hormones that are secreted directly into blood vessels.*

Adrenal Glands

Use Visuals

Figure 39–9 Point out the adrenal glands' location on top of the kidneys. Have students find the kidneys in Figure 39–2 if they do not know where they are located. Then, have students find the two parts of the adrenal gland in Figure 39–9. Tell them that the term *cortex* refers to the outer part of an organ or gland. Ask: **What do you think the term *medulla* refers to?** *(The inner part of an organ or gland)* **Besides location, what relationship is there between the kidneys and the adrenal glands?** *(The adrenal cortex secretes aldosterone, which regulates the reabsorption of sodium ions and the excretion of potassium ions by the kidneys.)*

Meet Diverse Needs

Challenge gifted students to research the complex mechanism by which the kidney controls the production of the adrenal cortex hormone aldosterone. Have students draw diagrams to illustrate the mechanism. Ask volunteers to explain their diagrams to the class or display them in the classroom. While doing their research, students are likely to encounter alternate names for epinephrine and norepinephrine—adrenaline and noradrenaline. **Learning modality: visual**

Make Connections

Health Science Explain to students that when someone is under constant stress, the adrenal medulla may be continually stimulated to produce its "fight-or-flight" hormones. Ask: **What effect do you think this might have on the body over the long run?** *(The increased heart rate and blood pressure and other responses to epinephrine and norepinephrine would put wear and tear on the body and could lead to illness.)*

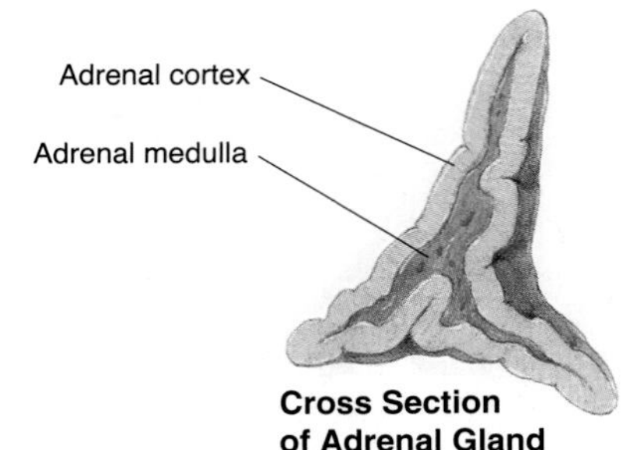

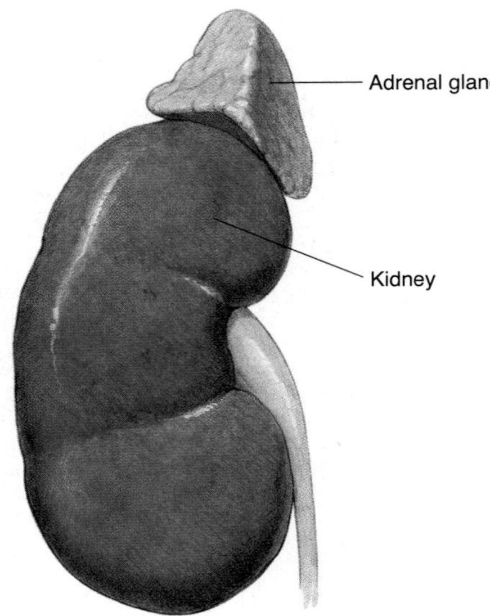

▲ **Figure 39–9** **The adrenal glands help the body prepare for and deal with stress.** The adrenal gland is divided into two parts: the adrenal cortex and the adrenal medulla.

Adrenal Glands

The adrenal glands are two pyramid-shaped structures that sit on top of the kidneys, one gland on each kidney, as shown in **Figure 39–9.** **The adrenal glands help the body prepare for and deal with stress.** An adrenal gland has an outer part called the adrenal cortex and an inner part called the adrenal medulla. These parts contain different types of tissues.

Adrenal Cortex About 80 percent of an adrenal gland is its adrenal cortex. The cortex produces more than two dozen hormones called corticosteroids (kawr-tih-koh-STEER-oydz). The hormone aldosterone (al-DAHS-tuh-rohn) regulates the reabsorption of sodium ions and the excretion of potassium ions by the kidneys. Another hormone, called cortisol, helps control the rate of metabolism of carbohydrates, fats, and proteins.

Adrenal Medulla The release of hormones from the adrenal medulla is regulated by the sympathetic nervous system. The two hormones released by the adrenal medulla are epinephrine and norepinephrine. Epinephrine, which is more powerful than norepinephrine, makes up about 80 percent of the total secretions of the adrenal medulla.

The adrenal medulla produces the "fight or flight" response to stress. This response is the feeling you get when you are excited or frightened. Nerve impulses from the sympathetic nervous system stimulate cells of the adrenal medulla. This stimulation causes the cells to release large amounts of epinephrine and norepinephrine. These hormones increase heart rate, blood pressure, and blood flow to the muscles. They cause air passageways to open wider, allowing for an increase in the intake of oxygen. They also stimulate the release of extra glucose into the blood to help produce a sudden burst of energy. The result of all these actions is a general increase in body activity, which can serve as preparation for intense physical activity. If your heart rate speeds up and your hands begin to perspire when you take a test, you are feeling the effects of your adrenal medulla!

CHECKPOINT *Which hormones are released from the adrenal cortex? From the adrenal medulla?*

HISTORY OF SCIENCE

From dog urine to crystals

In 1889, scientists removed the pancreas from laboratory dogs and found, by chance, that the dogs' urine attracted bees. The scientists inferred that the urine contained sugar, which was also known to be true of the urine of people with diabetes mellitus. The scientists concluded that the pancreas must produce a substance that was involved somehow in the disease. The substance was named insulin after *insula*, the Latin word for "island," because it was thought to be produced by the islets of Langerhans. In 1922, insulin was isolated and identified by Sir Frederick Banting and Charles Best. Banting received a Nobel prize for the discovery the following year. Banting and Best also determined insulin's role in carbohydrate metabolism and diabetes mellitus. In 1969, the English chemist Dorothy Crowfoot Hodgkin used crystallography to determine insulin's crystal structure.

Pancreas

The pancreas is an unusual organ. Located along the right side of and behind the stomach, the pancreas seems to be a single gland—but appearances can be deceiving! Recall that the pancreas is a digestive organ whose enzyme secretions help to break down food. This makes the pancreas an exocrine gland. However, different cells in the pancreas release hormones into the blood, making the pancreas an endocrine gland as well.

The hormone-producing portion of the pancreas consists of clusters of cells that resemble islands. These clusters of cells are called islets of Langerhans after their discoverer, the German anatomist Paul Langerhans. Each islet includes beta cells, which secrete a hormone called insulin, and alpha cells, which secrete another hormone called glucagon. **Insulin and glucagon released from the pancreas help to keep the level of glucose in the blood stable.** Insulin stimulates cells in the liver and muscles to remove sugar from the blood and store it as glycogen or fat. Glucagon stimulates the liver to break down glycogen and release glucose back into the blood. The actions of insulin and glucagon are summarized in **Figure 39–10.**

▼ **Figure 39–10** **Insulin and glucagon from the pancreas help keep the level of glucose in the blood stable.** The top half of the flowchart shows what happens when the level of glucose in the blood increases. The bottom half shows what happens when the level of glucose in the blood decreases.

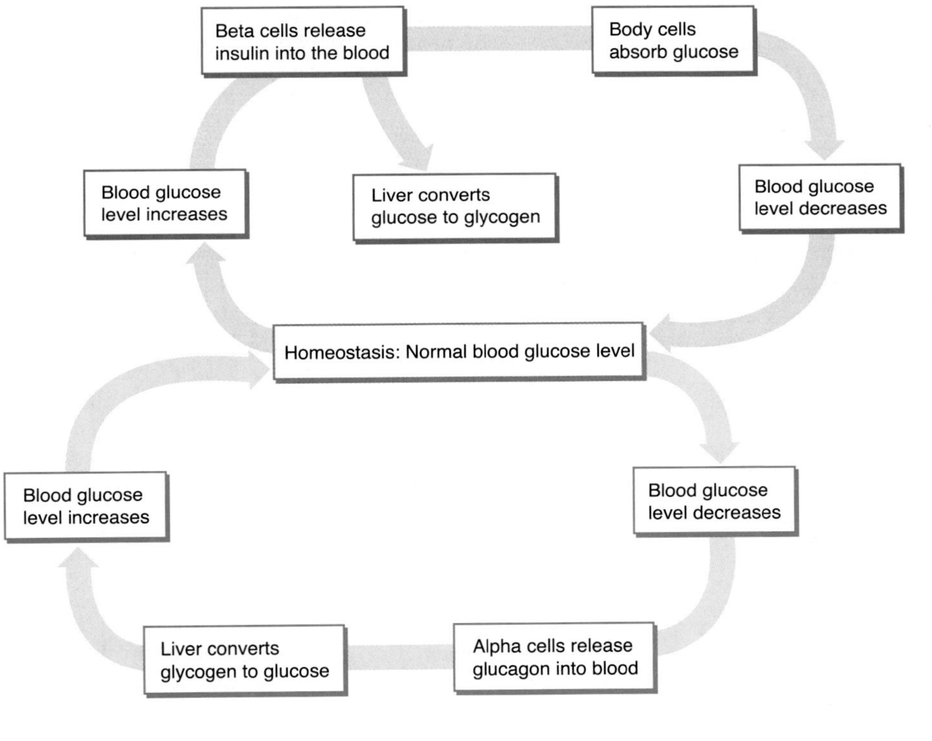

Pancreas

Address Misconceptions

Students are likely to have heard diabetes mellitus referred to simply as "diabetes." Point out that the term *diabetes* actually refers to any disease that is characterized by excessive urination and thirst and that there is more than one type of diabetes. For example, diabetes insipidus is a type of diabetes caused by lack of the pituitary hormone ADH and not by lack of insulin. Ask: **If diabetes mellitus is controlled by insulin injections, how do you think diabetes insipidus is controlled?** *(By ADH injections)*

Demonstration

Tell students that diabetes mellitus often is diagnosed by detecting sugar in the urine. Give students glucose test strips and explain how they are used. Then, have students use the test strips to test either a mixture of water, yellow food coloring, and sugar or a mixture of water and yellow food coloring alone. Ask: **Did your "urine" specimen contain sugar?** *(Answers will depend on which mixture was tested.)* Check that students have correctly interpreted their test results.

Use Community Resources

Ask a nurse or other medical professional who is knowledgeable about diabetes mellitus to visit your class. Have the visitor explain why and when people with diabetes mellitus must measure their blood glucose and why and when insulin must be taken. If possible, have the visitor demonstrate how a glucometer and an insulin kit are used. Urge students to prepare a list of questions in advance, such as: What dietary restrictions must diabetics follow? Is diabetes mellitus inherited?

TEACHER TO TEACHER

After students have read about the endocrine hormones, I check their comprehension by showing them pictures of situations in which a particular hormone is needed. Then, I have students identify the hormone and explain why it is produced. For example, if I show students a picture of someone eating candy, they should respond that insulin is produced by the pancreas to help control blood sugar levels. If I show them a picture of someone shivering on a winter day, they should respond that TSH is produced by the pituitary to stimulate the thyroid to increase body metabolism.

—*Ruth Gleicher*
Biology Teacher
Niles West High School, Skokie, IL

Answer to . . .

CHECKPOINT *Corticosteroid hormones, such as aldosterone and cortisol, are released from the adrenal cortex. Epinephrine and norepinephrine are released from the adrenal medulla.*

39–2 (continued)

Reproductive Glands

Address Misconceptions

Students are likely to think that testosterone is produced only by males and estrogen only by females. Tell students that the adrenal glands produce small amounts of estrogen and testosterone in both females and males. Ask: **Why do you think males do not show the effects of adrenal estrogen or females the effects of adrenal testosterone?** *(The amounts of hormones produced by the adrenal glands are small compared with the amounts produced by the gonads.)*

3 ASSESS

Evaluate Understanding

Call on students to identify hormones produced by each endocrine gland. Call on other students to describe the function of each hormone.

Reteach

Divide the class into two teams. Play a quiz game in which you act as moderator and require students on alternating teams to identify hormones based on a description.

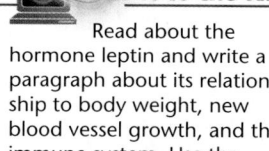

Take It to the NET

Leptin is produced by fat cells. It tells the hypothalamus how much fat the body contains. The hypothalamus, in turn, regulates appetite and controls body weight. Leptin also plays a role in reproduction and metabolism, and it may contribute to weight loss in people with cancer. In addition, leptin stimulates new blood vessel growth and helps white blood cells fight infection. For additional information, visit **www.phschool.com**

Use iText to review the key concepts in Section 39–2.

Answer to . . .

Figure 39–11 *Blood pressure rises.*

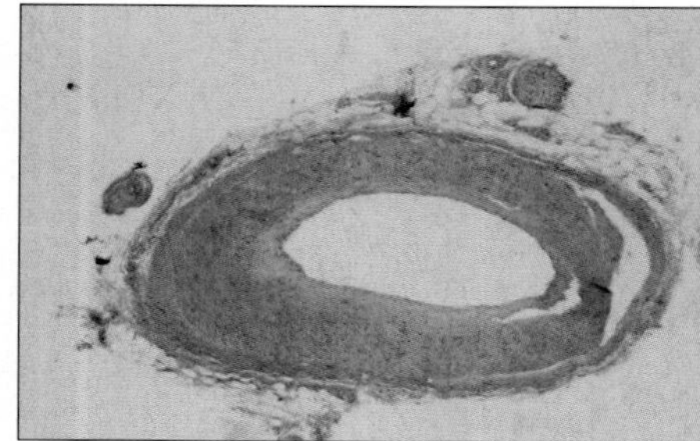

Normal Coronary Artery

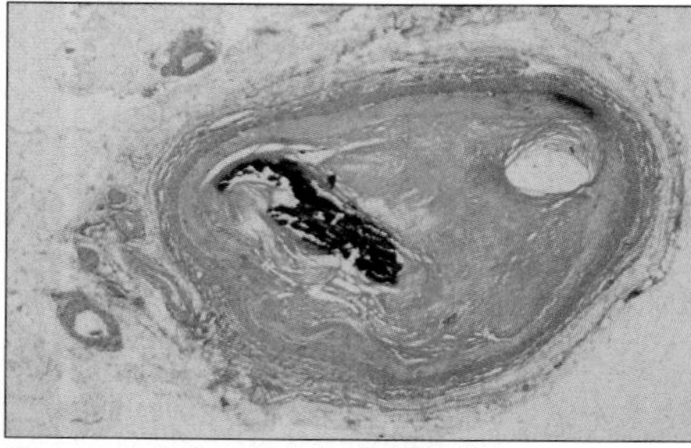

Coronary Artery Totally Blocked

▲ **Figure 39–11** Uncontrolled diabetes can increase the risk of blocked arteries. **Applying Concepts** *What effect do blocked arteries have on blood pressure?*

When the pancreas produces too little insulin, a condition known as **diabetes mellitus** occurs. In diabetes mellitus, the amount of glucose in the blood may rise so high that the kidneys actually excrete glucose in the urine. Very high blood glucose levels can damage many organs and tissues, including the coronary artery shown in **Figure 39–11.**

There are two types of diabetes mellitus. Juvenile-onset diabetes, also known as Type I, most commonly develops in people before the age of 15. In this type of diabetes, there is little or no secretion of insulin. People with this type of diabetes must follow a strict diet and get daily injections of insulin. Adult-onset diabetes, or Type II, most commonly develops in people after the age of 40. People with adult-onset diabetes produce low to normal amounts of insulin. However, their cells are unable to properly respond to the hormone because the interaction of the insulin receptors and the insulin is inefficient. Adult-onset diabetes, especially in its early stages, can often be controlled through diet and exercise.

Reproductive Glands

The gonads are the body's reproductive glands. **The gonads serve two important functions: the production of gametes and the secretion of sex hormones.** The female gonads—the **ovaries**—produce eggs (ova). The male gonads—the **testes** (singular: testis)—produce sperm. The gonads also produce sex hormones. You will read more about these hormones in the next section.

39–2 Section Assessment

1. **Key Concept** Describe the role of each major endocrine gland.
2. Why is the hypothalamus an important part of both the nervous system and the endocrine system?
3. What are the two types of diabetes mellitus?
4. What endocrine gland goes to work when you are surprised with a pop quiz?
5. **Critical Thinking Predicting** Suppose the secretion of a certain hormone causes an increase in the concentration of substance X in the blood. What is the effect on the rate of hormone secretion if an abnormal condition causes the level of X in the blood to remain very low?

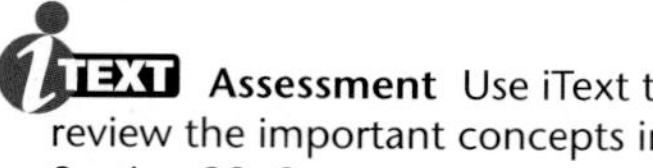

Assessment Use iText to review the important concepts in Section 39–2.

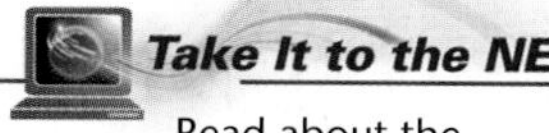

Read about the hormone leptin and write a paragraph about its relationship to body weight, new blood vessel growth, and the immune system. Use the links provided in the Biology area at the Prentice Hall Web site for help in completing this activity: **www.phschool.com**

39–2 Section Assessment

1. Pituitary: regulates functions such as growth and actions of other glands; hypothalamus: controls the pituitary gland; parathyroids and thyroid: metabolism and level of calcium in blood; adrenals: metabolism, salt excretion, and response to stress; pancreas: level of blood glucose; ovaries and testes: production of gametes and secretion of sex hormones.
2. It monitors sensory input from the nervous system and uses it to control the endocrine system via the pituitary gland.
3. Type I, or juvenile onset (before age 15), and Type II, or adult onset (after age 40)
4. The adrenal gland
5. Rate of hormone secretion remains high.

39–3 The Reproductive System

Reproduction is the formation of new individuals. This makes the reproductive system unique among the systems of the body. If any other body system, such as the nervous or circulatory system, failed to function, the result would be fatal in most animals. This is not the case for the reproductive system because an individual can lead a healthy life without reproducing. However, the reproductive system could be thought of as the single most important system for the continuation of a species—without it, no species could produce another generation.

In humans, as in other vertebrates, the reproductive system produces, stores, and releases specialized sex cells known as gametes. These cells are released in ways that make possible the fusion of sperm and egg to form a zygote, the single cell from which all cells of the human body develop.

Sexual Development

For the first six weeks of development, human male and female embryos are identical in appearance. Then, during the seventh week, major changes occur. The primary reproductive organs—the testes in males and the ovaries in females—begin to develop. The testes produce testosterone, a male sex hormone. Testosterone is required for sperm production and the development of male physical characteristics. The ovaries produce the female sex hormones estrogen and progesterone. Estrogen is required for the development of eggs and for the formation of female physical characteristics. Progesterone prepares the uterus for the arrival of a developing embryo. Although the male and female reproductive organs develop from the same tissues in the embryo, these hormones determine whether the embryo will develop into a male or a female.

After birth, the gonads produce small amounts of sex hormones that continue to influence the development of the reproductive organs. However, neither the testes nor the ovaries are capable of producing active reproductive cells until puberty. **Puberty** is a period of rapid growth and sexual maturation during which the reproductive system becomes fully functional. At the completion of puberty, the male and female reproductive organs are fully developed. The onset of puberty varies considerably among individuals. It may occur any time between the ages of 9 and 15, and, on average, begins about a year earlier in females than in males.

Guide for Reading

Key Concepts
- What are the roles of the male and female reproductive systems?
- What are the four phases of the menstrual cycle?

Vocabulary
puberty • scrotum
seminiferous tubule
epididymis • vas deferens
urethra • penis • follicle
ovulation • Fallopian tube
uterus • vagina
menstrual cycle
corpus luteum • menstruation

Reading Strategy: Outlining Before you read, use the headings in this section to make an outline about the reproductive system. As you read, fill in subtopics. Then, add phrases or a sentence after each subtopic to provide key information showing how the reproductive system is important.

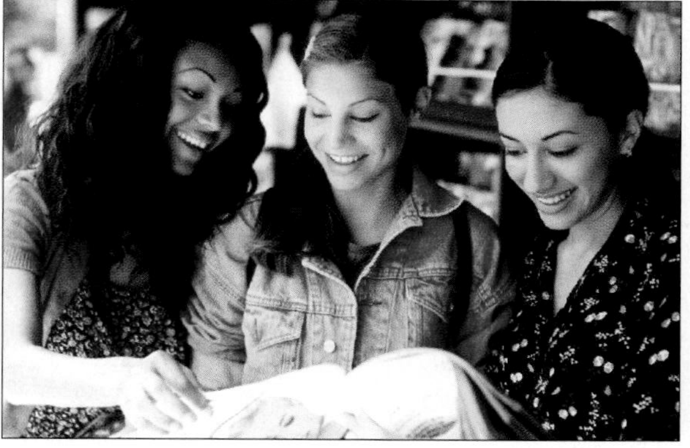

▼ **Figure 39–12** Many changes in your life—both social and physical—are dependent on your age.

SECTION RESOURCES

Print:
- ***Laboratory Manual A,*** Chapter 39 Lab
- ***Laboratory Manual B,*** Chapter 39 Lab
- ***Teaching Resources,*** Section Review 39–3
- ***Guided Reading and Study Workbook,*** Section 39–3

Technology:
- ***iText***, Section 39–3

Section 39–3

1 FOCUS

Objectives

39.3.1 ***Describe*** sexual development.
39.3.1 ***Explain*** the role of the male and female reproductive systems.
39.3.1 ***Identify*** the four phases of the menstrual cycle.

Guide for Reading

Vocabulary Preview

Tell students that all the vocabulary words, except puberty, refer to either the male or the female reproductive system. Challenge students to identify which words refer to each system. They should check to see if they were right as they read the section.

Reading Strategy

Before students read the section, have them find and rewrite each boldfaced sentence in a question-and-answer format. After students read the section, they should check their comprehension by trying to answer the questions.

2 INSTRUCT

Sexual Development

Meet Diverse Needs

Encourage at-risk students to reread the first paragraph on the pituitary and hypothalamus in Section 39–2. Also have them read about LH and FSH in Figure 39–7. Check their understanding by asking: **What are the roles of LH and FSH?** *(LH stimulates ovaries and testes and prepares the uterus for implantation of a fertilized egg. FSH stimulates the production of eggs and sperm.)* **What controls the pituitary's production of LH and FSH?** *(Hormones produced by the hypothalamus)* **Limited English proficiency**

39–3 (continued)

Meet Diverse Needs

Challenge gifted students to write a short story for girls or boys aged 8 to 10 about what it is like to grow into an adult. In their stories, they should provide facts that children of this age should know in order to understand the developments of puberty. Ask volunteers to read their stories to the class. **Learning modality: verbal**

Make Connections

Environmental Science Tell students that many compounds released into the environment by human activities mimic estrogen if they enter the body through contaminated water or food. Ask: **What effect do you think these "environmental estrogens" might have on males?** *(Students might speculate that the estrogens could cause the development in males of female traits such as enlarged breasts and inhibit the development of normal male traits and the production of sperm.)*

The Male Reproductive System

Demonstration

Obtain a prepared slide of a sperm cell. Focus the slide under the microscope and invite students to take turns viewing it or use a microprojector. Have students locate the three main parts of the sperm cell *(Head, midpiece, and tail)* and draw a sketch of the cell with the three parts labeled. Ask: **Why do you think the sperm cell has a tail?** *(To help the sperm "swim" through the female reproductive tract)*

▼ **Figure 39–13** The sperm is the male gamete, or sex cell. **Interpreting Graphics** *What are the three sections of a sperm cell?*

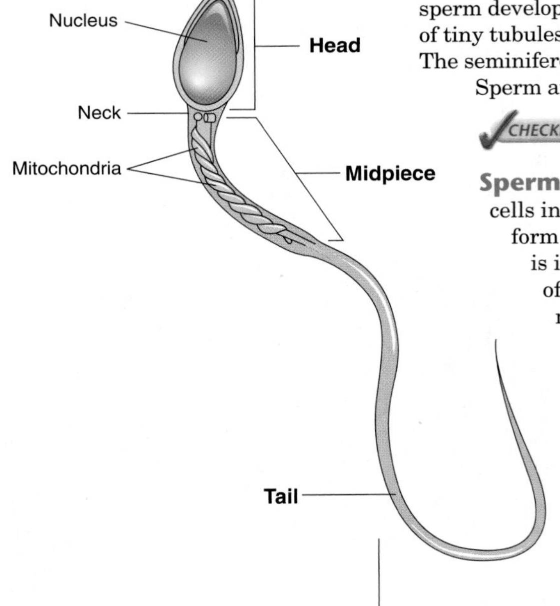

Puberty begins when the hypothalamus signals the pituitary to produce increased levels of two hormones that affect the gonads. These hormones are follicle-stimulating hormone (FSH) and luteinizing hormone (LH).

The Male Reproductive System

The release of FSH and LH stimulates cells in the testes to produce testosterone (tes-TAHS-tuh-rohn), a steroid that is the principal male sex hormone. Target cells for testosterone are found all over the body. Testosterone produces a number of secondary sex characteristics that appear in males at puberty. These characteristics include the growth of facial and body hair, increase in body size, and deepening of the voice.

FSH and testosterone stimulate the development of sperm. Once large numbers of sperm have been produced in the testes, the developmental process of puberty is completed. The reproductive system is now functional, meaning that the male can produce and release active sperm.

The main structures of the male reproductive system are the testes, the epididymis, the vas deferens, the urethra, and the penis. These structures work together to produce and deliver sperm. Just before birth (or sometimes just after), the testes descend from the abdomen through a canal into an external sac called the **scrotum.** The testes remain in the scrotum, outside the body cavity, where the temperature is about one to three degrees lower than the internal temperature of the body (37°C). The lower temperature is important for proper sperm development. Within each testis are clusters of hundreds of tiny tubules called **seminiferous tubules** (sem-uh-NIF-ur-us). The seminiferous tubules are tightly coiled and twisted together. Sperm are produced in the seminiferous tubules.

CHECKPOINT *What is the role of testosterone?*

Sperm Development Sperm are derived from special cells in the testes that undergo the process of meiosis to form the haploid nuclei of mature sperm. A sperm cell is illustrated in **Figure 39–13.** A sperm cell consists of a head, which contains a highly condensed nucleus; a midpiece, which is packed with energy-releasing mitochondria; and a tail, or flagellum, which propels the cell forward. At the tip of the head is a small cap that contains an enzyme vital to the process of fertilization.

Figure 39–14 shows the structures of the male reproductive system. Sperm produced in the seminiferous tubules are moved into the **epididymis** (ep-uh-DID-ih-mis). This is the structure in which sperm fully mature and are stored. From the epididymis, some sperm are moved into a tube called the **vas deferens.**

TIME SAVER **PRESENTATIONS MADE EASY!**

The Presentation Assistant Plus contains the Prentice Hall Presentation Pro and the Transparencies, which provide easy-to-follow visual support for every step of this section. If you have a computer presentation station, use Prentice Hall Presentation Pro for Section 39–3, or use the transparencies listed here.

Section 39–3:

Interest Grabber
Section Outline
Menstrual Cycle
Figure 39–14
Figure 39–15

The vas deferens extends upward from the scrotum into the abdominal cavity. Eventually, the vas deferens merges with the **urethra,** the tube that leads to the outside of the body through the **penis.**

Glands lining the reproductive tract—including the seminal vesicles, the prostate, and the bulbourethral (bul-boh-yoo-REE-thrul) glands—produce a nutrient-rich fluid called seminal fluid. The combination of sperm and seminal fluid is known as semen. The number of sperm present in even a few drops of semen is astonishing. Between 50 and 130 million sperm are present in 1 milliliter of semen. That's about 2.5 million sperm per drop!

Sperm Release When the male is sexually excited, the autonomic nervous system prepares the male organs to deliver sperm. Sperm are ejected from the penis by the contractions of smooth muscles lining the glands in the reproductive tract. This process is called ejaculation. Because ejaculation is regulated by the autonomic nervous system, it is not completely voluntary. About 2 to 6 milliliters of semen, containing more than 200 to 600 million sperm, are released in an average ejaculation. If these hundreds of millions of sperm are released in the reproductive tract of a female, the chances of a single sperm fertilizing an egg, if one is available, are quite good.

▼ **Figure 39–14 The main structures of the male reproductive system are the testes, epididymis, vas deferens, urethra, and penis.** The testes descend into the scrotum just before or just after birth.

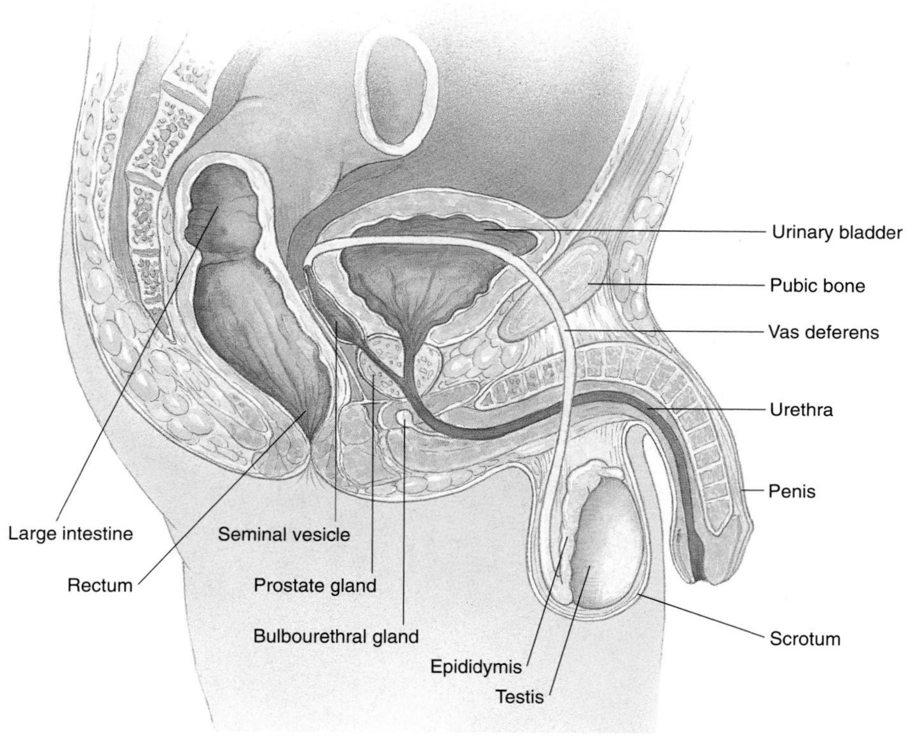

Meet Diverse Needs

Provide each student with a simple, unlabeled drawing of the male reproductive system. Then, using a large anatomical chart or model, point out each of the male reproductive organs and describe its function. As you discuss each organ, have students find the organ on their drawing and label the drawing with the organ's name and function. Suggest that students save their labeled drawings for study guides. **Learning modality: tactile**

Build Science Skills

Inferring Point out the huge number of sperm present in each milliliter of semen. Then, ask: **Why do you think so many sperm are produced?** *(To increase the chances that one will be able to reach the egg and fertilize it)*

Use Visuals

Figure 39–14 Have students study the figure and read the caption. Then, ask: **Where are sperm produced?** *(In the testis)* **Where are sperm stored?** *(In the epididymis)* **How do sperm get from the epididymis to the urethra?** *(Through the vas deferens)* **Which other reproductive organs or glands must sperm pass by or through to reach the urethra?** *(Seminal vesicle, prostate gland, and bulbourethral gland)*

FACTS AND FIGURES

Not too hot, not too cold

Testes do not always descend into the scrotum at birth. When they remain undescended, the condition is called cryptorchidism. It can be corrected with surgery or hormones administered before puberty. If the condition is not corrected, sterility is likely to result because sperm need the cooler temperatures outside the body to develop. Even in males with both testes descended, hot baths or tight clothing may increase the temperature of the testes enough to inhibit sperm production and cause temporary sterility. Sperm production may also be inhibited if the temperature of the testes becomes too cold. This is why, in cold weather, involuntary muscular contractions move the testes closer to the warmth of the body. Sperm are among the smallest human cells. For a clump of sperm to be visible with the unaided eye, it would have to contain about 100,000 cells.

Answers to . . .

CHECKPOINT *Testosterone produces a number of secondary sex characteristics that appear in males at puberty and, with FSH, it stimulates the development of sperm.*

Figure 39–13 *Head, midpiece, and tail*

The Female Reproductive System

Address Misconceptions

Students may have the misconception that a female is able to reproduce from the time she has her first menstrual period at menarche until she has her last menstrual period at menopause. Inform students that menstrual cycles at both ends of the reproductive period may occur without the release of an egg. Cycles that do not produce eggs may also occur at other times, for example, at times of stress or illness.

Use Visuals

Figure 39–15 Explain that the left-hand drawing in the figure is a side view and that the right-hand drawing is a view from the front. Point out the fingerlike projections, called fibula, at the ends of the Fallopian tubes nearest the ovaries. Explain how the fibula move in a beckoning motion that helps draw eggs into the Fallopian tubes. Ask: **What happens to an egg after it enters a Fallopian tube?** *(It travels through the Fallopian tube to the uterus.)*

Make Connections

Mathematics Have students use mathematics to improve their understanding of female reproduction. Ask: **If a female begins producing mature eggs at age 13 and continues uninterrupted until age 48, about how many mature eggs does she produce in a lifetime?** *(About one egg per month for 35 years, or a total of about 420 eggs)* **About how many eggs never mature?** *(The two ovaries together have about 800,000 immature eggs at birth, of which about 799,580 never mature.)*

The Female Reproductive System

As in males, puberty in females starts when the hypothalamus signals the pituitary gland to release FSH and LH. FSH stimulates cells within the ovaries to produce estrogen, the female steroid sex hormone. Interactions of estrogen with target cells produce female secondary sex characteristics. These characteristics include the development of the female reproductive system, widening of the hips, and development of the breasts.

The main structures of the female reproductive system are the ovaries, the Fallopian tubes, the uterus, and the vagina. In addition to producing eggs, the female reproductive system prepares the female's body to nourish a developing embryo. The structures of the female reproductive system are shown in **Figure 39–15.** In contrast to the millions of sperm produced each day in the male reproductive system, the ovaries usually produce only one mature ovum (plural: ova), or egg, between them each month.

Egg Development Each ovary contains about 400,000 primary **follicles,** which are clusters of cells surrounding a single egg. The function of a follicle is to help an egg mature for release into the reproductive tract, where it can be fertilized. Eggs mature within their follicles. Although a female is born with about 400,000 immature eggs (primary follicles)—and does not produce any new eggs during her lifetime—only about 400 eggs will actually be released.

▼ **Figure 39–15** **The main structures of the female reproductive system are the ovaries, Fallopian tubes, uterus, and vagina.** After puberty, a mature egg is released from an ovary about once a month.

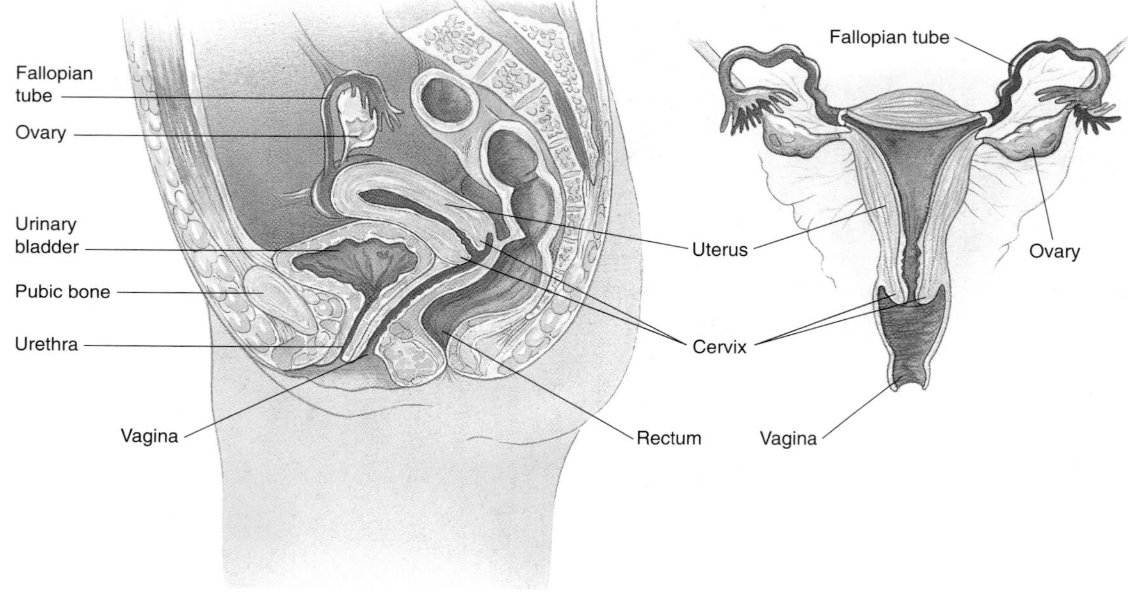

FACTS AND FIGURES

Treating female infertility

Female infertility is usually due to failure of the ovaries to release mature eggs or to blockage of the Fallopian tubes, which prevents eggs from being fertilized and reaching the uterus. Scientists have developed techniques that address each of these problems. Human menopausal gonadotropins can be injected to stimulate the follicles to develop, and drugs such as clomiphene can be given to promote ovulation. To bypass blocked Fallopian tubes, eggs can be harvested as they are ovulated, fertilized with sperm in a test tube, and placed in the uterus, a procedure that is called *in vitro fertilization*, or *IVF*. In a similar procedure, called *gamete intrafallopian tube transfer*, or *GIFT*, the sperm and unfertilized egg are placed in a Fallopian tube. GIFT is used for women who ovulate and have normal Fallopian tubes but still fail to conceive.

Roughly once a month, under the influence of FSH, a follicle gets larger and the egg passes through the early stages of meiosis. When meiosis is complete, a single large haploid egg and three smaller cells called polar bodies will be produced. The polar bodies have very little cytoplasm and soon disintegrate.

CHECKPOINT *Where do eggs develop?*

Egg Release When a follicle has completely matured, its egg is released in a process called **ovulation.** The follicle breaks open, and the egg is swept from the surface of the ovary into the opening of one of the two **Fallopian tubes,** as shown in **Figure 39–16.** The egg moves through the fluid-filled Fallopian tube, pushed along by microscopic cilia lining the walls of the tube. During its journey through the Fallopian tube, an egg can be fertilized. After a few days, the egg passes from the Fallopian tube into the cavity of an organ known as the **uterus.** The lining of the uterus is ready to receive a fertilized egg, if fertilization has occurred. The outer end of the uterus is called the cervix. Beyond the cervix is a canal—the **vagina**—that leads to the outside of the body.

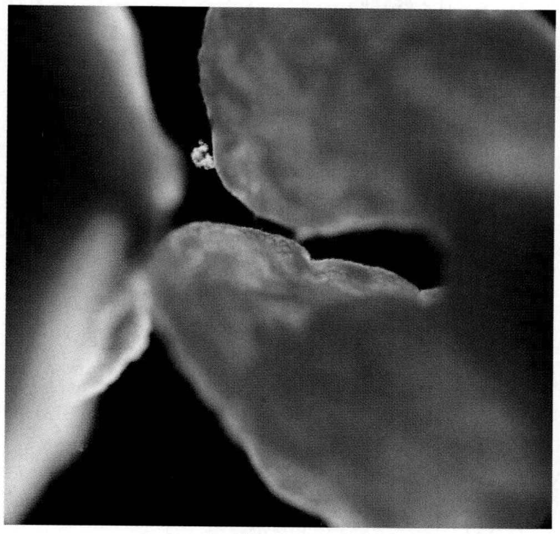

▲ **Figure 39–16** This photograph shows an ovum being released from an ovary. **Applying Concepts** *What is this process called?*

The Menstrual Cycle

After puberty, the interaction of the reproductive system and the endocrine system in females takes the form of a complex series of periodic events called the menstrual cycle. The cycle takes an average of about 28 days. The word *menstrual* comes from the Latin word *mensis,* meaning "month." The menstrual cycle is regulated by hormones that are controlled by negative-feedback mechanisms.

During the **menstrual cycle,** an egg develops and is released from an ovary. In addition, the uterus is prepared to receive a fertilized egg. If the egg is fertilized after ovulation, it is implanted in the uterus and embryonic development begins. If an egg is not fertilized, it is discharged, along with the lining of the uterus. **The menstrual cycle has four phases: follicular phase, ovulation, luteal phase, and menstruation.** Refer to **Figure 39–17** on page 1014 as you read about what happens during each phase.

Follicular Phase The follicular phase begins when the level of estrogen in the blood is relatively low. The hypothalamus reacts to low estrogen levels by producing a releasing hormone that acts on the pituitary gland. The releasing hormone stimulates the anterior pituitary to secrete FSH and LH. These two hormones travel through the circulatory system to the ovaries, where they cause a follicle to develop to maturity. Generally, just a single follicle develops, but sometimes two or even three mature during the same cycle.

Demonstration

Draw a simple diagram on the chalkboard to demonstrate how an immature egg undergoes meiosis to form a single large mature egg and three small polar bodies. Include at least one pair of chromosomes in your diagram to show how meiosis produces haploid cells. Ask: **Why is the mature egg called a haploid cell?** *(Because it contains half the usual number of chromosomes)* **What cells in males are haploid cells?** *(Sperm cells)* **Why must eggs and sperm both be haploid cells?** *(So that when they join together at fertilization, they produce a cell with the diploid number of chromosomes)* Add to your diagram to illustrate fertilization and how it affects chromosome number.

The Menstrual Cycle

Build Science Skills

Using Models Challenge students to create a diagram to model the feedback inhibition mechanisms that regulate the menstrual cycle when the egg is not fertilized. Students' diagrams should show how levels of LH, FSH, estrogen, and progesterone change during the cycle and how they affect target organs and glands. Call on volunteers to share their diagrams with the class. Ask: **What would happen to hormone levels if the egg were fertilized?** *(The corpus luteum would continue to produce estrogen and progesterone, but the pituitary would not produce LH and FSH because of the high estrogen level.)*

BIOLOGY UPDATE

Mice grow human eggs

Women facing the prospect of infertility due to disease or surgery used to have only one option if they eventually wanted to have children. They could arrange to have their mature eggs frozen and later thawed, fertilized, and implanted, using in vitro fertilization. Unfortunately, this option is not very satisfactory, because mature, unfertilized eggs are often damaged by the low temperatures needed to preserve them. To overcome this problem, scientists recently transplanted small pieces of previously frozen ovarian tissue into the backs of mice. The mice were then injected with FSH to promote growth of ovarian follicles. Later, the mice were injected with human chorionic gonadotropin to stimulate ovulation, so that the eggs could be retrieved for further maturation in the lab. The scientists hope eventually to bypass the mice and mature the eggs using only lab equipment.

Answers to . . .

CHECKPOINT *Eggs develop in the ovaries.*

Figure 39–16 *The process is called ovulation.*

Meet Diverse Needs

Have students summarize the detailed text on the menstrual cycle by drawing a cycle diagram of its four phases. Diagrams should show the order in which the phases occur, their relative lengths, and the major events that occur in each phase. Display students' completed diagrams in the classroom. **Learning modality: visual**

Use Visuals

Figure 39–17 Guide students in interpreting the chart by asking: **On which days of the menstrual cycle does menstruation occur?** *(Days 1 to 5)* **What happens to the uterine lining between days 5 and 24?** *(It increases)* **On what day of the cycle is the egg released from the follicle?** *(Around day 14)* **When is the level of estrogen highest?** *(Around day 12, just before ovulation)* **When does the amount of progesterone plateau?** *(Around day 24, toward the end of the luteal phase)*

Address Misconceptions

Students may have the misconception that the average length of the menstrual cycle, which is 28 days, is also the normal length and that shorter or longer cycles are abnormal. Explain the difference between average and normal. Point out that normal cycles can range from 20 to 36 days and normal menstrual periods from 3 to 6 days.

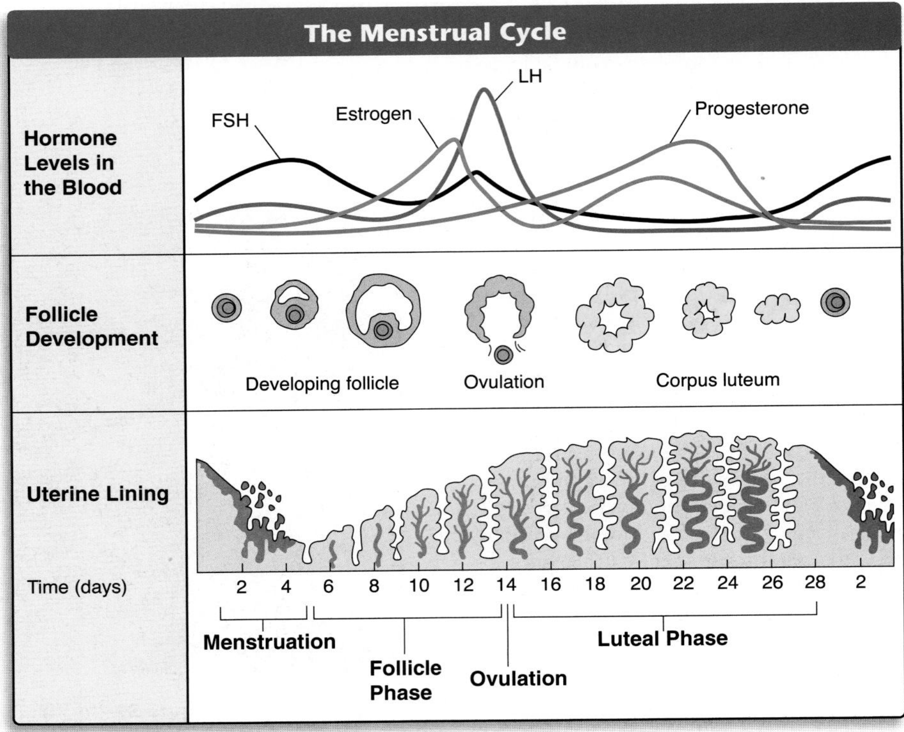

▲ **Figure 39–17**  **The menstrual cycle is divided into four phases: menstruation, follicular phase, ovulation, and luteal phase.** Notice the changes in hormone levels in the blood, the development of the follicle, and the changes in the uterine lining during the menstrual cycle.

As the follicle develops, the cells surrounding the egg enlarge and begin to produce increased amounts of estrogen. As the follicle produces more and more of the hormone, the estrogen levels in the blood rise dramatically. Estrogen causes the lining of the uterus to thicken in preparation for receiving a fertilized egg. The development of an egg in this stage of the cycle takes about 10 days.

Ovulation This phase is the shortest in the cycle. It occurs about midway through the cycle and lasts three to four days. During this phase, something (no one is certain what) causes the hypothalamus to send a large amount of releasing hormone to the pituitary gland. This in turn causes the pituitary gland to produce a sudden rush of FSH and LH. The release of these hormones has a dramatic effect on the follicle: It ruptures, and a mature egg is released into one of the Fallopian tubes.

✓CHECKPOINT *What happens during ovulation?*

Luteal Phase The luteal phase of the cycle begins after the egg is released. As the egg moves through the Fallopian tube, the cells of the ruptured follicle undergo a change. The follicle turns yellow and is now known as the **corpus luteum** (KAWR-pus LOOT-ee-um), which means "yellow body" in Latin. The

BIO INSIGHTS

BIOLOGY UPDATE

Solving the puzzle of menstruation

Scientists have long puzzled over the occurrence of menstruation in human females, which is unique among primates. The occurrence of menstruation seems to fly in the face of natural selection, because it limits the amount of time available to a female for reproduction and also costs her blood and energy. If anything, menstruation seems to be wasteful and even potentially dangerous. An answer to this puzzling situation was recently suggested by University of California professor Margie Profet, who hypothesized that menstruation might help the uterus rid itself of bacteria and viruses introduced during sexual intercourse. Profet's hypothesis has not been tested, but it does offer a reason why menstruation could be a benefit and not just a drawback and, therefore, why it might be favored by natural selection.

corpus luteum not only continues to release estrogen but also begins to release progesterone. During the first 14 days of the cycle, rising estrogen levels stimulate cell growth and tissue development in the lining of the uterus. Progesterone adds the finishing touches to that lining. Blood supply increases, the tissue matures, and the lining is fully prepared to accept a fertilized egg.

During the first two days of the luteal phase, immediately following ovulation, the chances that an egg will be fertilized are the greatest. This is usually from 10 to 14 days after the completion of the last menstrual cycle. If an egg is fertilized by a sperm, it will start to divide. After several divisions, a ball of cells will form and implant itself in the lining of the uterus. Within a few days of implantation, the uterus and the growing embryo will release hormones that keep the corpus luteum functioning for several weeks. This allows the lining of the uterus to nourish and protect the developing embryo.

Menstruation What happens if fertilization does not occur? Within two to three days of ovulation, the egg will pass through the uterus without implantation. The corpus luteum will begin to disintegrate. As the old follicle breaks down, it releases less and less estrogen and progesterone. The result is a decrease in the level of these hormones in the blood.

When the level of estrogen falls below a certain point, the lining of the uterus begins to detach from the uterine wall. This tissue, along with blood and the unfertilized egg, are discharged through the vagina. This phase of the cycle is called **menstruation.** Menstruation lasts about three to seven days on average. A new cycle begins with the first day of menstruation.

A few days after menstruation ends, levels of estrogen in the blood are once again low enough to stimulate the hypothalamus. The hypothalamus produces a releasing hormone that acts on the pituitary gland, which then starts to secrete FSH and LH, and the menstrual cycle begins again.

39–3 Section Assessment

1. **Key Concept** Describe the functions of the male and female reproductive systems.
2. **Key Concept** What happens during each of the four phases of the menstrual cycle?
3. What is puberty?
4. What is the function of testosterone? What is the function of progesterone?
5. **Critical Thinking Interpreting Graphics** Which hormone is at its peak during ovulation? (*Hint:* You may wish to refer to **Figure 39–17.**)

iTEXT **Assessment** Use iText to review the important concepts in Section 39–3.

MAKING CONNECTIONS

Chromosomes

How many chromosomes are there in a human egg cell or in a sperm? How many are there in a fertilized egg? (*Hint:* You may wish to refer back to Section 14–1.)

39–3 Section Assessment

1. To produce, store, and release gametes
2. Follicle phase—egg develops; ovulation—egg is released; luteal phase—egg travels through Fallopian tube where it may be fertilized, and uterus is prepared to accept and nourish egg; menstruation—lining of uterus, blood, and egg are discharged through vagina
3. A period of rapid growth and sexual maturation during which the reproductive system becomes fully functional
4. Testosterone produces secondary sex characteristics in males and stimulates production of sperm. Progesterone helps prepare the uterus for implantation of a fertilized egg.
5. Luteinizing hormone, or LH

Meet Diverse Needs

Challenge interested students to learn more about menopause, or the ending of the reproductive period in females. Suggest that they try to find answers to such questions as: When does menopause usually occur? What causes menopause? How does menopause affect women both physically and emotionally? Have students write a summary of what they learn. **Learning modality: verbal**

3 ASSESS

Evaluate Understanding

Call on students at random to define each of the vocabulary words. Call on other students to correct any errors.

Reteach

Have students use Figure 39–14 to trace the path of sperm through the male reproductive system and Figure 39–15 to trace the path of an egg through the female reproductive system.

MAKING CONNECTIONS

There are 23 chromosomes in a human egg or sperm and 46 in a fertilized egg.

Use iText to review the key concepts in Section 39–3.

Answer to . . .

CHECKPOINT *A mature egg is released from a follicle of an ovary.*

Section 39–4

1 FOCUS

Objectives

39.4.1 ***Describe*** fertilization.

39.4.2 ***State*** what happens during gastrulation.

39.4.3 ***Describe*** the function of the placenta.

39.4.4 ***Outline*** the life cycle after birth.

Guide for Reading

Vocabulary Preview

Challenge students to predict what the vocabulary words mean by writing a definition for each word. As they read the section, students should check their predictions and revise their definitions as needed.

Reading Strategy

Before they read the section, have students use the headings and subheadings to make an outline. Then, as they read, they should fill in phrases under the headings and subheadings to provide key information.

2 INSTRUCT

Fertilization

Meet Diverse Needs

Have students create a flowchart to summarize the process of fertilization. *(Their flowcharts should show an egg and sperm uniting to form a zygote.)* Then, ask: **What forms as a result of fertilization?** *(A zygote)* **How does a zygote differ from a sperm or an egg?** *(It is a diploid rather than a haploid cell.)* Suggest that students add to their flowcharts as they read the section to show what happens to the zygote during gestation. **Learning modality: visual**

39–4 Fertilization and Development

Guide for Reading

Key Concepts
- What is fertilization?
- What is the function of the placenta?

Vocabulary
zygote
implantation
gastrulation
placenta
fetus

Reading Strategy: Using Graphic Organizers
As you read, draw a flowchart that shows the steps from fertilized egg to newborn baby.

When an egg is fertilized, the remarkable process of human development begins. In this process, a single cell no larger than the period at the end of this sentence undergoes a series of cell divisions that results in the formation of a new human being.

Fertilization

If an egg is to become fertilized, sperm must be present in the female reproductive tract—more specifically, in a Fallopian tube. Sperm are released during sexual intercourse, when semen is ejaculated through the penis into the vagina. The penis generally enters the vagina to a point just below the cervix, which is the opening that connects the vagina to the uterus. Sperm swim actively through the uterus into the Fallopian tubes. Although hundreds of millions of sperm are released during an ejaculation, only about one percent will reach the upper region of each Fallopian tube. If an egg is present in one of the Fallopian tubes, its chances of being fertilized by a sperm are very good.

The egg is surrounded by a thick protective layer that contains binding sites to which sperm can attach. When a sperm attaches to a binding site, as shown in **Figure 39–18,** a sac in the sperm head ruptures and releases powerful enzymes that break down the protective layer of the egg. Once the sperm enters the egg, the membranes around the egg and sperm nuclei rupture and the nuclei are joined. **The process of a sperm joining an egg is called fertilization.**

The fertilized egg, called a **zygote** (ZY-goht), undergoes cell division to produce a two-celled embryo. These cells divide again and again to form a ball of cells. The ball of cells attaches itself to the wall of the uterus and continues to divide.

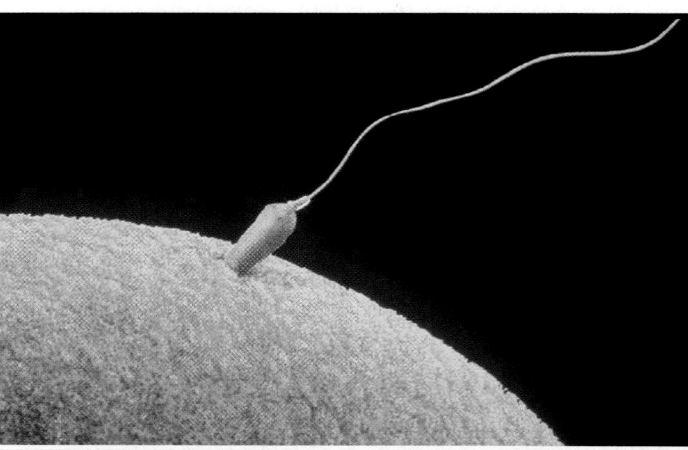

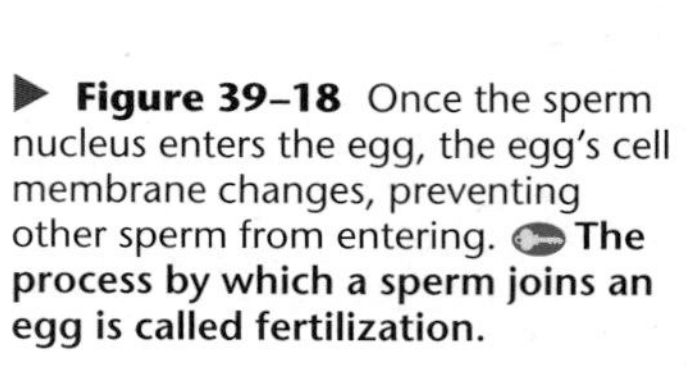

▶ **Figure 39–18** Once the sperm nucleus enters the egg, the egg's cell membrane changes, preventing other sperm from entering. **The process by which a sperm joins an egg is called fertilization.**

SECTION RESOURCES

Print:
- ***Teaching Resources,*** Section Review 39–4, Chapter 39 Exploration
- ***Guided Reading and Study Workbook,*** Section 39–4

Technology:
iText, Section 39–4

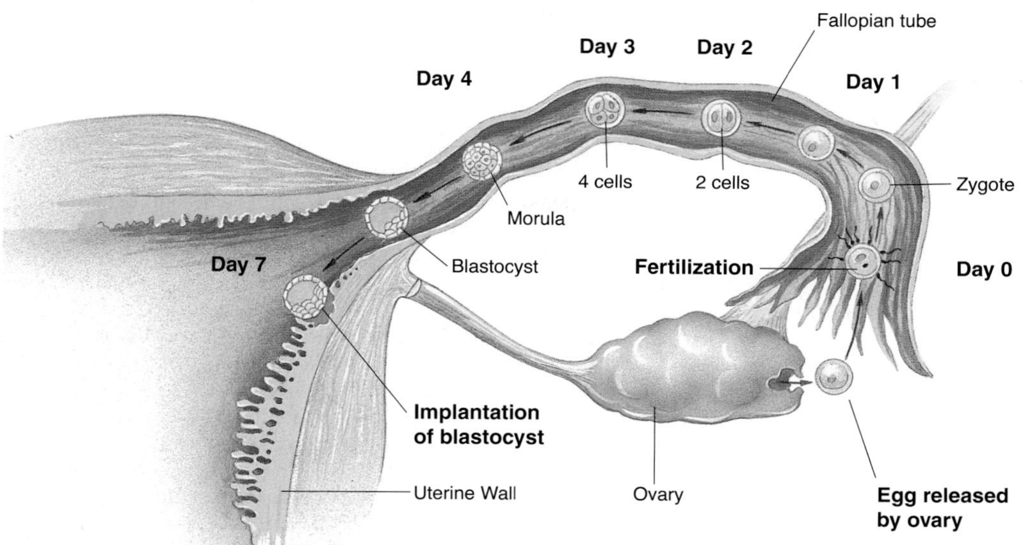

▲ **Figure 39–19** If an egg is fertilized, a zygote forms and begins to undergo cell division as it travels to the uterus. (The size of the egg has been greatly exaggerated.) **Interpreting Graphics** *How much time passes before the blastocyst is attached to the uterine wall?*

Early Development

The first few cell divisions take place while the zygote is still in the Fallopian tube, as shown in **Figure 39–19.** Four days after fertilization, the embryo is a solid ball of about 50 cells called a morula (MAWR-yoo-luh). As the embryo grows, a fluid-filled cavity forms in the center, transforming the embryo into a hollow structure called a blastocyst. About six or seven days after fertilization, the blastocyst attaches itself to the wall of the uterus. The embryo secretes enzymes that digest a path into the soft tissue. This process is known as **implantation.**

Gastrulation A cluster of cells gradually forms within the cavity of the blastocyst. This cluster sorts itself into two layers, which then produce a third layer by a process of cell migration known as **gastrulation** (gas-troo-LAY-shun). The result of gastrulation is the formation of three cell layers known as the ectoderm, mesoderm, and endoderm. These three layers are referred to as the primary germ layers, because all of the organs and tissues of the embryo will be formed from them.

Shortly after implantation, the outer layer of cells of the blastocyst produces important membranes that surround, protect, and nourish the developing embryo. Two of these membranes are the amnion and the chorion.

CHECKPOINT *What is gastrulation?*

Word Origins

Zygote comes from the Greek word *zygon,* meaning "yoke." A yoke is a frame used to harness a pair of oxen together. **Why is *zygote* an appropriate name for a fertilized egg?**

Early Development

Build Science Skills

Using Models Challenge students to use illustrations in reference books to create three-dimensional clay models of the zygote, morula, and blastocyst stages. Have students show their models to the class. Ask: **What changes have occurred at each stage?** *(From the single-celled zygote to the morula stage, cell divisions have produced a solid mass of cells. By the blastocyst stage, the mass of cells has become a hollow, fluid-filled ball.)*

Use Visuals

Figure 39–19 Ask: **Where does fertilization occur?** *(In the Fallopian tube)* **How does the zygote differ from the egg that has just been released from the ovary?** *(It has been fertilized by a sperm, making it a diploid cell.)* **What happens to the zygote before it reaches the uterus?** *(It undergoes many cell divisions.)* **At what stage does implantation occur?** *(At the blastocyst stage)*

Meet Diverse Needs

Point out that in about one percent of pregnancies, the blastocyst implants in the Fallopian tube or in the abdominal cavity instead of in the wall of the uterus. This is called an ectopic pregnancy. Challenge interested students to find out what causes an ectopic pregnancy, how it is diagnosed, the risks it poses for both fetus and mother, and how it is treated. Ask students to share what they learn with the class in an oral report. **Learning modality: verbal**

Word Origins

Zygote is an appropriate name because two gametes are joined together when a fertilized egg forms.

TIME SAVER PRESENTATIONS MADE EASY!

The Presentation Assistant Plus contains the Prentice Hall Presentation Pro and the Transparencies, which provide easy-to-follow visual support for every step of this section. If you have a computer presentation station, use Prentice Hall Presentation Pro for Section 39–4, or use the transparencies listed here.

Section 39–4:

Interest Grabber
Section Outline
Fertilization and Implantation of the Egg
Figure 39–20

Answers to . . .

CHECKPOINT *The process of cell migration by which the three primary germ layers of the embryo are formed*

Figure 39–19 *7 days*

39–4 (continued)

Make Connections

Health Science Help students understand the health significance of keeping the fetal and maternal blood supplies separate by discussing Rh incompatibility. Remind students that Rh blood type refers to the presence or absence on the surface of the red blood cells of an antigen called the rhesus antigen. A woman with Rh negative blood lacks the antigen, but her fetus could have Rh positive blood that contains the antigen. If the mother's blood is exposed to the antigen in the fetal blood, her immune system will recognize it as foreign and attack it. Ask: **How does the placenta prevent this from happening?** *(The placenta allows some substances to cross the membranes between the fetal and maternal blood supplies but prevents the two blood supplies from actually mixing.)*

Use Visuals

Figure 39–20 Guide students in tracing the umbilical artery and vein as they branch in the placenta and come into contact with the maternal blood supply. Ask: **What substances travel through the umbilical artery?** *(Oxygen and nutrients)* **What substances travel through the umbilical vein?** *(Carbon dioxide and wastes)*

Demonstration

Demonstrate the important role played by the amnion. Put a raw egg inside a gallon-size resealable plastic storage bag, fill the bag with water, and seal it shut. Challenge one or more students to try to break the egg without removing the egg or water from the bag. Then, ask: **If the amnion is like the storage bag, what role does it play in fetal development?** *(It cushions the developing fetus from outside injuries.)* **When might this be important?** *(Possible answers might include in case the mother falls or is in an automobile accident.)*

The Placenta By the end of the third week of development, the nervous and digestive systems have begun to form. The chorion has grown into the uterine tissue to form a vital organ called the **placenta.** The placenta is the connection between mother and developing embryo. The developing embryo needs a supply of nutrients and oxygen. It also needs a means of eliminating carbon dioxide and other metabolic wastes. At first thought, it seems that this task could be accomplished by having the blood supply of the embryo joined to that of the mother. But such an arrangement would allow disease to spread from mother to embryo. It would also cause a problem if the mother and embryo had different blood types.

Figure 39–20 shows that the blood of the mother and that of the embryo flow past each other, but they do not mix. They are separated by the placenta. Across this thin barrier, gases are exchanged and food and waste products diffuse. **The placenta is the embryo's organ of respiration, nourishment, and excretion.** Almost everything that the mother takes into her body passes through the placenta to the embryo.

This early period of development is particularly important because a number of external factors can disrupt development at this time. The placenta acts as a barrier to some harmful or disease-causing organisms. Others, such as rubella (German measles), can penetrate the placenta and affect development. So can drugs—including alcohol and prescription medications.

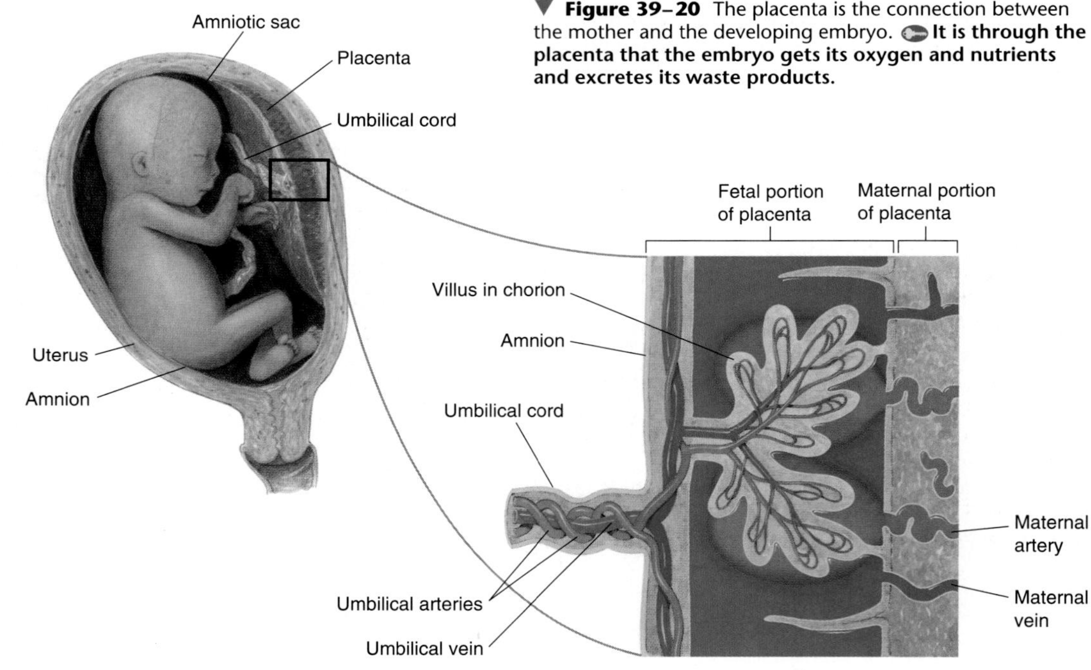

▼ **Figure 39–20** The placenta is the connection between the mother and the developing embryo. **It is through the placenta that the embryo gets its oxygen and nutrients and excretes its waste products.**

HISTORY OF SCIENCE

Observing fertilization

Scientists of antiquity could not observe fertilization, so they had no direct evidence for how it occurs. Aristotle thought that semen was a seed that gave rise to a new individual and that the female body was simply the place where the seed was nourished. In the mid-1600s, when microscopes were invented, scientists were able to see human sperm for the first time. Even then, however, some claimed they saw a tiny human, called a homunculus, within each sperm. Scientists of the 1700s and 1800s studied frog eggs, because amphibian eggs are large enough to be seen with a magnifying glass. They did not observe fertilization, but they were able to see how fertilized eggs developed from zygote to morula and blastocyst stages. Human eggs were first viewed in the early 1900s, but it was not until the 1940s that the fertilization of human eggs was observed directly.

After eight weeks of development, the embryo is called a **fetus.** By the end of three months of development, most of the major organs and tissues of the fetus are fully formed. During this time, the umbilical cord also forms. The umbilical cord connects the fetus to the placenta. The muscular system of the fetus is by now well developed, and the fetus may begin to move and show signs of reflexes. After three months the average fetus is about 8 centimeters long and has a mass of about 28 grams. The amnion has developed into a fluid-filled amniotic sac, which cushions and protects the developing fetus.

CHECKPOINT *What is the umbilical cord?*

Later Development

During the fourth, fifth, and sixth months after fertilization, the tissues of the fetus become more complex and specialized, and more tissues begin to function. A skeleton forms, and the fetal heartbeat becomes strong enough to be heard with a stethoscope. A layer of soft hair grows over the fetus's skin. As the fetus increases in size, the mother's abdomen swells to accommodate it. The developing fetus is about 35 centimeters long and has a mass of about 850 grams after seven months.

After six months, the fetus may be able to survive outside the uterus if life-supporting equipment is available. However, its chances of survival are much better after three more months in the uterus. The fetus doubles in mass, and the lungs and other organs undergo a series of changes that prepare them for life outside the uterus. Premature babies—those born before eight months of development—often have severe breathing problems because of incomplete lung development. **Figure 39–21** shows an embryo and a fetus at different stages of development.

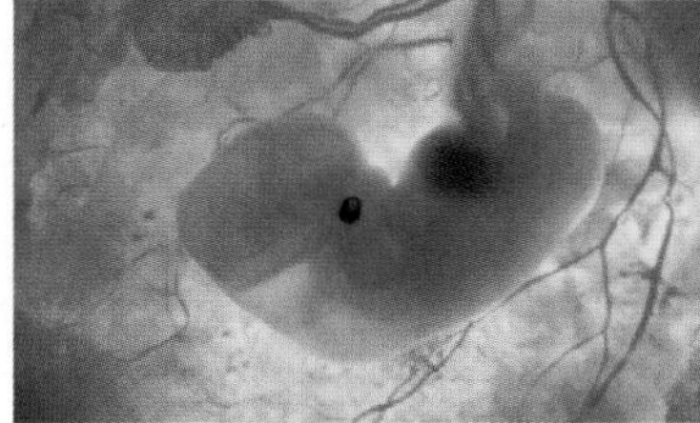
Embryo at 7 Weeks

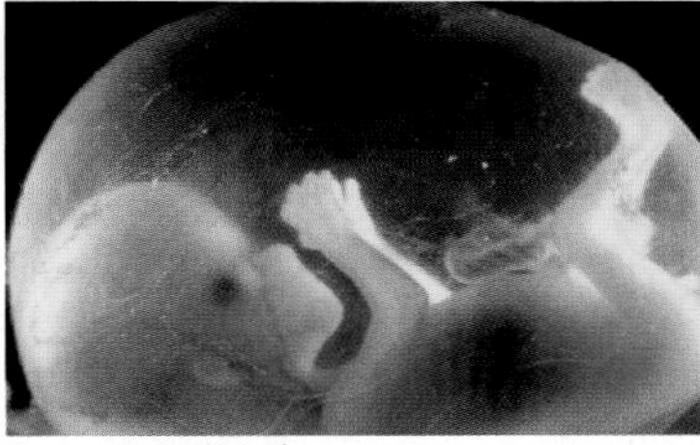
Fetus at 14 Weeks

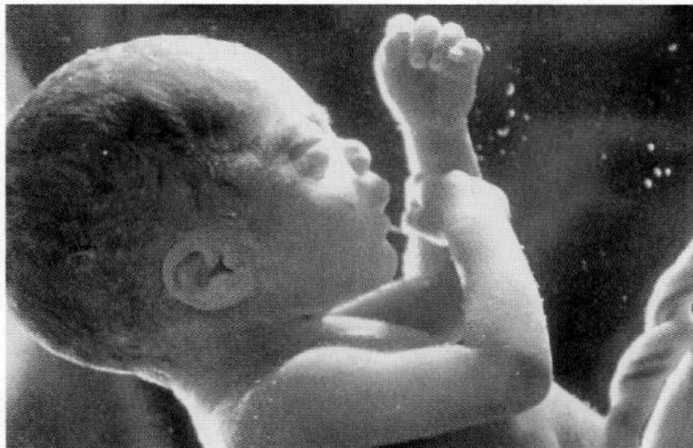
Fetus at Full Term

Figure 39–21 At 7 weeks, most of the organs have begun to form. The heart—the dark rounded structure—is beating. By 14 weeks, the hands, feet, and legs have reached their birth proportions. The eyes, ears, and nose are well developed. When the fetus is full-term, it is fully developed and capable of living on its own. **Interpreting Graphics** ***What significant changes do you see from 7 weeks to 14 weeks?***

BIO INSIGHTS

BIOLOGY UPDATE

Fetal surgery for spina bifida

About 1 in every 1,000 children is born with spina bifida, a condition in which some of the vertebrae do not develop normally, leaving part of the spinal cord exposed to damage from amniotic fluid before birth and from infection and injury during and after birth. Symptoms of spina bifida depend on the extent to which the spinal cord is exposed and damaged. In severe cases, the condition may cause hydrocephalus (water on the brain), mental retardation, abnormalities of the kidneys and bladder, and physical deformities. In the mid-1990s, doctors performed the first successful human fetal surgery to help correct spina bifida in utero. Since then, many more fetal surgeries for spina bifida have been performed with good results. Spina bifida babies who have fetal surgery require fewer postnatal shunt procedures to control hydrocephalus, and they are less likely to develop malformations of the hindbrain.

Meet Diverse Needs

Give gifted students an extra challenge by having them research dangers to the embryo during each week of early development, from week four through week nine. Students should find out which substances are toxic and how they affect the embryo at each week of development. *(Students may find out, for example, that infectious agents can cause heart defects in week five and blindness in week six.)* Invite volunteers to share their research with the class. **Learning modality: verbal**

Later Development

Make Connections

Mathematics Guide students in using mathematics to appreciate how quickly a fetus grows. Draw a small dot on the chalkboard and tell students that the dot represents a fertilized egg. Point out that an actual human egg is smaller, about 0.1 mm in diameter and barely visible with the unaided eye. Then, show students a baby doll that is about the same size as a newborn, or about 50 cm in length. Ask: **How fast must the fetus grow to change from the size of an egg to the size of a newborn in nine months of gestation?** *(About 56 mm per month)* Ask: **How tall would the individual be by age 15 if growth continued at that rate?** *(About 10 meters tall)*

Use Community Resources

Ask a physician's assistant, nurse, or medical technician who does pregnancy ultrasound scans to speak to the class about the procedure. Suggest that the speaker address such topics as why and when ultrasound scans are performed during pregnancy and what can be learned from them. If possible, have the speaker bring sample ultrasound scans of fetuses at different stages of development to show the class. Ask students to write a brief summary of what they learn.

Answers to . . .

CHECKPOINT *A cord that connects the fetus to the placenta*

Figure 39–21 *The hands, feet, and legs have reached their birth proportions, and the eyes, ears, and nose are well developed.*

Quick Lab

Objective Students will be able to observe frog embryos and conclude at which stage they start to show developmental changes.

Skills Focus Observing, Drawing Conclusions

Materials dropper pipette, early-stage frog embryos, depression slide, dissecting microscope, prepared slides of frog embryos

Time 20 minutes

Safety Remind students to handle microscope slides carefully.

Advance Prep Order frog eggs so they arrive just before you need them, because they develop into tadpoles within a week.

Strategy
Guide students in looking for visible differences such as cell size and shape.

Expected Outcome
After observing cells, students should conclude that frog embryos start to show developmental changes in the late gastrula or early neurula stage.

Think About It

1. Differences in cell size are visible at the gastrula stage.
2. The body plan becomes visible after neurulation, as the embryo elongates and the head and tail become recognizable.
3. Organ formation is first visible at the neurula stage, as the neural tube takes shape.

Childbirth

Make Connections

Health Science Tell students that the health status of a newborn is assessed at one minute after birth with a procedure called the Apgar test. The infant is given a score of 0, 1, or 2 on each of the following five items: heart rate, respiration, muscle tone, response to stimuli, and color. The maximum score is 10, and a score of 7 to 10 is considered normal. Infants with lower scores need immediate medical attention. Ask: **Which body systems are assessed with the Apgar test?** *(Cardiovascular, respiratory, muscular, and nervous systems)*

Quick Lab

How do embryos develop?

Materials dropper pipette, early-stage frog embryos, depression slide, dissecting microscope, prepared slides of frog embryos

Procedure 

1. Use a dropper pipette to transfer several early-stage frog embryos in water to a depression slide. **CAUTION:** *Microscopes and slides are fragile. Handle them carefully. Tell your teacher if you break any glass.*
2. Look at the embryos under the dissecting microscope at low power. Sketch what you see.
3. Look at prepared slides of the early embryonic stages of a frog. Make sketches of what you see.

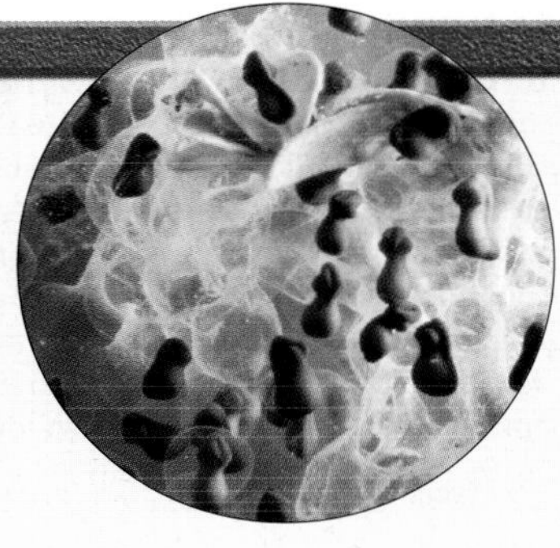

Frog Embryos

Analyze and Conclude

1. **Observing** Describe any differences you saw among the cells. At what stage is cell differentiation visible?
2. **Observing** Were you able to see a distinct body plan? At what stage did the body plan become visible?
3. **Drawing Conclusions** Describe any organs you saw. At what stage did specific organs form?

▼ **Figure 39–22** A newborn baby takes its first breath of air.

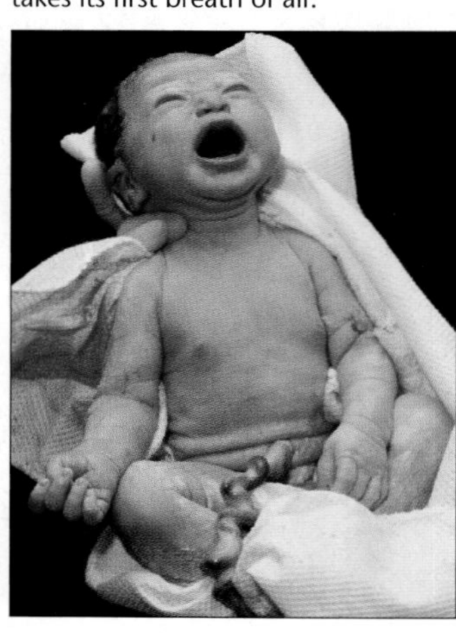

Childbirth

About nine months after fertilization, the fetus is ready for birth. A complex set of factors affect the onset of childbirth. One factor is the release of the hormone oxytocin from the posterior pituitary gland. Oxytocin affects a group of large involuntary muscles in the uterine wall. As these muscles are stimulated, they begin a series of rhythmic contractions known as labor. The contractions become more frequent and more powerful. The opening of the cervix expands until it is large enough for the head of the baby to pass through it. At some point, the amniotic sac breaks, and the fluid it contains rushes out of the vagina. Contractions of the uterus force the baby, usually head first, out through the vagina.

As the baby meets the outside world, he or she may begin to cough or cry, which rids the lungs of fluid. Breathing starts almost immediately, and the blood supply to the placenta begins to dry up. The umbilical cord is clamped and cut, leaving a small piece attached to the baby. This piece will soon dry up and fall off, leaving a scar known as the navel—or in its more familiar term, the belly button. In a final series of uterine contractions, the placenta itself and the now-empty amniotic sac are expelled from the uterus as the afterbirth.

The baby now begins to lead an independent existence. Most newborn babies are remarkably hardy. Their systems quickly switch over to life outside the uterus, supplying their own oxygen, excreting wastes on their own, and maintaining their own body temperatures.

BIO INSIGHTS — HISTORY OF SCIENCE

Caesarian section
Caesarian section is an operation in which a baby is removed from a mother's body through incisions in her abdominal wall and uterus. It is an ancient procedure that is referred to in folklore from around the world. The name *caesarian* may have come from a Roman law, under Julius Caesar, that required all women dying in childbirth to undergo the procedure in order to save their offspring. The law was apparently part of an imperialistic effort to increase the Roman population. Until the development of anesthetics, antibiotics, and modern surgical procedures over the past two centuries, caesarian sections were extremely painful and had a high risk of death for both mother and infant. Therefore, a caesarian section was almost always a last resort, performed only when the mother was dead or dying and for the sole purpose of trying to save her infant's life.

Within a few hours after birth, the pituitary hormone prolactin stimulates the production of milk in the breast tissues of the mother. Nutrients packed into that milk contain everything the baby needs for growth and development during the first few months of life.

Sometimes more than one baby develops during a pregnancy. Multiple births can happen for one of two reasons: (1) When two eggs are released and fertilized during the same cycle, fraternal twins result. Such twins are not identical because each has been formed by the fusion of a different sperm and egg cell. (2) Identical twins are formed when a single zygote splits apart to produce two embryos. Identical twins are formed by the fusion of the same sperm and egg cell and, therefore, are genetically identical.

✔CHECKPOINT *What is oxytocin?*

Early Years

Although the most spectacular developments of the human body occur before birth, development is a continuing process—it lasts throughout the life of an individual. In the first weeks of a baby's life, the systems that developed before birth move into high gear, supporting rapid growth that generally triples a baby's birth weight within 12 months.

Infancy Infancy, the period from four weeks after birth until about two years of age, is a period of rapid growth and development. The nervous system develops coordinated body movements as the infant begins to crawl and then to walk. A baby's first teeth appear and he or she begins to eat solid food. Infants also begin to understand and use language. Growth in the skeletal and muscular systems is especially rapid, demanding good nutrition to support proper development.

Childhood Childhood lasts from infancy until the onset of puberty, typically around the age of 12 or 13. During this time language is acquired and motor coordination is perfected. Permanent teeth begin to appear and the long bones of the skeletal system reach 80 percent of their adult length. The key elements of personality and human social skills are formed, and reasoning skills are developed to a high level.

Figure 39–23 During infancy, an infant learns to stand, walk, speak a few words, and imitate others. From ages 5 to 12, children grow to about 70 percent of their adult height and weight.

FACTS AND FIGURES

Multiple births

Multiple births occur normally in many species of mammals, but they are relatively uncommon in humans. Human twins are born in one out of about 90 births, triplets in one out of about 8,000 births, and quadruplets in one out of about 750,000 births. Approximately 70 percent of twins are dizygotic, or two-egg, twins. The chances of having dizygotic twins is greater in women who take the fertility drug clomiphene, which stimulates the ovaries to produce eggs. The chances are also greater in women who have a family history of multiple births, are in their later childbearing years, or are of African ancestry. The chances of having monozygotic, or one-egg, twins, in contrast, appear to be the same in most women, regardless of family history, age, or race.

Use Community Resources

Arrange for a Lamaze instructor to visit the class to demonstrate the Lamaze method for helping women cope with the pain of childbirth. Have the instructor explain the philosophy behind the Lamaze method and describe what else is taught in Lamaze classes. After the visit, ask students: **Under what other circumstances might the Lamaze method be useful?** *(Whenever a person has to cope with severe stress or pain)*

Early Years

Demonstration

Have students bring in photographs of themselves when they were less than two years of age. Display the unlabeled photos in the classroom and challenge students to identify as many of their classmates as they can. Then, ask: **In what ways do people change physically between infancy and adolescence?** *(People change in body size and proportions. Their facial features also become larger and more mature looking.)* **What are some of the features that remain constant enough that we can use them for identification?** *(Students might mention skin or eye color or the shape of certain distinctive facial features, such as the nose, chin, or eyes.)* Point out that features such as eye color and skin tone can change during infancy.

Meet Diverse Needs

Challenge interested students to create an illustrated chart showing the major physical and cognitive developments that occur from birth to age two. Their charts should include the eruption of teeth, the development of motor skills such as crawling and walking, and the development of language abilities. Charts should also show how much the average infant increases in length and weight during the first two years. Display students' completed charts in the classroom. **Learning modality: visual**

Answer to . . .

✔CHECKPOINT *Oxytocin is a hormone released from the pituitary gland that stimulates a group of large involuntary muscles in the wall of the uterus to begin labor contractions.*

39–4 (continued)

Adulthood

Use Community Resources

Suggest that students consult local libraries, senior centers, and government agencies to find out what services are available in their area for seniors. (Services might include meal delivery, social programs, transportation, and nursing care.) Ask: **What special needs of seniors are met by these services?** *(Students might mention disabling health problems, physical limitations, and the need for social interactions.)*

3 ASSESS

Evaluate Understanding

Call on students at random to name the stages of development of the embryo and fetus. Call on other students to describe the features of the embryo or fetus at each stage.

Reteach

Using the chalkboard, work with students to develop a time line of important events from fertilization to birth.

ALTERNATIVE ASSESSMENT

The time lines should show that students can recognize important developmental milestones, such as walking, talking, learning to read, first permanent tooth, learning to share, and the first signs of puberty.

Use iText to review the concepts in Section 36–3.

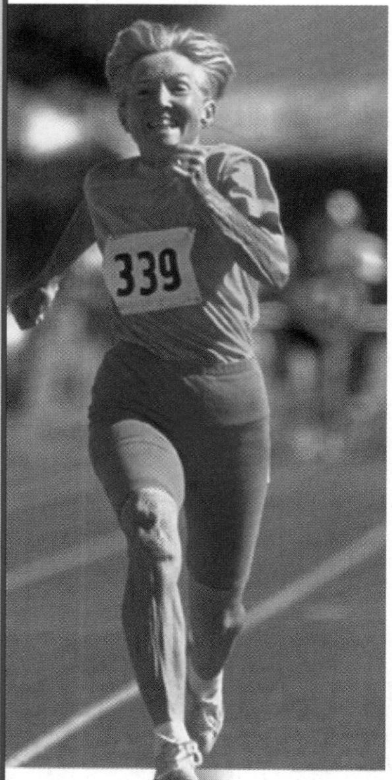

▲ **Figure 39–24** By maintaining a healthy lifestyle, you may be able to slow the aging process. **Applying Concepts** ***What factors contribute to a healthy life cycle?***

Adolescence Adolescence begins with puberty and ends with adulthood. The surge in sex hormones that starts at puberty produces a growth spurt that will conclude in mid-adolescence as the long bones of the arms and legs stop growing and complete their mineralization. The continuing development of intellectual skills is associated with personality changes that come with adult maturity.

Adulthood

Development continues during adulthood. By most measures, adults reach their highest levels of physical strength and development between the ages of 25 and 35. Peak childbearing years are those of early adulthood. During these years, most individuals assume the responsibilities of adulthood, including establishing careers.

In most individuals, the first signs of physiological aging appear in the 30s. Joints begin to lose some of their flexibility, muscle strength plateaus, and several body systems show slight declines in efficiency. By age 50, these changes, although generally still minor, are apparent to most individuals. In women, menopause greatly reduces estrogen levels. After menopause, ovulation stops, marking the end of the childbearing years. At around age 65, most systems of the body become less efficient, making homeostasis more difficult to maintain.

Although there are some changes in mental functioning during older adulthood, these changes usually have little effect on thinking, learning, or long-term memory. The brain remains open to change and to learning. In fact, evidence suggests that the aging process can be slowed by keeping the mind active and challenged. Most older adults are fully capable of continuing stimulating intellectual work. By practicing the habits of good health and regular exercise, as the woman is doing in **Figure 39–24,** every person can hope to be happy and productive at every stage of human development.

39–4 Section Assessment

1. **Key Concept** Describe the process of fertilization.
2. **Key Concept** Describe the role of the placenta.
3. What are the three germ layers that result from gastrulation?
4. Describe the early years of development.
5. **Critical Thinking Applying Concepts** Why do you think doctors recommend that women avoid most medications and alcohol during pregnancy?

iTEXT **Assessment** Use iText to review the important concepts in Section 39–4.

ALTERNATIVE ASSESSMENT

Creating a Time Line Starting with your birth date, create a time line of developmental milestones. As resources, you can use interviews, photographs, and memories.

39–4 Section Assessment

1. Sperm attaches to a binding site and releases enzymes that attack the egg's protective layer. Inside, membranes around the egg and sperm nuclei rupture and the nuclei merge.
2. The placenta is the embryo's organ of respiration, nourishment, and excretion.
3. Ectoderm, mesoderm, and endoderm
4. Infancy: rapid growth and development, first teeth, start of coordinated body movements; childhood: perfection of motor coordination, language acquisition, first permanent teeth, long bones reach 80 percent of adult length, development of personality, social skills, and higher level reasoning skills; adolescence: puberty, growth spurt, personality changes, continued development of intellect
5. Because these substances may cross the placenta and harm the embryo or fetus

Answer to . . .

Figure 39–24 *Factors include a well-balanced, low-fat diet and regular exercise.*

Exploration

Modeling Blood Glucose Regulation

Regulating the level of blood glucose is one of the body's most important jobs. Two hormones, insulin and glucagon, help to regulate the level of glucose in blood. Because these two hormones have opposite effects, it is important that a proper balance between them is maintained. In this investigation, you will simulate how this regulatory mechanism works.

Problem
How does the body regulate blood glucose levels?

Materials
- 3 pieces of construction paper of different colors
- scissors

Skills
Using Models, Posing Questions

Procedure

1. Work in groups of three students. Give each member of the group a number from 1 to 3.
2. Cut 15 cards out of construction paper of one color. On each card, print "10 mg glucose/100 mL blood" on the front and "glycogen" on the back. These are your glucose cards. Turning over a glucose card represents converting glucose into glycogen, or vice versa.
3. Cut out 2 cards of a second color. On each of these cards print "insulin." One of these insulin cards can convert 1 glucose card into glycogen.
4. Cut out 2 more cards of a third color. On each of these cards print "glucagon." One glucagon card can convert 1 glucose card from glycogen into glucose.
5. Place 9 glucose cards face up on the table. This represents the normal level of glucose in blood (90 mg glucose/100 mL blood). Student 1 should keep 2 more glucose cards face up.
6. Student 2 should keep the insulin and glucagon cards. Student 3 should keep the remaining 4 glucose cards face down, to represent stored glycogen.
7. To simulate the effect of a meal, student 1 should add a glucose card to the 9 on the table. Discuss how the body responds to this change.
8. Students 2 and 3 should use the cards to model how the body restores the normal blood glucose level after a meal.
9. To simulate the effect of exercise, student 1 should remove a glucose card from the 9 on the table. Repeat step 8.
10. To simulate what happens when a person has Type I diabetes, repeat steps 7 and 8 without using the insulin cards.

Analyze and Conclude

1. **Applying Concepts** What organ does student 2 represent? Explain your answer.
2. **Using Models** How did students 2 and 3 respond in step 8? In step 9? In step 10? Describe what happens in the body in each situation.
3. **Predicting** What do you think would happen if a person with diabetes ate a lot of sugar?

Go Further

Making a Model What do you think would happen if the body did not produce enough glucagon? Use your cards to model what would happen in this situation.

Exploration

Objective
Students will be able to use a model to gain an understanding of blood glucose regulation.

Skills Focus Using Models, Predicting

Time 40 minutes

Advance Prep You can save time by cutting out the cards before class, or by using colored index cards instead of cards cut from colored paper.

Teaching Tip Before students follow the procedure, review how blood glucose is regulated by insulin and glucagon. (See page 1007.)

Procedure
9. You may need to help students reason through the effects of exercise on blood glucose levels.

Go Further

If the body did not produce enough glucagon, it would not be able to convert glycogen into glucose. After exercise or several hours without food, the body's blood glucose level might become too low.

Analyze and Conclude

1. The pancreas, because the pancreas produces and releases insulin and glucagon

2. In step 8, student 2 placed an insulin card on the table and student 3 turned over one of the glucose cards. In the body, insulin is released, causing glucose to be converted into glycogen. In step 9, student 2 placed a glucagon card on the table and student 3 turned over one of the glycogen cards. In the body, glucagon is released, causing glycogen to be converted into glucose. In step 10, students 2 and 3 did not respond. In the body, insulin is not released and glucose increases instead of being converted to glycogen and lipids.

3. His or her blood glucose level would rise.

Chapter 39 Study Guide

Study Tip

Have students work in pairs to make flashcards for the Vocabulary terms and Key Concept questions and use the cards to quiz each other on the chapter.

Thinking Visually

Students' charts should include the following: pituitary gland (ADH, oxytocin, FSH, LH, TSH, ACTH, GH, prolactin, MSH), parathyroid glands (parathyroid hormone), thyroid gland (thyroxine, calcitonin), adrenal glands (epinephrine, norepinephrine, aldosterone, cortisol), pancreas (insulin, glucagon), ovary (estrogen, progesterone), and testis (testosterone).

Chapter 39 Assessment

Reviewing Content

1. b **2.** b **3.** b **4.** d **5.** c **6.** a **7.** b **8.** c **9.** c **10.** c

Understanding Concepts

11. A hormone binds to a specific chemical receptor site on a target cell. For example, progesterone binds to a receptor site on a cell in the uterus.

12. Prostaglandins are hormonelike substances that affect only nearby cells or tissues.

13. When a hormone increases in the blood, it "feeds back" to inhibit the gland that produced it.

14. The pituitary gland

15. Epinephrine increases heart rate, blood pressure, and blood flow to the muscles. It also causes air passageways to widen and stimulates the release of extra glucose into the blood to help produce a sudden burst of energy. These actions result in a general increase in body activity, which can serve as preparation for intense physical activity.

16. Diabetes mellitus may occur. Very high blood glucose levels can damage the circulatory system.

17. A period of rapid growth and sexual maturation during which the reproductive system becomes fully functional

Chapter 39 Study Guide

39–1 The Endocrine System

Key Concepts

- The endocrine system is made up of glands that release their products into the bloodstream. These products broadcast messages throughout the body.
- Like most systems of the body, the endocrine system is regulated by feedback mechanisms that function to maintain homeostasis.

Vocabulary
hormone, p. 997
target cell, p. 997
exocrine gland, p. 998
endocrine gland, p. 998
prostaglandin, p. 1000

39–2 Human Endocrine Glands

Key Concepts

- The pituitary gland secretes nine hormones that directly regulate many body functions and control the actions of several other endocrine glands.
- The hypothalamus controls the secretions of the pituitary gland.
- The thyroid gland has the major role in regulating the body's metabolism.
- Hormones from the thyroid gland and the parathyroid glands maintain homeostasis in blood calcium levels.
- The adrenal glands help the body prepare for and deal with stress.
- Insulin and glucagon released from the pancreas help to keep the level of glucose in the blood stable.
- The gonads serve two important functions: the production of gametes and the secretion of sex hormones.

Vocabulary
pituitary gland, p. 1003
diabetes mellitus, p. 1008
ovary, p. 1008
testis, p. 1008

39–3 The Reproductive System

Key Concepts

- The main structures of the male reproductive system are the testes, the epididymis, the vas deferens, the urethra, and the penis. These structures work together to produce and deliver sperm.
- The main structures of the female reproductive system are the ovaries, the Fallopian tubes, the uterus, and the vagina. In addition to producing eggs, the female reproductive system prepares the female's body to nourish a developing embryo.
- The menstrual cycle has four phases: follicular phase, ovulation, luteal phase, and menstruation.

Vocabulary
puberty, p. 1009 • scrotum, p. 1010
seminiferous tubule, p. 1010
epididymis, p. 1010 • vas deferens, p. 1011
urethra, p. 1011 • penis, p. 1011
follicle, p. 1012 • ovulation, p. 1013
Fallopian tube, p. 1013 • uterus, p. 1013
vagina, p. 1013 • menstrual cycle, p. 1013
corpus luteum, p. 1014 • menstruation, p. 1015

39–4 Fertilization and Development

Key Concepts

- The process of a sperm joining with an egg is called fertilization.
- The placenta is the embryo's organ of respiration, nourishment, and excretion.

Vocabulary
zygote, p. 1016
implantation, p. 1017
gastrulation, p. 1017
placenta, p. 1018
fetus, p. 1019

Thinking Visually

Use the information in this chapter to construct a chart listing the actions of each hormone discussed. Your chart should include three headings: Endocrine Gland, Hormone, and Action of Hormone.

CHAPTER RESOURCES

Print:

- ***Teaching Resources,*** Chapter Vocabulary Review, Graphic Organizer
- ***Chapter Tests: Levels A and B,*** Chapter 39 Test
- ***PH Assessment System,*** Practice Test

Technology:

- ***Computer Test Bank,*** Chapter 39 Test
- ***iText,*** Chapter 39 Assessment

Chapter 39 Assessment

Reviewing Content

Choose the letter that best answers the question or completes the statement.

1. Organs that release hormones into the blood are part of the
   a. digestive system.
   b. endocrine system.
   c. circulatory system.
   d. nervous system.
2. Which type of hormones are lipids produced from cholesterol?
   a. protein hormones
   b. steroid hormones
   c. nonsteroid hormones
   d. peptide hormones
3. Hormonelike substances produced by nearly all cells are called
   a. thyroxines.
   b. prostaglandins.
   c. steroids.
   d. androgens.
4. Hormones that help regulate blood calcium levels are produced in the
   a. adrenal gland.
   b. thymus gland.
   c. pancreas.
   d. parathyroid gland.
5. The rate of metabolism of all body cells is regulated by
   a. PTH.
   b. aldosterone.
   c. thyroxine.
   d. calcitonin.
6. The diagram shows the female reproductive system. Which structure is indicated by the X?
   a. uterus
   b. Fallopian tube
   c. ovary
   d. cervix

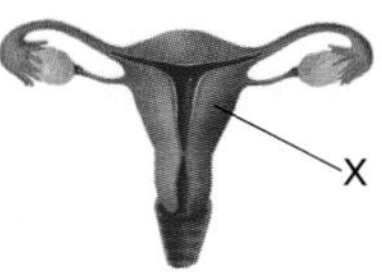

7. The principal male sex hormone is
   a. FSH.
   b. testosterone.
   c. estrogen.
   d. insulin.
8. Another name for a fertilized egg is a
   a. gastrula.
   b. placenta.
   c. zygote.
   d. fetus.
9. Fertilization usually occurs in the
   a. uterus.
   b. vagina.
   c. Fallopian tube.
   d. ovary.
10. After the eighth week of development, the human embryo is known as a(an)
    a. zygote.
    b. infant.
    c. fetus.
    d. zygote.

Understanding Concepts

11. What is the relationship between a hormone and a target cell? Use a specific example to explain your answer.
12. What are prostaglandins?
13. How does a feedback mechanism regulate the activity of the endocrine system?
14. What endocrine gland produces growth hormone?
15. How does the secretion of epinephrine prepare the body for emergencies?
16. What happens if blood glucose levels are not kept stable?
17. What is puberty?
18. What are the two hormones that stimulate production of hormones in the gonads?
19. List the secondary sex characteristics that appear in males at puberty.
20. Describe the structure of a sperm.
21. Trace the path of sperm from a testis until it leaves the body.
22. What are the functions of estrogen?
23. Trace the path of an unfertilized egg from a follicle until it leaves the body.
24. Explain why the menstrual cycle is an example of a feedback mechanism.
25. Trace the development of a zygote from fertilization through implantation.
26. Describe gastrulation and the importance of the primary germ layers.
27. What is the function of the placenta?
28. Describe what happens during childbirth.

TIME SAVER — HOMEWORK GUIDE

Section:	Questions:
Section 39–1	1–5, 11–13, 30, 37
Section 39–2	14–16, 29, 31, 32, 38
Section 39–3	6, 7, 17–24, 35, 36, 39, 40
Section 39–4	8–10, 25–28, 33, 34, 41

Chapter 39 Assessment (continued)

18. Follicle-stimulating hormone (FSH) and luteinizing hormone (LH)

19. Growth of facial and body hair, increase in body size, and deepening of the voice

20. A sperm cell consists of a head containing a highly condensed nucleus, a midpiece packed with mitochondria, and a flagellum that propels it forward.

21. Sperm travel from the seminiferous tubules in the testes into the epididymis, where they mature and are stored. Sperm then are moved into the vas deferens, where fluids from the seminal vesicle, prostate gland, and bulbourethral gland are added. The sperm and fluid are ejected from the penis through the urethra.

22. Development of the reproductive system and female secondary sex characteristics, regulation of the menstrual cycle, and preparation of the uterus for implantation

23. It passes through a Fallopian tube and the uterus and is discharged from the body through the vagina.

24. The menstrual cycle is regulated by hormones that are controlled by feedback inhibition mechanisms. For example, FSH and LH are released when the hypothalamus reacts to low estrogen levels in the blood by producing a releasing hormone that acts on the pituitary gland.

25. A zygote undergoes cell division as it passes through the Fallopian tube from a two-celled embryo on day 2 to a solid, 50-cell morula on day 4. As the embryo grows, a fluid-filled cavity forms in the center, transforming it into a hollow blastocyst. About six or seven days after fertilization, the blastocyst attaches itself to the wall of the uterus.

26. During gastrulation, the two layers of cells within the cavity of the blastocyst migrate to produce a third primary germ layer. All organs of the embryo form from these primary germ layers.

27. The placenta is the fetus's organ of respiration, nutrition, and excretion.

28. Childbirth begins when the pituitary gland releases oxytocin, which stimulates labor contractions. The contractions cause the opening of the cervix to expand enough for the baby's head to pass through it. The amniotic sac breaks, and contractions of the uterus force the baby out through the vagina.

Chapter 39 Assessment

Critical Thinking

29. The red line represents a person with diabetes, and the blue line represents a person who does not have diabetes. The person with diabetes has a high level of blood glucose for a longer period of time following a meal due to lack of insulin to help remove glucose from the blood.

30. Students' drawings should show that the level of thyroxine in the blood stimulates the pituitary gland to produce more or less thyroid stimulating hormone, which, in turn, leads to the production of more or less thyroxine by the thyroid gland.

31. Some hormones are taken orally because they are slow-acting. Other hormones, such as insulin, are injected because it is important for them to act quickly.

32. The heartbeat increases before a meet because nervousness or excitement leads to the production of "fight or flight" hormones by the adrenal gland. During the meet, the heartbeat increases to supply the muscles with extra oxygen.

33. The placenta is made up of two layers, the fetal portion and the maternal portion. This two-layered structure allows the blood of the mother and the embryo to flow past each other, but not to mix.

34. Because the Fallopian tube does not provide the fetus with enough room to grow and the tube could rupture

35. Because this keeps sperm at a cooler temperature than internal body temperature, which they need to develop normally

36. Insufficient amounts of FSH and LH would cause follicles to fail to develop to maturity and release mature eggs.

37. Traffic reports are similar to hormones because they broadcast messages that affect the activities of motorists. They act as a feedback control by inhibiting motorists from moving toward areas of traffic congestion.

38. A deficiency of iodine in the diet causes the thyroid gland to produce too little thyroxine, which causes an excess of THS, which causes the thyroid gland to swell.

Chapter 39 Assessment

Critical Thinking

29. Interpreting Graphics The graph below shows the levels of glucose in the blood of two people during a 5-hour period immediately following the ingestion of a typical meal. Which line represents a person with diabetes? Which line represents a person who does not have diabetes? Explain your answers.

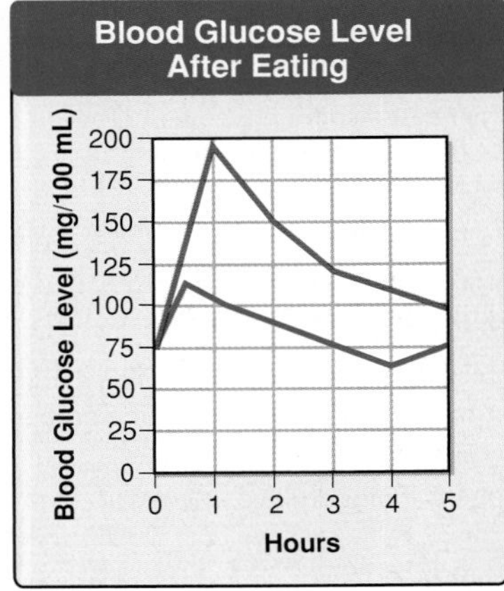

30. Using Models Make a diagram of a negative-feedback mechanism involving hormones that function to regulate the production of thyroxine.

31. Applying Concepts Explain why some hormones can be taken orally, whereas others, such as insulin, are injected directly into the body.

32. Applying Concepts The heartbeat of a swimmer increases significantly both before and during a swim meet. Explain why this happens.

33. Applying Concepts The placenta develops from tissues produced by both the embryo and the uterus. How does the structure of the placenta prevent the mother's blood from mixing with the blood of the developing embryo?

34. Inferring Occasionally, a zygote does not move into the uterus but attaches to the wall of a Fallopian tube instead. Why might this be a very dangerous situation for the mother?

35. Formulating Hypotheses Sperm are stored in the epididymis, which is located in the scrotum. Why is it advantageous for sperm to be stored in the scrotum?

36. Predicting Predict the effects that insufficient amounts of FSH and LH will have on the menstrual cycle.

37. Using Analogies In many areas during rush hour, radio stations broadcast traffic reports. How are traffic reports similar to hormones? How do the reports act as a feedback control mechanism for the flow of traffic?

38. Formulating Hypotheses Why do you think that the thyroid gland enlarges in response to a deficiency of iodine in the diet?

39. Applying Concepts Describe how each of the following represents an adaptation that helps to ensure successful fertilization: seminal fluid; production and release of millions of sperm; cilia lining the Fallopian tubes; long tail of a sperm.

40. Drawing Conclusions The menstrual cycle is suppressed during pregnancy. Explain why this is important to the success of a full-term pregnancy.

41. Making Connections Use what you learned about mitochondria in Section 7–2 to explain why sperm cells contain many mitochondria.

Performance-Based Assessment

In the Community Research the topic of fetal alcohol syndrome. Then, design a pamphlet to be used in a clinic informing women of the dangers of drinking alcohol during pregnancy. Your pamphlet must have a title, illustrations, and brief facts about fetal alcohol syndrome.

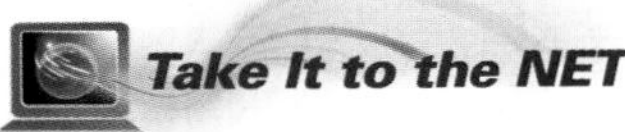

Who is at risk for diabetes? Visit the Prentice Hall Web site at **www.phschool.com** to find out the risk factors for the disease. Then, answer the following questions:

- Take the risk test. What is your current risk of having diabetes?
- What can you do to maintain or lower your risk?
- Why are questions about symptoms of diabetes left off the risk test?
- What data are the test questions based on?

Take It to the NET

- Answers will depend on students' responses.
- Behaviors that lower risk of diabetes include maintaining normal weight or losing weight if you are overweight; staying active most days of the week; and eating low-fat meals that are high in fruits, vegetables, and whole-grain foods.
- Questions about symptoms of the disease are left off the risk test because some people with diabetes do not have symptoms or their symptoms mimic those of other diseases. Symptoms are also difficult to define, quantify, and assess in self-administered questionnaires.
- The test questions are based on a study of diabetes risk factors that was conducted by the Centers for Disease Control and Prevention. For additional information, visit

www.phschool.com

Test-Taking Tip For questions containing words like NOT or EXCEPT, first rule out any choice that *does* fit the characteristic in question. Use this approach to eliminate four out of five choices. To check if your answer is correct, confirm that it *does not* fit the characteristic in question.

Directions: Choose the letter that best answers the question or completes the statement.

1. What is the correct path of semen out of the human male reproductive system?
   (A) vas deferens, urethra, epididymis
   (B) epididymis, vas deferens, urethra
   (C) vas deferens, epididymis, urethra
   (D) urethra, epididymis, vas deferens
   (E) epididymis, urethra, vas deferens
2. Each of these is a stage in the human menstruation cycle EXCEPT
   (A) ovulation (D) follicular phase
   (B) luteal phase (E) menstruation
   (C) corpus phase
3. Which of the following is NOT an endocrine gland?
   (A) thyroid gland (D) sweat gland
   (B) pituitary gland (E) adrenal gland
   (C) parathyroid gland

Questions 4–8 Each of the lettered choices below refers to the following numbered statements. Select the best lettered choice. A choice may be used once, more than once, or not at all.

(A) Ovary
(B) Follicle
(C) Hypothalamus
(D) Epididymis
(E) Cervix

4. Prepares an egg for release into the human female reproductive tract
5. Opening to the uterus
6. Produces estrogen and progesterone
7. Controls the secretions of the pituitary gland
8. Stores sperm in the human male reproductive system

Questions 9–11 The diagram below shows the human endocrine system. Use the diagram to answer the questions.

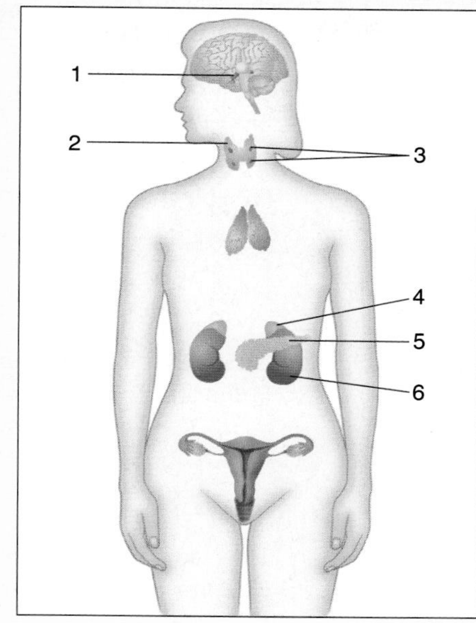

9. Which gland helps the body prepare for and deal with stress?
   (A) 1 (D) 5
   (B) 2 (E) 6
   (C) 4
10. Which gland is both an endocrine and an exocrine gland?
   (A) 2 (D) 5
   (B) 3 (E) 6
   (C) 4
11. Which gland secretes growth hormone?
   (A) 1 (D) 4
   (B) 2 (E) 5
   (C) 3

Standardized Test Prep

1. B 2. C 3. D 4. B 5. E 6. A 7. C 8. D 9. C 10. D 11. A

(continued from page 1026)

39. Seminal fluid provides a nutrient-rich medium in which sperm are nourished and transported. The production and release of millions of sperm help ensure that at least one sperm will reach and fertilize the egg. Cilia lining the Fallopian tubes push eggs, which are not motile, toward the uterus. The long tail of a sperm helps it to travel to the egg.

40. During pregnancy, an embryo is attached to the uterus wall and growing. If the menstrual cycle continued and a new egg cell was not fertilized, the corpus luteum could start to disintegrate, and the embryo could be discharged from the uterus.

41. Mitochondria release energy, and sperm cells need a lot of energy to reach an egg.

Performance-Based Assessment

Students' pamphlets should indicate that fetal alcohol syndrome refers to birth defects—such as low birth weight, facial abnormalities, heart defects, and lower-than-normal intelligence—caused by ingestion of alcohol during pregnancy. Pamphlets should make it clear that there is no safe level of alcohol consumption during pregnancy.

Chapter Planner 40 The Immune System and Disease

Section and Section Objectives	Time	Activities and Labs
40–1 Infectious Disease, pp. 1029–1033 **40.1.1** ***Identify*** the causes of disease. **40.1.2** ***Explain*** how infectious diseases are transmitted. **40.1.3** ***Describe*** how antibiotics fight infection.	1 period (1/2 block)	**SE:** ***Inquiry Activity***, How do diseases spread?, p. 1028 **TE:** ***Demonstration,*** p. 1030
40–2 The Immune System, pp. 1034–1040 **40.2.1** ***Identify*** the body's nonspecific defenses against invading pathogens. **40.2.2** ***Describe*** immunity.	2 periods (1 block)	**TE:** ***Demonstration,*** p. 1035 **TE:** ***Demonstration,*** p. 1036 **SE:** ***Quick Lab,*** How does cell-mediated immunity work?, p. 1039
40–3 Immune System Disorders, pp. 1041–1044 **40.3.1** ***State*** what happens when the immune system overreacts. **40.3.2** ***Explain*** what an autoimmune disease is. **40.3.3** ***Describe*** how HIV affects the immune system.	1 period (1/2 block)	**SE:** ***Analyzing Data,*** HIV Infection Among Women, p. 1043 **SE:** ***Issues in Biology,*** Slowing the AIDS Epidemic, p. 1045
40–4 Cancer, pp. 1046–1048 **40.4.1** ***Identify*** the basic mechanism of cancer. **40.4.2** ***Describe*** how cancer is treated.	1 period (1/2 block)	**TE:** ***Demonstration,*** p. 1046 **SE:** ***Real-World Lab,*** Testing the Specificity of Antibodies, p. 1049
Chapter Assessment, pp. 1050–1053	1 period (1/2 block)	

ACTIVITY PLANNER

SE: ***Inquiry Activity,*** p. 1028; (10 min.); Glo Germ oil or dilute fluorescein solution, ultraviolet lamp

TE: ***Demonstration,*** p. 1030; (5 min., 5 min.); bacterial culture, wire loop, 2 sterile petri dishes with nutrient agar, Bunsen burner

TE: ***Demonstration,*** p. 1035; (10 min.); microprojector, drop of pond water on slide

TE: ***Demonstration,*** p. 1036; (15 min.); posterboard, string, scissors, markers

SE: ***Quick Lab,*** p. 1039; (15 min.); 3 red balloons; 3 yellow balloons; 3 blue balloons; red, yellow, and white adhesive notes; toothpick

TE: ***Demonstration,*** p. 1046; (5 min.); microprojector, slides of normal and cancerous cells

SE: ***Real-World Lab,*** p. 1049; (45 min.); Strep A diagnostic kits with control samples for three tests, sterile water

PLANNING KEY

Ability Levels

B	**Basic**	For students who need additional help
A	**Average**	For all students
E	**Enriched**	For students who need to be challenged

Components

SE	Student Edition	**GRSW**	Guided Reading and Study Workbook	**IDM**	Issues and Decision Making
TE	Teacher's Edition	**CT**	Chapter Tests: Levels A and B	**CTB**	Computer Test Bank
LMA	Laboratory Manual A	**PHAS**	PH Assessment System	**PA**	Presentation Assistant Plus
LMB	Laboratory Manual B	**LA**	Lab Assessment with Scoring Guide	**BD**	BioDetectives Videotape
TR	Teaching Resources	**BTM**	BioTechnology Manual	**iT**	iText

Program Resources	Assessment	Media and Technology
LMA: Chapter 40 Lab A E **TR:** Section Review 40–1 B A **GRSW:** Section 40–1 B A	**SE:** 40–1 Section Assessment, p. 1033 **TR:** Section Review 40–1	**PA:** 40–1 Interest Grabber, Section Outline, Koch's Postulates, Figure 40–3 **iT:** Section 40–1
LMB: Chapter 40 Lab B A **TR:** Section Review 40–2 B A **GRSW:** Section 40–2 B A	**SE:** 40–2 Section Assessment, p. 1040 **TR:** Section Review 40–2	**PA:** 40–2 Interest Grabber, Section Outline, Primary and Secondary Infections, Figure 40–7, Figure 40–8, Figure 40–9, Figure 40–11 **iT:** Section 40–2
TR: Section Review 40–3 B A **GRSW:** Section 40–3 B A **IDM:** 40–1 A E	**SE:** 40–3 Section Assessment, p. 1044 **TR:** Section Review 40–3	**PA:** 40–3 Interest Grabber, Section Outline, Stages of HIV Infection **iT:** Section 40–3
TR: Section Review 40–4 B A Chapter 40 Real-World Lab B A E **GRSW:** Section 40–4 B A	**SE:** 40–4 Section Assessment, p. 1048 **TR:** Section Review 40–4	**PA:** 40–4 Interest Grabber, Section Outline, Concept Map **iT:** Section 40–4
	SE: Chapter 40 Assessment, pp. 1050–1053 **TR:** Chapter Vocabulary Review, Graphic Organizer **CT:** Chapter 40 Test **CTB:** Chapter 40 Test **PHAS:** Practice Test	**CTB:** Chapter 40 Test **iT:** Chapter 40 Assessment

PRESSED FOR TIME?

To Preview the Chapter
- Have students study the figures in Sections 40–1 and 40–2 and read the captions.
- Have students scan Sections 40–1 and 40–2 for boldface Vocabulary terms and read the definitions.

To Cover the Chapter Quickly
- Have students read all of Sections 40–1 and 40–2 and the introductions to Sections 40–3 and 40–4.
- Assign the Section Assessments 40–1 and 40–2, questions 1–9, 11–22, 27, 30, 32, 33, and 36 in Chapter 40 Assessment, and questions 1–8 in Chapter 40 Standardized Test Prep.

To Review the Chapter
- Assign Sections 40–1 and 40–2 in the Guided Reading and Study Workbook.
- Assign the Section Reviews for 40–1 and 40–2 and the Chapter Vocabulary Review for Chapter 40 in the Teaching Resources.

Chapter 40

ENGAGE/EXPLORE

Inquiry Activity

Objectives Students will be able to
- infer how a virus spreads;
- conclude that thorough hand washing helps prevent the spread of diseases.

Skill Focus **Inferring, Drawing Conclusions**

Materials Glo Germ oil or dilute fluorescein solution, ultraviolet lamp

Time 10 minutes

Advance Prep Apply the Glo Germ oil no more than 10 minutes before students arrive.

Safety Caution students to avoid getting the fluorescent substance in their eyes or mouths.

Strategy You can make sure the "virus" spreads to students' hands by applying the fluorescent substance to the classroom door knob and any other objects in the classroom that students are likely to touch.

Expected Outcomes
- Students should observe the "virus" in various areas of the classroom and on their hands.
- Students should find that thorough hand washing removes the "virus" from their hands.

Think About It

1. The "virus" spread by contact as students moved around the room and touched objects.
2. Thorough hand washing helps prevent the spread of diseases by removing disease-causing agents before they can be spread to other people.

Encourage students to view "Influenza: Tracking a Virus" from the Bio Detectives Videotape.

Chapter 40 The Immune System and Disease

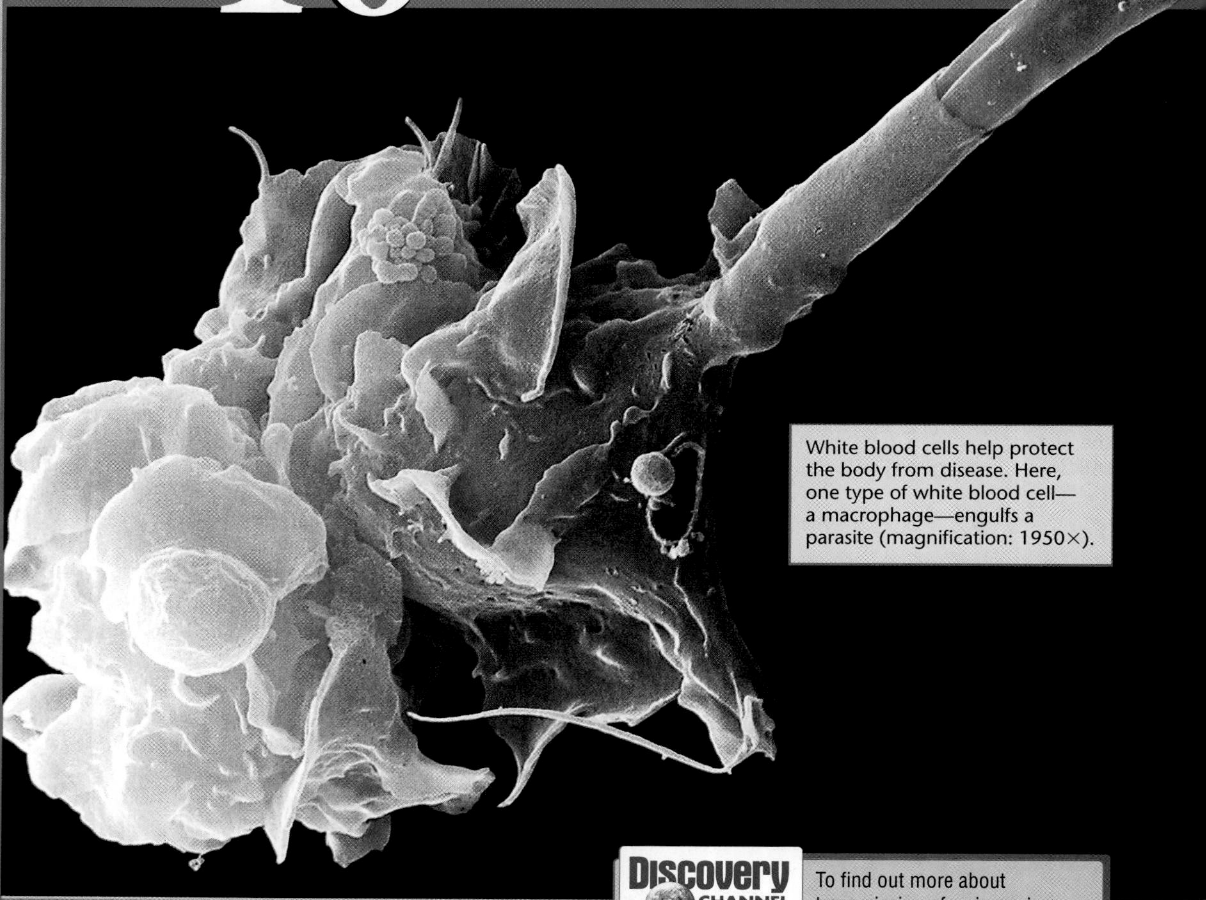

White blood cells help protect the body from disease. Here, one type of white blood cell—a macrophage—engulfs a parasite (magnification: 1950×).

To find out more about transmission of a virus, view the videotape "Influenza: Tracking a Virus."

Inquiry Activity

How do diseases spread?

Procedure

1. Your teacher has placed a fluorescent material in the classroom to simulate a virus. The material glows when exposed to ultraviolet radiation (UV). Use a UV lamp to check for "virus" on your hands and objects you touched since entering the classroom. **CAUTION:** *Ultraviolet light can harm your eyes. Do not look directly at the ultraviolet light.*
2. Exchange results with your classmates to determine how the "virus" spread through the classroom. Wash your hands with soap and water.

Think About It

1. **Inferring** What can you infer about how the "virus" spread through the classroom?
2. **Drawing Conclusions** How does thorough hand washing help prevent the spread of diseases?

HISTORY OF SCIENCE

Koch and his postulates

Robert Koch was a German surgeon born in 1843. Today, he is considered to be one of the founders of modern bacteriology, but when he developed his postulates he was just a country doctor. During a local anthrax epidemic, Koch tried to identify the cause of the disease. He isolated the pathogen from infected cattle, transferred it to mice, and recovered the same pathogen from the mice. Although Koch's postulates still guide bacteriology and epidemiology, there are some important exceptions to their use. For example, many pathogens, such as the pathogens that cause syphilis and AIDS, cannot be grown in culture. This makes it impossible to fulfill the second of Koch's postulates in linking these pathogens with a disease. In cases such as these, scientists must depend on circumstantial evidence, such as the presence of the organism in every individual diagnosed with the disease.

40–1 Infectious Disease

Good health is something that you might take for granted—until you, or someone close to you, gets sick. Then, the value of good health becomes all too obvious. Why do you get sick? How do you get better? What is the best way for you to avoid getting sick in the first place? These are questions that people have been asking for centuries. Today, in most cases, these questions can be answered.

A **disease** is any change, other than an injury, that disrupts the normal functions of the body. **Some diseases, such as hemophilia, are inherited. Others are caused by materials in the environment, such as cigarette smoke. Still others are produced by agents such as bacteria, viruses, and fungi.** Disease-causing agents such as bacteria are called **pathogens,** which means "sickness-makers." Diseases caused by pathogens are generally called infectious diseases because the agents that cause them usually enter, or infect, the body of the person who gets sick.

Guide for Reading

Key Concepts
- What causes disease?
- How are infectious diseases transmitted?

Vocabulary
disease
pathogen
germ theory of disease
Koch's postulates
toxin
vector
antibiotic

Reading Strategy: Using Prior Knowledge
Before you read, make a list of diseases that you have had. As you read, decide whether or not these diseases were infectious.

The Germ Theory of Disease

For thousands of years, people believed that diseases were caused by curses, evil spirits, or night vapors. In the mid-nineteenth century, a new explanation based on the work of the French chemist Louis Pasteur and the German bacteriologist Robert Koch was put forth. The observations of Pasteur and Koch led them to conclude that infectious diseases were caused by microorganisms, or germs. This conclusion is now known as the **germ theory of disease.** The world is filled with microorganisms of every shape and description. How can scientists be sure which organism causes a particular disease?

In 1975, Allen Steere of Yale University got a chance to ask exactly that question. In a small area of Connecticut, Steere found 39 children and several adults suffering from pain and joint inflammation. Their symptoms looked like a rare form of childhood arthritis. However, Steere thought that there were far too many cases for such a small population. The rural location of the outbreak, and the fact that most of the cases had started in summer or early fall, made Steere suspect that this could be an infectious disease carried by an insect.

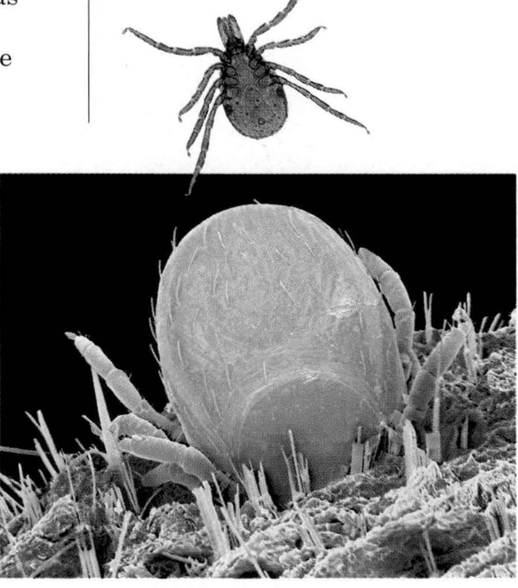

(magnification: about 30×)

Figure 40–1 Diseases can be inherited, caused by materials in the environment, or produced by pathogens. Ticks often carry bacteria, so when they come in contact with human skin, they often transmit pathogens.

SECTION RESOURCES

Print:
- ***Laboratory Manual A,*** Chapter 40 Lab
- ***Teaching Resources,*** Section Review 40–1
- ***Guided Reading and Study Workbook,*** Section 40–1

Technology:
- ***iText,*** Section 40–1

Section 40–1

1 FOCUS

Objectives

40.1.1 ***Identify*** the causes of disease.
40.1.2 ***Explain*** how infectious diseases are transmitted.
40.1.3 ***Describe*** how antibiotics fight infection.

Guide for Reading

Vocabulary Preview

Tell students that the term *pathogen* refers to an agent that causes disease. Ask: **How do you think the term *pathogen* is related to the germ theory of disease?** *(Germ is another term for pathogen. According to the theory, germs, or pathogens, cause disease.)*

Reading Strategy

Students are likely to list respiratory infections such as colds and flu and gastrointestinal infections that cause stomachaches and diarrhea.

2 INSTRUCT

Meet Diverse Needs

Make a concept map of the boldface text in the introduction. Include an example of a disease for each cause, such as hemophilia for inherited factors, lung cancer for materials in the environment, and athlete's foot for pathogens. **Learning modality: visual**

The Germ Theory of Disease

Demonstration

Help students appreciate the importance of the germ theory of disease by demonstrating how many deaths were caused by infectious diseases in Koch's and Pasteur's day. Show students death rates by cause of death in the United States population for the late 1800s and also for a recent year, such as 2000. Then, ask: **How did the number of deaths caused by infectious diseases change?** *(It fell dramatically.)* Add that identifying germs as the cause of infectious diseases was the first step in bringing these diseases under control.

Meet Diverse Needs

Have students who need extra challenges learn more about Lyme disease. Students might investigate the current distribution of the disease in the United States, the number of people who are infected, how the disease is treated, and whether it can be transmitted by other vectors. Students should share what they learn in an oral report illustrated with visuals, such as a map showing the distribution of Lyme disease or a diagram illustrating how Lyme disease is transmitted. **Learning modality: verbal**

Koch's Postulates

Demonstration

Demonstrate the importance of using sterile techniques when applying Koch's second postulate. Hold a wire loop in the flame of a Bunsen burner for a few seconds. Allow the loop to cool, dip it in a bacterial culture, and run it over sterile agar in a petri dish. (**CAUTION:** Use a safe strain of bacteria, such as *E. coli* from a scientific supply company, and apply sterile techniques to the handling of the bacterial culture.) Sterilize the loop again, let it cool, and run it over sterile agar in a second petri dish. Incubate both dishes at 37°C for 24 hours, and then have students observe the differences in the agar. (*Bacteria should be visible growing in the first petri dish but not the second.*) Ask: **Which step of the demonstration caused the different outcomes in the two petri dishes?** *(The resterilization of the wire loop)* **How does this demonstration relate to Koch's second postulate?** *(If you had been trying to isolate and grow a pathogen in the petri dishes, only the second dish would produce a pure culture. The first petri dish would have produced bacteria in addition to the pathogen.)*

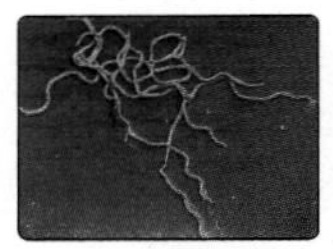

Pathogen (*Borrelia burgdorferi*) identified

↓

Pathogen grown in pure culture

↓

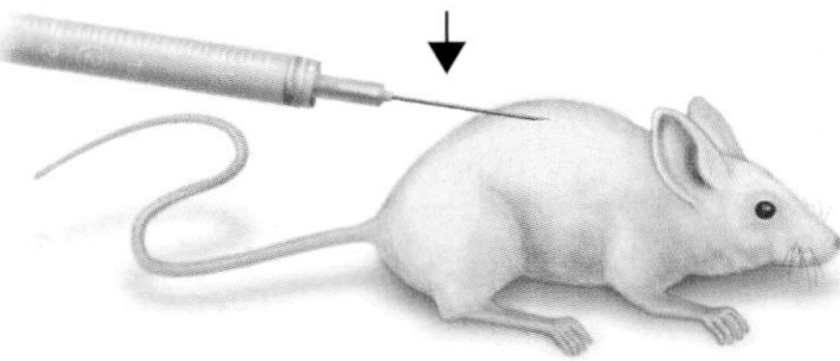

Pathogen injected into healthy lab mouse

↓

Healthy mouse becomes sick

↓

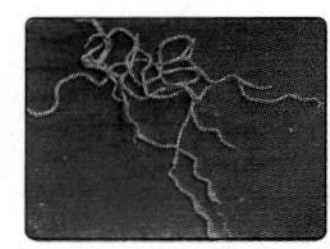

Pathogen (*Borrelia burgdorferi*) identified

▲ **Figure 40–2** Allen Steere followed Koch's postulates to test his theory that the bacterium *Borrelia burgdorferi* caused Lyme disease. **Inferring** ***Why must the pathogen be grown in a pure culture?***

Sure enough, many of the children reported that their problems had begun with what they thought was an insect bite. The bite was followed by an expanding skin rash. Steere called the infection Lyme disease after the town of Lyme, Connecticut, where it was first discovered.

Steere and his colleagues were able to link the skin rash to the bite of the tiny deer tick *(Ixodes scapularis)*. One of Steere's colleagues, Dr. Willy Burgdorfer, found an unusual spiral-shaped bacterium *(Borrelia burgdorferi)* in the ticks. Steere found the same bacterium in patients with Lyme disease. Could this bacterium be the cause of Lyme disease?

For ethical reasons, Steere did not try to infect healthy children with the bacterium. However, when the bacterium was injected into laboratory mice, they developed arthritis and other symptoms, just like the children. From the sick mice, Steere recovered the bacteria, which were then able to pass the infection along to healthy mice. Steere and his colleagues had found the organism that caused Lyme disease. The process Steere used is shown in **Figure 40–2.**

Koch's Postulates

The groundwork for Allen Steere's work with Lyme disease was actually laid more than a hundred years earlier by Robert Koch. From his studies with other bacteria, Koch developed a series of guidelines still used today to identify the microorganism that causes a specific disease. These rules are known as **Koch's postulates.** Koch's postulates state the following:

1. The pathogen should always be found in the body of a sick organism and should not be found in a healthy one.
2. The pathogen must be isolated and grown in the laboratory in pure culture.
3. When the purified pathogens are placed in a new host, they should cause the same disease that infected the original host.
4. The injected pathogen should be reisolated from the second host. It should be identical to the original pathogen.

With these rules, disease did not seem to be an unavoidable consequence of being alive. If a particular pathogen could be identified, maybe the disease it caused could be prevented or cured.

CHECKPOINT *What are Koch's postulates?*

TIME SAVER **PRESENTATIONS MADE EASY!**

The Presentation Assistant Plus contains the Prentice Hall Presentation Pro and the Transparencies, which provide easy-to-follow visual support for every step of this section. If you have a computer presentation station, use Prentice Hall Presentation Pro for Section 40–1, or use the transparencies listed here.

Section 40–1: Interest Grabber
Section Outline
Koch's Postulates
Figure 40–3

Agents of Disease

For many pathogens, the human body provides just the right conditions for growth—the right temperature, a watery environment, and an abundance of nutrients. The large intestine, for example, harbors dense colonies of bacteria. Bacteria and yeast are found in the mouth, throat, and in the tissues surrounding the eyeball. Fortunately, most of these organisms are harmless and many are actually beneficial.

If this is true, then exactly how do pathogens cause disease? Recall the pathogens you studied in Units 6 and 8. Bacteria can either break down the tissues in an infected organism or release toxins into the body. **Toxins** are poisons that produce illness by disrupting bodily functions. Some protists, fungi, and worms are parasites that live and feed inside an infected organism. Some remove nutrients from the digestive system. Others destroy blood cells and neurons. A virus, which is a nonliving pathogen, can use the materials of a host cell to make copies of the virus until the cell bursts. **Figure 40–3** gives examples of pathogens, the diseases they cause, and how the pathogens are transmitted.

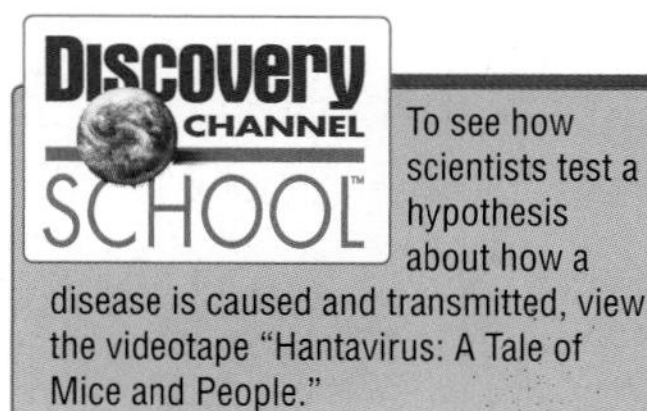

To see how scientists test a hypothesis about how a disease is caused and transmitted, view the videotape "Hantavirus: A Tale of Mice and People."

▼ **Figure 40–3** This table lists some of the viruses, bacteria, protists, worms, and fungi that cause disease. **Using Tables and Graphs** *What kind of pathogen causes athlete's foot?*

Pathogens and Disease

Pathogen Types	Disease	Agent That Causes Disease	Method of Transmission
Viruses	Common cold	Rhinovirus	Airborne; direct contact with infected person
	Influenza	Two types (A, B), plus subtypes	Airborne; droplet infection; direct contact with infected person
	Chicken pox	Varicella	Airborne; direct contact with infected person
	Measles	Paramyxovirus	Droplets in air; direct contact with secretions of infected person
Bacteria	Tuberculosis	*Mycobacterium tuberculosis*	Droplets in air; contaminated milk and dairy products
	Meningitis	*Neisseria meningitidis*	Direct contact with a carrier
	Cholera	*Vibrio cholerae*	Contaminated drinking water
	Tetanus	*Clostridium tetani*	Contaminated wound; usually puncture wound
Protists	African sleeping sickness	*Trypanosoma*	Spread by tsetse fly
	Malaria	*Plasmodium*	Spread by *Anopheles* mosquitoes
	Amoebic dysentery	*Entamoeba histolytica*	Contaminated drinking water
Worms	Schistosomiasis	*Schistosoma*	Freshwater streams and rice paddies
	Beef tapeworm	*Taenia saginata*	Contaminated meat
Fungi	Athlete's foot	Imperfect fungi	Contact with infected person; shower stalls
	Ringworm	Imperfect fungi	Exchange of hats, combs, or athletic head gear with infected person

BIO INSIGHTS — FACTS AND FIGURES

All about tetanus

Although tetanus was described by Hippocrates 2,400 years ago, its prevalence has been masked because it strikes individuals and does not cause epidemics. The organism that causes tetanus, the bacillus *Clostridium tetani,* is found mainly in soil. It can enter the body through any break in the skin, from a superficial scratch to a puncture wound. Because *C. tetani* is anaerobic, it grows best in deeper tissues, so puncture wounds are especially prone to developing tetanus infections. The bacterium produces one of the most powerful toxins known. It affects the nervous system and causes painful muscle contractions, especially in the muscles of the neck, jaw, and thorax. It frequently leads to death. Fortunately, tetanus can be prevented with a vaccine.

Agents of Disease

Build Science Skills

Drawing Conclusions Assign one student to research each of the pathogens in Figure 40–3. Students should find out how the pathogen causes disease and report back to the class. *(Findings will vary depending on the pathogen. For example, the bacterium that causes tetanus produces a toxin that causes involuntary muscle spasms, especially of the jaw.)* After all the students have reported, ask: **Based on these findings, what conclusions can you draw about different types of pathogens and how they cause disease?** *(Students might conclude, for example, that worms cause disease by removing nutrients from the digestive system or by injuring tissues.)*

Address Misconceptions

Explain that symptoms of infectious diseases are sometimes due to the response of the immune system to the presence of a pathogen. For example, the sneezing and runny nose associated with a cold are due to the production of histamines in response to the presence of the cold virus. Students may think that all infectious diseases are contagious. Contagious diseases are spread from person to person by direct or indirect contact. Measles and influenza are contagious; tetanus is not.

Use Visuals

Figure 40–3 Review with students the types of pathogens listed in the table. For example, remind students that protists are single-celled eukaryotic organisms and that bacteria are single-celled prokaryotic organisms. Check students' understanding of the table by asking: **How are viruses spread?** *(By direct contact or through the air)* **Which illnesses are spread by insects?** *(African sleeping sickness and malaria)*

Answers to . . .

CHECKPOINT *A series of guidelines used to identify the pathogen that causes a disease*

Figure 40–2 *To make sure that only the suspected pathogen has been transferred to the new host*

Figure 40–3 *Fungi*

How Diseases Are Spread

Meet Diverse Needs

Challenge groups of students to create posters illustrating some of the ways that infectious diseases can be spread and also how their spread can be prevented. For example, students might use a picture of two people shaking hands to illustrate the spread of diseases through direct contact and beside it a picture of someone washing hands to prevent the spread of disease in this way. Provide students with space in the classroom to display their posters. **Learning modality: visual**

Build Science Skills

Designing Experiments Challenge students to design an experiment to measure the effects of frequent hand-washing on the transmission of infectious diseases such as the common cold. Each experimental design should include a clearly stated research question, a description of the variables to be tested and how they will be measured, and an explanation of how other variables will be controlled.

Make Connections

Environmental Science List some vector-borne diseases found in the United States and the vectors that spread them, such as Rocky Mountain spotted fever, which is spread by ticks, and encephalitis, which is spread by mosquitoes. Ask: **What are some ways you could reduce the spread of these diseases?** *(Students are likely to say by eliminating the vectors, for example, by spraying with pesticides, or by avoiding contact with the vectors, for example, by wearing protective clothing.)* **Are there any drawbacks to these approaches?** *(Unless pesticides are pathogen-specific, they can harm other organisms.)*

How Diseases Are Spread

The best method for fighting any disease is to avoid it. Once a pathogen has been identified, biologists search for clues as to how it is passed from one person to the next. If a disease is thoroughly understood, how to prevent it usually becomes clear.

Infectious diseases are transmitted in a number of ways. **Some infectious diseases are spread from one person to another through coughing, sneezing, or physical contact. Other infectious diseases are spread through contaminated water or food. Still others are spread by infected animals.**

▲ **Figure 40–4** **Some infectious diseases are spread by insects.** This *Anopheles* mosquito may be a carrier of the protist that causes malaria.

Vectors Animals, such as ticks or the mosquito in **Figure 40–4,** spread many diseases. Animals that carry disease-causing organisms from person to person are called **vectors.** Vectors are often the key to stopping the diseases they spread. Avoiding tall grass and wooded areas where deer are present will limit your exposure to the ticks that carry Lyme disease. **Figure 40–5** shows another method of limiting people's exposure to vectors—spraying insecticides. Mosquito breeding areas can be sprayed with insecticides to fight malaria and West Nile virus.

The common cold, mumps, measles, and influenza are diseases that can spread from one person to another through coughing, sneezing, or even through hand-to-hand contact. Some habits can help to control transmission of these diseases. Simple measures such as covering your mouth with a tissue when you cough are often enough to limit infection. Washing your hands thoroughly helps to prevent the spread of many pathogens. You probably have noticed the signs in restaurant bathrooms reminding employees to wash their hands. This reminder is one way that restaurant owners try to prevent contamination of food.

Sexually Transmitted Diseases Some of the most dangerous pathogens are spread from one person to another by sexual contact. Sexually transmitted diseases, or STDs, are a serious health problem in the United States, infecting millions of people each year and accounting for thousands of deaths. Many of the most serious STDs—including syphilis and gonorrhea—are caused by bacteria. Others, including hepatitis B, hepatitis C, genital herpes, and AIDS, are caused by viruses. The consequences of infection can be severe. Gonorrhea and a disease called chlamydia, for example, can permanently damage the reproductive system. Other STDs, including syphilis and AIDS, can be fatal.

BIO INSIGHTS — HISTORY OF SCIENCE

The black death

Bubonic plague—or the black death, as it was referred to in the Middle Ages—is caused by a bacillus, *Yersinia pestis*, that is transmitted by fleas. *Y. pestis* is usually spread among wild rodent populations, but it can also spread to other mammals, including humans. Huge epidemics of bubonic plague have afflicted human populations throughout history. For example, in the mid-1300s, bubonic plague swept across Europe and killed a quarter of the human population. Between 1890 and 1930, more than 13 million people worldwide died of plague. Most people are surprised to learn that plague bacillus is still present today in wild rodent populations in many areas of the world, including some parts of the United States, and that local outbreaks of plague occasionally occur in human populations. Fortunately, the disease now can be treated successfully with antibiotics.

Fighting Infectious Diseases

If prevention fails, drugs have been developed for use against all sorts of pathogens. Perhaps the most useful single class of infection-fighting drugs are the antibiotics. **Antibiotics** are compounds that kill bacteria without harming the cells of humans or animals. Antibiotics work by interfering with the cellular processes of microorganisms. Many antibiotics are produced naturally by living organisms. Others are produced synthetically. Penicillin is, perhaps, the most well-known antibiotic.

Penicillin, the first antibiotic to be discovered, was found accidently in 1928 by the Scottish bacteriologist Alexander Fleming. Fleming had been growing *Staphylococcus* bacteria in a culture dish. One day, Fleming noticed that the culture of bacteria had been contaminated by a species of green mold called *Penicillium notatum.* This might simply have been annoying. However, Fleming noticed something exciting. The bacteria were not growing near the mold. Something produced by the mold was inhibiting the growth of the bacteria. Later, researchers discovered that penicillin—the name given to the antibiotic by Fleming—interferes with the synthesis of cell walls by bacteria, crippling fast-growing, walled bacteria.

Another antibiotic, streptomycin, interferes with the growth of bacteria by blocking protein synthesis on their ribosomes. Streptomycin was discovered by Russian American microbiologist Selman Waksman in 1943.

Antibiotics have no effect on viruses. However, antiviral drugs have been developed to fight certain viral diseases. These drugs generally inhibit the ability of viruses to invade cells and to multiply once inside of cells.

▲ **Figure 40–5** Spraying insecticides helps prevent the spread of disease. Because most insecticides can harm more than the target organism, they must be used with caution. Spraying is usually done at night when contact with humans and other animals is limited. **Applying Concepts** *How do insecticides help prevent the spread of disease?*

40–1 Section Assessment

1. **Key Concept** Describe some of the causes of disease.
2. **Key Concept** What are the ways in which infectious diseases are spread?
3. List Koch's postulates.
4. Give two examples each of diseases caused by viruses, bacteria, fungi, and protists.
5. How do vectors spread disease?
6. What are antibiotics?
7. **Critical Thinking Inferring** Louis Pasteur once stated, "In the fields of observation, chance favors only the mind that is prepared." How does this statement apply to the discovery of the antibiotic properties of penicillin?

iTEXT **Assessment** Use iText to review the important concepts in Section 40–1.

ALTERNATIVE ASSESSMENT

Designing a Graphic Organizer
Create a graphic organizer to show the different ways that infectious diseases are spread. Include at least four different routes of transmission in your graphic organizer.

Fighting Infectious Diseases

Make Connections

Health Science Introduce the concept of bacterial resistance to antibiotics. Explain that it occurs when people fail to take antibiotics long enough to kill all the bacteria that are causing an infection. Ask: **Why does this lead to the bacteria developing resistance to the antibiotic?** *(The remaining bacteria are those that have some resistance to the antibiotic. Through time, repeated selection in this way for the most resistant bacteria leads to bacteria that are almost completely resistant to a particular antibiotic.)*

3 ASSESS

Evaluate Understanding

Call on students at random to name the agents of disease. Call on other students to give an example of each agent.

Reteach

Have students write each of Koch's postulates, unnumbered, on an index card. Then, have students shuffle the cards and try to put them back in the correct order.

ALTERNATIVE ASSESSMENT

Students' graphic organizers should show that infectious diseases are spread through the air by coughing and sneezing, via contaminated food or water, by infected animal vectors, and through sexual contact. Suggest that students add examples of diseases spread in each of these ways.

Use iText to review the key concepts in Section 40–1.

40–1 Section Assessment

1. Inherited factors, materials in the environment, and pathogens
2. By coughing, sneezing, or physical contact; contaminated water and food; infected animals; and sexual contact
3. The pathogen should be found in a sick organism but not a healthy one. It must be isolated and grown in pure culture. The purified pathogen should cause the same disease in a second host. The same pathogen must be reisolated from the second host.
4. Students may list any disease in Figure 40–3.
5. By carrying pathogens from person to person
6. Compounds that kill bacteria without harming human or animal cells
7. Fleming did not discard a contaminated bacterial culture. Instead, he noted that the green mold prevented bacterial growth.

Answer to . . .

Figure 40–5 *Insecticides help prevent the spread of disease by killing insect vectors that carry pathogens from person to person.*

Section 40–2

1 FOCUS

Objectives

40.2.1 ***Identify*** the body's non-specific defenses against invading pathogens.
40.2.2 ***Describe*** immunity.

Guide for Reading

Vocabulary Preview

Explain that immunity means resistance to infection. Then, challenge students to fill in the blanks in the following statements with the correct Vocabulary terms containing the word *immunity*. **Immunity against pathogens in body fluids is called _____ immunity.** *(humoral)* **You will not get a disease to which you have _____ immunity.** *(permanent)* **Immunity involving killer T cells is called _____ immunity.** *(cell-mediated)* **When the body makes antibodies in response to an antigen, it is called _____ immunity.** *(active)* After students read the section, they should check to see if their answers were correct.

Reading Strategy

Have students preview the section by studying the figures and reading the captions.

2 INSTRUCT

Meet Diverse Needs

Challenge students to create a two- or three-dimensional model of the series of defenses that protects the body from pathogens. Suggest that students read the introductory paragraph for ideas but also encourage them to be creative. **Learning modality: tactile**

Nonspecific Defenses

Build Science Skills

Applying Concepts Ask: **If you eat food that contains bacteria, which nonspecific defenses will help protect your body from illness?** *(Lysozyme in saliva and stomach acid and digestive enzymes in the stomach)*

40–2 The Immune System

Guide for Reading

Key Concepts
- What are the body's non-specific defenses against invading pathogens?
- What is immunity?

Vocabulary
inflammatory response
fever
interferon
immune response
antigen
humoral immunity
antibody
cell-mediated immunity
permanent immunity
vaccination
active immunity

Reading Strategy: Finding Main Ideas Before you read, skim the section to identify the key ideas. Then, carefully read the section, making a list of supporting details for each main idea.

With pathogens all around us, it might seem like a miracle that you aren't sick all of the time. There's a reason, of course, why most of us enjoy good health. Our bodies have a protective system—a series of defenses that guard against disease. Some of these defenses, like the wall around a fortress, are simple barriers that keep all invaders out. Others, like security guards, are trained to spot invaders that have somehow slipped through the fortress walls. Once identified, such invaders can be rounded up and kept from doing damage.

Nonspecific Defenses

The immune system is the body's primary defense against pathogens. It consists of nonspecific and specific defenses against infection. Nonspecific defenses are the fortress walls of the system. They keep everything out and guard against all infections. Specific defenses work like security guards. They track down harmful pathogens that have managed to break through the body's nonspecific defenses.

First Line of Defense The job of the body's first line of defense is to keep pathogens out. This role is carried out by skin, mucus, sweat, and tears. **Your body's most important nonspecific defense is the skin.** Very few pathogens can penetrate the layers of dead cells at the skin's surface. Oil and sweat glands in the skin produce an acidic environment that kills many bacteria. The importance of the skin as a barrier against infection becomes obvious as soon as the skin is broken. As you know, even a small scrape or cut can become infected if it is not taken care of. The infections are caused by microorganisms normally present on the unbroken surface of your skin. When your skin is broken, pathogens can enter your body and multiply. As they grow, they cause the symptoms of an infection, such as swelling, redness, and pain.

Pathogens can also enter your body through your mouth and nose. Your body has other nonspecific defenses that protect these openings. Mucus in your nose and throat traps viruses and bacteria and cilia push them away from your lungs. Stomach acid and digestive enzymes destroy many pathogens that make their way to your stomach. Finally, many secretions of the body, including mucus, saliva, sweat, and tears, contain lysozyme, an enzyme that breaks down the cell walls of many bacteria.

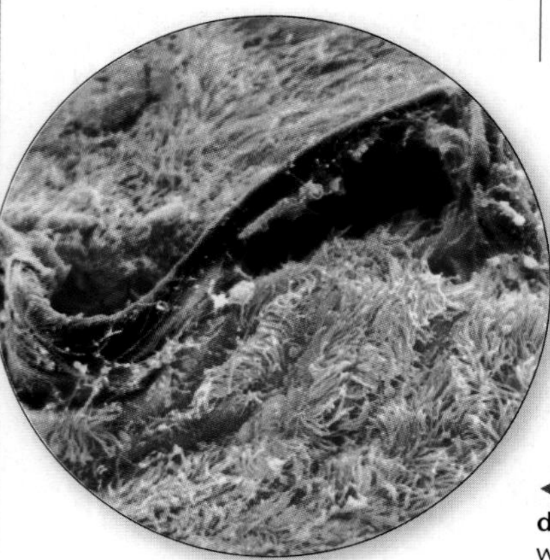

(magnification: 1100×)

◀ **Figure 40–6** **Mucus is another of your body's nonspecific defenses against infection.** Pathogens can get trapped in mucus the way the long brown strand of dirt in the photograph is trapped.

SECTION RESOURCES

Print:
- ***Laboratory Manual B,*** Chapter 40 Lab
- ***Teaching Resources,*** Section Review 40–2
- ***Guided Reading and Study Workbook,*** Section 40–2

Technology:
- ***iText,*** Section 40–2

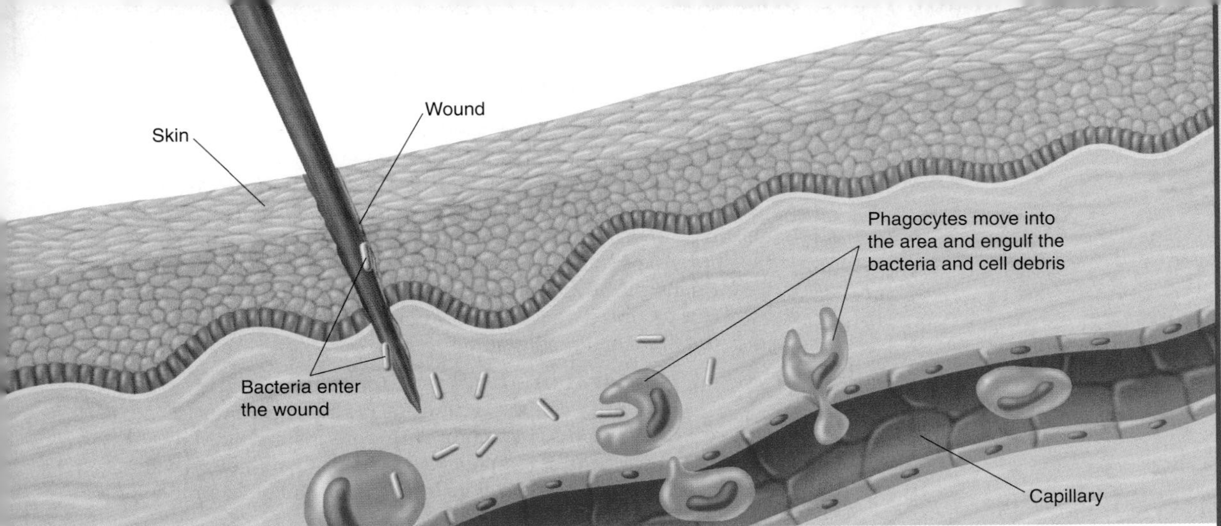
Skin
Wound
Phagocytes move into the area and engulf the bacteria and cell debris
Bacteria enter the wound
Capillary

▲ **Figure 40–7** **The inflammatory response is a nonspecific defense reaction to tissue damage caused by injury or infection.** When pathogens enter the body, phagocytes move into the area and engulf the pathogens. In addition, platelets and clotting factors leak from the capillaries.

Second Line of Defense If pathogens do manage to enter your body, they may multiply quickly, releasing toxins into your tissues. When this happens, the **inflammatory response**—a second line of defense—is activated. **The inflammatory response is a nonspecific defense reaction to tissue damage caused by injury or infection.** Blood vessels near the wound expand, and white blood cells leak from the vessels to enter the infected tissues. Many of these white blood cells are phagocytes, which engulf and destroy bacteria. The infected tissue may become swollen and painful. The battle between pathogens and phagocytes is illustrated in **Figure 40–7.**

When pathogens are detected, the immune system produces millions of white blood cells, which fight the infection. If a blood test reveals an increase in the number of white blood cells, the body is dealing with a serious infection. The immune system also releases chemicals that increase the core body temperature. You may have experienced this elevated body temperature, called a **fever**. Many pathogens can only survive within a narrow temperature range. An elevated temperature slows down or stops the growth of such pathogens. The higher temperature increases heart rate so that the white blood cells get to the sites of infection faster. An increased temperature also speeds the activities of the white blood cells and the rate of the chemical reactions that help repair damaged tissues.

Interferon In 1957, scientists discovered that virus-infected cells produce a group of proteins that help other cells resist viral infection. Scientists named these proteins **interferons** because they "interfere" with the virus. Interferons inhibit the synthesis of viral proteins in infected cells and help block viral replication. This slows down the progress of infection and often gives the specific defenses of the immune system time to respond.

CHECKPOINT *How do interferons help fight infection?*

Word Origins

Phagocyte comes from the Greek *phag*, meaning "eat," and *kutos*, meaning "cell." Thus, a phagocyte is a cell that eats or engulfs. **If the Greek prefix *macro*- means "large," what might the word *macrophage* mean?**

Meet Diverse Needs

Challenge students who are gifted in writing to create a short story or screenplay that correctly depicts the nonspecific defenses that challenge a pathogen entering the body. Their fictional accounts should take the point of view of the pathogen and correctly portray the action of the nonspecific defenses the pathogen must overcome and the order in which the defenses come into play. Urge students to read their stories or screenplays to the class. Have other students try to identify the nonspecific defenses as they are described in the fictional accounts. **Learning modality: verbal**

Demonstration

Use a microprojector and a drop of pond water on a slide to show students how amoebas feed. Point out the amoebas on the slide. As students watch their activity, ask: **What do amoebas do to consume their prey?** *(They engulf, or surround, their prey.)* Explain that phagocytes engulf bacteria and other pathogens in the same way.

Make Connections

Health Science Explain that since interferons were discovered in 1957, doctors have been excited about the possibility of using them to prevent disease. In 1980, an interferon became the first biopharmaceutical to be successfully mass-produced using genetic engineering. Mass production made interferons available for research purposes. Challenge interested students to find out the results of interferon research since 1980 and report back to the class on what they learn. *(Students will find that interferons show promise against many viral diseases and some cancers.)*

Word Origins

Macrophage means a large cell that eats or engulfs.

TIME SAVER — PRESENTATIONS MADE EASY!

The Presentation Assistant plus contains the Prentice Hall Presentation Pro and the Transparencies, which provide easy-to-follow visual support for every step of this section. If you have a computer presentation station, use Prentice Hall Presentation Pro for Section 40–2, or use the transparencies listed here.

Section 40–2:

Interest Grabber
Section Outline
Primary and Secondary Infections
Figure 40–7
Figure 40–8
Figure 40–9
Figure 40–11

Answer to . . .

CHECKPOINT *Interferons inhibit the synthesis of viral proteins and help block viral replication.*

Specific Defenses

Use Visuals

Figure 40–8 Point out that the drawings are greatly simplified abstractions of what are in reality complex molecules. Make sure students realize that the drawing on the right is just an enlargement of the drawing on the left with the antigens removed, making the antigen-binding sites easier to see.

Demonstration

Demonstrate to students how the immune system responds to specific pathogens. Select ten student volunteers. Have the students use poster board, string, scissors, and markers to make five signs (attached to string so they can be worn around the neck) labeled: Whooping Couth, Strep Throat, Bacterial Pneumonia, Diphtheria, and Tetanus. Also have the students cut five squares of poster board in half, each one in a different way so it forms two unique pieces that fit together like pieces of a jigsaw puzzle but that do not fit with any of the other pieces. Then, assign five of the students to wear the signs and play the roles of bacteria. Give each of them one half of a puzzle and have them line up at the back of the room. Assign the remaining five students to be B cells, give them the other halves of the puzzles, and have them line up at the front of the room. Finally, tell the bacteria to "invade" the room and the B cells to "attack" the bacterium that has the matching puzzle piece. When a B cell finds the bacterium that is its match, both should sit down. After the last pair sits down, ask: **What do the puzzle pieces carried by the "bacteria" represent?** *(Antigens)* **What do the puzzle pieces carried by the "B cells" represent?** *(Antibodies)*

Specific Defenses

If a pathogen is able to get past the body's nonspecific defenses, the immune system reacts with a series of specific defenses that attack the disease-causing agent. These defenses are called the **immune response.** A substance that triggers this response is known as an **antigen.** Carbohydrates, proteins, and lipids on the surfaces of viruses, bacteria, and other pathogens may serve as antigens that trigger responses by the immune system. The body can produce two different immune responses: humoral immunity and cell-mediated immunity.

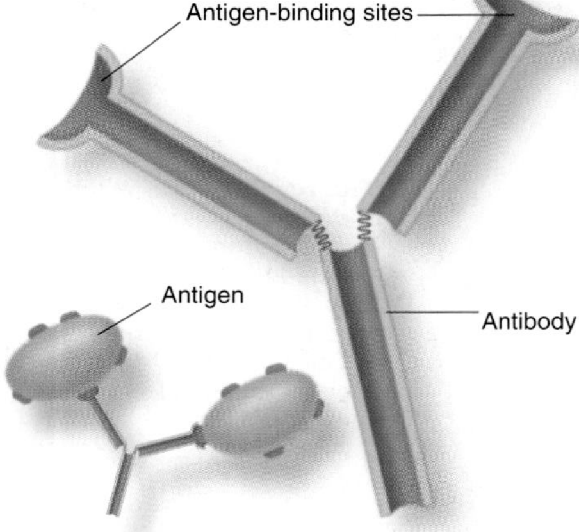

▲ **Figure 40–8** An antibody molecule has two identical antigen-binding sites. It is at these sites that one or two specific antigens bind to the antibody. **Applying Concepts** *How do antibodies help in the immune response?*

Humoral Immunity **Humoral immunity** is immunity against pathogens in the body fluids (blood and lymph). This immune response is produced by the actions of lymphocytes, a type of white blood cell. B lymphocytes, or B cells, are responsible for producing antibodies.

An antibody molecule is the basic functional unit of the humoral immune response. An **antibody** is a protein that helps destroy pathogens. As shown in **Figure 40–8,** an antibody is shaped like the letter Y and has two identical antigen-binding sites. These sites allow each antibody to bind to two antigens. Suppose the antigen is a protein found on the surface of the flu virus. Each flu virus particle is covered with many protein antigens. By attaching to the viral antigens, a group of antibody molecules can link the viruses together in a large mass. The clump of viruses and antibodies attracts phagocytes, which engulf and destroy the whole mass. If the immune system produces enough antibodies to a particular virus, it can prevent that virus from infecting cells.

Antibodies can fight bacterial infections as well. When antibodies bind to the surfaces of bacteria, they mark the cells for destruction by phagocytes and other white blood cells.

How does the immune system produce the specific antibodies that bind to antigens on the surface of pathogens? In a sense, they are custom made. As B cells develop early in life, the genes that code for antibodies rearrange themselves in slightly different ways in each B cell. When the development of B cells is complete, the immune system contains millions of B cells. Each of these B cells is capable of producing a slightly different antibody.

When a pathogen invades the body, its antigens are recognized by a small fraction of the body's B cells. These activated B cells grow and divide rapidly, producing large numbers of specialized B cells called plasma cells. Plasma cells release antibodies into the bloodstream to attack the pathogen that is causing the infection. Millions of plasma cells may form from just a few dozen B cells as a result of exposure to an antigen. The activation of plasma cells is assisted and regulated by lymphocytes known as T lymphocytes, or T cells. **Figure 40–9** summarizes the process of humoral immunity.

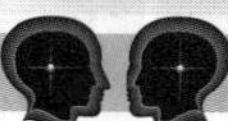

TEACHER TO TEACHER

After students have learned about nonspecific defenses and before they read about specific defenses, I challenge them to design a cell or cells to attack a particular pathogen. I have students work in groups and use a cold virus as the pathogen. Then, I have each group share its results by listing the cell specifications on the board and explaining them to the class. After the activity, as students read about specific defenses, they can see how their design compares with the "real thing." This activity helps students anticipate the complexity of specific defense cells before they actually read about them.

—Ruth Gleicher,
Biology Teacher
Niles West High School,
Skokie, IL

FIGURE 40–9 Humoral Immunity

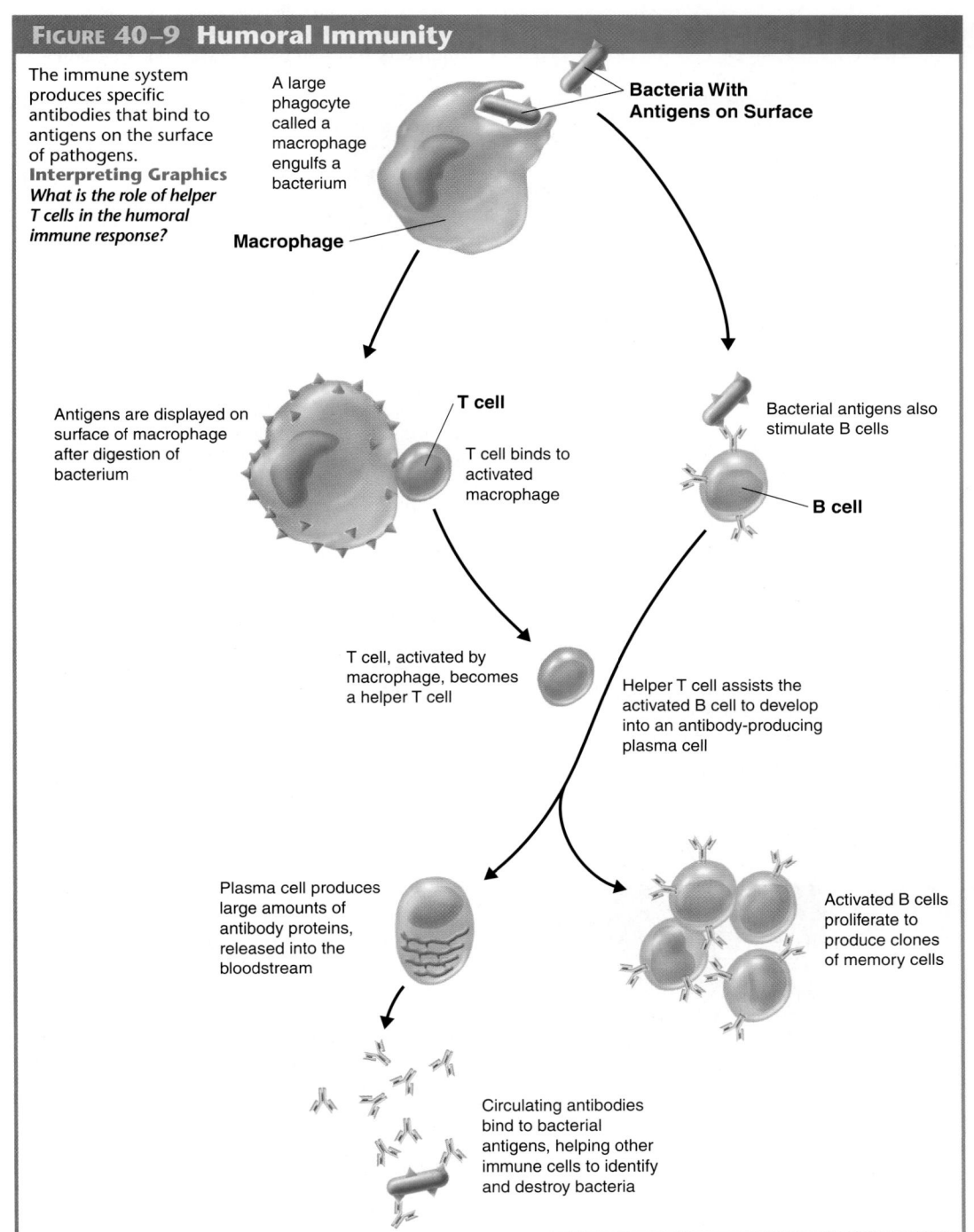

The immune system produces specific antibodies that bind to antigens on the surface of pathogens. **Interpreting Graphics** ***What is the role of helper T cells in the humoral immune response?***

A large phagocyte called a macrophage engulfs a bacterium

Bacteria With Antigens on Surface

Macrophage

Antigens are displayed on surface of macrophage after digestion of bacterium

T cell

T cell binds to activated macrophage

Bacterial antigens also stimulate B cells

B cell

T cell, activated by macrophage, becomes a helper T cell

Helper T cell assists the activated B cell to develop into an antibody-producing plasma cell

Plasma cell produces large amounts of antibody proteins, released into the bloodstream

Activated B cells proliferate to produce clones of memory cells

Circulating antibodies bind to bacterial antigens, helping other immune cells to identify and destroy bacteria

Meet Diverse Needs

Challenge groups of students to create a board game called "Pathogen Invaders." The game should have three players, each player representing either a B cell, a T cell, or a plasma cell. The play of the game should model the activation of a B cell by an invading pathogen. With the help of a T cell, a B cell develops into an antibody-releasing plasma cell. The goal of the game should be to produce antibodies to attack and destroy the invading pathogen. Allow time for groups to share and play their games. **Learning modality: kinesthetic**

Make Connections

Chemistry Explain that the stem of each Y-shaped antibody is essentially the same, but the end of each arm has a region that is unique. In this area, two polypeptide chains are folded to form a groovelike cavity that is complementary to the contour and electric charge of a particular antigen. Ask: **How do these differences in the antigen-binding sites of antibodies occur?** *(The genes that code for the two polypeptide chains rearrange themselves in slightly different ways in each B cell.)*

Use Visuals

Figure 40–9 Have students follow the flowchart as you read the captions, starting with, "A large phagocyte called a macrophage engulfs a bacterium." Make sure students can identify the cells involved in each step.

FACTS AND FIGURES

Phagocyte power

Phagocytes develop from stem cells in bone marrow. Types of phagocytes include neutrophils, eosinophils, and monocytes, which mature into macrophages. Phagocytes are drawn by altered chemical gradients into an area of damaged or invaded tissues. There, they engulf and destroy pathogens and other foreign substances by means of endocytosis. In endocytosis, the plasma membrane of the phagocyte encloses the pathogen at or near the cell surface of the phagocyte. Then, the membrane pinches off to form a closed endocytic vesicle around the pathogen. The endocytic vesicle provides a "traveling compartment" that enables the pathogen to be transported into the cytoplasm of the phagocyte. Once inside the cytoplasm, the endocytic vesicle fuses with lysosomes, and the pathogen is destroyed.

Answers to . . .

Figure 40–8 *By binding to antigens on the surfaces of pathogens and linking pathogens together in a large mass, which attracts phagocytes*

Figure 40–9 *To help B cells develop into antibody-producing plasma cells*

40–2 (continued)

Use Visuals

Figure 40–10 Check students' comprehension of the flowchart by asking: **What causes a T cell to become a helper T cell?** *(Activation by a macrophage)* **What causes a killer T cell to attack the infected cell?** *(Activation by a helper T cell)*

Build Science Skills

Applying Concepts Point out that cell-mediated immunity is particularly important for diseases caused by eukaryotic pathogens. Ask: **Which pathogens are eukaryotic, and what are some of the diseases they cause?** *(Protists, fungi, and worms are eukaryotic pathogens. Some of the diseases they cause include malaria, beef tapeworm, and athlete's foot. Refer students to Figure 40–3 for other diseases caused by eukaryotic pathogens.)*

Use Visuals

Figure 40–11 Have students read the caption, which points out how much stronger and quicker the second immune response is than the first. Then, ask: **Why is a quick immune response important when you are fighting an infection?** *(The sooner that antibodies are produced, the less chance the pathogen has to multiply.)*

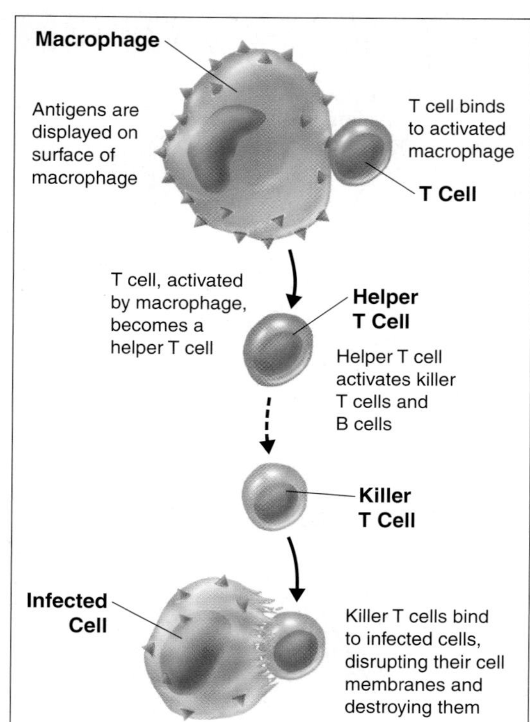

▲ **Figure 40–10** During the cell-mediated immune response, helper T cells stimulate killer T cells to divide. The killer T cells then attack the pathogen. **Comparing and Contrasting** *How are humoral immunity and cell-mediated immunity similar? How are they different?*

Cell-Mediated Immunity Sometimes immunity relies on lymphocytes, not antibodies. Helper T cells regulate the production of antibodies by B cells. However, other T cells can attack antigen-bearing cells directly. The most effective attacking cells in the immune system are killer T cells, or cytotoxic T cells. These killer cells transfer proteins into the cell membrane of a pathogen, causing fluid from inside the cell to leak out of the membrane. The rapid loss of material causes the cell to rupture and die. This immune response, called **cell-mediated immunity,** is particularly important in the case of diseases caused by eukaryotic pathogens. Cell-mediated immunity is summarized in **Figure 40–10.**

Killer T cells make it difficult to do organ transplants. Body cells have a set of marker proteins on their surfaces that allow the immune system to recognize the cells. When an organ from one person is transplanted into another person, the second person's immune system recognizes the transplanted organ as foreign, and attacks it. The immune system damages and destroys the transplanted organ. This process is known as rejection. To prevent organ rejection, doctors search for a donor whose markers are nearly identical to the markers of the recipient. Recipients must take drugs that suppress the cell-mediated immune response, usually for the rest of their lives. These drugs include cyclosporine and the steroid prednisone.

Permanent Immunity The growth of B cells and T cells in response to infection has an important consequence—one that people have been aware of for more than 2000 years. The Greek physician Hippocrates noted that people who survived certain diseases, such as measles and smallpox, never developed those diseases again. They had acquired a **permanent immunity** to the disease that had previously infected them.

Today we understand the nature of permanent immunity. **Once the body has been exposed to a pathogen, millions of memory B and T cells remain capable of producing specific antibodies to that pathogen.**

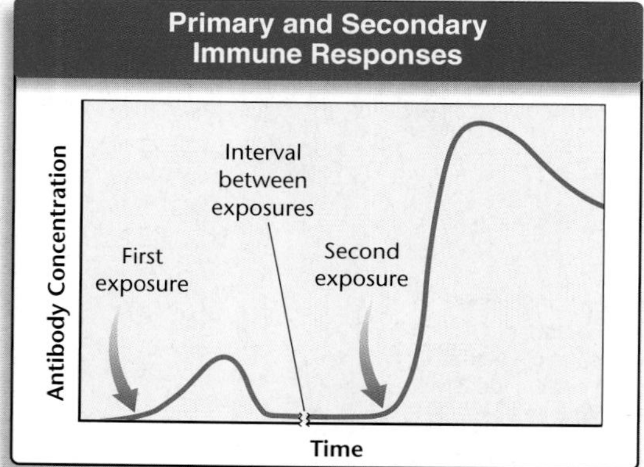

◀ **Figure 40–11** **Once the body has been exposed to a pathogen, it remains capable of producing specific antibodies to that pathogen.** Notice how much more strongly and quickly the immune system reacts to a second infection by the same pathogen.

BIO INSIGHTS — HISTORY OF SCIENCE

Cells that eat cells

A significant step in understanding the immune system came in 1883 with the work of Elie Metchnikoff. The Russian biologist was researching the cause of inflammation in animals, using starfish larvae as research subjects because they have transparent bodies that allow for clear observation of internal processes. Wondering how the organism's cells would react to a foreign body, Metchnikoff plucked a thorn from one of the roses in his rose garden and plunged it into a larva. A day later, he noticed the thorn was surrounded by a swarm of cells. Through further study, he identified similar cells in humans, specifically the white blood cells in pus. He recognized that these cells are able to digest foreign particles, and he named the cells phagocytes, from the Greek words meaning "to eat" and "cells."

Quick Lab

How does cell-mediated immunity work?

Materials 3 red balloons; 3 yellow balloons; 3 blue balloons; red, yellow, and white adhesive notes; toothpick

Procedure

1. Partially inflate and tie the balloons. The balloons represent pathogens. The different colors represent different surface antigens. Put the inflated balloons on the table.
2. The adhesive notes represent antibodies that can bind to antigens on the surface of a pathogen of the same color. Use the adhesive notes to model the binding of antibodies to antigens on pathogens.
3. The toothpick represents a killer T cell. Use the toothpick to burst any balloons marked by adhesive notes.

Analyze and Conclude

1. **Using Models** How did you model the binding of antibodies to matching antigens in step 2?
2. **Using Models** What signals a killer T cell to attack a pathogen?

These memory B cells ensure that the disease never gets a chance to develop a second time. **Figure 40–11** shows how antibody production differs between the first and second exposures.

What is cell-mediated immunity?

Active Immunity

More than 200 years ago, the English physician Edward Jenner wondered if it might be possible to produce permanent immunity against one of the deadliest diseases of the day—smallpox. Jenner knew of a mild disease called cowpox that was often contracted by milkmaids. Once they had contracted cowpox, the milkmaids were immune to smallpox. Was there a way, Jenner wondered, to deliberately infect a person with cowpox, thus protecting them from getting smallpox?

To answer this question, Jenner took fluid from one of the sores of a cowpox patient and put the fluid into a small cut that he made on the arm of a young farm boy named Jamie Phipps. As expected, Jamie developed a cowpox infection. Two months later, Jenner performed a daring experiment. He inoculated Jamie with fluid from a smallpox infection. Fortunately for Jamie, the experiment was a success—the boy did not develop smallpox. His cowpox infection had protected him from getting smallpox.

Quick Lab

Objective Students will be able to use a model to determine how cell-mediated immunity works.

Skill Focus **Using Models**

Materials 3 red balloons; 3 yellow balloons; 3 blue balloons; red, yellow, and white adhesive notes; toothpick

Time 15 minutes

Advance Prep To save time, you can inflate the balloons before class.

Strategy Ask: **What do the blue balloons and white adhesive notes represent in the model?** *(The blue balloons represent pathogens for which there are no antibodies. The white adhesive notes represent antibodies for which there are no pathogens.)*

Expected Outcome Students should break only the red and yellow balloons.

Analyze and Conclude

1. The binding of antibodies to matching antigens was modeled by attaching colored adhesive notes to balloons of the same color.
2. An antibody bound to an antigen on the surface of a pathogen signals a killer T cell to attack the pathogen.

Active Immunity

Use Community Resources

Have students contact a pediatrician's office or their local health department to obtain a schedule of recommended vaccinations from birth to adulthood. Then, have students create a poster to convey the information in an eye-catching way. If possible, arrange to have their posters displayed at a location in the community where families with young children are likely to see them, for example, at a public library or preschool.

FACTS AND FIGURES

So many flu strains, so little time

Influenza, or flu, is caused by an airborne virus. It occurs in periodic epidemics, which sometimes have a high death toll. For example, a 1968 flu epidemic killed almost 70,000 people worldwide in just six weeks. Scientists have developed fairly effective flu vaccines, but it takes at least six months to prepare a vaccine once the particular strain of flu virus is isolated. Mutations occur frequently in the flu virus, and new strains appear every couple of years, so scientists cannot predict for certain which strain of flu virus will strike in a given year. Therefore, a vaccine that is effective against this year's strain of flu virus may prove useless against next year's strain.

Answers to . . .

CHECKPOINT *Immunity in which killer T cells destroy infected cells*

Figure 40–10 *Both are specific defenses. In humoral immunity, B cells produce antibodies against the pathogen. In cell-mediated immunity, killer T cells attack infected cells.*

Passive Immunity

Build Science Skills

Inferring Ask: **Why does passive immunity last for only a few weeks or months?** *(Passive immunity occurs when antibodies are injected into the blood or ingested in milk. Because antigens are not included with the antibodies, the immune system does not "learn" how to make the antibody. Once the antibodies are destroyed, the person is no longer immune.)*

3 ASSESS

Evaluate Understanding

Have students make a concept map entitled "Defenses Against Pathogens," using the following terms: nonspecific defenses, specific defenses, humoral immunity, cell-mediated immunity, first-line defenses, and second-line defenses.

Reteach

Play a quiz game in which you read definitions of the Vocabulary terms and student contestants try to identify the terms from the definitions.

ALTERNATIVE ASSESSMENT

Students should find that medical professionals and public health officials strongly support vaccinations because they prevent epidemic outbreaks of disease and prevent deaths. However, vaccinations cause side effects in a small number of people. For this reason, some people do not think vaccinations should be mandatory. Assign several students to represent each viewpoint. Assign a moderator and a timekeeper to ensure that each side has the same amount of time to present its views.

Use iText to review the key concepts in Section 40–2.

Answer to . . .

Figure 40–12 *Vaccines stimulate production of specific antibodies.*

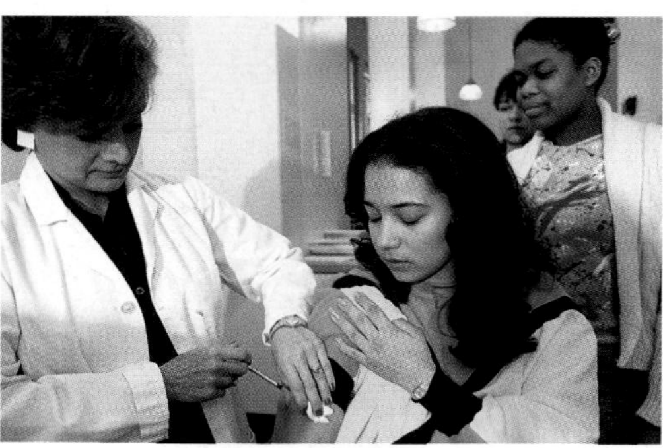

▲ **Figure 40–12** Vaccines are an important weapon in fighting disease. **Applying Concepts** *How do vaccines work?*

The injection of a weakened or mild form of a pathogen to produce immunity is known as a **vaccination.** *Vacca* is the Latin word for "cow," reflecting the history of Jenner's first vaccination experiment. The immunity produced by a vaccine is known as **active immunity** because the body of the recipient has the ability to mount an immediate active immune response against the pathogen.

Today, more than 20 serious human diseases can be prevented by vaccination. Like the vaccines developed by Jenner, modern vaccines stimulate the immune system to create millions of plasma cells ready to produce specific types of antibodies.

When you were very young, you were probably vaccinated against polio. Weakened polio viruses were used to stimulate the B cells in your body capable of making antipolio antibodies. As a result, should you ever be exposed to polio, your body is prepared to fight the virus with millions of plasma cells ready to make antipolio antibodies.

Passive Immunity

In active immunity, the body makes its own antibodies in response to an antigen. The body can also be protected from disease in another way. If antibodies produced by other animals for a pathogen are injected into the bloodstream, the antibodies produce a passive immunity against the pathogen as long as they remain in the circulation, usually for several weeks. Travelers are sometimes given antibodies against tropical diseases before they leave home. Passive immunity lasts only a short time because the body destroys the borrowed antibodies.

Another type of passive immunity is called maternal immunity. It occurs when antibodies from the mother are passed to the fetus through the placenta or to the infant in mother's milk. Maternal immunity protects a child against most infectious diseases for the first few months of its life, or longer if the infant is breast-fed.

40–2 Section Assessment

1. **Key Concept** Describe the body's nonspecific defenses against pathogens.
2. **Key Concept** Describe the process of immunity.
3. How do interferons protect the body against viruses?
4. How are antigens related to antibodies?
5. **Critical Thinking Comparing and Contrasting** How are active and passive immunity similar? How are they different?

iTEXT Assessment Use iText to review the important concepts in Section 40–2.

ALTERNATIVE ASSESSMENT

Conducting a Debate Vaccinations have benefits and risks. Collect various opinions about vaccinations. Then work with classmates to arrange a class debate that addresses both sides of the issue.

40–2 Section Assessment

1. Unbroken skin is a barrier to pathogens. If pathogens penetrate the skin, they cause an inflammatory response, which includes the release of phagocytes. Pathogens that enter through the mouth or nose are trapped in mucus, or attacked by lysozyme, digestive enzymes, and stomach acid. Viruses trigger the production of interferons.
2. The immune system reacts with a series of specific defenses that attack a pathogen.
3. Interferons inhibit the progress of viral infections, which may give specific defenses time to respond.
4. An antigen is a substance on the surface of a pathogen that triggers an immune response. Antibodies are molecules that are custom-made to bind to specific antigens.
5. They both provide antibodies against a specific pathogen. Active immunity is permanent; passive immunity is temporary.

40–3 Immune System Disorders

Although the immune system defends the body from a wide range of potential pathogens, sometimes disorders occur. There are two main types of disorders. In the first type, the immune system may overreact to an antigen, producing discomfort or even disease. In the second type, the cellular nature of the immune response is a potential weak point. What would happen if a disease attacked the lymphocytes, which are the heart of the immune system? As you will learn, the consequences can be disastrous.

Allergies

The most common overreactions of the immune system are known as allergies. **Allergies** result when antigens from allergens, such as those in **Figure 40–13,** bind to mast cells. Mast cells are a type of immune cell. They are especially common in the linings of the nasal passages.

When allergy-causing antigens attach themselves to mast cells, the activated mast cells release chemicals known as **histamines.** Histamines increase the flow of blood and fluids to the surrounding area. Histamines produce the sneezing, runny eyes and nose, and other irritations that make a person with allergies so uncomfortable. If you have allergies, you may have taken antihistamines. Antihistamines are drugs that are used to counteract the effects of histamines.

Guide for Reading

Key Concept
- What is an autoimmune disease?

Vocabulary
allergy
histamine
asthma

Reading Strategy: Using Prior Knowledge
Do you or someone you know have allergies? As you read this section, use what you learn to explain the cause and symptoms of allergies.

Figure 40–13 Many common objects including ragweed pollen, dust, and dust mites are allergens. In the SEM of the dust ball, notice the insect parts, gray spider webbing, and other dirt. Dust mites live in furniture, mattresses, and even pillows. **Inferring** *Why do you think it is recommended that people wash their sheets and bedding in hot water?*

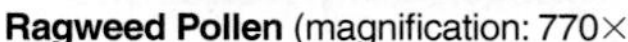

Ragweed Pollen (magnification: 770×)

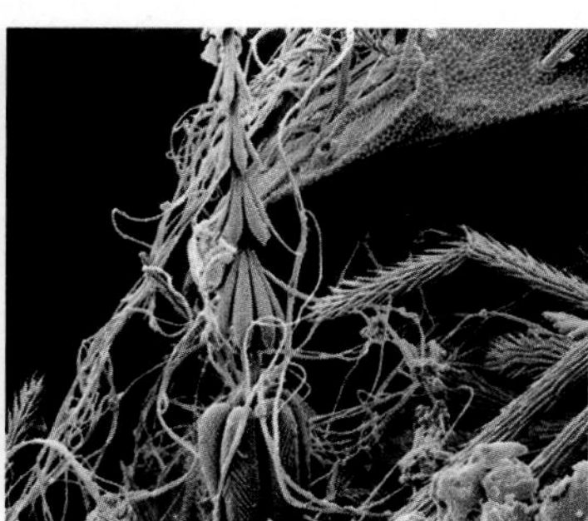

Dust Ball (magnification: 760×)

Dust Mite (magnification: 900×)

SECTION RESOURCES

Print:
- ***Teaching Resources,*** Section Review 40–3
- ***Guided Reading and Study Workbook,*** Section 40–3
- ***Issues and Decision Making,*** 40–1

Technology:
- ***iText,*** Section 40–3

Section 40–3

1 FOCUS

Objectives

40.3.1 ***State*** what happens when the immune system overreacts.
40.3.2 ***Explain*** what an autoimmune disease is.
40.3.3 ***Describe*** how HIV affects the immune system.

Guide for Reading

Vocabulary Preview

Suggest that students scan the section for the boldface Vocabulary terms and write a definition for each term based on the information in the text.

Reading Strategy

Have students read the figure captions and find the terms *allergens, autoimmune disease*, and *retrovirus.* Challenge students to define the terms based on the information in the captions.

2 INSTRUCT

Allergies

Build Science Skills

Using Tables and Graphs Have students design a simple allergy questionnaire that includes questions on whether the subject has allergies and which allergens are known or thought to be responsible. Then, have each student administer the questionnaire to at least five people, such as family members and neighbors, and summarize the results in a table that shows the number of people with allergies and the number allergic to each allergen. Assign a few students to pool the results for the whole class and use the data to create a bar graph showing the proportion of the total sample affected by the top three allergens.

Answer to . . .

Figure 40–13 *To kill dust mites that can cause allergies*

Use Community Resources

Arrange to have a nurse, physician's assistant, or other medical professional from an allergy practice or clinic visit the class. Ask the visitor to demonstrate allergy testing and to identify the allergens for which tests are most commonly performed. Encourage students to ask any questions they might have about allergies and allergy testing.

Autoimmune Disease

Meet Diverse Needs

Assign interested students to research each of the other autoimmune diseases listed in the text: juvenile-onset diabetes, myasthenia gravis, and multiple sclerosis. For each disease, students should find out the cause, number of people affected, symptoms, and treatment. Urge students to share what they learn by writing a short report on the disease. **Learning modality: verbal**

AIDS

Address Misconceptions

Point out that the terms HIV infection and AIDS are often used interchangeably. Explain that a person with an HIV infection may or may not have symptoms of the disease AIDS. In fact, an infected person may have no idea that he or she is even infected. Add that a person is diagnosed with AIDS only after the HIV infection has caused immune system damage leading to unusual infections, such as fungal infections in the mouth and rare forms of skin cancer.

▼ **Figure 40–14** **When the immune system makes a mistake and attacks the body's own cells, it produces an autoimmune disease.** Multiple sclerosis is one example of an autoimmune disease.

Allergic reactions can create a dangerous condition called **asthma** in which smooth muscle contractions reduce the size of air passageways in the lungs and make breathing very difficult. A particular antigen usually triggers an asthma attack. For people prone to asthma, the best way to avoid an attack is to avoid the antigen that produces the attack. Scientists do not fully understand the reasons why some individuals become oversensitive to certain antigens. Drugs that are inhaled or injected make it possible to provide immediate relief. These drugs relax the smooth muscles to make breathing easier.

CHECKPOINT *What happens in the lungs during an asthma attack?*

Autoimmune Disease

The immune system could not defend your body against a host of invading pathogens unless it was able to distinguish those pathogens from the cells and tissues that are part of your body. In other words, the immune system has the ability to distinguish "self" from "nonself." **When the immune system makes a mistake and attacks the body's own cells, it produces an autoimmune disease.**

Sometimes an infection can produce an autoimmune disease. This can happen when *Streptococcus* bacteria produce an infection known as strep throat. If the strep throat is left untreated, the immune system produces antibodies that destroy the bacteria. Because antigens on the surface of the bacteria are so similar to proteins on the surface of some cardiac cells, the immune system may attack the heart as well. This results in a condition known as rheumatic fever. In this disease, antibodies and killer T cells kill and scar cells of the heart lining and valves. Rheumatic fever can be prevented if the *Streptococcus* infection is promptly treated with antibiotics.

Other autoimmune diseases include juvenile-onset diabetes, myasthenia gravis, and multiple sclerosis. In juvenile-onset diabetes, an autoimmune reaction attacks the insulin-producing cells of the pancreas. In myasthenia gravis, antibodies attack neuromuscular junctions. Multiple sclerosis, or MS, is an autoimmune disease of the nervous system that results from the destruction of the myelin sheath that surrounds nerve fibers. The first symptoms of multiple sclerosis usually appear between the ages of 20 and 40. There is some evidence that suggests that this disease may be triggered by a viral infection.

AIDS

A dramatic example of what happens when cells of the immune system are weakened by infection is the disease called Acquired Immune Deficiency Syndrome, or AIDS. In the early 1980s, physicians began to see a number of unusual infections. The infections included protozoa in the lungs, severe fungal infections in the mouth and throat, and a rare form of skin cancer.

TIME SAVER

PRESENTATIONS MADE EASY!

The Presentation Assistant Plus contains the Prentice Hall Presentation Pro and the Transparencies, which provide easy-to-follow visual support for every step of this section. If you have a computer presentation station, use Prentice Hall Presentation Pro for Section 40–3, or use the transparencies listed here.

Section 40–3: **Interest Grabber**
Section Outline
Stages of HIV Infection

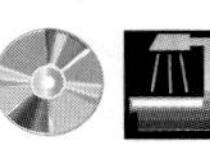

Analyzing Data

HIV Infection Among Women

Since the beginning of the AIDS epidemic, researchers at the Centers for Disease Control (CDC) in Atlanta have closely monitored the number of new AIDS cases each year. When an AIDS case is reported, investigators do their best to determine the source of the infection and report it along with the case itself. The data shown below are taken from a CDC report showing the number of new AIDS cases in adult and teenage women in the United States.

1. **Interpreting Graphics** From 1996 through 1998, did the overall number of AIDS cases among women increase, decrease, or remain the same?
2. **Drawing Conclusions** Which source of infection presents the greatest risk of AIDS for American women?
3. **Applying Concepts** If you were asked to design an educational program to decrease the risk of AIDS among women, which sources of infection would you stress? Which behaviors or activities seem to carry the greatest danger to women?
4. **Going Further** Use the library or the Internet and find the latest statistics on infections in men and adolescent boys. Analyze the differences between male and female patterns of HIV infection.

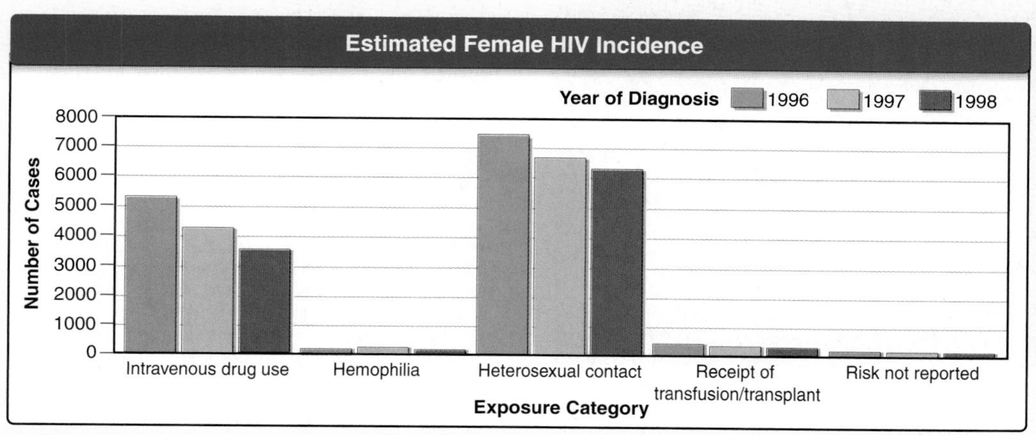

Normally, such infections are prevented by the immune system. Individual doctors realized that the symptoms were a signal that the immune systems of their patients had been weakened. However, doctors needed to see many similar cases before they were able to conclude that these weakened immune systems were characteristic of a new autoimmune disease.

The spread of the disease made scientists suspect that it was caused by a virus. In 1983, that virus—now known as HIV (human immunodeficiency virus)—was identified. Once HIV enters the body, it attaches to receptors on the surfaces of the T cells that help other lymphocytes respond to infection. The body does produce antibodies against HIV, but HIV replicates within cells of the immune system. Thus, it is less likely to bind to antibodies. Gradually, HIV kills off most of the helper T cells.

Analyzing Data

Point out that the table shows the number of new HIV infections and that AIDS may not develop for years in people who are infected with HIV. Challenge students to identify what the exposure categories in the table have in common. *(Exposure to blood or other body fluids)*

Answers

1. The overall number of AIDS cases among women decreased from 1996 through 1998.

2. Heterosexual contact presents the greatest risk of AIDS for American women.

3. Students should say they would stress heterosexual contact and intravenous drug use, because these two sources of infection carry the greatest risk for women.

4. Students should find data for males on the number of new cases of HIV infection by exposure category.

Make Connections

Health Science Explain that HIV infections can be detected with a blood test for the presence of antibodies to HIV. A positive test indicates that the antibodies are present, and a negative test indicates that the antibodies are not present. Ask: **What do you think a false negative result indicates?** *(That antibodies are present but not detected by the test)* Point out that someone who was very recently infected with HIV might have a false negative result because the immune system had not yet produced enough antibodies to be detected in the blood.

BIO INSIGHTS FACTS AND FIGURES

HIV and helper T cells

Two types of HIV virus are known: HIV–1 and HIV–2. In both types, each viral particle consists of a protein core that surrounds its RNA and several copies of the enzyme reverse transcriptase. When the virus attaches to a helper T cell, the protein core becomes wrapped in a lipid envelope derived from the T cell's plasma membrane. The virus progresses from the surface of the T cell to the cell interior. Once the virus is inside the T cell, the reverse transcriptase uses the viral RNA as a template for making DNA. This DNA is then inserted into a chromosome of the helper T cell. When the helper T cell is activated, it transcribes the HIV DNA along with portions of its own DNA, thus inadvertently producing copies of viral RNA. The viral RNA is translated into viral proteins, which assemble to form new viruses that go on to infect and destroy more helper T cells.

Answer to . . .

CHECKPOINT *Smooth muscle contractions reduce the size of the air passageways, which makes breathing difficult.*

40–3 (continued)

Use Visuals

Figure 40–15 Call students' attention to the drawing at the top of the figure. Explain that it is an abstract representation of HIV. Remind students that viruses are not complete cells. Ask students to locate the viral RNA in the drawing. Ask: **Where is the viral DNA?** *(There is none, because HIV is a retrovirus, so its genetic information is initially copied backward from RNA to DNA.)*

3 ASSESS

Evaluate Understanding

Have students write a concise, informative paragraph correctly using each of the Vocabulary terms.

Reteach

On the chalkboard or an overhead transparency, make a concept map with the following terms: immune system disorders, allergies, autoimmune diseases, and AIDS. Call on students to describe or give an example of each type of disorder listed in the concept map.

Take It to the NET

Additional autoimmune diseases students might include in their charts include Graves' disease, systemic lupus erythematosus, rheumatoid arthritis, scleroderma, and inflammatory bowel disease. For additional information, visit **www.phschool.com**

iTEXT

Use iText to review the key concepts in Section 40–3.

Answer to . . .

Figure 40–15 *White blood cell*

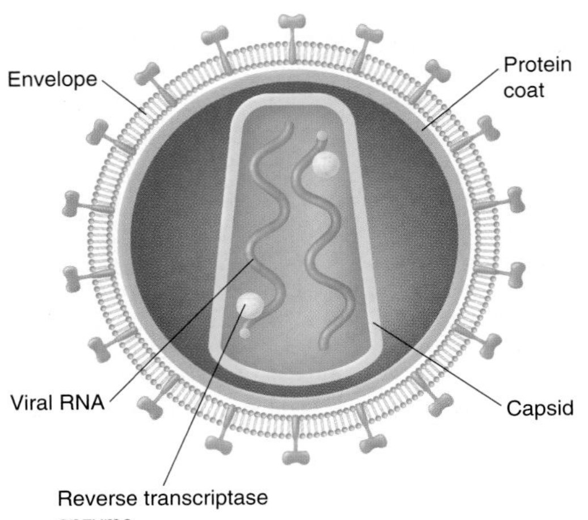

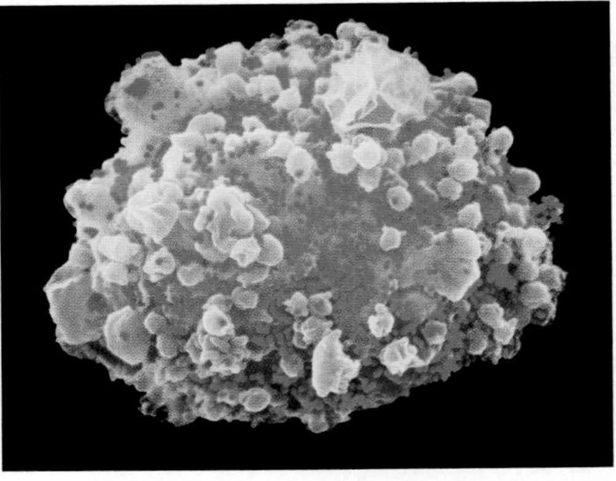

(magnification: about 5000×)

Figure 40–15 HIV is an example of a retrovirus, which contains RNA as its genetic material. Retroviruses get their name because their genetic information is first copied backward from RNA to DNA. **Interpreting Graphics** ***In the photograph, what type of blood cell are the red HIV particles attacking?***

By the year 2000, more than 350,000 Americans had died from AIDS. The death toll worldwide was more than 10 times as great. At present, there is no cure for AIDS. Some progress has been made in developing drugs that make it more difficult for HIV to infect cells and to reproduce. Fortunately, HIV does not spread easily from person to person. The way in which the virus is transmitted is now well understood.

To help slow down the spread of this deadly epidemic, people need to know how HIV is transmitted. HIV is spread only by contact with infected blood and other bodily fluids. It is not spread by casual contact. One way HIV is spread is by intravenous drug users who share needles, which is reason enough to avoid using drugs.

HIV is also spread by sexual contact. Any sexual contact carries some risk of contracting HIV. Some people may not know that they have the virus, or they may know but not tell. The safest course of conduct people can follow is to abstain from sexual contact before marriage and for both partners in a committed relationship to remain faithful. The next safest course is to use a latex condom, but even a latex condom does not provide 100 percent protection.

40–3 Section Assessment

1. **Key Concept** What happens in an autoimmune disease?
2. What are the two main types of immune system disorders?
3. What produces an allergy attack?
4. Why is it difficult for a person with HIV to fight off infections?
5. What are three ways in which HIV is spread?
6. **Critical Thinking Relating Concepts** In treating asthma, the first thing many physicians do is to ask a patient to make a list of times and places he or she has experienced asthmatic reactions. Why do you suppose doctors do this?

iTEXT Assessment Use iText to review the important concepts in Section 40–3.

Take It to the NET

Find out about three other autoimmune diseases. Then, construct a chart that contains the name of the disease, a description, symptoms, and treatments. Use the links provided in the Biology area at the Prentice Hall Web site for help in completing this activity: **www.phschool.com**

40–3 Section Assessment

1. In an autoimmune disease, the immune system attacks the body's own cells.
2. Overreaction of the immune system to an antigen and potential weakness of the immune system due to its cellular nature
3. When antigens attach to mast cells, the activated mast cells produce histamines.
4. HIV kills off most of the helper T cells, which weakens the immune system.
5. HIV is spread by the sharing of needles by intravenous drug users, sexual contact, and blood transfusions.
6. Doctors ask asthmatic patients where and when their asthmatic reactions occur in order to identify the antigens that trigger the asthma attacks.

Slowing the AIDS Epidemic

AIDS is a threat on every continent in the world, but nowhere has its effect been more devastating than in Africa. Seventy percent of the world's HIV-infected population lives in sub-Saharan Africa. Thirteen million Africans have already died of AIDS and another ten million are expected to die within the next 5 years. In some African countries, the HIV-infection rate is as high as one in three people.

Leaders from around the world disagree on how the AIDS epidemic should be handled. Some argue that anti-AIDS drugs should be distributed. Other leaders argue that the people should be given AIDS education in order to prevent future AIDS cases.

The Viewpoints

Spend Money for Treatment

Pharmaceutical companies holding patents on anti-HIV drugs should provide the drugs to those countries with high HIV-infection rates. In countries such as the United States, these drugs have dramatically cut the death rate from AIDS. In addition, these drugs have improved the lives of people living with HIV infection. If African countries had access to these drugs, the effects of this epidemic would be dramatically lessened. Therefore, money should be spent on treating those who are already HIV-infected.

Spend Money for Education

Intensive efforts to prolong the lives of HIV-infected people will only prolong the effects of the epidemic. Many people in the HIV-infected population do not have basic knowledge about AIDS, including how HIV is spread. Thus, what is really needed is an intensive program of public health and education to stop the spread of the virus. If people are educated about risk factors and modes of transmission, they will take some responsibility in the prevention of the disease. For this reason, the money should be spent on AIDS education.

You Decide

1. **Making Judgments** Given limited resources to fight HIV, how would you decide if those resources would be better spent on treatment or prevention education?
2. **Interpreting Graphics** Look at the world map showing the number of adults and children living with HIV/AIDS. What three regions have the highest number of people living with HIV/AIDS? Which three areas have the lowest?

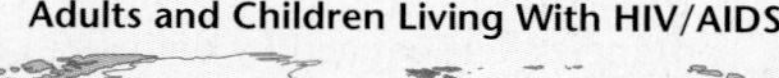

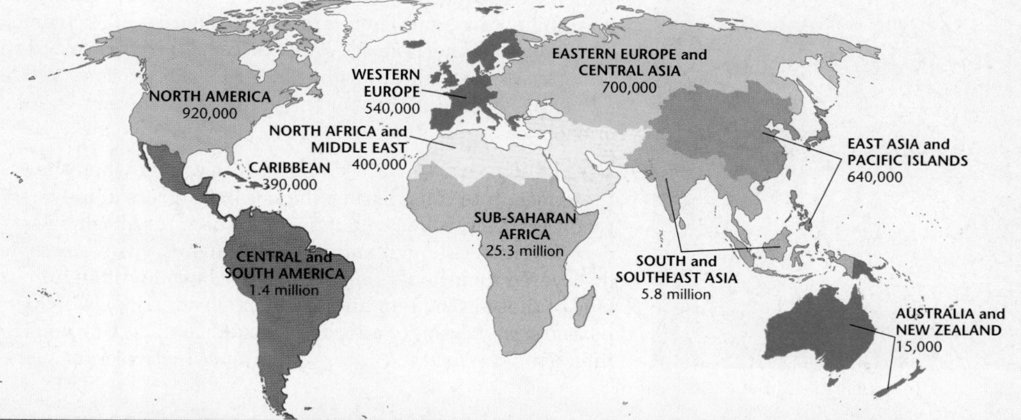

Have students role-play a conference about the issues. Assign students to play the following roles: representative of an American pharmaceutical company that manufactures anti-HIV drugs; minister of health of a sub-Saharan African country; president of the World Health Organization; and an expert consultant on AIDS prevention education. Students should research the issues and then take one of the viewpoints presented in the feature. In their role-play, students should present logical arguments, based on their research, in support of the viewpoint they have chosen.

You Decide

The issues focus on how the limited amount of money available should be spent to slow the AIDS epidemic in sub-Saharan Africa. Options include drug treatment for those infected with HIV and AIDS prevention education. Drug treatment cuts the death rate from AIDS but is unlikely to slow down the epidemic. AIDS prevention education does not reduce the death rate in the short term but should slow down the spread of HIV.

1. Students might say they would investigate to see how effective the two different options have been in other populations.

2. Sub-Saharan Africa, South and Southeast Asia, and Central and South America have the highest number. Australia and New Zealand, the Caribbean, and North Africa and the Middle East have the lowest number. Students might hypothesize that the differences in rates are due to variation in such factors as income, availability of health care, culture, or education.

BACKGROUND

Putting HIV and AIDS in context

No one knows why HIV appeared suddenly in the late 1970s, although most scientists believe it originated in Africa. It could have been a virus in monkeys that mutated and infected humans, but it has never been isolated from any animal source. In the United States and Europe, HIV has been transmitted most often among male homosexuals and intravenous drug users. In Africa, it has been transmitted almost solely among heterosexuals. Heterosexual transmission is also on the rise in Latin America. Besides education and treatment, a third way to slow the AIDS epidemic is through vaccination. Scientists have been working for years on a vaccine to prevent HIV infection, but developing a vaccine has been difficult because HIV mutates rapidly. Nonetheless, a vaccine may be available in the near future.

Section 40–4

1 FOCUS

Objectives

40.4.1 ***Identify*** the basic mechanism of cancer.

40.4.2 ***Describe*** how cancer is treated.

Guide for Reading

Vocabulary Preview

Explain that the word *tumor* comes from the Latin verb *tumere*, which means "to swell," and that a tumor is a swelling, or mass, of growing tissue.

Reading Strategy

Challenge students to predict what each of the terms means before they look for them in the section. Have visual learners preview the section by studying the figures and reading the captions.

2 INSTRUCT

A Cellular Disease

Demonstration

Point out that tumors can often be detected by physical exam or X-ray, but determining whether a tumor is cancerous usually requires a biopsy. Explain that a biopsy is the surgical removal of a few cells of a tumor so they can be examined under a microscope for evidence of cancer. Use a microprojector and show students slides of normal and cancerous cells. Alternatively, you can show students pictures of normal and cancerous cells from histology textbooks or Internet sites. Ask: **How do the normal and cancerous cells appear to differ?** *(Differences include cell size and shape.)*

40–4 Cancer

Guide for Reading

Key Concepts
- What is the basic mechanism of cancer?
- How is cancer treated?

Vocabulary
tumor
malignant
metastasis
chemotherapy

Reading Strategy: Predicting Before you read, hypothesize about how radiation can be both a cause and a treatment for cancer. As you read, list evidence that supports or rejects your hypothesis.

Cancer is a life-threatening disease in which cells multiply uncontrollably and destroy healthy tissue. Cancer is a unique disease because the cells that cause it are not foreign cells but the body's own cells. This fact has made cancer difficult to treat and to understand.

A Cellular Disease

Cancers begin when something goes wrong with the controls that normally regulate cell growth and division. A single cell or a group of cells begins to grow and divide uncontrollably, often resulting in the formation of a mass of growing tissue known as a **tumor.** Not all tumors are cancerous. Some tumors are benign, or noncancerous. A benign tumor does not spread to surrounding healthy tissue or to other parts of the body.

Cancerous tumors, on the other hand, are **malignant,** which means that they can invade and destroy surrounding healthy tissue. In some cases, cells from a malignant tumor break away and are carried by blood or lymph to other parts of the body. The spread of cancerous tumors beyond their original site is called **metastasis** (muh-TAS-tuh-sis).

As cancer cells like the one in **Figure 40–16** spread, they absorb the nutrients needed by other cells, block nerve connections, and prevent the organs they invade from functioning properly. Soon, the delicate balance of processes in the body is disrupted and a life-threatening illness results.

✓CHECKPOINT *What are benign tumors?*

▼ **Figure 40–16** **Cancers involve a breakdown in the control of cell growth.** The body recognizes cancer cells as foreign and tries to destroy them. In this color-enhanced SEM, a killer T cell (orange) is attacking a cancer cell (purple).

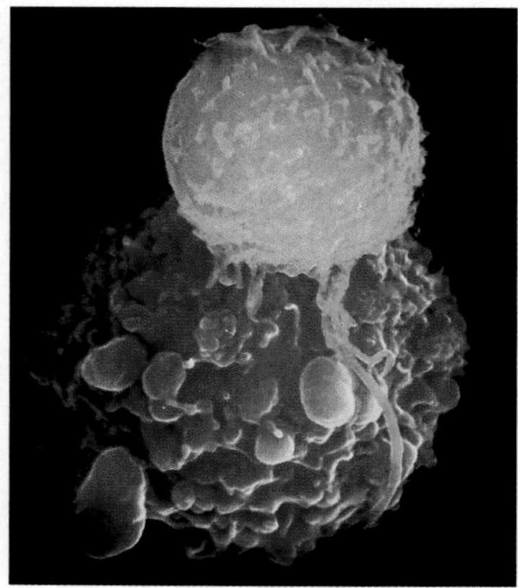

(magnification: about 3000×)

Causes of Cancer

Cancers are caused by defects in the genes that regulate cell growth and division. There are several sources of such defects: They may be inherited, they may be caused by viruses, or they may result from mutations in DNA. These mutations in DNA may occur spontaneously, or they may be produced by radiation or chemicals.

Viral Cancers Certain viruses cause cancer when the genes they inject into cells disrupt the normal process of mitosis. The result is uncontrolled cell division in the injured cell and its descendants. Although many cancer-causing viruses have been discovered in animals, only a few have been found in humans. One of these is the human papilloma virus (HPV), which is passed from person to person by sexual contact. Chronic HPV infections can lead to cancer of the reproductive organs.

SECTION RESOURCES

Print:
- ***Teaching Resources,*** Section Review 40–4, Chapter 40 Real-World Lab
- ***Guided Reading and Study Workbook,*** Section 40–4

Technology:
- ***iText,*** Section 40–4

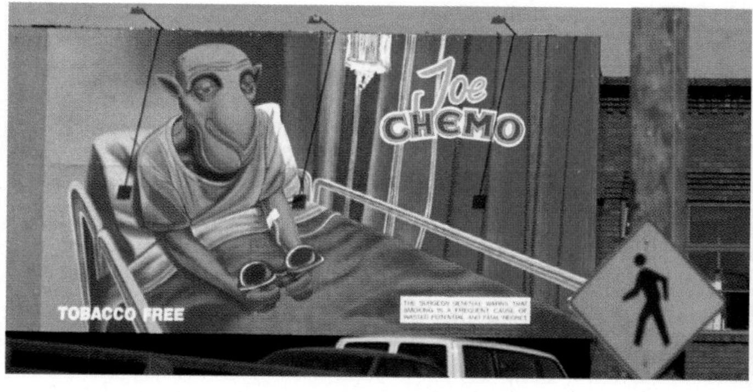

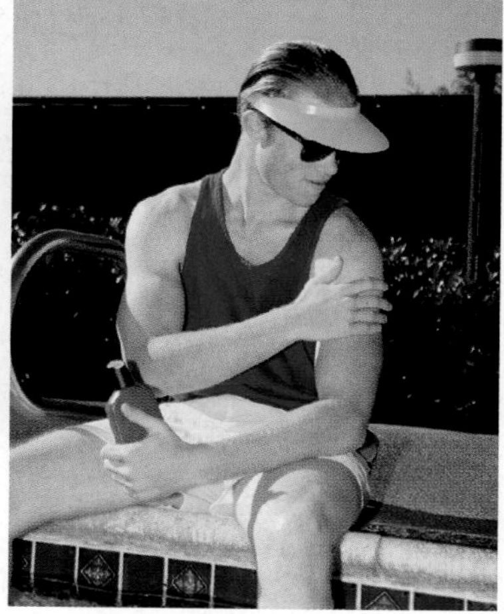

Figure 40–17 Radiation from sunlight and chemicals in tobacco smoke can lead to two of the most common forms of cancer. **Inferring** *How might applying sunscreen help reduce your risk of skin cancer?*

Radiation Most forms of radiation—including sunlight, X-rays, and nuclear radiation—can cause cancer by producing mutations in DNA. If mutations occur in genes that control cell growth, a normal cell may be transformed into a cancer cell. Most cases of skin cancer, for example, are caused by the ultraviolet radiation in sunlight. For this reason, it is important to use sunscreen and avoid prolonged exposure to the sun.

Chemicals Chemical compounds can also cause cancer, usually by triggering mutations in the DNA of normal cells. Chemical compounds that are known to cause cancer are called carcinogens. Some carcinogens are produced in nature. Others, such as chloroform and benzene, are synthetic compounds. Some of the most powerful chemical carcinogens are found in tobacco smoke. Cigarette smoking is responsible for at least 80 percent of all cases of lung cancer. Lung cancer is the most common fatal cancer in the United States.

Fighting Cancer

As with other diseases, the best way to fight cancer is to prevent it. The best way to do that is by protecting your DNA from agents that cause cancer. For example, you can dramatically reduce your risk of developing lung cancer by not smoking. In addition, regular exercise and a balanced diet with plenty of fruits and vegetables also can help to lower your cancer risk.

Physicians also stress that, if a cancer is detected early, the chances of treating it successfully may be as high as 90 percent. Regular checkups and tests are an important preventive measure. These tests depend on a person's age, gender, and family history. Self-examinations for skin, breast, or testicular cancer are also helpful when combined with regular checkups. Your doctor can give you instructions for performing these self-examinations.

Treatments for cancer fall into three general categories: surgery, radiation therapy, and drug therapy. In many cases, treatment consists of two or sometimes all three of these methods.

KEEP CURRENT WITH . . . SCIENCE NEWS®

To find out more about the topics in this chapter, go to: **www.phschool.com**

Causes of Cancer

Build Science Skills

Using Tables and Graphs Provide students with the following lung cancer death rates for the United States for 1960–1962 and 1990–1992: 40 and 74 per 100,000 for males and 6 and 32 per 100,000 for females. Have students construct a table and a bar graph to display the data. Then, have them calculate the percent increase in lung cancer death rates for males and females. *(About 85% for males and 433% for females)* Finally, ask: **Why do you think the death rate increased so much for females?** *(Students might hypothesize that more females began smoking cigarettes.)*

Fighting Cancer

Use Community Resources

Point out that being aware of the warning signs of cancer can help lead to early detection and successful treatment. Ask students to contact their local office of the American Cancer Society or a similar agency to find out the seven warning signs of cancer. *(A change in bowel or bladder habits; a sore that does not heal; any unusual bleeding or discharge; a thickening or lump in a breast or elsewhere; indigestion or difficulty swallowing; an obvious change in a wart or mole; a nagging cough or hoarseness)* Urge students to create a visual display, such as a poster, billboard, or brochure, of the seven warning signs. Provide students with an opportunity to share their work.

SCIENCE NEWS®

Encourage students to visit **www.phschool.com** for the most current information on this topic.

PRESENTATIONS MADE EASY!

The Presentation Assistant Plus contains the Prentice Hall Presentation Pro and the Transparencies, which provide easy-to-follow visual support for every step of this section. If you have a computer presentation station, use Prentice Hall Presentation Pro for Section 40–4, or use the transparencies listed here.

Section 40–4: **Interest Grabber** **Section Outline** **Concept Map**

Answers to . . .

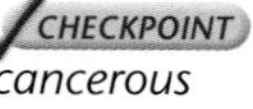 *Tumors that are noncancerous*

Figure 40–17 *Applying sunscreen protects your skin from the ultraviolet radiation in sunlight.*

Progress Against Cancer

Meet Diverse Needs

Ask students to collect articles about recent developments in cancer research. Have them arrange and mount the articles on posterboard. **Learning modality: visual**

3 ASSESS

Evaluate Understanding

Ask students to make a concept map of the causes of cancer.

Reteach

Using the chalkboard or an overhead transparency, work with students to make an outline of the section by writing the section headings and subheadings as outline topics and subtopics and calling on students to fill in important details.

MAKING CONNECTIONS

Cells would be most vulnerable to damage from radiation during the S phase of the cell cycle, when DNA is being replicated. Cancer cells would be especially vulnerable to radiation because cancer is characterized by rapid cell division.

Use iText to review the key concepts in Section 40–4.

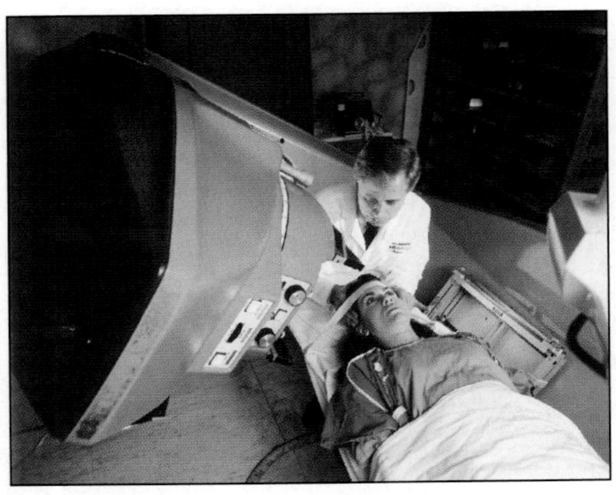

▲ **Figure 40–18** **Radiation is used to treat some cancers, as are surgery and chemotherapy.** The high-energy beam of radiation is focused on the cancer cells.

Localized cancerous tumors, or those that do not spread quickly, are often removed by surgery. If this can be done before the cancer has spread, the patient may be completely cured. **Figure 40–18** shows radiation therapy being used to attack cancer cells. Perhaps this seems confusing after you just learned that radiation is also a cause of cancer. However, controlled amounts of properly directed radiation destroy fast-growing cancer cells more quickly than normal cells, making this method a useful form of therapy.

Drug therapy, or **chemotherapy,** is the use of a combination of chemicals to destroy cancer cells. Although most anticancer drugs destroy cancer cells, many of these drugs also harm normal cells. In addition, patients undergoing chemotherapy may experience nausea, headaches, and hair loss.

Progress Against Cancer

In the last decade, genuine progress has been made in the war on cancer. In the United States since 1990, both the incidence of cancer and the rate of cancer deaths have declined steadily. Earlier detection, better treatment, and fewer people using tobacco have all been behind the decline. Researchers, however, still dream of a "magic bullet" that could destroy cancer cells the way that antibiotics kill bacteria. That day is not yet here, but there are hopeful indications that it may not be too far away. A number of researchers have found compounds that can block the growth of new blood vessels into tumors, thereby causing many tumors to shrink and disappear. Other researchers have sought ways to block the signals that cause cancer cells to grow, and still others have tried to stimulate the body's own immune system to attack cancer cells directly. We can all hope that sooner or later one of these approaches will be successful and cancer will join the list of other diseases that medical science has overcome.

40–4 Section Assessment

1. **Key Concept** Describe how cancer starts.
2. **Key Concept** What are three methods of treating cancer?
3. List some of the causes of cancer.
4. Why are regular medical checkups and self-examinations important?
5. **Critical Thinking Classifying** Is cancer an infectious disease? Explain your answer.

iTEXT Assessment Use iText to review the important concepts in Section 40–4.

MAKING CONNECTIONS

The Cell Cycle
Recall the cell cycle from Section 10–2. In which phase would cells be most vulnerable to damage from radiation? Explain your choice. What characteristic of cancer cells might make them especially vulnerable?

40–4 Section Assessment

1. Cancer starts when something goes wrong with the controls that normally regulate cell growth and reproduction, and a single cell or group of cells begins to grow and divide uncontrollably.
2. Surgery, radiation therapy, and drug therapy, or chemotherapy
3. Cancers are caused by defects in the genes that regulate cell growth and division. These defects may be inherited, caused by viruses, or result from mutations in DNA produced by radiation or chemicals.
4. Regular medical checkups and self-examinations are important for detecting cancer early so there is a better chance of treating it successfully.
5. Most cases of cancer are not infectious. However, cancer-causing viruses can be passed from person to person.

Real-World Lab

Testing the Specificity of Antibodies

Antibodies are very selective. They will bind only to specific antigens. An antibody that binds strongly to a certain protein or carbohydrate may not bind at all to another molecule that has a very similar structure. In this investigation, you will determine the specificity of an antibody.

Problem **How specific is the binding of antibodies to antigens?**

Materials

- Strep A diagnostic kits with control samples (materials for three tests)
- sterile water

Skills Predicting, Posing Questions

Procedure  

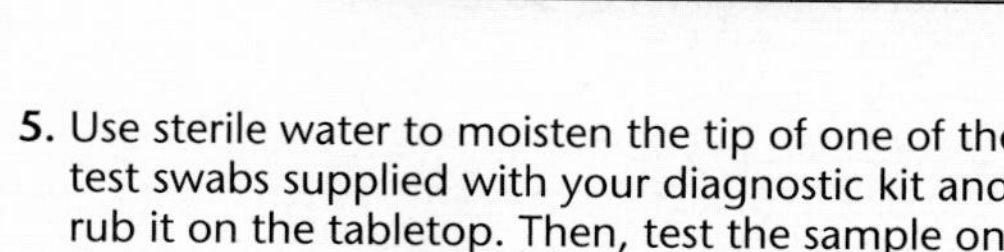

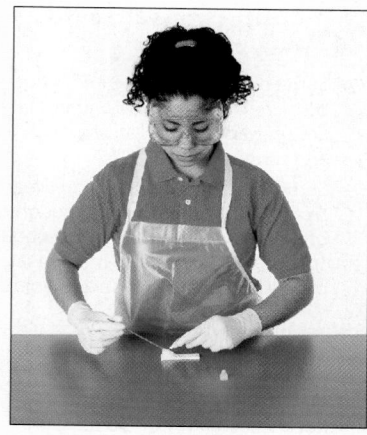

1. Make a copy of the data table shown. To see how the antibody-based Strep A diagnostic kit reacts to an antigen found in the cell wall of *Streptococcus* group A (the bacterium that causes the infection known as "strep throat"), follow the instructions in the kit to test the positive control sample. Record the result of this test.
2. **Predicting** *Streptococcus* group C is closely related to *Streptococcus* group A, but does not cause disease. Record your prediction of how the diagnostic kit will react to antigens from the cell wall of *Streptococcus* group C.
3. Test the *Streptococcus* group C sample as you did the *Streptococcus* group A sample in step 1. Record the result of this test.
4. **Predicting** Record your prediction of whether *Streptococcus* group A is present on the tabletops in your lab.
5. Use sterile water to moisten the tip of one of the test swabs supplied with your diagnostic kit and rub it on the tabletop. Then, test the sample on the swab and record your results.

Data Table

Sample	Result (positive or negative)
Streptococcus group A	
Streptococcus group C	
Tabletop swab	

Analyze and Conclude

1. **Observing** Did the antibody-based test react to the antigen of *Streptococcus* group A? To the antigen of group C?
2. **Analyzing Data** Did your results support the idea that an antibody can be used to distinguish between two similar antigens, such as those of *Streptococcus* group A and group C?
3. **Evaluating** Did the diagnostic kit detect any *Streptococcus* on the tabletop? Did your results in steps 1 through 3 support the idea that this is a reliable result? Explain your answer.
4. **Drawing Conclusions** Use what you have learned about the specificity of antibodies to explain what happens in autoimmune diseases such as rheumatic fever.

Go Further

Interviewing a Professional Interview a health professional to find out how antibody-based tests are used to determine blood types and to diagnose diseases.

Real-World Lab

Objective Students will be able to make and test predictions about the specificity of the Strep A antibody.

Skills Focus **Predicting, Posing Questions**

Time 40 minutes

Advance Prep You can obtain Strep A diagnostic kits from a pharmacy or a pharmaceutical distributor without a prescription. Before the activity, carefully read the instructions enclosed with the test kits.

Safety Students should wear disposable plastic gloves when working with the diagnostic kits. Be sure to collect and properly dispose of the gloves after the lab.

Teaching Tips Have students read the entire procedure. Then, ask: **What does it mean when a sample "tests positive" with the Strep A diagnostic kit?** *(A positive test result means that the sample is Strep A.)* **What causes the positive reaction to occur when Strep A is tested?** *(Strep A antibodies in the diagnostic kit bind with Strep A antigens in the sample.)*

Procedure

5. Students may not know that *Streptococcus* group A is not normally found on tabletops. Explain that it is more likely to be found in warm, dark, moist places like the human throat.

Go Further

Students might interview a laboratory technician or clinical nurse. Students will learn that antibody-based tests are used to help diagnose many different diseases, including AIDS, and to determine ABO and Rhesus blood types. In tests for blood types, the antibodies to the blood group antigens cause the red blood cells in the sample to clump together, or agglutinate. For example, the red blood cells in type A blood agglutinate when tested with anti-A antibodies.

Analyze and Conclude

1. The antibody-based test reacted to the antigen of *Streptococcus* group A but not to the antigen of *Streptococcus* group C.

2. Yes, the results supported the idea that an antibody can distinguish between two similar antigens.

3. It is unlikely that the diagnostic kit detected any *Streptococcus* group A on the tabletop. The ability of the diagnostic kit to distinguish between *Streptococcus* group A and *Streptococcus* group C in steps 1 through 3 supported the idea that this is a reliable result.

4. In autoimmune diseases such as rheumatic fever, the antibodies that form to fight a pathogen cannot distinguish between the pathogen's antigens and some of the body's own proteins. As a result, the antibodies attack body cells as well as the pathogen.

Chapter 40 Study Guide

Study Tip

Have students review the chapter by rereading all the boldfaced sentences. Suggest that pairs of students quiz each other on the Vocabulary terms.

Thinking Visually

1. Nonspecific defenses
2. Inflammatory response
3. Interferons
4. Cell-mediated immunity

Chapter 40 Assessment

Reviewing Content

1. a	**5.** a	**9.** b
2. c	**6.** d	**10.** c
3. b	**7.** a	
4. d	**8.** a	

Understanding Concepts

11. The germ theory of disease states that infectious diseases are caused by microorganisms. (Viruses can also cause infectious diseases.)

12. Koch's postulates can be used to identify the pathogen that causes a specific infectious disease.

13. The five types of pathogens are viruses, bacteria, fungi, worms, and protists. Refer to Figure 40–3 for examples of diseases.

14. Animals that carry disease-causing organisms from person to person.

15. The spread of disease can be stopped by such habits as hand washing and covering the mouth when coughing; by the use of pesticides to destroy vectors; and by avoidance of unprotected sexual contact.

16. Antibiotics kill bacteria by interfering with the synthesis of cell walls in fast-growing walled bacteria or by blocking the synthesis of proteins in bacterial ribosomes.

17. A fever slows down or stops the growth of many pathogens; increases heart rate so that white blood cells get to the site of an infection faster; and speeds up the activity of white blood cells and the reactions that help repair damaged tissues.

Chapter 40 Study Guide

40–1 Infectious Disease

Key Concepts

- Some diseases are inherited. Others are caused by materials in the environment. Still others are produced by organisms such as bacteria and fungi.
- Some infectious diseases are spread from one person to another through coughing, sneezing, or physical contact. Other infectious diseases are spread through contaminated water or food. Still others are spread by infected animals.

Vocabulary
- disease, p. 1029
- pathogen, p. 1029
- germ theory of disease, p. 1029
- Koch's postulates, p. 1030
- toxin, p. 1031
- vector, p. 1032
- antibiotic, p. 1033

40–2 The Immune System

Key Concepts

- Your body's most important nonspecific defense is the skin.
- The inflammatory response is a nonspecific defense reaction to tissue damage caused by injury or infection.
- Once the body has been exposed to a pathogen, millions of memory B and T cells remain capable of producing specific antibodies to that pathogen.

Vocabulary
- inflammatory response, p. 1035 • fever, p. 1035
- interferon, p. 1035 • immune response, p. 1036
- antigen, p. 1036 • humoral immunity, p. 1036
- antibody, p. 1036
- cell-mediated immunity, p. 1038
- permanent immunity, p. 1038
- vaccination, p. 1040 • active immunity, p. 1040

40–3 Immune System Disorders

Key Concept

- When the immune system makes a mistake and attacks the body's own cells, it produces an autoimmune disease.

Vocabulary
- allergy, p. 1041 • histamine, p. 1041
- asthma, p. 1042

40–4 Cancer

Key Concepts

- Cancers begin when something goes wrong with the controls that normally regulate cell growth and division.
- Treatments for cancer fall into three general categories: surgery, radiation therapy, and drug therapy.

Vocabulary
- tumor, p. 1046 • malignant, p. 1046
- metastasis, p. 1046 • chemotherapy, p. 1048

Thinking Visually

Using the information in this chapter, complete the following concept map:

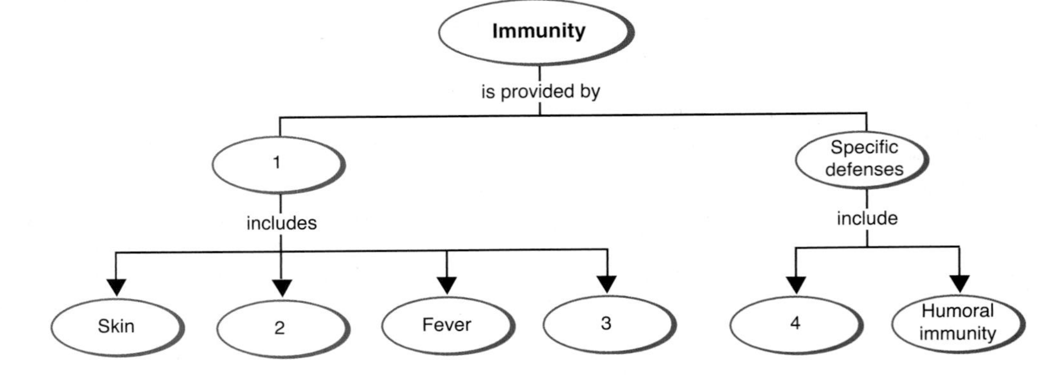

CHAPTER RESOURCES

TIME SAVER

Print:
- ***Teaching Resources,*** Chapter Vocabulary Review, Graphic Organizer
- ***Chapter Tests: Levels A and B,*** Chapter 40 Test
- ***PH Assessment System*** Practice Test

Technology:
- ***Computer Test Bank,*** Chapter 40 Test
- ***iText,*** Chapter 40 Assessment

Chapter 40 Assessment

Reviewing Content

Choose the letter that best answers the question or completes the statement.

1. Any change, other than an injury, that disrupts the normal functions of a person's body is a
 a. disease. c. toxin.
 b. pathogen. d. vector.
2. Disease-causing agents such as viruses, bacteria, and worms are known as
 a. antibodies. c. pathogens.
 b. antigens. d. toxins.
3. The germ theory of disease was established by
 a. Steere. c. Hooke.
 b. Koch. d. Salk.
4. The most important nonspecific defense against pathogens is your
 a. tears. c. saliva.
 b. mucus. d. skin.
5. A nonspecific defense reaction to tissue damage caused by injury or infection is known as the
 a. inflammatory response.
 b. active immunity.
 c. cell-mediated immunity.
 d. permanent immunity.
6. The swelling and pain associated with an inflammatory response are caused by
 a. secretion of antibodies.
 b. expansion of local blood vessels.
 c. secretion of antigens.
 d. white blood cells destroying bacteria.
7. A protein that helps other cells resist viral infection is
 a. interferon. c. prednisone.
 b. penicillin. d. histamine.
8. Label X is pointing to the
 a. antigen-binding sites. c. antibodies.
 b. antigens. d. interferons.

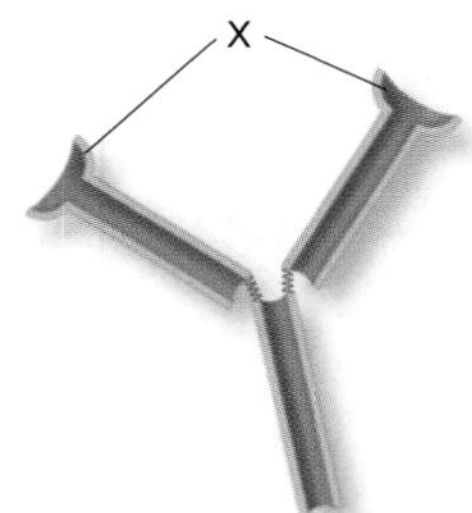

9. A substance that triggers the specific defenses of the immune system is a(an)
 a. antibody. c. B cell.
 b. antigen. d. pathogen.
10. Allergy-causing antigens attach themselves to mast cells that release chemicals known as
 a. antibodies. c. histamines.
 b. antigens. d. pathogens.

Understanding Concepts

11. What is the germ theory of disease?
12. What purpose do Koch's postulates serve?
13. List the five types of pathogens that are responsible for the spread of infectious disease. Give an example of a disease that each specific pathogen may cause.
14. What are vectors?
15. What are some ways by which the spread of disease can be stopped?
16. Describe how antibiotics work.
17. What is the function of a fever?
18. What are antibodies? Describe how they are formed.
19. Describe the roles of helper T cells and killer T cells.
20. Distinguish between humoral immunity and cell-mediated immunity.
21. How did people acquire immunity to a disease before the development of vaccines?
22. Explain why passive immunity lasts for only a short period of time.
23. Explain why allergies are not classified as autoimmune diseases.
24. How does the human body respond once HIV enters the body?
25. Distinguish between a malignant and a benign tumor.
26. Describe what is meant by the term *metastasis*.

TIME SAVER HOMEWORK GUIDE

Section:	Questions:
Section 40–1	1–3, 11–15, 27
Section 40–2	4–9, 16–22, 28, 30, 32, 33, 36
Section 40–3	10, 23, 24, 31, 34, 35
Section 40–4	25, 26, 29

Chapter 40 Assessment (continued)

18. Antibodies are proteins that help destroy pathogens. As B cells develop early in life, the genes that code for antibodies rearrange themselves in slightly different ways in each B cell. When the development of B cells is complete, the immune system contains millions of B cells, each capable of producing a slightly different antibody. When a pathogen invades the body, its antigens are recognized by a small portion of the body's B cells. These activated B cells produce plasma cells, which release antibodies into the bloodstream to attack the pathogen.

19. Helper T cells help activated B cells to develop into antibody-producing plasma cells. Killer T cells transfer proteins into the cell membrane of an infected cell, causing a rapid loss of fluid. This rapid loss of material causes the cell to rupture and die.

20. In humoral immunity, B cells secrete antibodies that bind to antigens. In cell-mediated immunity, killer T cells rupture infected cells.

21. Before vaccines, people acquired immunity to a disease by contracting the disease and surviving.

22. Passive immunity is short-lived because the body destroys the injected or ingested antibodies.

23. In an autoimmune disease, the immune system attacks the body's own cells. The allergens that cause allergies are foreign materials.

24. The body produces antibodies to HIV, but HIV replicates within cells of the immune system. Thus, HIV is less likely to bind to the antibodies. Because HIV attaches to receptors on helper T cells, the body is unable to fight infections that are normally prevented by the immune system.

25. A benign tumor is noncancerous and a malignant tumor is cancerous.

26. Metastasis is the spread of a cancerous tumor beyond its original site.

Chapter 40 Assessment

Critical Thinking

27. Students should suggest that if the same pathogen causing a disease in the original host is not isolated from the second host, there is no way to verify that the same pathogen caused illness in both host organisms.

28. Responses should reflect an understanding of vaccines and immunity.

29. As of 1995, prostate cancer has the highest survival rate, slightly higher than the rate for breast cancer. Lung cancer has the worst survival rate. Survival rates have increased due to the development of better treatments.

30. A slight fever means that the body is probably fighting an infection. The slight fever may be beneficial if it makes the body temperature too high for pathogens to survive.

31. Once HIV enters the body, it attaches to receptors on the surface of helper T cells. HIV replicates within the T cells and eventually kills the cells.

32. Benefits would include developing permanent active immunity naturally. Risks would include developing a serious, possibly deadly illness.

33. Both B cells and T cells are involved in antibody immunity. B cells are lymphocytes that produce antibodies. Helper T cells help stimulate the development of activated B cells. T cells are also involved in cell-mediated immunity. Killer T cells attack and destroy infected cells.

34. When people who are sensitive to bee venom are stung, they produce antibodies that bind to mast cells. When venom from a second sting attaches to the antibodies, the mast cells release histamines and other chemicals, which produce a systemic reaction called anaphylactic shock.

35. It could increase the number of T cells because T cells are made in the bone marrow. The new T cells could be rejected.

36. The immune system helps maintain homeostasis by protecting the body from disease-causing pathogens. Pathogens can disrupt homeostasis by releasing toxins or removing nutrients from the digestive system.

Chapter 40 Assessment

Critical Thinking

27. **Formulating Hypotheses** Why is the fourth step of Koch's postulates necessary to prove that a disease is caused by a specific pathogen?

28. **Making Judgments** The first vaccine was developed by Edward Jenner to fight smallpox. Jenner tested his immunization theory on an eight-year-old boy. Do you think Jenner was justified in using the child as an experimental test subject? Support your answer.

29. **Interpreting Graphics** The chart below shows the relative 5-year cancer survival rates in the United States. Which type of cancer has the best survival rate? The worst? Why do you think the five-year survival rates increased between the years 1974–1976, 1980–1982, and 1989–1995?

Relative 5-year Cancer Survival Rates (in %)

Site	1974–76	1980–82	1989–95
All sites	50	51	59
Brain	22	25	30
Breast (female)	75	76	85
Colon	50	55	62
Lung and bronchus	13	13	14
Leukemia	34	39	43
Prostate	67	73	92

30. **Inferring** Many people become alarmed if they have a slight fever. Why might a slight fever be considered beneficial, assuming it lasts for just a few days?

31. **Applying Concepts** The blood of a person with HIV often shows decreasing numbers of helper T cells. How do you explain this decrease?

32. **Problem Solving** Suggest some risks and benefits associated with gaining immunity to a disease by intentionally exposing yourself to it.

33. **Comparing and Contrasting** Compare the roles of B cells and T cells in the immune response.

34. **Applying Concepts** Why is a second bee sting more dangerous than the first for a person who is allergic to bee stings?

35. **Predicting** Bone marrow transplants are a method of treatment being considered for some AIDS patients. How might a bone marrow transplant benefit some AIDS patients? What might be some problems with this treatment?

36. **Making Connections** Use what you learned about homeostasis in Section 1–3 to explain how the immune system works to maintain homeostasis in the human body. Give a specific example.

Performance-Based Assessment

Oral Presentation Prepare a radio or television broadcast in which you explain how a specific infectious disease invades the body. Describe how the body's immune system responds to the infectious disease. Your broadcast must include the following:

- How the pathogen comes in contact with the body.
- A description of the first symptom of the disease and the first defense response of the body.
- A description of further symptoms and immune responses as the disease moves to different sites within the body.
- The final results of the disease conflict.
- Any long-term effects on the body from the disease.

The Internet is an excellent source of current information on cancer. Visit the Prentice Hall Web site at **www.phschool.com** to find out more about cancer prevention and awareness. Then, answer the following questions:

- What is a risk factor?
- What is the difference between prevention and early detection?
- How can you affect your risk of cancer by changing your diet?
- What are the two main steps in an environmental risk assessment?

Take It to the NET

- A risk factor is anything that increases a person's chance of developing a disease.
- Prevention stops cancer from developing; early detection finds cancer when it can be treated most effectively and with the fewest side effects.
- The risk of cancer can be reduced by a diet that includes a high proportion of plant foods and a limited amount of high-fat foods, such as meat.
- (1) Identify an environmental hazard's properties and its cancer-producing potential through clinical and epidemiological studies, and laboratory tests using animals or cells; (2) measure the hazard's concentration in the environment and the extent to which people are actually exposed to the hazard. For additional information, visit

www.phschool.com

Standardized Test Prep

Test-Taking Tip When evaluating multiple-choice answers, be sure to read all of the answer choices, even if the first answer choice seems to be the correct one. By doing so, you can make sure that the answer you chose is the best one.

Directions: Choose the letter that best answers the question or completes the statement.

1. All of the following prevent pathogens from entering the human body EXCEPT
   (A) red blood cells.
   (B) tears.
   (C) mucus.
   (D) skin.
   (E) sweat glands.
2. Which of the following is NOT a symptom of the inflammatory response?
   (A) White blood cells rush to infected tissues.
   (B) Blood vessels near the wound shrink.
   (C) Phagocytes engulf and destroy pathogens.
   (D) The wound becomes swollen.
   (E) The wound becomes red.
3. What is one effect of a fever?
   (A) It speeds up the growth of pathogens.
   (B) It decreases the heart rate.
   (C) It decreases the rate of chemical reactions.
   (D) It increases the heart rate.
   (E) It decreases the number of white blood cells.

Questions 4–8 Each of the lettered choices below refers to the following numbered statements. Select the best lettered choice. A choice may be used once, more than once, or not at all.

(A) Antibody
(B) Antigen
(C) B cells
(D) T cells
(E) Phagocytes

4. White blood cells that produce antibodies
5. White blood cells that activate plasma cells
6. Proteins that bind to surface antigens
7. White blood cells that can engulf pathogens
8. Substance that triggers an immune response

Questions 9–11

A researcher measured the concentrations of HIV and T cells in 120 HIV-infected patients over a period of 10 years. Her data are summarized in the graph.

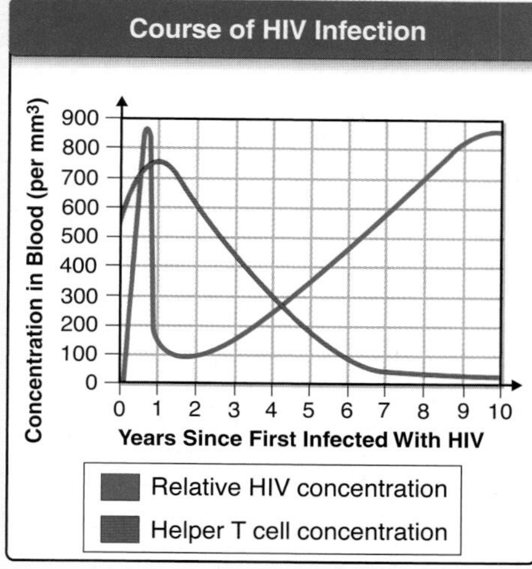

9. Why does the T cell concentration decrease after two years?
   (A) HIV dies off after two years.
   (B) HIV attacks T cells.
   (C) T cells produce toxins.
   (D) An inflammatory response occurs.
   (E) B cells increase.
10. What happened to the HIV concentration over years 2 through 9?
    (A) It stayed about the same, then suddenly increased.
    (B) It stayed about the same, then suddenly decreased.
    (C) It steadily increased.
    (D) It steadily decreased.
    (E) It constantly fluctuated.
11. What is probably responsible for the change in HIV concentration during the first year?
    (A) immune response
    (B) inflammatory response
    (C) permanent immunity
    (D) HIV vaccination
    (E) HIV stopped replicating

Standardized Test Prep

1. A	**5.** D	**9.** B
2. B	**6.** A	**10.** C
3. D	**7.** E	**11.** A
4. C	**8.** B	

Performance-Based Assessment

Students' presentations should reflect an understanding of pathogens and how the immune system responds to them.

Appendix A Science Skills

Basic Process Skills

During a biology course, you often carry out short lab activities as well as lengthier experiments. Here are some skills that you will use.

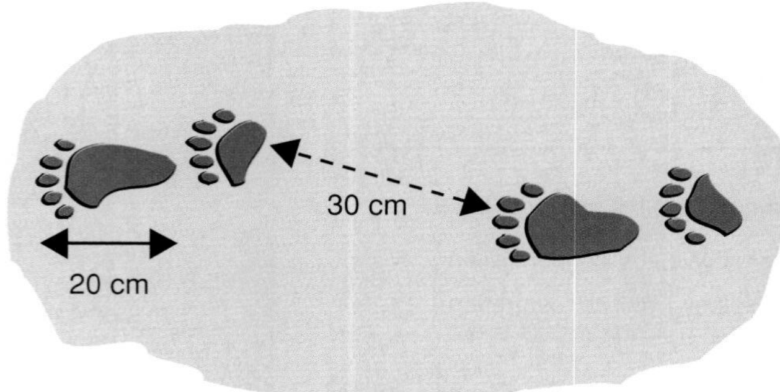

Observing

In every science activity, you make a variety of observations. Observing is using one or more of the five senses to gather information. Many observations involve the senses of sight, hearing, touch, and smell. On rare occasions in a lab—but only when explicitly directed by your teacher—you may use the sense of taste to make an observation.

Sometimes you will use tools that increase the power of your senses or make observations more precise. For example, hand lenses and microscopes enable you to see things in greater detail. Rulers, balances, and thermometers help you measure key variables. Besides expanding the senses or making observations more accurate, tools may help eliminate personal opinions or preferences.

In science, it is customary to record your observations at the time they are made, usually by writing or drawing in a notebook. You may also make records by using computers, cameras, videotapes, and other tools. As a rule, scientists keep complete accounts of their observations, often using tables to organize their observations.

Inferring

In science, as in everyday life, observations are usually followed by inferences. Inferring is interpreting an observation or statement based on prior knowledge. For example, suppose you're on a mountain hike and you see footprints in wet soil. Based on their size and shape, you might infer that a large mammal had passed by. In making that inference, you would use your knowledge about the shape of animals' feet. Someone who knew more about mammals might infer that a bear left the footprints. You can compare examples of observations and inferences in the table above.

Comparing Observations and Inferences

Sample Observations	Sample Inferences
The footprints in the soil each have five toes.	An animal made the footprints.
The larger footprints are about 20 cm long.	A bear made the footprints.
The space between each pair of footprints is about 30 cm.	The animal was walking, not running.

Notice that an inference is an act of reasoning, not a fact. An inference may be logical but not true. It is often necessary to gather further information before you can be confident that an inference is correct. For scientists, that information may come from further observations or from research done by others.

As you study biology, you may make different types of inferences. For example, you may generalize about all cases based on information about some cases: *All the plant roots I've observed grow downward, so I infer that all roots grow downward.* You may determine that one factor or event was caused by another factor or event: *The bacteria died after I applied bleach, so I infer that bleach kills bacteria.* Predictions may be another type of inference.

Predicting

People often make predictions, but their statements about the future could be either guesses or inferences. In science, a prediction is an inference about a future event based on evidence, experience, or knowledge. For example, you can say, *On the first day next month, it will be sunny.* If your statement is based on evidence of weather patterns in the area, then the prediction is scientific. If the statement was made without considering any evidence, it's just a guess.

Predictions play a major role in science because they provide a way to test ideas. If scientists understand an event or the properties of a particular object, they should be able to make accurate predictions about that event or object. Some predictions can be tested simply by making observations. At other times, carefully designed experiments are needed. You'll read more about the relationship between predictions and experiments on the next two pages.

Classifying

If you have ever heard people debate whether a tomato is a fruit or a vegetable, you've heard an argument about classification. Classifying is the process of grouping items that are alike according to some organizing idea or system. Classifying occurs in every branch of science, but it is especially important in biology because living things are so numerous and diverse.

You may have the chance to practice classifying in different ways. Sometimes you will place objects into groups using an established system. At other times, you may create a system of your own by examining a variety of objects and identifying their properties.

Classification can have different purposes. Sometimes it's done just to keep things organized, for example, to make lab supplies easy to find. More likely, though, classification helps scientists understand living things better and discover relationships among them. For example, biologists classify certain animal parts as bone or muscle and investigate how they work together. One way biologists determine how groups of vertebrates are related is to compare their bones.

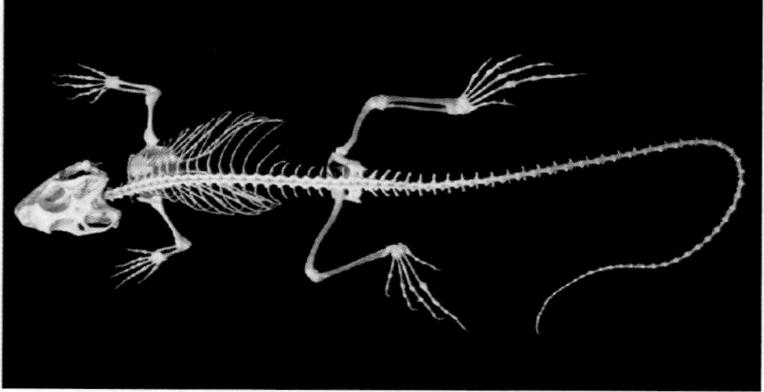

Using Models

Some cities refuse to approve any new buildings that could cast shadows on a popular park. As architects plan buildings in such locations, they use models that can show where a proposed building's shadow will fall at any time of day at any season of the year. A model is a mental or physical representation of an object, process, or event. In science, models are usually made to help people understand natural objects and processes.

Model of a Glucose Molecule

Models can be varied. Mental models, such as mathematical equations, can represent some kinds of ideas or processes. For example, the equation for the surface area of a sphere can model the surface of Earth, enabling scientists to determine its size. Physical models can be made of a huge variety of materials; they can be two-dimensional (flat) or three-dimensional (having depth). In biology, a drawing of a molecule or a cell is a typical two-dimensional model. Common three-dimensional models include a representation of a DNA molecule and a plastic skeleton of an animal.

Physical models can also be made "to scale," which means they are in proportion to the actual object. Something very large, such as an area of land being studied, can be shown at 1/100 of its actual size. A tiny organism can be shown at 100 times its size.

Conducting an Experiment

A science experiment is a procedure designed to test a prediction. Some types of experiments are fairly simple to design. Others may require ingenious problem solving.

Starting With Questions or Problems

A gardener collected seeds from a favorite plant at the end of the summer, stored them indoors for the winter, then planted them the following spring. None of the stored seeds developed into plants, yet uncollected seeds from the original plant germinated in the normal way. The gardener wondered: *Why didn't the collected seeds germinate?*

An experiment may have its beginning when someone asks a specific question or wants to solve a particular problem. Sometimes the original question leads directly to an experiment, but often researchers must restate the problem before they can design an appropriate experiment. The gardener's question about the seeds, for example, is too broad to be tested by an experiment, because there are so many possible answers. To narrow the topic, the gardener might think about related questions: *Were the seeds I collected different from the uncollected seeds? Did I try to germinate them in poor soil or with insufficient light or water? Did storing the seeds indoors ruin them in some way?*

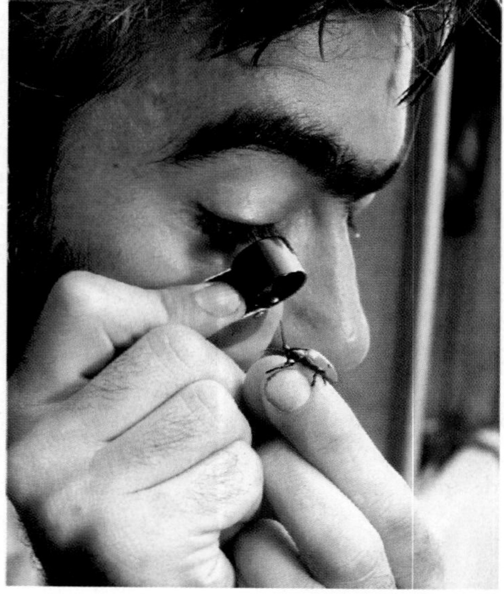

Developing a Hypothesis

In science, a question about an object or event is answered by developing a possible explanation called a **hypothesis.** The hypothesis may be developed after long thought and research, or it may come to a scientist "in a flash." How a hypothesis is formed doesn't matter; it can be useful as long as it leads to predictions that can be tested.

The gardener decided to focus on the fact that the nongerminating seeds were stored in the warm conditions of a heated house. That led the person to propose this hypothesis: *Seeds require a period of low temperatures in order to germinate.* The next step is to make a prediction based on the hypothesis, for example: *If seeds are stored indoors in cold conditions, they will germinate in the same way as seeds left outdoors during the winter.* Notice that the prediction suggests the basic idea for an experiment.

Designing an Experiment

A carefully designed experiment can test a prediction in a reliable way, ruling out other possible explanations. As scientists plan their experimental procedures, they pay particular attention to the factors that must be controlled.

The gardener decided to study three groups of seeds: (1) some that would be left outdoors throughout the winter, (2) some that would be brought indoors and kept at room temperature, and (3) some that would be brought indoors and kept cold.

Controlling Variables

As researchers design an experiment, they identify the **variables,** factors that can change. Some common variables include mass, volume, time, temperature, light, and the presence or absence of specific materials. An experiment involves three categories of variables. The factor that scientists purposely change is called the **manipulated variable.** A manipulated variable is also known as an **independent variable**. The factor that may change because of the manipulated variable and that scientists want to observe is called the **responding variable.** A responding variable is also known as a **dependent variable.** Factors that scientists purposely keep the same are called **controlled variables.** Controlling variables enables researchers to conclude that the changes in the responding variable are due exclusively to changes in the manipulated variable.

What Is a Control Group?

When you read about certain experiments, you may come across references to a control group (or "a control") and the experimental groups. All the groups in an experiment are treated exactly the same except for the manipulated variable. In the experimental group, the manipulated variable is being changed. The control group is used as a standard of comparison. It may consist of objects that are not changed in any way or objects that are being treated in the usual way. For example, in the gardener's experiment, the seeds left outdoors would be the control group, because they reveal what happens under natural conditions.

For the gardener, the manipulated variable is whether the seeds were exposed to cold conditions. The responding variable is whether or not the seeds germinate. Among the variables that must be controlled are whether the seeds remain dry during storage, the time of year the seeds are planted, the amount of water the planted seeds receive, and the type of soil used.

Forming Operational Definitions

In an experiment, it is often necessary to define one or more variables explicitly so that any researcher could measure or control the variable in exactly the same way. An **operational definition** describes how a particular variable is to be measured or how a term is to be defined. ("Operational" means "describing what to do.")

The gardener, for example, had to decide exactly what the indoor "cold" conditions of the experiment would involve. Would the seeds be kept in a refrigerator or in a freezer? Since winter temperatures often fell below freezing, the gardener decided that "cold" meant keeping the seeds in a freezer.

Interpreting Data

The observations and measurements that are made in an experiment are called **data.** Scientists usually record data in an orderly way. When an experiment is finished, the researcher analyzes the data for trends or patterns, often by doing calculations or making graphs, to determine whether the results support the hypothesis.

For example, after planting the seeds in the spring, the gardener counted the seeds that germinated and found these results: None of the seeds kept at room temperature germinated, 80 percent of the seeds kept in the freezer germinated, and 85 percent of the seeds left outdoors germinated. The overall trend was clear: The gardener's prediction was correct.

Drawing Conclusions

Based on whether the results support or refute the hypothesis, researchers make a final statement summing up the results of the experiment. That final statement is called the conclusion of the experiment. For example, the gardener's conclusion was: *Some seeds must undergo a period of freezing in order to germinate.*

Following Up an Experiment

When an experiment has been completed, one or more events often follow. Researchers may repeat the experiment to verify the results. They may publish the experiment so that others can evaluate and replicate their procedures. They may compare their conclusion with the discoveries made by other scientists. And they may raise new questions that lead to new experiments. For example, *Are the spores of fungi affected by temperature as these seeds were?*

Researching other discoveries about seeds would show that certain other plants in temperate zones require periods of freezing before they germinate. This pattern makes it less likely that the seeds will germinate before winter, so it increases the chances that the young plants will survive.

Appendix  SCIENCE SKILLS

Organizing Information

When you study or want to communicate facts and ideas, you may find it helpful to organize information visually. Here are some common graphic organizers you can use. Notice that each type of organizer is useful for specific types of information.

Concept Maps

Concept maps can help you organize a broad topic having many subtopics. A concept map begins with a main idea and shows how it can be broken down into specific topics. It makes the ideas easier to understand by presenting their relationships visually.

You construct a concept map by placing the concept words (usually nouns) in ovals and connecting the ovals with linking words. The most general concept usually is placed at the top of the map or in the center. The content of the other ovals becomes more specific as you move away from the main concept. The linking words, which describing the relationship between the linked concepts, are written on a line between two ovals. If you follow any string of concepts and linking words down through a map, they should sound approximately like a sentence.

Some concept maps may also include linking words that connect a concept in one branch to another branch. Such connections, called cross-linkages, show more complex interrelationships.

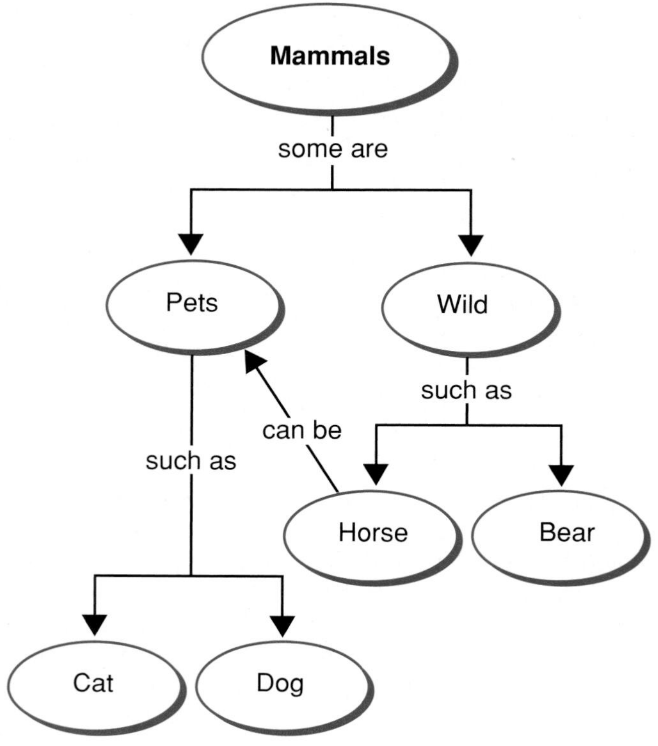

Compare-and-Contrast Tables

Compare-and-contrast tables are useful for showing the similarities and differences between two or more objects or processes. The table provides an organized framework for making comparisons based on specific characteristics.

To create a compare-and-contrast table, list the items to be compared across the top of the table. List the characteristics that will form the basis of your comparison in the column on the left. Complete the table by filling in information for each item.

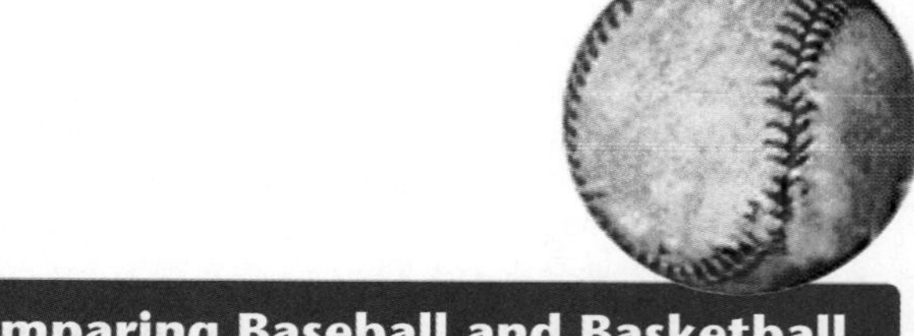

Comparing Baseball and Basketball

Characteristic	Baseball	Basketball
Number of Players	9	5
Playing Field	Baseball diamond	Basketball court
Equipment	Bat, baseball, mitts	Basket, basketball

Venn Diagrams

Another way to show similarities and differences between items is with a Venn diagram. A Venn diagram consists of two or more circles or ovals that partially overlap. Each circle or oval represents a particular object or idea. Characteristics that the objects share are written in the area of overlap. Differences or unique characteristics are written in the areas that do not overlap.

To create a Venn diagram, draw two overlapping circles or ovals. Label them with the names of the objects or the ideas they represent. Write the unique characteristics in the part of each circle or oval that does not overlap. Write the shared characteristics within the area of overlap.

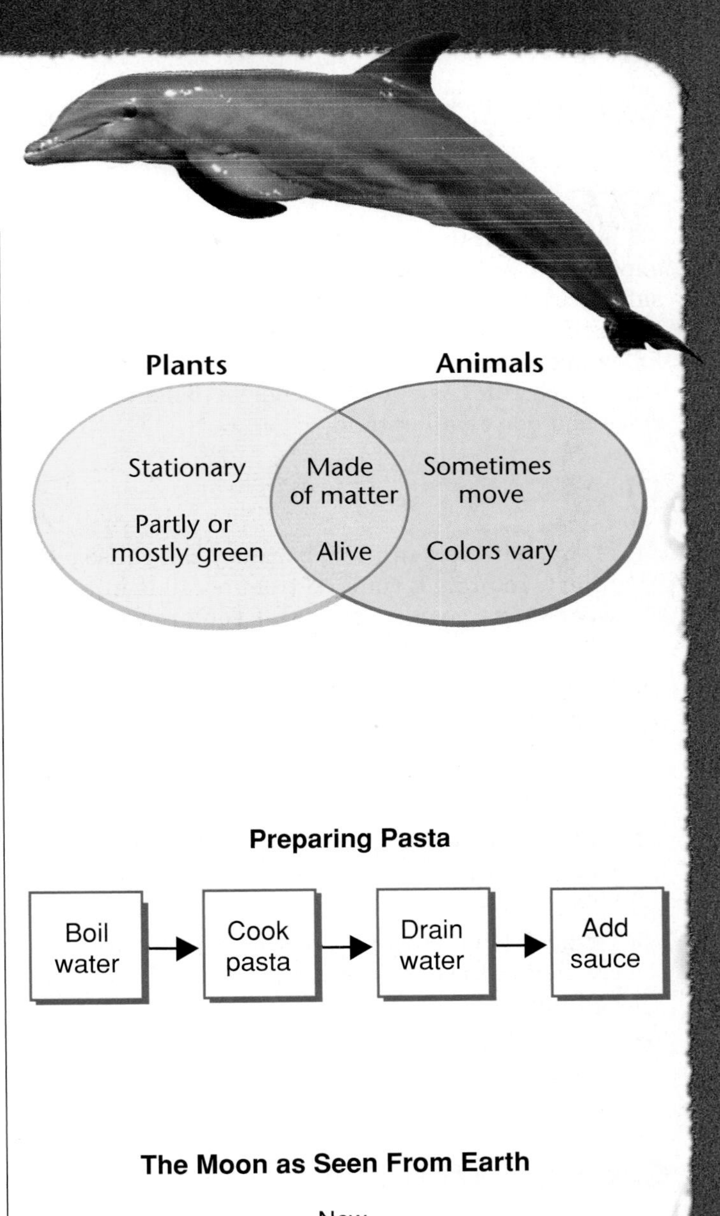

Flowcharts

A flowchart can help you represent the order in which a set of events have occurred or should occur. Flowcharts are useful for outlining the steps in a procedure or stages in a process with a definite beginning and end.

To make a flowchart, list the steps in the process you want to represent, and count the steps. Then, create the appropriate number of boxes, starting at the top of a page or on the left. Write a brief description of the first event in the first box, then fill in the other steps, box by box. Link each box to the next event in the process with an arrow. Then, add a title to the flowchart.

Cycle Diagrams

A cycle diagram shows a sequence of events that is continuous, or cyclical. A continuous sequence does not have a beginning or an end; instead, each event in the process leads to another event. The diagram shows the order of the events.

To create a cycle diagram, list the events in the process and count them. Draw one box for each event, placing the boxes around an imaginary circle. Write one of the events in a box, then draw an arrow to the next box, moving clockwise. Continue to fill in the boxes and link them with arrows until the descriptions form a continuous circle. Then, add a title.

The Moon as Seen From Earth

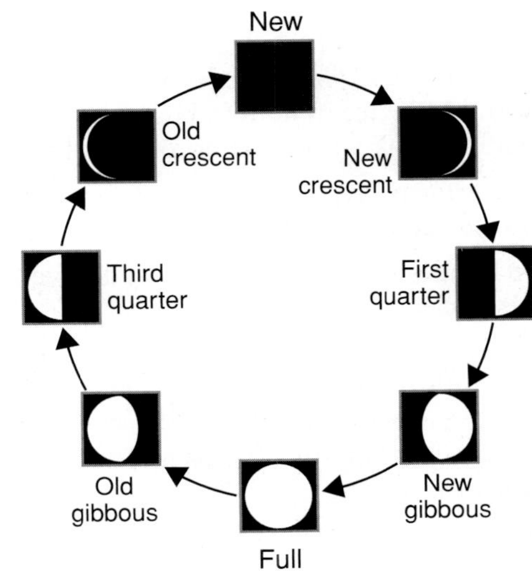

Appendix B SCIENCE SAFETY

Science Safety Rules

Working in the laboratory can be an exciting experience, but it can also be dangerous if proper safety rules are not followed at all times. To prepare yourself for a safe year in the laboratory, read the following safety rules. Make sure that you understand each rule. Ask your teacher to explain any rules you don't understand.

Dress Code

1. Many materials in the laboratory can cause eye injury. To protect yourself from possible injury, wear safety goggles whenever you are working with chemicals, burners, or any substance that might get into your eyes. Avoid wearing contact lenses in the laboratory. Tell your teacher if you need to wear contact lenses to see clearly, and ask if there are any safety precautions you should observe.
2. Wear a laboratory apron or coat whenever you are working with chemicals or heated substances.
3. Tie back long hair to keep it away from any chemicals, burners, candles, or other laboratory equipment.
4. Before working in the laboratory, remove or tie back any article of clothing or jewelry that can hang down and touch chemicals and flames.

General Safety Rules and First Aid

5. Read all directions for an experiment several times. Follow the directions exactly as they are written. If you are in doubt about any part of the experiment, ask your teacher for assistance.
6. Never perform investigations your teacher has not authorized.
7. Never handle equipment unless you have specific permission.
8. Take care not to spill any material in the laboratory. If spills occur, ask your teacher immediately about the proper cleanup procedure. Never pour chemicals or other substances into the sink or trash container.
9. Never eat, drink, or bring food into the laboratory.
10. Immediately report all accidents, no matter how minor, to your teacher.
11. Learn what to do in case of specific accidents, such as getting acid in your eyes or on your skin. (Rinse acids off your body with lots of water.)
12. Be aware of the location of the first-aid kit. Your teacher should administer any required first aid due to injury. Your teacher may send you to the school nurse or call a physician.
13. Know where and how to report an accident or fire. Find out the location of the fire extinguisher, fire alarm, and phone. Report any fires to your teacher at once.

Heating and Fire Safety

14. Never use a heat source such as a candle or burner without wearing safety goggles.
15. Never heat a chemical you are not instructed to heat. A chemical that is harmless when cool can be dangerous when heated.
16. Maintain a clean work area and keep all materials away from flames. Be sure that there are no open containers of flammable liquids in the laboratory when flames are being used.
17. Never reach across a flame.
18. Make sure you know how to light a Bunsen burner. (Your teacher will demonstrate the proper procedure for lighting a burner.) If the flame leaps out of a burner toward you, turn the gas off immediately. Do not touch the burner. It may be hot. Never leave a lighted burner unattended!
19. When you are heating a test tube or bottle, point the opening away from yourself and others. Chemicals can splash or boil out of a heated test tube.
20. Never heat a closed container. The expanding hot air, vapors, or other gases inside may blow the container apart, causing it to injure you or others.
21. Never pick up a container that has been heated without first holding the back of your hand near it. If you can feel the heat on the back of your hand, the container may be too hot to handle. Use a clamp or tongs when handling hot containers.

Using Chemicals Safely

22. Never mix chemicals for "the fun of it." You might produce a dangerous, possibly explosive substance.
23. Many chemicals are poisonous. Never touch, taste, or smell a chemical that you do not know for certain is harmless. If you are instructed to smell fumes in an experiment, gently wave your hand over the opening of the container and direct the fumes toward your nose. Do not inhale the fumes directly from the container.
24. Use only those chemicals needed in the investigation. Keep all container lids closed when a chemical is not being used. Notify your teacher whenever chemicals are spilled.
25. Dispose of all chemicals as instructed by your teacher. To avoid contamination, never return chemicals to their original containers.
26. Be extra careful when working with acids or bases. Pour such chemicals from one container to another over the sink, not over your work area.
27. When diluting an acid, pour the acid into water. Never pour water into the acid.
28. If any acids or bases get on your skin or clothing, rinse them with water. Immediately notify your teacher of any acid or base spill.

Using Glassware Safely

29. Never heat glassware that is not thoroughly dry. Use a wire screen to protect glassware from any flame.
30. Keep in mind that hot glassware will not appear hot. Never pick up glassware without first checking to see if it is hot.
31. Never use broken or chipped glassware. If glassware breaks, notify your teacher and dispose of the glassware in the proper trash container.
32. Never eat or drink from laboratory glassware. Thoroughly clean glassware before putting it away.

Using Sharp Instruments

33. Handle scalpels or razor blades with extreme care. Never cut material toward you; cut away from you.

34. Notify your teacher immediately if you cut yourself when in the laboratory.

Working With Live Organisms

35. No experiments that will cause pain, discomfort, or harm to animals should be done in the classroom or at home.
36. Your teacher will instruct you how to handle each species that is brought into the classroom. Animals should be handled only if necessary. Special handling is required if an animal is excited or frightened, pregnant, feeding, or with its young.
37. Clean your hands thoroughly after handling any organisms or materials, including animals or cages containing animals.

End-of-Experiment Rules

38. When an experiment is completed, clean up your work area and return all equipment to its proper place.
39. Wash your hands before and after every experiment.
40. Turn off all burners before leaving the laboratory. Check that the gas line leading to the burner is off as well.

Appendix B SCIENCE SAFETY

Safety Symbols

These symbols appear in laboratory activities to alert you to possible dangers and to remind you to work carefully.

Safety Goggles Always wear safety goggles to protect your eyes in any activity involving chemicals, flames or heating, or the possibility of broken glassware.

Lab Apron Wear a laboratory apron to protect your skin and clothing from injury.

Breakage Handle breakable materials such as thermometers and glassware with care. Do not touch broken glass.

Heat-Resistant Gloves Use an oven mitt or other hand protection when handling hot materials. Heating plates, hot water, and glassware can cause burns. Never touch hot objects with your bare hands.

Plastic Gloves Wear disposable plastic gloves to protect yourself from contact with chemicals or organisms that could be harmful. Keep your hands away from your face, and dispose of the gloves according to your teacher's instructions at the end of the activity.

Heating Use a clamp or tongs to hold hot objects. Do not touch hot objects with your bare hands.

Sharp Object Scissors, scalpels, pins, and knives are sharp. They can cut or puncture your skin. Always direct sharp edges and points away from yourself and others. Use sharp instruments only as directed.

Electric Shock Avoid the possibility of electric shock. Never use electrical equipment around water, or when the equipment or your hands are wet. Be sure cords are untangled and cannot trip anyone. Disconnect equipment when it is not in use.

Corrosive Chemical This symbol indicates the presence of an acid or other corrosive chemical. Avoid getting the chemical on your skin or clothing, or in your eyes. Do not inhale the vapors. Wash your hands when you are finished with the activity.

Poison Do not let any poisonous chemical get on your skin, and do not inhale its vapor. Wash your hands when you are finished with the activity.

Physical Safety This activity involves physical activity. Use caution to avoid injuring yourself or others. Follow instructions from your teacher. Alert your teacher if there is any reason that you should not participate in the activity.

Animal Safety Treat live animals with care to avoid injuring the animals or yourself. Working with animal parts or preserved animals may also require caution. Wash your hands when you are finished with the activity.

Plant Safety Handle plants only as your teacher directs. If you are allergic to any plants used in an activity, tell your teacher before the activity begins. Avoid touching poisonous plants and plants with thorns.

Flames Tie back loose hair and clothing, and put on safety goggles before working with fire. Follow instructions from your teacher about lighting and extinguishing flames.

No Flames Flammable materials may be present. Make sure there are no flames, sparks, or exposed sources of heat present.

Fumes Poisonous or unpleasant vapors may be produced. Work in a ventilated area. Avoid inhaling a vapor directly. Test an odor only when directed to do so by your teacher, using a wafting motion to direct the vapor toward your nose.

Disposal Chemicals and other materials used in the activity must be disposed of safely. Follow the instructions from your teacher.

Hand Washing Wash your hands thoroughly when finished with the activity. Use antibacterial soap and warm water. Lather both sides of your hands and between your fingers. Rinse well.

General Safety Awareness You may see this symbol when none of the symbols described earlier applies. In this case, follow the specific instructions provided. You may also see this symbol when you are asked to design your own experiment. Do not start your experiment until your teacher has approved your plan.

Appendix  THE METRIC SYSTEM

The Metric System

The metric system of measurement is used by scientists throughout the world. It is based on units of ten. Each unit is ten times larger or ten times smaller than the next unit. The most commonly used units of the metric system are given below. After you have finished reading about the metric system, try to put it to use. How tall are you in meters? What is your mass? What is your normal body temperature in degrees Celsius?

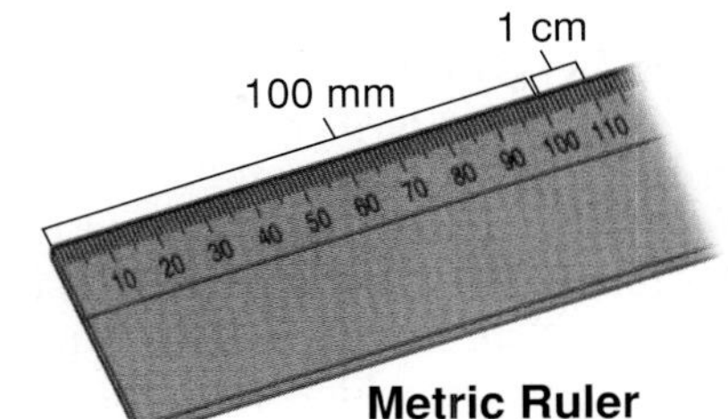

Metric Ruler

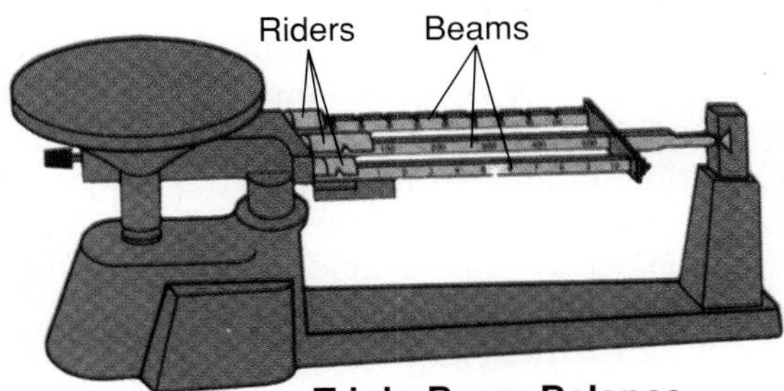

Triple-Beam Balance

Commonly Used Metric Units

Length The distance from one point to another

meter (m)	A meter is slightly longer than a yard.
	1 meter = 1000 millimeters (mm)
	1 meter = 100 centimeters (cm)
	1000 meters = 1 kilometer (km)

Volume The amount of space an object takes up

liter (L)	A liter is slightly more than a quart.
	1 liter = 1000 milliliters (mL)

Mass The amount of matter in an object

gram (g)	A paper clip has a mass equal to about one gram.
	1000 grams = 1 kilogram (kg)

Temperature The measure of hotness or coldness

degrees Celsius (°C)	0°C = freezing point of water
	100°C = boiling point of water

Metric–English Equivalents

2.54 centimeters (cm) = 1 inch (in.)
1 meter (m) = 39.37 inches (in.)
1 kilometer (km) = 0.62 miles (mi)
1 liter (L) = 1.06 quarts (qt)
236 milliliters (mL) = 1 cup (c)
1 kilogram (kg) = 2.2 pounds (lb)
28.3 grams (g) = 1 ounce (oz)
$°C = 5/9 \times (°F - 32)$

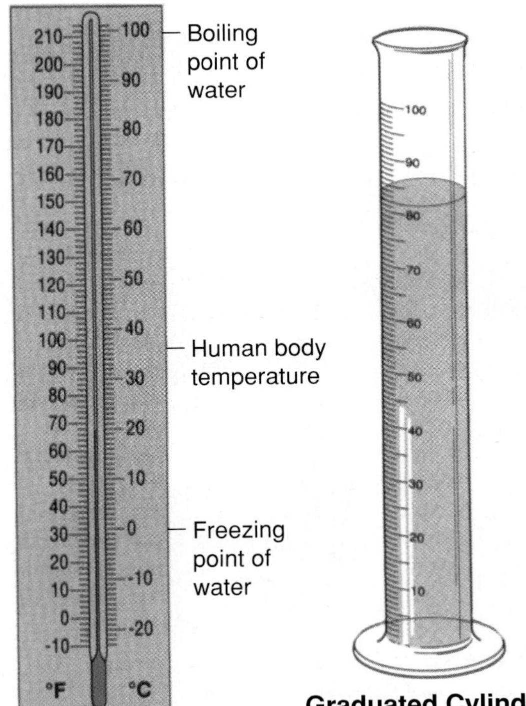

Thermometer

Graduated Cylinder

Appendix D USE OF THE MICROSCOPE

The Compound Microscope

The microscope used in most biology classes, the compound microscope, contains a combination of lenses. The eyepiece lens is located in the top portion of the microscope. This lens usually has a magnification of 10×. Other lenses, called objective lenses, are at the bottom of the body tube on the revolving nosepiece. By rotating the nosepiece, you can select the objective through which you will view your specimen.

The shortest objective is a low-power magnifier, usually 10×. The longer ones are of high power, usually up to 40× or 43×. The magnification is marked on the objective. To determine the total magnification, multiply the magnifying power of the eyepiece by the magnifying power of the objective. For example, with a 10× eyepiece and a 40× objective, the total magnification is 10 × 40 = 400×.

Learning the name, function, and location of each of the microscope's parts is necessary for proper use. Use the following procedures when working with the microscope.

1. Carry the microscope by placing one hand beneath the base and grasping the arm of the microscope with the other hand.
2. Gently place the microscope on the lab table with the arm facing you. The microscope's base should be resting evenly on the table, approximately 10 cm from the table's edge.
3. Raise the body tube by turning the coarse adjustment knob until the objective lens is about 2 cm above the opening of the stage.
4. Rotate the nosepiece so that the low-power objective (10×) is directly in line with the body tube. A click indicates that the lens is in line with the opening of the stage.
5. Look through the eyepiece and switch on the lamp or adjust the mirror so that a circle of light can be seen. This is the field of view. Moving the lever of the diaphragm permits a greater or smaller amount of light to come through the opening of the stage.
6. Place a prepared slide on the stage so that the specimen is over the center of the opening. Use the stage clips to hold the slide in place.
7. Look at the microscope from the side. Carefully turn the coarse adjustment knob to lower the body tube until the low-power objective almost touches the slide or until the body tube can no longer be moved. Do not allow the objective to touch the slide.

PARTS OF THE MICROSCOPE AND THEIR FUNCTION

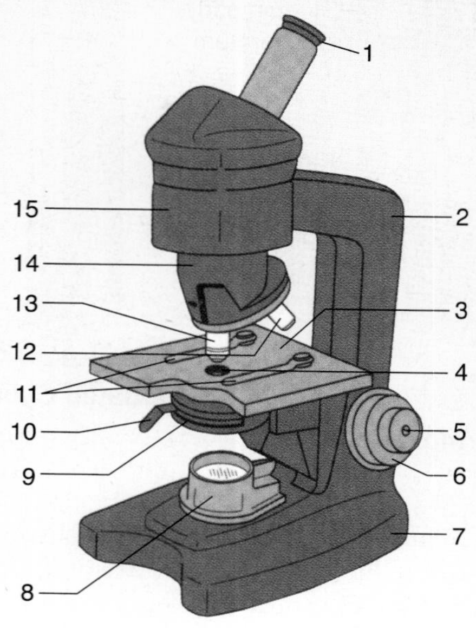

1. **Eyepiece** Contains a magnifying lens
2. **Arm** Supports the body tube
3. **Stage** Supports the slide being observed
4. **Opening of the stage** Permits light to pass up to the eyepiece
5. **Fine adjustment knob** Moves the body tube slightly to sharpen the image
6. **Coarse adjustment knob** Moves the body tube to focus the image
7. **Base** Supports the microscope
8. **Illuminator** Produces light or reflects light up toward the eyepiece
9. **Diaphragm** Regulates the amount of light passing up toward the eyepiece
10. **Diaphragm lever** Opens and closes the diaphragm
11. **Stage clips** Hold the slide in place
12. **Low-power objective** Provides a magnification of 10× and is the shortest objective
13. **High-power objective** Provides a magnification of 40× and is the longest objective
14. **Nosepiece** Holds the objectives and can be rotated to change the magnification
15. **Body tube** Maintains the proper distance between the eyepiece and the objectives

8. Look through the eyepiece and observe the specimen. If the field of view is out of focus, use the coarse adjustment knob to raise the body tube while looking through the eyepiece. **CAUTION:** *To prevent damage to the slide and the objective, do not lower the body tube using the coarse adjustment while looking through the eyepiece.* Focus the image as best you can with the coarse adjustment knob. Then use the fine adjustment knob to focus the image more sharply. Keep both eyes open when viewing a specimen. This helps prevent eyestrain.
9. Adjust the lever of the diaphragm to allow the right amount of light to enter.
10. To change the magnification, rotate the nosepiece until the desired objective is in line with the body tube and clicks into place.
11. Look through the eyepiece and use the fine adjustment knob to bring the image into focus.
12. After every use, remove the slide. Return the low-power objective into place in line with the body tube. Clean the stage of the microscope and the lenses with lens paper. Do not use other types of paper to clean the lenses; they may scratch the lenses.

Preparing a Wet-Mount Slide

1. Obtain a clean microscope slide and a coverslip. A coverslip is very thin, permitting the objective lens to be lowered very close to the specimen.
2. Place the specimen in the middle of the microscope slide. The specimen must be thin enough for light to pass through it.

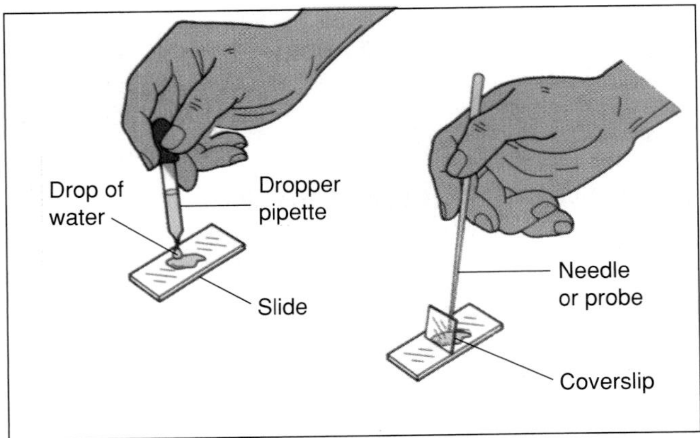

3. Using a dropper pipette, place a drop of water on the specimen.
4. Lower one edge of the coverslip so that it touches the side of the drop of water at about a 45° angle. The water will spread evenly along the edge of the coverslip. Using a dissecting needle or probe, slowly lower the coverslip over the specimen and water as shown in the drawing. Try not to trap any air bubbles under the coverslip. If air bubbles are present, gently tap the surface of the coverslip over the air bubble with a pencil eraser.
5. Remove any excess water at the edge of the coverslip with a paper towel. If the specimen begins to dry out, add a drop of water at the edge of the coverslip.

Staining Techniques

1. Obtain a clean microscope slide and coverslip.
2. Place the specimen in the middle of the microscope slide.
3. Using a dropper pipette, place a drop of water on the specimen. Place the coverslip so that its edge touches the drop of water at a 45° angle. After the water spreads along the edge of the coverslip, use a dissecting needle or probe to lower the coverslip over the specimen.

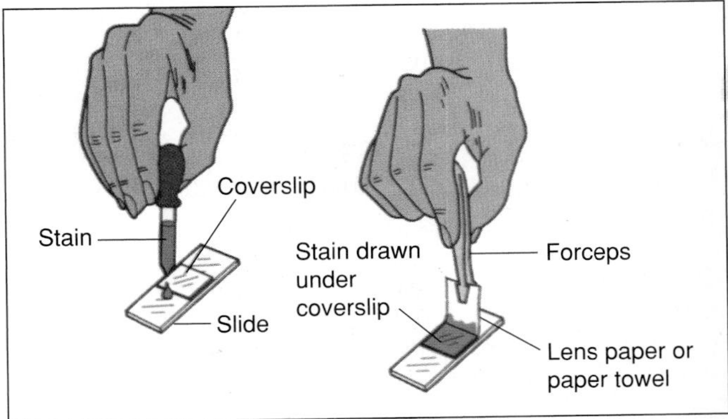

4. Add a drop of stain at the edge of the coverslip. Using forceps, touch a small piece of lens paper or paper towel to the opposite edge of the coverslip, as shown in the drawing. The paper causes the stain to be drawn under the coverslip and to stain the cells in the specimen.

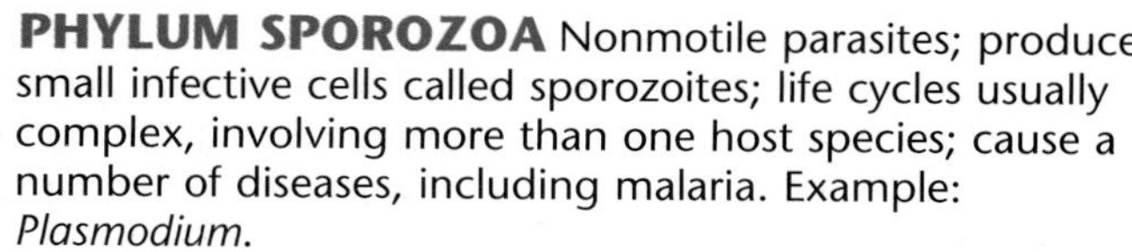

Appendix E Classification

DOMAIN ARCHAEA
Kingdom Archaebacteria

Single-celled prokaryotic organisms that lack peptidoglycan cell walls and have distinctive ribosomal RNA sequences.

The Archaebacteria include methanogens (organisms that produce methane gas, such as *Methanobacterium*), salt-loving bacteria (*Halococcus*), and thermoacidophilic bacteria (*Thermoplasma*), which grow in extremely high temperatures.

DOMAIN BACTERIA
Kingdom Eubacteria

Single-celled prokaryotic organisms; most have peptidoglycan cell walls. Sometimes form colonies of clumps or filaments.

The Eubacteria include the blue-green bacteria (cyanobacteria such as *Anabaena*), chemoautotrophs (*Nitrobacter*), spirochetes (*Treponema*), prochlorobacteria (*Prochloron*), spore-forming bacteria (*Bacillus*), and obligate internal parasites, such as the rickettsiae (*Rickettsia*).

DOMAIN EUKARYA
Kingdom Protista

Eukaryotic; usually unicellular; some multicellular or colonial; heterotrophic or autotrophic organisms.

ANIMALLIKE PROTISTS
Unicellular; heterotrophic; usually motile; also known as protozoa.

PHYLUM CILIOPHORA (ciliates) All have cilia at some point in development; almost all use cilia to move; characterized by two types of nuclei: macronuclei and micronuclei; most have a sexual process known as conjugation. Examples: *Paramecium, Didinium, Stentor.*

PHYLUM ZOOMASTIGINA (zooflagellates) Possess one or more flagella (some have thousands). Examples: *Trichomonas, Trichonympha.*

PHYLUM SPOROZOA Nonmotile parasites; produce small infective cells called sporozoites; life cycles usually complex, involving more than one host species; cause a number of diseases, including malaria. Example: *Plasmodium.*

PHYLUM SARCODINA Sarcodines use pseudopods for feeding and movement; some produce elaborate shells that contain silica or calcium carbonate; most free-living; a few parasitic; some involved in formation of sedimentary rock. Examples: *Amoeba*, foraminiferans.

PLANTLIKE PROTISTS
Mostly unicellular photosynthetic autotrophs that have characteristics similar to those of plants. A few species are multicellular or heterotrophic.

PHYLUM EUGLENOPHYTA (euglenophytes) Primarily photosynthetic; most live in fresh water; possess two unequal flagella; lack cell walls. Example: *Euglena.*

PHYLUM PYRROPHYTA (dinoflagellates) Two flagella; most live in salt water, are photosynthetic, and have rigid cell walls that contain cellulose; some are luminescent; many are symbiotic. Examples: *Gonyaulux, Noctilucans scintillans.*

PHYLUM CHRYSOPHYTA (chrysophytes) Mostly photosynthetic; aquatic; mostly unicellular; contain yellow-brown pigments. Example: *Thallasiosira.*

PHYLUM BACILLARIOPHYTA (diatoms) Photosynthetic; live in fresh and salt water; have unique glasslike cell walls; among the most abundant organisms on Earth. Example: *Navicula.*

PHYLUM CHLOROPHYTA (green algae) Live in fresh water and salt water; unicellular or multicellular; chlorophylls and accessory pigments similar to those in vascular plants; food stored as starch. Examples: *Ulva, Chlamydomonas, Spirogyra.*

PHYLUM PHAEOPHYTA (brown algae) Live almost entirely in salt water; multicellular; contain brown pigment fucoxanthin. Examples: *Fucus* (rockweed), kelp, *Sargassum.*

PHYLUM RHODOPHYTA (red algae) Live almost entirely in salt water; multicellular; contain red pigment phycobilins. Examples: *Chondrus* (Irish moss), coralline algae.

FUNGUSLIKE PROTISTS
Heterotrophs that have some characteristics similar to those of fungi, though they have centrioles and lack cell walls of chitin.

PHYLUM ACRASIOMYCOTA (cellular slime molds) Spores develop into independent free-living amoeba-like cells that may come together to form a multicellular structure; this structure forms a fruiting body that produces spores. Example: *Dictyostelium*.

PHYLUM MYXOMYCOTA (acellular slime molds) Spores develop into haploid cells that can switch between flagellated and amoeba-like forms; these haploid cells fuse to form a zygote that grows into a plasmodium, which ultimately forms spore-producing fruiting bodies. Example: *Physarum*.

PHYLUM OOMYCOTA (water molds) Unicellular or multicellular; mostly aquatic; cell walls contain cellulose. Example: *Phytophthora infestans*.

Kingdom Fungi

Eukaryotic; heterotrophic; unicellular or multicellular; cell walls typically contain chitin; mostly decomposers; some parasites; some commensal or mutualistic symbionts; asexual reproduction by spore formation, budding, or fragmentation; sexual reproduction involving mating types; classified according to structure and method of reproduction.

PHYLUM ZYGOMYCOTA (common molds) Cell walls of chitin; hyphae generally lack cross walls; sexual reproduction by conjugation produces diploid zygospores; asexual reproduction produces haploid spores; most parasites; some decomposers. Example: *Rhizopus stolonifer* (black bread mold).

PHYLUM ASCOMYCOTA (sac fungi) Cell walls of chitin; hyphae have perforated cross walls; most multicellular; yeasts unicellular; sexual reproduction produces ascospores; asexual reproduction by spore formation or budding; some cause plant diseases such as chestnut blight and Dutch elm disease. Examples: *Neurospora* (red bread mold), baker's yeast, morels, truffles.

PHYLUM BASIDIOMYCOTA (club fungi) Cell walls of chitin; hyphae have cross walls; sexual reproduction involves basidiospores, which are borne on club-shaped basidia; asexual reproduction by spore formation. Examples: mushrooms, puffballs, shelf fungi, rusts.

PHYLUM DEUTEROMYCOTA (imperfect fungi) Cell walls of chitin; sexual reproduction never observed; members resemble ascomycetes, basidiomycetes, or zygomycetes. Example: *Penicillium*.

Kingdom Plantae

Eukaryotic; multicellular and nonmotile; photosynthetic autotrophs; possess chlorophylls *a* and *b* and other pigments in organelles called chloroplasts; cell walls contain cellulose; food stored as starch; reproduce sexually; alternate haploid (gametophyte) and diploid (sporophyte) generations.

PHYLUM BRYOPHYTA (mosses) Generally small; multicellular plants; live on land in moist habitats; lack vascular tissue; lack true roots, leaves, and stems; gametophyte dominant; water required for reproduction.

PHYLUM HEPATICOPHYTA (liverworts) Generally small, flat, lobe-shaped; multicellular plants; live on land in moist habitats; lack vascular tissue and true roots, leaves, and stems; gametophyte dominant; water required for reproduction.

PHYLUM ANTHCEROPHYTA (hornworts) Generally small; multicellular plants; live on land in moist habitats; lack vascular tissue and true roots, leaves, and stems; gametophyte dominant; named for horn-shaped sporophyte; water required for reproduction.

PHYLUM LYCOPHYTA (club mosses) Primitive vascular plants; usually small; sporophyte dominant; possess roots, stems, and leaves; water required for reproduction. Examples: club moss, quillwort.

PHYLUM ARTHROPHYTA (horsetails) Primitive vascular plants; stems comprise most of mature plants and contain silica; produce only one kind of spore; motile sperm must swim in water. Only one living genus. Example: *Equisetum*.

PHYLUM PTEROPHYTA (ferns) Vascular plants well-adapted to live in predominantly damp or seasonally wet environments; sporophyte dominant and well adapted to terrestrial life; gametophyte inconspicuous; reproduction still dependent on water for free-swimming gametes. Examples: cinnamon fern, Boston fern, tree fern, maidenhair fern.

Appendix  Classification

PHYLUM CYCADOPHYTA (cycads) Evergreen, slow-growing, tropical and subtropical shrubs; many resemble small palm trees; palmlike or fernlike compound leaves; sexes are separate—individuals have either male pollen-producing cones or female seed-producing cones.

PHYLUM GINKGOPHYTA (ginkgoes) Deciduous trees with fan-shaped leaves; sexes separate; outer skin of ovule develops into a fleshy, fruitlike covering. Only one living species: *Ginkgo biloba* (ginkgo).

PHYLUM GNETOPHYTA (gnetophytes) Few species; mostly desert-living. Examples: *Welwitschia*, Mormon tea (*Ephedra*).

PHYLUM CONIFEROPHYTA (conifers) Seeds born on cones; predominantly wind-pollinated; most are evergreen; most are temperate and subarctic shrubs and trees; many have needlelike leaves; in most species, sexes are not separate. Examples: pine, spruce, cedar, cypress, yew, fir, larch, sequoia.

PHYLUM ANTHOPHYTA (angiosperms: flowering plants) Seeds develop enclosed within ovaries; leaves modified into flowers; flowers pollinated by wind or by animals, including insects, birds, and bats; occur in many different forms; found in most land and freshwater habitats; a few species found in shallow saltwater and estuarine areas.

CLASS MONOCOTYLEDONAE (monocots) Embryo with a single cotyledon; leaves with predominantly parallel venation; flower parts in multiples of three; vascular bundles scattered throughout stem. Examples: lily, corn, grasses, iris, palm, tulip.

CLASS DICOTYLEDONAE (dicots) Embryo with two cotyledons; leaves with venation in netlike patterns; flower parts in multiples of fours or fives; vascular bundles arranged in rings in stem. Examples: rose, maple, oak, daisy, apple.

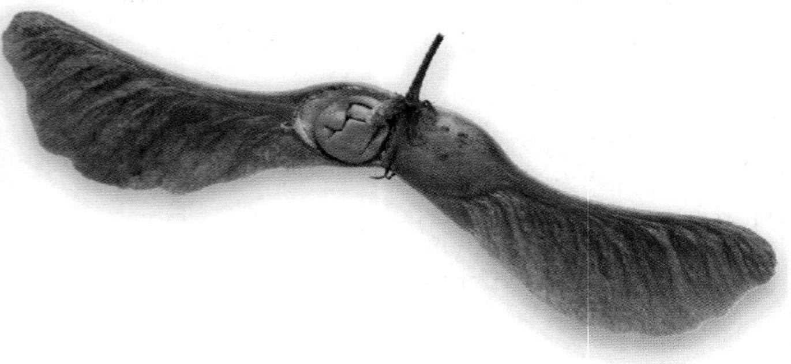

Kingdom Animalia

Multicellular; eukaryotic; typical heterotrophs that ingest their food; lack cell walls; in most phyla, cells are organized into tissues that make up organs; most reproduce sexually; development involves formation of a hollow ball of cells called a blastula.

PHYLUM PORIFERA (sponges) Aquatic; lack true tissues and organs; motile larvae and sessile adults; filter feeders; internal skeleton made up of spongin and/or spicules of calcium carbonate or silica. Examples: Venus' flower basket, bath sponge, tube sponge.

PHYLUM CNIDARIA (cnidarians) Previously known as coelenterates; aquatic; mostly carnivorous; two layers of true tissues; radial symmetry; tentacles bear stinging nematocysts; many alternate between polyp and medusa body forms; gastrovascular cavity.

CLASS HYDROZOA Spend most of their time as polyps; colonial or solitary; life cycle typically includes a medusa generation that reproduces sexually and a polyp generation that reproduces asexually. Examples: hydra, Portuguese man-of-war.

CLASS SCYPHOZOA Spend most of their time as medusas; some species bypass polyp stage. Examples: lion's mane jellyfish, moon jelly, sea wasp.

CLASS ANTHOZOA Colonial or solitary polyps; no medusa stage. Examples: reef coral, sea anemone, sea pen, sea fan.

PHYLUM PLATYHELMINTHES (flatworms) Three layers of tissues (endoderm, mesoderm, ectoderm); bilateral symmetry; some cephalization; acoelomate; free-living or parasitic.

CLASS TURBELLARIA (turbellarians) Free-living carnivores and scavengers; live in fresh water, in salt water, or on land; move with cilia. Example: planarians.

CLASS TREMATODA (flukes) Parasites; life cycle typically involves more than one host. Examples: *Schistosoma*, liver fluke.

CLASS CESTODA (tapeworms) Internal parasites; lack digestive tract; body composed of many repeating sections (proglottids). Example: tapeworms.

PHYLUM NEMATODA (roundworms) Digestive system has two openings—a mouth and an anus; pseudocoelomates. Examples: *Ascaris lumbricoides*, hookworms, *Trichinella*.

PHYLUM ANNELIDA (segmented worms) Body composed of segments separated by internal partitions; digestive system has two openings; coelomate; closed circulatory system.

CLASS POLYCHAETA (polychaetes) Live in salt water; pair of bristly, fleshy appendages on each segment; some live in tubes. Examples: sandworm, fanworm, feather-duster worm.

CLASS OLIGOCHAETA (oligochaetes) Lack appendages; few bristles; terrestrial or fresh water. Examples: *Tubifex*, earthworm.

CLASS HIRUDINEA (leeches) Lack appendages; carnivores or blood-sucking external parasites; most live in fresh water. Example: medicinal leech (*Hirudo medicinalis*).

PHYLUM MOLLUSCA (mollusks) Soft-bodied; often possess a hard, calcified shell secreted by a mantle; muscular foot; digestive system with two openings; coelomates.

CLASS BIVALVIA (bivalves) Two-part hinged shell; wedge-shaped foot; typically sessile as adults; primarily aquatic; some burrow in mud or sand. Examples: clam, oyster, scallop, mussel.

CLASS GASTROPODA (gastropods) Use broad, muscular foot in movement; most have spiral, chambered shell; some lack shell; distinct head; some terrestrial, others aquatic; many are cross-fertilizing hermaphrodites. Examples: snail, slug, nudibranch, sea hare, sea butterfly.

CLASS CEPHALOPODA (cephalopods) Foot is divided into tentacles; live in salt water; closed circulatory system. Examples: octopus, squid, nautilus, cuttlefish.

PHYLUM ARTHROPODA (arthropods) Exoskeleton of chitin; jointed appendages; segmented body; many undergo metamorphosis during development; open circulatory system; largest animal phylum.

Subphylum Trilobita (trilobites) Two furrows running from head to tail divide body into three lobes; one pair of unspecialized appendages on each body segment; each appendage divided into two branches—a gill and a walking leg; all extinct.

Subphylum Chelicerata (chelicerates) First pair of appendages specialized as feeding structures called chelicerae; body composed of two parts—cephalothorax and abdomen; lack antennae; most terrestrial. Examples: horseshoe crab, tick, mite, spider, scorpion.

Subphylum Crustacea (crustaceans) Most aquatic; most live in salt water; two pairs of antennae; mouthparts called mandibles; appendages consist of two branches; many have a carapace that covers part or all of the body. Examples: crab, crayfish, pill bug, water flea, barnacle.

Subphylum Uniramia Almost all terrestrial; one pair of antennae; mandibles; unbranched appendages.

CLASS CHILOPODA (centipedes) Long body consisting of many segments; one pair of legs per segment; poison claws for feeding; carnivorous.

CLASS DIPLOPODA (millipedes) Long body consisting of many segments; two pairs of legs per segment; mostly herbivorous.

CLASS INSECTA (insects) Body divided into three parts—head, thorax, and abdomen; three pairs of legs and usually one or two pairs of wings attached to thorax; some undergo complete metamorphosis. Examples: termite, ant, beetle, dragonfly, fly, moth, grasshopper.

PHYLUM ECHINODERMATA (echinoderms) Live in salt water; larvae have bilateral symmetry; adults typically have radial symmetry; endoskeleton; tube feet; water vascular system used in respiration, excretion, feeding, and locomotion; deuterostomes.

CLASS CRINOIDEA (crinoids) Filter feeders; feathery arms; mouth and anus on upper surface of body disk; some sessile. Examples: sea lily, feather star.

Appendix  CLASSIFICATION

CLASS ASTEROIDEA (sea stars) Star-shaped; carnivorous; bottom dwellers; mouth on lower surface. Examples: crown-of-thorns sea star, sunstar.

CLASS OPHIUROIDEA Small body disk; long armored arms; most have only five arms; lack an anus; most are filter feeders or detritus feeders. Examples: brittle star, basket star.

CLASS ECHINOIDEA Lack arms; body encased in rigid, box-like covering; covered with spines; most grazing herbivores or detritus feeders. Examples: sea urchin, sand dollar, sea biscuit.

CLASS HOLOTHUROIDEA (sea cucumbers) Cylindrical body with feeding tentacles on one end; lie on their side; mostly detritus or filter feeders; endoskeleton greatly reduced.

PHYLUM CHORDATA (chordates) Dorsal hollow nerve cord, notochord, pharyngeal pouches, and a muscular tail during at least part of development.

Subphylum Urochordata (tunicates) Live in salt water; tough outer covering; display chordate features during larval stages; many adults sessile, some free-swimming. Examples: sea squirt, sea peach, salp.

Subphylum Cephalochordata (lancelets) Fishlike; live in salt water; filter feeders; no internal skeleton. Example: Branchiostoma.

Subphylum Vertebrata Most possess a vertebral column (backbone) that supports and protects dorsal nerve chord; endoskeleton; distinct head with a skull and brain.

CLASS MYXINI (hagfishes) Mostly scavengers; live in salt water; short tentacles around mouth; rasping tongue; extremely slimy; open circulatory system.

CLASS CEPHALASPIDOMORPHI (lampreys) Larvae filter feeders; adults are parasites whose circular mouth is lined with rasping toothlike structures; many live in both salt water and fresh water during the course of their lives.

CLASS CHONDRICHTHYES (cartilaginous fishes) Have jaws, fins, and endoskeleton of cartilage; most live in salt water; typically several gill slits; tough small scales with spines; ectothermic; two-chambered heart; males possess structures for internal fertilization. Examples: shark, ray, skate, chimaera, sawfish.

CLASS OSTEICHTHYES (bony fishes) Bony endoskeleton; aquatic; ectothermic; well-developed respiratory system, usually involving gills; possess swim bladder; paired fins; divided into two groups—ray-finned fishes, which include most living species, and lobe-finned fishes, which include lungfishes and the coelocanth. Examples: salmon, perch, sturgeon, tuna, goldfish, eel.

CLASS AMPHIBIA (amphibians) Adapted primarily to life in wet places; ectothermic; most carnivorous; smooth, moist skin; typically lay eggs that develop in water; usually have gilled larvae; most have three-chambered heart; adults either aquatic or terrestrial; terrestrial forms respire using lungs, skin, and/or lining of the mouth.

Order Urodela (salamanders) Possess tail as adults; carnivorous; usually have four legs; usually aquatic as larvae and terrestrial as adults.

Order Anura (frogs and toads) Adults in almost all species lack tail; aquatic larvae called tadpoles; well-developed hind legs adapted for jumping.

Order Apoda (legless amphibians) Wormlike; lack legs; carnivorous; terrestrial burrowers; some undergo direct development; some viviparous. Example: caecilians.

CLASS REPTILIA (reptiles) As a group, adapted to fully terrestrial life, some live in water; dry, scale-covered skin; ectothermic; most have three-chambered hearts; internal fertilization; amniotic eggs typically laid on land; extinct forms include dinosaurs and flying reptiles.

Order Sphenodonta (tuataras) Lack internal ears; primitive scales; found only in New Zealand; carnivorous. One species: *Sphenodon punctatus*.

Order Squamata (lizards and snakes) Most carnivorous; majority terrestrial; lizards typically have legs; snakes lack legs. Examples: iguana, gecko, skink, cobra, python, boa.

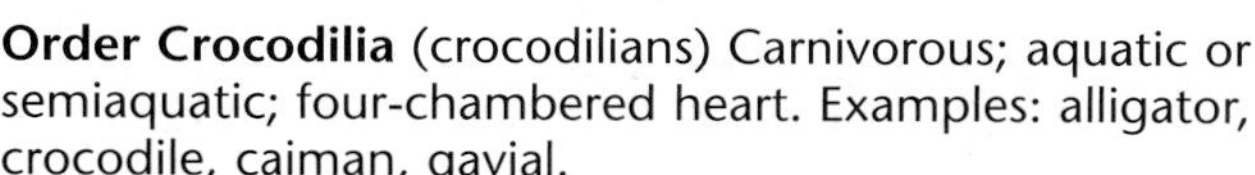

Order Crocodilia (crocodilians) Carnivorous; aquatic or semiaquatic; four-chambered heart. Examples: alligator, crocodile, caiman, gavial.

Order Testudines (turtles and tortoises) Bony shell; ribs and vertebrae fused to upper part of shell; some terrestrial, others semiaquatic or aquatic; all lay eggs on land. Examples: snapping turtle, tortoise, hawksbill turtle, box turtle.

Class Aves (birds) Endothermic; feathered over much of body surface; scales on legs and feet; bones hollow and lightweight in flying species; four-chambered heart; well-developed lungs and air sacs for efficient air exchange. Examples: owl, eagle, duck, chicken, pigeon, penguin, sparrow, stork.

Class Mammalia (mammals) Endothermic; subcutaneous fat; hair; most viviparous; suckle young with milk produced in mammary glands; four-chambered heart; most have four legs; use lungs for respiration.

Order Monotremata (monotremes) Exhibit features of both mammals and reptiles; possess a cloaca; lay eggs that hatch externally; produce milk from primitive nipple-like structures. Examples: duckbill platypus, short-beaked echidna.

Order Marsupialia (marsupials) Young develop in the female's uterus but emerge at very early state of development; development completed in mother's pouch. Examples: opossum, kangaroo, koala.

Order Insectivora (insectivores) Have long, narrow snouts and sharp claws for digging. Examples: shrew, mole, hedgehog.

Order Chiroptera (bats) Flying mammals, with forelimbs adapted for flight; most nocturnal; most navigate by echolocation; most species feed on insects, nectar, or fruits; some species feed on blood. Examples: fruit bat, flying fox, vampire bat.

Order Primates (primates) Highly developed brain and complex social behavior; excellent binocular vision; quadrupedal or bipedal locomotion; five digits on hands and feet. Examples: lemur, monkey, chimpanzee, human.

Order Edentata (edentates) Teeth reduced or absent; feed primarily on social insects, such as termites and ants. Examples: anteater, armadillo.

Order Lagomorpha (lagomorphs) Small herbivores with chisel-shaped front teeth; generally adapted to running and jumping. Examples: rabbit, pika, hare.

Order Rodentia (rodents) Mostly herbivorous but some omnivorous; sharp front teeth. Examples: rat, beaver, guinea pig, hamster, gerbil, squirrel.

Order Cetacea (cetaceans) Fully adapted to aquatic existence; feed, breed, and give birth in water; forelimbs specialized as flippers; external hindlimbs absent; many species capable of long, deep dives; some use echolocation to navigate; communicate using complex auditory signals. Examples: whale, porpoise, dolphin.

Order Carnivora (carnivores) Mostly carnivorous; live in salt water or on land; aquatic species must return to land to breed. Examples: seal, bear, raccoon, weasel, skunk.

Order Proboscidea (elephants) Herbivorous; have trunks; largest land animal. Examples: Asian elephant, African elephant.

Order Sirenia (sirenians) Aquatic herbivores; slow-moving; front limbs modified as flippers; hindlimbs absent; little body hair. Examples: manatee, sea cow.

Order Perissodactyla (odd-toed ungulates) Hoofed herbivores; odd number of digits on each foot; teeth, jaw, and digestive system adapted to plant material. Examples: horse, donkey, rhinoceros, tapir.

Order Artiodactyla (even-toed ungulates) Hoofed herbivores; hoofs derived from two digits on each foot; digestive system adapted to thoroughly process tough plant material. Examples: sheep, cow, hippopotamus, antelope, camel, giraffe, pig.

GLOSSARY

abdomen posterior part of an arthropod's body (p. 721)

abiotic factor physical, or nonliving, factor that shapes an ecosystem (p. 90)

abscission layer layer of cells at the petiole that seals off a leaf from the vascular system (p. 642)

accessory pigment compound other than chlorophyll that absorbs light at different wavelengths than chlorophyll (p. 506)

acellular slime mold slime mold that passes through a stage in which its cells fuse to form large cells with many nuclei (p. 516)

acetylcholine neurotransmitter that diffuses across a synapse and produces an impulse in the cell membrane of a muscle cell (p. 929)

acid compound that forms hydrogen ions (H^+) in solution (p. 43)

acid rain rain containing nitric and sulfuric acids (p. 148)

acoelomate animal lacking a coelom, or body cavity (p. 683)

actin a protein that mainly makes up the thin filaments in striations in skeletal muscle cells (p. 928)

action potential reversal of charges across the cell membrane of a neuron (p. 899)

activation energy energy needed to get a reaction started (p. 50)

active immunity immunity produced by a vaccine; so-called because the body has the ability to mount an active immune response against the pathogen (p. 1040)

active transport energy-requiring process that moves material across a cell membrane against a concentration difference (p. 189)

adaptation inherited characteristic that increases an organism's chance of survival (p. 380)

adaptive radiation process by which a single species or small group of species evolves into several different forms that live in different ways; rapid growth in the diversity of a group of organisms (pp. 437, 851)

addiction uncontrollable craving for more of a drug (p. 911)

adenosine triphosphate (ATP) one of the principal chemical compounds that living things use to store energy (p. 202)

adhesion attraction between molecules of different substances (p. 41); in plants: attraction between unlike molecules (p. 599)

aerobic process that requires oxygen (p. 226)

age-structure diagram graph of the numbers of males and females within different age groups of a population (p. 131)

aggression threatening behavior that one animal uses to gain control over another (p. 881)

agriculture the practice of farming (p. 141)

air sac one of several sacs attached to a bird's lungs into which air moves when a bird inhales; allows for the one-way flow of air through the respiratory system (p. 810)

algal bloom an immediate increase in the amount of algae and other producers that results from a large input of a limiting nutrient (p. 80)

allele one of a number of different forms of a gene (p. 265)

allergy overreaction of the immune system that results when antigens bind to mast cells (p. 1041)

alternation of generations process in which many algae switch back and forth between haploid and diploid stages of their life cycles (p. 512)

alveolus tiny air sac at the end of a bronchiole in the lungs that provides surface area for gas exchange to occur (pp. 859, 958)

amino acid compound with an amino group ($—NH_2$) on one end and a carboxyl group ($—COOH$) on the other end (p. 47)

amniotic egg egg composed of shell and membranes that create a protected environment in which the embryo can develop out of the water (p. 802)

amoeboid movement type of locomotion used by amoebas (p. 498)

amphibian vertebrate that, with some exceptions, lives in water as a larva and on land as an adult, breathes with lungs as an adult, has moist skin that contains mucus glands, and lacks scales and claws (p. 782)

amylase enzyme in saliva that breaks the chemical bonds between the sugar monomers in starches (p. 979)

anaerobic process that does not require oxygen (p. 224)

anal pore region of the cell membrane of a ciliate where waste-containing food vacuoles fuse and are then emptied into the environment (p. 500)

anaphase the third phase of mitosis, during which the chromosome pairs separate and move toward opposite poles (p. 248)

angiosperm flowering plant; bears its seeds within a layer of tissue that protects the seed (p. 564)

Animalia kingdom of multicellular eukaryotic heterotrophs whose cells do not have cell walls (p. 461)

annual flowering plant that completes a life cycle within one growing season (p. 572)

anther flower structure in which haploid male gametophytes are produced (p. 612)

antheridium male reproductive structure in some algae and plants (pp. 519, 559)

anthropoid humanlike primate (p. 835)

antibiotic compound that blocks the growth and reproduction of bacteria (pp. 480, 1033)

antibody specialized protein that helps destroy disease-causing organisms (p. 1036)

anticodon group of three bases on a tRNA molecule that are complementary to an mRNA codon (p. 304)

antigen substance that triggers an immune response (p. 1036)

anus opening through which wastes leave the digestive tract (pp. 661, 689)

aorta large blood vessel in mammals through which blood travels from the left ventricle to all parts of the body except the lungs (p. 946)

aphotic zone permanently dark layer of the oceans below the photic zone (p. 109)

apical dominance phenomenon in which the closer a bud is to the stem's tip, the more its growth is inhibited (p. 636)

apical meristem group of undifferentiated cells that divide to produce increased length of stems and roots (p. 580)

appendage structure, such as a leg or antenna, that extends from the body wall (p. 715)

aquaculture farming of aquatic organisms (p. 147)

Archaea domain of unicellular prokaryotes that have cell walls that do not contain peptidoglycan (p. 459)

Archaebacteria kingdom of unicellular prokaryotes whose cell walls do not contain peptidoglycan (p. 459)

archaeocyte specialized cell in a sponge that makes spicules (p. 665)

archegonium female reproductive structure in some plants, including mosses and liverworts (p. 559)

artery large blood vessel that carries blood from the heart to the tissues of the body (p. 946)

artificial selection selection by humans for breeding of useful traits from the natural variation among different organisms (p. 379)

ascospore haploid spore produced within the ascus of ascomycetes (p. 532)

ascus structure within the fruiting body of an ascomycete in which two nuclei of different mating types fuse (p. 532)

asexual reproduction process by which a single parent reproduces by itself (p. 17)

asthma allergic reaction in which smooth muscle contractions reduce the size of air passageways in the lungs and make breathing very difficult (p. 1042)

atherosclerosis condition in which fatty deposits called plaque build up on the walls of the arteries (p. 949)

atom basic unit of matter (p. 35)

ATP synthase large protein that uses energy from H^+ ions to bind ADP and a phosphate group together to produce ATP (p. 210)

atrium large muscular upper chamber of the heart that receives and holds blood that is about to enter the ventricle (pp. 776, 944)

autosome autosomal chromosome; chromosome that is not a sex chromosome (p. 341)

autotroph organism that can capture energy from sunlight or chemicals and use it to produce its own food from inorganic compounds; also called a producer (pp. 67, 201)

auxin substance produced in the tip of a seedling that stimulates cell elongation (p. 635)

axon long fiber that carries impulses away from the cell body of a neuron (p. 898)

bacillus rod-shaped prokaryote (p. 473)

Bacteria domain of unicellular prokaryotes that have cell walls containing peptidoglycans (p. 459)

bacteriophage virus that infects bacteria (pp. 289, 484)

bark tree structure that includes all tissues outside the vascular cambium, including phloem, the cork cambium, and cork (p. 593)

base compound that produces hydroxide ions (OH^+) in solution (p. 43)

base-pairing principle that bonds in DNA can form only between adenine and thymine and between guanine and cytosine (p. 294)

basidiospore spore in basidiomycetes that germinates to produce haploid primary mycelia (p. 535)

basidium spore-bearing structure of a basidiomycete (p. 534)

behavior the way an organism reacts to changes in its internal condition or external environment (p. 871)

behavioral isolation form of reproductive isolation in which two populations have differences in courtship rituals or other types of behavior that prevent them from interbreeding (p. 404)

benthos organisms that live attached to or near the ocean floor (p. 112)

biennial flowering plant that completes its life cycle in two years (p. 572)

bilateral symmetry body plan in which only a single, imaginary line can divide the body into two equal halves; characteristic of worms, arthropods, and chordates (pp. 662, 748)

binary fission type of asexual reproduction in which a prokaryote replicates its DNA, and divides in half, producing two identical daughter cells (p. 476)

binocular vision ability to merge visual images from both eyes, which provides depth perception and a three-dimensional view of the world (p. 834)

binomial nomenclature classification system in which each species is assigned a two-part scientific name (p. 448)

biodiversity biological diversity; the sum total of the variety of organisms in the biosphere (p. 150)

Glossary

biogeochemical cycle process in which elements, chemical compounds, and other forms of matter are passed from one organism to another and from one part of the biosphere to another (p. 74)

biological magnification increasing concentration of a harmful substance in organisms at higher trophic levels in a food chain or food web (p. 152)

biology science that seeks to understand the living world (p. 16)

biomass total amount of living tissue within a given trophic level (p. 72)

biome group of ecosystems that have the same climate and dominant communities (pp. 64, 98)

biosphere part of Earth in which life exists including land, water, and air or atmosphere (p. 63)

biotic factor biological influence on organisms within an ecosystem (p. 90)

bipedal term used to refer to two-footed locomotion (p. 835)

bird endothermic animal that has an outer covering of feathers, two legs covered with scales that are used for walking or perching, and front limbs modified into wings (p. 806)

blade thin, flattened section of a plant leaf that collects sunlight (p. 595)

blastula hollow ball of cells formed when a zygote undergoes a series of divisions (p. 661)

bone marrow soft tissue inside cavities within bones; two types are yellow marrow and red marrow (p. 922)

book lung organ that has layers of respiratory tissue stacked like the pages of a book; used by some terrestrial arthropods to exchange gases (p. 717)

Bowman's capsule cup-shaped structure in the upper end of a nephron that encases the glomerulus (p. 987)

brain stem structure that connects the brain and spinal cord; includes the medulla oblongata and the pons (p. 902)

bronchus passageway leading from the trachea to a lung (p. 958)

bryophyte nonvascular plant; examples are mosses and their relatives (p. 556)

bud plant structure containing undeveloped tissue that can produce new stems and leaves (p. 589)

budding process of attaching a bud to a plant to produce a new branch (p. 623)

buffer weak acid or base that can react with strong acids or bases to help prevent sharp, sudden changes in pH (p. 43)

calorie amount of energy required to raise the temperature of 1 gram of water by 1 Celsius degree (p. 221)

Calorie term used by scientists to measure the energy stored in foods; 1000 calories (p. 971)

Calvin cycle reactions of photosynthesis in which energy from ATP and NADPH is used to build high-energy compounds such as sugars (p. 212)

cancer disorder in which some of the body' s own cells lose the ability to control growth (p. 252)

canopy dense covering formed by the leafy tops of tall rain trees (p. 100)

capillary smallest blood vessel; brings nutrients and oxygen to the tissues and absorbs carbon dioxide and waste products (p. 947)

capillary action tendency of water to rise in a thin tube (p. 599)

capsid outer protein coat of a virus (p. 483)

carapace in crustaceans, the part of the exoskeleton that covers the cephalothorax (p. 721); in turtles and tortoises, the dorsal part of the shell (p. 805)

carbohydrate compound made up of carbon, hydrogen, and oxygen atoms; major source of energy for the human body (pp. 45, 972)

carnivore organism that obtains energy by eating animals (p. 69)

carpel innermost part of a flower that produces the female gametophytes (p. 612)

carrying capacity largest number of individuals of a population that a given environment can support (p. 122)

cartilage strong connective tissue that supports the body and is softer and more flexible than bone (pp. 773, 922)

Casparian strip waterproof strip that surrounds plant endodermis cells (p. 587)

caste group of individual insects specialized to perform particular tasks, or roles (p. 732)

catalyst substance that speeds up the rate of a chemical reaction (p. 51)

cell collection of living matter enclosed by a barrier that separates the cell from its surroundings; basic unit of all forms of life (pp. 17, 170)

cell body largest part of a typical neuron; contains the nucleus and much of the cytoplasm (p. 897)

cell culture group of cells grown in a nutrient solution from a single original cell (p. 27)

cell cycle series of events that cells go through as they grow and divide (p. 245)

cell division process by which a cell divides into two new daughter cells (p. 243)

cell fractionation technique in which cells are broken into pieces and the different cell parts are separated (p. 27)

cell-mediated immunity an immune response in which killer T cells attack antigen-bearing cells directly (p. 1038)

cell membrane thin, flexible barrier around a cell; regulates what enters and leaves the cell (p. 171)

cell specialization separate roles for each type of cell in multicellular organisms (p. 191)

cell theory idea that all living things are composed of cells, cells are the basic units of structure and function in living things, and new cells are produced from existing cells (p. 170)

cellular respiration process that releases energy by breaking down food molecules in the presence of oxygen; made up of glycolysis, the Krebs cycle, and the electron transport chain (p. 222)

cellular slime mold slime mold whose individual cells remain separated during every phase of the mold's life cycle (p. 516)

cell wall strong layer around the cell membrane in plants, algae, and some bacteria (p. 171)

central nervous system the brain and the spinal cord (p. 901)

centriole one of two tiny structures located in the cytoplasm of animal cells near the nuclear envelope (p. 246)

centromere area where the chromatids of a chromosome are attached (p. 244)

cephalization concentration of sense organs and nerve cells at the front of an animal's body (pp. 663, 748)

cephalothorax region of a crustacean formed by the fusion of the head with the thorax (p. 721)

cerebellum region of the brain that coordinates body movements (pp. 777, 902)

cerebral cortex outer layer of the cerebrum of a mammal's brain; center of thinking and other complex behaviors (p. 825)

cerebrospinal fluid fluid in the space between the meninges that acts as a shock absorber that protects the central nervous system (p. 901)

cerebrum area of the brain responsible for all voluntary activities of the body (pp. 777, 902)

chelicerae pair of mouthparts in chelicerates that contain fangs and are used to stab and paralyze prey (p. 722)

cheliped one of the first pair of legs of decapods (p. 721)

chemical bond link that holds together atoms in compounds (p. 38)

chemical reaction process that changes one set of chemicals into another set of chemicals (p. 49)

chemoautotroph prokaryote that obtains energy directly from inorganic molecules using chemical reactions (p. 474)

chemosynthesis process by which some organisms use chemical energy to produce carbohydrates (p. 68)

chemotherapy drug therapy; the use of a combination of chemicals to destroy cancer cells (p. 1048)

chitin complex carbohydrate that makes up the cell walls of fungi; also found in the external skeletons of arthropods (pp. 527, 715)

chlorophyll principal pigment of plants and other photosynthetic organisms; captures light energy (p. 207)

chloroplast organelle found in cells of plants and some other organisms that uses energy from sunlight to make energy-rich food molecules by photosynthesis (p. 180)

choanocyte specialized cell in sponges that uses a flagellum to move a steady current of water through the sponge (p. 665)

chordate member of the phylum Chordata; animal that has, for at least some stage of its life, a dorsal, hollow nerve cord; a notochord; pharyngeal pouches; and a muscular tail (p. 767)

chromatid one of two identical "sister" parts of a duplicated chromosome (p. 244)

chromatin granular material visible within the nucleus; consists of DNA tightly coiled around proteins (pp. 175, 297)

chromosome threadlike structure within the nucleus containing the genetic information that is passed from one generation of cells to the next (p. 175)

chyme mixture of stomach fluids and food produced in the stomach by contracting stomach muscles (p. 981)

cilium short hairlike projection similar to a flagellum; produces movement in many cells (p. 499)

circadian rhythm behavioral cycle that occurs in a daily pattern (p. 878)

cladogram diagram that shows the evolutionary relationships among a group of organisms (p. 453)

class group of similar orders (p. 449)

classical conditioning learning process in which an animal makes a mental connection between a stimulus and some kind of reward or punishment (p. 874)

climate average, year-after-year conditions of temperature and precipitation in a particular region (p. 87)

clitellum band of thickened, specialized segments in annelids that secretes a mucus ring into which eggs and sperm are released (p. 696)

cloaca a muscular cavity at the end of the large intestine through which digestive wastes, urine, and eggs or sperm leave the body (p. 748)

clone member of a population of genetically identical organisms produced from a single cell (p. 333)

closed circulatory system system in which blood is contained within a network of blood vessels (pp. 695, 754)

cnidocyte stinging cell located along the tentacles of cnidarians; used for defense and to capture prey (p. 669)

coastal ocean marine zone that extends from the low-tide mark to the end of the continental shelf (p. 110)

GLOSSARY

coccus spherical prokaryote (p. 473)

cochlea fluid-filled part of the inner ear; sends nerve impulses to the brain through the cochlear nerve (p. 908)

codominance situation in which both alleles of a gene contribute to the phenotype of the organism (p. 272)

codon three-nucleotide sequence on messenger RNA that codes for a single amino acid (p. 302)

coelom fluid-filled body cavity lined with mesoderm (pp. 683, 749)

coevolution process by which two species evolve in response to changes in each other (p. 437)

cohesion attraction between molecules of the same substance (p. 41)

collenchyma type of ground tissue cell with a strong, flexible cell wall; helps support larger plants (p. 583)

commensalism symbiotic relationship in which one member of the association benefits and the other is neither helped nor harmed (p. 93)

common descent principle that all living things have a common ancestor (p. 382)

communication passing of information from one organism to another (p. 881)

community assemblage of different populations that live together in a defined area (p. 64)

companion cell phloem cell that surrounds sieve tube elements (p. 583)

competitive exclusion principle ecological rule that states that no two species can occupy the same exact niche in the same habitat at the same time (p. 92)

complete metamorphosis type of insect development in which the larvae look and act nothing like their parents and also feed in completely different ways (p. 729)

compound substance formed by the chemical combination of two or more elements in definite proportions (p. 37)

compound light microscope microscope that allows light to pass through a specimen and uses two lenses to form an image (p. 26)

concentration the mass of solute in a given volume of solution, or mass/volume (p. 185)

cone in gymnosperms, a seed-bearing structure (p. 564); in the retina of the eye, a photoreceptor that responds to light of different colors, producing color vision (p. 907)

conidium tiny fungal spore that forms at the tips of specialized hyphae in ascomycetes (p. 532)

coniferous term used to refer to trees that produce seed-bearing cones and have thin leaves shaped like needles (p. 103)

conjugation form of sexual reproduction in which paramecia and some prokaryotes exchange genetic information (pp. 476, 500)

connective tissue tissue that holds organs in place and binds different parts of the body together (p. 894)

conservation wise management of natural resources, including the preservation of habitats and wildlife (p. 154)

consumer organism that relies on other organisms for its energy and food supply; also called a heterotroph (p. 68)

contractile vacuole cavity in the cytoplasm of some protists that collects water and discharges it from the cell (p. 500)

controlled experiment a test of the effect of a single variable by changing it while keeping all other variables the same (p. 9)

controlled variable factor in an experiment that a scientist purposely keeps the same (p. 1056)

convergent evolution process by which unrelated organisms independently evolve similarities when adapting to similar environments (p. 437)

coral reef diverse and productive environment named for the coral animals that makes up its primary structure (p. 111)

cork cambium lateral meristematic tissue that produces the outer covering of stems (p. 591)

corpus luteum name given to a follicle after ovulation because of its yellow color (p. 1014)

cortex spongy layer of ground tissue just inside the epidermis of a root (p. 585)

cotyledon seed leaf in a plant embryo (p. 570)

courtship type of behavior in which an animal sends out stimuli—such as sounds, visual displays, or chemicals—in order to attract a member of the opposite sex (p. 879)

covalent bond bond formed by the sharing of electrons between atoms (p. 38)

crop in earthworms, part of the digestive system in which food can be stored (p. 695); in birds, structure at the lower end of the esophagus in which food is stored and moistened (p. 809)

crossing-over process in which homologous chromosomes exchange portions of their chromatids during meiosis (p. 277)

cuticle in plants, a thick, waxy layer on exposed outer surfaces of cells that protects them against water loss and injury (p. 581)

cyclin one of a family of closely related proteins that regulate the cell cycle in eukaryotic cells (p. 251)

cytokinesis division of the cytoplasm during cell division (p. 248)

cytoplasm material inside the cell membrane—but not including the nucleus (p. 171)

cytoskeleton network of protein filaments within some cells that helps the cell maintain its shape and is involved in many forms of cell movement (p. 176)

data evidence; information gathered from observations (pp. 4, 1057)

deciduous term used to refer to a tree that sheds its leaves during a particular season each year (p. 100)

decomposer organism that breaks down and obtains energy from dead organic matter (p. 69)

deforestation destruction of forests (p. 146)

demographic transition change in a population from high birth and death rates to low birth and death rates (p. 130)

demography scientific study of human populations (p. 130)

dendrite extension of the cell body of a neuron that carries impulses from the environment or from other neurons toward the cell body (p. 898)

denitrification conversion of nitrates into nitrogen gas (p. 78)

density-dependent limiting factor limiting factor that depends on population size (p. 125)

density-independent limiting factor limiting factor that affects all populations in similar ways, regardless of population size (p. 127)

deoxyribonucleic acid (DNA) nucleic acid that contains the sugar deoxyribose (p. 47)

dependent variable factor in an experiment that a scientist wants to observe, which may change because of the manipulated variable; also known as a responding variable (p. 1056)

depressant drug that decreases the rate of functions regulated by the brain (p. 911)

derived character characteristic that appears in recent parts of a lineage, but not in its older members (p. 453)

dermis innermost layer of the skin (p. 935)

descent with modification principle that each living species has descended, with changes, from other species over time (p. 381)

desertification in areas with dry climates, a process caused by a combination of poor farming practices, overgrazing, and drought that turns productive land into desert (p. 145)

detritivore organism that feeds on plant and animal remains and other dead matter (p. 69)

detritus particles of organic material that provide food for organisms at the base of an estuary's food web (p. 108)

deuterostome animal whose anus is formed from the blastopore of a blastula (p. 661)

diabetes mellitus condition that occurs when the pancreas produces too little insulin, resulting in an increase in the amount of glucose in the blood (p. 1008)

diaphragm large, flat muscle at the bottom of the chest cavity that contracts during breathing, pulling the bottom of the chest cavity down and increasing its volume (pp. 824, 959)

dicot angiosperm whose seeds have two cotyledons (p. 570)

diffusion process by which molecules tend to move from an area where they are more concentrated to an area where they are less concentrated (p. 185)

diploid term used to refer to a cell that contains both sets of homologous chromosomes (p. 275)

directional selection form of natural selection in which the entire curve moves; occurs when individuals at one end of a distribution curve have higher fitness than individuals in the middle or at the other end of the curve (p. 398)

disease any change, other than an injury, that disrupts the normal functions of the body (p. 1029)

disruptive selection form of natural selection in which a single curve splits into two; occurs when individuals at the upper and lower ends of a distribution curve have higher fitness than individuals near the middle (p. 399)

DNA fingerprinting analysis of sections of DNA that have little or no known function, but vary widely from one individual to another, in order to identify individuals (p. 357)

DNA polymerase enzyme that "proofreads" new DNA strands, helping to ensure that each molecule is a nearly perfect copy of the original DNA (p. 299)

domain most inclusive taxonomic category; larger than a kingdom (p. 458)

dormancy period of time during which a plant embryo is alive but not growing (pp. 620, 641)

double fertilization fertilization in angiosperms, in which two distinct fertilization events take place between the male and female gametophytes (p. 616)

drug any substance, other than food, that causes a change in the structure or function of the body (p. 910)

drug abuse use of any drug in a way that most doctors would not approve (p. 914)

ecological pyramid diagram that shows the relative amounts of energy or matter within each trophic level in a food chain or food web (p. 72)

ecological succession gradual change in living communities that follows a disturbance (p. 94)

ecology scientific study of interactions among organisms and between organisms and their environment (p. 63)

ecosystem collection of all the organisms that live in a particular place, together with their nonliving environment (p. 64)

ecosystem diversity variety of habitats, living communities, and ecological processes in the living world (p. 150)

ectoderm outermost germ layer of most animals; gives rise to outer layer of the skin, sense organs, and nerves (p. 661)

ectotherm animal that relies on interactions with the environment to help it control body temperature (pp. 800, 855)

electron negatively charged particle; located outside the atomic nucleus (p. 35)

electron microscope microscope that forms an image by focusing beams of electrons onto a specimen (p. 26)

electron transport chain a series of proteins in which the high-energy electrons from the Krebs cycle are used to convert ADP into ATP (p. 228)

element substance consisting entirely of one type of atom (p. 36)

embryo early developmental stage of a sporophyte plant (p. 565)

embryo sac female gametophyte within the ovule of a flowering plant (p. 615)

emigration movement of individuals out of a population (p. 120)

emphysema disease in which the tissues of the lungs lose elasticity, making breathing very difficult (p. 962)

endangered species species whose population size is rapidly declining and will become extinct if the trend continues (p. 151)

endocrine gland gland that releases its secretions directly into the bloodstream (p. 998)

endocytosis process by which a cell takes material into the cell by infolding of the cell membrane (p. 189)

endoderm innermost germ layer of most animals; develops into the linings of the digestive tract and much of the respiratory system (p. 661)

endodermis layer of cells that completely encloses vascular tissue (p. 585)

endoplasmic reticulum internal membrane system in cells in which components of the cell membrane are assembled and some proteins are modified (p. 177)

endoskeleton structural support located inside the body of an animal (pp. 734, 757)

endosperm food-rich tissue that nourishes a seedling as it grows (p. 616)

endospore type of spore formed when a bacterium produces a thick internal wall that encloses its DNA and a portion of its cytoplasm (p. 476)

endosymbiotic theory theory that eukaryotic cells formed from a symbiosis among several different prokaryotic organisms (p. 427)

endotherm animal that generates its own body heat and controls its body temperature from within (pp. 808, 855)

enzyme protein that acts as a biological catalyst (p. 51)

epidermal cell cell that makes up the dermal tissue, which is the outer covering of a plant (p. 581)

epidermis outer layer of the skin (p. 934)

epididymis structure in the male reproductive system in which sperm fully mature and are stored (p. 1010)

epiphyte plant that grows directly on the body of another plant (p. 645)

epithelial tissue tissue that covers the surface of the body and lines internal organs (p. 894)

era one of several subdivisions of the time between the Precambrian and the present (p. 421)

esophagus food tube connecting the mouth to the stomach (p. 980)

estuary wetlands formed where rivers meet the ocean (p. 108)

ethylene plant hormone that stimulates fruits to ripen (p. 638)

Eubacteria kingdom of unicellular prokaryotes whose cell walls are made up of peptidoglycan (p. 459)

Eukarya domain of all organisms whose cells have nuclei, including protists, plants, fungi, and animals (p. 460)

eukaryote organism whose cells contain nuclei (p. 172)

evaporation process by which water changes from a liquid into an atmospheric gas (p. 75)

evolution change in a kind of organism over time; process by which modern organisms have descended from ancient organisms (pp. 20, 369)

evolutionary classification method of grouping organisms together according to their evolutionary history (p. 452)

exocrine gland gland that releases its secretions through tubelike structures called ducts (p. 998)

exocytosis process by which a cell releases large amounts of material (p. 189)

exon expressed sequence of DNA; codes for a protein (p. 302)

exoskeleton external skeleton; tough external covering that protects and supports the body of many invertebrates (pp. 715, 757)

exponential growth growth pattern in which the individuals in a population reproduce at a constant rate (p. 121)

external fertilization process in which eggs are fertilized outside the female's body (pp. 672, 758)

extinct term used to refer to a species that has died out (p. 417)

extinction disappearance of a species from all parts of its geographical range (p. 151)

extracellular digestion process in which food is broken down outside the cells in a digestive tract (p. 751)

eyespot group of cells that can detect changes in the amount of light in the environment (pp. 506, 685)

facilitated diffusion movement of specific molecules across cell membranes through protein channels (p. 188)

Fallopian tube one of two fluid-filled tubes in human females through which an egg passes after its release from an ovary (p. 1013)

family group of genera that share many characteristics (p. 449)

fat lipid; made up of fatty acids and glycerol (p. 972)

feather structure made mostly of protein that develops from a pit in a bird's skin (p. 806)

feedback inhibition process by which the product of a system shuts down the system or limits its operation (p. 895)

fermentation process by which cells release energy in the absence of oxygen (p. 224)

fetal alcohol syndrome group of birth defects caused by the effects of alcohol on a fetus (p. 913)

fetus name given to a human embryo after eight weeks of development (p. 1019)

fever elevated body temperature that occurs in response to infection (p. 1035)

fibrous root part of a root system in which roots branch to such an extent that no single root grows larger than the rest (p. 584)

filament in algae, a long threadlike colony formed by many green algae (p. 512); in plants, a long, thin structure that supports an anther (p. 612)

filtration process by which fluid from the blood filters into Bowman's capsule in the kidneys (p. 987)

fish aquatic vertebrate characterized by paired fins, scales, and gills (p. 771)

fission form of asexual reproduction in which an organism splits into two, and each half grows new parts to become a complete organism (p. 686)

fitness ability of an organism to survive and reproduce in its environment (p. 380)

flagellum whiplike structure on some cells that is used for movement (p. 473)

flame cell specialized cell that filters and removes excess water from the body of a flatworm (p. 684)

flower seed-bearing structure of an angiosperm (p. 564)

follicle cluster of cells surrounding a single egg in the human female reproductive system (p. 1012)

food chain series of steps in an ecosystem in which organisms transfer energy by eating and being eaten (p. 69)

food vacuole small cavity in the cytoplasm of protists that temporarily stores food (p. 498)

food web network of complex interactions formed by the feeding relationships among the various organisms in an ecosystem (p. 70)

foot muscular part of a mollusk (p. 702)

fossil preserved remains or evidence of an ancient organism (p. 371)

fossil record information about past life, including the structure of organisms, what they ate, what ate them, in what environment they lived, and the order in which they lived (p. 417)

founder effect change in allele frequencies as a result of the migration of a small subgroup of a population (p. 400)

frameshift mutation mutation that shifts the "reading" frame of the genetic message by inserting or deleting a nucleotide (p. 307)

frond large leaf of a fern (p. 562)

fruit thick wall of tissue surrounding an angiosperm seed (p. 569)

fruiting body reproductive structure of fungus that develops from a mycelium (p. 528)

Fungi kingdom composed of heterotrophs; many obtain energy and nutrients from dead organic matter (p. 460)

gametangium gamete-forming structure produced when the hyphae of opposing mating types of fungi meet (p. 529)

gamete specialized cell involved in sexual reproduction (p. 266)

gametophyte haploid, or gamete-producing, phase of an organism (pp. 514, 552)

ganglion group of nerve cells (p. 685)

gastrovascular cavity digestive chamber with a single opening, in which cnidarians, flatworms, and echinoderms digest food (p. 671)

gastrulation process of cell migration by which a third layer of cells is formed within the cavity of a blastocyst (p. 1017)

gel electrophoresis procedure used to separate and analyze DNA fragments by placing a mixture of DNA fragments at one end of a porous gel and applying an electrical voltage to the gel (p. 323)

gemma small cup-shaped structure in liverworts that contains many haploid cells; used for asexual reproduction (p. 557)

gemmule group of archaeocytes surrounded by a tough layer of spicules; produced by some sponges (p. 667)

gene sequence of DNA that codes for a protein and thus determines a trait (p. 265)

gene map diagram showing the relative locations of each known gene on a particular chromosome (p. 280)

gene pool combined genetic information of all the members of a particular population (p. 394)

genetic diversity sum total of all the different forms of genetic information carried by all organisms living on Earth today (p. 150)

genetic drift random change in allele frequencies that occurs in small populations (p. 400)

genetic engineering process of making changes in the DNA code of living organisms (p. 322)

genetic equilibrium situation in which allele frequencies remain constant (p. 401)

genetic marker gene that makes it possible to distinguish bacteria that carry a plasmid with foreign DNA from those that don't (p. 328)

genetics scientific study of heredity (p. 263)

genotype genetic makeup of an organism (p. 268)

genus group of closely related species, first part of the scientific name in binomial nomenclature (p. 448)

geographic isolation form of reproductive isolation in which two populations are separated physically by geographic barriers such as rivers, mountains, or stretches of water (p. 405)

geologic time scale scale used by paleontologists to represent evolutionary time (p. 421)

germ theory of disease idea that infectious diseases are caused by microorganisms, or germs (p. 1029)

germination early growth stage of a plant embryo (p. 621)

gibberellin growth-promoting substance produced by plants (p. 637)

gill filamentous organ in aquatic animals specialized for the exchange of gases with water (p. 696)

gizzard in earthworms, part of the digestive system in which food is ground into smaller pieces (p. 695); in birds, a muscular organ that helps in the mechanical breakdown of food (p. 809)

global warming increase in the average temperatures on Earth (p. 159)

glomerulus small network of capillaries encased in the upper end of a nephron (p. 987)

glycolysis first step in releasing the energy of glucose, in which a molecule of glucose is broken into two molecules of pyruvic acid (p. 221)

Golgi apparatus stack of membranes in the cell in which enzymes attach carbohydrates and lipids to proteins (p. 178)

grafting use of a stem as a scion (p. 623)

gravitropism tendency of a plant to grow in a direction in response to the force of gravity (p. 635)

green revolution introduction of intensive farming practices that lead to a substantial increase in crop yields (p. 142)

greenhouse effect natural situation in which heat is retained in Earth's atmosphere by carbon dioxide, methane, water vapor, and other gases (p. 87)

guard cell specialized cell in the epidermis of plants that controls the opening and closing of stomata by responding to changes in water pressure (p. 596)

gullet indentation in one side of a ciliate that allows food to enter the cell (p. 500)

gymnosperm seed plant that bears its seeds directly on the surfaces of cones (p. 564)

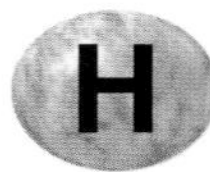

habitat the area where an organism lives, including the biotic and abiotic factors that affect the organism (p. 90)

habitat fragmentation splitting of ecosystems into small fragments (p. 151)

habituation learning process by which an animal decreases or stops its response to a repetitive stimulus that neither rewards nor harms it (p. 874)

hair follicle tubelike pocket of epidermal cells that extends into the dermis; cells at the base of hair follicles produce hair (p. 936)

half-life length of time required for half of the radioactive atoms in a sample to decay (p. 420)

haploid term used to refer to a cell that contains only a single set of chromosomes and therefore only a single set of genes (p. 275)

Hardy-Weinberg principle principle that allele frequencies in a population will remain constant unless one or more factors cause the frequencies to change (p. 401)

Haversian canal one of a network of tubes running through compact bone that contains blood vessels and nerves (p. 922)

heartwood older xylem near the center of a woody stem that no longer conducts water (p. 592)

hemoglobin iron-containing protein in red blood cells that transports oxygen from the lungs to the tissues of the body (p. 952)

herbicide compound that is toxic to plants (p. 636)

herbivore organism that obtains energy by eating only plants (p. 69)

hermaphrodite individual that has both male and female reproductive organs (p. 686)

heterotroph organism that obtains energy from the foods it consumes; also called a consumer (pp. 68, 201)

heterozygous term used to refer to an organism that has two different alleles for the same trait (p. 268)

histamine chemical released by activated mast cells that increases the flow of blood and fluids to the surrounding area (p. 1041)

histone globular protein molecule around which DNA is tightly coiled in chromatin (p. 297)

homeostasis process by which organisms maintain a relatively stable internal environment (p. 19)

hominid primate that walks upright, has opposable thumbs, and possesses a large brain; only living members are humans (p. 835)

hominoid member of a group of primates that includes apes and humans (p. 835)

homologous term used to refer to chromosomes that each have a corresponding chromosome from the opposite-sex parent (p. 275)

homologous structures structures that have different mature forms in different organisms but develop from the same embryonic tissues (p. 384)

homozygous term used to refer to an organism that has two identical alleles for a particular trait (p. 268)

hormone substance produced in one part of an organism that affects another part of the same individual (pp. 634, 997)

host organism that provides a source of nutritional needs for a parasite (p. 658)

hox genes series of genes that controls the organs and tissues that develop in various parts of an embryo (p. 312)

humoral immunity immunity against pathogens in the body fluids (p. 1036)

humus material formed from decaying leaves and other organic matter (p. 103)

hybrid offspring of crosses between parents with different traits (p. 264)

hybridization breeding technique that involves crossing dissimilar individuals to bring together the best traits of both organisms (p. 319)

hydrostatic skeleton layers of circular and longitudinal muscles, together with the water in the gastrovascular cavity, that enable movement (p. 671)

hypha tiny filament that makes up a multicellular fungus or a water mold (pp. 518, 527)

hypothalamus brain structure that acts as a control center for recognition and analysis of hunger, thirst, fatigue, anger, and body temperature (p. 903)

hypothesis possible explanation for a set of observations or possible answer to a scientific question (pp. 5, 1056)

immigration movement of individuals into an area occupied by an existing population (p. 120)

immune response the body's specific defenses that attack a disease-causing agent (p. 1036)

implantation process in which a blastocyst attaches itself to the wall of the uterus (p. 1017)

imprinting learning based on early experience; once imprinting has occurred, the behavior cannot be changed (p. 876)

inbreeding continued breeding of individuals with similar characteristics (p. 320)

incomplete dominance situation in which one allele is not completely dominant over another (p. 272)

incomplete metamorphosis type of insect development characterized by a similar appearance throughout all stages of the life cycle (p. 729)

independent assortment independent segregation of genes during the formation of gametes (p. 271)

independent variable factor in an experiment that a scientist purposely changes; also known as a responding variable (p. 1056)

index fossil distinctive fossil used to compare the relative ages of fossils (p. 419)

inference logical interpretation based on prior knowledge and experience (p. 4)

inflammatory response nonspecific defense reaction to tissue damage caused by injury or infection (p. 1035)

innate behavior instinct, or inborn behavior; behavior that appears in a fully functional form the first time it is performed (p. 873)

insight learning also called reasoning; learning process in which an animal applies something it has already learned to a new situation without a period of trial and error (p. 875)

interferon one of a group of proteins that help cells resist viral infection (p. 1035)

internal fertilization process in which eggs are fertilized inside the female's body (pp. 666, 690, 758)

internode region between nodes on plant stems (p. 589)

interphase period of the cell cycle between cell divisions (p. 245)

intracellular digestion process in which food is digested inside cells (p. 751)

intron intervening sequence of DNA; does not code for a protein (p. 302)

invasive species plants and animals that have migrated to places where they are not native (p. 153)

invertebrate animal that does not have a backbone or vertebral column (p. 657)

ion atom that has a positive or negative charge (p. 38)

ionic bond bond formed when one or more electrons are transferred from one atom to another (p. 38)

isotope atom of an element that has a number of neutrons different from that of other atoms of the same element (p. 36)

joint place where one bone attaches to another (p. 924)

karyotype set of photographs of chromosomes grouped in order in pairs (p. 341)

kelp forest coastal ocean community named for its dominant organism—kelp (p. 110)

keratin tough, fibrous protein found in skin (p. 934)

kidney organ that removes urea, excess water, and other waste products from the blood and passes them to the ureter (p. 985)

kingdom largest taxonomic group, consisting of closely related phyla (p. 449)

Koch's postulates series of guidelines used to identify the microorganism that causes a specific disease (p. 1030)

Krebs cycle second stage of cellular respiration, in which pyruvic acid is broken down into carbon dioxide in a series of energy-extracting reactions (p. 226)

language system of communication that combines sounds, symbols, or gestures according to a set of rules about word order and meaning (p. 882)

large intestine colon; organ that removes water from the undigested materials that pass through it (p. 984)

larva immature stage of an organism that looks different from the adult form (p. 666)

larynx structure in the throat containing the vocal cords (p. 958)

lateral bud meristematic area on the side of a stem that gives rise to side branches (p. 636)

lateral line system sensitive receptor system that enables fish to detect gentle currents and vibrations in the water (p. 777)

leaf photosynthetic organ that contains one or more bundles of vascular tissue (p. 561)

learning alterations in behavior as a result of experience (p. 873)

lens transparent object behind the iris that changes shape to help adjust the eye's focus to see near or distant objects (p. 907)

lichen symbiotic association between a fungus and a photosynthetic organism (p. 540)

ligament strip of tough connective tissue in a joint that holds bones together (p. 925)

light-dependent reactions reactions of photosynthesis that use energy from light to produce ATP and NADPH (p. 210)

lignin substance in vascular plants that makes cell walls rigid (p. 560)

limiting factor factor that causes the growth of a population to decrease (p. 124)

limiting nutrient single nutrient that either is scarce or cycles very slowly, limiting the growth of organisms in an ecosystem (p. 80)

lipid macromolecule made mainly from carbon and hydrogen atoms; includes fats, oils, and waxes (p. 46)

lipid bilayer double-layered sheet that forms the core of nearly all cell membranes (p. 184)

liver large organ just above the stomach that produces bile, a fluid loaded with lipids and salts (p. 982)

logistic growth growth pattern in which a population's growth rate slows or stops following a period of exponential growth (p. 122)

long-day plant plant that flowers when days are long (p. 641)

loop of Henle section of the nephron tubule that conserves water and minimizes the volume of urine (p. 988)

lymph fluid lost by the blood into surrounding tissue (p. 954)

lysogenic infection process by which a virus embeds its DNA into the DNA of the host cell and is replicated along with the host cell's DNA (p. 485)

lysosome cell organelle filled with enzymes needed to break down certain materials in the cell (p. 178)

lytic infection process in which a virus enters a cell, makes a copy of itself, and causes the cell to burst (p. 485)

macroevolution large-scale evolutionary changes that take place over long periods of time (p. 435)

macronucleus the larger of a ciliate's two nuclei, contains multiple copies of most of the genes that the cell needs in its day-to-day existence (p. 499)

madreporite sievelike structure through which the water vascular system of an echinoderm opens to the outside (p. 735)

malignant term used to describe cancerous tumors, which can invade and destroy surrounding healthy tissue (p. 1046)

Malpighian tubule saclike organ in most terrestrial arthropods that extracts wastes from the blood and adds them to feces that move through the gut (p. 717)

mammary gland gland in mammals that produces milk to nourish the young (p. 821)

mandible mouthpart adapted for biting and grinding food (p. 721)

mangrove swamp coastal wetland dominated by mangroves, salt-tolerant woody plants (p. 108)

manipulated variable factor in an experiment that a scientist purposely changes; also known as independent variable (pp. 9, 1056)

mantle thin layer of tissue that covers most of a mollusk's body (p. 702)

marsupial mammal which bears live young that complete their development in an external pouch (p. 829)

mass extinction event in which many types of living things become extinct at the same time (p. 431)

medulla oblongata area of the brain that controls the functioning of many internal organs (p. 777)

medusa motile stage of the life cycle of a cnidarian that has a bell-shaped body (p. 670)

meiosis process by which the number of chromosomes per cell is cut in half through the separation of homologous chromosomes in a diploid cell (p. 276)

melanin dark-brown pigment found in skin (p. 934)

meninges three layers of connective tissue in which the brain and spinal cord are wrapped (p. 901)

menstrual cycle cycle during which an egg develops and is released from an ovary and the uterus is prepared to receive a fertilized egg (p. 1013)

menstruation last phase of the menstrual cycle, during which the lining of the uterus, along with blood and the unfertilized egg, is discharged through the vagina (p. 1015)

meristematic tissue plant tissue found only in the tips of shoots and roots; responsible for plant growth (p. 580)

mesoderm middle germ layer of most animals; gives rise to muscles and much of the circulatory, reproductive, and excretory systems (p. 661)

mesophyll specialized ground tissue that makes up the bulk of most leaves; performs most of a plant's photosynthesis (p. 596)

messenger RNA (mRNA) RNA molecule that carries copies of instructions for the assembly of amino acids into proteins from DNA to the rest of the cell (p. 301)

metabolism set of chemical reactions through which an organism builds up or breaks down materials as it carries out its life processes (p. 18)

metaphase second phase of mitosis, during which the chromosomes line up across the center of the cell (p. 248)

metastasis spread of a cancerous tumor beyond its original site (p. 1046)

metric system decimal system of measurement based on certain physical standards and scaled on multiples of 10 (p. 24)

microclimate climate within a small area that differs significantly from the climate of the surrounding area (p. 98)

microfilament long, thin fiber that functions in the movement and support of the cell (p. 176)

microfossil microscopic fossil (p. 426)

micronucleus the smaller of a ciliate's two nuclei; contains a "reserve copy" of all of the cell's genes (p. 499)

microscope device that produces magnified images of structures that are too small to see with the unaided eye (p. 25)

microtubule hollow tube of protein that maintains cell shape and can also serve as a "track" along which organelles are moved (p. 176)

migration periodic movement and return of animals from one place to another (p. 878)

mineral inorganic nutrient the body needs, usually in small amounts (p. 975)

mitochondrion cell organelle that releases energy from stored food molecules (p. 180)

mitosis part of eukaryotic cell division during which the cell nucleus divides (p. 245)

mixture material composed of two or more elements or compounds that are physically mixed together but not chemically combined (p. 41)

molecular clock model that uses DNA comparisons to estimate the length of time that two species have been evolving independently (p. 455)

molecule smallest unit of most compounds (p. 38)

molting process in which an arthropod sheds its exoskeleton and manufactures a larger one to take its place (p. 719)

monocot angiosperm whose seeds have one cotyledon (p. 569)

monoculture farming strategy in which large fields are cleared, plowed, and planted with a single, highly productive crop year after year (p. 142)

monomer small unit that can join together with other small units to form polymers (p. 45)

monosaccharide single sugar molecule (p. 46)

monotreme egg-laying mammal (p. 828)

multiple alleles three or more alleles of the same gene (p. 273)

muscle tissue tissue that controls the internal movement of materials in the body, as well as external movement of the entire body or body parts (p. 894)

mutation change in a DNA sequence that affects genetic information (p. 307)

mutualism symbiotic relationship in which both species benefit from the relationship (p. 93)

mycelium many hyphae tangled together into a thick mass; comprises the bodies of multicellular fungi (p. 528)

mycorrhiza symbiotic association of plant roots and fungi (p. 541)

myelin sheath insulating membrane surrounding the axon in some neurons (p. 898)

myocardium thick middle muscle layer of the heart; pumps blood through the circulatory system (p. 944)

myosin protein that makes up the thick filaments in striations in skeletal muscle cells (p. 928)

NAD^+ (nicotinamide adenine dinucleotide) electron carrier involved in glycolysis (p. 223)

$NADP^+$ (nicotinamide adenine dinucleotide phosphate) one of the carrier molecules that transfers high-energy electrons from chlorophyll to other molecules (p. 209)

natural selection process by which individuals that are better suited to their environment survive and reproduce most successfully; also called survival of the fittest (p. 381)

natural variation differences among individuals of a species (p. 379)

nematocyst stinging structure within each cnidocyte of a cnidarian that is used to poison or kill prey (p. 669)

nephridium excretory organ of an annelid that filters fluid in the coelom (p. 696)

nephron small independent blood-filtering unit in the renal cortex of the kidney (p. 986)

nerve net loosely organized network of nerve cells that together allow cnidarians to detect stimuli (p. 671)

nervous tissue tissue that receives messages from the body's external and internal environment, analyzes the data, and directs the response (p. 894)

neuromuscular junction point of contact between a motor neuron and a skeletal muscle cell (p. 929)

neuron cell that carries messages throughout the nervous system (p. 897)

neurotransmitter chemical used by a neuron to transmit an impulse across a synapse to another cell (p. 900)

niche full range of physical and biological conditions in which an organism lives and the way in which the organism uses those conditions (p. 91)

nicotine stimulant drug in tobacco that increases heart rate and blood pressure (p. 961)

nictitating membrane movable transparent membrane in amphibians located inside the regular eyelid; protects the surface of the eye from damage under water and keeps it moist on land (p. 787)

nitrogen fixation process of converting nitrogen gas into ammonia (pp. 78, 478)

node point on a stem where a leaf is attached (p. 589)

nondisjunction error in meiosis in which homologous chromosomes fail to separate (p. 352)

nonrenewable resource resource that cannot be replenished by natural processes (p. 144)

notochord long supporting rod that runs through a chordate's body just below the nerve cord (pp. 767, 849)

nuclear envelope double-membrane layer that surrounds the nucleus of a cell (p. 176)

nucleic acid macromolecule containing hydrogen, oxygen, nitrogen, carbon, and phosphorus (p. 47)

nucleolus small, dense region within most nuclei in which the assembly of ribosomes begins (p. 176)

nucleotide monomer of nucleic acids made up of a 5-carbon sugar, a phosphate group, and a nitrogenous base (pp. 47, 291)

nucleus the center of the atom which contains the protons and neutrons (p. 35); in cells, large structure inside some cells that contains the cell's genetic material (DNA) and controls the cell's activities (p. 171)

nutrient chemical substance that an organism requires to live (p. 76)

nymph immature form that lacks functional sex organs and other adult structures (p. 729)

O

observation use of one or more of the senses—sight, hearing, touch, smell, and sometimes taste—to gather information (p. 4)

omnivore organism that obtains energy by eating both plants and animals (p. 69)

oogonium specialized structure formed by hyphae that produces female nuclei (p. 519)

open circulatory system system in which blood is not always contained within a network of blood vessels (pp. 703, 754)

operant conditioning learning process in which an animal learns to behave in a certain way through repeated practice, in order to receive a reward or avoid punishment; also called trial-and-error learning (p. 875)

operational definition description of how a particular variable is to be measured or how a term is to be defined (p. 1057)

operator region of chromosome in an operon to which the repressor binds when the operon is "turned off" (p. 310)

operon group of genes operating together (p. 309)

opposable thumb thumb that enables grasping objects and using tools (p. 835)

order group of similar families (p. 449)

organ group of tissues that work together to perform closely related functions (p. 193)

organ system group of organs that work together to perform a specific function (p. 193)

organelle specialized structure that performs important cellular functions within a eukaryotic cell (p. 172)

osmosis diffusion of water through a selectively permeable membrane (p. 186)

ossification process of bone formation, during which cartilage is replaced by bone (p. 922)

ovary in plants, a flower structure that contains one or more ovules from which female gametophytes are produced (p. 612); in animals, the female gonad that produces eggs (p. 1008)

oviparous term used to refer to animals whose eggs hatch outside the mother's body (p. 778)

ovoviviparous term used to refer to animals whose young are born alive after developing in eggs inside the mother's body (p. 778)

ovulation process in which an egg is released from the ovary (p. 1013)

ovule structure in seed cones in which female gametophytes develop (p. 610)

ozone layer band of ozone, a gas made up of three oxygen atoms (p. 157)

pacemaker small group of cardiac muscle cells in the right atrium that "set the pace" for the heart as a whole; also known as the sinoatrial node (p. 946)

paleontologist scientist who studies fossils (p. 417)

palisade mesophyll layer of tall, column-shaped mesophyll cells just under the upper epidermis of a leaf (p. 596)

pancreas gland that produces hormones that regulate blood sugar; enzymes that break down carbohydrates, proteins, lipids, and nucleic acids; and sodium bicarbonate, a base that neutralizes stomach acid (p. 982)

parasite organism that lives within or on another organism and harms that organism by feeding on it (p. 658)

parasitism symbiotic relationship in which one organism lives in or on another organism and harms it (p. 93)

parenchyma type of ground-tissue cell with a thin cell wall and large central vacuole (p. 583)

pathogen disease-causing agent, such as a bacterium or fungus (pp. 479, 1029)

pedigree chart that shows the relationships within a family (p. 342)

pedipalps pair of mouthparts in chelicerates that are usually modified to grab prey (p. 722)

pellicle cell membrane in euglenas (p. 506)

penis external male reproductive organ that connects the urethra to the outside of the body (p. 1011)

peptic ulcer hole in the stomach wall (p. 981)

perennial flowering plant that lives for more than two years (p. 572)

period unit of time into which eras are subdivided (p. 422)

periosteum tough layer of connective tissue surrounding a bone (p. 922)

peristalsis rhythmic muscular contractions that squeeze food through the esophagus into the stomach (p. 980)

permafrost layer of permanently frozen subsoil in the tundra (p. 104)

permanent immunity condition in which people who have survived exposure to a disease never develop it again (p. 1038)

petal brightly-colored structure just inside the sepals; attracts insects and other pollinators to a flower (p. 612)

petiole thin stalk by which a leaf blade is attached to a stem (p. 595)

pH scale measurement system used to indicate the concentration of hydrogen ions (H^+) in solution; ranges from 0 to 14 (p. 43)

phagocyte white blood cell that engulfs and digests foreign cells (p. 952)

phagocytosis process in which extensions of cytoplasm surround and engulf large particles and take them into the cell (p. 189)

pharyngeal pouch one of a pair of structures in the throat (pharynx) region of a chordate (p. 767)

pharynx muscular tube at the end of the gastrovascular cavity, or throat, that connects the mouth with the rest of the digestive tract and serves as a passageway for air and food (pp. 684, 956)

phenotype physical characteristics of an organism (p. 268)

pheromone specific chemical messenger that affects the behavior or development of other individuals of the same species (p. 731)

phloem vascular tissue responsible for the transport of nutrients and the carbohydrates produced by photosynthesis (p. 560)

photic zone well-lit upper layer of the oceans (p. 109)

photoautotroph prokaryote that carries out photosynthesis in a manner similar to that of plants (p. 474)

photoheterotroph prokaryote that is photosynthetic but also needs organic compounds for nutrition (p. 474)

photoperiodism response of plants to periods of light and darkness (p. 641)

photosynthesis process by which plants and some other organisms use light energy to power chemical reactions that convert water and carbon dioxide into oxygen and high-energy carbohydrates such as sugars and starches (pp. 68, 204)

phototropism tendency of plants to grow toward a source of light (p. 634)

phycobilin accessory pigment found in red algae that is especially good at absorbing blue light (p. 510)

phylum group of closely related classes (p. 449)

phytochrome plant pigment responsible for photoperiodism (p. 641)

phytoplankton population of algae and other small, photosynthetic organisms found near the surface of the ocean and forming part of plankton (pp. 107, 508)

GLOSSARY

pigment light-absorbing colored molecule (p. 207)

pioneer species first species to populate an area during primary succession (p. 94)

pith parenchyma cells inside the ring of vascular tissue in dicot stems (p. 590)

pituitary gland gland in the base of the skull that secretes nine hormones that directly regulate many body functions and control the actions of several other endocrine glands (p. 1003)

placenta organ in placental mammals through which nutrients, oxygen, carbon dioxide, and wastes are exchanged between embryo and mother (pp. 829, 1018)

plankton tiny, free-floating, weakly swimming organisms that occur in aquatic environments (p. 107)

Plantae kingdom of multicellular photosynthetic autotrophs that have cell walls containing cellulose (p. 461)

plasma straw-colored fluid that makes up about 55 percent of blood; consists of about 90 percent water and about 10 percent dissolved gases, salts, nutrients, enzymes, hormones, waste products, and plasma proteins (p. 951)

plasmid circular DNA molecule found in bacteria (p. 327)

plasmodium structure with many nuclei formed by acellular slime molds (p. 518)

plastron ventral part of a turtle's or tortoise's shell (p. 805)

platelet cell fragment released by bone marrow (p. 953)

point mutation mutation that affects a single nucleotide, usually by substituting one nucleotide for another (p. 307)

polar zone cold climate zone where the sun's rays strike Earth at a very low angle (p. 188)

pollen cone cone in gymnosperms that produces male gametophytes in the form of pollen grains (p. 610)

pollen grain male gametophyte in seed plants (p. 565)

pollen tube structure grown by a pollen grain; contains two haploid sperm nuclei (p. 611)

pollination transfer of pollen from the male gametophyte to the female gametophyte (p. 565)

pollutant harmful material that can enter the biosphere through the land, air, or water (p. 148)

polygenic trait trait controlled by two or more genes (pp. 273, 343, 396)

polymer large compound formed from combinations of many monomers (p. 45)

polymerase chain reaction (PCR) technique that allows molecular biologists to make many copies of a particular gene (p. 325)

polyp usually sessile stage of the life cycle of a cnidarian that has a cylindrical body with armlike tentacles (p. 670)

polyploid having many sets of chromosomes (p. 321)

polysaccharide large macromolecule formed from monosaccharides (p. 46)

population group of individuals of the same species that live in the same area (p. 64)

population density number of individuals per unit of area (p. 119)

predation interaction in which one organism captures and feeds on another organism (p. 93)

predator-prey relationship mechanism of population control in which a population is regulated by predation (p. 126)

prehensile term used to refer to a long tail that can grasp branches (p. 835)

pressure-flow hypothesis hypothesis that considers plants in terms of where they produce and use materials from photosynthesis (p. 602)

primary growth type of plant growth that occurs at the tips of roots and shoots (p. 590)

primary productivity rate at which organic matter is created by producers in an ecosystem (p. 80)

primary succession succession that occurs on surfaces where no soil exists (p. 94)

prion infectious particle made up of protein rather than RNA or DNA (p. 487)

probability likelihood that a particular event will occur (p. 267)

producer organism that can capture energy from sunlight or chemicals and use it to produce food from inorganic compounds; also called an autotroph (p. 67)

product element or compound produced by a chemical reaction (p. 49)

proglottid one of the segments that make up most of a tapeworm's body (p. 688)

prokaryote single-celled microorganism that lacks a nucleus (pp. 172, 471)

promoter region of DNA that indicates to an enzyme where to bind to make RNA (p. 301)

prophase first and longest phase of mitosis, during which the chromosomes become visible and the centrioles separate and take up positions on the opposite sides of the nucleus (p. 246)

prosimian with few exceptions, small, nocturnal primate that has large eyes for seeing in the dark (p. 834)

prostaglandin hormonelike modified fatty acid produced by a wide range of cells; generally affects only nearby cells and tissues (p. 1000)

protein macromolecule that contains carbon, hydrogen, oxygen, and nitrogen; needed by the body for growth and repair and to make up enzymes (pp. 47, 973)

proteinoid microsphere tiny bubble, formed of large organic molecules, that has some characteristics of a cell (p. 425)

protist any eukaryote that is not a plant, an animal, or a fungus (p. 495)

Protista kingdom composed of eukaryotes that are not classified as plants, animals, or fungi (p. 460)

protonema mass of tangled green filaments in mosses that forms during germination (p. 558)

protostome animal whose mouth is formed from its blastopore (p. 661)

pseudocoelom body cavity between the endoderm and mesoderm tissues that is partially lined with mesoderm tissue (p. 689)

pseudopod projection of cytoplasm, or false foot, used by some protists for feeding or movement (p. 498)

puberty period of rapid growth and sexual maturation during which the reproductive system becomes fully functional (p. 1009)

pulmonary circulation pathway in which the right side of the heart pumps blood to the lungs (p. 944)

punctuated equilibrium pattern of evolution in which long stable periods are interrupted by brief periods of more rapid change (p. 439)

Punnett square diagram showing the gene combinations that might result from a genetic cross (p. 268)

pupa stage of metamorphosis in which an insect changes from a larva into an adult (p. 729)

pupil small opening in the middle of the iris through which light enters the eye (p. 906)

radial symmetry body plan in which body parts repeat around the center of the body; characteristic of sea anemones and sea stars (pp. 662, 748)

radioactive dating technique in which scientists calculate the age of a sample based on the amount of remaining radioactive isotopes it contains (p. 420)

radula tongue-shaped structure used for feeding by snails and slugs (p. 702)

reabsorption process by which most of the material removed from the blood at Bowman's capsule makes its way back into the blood (p. 987)

reactant element or compound that enters into a chemical reaction (p. 49)

recombinant DNA DNA produced by combining DNA from different sources (p. 324)

reflex quick automatic response to a stimulus (p. 903)

relative dating method of determining the age of a fossil by comparing its placement with that of fossils in other layers of rock (p. 419)

relative frequency number of times an allele occurs in a gene pool compared with the number of times other alleles occur (p. 394)

renewable resource resource that can regenerate quickly and that is replaceable (p. 144)

replication copying process by which a cell duplicates its DNA (p. 299)

reproductive isolation separation of species or populations so that they cannot interbreed and produce fertile offspring (p. 404)

reptile any vertebrate that has dry scaly skin, lungs, and terrestrial eggs with several protective membranes (p. 797)

resource any necessity of life, such as water, nutrients, light, food, or space (p. 92)

responding variable factor in an experiment that a scientist wants to observe, which may change in response to the manipulated variable; also known as a dependent variable (pp. 9, 1056)

response single, specific reaction to a stimulus (p. 871)

resting potential difference in electrical charge across the cell membrane of a resting neuron (p. 898)

restriction enzyme enzyme that cuts DNA at a specific sequence of nucleotides (p. 323)

retina innermost layer of the eye (p. 907)

retrovirus virus that contains RNA as its genetic information (p. 487)

rhizoid in fungi, a rootlike hypha that penetrates the surface of an object (p. 530); in mosses, a long, thin cell that anchors the moss to the ground and absorbs water and minerals from the surrounding soil (p. 557)

rhizome creeping or underground stem in ferns (p. 562)

ribonucleic acid (RNA) single-stranded nucleic acid that contains the sugar ribose (p. 47)

ribosomal RNA (rRNA) type of RNA that makes up the major part of ribosomes (p. 301)

ribosome small particle in the cell on which proteins are assembled; made of RNA and protein (p. 177)

RNA polymerase enzyme similar to DNA polymerase that binds to DNA and separates the DNA strands during transcription (p. 301)

rod photoreceptor in eye that is extremely sensitive to light (p. 907)

root underground organ in plants that absorbs water and minerals (p. 561)

root cap tough structure that protects a root as it forces its way through the soil (p. 585)

root hair tiny projection from the outer surface, or epidermis, of a root (p. 585)

rumen stomach chamber in cows and related animals in which newly swallowed plant food is stored and processed (p. 823)

salt marsh temperate-zone estuary dominated by salt-tolerant grasses above the low-tide line and by seagrasses under water (p. 108)

saprobe organism that obtains food from decaying organic matter (p. 537)

sapwood area in plants that surrounds heartwood and is active in fluid transport (p. 592)

science organized way of using evidence to learn about the natural world; also, the body of knowledge that scientists have built up after years of using this process (p. 3)

sclerenchyma type of ground-tissue cell with an extremely thick, rigid cell wall that makes ground tissue tough and strong (p. 583)

scolex head of an adult tapeworm; can contain suckers or hooks (p. 688)

scrotum external sac containing the testes (p. 1010)

secondary growth pattern of plant growth in which stems increase in width (p. 95)

secondary succession succession following a disturbance that destroys a community without destroying the soil (p. 95)

seed embryo of a living plant that is encased in a protective covering and surrounded by a food supply (p. 565)

seed coat structure that surrounds and protects a plant embryo and keeps it from drying out (p. 565)

seed cone cone that produces female gametophytes (p. 610)

segregation separation of alleles during gamete formation (p. 266)

selective breeding method of improving a species by allowing only those individual organisms with desired characteristics to produce the next generation (p. 319)

selective permeability property of biological membranes that allows only certain substances to pass through them (p. 186)

semicircular canal one of three structures within the inner ear that help an organism maintain balance (p. 908)

seminiferous tubule one of hundreds of tiny tubules in the testes in which sperm are produced (p. 1010)

sensory receptor neuron that reacts directly to light, sound, or other stimuli by sending impulses to other neurons and eventually to the central nervous system (p. 906)

sepal outermost circle of flower parts that encloses a bud before it opens and protects the flower while it is developing (p. 612)

septum internal wall between the segments of an annelid's body (p. 694)

seta bristle attached to the segments of many annelids (p. 694)

sex chromosome one of two chromosomes that determine an individual's sex; females have two X chromosomes; males have one X chromosome and one Y chromosome (p. 341)

sex-linked gene gene located on the X or Y chromosome (p. 350)

sexual reproduction process by which two cells from different parents unite to produce the first cell of a new organism (p. 17)

shell structure in mollusks made by glands in the mantle that secrete calcium carbonate (p. 702)

short-day plant plant that flowers when daylight is short (p. 641)

sieve tube element phloem cell that is joined end-to-end to similar cells to form a continuous sieve tube (p. 582)

single-gene trait trait controlled by a single gene (p. 395)

siphon tubelike structure through which water enters and leaves a mollusk's body (p. 703)

small intestine digestive organ in which most chemical digestion takes place (p. 981)

smog gray-brown mixture of chemicals that occurs as a haze in the atmosphere (p. 148)

society group of closely related animals of the same species that work together for the benefit of the group (p. 732)

soil erosion wearing away of surface soil by water and wind (p. 145)

solute substance that is dissolved in a solvent to make a solution (p. 42)

solution mixture of two or more substances in which the molecules of the substances are evenly distributed (p. 42)

solvent substance in which a solute is dissolved to form a solution (p. 42)

sorus cluster of sporangia on the underside of a fern frond (p. 562)

speciation formation of new species (p. 404)

species group of similar organisms that can breed and produce fertile offspring (p. 64)

species diversity number of different species in the biosphere (p. 150)

spicule spike-shaped structure that makes up the skeletons of harder sponges; made of either chalklike calcium carbonate or glasslike silica (p. 665)

spindle fanlike microtubule structure that helps separate the chromosomes during mitosis (p. 247)

spinneret organ in spiders that contains silk glands (p. 723)

spiracle small opening located along the side of the body through which air enters and leaves the body of many terrestrial arthropods (p. 717)

spirillum spiral or corkscrew-shaped prokaryote (p. 473)

spongy mesophyll loose tissue beneath the palisade layer of a leaf; has many air spaces between its cells (p. 596)

spontaneous generation hypothesis (disproven) stating that life could arise from nonliving matter (p. 8)

sporangiophore specialized hyphae where sporangia are found (p. 528)

sporangium structure in ferns and some fungi that contains spores (pp. 528, 562)

spore haploid reproductive cell (p. 514)

sporophyte diploid, or spore-producing, phase of an organism (pp. 514, 552)

stabilizing selection form of natural selection by which the center of the curve remains in its current position; occurs when individuals near the center of a distribution curve have higher fitness than individuals at either end (p. 399)

stamen male part of the flower; made up of an anther and a filament (p. 612)

stem supporting structure that connects roots and leaves and carries water and nutrients between them (p. 561)

sterilization process of destroying bacteria using great heat or chemical action (p. 481)

stigma sticky portion at the top of the style where pollen grains frequently land (p. 612)

stimulant drug that speeds up the actions regulated by the nervous system (p. 910)

stimulus any kind of detectable signal that carries information (p. 871)

stolon in fungi, a stemlike hypha that runs along the surface of an object (p. 530); in plants, a long, trailing stem that produces roots when it touches the ground (p. 622)

stoma opening in the underside of a leaf that allows carbon dioxide and oxygen to diffuse into and out of the leaf (p. 596)

stomach large muscular sac that continues the mechanical digestion of food (p. 980)

stroma region outside the thylakoid membranes in chloroplasts (p. 208)

struggle for existence competition among members of a species for food, living space, and the other necessities of life (p. 380)

style narrow stalk of the carpel in a flower (p. 612)

subcutaneous fat layer of fat cells beneath the skin (p. 822)

subsistence hunting hunting only to acquire basic necessities for survival; makes relatively few demands on the environment (p. 140)

substrate reactant of an enzyme-catalyzed reaction (p. 52)

survival of the fittest process by which individuals that are better suited to their environment survive and reproduce most successfully; also called natural selection (p. 381)

suspension mixture of water and nondissolved materials (p. 42)

sustainable use using natural resources at a rate that does not deplete them (p. 145)

swim bladder internal gas-filled organ in many bony fishes that adjusts their buoyancy (p. 777)

swimmerets flipperlike appendages used by decapods for swimming (p. 721)

symbiosis relationship in which two species live closely together (p. 93)

synapse location at which a neuron can transfer an impulse to another cell (p. 900)

systemic circulation pathway in which the left side of the heart pumps blood to all of the body except the lungs (p. 944)

taproot primary root found in some plants that grows longer and thicker than other roots (p. 584)

target cell cell affected by a particular hormone (pp. 634, 997)

taste bud sense organ that detects the flavor of a substance (p. 909)

taxon group or level of organization into which organisms are classified (p. 449)

taxonomy discipline of classifying organisms and assigning each organism a universally accepted name (p. 447)

telophase fourth and final phase of mitosis, during which the chromosomes begin to disperse into a tangle of dense material (p. 248)

temperate zone moderate climate zone between the polar zones and the tropics (p. 88)

temporal isolation form of reproductive isolation in which two populations reproduce at different times (p. 405)

tendon tough connective tissue that joins skeletal muscles to bones (p. 930)

territory specific area occupied and protected by an animal or group of animals (p. 881)

testis male gonad that produces sperm (pp. 688, 1008)

tetrad structure containing 4 chromatids that forms during meiosis (p. 276)

thalamus brain structure that receives messages from the sense organs and relays the information to the proper region of the cerebrum for further processing (p. 903)

theory well-tested explanation that unifies a broad range of observations (pp. 14, 369)

thigmotropism response of plants to touch (p. 639)

thorax body part of a crustacean that lies just behind the head and houses most of the internal organs (p. 721)

threshold minimum level of a stimulus required to activate a neuron (p. 899)

thylakoid saclike body in chloroplasts made of photosynthetic membranes that contain photosystems (p. 208)

tissue group of similar cells that perform a particular function (p. 192)

toxin poison that produces illness by disrupting bodily functions (p. 1031)

trachea windpipe; tube through which air moves (p. 956)

tracheal tube one of many branching, air-filled tubes that extend throughout the bodies of many terrestrial arthropods (p. 717)

tracheid hollow plant cell in xylem tissue with thick cell walls that resist pressure (p. 560)

trait specific characteristic that varies from one individual to another (p. 264)

transcription process in which part of the nucleotide sequence of DNA is copied into a complementary sequence in RNA (p. 301)

transfer RNA (tRNA) type of RNA molecule that transfers amino acids to ribosomes during protein synthesis (p. 301)

transformation process in which one strain of bacteria is changed by a gene or genes from another strain of bacteria (p. 288)

transgenic term used to refer to an organism that contains genes from other organisms (p. 331)

translation decoding of a mRNA message into a polypeptide chain (p. 304)

transpiration loss of water from a plant through its leaves (pp. 75, 596)

trichocyst small, bottle-shaped structures used for defense by paramecia (p. 499)

trichome tiny cellular projection on the surfaces of some leaves that helps protect the leaf and also gives it a fuzzy appearance (p. 581)

trochophore free-swimming larval stage of an aquatic mollusk (p. 701)

trophic level step in a food chain or food web (p. 70)

tropical zone warm climate zone that receives direct or nearly direct sunlight year round (p. 88)

tropism response of a plant to an environmental stimulus (p. 639)

true-breeding term used to describe organisms that produce offspring identical to themselves if allowed to self-pollinate (p. 263)

tube foot suction cup-like structure attached to radial canals of echinoderms; used to walk and to open shells (p. 735)

tumor mass of growing tissue that may form when a cell or group of cells begins to grow and divide uncontrollably (p. 1046)

tympanic membrane eardrum of amphibians inside the skull; vibrates in response to sound, allowing hearing (p. 787)

understory layer in a rain forest formed by shorter trees and vines (p. 100)

ureter tube that carries urine from the kidney to the urinary bladder (p. 985)

urethra tube through which urine and semen are released from the body (pp. 988, 1011)

urinary bladder saclike organ in which urine is stored before being excreted (p. 985)

uterus organ of the female reproductive system in which a fertilized egg can develop (p. 1013)

vaccination injection of a weakened or mild form of a pathogen to produce immunity (p. 1040)

vacuole cell organelle that stores materials such as water, salts, proteins, and carbohydrates (p. 179)

vagina canal in the human female reproductive system that leads from the uterus to the outside of the body (p. 1013)

valve flap of connective tissue between an atrium and a ventricle, or in a vein, that prevents backflow of blood (p. 945)

van der Waals forces a slight attraction that develops between the oppositely charged regions of nearby molecules (p. 39)

variable factor in an experiment that can change (p. 1056)

vas deferens tube that carries sperm from the epididymis to the urethra (p. 1010)

vascular bundle plant stem structure that contains xylem and phloem tissue (p. 590)

vascular cambium lateral meristematic tissue that produces vascular tissues and increases the thickness of the stem over time (p. 591)

vascular cylinder central region of a root that includes the vascular tissue—xylem and phloem (p. 585)

vascular tissue type of plant tissue specialized to conduct water (p. 560)

vector animal that carries disease-causing organisms from person to person (p. 1032)

vegetative reproduction method of asexual reproduction used by many flowering plants (p. 622)

vein in plants, a cluster of vascular tissue in leaves (p. 561); in animals, a blood vessel that returns blood to the heart (p. 947)

ventricle thick-walled lower chamber of the heart that pumps blood out of the heart (pp. 776, 944)

vertebra individual segment of the backbone; encloses and protects the spinal cord (p. 768)

vertebrate animal that has a vertebral column, or backbone (p. 657)

vessel element in angiosperms; xylem cell that forms part of a continuous tube through which water can move (p. 582)

vestigial organ organ that serves no useful function in an organism (p. 385)

villus folded projection that increases the surface area of the walls of the small intestine (p. 983)

virus particle made up of nucleic acid, protein, and in some cases lipids that can replicate only by infecting living cells (p. 482)

visceral mass area beneath the mantle of a mollusk that contains the internal organs (p. 702)

vitamin organic molecule that helps regulate body processes (p. 974)

viviparous term used to refer to animals that bear live young that are nourished directly by the mother's body as they develop (p. 778)

water vascular system system of internal tubes in echinoderms that carries out essential functions such as feeding, respiration, circulation, and movement (p. 735)

weather condition of Earth's atmosphere at a particular time and place (p. 87)

wetland ecosystem in which water either covers the soil, or is present at or near the surface of the soil for at least part of the year (p. 107)

xerophyte desert plant (p. 644)

xylem vascular tissue that carries water upward from the roots to every part of a plant (p. 560)

zonation prominent horizontal banding of organisms that live in a particular habitat (p. 110)

zooplankton tiny animals that form part of the plankton (p. 107)

zoosporangium spore case (p. 518)

zygospore resting spore that contains zygotes formed during the sexual phase of a mold's life cycle (p. 530)

zygote fertilized egg (p. 1016)

INDEX

B

INDEX

F

G

N

O

INDEX

Q

R

INDEX

S

T

Credits

Staff Credits

The people who made up the *Prentice Hall Biology* team—representing design services, editorial, editorial services, market research, marketing services, online services & multimedia development, production services, project office, and publishing processes—are listed below. Bold type denotes the core team members.

Laura Baselice, Diane Braff, **Kristen Cetrulo Braghi,** Jonathan D. Cheney, Christine Cuccio, Patricia M. Dambry, Robert Danielenko, **Irene Ehrmann,** Holly Gordon, **Maureen Grassi,** Jon Greenberg, Kristan Hoskins, Anne Jones, Carol Lavis, **Ellen Levinger, Sandra McGloster,** Chris Maniatis, Natania Mlawer, Carrie O'Connor, **Steve Palme, Rachel Avenia-Prol, Maureen Raymond,** Amy Rosen, Robin Santel, Annette Simmons, **Dori Steinhauff,** Janna Wasilewski, Mike Wevrick

Additional Credits

Greg Abrom, Ernest Albanese, Robert Aleman, Diane Alimena, Gabriella Apolito, Penny Baker, Michele Bigness, Anthony Barone, Barbara Blecher, Chris Callaway, Rui Camarinha, Catherine Caradonna, John Carle, Martha Conway, Lisa Del Gatto, Paul DelSignore, Yvonne Favaro, Elizabeth Forsyth, Catalina Gavilanes, Michael Ginsberg, Evan Holstrom, Beth Hyslip, Helen Issackedes, Catherine Johnson, Susan Karpin, Vicki Lamb, Marguerite McCartney, Vickie Menanteaux, Kathleen Mercandetti, Art Mkrtchayn, LaShonda Morris, Kenneth Myett, Raymond Parenteau, Linda Punskovsky, Bruce Rolff, Laura Ross, Gerry Schrenk, Mildred Schulte, Nancy Sharkey, Lou Suffredini, Kathleen Ventura

t. = Top, b. = Bottom; l. = Left; r. = Right; m. = Middle

Art Credits

Charts and Graphs: Ernest Albanese and Studio A Aleman, Rob **400, 440, 460** (fungi icons), **461, 610, 612, 630** Art and Science **767, 769, 770** Articulate Graphics **71, 72, 73, 109, 115, 243** (cubes; with E. Albanese), **245, 246–247, 248, 250, 251, 257, 258, 259, 266, 268** t., **269, 270, 271, 272, 276, 277, 278, 283, 284, 285, 290, 291, 294, 295, 298, 300, 301, 302, 303, 304, 305, 306, 307, 308, 309, 310, 311, 312, 315, 316, 322, 323, 324, 325, 326, 327, 328, 329, 332, 337, 338, 342, 343, 347, 349, 350, 352, 356, 358, 360, 361, 363, 365, 472, 483, 484, 485, 498, 499, 500, 506, 523, 524, 661, 679, 680, 718, 852, 944, 953, 959, 999, 1035, 1037, 1038, 1044** Bechtold, Glory **264** (from Biology, The Living Science), **265** (from Biology, The Living Science), **379** (from Science Exporer), Cavallo, Tamara **514, 517, 518, 519, 527, 528, 531, 533, 534, 540, 545, 973, 974, 975** Cummings, Sally **193** r., **979, 980, 995** Dorling Kindersley Publishers **892–893, 903, 922, 933** t.r., **924, 927** t.r., **945** t.r., **955** Duray-Bito, Cecile **414, 436, 450, 450, 465, 467** Gagliano, Tom **35, 36, 38, 39, 40, 41, 42, 44, 45, 46, 47, 48, 52, 57, 92, 153, 163, 184, 185, 186, 187, 188, 189, 193** l. (from Science Explorer), **198, 202, 203, 206, 209** t., **211, 212, 217, 219, 222, 223, 225, 227, 228, 230, 652, 653, 701, 878** (turtles in map), **892–893, 897–900, 902, 907, 908, 917, 998, 1025, 1027** Imagineering **9, 11, 12, 21, 24, 25, 64, 68, 75, 77, 78, 79, 85, 87, 88, 148, 152, 159, 160, 237, 297**(with Articulate Graphics), **299** (with Articulate Graphics), **312, 369, 389, 418, 419, 422, 424, 425, 443, 566, 580** (with Patrice Rossi Calkin), **586** (leaf art), **588, 591, 597, 599, 602, 683, 763, 777, 793, 810**t.l., **811, 817, 825, 858, 859** b., **862** Iverson, Carlyn **69, 384, 501, 513, 517, 518, 685, 687, 688, 689, 694, 697, 702, 703, 711, 772, 773, 774, 776, 782, 783, 786, 803, 823, 826–827, 837, 838, 845, 859** t., **867, 868, 934** Levine, Andy **182, 209** b. Mapping Specialists **89, 91, 99, 101, 148, 153, 156, 159, 165, 348, 371, 383** (with Wendy Smith), **405, 410** (with Ernest Albanese), **700, 724, 832** (with Wendy Smith), **878, 1045** McGregor, Malcolm **423** Miller, Mark **923, 931, 947, 951, 1030, 1036, 1051** Mkrtchyan, Art **195, 460, 461, 807** (icons), **836, 869** Morales, Elizabeth **904, 1010, 1011, 1012, 1014, 1017** (from Biology, The Living Science) Oh, Steve **169, 172, 174, 175, 176, 177, 178, 180, 181, 208, 427, 551** O'Keefe, Laurie **376, 382, 391, 406, 439** (modern horse), **452, 552, 557, 558, 609, 611, 612, 634, 635, 636, 641, 662, 665, 666, 669, 670, 672, 717, 718, 721, 722, 728, 729, 732, 733, 735, 741, 784, 785, 798, 799, 801, 806, 809, 810**b., **812, 824, 849, 860, 862, 874, 885** Phippin, Spencer **901, 902, 925, 927, 928, 945, 946, 957, 958, 969, 978, 981, 983, 986, 987, 989, 1003, 1005, 1006, 1018** Precision Graphics **111, 280, 288, 290, 334, 461, 554** b., **555, 625, 627, 640, 649, 660, 726, 747, 768, 790, 807** (icons), **850** (icons), **905, 915, 930, 964** Rossi-Calkin, Patrice **280, 511, 554** t., **563, 565, 570, 575, 576, 580** (with Imagineering, Inc.), **581, 582, 584, 585, 587, 589, 590, 593, 595, 596, 600, 602** (with Imagineering, Inc.), **616, 621, 629, 642, 651, 671, 745, 746, 752, 753, 754, 755, 756, 757** Rothman, Michael **96, 97** Smith, Wendy **64, 68, 69, 83, 84, 383** (animals), **692, 832** Woolsey Associates, J/B **41, 209, 226, 259** Adapted from Neil A. Campbell, Jane B. Reece, and Lawrence G. Mitchell, Biology: Concepts and Connections, 3rd ed. (Menlo Park, CA: Benjamin/Cummings, 2000) **973**

Photo Credits

Photo Research: Slip Jig

Cover ©Tim Fitzharris 1996/Minden Pictures, Inc. **Title Page** ©Tim Fitzharris 1996/Minden Pictures, Inc. **ii** F. Rauschenbach/ Natural Selection Stock Photography, Inc. **iii** t. Courtesy of Ken Miller; b. Russ Lappa/PH School **vi** ©Gregory Ochocki/Photo Researchers, Inc. **vii** t. Joseph Van Os/The Image Bank; b. ©XX NCI/CNRI/Phototake NYC/Phototake **ix** Lee Rentz/Bruce Coleman, Inc. **x** t. ©Dorling Kindersley; b. ©Kjell B. Sandved/Visuals Unlimited **xi** t. Courtesy of Wolfgang Kaehler; b. ©Wayne Lankinen/DRK Photo **xiii** t. Manny Millan/Sports Illustrated; b. ©Michael Fogden/DRK Photo **xiv** t. Pearson Education/PH School; b.l. Pearson Education/PH School; b.r. ©William Leonard/DRK Photo **xv** t. Pearson Education/PH School; b. Pearson Education/PH School **xvi** Runk/Schoenberger/Grant Heilman Photography **xvii** t.l. ©Andy Rouse/DRK Photo; b.l. ©Dan McCoy/ Rainbow; b.r. Richard Anderson/PH School **xviii** b. Courtesy of Ken Miller **xix** Russ Lappa/PH School **xxi** t.l. ©Harold Hoffman/Photo Researchers, Inc.; t.r. ©Steve Kaufman/DRK Photo **xxii–1** ©Steve Wolper/DRK Photo **2** ©Andrew Syred/Science Photo Library/Photo Researchers, Inc. **3** 35464/13 "Creation of North Sacred Mountain" by Harrison Begay, Navajo. In the Collections of the Museum of Indian Arts and Culture/Laboratory of Anthropology, Museum of New Mexico. Photograph by Blair Clark. **4** t. ©The Stock Market/Douglas Faulkner; b. ©The Stock Market/John Zoiner **5** ©Jim Sugar Photography/CORBIS **6** CORBIS Sygma **7** ©Thierry Orban/CORBIS Sygma **9** Animals Animals/©Breck P. Kent **10** ©James L. Amos/CORBIS **12** t. ©Bettmann/CORBIS; b.l. ©CORBIS; b.r. Courtesy of the National Portrait Gallery, London **13** t. ©CORBIS; b.l. ©Julia Cameron/ CORBIS; b.r. ©A. Barrington Brown/Science Source/Photo Researchers, Inc. **14** ©Frans Lanting/Minden Pictures, Inc. **15** l. Eric and David Hosking/CORBIS; r. ©Tom McHugh/Photo Researchers, Inc. **16** t. ©Chris Bjornberg/Photo Researchers, Inc.; b. ©Marty Cordano/ DRK Photo **17** t. Animals Animals/©Robert Maier; m. ©Dwight R. Kuhn/ DRK Photo; b. ©Biophoto Associates/ Photo Researchers, Inc. **18** l–r: #1 Animals Animals/©E.R. Degginger; l–r: #2 Animals Animals/©Jennifer Loomis; l–r: #3 Animals Animals/©Patti Murray; l–r: #4 Animals Animals/ ©Patti Murray; b. Animals Animals/©Bruce Davidson **19** ©Ron Spomer/Visuals Unlimited **20** l. ©Michael Fogden/DRK Photo; r. ©Michael Fogden/DRK Photo **22** ©Zigy Kaluzny/ Stone **23** Stephff/Cartoonists & Writers Syndicate **26** t. ©Kevin and Betty Collins/Visuals Unlimited; m. ©M.I. Walker/Photo Researchers, Inc.; b. ©Oliver Meckes/Photo Researchers, Inc. **27** ©The Stock Market/Charles Gupton **28** ©Paul Chelsley/ Stone **31** Anthony Bannister; Gallo Images/CORBIS **34** Animals Animals/©Patti Murray **37** t.l. ©PhotoDisc, Inc., 2001; t.r. Richard Anderson/Pearson Education/PH School **39** t.l. Kellar Autumn & Ed Florance; t.r. ©Mark Moffett/Minden Pictures, Inc.; b. ©Mark Moffett/Minden Pictures, Inc. **40** Wood Sabold/Index Stock Photography, Inc. **41** ©Mark Moffett/Minden Pictures, Inc. **45** ©Bill Bachmann/Photo Network/PictureQuest **46** ©Ricardo Arias, Latin Stock/Science Photo Library/Photo Researchers, Inc. **49** Richard Megna/Fundamental Photographs **53** t. Thomas Steitz, Yale University; b. Thomas Steitz, Yale University **54** Pearson Education/PH School **55** Pearson Education/PH School **56** Wood Sabold/Index Stock Photography, Inc. **60–61** Corel Professional Photos CD-ROM™ **62** ©Bruce Coleman, Ltd./Natural Selection **63** ©Gerry Ellis/Minden Pictures, Inc. **65** ©Mark Moffett/Minden

Pictures, Inc. **66** t.l. U.S. Department of the Interior/ U.S. Geological Survey; t.r. U.S. Department of the Interior/ U.S. Geological Survey; b. Provided by the SeaWiFS Project, NASA/Goddard Space Flight Center, and ORBIMAGE **67** ©Gregory Ochocki/Photo Researchers, Inc. **69** ©Rod Planck/Photo Researchers, Inc. **70** Pearson Education/ PH School **74** l. ©Bill Frymire/Masterfile Stock Image Library; b. ©Ron Sanford & Mike Agliolo/Photo Researchers, Inc. **76** Rod Wiliams/Bruce Coleman, Inc. **80** ©Larry Ulrich/DRK Photo **81** Pearson Education/ PH School **82** ©Richard Matthews/Masterfile Stock Image Library **86** ©Frans Lanting/Minden Pictures, Inc. **90** ©Kenneth H. Thomas/ Photo Researchers, Inc. **91** ©Ray Ellis/Photo Researchers, Inc. **93** t. ©Nuridseny et Perennou/Photo Researchers, Inc.; m. ©Fred Bavendam/Minden Pictures, Inc.; b. ©Ken Wagner/Phototake **95** t. ©J.B. Diederich/Contact Press Images/PictureQuest; b.l. ©PhotoDisc, Inc., 2001; b.r. Courtesy of Belva Fry **97** University of Hawaii at Manoa School of Ocean and Earth Science and Technology **100** t. ©Luiz C. Marigo/Peter Arnold, Inc.; inset: t.l. ©Tom & Pat Leeson/ Photo Researchers, Inc.; inset: t.r. ©Wayne Lynch/DRK Photo; b. ©E. Hanumantha Rao/Photo Researchers, Inc.; inset: b.l. ©Belinda Wright 1984/DRK Photo; inset: b.r. ©1994 Chamberlain, MC/DRK Photo **101** t. Courtesy of Wolfgang Kaehler inset: t.l. ©Barbara Gerlach/DRK Photo **101** inset: t.r ©Stephen J. Krasemann/DRK Photo; b. ©Larry Ulrich/DRK Photo; inset: b.l. ©Marty Cordano/DRK Photo; inset: b.r. ©Stephen J. Krasemann/DRK Photo **102** t. ©Tom Bean 1996/DRK Photo; inset: t.l. ©Wayne Lankinen/DRK Photo; inset: t.r ©Tom & Pat Leeson/DRK Photo; b. ©Walter H. Hodge/Peter Arnold, Inc.; inset: b.l. ©Gary R. Zahm/DRK Photo; inset: b.r. ©Mark Smith/Photo Researchers, Inc. **103** t. ©Michael P. Gadomski/ Photo Researchers, Inc.; inset: t.l. ©Noble Proctor/Photo Researchers, Inc.; inset: t.r ©Stephen J. Krasemann /DRK Photo; b. ©Gerry Ellis/Minden Pictures, Inc.; inset: b.l. ©Stephen Dalton/Photo Researchers, Inc.; inset: b.r. Animals Animals/©Leo Keeler **104** t. ©Tom Bean/CORBIS; inset: t.l. ©Lynn M. Stone 1997/DRK Photo; inset: t.r. Daniel J. Cox/naturalexposures.com; b. ©Kim Heacox Photography/DRK Photo; inset: b.l. Daniel J. Cox/ naturalexposures.com; inset: b.r. ©Steve Kaufman 1991/DRK Photo **105** ©Dennis Flaherty/ Photo Researchers, Inc. **106** Animals Animals/©Richard & Susan Day **107** t. ©Roland Birke/Peter Arnold, Inc.; b. ©Clint Farlinger/Natural Selection **108** l. Animals Animals/©Fred Whitehead; r. ©Belinda Wright/DRK Photo **109** ©Andrew J. Martinez/Photo Researchers, Inc **110** t. ©Frans Lanting/ Photo Researchers, Inc.; b. ©Flip Nicklin/Minden Pictures, Inc. **111** ©Fred Bavendam/Minden Pictures, Inc. **112** t. ©Dough Perrine 1990/DRK Photo; b. ©Norbert Wu/DRK Photo **113** ©Spike Walker/ Stone **118** ©Frans Lanting/Minden Pictures, Inc. **119** ©Terry Donnelly **120** Joseph Van Os/The Image Bank **121** t. ©CNRI/Phototake; b. ©Frans Lanting/ Minden Pictures, Inc. **123** Bernard W. Knott, Ed. D. 124 l-r: #1 ©Lee F. Snyder/Photo Researchers, Inc. **124** l-r: #2 ©Stephen J. Krasemann/ DRK Photo; l-r: #3 John Gerlach/Tom Stack & Associates; l-r: #4 ©Ford Kristo/Masterfile Stock Image Library; l-r: #5 ©Gerry Ellis/Minden Pictures, Inc. **125** ©Lee F. Snyder/Photo Researchers, Inc. **126** t.l. ©Patrick J. Endres/Visuals Unlimited; t.r. ©Andy Rouse/ DRK Photo; b. John Gerlach/Tom Stack & Associates **127** ©Ford Kristo/Masterfile Stock Image Library **128** ©Roy Corral/ Stone **130** t.l. Black Star; t.r. Bett Press/Woodfin Camp & Associates **132** ©Paul Harris/Stone **133** ©M. Abbey/Photo Researchers, Inc. **138** ©Sun Star/Stock Photos Hawaii **139** ©Frans Lanting/Minden Pictures, Inc. **140** t. Gallery of Prehistoric Art; b. ©BIOS (A. Compost)/Peter Arnold, Inc. **141** University of Reading ©Rural History Centre **142** ©Mitch Kezar/Stone **143** t. ©Jake Rajs/Stone; b. ©Murray & Associates, Inc./ Picturesque/PictureQuest **144** ©Holt Studios International (Miss P. Peacock)/Photo Researchers, Inc. **145** t. Animals Animals/ ©James H. Robinson; b. ©Mark Edwards/ Still Pictures/Peter Arnold, Inc. **146** ©Peter Christopher/ Masterfile Stock Image Library **147** ©Labat/Jacana/Photo Researchers, Inc. **148** ©Gary Milburn/ Tom Stack & Associates **149** ©David Woodfall/Stone **151** ©Academy of Natural Sciences of Philadelphia/ CORBIS **152** ©Scott Camazine/Photo Researchers, Inc. **153** ©Tom Vezo/Peter Arnold, Inc. **154** t. Portrait of Mrs. Augustus Hemenway, John Singer Sargent, Private Collection; Photo courtesy Adelson Galleries, Inc., New York; b.l. Bobbe' Z. Christopherson; b.r. ©Doug Armand/Stone **155** t. Kjell Sandved/Bruce Coleman, Inc.; b.l. NASA; b.r. Graeme Ellis-Ursus/Ursus Photography, Vancouver **156** cw: 1 ©Joe McDonald/DRK Photo; cw: 2 ©Doug Cheeseman/Peter Arnold, Inc.; cw: 3 ©Simon D. Pollard/Photo Researchers, Inc.; cw: 4 ©E. Hanumantha Rao/Photo Researchers, Inc.; cw: 5 Kjell B. Sandved/ Butterfly Alphabet, Inc.; cw: 6 ©R. Ian Lloyd/ Masterfile Stock Image Library; cw: 7 ©Ted Schiffman/Peter Arnold, Inc.; cw: 8 Animals Animals/©Fabio Colombini **157** ©NASA/Science Photo Library/Photo Researchers, Inc. **158** ©James Darell/Stone **161** ©Impact Visuals/ Phototake **162** ©Joe McDonald/DRK Photo **166–167** ©Dr. Brian Eyden/ Science Photo Library/Photo Researchers, Inc. **168** ©Quest/ Science Photo Library/Photo Researchers, Inc. **170** t. ©Martha J. Powell/Visuals Unlimited; m. ©Spike Walker/Stone; b.l. ©Robert Hooke/Visuals Unlimited; b.r. Bausch & Lomb Incorporated **171** t. Courtesy National Archives; b. ©Biophoto Associates/Photo Researchers, Inc. **173** ©Dr. Dennis Kunkel/Phototake **175** ©Professors P. Motta & T. Naguro/Science Photo Library/Photo Researchers, Inc. **176** ©Albert Tousson/Phototake **177** l. ©Science Source/Photo Researchers, Inc.; r. ©Professors P. Motta & T. Naguro/Science Photo Library/Photo Researchers, Inc. **178** ©Professors P. Motta & T. Naguro/Science Photo Library/Photo Researchers, Inc. **179** t. Pearson Education/PH School; b. ©Newcomb & Wergin/BPS/Stone **180** ©Biophoto Associates/Science Source/ Photo Researchers, Inc. **181** ©Professors P. Motta & T. Naguro/Science Photo Library/Photo Researchers, Inc. **190** l. ©David M. Phillips/Visuals Unlimited; r. ©CNRI/Science Photo Library/Photo Researchers, Inc.; m. ©Cabisco /Visuals Unlimited **191** t.r. ©Dr. Dennis Kunkel/Phototake; b.l. ©Don Fawcett/Photo Researchers, Inc.; b.r. ©John D. Cunningham/ Visuals Unlimited; m.b. ©Dr. Dennis Kunkel/Phototake **192** l. ©PhotoDisc, Inc., 2001; r. Patricia Greer **194** Pearson Education/PH School **197** cw: 1 ©CNRI/Science Photo Library/Photo Researchers, Inc.; cw: 2 ©Stan Flegler/Visuals Unlimited; cw: 3 ©Dr. Dennis Kunkel/Phototake; cw: 4 ©John D. Cunningham/Visuals Unlimited **200** ©Stone **201** l. Pearson Education Corporate Digital Archive; r. A. Shah/ABPL Anthony Bannister's Photo Library **202** ©The Stock Market/Ed Bock **204** t. The Granger Collection, New York; b. The Granger Collection, New York **205** t.l. Dwight Kuhn Photography; t.r. ©Bettmann/CORBIS; b. Lawrence Berkley Nat'l Lab **206** Pearson Education/PH School **208** t.l. ©Clyde H. Smith/Peter Arnold, Inc.; b.l. ©John Durham/Science Photo Library/Photo Researchers, Inc.; b.r. ©Newcomb & Wegin/ Stone **210** ©David Muench 2000 **214** t. ©Larry Brownstein/ Rainbow/PictureQuest; b. ©PhotoDisc, Inc., 2001 **215** Pearson Education/ PH School **216** ©David Muench 2000 **218** ©Ken Wagner/Phototake/ PictureQuest **220** Duomo Photography, Inc. **221** l. ©Bob Gurr/DRK Photo; r. ©Keith Porter/Photo Researchers, Inc.; m.t. ©Ron Boardman/Stone; m.b. ©John Durham/Science Photo Library/Photo Researchers, Inc. **224** ©Becky Luigart-Stayner/CORBIS **226** ©Science Photo Library/ Photo Researchers, Inc. **230** ©Allsport/Ross Kinnaird **231** Pearson Education/PH School **233** ©Dan Smith/Stone **234** Pearson Education/PH School **235** Pearson Education/PH School **236** t. ©Dan Smith/Stone; b. ©Bob Gurr/DRK Photo **240** ©CAMR/A.B. Dowsett/Science Photo Library/Photo Researchers, Inc. **241** ©Kevin Summers/ Stone **242** Pearson Education/PH School **244** ©Gunther F. Bahr/AFIP/ Stone **246** t. ©Ed Reschke/Peter Arnold, Inc. l. ©Ed Reschke/Peter Arnold, Inc.; b. ©Ed Reschke/Peter Arnold, Inc. **247** t. ©Ed Reschke/ Peter Arnold, Inc.; b.l. ©Ed Reschke/Peter Arnold, Inc. b.r. ©Ed Reschke/Peter Arnold, Inc. **248** ©R. Calentine/ Visuals Unlimited **252** ©Dr. Gopal Murti/Science Photo Library/Photo Researchers, Inc. **253** t.l. ©CAMR/A.B. Dowsett/Science Photo Library/ Photo Researchers, Inc.; t.r. ©Dr. Dennis Kunkel/Phototake; b.l. ©Stan Flegler/Visuals Unlimited; b.r. ©Professor P.M. Motta & E. Vizza/Science Photo Library/Photo Researchers, Inc. **254** ©Ed Reschke/Peter Arnold, Inc. **255** Pearson Education/PH School **260–261** ©Tom & Pat Leeson **262** ©Dan McCoy/Rainbow **263** CORBIS **267** ©Al Francekevich/The Stock Market **270** ©James W. Richardson/Visuals Unlimited **271** Runk/Schoenberger/Grant Heilman Photography **273** t.l. ©John Gerlach/Visuals Unlimited; t.r. Animals Animals/©Richard Kolar; b.l. ©Jane Burton/Bruce Coleman, Inc.; b.r. ©Hans Reinhard/Bruce Coleman, Inc. **274** Kim Taylor/Bruce Coleman, Inc. **279** Animals Animals/©George Bernard **281** Pearson Education/PH School **284** ©S. Nielsen/DRK Photo **286** Jacob Halaska/Index Stock Imagery, Inc.; Jacob Halaska/Index Stock Imagery, Inc. **287** ©Klaus Guldbrandsen/ Science Photo Library/Photo Researchers, Inc. **289** ©Lee D. Simon/Science Source/Photo Researchers, Inc. **292** t.l. ©Science Source/Photo Researchers, Inc.; t.r. ©Cold Spring Harbor Laboratory Archives/Peter Arnold, Inc.; b. ©Bettmann/ CORBIS **293** t. ©2000 Kay Chernush/ Howard Hughes Medical Institute; b.l. ©A. Barrington/ Photo Researchers, Inc.; b.r. Jane Reed/Harvard University **296** Science Photo Library/Custom Medical Stock Photo, Inc. **298** ©Dr. Gopal Murti/Science Photo Library/Photo Researchers, Inc. **301** From J. Frank, American Scientist 86 (2000), 428–439, Courtesy of Joachim Frank, All Rights Reserved. **313** Pearson Education/PH School **318** ©Geoff Tompkinson/Science Photo Library/Photo Researchers, Inc. **319** ©Darrell

Credits

Gulin/DRK Photo **320** t. ©Mitsuaki Iwago/Minden Pictures, Inc.; b. ©Manfred Kage/Peter Arnold, Inc. **321** Runk/Schoenberger/Grant Heilman Photography **326** Pearson Education/PH School **330** N. Cobbing. ©Still Pictures/Peter Arnold, Inc. **331** ©Keith V. Wood/Visuals Unlimited **333** "PA" News **335** Pearson Education/PH School **340** ©The Stock Market/Rob Lewine **341** ©CNRI/Science Photo Library/Photo Researchers, Inc. **343** ©Craig Farraway **344** ©The Stock Market/Charles Gupton **346** ©Simon Fraser/RVI, Newcastle-Upon Tyne/ Science Photo Library/Photo Researchers, Inc. **347** ©Omikron/ Photo Researchers, Inc. **349** Leslie Jones/CORBIS **352** ©PhotoDisc, Inc., 2001 **353** t.l. ©Lawrence Migdale; t.r. ©Dr. Dennis Kunkel/CNRI/ Phototake **354** AP/Wide World Photos **355** t. ©James King-Holmes/ Science Photo Library/ Photo Researchers, Inc.; b. AP/Wide World Photos **356** l. ©Leonard Lessin/Peter Arnold, Inc.; r. ©D. VoTrung/Phototake **357** Paul Hosefros/NYT Permissions **359** t.l. ©PhotoDisc, Inc., 2001; t.r. ©2000 Ron Caesar **362** ©CNRI/Science Photo Library/Photo Researchers, Inc. **366–367** ©1996 Jack S. Grove c/o Mira **368** Art Wolfe Incorporated **370** l. Syndics of Cambridge University Library; r. ©Joe McDonald/Bruce Coleman, Inc./PictureQuest **371** t. ©D. Cavagnaro/ DRK Photo; m. ©M. Cavagnaro/DRK Photo; b. ©D. Cavagnaro/DRK Photo **372** ©Frans Lanting/Photo Researchers, Inc. **373** ©Jean-Loup Charmet **374** t. ©Tom Bean/DRK Photo; m. The Granger Collection, New York; b. Stock Montage, Inc. **375** t.l. The Granger Collection, New York; t.r. Brown Brothers; b. ©2000 North Wind Picture Archives **377** Archiv für Kunst und Geschichte, Berlin **378** Mark Downey/Index Stock Photography, Inc. **379** Pearson Education/PH School **380** ©J. Sneesby/B. Wilkins/Stone **381** ©Ron Austing/Photo Researchers, Inc. **382** Neil Fletcher/©Dorling Kindersley **385** t. Harry Taylor/©Dorling Kindersley; b.l. ©George Whiteley/Photo Researchers, Inc.; m.b. Animals Animals/©Keith Gillett; b.r. ©David Spears/ Science Photo Library/Photo Researchers, Inc. **386** ©ARCHIV/Photo Researchers, Inc. **390** t. ©M. Cavagnaro/ DRK Photo; b. ©D. Cavagnaro/DRK Photo **392** ©J. Eastcott & Y. Momatiuk/Masterfile Stock Image Library **393** ©Melanie Carr/ Zephyr Photos **395** l. ©David Young-Wolff/PhotoEdit/PictureQuest; r. ©David Young-Wolff/PhotoEdit/ PictureQuest **396** New York Public Library, (Rare Book Division or Print Collection. Miriam and Ira D. Wallach Division of Art, Prints and Photographs); Astor, Lenox and Tilden Foundations **397** ©Charlie Ott/Photo Researchers, Inc. **399** ©Melanie Carr/Zephyr Photos **401** Pearson Education/PH School **402** ©Lee F. Snyder/Photo Researchers, Inc. **403** ©David R. Frazier/Photo Researchers, Inc. **404** l. ©Harold Hoffman/ Photo Researchers, Inc.; r. ©Steve Kaufman/DRK Photo **405** t. ©Danny Lehman/CORBIS; inset: l. Animals Animals/©Breck P. Kent; inset: r. ©Tom & Pat Leeson/DRK Photo **407** t. Photograph by B.R. Grant; b. Photograph by P.R. Grant **409** Yahn Arthus-Bertrand/CORBIS **411** Pearson Education/PH School **416** Jackie Beckett/American Museum of Natural History **417** Ira Block/National Geographic Society **419** l. ©David Hanson/Stone; r. CORBIS **425** ©Sidney Fox/Visuals Unlimited **426** ©Fred Bavendam/Peter Arnold, Inc. **428** British Museum of Natural History, London **429** ©D.W. Miller **430** British Museum of Natural History, London/J. Sibbick **431** t. The Field Museum, Chicago, Il; b. Lefever/ Grushow/ Grant Heilman Photography **432** 1989 Mark Hallett **433** t. The Natural History Museum London/M. Long; b.l. ©PhotoDisc, Inc., 2001; b.r. Dan Olson/Pearson Education/PH School **434** ©Douglas Henderson **435** ©D. Van Ravenswaay/Science Photo Library/ Photo Researchers, Inc. **437** t. ©PhotoDisc, Inc., 2001; m. ©Wayne Lynch/ DRK Photo; b. Mike Bacon/Tom Stack & Associates **438** t. The Natural History Museum, London; b. ©Charles Marden Fitch **439** t-b: 2 Sean Milne/©Dorling Kindersley; t-b: 3 Sean Milne©Dorling Kindersley; t-b: 4 Sean Milne/©Dorling Kindersley; t-b: 5 Sean Milne/©Dorling Kindersley **441** Pearson Eduction/School Division **446** Steve Winter **447** ©Jeff Lepore/Photo Researchers, Inc. **448** ©Kenneth W. Fink/Photo Researchers, Inc. **449** t. CORBIS; bl. ©Art Wolfe/Photo Researchers, Inc.; mb. Animals Animals/©Norbert Rosing; br. Daniel J. Cox/naturalexposures.com **451** t.l. Animals Animals/©Rudolf Ingo Riepl ;b.l. ©Peter Howorth/Mo Yung Productions/ www.norbertwu.com; b.r. ©Nancy Sefton/Photo Researchers, Inc. **454** t. ©Barbara Gerlach/ DRK Photo; b. ©D. Parer & E. Parer-Cook/ Auscape International Photo Library **456** t. ©Marie Selby Botanical Gardens; b. ©Marie Selby Botanical Gardens **457** l. ©Michael Abbey/ Photo Researchers, Inc.; r. ©CNRI/ Phototake **463** cw:1 Matthew Ward/©Dorling Kindersley; cw:2 ©Dorling Kindersley; cw:3 Matthew Ward/©Dorling Kindersley; cw:4 ©Dorling Kindersley; cw:5 ©Dorling Kindersley; cw:6 Matthew Ward/©Dorling Kindersley; m. Matthew Ward/©Dorling Kindersley **468–469** ©David M. Dennis **470** ©Beth Donidow/Visuals Unlimited **471** Esther R. Angert, Harvard University **472** ©M. Wurtz/Biozentrum, University of Basel/Science Photo Library/Photo Researchers, Inc. **473** t.l. ©David Scharf/Peter Arnold, Inc.; t.r. ©Scott Camazine/Photo Researchers, Inc.; m.t. ©David M. Phillips/Visuals Unlimited; m.r. ©Biodisc/Visuals Unlimited; b. ©CNRI/Phototake **474** ©Fred McConnaughey/Science Source/Photo Researchers, Inc. **475** l. ©PhotoDisc, Inc., 2001; r. Courtesy of Elizabeth Lawton; b. ©Dr. Dennis Kunkel/ Phototake **476** t. ©Dr. Dennis Kunkel/Phototake; b. ©Dr. Dennis Kunkel/Phototake **477** ©Michael P. Gadomski/Photo Researchers, Inc. **478** t. ©Richard L. Carlton/Visuals Unlimited; m. W. J. Short; b. Hulton-Deutsch Collection/CORBIS **479** t. Brown Brothers; b. Chris Ware/Liaison Agency **480** SuperStock **482** ©Norm Thomas/Photo Researchers, Inc. **483** l. ©M. Wurtz/Biozentrum, University of Basel/Science Photo Library/Photo Researchers; m. ©Dr. O. Bradfute/Peter Arnold, Inc.; r. ©National Institute for Biological Standards and Control, England/Photo Researchers, Inc. **486** Pearson Education/PH School **487** Sinclair Stammers/Science Photo Library/ Photo Researchers, Inc. **488** ©Meckes/Ottawa/Photo Researchers, Inc. **489** Pearson Education/PH School **490** t. ©M. Wurtz/Biozentrum, University of Basel/Science Photo Library/Photo Researchers, Inc.; b. ©Dr. Dennis Kunkel/ Phototake **491** t.l. ©M. Wurtz/Biozentrum, University of Basel/Science Photo Library/Photo Researchers, Inc.; t.r. ©David M. Phillips/Visuals Unlimited; b.l. ©David Scharf/Peter Arnold, Inc.; b.r. ©Scott Camazine/Photo Researchers, Inc. **494** ©Biophoto Associates/Photo Researchers, Inc. **495** l. ©Manfred Kage/Peter Arnold, Inc.; m. ©Manfred Kage/Peter Arnold, Inc.; r. ©M.I. Walker/Photo Researchers, Inc. **496** ©T.E. Adams/Visuals Unlimited **497** l. ©Michael Abbey/Photo Researchers, Inc.; r. ©Oliver Meckes/Photo Researchers, Inc. **498** Runk/Schoenberger/ Grant Heilman Photography **499** ©Eric V. Grave/Photo Researchers, Inc. **501** ©Oliver Meckes/Photo Researchers, Inc. **502** ©Robert Brons/Biological Photo Service **503** l. ©Dr. Dennis Kunkel/ Phototake; r. ©Eric Grave/Science Source/Photo Researchers, Inc. **504** ©Garry D. McMichael 1987/Photo Researchers, Inc. **505** ©A. Flowers & L. Newman/Photo Researchers, Inc. **506** ©M. Abbey/Visuals Unlimited **507** t. ©Dr. Dennis Kunkel/Phototake; b. ©Dr. Dennis Kunkel/Phototake **509** t. ©Bill Bachman/Photo Researchers, Inc.; inset ©David M. Phillips/ Visuals Unlimited **510** ©G. Robinson/Visuals Unlimited **512** t. Biophoto Assoc./Photo Researchers, Inc.; m. ©James W. Richardson/Visuals Unlimited; b. ©Laurie Campbell/ NHPA **515** t. ©StockFood America/Eising; b. ©StockFood America/DeSanto **516** ©L. West/Photo Researchers, Inc. **517** ©Matt Meadows/Peter Arnold, Inc. **518** ©Dr. Dennis Kunkel/Phototake **520** t. The Granger Collection, New York b.l. ©E. Webber/Visuals Unlimited; b.r. ©Holt Studios Int./Photo Researchers, Inc. **521** Pearson Education/PH School **526** ©D. Cavagnaro/DRK Photo **528** t. ©Sarah J. Frankling/ Stone; b. Robert & Linda Mitchell Photography **529** ©Jeff Lepore/Photo Researchers, Inc. **532** Lee Rentz/Bruce Coleman, Inc. **535** t.l. ©Jeff Lepore/Photo Researchers, Inc.; t.r. ©Laurie Campbell/ Stone; m.t. ©Robert W. Domm/Visuals Unlimited; m.b. ©Michael Fogden/DRK Photo; b.l. ©Michael Fogden/DRK Photo; b.r. ©Ed Reschke/Peter Arnold, Inc. **536** t. ©Jack M. Bostrack/Visuals Unlimited; b. ©David Scharf/Peter Arnold, Inc. **537** D. Redecker (B-E), R. Kodner (A); ©Science, 2000 **538** ©Stephen G. Maka/DRK Photo **539** t.l. ©Astrid & Hanns-Frieder Michler/Science Photo Library/Photo Researchers, Inc.; m.t. ©Holt Studios International/Nigel Cattlin/Photo Researchers, Inc.; t.r. ©Dr. P. Marazzi/Photo Researchers, Inc.; b. ©Michael Fogden/DRK Photo **540** t. ©Courtney Milne; m. ©Jack Dermid; b. ©L. West/Photo Researchers, Inc. **541** ©Phil Matt/Stone **542** t. ©John D. Cunningham/Visuals Unlimited; b. Runk/Schoenberger/Grant Heilman Photography **543** Pearson Education/PH School **548–549** ©Clyde H. Smith/Peter Arnold, Inc. **550** ©Frans Lanting/ Minden Pictures, Inc. **551** Runk/Schoenberger/Grant Heilman Photography **552** ©Russell D. Curtis/Photo Researchers, Inc. **553** t. Jane Grushow/Grant Heilman Photography; b. Animals Animals/ ©Joyce & Frank Burek **554** Hans Steur, The Netherlands **555** cw: 1 ©Dorling Kindersley; cw: 2 ©Ed Reschke/Peter Arnold, Inc.; cw: 3 ©Ed Reschke/ Peter Arnold, Inc.; cw: 4 ©Pat Lynch/Photo Researchers, Inc. **556** ©Terry Donnelly/Stone **557** l. ©Alvin E. Staffan/National Audubon Society/Photo Researchers, Inc. r. Robert & Linda Mitchell Photography **559** ©Farrell Greham/Photo Researchers, Inc. **560** t. Peter Chadwick/©Dorling Kindersley; b. Photo Researchers, Inc. **561** l. ©Gary W. Carter/Visuals Unlimited; r. ©Ed Reschke/Peter Arnold, Inc. **562** t. ©Peter Chadwick/Dorling Kindersley; b.l. ©Biophoto Associates/ Photo Researchers, Inc.; b.r. ©Ed Reschke/Peter Arnold, Inc. **564** Animals Animals/©Erwin & Peggy Bauer **565** ©PhotoDisc, Inc., 2001 **566** t. Dr. E.R. Degginger; b. Peter Chadwick/©Dorling Kindersley **567** t. ©Gerald & Buff Corsi/Visuals Unlimited; m. ©Jeff Lepore/Photo Researchers, Inc.; b. ©Walter H. Hodge/Peter Arnold, Inc. **568** l. ©Stephen G. Maka/ DRK Photo; r. Larry Lefever/Grant Heilman Photography **569** l. Hans Reinhard/ Bruce Coleman, Inc.; r. ©PhotoDisc, Inc., 2001 **571** l. ©PhotoDisc, Inc., 2001; r. Meoy Gee **572** l. Joy Spurr/Bruce Coleman, Inc.; m. Jonathan Buckley/©Dorling Kindersley; r. Larry Lefever/Grant Heilman Photography **573** ©Fritz Polking/Visuals Unlimited **574** ©Dorling Kindersley **576** Brian Parker/Tom Stack & Associates **578** ©Manfred Kage/Peter Arnold, Inc. **581** t.l. Ray F. Evert, University of Wisconsin; t.r. Ray F. Evert, University of Wisconsin; b. ©Andrew Syred/Science Photo Library/Photo Researchers, Inc. **582** Ray F. Evert, University of Wisconsin **583** l. ©Ed Reschke/Peter Arnold, Inc.; m. ©Ed Reschke/Peter Arnold, Inc.; r. ©George Wilder/Visuals Unlimited **585** ©Carolina Biological Supply/Phototake **590** l. ©Ed Reschke/Peter Arnold, Inc.; r. ©Ed Reschke/Peter Arnold, Inc. **592** ©Manfred Kage/Peter Arnold, Inc. **594** t.l. Barry L. Runk/Grant Heilman Photography; t.r. ©Dorling Kindersley; b.l. ©Geoff Dann/Dorling Kindersley; b.r. ©Dorling Kindersley **597** ©Dr. Jeremy Burgess/Science Photo Library/Photo Researchers, Inc. **598** l. ©Kjell B. Sandved/Visuals Unlimited; m. ©Doug Sokell/Visuals Unlimited; t.r. ©Brian P. Foss/ Visuals Unlimited; b.r. ©Kjell B. Sandved/Visuals Unlimited **600** ©Jack M. Bostrack/Visuals Unlimited **601** Pearson Education/PH School **608** ©Carl R. Sams II/Peter Arnold, Inc. **610** t. ©Walter H. Hodge/Peter Arnold, Inc.; b.l. ©Martha Cooper/Peter Arnold, Inc.; b.r. ©Manfred Kage/Peter Arnold, Inc. **612** l. ©Nigel Cattlin/H.S.I./Photo Researchers, Inc.; r. ©Rod Planck/Photo Researchers, Inc. **613** t. Pearson Education/PH School; b.l. Geoff Dann©Dorling Kindersley; b.r. CORBIS 615; t.r. ©Geoff Bryant/Photo Researchers, Inc. **615** b.l. Animals Animals/©Carroll W. Perkins; b.r. ©M. H. Sharp/Photo Researchers, Inc. **617** t. Florigene Limited; b. Florigene Limited **618** t. ©Dorling Kindersley; b.l. ©Dorling Kindersley; b.r. ©Dorling Kindersley **619** t. ©Gregory K. Scott/Photo Researchers, Inc.; b. ©Stephen J. Krasemann/Photo Researchers, Inc. **620** ©L. Linkhart /Visuals Unlimited **622** Runk/Schoenberger/Grant Heilman Photography **623** t. ©Michael P. Gadomski/Photo Researchers, Inc.; b. ©Holt Studios Int./Photo Researchers, Inc. **624** t. ©Wolfgang Kaehler/CORBIS; m.l. ©PhotoDisc, Inc., 2001; m.r. SBG; b.l. ©Werner H. Muller/Peter Arnold, Inc.; b.r. ©Karen Su/CORBIS **625** t.l. ©Holt Studios Int./Nigel Cattlin/Photo Researchers, Inc.; t.r. ©David Cavagnaro/Peter Arnold, Inc.; b. ©PhotoDisc, Inc., 2001 **626** ©Michael P. Gadomski/Photo Researchers, Inc. **628** ©Walter H. Hodge/Peter Arnold, Inc. **632** ©Dr. Paul A. Zahl/Photo Researchers, Inc. **633** Animals Animals/©Dani/ Jeske **635** Dr. E.R. Degginger **637** ©Sylvan Wittwer/Visuals Unlimited **638** Courtesy of Stephen Gladfelter, Stanford University **639** ©Charles D.Winters/ Photo Researchers, Inc. **640** t. ©Ed Reschke/Peter Arnold, Inc.; b. ©Ed. Reschke/Peter Arnold, Inc. **642** ©Ed. Reschke/Peter Arnold, Inc. **643** ©Paul A. Souders/CORBIS **644** ©Doug Sokell/Visuals Unlimited **645** t. Sean Morris/©Oxford Scientific Films; b. ©Ray Pfortner/ Peter Arnold, Inc. **646** l. ©Bill Ivy/Stone; r. ©Rod Planck/Photo Researchers, Inc. **647** ©David Cavagnaro/Peter Arnold, Inc. **648** ©Jack Bostrack/Visuals Unlimited **654–655** ©Wayne Lynch/DRK Photo **656** ©Jeff Greenberg/Photo Researchers, Inc. **657** ©Ken Highfill/Photo Researchers, Inc. **658** t.l. ©John Cancalosi/ DRK Photo; m.l. SuperStock; b.l. ©BIOS (F. Marquez)/Peter Arnold, Inc.; b.r. ©Roger Eriksson **659** l. ©Anthony Bannister/Photo Researchers, Inc.; r. ©Kevin Schafer/Stone; b. ©Tom & Pat Leeson/Photo Researchers, Inc.; t. ©Carolina Biological Supply/Phototake **661** m. ©Carolina Biological Supply/ Phototake; b. ©Carolina Biological Supply /Phototake **663** F. Rauschenbach/Natural Selection Stock Photography, Inc. **664** l. ©Mary Beth Angelo/Photo Researchers, Inc.; r. ©Charles V. Angelo/Photo Researchers, Inc. **667** ©Fred McConnaughey/Photo Researchers, Inc. **668** ©Larry Dunmire/Photo Network/PictureQuest **671** l. Jeffrey L. Rotman; r. ©Mary Beth Angelo/Photo Researchers, Inc. **673** t.l. Copyright ©2000 Harbor Branch Oceanographic/E. Widder; t.r. Copyright ©2000 Harbor Branch Oceanographic; b. ©2001 Norbert Wu/ www.norbertwu.com **674** ©Doug Perrine/Innerspace Visions **675** ©2001 Norbert Wu/www.norbertwu.com **676** t. Pearson Education/PH School; b. ©Science Pictures Limited/CORBIS **682** ©Jeffrey L. Rotman **683** ©Fred McConnaughey/Photo Researchers, Inc. **684** ©Drs. Kessel and Shih/ Peter Arnold, Inc. **685** ©Carolina Biological Supply Company/Phototake **686** l. ©Jeffrey L. Rotman/Peter Arnold, Inc.; r. ©Brian Rogers/Visuals Unlimited **688** ©Oliver Meckes/Photo Researchers, Inc. **689** ©Cabisco/Visuals Unlimited **690** t. ©Oliver Meckes/Photo Researchers, Inc.; b. ©David Scharf/ Peter Arnold, Inc. **691** t.l. ©PhotoDisc, Inc., 2001; t.r. Jim Foster/ Pearson Education/PH School; b. ©R. Umesh Chandran, TDR, WHO/Science Photo Library/Photo Researchers, Inc. **692** ©C. James Webb/Phototake NYC **693** l. ©Sinclair Stammers/Science Photo Library/Photo Researchers, Inc.; r. ©Fernand Ivaldi/Stone **694** ©Kjell B. Sandved/Visuals Unlimited **695** t. Pearson Education/PH School; b. Animals Animals/©Raymond A. Mendez **696** t. ©Aldo Brando/Peter Arnold, Inc.; b. Bruce Coleman, Inc. **698** t.l. ©C.P. Hickman/Visuals Unlimited; t.r. National Archives; b. ©Hal Beral/Visuals Unlimited **699** ©Robert Pickett/CORBIS **701** ©Kelvin Aitken/Peter Arnold, Inc. **704** left: 1 ©Jane Burton/Dorling Kindersley; left: 2 Jane Burton/©Dorling Kindersley; left: 3 ©Jane Burton/Dorling Kindersley; left: 4 ©Jane Burton/Dorling Kindersley; b. ©Fred Bavendam/Peter Arnold, Inc. **705** t.l. ©A. Flowers and L. Newman/Photo Researchers, Inc.; t.r. ©William J. Weber/Visuals Unlimited; b.r. ©Alexandra Edwards/Peter Arnold, Inc. **706** t. ©Fred Bavendam/Peter Arnold, Inc.; b. ©Dave B. Fleetham/ Visuals Unlimited **707** ©Frank Greenway/Dorling Kindersley **708** ©Heather R. Davidson **710** ©Jeffrey L. Rotman/Peter Arnold, Inc. **712** ©Marty Snyderman/Visuals Unlimited **713** ©T.E. Adams/Visuals Unlimited **714** ©Leroy Simon/Visuals Unlimited **715** ©Carolina Biological Supply/Phototake **716** t. ©John Cancalosi/DRK Photo; b. ©Dorling Kindersley **719** Barry L. Runk/Grant Heilman Photography **720** ©Rod Planck/Photo Researchers, Inc. **723** t. ©Franz Lanting/Minden Pictures, Inc.; b. ©Dorling Kindersley **724** t. ©R. Calentine/Visuals Unlimited b. ©BIOS (X. Eichaker)/Peter Arnold, Inc. **725** t. ©Tom McHugh/Photo Researchers, Inc.; b. ©Michael & Patricia Fogden/ DRK Photo **726** t. Wolfgang Kaehler Photography; b.l. ©Dorling Kindersley; b.r. ©M.C. Chamberlain/DRK Photo **727** ©Dorling Kindersley **728** ©Stephen Dalton/Photo Researchers, Inc. **730** t. ©Martin Dohrn/Science Photo Library/Photo Researchers, Inc.; b.l. ©David Scharf/Peter Arnold, Inc.; b.r. ©Galen Rowell/CORBIS **731** t. ©E. R. Degginger/Photo Researchers, Inc.; b. AP/Wide World Photos/David Jennings **734** ©Glenn M. Oliver/Visuals Unlimited **736** ©Dorling Kindersley **737** t. ©Charles V. Angelo/Photo Researchers, Inc. m. Animals Animals/©Clay Wiseman b.l. ©Fred Bavendam/Peter Arnold, Inc. b.r. ©Andrew J. Martinez/Photo Researchers, Inc. **738** t. ©M.C. Chamberlain/DRK Photo; b. ©James Amos/Photo Researchers, Inc. **744** ©Doug Perrine/Innerspace Visions **746** Chip Clark/National Museum of Natural History, Smithsonian **751** ©Ray Coleman/Photo Researchers, Inc. **753** Pearson Education/PH School **757** ©Lawrence Naylor/Photo Researchers, Inc. **758** l. ©Brandon D. Cole; r. ©Kelvin Aitken/Peter Arnold, Inc. **759** Pearson Education/PH School **764–765** ©Merlin D. Tuttle/Bat Conservation International **766** ©Art Wolfe/ Stone **769** Animals Animals/©W. Gregory Brown **770** Runk/Schoenberger/Grant Heilman Photography **771** ©Labat-Lanceau/AUSCAPE International **773** Dr. Michael E. Williams/Cleveland Museum of Natural History **774** ©Peter David/Masterfile Stock Image Library **775** t. Pearson Education/PH School; b. Animals Animals/©A. Root **777** ©Richard T. Nowitz/Photo Researchers, Inc. **778** t. ©Natalie Fobes/Stone m. Animals Animals/©Zig Leszczynski b. ©Brian Parker/Tom Stack & Associates **779** t. Howard Hall Productions; m. Animals Animals/©Herb Segars; b. ©Stephen Frink/Stone **780** t.l. ©Fred Bavendam/Minden Pictures, Inc.; m.t. ©Fred Bavendam/ Minden Pictures, Inc.; t.r. ©Norbert Wu/DRK Photo; m.l. ©Stephen Frink/Waterhouse Stock; m.r. Howard Hall Productions; b. ©Mark Erdmann/Innerspace Visions **781** ©Ralph A. Clevenger/CORBIS **787** Animals Animals/©Bill Beatty **788** t.l. ©William Leonard/DRK Photo; b.l. Animals Animals/©Juan Manuel Renjifo; b.r. ©Dorling Kindersley **789** Animals Animals/©Stephen Dalton **790** t. ©RogerTreadwell/Visuals Unlimited; b. Animals Animals/©M. Gibbs **791** Pearson Education/PH School **792** t. ©William Leonard/ DRK Photo; b. ©Labat-Lanceau/AUSCAPE International **796** ©Bruce Coleman, Ltd./Natural Selection **797** ©David A. Northcott/CORBIS **800** ©Joe McDonald/Natural Selection **801** ©Michael Fogden/DRK Photo **802** t.l. ©Michael Fogden/DRK Photo; t.r. ©Michael Fogden/DRK Photo; b. ©E.R. Degginger/Photo Researchers, Inc. **803** ©K.H. Switak/Photo Researchers, Inc. **804** t.l. ©Dorling Kindersley; t.r. ©Anup Shah/DRK Photo; m. Michael & Patricia Fogden/ CORBIS; b.l. ©John Cancalosi/ Peter Arnold, Inc.; b.r. ©Gary Retherford/Photo Researchers, Inc. **805** Gerry Ellis/gerryellis.com **807** ©Sinclair Stammers/Science Photo Library/Photo Researchers, Inc. **808** t–b:1 Steve Gettle/gerryellis.com; t–b: 2 ©Joe McDonald/DRK Photo; t–b: 3 Gerry Ellis/gerryellis.com; t–b: 4 ©Michael Fogden/DRK Photo; t–b: 5 ©Joe McDonald/ DRK Photo; t–b: 6 ©Frans Lanting/Minden Pictures, Inc. **813** cw: 1 ©Stephen J. Krasemann/DRK Photo; cw: 2 Michael Gore; Frank Lane Picture Agency/CORBIS; cw: 3 ©Tim Davis/Photo Researchers, Inc.; cw: 4 ©M.H. Sharp/Photo Researchers, Inc.; cw: 5 ©PhotoDisc, Inc., 2001; cw: 6

Credits

Seldon Jr., W. Lynn/Omni-Photo Communications, Inc.; m. ©2000, Gail Shumway/FPG International LLC **814** ©Wayne Lankinen/DRK Photo **815** AP/Wide World Photos **816** ©Dorling Kindersley **820** Animals Animals/©Zig Leszczynski **821** ©Frans Lanting/ Minden Pictures, Inc. **822** t. Daniel J. Cox/naturalexposures.com; b. ©Flip Nicklin/Minden Pictures, Inc. **824** ©The Stock Market/ Keenan Ward **826** t.l. ©Jany Sauvanet/Photo Researchers, Inc.; t.r. ©Mitsuaki Iwago/Minden Pictures, Inc.; b. ©Thomas Mangelsen/ Minden Pictures, Inc. **827** l. ©Manfred Danegger/OKAPIA/Photo Researchers, Inc.; m. ©Stephen Dalton/Photo Researchers, Inc.; r. ©Gregory Ochocki/Photo Researchers, Inc. **828** ©Tom McHugh/ Photo Researchers, Inc. **829** t.r. ©Art Wolfe/Stone; m. ©D. Parer and E. Parer-Cook/Stone; b. Nicole Galeazzi/Omni-Photo Communications, Inc. **830** cw: 1 ©Merlin D. Tuttle/ Bat Conservation International/Photo Researchers, Inc.; cw: 2 ©Wayne Lawler/ Photo Researchers, Inc.; cw: 3 ©Stone; cw: 4 Graeme Ellis-Ursus/ Ursus Photography, Vancouver; cw: 5 ©Doug Perrine/Innerspace Visions; cw: 6 ©Anthony Mercieca/Photo Researchers, Inc. **831** t.l. ©Tui De Roy/Minden Pictures, Inc.; t.r. Daniel J. Cox/naturalexposures.com; m.l. Animals Animals/©Michael Dick; m.r. Daniel J. Cox/naturalexposures.com; b.l. ©Thomas Kitchin/Natural Selection; b.r. ©Frans Lanting/Minden Pictures, Inc. **833** ©Gerry Ellis/Minden Pictures, Inc. **834** l–r #1 ©Mitsuaki Iwago/Minden Pictures, Inc.; l-r #2 ©Frans Lanting /Minden Pictures, Inc.; l–r #3 ©Tom McHugh/ Photo Researchers, Inc.; l–r #4 Kevin Schafer; l–r #5 Daniel J. Cox/naturalexposures.com; l–r #6 ©Tim Davis/Photo Researchers, Inc.; l–r #7 ©Mark Newman/Photo Researchers, Inc.; l–r #8 ©Frans Lanting/Minden Pictures, Inc.; l–r #9 ©Tim Davis/Photo Researchers, Inc.; l-r #10 ©PhotoDisc, Inc., 2001 **836** t. ©John Reader/Science Photo Library/ Photo Researchers, Inc.; m. (c)Archivo Iconograpico, S.A./CORBIS; b. ©Science Photo Library/Photo Researchers, Inc. **837** t. Institute of Human Origins; b.l. ©David L. Brill Photography; b.r. ©John Reader/ Photo Researchers, Inc. **838** Fred Spoor, copyright National Museums of Kenya **839** Animals Animals/©E. R. Degginger **840** Laurie Grace & Janna Brenning/ Scientific American Magazine **841** ©De Sazo/Photo Researchers, Inc. **842** t. Runk/Schoenberger/Grant Heilman Photography; m. Dwight Kuhn Photography, ©1986; b. Runk/Schoenberger/ Grant Heilman Photography **844** ©The Stock Market/ Keenan Ward **848** ©Michael & Patricia Fogden/Fogden Wildlife **849** S. Conway Morris, University of Cambridge **851** cw: 1 ©Dorling Kindersley; cw: 2 ©Dorling Kindersley; cw: 3 ©Dorling Kindersley; cw: 4 ©Dorling Kindersley **852** cw: 1 ©Hal Beral/Visuals Unlimited; cw: 2 ©Tom & Pat Leeson/Photo Researchers, Inc.; cw: 3 ©Roger Treadwell/Visuals Unlimited; cw: 4 Nicole Galeazzi/ Omni-Photo Communications, Inc.; cw: 5 ©Stephen J. Krasemann/DRK Photo; cw: 6 ©Tom McHugh/ Photo Researchers, Inc. **853** ©Bob Daemmrich/Stock, Boston/PictureQuest **854** ©Frans Lanting/Minden Pictures, Inc. **856** Animals Animals/ ©Marian Bacon **857** ©Art Wolfe/Photo Researchers, Inc. **863** t.l. ©PhotoDisc, Inc., 2001; t.r. Courtesy of Verda Davis b. ©E.R. Degginger/Photo Researchers, Inc. **864** t.l. ©Fred Bavendam/Minden Pictures, Inc.; t.m. ©Stephen J. Krasemann/ Photo Researchers, Inc.; t.r. Daniel J. Cox/naturalexposures.com **866** t. Animals Animals/©Marian Bacon; b. Daniel J. Cox/naturalexposures.com **870** Daniel J. Cox/naturalexposures.com **871** ©Heather Angel/Biofotos **872** t. ©Joe McDonald/DRK Photo; b.l. ©Rod Planck/Photo Researchers, Inc.; b.r. ©Rod Planck/Photo Researchers, Inc. **873** Courtesy of Wolfgang Kaehler **876** William Lishman & Associates Limited **877** ©Flip Nicklin/Minden Pictures, Inc. **879** Courtesy of Wolfgang Kaehler **880** Michael K. Nichols/National Geographic Society **881** t. ©Gregory Dimijian/Photo Researchers, Inc.; b. ©Fred McConnaughey/Photo Researchers, Inc. **882** ©Francois Gohier/ Photo Researchers, Inc. **883** Anne et Jacques Six **884** ©Francois Gohier/Photo Researchers, Inc. **888–889** ©Orion Press/Black Sheep **890** ©Quest/Science Photo Library/Photo Researchers, Inc. **891** l. Corel Professional Photos CD-ROM™; r. ©Jim Cummins/FPG International LLC **894** t.l. ©David M. Phillips/Visuals Unlimited; t.r. ©Michael Abbey/Photo Researchers, Inc.; b.l. ©Dr. Dennis Kunkel/Phototake; b.r. Quest/Science Photo Library/Photo Researchers, Inc. **895** Ken Karp **906** Quest/Science Photo Library/ Photo Researchers, Inc. **908** ©Prof. P. Motta, Dept. of Anatomy, University La Sapienza, Rome/Science Photo Library/Photo Researchers, Inc. **909** ©Prof. P. Motta/Dept. of Anatomy/University La Sapienza, Rome/Science Photo Library/Photo Researchers, Inc. **910** l. Pearson Education Corporate Digital Archive; r. ©PhotoDisc, Inc., 2001 **911** t. ©Dr. Morley Read/Science Photo Library/Photo Researchers, Inc.; b. Dr. E.R. Degginger **912** ©David Young-Wolff/PhotoEdit/PictureQuest **920** ©Prof. P. Motta/Dept. of Anatomy/University La Sapienza, Rome/ Science Photo Library /Photo Researchers, Inc. **921** Manny Millan/ Sports Illustrated **923** ©Andrew Syred/ Science Photo Library/Photo Researchers, Inc. **926** l. ©Eric Graves/Phototake; m. ©Biophoto Associates/Photo Researchers, Inc.; r. ©John D. Cunningham/Visuals Unlimited **929** t. ©Ed Reschke/ Peter Arnold, Inc.; b. ©James Balog/ Stone **932** t. ©Dan McCoy/Rainbow; b. ©Dan McCoy/Rainbow **933** t. ©Dr. Jeremy Burgess/Science Photo Library/Photo Researchers, Inc.; b. ©1996 Jim Cummins/ FPG International LLC **936** ©Quest/Science Photo Library/Photo Researchers, Inc. **937** Pearson Education/ PH School **939** t.l. ©Eric Graves/Phototake; t.r. ©Biophoto Associates/ Photo Researchers, Inc.; b.l. ©John D. Cunningham/Visuals Unlimited; b.r. ©Andrew Syred/Science Photo Library/Photo Researchers, Inc. **940** ©Salisbury District Hospital/Science Photo Library /Photo Researchers, Inc. **942** ©Image Shop/Phototake **943** ©Will & Deni McIntyre/Photo Researchers, Inc. **948** t. ©Joseph Nettis/Photo Researchers, Inc.; b. Brown Brothers **949** t. AP/Wide World Photos; b.r. ©Hank Morgan/Science Source/Photo Researchers, Inc. **952** ©Yorgos Nikas/ Stone **953** ©Dr. Dennis Kunkel/Phototake **956** ©Prof. Motta, Correr & Nottola/University La Sapienza, Rome/Science Photo Library/ Photo Researchers, Inc. **959** l. ©PhotoDisc, Inc., 2001; r. Steve Downing **960** Pearson Education/PH School **961** ©George Hall/ Check Six/PictureQuest **962** ©A. Glauberman/Photo Researchers, Inc. **963** t. ©Science Photo Library/Photo Researchers, Inc.; b. ©Science Photo Library/Photo Researchers, Inc. **965** t. Pearson Education/PH School; b. Pearson Education/PH School **966** ©Yorgos Nikas/Stone **967** ©Dr. Dennis Kunkel/Phototake **970** ©Fred Hossler/ Visuals Unlimited **971** Bob Daemmrich/Stock, Boston **972** t. ©Chris Harvey/Stone; b. ©Don & Pat Valenti/DRK Photo **973** t.l. Grant Heilman Photography; t.r. United States Department of Agriculture **982** Pearson Education/ PH School **983** ©David Scharf/Peter Arnold, Inc. **984** ©Sovereign/Phototake **985** John McDonough/Sports Illustrated **990** Pearson Education/PH School 992 t. Bob Daemmrich/ Stock, Boston **992** b. ©David Scharf/Peter Arnold, Inc. **996** ©P. Motta/Photo Researchers, Inc. **997** ©Jeff Greenberg/Visuals Unlimited **1001** David Young-Wolff/ PhotoEdit **1008** t. ©Sloop-Ober/Visuals Unlimited; b. ©Sloop-Ober/ Visuals Unlimited **1009** SuperStock **1013** Lennart Nilsson/Albert Bonnier Förlag AB, A CHILD IS BORN, Dell Publishing Company **1016** ©Leroy Francis/Photo Researchers, Inc. **1019** t. ©Petit Format/ Nestle/Science Source/Photo Researchers, Inc.; b.l. ©Petit Format/Nestle/Science Source/Photo Researchers, Inc.; b.r. ©Petit Format/Nestle/ Science Source/Photo Researchers, Inc. **1020** t. ©T. Wiewandt/DRK Photo; b. Keith/Custom Medical Stock Photo **1021** t. ©Jose Luis Pelaez Inc./The Stock Market; b. ©William Campbell/ DRK Photo **1022** ©Bob Daemmrich/Stock, Boston/PictureQuest **1023** Pearson Education/PH School **1028** ©Juergen Berger/Max-Plank Institute/Science Photo Library/Photo Researchers, Inc. **1029** t. ©Carolina Biological Supply/ Phototake; b. ©Volker Steger/Science Photo Library/Photo Researchers, Inc. **1030** t. ©Microworks/Phototake; b. ©Microworks/Phototake **1032** ©Oliver Meckes/Photo Researchers, Inc. **1033** AP/Wide World Photos **1034** Lennart Nilsson/Albert Bonniers Forlag **1039** Pearson Education/PH School **1040** ©Zeva Delbaum/Peter Arnold, Inc. **1041** l. ©David Scharf/Peter Arnold, Inc.; m. ©David Scharf/Peter Arnold, Inc.; r. ©Oliver Meckes/Ottawa/Photo Researchers, Inc. **1042** ©Rodolfo Gonzalez/Rocky Mountain News/ CORBIS Sygma **1044** ©National Institute for Biological Standards and Control, England/Science Photo Library/Photo Researchers, Inc. **1046** ©Dr. Andrejs Liepins/Science Photo Library/Photo Researchers, Inc. **1047** l. AP/Wide World Photos; r. Tom Prettyman/PhotoEdit **1048** ©Yoav Levy/Phototake **1049** Pearson Education/PH Schoo **1055** ©E.R. Degginger/Photo Researchers, Inc. **1056** ©Mark Moffett/ Minden Pictures, Inc. **1057** t. ©Nigel Cattlin/Holt Studios Int'l/Photo Researchers, Inc.; b. ©Jeff Lepore/Photo Researchers, Inc. **1058** l. ©Dan Smith/Stone; r. ©PhotoDisc, Inc., 2001 **1059** ©Francois Gohier/ Photo Researchers, Inc. **1061** t. Pearson Education/PH School; b. Pearson Education/PH School **1066** t. ©Fr. Westall/Eurelios/Phototake; m. ©David Scharf/Peter Arnold, Inc.; b. ©Manfred Kage/Peter Arnold, Inc. **1067** l. Lee Rentz/Bruce Coleman, Inc.; r. ©Ed Reschke/ Peter Arnold, Inc. **1068** l. Geoff Dann/©Dorling Kindersley; r. ©Charles V. Angelo/Photo Researchers, Inc. **1069** l. ©R. Calentine/ Visuals Unlimited; r. ©John Cancalosi/DRK Photo **1070** t. ©Labat/ Jacana/Photo Researchers, Inc.; b.l. Animals Animals/©Marian Bacon; b.r. ©William Leonard/DRK Photo **1071** t. Merlin D. Tuttle/Bat Conservation International b Kevin Schafer

Note: *Every effort has been made to locate the copyright owner of material reprinted in this book. Omissions brought to our attention will be corrected in subsequent editions.*